REAL ESTATE TRANSFER, FINANCE, AND DEVELOPMENT

CASES AND MATERIALS

Ninth Edition

■ ■ ■

by

Grant S. Nelson
William H. Rehnquist Professor of Law
Pepperdine University

Dale A. Whitman
James E. Campbell Missouri Endowed Professor of Law Emeritus
University of Missouri

Ann M. Burkhart
Curtis Bradbury Kellar Professor of Law
University of Minnesota

R. Wilson Freyermuth
John D. Lawson Professor of Law and Curators' Teaching Professor
University of Missouri

AMERICAN CASEBOOK SERIES®

American Casebook Series is a trademark registered in the U.S. Patent and Trademark Office.

COPYRIGHT © 1976, 1981, 1987, 1992 WEST PUBLISHING CO.
© West, a Thomson business, 1998, 2003, 2006
© 2009 Thomson Reuters
© 2015 LEG, Inc. d/b/a West Academic
    444 Cedar Street, Suite 700
    St. Paul, MN 55101
    1-877-888-1330

West, West Academic Publishing, and West Academic are trademarks of West Publishing Corporation, used under license.

Printed in the United States of America

ISBN: 978-0-314-28860-8

To
Judy, Marge, Chris, and Shari

PREFACE

This is the ninth edition of a book on which Grant Nelson and Dale Whitman began collaboration 41 years ago. Six years have passed since the publication of the Eighth Edition of this book in 2009. At the time, we noted: "[R]eal estate finance law is undergoing the greatest upheaval of our lifetimes." Indeed, this upheaval has continued, to a significant extent, over these past six years. Residential and commercial real estate values plummeted, with only a partial recovery in many markets. Default and foreclosure rates skyrocketed, particularly in the residential sector. Fannie Mae and Freddie Mac became insolvent, received an enormous public bailout, and were placed in federal conservatorship—yet are now once again earning enormous profits and have largely repaid the public bailout. Enormous sums have been spent to implement mortgage modification programs designed to keep distressed borrowers in their homes, yet substantial doubt remains about the overall effectiveness of these efforts.

More significantly, the foreclosure crisis produced by this upheaval has revealed a real estate finance system that is significantly broken, both for borrowers and lenders. On the one hand, the crisis has exposed that securitization fostered appallingly inadequate recordkeeping and servicing practices. Original promissory notes that ostensibly were to end up in securitization pools were frequently lost, destroyed, or improperly negotiated, raising unnecessary legal doubt regarding the ability to enforce the underlying obligation of the borrowers. The MERS system—conceptually intended to streamline the securitization process by avoiding the need for a recorded chain of mortgage assignments—became a lightning rod for criticism for permitting MERS members to institute foreclosures in the name of MERS rather than in the name of the actual beneficial owner of the mortgage note, contributing to a perceived lack of transparency in the foreclosure process. Some servicers overwhelmed by the volume of foreclosures produced misleading or fraudulent affidavits ostensibly designed to validate the lender's right to foreclose despite sloppy recordkeeping practices. On the other hand, the crisis has also exposed that the foreclosure process itself needs major repair. In many states, the judicial foreclosure process has crawled to a stop; Federal Housing Finance Agency data suggests that foreclosure in some judicial-foreclosure-only states takes three years or more. This type of delay imposes unjustifiable costs on financially responsible borrowers.

Further, while the law governing foreclosure of personal property security enjoys nationwide consistency under UCC Article 9, the law of real estate finance remains frustratingly nonuniform. While state courts and legislatures have begun experimenting with the implementation of mediation and loss mitigation programs designed to facilitate mortgage modification for distressed borrowers, these efforts remain haphazard. The crisis has prompted the Uniform Law Commission to renew its efforts to promote a uniform law governing foreclosure, but the outlook for its success remains quite unclear.

While the full consequences of the real estate crisis remain an open question, the Ninth Edition seeks to catalogue these recent developments and places them in the appropriate context of the history and practice of mortgage law. Given the major upheaval in the securitization markets, the Ninth Edition reflects a thorough revision of the material on the law and practice governing transfer of mortgage notes and securitization. It likewise provides thorough treatment of the foreclosure crisis and its impact on the foreclosure process, including substantial treatment of federal and state loss mitigation programs spawned by the crisis. This edition also features a thorough structural revision of the material on bankruptcy and its impact on the rights of the mortgagee. Finally, this edition comprehensively addresses new governmental intervention in the mortgage market, including the new and developing role of the Consumer Financial Protection Bureau.

While these are sobering times for real estate and mortgage lawyers, they are also exciting. The economic crisis has provided an opportunity for reevaluation of old rules, standards, and regulations, and we have tried to take advantage of this chance to reflect on and reevaluate the traditional modes of thinking about property and mortgages.

At the same time, this process of reflection and rethinking continues throughout the country as courts, legislators, and policymakers act in response to the mortgage crisis. Almost daily, new legislative proposals are introduced and debated. While the information in this edition is accurate as of the time this book went to press in June 2015, we expect additional legislative action will occur as the economic uncertainty continues. If substantial new legislative developments warrant, we expect to provide and distribute electronic updates to these materials through www.westacademic.com.

Despite the incorporation of much new material, order of coverage and basic organization of this edition remain identical to previous editions. Hence, teachers who have used the book in the past will find the transition to this edition easy. Because there is far more here than can be used in a single law school course, a few comments about ways law teachers can employ the book may be helpful. Chapters three through seven, which deal with basic mortgage law concepts, can form the basis for a 3-credit course in "real estate finance." Alternatively, selected portions of the first two chapters can be added to the material in chapters three through seven to support a three-credit or four-credit "real estate transactions" course.

There are several other possible configurations. The first two chapters, dealing with sale contracts and conveyances, can form the basis of a short "Property II" course for students whose first-year property class did not cover conveyancing. The material in chapters eight through eleven, which cover government regulation and real estate development, can be covered in a separate "real estate development" course or can be selectively added to the basic mortgage material in chapters three through seven.

There are three other books, all available through West Academic Publishing, that both students and teachers (especially those teaching this material for the first time) may find useful. Nelson, Whitman, Burkhart, and Freyermuth's treatise, Real Estate Finance Law, now in its sixth edition, closely parallels the organization of the mortgages material in this casebook. It is available in both a student edition and a two-volume practitioner's edition; the latter includes more complete coverage of subrogation and marshaling, material on financing of condominium and planned communities, and an extensive collection of forms that is not found in the student edition.

Land Transactions and Finance, a book in West's "Black Letter" series, is more succinct and less costly but follows an order of presentation similar to that of the treatise. Finally, the Restatement (Third) of Property (Mortgages) (1997), of which Nelson and Whitman were the reporters, provides an authoritative discussion of most important mortgage law concerns in a traditional restatement format.

In the present casebook we have edited the cases liberally to focus on the significant property and mortgage law issues. Ellipses denote omissions in the text of the cases, but we have not indicated omissions of footnotes. Where footnotes are retained, they keep their original superscript numbers. Each of the notes following the cases begins with an italicized topic heading to guide the reader in studying them.

We are most appreciative of all those whose work we have built on here: the judges, clerks, and lawyers who contributed to the judicial opinions we have reprinted, and the countless people with whom we have discussed the concepts of real estate law with which this book deals: students, faculty colleagues, practicing lawyers, and members of The American Law Institute, the American College of Real Estate Lawyers, the American College of Mortgage Attorneys, and the Section of Real Property, Trust and Estate Law of the American Bar Association.

A special word of thanks is in order to two colleagues, Professor Roger Bernhardt of Golden Gate University and the late Professor Patrick Randolph of the University of Missouri-Kansas City, who have worked so effectively to analyze new developments in property and mortgage law and engage other scholars and lawyers in debating these developments. Each of these people has helped us clarify our thinking and formulate strategies for teaching the concepts in this book. A special thanks also is owed to John E. Rent, Vice President, Commercial Real Estate, Wells Fargo Bank, N.A., for his detailed and comprehensive remarks concerning the chapters on construction lending and income-producing properties. We must take full responsibility for any errors, but others are due much credit for the good that may be found in the book.

Finally, we thank our families and especially our spouses for their enduring support and patient understanding during the hours we spent in preparing this new edition.

GRANT S. NELSON

DALE A. WHITMAN

ANN M. BURKHART

R. WILSON FREYERMUTH

June 2015

SUMMARY OF CONTENTS

TABLE OF CONTENTS

PART 2. REAL ESTATE FINANCE

PART 3. REAL ESTATE DEVELOPMENT

TABLE OF CASES

The principal cases are in bold type.

REAL ESTATE TRANSFER, FINANCE, AND DEVELOPMENT

CASES AND MATERIALS

Ninth Edition

PART 1

THE TRANSFER OF OWNERSHIP

■ ■ ■

CHAPTER ONE

CONTRACTS FOR THE SALE OF LAND

∎ ∎ ∎

The first two chapters of this book deal with the processes through which real estate is bought and sold. Although there are many possible variations, even the simplest of realty transfers usually takes place through a series of well-defined steps: (1) the execution of a contract of sale; (2) inspections of the property and examination of the seller's title by the buyer; (3) the arranging of financing by the buyer, if needed; (4) the closing or "settlement"; (5) the recording of the deed and any mortgage or other security instrument that the buyer has executed; and (6) the issuance of title insurance. The first three steps are the subject of Chapter One. The latter three steps will be covered in Chapter Two.

A. REAL ESTATE BROKERS

A large proportion of all real estate on the market is "listed" with real estate brokers. The listing process involves the execution by the seller of a contract appointing the broker to be the seller's agent in obtaining a buyer. If the broker is successful (and the definition of "success" may be a matter of dispute, as we will see below), the seller will be obligated to pay the broker a commission, usually computed as a percentage of the actual sales price. A typical listing contract, this one prepared by the Nebraska Real Estate Commission for (optional) use by real estate agents in that state, is reproduced below.[1] The footnotes are not part of the listing contract, but are provided to aid your understanding of the contract.

THIS IS A LEGALLY BINDING AGREEMENT, IF NOT UNDERSTOOD, SEEK LEGAL ADVICE.
EXCLUSIVE RIGHT-TO-SELL LISTING CONTRACT

_____(Seller)

(Seller's Name)

Contracts with _____(Broker)

(Broker's Name or Firm and Address)

for the purposes and under the terms set forth below, with my specific Seller's Limited Agent, _____(Name of Agent)_____,

---

[1] The form is updated from time to time and is available on the Commission's web site, www.nrec.ne.gov/pdf/forms/RIGHT2SL.pdf.

and such other affiliated licensees of Broker[2] as may be assigned by Broker in writing, if needed as exclusive Seller's Limited Agents.[3] The affiliated licensee(s) named in this paragraph and the Seller's Limited Agents who may be appointed by the Broker are collectively referred to in this Listing Contract as Seller's Limited Agents. All responsibilities and duties of Broker shall also be the responsibilities and duties of the Seller's Limited Agent:

1.   **Purpose of Agency**. The purpose of this sole and exclusive right-to-sell agency contract ("Listing Contract") is to engage the efforts of Broker to accomplish the Sale of the Real Property legally described

_____ (Legal Description) _____ also known as:

_____ (Street Address) _____ (City) _____ (State) _____

together with any items of Personal Property to be conveyed pursuant to Paragraph 5 (collectively referred to as the "Property").

2.   **Effect of this Listing Contract**. By contracting with Broker, Seller agrees to conduct all negotiations for the Sale of the Property through Seller's Limited Agent and to refer to Seller's Limited Agent all inquiries received in any form from any source during the term of this Contract.

3.   **The Listing Period**. This Contract shall begin _____, _____, and shall continue through _____, _____. (This is referred to as the "Listing Period.")

4.   **Price and Terms**. The Offering Price for the Property shall be $_____ on the following Terms:

_____

5.   **Price to Include**. The Price shall include all attached fixtures, except: _____

The following Personal Property is also included:

_____

6.   **Title**. Seller represents to Broker that title to the Property is solely in Seller's name. Seller shall deliver to Broker, upon request, copies of all relevant title materials. Seller represents that there are no known encroachments affecting this Property, except (If none, state "None"):

_____

_____

Seller agrees to convey marketable record title by warranty deed or

_____.

---

[2]   This is a reference to other salespeople who operate out of the broker's office and under the broker's supervision.

[3]   The agents are "limited" in the sense that they are required to perform only specific duties. Those duties are spelled out in Neb. Stat. § 76–2417, and are repeated in Paragraph 20 of this listing contract.

If the Property has been or will be assessed for local improvements installed, under construction or ordered by public authority at the time of signing a Purchase Agreement, Seller will be responsible for payment of same. Broker may terminate this Listing Contract upon written notice to Seller that title is not satisfactory to Broker.

7.   Evidence of Title. Seller agrees to convey a marketable title to Buyer, evidenced by a policy of title insurance or an abstract certified to date.

8.   Possession. Possession of the Property shall be delivered to Buyer on (Date)_____.

9.   Material Defects and Indemnification. Seller represents to the Broker solely for the purposes of this Listing Contract that he or she has completed or will promptly complete the Seller Property Condition Disclosure Statement fully and correctly to the best of the Seller's knowledge. Seller further states that all oral representations made to Seller's Limited Agent are accurate. Seller's Limited Agent shall not receive any offers to purchase until the Seller Property Condition Disclosure Statement is complete.

Seller agrees to indemnify and hold harmless Broker (Listing Company) and any subagents, from any claim that may be made against the Listing Company or subagents by reason of the Seller having breached the terms of this paragraph. In addition, Seller agrees to pay attorney fees and associated costs reasonably incurred by Broker to enforce this indemnity. Seller agrees that any defects of a material nature (including, but not limited to, structural defects, soil conditions, violations of health, zoning or building laws, and nonconforming uses or zoning variances) actually known by Seller's Limited Agent must be disclosed by Seller's Limited Agent to any prospective Buyer.

10. Compensation of Broker. In consideration of services to be performed by Seller's Limited Agent, Seller agrees to pay Broker a commission[4] of _____, payable upon the happening of any of the following:

(a) If during the term of the listing, Seller, Broker or any other person:

(1)   sells the Property; or

(2)   finds a Buyer who is ready, willing and able to purchase the Property at the above price and terms or for any other price and terms to which Seller agrees to accept; or

---

[4]   The commission is usually expressed as a percentage of the selling price. Under Nebraska law, as in many states, there is nothing to prevent the parties from agreeing to a flat-fee commission or computing the commission on some other basis.

(3) finds a Buyer who is granted an option to purchase or enters into a lease with option to purchase and the option is subsequently exercised; or

(b) If this agreement is revoked or violated by Seller; or

(c) If Broker is prevented in closing the Sale of this Property by existing claims, liens, judgments, or suits pending against this Property, or Seller thereof; or

(d) If Broker is unfairly hindered by Seller in the showing of or attempting to sell this Property; or,

(e) If within (180)[5] days after the expiration of this Listing Contract, Seller sells this Property to any person found during the term of this listing, or due to Broker's efforts or advertising, under this Listing Contract, unless this Property is listed with another Broker.

11. Limitation on Broker's Compensation. Broker may accept compensation when Broker or affiliated licensee (other than Seller's Limited Agent), is serving as a Buyer's Agent. In all other cases, Broker shall not accept compensation from the Buyer, the Buyer's agent, or any entity participating in or providing services for the Sale without written agreement of Seller.

12. Cooperating with Other Brokers. Broker may accept the assistance and cooperation of other brokers who will be acting as subagents of the seller or as agents for a Buyer. If Broker participates in a local multiple listing service Broker shall submit the Property to such listing service. Seller authorizes Broker to compensate from the amount described in paragraph 10:

☐ seller's sub-agent; ☐ buyer's agent; ☐ agents acting for both the buyer and the seller-dual agents.[6]

13. Forfeiture of Earnest Money. In the event of forfeiture of the earnest money made by a prospective Buyer, the monies received, after expenses incurred by Broker, shall be divided between Broker and Seller, one-half thereof to Broker, but not to exceed the commission agreed upon herein, and the balance to Seller.

14. Cost of Services. Broker shall bear all expenses incurred by Broker, if any, to market the Property and to compensate cooperating brokers, if any. Broker will not obtain or order any products or services to be paid by Seller unless Seller agrees. Broker shall not be obligated to advance funds for the benefit of Seller.

---

[5] The 180-day figure is not in the contract form, but is probably representative of the time period that is usually filled in this blank.

[6] It is likely that in the great majority of cases, all three blanks are checked, so that other agents can receive a split of the commission whether they technically represent the seller, the buyer, or both.

15. Maintenance of the Property. Seller agrees to maintain until delivery of possession, the heating, air conditioning, water heater, sewer, plumbing and electrical systems and any built-in appliances in good and reasonable working condition. Seller further agrees to hold Broker harmless from any and all causes of action, loss, damage, or expense Broker may be subjected to arising in connection with this section. Seller also agrees that Broker shall not be responsible for maintenance of the Property.

16. Nondiscrimination. The undersigned Seller and Broker acknowledge, by their respective signature hereon, that the law prohibits discrimination for or against any person because of race, color, religion, sex, handicap, familial status, or national origin.

17. Escrow Closing. Seller agrees that the closing of any sale made by Broker may be handled by an Escrow Agent and authorizes Broker to transfer all earnest monies, down payments and other trust funds to the Escrow Agent along with documents and other items received by Broker related to the sale. The cost of the Escrow Closing shall be paid by Seller or as negotiated with the Buyer in the Purchase Agreement.

18. Smoke Detectors. Seller agrees to install at Seller's expense any smoke detectors required by law.

19. "For Sale" Sign Permitted. Seller gives permission to Broker to place a "For Sale" and a "Sold" sign on the Property and to use a "Lock Box."

20. Duties and Responsibilities of Seller's Limited Agent. Seller's Limited Agent shall have the following duties and obligations:

a. To perform the terms of this agreement;

b. To exercise reasonable skill and care for Seller;

c. To promote the interest of Seller with the utmost good faith, loyalty and fidelity including:

    1.   Seeking the price and terms which are acceptable to Seller except that Seller's Limited Agent shall not be obligated to seek additional offers to purchase the property while the property is subject to a contract for sale;

    2.   Presenting all written offers to and from Seller in a timely manner regardless of whether the property is subject to a contract for sale;

    3.   Disclosing in writing to Seller all adverse material facts actually known by Seller's Limited Agent; and

    4.   Advising Seller to obtain expert advice as to material matters of that which Seller's Limited Agent knows but the specifics of which are beyond the expertise of Seller's Limited Agent;

d. To account in a timely manner for all money and property received;

e. To comply with the requirements of agency relationships as defined in Neb. Rev. Stat. § 76–2401 through § 76–2430, the Nebraska Real Estate License Act,[7] and any rules or regulations promulgated pursuant to such sections or act; and

f. To comply with any applicable federal, state, and local laws, rules, regulations, and ordinances, including fair housing and civil rights statutes and regulations.

21. Confidential Information. Seller's Limited Agent shall not disclose any confidential information about Seller, without Seller's written permission, unless disclosure is required by statute, rule, or regulation, or failure to disclose the information would constitute fraudulent misrepresentation. Seller's Limited Agent is required to disclose adverse material facts to any prospective buyer. Adverse material facts may include any environmental hazards affecting the property which are required by law to be disclosed, physical condition of the property, any material defects in the property, any material defects in the title to the property, or any material limitation on Seller's ability to perform under the terms of the contract.

22. Modification of this Listing Contract. No modification of this Listing Contract shall be valid, unless made in writing and signed by the parties.

23. Release of Information. Seller authorizes Broker to obtain any information relating to utility expenses and all pertinent information regarding the present mortgage(s) or Deed(s) of Trust on this Property including existing balance, interest rate, monthly payment, balance in escrow account and pay off amount. Seller authorizes the dissemination of sales information including selling price and terms after closing of the transaction.

24. Entire Agreement. This Listing Contract constitutes the entire Contract between the parties and any prior negotiations or agreements, whether oral or written, are not valid unless set forth is this Contract.

25. Copies of Agreement. This Listing Contract is executed in multiple copies and Seller acknowledges receipt of a copy signed by the Broker or Broker's affiliated licensee.

Signed this _____ day of _____, _____.

_____   _____
Broker's Name, Address   Seller's Name, Address
& Signature   & Signature

---

[7] The main burden of these provisions is disclosure of the agency relationship to the parties to the sale.

NOTES AND QUESTIONS

1. *The broker's authority.* What, exactly, does the broker have legal authority to do? Is it merely to show, advertise, and market the property, or to enter into an actual contract of sale? The usual view is that only the former authority is contemplated, and the broker cannot force the sale to take place if the seller refuses to go forward (although the seller may nonetheless be liable for the commission). See Forbis v. Honeycutt, 301 N.C. 699, 273 S.E.2d 240 (1981); Davito v. Blakely, 96 Ill. App. 2d 196, 238 N.E.2d 410 (1968); cf. Ward v. Mattuschek, 134 Mont. 307, 330 P.2d 971 (1958). See also Diversified Devel. & Inv., Inc. v. Heil, 119 N. M. 290, 889 P.2d 1212 (1995) (broker did not have "apparent authority" to grant extension of time for exercise of option).

2. *Power to consummate a sale?* Of course, if the language of the listing agreement is specific enough, it may give the broker a "power of attorney" to enter into a sales contract and consummate sale. Does the following language, taken from another printed listing agreement, do so?

> In consideration of the services to be performed by the undersigned Agent, the undersigned Seller does hereby grant to the agent commencing with date hereof and expiring at midnight on _____, 20__ the exclusive right to sell or contract to sell and to receipt for deposit in connection therewith, the following described property * * * .

The phrase "or contract to sell" was probably inserted because the form is used in an area where property is frequently sold by installment land contract, a device by which the seller finances the buyer's purchase. In such a transaction, the contract is the vehicle of sale. But does the language quoted above suggest that the broker herself has authority to execute the contract on behalf of the principal? See Roskwitalski v. Reiss, 338 Pa. Super. 85, 487 A.2d 864 (1985) (holding similar language gave the broker no power to form a contract). If a power of attorney to the broker is desired, it must be very clearly stated.

3. *Types of listings.* The Statute of Frauds in nearly all states requires listing agreements to be written. See, e.g., Bishop v. Hansen, 105 Wash. App. 116, 19 P.3d 448 (2001). New York is a notable exception; N.Y. General Obligations Law § 5–701(10) specifically exempts real estate listing agreements from the Statute of Frauds. See Miranda v. Aliotta, 980 N.Y.S.2d 236 (N.Y. Sup. Ct. 2013) (if agreement does not state commission rate, broker is entitled to a reasonable commission). But obviously, it is wise to use a writing in New York. An oral listing might be brought into compliance with the Statute of Frauds if it is sufficiently described in some other written document, such as the contract of sale. See C. Porter Vaughn, Inc. v. Dilorenzo, 689 S.E.2d 656 (Va. 2010).

The common types of listings are described in Real Estate Listing Service, Inc. v. Connecticut Real Estate Comm'n, 179 Conn. 128, 425 A.2d 581 (1979):

> [O]nly three types of real estate listing agreements have traditionally been used in this state * * * . Those categories are: the open listing, under which the property owner agrees to pay to the listing broker a commission if that broker effects the sale of the property but retains the right to sell the property himself as well as the right to procure the services of any other broker in the sale of the property; the exclusive agency listing, which is for a time certain and authorizes only one broker to sell the property but permits the property owner to sell the property himself without incurring a commission; * * * and the exclusive right to sell listing, under which the sale of the property during the contract period, no matter by whom negotiated, obligates the property owner to pay a commission to the listing broker.

Which type of listing is represented by the Nebraska Real Estate Commission form reproduced at the beginning of this chapter? Nearly all residential properties are listed on an "exclusive right to sell" basis. Hence, a broker who is effective in obtaining listings may do very well financially without ever selling a house! See Ellis, Preparing the Listing Agreement between Owner and Broker (with Form), 2 Prac. Real Est. Law., 51 (No. 4, July 1986).

4. *The relationship of commissions to selling price.* The standard rationale for basing real estate commissions on selling prices is that, because higher prices will result in larger commissions, agents have an incentive to obtain the highest possible prices for their clients, the sellers. Two economists at the University of Chicago, Steven D. Levitt and Chad Syverson, questioned this relationship. They noted that in a Chicago suburb, properties owned by real estate agents personally tended to remain on the market longer and sell for higher prices than properties owned by clients of agents.

> Real estate agents have a better sense than others of the best price a home can command. But when they work for others, they don't have the financial incentive to pursue it. Most home sales generate a 6 percent commission, split between the brokerage firms representing the buyer and seller. The agent generally receives half of the firm's draw, or 1.5 percent of the sale. So if a home sells for $500,000, the agent personally receives $7,500. Not bad for what may be just a few days of work. If the agent works for an additional week and urges the seller to hold out for $515,000, that's an extra $15,000 for the seller, but only an extra $225 for the agent. Because every additional dollar throws only a penny and a half into the pocket of the agent, the economists reason, the agent may push clients to accept lowball offers.

Daniel Gross, Why a Real Estate Agent May Skip the Extra Mile, N.Y. Times, Feb. 20, 2005.

5.   *Multiple listing services and discount brokers.* In addition to a listing agreement, the seller and the broker also will prepare a form on which detailed information about the house or other property is given. Such information will include the number of rooms and baths, heating system, sewer system, appliances, and existing financing. This information will find its way into the publication of the multiple listing service (the "MLS"), which is operated by a local board of realtors, where all member brokers and their salespeople will see it. Photographs of the property are often included as well. Multiple listing services today usually maintain this information on an on-line data base instead of a printed book.

Access to the multiple listing service often is essential to the successful marketing of the property. Indeed, the listing broker's main function may be to provide such access, because nonbrokers and nonmembers of the local board of realtors are not permitted to list property directly with the MLS. Of course, the local board's members generally feel that they have every right to exclude listings by nonmembers or agents they consider marginal. Do you see antitrust problems with this attitude? The court found no antitrust violation in restricting access to the MLS to members of the local board of realtors in Supermarket of Homes, Inc. v. San Fernando Valley Board of Realtors, 786 F.2d 1400 (9th Cir.1986). In most other cases, efforts to impose Sherman Act liability on MLSs have similarly failed.

However, in Regional Multiple Listing Service of Minnesota, Inc. v. American Home Realty Network, Inc., 9 F.Supp.3d 1032 (D.Minn. 2014), a regional MLS sued a privately owned firm that operated an online residential real estate service called Neighborcity that connected prospective buyers with buy-side real estate agents. The MLS claimed that Neighborcity had violated copyright law by reproducing photographs and descriptions of houses taken from the MLS. Neighborcity counterclaimed, asserting that the MLS and its members were engaged in a conspiracy in restraint of trade in violation of the Sherman Act. The court found that there were no other complete sources of data on properties for sale except the MLS, and that its refusal to license that data to other companies had anticompetitive effects. Thus, the Sherman Act counterclaim survived a motion to dismiss. This pot is likely to continue to bubble.

6.   *Minimum service laws.* About half of U.S. states have enacted "minimum service" statutes. Their purposes is to require that real estate brokers provide a full panoply of services, and thus to prevent the operation of "fee for service" brokers who sell each service individually, with a separate charge for each. Traditional real estate agents have been strong advocates for these statutes. The Antitrust Division of the U.S. Department of Justice has condemned such laws, noting that they diminish consumer choice and raise the cost of selling a house. In a 2008 press release, it commented as follows:

> Fee-for-service brokers "unbundle" the package of real estate services typically offered by traditional full-service real estate brokers and charge a fixed or hourly fee for specific services, such as

listing the house in the MLS, negotiating or closing contracts, and pricing the home. These brokerage models enable consumers to save thousands of dollars by allowing them to purchase only those services they want.

Why would some consumers use a fee-for-service broker? Most consumers want to make as much money as possible on the sale of their home and spend no more than necessary when purchasing a home. In many cases, the standard broker's commission can offset a portion of the equity value that has been building up in a seller's home or push the price of a home beyond a buyer's purchasing power. Consumers who want to perform some of the steps involved in selling a home can reap significant financial savings by purchasing only those real estate brokerage services they actually want. * * *

Although many consumers do want to buy all the services these provisions require a broker to provide, other consumers prefer to save money by performing some services themselves. * * *

Do minimum service laws result in better service for consumers? Minimum service laws do not ensure quality. They merely require that real estate brokers provide—and consumers purchase—more services. State policymakers concerned with ensuring quality real estate brokerage services can help in other ways—by fostering competition among real estate brokers and by enforcing existing state licensing, continuing education, and disciplinary rules.

See Muller, Encouraging Price Competition among New Jersey's Residential Real Estate Brokers: Reforms to Promote the Growth of Alternative Brokerages and Reduce Transaction Costs, 39 Seton Hall L. Rev. 665 (2009).

DRAKE v. HOSLEY

Supreme Court of Alaska, 1986
713 P.2d 1203

MOORE, JUSTICE

This is an appeal from a summary judgment granted in favor of Charles Hosley, entitling him to a real estate broker's commission under a contract with the seller. The superior court concluded that Hosley had fulfilled the terms of a written agreement with the seller by finding a buyer who entered into a contract to purchase in accord with the seller's terms. We affirm.

On March 5, 1984, Paul Drake signed an exclusive listing agreement with The Charles Hosley Company, Realtors (hereafter "Hosley"). The agreement authorized Hosley to act as Drake's agent until March 30, 1984, to sell some land Drake owned in North Pole, Alaska. The agreement provided for payment of a ten percent commission if, during the period of the listing agreement, (1) Hosley located a buyer "willing and able to purchase at the terms set by the seller," or (2) the seller entered into a "binding sale" during the term set by the seller.

Hosley found a group of three buyers, Robert Goldsmith, Dwayne Hofschulte and David Hystrom (hereafter "buyers"), who were interested in the property. On March 23, 1984, Drake signed a purchase and sale agreement, entitled "earnest money receipt," in which he agreed to sell the land to the buyers at a specified price and terms. The buyers also signed the agreement. It provided that closing would occur "within 10 days of clear title" and "ASAP, 1984." A typed addendum stated that Drake agreed to pay Hosley a commission of ten percent of the price paid for the property. Both Drake and Hosley signed the addendum.

On April 3, 1984, Hosley received a preliminary commitment for title insurance. The title report listed a judgment in favor of Drake's ex-wife as the sole encumbrance on the title. The next day Hosley called Drake's attorney, Tom Wickwire, to ask about the judgment. Wickwire stated that the judgment would be paid with the cash received at closing.

Two or three days later, attorney Wickwire called Hosley and stated that his client (Drake) wanted the sale closed by April 11. Wickwire explained that he had negotiated a discounted settlement with Drake's ex-wife that required payment by April 11. Wickwire claims that Hosley agreed to close by April 11. Hosley disagrees, and claims that he merely stated that he would try to close as quickly as possible.

When Hosley became concerned that the buyers would not be able to close on April 11, he telephoned the attorney for Drake's ex-wife and learned that the April 11 deadline for payment of the judgment had been extended until the end of the month.

On April 11, Wickwire called Hosley to set up the closing. Hosley told Wickwire that the buyers could not close that day because they did not have the money and would not have it before May 1. Wickwire indicated that he would advise Drake to call off the sale because the buyers had refused to perform. Wickwire mailed a letter to Hosley, dated April 11, stating that Drake's offer to sell was withdrawn. Hosley received the letter on approximately April 18. On April 12, Drake sold his property through another broker to different buyers.

On April 12, Hosley went to Wickwire's office to close the sale and submitted checks from the buyers totaling $33,000 for the down payment. Wickwire refused the checks, stating that another buyer already had purchased the property.

Hosley filed a complaint, alleging he had fulfilled the terms of the exclusive listing agreement and was entitled to payment of a commission. The parties filed cross-motions for summary judgment. The trial court granted Hosley's motion and denied Drake's. Drake appeals.

I.

Drake contends he does not owe a commission to Hosley and that entry of judgment in favor of Hosley was improper. In reviewing a summary judgment, we must determine whether there are any genuine issues of material fact, and whether the moving party is entitled to judgment as a matter of law. Moore v. State, 553 P.2d 8, 15 (Alaska 1976). See Alaska R. Civ. P. 56(c).

Alaska Statute § 08.88.361 provides that "[a] commission is earned when the real estate broker fulfills the terms of a written personal services contract." The exclusive listing agreement between Drake, as seller, and Hosley, as broker, provided that a ten percent commission would be paid to Hosley if one of three conditions occurred:

a) if a property is sold or a *binding sale or lease agreement is entered into by Seller* during the term set by seller; or

b) if during the term of this Agreement [Hosley] *finds a buyer willing and able to purchase* at the terms set by Seller; or

c) if a buyer located by [Hosley] enters into a binding sale or lease agreement within 120 days after the expiration of this Agreement.

(Emphasis added.)

It is undisputed that during the term of the agreement, Hosley found a group of three buyers, and that Drake entered into a purchase and sale agreement ("earnest money receipt") with the buyers. The earnest money agreement signed by Drake stated: "I hereby approve and accept the above sale for said price and on said terms and conditions and agree to consummate the same as stated." A typed addendum to the earnest money agreement provided: "Seller agrees to pay a Realtors' commission in the amount of 10% of price to be paid by partial assignment of the deed of trust at the rate of $1,000/month."

On the basis of these facts, the trial court concluded that Hosley had performed the terms of his agreement with Drake. The court found that, within the terms of the listing agreement, Hosley located a group of buyers who entered into a binding sale agreement with Drake. The court ruled that Hosley therefore was entitled to his commission.

Drake invites this court to adopt the reasoning of *Ellsworth Dobbs, Inc. v. Johnson*, 50 N.J. 528, 236 A.2d 843 (1967), and hold that a real estate broker does not earn a commission unless the contract of sale is performed.

The traditional rule followed by a majority of jurisdictions is that a broker is entitled to a commission when he produces a buyer ready, willing and able to purchase the property on the seller's terms, even if the sale is not completed. Sowash v. Garrett, 630 P.2d 8, 12 (Alaska 1981). See generally Annot., 12 A.L.R. 4th 1083 (1982). The rationale for concluding that a potential purchaser is deemed "willing and able" the instant the purchaser signs a contract with the seller is explained in *Kopf v. Milam*, 60 Cal. 2d 600, 35 Cal. Rptr. 614, 617, 387 P.2d 390, 393 (1963):

> When a vendor enters a valid unconditional contract of sale with a purchaser procured by a broker, the purchaser's acceptability is conclusively presumed because the vendor is estopped to deny the qualifications of a purchaser with whom he is willing to contract.

Drake suggests that the rule of *Dobbs* is better reasoned because it emphasizes that a broker has not produced a ready, willing and able buyer if the buyer refuses or is unable to perform at closing. Dobbs, 236 A.2d at 853. In a practical world the true test of a willing buyer is not met at the time a purchase agreement is signed, but at the time of closing of title. Id. Since the broker's duty to the owner is to produce a buyer who is financially able to pay the purchase price, it is reasonable to allow the owner to accept the buyer and enter into a sales contract without becoming liable for a broker's commission unless the sale is consummated. Id.

The *Dobbs* court also noted that when an owner of property lists it for sale with a broker, the owner usually expects that money for payment of a commission will come from the sale proceeds. Id. at 854. For these reasons, the *Dobbs* court concluded that:

> public policy requires the courts to read into every brokerage agreement or contract of sale a requirement that barring default by the seller, commissions shall not be deemed earned against him unless the contract of sale is performed.

Id. at 857.

We find such reasoning persuasive. We also note that several jurisdictions recently have adopted the *Dobbs* rule, or modified versions of it. See Annot., 12 A.L.R. 4th 1083, 1088, 1094–1103 (1982). However, adoption of the rule does not assist Drake in this case. The *Dobbs* court specifically held that "in the *absence of default by the seller,* the broker's right to commission * * * comes into existence only when his buyer performs in accordance with the contract of sale." Dobbs, 236 A.2d at 855 (emphasis added). A broker still is entitled to a commission if "improper or frustrating conduct" by the owner prevents title from passing. Id. at 853.

Drake claims that there is a genuine issue of fact regarding whether the buyer or seller refused to perform. In particular he argues that there is a material factual dispute "whether Hosley, acting for the buyers, first agreed with Wickwire to close the sale on April 11, 1984, then * * * refused to close on that day * * * ." Drake is correct that the existence of an agreement is disputed. However, there is no genuine issue as to whether Hosley was acting for the buyers. Other than a bare allegation in Drake's pleadings, the record is devoid of any evidence that Hosley was representing the buyers. Hence, the buyers could not be bound whether or not an agreement to expedite closing was made by Hosley and Wickwire.

Drake points to the fact that Hosley told Drake's attorney that the buyers could not close on April 11 because they did not have the money. The fact that Hosley communicated a message from the buyers does not make him their agent. Further, the affidavit of Drake's attorney, Wickwire, does not state that Hosley ever claimed or intimated that he was acting in any role other than as Drake's broker.

In short, Drake failed to make any showing that Hosley was the buyers' agent and had authority to modify their contract. In the absence of such evidence, any agreement between Drake's attorney and Drake's broker could not modify the contractual obligations of the buyers. Since Hosley's right to a commission does not turn on whether he and Drake's attorney agreed to expedite closing, the disputed agreement was not a material fact that would preclude summary judgment.

Under the terms of the earnest money agreement, the buyers were required to close within ten days after evidence of clear title was furnished. Hosley stated that he received a report from the title insurance company on April 3. The report carried a typist's date of April 2. We agree with the trial court that the buyers met the terms of the earnest money agreement by submitting checks for the down payment to Drake's agent on April 12—which was within ten days of either the April 2 or April 3 date. Thus, it was not the buyers who prevented the sale from going through.

* * *

To summarize, Hosley found a group of buyers who were willing and able to perform in accord with the terms set by the seller, but they were prevented from doing so by the seller's frustrating conduct. The buyers tried to perform by tendering checks for the down payment "within 10 days of clear title," as required by the earnest money agreement. The sale did not take place because the seller, Drake, sold the property to a third party during the ten-day closing period. Thus, even under the *Dobbs* rule, Hosley is entitled to his commission.

The judgment in favor of Hosley is AFFIRMED.

NOTES AND QUESTIONS

1. *Is the commission owed if no closing occurs?* The common law rule recognizing the broker's claim for the commission despite the failure to close is still alive and well, despite the inroads of *Dobbs*-like cases. See, e.g., Fairbourn Commercial, Inc. v. American Housing Partners, Inc., 94 P.3d 292 (Utah 2004):

> [T]he general rule in Utah is that a real estate broker is entitled to its commission when it has procured a buyer who is "ready, willing and able and who is accepted by the seller." Bushnell Real Estate, Inc. v. Nielson, 672 P.2d 746, 751 (Utah 1983). American urges us to discard this rule in favor of the rule first enunciated in *Ellsworth Dobbs, Inc. v. Johnson*, 50 N.J. 528, 236 A.2d 843 (1967), which imbues all broker listing agreements with the implied condition that commission is due only if the underlying real estate transaction is consummated. Id. at 855. We decline to adopt this rule because absent a contractual provision conditioning a broker's commission on a buyer's performance, "[t]he broker is not an insurer of the subsequent performance of the contract." Bushnell, 672 P.2d at 751.

Is the Utah court's "reason" for refusing to adopt the *Dobbs* rule really a reason? If the *Dobbs* rule is adopted and the agent cannot collect a commission from the seller, can the agent recover from the breaching buyer who refuses to close? See Bailey v. Montgomery, 31 Ark. App. 1, 786 S.W.2d 594 (1990) (rejecting such a claim on the ground that the agent, whose listing agreement was with the sellers, had no contractual relationship with the buyers). Could language obligating the buyers on these facts be inserted, not in the listing agreement, but in the contract of sale? Bear in mind, too, that the agent may well have the right to share any earnest money retained by the seller if the buyer breaches the sales contract. See paragraph 13 of the Nebraska listing agreement, supra.

Refer to paragraph 10(a)(2) of the Nebraska listing. Does it entitle the agent to a commission if the buyer signs a contract of purchase but later backs out of it? If you were the seller and your jurisdiction had not adopted the *Dobbs* rule, how would you modify the contract form to ensure that you would not have to pay a commission unless an actual closing of the sale occurred?

2. *Variations in listing agreements.* Even if the particular jurisdiction has not adopted the *Dobbs* rule, the parties can do so by adding appropriate language to the listing agreement. For example, in Graff v. Billet, 477 N.E.2d 212 (N.Y. 1984), the agreement said, "The commission is payable only as, if, and when title passes, except for willful default on the part of the seller."

Such language is commonly included in New York. The broker obtained a full price offer for the property, but the seller rejected it and refused to enter into a contract of sale. The court concluded that the broker was not entitled to a commission. In effect, it held that "willful default" after a contract of sale was signed was not the same as willful refusal to enter into a contract in the first place! For a similar result, but not based on such specific language, see RealPro, Inc. v. Smith Residual Co., LLC, 138 Cal. Rptr. 3d 255 (Cal.App. 2012). How can a broker modify the language quoted above to eliminate this problem?

For a contrasting point of view, see E. Kendall Investments, Inc. v. Bankers Real Estate Partners, 742 So. 2d 302, 306 (Fla. App. 1999):

> The broker's undertaking here was to produce a ready, willing, and able buyer. When the buyer met the asking price, the seller raised the price, even though there was no competing bid. The buyer met the higher price, and the seller orally accepted the letter of intent. Thereafter the seller simply refused to proceed. The record supports the trial court finding that seller was responsible for the failure to consummate the sale.

Shouldn't a court take the same view even if the listing agreement provides that the commission is payable only upon passage of legal title?

Assume that the jurisdiction has not adopted the *Dobbs* rule, but that the listing agreement states that the broker's commission will be paid "from the proceeds at closing." Is this language sufficient to deny the broker the commission if no closing ever occurs? Compare Arvida Realty Sales, Inc. v. William R. Tinnerman & Co., 536 So. 2d 1041 (Fla. App. 1988) and Chamberlain v. Porter, 562 A.2d 675 (Me. 1989) (seller not liable for commission) with Fairbourn Commercial, Inc. v. American Housing Partners, Inc., supra note 1, and Realty Associates of Sedona v. Valley National Bank of Arizona, 153 Ariz. 514, 738 P.2d 1121 (App. 1986) (seller liable for commission).

If the purchase price is to be paid in installments, can the seller avoid paying part of the commission (or recover some of what has already been paid) if the purchaser pays some installments, but then defaults? Or suppose the listing was for a lease, and the tenant signs the lease, but later defaults on the rent? Is the full commission still owed? The general answer is that the full commission is payable, even in a jurisdiction that has adopted the *Dobbs* rule. See Hildebrandt v. Anderson, 180 Or. App. 192, 42 P.3d 355 (2002). However, it is quite possible for the listing agreement to provide that the broker will be paid only if and as the installments are paid. See Ferrara v. Firsching, 91 Nev. 254, 533 P.2d 1351 (1975). From the seller's viewpoint, such a provision in the listing agreement with the broker is an excellent idea.

3.   *Licensing.* All U.S. states license and regulate the real estate brokerage industry. Typically there are two classes of licensees: brokers and salespersons. The salesperson is the entry level license. It requires no prior

experience and the passage of a fairly simple examination. The broker's license is harder to obtain. There's a requirement of prior experience as a salesperson, commonly for 3 to 5 years, and a much more difficult examination. The functional difference between the two types of license is this: salespersons must work only under the supervision of a broker, and any commissions must be paid to the broker (who will then divide them with salespersons as appropriate). See Maclay v. Idaho Real Estate Com'n, 300 P.3d 616 (Idaho 2012).

Acting as a broker without a license is forbidden, and may result in denial of any claim for a commission; see, e.g., Bus. Advisors, Inc. v. Chicago Title Ins. Co., 2013 WL 2325124 (Cal. App. 2013) (not published in Cal.Rptr.). In some states licensed attorneys may act as brokers, although they usually are not allowed to supervise other salespersons. However, the attorney who occupies such a dual role is in a tricky position; duties of confidentiality as a lawyer may well conflict with duties of disclosure as a broker.

4.   *Conflicts of interest.* Unless agreed to by all parties after full disclosure, conflicts of interest by a broker can give rise to private liability as well as public discipline from the state licensing body. The agent who causes loss to the principal by virtue of the conflict may lose the commission and be subjected to a judgment for damages. See, e.g., Meerdink v. Krieger, 15 Wash. App. 540, 550 P.2d 42 (1976).

The conflict of interest problem is remarkably pervasive, mainly because of the operation of multiple listing services. Suppose Broker #1 obtains a listing on B's house. Broker #2 sees the listing on the MLS and knows just the customer who would like to buy it. Broker #2 writes an offer, her customer signs it, and Broker #2 transmits the offer to Broker #1 for submission to the seller.

If the seller accepts the offer and the sale closes, the commission will be divided between the two brokers according to the bylaws or rules of the MLS or local custom. Splits of 50–50 or 60–40 are common.

On these facts, it is clear that Broker #1 is the seller's agent, but whose agent is Broker #2? Her commission is being paid by the seller, but her time and efforts have been spent largely with the buyer, and it is in that direction that her real loyalties probably lie. For example, if we could overhear all of her conversations, we would be much more likely to hear her say to the buyer, "I'll see if I can get the seller to come down $1,000," than to say to the seller, "I'll see if I can get the buyer to come up $1,000."

Is this a violation of Broker #2's fiduciary duty? If so, should that duty be redefined? Traditionally, the selling agent is considered a subagent of the listing agent, and hence an agent of the seller. Does any language in the Nebraska listing agreement bear on the issue? See generally Brown & Grohman, Real Estate Brokers: Shouldering New Burdens, Probate & Property, May/June 1997, at 14; Black, Proposed Alternatives to Traditional

Real Property Agency: Restructuring the Brokerage Relationship, 22 Real Est. L.J. 201 (1994).

5. *Agency disclosure requirements.* In a large number of states, statutes or regulations now require real estate brokers to disclose in writing whether they represent the buyer or seller. In the absence of a specific disclosure, many consumers are unaware of the traditional principle that the selling agent is a subagent of the seller. A 1983 Federal Trade Commission survey concluded that 72 percent of buyers believed that the selling brokers who helped them find property were representing them rather than the sellers. See Federal Trade Commission, The Residential Real Estate Brokerage Industry: A Staff Report by the Los Angeles Regional Office 69 (1983). Does the typical buyer know or care whom the agent represents? Does it really matter? See Brown, Grohman, & Valcarcel, Real Estate Brokerage: Recent Changes in Relationships and a Proposed Cure, 29 Creighton L. Rev. 25 (1995).

6. *Buyers' brokers.* There has been considerable growth in the use of "buyers' brokers" in residential real estate. How are such brokers compensated? Obviously most buyers are not eager to pay these brokers direct commissions; they assume that a "full" commission is already built into the price of the house and will be paid by the seller. In most cases, listing brokers concede that it is appropriate to split their commissions with selling brokers who represent buyers. Hence, the buyer is not "out of pocket" for the buyer's agent's commission. What happens if, after signing a contract to purchase, the buyer backs out of the transaction and no closing occurs. Under the *Dobbs* rule, the seller will owe no commission, so there is nothing to split with the buyer's broker. Should the buyer's broker be entitled to recover her or his split (say, 3 percent of the contract price) from the buyer directly? See Hamilton v. Hopkins, 834 So. 2d 695 (Miss. 2003) (buyer's broker entitled to commission from breaching buyer). Of course, the sale may not close for reasons other than a breach by the buyer. Perhaps the seller is unable to satisfy some of the contract's conditions, thus allowing the buyer to terminate the contract. Is the buyer's broker entitled to a commission, to be paid by the buyer? A typical buyer's broker agency agreement will say something like this:

> COMPENSATION. Broker's compensation is earned when, during the term of this agreement, Buyer contracts to acquire real property as specified in this agreement. Buyer will be responsible for paying Broker $_____ or ___% of the total purchase price, but will be credited with any amount Broker receives from a seller or a real estate licensee who is working with a seller.

Under this clause, if there is no "amount" received from the seller or the listing broker (because the closing never occurs), the buyer seems to be left with full liability for the commission. Moreover, the commission is earned, according to this clause, when the buyer "contracts to acquire real property," whether the contract is ever performed or not.

In RC Royal Development and Realty Corp. v. Standard Pacific Corp., 100 Cal. Rptr. 3d 115 (Cal. App. 2009), the buyer hired a buyer's broker and then signed a contract to purchase a condominium project that was under construction. The issuance of a certificate of occupancy by the local government was made a condition of the buyer's obligation to purchase the property. Due to construction delays, the certificate was not issued within the time frame allowed by the contract. The buyer, recognizing that condominium prices were now falling in the area, withdrew from the contract (as the buyer had a right to do). The brokerage agreement provided that a commission would be owed if the buyer acquired any "beneficial interest in the property." The court held that simply signing a contract of sale gave the buyer a "beneficial interest," and thus that the buyer owed the commission even though the buyer never acquired legal title to the property.

The similarity of these cases to the *Ellsworth Dobbs* issue is obvious. They seem to suggest that a buyer would be well-advised to protect against the risk of being liable for a commission to a buyer's broker if no closing occurs. Can you craft language that would modify the "Compensation" clause reproduced above to do so?

Suppose the Compensation clause above contained a sentence providing that "Broker's compensation will be paid at the time of closing." Would this language be sufficient to establish that, if there is no closing, no commission need be paid to the broker? By analogy, see the cases cited in Note 2 above.

7. *Other forms of representation.* It is theoretically possible for a broker to represent both the buyer and the seller quite explicitly. A number of states now expressly allow dual agency by statute or regulation.

> "[D]ual agency was, and is, perilous because it requires identical loyalties to parties with different, often opposite, wishes and needs. The dual agent must not violate the duty of loyalty to one party by fulfilling the duty of loyalty to the other. Brokers who inadvertently became dual agents have little chance of avoiding a breach of their duties. In particular, a dual agent must disclose the existence of the dual agency to both principals."

Brown & Grohman, supra note 4.

In Brown v. FSR Brokerage, Inc., 62 Cal. App. 4th 766, 72 Cal. Rptr. 2d 828 (1998), the broker was a dual agent but failed to disclose that fact to the seller, who believed that the agent represented only him. The agent told the buyer that he thought he could "talk down" the seller's price, and then proceeded to do so. The sale closed, and only at the closing was the dual agency disclosed to the seller. The court held that the agent could be held liable for damages to the seller on account of the failure to disclose.

Another novel form of representation now authorized in perhaps a dozen states is the "transaction broker" or "nonagent broker," who does not represent either party to the exclusion of the other, but has a duty to facilitate the transaction for both sides. Both dual agents and transaction brokers have a duty of evenhandedness toward the parties, and cannot disclose confidential information obtained from either party to the other. Beyond this duty of even-handedness, however, there are many uncertainties in the scope of duties of such brokers. Sieverling, The Changing Face of the Real Estate Professional: Keeping Pace, 63 Mo. L. Rev. 581 (1998); Mariea, Transaction Brokerage Enters the Playing Field for Real Estate Brokers and Licensees, J. Mo. Bar, July/Aug. 1999, at 196. Despite the duty of evenhandedness, dual agents and transaction brokers continue to be paid as a percentage of the selling price, which obviously gives them an economic incentive to maximize the price and thereby favor the seller. See Wilson, Nonagent Brokerage: Real Estate Agents Missing in Action, 52 Okla. L. Rev. 85 (1999).

8. *Duty to disclose material facts.* It has long been widely recognized that a broker has a duty to disclose to a buyer material defects known to the broker but unknown to and unobservable by the buyer. This is true even if the broker is the agent only of the seller. In Easton v. Strassburger, 152 Cal. App. 3d 90, 199 Cal. Rptr. 383 (1984), the court greatly extended this duty. The house for sale had been damaged by an earlier earthslide, and repairs would have cost several hundred thousand dollars. The agent did not disclose this fact to the buyer, but there was no direct evidence that the agent knew it. The court held the agent liable for damages anyway, holding that the agent had a duty "to conduct a reasonably competent and diligent inspection of the residential property listed for sale and to disclose to prospective purchasers all facts materially affecting the value or desirability of the property that such an investigation would reveal."

California real estate brokers were understandably exercised about *Easton.* In response to their lobbying efforts, in 1985 the California legislature revised the California Civil Code to "codify and make precise" the holding of *Easton,* and to provide "a definition of the duty of care found to exist" by that case.

Cal. Civ. Code § 2079

It is the duty of a real estate broker or sales person . . . [owed] to a prospective purchaser of residential real estate comprising one to four dwelling units, or a manufactured home * * * to conduct a reasonably competent and diligent visual inspection of the property offered for sale and to disclose to that prospective purchaser all facts materially affecting the value or desirability of the property that such an investigation would reveal * * * .

Cal. Civ. Code § 2079.2

The standard of care owed by a broker [under Section 2079] is * * * the degree of care that a reasonably prudent real estate licensee would exercise and is measured by the degree of knowledge through education, experience, and examination, required to obtain a license [as a broker or salesperson].

Under these statutory requirements, the scope of the inspection required does not include an inspection of areas that are normally inaccessible. Cal. Civ. Code § 2079.3. The statute imposes a two-year statute of limitations period that runs from the date of the purchaser's possession of the property. Cal. Civ. Code § 2079.4. Under Cal. Civ. Code § 2079.5, the statute expressly does not relieve the buyer "of the duty to exercise reasonable care to protect himself or herself, including those facts which are known to or within the diligent attention and observation of the buyer or a prospective buyer."

How do these statutory provisions assist brokers? Is the California approach a reasonable accommodation of the rights of purchasers and brokers? Where does it leave the buyer of nonresidential property?

9. The influence of Easton. The *Easton* decision, by imposing a duty of investigation on the broker, went farther than most recent cases. Cases holding the broker liable for affirmative statements that turn out to be false (even though the broker did not realize it at the time) are quite common. See, e.g., Shaffer v. Earl Thacker Co., 6 Haw. App. 188, 716 P.2d 163 (1986) (broker made incorrect statements about boundaries and encroachments). Contra, Hoffman v. Connall, 108 Wash. 2d 69, 736 P.2d 242 (1987). So are cases finding liability where the broker was silent in the face of actual knowledge of a material fact concerning the property. See, e.g., Strawn v. Canuso, 140 N.J. 43, 657 A.2d 420 (1995) (failure to disclose existence of nearby toxic waste dump); Hermansen v. Tasulis, 48 P.3d 235 (Utah 2002) (failure to disclose unstable soil). It is unlikely that a broker can escape this sort of liability by an exculpatory clause in the sale contract. See Syvrud v. Today Real Estate, Inc., 858 So. 2d 1125 (Fla. Ct. App. 2003).

However, courts outside California generally have been unwilling to hold brokers liable when they were silent about defects of which they had no actual knowledge, but that could have been found by inspection. See Blackmon v. First Real Estate Corp., 529 So. 2d 955 (Ala. 1988); Harkala v. Wildwood Realty, Inc., 200 Ill. App. 3d 447, 146 Ill. Dec. 232, 558 N.E.2d 195 (1990); Teter v. Old Colony Co., 190 W. Va. 711, 441 S.E.2d 728 (1994).

10. What must be disclosed? The duty to disclose is not necessarily limited to facts about the physical property itself. In Silverman v. Pitterman, 574 So. 2d 275 (Fla. App. 1991), a married couple obtained a divorce. The court's judgment ordered that their house be sold and the proceeds divided. At the husband's suggestion, they listed the house with a broker who (unbeknownst to the wife) had a romantic relationship with the husband's divorce lawyer. When the wife discovered this, she sued the broker, claiming a breach of fiduciary duty. The court agreed and held that she might recover both compensatory and punitive damages, and that the broker also might be required to forfeit the commission.

The agent's disclosure obligations may include financial matters. In Holmes v. Summer, 116 Cal. Rptr. 3d 419 (Cal. App. 2010), the agent knew that the property was overencumbered (or "under water") with mortgages that greatly exceeded the amount of the sale price. Hence, the seller could not complete the transaction unless the existing mortgage lenders were willing to accept less than the outstanding balances of their loans (a process known as a "short sale"), or unless the seller was willing and able to put nearly $400,000 cash into the transaction to make up the difference between the selling price and the encumbrances and expenses of sale. (Neither of these conditions was met.) The court held that the agent should have realized that these facts made it likely that the seller would breach the contract of sale, and had a duty to disclose them to the buyer before the buyer signed the contract. The agent's duty was not lessened by the fact that a title search would have revealed the existence of the mortgages.

The duty of disclosure can run in favor of a seller as well. In Lombardo v. Albu, 199 Ariz. 97, 14 P.3d 288 (2000), a buyer's broker was held liable for failing to disclose to the sellers adverse financial information about the buyer, actually known to the broker, that resulted in the buyer's being unable to qualify for a mortgage loan and therefore failing to close on the purchase.

However, the broker may not be held liable if the buyer misconstrues true information that the broker provides. In Saffie v. Schmeling, 224 Cal.App.4th 563 (Cal.App. 2014), the broker told the buyer in a 2006 transaction that the land had been certified as "buildable" under geological regulations, and provided the buyer with a 1986 report of the geologist so stating. The buyer assumed that the report was still valid, but the applicable regulations had changed and the land could no longer be built on. The court found that everything the broker said was true, and that he was not responsible for the buyer's mistaken assumptions.

B. THE STATUTE OF FRAUDS AND PART PERFORMANCE

No law says the parties must have a contract at all. If P is merrily walking down the street one day, spots V's house with a "For Sale" sign in the front yard, and decides she would like to buy it, she can simply knock on V's door and begin haggling with him about the price.[8] If they can agree, P can pull out her checkbook and write V a check, in return for which V can write a deed to the property (the back of an old envelope will do) and immediately hand it to P. Presto, the transaction is completed! Even here a purist might argue that there was an (oral) executory contract of sale for a few brief moments, but if so it was an exceedingly ephemeral and unimportant one.

In real life events seldom happen this way. Instead there is usually a rather detailed written agreement of sale, often filled in on a printed form. Considerable time—say, 30 to 90 days or more—commonly passes between the contract's execution and its performance at the "closing," at

---

[8] In this and the following sections, we use the feminine gender to describe the buyer and the masculine to describe the seller. —Eds.

which time V receives his money and P receives legal title by a deed to her.

Why the delay, and why the need for a detailed contract? Two reasons stand out:

1.   P wants to be certain that V really owns the property, and that V's title is "good" or "clear" or "marketable." This determination takes time and money, and P does not want to go to the trouble unless she is confident that V is committed to completing the sale at the agreed price.

title clearing

2.   P needs to borrow part (usually most) of the money needed to buy the house. Again, obtaining a loan involves time, trouble, and some expense. Moreover, most institutional lenders won't even consider P's application for a loan unless she has a signed contract of purchase.

financing

These are the two most pervasive reasons a contract and an "executory period" are needed. You may be able to think of many more. Here are a few possibilities:

3.   P needs time to sell her previous house or terminate her existing lease and to arrange to move her personal effects.

4.   V needs time to find another home and to arrange to buy or rent it.

5.   P is concerned about the physical condition of the house— the roof, plumbing, furnace, foundation, etc.—and wants an expert to inspect them and report to her.

You may think it odd that contract law is included in this course, given that you are probably taking, or may already have taken, a course labeled "Contracts." Of course, the standard contract doctrines—offer, acceptance, consideration, and so forth—apply equally to realty contracts. But real estate sales contracts have a number of unique features that justify separate treatment in a Property course. These features are often termed the law of "vendor and purchaser."

Types of contracts. As we begin to examine real estate sales contracts, it is important to recognize that there are two quite different types of contracts that are, used for very different purposes. The first type, described above and explored in some depth in this chapter, is usually termed a "short-term," "earnest-money," "deposit receipt," "binder," or "marketing" contract. Its function is simply to permit the parties to prepare for the transfer of title by making the arrangements described above. It usually provides for the closing—the delivery of a deed and the payment of the purchase price—to occur within a few weeks or months after the contract is signed. Usually, the buyer takes possession on the closing date. The buyer will typically give the seller some "earnest money"—anywhere from a few hundred dollars to as much as 10% of the purchase price—at the time the contract is signed. If the seller is to accept something other than cash for part of the purchase price, such as the buyer's promissory note secured by a mortgage, this fact will be mentioned in the earnest money contract, but the note and mortgage themselves will be separate documents, usually signed at or just prior to the closing.

The second type of sales contract is often called a "real estate installment contract," or (especially in the Midwest) a "contract for deed." It contemplates that the buyer will go into possession immediately, make payments to the seller on a regular basis (say, monthly) over a long time period (say, ten to twenty-five years), and finally receive a deed when the last installment is paid. The seller is financing the purchase and the contract is being used much like a mortgage, to secure the buyer's obligation to pay the installments as they fall due. See Nelson, The Contract for Deed as a Mortgage: The Case for the Restatement Approach, 1998 B.Y.U. L. Rev. 1111.

This latter type of contract presents different problems than the earnest-money contract. It is, in effect, a "mortgage substitute." Unfortunately, courts sometimes cite cases dealing with one type of real estate sales contract to attempt to resolve litigation dealing with the other type. The results are sometimes satisfactory and sometimes disastrously confusing. Be careful not to fall into this trap.

The requirement of a writing. The great majority of real estate sales contracts are in writing. This is almost invariably so when a real estate broker is involved, for two reasons. First, the broker does not want the deal to "fall through," and an experienced broker knows that there is more pressure on the parties, both legally and psychologically, to complete the transaction if the contract is written.

Second, most printed form contracts are prepared by brokers or their trade associations. Such printed form contracts often include clauses that reconfirm the seller's obligation to pay the sales commission and allow the broker to recover it out of the "earnest money" deposit paid by the buyer if the buyer reneges on the deal and the deposit money is forfeited. Never mind that the payment of a commission has nothing directly to do with the agreement for sale between the buyer and seller; brokers find the clause useful anyway. A typical clause, which tracks some of the material contained in Paragraphs 10 and 13 of the Nebraska listing agreement reproduced at the beginning of this chapter, might read as follows:

> Seller agrees to pay a commission of ___% of the sales price or $_____ to agent _____. Seller assigns to Agent a portion of sales proceeds equal to commission. The closing agent shall

apportion the commission between listing and selling agents as specified in the listing, or as specified by selling agent if there is no written listing. If earnest money is retained as liquidated damages, any advance by Agent for Buyer or Seller shall be reimbursed and the balance shall be divided equally between Seller and Agent.

A legally binding sale contract can be very brief, but most printed form contracts are several pages in length and cover a variety of "standard" issues. The following form is typical, if a bit simplified.

Contract for the Purchase and Sale of
Real Estate (Single-family Residence)

THIS CONTRACT, made and entered into this _____ day of _____, 20___ by and between _____("the Seller") and _____("the Buyer").

WITNESSETH: For and in consideration of the mutual obligations of the parties hereto, the Seller hereby agrees to sell and convey unto the Buyer and the Buyer agrees to purchase from Seller, upon the terms and conditions hereinafter set forth, the following described real estate situated in the County of _____, State of _____, to wit:

[INSERT LEGAL DESCRIPTION HERE]

[LIST ANY PERSONAL PROPERTY TO BE INCLUDED WITH THE REAL ESTATE.]

PRICE. The price for said property shall be $_____, to be paid by Buyer as follows: $_____ at the time of the execution and delivery of this contract, the receipt of which is hereby acknowledged by the Seller, and which is deposited with the Seller, as earnest money, and as a part of the purchase price and consideration for this agreement; and by delivery to Seller of the remaining balance of the purchase price, if any, in cash or by certified check.

In the event of a material breach of this contract by the Buyer, the Seller may retain the earnest money deposit as liquidated damages for the Buyer's breach, or in the alternative may waive the right to liquidated damages and obtain such other remedies as are available in law or equity.

TITLE QUALITY. Title shall be marketable of record, subject to existing street and utility easements, the lien of the current year's property taxes and any special assessments, zoning ordinances and codes, and covenants, conditions, or restrictions (CC & Rs) that do not materially affect the value of the property for use as a residence.

TITLE APPROVAL. Seller shall, within ten days after the execution of this contract, obtain and forward to Buyer a preliminary title report on the property issued by a title insurance company doing business in

_____. Within ten days after receipt of that report, Buyer will notify Seller in writing of any objections to matters shown thereon which, in Buyer's opinion, make title unmarketable as defined above. Seller shall within five days of receipt of such objections notify Buyer whether Seller elects to (1) terminate the contract at that time and refund Buyer's earnest money deposit, or (2) attempt to cure the title matters to which Buyer has objected. If Seller elects to attempt to cure such title matters, Seller shall effect such cure before the date of closing. In the event of Seller's failure to effect such cure within that time, Buyer may elect (1) to terminate the contract and receive a return of Buyer's earnest money deposit, or (2) to complete the purchase with an abatement of the purchase price in an amount equivalent to the reduction in value of the property resulting from the title defects objected to.

TITLE INSURANCE. Seller will provide Buyer at closing or immediately after closing with an ALTA owner's policy of title insurance, showing marketable title in Buyers subject only to the matters mentioned above.

FINANCING. The Buyer's obligation to purchase the property under this contract is conditioned upon the Buyer's obtaining of a [conventional] [FHA] [VA] mortgage loan in the amount of $_____ payable over a period of not less than ___ years and bearing interest at a rate of not more than ___ percent and ___ origination fee (points) payable by the Buyer. Said loan shall carry ❏ a fixed interest rate ❏ an adjustable interest rate which adjusts on a _____-year basis. The Buyer agrees to use reasonable efforts to obtain such a loan. In the event Buyer is unable to obtain a commitment from an institutional lender in _____ County for such a loan by _____, 20__, Buyer, at Buyer's option, may terminate this contract by notice to Seller on or before that date, and Buyer's earnest money deposit shall immediately be refunded. If Seller is given no notice by the stated date of Buyer's inability to obtain a loan commitment, this condition shall be deemed satisfied.

SELLER DISCLOSURE and BUYER'S INSPECTION. With seven days after acceptance of this contract, Seller will complete and submit to the Buyer the Seller's Disclosure Form attached to this contract. Buyer may, at Buyer's expense, obtain such inspections, engineering reports, and other analyses of the property as Buyer shall deem desirable. In the event any information in the Seller's Disclosure Form, or any inspection or report obtained by Buyer, shall disclose conditions unacceptable to Buyer, Buyer shall notify Seller within 21 days after acceptance of this contract of Buyer's objection to such conditions, together with a copy of any inspection or report obtained by Buyer disclosing those conditions. Any objection shall be made in good faith and shall specify the specific condition or conditions objected to. Seller shall notify Buyer within five days after receipt of such objections whether Seller elects (1) to terminate the contract at that time and refund Buyer's earnest money deposit, or (2) to cure, at Seller's expense, the conditions to which Buyer has objected. If Seller elects to attempt to cure such conditions, Seller shall be obligated to effect such cure before the date of closing.

Buyer shall indemnify and hold Seller harmless from any liability, costs (including reasonable attorneys' fees), liens, and damages to Seller or other occupants of the property arising from Buyer's inspections, studies, and analyses of the property, and the entry onto the property of Buyer or persons employed or contracted by Buyer. Following each entry on the property by such persons, Buyer shall leave the property in substantially the same condition as it was in prior to the entry and inspection.

[ALTERNATIVE 1] SELLER WARRANTIES. Seller warrants that: (a) Seller has received no claim or notice of any building or zoning violation concerning the property which has not or will not be remedied prior to closing; (b) there is, to the best of Seller's knowledge, no action pending by any governmental authority to take the property by power of eminent domain; (c) all obligations against the property including taxes, assessments, liens and other encumbrances of any nature shall be paid or brought current on or before closing; and (d) the plumbing, heating, air conditioning and ventilating systems, electrical system, and appliances shall be in satisfactory working condition, and there will be no leaks on the roof or basement, at the time of closing.

[ALTERNATIVE 2] NO WARRANTIES BY SELLER. Buyer acknowledges that, with the exception of the Seller's Disclosure Form attached to this contract, neither Seller nor any agent or broker has made any representations, guaranties, warranties, or covenants of any kind, express or implied, relative to the property, its use or value, or the transaction contemplated by this contract, including without limitation the condition or quality of the property or the improvements on it, compliance with zoning ordinances, building or housing codes, or compliance with other federal, state, or local law. Buyer agrees to take the property "as is," and subject to all faults and conditions existing thereon.

RISK OF LOSS. All risk of loss or damage to the property shall be borne by the Seller until closing. In the event there is loss or damage to the property between the date of this contract and the date of closing, by reason of fire, vandalism, flood, earthquake, or acts of God, and the cost to repair such damage shall exceed ten percent (10%) of the purchase price of the property, Buyer may, at Buyer's option, either proceed with this transaction if Seller agrees in writing to repair or replace damaged property before the date of closing, or declare this Agreement null and void and receive a refund of Buyer's earnest money deposit. If damage to property is less than ten percent (10%) of the purchase price and Seller agrees in writing to repair or replace and does actually repair and replace damaged property prior to the agreed closing date (or such additional time period as the parties may mutually agree upon), this transaction shall proceed as agreed; but if Seller fails so to agree in writing, Buyer may declare this Agreement null and void and receive a refund of Buyer's earnest money deposit.

ADJUSTMENTS AT CLOSING. At the date of closing property taxes and special assessments for the current year shall be prorated between Buyer and Seller. Seller will pay the cost of the owner's policy of title insurance and any applicable transfer tax. Buyer will pay the cost of recording the deed and the deed of trust, and will pay all costs associated with Buyer's mortgage loan applications and financing. The escrow or closing fee and all other expenses of sale shall be shared equally by Buyer and Seller.

CLOSING. Closing shall occur, and legal title shall pass by warranty deed to Buyer on the ___ day of _____, 20__ at 2 o'clock pm or at such other time and place as the parties may mutually agree. Time is of the essence in all provisions of this contract.

POSSESSION. Possession shall be delivered to the Buyer at the time of closing.

REAL ESTATE COMMISSIONS. The Buyer and Seller hereby represent to one another that neither has contracted for representation by any real estate broker in connection with this sale, and each will indemnify and hold harmless the other from any liability for any real estate commission for which he or she has contracted in connection with this sale.

COMPLETE AGREEMENT. This contract constitutes the entire agreement between Buyer and Seller with regard to the property, and supersedes and replaces all prior discussions, negotiations, and agreements between them, whether written or oral.

IN WITNESS WHEREOF, the Buyer has executed this agreement on the day and year first above written and acknowledges receipt of one copy of this contract.

[EXPIRATION OF OFFER (to be used if this is an offer to purchase)]. The Buyer's offer to purchase as set forth herein shall automatically expire on the _____ day of _____ at 12:00 noon if not accepted by Seller or withdrawn by Buyer prior to that time.

Buyer._____

Date _____ Time _____

Seller hereby accepts the foregoing offer.

Seller _____

Date _____ Time _____

Even real estate brokers do not always do a thorough or careful job of writing the sales contract. Often they are in a hurry to have the sales contract signed by the parties before the buyer or the seller has second thoughts about the terms of the deal. Sometimes a deal is so complex that it is beyond the capacity of the parties to describe clearly. When no broker or lawyer is involved, contracts tend to be even sketchier and sloppier. There may be no writing at all, or someone who should sign the sales contract may fail to do so, or a key term may be left blank.

JOHNSTON v. CURTIS
Court of Appeals of Arkansas, 2000
70 Ark. App. 195, 16 S.W.3d 283

BIRD, JUDGE

Appellants Gerald Johnston and Bebe Dare Johnston bring this appeal from the Circuit Court of Lonoke County contending that the court erred in finding that the parties orally modified a written real estate contract and that their nonperformance of the contract was not excused. Appellees Glen Curtis and Deanna Curtis have cross-appealed, stating that the court should have awarded them "expectancy" and punitive damages. We affirm the decision of the trial court on direct appeal and cross-appeal.

On October 9, 1997, the parties entered into a written real estate contract, whereby the Curtises offered to sell and the Johnstons agreed to buy a house in Cabot for $114,000. A real estate agent was not involved. Under the terms of the contract, the transaction was subject to the Johnstons obtaining a home loan of $102,600, which was 90 percent of the purchase price. Specifically, the contract provided that the Johnstons' obligation was subject to:

> The Buyer's ability to obtain a loan secured by the property in an amount no less than $102,600, with Jan Turbeville at Arkansas Fidelity Mortgage Co., payable over a period of not less than ____ Years, with interest not to exceed ____% per annum.

Deanna Curtis testified that after the Johnstons told her and her husband that they had been pre-approved for their loan, the Curtises purchased a home in Searcy, and they moved out of the home in Cabot after they signed the contract with the Johnstons. However, because the house appraised for only $110,000, the mortgage company denied the loan to the Johnstons. Thereafter, the parties entered into an oral agreement whereby the Johnstons agreed to buy and the Curtises agreed to sell the house for $110,000. On November 3, 1997, after the lease on the

Johnstons' home in Hot Springs expired but before the parties closed on the house in Cabot, the Johnstons paid the Curtises $500, took "early possession" of, and moved into, the home in Cabot. Deanna Curtis testified that she and her husband allowed the Johnstons to move into the home before closing only after they had made "some kind of a show of good faith." The Johnstons tendered a check for $500 to the Curtises for the Curtises to hold until closing.

Jan Turbeville, a mortgage loan originator, testified that she had a difficult time obtaining a loan for the Johnstons, but that a loan for ninety percent of the purchase price was finally approved at the reduced price of $110,000, and the transaction was set for closing on November 17. She testified that when the loan was approved, the Johnstons were informed of the terms. She also testified that one of the terms of the loan was that Bebe Dare Johnston's name would not be on the title of the home, but that the title of the home would be in Gerald Johnston's name only. She also testified that during the initial meeting that she had with the Johnstons, Gerald Johnston did not put any parameters on the type of financing that he would accept. In addition, she testified that he accepted the terms of the final loan for which he was approved. She stated that had Gerald Johnston not approved the terms of the loan, she would have neither set a closing date nor ordered any of the documents needed for closing.

Deanna Curtis testified that the parties were to close on the house on November 17, but that they were informed that day that the Johnstons had refused to close. Thereafter, the Curtises demanded that the Johnstons vacate the premise. The Curtises then listed the home with a realtor and sold the property in March 1998 for $100,000. Deanna Curtis testified that after deducting the six-percent commission, they received $94,000, less closing costs.

Gerald Johnston testified that the parties had entered into a real estate contract, but stated that the terms of the agreement were that he purchase the home for $110,000 if he could obtain a loan at an acceptable rate of interest and acceptable closing costs. He stated that he had been led to believe by a mortgage lender that the interest rate would be between nine and ten percent. However, he admitted that the written real estate contract did not state that the offer was contingent upon obtaining a loan with an interest rate between nine and ten percent. Johnston testified that he and his wife were originally set to close on the house on November 8 or 9, and that they showed up at the office to close, but that the papers were not ready. He said that he was told on November 17 that the closing would take place that afternoon, but at that time the mortgage company did not know the amount of the closing costs or the interest rate. He said that someone by the name of Brown called him later that afternoon and told him the interest rate and the amount of the closing costs and that they were beyond what he had discussed. Gerald Johnston told Brown that he and his wife were not interested. He said that he was quoted an interest rate of 10.75%, but that it was too high and that he was only interested in purchasing the house if he would obtain an acceptable interest rate. Gerald Johnston also stated that he was never informed, until the trial, that his wife was not going to be named on the deed, and he said that he would not have purchased the home without her name being included on the deed. He denied that Turbeville had several conversations with him concerning the transaction. Gerald Johnston stated that the $500 check he wrote to the Curtises when they moved into the home was not earnest money, but was given to cover any damages that they might cause to the home. He stated that he stopped payment on the check because the Curtises were not acting in good faith.

The trial court found that the parties had orally modified their agreement to reduce the price from $114,000 to $110,000, but subject to all the other terms of the original contract, that the oral modification to the contract was not subject to the requirements of the statute of frauds, and that the Johnstons had breached the contract by their failure to close. Damages were awarded to the Curtises in the amount of $10,000, representing the difference between the modified contract price and the amount for which the Curtises later sold the house to someone else.

For appellants' first point on appeal, they argue that the court erred in finding that the parties had orally modified the written contract and that the oral modification was not barred by the statute of frauds. Appellants argue that there was not a meeting of the minds between the parties because they had not agreed on an acceptable loan amount, interest rate or closing costs. In the alternative, they argue that even if an oral contract existed, it violated the statute of frauds.

A meeting of the minds, or what is more commonly known as an objective indicator of agreement, see Fort Smith Serv. Fin. Corp. v. Parrish, 302 Ark. 299, 789 S.W.2d 723 (1990), does not depend upon the subjective understanding of the parties, but instead requires only objective manifestations of mutual assent for the formation of a contract. Hagans v. Haines, 64 Ark. App. 158, 984 S.W.2d 41 (1998). The meeting of the minds is essential to the formation of a contract and is determined by the expressed or manifested intention of the parties. Id. The question of whether a contract has been made must be determined from a consideration of the parties' expressed or manifested intention determined from a consideration of their words and acts. Id.

The Johnstons argue that the oral contract between the parties provided that they would purchase the home for $110,000 if they were given an acceptable interest rate and closing costs. After a consideration of the parties' words and acts, it is clear that the contract was modified from $114,000 to $110,000. Through their testimony, both parties admit that they changed the terms of the agreement from the purchase prices of $114,000 to $110,000. They also state that those were the only terms changed. The original real estate contract was silent as to what would constitute an acceptable rate of interest or acceptable closing costs. In addition, Turbeville testified that the Johnstons did not discuss with her what interest rate or amount of closing costs would be acceptable to them.

The Curtises argue that the statute of frauds is an affirmative defense and that the Johnstons are barred from arguing it as a defense because they did not specifically plead such in their answer. While it is true that the statute of frauds is an affirmative defense, see Ark. R. Civ. P. 8, the court in this case amended the pleadings to conform to the proof. Arkansas Rule of Civil Procedure 15(b) states, "When issues not raised by the pleadings are tried by express or implied consent of the parties, they shall be treated in all respects as if they had been raised in the pleadings." In the case at bar, after the Curtises presented their case, the Johnstons made a motion to dismiss the case, the court denied the motion, stating that the pleadings were amended to conform to the proof, and it considered the issues of the applicability of the statute of frauds. Therefore, even though it was not raised in the Johnstons' answer, this court can address the defense of the statute of frauds.

A contract for the sale of land comes within the statute of frauds and must be in writing to be enforceable. Ark. Code Ann. § 4–59–101 (Repl. 1996). A material modification of a contract comes within the statute of frauds and must be in writing in order to be valid and binding. Shumpert v. Arko Telephone Communications Inc., 318 Ark. 840, 888 S.W.2d 646 (1994). Such a contract cannot be modified in essential parts by parol agreement so as to be valid against a plea of invalidity under the statute of frauds. Id. See also Arkmo Lumber Co. v. Cantrell, 159 Ark. 445, 252 S.W. 901 (1923); J.W. Davis v. Patel, 32 Ark. App. 1, 794 S.W.2d 158 (1990). The court found that the statute of frauds did not apply in this case because a written agreement may be modified by an oral agreement. We disagree, but we affirm the court because, even though the trial court applied the wrong reason, it reached the correct result. Van Camp v. Van Camp, 333 Ark. 320, 969 S.W.2d 184 (1998).

In the case at bar, the statute of frauds is not applicable because of the Johnstons' part performance of the contract. In order to remove an oral agreement from the statute of frauds, it is necessary to prove both the making of the oral agreement and its part performance by clear and convincing evidence. Langston v. Langston, 3 Ark. App. 286, 625 S.W.2d 554 (1981). A requirement that the evidence be clear and convincing does not mean that the evidence be uncontradicted. Freeman v. Freeman, 20 Ark. App. 12, 722 S.W.2d 877 (1987). Partial performance of a contract by payment of a part of the purchase price and placing a buyer in possession of land pursuant to an agreement of sale and purchase is sufficient to take the contract out of the statute of frauds. Sossamon v. Davis, 271 Ark. 156, 607 S.W.2d 405 (1980). In the case at bar, the parties orally modified the contract by changing the purchase price from $114,000 to $110,000. The Johnstons admit that they took possession of the home, and they admit to tendering a check to the Curtises for $500. In addition, Deanna Curtis testified that when the Johnstons requested to take possession of the home prior to closing, she and her husband asked the Johnstons to show their good faith by tendering the check for $500 before they allowed the Johnstons to take early possession of the home. The Johnstons' acts of taking possession of the property and paying a portion of the purchase price are sufficient to take the oral modification to the contract out of the statute of frauds.

For appellants' second point on appeal, they argue that the court erred in not finding that the contract between the parties was subject to conditions precedent that appellants obtain acceptable financing and acceptable closing costs. In addition, they argue that because Mrs. Johnston's name was not going to appear on the deed, another condition of their contract was not satisfied. They contend that because all of these conditions precedent were not satisfied, their failure to perform was excused.

Whether a provision of a contract amounts to a condition precedent is generally dependent on what the parties intended, as adduced from the contract itself. Stacy v. Williams, 38 Ark. App. 192, 834 S.W.2d 156 (1992). When the terms of a written contract are ambiguous and susceptible to more than one interpretation, extrinsic evidence is permitted to establish the intent of the parties and the meaning of the contract then becomes a question of fact. Id. Furthermore, evidence of a parol agreement that a written agreement is being delivered conditionally constitutes an exception to the parol evidence rule. Id.

For this argument, the Johnstons rely on Stacy v. Williams, supra. However, that case is distinguishable from the one at bar because in Stacy, the parties made obtaining financing a condition precedent to the contract, and the appellees were never approved for any financing. In the case at bar, the Johnstons were approved for financing, but refused to close because they found the rate and the closing costs unacceptable. However, the original contract stated only that the Johnstons would receive a loan for $102,600, which was ninety percent of the purchase price. Although the contract form that the parties used contained a blank space where a limitation on the interest rate of their loan could have been inserted, it was left blank. The contract contained no mention of any limitation in the amount of the closing costs.

The Johnstons also argue that they should be excused from performing the contract because Mrs. Johnston's name was not going to be on the deed. However, the Johnstons did not become aware of that fact until the day of the trial, more than a year after they refused to perform the contract. They cannot rely on a fact of which they were unaware at the time of their breach as an excuse for their failure to perform. See Barbara Oil Co. v. Patrick Petroleum Co., 1 Kan. App. 2d 437, 566 P.2d 389 (1977).

The Curtises have cross-appealed, contending that the court erred in not awarding them special and punitive damages. The court found that the Johnstons had breached the contract, and it awarded the Curtises $10,000, which represented the difference between the $110,000 purchase price agreed upon between the two parties and the $100,000 sale price that the Curtises accepted from another buyer several months later. The Curtises argue that they should also have been awarded damages for the $6,000 realtor's commission fee that they paid when their house eventually sold, that they should recover damages for interest on the mortgage, as well as taxes, hazard insurance and mortgage insurance that they were obligated to pay on their Cabot house until it was eventually sold, and that they should recover the rent they expended on their new residence in Searcy up until the time the Cabot house was sold.

The measure of damages for a vendee's breach of an executory contract for the sale of land is the difference between the contract price of the land and its market value at the time of the breach, less the portion of the purchase price already paid. Williams v. Cotten, 14 Ark. App. 80, 684 S.W.2d 837 (1985) (citing McGregor v. Echols, 153 Ark. 128, 239 S.W. 736 (1922)). In *McGregor*, the court wrote:

> In actions against a vendee on a contract for the purchase of real estate, we had supposed it to be a well settled rule that when a party agreed to purchase real estate at a certain stipulated price and subsequently refuses to perform his contract, the loss in the bargain constitutes the measure of damages, and that is the difference between the price fixed in the contract and the salable value of the land at the time the contract was to be executed.

153 Ark. at 132, 239 S.W. at 736.

The court in *Williams v. Cotten*, supra, went on to state that the general rule does not prevent a party from ever recovering other damages flowing directly from a breach, and cited the expenses of abstracts of title and title opinions as examples of expenses that might be incurred in preparation for the sale for which a seller might recover damages. But the court specifically excluded expenses connected with the resale to third parties, such as a real estate commission, monthly house payments, and utilities. The court in *Williams v. Cotton* found that these types of damages were not directly connected with a party's breached sale and were remote and speculative in that the ultimate or total amount for these items depends solely upon when the party consummated a resale. Because the Curtises were awarded the difference between the contract price with the Johnstons and the amount for which the Curtises eventually sold their Cabot house, we do not find that the Curtises are entitled to any other damages.

Regarding the Curtises's argument on cross-appeal that they should recover punitive damages, their complaint contained no prayer for punitive damages, they made no argument in the trial court that punitive damages should be awarded, and no authority is cited to this court why punitive damages should be awarded in an action for breach of contract. We do not consider arguments made for the first time on appeal, Dobie v. Rogers, 339 Ark. 242, 5 S.W.3d 30 (1999), or arguments not supported by convincing authority, National Bank of Commerce v. Dow Chem. Co., 338 Ark. 752, 1 S.W.3d 443 (1999).

Affirmed on direct appeal and on cross-appeal.

NOTES AND QUESTIONS

1.   *What sort of writing?* The Arkansas Court of Appeals says, "A contract for the sale of land comes within the statute of frauds and must be in writing to be enforceable." But that is not quite accurate. The Arkansas Statute of Frauds, which is entirely typical, states:

Ark. Code Ann. § 4–59–101

Unless the agreement, promise, or contract, *or some memorandum or note thereof*, upon which an action is brought is made in writing and signed by the party to be charged therewith, or signed by some other person properly authorized by the person sought to be charged, no action shall be brought to charge any * * * person upon any contract for the sale of lands, tenements, or hereditaments, or any interest in or concerning them.

Thus, putting the contract in writing is only one way of satisfying the statute's demands. Any "memorandum" that contains the necessary information about the contract and is properly signed will do; it does not have to be the contract itself. The writing will suffice even though:

(a) it is a letter, a check, or some other type of document not drawn for the purpose of memorializing the contract. See Collins v. Morris, 122 Md. App. 764, 716 A.2d 384 (1998) (will executed by vendor); Putt v. City of Corinth, 579 So. 2d 534 (Miss.1991) (minutes of city utilities commission); Hines v. Tripp, 263 N. C. 470, 139 S.E.2d 545 (1965) (exchange of letters); Timberlake v. Heflin, 180 W. Va. 644, 379 S.E.2d 149 (1989) (complaint filed in divorce action); Richardson v. Schaub, 796 P.2d 1304 (Wyo. 1990) (financial statement filed with

Department of HUD); Annot., 9 A.L.R. 4th 1009 (1981). Indeed, "almost any form of writing will satisfy the statute of frauds, including receipts, letters, record books, or computer entries"; McClare v. Rocha, 86 A.3d 22 (Me. 2014).

(b) it consists of several related documents which can be tied together by the court to embody, in toto, the necessary elements. See Rohlfing v. Tomorrow Realty & Auction Co., 528 So. 2d 463 (1988); Pee Dee Oil Co. v. Quality Oil Co., 80 N. C. App. 219, 341 S.E.2d 113 (1986).

(c) it has been destroyed prior to trial, or is otherwise unavailable for introduction into evidence, if there is credible proof that it once existed. See Reed v. Hess, 239 Kan. 46, 716 P.2d 555 (1986); Brawley v. Brawley, 87 N. C. App. 545, 361 S.E.2d 759 (1987).

(d) it was written long after the contract was formed.

(e) although signed by one party, it has never been delivered to the other party. See D'Angelo v. Schultz, 306 Or. 504, 760 P.2d 866 (1988).

(f) the person seeking to enforce the contract did not know the writing existed until after the litigation was commenced. See Smith v. McClam, 289 S.C. 452, 346 S.E.2d 720 (1986).

The signature requirement also is interpreted fairly loosely. It need not be handwritten; any written identification of the party, signifying his or her assent, will do. See, e.g. Hessenthaler v. Farzin, 388 Pa. Super. 37, 564 A.2d 990 (1989) (mailgram was a "signed writing"). Cf. Durham v. Harbin, 530 So. 2d 208 (Ala. 1988) (printed letterhead and typed name of seller do not suffice as a "signature" unless the seller placed or used them "for the purpose of authenticating the writing as binding on him"). All of the owners must sign (assuming that the contract is for the sale of the entire property, and not merely a fractional interest in it); see Johnson v. Cook, 167 S.W.3d 258 (Mo. App. 2005).

2.   *Electronic communication.* In 2000 Congress enacted the Electronic Records in Global and National Commerce Act (popularly called "E-Sign"), which makes a major and preemptive modification of the states' statutes of frauds:

15 U.S.C. § 7001

Notwithstanding any statute, regulation, or other rule of law, * * * with respect to any transaction in or affecting interstate or foreign commerce—

(1) a signature, contract, or other record relating to such transaction may not be denied legal effect, validity, or enforceability solely because it is in electronic form; and

(2) a contract relating to such transaction may not be denied legal effect, validity, or enforceability solely because an electronic signature or electronic record was used in its formation.

Under E-Sign, the term "electronic signature" means an electronic sound, symbol, or process, attached to or logically associated with a contract or other record and executed or adopted by a person with the intent to sign the record. 15 U.S.C. § 7006(5). Similar language appears in the Uniform Electronic Transactions Act (UETA), promulgated in 1999 and enacted in nearly all states. Under E-Sign and UETA, it is perfectly clear that an enforceable contract of sale can result from an exchange of faxes, texts, or e-mails. See McClare v. Rocha, 86 A.3d 22 (Me. 2014).

3. *What must the writing contain?* The Statute of Frauds does not require the writing to include the entire contract, but only its "essential" terms. This means identification of the parties and a description of the land to be sold, along with words indicating that a sale is intended. Most (but not all) courts require that the price be stated. See MacThompson Realty, Inc. v. City of Nashua, 993 A.2d 773 (N.H. 2010) (price is essential, but may be fixed by a future appraisal). Cf. Pettigrew v. Collins, 539 S.E.2d 214 (Ga.App. 2000) (contract that provided for sale for "appraised value" without specifying a method of appraisal held ambiguous and unenforceable). If part of the price is to be paid in installments or represented by a note and mortgage, the writing may be deemed insufficient if it does not spell out the details of payment. See Trotter v. Allen, 285 Ala. 521, 234 So. 2d 287 (1970); de Vaux v. Westwood Baptist Church, 953 So. 2d 677 (Fla. App. 2007).

Courts usually will assume that the price is to be paid in cash if there is no contrary statement, see Busching v. Griffin, 465 So. 2d 1037 (Miss. 1985), and they will assume that the closing is to occur within a reasonable time if the writing contains no agreed date. see Guel v. Bullock, 127 Ill. App. 3d 36, 82 Ill. Dec. 264, 468 N.E.2d 811 (1984). The remedy sought may bear on the court's attitude. Specific performance is usually thought to demand greater specificity than damages. See Booras v. Uyeda, 295 Or. 181, 666 P.2d 791 (1983); ULTA §§ 2–201(a), 2–202.

The identification of the land is a frequent point of dispute. Technical legal descriptions are sometimes not used because it would be too time-consuming or bothersome to obtain them. Most courts find street addresses to be adequate if the city and state are given and there is no ambiguity. See, e.g., Park West Village, Inc. v. Avise, 714 P.2d 1137, 1141 (Utah 1986); French v. Bank of New York Mellon, 729 F.3d 17 (1st Cir. 2013). The use of street addresses is not a good practice, however, because they are often quite ambiguous as land descriptors. See, e.g., Boyer v. Sinclair & Rush, Inc., 67 S.W.3d 627 (Mo. Ct. App. 2002) (contract contained a single street address but also described two parcels of land known by two addresses); Maryland State Housing Co. v. Fish, 208 Md. 331, 118 A.2d 491 (1955) (property was a double house on a single parcel of land, known by two distinct street addresses).

Some courts are quite strict, refusing to enforce vague land descriptions. See Calvary Temple Assembly of God v. Lossman, 200 Ill. App. 3d 102, 146 Ill. Dec. 122, 557 N.E.2d 1309 (1990) ("the residence which [purchaser] occupies on the subject property" held to be an insufficient description because it was unclear how much land or other structures around the home were to be included); Cousar v. Shepherd-Will, Inc., 300 S.C. 366, 387 S.E.2d 723 (App. 1990) ("5 acres land adjoining property owned by the purchaser" held unenforceable). Washington and Idaho are perhaps the most strict jurisdictions in the nation, requiring an accurate and complete legal description, and rejecting entirely the use of street addresses. See Ray v. Frasure, 200 P.3d 1174 (Idaho 2009); Martin v. Seigel, 35 Wash. 2d 223, 212 P.2d 107 (1949). See generally Annot., 73 A.L.R. 4th 135; ULTA § 1–312.

Sometimes a court will consider existing fence lines or other ground markings in interpreting an otherwise vague description. In Schreck v. T & C. Sanderson Farms, Inc., 37 P.3d 510 (Colo. Ct. App. 2001), the contract contained a clear description of a parcel, but then stated "excluding the house and out buildings" without defining the excluded land. The court nonetheless enforced the contract, holding that the contract "sufficiently described a specific parcel of land that was set off by fences and the [sellers] had farmed for the 1997 growing season." Is this a fair application of the Statute of Frauds?

An alternative method of describing the land to be sold was explained by the Texas Court of Appeals as follows:

> Land is identified with reasonable certainty whenever the two-part test enunciated in *Pickett v. Bishop*, 148 Tex. 207, 223 S.W.2d 222 (1949) is satisfied. Under *Pickett*, land is identified with reasonable certainty when: (1) the contract contains a "statement of ownership" such as "my property," "my land," or "owned by me"; and (2) it is shown by extrinsic evidence that the party to be charged owns only one tract of land fitting the property description in the contract.

Moudy v. Manning, 82 S.W.3d 726 (Tex. App. 2002). For example, the phrases "stable property" and "3.78 Acre tract" were sufficient where the vendor only owned one tract meeting those descriptors; Dittman v. Cerone, 2013 WL 5970356 (Tex. App. 2013).

A reference to a county tax map or an existing survey, even one that has not been recorded, may well suffice; see Nguyen v. Yovan, 317 S.W.3d 261 (Tex. App. 2009). But a description by reference to a survey will not suffice if the survey has not been completed when the contract is signed; Min Quin Shao v. Corley, 95 So. 3d 14 (Ala. Civ. App. 2012).

The writer of the following letter owned a cottage on Rabbit Bay. Does her letter contain the "essential" elements to satisfy the statute? See Zurcher v. Herveat, 238 Mich. App. 267, 605 N.W.2d 329 (1999).

Dear Diane & Jim,

I have decided to sell Rabbit Bay. I had it appraised last summer. It was valued at $59,900, so that's what I'm asking. I promised you first chance. Please let me know if you're interested, if possible by July 5. I want to sell this summer. If you aren't interested, I want to get it on the market fast.

Love Barb

Among the items that need *not* be included in the writing are the date and place of closing, provisions for apportionment of property taxes, a statement as to the type of deed to be delivered, an acknowledgment before a notary public, and the signatures of witnesses. See Kane v. McDermott, 191 Ill. App. 3d 212, 138 Ill. Dec. 541, 547 N.E.2d 708 (1989).

4.   *Who must sign?* The English version of the Statute of Frauds and most American versions require a signature by the "party to be charged"— that is, the person who is resisting enforcement of the contract, usually the defendant in the lawsuit. See, e.g., Ark. Code Ann. § 4–59–101 (quoted in Note 1 following *Johnston v. Curtis*, supra). However, in a few United States jurisdictions, the signature must be that of "the vendor." This statutory language seems to suggest that in such states a vendor could simply make up her own writing, sign it, and enforce the contract against the purchaser. However, case law in those states usually requires evidence that the signed writing was in some way delivered to, accepted by, or otherwise acknowledged by the purchaser. See Schwinn v. Griffith, 303 N.W.2d 258 (Minn. 1981).

5.   *Modifications and rescissions.* As *Johnston v. Curtis* holds, an oral modification of a contract of sale falls within the Statute of Frauds and must be supported by a writing, whereas an oral rescission does not. See Sabot v. Rykowsky, 363 N.W.2d 550 (N.D. 1985). Is this distinction sensible? Are modifications more likely to be falsely invented by a party than rescissions? A modification that is not evidenced by a writing and is therefore unenforceable is simply ignored by the courts, leaving the original contract in effect. But part performance of the contract as modified may take the modification out of the Statute of Frauds and make it binding, as *Johnston v. Curtis* indicates. See ULTA § 1–310; Annot., 42 A. L. R.3d 242 (1972).

Should courts be more lenient in recognizing an oral modification if it covers a point that the Statute of Frauds would not have required to be included in the original written memorandum? See Garcia v. Karam, 154 Tex. 240, 276 S.W.2d 255 (1955).

6.   *Modifying time of performance.* Oral modifications or waivers of the contract clause that states the time of performance are widely upheld. See, e.g., Johnson v. Sellers, 798 N.W.2d 690 (S.D. 2011); Tiedemann v. Cozine, 297 N. J. Super. 579, 688 A.2d 1056 (1997). This is often justified on a reliance theory. If V orally tells P, "Don't worry about closing on time; I'll give you an extra two weeks," and P in fact delays getting ready to close for two

additional weeks, it is almost irresistible for a court to recognize the validity of the modification and allow P to enforce the contract despite P's late tender of performance.

7.   *Can an admission substitute for the writing?* Suppose there is no writing that evidences the parties' agreement. Can the defendant admit in pleadings, depositions, or on the witness stand that there was a sales contract (albeit oral), yet still avoid its enforcement by raising the Statute of Frauds as a defense? The traditional answer was a defendant could do so, but numerous courts have been uncomfortable with that position. See Anchorage-Hynning & Co. v. Moringiello, 697 F.2d 356 (D. C. Cir. 1983); Kolodziej v. Kolodziej, 54 A.D.2d 228, 388 N.Y.S.2d 447 (1976); Powell v. City of Newton, 703 S.E.2d 723 (N.C. 2010). Does a reversal of the traditional rule create an undesirable incentive for perjury? See Nix v. Wick, 66 So. 3d 209 (Ala. 2010); Stevens, Ethics and the Statute of Frauds, 37 Cornell L. Q. 355 (1952); Uniform Commercial Code § 2–201.

8.   *Remedies in the absence of a writing.* Even if the Statute of Frauds is not satisfied, the purchaser can still rescind and recover her earnest money (since that is not "enforcement" of the contract). See Fourteen West Realty, Inc. v. Wesson, 167 Ga. App. 539, 307 S.E.2d 28 (1983). Should she also get back her expenses of title examination? Any improvements she has made on the property? The value of any services rendered to the vendor? See Troj v. Chesebro, 30 Conn. Supp. 30, 296 A.2d 685 (1972).

ADDITIONAL NOTES AND QUESTIONS ON THE PART PERFORMANCE DOCTRINE

1.   *The part performance doctrine.* If you had not read *Johnston v. Curtis*, you might assume that when no sufficient writing can be found, a contract for the sale of real estate is simply unenforceable. But as *Johnson* illustrates, the doctrine of part performance may allow enforcement with no writing at all. What acts, performed before the closing, are necessary to comprise part performance? The three most often mentioned by the courts are the purchaser's:

- payment of part (or all) of the purchase price
- going into possession of the realty
- making substantial improvements

The first two factors were present in *Johnson*. The courts require these factors in various combinations. A few might treat one factor alone as sufficient, but most demand that two or all three factors must be present for an unwritten sales contract to be enforced. Nearly all the courts agree that partial payment alone is not sufficient. See Tikvah Realty, LLC v. Schwartz, 841 N.Y.S.2d 616 (App. Div. 2007); Zappa v. Basden, 188 Ga. App. 472, 373 S.E.2d 246 (1988). If improvements are used as a factor, presumably they must actually make the property more valuable. See Johnson v. Cook, 167 S.W.3d 258 (Mo. Ct. App. 2005) (court refused to find part performance on the basis of "improvements" that actually "devalued the land and caused damage that cannot be repaired").

2. *Are these acts really "performance?"* Is "part performance" an apt name for the doctrine? Which of the factors listed in Note 1 above can fairly be termed "performance" of the contract?

3. *A contract must be proven.* Do not become confused as to the function of the part performance doctrine. It simply takes the contract "out of" the Statute of Frauds, thereby permitting enforcement of the terms of the contract in equity despite the absence of a suitable writing. Part performance is *not* a substitute for the contract itself, whose formation must still be proven, even though it is oral. See Kiernan v. Creech, 268 P.3d 312 (Alaska 2012). Often, as the *Johnson* court noted, courts hold that proof of the existence of a contract must be by "clear and convincing" evidence. And although part performance is similar to promissory estoppel (Restatement, Contracts § 90), its purpose is not to overcome a lack of consideration, but rather to overcome the lack of a writing.

4. *Theories of part performance: Reliance.* There are two traditional theoretical justifications for part performance. The first theory is based on estoppel or reliance notions, and is articulated in Section 129 of the Restatement (Second) of Contracts:

Restatement (Second) of Contracts § 129

A contract for the transfer of an interest in land may be specifically enforced notwithstanding failure to comply with the Statute of Frauds if it is established that the party seeking enforcement, in reasonable reliance on the contract and on the continuing assent of the party against whom enforcement is sought, has so changed his position that injustice can be avoided only by specific enforcement.

Note that the Restatement language is not limited to the "big three" acts—payment, possession, and improvements—but seems to suggest that a much broader range of actions could constitute "reasonable reliance." For example, suppose the purchaser gives up her previous business location and terminates her lease there in reliance on the contract. These acts were held to constitute part performance in Payne v. Mill Race Inn, 504 N.E.2d 193 (Ill. App. 1987). Can you think of other acts by a purchaser that would satisfy the Restatement's test? What about acts by a vendor? Note that under the Restatement, a vendor as well as a purchaser can use the doctrine of part performance. See Restatement (Second of Contracts § 197 comm. (e). When the acts of reliance are not the three standard acts of payment, possession, and improvements, courts that follow the broader view of Restatement (Second) of Contracts § 197 sometimes call the doctrine "promissory estoppel" rather than "part performance." See, e.g., Jacobson v. Gulbransen, 623 N.W.2d 84 (S. D. 2001).

5.	*Theories of part performance: Evidentiary.* The other theoretical justification for the doctrine of part performance grows out of the idea that the Statute of Frauds mainly serves an evidentiary role; we demand a writing because it is otherwise too easy for one of the parties to invent a contract where none existed. If this is the Statute's role (is it?), then alternative types of evidence, such as the purchaser's acts of part performance, ought to be equally satisfactory proof of the contract's existence if they are strong and unequivocal enough. Consider Justice Cardozo's famous statement of this view:

> Not every act of part performance will move a court of equity, though legal remedies are inadequate, to enforce an oral agreement affecting rights in land. There must be performance "unequivocally referable" to the agreement, performance which alone and without the aid of words of promise is unintelligible or at least extraordinary unless as an incident of ownership, assured, if not existing. An act which admits of explanation without reference to the alleged oral contract or a contract of the same general nature and purpose is not, in general, admitted to constitute a part performance.

Burns v. McCormick, 233 N.Y. 230, 135 N.E. 273 (1922). See also Winecellar Farm, Inc. v. Hibbard, 27 A.3d 777 (N.H. 2011) (holding that payments made by a putative purchaser could be explained as rent under a lease rather than under a contract or sale); Martin v. Scholl, 678 P.2d 274 (Utah 1983) (where the putative purchaser worked long hours as a ranch foreman for nearly 30 years, a sharply divided court held that his labors were held not sufficiently referable to a contract of purchase).

Can Cardozo be taken literally? Is there any act of part performance that cannot be explained plausibly on noncontract grounds—e.g., that the "buyer" was merely a tenant? Indeed, if the buyer in fact starts out as a tenant, doesn't Cardozo's rule, applied strictly, make part performance almost impossible to establish? In truth, the "unequivocal referability" rule is often not applied very strictly. See Sutton v. Warner, 12 Cal. App. 4th 415, 15 Cal. Rptr. 2d 632 (1993); Collins v. Morris, 122 Md. App. 764, 716 A.2d 384 (1998).

6.	*Mixing the theories.* Some courts clearly emphasize either the reliance-estoppel theory or the evidentiary theory, but there are plenty of opinions that mix the two theories or seem to apply both together. See, e.g., Blackwell v. Mahmood, 992 A.2d 1219 (Conn.App. 2010). Should a court demand "unequivocal referability" if it adopts the fraud-estoppel theory? Should it demand proof of significant harm to the purchaser if it adopts the evidentiary theory?

7.	*Can a seller use part performance?* Most plaintiffs who rely on part performance are purchasers. Is there any reason not to let a *seller* assert the doctrine if the purchaser reneges on the contract after making a down payment, taking possession, and making improvements? Or should the seller be required to show his *own* acts of "part performance"? Should the answer depend on the theoretical rationale for part performance used by the particular court? Logically, if the evidentiary theory is adopted by the court, once the evidence is presented either party should be able to use it. On the other hand, if the court adopts the reliance theory, only the party who engages in the acts of reliance should be in a position to use them to enforce the contract. Compare Pearson v. Gardner, 202 Mich. 360, 168 N.W. 485 (1918), with Palumbo v. James, 266 Mass. 1, 164 N. E. 466 (1929).

8. *Damages as a remedy.* If a contract is established by use of the part performance doctrine, it's usually said that only equitable remedies (usually specific performance) can be obtained; damages is not an available remedy. See, e.g. Miller v. McCamish, 78 Wash. 2d 821, 479 P.2d 919 (1971) (one of the few cases granting damages). Does the Restatement (Second) of Contracts § 197, quoted in Note 4 above, limit the available remedy to specific performance? Does this limitation make sense? Is there any rational objection to the use of the doctrine in an action for damages? Compare ULTA § 2–201, Commissioners' Comment No. 3.

9. *Part performance and judicial authority.* In most states, part performance is not mentioned in the Statute of Frauds. Is the doctrine of part performance a judicial usurpation of legislative power? Does it permit courts to contradict the legislature? If, as courts often say, the Statute of Frauds is sometimes employed in an attempt to commit a fraud (by escaping from a genuine but oral contract), is this criticism also true of the doctrine of part performance? Would society be better off without the doctrine?

C. REMEDIES AND REAL ESTATE CONTRACTS

The two most widely employed remedies for the breach of a real estate sale contract are damages and specific performance. A third remedy, rescission, also is available, although it seems not to be requested very often. See, e.g., Greenstreet v. Fairchild, 313 S.W.3d 163 (Mo. App. 2010) (allowing the purchasers to rescind a long-term installment contract because the vendors persistently breached it by trespassing on the property).

An award of damages usually contemplates that the vendor will keep the property, or will sell it to someone else. An order of specific performance, on the other hand, means that the vendor will convey the property to the contract purchaser, who in turn must pay the full agreed price. In general, both the buyer and seller may seek either of these remedies if the other party breaches the sales contract.

Loss of bargain damages resulting from a breach of the sales contract traditionally are measured as the difference between the contract price and the market value of the land on the date of the breach. Under this measure, the vendor will recover nothing if the property's value has risen higher than the contract price, and the purchaser will recover nothing if the property is worth less than the contract amount. See Kuish v. Smith, 105 Cal. Rptr. 3d 475 (Cal.App. 2010). But the "pure" loss of bargain computation may be only the beginning of a total claim for damages, as the following case and the notes afterwards illustrate.

DONOVAN V. BACHSTADT

Supreme Court of New Jersey, 1982
91 N.J. 434, 453 A.2d 160

[Defendant Bachstadt contracted to sell real estate to plaintiffs Donovans for $58,900. The contract provided that Bachstadt would finance $44,000 by way of a purchase money mortgage, thus helping the Donovans avoid the necessity of bank financing, which at the time was available only at very high interest rates. Under applicable usury statutes, the purchase money mortgage could not have borne an interest rate exceeding 10.5%. It developed that Bachstadt did not have and could not obtain marketable title to the property.]

When defendant could not obtain marketable title, the Donovans commenced this suit for compensatory and punitive damages. * * * [T]he trial court granted plaintiffs' motion for summary judgment. It was indisputable that the defendant had breached the agreement. The only issue was damages. The trial court held that plaintiffs were entitled under N.J.S.A. § 2A:29–1 to recovery of their costs for the title search and survey. Plaintiffs had apparently in the interim purchased a home in Middlesex County and obtained a mortgage loan bearing interest at the rate of 13¼ per annum. Plaintiffs sought the difference between 10½ and 13¼ as compensatory damages, representing their loss of the benefit of the bargain. The trial court denied recovery because the contract was for the sale of the property and the financing "was only incidental to the basic concept."

The Appellate Division reversed. 181 N. J. Super. 367, 437 A.2d 728 (1981). It held that N.J.S.A. § 2A:29–1 was declarative of the general common law right to recover consequential damages for breach of a contract and that the statute modified the preexisting law, which limited a realty purchaser to recovery of his deposit upon a seller's breach due to a defective title. The court concluded the statute intended that the general law of damages for breach of a contract applies and stated that the difference in interest rates could be the basis for a measure of damages depending on whether the plaintiffs "have entered into a comparable transaction for another home * * * or are likely to do so in the near future * * * ." Id. at 376, 437 A.2d 728. The Appellate Division cautioned that any award of future damages should represent the true life of the mortgage and be reduced to present value. Further, the plaintiffs should be held to a duty to mitigate. Lastly, if the proofs should demonstrate that plaintiffs have not purchased and are not likely to purchase a home in the near future, their damages would be remote and speculative. The cause was remanded for a plenary hearing.

I

The initial inquiry is whether plaintiffs are entitled to compensatory damages. We had occasion recently to discuss the measure of damages available when a seller breaches an executory contract for the sale of real property. St. Pius X House of Retreats v. Diocese of Camden, 88 N.J. 571, 582–87, 443 A.2d 1052 (1982). We noted that New Jersey follows the English rule, which generally limits a buyer's recovery to the return of his deposit unless the seller wilfully refuses to convey or is guilty of fraud or deceit. The traditional formulation of the English rule has been expressed by T. Cyprian Williams, an English barrister, as follows:

> Where the breach of contract is occasioned by the vendor's inability, without his own fault, to show a good title, the purchaser is entitled to recover as damages his deposit, if any, with interest, and his expenses incurred in connection with the agreement, but not more than nominal damages for the loss of his bargain. T.C. Williams, The Contract of Sale of Land 128 (1930).

In *St. Pius*, we found no need to reexamine the English rule, though we raised the question whether the American rule that permits a buyer to obtain benefit of the bargain damages irrespective of the nature of the reasons for the seller's default might not be more desirable.

* * *

We are satisfied that the American rule is preferable. The English principle developed because of the uncertainties of title due to the complexity of the rules governing title to land during the eighteenth and nineteenth centuries. Oakley, Pecuniary Compensation for Failure to Complete a Contract for the Sale of Land, 39 Cambridge L.J. 58, 69 (1980). At that time the only evidence of title was contained in deeds that were, in a phrase attributed to Lord Westbury, "difficult to read, disgusting to touch, and impossible to understand." The reason for the English principle that creates an exception to the law governing damages for breaches of executory contracts for the sale of property is no longer valid, and the exception should be eliminated. *Cessante ratione legis, cessat et ipsa lex* (the reason for a law ceasing, the law itself ceases). See Fox v. Snow, 6 N. J. 12, 14, 22–23, 76 A.2d 877 (1950) (Vanderbilt, C. J., dissenting). Indeed, in England the rule has been modified by placing the burden of proof on the vendor to establish that he has done everything within his power to carry out the contract. Malhotra v. Choudhury, [1978] 3 W.L.R. 825; [1979] 1 All E.R. 186 (C.A.).

Whether titles are clear may be ascertained by record searches. See N. J. S. A. § 46:21–1; Jones, The New Jersey Recording Act—A Study of its Policy, 12 Rutgers L. Rev. 328, 329–30 (1957). Moreover, limitation periods may be applicable. See N.J.S.A. § 2A:14–30; 13A N.J. Practice (Lieberman, Abstracts and Titles) § 1643 at 140 (3d ed. 1966). Thus, it is standard practice for title examiners to search the back title for 60 years and until a warranty deed is found in the chain of title. Palamarg Realty Co. v. Rehac & Piatkowski, 80 N.J. 446, 460, 404 A.2d 21 (1979). Further, the parties may insert appropriate provisions in their agreements protecting them from title defects so that to a very large extent sellers may control the measure of redress.

There is no sound basis why benefit of the bargain damages should not be awarded whether the subject matter of the contract is realty or personalty. Serious losses should not be borne by the vendee of real estate to the benefit of the defaulting vendor. This is particularly so when an installment purchase contract is involved that extends over a period of years during which the vendee makes substantial payments upon the principal, as well as extensive improvements to the property. * * *

We are satisfied that a buyer should be permitted to recover benefit of the bargain damages when the seller breaches an executory contract to convey real property. Here the defendant agreed to convey marketable title. He made that bargained-for promise and breached it and is responsible to the plaintiff for the damages occasioned thereby. The next question is how to compute those compensatory damages.

II

Judicial remedies upon breach of contract fall into three general categories: restitution, compensatory damages and performance. Separate concepts undergird each of these remedial provisions. The rationale for restitution is to return the innocent party to his status before the contract was executed. Compensatory damages are intended to recompense the injured claimant for losses due to the breach, that is, give the innocent party the benefit of the bargain. Performance is to effect a result, essentially other than in terms of monetary reparation, so that the innocent party is placed in the position of having had the contract performed. We have now adopted the American rule providing for compensatory damages upon the seller's breach of an executory contract to sell realty and we must examine the appropriate elements that should properly be included in an award.

"Compensatory damages are designed to put the injured party in as good a position as he would have had if performance had been rendered as promised." 5 Corbin, Contracts § 992, p. 5 (1951). * * * What that position is depends upon what the parties reasonably expected. It follows that the defendant is not chargeable for loss that he did not have reason to foresee as a probable result of the breach when the contract was made. Hadley v. Baxendale, 9 Exch. 341, 5 Eng. Rul. Case 502 (1854); accord Crater v. Binninger, 33 N.J.L. 513 (E. & A. 1869). The oft-quoted language in *Hadley* for this proposition is:

> Where two parties have made a contract, which one of them has broken, the damages which the other party ought to receive, in respect of such breach, should be such as may fairly be considered either arising naturally, i.e., according to the usual course of things, from such breach of contract itself, or such as may reasonably be supposed to have been in the contemplation of both parties at the time they made the contract, as the probable result of the breach of it. 5 Eng. Rul. Case at 504.

See Restatement (Second) of Contracts § 351 (1981); see also Weiss v. Revenue Building & Loan Ass'n, 116 N.J.L. 208, 210, 182 A. 891 (E. & A. 1936). Further, the loss must be a reasonably certain consequence of the breach, although the exact amount of the loss need not be certain. Kozlowski v. Kozlowski, 80 N. J. 378, 388, 403 A.2d 902 (1979); Tessmar v. Grosner, 23 N.J. 193, 203, 128 A.2d 467 (1957).

The specific elements to be applied in any given case of a seller's breach of an executory agreement to sell realty may vary in order to achieve the broad purposes of reparations; some items, however, will almost invariably exist. Thus, the purchaser will usually be entitled to the return of the amount paid on the purchase price with interest thereon. Costs and expenses incurred in connection with the proposed acquisition, such as for the title search and survey, would fall in the same category. The traditional test is the difference between the market price of the property at the time of the breach and the contract price. Ganger v. Moffett, 8 N.J. 73, 79, 83 A.2d 769 (1951); King v. Ruckman, 24 N. J. Eq. 298 (Ch.), aff'd, 24 N.J. Eq. 556 (E. & A. 1873). See cases cited in Annotation, Measure of Recovery by Vendee Under Executory Contract for Purchase of Real Property Where Vendor is Unable to Convey, 48 A. L. R. 12, 15–17 (1927). Under this standard, the buyer who had taken possession before title passed would be entitled to recover for improvements he made that increased the value of the property. Sabaugh v. Schrieber, 87 Ind. App. 588, 162 N.E. 248 (1928).

The difference between market and contract price may not be suitable in all situations. Thus, where a buyer had in turn contracted to sell the realty, it is reasonable to measure his damages in terms of the actual lost profit. See Bonhard v. Gindin, 104 N.J.L. 599, 142 A. 52 (E. & A. 1928) (awarding the consideration paid, search fees, taxes and assessments paid, and lost profits from a sale to a third person); see also Giumarra v. Harrington Heights, 33 N. J. Super. 178, 109 A.2d 695 (App. Div. 1954) (awarding contract buyer of realty lost profits in action against contract buyer's assignee). What the proper elements of damage are depend upon the particular circumstances surrounding the transaction, especially the terms, conditions and nature of the agreement.

The plaintiffs here assert that their damages are equivalent to the difference in interest costs incurred by them in purchasing a different home at another location. This claim assumes that the financial provision of the contract concerning the purchase money mortgage that the defendant agreed to accept was independent and divisible from the purchase of the land and house. The defendant contends that he did not agree to loan these funds in connection with the purchase of some other property, but that this provision was incidental to the sale of the house. Neither position is entirely sound. This financing was an integral part of the transaction. It can be neither ignored nor viewed as an isolated element.

The relationship of the financing to the purchase of a home has changed in recent years. As interest rates rose and the availability of first mortgage funds was sharply reduced, potential homeowners, though desirous of purchasing homes, found financing difficult to obtain. The seller's acceptance of a purchase money mortgage became an important factor in effecting a sale. See Rand, Home Resale Market: Pattern Shift, N.Y. Times, March 22, 1981, § 11, at 18, col. 3. In evaluating a contract such a financial arrangement could play an important part in determining price. The rise in interest rates, the expense of mortgage credit and the availability of funds has rendered traditional methods of financing acquisition of homes impractical. Walleser, The Changing Complexion of Home Mortgage Financing in America, 31 Drake L. Rev. 1, 2 (1981). Favorable vendor financing could lead to increased market value. Only then might a buyer be able to purchase. Iezman, Alternative Mortgage Instruments: Their Effect on Residential Financing, Real Est. L.J. 3, 4 (1981). The importance of a seller's purchase money mortgage to the overall agreement to convey property was recognized in *King v. Ruckman*, 24 N.J. Eq. 298 (Ch.), aff'd, 24 N.J. Eq. 556 (E. & A. 1873). The seller agreed to convey certain property and to accept as part of the purchase price a purchase money mortgage with 6% interest payable in five annual installments. The seller refused to convey. The buyer obtained a final decree for specific performance including the purchase money mortgage. The Chancery Court's view of the mortgage confirmed by the Court of Errors and Appeals on review was:

> The benefit accruing to the purchaser from having time for the payment of the bulk of the principal, and of the rate agreed on for interest, is apparent. It is a material ingredient of the bargain, as much so in reality, though not in degree, as the price, and cannot be withheld from the purchaser in this case by the willful misconduct of the vendor, for the sole benefit of the vendor himself. 24 N.J. Eq. at 303.

The interest rate is not sufficiently discrete to calculate damages in terms of it alone under these circumstances.

In some circumstances, interest rate differentials are an appropriate measure of damages. Where the buyer has obtained specific performance, but because of the delay has incurred higher mortgage rates, then his loss clearly should include the higher financing cost. *Godwin v. Lindbert*, 101 Mich. App. 754, 300 N.W.2d 514 (1980), is illustrative. The buyers lost their commitment for a mortgage with an interest rate of 8¾ when the seller refused to convey. The buyers succeeded in obtaining specific performance but were compelled to borrow funds at 11½. They were awarded the difference reduced to present value. See also Reis v. Sparks, 547 F.2d 236 (4th Cir. 1976). Moreover, we are not unmindful of the possibility that a buyer might demonstrate that a lending institution's commitment to advance the funds initially at a certain interest rate was due to the buyer's financial condition. The particular realty might well be a secondary and incidental consideration for the loan. Therefore, an interest differential occasioned by the seller's default might be a proper factor in fixing damages where the buyer shortly thereafter purchased another property financed at a higher interest rate.

This is not such a situation. The defendant's motive was to sell a house and not to lend money. In measuring the plaintiffs' loss there should be a determination of the fair market value of the property and house that could be acquired with a purchase money mortgage in the principal amount of $44,000 at an interest rate of 10½ (no appeal was taken from the judgment of reformation) for a 30-year term. The valuation should be at the time the defendant failed to comply with the judgment of specific performance. The plaintiffs would be entitled to the difference between $58,900 and that fair market value. If the fair market value was not more than the contract price, the plaintiffs would not have established any damage ascribable to the loss of the bargain. They are also entitled to their expenditures for the survey, search, and counsel fees for services rendered in preparation of the aborted closing. The plaintiffs have hitherto received the return of the deposit.

NOTES AND QUESTIONS

1. *Limiting the buyer's remedy for a defective title to rescission.* The English rule, discussed in *Donovan,* limiting the purchaser to restitutionary recovery when the seller's title is defective but the seller has acted in good faith, is followed in about half the American jurisdictions. It does not apply, however, if the vendor breaches the contract, even in good faith, for reasons unrelated to the title. See Beard v. S/E Joint Venture, 321 Md. 126, 581 A.2d 1275 (1990).

2. *Incidental and consequential damages.* In addition to the traditional loss-of-bargain damages, available to a buyer only if the property's value is

higher than the contract price, what other elements of damage ("incidental" or "consequential") might an innocent buyer attempt to recover?

(a) Expenditures for title examination, survey, and attorneys' fees in preparation for the closing? See *Donovan*, supra. *Yes*

(b) Airfare for travel to negotiate and execute the contract which the seller subsequently breached? See Fountain v. Mojo, 687 P.2d 496 (Colo. App. 1984). *No*

(c) Additional rent, taxes, mortgage interest, and other carrying costs at her present location while she locates and purchases substitute property? *most likely not*

(d) Loss of particularly favorable financing from a bank or savings association, no longer available as a result of an increase in market interest rates? See Wall v. Pate, 104 N. M. 1, 715 P.2d 449 (1986). *Yes*

(e) The cost of leasing temporary quarters elsewhere, including rent, advertising for a place to lease, and the expense of moving to the leased premises? See Ruble v. Reich, 259 Neb. 658, 611 N.W.2d 844 (2000) (allowing the buyers to recover the rent they paid for temporary quarters, but deducting the amount of property taxes and interest they would have paid after closing if the sale had closed on time, and that they saved by renting instead).

(f) Lost profits if the purchaser planned to use the property for business purposes or build on or renovate and resell it? See Greenwich S. F., LLC v. Wong, 118 Cal. Rptr. 3d 531 (Cal. App. 2010) (evidence of lost profits was too uncertain and speculative). Cf. Hoang v. Hewitt Ave. Assoc., LLC, 936 A.2d 915 (Md. App. 2007) (purchaser's 25-year track record of building and marketing homes in the area made its claim for lost profits reasonably certain).

If these items are recoverable as damages, should they (or any of them) be offset by the fact that the purchaser still has the purchase money, and may have earned interest on it (if it was to have been paid in cash) or has saved the interest which she would have paid on it (if she intended to borrow it)?

3. *Damages resulting from higher interest rate.* The final paragraph in the *Donovan* opinion seems to say that the court will not allow the buyers any additional damages to account for the higher interest rate they had to pay in purchasing another house. But query if that is really the result of its analysis. It states that "In measuring the plaintiffs' loss [that is, applying the standard damages measure, the difference between the contract price and the market value on the date of breach] there should be a determination of the fair market value of the property and house that could be acquired with a purchase money mortgage in the principal amount of $44,000 at an interest rate of 10½%." Is this value greater than the value of the house with no financing attached to it? It seems obvious that it is. The Donovans surely would not have been willing to pay as much for the house with no accompanying financing, given the much higher interest rates prevailing in

the market at the time. It should be possible to estimate the added amount they were willing to pay for the favorable financing. Doesn't including that amount in the estimate of the house's fair market value add the equivalent amount to their damages?

4. *Date of valuation.* Consider the damages recoverable by the seller when the buyer breaches. The traditional measure of loss of bargain damages measures the property's market value as of the date of the breach, but as the *Donovan* case suggests, this may not be a fair or relevant date. Frequently the seller will be forced to put the property back on the market and may wait for months or even years before another buyer is found. In a declining market, the ultimate sale price may be much lower than the value on the date of the breach. Assuming that the seller has continued to make a diligent effort to resell, should the actual resale price be the relevant value for purposes of computing damages? The court so held in Kuhn v. Spatial Design, Inc., 245 N.J. Super. 378, 585 A.2d 967 (1991), following the rule for sales of goods found in UCC § 2–706, –708. Contra, see Jones v. Lee, 126 N. M. 467, 971 P.2d 858 (App. 1998). Courts frequently seem to assume that the resale price is good evidence (perhaps the "best" or only available evidence) of market value, and often use it without much discussion of the matter. See White v. Farrell, 964 N.Y.S.2d 467, 987 N.E.2d 244 (N.Y. 2013) ("the resale price, in a particular case, may be very strong evidence of fair market value at the time of the breach").

When the purchaser seeks damages, an argument can be made that the property should be valued as of the time of trial in the damages action, rather than at the date of the breach. In a market in which prices are rising, the purchaser can argue that, but for the seller's breach, the purchaser would have owned property worth much more by the time of trial, and hence that the breach damaged the purchaser that much more. The court seemed sympathetic to this view, but rejected it because a statute mandated the standard date-of-breach valuation, in Reese v. Wong, 93 Cal. App. 4th 51, 112 Cal. Rptr. 2d 669 (2001).

5. *Measurement of value.* A further reason why the courts may prefer to rely on the actual reselling price as the relevant measure of value is that otherwise they must act on the basis of appraisal testimony, which can be notoriously imprecise. For example, in Askari v. R & R Land Co., 179 Cal. App. 3d 1101, 225 Cal. Rptr. 285 (1986), the appraisers for the two parties were $400,000 apart in their estimates of value as of the trial date—an amount that was 32 percent of the original contract price of $1.25 million. Such variations in appraisals are not unusual and scarcely build one's confidence in the measurement of damages.

6. *Seller's damages.* Consider now the "incidental" and "consequential" damages recoverable by a seller. Should they include the following?

(a) Carrying costs of the property until it is resold (assuming continuing reasonable efforts to resell)? Such costs might include property taxes, insurance, utilities, maintenance, and interest on existing mortgage loans. See Mueller v. Johnson, 60 Wash. App. 683, 806 P.2d 256 (1991); Ner Tamid Congregation of North Town v. Krivoruchko, 660 F.Supp.2d 927 (N.D.Ill. 2009) (approving recovery of these items). But other courts refuse such claims; see DiScipio v. Sullivan, 816 N.Y.S.2d 578 (N.Y. App. Div. 2006); Quigley v. Jones, 334 S.E.2d 664 (Ga. 1985)

(b) Interest income the seller expected to earn on the purchase price, or on purchase-money mortgage financing he was obligated under the contract to provide to the purchaser? See Askari v. R & R Land Co., 179 Cal. App. 3d 1101, 225 Cal. Rptr. 285 (1986) (approving recovery of lost interest on purchase-money financing); Van Moorlehem v. Brown Realty Co., 747 F.2d 992 (10th Cir.1984) (denying recovery for interest seller expected to earn on cash purchase price).

(c) The cost of a second real estate broker's commission on the resale, if the seller was obliged to pay a commission on the first sale even though it did not close? Compare Mueller v. Johnson, 60 Wash. App. 683, 806 P.2d 256 (1991) (approving recovery of resale expense) with Johnston v. Curtis, 70 Ark. App. 195, 16 S.W.3d 283 (2000) (rejecting such recovery). Other resale expenses (e.g., advertising) presumably would be treated similarly.

Is it bad policy to permit the seller to recover carrying costs of the property until it is resold? One court put it this way:

Allowing such damages to be recovered * * * could incent the seller to hold the property indefinitely while waiting for market conditions to change, or for a purchaser willing to pay a specific price, because the seller knows his breaching buyer is responsible for all costs the seller is incurring by continuing to own the property.

Goldman v. Olmstead, 414 S.W.3d 346, 352 (Tex. App. 2013). Do you agree?

What about the use value of the property during the period the seller is attempting to resell? If the seller in fact rents the property to a tenant during the interim, it seems obvious that the rent collected should offset the seller's claim for incidental and consequential damages. Should a similar result follow, with an offset for fair rental value, if the seller continues to use the land himself? Suppose the seller does not in fact use the property, but it remains available and adaptable to the seller's use?

7. *Specific performance plus damages?* Even if the contract is eventually performed, either under a decree of specific performance or voluntarily (but after an unjustified delay), should the nonbreaching party also be permitted to recover some or all of the elements mentioned in the above Notes as damages? See Houston v. Willis, 24 So. 3d 412, 420 (Miss. App. 2009) (where purchaser breached and was ordered to specifically perform, vendor could also recover damages for mortgage payments, insurance, and taxes purchaser should have been paying during the period of

delay); Shelter Corp. of Canada, Ltd. v. Bozin, 468 So. 2d 1094 (Fla. App. 1985) (where vendor breached and was ordered to specifically perform, it could recover damages for interest and taxes, but only to the extent offset by purchaser's claim for damages for loss of fair rental value); III Lounge, Inc. v. Gaines, 227 Neb. 585, 419 N.W.2d 143 (1988); Annot., 74 A.L.R. 2d 578 (1960). Cf. McCoy v. Alsup, 94 N. M. 255, 609 P.2d 337 (App. 1980).

Other examples of damage awards despite ultimate performance of the contract include Woliansky v. Miller, 146 Ariz. 170, 704 P.2d 811 (App.1985) (damages for deterioration to improvements on the land during five-year delay), and Bravo v. Buelow, 168 Cal. App. 3d 208, 214 Cal. Rptr. 65 (1985) (damages resulting from rise in cost to purchaser of constructing a house on the land). During periods of rapidly rising interest rates, courts have awarded damages for the higher cost of mortgage financing that the purchaser must pay because interest rates have risen during the period of delay. See, e.g., Appollo v. Reynolds, 364 N.W.2d 422 (Minn. App. 1985). See also Garland, Purchaser's Interest Rate Increase: Caveat Venditor, 27 N.Y.L. Sch. L. Rev. 745 (1982); Note, 12 Seton Hall L. Rev. 916 (1982); W. Stoebuck & D. Whitman, The Law of Property § 10.5 nn. 20–22 (3d ed. 2000).

SCHWINDER V. AUSTIN BANK OF CHICAGO

Illinois Court of Appeals, 2004
348 Ill. App. 3d 461, 809 N.E.2d 180, 284 Ill. Dec. 58

JUSTICE GORDON delivered the opinion of the court.

The instant suit arises from a chancery action filed by plaintiffs, Thomas F. Schwinder and Susan L. Londay, seeking specific performance of a condominium purchase contract against defendants, Austin Bank of Chicago and Marian Baginski. Baginski subsequently filed a counterclaim, seeking possession of the condominium unit and claiming a rental rate of $1,500 per month. Following a bench trial, the trial court entered judgment for plaintiffs, granting specific performance and returning to plaintiffs a portion of rent they paid to defendant for November 2000. * * *

BACKGROUND

The record and testimony in this case reveal that on June 21, 2000, plaintiffs, Thomas F. Schwinder and Susan L. Londay, tendered an offer to purchase a condominium unit located at 3117 South Benson, in Chicago, Illinois, which was owned by defendants, Austin Bank of Chicago, trustee under trust agreement dated February 24, 1978, known as trust No. 5861 (hereinafter Trustee), and Marian Baginski. As the sole beneficiary of this land trust, Baginski was thus authorized to convey the title to plaintiffs.

On July 5, 2000, Baginski accepted the offer from plaintiffs to purchase the condominium unit. The purchase contract between the parties was a form real estate contract prepared by Baginski's attorney and utilized for all real estate transactions in the Bridgeport Crossing Condominium complex in which the condominium unit was located. * * *

[Baginski failed to tender a deed on the agreed closing date because he was in the process of obtaining a divorce and was uncertain whether the court in the divorce action would require him to make some particular disposition of the condominium unit. He signed an agreement permitting the buyers to move in without a closing, upon their promise to pay a fee of $1,500 per month "until such time as Seller is able to close on the sale of the property." After the divorce court approved the sale of the condominium, and despite repeated efforts by the buyers to get Baginski to schedule a closing of the sale, he refused to do so. The buyers then brought this action for specific performance of the contract. The court reviewed the terms of the original contract and the agreement for possession, which modified the contract, and concluded that the contract, as modified, was valid and enforceable.]

ANALYSIS

Finding the purchase contract valid and enforceable, we must now consider whether the grant of specific performance was proper in this case. The principle underlying the specific performance remedy is to grant equitable relief where the damage remedy at law is inadequate. See Geist v. Lehmann, 19 Ill. App. 3d 557, 561, 312 N.E.2d 42, 46 (1974). At the time this branch of equity jurisdiction was evolving in England, the presumed uniqueness of land, as well as its importance to the social order, led to the conclusion that damages at law could never be adequate to compensate for the breach of a contract to transfer an interest in land. Hence, specific performance became a fixed remedy in this class of transactions. See 11 S. Williston on Contracts § 1418A (3d ed.1968); 5 Corbin on Contracts § 1143 (1964).

> Two distinct elements enter into the application of [specific performance]: first, the extent to which the evidentiary function of the statutory formalities is fulfilled by the conduct of the parties; second, the reliance of the promisee, providing a compelling substantive basis for relief in addition to the expectations created by the promise. Restatement (Second) of Contracts § 129, comm. b, at 322 (1981). The evidentiary element can be satisfied by a meticulous examination of the evidence and realistic appraisal of the probabilities on the part of the trier of fact; commonly summarized in a standard that calls upon the trier of fact to be satisfied by "clear and convincing evidence.

Restatement (Second) of Contracts § 129, comm. b, at 322 (1981). The substantive element requires consideration of the adequacy of the remedy of restitution. Restatement (Second) of Contracts § 129, comm. b, at 322 (1981).

Illinois courts have long held that where the parties have fairly and understandingly entered into a valid contract for the sale of real property, specific performance of the contract is a matter of right and equity will enforce it, absent circumstances of oppression and fraud. Giannini v. First National Bank of Des Plaines, 136 Ill. App. 3d 971, 981, 91 Ill. Dec. 438, 483 N.E.2d 924, 933 (1985). Contracts to devise or convey real estate are enforced by specific performance on the ground that the law cannot "do perfect justice." Giannini, 136 Ill. App. 3d at 981, 91 Ill. Dec. 438, 483 N. E.2d at 933; Hagen v. Anderson, 317 Ill. 173, 177, 147 N.E. 791, 793 (1925). Generally, a party will be entitled to specific performance of a contract for conveyances of real estate only upon establishing either that the party has performed according to the terms of the contract or that the party was ready, willing and able to perform but was prevented, and thus excused from doing so by the acts or conduct of the other party. Omni Partners, 246 Ill. App. 3d at 63, 185 Ill. Dec. 657, 614 N.E.2d at 1346; Tantillo v. Janus, 87 Ill. App. 3d 231, 234, 42 Ill. Dec. 291, 408 N.E.2d 1000, 1003 (1980).

Specific performance is a matter of sound judicial discretion controlled by established principles of equity and exercised upon a consideration of all the facts and circumstances of a particular case. Omni Partners, 246 Ill. App. 3d at 62, 185 Ill. Dec. 657, 614 N.E.2d at 1345; Djomlija v. Urban, 107 Ill. App. 3d 960, 967, 63 Ill. Dec. 627, 438 N.E.2d 558, 563 (1982). In this regard, the trial court should balance the equities between the parties. Hild v. Avland Development Co., 46 Ill. App. 3d 173, 179, 4 Ill. Dec. 672, 360 N.E.2d 785, 790 (1977). Accordingly, a court using its equitable powers may refuse to grant specific performance where the remedy would cause a peculiar hardship or inequitable result. Geist, 19 Ill. App. 3d at 561, 312 N.E.2d at 46. A court's decision to grant such relief will not be disturbed absent an abuse of discretion. Omni Partners, 246 Ill. App. 3d at 62, 185 Ill. Dec. 657, 614 N.E.2d at 1345; Tantillo, 87 Ill. App. 3d at 239, 42 Ill. Dec. 291, 408 N.E.2d at 1003.

In applying the requirements needed for specific performance, first, we must set forth that both plaintiffs and defendants freely and understandingly entered into a purchase contract for the sale of the condominium unit. There is no question from the facts in this case that there was no fraud or oppression by either party upon the other at the time of execution of the purchase contract. In fact, defendants note multiple times in their brief that both parties fully understood the purchase contract before they executed it.

Next we must turn to whether a condominium is the proper subject of specific performance. Although neither of the parties contends that specific performance cannot be granted when dealing with a condominium unit, the question of uniqueness is an issue of concern for courts. On one side is the argument that condominium units are real estate, per se unique and thus entitled to a remedy in equity. See Giannini, 136 Ill. App. 3d at 981, 91 Ill. Dec. 438, 483 N.E.2d at 933–34. On the other side is the argument that a condominium unit is but one of thousands with the same layout, typically in the same building, and therefore are only entitled to remedies at law. See Centex Homes Corp. v. Boag, 128 N.J. Super. 385, 389, 320 A.2d 194, 196 (1974). However, using either argument, there is no question that the condominium unit in this case is unique. Giannini, 136 Ill. App. 3d at 980–81, 91 Ill. Dec. 438, 483 N.E.2d at 932–33 (although there has been debate over whether condominium units are unique and thus are the proper subject of specific performance, this court held that condominiums are "real property" for the purposes of specific performance); but see Centex Homes, 128 N.J. Super. at 389, 320 A.2d at 196 (finding that except upon a showing of unusual circumstances or a change in the vendor's position, such as where the vendee has entered into possession, the vendor's damages are usually measurable, his remedy at law is adequate and there is no jurisdictional basis for equitable relief). The condominium unit in this case is obviously unique under the *Giannini* argument, and it meets the exact exception making it unique under the *Centex Homes argument*. Giannini, 136 Ill. App. 3d at 980–82, 91 Ill. Dec. 438, 483 N.E.2d at 932–34; Centex Homes, 128 N.J. Super. at 389, 320 A.2d at 196. The condominium unit was not sold as a sample; it was substantially upgraded to plaintiffs' specifications. Furthermore, plaintiffs themselves have made improvements to the condominium unit. Lastly, and most importantly, the condominium unit in this case has been plaintiffs' home for the past two years. The uniqueness of this condominium unit to the plaintiffs makes it an unquestionably proper subject for specific performance and makes the remedy at law inadequate.

Finding that a remedy at law was inadequate, the trial court found, and we agree, that it would be inequitable to deny specific performance in this case. The above-enumerated facts bear this out. Notably, plaintiffs paid the earnest money to defendants, took possession of the condominium unit, withdrew their 401(k) for a down payment, obtained mortgage commitment papers and made substantial improvements to the condominium unit. It would be inequitable for the court to allow plaintiffs to bear all the loss they suffered and move them out of their home when they complied with all of the terms of the agreement.

Furthermore, at all times during the pendency of the sales contract, plaintiffs were ready, willing and able to perform but were prevented, and thus excused, from doing so by Baginski's refusal to schedule a closing date. Plaintiffs were ready with a mortgage approval and a down payment in hand to close on the condominium unit the very instant Baginski assigned a closing date. However, Baginski repeatedly refused to schedule the closing date, and thus, plaintiffs never consummated the sale of the condominium unit.

Based on the foregoing, the trial court's determination to grant specific performance of the purchase contract was proper in this case.

CONCLUSION

For the foregoing reasons, the judgment of the trial court is affirmed.

NOTES AND QUESTIONS

1. *Specific performance for the vendor?* The *Schwinder* case involved a prayer for specific performance by the purchasers. In such cases, specific performance seems easy to justify, since the purchasers are obtaining title to the very real estate they contracted to buy, and no other real estate would be exactly the same. Specific performance for a *vendor* seems harder to justify because the vendor is simply receiving money—the purchase price. Why do most courts, most of the time, grant specific performance to vendors? The New Jersey court in *Centex Homes, Inc. v. Boag,* discussed in the *Schwinder* opinion, disparages doing so, putting it down to a slavish following of mutuality of remedy. But is there a better reason? Real estate is notoriously illiquid. In a slow market, a seller who has suffered a breach of contract may take many months or even years to resell the property. Moreover, the price at which it will finally sell may not be known at the time of a damages action— which is one reason damages will be computed on the basis of market value at the date of breach instead.

As you can see, vendors who can recover only damages are subjected to the very substantial risks associated with resale. Yet those are precisely the risks they bargained out of by entering into the original contract of sale. In view of this fact, confining a vendor to damages may be quite unfair, and the unfairness results directly from the "uniqueness" of real estate and the absence of a liquid market for it. That seems to us a better justification for awarding specific performance.

2. *Vendors of large projects containing many similar units.* If you are convinced by the foregoing note, ask yourself whether a case like *Centex,* involving a condominium project, is different. The court in *Centex* made a good deal of the fact that the condominium units were numerous and very similar. Given the fact that Centex Homes had an ongoing sales program and a clearly defined price schedule for its condominium units, would it not have been able to establish their current market value easily and reliably? Moreover, would not its success (or lack of success) in that sales program make it quite easy to estimate how long it would take Centex to remarket the unit the Boags refused to buy, and for that matter, what the cost of remarketing it would be? Do you suppose these factors influenced the court in *Centex* in reaching its conclusion that specific performance was unnecessary?

A few other cases have cast doubt on the usual assumption that a vendor may have specific performance as a matter of course. See Seabaugh v. Keele, 775 S.W.2d 205 (Mo. App. 1989); Wolf v. Anderson, 334 N.W.2d 212 (N. D. 1983); and Perron v. Hale, 108 Idaho 578, 701 P.2d 198 (1985).

3. *Grounds for denial of specific performance.* Unlike the *Centex* court, most courts routinely grant specific performance for either party. See, e.g., BD Inns v. Pooley, 218 Cal. App. 3d 289, 266 Cal. Rptr. 815 (1990). There are, however, several situations in which specific performance may be denied and the plaintiff relegated to other remedies:

(a) Due to the fact that specific performance is an equitable remedy, it will be refused if it would produce unjust or unconscionable results, as the court in *Schwinder* indicated. See 6A Powell, Real Property, ¶ 930; Kilarjian v. Vastola, 877 A.2d 372 (N.J. Ch. Div. 2004) (specific performance for purchasers denied, where vendor wished to remain in her home because of severely deteriorating health). Likewise, a contract that appears excessively vague may be denied specific enforcement, even if damages could be awarded. See Homart Devel. Co. v. Sigman, 868 F.2d 1556 (11th Cir.1989).

(b) If the vendor has resold the land to a purchaser who had no notice of the prior contract, the court will not force the innocent purchaser to give up the land in order to give the original buyer specific performance. See UFG, LLC v. Southwest Corp., 848 N.E.2d 353 (Ind. App. 2006). But a purchaser who takes with notice of the previous contract is bound by it, and must give up the land if the original purchaser obtains an order of specific performance. Wilde v. O'Leary, 374 N. J. Super. 582, 866 A.2d 205 (2005).

(c) Neither party will be ordered to perform the contract if performance would be impossible. For example, the vendor will not be ordered to perform if his title is missing or defective. The purchaser may waive the defect, however, and obtain specific performance. See Anderson v. Onsager, 455 N.W.2d 885 (Wis. 1990). Likewise, the purchaser may assert that she is incapable of paying the purchase price, and hence that her performance is impossible. But a court may be hard to convince on this score. In Ash Park, LLC v. Alexander & Bishop, Ltd., 783 N.W.2d 294 (Wis. 2010), the purchasers planned to build a shopping center on the land, but their primary tenant refused to enter into a lease. They argued that this made their performance of the contract impossible, but the court was unpersuaded and ordered specific performance.

(d) If the purchaser was buying the land for the purpose of immediate resale at a profit, its supposed uniqueness is of no real consequence to her, and damages are sometimes considered an adequate remedy. See Watkins v. Paul, 95 Idaho 499, 511 P.2d 781 (1973). Cf. Chan v. Smider, 31 Wash. App. 730, 644 P.2d 727 (1982). See also Brenner, Specific Performance of Contracts for the Sale of

Land Purchased for Resale or Investment, 24 McGill L. J. 513 (1978).

(e) Both specific performance and other remedies may be denied if the sales contract contains precedent or concurrent conditions that have not been fulfilled or if the plaintiff is in substantial breach. (Precedent and concurrent conditions in sales contracts are discussed later in Section G of this chapter.)

(f) If the contract gives the vendor the right to forfeit the purchaser's earnest money as liquidated damages, the clause may be treated as the vendor's sole remedy, barring him from specific performance. See Hatcher v. Panama City Nursing Center, Inc., 461 So. 2d 288 (Fla. App. 1985). Cf. Rubinstein v. Rubinstein, 23 N.Y.2d 293, 296 N.Y.S.2d 354, 244 N.E.2d 49 (1968). Most decisions allow the vendor to elect between the two remedies unless the clause is, by its own terms, the sole remedy.

4. *Specific performance with abatement of the price.* If the seller does not own all the property covered by the contract, the purchaser may desire, and can generally obtain, specific performance with an abatement of the price to reflect the shortage in the land. See, e.g., Burk v. Hefley, 32 Ark. App. 133, 798 S.W.2d 109 (1990); Ewing v. Bissell, 105 Nev. 488, 777 P.2d 1320 (1989). The same principle is applied if the seller owns only a fractional undivided interest in the property he contracted to sell. See Chastain v. Schomburg, 258 Ga. 218, 367 S.E.2d 230 (1988).

5. *The vendee's lien.* If the vendor breaches but refuses to return the purchaser's earnest money, some states give the purchaser a "vendee's lien" on the property to secure its recovery. See Sparks v. Charles Wayne Group, 568 So. 2d 512 (Fla. App. 1990) (purchaser may file a notice of lis pendens in support of his vendee's lien); Cox v. RKA Corp., 164 N. J. 487, 753 A.2d 1112 (2000) (vendee's lien would be subordinate to a construction mortgage on the property, to the extent of payments made by vendee after gaining notice of construction mortgage). Unless the contract is recorded (which is unlikely), a conveyance by the vendor to a good faith purchaser without notice of the contract will free the land of the lien. See State Sav. & Loan Ass'n v. Kauaian Development Co., 50 Haw. 540, 445 P.2d 109 (1968). Cf. In re Pearl, 40 B. R. 860 (Bankr. D. N.J. 1984).

6. *The vendor's lien.* If the purchaser breaches after the vendor has transferred title to her (not a very common situation), there is a "vendor's lien" (perhaps more aptly a "grantor's lien") in most states to secure payment to the grantor of the remaining purchase price. See, e.g., Bolen v. Bolen, 169 S.W3d 59 (Ky. Ct. App. 2005). Again, however, a further transfer by the purchaser to a good faith purchaser for value will defeat the lien. See Cooksey v. Sinder, 682 S.W.2d 252 (Tex. 1984).

The vendee's lien is an aid to rescission and restitution, whereas the vendor's lien is an aid to specific enforcement of the contract. In both cases a personal "deficiency" judgment can probably be obtained if the foreclosure of the lien does not produce sufficient funds to pay the plaintiff fully. See Quintana v. Anthony, 109 Idaho 977, 712 P.2d 678 (App. 1985).

7.   *Earnest money.* A purchaser is nearly always expected to make an "earnest money" deposit when submitting an offer to buy real estate. If the offer is accepted, the money may be taken directly by the seller, or held until the closing by the broker or the seller's attorney. (Which would you prefer as a buyer? As a broker?)

It is sometimes asserted that earnest money is essential to the formation of an enforceable contract, as otherwise there would be a lack of consideration. This is obviously wrong. What is the consideration for each party's promise in a real estate sale contract? The other party's promise! From a vendor's viewpoint, getting earnest money from the purchaser is obviously a sensible and desirable move, but it is not in the slightest legally essential.

Customs with respect to earnest money vary widely. In the Northeastern states, it may be very substantial—typically 10 percent or so of the total price. In the South and West it is often much smaller, and may be as little as a few hundred dollars, especially in lower-priced tract subdivisions. The amount is entirely a matter of negotiation. An illustrative clause, taken from the sales contract form reprinted in Section B of this chapter, reads as follows:

In the event of a material breach of this contract by the Buyer, the Seller may retain the earnest money deposit as liquidated damages for the Buyer's breach, or in the alternative may waive the right to liquidated damages and obtain such other remedies as are available in law or equity.

Depending on the circumstances, the amount of the deposit may be either smaller or greater than the vendor's actual damages. Hence the liquidated damages clause raises three common questions:

- May the vendor be compelled, notwithstanding the clause, to return some or all of the deposit if it exceeds his actual loss?

- Does the clause preclude an action by the vendor for additional damages if the deposit is too small to cover his actual loss?

- Does the clause preclude assertion of alternate remedies by the vendor, such as actual damages or specific performance? See Note 3(f), supra.

ORR V. GOODWIN

Supreme Court of New Hampshire, 2008
157 N.H. 511, 953 A.2d 1190

GALWAY, J.

The plaintiffs, Suzanne Orr and Nelson Bolstridge, appeal an order of the Superior Court (Houran, J.) granting summary judgment to the defendants, David A. Goodwin, Ann Goodwin, Aaron Goodwin and Kylie Goodwin. We affirm.

The parties do not dispute the relevant background facts. In October 2004, the parties executed a sales agreement in which the defendants agreed to purchase real and personal property in Madbury from the plaintiffs for $1,020,000. Upon execution of the agreement, the defendants paid a deposit of $10,000. The parties' sales agreement contained a clause titled "Liquidated Damages," which stated: "If the Buyer shall default in the performance of their [sic] obligation under this agreement, the amount of the deposit may, at the option of the Seller, become the property of the Seller as reasonable." In February 2005, an addendum was executed confirming that the defendants had paid an additional $15,000 as a deposit. The addendum also provided that the sale was to close by October 15, 2005.

In October 2005, the defendants informed the plaintiffs that they were not able to sell their home and, therefore, could not afford to purchase the plaintiffs' property. The plaintiffs retained the $25,000 deposit and it appears that there was virtually no further contact between the parties until early 2007.

Despite retaining the deposit, the plaintiffs instituted this suit in February 2007 to recover various damages, including carrying costs on the Madbury property and costs incurred in purchasing and carrying other property, as a result of the defendants' failure to consummate their agreement. The defendants moved for summary judgment, which the trial court granted. After their motion for reconsideration was denied, the plaintiffs filed this appeal.

* * *

On appeal, the plaintiffs first contend that the trial court erred in concluding that the liquidated damages clause of the parties' contract was enforceable. Interpretation of the parties' written agreement is a question of law, which we review de novo. Czumak v. N.H. Div. of Developmental Servs., 155 N.H. 368, 373, 923 A.2d 208 (2007). When interpreting a written agreement, we give the language used by the parties its reasonable meaning, considering the circumstances and the context in which the agreement was negotiated, and reading the document as a whole. Id.

According to the plaintiffs, the liquidated damages clause fails two of the three criteria for a valid liquidated damages provision and, therefore, cannot be enforced against them. Before a liquidated damages clause will be enforced, three conditions must be met: (1) the damages anticipated as a result of the breach are uncertain in amount or difficult to prove; (2) the parties intended to liquidate damages in advance; and (3) the amount agreed upon must be reasonable and not greatly disproportionate to the presumable loss or injury. Shallow Brook Assoc's v. Dube, 135 N.H. 40, 46, 599 A.2d 132 (1991). The plaintiffs concede that the damages were uncertain in amount. Accordingly, the first factor is met.

As to the second factor, the plaintiffs contend that it was not their intention or belief that "their damages would be limited to the $25,000.00 deposit." The amount of damages, however, is not at issue in considering this factor. The relevant consideration is whether there is evidence that the parties intended to liquidate their damages in advance. Here, the contract contains a clause specifically titled "Liquidated Damages," which initially demonstrates an intent to liquidate damages. The plaintiffs contend, however, that because the clause does not use the term "liquidated damages" outside the title, it is insufficient to demonstrate an intent to provide for such damages. At oral argument, the plaintiffs also contended that the term "reasonable" as used in the clause applies to the term "property," and thus does not demonstrate an intent to define liquidated damages. We are not persuaded by either argument.

Although the term "liquidated damages" appears only in the title, the language of the clause defines how damages are handled by delineating the rights of the sellers relative to the buyers' deposit in the event of default, a result that would not change had the term been repeated in the body of the clause. Further, to interpret the clause as suggested by the plaintiffs would allow them to retain the deposit as "reasonable property." The plaintiffs, however, do not indicate what the term "reasonable property" means. The interpretation advanced by the defendants, in contrast, regards the term "reasonable" as defining the liquidated damages referenced in the title. We believe the defendants' interpretation to be sounder and in line with the apparent intent of the clause. Given the title of the clause and the rights it defines, we conclude that the clause was intended to provide for liquidated damages and, therefore, that this provision evinces an intent by the parties to liquidate damages in advance. See id. Therefore, the second factor has been met.

"The third prong of the test requires that the amount stipulated was a reasonable one, that is to say, not greatly disproportionate to the presumable loss or injury." Id. at 47, 599 A.2d 132. In determining whether the stipulated amount is reasonable, "[o]ur function on appeal is to determine whether a reasonable person could have arrived at the same determination as the trial court, based on the evidence, and we will not upset the trial court's finding as long as it is substantiated by the record and is not erroneous as a matter of law." Id. "Thus, it is not enough that we might have ruled differently had we been asked to decide this question in the first instance. Rather we must affirm the trial court's finding unless it is unsupported by the evidence." Id.

While we have stated that the relevant consideration is whether the amount stipulated is not disproportionate to the presumable loss, we have also stated that it is proper to look at the actual damages suffered in determining whether the amount is reasonable. Id. at 47–48, 599 A.2d 132. Therefore, we have adopted a two-part test for assessing the reasonableness of the amount stipulated whereby we "first judge whether the provision was a reasonable estimate of difficult-to-ascertain damage at the time the parties agreed to it." Id. at 48, 599 A.2d 132. If it is a reasonable estimate, we must then conduct a retrospective appraisal of the liquidated damages provision, and if the actual damages turn out to be easily ascertainable, we must then consider whether the stipulated sum is unreasonable and grossly disproportionate to the actual damages from a breach. Id. at 48–49, 599 A.2d 132. If so, the liquidated damages provision will be deemed unenforceable as a penalty, and the aggrieved party will be awarded no more than the actual damages. Id. at 49, 599 A.2d 132. Thus, "even if the liquidated sum is reasonable in light of the anticipated or presumable loss, the provision will not be enforced if the actual loss to the party is minimal and easy to prove." Id. at 48, 599 A.2d 132; see also Restatement (Second) of Contracts § 356 comment b at 157–58 (1981). As the parties alleging that the liquidated damages amount is unreasonable, the plaintiffs bear the burden of proof. Dube, 135 N.H. at 50, 599 A.2d 132.

In conducting the above analysis, we note that in a land sale contract the proper measure of damages is the seller's loss of bargain; that is, the difference between the contract price and the actual value of the real estate at the time of the breach. Id. at 49, 599 A.2d 132. Additionally, while, generally, damages may be recovered for those harms that are reasonably foreseeable at the time the parties entered into the contract, see Indep. Mechanical Contractors v. Gordon T. Burke & Sons, 138 N.H. 110, 114, 635 A.2d 487 (1993), much of the damages claimed by the plaintiffs arise from costs associated with various transactions related to other properties, and undertaken by the plaintiffs months after the parties here signed their agreement. Because those costs were not reasonably foreseeable at the time the contract was made, we do not consider those alleged damages in determining whether the liquidated damages clause is reasonable.

Turning to the first consideration, we note, as we did in *Dube*, that no evidence was presented to suggest that the liquidated damages provision was an unreasonable estimate of difficult-to-ascertain damages at the time the parties agreed to it, see Dube, 135 N.H. at 49, 599 A.2d 132; nor do the plaintiffs argue that the provision was an unreasonable estimate. Thus, the first consideration is satisfied.

Second, the plaintiffs did not present evidence about the actual value of the real estate at the time of the breach. Thus, the plaintiffs did not demonstrate that their actual damages are easily ascertainable. Also, the plaintiffs' response to interrogatories state that the property had since been re-listed for approximately $20,000 less than the amount the defendants had offered to pay, indicating that any actual loss of bargain damages are not grossly disproportionate to the liquidated damages amount.

Furthermore, as stated above, the basis upon which a liquidated damages clause may be invalidated under this consideration is if it is excessive or punitive. Id. We are not aware of, and the plaintiffs do not point to, any authority supporting their proposition that a liquidated damages clause ought to be invalidated as being insufficient, particularly where the liquidated damages are retained only at the option of the injured party. Because the plaintiffs did not demonstrate that their damages were easily ascertainable at the time the contract was made or breached, and because the amount at issue is not a penalty or grossly disproportionate to any actual loss from the breach, we conclude that the third factor has been satisfied. Accordingly, the trial court did not err in upholding the liquidated damages provision.

The plaintiffs contend that even if the liquidated damages provision is valid, it does not limit them to receiving the liquidated damages as their sole and exclusive remedy. This is so because, according to the plaintiffs, the clause does not define liquidated damages as the sole available remedy, and their retention of the liquidated damages does not bar a suit for their actual damages. The trial court concluded that even if there was a genuine dispute over the exclusivity of the liquidated damages remedy, it was immaterial because the plaintiffs' retention of the deposit as liquidated damages constituted an election of remedies.

We are not aware of, and the parties do not point to, any case in New Hampshire directly addressing this issue. Other courts have found that the designation of a deposit as "liquidated damages" evidences the parties' intention to limit the seller's recovery to the stipulated amount. Annotation, Provision in Land Contract for Liquidated Damages upon Default of Purchaser as Affecting Right of Vendor to Maintain Action for Damages for Breach of Contract, 39 A.L.R. 5th 33, 54–55 (1996). Moreover, the absence of a provision expressly permitting the recovery of actual damages has been held to prevent a seller from pursuing such a remedy. Id. at 58–61. There are, however, instances where courts have found that use of permissive terms, such as "option," permit a seller to sue for actual damages despite the existence of a valid liquidated damages provision. Id. at 67–69. Likewise, there are courts that have permitted a non-breaching party to retain liquidated damages and then to pursue an additional claim for actual damages, even in the absence of permissive language. Id. at 77–79. We are persuaded that the rule most in line with our jurisprudence is that liquidated damages and actual damages are, absent express language permitting recovery of both, mutually exclusive remedies, and that where an election is permitted, the election of one remedy bars pursuit of the other.

In *General Linen Services, Inc. v. Franconia Investment Associates, L.P.*, 150 N.H. 595, 599–600, 842 A.2d 105 (2004), we concluded that because a provision for liquidated damages was unenforceable, the plaintiff was entitled to recover actual damages. Thus, the plaintiff could seek actual damages only because liquidated damages were unavailable. We reached a similar conclusion in *Technical Aid Corp. v. Allen*, 134 N.H. 1, 22–23, 591 A.2d 262 (1991). These decisions indicate that the right to recover liquidated damages and the right to recover actual damages are mutually exclusive remedies. This conclusion comports with the general purpose of a liquidated damages provision to eliminate the right and responsibility of a plaintiff to prove actual damages. 24 R. Lord, Williston on Contracts § 65:31, at 359–60 (4th ed. 2002). Thus, although the clause does not specifically define liquidated damages as the plaintiffs' sole remedy, when the plaintiffs availed themselves of it, they foreclosed their pursuit of actual damages. To conclude otherwise would permit recovery of both liquidated and actual damages, a result contrary to the purpose of a liquidated damages clause and decisions of this court.

The plaintiffs contend that any "mistake" they may have made in retaining the deposit as liquidated damages should not operate to bar them from pursuing their actual damages. The trial court, relying upon the Restatement (Second) of Contracts § 378, at 228 (1981), concluded that the plaintiffs' election of liquidated damages was final. The plaintiffs argue, based upon the same provision of the Restatement, that because the defendants have not materially changed their position based upon their election and because their election was made with ignorance of material facts, they are not precluded from seeking their actual damages. Assuming for purposes of this opinion that the Restatement applies, we disagree.

First, the plaintiffs do not allege any material facts of which they were ignorant in making their election. They allege only that they interpreted the contract to permit recovery of liquidated damages and actual damages. As such, we do not find this argument availing.

The plaintiffs' argument that they are not bound by their election because there has been no material change by the defendants is in accord with general principles of contract law that when a party has a choice of remedy and elects one, he or she is not bound by his or her first choice in some instances. See id.; see also 13 R. Lord, Williston on Contracts § 39:34, at 650 (4th ed. 2000). The electing party, however, will be bound by his or her choice when there has been justifiable reliance or a material change by the other party such that a new selection would be unfairly prejudicial. 13 R. Lord, Williston on Contracts § 39:34, at 650; 12 Corbin on Contracts § 1220, at 495, 503–04 (Interim ed. 2002). According to the Restatement, "[a] change of position is 'material' within the meaning of this Section if it is such that in all the circumstances a shift in remedies would be unjust." Restatement (Second) of Contracts § 378 comment at 228.

The trial court concluded that the plaintiffs' election prevented them from pursuing a claim for their actual damages. Although the trial court did not specifically find that permitting the plaintiffs to seek a shift in remedies would be unjust, we assume that it made all subsidiary findings necessary to support its ruling that the plaintiffs are precluded from pursuing a claim for their actual damages. See N.H. Dep't of Envtl. Servs. v. Mottolo, 155 N.H. 57, 63, 917 A.2d 1277 (2007). Here, the trial court had evidence that the plaintiffs retained the deposit, an act indicating that they had elected the liquidated damages as their remedy and had, therefore, opted not to pursue a claim for their actual damages. Further, the plaintiffs retained the deposit, without communication to the defendants, for nearly a year and a half before instituting this suit. Indeed, the plaintiffs have never indicated that they would return the liquidated damages prior to seeking to recover their alleged actual damages. Thus, the defendants have been deprived of the use of $25,000 for a substantial time without any indication that it might be returned and the plaintiffs have had the benefit of the money without any offer to return it prior to seeking additional damages. Under these circumstances, we conclude that the trial court did not err in determining that the plaintiffs' election was final, precluding a claim for their actual damages.

Finally, the plaintiffs contend that the parties' contract should be construed against the defendants because the parties had unequal bargaining power, and because the defendants did not disclose a material contingency. Based upon the record before us, we are not persuaded by the plaintiffs' arguments, nor are we convinced that they have any impact on the validity or enforceability of the parties' contract and its liquidated damages clause. Accordingly, because the parties' liquidated damages clause is valid, and because the plaintiffs are bound by their election of the liquidated damages pursuant to that clause, we hold that the trial court did not err in granting summary judgment to the defendants.

Affirmed.

NOTES AND QUESTIONS

1. *Election of remedies.* The *Orr* opinion reads as if it were written by two different judges. The first seems to have believed that the liquidated damages clause was enforceable, and hence was the sole damages remedy available to the plaintiff vendors. The second seems to have believed that the vendors had a choice of liquidated or actual damages, but made that choice (or "elected their remedy") by retaining the $25,000 earnest money. But under the first view, because there was only one available damages remedy, any discussion of "election of remedies" would be irrelevant. Of course, both views lead to the same conclusion on these facts, but which of them represents the court's holding? *good a*

2. *Contesting the liquidated damages clause.* It may seem odd that in the *Orr* case it was the vendor, the party for whose primary benefit the liquidated clause was probably included in the contract, who was attempting to characterize the clause as an unenforceable "penalty." Such an argument is more typically made by the purchaser, who often argues that the liquidated amount greatly exceeds the vendor's actual damages, and thus should not be enforced. The New Hampshire court rejected the vendor's argument in *Orr*, but the vendor's argument worked (and gave the vendor a far greater recovery than mere retention of the earnest money) in Community Development Service, Inc. v. Replacement Parts Manufacturing, Inc., 679 S.W.2d 721 (Tex. App. 1984).

3. *When is reasonableness determined?* Courts usually say that the reasonableness of the amount of liquidated damages should be judged as of the time the contract is entered into, not necessarily at the date of breach. At least two other judicial approaches, however, can be found in the case law. Some courts assess reasonableness as of the date of the breach, and hold that the forfeited amount must not be unreasonably disproportionate to the actual damages suffered. See Hershey v. Simpson, 111 Idaho 491, 725 P.2d 196, 200 (App. 1986). Others, like *Orr*, require reasonableness *both* at the date of contracting and the date of breach. See Mason v. Fakhimi, 109 Nev. 1153, 865 P.2d 333 (1993) (finding that a forfeiture of three times the vendor's actual damages was not unduly disproportionate). There is no doubt that the first approach is gaining ground and is likely the majority view. See, e.g., Hong v. Somerset Associates, 161 Cal. App. 3d 111, 207 Cal. Rptr. 597 (1984); Fuqua Constr. Co. v. Pillar Devel., S.E.2d 633 (Ga. App. 2008); Kelly v. Marx, 428 Mass. 877, 705 N.E.2d 1114 (1999); Watson v. Ingram, 124 Wash. 2d 845, 881 P.2d 247 (1994). The Appendix to the majority opinion in Kelly v. Marx, 44 Mass. App. Ct. 825, 694 N.E.2d 869 (1998) lists 22 jurisdictions as determining reasonableness only as of the date of the contract, and 20 jurisdictions as also requiring reasonableness at the date of the breach.

A few courts that look only to reasonableness at the time of contracting take the view that the vendor may not retain the deposit if he suffered no damages at all. See Stabenau v. Cairelli, 22 Conn. App. 578, 577 A.2d 1130 (1990); Shanghai Investment Co. v. Alteka Co., 92 Hawai'i 482, 993 P.2d 516

(2000) (proof of actual damages must be considered to justify a forfeiture of a $5 million deposit on a $35 million purchase), overruled by Blair v. Ing, 96 Hawaii 327, 31 P.3d 184. Section 356 of the Restatement (Second) of Contracts appears to support this position, but there is not much support for it in the cases. See Restatement (Second) of Contracts § 356, cmt. B illus. 4; Note, "Keep the Change!": A Critique of the No Actual Injury Defense to Liquidated Damages, 65 Wash. L. Rev. 977 (1990).

From an economic viewpoint, a liquidated damages provision is a form of insurance bought by the purchaser from the vendor. The buyer says, in effect, "If I fail to perform this contract, I realize that I may be liable for actual damages. Whether those damages will be large or small is impossible to predict, since they will depend on future changes in market values that are inherently uncertain. Because I'm averse to that sort of risk, I would prefer to fix in advance a sum that I will have to pay if I breach. Whether your actual damages are high, low, or nonexistent, I will pay the agreed amount instead."

If the liquidated damage amount is fairly bargained between the parties, it presumably represents a result that both of them prefer when they contract. Hence, any court decision that overrides this outcome will have the effect of undermining the bargaining process, giving one party a windfall for which he or she did not bargain, and producing a result that is economically inefficient. As the Washington court put it, "The negotiated liquidated damages sum represents the parties' best estimate of the value of the breach and permits the parties to allocate and incorporate these risks in their negotiations." Watson v. Ingram, 124 Wash. 2d 845, 881 P.2d 247 (1994).

Thus economists usually argue that liquidated damages clauses should always be enforced, even when they allow the vendor to recover much more than actual damages or when there are no damages at all. The only inquiry should be the *prospective* reasonableness of the clause, at the time of contracting—or perhaps better yet, the inquiry should merely be whether the clause was the result of fair negotiation, irrespective of its amount. See Rea, Efficiency Implications of Penalties and Liquidated Damages, 13 J. Legal Stud. 147 (1984); Guiliano v. Cleo, Inc., 995 S.W.2d 88 (Tenn. 1999) (only prospective reasonableness required; a convenient survey of other jurisdictions is included in the opinion).

4.   *How large a forfeiture is reasonable?* Many courts have been willing to permit retention of quite large deposits despite the fact that they plainly exceeded the vendor's actual damages. See, e.g., U.S. v. Ponnapula, 246 F.3d 576 (6th Cir. 2001) (15% of price); Leeber v. Deltona Corp., 546 A.2d 452 (Me. 1988) (under Florida law, 15% of price); Siegel v. Levy Organization Development Co., Inc., 182 Ill. App. 3d 859, 131 Ill. Dec. 340, 538 N.E.2d 715 (1989) (20 percent of price); Wallace Real Estate Inv., Inc. v. Groves, 124 Wash. 2d 881, 881 P.2d 1010 (1994) (17 percent of price). Amounts up to ten percent of the purchase price are nearly always acceptable to the courts. Cf. McIlvenny v. Horton, 227 Ark. 826, 302 S.W.2d 70 (1957) (forfeiture of 16 percent of price was an unenforceable penalty).

New York appeared at first to adopt a ten percent rule of thumb in Maxton Builders, Inc. v. Lo Galbo, 68 N.Y.2d 373, 509 N.Y.S.2d 507, 502 N.E.2d 184 (1986). Later, in Uzan v. 845 UN Limited Partnership, 10 A.D.3d 230, 778 N.Y.S.2d 171 (App. Div. 2004), two Turkish billionaires contracted to buy two apartments in a building being constructed by Donald Trump for $32 million. A few weeks before the scheduled closing the World Trade Center was attacked and destroyed by terrorists, and the buyers changed their minds, refusing to close. Their earnest money deposit was a whopping 25 percent of the price, or nearly $8 million. The court thought that amount might well be considered a reasonable estimate of probable damages, but ultimately held that "reasonableness" did not matter—*any* deposit, even an unreasonable one, can be retained by the vendor under New York law. The New York court noted that "real estate down payments have been subject to limited supervision. They have only been refunded upon a showing of disparity of bargaining power between the parties, duress, fraud, illegality or mutual mistake."

Several states have adopted statutes setting a presumptively valid level of liquidated damages as a percentage of the sales price. These statutes typically apply only to sales of single-family residences and do not prevent the vendor's retention of a larger amount if the vendor can satisfy the usual common law approaches described in Note 2, supra. See, e.g., Calif. Civ. Code § 1675 (3% of sales price); Wash. Rev. Code § 64.04 (5% of sales price).

5. *Does the presence of a liquidated damages clause bar other remedies?* If a liquidated damages clause does not address the issue of other remedies, the usual rule, as stated in the *Orr* opinion, is that the vendor may not seek actual damages in addition to liquidated damages, but may seek specific performance (because a limitation on *damages* does not imply a limitation on nondamage remedies like specific performance). See Conner v. Auburn Partners, L.L.C., 852 So. 2d 755 (Ala. Civ. App. 2002); Stoebuck & Whitman, The Law of Property § 10.4 (3d ed. 2000). But if the liquidated damages clause specifies that the vendor may elect either actual damages or the liquidated sum, or if the clause provides that retention of the deposit is optional with the vendor, many courts indeed allow the vendor to make the election after the breach has occurred. See, e.g., Gaskins v. Young, 2004 WL 1178278 (Ohio Ct. App. 2004); Alexsey v. Kelly, 205 A.D.2d 649, 614 N.Y.S.2d 734 (1994).

Other courts, however, hold that such a clause is not really a liquidated damage clause at all, but rather is inherently a penalty clause and hence is unenforceable. See Catholic Charities of Archdiocese of Chicago v. Thorpe, 318 Ill. App. 3d 304, 251 Ill. Dec. 764, 741 N.E.2d 651 (2000) (holding that such a clause is an attempt by the vendor "to have his cake and eat it too."). Accord, Real Estate World, Inc. v. Southeastern Land Fund, Inc., 227 S.E.2d 340 (Ga. 1976); Lefemine v. Baron, 573 So.2d 326 (Fla. 1991). See generally Annot., 39 A.L.R. 5th 33 (1996).

Even if the presence of liquidated clause does not bar other remedies, the exercise of the clause may do so. Some courts hold that, if the vendor wishes to pursue other remedies, the earnest money (as a liquidated damage sum) must be returned to the purchaser within a reasonable time; otherwise, the vendor will be viewed as having elected the remedy of liquidated damages, and all other remedies will be barred. See, e.g., Heflin v. Brackelsberg, 374 S.W.3d 755 (Ark. 2010); McKeon v. Crump, 53 P.3d 494 (Ut.App. 2002).

6. *Limitations on the purchaser's remedies.* In several cases involving sales of new condominium units, courts have dealt with contracts that gave the developer the usual right to retain the purchaser's earnest money deposit as liquidated damages, or to assert other legal or equitable remedies. But these contracts were unusual in that they made the *purchaser's* sole remedy, in the event of a breach by the developer, a termination of the contract and refund of the deposit—in effect, rescission and restitution.

In a condominium development, sales contracts are often signed before construction of the project commences. As a result, the executory period of the contracts can be quite lengthy. The obvious purpose of this sort of clause is to permit the developer, if the units' values rise during construction, to cancel the original contracts and sell to other buyers at higher prices. Such clauses have aroused considerable disfavor in the Florida courts. Consider the following language from Ocean Dunes of Hutchinson Island Dev. Corp. v. Colangelo, 463 So. 2d 437 (Fla. App. 1985):

> There is no question that parties to a contract may agree to limit their respective remedies and that those remedies need not be the same. Jay Vee Realty Corp. v. Jaymar Acres, Inc., 436 So. 2d 1053 (Fla. 4th DCA 1983); Wright & Seaton v. Prescott, 420 So. 2d 623 (Fla. 4th DCA 1982). Such contractual provisions, however, must be reasonable to be enforced. * * * There is nothing reasonable about the foregoing default provisions. In this contract, the seller's obligations are wholly illusory, while the buyers' are quite real. The developer can opt to sell the unit to any new buyer willing to pay a higher price than the existing contract price, or even fail to show title to be vested in the developer as required by paragraph 5 of the Agreement, with absolutely no harmful consequences; the developer must only return the buyer's *own* money. A return of one's own money hardly constitutes damages in any meaningful sense. It is especially unconscionable in this case in light of the buyers' deprivation of the use of their money for several years.

If the seller's obligations are illusory, as the *Ocean Dunes* court holds, what is the result? Traditionally, courts held that if one party had no meaningful obligation, the contract was unenforceable by either party for lack of consideration. But increasingly in modern times, the courts are likely to restructure such contracts to make the obligation meaningful. See I Farnsworth, Contracts § 2.13 (1990). That is what the court did in *Ocean Dunes*. It imposed a duty on the part of the seller to grant specific performance, despite that contract's disclaimer of that remedy. See also Embree v. Bank of New York Mellon, 2013 WL 6384776 (D.N.H. 2013), where the court concluded that the limitation to a return of earnest money should be enforced only if the vendor's breach was unintentional.

D. TIME OF PERFORMANCE AND TENDER

Closings of real estate sales often occur later than the parties agreed. There are manifold reasons, simply because so many things can go wrong or need to be resolved. Often the real estate broker or brokers, who have an obvious and strong interest in getting to the closing, will work energetically at solving the problems. But when the closing does not occur by the agreed time, one of the parties may get "cold feet" and refuse to close, claiming that the other party's lateness is a material breach of the real estate sales contract. At this point, several facts take on critical importance. Did the original contract make "time of the essence?" If it did not, has one of the parties properly made "time of the essence" unilaterally? If time is not "of the essence," how far beyond the agreed closing date is the late party permitted to perform? As the agreed closing date approaches, it is common to have a flurry of communications, some of which may lack precision and clarity. The following case is illustrative.

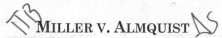

MILLER v. ALMQUIST

New York Supreme Court, Appellate Division, 1998
241 A.D.2d 181, 671 N.Y.S.2d 746

TOM, JUSTICE

This case arises out of a proposed sale of a cooperative unit between next door neighbors. The plaintiff-buyers live in Apartment 4S at 150 East 69th Street in Manhattan. The defendant-sellers lived in Apartment 4T (the "Premises"). The buyers anticipated buying the sellers' apartment with the goal of consolidating the two apartments into a single living unit for their growing family.

On February 25, 1997, the parties entered into a contract of sale for the Premises at a purchase price of $545,000 to be paid in cash. The contract provided for a 10% down payment and contained no financing contingency clause. However, the buyers did not represent that they would not seek financing, and they did apply for a loan. The contract specified a closing date of April 1, 1997, but did not specify that time was of the essence. At the time of contract, the buyers paid a down payment of $54,500 to be held in escrow by the sellers' attorney. The contract further provided that in the event the buyers defaulted, the sellers would be permitted to terminate the contract and the buyers would forfeit their down payment.

The cooperative Board of Directors approved the sale on March 25, 1997, six days prior to the scheduled closing date. Thereafter, the buyers experienced delays arising from loan clearance and documentation. By letter dated March 31, 1997, the buyers' attorney sought an adjournment of the closing until April 16, 1997, subject to the availability of the cooperative's transfer agent. As a consequence, neither party appeared on April 1st. By responsive letter dated April 2, 1997, the sellers' attorney agreed to the adjournment, but claimed that time was now of the essence.

On April 14, 1997, the buyers' attorney contacted the lender to arrange for apportionment of the proceeds for the April 16th closing. For the first time, the lender's attorney asked how certain tax liens* would be resolved. The buyers' attorney contacted his client, who indicated that the liens had been satisfied years ago, but that they could not immediately locate canceled checks evidencing satisfaction of the liens. The lender required proof of payment by the next morning, April 15th, indicating that otherwise the April 16th closing would have to be adjourned pending receipt of proof. The buyers received a faxed copy of the satisfaction of lien from the New York State Department of Taxation and Finance. This documentation had been sent to the buyers' office at 5:22 PM on April 14th, followed by written confirmation dated April 15th. The clients provided the documentation to their attorney, who then provided it to the lender enclosed with a letter faxed to the lender's attorney at 11:24 AM on April 15th. This evidence of satisfaction was acceptable to the lender. However, a closing could not be scheduled with the lender at this time for the following day due to the delay in obtaining the satisfaction. The lender indicated that it was available to close on April 18th.

Also on April 15th, several communications went back and forth between the buyers and sellers. Initially, the buyers' attorney contacted the sellers' attorney, and indicated that the buyers' lender had just informed the buyers about the results of the lien search. This was followed by a faxed letter at 5:58 PM to the sellers' attorney confirming a prior conversation that the buyers could not attend the closing scheduled for the next day. This letter also confirmed the buyers' willingness to pay the sellers $300 per day for maintenance and opportunity cost, which counsel characterized as being well in excess of that calculated by the sellers' attorney. The buyers' attorney initially indicated that the buyers would be able to close in seven days, and asked for a response.

The buyers did not appear on April 16, 1997 for the scheduled closing. By certified mail dated April 16, 1997, the sellers' attorney informed the buyers' attorney that as a consequence of the buyers' failure to appear that day, and the prior declaration that time was of the essence,

---

* These were apparently liens for state income taxes owed by the buyers, which might have had priority over the new mortgage if they were not satisfied prior to or at the closing.— Eds.

the buyers were in default and the down payment would be delivered to the sellers. By faxed letter dated April 16, 1997, at 12:58 PM, the buyers' attorney now sought to confirm the assurance given in a prior conversation that the buyers were now ready, willing and able to close on April 18, 1997, again subject to the availability of the cooperative's transfer agent. By letter faxed at 5:26 PM on April 16, 1997, the buyers' attorney confirmed a conversation with the sellers' attorney that the sellers would not appear on April 18th and had declined to agree to any other date. By letter faxed and hand delivered on April 18th, the buyers' attorney informed the sellers' attorney that a closing date was reserved for April 23, 1997 since this was the first available date for the cooperative's transfer agent. This letter also advised the sellers that the time of the essence clause had not been contemplated in the contract and constituted only a unilateral declaration by the sellers' attorney. By a second letter that day, faxed at 5:01 PM, the buyers' attorney again confirmed that his clients were ready, willing and able to close on April 23rd, but that the sellers had stated an unwillingness to attend. By letter dated April 21, 1997, the buyers' attorney rejected the default notice and again confirmed his clients' willingness to close; the letter demanded that the down payment remain escrowed. The same letter also indicated that the buyers had been willing to make several concessions to keep the deal alive, that the sellers had suffered no prejudice, and that the sellers' attorney would be acting in bad faith if the closing did not take place. By an April 22, 1997 letter, the sellers' attorney then contacted the transfer agent to cancel the April 23, 1997 reservation. The buyers warrant that they appeared for closing on April 23, 1997 with all necessary documentation and a check for $490,000.

The buyers commenced this action on or about April 27, 1997, seeking to enjoin the sellers from terminating the contract, from implementing a forfeiture of the down payment and from contracting to sell the apartment to any other party. The sellers cross-moved for summary judgment dismissing the complaint on the basis that the contract already had been terminated, after which the buyers also sought summary judgment. By order and judgment entered June 5, 1997, the Supreme Court, New York County (Harold Tompkins, J.), noting the absence of a financing contingency clause and finding that the sellers had made time of the essence, granted the sellers' cross-motion for summary judgment dismissing the complaint. Plaintiffs-buyers appeal and we now reverse.

We have long been guided by the rule that "every contract contains an implied obligation by each party to deal fairly with the other and to eschew actions which would deprive the other party of the fruits of the agreement." Greenwich Village Associates v. Salle, 110 A.D.2d 111, 115, 493 N.Y.S.2d 461; Gross v. Neuman, 53 A.D.2d 2, 5, 385 N.Y.S.2d 46, in furtherance of the covenant of good faith implied in every contract, Dalton v. Educational Testing Service, 87 N.Y.2d 384, 639 N.Y.S.2d 977, 663 N.E.2d 289.

When a contract for sale of real property does not specify that time is of the essence, either party is entitled to a reasonable adjournment of the closing date. In granting an adjournment, the other party may unilaterally impose a condition that time be of the essence as to the rescheduled date. The effectiveness of this condition, though, is contingent on the specificity of the notice and on the reasonableness of the time period. The notice in this case was sufficiently clear and unequivocal. The question is whether it afforded the buyers a reasonable time to close. What constitutes a reasonable time to close depends on the facts and circumstances of the particular case. Among the factors to be considered are the nature and object of the contract, the previous conduct of the parties, the presence or absence of good faith, the experience of the parties and the possibility of hardship or prejudice to either one, as well as the specific number of days provided for the performance. Reasonableness in this case turns on whether the post-notice time period provided a reasonable time period in which to close especially when the time of the essence provision was unilaterally made by the sellers after the buyers had selected a very short adjourned closing date.

We initially note that the time period from the initial scheduled closing date of April 1st to the time when the buyers were ready, willing and able to close was very short. From the receipt of the time of the essence letter dated April 2, 1997 to the April 15th request for an adjournment was a matter of days, and this entire period was only six weeks after the contract was signed. The very brevity of the additional adjournment—two days for the buyers' purposes—supports the conclusion that the few days initially allowed were not reasonably sufficient to achieve the buyers' purpose. Parenthetically, although the buyers requested 15 days for the initial adjournment, they reasonably could have requested a longer period. Insofar as time was not of the essence for the contract's law date, and in the absence of discernible prejudice, the sellers could not have rejected a moderately longer adjournment period. A moderately longer adjournment period, as it turns out, would have avoided the very problem that arose in this case. The delay was occasioned only by the usual sort of documentation glitch that is not uncommon in residential closings. If the sellers had extended the usual courtesies under these circumstances, there is every indication that the buyers, after the very minor adjournment sought, would have presented a check for the entire purchase price, and neighbors could have parted as friends.

The previous conduct of the parties, as well as the time periods involved, does not reveal extensive delays or acts of bad faith on behalf of the buyers. The buyers' attorney explained the delay and communicated regularly with the sellers' counsel; his explanation, which is a reasonable one, is well documented in the record. By April 14th, counsel knew that the financing was already approved; he was calling in regard to apportioning the check. The delay was merely to finalize the documentation required in connection with the lender's lien search and to reschedule for those parties appearing in a representative capacity. Hence, the sellers were assured that the sale would close in the immediate future.

The evidence in this case clearly shows that the buyers were not experienced in the real estate field. They suffered hardship as a result of their inability to close under the facts and circumstances of this case. They sought to acquire the next door apartment to break through so as to make adequate room for their growing family, which included two young children (ages two and four years old), and the wife's mentally retarded sister, whom they expected to move in with them. Because of the short delay, the buyers have lost not only their opportunity to purchase the adjacent apartment, but also their $54,500 deposit. Conversely, the sellers have failed to show how the delay of a few days would have prejudiced them, since they would have received the all-cash deal they had bargained for, as well as several thousand dollars in expenses dating back to April 1, 1997. It is undisputed that the sellers subsequently sold the premises to a third party at a higher sale price.

Taking all of these factors into consideration, we cannot conclude that the time allotted in the time of the essence letter in response to a short adjourned closing date chosen by the buyers was reasonable so as to inflexibly bind the buyers to an April 16th closing date.

* * *

In the various cases claimed by the sellers to support their position, there were significant warnings during the course of unreasonable delays that the delays had to end. The time periods allowed in tandem with the conduct of the parties factored into the determination whether the time to which the delaying party would be held was unreasonable. By sharp contrast, it was unreasonable under the unusual circumstances of the present case for the sellers, having unilaterally declared time to be of the essence, to have held the buyers to the very limited time period in issue, especially since time had not been made of the essence when the buyers had selected the date only days before. Under the present circumstances, in which only a single adjournment had been sought during a two-week period, it would be unreasonable to inflexibly hold the buyers to that date on the basis that the buyers had made the initial selection.

Accordingly, the order and judgment (one paper) of Supreme Court, New York County (Harold Tompkins, J.) entered June 5, 1997, granting defendants' motion for summary judgment dismissing the complaint, should be reversed, on the law, without costs, the motion denied, the complaint reinstated and, upon a search of the record, summary judgment should be granted to plaintiffs to the extent of directing that plaintiffs recover $54,000 plus interest from defendants. The Clerk is directed to enter judgment accordingly.

NOTES AND QUESTIONS

1.   *The significance of time being "essential."* It is usually said that, unless the contract itself or the circumstances make time "essential" or "of the essence," it is not such in equity, but that time is always of the essence at law, See II Am. L. Prop. § 11.45 (1952). This rather glib statement does not hold up well under close scrutiny, at least as applied to real estate sales contracts.

Assume that the time in question under a sales contract is the "closing date," and with the buyer's tender of the remaining purchase price and the seller's tender of a deed as concurrent conditions. If the sales contract does not expressly make "of the essence," what rules apply if one party is unable to perform on the specified closing date?

(1) The party who is late, but who tenders her own performance within a reasonable time after the agreed closing date, may nevertheless: (a) enforce the contract by specific performance; or (b) rescind the contract and recover her earnest money if the other party refuses to perform.

(2) The party who is late in tendering performance is, however, liable for "interim" damages caused by the delay.

(3) The party who is late is barred from recovering damages against the other party if the latter repudiates the contract (the late party's tender of performance on time being a concurrent condition to the other party's duty to perform "at law.")

For the first proposition above, that a party whose performance is late but is tendered within a reasonable time can have specific performance of the sales contract if time is not of the essence, there is abundant case support. See, e.g., Marioni v. 94 Broadway, Inc., 866 A.2d 208 (N.J. Super. App. Div. 2005); Parker v. Byrne, 996 A.2d 627 (R.I. 2010). In the *Miller* case above, the buyers could have obtained specific performance if they had wanted it. Likewise, *Miller* illustrates that the party who is reasonably late can rescind and recover her earnest money if the other side later refuses to perform.

On the other hand, if time *is* of the essence, one who is late cannot enforce the contract in equity or at law; the delay is treated as a material breach, and the innocent party's duty of performance is discharged. Hence, the innocent party is entitled to rescission, damages, or (if that party is the seller) retention of the buyer's earnest money as liquidated damages if the usual tests are met; see Grace v. Nappa, 46 N.Y.2d 560, 415 N.Y.S.2d 793,

389 N.E.2d 107 (1979); Joseph v. MTS Inv. Corp., 964 So. 2d 642 (Ala. 2006); ULTA § 2–302(b). Even a very slight delay is sufficient to discharge the innocent party; see Miceli v. Dierberg, 773 S.W.2d 154 (Mo. App. 1989) (purchaser's tender 3½ hours late discharged vendor). There's generally no "good faith" duty to give a time extension; see Lafayette Place Associates v. Boston Redevelopment Authority, 427 Mass. 509, 694 N.E.2d 820 (1998). If the contract sets a date but not an hour, tender any reasonable time on that date is sufficient; see Elm Land Co., Inc. v. Glasser, 174 A.2d 233 (N.J. Super. App. Div. 1961).

There also is abundant authority for the second proposition, that the late party may be liable for "interim" damages resulting from the delay. See, e.g., Richardson v. Van Dolah, 429 F.2d 912 (9th Cir. 1970); 6 Williston, Contracts § 846 (3d ed. 1957). If the late party does ultimately perform within a reasonable time, the damages in question are not based on "loss of bargain" because the innocent party eventually receives the bargained-for performance of the contract. Only the damages resulting from the delay *per se* should be recoverable, and in many cases the net amount will be quite small. For example, if the seller delays in conveying an apartment building, the buyer will have lost the rental income for that period, but also will have avoided the property taxes, insurance, maintenance expenses and mortgage interest that accrued during the same period. The buyers' offer to pay $300 per day for the delay in closing in the *Miller* case was an apparent recognition of their duty to pay these interim damages.

The third proposition listed above is the most doubtful. If time is not of the essence and one party is reasonably late in tendering performance, but the other party then repudiates the contract entirely, why is the late party not entitled to choose loss of bargain damages, rather than just specific performance or rescission? It is very hard to find any authority that strictly limits the late party to equitable remedies, and at least one case expressly allows damages as well. See Tanenbaum v. Sears, Roebuck and Co., 265 Pa. Super. 78, 401 A.2d 809 (1979). The original Restatement of Contracts § 276(e) appeared to limit the late party to specific performance. The Restatement (Second) of Contracts § 242 contains no such limit on its face, although its example (Illustration 5) speaks only of the late party's right to specific performance. We think the supposed distinction between law and equity in this area is simply a red herring.

Compare these rules, which favor the late-performing party, with the consequences for the late party if the sales contract affirmatively makes "time of the essence." If time *is* of the essence, one who is late cannot enforce the contract in equity or at law. The delay is treated as a material breach, and the innocent party's duty of performance is discharged. Consequently, the innocent party is entitled to rescission, damages, or (if that party is the seller) retention of the buyer's earnest money if the usual common law tests are met. See Grace v. Nappa, 46 N.Y.2d 560, 415 N.Y.S.2d 793, 389 N.E.2d 107 (1979); ULTA § 2–302(b). Even a very slight delay is sufficient to discharge the innocent party. See Miceli v. Dierberg, 773 S.W.2d 154 (Mo.

App. 1989) (purchaser's tender 3½ hours late discharged vendor). In the context of real estate sales contracts, generally there is no "good faith" duty to give the late party a time extension. See Lafayette Place Associates v. Boston Redevelopment Authority, 427 Mass. 509, 694 N.E.2d 820 (1998). If the sales contract sets a date but not an hour, tender any reasonable time on that date is sufficient. See Elm Land Co., Inc. v. Glasser, 174 A.2d 233 (N.J. Super. App. Div. 1961).

As noted above, the nonbreaching party may seek damages for the delay in performance of the sales contract. When the sales contract makes "time of the essence," any delay at all is a material breach and may give rise to damages. Of course, it is quite possible that no damages can be proven. For example, suppose the purchaser is late and the vendor is unwilling to extend the closing date precisely because the vendor has received a higher offer from someone else and wants to accept the higher offer. In this situation the vendor has not suffered "loss of bargain" damages from the purchaser's inability to close on time. If the vendor is the late party, the purchaser can recover any interim damages flowing from the delay even if she or he has accepted delivery of a deed. See Brogden v. Durkee, 16 So. 3d 113 (Ala. Civ. App. 2009).

To summarize, if time is not of the essence, a late (but reasonably late) tender of performance is a breach of the real estate sales contract, but it is not a material breach. One who commits an immaterial breach must pay the damages caused by the breach, but continues to have the power to enforce the contract. On the other hand, if time is not of the essence and a party tenders performance that is unreasonably late, or if time *is* of the essence and a party is late *at all*, the breach is material and the other party's duty of performance is discharged. See R & S Investments v. Howard, 95 Nev. 279, 593 P.2d 53 (1979). When we say "at all," we mean it—see the rather famous case of Doctorman v. Schroeder, 92 N. Eq. 676, 114 A. 810 (1921) (a delay of 30 minutes in performance was fatal where time was of the essence and the contract fixed a specific hour for closing).

2. *How much delay is unreasonable?* Even if time is not of the essence, an *unreasonable* delay will put the late party in material breach and deny him or her enforcement of the contract. See Ronne v. Ronne, 568 P.2d 1021 (Alaska 1977) (one month delay reasonable); E. Shepherdstown Developers, Inc. v. J. Russell Fritts, Inc., 183 W. Va. 691, 398 S.E.2d 517 (1990) (three year delay unreasonable); ULTA § 2–302(e). One of the champion cases is Krotz v. Sattler, 586 N.W.2d 336 (Iowa 1998), finding a ten-year delay reasonable! As a rule of thumb, the courts routinely find delays of 30 to 90 days to be reasonable.

3. *Circumstances making time essential.* Merely stating a precise date and time for the closing in the sales contract will not make time essential. A further statement (e.g., "Time is of the essence in the performance of this contract") is necessary. But even if the contract contains no such statement, time may be considered of the essence by courts due to special circumstances,

such as rapidly fluctuating values or evidence that one of the parties was particularly concerned with an on-time performance and the other party was aware of this fact. See Gunn v. Heggins, 964 So. 2d 586, 593 (Miss. App. 2007); Woodhull Corp. v. Saibaba Corp., 234 Ga. App. 707, 507 S.E.2d 493 (1998); 3A Corbin, Contracts § 716 (1960).

4. *Unilateral notice making time essential.* As the *Miller* case illustrates, even if time was not originally of the essence, either party can unilaterally make it so by giving the other notice to that effect and by fixing a date for performance that is a reasonable time beyond the date of the notice. According to the New York view, the notice must "clearly and distinctly set a new date and time for closing," and inform the other party that "[he] would be considered in default if [he] did not perform by a given date;" see Latora v. Ferreira, 958 N.Y.S.2d 727 (N.Y. App. Div. 2013). Once such notice is given, it binds both parties. Does the recognition of such unilateral notices (which probably need not be in writing) violate the underlying principle of the Statute of Frauds? Does their recognition give one party alone the right to modify the contract?

If we assume that the sellers' April 2 letter in the *Miller* case was faxed to the buyers, it made time of the essence and gave the buyers 14 days to close. Can you identify the factors that made this allowance of time unreasonable? A period of 18 days was found reasonable in EC, L.L.C. v. Eaglecrest Manufactured Home Park, 275 A.D.2d 898, 713 N.Y.S.2d 391 (2000).

5. *Waiver of timely performance.* Even if time is of the essence, either party can waive the other's duty to perform strictly on time. For example, the vendor may tell the purchaser and say, "I know you've been having trouble getting your financing arranged, but don't worry about being ready to close next Friday (the date fixed in the contract). I'll work with you on this." See, e.g., Livas v. Kodrick, 143 Ill. App. 3d 1097, 98 Ill. Dec. 85, 493 N.E.2d 1106 (1986); Dellicarri v. Hirschfeld, 210 A.D. 584, 619 N.Y.S.2d 816 (1994). A waiver also may be inferred from the circumstances, without a formal statement; see Marioni v. 94 Broadway, Inc., 374 N.J. Super. 588, 866 A.2d 208 (2005) (waiver found when parties continued to negotiate about a closing date after time set for closing had elapsed); Quirk v. Schenk, 34 Mass. App. Ct. 931, 612 N.E.2d 1194 (1993) (waiver inferred from party's readily giving multiple extensions). Contra, see Miami Child's World, Inc. v. City of Miami Beach, 688 So. 2d 942 (1997) (multiple extensions do not amount to a waiver).

After giving a waiver, a party may reinstate a "time is of the essence" requirement but must, as in *Miller*, give a reasonable time for the other party to prepare to close. See Tarlow v. Kelly, 158 Or. App. 7, 970 P.2d 688 (1999). The parties also may enter into a formal extension of time, but provide that (the new) time remains essential. See Enclave, Inc. v. Resolution Trust Corp., 986 F.2d 131 (5th Cir. 1993).

6. *When tender is excused.* Ordinarily the obligations of the seller to tender a deed conveying marketable title, and of the buyer to tender the

unpaid balance of the purchase price, are concurrent conditions. Neither party can regard the other as in breach, or sue for breach, without first tendering her or his own performance. Radkiewicz v. Radkiewicz, 353 Ill. App. 3d 251, 288 Ill. Dec. 723, 818 N.E.2d 411 (2004) (vendor who never tendered deed cannot forfeit earnest money deposited by purchaser); Steinberg v. Linzer, 27 A.D. 3d 450, 812 N.Y.S.2d 565 (App. Div. 2006) (purchaser who never tendered purchase price cannot recover her earnest money unless seller's title is incurably defective). A "tender" is defined as an offer to perform immediately, coupled with the ability to carry out the offer. Some courts say that the party tendering must actually have the necessary documents (the deed, the check, etc.) in hand and offer to deliver them, conditioned of course on the other party's performance. See Miller v. Johnson, 125 N.M. 175, 958 P.2d 745 (App. 1998). A formal offer of tender by a party may be excused, however when:

(a) the other party has anticipatorily repudiated the contract. See Internacional Realty, Inc. v. 2005 RP W., Ltd., 2014 WL 5025950 (Tex. App. 2014).

(b) even without a repudiation, it is apparent that the other party will not perform, or is obstructing the attempted tender. See Bacchetta v. Conforti, 107 A.D 2d 616, 484 N.Y.S.2d 1 (1985), affirmed without opinion, 65 N.Y.2d 627, 491 N.Y.S.2d 157, 480 N.E.2d 746 (1985). See also Bourke v. Webb, 627 S.E.2d 454 (Ga.App. 2006) (purchasers not required to tender, where time was of the essence and seller had not completed construction of the house on time).

(c) the other party's performance has become impossible (for example, the vendor has sold the property to another or his or her title is incurably defective). See Kessler v. Tortoise Development, Inc., 134 Idaho 264, 1 P.3d 292 (2000). Cf. Esplendido Apartments v. Olsson, 144 Ariz. 355, 697 P.2d 1105 (App. 1984) (vendor's title defects were no excuse for purchaser's failure to tender where purchaser was unaware of defects).

7.   *Mutual failure to tender*. If time is not of the essence and neither party tenders on the agreed date, neither is in breach; the closing is automatically extended until one sets a date and notifies the other. Again, the notice must be given a reasonable period prior to the date it sets as the new closing date. See Fisher v. Applebaum, 947 A.2d 248 (R.I. 2008); Limpus v. Armstrong, 3 Mass. App. Ct. 19, 322 N.E.2d 187 (1975); III Am. L. Prop. § 11.44; ULTA § 2–302(e). A remarkable example is Barber v. Fox, 36 Mass. App. Ct. 525, 632 N.E.2d 1246 (1994), in which a party to an intrafamily sale of land demanded (and got an order of) performance nearly 20 years after the contract date. No earlier demand had ever been made!

But suppose time *is* essential and neither party tenders on the date fixed for closing. There is a good deal of authority for the view that both parties are discharged on the ground that it is impossible to make a tender of substantial performance after that date has passed. See, e.g., Gunn v. Heggins, 964 So. 2d 586 (Miss. App. 2007); Pittman v. Canham, 2 Cal. App. 4th 556, 3 Cal. Rptr. 2d 340 (1992) ("When is a contract no longer a contract? When [time is of the essence,] it contains concurrent conditions and neither party tenders timely performance. Unlike love or taxes, concurrent conditions do not last forever.").

If both parties act as if the contract is still in force (e.g., by continuing efforts to prepare for a closing) despite the delay, should a court consider their behavior as evidence of a mutual intent to waive the essentiality of the original time clause and keep the sales contract intact? See Galdjie v. Darwish, 7 Cal. Rptr. 2d 178 (Cal. App. 2004) (so holding).

E. TITLE TO BE CONVEYED

In this section we consider whether a buyer of real estate may be justified in refusing to complete the purchase because the buyer is dissatisfied with the quality of the title the seller proposes to convey. Note that we have not yet investigated the mechanics of title search and examination—the process through which the buyer learns what the quality of the seller's title is. A thorough discussion of that topic will come in the next chapter.

For present purposes, it is enough to say that there are two main methods that buyers employ, depending on the conditions and customs of the locality, to ascertain the quality of the seller's title. One method (the older of the two) is to obtain a written attorney's opinion as to the title. The attorney may base that opinion on a personal search of the official public records in the county courthouse, or may instead review an *abstract,* a copy or summary of the instruments filed in the courthouse, but prepared and sold by a privately owned abstract company. Personal search is most common in the South and along the Atlantic seaboard, especially outside major urban areas; abstracts are more commonly used in rural areas of the Midwest and West.

The second method (used throughout the West and in larger cities nationwide) is to obtain a title report, sometimes called a "commitment" or "binder" (and ultimately, after the closing, a title insurance policy) from a title insurance company. The company may base its report on a search of its own internal records (called a "title plant") or, less commonly, a search of the public records. The title report does not necessarily claim to be a complete statement of the findings of the company's search. Technically, it merely states that the company is willing to issue a policy insuring that the land's title is as stated in the report, and thus to be liable to indemnify the insured if she or he suffers a loss due to any title defect not disclosed in the report. As a practical matter, buyers treat the title report as stating the results of a title search. There is little doubt that attorneys' opinions of title are gradually fading from use (except with respect to oil, gas, and mining interests), and that title insurance is becoming increasingly widespread.

HAISFIELD V. LAPE

Virginia Supreme Court, 2002
264 Va. 632, 570 S.E.2d 794

Opinion by JUSTICE DONALD W. LEMONS.

In this consolidated appeal, we consider whether a "line-of-sight" or "view" easement* renders title to the property at issue unmarketable, thereby justifying the buyers' refusal to close the transaction.

I.   FACTS AND PROCEEDINGS BELOW

On February 14, 2000, Audrey Lea Haisfield and Laurel Ridge, LLC (collectively, "Haisfield") entered into a land sale contract ("Purchase Agreement") with Kenneth R. Lape, Trustee of the Kenneth R. Lape living trust and Barbara Gsand Lape, Trustee of the Barbara Gsand Lape living trust (collectively, the "Lapes"). The Purchase Agreement was for the sale of approximately 99 acres in Albemarle County owned by the Lapes and referred to as Laurel Ridge Farm ("Laurel Ridge"). Laurel Ridge was once part of a larger piece of land that encompassed approximately 148 acres owned by the Lapes known as Oakmont Farm. In 1994, the Lapes conveyed approximately 48 acres ("Oakmont") of Oakmont Farm to Dr. Hamilton Moses, III and Alexandra G. Moses (the "Moseses"). At the time of the Purchase Agreement, Oakmont Farm was two separate parcels: Oakmont, owned by the Moseses and Laurel Ridge, owned by the Lapes.

The Purchase Agreement required Haisfield to deposit $50,000 with McLean Faulconer, Inc., a real estate firm, as an earnest money deposit to be held in escrow. Further, the Purchase Agreement provided that "[s]hould Purchaser default and/or breach this [Purchase Agreement], the Seller shall be entitled to retain the earnest money deposit of $50,000.00 as liquidated damages in lieu of all other remedies provided at law or in equity against the Purchaser."

A closing date of June 30, 2000 was set. On June 29, 2000, through an agent, Haisfield notified the Lapes that the chain of title to Laurel Ridge contained a restrictive covenant that rendered title to the property unmarketable. The line-of-sight easement, discovered by Haisfield just prior to closing, was found in the 1994 deed conveying Oakmont to the Moseses from the Lapes. In part, the Oakmont deed contained the following covenant:

---

* The trial court and the parties have used interchangeably the terms "line-of-sight easement," "view easement" and "restrictive covenant."—Eds.

[F]or a period of thirty (30) years from the date of this deed [May 3, 1994], no building shall be built on the current Albemarle County Tax Map Parcel 111–5A [Laurel Ridge] . . . which may be visible from the main residence (Oakmont) located on the property conveyed by this deed.

Haisfield gave the Lapes 60 days pursuant to Paragraph 14 of the Purchase Agreement to cure the defect created by the Moseses' line-of-sight easement. Further, she maintained that she was justified in refusing to close the transaction and was entitled to the return of her $50,000 earnest money deposit if the defect was not cured. Paragraph 14 states the following:

> At settlement Seller shall convey the Property to the Purchaser by a general warranty deed containing English covenants of title, free of all encumbrances, tenancies, and liens (for taxes and otherwise), but subject to such restrictive covenants and utility easements of record which do not materially and adversely affect the use of the Property for residential purposes or render the title unmarketable. * * * If the examination reveals a title defect of a character that can be remedied by legal action or otherwise within a reasonable time, Seller, at its expense, shall promptly take such action as is necessary to cure such defect. If the defect is not cured within 60 days after Seller receives notice of the defect, then Purchaser shall have the right to (1) terminate this Contract, in which event the Deposit shall be returned to Purchaser, and Purchaser and Seller shall have no further obligations hereunder[.] * * *

The Lapes disagreed that the line-of-sight easement rendered title to Laurel Ridge unmarketable, and efforts between the parties to reach a settlement in the matter were unsuccessful.

Consequently, on July 28, 2000, the Lapes filed a motion for judgment claiming that Haisfield breached the Purchase Agreement and claiming the $50,000 earnest money deposit plus interest as liquidated damages for the breach. Subsequently, Haisfield filed a grounds of defense and counterclaims against the Lapes maintaining that the Lapes failed to deliver marketable title and asking the court to return to her the $50,000 earnest money deposit.

A trial was held without a jury on May 24, 2001. Evidence was submitted by both parties, and the court conducted a view of the property. In a letter opinion dated June 14, 2001, the trial court held that the line-of-sight easement did not materially or adversely affect the use of the Laurel Ridge property for residential purposes nor did it render title unmarketable under the terms of the Purchase Agreement.

The trial court granted judgment in favor of the Lapes against Haisfield in the amount of $50,000 with interest, but refused any award of attorneys' fees to the Lapes. From this judgment, Haisfield appeals the trial court's holding that she was in breach of the contract and the judgment entered. The Lapes appeal the denial of attorneys' fees.

II. ANALYSIS

The plain language of Paragraph 14 of the Purchase Agreement requires the seller to convey the property by a general warranty deed containing English covenants of title free of all encumbrances but subject to such restrictive covenants and utility easements of record "which do not materially and adversely affect the use of the Property for residential purposes or render the title unmarketable." In this appeal, we are only concerned with the marketability of title. In the interpretation of this provision of the Purchase Agreement, we are guided by an oft-cited principle of contract interpretation:

> Words that the parties used are normally given their usual, ordinary, and popular meaning. No word or clause in the contract will be treated as meaningless if a reasonable meaning can be given to it, and there is a presumption that the parties have not used words needlessly.

D.C. McClain, Inc. v. Arlington County, 249 Va. 131, 135–36, 452 S.E.2d 659, 662 (1995).

The plain meaning of Paragraph 14 is that, if a particular restrictive covenant or utility easement does render the title unmarketable, the seller will have failed to perform in accordance with its terms unless the defect is remedied within a reasonable time. While it is true that Paragraph 14 of the Purchase Agreement operates as a waiver of objection to certain easements or restrictive covenants, a restrictive covenant that renders title unmarketable is not one of them. If the line-of-sight easement constitutes a restrictive covenant that renders title unmarketable, and the defect is not removed within a reasonable time, Haisfield is entitled to terminate the contract without penalty.

In *Madbeth, Inc. v. Weade*, 204 Va. 199, 202, 129 S.E.2d 667, 669–70 (1963), we stated:

> A marketable title is one which is free from liens or encumbrances; one which discloses no serious defects and is dependent for its validity upon no doubtful questions of law or fact; one which will not expose the purchaser to the hazard of litigation or embarrass him in the peaceable enjoyment of the land; one which a reasonably well-informed and prudent person, acting upon business principles and with full knowledge of the facts and their legal significance, would be willing to accept, with

the assurance that he, in turn, could sell or mortgage the property at its fair value.

However, not all liens and encumbrances render a title unmarketable. In *Sachs v. Owings*, 121 Va. 162, 170, 92 S.E. 997, 1000 (1917), we held that:

> A vendee cannot elect to rescind and treat the contract as rescinded on the ground that the title is not a marketable title because there are encumbrances on the land purchased, if they are of such character and amount that he can apply the unpaid purchase money to the removal of the encumbrances. This can be done where the amount of the encumbrance is definite, does not exceed the unpaid purchase money due, is presently payable (as was the case with the delinquent tax lien in the instant case), and its existence is not a matter of doubt or dispute, or the situation is not such with respect thereto as to expose the vendee to litigation on the subject.

See also Davis v. Beury, 134 Va. 322, 338, 114 S.E. 773, 777 (1922).

In this case, the amount of the encumbrance is not definite, such as a tax lien or judgment lien. The line-of-sight easement acts as a building restriction upon the property, much like the building restrictions found to render title unmarketable in *Scott v. Albemarle Horse Show Ass'n*, 128 Va. 517, 104 S.E. 842 (1920). In *Scott*, we agreed with the purchaser's assertion that the building restrictions in the tendered deed were not in compliance with the terms of the contract and rendered title unmarketable. Id. at 529–30, 104 S.E. at 846. Finally, the line-of-sight easement in this case is not an "open, visible, physical [e]ncumbrance of the property [that] must have been taken into consideration in fixing the price of the property. . . ." Riner v. Lester, 121 Va. 563, 572, 93 S.E. 594, 597 (1917). In *Riner*, we stated that:

> where the circumstances and the conduct of the parties show that the existence of an open, visible, physical [e]ncumbrance of the property must have been taken into consideration in fixing the price of the property, the purchaser can neither refuse to complete the purchase nor require an abatement of the [purchase] price.

Id.

The line-of-sight easement in this case is clearly an encumbrance upon the property restricting its use in such a manner as to render the title unmarketable. The existence of the easement is not an open, visible, physical encumbrance of the property that might have been considered in the establishment of a purchase price. The existence of a restrictive covenant that renders title to the property unmarketable is not excepted under the provisions of Paragraph 14 of the Purchase Agreement. Under these circumstances, Haisfield was not in breach of the Purchase Agreement by refusing to close the transaction. The trial court erred in holding that Haisfield was in breach and ordering the payment of $50,000 in liquidated damages plus interest. Because we hold that Haisfield was not in breach of the Purchase Agreement, it is unnecessary to resolve the issue of attorneys' fees presented in the Lapes' separate appeal, and we will dismiss the appeal. With respect to Haisfield's appeal, we will reverse the judgment of the trial court and enter final judgment in favor of Haisfield.

NOTES AND QUESTIONS

1. *The implied covenant of marketable title.* In *Haisfield*, the contract of sale expressly provided that title must be marketable. Even in the absence of such an express statement, every contract for the sale of real estate is deemed to contain an implied covenant that title will be "marketable," unless the parties agree otherwise. See, e.g., Wallach v. Riverside Bank, 206 N.Y. 434, 100 N.E. 50 (1912) ("When a vendor agrees to sell a piece of land, the law imputes to him a covenant that he will convey a marketable title unless the vendee stipulates to accept something less"); Osswald v. Osswald, 703 N.W.2d 383 (Wis. App. 2005); Conklin v. Davi, 388 A.2d 598, 600 (N.J. 1978).

One common alternative is to provide that the title must be insurable by using the following in the sales contract:

Purchaser agrees to accept a title such as any reputable title company, subject to the exceptions in this contract provided, would approve and insure.

E.g., Patten of New York Corp. v. Geoffrion, 193 A. D.2d 1007, 598 N.Y.S.2d 355 (1993). Such language is actually a bit sloppy because it does not identify the particular title insurance policy form to be used, and some policy forms contain standard exclusions that might seriously disadvantage the purchaser. Nevertheless, the concept of "insurable title" is quite desirable because it adds considerable flexibility to the transaction. If the title insurance company identifies a fairly minor defect in its search, it may be persuaded to "insure over" the defect when it issues its policy—that is, to refrain from showing the defect as an exception to the policy's coverage. If the defect is one that arguably makes the title unmarketable, using the "insurable title" standard instead may allow a transaction to proceed that would otherwise falter. Of course, the contract might provide that title will be both marketable and insurable too. See Nelson v. Anderson, 286 Ill. App. 3d 706, 676 N.E.2d 735 (1997).

It is clear that "insurable" is a lower standard than "marketable," since it is entirely possible that a title company will be willing to "insure over" a defect that would make the title unmarketable. As one court put it,

Standards for marketable title and insurable title are markedly different, with marketable title being title that is "... reasonably free from any doubt which would interfere with its market value." For title to be insurable, it need only be that which a title insurer would insure, a far lower standard and one which seems elusive at best.

Auroa Loan Servs. LLC v. Scheller, 992 N.Y.S.2d 157 (N.Y. Sup. Ct. 2014). To the same effect, see De Paz v. First Am. Title Ins. Co., 2010 WL 2856089 (Cal. App. 2010). A buyer might well be dissatisfied with accepting title that was insurable but not marketable, since the buyer might anticipate difficulty getting another title company to insure that title when the buyer was ready to resell the property at a later time. If the buyer has bargained for a marketable title, the court will not force him or her to accept one that is insurable but not marketable; see Nelson v. Anderson, 676 N.E.2d 735 (Ill.App. 1997); U.S. Bank v. Smith, 801 N.Y.S.2d 243 (N.Y. Sup. Ct. 2005).

Haisfield only wanted to rescind the contract and get her deposit back. Suppose land prices in the area had gone up since the contract was formed, and she had sought loss of bargain damages instead. About half the states deny such damages if the vendor acted in good faith. Do you think the Lapes' conduct met the "good faith" standard?

2. *Defects making title unmarketable.* There is a large body of lore dealing with the question of whether a particular legal problem relating to land involves *title* or not, as that term is used in the implied covenant of marketable title or in similar express covenants. The results of this sort of litigation are not particularly predictable, so the list below should be taken only as a general guide to the issue.

(a) *Encumbrances.* The traditional types of real estate encumbrances (leases, covenants, mineral reservations, mortgages, easements and liens) are usually considered to be title matters. If the contract of sale does not expressly provide that the purchaser will take subject to them, they violate the implied covenant of marketable title. See Hastings v. Gay, 55 Mass. App. Ct. 157, 770 N. E.2d 11 (2002) (mortgage, lease and lien); Turner v. Taylor, 268 Wis. 2d 628, 673 N.W.2d 716 (2003) (easement). This fact emphasizes the need for careful contract drafting. Too frequently the contract either makes no attempt to mention or itemize the existing encumbrances, which exist in some measure on almost every parcel of real estate, or it merely contains a general statement such as "subject to all encumbrances of record." Either approach can be highly dangerous, the former to the seller and latter to the buyer.

For example, in Stevenson v. Baum, 65 Cal. App. 4th 159, 75 Cal. Rptr. 2d 904 (1998), the buyer of a mobile home park agreed in the contract to take "subject to easements of record." It turned out that there was an oil company pipeline easement, and that the oil company had the right to force removal of several mobile homes if necessary to get access to its pipeline. Because of the sales contract language, the buyer was "stuck" with this burden.

In many cases, of course, both parties are fully aware of the encumbrances that exist, and the buyer is perfectly willing to take subject to them. If the contract makes no mention of a certain encumbrance, but there is proof that the buyer was well aware of it when she signed the contract, should she later be permitted to raise an objection to it? The *Haisfield* court seemed to think not. But other courts have usually found that the purchaser's knowledge of an encumbrance did not waive the right to object to it as making title unmarketable; see Create 21 Chuo, Inc. v. Southwest Slopes, Inc., 918 P.2d 1168 (Haw. App. 1996); 325 Schermerhorn, LLC v. Nevins Realty Corp., 23 Misc. 3d 1109(A), 886 N.Y.S.2d 69 N.Y. (Sup. Ct. 2009) aff'd, appeal dismissed, 76 A.D.3d 625, 906 N.Y.S.2d 339 (App. Div. 2010).

(b) *Visible or beneficial encumbrances*. In the same vein, courts sometimes hold that an easement does not make the title unmarketable if it is obviously visible and is beneficial to the land. A typical example would be a power line easement for electrical distribution along the back property line of a residential lot. Compare Ford v. White, 179 Or. 490, 172 P.2d 822 (1946) (visible power line easement; title held to be marketable) with Atlas Realty of East Meadow, Inc. v. Ostrofsky, 56 Misc. 2d 787, 289 N.Y.S.2d 784 (1967) (2.5 foot easement for visible wires and poles; title not marketable.) Open and visible public road easements do not render title unmarketable. See Whitman v. Larson, 172 A.D.2d 968, 568 N.Y.S.2d 485 (1991). Cf. Egeter v. West and North Properties, 92 Or. App. 118, 758 P.2d 361 (1988) (if road is not open and visible, title is unmarketable).

(c) *Access*. Perhaps surprisingly, a complete lack of access to a public road usually has been held to make the title unmarketable, presumably on the theory that it would subject the purchaser to the risk of a suit to establish an easement of necessity. See Regan v. Lanze, 40 N.Y.2d 475, 387 N.Y.S.2d 79, 354 N.E.2d 818 (1976); Hinton Hardwoods, Inc. v. Cumberland Scrap Processors Transp., LLC, 2008 WL 5429569 (Ky. App. 2008) (unpublished). But the access, to be legally sufficient, need not be particularly convenient or direct. See Kirkwall Corp. v. Sessa, 39 A.D.2d 185, 333 N.Y.S.2d 108 (1972), reversed on other grounds, 48 N.Y.2d 709, 422 N.Y.S.2d 368, 397 N.E.2d 1172 (1979).

(d) *Encroachments*. An encroachment (a structure built by a neighboring property owner which overlaps the property boundary) is usually considered to affect marketability of title. See, e.g., Azat v. Farruggio, 162 Md. App. 539, 875 A.2d 778 (2005). The same is true if a structure built by the owner of the property in question extends onto adjoining land; see Sydelman v. Marici, 56 A.D.2d 866, 392 N.Y.S.2d 333 (1977); Klavens v. Siegel, 256 Md. 476, 260 A.2d 637 (1970). The encroachment need not be a permanent structure to render title unmarketable.

(e) *Title by adverse possession.* If the vendor's title is based exclusively on his or her own adverse possession, the title is usually thought not to be marketable, although it may be perfectly good. The difficulty is that a lawsuit might require detailed factual proof of the vendor's possession and its attributes, an unreasonable risk to impose on the purchaser. See Tri-State Hotel Co. v. Sphinx Inv. Co., 212 Kan. 234, 510 P.2d 1223 (1973). Cf. Conklin v. Davi, 76 N. J. 468, 388 A.2d 598 (1978). The same principle is applied to other nondocumented methods of acquiring land, such as accretion of soil to land abutting a river. See Gaines v. Dillard, 545 S.W.2d 845 (Tex. Civ. App. 1976).

(f) *Ordinance violations.* A variety of local zoning, environmental, and other land use ordinances may affect an owner's ability to use the real estate. Traditionally, the mere existence of such ordinances has not been regarded as affecting the marketability of title. See, e.g., Haw River Land & Timber Company, Inc. v. Lawyers Title Insurance Corp., 152 F.3d 275 (4th Cir.1998) (ordinance prohibiting cutting timber); Gloucester Landing Assocs. v. Gloucester Redevelopment Authority, 802 N.E.2d 1046 (Mass. App. 2004) (inability to obtain waterways license from state agency). The court in *Gloucester Landing* noted that "There is a difference between economic lack of marketability, which concerns conditions that affect the use of land, and title marketability, which relates to defects affecting legally recognized rights and incidents of ownership. * * * Thus, "[a]n individual can hold clear title to a parcel of land, although the same parcel is valueless or considered economically unmarketable because of some restriction or regulation on its use." See also 6 Powell, Real Property ¶ 928.1 (1979).

Some courts have concluded that *existing* structures or conditions that are in violation of zoning or other land use ordinances would be sufficient to make title unmarketable. See Radovanov v. Land Title Co. of Am. Inc., 189 Ill. App. 3d 433, 545 N.E.2d 351 (1989) (pending suit for violation of housing code renders title unmarketable); Venisek v. Draski, 35 Wis. 2d 38, 150 N.W.2d 347 (1967); Note, 1958 Wis. L. Rev. 128 (1958); Allison Dunham, Effect on Title of Violation of Building Covenants and Zoning Ordinances, 27 Rocky Mt. L. Rev. 255 (1955). But see Cone v. Stranahan, 843 N.Y.S.2d 717 (N.Y. App. Div. 2007) (violation of wetlands regulation did not make title unmarketable); Fernandes v. Jamron, 780 N.Y.S.2d 164 (N.Y. App. Div. 2004) (lapse of subdivision approval did not make title unmarketable); Elysian

Investment Group v. Stewart Title Guaranty Co., 105 Cal. App. 4th 315, 129 Cal. Rptr. 2d 372 (2002) (recorded notice of building code violations did not make title unmarketable).

(g) *Hazardous waste.* What is effect on title marketability of the presence of illegal hazardous waste on the property? The standard answer is none at all; physical conditions by themselves have no title implications. See Humphries v. Ables, 789 N.E.2d 1025 (Ind. Ct. App. 2003) (contaminated soil); Badding v. Inglis, 977 N.Y.S.2d 829 (N.Y. App. Div. 2013) (defective exterior bricks). In some states, hazardous waste statutes affirmatively require disclosure of the land's status in the contract. See Johnson Machinery Co. v. Manville Sales Corp., 248 N. J. Super. 285, 590 A.2d 1206 (1991) (permitting a purchaser to rescind the sale because the contract failed to state that the land had been used as a sanitary landfill, as required by statute).

Under the law of many states, a lien, or even a "superlien" (having a priority superior to all other interests) can be imposed on the property to reimburse the government for the cost of cleanup. If the lien has already been imposed (and not yet discharged), title is obviously unmarketable. But if the lien is merely a possibility, and not yet a reality, at the time of the sale, title will probably be considered marketable. See Chicago Title Ins. Co. v. Kumar, 24 Mass. App. Ct. 53, 506 N.E.2d 154, 156–57 (1987); Lick Mill Creek Apartments v. Chicago Title Ins. Co., 231 Cal. App. 3d 1654, 283 Cal. Rptr. 231 (1991).

It may not be the responsibility of a title examiner to inspect land for hazardous material, but anyone purchasing land that has been used for commercial, industrial, or agricultural purposes is well-advised to have an environmental assessment made by a qualified engineer or consultant. Even though federal environmental laws do not impose a "superlien" on the contaminated property, such laws may create a duty of cleanup on the current owner of a hazardous waste site, even though that owner may not have caused the contamination and had no knowledge that the property was contaminated when it was acquired. See Comprehensive Environmental Response, Compensation and Liability Act of 1980 (CERCLA), § 107(a), 42 U.S.C. § 9607(a); New York v. Shore Realty Corp., 759 F.2d 1032 (2d Cir. 1985). There is an "innocent landowner" exemption in CERCLA, but its requirements are difficult to meet. See, e.g., U.S. v. Serafini, 706 F. Supp. 346 (M.D. Pa. 1988). In the absence of a satisfactory environmental assessment, a contaminated site may well be unmarketable from a practical point of view, whether its legal title is unmarketable or not.

(h) *Existing adverse possessors.* Obviously the vendor's title is unmarketable if an adverse possessor has completed acquisition of the title. See Lake Forest, Inc. v. Bon Marche Homes, Inc., 356 So. 2d 1133 (La. App. 1978). What should the result be if the adverse possessor is still on the land, but the statute of limitations has not yet run? See Double L. Properties, Inc. v. Crandall, 51 Wash. App. 149, 751 P.2d 1208 (1988) (holding that the presence of an adverse possessor breaches a covenant of seisin in a deed, even though the adverse possession is incomplete). Should the same rule apply to the covenant of marketable title in a contract?

(i) *Violations of covenants.* Even if the purchaser has agreed to take title subject to restrictive covenants, she may still claim that the title is unmarketable if there is an existing violation of those covenants. The cases on this point are divided. See Coons v. Carstensen, 15 Mass. App. Ct. 431, 446 N.E.2d 114 (1983); Camp v. Commonwealth Land Title Ins. Co., 787 F.2d 1258 (8th Cir. 1986).

(j) *Title links not of record.* Suppose a link in the chain of title (e.g., a deed or will) exists or once existed, but cannot be found in the public records. Is the title unmarketable? In general, the "muniments of title" (i.e., the documents that comprise the links in the chain) need not be recorded unless the contract provides for "marketable title of record." See Lucas v. Ind. Sch. Dist. No. 284, 433 N.W.2d 94 (Minn. 1988). But if there is an actual break in the chain of title—that is, a deed that is not only unrecorded but missing—title will, of course, be considered unmarketable. See Ferrara v. Walters, 919 So. 2d 876 (Miss. 2005).

(k) *Unreasonable risk of litigation.* If the property's title is currently being contested in litigation, the title is obviously unmarketable; see Muniz v. Crystal Lake Project, LLC, 947 So. 2d 464 (Fla.App. 2006). Similarly, if one of the matters listed in the foregoing notes as making title unmarketable is not firmly established, but represents a risk of litigation that a reasonable buyer would find unacceptable, then the title is unmarketable. See Stewart Title Guaranty Co. v. Greenlands Realty, L.L.C., 58 F. Supp. 2d 360 (D.N.J. 1999). The mere threat of litigation concerning nontitle aspects of the land, however, will not make title unmarketable. See Humphries v. Ables, 789 N.E.2d 1025 (Ind. Ct. App. 2003) (possibility of litigation over contamination by hazardous waste does not make title unmarketable).

3. *Notice to the vendor of title defects.* The buyer is expected to examine the title before the closing and delivery of the deed. If the buyer finds a basis for objection to the quality of the title, she must notify the seller and give a fair opportunity for the defect to be cured unless the defect is, by its nature, incurable. This means that the notice must not be given a mere day or two prior to the date of closing. If it is, an automatic extension will be given to the

seller for a reasonable time to effect a cure of the title defects. See Pederson v. McGuire, 333 N.W.2d 823 (S.D. 1983). The extension must be given even if time is of the essence; see Chin v. Zoet, 418 N.W.2d 191 (Minn. Ct. App. 1988); III Am. L. Prop. § 11.51 (1952). Upon receiving notice of the title defect, the seller has a duty to make a reasonable (or "good faith") effort to cure the defect unless a cure would be impossible. See Snowdon Farms v. Jones, 8 Neb. App. 599, 599 N.W.2d 845 (1999); Johnson v. Lambros, 143 Idaho 468, 147 P.3d 100 (2006); Harris v. Hosten, 17 Misc. 3d 1123, 351 N.Y.S.2d 69 (2007).

4. *Time of title marketability.* When must the vendor's title be in marketable condition? The usual answer is not until the closing. *See* Wright v. Bryan, 226 Va. 557, 311 S.E.2d 776 (1984). Indeed, at the time the vendor signs the contract he need not have title at all, so long as it appears possible for him to obtain it by the closing date. This rule is probably unobjectionable in short-term earnest money contracts. It gives rise to more serious problems with long-term installment contracts, where the purchaser may make payments for many years with no assurance that the vendor will be able to cure the title problem by the time the last payment is made and the vendor delivers a deed. Some cases give the purchaser under such a contract an immediate right of rescission if the vendor is unable to provide reasonable assurances that a cure will be effected. See Leavitt v. Blohm, 11 Utah 2d 220, 357 P.2d 190 (1960).

5. *Satisfying liens at closing.* As *Haisfield v. Lape* indicates, if the property is subject to a mortgage or other lien that the vendor must satisfy in order to give marketable title, it can usually be discharged with the proceeds of the sale. If this can be done, the purchaser cannot object to the mortgage or lien as making title unmarketable because it will be paid off and extinguished by the time title passes to the purchaser. Ordinarily the closing agent (a lawyer, escrow company, or title company) will be instructed to record and deliver the deed to the purchaser and simultaneously to record the instrument that satisfies the mortgage, at the same time disbursing the funds necessary to satisfy outstanding balance of the lien to the lienholder. There is ancient authority for the notion that this is impermissible, and that the title must be marketable without consideration being given to the payoff that will be made out of the proceeds of the sale. Such an approach is entirely unrealistic, and most courts in recent years have followed the more practical approach, treating the title as marketable if it will become so at the closing. See, e.g., New York Prop. Holding Corp. v. Rosa, 809 N.Y.S.2d 34, 35 (N.Y. App. Div. 2006); Lone Star Development Corp. v. Miller, 564 F.2d 921 (10th Cir. 1977); see generally III Am. L. Prop. § 11.49 (1952).

Of course, this approach does not always work. If the aggregate balance owing on the liens on the property exceeds the net proceeds of sale (after payment of the various expenses of the transaction, such as brokerage commissions, escrow fees, and recording costs), there are only two ways to clear the liens. One is for the vendor to provide the needed additional cash—money that the vendor may not have or may not want to part with. The other is to persuade the holders of one or more of the liens to release the liens for a payment of less than the full amount owing (sometimes called a "short sale"). But if neither solution is available, the vendor will be in breach of the sales contract due to the remaining liens (unless the purchaser agrees to waive and take title subject to the remaining liens, usually in exchange for a reduced sale price).

6. *Bringing the title examination "down" to the closing date.* Even though the buyer will have obtained a title examination or title report from her attorney or title insurance company several days or weeks prior to the closing, the buyer understandably will not wish to tender the cash purchase price unless she can first check the public records immediately prior to accepting delivery of and recording the deed. If this is not done, the buyer may later discover that a last-minute title defect (e.g., a judgment lien against the seller) has been recorded, thereby impairing the buyer's title. This scenario actually happened in Prochaska v. Midwest Title Guarantee Co., 85 Wash. App. 256, 932 P.2d 172 (1997), when a judgment lien was recorded against the seller nine minutes before the buyer's deed was recorded. The title company missed the lien in the downdate of the buyer's title search. The appellate court originally held that the buyer had taken the property subject to the lien. After the Washington Supreme Court granted review, the parties jointly moved to vacate the appellate court's original opinion. The appellate court granted the motion, vacated and withdrew its opinion, and dismissed the case. See 950 P.2d 497 (Wash. Ct. App. 1997). Nonetheless, the opinion seems correct.

7. *Merger of title covenants.* A well-known doctrine termed "merger" holds that if the purchaser has some objection to the title on the basis of the implied covenant of marketable title (or an express contract covenant concerning title), the purchaser must raise the title defect prior to accepting delivery of the deed. Unless the sales contract provides otherwise, once the purchaser accepts the deed she is deemed to be satisfied with the quality of the title received, so far as the contract is concerned. Any future objection based on a defect in the legal title must be based on a breach of the covenants of title contained in the deed itself. See Donchi, Inc. v. Robdol, LLC, 640 S.E.2d 719 (Ga. App. 2007); Dansie v. Hi-Country Estates Homeowners Ass'n., 987 P.2d 30 (Ut. 1999). In particular, the buyer cannot rescind the sale after accepting the deed based on a defect in title, since the only remedy for a breach of most of the deed's covenants of title is damages. See III Am. L. Property § 11.65 (1952). Deed covenants of title are covered later in Chapter Seven.

The doctrine of merger does not apply to most nontitle matters, such as warranties or covenants in the sales contract regarding the physical condition of the property. See Campbell v. Rawls, 381 So. 2d 744 (Fla. App. 1980) (warranty that air conditioning system would be in working order); Williams v. Runion, 173 Ga. App. 54, 325 S.E.2d 441 (1984) (builder's warranty of quality on new house). See also In re Tribby, 241 B.R. 380 (E. D. Va. 1999) (merger doctrine does not prevent buyers who accepted a late-tendered deed from recovering damages for the delay); Bruggeman v. Jerry's Enterprises, Inc., 583 N.W.2d 299 (Minn. App. 1998) (merger doctrine does not prevent enforcement by vendor of a repurchase option contained in the contract of sale).

The merger concept won't be applied where there was fraud, mutual mistake, or perhaps even unilateral mistake by the purchaser; see Czarobski v. Lata, 862 N.E.2d 1039 (Ill.App. 2007) aff'd, 882 N.E.2d 536 (Ill. 2008); Munawar v. Cadle Co., 2 S.W.3d 12, 15 (Tex. App. 1999).

8. *Type of deed to be delivered.* The covenant in the sales contract that the title delivered at the closing will be marketable says nothing about the nature of the deed to be tendered to the buyer at the closing. In a well-drafted sales contract, the parties will specify the type of deed to be delivered. A deed may contain a broad range of covenants of title, a more limited range, or none at all (a "quitclaim" deed). These distinctions are covered in the next chapter. But any deed, whether it contains covenants of title or not, will transfer whatever title the grantor has. Thus, there is no logical basis for an assumption that a covenant in the contract calling for marketable title necessarily implies that a warranty deed will be given. See Department of Public Works and Bldgs. v. Halls, 35 Ill. 2d 283, 220 N.E.2d 167 (1966); Lininger v. Black Hills Greyhound Racing Ass'n, 82 S.D. 507, 149 N.W.2d 413 (1967). Similarly, a contract clause providing that conveyance at the closing will be by a quitclaim deed does not logically negate the implied covenant that title will be marketable. See, e.g., Wallach v. Riverside Bank, 206 N.Y. 434, 100 N.E. 50 (1912).

F. EQUITABLE CONVERSION

Even if the time between execution and performance of a real estate sale contract is brief—a few weeks or even a few months—many events can occur during that period that raise legal questions. The traditional method of dealing with most of these questions is to employ a doctrine called *equitable conversion,* as a sort of labeling technique. In brief, this doctrine holds that "equitable" title passes to the purchaser as soon as an enforceable contract to sell real estate is formed, even though it is clear that the "legal" title will remain with the seller until the closing and the delivery of a deed to the purchaser.

The situations where the equitable conversion doctrine is used can be divided into two categories. The first situation involves a *characterization* issue. During the executory period for a real estate sales contract, should we characterize a given party (either the vendor or the purchaser) as owning a *real* property or a *personal* property interest? Characterization questions can arise in many contexts. Consider the following examples:

- A party to the sales contract dies, leaving a will that devises the deceased party's real estate to A, but bequeaths all personal property to B.

- A judgment (by statute, a lien against realty) is entered against a party to the sales contract.
- A tax is imposed on either realty or personalty.
- A party wishes to make a claim (e.g., a homestead exemption from creditors) or file an action (e.g., trespass) available only to an owner of real estate.

These and similar cases require that we label each party's interest as either real estate or as personal property. This "labeling" is precisely the function of the doctrine of equitable conversion.

The second situation typically involves a risk issue. For example, during the executory period of the sales contract, a casualty event occurs that jeopardizes the property's value or usefulness. Which party to the sales contract must absorb the risk or sustain the loss? Must the buyer complete the purchase despite the loss, or may the buyer rescind or at least insist on reduction of the price?

Risk questions can take a variety of forms. Some risks are physical: fire, earthquake, hurricane, flood, or frost damage to crops. Other risks flow from changes in the land's legal status: an amendment to the zoning ordinance, a new building code with retroactive impact on existing structures, a lien for a public assessment for a new sewer system, or a taking of the property by eminent domain with a resulting award from the government that is less than the contract price. Of course, the parties may agree expressly in the sales contract as to how such risks will be allocated, but they often fail to do so, or the loss that occurs is not a type they thought to address. The law must supply some rule to resolve these disputes, and it is usually the doctrine of equitable conversion that is used to do so.

As you read *Grant v. Kahn* and the materials that follow, consider whether the underlying issue involves *characterization* or *risk*. Is equitable conversion a suitable way of resolving the issue?

GRANT V. KAHN   *not part of sale K but Had lien on property*

Maryland Court of Appeals, 2011
198 Md. App. 421, 18 A.3d 91

[On May 29, 2007, Kareem Grant contracted to purchase a house in Wheaton, Maryland from Jeffrey Ganz for $320,000. The contract contained the following provision:

This contract is contingent on Buyer obtaining approval for loan(s) to purchase the Property (the "Financing Contingency"). This contract is contingent until 9 p.m. 45 Days after Date of

Ratification ("Financing Deadline") upon Buyer Delivering Notice to Seller on the Regional Form #100 removing this Financing Contingency.

Grant never provided Ganz with Regional Form #100, indicating that he had obtained a loan approval and was removing the contingency. He apparently did in fact obtain a suitable loan because on July 31, 2007, Grant and Ganz closed on the sale of the property.]

* * *

At the time of closing, Grant did not realize that a short time earlier, on July 20, the Kahns had obtained a money judgment against Ganz for about $172,000. About eight months after the closing, on March 27, 2008, the Kahns filed a petition pursuant to Maryland Rule 2–641, in which the Kahns asked the circuit court to issue a Writ of Execution directing the sheriff to levy upon the property. Grant then filed a motion to release the property from the levy. In Maryland, as in most states, a judgment becomes a lien on the real property of the judgment debtor. In some states, the lien attached only when the judgment or some record of it is recorded in the real property records, but this is not necessary in Maryland; the lien takes effect as soon as the judgment is entered in the court's docket records.

Given that a the judgment lien attaches only to real property owned by the debtor, a principal issue in the case was whether Ganz's interest in the house and land should be considered to be real property as of July 20. 2007, the date that the judgment was entered.

Grant argues that the doctrine of equitable conversion prevented the judgment against Ganz from attaching to the property. Specifically, Grant contends that, under the doctrine of equitable conversion, on May 29, 2007, when Grant and Ganz entered into the contract of sale, Grant became the equitable owner of the property and Ganz held only bare legal title. According to Grant, because a judgment creditor's lien cannot attach to bare legal title, the judgment against Ganz could not attach to the property after the execution of the contract of sale. Grant rejects the theory that the financing contingency in the contract of sale prevented the doctrine of equitable conversion from applying, because Grant could have waived the contingency and sought specific performance. Additionally, Grant contends that language in this Court's opinion in *Chambers v. Cardinal*, 177 Md. App. 418, 935 A.2d 502 (2007), which is contrary to his position, is merely dicta. Lastly, Grant submits that sound public policy supports a determination that equitable conversion occurred despite the financing contingency, because to hold otherwise would expose buyers who commonly rely on such contingencies to significant risks "associated with the seller's creditworthiness or lack thereof."

Δ argument

The Kahns counter that the circuit court was correct in its determination that the doctrine of equitable conversion was not applicable under the circumstances of the instant case. According to the Kahns, "[t]he ability of a buyer to specifically enforce a contract for realty is the lynchpin upon which rests the determination of whether equitable conversion has occurred." The Kahns contend that Grant could not have obtained specific performance of the contract of sale, because "specific performance requires that all contingencies and conditions precedent be satisfied by the party demanding the same." Here, according to the Kahns, the financing contingency remained unsatisfied and unremoved at the time that the confessed judgment was entered against Ganz, and thus equitable conversion had not occurred to prevent the judgment from attaching to the property. The Kahns also assert that Grant could not waive the financing contingency, because such contingency benefitted both Ganz, as seller, and Grant, as buyer. Finally, the Kahns contend that sound public policy supports affirming the circuit court, because fault lies with the title company that failed to bring the title examination up-to-date prior to closing. The Kahns conclude that a contrary holding would allow judgment debtors to shelter property from liens by entering into nonbinding contracts of sale. * * *

EQUITABLE CONVERSION

"Equitable conversion . . . is a theoretical change of property from realty to personalty, or vice versa, in order that the intention of the parties, in the case of a contract of sale, or the directions of the testator, in the case of directions in a will, may be given effect." Coe v. Hays, 328 Md. 350, 358, 614 A.2d 576 (1992). "The doctrine of equitable conversion and, more particularly, by contract, is well-established in Maryland." DeShields v. Broadwater, 338 Md. 422, 437, 659 A.2d 300 (1995). Our courts have routinely cited Thompson on Real Property's treatment of the topic:

> The legal cliché, that equity treats that as being done which should be done, is the basis of the theory of equitable conversion. Hence, when the vendee contracts to buy and the vendor to sell, though legal title has not yet passed, in equity the vendee becomes owner of the land, the vendor of the purchase money.

11 Thompson on Real Property § 96.06(a) (David A. Thomas ed., 2002 & Supp. 2008) (footnote omitted). See DeShields, 338 Md. at 437; Coe, 328 Md. at 358, 614 A.2d 576; Himmighoefer v. Medallion Industr., Inc., 302 Md. 270, 278, 487 A.2d 282 (1985).

Speaking for the Court of Appeals in *Watson v. Watson*, 304 Md. 48, 61, 497 A.2d 794 (1985), Judge Lawrence Rodowsky wrote:

> The doctrine of equitable conversion by contract rests on the maxim that equity considers as done that which ought to be

done. Hence, an equitable conversion will place equitable title in the purchaser only if the contract is one under which the vendor would be subject to a decree for specific performance. As explained by Chief Judge Jeremiah Townley Chase for the Court in *Hampson v. Edelen*, [2 H. & J. 64, 66 (1807)],

> [a] contract for land, bona fide made for a valuable consideration, vests the equitable interest in the vendee from the time of the execution of the contract, although the money is not paid at that time. When the money is paid according to the terms of the contract, the vendee is entitled to a conveyance, and to a decree in Chancery for a specific execution of the contract, if such conveyance is refused.

> The commentators are in accord that equitable conversion by contract takes place only if the contract is specifically enforceable.

Judge Rodowsky went on to discuss the legal effect of a judgment entered against a vendor after the contract has been made:

> One result of the doctrine is that a *judgment entered against the vendor after the contract has been made does not become a lien on the realty*. A vendor's judgment creditor may not execute on the realty because the vendor, sometimes described as trustee for the purchaser, has a right to the balance of the purchase money but has no beneficial interest in the property. Equitable title is superior to a later judgment lien.

Watson, 304 Md. at 60, 497 A.2d 794 (emphasis added); accord, Caltrider v. Caples, 160 Md. 392, 396, 153 A. 445 (1931) (stating that " '[a] judgment obtained by a third person against the vendor, mesne the making [of] the contract and the payment of the money, cannot defeat or impair the equitable interest thus acquired, nor is it a lien on the land to affect the right of such cestui que trust.' ") (quoting Hampson, 2 H. & J. at 66)).

In *Himmighoefer*, the Court of Appeals elaborated on this aspect of the doctrine:

> It is a general rule that the holder of an equitable title or interest in property, by virtue of an unrecorded contract of sale, has a claim superior to that of a creditor obtaining judgment subsequent to the execution of the contract. . . . The effect of such a contract is to vest the equitable ownership of the property in the vendee, subject to the vendor's lien for unpaid purchase money, and to leave only the legal title in the vendor pending the fulfillment of the contract and the formal conveyance of the estate. The right of the vendee to have the title conveyed upon

full compliance with the contract of purchase is not impaired by the fact that the vendor, subsequently to the execution of the contract, incurred a debt upon which judgment was recovered. A judgment creditor stands in the place of his debtor, and he can only take the property of his debtor subject to the equitable charges to which it is liable in the hands of the debtor at the time of the rendition of the judgment.

302 Md. at 279, 487 A.2d 282 (emphasis added) (citations and quotations omitted) (quoting Stebbins-Anderson Co. v. Bolton, 208 Md. 183, 187–88, 117 A.2d 908 (1955)).

"[I]t is elementary that either party to a contract may waive any of the provisions made for his benefit." Twining v. Nat'l Mortg. Corp., 268 Md. 549, 555, 302 A.2d 604 (1973). " '[A]lthough a party may waive a provision included in a contract for that party's sole benefit, a party cannot waive a contractual requirement that benefits both sides to the transaction.' " Cattail Assoc., Inc. v. Sass, 170 Md. App. 474, 500, 907 A.2d 828 (2006) (quoting Citadel Equity Fund Ltd. v. Aquila, Inc., 371 F. Supp. 2d 510, 520 (S.D.N.Y. 2005)). "Accordingly, the application of the doctrine of waiver when one party seeks to enforce a contract . . . ordinarily requires a determination whether the condition was inserted in the contract solely for the benefit of the party seeking to enforce the contract despite its nonoccurrence." Id. (quoting 25 Samuel Williston, A Treatise on the Law of Contracts § 39:24 (Richard A. Lord ed., 4th ed.1992, Supp. 2006)).

ANALYSIS

In the instant case, there is no question that the parties entered into a valid contract for Grant to purchase the property from Ganz and that the judgment lien against Ganz was entered after the execution of the contract but before settlement thereon. The central issue is whether the financing contingency in the contract of sale prevented equitable conversion from occurring at the time that the contract was made. Specifically, we need to decide whether the financing contingency prevented specific enforcement of the contract by Grant, which thereby would have precluded equitable conversion. See Watson, 304 Md. at 61, 497 A.2d 794 (stating that "[t]he commentators are in accord that equitable conversion takes place only if the contract is specifically enforceable.").[3]

---

[3]   Although not raised by Grant, the Court of Appeals in *Caltrider v. Caples*, 160 Md. 392, 397–98, 153 A. 445 (1931), rejected the judgment creditor's argument that the contract of sale was not specifically enforceable, holding that the judgment creditor had no standing to raise that argument. The Court reasoned that the judgment creditor acquired no more rights than those retained by the vendor/judgment debtor, and the vendor had obviated the necessity of deciding the question of specific performance by carrying out the agreement. Id.

Our review of the financing contingency in the contract indicates that it unquestionably benefitted Grant by making the contract contingent on his ability to secure the necessary financing. On the other hand, the financing contingency gave Ganz only the power, after the initial 45 day period, to impose a time limit for Grant to either remove the contingency or let the contract terminate, without liability. Therefore, the financing contingency benefitted only Grant, and because Grant could waive the contingency at any time, the contract was specifically enforceable by Grant.

In addition, according to the financing contingency, from May 29, 2007 to July 13, 2007 (the 45 day period following the date of the contract ratification), the contract was "contingent on [Grant] obtaining approval for [a] loan[ ] to purchase the [p]roperty." Grant did not exercise that option, and the contract was not terminated by him. After 9 p.m. on July 13, 2007 (the "deadline" for providing Ganz notice by Form #100 removing the financing contingency), the contingency, by its express terms, continued unless it was satisfied. After passage of the deadline, Ganz had the option to give notice to Grant that the contract would become void if Grant failed to deliver Form #100 within three days. Ganz did not exercise this option, and the contract continued to be in effect.

Instead, on July 31, 2007, Grant and Ganz met for settlement on the property, and Grant tendered the full amount of the purchase price. At that time Ganz had no option or discretion under the contract not to convey the property to Grant. Thus, if Ganz had refused such conveyance, specific performance of the contract was available to Grant. See Watson, 304 Md. at 61, 497 A.2d 794 (stating that "[w]hen the money is paid according to the terms of the contract, the vendee is entitled to a conveyance, and to a decree in Chancery for a specific execution of the contract, if such conveyance is refused").

We conclude that the financing contingency consisted of conditions subsequent. Neither party took advantage of the conditions permitting termination of the contract, so that the contract continued in effect. Therefore, the financing contingency did not prevent the occurrence of equitable conversion at the time of the execution of the contract. Accordingly, on July 24, 2007, when the circuit court entered a confessed judgment against Ganz, equitable title to the property was held by Grant, and the judgment could not attach as a lien on the property. Grant's claim of equitable title was superior to that of the Kahns as judgment creditors. The circuit court erred in coming to a contrary conclusion. * * *

PUBLIC POLICY

Finally, Grant claims that "sound public policy" dictates that the decision of the circuit court be reversed. Grant reasons that the trial court's decision "endangers the free transferability of residential real property" by exposing buyers to significant risks associated with sellers who have "poor credit histories or financial difficulties." The Kahns counter that a reversal of the circuit court's decision "would implicitly allow judgment debtors to remove their real estate assets from the grasp of their judgment creditors by entering into non-binding contracts of sale which can be unilaterally nullified by their putative purchasers simply by giving notice." We agree with Grant.

Under the Kahns' theory, a buyer entering into a contract of sale with a financing contingency would be exposed to the risk of judgment liens entered against the seller after the execution of the contract. These liens could affect the sale itself where, for example, the total of all liens or encumbrances on the property exceed the purchase price, and the judgment creditor challenges the sufficiency of the purchase price. Such uncertainty, in our view, would adversely affect the free transferability of real property. The Kahns' concern over a debtor using a pretextual sale to avoid the anticipated lien of a judgment creditor is addressed by the doctrine of equitable conversion. Equitable conversion requires a "contract for land, bona fide made for a valuable consideration." Watson, 304 Md. at 61, 497 A.2d 794; see Birckner v. Tilch, 179 Md. 314, 323, 18 A.2d 222 (stating that "[i]n order to work a conversion, the contract must be valid and binding"), cert. denied, 314 U.S. 635, 62 S.Ct. 68, 86 L. Ed. 509 (1941). Therefore, we conclude that sound public policy supports the application of the doctrine of equitable conversion to the case sub judice.

JUDGMENT REVERSED; COSTS TO BE PAID BY APPELLEE.

NOTES AND QUESTIONS

1. *Two types of contracts.* The contract of sale in *Grant* was a short-term "earnest money" contract, which contemplates only a short executory period—a few weeks or a few months. It was in fact performed just two months after being entered into by the parties. There are no installment payments on such a contract, but usually just a single payment of the purchase price (less any earnest money already paid) on the closing date. The buyer ordinarily does not take possession until the closing. The other type of contract is a long-term installment contract (called in some states a "contract for deed"), in which the purchaser takes possession of the land when the contract is signed, makes payments (monthly, quarterly, or annually) for a number of years, and receives a deed only when the last payment is made.

Equitable conversion is typically applied without distinction to both types of contracts. But it is much easier to visualize the buyer as an "owner of real estate" in the long-term installment contract case because the buyer has possession and is making payments that are similar to the payments that would be due under a mortgage loan. Even in short term earnest money contracts, should the buyer's rights in the real estate be considered sufficient to regard the buyer as an equitable owner?

2. *Acceptance of equitable conversion.* Equitable conversion is widely, but not universally, accepted by American courts. One article cites 32 jurisdictions as having adopted the doctrine in some context or other. Nock, Strait & Weaver, Equitable Conversion in Washington: The Doctrine That Dares Not Speak Its Name, 1 U. P. S. L. Rev. 121 (1977). Its historical background is recounted in Harlan Stone, Equitable Conversion by Contract, 13 Colum. L. Rev. 369 (1913); C.C. Langdell, A Brief Survey of Equity Jurisdiction, 1 Harv. L. Rev. 355 (1887).

3. *Necessity of a contract.* Conversion occurs only if there is a contract that equity would specifically enforce. There is no equitable conversion if, at the relevant time, there is only an unaccepted offer or an unexercised option. See Riddle v. Elk Creek Salers, Ltd., 52 S.W.3d 644 (Mo. Ct. App. 2001). But if an enforceable contract exists at the time in question, it is immaterial in characterization cases that the contract is later rescinded, abandoned, or never enforced. See III Am. L. Prop. § 11.23 (1952); Frietze v. Frietze, 78 N.M. 676, 437 P.2d 137 (1968) (contract was in force at time of purchaser's death, and equitable conversion governed passage of his title, even though contract was never performed). On the other hand, if the contract has expired at the time in question, no equitable conversion will be found. See Lewis v. Muchmore, 26 S.W.3d 632 (Tenn. Ct. App. 2000).

4. *When conversion is inapplicable.* Courts occasionally have developed other "exceptions" to equitable conversion, perhaps manipulating them to avoid results they consider unfair. For example, equitable conversion will not have occurred if the vendor's title is unmarketable as of the date that conversion is in issue. See Bleckley v. Langston, 112 Ga. App. 63, 143 S.E.2d 671 (1965); Coe v. Hays, 328 Md. 350, 614 A.2d 576 (1992). This exception is consistent with the rule that equitable conversion can occur only if there is a contract that equity would specifically enforce. Obviously, a court would not order specific performance of the contract if the seller could not convey marketable title to the buyer. As *Grant* suggests, some courts hold that there is no conversion until all conditions precedent to the transfer of legal title have been fulfilled. See Southport Congregational Church—United Church of Christ v. Hadley, 98 A.3d 99 (Conn. App. 2014) (financing condition not satisfied); Sanford v. Breidenbach, 173 N.E.2d 702 (Ohio App. 1960) (sellers had not yet provided easement for septic tank to purchasers as required by contract).

5. *Judgment liens.* The issue in *Grant* was whether equitable conversion changes the vendor's interest to personal property, and therefore prevents a judgment lien from attaching to it. The case law on this point is split. Compare Bank of Hawaii v. Horwoth, 787 P.2d 674 (Haw. 1990) and Cannefax v. Clement, 818 P.2d 546 (Ut. 1991) (recognizing equitable conversion and finding no judgment lien on the vendor's interest) with Bedortha v. Sunridge Land Co., 822 P.2d 694 (Or. 1991) and Schleuter Co. v. Sevigny, 546 N.W.2d 309 (S.D. 1997) (rejecting equitable conversion and finding a judgment lien). See generally W. Stoebuck & D. Whitman, The Law of Property § 10.13 (3d ed. 2000).

Does the Maryland court's rationale in *Grant* for refusing to recognize the judgment lien make any sense? If the lien is "docketed" (i.e., entered into the court's records) during a short-term earnest money contract's executory period, it normally will be found prior to the closing when the title company or attorney will bring the title search "down to date." How can the *Grant* court assert that the buyer is exposed to significant risks in this situation? A competent title searcher will identify the lien, and either the seller will pay it off from the proceeds of the sale, or if the proceeds are insufficient and the seller has no other funds to pay it, the sale will be rescinded and the buyer's earnest money refunded. Thus, a judgment lien against the seller is really no different than any other lien that might attach to the property during the executory period.

If the sales contract is a long-term installment contract instead, the attachment of a judgment lien to the vendor's interest presents a more significant problem. The purchaser may be unaware of the lien's attachment and continue to make payments on the contract price, possibly ending up paying more than the encumbered property is worth. Of course, the purchaser could procure another title search before making each payment, but this would be ludicrously burdensome and costly. See the Utah court's discussion of this issue in *Cannefax v. Clement*, supra. One solution is for the court to treat the installment sale purchaser as a bona fide purchaser who is protected in making payments to the vendor unless and until the purchaser receives actual notice that the lien has been docketed. See Burke v. Johnson, 16 P. 204 (Kan. 1887); W. Lawrence Church, Equitable Conversion in Wisconsin, 1970 Wis. L. Rev. 404.

 What about a judgment lien that is docketed against the *purchaser* during the executory period of the sales contract? Here, equitable conversion is very widely applied to make the judgment a lien on the purchaser's interest. See Fulton v. Duro, 687 P.2d 1367 (Idaho App. 1984); Hannah v. Martinson, 232 Mont. 469, 758 P.2d 276 (1988); Farmers State Bank v. Slaubaugh, 366 N.W.2d 804 (N.D. 1985); Bank of Santa Fe v. Garcia, 102 N.M. 588, 698 P.2d 458 (App. 1985), certiorari denied 102 N.M. 613, 698 P.2d 886 (1985); Butler v. Wilkinson, 740 P.2d 1244 (Utah 1987).

6.   *Death of a contracting party.* Probably the most-discussed equitable conversion characterization issue is devolution of a party's interest upon his or her death during the executory period. If a court concludes that equitable conversion has occurred at the time of the vendor's death, the vendor's interest descends as personal property to his legatees or, if intestate, his statutory next-of-kin. If it is the purchaser who dies, her interest descends as realty to her devisees or, if intestate, her statutory heirs.

In the case of the vendor's death, the foregoing means that "bare" legal title descends to the devisees or heirs, who have a duty to convey it to the purchaser at the closing. See Mackiewicz v. J.J & Assoc., 245 Neb. 568, 514 N.W.2d 613 (1994). The deceased vendor's personal property legatees or next-of-kin will be entitled to the purchase price, and the devisees or heirs who were forced to convey away the legal title to the real estate receive nothing. See In re Estate of Line, 122 Ohio App. 3d 387, 701 N.E.2d 1028 (1997).

On the other hand, if the purchaser dies prior to the closing, the purchaser's devisees or heirs will be entitled to delivery of the deed at the closing, but the purchase price will be paid out of the personal property estate of the deceased purchaser, and will reduce the assets going to the purchaser's personal property legatees or heirs. See Timberlake v. Heflin, 180 W. Va. 644, 379 S.E.2d 149 (1989); III Am. L. Prop. § 11.26–.27 (1952).

Equitable conversion is usually unimportant if the decedent (whether the vendor or the purchaser) is intestate, because modern intestacy statutes commonly make the same person or group of persons heirs of the real property and next-of-kin takers of the personal property of the intestate decedent. The issue is more critical if the decedent left a will that designates different individuals as devisees and legatees. For example, suppose the decedent was the purchaser, and her will provides, "I leave all my personal property to John and all my real property to Mary." Is it plausible to suppose the decedent intended Mary to get the land and John to suffer the payment of the price out of the personal property he is to receive? Does it matter whether the will was executed before or after the contract? Whether the will mentions the specific land in question?

Is the real problem here that the so-called "doctrine of exoneration," which forces the decedent's debts—even contractual debts secured by a real estate sales contract—to be paid out of the decedent's personal property estate? The doctrine of exoneration is plainly weakening in the United States. Increasingly, courts are holding that property subject to a mortgage, for example, will pass pursuant to a decedent's will with the mortgage still encumbering it, rather than requiring that the mortgage must be paid off from the personal property estate, unless the testator's will expressly requires exoneration. See In re Estate of Vincent, 98 S.W.3d 146 (Tenn. 2003) (testator's statement in will, that executor was to pay his "just debts," was insufficiently specific to require exoneration of a mortgage on land). The Uniform Probate Code abolishes exoneration with respect to mortgages, although it makes no reference to exoneration of an obligation to pay the purchase price of land pursuant to a real estate sales contract. See UPC § 2–609.

Would it be more fair for Mary to take the land, but subject to the "vendor's lien" for the unpaid price, so that Mary would have to pay the remainder of the purchase price in order to keep the land? Disposition of the decedent's property pursuant to the terms of a will is always a matter of intent, if the decedent's intent can be discerned, but too often the decedent expressed no clear intent and court is left to speculate. See, e.g., First Camden Nat. Bank & Trust v. Broadbent, 66 N.J. Super. 199, 168 A.2d 677 (1961).

Similar concerns can arise in the event of the vendor's death. Suppose the vendor's will leaves his personal property to John and his real estate to

Mary. If the will was made at a time when the land in question was already under contract, and especially if that land was the only real estate the vendor owned, how likely is it that the vendor intended the contract to cut Mary out of receiving the financial benefits of the real estate contract? Yet this is the result under the doctrine of equitable conversion. See Father Flanagan's Boys' Home v. Graybill, 178 Neb. 79, 132 N.W.2d 304 (1964). If the will predates the contract, cutting Mary out seems easier to accept as a result. Arguably, the vendor expected that would be the result of his signing the contract. See In re Estate of Pickett, 879 So. 2d 467 (Miss. Ct. App. 2004) (where vendor's will made a specific devise of the property, but vendor then entered into a contract of sale before he died, the contract was enforceable. and under the doctrine of equitable conversion, the vendor's rights were converted into personal property; hence, the specific devise was adeemed and no rights to the property or its proceeds passed to the devisees).

Given the inherent ambiguities involved in these characterization situations, a few states have changed the foregoing rules for disposition of the parties' interests by statute. See, e.g., Rowe v. Newman, 290 Ala. 289, 276 So. 2d 412 (1972). If you were a state legislator, would you adopt a statutory rule to address these characterization issues? Or would you prefer to allow the courts discretion to continue to apply the doctrine of equitable conversion (or not) on a case by case basis?

7. *Risk of loss.* In situations where the property is damaged during the executory period of the contract, equitable conversion imposes the loss on the purchaser. The purchaser is treated as the owner of the property, and therefore is subject to a decree of specific performance, forcing the purchaser to pay the full price, even though the real estate has been devalued by the loss. Which party had possession of the property at the time of the loss is said to be irrelevant. See 6A Powell, Real Property ¶ 933 (1979). Consider whether this result fulfills the following policy objectives:

- Is it consistent with the probable expectation of the parties as to their rights?

- Does it place the risk on the party who is best able to oversee the property and guard against loss?

- Does it place the risk on the party who is most likely to carry insurance against it?

See generally Fineberg, Risk of Loss in Executory Contracts for the Sale of Real Property, 14 Colum. J.L. & Soc. Prob. 453 (1979). It seems to us that application of the doctrine of equitable conversion in a casualty loss situation fails all three of these tests. But whatever its merits, the doctrine continues to be strongly supported in "risk of loss" cases. See, e.g., Continental Ins. Co. v. Brown, 630 F. Supp. 302 (W. D. Va. 1986); Ambrose v. Harrison Mut. Ins. Ass'n, 206 N.W.2d 683 (Iowa 1973); Bleckley v. Langston, 112 Ga. App. 63, 143 S.E.2d 671 (1965). It is clear, however, that the parties can modify this risk allocation as they wish in the sales contract. See, e.g., Holscher v. James,

124 Idaho 443, 860 P.2d 646 (1993). Printed form contracts routinely shift the risk of loss back to the vendor until the closing, or perhaps until the purchaser takes possession. It is clear that appropriate contract language can prevent equitable conversion from occurring; see Noor v. Centreville Bank, 996 A.2d 928, 933 (Md. App. 2010). Hence, the litigated cases usually involve situations where the sales contract is silent on the risk of loss issue. See Rector v. Alcorn, 241 N.W.2d 196 (Iowa 1976). For example, in Munshower v. Martin, 641 So. 2d 909 (Fla. App. 1994), the contract stated "the risk of loss or damage by fire or other cause is assumed by the seller." The court held that this language was sufficient to override the equitable conversion doctrine and require the seller to pay for roof damage caused by Hurricane Andrew.

Both the equitable conversion doctrine and any contract terms reversing it are predicated on the assumption that the loss in question is not the fault of either party to the contract. For example, if the contract imposes the risk of loss on the vendor, but the purchaser takes possession and negligently or intentionally starts a fire that damages the premises, the purchaser will be legally responsible for the loss despite the contract provision. See Voorde Poorte v. Evans, 66 Wash. App. 358, 832 P.2d 105 (1992). Likewise if, under equitable conversion, the risk is on the purchaser, but the property is damaged through the vendor's fault, the vendor must stand the loss. See Sposit v. Navratil, 72 Ohio App. 3d 493, 595 N.E.2d 467 (1991) (vendor negligent in allowing water pipes to freeze prior to closing).

8.   *The minority view: Risk remains on the vendor.* A few courts have refused to follow equitable conversion in risk of loss cases; they usually place the risk on the seller until legal title or possession is transferred, and permit the buyer to rescind in the event of a loss or (at the purchaser's option) to get specific performance with an abatement of the price to account for the land's reduced value. See Libman v. Levenson, 236 Mass. 221, 128 N.E. 13 (1920); Anderson v. Yaworski, 120 Conn. 390, 181 A. 205 (1935); Lampesis v. Travelers Ins. Co., 101 N.H. 323, 143 A.2d 104 (1958). Consider the following excerpt from Skelly Oil Co. v. Ashmore, 365 S.W.2d 582, 588 (Mo. 1963), quoting with approval from Dean Stone's article, supra Note 2:

> The *non sequitur* involved in the proposition that performance may be had because of the equitable ownership of the land by the vendee, which in turn depends upon the right of performance, is evident. The doctrine of equitable conversion, so far as it is exemplified by the authorities hitherto considered, cannot lead to the result of casting the burden of loss on the vendee, since the *conversion depends upon the question whether the contract should in equity be performed.* In all other cases where the vendee is treated as the equitable owner of the land, it is only because the contract is one which equity first determines should be specifically performed. (emphasis in original.)

See also Linda Hume, Real Estate Contracts and the Doctrine of Equitable Conversion in Washington; Dispelling the *Ashford* Cloud, 7 U. Puget Sound L. Rev. 233 (1984).

Perhaps the most sensible approach is represented by Brush Grocery Kart, Inc. v. Sure Fine Market, Inc., 47 P.3d 680 (Colo. 2002). The court held that equitable conversion would impose the risk of loss on the purchaser only in cases where the purchaser had taken possession of the property at the time of the loss. This result is similar to that reached by the Uniform Vendor and Purchaser Risk Act, discussed in Note 11 infra. A similar approach was taken in Alley v. McLain's Inc. Lumber and Construction, 182 S.W.3d 312 (Tenn. Ct. App. 2005) (where purchaser had timber cut on the property, person cutting timber might be shielded from liability to vendor by equitable conversion doctrine, but only if purchaser was entitled to possession at the time timber was cut).

9. *Types of losses.* Although the losses that equitable conversion imposes on the purchaser are usually the result of fire, flood, wind, or other physical hazards, the risk of change in the property's *legal* status is sometimes allocated to the purchaser in the same way. The following situations are illustrative:

(a) *Zoning change.* Mohave County v. Mohave-Kingman Estates, Inc., 120 Ariz. 417, 586 P.2d 978 (1978); J.C. Penney Co. v. Koff, 345 So. 2d 732 (Fla. App. 1977); cf. Clay v. Landreth, 187 Va. 169, 45 S.E.2d 875 (1948) (contract will not be enforced if zoning change has made property unusable for purchaser's intended purpose).

(b) *Building code change.* Cox v. Supreme Sav. & Loan Ass'n, 126 Ill. App. 2d 293, 262 N.E.2d 74 (1970).

(c) *Eminent domain action.* Arko Enterprises, Inc. v. Wood, 185 So. 2d 734 (Fla. App. 1966); Annot., 27 A.L.R. 3d 572 (1969).

(d) *Liability for the cost of cleanup of hazardous waste.* United States v. Capital Tax Corp., 545 F.3d 525 (7th Cir. 2008).

10. *Loss from title defects.* Suppose the event that occurs during the executory period of the sales contract and causes a loss also is a title defect, such as the imposition by the city of a lien for a sewer improvement assessment. Should this event be treated as a breach of the covenant of marketable title (imposing the risk on the seller) or handled under equitable conversion (imposing the risk on the purchaser)? See Byrne v. Kanig, 231 Pa. Super. 531, 332 A.2d 472 (1974). The eminent domain cases raise a similar issue (although the courts do not always recognize it), because a pending eminent domain action is a defect in marketable title. See III Am. L. Prop. § 11.49 n. 52 (1952).

11. *The Uniform Vendor and Purchaser Risk Act.* Eleven states have adopted the Uniform Vendor and Purchaser Risk Act (Act), which changes the impact of equitable conversion on the risk of certain types of losses. The adopting states include California, Hawaii, Michigan, Oklahoma, Oregon,

South Dakota, Texas, Wisconsin, Illinois, New York, and North Carolina (the latter three with some modifications of the official text). The Act was inspired by Professor Samuel Williston; its background and the New York modifications are discussed in Frank Lacy, The Uniform Vendor and Purchaser Risk Act and the Need for a Law-Revision Commission in Oregon, 36 Or. L. Rev. 106 (1957). See also W. Stoebuck & D. Whitman, The Law of Property § 10.13 (3d ed. 2000).

UNIFORM VENDOR AND PURCHASER RISK ACT

§ 1. Risk of Loss. Any contract hereafter made in this State for the purchase and sale of realty shall be interpreted as including an agreement that the parties shall have the following rights and duties, unless the contract expressly provides otherwise:

(a) If, when neither the legal title nor the possession of the subject matter of the contract has been transferred, all or a material part thereof is destroyed without fault of the purchaser or is taken by eminent domain, the vendor cannot enforce the contract, and the purchaser is entitled to recover any portion of the price that he has paid;

(b) If, when either the legal title or the possession of the subject matter of the contract has been transferred, all or any part thereof is destroyed without fault of the vendor or is taken by eminent domain, the purchaser is not thereby relieved from a duty to pay the price, nor is he entitled to recover any portion thereof that he has paid.

QUESTIONS

(a) What sorts of losses are covered by the Act? What about the "legal" losses mentioned in Notes 9 and 10, supra.

(b) How much is a "material part"? If the property is a house worth $150,000, what about damage of $100? $1,000? $10,000? See National Factors, Inc. v. Winslow, 52 Misc. 2d 194, 274 N.Y.S.2d 400 (1966).

(c) If the damage is less than "material," the purchaser has no right under the Act to rescind. But can the purchaser insist on an abatement of price in the amount of the damage?

(d) If the damage to the property is clearly "material," the Act will allow the purchaser to rescind. Suppose the purchaser prefers to specifically enforce the contract with an abatement of the price. Can the purchaser do so? See Or Home, Inc. v. Purrier, 851 N.Y.S.2d 71 (N.Y. Sup. Ct. 2007); Lucenti v. Cayuga Apartments, Inc., 59 A.D.2d 438, 400 N.Y.S.2d 194 (1977).

(e) What does it mean for "possession" to be "transferred"? Has possession been transferred if the purchaser, at the time of the loss, has the legal right to possession but has not actually gone into occupancy yet? See Unger v.

Nunda Township Rural Fire Protection Dist., 135 Ill. App. 3d 758, 90 Ill. Dec. 416, 482 N.E.2d 123 (1985).

(f) The Act's results can be varied by the contract's terms. Caulfield v. Improved Risk Mutuals, Inc., 66 N.Y.2d 793, 497 N.Y.S.2d 903, 488 N.E.2d 833 (1985). Suppose the sales contract says that the purchaser will accept the property "as is." Does such language shift the risk of loss to the purchaser? See Redner v. New York, 53 Misc. 2d 148, 278 N.Y.S.2d 51 (1967).

(g) In a state without the Act, it is obviously crucial to have a contract clause covering the risk of loss issue. How should such a clause be worded? Is it sufficient to say "Risk of loss shall be on the vendor until legal title is transferred"? Should the clause track the language of the Act? See M. Friedman, Contracts and Conveyances of Real Property 382 (3d ed. 1975). As a legal drafting skills exercise, try your hand at writing a sales contract clause that deals clearly with all of the issues raised in this set of Notes on equitable conversion.

NOTE ON THE IMPACT OF CASUALTY INSURANCE

It is very common for the vendor to have a casualty insurance policy in force because the vendor usually has owned the property for some time before putting it on the market. The purchaser usually applies for a new casualty insurance policy that will take effect on the date of closing. Hence, there is a lack of correspondence between the insurance coverage and the risk of loss, which may be on the purchaser under the doctrine of equitable conversion, or because the purchaser has gone into possession and thus has assumed the risk of a casualty loss under the UVPRA or a contract clause.

Casualty insurance is a personal contract between the insurer and the insured. Thus, the insurer is not obligated to pay the proceeds to anyone except the insured under the policy. But to let the vendor keep the insurance proceeds and, at the same time, enforce the contract of sale for the full purchase price, obviously results in the unjust enrichment of the vendor. You can imagine a vendor in these circumstances saying, "This is one of the best fires I ever had!"

To avoid this unjust enrichment, many courts require the vendor to pay or credit the insurance proceeds to the purchaser, up to the full purchase price. Here is one court's explanation for such a holding. The vendors were the defendants, who had an existing mortgage on the real estate at the time the contract of sale was entered into.

> Looked at as a practical matter, there is no manifest disruption of the law if the equitable result is favored, especially if the vendee is required to reimburse the vendor for his cost of maintaining the insurance during the vendee's possession and the insurance proceeds are credited to the unpaid purchase price only to the extent of the market value of the dwelling immediately before the loss. Here, defendants had carried insurance on the property,

presumably as required by their mortgage. The property was sold at a value that met the mortgage demand. If the property had not been destroyed, the purchase price would have satisfied the mortgage; having been destroyed, the insurance proceeds satisfy the mortgage. If he does not credit the proceeds to the balance due, the vendor profits by a fortuitous event, thus unreasonably forcing the vendee to rescind even though, as here, he elects to compel specific performance presumably because the land, and not the dwelling upon it, was the motivating reason for his purchase. And even if the proceeds are credited to the purchase price, the burden of the loss in the sense of replacing the dwelling rests on the vendee. It does not answer the problem to say the vendee could have carried insurance. The parties both have insurable interests in the property which are at best difficult to allocate out of the total property.

While the legal relations between vendor and his insured and vendor and his vendee are personal, beneath this external form the essence of the agreement before the sale is completed is that the purchase price ought to be paid to the vendor and the land ought to be conveyed to the vendee. Where the final acts contemplated by the parties can be achieved by requiring that the proceeds be applied to reduce the purchase price, it ought to be regarded as done.

Gilles v. Sprout, 293 Minn. 53, 196 N.W.2d 612 (1972). See also Hillard v. Franklin, 41 S.W.3d 106 (Tenn. Ct. App. 2000) (same result). The vendor is sometimes said to hold the insurance proceeds in "constructive trust" for the purchaser, but this normally means simply that the purchaser is credited with them. See, e.g., New Hampshire Ins. Co. v. Vetter, 326 N.W.2d 723 (S.D. 1982); Fellmer v. Gruber, 261 N.W.2d 173 (Iowa 1978); Chapline v. North American Acceptance Corp., 25 Ariz. App. 465, 544 P.2d 682 (1976). Cf. Long v. Keller, 104 Cal. App. 3d 312, 163 Cal. Rptr. 532 (1980). See James Fischer, The Presence of Insurance and the Legal Allocation of Risk, 2 Conn. Ins. L. J. 1, 27 n. 107 (1996).

New York generally has refused to credit the purchaser with the insurance proceeds, but does so if the purchaser was obligated to and did pay the premiums. See Raplee v. Piper, 3 N.Y.2d 179, 164 N.Y.S.2d 732, 143 N.E.2d 919 (1957); accord, Wilson v. Fireman's Ins. Co., 403 Mich. 339, 269 N.W.2d 170 (1978) (construing the policy as benefitting both vendor and purchaser, where the premiums were paid by the purchaser). See generally Allen Fineberg, Risk of Loss in Executory Contracts for the Sale of Real Property, 14 Colum. J. L. & Soc. Prob. 453, 476 (1979); Annot., Rights of Vendor and Purchaser, As Between Themselves, In Insurance Proceeds, 64 A.L.R. 2d 1402 (1959).

Suppose the buyer willingly pays the full price despite the fire or other damage (perhaps because the buyer planned to demolish the structure anyway), and makes no claim to the insurance proceeds. Can the insurer refuse to pay the insured vendor's claim on grounds that; (1) insurance is a contract of indemnity, and on these facts the vendor has no loss to be indemnified, or; (2) the vendor, having contracted to sell the property, no longer had an insurable interest in it at the time of the damage? Compare Wolf v. Home Ins. Co., 100 N.J. Super. 27, 241 A.2d 28 (1968) (vendor can collect claim) with Westfall v. Am. States Ins. Co., 43 Ohio App. 2d 176, 334 N.E.2d 523 (1974) (vendor had no insurable interest). Does payment of the insurance proceeds in such a situation give the vendor an unjustifiable windfall? See Banks McDowell, Insurable Interest in Property Revisited, 17 Cap. U. L. Rev. 165 (1988).

Suppose instead that it is the purchaser who carries the insurance, is named as insured, and has the risk of loss. Obviously, in the event of a casualty loss the purchaser is entitled to claim the insurance proceeds. If the risk is on the seller, however, the purchaser arguably has no loss and no insurable interest. As a result, the insurer in this situation may entirely avoid payment under the policy. See Sanford v. Breidenbach, 111 Ohio App. 474, 173 N.E.2d 702 (1960).

In general, the vendor has no right to the insurance proceeds when the purchaser is the insured under the policy. But if the sales contract specified that the purchaser was to carry insurance, the courts often infer that the parties intended for the vendor to have the benefit of the policy, up to the outstanding balance on the contract, and permit the vendor to claim it. See Nevada Refining Co. v. Newton, 88 Nev. 333, 497 P.2d 887 (1972); Marbach v. Gnadl, 73 Ill. App. 2d 303, 219 N.E.2d 572 (1966). Cf. Phillips v. Bacon, 245 Ga. 814, 267 S.E.2d 249 (1980). This right of the vendor is even more clear if the purchaser expressly promised to carry casualty insurance on the property for the vendor's benefit. See Rosario-Paolo, Inc. v. C & M Pizza Restaurant, Inc., 84 N.Y.2d 379, 618 N.Y.S.2d 766, 643 N.E.2d 85 (1994).

G. CONDITIONS IN CONTRACTS

The provisions of a contract for the sale of real estate may contain covenants, conditions, or both. For present purposes, it is highly important to distinguish among them, although this is a matter that the laypersons who usually prepare such contracts often forget or ignore.

A covenant, of course, is a promise. One who enters into it is obligated to perform, and one who does not do so may be subject to a suit for breach, with such remedies as damages, specific performance, and rescission potentially available to the nonbreaching party.

A condition, on the other hand, is not a promise at all; instead, it is merely a statement that a party's obligation to perform some covenant is dependent upon the happening of a specified event or occurrence. For example, V may covenant with P to sell his house to P, but may add the condition that he is obligated to do so only if it does not rain on the following Tuesday. Of course, that particular condition is rather unusual and probably has little utility, but it does illustrate that conditions may involve events that no one promises will occur, and indeed that may be entirely outside the control of the parties.

In many cases a particular statement in a sales contract can be both a covenant and a condition. Consider the clauses concerning V's delivery of the deed transferring marketable title and P's payment of the purchase price at the closing. These are obviously covenants because each party is promising to perform and will be liable for breach for failure to do so. But such clauses also are conditions, and, as we have already seen, are usually construed to be concurrent conditions. As a result, neither party is obligated to perform until the other tenders his or her own promised performance.

Not all conditions in a sales contract are concurrent. By its terms or context within the body of the sales contract, it may be apparent that a particular condition is precedent, which means that it stands on its own, and that the other party's duty to perform certain covenants under the contract depends on that condition being fulfilled first. Purchasers of real estate often try to protect themselves with various conditions precedent, so that they can rescind the contract and receive a refund of their earnest money deposit under certain circumstances. Without doubt, the most common condition precedent is the arrangement of satisfactory financing to permit the purchase. Obviously, the buyer does not want to be bound to complete the deal unless it is possible to borrow the necessary money to purchase the property on satisfactory terms. Other common kinds of conditions precedent might relate to the purchaser's sale of other real estate, the successful procurement of a zoning change for the property, satisfactory completion of certain physical tests (e.g., an inspection of the physical condition of the property for defects, a soil test for strength or water percolation, a survey, an appraisal, etc.), or the obtaining of an easement to benefit the land.

Conditions also may be used to protect the vendor of the land. For example, if the vendor is providing financing for part of the purchase price, he may condition his duty on the receipt of a credit report and financial statement from the purchaser that meets certain standards.

The use of conditions is not the only way to handle the purchaser's problem of hoped-for, but as yet unassured, future events such as obtaining financing or procuring a zoning change. One alternative is the use of an option to purchase the property in the future. Under this method, the optionor (the seller-to-be) grants to the optionee (the buyer-to-be) an irrevocable offer to sell the property, usually at a fixed price for a specific period of time. The optionee pays consideration for the optionor's promise to leave the offer open for the time specified. This promise becomes contractually binding, and the offer itself becomes irrevocable. The optionee can decide for herself (after making the necessary investigations and inquiries) whether to buy the property or not. The holder of the option right "exercises" the option by accepting the offer to buy the real estate. If the optionee decides not to purchase, she merely lets the option lapse without any further liability.

The option's advantage is that it is unnecessary to spell out in advance all of the conditions precedent that must be satisfied before the purchaser must buy the real estate. It is entirely up to the buyer whether to exercise the option right or not. The disadvantage of the option method is that one generally must pay for an option, and the money paid is permanently lost if the option right is not exercised. Options are not used very frequently in single-family residence transactions, but are a common method for the acquisition of land for the development of subdivisions or for commercial development. See Temkin, Too Much Good Faith in Real Estate Purchase Agreements? Give Me an Option, 34 Kan. L. Rev. 43 (1985).

Let us return to conditions, and specifically to the most common type, the condition relating to the financing of the purchase. Financing clauses in real estate sales contracts often are stated in incredibly loose language, such as "Subject to the buyer's obtaining suitable financing" or the like. Forgetting for the moment about the question of what sort of financing will be "suitable", what do the words "subject to" mean? Do they impose a condition, a covenant, or both? More specifically, do they excuse a party (and if so, which party?) from performance if financing is not obtained? Do they impose on a party (again, which party?) an obligation to seek financing? Another favorite word of lay drafters in the financing clause context is "contingent", as in "contract contingent on obtaining financing." The same questions apply. Moreover, do not assume that preprinted form contracts are models of professional drafting; many of them are simply dreadful. Phrases like "subject to" and "contingent on" are vague and can easily provoke litigation. Although many lawyers, judges, and real estate agents may use these phrases, you should not. If your client desires a condition precedent, call it a condition.

Recall that the point of the financing condition is that if the purchaser is unable to obtain the described financing, the purchaser can rescind the contract and have the earnest money deposit refunded. See Saulcy Land Co. v. Jones, 983 P.2d 1200 (Wyo. 1999). Although conditions concerning financing usually are inserted for entirely legitimate reasons, they may become a pretext for the purchaser to rescind the sales contract for reasons that have nothing to do with financing.

NOTES AND QUESTIONS

1. *"Obtaining" financing.* It is one thing to obtain a loan commitment from a lender, and quite another to obtain the loan itself. A lender may

withdraw a preclosing loan commitment because of changes in the circumstances of the proposed borrower. Common language used in loan commitments allows for cancellation "if prior to funding, your financial condition or employment status adversely changes." If the borrower cannot actually obtain the money, having once had a clean commitment is pretty cold comfort. But unless the financing condition expressly provides that it is met only by the actual funding of the loan, the courts usually find that a financing condition is satisfied by the issuance of a loan commitment, even if it is later withdrawn. See, e.g., Malus v. Hager, 312 N. J. Super. 483, 712 A.2d 238 (1998) (borrower lost his job after commitment was issued); Bruyere v. Jade Realty Corp., 117 N. H. 564, 375 A.2d 600 (1977) (borrower couple decided to divorce after commitment was issued).

As a practical matter, the buyer in this unfortunate situation usually will forfeit his or her earnest money deposit (typically pursuant to a liquidated damages clause in the sales contract). Compare the result in Aubin v. Miller, 64 Conn. App. 781, 781 A.2d 396 (2001). In *Aubin*, the purchaser lost his job shortly after he applied for the loan. The contract was "conditioned on the Purchaser being able to obtain a mortgage loan"—not merely a commitment for a loan. The court allowed the purchaser to rescind the sales contract and to recover the earnest money due to the failure of the financing condition precedent. In fairness, which party do you think should bear the risk that the purchaser will become uncredit worthy after obtaining a loan commitment? Does your answer depend on whether you represent the buyer or the seller?

2.   *Waiving the condition.* Generally, a condition that has been inserted for the benefit of one party may be waived voluntarily by that party if he or she wants to proceed despite the failure of the condition. A financing condition ordinarily is intended to benefit the buyer. Therefore, the buyer can waive it and the seller remains bound to perform under the sales contract. See Pelligreen v. Wood, 111 S.W.3d 446 (Mo. Ct. App. 2003). If the condition makes the contract "null and void" in the event that satisfactory financing is not obtained, does this language eliminate the possibility of a waiver by the buyer? See Koedding v. Slaughter, 481 F. Supp. 1233 (E.D. Mo. 1979).

Of course, if the seller is taking the purchaser's note as secondary financing for part of the price, the seller has a legitimate concern about the nature of the purchaser's primary financing. In this situation, the financing clause benefits the seller as well as the buyer. See Fleischer v. McCarver, 691 S.W.2d 930 (Mo. App. 1985). Even if the seller is not "carrying back" part of the financing, is it arguable that the seller has a stake in the buyer's obtaining of financing because if none is obtained there is a greatly increased risk to the seller that the buyer will be unable to close? In Watson v. Gerace, 175 Fed. Appx. 528 (3d Cir. 2006), the financing condition described the loan to be obtained, but also said "Any mortgage commitment signed by the buyer will satisfy this mortgage contingency." The commitment obtained by the buyer contained several somewhat unusual conditions of its own, including that the buyer pass the lender's financial analysis and qualify for a second mortgage loan from the same lender for $32,000. The seller was dissatisfied with these extra requirements and attempted to avoid the sale, claiming that the loan obtained did not conform to the contract's language. The court rejected this view on the basis of the language quoted above, which seemed to say that the buyer could waive the financing condition. But if that language had been absent, would the seller have had the right to rescind the sales contract, in order to escape being subjected to the delay and uncertainty of the buyer's meeting the additional loan requirements?

H. INTRODUCTION TO MORTGAGE FINANCING

It is fairly rare for a buyer of real estate to pay cash. In the majority of real estate transactions a buyer must obtain financing from some source to complete the purchase. Although financing can take a wide variety of forms, it is usually one or a combination of the following:

- a loan from a third-party lender (e.g., a bank) to the buyer;
- the "taking over" by the buyer of the payments on an existing loan that the seller or some former owner obtained from a third-party lender; and
- financing provided by the seller, usually in the form of a deferral of receipt of some portion of the purchase price.

The obligation to repay the financing in all of the above cases is generally represented by a promissory note (or sometimes by a bond or contract) requiring monthly or other regular installment payments. Real estate usually is considered to be excellent security for a loan. Consequently, most financing that is extended to enable the purchase of realty is secured by that same realty, commonly by means of an instrument known as a mortgage (or, where permitted by state statute, a deed of trust). A mortgage involves a transfer by a debtor-mortgagor to a creditor-mortgagee of a real estate interest, to be held as security for the performance of an obligation, which normally is the payment of a debt evidenced by a promissory note. If the debtor defaults on the note, the mortgagee can have the real estate sold and the proceeds applied toward payment of the debt through a process known as foreclosure.

Of course, not all mortgages are related to the acquisition of real property. An owner of real estate may borrow money to start a new business or to send his or her children to college, and may give a mortgage to secure repayment of the loan. In American law, the characterization of a mortgage as "purchase money" in nature (i.e., the money was borrowed in order to raise funds to buy the property) has important consequences with respect to its priority as against competing liens, and in some states with respect to the ability of the lender to obtain a "deficiency judgment" if the borrower defaults and the sale of the real estate through foreclosure does not bring enough to pay the debt.

"amortized"

Today, most mortgages are amortized or repaid over a substantial number of years. Until the 1930s, most mortgages were of the "balloon-note" type. Typically these were short-term mortgages for three to five years, with borrowers only making interest payments until the loan came due. At that point, if the borrower had not saved enough to pay the entire principal, it would be necessary to ask the lender to renew the loan or to attempt to refinance the balance due with another lender. During the Great Depression of the 1930s, many lenders were forced to demand full payment and to foreclose on properties when mortgagors could not pay off their balloon mortgages. With the encouragement of Congress and the Federal Housing Administration, lenders during this period developed the amortized mortgage loan, which allows mortgagors to repay loans over many years by making monthly principal and interest payments. No large lump sum of principal ever comes due on an amortized mortgage loan because the regular monthly payments are sufficient to cover the repayment of both full principal and all interest over the term of the loan.

Characteristics of amortized loans.

Because the level monthly payment, fully amortized loan is so commonly employed in modern real estate financing, its characteristics are important to understand. The monthly payment is set so that only a portion (though it is a relatively large portion in the early years) is needed to cover the interest that has accrued since the last preceding payment. The remainder of each monthly payment is applied to reduce the outstanding principal balance of the loan. Thus, the interest that accrues in each month will be less than the interest for the preceding month because interest is being computed on a continually declining principal amount.

100K × .5% (.005) = 500.

These concepts are best understood by means of an example. Suppose a borrower signs a promissory note to repay $100,000 over a period of thirty years, with interest at the rate of 6% per annum. The loan is made on January 1, 2016, with level repayment installments to be made monthly by the borrower. Thus, the first monthly payment will be due February 1, 2016. Interest alone at the end of that first month would be $100,000 times 1/2 of 1% (the monthly equivalent of 6% per annum), or $500. Consultation of a standard table of mortgage payments reveals that the full payment due (including both interest and amortization of the principal) is $599.55. The amortization schedule below shows the effect of the borrower's first payment and the next few payments that follow it.

Amortization Schedule
($100,000 loan @ 6% for 30 years)

Payment Date		Period	Total Payment	Interest Payment	Principal Payment	Remaining Balance
February	2016	1	599.55	500.00	99.55	99,900.45
March	2016	2	599.55	499.50	100.05	99.800.00
April	2016	3	599.55	499.00	100.55	99.699.85
May	2016	4	599.55	498.50	101.05	99,598.80
June	2016	5	599.55	497.99	101.56	99,497.24
July	2016	6	599.55	497.49	102.06	99,395.18
August	2016	7	599.55	496.98	102.57	99,292.61
September	2016	8	599.55	496.46	103.09	99,189.52
October	2016	9	599.55	495.95	103.06	99,085.92
November	2016	10	599.55	495.43	104.12	98,981.79
December	2016	11	599.55	494.91	104.64	98,877.15

The last payment, which would be made at the end of the 360th month of the loan on January 1, 2046, will be approximately the amount necessary to discharge entirely the small sum still remaining on the principal balance. Of course, filling in the schedule above for a full 360 months is a tedious process unless you use a computer, but if you did so you would see that the amount we originally specified as the monthly payment, $599.55, is precisely the amount necessary to amortize the loan's balance fully over a 30-year period.

The amount of the regular monthly payments necessary to amortize a loan over a given period of time depends on several factors: (1) the frequency of payments (usually monthly for mortgage loans); (2) the term or period of repayments; (3) the interest rate; and (4) the amount borrowed. The table below shows the monthly payments for each one thousand dollars borrowed at various interest rates and terms. You can apply the table to any principal amount simply by multiplying the factor shown by the number of thousands of dollars borrowed.

Monthly Payment Factors (per $1,000 of debt) (rounded)
Term of Loan

Interest Rate	20 years	30 years	40 years
3%	5.55	4.22	3.58
4%	6.06	4.77	4.18
5%	6.60	5.37	4.82
6%	7.16	5.99	5.50
7%	7.75	6.65	6.21
8%	8.36	7.34	6.95
9%	9.00	8.05	7.71
10%	9.65	8.78	8.49
11%	10.32	9.52	8.28
12%	11.01	10.29	10.08
13%	11.72	11.06	10.90
14%	12.44	11.85	11.71
15%	13.17	12.64	12.53

Several observations can be made about the level payment, fully amortized loan. The principal balance declines quite slowly during the early years. After five years of regular payments on the loan in the foregoing example, the principal would be reduced to $92.920, a reduction of only $7,080. This is illustrated in the graph on the following page.

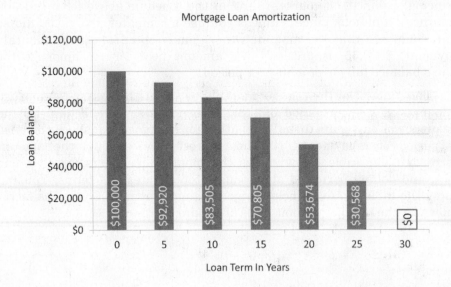

As noted above, each monthly payment is partly allocated to interest and partly to principal. These allocations change over time; in the early years the bulk of each payment is applied toward interest, as the amortization schedule above shows. In later years, more and more of each payment is applied to principal. The graph below shows these changes.

Principal and Interest
Components of Monthly Payment

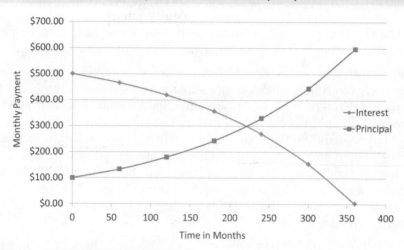

The effect of higher interest rates on the payment can be quite startling. In our example, an interest rate of 7% (rather than the 6% we assumed) would raise the monthly payment by $65, to $665. These figures suggest something of the adverse impact high interest rates can have on the demand for housing. Lengthening the loan term can reduce the monthly payments, but beyond about 30 or 40 years, the impact is not very great. In our example (with a 6% interest rate), increasing the maturity from 30 to 40 years would lower monthly payments by only $50, to $550. Further increases in maturity would bring the monthly payments somewhat closer to $500 per month, the interest-only level, which forms a "floor" below which payments could not go no matter how long the loan term.

The level payment, fully amortized loan is very widely used in single family home financing, and quite commonly employed with commercial and industrial property as well. Beginning in the late 1970s, both federal and state regulators of lending institutions began to permit lenders to use other "innovative" loan repayment formats on home loans. For example, adjustable rate mortgages (ARMs) permit modification of the interest rate during the life of the loan (with concomitant changes in maturity or monthly payment).

Principal amortization is in a sense a form of forced savings. Some households might prefer to minimize, or even eliminate entirely, the amortization component. The lender, however, generally will prefer a relatively more rapid reduction in principal because the loan is seen as a safer investment if the borrower is accumulating equity in the property. During the first half of the 2000s, "interest only" mortgages i.e., with no portion of the monthly payments allocated to the amortization of principal, once again became fairly common because sharp increases in housing prices in some areas of the United States made it difficult for home buyers to afford the payments on fully amortized mortgage loans. As in the Great Depression, beginning in 2008 these loans indeed proved riskier, and went into default more often, than fully amortized loans.

When interest rates are falling or have stabilized at low levels, buyers prefer to finance most home sales with new mortgage loans from institutional lenders such as banks, savings associations, and mortgage companies. When interest rates are rising or have stabilized at high levels, buyers and sellers are more willing to seek alternative or "creative" financing techniques. The variations on these alternative financing methods are virtually endless, but the following list suggests the major ways in which home sales can be financed. Many of these techniques assume that the seller is willing to defer the receipt of all or part of the sale price.

- *All cash sale.* Buyer pays all cash to seller. Buyer may have cash from savings, from gifts from relatives, or by borrowing under a new mortgage loan from an institutional lender.

- *Assumption or taking subject to existing mortgage.* Buyer "takes over" the seller's existing mortgage financing and pays cash equal to the difference between the sales price of the property and the principal balance that remains on the existing loan. The buyer may "take over" the loan either by signing an "assumption agreement" that makes her personally liable on the mortgage debt, or merely by taking "subject to" the loan without any express promise to pay it. In the latter case, the buyer is not personally liable for the repayment of the remaining debt, but will still have a powerful economic incentive to repay the mortgage loan in full to avoid foreclosure and the possible loss of the buyer's cash investment in the property.

- *Seller financing.* Buyer enters into a mortgage loan or an installment contract with seller for all or a large portion of the total purchase price. This is the only debt obligation involved in the transaction. The loan will bear interest and require regular installments payments that are similar to an institutional loan. The seller treats the obligation as an investment. This technique is feasible only if the seller does not need to receive the full amount of the sale price in cash immediately upon the sale of the property.

- *Combination of assumption/subject to and seller financing.* In this combination, the buyer "takes over" the seller's existing mortgage financing, but cannot raise enough cash to pay the entire difference between the sale price and the loan balance. The buyer gives the seller a promissory note secured by a second mortgage on the real estate for part of this difference, thereby reducing the cash demanded of the buyer to a manageable level.

- *Wrap-around financing.* In a "wraparound" financing arrangement, the transaction between the buyer and the seller is structured as seller financing. The seller, however, has a preexisting mortgage loan on the property (usually in the form of an institutional mortgage loan), and does not pay off this preexisting mortgage at the time of the transfer to the buyer. Instead, the seller continues to make payments on the "underlying" institutional loan while the buyer makes payments to the seller on the new (or "wraparound") loan. The interest rate on the wraparound loan often is higher than on the preexisting mortgage loan, resulting in a tidy profit for the seller. From the seller's viewpoint, one of the advantages of the wraparound arrangement over an assumption/subject to financing arrangement is that the seller will not be caught unaware of a default on the preexisting first mortgage because the payments on it are made directly by the seller rather than by the buyer.

[handwritten margin note: Wraparound loan.]

Note that any loan assumption, taking subject to a preexisting mortgage, or "wraparound" of the preexisting institutional mortgage will be problematic if the preexisting mortgage agreement contains an enforceable due-on-sale clause. Such a clause permits the lender to demand an immediate payoff of the loan if the real estate is transferred. In most cases, a due-on-sale clause is indeed enforceable in an arm's length sale transaction. If the lender chooses to enforce the due-on-sale clause, the parties' contract of sale may be frustrated if the buyer is unable to obtain financing sufficient to pay off the preexisting mortgage debt.

ADDITIONAL NOTES ON WRAPAROUND FINANCING

1. *Drafting a sale contract when the existing mortgage contains a due-on-sale clause.* It is remarkable how frequently buyers and sellers enter into sale contracts which contemplate a continuation of existing mortgage financing (by assumption, taking subject to, or wraparound) without thinking through the possible results of an existing mortgage lender's assertion of its due-on-sale clause. Often they do not even check to see whether such a clause exists or inquire under what conditions the lender might assert or waive it. See, e.g., Schrader v. Benton, 635 P.2d 562 (Haw. App. 1981).

2. *Default by the wrap seller.* Suppose you represent a purchaser who is buying real estate by means of a wraparound purchase-money mortgage.

Your client, the buyer, will be making a monthly payment to the seller on the wraparound loan, and the seller is obligated to make a corresponding, but smaller, payment each month to the lender who holds the underlying loan. What will happen if the seller fails to do so? The underlying lender will experience a default, and will ultimately decide to foreclose its mortgage. But the buyer may not learn of the default until several months of payments have been missed, and perhaps not until foreclosure proceedings are commenced. By then, it may be too late for the buyer to merely make up the missed payments; the lender may have accelerated the loan, making the entire balance due and payable, and the buyer may be financially incapable of paying off or refinancing the loan.

How can the buyer avoid getting into this mess? One way is to ask the underlying lender to notify the buyer immediately if the lender experiences a default. For example, the buyers did this, through their counsel, in Illinois State Bank v. Yates, 678 S.W.2d 819 (Mo. App. 1984). But the lender may not agree to this obligation, and may not perform it even if it agrees.

An alternative, and perhaps better, approach is to set up a "payment escrow" with a local bank or title company. Each month the escrow holder will receive the buyer's payment and split it into two parts, with the underlying lender receiving the amount due on the old loan and the seller receiving the balance. Under this arrangement, the buyer can be certain that the underlying lender actually receives the payments owed to it. For an illustration, see Adams v. George, 812 P.2d 280 (Idaho 1991).

NOTE ON THE FORECLOSURE PROCESS: HISTORY AND MODERN APPROACHES

Mortgage foreclosures. When a mortgage loan goes into default, the mortgagee normally has the right to "accelerate," which has the effect of making the entire debt due and payable. The mortgagee may, under some circumstances, simply decide to proceed against the mortgagor personally in a personal action to recover the debt, and forego reliance on the mortgage security. Usually, however, the mortgagee will choose (and in some states will be required by law) to foreclose the mortgage first. Although methods of foreclosure vary, under most circumstances there will be a sale of the mortgaged premises. The proceeds of the sale will be used to pay off the mortgage debt and the surplus, if any, will go to any subordinate lienholders and the mortgagor. If the sale does not yield enough to cover the debt, the mortgagee will usually be able to obtain a personal judgment for the deficiency against the mortgagor.

Where more than one mortgage exists on the same property, questions of priority become paramount. Suppose, for example, the mortgagor gave a $65,000 long-term first mortgage to a savings association on Blackacre, which then was worth $75,000. Assume that after paying the mortgage down to about $60,000, the mortgagor borrows $12,000 from another lender and gives that lender a mortgage to secure the $12,000 debt. This is a second mortgage. Suppose that the first mortgage is foreclosed. What will the purchaser at the foreclosure sale get and what will she pay for it? Here it is important to remember one of the basic functions of foreclosure—to put the foreclosure sale purchaser in the shoes of the mortgagor as of the time of execution of the mortgage being foreclosed. Thus, the purchaser will obtain a title that is free and clear of all mortgages or other liens junior or subordinate to the mortgage being foreclosed. Accordingly, a sale purchaser, assuming that the market value of Blackacre free and clear of liens is still $75,000, will be willing to pay, at most $75,000. For this she will get title free of the second mortgage. In other words, any junior liens are wiped out. If, however, the sale brings more than the $60,000 first mortgage debt, the second mortgagee should ~~normally have a claim to the surplus superior to that of~~ the ~~mortgagor.~~

Suppose, instead, that the first mortgage is not in default but that the second mortgage is and that the second mortgagee forecloses. What will the sale purchaser get and what will she pay for it? Again, remembering one of the basic functions of foreclosure discussed above, the sale should put the purchaser in the shoes of the mortgagor as of the time the mortgage being foreclosed was executed. Thus a purchaser will obtain fee title to Blackacre subject to the first mortgage. In other words, the foreclosure of a junior mortgage normally will not affect the status of a senior mortgage on the property. Therefore, in calculating what a purchaser will bid, she will, at the very least, subtract from the market value of Blackacre free and clear of liens the amount of the first mortgage. Thus, assuming that this market value is still $75,000, the most the purchaser should bid is $15,000, the fair market value less the amount of the senior lien. Although the sale purchaser will not usually be personally liable on the first mortgage debt, if she does not pay it off she runs the risk that the first mortgage will be foreclosed and that she will lose her title to Blackacre.

The impact of English history. An understanding of the modern real estate mortgage requires, at least, a limited consideration of its historical antecedents. Although the mortgage has its roots in both Roman law and in early Anglo-Saxon England, the most significant developments for our purposes are the English common law mortgage and the effects on that mortgage of the subsequent intervention of English equity courts. These developments not only substantially influenced the substance of American mortgage law, but they are responsible for much of its terminology as well.

Although the common law mortgage as it developed in the 14th and 15th centuries varied, in form it was essentially a conveyance of fee simple ownership, but the conveyance was expressly on condition subsequent. For example, assume B loaned A $1,000. A would convey Blackacre to B and his heirs, but on the condition that, if A repaid the $1,000 to B on a specified day, A would have the right to reenter and terminate B's estate. There were several important attributes to this transaction. B, the mortgagee, received legal title to the land and the normal incidents of that title. Perhaps the most striking and important feature of this mortgage was that the grantee, having legal title from the outset, got the incidents of that title even though unnecessary or even antagonistic to the sole purpose of the conveyance, namely, security for the performance of an act by the grantor. The most significant of these incidents was possession. Originally, the mortgagee used possession and the right to collect rents and profits as a method to get a return on the loan, since the taking of any interest was then considered to be usurious and unlawful. Later the custom developed to leave the mortgagor in possession, although the mortgagee nevertheless retained the right to obtain possession. If the lender did obtain possession, however, he or she was required to account for the rents and profits on the mortgage debt.

The condition with provision for reentry was gradually displaced by a covenant by the mortgagee to reconvey upon full performance by the mortgagor. This covenant had a double operation. It was effective at law as a condition, and also was a promise which equity would enforce specifically. Its development apparently coincided with that of the equity of redemption referred to below, and its popularity was based upon the practical advantages of getting back by a reconveyance, instead of by reentry, the interest conveyed to the mortgagee. Regardless of which form was used, if the mortgagor failed to perform on the day set, the mortgagee's estate became absolute.

This common law mortgage was especially harsh on the mortgagor. The payment date was called the law day. Under the common law, if for any reason the payment was not made on that day, the mortgagor forfeited all interest in Blackacre. This was an absolute rule. It applied even if the mortgagor could not find the mortgagee to make the payment. Time was strictly of the essence.

The intervention of equity. The excesses and harshness of the common law mortgage inevitably yielded to the moderating influence of English Chancery. Initially, equity intervened to aid the mortgagor who had failed promptly to perform on law day where the mortgagor could establish such traditional equitable grounds for relief as fraud, accident, misrepresentation, or duress. In other words, even though the mortgagee's rights at law were absolute, the mortgagor who had the financial capability to tender the amount due and owing could get the property back after law day so long as he or she could fit within the grounds described above. However, by the 17th century, the granting of such relief by equity became much more routine so that the mortgagor was able, as a matter of course and right, to redeem the land from the mortgagee by tendering the principal and interest within a reasonable time after law day. It was no longer necessary to establish any more specific equitable grounds for relief. This right to tardy redemption was referred to as the mortgagor's equity of redemption and became recognized as an equitable estate in land.

The mortgagor's right to tardy redemption obviously created a substantial problem for the mortgagee. Even though the mortgagor had defaulted, the mortgagee could never be reasonably sure that the mortgagor would not sue in equity to redeem. The mortgagee obviously needed to be relieved at some point of the threat of redemption. Thus, this same period saw the concurrent development in equity of the mortgagee's right to foreclosure. When the mortgagor failed to pay on law day or to bring a suit to redeem, at the request of the mortgagee in a bill setting forth the details of the mortgage and default, equity would order the mortgagor to pay the debt, interest and costs within a fixed period. Failure to comply with the decree meant that the mortgagor's right to redeem was forever barred. This type of foreclosure, which is little used today, is known as strict foreclosure because the land is forfeited to the mortgagee no matter what its value in relation to the original mortgage debt. No sale of the land is involved.

Whatever the original reasons for the chancellor's interventions, clearly the later equity view was that the mortgagee's interest was only security and intercession needed no other justification than to limit and protect it for that purpose. It is unlikely that the law courts did not recognize just as clearly as did the courts of equity that the parties intended the transaction to be one for security purposes only. The difficulty was that, although they saw it, they felt powerless to alter the design of the legal device chosen by the parties to achieve their purpose. So far as the law courts were concerned, since the parties had seen fit to have the entire legal title given as security (not absolutely, since the mortgagor could get it back by paying on a certain day), that was that. No such limitations were felt by the courts of equity, and they felt free to superimpose upon the legal device various restrictions or additions so as to give to the mortgagee only that protection in regard to the property which they thought it necessary or desirable for the protection of the security. What this protection should be inevitably would be a compound of conflicting economic interests, contradictory social ideals, business expediency, feelings of "fairness" in the particular case, and attempts, justifiable or otherwise, at logical consistency with other legal rules, plus other miscellaneous considerations.

In developing this view of the mortgage as a security transaction the equitable theory of the nature and incidents of the mortgagor's interest in the property before default underwent considerable change. For one thing, the term "equity of redemption," which had previously and appropriately been applied to the mortgagor's right to get back the property after default, was applied somewhat inappropriately to this entirely distinct equitable ownership before default. This, however, is merely a matter of nomenclature. But the analytical nature of the interest itself was the subject of serious and important inquiry and decision.

At first the mortgagor's interest was looked upon as a purely in personam right against the mortgagee, but soon it was perceived to be in rem, and finally was regarded as an equitable estate, a conception conforming to both popular and legal notions. For example, it could be cut into lesser estates; it had to be conveyed by a formal conveyance with formal limitations; it descended on to the heirs of the mortgagor; it could be devised, mortgaged, or entailed; and it prevailed against heirs, purchasers, and other successors of the mortgagee. In other words, it came to be treated, for all practical purposes, as ownership of the land—subject, of course, to the mortgage.

The American development. While strict foreclosure is actually used in a few states and is theoretically available in some special situations in others, the major method of foreclosure in the United States today involves a public sale of the premises. There are two main types of sale foreclosure used in the United States today. The most common type is judicial foreclosure where a public sale results after a full judicial proceeding in which all interested persons must be made parties. In many states this is the sole method of foreclosure. It is time-consuming and costly. The other method of foreclosure is by power of sale. Under this method, after varying types and degrees of notice to the parties, the property is sold at a public sale, either by some public official such as a sheriff, by the mortgagee, or by some other third party. No judicial proceeding is required in a power of sale foreclosure. It is generally available only where both the mortgage instrument and a state statute authorize it.

It is important to remember that as a general proposition, the mortgagor cannot lose his or her equity of redemption (or equity of tardy redemption, as it is sometimes called) unless there has been a valid foreclosure of the mortgage. In other words, even though the mortgage is in substantial default, normally no agreement of the parties in the mortgage, or contemporaneous with it, can cut off a recalcitrant mortgagor's rights in the mortgaged property without the mortgagee resorting to foreclosure. This concept, which will be considered in greater detail later, is sometimes referred to as the *prohibition against clogging the mortgagor's equity of redemption.*

Suppose, however, that there has been a valid foreclosure and that the mortgagor's equity of redemption has been cut off. About 20 states, by a variety of legislative methods, have created something called *statutory redemption.* This type of redemption becomes available *only* when the equity of redemption has been effectively cut off by a valid foreclosure. Statutory redemption, as we will see later, varies widely from state to state. In general, however, these statutes permit the mortgagor, and sometimes junior lienors or the holders of other subordinate interests, to redeem for some fixed period after the sale. The time periods vary from as short as a few months in some states to as long as 18 months or more in a few others. The statutory right of redemption was created, in part, to afford the mortgagor or other person entitled to exercise the right additional time to refinance and save the property, but mainly to put pressure on the mortgagee to bid the value of the property at the foreclosure sale, at least up to the amount of the mortgage debt. To enforce this purpose the redemption amount is usually the *sale price* and *not the mortgage debt.* A secondary purpose of these statutes in some states is to allow an additional period of possession to a hard-pressed mortgagor. It's important to remember that statutory redemption normally begins *only* after the mortgagor's equity of redemption has been validly terminated by foreclosure.

The deed of trust as a mortgage variant. In many states the deed of trust represents the most commonly used mortgage instrument. This device normally involves a conveyance of the realty to a third person (often the lender's lawyer, employee, or subsidiary corporation) in trust to hold as security for the payment of the debt to the lender-noteholder whose role is analogous to that of the mortgagee. Deeds of trust will almost always contain a power of sale in the trustee to be exercised after a default at the request of the lender-noteholder. Such a deed of trust is essentially similar to a mortgage with a power of sale. Indeed, in some states the same statutes regulating foreclosure of power of sale mortgages are applicable to deeds of trust as well. In other states, mortgages are required to be foreclosed by judicial process, and only the deed of trust can employ a power of sale. Other differences may also exist in a particular state; for example, deficiency judgments or post-sale redemption may be treated differently with deeds of trust than with mortgages.

CHAPTER TWO

DEEDS AND TITLES

• • ▪

A. DEEDS

The preceding chapter dealt with contracts of sale. Even though such contracts create an "equitable title" in the purchaser under the doctrine of equitable conversion, the parties to a real estate contract always understand that the contract is preliminary in nature, and that if it is performed as agreed, the seller will deliver a deed to the buyer. The deed will transfer legal title, and it is that sort of transfer that is the subject of this chapter.

Although deeds are surely the most common mode of conveying legal title, they are not the only way. Title to real property also is transferred by wills, by intestate succession, and by court decrees. It can even be (and in the case of government land, often has been) transferred by legislative acts. Although technically not transfers, such events as adverse possession and death of a joint tenant have much the same effect. But the delivery of deeds surpasses all of these other ways of transferring title in frequency and importance, and in cases involving negotiated sales of real property the delivery of a deed is nearly always the object of the parties' agreement.

1. HISTORY OF THE DEED

HISTORY OF THE ENGLISH SYSTEM OF CONVEYANCING,
IN PATTON, TITLES
Vol. 1 at 3–8 (2d ed. 1957)

We do not know the origin of the practice of transferring title to real estate by a written instrument. It may have been in existence and quite highly developed at the very dawn of written history. It appears to have passed from one predominating civilization to the next till it reached the Roman era, and from the latter into the legal systems of continental Europe. But Roman law did not, directly at least, exercise any appreciable influence on English land law. Instead, therefore, of finding transfers of title in England made from the time of the Roman occupation by the execution and delivery of a deed, we find that at no very remote date, possession was the only evidence of title, and that proof of a transfer of title existed solely in the memory of witnesses present at the time when the change of possession occurred. As to estates for years, a transfer of title was effected by a mere entry of the new owner, but in the case of freehold estates the change had to be in the form of a symbolic ceremony known as livery of seisin. This was a ceremony consisting of a symbolical delivery of the corporeal possession of land by the grantor, or "feoffor," as he was called, to the grantee, or "feoffee." The parties, with their witnesses, went upon the land, and the feoffor gave to the feoffee a stick, twig, piece of turf, or a handful of earth taken from the land. Sometimes a ring, a cross, or a knife was handed over, anything, in fact, as a token of the delivery. As a further part of the ceremony, the feoffor used proper, and technical, words which were to show that he intended to transfer the land to the feoffee, and which also marked out, or limited, the estate, or the interest, in the land which the feoffor intended the feoffee to have. The words "I give" (Latin, "do") were the proper words to use for the conveyance, while the words "to him" (i.e., the feoffee) "and his heirs," or "to him and the heirs of his body," (designating the limitation, either as a fee simple or a fee tail) indicated the estate conveyed. A distinction was made between livery in deed and livery in law. The former arose when the livery of seisin took place on the land itself; the latter when the parties were not actually on the land—as when the transfer was made in sight of the premises, but without an actual entry on them. In the latter case, the feoffor, pointing out the land, bade the feoffee enter and take possession of it. Should the feoffee do so within the lifetime of the parties, the feoffment was valid in law. Livery of seisin also required an abjuration of the land by the donor, or feoffor; that is, he had to leave, or vacate, the land, leaving the feoffee in possession. No writing was necessary to give evidence to livery of seisin, although writings became customary in very early times. In later times, however, livery of seisin was usually accompanied by a written deed, especially when the limitations of the estate granted were numerous. Such a deed was, however, only an evidence of title, and not a conveyance itself. A writing was not legally required till the statute of frauds.

Later, as the art of writing became common among our ancestors, there might also have been a deed in order to more definitely designate the nature and extent of the estate granted, and its various conditions and limitations. But the use of a writing remained optional with the parties till the passage in 1677 of the Statute of Frauds. It was only incorporeal interests and future estates, which were not capable of livery of seisin because of an absence of the element of possession, as to which a transfer of title could be made by a deed alone. The latter was called a deed of grant and was responsible for the common-law distinction between things which "lie in livery" and those which "lie in grant." In the case of freehold estates in corporeal real property, the deed required by the Statute of Frauds did not operate to transfer the title and livery of seisin remained essential in England, theoretically at least, till dispensed with by the Real Property Act 1845, § 3. But the enactment of the Statute of Uses in 1535 had practically that effect in that it brought into almost universal use modes of alienation which did not require the symbolic ceremony. Aside from a more common form of conveyance which indirectly resulted from the statute, as set forth in the next paragraph, those directly resulting from the statute were, (1) a contract in the form of a covenant to stand seized of property for the benefit of a beneficiary related to the covenantor by blood or marriage, and (2) a contract, or deed, of bargain and sale of lands "whereby the bargainor for some pecuniary consideration bargains and sells, that is, contracts to convey, the land to the bargainee; and becomes by such bargain, a trustee for, or seised to the use of the bargainee." The statute executed the contract in both cases, and thus the purchaser acquired the seisin and possession of the same as though there had been a livery of seisin.

But since the statute enabled a landowner by a mere contract of sale to vest the title in another without livery of seisin or other publicity, the same parliament passed a companion act for the express purpose of preventing clandestine conveyances. This was the Statute of Enrollments. It made a deed of bargain and sale of a freehold interest void unless within six months it was enrolled in a court of record at Westminster, or in certain other public offices. These two statutes were merely part of a plan to provide a general scheme for the transfer of title by deed, and for the recording or registry of land conveyances. But because of a general disposition of the landholding aristocracy to withdraw the details of their family settlements and domestic arrangements from the curiosity of the public, their conveyancers welcomed the first part of the plan and set themselves to work to frustrate the second. A common-law deed of "lease and release" had previously been somewhat used to effect a transfer of title without the formal livery of seisin; it was now brought into general use to effect a conveyance which would not be within the terms of the Statute of Enrollments. * * * All that the conveyancer had to do was to have the owner execute a lease (usually in the form of a bargain and sale deed of an estate for one year), followed at once by a release of the reversion to the lessee. This cumbersome use of two instruments for every transfer continued in England till the necessity for the fictitious lease was abolished in 1841. Four years later the Real Property Act was passed, making a simple deed of grant sufficient to convey all estates.

NOTE ON DEEDS IN MODERN AMERICAN
REAL ESTATE PRACTICE

The significance of the forms of deeds used historically in England has been almost completely discarded in the United States. Here, a simple deed need contain only the following written elements: Identification of the grantor and grantee, a description of the land being conveyed, some words indicating that title is to pass (such as "hereby conveys title" or the like), and the grantor's signature. A writing is necessary in every state under the Statute of Frauds.

Nonetheless, the use of the old English terms often persists, even though the terms no longer carry their historic meaning. A few pages later in this book you will see a good example: the Washington state statute authorizing the use of a "bargain and sale" deed (Rev. Code of Wash. § 64.04.040), even though the meaning of the term "bargain and sale," referring to a deed in the form of a contract of sale that was "executed" by the Statute of Uses, has long been lost. Another example is the word "grant," which is very often used as a term of conveyance in American deeds. It originated in England as referring to a conveyance of a nonpossessory interest, such as a future interest or an easement. But today it has entirely lost that connotation, and may be used to pass any interest in land, possessory or nonpossessory.

Modern deeds may and often do contain covenants of title by which the grantor assures the grantee that he or she has title to pass. A deed that contains a broad statement of such covenants is usually called a "general warranty deed." Sometimes the grantor will be willing to covenant that she or he personally has done nothing to impair the title, but is unwilling to assure the grantee that previous owners have not done so. Such a deed, warranting only against the acts of the grantor and not the grantor's predecessors in title, is often termed a "special warranty deed." Finally, a deed that contains no covenants of title at all is usually in the form of a "quitclaim" deed, in which the grantor will typically "remise, release, and quitclaim" the described land to the grantee. (Once again, we see a "repurposing" of an ancient term: the "release" portion of an old deed of "lease and release.")

Sometimes the old English deed terminology has been adapted by modern statutes as a way of automatically importing certain warranties of title into deeds. For example, the Washington statute mentioned above has the effect of imposing a "special warranty" if the deed uses the term "bargains and sells." Likewise, in California the use of the word "grant" will make the deed a special warranty deed; see Cal. Civ. Code § 1113. There are many other examples around the country.

None of this is to say that the historic deed forms used in England would not work in the United States in their original contexts. Since most states treat the Statute of Uses as having been received at the inception of statehood, there is every reason to expect that a "covenant to stand seized" or a "bargain and sale" deed in the traditional English form would be given effect. See, e.g., Brevard County v. Ramsey, 658 So.2d 1190 (Fla.App.1995), indicating that Florida courts would enforce such deeds; Robertson v. Robertson, 47 So. 675 (Miss.1908), where the court construed a rather confused agreement between a husband and wife as a covenant to stand seized. Likewise, there is nothing today that would prevent a grantor from using the "lease and release" technique to convey a fee simple estate. But it is hard to imagine why anyone would bother to go through these contortions when the simple statement that "A hereby grants to B the following described land" will do the job perfectly well.

BALE V. ALLISON

Court of Appeals of Washington, 2013
294 P.3d 789

LAU, J.

Robert E. Fletcher used a quitclaim deed to gift his Winthrop cabin to his nephews, John and Robert G. Fletcher. John and Robert appeal the trial court's determination that the failure to recite consideration invalidated the deed. We conclude the deed is valid because it met all statutory requirements and no recital is required to effectively gift real property. Accordingly, we reverse the judgment awarding title to Denny and Allen Bale. On cross appeal, the Bales challenge the trial court's use of the clear, cogent, and convincing standard of proof to find that the Bales failed to establish an oral contract to devise existed between Bob and the Bales. We conclude the trial court applied the correct standard of proof at trial to determine insufficient evidence of an oral contract to devise existed. We remand to the trial court to consider an award of attorney fees and costs to John and Robert but deny fees and costs on appeal.

FACTS

Neither party assigns error to the trial court's findings of fact and, thus, they are verities on appeal. *Moreman v. Butcher,* 126 Wash.2d 36, 40, 891 P.2d 725 (1995).

Bob Fletcher owned a parcel of real property including a cabin in Winthrop, Washington. John and Robert Fletcher were Bob's nephews. Starting around 1960, Bob took his nephews to visit the cabin two or three times a year. John and Robert's father (Bob's brother) died in 1964 when the boys were young, so Bob "took [them] under his wing." Report of Proceedings (RP) (June 9, 2011) at 508. Bob lived with John and Robert for two years and married their mother (Bob's brother's widow) in 1968. That marriage lasted only two years. Until 1971, John continued visiting the cabin property two or three times a year.

Bob married Edna Fletcher in 1971. Denny and Allen Bale ("the Bales") are Edna's adult sons from a previous marriage. When Bob and Edna married, the cabin on the Winthrop property was a small, rustic Forest Service cabin that lacked indoor plumbing and running water.

Bob and Edna were married 28 years. During that time, the Bales made numerous improvements to the Winthrop property, including

> building a woodshed; installing exterior lighting; building a storage shed; clearing a parking area near the cabin; clearing and seeding lawn areas near the cabin; cutting down trees and removing tree stumps; planting ornamental bushes, evergreen trees, and fruit trees; rebuilding, grading, and graveling the driveway; and building a horse coral; adding on a bedroom, a bathroom, and a porch to the cabin; installing a complete water system to the cabin property, including a well; adding complete interior plumbing and septic systems to the cabin property; remodeling the living room; extending and enlarging the kitchen space; installing countertops and cabinets to the kitchen; rewiring the entire electrical system; replacing the roof on the old section of the cabin and roofing the new additions to the cabin; insulating all of the original walls and ceiling portions, plus the new additions; replacing all the windows; installing new flooring and related structural supports; re-sheeting the exterior walls; installing a new water heater; making major repairs to the wood burning and cooking stoves; installing a propane fireplace; and replacing the two chimneys.

They also contributed furnishings and appliances to the cabin. They "provided the time and labor, and materials and payments necessary for these extensive renovations, improvements, and maintenance in reliance on their understanding that they would own the Winthrop property after [Bob] died." John and Robert stopped visiting the cabin during Bob and Edna's marriage because Edna did not "appreciate" them.

Edna died in 1999 and Bob again invited John and Robert to visit the cabin. John visited the property a couple times a year. He did maintenance work each time: "I did as much as I had to do to maintain the property while I was there and leave it like it was better than it was when I got there, just like [Bob] always told everyone to do." RP (June 7, 2011) at 385. About a year and a half after Edna died, Bob married Garry Allison.

Bob executed a will in October 2003 in which he made three bequests: (1) to his stepsons, "Dennis Bale and [Allen] Bale, I give my property in Winthrop, WA, share and share alike"; (2) $2,000 to his adopted daughter; and (3) the rest, residue, and remainder of his estate to Garry Allison. Resp't's Reply Br. at Appendix A. In devising the Winthrop property to the Bales, Bob indicated his desire that they allow Garry Allison, John, and Robert to use the property for their enjoyment " 'at the discretion of Dennis Bale and [Allen] Bale.' " Resp't's Reply Br. at Appendix A.

Bob was diagnosed with terminal lung cancer in the fall 2008. John testified that after the diagnosis, Bob invited him and Robert over for lunch. Garry Allison was also present at the lunch. John and Robert both testified that Bob told them at that time, "I want you boys to have the cabin." RP (June 9, 2011) at 559, 587. John found a preprinted quitclaim deed online and filled it out. John and Robert then took Bob to Bank of America to get the deed notarized. Bob signed the deed, and the notary acknowledged his signature. John recorded the deed in Okanogan County on December 19, 2008.

The deed "conveys and quitclaims" the cabin property to John and Robert. The spaces after "in consideration of" and "quit claims to" are blank. Ex. 2. Handwritten at the top of the deed after "Grantee" are the names "Robert Gary Fletcher" and "John Franklin Fletcher" and "Robert Ernest Fletcher" after the word "Grantor." Ex. 2. In the preprinted real estate excise tax affidavit (REETA) and supplemental statement, under the heading "Gifts without consideration," Bob checked the box indicating, "There is no debt on the property; Grantor (seller) has not received any consideration towards equity. No tax is due." Ex. 4. Also handwritten after "Reason for exemption" is "gift, w/no debt." Ex. 4. The REETA also lists Bob as grantor and John and Robert as grantees. The Okanogan County treasurer stamped the REETA "Not Subject to Excise Tax." Ex. 4.

Bob died in April 2009 and Garry Allison was named personal representative under the 2003 will. After Bob's death, John amended the previously recorded quitclaim deed by adding "for love and affection" and also wrote in his name and Robert's name in the "quit claim to" blank.[2] Resp't's Br. at App. C; RP (June 7, 2011) at 390. John also prepared a new REETA to include considerable personal property in and around the cabin. Garry Allison signed the REETA in her capacity as personal representative of Bob's estate. John rerecorded the quitclaim deed on June 26, 2009.

When the Bales learned that Bob quitclaimed the Winthrop property to John and Robert, they filed a "complaint for specific performance, damages and further equitable relief" against John, Robert, and Garry Allison, requesting that the Winthrop property be transferred from John

---

[2] When asked why he altered the language, John testified that in February 2009, he had discussed the deed with an attorney friend. The friend advised him to rerecord the deed because the original deed failed to recite consideration. John asked the friend "if it was standard to correct verbiage on a quitclaim and rerecord it, and she said yes, we do it all the time." RP (June 9, 2011) at 564. John decided to rerecord the deed and did so in June 2009, two months after Bob died.

and Robert to them. (Capitalization omitted.) They alleged numerous claims, including breach of oral contract, breach of implied contract, promissory estoppel, undue influence, and tortious interference.

Garry Allison moved for summary judgment on all claims. The court granted summary judgment dismissal on the undue influence, tortious interference, and promissory estoppel claims but denied summary judgment on the oral and implied contract issues. The trial evidence related primarily to the Bales' oral contract to devise claim.

The court entered a judgment awarding clear title to the Bales and entered written findings and conclusions. Regarding the quitclaim deed, the court's conclusions of law state:

> 1.   The quit claim deed executed by [Bob] in December 2008 lacks specific and necessary terms to effectively transfer title. The quit claim deed is incomplete and fails to state what consideration, if any, was given for the deed. There were blanks left as to whom the property was conveyed. Because of the fatal defects as to consideration, the quit claim deed is ineffective and did not transfer title to John and Robert G. Fletcher.

> 2.   The quit claim deed executed by [Bob] in December 2008 does not meet the fundamental statutory requirements for a "good and sufficient conveyance, release and quitclaim to the grantee[s]" pursuant to RCW 64.04.050, and therefore, is ineffective to transfer the Winthrop property to John and Robert G. Fletcher.

> 3.   Because [Bob] is deceased and died testate, the December 2008 quit claim deed cannot be reformed by the personal representative, and the post-death alterations to the December 2008 deed are improper and of no legal effect.

(Third alteration in original.) The court concluded that given the deed's invalidity, Bob's October 2003 will controlled distribution of his estate and the property passed to the Bales.

The court rejected the Bales' oral contract to devise and implied contract claims. The relevant conclusions state:

> 6.   [The Bales] were unable to establish [by] clear, cogent and convincing evidence that there was an implied contract between themselves and [Bob] to transfer the Winthrop property in exchange for the work that the Bales performed.

> 7.   [The Bales] were unable to establish that Defendant Ms. Garry Allison had knowledge of any contract, oral or implied, or that she took any actions that would have breached either agreement. * * *

10. Although [the Bales] established that they performed significant work to improve the Winthrop property, they did not establish by clear, convincing and cogent evidence the existence of an oral contract to devise.

11. [The Bales] did not establish that [John or Robert] had knowledge of any oral contract that might have existed between them and [Bob]. Therefore, [the Bales] did not establish that [John or Robert] took action that interfered with any alleged contract.

12. [The Bales] did not establish that [John or Robert] exerted undue influence on [Bob], nor was there sufficient evidence that [Bob] lacked testamentary capacity.

The court ordered John and Robert to transfer all rights and title to the Winthrop property to the Bales under a quitclaim deed.

John and Robert appeal the trial court's conclusion that the quitclaim deed was invalid for failure to recite consideration. The Bales cross appeal the court's conclusion that they failed to establish an oral contract to devise.

ANALYSIS

Quitclaim Deed Validity

John and Robert contend the trial court erred in ruling that "fatal defects as to consideration" rendered the quitclaim deed ineffective. They argue that transfer of real property intended as a gift requires no recital of consideration under Washington law.

Construction of deeds is a matter of law. *Niemann v. Vaughn Cmty. Church,* 154 Wash.2d 365, 374, 113 P.3d 463 (2005). Whether the trial court properly determined the legal consequences of the deed's failure to recite consideration is subject to de novo review. The goal of deed construction is to effectuate the parties' intent. *Niemann,* 154 Wash.2d at 374, 113 P.3d 463. "In other words, 'it is a factual question to determine the intent of the parties' with the court then 'apply[ing] the rules of law to determine the legal consequences of that intent.'" *Niemann,* 154 Wash.2d at 374–75, 113 P.3d 463 (alteration in original) (quoting *Veach v. Culp,* 92 Wash.2d 570, 573, 599 P.2d 526 (1979)).

Real property conveyances, including gifts, must be accomplished by deed. RCW 64.04.010; *Oman v. Yates,* 70 Wash.2d 181, 185–86, 422 P.2d 489 (1967) (gifts in general); *Holohan v. Melville,* 41 Wash.2d 380, 385, 249 P.2d 777 (1952) (gift of real property). "Every deed shall be in writing, signed by the party bound thereby, and acknowledged by the party before some person authorized ... to take acknowledgment of deeds." RCW

64.04.020. Deeds also require a complete legal description of the property conveyed. *Berg v. Ting,* 125 Wash.2d 544, 551, 886 P.2d 564 (1995).

Washington courts have affirmed both real property gifts and gifts without consideration. *See Kessler v. Kessler,* 55 Wash.2d 598, 600, 349 P.2d 224 (1960) ("It was not against public policy, under the facts of this case, for the competent and grateful mother to have executed a deed of gift to her son of her residence property."); *Stringfellow v. Stringfellow,* 53 Wash.2d 639, 641, 335 P.2d 825 (1959) (father gifted stocks to son by "caus[ing] the issuance of the stock certificate in the son's name" no consideration recited) (italicization omitted); *State v. Superior Court of Snohomish County,* 165 Wash. 648, 650, 5 P.2d 1037 (1931) (parents could have deeded their home to their daughter "without any consideration at all," but never made that argument). The real estate tax regulation WAC 458–61A–201(1) treats a gift of real property as a nontaxable event. It provides:

> Generally, a gift of real property is not a sale, and is not subject to the real estate excise tax. A gift of real property is a transfer for which there is no consideration given in return for granting an interest in the property. If consideration is given in return for the interest granted, then the transfer is not a gift, but a sale, and it is subject to the real estate excise tax to the extent of the consideration received.

(Emphasis added.)

Bob used a quitclaim deed to gift the Winthrop property to John and Robert without any recital of consideration. RCW 64.04.050 provides a sample quitclaim deed form containing a blank for consideration:

Quitclaim deeds *may* be in substance in the following form:

> The grantor (here insert the name or names and place of residence), *for and in consideration of (here insert consideration)* conveys and quitclaims to (here insert grantee's name or names) all interest in the following described real estate (here insert description), situated in the county of . . . , state of Washington. Dated this . . . day of . . . , 19 . . .

> Every deed in substance in the above form, when otherwise duly executed, shall be deemed and held a good and sufficient conveyance, release and quitclaim to the grantee, his or her heirs and assigns in fee of all the then existing legal and equitable rights of the grantor in the premises therein described, but shall not extend to the after acquired title unless words are added expressing such intention.

(Emphasis added.) In *Newport Yacht Basin Ass'n of Condominium Owners v. Supreme Northwest, Inc.,* 168 Wash.App. 56, 277 P.3d 18 (2012), we explained that "a quitclaim deed need not precisely match the form described in RCW 64.04.050 in order to convey fee title." *Newport Yacht,* 168 Wash.App. at 67, 277 P.3d 18. We further explained that "the operative words of a quitclaim deed are 'conveys and quitclaims.'" *Newport Yacht,* 168 Wash.App. at 67, 277 P.3d 18 (quoting 18 *William B. Stoebuck & John W. Weaver, Washington Practice: Real Estate: Transactions* § 14.2, at 116 (2d ed. 2004)).

In *Newport Yacht,* we discussed consideration in the context of quitclaim deeds:

> As our Supreme Court has long recognized, "[g]enerally speaking, inadequacy of price is not sufficient, standing by itself, to authorize a court of equity to set aside a deed." *Downing v. State,* 9 Wash.2d 685, 688, 115 P.2d 972 (1941). Only where the inadequacy of consideration for conveyance of realty is so great as to shock the conscience may a court invoke its equitable power to set aside the conveyance. *Downing,* 9 Wash.2d at 688, 115 P.2d 972; *see also Binder v. Binder,* 50 Wash.2d 142, 150, 309 P.2d 1050 (1957). *However, quitclaim deeds are commonly used in transactions that are not the result of a sale for value.* 17 *Stoebuck & Weaver, supra,* § 7.2, at 472. *Such instruments are* "used in donative transactions, in which, despite the recital of consideration in the deed, no actual consideration passes except perhaps love and affection." 17 *Stoebuck & Weaver, supra,* § 7.2, at 472. Similarly, quitclaim deeds are often used "to clear title, to correct errors in prior deeds, and to adjust disputed boundaries between adjoining landowners." 17 *Stoebuck & Weaver, supra,* § 7.2, at 472. In such circumstances, "the common practice in Washington . . . to recite consideration of 'ten dollars and other good and valuable consideration' is sufficient to support a conveyance by deed." 17 *Stoebuck & Weaver, supra,* § 7.7, at 483.

Newport Yacht, 168 Wash.App. at 82–83, 277 P.3d 18 (alteration in original) (emphasis added).

No Washington case addresses whether a quitclaim deed must recite consideration when the grantor intends to convey real property as a gift. Professors Stoebuck and Weaver address this question in their authoritative real property treatise:

> The Washington statute that gives the general form of a deed, RCWA 64.04.020, does not say that the deed must recite consideration. However, the statutes that set out the three statutory forms all say, "for and in consideration of (here insert

consideration).” Two questions arise: Must consideration in fact be given? Must a Washington deed recite consideration?

Washington authority on the question is not as clear as might be wished, but *the Supreme Court of Washington does seem to have adopted the rule that a deed is valid without valuable consideration.* In other words, land may be conveyed by deed as a gift. The gift cases involve gifts between close relatives, such as spouses or parent to child, but gifts should be possible between non-relatives, though perhaps more subject to being set aside on grounds of fraud or some related equitable ground than are gifts to close relatives. Gift deeds have been upheld between wife and husband and between parent and child. Dictum in two other gift cases that a gift may be supported by “consideration” in the form of love and affection or of past consideration is confusing, since a true gift need not be supported by any form of consideration. When some consideration is given, it need not be in an “adequate” amount; *i.e.,* mere inadequacy of consideration is not ground to set aside a deed. Thus, the common practice in Washington, as in other states, to recite consideration of “ten dollars and other good and valuable consideration” is sufficient to support a conveyance by deed. However, the lack of consideration or inadequacy of consideration, along with other suspicious circumstances, may give grounds to set a deed aside for fraud or upon some related equitable theory. That subject will be discussed later in this chapter.

A deceptively simple question in Washington is, what is the correct form of deed to make a gift? In the gift cases reported in the preceding paragraph, or in any Washington appellate decision that can be found, the courts either did not quote the language of a gift deed or described a deed that recited nominal consideration. *The problem is that Washington lawyers habitually use one of the three special statutory deed forms, and, as previously noted, those forms all call for at least a recital of consideration.* A common practice is to use one of the statutory forms, usually the quitclaim deed form, so that the grantor will not “donate” warranties as well as title, and to recite as consideration the rote phrase, “ten dollars and other good and valuable consideration,” or the phrase, “ten dollars, love and affection, and other good and valuable consideration.” Aside from the fact that the deed contains a false recital, this works, but on its face, the deed is subject to a small amount of the excise tax imposed on real estate sales by RCWA Chapter 82.45. To get around that slight embarrassment, some Washington lawyers insert a recital, a sort of “P.S.,” in some convenient blank space in the deed, reciting that the deed is one of gift, and no consideration of money value actually passed. Since no excise tax is due on gifts, this moves the county treasurer to stamp the deed "No Tax Due," but it compounds the falsity of the previous recital of consideration. Cautious draftsmen, who tend to be fussy about such details, may wonder if there is a better, truer way to draft a gift deed.

It should be possible to rely upon the general deed statute, RCWA 64.04.020, and to draft a deed that meets the three essentials, in writing, signed by the grantor, and acknowledged, without any recital of consideration, since the statute does not require it. In fact, such deeds are used to grant easements in Washington, and easements, being "interests" in land, are just as much within the deed statutes as are conveyances in fee simple. Of course the deed needs to name the grantor and grantee, describe the land, and contain appropriate words of conveyance. The general deed statute does not give words of conveyance, and the draftsman wants to avoid using the words of any of the three special deed forms; so, the word "conveys" or the phrase "grants and conveys" might be used. Assuming the donor does not want to make warranties, it would be well to add a disclaimer of warranties, to avoid any argument that the grantor intended one of the special statutory forms. The following is a form of deed that should be sufficient to make a gift of a fee simple estate in Washington:

Grantors, John Doe and Jane Doe, husband and wife, hereby grant and convey as a gift, without warranties, to Richard Roe and Mary Roe, husband and wife, the following described real estate in fee simple absolute: (legal description), situated in the County of _____, State of Washington.

Dated this _____ day of _____, 20____.

17 *Stoebuck & Weaver* § 7.7, at 482–84 (footnotes omitted).[4]

The Bales rely exclusively on RCW 64.04.050, quoted above, to argue that the December 2008 quitclaim deed was ineffective because it was "devoid of any statement of consideration." Resp't's Reply Br. at 9. The Bales do not dispute that Bob intended to gift the real property to John and Robert. They cite no statute or case authority requiring a deed to recite consideration when the grantor intends to convey the real property as a gift. *See State v. Logan,* 102 Wash.App. 907, 911 n. 1, 10 P.3d 504 (2000) (" 'Where no authorities are cited in support of a proposition, the court is not required to search out authorities, but may assume that counsel, after

---

4   We agree with Professors Stoebuck and Weaver's comment that dictum in gift cases that a gift may be supported by consideration in the form of love and affection or of past consideration promotes confusion. See Whalen v. Lanier, 29 Wash.2d 299, 308–11, 186 P.2d 919 (1947) (past consideration; dictum); Lehman v. Columbia Fire Ins. Co., 188 Wash. 640, 643, 63 P.2d 442 (1936) (love and affection; dictum).

diligent search, has found none.'") (quoting *DeHeer v. Seattle Post-Intelligencer,* 60 Wash.2d 122, 126, 372 P.2d 193 (1962)). The Bales' reliance on RCW 64.04.050 is questionable because the statute's use of the term "may" is permissive, not mandatory. Nor do they challenge Professors Stoebuck and Weaver's analysis discussed above. For the reasons discussed above, we hold no recital of consideration is required to effectively gift real property. The trial court erred when it concluded the deed's invalidity premised on the recital of consideration omission.

The Bales also claim the deed's invalidity because "the notary failed to enter in her acknowledgment the identity of the person appearing before her." Resp't's Br. at 13. They offer no additional argument on this issue and cite no authority supporting their claim that this omission invalidated the deed, and we can decline to address it. *See Palmer v. Jensen,* 81 Wash.App. 148, 153, 913 P.2d 413 (1996) ("Passing treatment of an issue or lack of reasoned argument is insufficient to merit judicial consideration."). Even if we consider this argument, it fails.[6] Review of the disputed deed shows that the grantor's and grantees' names appear on the document. Bob signed and dated the deed. The notary's signature appears directly beneath Bob's signature. The deed contains a blank in the certification: "I certify that I know or have satisfactory evidence that ____, the person(s) who appeared before me. . . ." Ex. 2. Despite this omission, it is clear that the notary acknowledged Bob's signature because he was the only person who signed the deed. The notary's uncontroverted trial testimony supports this conclusion.[7] *See* RP (June 9, 2011) at 458–69.

[The court also concluded that the Bales had not presented sufficient evidence of an oral contract by Bob to devise the cabin to them.]

NOTES

1. *Consideration.* The modern cases generally agree with *Bale* that a deed is not a contract, and that no consideration is necessary to the validity of a deed. See, e.g., Celtic Corp. v. Tinnea, 254 S.W.3d 137 (Mo. App. 2008); Estate of Dykes v. Estate of Williams, 864 So. 2d 926 (Miss. 2003); Cox v. Cox, 138 Idaho 881, 71 P.3d 1028 (2003); Chase Fed. Sav. & Loan Ass'n v. Schreiber, 479 So. 2d 90 (Fla. 1985). "If, however, a person has been induced to part with a thing of value for little or no consideration, equity will seize upon the slightest circumstance of oppression, fraud, or duress for the

---

[6] Given our decision, we need not address the Bales' argument that John and Robert knew the deed was defective when they attempted to rerecord it after Bob's death. We also need not address whether the attempted alteration cured the allegedly defective deed. Regardless, John and Robert do not argue that the rerecorded deed cured any alleged error. They argue that the original December 2008 deed was valid as written and recorded

[7] To the extent the Bales also argue that the failure to enter the grantees' names in the middle part of the deed results in invalidity, the above reasoning applies. Again, the Bales cite no authority for their argument that such an omission invalidates the deed. And as discussed above, the deed elsewhere makes clear that John and Robert are the grantees. We construe the deed to give effect to the grantor's intent. *Zunino,* 140 Wash.App. at 222, 165 P.3d 57.

purpose of administering justice in the case at hand.", In re Estate of Bontkowski, 337 Ill. App. 3d 72, 785 N.E.2d 126 (2003).

Notwithstanding the foregoing courts' clear holdings that consideration is not essential to a valid deed, one still finds opinions purporting to set aside deeds for lack of consideration. See, e.g., West America Housing Corp. v. Pearson, 171 P.3d 539 (Wyo. 2007). Almost invariably, however, there is some element of fraud, deceit, or mistake in the transaction, and not merely the absence of consideration.

2. *Modifying a deed after delivery.* You will notice that neither the Fletchers nor the court gave any weight to the alteration and re-recording of the deed after it had been delivered. That's correct, of course; changes made to a deed by its grantee after its delivery are of no legal consequence. See Julian v. Peterson, 966 P.2d 878 (Utah App. 1998) (adding the name of an additional grantee after delivery of deed was ineffective); Lee v. Lee, 97 Cal. Rptr. 3d 516 (Cal.App. 2009) (similar).

However, courts will sometimes allow the *grantor* to make changes to the deed and redeliver it, and if the changes do not conflict with the original grant, they will be given effect. For example, if the original deed contained a faulty legal description, the grantor can correct the description and redeliver the deed. See Green v. Crane, 386 S.E.2d 757 (N.C.App. 1990), construing N.C. Gen. Stat. § 47–36.1 to allow such a procedure only if the error was "an obvious typographical or other minor error." Texas has allowed correction of an improper acreage description, an inaccurate metes and bounds description, and a defective description of the grantor's capacity, but not a correction adding to the originally-described land; see Myrad Properties, Inc. v. LaSalle Bank Nat. Ass'n, 300 S.W.3d 746 (Tex. 2009). In all events, it is obvious that such a "correction" signed only by the grantor cannot deprive the grantee of the rights granted by the original deed; see Hilterbrand v. Carter, 27 P.3d 1086 (Or. App. 2001); Knapp v. Hughes, 808 N.Y.S.2d 791 (N.Y.App.Div. 2006).

---

2.   REQUIREMENTS FOR A DEED

The minimum requirements for a valid written deed are determined by state statutes and can vary by jurisdiction. The Washington state statute reproduced below provides a useful model to study.

Revised Code of Washington

64.04.020 Requisites of a Deed. Every deed shall be in writing, signed by the party bound thereby, and acknowledged by the party before some person authorized by this act to take acknowledgments of deeds.

or notarized

64.04.030 Warranty Deed—Form and Effect. Warranty deeds for the conveyance of land may be substantially in the following form, without express covenants:

The grantor (here insert the name or names and place of residence) for and in consideration of (here insert consideration) in hand paid, conveys and warrants to (here insert the grantee's name or names) the following described real estate (here insert description), situated in the county of _____, state of Washington. Dated this _____ day of _____, 19__.

Every deed in substance in the above form, when otherwise duly executed, shall be deemed and held a conveyance in fee simple to the grantee, his heirs and assigns, with covenants on the part of the grantor: (1) That at the time of the making and delivery of such deed he was lawfully seized of an indefeasible estate in fee simple, in and to the premises therein described, and had good right and full power to convey the same; (2) that the same were then free from all encumbrances; and (3) that he warrants to the grantee, his heirs and assigns, the quiet and peaceable possession of such premises, and will defend the title thereto against all persons who may lawfully claim the same, and such covenants shall be obligatory upon any grantor, his heirs and personal representatives, as fully and with like effect as if written at full length in such deed.

64.04.040 Bargain and Sale Deed—Form and Effect. Bargain and sale deeds for the conveyance of land may be substantially in the following form, without express covenants: The grantor (here insert name or names and place of residence), for and in consideration of (here insert consideration) in hand paid, bargains, sells and conveys to (here insert the grantee's name or names) the following described real estate (here insert description) situated in the county of _____, state of Washington. Dated this _____ day of _____, 19__.

Every deed in substance in the above form when otherwise duly executed shall convey to the grantee, his heirs or assigns an estate of inheritance in fee simple, and shall be adjudged an express covenant to the grantee, his heirs or assigns, to wit: That the grantor was seized of an indefeasible estate in fee simple, free from encumbrances, done or suffered from the grantor, except the rents and services that may be reserved, and also for quiet enjoyment against the grantor, his heirs and assigns, unless limited by express words contained in such deed; and the grantee, his heirs, executors, administrators and assigns may recover in any action for breaches as if such covenants were expressly inserted.

NOTES AND QUESTIONS

1. *Multiple deeds to the same land.* Laypersons (and even law students) often have the misconception that there is only a single piece of paper that is the "official" deed to a given parcel of land. The truth is quite the contrary; anyone (whether the owner or not) may make up and sign as many deeds to a parcel as he or she[1] wishes. Indeed, one can literally run them off on a photocopy machine!

Of course, once one of those deeds is signed by the owner of the land and delivered to a grantee, the grantor no longer has title. Any deed that the grantor might subsequently give to another grantee will convey nothing (assuming that the first deed was recorded—about which we will have more to say later), and will have no legal significance apart from possibly subjecting the grantor to liability on the covenants of title if the later deed contains such covenants.

Implicit in the last statement is the fact that there is no inherent legal wrong in the execution and delivery of a deed by one who owns no interest in the land. In fact, if any reader would like a deed to the Space Needle in Seattle (or any other piece of valuable real estate except our houses—be as choosy as you wish), you may simply write to one of the authors and we will be happy to send you one! Needless to say, the deed we send you will be a quitclaim deed, containing no covenants of title, and because we do not own the Space Needle, the deed will in fact convey nothing at all to you. We will use a quitclaim deed so that you cannot hold us liable for damages when you determine that you failed to acquire any title to the Space Needle through the deed.

A common related misconception is that "the" deed is passed down from one owner to another in succession indefinitely. What actually occurs is that each owner, as he or she is ready to make a sale or gift of the property, prepares and executes a brand-new deed and delivers it to the grantee. Assuming that the deed from the previous transfer was recorded (so that one can obtain a copy of it from the courthouse if a dispute about its existence or content arises), it is really quite irrelevant whether that prior deed is even in existence any longer. People commonly retain deeds by which they have acquired property in their files or safety-deposit boxes, but except in very rare cases (e.g., the need to have them examined by questioned documents experts to detect a forgery) there would be nothing alarming about throwing them out in the trash (after recording, of course.)

2. *Using old terminology in new ways.* Many states have statutes that are designed to make certain specific covenants of title a part of a deed if it uses specified "magic" words. The Washington statutes reproduced above illustrate that phrases which originated in medieval deeds continue to be used in the United States, but are often given new and different meanings and are employed in ways the old English lawyers would have thought wholly

---

[1] In the notes in this chapter, the male gender will often be used to refer to the grantor, and the female gender to refer to the grantee. —Eds.

inappropriate. Can you see the difference between a "warranty deed" and a "bargain and sale deed" in Washington? That difference is purely a product of the Washington legislature's creative definitions, and has nothing to do with the ways the same terms were used at common law.

3. *The writing requirement.* The application of the Statute of Frauds to conveyances (as distinct from contracts of sale or brokerage listing agreements already studied) requires further explanation.

(a) Although the Washington statute of frauds refers to "deeds", many states require a writing for "conveyances of interests in land" or the like, but then exempt certain types of conveyances, such as those of interests having a duration of one year or less. The point of such an exemption is to legitimize short-term oral leases.

(b) There is, surprisingly, some authority that an oral gift of land is effective if the donee takes possession and engages in other acts of detrimental reliance. The principle involved is not well-defined, but seems to be analogous to the doctrine of "part performance" of land sale contracts. See Troxel v. Bishop, 201 S.W.3d 290 (Tex. App. 2006); Lynch v. Lynch, 239 Iowa 1245, 34 N.W.2d 485 (1948); Patrick McFadden, Oral Transfers of Land in Illinois, 1988 U. Ill. L. Rev. 667. The drafters of the Restatement (Second) of Property: Donative Transfers did not find this idea appealing. Section 31.4 provides as follows.

Except to the extent allowed by the State of Frauds, the owner of an interest in land cannot make an effective donative transfer thereof * * * to another person (the donee) by delivering the land to the donee * * * with the manifested intention that the donee be the recipient of a gift.

(c) Ordinarily, only the grantor is required to sign the deed. Even if the deed contains covenants that will bind the grantee, the grantee is not required to sign; her acceptance of the deed will be regarded as sufficient evidence of assent. A deed signed only by the grantor was known in England as a deed poll. A deed that the grantee also signed was known as a deed of indenture, a term apparently derived from the practice of having the grantee sign on a portion of the paper, which would then be cut off with a wavy or zig-zag cut (thus, "indented") and retained by the grantor as a sort of receipt, with the grantee receiving the portion the grantor had signed.

(d) Most Statutes of Frauds (unlike Washington's statute) do not require acknowledgment by a notary or other officer for validity of the deed. In a few states, acknowledgment is required; see, e.g., Fla. Stat. § 689.04 (warranty deeds); Ariz. Rev. Stat. § 33–401; Neb. Rev. Stat. § 76–211. However, acknowledgment is almost uniformly required for *recordation* in the public records. Thus (as our subsequent discussion of recording acts will reveal), acknowledgment is unnecessary as between the parties themselves in most states, but it (and recording) are essential in order to protect the grantee against further adverse conveyances by the grantor to third parties.

$176,000   571708

AFTER RECORDING Mail To
Troy Osborn and Sara Osborn
2018 Rockefeller Avenue
Everett, WA 98201

2006042B0875   1   PG
04/28/2006 1:17pm $32.00
SNOHOMISH COUNTY, WASHINGTON

Filed for Record at Request of : Ticor Title Company

STATUTORY WARRANTY DEED

THE GRANTOR(S)

     John D Jones and Vicky L Jones, husband and wife

for and in consideration of Ten dollars and other good and valuable consideration in hand paid, conveys, and warrants to

     Troy Osborn and Sara Osborn, husband and wife

the following described real estate, situated in the County of Snohomish, State of Washington

Lot 57 of Cedarcrest park, according to the Plat recorded December 8, 1998 under Recording No 9812085003, in Snohomish County, Washington

Tax Parcel Number 008877-000-057-00Subject to easements, covenants, conditions and restrictions shown on Exhibit "A" as hereto attached and by this reference made a part hereof

Assessor's Property Tax Parcel/Account Number 00887700005700

Dated   April 25, 2006

_____
John D Jones

_____
Vicky L Jones

Talon Group
745003
A division of First
American Title Insurance
Company   1/33

STATE OF WASHINGTON

COUNTY OF SNOHOMISH

On this day personally appeared before me John D Jones and Vicky L Jones to me known to be the individual(s) described in and who executed the within and foregoing instrument, and acknowledged that he/she/they signed the same as his/her/their free and voluntary act and deed, for the uses and purposes therein mentioned

Given under my hand and official seal, this the 26, April 2006

_____
Notary Public in and for the State of Washington
residing at Snohomish
     Sammamish
My Commission Expires 2-19-07

(SEAL)

Escrow No 6368614-   LPB-10 7/97

4.   *Elements of a deed.* The essential components of a deed are few: it must identify the grantor(s) and grantee(s), identify the land being conveyed, contain some words indicating title is to pass (so-called "words of grant"), and be signed by the grantor(s). In a few states acknowledgment or witnesses are necessary.

Now refer to the modern deed reprinted on the previous page, and see if you can find and interpret the following items:

(a) The grantor's name and signature.

(b) The grantees' names and an indication of the manner in which they are taking title. (Washington is a community property state.)

(c) The recitation of consideration. As you saw in *Bale v. Allison*, supra, in most states neither the actual payment of consideration nor its recitation are necessary to the validity of the deed. Still, the recitation continues to be found in virtually every American deed. It is a historical artifact, left over from the post-Statute of Uses era when covenants to stand and bargain and sale deeds were used.

(d) The description of the real estate, here accomplished by reference to a previously recorded subdivision plat.

(e) A statement of "exclusions"—matters to which the fee simple title will be subject, and therefore prevent the conveyance of a "pure" fee simple absolute title in the real estate. The main purpose of the statement in the deed is not to inform the grantee of the nature of the exceptions (the statement comes too late in the due diligence process and is too broadly worded for that), but to preclude the grantor from becoming liable based on a breach of deed covenants of title as a result of the existence of the matters mentioned as exclusions. The buyer should already have learned about these exclusions from a title report, title commitment, attorney's opinion, or the like, and will have satisfied herself (if she is well-advised) that they are acceptable.

(f) Language indicating an intent to make a conveyance—or "words of grant." A variety of words have been held sufficient by various courts, including alienate, assign, assure, convey, enfeoff, give, quitclaim, set over, and transfer. But sometimes a grantor will use words that simply do not indicate an intent to transfer anything. Such a deed is ineffective. See Raley v. Raley, 121 Miss. 555, 83 So. 740 (1920) (the words "warrant and defend" are not words of grant and convey nothing). See also III Am. L. Prop. § 12.44 (1952).

The words of grant in the Washington deed also trigger the warranties of title described in the Washington statutes set out above. We will investigate deed warranties in general later in this chapter, but you should be able to understand from the statutory language the basic notion behind the two types of warranties.

Note that the deed reprinted above does not contain any statement about the duration of the estate being transferred. You will recall that at common law, the words "and her heirs" were necessary to give the grantee a fee simple. Today, however, virtually every state presumes that a fee simple is intended unless contrary language appears; hence, no specific statement of the estate's duration is required.

In states that continue to use more archaic deed forms, it is common to include a "habendum" clause (from the Latin "habendum et tendendum"—"to have and to hold"), which states the quality of the estate, especially if it is less than a fee simple. For example, language indicating a life estate might read, "To have and to hold for his life only"

(g) The date. Although a date is not essential, it is usually included. The critical date is not the date of execution of the deed, but rather the date of delivery (because delivery is when the deed "speaks"). Nevertheless, the execution date is the one normally inserted in the deed itself.

(h) The notary public's certificate of acknowledgment.

(i) The stamp of the public official (in Washington known as the auditor, but in most states, the county recorder) indicating that the deed has been officially recorded.

(j) The auditor's stamp indicating that the recording fee (here, $3.00) has been paid.

(k) Stamps indicating the payment of the transfer taxes. Washington state charges 1.28 percent of the sale price and Snohomish County an additional 0.5 percent, for a total of $3,738 on a house selling for $210,000. Washington is a rather expensive place to transfer land! At least 37 states impose a real estate transfer tax. Most apply a flat percentage rate, though a few apply a higher rate for higher value transactions. The rate varies widely by state, from 0.01 percent up to 2 percent, with the median of the states applying the tax being 0.4 percent. The National Conference of State Legislatures maintains a list of transfer taxes; see http://www.ncsl. org/issues-research/budget/real-estate-transfer-taxes.aspx.

5. *Does the deed convey an estate or something less?* A deed is presumed to convey a fee simple absolute estate (if the grantor has one) unless a contrary intent is expressed. But drafters of deeds sometimes insert language that leaves the reader uncertain as to whether something less than a fee simple estate is intended, and if so, exactly what is being conveyed.

For example, a conveyance of "a strip of land for a right of way" or "a right of way over a strip of land" may be thought to grant only an easement and not an estate. See Severns v. Union Pac. R.R. Co., 125 Cal. Rptr. 2d 100 (Cal.App. 2002); Little Miami, Inc. v. Wisecup, 13 Ohio App. 3d 239, 468

N.E.2d 935 (1984). There are hundreds of such cases, mostly dating from the late 19th and early 20th centuries, when agents for railroads acquired land interests for tracks, and were often careless or imprecise in describing the nature of the interests they obtained. The outcomes of the cases are variable and hard to predict; they turn on the precise language used in the deed.

The issue has become important for several reasons. One is that in the late 20th and early 21st centuries, railroads have wished to allow communication companies to install fiber optic lines along their tracks. This is perfectly permissible if the railroad has a fee simple estate, but may violate the rights of the underlying landowner if the railroad has only an easement. Another reason is that an easement may be terminated by abandonment, while a fee simple estate cannot. See Union Pac. R. Co. v. Ameriton Properties Inc., 2014 WL 4928778 (Tex.App. 2014); Kershaw Sunnyside Ranches, Inc. v. Yakima Interurban Lines Ass'n, 126 P.3d 16 (Wash. 2006).

Even a reference to an "easement" or "license" may be subject to reinterpretation if a court feels the word does not describe the legal result the parties desired. See Ouellette v. Butler, 125 N.H. 184, 480 A.2d 76 (1984). Good drafting thus requires careful and unambiguous expression of the parties' intentions.

6.   *Exceptions and reservations.* Another problem arises from the use of "exceptions" and "reservations" in deeds. In theory, an "exception" is a holding back of some previously existing interest in or portion of the land, while a "reservation" creates and leaves with the grantor a newly formed interest in the land. Thus, it would be proper to "except the south fifty feet" but to "reserve a life estate." In practice the two terms are used almost interchangeably, and the distinction between them has little significance. See O'Brien v. Village Land Co., 794 P.2d 246 (Colo. 1990).

A common law rule states that a deed may not create an interest in a *third party* by way of an exception or reservation; such clauses may operate only in favor of the grantor. (Of course, the grantor could then transfer the interest, so reserved or excepted, to another party by a second deed.) See Shirley v. Shirley, 259 Va. 513, 525 S.E.2d 274 (2000). This rule is so obviously artificial and apt to defeat intention that many modern cases have refused to follow it; see Simpson v. Kistler Inv. Co., 713 P.2d 751 (Wyo. 1986); Malloy v. Boettcher, 334 N.W.2d 8 (N.D. 1983), Note, 60 N.D. L. Rev. 317 (1984). But the wise drafter will avoid the problem.

7.   *The need for an existing grantee.* A deed that conveys a present (as distinct from a future) interest must have an ascertainable grantee—that is, a living person or an existing juridical entity, such as a corporation, partnership, trust, or governmental unit. See, e.g., In re Estate of Savich, 671 N.W.2d 746 (Minn. App. 2003) (deed purportedly delivered to grandmother after her death was void). Thus courts often hold deeds void if the grantee is a corporation or other entity that has not yet been formed or that has been dissolved. See, e.g., United States v. Miller, 1999 WL 675328 (W.D. Wash. 1999) (not reported in F.Supp.) (deed to purported entity with no legal

existence was void); Stone v. Jetmar Properties, LLC, 733 N.W.2d 480 (Minn. App. 2007) (deed to LLC not yet formed is void); Haney's Chapel United Methodist Church v. United Methodist Church, 716 So. 2d 1156 (Ala. 1998) (deed to "this community for a Union Church" is void); Piedmont and Western Inv. Corp. v. Carnes-Miller Gear Co., 96 N.C. App. 105, 384 S.E.2d 687 (1989) (deed to dissolved corporation is void); Myers v. Francis, 548 So. 2d 833 (Fla. App. 1989) (deed that fails to name a grantee is void).

Trusts are a little different. A deed to a trustee is valid even though the trust has not yet been formed, since the trustee can hold title in her or his individual capacity until the trust is created; see Luna v. Brownell, 110 Cal. Rptr. 3d 573 (Cal.App. 2010).

8. *Returning title by handing deed back.* A grantee will sometimes hand a deed back to the grantor with the intent of reconveying title to the land to the grantor. But of course the deed's wording is completely inapt for this purpose, and no reconveyance is accomplished. See Stockwell v. Stockwell, 790 N.W.2d 52 (S.D. 2010). See also Ward v. Ward, 874 N.E.2d 433 (Mass. App. 2007) (grantor could not revoke deed after delivering it). Delivering a deed is like squeezing toothpaste out of a tube; you can't put it back in again!

B. LAND DESCRIPTIONS

BROWN, BOUNDARY CONTROL AND LEGAL PRINCIPLES
2–3, 5–9 (1957)

Land is fixed in place. If it is to be divided among various people, it must be marked by monuments where they exist or directions must be given explaining how it is or can be monumented. The earliest land holdings were dependent upon found or set monuments that delineated limits of ownership. But monuments and marks on the earth's surface are subject to destruction or movement by intentional or unintentional means. Trees die, wooden stakes rot, rivers change their course, and ploughs remove stakes. Certainty of boundary lines dependent upon monuments may be destroyed with the destruction of the monuments marking them. To cope with the problem of replacing lost or destroyed monuments, especially in the Nile valley of Egypt where frequent floods destroyed many land markers, man invented measuring methods that would enable him to reset new monuments reasonably close to the spot occupied by the old monuments. Measurements start from some definite point, a monument, and go a fixed distance in a given direction. By relating numerous monuments to one another by measurements, a lost monument can be replaced by distance and direction from other monuments.

Land ownerships have shape, size, and location. The shape and size of a parcel of land may be defined without the aid of monuments, i.e., a square, a parallelogram, a circle, or an irregular parcel by bearings and distances. But the place where the particular shape is located is related to a fixed monument on the face of the earth. Theoretically the position of land can be defined by latitude and longitude without the aid of monuments, but, because of technical difficulties in pinpointing a particular latitude and longitude, it is rarely done. All the advancements in land location technique have not eliminated the monument as the ultimate means by which land is controlled.

In the early days in the United States *free surveys* often existed. A surveyor could start at any point, survey a selected quantity of land, monument, and describe it. He was not limited by previous ownerships or previous surveys. Today practically all boundary surveys are dependent partly or wholly upon monuments or points previously established on the earth. If a new parcel is described, it is related to existing boundaries which in turn are related somehow to a fixed monument. If a new parcel is established by survey, it is done by measurements from fixed monuments. Monuments are the backbone in relation to which land is located.

From early Colonial times down to the present, various systems have been adopted to describe real property relative to monuments, said systems being dependent upon either local laws, common laws, state laws, Colonial laws, or Federal laws. Townships, ranges, and sections of land as first defined by the Continental Congress and later enacted into Federal law represent the most widespread system used to mark and describe land within the United States.

The government survey system which governs land descriptions in most of the midwestern and western United States had its inception with a committee headed by Thomas Jefferson, an experienced surveyor. The committee recommended the system to the Continental Congress, which adopted it on April 26, 1785. Most of the land added to the United States subsequent to that time has been surveyed under the system. The map on the next page shows the modern coverage of the system, and also illustrates the network of Base Lines and Principal Meridians which it superimposes on the nation.

The Principal Meridian lines run North–South and the Base Lines run East–West. Spaced out parallel to the Base Line, and running East–West, are lines dividing the land into "Townships." As the diagram below shows, the second Township south of the Base Line would be called

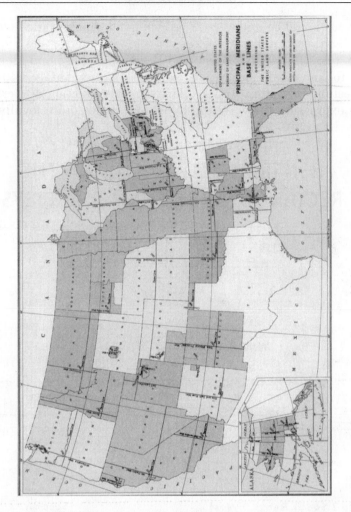

"Township 2 South." Each township has a side about 6 miles in length. Similarly, the North–South lines running parallel to the Principal Meridian divide the land into "Ranges;" the third Range West of the Principal Meridian would be called "Range 3 West." Note carefully that the term "Township" has a double meaning here; it refers both to the distance north or south of the Base Line, and also to the individual square parcel of land, six miles on a side, which is identified by stating both a Township and a Range number, as in "Township 2 South, Range 3 West."

Each Township (using the latter meaning of the term) is further subdivided into 36 "Sections", each about one mile square. Note the numbering system, which begins in the Northeast corner of the Section and continually loops back and forth, winding up with Section 36 in the Southeast corner. Each Section may be further divided as the owners or their surveyors desire into quarters, quarter-quarters, and so on. On the diagram you should be able to pick out the land which would be described as "The Southeast quarter of the Northwest quarter of Section 14, Township 2 South, Range 3 West, San Bernardino Base and Meridian." It is useful to know that a Section contains approximately 640 acres, a quarter-section 160 acres, and a quarter-quarter-section 40 acres. Thus, while the expression "plowing the South 40" is not quite legally explicit, we can see its origin.

GENERALIZED DIAGRAM OF THE RECTANGULAR SYSTEM OF SURVEYS

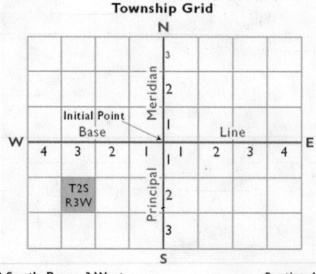

We have described the government survey system only superficially here; for more detailed information on its history and modern operation, see Brown & Eldridge, Evidence and Procedures for Boundary Location

101 (1962); U.S. Department of the Interior, Restoration of Lost or Obliterated Corners & Subdivision of Sections: A Guide for Surveyors (1974).

If land in a government survey state is being broken into smaller parcels for agricultural use, the fractional-section method of description illustrated above may be quite satisfactory. However, if land is to be developed for urban uses, such as businesses, homes, and apartments, the parcels are likely to be so small and so irregularly-shaped that they cannot be described satisfactorily as fractions of sections. Two other methods therefore come into common usage for urban property (and for rural property in states without the government survey system.) One is the recorded subdivision plat; the other, older and somewhat diminishing in use, but still very important, is the "metes and bounds" description. Both of these methods often use the government survey system as an initial starting point or framework; indeed, descriptions which rely to some degree on all three methods are quite common.

A subdivision plat is a map, generally prepared by an engineer or surveyor at the request of the landowner, which meets certain publicly-promulgated standards for format and accuracy, and which is filed as a permanent record in the appropriate government office, usually that of the county recorder. The plat must usually be approved by the governing body of the local government (e.g., the city council or the county commission) before the recorder will accept it for filing, and that approval is usually conditioned on compliance with a "subdivision ordinance" which imposes various technical standards (street width, lot size, installation of curb and gutter, etc.) and may compel dedication to the local government of streets, utility easements, and even school sites. See J. Juergensmeyer & T. Roberts, Land Use Planning and Development Regulation Law, ch. 7 (2d ed. 2007).

A subdivision plat may include hundreds of lots, or only two or three. It will normally show a reference to some preexisting monument or to an element of the government survey system, such as a section corner. Once it has been officially filed, it can form the basis for legal descriptions of its individual lots; the description need not go "behind" the plat or recite the underlying monument references, so the description of a lot can be very brief: "Lot 3, Block K, Ridgefield Acres Subdivision, as shown in Plat Book D, page 23, Official Records of Orange County." Nearly all modern single-family residential developments are built on land which is covered by platted subdivisions, and they are fairly common with commercial property, such as shopping centers, as well.

The other major type of land description is "metes and bounds." It involves a written description of the property's boundaries, usually by a series of "calls", each of which states the location of an individual boundary line. Of course, the point of beginning of the calls must be monumented somehow. This may be done by direct reference to a monument. Alternatively, the metes and bounds description may lie within (and make reference to) a lot in a platted subdivision or a section in the government survey system.

———————

Types of Metes and Bounds Conveyances. Several types of metes and bounds descriptions * * * exist, some being so closely related to subdivision descriptions that they could be considered as a quasi-subdivision description.

Described by Successive Bounds. In the most common metes and bounds description, and the one normally considered to be the true metes and bounds description, all the bounds are described in successive order, the bounds being fixed by reference to a map or document, by bearing and distance, by monuments, or by all three. The purpose of any description is to convey, by written language, a parcel of land of the exact shape, size, and location offered for sale by the grantor. Although it is desirable to use as short a description as possible, it is often necessary, when a clear intent is expressed, to use many words describing each bound. All too often a short description can alter the meaning of a deed, and a long description written by an unskilled person frequently shows conflicts among the terms of a deed. The following quasi-metes and bounds descriptions are discussed along with true metes and bounds descriptions. * * *

Direction of Travel. True metes and bounds descriptions and many quasi-metes and bounds descriptions have a direction of travel. A bearing may be stated in either of two directions on a map or plat but only one can be utilized in a written perimeter description. In the figure below, starting at the point of beginning, the direction of travel is to the southeast, making the first written bearing in the description S 45°00′E, not N 45°00′ W. Because the relationship of one line to another is shown by the plotting of the lines in the figure below, it is immaterial whether the bearing on the plat is written S 45°00′E or N 45°00′W.

DIRECTION OF TRAVEL

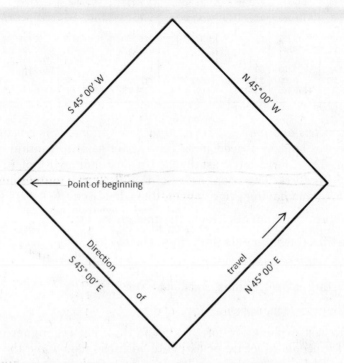

Monuments. Monuments are classified as either *natural, artificial, record, or legal.* Naturally occurring monuments such as rivers, lakes, oceans, bays, sloughs, cliffs, trees, hills, and large boulders are permanent objects found on the land as they were placed by nature and are usually considered controlling over *artificial monuments* (man-made) such as iron stakes, wooden stakes, rock mounds, stones and wooden fences, but, if the writings clearly indicate a contrary intent, especially where the lines of a survey are called for, the control might be reversed. Some man-made monuments, because of the certainty of location, visibility, stability, and permanence, are considered equal in rank to natural monuments. In this classification would fall sidewalks, street paving, curbs, wells, canals, concrete buildings, and concrete fences.

NOTES

1. *Units of measurement.* The following table, published by the National Bureau of Standards, may help you deal with the various units of length sometimes used in legal descriptions.

Units	Inches	Links	Feet	Yards	Rods	Chains	Miles	Meters
1 inch	1	0.126 263	0.083 333 3	0.027 777 8	0.005 050	0.001 262	0.000 015 783	0.025 400.05
1 link	7.92	1	0.66	0.22	0.04	0.01	0.000 125	0.201 168 4
1 foot	12	1.515 152	1	0.333 333	0.060 606	0.015 151	0.000 189 394	0.304 800 6
1 yard	36	4.545.45	3	1	0.181 818	0.045 454	0.000 568 182	0.914 401 8
1 rod	198	25	16.5	5.5	1	0.25	0.003 125	5.029 210
1 chain	792	100	66	22	4	1	0.0125	20.116 84
1 mile	63 360	8 000	5 280	1 760	320	80	1	1 609.347 2
1 meter	39.37	4.970 960	3.280 833	1.093 611 1	0.198 838	0.049 710	0.000 621 370	1

2.   *Conflicts and ambiguities in land descriptions.* It is not unusual for a description of land in a deed (or a contract of sale) to contain conflicting information. The courts have established a descending list of priorities to resolve such conflicts. The usual order of this list (with items higher on the list controlling, and having priority over, items lower on the list) is as follows:

- Natural monuments (trees, streams, rocks, etc.)

- Artificial monuments (buildings, curbs, etc.)

- Courses (directions in relation to true North)

- Distances (feet, chains, rods, etc.)

- Quantity (e.g., acres)

Perhaps the best explanation for this list is that matters higher on the list are easier for people to locate or estimate with the naked eye than matters lower down. Thus, it is easier to locate a tree than to estimate a course (direction), which in turn is easier to estimate than the acreage of a plot of land.

Do not assume that, because natural monuments are given the highest priority, it is desirable to use them whenever possible. Quite the contrary is true. Suppose you were searching a title and got back to a deed that made a reference to "the big white rock beside Perkins Creek." Unfortunately, the creek is now in a concrete culvert and the rock is long gone, removed to make room for the construction of a shopping center. Because natural monuments are impermanent, it may be impossible to locate them when someone needs them in the future.

3.   *Sketching a metes and bounds description.* As a lawyer, you should not attempt to fulfill the role of a surveyor or engineer (unless, of course, you have actually been trained to do so). But you can and should examine legal descriptions with a critical eye. In most cases, you can sketch a metes and bounds description by hand and see if it makes sense. Here's a real one to try:

A 1.1608 acre tract of land more or less, in the northwest quarter of the southwest quarter of Section 34, Block Y, Arnold and Barrett Survey, Hutchinson County, Texas, said tract being more particularly described as follows:

Beginning at a ½" iron rebar marking the southwest corner of said tract, being S. 89 degrees 55' 08" E. a distance of 852.31 feet from a 5/8 inch rod marking the southwest corner of the said northeast quarter of the southwest quarter of Section 34;

Thence S. 89 degrees 55' 08" E. along the south line of said northeast quarter of the southwest quarter of Section 34 a distance of 224.94 feet.

Thence N. 13 degrees 52' 47" W. a distance of 270.96 feet;

Thence S. 89 degrees 52' 00" W. a distance of 160 feet;

Thence S. 0 degrees 00' 47" E. a distance of 262.37 feet to a point of beginning.

If your sketch is correct, the resulting land parcel should look like this. It is easy for transcription errors to creep into metes and bounds descriptions as they are copied from one document to another. Your sketch may well reveal such an error, particularly if it is a fairly gross one (such as substituting "east" for "west" or the like).

Modern surveyors and engineers use computer programs to prepare such drawings. The program will also determine whether the description "closes"—that is, whether the termination of the final "call" returns to the point of beginning. (If it does not, the description contains an error.) If you discover an error, don't try to correct it yourself; get the assistance of an engineer or surveyor.

C. DELIVERY AND ESCROWS

1. DELIVERY AND TESTAMENTARY TRANSFER

The expression "signed, sealed, and delivered" once applied quite literally to deeds. As we have already seen, the grantor's signature is still required. A seal was traditionally a blob of wax into which an impression of the grantor's ring or other insignia had been pressed. Later, it became permissible to simply write the word "seal" or the letters "l.s." (for locus sigilium, the place of the seal) beside the grantor's signature. In most states, the necessity of a seal has now been abolished. See III American Law of Property § 12.58 (1952).

Delivery continues to be a crucial requirement, and one that is frequently litigated. As between the parties, it is delivery that makes the deed operative, and a deed which has not been delivered is said to be entirely void. An undelivered deed (purloined by the grantee, for example) can be recorded and appear to be perfectly valid. The cheating grantee might then be able to purport to make a further conveyance to a bona fide purchaser. But even if this occurs, the purchaser gets no title. See Lange v. Wyoming Nat. Bank of Casper, 706 P.2d 659 (Wyo. 1985).

A valid delivery requires the coincident presence of two factors: an intent by the grantor to pass title immediately, and some act or behavior on the grantor's part to evidence that intent. The act is often the manual handing over of the deed to the grantee, but that is not the only proper method; any act which sufficiently evidences the requisite intent will do. Occasionally a court may even say that no act at all is necessary if the intent is sufficiently clear, but the standard doctrine is that both the intent and the act must exist. See Johnson v. Johnson, 760 S.E.2d 618 (Ga.App. 2014) (without an act of delivery, no title could pass).

Delivery is seldom an issue in the context of real estate sales (as distinguished from gifts) because the sales transaction generally is supervised by an attorney, escrow agent, title insurance company, or other professional who understands the delivery requirement. Problems tend to arise in intrafamily transfers and most often, it seems, when the grantor is contemplating his or her own death.

IN RE ESTATE OF WARD

Texas Court of Appeals, 2011
2011 WL 3720829

In this will-contest case, appellant, Bobby Ward, challenges the jury's verdict that: (1) the will of his now-deceased wife, Doris Ward, is unenforceable because he exerted undue influence; and (2) Doris conveyed a seventy-seven-acre tract of land to her daughter, Dwana Phillips, several months before the will in question was executed. In five issues, Bobby complains that the evidence supporting the jury's verdict is legally and factually insufficient and that the attorney's fees award was not allowed by statute, inequitable, and unjust. We affirm.

Doris and Bobby married in 1978. Both had children from previous marriages, but they did not have children together. The Wards lived in a house constructed on 4.44 acres that was conveyed to them by Doris's parents, the Dunns, in 1997. On an adjacent 2.57-acre tract of land, Dwana and her husband live in a house that apparently was updated by Doris and Bobby after the Phillipses agreed to move from Arkansas to Cleburne, Texas, to care for Doris and her father. At the time the Phillipses moved to Cleburne, Doris and her father "were in failing health."

Dwana is Doris's daughter from her first marriage and, by all accounts, was very close to Doris. The two spoke on the telephone frequently and saw each other virtually every day. Dwana actively took care of Doris to the extent that, at one point in time, Doris granted Dwana a power of attorney to make medical decisions for her.

On January 1, 2009, Doris was taken to the hospital for various medical issues. At the time, she was suffering from Parkinson's disease, had numerous problems with her back, and had lost most of the sight out of one of her eyes due to a fungal infection. Shortly thereafter, Doris was transferred to Ridgeview Rehabilitation & Skilled Nursing facility. Doris's health continued to decline, and she ultimately passed away on March 21, 2009.

On April 17, 2009, Bobby filed an application to probate Doris's will and for issuance of letters testamentary. The will Bobby sought to probate had been executed by Doris on December 11, 2008. In this will, Doris left all her real property to Bobby upon her death, including a seventy-seven-acre tract of land that Doris had inherited from her parents. The trial court probated Doris's will and, in accordance with the will, appointed Bobby as independent executor.

On June 10, 2009, Dwana filed her lawsuit, requesting a declaration from the trial court as to the rights of the parties under a purported deed and alleging that Doris's will was executed as the result of undue influence exerted by Bobby and that the will contained a mistake as to the disposition of the seventy-seven-acre tract of land commonly referred to as the family farm. Dwana asserted in the trial court that Doris had conveyed the seventy-seven-acre family farm in a deed that was delivered before Doris and Bobby went to Europe and was destroyed by someone a few days after the couple had returned from their trip.

This matter was tried to a jury, and at the conclusion of the trial, the jury determined that: (1) Doris had signed a deed to the family farm and had delivered the deed to Dwana; and (2) Bobby exerted undue influence over Doris in the execution of the December 11, 2008 will. [Based on evidence from Dwana and Doris' nurses that Bobby was domineering and abusive to Doris, the court sustained the jury's verdict that the will had been executed under Bobby's undue influence.] * * *

In his third issue, Bobby alleges that the evidence is legally and factually insufficient to prove that a valid deed conveying the family farm to Dwana existed. In his fourth issue, Bobby asserts that if such a deed was valid and existed, the evidence supporting the jury's finding that Doris delivered the deed to Dwana is legally and factually insufficient.

A.　WHETHER A VALID DEED EXISTED

Section 5.021 of the property code requires that a deed be in writing and must be subscribed or delivered by the conveyor or the conveyor's agent. Tex. Prop. Code Ann. § 5.021 (West 2004). However, as noted by the Fourteenth Court of Appeals,

> there is no longer a requirement, as there was at common law, that a deed or instrument to effect conveyance of real property have all the formal parts of a deed formerly recognized at common law or contain technical words. If from the whole

instrument a grantor and grantee can be ascertained, and there are operative words or words of grant showing an intention by the grantor to convey title to a real property interest (which is sufficiently described) to the grantee, and is signed and acknowledged by the grantor[,] it is a deed which accomplishes a legally effective conveyance.

Green v. Canon, 33 S.W.3d 855, 858 (Tex. App. Houston [14th Dist] 2000, pet. denied). "A property description is sufficient if the writing furnishes within itself, or by reference to some other existing writing, the means or data by which the particular land to be conveyed may be identified with reasonable certainty." AIC Mgmt. v. Crews, 246 S.W.3d 640, 645 (Tex. 2008).

In this case, the purported deed has been lost or destroyed. In such a case, the existence of the writing can be proven by parol evidence only if the witness saw the writing and can testify clearly as to its contents. Placer Energy Corp. v. E & S Oil Co., 692 S.W.2d 197, 199–200 (Tex. App.-Fort Worth 1985, no writ) (citing Arreguin v. Cantu, 609 S.W.2d 639, 641 (Tex. Civ. App.-San Antonio 1980, no writ); Crosby v. Davis, 421 S.W.2d 138, 142–43 (Tex. Civ. App.-Tyler 1967, writ ref'd n.r.e.)); Hutchison v. Massie, 226 S.W. 695, 696 (Tex. Civ. App.-Amarillo 1920, writ dism'd w.o.j.).

B. DELIVERY OF THE DEED

Conveyance by deed requires delivery of the deed. See Tex. Prop. Code Ann. § 5.021; see also Noell v. Crow-Billingsley Air Park Ltd. P'ship, 233 S.W.3d 408, 415 (Tex. App.-Dallas 2007, pet. denied). Delivery of a deed has two elements: (1) the grantor must place the deed within the control of the grantee (2) with the intention that the instrument becomes operative as a conveyance. Noell, 233 S.W.3d at 415. The question of delivery of the deed is controlled by the intent of the grantor, and it is determined by examining all the facts and circumstances preceding, attending, and following the execution of the instrument. Id. Recording a deed is not necessary to pass title; an unrecorded deed is binding on the parties to the conveyance. Id. at 416–17 (citing Tex. Prop. Code Ann. § 13.001(b) (West 2004) ("The unrecorded instrument is binding on a party to the instrument, on the party's heirs, and on a subsequent purchaser who does not pay a valuable consideration or who has notice of the instrument.")).

C. DISCUSSION

In the present case, only three people knew the contents of the purported deed: Dwana, Doris, and Bobby. Dwana testified that Doris handwrote the deed and placed it on the kitchen table before she and Bobby went on vacation to Europe. Dwana recalled that the deed described the property and that she understood the document to mean that Doris was conveying the family farm to her. The family farm was Doris's separate property to convey as she wished considering she had inherited it from her parents. See Tex. Fam. Code Ann. § 3.001(2) (West 2006) (providing that "the property acquired by the spouse during marriage by gift, devise, or descent" is the spouse's separate property). Bobby remembered the document as well and admitted that the document referenced the seventy-seven-acre tract of land commonly referred to as the family farm. He also admitted that, at one point, Doris intended to give Dwana the family farm but that Doris changed her mind shortly thereafter. When Doris and Bobby left for Europe, Dwana read the document and left it on the kitchen table where Doris had originally put it. Shortly after the Wards returned from Europe, the document was destroyed. Bobby alleged that, after changing her mind about conveying the family farm to Dwana, Doris shredded the document. Dwana testified that when the document disappeared off of the kitchen table, Doris asked her if she had received the document, to which Dwana responded, "No, mother, I did not get it. But it's not on the table. . . . " Both Dwana and Bobby recognized that the document had been signed by Doris and had been given to Dwana. However, Bobby contended in the trial court that the document was not a valid deed because it had not been notarized.

Dwana proffered additional testimony to prove the existence and delivery of the deed. David Paul Holibaugh, Doris's brother in law, testified that he had leased a portion of the family farm in the past. Holibaugh recounted that Doris told him to make out his 2009 lease payment to Dwana. Arden Lockett witnessed Doris sign the deed conveying the family farm to Dwana, and Helen Herron attended a celebratory lunch at the Cotton Patch restaurant with Doris and Bobby where Doris told her that "they were selling the farm to Dwana" because Dwana was "going to get it when [Doris was] gone anyway." Whitworth noted that Bobby and Doris attended his church for approximately ten years and that he visited Doris while she was in the hospital. Whitworth heard Doris exclaim that "Bobby was going to take the farm. She apologized to Dwana over and over again." Doris told Whitworth, "You are my witness, you're my witness. Don't let him [Bobby] take the farm." Whitworth also recalled a Wednesday night prayer meeting where Doris made a praise report indicating that Dwana was the owner of the family farm.

The jury charge contained the following instructions regarding the purported deed:

Question 2: Did Doris Ward execute a deed for the 77-acre tract to Dwana that was subsequently lost or destroyed?

You are instructed that a "Deed" is a writing that must be subscribed by the grantor which contains the description of the property conveyed.

You are further instructed to consider all the facts and circumstances preceding, attending, and following the execution, if any, of the deed.

Question 3: Did Doris Ward deliver a deed for the 77-acre tract of land to Dwana Phillips?

You are instructed that a Grantor may deliver a deed to the grantee or to an [sic] third person. When a grantor delivers a Deed to a third person, without any reservation on his or her part of the right to recall it, he or she makes an effective delivery of the Deed when he or she instructs the third person to:

    a.   deliver the deed to the grantee;

    b.   deliver the deed to the grantee upon the grantor's death; or

    c.   file the deed with the property records of the county where the property is located."

On appeal, Bobby complains that "the charge was exceedingly bare-bones." However, in making the argument, Bobby does not adequately explain the deficiencies in the jury charge. Furthermore, the record does not reflect that Bobby objected to questions 2 or 3 of the jury charge. See In re B.L.D., 113 S.W.3d 340, 349 (Tex. 2003) ("[A]ny complaint to a jury charge is waived unless specifically included in an objection.") (citing Tex. R. Civ. P. 274; Tex. R. App. P. 33.1(a)(1)).

Based on the charge submitted, the jury concluded that Doris had conveyed the family farm to Dwana via a deed and that the deed had been delivered to Dwana. It is undisputed that the purported deed described the property as the seventy-seven acre family farm and that the family did not own another seventy-seven acre tract of land referred to as the family farm. By finding in favor of Dwana regarding the deed, the jury believed, through the testimony of Dwana, Holibaugh, Lockett, Herron, and Whitworth, that Doris conveyed the family farm to Dwana, the deed was valid, and the deed had been delivered to Dwana. See Carr, 867 S.W.2d at 28; see also McGalliard, 722 S.W.2d at 697. And the jury clearly rejected Bobby's testimony that Doris changed her mind about conveying the family farm to Dwana and subsequently shredded the deed herself. See Carr, 867 S.W.2d at 28; see also McGalliard, 722 S.W.2d at 697.

Based on our review of the record, there is legally sufficient evidence to indicate that Doris, the grantor, handwrote a deed conveying the family farm to Dwana, the grantee; that it was Doris's intent that Dwana receive the family farm; and that Doris delivered the deed, as defined by the charge, to Dwana. See Green, 33 S.W.3d at 858; Crews, 246 S.W.3d at 645; Noell, 233 S.W.3d at 415; see also Chapman, 118 S.W.3d at 751; City of Keller, 168 S.W.3d at 807, 827. In addition, we cannot say that the jury's findings in questions 2 and 3 are so contrary to the overwhelming weight of the evidence as to be clearly wrong and manifestly unjust; thus, the evidence is factually sufficient to support the jury's findings as to this issue. See Francis, 46 S.W.3d at 242; Cain, 709 S.W.2d at 176.

NOTES AND QUESTIONS

1. *Physical delivery.* In *Ward* there is certainly evidence of Doris's intent to deed the farm to Dwana. But what was the physical act that accompanied that intent? Was it simply placing the deed on the kitchen table? To be an effective delivery, must Doris's actions have at least been accompanied by some contemporaneous expression indicating that the deed was now in force, such as "Now the farm belongs to Dwana"?

The physical act of delivery often is subordinated to the issue of the grantor's intent. For example, if the grantor clearly has the requisite intent, but is physically incapacitated, gestures or nods can be an adequate delivery. See Arwe v. White, 117 N.H. 1025, 381 A.2d 737 (1977). In Barker v. Nelson, 306 Ark. 204, 812 S.W.2d 477 (1991), the grantor showed the deed to the grantees and gave them photocopies of it, but kept the original. Nevertheless, the court found a delivery. On various modes of delivery, see Note, The Issue of Delivery Raised by "Dispositive" Conveyances, 18 Drake L. Rev. 67 (1968).

The mere fact that a deed had been handed over does not always establish delivery because the requisite intent on the part of the grantor may be lacking. For example, there is no delivery if the deed is merely handed to the grantee so that she can inspect it, or for some other temporary purpose. See Martinez v. Martinez, 678 P.2d 1163 (N.M. 1984) (deed handed to grantees so they could place it in escrow at bank). Similarly, if the grantor announces that he intends to remain on the land, or if he in fact remains on it after handing over the deed, or if other circumstances indicate lack of intent to make an immediate transfer, the courts may find lack of delivery. See, e.g., Cusick v. Meyer, 124 Or. App. 515, 863 P.2d 486 (1993); Den-Gar Enterprises v. Romero, 94 N.M. 425, 611 P.2d 1119 (App. 1980); Avery v. Lillie, 260 Iowa 10, 148 N.W.2d 474 (1967). Cf. Corkins v. Corkins, 358 Mich. 691, 101 N.W.2d 362 (1960).

2. *Recordation of the deed.* Courts widely hold that a deed that has been recorded is presumed to have been delivered. See In re Estate of Hardy, 910 So. 2d 1052 (Miss. 2005). There is some indication that the presumption arises only if the grantor records the deed, but in most states it applies irrespective of which party records. See Rausch v. Devine, 80 P.3d 733 (Alaska 2003). A few states make the presumption of valid delivery if the deed is recorded conclusive. See Ann. L. Mass., Ch. 183, § 5; Mattox v. Mattox, 777 So.2d 1041 (Fla.App. 2001) (recording is delivery *per se* in the absence of fraud on the grantor). In most states, however, the presumption is rebuttable. See, e.g., Hoefer v. Musser, 417 S.W.3d 330 (Mo.App. 2013); Estate of Skvorak v. Security Union Title Ins. Co., 140 Idaho 16, 89 P.3d 856 (2004). From the standpoint of title examination, the conclusive presumption

is very comforting. Title searchers dislike having to worry about whether a recorded deed was validly delivered or not, since an undelivered deed is void.

If recording raises a rebuttable presumption of delivery, what sort of evidence will rebut the presumption? The cases are varied and unpredictable. Courts sometimes hold that delivery has occurred even though the grantor retained the recorded deed itself, see LeMehaute v. LeMehaute, 585 S.W.2d 276 (Mo. App. 1979), or retained possession of the land, see Hartley v. Stibor, 96 Idaho 157, 525 P.2d 352 (1974). Adding to the uncertainty, the doctrines relating to grantor retention of the deed or of possession also are sometimes stated as presumptions, leading to cases that devolve into battles over presumptions and burdens of proof.

Finally, bear in mind that although recording may help prove that a delivery has occurred, recording is not essential to the validity of any deed, and it is clear that a delivery can occur without recording; see Johannes v. Idol, 181 P.3d 574 (Kan.App. 2008). Nevertheless, many laypeople mistakenly believe that the recording of the deed is necessary for a conveyance of title to occur. If the grantor hands the deed to the grantee, but instructs the grantee not to record it until some future date or event, should that be treated as evidence that the grantor did not intend a delivery? See Blancett v. Blancett, 136 N.M. 573, 102 P.3d 640 (2004) (treating such an instruction as relevant evidence of intent not to deliver).

3. *Acceptance.* Most courts agree that acceptance of the delivery by the grantee is an essential element in the conveyance of title. Of course, acceptance is rarely an issue because the grantee ordinarily is happy to receive the land. Most courts say that acceptance is presumed, at least if the deed is beneficial to the grantee. See Collins v. Columbia Gas Transmission Corp., 188 W. Va. 460, 425 S.E.2d 136 (1992). But if acceptance of the land would be burdensome, the presumption does not apply. See Messer v. Laurel Hill Assoc., 93 N.C. App. 439, 378 S.E.2d 220 (1989) (no presumption of acceptance, where deed contained a covenant requiring grantee to construct a street). Even if the presumption applies, the grantee can overcome the presumption by expressly declining to accept the deed if she does not want it. See State v. Thomason, 845 N.W.2d 640 (S.D. 2014); Hood v. Hood, 384 A.2d 706 (Me. 1978). See generally III Am. L. Prop. § 12.70 (1952); Annot., 74 A.L.R. 2d 992 (1960).

4. *Deeds conveying future interests.* For an effective delivery, the intent must be to make the deed immediately operative. But the deed itself need not pass title to a presently possessory estate; it may convey a future interest instead. Thus, the courts distinguish the following two scenarios:

- Grantor signs a deed which purports to grant fee simple title and hands it to the grantee, stating, "This grant is yours, but it does not take effect until next January 1." The deed is wholly ineffective.

- Grantor signs a deed which, by its terms, provides that possession is to remain in the grantor until next January 1, at which time the grantee is to have possession. Such language creates a springing executory interest in the grantee. If the grantor hands the deed to the grantee, she immediately becomes the owner of that interest, and the deed is valid.

Will the second scenario work even if the grantor also reserves in the deed itself a power to revoke the future interest? See Tennant v. John Tennant Memorial Home, 167 Cal. 570, 140 P. 242 (1914) (holding that it will).

Any number of other types of conditions may be inserted in a deed. If the conditions have not been satisfied, a court may say that the deed is "void" or "invalid." See Valley Honey Co. LLC v. Graves, 666 N.W.2d 453 (N.D. 2003). The better view, however, is that the deed conveys a future interest, and that the interest does not become possessory until the conditions are satisfied.

––––––––––

Frequently the grantor wishes to make an *ambulatory* disposition of the property—that is, one that is not finalized until death, and that can be revoked so long as the grantor remains alive. Of course, the "correct" instrument to accomplish this is a will, which has by its very nature precisely the characteristics just described. But many grantors have been told (sometimes with considerable accuracy) that a will must be probated, and that probate is costly and time-consuming, and hence is to be avoided.

There are other alternatives, such as joint tenancies and inter vivos trusts, that the grantor might consider in order to make an ambulatory disposition of real property without the necessity of probate, but many grantors take the easier tack—they use a deed!

WIGGILL V. CHENEY

Supreme Court of Utah, 1979
597 P.2d 1351

MAUGHAN, JUSTICE

This case involves the disposition of certain real property located in Weber County, State of Utah. The judgment before us invalidated a Warranty Deed, because of no valid delivery. We affirm. No costs awarded.

The material facts are undisputed. Specifically, on the 25th day of June, 1958, Lillian W. Cheney signed a deed to certain real property located in the city of Ogden, Utah, wherein the defendant, Flora Cheney, was named grantee. Thereafter Lillian Cheney placed this deed in a sealed envelope and deposited it in a safety deposit box in the names of herself and the plaintiff, Francis E. Wiggill. Following the deposition of the deed, Lillian Cheney advised plaintiff his name was on the safety deposit box and instructed plaintiff that upon her death, he was to go to the bank where he would be granted access to the safety deposit box and its contents. Lillian Cheney further instructed, "in that box is an envelope addressed to all those concerned. All you have to do is give them that envelope and that's all." At all times prior to her death, Lillian Cheney was in possession of a key to the safety deposit box and had sole and complete control over it. Plaintiff was never given the key to the safety deposit box.

Following the death of Lillian Cheney, plaintiff, after gaining access to the safety deposit box, delivered the deed contained therein to Flora Cheney, the named grantee.

The sole issue presented here on appeal is whether or not the acts of plaintiff constitute a delivery of the deed such as will render it enforceable as a valid conveyance.

The rule is well settled that a deed, to be operative as a transfer of the ownership of land, or an interest or estate therein, must be delivered. It was equally settled in this and the vast majority of jurisdictions that a valid delivery of a deed requires it pass beyond the control or domain of the grantor. The requisite relinquishment of control or dominion over the deed may be established, notwithstanding the fact the deed is in possession of the grantor at her death, by proof of facts which tend to show delivery had been made with the intention to pass title and to explain the grantor's subsequent possession. However, in order for a delivery effectively to transfer title, the grantor must part with possession of the deed or the right to retain it.

The evidence presented in the present case establishes Lillian Cheney remained in sole possession and control of the deed in question until her death. Because no actual delivery of the deed occurred prior to the death of the grantor, the subsequent manual delivery of the deed by plaintiff to defendant conveyed no title to the property described therein, or any part thereof, or any of its contents.[5]

NOTES AND QUESTIONS

1. *No delivery if the grantor's intent is testamentary.* The fact that Lillian Cheney wanted the real estate to pass to Flora Cheney upon Lillian's

---

[5] Concerning the contention that the grantor intended title to pass, the applicable rule was explained in *Singleton v. Kelly*, [61 Utah 277, 212 P. 63, 66 (1922)], where this court stated,

"that is true (the courts will carry out the grantor's intention whenever this is possible), but without any evidence of delivery, it can be of no importance whatever what the intentions of the grantor in this case were. One may have an intention to convey his property to another, but unless the deed is delivered to the grantee, or someone for him, title cannot pass, and the undelivered deed is a nullity."

death seems unassailable. Why should the law stand in the way of that result? The answer lies in the law's extensive formality requirements for wills. For a valid will, at least two witnesses must sign in the presence of the testator and each other. Why are the formal signature requirements for a will so much greater than for a deed? Because almost invariably, when the authenticity of a will is disputed, the testator is dead and cannot testify to her or his own intent.

Could the deed in the principal case be upheld as a will? Or would that be improper because a deed does not read like a will—on its face a deed appears to convey title to the property that is the subject of the deed immediately and not at the grantor's death? In any event, a deed ordinarily will not have the signatures of two witnesses, executed in the manner required for a will.

Could the conveyance in the principal case be upheld on an agency theory? After Lillian died, the plaintiff (who was executor of Lillian's estate) handed the deed to Flora. Was the plaintiff arguably acting as Lillian's agent, consummating the transaction by delivery? Does the fact that the principal was dead foreclose this argument? Cf. Womack v. Stegner, 293 S.W.2d 124 (Tex. Civ. App. 1956) (where grantor delivered deed with grantee's name left blank, but authorized the person receiving delivery to fill in any name he wished, the agency was irrevocable and could be exercised after the grantor died).

Did the delivery in the principal case fail due to lack of a sufficient manual act or lack of the appropriate intent? Compare the facts of *Estate of Dittus*, 497 N.W.2d 415 (N.D. 1993), which was similar to *Wiggill v. Cheney*, except that the grantor gave the grantee one of two keys to the safe-deposit box. The court was unimpressed and refused to find a delivery, finding that "the delivery of but one of two keys * * * is inconclusive, without other evidence, of intent to presently transfer title."

2. *What actions evidence an intent to make a present delivery?* Suppose the safety-deposit box had been rented in the joint names of Lillian and Flora, and that both had keys from the outset. Would placing the deed in the box constitute delivery? See Moseley v. Zieg, 180 Neb. 810, 146 N.W.2d 72 (1966) (finding no delivery on similar facts). On the other hand, if the deed had been placed (during the grantor's life) in a safety-deposit box rented *exclusively* in the grantee's name, a delivery very likely would have been found. See Estate of Blettell v. Snider, 114 Or. App. 162, 834 P.2d 505 (1992).

In sum, intent to make a *present* conveyance is critical. If the intent is to make the transfer effective only at the grantor's death, there is no delivery and the deed is void. See Tafolla v. Tafolla, 2011 WL 1466472 (Cal.App. 2011) (not published in Cal. Rptr.).

3. *Oral reservation of a life estate.* Suppose the grantor hands the deed to the grantee directly, but simultaneously makes an oral statement that it is

to be effective to give possession only upon the grantor's death, and that the grantor will keep the land during his life. As we have already suggested, such conduct is often taken as evidence that the grantor does not intend a *present* transfer of any interest, and thus that nothing passes at all. See, e.g., Broomfield v. Broomfield, 242 Ark. 355, 413 S.W.2d 657 (1967). Suppose the grantor merely says "The land is yours, but I'll take care of it for the rest of my life"? See Corkins v. Corkins, 358 Mich. 691, 101 N.W.2d 362 (1960).

By contrast, it is perfectly clear that the grantor can reserve a life estate *in the deed itself*, and make a valid delivery that will convey title subject to the retained estate. Indeed, such conveyances are so commonly accepted as hardly to be worth commenting on. See, e.g., Farina v. Bastianich, 984 N.Y.S.2d 46 (N.Y. App. Div. 2014); Lanford v. Cornett, 415 P.2d 984 (Okl. 1966).

4.   *Death escrow.* Another common variant is the handing of the deed by the grantor to a third party, with instructions to give it to the grantee upon the grantor's death. This arrangement is sometimes termed a "death escrow" and perhaps surprisingly, it can work. The courts have had a good deal of difficulty deciding which delivery (to the third party, or to the grantee) is the one that really counts, but when they select the latter, they usually say that it "relates back" to the date of the former; see Pipes v. Sevier, 694 S.W.2d 918 (Mo.App. 1985). (Otherwise, the courts are put in the awkward position of sustaining a delivery by a dead grantor.) The death escrow is an apparent exception to the usual rule (which we will study presently) that for a "true" escrow with relation-back effect, there must be an underlying contract of sale.

The death escrow will be ineffective if the grantor reserves the right to revoke the deed (whether he exercises that right or not), because such a power would indicate an intent not to make a present transfer. See Albrecht v. Brais, 324 Ill. App. 3d 188, 754 N.E.2d 396 (2001); Rausch v. Devine, 80 P.3d 733 (Alaska 2003); III Am. L. Prop. § 12.67 (1952). Of course, if the third party is a trusted friend of the grantor, and if the grantee is not told about the deed, the grantor has a practical power to revoke whether it is stated explicitly or not. But that fact will not stand in the way of the validity of the arrangement. See Vasquez v. Vasquez, 973 S.W.2d 330 (Tex. App. 1998).

The usual judicial interpretation of the death escrow is that the grantor continues to have the right to possess the land for the remainder of his life, despite the fact that the language of the deed itself does not expressly reserve a life estate, and that the grantee immediately obtains title subject to the retained life estate. See Garrett v. Garrett, 302 P.3d 1061 (Idaho 2013); Herman v. Mortensen, 72 Cal. App. 2d 413, 164 P.2d 551 (1945). How can this result be explained? Does it follow inevitably from the fact that, by the terms of the conditional delivery, the grantee cannot take possession until the grantor dies, and possession must be with somebody in the meantime?

Be careful not to confuse the death escrow cases with two other categories:

(a) cases like those described in Note 3 above, where a condition is orally imposed but the deed is manually handed to the grantee directly.

(b) cases where there is an unconditional delivery to a third party who is simply the agent of the grantee. There is no doubt that a delivery to the grantee's properly authorized agent (for example, the grantee's attorney) is effective. See DiMaio v. Musso, 2000 Pa. Super 326, 762 A.2d 363 (2000). Of course, there may be a dispute about whose agent the individual is. See, e.g., Capozzella v. Capozzella, 213 Va. 820, 196 S.E.2d 67 (1973). Even a delivery to the grantor's own attorney can suffice if the attorney is also instructed to record the deed. See Caruso v. Parkos, 637 N.W.2d 351 (Neb. 2002).

5. *"Beneficiary deeds" or "Transfer on Death" deeds.* The desire of people to leave their land to others at death without making a will or a trust is obvious from the materials above. Why not let them do it? That is precisely the purpose of the "beneficiary" or "transfer on death" (TOD) deed. At this writing, about twenty U.S. jurisdictions have authorized TOD deeds.

must recd formalities needed

A TOD deed is executed and recorded during the lifetime of the grantor, but becomes effective only at death. There is no interest of any kind, present or future, in the grantee until the grantor dies. The grantor can revoke the deed at any time before death, typically by recording a notice of revocation or by deeding the property to someone else prior to death. If the deed is not revoked, it will pass whatever interest the grantor holds in the property at the time of death, subject to any mortgages, liens, or other encumbrances imposed on the property during the grantor's life.

The TOD deed fills an obvious need, and is likely to become more popular in the future. Several additional state legislatures are considering adoption of statutes authorizing TOD deeds at this writing, and in 2009 the Commissioners on Uniform State Laws released the "Uniform Real Property Transfer on Death Act," which has been adopted by thirteen states and the District of Columbia.

Yet the TOD deed raises a question. It is clearly "testamentary" in the sense that, like a will, it speaks only at the grantor's death. Hence questions about the grantor's capacity and intent are likely to be raised only after the grantor is dead and cannot testify. Yet TOD deeds, like other deeds, are required to be executed with only minimal formalities: a signature, acknowledgment, and recording. Is this adequate, or should the law require execution like a will, with two witnesses who sign in the presence of the grantor and each other?

Assume in a jurisdiction that has adopted a TOD deed statute, a grantor delivers a deed with an express (oral) statement that it is to be effective only upon the grantor's death. Does it still make sense for a court to hold, as in *Wiggill,* that the deed is void because the grantor's intent is testamentary? Or does the existence of the TOD statute signal that the policy underlying the Statute of Wills, with its accompanying formalities, is no longer important enough to demand strict adherence?

2. DEFECTIVE DEEDS

One suspects that the actual outcomes of cases of disputed delivery or acceptance are often influenced by whether the land has passed into the hands of a bona fide purchaser (BFP), although most courts would say that any such consideration is legally irrelevant, and that an undelivered deed is entirely void and cannot pass title, even to a BFP. This brings us to a more general discussion of the impact of the presence of a subsequent BFP on an otherwise defective deed.

If there is a legal defect in the drafting, execution, or delivery of a deed, we need to consider what legal consequences will ensue. Of course, if the error is simply a mistake or inadvertence, equity will reform the deed at the instance of one of the parties. If the defect is very minor, such as the omission of a seal or an acknowledgment (in the few states that require them for validity), it is often possible to find a "curative act" passed by the legislature which restores such deeds to full validity after the passage of a few years.

Our concern here is with defects that are more substantial, including such matters as the grantor's incapacity and the grantee's fraud or forgery. Here there are two possible classifications: the deed may be either *void* or *voidable.* In either case, if the grantee has not made a further conveyance, a court will set aside the deed upon the grantor's request. The distinction between a void deed and a deed that is merely voidable arises if the grantee has subsequently transferred the land to a bona fide purchaser who has paid value and has taken title from the grantee without notice of the defect. If the court treats the defect as rendering the deed void, even the BFP will have no title. If, however, the deed is merely voidable, then the title will be unassailable in the hands of the BFP.

Obviously, one can be a BFP without notice that title is based on a void deed. Frequently, the defect making the deed void will be of such a nature that even the most careful inspection of the recorded deed will not reveal it (as in the case of lack of delivery, for example). Those who search and insure titles would probably prefer that the law treat all defects as making the grantee's title merely voidable, thus protecting innocent future buyers (and their lawyers and title insurers).

Incidentally, in cases in which the grantor continues to possess the land, his or her very presence will serve as notice to future buyers, and one who fails to make inquiry of the person in possession will generally be held to have whatever knowledge a reasonable inquiry would have produced. Hence, it is nearly impossible to become a BFP in such circumstances. See, e.g., Houston v. Mentelos, 318 So.2d 427 (Fla. App. 1975); Stevens v. American Sav. Inst., Inc., 289 Or. 349, 613 P.2d 1057 (1980). But of course grantors are not always in possession of their land.

Of all the categories of defects in deeds, perhaps the one as to which the law is clearest is forgery—a false signature, or an addition, deletion, or alteration to the essential language of the deed after it is signed. Such a deed is void, and unavailing even in the hands of a BFP who has no notice of the forgery. In *Harding v. Ja Laur Corp.*, 20 Md. App. 209, 315 A.2d 132 (1974), the grantee obtained the grantor's signature on a blank piece of paper, and later affixed it to a deed. The court classified it as a forgery, and observed:

> [T]he common law rule that a forger can pass no better title than he has is in full force and effect in this State. * * * A forger, having no title can pass none to his vendee. * * * Consequently, there can be no bona fide holder of title under a forged deed. A forged deed, unlike one procured by fraud, deceit or trickery is void from its inception. The distinction between a deed obtained by fraud and one that has been forged is readily apparent. In a fraudulent deed an innocent purchaser is protected because the fraud practiced upon the signatory to such a deed is brought into play, at least in part, by some act or omission on the part of the person upon whom the fraud is perpetrated. He has helped in some degree to set into motion the very fraud about which he later complains. A forged deed, on the other hand, does not necessarily involve any action on the part of the person against whom the forgery is committed. So that if a person has two deeds presented to him, and he thinks he is signing one but in actuality, because of fraud, deceit or trickery he signs the other, a bona fide purchaser, without notice, is protected. On the other hand, if a person is presented with a deed, and he signs that deed but the deed is thereafter altered e.g. through a change in the description or affixing the signature page to another deed, that is forgery and a subsequent purchaser takes no title.

Nearly all courts agree that forged deeds are void. See Zurstrassen v. Stonier, 786 So. 2d 65 (Fla. App. 2001); Northlake Dev. L.L.C. v. BankPlus, 60 So. 3d 792 (Miss. 2011); Scott D. Erler, D.D.S. Profit Sharing Plan v. Creative Fin. & Investments, L.L.C., 203 P.3d 744 (Mont. 2009) (forged deed void, but could be ratified by purported grantor); Neuman v. Neumann, 971 N.Y.S.2d 322 (N.Y. App. Div. 2013) (deed given by grantor with forged power of attorney was void).

Strangely, forged releases of mortgages are not necessarily treated as strictly; see Schiavon v. Arnaudo Bros., 100 Cal. Rptr. 2d 801 (Cal.App. 2000) (reconveyance of deed of trust was voidable, and good in the hands of a BFP, although it was based on a forged request for reconveyance); Bank of New York v. Langman, 986 N.E.2d 749 (Ill. App. 2013) (forged release of mortgage was voidable).

The Maryland court's statements about fraud making a deed merely voidable bear further scrutiny. Many cases distinguish two types of fraud. One type, sometimes termed "fraud in the inducement," involves misrepresentations which persuade the grantor to sign the deed, such as the tender of a worthless check or false statements about the grantee's financial position. In such cases the deed is nearly always held voidable, not void. See Malcom v. Wilson, 534 So. 2d 241 (Ala. 1988) (grantee induced grantor to sign deed by falsely asserting that she was pregnant with his child and by threatening him with legal action and bodily harm).

On the other hand, the fraud may consist of a false statement to the grantor about the nature of the instrument itself, such as telling him that it is a letter, a lease or a contract, or it may involve slipping a deed in among other innocuous papers which the grantor is signing. Such behavior is sometimes called "fraud in the factum." Here the cases diverge, with some holding the deed void, especially if the grantor is old, illiterate, disabled, confused, or has reason to place particular reliance on the trustworthiness of the grantee. See Tafolla v. Tafolla, 2011 WL 1466472 (Cal. App. 2011) (not reported in Cal. Rptr.); Valle v. Washington Mut. Bank, 2009 WL 1919392 (Cal. App. 2009) (referring to a fraud in the factum execution as a "forgery"); Houston v. Mentelos, 318 So. 2d 427 (Fla. App. 1975); Hoffer v. Crawford, 65 N.W.2d 625 (N.D. 1954). Such cases seem to the courts to be tantamount to forgery. But if the grantor is competent and alert, and deals with the grantee at arm's length, the court is more likely to paste the "voidable" label on the deed, protecting the later BFP. The court may even call the grantor negligent for his failure to examine more closely the documents he signed. Compare Dines v. Ultimo, 532 So. 2d 1131 (Fla. App. 1988) (grantors were told they were signing credit references; conveyance valid in hands of a BFP) with Fronning v. Blume, 429 N.W.2d 310 (Minn. App. 1988) (grantors were told they were signing a description of their farm; conveyance held void).

Finally, there are cases in which the grantee knows that the instrument is a deed, but its contents or details are falsely represented to him by the grantor. Here, the usual result is like that of fraud in the inducement, and the deed is merely voidable, even if the grantor is illiterate or feeble. See Jenkins v. Maint., Inc., 76 N.C. App. 110, 332 S.E.2d 90 (1985); McCoy v. Love, 382 So. 2d 647 (Fla. 1979).

Lack of delivery is the other defect which traditionally makes a deed absolutely void. See Stone v. French, 37 Kan. 145, 14 P. 530 (1887) (a classic case); Blancett v. Blancett, 136 N.M. 573, 102 P.3d 640 (2004). But here too, the desire of the courts to protect the BFP is sometimes irrepressible. For example, in Webb v. Stewart, 255 Or. 523, 469 P.2d 609 (1970), the grantor handed the deed to the grantee to place in escrow; the escrow company was expected to deliver the deed later when the grantee paid for the land. Instead, the grantee took the deed to the courthouse and recorded it, and then gave a mortgage on it. The court thought the deed should be deemed voidable rather than void. Ultimately, it made no difference in the outcome because the mortgagee had constructive notice of the grantor's continued interest from his possession of the property and hence was held not to be a BFP without notice of the deed's defect. Compare this result with the situation where an escrow agent wrongfully delivers a deed out of escrow to a grantee. See the discussion infra at Section C.3, Note 9.

Numerous other types of defects are fairly uniformly held to make deeds merely voidable. These include the incompetency or incapacity of the grantor (unless it is a matter of public record), duress or undue influence exercised by the grantee, and infancy. See, e.g., Matter of LeBovici, 171 Misc. 2d 604, 655 N.Y.S.2d 305 (1997); First Interstate Bank v. First Wyoming Bank, 762 P.2d 379 (Wyo. 1988). Contra, see Scott v. Nelson, 820 So. 2d 23 (Miss. App. 2002) (deed by grantor who was incompetent and under conservatorship held void). All in all, the courts seem to be drifting toward an increasingly pro-BFP position. Is there anything wrong with that? Should the rule simply be that any recorded deed is conclusively presumed good if necessary to protect a BFP? Or should forgery be the sole exception to such a rule?

3. ESCROW CLOSINGS

We have already intimated that an *escrow* may be used to effect the closing of a real estate sale and the delivery of a deed. Literally, an escrow is a delivery of a deed by the grantor to an independent third party with instructions that it be delivered to the grantee upon the occurrence of certain stated conditions. The deed is "made out" to the grantee, not the escrow agent. The conditions may be as complex as desired, but the most common is the payment to the escrow agent by the grantee of the remainder of the cash purchase price. The escrow agent is usually responsible for disbursing the funds thus deposited in an appropriate manner—i.e., by paying off and discharging any existing mortgages and other encumbrances to which the buyer is not taking subject, by sending checks to the title insurer, surveyor, property inspector, and other providers of ancillary services in connection with the transfer (including the escrow agent's own fee), and finally by remitting the balance of the funds to the seller.

There is obviously no legal requirement that any real estate transaction be closed through escrow, and in some areas of the nation escrows are almost unheard of. They are widely used in larger urban areas throughout much of the country, and are virtually universal for property sales in the West Coast states and Mountain West states.

The escrow concept is useful in several respects. First, it places a person or entity with considerable expertise in the role of computing the flows of funds, assembling and recording the necessary documents, and performing the other mechanical (but rather complex) functions necessary to complete a real estate sale. Of course, other entities such as lawyers and lenders could do this as well, and in fact they do so in many areas. But the escrow has further advantages. It avoids the inconvenience of a face-to-face closing, in which all of the parties must gather in the same room to "pass the papers." When an escrow is used, the documents and checks may be signed by the parties at any convenient time and left with the escrow agent. Then on the designated closing date, he or she "closes" the escrow simply by recording the conveyances.

The escrow device provides an easy method of making sure that the seller's title remains clear down to the very moment of closing, since the escrow agent can perform a "down-date" of the title search just before recording, and can refrain from closing if a recently recorded adverse conveyance is found. In jurisdictions which do not use escrows, there is often a gap of a few days or a week between the time of the title search and the closing. Sometimes lawyers in these jurisdictions deal with the problem by actually closing in or near the courthouse, and doing a title down-date immediately before or after the closing, but this can be inconvenient as well.

Finally, if the legal prerequisites are met, the escrow has a "relation back" feature. The ultimate delivery to the grantee by the escrow agent is usually deemed to relate back to the date the grantor placed the deed in escrow. Particularly in cases of the grantor's intervening incompetence or death, "relation back" makes the delivery valid. In jurisdictions which do not use escrows, such events are not fatal to the transaction, but they can bog the grantee down in a search for the grantor's heirs or devisees (if the grantor has died) or the appointment of a guardian or conservator (if the grantor has become incompetent). Escrow makes these efforts unnecessary.

Despite these advantages, escrows are a mixed blessing. On the West Coast, where "independent" escrow companies (having no other connection with the transaction) are commonly used, the cost of the escrow company's services can be very substantial. For the sale of an ordinary home, the escrow fee may range from a few hundred dollars to (in California) more than $1,000. Plainly the use of independent escrow agents can contribute to high overall settlement costs. It is probably more efficient to use an entity already involved in the transaction, such as the lending institution which is providing the financing or the title insurer.

It is common, and certainly a desirable practice, for the parties to submit written escrow instructions to the escrow agent. They may each submit their own, or may both sign the same set of instructions. It is important, of course, that there be no conflict between the instructions of the buyer and the seller, and no conflict between the escrow instructions and the contract of sale.

NOTES AND QUESTIONS

1. *Additional readings.* By far the best treatment of escrows (although now somewhat dated and oriented toward Illinois law) is Mann, Escrows— Their Use and Value, 1949 U. Ill. L. F. 398. See also Note, Escrow Agreements, 8 Miami L.Q. 75 (1953); Note, Survey of Escrow—A Legal Adolescent, 8 Ark. L. Rev. 164 (1954).

2. *Attorneys as escrow agents.* It is clear that the escrow agent must be a "third" party, and not one of the parties to the transaction itself. There seems to be no legal objection in most jurisdictions to an attorney for one or both of the parties serving as their escrowee. See Fisk v. Peoples Liberty Bank & Trust Co., 570 S.W.2d 657 (Ky. App. 1978). But see Galvanek v. Skibitcky, 55 Conn. App. 254, 738 A.2d 1150 (1999); Patel v. Gannaway, 726 F.2d 382 (8th Cir. 1984) (court cautioned lawyers about the ethical risks of serving as an escrowee while at the same time representing one of the parties as an attorney). Do you think this is a good practice? Can you envision situations where there is an irreconcilable conflict between the duty of fairness to both parties that an escrow agent is expected to fulfill and the attorney's professional responsibilities in the representation of her or his client?

3. *Requirements for a "true" escrow.* In order to have a "true" escrow (the significance of which will be discussed below), at least two additional requirements usually are imposed:

(a) The grantor, when depositing the deed with the escrow agent, must not reserve any power to recall it. See Malcolm v. Tate, 125 Or. 419, 267 P. 527 (1928); Loubat v. Kipp & Young, 9 Fla. 60 (1860).

(b) The parties must have entered into an enforceable contract of sale. See Merry v. County Bd. of Educ., 264 Ala. 411, 87 So. 2d 821 (1956), noted 9 Ala. L. Rev. 130 (1956); Johnson v. Wallden, 342 Ill. 201, 173 N.E. 790 (1930); Jozefowicz v. Leickem, 174 Wis. 475, 182 N.W. 729 (1921).

4. *Characteristics of a "true" escrow.* If a "true" escrow exists, the most important result is that the second delivery (to the grantee) will relate back in time to the first delivery (to the escrowee), and hence will be valid irrespective of the grantor's intervening death or incompetence. See, e.g., Donnelly v. Robinson, 406 S.W.2d 595 (Mo. 1966); Morris v. Clark, 100 Utah 252, 112 P.2d 153 (1941). This "relation back" is obviously fictitious, and will not inevitably apply in all situations. Its purpose is to prevent injustice and effectuate the intention of the parties. See Clodfelter v. Van Fossan, 394 Ill. 29, 67 N.E.2d 182 (1946); Mann, supra note 1, at 413.

In addition, a "true" escrow puts the deed beyond the grantor's control pending the second delivery. The grantor has no right to withdraw it from the escrow, and if he or she purports to give a second deed to another grantee who has notice of the escrow, that deed will pass nothing. See Chaffin v. Harpham, 166 Ark. 578, 266 S.W. 685 (1924); DeBoer v. Oakbrook Home Ass'n, Inc., 218 Neb. 813, 359 N.W.2d 768 (1984). This insulation of the grantor from the deed applies only so long as the underlying sales contract remains enforceable. If the underlying sales contract is terminated by agreement or breached by the purchaser, the grantor can then get the deed back.

If the purported escrow is not a "true" escrow as defined by the concepts of note 3, supra, contrary results follow. There is no relation back, and the grantor may reclaim the deed from the escrow at any time prior to the second delivery, presumably whether any express right to do so has been reserved or not. Nonetheless, the escrow is not void, and if the grantor remains alive and competent, and makes no attempt to withdraw the deed, there is no reason why the second delivery should not constitute a valid transfer of title.

It is perhaps plausible that the relation back concept should be defeated if the grantor has a power to recall the deed, since on such facts we cannot really be certain that he or she intended to go through with the transfer until it actually occurs. But what is the justification for the requirement that there be an underlying enforceable contract? Would any policy be disserved if even pure gifts through escrow, with no contract of sale at all, were allowed to relate back? (Indeed, they are in the limited context of the death escrow, discussed earlier in this section.) The contract requirement was vigorously criticized by Ralph Aigler, Is a Contract Necessary to Create an Effective Escrow?, 16 Mich. L. Rev. 569 (1918).

5. *Escrow instructions and the Statute of Frauds.* Somewhat ironically, the very presence of an escrow may make a contract enforceable. If the contract was oral, and hence out of compliance with the Statute of Frauds, the written escrow instructions may supply the requisite memorandum. See Wood Bldg. Corp. v. Griffitts, 164 Cal. App. 2d 559, 330 P.2d 847 (1958). Incidentally, the Statute of Frauds does not apply to the escrow instructions themselves, since they do not constitute a contract for the sale of realty; thus, they are enforceable though oral; see Lewis v. Shawnee State Bank, 226 Kan. 41, 596 P.2d 116 (1979); Young v. Bishop, 88 Ariz. 140, 353 P.2d 1017 (1960).

Moreover, the courts are fairly lenient in supplying omitted terms or correcting confusing instructions, even if there is a writing; see, e.g., Animalfeeds Int'l Inc. v. Banco Espirito Santo E Comercial De Lisboa, 101 Misc. 2d 379, 420 N.Y.S.2d 954 (1979); Shaheen v. American Title Ins. Co., 120 Ariz. 505, 586 P.2d 1317 (App. 1978) (escrowee had authority to disburse sale proceeds to seller, although instructions did not so state.) But of course the better practice is to prepare careful, thorough written instructions.

Yet written escrow instructions can also pose problems. Suppose there is a conflict between the original contract and the instructions; which should prevail? If the contract did not make time of the essence, but the escrow instructions do, what is the result? Should lawyers advise incorporating the contract by reference into the instructions, or combining both into a single document?

6. *When does title pass?* The very essence of an escrow is that the "closing" (i.e., the second delivery) cannot occur until various conditions have been met. Suppose they have been met, but the escrow agent has not yet recorded the deed or manually delivered it to the grantee. Has legal title passed? The question might be important if, for example, a creditor of the grantor attempts to attach the property at that point; see Lowry v. C.I.R., 171 F. App'x 6 (9th Cir. 2006), Matter of Berkley Multi-Units, Inc., 69 B.R. 638 (Bankr. M.D. Fla. 1987), and Sturgill v. Indus. Painting Corp., 82 Nev. 61, 410 P.2d 759 (1966), holding that title passes when the last condition occurs, irrespective of recording or physical delivery; Cf. TDNI Properties, LLC v. Saratoga Glen Builders, LLC, 914 N.Y.S.2d 746 (N.Y. App. Div. 2011) (title passes only when escrow agent delivers deed); Roberts v. Osburn, 589 P.2d 985 (Kan.App. 1979) (same). Does the doctrine of relation back make this point irrelevant?

7. *Duties of escrow agents.* An escrow agent occupies a fiduciary position with respect to the parties, and will be held liable for negligence or breach of instructions. See, e.g., Banville v. Schmidt, 37 Cal. App. 3d 92, 112 Cal. Rptr. 126 (1974) (negligence); Miller v. Craig, 27 Ariz. App. 789, 558 P.2d 984 (1976) (instructions). Cf. Jafari v. F.D.I.C., 2 F.Supp.3d 1125 (S.D.Cal. 2014) (no duty owed to third party who expected to receive proceeds of escrow).

Closer questions arise when the escrow agent fails to disclose to one of the parties information it obtains from the other party, or from its general business dealings. See Karen Jacobsen, California Escrow Agents: A Duty to Disclose Known Fraud?, 17 Pac. L. J. 309 (1985). This issue is most common when the escrowee is also a title insurance company and has particular knowledge of title problems with the property, but has not been specifically instructed to investigate the title or write an insurance policy on it. See, e.g., Axley v. Transamerica Title Ins. Co., 88 Cal. App. 3d 1, 151 Cal. Rptr. 570 (1978) (no duty to warn seller that she was undersecured by deeds of trust); Shaheen v. American Title Ins. Co., 120 Ariz. 505, 586 P.2d 1317 (App. 1978) (no duty to inform party of title defects, where no title insurance purchased);

Gordon v. New Mexico Title Co., 77 N.M. 217, 421 P.2d 433 (1966) (no duty to investigate presence of unfiled mechanic's liens.)

There is a good deal of authority that an escrow agent who discovers fraud, or facts which suggest fraud, by one party has a duty to disclose them to the other party. See Mark Props. v. Nat'l Title Co., 116 Nev. 1158, 14 P.3d 507 (2000); Manley v. Ticor Title Ins. Co., 168 Ariz. 568, 816 P.2d 225 (1991); Sargeant & Hill, Recent Developments in Title Insurance Law, 36 Tort & Ins. L.J. 605 (2001). Do you think escrow agents should be forced into the "traffic cop" mode by the courts?

Suppose the escrowee purports (in the printed instructions) to exculpate itself from liability for negligence or failure to follow instructions. A California court held such an attempt ineffective in Akin v. Business Title Corp., 264 Cal. App. 2d 153, 70 Cal. Rptr. 287 (1968). Should this result follow if the escrowee is not generally in the escrow business, and is merely serving as an accommodation to the parties?

8.   *Risk of loss from an escrow agent's default.* If an escrow agent absconds with the funds and is unavailable for suit, who stands the loss? The usual answer depends on whether title has passed or not. If it has, the money belongs to the seller, who must stand the loss; if title has not passed, it was the buyer's money that was stolen. See, e.g., In re Brown, 28 Fed. Appx. 725 (9th Cir. 2002) (Washington law); Bixby Ranch Co. v. United States, 35 Fed. Cl. 674 (1996). Here is a situation in which the time of passage of title, discussed in note 6 supra, clearly matters! The same rule is usually applied to closings handled by attorneys or others which are not technically escrows, but which raise the same problems when the closing agent decamps with the dollars. See, e.g., Lawyers Title Ins. Corp. v. Edmar Const. Co., Inc., 294 A.2d 865 (D.C.App. 1972). Does this insistence in placing all of the loss on one party or the other make sense? After all, the crook was really employed by both parties.

If title insurance is being issued in connection with the escrow, the title insurer may provide a "closing protection letter" to the insured, in effect promising to indemnify the insured if the escrow holder embezzles funds. See, e.g., GE Capital Mortg. Services, Inc. v. Privetera, 346 N.J. Super. 424, 788 A.2d 324 (App. Div. 2002), holding that such a letter did not protect the holder of a prior mortgage, who was not being insured by the title company.

Where the escrow or closing agent is a lawyer for one of the parties, the normal loss allocation rule mentioned above might not be followed. In *Johnson v. Schultz*, 691 S.E.2d 701 (N.C. 2010), the attorney embezzled the sale proceeds after the closing occurred. The court noted that the custom in North Carolina was for the attorney to represent the buyer, even though he might also prepare a deed or perform other services for the seller as well. The court also thought the buyer was in a better position than the seller to protect against the lawyer's default by obtaining a closing protection letter from the title insurance company. Hence it imposed the loss on the buyer.

9. *Wrongful delivery by escrow agents.* Perhaps the most interesting legal issue arising from escrows involves a wrongful second delivery. Suppose the essential conditions have not yet been fulfilled, but the grantee somehow obtains the deed from the escrowee—by theft, fraud, or perhaps by bribing the escrow holder. Everyone would agree that the grantee cannot claim title, for there is no intent on the part of the grantor to make a delivery yet. See Allen v. Allen Title Co., 77 N.M. 796, 427 P.2d 673 (1967). But if the grantee nevertheless records the deed and immediately resells to a bona fide purchaser, who will prevail as between the BFP and the grantor? From the BFP's viewpoint the title appears perfect (assuming the grantor is not in possession of the land). Is the grantor equally innocent? To put the question slightly differently, is the purported transfer void or voidable? The prevailing view (from which there is considerable dissent, both scholarly and judicial) is that the deed is void (just as in the case of an undelivered deed stolen directly from the grantor.) See, e.g., Miguel v. Belzeski, 797 F. Supp. 636 (N.D. Ill. 1992) (Illinois law); Clevenger v. Moore, 126 Okl. 246, 259 P. 219, 54 A.L.R. 1237 (1927); Watts v. Archer, 252 Iowa 592, 107 N.W.2d 549 (1961). The contrary cases are collected in Am. Jur. 2d Escrow § 26; see also Annot., 54 A.L.R. 1246 (1928).

D. LIABILITY OF SELLERS FOR PROPERTY DEFECTS

Traditional case law held that mere silence concerning defects by the seller of real estate was not actionable unless the seller engaged in other conduct, such as active concealment efforts, that made the silence misleading. See, e.g., Swiedler v. Ferguson, 393 S.E.2d 456 (Ga. App. 1990). The following case illustrates that this view is rapidly evolving, with courts becoming quite willing to impose liability for silence if the matter not disclosed is "material," is not known to the buyer or obvious on a routine inspection, and the seller is aware of it.

JENSEN V. BAILEY
Florida Court of Appeals, 2011
76 So. 3d 980

WALLACE, JUDGE

Eric Jensen and Joyce Jensen appeal a final judgment awarding damages against them and in favor of Cynthia Bailey on her claim for the Jensens' failure to disclose material defects in their residence to Mrs. Bailey under *Johnson v. Davis*, 480 So. 2d 625 (Fla.1985). Because the circuit court found that the Jensens had no knowledge of the defects but improperly found the Jensens liable to Mrs. Bailey under a "should have known" standard, we reverse the final judgment.

I. The Facts and the Procedural Background

In June 2005, the Jensens entered into a contract with Gene Bailey and Cynthia Bailey for the sale and purchase of the Jensens' residence in St. Petersburg. Before the parties signed the contract, the Jensens filled out a property disclosure statement for the Baileys' review. One of the questions on the disclosure statement asked whether the sellers were aware "of any improvements or additions to the property, whether by you or by others, that have been constructed in violation of building codes or without necessary permits?" In response to this question, the Jensens checked the "NO" box. The parties closed the sale in July 2005, and the Baileys took possession of the property.

Approximately two years later, the Baileys filed an action for damages against the Jensens. In their complaint, the Baileys alleged claims for breach of contract, nondisclosure of material defects in the residence under Johnson, and fraudulent concealment. The Jensens filed an answer denying the material allegations of the complaint and raised affirmative defenses. Mr. Bailey died while the action was pending in the circuit court, and Mrs. Bailey continued the action as the sole plaintiff.

II. The Circuit Court's Verdict and the Final Judgment

After a bench trial that lasted two days, the circuit court entered a detailed verdict in favor of Mrs. Bailey on her nondisclosure claim under *Johnson*. In the verdict, the circuit court ruled, in pertinent part, as follows:

> At trial two main categories of problems emerged. One was the alleged defective sanitary sewer which caused reoccurring backups into the home. The other was a trio of unpermitted changes in the home which were discovered to be not in conformity with building codes and would thus require reconstruction.

> After careful consideration the court finds the evidence insufficient to support [Mrs. Bailey's] claims regarding the sewer system. On the other hand, the evidence was that . . . the [Jensens] had substantial remodeling work done in their master bath, their kitchen, and in the bedroom by the installation of French doors. It was uncontroverted that these three jobs required proper permits. The evidence supports the conclusion that neither the [Jensens] nor those who they hired obtained the permits. Expert testimony indicated that the work was not properly done, did not conform to the codes applicable when done, and would require reconstruction in full conformity with newer, more stringent codes.

There was no evidence that the [Jensens] actually knew about the failure to obtain permits or the improper work. They, like perhaps many trusting people, relied upon the individuals or companies they hired to do the work legally and in a proper fashion.

These facts presented a difficult question regarding the extent to which Florida law will protect a buyer in a residential real estate transaction from material defects which are not actually known to the seller but should have been known by them. As a practical matter, homeowners have a responsibility to obtain proper permits and generally can find no protection from their failure to do so because they merely relied on someone else to do so. Since such permits are required, it does not seem an unreasonable conclusion that the homeowner is likewise expected to know whether the permits were actually issued and posted for the construction. These logical assumptions appear to be the foundation for the questions presented to sellers in the typical real property disclosure forms. That is, the owner is expected to know about these important matters with regard to their property because they are in a position to need to know.

The circuit court concluded "that the proofs support a *Johnson v. Davis* claim [that] the [Jensens] should have known about the absence of permits and reported same in the disclosure statement. As a result [, Mrs. Bailey is] entitled to relief." Based on the verdict, the circuit court entered a final judgment in favor of Mrs. Bailey and against the Jensens for $33,370 in damages, plus $13,787.31 in prejudgment interest. The Jensens' appeal followed, and Mrs. Bailey filed a cross-appeal.

III. The Parties' Arguments

On their direct appeal, the Jensens make several arguments. However, we need only address the Jensens' argument that the circuit court erred in finding them liable to Mrs. Bailey on her nondisclosure claim based on a "should have known" standard. On the cross-appeal, Mrs. Bailey contends that the circuit court erred in finding that the Jensens did not have actual knowledge of the asserted material defects in the residence.

IV. Framing the Issues

This case requires us to decide whether liability under the rule in *Johnson* may be based on a finding of the seller's constructive knowledge of an undisclosed material defect instead of his or her actual knowledge. We conclude that to hold the seller liable under *Johnson*, the buyer must prove the seller's actual knowledge of an undisclosed material defect. Accordingly, on the direct appeal, we reverse the circuit court's final judgment finding the Jensens liable to Mrs. Bailey under a "should have known" standard.

On the cross-appeal, we affirm. The circuit court's finding that the Jensens did not have actual knowledge of the asserted undisclosed material defects is supported by substantial, competent evidence, and the issue raised on the cross-appeal does not warrant further discussion. We turn now to an examination of the issue raised on the Jensens' direct appeal concerning the knowledge element under *Johnson*.

V. Discussion

A nondisclosure claim under *Johnson* has four elements: (1) the seller of a home must have knowledge of a defect in the property, (2) the defect must materially affect the value of the property, (3) the defect must be not readily observable and must be unknown to the buyer, and (4) the buyer must establish that the seller failed to disclose the defect to the buyer. 480 So. 2d at 629. Here, we address the first element, the seller's knowledge of a defect in the property.

Notably, the only consideration pertinent to the seller's state of mind under *Johnson* is knowledge of a defect materially affecting the value of the property at the time the seller enters into the contract with the buyer. Billian v. Mobil Corp., 710 So. 2d 984, 988 (Fla. 4th DCA 1998). As the Fourth District has explained:

> *Johnson* does not specify any state of mind element with regard to the act of non-disclosure for the cause of action it identifies. . . . Significantly, *Johnson* casts the cause of action in terms of "duty," a concept drawn from the law of negligence. If the facts of a case give rise to a duty to disclose under *Johnson*, the seller's state of mind motivating the failure to disclose is immaterial; the forgetful or unsophisticated seller is just as liable as the knowing dissembler.

Id. Thus the critical issue under the first element of liability under *Johnson* is the seller's knowledge, not his or her intent. The question raised by this case is whether anything less than actual knowledge is sufficient to satisfy the first element.

The late Chief Justice Joseph Boyd dissented in *Johnson*, and he raised this question in his dissent. Chief Justice Boyd expressed his fear that the majority's holding in *Johnson* would lead to "making the seller a guarantor of the good condition of the property" and thus "significantly burden the alienability of property." 480 So. 2d at 631 (Boyd, C.J., dissenting). He predicted that the courts would ultimately construe *Johnson*'s requirement of actual knowledge to permit a finding of liability based on constructive knowledge:

The trend will proceed somewhat as follows. At first, the cause of action will require proof of actual knowledge of the undisclosed defect on the part of the seller. But in many cases the courts will allow it to be shown by circumstantial evidence. Then a rule of constructive knowledge will develop based on the reasoning that if the seller did not know of the defect, he should have known about it before attempting to sell the property. Thus the burden of inspection will shift from the buyer to the seller. Ultimately the courts will be in the position of imposing implied warranties and guaranties on all sellers of real property.

Id. This case proves that Chief Justice Boyd's fear about the eventual effect of the majority's holding in *Johnson* was not completely unjustified. Here, the circuit court found the Jensens liable to Mrs. Bailey in the absence of proof of their actual knowledge of the asserted material defects based on a "should have known" standard.

However, this court has consistently reversed judgments in favor of the buyer for nondisclosure under *Johnson* in the absence of proof of the seller's actual knowledge of the defect. See Brown v. Carter, 13 So.3d 111, 113–14 (Fla. 2d DCA 2009); Spitale v. Smith, 721 So. 2d 341, 345 (Fla. 2d DCA 1998); Slitor v. Elias, 544 So. 2d 255, 258–59 (Fla. 2d DCA 1989). In *Slitor*, we said:

> *Johnson* does not convert a seller of a house into a guarantor of the condition of the house. As we have said, to prove a cause of action under *Johnson*, a buyer of a house must prove the seller's knowledge of a defect which materially affected the value of the house. While knowledge in this regard can be proven by circumstantial evidence, it must nevertheless be proven by competent, sufficient evidence which, as we have explained, did not exist here.

Id. (citation omitted). Other Florida courts have recognized that liability for nondisclosure under *Johnson* requires proof of the seller's actual knowledge of the defect. See Billian, 710 So. 2d at 988 ("*Johnson* creates a duty to disclose where a seller knows of certain facts under circumstances giving rise to the duty"); Haskell Co. v. Lane Co., 612 So. 2d 669, 674 (Fla. 1st DCA 1993) (quoting Slitor, 544 So. 2d at 258, for the proposition that "*Johnson* does not convert a seller of a house into a guarantor of the condition of the house").

In reaching a contrary conclusion, the circuit court relied on two cases, *Nystrom v. Cabada*, 652 So. 2d 1266 (Fla. 2d DCA 1995), and *Revitz v. Terrell*, 572 So. 2d 996 (Fla. 3d DCA 1990). The circuit court concluded that each of these cases supported the use of a "should have known" liability standard for nondisclosure claims under *Johnson*. We read these cases differently.

In the *Nystrom* case, Mr. Nystrom, acting as his own contractor, had constructed the residence in question and had occupied it for one year before selling it. 652 So. 2d at 1267. Although Mr. Nystrom was not a licensed contractor, he had extensive experience in the construction industry and had performed all of the carpentry work in the house. Id. at 1268. After the buyer moved into the house, she discovered that it had numerous structural defects. Id. at 1267. An engineering firm issued a report concluding that the house "was a 'hazardous building' in regard to high-wind resistance." Id. In the buyer's action against Mr. and Mrs. Nystrom, the trial court ruled in favor of the buyer. Id. at 1268.

On appeal, this court affirmed the trial court's finding of liability in favor of the buyer. Id. In upholding the trial court's determination of the Nystroms' liability, this court said:

> Since the serious structural defects which the experts found to exist all arose from the carpentry, the record supports the finding that Mr. Nystrom *knew or should have known* of these defects and had a duty to disclose them to [the buyer] under *Johnson v. Davis*, 480 So.2d 625 (Fla. 1985).

Id. at 1268 (emphasis added).

To be sure, the *Nystrom* court used the questionable "should have known" language in stating its conclusion in favor of the buyer on the liability issue. However, the facts in *Nystrom* showed that Mr. Nystrom, who had extensive experience in construction, built the residence, performed all of the carpentry work, and lived in the residence for one year before selling it to the buyer. The problems in the house resulted directly from the defective carpentry that Mr. Nystrom personally performed. It follows that Mr. Nystrom certainly had to know about the serious defects in the home because he had built it and lived in it before selling it to the buyer. Under these circumstances, the *Nystrom* court's use of the phrase "should have known" is a convenient or shorthand way to express the conclusion that the buyer established Mr. Nystroms' actual knowledge of the defects in the property through circumstantial evidence. *Nystrom* does not support using a "should have known" standard to find the Jensens liable for nondisclosure under *Johnson* on the very different facts in this case.

Revitz, the other case relied upon by the circuit court, involved a failure by the sellers' real estate agent to disclose to the buyer defects in a residence relating to building code violations and the availability of low-cost flood insurance for the property. 572 So. 2d at 996–97. The trial court ruled in favor of the sellers based on a finding that the undisclosed defects were not material as a matter of law. Id. at 998. On appeal, the Third District found that the trial court had used an incorrect test in determining that the undisclosed items were immaterial. Id. at 998–99.

For this reason, the Third District reversed the final judgment for the sellers and remanded the case to the trial court for further proceedings. Id. at 999.

In *Revitz*, the trial court did not make any findings concerning the real estate agent's knowledge of the undisclosed defects. Id. at 998 n. 6. Referring to the undisclosed problems, the Third District said that "[a]ssuming that the seller[s'] agent knew, or reasonably should have known, . . . there was a duty to disclose that fact to the buyer." Id. at 998. The Third District emphasized the evidence in the record tending to establish that the sellers' agent must have known of the undisclosed defects. Id. at 998 n. 6. The emphasis in the opinion on this evidence suggests that the *Revitz* court, like the *Nystrom* court, was using the phrase "should have known" as a shorthand reference to circumstantial evidence establishing the agent's actual knowledge. However, this question need not detain us. As the Third District said in its opinion, the basis for the reversal of the final judgment was "the trial court's misinterpretation of Florida law" on the issue of whether the undisclosed defects were material. Id. It follows that the Third District's discussion of the agent's knowledge of the undisclosed defects was dicta. Accordingly, *Revitz* does not support the circuit court's decision to base a determination of the Jensens' liability on a "should have known" standard. Furthermore, the circuit court was obligated to follow this court's decisions in *Brown*, *Spitale*, and *Slitor*, which require proof of the seller's actual knowledge of the defect to establish liability under *Johnson*.

VI. Conclusion

On the direct appeal, we reverse the final judgment in favor of Mrs. Bailey and remand for the entry of a final judgment in favor of the Jensens. On the cross-appeal, we find no error and affirm the circuit court's finding that the Jensens had no actual knowledge of the asserted material defects.

Affirmed in part, reversed in part, and remanded with directions.

NOTES AND QUESTIONS

1. *Types of real estate.* The ruling in the principal case is couched in terms of houses or residences. Doubtless most cases that arise do indeed deal with houses, but there is no reason that the principle of fraudulent concealment need be limited in that way. In *Johnson v. Davis*, the original 1985 Florida Supreme Court decision establishing the duty of disclosure in Florida, the court noted, "This duty is equally applicable to all forms of real property, new and used."

But there are contextual differences in the marketing and sale of residential and nonresidential real estate. First, it is much less probable that a seller will fill out a lengthy disclosure questionnaire for nonresidential property. Second, there is a much greater probability that the contract of sale for a nonresidential property will contain an "as is" clause, or perhaps a much more extensive clause disclaiming any duty on the seller's part to disclose anything. Whether such a clause will be effective in barring the seller's liability is open to serious question. These issues are explored in the following Notes.

2.   *Imputed knowledge of the seller.* Do you agree that it is unjust to charge a seller with liability for failure to disclose based on imputed knowledge—i.e., that the seller ought to have known, or had a duty to know, of the defect? See Anderson v. Kriser, 266 P.3d 819 (Utah 2011) (only actual knowledge will give rise to liability); Cook's Pest Control, Inc. v. Rebar, 28 So. 3d 716 (Ala. 2009) (same).

3.   *Reliance must be reasonable.* The case law is in general agreement that the plaintiff's reliance on the nondisclosure must be reasonable. As the *Jensen* opinion above puts it, "the defect must be not readily observable and must be unknown to the buyer." But many courts go well beyond the "not readily observable" standard. For example, in *Jackowski v. Borcheit*, 209 P.3d 514 (Wash. App. 2009), the court stated that "[i]n a fraudulent concealment claim, the plaintiff must prove the defect would not have been disclosed by a careful, reasonable inspection by the purchaser." Id. at 522. (imposing an expectation that the buyer will obtain professional inspections).

In Khindri v Getty Petroleum Mktg., Inc., 33 Misc. 3d 1208(A), 2011 WL 4904403 (N.Y. Sup. 2011), the state scheduled a hearing while the contract was pending on widening the road in front of the property, which would have prevented its use as a gas station as the purchasers intended. The court found that the reliance by the purchasers was insufficient. "Reliance is not 'justified' as required when the plaintiff reasonably could have discovered the true facts with due diligence. The prevailing rule today is that justifiable reliance does not exist when plaintiff has failed to inspect public records, meaning that such party had the means to discover the true nature of the transaction entered into by the exercise of ordinary intelligence and failed to make use of such means."

4.   *Active concealment.* An even stronger case for liability exists where the seller is shown to have taken active steps to hide the defect. See, e.g., Van Deusen v. Snead, 247 Va. 324, 441 S.E.2d 207 (1994) (seller put new mortar over foundation cracks to conceal them); Andreychak v. Lent, 257 N.J. Super. 69, 607 A.2d 1346 (1992) (seller of existing house with defective septic system had falsely obtained a city certification of the system, which buyers relied upon); George v. Lumbrazo, 184 A.D.2d 1050, 584 N.Y.S.2d 704 (1992) (seller paneled over wall to conceal cracks).

5.   *Additional risk factors.* Additional factors that tend to increase the probability of seller liability include the following:

- the property is a personal residence, purchased by an unsophisticated person.

- the defect is dangerous to health or safety. See, e.g., Roberts v. C & S Sovran Credit Corp., 621 So.2d 1294 (Ala. 1993) (seller could be liable for defective septic system as a "specific defect" that affects "health or safety").

- the seller personally created the defect, or previously attempted to repair it and failed to do so. See Anderson v. Harper, 424 Pa. Super. 161, 622 A.2d 319 (1993) (sellers had ineffectively attempted to repair septic system).

- the seller gave reassurances to the buyer about the quality of the improvements (e.g., "You have nothing to worry about so far as the roof is concerned.") See Brewer v. Brothers, 82 Ohio App. 3d 148, 611 N.E.2d 492 (1992). If the seller knows the statement to be false, the buyer may have a claim for affirmative misrepresentation. Even if the seller believes the statement to be true, the buyer may have a claim for rescission based on mutual mistake. See Harding v. Willie, 458 N.W.2d 612 (Iowa App. 1990).

6.   *Implied warranties on existing housing.* You will see when you read the next case that the courts have created implied warranties of quality in the sale of a *new* house by a builder-vendor. The courts have consistently refused to imply similar warranties in the sale of *existing* houses by ordinary consumers to one another. See Everts v. Parkinson, 147 N.C. App. 315, 555 S.E.2d 667 (2001). Thus, buyers of existing housing are limited to claims based on: (1) affirmative fraudulent misrepresentations; (2) nondisclosure claims under a *Johnson*-type standard; and (3) any express warranties or contractual covenants concerning the physical condition of the property that the seller may have given in the sales contract.

7.   *"Psychologically impacted" housing.* Is the supposed presence of ghosts in a house a "defect" that must be disclosed to the buyer? There has been a good deal of debate about "psychologically impacted" real estate, in which some past event or the characteristics of some past occupant are alleged to make the property undesirable. For example, in Reed v. King, 145 Cal. App. 3d 261, 193 Cal. Rptr. 130 (1983), the purchaser learned that the home she had bought was the site of a multiple murder ten years earlier. The court held that she had the opportunity to establish, at trial, that this was a material fact, in the sense that it had a significant effect on market value. If she could do so, she would be entitled to rescission and damages under the California law that requires affirmative disclosure of material facts. Compare this result with Stambovsky v. Ackley, 169 A.D.2d 254, 572 N.Y.S.2d 672 (1991), a case decided under New York law. The New York courts at the time followed the doctrine of caveat emptor, which is a minority approach, and imposed no duty of affirmative disclosure upon the seller regarding the physical condition of the premises. In *Stambovsky,* the court created an exception and imposed a duty on the seller to disclose to the out-of-town buyers that the house was "haunted," a belief that had been "deliberately

fostered" by the seller of the home to the local citizens for nine years prior to the sale of the home.

Other forms of past criminal activity may have more significant effects than ghosts. For example, if the site formerly was used for extensive illegal drug dealing or as a house of prostitution, the old customers may continue to return. (A relative of one of the authors once purchased a house in the latter category, and subsequently had a number of very interesting conversations with former "clients" who did not know the property had changed hands and uses.) Are these prior activities "material facts" that must be disclosed to the buyer?

Some courts have balked at the whole notion of "psychologically impacted" houses. In Milliken v. Jacono, 96 A.3d 997 (Pa. 2014), the house had been the site of a murder/suicide 14 months before the sellers placed it on the market. The court exonerated them for their failure to disclose it, finding that it was not a "material defect." The court commented:

> Regardless of the potential impact a psychological stigma may have on the value of property, we are not ready to accept that such constitutes a material defect. The implications of holding that non-disclosure of psychological stigma can form the basis of a common law claim for fraud or negligent misrepresentation, or a violation of the [Unfair Trade Practices statute's] catch-all, even under the objective standard posited by appellant, are palpable, and the varieties of traumatizing events that could occur on a property are endless. Efforts to define those that would warrant mandatory disclosure would be a Sisyphean task. One cannot quantify the psychological impact of different genres of murder, or suicide—does a bloodless death by poisoning or overdose create a less significant "defect" than a bloody one from a stabbing or shooting? How would one treat other violent crimes such as rape, assault, home invasion, or child abuse? What if the killings were elsewhere, but the sadistic serial killer lived there? What if satanic rituals were performed in the house?
>
> It is safe to assume all of the above are events a majority of the population would find disturbing, and a certain percentage of the population may not want to live in a house where any such event has occurred. However, this does not make the events defects in the structure itself. The occurrence of a tragic event inside a house does not affect the quality of the real estate, which is what seller disclosure duties are intended to address. We are not prepared to set a standard under which the visceral impact an event has on the populace serves to gauge whether its occurrence constitutes a material defect in property. Such a standard would be impossible to apply with consistency and would place an unmanageable burden on sellers, resulting in disclosures of tangential issues that threaten

to bury the pertinent information that disclosures are intended to convey.

Many states have adopted statutes that preclude liability of sellers for failure to disclose that a home is "psychologically impacted." The real estate brokerage industry has pressed aggressively for such statutes. The Idaho statute reproduced below is typical.

Idaho Code § 55–2801

"[P]sychologically impacted" means the effect of certain circumstances surrounding real property which include, but are not limited to, the fact or suspicion that real property might be or is impacted as a result of facts or suspicions including, but not limited to the follow:

(1) That an occupant or prior occupant of the real property is or was at any time suspected of being infected or has been infected with a disease which has been determined by medical evidence to be highly unlikely to be transmitted through the occupancy of a dwelling place;

(2) That the real property was at any time suspected of being the site of suicide, homicide or the commission of a felony which had no effect on the physical condition of the property or its environment or the structures located thereon; or

(3) That a registered or suspected sex offender occupied or resides near the property.

See also Shelley Ross Saxer, "Am I My Brother's Keeper?": Requiring Landowner Disclosure of the Presence of Sex Offenders and Other Criminal Activity, 80 Neb. L. Rev. 522 (2001); Williams, Stigmatized Property Law, 85 Mich. B. J. 34 (Feb. 2006); Fisk, Stigma Damages in Construction Defect Litigation: Feared by Defendants, Championed by Plaintiffs, Awarded by (Almost) No Courts—What Gives?, 53 Drake L. Rev. 1029 (2005).

8. *Discrimination based on handicap status.* Consider the impact of the federal Fair Housing Act, as amended in 1988.

42 U.S.C.A. § 3604(f)(1)

[It shall be unlawful to] discriminate in the sale or rental, or to otherwise make unavailable or deny, a dwelling to any buyer or renter because of a handicap of

(A) that buyer or renter;

(B) a person residing in or intending to reside in that dwelling after it is so sold, rented, or made available; or

(C) any person associated with that buyer or renter.

Suppose the seller of a house has AIDS. This illness is a "handicap" under the Fair Housing Act. See Baxter v. City of Belleville, 720 F. Supp. 720

(S.D. Ill. 1989); Association of Relatives and Friends of AIDS Patients (A.F.A.P.S.) v. Regulations and Permits Administration (A.R.P.E.), 740 F. Supp. 95 (D.P.R. 1990). If you were advising a real estate agent who was showing this house to a prospective purchaser, would you advise the agent to disclose the seller's illness? If you did so, would you be in violation of Section 3604(f)(1) of the Fair Housing Act? Or would disclosure be a violation of Section 3604(c), which makes it unlawful "to make. . .any statement. . .with respect to the sale. . .of a dwelling that indicates any preference, limitation, or discrimination based on race, color, religion, sex, handicap, familial status, or national origin, or an intention to make any such preference, limitation, or discrimination." See Tex. Atty. Gen. Op. Jm–1093 (1989) (concluding that a proposed Texas statute requiring a broker to disclose the seller's HIV/AIDS status would violate § 3604(c) of the Fair Housing Act). See generally Note, Secrets Worth Keeping: Toward a Principled Basis for Stigmatized Property Disclosure Statements, 58 U.C.L.A. L. REV. 281 (2010).

9. *Off-site conditions.* What is the effect of the seller's failure to disclose material off-site conditions—matters located elsewhere and affecting the property's surroundings or neighborhood? In Strawn v. Canuso, 140 N.J. 43, 657 A.2d 420 (1995), the New Jersey Supreme Court held a subdivision developer liable for failing to disclose to its customers the existence of a hazardous waste dump site located within a half-mile from some of the houses. Do you think the disclosure duty should extend to such conditions?

The statutes mentioned in Note 7 above dealing with "psychologically impacted" properties do not cover all possible concerns of sellers and their agents, particularly with respect to off-site conditions. For example, suppose you are selling your house, and the house next door is a licensed group home for mentally handicapped persons. Must the seller disclose this fact to prospective purchasers? Or would such a disclosure violate Section 3604(c) of the Fair Housing Act? Alternatively, suppose the group home is for delinquent youths, young single mothers with infant children, recovering alcoholics, or recently released felons. Does each of these present distinct legal issues? Which ones raise a concern under the Fair Housing Act?

10. *Liability to remote purchasers.* Should a seller be liable to a remote purchaser (one who buys from the party who dealt with the seller) for failure to disclose material facts? The traditional answer would be "no" on the ground that there is no contractual privity between the plaintiff and the defendant. But in Geernaert v. Mitchell, 31 Cal. App. 4th 601, 37 Cal. Rptr. 2d 483 (1995), the court held that liability should be found if the seller had "reason to expect" that subsequent buyers in the chain of title would be affected by the nondisclosure. When, if ever, would the "reason to expect" standard *not* be satisfied? After all, if A does not tell B about the termite damage to the property (or the faulty septic system, or whatever the hidden defect might be), when would it *not* be reasonable to expect that B might not tell C about the hidden defect?

11. *Disclaiming the duty to disclose.* Can a seller avoid liability for failure to disclose defects by expressly disclaiming the duty in the sales contract? The cases are reasonably clear that a specific disclaimer identifying the type of defect in question will be effective. See, e.g., Rice v. Patterson Realtors, 857 P.2d 71 (Okl. 1993) ("Buyer accepts the flood and water risk attendant to the Property"). With respect to "generic" clauses (e.g., "Buyer takes the property 'as is'") the picture is mixed. Many recent cases refuse to give effect to "as is" clauses. As one court put it, "An 'as is' clause relives the seller of liability for defects in the property unless the seller, through fraud or misrepresentation conceals material defects not otherwise known or observable to the buyer." Shahram Holdings, Inc. v. Environmental Geotechnology Laboratory, Inc., 2011 WL 1368542 (Cal. App. 2011). Not much comfort, is it? On the other hand, a fairly elaborate, well-drafted "as is" clause was enforced in Alires v. McGehee, 277 Kan. 398, 85 P.3d 1191 (2004). If an "as is" clause may not relieve the seller from an affirmative duty of disclosure, why would a seller bother to include such a clause in the sales contract?

12. *Statutory disclosure requirements.* In recent years many states have adopted statutes requiring home sellers to disclose specific information to their purchasers. A typical example is Section 10–702 of the Maryland Code Annotated, Real Property, which became effective January 1, 1994. It applies to sellers of existing (not newly constructed) one- to-four-family homes. On or before the date a contract of sale is signed, the seller must either give a disclaimer of all warranties and representations, or a disclosure of any defects of which the seller has knowledge in a "laundry list" of the house's systems and features. The purchaser can rescind the sales contract if the required statement is not given, but cannot rescind on the basis of the information in the disclosure statement.

Some of the statutes do not expressly state that a knowingly false disclosure statement is grounds for damages or rescission. See Iadanza v. Mather, 820 F. Supp. 1371 (D. Utah 1993) (finding liability for such a false disclosure statement). Cf. Brasier v. Sparks, 17 Cal. App. 4th 1756, 22 Cal. Rptr. 2d 1 (1993) (finding no liability where the disclosure statement expressly recited that "it is not a warranty of any kind by the sellers * * * and is not intended to be part of any contract between the buyer and seller"). What is a disclosure of that sort worth? One answer, illustrated by the principal case, *Jensen v. Bailey*, is that a seller who checks "no" or "no knowledge" when the seller in fact actually does know of the defect is providing documentary proof of his or her concealment. Such proof may provide the evidence necessary to establish a fraudulent misrepresentation and concealment claim.

Some jurisdictions expressly permit rescission for noncompliance with the requirements of a disclosure statement statute. See, e.g., Little v. Stogner, 162 N.C. App. 25, 592 S.E.2d 5 (2004) (rescission is sole remedy). Other statutes provide, either directly or by judicial construction, for the recovery of damages by the buyer for a false disclosure. Perhaps surprisingly, several courts have granted damages in such cases even when the buyer had actual knowledge of the falsity of the disclosure. See, e.g., Woods v. Pence, 303 Ill. App. 3d 573, 236 Ill. Dec. 977, 708 N.E.2d 563 (1999); Bohm v. DMA Partnership, 8 Neb. App. 1069, 607 N.W.2d 212 (2000). Of course, that knowledge might be reflected in the price the buyer paid, and to that extent would reduce the damages the buyer could recover.

New York's disclosure statute, which was not adopted until 2002 (well after the *Stambovsky* case cited in Note 7 was decided), allows a seller to opt out of all disclosure obligations by crediting the buyer with $500 toward the selling price. If this is done, the seller can be held liable only for common law fraud (not fraudulent concealment). In the absence of any other affirmative disclosures or representations, fraud will be virtually impossible to prove. See Bishop v. Graziano, 10 Misc. 3d 342, 804 N.Y.S.2d 236 (N.Y.Dist. Ct. 2005).

The principal proponent of disclosure statement statutes for residential properties has been the real estate brokerage industry. Brokers have been (understandably) worried about their liability for failure to disclose material facts, and statutes such as this are designed to get them "off the hook." The Maryland statute, for example, provides that brokers have a duty to inform buyers and sellers of their rights and obligations under the statute, and that if a broker does so, he or she "shall have no further duties under this section to the parties to a residential real estate transaction; and is not liable to any party to a residential real estate transaction for a violation of this section." California, Illinois and Rhode Island have adopted similar statutes. See Cal. Civ. Code § 1102 et seq.; Ill. Stat. Ch. 765 § 77/1 et seq.; R.I. Gen. L. § 5–20.8–1 et seq.

The duty of disclosure applies, at least in concept, to all sorts of real estate—not merely to residential property. Moreover, it applies whether the improvements on the real estate are newly constructed or have existed for many years. We now turn our attention to an additional theory of seller liability, usually termed an "implied warranty." This theory generally is limited to new residences where the seller is a builder-vendor. It also may apply where extensive repairs, renovations or improvements have been made to an existing home by a contractor. Although applicable to a more narrow category of real estate, this theory may allow recovery on the basis of much less stringent proof by the purchaser. The overwhelming majority of U.S. jurisdictions have adopted have adopted some form of this implied warranty. Utah, long a holdout, may have become the final state to do so; see Davencourt at Pilgrims Landing Homeowners Ass'n v. Davencourt at Pilgrims Landing, LC, 221 P.3d 234 (Ut. 2009).

SPEIGHT V. WALTERS DEVELOPMENT CO., LTD.
Supreme Court of Iowa, 2008
744 N.W.2d 108

LARSON, JUSTICE

The plaintiffs, Robert and Beverly Speight, appeal from a summary judgment entered against them in their suit for breach of implied warranty of workmanlike construction against the builder of their home. The court of appeals affirmed. Both the district court and the court of appeals expressly declined to recognize an implied warranty claim in favor of third-party purchasers, deferring for such a decision to this court. We now extend our common law of implied warranty to cover such parties and therefore vacate the decision of the court of appeals, reverse the judgment of the district court, and remand for further proceedings.

I.   Facts and Prior Proceedings

The Speights are the present owners of a home in Clive, Iowa, which was custom-built in 1995 by the defendant, Walters Development Company, Ltd. It was built for use by the original buyers, named Roche. The Roches sold the home to people named Rogers, who in turn sold it to the Speights on August 1, 2000. Sometime after purchasing the home, the Speights noticed water damage and mold. A building inspector determined that the damage was the result of a defectively constructed roof and defective rain gutters. Nothing in the record indicates that any of the owners between the original builder and the Speights had actual or imputed knowledge of these defects.

The Speights filed suit against Walters on May 23, 2005, alleging a breach of implied warranty of workmanlike construction and general negligence in construction of the home. Both the Speights and Walters moved for summary judgment raising the issue of whether the Speights, as remote purchasers, could pursue a claim for breach of an implied warranty of workmanlike construction. Walters also raised the issue of whether the plaintiffs' claim for breach of implied warranty was barred by Iowa Code section 614.1(4) (2005), the applicable statute of limitations. The district court concluded that, under the present state of the law, the Speights could not maintain an implied warranty claim and, in any event, such claim would be barred by the statute of limitations. The district court also concluded that the Speights could not bring a general negligence claim because they did not assert an accompanying claim for personal injury—a ruling the plaintiffs do not challenge on appeal.

II.   The Implied Warranty Claim

The implied warranty of workmanlike construction is a judicially created doctrine implemented to protect an innocent home buyer by holding the experienced builder accountable for the quality of construction. See 17 Richard A. Lord, Williston on Contracts § 50:30 (4th ed. 2007) [hereinafter Lord]. Home buyers are generally in an inferior position when purchasing a home from a builder-vendor because of the buyer's lack of expertise in quality home construction and the fact that many defects in construction are latent. These defects, even if the home were inspected by a professional, would not be discoverable. See Sean M. O'Brien, Note, Caveat Venditor: A Case for Granting Subsequent Purchasers a Cause of Action Against Builder-Vendors for Latent Defects in the Home, 20 J. Corp. L. 525, 529 (Spring 1995).

The implied warranty of workmanlike construction addresses the inequities between the buyer and the builder-vendor by requiring that a building be constructed "in a reasonably good and workmanlike manner and . . . be reasonably fit for the intended purpose." Kirk v. Ridgway, 373 N.W.2d 491, 492 (Iowa 1985). In *Kirk* this court applied the doctrine of implied warranty of workmanlike construction to the sale of a home by the builder to the first owner. 373 N.W.2d at 496. In doing so, we noted that interest in consumer protection had increased, and the complexity of homes had increased, making it difficult for a buyer to discover defects in the construction. Id. at 493–94. In *Kirk* we rejected the application of the doctrine of caveat emptor under which "it has been observed, courts considered purchasing as a game of chance." Id. at 493 (citing Roberts, The Case of the Unwary Home Buyer: The Housing Merchant Did It, 52 Cornell L.Q. 835, 836 (1967)). We noted that home buyers are ill-equipped to discover defects in homes, which are increasingly complex, and therefore must rely on the skill and judgment of the vendor. Id. at 494.

In *Kirk* we held that, in order to sustain a claim that a builder-vendor has breached the implied warranty of workmanlike construction, the buyer must show:

> (1) [t]hat the house was constructed to be occupied by the [buyer] as a home;
>
> (2) that the house was purchased from a builder-vendor, who had constructed it for the purpose of sale;
>
> (3) that when sold, the house was not reasonably fit for its intended purpose or had not been constructed in a good and workmanlike manner;
>
> (4) that, at the time of purchase, the buyer was unaware of the defect and had no reasonable means of discovering it; and
>
> (5) that by reason of the defective condition the buyer suffered damages.

Id. at 496; see also Flom v. Stahly, 569 N.W.2d 135, 142 (Iowa 1997).

In *Kirk* we defined a "builder" as

a general building contractor who controls and directs the construction of a building, has ultimate responsibility for completion of the whole contract and for putting the structure into permanent form thus, necessarily excluding merchants, material men, artisans, laborers, subcontractors, and employees of a general contractor.

373 N.W.2d at 496 (quoting Jeanguneat v. Jackie Hames Constr. Co., 576 P.2d 761, 762 (Okla. 1978)).

The plaintiffs ask this court to take the cause of action recognized in *Kirk* one step further by applying it to the case of a subsequent purchaser. Jurisdictions outside of Iowa are split on this issue.

Many jurisdictions do not permit subsequent purchasers to recover for a breach of the implied warranty of workmanlike construction.[1] This holding stems from the lack of a contractual relationship between the subsequent purchaser and the builder-vendor. Michael A. DiSabatino, J.D., Annotation, Liability of Builder of Residence for Latent Defects Therein as Running to Subsequent Purchasers from Original Vendee, 10 A.L.R. 4th 385, 388 (1981) [hereinafter DiSabatino]. The implied warranty of workmanlike construction is contractual in nature, and because privity is traditionally required in order to maintain a contract action, some courts have concluded that the lack of privity between the subsequent purchaser and the builder-vendor prevents the subsequent purchaser's implied-warranty claim. O'Brien, 20 J. Corp. L. at 537; see also Mary Dee Pridgen, Consumer Protection and the Law § 18:19 (2006) [hereinafter Pridgen] (discussing the holding in Crowder v. Vandendeale, 564 S.W.2d 879, 881 (Mo. 1978)); 2 James Acret, Construction Law Digests § 14:12 (2007) [hereinafter Acret] ("The implied warranty of habitability arises out of a contract between the builder and the initial buyer. There is no hint in the case law that it arises out of the general duty to build a reasonably fit house, by reason of which the builder would

---

[1] See, e.g., Lee v. Clark & Assocs. Real Estate, Inc., 512 So. 2d 42 (Ala. 1987); Aas v. Super. Ct., 24 Cal. 4th 627, 101 Cal. Rptr. 2d 718, 12 P.3d 1125 (Cal. 2000) (superseded by statute on other grounds); Cosmopolitan Homes, Inc. v. Weller, 663 P.2d 1041 (Colo. 1983); Coburn v. Lenox Homes, Inc., 173 Conn. 567, 378 A.2d 599 (Conn. 1977); Council of Unit Owners of Sea Colony East, Phases III, IV, VI & VII v. Carl M. Freeman Assocs., Inc., 1989 WL 48568 (Del. Super. 1989); Drexel Props., Inc. v. Bay Colony Club Condo., Inc., 406 So. 2d 515 (Fla. Dist. Ct. App. 1981), disapproved of on other grounds by Casa Clara Condo. Ass'n, Inc. v. Charley Toppino & Sons, Inc., 620 So. 2d 1244 (Fla. 1993); Dunant v. Wilmock, Inc., 176 Ga. App. 48, 335 S.E.2d 162 (Ga. Ct. App. 1985); Miles v. Love, 1 Kan. App. 2d 630, 573 P.2d 622 (Kan. Ct. App. 1977); Real Estate Mktg., Inc. v. Franz, 885 S.W.2d 921 (Ky. 1994); Tereault v. Palmer, 413 N.W.2d 283 (Minn. Ct. App. 1987); John H. Armbruster & Co. v. Hayden Co.-Builder Developer, Inc., 622 S.W.2d 704 (Mo. Ct. App. 1981); Butler v. Caldwell & Cook, Inc., 122 A.D.2d 559, 505 N.Y.S.2d 288 (N.Y. App. Div. 1986); [Conway v. Cutler Group, Inc., 99 A.3d 67 (Pa. 2014) —added by Eds]; Brown v. Fowler, 279 N.W.2d 907 (S.D. 1979); Briggs v. Riversound Ltd. P'ship, 942 S.W.2d 529 (Tenn. Ct. App. 1996); Schafir v. Harrigan, 879 P.2d 1384 (Utah Ct. App. 1994); Northridge Co. v. W.R. Grace & Co., 162 Wis. 2d 918, 471 N.W.2d 179 (Wis. 1991).

be liable to remote purchasers, that is, the general public, having no privity with it." (discussing the holding in Foxcroft Townhome Owners Ass'n v. Hoffman Rosner Corp., 96 Ill. 2d 150, 70 Ill. Dec. 251, 449 N.E.2d 125 (Ill. 1983)). Further, because there is a lack of privity between the subsequent purchaser and the builder-vendor, there is no reliance by the subsequent purchaser on any representations made by the builder-vendor regarding the quality of construction. See Pridgen, § 18:19. Finally, some courts have concluded that the justifications for eliminating the privity requirement in products liability cases do not exist in the sale of real estate. See DiSabatino, 10 A.L.R. 4th at 397–98 ("The court reasoned that a house which is not the product of a mass marketing scheme or which is not designed as a temporary dwelling differs from the usual item to which the principles of strict liability have generally been applied, in that it is not an item which generally changes owners or occupants frequently." (discussing Coburn v. Lenox Homes, Inc., 173 Conn. 567, 378 A.2d 599 (Conn.1977)).

Other jurisdictions do permit subsequent purchasers to recover for a breach of the implied warranty of workmanlike construction.[2] The purpose of the implied warranty of workmanlike construction is to ensure that innocent home buyers are protected from latent defects. This principle is "equally applicable to subsequent purchasers" who are in no better position to discover those defects than the original purchaser. Acret, § 14:12 (discussing and quoting the holding in Lempke v. Dagenais, 130 N.H. 782, 547 A.2d 290 (N.H. 1988)); see also Pridgen, § 18:19 ("The purpose of a warranty is to protect innocent purchasers and hold builders accountable for their work. With that object in mind, any reasoning which would arbitrarily interpose a first buyer as an obstruction to someone equally as deserving of recovery is incomprehensible." (quoting Moxley v. Laramie Builders, Inc., 600 P.2d 733, 736 (Wyo. 1979))). Thus, the public policy justifications for eliminating the doctrine of caveat emptor for original purchasers of new homes similarly support allowing subsequent purchasers to recover on a theory of a breach of the implied warranty of workmanlike construction. See O'Brien, 20 J. Corp. L. at 531–32 ("[B]y

---

[2] See, e.g., Richards v. Powercraft Homes, Inc., 139 Ariz. 242, 678 P.2d 427 (Ariz. 1984); Blagg v. Fred Hunt Co., 272 Ark. 185, 612 S.W.2d 321 (Ark. 1981); Tusch Enters. v. Coffin, 113 Idaho 37, 740 P.2d 1022 (Idaho 1987); Redarowicz v. Ohlendorf, 92 Ill. 2d 171, 65 Ill. Dec. 411, 441 N.E.2d 324 (Ill. 1982); Barnes v. Mac Brown & Co., 264 Ind. 227, 342 N.E.2d 619 (Ind. 1976); Degeneres v. Burgess, 486 So. 2d 769 (La. Ct. App. 1986); Dunelawn Owners' Ass'n v. Gendreau, 750 A.2d 591 (Me. 2000) (citing 33 M.R.S.A. § 1604–113(f)); Keyes v. Guy Bailey Homes, Inc., 439 So.2d 670 (Miss. 1983); Moglia v. McNeil Co., 270 Neb. 241, 700 N.W.2d 608 (Neb.2005); Lempke v. Dagenais, 130 N.H. 782, 547 A.2d 290 (N.H. 1988); Hermes v. Staiano, 181 N.J. Super. 424, 437 A.2d 925 (N.J. 1981); Gaito v. Auman, 313 N.C. 243, 327 S.E.2d 870 (N.C. 1985); Baddour v. Fox, 2004 WL 1327925 (Ohio Ct. App. 2004); Elden v. Simmons, 631 P.2d 739 (Okla. 1981); Nichols v. R.R. Beaufort & Assocs., Inc., 727 A.2d 174 (R.I. 1999); Terlinde v. Neely, 275 S.C. 395, 271 S.E.2d 768 (S.C.1980); Gupta v. Ritter Homes, Inc., 646 S.W.2d 168 (Tex. 1983), overruled in relevant part in Amstadt v. U.S. Brass Corp., 919 S.W.2d 644 (Tex. 1996); Sewell v. Gregory, 179 W.Va. 585, 371 S.E.2d 82 (W. Va. 1988); Moxley v. Laramie Builders, Inc., 600 P.2d 733 (Wyo. 1979).

definition, latent defects are not discoverable by reasonable inspection. Thus, home buyers are left with the choice of relying on a builder-vendor's expertise, or not buying a home at all. As one court stated, "[t]o apply the rule of caveat emptor to an inexperienced buyer, and in favor of a builder-vendor who is daily engaged in the business of building and selling houses is manifestly a denial of justice." Further, the purpose of the implied warranty of workmanlike construction is to ensure the home "will be fit for habitation, a matter that depends upon the quality of the dwelling delivered not the status of the buyer." Pridgen, § 18:19.

The lack of privity between the subsequent purchaser and the builder-vendor is not an impediment, in these jurisdictions, to allowing a subsequent purchaser to recover on an implied-warranty claim. Though the implied warranty of workmanlike construction "has roots in the execution of the contract for sale," it exists independently of the contract by its very nature. O'Brien, 20 J. Corp. L. at 538 (citations omitted). Additionally, requiring privity to sue for a breach of an implied warranty has been disfavored in products liability cases in some jurisdictions. Many jurisdictions find similar justifications for extinguishing the privity requirement in the purchase of a home. See O'Brien, § 50:30 ("[T]he builder was in the same position as a manufacturer who sells an article which, if defective, will be imminently dangerous to persons who come in contact with it, 'and liability is not limited to those with whom the manufacturer contracts.'" (quoting Leigh v. Wadsworth, 361 P.2d 849 (Okla.1961))). From a practical perspective, these jurisdictions note that many latent defects "are often not discoverable for some time after completion of the house. By the time the defects come to light, the original purchasers may have sold the home. For that reason, subsequent purchasers need protection for faulty construction." Pridgen, § 18:19. Additionally, the reality is that our society is increasingly mobile, and as a result, a home's ownership is likely to change hands a number of times. See O'Brien, 20 J. Corp. L. at 526 (noting that, at the time the note was written, "[n]early four million single-family used homes [were] sold in the United States every year"). A blanket rule prohibiting subsequent purchasers from recovering for a breach of the implied warranty of workmanlike construction would do injustice to those who purchase a home from a previous buyer shortly after the home was constructed when the subsequent purchaser later discovers that the home was defectively constructed. See id. at 538. Finally, one author posits that the doctrine of assignment allows for the transfer to the subsequent purchaser of the original purchaser's right to sue for breach of the implied warranty of workmanlike construction. Id. at 538–40.

We believe that Iowa law should follow the modern trend allowing a subsequent purchaser to recover against a builder-vendor for a breach of the implied warranty of workmanlike construction. As in many jurisdictions, this court has eliminated the privity requirement in products liability cases raising a breach of implied warranty claim. See State Farm Mut. Auto. Ins. Co. v. Anderson-Weber, Inc., 252 Iowa 1289, 110 N.W.2d 449, 456 (Iowa 1961). As the court discussed in *State Farm*, the privity requirement was eliminated in other jurisdictions to "ameliorate the harsh doctrine of caveat emptor," and because "the [implied warranty] obligations on the part of the seller were imposed by operation of law, and did not depend for their existence upon express agreement of the parties," privity was not necessary. Id. at 454 (quoting Henningsen v. Bloomfield Motors, Inc., 32 N.J. 358, 161 A.2d 69 (N.J. 1960)). The same is true in a case such as the present one in which a home buyer raises an implied warranty claim. Further, the implied warranty of workmanlike construction is a judicial creation and does not, in itself, arise from the language of any contract between the builder-vendor and the original purchaser. Thus, it is not extinguished upon the original purchaser's sale of the home to a subsequent purchaser. The builder-vendor warrants that the home was constructed in a workmanlike manner, not that it is fit for any particular purpose the original owner intended. As such, there is no contractual justification for limiting recovery to the original purchaser.

Additionally, the public policy justifications supporting our decision to recede from the doctrine of caveat emptor in the sale of new homes by builder-vendors equally apply to the sale of used homes to subsequent purchasers. As discussed above, latent defects are, by definition, undiscoverable by reasonable inspection. Thus, the subsequent purchaser is in no better position to discover those defects than the original purchaser. It is inequitable to allow an original purchaser to recover while, simultaneously, prohibiting a subsequent purchaser from recovering for latent defects in homes that are the same age.

Walters contends that allowing the recovery the Speights seek would lead to increased costs for builders, increased claims, and increased home prices. However, builder-vendors are currently required to build a home in a good and workmanlike manner. The implied warranty of workmanlike construction reasonably puts the risk of shoddy construction on the builder-vendor. The builder-vendor's risk is not increased by allowing subsequent purchasers to recover for the same latent defects for which an original purchaser could recover. As discussed more fully below, the statute of limitations and statute of repose are the same for original purchasers and subsequent purchasers, thus eliminating any increased time period within which a builder-vendor is subject to suit.

Walters argues that allowing subsequent purchasers to recover for a breach of the implied warranty of workmanlike construction would subject builder-vendors to unlimited liability; however, we are not persuaded. Iowa Code section 614.1(11) provides a safety net—a statute of repose for potential plaintiffs seeking to recover for breach of an implied warranty on an improvement to real property. A statute of repose works to "terminate[ ] any right of action after a specified time has elapsed, regardless of whether or not there has as yet been an injury." Bob McKiness Excavating & Grading, Inc. v. Morton, 507 N.W.2d 405, 408 (Iowa 1993) (quoting Hanson v. Williams County, 389 N.W.2d 319, 321 (N.D. 1986)). Section 614.1(11) applies to an action for breach of the implied warranty of workmanlike construction in the purchase of a building. See id. at 409. That section provides:

> An action arising out of the unsafe or defective condition of an improvement to real property based on tort and implied warranty . . . and founded on injury to property, real or personal, or injury to the person or wrongful death, shall not be brought more than fifteen years after the date on which occurred the act or omission of the defendant alleged in the action to have been the cause of the injury or death.

Pursuant to section 614.1(11), the period of repose begins to run on the date of the act or omission causing the injury. In cases involving the construction of a building, such as this home, that period begins upon completion of the construction of the building. See Bob McKiness Excavating & Grading, Inc., 507 N.W.2d at 409. As a result, builder-vendors are not liable on an implied warranty claim after the statute of repose has run, regardless of who owns the home. In summary, we adopt what we view to be the emerging and better view that subsequent purchasers may recover for breach of implied warranty of workmanlike construction against a builder-vendor as recognized in *Kirk* for first-party purchasers. Subsequent purchasers, of course, may not be afforded greater rights of recovery than the original purchasers.

III. The Statute of Limitations

The defendant contends that, even if we recognize a cause of action under these circumstances, it would be barred by the statute of limitations under Iowa Code section 614.1(4). The district court and the court of appeals agreed and concluded that this suit was time barred. We disagree. Under Iowa Code section 614. 1:

> Actions may be brought within the times herein limited, respectively, *after their causes accrue*, and not afterwards, except when otherwise specially declared: * * *

> 4. *Unwritten contracts—injuries to property—fraud—other actions.* Those founded on unwritten contracts, those brought for injuries to property, or for relief on the ground of fraud in cases heretofore solely cognizable in a court of chancery, and all other actions not otherwise provided for in this respect, within five years. . . .

(Emphasis added).

The question in this case is when the plaintiffs' cause of action accrued. The defendant argues, and the district court held, that the cause of action accrued in 1995, when the house was sold by the defendant to the original purchasers. The Speights filed this suit in 2005, which was well beyond the five-year statute of limitations, according to the defendant. The defendant's time-bar argument relies on Iowa Code section 554.2725(2), under which all actions for breach of implied warranty accrue at the time of delivery, not at the time the damage is discovered. The Speights counter that their claim is not based on the sale of goods and, therefore, section 554.2725(2), which is part of the Uniform Commercial Code (UCC), does not apply. We agree with the Speights' position. Article 2 of the UCC applies only to transactions involving the sale of goods. Iowa Code § 554.2102. Goods are "all things . . . which are movable at the time of identification to the contract for sale." Id. § 554.2105(1). Clearly, the construction of a home is not a transaction for the sale of goods to which the UCC applies. Therefore, the limitation provided in section 554.2725(2) does not apply to cases such as the present one. We made that clear in *Brown v. Ellison*, 304 N.W.2d 197 (Iowa 1981), in which we distinguished cases involving breach of implied warranties of workmanship from those under the UCC.

> We hold that the discovery rule is applicable to cases arising from express and implied warranties. This holding, of course, does not apply to situations in which statutes expressly provide that a cause of action accrues when the breach occurs, regardless of the aggrieved party's lack of knowledge of the breach. See, e.g., Iowa Uniform Commercial Code, § 554.2725. . . . The trial court was, therefore, correct in applying the discovery rule.

Brown, 304 N.W.2d at 201.

We reject the defendant's argument that the plaintiffs' cause of action accrued in 1995 when the house was originally sold. Under the discovery rule, a cause of action does not accrue until the injured party has actual or imputed knowledge of the facts that would support a cause of action. We have said:

> Knowledge is imputed to a claimant when he gains information sufficient to alert a reasonable person of the need to investigate. As of that date he is on inquiry notice of all facts that would have been disclosed by a reasonably diligent investigation.

Perkins v. HEA of Iowa, Inc., 651 N.W.2d 40, 44 (Iowa 2002). The Speights' suit was filed on May 23, 2005, which was within five years of their purchase of the home. It cannot, therefore, be credibly argued that the plaintiffs had knowledge—either actual or imputed—of the defect more than five years before their suit was filed because they did not even own the property at that time.

We adopt and apply the doctrine of implied warranty of workmanlike construction to subsequent, as well as initial, purchasers. We conclude as a matter of law that the plaintiffs could not have gained actual or imputed knowledge of the defect in their home more than five years prior to commencing this action, and their suit is therefore not time-barred under Iowa Code section 614.1(4). We vacate the decision of the court of appeals, reverse the judgment of the district court, and remand for further proceedings.

NOTES AND QUESTIONS

1. *Severity of defects.* Obviously few, if any, new houses are perfectly constructed. How serious must the defects be in order to breach the implied warranty? The cases present a wide range of answers. Recall from *Speight* that in Iowa the standard is that the house must be constructed "in a reasonably good and workmanlike manner and . . . be reasonably fit for the intended purpose." This is a relatively pro-buyer standard, and could cover a wide range of possible defects, such as the defective roof and rain gutters involved in *Speight*. See Deisch v. Jay, 790 P.2d 1273 (Wyo. 1990) (builder liable for "minor construction defects causing temporary injury"—in this case, a damp basement that caused articles stored there to become moldy); Roper v. Spring Lake Dev. Co., 789 P.2d 483 (Colo. App. 1990) (foul odor in garage, apparently caused either by sour drywall, dead animals in the soil, or a nearby gas line, breached the implied warranty).

Other courts are much less pro-purchaser, and require much more serious defects. See, e.g., Stuart v. Coldwell Banker Commercial Group, Inc., 109 Wash. 2d 406, 417, 745 P.2d 1284, 1290 (1987) (warranty breached only by structural defects that "profoundly compromise" the dwelling); Samuelson v. A.A. Quality Construction, Inc., 230 Mont. 220, 749 P.2d 73 (1988) (warranty "limited to defects which are so substantial as reasonably to preclude the use of the dwelling as a residence"). The extremely narrow view of the warranty taken by the Washington Supreme Court in *Stuart* was widely criticized. See Hansen v. Residential Development, Ltd., 128 Wash. App. 1066 (2005).

2. *Time limitations on actions.* If the courts overcome the privity problem and permit remote grantees to sue the builder or contractor, the period of potential liability lasts for a much longer time, on the average, than under the older cases that required direct privity between the plaintiff and the builder or contractor who performed the work. One way to limit this liability is to require that the suit be brought within a "reasonable time," and several of the cases cited above impose such a limitation. See Bankston v. Pulaski County School District, 281 Ark. 476, 665 S.W.2d 859 (1984); Redarowicz v. Ohlendorf, 92 Ill. 2d 171, 65 Ill. Dec. 411, 441 N.E.2d 324 (1982). But from whose viewpoint is "reasonableness" to be judged? Suppose

the property is sold for the fifth time, 20 years after the house was built, to an owner who immediately thereafter notices the defect and files a lawsuit against the original builder?

In response to lobbying efforts by the construction and remodeling industries, many states have responded to the issue of time limitations on claims against builders and contractors by enacting special statutes of repose. Statutes of limitation usually are construed as incorporating the "discovery rule," meaning that their time periods do not begin to run until the injury was or should have been discovered. See, e.g., Haidar v. Nortey Foundation Designs, Inc., 239 S.W.3d 924 (Tex. App. 2007). On the other hand, a statute of repose fixes a time period (usually commencing from the date construction is completed or the house is sold) after which claims are cut off, irrespective of discovery. See Alsenz v. Twin Lakes Village, Inc., 108 Nev. 1117, 843 P.2d 834 (1992). For example, in North Carolina a general three-year limitation period is imposed for negligence actions by Section 1–52 of the North Carolina General Statutes. A further statute of repose found in Subsection 1–52(5), cuts off all claims, irrespective of the time of discovery.

N.C. Gen. Stat. § 1–50(5)

(5)(a) No action to recover damages based upon or arising out of the defective or unsafe condition of an improvement to real property shall be brought more than six years from the later of the specific last act or omission of the defendant giving rise to the cause of action or substantial completion of the improvement.

* * *

(5)(f) This subdivision prescribes an outside limitation of six years from the later of the specific last act or omission or substantial completion, within which the limitations prescribed by G.S. 1–52 and 1–53 continue to run. For purposes of the three-year limitation prescribed by G.S. 1–52, a cause of action based upon or arising out of the defective or unsafe condition of an improvement to real property shall not accrue until the injury, loss, defect or damage becomes apparent or ought reasonably to have become apparent to the claimant. However, as provided in this subdivision, no action may be brought more than six years from the later of the specific last act or omission or substantial completion.

Note that a statute of repose (which ignores the discovery rule) and a statute of limitations (which incorporates the discovery rule can operate side by side. See, e.g., Gomez v. David A. Williams Realty & Const., Inc., 740 N.W.2d 775 (Minn. App. 2007) (2-year statute of limitations, 10-year statute of repose).

Even a statute of repose is not always a safe harbor for a builder. In Pfeifer v. City of Bellingham, 112 Wash. 2d 562, 772 P.2d 1018 (1989), a plaintiff was injured in a fire in a condominium project that was allegedly built improperly. She sued the builder, not for the defects per se, but for the tort of intentionally concealing a known and dangerous condition. The court held that the statute of repose did not bar this sort of tort action. Similarly, in Boghossian v. Ferland Corp., 600 A.2d 288 (R.I. 1991), the statute of repose expressly barred "tort actions." The court characterized the plaintiff's action against the builder as sounding in contract, not in tort, and thereby disregarded the statute.

3. *Does a specific express warranty disclaim an implied warranty?* Given the rule that a disclaimer of the implied warranty must appear in "clear and unambiguous language," should a court find that a specific written warranty with a one-year term supplants the implied warranty? Several courts have refused to do so. See Graham Constr. Co. v. Earl, 208 S.W.3d 106 (Ark. 2005); Bridges v. Ferrell, 685 P.2d 409 (Okl. App. 1984).

4. *Drafting effective disclaimers.* There is general agreement that an express disclaimer can negate the implied warranty. As the Hawaii Supreme Court explained in Association of Apartment Owners of Newtown Meadows v. Venture 15, Inc., 115 Hawaii 232, 167 P.3d 225 (2007):

> [T]he burden on [the builder] to establish that it disclaimed the implied warranty of habitability is "very high," * * * and such disclaimers are strictly construed against the defendant; see also Tusch Enters. v. Coffin, 113 Idaho 37, 740 P.2d 1022, 1030 (1987) (observing that "[t]he majority of states permit a disclaimer of an implied warranty of habitability, but the disclaimer must be clear and unambiguous and such disclaimers are strictly construed against the [defendant].")

Id. at 256, 167 P.3d at 249. See Board of Managers v. Wilmette Partners, 760 N.E.2d 976 (Ill. 2001), where the disclaimer wasn't specific enough. As legal counsel for builders and contractors become increasingly sophisticated at drafting effective disclaimers, will there be a gradual erosion of the protections that the courts have provided to consumers in the form of an implied warranty? Although writing an effective disclaimer is difficult, it is not impossible. See Hicks v. Superior Court, 8 Cal. Rptr. 3d 703 (Cal. App. 2004); Jones v. Centex Homes, 939 N.E.2d 1294 (Ohio App. 2010); Mattingly v. Palmer Ridge Homes LLC, 238 P.3d 505 (Wash. App. 2010) (all of which found disclaimers to be effective). The *Hicks* case later was superseded by the passage in 2002 of a California statute, Cal. Civil Code § 895 et seq., that provides for "notice and opportunity to repair" certain nonwaivable warranties. Notice and opportunity to repair statutes are discussed in the following note.

5. *Notice and opportunity to repair statutes.* In some states, such as California, construction defect litigation reached what builders considered to be epidemic proportions. In an attempt to stem the tide, approximately 30 states adopted "NOR" (short for "notice and opportunity to repair") statutes in the 1990s and 2000s. These NOR Statutes require property owners to put builders on notice of construction defect claims and give them an opportunity to cure the defects. Such statutes, which have been vigorously supported by

the National Association of Home Builders and other builder groups, usually prohibit the filing of a suit until some fixed time (e.g., 60 days) after the builder is given notice, and they require the builder to respond to the notice either by disputing it, inspecting the property, or making a cash offer of settlement. See Standard Pacific Corp. v. Superior Court, 98 Cal. Rptr. 3d 295 (Cal. App. 2009) (homeowners must give builder notice and opportunity to cure, as a prerequisite to filing suit, unless builder has failed to give them proper documentation); Hoch, The Kansas Residential Construction Defect Act: A Schematic Blueprint for Repairs, 74 J. Kan. Bar Assn. 20 (Mar. 2005).

6. *Nonresidential real estate.* Should the implied warranty be extended to nonresidential properties as well? Is the average landlord or small business owner better able to protect himself or herself than the average home buyer? A few courts have extended the protection to commercial properties. See Hayden Bus. Ctr. Condominiums Ass'n v. Pegasus Dev. Corp., 105 P.3d 157 (Ariz.App. 2005), disapproved on other grounds by Lofts at Fillmore Condo. Ass'n v. Reliance Commercial Const., Inc., 190 P.3d 733 (Ariz. 2008) (business center condominiums); Pollard v. Saxe & Yolles Development Co., 12 Cal. 3d 374, 115 Cal. Rptr. 648, 525 P.2d 88 (1974) (apartment buildings); Hodgson v. Chin, 168 N.J. Super. 549, 403 A.2d 942 (1979) (stores purchased for business use). But see Dawson Industries, Inc. v. Godley Const. Co. Inc., 29 N.C. App. 270, 224 S.E.2d 266 (1976) (refusing to apply the warranty to commercial property). See Tomcho, Commercial Real Estate Buyer Beware: Sellers May Have the Right to Remain Silent, 70 S. Cal. L. Rev. 1571 (1997). Only a handful of the NOR statutes apply to nonresidential construction.

E. TITLE COVENANTS IN DEEDS

With this section we begin our consideration of *title assurance*—that is, the set of mechanisms that buyers of land use to: (1) learn in advance whether their sellers have and can convey the quality of title they claim; and (2) obtain recovery if the title, after the transfer, turns out not to be as represented. The first of these mechanisms, covered in this section, is the concept of the deed covenant; in essence it is simply a statement in (or a legal inference from) the deed itself that gives the grantee rights against the grantor if the title is not as promised. In subsequent sections we will examine three other mechanisms: (1) the recording system; (2) the Torrens or title registration system; and (3) title insurance.

DALE A. WHITMAN, OPTIMIZING LAND TITLE ASSURANCE SYSTEMS
42 George Washington Law Review 40, 41–42 (1974)

Perhaps the problem will be clarified by a discussion of a generalized title assurance system. The description offered here is broad enough to encompass all of the diverse methods of title assurance in use in the

United States and in most other industrialized nations. It proceeds from the view that the system is in reality a combination of four subsystems that are expected to work in harmony to provide the desired result.

One subsystem must exist to record, retrieve, and aggregate data disclosing legal interests in the property in question. It is referred to below as the "data subsystem." In the United States, this subsystem is typically operated and maintained by lawyers, abstracters, or title companies, working in cooperation with the local custodians of public records. Another subsystem interprets the data and makes judgments about the current state of the title in question. Lawyers and title insurers usually perform these tasks, although officials of local government may also be involved. A third subsystem of law and custom must exist to allocate risks which result from the existence of legal interests that are collateral to the record, and therefore outside the data subsystem, but may affect the validity of title, or from any errors in the processes of recordation, retrieval, aggregation, and interpretation of the data. A final subsystem indemnifies persons whose legal interests are impaired by the risks allocated by the third subsystem. It includes title insurance, suits and claims based on title covenants in deeds, recovery from negligent abstracters or attorneys, and Torrens indemnification funds.

All systems of title assurance used in the United States contain some form of each of the subsystems described above, but variations in the performance of individual subsystems result in differences in the overall effectiveness of title assurance systems from place to place.

Of all of the title assurance mechanisms in use in the United States, the deed covenant is by far the crudest and least effective. Its "data subsystem" consists simply of whatever knowledge the grantor has and is willing to reveal about the title, and hence may be highly inaccurate. It provides no method of obtaining interpretation or judgment concerning the data except that which the grantee or his or her attorney may bring to bear. It does, as we will see, allocate among the parties the risk of title defects which were not disclosed to the grantee, but it provides no external financial resource for indemnification of the party on whom the risk falls; instead, it either makes the grantee absorb the loss without further recovery, or it gives the grantee a claim against the grantor, whose ability to respond by payment of damages may range from handsome to insignificant.

For these reasons, the deed covenant is a weak and ineffective means of title assurance, and few buyers of real estate today rely on it exclusively. But it is still important, for most deeds do contain covenants of title, and suits on them do continue to be brought and litigated. Even when the grantee has placed principal reliance on another form of title assurance, such as title insurance, the deed covenant may still be of consequence; the title insurer may pay the grantee's claim, indemnifying her for the loss resulting from the defect, and may then sue the grantor on the deed covenant, being subrogated to the grantee's rights. A nice illustration is Kelly v. National Attorneys Title Assurance Fund, 955 N.E.2d 224 (Ind. App. 2011).

Of course, a deed may contain no covenants of title at all. Such a deed is usually termed a "quitclaim" deed, and no covenants of title are implied in it. As the Texas Supreme Court explained,

> Quitclaim deeds are commonly used to convey "interests of an unknown extent or claims having a dubious basis." A quitclaim deed conveys upon its face doubts about the grantor's interest; any buyer is necessarily put on inquiry as to those doubts. Thus, a quitclaim deed *without warranty of title* cannot be a warranty (or "misrepresentation") of title.

Geodyne Energy Income Production Partnership I-E v. Newton Corp., 161 S.W.3d 482, 487 (Tex. 2005) (emphasis in original). Note carefully that a quitclaim deed is just as effective as a warranty deed in actually transferring *whatever title the grantor has.* The only distinction between warranty deeds and quitclaim deeds lies in the remedies (or lack of remedies) the grantee has if the title fails; there is no difference in the quality of the title conveyed. This is a point of common misconception.

Instead of a quitclaim, which contains no covenants of title, the grantor may include some covenants. American law generally recognizes six distinct types of title covenants in deeds. A "full warranty" deed (something of a misnomer, since the term "warranty" is also the name of one of the six specific covenants) will include all six. In some states, it is customary to spell out each warranty in detail on the face of the deed, but in many jurisdictions there are statutes that impose certain deed covenants whenever specific words (like "grant", "convey and warrant", or the like) are used in a deed. The Washington statute set out in Section A of this chapter is an example of one such "statutory warranty deed" jurisdiction.

The first three of the six possible covenants are usually termed "present" covenants, because they can be breached, if at all, only at the moment the deed is delivered:

(1) *Covenant of Seisin.* "Seisin" is a now-obsolete medival term that represented the legal possession of law. Hence, in substance the covenant of seisin is a promise by the grantor that he or she owns and is in possession of the land, although not necessarily free of encumbrances. See Estate of Patterson v. Palmetto Bank, 646 S.E.2d 885 (S.C. App. 2007). A few states treat it as a covenant that the grantor possesses the land, whether or not by

legal right, but this is a minority view. The distinction is important if the land is transferred while an adverse possessor or holdover tenant is in possession. Compare Boatmen's Nat. Bank v. Dandy, 804 S.W.2d 783 (Mo. App. 1990) (deed covenants of title are not violated by presence of an adverse possessor) with Double L. Properties, Inc. v. Crandall, 51 Wash. App. 149, 751 P.2d 1208 (1988) (presence of adverse possessor breaches covenant of seisin).

(2) *Right to Convey*. This covenant usually overlaps with the covenant of seisin, but not always. For example, a grantor who is attorney in fact for the owner of the land under a valid power of attorney would have the right to convey, but would not have seisin.

(3) *Covenant Against Encumbrances*. This is a promise that title is passing free of mortgages, liens, easements, future interests in others, covenants running with the land, etc. See Ensberg v. Nelson, 320 P.3d 97 (Wash. App. 2013), holding that a judgment against the homeowners association of which the property was a part did not constitute an encumbrance on the property itself. Note that in many cases, the grantee is aware of and intends to take the real estate "subject to" some encumbrances. The careful lawyer who prepares a deed for a grantor containing this covenant will list on the face of the deed, as "subject to" exceptions to the covenant, the encumbrances on the property that the grantee has agreed to accept, and hence that cannot be a basis for a later suit on this covenant.

The next three types of covenants are usually termed "future" covenants, because they are by definition breached only when an *eviction* of the grantee occurs, and this may occur some time after the delivery of the deed itself.

Next 3: "future" cov's.

(4) and (5) *Warranty* and *Quiet Enjoyment*. In substance, these two covenants are identical. They amount to a promise by the grantor to compensate the grantee for the loss if the title turns out to be defective or subject to an encumbrance, and the grantee thereby suffers an eviction.

(6) *Further Assurances*. This is a promise by the grantor to execute such further documents as may be necessary to perfect the grantee's title. For example, if the grantor did not have title at the time he made the original deed to the grantee, but later obtained title, he could be compelled to execute a further deed to the grantee. The covenant is enforceable in equity by a decree of specific performance. It will also prevent the grantor from later

claiming title against the grantee by adverse possession. See Carrozza v. Carrozza, 944 A.2d 161 (R.I. 2008).

Most of the covenants above are nicely summarized in Lloyd v. Estate of Robbins, 997 A.2d 733 (Me. 2010). Whether the distinctions among these various covenants are useful or serve sound policy is debatable. See Levin, Warranties of Title—A Modest Proposal, 29 Vill. L. Rev. 649 (1984). Nevertheless, the distinctions continue to be relevant, as demonstrated by the explanatory material below and the next principal case, *Brown v. Lober*. For further discussion of the six types of title covenants, see W. Stoebuck & D. Whitman, The Law of Property § 11.13 (3d ed. 2000); Cribbet, Property 268 (2d ed. 1975); 6A Powell, Real Property ¶ 904ff (1979); III American Law of Property § 12.124ff (1952).

A grantor may limit the coverage of the title covenants he makes by adding further language. For example, we have already noted that it is common in some areas for grantors to give a full set of covenants, but only "against the lawful claims of all persons claiming by, through or under them," but not those created by their predecessors in title. Such a deed is sometimes termed a "special warranty" or "limited warranty" deed. The second of the two Washington statutes reprinted in Section A above appears to have this effect when the deed uses the terms "bargains, sells, and conveys."

Under a "special warranty" deed, questions can arise about whether the title defect in question was created by the grantor or arose while the grantor owned the property. For example, if the grantor has engaged in conduct that reduced the size of the land parcel under the doctrine of "boundary by acquiescence," is the grantor liable under the deed? Compare Egli v. Troy, 602 N.W.2d 329 (Iowa 1999) (grantor liable) with Mason v. Loveless, 24 P.3d 997 (Utah App. 2001) (grantor not liable). See also Greenberg v. Sutter, 173 Misc. 2d 774, 661 N.Y.S.2d 933 (1997) (holding that a grantor who permitted an adverse possessor to acquire a portion of her land would be in violation of her subsequent special warranty deed, even though she had no actual knowledge of the adverse possession).

It may be useful at this point to compare the deed covenants mentioned above with the covenant of marketable title, discussed in Chapter Six, that is implied in contracts for the sale of land. The most obvious point of similarity between deed covenants and the implied covenant of marketable title is that both are concerned with *title*. In general, the same sorts of title defects that might breach the contractual covenant will be breaches of the deed covenants as well—failures of title, encumbrances, and so on. The courts are split, however, as to whether the presence of known or visible easements will violate a covenant against encumbrances in a deed. Compare Marathon Builders, Inc. v. Polinger,

263 Md. 410, 283 A.2d 617 (1971) with Gill Grain Co. v. Poos, 707 S.W.2d 434 (Mo. App. 1986). For other types of title defects, the grantee's knowledge at the time the deed is delivered is probably irrelevant. See Midfirst Bank v. Abney, 850 N.E.2d 373 (Ill. App. 2006) ("The fact that a purchaser may have actual knowledge of an encumbrance does not relieve the vendor of his liability upon the covenants contained in his deed. Such knowledge on the part of the purchaser does not operate as a release or discharge of a covenant"). Cf. In re Estate of Hennel, 967 N.Y.S.2d 625 (N.Y. Sur.Ct. 2013) (where grantees had knowledge of mortgage on land when they accepted deed, they could not recover for breach of warranty; there was no separate covenant against encumbrances).

Unlike the implied covenant of marketable title in a sales contract, deed covenants of title are not breached by legal violations that do not themselves affect title. Thus, existing conditions that breach local zoning or other ordinances usually are not considered to violate deed covenants of title. See Arnell v. Salt Lake County Bd. of Adjustment, 112 P.3d 1214 (Utah App. 2005); Barnett v. Decatur, 261 Ga. 205, 403 S.E.2d 46 (1991). Cf. Bianchi v. Lorenz, 166 Vt. 555, 701 A.2d 1037 (1997) (holding, rather bizarrely, that a zoning violation resulting from failure of grantor to obtain septic system permit constituted an encumbrance, breaching a deed covenant against encumbrances); War Eagle, Inc. v. Belair, 694 S.E.2d 497 (N.C. App. 2010) (existing zoning violation breached covenant against encumbrances). Likewise, the presence of illegal hazardous waste on the land is not a breach of a deed covenant against encumbrances, unless the condition has actually triggered the assertion of a lien for cleanup expenses by a federal or state agency. See Cameron v. Martin Marietta Corp., 729 F. Supp. 1529 (E.D.N.C. 1990).

There are other important differences between the contractual covenant of marketable title and deed covenants. One is the available remedy. If a buyer of land discovers prior to closing that title is unmarketable, her usual remedy is to rescind, although she may also receive specific performance with abatement of part of the purchase price, if desired, and in some cases, damages. Under a deed covenant, damages are usually the only remedy unless the covenant of further assurances can be used to compel a further conveyance that will perfect the title. Rescission of the transaction generally is not available. Another difference lies in the standard of quality that the title must meet. Under the implied covenant of marketable title in a sales contract, the title must be not only good, but marketable as well, meaning that it must not be subject to an unreasonable risk of litigation. There is no such requirement in the context of deed covenants, where a title that is good in fact will suffice despite the possibility that numerous questions could reasonably be raised or litigated about it. For example, in Fong v. Batton, 214 So. 2d 649 (Fla. App. 1968), there was a gap in the public records in the grantor's chain of title. Such a condition would probably make title unmarketable, but the court held that it did not constitute a breach of the covenant of seisin, because the grantee had received actual title notwithstanding the record gap.

A further illustration of the difference between a good title (which is all that deed covenants of title promise) and a marketable one is Elliott v. Elliott, 252 Ark. 966, 482 S.W.2d 123 (1972), where the *grantors* sued their own grantee, claiming a half interest in the mineral rights to the land they previously had deeded to him. The grantee won the suit, and then brought an action against the grantors under the covenant of warranty in the deed for the expenses of defending the grantors' action. Here, the grantee lost. The court held that because the grantee had good title all along, he could not recover based on the theory that a deed warranty had been breached.

Present Versus Future Covenants. The distinction between the present and future deed covenants is important for several reasons. One is the application of the statute of limitations. A breach of the present covenants occurs, if at all, at the time the deed is delivered. Consequently, the statute of limitations for a claimed breach of a present covenant commences at the moment of delivery. See Lloyd v. Estate of Robbins, 997 A.2d 773 (R.I. 2010). Often, of course, the grantee is unaware of the title defect, and may not learn of it until some months or years later, at which point the statute of limitations may have cut off her claim based on a breach of the present covenant. Thus, a deed containing only present covenants gives a highly ephemeral form of protection. Fortunately, this problem does not exist with a future covenant because the statute of limitations for a future covenant runs only from the date of an eviction resulting from the breach. One can hardly be evicted without knowing about it. See Annot., 95 A.L.R. 2d 913 (1964).

Real estate lawyers say that the future covenants "run with the land," whereas the present covenants do not. What does it mean for a covenant to "run with the land"? To illustrate, suppose A deeds land to B with all six covenants. B subsequently conveys the land to C (whether with or without title covenants), and C then discovers a title defect that predates the original conveyance by A. May C recover against A? So far as the present covenants are concerned, the breach occurred when the A–B deed was delivered. Unless B expressly assigned to C the cause of action that B has against A based on the breach of a present deed covenant, according to the weight of authority C has no claim against A based on the present covenants because the present covenants in the A–B deed do not "run" to the more remote grantee in the chain of title, C. A few courts have circumvented this difficulty by the simple expedient of holding the B–C deed to constitute an implied assignment to C of B's cause of action against A. See III American Law of Property § 12.127 (1952).

With respect to the future covenants, C's position is much brighter, for they are uniformly held to run with the land, and hence to permit the more remote grantee C to recover directly from A. See, e.g., Holmes Devel., LLC v. Cook, 48 P.3d 895 (Ut. 2002); Bridges v. Heimburger, 360 So. 2d 929 (Miss. 1978). Does this distinction between present and future covenants serve any policy function? Is it desirable to have a "smorgasbord" of covenants, with differing legal consequences, so that the parties may select those covenants that suit them? Do you suppose it is common for parties to a deed to discuss or negotiate about the particular covenants to be included?

Given that a future deed covenant can be breached only by an eviction, it becomes important to know what sorts of occurrences will amount to an eviction. If the holder of the paramount title asserts it directly and forcibly, as by "throwing out" the grantee by force, no one would doubt that an "eviction" has occurred. But this is a rare circumstance.

BROWN V. LOBER

Supreme Court of Illinois, 1979

75 Ill.2d 547, 27 Ill. Dec. 780, 389 N.E.2d 1188

[Plaintiffs purchased the land in question in 1957, receiving a deed containing covenants of seisin, right to convey, against encumbrances, warranty, and quiet enjoyment. In 1974, they negotiated the sale of the coal rights to the land to Consolidated Coal Company for $6,000. The coal company later discovered that a prior owner had reserved a two-thirds interest in the coal rights, and that the plaintiffs had only one-third. The plaintiffs one-third mineral interest was sold to the coal company for $2,000. The plaintiffs then brought this action against the estate of their grantor, claiming a breach of the covenants of title in the deed and seeking $4,000 in damages. The court held that the plaintiffs' action on the present covenants was barred by the jurisdiction's 10-year statute of limitations. Plaintiffs appealed.]

This court has stated on numerous occasions that, in contrast to the covenant of seisin, the covenant of warranty or quiet enjoyment is prospective in nature and is breached only when there is an actual or constructive eviction of the covenantee by the paramount titleholder. * * *

The cases are also replete with statements to the effect that the mere existence of paramount title in one other than the covenantee is not sufficient to constitute a breach of the covenant of warranty or quiet enjoyment: "[T]here must be a union of acts of disturbance and lawful title, to constitute a breach of the covenant for quiet enjoyment, or warranty * * * ." Barry v. Guild, 126 Ill. 439, 446, 18 N.E. 759, 761 (1888).

"[T]here is a general concurrence that something more than the mere existence of a paramount title is necessary to constitute a breach of the covenant of warranty." Scott v. Kirkendall, 88 Ill. 465, 467 (1878). "A mere want of title is no breach of this covenant. There must not only be a want of title, but there must be an ouster under a paramount title." Moore v. Vail, 17 Ill. 185, 189 (1855).

The question is whether plaintiffs have alleged facts sufficient to constitute a constructive eviction. They argue that if a covenantee fails in his effort to sell an interest in land because he discovers that he does not own what his warranty deed purported to convey, he has suffered a constructive eviction and is thereby entitled to bring an action against his grantor for breach of the covenant of quiet enjoyment. We think that the decision of this court in *Scott v. Kirkendall*, 88 Ill. 465 (1878), is controlling on this issue and compels us to reject plaintiffs' argument.

In *Scott,* an action was brought for breach of the covenant of warranty by a grantee who discovered that other parties had paramount title to the land in question. The land was vacant and unoccupied at all relevant times. This court, in rejecting the grantee's claim that there was a breach of the covenant of quiet enjoyment, quoted the earlier decision in *Moore v. Vail*, 17 Ill. 185, 191 (1855):

> Until that time, (the taking possession by the owner of the paramount title,) he might peaceably have entered upon and enjoyed the premises, without resistance or molestation, which was all his grantors covenanted he should do. They did not guarantee to him a perfect title, but the possession and enjoyment of the premises. 88 Ill. 465, 468.

Relying on this language in *Moore,* the *Scott* court concluded:

> We do not see but what this fully decides the present case against the appellant. It holds that the mere existence of a paramount title does not constitute a breach of the covenant. That is all there is here. There has been no assertion of the adverse title. The land has always been vacant. Appellant could at any time have taken peaceable possession of it. He has in no way been prevented or hindered from the enjoyment of the possession by anyone having a better right. It was but the possession and enjoyment of the premises which was assured to him, and there has been no disturbance or interference in that respect. True, there is a superior title in another, but appellant has never felt "its pressure upon him." 88 Ill. 465, 468–69.

Admittedly, *Scott* dealt with surface rights while the case before us concerns subsurface mineral rights. We are, nevertheless, convinced that the reasoning employed in *Scott* is applicable to the present case. While plaintiffs went into possession of the surface area, they cannot be said to have possessed the subsurface minerals. * * * "To possess the mineral estate, one must undertake the actual removal thereof from the ground or do such other act as will apprise the community that such interest is in the exclusive use and enjoyment of the claiming party." Failoni v. Chicago & North Western Ry. Co., 30 Ill. 2d 258, 262, 195 N.E.2d 619, 622 (1964).

Since no one has, as yet, undertaken to remove the coal or otherwise manifested a clear intent to exclusively "possess" the mineral estate, it must be concluded that the subsurface estate is "vacant." As in *Scott,* plaintiffs "could at any time have taken peaceable possession of it. [They have] in no way been prevented or hindered from the enjoyment of the possession by anyone having a better right." 88 Ill. 465, 468. Accordingly, until such time as one holding paramount title interferes with plaintiffs' right of possession (e.g., by beginning to mine the coal), there can be no constructive eviction and, therefore, no breach of the covenant of quiet enjoyment.

What plaintiffs are apparently attempting to do on this appeal is to extend the protection afforded by the covenant of quiet enjoyment. However, we decline to expand the historical scope of this covenant to provide a remedy where another of the covenants of title is so clearly applicable. As this court stated in *Scott v. Kirkendall*, 88 Ill. 465, 469 (1878):

> To sustain the present action would be to confound all distinction between the covenant of warranty and that of seizin, or of right to convey. They are not equivalent covenants. An action will lie upon the latter, though there be no disturbance of possession. A defect of title will suffice. Not so with the covenant of warranty, or for quiet enjoyment, as has always been held by the prevailing authority.

The covenant of seisin, unquestionably, was breached when the Bosts delivered the deed to plaintiffs, and plaintiffs then had a cause of action. However, despite the fact that it was a matter of public record that there was a reservation of a two-thirds interest in the mineral rights in the earlier deed, plaintiffs failed to bring an action for breach of the covenant of seisin within the 10-year period following delivery of the deed. The likely explanation is that plaintiffs had not secured a title opinion at the time they purchased the property, and the subsequent examiners for the lenders were not concerned with the mineral rights. Plaintiffs' oversight, however, does not justify us in overruling earlier decisions in order to recognize an otherwise premature cause of action. The mere fact that plaintiffs' original contract with Consolidated had to be modified due to their discovery that paramount title to two-thirds of the subsurface minerals belonged to another is not sufficient to constitute the constructive eviction necessary to a breach of the covenant of quiet enjoyment.

Finally, although plaintiffs also have argued in this court that there was a breach of the covenant against incumbrances entitling them to recovery, we decline to address this issue which was argued for the first time on appeal. It is well settled that questions not raised in the trial court will not be considered by this court on appeal. Kravis v. Smith Marine, Inc., 60 Ill. 2d 141, 324 N.E.2d 417 (1975); Ray v. City of Chicago, 19 Ill. 2d 593, 169 N.E.2d 73 (1960).

Accordingly, the judgment of the appellate court is reversed, and the judgment of the circuit court of Montgomery County is affirmed.

NOTES AND QUESTIONS

1. *What constitutes eviction?* Obviously the mere fact that a deed grantee believes someone else has better title will not constitute an eviction, giving rise to an action on the future covenants in the deed; see Green Harbour Homeowners Ass'n, Inc. v. Ermiger, 898 N.Y.S.2d 302 (N.Y. App. Div. 2010). The following acts by the holder of paramount title have been held to constitute an eviction (sometimes termed a "constructive eviction") of the grantee, and thus to breach the future covenants:

(a) When the grantee takes the deed, the paramount titleholder is already in possession of the land or has constructed encroachments on it. Riddle v. Udouj, 267 S.W.3d 586 (Ark. 2007).

(b) The paramount titleholder obtains a decree of specific performance, ejectment, or other order giving him possession or confirming his title to the land. Foley v. Smith, 14 Wn. App. 285, 539 P.2d 874 (1975).

(c) The paramount titleholder orders the grantee off the land and threatens litigation against her. McCleary v. Bratton, 307 S.W.2d 722 (Mo. App. 1957).

(d) The grantee buys the paramount title in order to avoid being evicted by its holder. Greenwood v. Robbins, 108 N.J. Eq. 122, 154 A. 333 (1931).

(e) The grantee surrenders her claim to the holder of the paramount title and moves off the land. Solares v. Solares, 232 S.W.3d 873 (Tex. App. 2007); Brewster v. Hines, 185 S.E.2d 513 (W.Va. 1971) (noted in Case Comment, 74 W.Va. L. Rev. 415 (1972)).

(f) The grantee is sued by the person with paramount title, and enters into a reasonable settlement of the suit in which the grantee is left with only a part of the land originally granted by the deed in question. Garcia v. Herrera, 125 N.M. 199, 959 P.2d 533 (1998).

Obviously, physical interference by the holder of paramount title with the possession of the grantee will be an actual eviction. See, e.g., Jackson v. Smith, 80 S.W.3d 443 (Ark. 2010) (paramount title holder cut off electricity to grantee). This might occur because the paramount titleholder is already in possession of the property when the deed is delivered to the grantee, as noted above. Or the holder of paramount title may come onto the land later and attempt to take possession, or attempt to use an easement after the grantee has taken possession; see McMurray v. Housworth, 638 S.E.2d 421 (Ga.App. 2006). Incidentally, if the government is the holder of paramount title, that fact alone will comprise an eviction, and no further action by the government is necessary. See Cover v. McAden, 112 S.E. 817 (N.C. 1922).

2. *Limits on recovery.* There is nearly universal agreement that the recovery by the grantee under a deed's covenants of title cannot exceed the consideration received by the covenantor-grantor plus interest. See Bedard v. Martin, 100 P.3d 584 (Colo. Ct. App. 2004); Annot., 100 A.L.R. 1194 (1937). If the land has risen in value, or the grantee has made improvements on it, this rule can result in the grantee's bearing a substantial share of the total loss, particularly if there is a total failure of title. The limitation has been criticized. See Jon Groetzinger, Breach of the Warranty Covenants in Deeds and the Allowable Measure of Damages, 17 N.H. Bar J. 1 (1975). An occasional court decision and a few statutes remove the limitation and permit recovery based on the current land value. See Bridwell v. Gruner, 212 Ark. 992, 209 S.W.2d 441 (1948); 6A Powell, Real Property ¶ 908 n. 24 (1979).

The limitation on recovery to the amount the grantor received applies equally to all of the covenants. For example, if the property turns out to have been encumbered by a mortgage with a balance greater than the price the grantor received for the land, the grantor's liability on the covenant against encumbrances is limited to the purchase price. Forrer v. Sather, 595 P.2d 1306 (Utah 1979).

3. *What did the grantor receive?* In some cases the "consideration received" by the grantor is not so easy to measure. If the land was transferred in exchange for other land, what is the amount of the consideration? See Maxwell v. Redd, 209 Kan. 264, 496 P.2d 1320 (1972). Or suppose the land was transferred as a gift, with no consideration or only a nominal amount? Does this preclude recovery entirely? Compare Smith v. Smith, 243 Ga. 56, 252 S.E.2d 484 (1979) (full value of land is measure of damages) with Ragsdale v. Ragsdale, 172 S.W.2d 381 (Tex. Civ. App. 1943) (no recovery).

4. *Measuring damages.* It is usually said that the damages for a breach of a covenant against encumbrances are equal to the amount required to remove the encumbrance, if this is possible, and otherwise the diminution it causes to the value of the land. See Yonkers City Post No. 1666, VFW v. Josanth Realty Corp., 67 N.Y.2d 1029, 503 N.Y.S.2d 321, 494 N.E.2d 452 (1986). In Ellison v. F. Murray Parker Builders, Inc., 573 S.W.2d 161 (Tenn. App. 1978), the grantees bought their house by warranty deed for $46,500. A few years later they contracted to sell it for $59,500. However, a title examination disclosed that a previously unknown sewer easement ran under the house. They did not remove the easement, but instead reduced the selling price by $3,000, to $56,500, and completed the sale. They then brought an action against their grantor for breach of the covenant against encumbrances.

An expert appraiser testified that the easement reduced the land's value by $6,700 as of the date the plaintiffs bought it. What should their recovery be? The $6,700 reduction in value? The $3,000 reduction in the actual selling price? Zero, on the ground that, notwithstanding the encumbrance, they still sold the property for much more than they had paid? The court opted for the first figure.

5. *Limitation to actual loss.* The damages that a grantee-covenantee recovers must be related to her actual outlay or loss. Thus, if there is an encumbrance but the grantee does not clear it or pay it off, and it causes her no physical inconvenience, her recovery on the covenant will be merely nominal. See In re Meehan's Estate, 30 Wis. 2d 428, 141 N.W.2d 218 (1966). Similarly, if the grantee is able to persuade the holder of the outstanding encumbrance or paramount title to deed or release it to her without cost, she has only nominal damages. See, e.g., Creason v. Peterson, 24 Utah 2d 305, 470 P.2d 403 (1970).

6. *Recovery by remote grantees.* Consider the problems of measuring damages in a "leap-frog" action. Assume that A conveys to B (with a deed containing future covenants) for $20,000. Later, when prices have fallen, B conveys to C (via a deed with or without covenants) for $15,000. As matters turn out, A's title was wholly defective, and C is evicted. C can maintain an action against A because the future covenants run with the land. Is his recovery $20,000 (the amount A received) or $15,000 (the amount C paid)? Would it matter if C could show that, by the time of the suit, the land's value had risen again to $20,000 or more? See Cribbet, Property 275–76 (2d ed. 1975); ULTA § 2–513, Commissioners' Comment 2. In Patrick v. Meachum, 2007 WL 286712 (Ky. App. 2007) (not reported in S.W.3d), the court found that the covenant of warranty ran with the land and protected a remote purchaser, but limited the damages to land's value at the time the original covenant was given.

7. *Defending the grantee's title: Interest, costs and attorneys' fees.* Under the covenants of warranty and quiet enjoyment, the grantee can "tender" the defense of title to the grantor, who then has the obligation to defend against the claim of the putative paramount titleholder. See, e.g., Erickson v. Chase, 231 P.3d 1261 (Wash. App. 2010); Coco v. Jaskunas, 986 A.2d 531 (N.H. 2009). In Edmonson v. Popchoi, 256 P.3d 1223 (Wash. 2011), the court held that this meant an active, good faith defense, and not merely a "quickie" settlement, followed by the payment of damages to the grantee.

If the grantor fails to accept the obligation to defend the title, the grantor becomes liable for the court costs and (usually) the attorneys' fees expended by the grantee in negotiating or litigating in good faith against the person claiming paramount title. See Dionne v. LeClerc, 896 A.2d 923 (Me. 2006); Creason v. Peterson, 470 P.2d 403 (Utah 1970). Some courts will allow recovery of these expenses even if the grantee does not first demand that the grantor defend the title. In addition, the grantee usually can obtain interest on her recovery, at least if she was deprived of the use or profits of the land by the acts of the paramount titleholder.

Suppose the grantee litigates the title against a putative paramount titleholder and *wins*. Has the grantee, by winning, thereby established that there was no title defect, and thus that the covenantor is not liable to her for anything, either damages or attorney fees? This is the usual view. See Nunes v. Meadowbrook Devel. Co., 24 A.3d 539 (R.I. 2011); Stumhoffer v. Perales, 2014 WL 4776153 (Tex. App. 2014); Sanpete Am., LLC v. Willardsen, 269 P.3d 118 (Ut. 2011); Black v. Patel, 594 S.E.2d 162 (S.C. 2004). Given the costs associated with her title defense, is such a result the ultimate "Catch-22" for the winning grantee?

8. *After-acquired title.* Covenants in deeds are of importance in the operation of the doctrine known as "after-acquired title" or "estoppel by deed." Suppose A purports to convey land to B by full warranty deed, but at the time A really has no title at all. Obviously, B gets nothing (except a claim against A on the covenants of title). Later, however, A acquires the title from the true owner. The doctrine of after-acquired title holds that the title then inures instantly and automatically to B. See Mack Oil Co. v. Garvin, 39 P.3d 775 (Okla. 2001); 6A Powell, Real Property ¶ 937 (1979).

This passage of title to B can be explained in terms of estoppel. If A has given B covenants of title, the grantor A ought to be estopped to deny, when A later acquires title, that it has passed to B. Under this reasoning, a quitclaim deed ordinarily will not cause the doctrine to operate, unless it also contains some specific representation by A that he has the title. See Carkuff v. Balmer, 795 N.W.2d 303 (N.D. 2011); Kennedy Oil v. Lance Oil & Gas Co., Inc., 126 P.3d 875 (Wyo. 2006); Sorenson v. Wright, 268 N.W.2d 203 (Iowa 1978).

The operation of the doctrine is not limited to deeds. For example, a mortgage on land given by A, who has no title, to B (if it contains covenants of title, as mortgages almost invariably do) will become effective if A later obtains title to the land. See Rabo Agrifinance, Inc. v. Terra XXI, Ltd., 336 P.3d 972 (N.M. App. 2014); Guess v. Gathings, 728 So. 2d 1038 (La. App. 1999).

Estoppel by deed situations can raise a number of hard questions. Suppose the grantee has changed her mind, no longer wants the land, and prefers to seek damages for the breach of title covenants instead. May she do so? See W. Stoebuck & D. Whitman, The Law of Property § 11.5 (3d ed. 2000). Must the grantee who claims title under estoppel by deed show actual detrimental reliance, as in an ordinary estoppel? See Shell Oil Co. v. Trailer & Truck Repair Co., 828 F.2d 205 (3d Cir. 1987) (applying New Jersey law). What about interests that normally would attach to A's title the moment he acquired title to the land, such as a preexisting lien of a judgment creditor or his spouse's marital rights? On its face, the doctrine of after-acquired title leaves these matters unsettled, leaving it up to the courts to deal with such issues on an *ad hoc* basis.

A number of states have adopted statutes on the subject. They usually appear to restate the common law rule, but often limit themselves to cases in which the first conveyance purports to be a fee simple transfer; in addition, they appear to make the "inurement" of title to the grantee automatic, even if that would be contrary to the grantee's wishes or the interests of third parties. Moreover they often leave unclear whether the legislature intended to preempt the field, or whether the common law doctrine of estoppel by deed continues to operate in cases not covered by the statute. See generally Robert Swenson, Statutory Estoppel by Deed, 1950 Wash. U.L.Q. 361 (1950).

Estoppel by deed can cause serious problems for title examiners, for the deed that contains the covenants and therefore creates the estoppel is obviously out of time sequence in the chain of title, and hence may be very hard to locate in the public records. Moreover, if the party who is relying on the doctrine is not a bona fide purchaser, his or her interest may be defeated by the operation of the recording acts; see F.D.I.C. v. Taylor, 267 P.3d 949 (Ut. App. 2011). These and other problems encountered by title searchers are addressed in the next section.

F. TITLE ASSURANCE METHODS

1. INTRODUCTION

In this section we treat what might be considered the central issue in the transfer of real estate: proof of title. Obviously, no one wants to advance very much cash (or credit) toward the purchase of property without first being certain that the purported seller really owns the land or otherwise has the right to convey it. Even if individual buyers might sometimes be fairly casual in this respect, they usually find that they must borrow some or all of the purchase price, and their institutional lenders (who usually insist on a mortgage or other security interest in the real estate being purchased) most assuredly are not casual at all. Nobody wants a mortgage on the proverbial Brooklyn Bridge!

How does one find out whether the person who claims to own land really owns it?[2] Most laypeople would answer by saying that one must "search the title," but laypeople often have quite an erroneous idea of what a "title search" means. It is widely understood that the county court house (or other local government depository) contains some records, and that the search is made by using those records. But many people probably assume that the "search" is simply a matter of going to the proper officials in the courthouse and *asking* them who owns the land in question. In other words, the notion is widespread that someone in local government

---

[2] The simplest answer, of course, is to ask the seller. But the seller might be mistaken or crooked, and our study of covenants of title in the previous section should have convinced you that recoveries on such covenants are problematic at best. What buyers need is an independent source of title information.

somehow keeps track of the ownership of each parcel of land, and has the duty of answering the public's questions about title.

If we were concerned with motor vehicles instead of land, that concept would be quite accurate. In most states there is some statewide authority (say, a Department of Motor Vehicles) that can provide computerized and virtually instantaneous data about the ownership of a particular car or truck. There is, in fact, a similar (though considerably more complex) system for land in nine states, but it is widely used in only a handful of localities. It is called the Torrens or title registration system, and we will take a brief look at it later in this section. But it is not a popular approach.

For the most part in the United States, local governments take no active role in determining or averring the state of the title to land, but instead merely act as passive depositories for the instruments affecting title that people choose to "record" by having them copied by the relevant public official. To one who wishes to know the state of the title to a parcel, the local government (typically, at the county level) says not "We will tell you who owns it," but rather "Here are all of the deeds, mortgages, liens, and other documents that have been left with us. You are welcome to look through them and draw your own conclusions about the title." If the searcher reaches erroneous conclusions about the title after examining the documents on file, that is his or her own problem. The county simply is not liable unless its employees have made a mechanical or clerical error in copying or indexing the papers.[3]

In most American jurisdictions, recording is done at the county level, but there are exceptions. In Hawaii and Alaska recording is administered by the state. In several New England states, towns rather than counties operate recording systems. Connecticut, for example, has about 170 recording offices. The recording function may be carried out by the clerk of the local trial court, the county clerk, or by a separate official known as the "county recorder," the "register of deeds," or the like. All told, there are about 3,600 recording jurisdictions in the country. There is a nice summary of the systems in Hone, Land and Property Research in the United States 184 (1997).

"Well," you may say, "if I must look at all of these musty old documents and then decide for myself who has the title, can I at least be

---

[3] In some states the responsible official can be held liable for negligence. See, e.g., Badger v. Benfield, 337 S.E.2d 596 (N.C.App. 1985) (clerk is liable if negligence is the proximate cause of plaintiff's injury). Cf. Antonis v. Liberati, 821 A.2d 666 (Pa. Commw. Ct. 2003) (clerk held immune from liability for negligence for incorrectly indexing a mortgage). In most states, recording officials are required by law to be bonded, but the bond is often for a limited amount, usually considerably less than the value of the average parcel of real estate. Recovery against the local government itself may be barred by sovereign immunity, and courts obviously will be reluctant to levy large personal judgments against public officials or employees. For all of these reasons, negligence suits against recorders often result in an inadequate recovery. We will address later the question of who, as between the party recording the instrument and the party searching for it, will prevail as to the title when the recorder has made an error.

certain that all of the legally relevant documents are here?" The answer depends on your status as a buyer of land (or your client's status, if you search titles as a lawyer). If the buyer fulfills certain criteria, he or she can be confident that *most* of the legally relevant documents are in the courthouse. What status is necessary? In nearly all states, the buyer must be a good faith purchaser for value (a label that we will explore in the next subsection). In about half of the states, a good faith purchaser must also record his or her own conveyance in the public records before anyone else having an adverse claim to the title does so. If the buyer qualifies as a good faith purchaser, he or she can be confident in ignoring the possibility that certain types of adverse claims exist, due to the protection offered by the *recording act* of the state where the land is located.

Unfortunately, recording acts only protect against certain types of adverse claims. There are other types of adverse claims to the title that are entirely outside the coverage of the recording acts system, and thus might have full validity even though a title searcher, despite meticulous examination, cannot find a trace of them in the courthouse. Such adverse claims include claims that do not arise out of a written instrument at all (such as adverse possession, prescriptive easements, implied easements, and oral boundary line agreements), and claims that cause the written and recorded documents to have less than their facial efficacy, which cannot be discerned by looking at the documents in question. (A forged deed is the most obvious example of this category, but there are others, as we will see.)

At this point you may be ready to throw up your hands and exclaim that you want no part of such a defective system of title assurance. You will probably take little comfort in the assertion that these "unfindable" adverse claims crop up rather infrequently. After all, the fact that the chances are one in a thousand is pretty cold comfort if *your* client happens to be the one who "wins" the adverse claim lottery. The truth is that our system is defective, and that if one looks only at the formal legal structure one would probably conclude that in modern, mobile society it presents unacceptable risks. For precisely that reason, an unofficial, privately owned system of title assurance, called "title insurance," has arisen to absorb and spread most of the risks that the public records system presents. In terms of speed, accuracy, and effective risk-spreading it is quite successful, although it operates in a market environment that is characterized by little price competition, and hence probably imposes excessive costs on consumers.[4]

Ironically, the very existence of the private title insurance industry has made reform of the public records system more difficult, because the title insurers are highly antagonistic to any institutional changes which

---

[4] On the economics of the title insurance industry, see Owen, Kickbacks, Specialization, Price Fixing, and Efficiency in Residential Real Estate Markets, 29 Stan. L. Rev. 931 (1977); Whitman, Home Transfer Costs: An Economic and Legal Analysis, 62 Geo. L. J. 1311 (1974).

would render their own services obsolete or in less demand. Thus, reform has moved with glacial speed. For example, the Uniform Simplification of Land Transfers Act, promulgated by the National Conference of Commissioners on Uniform State Laws in 1976 and 1977, largely reflects the work done and published by Lewis Simes and Clarence Taylor nearly 20 years earlier. Its concepts are scarcely radical, but they were a long time coming, and there has never been any great outpouring of interest in them.

But we are ahead of our story. Before we study reform of the existing system or the efforts of private industry to supplement it, we need to understand how the current system operates.

2.　RECORDING ACTS

Why do people who enter into real estate transactions bother to take their papers to the courthouse to be recorded? It is clear in virtually every state that recording is unnecessary to the validity of a deed. As between the grantor and the grantee, the deed is effective upon delivery to the grantee whether filed in the public records or not. Yet the law gives certain incentives for filing, and most people respond by doing so. To understand the incentives, imagine the simple case in which Oscar (O) is the owner in fee simple of land. On day one, O sells the land to Alice (A), giving A a deed and receiving a handsome price. On day two, feeling greedy and a bit corrupt, O decides to sell *the same land* to Betty (B)! Obviously, this scam is likely to work only if A has not taken possession of the land yet, because A's presence would tip off B that O is no longer the owner of the land. We can diagram our hypothetical series of transactions this way:

Deed

Day 1: O ⸻⟶ A

Deed

Day 2: O ⸻⟶ B

Do not be disturbed by the fact that there are two deeds in this picture! Recall that a deed is not a unique piece of paper, and O can make up as many of them (to the same land) as O wishes. The question, of course, is who holds the superior claim of title to the land? In a jurisdiction without a recording act (and there are none in the United States, so we must imagine one hypothetically), strict legal logic would tell us that A is the owner. B cannot prevail in a title dispute with A because at the time O purported to deed the land to B, O had nothing. So B has nothing either. In other words, the common law principle of "first in time, first in right" governs.

Astounding as it may seem, statutory recording acts can (and often do) change this result. In effect, a recording act gives O the power, under certain circumstances, to convey superior title to B notwithstanding the prior conveyance to A. This is a strange concept—that one with no title can still transfer good title—and it takes a little getting used to. Under what circumstances can this result occur? First (and this is true under every American recording act), it can occur only if A fails to record her deed before B buys the land from O. You can immediately see that this provides a powerful incentive for A to record her deed immediately. The law tells A that, although she now has title, she may lose it if her grantor makes a later conveyance of the same land *unless she records.* True, A will probably have a claim for damages against O if this occurs (particularly if she received a deed containing full covenants of title), but this is much less satisfactory to A than keeping the land she bought. So A will usually be very careful to record her deed immediately, thereby cutting off O's power to deprive A of her title.

Even if A fails to record, B will not always prevail, for the recording acts of the various states impose certain criteria upon B's status and behavior as well. There are three categories of such acts, and by oversimplifying a little we can present some basic information about them in the form of a table. The table's purpose is to answer the question, "Assuming that A has failed to record, what must B do to qualify as having superior title under the recording act and thereby prevail in a title dispute as against A?"

What must B do to prevail against A?	Type of Act	Prevalence of this type of act
1. B must be a purchaser for value and without notice.	Notice	About half of the states
2. B must record his own conveyance before A records.	Race	Only three states: Delaware, Louisiana and North Carolina[5]
3. B must both be a purchaser for value and without notice, and also record before A.	Notice-Race	About half the states

The requirements that the recording act statutes impose on B have a moralistic ring about them. The "notice" and "notice-race" states seem to say, "Why should we let B take advantage of A's failure to record if B

---

[5]   A few other states have specialized race-type statutes that apply to specific types of conveyances. These include, for example, Arkansas (mortgages), Ohio (mortgages and oil and gas leases), and Pennsylvania (mortgages except for purchase money.)

knew about A anyway, or if B paid nothing for the land (so that she has nothing to lose)?" The "race" and "notice-race" states seem to say, "Why should we let B take advantage of A's failure to participate in the public recording process if B herself also fails to participate?" Pause for a moment and consider whether either the notice or recording-first requirements are really essential to a rational and workable recording system. Would it be equally satisfactory (and more simple) if the statutes allowed *all* subsequent grantees to prevail against A's unrecorded deed? Or, should we take the next logical step, and simply announce that all unrecorded conveyances are void until recorded? No American recording system goes this far.

Our example above assumed that both A and B were given deeds purporting to convey fee simple title, but the same principles apply if one or both of them transfer lesser interests in the land. For example, if both are mortgages, the common law would say that A has the first mortgage, and that B's mortgage is junior or subordinate to it. A notice-type recording act will reverse those priorities if A failed to record and B is a good faith "purchaser" (many of the statutes add the words "or creditor" just to take care of mortgagees, but they are universally considered to be included anyway unless there is a special recording statute for mortgages) for value (a "BFP") who acquired the mortgage interest without notice of A's prior mortgage on the land. Similarly, if the deed to A granted A only an easement across O's land, the question becomes whether B (whose deed conveys a fee simple) takes free of A's easement or takes the land subject to it. In general, we can say that the recording acts may give B, the subsequent purchaser, priority over an interest to which B would otherwise be subordinate.

At this point it is appropriate to examine a few recording act statutes in some depth. We will omit language defining terms, setting up the recording office, authorizing the recorder to perform his or her duties, and so forth, and concentrate instead on the operative language of the statute divesting the title of transferees who fail to record. Perhaps the most common format is represented by the Washington statute reproduced below.

Wash. Rev. Code § 65.08.070

Every * * * conveyance not * * * recorded is void as against any subsequent purchaser or mortgagee in good faith and for valuable consideration from the same vendor * * * whose conveyance is first duly recorded.

The Washington statute is of the "notice-race" type because the subsequent purchaser, in order to prevail, must both be a BFP and record first. The legislature could easily amend the statute to make it a pure "notice" type by deleting the last phrase quoted, " * * * whose conveyance is first duly recorded." Many "notice" type statutes follow this format. The Arkansas statute, for example, reads this way; see Ark. Code Ann. § 16–115. An alternative type of wording for a "notice" statute, and one that also is very common, is represented by the Iowa Statute reproduced below.

Iowa Code § 558.41

No instrument affecting real estate is of any validity against subsequent purchasers for a valuable consideration, without notice, unless filed in the office of the recorder * * * .

Although most recording acts are worded in a straightforward manner, a few are ambiguous or confusing. Colorado, New Hampshire, and Missouri have been particularly problematic, requiring clarification by courts or legislatures.

The operational difference between the notice and race-notice types of statutes is illustrated by the following facts:

Day 1	O —Deed→	A (Unrecorded)
Day 2	O —Deed→	B (Unrecorded, but B is a BFP)
Day 3	A records	
Day 4	B records	

Under a notice statute, B will prevail because she lacked notice of A's claim and paid value at the time of her conveyance. Under a race-notice statute, A will prevail; B is disqualified, despite her BFP status, because she did not record her deed from O first. Is either type of statute superior to the other in policy terms? The Colorado Court of Appeals thought so:

Our decision is buttressed by the fact that a pure notice statute serves to protect subsequent purchasers, allowing them to rely on the record title as it exists at the time of their purchase. The danger of a race-notice statute is that a prior interest holder who has failed to record may cut off the claim of a subsequent purchaser who relied on the record at the time of his closing but has not yet had time to record his own instrument. See Note, The Colorado Recording Act: Race-Notice or Pure Notice? 51 Den. L. J. 115 (1974). Characterizing the statute as a pure notice rather than race-notice statute will encourage purchasers to record their interests as soon as acquired. Although a subsequent purchaser need not record to protect his interest against prior unrecorded interests, unless he does record, his interest may be cut off by a purchaser subsequent to him.

Fees-Krey, Inc., v. Page, 42 Colo. App. 8, 12, 591 P.2d 1339, 1343 (1978).

Finally, examine the North Carolina statute reproduced below.

N.C. Gen. Stat. § 47–18

No * * * conveyance of land * * * shall be valid to pass any *Race* property interest as against lien creditors or purchasers for a valuable consideration from the donor * * * but from the time of registration thereof.

If you compare this statute with those of Washington and Iowa above, you will note that the word "subsequent" does not appear before "creditors or purchasers" in the North Carolina version. You might think of the North Carolina statute as working "both ways"—that is, denying unrecorded conveyances validity both as against subsequent *and prior* purchasers. Nobody is safe from anybody else until he or she records! Of course, the statute is not quite a "pure" race statute because to prevail against a prior unrecorded conveyance, one must have paid value. The point is that in our A–B example, under North Carolina law B can prevail against A if B records before A does (assuming B pays value), even though B knows all about O's prior conveyance to A.

Incidentally, the "race" designation applied to the North Carolina and similar statutes is a bit misleading in another sense. It seems to suggest that A and B are literally racing one another to the courthouse, and the first one to arrive and record will own the land. In reality, each of them is usually entirely unaware of the other for many months or years, and there is no race going on at all. Still, the first one to record will win (assuming that B is a BFP who paid value and not a donee).

Bear in mind that, under all three types of recording statutes, A always will prevail over subsequent purchasers if A records immediately. To illustrate, consider the facts of Prochaska v. Midwest Title Guarantee Co., 85 Wash. App. 256, 932 P.2d 172 (1997). A plaintiff who had obtained a judgment against the property owner recorded a certified copy of the judgment at 10:05 am. (Recording the judgment made it operative as a lien against the owner's real estate located in the county where the judgment was rendered.) Nine minutes later, at 10:14 am, the deed by which the owner was selling his property was recorded by the buyers' escrow company. The court held, quite correctly, that because the judgment was recorded first (though not by much), it had priority over the deed under Washington's race-notice statute. As a result, the title received by the buyers was subject to the judgment lien. They had title insurance (fortunately) and their title company ended up having to pay off the lien. The title company argued that it could not have found the judgment in its search—the judgment had obviously not yet been indexed by the recorder's staff, and it was probably lying in an "in-box" waiting to be processed. The court took the view that indexing the judgment was not part of "recording" it, and that once the judgment had been accepted and date-and-time stamped by the recorder of deeds, it was considered to be "recorded." Perhaps the title company should have thumbed through the documents in the in-box! In jurisdictions with large recording volumes, however, this approach might be completely impractical, resulting in a risk that the title company must bear as part of its business.

A fascinating problem is presented by the facts of First Bank v. East West Bank, 132 Cal. Rptr. 3d 267 (Cal.App. 2011), in which an owner executed and delivered two conflicting mortgages on his property to two different lenders, neither of which knew of the other. Both mortgages were recorded, by two different title companies, on the same day. Because of the peculiar California practice of allowing title companies to present documents for recording before the opening of business hours at the recorders' offices, both were submitted in the early morning hours and were time-stamped at exactly 8:00 am on the same day. Thus for legal purposes, both mortgages were recorded simultaneously! The court held, apparently quite correctly, that neither one was a "subsequent" conveyance. The court then concluded that the two mortgages had equal priority. Does this conclusion logically follow? Would a better analysis be that, because neither mortgage was subsequent, the California notice-race recording act simply did not apply; therefore, that the common law rule of "first in time, first in right" governed the priority of the two mortgages? And wouldn't that mean that the first mortgage to be executed and delivered by the mortgagor had priority?

Given that under the recording acts a subsequent conveyance by O to a BFP (who, in half the states, also must record first), coupled with A's failure to record, has the effect of cutting off A's rights, you might wonder whether A can recover damages against O for the loss. In a sense, A brought the loss on himself or herself by failing to record. But in another sense, A would have suffered no loss if O had not made a subsequent conveyance of land that O no longer owned. Should O be liable to A for making the subsequent conveyance to a BFP? Several cases suggest that such liability should indeed arise, although on a variety of theories. See, e.g., Bardwell v. White, 762 So. 2d 778 (Miss. App. 2000) (recovery based on breach of duty of good faith and fair dealing); Jones v. Garden Park Homes Corp., 393 S.W.2d 501 (Mo. 1965) (recovery in tort permitted); Patterson v. Bryant, 216 N.C. 550, 5 S.E.2d 849 (1939) (restitution permitted to avoid unjust enrichment).

3. INTERESTS AND CONVEYANCES OUTSIDE THE RECORDING ACT SYSTEM

So far we have treated the recording acts as though they applied equally to all types of interests in land transferred in all possible ways. Unfortunately, life is not so simple. First, consider the matter of what interests are within the scope of the recording act system. By their terms, the acts usually exclude short-term leases (typically those for less than one to three years)—usually those that are not required to be in writing pursuant to the Statute of Frauds. Consequently, a tenant for a short term need not record the lease in order to protect herself against a future transfer of the property by her landlord to a BFP. In many cases, the tenant's possession would give notice to the purchaser in any event, but the rule described above operates even if the tenant is not in possession.

With this one exception, virtually all interests in land that are evidenced by a writing are within the recording acts[6] (although, as we shall see below, the manner of their conveyance may not be). Specifically, there is no doubt today that express easements, restrictive covenants, contracts of sale, and even options to sell[7] are covered, and one who takes an interest of any of these types can best protect himself or herself by recording. On the other hand, documents that do not create or transfer interests in land are often held to be nonrecordable; the records, after all, are not a public bulletin board. For example, if a purchaser under an installment land contract (in general, clearly a recordable instrument) finds that the contract itself cannot be recorded (because, for example, the vendor's signature was not acknowledged before a notary), she may try to record a "notice of interest" or an affidavit of ownership instead. Such a paper is not a conveyance, and may be held technically unrecordable;[8] but as a practical matter, the recorder may well accept it, and future searchers will probably find it.

More serious difficulties arise with interests in land which the law recognizes, but that are not created by a written document. The classic example is adverse possession. It gives rise to no paper to be recorded. Thus, it is entirely possible for the adverse possessor to complete

---

[6] See 6A Powell, Real Property ¶ 914 (1979). Interests in land owned by the Federal government cannot be defeated by operation of state recording acts, and conveyances by the Federal government (and many states) need not be recorded in order to be protected from a subsequent BFP. See III Am. L. Prop. § 17.8 (1952).

[7] Is an option a conveyance of an interest in land? Technically, it is not, but as a practical matter it is highly desirable that options be recordable, and most cases have held that they are. See, e.g., Strong v. Clark, 56 Wn. 2d 230, 352 P.2d 183 (1960).

[8] Coggins v. Mimms, 373 So. 2d 964 (Fla. App. 1979). If the instrument is legally unrecordable but is in fact placed in the records, it gives no constructive notice to those who should have searched for it but failed to do so. See, e.g., In re Ryan, 851 F.2d 502 (1st Cir. 1988) (under Vermont law, a deed lacking one of two required witnesses was not entitled to be recorded, and hence gave no constructive notice). It may, however, well give actual notice to those who search and therefore see it in fact. See Annot., 3 A.L.R. 2d 589 (1949).

possession for the statutory period, then vacate the land (so that his presence will no longer warn a buyer of his title), and yet prevail over a subsequent BFP from the record owner. Mugaas v. Smith, 33 Wash. 2d 429, 206 P.2d 332, 9 A.L.R. 2d 846 (1949). The same sort of thing can occur with prescriptive easements. See In re Boston Regional Medical Center, Inc., 240 B.R. 813 (Bankr. D. Mass.1999) (BFPs take subject to prescriptive easements under Massachusetts law). Most recent cases give title to BFPs free of unrecorded implied easements; see, e.g., Tiller v. Hinton, 19 Ohio St. 3d 66, 482 N.E.2d 946 (1985). But see Otero v. Pacheco, 94 N.M. 524, 612 P.2d 1335 (App. 1980), (court found that the purchasers had constructive notice from the "visibility" of a buried sewer line). In many states the status of unrecorded prescriptive and implied easement is unclear.

Marital rights provide another example. Common law dower and curtesy and some of their modern statutory counterparts apply not solely to land owned at the decedent's death, but to all land owned during the marriage. Yet there is no practical way that a title searcher can tell whether a former owner of the land was married or not. Most courts today would protect subsequent BFP's from such dower and curtesy claims, as the court did in Petta v. Host, 115 N.E.2d 881 (Ill. 1953). Bankruptcy presents another example. The property of one who is declared bankrupt is automatically transferred to the trustee in bankruptcy. There is no deed representing this transfer, and therefore nothing to record in the county records (although the federal court having jurisdiction of the case will reflect the matter in its docket records).

A similar problem is raised by mechanic's liens, which are intended to help those who supply labor or materials for building projects to recover the money they are owed if the owner or builder does not pay them. Laborers and suppliers are permitted to file claims of lien on the real property, and ultimately to have it sold to raise the necessary funds to pay their claims. Title search difficulties arise because the claimant generally is given some amount of time after *completion* of the work to file the claim in the public records. Once filed, the priority of the lien relates back in time, under many statutes, to the date the particular work or the entire project *commenced*. Consequently, one who purchases the land between these two dates (the beginning of the work or project and the end of the lien filing period) cannot be certain of taking free of such liens. The problem is particularly acute when the work has been fairly minor in nature, so that the buyer of the property may not even realize that it has been done. The relation-back feature of a mechanic's lien is obviously very attractive to lien claimants, whose claims otherwise would be cut off by a transfer of the property to a BFP, but it also tends to sap the public records of their reliability.

In addition to interests that need not be recorded at all (like adverse possession) and those that need be recorded only after the fact (like mechanic's liens), additional title search problems are raised by claims, judgment liens or other encumbrances that are allowed to be (and normally are) recorded in places other than the county recorder's office. The nature of these items varies from state to state, but the following are typical: (1) real property tax liens recorded in the county treasurer or tax collector's office; (2) assessment liens for street, sewer, and other improvements in various city offices; (3) wills in the office of the clerk of the probate or other relevant court;[9] (4) judgment liens in the office of the municipal, district, county or state clerk of court; (5) bankruptcies and federal condemnations in the office of the federal district court clerk; and (6) zoning or other land use information (technically not an aspect of title, but equally important to real estate purchasers) in a city or county zoning administrator's office. This list is merely illustrative, and in some localities many more sources of information must be checked. One compilation for Cleveland, Ohio, listed 76 types of records in 16 different public offices that might contain land title data. See Johnstone & Hopson, Lawyers and Their Work 274–75 (1967). This is surely an extreme example, but the point is that a searcher may spend a great deal of time and effort in a very inefficient process!

Until now, we have been discussing the problem of title data that is not recorded or is hard to find. Now consider the other side of the coin: there is no assurance that the records one does find are authentic or reliable. When the title searcher examines a deed in the records that appears to be valid on its face, the searcher must remember that the deed may be subject to numerous objections. For example, the deed might be forged, have a defective acknowledgment, or never may have been delivered to its grantee. The deed may have been given by a grantor who was without capacity or have been executed by an attorney in fact whose power of attorney had been revoked. The recorder's office makes no representation that the instruments it preserves are correct, and in many cases one cannot detect such defects by examining the document itself. Some defects may make the conveyance void whereas others make it only voidable, but even in the latter case the BFP may be forced to litigate to prove the superiority of his or her title, hardly an attractive prospect.

Even if none of these technical problems arise, it is all too easy for a searcher to make a mistake. In theory, one can construct a complete title history of any parcel back to the original conveyance from the sovereign, but in many jurisdictions, especially in the East, this is impractically burdensome, and searches are often limited to periods of 30 to 60 years.

---

[9] Although a will is obviously a conveyance, most states' recording acts do not cover wills; instead, the records of the probate court in which the will was proved constitute public notice of its existence and contents. See III Am. L. Prop. § 17.8 (1952).

Of course, this is a calculated risk because earlier defects in the title could come to light. Even within the period searched, it is not unusual to miss an entry, misread a document, or misplace a sheet of notes. These kinds of mistakes may result in liability for damages if the searcher is a lawyer or an abstractor, but damages are sometimes hard to collect, and in any event are a poor substitute for the land itself.

Professor Ted Fiflis, after surveying all of the problems we have just described, listed nineteen specific ways in which a title search in the public records might produce erroneous results. Fiflis, Land Transfer Improvement: The Basic Facts and Two Hypotheses for Reform, 38 U. Colo. L. Rev. 431, 453–54 (1966). See also R. Lynwood Straw, Off-Record Risks for Bona Fide Purchasers of Interests in Real Property, 72 Dick. L. Rev. 35 (1967); Stroup, The Unreliable Record Title, 60 N.D. L. Rev. 203 (1984). Other writers have arrived at different numbers, but the point is clear: a search of the records, even if diligently made, still leaves a buyer or mortgagee of the land open to serious title risks.

4. BONA FIDE PURCHASERS

Except in Delaware, North Carolina and Louisiana, the only subsequent purchasers who are protected by the recording acts against prior unrecorded conveyances are bona fide purchasers. BFP status encompasses two elements: paying value and lacking notice of the prior conveyance. There is a good deal of legal lore on each of these elements.

Paying value is a requirement that obviously excludes mere donees of gifts. The recipient of the land must give up something in return. Most courts require more than nominal or "grossly inadequate" consideration, but do not necessarily demand that the price paid be comparable to the land's fair value. See, e.g., Phillips v. Latham, 523 S.W.2d 19 (Tex. Civ. App. 1975). A mere promise to pay in the future (unless it is a negotiable note) will not count until at least some payment is made in fact. Even if negotiable, the note is not regarded as value unless it has in fact been negotiated to a holder in due course (who could enforce it against its maker without regard to most of the defenses the maker might raise). See IV Am. L. Prop. § 17.10 n. 14 (1952). Due to the fact that nearly all of the statutes, either explicitly or by judicial interpretation, protect subsequent creditors as well as purchasers, a lender who advances a loan and takes a mortgage or deed of trust as security has given "value," even though it is expected that the loan will be fully repaid.

A common problem is raised by the creditor who takes a mortgage or other security interest in land to secure a preexisting debt. For example, a bank may make an unsecured loan and later ask the debtor to give it a mortgage as security. Unless the bank somehow changes its position detrimentally in return for the mortgage (e.g., by granting an extension of time for repayment), the majority view is that the bank has not given value under the recording acts, and its mortgage will be subordinate to any prior unrecorded conveyances the debtor has made of the land. Gabel v. Drewrys Ltd., U.S.A., Inc., 68 So. 2d 372 (Fla. 1953); see Annot., 39 A.L.R. 2d 1088 (1955). The same is true of a mechanic's lien claimant who originally performed his work without taking any interest in the land as security, and who gives up no further value in return for the lien when it arises. See Stout v. Lye, 103 U.S. (13 Otto) 66, 26 L. Ed. 428 (1880). In many cases, however, the "relation back" feature of mechanic's liens provides the lien claimant with greater priority than he would gain through the recording acts. The notion, then, is that the "value" ought to be paid contemporaneously or subsequent to the conveyance. Compare the case of the creditor who previously has made an unsecured loan, and who later takes a *deed* of the land as satisfaction for the debt. This situation is vastly different from that of a creditor who takes a mortgage, for here the creditor has incurred a huge detriment—it has deemed the debt satisfied, and given up its claim against the debtor. Surprisingly, quite a few courts have misunderstood this distinction. Clearly, the latter case is one in which value has been given, and the creditor should be protected. See IV Am. L. Prop. § 17.10 n. 29 (1952) (collecting calls). Cf. Wight v. Chandler, 264 F.2d 249 (10th Cir. 1959).

The timing of the payment of "value" can become a critical issue. To be a BFP, one must have no notice of the prior unrecorded instrument at the time the value is paid. This is simple enough when the sale is for cash, but is more complicated with an installment contract sale. Suppose the buyer begins making monthly payments while entirely innocent of notice, but later learns of the prior conveyance after paying, say, half of the total price. Some sort of *pro tanto* protection seems in order here. The most common method of accomplishing it is to give the contract purchaser a lien on the real estate for the amount she paid before getting notice of the prior transferee's rights. See, e.g., Westpark, Inc. v. Seaton Land Co., 225 Md. 433, 171 A.2d 736 (1961). Should the buyer also get a lien for any improvements he has made?

Giving the contract purchaser a lien for the amount paid probably will enable her to recover the payments, but one might well ask whether other approaches are more just. Should the buyer simply be permitted to complete her payments as per the contract, except with the payments accruing after she receives notice being made to the holder of the unrecorded title? See 5 Tiffany, Real Property § 1305 n. 41 (3d ed.1939) (describing cases taking this position).

Finally, consider the plight of the judgment creditor whose defendant-debtor has made unrecorded transfers of his real estate. The creditor, relying on the records, may assume that the debtor has substantial assets. He retains legal counsel, pays court costs and witness fees, obtains a judgment, and then discovers that the unrecorded deeds have left the defendant without assets. Can he claim the protection of the recording acts? The typical answer is negative, on the ground that he has not paid any contemporaneous consideration for his judgment lien. See ABN AMRO Mortg. Group, Inc. v. American Residential Serv., LLC, 845 N.E.2d 209 (Ind. App. 2006); In re Brosnahan, 312 B.R. 220 (Bankr.W.D.N.Y. 2004); Texas American Bank/Levelland v. Resendez, 706 S.W.2d 343 (Tex. App. 1986); IV Am. L. Prop. § 17.10 n. 24, § 17.29 (1952); Note, Status of Judgment Creditors Under the Recording Acts, 32 Notre Dame L. Rev. 471 (1957). On the other hand, if a property is subject to a recorded judgment lien and the judgment creditor executes the lien through a foreclosure sale, any BFP who purchases the property at the execution sale before the prior conveyances are recorded usually will be protected. See IV Am. L. Prop. § 17.30 (1952); Valley Nat. Bank v. Avco Development Co., 14 Ariz. App. 56, 480 P.2d 671 (1971). Does this distinction make sense? Suppose the judgment creditor himself is the BFP at the execution sale. Should he be protected?

The second aspect of BFP status is lack of notice of the prior unrecorded conveyance. Thus, it is necessary to consider what sorts of notice might be imputed to a purchaser of real estate. Actual knowledge of the prior conveyance obviously constitutes notice. Rumors or gossip in the community, however, usually are not sufficient, but if the buyer has heard some apparently reliable information about an adverse claim, she is expected to make a reasonable investigation. See 6A Powell, Real Property ¶ 916 n. 11 (1979); Annot., 109 A.L.R. 746 (1937); Furnari v. Wells Fargo Bank, 2006 WL 664843 (Mich. App. 2006) (not reported in N.W.2d) (mortgage to vendor was subordinate to earlier mortgages to banks, where the earlier mortgages were mentioned in the mortgage to the vendor, giving him actual knowledge of them); Caruso v. Parkos, 262 Neb. 961, 637 N.W.2d 351 (2002) (subsequent purchaser was not a BFP, where he learned of prior deed from conversations with family members). Information given to the purchaser's attorney will also suffice if a reasonable person would further investigate it. See First Alabama Bank of Huntsville v. Key, 394 So. 2d 67 (Ala. Civ. App. 1981).

In general, the principle is this: "if the purchaser had knowledge of circumstances which ought . . . to have put a person of ordinary prudence on inquiry, he will be presumed to have made such inquiry and will be charged with notice of all facts which such an investigation would in all probability have disclosed if it had been properly pursued." Beins v. Oden, 843 A.2d 147 (Md. App. 2004).

Investigation requires that the purchaser must make an inquiry of the adverse claimant himself (if he can be identified and located by reasonable effort). It is plainly not enough for the purchaser to inquire of the seller, who in this context is in effect presumed to be a crook. Note carefully that the purchaser will be deemed to have whatever knowledge a proper and reasonable investigation would have turned up, whether she in fact makes any investigation or not. The courts may describe this imputation of knowledge to the purchaser as either "constructive" notice or "inquiry" notice.

The public records are sometimes said to be notice of their contents to "all the world," but this is surely an overstatement, for the public records give no notice to people who have no thought of buying any interest in the land in question, and who consequently have no reason to search the records. For example, a construction contractor who damaged a telephone company's underground cable was held not to have had constructive notice of the cable's existence despite the fact that the company had a recorded easement for it. *See* Mountain States Telephone & Tel. Co. v. Kelton, 79 Ariz. 126, 285 P.2d 168 (1955). The public records *are* notice to subsequent purchasers, but even this statement must be tempered by the concept of reasonableness. Suppose installment contract purchaser B (whose crooked vendor O has made a prior unrecorded deed to A) agrees to pay for the land in monthly installments over ten years. After two years of such payments A, the grantee of the prior deed, records it. This recording is certainly not automatically deemed notice to the installment contract purchaser B, for to say this would require B to search the title before each monthly payment, an intolerable burden. In this situation, B will not be held to have notice of the deed until some actual information concerning it reaches her. See, e.g., Dame v. Mileski, 80 Wyo. 156, 340 P.2d 205 (1959); Giorgi v. Pioneer Title Ins. Co., 85 Nev. 319, 454 P.2d 104 (1969). But see Alexander v. Andrews, 135 W.Va. 403, 64 S.E.2d 487 (1951).

On its face, the doctrine that the public records give constructive notice to later purchasers seems almost of trivial importance, because once a prior conveyance is recorded, it cannot be divested by the operation of any type of recording act. But a recorded instrument may refer to or describe a prior unrecorded one, or may otherwise state facts that would lead a prudent buyer to inquire, and hence may give constructive notice to a potential purchaser. For example, suppose a deed in the chain of title recites that the title is being transferred "subject to an easement previously granted to J.A. Jones for an irrigation ditch over the westerly ten feet." Even though the prior grant of the easement itself is unrecorded, the majority view is that a reference to it in a recorded deed will give a later buyer notice of whatever facts an inquiry of J.A. Jones would have adduced (assuming that Jones could be located by reasonable effort.) See Powell, supra; Clancy v. Recker, 455 Pa. 452, 316 A.2d 898 (1974); IV Am. L. Prop. § 17.28 (1952). Not all courts agree with the majority view. See Kalange v. Rencher, 136 Idaho 192, 30 P.3d 970

(2001). The majority rule is obviously burdensome to title examiners, and the Colorado legislature disliked it so much that it was revoked.

Colo. Rev. Stat. § 38–35–108

[When a recorded document] contains a recitation of or reference to some other instrument purporting to affect title to said real property, such recitation or reference shall bind only the parties to the instrument and shall not be notice to any other person whatsoever unless the instrument mentioned or referred to in the recital is [recorded].

Should other states adopt similar statutory provisions?

Incidentally, the types of public records that give notice are not limited to those in the county recorder's office. It is often held that other documents, such as property tax and assessment records and the docket records of the clerk of court, also are deemed to be constructive notice to the public, but records in zoning and planning offices usually are not. Cf. Story Bed & Breakfast v. Brown County Area, 794 N.E.2d 519 (Ind. App. 2003) (covenants filed with county planning office give no constructive notice); Ioannou v. Southold Town Planning Bd., 304 A.D.2d 578, 758 N.Y.S.2d 358 (2003) (same); First American Title Ins. Co. v. J.B. Ranch, Inc., 966 P.2d 834 (Utah 1998) (map filed in county clerk's office, rather than county recorder's office, gives no constructive notice); Island Venture Associates v. New Jersey Dept. of Environmental Protection, 359 N.J. Super. 391, 820 A.2d 88 (App. Div. 2003) (restrictive covenant filed only with state environmental agency gives no constructive notice). The court records that give constructive notice are not limited to judgments, which generally are liens on the defendant's real estate. The very filing of a lawsuit in which land title is in issue gives notice to prospective purchasers under the doctrine of lis pendens. In a number of states there are now statutory provisions for the filing of a "notice of lis pendens" in the county recorder's office, where a title searcher is much more likely to find it. But these statutes do not usually preempt fully the common law notion that the pendency of a suit involving land title is itself notice; see Chrysler Corp. v. Fedders Corp., 670 F.2d 1316 (3d Cir. 1982); IV Am. L. Prop. § 17.11. Consequently, court records always must be searched. For a comparison of common law and statutory lis pendens procedures, see Kelly v. Perry, 111 Ariz. 382, 531 P.2d 139 (1975), and Ravitch v. Stollman Poultry Farms, Inc., 162 Conn. 26, 291 A.2d 213 (1971).

Some cases hold that a grantee will lose BFP status due to certain characteristics of the transfer he receives. Thus, there is older authority that one who takes a quitclaim deed cannot be a BFP, because the form of deed indicates that the grantor is uncertain of his own title. Most of the recent cases protect grantees under quitclaim deeds if they are otherwise without notice. See, e.g., Sabo v. Horvath, 559 P.2d 1038 (Alaska 1976);

Note, Deeds—Quitclaim Grantee as a Bona Fide Purchaser, 28 Ore. L. Rev. 258 (1949); Annot., 162 A.L.R. 556 (1946); IV Am. L. Prop. § 17.16 (1952). Cf. Martinez v. Affordable Housing Network, Inc., 123 P.3d 1201 (Colo.2005) (back-to-back quitclaim deeds should raise a suspicion in the ultimate grantee's mind as to the legitimacy of the title). Similarly, some cases hold that one whose grantor's deed is unrecorded cannot be a BFP. See, e.g., Zimmer v. Sundell, 237 Wis. 270, 296 N.W. 589 (1941). Perhaps the best (or worst) example is Messersmith v. Smith, 60 N.W.2d 276 (N.D. 1953), in which a grantee was held not to be a BFP because the deed to his predecessor in title, although recorded, was improperly acknowledged and thus not entitled to recordation. (The grantor of that deed had not physically appeared before a notary, but merely had talked with the notary by telephone.) This defect, of course, was entirely indiscernible to a title searcher. See IV Am. L. Prop. § 17.10 n. 31 (1952); Maxwell, The Hidden Defect in Acknowledgment and Title Security, 2 U.C.L.A. L. Rev. 83 (1954). These decisions are not strictly logical, and it is very hard to justify them in terms of constructive or inquiry notice, for the facts of the cases give no clue as to whom an inquiry should be made by the prospective purchaser.

Undoubtedly, the most litigated aspect of notice is the rule that a purchaser of an interest in land is deemed to view it physically before buying, and that the purchaser is held to inquiry notice of facts that an inspection and inquiry of those in possession would disclose. This rule of "inquiry notice" is almost universally accepted. See, e.g., Mazza v. Realty Quest Brokerage Corp., 185 Misc. 2d 162, 712 N.Y.S.2d 288 (Civ. Ct. 2000); In re Crowder, 225 B.R. 794 (Bankr. D.N.M. 1998); Mazza v. Realty Quest Brokerage Corp., 185 Misc. 2d 162, 712 N.Y.S.2d 288 (Civ. Ct. 2000) (court concluded that possession by the owner of one unit in a duplex gave constructive notice of her rights). Cf. Madison v. Gordon, 39 S.W.3d 604 (Tex. 2001) (possession by unrecorded titleholder of one apartment in a four-plex gave no constructive notice of his rights; his possession was "neither exclusive nor unequivocal," because he appeared to be merely an ordinary tenant). A few recording act statutes speak only of "actual notice." If this language is construed literally, no inquiry notice arises from possession or other physical attributes of the property. See, e.g., Ann. L. Mass. c. 183 § 4; Comment, Possession as Notice under Missouri Recording Act, 16 Mo. L. Rev. 142 (1951).

Trouble arises in determining what is possession and what sorts of facts would lead a reasonable buyer to make further inquiry. For example, if the possession of the land is consistent with the record title (e.g., the grantor and his or her family are residing there), no inquiry is necessary. See, e.g., Diamond v. Wasserman, 8 A.D.2d 623, 185 N.Y.S.2d 411 (1959). But see Yancey v. Harris, 234 Ga. 320, 216 S.E.2d 83 (1975) (possession of grantor's family members does give notice of their rights);

Martinez v. Affordable Housing Network, Inc., 123 P.3d 1201 (Colo. 2005) (continued possession of former owner under lease with option to repurchase gave constructive notice to purchaser); Tompkins County Trust Co. v. Talandis, 176 Misc. 2d 632, 673 N.Y.S.2d 301 (1998) (possession of house by owner's ex-wife gave notice of her right to possession under unrecorded separation agreement). See generally 5 Tiffany, Real Property § 1290 (3d ed. 1939); IV Am. L. Prop. § 17.13 (1952); Comment, Grantor's Possession as Constructive Notice, 34 Miss. L. J. 325 (1963).

At the other extreme, suppose the property is a commercial store, and the tenant under an unrecorded lease puts a sign on the front of the building advertising his name and business. Here, a purchaser is surely expected to go inside and ask the tenant what his rights are. The sign, of course, is not essential; it is possession by the tenant that does the trick. There are dozens of cases. See, e.g., Apex Fin. Corp. v. Garza, 155 S.W.3d 230 (Tex. Ct. App. 2004); Grand Island Hotel Corp. v. Second Island Development Co., 191 Neb. 98, 214 N.W.2d 253 (1974); New Freedom Corp. v. Brown, 260 Md. 383, 272 A.2d 401 (1971). Incidentally, if the buyer does inquire of the party in possession, and the latter falsely denies his own interest in the land, he will be estopped to assert it later. See Losey v. Simpson, 11 N.J. Eq. 246 (1856). There also are many cases in which the facts are more ambiguous, and it is hard to predict the results. This is especially true where the holder of the unrecorded interest makes only sporadic or limited use of the property, such as camping or vacationing, running grazing stock, cutting timber, or parking motor vehicles. Compare Bradford v. Kimbrough, 485 So. 2d 1114 (Ala. 1986) with White v. Boggs, 455 So. 2d 820 (Ala. 1984). See IV Am. L. Prop. § 17.15 (1952). If the owner of the unrecorded interest places a sign on the property giving his name and address or telephone number, its presence will probably give inquiry notice to prospective purchasers even if his personal possession is dubious or weak. See, e.g., Chaffin v. Solomon, 255 Or. 141, 465 P.2d 217 (1970); Wineberg v. Moore, 194 F. Supp. 12 (N.D. Cal.1961), affirmed 349 F.2d 685 (9th Cir. 1965).

Suppose an instrument is filed by mistake, in the sense that it was defectively acknowledged, no recording fee or tax was paid, or in some other fashion it failed to meet the requirements for proper recording. Nevertheless, the instrument may contain accurate and highly important information about the title. The instrument, although it may exist in the public records, is legally "unrecorded." But what is its notice impact? The common attitude of the courts is that such an "unrecorded" filing gives no constructive notice, because it is really not entitled to be present in the records at all. See IV Am. L. Prop. §§ 17.27, 17.31 n. 16 (1952); In re Crim, 81 S.W.3d 764 (Tenn. 2002); Allen v. Allen, 86 Mass. App. Ct. 295 (Mass.App. 2014). In a few states, by statute, even improperly filed instruments do give constructive notice. See In re Wonderfair Stores, Inc., of Arizona, 511 F.2d 1206 (9th Cir. 1975) (Arizona law). Some courts seem to distinguish between recording defects that are evident on the face of the instrument (e.g., absence of any acknowledgment) and those that are latent (e.g., a false acknowledgment), giving constructive notice effect to the latter. See Hildebrandt v. Hildebrandt, 9 Kan. App. 2d 614, 683 P.2d 1288 (1984); Annot., 59 A.L.R. 2d 1299, 1316 (1958). Cf. In re Marsh, 12 S.W.3d 449 (Tenn. 2000) (recorded deed lacking notary's seal is treated as unrecorded); In re Rice, 133 B.R. 722 (Bankr. E.D. Pa. 1991) (recorded mortgage, notarized without the signers appearing personally before the notary, is treated as unrecorded). If a title searcher in fact finds and reads the document, he or she will gain actual knowledge, and hence will be held to have notice of whatever information it provides, and may well be under a duty to make further reasonable inquiries based on that information. See Chandler v. Cameron, 229 N.C. 62, 47 S.E.2d 528 (1948); 6A Powell, Real Property ¶ 914 n. 3; 5 Tiffany, Real Property § 1264 n. 65 (3d ed. 1939); Annot., 59 A.L.R. 2d 1299, 1318 (1958). Similarly, a purchaser whose lawyer examines an abstract showing an instrument that should not have been recorded, and reports it to the purchaser, will have actual notice of its contents. See Mulligan v. Snavely, 117 Neb. 765, 223 N.W. 8 (1929).

In many states curative statutes have been enacted providing that after the passage of some number of years, instruments lacking seals, acknowledgments, or other technical requirements are deemed to have been properly recorded. See generally Simes & Taylor, The Improvement of Conveyancing by Legislation 17–27 (Univ. of Mich. Law School 1960). Such statutes remove uncertainty from a title examiner's life, but they also raise a more fundamental question: is acknowledgement of the signature(s) on the deed by a notary public really necessary in terms of good policy? Acknowledgment before a notary public is supposed to be a protection against forgery, but because of the casual way in which many notaries approach their duties, it is not a very effective protection. Why not do away with the acknowledgment requirement entirely? The Uniform Simplification of Land Transfers Act (USLTA) does so in Section 2–301(b). In fact, the USLTA even does away with the need for a signature!

Consider now another type of mistake—one made by the recorder's office personnel. It is generally agreed that if they fail entirely to file a copy of an instrument in the appropriate book or microfiche card, the instrument is simply not "recorded." This means that a careful grantee, after recording the deed, should return to the courthouse a few days later and check to see that it has been properly filed in the system (and hence, "recorded"). Should an attorney check back with the recorder's office after recording a document, to make sure it has been properly indexed? This is certainly not a common practice among lawyers, but an attorney was held liable in malpractice for failing to do so in Antonis v. Liberati, 821 A.2d 666 (Pa. 2003).

There is much less agreement if the recorder's employees file the instrument properly, but fail to index it, or index it improperly. As we will see, a misindexed or unindexed document is virtually worthless to a title searcher because the indexes are essential to the title search process. A filed but improperly indexed instrument is, in effect, a needle in a haystack. These indexing cases turn in part on the specific language of the statute. There are numerous cases on both sides of the issue, but the modern trend is to treat misindexed instruments as if they were unrecorded, and hence as failing to give constructive notice. See Dyer v. Martinez, 147 Cal. App. 4th 1240, 54 Cal. Rptr. 3d 907 (2007); Coco v. Ranalletta, 189 Misc. 2d 535, 733 N.Y.S.2d 849 (2001); Keybank Nat'l Ass'n v. NBD Bank, 699 N.E.2d 322 (Ind. App. 1998); Hanson v. Zoller, 187 N.W.2d 47 (N.D. 1971); Mortensen v. Lingo, 13 Alaska 419, 99 F. Supp. 585 (1951). But see Miller v. Simonson, 140 Idaho 287, 92 P.3d 537 (2004); finding that a misindexed document can still impart constructive notice; Anderson v. North Florida Production Credit Ass'n., 642 So.2d 88 (Fla. App. 1994); In re Harris, 183 B.R. 657 (D.D.C. 1995).

In First Citizens Nat'l Bank v. Sherwood, 817 A.2d 501 (Pa. Super. 2003), the court took an intermediate position, holding that although a misindexed document ordinarily would not give constructive notice, it might do so if a computerized search facility provided by the recorder allowed full text searches of the recorded documents. See also Baccari v. De Santi, 70 A.D.2d 198, 431 N.Y.S.2d 829 (1979) (holding quite remarkably that an unindexed document imparts constructive notice, but a misindexed document does not).

Although the courts usually deal with the issue in terms of whether a misindexed deed gives constructive notice to subsequent purchasers, the first question really should be whether the deed should be treated as recorded or not, since if the deed is "recorded" it cannot be divested by a subsequent transfer, no matter how innocent the transferee. See generally Annot., 63 A.L.R. 1057 (1929); IV Am. L. Prop. § 17.31 (1952).

5. SEARCHING A TITLE

With the foregoing basic knowledge of recording acts and the public records system, we are now ready to discuss how titles are searched. If you practice law in the Northeastern United States, there is a good chance that you will use this information directly in your practice. In other areas of the country, abstract or title insurance companies perform most searches, but an understanding of the process is still very helpful to real estate attorneys. For a good description of abstract companies and their work, see Ford v. Guarantee Abstract & Title Co., 220 Kan. 244, 553 P.2d 254 (1976).

All privately held land titles (except those derived from accretion or adverse possession) can be traced back through a chain of owners to some original conveyance from a sovereign, typically the federal government or a state. Set forth below is a hypothetical chain of title that we can use as the basis for illustration of title search problems. You may wish to sketch it out on a separate piece of paper so you can keep it before you as you read the remainder of this section.

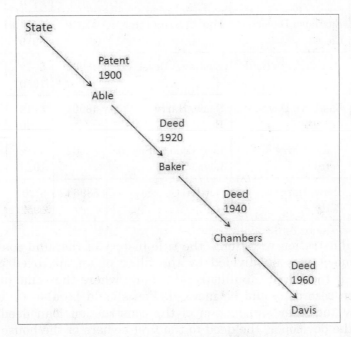

The patent is merely a grant of title by the state. The present owner of the land is Davis, and we will assume that he proposes to sell it to your client, who has asked you to search and examine the title. When you receive this assignment, you know nothing about the prior title history of the land; you are merely told its legal description, (Lot 4, Block G, Suburban Acres) and the fact that Donald Davis presently claims to own it.

How will you proceed? The answer depends on the type of indexing system used by the recorder's office in your jurisdiction. From the title searcher's viewpoint, indexing by tract or parcel is by far the better method. This approach allocates a separate page or set of pages in the index books to each parcel of land, or perhaps to each tract (such as a quarter-quarter section), even though it might contain several parcels. As each instrument is brought into the courthouse for recordation, an entry is made on the appropriate page for each parcel affected by the instrument. A brief example is set forth below.

Parcel Index					
Lot 3, Block L. Eastlawn Estates Subdivision					
Type of Instrm't	Grantors, etc.	Grantees, etc.	Doc. No.	Date Files	Book & Page
(Note: for prior instruments, see SE1/4 of NW1/4, T4N,R2E.)					
Subdiv. Plat	Eastlawn Devel. Co.	- - - - - - -	45872	9–15 1949	34–17 Plat Bk
Deed of Trust	Eastlawn Devel. Co.	Fourth State Bank	47339	10–10 1949	117–667
Reconv.	Fourth State Bank	Eastlawn Devel. Co.	48960	5–12 1950	119–88
Deed	Eastlawn Devel. Co.	Shaw, Harry & Betty	48961	5–12 1950	119–89
Deed of Trust	Shaw, Harry & Betty	Last Federal Sav. & Loan	48962	5–12 1950	119–90
Lis Pen	Shaw, Harry & Betty	Gotcha, George	53964	8–30 1952	124–733

This illustration represents the title history of the land commencing at the time it was subdivided by the filing of an approved plat. The reference at the top of the illustration shows where the same land's pre-subdivision records would be indexed. You should be able to follow the imposition and later satisfaction of the construction loan deed of trust given by the developer, the deed to the first owners of the house that the developer built on the land, and their deed of trust to the lender who made the loan with which first owners bought the house. Finally, you can see that they apparently had a dispute concerning title to their land, and were sued in connection with it by George Gotcha in 1952.

With a tract index, the construction by the title examiner of a chain of title is relatively easy because all of the relevant information is together on a single page or pages. Of course, it may be necessary to consult other records in other offices (e.g., for wills, intestacies, judgments, property taxes, etc.), but in most cases the chain of title can be determined without much trouble. The tile examiner must then pull the books from the shelves, or check the microfilm or computer-scanned copies, and examine the actual copies of the instruments themselves to see if they appear to be regular and indeed affect the land in question. The references in the last column on the right in the index book tell the searcher the exact book and page number where each document will be found. If any prior owner has made an "adverse conveyance"—one that impairs the present quality of the title or makes it unmarketable—this fact will be very easy to see. For example, a lis pendens would be considered such an adverse conveyance unless it had been removed later or a statute of limitations had cut it off.

The tract index is very convenient for title searchers, but it does require a reasonable amount of skill on the part of the recording office personnel, who must read every instrument with some care to determine what land it affects, and properly index it, perhaps under multiple parcels. This is not difficult when the legal description is based on a recorded subdivision plat as in our illustration, but it can be formidable with descriptions based on natural monuments (e.g., "to the old white oak tree"). Perhaps for this reason, only a few American states provide in their recording statutes for the maintenance of tract or parcel indexes.[10]

In the great majority of states, the only official indexes available to title searchers in the courthouse are "name" or "grantor-grantee" indexes—those based on the names of the parties to a given instrument. A name index is easier to construct and maintain, but much more difficult to search than a tract index. The overall advantages of the tract index are attested by the fact that virtually every privately owned set of title records ("title plant") in the nation employs tract indexing.

For many years there was little pressure from any organized group—recorders, lawyers, title companies, or the public—for reform of the traditional name index system. In recent years, however, a movement has taken root, with the encouragement of a few progressive county recorders and of Fannie Mae and Freddie Mac (the two principal federally sponsored secondary market purchasers of mortgage loans), to develop and implement computer-based tract indexing systems.[11] The organization most actively involved in this movement is the Property Records Industry Association (PRIA). A new uniform act, the Uniform Real Property Electronic Recording Act (URPERA), endorsed by the PRIA, has been adopted by the Commissioners on Uniform Laws to authorize recorders to accept electronic filings. The PRIA web site is found at http://www.pria.us/. The URPERA, promulgated by the Commissioners in 2005 because of concern that the authorization in the

---

[10] See generally Note, The Tract and Grantor-Grantee Indices, 47 Iowa L. Rev. 481 (1962). The USLTA mandates a tract index, but it has not been adopted by any state legislature. See § 6–207. The USLTA also contains an interesting and apparently unprecedented feature requiring those who present instruments for recordation to supply "information fixing the location sufficiently to enable the recording officer to determine where in the geographic index the document is to be indexed." USLTA § 2–302(a)(4).

[11] See Whitman, Digital Recording of Real Estate Documents, 32 John Marshall L. Rev. 227 (1999). Recorders are authorized (but not required) to accept electronic documents for recording by the Uniform Electronic Transactions Act (UETA) § 17–19, promulgated in 1999 and adopted in every state except Illinois, New York, and Washington.

Uniform Electronic Transactions Act was not specific and concrete enough, has been adopted in 28 jurisdictions.

Such filings can be indexed and therefore searched by any item of information—names, tract, type of document, date, or other relevant information. To service this new demand, a number of commercial firms are providing software (and as needed, hardware) to permit recorders to accept electronic documents, record them in a quasi-automated fashion, and make them searchable by members of the public and the title insurance industry via the Internet. A fair number of recorders' offices, usually in populous counties, have already made this shift, and others are seriously considering it. Thus, it seems possible that within a few years, a truly modern system of public land title records will be available in much of the United States (though with all of the legal limitations of the recording system still intact, of course).

Suppose you are not fortunate enough to practice in a state with an official tract index. (Ironically, in those states few lawyers perform searches in the public records.) Instead, you find that you must search in the name indexes in your courthouse. How can you construct a chain of title to the land your client wishes to buy from Davis? There are dual sets of name indexes; one set is arranged alphabetically by the name of the grantee(s) to each instrument, and the other alphabetically by the name of the grantor(s). You will begin your work in the grantee index, which might take a form like this:

| Grantee Index   Year <u>1960</u> | | | | | | |
| Grantee's Names beginning with   <u>Da</u> | | | | | | |
Type of Instrm't	Grantee's Name	Grantor's Name	Doc. No.	Date Filed	Book & Page	Brief Legal Description
Release of Easm't	Davis, Abner	Voltzman Elect. Power Co.	2243	5–22 1960	344–221	Lt. 14, Block B Ridge Estates
Mech's Lien	Damion Plumbing & Heating	Fish, Frederick	4322	8–16 1960	346–132	E ½ of SE ¼ Sec. 22, R2E T3N
Deed	Davis, Donald	Chambers, Elaine	2089	8–19 1960	346–367	Lot 4, Block G Suburban Acres
Lease	Dalton's Men's Wear	Watson Real Estate, Inc.	4531	8–28 1960	346–451	Lots 3–4, Brown's Addition No. 2

There are several interesting features of the grantee index page above. The grantees' names are not in exact alphabetical order, because they are entered on the page (this one is labeled "Da") as they come into the office for recordation. In some sophisticated offices, a computer program may be used to resort and reprint the pages periodically in accurate alphabetical order. Note that all entries are during the year 1960. In large urban counties, a new set of index books is generally made up each year. If this were not done, the books would soon become so large as to be physically unmanageable. In rural counties with few transactions, the indexes might be allowed to accumulate over five or even ten years before a new set is begun.

Now, to search Donald Davis's title, we must begin by looking for his name in the grantee index, because if Davis owns the land he must have been a grantee under a deed at some point in time. Unless we can get a copy of Davis's deed from him or he tells us when he acquired the land, we will not know which one of the grantee books to check, so we must start with the present year and work our way backwards, looking for Davis's name as a grantee. When we finally get to 1960 and read the page reproduced above, we will find him. Scanning across to the "Brief Legal Description" column will verify that the entry does in fact affect the land we are searching. Unfortunately, in some states there is no such column, and we would have to look up in the actual record books each deed that is indexed with Davis as a grantee to see what land it covers. If Davis had bought a good deal of real estate in the county, this could become exceedingly tedious. Even where the indexes carry this column, there may be a serious but rarely litigated question as to whether a title searcher can safely rely upon it. As a practical matter, however, searchers obviously do so.

We must now look for the next link (going backward in time) in the chain of title. We do so by looking for Elaine Chambers's name in the grantee index, because the entry that we found under Davis's name told us that Chambers was Davis's grantor. We assume that Chambers received title to the land prior to the time she deeded it to Davis (although this need not always be true under the doctrine of estoppel by deed), and begin looking for her name as a grantee in 1960. Searching back year by year, we will find her as a grantee from Baker in 1940. We then search for Baker as a grantee, and so on, until we come back to the original patent from the state in 1900.

We now have a complete chain of title to the land, but that is only the first of three major steps in searching the record title. The second step involves determining whether any one of the owners we have identified has made any adverse conveyances. Suppose, for example, that Able (who obtained the land in 1900) granted an easement to Zoller in 1910. You might wish to pencil in such a grant on the diagram of the chain of title. We would certainly want to advise our client that the easement exists. How can we discover such conveyances? We must use the other set of name indexes, those arranged alphabetically by the name of the grantor. A part of a typical page might look as follows:

Grantor Index   Year <u>1960</u>
Grantor's Names beginning with <u>Aa through Ac</u>

Type of Instrm't	Grantor's Name	Grantor's Name	Doc. No.	Date Filed	Book & Page	Brief Legal Description
Mortg.	Ackerman, Alan	Third Nat'l Bank	2276	1-14 1910	22-889	Pt. of N ½ Sec. 5 R3E T6S
Grant of Easement	Abie, Abner	Zoller, Charles	2298	2-21 1910	22-970	Lot 4, Block G Suburban Acres
Assign. of Mtg.	Abbott Mortgage Co.	Philadelphia Soc. for Savings	2375	4-12 1910	23-29	Lot 18, Summit Ridge Add'n
Release of Mtg.	Abbott Mortgage Co.	Weller, Frank Martha	2418	7-7 1910	23-445	S ½ of NE 1/4 Sec. 12, R3E T5S

We will begin with Able's name.[12] Able acquired the land in 1900 and deeded it away to Baker in 1920. Therefore, we will look for any conveyances with Able as a grantor during that period. (We will discuss later whether a title searcher also needs to look under Able's name prior to 1900 or after 1920). Again, we check the records year by year, this time in the grantor index. The page reprinted above shows that in 1910 Able was a grantor to Zoller of an easement. Unless we subsequently find a release of the easement by Zoller (which we can find by looking in the grantor index under his name), we must conclude that the easement still exists and report it to our client as affecting the current state of the title. Of course, some off-record circumstances, such as a stone wall that has blocked the path of the easement for 30 years, might convince us that despite the records the easement is no longer viable but has been terminated by prescription.

---

[12] Why not begin with the state itself? It is surely possible that the state land office inadvertently issued two patents on the same land. If our chain of title derives from the second, then it presumably has no validity at all. In some states, the recording acts or other statutes specifically treat state patents in the same manner as other deeds. Thus, if the first patent were unrecorded in the county records, the second one would prevail in the hands of a BFP. See 2 Patton, Titles § 296 (2d ed. 1957), (listing 16 states with such statutes); Meacham v. Stewart, 19 Or. 285, 24 P. 241 (1890). In other jurisdictions there is no applicable statute, and the records of the state land office are sufficient to sustain the first patent even against a BFP holder of the second. See, e.g., United States v. Buras, 332 F. Supp. 1017 (E.D. La. 1970), reversed 458 F.2d 346 (5th Cir. 1972); Moran v. Palmer, 13 Mich. 367 (1865). In these states, a careful title searcher ought to review the records in the land office to make certain that no earlier patent covers the land in question. The same is true of federal patents because state recording statutes cannot divest them. Patton, supra; Lomax v. Pickering, 173 U.S. 26, 19 S. Ct. 416, 43 L. Ed. 601 (1899); Sayward v. Thompson, 11 Wash. 706, 40 P. 379 (1895); 8A Thompson, Real Property § 4348 (1963). Even though the records of the United States patent offices are constructive notice to subsequent purchasers, and many states would probably take the same position with respect to state-issued patents, it is doubtful that many title searchers attempt to check for duplicate or overlapping patents. On federal patent procedures generally, see III Am. L. Prop. § 12.20 (1952).

We must check the grantor index in a similar fashion for Baker, Chambers, and Davis to see if any of them made adverse conveyances. We are very likely to find, for example, that one or more of them gave mortgages or deeds of trust on the land. We must then use the grantor index to trace any further transfers or releases of these interests to determine whether they still affect the title today. We might even discover that Baker was a crook, and gave a deed to some person outside our chain of title (say, Zobell), in 1930. Zobell, in turn, might have started a chain of further conveyances leading down to a present owner who would claim title as against Davis.

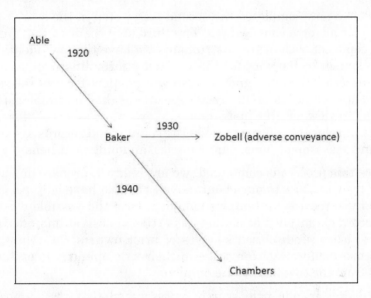

If the deed from Baker to Zobell is recorded, it (and persons claiming under it) would have priority over the chain of title we have discovered from Baker through Chambers to Davis, and Davis would own nothing. Fortunately, because the deed to Zobell was recorded, we will be able to find it by our normal search process, and thus can warn our client not to buy the land from Davis. On the other hand, if the deed from Baker to Zobell is not recorded, then we would need only to show that Chambers, Davis, or our own client was a BFP in order to cut off Zobell by operation of the recording acts. Incidentally, if Chambers, for example, were a BFP, then Davis (and our client) could take the land safely even though they were aware of the unrecorded adverse conveyance to Zobell. This is so because of the so-called "shelter rule," which says that once title has come into the hands of a BFP who is protected by the recording acts, the BFP can pass that protection on to grantees even if they have notice of the prior adverse conveyance. See Hendricks v. Lake, 12 Wn. App. 15, 528 P.2d 491 (1974); IV Am. L. Prop. § 17.11 nn. 18–20 (1952); 3 Pomeroy, Equity Jurisprudence 55–57 (5th ed. 1941). The one exception is that if title is transferred back to one who had previously held it with notice of the adverse conveyance before it was "cleansed" by the BFP, he will not be protected. Thus, one cannot "clean up" one's own title merely by running it through a BFP. See Rose v. Knapp, 153 Cal. App. 2d 379, 314 P.2d 812 (1957). If the shelter rule did not exist and the news of Baker's adverse conveyance to Zobell became common knowledge in the community after Baker's conveyance to Chambers, Chambers might find that she owned the land but could not as a practical matter sell it to anyone, because no one else could qualify as a BFP without notice of the adverse conveyance.

We have now completed the second major step in the search process, checking for adverse conveyances. The third step requires that we look at the full copies of each of the instruments we have thus far identified. We will check each instrument for the necessary formalities, the consistency of legal descriptions, etc., and we also will be alert for any references to unrecorded documents or interests. Assuming that no problems emerge from this review of the instruments, next we will check for adverse interests in relevant sources outside the county land records system, such as tax and assessment liens, bankruptcies, and judgment liens.

Once this process is completed, we are ready to prepare an opinion of title for transmission to our client. Given that we have only performed a search of the records system, we cannot negate the possible existence of an off-record claim, such as claims by parties in possession under a short-term oral lease, undisclosed spouses of prior owners, etc. Many careful lawyers use "boilerplate" language in their title opinions to exclude such matters from the coverage of the opinion.

Note that in our title search we assumed that the names of the various prior owners are unambiguous and readily found in the indexes. But this is not always the case. One Connecticut lawyer gave the following examples to the authors:

> In the Town of New Milford, Connecticut, all documents which appear to concern a religious organization are indexed under "C" for "Church" even if the word "church" doesn't appear in the name (e.g., First Lutheran Society). Likewise, in New Milford all Federal agencies are indexed under "U" for "United States of America" (a deed from "John Smith, Secretary of Housing and Urban Development" will be indexed under "U" as "United States of America—HUD." In the Town of Farmington for many years, all documents pertaining to financial institutions were indexed under "B" for "Bank" (e.g., Society for Savings).

Obviously, as with politics, never forget that all recording systems are local!

Computerized alphabetization of the indexes may not help, and may actually make things worse. The Connecticut lawyer mentioned above referred to a case in which "The property owner is X. Y. Z. Corporation, Inc., and I didn't find the $20,000,000.00 mortgage because it was indexed 5 pages away under XYZ Corp." Searching titles is not for out-of-towners or the faint of heart!

6. CHAIN OF TITLE PROBLEMS

There are certain types of adverse conveyances that are difficult or impossible to find, even though they are in fact recorded. Your teacher may want you to go over them in detail, and may assign additional reading for that purpose. We will merely summarize them below:

1. *The wild deed.* Assume there is a chain of two adverse conveyances in a row. The first one is unrecorded but the second is recorded (perhaps because it has never been filed at all, or it has been filed but misindexed by the reader's office). The second instrument is essentially impossible to find in a name index system. This is because the title searcher has no knowledge of the name of either the grantor or grantee of the second deed—it is a needle in a haystack. We call the second instrument a "wild deed" because it is not connected into the chain of title through the name of either a grantor or grantee. It is universally agreed that a wild deed should be treated as if it were unrecorded.

2. *The late-recorded deed.* Suppose a previous owner executed and delivered an adverse conveyance, but its grantee did not record it until many years after receiving it—perhaps, not until long after the subsequent deed in the chain of title was recorded, and therefore after the grantor of the adverse conveyance appears from the records to have parted with title. Should a title searcher be expected to look for the adverse conveyance not only during the period each previous owner had title, but also thereafter . . . potentially down to the present time? Such a search is not impossible to do, but it adds greatly to the title searcher's burden. Nearly half of the cases on this point treat the adverse conveyance as if it were unrecorded, thereby sparing title searchers additional work.

3. *The early-recorded deed.* You may think an "early-recorded deed" is a typographical error—how can a deed be recorded before it is effective? But under the doctrine of after-acquired title, this is exactly what can happen. Suppose someone with no title at all executes and delivers a warranty deed, and his grantee records it. Many years later the grantor actually obtains title through a legitimate chain, and then purports to pass it down the chain of title to your client's immediate predecessor. If you are performing a search, do you need to look under the grantor's name in the records, not only during the period he appears to have held

the title, but also during earlier periods—potentially back 70 years or so if the grantor is a natural person? About three-quarters of the cases on this issue excuse the title searcher from performing the extra work, holding instead that the early-recorded deed is treated as if it were unrecorded.

4.   *The deed for one parcel encumbers another parcel.* Suppose a former owner held two lots, side by side, and sold one while retaining the other. The deed contained a covenant that neither lot would ever be used except for a single-family residence. Now suppose your client has agreed to buy the lot that the former owner retained, and you are searching its title. The retained lot is encumbered by the single-family residence covenant, but how can you discover that fact? The covenant encumbering the retained lot is contained in a recorded deed, but it is in the deed for a *different lot* than the lot you are searching. *If* the grantor index in your county includes a "brief description" column, and *if* the recorder's office personnel indicated in that column that the deed for the first lot affected both lots, you can easily find the covenant that encumbers the title to the lot you are searching. If either of these facts is not true, you will find the encumbrance on the retained lot only by reading in detail *every deed* the former owner ever recorded. Note that if the former owner was a real estate developer, that might be a very large number of deeds! About half of the cases considering this problem save the title searcher the extra work by treating the encumbrance on the retained lot as if it were unrecorded.

These are the four standard "chain of title" issues. All of these issues are intrinsic to a name indexing system, and will not arise in a properly maintained tract indexing system.

In many areas of the nation, particularly in the Midwest and on the West Coast, there is little search activity in the typical recorder's office. Instead, most title searches are conducted in private "title plants" owned by abstract or title insurance companies. Because these title plants are invariably arranged on a tract index basis, the chain of title problems we have examined above are, for the most part, of no practical importance in such areas. How should a court deal with a chain of title issue in a state where few searchers will ever encounter it in practice? And what of the importance of reform of the public records, by computerization and tract indexing, in such states? Is it worthwhile to encourage expensive changes of this kind in the public sector, if the private sector is already providing the needed services?

7.   MARKETABLE TITLE ACTS

Although the idea of the computerized tract index is an important and far-reaching type of reform of the recording system, it is not the only reform possible. We have already mentioned the very modest step of "curative acts" that have been adopted in many states. Curative acts typically provide that instruments which are defective due to the lack of proper acknowledgment of the deed's signatures by a notary public, a seal (where still required for a valid deed) or a deed that was not delivered will be conclusively presumed valid as against such defects after they have been of record for some specified period (say, two years or five years.).[13] These acts reduce the burden on title examiners, while at the same time rarely impairing any substantive rights of claimants to the land.

Another practical reform is the development (usually by real property committees of state bar associations) of so-called "title standards." Title standards allow attorneys who examine titles to pass certain minor or trivial title defects without being concerned that some later attorney will attack the title as unmarketable on the same grounds. Title standards also provide suggested procedures for curing certain common defects. A collection of about 30 states' title standards, along with worthwhile discussion and analysis, is found at http://www.realpropertytitle standards.org/, the web site of the National Title Examination Standards Resource Center, funded by the American Bar Association and maintained by the Oklahoma City University School of Law.

A step beyond title standards and curative acts are specialized statutes that cut off certain old rights in land after the passage of a certain period of time (typically 20 to 50 years). The rights specified are of a type that few claimants are likely to rely upon or assert after the passage of so much time. If the owner of the rights wishes to keep those rights alive, he is generally permitted to do so by re-recording the original instrument creating them, or alternatively recording a notice of their existence, before the running of the statute terminates them. The rights mentioned in the statutes vary from state to state, but those commonly covered include rights of entry and possibilities of reverter, judgment liens, mortgages, and even restrictive covenants.[14] Statutes of this type are not comprehensive, but again they make the examiner's task a little simpler.

The final step in this progression of reform legislation is the advent of "marketable title acts." See generally Basye, Clearing Land Titles, Ch. 5 (3d ed. 2014); Barnett, Marketable Title Acts—Panacea or Pandemonium, 53 Cornell L. Rev. 45 (1967); Swenson, Utah Marketable

---

[13] See the Model Curative Act, discussed in Simes & Taylor, The Improvement of Conveyancing by Legislation 17–27 (U. Mich. L. School 1960). The topic is dealt with in its fullest detail in Basye, Clearing Land Titles §§ 201–364 (2d ed. 1970). See USLTA § 3–401 for a compact, comprehensive curative statute.

[14] See Basye, Clearing Land Titles §§ 51–165. The New York statute barring possibilities of reverter and rights of entry was held unconstitutional as a taking of property in Board of Education of Central School District No. 1 v. Miles, 15 N.Y.2d 364, 259 N.Y.S.2d 129, 207 N.E.2d 181 (1965). All of the other decisions have been favorable to constitutionality. See, e.g., Presbytery of Southeast Iowa v. Harris, 226 N.W.2d 232 (Iowa 1975); Hiddleston v. Nebraska Jewish Educ. Soc., 186 Neb. 786, 186 N.W.2d 904 (1971).

Title Act, 8 Utah L. Rev. 200 (1963). Marketable title acts are found in California, Connecticut, Florida, Illinois, Indiana, Iowa, Kansas, Michigan, Minnesota, Nebraska, North Carolina, North Dakota, Ohio, Oklahoma, South Dakota, Utah, Vermont, Wisconsin, and Wyoming. The name for these statutes is unfortunate, for marketable title acts neither declare anyone's title to be marketable nor define marketability. Instead, such acts attempt to limit the required period of title search by cutting off virtually *all* interests in land that appear in the public records prior to a given point, unless some reference is made to them in a more recently recorded instrument. The title searcher is expected to go back to the "root of title," usually defined as a deed recorded earlier than some fixed number of years before the search being made. The number of years varies among the states that have adopted marketable title acts. The shortest period is 22 years and the longest period is 50 years, with 40 years being most common. Suppose a title searcher in 2014 found a chain of deeds to the land, with one recorded in each decade. In a 40-year state, the title searcher would go back to the most recent deed that was at least 40 years old. Thus, a deed recorded in 1974 could be the root of title, and no search of the records prior to 1974 would be necessary.

Unfortunately, the existing marketable title acts contain a number of exceptions for interests that are permitted to survive despite the fact they are mentioned only in documents predating the root of title. These include rights of the United States government (which state law has no power to cut off, of course), rights of state and local governments, visible easements, roads or highways, utility or railroad easements, mineral rights, and so on. The exceptions are usually the result of political pressures brought by lobbyists for the groups or industries affected; they obviously make the acts much less effective in reducing search periods, because they make stopping at the root of title more risky. See, e.g., Note, Property Law—North Carolina's Marketable Title Act—Will the Exceptions Swallow the Rule?, 52 N.C.L. Rev. 211 (1973).

Marketable title acts were given a considerable boost by the development of a model act by Lewis Simes and Clarence Taylor at the University of Michigan in 1960. See Simes, A Handbook for More Efficient Conveyancing (U. Mich. L. School 1960). Half of the existing marketable title acts have been passed since that time. Most marketable title acts are found in Midwestern states where title searches commonly are performed by abstract companies who work in their own private tract-indexed title plants. But two New England states, Connecticut (1967) and Vermont (1969), and two Southern states, North Carolina (1973) and Florida (1963), have passed marketable title acts. Tract indexes are not widely used in these four states, a fact that makes it possible for two or more chains of title to exist simultaneously, each of which is apparently valid under the language of the marketable title act. This could easily occur if a purported grantor 50 or more years ago gave two forged deeds of the same land to two grantees. Even a forged deed can be a valid root of title. See Marshall v. Hollywood, Inc., 236 So. 2d 114 (Fla. 1970), affirming 224 So. 2d 743 (Fla. App. 1969), noted 22 U. Fla. L. Rev. 669 (1970). A tract index would almost certainly disclose this problem to a title searcher, but a name index system in a marketable title act state might not. The existing marketable title acts contain no mechanism for solving this conflict. See Medway Associates v. Shoneck, 1992 WL 156142 (Conn. Super. 1992); Cheadle v. County Bd. of School Trustees, 20 Ill. App. 3d 212, 313 N.E.2d 196 (1974); Whaley v. Wotring, 225 So. 2d 177 (Fla. App. 1969).

Moreover, one might argue that marketable title acts operate unfairly on persons whose rights in land are old, but are still perfectly valid and valuable. See, e.g., H & F Land, Inc. v. Panama City-Bay County Airport, 736 So. 2d 1167 (Fla. 1999), in which a marketable title act cut off an easement of necessity because no notice or transaction reflecting it had been recorded for more than 30 years. Should such persons be put to the trouble of re-recording their documents every few decades? The burden might be particularly heavy on those who own numerous interests in the land of others, such as mining or utility companies. They often argue that re-recording is totally impractical for them, the original documents having been lost or being filed in such a manner that they cannot be retrieved for this purpose. Many of the exceptions found in the existing marketable title acts are the products of these arguments.

8. THE TORRENS SYSTEM FOR TITLE REGISTRATION

Even a modern, computerized, tract-indexed recording system aided by marketable title and curative acts still leaves much to be desired. Two main defects are noteworthy. First, such a system does not directly inform anyone what the state of the title actually is for a parcel of land. The current records system presents a mass of old documents and lets the searcher determine the state of the title, with all of the potential for error that such a process implies. Second, determining title by a search of the records allows the existence of a large number of "off-record" interests that cannot be found but nonetheless may affect the title. Some of these adverse claims might be identified by inspection of the land or other means, but many cannot be discovered with any reasonable degree of effort.

Is there a better system, one that will solve these problems without introducing others that are equally objectionable? The solution adopted by most other nations is the "Torrens" or title registration system. It was originally developed in 1858 in Australia by Sir Robert Torrens, who modeled it on the English system of maintenance of title records for ships.

The Torrens system spread throughout Australia, New Zealand, and other members of the British commonwealth, and is now in widespread use in the United Kingdom itself. See Fiflis, English Registered Conveyancing: A Study in Effective Land Transfer, 59 N.W. L. Rev. 468 (1964); Pamela O'Connor, Registration of Title in England and Australia: A Theoretical and Comparative Analysis, in Cooke, Modern Studies in Property Law 81–99 (2007); C. Dent Bostick, Land Title Registration: An English Solution to an American Problem, 63 Ind. L.J. 55 (1988). By 2004, all of England and Wales was covered by the registration system and about four-fifths of the land was actually registered. See Elizabeth Cooke & Pamela O'Connor, Purchaser Liability to Third Parties in the English Land Registration System: A Comparative Perspective, 120 Law Q. Rev. 640, 651 (2004). Similar title registration systems are widely used today in other countries.

The fundamental principle of the Torrens system is that government ought to be more than a mere custodian of the records of title. Rather, the government should take the next logical step of averring the condition or state of the title to interested parties. We take this idea for granted with motor vehicles in the United States, but as applied to land titles it is a radical departure from accustomed methods. Interest in the Torrens system blossomed in the United States around the turn of the 20th century, and about 20 states adopted statutes implementing it, beginning with Illinois in 1895.[15] But the system's weaknesses as implemented, and the strong opposition of the existing conveyancing industry (principally lawyers and title insurers) combined with the result that only nine states retain the system today for new registrations.

The Torrens system is used extensively in only four states. The areas of largest use in the United States are: (1) Hennepin County, Minnesota (Minneapolis), with 40 percent to 45 percent of the parcels registered under the system; (2) Cook County, Illinois, with about one-third of the land registered; (3) the Southern District Registry of Middlesex County, Massachusetts (Cambridge) with about 20 percent of the land registered; and (4) Hawaii, with about 45 percent of the land registered. The system is legislatively authorized today in Colorado, Georgia, Hawaii, Massachusetts, Minnesota, North Carolina, Ohio, Virginia, and Washington, but in several of those states activity under it is virtually nil. The system was repealed, with respect to new registrations, effective in

---

[15] The United States statutes are described in Patton, Evolution of Legislation on Proof of Title to Land, 30 Wash. L. Rev. 224 (1956); 6A Powell, Real Property ¶ 919ff (1979); Shick & Plotkin, Torrens in the United States (1978); The latter book's authors were employed as consultants to the title insurance industry, historically a vigorous foe of the Torrens system; the book might fairly be described as a "hatchet job" on Torrens. The English approach is compared to the U.S. system in Bostick, Land Title Registration: An English Solution to an American Problem, 63 Ind. L. J. 55 (1988).

1997, in both New York and Illinois, although existing registrations in those states continue to be effective.

In the American version of the Torrens system, registration is completely voluntary and usually quite costly. The owner brings what is in substance a quiet title action before a court or a quasi-judicial tribunal. Doing so might be expected to cost several thousand dollars. Notice is sent to all persons having apparent claims to the land, and a hearing is held. If the registrant's title appears sound, the court orders the land registered. A certificate of title is created and held in the registration office, and a duplicate copy may be given to the owner. The certificate amounts to a governmental averment that the registered owner is indeed the owner of the land, and that his or her title is not subject to any claims or encumbrances other than those shown as "memorials" on the certificate.

From that point forward, all title transactions affecting the land must be memorialized on the registry's copy of the certificate of title or they will not be binding. Memorials may be added (e.g., if the owner gives a neighbor an easement) or deleted (e.g., if the owner satisfies a mortgage). If the owner transfers the fee title, a new certificate is made up, carrying over the memorials that represent interests still in effect and discarding those that have become obsolete. Thus, anyone can determine the state of the title by simply looking at the official copy of the certificate in the registry, and by then examining the underlying documents referred to in the current memorials on the certificate. These documents are retained by the registry. No historical search of the title is ever required, for only the current certificate and the instruments memorialized on it are relevant.

An interesting and largely unresolved question is whether a person holding a certificate of title is bound by conveyances of prior interests that are not memorialized on the certificate, but of which the holder has actual notice. In In re Collier, 726 N.W.2d 799 (Minn. 2007), the Minnesota Supreme Court noted that a holder of a certificate, by the terms of the statute, had to be in "good faith" to be protected by the Torrens act. Hence, the court concluded that although a holder would not be subject to the doctrine of constructive notice, one who had *actual* notice of a prior but unmemorialized interest would be subject to it. The Supreme Court of Canada agreed with this view in United Trust Co. v. Dominion Stores Ltd., [1977] 2 S.C.R. 915.

Once a parcel is brought within the Torrens system, transfers are very inexpensive and (if the system is well administered) quick and easy. But the initial cost of title registration has been a serious detriment, because most landowners have little interest in spending a large sum today so that future owners will be able to consummate transfers cheaply.

Two additional problems have impeded the expansion of the Torrens system. One is the fact that existing American Torrens systems (much like marketable title acts) have numerous statutory exceptions to their coverage, so that the certificate is not really the complete statement of the title that users might desire. In addition to federal government claims (which are beyond the power of the states to bring under the system), common exceptions are made for persons in possession, mineral claims, observable easements, public roads, and so on—generally the same sorts of exceptions found in the marketable title acts, and for the same basic reasons. Compare Tetrault v. Bruscoe, 398 Mass. 454, 497 N.E.2d 275 (1986) (prescriptive easement does not affect registered land unless it is noted on certificate of title) with Henmi Apartments, Inc. v. Sawyer, 3 Haw. App. 555, 655 P.2d 881 (1982) (valid implied easement can arise upon registered land).

The other major impediment to the expansion of the Torrens system relates to the registry's liability if its administrators make a mistake. Recall that the certificate is conclusive as to the fee title it displays. Consequently, an error by registration officials might result in a mortgage or easement being cut off, or even the vesting of title in a person who had no right to it. The American Torrens systems all include funds out of which persons who lose their interests by such errors can be compensated, but the funds often are absurdly small in comparison to the potential liability, and in general the full faith and credit of the state or county does not back the Torrens system registry. For example, in Gill v. Johnson, 21 Cal. App. 2d 649, 69 P.2d 1016 (1937), a plaintiff against the California state fund was held entitled to a $48,000 judgment. Unfortunately, this completely exhausted the fund's meager resources and left it $8000 in debt! New registrations under the California law virtually ceased after this decision, and the statute was repealed in 1955. Moreover, claims against the registry are allegedly slow to be paid, some of the statutes require exhaustion of all other possible sources of recovery, and administration of the Torrens system is often less than a model of efficiency. For all of these reasons, it is not hard to see why the Torrens system of title registration has not been an astounding success in the United States. Its future is dim, and reforming the predominant recording system seems a more fruitful endeavor. See McCormack, Torrens and Recording: Land Title Assurance in the Computer Age, 18 Wm. Mitchell L. Rev. 61 (1992).

G. TITLE INSURANCE

Title insurance is the predominant method of assuring real estate titles in the United States today. It was developed more than one hundred years ago, and is an exclusively American invention. Title insurance attempts to solve the problems we have discussed in connection with the recording system. In substance, a title insurance policy is the insurer's promise that, if the title is not in the condition described by the policy on its effective date, the insurer will attempt to fix the problem or will indemnify the insured for resulting loss.

There are two kinds of title insurance policies: those insuring the interests of lenders and those insuring the interests of owners. The lender's policy is far more significant in economic terms, because it is really lenders and secondary market mortgage investors who have made title insurance the important force in real estate conveyancing that it is today. The secondary market, in which financial institutions (e.g., life insurance companies, savings banks, and federally chartered corporations such as Fannie Mae and Freddie Mac) and mortgage securitizers buy mortgages from local lenders, has been particularly insistent on title insurance. This is a reasonable insistence, because an investor who is acquiring mortgages from many states and localities is understandably reluctant to rely on the opinions and malpractice insurance policies of numerous local lawyers whose qualifications and experience are hard to judge and police. Title insurance provides a standardized, fungible nationwide means of assuring titles, and thus is a far more attractive option.

Nearly all title insurers obtain title searches and examinations before issuing policies. In some states this is legally mandated, and it is generally considered foolish to do otherwise. The search may be done by a local lawyer who is approved by the title company. In this setting, the title company is paid only a "risk premium", because it is not required to perform the title search and the attorney is separately compensated by the client for the title examination work. In other areas or among other companies, the insurer's own employees may perform title searches, either in the company's private title plant or in the public records. Under this method, the company generally charges an "all-inclusive" premium to the insured that covers both the search and the risk-assumption aspects. The "approved attorney" approach is predominant in the East and the Midwest, especially outside major cities. The "all-inclusive" approach is widely used in the West and in major cities throughout the rest of the United States.

Under the "all-inclusive" method, the company or its agent usually issues a "preliminary report" or "binder" that shows the matters disclosed by its search, which will be listed as exceptions in the policy. The purchaser treats this report much like a lawyer's title opinion based on a record search.

For the reasons mentioned above, the vast majority of lenders now insist on the issuance of a lender's policy whenever a new mortgage loan is made. It is the nearly universal custom that the borrower must pay the premium for this policy. Owners' policies are not issued quite as frequently. They may be paid for by the buyer of the property (commonly in the East) or by the seller (commonly in the West). As we will see below, there are often significant differences between the coverage of lender's and owner's policies, with the former usually having fewer exceptions and thus absorbing a broader range of risks.

Virtually all title insurance underwriters and many agents and abstractors are members of the American Land Title Association (ALTA), a trade association headquartered in Washington, D.C. For many years ALTA has promulgated title insurance policy forms that are very widely used throughout the United States.

The form below is standard ALTA owner's policy form. (Some of the "conditions" in the form are summarized or omitted for the sake of brevity.)

OWNER'S POLICY OF TITLE INSURANCE

Issued by

BLANK TITLE INSURANCE COMPANY

Adopted by the American Land Title Association June 17, 2006

Any notice of claim and any other notice or statement in writing required to be given to the Company under this Policy must be given to the Company at the address shown in Section 18 of the Conditions.

COVERED RISKS

SUBJECT TO THE EXCLUSIONS FROM COVERAGE, THE EXCEPTIONS FROM COVERAGE CONTAINED IN SCHEDULE B, AND THE CONDITIONS, BLANK TITLE INSURANCE COMPANY, a Blank corporation (the "Company") insures, as of Date of Policy and, to the extent stated in Covered Risks 9 and 10, after Date of Policy, against loss or damage, not exceeding the Amount of Insurance, sustained or incurred by the Insured by reason of:

1.   Title being vested other than as stated in Schedule A.

2.   Any defect in or lien or encumbrance on the Title. This Covered Risk includes but is not limited to insurance against loss from

   (a)   A defect in the Title caused by

     (i)   forgery, fraud, undue influence, duress, incompetency, incapacity, or impersonation;

     (ii)   failure of any person or Entity to have authorized a transfer or conveyance;

(iii) a document affecting Title not properly created, executed, witnessed, sealed, acknowledged, notarized, or delivered;

(iv) failure to perform those acts necessary to create a document by electronic means authorized by law;

(v) a document executed under a falsified, expired, or otherwise invalid power of attorney;

(vi) a document not properly filed, recorded, or indexed in the Public Records including failure to perform those acts by electronic means authorized by law; or

(vii) a defective judicial or administrative proceeding.

(b) The lien of real estate taxes or assessments imposed on the Title by a governmental authority due or payable, but unpaid.

(c) Any encroachment, encumbrance, violation, variation, or adverse circumstance affecting the Title that would be disclosed by an accurate and complete land survey of the Land. The term "encroachment" includes encroachments of existing improvements located on the Land onto adjoining land, and encroachments onto the Land of existing improvements located on adjoining land.

3.   Unmarketable Title.

4.   No right of access to and from the Land.

5.   The violation or enforcement of any law, ordinance, permit, or governmental regulation (including those relating to building and zoning) restricting, regulating, prohibiting, or relating to

(a)   the occupancy, use, or enjoyment of the Land;

(b)   the character, dimensions, or location of any improvement erected on the Land;

(c)   the subdivision of land; or

(d)   environmental protection

if a notice, describing any part of the Land, is recorded in the Public Records setting forth the violation or intention to enforce, but only to the extent of the violation or enforcement referred to in that notice.

6.   An enforcement action based on the exercise of a governmental police power not covered by Covered Risk 5 if a notice of the enforcement action, describing any part of the Land, is recorded in the Public Records, but only to the extent of the enforcement referred to in that notice.

7. The exercise of the rights of eminent domain if a notice of the exercise, describing any part of the Land, is recorded in the Public Records.

8. Any taking by a governmental body that has occurred and is binding on the rights of a purchaser for value without Knowledge.

9. Title being vested other than as stated in Schedule A or being defective

    (a) as a result of the avoidance in whole or in part, or from a court order providing an alternative remedy, of a transfer of all or any part of the title to or any interest in the Land occurring prior to the transaction vesting Title as shown in Schedule A because that prior transfer constituted a fraudulent or preferential transfer under federal bankruptcy, state insolvency, or similar creditors' rights laws; or

    (b) because the instrument of transfer vesting Title as shown in Schedule A constitutes a preferential transfer under federal bankruptcy, state insolvency, or similar creditors' rights laws by reason of the failure of its recording in the Public Records

        (i) to be timely, or

        (ii) to impart notice of its existence to a purchaser for value or to a judgment or lien creditor.

10. Any defect in or lien or encumbrance on the Title or other matter included in Covered Risks 1 through 9 that has been created or attached or has been filed or recorded in the Public Records subsequent to Date of Policy and prior to the recording of the deed or other instrument of transfer in the Public Records that vests Title as shown in Schedule A.

The Company will also pay the costs, attorneys' fees, and expenses incurred in defense of any matter insured against by this Policy, but only to the extent provided in the Conditions.

BLANK TITLE INSURANCE COMPANY

BY: _____ **PRESIDENT**

BY: _____ **SECRETARY**

EXCLUSIONS FROM COVERAGE

The following matters are expressly excluded from the coverage of this policy, and the Company will not pay loss or damage, costs, attorneys' fees, or expenses that arise by reason of:

1.   (a) Any law, ordinance, permit, or governmental regulation (including those relating to building and zoning) restricting, regulating, prohibiting, or relating to

       (i)   the occupancy, use, or enjoyment of the Land;

       (ii) the character, dimensions, or location of any improvement erected on the Land;

       (iii) the subdivision of land; or

       (iv) environmental protection;

       or the effect of any violation of these laws, ordinances, or governmental regulations. This Exclusion 1(a) does not modify or limit the coverage provided under Covered Risk 5.

     (b) Any governmental police power. This Exclusion 1(b) does not modify or limit the coverage provided under Covered Risk 6.

2.   Rights of eminent domain. This Exclusion does not modify or limit the coverage provided under Covered Risk 7 or 8.

3.   Defects, liens, encumbrances, adverse claims, or other matters

     (a) created, suffered, assumed, or agreed to by the Insured Claimant;

     (b) not Known to the Company, not recorded in the Public Records at Date of Policy, but Known to the Insured Claimant and not disclosed in writing to the Company by the Insured Claimant prior to the date the Insured Claimant became an Insured under this policy;

     (c) resulting in no loss or damage to the Insured Claimant;

     (d) attaching or created subsequent to Date of Policy (however, this does not modify or limit the coverage provided under Covered Risk 9 and 10); or

     (e) resulting in loss or damage that would not have been sustained if the Insured Claimant had paid value for the Title.

4.   Any claim, by reason of the operation of federal bankruptcy, state insolvency, or similar creditors' rights laws, that the transaction vesting the Title as shown in Schedule A, is

     (a) a fraudulent conveyance or fraudulent transfer; or

     (b) a preferential transfer for any reason not stated in Covered Risk 9 of this policy.

5.   Any lien on the Title for real estate taxes or assessments imposed by governmental authority and created or attaching between Date of Policy and the date of recording of the deed or other instrument of

transfer in the Public Records that vests Title as shown in Schedule A.

SCHEDULE A

Name and Address of Title Insurance Company: _____

[File No.:_____]   Policy No.: _____

Address Reference: _____

Amount of Insurance: $ _____ [Premium: $ _____]

Date of Policy: _____ [at a.m./p.m.]

1. Name of Insured:

2. The estate or interest in the Land that is insured by this policy is:

3. Title is vested in:

4. The Land referred to in this policy is described as follows:

SCHEDULE B

EXCEPTIONS FROM COVERAGE

This policy does not insure against loss or damage, and the Company will not pay costs, attorneys' fees, or expenses that arise by reason of:

1.   [Policy may include regional exceptions if so desired by the issuing Company.]

2.   [Variable exceptions such as taxes, easements, CC&R's, etc., shown here]

CONDITIONS

1. DEFINITION OF TERMS

The following terms when used in this policy mean:

(a)   "Amount of Insurance": The amount stated in Schedule A, as may be increased or decreased by endorsement to this policy, increased by Section 8(b), or decreased by Sections 10 and 11 of these Conditions.

(b)   "Date of Policy": The date designated as "Date of Policy" in Schedule A.

(c)   "Entity": A corporation, partnership, trust, limited liability company, or other similar legal entity.

(d)   "Insured": The Insured named in Schedule A.

    (i)   the term "Insured" also includes

(A) successors to the Title of the Insured by operation of law as distinguished from purchase, including heirs, devisees, survivors, personal representatives, or next of kin;

(B) successors to an Insured by dissolution, merger, consolidation, distribution, or reorganization;

(C) successors to an Insured by its conversion to another kind of Entity;

(D) a grantee of an Insured under a deed delivered without payment of actual valuable consideration conveying the Title

(1) if the stock, shares, memberships, or other equity interests of the grantee are wholly-owned by the named Insured,

(2) if the grantee wholly owns the named Insured,

(3) if the grantee is wholly-owned by an affiliated Entity of the named Insured, provided the affiliated Entity and the named Insured are both wholly-owned by the same person or Entity, or

(4) if the grantee is a trustee or beneficiary of a trust created by a written instrument established by the Insured named in Schedule A for estate planning purposes.

(ii) with regard to (A), (B), (C), and (D) reserving, however, all rights and defenses as to any successor that the Company would have had against any predecessor Insured.

(e) "Insured Claimant": An Insured claiming loss or damage.

(f) "Knowledge" or "Known": Actual knowledge, not constructive knowledge or notice that may be imputed to an Insured by reason of the Public Records or any other records that impart constructive notice of matters affecting the Title.

(g) "Land": The land described in Schedule A, and affixed improvements that by law constitute real property. The term "Land" does not include any property beyond the lines of the area described in Schedule A, nor any right, title, interest, estate, or easement in abutting streets, roads, avenues, alleys, lanes, ways, or waterways, but this does not modify or limit the extent that a right of access to and from the Land is insured by this policy.

(h) "Mortgage": Mortgage, deed of trust, trust deed, or other security instrument, including one evidenced by electronic means authorized by law.

(i) "Public Records": Records established under state statutes at Date of Policy for the purpose of imparting constructive notice of matters relating to real property to purchasers for value and without Knowledge. With respect to Covered Risk 5(d), "Public Records" shall also include environmental protection liens filed in the records of the clerk of the United States District Court for the district where the Land is located.

(j) "Title": The estate or interest described in Schedule A.

(k) "Unmarketable Title": Title affected by an alleged or apparent matter that would permit a prospective purchaser or lessee of the Title or lender on the Title to be released from the obligation to purchase, lease, or lend if there is a contractual condition requiring the delivery of marketable title.

2. CONTINUATION OF INSURANCE

The coverage of this policy shall continue in force as of Date of Policy in favor of an Insured, but only so long as the Insured retains an estate or interest in the Land, or holds an obligation secured by a purchase money Mortgage given by a purchaser from the Insured, or only so long as the Insured shall have liability by reason of warranties in any transfer or conveyance of the Title. This policy shall not continue in force in favor of any purchaser from the Insured of either (i) an estate or interest in the Land, or (ii) an obligation secured by a purchase money Mortgage given to the Insured.

3. NOTICE OF CLAIM TO BE GIVEN BY INSURED CLAIMANT

The Insured shall notify the Company promptly in writing (i) in case of any litigation as set forth in Section 5(a) of these Conditions, (ii) in case Knowledge shall come to an Insured hereunder of any claim of title or interest that is adverse to the Title, as insured, and that might cause loss or damage for which the Company may be liable by virtue of this policy, or (iii) if the Title, as insured, is rejected as Unmarketable Title. If the Company is prejudiced by the failure of the Insured Claimant to provide prompt notice, the Company's liability to the Insured Claimant under the policy shall be reduced to the extent of the prejudice.

4. PROOF OF LOSS * * * [Company may require insured to provide a written proof of loss.].

5. **DEFENSE AND PROSECUTION OF ACTIONS * * *** [Company must provide a defense of the insured in litigation in which a third party asserts a claim covered by the policy. Company may also institute an action to establish the insured's title or prevent or reduce loss to the insured.]

6. **DUTY OF INSURED CLAIMANT TO COOPERATE * * ***

7. **OPTIONS TO PAY OR OTHERWISE SETTLE CLAIMS; TERMINATION OF LIABILITY * * ***

8. **DETERMINATION AND EXTENT OF LIABILITY**

This policy is a contract of indemnity against actual monetary loss or damage sustained or incurred by the Insured Claimant who has suffered loss or damage by reason of matters insured against by this policy.

(a) The extent of liability of the Company for loss or damage under this policy shall not exceed the lesser of

(i) the Amount of Insurance; or

(ii) the difference between the value of the Title as insured and the value of the Title subject to the risk insured against by this policy.

(b) If the Company pursues its rights under Section 5 of these Conditions and is unsuccessful in establishing the Title, as insured,

(i) the Amount of Insurance shall be increased by 10%, and

(ii) the Insured Claimant shall have the right to have the loss or damage determined either as of the date the claim was made by the Insured Claimant or as of the date it is settled and paid.

(c) In addition to the extent of liability under (a) and (b), the Company will also pay those costs, attorneys' fees, and expenses incurred in accordance with Sections 5 and 7 of these Conditions.

9. **LIMITATION OF LIABILITY * * *** [Company is deemed to have fulfilled its obligations under the policy if it cures the title defect.]

10. **REDUCTION OF INSURANCE; REDUCTION OR TERMINATION OF LIABILITY**

All payments under this policy, except payments made for costs, attorneys' fees, and expenses, shall reduce the Amount of Insurance by the amount of the payment.

11. LIABILITY NONCUMULATIVE

The Amount of Insurance shall be reduced by any amount the Company pays under any policy insuring a Mortgage to which exception is taken in Schedule B or to which the Insured has agreed, assumed, or taken subject, or which is executed by an Insured after Date of Policy and which is a charge or lien on the Title, and the amount so paid shall be deemed a payment to the Insured under this policy.

12. PAYMENT OF LOSS * * *

13. RIGHTS OF RECOVERY UPON PAYMENT OR SETTLEMENT
* * * [If Company pays a claim, it is subrogated to the rights of the insured against other parties.]

14. ARBITRATION * * *

15. LIABILITY LIMITED TO THIS POLICY; POLICY ENTIRE CONTRACT * * *

16. SEVERABILITY * * *

17. CHOICE OF LAW; FORUM * * *

18. NOTICES, WHERE SENT * * *

The "Variable Exceptions" listed in Schedule B of the policy are, in essence, the outstanding interests in the land held by others as disclosed by the title search. Typical of such claims would be existing mortgages (in an owner's policy) or prior mortgages (in a lender's policy), utility easements, the lien of the current year's property taxes if they have not been paid, and so on. In most cases the company will have issued a preliminary title report or binder prior to the issuance of the policy itself. The preliminary title report will indicate the matters that the company expects to show as "Exceptions" on Schedule B of the policy based on the results of its title search. Sometimes the title insurance company can be persuaded that one or more of these matters is so old or so unlikely to be asserted that the company can safely "insure over" it, dropping it from Schedule B. In some areas, the title company may charge an additional premium (to cover the added risk) when they do so.

Although the standard owner's policy reproduced above is very widely used, there are many variations in policy forms. For example, in 2008 ALTA promulgated an enhanced homeowner's policy, which is available only for one-to-four-family residences. It provides many types of coverage not available under the standard policy, including failure of a prior owner to obtain a proper building permit or subdivision approval, violations of restrictive covenants, damage from mineral extraction, inconsistencies between the map attached to the policy and the public records, and lack of both pedestrian and vehicular access.

Remarkably, the enhanced homeowner's policy also covers certain events occurring *after* the policy is issued—a form of protection completely foreign to traditional title insurance. These events include forged documents, construction of encroaching structures, adverse possession, prescriptive easements, and enforcement of zoning ordinances that require removal of structures or prevent use of the land as a single-family residence. In addition, the enhanced homeowner's policy applies an automatic percentage increase to the original policy amount (say, 10 percent per year) for each of the first five years after the policy is issued. This automatic coverage increase helps to cover increases in the value of the property. Moreover, the enhanced policy automatically covers a spouse who acquires the property pursuant to a divorce, inheriting heirs, related family trusts and their beneficiaries. None of these parties is covered by the standard policy.

In contrast, title insurance companies in some states commonly use policies prepared by state trade associations or customized by individual companies that provide *less* coverage than the standard ALTA owner's policy. Among the types of coverage that may be missing from these policies are rights of access, encroachments and boundary discrepancies, unfiled mechanic's liens, and unrecorded easements, liens, or other encumbrances. Such limited-coverage policies usually fail to insure marketability of the title as well. Of course, these variations in coverage are reflected in the premium charged for the policy, with the enhanced homeowner's policy costing more (perhaps 20 percent more than the standard policy) and the limited-coverage policy costing less. In addition to providing greater coverage, issuance of an ALTA policy usually requires a physical inspection of the property, and perhaps a survey, whereas a limited-coverage policy may not.

———————

Lenders' policies differ from owners' policies in that the insuring language at the beginning of the policy is generally broader in scope. For example; the standard ALTA lender's policy, adopted June 17, 2006, tracks the general coverage of the owner's policy reprinted above, but adds the following items:

9. The invalidity or unenforceability of the lien of the Insured Mortgage upon the Title. This Covered Risk includes but is not limited to insurance against loss from any of the following impairing the lien of the Insured Mortgage

(a) forgery, fraud, undue influence, duress, incompetency, incapacity, or impersonation;

(b) failure of any person or Entity to have authorized a transfer or conveyance;

(c) the Insured Mortgage not being properly created, executed, witnessed, sealed, acknowledged, notarized, or delivered;

(d) failure to perform those acts necessary to create a document by electronic means authorized by law;

(e) a document executed under a falsified, expired, or otherwise invalid power of attorney;

(f) a document not properly filed, recorded, or indexed in the Public Records including failure to perform those acts by electronic means authorized by law; or

(g) a defective judicial or administrative proceeding.

10. The lack of priority of the lien of the Insured Mortgage upon the Title over any other lien or encumbrance.

11. The lack of priority of the lien of the Insured Mortgage upon the Title

(a) as security for each and every advance of proceeds of the loan secured by the Insured Mortgage over any statutory lien for services, labor, or material arising from construction of an improvement or work related to the Land when the improvement or work is either

(i) contracted for or commenced on or before Date of Policy; or

(ii) contracted for, commenced, or continued after Date of Policy if the construction is financed, in whole or in part, by proceeds of the loan secured by the Insured Mortgage that the Insured has advanced or is obligated on Date of Policy to advance; and

(b) over the lien of any assessments for street improvements under construction or completed at Date of Policy.

12. The invalidity or unenforceability of any assignment of the Insured Mortgage, provided the assignment is shown in Schedule A, or the failure of the assignment shown in Schedule A to vest title to the Insured Mortgage in the named Insured assignee free and clear of all liens.

13. The invalidity, unenforceability, lack of priority, or avoidance of the lien of the Insured Mortgage upon the Title

(a) resulting from the avoidance in whole or in part, or from a court order providing an alternative remedy, of any transfer of all or any part of the title to or any interest in the Land occurring prior to the transaction creating the lien of the Insured Mortgage because that prior transfer constituted a fraudulent or preferential transfer under federal bankruptcy, state insolvency, or similar creditors' rights laws; or

(b) because the Insured Mortgage constitutes a preferential transfer under federal bankruptcy, state insolvency, or similar creditors' rights laws by reason of the failure of its recording in the Public Records

    (i)   to be timely, or

    (ii) to impart notice of its existence to a purchaser for value or to a judgment or lien creditor.

14. Any defect in or lien or encumbrance on the Title or other matter included in Covered Risks 1 through 13 that has been created or attached or has been filed or recorded in the Public Records subsequent to Date of Policy and prior to the recording of the Insured Mortgage in the Public Records.

————————

Lenders' policies, unlike owners' policies, are generally assignable. Thus, a secondary market purchaser of the mortgage gets the benefit of the original lender's policy. If the mortgagee purchases at a foreclosure sale of the mortgage, the policy's protection continues (although only for the amount of the previous mortgage loan). Although lenders' policies are very useful to mortgagees, they do not solve all possible problems. A lender's policy will not, for example, protect against the eventuality that the debt itself is unenforceable because the promissory note was a forgery, because the lender failed to disburse the loan funds to the mortgagor, or because the note was not delivered to an assignee of the mortgage. See Lawyers Title Ins. Co. v. Novastar Mortg., Inc., 862 So.2d 793 (Fla. Ct. App. 2003).

NOTES AND QUESTIONS

1.   *Additional readings.* Two excellent works on the subject of title insurance are B. Burke, Law of Title Insurance (1986) and J. Palomar, Title Insurance Law (2014). For a highly useful compendium of information on title insurance, including discussion of coverage and claims procedures with sample policy forms, see Gosdin, Title Insurance: A Comprehensive Overview (American Bar Ass'n 2007).

2.   *Practice of law?* Consider the policy forms reproduced above before answering this and the following questions. Is a title policy really a legal opinion as to the state of the title, and thus the unauthorized practice of law? See Payne, Title Insurance and the Unauthorized Practice of Law Controversy, 53 Minn. L. Rev. 423 (1969).

3.   *Must the insurer do a search?* Must the company represent that it has searched the title? Some states have statutes so requiring. See, e.g., Fla. Stat. § 627.7845; N.J. Stat. Tit. 17 § 46–B9; 2B N.C. Gen. Stat. § 58–132; 20 Ariz. Rev. Stat. § 1567A. In a state with no statute, is there any remedy

(beyond a claim on the policy itself if a defect arises) for the title company's failure to search? See Note, Title Insurance: The Duty to Search, 71 Yale L.J. 1161 (1962).

Several courts have held that the title company may be liable as an abstractor for a negligent (or, presumably, nonexistent) search, irrespective of the language of the policy. See, e.g., Bank of California v. First American Title Ins. Co., 826 P.2d 1126 (Alaska 1992); Garton v. Title Ins. and Trust Co., 106 Cal. App. 3d 365, 165 Cal. Rptr. 449 (1980); Moore v. Title Ins. Co. of Minn., 148 Ariz. 408, 714 P.2d 1303 (App.1985); Tess v. Lawyers Title Ins. Corp., 251 Neb. 501, 557 N.W.2d 696 (1997). Cf. Focus Inv. Assoc. v. American Title Ins. Co., 992 F.2d 1231 (1st Cir.1993) (no liability for negligence where title company did not issue a preliminary report to insured). There are also several cases finding no tort liability. See Davis, More Than They Bargained For: Are Title Insurance Companies Liable in Tort for Undisclosed Title Defects?, 45 Cath. U. L. Rev. 71 (1995); Palomar, Title Insurance Companies' Liability for Failure to Search Title and Disclose Record Title, 20 Creighton L. Rev. 455 (1987).

Why would a plaintiff prefer to rely on a negligence theory rather than a claim or suit on the title insurance policy itself? Several reasons may exist:

(a) The period provided in the policy for filing a claim (often 90 days) may have expired.

(b) The insured may wish to claim consequential or punitive damages that are permitted in tort, but not in contract. See, e.g., Red Lobster Inns of America, Inc. v. Lawyers Title Ins. Corp., 492 F. Supp. 933 (E.D. Ark. 1980). Or, the insured may wish to claim damages for emotional distress. See Jarchow v. Transamerica Title Ins. Co., 48 Cal. App. 3d 917, 122 Cal. Rptr. 470, 486 (1975) (subsequently overruled by statute).

(c) An outstanding title interest was not shown on the preliminary title report, and hence the insured was not warned of its existence, but it was shown as a Schedule B exception when the policy itself was issued. See Heyd v. Chicago Title Ins. Co., 218 Neb. 296, 354 N.W.2d 154 (1984); Garton v. Title Ins. & Trust Co., 106 Cal. App. 3d 365, 165 Cal. Rptr. 449 (1980); Shotwell v. Transamerica Title Ins. Co., 16 Wn. App. 627, 558 P.2d 1359 (1976).

(d) The party making the claim was not insured, but nonetheless relied on the policy. For example, in Barrington Reinsurance Ltd., LLC v. Fidelity Nat'l Title Ins. Co., 143 N.M. 31, 172 P.3d 168 (N.M. App. 2007), the title company issued a policy to A. Shortly thereafter, A sold the property to B, and the title company advised B not to bother getting a new title policy since the old one was still quite fresh. The court held that under the circumstances it was entirely foreseeable that B would rely on the policy, and held the insurer liable.

Paragraph 15 of the "Conditions" section of the owner's policy contains the following restriction on claims,

> This policy * * * is the entire policy and contract between the insured and the Company. * * * Any claim or loss or damage that arises out of the status of the Title or by any action asserting such claim shall be restricted to this policy.

Does this language make it impossible to assert a claim based on negligence, that is not covered by the policy language? Several cases have so held. See, e.g., Reflections Townhomes v. First American Title Ins. Co., 2010 WL 445521 (Ariz. App. 2010) (where policy claim was barred by failure to notify company of claim within 90 days, insured could not maintain negligence claim).

4. *Must the insurer cure the title defects?* Does the policy impose an affirmation duty on the title company to make affirmative efforts to cure title defects that come to light, or may the company merely wait until a loss is sustained and then compensate the insured? Policy language usually purports to give the insurer the choice on this point, but there is a great deal of judicial authority that the insurer must actually attempt to cure the alleged defeat and clear the title if it is feasible to do so. See Stewart Title Guar. Co. v. West, 110 Md. App. 114, 676 A.2d 953 (1996); Shada v. Title & Trust Co., 457 So. 2d 553 (Fla. App. 1984); Summonte v. First American Title Ins. Co., 180 N.J. Super. 605, 436 A.2d 110 (1981).

5. *What sorts of claims are covered?* Consider whether the ALTA owner's policy, supra, covers the insured against the following items (which are not mentioned in Schedule B of the policy):

(a) A mechanic's lien, filed by a plumber who has worked on the property before the sale of the property and the issuance of the policy, but whose lien is not filed until after the sale occurs. By statute, the lien's priority "relates back" to the date the work was commenced.

(b) A set of restrictive covenants limiting the use of the property to single-family dwellings only.

(c) A reservation of oil and gas rights, made by the grantor of a deed 100 years ago.

(d) Lack of delivery of a deed in the chain of title for the insured property.

(e) A dower right or other marital property claim by the (until now undisclosed) wife of a former owner.

(f) A claim against the insured owner, made by a grantee of a deed from that owner based on a warranty in the deed. See Stewart Title Guar. Co. v. Lunt Land Corp., 162 Tex. 435, 347 S.W.2d 584 (1961).

(g) A zoning ordinance that prevents the most economical use of the property (although the current use does not violate the ordinance).

(h) Failure of the subdivider who developed the property to obtain the necessary local government approvals for the subdivision. See Hocking v. Title Ins. & Trust Co., 37 Cal. 2d 644, 234 P.2d 625 (1951).

(i) An easement that runs along one side of the property for storm drainage purposes. The ditch was visible to the insured when he or she inspected the property before purchasing it. Cf. Jones v. Grow Inv. & Mortg. Co., 11 Utah 2d 326, 358 P.2d 909 (1961).

(j) An easement for a buried pipeline running across the property. The pipeline is recorded, but it is not visible from the surface. See Guarantee Abstract & Title Ins. Co. v. St. Paul Fire & Marine Ins. Co., 216 So. 2d 255 (Fla. App. 1968).

(k) The rights of a tenant who is occupying the property under an unrecorded one-year lease. See Annot., 94 A.L.R. 3d 1188.

6. *Claims against title insurers.* Title insurance is quite different than most other insurance products. Title companies that operate by the "all-inclusive" method spend a great deal of money in *loss avoidance*—that is, in searching titles in order to identify existing encumbrances and defects, so that these items can be excluded from the coverage of the insurance policies to be written. For this reason, the operating expenses of title insurers constitute a much higher percentage of their total operating revenue, roughly 90 percent, than is the case with other insurance products. Likewise, because the efforts of title insurers at loss avoidance are generally successful, title insurers spend a much lower percentage, roughly 8 percent, of their operating revenue on loss payments and loss adjustment expense (litigation and negotiation costs) than other types of insurers. See J. Palomar, Title Insurance § 1.04[1] (2007).

What are the main types of losses title companies experience? Among the important ones are the following:

- Mechanic's liens
- Plant search errors
- Examination and opinion errors
- Forgeries
- Property taxes

Mechanic's liens are a particular problem for title insurers. A mechanic's lien can be filed by a contractor or materials seller who supplies labor or materials to improvements on a parcel of real estate and is not paid. Typically the claim or notice of lien must be recorded in the public records within a fixed period (usually, six to 12 months, depending on the jurisdiction). The difficulty arises from the fact that the lien's priority date then "relates back," commonly to the date that work on the project commenced. If some other party buys the property or accepts a mortgage on it between the time work commenced and the time the notice of lien is recorded, she or he may be "stuck" with the lien despite the fact that no search in the public records could have disclosed it. This is, of course, an outrageously bad system (unless you happen to be a contractor or materials supplier, in which case you may consider it eminently reasonable).

Many title insurance companies refuse to insure against unfiled mechanic's liens, or insure against them only for an extra premium, due to their "unfindable" nature. Mechanic's lien claims often result from cost overruns and developer insolvencies in commercial or residential construction projects. These insolvency situations tend to occur during periods when interest rates are high and construction costs are rising rapidly. As a result, title insurance claims arising from mechanic's liens tend to be cyclical, following national economic trends.

H. SETTLEMENT

1. OVERVIEW OF SETTLEMENT PROCEDURES

Once the title has been examined, financing arranged, and other necessary conditions satisfied and investigations completed, the buyer and seller will exchange a deed converging title for the purchase price in a process called "closing" or "settlement." Settlement procedures are straightforward, although somewhat complex. Usually a designated "closing agent"—who may be an attorney, a title insurance company, an escrow company, or (less commonly) a real estate broker or mortgage lender—will handle the settlement process. The closing agent's tasks may include the following:

1. Reviewing the preliminary title report to determine what liens or encumbrances exist on the property, and then inquiring of their holders (e.g., existing lending institutions) the exact amount that will be necessary to pay them off as of the closing date.

2. Obtaining executed copies of the deed, the new note and mortgage or other security device if any, and a multitude of other forms and documents, including written and recordable satisfactions of mortgages or liens that will be paid off at the closing.

3. Obtaining funds from the buyer and the new lender.

4. Arranging for or verifying completion of some miscellaneous ancillary services, such as surveys, pest inspections, etc.

5.   Computing the necessary pro ration adjustments between buyer, seller, and old and new lienholders for such matters as property taxes, insurance, and local assessments.

6.   Seeing that appropriate documents are recorded and mailed to the persons entitled to receive a copy of them.

7.   Disbursing funds to the providers of ancillary services, to taxing authorities if any, and to the seller and prior lienholders who are being paid off.

There is great national variation in the filling of the roles of title examiner and closing agent. Along most of the East Coast (with exceptions in New York City and Washington, D.C.) attorneys commonly do both jobs; in fact, they frequently do the actual searches in the public records, although the more sophisticated members of the bar employ lay assistants or independent contractors for this phase of their work. In the Mountain West, the West Coast, and Texas, the examination of titles is generally done by private title insurance companies, often in their own private title plants. In these areas of the United States, the closing agent is usually an "escrow agent"—a private corporation (sometimes affiliated with a title company or lending institution) set up to receive and disburse documents and funds in real estate transactions.

In rural areas of the Midwest, title assurance was traditionally in the form of an "abstract," a book or sheaf of documents that summarized or set forth in full each instrument in the public records relating to the land in question. Abstracts were prepared by specialized "abstract companies." They were usually passed down from one owner to the next, and were updated with each transfer, thus saving a great deal of time and duplication that would be necessary if a complete record search had to be made each time land was sold. Under the Midwestern practice, the abstract was typically examined by an attorney, who provided his or her opinion of the title to the new lender and the buyer. The attorney might also handle the closing function. Today, in urban areas of the Midwest the use of abstracts has now largely been supplanted by "all-inclusive" title insurance.

Would consumers be better off if attorneys were more involved in the real estate sale and settlement process? Consider In re Opinion No. 26 of Committee on Unauthorized Practice of Law, 139 N.J. 323, 654 A.2d 1344 (1995), in which the New Jersey Supreme Court approved the practice commonly followed in South Jersey, where brokers and title insurance companies handle virtually all aspects of home sales with no attorney representing either party. Although the court felt that having lawyers represent both sides of the sale was wise and desirable, it noted:

The record fails to demonstrate that the public interest has been disserved by the South Jersey practice over the many years it has been in existence. While the risks of non-representation are many and serious, the record contains little proof of actual damage to either buyer or seller. Moreover, the record does not contain proof that, in the aggregate, the damage that has occurred in South Jersey exceeds that experienced elsewhere. In this case, the absence of proof is particularly impressive, for the dispute between the realtors and the bar is of long duration, with the parties and their counsel singularly able and highly motivated to supply such proof as may exist. The South Jersey practice also appears to save money. For the record demonstrates what is obvious, that sellers and buyers without counsel save counsel fees.

2. REAL ESTATE SETTLEMENT PROCEDURES ACT

Congressional concern with the high costs of settlement services and with allegedly abusive practices in the settlement industry resulted in the enactment of the Real Estate Settlement Procedures Act, 12 U.S.C. § 2601 et seq. (RESPA). RESPA has been amended substantially by Congress several times since its original enactment in 1974. Its basic thesis is that if consumers are given advance information about settlement services and costs, they will shop more vigorously and will bargain down prices to competitive levels. Section 5 of RESPA requires lending institutions to give to loan applicants a "special information booklet" prepared by HUD, and a written "good faith estimate" of the settlement costs the borrower is likely to incur, within three days after the loan application is received. Given that this information is provided *after* the loan application has been made, do you think that this information has much impact on shopping behavior or prices? If accurately prepared, the "good faith estimate" of the settlement costs does inform borrowers well in advance of the closing date of the amount of cash they must bring to the closing so that they are unlikely to arrive without sufficient funds to close.

Perhaps the most controversial aspect of RESPA is Section 8, which prohibits referral fees and fee-splitting among providers of settlement services, except to the extent that the fee is for the reasonable value of services actually performed. The core language of Section 8 is set forth below:

RESPA § 8

No person shall give and no person shall accept any fee, kickback, or thing of value pursuant to any agreement or understanding, oral or otherwise, that business incident to or a part of a real estate settlement service involving a federally related mortgage loan shall be referred to any person.

Both civil and criminal penalties are provided for violations. Such fees for referrals were very widespread prior to the enactment of RESPA, and there is no doubt that their frequency has declined. Today, they are much more likely to take the form of free services, trips, information, food and beverages, tickets to concerts and sporting events, office space, and so on, rather than in the form of cash.

Most of the entities that formerly were involved in paying referral fees, such as title insurers, were pleased with the passage of Section 8 of RESPA. Yet there is by no means universal agreement that Section 8's prohibition on referral fees is a good thing, even if it is effectively enforced. See Owen, Kickbacks, Specialization, Price Fixing, and Efficiency in Residential Real Estate Markets, 29 Stan. L. Rev. 931 (1977), arguing that because real estate brokers are more price-competitive than title insurers, the "monopoly profits" earned by the latter are more likely to filter down to consumers (in the form of lower brokerage commissions) if the title insurers are permitted to pay referral fees to brokers. If this is so (and it appears to be), the referral fee prohibition in RESPA is counterproductive.

After the passage of Section 8 of RESPA, a number of real estate brokers, attorneys, and lenders attempted to circumvent it by establishing or purchasing title insurance companies of their own. This practice, known as "controlled business," permits an attorney or broker (for example) who is a part owner of a title company to refer customers to the title company and to recover the profits in the form of dividends or partnership distributions rather than illegal referral fees. The major title insurance underwriters consider this referral of controlled business highly objectionable, because it allows new or "upstart" title companies, particularly those controlled by large real estate brokers, to divert business away from older and more established title insurance companies.

In 1983, Congress attempted to resolve the "controlled business" issue by an amendment to RESPA. It permits the referral of business to a controlled entity if:

(a) a timely disclosure of the relationship is made to the consumer,

(b) an estimate is given of the charges generally made by the controlled entity,

(c) the consumer is not required to use the controlled entity, and

(d) the referring entity receives nothing of value for the referral except a return on its ownership interest.

Do you suppose these restrictions have inhibited the referral of business to controlled entities?

NOTES AND QUESTIONS

1. *Expansion of RESPA's scope.* In 1992, Congress amended RESPA again, expanding its coverage from traditional first lien home purchase loan transactions to include refinancings and subordinate lien transactions (e.g., "home equity" and "home improvement" loans) as well. See Housing and Community Development Act of 1992, Pub. L. No. 102–550, § 908. HUD regulations interpreting and applying these changes were issued in 59 Fed. Reg., 6513, effective August 9, 1994. The statutory amendment also made it clear that the making of a mortgage loan was itself a "real estate settlement service" subject to RESPA. The original statute was unclear on this point.

2. *Fees to attorneys.* Because attorneys act as agents for title insurance underwriters in many areas of the country, there has been concern that an attorney might receive a fee from a title company that purported to compensate for the attorney's work as agent, but that would in fact constitute payment for referring business to the title company. If the latter were shown, it would, of course, violate Section 8 of RESPA. In a 1992 regulation, HUD attempted to deal with this issue by providing that "for an attorney of the buyer or seller to receive compensation as a title agent, the attorney must perform core title agent services (for which liability arises) separate from attorney services, including the evaluation of the title search to determine the insurability of the title, the clearance of underwriting objections, the actual issuance of the policy or policies on behalf of the title insurance company, and, where customary, issuance of the title commitment, and the conducting of the title search and closing." 57 Fed. Reg. 49600 (Nov., 2, 1992). Does it strike you as odd that a federal agency would need to adopt a regulation to prevent lawyers from profiting by referring their clients' business to title companies?

3. *What is "fee-splitting"?* Section 8 of RESPA prohibits the payment or receipt of a division of fees or charges made for a settlement service, other than for services actually performed. This rule against fee-splitting was asserted by the plaintiff-borrower in Mercado v. Calumet Federal Sav. & Loan Ass'n, 763 F.2d 269 (7th Cir. 1985). The case involved a lender who, without clear authority in the mortgage documents, demanded that an existing borrower refinance at a higher interest rate and with payment of various new loan charges. The court held that, because there was no third party with whom the asserted borrower's fees were being split, Section 8 was

not violated. RESPA, the Seventh Circuit noted, is not a "general mortgage loan antifraud provision." It left the plaintiff to her state court remedies based on the contract documents.

The question of "mark-ups" by lenders or other settlement service providers has been controversial. For example, suppose the lender pays a recording fee of $25, but charges the borrower $50 for it. Is this illegal "fee-splitting"? In Freeman v. Quicken Loans, Inc., 132 S. Ct. 2034 (2012), the United States Supreme Court held, in a unanimous opinion, that Section 8(b) of RESPA does not prevent the retention of an unearned fee by a single settlement-service provider. Rather, Section 8(b) applies only when a fee is divided among two or more persons. *Quicken Loans* rejected HUD's Policy Statement 2001–1, 66 Fed. Reg. 53052 (2001), which took the position that mark-ups and unearned fees violate Section 8(b) of RESPA.

4. *Requiring use of a specific title insurer.* Section 9 of RESPA prohibits sellers of real estate from requiring buyers to purchase title insurance from any particular company. One might think this sort of rule is so clear-cut that no one would think of violating it, but in Weisberg v. Toll Brothers, Inc., 617 F. Supp. 539 (E.D. Pa. 1985) the court approved a $265,000 settlement in a class action under Section 9 brought by 334 home buyers in Bucks County, Pennsylvania against 17 defendant builders. Each of the class members was awarded approximately 105 percent of the amount he or she originally spent on the title insurance, despite the court's observation that the violation of RESPA had in fact cost them nothing, because the title companies to which they were directed by the builders charged virtually the same rates as all other title companies in the area!

Note that there is no similar rule prohibiting lawyers or lenders from requiring the use of a particular title company, although if they do so, and if they also have a financial interest in the title company, they will have to provide the "controlled business" disclosure statement described above.

5. The *standard settlement statement and the development of the Integrated Mortgage Disclosures.* Section 4 of RESPA requires that closing agents on residential loans use a standard settlement statement form. The original from was released by HUD in the early 1970s and was known as the HUD–1 form. It was designed to make an inherently complex transaction as intelligible as possible to consumers, and has been used in millions of transactions.

The Dodd-Frank Wall Street Reform and Consumer Protection Act, Public Law 111–203 (Dodd-Frank), enacted by Congress in 2010, transferred enforcement authority for RESPA from HUD to the newly created Consumer Financial Protection Bureau (CFPB). It also transferred the power to enforce the federal Truth in Lending Act from the Federal Reserve Board to the CFPB. See Dodd-Frank, §§ 1032(f), 1098, and 1100A. Due to the fact that both of these statutes require lenders to make written disclosures to residential borrowers, Dodd-Frank instructed CFPB to issue a set of combined disclosure forms that would satisfy both acts.

This undertaking was, to put it mildly, complex. The CFPB's final rule, along with its preamble and interpretations, runs 1887 pages in double-spaced typescript! The rule was issued Nov. 30, 2013 and applies to loans for which an application is received on or after Nov. 1, 2015. It replaced the "Good Faith Estimate" of settlement costs mandated by RESPA at the time of loan application, as well as the "early" or preliminary Truth in Lending disclosure form, with a single new disclosure entitled the "Loan Estimate." The rule also replaced the HUD–1 form with a "Closing Disclosure" form, and combined it with a final Truth in Lending disclosure that must be provided to the borrower no later than three business days before the borrower closes on the loan.

The core content of the "Closing Disclosure" form remains similar to the traditional HUD–1 form, but it contains a great deal more information about the mortgage loan. Because of the limited size of the pages in this book, it isn't feasible to reprint the Loan Estimate or the Closing Disclosure in legible form here. Both are available in blank and filled-in versions on the CFPB's web site, along with compliance guides, and links to the rule itself. See http://www.consumerfinance.gov/regulatory-implementation/tila-respa/. We recommend that you download the forms and become familiar with them.

PART 2

REAL ESTATE FINANCE

■ ■ ■

CHAPTER THREE

THE USE OF MORTGAGE SUBSTITUTES

. . .

A. THE ABSOLUTE DEED, THE CONDITIONAL SALE, AND RELATED TRANSACTIONS

The material in this chapter is concerned with financing devices employed by mortgagees in attempting to circumvent the mortgagor's equity of redemption and other substantive mortgage law protections. The impetus for using such "mortgage substitutes" can in large measure be traced to a traditional judicial intolerance toward attempts to "clog the equity of redemption." The language of the court in Humble Oil & Refining Co. v. Doerr, 123 N.J.Super. 530, 303 A.2d 898 (1973), reflects this pervasive "anti-clogging" rule:

> For centuries it has been the rule that a mortgagor's equity of redemption cannot be clogged and that he cannot, as a part of the original mortgage transaction, cut off or surrender his right to redeem. Any agreement which does so is void and unenforceable as against public policy. A classic statement of the rule appears in 4 Pomeroy, Equity Jurisprudence (5th ed. 1941), § 1193 at 568 et seq.:
>
>> § 1193. *Once a Mortgage, Always a Mortgage; Collateral Agreements and Agreements Clogging the Equity of Redemption.*—In general, all persons able to contract are permitted to determine and control their own legal relations by any agreements which are not illegal, or opposed to good morals or to public policy; but the mortgage forms a market exception to this principle. The doctrine has been firmly established from an early day that when the character of a mortgage has attached at the commencement of the transaction, so that the instrument, whatever be its form, is regarded in equity as a mortgage, that character of mortgage must and will always continue. If the instrument is in its essence a mortgage, the parties cannot by any stipulations, however express and positive, render it anything but a mortgage, or deprive it of the essential attributes belonging to a mortgage in equity. The debtor or mortgagor cannot, in the inception of the instrument, as a part of or collateral to its execution, in any manner deprive

himself of his equitable right to come in after a default in paying the money at the stipulated time, and to pay the debt and interest, and thereby to redeem the land from the lien and encumbrance of the mortgage; the equitable right of redemption, after a default is preserved, remains in full force, and will be protected and enforced by a court of equity, no matter what stipulations the parties may have made in the original transaction purporting to cut off this right.

See also 4 American Law of Property (1952), §§ 16.58–16.61 at 106 et seq.; Osborne, Handbook on the Law of Mortgages, (2nd ed. 1970), §§ 96–99 at 144 et seq.; 1 Glenn on Mortgages (1943), § 44 at 278; Jones on Mortgages (6th ed. 1904), §§ 250, 251 at 185–187; 55 Am.Jur.2d, Mortgages, § 514 at 504, and § 1220 at 1001.

As indicated by the above authorities, the doctrine is universally applied, both in the United States and England, * * * .

* * *

As a part of the doctrine it is well settled that an option to buy the property for a fixed sum cannot be taken contemporaneously by the mortgagee. As stated in 4 American Law of Property, § 16.59 at 108:

* * * By a parity of reasoning, an agreement allowing the mortgagee to keep any part of the mortgaged property, redemption being limited to the balance, fails. Nor is the mortgagee allowed at the time of the loan to enter into an option or contract for the purchase of the mortgaged property. This rule was established early and still continues to be the law.

* * *

So strong is the policy behind the rule that it is applied to hold such options absolutely void and unenforceable regardless of whether there is actual oppression in the specific case. In 1904, in the leading case of Samuel v. Jarrah Timber and Wood Paving Corp., [(1904) A.C. 323], the question of whether it should continue to be so applied was squarely presented to the House of Lords for reconsideration and possible change. The House affirmed the Court of Appeals and held that an option to purchase for a fixed sum taken by a mortgagee as a part of the original transaction was void as a clog on the equity of redemption regardless of fairness. Although it acknowledged that the rule might be used as a 'means of evading a fair bargain come to between persons dealing at arms' length and negotiating on equal terms,' it nevertheless concluded that, in view of the long line of precedents applying the doctrine as a fixed rule without deviation, there should be no change therefrom. Noting that the virtue of such a fixed rule is that it serves 'to obviate the necessity of inquiry and investigation in cases where suspicion may be probable and proof difficult,' Lord Macnaghten said:

Having regard to the state of authorities binding on the Court of Appeals, if not this House, it seems to me that they could not have come to any other conclusion, although the transaction was a fair bargain between men of business without any trace or suspicion of oppression, surprise or circumvention. [(1904) A.C. 323, 325]

The same rule was applied in the recent case of Lewis v. Frank Love, Ltd., supra, where Judge Plowman for the English Chancery Division, holding that 'an option to purchase, if exercised, indubitably does stop a mortgagor from redemption,' followed the *Samuel* case and ruled:

* * * the doctrine of a clog on the equity of redemption is a technical doctrine which is not affected by the question whether in fact there has been oppression, and which applies just as much where parties are represented, as they were here, by solicitors. [(1961) 1 All.E.R. 446, 454].

NOTES

1. *Is the clogging doctrine justified in the option context?* Is it sound policy to hold such contemporaneous options "absolutely void and unenforceable regardless of whether there is actual oppression in the specific case"? Consider the following analysis of this question:

An overly dogmatic approach to such options may * * * unduly discourage the flow of capital to a variety of socially useful projects. For example, the prospect of being able to share in the success of a corporate mortgagor may very well induce a mortgagee to consider use of a variety of techniques that afford the mortgage lender the opportunity to acquire equity ownership in the mortgagor's real estate. In this connection, corporate mortgagors commonly grant their lenders warrants to purchase their stock. Conceivably a rigid application of the clogging principle could render such warrants unenforceable because they enable a mortgage lender to acquire an interest in the mortgaged corporate assets without having to resort to foreclosure. Even assuming that a court would be reluctant to apply the anti-clogging concept where the mortgagee acquires such an indirect interest in the mortgaged assets, it is not difficult to envisage its application in a variety of other settings where a mortgage lender is encouraged to provide capital by the prospect of sharing more directly in any future success of mortgagor. For example, suppose that part of the inducement to a mortgage lender to provide long term financing for several of borrower's shopping center developments is the prospect of being able later to acquire one or more of those projects or at least a significant interest in them, should the projects prove successful. A strict application of the anti-clogging doctrine could frustrate the use of options in such situations even though the lender's primary motivation is to share in the mortgagor's success rather than to avoid foreclosure when the mortgagor's venture proves to be a failure.

* * *

Thus, it seems preferable to reject the inflexible position that all mortgagee attempts to enforce such options are invalid in favor of an approach which validates them unless their enforceability is expressly tied to mortgagor default. Such an approach recognizes that the essence of the equity of redemption is the right of the mortgagor in default to insist that she be deprived of the mortgaged real estate only by a foreclosure process that tests its value at a public sale.

Notwithstanding the foregoing, it may be justifiable in extreme cases to protect even nondefaulting residential and small business mortgagors from inequitable attempts by mortgagees to profit by acquiring appreciated and improved real estate via the option route. Such mortgagors are more liable to be unrepresented by counsel and less commercially sophisticated than their more substantial business counterparts, and close judicial scrutiny is therefore probably justified. One Wisconsin case is illustrative in this regard.[1] There, mortgagee advanced approximately $8,500 to mortgagor, a good friend, to acquire a tavern property. Mortgagee took back a promissory note payable in six years secured by a mortgage on the tavern property. In addition, mortgagor, who was unrepresented by counsel, gave mortgagee, who had legal representation, a ten-year option to purchase the mortgagee's property for $8,000. The option was silent both as to refund of payments made by mortgagor on the indebtedness and as to reimbursement for improvements made on the property. Exercise was not tied to default. Two years later, after significant payments on the note and $3,000 in repairs and improvement, mortgagee exercised the option to purchase. Mortgagor was not in default on the note, and the mortgaged real estate at the time of exercise was worth between $14,000 and $18,000. The Wisconsin Supreme Court affirmed a denial of specific performance of the option. While the court's rationale was not entirely clear, it seemed to rely not only on the anti-clogging

---

[1]   Barr v. Granahan, 255 Wis. 192, 38 N.W.2d 705 (1949).

concept, but also on its inherent discretion to deny equitable relief under harsh and unequitable circumstances. This latter ground is the preferable one in our view.

Nelson, Whitman, Burkhart & Freyermuth, Real Estate Finance Law 44–45 (6th ed.2014).* There are several decisions upholding the enforceability of options against clogging attacks, finding that the option in question was not being used to circumvent foreclosure. See e.g., MacArthur v. North Palm Beach Utils., Inc., 202 So.2d 181 (Fla.1967); Blackwell Ford, Inc. v. Calhoun, 219 Mich.App. 203, 555 N.W.2d 856 (1996). For further consideration of this problem, see John C. Murray, Clogging Revisited, 33 Real Prop.Prob. & Tr. J. 279 (1998); James D. Cooper-Hill & Joseph J. Slama, The Convertible Mortgage: Can It Be Separated from the Clogging Rule?, 27 S. Tex.L.Rev. 407 (1986).

2. *Legislation modifying the clogging doctrine.* Several states have enacted legislation limiting the impact of the clogging rule in the option-mortgage context. New York legislation specifies that an option to acquire an equity or other ownership in property granted to a mortgagee simultaneously, or in connection with, a mortgage is not "unenforceable" so long as the "power to exercise such option or right is not dependent upon the occurrence of a default" in the mortgage transaction and the mortgage obligation is $2.5 million or more. N.Y. Gen. Oblig. Law § 5–334 (1985). California and Virginia have similar legislation—the statutes in those two states avoid a monetary limitation, but apply to mortgages on all property other than residential real estate containing four or fewer units. West's Ann.Cal.Civ.Code § 2906; Va. Code Ann. § 55–57.2. Finally, under the Restatement approach such an option is normally enforceable "unless its effectiveness is expressly dependent on mortgagor default." Restatement (Third) of Property (Mortgages) § 3.1(c) (1997).

Would a better approach be to treat as an unenforceable clog any attempt by the mortgagee to enforce the option after default by the mortgagor, irrespective of whether "its effectiveness is expressly dependent on mortgagor default"? Would such an approach encourage a mortgagor intentionally to go into default in order to avoid performance under the option where market conditions have otherwise made exercise of the option advantageous for the mortgagee? According to the Restatement, to "confer such discretion over the effectiveness of the option on the mortgagor might render its enforcement so unpredictable as to jeopardize its usefulness as a mortgage financing incentive." Id. cmt. d. Do you agree?

3. *The deed in escrow as a clog.* Sometimes, in conjunction with the execution of a "traditional" mortgage, the mortgagor will deliver to mortgagee or an escrow agent a deed to the mortgaged real estate. The understanding is that if the debt is satisfied, the deed will be returned to the mortgagor; however, in the event of default, the mortgagee or escrow agent is authorized to record the deed as a substitute for foreclosing the mortgage. The deed

---

* Reprinted with permission of LEG, Inc. d/b/a/ West Academic.

represents an invalid clog on the equity of redemption. See C. Phillip Johnson Full Gospel Ministries, Inc. v. Investors Financial Services, LLC., 418 Md. 86, 12 A.3d 1207 (Md.2011); In re Greene, 2007 WL 1309047 (Bankr. E.D. Va. 2007); Panagouleas Interiors, Inc. v. Silent Partner Group, Inc., 2002 WL 441409 (Ohio App.2002); Oakland Hills Dev. Corp. v. Lueders Drainage Dist., 212 Mich.App. 284, 537 N.W.2d 258 (1995); Vitvitsky v. Heim, 860 N.Y.S.2d 305 (2008); Basile v. Erhal Holding Corp., 148 A.D.2d 484, 538 N.Y.S.2d 831 (1989); Marple v. Wyoming Prod. Credit Ass'n, 750 P.2d 1315 (Wyo.1988); Nelson, Whitman, Burkhart & Freyermuth, Real Estate Finance Law § 3.1 (6th ed. 2014). See John C. Murray, Mortgage Workouts: Deeds in Escrow, 41 Real Prop. Prob. & Tr. J. 185, 187–189 (2006).

4. *Subsequent conveyances as clogs.* The "anti-clogging" doctrine is generally inapplicable to transactions that are *subsequent* to the execution of the mortgage. For example, courts routinely uphold the "deed in lieu of foreclosure," which amounts to a conveyance of the equity of redemption to the mortgagee when the mortgagor is in default and is threatened with foreclosure. See C. Phillip Johnson Full Gospel Ministries, Inc. v. Investors Financial Services, LLC., 418 Md. 86, 12 A.3d 1207 (Md.2011) ("After a mortgagor defaults on a note, she may legitimately contract with the noteholder to execute a conveyance, in exchange for adequate consideration, so long as there is no overreaching."); Nelson, Whitman, Burkhart & Freyermuth, Real Estate Finance Law § 3.3 (6th ed. 2014). Nevertheless, this type of "subsequent" transaction can receive close judicial scrutiny for a variety of other reasons which we examine in detail later in this volume. See Chapter 5, Section E, infra. In re Greene, 2007 WL 1309047 (Bankr. E.D. Va. 2007).

Should subsequent *executory* agreements between mortgagor and mortgagee be similarly shielded from the clogging principle? Suppose that after mortgagor goes into default, the parties negotiate an agreement whereby mortgagor delivers a quitclaim deed to the mortgaged real estate. The parties agree that if the debt is paid off within six months, the deed is to be returned to the mortgagor, but if the mortgagor fails to do so, the mortgagee is authorized to record the deed. Suppose the mortgagor does not pay off the debt within the six month period and mortgagee records the deed. If mortgagor, a few months later, tenders to mortgagee the full amount of the mortgage debt, will such a redemption attempt be effective? For the view that "the policy supporting the rule against clogging in contemporaneous agreements also has force where a subsequent transaction provides for a future waiver of mortgagor's redemption rights," see Restatement (Third) of Property (Mortgages) § 3.1, cmt. f and illus. 15 (1997); Patmos Fifth Real Estate, Inc. v. Mazl Building, LLC, 2 N.Y.S.3d 83 (App. Div. 2015). Do you agree? See Nelson, Whitman, Burkhart & Freyermuth, Real Estate Finance Law § 3.3 (6th ed.2014). For a contrary view, see Bradbury v. Davenport, 120 Cal. 152, 52 P. 301 (1898); Rothschild Reserve Int'l, Inc. v. Silver, 830 So.2d 224 (Fla.App.2002); Ringling Joint Venture II v. Huntington Nat'l Bank, 595 So.2d 180 (Fla.App.1992) (subsequent transaction that placed deed in escrow held not a clog; however, court stressed that the "agreements used in this case could easily result in abuse or inequity in another case under other facts. Such arrangements should be carefully scrutinized to assure that they do not violate the favored right of redemption."). Cf. Guam Hakubotan, Inc. v. Furusawa Inv. Corp., 947 F.2d 398 (9th Cir.1991); Wensel v. Flatte, 27 Ark.App. 5, 764 S.W.2d 627 (1989).

If the mortgagee cannot effectively shortcut the necessity to foreclose by taking a deed along with the mortgage, to what extent can he or she accomplish the same goal by dispensing with the mortgage entirely and merely taking a deed? The material that immediately follows deals with this and related questions.

ROGER A. CUNNINGHAM & SAUL TISCHLER, DISGUISED REAL ESTATE SECURITY TRANSACTIONS AS MORTGAGES IN SUBSTANCE

26 Rutgers L.Rev. 1, 1–4, 6–13, 14, 15–19, 21, 22–24 (1972)*

Ever since the English Chancellors regularly began to allow redemption of mortgages after default, creditors have sought ways to have real property serve as security free from any right in the debtor to redeem. As one writer put it, "[T]he big idea is to find a form of a transaction that will have the practical effect of security, yet will be held not to be a security but to belong to a wholly different jural species and so be held immune from security law."

Creditors may use two devices to create real property security without appearing to enter into a security transaction. A creditor may require his debtor to grant him land by absolute deed, under oral agreement or tacit understanding that he will reconvey only if the debtor pays the debt when due. Alternatively, a creditor may obtain from his debtor an absolute deed to real property and execute to his debtor some sort of written agreement (almost invariably withheld from public record) to reconvey the property to the debtor upon receiving payment of the debt. The written agreement to reconvey may take the form of an option to repurchase, an unconditional contract obligating the grantee to reconvey and the grantor to repurchase, or a lease back to the grantor with an option to repurchase at or before the end of the lease term. Some such options or contracts provide for the deposit in escrow of a deed of reconveyance.

The use of an absolute deed to secure a debt, with or without a written collateral agreement for reconveyance upon satisfaction, is designed to eliminate the "grantor's" equity of redemption and the necessity of foreclosure if the debtor defaults. The written instrument,

---

* Reprinted with permission of Rutgers University, The State University of New Jersey, West Publishing Co. and the authors.

whether option to repurchase, contract to reconvey, or other arrangement, usually contains provisions making time "of the essence" and forfeiting the grantor's right in case he fails to exercise the option or tender payment under the contract within the time limited.

Besides avoiding the expense and delay involved in foreclosure, the creditor often expects to gain other advantages by securing his interest with an absolute deed rather than a regular mortgage. These other advantages include the right to possession of the land prior to default, the right to possession of chattels severed from the land by the debtor or third parties, preventing the debtor from encumbering the land with further mortgages or judgment liens, and the possibility of enlarging the creditor's security interest to cover future advances to the debtor without the execution of a new security instrument.

* * *

It is important to keep in mind that the crucial question is *not* whether the parties to a deed absolute on its face intended to create the relation of mortgagor and mortgagee, but whether they intended the deed to stand as security for a debt. Where the parties cast their transaction in the form of an absolute conveyance instead of a mortgage, they do *not* intend to create the relation of mortgagor and mortgagee. Thus, the real issue is whether the circumstances are such as to justify treating the transaction as a mortgage in substance though the parties did not so intend. If the purpose of a conveyance was security, it will be treated as a mortgage even though the parties may have agreed or understood that the debtor should have no right to redeem. The right to redeem after default is an inseparable incident of the mortgage relationship and, as with ordinary mortgages, the parties cannot contract against its exercise where their relationship is in substance that of mortgagor and mortgagee.

PERRY V. QUEEN

United States District Court, M.D. Tennessee, 2006
2006 WL 481666

TRAUGER, J.

* * *

The plaintiff, a low income homeowner with a high school education, has resided at 3013 Capps Drive, Nashville, TN 37207 since 1977. This property is encumbered by two mortgages, both of which have been held in his name at all times relevant to this case. In 2004, the plaintiff received notice that the second mortgagee was going to institute foreclosure proceedings because the plaintiff had become delinquent on that account.

On or about August, 12, 2004, the plaintiff received a letter in the mail from defendant Sean Queen ("defendant Queen"), the President of Royalty Properties, LLC. The letter stated the following:

HELP Has Arrived!

You Can Stop your Foreclosure Now!

Dear Homeowner,

We are here to help people just like you. You can STOP your foreclosure in 5 days or less by letting us help you keep your home or by Selling your house for all CA$H.

"YES" we do have the CA$H to bring your payments current and "YES" we do have the CA$H to buy your house. It's your choice if you want to stay or move on. We can Help!

Here is a $2,000.00 check to show you we are serious about helping you. All you have to do is call us at 456–7000 and ask for Sean Queen so we can be on our way to signing it along with a 2nd check for the rest of the amount needed.

Don't file for bankruptcy and ruin your credit! Let us provide a better solution in keeping your home.

It doesn't matter what may have happened for you to be in the present situation, what does matter is that you are treated right and with respect.

Just ask the Taylors how we helped them keep their home and how they were able to say "Thanks so much for being honest and acting quick in a very distressful situation. Without your help we would have lost our home. Thanks a million!"

Or just ask the Troups how we were able to buy their home in less than 5 days and how they were able to say "We appreciate so much working with someone straight forward. Thanks so much for acting quick to buy our house and for keeping the foreclosure off our credit. Now we can start over fresh. Thanks again."

These folks are real people just like you that you can call for yourself.

Even if you are working on a solution for yourself, we encourage you to give us a call so we can be your "back up" plan in case your solution falls through.

HELP has arrived and it's just a phone call away! . . .

Shortly after receiving the letter, the plaintiff contacted defendant Queen by telephone. Soon thereafter, defendant Queen visited plaintiff at plaintiff's home. Defendant Queen gave plaintiff $11,113.99, to be used as follows: approximately $3,841.99 would be used to bring plaintiff's mortgage payments current, approximately $2,272 would be used to make mortgage payments through January 2005, and approximately $5,000 would go directly to the plaintiff. In exchange, the plaintiff executed a warranty deed, a Residential Lease Agreement, a Lease and Option Disclosure, and a Memorandum of Understanding.

The warranty deed deeded to the defendants the title to the plaintiff's property. Under the Residential Lease Agreement, the plaintiff agreed to lease this property back from the defendants for one year, beginning on August 30, 2004. As of January 5, 2005, the plaintiff was to pay the defendant $667.98 per month in rent. Finally, under the Lease Option and Disclosure and the Memorandum of Understanding, the plaintiff had an option to repurchase the property from the defendants. The plaintiff was required to pay approximately $44,708.71 by the end of his lease term in order to exercise the option.[2]

According to the Davidson County Property Assessor's Office, the Property is currently valued at $94,500. It is estimated that, at the time of the transaction, the outstanding balance of the two mortgage loans was $26,000, which means that the plaintiff had approximately $68,500 in equity in his property at the time of the transaction in question. By August 30, 2005, when his lease ended, the plaintiff had not exercised his option to repurchase. On September 7, 2005, the defendants served the plaintiff with a detainer warrant in an attempt to regain possession of the property.

On August 1, 2005, the plaintiff filed a Complaint alleging that the transaction described above was actually a mortgage loan transaction, with the property acting as security for the $11,113.99 the defendants gave to him. The plaintiff argued that, because this was a mortgage loan transaction, the defendants were subject to certain disclosure and other requirements under the federal Truth in Lending Act ("TILA"). According to the plaintiff, the defendants had failed to comply with all of these requirements. Such failure, the plaintiff claimed, entitled him to actual and statutory damages and gave him a right to rescind the transaction up to three years after its consummation.

ANALYSIS

* * *

The defendants here factually dispute the existence of subject matter jurisdiction. They claim that this court does not have jurisdiction to hear the plaintiff's claims because he has failed to state a federal cause of

---

[2] The $44,708.81 amount included the $11,113.99 the defendants gave to the plaintiff, a $10,000 fee, and the balance of the two mortgages that continued to encumber the property. The option price was to be adjusted to reflect the payoff amount of the two mortgages at the time plaintiff exercised the option.

action. Specifically, the defendants assert that TILA does not apply to the plaintiff's case and that, because each of the plaintiff's federal claims turns on TILA, they are not properly before the court.[6]

* * *

In evaluating whether TILA governs the sale/leaseback transaction at issue in this case, the court must determine whether it qualifies as an equitable mortgage.[7] Both parties agree that, if the transaction does so qualify, it is subject to the provisions of TILA. A consumer credit transaction qualifies as a mortgage under TILA if two contingencies are met: (1) the transaction is secured by the consumer's principal dwelling; and (2) the annual percentage rate at the consummation of the transaction exceeds a particular amount or the total points and fees payable by the consumer at or before closing exceeds the greater of a) 8 percent of the total loan amount; or b) $400.[8] See 15 U.S.C. § 1602(aa)(1).

The latter of these qualifications is not disputed in the case at hand. Defendant Queen gave the plaintiff $11,113.99. If and when the plaintiff paid off that loan, the plaintiff was required to pay a $10,000 fee, which is well in excess of the amount required under TILA. See 15 U.S.C. § 1602(aa)(1). Accordingly, the court must focus its analysis on whether the transaction between the plaintiff and the defendants was secured by the plaintiff's principal dwelling.

In Tennessee, proof that a conveyance was intended as a security must establish that (1) the grantor was indebted to the grantee; and (2) the grantor intended his conveyance to serve as a security device. *Hensley v. Britt*, No. 01A01–9607–CH–00296, 1996 WL 709375, at 5 (Tenn.Ct.App. Dec.11, 1996); *see also Flack v. McClure*, 206 Ill.App.3d 976, 151 Ill.Dec. 860, 565 N.E.2d 131, 136 (Ill.App.Ct.1990). The party asserting that a security interest was intended must prove that fact by clear and convincing evidence. *See, e.g.*, Swenson v. Mills, 198 Or.App. 236, 108 P.3d 77, 80 (Or.Ct.App.2005); *Flack*, 151 Ill.Dec. 860, 565 N.E.2d at 135. Additionally, "the evidence that security only was intended may be written or oral. The statute of frauds is not a bar to proof by parol that a deed absolute on its face was meant as a mortgage." *Hensley*, 1996 WL 709375, at 5.

---

[6]   Federal courts have jurisdiction over claims arising under TILA. *See* Truth in Lending Act, 15 U.S.C. § 1640(e) (2000) ("Any action under [TILA] . . . may be brought in any United States district court, or in any other court of competent jurisdiction, within one year from the date of the occurrence of the violation.").

[7]   Under Tennessee law, an equitable mortgage exists when "deeds purporting to convey an absolute legal and equitable title were, in fact, meant to grant only a security interest." *Hensley v. Britt*, No. 01A01–9607–CH–00296, 1996 WL 709375, at 5 (Tenn.Ct.App. Dec.11, 1996).

[8]   For 2004, the year in which the instant transaction was executed, the $400 figure was adjusted to $499 to account for inflation. *See* 12 C.F.R. § 226.32(a)(1)(ii)(2) (2005).

The defendants here argue that the plaintiff was not indebted to them because he was not obligated to repurchase the property or pay any money to the defendants but, instead, could keep the money they had lent him in return for the deed to his home. Other courts have rejected similar arguments. For instance, in *Flack*, the plaintiff signed a contract to sell her house to the defendants for $80,000. See *Flack*, 151 Ill.Dec. 860, 565 N.E.2d at 132. On the day that the contract was signed, the plaintiff asked the defendants for an advance payment of $9,000. *Id.* The defendants loaned the money to the plaintiff in exchange for a quitclaim deed to her house. *Id.* The sale of the plaintiff's house to the defendants was never completed, however, because the defendants were unable to obtain the necessary financing. *Id.* The holder of the first mortgage on the property later instituted a foreclosure action, and the house was purchased at the foreclosure sale by a third party. *Id.* In an effort to prevent the sale from being finalized, the defendants recorded their quitclaim deed and subsequently redeemed the property. *Id.* The court found that, because the defendants had agreed to return the quitclaim deed to the plaintiff when the $9,000 was repaid, the plaintiff was indebted to the defendants and the quitclaim deed served only as security for the $9,000 loan. *Id.* at 136–37.

Here, the defendants similarly had agreed to return the warranty deed to the plaintiff once he repaid to the defendants the $11,113.99 they had lent him plus defendant Queen's $10,000 fee and the $23,594.72 that approximately represented the aggregated principal amount of the two mortgages that encumbered the property. In both *Flack* and the case at hand, the plaintiffs were not obligated to repay the defendants in an absolute sense, but they were required to do so if they wanted to retain ownership of their property. Accordingly, like the Flack plaintiff, the plaintiff here was indebted to the defendants. Having established the existence of a debt, the court now must evaluate whether the plaintiff intended his conveyance of the warranty deed to serve as a security device. See *Hensley*, 1996 WL 709375 at 5.

Tennessee courts consider a number of factors in determining the grantor's intent. Among these considerations are the following: (1) the relationship between the parties; (2) whether the parties had access to legal counsel; (3) the sophistication and circumstances of the parties; (4) the adequacy of consideration; and (5) whether the grantor retained possession of the property. *Hensley*, 1996 WL 709375, at 5. A number of the factors delineated in Hensley are material to the court's determination as to the plaintiff's intent.

The disparity between the parties as to their sophistication and the circumstances under which they were operating is particularly relevant. Courts view grantors who are lacking in sophistication or who are laboring under stressful circumstances as more likely to have intended their conveyances to serve as security devices, as opposed to as transfers of their land. *See, e.g., Robinson v. Builders Supply & Lumber Co.,* 223 Ill.App.3d 1007, 166 Ill.Dec. 358, 586 N.E.2d 316, 322 (Ill.App.Ct.1991) (finding that a genuine issue of material fact existed as to the presence of an equitable mortgage in part because the plaintiff, a relatively unsophisticated party who had "never conducted any business affairs" was in "desperate circumstances" at the time that she completed her transaction with the defendant, who "was in the business of buying and rehabilitating distressed properties"); *Flack,* 151 Ill.Dec. 860, 565 N.E.2d at 137 (finding that an equitable mortgage existed based, in part, on evidence that plaintiff needed to raise money quickly because she was significantly behind on mortgage and school tuition payments). The plaintiff here has a high school education and has worked in the printing industry most of his life. There is no evidence in the record that indicates that he has experience in dealings involving property. Additionally, at the time of his transaction with the defendants, the plaintiff faced foreclosure on his second mortgage and felt "extremely desperate" about his financial situation. The defendants, on the other hand, work in a business dedicated, at least in part, to arranging the type of transaction that is being questioned in this case. The fact that the plaintiff is a relatively unsophisticated party who faced dire circumstances at the time of the transaction helps to compel the conclusion that he intended his conveyance to serve as a security device. *See Robinson,* 166 Ill.Dec. 358, 586 N.E.2d at 322.

Similarly, the relatively low amount of consideration paid by the defendants in exchange for the plaintiff's warranty deed here furthers a determination that the plaintiff intended the deed to serve as security for the loan. Where consideration received by the grantor is much less than the value of his property, there is an inference that a security device, as opposed to an outright sale, was intended. *Hensley,* 1996 WL 709375, at 5. The plaintiff's property is currently valued at approximately $94,500. At the time of his transaction with the defendants, the plaintiff purportedly had approximately $68,500 worth of equity in his house. Comparatively, the consideration paid by the defendants to the plaintiff was $11,113.99, or approximately 12% of the property's estimated value. The discrepancy between the value of the property and the price paid by the defendants is indicative of the plaintiff's intent to convey it as a security device. *See Hensley,* 1996 WL 709375, at 5, *Flack* at 151 Ill.Dec. 860, 565 N.E.2d at 137 (finding consideration to be inadequate where the plaintiff relinquished to the defendants a quitclaim deed on her $80,000 home in exchange for $9,000).

Also indicating the plaintiff's intent in this case is the fact that he retained physical possession of his house after he gave the defendants the warranty deed. Where a grantor continues to occupy the premises, there is an inference that a security device was intended. See *Hensley,* 1996 WL 709375, at 5. The evidence that the plaintiff paid rent to the defendants while he lived on the property following their transaction, which might otherwise tend to indicate the defendants' possession of such is mitigated by the fact that the two mortgages on the property remained in plaintiff's name, thus rendering him liable on them. See *Hensley,* 1996 WL 709375, at 5 (suggesting that the payment of property-related costs serves as indicia of possession).

The last of the relevant *Hensley* factors directs the court to consider whether the parties to the transaction in question were represented by legal counsel. * * * While the plaintiff did not have access to legal advice at the time the deal was executed, the defendant did. (*See* Perry Aff., Docket No. 10, Ex. 1 at 2 ("Mr. Queen drove me to an office where we met with a man who Mr. Queen identified as his attorney. The attorney handed me a stack of papers and told me to sign them.")) Like the other factors, this one also leads the court to a determination that the plaintiff intended his deed to serve as a security device. See *Flack,* 151 Ill.Dec. 860, 565 N.E.2d at 137 (upholding the finding of an equitable mortgage in part because the plaintiff did not have the advice of counsel upon executing the contested transaction, whereas the defendant did).

Outside of these factors, the defendants argue that the plaintiff must have understood the instant transaction to be a sale-leaseback with an option to repurchase because the plaintiff sent the defendants a letter indicating his intent to exercise the option on or about May 31, 2005. The court finds this argument unpersuasive because this letter was sent approximately nine months after the instant transaction was executed. The letter thus has little bearing on the intent of the plaintiff at the time the transaction was executed, which must be the relevant consideration here.

Accordingly, because the plaintiff was indebted to the defendants and because each of the *Hensley* factors considered by the court compels a finding that the plaintiff intended his conveyance to serve as a security device, the court finds that the plaintiff has shown by clear and convincing evidence that the sale-leaseback transaction in question qualifies as an equitable mortgage. * * * As such, TILA applies. *See* 15 U.S.C. §§ 1602(aa)(1), 1640(e). Thus, the plaintiff has met his burden of demonstrating, by a preponderance of the evidence, that this court has subject matter jurisdiction to hear his claims. * * *

NOTES

1. *Difference between absolute deed and conditional sale.* Note that *Flack v. McClure,* relied upon in *Perry,* represents a pure *"absolute deed"* transaction. The only writing we are confronted with is a deed from the grantor to the grantee. On the face of things, it appears that the grantor has

"sold" the real estate to the grantee. Here parol evidence is used to establish that the deed did not reflect a sale transaction, but rather was intended as security for a loan or obligation. If grantor succeeds, she will be permitted to "redeem" the land by paying the obligation.

Perry, on the other hand, is usually described as a *"conditional sale"* transaction. In this latter situation there not only is a deed to the grantee, but a second written document that normally purports to confer on the grantor the obligation or option to purchase the real estate described in the deed. Thus, unlike in the absolute deed setting, here it is clear from the second writing that the grantor has the right to reacquire the real estate. To do so the grantor need only comply with the terms of the option. Suppose, however, the option has already expired. Here the law gives the grantor a second shot at recovering the real estate by permitting him to establish that the deed was intended to serve as security for a loan or obligation and should therefore be treated as a mortgage. If successful, grantor will be permitted to "redeem" the land from the "mortgage."

Note that there is a third transaction that is less complex and thus need be mentioned only briefly. Here the deed is accompanied by a second written document, but unlike in the latter situation, it does not purport to give the grantor an option to purchase the real estate, but instead *makes it clear* that the deed was intended to serve as security for an obligation. For example, suppose this second writing is a letter from grantee to grantor that contains language that says "if you pay off the $5,000 you owe me with 10 percent interest by the end of next year, I will reconvey the real estate to you." Here the court will treat the deed and letter together as a mortgage. The letter simply provides the "defeasance" language that is found in a normal mortgage. For relatively straight-forward examples of this third type of transaction, see BMBT, LLC, v. Miller, 322 P.3d 1172 (Utah App.2014); Leona Bank v. Kouri, 3 A.D.3d 213, 772 N.Y.S.2d 251 (2004). For a somewhat more complicated version, see APAC-Mississippi, Inc. v. JHN, Inc., 818 So.2d 1213 (Miss.App.2002).

2.   *Parol evidence rule and Statute of Frauds.* At this point, you might be wondering why attempting to recharacterize an absolute deed or conditional sale does not run afoul of both the parol evidence rule and the Statute of Frauds. The former rule normally bars extrinsic evidence that would vary the terms of a written document executed with the intent that it embody the complete agreement of the parties. The Statute of Frauds, on the other hand, requires that the transfer of interests in land normally be in writing. Suffice it to say that courts usually do not permit either the parol evidence rule or the Statute of Frauds to stand in the way of attempts to establish that an absolute deed or conditional sale were intended as security transactions. However, should you wish to pursue these questions further, see 1 Nelson, Whitman, Burkhart & Freyermuth, Real Estate Finance Law § 3.15 (6th ed. Practitioner Series 2014); Restatement (Third) of Property (Mortgages) § 3.2, cmts. c & d (1997).

3.   *Nature of obligation.* In determining whether an absolute deed or conditional sale should be treated as a mortgage, courts look to the totality of the circumstances surrounding the transaction. Although no one factor is usually dispositive, most courts require that there be an obligation or debt owed to the grantee and that the conveyance was intended as security for that obligation. However, significant confusion exists concerning the nature and form of that obligation or debt. More specifically, there is disagreement as to whether the grantor must be personally liable for its payment. Many decisions require that "a specific debt" be due "from mortgagor to mortgagee" or that "there must be a right of the grantee to demand and enforce his debt and the obligation of the grantor to pay." See Hall v. Livesay, 473 So.2d 493 (Ala.1985); Toulouse v. Chilili Coop. Ass'n, 108 N.M. 220, 770 P.2d 542 (App.1989). Such language strongly suggests that the grantor must be personally liable on the underlying debt or obligation. An extreme version of this approach may require the production of a promissory note or at least some written evidence of the debt or obligation.

Other jurisdictions are much less demanding in this regard. For these courts, the terms "debt" or "obligation" seem to encompass the mere "expectation or assumption" on the part of the parties that a repayment of the consideration will occur and do not require a formal personal obligation of the grantor to repay. According to the United States Court of Appeals for the Eleventh Circuit, requiring a personal obligation,

> overlooks the fact that numerous secured real estate loan transactions are nonrecourse loans. Express creation of a recourse obligation—or the absence thereof—is undoubtedly an important fact to consider, but it cannot be the determinative factor. Instead, a court must look at the intent of the parties in light of *all* the circumstances surrounding the transaction.

In re Cox, 493 F.3d 1336 (11th Cir. 2007). See also Hatchett v. W2X, INC., 993 N.E.2d 944, 960–61 (Ill.App. 2013) ("While a debt relationship is essential to establish and equitable mortgage, direct evidence is not necessary to prove the relationship and no particular *type* of evidence is required.").

Moreover, the existence of a debt or obligation will be imputed where there is evidence the parties intended a loan transaction and other factors suggest a mortgagor-mortgagee relationship. See Johnson v. Cherry, 726 S.W.2d 4 (Tex.1987).

Consider, in this regard, the approach of Restatement (Third) of Property (Mortgages) §§ 3.2, 3.3 (1997):

§ 3.2   The Absolute Deed Intended as Security[*]

(a) Parol evidence is admissible to establish that a deed purporting to be an absolute conveyance of real estate was intended

---

[*]   © 1997 by The American Law Institute. Reprinted with permission.

to serve as security for an obligation, and should therefore be deemed a mortgage. The obligation may have been created prior to or contemporaneous with the conveyance and need not be the personal liability of any person.

(b) Intent that the deed serve as security must be proved by clear and convincing evidence. Such intent may be inferred from the totality of the circumstances, including the following factors:

(1) Statements of the parties;

(2) The presence of a substantial disparity between the value received by the grantor and the fair market value of the real estate at the time of the conveyance;

(3) The fact that the grantor retained possession of the real estate;

(4) The fact that the grantor continued to pay real estate taxes;

(5) The fact that grantor made post-conveyance improvements to the real estate; and

(6) The nature of the parties and their relationship prior to and after the conveyance.

(c) Where, in addition to the deed referred to in subsection (a) of this section, a separate writing exists indicating that the deed was intended to serve as security for an obligation, parol evidence is admissible to establish that the writings constitute a single security transaction.

§ 3.3 The Conditional Sale Intended as Security

(a) Parol evidence is admissible to establish that a deed purporting to be an absolute conveyance of real estate accompanied by a written agreement conferring on the grantor a right to purchase the real estate, was intended to serve as a security for an obligation, and should therefore be deemed a mortgage. The obligation may have been created prior to or contemporaneous with the conveyance and need not be the personal liability of any person.

(b) [Subsection (b) is identical to § 3.2(b) except that it includes, as an additional factor, the "terms on which the grantor may purchase the real estate."]

Does the Restatement approach require that the grantor in an absolute deed or conditional sale situation be personally liable on an obligation? Is a promissory note or other written evidence of the obligation required? See id. § 3.2, cmt. e, illus. 3–5 and § 3.3, cmt. c, illus. 3–6 (1997).

DOWNS V. ZIEGLER
Court of Appeals of Arizona, Division 1, 1970
13 Ariz.App. 387, 477 P.2d 261

HAIRE, JUDGE.

Plaintiffs Claude and Mary Downs, commenced an action to foreclose a real estate mortgage and to hold Albert Ziegler, the mortgagor, and three doctors alleged to have subsequently agreed to pay the mortgage, liable for any deficiency remaining after the foreclosure sale of the mortgaged property. The case was tried to the court sitting without a jury, and the court entered judgment for plaintiffs on the issue of foreclosing the subject mortgage, and for the defendant doctors on the issue of their liability for any resulting deficiency. Plaintiffs appealed from that judgment.

The facts necessary for a determination of this appeal are as follows: Defendant Ziegler was in the construction business, having built and owned four apartment buildings. One of the apartments was built on land conveyed to Ziegler by the plaintiffs. Ziegler paid for this land by giving the plaintiffs an installment promissory note in the sum of $75,000.00, secured by a mortgage on the land. Some two years after the purchase of the land Ziegler encountered financial difficulties. At that time Ziegler was unable to meet his financial obligations, including a $30,000.00 promissory note for a personal loan from the Continental National Bank. One of the bank's officers contacted his own brother, Dr. Howland (one of the defendant doctors), and advised him of Ziegler's situation, suggesting that he, in association with two other doctors (Drs. Zemer and Sadler), undertake a refinancing of the property owned by Ziegler. The plan was that the doctors would collectively make available their credit so that $21,000.00 could be obtained to prevent foreclosure on the property, and also that they would guarantee payment of Ziegler's obligation to the bank in the sum of $30,000.00.

The arrangement was consummated under an agreement dated April 15, 1965, pursuant to which Ziegler agreed to convey to the doctors his interest in the mortgaged parcel here involved, in exchange for the doctors' agreement to advance funds to bring current the various secured indebtednesses against the property, and to guarantee payment of Ziegler's promissory note to the bank in the amount of $30,000.00. The agreement also provided for the "assumption of payment [by the doctors] of the balance due and owing * * * on any obligations secured by mortgages of record with respect to * * * "the property here involved. The agreement further provided that Ziegler could "repurchase" the property before the expiration of a year by paying to the doctors an amount calculated to reimburse the doctors for their expenditures, plus $10,000.00. In conjunction with this agreement the deeds were executed for the different properties involved, none of which purported to bind the doctors to pay Ziegler's debts, but transferred title "subject to" enumerated encumbrances.

Defendant Ziegler cross-claimed against the defendant doctors, seeking judgment against them for any deficiency which might be rendered against him in favor of the plaintiffs. In turn, the doctors cross-claimed against the defendant Continental National Bank alleging fraud and deceit on the part of the bank in inducing them to enter into the agreement of April 15, 1965. The trial court severed the doctors' cross-claim against the bank for trial at a later time.

At the trial the court admitted, over plaintiffs' objection, extrinsic evidence which tended to show that the April 15, 1965 agreement was in reality a mortgage rather than a contract of sale.

The principal issues raised on appeal are (1) whether the trial court properly admitted extrinsic evidence to show that the agreement of April 15, 1965 was actually a mortgage; (2) if extrinsic evidence was admissible, whether that evidence was sufficient to support the trial court's determination that the agreement was a mortgage rather than an agreement of sale; and (3) whether the trial court erred in admitting into evidence certain requests for admissions made by Ziegler and the bank. Collateral issues are raised in addition to these and will be considered elsewhere in this opinion.

There is no dispute between the parties that if the subject agreement be construed as an agreement of sale, then the defendant doctors would be personally liable for the payment of the mortgages here involved. There is additionally no assertion that the doctors would be liable for those sums if the court properly found a mortgage, and indeed the contrary has been affirmed by the appellants in their reply brief, acknowledging therein that a first mortgagee, absent consideration for the alleged assumption of liability in the second mortgage, cannot recover from a second mortgagee. See, e.g., Garnsey v. Rogers, 47 N.Y. 233, 7 Am.Rep. 440 (1872); Savings Bank of Southern California v. Thornton, 112 Cal. 255, 44 P. 466 (1896); and G. Osborne, Mortgages § 266 (2d ed. 1970). Further, no claim has been made that there was consideration given for the assumption of liability in the agreement if properly held to constitute a second mortgage. Indeed, the dispute between the parties has not touched upon the *effect* of the trial court's finding of a mortgage, but has centered on the propriety of making such a finding in light of an instrument purporting on its face to be an agreement of sale.

In addition to the assumption language previously quoted, the agreement states:

"8. Nothing herein contained shall be construed to involve a loan from Buyers to Sellers or to create the relationship of mortgagors and mortgagees between the parties hereto, it being understood and agreed between Buyers and Sellers that the transaction provided for are a sale and a conveyance of real property and option for a valuable consideration to purchase real property under specified conditions and on specified terms."

Although there is case authority in other jurisdictions that if an agreement for reconveyance expressly recites that the transaction is not a mortgage such a recital is conclusive of the matter, it has also been held that such a recital is not conclusive, and that a deed intended as security for a debt will be found a mortgage *no matter how strong* the language of the deed or of any accompanying instrument. 59 C.J.S. Mortgages § 27b at 64 (1949). We believe that the provisions of A.R.S. § 33–702 are pertinent to the decision of this question in Arizona. That statute provides:

> "Every transfer of an interest in property, other than in trust, made only as a security for the performance of another act, is a mortgage, except a transfer of personal property accompanied by an actual change of possession, which is deemed a pledge. *The fact that a transfer was made subject to defeasance on a condition, may, for the purpose of showing that the transfer is a mortgage, be proved except against a subsequent purchaser or encumbrancer for value and without notice, notwithstanding that the fact does not appear by the terms of the instrument.*" (Emphasis supplied).

Additionally, there is abundant Arizona case authority holding that parol evidence is admissible to show that a conveyance absolute on its face was intended as a mortgage even though the instrument was knowingly cast in the form of a conveyance, and that the true nature of the transaction is a question of intention to be inferred from all the facts and circumstances surrounding the transaction. See Merryweather v. Pendleton, 90 Ariz. 219, 367 P.2d 251 (1961); Britz v. Kinsvater, 87 Ariz. 385, 351 P.2d 986 (1960); Charter Gas Engine Co. v. Entrekin, 30 Ariz. 341, 246 P. 1038 (1926); and Coffin v. Green, 21 Ariz. 54, 185 P. 361 (1919). We therefore hold that in this case the trial court properly admitted extrinsic evidence for the purpose of showing that the parties intended an arrangement to secure the repayment of the defendant doctors rather than a sale. However, this extrinsic evidence must be clear and convincing in order to show that a deed absolute and a separate option to repurchase together constitute a mortgage. Merryweather v. Pendleton, supra, 90 Ariz. at 223, 224, 367 P.2d at 253. In the case under consideration, we are of the opinion that the defendant doctors sustained this burden.

Our Supreme Court has said that:

> "Whether a transaction ostensibly a conditional sale is in fact an equitable mortgage or pledge depends ultimately upon the intent of the parties. Where, as in this case, the parties' testimony as to their intentions is wholly contradictory, such intentions must be determined from and in light of all the circumstances surrounding the transaction." (Merryweather v. Pendleton, supra, 90 Ariz. at 226, 367 P.2d at 255).

Of primary importance in Arizona in determining whether a transaction was intended to be a security device, i.e., a mortgage, or an absolute conveyance is the presence of a subsisting obligation. Our Supreme Court has drawn a firm distinction between a deed of conveyance coupled with an option to purchase, from which there cannot be inferred from the surrounding facts an intended obligation to repay, and a security device through which the sum paid was actually intended as a loan. Merryweather v. Pendleton, supra; and Charter Gas Engine Co. v. Entrekin, supra. This indeed is the prevailing rule. See 59 C.J.S. Mortgages § 28 (1949). Certain criteria which have been considered by the courts in determining whether a security device was intended have been succinctly enumerated in Merryweather, supra. These criteria are:

> "(1) the prior negotiations of the parties, to discern if such negotiations contemplated a mere security for a debt; (2) the distress of the maker; (3) the fact that the amount advanced was about the amount that the 'grantor' needed to pay an existing indebtedness; (4) the amount of the consideration paid in comparison to the actual value of the property in question; (5) a contemporaneous agreement to repurchase; and (6) the acts of the parties in relation to each other, i.e., whether their acts are ordinarily indicative of a vendor-purchaser relationship or that of a mortgagor and mortgagee." (90 Ariz. at 239, 367 P.2d at 264). (Footnotes omitted).

The parol testimony is without contradiction that in their negotiations the parties contemplated security for the repayment of funds advanced by the doctors. The presence of other facts surrounding the agreement also furnish sufficient support in the record to find a mortgage. It is undisputed that at the time of the agreement, Ziegler was in severe financial distress, being threatened with foreclosures. The defendant doctors, further, guaranteed Ziegler's note to the bank in the amount of $30,000.00, which was about to be recalled, and the additional obligations undertaken by the doctors were for the amounts required to make current mortgage payments. In addition to these facts, there is uncontradicted testimony in the record that the doctors never as much as inspected the premises, never took possession of or occupied the same, and never collected any rents accruing therefrom. These surrounding facts are more consistent with a mortgagor-mortgagee relationship than with a seller-buyer relationship, and together with the doctors' testimony as to intent, furnish ample support for the trial court's conclusions.

* * *

The judgment of the trial court is affirmed.

EUBANK, P.J., and JACOBSON, J., concur.

NOTES

1. *Assumptions of liability by junior mortgagees.* The key to understanding the *Downs* case lies in the paragraph of the opinion that cites *Garnsey v. Rogers.* The court there refers to the old rule that holds that, if a junior mortgagee enters into an assumption agreement, promising to pay a senior mortgage debt, the "first mortgagee, absent consideration for the alleged assumption of liability in the second mortgage, cannot recover from a second mortgagee." The doctors argued that (1) their deed should be recharacterized as a mortgage; (2) hence, it was a junior mortgage, subordinate to the Downs mortgage; (3) Downs had given them no consideration for their assumption agreement; (4) and therefore Downs could not enforce the assumption agreement against them by recovering a deficiency from them. If the court had refused to recharacterize the deed as a mortgage, this line of defense by the doctors would have fallen apart, since it is perfectly clear that when a grantee of a deed assumes a preexisting mortgage, the mortgagee can directly enforce the assumption agreement.

Of course, the underlying rule is silly, although apparently Downs did not attack it on the merits. Why should an assumption agreement by a grantee be enforceable by the mortgagee (irrespective of whether the mortgagee gave consideration for it), while an assumption agreement by a junior mortgagee cannot be enforced unless the mortgagee gave consideration for it? We think there is no sensible answer to this question. The Restatement rejects the rule that insulates junior mortgagees from liability for their assumption agreements. See Restatement (Third) of Property (Mortgages) § 5.1(c) (1997) and especially comment f: "Whether the senior mortgagee gave any consideration for the junior's assumption should be entirely irrelevant."

Incidentally, can you construct an argument that Downs actually *did* give consideration for the doctors' assumption agreement? In fact, why would a junior mortgagee ever give an assumption agreement benefitting the senior lender, unless the senior were giving up something of value in return—typically forbearance in foreclosing even though the senior debt is in default.

2. *Dangers in using the absolute deed as security.* Although most jurisdictions permit the grantor in the absolute deed or the conditional sale situation to establish by extrinsic evidence, parol or otherwise, that a security

transaction was intended, there is always the strong possibility that the grantor will be unable to sustain the heavy burden of producing clear and convincing evidence of that intent. In that event the land is lost. Moreover, the grantor always runs the substantial risk that if the grantee (mortgagee) records the conveyance, the land will be sold to a bona fide purchaser, and the grantor's interest in the land be terminated. See, e.g., Mansfield v. Roy, 1999 WL 1015543 (Tex.App.1999, not reported in S.W.3d) (grantor was successful in establishing a security transaction, but was unable to recover the land because it was now owned by a BFP); Martinez v. Affordable Housing Network, Inc., 123 P.3d 1201 (Colo.2005) (grantor established that deed was a disguised mortgage—however, purchaser was not a BFP because it had constructive notice of grantor's rights from grantor's possession); Finstad v. Gord, 844 N.W.2d 913 (N.D.2014) (because the recorded deed from Finstad to Beresford gave the latter all of Finstad's rights in the property," the deed did not provide the Gords, a third party to the Finstad-Beresford transactions, with notice of any equitable mortgage between the Finstads and Beresford"); Roger A. Cunningham & Saul Tischler, Disguised Real Estate Security Transactions as Mortgages in Substance, 26 Rutgers L.Rev. 1, 26–27 (1972).

Of course, in most states the grantor will be protected if he or she remains in possession because this will constitute constructive notice of the grantor's claim to any potential purchaser. However, in a few states, possession can only provide *actual* and not constructive notice, so that a purchaser who does not inspect the land or have actual knowledge of grantor's interest by some other means may take free and clear of the grantor's interest. See e.g., Drey v. Doyle, 99 Mo. 459, 12 S.W. 287 (1889); Note, 16 Mo.L.Rev. 142.

On the other hand, use of the absolute deed as security may, under some circumstances, seriously disadvantage the grantee-mortgagee. Suppose the grantee is willing to concede that the transaction was actually a mortgage. The essential terms may be difficult to establish. May an acceleration clause be established by parol testimony? Even more important is the absence of a power of sale in jurisdictions that recognize the concept of nonjudicial foreclosure. In all likelihood, if a grantee seeks to treat the transaction as a mortgage, judicial foreclosure will be necessary because of that absence. See Nelson, Whitman, Burkhart & Freyermuth Real Estate Finance Law § 3.9 (6th ed.2014).

3.   *Other reasons for using an absolute deed as security.* While the lender in both the absolute deed and conditional sale situations seeks, among other things, to avoid the consequences of the mortgagor's equity of redemption and certain substantive rules of mortgage law, the conditional sale is sometimes used for certain additional reasons. "The lender often seeks to avoid the consequences of the usury law. In other words, the lender will seek to characterize the difference between the 'sale' price and the repurchase price as simply part of the repurchase price and not as interest. Finally, an income tax motive may be present. For example, the grantee may seek to

mask the difference between the sale price and the repurchase price as a capital gain rather than as ordinary interest income." Id. at § 3.17.

4. *Burden of proof.* Should the same burden of proof to establish a mortgage be applicable in both absolute deed and conditional sale settings? While a "clear and convincing" standard is the norm in absolute deed situations, it has been less broadly accepted in the conditional sale context. Many courts follow a "preponderance of the evidence" standard in the latter situation. These courts reason that since the written documents in the conditional sale on their face establish that the grantor has the right to regain title to the real estate, permitting grantor to establish that the transaction was intended as a security transaction does not "contradict the written documentation in the same degree as in the absolute deed setting. The grantee's expectations arguably are disturbed to a much lesser extent where a formal agreement expressly provides for grantor's reacquisition of the real estate than where grantee is compelled to part with title that he or she may well have assumed to be indefeasible." Restatement (Third) of Property (Mortgages) § 3.3, cmt. b (1997).

By contrast, in the conditional sale situation the use of extrinsic evidence not only contradicts the deed to the grantee, but also contravenes a second written document as well. Should it therefore be more difficult to justify the use of extrinsic evidence in the conditional sale than where it simply is used to supply an element of the transaction that the parties did not delineate in the absolute deed? Should this latter consideration at least justify the application of the same standard to both types of transaction? See id. § 3.3, cmt. b; Nelson, Whitman, Burkhart & Freyermuth, Real Estate Finance Law § 3.18 (6th ed.2014).

5. *Burden of proof for grantees.* The *Downs* case is unusual in that the grantee rather than the grantor is attempting to establish a mortgage transaction. Should the burden of proof be the same for the grantee as for the grantor?

Additional reasons, beyond the rather odd one involved in *Downs*, may occasionally motivate a grantee to seek to characterize an absolute deed or conditional sale as a mortgage transaction. Suppose, for example, a third party is injured on the real estate and the grantee is sued on a negligence theory in his or her status as a "landowner." Because a mortgagee normally will not be liable to third parties for unsafe conditions on mortgaged real estate unless he or she exercises dominion and control over it, a grantee in such circumstances may well be delighted to eschew ownership for the benefits of mortgagee status. See, e.g., Smith v. Fried, 98 Ill.App.3d 467, 53 Ill.Dec. 845, 424 N.E.2d 636 (1981).

6. *Language disclaiming mortgage intent.* Note that the grantees in *Downs* included specific mortgage-negating language in the documents. Should such language have been case-dispositive? If courts were to treat such provisions as determinative of the parties' intent, what would be the impact on the substantive rules considered in this Section? Would it make more

sense to treat such provisions as merely relevant to the issue of intent? See Fraser v. Fraser, 702 N.W.2d 283 (Minn.Ct.App.2005) (language in agreement that it "shall not be construed and interpreted as an 'equitable mortgage' as that term is defined by Minnesota law" not deemed conclusive as to the question of intent). Should it have made a difference in *Downs* that the grantees were attacking the provision that *they* probably insisted on including in the agreement? Were they successful in being able to "have their cake and eat it too"? See Restatement (Third) of Property (Mortgages) § 3.3, illus. 7 and cmt. d (1997) ("If the grantee was the party who insisted on insertion of the mortgage-negating language, the grantee probably should be estopped from attacking his or her own attempt to negate mortgage intent.").

B. THE INSTALLMENT LAND CONTRACT

The most commonly used substitute for the mortgage or deed of trust as a land financing device is the installment land contract. This device is also known variously as the "contract for deed" or the "long term land contract." The installment land contract carries out the same economic function as a purchase money mortgage—financing by the seller of the unpaid portion of the purchase price of the real estate. Under the installment land contract, the vendee normally goes into possession and agrees to make monthly installment payments of principal and interest until the principal balance is paid off. The vendor retains legal title until the final payment is made, at which time he has a duty to execute a deed to the land. Such contracts may be amortized over varying time periods as short as two or three years or as long as twenty years or more. Even if a long amortization period is used, the vendee may be required to pay off the balance by a "balloon payment" after three to five years. During the period of the contract, the vendee will usually be required to pay the taxes, maintain casualty insurance and keep the premises in good repair.

The installment land contract should be distinguished from the ordinary executory contract for the sale of land, variously known as an "earnest money contract," a "binder", or a "marketing contract." The latter type of contract is used primarily to establish the rights and liabilities of the parties during the time period between the date the bargain was entered into and the date of closing, at which time title passes and security agreements, if any, are executed. The installment land contract governs the parties throughout the life of the debt, whereas in the binder type of contract, the debt relationship after the closing date is governed by the security device and the binder contract no longer has a function. Indeed, it is not uncommon for a binder contract to state that the parties will enter into an installment land contract at the closing date of the binder contract.

When a vendee under an installment land contract defaults, the vendor, under traditional remedies, may sue "(1) for the installments which are due with interest thereon; (2) for specific performance of the contract; (3) for damages for the breach; (4) to foreclose his vendee's rights; (5) to quiet title; or if he should desire, he may merely rescind the contract." See Comment, Installment Contracts for the Sale of Land in Missouri, 24 Mo.L.Rev. 240, 243 (1959). Most of these remedies, however, tend to be slow and expensive, and some of them depend on the vendee's being able to satisfy a money judgment. As a consequence vendors most frequently rely on the forfeiture clause which is contained in virtually every installment land contract. This clause typically will provide that "time is of the essence" and that when a vendee defaults under the contract, the vendor has the option to declare the contract terminated, to retake possession of the premises, and to retain all payments under the contract as liquidated damages. Moreover, this clause also purports to relieve the vendor from further obligations under the contract.

"Resort to the installment contract device is usually attributed to the unavailability of mortgage financing for very low down payment sales and to the supposed ease of terminating the purchaser's interest in the property in the event of default." Frank R. Lacy, Land Sale Contracts in Bankruptcy, 21 U.C.L.A.Rev. 477 (1973). Indeed, as high loan-to-value-ratio (95% to 100%) loans from institutional lenders have become more widely available over the past several decades, the use of real estate installment contracts has declined. But they have not faded away, since vendors are often willing to supply credit to purchasers whose poor credit scores and relatively low incomes would disqualify them from getting institutional loans.

Vendors view the long term land contract as a "pro-vendor" financing device. It is especially heavily used in jurisdictions where the substantive law governing the normal mortgage transaction is perceived to be weighted in favor of the mortgagor. In considering the following material, you should focus on the remedies available to the installment contract vendor and on the rights of the vendee. These remedies and rights will vary greatly from jurisdiction to jurisdiction. Additional questions should be raised after an examination of the material. Is the installment contract device, in fact, really as "pro-vendor" as the common perception of it? Or does it perhaps seriously disadvantage the vendee without giving the vendor the swift and sure creditor's security device that he or she was counting on?

RUSSELL V. RICHARDS

Supreme Court of New Mexico, 1985
103 N.M. 48, 702 P.2d 993

WALTERS, JUSTICE.

Mary V. Russell filed this action against John R. and Beth Richards for damages resulting from the default and forfeiture of her interest in a real estate contract * * * . The trial court entered judgment for Russell and awarded damages * * * . The Richardses filed this appeal. * * *

The Richardses present the following issues on appeal: (1) whether the trial court's refusal to enforce the forfeiture was an abuse of discretion; and (2) whether the trial court erred in awarding damages.

Russell was an assignee-purchaser under a standard form real estate contract with the Richardses, who were the original sellers of the real property. Russell paid $11,188 to the assignors and assumed $37,938 under the contract. At the time of her default, Russell had made 72 payments to the Richardses and had reduced the principal owed by $10,782, leaving a principal amount of $26,504. The real property, by that time, had increased in value from $48,989 at time of purchase to $82,735.

At trial, Russell presented evidence on the circumstances of her default, the valuation of the real property subject to the contract and the value of her personal property not recovered after default. She asserted that the forfeiture of her interest under the contract should shock the conscience of the trial court. Although the trial court found that Russell's interest under the contract was forfeited, it also found that the forfeiture shocked its conscience. The trial court entered judgment in favor of Russell, awarding damages of $56,724 for her equity in the real property * * * .

The Richardses contend that the trial court's failure to enforce the forfeiture of Russell's interest under the contract was an abuse of discretion. We agree. The rule is well settled in New Mexico that the forfeiture provision in this type of real estate contract is enforceable, *Eiferle v. Toppino,* 90 N.M. 469, 565 P.2d 340 (1977), absent unfairness which shocks the conscience of the court. *Bishop v. Beecher,* 67 N.M. 339, 355 P.2d 277 (1960). To determine whether a forfeiture shocks the conscience of the court, this Court has applied the following equitable considerations: the amount of money already paid by the buyer to the seller; the period of possession of the real property by the buyer; the market value of the real property at the time of default compared to the original sales price; and the rental potential and value of the real property. *See Huckins v. Ritter,* 99 N.M. 560, 661 P.2d 52 (1983).

Russell's reliance on the equitable exception to enforcement of forfeiture is misplaced. Not every case of default and forfeiture presents circumstances which shock the conscience of a court. *Compare Huckins v. Ritter,* 99 N.M. 560, 661 P.2d 52 (1983) (forfeiture not enforced), with *Manzano Industries, Inc. v. Mathis,* 101 N.M. 104, 678 P.2d 1179 (1984) (forfeiture enforced). The parties to a real estate contract and their assignees agree to be bound by its terms and provisions, and to accept the burdens of the contract together with its benefits. A subpurchaser takes the land subject to the terms of the contract of which he has knowledge. *Campbell v. Kerr,* 95 N.M. 73, 618 P.2d 1237 (1980). The courts will enforce a real estate contract except where enforcement, under the equitable circumstances of the case, would result in an unconscionable forfeiture. *Huckins v. Ritter.* Such equitable circumstances as would avoid forfeiture are not present here.

In this case, Russell was in possession of the premises approximately 6 years and paid a total of $10,782 on the contract principal to the Richardses over that period; and the trial court properly considered that amount. The trial court's further consideration of Russell's down payment was not proper, however, because that amount was paid to Russell's assignors. The Richardses received no part of that payment. The trial court's inclusion of the down payment in the damage amount placed the financial responsibility on the Richardses to return money that was never paid to them.

Similarly, the trial court's consideration of the increased market value of the real property was erroneous. The inclusion of any portion of the market value amount in the damage amount gave Russell the benefit of the enhancement in the value of the property, contrary to established law. This court has held that "during the life of the real estate contract any risk of loss or enhancement in value accrues to the purchaser." *MGIC Mortgage Corp. v. Bowen,* 91 N.M. 200, 202, 572 P.2d 547, 549 (1977). Upon default and forfeiture, the buyer's interest is terminated and there is no enhancement value to be recovered by the buyer. *Id.*

We note that Russell had received benefit and profit during her possession. She rented out three units of the property and, at the time of default, the entire property was leased for a monthly payment far in excess of the payment due under the contract. Russell had been in default several times before the forfeiture and each time she had cured the default. She knew the consequences of default.

We also agree with the Richardses that the trial court erred in awarding damages for Russell's loss of her interest under the contract. In order to recover damages there must be a right of action for a wrong inflicted on the party claiming damages; damage without wrong does not constitute a cause of action. *See Jomack Lumber Co. v. Grants State Bank,* 75 N.M. 787, 411 P.2d 759 (1966). Russell's loss of her interest under the contract did not result from a wrong committed by the

Richardses, but from her default under the real estate contract for failure to make timely payment. The usual consequence of default, as clearly stated in the contract assumed by Russell, is forfeiture of all interest; only unusual equitable circumstances create an exception to that rule. *Bishop v. Beecher.*

* * *

* * * [T]he award of $56,724 in * * * damages is reversed. The case is remanded for modification of the judgment accordingly.

IT IS SO ORDERED.

FEDERICI, C.J., SOSA, SENIOR J., and RIORDAN, J., concur.

STOWERS, J., concurs in part, dissents in part.

NOTES

1. *The strict enforcement approach.* For an equally unsympathetic response to a vendee attempt to avoid forfeiture, consider Burgess v. Shiplet, 230 Mont. 387, 750 P.2d 460 (1988). In that case, vendees had paid slightly more than 20% of the purchase price on one contract and slightly less than that amount on another. In reversing a trial court decision that found vendees in default, but that granted them a one year right to redeem the contracts, the Montana Supreme Court stated:

> When a purchaser enters into a contract for deed with a seller, he or she runs the risk of defaulting on the required payments and facing the consequences of losing the property along with forfeiting the amount already paid. If this produces a harsh or unwanted result, it is for the legislature to remedy and not the job of this court to change the plain meaning of the contract.
>
> In the case before us, the contract for deed provides that upon their default buyers have 30 days in which to correct the default or sellers are entitled to demand, within 30 days, full payment of the unpaid balance of the purchase price plus accrued interest. If the buyer fails to pay the total unpaid balance in 30 days, the agreement terminates and the property is returned to the seller.
>
> The District Court found that buyers defaulted on both contracts which they had with sellers. The default provisions under the contract for deed spells out the remedies available to sellers. Buyers cannot look to mortgage law for alternative remedies but must accept the remedies set forth in their contract with sellers.

2. *Relaxing strict enforcement.* While *Russell* and *Burgess* illustrate that forfeitures are sometimes enforced, they hardly represent a mainstream approach. Many courts have proven more receptive to the argument that forfeiture would be unconscionable. Moreover,

during the past several decades, an increasing number of courts and legislatures have been focusing on the installment land contract and its forfeiture clause with a mortgage law analogy in mind. As one court recently asked, "if the absolute deed kind of forfeiture may not be enforced by the grantee according to the express terms of the agreement, why then, should a forfeiture under a land sale contract be so enforced?"[2] The foregoing process, however, has hardly produced either an analytical or practical consensus. Consequently, the law in this area is not susceptible to orderly analysis: "Not only does the law vary from jurisdiction to jurisdiction, but within any one state results may vary depending upon the type of action brought, the exact terms of the land contract, and the facts of the particular case."[3] The interplay of these various factors makes it extremely difficult to predict whether the buyer's interest will be forfeited. While forfeitures are still sometimes judicially enforced, it nevertheless can be safely stated that in no jurisdiction today will a vendor be able to assume that forfeiture provisions will be automatically enforced as written. This change is the result of both legislative and judicial intervention to ameliorate the harsh impact of automatic forfeiture.

* * *

[N]umerous state courts have in recent years refused to enforce against a defaulting vendee forfeiture clauses that the courts have deemed unreasonable or inequitable. These courts have employed several approaches to save the vendee from forfeiture. Some cases, for example, have in effect conferred on the vendee a mortgagor's equity of redemption, permitting him to tender the remainder of the purchase price (or even his arrearages) in a suit or counterclaim for specific performance of the contract. Where the vendee was unable or unwilling to redeem, courts have occasionally ordered the judicial foreclosure of the land contract. Finally, some courts, after determining that a particular forfeiture clause is unfair, have extended to the defaulting vendee the right to restitution—the right to recoup his payments to the extent that they exceed the vendor's damages caused by the vendee's default. Of course, many state courts have not considered the forfeiture clause in all of the remedial contexts described above, nor have they always been theoretically precise. Some courts have utilized contract principles to protect the defaulting vendee from an inequitable forfeiture provision. Other courts have gone a long way toward simply treating the installment land contract as a mortgage * * *. Still

---

[2] Braunstein v. Trottier, 54 Or.App. 687, 635 P.2d 1379, 1382 (1981), review denied 292 Or. 568, 644 P.2d 1129 (1982).

[3] Nelson, The Contract for Deed as a Mortgage: The Case for the Restatement Approach, 1998 BYU L. Rev. 1111. * * *

others have employed a confusing amalgam of mortgage and contract law.

Nelson, Whitman, Burkhart & Freyermuth, Real Estate Finance Law 70–71, 76 (6th ed. 2014).*

Would the forfeiture provision in the principal case have been equally effective had Russell sought specific performance of the contract (that is, the right to pay off the balance owing and keep the property, despite the fact that she was late and in default) rather than damages? Keep this question in mind in connection with the following material.

PETERSEN V. HARTELL

Supreme Court of California, 1985
40 Cal.3d 102, 219 Cal.Rptr. 170, 707 P.2d 232

REYNOSO, JUSTICE.

* * *

I

Defendant is administratrix of the estate of Juanita Gaspar who, upon the death of her first husband in 1946, succeeded to sole ownership of a 160-acre tract of unimproved land southeast of Fort Bragg in Mendocino County. In the late 1960's she entered into agreements with three of her grandchildren to sell small portions of the land at $1,500 per acre, with no down payment and monthly installments of $50 or less. The agreement now relied on by plaintiffs was embodied in a written contract, executed in November 1967, providing for the sale to granddaughter Kathy Petersen and her husband, Richard Petersen, of slightly more than six acres for a total purchase price of $9,162, payable at $50 per month. The buyers were given the right to pay the entire balance of the purchase price at any time. There was no provision making time of the essence or specifying remedies in the event of default.

Although the contract was drafted by Richard Petersen, who was then a recent law school graduate, the trial court found that no undue influence or overreaching was employed by either of the Petersens in the preparation or execution of the agreement. The price of $1,500 per acre was set by Mrs. Gaspar, who wished to give her grandchildren the opportunity to acquire small portions of her property. She was dependent, however, on income from the land contract payments, along with her social security benefits, to make ends meet.

The Petersens missed occasional payments in 1968, 1969, 1971, and 1972. Of the 65 payments due from November 1967 through March 1973, they made 58 payments totaling $2,900. In April 1973 the couple

---

    *   Reprinted with permission of LEG, Inc. d/b/a West Academic.

separated and their payments ceased. Kathy Petersen testified that about that time she spoke about the separation to her grandmother, who said it was important to take care of the children first and that she (the grandmother) would "get by."

In September 1975 Kathy Petersen sent Mrs. Gaspar a check for $250 as "back payments." Mrs. Gaspar's attorney then wrote the Petersens, stating that Mrs. Gaspar elected to terminate the contract. In February 1976 Mrs. Gaspar wrote to Kathy Petersen, returning the latter's check and explaining that she considered the contract broken. In September 1976 Richard Petersen wrote to the attorney requesting reinstatement of the contract and a statement of the amounts due, and enclosing a $250 money order, which the attorney promptly returned on instructions from Mrs. Gaspar.

In October 1976, Mrs. Gaspar died. Kathy Petersen then assigned all her interest under the contract to Carol Ranta as trustee for the two minor children of the Petersen marriage. Thus, the plaintiffs in the present action are Richard Petersen and the two children, who appear through Ranta as their guardian ad litem. By their amended complaint against Mrs. Gaspar's administratrix, plaintiffs seek specific performance, declaratory relief, damages, and the quieting of title to an easement of necessity to connect the property with a public road. They further tender the entire balance due under the contract on condition that defendant deliver a good and sufficient deed.

After a nonjury trial, the trial court denied plaintiffs' prayer for specific performance. It concluded that (1) plaintiffs' breach of the contract was grossly negligent and wilful, (2) plaintiffs failed to tender full performance until April 1, 1977, when the action was commenced, (3) defendant is entitled to restitution of the property, and (4) plaintiffs are entitled to restitution of $2,900 plus interest from April 1, 1977. Judgment was entered accordingly with costs to defendant.

II

In *MacFadden v. Walker,* 5 Cal.3d 809, 97 Cal.Rptr. 537, 488 P.2d 1353, this court affirmed a judgment for specific performance in favor of a vendee whose default in monthly payments we found wilful as a matter of law. The trial court had found the default to be neither wilful nor grossly negligent and so had granted relief under Civil Code section 3275, which provides that a party may be relieved from a forfeiture incurred for nonperformance of a contractual obligation "upon making full compensation to the other party, except in case of a grossly negligent, willful, or fraudulent breach of duty." That section was the basis for the prior holding in *Barkis v. Scott* (1949) 34 Cal.2d 116, 208 P.2d 367, that a vendee who had made substantial payments and improvements on the property and then as a result of simple negligence defaulted in two payments was entitled to have the contract reinstated. In *MacFadden,* however, this court concluded that relief under section 3275, as construed in *Barkis,* was not available because the trial court's finding that the vendee's default had been nonwilful was not supported by evidence. The issue on appeal, therefore, was "whether a vendee who would otherwise be entitled to specific performance of an installment land sale contract in which time is declared to be of the essence forfeits the right to that remedy because of her wilful failure to make installment payments when due after there has been substantial part performance of the contract." (5 Cal.3d at p. 811, 97 Cal.Rptr. 537, 488 P.2d 1353.)

To resolve that issue, *MacFadden* turned to *Freedman v. The Rector* (1951) 37 Cal.2d 16, 230 P.2d 629, explaining that there, "we held that section 3275 is not the exclusive source of the right to relief from forfeiture. We concluded that the prohibition of punitive damages for breach of contract (Civ.Code, § 3294), the strict limitations on the right to provide for liquidated damages (Civ.Code, §§ 1670, 1671), and the provision that 'Neither specific nor preventive relief can be granted to enforce a penalty or forfeiture in any case * * * '(Civ.Code, § 3369) together established a policy that precludes any forfeiture having no reasonable relation to the damage caused by the vendee's breach even when that breach is wilful. (See also *Baffa v. Johnson* (1950) 35 Cal.2d 36, 37–39 [216 P.2d 13].) Since in the *Freedman* case, however, the vendor had sold the property to a third party in reliance on the vendee's repudiation of the contract, specific performance was not an available remedy, and relief from forfeiture was necessarily limited to awarding the defaulting vendee restitution in the amount of the excess of his part payment over the damages caused by his breach. We believe that the anti-forfeiture policy recognized in the *Freedman* case also justifies awarding even wilfully defaulting vendees specific performance in proper cases. * * * "

* * *

Unlike the trial court in *MacFadden,* the trial court below denied plaintiff vendees specific performance. Since that remedy is discretionary (*Pasqualetti v. Galbraith* (1962) 200 Cal.App.2d 378, 382, 19 Cal.Rptr. 323; *Lind v. Baker* (1941) 48 Cal.App.2d 234, 245, 119 P.2d 806), we must consider whether the denial was an abuse of discretion and, if not, whether plaintiffs are entitled to relief on some other ground.

To be entitled to specific performance of a contract, a plaintiff must plead and prove that the contract is just and reasonable and the consideration adequate, as required by section 3391 (fn. 2, ante). (*Lucientes v. Bliss* (1958) 157 Cal.App.2d 565, 568, 321 P.2d 526.) Yet here, the trial court's findings of fact and conclusions of law fail to decide those issues even though they were properly raised in the complaint.

There are indications in the findings and the trial court's memorandum of intended decision, however, that had the court reached those issues, it would have resolved them in plaintiffs' favor. * * * Accordingly, we infer that the trial court omitted any determination that the contract was just and reasonable and the consideration adequate not because of any lack of support for those conclusions in the record but because, in the court's view, those determinations would not have altered the court's ultimate conclusion that specific performance should be denied.

* * *

The more likely connection between the [trial court's] findings of the Petersens' derelictions as to payments and the denial of specific performance is that the trial court weighed the seriousness of plaintiffs' defaults against them in a balancing of equities. That that was the court's theory seems likely from its citation of *Kosloff v. Castle* (1981) 115 Cal.App.3d 369, 171 Cal.Rptr. 308, where the Court of Appeal declared that whereas the wilfully defaulting vendee's right to restitution of installment payments made in excess of the seller's damages is unqualified, such vendee's right to specific performance is discretionary and dependent on a balancing of equities that include the seriousness of the vendee's defaults. (*Id.,* at p. 376, 171 Cal.Rptr. 308. Accord, *Bartley v. Karas* (1983) 150 Cal.App.3d 336, 344–345, 197 Cal.Rptr. 749.)

If that theory were correct, there would be ample basis in the evidence and findings to support the denial of specific performance. The Petersens' monthly payments were erratic and delinquent almost from the beginning even though the seller made clear her need of the payments for her support. By April 1973 the Petersens had made only 58 out of the 65 payments then due, and their first attempt to reinstate the contract was not until 29 months later, when they tendered only $250 out of the $1,800 that was by then overdue and unpaid.

The issue, therefore, is whether plaintiffs, despite their wilful defaults in payments, now have an absolute right to a conveyance of the property in exchange for payment of the entire balance of the purchase price (together with interest and any other damages) in light of their substantial part performance and the seller's notice of election to terminate the contract on account of such defaults.

III

Although we treated factors mitigating the seriousness of the vendee's default as relevant in upholding the judgment of specific performance in *MacFadden v. Walker,* supra, 5 Cal.3d 809, 813, 97 Cal.Rptr. 537, 488 P.2d 1353, we took care to explain that "[s]ince we have concluded * * * that Mrs. Walker [the vendee] is entitled to the remedy of specific performance, we need not decide whether she might also be entitled to some other remedy under the law governing security transactions" (*id.,* at p. 816, 97 Cal.Rptr. 537, 488 P.2d 1353). For at least a century in this state, a seller of land being sold under an installment contract who sues to quiet title because of the vendee's default in installment payments has been required to give the vendee a reasonable opportunity to complete performance. * * *

In those early cases, however, the vendee who failed to exercise the right to redeem by completing the payments forfeited payments already made, apparently without regard to whether the amounts paid exceeded the seller's damages. * * * Thereafter, this court decided that even a wilfully defaulting vendee may be entitled to restitution under section 3369, which provides that "[n]either specific nor preventive relief can be granted to enforce a penalty or forfeiture in any case." That section "precludes the court from quieting the vendor's title unless he refunds the excess of the part payments over the damage caused by the vendee's breach." (*Freedman v. The Rector* (1951) 37 Cal.2d 16, 22, 230 P.2d 629.) Such restitution is a matter of right for the wilfully defaulting vendee who proves that the payments made to the seller exceed the amount necessary to give the seller the benefit of his bargain. (*Honey v. Henry's Franchise Leasing Corp.,* supra, 64 Cal.2d 801, 805, 52 Cal.Rptr. 18, 415 P.2d 833; *Bartley v. Karas,* supra, 150 Cal.App.3d 336, 345, fn. 5, 197 Cal.Rptr. 749; *Kosloff v. Castle,* supra, 115 Cal.App.3d 369, 376, 171 Cal.Rptr. 308.)

While recognizing that the wilfully defaulting vendee's right to restitution is unqualified, some post-*Freedman* decisions have treated such vendee's right to a reasonable opportunity to redeem the property by paying the entire balance owed, plus damages, before title is quieted in the seller, as merely discretionary. Thus, in *Bartley v. Karas,* supra, 150 Cal.App.3d 336, 197 Cal.Rptr. 749, the court interpreted the *Keller* line of cases as allowing such relief "*where the circumstances indicated* that it would be 'in consonance with equity' " (*id.,* at p. 344, 197 Cal.Rptr. 749, emphasis added) and as holding that the relief "*may* * * * be proper where the seller's conduct contributed to the default and where there is some good faith, but imperfect excuse, for the buyer's conduct" (*id.,* at p. 345, 197 Cal.Rptr. 749, emphasis added). Other decisions similarly have weighed the seriousness of the vendee's defaults in determining the propriety of granting the relief. * * *

We think that as a matter both of stare decisis and of sound public policy, a vendee who has made substantial payments on a land installment sale contract or substantial improvements on the property, and whose defaults, albeit wilful, consist solely of failure to pay further amounts due, has an unconditional right to a reasonable opportunity to complete the purchase by paying the entire remaining balance plus damages before the seller is allowed to quiet title. We read *Keller* and its earlier progeny as so holding. As *Keller* itself observes, "the legal title is retained by the vendor as security for the balance of the purchase money, and if the vendor obtains his money and interest he gets all he expected when he entered the contract." (53 Cal. at p. 118.) To that statement we add that the seller may be entitled to damages in addition to interest.[4] Whatever the amounts due, their payment in full makes the seller whole regardless of the nature of the vendee's defaults in payments.

In the present case, of course, the seller did not sue to quiet title but instead gave the vendees written notice of election to terminate the contract because of their failure to make timely payments. When plaintiffs sued for specific performance, defendant merely answered, praying that plaintiffs take nothing. Thus, the right of redemption asserted by plaintiffs cannot be justified as a condition to the granting of relief sought in this action by the seller.

If Mrs. Gaspar had been entitled to foreclose the Petersens' interest in the land by a unilateral declaration of termination on account of wilful default, leaving the Petersens with only a right to monetary restitution of payments in excess of seller's damages, there would appear no basis for allowing plaintiff vendees to enforce an absolute right of redemption in an action in which defendant sought no affirmative relief. Arguably supporting the trial court's apparent conclusion that the seller had such a right of nonjudicial foreclosure were (1) the absence of equities requisite to a vendee's right of specific performance under *MacFadden* and (2) facts that appear to have empowered the seller to convey to a bona fide purchaser: the contract was not recorded; the land was unoccupied; and the seller paid the property taxes.

Other circumstances, however, both factual and legal, lead us to conclude that Mrs. Gaspar had only a security interest (see Note, *Contracts: Forfeiture Clauses: Relief to Vendee in Default in California* (1952) 40 Calif.L.Rev. 593, 597), and that the vendees' right to purchase the property by completing payment of the purchase price and any other amounts due could be terminated only by a foreclosure sale or by strict foreclosure, i.e., a judicial proceeding quieting the seller's title against the vendees' right of redemption. Seller's counsel acknowledged at least the possibility that such foreclosure might be necessary by (1) accompanying the formal notices of termination with requests for a quitclaim deed and (2) including in the judgment prepared for, and signed by, the trial judge, a provision that "plaintiffs have no right, title, or interest in" the property.

---

[4]   Compare Code of Civil Procedure section 726, subdivision (a), providing for application of the proceeds of a mortgage foreclosure sale to "the payment of the costs of court, the expenses of levy and sale, and the amount due plaintiff, including, where the mortgage provides for the payment of attorney's fees, such sum for attorney's fees as the court shall find reasonable, not exceeding the amount named in the mortgage."

Moreover, sections 2985 and 2985.1, enacted in 1961 and 1963, prohibit one who has contracted to sell land under a long-term installment contract from conveying title in complete disregard of the vendees' interest. Section 2985 defines a "real property sales contract" as "an agreement wherein one party agrees to convey title to real property to another party upon the satisfaction of specified conditions set forth in the contract and which does not require conveyance of title within one year from the date of formation of the contract." Section 2985.1 provides in pertinent part: "A real property sales contract may not be transferred by the fee owner of the real property unless accompanied by a transfer of the real property which is the subject of the contract, and real property may not be transferred by the fee owner thereof unless accompanied by an assignment of the contract." The seller is thus prohibited from making any transfer that would sever the direct contractual relationship between the vendee and the owner of the fee. The intended protection of the vendees' interest is best served by interpreting section 2985.1 to require continuation of that linkage between seller's title and vendee's contractual interest until the latter has been affirmatively terminated by conveyance of title to the vendee, by a foreclosure sale (see fn. 4, ante), or by strict foreclosure.

Finally, we think that to retain specific performance under *MacFadden v. Walker,* supra, 5 Cal.3d 809, 97 Cal.Rptr. 537, 488 P.2d 1353, as the utmost remedy available in a suit initiated by a wilfully defaulting vendee unduly burdens courts and litigants with time-consuming and expensive legal proceedings. The present case is illustrative. To settle a dispute over land sold for a total price of only $9,162 required two days of nonjury trial in which eight witnesses (only two of whom were parties) testified to circumstances bearing on whether the vendees' defaults were sufficiently egregious to bar them from specific performance under *MacFadden.* Yet, as already explained, if defendant seller had sued to quiet title, plaintiffs would have been entitled as a matter of right to a conveyance of title in exchange for payment of the balance of the purchase price with interest and damages. Such redemption by plaintiff would give defendant the entire benefit bargained for, free of any dependence on further performance by plaintiff vendees. The outcome will be no less fair to both parties if, as we hold, the vendees under a real property sales contract, as defined in section 2985, are entitled to judicial enforcement of the same absolute right of redemption in response to the seller's notice of election to terminate the contract for default in payments. The complaint initiating the vendee's action for that purpose, rather than being designated as one for specific performance, is more appropriately referred to as one to redeem the vendee's interest in real property.

Accordingly, we conclude that plaintiffs are entitled to a conveyance of title to the property in exchange for payment of the entire remaining balance due under the contract together with interest and any consequential damages as determined by the court. Should plaintiffs fail to make such payments within a reasonable time fixed by the court, the adjudication that plaintiffs have no further interest in the property should become effective only upon defendant's payment of the sums due to plaintiffs as restitution. Statements in *Bartley v. Karas,* supra, 150 Cal.App.3d 336, 197 Cal.Rptr. 749, and *Kosloff v. Castle,* supra, 115 Cal.App.3d 369, 171 Cal.Rptr. 308, inconsistent with this conclusion are disapproved.

The judgment is reversed.

GRODIN, BROUSSARD and KAUS, JJ., concur.

BIRD, CHIEF JUSTICE, concurring and dissenting.

I agree with the majority that an unconditional right of redemption exists for most wilfully defaulting vendees under security device installment land sale contracts.

However, there is no reason to deny the right of redemption to vendees whose payments prior to default amount to less than "a substantial part of the purchase price."

* * *

The majority also fail to discuss the cogent arguments raised by Professor Hetland, who appeared as amicus curiae for plaintiffs. Professor Hetland argues that the installment land sale contract, when employed as a security device, is the functional equivalent of a mortgage or deed of trust and should generally be subject to the same rules. This view has much to recommend it.

Treating the installment land sale contract as the equivalent of a mortgage under Civil Code section 2924[1] would bring the procedures for foreclosure of the vendee's equity of redemption into line with those permitted for foreclosure under a mortgage or deed of trust. (See Civ.Code, § 2924 [private foreclosure sale]; Code Civ.Proc., § 700.010 et seq. [judicial foreclosure sale].) Moreover, the vendee, like a mortgagor or trustor under a deed of trust, would not be restricted to an equity of *redemption,* i.e., the right to conveyance of title only upon payment of the *full* amount of the debt. The vendee would also be entitled to *reinstatement* of the contract upon payment of any *delinquent* amounts. (See Civ.Code, § 2924c.)

---

[1] Section 2924 provides in part that "Every transfer of an interest in property, other than in trust, made only as a security for the performance of another act, is to be deemed a mortgage. * * * * " * * *

* * *

In *MacFadden* a unanimous court took note of Professor Hetland's "persuasive arguments that installment land sale contracts should be treated as security devices substantially on a par with mortgages and deeds of trust, and that therefore 'the law governing those security devices should be adopted with appropriate modifications in determining the remedies for breaches of installment contracts.' " (*MacFadden, supra,* 5 Cal.3d 809, 816, 97 Cal.Rptr. 537, 488 P.2d 1353, citing *Honey v. Henry's Franchise Leasing Corp.* (1966) 64 Cal.2d 801, 804, 52 Cal.Rptr. 18, 415 P.2d 833; Hetland, Cal.Real Estate Secured Transactions, *supra,* §§ 3.58–3.81, pp. 100–134.)

Specifically, the court observed that the law governing mortgages "affords even the wilfully defaulting debtor an opportunity to *cure* his default before losing his interest in the security." (*MacFadden, supra,* 5 Cal.3d at p. 816, 97 Cal.Rptr. 537, 488 P.2d 1353, italics added; see also *County of Los Angeles v. Butcher* (1957) 155 Cal.App.2d 744, 747, 318 P.2d 838 ["it is clear that where parties enter into a written contract for the purchase and sale of real property pursuant to which the * * * seller retains the legal title as security for the purchase price, the [seller] 'has no greater rights than he would possess if he had conveyed the land and taken back a mortgage' "].)

The predominant use of installment land sale contracts has been to finance the purchase of housing by low income families and individuals unable to qualify for conventional mortgage financing or government loan guarantee programs. (See Note, *Reforming the Vendor's Remedies for Breach of Installment Land Sale Contracts, supra,* 47 So.Cal.L.Rev. at pp. 193–198.)

Providing installment contract vendees the same protections that are afforded to mortgagors would eliminate some abusive practices of vendors, who have exploited the lack of legal sophistication and limited capacity to litigate of their low-income clients. (See *id.,* at pp. 197, fn. 36, 205–206, 211.) Most important, defaulting vendees would be able to avoid the loss of their homes by paying only the delinquent amounts. Under the majority's holding, a wilfully defaulting vendee may avoid this fate only by paying the outstanding balance in full. This is an unjustifiably harsh burden to place on the low-income and middle-income families and individuals who will be most affected.*

---

*   The majority opinion responded to the Chief Justice as follows:

The Chief Justice urges us to extend wilfully defaulting vendees' rights beyond those articulated in this opinion by reaching issues not presented by this case. Thus, she would give an absolute right of redemption to wilfully defaulting vendees who have not yet paid a substantial part of the purchase price. She further advocates that the land installment sale contract be treated as the equivalent of a mortgage under section 2924 (though conceding that section does not "literally" apply), thus limiting the seller's

[The dissenting opinion of MOSK, J. is omitted.]

NOTES

1. *Judicial recognition of a right of redemption.* A substantial number of states, like California, afford the tardy vendee a final opportunity to tender the contract balance before losing the land. See Lewis v. Premium Inv. Corp., 341 S.C. 539, 535 S.E.2d 139 (2000); Lamberth v. McDaniel, 131 N.C.App. 319, 506 S.E.2d 295 (1998). This specific performance or "equity of redemption" right is sometimes viewed as unconditional, while other courts enforce it only if the vendee has paid a "substantial" amount of the contract price. See Nelson, Whitman, Burkhart & Freyermuth Real Estate Finance Law § 3.29 (6th ed.2014). Moreover, many courts impose a "good faith" requirement on the vendee. According to the Hawaii Supreme Court, for example, specific performance should be available where "the vendee's breach has not been due to gross negligence, or to deliberate or bad-faith conduct on his part, and the vendor can reasonably and adequately be compensated for his injury." Jenkins v. Wise, 58 Hawaii 592, 574 P.2d 1337 (1978). For a clear-cut example of the denial of specific performance to a grossly negligent vendee, see Curry v. Tucker, 616 P.2d 8 (Alaska 1980), where the Alaska Supreme Court affirmed a forfeiture decree where vendee made

> no good faith efforts to fulfill his obligations under the contracts. Despite numerous reminders of his duty to make monthly payments, Curry made no such payments in 1968, 1969, 1970, 1971, 1972, 1974, 1975 and only minimal payments in the form of retained wages in 1973. During this period, Curry lived rent free on the property, first in the fourplex and then in a 1715 square foot one bedroom apartment built primarily with money, material and labor supplied by Tucker in order to complete the fourplex. Furthermore, from the time he was first served with the notice of forfeiture until the date of trial, Curry made absolutely no effort to tender the purchase price or in any other way fulfill his contractual obligations. Tucker, on the other hand, has seemingly done everything humanly possible to assist Curry, even to the point of endangering his own

---

remedy against a wilfully defaulting vendee to foreclosure by judicial sale, or by private sale if there is a power of sale in the contract, all subject to the wilfully defaulting vendee's right to reinstate the contract by paying only the delinquent amounts plus costs and attorney's fees. None of these far-reaching changes in the law are sought by the present plaintiffs, who have already paid a substantial part of the price and who now tender the entire balance due under the contract.

This court has twice declined similar invitations to consider such innovations in the law on the ground that considering them was unnecessary to proper disposition of the cases then before us. (*MacFadden v. Walker,* (1971) 5 Cal.3d 809, 816, 97 Cal.Rptr. 537, 488 P.2d 1353; *Honey v. Henry's Franchise Leasing Corp.* (1966) 64 Cal.2d 801, 804–805, 52 Cal.Rptr. 18, 415 P.2d 833.) We again conclude that sound development of the law in this complex area can best be assured by limiting our holdings to the issues necessarily presented for decision.

Maj. Opn., ante at 219 Cal.Rptr. at 172, n. 1, 707 P.2d at 234, n. 1.

financial status. Indeed, it was only after Tucker had been pushed to the brink of bankruptcy that he refused to continue to meet Curry's obligations. Even then Tucker suggested various alternatives which would have allowed Curry to keep all or a part of the property, all of which Curry summarily rejected. Under the circumstances, it does not seem inequitable to allow the contract to be enforced according to its terms.

2. *Restitution as an alternative form of relief for the vendee.* Suppose a vendee is in a jurisdiction where the "equity of redemption" approach has not been adopted or she is simply unable or unwilling to redeem. An alternative remedy endorsed by the *Petersen* court is restitution. Increasingly, many courts are holding that "forfeiture may not be 'free' and that the vendor must return the payments he has received insofar as they exceed his actual damages. Some courts * * * take this position only in cases in which they conclude that an outright forfeiture would be 'unconscionable' but this may simply mean that the purchaser would suffer a substantial net loss if no restitution were ordered." Nelson, Whitman, Burkhart & Freyermuth, Real Estate Finance Law 84 (6th ed.2014). See, e.g., Moran v. Holman, 501 P.2d 769 (Alaska 1972); K.M. Young & Assocs., Inc. v. Cieslik, 4 Hawaii App. 657, 675 P.2d 793 (1983); Bellon v. Malnar, 808 P.2d 1089 (Utah 1991).

The restitutionary remedy seems deceptively simple. However, vendees have often found it to be frustratingly difficult, as Clampitt v. A.M.R. Corp., 109 Idaho 145, 706 P.2d 34 (1985), illustrates. In that case, after forfeiting under a $2.3 million dollar installment land contract for the purchase of a farm (which vendor resold two years later for $3.8 million), vendee sought restitution of over $750,000 expended in connection with the contract. Consider the language of the Idaho Supreme Court in affirming a trial court denial of restitutionary relief:

> * * * the amounts paid by purchaser which were forfeited as liquidated damages are:

Amounts forfeited by purchaser	
Principal	$510,000
Interest	221,753
Taxes	13,783
Irrigation equipment	7,338
Total	$752,874

Actual Damages

A. *Market Value*

> In addition to A.M.R.'s claim that the amount forfeited exceeded the reasonable rental value of the property and other allowable damage items, A.M.R. alleges that the market value of the premises increased from the date of execution of the contract until the time of the breach, and that gain should have been considered by the trial court in determining the amounts

forfeited by the purchaser. * * * Where there is a liquidated damage clause, a * * * determination of the difference between contract price and market value of the premises should be made to determine whether or not what the seller is acquiring back as a result of the forfeiture is more valuable than what he contracted to sell. While the rule is generally stated as the difference in values *at the time of the breach,* "this rule necessarily presupposes that the vendor is free to use or dispose of the property on the date of breach. Accordingly, if the vendee has interfered with the vendor's freedom in this respect, by retaining possession or asserting an interest in the property, the vendor may include any additional damages caused thereby in the amount necessary to give him the benefit of his bargain." 77 Am.Jur.2d Vendor and Purchaser § 489, p. 614. *See also Honey v. Henry's Franchise Leasing Corp.,* 64 Cal.2d 801, 52 Cal.Rptr. 18, 415 P.2d 833 (1966).

In this case the trial court found that there was no increase in market value. The trial court determined the relevant period to be from July of 1974 when A.M.R. purchased the property until July of 1976 when the seller actually terminated the contract for failure of the vendee to cure the default. We find no merit in A.M.R.'s argument that the trial court should have used an earlier date in December, 1975, the date of breach when it actually failed to make the payments. * * * The trial court's findings are supported by substantial competent evidence and are not clearly erroneous, and therefore are affirmed.

B. *Rental Value*

In determining whether a liquidated damages provision on default constitutes an unreasonable forfeiture, one element of damage to consider is the loss of rental value during the time the defaulting purchaser was in possession. *Anderson v. Michel,* 88 Idaho 228, 398 P.2d 228 (1965). The trial court determined that the reasonable rental value for the entire farm for the two-year period that the vendees were in possession to be the sum of $447,518.51. The trial court calculated that rental value by first determining that the rental value for the portion of the acreage under cultivation was $401,252, using the landlord's crop share for those acres based upon average prices and average yields of the area. The trial court then determined the rental value of the undeveloped land to be $46,266.51, based upon what a reasonable return on investment or equity would yield for the entire farm, less the $401,252 allocable to the irrigated acreage under cultivation. The purchaser, who presented conflicting evidence suggesting that the actual rental proceeds were lower, argues that the trial court's consideration of evidence of return on investment in arriving at rental value was improper. However, return on investment in property is circumstantial evidence relevant to determining a property's rental value. Neither the actual rental received nor the average rental received on comparable properties is conclusive evidence as to what is a reasonable rental value. Both values are relevant evidence upon which to base a finding of reasonable rental value, as is evidence of return on investment. * * *

C.   *Costs of Repossession, Refinancing and Resale*

The costs which a seller incurs in repossessing the property from a defaulting purchaser are actual damages suffered by the seller. *See Williamson v. Smith,* 74 Idaho 79, 256 P.2d 784 (1953). A vendor may also claim as actual damages any costs which flow from the breach and which could have been within the contemplation of the parties at the time of contracting. *See* Annot. 52 A.L.R. 1511, 1512 (1928). It is possible that these additional damages could include, in the proper case with proper findings of fact, the costs of refinancing or reselling the property. This Court noted in *Anderson v. Michel, supra,* that "the possible expense of resale of the property" may be considered as actual damages to a vendor in determining whether an unreasonable forfeiture has occurred.

In the present case the trial court found that the costs of repossessing, refinancing and reselling the property were "intertwined and must be considered together." This finding of fact was supported by substantial and competent evidence. At the time of executing the purchase agreement, purchaser was aware of the underlying indebtedness and the necessity of improving the unirrigated land. Purchaser was aware that a breach on its part could cause a breach on the underlying contract and therefore jeopardize the loss of the entire property. Purchaser was also aware that the failure to develop the unirrigated land and apply water rights to beneficial use might result in the loss of the water rights. At trial both parties testified as to the urgency for someone to cure the defaults on the underlying contracts and to apply the water rights to beneficial use prior to expiration. Prior to losing possession, the purchaser was also trying to obtain refinancing in order to cure the defaults, develop the irrigation system and hopefully subdivide and resell the property. Therefore, we find no error in the trial court's considering these costs as damages to the vendors in determining the unreasonableness of the forfeiture.

* * *

D. *Miscellaneous Damages*

There were several other various items of alleged damage, some of which the trial court included in the actual damage sum, others of which the trial court did not include, and still others which it is not certain whether they were included or not. After considering each item and the objections to them, and eliminating some of them from our consideration on this appeal, we nevertheless conclude that the vendors' actual damages approximated the amount forfeited as reflected in the following schedule:

Vendors actual damages:	
Reasonable rental	$447,518.00
Damage to sprinkler pipes	
Costs of repossession and refinancing:	800.00
Loan commitment	600.00
Loan commitment	11,000.00
Loan fee & interest	44,908.00
Title policy & fees	5,954.00
Appraisal	250.00
Attorney fees	4,500.00
Attorney fees	6,730.00
Title fees	200.00
Costs of resale:	
Realtor's commission	224,640.00
Total	$747,100.00

When comparing the $747,100 in actual damages to $752,874, the amount forfeited under the liquidated damage clause, the application of the liquidated damage clause in this case appears fair and reasonable.

* * *

We conclude that the trial court's determination that the forfeiture clause in the contract does not operate as an unconscionable forfeiture in this case is supported by substantial and competent evidence and is not clearly erroneous.

WATKINS V. EADS

Court of Appeals of Kentucky, 2014
2014 WL 2154901

Before LAMBERT, TAYLOR, and VANMETER, JUDGES.

OPINION

TAYLOR, JUDGE.

On September 24, 1998, Joe (Jody) S. Watkins entered into an installment land sale contract with Elizabeth Stipp Eads for the purchase of residential property owned by Elizabeth located at 531 Main Street, Paris, Kentucky. Although not documented in the record, Elizabeth subsequently conveyed her interest in the property to Richard and Deanna Eads. The contract stated a total purchase price of $125,000 with a down payment of $5,000 to be paid upon execution of the contract. The $120,000 balance was to accrue interest at the rate of 9.5 percent per annum, simple interest, and was to be paid in 180 equal monthly installments of $1,253.07. Watkins was also responsible for paying the *ad valorem* taxes on the property conveyed under the contract. The contract further provided that in the event of default, the Eads could declare the total balance due, and if such balance was not paid within ten days, the contract could be terminated. The contract also contained the following forfeiture clause which is the genesis of this appeal:

> [I]n the event that the amount then owing is not paid within ten (10) days payments made by Purchaser hereunder and the value of any repairs and/or improvements made by Purchaser may retained to the benefit of the Seller as fixed and liquidated damages for nonperformance by Purchaser of this agreement and as rent and compensation for use and occupancy of said property by Purchaser, as Purchaser specifically waives their right to foreclosure sale of the property.

> However, if the above remedy of Seller, upon default by Purchaser, is determined to be unenforceable by a court of competent jurisdiction, then in that event Seller may, at his option, declare all of the unpaid purchase money herein, the interest due thereon and all other amounts due hereunder to be immediately due and payable without further notice of demand to Purchaser, and Seller may thereupon institute proceedings to collect the same as if Seller had a purchase money lien on said property, pursuant to the holding and guidelines of *Sebastian v. Floyd,* Ky., 585 S.W.2d 381 (1979), and Purchaser agrees to pay all costs thereof, including reasonable attorney's fees.

It is undisputed that Watkins eventually defaulted under the terms of the contract. On June 4, 2010, the Eads sent Watkins a letter notifying him the contract would be terminated in ten days unless all arrearages (payments, taxes, and interest) were paid in full. There is a dispute between the parties as to the actual amount owed including interest. The arrearages were not paid; consequently, the Eads filed a complaint in Bourbon Circuit Court in June of 2011. Therein, the Eads alleged that Watkins was in default under the terms of the contract, and that per the contract's forfeiture clause, Watkins forfeited any right to a foreclosure sale or recoupment of payments made thereunder.

Watkins filed an answer and counterclaim, asserting that he had not forfeited the right to a foreclosure sale and was entitled to recoupment of payments made under the land contract. Specifically, Watkins argued that a foreclosure sale of the real property was legally mandated * * * .

By opinion and order entered April 17, 2012, the circuit court granted summary judgment in favor of the Eads. The circuit court determined that Watkins was in default, had forfeited his right to a foreclosure sale per the contract, and waived any payments made under the land contract. * * * These appeals follow.

Watkins contends the circuit court erred by concluding that the forfeiture clause in the contract was enforceable and that he waived his right to a foreclosure sale of the real property. Watkins relies upon *Sebastian v. Floyd,* 585 S.W.2d 381 (Ky.1979), for the proposition that a forfeiture clause in an installment land contract is *per se* invalid. The Eads respond that Watkins voluntarily waived his right to a foreclosure sale of the real property under the contract and, therefore, *Sebastian,* 585 S.W.2d 318, is inapposite. The circuit court concluded Watkins' waived his right to a judicial foreclosure sale. * * *

Installment land sale contracts, also commonly referred to as contracts and bond for deed, are recognized as valid and enforceable contracts to finance the purchase of real property. *Sebastian,* 585 S.W.2d 381. These contracts are common in owner-financed transactions. Upon execution of an installment land sale contract, legal title to the real property remains with the seller, and equitable title to the real property passes to the purchaser. *Id.* However, Kentucky law is clear that upon default by the purchaser in an installment land contract, the purchaser does not "forfeit" his interest in the real property and, most importantly, a purported forfeiture clause stating otherwise is considered void and unenforceable. *Sebastian,* 585 S.W.2d 381.

This Court recently revisited *Sebastian* in *Slone v. Calhoun,* 386 S.W.3d 745 (Ky.App.2012). As noted in *Slone, Sebastian* remains the controlling precedent in Kentucky regarding installment land sale contracts. Under the *Sebastian* rule, a real estate purchaser, who defaults under an installment land sale contract, still retains an equitable interest in the real property and further possesses redemption rights therein pursuant to Kentucky Revised Statutes (KRS) 426.530. The Kentucky Supreme Court held in *Sebastian* that the forfeiture provision in an installment land sale contract that provided for the forfeiture of the buyers' payment upon the buyers' default was invalid and otherwise not enforceable in Kentucky. The Supreme Court noted that there was no practical distinction between a land sale contract and a purchase money mortgage. The Court made the following observation regarding this issue:

> There is no practical distinction between the land sale contract and a purchase money mortgage, in which the seller conveys legal title to the buyer but retains a lien on the property to secure payment. The significant feature of each device is the seller's financing the buyer's purchase of the property, using the property as collateral for the loan.
>
> Where the purchaser of property has given a mortgage and subsequently defaults on his payments, his entire interest in the property is not forfeited. The mortgagor has the right to redeem the property by paying the full debt plus interest and expenses incurred by the creditor due to default. In order to cut off the mortgagor's right to redeem, the mortgagee must request a court to sell the property at public auction. *See* Lewis, Reeves, How the Doctrine of Equitable Conversion Affects Land Sale Contract Forfeitures, 3 Real Estate Law Journal 249, 253 (1974). *See also* KRS 426.005, 426.525. From the proceeds of the sale, the mortgagee recovers the amount owed him on the mortgage, as well as the expenses of bringing suit; the mortgagor is entitled to the balance, if any.

Sebastian, 585 S.W.2d at 383.

Effectively, grantors who finance the sale of real property are treated like banks or mortgage institutions that finance real estate transactions and retain mortgages against the property to secure the payment of the indebtedness owed. This public policy is consistent with the legislative mandate that "strict foreclosure" in Kentucky has been abolished, regardless of the method of financing. KRS 426.525. Prior to passage of this statute at common law, a lien holder could unilaterally take possession and control of mortgaged property, thereby eliminating any equity of the mortgagor or owner of the property, as well as extinguishing statutory redemption rights provided for in KRS 426.530. *Sebastian* extended the policy of strict foreclosure prohibition to installment land sale contracts.

The forfeiture clause at issue in this case clearly violates the holding in *Sebastian* and *Slone* and also contravenes KRS 426.525 and KRS 426.530. The forfeiture clause in Watkins' contract is void and of no effect. The circuit court erred as a matter of law in enforcing the same.

We would further note that the circuit court's conclusion that the contract states that "he [Watkins] is waiving his rights that were established by *Sebastian v. Floyd. . . .*" is also erroneous on its face for two reasons. First, the contract does not contain any language whatsoever regarding the waiver of "*Sebastian* rights." Second, had the contract expressly waived any "rights" from *Sebastian,* this waiver would also have been void on its face. We must emphasize that *Sebastian* did not create "rights" that are subject to waiver. Rather, *Sebastian* established and applied the long-standing law in Kentucky that strict foreclosure is prohibited in any real estate financing transaction, including owner-financed transactions that utilize installment land sale contracts. Until the Supreme Court directs otherwise, any attempt to waive the protections afforded by *Sebastian* are void as a matter of law and the only judicial remedy available to address the alleged breach of an installment land sale contract is a judicial sale of the property. *Sebastian,* 585 S.W.2d 381.

Under the authority of *Sebastian,* 585 S.W.2d 381, a forfeiture clause in an installment land contract is void and will not be given legal effect in this Commonwealth. *See also Slone,* 386 S.W.3d 745. * * *

Upon remand and entry of judgment, the circuit court shall direct that a judicial sale of the real property be conducted in accordance with applicable law, and from the proceeds, the Eads are entitled to recover the balance owed under the land contract as determined by the circuit court in accordance with this opinion. Any remaining balance will be paid to Watkins.

    * * *

ALL CONCUR.

NOTES

1. *Treating the installment land contract as a mortgage. Watkins* and *Sebastian* represent the most straight-forward judicial treatment of the installment land contract as a mortgage for remedy purposes. Indiana (see Skendzel v. Marshall, 261 Ind. 226, 301 N.E.2d 641 (1973)) is similar to Kentucky, but there courts still recognize that forfeiture can occur in two exceptional circumstances: (1) where the vendee has abandoned the premises or (2) where the vendee has paid only a minimal amount toward the contract price and the security has been jeopardized. Consider how a recent Indiana decision approached these two exceptions:

> [F]or there to be an abandonment of a conditional land sales contract one must actually and *intentionally* relinquish possession of the land and act in a manner which is unequivocally inconsistent with the existence of a contract. *McLendon v. Safe Realty Corp.,* 401 N.E.2d 80, 83 (Ind.Ct.App.1980) (emphasis added). Here, the trial

court seems to have relied upon its findings that Brian [the vendee] told Morris [the vendor] to "stick it up your ass" and that he directed tenants to make all future rent payments to Morris as evidence of his intent to abandon the contract.* * * The right to collect rents on the property is an incident of ownership, which accrued to Brian when the parties entered the contract. * * * The relinquishment of this right could reasonably be viewed as an act "inconsistent with the existence of a contract." *McLendon*, 401 N.E.2d at 83.

However, the record clearly establishes that Brian did not leave the property until Morris changed the locks, and the trial court specifically found that he "abandoned and vacated" the property "[c]ontemporaneously" with the delivery of the rent notice to tenants on October 4, 2001. * * * This does not support a conclusion that Brian "actually and intentionally relinquish[ed] possession of the land[.]" *McLendon*, 401 N.E.2d at 83. * * *

The trial court's findings do not support its conclusion that Brian abandoned the land sales contract. Moreover, to allow Morris the remedy of forfeiture because of abandonment when he forced Brian to relinquish possession of the property by locking him out would hardly be "consonant with notions of fairness and justice" as set forth in *Skendzel*.* * *

Next, Brian argues that the trial court erred by finding he fell within the second *Skendzel* exception, which requires a showing of both that the vendee has paid only a minimal amount toward the contract price and that the vendor's security interest has been jeopardized.* * * Whether a particular sum paid toward a contract price is minimal depends upon the totality of the circumstances surrounding the contract and its performance. * * *

Morris contends that forfeiture was the appropriate remedy for breach because the contract called for forfeiture of any payment as liquidated damages until Brian had paid a "substantial amount" on the principal purchase price. The contract defined that "substantial amount" as "when the fair market value of the real estate at the time of default exceeds the sum of (a) the then remaining unpaid balance of the purchase price with accrued interest thereon, (b) the estimated cost of resale, (c) the amount of any additional liens on the real estate, and (d) reasonable attorney fees for the enforcement of the contract[.]" * * * Morris asserts that Brian had not paid a "substantial amount" under this formula, while Brian contends that he had.

We have previously rejected contract provisions purporting to establish a minimal equity threshold by agreement of the parties. In *Parker v. Camp*, 656 N.E.2d 882 (Ind.Ct.App.1995), we held that a contract provision permitting the vendor to seek forfeiture until the vendee attained "substantial equity" in the property, defined as 75% of the purchase price, to be void as against the public policy of this state as set forth in Skendzel. Id. at 885. Likewise, in *Johnson*, 472 N.E.2d at 620, the vendors argued that forfeiture was warranted by virtue of a contract provision requiring $12,000 payment on a purchase price of $52,000 as the "minimal equity threshold." However, we concluded that the vendee's payment of $11,000 toward the principal constituted more than minimal payment and that foreclosure was the appropriate remedy. Id. at 626.

The trial court found that Brian had paid "a mere 10% of the total contract price." * * * The trial court's findings and conclusions offer no indication how it reached this figure. It is undisputed that Brian paid a total of $96,363.48, of which $33,727.83 was applied to principal. The amount applied to the principal is computed to be 18.2% of the contract price of $185,000.

Courts determining whether a vendee has made more than minimal payment have looked at payments toward both principal and interest. * * * In addition to the amount paid, this court has also considered the length of time and the number of payments made in determining whether a vendee had made minimal payment. See *S.B.D. v. Sai Mahen, Inc.*, 560 N.E.2d 86, 88 (Ind.Ct.App.1990). The *Skendzel* court did not provide a minimum threshold that would permit forfeiture, but held that a vendee who had paid 29% of principal had made more than minimal payment. See also *Morris*, 270 Ind. at 122, 383 N.E.2d at 342 (29.7% of contract price was substantial amount); *S.B.D., Inc.*, 560 N.E.2d at 88 (28% of contract price was substantial amount). We also note that a panel of this court observed in dicta that a payment of 18.6% of the contract principal would be more than minimal payment. See *Oles*, 444 N.E.2d at 879.

Here, there is no dispute that Brian made regular payments for roughly three years in a total amount of $96,363.48, and had paid 18.2% of the principal. Although he failed to make one year's property tax payment, Brian continued to make monthly payments and maintained insurance on the property until Morris effectively dispossessed him by changing the locks. Under all these facts and circumstances, we conclude that Brian had made more than minimal payment for purposes of *Skendzel*.

Even if only a minimal amount has been paid on the contract price, forfeiture is not appropriate unless the vendor's security interest is jeopardized by the vendee's acts or omissions. Morris, 270 Ind. at 125, 383 N.E.2d at 344. Nothing in the record suggests that foreclosure on the property would not have satisfactorily protected the interests of both parties. Although the trial court found that Morris had to pay $3000 to have trash and debris removed from the premises, Morris testified that the property was worth "probably the same" as in 1998. * * * Upon foreclosure, the vendee retains a vendee's lien upon the sale, and once the balance owed under the contract has been paid to the vendor, the vendee may retain the proceeds from the sale. If the foreclosure does not net a sufficient amount to satisfy the vendor's remaining security interest in the property, a damage judgment for waste caused by the vendee equivalent to the amount recoverable by a mortgagee as a deficiency judgment would be appropriate. * * * Thus, Morris's security interest in the property was not jeopardized. However, because the trial court also found that Morris had to pay $3000 to have trash and debris removed from the premises, Morris is entitled to recover that sum from Brian.

Under these facts and circumstances, the trial court erred when it ordered forfeiture rather than foreclosure as the remedy for Brian's breach of the land sales contract.

McLemore v. McLemore, 827 N.E.2d 1135, 1141–1143 (Ind.App.2005).

If anything, *Skendzel* has produced more litigation and uncertainty—Indiana continues to be bedeviled by installment land contract cases. See Huber v. Sering, 867 N.E.2d 698 (Ind.App.2007) (forfeiture affirmed where less than 20% of contract price had been paid and vendee had violated insurance and maintenance covenants); Franks v. Andre Trust, 886 N.E.2d 698 (Ind.App.2008) (forfeiture affirmed where 20% of contract price had been paid and vendee had abandoned the premises); Williams v. Hilycord, 886 N.E.2d 119 (Ind.App.2008) (forfeiture reversed where 28.5% of the contract price had been paid). Would Indiana be better off if its supreme court simply held that all installment land contracts should be treated as mortgages irrespective of the amount paid on the contract or such issues as abandonment or security impairment? Or should the legislature regulate when forfeitures are permissible and otherwise institutionalize the installment land contract?

While the Florida Supreme Court has not yet held that a vendee has an absolute right to insist on foreclosure of an installment land contract, numerous Florida appellate decisions state that such a contract is a mortgage and must be foreclosed by judicial sale. See, e.g., Kubany v. Woods, 622 So.2d 22 (Fla.App.1993) ("This agreement for deed is treated under Florida law as a mortgage and is subject to the same rules of foreclosure."); Luneke v. Becker, 621 So.2d 744 (Fla.App.1993) ("[T]he vendor * * * has no right to repossess the property; the vendor must proceed with a foreclosure action * * * . Accordingly, the proper remedy in this case was not ejectment, but a foreclosure action"); White v. Brousseau, 566 So.2d 832 (Fla.App.1990) (same). Similarly, the New York Supreme Court, Appellate Division, in a 1983 case where vendees had paid almost half of the contract purchase price of a house, reversed a trial court forfeiture decree, found "no reason why these vendees should be treated any differently than the mortgagor at common law," and held that "vendors may not summarily dispossess the vendees of their equitable ownership without first bringing an action to foreclose the vendees' equity of redemption." Bean v. Walker, 95 A.D.2d 70, 464 N.Y.S.2d 895 (1983). See also Call v. LaBrie, 116 A.D.2d 1034, 498 N.Y.S.2d 652 (1986) (payment by vendee of over 12% of the contract price deemed sufficient to convert contract for deed into an equitable mortgage).

The Nebraska Supreme Court, while not yet holding that installment land contracts are mortgages for all purposes, has increasingly subjected them to mortgage law analysis. See, e.g., Mackiewicz v. J.J. & Associates, 245 Neb. 568, 514 N.W.2d 613 (1994) ("We have refused to strictly enforce the traditional remedy of forfeiture * * * in favor of recognizing the right of the seller to foreclose as if the contract were a mortgage. * * * Because this court has uniformly recognized that a seller in a land contract retains the title as security for the unpaid purchase money and has an equitable lien on the land to the extent of the debt, a seller has, for all intents and purposes, a purchase-money mortgage."). See also Clark v. Clark, 275 Neb. 276, 746 N.W.2d 132 (2008).

In Colorado, trial courts have the discretion to require that a contract for deed be foreclosed as a mortgage. See Grombone v. Krekel, 754 P.2d 777 (Colo.App.1988) ("The decision whether an installment land contract is to be treated as a mortgage is committed to the sound discretion of the trial court, based on facts presented. * * * There are numerous Colorado decisions which have required that an installment land contract must be foreclosed as a mortgage. * * * The factors to be used by the trial court in determining whether to treat an installment land contract as a mortgage include the amount of the vendee's equity in the property, the length of the default period, the willfulness of the default, whether the vendee has made improvements, and whether the property has been adequately maintained.").

Under the Restatement approach, an installment land contract "creates a mortgage." Restatement (Third) of Property (Mortgages) § 3.4(b) (1997). As a result, in any jurisdiction adopting the latter section, an installment land contract will be "governed procedurally and substantively by the law of mortgages." Id. at cmt. c. See also Mike Lee, Note, Contracts for Deed: Extinction Long Overdue, 37 Tex. Tech. L. Rev. 1231 (2005).

Vermont's approach is consistent with the Restatement. See Prue v. Royer, 193 Vt. 267, 67 A.3d 895 (2013).

Texas legislation treats many installment land contracts as mortgages. Consider the following description of its legislation:

> First, it applies only to contracts for deed on real estate "used or to be used as the purchaser's residence * * * . If the purchaser "has paid 40 percent or more of the amount due or the equivalent of 48 monthly payments" under the contract for deed, forfeiture or rescission is unavailable to the vendor. Rather, the vendor is granted a power of sale and his or her sole remedy is to appoint a

> trustee who must conduct a foreclosure sale in accordance with Texas legislation governing the nonjudicial foreclosure of mortgages and deeds of trust. As a practical matter, once the purchaser's payments have satisfied the statutory threshold, the contract for deed becomes a mortgage or deed of trust with power of sale.

Nelson, Whitman, Burkhart & Freyermuth, Real Estate Finance Law 131 (6th ed. 2014). Illinois has similar legislation although the purchaser is entitled to mortgage treatment when the amount due is less than 80% of the contract price. Id. at 130. See also Md.Code Ann. Real Prop. § 10–105 (West) (foreclosure required after 40% of contract price paid).

2. *Waiver or estoppel as a defense against forfeiture.* An additional ameliorative judicial approach, conceptually less drastic than the foregoing theories, is the waiver concept:

> Frequently a vendor will accept one or several late payments from the vendee without taking action to declare a forfeiture. When the vendor finally runs out of patience and informs the vendee that forfeiture has occurred, the vendee may argue that the vendor's prior behavior constitutes a waiver of the time provisions of the contract and that the vendor is legally bound to accept the late payments. This dispute often surfaces in a vendee's suit or counterclaim for specific performance of the contract. The vendee may be willing to tender the entire purchase price, or he may insist upon an opportunity to make up his arrearages and resume the original payment schedule.
>
> Many courts have adopted the vendee's position in this situation. In effect, these courts hold that the vendor's waiver avoids the effect of the forfeiture clause and creates in the vendee a right analogous to an equity of redemption. According to this view, if the vendor had given the vendee clear notice that no further delinquencies would be tolerated, and if this notice had been given in adequate time to allow the vendee to get back on schedule, the vendor might thereby have preserved his right of forfeiture as to future installments. Since the vendor did not do so, the court itself will generally fix a reasonable time within which the vendee must cure the delinquencies.

Nelson & Whitman, Installment Land Contracts—The National Scene Revisited, 1985 B.Y.U.L.Rev. 1. See Turley v. Staley, 372 S.W.3d 821 (Ark.App.2009) (vendor waived the forfeiture remedy by accepting late payments over a ten year period).

Even where there is no prior pattern of forbearance, a vendor may occasionally be *estopped* to invoke forfeiture based on a single transaction. In Danelson v. Robinson, 317 Mont. 462, 77 P.3d 1010 (2003), a defaulting vendee asserted that the vendor, in response to the vendee's offer to cure the contract by obtaining a loan from vendee's mother-in-law, assured vendee that "he was not worried about the payment and that taking out a loan from [vendee's] mother-in-law was not necessary." Id. at 1011. Two months later vendor initiated a forfeiture of the contract. Vendee then sought a judicial declaration that vendor was estopped to assert a forfeiture. The trial court rejected vendee's estoppel argument. However, the Montana Supreme Court reversed, holding that the vendee should be permitted "to show that the [vendor] * * * waived [the right to forfeiture] for at least a period of time; that the [vendee] relied on this waiver; and that the [vendor] should be estopped thereby." Id. at 1013.

3.   *Oklahoma statute.* Consider the impact of the following Oklahoma statute, under which installment land contracts

> for purchase and sale of real property made for the purpose or with the intention of receiving the payment of money and made for the purpose of establishing an immediate and continuing right of possession of the described real property, whether such instruments be from the debtor to the creditor or from the debtor to some third person in trust for the creditor, shall to that extent be deemed and held mortgages, and shall be subject to the same rules of foreclosure and to the same regulations, restraints and forms as are prescribed in relation to mortgages.

Okla.Stat.Ann. tit. 16, § 11A (1998). Does this legislation render the installment land contract obsolete in Oklahoma? See Drew L. Kershen, Contracts for Deed in Oklahoma: Obsolete, But Not Forgotten, 15 Okla.City L.Rev. 715 (1990) ("If attorneys use contracts for deed to transfer Oklahoma real estate, they have not accomplished legally anything different under Oklahoma law than if they had used a deed and mortgage"); G. Booker Schmidt, Comment, The Decline of the Contract for Deed in Oklahoma, 14 Tulsa L.J. 557 (1979).

MINN.STAT.ANN.
§ 559.21

Subd. 2a. For post 7/31/1985 contract. If a default occurs in the conditions of a contract for the conveyance of real estate or an interest in real estate executed on or after August 1, 1985, that gives the seller a right to terminate it, the seller may terminate the contract by serving upon the purchaser or the purchaser's personal representatives or assigns, within or outside of the state, a notice specifying the conditions in which default has been made. The notice must state that the contract will terminate 60 days, or a shorter period allowed in subdivision 4, after the service of the notice, unless prior to the termination date the purchaser:

(1) complies with the conditions in default;

(2) makes all payments due and owing to the seller under the contract through the date that payment is made;

(3) pays the costs of service of the notice, including the reasonable costs of service by sheriff, public officer, or private process server; except payment of costs of service is not required unless the seller notifies the purchaser of the actual costs of service by certified mail to the purchaser's last known address at least ten days prior to the date of termination;

(4) except for earnest money contracts, purchase agreements, and exercised options, pays two percent of any amount in default at the time of service, not including the final balloon payment, any taxes, assessments, mortgages, or prior contracts that are assumed by the purchaser; and

(5) if the contract is executed on or after August 1, 1999, pays an amount to apply on attorneys' fees actually expended or incurred, of $250 if the amount in default is less than $1000, and of $500 if the amount in default is $1000 or more; or if the contract is executed before August 1, 1999, pays an amount to apply on attorneys' fees actually expended or incurred, of $125 if the amount in default is less than $750, and of $250 if the amount in default is $750 or more; except no amount for attorneys' fees is required to be paid unless some part of the conditions of default has existed for at least 30 days prior to the date of service of the notice.

Subd. 3. **Notice defined.** For purposes of this section, the term "notice" means a writing stating the information required in this section, stating the name, address and telephone number of the seller or of an attorney authorized by the seller to accept payments pursuant to the notice and the fact that the person named is authorized to receive the payments, and including the following information in 12-point or larger underlined upper-case type, or 8-point type if published, or in large legible handwritten letters:

THIS NOTICE IS TO INFORM YOU THAT BY THIS NOTICE THE SELLER HAS BEGUN PROCEEDINGS UNDER MINNESOTA STATUTES, SECTION 559.21, TO TERMINATE YOUR CONTRACT FOR THE PURCHASE OF YOUR PROPERTY FOR THE REASONS SPECIFIED IN THIS NOTICE. THE CONTRACT WILL TERMINATE ___ DAYS AFTER (SERVICE OF THIS NOTICE UPON YOU) (THE FIRST DATE OF PUBLICATION OF THIS NOTICE) UNLESS BEFORE THEN:

(a) THE PERSON AUTHORIZED IN THIS NOTICE TO RECEIVE PAYMENTS RECEIVES FROM YOU:

(1) THE AMOUNT THIS NOTICE SAYS YOU OWE; PLUS

(2) THE COSTS OF SERVICE (TO BE SENT TO YOU); PLUS

(3) $_____ TO APPLY TO ATTORNEYS' FEES ACTUALLY EXPENDED OR INCURRED; PLUS

* * *

(5) FOR CONTRACTS, OTHER THAN EARNEST MONEY CONTRACTS, PURCHASE AGREEMENTS AND EXERCISED OPTIONS, EXECUTED ON OR AFTER AUGUST 1, 1985, $_____ (WHICH IS TWO PERCENT OF THE AMOUNT IN DEFAULT AT THE TIME OF SERVICE OTHER THAN THE FINAL BALLOON PAYMENT, ANY TAXES, ASSESSMENTS, MORTGAGES, OR PRIOR CONTRACTS THAT ARE ASSUMED BY YOU); OR

(b) YOU SECURE FROM A COUNTY OR DISTRICT COURT AN ORDER THAT THE TERMINATION OF THE CONTRACT BE SUSPENDED UNTIL YOUR CLAIMS OR DEFENSES ARE FINALLY DISPOSED OF BY TRIAL, HEARING OR SETTLEMENT. YOUR ACTION MUST SPECIFICALLY STATE THOSE FACTS AND GROUNDS THAT DEMONSTRATE YOUR CLAIMS OR DEFENSES.

IF YOU DO NOT DO ONE OR THE OTHER OF THE ABOVE THINGS WITHIN THE TIME PERIOD SPECIFIED IN THIS NOTICE, YOUR CONTRACT WILL TERMINATE AT THE END OF THE PERIOD AND YOU WILL LOSE ALL THE MONEY YOU HAVE PAID ON THE CONTRACT; YOU WILL LOSE YOUR RIGHT TO POSSESSION OF THE PROPERTY; YOU MAY LOSE YOUR RIGHT TO ASSERT ANY CLAIMS OR DEFENSES THAT YOU MIGHT HAVE; AND YOU WILL BE EVICTED. IF YOU HAVE ANY QUESTIONS ABOUT THIS NOTICE, CONTACT AN ATTORNEY IMMEDIATELY.

Subd. 4. Law prevails over contract; procedure; conditions. (a) The notice required by this section must be given notwithstanding any provisions in the contract to the contrary, except that earnest money contracts, purchase agreements, and exercised options that are subject to this section may, unless by their terms they provide for a longer termination period, be terminated on 30 days' notice or may be cancelled under section 559.217. The notice must be served within the state in the same manner as a summons in the district court, and outside of the state, in the same manner, and without securing any sheriff's return of not found, making any preliminary affidavit, mailing a copy of the notice or doing any other preliminary act or thing whatsoever. Service of the notice outside of the state may be proved by the affidavit of the person making the same, made before an authorized officer having a seal, and within the state by such an affidavit or by the return of the sheriff of any county therein.

(b) If a person to be served is a resident individual who has departed from the state, or cannot be found in the state; or is a nonresident individual or a foreign corporation, partnership, or association, service may be made by publication as provided in this paragraph. Three weeks published notice has the same effect as personal service of the notice. The published notice must comply with subdivision 3 and state (1) that the person to be served is allowed 90 days after the first date of publication of the notice to comply with the conditions of the contract, and (2) that the contract will terminate 90 days after the first date of publication of the notice, unless before the termination date the purchaser complies with the notice. If the real estate described in the contract is actually occupied, then, in addition to publication, a person in possession must be personally served, in like manner as the service of a summons in a civil action in state district court, within 30 days after the first date of publication of the notice. If an address of a person to be served is known, then within 30 days after the first date of publication of the notice a copy of the notice must be mailed to the person's last known address by first class mail, postage prepaid.

(c) The contract is reinstated if, within the time mentioned, the person served:

(1) complies with the conditions in default;

(2) * * * makes all payments due and owing to the seller under the contract through the date that payment is made;

(3) pays the costs of service as provided in subdivision * * * 2a;

(4) if subdivision 2a applies, pays two percent of the amount in default, not including the final balloon payment, any taxes, assessments, mortgages, or prior contracts that are assumed by the purchaser; and

(5) pays attorneys' fees as provided in subdivision * * * 2a.

(d) The contract is terminated if the provisions of paragraph (c) are not met.

(e) In the event that the notice was not signed by an attorney for the seller and the seller is not present in the state, or cannot be found in the state, then compliance with the conditions specified in the notice may be made by paying to the court administrator of the district court in the county wherein the real estate or any part thereof is situated any money due and filing proof of compliance with other defaults specified, and the court administrator of the district court shall be deemed the agent of the seller for such purposes. A copy of the notice with proof of service thereof, and the affidavit of the seller, the seller's agent or attorney, showing that the purchaser has not complied with the terms of the notice, may be recorded with the county recorder or register of titles, and is prima facie evidence of the facts stated in it; but this section in no case applies to contracts for the sale or conveyance of lands situated in another state or in a foreign country. If the notice is served by publication, the affidavit must state that the affiant believes that the party to be served is not a resident of the state, or cannot be found in the state, and either that the affiant has mailed a copy of the notice by first class mail, postage prepaid, to the party's last known address, or that such address is not known to the affiant.

Subd. 5. If required, notify commissioner. When required by and in the manner provided in section 270C.63, subdivision 11, the notice required by this section shall also be given to the commissioner of revenue.

NOTE

Statutory institutionalization of the forfeiture remedy. There have been several legislative attempts, of which the above Minnesota statute is typical, to ameliorate the harshness of the forfeiture clause. Most of these statutes provide for varying degrees of notice to the defaulting vendee of the vendor's intent to terminate the contract as well as a "grace period" during which the tender of late payments will reinstate the contract. See, e.g., Ariz.Rev.Stat. §§ 33–741–742 (1974); Iowa Code Ann. §§ 656.1–656.6; N.D.Cent.Code 32–18–01 to 32–18–06; Ohio Rev.Code §§ 5313.01–5313.10; Or.Rev.Stat. 93.905–93.940; Tex.Prop. Code §§ 5.061–5.066; West's Wash.Rev.Code 61.30.010. In addition to moderating the impact of forfeiture, this legislation has to some extent resulted in the institutionalization of the forfeiture concept. See, e.g., Goodale v. Bray, 546 N.W.2d 212 (Iowa 1996).

To be sure, courts in states having such statutes sometime suggest that judicial relief from an "unconscionable forfeiture" may be available. See, e.g., Coddon v. Youngkrantz, 562 N.W.2d 39 (Minn.App.1997) (recognizing that equity may intervene where strict application of statutory cancellation would be "unjust"). Moreover, statutory forfeiture may sometimes be held inappropriate for certain relatively minor defaults. Compare Lett v. Grummer, 300 N.W.2d 147 (Iowa 1981) (statutory forfeiture refused where failure to make minor repairs did not threaten security) with Miller v. American Wonderlands, Inc., 275 N.W.2d 399 (Iowa 1979) (upholding forfeiture based on a $10.48 default on a $30,000 contract and vendee's allowing liens to be filed against the premises) and ExtraOrdinary Learning and Educ. Complex/Minneapolis Communiversity, Inc. v. New Bethel Baptist Church, 430 N.W.2d 184 (Minn.App.1988) (forfeiture upheld where vendee was, at most, one day late).

Nevertheless, judicial intervention in such statutory termination contexts tends more often to focus more on technical statutory compliance than on the inherent fairness of the forfeiture itself. See Nelson, Whitman, Burkhart & Freyermuth, Real Estate Finance Law § 3.28 (6th ed. 2014). Indeed, Professor Durham's observations with respect to Ohio legislation may well have national relevance: "[u]nlike defaults on land contracts not covered by [Ohio Rev.Code §§ 5313.01–5313.10] where Ohio courts have clearly been inclined to give vendees equitable relief, the vendee subject to statutory forfeiture may find himself faced with a judge who either feels constrained by the statute from granting equitable relief or takes comfort in the simplicity of the statute and ignores the possibility of equitable action." James Geoffrey Durham, Forfeiture of Residential Land Contracts in Ohio: The Need for Further Reform of a Reform Statute, 16 Akron L.Rev. 397 (1983).

GRANT S. NELSON, THE CONTRACT FOR DEED AS A
MORTGAGE: THE CASE FOR THE RESTATEMENT APPROACH
1998 B.Y.U. Rev. 1111, 1131–1135

OTHER VENDOR REMEDIES

Even where forfeiture is available, it will sometimes be an undesirable option for the vendor. This will be the case where the real estate is now worth less than the contract price. Of course, were the vendor a mortgagee under a mortgage or deed of trust, or should a court choose to apply mortgage law to the contract, the alternative remedies normally would be clear. The vendor could opt to foreclose and if the foreclosure sale yields less that what was owing, a deficiency judgment would be available for the difference between the sale price and the obligation. Alternatively, the vendor could sue on the contract obligation, obtain a judgment for that amount and collect the judgment out of all of the purchaser's assets, including the contract land.

Unfortunately, in most states, the vendor's options will hardly be so unambiguous. Courts commonly apply either contract law or a confusing combination of mortgage and contract principles. Moreover, even in states that largely utilize a mortgage law analogue in interpreting contracts for deed, courts have yet to confront or work through the myriad of collateral issues and implications that a mortgage characterization creates. However, sometimes contract remedies permit a vendor to achieve indirectly what is usually available as a matter of course in the mortgage law context. Also, sometimes a court will allow a vendor to opt for a mortgage remedy where forfeiture and contract law are not to his liking— in effect, he is permitted to "have his cake and eat it too." What follows is a description and analysis of some of these nonforfeiture remedies.

A.   Specific Performance for the Price

Suppose a contract purchaser goes into default because the value of the real estate has dropped significantly below the remaining contract balance. In other words, the purchaser, who is otherwise able to pay, has made a rational decision "not to throw good money after bad." From the vendor's perspective, the ideal remedy would be specific performance. Under this approach, the vendor tenders title to the land and seeks an equitable decree compelling the purchaser to pay the balance of the contract price. The analogue, of course, is a vendor's action for specific performance where a purchaser fails or refuses to perform under an earnest money contract for the sale of land. In this latter setting, specific performance is almost always granted. Should this remedy also be routinely available in the contract for deed setting?

In fact, vendors are frequently successful in their quest for specific performance, although, in a few cases, as in the earnest money context, courts require the vendor to establish that the remedy at law is inadequate. Where this remedy is available, the court enters a decree against the purchaser for the full contract balance which is collectible by a judicial sale of the purchaser's assets, including the contract property. Note, however, that the conceptual roadblocks to specific performance are more troublesome in the contract for deed setting than with respect to its earnest money contract counterpart. The latter contract, because it is executory, typically provides for the payment of the balance of the contract price on one closing date, while the contract for deed, as a long term financing device, is usually amortized in installments over a longer period of time. Consequently, when a purchaser under an earnest money contract defaults on the closing date, the contract can be treated as completely repudiated, and a specific performance decree for the full contract price is hardly conceptually difficult. On the other hand, when a contract for deed purchaser defaults, a suit for more than the past due installments can be problematic for the vendor. This is because many contracts for deed, unlike most mortgage documents, contain no acceleration clause which permits the vendor to declare the entire contract balance due and payable upon purchaser default. Where this is the case, the vendor may only be able to sue for the past due installments plus interest. To be sure, a court may occasionally come to the vendor's rescue by applying the contract doctrine of anticipatory repudiation as a basis for acceleration. Nevertheless, the absence of an acceleration provision surely presents a substantial obstacle for the vendor seeking specific performance.

B. Action for Damages

In theory, a contract for deed vendor, like his earnest money contract counterpart, should be able to sue the purchaser in default for damages for breach of contract. Using the earnest money analogy, the vendor's damages should be measured by the difference between the contract balance and the fair market value of the property as of the date of the purchaser's breach. However, the damages remedy may only be available where the purchaser has abandoned the land. This is the case because where forfeiture is necessary to regain the property, an action for damages could well be barred by the election of remedies doctrine * * * . Perhaps more important, the vendor faces a significant pragmatic problem—the factfinder (very often a jury) must be convinced that the property, as of the date of the breach, was worth less than the contract price. In other words, the vendor may be in the unenviable position of persuading the fact finder that he or she convinced the purchaser to enter into a "bad deal." Obviously, where a purchaser is capable of satisfying a judgment, the vendor would confront fewer obstacles in suing for specific performance for the price. Not only is the election of remedies problem obviated, so too is the burden of proving damages.

C. Foreclosure of Purchaser's Rights

As * * * explained earlier, several jurisdictions treat the contract for deed as a mortgage for most purposes. Where this is the case, the vendor generally must foreclose the contract as a mortgage. However, in jurisdictions where the mortgage status of the contract for deed is less clear, courts sometimes give the vendor the option to foreclose the contract for deed by judicial sale. This approach seems conceptually problematic because the vendor is seeking a mortgage remedy under a device that, to a greater extent, is governed by contract law. In any event, where this approach is followed, to the extent the sale yields more than the contract balance, the purchaser is entitled to the surplus. Where the sale brings less than the contract balance, the vendor normally will be entitled to a deficiency judgment. Note that this foreclosure route is economically similar to the specific performance remedy. In each situation, the vendor obtains a judgment for the full contract balance, and that judgment may be satisfied out of the contract real estate. In addition, the purchaser in each setting bears the risk of postcontract decline in the value of the real estate.

Moreover, as we saw earlier in the specific performance context, a judgment for the remaining contract balance usually is unavailable unless the contract contains an acceleration clause. The same problem exists when the vendor opts for foreclosure. Unless a court is willing to employ the anticipatory repudiation concept to make the remaining balance due and owing, the vendor will be faced with the undesirable option of foreclosing for the past due installments.

To what extent then do the foreclosure and specific performance remedies differ? In the former context, "the vendor will have the protection of a lien on the contract real estate dating from the execution or recording of the contract." This may not be the case in the specific performance setting. Here the vendor's lien may become effective only when the specific performance decree is entered. Consequently, this lien may well be subordinate to other postcontract liens created by, or arising against, the purchaser.

In some states, including a few that have no tradition of foreclosing contracts for deed by judicial sale, the vendor will be able to obtain strict foreclosure of the purchaser's interest. Under this approach, the contract is canceled and title to the land is quieted in the vendor. However, this remedy is subject to an important qualification. The purchaser is entitled to specific performance of the contract if he or she tenders the balance due on the contract within a "redemption period" set by the court. Note that a failure to redeem deprives the purchaser of any "equity" in the real estate. Consequently, some courts will award strict foreclosure only if the vendor establishes that the value of the real estate does not exceed the contract balance. Where such an excess exists, the court may instead order judicial foreclosure by sale.

NOTE

1. *Mortgagee remedies when the contract is recharacterized as a mortgage.* Whenever a jurisdiction chooses to treat the installment land contract substantively and procedurally as a mortgage, the vendor's contract remedies described above will, as such, be unavailable. However, the vendor-mortgagee is not being prejudiced because mortgage law affords him or her functionally equivalent remedies:

> For example, just as the mortgagee normally has the right to defer or forgo foreclosure in favor of a suit on the obligation, the contract vendor will be able to do likewise for an amount equal to the contract price. * * * The net effect is that the vendor *qua* mortgagee will be entitled to a remedy that differs in name only from specific performance for the price. Moreover, to the extent that a deficiency judgment is available to a mortgagee where the foreclosure sale yields less than the mortgage obligation, so too will such a judgment be granted to a contract vendor after a foreclosure sale produces similar results. This mortgage remedy not only affords the vendor a practical substitute for a contract action for damages, but also gives the vendor the advantage of not having to prove the fair market value of the real estate, as would be required in an action for damages.

Restatement (Third) of Property (Mortgages) § 3.4, cmt. e (1997).*

2. *Premises liability of vendors.* To what extent should an installment land contract vendor be liable to third parties for the condition of the premises or personal injuries that occur on them? Compare Kreher v. Bertucci, 814 So.2d 614 (La.App.2002) (vendor not liable in tort to tenant of vendee who is injured on premises); Jackson v. Scheible, 902 N.E.2d 807 (Ohio 2009) (contract vendor not liable for injuries where bicyclist's view is blocked by failure to trim tree located on contract premises—vendor is not liable as owner under ordinance requiring tree trimming). Flint v. Holbrook, 80 Ohio App.3d 21, 608 N.E.2d 809 (1992) (installment land contract vendor not liable in tort to party bitten by vendee's pit bull even assuming contract was chronically in default and vendor knew vendee was keeping a vicious dog

---

on the premises); and Romel v. Reale, 155 A.D.2d 747, 547 N.Y.S.2d 691 (1989) (vendor has no liability for injury to guest of vendee who fell on contract premises after possession had been delivered to vendee) with City of Webster Groves v. Erickson, 763 S.W.2d 278 (Mo.App.1988) (vendor liable as "owner" under public nuisance ordinance for failing to clear premises of debris even though vendee was in possession). Normally, a mortgagee will not be liable for unsafe conditions on mortgaged real estate unless she is in possession or otherwise exercises dominion and control over it. See, e.g., Smith v. Fried, 98 Ill.App.3d 467, 53 Ill.Dec. 845, 424 N.E.2d 636 (1981).

GRANT S. NELSON & DALE A. WHITMAN, INSTALLMENT LAND CONTRACTS—THE NATIONAL SCENE REVISITED
1985 B.Y.U.L.Rev. 1, 40

To the extent that a jurisdiction recognizes forfeiture as a valid remedy, a vendor faces an election of remedies problem. Once forfeiture has been accomplished, the vendor typically is barred from seeking to recover the equivalent of a mortgage deficiency judgment.[140] Suppose, for example, that under an installment land contract the total purchase price was $50,000, of which the vendee paid $5,000 in cash at the date of contract execution and agreed to pay the balance in nine equal annual installments of $5,000, together with accrued interest at twelve percent per annum. Suppose further that the vendee never makes a further payment on the contract and that the vendor chooses to invoke forfeiture. Later the vendor discovers that the land is worth only $30,000. Under the election of remedies doctrine the vendor cannot collect from the vendee the difference between the balance due on the contract ($45,000) and the fair market value of the land. Moreover, the same result will be reached even when the contract obligation to the vendor is evidenced by a separate promissory note.[141] Occasionally a state will reject the election of remedies doctrine but reach the same result on the ground that it "flows from the fact that the contract between the parties has been terminated, thereby extinguishing any right to recover the unpaid purchase price."[142]

---

[140] See Zirinsky v. Sheehan, 413 F.2d 481 (8th Cir.1969); Nemec v. Rollo, 114 Ariz. 589, 562 P.2d 1087 (Ariz.Ct.App.1977); Hepperly v. Bosch, 172 Ill.App.3d 1017, 123 Ill.Dec. 70, 527 N.E.2d 533 (1988); Community Insurance Agency, Inc. v. Kemper, 426 N.W.2d 471 (Minn.App.1988); Covington v. Pritchett, 428 N.W.2d 121 (Minn.App.1988); Langenes v. Bullinger, 328 N.W.2d 241 (N.D.1982); Butler v. Michel, 14 Ohio App.3d 116, 470 N.E.2d 217 (1984); Trans West Co. v. Teuscher, 27 Wash.App. 404, 618 P.2d 1023 (1980).

[141] See Nemec v. Rollo, 114 Ariz. 589, 562 P.2d 1087 (Ariz.Ct.App.1977).

[142] Gray v. Bowers, 332 N.W.2d 323, 325 (Iowa 1983).

SUMMIT HOUSE CO. v. GERSHMAN

Court of Appeals of Minnesota, 1993
502 N.W.2d 422

ANDERSON, CHIEF JUDGE.

* * *

In 1986, respondents Bruce and Karen Gershman (Gershmans) entered into a contract for deed to sell their condominium to appellant Summit House Co., a Minnesota general partnership consisting of Melvin C. Gittleman and Donald W. Anderson (Summit). The contract required Summit to make a balloon payment on October 31, 1987. On September 10, 1987, with the market value of condominiums declining, Summit sued to terminate the contract. The Gershmans counterclaimed for specific performance of the contract and were awarded summary judgment in the amount of $107,605.25. The district court stated the Gershmans were to convey the property to Summit upon payment of the judgment.

Summit failed to pay the judgment. The Gershmans proceeded to levy execution on Summit's contract for deed vendee's interest in the condominium and purchased that interest for $73,130.18 at a sheriff's sale on February 22, 1991. Summit failed to bid at the sheriff's sale and failed to redeem the condominium within the one-year redemption period provided by Minn.Stat. § 550.25 (1990). On May 14, 1992, Summit moved for an order that the judgment had been satisfied by the sheriff's sale. The district court denied Summit's motion, concluding the execution sale had not canceled the contract.

The district court held the judgment against Summit for $107,605.25 was only partially satisfied by the sheriff's sale of the condominium for $73,130.18, and that Summit still owed the Gershmans $34,475.07, the balance of the judgment. The district court stated there is no reason why the Gershmans should be treated differently from any other creditor. It noted the sheriff's sale was an execution on a money judgment and that Summit had a full year to redeem its contract for deed vendee's interest, but failed to exercise that option. The district court held that Summit would be entitled to a satisfaction of the judgment under Minn.Stat. § 548.15 (1990) as soon as it satisfied the balance of the judgment.

* * *

ISSUE

Did the Gershmans' execution on Summit's contract for deed vendee's interest at a sheriff's sale, after having obtained a judgment for specific performance of the contract for deed, constitute a cancellation of the contract for deed that satisfied the judgment?

* * *

A contract for deed vendor has a choice of remedies when the contract for deed vendee defaults on the contract. Kosbau, 400 N.W.2d at 108. The vendor may either seek specific performance on the contract or may cancel the contract. Id. The doctrine of election of remedies is designed to prevent double recovery for a single wrong, and therefore the vendor cannot seek both specific performance and contract cancellation. Covington v. Pritchett, 428 N.W.2d 121, 124 (Minn.App.1988). A contract can be canceled either by judicial termination or by statutory cancellation under Minn.Stat. § 559.21 (1990). Blythe v. Kujawa, 177 Minn. 79, 224 N.W. 464 (1929); Kosbau, 400 N.W.2d at 108.

The Gershmans chose the remedy of specific performance in response to Summit's attempt to rescind the contract. The district court entered a judgment in favor of the Gershmans' claim for specific performance. By pursuing specific performance to a determinative conclusion, the Gershmans chose not to cancel the contract, but to affirm it. See id.

Summit claims the Gershmans, by executing on Summit's interest in the condominium at the sheriff's sale, obtained all that they were equitably entitled to under the contract for deed. It argues that, because the Gershmans have resold the property, they would be unable to convey title to Summit in the event that Summit satisfied the balance of the judgment. Summit further argues that paragraph 5 of the district court's order of November 30, 1988 requires the Gershmans to convey the condominium to Summit upon payment of the judgment in full. This argument fails because it ignores the sequence of events which led to the execution sale.

Had Summit satisfied the money judgment prior to the sheriff's sale, it would have retained the right to receive title to the condominium. Summit's failure to pay the judgment forced the Gershmans to seek satisfaction of the judgment at an execution sale which netted less than the amount of the judgment. Summit had the opportunity to bid for the condominium at the sheriff's sale and could have exercised its right to redeem the condominium within the statutory period of one year from the date of sale. It failed to pursue either option. Once the execution sale took place in an attempt to satisfy a money judgment and the condominium was not redeemed within the one-year redemption period, the action was taken out of the context of a contract for deed. It then became an action to enforce a money judgment.

Summit argues that because the Gershmans reacquired the property as a result of the sheriff's sale, the contract was canceled and the judgment has been satisfied. We disagree. Summit has provided no authority to support its contention that the sheriff's execution sale, which was to enforce a money judgment against a defaulting buyer on a contract for deed, cancels the contract which formed the basis of the money judgment.

* * *

To hold that the Gershmans' judgment for specific performance was satisfied because they bought the condominium at an open sheriff's sale after Summit refused to satisfy the judgment would be an incongruous result. Such a result would in effect eliminate specific performance as a viable remedy for a contract for deed vendor and eviscerate the election of remedies doctrine. The choice of remedies would be effectively eliminated if the vendor knew that the vendee could simply refuse to pay a money judgment and force the seller to accept the return of the property as full satisfaction of the judgment. Summit asks us to hold, in effect, that cancellation of the contract and the return of the property is the vendor's only remedy against the defaulting vendee. We agree with the district court and refuse to follow that line of reasoning.

* * *

The district court properly denied Summit's motion for an order that the judgment was satisfied by the sheriff's execution sale. * * *

NOTES

1. *The election of remedies doctrine.* Some courts alleviate the harshness of the election of remedies concept by means of their determination of when an election takes place. For example, the Michigan Supreme Court has held that "while the [vendor] may not accept or take possession and still seek money damages, he may, even after sending notice of forfeiture, refuse tender of possession and either commence an action for money damages or for foreclosure of the land contract." Gruskin v. Fisher, 405 Mich. 51, 273 N.W.2d 893 (1979). But see Mazur v. Young, 507 F.3d 1013 (6th Cir. 2007) (guarantors' obligations to vendor did not survive forfeiture—applying Michigan law). For a full explanation of Michigan law, see Mayes v. Mathews, 2011 WL 5964615 (Mich.Ct.App. 2011). See also Kaufman Bros. v. Home Value Stores, Inc., 365 Mont. 196, 279 P.3d 157 (2012) (specific performance unavailable after termination of contract).

Some state statutes ameliorate somewhat the vendor's election of remedies dilemma by authorizing, in certain limited circumstances, the award of damages to the vendor even though a contract termination election has already been made. For example, Ohio Rev.Code § 5313.10 provides that even though a judgment for cancellation of the contract has taken place, a damage award may be entered against the vendee if the latter "has paid an amount less than the fair rental value plus deterioration or destruction of the property occasioned by the vendee's use. In such case the vendor may recover the difference between the amount paid by the vendee on the contract and the fair rental value of the property plus an amount for the deterioration or destruction of the property occasioned by the vendee's use." For a thoughtful analysis see James Geoffrey Durham, Forfeiture of Residential Land Contracts in Ohio: The Need for Further Reform of a Reform Statute, 16 Akron L.R. 397 (1983).

Iowa rejects the election of remedies doctrine, but reaches the same result on the ground that it "flows from the fact that the contract between the parties has been terminated, thereby extinguishing any right to recover the unpaid purchase price." Gray v. Bowers, 332 N.W.2d 323, 325 (Iowa 1983).

Finally, some courts reject the election rule entirely in the installment land contract context and has substituted for it an estoppel concept. Under this approach, "the proper inquiry should be whether the [vendee] has relied on [acts or statements by the vendor] and therefore would be unfairly prejudiced by assertion of a different inconsistent remedy. If so, the [vendor] should be bound to the remedy earlier chosen. * * * Absent estoppel, he should be free to choose a different remedy." Keesee v. Fetzek, 106 Idaho 507, 681 P.2d 600 (App.1984).

2. *Does election of remedies bar the vendor's recovery for waste?* Should an election to enforce forfeiture bar a subsequent attempt by vendor to recover from vendee for physical damage caused to the premises? See Rudnitski v. Seely, 452 N.W.2d 664 (Minn.1990) (election of remedies doctrine barred vendors' action against vendee for waste where contract did not prohibit waste); Hepperly v. Bosch, 172 Ill.App.3d 1017, 123 Ill.Dec. 70, 527 N.E.2d 533 (1988) (after vendors elected forfeiture remedy, they could not recover for damage to the premises for vendees' failure to "maintain, repair and renovate the premises" as required by the contract). But see Voska v. Coffman, 2013 WL 6579576 (Ohio App.2013) (forfeiture and waste recovery permitted under Ohio statute quoted in Note 1, supra). Should the election of remedies concept prevent vendor's post-forfeiture attempt to collect delinquent real estate taxes that vendee was obligated to pay under the contract? For an affirmative answer, see Michigan Nat'l Bank v. Cote, 451 Mich. 180, 546 N.W.2d 247 (1996).

JOHN MIXON, INSTALLMENT LAND CONTRACTS: A STUDY OF LOW INCOME TRANSACTIONS WITH PROPOSALS FOR REFORM AND A NEW PROGRAM TO PROVIDE HOME OWNERSHIP IN THE INNER CITY
7 Houston L.Rev. 523, 545–548 (1970)*

When a buyer finances his purchase by a mortgage, one of the transactional costs covers title search or a title insurance policy guaranteeing that the buyer will get good title to the land. The system of land titles in this country is such that a purchaser cannot easily tell who owns or claims title to the land. Unless he is willing to take the seller's word that title is good, a purchaser must get expert assistance. Failure to

---

*   Reprinted with permission of Houston Law Review.

do so can result in his paying the full purchase price for land and then losing it to a superior claimant.

Although individual middle income purchasers might be willing to take the title risk, or they might lack knowledge about the weakness of the system, their mortgagees are neither willing to take the risk nor do they lack knowledge. Hence, before a mortgagee will lend money for the purchase, the borrower will have to produce a policy of title insurance or other reliable assurance that title is good. The title policy brings title up to date at the time of the sale, and it offers considerable assurance to the buyer that he will be able to keep and enjoy the land which he buys. It also guarantees to the mortgagee that his lien has priority over any other claims.

On the other hand, the low income installment land contract buyer does not know about the need for title insurance, and he would be unlikely to persuade his seller to pay for a policy or for a title search. Without title insurance or other protection, the installment purchaser runs the risk that the seller's title is no good. In the case of older housing which the vendor may have bought as a purely speculative venture, this risk can be very high. On the other hand, title to a large tract of land which the seller puts together as a new housing development is likely to be good into the seller, but it will probably have another defect, that of development cost financing.

When an installment land seller puts together a subdivision, he borrows money to finance both his purchase and construction of the houses he plans to sell. His mortgagee will probably require a title insurance policy or other means of title assurance be provided. Even without the mortgagee's insistence, the developer would be knowledgeable enough to get good title to the land. The contract vendee in a large scale development therefore probably need not worry too much about title into his vendor. Title out of the vendor, however, is another matter. The vendor will develop the subdivision, and build his houses with money borrowed from a mortgagee. He will plan to sell the houses on contracts and use the cash flow from contract receipts to pay off the purchase price and construction mortgages. If the payoff occurs as indicated, the vendee may indeed get good title because the vendor's debt will eventually be extinguished. However, if the subdivision does not succeed, all contract vendees may lose their entire investment. This will occur if the vendor does not get enough cash flow in receipts from his sales to make his payments, or if he pockets the cash and skips town. In either event, the mortgagee will foreclose. Because the mortgagee's rights are prior in time to the rights of the contract vendees, they will lose their rights or claims in the foreclosure, whether they are current on their payment or not.*

Another title problem which can plague an installment contract vendee is the operation of the real property recording act. When a buyer purchases under a mortgage-financed transaction, his deed is immediately recorded to show he has claim to the land. The public record protects the buyer from anyone who might later deal with the former owner. However, if the buyer's claim is not recorded, a later purchaser who takes a deed from the former owner may cut off the interest of the first (unrecorded) purchaser. Installment land contracts are virtually never recorded. Thus, the vendee's claim is vulnerable to a later purchaser from the vendor. Although in the study area, the vendee's possession would give him legal protection against a subsequent purchaser, the conflict presented by such a conveyance almost certainly would require a lawsuit to establish that the vendee had good title. The reason for lack of recordation of installment contracts is that the vendor anticipates the vendee probably will miss a payment, and the property will eventually be repossessed. In that situation the vendor will not want any indication on the record that there was once an installment contract to a prior claimant. If the record title is clear (that is, if the installment contract has not been recorded), the only concern a vendor has is evicting the defaulting vendee from the land. This he usually is able to do either by threats or by the tenant eviction procedure. The vendor then has clear record title which he can convey or contract to sell to some new buyer.

Even if an installment vendee were willing to spend the money to have a title search made, he could not protect himself from most of the potential title difficulties under an installment land contract. For example, the vendee would still run the risk that his seller might go bankrupt, suffer a tax lien, or make title questionable by conveying to a subsequent purchaser. The title search would, of course, turn up prior liens which the vendor had placed on the property, and it would show whether the base title into the seller was good.

NOTES

1.   *When must the vendor perfect the title?* Suppose the vendor does not have marketable title at the time the contract is entered into. Is the vendor in default if the title is defective? The usual view is that the vendor has no duty to perfect the title until the vendee makes the final payment. See Weeks v. Rowell, 289 Ga.App. 507, 657 S.E.2d 881 (2008); Luette v. Bank of Italy, 42 F.2d 9 (9th Cir.1930). But consider Marlowe Inv. Corp. v. Radmall, 26 Utah 2d 124, 485 P.2d 1402, 1403 (1971):

---

*   Does this depend on when the contracts were entered into?

It is true that ordinarily such a vendor does not necessarily have to have marketable title until the purchaser has made his payments. Nevertheless, if it plainly appears that he has so lost or encumbered his ownership or his title that he will not be able to fulfill his contract, he cannot insist that the purchaser continue to make payments when it is obvious that his own performance will not be forthcoming.

2. *Clearing the vendor's title after a forfeiture.* Installment land contracts may also pose title problems of a sort for the vendor. Suppose we are in a state that does not have a statutory non-judicial method for terminating a contract vendee's interest. Suppose further that the vendee records his contract and then goes into default. Even assuming that a court will find that forfeiture is valid under the circumstances, as a practical matter it will take a judicial proceeding to make that determination. The reason is that most title examiners will not accept title for a subsequent purchaser on the mere affidavit from the vendor that the vendee has defaulted under the contract. Absent some type of valid release by the vendee, the title is clouded to such an extent that a judicial action may be necessary. In this situation, even a vendee with little or no equity has enough bargaining position to demand something of a *quid pro quo* from the vendor. See Nelson, Whitman, Burkhart & Freyermuth, Real Estate Finance Law § 3.33 (6th ed.2014).

Many vendors seek to avoid the above predicament by making sure that the contract is not recordable. This is attempted by not providing for an acknowledgment of the parties' execution of the contract. Some vendors, according to Professor Warren, will include a contractual provision which states "that the agreement is avoided upon recording the contract. It is doubtful that this clause is effective to attain anything more than the hostility of the judge who has to interpret the contract." Warren, California Installment Land Sales Contracts: A Time for Reform, 9 U.C.L.A.L.Rev. 609, 629 (1962).

Vendees frequently attempt to overcome the foregoing obstacles by recording an affidavit or notice that incorporates the essential terms of the contract, including the legal description, parties, and the important terms. Such a document contains vendee's signature and acknowledgment only. In addition, some vendees record an acknowledged "assignment" of interest in the contract to a straw party. While the above recording tactics or some variant thereof often puts a practical cloud on the vendor's interest, jurisdictions may differ as to whether such recording constitutes valid constructive notice to subsequent persons whose interests arise through the vendor. See Coggins v. Mimms, 373 So.2d 964 (Fla.App.1979) (recording of an affidavit by vendee reciting the existence of agreements to convey land to vendee held not an instrument entitled to recordation as constructive notice to other potential buyers because of the absence of an acknowledgment by the vendors).

Iowa has legislation requiring that residential installment land contract vendors record their contracts within 180 days of signing. Failure to record will result in daily fines and loss of the right to enforce forfeiture provisions in such contracts. Iowa Code Ann. § 558.46 et. seq. (1998).

3. *The vendee's possession as notice.* Suppose vendee does not record the contract but takes possession of the real estate. To what extent is the vendee protected against subsequent liens arising through the vendor? As Professor Mixon suggests, possession by the vendee normally will prevent such a lien from attaching to the vendee's interest. See, e.g., Hentges v. P.H. Feely & Son, Inc., 436 N.W.2d 488 (Minn.App.1989) ("Possession by a vendee under a contract for deed operates as full notice of his rights to creditors of the vendor."). However, in a few states, possession can only provide *actual* and not constructive notice, so that a mortgagee or judgment creditor of the vendor who acquires her interest without actual knowledge of the vendee's interest, may take free and clear of the vendee's interest. See, e.g., Drey v. Doyle, 99 Mo. 459, 12 S.W. 287 (1889); Note, 16 Mo.L.Rev. 142 (1951).

4. *Installment contract purchase subject to a blanket mortgage.* Suppose you represent a potential installment land contract vendee who desires to purchase a lot from a developer. Suppose, further, that there is a blanket first mortgage on the subdivision, and the lot in question is not released from the lien of the blanket mortgage when the contract is entered into. Can the vendee be protected in the event the first mortgage is foreclosed? What would you advise?

5. *Use of deeds in escrow.* Vendors frequently attempt to avoid the uncertainty and pro-vendee implications of the foregoing case law and attendant title problems by utilizing a deed in escrow. Under this procedure, the vendee, at the time of the execution of the installment land contract, delivers to an escrow agent an executed quitclaim deed to the real estate. If vendee defaults, the vendor notifies the escrow agent of termination of the contract, and the latter, pursuant to the escrow agreement, records the deed. From the vendor's perspective this approach presumably terminates the vendee's contract rights and clears up any title problems occasioned by vendee's recording of the contract. Is this a sensible solution for vendors? To what extent is the "anti-clogging" doctrine we studied earlier in this chapter relevant to this problem? See Nelson, Whitman, Burkhart & Freyermuth, Real Estate Finance Law § 3.31 (6th ed. 2014).

6. *Bankruptcy of a party to the contract.* When either vendor or vendee goes into bankruptcy prior to the conveyance of legal title to the vendee, it can have important consequences for the other party. Because they are better understood in the context of a more extensive consideration of the impact of the Bankruptcy Code on real estate security, such problems are explored in Chapter 6, Section J infra. As to the effect on the vendee of federal tax liens against the vendor, see Nelson, Whitman, Burkhart & Freyermuth, Real Estate Finance Law § 3.33 (6th ed. 2014); William T. Plumb, Federal Tax Liens 73 (3rd ed. 1972).

As a vendee pays off the installments under the contract and particularly if the land increases in value, the vendee's interest can become a significant economic asset. For example, suppose vendee's original contract balance was $100,000 and now it has been paid down to $50,000. Assuming the land is worth $150,000, vendee has a $100,000 equity in it. Suppose vendee needs to send her son or daughter to college. Will she be able to borrow the college tuition by using her vendee's interest as security for the loan? Fortunately for her, virtually all cases hold that her interest is mortgageable. See Nelson, Whitman, Burkhart & Freyermuth, Real Estate Finance Law § 3.35 (6th ed. 2014). Note that functionally a mortgage on the vendee's interest is the economic equivalent of a second mortgage because the vendor holds an interest analogous to a first purchase money mortgage on the land.

NOTES

1. *Protecting the vendee's mortgagee from forfeiture or foreclosure by the vendor.* While it may be well and good to know that the vendee's interest is mortgageable, this fact is of little benefit to vendee's mortgagee unless it has some way to protect itself against a vendor's declaration of forfeiture. The cases provide some measure of protection for the mortgagee. Almost all cases, for example, hold that where a vendor has actual knowledge of the vendee's mortgagee, he cannot invoke forfeiture of the contract without giving the vendee's mortgagee "notification of intent to forfeit and an opportunity to protect himself." See e.g., Credit Fin., Inc. v. Bateman, 135 Ariz. 268, 660 P.2d 869 (App.1983); Fincher v. Miles Homes of Missouri, Inc., 549 S.W.2d 848 (Mo.1977); Yu v. Paperchase Partn., 114 N.M. 635, 845 P.2d 158 (1992).

Suppose, however, that the vendor has no actual knowledge of the mortgagee's interest, but the mortgage has been recorded. The Washington Supreme Court held that under such circumstances there is no duty to notify the mortgagee of the vendor's intent to terminate the contract. See Kendrick v. Davis, 75 Wash.2d 456, 452 P.2d 222 (1969). Accord: Dirks v. Cornwell, 754 P.2d 946 (Utah App.1988); Shindledecker v. Savage, 96 N.M. 42, 627 P.2d 1241 (1981). However, subsequent Washington legislation requires that notice "shall be given to each person who at the time the notice to forfeit is recorded has recorded [in the county in which the property is located." West's Rev.Code Wash. 61.30.040 (3). Which approach is preferable? Consider, in this regard, the following argument:

> The better policy would be to protect the mortgagee's interest if the mortgage has been recorded. If the burden of providing actual notice to the vendor is placed on the mortgagee and the mortgagee fails to prove such notice, his rights will be lost. As one commentator pointed out: "It would be far more equitable to place a burden of notification on the party who seeks to extinguish the

rights of another completely, than to penalize for failure to give notice one who seeks only the opportunity to perform obligations under the contract." There are other reasons why the constructive notice rule would be preferable. When a vendor seeks forfeiture he usually consults an attorney. Mortgagees, however, quite commonly give and record mortgages without the benefit of counsel. The vendor's lawyer would have knowledge of a constructive notice rule and would search the record for potential mortgages. A mortgagee acting alone would lose his interest in the land by relying on the commonly accepted tenet that recording provides protection. Adoption of the actual notice rule would reward ignorance. A vendor who did not search the public record would be in a better position than one who checked the record and discovered the mortgage.

Note, Mortgages—Mortgage of a Vendee's Interest in an Installment Land Contract—Mortgagee's Rights Upon Default, 43 Mo.L.Rev. 371, 373–374 (1978).*

2.   *The rights of the vendee's mortgagee.* When a forfeiture occurs under circumstances where prior notice to the mortgagee is required, courts find that the rights of the mortgagee remain unimpaired. There can be substantial disagreement, however, as to what those rights are. Some courts indicate that the mortgagee can acquire title to the land, free and clear of all liens, simply by paying the vendor the balance due under the installment land contract. As a result the mortgagee acquires the title without going through the usual process of purchasing it at his own foreclosure sale. See e.g., First Mortg. Corp. of Stuart v. deGive, 177 So.2d 741 (Fla.App.1965); Shindledecker v. Savage, 96 N.M. 42, 627 P.2d 1241 (1981). Does this approach overcompensate the mortgagee? If we treat the vendor as a functional equivalent of a first mortgagee, shouldn't the vendee's mortgagee's rights be analogous to those of a second mortgagee? In other words, if the mortgagee is not provided with notice of a contract forfeiture, should its rights be analogous to those of an omitted lienor (second mortgagee) in a judicial foreclosure proceeding? See Note, Mortgages—Mortgage of a Vendee's Interest in an Installment Land Contract—Mortgagee's Rights Upon Default, 43 Mo.L.Rev. 371, 374–376 (1978); Nelson, Whitman, Burkhart & Freyermuth, Real Estate Finance Law § 3.32 (6th ed.2014). Because the rights of an omitted lienor entail highly complex and difficult concepts that are covered in detail later in this volume, it is probably preferable to defer further consideration until you reach that point. However, for those who wish to pursue the matter now, see Chapter 6, Section C infra.

3.   *Documents to be used in mortgaging the vendee's interest.* What type of documents typically are used to mortgage a vendee's interest? Because lenders are often unclear about the nature of the vendee's interest and because the law governing installment land contracts varies so significantly from state to state, there are a wide variety of security devices in use.

---

* Reprinted with permission of the Missouri Law Review.

Unfortunately, many lenders employ a variety of problematic and nonstandard devices. Some simply may use an "assignment of purchaser's interest for security purposes." Here it is apparent from the face of the document that the "assignment" represents a mortgage on the vendee's interest. Other lenders, however, attempt to disguise the true nature of the transaction by characterizing it as a sale rather than a mortgage of the vendee's interest. As a result, they may take from the vendee both an assignment (containing no security language) and a quitclaim deed. They assume that, in the event of vendee default, recording the quitclaim deed will obviate the need for foreclosure. However, as we have seen earlier in this Chapter, both the "clogging" and "absolute deed as mortgage" doctrines can be used to defeat such attempts to avoid mortgage law. Moreover, because power of sale language will invariably be absent from the documents in each of the foregoing nonstandard approaches to vendee financing, lenders will be required to use costly and time-consuming judicial foreclosure to enforce their security interests.

Prudent lenders instead will use standard financing forms such as a mortgage or a deed of trust to effectuate a security interest in the vendee's interest. Moreover, where local law permits, they make sure the forms contain a power of sale to obviate the need for judicial foreclosure in the event of vendee default.

4. *Prohibition on assignment by the vendee.* An installment land contract may purport to deny the vendee the power to assign or mortgage his or her interest without the vendor's consent. Such a provision is conceptually similar to so-called "due-on-sale" or "due-on-encumbrance" clauses in mortgages, discussed at Chapter 5, Section B infra. The courts tend to construe such prohibitions on assignment very narrowly. See, e.g., Murray First Thrift & Loan Co. v. Stevenson, 534 P.2d 909 (Utah 1975) (prohibition on "assignment" did not disable the vendee from assigning, but merely gave rise to an action for damages; in any event, the prohibition did not apply to a collateral or security assignment, as distinct from an outright assignment). Such a prohibition may even be struck down as an unreasonable restraint on alienation. See, e.g., Terry v. Born, 24 Wash.App. 652, 604 P.2d 504 (1979) (where contract prohibited both assignment and prepayment, so that vendee could not transfer the land either subject to or free of the contract, an unreasonable restraint on alienation existed).

CASCADE SECURITY BANK V. BUTLER

Supreme Court of Washington, 1977
88 Wash.2d 777, 567 P.2d 631

BRACHTENBACH, ASSOCIATE JUSTICE.

The issue here is whether the interest of a real estate contract purchaser constitutes "real estate" within the meaning of the judgment lien statutes, RCW 4.56.190 and 4.56.200. Those statutes provide:

RCW 4.56.190:

> The *real estate* of any judgment debtor, and such as he may acquire, not exempt by law, shall be held and bound to satisfy any judgment of the district court of the United States rendered in this state, any judgment of the supreme court, court of appeals, or superior court of this state, and any judgment of any justice of the peace rendered in this state * * * .

(Italics ours.)

* * *

We hold, prospectively, that judgments are liens upon the interest of a real estate contract purchaser within the meaning of those statutes. This holding, at long last, constitutes the demise of Ashford v. Reese, 132 Wash. 649, 233 P. 29 (1925).

The facts are that in 1968 the judgment debtors (defendants) became contract vendees of real estate. In March of 1973 the plaintiff obtained a judgment against those vendees-defendants who were then in possession of the property with their contract in good standing. Ten days later, for good consideration, the vendees' interest was assigned to third parties who are not involved here. Some months later the then vendees-assignees assigned their interest to the respondent-intervenors, who are now the holders of the contract vendees' interest. Almost a year after the present contract vendees-respondent intervenors acquired all of the vendees' interest in the contract, the judgment creditor-plaintiff applied for a writ of execution on the judgment and against the vendees' interest. The sheriff executed and published notice of sale. The respondents intervened. The trial court granted their motion for summary judgment and enjoined the sale.

The trial court based its decision in favor of the contract vendees upon Ashford v. Reese, supra, wherein we said at page 650, 233 P. at page 29:

> [A]n executory contract of sale in this state conveys no title or interest, either legal or equitable, to the vendee * * * .

If the holding of Ashford v. Reese, supra, were still the law, the contract vendee did not hold a real estate interest within the scope of the judgment lien statute. It would follow that the judgment debtor's interest was not subjected to the automatic lien when the judgment was entered and, because the debtor's interest had been assigned to another before execution, that interest was free from the lien. We overrule Ashford v. Reese, supra, but only prospectively, and therefore affirm.

From its inception the doctrine of Ashford v. Reese, supra, has been criticized. Schweppe, Rights of a Vendee Under an Executory Forfeitable

Contract for the Purchase of Real Estate: A Further Word on the Washington Law, 2 Wash.L.Rev. 1 (1926); Oles, The Vendor-Purchaser Relationship in Washington, 22 Wash.L.Rev. 110 (1947). Despite our failure to specifically overrule *Ashford,* we have distinguished it in so many ways that its sweeping language has become virtually meaningless.

We have identified the vendee's interest as "substantial rights", as a "valid and subsisting interest in property", as a "claim or lien" on the land and as rights "annexed to and * * * exercisable with reference to the land." Oliver v. McEachran, 149 Wash. 433, 438, 271 P. 93 (1928) * * * .

These characterizations are patently at odds with the *Ashford* language. Additionally, we have held the vendee to have certain rights totally inconsistent with the concept that a vendee has no title or interest, legal or equitable. For example, we have held [citations omitted] that: a vendee may contest a suit to quiet title; under the traditional land sale contract, the vendee has the right to possession of the land, the right to control the land, and the right to grow and harvest crops thereon; a vendee has the right to sue for trespass; a vendee has the right to sue to enjoin construction of a fence; a vendee's interest constitutes a mortgageable interest; a vendee is a necessary and proper party for purposes of a condemnation proceeding; a vendor's interest for inheritance tax purposes is personal property; a vendor's interest for purposes of succession and administration is personal property; a vendee may claim a homestead in real property; a vendee is a real property owner for attachment purposes.

Specifically we here hold that a real estate contract vendee's interest is "real estate" within the meaning of the judgment lien statute. Other jurisdictions have so held, for example, Mutual Bldg. & Loan Ass'n v. Collins, 85 N.M. 706, 516 P.2d 677 (1973), and Fridley v. Munson, 46 S.D. 532, 194 N.W. 840 (1923).

We are urged to embrace the doctrine of equitable conversion as the proper characterization of the respective interests of the vendor and vendee. That is a theory by which the vendee's interest is at once converted into real property and the vendor's interest is strictly personal property. It is premised upon the maxim that equity regards that as done which ought to be done. 2 S. Spencer, Pomeroy's Equity Jurisprudence §§ 370–372, pages 31–33 (5th ed. 1941). To adopt that doctrine would merely substitute a new set of uncertainty for the confusion which has followed *Ashford*.

It is true that many jurisdictions have adopted it. It cuts a wide swath for it is deemed applicable to contracts, devolution, wills and trusts. It is the uncertainty of the doctrine which is of concern to us. Its application theoretically depends upon the intent of the parties. Parr-Richmond Indus. Corp. v. Boyd, 43 Cal.2d 157, 272 P.2d 16 (1954);

Atkinson v. VanEchaute, 236 Ark. 423, 366 S.W.2d 273 (1963). Some states do not favor it. In re Shareff's Estate, 143 Pa.Super. 465, 17 A.2d 623 (1941). Its nebulous character is evidenced by those decisions which hold that it applies only when necessity and justice require it, or that it applies only to the extent necessary to accomplish equity. National Bank of Topeka v. Saia, 154 Kan. 740, 121 P.2d 251 (1942); Chicago v. Salinger, 384 Ill. 515, 52 N.E.2d 184 (1943). It has been held that the parties may contract away application of the doctrine. Eade v. Brownlee, 29 Ill.2d 214, 193 N.E.2d 786 (1963).

Wisconsin has applied the doctrine for more than a century. After an analysis of that jurisdiction's case law, a law review writer concluded:

In Wisconsin, the doctrine seems to have served more to confuse than to clarify the law.

* * * [T]he history of equitable conversion in Wisconsin indicates that perhaps the law would be simpler and clearer, as well as more responsive to the individual issues and policies raised in each case, if reference to the doctrine were eliminated altogether.

Church, Equitable Conversion in Wisconsin, 1970 Wis.L.Rev. 404, 429.

The eminent Dean (and later Chief Justice) Harlan F. Stone has said:

Most of the difficulties and perplexities which attend the disposition of rights arising under contracts from the sale of land would never have arisen had this fiction never been invented.

Stone, Equitable Conversion by Contract, 13 Colum.L.Rev. 369, 388 (1913).

To base our decision upon this fiction would embark us upon a case-by-case determination of the boundaries of the doctrine in this State. Rather we are content to limit ourselves to the pertinent issue at hand, which is to overrule Ashford v. Reese, supra, and declare that a vendee's interest is real estate within the meaning of the judgment lien statutes. It is apparent from our many cases cited above that we have defined and classified the interests of vendors and vendees for a variety of purposes. That body of case law is based upon a realistic examination of the nature of the interest in a particular context. We need not adopt a fiction to buttress the rationale of those cases or the present one.

* * *

* * * Nevertheless, we are satisfied that to permit unlimited retroactive effect of the overruling of Ashford v. Reese could conceivably produce in some instances unnecessary hardship and injustice.

Accordingly, we hold that our decision here will apply prospectively only * * * .

* * *

WRIGHT, C.J., and STAFFORD, ROSELLINI and DOLLIVER, JJ., concur.

NOTES

1. *Is the vendee's interest real estate?* Most courts hold that a vendee's interest is real estate for purposes of judgment lien legislation and that a lien arises on that interest as soon as the judgment is docketed or recorded. See Nelson, Whitman, Burkhart & Freyermuth, Real Estate Finance Law § 3.36 (6th ed. 2014). See also In re Griffin, 397 B.R. 356 (Bankr.W.D.Va. 2008) (in Virginia, a judgment lien attaches to a vendee's equitable interest regardless of whether he also possesses legal title). However, there is some case law that holds that a judgment lien does not attach to equitable interests in real estate and, accordingly, that a vendee's interest, being equitable, is not subject to the lien. See Annot., 1 A.L.R.2d 717.

2. *The impact of a judgment against the vendee.* Witt executed an installment land contract as vendee. Thereafter Bank obtained a judgment against Witt. Witt then assigned his interest in the contract real estate to the Espinozas, who had actual knowledge of the Bank's lien. The Espinozas then made substantial improvements to the real estate. The Bank then filed suit to foreclose its lien. What will a purchaser at the foreclosure sale acquire? Note that if the Espinozas had been fee owners instead of purchasers of a contract vendee's interest, the answer would be clear, for as one early case stated, "no one ever doubted that a mortgage of land bound a house subsequently built upon it * * * ." Hoyle v. Plattsburgh & M.R.R., 54 N.Y. 314 (1873). However, in connection with our facts, consider the approach of the Court of Appeals of New Mexico in Bank of Santa Fe v. Garcia, 102 N.M. 588, 698 P.2d 458 (1985):

> [The Espinozas] do not deny that valid judgment liens have attached to the Witts' interest in the real estate. Relying on *Romero v. State,* 97 N.M. 569, 573, 642 P.2d 172, 176 (1982), however, [they] contend that the liens do not attach to the full value of the property at the time of foreclosure. *Romero* states that "a judgment lien can attach only to whatever interest the debtor has in the property." [They] urge us to limit a "debtor's interest" under these circumstances to the value of payments and improvements made by that debtor, or the amount commonly referred to as his or her "equity." Under [the Espinozas'] definition of a debtor's "interest," the trial court should have determined the amount of the Witts' equity and precluded their judgment lien creditors from reaching any of the proceeds in excess of that amount. While the issue has not been specifically addressed in New Mexico, the answer depends upon the terms and construction of the statute's provisions. 3 R.

Powell, *Powell on Real Property* ¶ 479 (1984). *See generally* Note, *Rights of a Judgment Creditor Against a Vendor or Vendee Following an Executory Contract for the Sale of Land,* 43 Iowa L.Rev. 366 (1958). The case law regarding the relationship between judgment liens and real estate contracts, together with the plain statutory language, indicates that defendants' position is incorrect.

Under a real estate contract, the purchaser holds equitable title, while the seller retains legal title in trust until the contract is paid. A judgment lien against the purchaser attaches to the equitable interest under the contract.

The seller's interest is considered personalty. * * * During the life of a real estate contract any risk of loss or enhancement of value accrues to the purchaser. *MGIC Mortgage Corp. v. Bowen,* 91 N.M. 200, 572 P.2d 547 (1977). In short, when the vendor has not exercised his contractual rights to declare a forfeiture, our cases support recognizing that the debtor's estate in the property is an equitable fee simple, subject to the vendor's lien for the unpaid purchase price. *See generally* III A. Casner, *American Law of Property* ¶ 11.29 (1952). Therefore, because a judgment lien is a lien on the real estate of the debtor from the date of filing of the transcript of judgment, Section 39–1–6, and a purchaser under a real estate contract is treated as the owner of the property, the debtor's interest in the property to which the lien attaches, when he holds equitable title under a real estate contract, is the full value of his estate in the property, not just the amount of his payments and the value of improvements as defendants here contend.

The same result has been reached elsewhere in comparable situations; courts in other jurisdictions have not restricted judgment lien creditors of a mortgagor to the amount of his or her payments and improvements at the date of foreclosure. *Belnap v. Blain,* 575 P.2d 696 (Utah 1978); *Kinney v. Vallentyne,* 124 Cal.Rptr. at 899, 541 P.2d at 539; *Gray v. Stevens,* 5 Utah 2d 361, 302 P.2d 273 (1956). The rule is consistent with the strong public policy in favor of satisfaction of judgments. *See Mutual Building & Loan Association of Las Cruces v. Collins.* The language of *Cochran v. Cutler,* 39 Ill.App.3d 602, 350 N.E.2d 59 (1976), in an analogous situation, is applicable to the Espinozas here. "By failing to make arrangements for the satisfaction of the lien at the time of the conveyance, they took the risk that the property might increase in value and that such increase might be reached by the judgment creditors should they choose to enforce the lien." 39 Ill.App.3d at 609, 350 N.E.2d at 64. Knowing that risk, they contributed to the equity in the property at their peril.

Would the result have been any different if the Espinozas had not had actual knowledge of the judgment lien? On the other hand, a divided Wisconsin appellate court held that a judgment lien on a vendee's interest was terminated after strict foreclosure and when vendees deeded their interest to the vendor. See Republic Bank of Chicago v. Lichosyt, 303 Wis.2d 474, 736 N.W.2d 153 (2007). According to the dissent, "I would have concluded that the distinction between land contracts and mortgages is one of name only. I would have concluded that the trial court erroneously exercised its equitable discretion by holding * * * that the [judgment lien against vendees] did not survive the strict foreclosure." Id. at 171 (dissenting opinion).

3. *Perfection of security interests in vendors' rights under installment contracts.* Suppose a creditor makes a loan, and takes as security the borrower's interest as a vendor under a real estate installment contract. The question arises as to how the creditor should "perfect" this security interest. Perfection is important in two contexts. (1) If the vendor makes a second security assignment to a different creditor, the first creditor will prevail over the second only if the first creditor is "perfected." (2) If the vendor becomes bankrupt after making the security assignment, the trustee in bankruptcy will have the rights of a perfected lien creditor of the bankrupt vendor. See Bankruptcy Code § 544(a). Hence if the creditor taking the security assignment has not perfected, the trustee in bankruptcy will have superior rights to the collateral, and will defeat the creditor.

Prior to 2000, the correct method of perfection was uncertain and the cases were in disarray. Some courts held that the vendor's interest under a real estate installment contract was essentially a personal property asset, and could be perfected simply by filing a financing statement under UCC Article 9. See In re Huntzinger, 268 B.R. 263 (Bkrtcy.D.Kan.2000); In re Northern Acres, Inc., 52 B.R. 641 (Bkrtcy.E.D.Mich.1985); Matter of Equitable Dev. Corp., 617 F.2d 1152 (5th Cir.1980). Other courts held that the primary asset involved was an interest in real property, so that perfection could be accomplished only by recording the security assignment in the local real estate records. See In re Hoeppner, 49 B.R. 124 (Bkrtcy.E.D.Wis.1985); Reardon v. Alsup, 114 N.M. 95, 835 P.2d 811 (1992); In re Shuster, 784 F.2d 883 (8th Cir.1986). Still other courts held that either method was sufficient; see Security Bank v. Chiapuzio, 304 Or. 438, 747 P.2d 335 (1987); or that both methods had to be employed together; see Bullitt, Trustee for Heide v. Mading King County Enters., Inc., 915 F.2d 531 (9th Cir.1990); Southwest Nat'l Bank v. Southworth, 22 B.R. 376 (Bkrtcy.D.Kan.1982). Finally, a group of courts held that the right to the contract payments was a personal property right, perfectable under Article 9, while the right to assert the security interest in the real estate was a real property right, separately perfectable by recording in the real estate records. See In re Freeborn, 94 Wash.2d 336, 617 P.2d 424 (1980). Article 9 was simply unclear on the point, and the law was a mess.

The issue was greatly clarified by Revised UCC Article 9, promulgated in 2000 and adopted by most states in 2001 or 2002. Under Revised § 9–308(e), perfection of a security interest in a right to payment or performance also perfects a security interest in a security interest, mortgage, or other lien on personal or real property securing the right, notwithstanding other law to the contrary.

Consequently one who takes a security interest in a vendor's interest in an installment land contract need not record in the real estate records to be validly perfected. But when and how does a lender to a vendor perfect under the Revised Article 9? Consider carefully the following analysis:

Under the previous version of Article 9, a vendor's interest under an installment contract was a "general intangible" (a sort of catch-all category), and a security interest in it was perfected by filing. In Revised Article 9, the definition of an "account" has been broadened. An "account" is now defined as "a right to payment of a monetary obligation, whether or not earned by performance, * * * *for property* that has been or is to be sold, leased, licensed, or otherwise disposed of." The old definition said "personal property," but the new definition includes a sale of real property. Hence, a vendor's interest in an installment contract is now an "account" rather than a "general intangible."

However, the method of perfecting a security interest in the vendor's interest remains the same. The assignee must file a financing statement unless Revised § 9–309(2) applies. The latter section provides that a security interest in an account is automatically deemed perfected when it attaches if the assignment of the account "does not by itself or in conjunction with other assignments to the same assignee transfer a significant part of the assignor's outstanding accounts or payment intangibles." Otherwise, filing a financing statement is required. Thus, the proper method of perfection depends on whether the account "is a significant part of the assignor's outstanding accounts."

This would seem to create a distinction (for example) between an individual who sold a home on an installment contract, and then pledged his rights to a bank as collateral for a loan, and someone who had sold a number of real estate parcels and then pledged his rights under one of those contracts to the same bank. The bank would arguably need to file in the former case but not the latter. In the first case, the contract in question is the only one the vendor has, so it appears to be a "significant part"—perhaps 100%—of the accounts the vendor has. This seems an odd and unexpected result (for real estate lenders).

On the other hand, the Official Comment [Rev. § 9–309, Official Comment 4] to the above section states that its purpose "is to save from *ex post facto* invalidation casual or isolated assignments— assignments which no one would think of filing. Any person who regularly takes assignments of any debtor's accounts or payment intangibles should file." If the language of the comment, rather than the Code itself, governs, it suggests that the result is the opposite from that described in the last paragraph. Filing would not be required where the vendor sold his or her home, but will be required where the vendor has sold a number of real estate parcels.

What are we to make of the foregoing ambiguity? One thing seems clear—the prudent lender who wants valid security in a vendor's interest will *always* file a financing statement. [If a lender fails to do so,] there may be a slight chance it will be held to have perfected anyway.

Nelson, Whitman, Burkhart & Freyermuth, Real Estate Finance Law 185–186 (6th ed.2014).

Assuming that the secured lender files under Article 9, should it also record an assignment of the vendor's contract interest in the real estate records? From the viewpoint of Article 9, such a recording is unnecessary and irrelevant. But as a practical matter, recording is important and desirable for three reasons:

(1) If the vendor defaults on the debt to the lender, the lender steps into the vendor's shoes, and thereafter the contract purchaser pays off the contract, the lender will need to give the purchaser a fulfillment deed. Unless there is also a recorded assignment to the lender, the lender's fulfillment deed will appear in the public records to be "wild"—i.e., not connected with the preexisting chain of title—and hence the purchaser's title may be considered unmarketable.

(2) If no assignment to the lender is recorded, the original vendor (without informing or consulting the lender) might declare a forfeiture of the land contract on account of the purchaser's default. After the forfeiture, the vendor might purport to make a competing outright sale of the real estate by deed to some other purchaser. A court might well hold that, once the land contract has been forfeited, there is no longer an "account" in existence in UCC terms, and hence Article 9 no longer applies at all. Thus, if the vendor didn't record its assignment in the real estate records, and the subsequent purchaser did record, the subsequent purchaser might prevail over the lender under the normal operation of the recording act.

(3) A third reason the lender should record the assignment in the land records arises if the vendor, after making the assignment, is tempted to collude with the contract purchaser to improperly release the vendor's interest to the purchaser—typically by recording a fulfillment deed. Obviously such a deed is highly improper if the assignee-lender has not consented to it. However, if the land records contain no indication that the assignment exists, it will appear from the records that the fulfillment deed is proper, and

hence that the purchaser now has unencumbered legal title. The purchaser may then enter into a further sale to (or mortgage loan from) a bona fide purchaser. Based on the normal operation of the recording act, there is little doubt that such a BFP will be protected by the courts, and will prevail against the claim of the unrecorded assignee. The only way the assignee can guard against this result is to record the assignment.

See Dale A. Whitman, Transfers By Vendors of Interests in Installment Land Contracts: The Impact of Revised Article 9 of the Uniform Commercial Code, 38 Real Prop., Prob. & Tr. J. 421, 443 (2003); Larry M. Wertheim, Revised Article 9 of the U.C.C. and Minnesota Contracts for Deed, 28 Wm. Mitchell L. Rev. 1483 (2002).

4. *Is the vendor's interest real estate for purposes of judgment liens?* Suppose the lien claimant is a holder of a judgment against the vendor. To what extent should the vendor's interest be treated as personalty in this context? Consider the language of First Sec. Bank of Idaho, Nat'l Ass'n v. Rogers, 91 Idaho 654, 429 P.2d 386 (1967):

> The doctrine of equitable conversion generally does not apply to the facts of [such cases]. The majority rule is that a judgment lien against a vendor after the making of the contract of sale, but prior to making and delivery of the deed, extends to all of the vendor's interest remaining in the land and binds the land to the extent of the unpaid purchase price. Chain O'Mines v. Williamson, 101 Colo. 231, 72 P.2d 265 (1937); Heider v. Dietz, 234 Or. 105, 380 P.2d 619 (1963); May v. Emerson, 52 Or. 262, 96 P. 454 (1908); Heath v. Dodson, 7 Wash.2d 667, 110 P.2d 845 (1941); Annot., 87 A.L.R. 1505 (1933); 30A Am.Jur.Judgments § 505; Simpson, Equitable Conversion, 44 Yale L.J. 559, 575 (1935).

Despite the foregoing, there is a significant body of case law that treats the vendor's lien as personalty for judgment lien purposes. See Nelson, Whitman, Burkhart & Freyermuth Real Estate Finance Law § 3.36 (6th ed.2014).

5. *Vendee vs. holder of judgment lien against vendor.* Suppose the vendee has recorded the contract and has paid a significant amount on the contract. Then two different creditors obtain judgments against the vendor. What are the vendee's rights and obligations vis a vis the vendor and the judgment creditors? A recent Indiana case analyzes this situation as follows:

> [prior case law] * * * teaches that judgment liens entered after [vendee] acquired equitable title to the real estate conferred upon the Lien Holders only such right in the real estate as [vendor] then possessed. This means that the Lien Holders acquired [vendor's] right to receive installment payments from [vendee]. Both parties proceed on the assumption, and the trial court so held, that the Lien Holders' right in this regard was not chargeable to [vendee] unless and until [vendee] became aware of the existence of the liens. [This]

is a reasonable [interpretation of prior case law]. * * * This means that, at a minimum, if [vendee] had made payments to [vendor] after she discovered the existence of the liens, she would have been liable to the Lien Holders for the same amount if [vendor] did not subsequently satisfy his debts to the Lien Holders.

If the law were as [vendor] urges, then [vendee] would have been forced to choose between, on the one hand, breaching the contract and, on the other, making what amounted to double payments * * * for the balance of the contract. It is that harsh scenario that the holding in [prior case law] prevented. Viewed thus, [prior case law] established a procedure for parties such as [vendee] to follow upon discovery of a judgment lien entered against property they are purchasing under an installment contract. Such party should: (1) cease making payments to the seller/judgment debtor; (2) initiate a separate action to resolve questions related to the right to the unpaid balance of the purchase amount; and (3) arrange to pay the balance due under the contract to the court and so notify the court.

Splittorff v. Fehn, 810 N.E.2d 385 (Ind.App.2004).

GRANT S. NELSON, THE CONTRACT FOR DEED AS A MORTGAGE: THE CASE FOR THE RESTATEMENT APPROACH
1998 B.Y.U.L.Rev. 1111, 1164–1166

Advocacy of the judicial adoption of the Restatement approach to contracts for deed clearly should not be interpreted as rejecting the idea that it is socially advantageous for the law to provide a relatively quick and inexpensive mechanism for a land seller to realize on his or her security in the event of default by a purchaser. The availability of such a procedure probably encourages the extension of credit to individuals whose credit-worthiness is so poor that institutional or other third party financing would be unavailable. Indeed, the law has traditionally encouraged the extension of credit by the land sellers in other contexts. For example, under the "purchase money mortgage" doctrine, the vendor and other purchase money mortgagees are given lien priority over other liens or interests previously arising through the purchaser-mortgagor. However, the solution to this need for special incentives to land sellers should not be the contract for deed. In most states this device has proved to be unreliable for the vendor and purchaser alike. Instead, the solution lies within the confines of traditional mortgage law. The first step would be judicial adoption of the Restatement approach. Legislatures may then have to act. In those states that currently permit only foreclosure by judicial action, legislatures should authorize power of sale foreclosure of mortgages and deeds of trust. States that already have nonjudicial foreclosure legislation should amend it to provide special incentives for land seller financing. A dual track foreclosure process could permit quicker foreclosure of a vendor purchase money mortgage where the mortgagor has not satisfied a specified minimum percentage of the original mortgage obligation. Moreover, other mortgagor protections could be modified. For example, in those states that afford mortgagors a statutory redemption period after the foreclosure sale, that redemption right would be unavailable unless the requisite percentage of the mortgage obligation had been satisfied.

The use of contracts for deed in states that have institutionalized the forfeiture remedy by statute pose a more difficult question. In these states, the contract for deed "works"—forfeiture not only is enforced, but it produces a marketable title in the vendor relatively cheaply and efficiently. Why "mess with success?" Why not leave well enough alone? The Minnesota legislation, especially, triggers these questions. It works relatively efficiently. Forfeiture is enforced, but its harshness is ameliorated by giving the purchaser a thirty- or sixty-day period after notice of default to pay arrearages and certain other costs. However, once forfeiture occurs, no post-forfeiture redemption is permitted. This latter feature makes the statute attractive to sellers because a six month redemption period applies to power of sale foreclosure of mortgages. * * *

While it is true that the Minnesota system and others like it work well with respect to the forfeiture remedy, the "third party" problems with the contract for deed are just as serious and perplexing in these states as they are in states that have not institutionalized the forfeiture process. The rights of third party creditors, secured and unsecured, are just as problematic. This is because the contract for deed conceptually is both a contract and financing device, "fish as well as fowl." These problems would be obviated if all states, including Minnesota, returned to a unitary land finance system, with mortgage law and the power of sale mortgage or deed of trust as its foundation. Of course, in states like Minnesota this process cannot begin with a judicial adoption of the Restatement approach. Where the contract for deed is regulated by statute and authorizes forfeiture, absent constitutional deficiencies, courts may not supplant what legislatures have mandated. Rather, the answer in such states lies in the legislature. In Minnesota, for example, the path to a unitary system seems relatively simple. First, the contract for deed termination statute should be repealed. Its substance should be incorporated into that state's power of sale mortgage foreclosure legislation. Thus, land sellers who take back a purchase money mortgage would be able to obtain a nonjudicial foreclosure sale subject to the same notice requirements and the same postdefault grace period now mandated under the current contract for deed termination statute. The same arrearages provisions would be applicable. No postsale redemption would be permitted. Even though the current contract for deed legislation does not distinguish between purchasers who have substantially reduced the contract balance and those who have not, the new "mortgage law" version should make the "fast track" available only when a minimum specified percentage of the mortgage obligation is unpaid. In all other situations, the "normal" power of sale requirements would be triggered, including the current six month post-sale redemption period. The only significant change from current Minnesota contract for deed procedure would be that the defaulting purchaser would have the right to a public foreclosure sale of the property. This public sale and valuation of the land could in some instances result in a surplus for the purchaser-mortgagor. The vendor would not automatically regain the land via forfeiture—he or she would be required to purchase at the sale.

C. THE NEGATIVE COVENANT AS A MORTGAGE

DALE A. WHITMAN, MORTGAGE DRAFTING: LESSONS FROM THE RESTATEMENT OF MORTGAGES
33 Real Prop. Prob. & Tr. J. 415, 429–30 (1998)

Rather than obtaining a mortgage, creditors sometimes require the borrower to covenant not to convey or encumber certain real estate held by the borrower. A creditor may consider covenants not to convey or encumber real estate superior to a mortgage because they are not supposed to be subject to the jurisdiction's antideficiency, one-action, or other similar procedural limitations on recovery against defaulting borrowers.[41] If the creditor, at its option, may later characterize the negative pledge as a mortgage, then it seems to have an opportunity to have its cake and eat it too.[42]

However, under the Mortgages Restatement a negative covenant is not a mortgage.[43] The case law widely agrees.[44] Thus, the covenant cannot be foreclosed. Indeed, whether the creditor has any satisfactory

---

[41] *See* Nelson, Whitman, Burkhart & Freyermuth, Real Estate Finance Law, § 3.39 (6th ed.2014).

[42] *See* John R. Hetland, Secured Real Estate Transactions 73 (1974).

[43] According to the Restatement (Third) of Property (Mortgages) sec. 3.5 (1997), absent "other evidence of intent to create a mortgage, a promise by a debtor to a creditor not to encumber or transfer an interest in real estate does not create a mortgage, equitable lien, or other security interest in that real estate." Only if the promise "is accompanied by specific language of grant or conveyance or by words such as 'mortgage,' 'security,' 'security interest,' 'lien,' or language of similar import to refer to the lender's interest, will extrinsic evidence normally be admissible to establish that a mortgage in real estate was intended." Id., cmt. b.

[44] *See, e.g.*, Chase Manhattan Bank v. Gems-By-Gordon, Inc., 649 F.2d 710 (9th Cir. 1981); Sorran Bank v. United States (*In re* Aumiller), 168 B.R. 811 (Bankr. D.C. 1994); Crystal City State Bank v. Goldstein (*In re* Slover), 71 B.R. 9 (Bankr. E.D. Mo. 1986); *In re* Friese, 28 B.R. 953 (Bankr. D. Conn. 1983); Weaver v. Tri City Credit Bureau, 557 P.2d 1072 (Ariz. Ct. App. 1976); Tahoe Nat'l Bank v. Phillips, 480 P.2d 320 (Cal. 1971); Equitable Trust Co. v. Imbesi, 412 A.2d 96 (Md. 1980); Perpetual Fed. Sav. & Loan Ass'n v. Willingham, 370 S.E.2d 286 (S.C. Ct. App. 1988).

remedy for breach of a negative covenant is unclear. Of course, the creditor may sue for damages if the borrower breached the covenant by conveying or encumbering the real estate. But if the original debt was recourse in nature, a suit for damages adds nothing significant to the creditor's action on the debt.[45] That a court would order specific performance of a negative covenant by literally preventing the borrower from transferring the land is highly unlikely because doing so would require the court to impose a direct and egregious disabling restraint on alienation.[46]

In light of the limited and dubious nature of the remedies available to a lender on a negative pledge, the wisest course is simply not to use them. They are subject to the charge of being too cute. An ordinary mortgage or deed of trust is almost certainly a better choice, regardless of the procedural limitations imposed upon them by local law.

---

[45]   Professor Gilmore stated it as follows:

[t]he debtor's covenant not to encumber property . . . should be treated, as on the whole case law has done, as a covenant "merely personal"—good enough to give rights against the covenantor for breach, to bring an acceleration clause into play, to constitute an "event of default" under a loan agreement, but not good enough to give rights, whether they be called legal or equitable, in property.

Grant Gilmore, Security Interests in Personal Property 1017 (1965).

[46]   The closest any court has come to granting specific performance of a negative covenant is the California Supreme Court's dictum in *Coast Bank v. Minderhout*, 392 P.2d 265, 268 (Cal. 1969), *overruled by Wellenkamp v. Bank of America*, 582 P.2d 970 (Cal. 1978):

Whether the promise not to transfer or encumber the property would be directly [enforceable] by injunction, specific performance or an action for damages is another question. It is open to doubt whether such a promise would be a reasonable restraint when, as in this case, plaintiff had the additional protection of a security interest and the right to declare the entire debt due in the event of default. It is unnecessary, however, to decide this question now.

This is not a ringing endorsement of specific enforcement of the negative covenant.

CHAPTER FOUR

RIGHTS AND DUTIES OF THE PARTIES PRIOR TO FORECLOSURE: SOME PROBLEM AREAS

• • •

A. THEORIES OF TITLE: POSSESSION, RENTS, AND RELATED CONSIDERATIONS

RESTATEMENT (THIRD) OF PROPERTY (MORTGAGES)
§ 4.1, COMMENT a (1997)*

[handwritten: 3 types of mort. law.]

American courts have traditionally recognized one of three theories of mortgage law. Under the title theory, legal "title" to the mortgaged real estate remains in the mortgagee until the mortgage is satisfied or foreclosed; in lien theory jurisdictions, the mortgagee is regarded as owning a security interest only and both legal and equitable title remain in the mortgagor until foreclosure. Under the intermediate theory, legal and equitable title remain in the mortgagor until a default, at which time legal title passes to the mortgagee. * * *

(1) *The title theory.* English legal history is crucial to understanding the title theory. * * * [W]hen the mortgage transaction became the conveyance of a fee on condition subsequent, with defeasance based on performance by the mortgagor on law day, the mortgagee obtained legal title to the land, and, with it, acquired the right to possession and to collect rents and profits. Thus, actual possession became the norm. * * * [U]nder English law at this time, any collection of interest was deemed usurious. Consequently, possession and its access to rents and profits proved to be an economic substitute for interest. Indeed, until the middle of the 17th century the usual practice was for the mortgagee to take possession upon execution of the mortgage; only thereafter did it become common for the mortgagor to be left in possession.

In all probability, the development of mortgagor possession coincided with the creation by equity of the mortgagor's equity of redemption. * * * This was a logical development because, with the acceptance of the mortgagor as the equitable owner of the real estate, there was an implicit

---

recognition that, notwithstanding the mortgagee's legal title, its major interest in the real estate was that of security. With the acceptance of this view, the mortgagee who actually exercised the right to possession was held to strict standards of accountability. Consequently, the exercise of the possessory right became relatively infrequent. Nevertheless, while seldom used, the right to possession was, as it still is in a few states today, a fundamental element of the mortgagee's legal title. As a result, the mortgagee could maintain ejectment against the mortgagor until the mortgage was satisfied * * * .

The American states initially adopted the title theory in substantially the same form it had developed in England. Usually, however, there was an express agreement permitting the mortgagor to stay on the mortgaged real estate. * * * Even without such express agreements, courts often found from the other terms and conditions of the mortgage documents an implicit right in the mortgagor to remain in possession.

Today, however, title jurisdictions differ in only a few respects from their lien theory counterparts. Such states recognize that mortgagees hold title for security purposes only, and for both practical and theoretical purposes they usually view the mortgagor as the owner of the land. * * * In addition, two other developments have placed significant limitations on the title theory. First, statutes in some title states give the mortgagor the right to possession until default. Second, commonly used mortgage forms containing similar provisions achieve the same result.

This is not to say that the title theory is now irrelevant. As legal titleholder, in the absence of agreement to the contrary, the mortgagee has a right to immediate possession against the mortgagor. This right is occasionally asserted after the mortgagor has defaulted and incident to the commencement of foreclosure. Its assertion can be important where a lengthy foreclosure proceeding could mean a substantial period during which mortgagor could divert the rents and profits of the land to purposes other than service of the mortgage obligation. * * * However, these advantages for the title theory mortgagee are more apparent than real, since a lien theory mortgagee is often able to accomplish similar results through the appointment of a receiver or enforcement of an assignment of rents agreement. * * *

(2) *The lien theory.* The substantial majority of American jurisdictions follow the lien theory. Under this theory, the mortgagee acquires only a "lien" on the mortgaged real estate and the mortgagor retains both legal and equitable title and the right to possession until foreclosure or a deed in lieu of foreclosure. Given the early acceptance of the title theory by American courts, the adoption of the lien theory was largely the product of legislation. Some lien theory statutes provide that

the mortgagee is not entitled to maintain a possessory action for the mortgaged real estate; some also state that the "mortgagor shall be deemed to be the owner of the land." Others accomplish the same result by slightly different terminology. Several statutes state that a mortgage shall not be deemed a conveyance so as to allow the mortgagee to obtain possession other than by foreclosure. Identical results usually follow even if a deed of trust, rather than a mortgage, is employed, and likewise where an absolute deed or conditional sale is intended as a security device.

Lien theory jurisdictions have been far from uniform as to the effect of mortgage language that purports to give the mortgagee a right to possession of the mortgaged real estate before foreclosure. While some states enforce such agreements, others invalidate them on the theory that they contravene the public policy in favor of mortgagor possession underlying lien theory statutes. However, where such language is either absent or ineffective, the lien theory means that a mortgagor, prior to foreclosure, may prevail against the mortgagee for any interference with the mortgagor's possession of the mortgaged real estate to the same extent that any owner of land would prevail against a trespasser.

(3) *The intermediate theory.* A few states purport to follow a compromise position between the title and lien theories. Under this "intermediate" approach, the mortgagor is deemed to have legal title until default occurs; after default, legal title passes to the mortgagee. In other words, the mortgagee has the right to possession and to collect rents and profits after mortgagor default. This approach is grounded variously in statutes and case law. Since it is uncommon for title theory mortgagees to assert a right to possession prior to default, in practice the intermediate theory seems to differ, little, if at all, from its title theory counterpart.

NOTES

1. *Classification of states.* At least 32 states follow the lien theory, with the balance adhering either to the title or intermediate theory. The Restatement adopts the lien theory. See Restatement (Third) of Property (Mortgages) § 4.1(a) (1997) ("A mortgage creates only a security interest in real estate and confers no right to possession of that real estate on the mortgagee.").

2. *Mortgagee in possession in lien states.* Even in a lien theory jurisdiction, a mortgagee may sometimes acquire possession of the mortgaged property legally by means other than foreclosure. First, the mortgagee may acquire possession with the consent of the mortgagor. See, e.g., Kelley/Lehr & Assoc., Inc. v. O'Brien, 194 Ill.App.3d 380, 141 Ill.Dec. 426, 551 N.E.2d 419 (1990). Second, a mortgagee who enters into peaceable possession in good faith after purchasing at an invalid foreclosure sale may remain in possession until a valid foreclosure takes place. Finally, where the mortgagor abandons

the mortgaged real estate, the mortgagee's security interest is usually deemed sufficient to permit the mortgagee to take and retain possession until foreclosure. In this setting, public policy clearly supports possession by the mortgagee to protect the abandoned real estate against vandalism and deterioration. Moreover, society is benefited by its productive use. See generally, Nelson, Whitman, Burkhart & Freyermuth, Real Estate Finance Law § 4.24 (6th ed.2014). The Restatement authorizes mortgagee possession in each of the foregoing situations. See Restatement (Third) of Property (Mortgages) § 4.1(c) (1997). Note, however, that the mortgagee's claim to possession must be *qua* mortgagee, by virtue of the security interest. Thus, mortgagee in possession status does not arise where the mortgagee acquires possession as a tenant or agent of the mortgagor.

    3.   *Mortgagee taking possession without judicial process.* The improper taking of possession by a mortgagee can sometimes prove costly. Consider the language of Wheeler v. Community Fed. Sav. & Loan Ass'n, 702 S.W.2d 83 (Mo.App.1985):

> Defendants-appellants Community Federal Savings and Loan Association, Charles W. Noel and David T. Mayhew appeal from an adverse judgment entered on a jury verdict awarding plaintiffs-respondents, Billy J. Wheeler, his wife Mary Wheeler and her daughter, Mary Jo Ridings, $500 actual and a total of $100,000 punitive damages for an intentional unlawful entry into the plaintiffs' home. We affirm.

> At the time of the incident, Community Federal held a note secured by a deed of trust on the plaintiffs' residential property. Also at that time, Community Federal employed Charles Noel as a loan officer. The jury assessed $40,000 and $60,000 punitive damages against Community Federal and Noel, respectively. Daniel Mayhew, a carpenter, actually entered the plaintiffs' home at the direction of Noel.

> Mayhew intentionally entered the plaintiffs' home on January 11, 1982. On the previous day, the Wheelers and Mary Jo Ridings left their home in Macon County, Missouri for Kansas City so Mr. Wheeler could pursue an employment prospect. Mr. Wheeler had been a bulldozer operator with a local coal mining company prior to being laid off in July 1979. During the next two and half years he and his wife worked numerous odd jobs to pay their mortgage and care for Mary Jo who had been confined to a wheelchair with totally debilitating injuries after being injured in an auto accident in 1969. As of January 11, 1982, there were only two mortgage payments in arrears, totaling approximately $727.00.

> On the day of the intentional entry, Mayhew changed the locks on the Wheeler home as he was directed to do by Noel. Defendants maintain that such actions were necessary to "secure the property" from the severe sub-zero winter weather. Furthermore, they claim

their actions stemmed from a belief that the Wheelers had abandoned their home. This belief purportedly resulted from assertions made by Wheelers' neighbors to Noel. At trial, however, these neighbors, Jim Foley and Roger Koll, denied making such assertions to Noel. We note that defendant, Community Federal, had not foreclosed their deed of trust as of January 11, 1982.

Prior to departing for Kansas City, the Wheelers arranged to have their home watched by their nearest neighbors, the Stroppels. They left keys to the house with both the Stroppels and Elmer Kruel, their brother-in-law.

Kruel was supposed to water the plants and fuel the furnace. On January 13, he unsuccessfully attempted to enter the Wheeler home. He subsequently called the Wheelers in Kansas City to inform them that he believed their locks had been changed. * * *

After speaking to Kruel, Mr. Wheeler contacted Jim Foley, the prosecuting attorney for Macon County, to notify him of a possible break-in. An investigation revealed that Mayhew had entered the Wheeler home at the direction of Noel on behalf of Community Federal.

* * *

[D]efendants cite *Pine Lawn Bank and Trust Co. v. M.H. & H. & Inc.,* 607 S.W.2d 696, 700 (Mo.App.1980) which states as a general rule "a mortgagee after default by a mortgagor has the right to possession of the mortgaged premises for the purposes of applying the rent and profits to discharge of the mortgage debts." We agree with defendants that *Pine Lawn* accurately reflects the rights of a mortgagee of a loan in default. However, defendants adduced no evidence indicating their intent to collect any rents and profits from the Wheeler home to discharge the mortgage debt. Moreover, defendants assert as a defense that they acted merely to prevent an impairment of their security by securing the Wheeler home from the severe winter weather.

As to point I(b), defendants' deed of trust contains certain clauses granting defendants a right of entry (after notice to plaintiffs) for "reasonable entries upon and inspection of the property" or "entry upon the property to make repairs." Defendants concede that no actual notice was given to plaintiffs prior to defendants' entry of the premises.

A reasonable entry upon and inspection of the plaintiffs' property would have revealed steam heat vapors coming from the Wheelers' furnace, negativing abandonment of the home. Also, no evidence adduced at trial indicates that the Wheeler home was in a state of disrepair. Defendants' provisions in the deed of trust do not provide them with the right to "secure the property" against inclement weather. Any impairment of their security caused by the harsh winter weather could only have been remedied by an action for waste. *Randolph v. Simpson,* 500 S.W.2d 289, 292 (Mo.App.1973). See also, 59 C.J.S. Mortgages § 334. * * *

The judgment is affirmed.

Is the foregoing decision correct? Is it perhaps implicitly recognizing a "residential-nonresidential" distinction?

4. *Liability of a mortgagee in possession.* Even where the mortgagee has the right to take possession, the decision whether to exercise that right must be influenced by a careful consideration of the rights and liabilities of a mortgagee in possession. For example, mortgagee-in-possession status makes the mortgagee liable in tort "for injuries resulting either through its actionable fault in utilizing the property or by reason of its failure to perform duties imposed by law upon the owner of land." Nelson, Whitman, Burkhart & Freyermuth, Real Estate Finance Law § 4.26, at 211 (6th ed.2014). One court recently held that "where a mortgagee lawfully takes possession * * *, he or she takes the rents received from the use of the premises in the quasi character of trustee or bailiff of the mortgagor." Mandel v. Strickland, 287 A.D.2d 695, 735 N.Y.S.2d 553 (2001). As a result, the mortgagee must operate the property "not only to protect its own interest but also for the benefit of the mortgagor to pay off the debt." In re Dupell, 235 B.R. 783, 792 (Bkrtcy.E.D.Pa.1999). See also Watergate West v. Barclays Bank, S.A., 759 A.2d 169 (D.C.2000); Gasco Corp. v. Tosco Props. Ltd., 236 A.D.2d 510, 653 N.Y.S.2d 687 (1997). In addition, the mortgagee in possession bears a significant responsibility to the mortgagor for maintenance of the mortgaged premises. In this connection, consider the language of the court in New York & Suburban Fed. Sav. & Loan Ass'n v. Sanderman, 162 N.J.Super. 216, 392 A.2d 635 (Ch.Div.1978). In that case, the first mortgagee sought reimbursement for various expenditures it had made in caring for the property while in possession.

> [The mortgagee] urges that under the decisions in Zanzonico v. Zanzonico, 2 N.J. 309, 66 A.2d 530 (1949), cert. den. 338 U.S. 868, 70 S.Ct. 143, 94 L.Ed. 532 (1949); Newark v. Sue Corp., 124 N.J.Super. 5, 7–8, 304 A.2d 567 (App.Div.1973), a mortgagee in possession has a duty to protect against vandalism or be held liable for loss or destruction of the property. It points to the following statement in *Zanzonico:*

>> A mortgagee who goes into possession of the mortgaged lands assumes a grave responsibility for the management and preservation of the property. It is notorious that in Newark untenanted property is apt to be wrecked by vandals. When the tenants in the six-family house vacated the premises on the order of the public authorities [Tenement House Commission— ed.], complainant could have surrendered the house to [mortgagor's] devisee or he could have made the necessary

repairs and alterations and charged the cost against future rents. But he did neither; he allowed the house to remain empty and took inadequate means to protect it. He is liable for the resulting damage. * * * [at 316, 66 A.2d at 533]

A mortgagee who goes into possession is under a duty to maintain and preserve the property. The standard by which the discharge of that duty should be judged is that of a provident owner. Essex Cleaning Contractors, Inc. v. Amato, 127 N.J.Super. 364, 366, 317 A.2d 411 (App.Div.1974), certif. den. 65 N.J. 575, 325 A.2d 709 (1974); * * * . However, until the mortgagee has foreclosed he is not the owner and must act with due regard to the interests of the junior encumbrancers and the holder of the equity of redemption. Shaeffer v. Chambers, 6 N.J.Eq. 548 (Ch.1847); cf. Taylor v. Morris, 1 N.J.Super. 410, 61 A.2d 758 (Ch.Div.1948).

It is suggested in 4 American Law of Property, § 16.100 at 190, that there is a limit on the duty of the mortgagee in possession:

> He must, therefore, conserve its value by making repairs, and this duty is recognized on the one hand by charging him for any loss that flows from his failure to act and, on the other hand, by allowing him credit for expenditures in carrying it out. There are, however, limitations on this. One is that he is not bound to dig into his own pocket and so need not expend more than the rents and profits he receives. Another is that he does not have to make good or prevent the depreciation caused by ordinary wear and tear—"the silent effect of waste and decay from time." Indeed, in casting upon him this duty of affirmative conduct the standard for its invocation is "willful default," "gross negligence," or "recklessness and improvidence," a rather low standard of responsibility whose [sic] mildness is explained by the fact that the mortgagor, the owner, also should look after the upkeep of his own property.

* * *

Judge Bigelow, who wrote the language quoted by the Supreme Court in *Zanzonico,* supra, in essence gave the mortgagee an option either to take possession, expending funds and collecting the expenditures from future rents, or not take possession but proceed quickly to foreclosure and sale of the real property. Under the first alternative the mortgagee, like a provident owner, would have to weigh the probability of collecting rents against the cost of repairs, taxes, insurance and the mortgagor redeeming the property. Under the second the mortgagee could proceed to foreclosure quickly and rely upon the right to collect any deficiency from the mortgagor. In no circumstance was the mortgagee to take possession and then allow the real property to be dissipated before foreclosure. In other words, the mortgagee was under a duty to evaluate what to do in the same manner as a provident owner would do.

For further consideration of this problem, see Myers-Macomber Engrs. v. M.L.W. Constr. Corp., 271 Pa.Super. 484, 414 A.2d 357 (1979); Nelson, Whitman, Burkhart & Freyermuth, Real Estate Finance Law §§ 4.24–4.29 (6th ed.2014).

5.   *Avoiding mortgagee in possession status.* Because of the foregoing responsibilities and liabilities associated with being a mortgagee in possession, mortgagees frequently use other mechanisms, such as receiverships, to gain access to the rents and profits and control over the mortgaged real estate pending foreclosure. We consider these matters in Section B of this Chapter.

DOVER MOBILE ESTATES V. FIBER FORM PRODUCTS, INC.
California Court of Appeal, Sixth District, 1990
220 Cal.App.3d 1494, 270 Cal.Rptr. 183

ELIA, ASSOCIATE JUSTICE.

* * *

In 1985, tenant Fiber Form entered into a five year lease with landlord Old Town Properties, Inc. The lease provided that it was subordinate to any deeds of trust or mortgages placed on the property unless the mortgagee or beneficiary elected to have the lease be superior.

Old Town subsequently encumbered the property with a second deed of trust to Saratoga Savings & Loan Association. Old Town defaulted. Saratoga Savings & Loan foreclosed and, at a December 3, 1986 trustee's sale, Income Property Investments, Inc. (hereafter Dover) purchased the property. Dover knew of Fiber Form's lease before it purchased the property. In fact, the lease was of "supreme importance to its decision to purchase." A trustee's deed was recorded on December 5, 1986.

On December 4, 1986, Dover notified Fiber Form that it had purchased the property. It told Fiber Form to direct future rent payments to Dover's management company. The parties did not enter into a new lease but Fiber Form continued to pay rent per the lease.

On March 9, 1987, Fiber Form and Dover discussed reducing the monthly rental. The discussion was prompted by a downturn in Fiber Form's business. Fiber Form allegedly advised Dover that the foreclosure extinguished the lease and contended that it was operating under a month to month lease. Dover denies that such notice occurred but alleges that Fiber Form requested a one-year delay in the rent increase scheduled to take effect, pursuant to the lease, on May 1, 1987. Dover offered to delay the increase if Fiber Form extended the lease an additional year. This proposal was never accepted.

On June 1, 1987, Fiber Form gave Dover 30 days written notice of its intent to vacate. Fiber Form subsequently vacated the premises and stopped paying rent.

Dover filed suit against Fiber Form for rent and conversion. The trial court determined that the trustee's sale terminated the lease and entered judgment for Fiber Form in the action to recover rent. Costs for attorney's fees in the amount of $7,255.95 were awarded to Fiber Form. This appeal ensued.

* * *

Fiber Form argues that it became a month to month tenant after the trustee's sale because the sale extinguished the lease. Dover, on the other hand, contends that the lease was not terminated but was ratified because Fiber Form continued to pay rent after the trustee's sale. For reasons we shall state, we conclude that the trustee's sale extinguished the lease so that Fiber Form became a month to month tenant, thereby allowing Fiber Form to terminate on 30 days notice.

Title conveyed by a trustee's deed relates back to the date when the deed of trust was executed. (*Bank of America v. Hirsch Merc. Co.* (1944) 64 Cal.App.2d 175, 184, 148 P.2d 110.) The trustee's deed therefore passes the title held by the trustor at the time of execution. (*Hohn v. Riverside County Flood Control etc. Dist.* (1964) 228 Cal.App.2d 605, 612, 39 Cal.Rptr. 647.) Liens which attach after execution of the foreclosed trust deed are extinguished. The purchaser at the trustee sale therefore takes title free of those junior or subordinate liens. (*Id.* at p. 613, 39 Cal.Rptr. 647; *Carpenter v. Smallpage* (1934) 220 Cal. 129, 133, 29 P.2d 841; see generally, Mortgage & Deed of Trust Practice, (Cont.Ed.Bar, 2d ed. 1990) pp. 90–92.)

A lease is generally deemed to be subordinate to a deed of trust if the lease was created after the deed of trust was recorded. (*Bank of America v. Hirsch Merc. Co., supra,* 64 Cal.App.2d at p. 184, 148 P.2d 110; Miller & Starr, Cal.Real Estate 2d; § 8:82, p. 422.) On the other hand, "when the lease was executed and recorded prior to the recordation of the deed of trust, or if the beneficiary of the deed of trust had notice of an unrecorded lease at the time the trust deed was recorded, the lien of the trust deed is junior to the estate of the lessee. * * *" (Miller & Starr, Cal.Real Estate 2d; § 8:82, p. 422, fn. omitted.)

A lease may also be deemed subordinate by virtue of a subordination agreement. (See e.g. *Tanner v. Title Insurance & Trust Co.* (1942) 123 P.2d 497, 500, mod. 20 Cal.2d 814, 129 P.2d 383; *Bank of America v. Hirsch Merc. Co., supra,* 64 Cal.App.2d at p. 182, 148 P.2d 110; *Security-First Nat. Bank v. Marxen* (1938) 28 Cal.App.2d 446, 453, 82 P.2d 727; Civ.Code, § 2934.) "Subordination agreements are often used to adjust the priorities between commercial tenants and the mortgagee of the real estate, * * * Absent such an adjustment, priorities will be governed by the recording acts and related common law principles." (Nelson & Whitman, Real Estate Finance Law (2d ed. [Lawyer's Ed.] 1985) § 15.11, p. 1114.)

A lease which is subordinate to the deed of trust is extinguished by the foreclosure sale. (*Bank of America v. Hirsch Merc. Co., supra,* 64 Cal.App.2d at p. 182, 148 P.2d 110; *Dugand v. Magnus* (1930) 107 Cal.App. 243, 247, 290 P. 309; *McDermott v. Burke* (1860) 16 Cal. 580, 590; Miller & Starr, Cal.Real Estate 2d; § 8:82, p. 422–424.) A foreclosure proceeding destroys a lease junior to the deed of trust, as well as the lessee's rights and obligations under the lease. (Nelson & Whitman, Real Estate Finance Law (2d ed. [Lawyer's Ed.] 1985) § 15.11, p. 1114.) As stated in section 15.1 of the Restatement Second of Property, "[i]f the sale of the landlord's interest is forced by one having a paramount title to that of the tenant, such as a mortgagee whose interest existed at the time the lease was made, the tenant's interest will be defeated by the sale." (*Id.* at p. 90.)

In this case the lease itself provides that it is subordinate to the deed of trust. Section 21.1 provides, "[t]enant agrees that this Lease shall be subordinate to any mortgages or deeds of trust * * * that may hereafter be placed upon the premises, * * *" Although section 21.1 does give the mortgagee or beneficiary the option to elect "to have this Lease superior to its mortgage or deed of trust * * *", that option was never exercised. Accordingly, it is clear that the lease is subordinate to the deed of trust and was therefore extinguished by the trustee's sale.

* * *

We find no reason to question the continued validity of this rule. The fact that foreclosure terminates a subordinate lease comports with basic notions of priorities and notice. If the trust deed is recorded before the lease is created, then the tenant enters into the lease with notice that the lease will be subordinate. Alternatively, if the tenant and landlord expressly agree that the lease should be subordinate, as is the case here, then the tenant is aware of the possibility that its lease could be extinguished by foreclosure. Indeed, Fiber Form expressly agreed that the lease was subordinate to any trust deeds and therefore it risked having foreclosure terminate the lease. That Fiber Form, rather than Dover, ultimately desired that the lease be terminated upon foreclosure should be of no import.

Dover argues that foreclosure should not automatically terminate the lease but should give the purchaser the option of terminating it. However, if this were the rule, then the purchaser could evict the tenant if rent values increased or hold the tenant to the lease if rent values decreased. In other words, the purchaser could do whatever was most profitable. We decline to allow the purchaser this option. To the contrary, we think it more equitable to follow the rule that the trustee's sale automatically terminates the lease. Of course, even though the lease is extinguished, the tenant and purchaser are not precluded from entering into a new lease agreement.

Finally, we note that the tenant under a subordinate lease can obtain some protection by requiring the landlord to obtain from its lender a nondisturbance agreement in favor of the tenant. Such an agreement provides that the lender with a superior lien will not, "by foreclosure or otherwise, disturb the tenant's possession, as long as the tenant is not then in default under the lease." (Johnson & Moskovitz, Cal.Real Estate Law & Practice, § 153.50, p. 153–94.) In addition, the tenant could bargain with its landlord for the right to cure the landlord's default. (*Ibid.*)

We next consider what Fiber Form's status was once the lease was terminated. Did Fiber Form become a tenant under a new lease agreement? There was evidence that in March 1987 Fiber Form notified Dover that it had been advised by counsel that the foreclosure extinguished the lease and therefore it was operating under a month to month tenancy. In addition, there was evidence that Dover believed the prior lease continued in effect after the foreclosure sale and, as a consequence, Dover did not attempt to obtain a new lease. We conclude that the foregoing constitutes substantial evidence in support of the trial court's conclusion that the parties did not enter into a new lease.

Having determined that no new lease agreement was reached, we conclude that Fiber Form was a month to month tenant. The prior lease was extinguished and a new lease was not entered into. Fiber Form paid rent monthly, with Dover's consent, but there was no agreement reached regarding the term of the hiring. Accordingly, Fiber Form must be deemed a month to month tenant, thereby entitled to terminate upon 30 days notice. (Civ.Code, § 1944; Civ.Code, § 1946; *Linnard v. Sonnenschein* (1928) 94 Cal.App. 729; *Vavuris v. Pinelli* (1957) 147 Cal.App.2d 390, 394, 305 P.2d 149.) Fiber Form gave such notice, vacated the premises and therefore was not obligated to pay any further rental.

* * *

The judgment is affirmed.

PREMO, Acting P.J., and COTTLE, J., concur.

NOTES

1.   *Senior vs. subordinate leases.* As the principal case indicates, whether a lease is senior or subordinate to a foreclosing mortgage can have significant consequences for both the lessee and the foreclosure sale

purchaser. Moreover, the interplay between lease-mortgage priority and the mortgage theory followed by the jurisdiction can also sometimes be important outside the context of foreclosure. Consider, in this regard, the following analysis:

LEASES PRIOR TO MORTGAGE

A lease that antedates a mortgage, if duly recorded, is prior and superior to the mortgage. In most states this would also be the case even if the lease were not recorded, for normally the lessee is in possession and in most states possession gives all the world notice of the tenant's rights. With respect to these prior leases the following points should be kept in mind:

1.   Such a lease, since it is prior and superior to the mortgage, cannot be extinguished by foreclosure of the mortgage.

2.   If such a lease contains an option to purchase the property, the option must be subordinated to the mortgage. Otherwise there is danger that exercise of the option would extinguish the mortgage.

3.   Complete subordination of a prior lease to a subsequent mortgage is legally possible. A subordination agreement signed by the lessee makes his lease junior to the mortgage, subject to extinguishment by foreclosure of the mortgage, just as if the lease had been signed after the recording of the mortgage. Oddly enough subordination of the lease to the mortgage in some respects weakens the mortgagee's position, as is evident from the subsequent discussion.

4.   In title and intermediate states, on default in the mortgage payments, the mortgagee has the right to serve a demand on a senior lessee (one whose lease antedates the mortgage) and the lessee must thereafter pay rent to the mortgagee.* The lessee has no right to move out, as is true of junior lessees, as hereinafter explained. This rule stems from the notion in title and intermediate states that the mortgage is a transfer of some sort of title to the mortgagee, a notion previously referred to herein. Because of this mysterious transfer of title, there is created between the lessee and the subsequent mortgagee an equally mysterious link called "privity of estate." It is this privity of estate that makes the lessee liable to a subsequent mortgagee for rents. While it has its benefits, this rule also carries some burdens as we shall subsequently see. This rule, it is evident, has one unusual consequence, namely, it helps the mortgagee collect rent where his mortgage is junior to the lease. Naturally, the tenant has no obligation to pay rent to such

---

*   A mortgagee in a title state has a common law right to collect rents as soon as its mortgage becomes effective. The text accompanying this footnote assumes that the mortgagee's right has been modified as described in the Restatement excerpt at the beginning of this chapter. Eds.

mortgagee until the mortgagee serves a demand on the tenant to pay such rent.

In lien theory states, the mortgagee ordinarily is not entitled to make such a demand on the tenant. This follows from the fact that in these states a mortgage conveys no title; hence privity of estate is lacking.

LEASES JUNIOR TO THE MORTGAGE

With respect to leases that are junior to the mortgage (e.g., leases made by the mortgagor after the recording of the mortgage) the following rules are applicable:

1. Such a lease can be extinguished by foreclosure of the mortgage.

2. Occasionally a mortgagee will wish to foreclose his mortgage without extinguishing the lease. In some states this is possible and in others not. In states where it is legally impossible to preserve a junior lease when a mortgage is foreclosed, a mortgagee must be wary of placing reliance on such leases.

3. In title and intermediate states the mortgagee has the right to evict junior leases as soon as default occurs in the mortgage payments.* This is also true in lien states where a clause is inserted in the mortgage giving the mortgagee the right to possession on default and the state is one that recognizes the validity of such a provision. Alternatively the mortgagee may serve a demand which gives the tenant a choice as between moving out or paying rent to the mortgagee. However, the mortgagee cannot compel the tenant to remain and pay rent to him. This is so because where the lease is subsequent to the mortgage, there is no privity of estate between the mortgagee and the lessee. For this reason, it is better for the mortgagee to proceed in such a situation under the assignment of rents, for then the tenant must stay and pay rent to the mortgagee.

4. If the mortgagee enters under his mortgage, as stated in paragraph three, and the tenant chooses to remain and pay rent, in many states the result is to terminate the lease and create a month-to-month or year-to-year tenancy. Here again if the mortgagee wishes to preserve the leases it is best for him to proceed under his assignment of rents rather than under the mortgage.

Robert Kratovil, Mortgages—Problems in Possession, Rents and Mortgagee Liability, 11 DePaul L.Rev. 1, 8–10 (1961).**

2. *Priority preferences.* As *Dover* illustrates, it is problematic to generalize about the priority preferences of the parties in commercial lease

---

* This statement again assumes that the title state mortgagee's common law rights have been modified. —Eds.

** Reprinted with permission of DePaul University and the author.

settings. Our first reaction probably is to assume that a tenant normally desires protection against a foreclosure wiping out its lease rights. After all, a tenant often makes a substantial investment in the leasehold and he or she would seem to have a strong interest in ensuring that the investment is fully realized over the complete term of the lease. On the other hand, as *Dover* illustrates, where the tenant's business is precarious or the rent or other lease terms prove to be unduly pro-landlord, the tenant may be only too willing to see the lease and its attendant liabilities destroyed by foreclosure.

So too, the mortgagee's self-interest is not always readily apparent. In many cases it may prefer senior status for its mortgage because if foreclosure occurs, the foreclosure purchaser often wants to have the option of compelling a renegotiation of leases that it desires to retain. On the other hand, if a prime tenant is bound by a long term lease that is very favorable to the landlord, the last thing the mortgagee desires is for foreclosure to take the tenant "off the hook."

3.   *Varying priorities by agreement.* A variety of devices are used to readjust the rights and responsibilities of the mortgagee and lessee in the commercial lease context. Two of these, the *subordination agreement* and the *nondisturbance agreement,* are described in *Dover. Subordination* is an act by which one having an interest in particular real estate consents to a reduction in priority as against another holding an interest in the same real estate. See Miscione v. Barton Dev. Co., 52 Cal.App.4th 1320, 61 Cal.Rptr.2d 280, 285 (1997). In the mortgage-lease setting, for example, the subordination agreement may provide that "the Lease, the leasehold estate created thereby, together with all rights and privileges of Tenant thereunder, are hereby unconditionally subjected, and made subordinate, to the lien or charge of the Mortgage." Note that usually such a subordination is contained in a separate document executed by the tenant and the mortgagee. However, as in *Dover*, sometimes boilerplate language in the lease accomplishes the same result.

In a *nondisturbance* agreement, a mortgagee holding a senior lien agrees that "in the event of foreclosure, the foreclosure purchaser will permit the lease to continue and allow the tenant to remain on the leased premises so long as the tenant continues to comply with the terms of the lease and is not in default."

The *attornment* is a third device used to readjust the relationship of the parties. It is an agreement by which a tenant agrees with the mortgagee that "if the interest of the Landlord under the Lease shall be transferred by reason of foreclosure or deed in lieu thereof, Tenant shall be bound to the Purchaser under all of the terms, covenants and conditions of the Lease for the balance of the term thereof with the same force and effect as if the Purchaser were the original landlord under the lease." It may further provide that "Tenant does hereby attorn to Purchaser, including Lender if it be Purchaser, as the landlord under the lease, said attornment to be effective and self-operative without the execution of any further instruments upon Purchaser's succeeding to the interest of the landlord under the Lease."

All three of these devices may be combined in a *Subordination, Nondisturbance, and Attornment Agreement*. This agreement is normally executed by the lessee and mortgagee, but sometimes by the landlord-mortgagor as well. Note carefully the impact of this agreement. First, the lessee specifically subordinates the lease to the mortgage. Next, the mortgagee grants the lessee the protection of a nondisturbance clause so that any foreclosure purchaser agrees to recognize lessee's rights under the lease. Finally, the lessee, by attorning, agrees to be bound under the terms of the lease to any foreclosure purchaser even though, as junior party, a foreclosure would otherwise terminate his or her leasehold obligations.

Does a combination of subordination and nondisturbance make sense? Why would a mortgagee insist that its mortgage be senior to the lease and then agree not to "disturb" the tenant's leasehold in the event of foreclosure? Stated another way, one might reasonably ask why a mortgagee who is willing to grant a tenant a nondisturbance provision should not also be willing to allow the lessee to retain seniority? One explanation is largely historical. Until recently (and still today under some state regulatory schemes), government regulations frequently required institutional lenders to hold "first" mortgages only. Thus, the foregoing arrangement was used to keep the mortgage technically "senior," but practically "junior" to the lease. Most such regulations, however, no longer exist. However, other reasons have been advanced for the use of the "tripartite" agreement. Consider the following commentary:

> Even if a prior lease is economically beneficial, the lender may still find it wise to obtain a [Subordination, Nondisturbance and Attornment Agreement] ("Attornment Agreement") for several reasons. First, an Attornment Agreement puts the tenant and lender in direct privity of contract, thus giving the lender the right to make demands directly on the tenant (such as the demand to pay rent directly to the lender after default and to obtain the lender's consent to any modification of the lease). Second, the Attornment Agreement provides the lender with a specific covenant from the tenant that, after foreclosure, the tenant will perform for the benefit of the lender upon demand to do so. Third, to the extent there are conflicting provisions in the lease and [mortgage] regarding insurance proceeds and the like, the Attornment Agreement provides a vehicle for addressing and, hopefully, resolving those conflicts.

Roy S. Geiger & Patricia Frobes, Lenders and Leases, 7 Cal.Real Prop.J. 1, 15 (1989). Let us consider a concrete problem. Suppose the lease provides that in the event of a casualty loss, all insurance proceeds shall be used to reconstruct the leased premises. The mortgage, on the other hand, requires that any insurance proceeds on the premises be used to prepay the mortgage obligation. Which provision governs? If the mortgage is senior to the lease, the mortgage insurance provision will trump its lease counterpart. If the lease is senior, the opposite will be the case. While the nondisturbance provision clearly gives the tenant the right to continue under the lease after foreclosure, it alone does not make the lease senior to the mortgage in a variety of contexts not directly dealing with the tenant's right to possession. Stated another way, in subordinating its lease to the mortgage, the lessee gives up more than it receives back via the nondisturbance provision. Thus, in our insurance problem, in formally subordinating the lease to the mortgage, the lessee makes the lease insurance provision junior to its mortgage counterpart, a result which is not altered by the nondisturbance agreement.

From a mortgagee's perspective, the ideal world would be one in which it would have the option to treat any leases on the real estate as junior or senior to its mortgage. For example, it could insist that all present and future leases on the mortgaged real estate contain language giving the mortgagee "the option to have this Lease senior or subordinate to its mortgage." In fact the lease in *Dover* contained similar language. Why was it ineffective?

Suppose we have a lease that is unquestionably junior to a mortgage in default. On the other hand, the lease is definitely "pro-landlord." Should a foreclosing mortgagee be able to make the lease survive foreclosure by the expedient of not making the lessee a party-defendant in a judicial foreclosure? Should the mortgagee be able to accomplish the same thing in a power of sale foreclosure context? These are difficult questions which we consider later in this volume. See Chapter 6, Sections C & D, infra.

4. *Junior residential leases and the Great Recession.* The overwhelming increase in foreclosures during the Great Recession caused legislatures to protect junior residential lessees whose leases would otherwise be destroyed by foreclosure of senior mortgages. Consider the following 2013 California statute:

(a) * * * a tenant or subtenant in possession of a rental housing unit under a month-to-month lease or periodic tenancy at the time the property is sold in foreclosure shall be given 90 days' written notice to quit pursuant to Section 1162 before the tenant or subtenant may be removed from the property as prescribed in this chapter.

(b) In addition to the rights set forth in subdivision (a), tenants or subtenants holding possession of a rental housing unit under a fixed-term residential lease entered into before transfer of title at the foreclosure sale shall have the right to possession until the end of the lease term, and all rights and obligations under the lease shall survive foreclosure, except that the tenancy may be terminated upon 90 days' written notice to quit pursuant to subdivision (a) if any of the following conditions apply:

(1) The purchaser or successor in interest will occupy the housing unit as a primary residence.

(2)   The lessee is the mortgagor or the child, spouse, or parent of the mortgagor.

(3)   The lease was not the result of an arms' length transaction.

(4)   The lease requires the receipt of rent that is substantially less than fair market rent for the property, except when rent is reduced or subsidized due to a federal, state, or local subsidy or law.

(c)   The purchaser or successor in interest shall bear the burden of proof in establishing that a fixed-term residential lease is not entitled to protection under subdivision (b).

(d)   This section shall not apply if any party to the note remains in the property as a tenant, subtenant, or occupant.

(e)   Nothing in this section is intended to affect any local just cause eviction ordinance. This section does not, and shall not be construed to, affect the authority of a public entity that otherwise exists to regulate or monitor the basis for eviction.

(f)   This section shall remain in effect only until December 31, 2019, and as of that date is repealed, unless a later enacted statute, that is enacted before December 31, 2019, deletes or extends that date.

West's Ann.Cal.C.C.P. § 1161b. In May 2009, Congress enacted the Protecting Tenants at Foreclosure Act of 2009 (PTFA or Act) (Pub.L. 111–22, Div. A, Title VII, §§ 702–704, May 20, 2009, 123 Stat. 1660) and, in 2010, Congress amended it (Pub.L. 111–203, Title XIV, § 1484, July 21, 2010, 124 Stat. 2204). The Act provides protections for bona fide tenants of residential real property at foreclosure following the date of its enactment until its sunset at the end of 2019. (PTFA, §§ 702, 704.). For a consideration of the California and Congressional enactments, see Nativi v. Deutsche Bank Nat'l Trust Co., 223 Cal.App.4th 261, 167 Cal.Rptr.3d 173 (2014).

Security Interests in Rents

Mortgage lenders frequently view real property as providing two separate and distinct sources of security for the mortgage obligation. They rely not only on the real property itself, but also on the rents it produces. However, in lien theory states, it is important to realize that simply taking a garden-variety mortgage on the debtor's fee simple absolute will not adequately protect the lender with respect to rents and profits. As one federal judge aptly observed, "[i]n such instances, the logic is that the borrower has retained all the incidents of possession, including the right to rents, profits and crops, and these he may do with as he pleases. It is only when the lender takes possession, or does so constructively, as by having a receiver appointed, that he is entitled to the ordinary incidents of possession, like rents, profits and crops." First Fed. Sav. of Arkansas, F.A. v. City Nat'l Bank of Fort Smith, 87 B.R. 565, 566 (W.D.Ark.1988).

Consequently, mortgagees commonly require mortgage language or collateral agreements by which the mortgagor "assigns" or "mortgages" the rents as additional security for the mortgage loan. In relatively rare situations, such agreements give the mortgagee immediate access to the rents. In these situations, the mortgagee may, from the inception of the loan, actually collect the rents from mortgagor's tenants and apply them to the mortgage indebtedness. More commonly, however, the mortgagee's right of access to the rents is triggered by mortgagor default. See generally, Keith D. Haroldson, Perfecting a Security Interest in Future Rents from Mortgaged Real Property, 40 Drake L.Rev. 287 (1991).

Today an assignment of rents agreement is enforceable in every jurisdiction, whether it follows the lien or title theory of mortgage law. This unanimity ends, however, as soon as courts confront the question of when such assignments become effective and at what point the mortgagee acquires the actual right to commence collection of the rents. As to these latter questions, mortgage law theory can sometimes play a significant role, as the following material illustrates.

What recording or filing requirements must be followed with respect to an assignment of rents? Perhaps out of an excess of caution, mortgagees frequently not only record in the real estate records, but attempt to perfect a Uniform Commercial Code security interest in rents as well. This "belt and suspenders" approach stems from a concern that rents may be characterized as "personalty" and that recordation of an assignment in the real estate records will not provide the mortgagee with sufficient protection. In theory this concern is misplaced. Under Article 9 of the UCC, the Code is inapplicable "to the creation or transfer of an interest in or lien on real property, including a lease or rents thereunder." U.C.C. § 9–109(d)(11). Thus, any attempted perfection under the UCC seems both unnecessary and ineffective, although it probably does no harm so long as the assignment is also properly recorded in the real estate records.

IN THE MATTER OF MILLETTE

United States Court of Appeals, Fifth Circuit, 1999
186 F.3d 638

Before JONES and STEWART, CIRCUIT JUDGES, and DUPLANTIER, DISTRICT
JUDGE.

EDITH H. JONES, CIRCUIT JUDGE:

* * *

BACKGROUND

Thomas Millette, Ted Millette, William Millette, and Charles Fridge own a commercial building in Pascagoula, Mississippi known as the "Market Street Building." In August 1992, the owners executed a promissory note in favor of Eastover Bank in the principal amount of $445,198.71. As security for the note, the owners executed a deed of trust in favor of Eastover that contained the following assignment of rents clause:

> As additional security, Debtor hereby assigns to Secured Party all rents accruing on the Property. Debtor shall have the right to collect and retain the rents as long as Debtor is not in default as provided in Paragraph 9. In the event of default, Secured Party in person, by an agent or by a judicially appointed receiver shall be entitled to enter upon, take possession of and manage the Property and collect the rents. All rents so collected shall be applied first to the costs of managing the Property and collecting the rents, including fees for a receiver and an attorney, commissions to rental agents, repairs and other necessary related expenses and then to payment of the indebtedness.

The parties stipulated that the deed of trust securing the Market Street Building was properly recorded in the Jackson County property records. MTGLQ Investment, L.P. subsequently purchased the note and deed of trust from Eastover and retained Security National to service the loan.

In November 1993, O'Neal Steel obtained an Alabama judgment against Thomas, William, and Ted Millette in the amount of $164,335.89 plus interest. O'Neal enrolled the judgment in Jackson County, Mississippi on January 10, 1994. In May 1994, the Millettes, doing business as "Millette & Associates," entered into a commercial lease with Jackson County, which became the sole tenant in the Market Street Building. After discovering that the Millettes owned the building and were receiving rental income from it, O'Neal instituted a garnishment action in the Mississippi Circuit Court and served a writ of garnishment on Jackson County. As required by Mississippi law, the County answered the writ of garnishment, admitting it owed a debt to "Millette & Associates" under the lease. The County further stated that Security National claimed a prior interest in the rents pursuant to the recorded assignment of rents clause contained in the deed of trust.

When Security National learned of the garnishment action on January 4, 1995, it immediately served written notice and demand on Jackson County and ultimately intervened as a party in the garnishment action. Months later, Security National instituted foreclosure proceedings, but before it could complete the foreclosure, Thomas Millette filed for Chapter 7 bankruptcy, staying the foreclosure and all activity in the state court garnishment proceeding. The present adversary proceeding was commenced in bankruptcy court to determine the extent and priority of the competing liens on the rents.

O'Neal argues here * * * that it had a perfected interest in the Market Street Building's rents from the date it served its writ of garnishment on Jackson County. O'Neal contends that its lien has priority over Security National's lien because Security National failed to take the necessary steps to perfect its interest. According to O'Neal, under Mississippi law, a mortgagee must not only record its assignment of rents, but must also take "additional action," like appointing a receiver, to perfect its interest in rents. Therefore, because O'Neal served its writ of garnishment before Security National took the requisite additional action, O'Neal's interest in the rents should be superior.

The bankruptcy court disagreed with O'Neal's construction of Mississippi law and granted summary judgment in favor of Security National, holding that, based upon a then-recent Mississippi Supreme Court decision, Security National had a perfected interest in the rents when it recorded its deed of trust containing the assignment of rents clause. Although the district court disagreed with the bankruptcy court's legal analysis, it reached the same result. It held that an assignment of rents clause is not perfected upon recordation; instead, a mortgagee must take "additional steps" to perfect its interest. According to the district court, Security National's actions upon learning of the garnishment were sufficient to perfect its previously recorded assignment of rents. * * *

DISCUSSION

Whether a Mississippi mortgagee, which has obtained an assignment of rents, is perfected in the rents when the assignment is recorded, or whether it must take additional steps to perfect its interest in the rents, is an issue of first impression both in this court and the courts of Mississippi. This court must anticipate what the Mississippi Supreme Court would decide if the issue were before it. See *Free v. Abbott Labs.*, 176 F.3d 298, 299 (5th Cir.1999); *F.D.I.C. v. Abraham*, 137 F.3d 264, 268 (5th Cir.1998). * * *

O'Neal * * * advocates the older common law approach, which a minority of states continue to follow.[6] Under the older rule, an assignment of rents gives the mortgagee an inchoate lien which is perfected only when the mortgagee takes additional action to enforce it. In Texas, for instance, "an assignment of rentals does not become operative until the mortgagee obtains possession of the property, or impounds the rents, or secures the appointment of a receiver, or takes some other similar action." *Taylor v. Brennan*, 621 S.W.2d 592, 594 (Tex.1981).

Several federal courts, while interpreting state law, have also followed the old rule. *See, e.g., In re Century Inv. Fund VIII L.P.*, 937 F.2d 371, 377 (7th Cir.1991) (Wisconsin law); *In re 1301 Conn. Ave. Assocs.*, 126 B.R. 1, 3 (D.D.C.1991) (District of Columbia law); *First Federal Savings and Loan Assoc. of Toledo v. Hunter (In re Sam A. Tisci, Inc.)*, 133 B.R. 857, 859 (N.D.Ohio 1991) (Ohio law); *Condor One, Inc. v. Turtle Creek, Ltd. (In re Turtle Creek, Ltd.)*, 194 B.R. 267, 278 (Bankr.N.D.Ala.1996) (Alabama law); *In re Mews Assocs., L.P.*, 144 B.R. 867, 868–69 (Bankr.W.D.Mo.1992) (Missouri law); *Drummond v. Farm Credit Bank of Spokane (In re Kurth Ranch)*, 110 B.R. 501, 506 (Bankr.D.Mont.1990) (Montana law); *Armstrong v. United States (In re Neideffer)*, 96 B.R. 241, 243 (Bankr.D.N.D.1988) (North Dakota law); *Ziegler v. First Nat'l Bank of Volga (In re Ziegler)*, 65 B.R. 285, 287 (Bankr.D.S.D.1986) (South Dakota law).

The majority of courts and legislatures have abandoned the "additional action" rule in favor of a rule analogous to those governing perfection of secured interest in personal property under the Uniform Commercial Code. Under the modern approach, the recording of a mortgage document containing an assignment of rents "gives the mortgagee rights superior to any subsequent third party who would seek to take a security interest in the leases and rentals pertaining thereto as a type of collateral." *O'Neil v. Carlson*, 135 N.H. 459, 608 A.2d 858, 861 (1992) (quoting *In re Rancourt*, 123 B.R. 143, 147 (Bankr.D.N.H.1991) (quotations omitted)). Several state legislatures have also rejected the old common law rule.[8] * * *

The recently published ALI *Restatement of Mortgages* has also adopted the position that a mortgage on rents is perfected when recorded.

---

[6] *See, e.g., Bevins v. Peoples Bank & Trust Co.*, 671 P.2d 875, 879 (Alaska 1983) ("The beneficiary must take some action to acquire possession of the property or the rents before the rent clause becomes operative."); *Martinez v. Continental Enter.*, 730 P.2d 308, 316 (Colo.1986) (en banc) ("[U]ntil the mortgagee takes some effectual step to subject the rents to the payment of the debt, . . . the mortgagee has but an inchoate right to the rents.").

[8] See, e.g., Cal. Civ.Code § 2938(a) (West 1993); Del.Code Ann. tit. 25, § 2121(a) (Supp.1998); Kan. Stat. Ann. § 58–2343(b) (1994); Md.Code Ann., Real Prop. § 3–204 (1996); Neb.Rev.Stat. § 52–1704 (1998); N.C. Gen.Stat. § 47–20(c) (Supp.1998); Tenn.Code Ann. § 66–26–116(a) (1993); Va.Code Ann. § 55–220.1 (Michie 1995); Wash. Rev.Code Ann. § 7.28.230(3) (West 1992).

See Restatement (Second) of Property—Mortgages § 4.2(b) (1997). Under the Restatement, a mortgage on rents "is effective as against the mortgagor and, subject to the operation of the recording act, as against third parties, upon execution and delivery." *Id.* The Restatement's comments make it clear that, upon recordation, the mortgagee will be protected against competing claims by third parties and others claiming priority over the rents. *See id.* at § 4.2 cmt. b.

Public policy considerations weigh in favor of rejecting the old rule. The modern rule best protects diligent mortgagees from competing liens filed by subsequent creditors. Under the prior approach, a mortgagee with a lien on rents or an assignment of rents clause will nearly always lose a priority battle with a judgment creditor when the debtor has not defaulted on its payments under a mortgage. A judgment creditor can perfect its interest at any time by properly serving a writ of garnishment, while a mortgagee is prohibited from taking the requisite "additional action" to perfect until the debtor has defaulted. This leads to a bizarre result: A mortgagee, which has done all it could to secure its interest in the rents, loses priority to a judgment creditor who had constructive knowledge by the recordation of the mortgagee's assignment of rents. The case at hand illustrates this result.

Security National was unaware of O'Neal's judgment against the Millettes until after the writ of garnishment had already been served. Once Security National learned of the garnishment, it immediately served notice of its interest and intervened in the garnishment action. Before O'Neal served the writ of garnishment, the Millettes were not in default on the lease, and Security National had no justification for "further action" to perfect its assignment of rents. In spite of Security National's post-garnishment diligence, its interest would be subordinate to O'Neal's under the old common law rule.

Recognizing the inequity resulting from the application of the old rule, courts that continue to apply it have occasionally escaped its harsh result by liberally finding "additional action" of a mortgagee that sufficiently satisfied the rule. *See, e.g., In re Keller,* 150 B.R. 835, 839 (Bankr.N.D.Ga.1993) (holding that a mortgagee perfected its right to rents upon filing of a motion for relief from the automatic stay); *In re Mariner Enterprises of Panama City, Inc.,* 131 B.R. 190, 193 (Bankr.N.D.Fla.1989) (holding that a mortgagee's demand that the borrower turn over the rents is sufficient); *In re McCann,* 140 B.R. 926, 928–29 (Bankr.D.Mass.1992) (holding that filing a state foreclosure action is sufficient). The district court's opinion in this case typifies the approach. The court held that, although Security National was not perfected at the time O'Neal served its writ of garnishment, it soon became perfected by taking immediate steps to protect its interest in the rents.

Courts also avoid the old rule when it appears that, instead of receiving an inchoate lien on rents, the mortgagee received an "absolute assignment" of the rents. An absolute assignment passes title to the rents instead of granting a security interest and "operates to transfer the right to rentals automatically upon the happening of a specified condition, such as default." *Taylor,* 621 S.W.2d at 594. To be absolute, however, there must be "especially clear evidence that the parties intended to create such an assignment." *F.D.I.C. v. International Property Management, Inc.,* 929 F.2d 1033, 1036 (5th Cir.1991); *see also In re Century Investment Fund VIII L.P.,* 937 F.2d 371, 377 (7th Cir.1991) (Wisconsin law). Words such as "security" or "pledge" in the loan documents are insufficient to effect an absolute assignment. *FDIC,* 929 F.2d at 1036.

Because the perfection-upon-recordation rule for a mortgagee's security interests in rents is consistent with modern secured transaction law and unencumbered by the complexities, distinctions, and harsh results of the common law, we conclude that the Mississippi Supreme Court would reject the old rule and reward a diligent creditor, which records its assignment of rents and protects its lien by giving constructive notice to hypothetical third-parties. *See Mills v. Damson Oil Corp.,* 720 F.2d 874, 875 (5th Cir.1983) (recognizing that a recorded deed in Mississippi, even if defective, gives constructive notice of the deed's contents); *McMahon v. McMahon,* 247 Miss. 822, 157 So.2d 494, 500–01 (1963) (same).

There is no contrary Mississippi authority. * * * Two Mississippi bankruptcy courts have addressed perfection of an assignment of rents clause under Mississippi law and followed the old rule. *See In re Crossroads Market, Inc.,* 190 B.R. 269, 271 (Bankr.N.D.Miss.1994); *Delta Plaza Partners v. Minnesota Mut. Life Ins. Co. (In re Delta Plaza Partners),* 133 B.R. 355, 357–58 (Bankr.N.D.Miss.1991). Both *Crossroads Market* and *Delta Plaza,* however, relied on Fifth Circuit cases interpreting Texas law that do not control a case governed by Mississippi law. Moreover, the only independent justification noted for the bankruptcy court's holding that Mississippi would adopt the old common law rule is that Mississippi, like Texas, is a "lien theory" state. * * * That premise appears to have been rejected by the en banc Mississippi Court of Appeals in a recent decision concluding that Mississippi is an "intermediate theory" state. *See Anderson v. Kimbrough,* No. 97–CA–01169–COA, 1999 WL 435649, at 6 (Miss.Ct.App. June 29, 1999) (en banc) (slip opinion); Miss.Code Ann. § 89–1–43 (Rev.1991). Application of the modern rule is particularly appropriate in an intermediate theory state.

CONCLUSION

Security National's interest in the rents was perfected when it recorded its deed of trust containing the assignment of rents clause. Accordingly, that interest primes the later garnishment lien asserted by O'Neal against the rents.

The judgments of the district and bankruptcy courts are, for the foregoing reasons, AFFIRMED.

NOTES

1. *State approaches to assignments.* As we noted earlier, every jurisdiction holds that rent assignments are valid and enforceable. However, this unanimity gives us cold comfort. The problem is that courts approach assignments in a variety of ways and are often hopelessly confused. To say that judicial and legislative treatment of assignments of rents lacks both uniformity and precision is a vast understatement. In trying to make sense of this bewildering situation, we need first to identify three crucial focal points in the creation and enforcement of a rents assignment. First, we need to ask ourselves when the assignment becomes *effective* between the mortgagor and mortgagee. In other words, when is a valid lien created as between those two parties? Next, we must determine when this lien becomes effective ("*perfected*") against others who acquire interests in the real estate or its rents. This is the issue confronted by the *Millette* court. Finally, we must identify when the mortgagee has the right to *collect* (to realize on or foreclose upon) the rents and profits. Unfortunately, while a growing number of courts and legislatures focus carefully on these three crucial issues, too many continue either to confuse or conflate them.

Some jurisdictions, as noted by *Millette,* claim to recognize the validity of so-called "absolute assignments" in situations where the language of the assignment is sufficiently sweeping. In such an assignment the mortgagee obtains a present title to the rents even though the assignment itself postpones the right to collect until mortgagor defaults. As one federal court stressed in interpreting New Jersey law:

> An absolute assignment transfers title to the assignee upon its execution. * * * An assignment is absolute if its language demonstrates an intent to transfer immediately the assignor's right and title to the rents. * * * The instant assignment was quintessentially absolute, because it was a total assignment in *per verba de praesenti:* Jason Realty "hereby grants, transfers and assigns to the assignee the entire lessor's interest in and to those certain leases ... Together with all rents." * * * This exchange inescapably and unambiguously expressed an agreement to assign present title.

* * *

> We are not moved by the fact that the assignment was part of a financing transaction and served as additional security for repayment of the note. An assignment clause within a mortgage may be independent of the mortgage security. * * * Moreover, we are impressed that the instant assignment was contained in an agreement separate from the mortgage.

In re Jason Realty, L.P., 59 F.3d 423, 427–28 (3d Cir.1995). For similar reasoning, see, e.g., First Fed. Sav. of Arkansas, F.A. v. City Nat'l Bank of Fort Smith, 87 B.R. 565 (W.D.Ark.1988); First Fidelity Bank v. Eleven Hundred Metroplex Assoc., 190 B.R. 510 (S.D.N.Y.1995); In re Ventura-Louise Props., 490 F.2d 1141 (9th Cir.1974); HomeCorp v. Secor Bank, 659 So.2d 15 (Ala.1994); MDFC Loan Corp. v. Greenbrier Plaza Partners, 21 Cal.App.4th 1045, 26 Cal.Rptr.2d 596 (1994); In re Gould, 78 B.R. 590 (D.Idaho 1987); 801 Nolana, Inc. v. RTC Mortg. Trust 1994–S6, 944 S.W.2d 751 (Tex.App.1997) ("An absolute assignment * * * operates to transfer the right to rents automatically upon the happening of a specified condition, such as default. It is a *pro tanto* payment of the obligation."). This approach supposedly requires no further affirmative action on the mortgagee's part either to perfect its interest or to commence collection.

The "absolute assignment" concept used in these cases is an unfortunate development that has created needless confusion. None of the foregoing decisions involve an outright sale or transfer of the rents. Indeed, the documents in most "absolute assignment" cases provide that, until default, the mortgagor has a "privilege," "license," or other right to collect the rents, or designates the mortgagor as the mortgagee's "agent" or "trustee" for purposes of rent collection. The fact is that the assignment in each instance is intended for security purposes only and not to make the mortgagee absolute owner of the rents. A growing number of courts have rejected the casuistry of the "absolute assignment" theory. Indeed, as one court aptly observed:

> To borrow a concept from tort law, but for the loan transaction, the Debtors would not have assigned rents to the Bank. No independent consideration was given for the assignments. The fact that the assignments are conditioned upon default and will terminate upon satisfaction of the debt indicates that they are merely additional security for the loan, and not an absolute transfer of the Debtor's interest in the rents to the Bank.

In re Lyons, 193 B.R. 637 (Bankr.D.Mass.1996). Accord: In re S. Side House, LLC, 474 B.R. 391 (Bankr.E.D.N.Y. 2012)("the majority of New York state cases are of the view that an absolute assignment is not permitted, regardless of the language in the agreement."); In re Cavros, 262 B.R. 206 (Bankr.D.Conn.2001). In any event, many courts that purport to recognize "absolute assignments" start with a presumption an assignment of rents creates only a pledge of rents or a security interest in rents. See, e.g., In re 5877 Poplar, L.P., 268 B.R. 140 (Bankr.W.D.Tenn.2001).

A significant number of states represent an opposite extreme that is sometimes referred to as the "American common law" view, an approach that was rejected by the *Millette* court. According to one Colorado court:

> [M]ortgages, trust deeds, and assignments of rents do not convey title to real property, but merely create liens against the property. Until a mortgagor defaults and a lender takes some "effectual step" subjecting the assigned rents toward the payment of the debt, for example, by gaining rightful possession of the property or by filing a foreclosure action, the lender has only an inchoate right to the rents. This is so even if the terms in a deed of trust grant the lender the right to receive rents in the event of default. * * * An inchoate interest is an interest in real estate which is not a present interest, but which may ripen into a vested estate, if it is not barred, extinguished, or divested.

Galleria Towers, Inc. v. Crump Warren & Sommer, Inc., 831 P.2d 908, 911 (Colo.App.1991). What are we to make of this approach? Professor Glenn once stated:

> It must be an equitable right of some sort; but equitable obligations vary in that they may confer a specific right to a specific thing from the outset; or they may create no such specific right, but merely confer protection upon the party if he takes affirmative action in his own behalf and assumes dominion over the thing that is described in the instrument. . . . [W]ith the rights of the [latter] class there is no specific equity that will prevail, just so, against later liens. The "equitable lien" or "equitable pledge" of this variety becomes effective only when the one who asserts it follows up his claim by assuming dominion over the thing that he demands. Having taken possession, one will be protected by the fact that he had an "equitable lien" or "equitable pledge," but unless and until he thus follows up his right, he has nothing.

2 Garrard Glenn, Mortgages 939–40 (1943). For other examples of this approach, see The Cadle Co. v. Collin Creek Phase II Assocs., Ltd., 998 S.W.2d 718 (Tex.App.1999); Bevins v. Peoples Bank & Trust Co., 671 P.2d 875 (Alaska 1983); In re Kurth Ranch, 110 B.R. 501 (Bankr.D.Mont.1990); Saline State Bank v. Mahloch, 834 F.2d 690 (8th Cir.1987) (interpreting Nebraska law); In re Constable Plaza Assocs., L.P., 125 B.R. 98 (Bankr.S.D.N.Y.1991); Wuorinen v. City Fed. Sav. & Loan Ass'n, 52 Wis.2d 722, 191 N.W.2d 27 (1971). Under the analysis of many of these "American common law" decisions, none of the three crucial steps we outlined in the first paragraph of this Note is regarded as satisfied until step three (the requisite "affirmative action") is accomplished by the mortgagee. For criticism of this approach, see In re Baltic Assocs., L.P., 170 B.R. 568 (E.D.Pa.1994) (the foregoing view "confuses the issues of *perfection* of a security interest and *enforcement* of a security interest.").

Note also that the affirmative action required by this latter approach can sometimes be nominal. For example, some courts have held that a refused demand for possession or simply filing a request for a receivership (as opposed to obtaining its appointment) suffices. See Matter of Century Investment Fund VIII Ltd. Partn., 937 F.2d 371 (7th Cir.1991); Long Island Bond & Mortg. Guarantee Co. v. Brown, 171 Misc. 15, 11 N.Y.S.2d 793 (1939); In re Flower City Nursing Home, Inc., 38 B.R. 642 (Bankr.W.D.N.Y.1984). Sometimes it is enough that the mortgagee notify the mortgagor of default and demand payment of the rents. See, e.g., In re Fluge, 57 B.R. 451 (Bankr.D.N.D.1985).

Between the foregoing extreme approaches, most states occupy a broad "middle ground" with respect to rent assignments. While there is great variety in this approach, most decisions and statutes focus on the three steps we outlined above. In general these jurisdictions hold that an assignment of rents is effective between the original parties upon execution and is perfected against third parties upon recording, but the right to commence collection (enforcement) requires subsequent affirmative action, albeit often relatively nominal, by the mortgagee. The Florida statute exemplifies this approach:

> (2) If such an assignment is made, the mortgagee shall hold a lien on the rents, and the lien created by the assignment shall be perfected and effective against third parties upon recordation of the [assignment].

> (3) Unless otherwise agreed to in writing by the mortgagee and mortgagor, the assignment of rents shall be enforceable upon the mortgagor's default and written demand for the rents made by the mortgagee to the mortgagor, whereupon the mortgagor shall turn over all rents in the possession of the mortgagor at the time of the written demand or collected thereafter.

Fla.Stat. § 697.07(2),(3); Ginsberg v. Lennar Florida Holdings, Inc., 645 So.2d 490 (Fla.App.1994) ("According to the statute an assignment of rents creates a lien on the rents in favor of the mortgagee, and the mortgagee will have the right to foreclose that lien and collect the rents without the necessity of foreclosing on the underlying mortgage."). See In re Bethesda Air Rights Ltd. Partn., 117 B.R. 202 (Bankr.D.Md.1990); New York Life Ins. Co. v. Bremer Towers, 714 F.Supp. 414 (D.Minn.1989) (in construing Minn.Stat.Ann. § 559.17, which authorizes assignments of rents and profits in mortgages exceeding $500,000 on non-homestead and non-agricultural real estate, the court stated that "an agreement between the parties creates an initial security interest in the property. The secured interest is then perfected by recording the assignment with the appropriate authority. The mere perfection of the interest, however, does not give the creditor immediate access to the property. If the debtor defaults on its obligations, though, the creditor can take action to enforce its security interest."); In re Fluge, 57 B.R. 451 (Bankr.N.D.1985) ("Under applicable North Dakota case law, an assignment of rents clause may be enforced apart from the security in the property itself and in advance of foreclosure by affording either the lessee or mortgagor/lessor notification of an intention to invoke the assignment of rents clause."); Tenn.Code Ann. § 66–26–116 (upon recordation of any instrument assigning leases or rents, the interest of the assignee "shall be fully perfected as to the grantor * * * and all third parties without the necessity of furnishing notice to the assignor or lessee, obtaining possession of the real property, impounding the rents, securing the appointment of a receiver, or taking any other affirmative action. * * * The lessee is authorized to pay the assignor until the lessee receives notification that rents due or to become due have been assigned and that payment is to be made to the assignee."); In re McCutchen, 115 B.R. 126 (Bankr.W.D.Tenn.1990) (foregoing statute "makes it clear that the perfected secured creditor is not entitled to the possession of the rents until a proper notice is received by the lessee, directing the lessee to pay the assignee.").

Note, however, that in some of these "middle ground" jurisdictions the affirmative action requirements that must be satisfied by the mortgagee to commence collection of the rents can be more substantial. See, e.g., 641 Avenue of the Americas Ltd. Partn. v. 641 Assocs., Ltd., 189 B.R. 583 (S.D.N.Y.1995) ("a security interest in rents is perfected upon recordation;" however, "[it] becomes enforceable when the assignee takes affirmative steps to assert his rights, such as appointing a receiver to collect the rents, taking possession of the property, commencing foreclosure proceedings, or seeking an order for sequestration of the rents"); In re Park at Dash Point L.P., 121 B.R. 850 (Bankr.W.D.Wash.1990) (In Washington, "assignments of rents are perfected by recording, and the mortgagee obtains the right to collect rents only after enforcing its security interest, which may be accomplished either by obtaining possession of the real property, or by the appointment of a receiver."); In re Rancourt, 123 B.R. 143 (Bankr.D.N.H.1991); In re Raleigh/ Spring Forest Apts. Assocs., 118 B.R. 42 (Bankr.E.D.N.C.1990) (assignment is perfected upon recording, but the right to rents is incomplete until mortgagee takes some affirmative action to enforce collection of them, such as obtaining the appointment of a receiver or taking possession of the premises).

2. *Restatement approach.* Consider the Restatement approach to taking a security interest in rents:

§ 4.2   Mortgaging Rents

* * *

(b) A mortgage may be given on the rents of real property. Such a mortgage may be included in a mortgage on the real property or may be a separate instrument. The mortgage is effective as against the mortgagor and, subject to the operation of the recording act, as against third parties, upon execution and delivery.

(c) The mortgage may provide that the mortgagee may commence collection of the rents at any time or, in any event, upon mortgagor default. The mortgagee's right to actual possession of the rents arises upon:

(1) satisfaction of any conditions in the mortgage; and

(2) delivery of a demand for the rents to the mortgagor, the holder of the equity of redemption, and each person who holds a mortgage on the real property or on its rents of which the mortgagee has notice.

(d) The delivery referred to in Subsection (c) is effective upon receipt and may be accomplished by personal service, the United States Mail, or any other means reasonably calculated to afford an addressee actual notice of the demand.

Restatement (Third) of Property (Mortgages) § 4.2 (1997)*. Where does the Restatement fit with respect to the approaches to assignments outlined above? Is it significant that the Restatement uses the term "mortgages" rather than "assigns?" What type of "affirmative action" is required to commence collection of the rents?

3. *California legislation.* California enacted sweeping and important assignment of rents legislation that became effective with assignments created on and after January 1, 1997. The statute is almost six pages long and is more comprehensive than any counterpart previously enacted in California or elsewhere. The following excerpts are probably its most significant provisions:

(a) A written assignment of an interest in leases, rents, issues, or profits of real property made in connection with an obligation secured by real property, irrespective of whether the assignment is denoted as absolute, absolute conditioned upon default, additional security for an obligation, or otherwise, shall, upon execution and delivery by the assignor, be effective to create a present security interest in existing and future leases, rents, issues, or profits of that real property. As used in this section, "leases, rents, issues, and profits of real property" include the cash proceeds thereof. The term "cash proceeds" means cash, checks, deposit accounts, and the like.

(b) An assignment of an interest in leases, rents, issues, or profits of real property may be recorded in the records of the county recorder in which the underlying real property is located in the same manner as any other conveyance of an interest in real property, whether the assignment is in a separate document or part of a mortgage or deed of trust, and when so duly recorded in accordance with the methods, procedures, and requirements for recordation of conveyances of other interests in real property, (1) the assignment shall be deemed to give constructive notice of the content of the assignment with the same force and effect as any other duly recorded conveyance of an

---

* © 1997 by The American Law Institute. Reprinted with permission.

interest in real property and (2) the interest granted by the assignment shall be deemed fully perfected as of the time of recordation with the same force and effect as any other duly recorded conveyance of an interest in real property, notwithstanding any provision of the assignment or any provision of law that would otherwise preclude or defer enforcement of the rights granted the assignee under the assignment until the occurrence of a subsequent event, including, but not limited to, a subsequent default of the assignor, or the assignee's obtaining possession of the real property or the appointment of a receiver.

(c) Upon default of the assignor under the obligation secured by the assignment of leases, rents, issues, and profits, the assignee shall be entitled to enforce the assignment in accordance with this section. On and after the date the assignee takes one or more of the enforcement steps described in this subdivision, the assignee shall be entitled to collect and receive all rents, issues, and profits that have accrued but remain unpaid and uncollected by the assignor or its agent or for the assignor's benefit on that date, and all rents, issues, and profits that accrue on or after the date. The assignment shall be enforced by one or more of the following:

(1) The appointment of a receiver.

(2) Obtaining possession of the rents, issues, or profits.

(3) Delivery to any one or more of the tenants of a written demand for turnover of rents, issues, and profits in the form specified in subdivision (k), a copy of which demand shall also be delivered to the assignor; and a copy of which shall be mailed to all other assignees of record of the leases, rents, issues, and profits of the real property at the address for notices provided in the assignment or, if none, to the address to which the recorded assignment was to be mailed after recording.

(4) Delivery to the assignor of a written demand for the rents, issues, or profits, a copy of which shall be mailed to all other assignees of record of the leases, rents, issues, and profits of the real property at the address for notices provided in the assignment or, if none, to the address to which the recorded assignment was to be mailed after recording.

* * *

(d) If an assignee elects to take the action provided for under paragraph (3) of subdivision (c), the demand provided for therein shall be signed under penalty of perjury by the assignee or an authorized agent of the assignee and shall be effective as against the tenant when actually received by the tenant at the address for notices provided under the lease or other contractual agreement under which the tenant occupies the property or, if no address for notices is so provided, at the property. Upon receipt of this demand, the tenant shall be obligated to pay to the assignee all rents, issues, and profits that are past due and payable on the date of receipt of the demand, and all rents, issues, and profits coming due under the lease following the date of receipt of the demand, unless either of the following occurs:

> (1) The tenant has previously received a demand which is valid on its face from another assignee of the leases, issues, rents, and profits sent by the other assignee in accordance with this subdivision and subdivision (c).

> (2) The tenant, in good faith and in a manner which is not inconsistent with the lease, has previously paid, or within 10 days following receipt of the demand notice pays, the rent to the assignor.

West's Ann.Cal.Civ.Code § 2938 (2009). Prior to this statute California legislation and case law recognized the validity of "absolute assignments." What is the effect of the above statute on such assignments? Note that the statute applies to an assignment "irrespective of whether [it] is denoted as absolute, conditioned upon default, additional security for an obligation or otherwise." Moreover, according to the statute's legislative history, it "would revise and recast [prior statutes] to apply to a written assignment * * * made in connection with an obligation secured by real property, regardless of how the assignment is denoted, and would specify requirements regarding these assignments." Legislative Counsel's Digest, S.B. No. 947 (1996).

Is California now a type of "middle ground" jurisdiction with respect to rents assignments? If so which kind? Are the requirements for triggering the right to collect the rents onerous?

4. *The Uniform Assignment of Rents Act.* In 2005 the National Conference of Commissioners on Uniform State Laws promulgated the Uniform Assignment of Rents Act (UARA). Professor Freyermuth, its reporter, describes UARA as follows:

> (UARA) * * * provides a comprehensive framework to govern the creation, perfection, and enforcement of security interests in rents arising from mortgaged real property. Without such a comprehensive statutory framework, courts (particularly bankruptcy courts) have struggled to establish clear and consistent rules governing security interests in rents—thereby encouraging needless and wasteful litigation over control of rents arising from mortgaged real property. Enactment of UARA in each state will provide much-needed clarity by establishing the following rules:

> ▪ "Rents" include sums payable for the right to possess or occupy the real property of another person, even if the occupant does not technically constitute a "tenant" under real property law. In

some commercial real estate developments (such as hotels and marinas), the occupants or "end-users" are not tenants under real property law, because their occupancy agreement does not create a sufficiently "exclusive" or "possessory" right. For this reason, some courts have refused to treat hotel room charges as "rents" and have thus concluded that hotel room charges would not be covered by an assignment of rents—even though such charges are functionally analogous to rents and parties often executed an assignment of rents believing that it covered such charges. UARA helps to resolve this documentary "trap," by providing that "rents" includes any sums payable for the right to possess or occupy the real property of another person. UARA § 2(12).

- A mortgage automatically creates a security interest in rents. Under the title theory of mortgages, a mortgage automatically effected an assignment of rents from the mortgaged real property. Under the lien theory of mortgages, however, a mortgage did not automatically create an assignment of rents. By contrast, under Article 9 of the Uniform Commercial Code, a security interest in collateral automatically extends to all identifiable proceeds of the collateral (including sums received from leasing collateral). Recognizing the functional similarity between "rents" and "proceeds," UARA provides that an effective mortgage automatically creates a security interest in rents arising from the mortgaged real property, unless the mortgage expressly provides otherwise. UARA § 4(a).

- A security interest in rents is perfected (and thus enforceable against creditors and purchasers) upon recording of the document creating an assignment of rents. Under Article 9, the filing of a financing statement is sufficient to perfect a security interest in most forms of personal property. By contrast, some courts have held that even if a creditor held a recorded assignment of rents, the creditor held only an "inchoate" lien until the creditor actually collected the rents after default. Many of these courts further held that if the debtor filed for bankruptcy before the creditor took effective steps to collect the rent after default, the creditor's interest was unperfected and the bankruptcy trustee could set aside the creditor's interest in rents using the trustee's strong-arm power. UARA overrules these decisions, providing that the recording of a document creating an assignment of rents is sufficient to perfect the creditor's security interest in rents and thereby make that interest enforceable against subsequent creditors and purchasers. UARA § 5(a)–(c).

- A security interest in rents is separate and distinct from a security interest in the underlying real property. The primary purpose of an assignment of rents is to create an effective security interest in rents that accrue after the assignor's default and prior to the assignee's completion of a foreclosure sale of the mortgaged real property. Most courts have treated these rents as a source of collateral that is separate and distinct from the underlying land. A few notorious bankruptcy court decisions, however, have held that rents are "subsumed within the land" such that a debtor need not provide adequate protection of the assignee's security interest in rents. UARA would overrule these decisions (to the extent that they rely upon state law), providing that a security interest in rents is an additional source of collateral that is distinct from the underlying real estate. UARA § 4(b).

- There is no such thing as an "absolute assignment of rents" in the context of a mortgage transaction; an assignment of rents creates only a security interest in the rents. Properly understood, an assignment of rents creates only a security interest in rents as collateral for the mortgage debt. Courts in some states, however, have held (and continue to hold) that an assignment of rents that purports to be an "absolute assignment" passes full title to the rents to the assignee, even prior to the assignor's default. UARA would overrule these decisions, providing that any assignment of rents granted in the context of a mortgage transaction creates only a security interest in rents (regardless of its form). UARA § 4(b).

- In a mortgage or assignment of rents, a provision granting the assignee the right to obtain a receiver following the assignor's default is enforceable. In many states, statutes provide few (if any) standards to inform a court's exercise of discretion whether to appoint a receiver to collect rents from mortgaged real property. UARA establishes consistent standards to govern the appointment of a receiver for mortgaged real property. UARA § 7(a). In particular, UARA establishes the enforceability of a clause by which the assignor has agreed that the assignee can obtain the appointment of a receiver after the assignor's default. UARA § 7(a)(1)(A).

- Upon default by the assignor (or as otherwise agreed by the assignor), the assignee may collect all rents that have accrued but remain unpaid and all rents that accrue thereafter. UARA § 6(b). By its terms, UARA does not allow the assignee to require the assignor to turn over sums already collected from its tenants prior to enforcement by the assignee. However, an assignee could create, perfect, and enforce a security interest in such monies under the provisions of UCC Article 9.

- The assignee may enforce an assignment of rents by obtaining the appointment of a receiver, by notification to the assignor, by notification to the assignor's tenants, or by any other method permitted by other law. UARA provides specific rules governing the collection of rents by receivership, by notification to the assignor, and by notification to tenants. UARA also provides that an assignee could collect rents by any other method permitted by law (including by becoming a mortgagee-in-possession). UARA §§ 6(a), 7, 8, 9.

- The assignee's enforcement of its rights and remedies under UARA does not render the assignee as a "mortgagee in possession" or trigger other adverse statutory consequences. At common law, a creditor that collected rents after default risked a possible argument that the creditor had become a "mortgagee in possession"—thereby triggering fiduciary obligations to the assignor and potential tort liability to third parties. UARA provides that the assignee's mere exercise of UARA's statutory remedies does not render the assignee as a mortgagee in possession. UARA § 11(1). Further, it does not constitute an election of remedies, render the mortgage debt unenforceable, violate a state's "one-action" principle, or trigger the application of a state's anti-deficiency statute. UARA § 11(2)–(7).

- An assignor that collects rents after it receives notification that the assignee has enforced its security interest in rents must turn over to the assignee the rents collected; if the assignor fails to do so, it is liable to the assignee for the amount not turned over. At common law, an assignor that refused to turn over rents to the assignee despite proper demand by the assignee could be held liable for "waste" (or conversion) of rents. The amount of such liability, however, varied depending upon whether the jurisdiction followed the lien theory of mortgages (damages recoverable only to the extent assignee was harmed) or the title theory of mortgages (damages measured by amount of rents collected and not turned over). UARA provides that the assignor that fails to turn over collected rents following a proper demand by the assignee is liable to the assignee for all sums collected by the assignor. UARA § 14(b), (d). Any damages recovered by the assignee in an action under § 14, however, constitute security for the mortgage debt and must therefore be applied to the mortgage debt. UARA § 12.

- Most tenants that receive notification to make rent payments to the assignee cannot thereafter discharge their rental obligation by paying the assignor. Under the common law of contracts, the obligor can discharge its obligation by payment to the obligee until the obligor receives notification that the obligee has assigned the right to payment and the assignee directs the obligor to make payment to the assignee. UARA primarily tracks existing common law, providing that a tenant that receives notification to pay the assignee can only discharge its obligation by paying the assignee. UARA § 9(c)(1)–(2). UARA does provide an exception for a tenant that occupies the premises as its primary residence, permitting such a tenant to satisfy its rental obligation by payment to either the assignee or the assignor. UARA § 9(c)(2).

- An assignee that collects rents from the tenants or the assignor can apply the collected sums to the mortgage debt and need not apply the rents to the payment of expenses of maintaining the mortgaged real property (unless otherwise agreed by the mortgagee). Tenants under commercial leases often pay sums called "rent" or "additional rent" based upon the tenant's proportionate share of real property taxes, insurance, and maintenance. An assignment of rents typically assigns the assignor's right to collect these payments to the assignee as security for the mortgage debt. Under prevailing law, an assignee that collects such rents can apply them to the debt, without obligation to use those sums for the payment of property-related expenses (unless the assignee has so agreed). UARA follows this prevailing view. UARA § 13(a). UARA preserves any claims or defenses that a tenant may have by virtue of the landlord's nonperformance of the lease, and also permits a tenant to seek appointment of a receiver if the assignee's nonpayment of property-related expenses causes or threatens harm to the tenant's interest in the mortgaged real property. UARA § 13(b), (c).

- UARA establishes priority rules that govern disputes between interests created by real property law (a security interest in the cash proceeds of rents) and interests in the same property created under Article 9. A perfected security interest in rents extends to the identifiable proceeds of those rents—typically, cash collections. Because cash monies—and the deposit accounts in which cash is typically maintained—are personal property in which a competing security interest can be created under Article 9, UARA provides coordinating priority rules to govern such priority disputes.

R. Wilson Freyermuth, Modernizing Security in Rents: The New Uniform Assignment of Rents Act, 71 Mo.L.Rev. 1, Appendix (2006).* To what extent is UARA similar to the Restatement and California approaches? To date, five

---

* Reprinted with permission of the Missouri Law Review.

states, (Nevada, New Mexico, North Dakota, Texas and Utah) have adopted UARA.

COLEMAN V. HOFFMAN

Court of Appeals of Washington, 2003
115 Wash.App. 853, 64 P.3d 65

BRIDGEWATER, J.

* * *

In July 1997, Roberta Coleman lived with her six-month-old daughter, Makaliah Paige, at the Sound View II apartment complex in Pierce County. On July 4, as Coleman prepared food for the evening's celebration, an unrelated child named Paris, age 9 years, walked Makaliah in a stroller along the balcony. The offending balcony was located outside of Coleman's apartment and was thus part of a common area. As Paris pushed Makaliah, the stroller's wheel caught in a rotten portion of carpet, causing the stroller to lurch forward into the balcony's rotten railing. Makaliah fell through the broken railing and onto the ground one story below. She sustained a broken arm, fractured skull and other injuries.

OCI brokers secured real estate investments. In late 1996, OCI arranged a loan to David Brown and Steve Clem, who owned and were refinancing Sound View II. The loan was secured by a deed of trust, of which OCI was beneficiary, which carried a standard assignment of rents provision. Anderson Hunter, a law firm, funded the loan.

In early April, after Brown and Clem's default, Anderson Hunter commenced judicial foreclosure proceedings and directed that OCI begin collecting and forwarding rents (OCI remained as beneficiary under the deed of trust). To comply, OCI instructed Sound View II tenants to begin making payments to OCI rather than Brown and Clem. And, to protect its investment, Anderson Hunter began paying utility and repair costs.

Sometime before Makaliah's injury, although disputed, Anderson Hunter hired Craig Hoffman to make repairs and manage the apartment complex. Hoffman previously tried to purchase the complex from Brown and Clem, but the transaction never closed. When Anderson Hunter hired Hoffman, which apparently occurred after the failed transaction, Hoffman expected to purchase the complex at the foreclosure sale.

On July 22, 1997, deciding against judicial foreclosure, Anderson Hunter sent a notice of default and of trustee's sale to Brown and Clem. The sale occurred on October 31, 1997. Hoffman was the purchaser.

Coleman, individually and as parent and guardian of Paige, sued Anderson Hunter, Hoffman, and OCI. She alleged several causes of action, including a common law premises liability claim. The trial court granted the defendants' summary judgment motions on all claims. * * *

Coleman appeals only the summary dismissal of her common law premises liability claim. Her theory is that the various respondents were mortgagees in possession and therefore can be held liable for the condition of the premises.

In an action for negligence, a plaintiff must prove four basic elements: (1) the existence of a duty, (2) breach of that duty, (3) resulting injury, and (4) proximate cause. Tincani v. Inland Empire Zoological Soc'y, 124 Wash.2d 121, 127–28, 875 P.2d 621 (1994). The threshold determination of whether a duty exists is a question of law. * * *

Although no Washington case is directly on point, other jurisdictions impose a duty of care on mortgagees in possession. See Mollino v. Ogden & Clarkson Corp., 243 N.Y. 450, 154 N.E. 307 (1926). Various treatises also support mortgagee liability:

"A mortgagee who properly acquires 'mortgagee in possession' status is held accountable for that possession . . . to third parties. In general, the mortgagee in possession is held to the standard of the provident owner to use reasonable diligence to keep the property . . . in a good state of repair." RESTATEMENT OF PROPERTY (THIRD), MORTGAGES, § 4.1, at 189 (1997).

In order for a mortgagee to be responsible for damages to third parties caused by unsafe conditions on the property, the mortgagee must exercise dominion and control over the property; a mortgagee out of possession of the mortgaged premises, with no management or control, is not liable for defects therein. Constructive possession is not sufficient to constitute control. 62 AM.JUR.2D Premises Liability, § 8, 356 (1990). * * *

"A possessor of land is (a) a person who is in occupation of the land with intent to control it or (b) a person who has been in occupation of land with intent to control it, if no other person has subsequently occupied it with intent to control it, or (c) a person who is entitled to immediate occupation of the land, if no other person is in possession under Clauses (a) and (b)." Ingersoll v. DeBartolo, Inc., 123 Wash.2d 649, 655, 869 P.2d 1014 (1994) (citing Restatement (Second) of Torts § 328E (1965)).

A. Anderson Hunter

By its affidavits, Anderson Hunter established that it collected rents from the tenants after Brown and Clem's default. Clise v. Burns involved a trustee who, under a deed of trust, received rents, issues, and profits from mortgaged property. Clise v. Burns, 175 Wash. 133, 26 P.2d 627 (1933). The *Clise* court stated that the trustee's actions did not constitute possession and control for mortgagee in possession purposes. Clise, 175 Wash. at 136–37, 29 P.2d 1119.

However, Coleman produced two relevant letters and the deposition testimony of an Anderson Hunter attorney that, together, weigh heavily in our analysis. First, a May 24, 1999 letter prepared by Paul Carpenter, a member of the Anderson Hunter firm and Hoffman's attorney, states, "at the time of the alleged accident (7/4/97) we, together with [OCI], had, for all practical purposes taken over control of [the premises] in that we could not locate and/or communicate with [Brown and Clem]." (Emphasis added). * * * Although conclusory as to control, the letter is in the nature of an admission by Anderson Hunter and therefore factors into our analysis. Second, an October 1997 letter from OCI's senior vice-president to Carpenter states "that Craig Hoffman had been heading the 'facelift' since last April and Anderson Hunter pool was advancing funds to him for that purpose." * * * Finally, Carpenter indicated at his deposition that Anderson Hunter began paying utility bills on June 11 and paid repair costs to a plumbing company in May or June 1997.

B.   Hoffman

In his affidavit, Hoffman stated that he did not own the premises until November 1997, that he did not make any repairs or collect rents at the premises until August 1997, and that he did not fire the apartment manager until September 1997.

But Coleman produced several other documents that bear on our analysis of Hoffman's possession. First, the October 1997 letter stated that Hoffman had been making repairs since April 1997, which was before the accident. Second, in her declaration in opposition to summary judgment, Coleman states that, in May or June 1997, "Mr. Hoffman and Billy began tearing up the floorboard in front of my apartment. The work lasted for about two days. By the time they ended, the sinkhole was repaired[.]" * * * Third, in his deposition, Carpenter stated that "[m]y recollection is Craig Hoffman terminated [the apartment manager's] service." * * * Although the record does not reflect the specific date of termination, the line of questioning at the deposition indicates that Hoffman fired the manager sometime in May, June, or July 1997.

C.   OCI

OCI carried its burden of establishing the absence of an issue of material fact regarding its possession. In its summary judgment motion, OCI stated that it has never had an ownership interest in the premises; that it had no involvement in the repair, maintenance, control, or operation of the premises; and that, in servicing Anderson Hunter's loan to Brown and Clem, it activated the assignment of rents provision contained in the deed of trust and collected those rents during May, June, and July 1997. Coleman establishes no other issue of fact as to OCI's possession.

The mortgagee possession issue was addressed in two cases from other jurisdictions that involved facts similar to those presented here. Scott v. Hoboken Bank for Sav. in City of Hoboken, 126 N.J.L. 294, 19 A.2d 327 (1941), was a premises liability case where the plaintiff sued the mortgagee bank for injuries received in a fall on an ill-maintained stairway. The court stated that the bank "had in fact assumed complete control over the premises not alone as to the collection of rents and payment of bills but also as to the making of repairs . . . and . . . the owner, in the position of a rent paying tenant, had no control." 19 A.2d at 330.

Scott aligns perfectly with Pantano v. Erie County Sav. Bank of Buffalo, 257 A.D. 451, 13 N.Y.S.2d 932 (N.Y.App.Div.1939), which was also a personal injury suit against a mortgagee bank. In *Pantano*, the bank had "the exclusive right to lease the property, to bring, prosecute and settle summary proceedings for the removal of tenants, or actions at law for the recovery of rents or of any damage done premises or for the abatement of any nuisance thereon, [and] to make necessary repairs and alterations to the building." Pantano, 13 N.Y.S.2d at 934. The court allowed suit against the bank, holding that the bank possessed and controlled the premises. Pantano, 13 N.Y.S.2d at 934.

In an apartment building, factors indicating a mortgagee's possession include the indicia of control that landlords normally exhibit. *Scott* and *Pantano* demonstrate certain such factors: leasing, making repairs, and paying bills. Additional factors could include making management decisions and receiving and responding to tenant complaints.

Hoffman performed two acts that show possession and control: he made repairs and a managerial decision. Similarly, Anderson Hunter performed acts indicating possession and control: it paid utility bills and repair costs, collected rents, and hired Hoffman. But the facts show that OCI only collected rents; under *Clise*, this action alone does not establish possession and control. Thus, as to Hoffman and Anderson Hunter, Coleman carried her burden in establishing genuine issues of fact regarding possession of the Sound View II. On her claim against OCI, Coleman has failed to establish an issue of fact. Therefore, the trial court erred in granting summary judgment in favor of Hoffman and Anderson Hunter, but it did not err in granting summary judgment to OCI.

* * *

The trial court's order of summary judgment on Coleman's common law premises liability claim is reversed as to Hoffman and Anderson Hunter but affirmed as to OCI.

We concur: HOUGHTON, P.J., and ARMSTRONG, J.

NOTES

1. *Does enforcing an assignment of rents create "mortgagee in possession" status?* Mortgagees are often concerned that they will become a "mortgagee in possession" simply because they enforce an assignment of rents provision. Under the Restatement, "the mere collection of rents pursuant to [an assignment of rents] does not constitute the mortgagee a 'mortgage in possession' with the duties and liabilities attendant to that status." Restatement (Third) of Property (Mortgages) § 4.2, comment c (1997). California takes the same position. See West's Ann.Cal.Civ.Code § 2938(e)(1). Accord: In re Olick, 221 B.R. 146 (Bankr.E.D.Pa.1998). UARA § 11(1). But see United Nat'l Bank v. Parish, 330 N.J.Super. 654, 750 A.2d 238 (1999) (assuming that mortgagee who collected rents pursuant to a rental assignment was a mortgagee in possession and therefore liable to pay real estate taxes during the period it collected rents). Consider the language of a recent Supreme Court of New Hampshire decision:

> Whether a mortgagee has exercised dominion and control over the property and, thus, possessed it, "is a factual issue." * * * For instance, collection of rent alone by a mortgagee may not render the mortgagee a mortgagee in possession; however, the collection of rent and active management of the real estate "will probably suffice." "In an apartment building, factors indicating a mortgagee's possession include the indicia of control that landlords normally exhibit," such as "leasing, making repairs, and paying bills." *Coleman v. Hoffman,* 115 Wash.App. 853, 64 P.3d 65, 69 (2003). "Additional factors could include making management decisions and receiving and responding to tenant complaints." *Id.;* see *Citizens' Savings & Trust Co. v. Rogers,* 162 Wis. 216, 155 N.W. 155, 159–60 (1915) (Mortgagee who "employed janitors, provided fuel and elevator service, and . . . collected rents from the tenants of the buildings" exercised "the dominion and control over the property that is usually . . . exercised by a landlord," and was mortgagee in possession.).

Case v. St. Mary's Bank, 164 N.H. 649, 656, 63 A.3d 1209, 1215 (2013).

Coleman illustrates a major problem with enforcing an assignment of rents clause. If the mortgagee actually collects the rents, won't tenants invariably hold the mortgagee accountable for repairs and other management problems concerning the real estate? If the mortgagee responds to tenant concerns by making repairs or the like, then won't the mortgagee be treated as a mortgagee in possession? You should revisit these questions after we consider the receivership remedy in the next section.

2. *Bankruptcy.* Assignment of rents issues become especially important when the mortgagor seeks the protection of the Bankruptcy Code. When this occurs, the rents mortgagee and the trustee (or the debtor-in-

possession) will each claim priority as to rents collected during the bankruptcy proceeding. State law will often be determinative of that controversy. Thus, we will consider rent assignments again in the bankruptcy context. See Chapter 6, Section J infra.

B. RECEIVERSHIPS

A mortgagee in the pre-foreclosure stage may prefer an equitable receivership either to attempting to obtain possession as mortgagee or to reliance on an assignment of rents provision. While the scope of an equitable receivership varies from jurisdiction to jurisdiction, it typically involves a judicial appointment of a third party to take possession of the mortgaged property, to repair or preserve the property, and to collect rents.

A title state mortgagee, as we have seen, in theory may successfully obtain possession by an action at law for ejectment. However, such an action is often drawn out and time-consuming. By comparison, a receiver may often be appointed promptly incident to a foreclosure suit. Moreover, by utilizing a receivership, a mortgagee avoids some of the strict accounting responsibilities associated with being a mortgagee in possession. Robert Kratovil, Mortgages—Problems in Possession, Rents, and Mortgagee Liability, 11 DePaul L.Rev. 1, 7 (1961). The receivership means that the mortgagee need not shoulder this burden. Also, "entry by a mortgagee may automatically terminate leases executed by the mortgagor [if they are subordinate to the mortgage—ed.], and if these leases are favorable to the landlord, such a course is to be avoided. Appointment of a receiver will ordinarily not have such a result." Id. Finally, the receivership generally will insulate a mortgagee from tort and related landowner-type liabilities normally imposed on mortgagees in possession. See Nelson, Whitman, Burkhart & Freyermuth, Real Estate Finance Law § 4.33 (6th ed.2014). In lien theory states, the receivership may be an even more important remedy to the mortgagee because of the unavailability of ejectment to obtain possession for the mortgagee.

A receivership may also sometimes be preferable to reliance on enforcement of an assignment of rents provision. What if there are now no tenants paying rents? It may well be that such an assignment provision is of no practical remedy to the mortgagee. On the other hand, a receiver can take possession and attempt to re-establish a cash flow from the mortgaged premises.

DART V. WESTERN SAVINGS & LOAN ASSOCIATION

Supreme Court of Arizona, 1968
103 Ariz. 170, 438 P.2d 407

STRUCKMEYER, JUSTICE.

These two appeals, consolidated for this decision only, arise out of an action to foreclose a mortgage on a trailer park. Dart and his wife, together with Inland Western Mortgage Company, second mortgagee, were sued by Western Savings and Loan Association to foreclose a first mortgage. Western also sought the appointment of a receiver. Inland cross-claimed to foreclose its second mortgage and to foreclose a first mortgage on the Darts' home. It also sought a receiver.

William J. Dart, in answer to the complaint for foreclosure by Western, asserted that he was the beneficiary of a trust whose res was the subject matter of the foreclosure suit and he cross-claimed against Union Title Company, as trustee, alleging conversion of trust moneys (income from the trailer park deposited in escrow) so that the trust res was jeopardized. Union answered the cross-claim, admitting that it had converted trust moneys and stated there was an arrearage of $18,500 on the first mortgage. It further alleged that the Darts had, in March, 1964, unlawfully assumed the management and control of the trust estate. Union also urged the appointment of a receiver.

At the time of the hearing on the application by Western for a receiver, the property was of the estimated value between $500,000 and $800,000, and $244,478.69 was owed on the first mortgage and $55,000 on the second mortgage. A federal tax lien had been placed against the property in the approximate amount of $187,000. It is conceded, however, that this tax lien is junior to both mortgages. Real and personal property taxes are accruing against the trailer park at the rate of $1700 a year and interest on the first mortgage is accruing at the rate of $1600 a month.

William J. Dart, the residuary beneficiary of the trust, and his wife Dorothy entered into possession of the real property after it became known that Union had embezzled the trailer park income. Thereafter, they collected rentals at the rate of approximately $5,000 a month. Although some of the income was used by the Darts to improve the trailer court, none was applied to meet the payments due on either the first or second mortgages.

The Inland mortgage provides for an assignment of rents and profits as security for the mortgage. In addition, both mortgages provide that if an action to foreclose is brought, a receiver "shall be appointed" to take charge of the property and to receive and collect rents, issues and profits and apply them to the payment of the mortgages, taxes and other charges. The court, acting upon the above stated facts, did appoint receivers, first at the instigation of Western and later at the instigation of

Inland. The appeals question the propriety of the trial court's actions in that respect.

It is clear that the appointments of the receivers were improvident.

A.R.S. § 33–703, subsec. A provides:

"A mortgage is a lien upon everything that would pass by a grant of the property, but does not entitle the mortgagee to possession of the property unless authorized by the express terms of the mortgage. * * * "

Of this section, we have said:

"The title to mortgaged property under our law remains in the mortgagor. The mortgagee's interest is that of a lienor." Mortgage Investment Co. of El Paso, Tex. v. Taylor, 49 Ariz. 558, 563, 68 P.2d 340, 342.

The principle applicable here has been discussed in 2 Glenn on Mortgages, § 173:

"The mortgagee's equitable right to have a receiver, therefore, arises only when he shows something more than a default; * * * . Such, at least, is the prevailing rule with which we are now dealing; and so it remains to ask what is the 'something more' that is required.

"The first point on which all are agreed, is that there should be no receivership if the security is adequate and no waste is threatened which is apt to impair the mortgagee's safety."

The reason for the rule that a mortgagee is not entitled to a receiver if the security is adequate and no waste is threatened is that, the mortgage being but a lien, the mortgagor is entitled to possession and to all the benefits, such as the income, which the possessor of property ordinarily enjoys. * * *

The evidence introduced at the hearing on the application by Western for a receiver makes it abundantly clear that the security is adequate. According to the uncontradicted statement of counsel for the Darts to the court at the hearing for the appointment of a receiver, the property is appraised at between $550,000 and $780,000. The attorney for Western made this statement to the court:

"At this particular time it's obvious to Counsel here that the property at the present time, under the way in which it's being managed is probably not jeopardizing our particular loan in the amount of 250 some odd thousand dollars. * * * "

And:

> "As to the receivership at the present time, I think Mr. Bayham has made his point that the property is not in jeopardy at the present time as to our security."

It is, however, Western's position that because its mortgage provides a pledge of the rents and profits and an agreement for the appointment of a receiver that the court acted properly and within its discretion. Here again appellee's position runs counter to the weight of reason.

> "We have seen that a receiver will not be appointed when the security is adequate and there is no danger of waste. The reason, of course, is that when the mortgagee does not stand in need of this interim measure an equity court will not deprive the mortgagor of the possession to which he is absolutely entitled under the lien theory; * * * . The question now is, whether the income and receivership clauses can overcome this rule. To say yes, would mean that although an equity court would properly refuse to thrust a mortgagee into possession when there is no necessity for it, yet the court should do that very thing if the mortgage so provides.

> "The answer is that no such contract provision should force a court of equity to exercise its discretion in favor of a party who stands in no need of aid. * * * If the security is plainly adequate, a receiver will not be appointed, despite the presence, in the mortgage, of a rent pledge or receivership clause, or both." 2 Glenn, Mortgages, § 175.1.

It is urged that the failure to pay taxes constitutes waste. But while it is true that taxes are accruing at the rate of $1700 a year, there is no evidence whatsoever that there has been a failure to pay taxes. And finally, Western suggests that the accrual of interest at the rate of $1600 a month is grounds for a receiver. We do not think so. Here again there is no showing that the security is insufficient to provide recoupment of interest.

The record is clear. The Union Title Company, as trustee, converted income from the property which if applied to the mortgages would have been sufficient to prevent them from being in default. Upon the failure of Union Title to make the mortgage payments, and it appearing that the property was being mismanaged by being permitted to fall into disrepair, appellant Dart, the residuary beneficiary of the trust, entered into possession. The testimony discloses, from Western's witness, Glenn Erickson, that when he first checked the property it was "badly run down. The recreation facilities were not operating. The pool was not operating, and it showed neglect throughout and they had quite a few vacancies out there." This was the condition of the property under the management of

Union Title shortly before July 3, 1964. Thereafter, under the appellants' management and by September 3rd, the date of the receivership hearing, Erickson found "all the facilities operating nicely. The landscaping is well taken care of. It's neat and there seems—I talked to several people and there is lots of harmony out there now, and I would say it was running in first class condition right now" with "very few" vacancies.

We think it was within the prerogative of the residuary beneficiary to attempt to save the trust res and that he had sufficient equitable interest to enter upon the property for that purpose under the peculiar circumstances of this case. The operative facts which would empower the court below to appoint a receiver to take charge of the property were not present. It should have directed either that Union Title be immediately superseded as trustee and that the successor trustee take charge of the property, applying the income in accordance with the trust agreement; or, if it determined that appellant had been properly managing the property, it should have placed him in possession, under bond, to preserve the property with directions to distribute the income in accordance with the trust agreement. * * * Irrespective, the lower court must direct that the net income of the trust property, both past and future, be distributed pursuant to the terms of the trust agreement.

The orders appointing the receivers are set aside and vacated and the cause is remanded for further proceedings consistent with this decision.

MCFARLAND, C.J., UDALL, V.C.J., and BERNSTEIN and LOCKWOOD, JJ., concur.

NOTES

1. *Standards for receivership.* In theory one would suppose that a receivership is more readily obtainable in a title than in a lien jurisdiction, since the title jurisdiction mortgagee has possessory rights not afforded its lien counterpart. Ironically, however, in some title jurisdictions this possessory right may traditionally have been an obstacle to rather than a reason for granting a receivership. Some of these courts have required that the legal remedy of ejectment be shown to be inadequate. See Nelson, Whitman, Burkhart & Freyermuth, Real Estate Finance Law § 4.34 (6th ed.2014).

However, today the articulated standard for the appointment of a receiver varies little among title, intermediate, and lien jurisdictions. Under the most common statement of the rule, insolvency of the mortgagor and inadequacy of the security are not enough to justify the receivership. Rather, "there must be shown some additional, distinct equitable ground, such as danger of loss, waste, destruction, or serious impairment of the property, to warrant the appointment." Grether v. Nick, 193 Wis. 503, 508, 213 N.W. 304, 306 (1927). See Atco Constr. & Dev. Corp. v. Beneficial Sav. Bank, F.S.B., 523

So.2d 747 (Fla.App.1988) (appointment of receiver constitutes abuse of discretion in the absence of a showing of waste or serious risk of loss).

Under the Restatement, a "mortgagee is entitled to the appointment of a receiver * * * if: (1) the mortgagor is in default under the mortgage; (2) the value of the real estate is inadequate to satisfy the mortgage obligation; and (3) the mortgagor is committing waste." Restatement (Third) of Property (Mortgages) § 4.3(a) (1997). Note that while, in some jurisdictions, "waste" means affirmative physical destruction or at least failure to repair, in others the term has a much broader meaning. For example, under the Restatement approach, waste includes not only failing "to pay real estate taxes," but, in addition, "the failure to pay insurance premiums, if payment is required by the mortgage documents." Id., cmt. b. Finally, waste can even encompass "the improper taking by the mortgagor of rents which should be paid to the mortgagee" under an assignment of rents provision. Id.

2. *Impact of receivership and rent assignment clauses.* As *Dart* illustrates, some courts hold that they will not enforce a receivership clause where the circumstances do not justify such an appointment in the absence of such a clause. See Nelson, Whitman, Burkhart & Freyermuth, Real Estate Finance Law 229 (6th ed. 2014). On the other hand, some courts will enforce receivership clauses irrespective of whether a receivership would be justified in their absence. See, e.g., Dover Assocs. Joint Venture v. Ingram, 768 A.2d 971 (Del.Ch.2000); Fleet Bank of Maine v. Zimelman, 575 A.2d 731 (Me.1990); Metropolitan Life Ins. Co. v. Liberty Center Venture, 437 Pa.Super. 544, 650 A.2d 887 (1994); Federal Home Loan Mortg. Corp. v. Nazar, 100 B.R. 555 (D.Kan.1989). Indeed, by statute, Arizona has now overruled *Dart* at least in cases where the mortgage contains an assignment of rents. See Ariz.Rev.Stat.Ann. § 33–702(B) (assignment of rents may be enforced by appointment of receiver "without regard to the adequacy of the security or the solvency of the mortgagor").

Under the Restatement, a mortgagee is entitled to a receivership "if the mortgagor is in default * * * and the mortgage or other agreement contains either a mortgage on the rents or a provision authorizing appointment of a receiver to take possession and collect rents upon mortgagor default." Restatement (Third) of Property (Mortgages) § 4.3(b) (1997).

Some courts, while not willing to enforce receivership agreements automatically, are favorably disposed toward them. See, e.g., Barclays Bank of California v. Superior Court, 69 Cal.App.3d 593, 137 Cal.Rptr. 743 (1977) ("[A]lthough a recital that upon default the [mortgagee] shall be entitled to the appointment of a receiver is not binding upon the courts, such a recital nevertheless has some evidentiary weight. * * * [I]t reasonably follows that it presents a prima facie, but rebuttable, evidentiary showing of the [mortgagee's] entitlement to appointment of a receiver."); Wellman Sav. Bank v. Roth, 432 N.W.2d 697 (Iowa App.1988); Riverside Props. v. Teachers Ins. & Annuity Ass'n, 590 S.W.2d 736 (Tex.Civ.App.1979).

In several states, statutes make receivership clauses enforceable upon default without the necessity of establishing the normal equitable conditions precedent. See, e.g., 735 Ill.Comp.Stat. 5/15–1701–15–1706; West's Ann.Ind.Code § 34–1–12–1(4)(c); Minn.Stat.Ann. § 559.17(2) (authorizing the enforcement of a receivership clause upon default in mortgages of $100,000 or more not involving homestead or agricultural property). N.Y.Real Prop.Law § 254(10); 366 Fourth Street Corp. v. Foxfire Enters., Inc., 149 A.D.2d 692, 540 N.Y.S.2d 489 (1989) (statute makes it proper to enforce receivership clause without regard to adequacy of security); Febbraro v. Febbraro, 70 A.D.2d 584, 416 N.Y.S.2d 59 (1979) (no showing of need required where mortgage contains receivership clause).

Receivership clauses in federally-insured mortgages tend to be given substantial weight, especially when they are being interpreted by federal courts. Some courts have indicated that such clauses alone may justify the appointment of a receiver in situations where the mortgagee is unable to establish the traditional equitable conditions precedent for such an appointment. See, e.g., United States v. Berk & Berk, 767 F.Supp. 593 (D.N.J.1991); United States v. Mountain Village Co., 424 F.Supp. 822 (D.Mass.1976). Cf. New York Life Ins. Co. v. Watt West Inv. Corp., 755 F.Supp. 287 (E.D.Cal.1991) (receivership clause entitled to "great weight"). It should be noted, however, that such cases are largely the product of the federal courts applying a "federal common law" instead of the substantive mortgage law of the forum state, a problem we will consider later in this volume. See Chapter 8, Section F infra.

3. *Ex parte receivership.* In some jurisdictions it is common for courts to appoint receivers by *ex parte* order. This entails the appointment of a receiver, usually pending judicial foreclosure, without providing either notice or a hearing for the mortgagor and other interested parties. On the other hand, some jurisdictions reject this remedy unless the mortgage documents specifically authorize the appointment of a receiver without notice. See, e.g., GE Life & Annuity Assurance Co. v. Fort Collins Assemblage, Ltd., 53 P.3d 703 (Colo.App.2001). In any event, does such a practice violate the due process clause of the 14th Amendment? Consider the response of the court in Friedman v. Gerax Realty Assocs., 100 Misc.2d 820, 420 N.Y.S.2d 247 (1979):

> Since the mortgage provides for the appointment of a receiver, the mortgage under Section 254(10) of the Real Property Law is considered as providing for the appointment of a receiver without notice. (Wolf v. 120 Middleton Realty, 31 Misc.2d 668, 221 N.Y.S.2d 110). That statute provides as follows:
>
> > "Where the action is for foreclosure of a mortgage providing that a receiver may be appointed without notice, notice of motion for such appointment shall not be required."

Thus, the prior ex-parte order was not in violation of New York Law. * * *

While it is true that United States Supreme Court has invalidated State statutes permitting ex-parte orders in replevin cases as a violation of due process (See Fuentes v. Shevin, 407 U.S. 67, 92 S.Ct. 1983, 32 L.Ed.2d 556; North Georgia Finishing v. Di-Chem Inc., 419 U.S. 601, 95 S.Ct. 719, 42 L.Ed.2d 751), there is no violation of due process where the appointment of the receiver is based upon sworn ex-parte documents under judicial supervision and followed by an early opportunity by debtor to put the creditor to his test. * * *

Here, this Court holds that the statutes are not violative of the due process rights of defendants. The appointment of the receiver, while ex parte, is under judicial supervision and, in this case, was supported by an affidavit of one of the plaintiffs, in addition to the verified complaint and supporting documents thereof including a copy of the mortgage and note. A bond in the sum of $312,000 was required to be filed. CPLR 6405 and 6401(b) enable an aggrieved party to immediately move to vacate the receivership and to limit his powers, (Security National Bank v. Village Mall at Hillcrest, 79 Misc.2d 1060, 361 N.Y.S.2d 977) and this Court has the power to deny the appointment if it is not supported to our satisfaction, and to limit his powers or to vacate the appointment with the opportunity for the mortgagor and mortgagee to be heard as to the validity of the underlying claim.

* * *

Accordingly, this Court holds that in view of the fact that the ex-parte appointment is under judicial supervision and that the law provides for an opportunity to an aggrieved party for an immediate hearing on the validity or probable validity of the underlying claim, these statutes are not unconstitutional.

Accord: Hartford Fed. Sav. & Loan Ass'n v. Tucker, 196 Conn. 172, 491 A.2d 1084 (1985). Even assuming that such a practice is otherwise unconstitutional, does the presence of a receivership clause constitute a waiver by the mortgagor of the constitutional objection? See Manufacturers Life Ins. Co. v. Patterson, 51 Ohio App.3d 99, 554 N.E.2d 134 (1988) (mortgage provision authorizing the appointment of a receiver without notice constitutes waiver by mortgagor of due process objections). See generally, Nelson, Whitman, Burkhart & Freyermuth, Real Estate Finance Law § 4.36 (6th ed.2014).

4. *Ability of receiver to terminate leases.* Suppose a receiver is appointed for rental property. To what extent should he or she be bound by rental prepayments or other collusive arrangements ("sweetheart" deals) between lessees and mortgagor? For an example of how New York, a lien jurisdiction, approaches this question, consider the following language from

New York City Community Preservation Corp. v. Michelin Assocs., 115
A.D.2d 715, 496 N.Y.S.2d 530 (1985):

> As a general rule, a receiver of rents and profits in a mortgage
> foreclosure action is bound by the agreement between the tenant
> and the mortgagor landlord, and notwithstanding that the amount
> fixed as rent under the terms of the lease is less than the fair and
> reasonable rental value of the premises, the tenant may not be
> required to pay to the receiver a greater amount, even though the
> lease is subordinate to the lien of the mortgage (*see, Prudence Co. v.
> 160 West 73rd St. Corp.*, 260 N.Y. 205, 213, 183 N.E. 365; *see also,
> Markantonis v. Madlan Realty Corp.*, 262 N.Y. 354, 186 N.E. 862;
> *Central Sav. Bank v. Chatham Assoc.*, 54 A.D.2d 873, 388 N.Y.S.2d
> 908; *Bank for Savings in City of N.Y. v. Shenk Realty & Constr. Co.*,
> 265 App.Div. 72, 37 N.Y.S.2d 597; *Bank of Manhattan Trust Co. v.
> 2166 Broadway Corp.*, 237 App.Div. 734, 262 N.Y.S. 730; *Flatbush
> Sav. Bank v. Levy*, 109 N.Y.S.2d 247; 15 Carmody-Wait 2d, NY
> Prac, § 92:490, p 461). However, this rule presupposes the existence
> of a bona fide lease, and a court has "broad power" to prevent
> frustration of an order appointing a receiver of rents "by a collusive
> or fraudulent lease for an inadequate rental or advance payment of
> rent in anticipation of a foreclosure action" (*Prudence Co. v. 160
> West 73rd St. Corp., supra*, 260 N.Y. at p. 213, 183 N.E. 365).

See generally, Nelson, Whitman, Burkhart & Freyermuth, Real Estate
Finance Law § 4.42 (6th ed.2014).

Under the Restatement, which adopts the lien theory of mortgages, a
receiver generally has no authority to disaffirm pre-receivership leases. See
Restatement (Third) of Property (Mortgages) § 4.4(a) (1997). Nevertheless,
the receiver may "disaffirm any lease or related agreement between the
mortgagor and a tenant that contravenes a provision of a prior recorded
mortgage" or was "made while the mortgagor is in default under the
mortgage that was not commercially reasonable when it was consummated."
Id. § 4.4(b) & (c).

For an example of disaffirmance of a lease that violated language of a
prior mortgage, see Dime Sav. Bank of New York, FSB v. Montague St.
Realty Assocs., 229 A.D.2d 461, 645 N.Y.S.2d 533 (1996) (mortgagor's lease
extension agreement with tenant requiring tenant to pay one year's rent in
advance violated provision in senior mortgage that prohibited any
prepayment of rent without mortgagee's written consent; tenant was
therefore held liable to receiver for the advance rent previously paid to
mortgagor). Suppose the post-default prepayment of rent had not been
prohibited by the senior mortgage. Would the prepayment be binding on the
receiver? See Restatement (Third) of Property (Mortgages) § 4.4, cmt. c (1997)
("[P]repayments of rent that are not authorized by the original lease will be
treated as presumptively not commercially reasonable and, accordingly, not
binding on the receiver.").

5. *Competing receivers.* Suppose a junior mortgagee obtains the appointment of a receiver. Must rents collected by that receiver be utilized to reduce senior mortgage debt? Consider the language of the court in Vechiarelli v. Garsal Realty, Inc., 111 Misc.2d 157, 443 N.Y.S.2d 622 (1980):

> A receiver appointed at the instance of one mortgagee acts on behalf of that mortgagee and not generally on behalf of all lienholders. *Sullivan v. Rosson*, 223 N.Y. 217, 119 N.E. 405; *Collins v. Wallens*, 143 Misc. 329, 256 N.Y.S. 453. Therefore the senior mortgagee must either obtain the appointment of his own receiver or an extension of the junior receivership before rents may be collected for his benefit. *Sullivan v. Rosson, supra; Kroehle v. Olcott*, 148 A.D. 54, 132 N.Y.S. 1056.

Similarly, the Restatement provides that "[w]hen a junior mortgagee obtains the appointment of a receiver, that receiver has the right, until a receiver is appointed under a senior mortgage, to collect rents from the mortgaged real estate and, after first using them to pay real estate taxes and other reasonable expenses associated with the maintenance and repair of the real estate, to apply the balance to the junior mortgage obligation." Restatement (Third) of Property (Mortgages) § 4.5(b) (1997). Is this sound policy? See id. cmt. b.

6. *Sale of Mortgaged Real Estate by Receiver.* The case law is unclear as to whether a receiver may sell mortgaged real estate and have that sale operate as a foreclosure.

> In the context of the recent real estate crisis, however, some commentators have advocated that receivership can be an effective way to dispose of real estate—and particularly, that it may in some cases provide a more effective way of disposing of mortgaged real property that the foreclosure process. * * * A receiver of mortgaged commercial real property could readily market that property to potential buyers in the context of operating the property during the receivership. Such marketing could permit potential buyers to perform more meaningful and complete due diligence. Further, a sale subject to judicial review and confirmation could produce greater finality regarding the title acquired by the buyer at the sale. Thus, there is certainly reason to expect that at least in some contexts, receiver sales of mortgaged real estate might produce higher sale prices than public foreclosure sales.

> * * *

> An existing federal statute explicitly authorizes a receiver appointed by a federal court to sell mortgaged property.[663]

---

[663] 28 U.S.C.A. § 2001. While the statute does not explicitly state that such a sale would be free of subordinate liens (and thus serve the same title-clearing function as a foreclosure sale), section 2001(a) provides that the receiver may sell "upon such terms and conditions as the court directs." Thus, it seems clear that if the court orders a sale free and clear of subordinate liens, that sale would have the effect of extinguishing any subordinate lien (unless the holder of that

Furthermore, the statute permits the receiver to sell the property in a private sale:

> After a hearing, of which notice to all interested parties shall be given by publication or otherwise as the court directs, the court may order the sale of such realty or interest or any part thereof at private sale for cash or other consideration and upon such terms and conditions as the court approves, if it finds that the best interests of the estate will be conserved thereby.[664]

As a result, mortgagees can in appropriate cases seek the appointment of a federal court receiver, ancillary either to an action to foreclose the mortgage or for specific performance of the borrower's assignment of rents. Nevertheless, one could typically obtain a federal court receiver only if there existed sufficient diversity of citizenship among the parties to warrant federal jurisdiction.

By contrast, under existing state laws, the authority for receiver sales is much less clear. There are a few states with statutory provisions that explicitly grant the power of sale to a receiver.[665] In most states, however, there is no comprehensive statute governing real estate receiverships, or the applicable statutes do not explicitly address whether the receiver has a power of sale. As a result, in some states, there is doubt as to whether or in what circumstances a state court receiver could conduct a sale of mortgaged property, and whether such a sale would be free and clear of liens and any applicable statutory redemption rights. The litigation in *Shubh Hotels Boca, LLC v. Federal Deposit Insurance Corp.*[666] provides a good example. Shubh Hotels Boca, LLC (Shubh) owned a 180-room hotel in Boca Raton, subject to $28.8 million mortgage loan. In May 2009, the mortgagee instituted a judicial foreclosure proceeding following financial defaults by Shubh, and the lender obtained the appointment of a receiver to collect rents during the foreclosure proceeding. By January 2010, hotel

---

lien did not receive notice and a reasonable opportunity to challenge the appointment of the receiver or the sale itself). See generally Toni Pryor Wise, Federal Receiverships—A New Old Tool for Selling Distressed Commercial Properties?, ACREL Papers (March 2011).

[664] 28 U.S.C.A. § 2001(b).

[665] See, e.g., Ind. Code § 32–30–5–7 (receiver may "sell property in the receiver's own name, and generally do other acts respecting the property as the court or judge may authorize"); N.C.Gen.Stat. § 1–505 (receiver may sell property "upon such terms as appear to be to the best interests of the creditors affected by the receivership"); Wash. Rev. Code Ann. § 7.60.260 (granting receiver the power to sell mortgaged property with the court's approval after notice and hearing). Minnesota's comprehensive receivership statute distinguishes between a general receiver (i.e., a receiver appointed to liquidate and administer all of a person's nonexempt property) and a limited (or custodial) receiver, Minn.Stat.Ann. § 576.21(h), (k), and recognizes a receiver's power to sell free and clear of liens only in a general receivership. Minn.Stat.Ann. §§ 576.29(b), 576.46.

[666] 46 So.3d 163 (Fla.Dist.Ct.App.2010).

operations were losing $28,000 each month and the receiver was unable to raise borrowed funds to continue operating the hotel. The mortgagee immediately moved to have the property sold as soon as a buyer could be identified. The trial court granted this motion, and the receiver identified a buyer willing to pay $9 million for the hotel, but Shubh objected to the proposed sale on the ground that the receiver had no legal authority to sell the hotel and could not convey title. The trial court rejected this objection and entered an order authorizing the sale, but the Florida District Court of Appeal reversed, noting that no Florida statute authorized a court-appointed receiver in a foreclosure case to sell the mortgaged property.[667] The court also noted that the mortgage itself did not specifically authorize the receiver to sell the property, but only "to protect and preserve" the mortgaged property, to "operate [it] preceding foreclosure or sale," and to collect rents and apply them against the debt.[668] More generally, the court noted that "the mere appointment of a receiver does not itself confer any of the owner's power or authority to sell such property," that "the role of a receiver in a foreclosure action is only to preserve the property's value," and that implying a power of sale would be inconsistent with that limited role.[669] Finally, the court noted that under Florida law, every mortgagor has a statutory right of redemption until the issuance of a certificate of sale by the clerk of court, and held that "[r]ecognizing a general interim power of a receiver to sell mortgaged property in a foreclosure case would contravene" that redemption right.[670]

Decisions in several other states have raised similar doubts about the effective power of a receiver to sell mortgaged property outside of the foreclosure context. For example, in South Carolina, courts have held that the purpose of a receiver is to preserve the status quo, and do not permit receivers to sell receivership property.[671] Likewise, a Minnesota court reversed a trial court's order authorizing a receivership sale free and clear of the borrower's statutory right of redemption, holding that such a result was contrary to the state's mortgage foreclosure statute, which affords the mortgagor a statutory redemption right.[672]

---

[667] *Shubh*, 46 So.3d at 165–166.

[668] *Shubh*, 46 So.3d at 166.

[669] *Shubh*, 46 So.3d at 167 (citing Eppes v. Dade Devs., Inc., 126 Fla. 353, 170 So. 875 (1936); Cone-Otwell-Wilson Corp. v. Commodore's Point Term Co., 94 Fla. 448, 114 So. 232 (1927); and Alafaya Square Ass'n Ltd. v. Great Western Bank, 700 So.2d 38 (Fla.Dist.Ct.App.1997)).

[670] *Shubh*, 46 So.3d at 167.

[671] See, e.g., Kirven v. Lawrence, 244 S.C. 572, 137 S.E.2d 764 (1964); Andrick Dev. Corp. v. Maccaro, 280 S.C. 103, 311 S.E.2d 95 (Ct.App.1984).

[672] Todd Enters., LLC v. MidCountry Bank, 2013 WL 4045765 (Minn.Ct.App.2013) (not reported in N.W.2d).

By contrast, courts in several other states have upheld receiver sales free and clear of liens and statutory redemption rights. In *CSB Bank v. Christy*,[673] the Michigan Court of Appeals upheld a receiver's sale of mortgaged property, rejecting challenges by a mortgagor that sale violated Michigan's foreclosure requirements. Likewise, several decisions in Ohio have concluded that a receiver may sell mortgaged property free and clear of liens and encumbrances in a private sale where authorized by the court in the order of appointment.[674] Interestingly, the Ohio decisions rely on the fact that the Ohio statute empowers the receiver to "do such acts respecting the property as the court authorizes" and does not contain any restrictions on what the court may authorize when it issues orders regarding receivership property.[675] In this regard, the Ohio decisions take the opposite interpretive approach from the Florida court in *Shubh*. A Pennsylvania court has held that a receiver may sell real estate free and clear of liens if there is "a reasonable prospect that a surplus will be left to be distributed among general creditors."[676]

This uncertainty is a lamentable by-product of the outdated and inadequate state statutory provisions governing receiverships. As one judge has noted, "[i]n today's volatile real estate climate, many distressed properties could be hopelessly encumbered by liens based on bad investment decisions. The receiver's authority, with the consent of the trial judge, provides a venue out of this problem in some circumstances."[677] Statutory reform could provide much needed clarity.

Nelson, Whitman, Burkhart & Freyermuth, Real Estate Finance Law 234–238 (6th ed. 2014) (reprinted with permission of LEG, Inc. d\b\a West Academic). See also U.S. Bank v. Pamilla Dev. Co., Inc., 343 P.3d 603 (Nev. 2015).

In 2012 the Uniform Law Commission created a drafting committee to prepare a new Model Act governing the appointment and powers of real estate mortgage receivers. Final approval is contemplated in the middle of

---

[673] CSB Bank v. Christy, No. 305869 (Mich.Ct.App. Oct. 18, 2012) (unpublished). The court rejected the mortgagor's circumvention argument out of hand, observing "this was not a sale pursuant to foreclosure; it was a receivership sale. The sale was being conducted pursuant to the prior order appointing a receiver—not a judicial foreclosure. Thus, the various requirements for a sale by foreclosure are simply inapplicable . . ."). *Christy*, slip op. at 5.

[674] Park Nat'l Bank v. Cattani, Inc., 187 Ohio App.3d 186, 931 N.E.2d 623 (2010); Huntington Nat'l Bank v. Motel 4 BAPS, Inc., 191 Ohio App.3d 90, 944 N.E.2d 1210 (2010); but see Director of Transp. v. Eastlake Land Dev. Co., 177 Ohio App.3d 379, 894 N.E.2d 1255 (2008) (holding, over a dissent, that court lacked the authority to order a receiver sale of mortgaged property without lienholder consent).

[675] *Cattani*, 931 N.E.2d at 625–626; *Motel 4 BAPS*, 944 N.E.2d at 1213.

[676] Bogosian v. Foerderer Tract Committee, Inc., 264 Pa.Super. 84, 399 A.2d 408 (1979).

[677] Director of Trans. v. Eastlake Land Dev. Co., 177 Ohio App.3d 379, 894 N.E.2d 1255, 1264 (Gallagher, J., dissenting).

2015. Consider the following proposed language of section 16(c) dealing with the power of a receiver to sell the mortgaged real estate:

(c) With court approval, a receiver may transfer receivership property other than in the ordinary course of business by sale, lease, license, exchange or other disposition. Unless the agreement of sale provides otherwise, a sale under this section is free and clear of a lien of the person that obtained the appointment of the receiver, any subordinate lien, and any rights of redemption, but is subject to a senior lien.

TRUSTCO BANK, NATIONAL ASSOCIATION V. EAKIN
Supreme Court, New York, Appellate Division, 1998
256 A.D.2d 778, 681 N.Y.S.2d 410

Before CARDONA, P.J., MERCURE, WHITE, SPAIN and CARPINELLO, JJ.

CARPINELLO, JUSTICE.

* * *In 1993, defendants Robert J. Eakin Jr. and Christine M. Eakin (hereinafter collectively referred to as defendants) purchased two connecting, three-story walk-up apartment buildings in the City of Troy, Rensselaer County, for $188,000. In 1995, defendants executed a mortgage on the premises in favor of plaintiff in the amount of $157,000. In the fall of that year, defendants contracted to sell the property for $160,000 * * *. Shortly thereafter, in February 1996, defendants defaulted on the mortgage.

The instant foreclosure action was commenced in June 1996. The following month, Supreme Court appointed a receiver of rents who, by the terms of the court's order, was "totally responsible to protect and preserve the Mortgaged Premises". For reasons not entirely clear from the record, the receiver did not qualify to serve until the posting of his bond in September 1996, at which time the premises were entirely vacant, having been abandoned by defendants. Although defendants did, at the receiver's request, drain the water pipes in anticipation of winter, they refused his specific request for additional funds to further secure the property. During the entire receivership, the total amount of rent proceeds turned over to the receiver by defendants was $84.46.

In January 1997, the receiver wrote to plaintiff's attorney stating:

The property has been secured as well as possible. The gas, water, and electricity have all been turned off. The Defendant and his counsel had the water pipes drained. There are no tenants and to my knowledge there are no occupants in these apartments. The accesses and lower windows should be boarded up. Unfortunately, there are no funds to do so.

Plaintiff declined to provide any funds to assist the receiver in preserving the premises. Apparently, the property remained unsupervised, unlet and unsecured until plaintiff's purchase of same at the foreclosure sale in May 1997 with a bid of $75,000. The premises were subsequently sold by plaintiff to a third party for $27,500. * * *

[D]efendants argued that no deficiency judgment should be awarded at all based upon plaintiff's refusal to advance funds to the receiver to secure the property, and that the receiver himself should be surcharged for his failure to protect the property during the term of his receivership. Plaintiff appeals from Supreme Court's determination denying its application for a deficiency judgment in its entirety and assessing costs against it.

We begin our analysis by noting that a court-appointed receiver in a foreclosure action is an officer of the court and not an agent of the party who procured the appointment (see, Kaplan v. 2108–2116 Walton Ave. Realty Co., 74 A.D.2d 786, 425 N.Y.S.2d 817). During the pendency of the receivership, the property is, in essence, in the possession of the court itself (see, Walling v. Miller, 108 N.Y. 173, 178, 15 N.E. 65) and we assess the legal consequences of any diminution in the value of the property in this context.

While it may have been more prudent for the receiver to have applied to the court to terminate the receivership upon discovering that the premises were vacant at the time of qualification (see, Emigrant Indus. Sav. Bank v. Feldblum Realty Corp., 238 App.Div. 231, 232, 264 N.Y.S. 104), we cannot disagree with Supreme Court's conclusion that the receiver should not be surcharged. Ordinarily, a receiver "should not be put in jeopardy personally as to his or her own financial status merely because the property is one which cannot readily be administered" (91 N.Y. Jur 2d, Receivers, § 49, at 582; cf., Griffo v. Swartz, 61 Misc.2d 504, 514, 306 N.Y.S.2d 64).

We also note that in this case plaintiff was not a mortgagee in possession (compare, Aetna Life Ins. Co. v. Avalon Orchards, 118 A.D.2d 297, 300, 505 N.Y.S.2d 216, appeal dismissed 68 N.Y.2d 997, 510 N.Y.S.2d 1028, 503 N.E.2d 125), for only then would plaintiff have been obliged "to use reasonable means to preserve the property from loss and injury and to conserve its value" (id., at 300, 505 N.Y.S.2d 216). In hindsight, it may have also been more prudent for plaintiff, instead of doing nothing, to have petitioned Supreme Court for authority to expend its own funds in aid of the court's receiver to secure the property and add that expenditure to the amount of its judgment. Nonetheless, we find no authority—and Supreme Court cites none—imposing upon a mortgagee, other than a mortgagee in possession, any legal obligation or duty to expend funds to preserve mortgaged premises, the default of which can affect its entitlement to a deficiency judgment.*

Indeed, in the absence of action by all parties—mortgagee, mortgagors and receiver—it was defendants who had the most to lose and therefore the greatest incentive (and legal right) to act because the amount of any potential deficiency judgment is the difference between the judgment of foreclosure and the greater of the highest bid at the foreclosure sale or the fair market value of the property at the time of the sale (see, RPAPL 1371). Defendants justify their own inactivity by pointing to language in the order appointing the receiver that they were not to "interfer[e] in any manner with the [subject] property". More to the point is the fact that the receiver specifically requested their assistance in securing the property, which they refused. It is axiomatic that defendants' title and right to possession of the mortgaged premises (except at it may have been affected by the receivership order) continued until the equity of redemption was extinguished at the foreclosure sale (see, Barson v. Mulligan, 191 N.Y. 306, 84 N.E. 75). Since defendants admit in their brief that "the damage to the premises occurred following the appointment of the Receiver and prior to the sale of the property", defendants must suffer the consequences caused by their failure or refusal to secure the property titled in their name.

* * *

ORDERED that the order is reversed, on the law, with costs, motion granted and deficiency judgment entered in favor of plaintiff * * * .

CARDONA, P.J., and MERCURE, WHITE and SPAIN, JJ., concur.

NOTE

The foregoing case illustrates that a receivership insulates the mortgagee from the obligations associated with being a mortgagee in possession. Where available, should a mortgagee always prefer a receivership?

---

* In fact, one of the incentives to seek a court-appointed receiver is to "insulate a mortgagee from tort and related landowner-type liabilities" (Restatement [Third] of Property § 4.3, comment a).

C. WASTE

PRUDENTIAL INSURANCE COMPANY OF AMERICA V. SPENCER'S KENOSHA BOWL, INC.

Court of Appeals of Wisconsin, 1987
137 Wis.2d 313, 404 N.W.2d 109

Before SCOTT, C.J., BROWN, P.J., and NETTESHEIM, J.

NETTESHEIM, JUDGE.

Spencer's Kenosha Bowl, Inc. (Spencer's) appeals from a judgment awarding $369,188.21 in damages to the Prudential Insurance Company of America (Prudential). The award is for waste committed by Spencer's upon real estate against which Prudential holds a mortgage.

* * *

The property involved in this litigation is a commercial building constructed in 1970 and situated on real estate located in the city of Kenosha. Spencer's purchased the property in 1975 from Delco Development Co. (Delco) which had previously mortgaged the property to Prudential. It is undisputed that Spencer's did not assume Delco's mortgage indebtedness when it purchased the property. Prudential subsequently foreclosed on the property after the mortgage note was in default.

In April, 1983, the Honorable Frederick Kessler, the judge then assigned to the case, granted Prudential's request for foreclosure of the property. The amount owed on the mortgage note at the time of the sheriff's sale was fixed at $994,497.80. The property sold for $635,000 in May, 1984. Following the sale, the Honorable Richard G. Harvey, Jr., the judge subsequently assigned to the case, held a hearing on Prudential's claim that Spencer's had committed waste upon the property. In his decision on the waste issue, Judge Harvey found that Spencer's had committed waste in the following amounts:

Property Taxes	$198,743.34
Roof	37,890.00
Ceiling Tile and Grid	103,064.52
Electric Facilities	14,647.16
Drywall-wood	36,251.85
Restroom	766.66
Exterior Canopy	13,090.83
Cleanup Costs	16,381.00
Floor Tile Damage	24,000.00
	$444,835.36

However, because the amount of the waste exceeded the amount of the debt less the foreclosure sale proceeds, Judge Harvey lowered Prudential's waste award so that it equaled the amount of the debt deficiency.

Spencer's initially argues that a grantee who does not assume the mortgage of a grantor-mortgagor cannot be held liable for any waste committed on the mortgaged property. Whether a mortgagee has a cause of action for waste is a question of law. *See Williams v. Security Savings & Loan Ass'n,* 120 Wis.2d 480, 482, 355 N.W.2d 370, 372 (Ct.App.1984). As a result, we review this question independently of any conclusions made by the trial court. *Id.*

Waste is a species of tort. *See Jaffe-Spindler Co. v. Genesco, Inc.,* 747 F.2d 253, 256 (4th Cir.1984). It is defined as "the unreasonable conduct by the owner of a possessory estate that results in physical damage to the real estate and substantial diminution in the value of the estates in which others have an interest." *Pleasure Time, Inc. v. Kuss,* 78 Wis.2d 373, 381, 254 N.W.2d 463, 467 (1977). Although a mortgagee only has a lien on the mortgaged property, *see* sec. 708.01, Stats.; *State v. Phillips,* 99 Wis.2d 46, 50, 298 N.W.2d 239, 241 (Ct.App.1980), he or she is entitled to maintain a legal action for waste against a mortgagor. *See Jones v. Costigan,* 12 Wis. 757 (677), 760–65 (1860).

We conclude that the waste doctrine permits a mortgagee to maintain an action for waste against a non-assuming grantee of a mortgagor. In *Scott v. Webster,* 50 Wis. 53, 6 N.W. 363 (1880), the supreme court held that senior mortgagees in possession of property were accountable to a junior mortgagee for waste committed on the property. *Id.* at 64, 6 N.W. at 365. There, the senior mortgagees removed a large amount of timber from the property which substantially diminished its value. *Id.* at 60–61, 6 N.W. at 363. Prior to the timber removal, the senior mortgagees purchased an equity of redemption which entitled them to possession of the property. *Id.* at 62, 6 N.W. at 364. Consequently, the senior mortgagees were both owners and mortgagees of the property. *Id.* at 63, 6 N.W. at 364–65. The court reasoned that with respect to the junior mortgagee, the senior mortgagees were mortgagees in possession and as such must be held liable for the waste they committed while in possession of the property. *Id.* at 63–64, 6 N.W. at 365.

Here, as in *Scott,* Spencer's legally had possession of the property and, under the trial court's findings, committed acts which resulted in a substantial diminution in the property's value. It is undisputed that Prudential, as a mortgagee, had an interest in the property. *See Phillips,* 99 Wis.2d at 50, 298 N.W.2d at 241. As a result, all of the essential ingredients for a waste cause of action as set out in *Pleasure Time* are met. *See Pleasure Time,* 78 Wis.2d at 381, 254 N.W.2d at 467. Moreover, we consider the court's reasoning in *Scott* as an indication of the liberality to be allowed a mortgagee when enforcing or protecting the lien interest. *See also Atkinson v. Hewett,* 63 Wis. 396, 23 N.W. 889 (1885) (mortgagee allowed to recover for wasteful conduct of trespasser). We do not deem the non-assuming grantee's status so unique that it warrants insulation from a waste action and prevents the mortgagee from preserving and protecting a security interest.

Our conclusion is also supported by the supreme court's language in *Edler v. Hasche,* 67 Wis. 653, 659–61, 31 N.W. 57, 59–61 (1887). There, Edler and Brandt were mortgagee and mortgagor, respectively. As in this case, Hasche purchased the mortgaged property from Brandt "subject to the mortgage." *Id.* at 659, 31 N.W. at 59. While the court left for a later proceeding the question of Hasche's liability for the mortgage debt and strongly suggested that the evidence might not support a finding that Hasche had assumed the mortgage, the court nonetheless recognized that Hasche's removal of a building was waste for which he was liable to Edler. The court stated that "Hasche's liability for waste . . . upon every principle of justice is clear and must be affirmed." *Id.* at 661, 31 N.W. at 60–61.

The import of *Edler* on this case is clear. Regardless of successor liability on the mortgage debt, the court in *Edler* affirms the principle that a non-assuming grantee can be liable to a mortgagee for waste committed to the secured property. Consequently, Spencer's non-assuming grantee status does not affect its liability for waste.

As an extension of this issue, Spencer's attempts to draw a distinction between its liability for active and passive waste.[2] Passive or permissive waste results from negligence or omission to do that which would prevent injury. *See Finley v. Chain,* 176 Ind.App. 66, 374 N.E.2d 67, 79 (1978) (overruled on other grounds by *Morris v. Weigle,* 383 N.E.2d 341, 345 n. 3 (Ind.1978)). Active or voluntary waste requires an affirmative act which results in the destruction or alteration of property. *See Jowdy v. Guerin,* 10 Ariz.App. 205, 457 P.2d 745, 748 (1969). At common law, an individual could be held liable for waste only if the acts were tortious and intentional. *See* Leipziger, *The Mortgagee's Remedies for Waste,* 64 Calif.L.Rev. 1086, 1093–94 (1976). No waste cause of action lay for negligent waste. *Id.* at 1094, 1130–32.

Whether a particular act is waste depends upon the circumstances. *Pleasure Time,* 78 Wis.2d at 381, 254 N.W.2d at 467. Modern Wisconsin

---

[2] Spencer's bases its passive waste argument on *Camden Trust Co. v. Handle,* 132 N.J.Eq. 97, 26 A.2d 865 (1942), which recognized the common law rule that a non-assuming grantee cannot be liable for passive or permissive [waste]. We agree with the Indiana court that there is no logical or practical reason for support of this rule. *See Finley v. Chain,* 374 N.E.2d 67, 79 n. 7 (Ind.Ct.App.1978) (overruled on other grounds by *Morris v. Weigle,* 383 N.E.2d 341, 345 n. 3 (Ind.1978)).

law does not distinguish between passive and active waste. However, early Wisconsin law recognized that waste could "be either voluntary or permissive." *Melms v. Pabst Brewing Co.,* 104 Wis. 7, 9, 79 N.W. 738, 739 (1899). Moreover, Wisconsin law has dealt with fact situations where the actions characterized as waste can be described as either active or passive. *See, e.g., Scott,* 50 Wis. at 53, 6 N.W. at 363 (waste resulting from removal of timber); *Jones,* 12 Wis. at 757 (removal of doors and windows from house); *Pleasure Time,* 78 Wis.2d at 381, 254 N.W.2d at 467–68 (waste alleged involved demolished and deteriorated buildings); *First Nat'l Bank v. Clark & Lund Boat Co.,* 68 Wis.2d 738, 741, 229 N.W.2d 221, 223 (1975) (failure to pay taxes).

We conclude that the modern waste definition is broad enough in Wisconsin to include both active and passive waste. The common law "limitations are not well rationalized in the cases and seem to have come about largely by accident." Leipziger, *supra*, at 1094. Conduct which results either in active or passive waste "may injure or threaten property rendering the debt unsafe." *Finley,* 374 N.E.2d at 79. Consequently, the mortgagee's security may be impaired by either passive or active waste and the policy for allowing the mortgagee recovery is the same regardless of the type of waste involved.

Next, Spencer's argues that the entry of judgment was not warranted because the amount of the waste found to have been committed was less than the amount obtained from the sale of the property. Spencer's, however, cites no legal authority for this proposition and, as a result, we are not required to consider it. *See State v. Shaffer,* 96 Wis.2d 531, 545–46, 292 N.W.2d 370, 378 (Ct.App.1980). Moreover, Spencer's argument seems to be a distortion of the common law rule that, in lien jurisdictions, a mortgagee cannot recover until his security has been substantially impaired which occurs only when waste has reduced the value of the encumbered property to less than the unpaid balance of the debt. *See* Leipziger, *supra*, at 1097. It is undisputed in this case that the waste found by the trial court reduced the value of the encumbered property in the fashion required by this rule.

Spencer's also challenges the trial court's calculation of the damages based on the debt deficiency. Spencer's argues that this is in fact an award of a deficiency judgment on a mortgage which it never assumed. However, in lien jurisdictions, a trial court must determine the extent of reduction in the value of the security interest in the property, not just the amount of injury to the real estate. *See Finley,* 374 N.E.2d at 78. Where, as here, the amount of waste committed on the property is greater than the amount of the debt deficiency, the extent of reduction in the value of the mortgagee's security interest will always be equal to the debt deficiency. Consequently, we do not view the trial court's award as a deficiency judgment but, rather, as an independent award litigated within the context of a foreclosure proceeding.

* * *

Judgment affirmed.

NOTES

1. *What constitutes waste?* As *Spencer's* suggests, waste was historically limited to cases of affirmative and intentional physical damage to the mortgaged real estate. Modern case law has expanded the concept markedly. The Restatement provides:

> Waste occurs when, without the mortgagee's consent, the mortgagor:
>
> (1) physically changes the real estate, whether negligently or intentionally, in a manner that reduces its value;
>
> (2) fails to maintain and repair the real estate in a reasonable manner, except for repair of casualty damage or acts of third parties not the fault of the mortgagor;
>
> (3) fails to pay before delinquency property taxes or governmental assessments secured by a lien having priority over the mortgage;
>
> (4) materially fails to comply with covenants in the mortgage respecting the physical care, maintenance, construction, demolition, or insurance against casualty of the real estate or improvements on it; or
>
> (5) retains possession of rents to which the mortgagee has the right of possession * * *

See Restatement (Third) of Property (Mortgages) § 4.6(a) (1997).*

Spencer's clearly supports categories (1) and (2). How should damage from natural disasters, such as earthquakes and floods be treated? Is it really different from routine wear and tear caused by the elements? What about the mortgagor's failure to repair damage resulting from such disasters?

Case support exists for (3), failure to pay property taxes, although it is not copious. See Travelers Ins. Co. v. 633 Third Assocs., 14 F.3d 114 (2d Cir.1994) (New York law); North Am. Sec. Life Ins. Co. v. Harris Trust & Sav. Bank., 859 F.Supp. 1163 (N.D.Ill.1994) (Illinois law). Considerable contrary authority also exists. See Chetek State Bank v. Barberg, 170 Wis.2d 516, 489 N.W.2d 385 (App.1992); FGH Realty Credit Corp. v. Bonati, 226 A.D.2d 188, 641 N.Y.S.2d 12 (1996) (failure to pay taxes is waste only if "fraudulent"). If failing to pay prior property taxes is waste, why isn't failure to pay other

---

*   © 1997 by The American Law Institute. Reprinted with permission.

prior liens, including prior mortgages, also waste? No substantial authority suggests that it is.

While damaging the property is waste, failing to take actions to maintain its value may not be. In Boucher Inv., L.P. v. Annapolis-West Ltd. Partn., 141 Md.App. 1, 784 A.2d 39 (2001), the mortgaged property was an office building. Its tenants had the use of an adjacent parking lot that was leased to the mortgagor. When the lease expired, the new owner of the office building made no attempt to renegotiate it. The mortgagee claimed waste because "the lack of parking resulted in a loss of tenants [and] . . . income to the property." The court characterized this argument as a "string of shaky inferences" and refused to find waste.

2. *Waste liability of non-assuming grantees.* In most jurisdictions, when a foreclosure sale yields less than the mortgage debt, the mortgagee may obtain a deficiency judgment against anyone who is personally liable on the mortgage obligation. However, a grantee of mortgaged real estate is not personally liable if she took title "subject to" the existing mortgage but did not "assume" the debt. See Chapter 5, Section A infra. Thus, deficiency judgments are unavailable against non-assuming grantees. Does *Spencer's* suggest that a mortgagee can avoid this prohibition by successfully bringing an action for waste? If so, this can be an extremely important application of the concept of waste.

One of the largest items of waste in *Spencer's* was failure to pay real estate taxes. Is it different to hold a non-assuming grantee liable for demolishing a building on the mortgaged real estate than to hold the grantee liable for failing to pay real estate taxes? Does it help a mortgagee's case against a non-assuming grantee if the mortgage, as is almost always the case, contains a specific covenant to pay taxes? See generally Nelson, Whitman, Burkhart & Freyermuth, Real Estate Finance Law §§ 4.4, 4.5, 4.11 (6th ed.2014). What about other mortgage covenants that seem to expand the liability that would otherwise exist for waste? For example, suppose a mortgage covenant requires a particularly stringent type or level of maintenance of the property, failure of which would not be common-law waste. Is there a theory on which even a non-assuming grantee could be held liable for breach of such covenants? Couldn't they be said to "run with the land," so as to bind even non-assuming grantees? Almost no authority exists on this point, but a Maryland court has held that such covenants do run with the land. See Union Trust Co. v. Rosenburg, 171 Md. 409, 189 A. 421 (App.1937).

3. *Waste liability when a mortgage clause or statute bars a deficiency judgment.* Can a mortgagee recover damages for waste if the mortgage note is "non-recourse"—that is, the mortgagor has no personal liability on the debt? The answer may depend on the exact wording of the non-recourse clause. See The Travelers Ins. Co. v. 633 Third Assocs., 973 F.2d 82 (2d Cir.1992), in which the court held that the particular non-recourse clause was broad enough to bar an action for waste. Carefully drafted non-recourse clauses

often "carve out" liability for waste, making the mortgagor liable for waste though he is not liable for the mortgage debt. In Aozora Bank, Ltd. v. 1333 North California Blvd., 119 Cal.App.4th 1291, 15 Cal.Rptr.3d 340 (2004), the clause clearly made the mortgagor liable for waste, but it did not provide that the mortgagee could recover its attorneys' fees in the waste action, which was a rather glaring error by the mortgagee's counsel. The court refused to award the fees.

What about recovery of waste damages in a state with a statute barring deficiency judgments against mortgagors? In Cornelison v. Kornbluth, 15 Cal.3d 590, 125 Cal.Rptr. 557, 542 P.2d 981 (1975), the California court held that no damages for waste should be imposed unless the waste was committed "in bad faith," which the court defined as "reckless" or "malicious," rather than merely as a result of "economic pressures." The court reasoned that a mortgagor in financial distress often must choose between paying the mortgage debt service and keeping the property in repair. The policy of the California antideficiency statute clearly was to avoid personal liability if the mortgagor defaulted in mortgage payments. The court concluded that the mortgagor also should not be liable for failing to make repairs. While Cornelison represents a barrier to recovery for waste in California, it is not insuperable. See Nippon Credit Bank v. 1333 North Cal. Blvd., 86 Cal.App.4th 486, 103 Cal.Rptr.2d 421 (2001) (mortgagor's failure to pay property taxes though it had the money to do so was bad faith waste and justified award of punitive damages!).

4. *Waste committed by non-owners.* Suppose a third party that has no possessory interest in the mortgaged real estate, such as a trespasser, a licensee, or an easement holder, commits waste. If a person who has a present estate in the mortgaged real estate is liable for waste, shouldn't those who hold lesser interests also be liable? They normally are liable. See Turner v. Kerin & Assocs., 283 Mont. 117, 938 P.2d 1368 (1997) (mortgagee could recover in waste against contractor who installed water main line in noncompliance with code standards); McCorristin v. Salmon Signs, 244 N.J.Super. 503, 582 A.2d 1271 (1990) (mortgagee could recover for waste against a third party who caused damage while installing a billboard on the mortgaged premises).

However, suppose the third party is a demolition contractor that the owner hired to destroy a house or other improvements on the real estate. Obviously, the owner may be liable for waste, but what about the contractor? Restatement (Third) of Property (Mortgages) § 4.6(d) provides: "If the waste was committed with the mortgagor's consent, liability exists only if the person committing it had actual knowledge of the existence of the mortgage." In other words, the recorded mortgage does not give constructive notice, and demolition contractors don't have a duty to search the title of the real estate they work on. But should the contractor be liable if it *knows* that the land is mortgaged? Or can the contractor successfully argue that the owner's consent made the contractor's acts entirely legal and not actionable? See Stevensen v. Goodson, 924 P.2d 339 (Utah 1996) (adopting this argument).

5. *Limitations on recovery of damages for waste.* The mortgagee's recovery of waste damages may not exceed the least of:

(a) The actual harm caused by the waste, which normally is either the cost of repair or the diminution in the property's value;

(b) The mortgage debt amount or, if foreclosure has already occurred, the amount of any unpaid deficiency. The mortgagee must apply *all* waste damages it recovers against the mortgage debt. Also, if the mortgagee entered a "full credit bid" and bought the property at the foreclosure sale, it cannot recover anything for waste, because its debt is considered to have been fully paid. See Cornelison v. Kornbluth, 15 Cal.3d 590, 125 Cal.Rptr. 557, 542 P.2d 981 (1975); or

(c) The amount by which the mortgagee's security has been impaired. This limitation is asserted mainly in lien theory states and is discussed in the next note.

6. *Measuring impairment of security.* To grasp this issue, you must first understand that most mortgage loans are made for less than the full appraised value of the real estate. The ratio of the loan amount to the property's value, the "loan-to-value ratio" ("LTV ratio"), is an important indicator of the likelihood that the lender will suffer a loss on the loan. Lower ratios are safer. Thus, a loan with a 75% LTV ratio is much more secure than a loan with a 95% LTV ratio. A loan's LTV ratio generally improves (declines) gradually over time if the property's value is stable and the loan balance is gradually paid down by regular amortization payments.

This brings us to the problem of how to measure impairment of security resulting from waste. The courts have had considerable difficulty with this question and have used several approaches. The "hard-nosed" definition runs along these lines: "If the injury to the property does not reduce its value below the amount required to secure the debt, the mortgagee has suffered no injury." Frio Investments, Inc. v. 4M-IRC/Rohde, 705 S.W.2d 784 (Tex.App.1986). The difficulty with this definition is that it leaves no "cushion" or margin of security for the mortgagee. In effect, it makes the LTV ratio 100%, even though the original loan nearly always was made at a lower LTV ratio. Other courts, more sensitive to this issue, have said that the mortgagee is entitled to a "reasonable" margin of security or to the same LTV ratio that existed before the waste.

The Restatement's approach is novel. It provides that "an impairment of security exists if the ratio of the mortgage obligation to the real estate's value is above its scheduled level." Restatement (Third) of Property (Mortgages) § 4.6(c). In other words, the waste damage award should be sufficient, when applied to the mortgage balance, to maintain the LTV ratio as "scheduled"— that is, the ratio that would have existed if all payments had been made on schedule and if the property's value had remained stable over the life of the loan.

See if you can compute the amount of damages the lender should recover by applying this approach to the following facts. ME makes a mortgage loan of $80,000 to MR that is secured by land worth $100,000. During the next five years, scheduled amortization payments are timely made and reduce the loan balance to $70,000 while the land's value increases to $120,000. MR then commits waste, which reduces the land's value by $30,000 to $90,000.

Here's the analysis under the Restatement approach. The scheduled LTV ratio at the time of the waste is $70,000/$100,000 or 70%. After the waste is committed, the property's value is reduced to $90,000. Seventy percent of $90,000 is $63,000. The mortgagee is entitled to recover enough damages to reduce the loan balance from its present level ($70,000) to $63,000. Note that the $7,000 damage award is less than the total loan balance and also is less than the waste damage ($30,000). Thus, of the three limitations mentioned in Note 5, the impairment of security limitation is controlling.

An interesting feature of the Restatement approach is that the mortgagor who commits waste gets the benefit of increases in the property's value. As the value rises, more waste can be committed before damages begin to accrue. But the owner is disadvantaged if the property falls in value, because less waste can be committed before damages begin to accrue. If the lender has foreclosed before bringing the waste action, the "impairment of security" test and the scheduled LTV ratio are irrelevant, because the land is no longer security for the loan. Therefore, only the first two limitations mentioned in Note 5 are applicable.

Whether the courts will follow the Restatement approach to impairment of security is still unclear. In McNeese v. Hutchinson, 724 So.2d 451 (Miss.Ct.App.1998), the court called the Restatement analysis "helpful" but opted for the simpler approach of finding impairment if the waste diminished the property's value from when the loan was made.

7.   *Other remedies.* The discussion above has focused on damages, but two other remedies are also generally available—an injunction and mortgage foreclosure. An injunction, which can prohibit further waste or order the mortgagor to correct the waste and thereby eliminate the impairment of security, may be thought of as a substitute for damages. But most mortgagees would probably rather have the money. Foreclosure isn't permitted if a third party committed the waste without the mortgagor's consent.

8.   *Waste of rents.* The fifth type of waste mentioned in the Restatement, quoted in Note 1 above, might be termed "waste of rents." Of course, a mortgagor who retains the rents is committing waste only if the mortgagee has actuated its security interest in the rents (a so-called "assignment of rents"), as discussed in Sections A and B of this chapter. See, e.g., Ginsberg v. Lennar Florida Holdings, Inc., 645 So.2d 490 (Fla.App.1994) (rejecting a mortgage holder's claim of waste of rents because the mortgage

holder had not demanded the rents, as required by the Florida statute, Fla.Stat.Ann. § 697.07).

Sometimes, unscrupulous persons buy real estate subject to an existing mortgage and then rent it, intending from the outset to retain all the rents and to pay nothing on the mortgage or for property maintenance. This practice, known as "rent skimming," can be particularly tempting in states that bar deficiency judgments. Rent skimming is a crime in California, Cal Civ. Code §§ 890–94, Colorado, Colo. Rev. Stat. § 18–5–802, Florida, Fla. Stat. Ann. § 697.08, Kansas, Kan. Stat. Ann. § 60–1011, and Washington, Wash. Rev. Code § 61.34.020–61.34.030.

The California law applies to a person who acquires five or more parcels of residential real property in any two-year period. Section 890 defines "rent skimming" as "using revenue from the rental of a parcel of residential real property at any time during the first year period after acquiring that property without first applying the revenue or an equivalent amount to the payments due on all mortgages and deeds of trust encumbering the property." This is a remarkable extension of the concept of "waste of rents;" it makes the waste a *crime* and applies even if the mortgagee has not actuated an assignment of rents clause or even if an assignment of rents does not exist! In People v. Bell, 45 Cal.App.4th 1030, 53 Cal.Rptr.2d 156 (1996), the court upheld the law against a variety of constitutional challenges. It noted that "the rent skimming sections contain no language requiring the defined acts be done with any fraudulent or larcenous intent, nor do the sections require the defendant intend any additional act or future consequence. The offense is thus one requiring general and not specific criminal intent." 53 Cal.Rptr.2d at 163.

D. MORTGAGEE LIABILITY FOR ENVIRONMENTAL PROBLEMS

Traditionally, a lender is not responsible to third parties, private or governmental, for the physical condition of the mortgaged real estate or injuries that occur on it. See, e.g., Solecki v. United States, 693 F.Supp. 770 (N.D.Iowa 1988) (mortgagee not liable for injury sustained by mortgagor's tenant in fall on mortgaged premises); Cantrell v. DuQuoin State Bank, 271 Ill.App.3d 291, 207 Ill.Dec. 621, 647 N.E.2d 1114 (1995) (mortgagee of building containing liquor establishment not liable under Dram Shop Act as "owner" where it exercises no dominion or control over the premises); Smith v. Fried, 98 Ill.App.3d 467, 53 Ill.Dec. 845, 424 N.E.2d 636 (1981) ("for a mortgagee to be responsible for damages to third parties caused by unsafe conditions on the property, the mortgagee must exercise dominion and control over the property"); Commonwealth v. Advantage Bank, 406 Mass. 885, 550 N.E.2d 1388 (1990) (mortgagee that was collecting rents pursuant to an assignment of rents clause not deemed an "owner" so as to be criminally liable under lead paint statute);

Greenpoint Bank v. John, 256 A.D.2d 548, 682 N.Y.S.2d 438 (1998) (mortgagee who is not in possession is not liable to mortgagor's tenant for repairs under Multiple Dwelling Law); Edwards v. Van Skiver, 256 A.D.2d 957, 681 N.Y.S.2d 893 (1998) (installment land contract vendor not liable to tenant of vendee for injuries sustained on the contract premises); Hausman v. Dayton, 73 Ohio St.3d 671, 653 N.E.2d 1190 (1995) (even though mortgagee in an "intermediate" state acquires "title" after default, it is not liable for a nuisance on the premises unless it is in possession). Only by becoming a mortgagee in possession (as discussed earlier in this chapter) or by acquiring title and the right to possession through foreclosure or a deed in lieu of foreclosure does a mortgagee assume the normal responsibilities of an owner or possessor of real estate. See Kubczak v. Chemical Bank & Trust Co., 456 Mich. 653, 575 N.W.2d 745 (1998) (mortgagee foreclosure purchaser not liable for torts on mortgaged premises during statutory redemption period where mortgagor retained possession until the expiration of that period).

However, the federal Comprehensive Environmental Response, Compensation, and Liability Act ("CERCLA") and similar state legislation significantly increased the potential for mortgagee liability. See 42 U.S.C.A. §§ 9601–9675. The essence of this legislation has been summarized as follows:

> Congress enacted CERCLA to deal with hazardous waste dump sites that are polluting neighboring lands or water sources. The Act and its related regulations authorize EPA either to order the responsible parties to contain the hazardous waste on the site or to clean the site and charge the responsible parties for EPA's response costs. The statutorily defined response costs include the cost of cleaning the site, any damages for injuries to natural resources, and the costs of any health assessment or health effects studies conducted pursuant to statutory authority. If EPA cleans the site, it may recover its response costs from any one or more of the persons enumerated in subsections 107(a)(1)–(4) of the Act, including: (1) the current "owner and operator" of the waste site, (2) any person who owned or operated the waste site when any hazardous dumping occurred; (3) the hazardous waste generators; and (4) the hazardous waste transporters. Liability for response costs is strict, joint, and several with limited exception.

Ann M. Burkhart, Lender/Owners and CERCLA: Title and Liability, 25 Harv.J.Legis. 317, 327 (1988).*

---

* Permission granted by the Harvard Journal on Legislation. Copyright © 1988 by the President and Fellows of Harvard College.

Why should a mortgagee be concerned about CERCLA? Mortgagees appear to be exempt from liability because CERCLA's definition of "owner and operator" excludes a "person, who, without participating in the management of a * * * facility, holds indicia of ownership primarily to protect his security interest in the * * * facility." 42 U.S.C.A. § 9601(20)(A).

Mortgagees were concerned for at least two reasons. The first is the preforeclosure period. Although the common law does not normally impose liability on the mortgagee for the mortgaged premise's physical condition, CERCLA could upset this normal assumption if the mortgagee's "participation in management" destroys its exemption from liability. To what extent does mortgagee oversight of the mortgagor's operations, which is common, represent impermissible "participation in management"?

The second potential liability problem for the mortgagee arises when it acquires ownership through foreclosure or by taking a deed in lieu of foreclosure. Clearly, the mortgagee is now the "owner" of the premises. At first blush, we would assume that the mortgagee takes on all liability that is inherent in being an owner in possession of real estate. However, the mortgagee may nevertheless be protected from liability if it can establish that even post-foreclosure ownership is held "primarily to protect his security interest in the * * * facility."

Avoiding CERCLA liability is critically important for mortgagees because the hazardous waste cleanup costs can far exceed the land's value even after it has been cleaned. Additionally, many insurance companies have refused to indemnify these costs. They argued that their comprehensive general liability policies did not insure against damages caused by hazardous waste. The specter of such large liabilities caused many lenders to refuse to extend credit against any land that is or could be contaminated, including for cleanup costs. On the other hand, in determining whether mortgagees should be liable, the economic benefit that they enjoy from a cleanup is incontrovertible whether they own the land or hold only a mortgage.

Largely as a result of these competing considerations, the judicial decisions concerning lender liability for hazardous waste cleanup costs have varied greatly. With respect to a mortgagee's preforeclosure liability, courts have differed concerning the types of actions that constitute "participation in management." In one leading case, United States v. Mirabile, 15 Envtl. L. Rep. (Envtl. L. Inst.) 20992, 20995 (E.D.Pa. Sept. 6, 1985), the court said that a mortgagee was liable only if it participated in "operational, production, or waste disposal activities." In marked contrast, the Eleventh Circuit Court of Appeals stated that a mortgagee would be liable if it had the "capacity to influence the [borrower's] treatment of hazardous wastes" even if it did not "actually ... involve itself in the day-to-day operations of the facility." United States v. Fleet Factors Corp., 901 F.2d 1550, 1557 (11th Cir.1990).

The courts also have markedly differed in considering the CERCLA liability of a mortgagee that has acquired the fee title to the mortgaged land. Some courts held that a mortgagee that acquired the land could have done so solely to protect its security interest. E.g., *Mirabile*. Other courts rejected that view. They held that, as a matter of straightforward statutory construction, a lender that acquires fee title is an "owner." These courts were also concerned with unjustly enriching the mortgagee. E.g., United States v. Maryland Bank & Trust Co., 632 F.Supp. 573 (D.Md.1986).

To provide clearer guidance on these issues, Congress enacted the Asset Conservation, Lender Liability, and Deposit Insurance Protection Act of 1996 ("1996 Statute"). As you review the following provisions from the 1996 Statute concerning mortgagee liability, consider which policies Congress considered to be most important and why. For example, what incentives was Congress attempting to create?

(E) Exclusion of lenders not participants in management

(i) Indicia of ownership to protect security

The term "owner or operator" does not include a person that is a lender that, without participating in the management of a * * * facility, holds indicia of ownership primarily to protect the security interest of the person in the * * * facility.

* * *

(ii) Foreclosure

The term "owner or operator" does not include a person that is a lender that did not participate in management of a * * * facility prior to foreclosure, notwithstanding that the person—

(I) forecloses on the * * * facility; and

(II) after foreclosure, sells, * * * or liquidates the * * * facility, maintains business activities, winds up operations, undertakes a response action * * * with respect to the * * * facility, or takes any other measure to preserve, protect, or prepare the * * * facility prior to sale or disposition,

if the person seeks to sell * * * or otherwise divest the person of the * * * facility at the earliest practicable, commercially reasonable time, on commercially reasonable terms, taking into account market conditions and legal and regulatory requirements. [The terms "foreclosure" and "foreclose" include acquiring title by a deed in lieu of foreclosure. § 9601(20)(G)(iii).]

(F) Participation in management

For purposes of subparagraph (E)—

(i) the term "participate in management"—

(I) means actually participating in the management or operational affairs of a * * * facility; and

(II) does not include merely having the capacity to influence, or the unexercised right to control, * * * facility operations;

(ii) a person that is a lender and that holds indicia of ownership primarily to protect a security interest in a * * * facility shall be considered to participate in management only if, while the borrower is still in possession of the * * * facility encumbered by the security interest, the person—

(I) exercises decisionmaking control over the environmental compliance related to the * * * facility, such that the person has undertaken responsibility for the hazardous substance handling or disposal practices related to the * * * facility; or

(II) exercises control at a level comparable to that of a manager of the * * * facility, such that the person has assumed or manifested responsibility—

(aa) for the overall management of the * * * facility encompassing day-to-day decisionmaking with respect to environmental compliance; or

(bb) over all or substantially all of the operational functions (as distinguished from financial or administrative functions) of the * * * facility other than the function of environmental compliance;

(iii) the term "participate in management" does not include performing an act or failing to act prior to the time at which a security interest is created * * *; and

(iv) the term "participate in management" does not include—

(I) holding a security interest or abandoning or releasing a security interest;

(II) including in the terms of an extension of credit, or in a contract or security agreement relating to the extension, a covenant, warranty, or other term or condition that relates to environmental compliance;

(III) monitoring or enforcing the terms and conditions of the extension of credit or security interest;

(IV) monitoring or undertaking 1 or more inspections of the * * * facility;

(V) requiring a response action or other lawful means of addressing the release or threatened release of a hazardous substance in connection with the * * * facility prior to, during, or on the expiration of the term of the extension of credit;

(VI) providing financial or other advice or counseling in an effort to mitigate, prevent, or cure default or diminution in the value of the * * * facility;

(VII) restructuring, renegotiating, or otherwise agreeing to alter the terms and conditions of the extension of credit or security interest, exercising forbearance;

(VIII) exercising other remedies that may be available under applicable law for the breach of a term or condition of the extension of credit or security agreement; or

(IX) conducting a response action * * *,

if the actions do not rise to the level of participating in management (within the meaning of clauses (i) and (ii)).

42 U.S.C.A. § 9601(20)(E), (F).

NOTES

1. *Petroleum and underground storage tanks.* Note that petroleum products and underground petroleum storage tanks are not covered by CERCLA, but rather by the Resource Conservation and Recovery Act ("RCRA"). The 1996 Statute extended the protections afforded CERCLA mortgagees to their RCRA counterparts. It amended RCRA to provide that the terms "owner" and "operator" "do not include a person that, without participating in the management of an underground storage tank and otherwise not engaged in petroleum production, refining, or marketing, holds indicia of ownership primarily to protect the person's security interest." 42 U.S.C.A. § 6991b(h)(9)(A). Moreover, the 1996 Statute makes it clear that the specific CERCLA provisions that protect mortgagees against being characterized as "participating in management" and that extend the "protecting security interest" exemption to the post-foreclosure period also apply to RCRA mortgagees. 42 U.S.C.A. § 6991b(h)(9)(B).

2. *Does CERCLA overprotect the mortgagee-purchaser?* Suppose a mortgagee forecloses a mortgage on a large apartment building and purchases at the sale. A few weeks later, government authorities determine that the building's electrical wiring system is defective and dangerous and must be replaced. As the building owner, the mortgagee-purchaser would normally be liable for the cost of replacement or repair. Similarly, if a person is injured on real estate owned by a mortgagee-purchaser who is in the process of reselling it, the mortgagee is liable. Travelers Property Casualty Co. of Am. v. Liberty Mut. Ins. Co., 444 F.3d 217, 222 (4th Cir.2006) (mortgagee that purchased a residential duplex at foreclosure sale and was in process of reselling it held liable to injured third party for negligent failure to maintain stairway). Is there a good reason why a mortgagee-purchaser should not also be liable for removal of toxic substances? Does CERCLA afford too much protection for the mortgagee-purchaser?

3. *Advising the mortgagee.* Suppose you represent a mortgage lender. What advice will you give with respect to future loans? Assuming that you are satisfied that a proposed borrower's real estate is now free of environmental contamination, how can the lender protect itself as to the future? What provisions, if any, should be included in the mortgage documents to deal with potential environmental problems? See Fannie Mae/Freddie Mac Uniform Covenant No. 21 in Appendix A, Form 2 infra. Is this language adequate?

Suppose, instead, that you represent a lender whose mortgage is already in default and you have a strong suspicion that the mortgaged real estate is contaminated. Assuming it is permitted in your jurisdiction, should the lender become a mortgagee in possession or should the mortgagee seek the appointment of a receiver? According to one commentator, the "benefit of having a receiver appointed is that the lender is arguably shielded by the fact that the receiver is the agent of the appointing court rather than the agent of the lender or property owner." Matthew L. Kimball, Environmental Strategies for the Real Estate Lender, 7 Real Est.Fin. 13, 22 (1991). Note also that a receiver is characterized under the 1996 Statute as a "fiduciary" and, as such, liability "for the release or threatened release of a hazardous substance at, from, or in connection with a * * * facility held in a fiduciary capacity shall not exceed the assets held in the fiduciary capacity." 42 U.S.C.A. § 9607(n)(1).

4. *CERCLA lien.* If the United States is not reimbursed for clean-up costs that it incurred, CERCLA gives it a lien on the real estate that was subject to the clean-up action if it belongs to a person who is liable for those costs. See 42 U.S.C.A. § 9607(*l*). Note that this lien is not given "superpriority" status vis á vis other security interests and liens on the real estate. Rather, it is "subject to the rights of any purchaser, holder of a security interest, or judgment lien creditor whose interest is perfected under applicable State law before notice of the lien has been filed in the appropriate office within the State." 42 U.S.C.A. § 9607(*l*)(3). Thus, the CERCLA lien is a "standard lien;" its priority "is determined under traditionally applicable

rules of lien priority. Thus, a CERCLA lien will be superior to liens held by unsecured creditors and those filed subsequently but will remain inferior to pre-existing liens." Jonathan Remy Nash, Environmental Superliens and the Problem of Mortgage-Backed Securitization, 59 Wash. & Lee L.Rev. 127, 146 (2002).

5.   *State legislation.* More than forty states have enacted legislation similar to CERCLA. See, e.g., Mass.Gen.Laws Ann. c. 21C; Minn.Stat.Ann. § 115B.20; N.Y.—McKinney's State Finance Law § 97–b; Or.Rev.Stat. § 466.670. The statutes in a few of these states, unlike CERCLA, create "superliens" in favor of the state on real estate for which there are unreimbursed clean-up costs. These liens, like many real estate tax liens, are senior to pre-existing perfected mortgages on real estate. See, e.g., Mass.Gen.Laws Ann. c. 21E, § 13 (lien "shall have priority over any encumbrance theretofore recorded, registered or filed * * * other than on real property the greater part of which is devoted to single or multi-family housing."); N.J.Stat.Ann. 58:10–23.11f(f) (lien shall have priority "over all other claims or liens which are or have been filed against the property, except if the property comprises six dwelling units or less and is used for residential purposes"). How should mortgage lenders react to the "superlien" approach? Should a state's superlien trump a pre-existing recorded purchase money mortgage? Consider Professor Nash's analysis:

> The underlying motive for these superlien statutes is manifest. Absent such a statute, the traditional rules of lien priority would allow a state to expend funds to clean up a contaminated property, with some or all of the benefit from those expenditures inuring to the senior secured lenders. These lenders would see the value of their security increase by virtue of the increase in property value resulting from the cleanup. If a state cannot recover its cleanup expenditures from the contaminating parties, it would be left to pursue any remaining equity in the property and other unencumbered assets of the property owner to recoup its expenses. Because environmental cleanup costs are generally quite large and the property owner is probably insolvent, the state, under these circumstances, will probably not recover much, if any, of the expenditures.

Jonathan Remy Nash, Environmental Superliens and the Problem of Mortgage-Backed Securitization, 59 Wash. & Lee L.Rev. 127, 148–49 (2002). Are there constitutional problems with superliens because they can trump previously recorded and perfected mortgages? See *id.* at 149–51.

How can mortgage lenders protect themselves against such liens? Can they require mortgagors to "escrow" for these liabilities as lenders normally do for real estate taxes? See Section E of this chapter. Can lenders predict potential environmental costs to the same extent that they can for real estate taxes?

EDWARDS V. FIRST NATIONAL BANK OF NORTH EAST

Court of Special Appeals of Maryland, 1998
122 Md.App. 96, 712 A.2d 33

Argued before HARRELL, SALMON and BYRNES, JJ.

BYRNES, JUDGE.

* * *

Randy and Cynthia Edwards are the owners of residential real property in North East, Maryland known as 505 Mechanics Valley Road. Their property is adjacent to and downgrade from commercial property known as 513 Mechanics Valley Road. For approximately twenty years, the 513 Mechanics Valley Road site was used for a gasoline service station. During part of that time, from 1981 until 1994, the property was owned by Jacqueline C. Yerkes. Mrs. Yerkes and her husband added a mini-market to the gasoline service station. The property came to be called the "T & C Mini Market."

First National Bank of North East ("the Bank") held a mortgage on the T & C Mini Market property. When Mrs. Yerkes defaulted on the mortgage, the Bank foreclosed on the property. Thereafter, on May 10, 1994, it purchased the property at the foreclosure sale and took possession of it. A few weeks later, the Bank conducted "tank tightness tests" on two 6,016 gallon underground storage tanks ("USTs") and one 3,000 gallon UST on the property. The tanks passed all of the tests and were judged to be tight.

The Bank then contracted with Edwards Service Station Equipment, Inc. ("ESSE") to remove the USTs. ESSE did so on October 24, 1994, under the watchful eyes of Maryland Department of the Environment ("MDE") employees. Removal of the USTs produced a strong smell of petroleum. Tests that were later performed on the property by MDE revealed the presence of petroleum byproducts in the soil at levels greater than permitted by law. MDE arranged for three testing wells to be installed on the T & C Mini Market property and ordered further testing to be undertaken. Those tests showed the continued presence of petroleum byproducts in the land.

In the meantime, on May 5, 1994, shortly before the Bank took possession of the T & C Mini Market property, Mr. and Mrs. Edwards installed a new deep well on their property. They did so in part because Mrs. Edwards was operating a day care center in their home and she needed to comply with certain local health regulations. The new well was approved by the Cecil County Health Department on September 9, 1994, after officials "completed multiple tests and personal inspections."

In late November, 1994, Mr. and Mrs. Edwards noticed the smell of gasoline in their house. When the smell intensified, they had their well-water tested. Tests performed on January 23, 1995 came up positive for PH-petroleum hydrocarbons. The MDE performed additional tests that confirmed the presence of petroleum byproducts in the Edwards's well.

On August 20, 1996, Mr. and Mrs. Edwards filed suit for damages against the Bank and against ESSE for injury to their real and personal property, in the Circuit Court for Cecil County. They pleaded causes of action against both defendants for * * * negligence, nuisance, trespass, and strict liability. On December 20, 1996, the Bank filed a motion to dismiss for failure to state a claim for which relief could be granted * * * . After hearing argument of counsel, the trial court granted the Bank's motion, from the bench. It subsequently issued a written order dismissing the Bank from the case and entering final judgment against Mr. and Mrs. Edwards in favor of the Bank * * * . Mr. and Mrs. Edwards then noted this appeal.

DISCUSSION

* * *

[Mr. and Mrs. Edwards] maintain * * * that the circuit court erred in ruling that the Water Pollution Control and Abatement Act in its entirety, and Env. § 4–401(i)(2)(i)(2) specifically, abrogated their common law causes of action for negligence, nuisance, trespass, and strict liability in tort.

Env. § 4–401 sets forth definitions for certain terms that are used in the Act. "Person responsible for the discharge," one such term, is defined at Env. § 4–401(i)(1) to include:

(i) The owner of the discharged oil;[4]

(ii) The owner, operator, or person in charge of the oil storage facility, vessel, barge, or vehicle involved in the discharge at the time of or immediately before the discharge; and

(iii) Any other person who through act or omission causes the discharge.

The statutory language at issue in this case appears in Env. § 4–401(i)(2), which defines those who do *not* fall into the category of "Person responsible for the discharge:"

(i) A person who, without participating in the management of an underground oil storage tank, and who otherwise is not engaged in petroleum production, refining, or marketing, holds indicia of

---

4 "Oil" is defined to include, inter alia, petroleum, petroleum by-products, and gasoline. Env. § 4–401(g).

ownership in an underground oil storage tank primarily to protect its security interest in that underground oil storage tank if that person [. . .]

2. Abandoned that underground oil storage tank under regulations of the Department within 180 days of acquiring the tank through foreclosure or other means.[5]

The Bank contends that, on the facts alleged in the complaint and within the meaning of Env. § 4–401(i)(2)(i)(2), it "abandoned" the USTs at the T & C Mini Market site within 180 days of acquiring the property through foreclosure and thus it is not a "Person responsible for the discharge" under the Act. It argues further that because the legislative intent behind Env. § 4–401(i)(2)(i)(2) is, to use its words, "to protect a foreclosing lender from liability if the lender removes an underground storage tank within 180 days following foreclosure," the trial court properly ruled that the Act abrogated all common law causes of action against it arising out of contamination of adjacent property by oil kept in the USTs on the T & C Mini Market property. We disagree.

In determining the legislative intent of a statute, " '[t]he primary source . . . is, of course, the language of the statute itself.' " *State v. Pagano*, 341 Md. 129, 133, 669 A.2d 1339 (1996) * * * . "In some circumstances, [the courts] need not look beyond the statutory language

---

[5] The February 27, 1997 amendment to Env. § 4–401(i)(2) added the following to those who are not included in the category of "Person not responsible for the discharge:"

(ii) A holder of a mortgage or deed of trust who acquires title to a property that is subject to a corrective action plan approved by the Department under this subtitle provided that the holder complies with the requirements, prohibitions, and conditions of the plan;

(iii) Subject to paragraph (3) of this subsection, a lender who extends credit for the performance of removal or remedial actions conducted in accordance with requirements imposed under this title who:

1. Has not caused or contributed to a discharge of oil; and

2. Previous to extending that credit, is not a person responsible for the discharge at the site; or

(iv) Subject to paragraph (3) of this subsection, a lender who takes action to protect or preserve a mortgage or deed of trust on a site or a security interest in property located on a site at which a discharge of oil has occurred, by stabilizing, containing, removing, or preventing the discharge of oil in a manner that does not cause or contribute to a discharge of oil if:

1. The lender provides advance written notice of its actions to the Department or in the event of an emergency in which action is required within 2 hours, provides notice by telephone;

2. The lender, previous to taking the action, is not a person responsible for the discharge at the site; and

3. The action does not violate a provision of this article.

The amendment also added a new subsection, at Env. § 4–401(i)(3), which provides: "A lender taking action to protect or preserve a mortgage or deed of trust or security interest in property located on a site, who causes or contributes to a discharge of oil shall be liable solely for costs incurred in response to the discharge which the lender caused or to which the lender contributed unless the lender was a person responsible for the discharge before acquiring a mortgage, deed of trust, or security interest in the site or property located on the site."

to determine the legislative purpose. 'Sometimes the language in question will be so clearly consistent with apparent purpose (and not productive of any absurd result) that further research will be unnecessary.'" *Pagano,* 341 Md. at 133, 669 A.2d 1339 (quoting *Kaczorowski v. City of Baltimore,* 309 Md. 505, 515, 525 A.2d 628 (1987)).

The Bank urges us to construe Env. § 4–401(i)(2)(i)(2) broadly, as a general grant of immunity from suit in favor of commercial lenders. Yet, the statutory language states only that, under certain limited and defined circumstances, a lender is not a "Person responsible for the discharge." To the extent that a lender could face exposure to liability as a "Person responsible for the discharge," within the meaning of the Act, its exclusion from that category under Env. § 4–401(i)(2)(i)(2) would insulate it. To interpret Env. § 4–401(i)(2)(i)(2) to confer blanket immunity for lenders against common law liability for groundwater contamination, we would have to disregard the narrowly circumscribed language of the statute and illogically generalize its meaning. In interpreting the language of a statute, we must apply common sense and avoid unreasonable constructions. * * * We decline to find in the limited and specific exclusion spelled out in Env. § 4–401(i)(2)(i)(2) the overarching and sweeping meaning that the Bank suggests.

In addition, Env. § 4–401(i)(2)(i)(2) must be read in conjunction with the remainder of the Act, * * * which includes a purpose clause expressly prohibiting any construction of the Act so as to abrogate or preempt common law remedies. Env. § 4–403, entitled "Construction and purpose of subtitle; remedies additional and cumulative," is explicit:

> . . . It is the purpose of this subtitle to provide additional and cumulative remedies to prevent, abate, and control the pollution of the waters of the State. This subtitle may not be construed to abridge or alter rights of action or remedies in equity under existing common law, statutory law, criminal or civil, nor may any provision of this subtitle, or any act done pursuant to it, be construed as estopping any person, as riparian owner or otherwise, in the exercise of his rights in equity, under the common law, or statutory law to suppress nuisances or abate pollution.

The meaning of Env. § 4–403 is plainly apparent from its language. The words of the statute reflect the General Assembly's intention that the Act, which comprises subtitle 4 of the Environment Article, not be read to affect common law remedies. We need not search further for statutory meaning * * * . Moreover,

> Maryland courts adhere to the policy that statutes are not to be construed to alter the common-law by implication. The reason for this protection of common-law principles from statutory erosion

is based on Article 5 of the Maryland Declaration of Rights, which guarantees to Maryland citizens the common-law of England. Thus, there is a presumption against statutory preemption of the common-law. The presumption is easily dissipated if the statute expressly overrides a common-law principle.

Hardy v. State, 301 Md. 124, 131–32, 482 A.2d 474 (1984) (citations omitted). * * * In this case, not only does the statute in question not expressly override the common law, it expressly states that it shall not be interpreted to override the common law.

Without making mention of Env. § 4–403 in its brief, the Bank argues that Env. § 4–401(i)(2)(i)(2) must be interpreted broadly so as to protect lenders against common law liability for two reasons: first, any other interpretation of the subsection would render it superfluous * * * and second, the legislative history surrounding the passage of the section evidences an intention on the part of the General Assembly to extend a broad grant of immunity to commercial lenders.

We agree that statutes should not be read so as to render their language superfluous. *See Bell Atlantic*, 346 Md. at 178, 695 A.2d 171; *City of Baltimore v. Hackley*, 300 Md. 277, 283, 477 A.2d 1174 (1984). * * * We disagree, however, that to give meaning to Env. § 4–401(i)(2)(i)(2), we must read it to abrogate common law causes of action against lenders, in direct contravention of the statutory purpose stated in Env. § 4–403. * * *

The legislative history that the Bank cites and the policy observations that it makes are not persuasive. To be sure, the 1992 enactment of what is now Env. § 4–401(i)(2)(i)(2) and the 1997 amendments to that section evidence legislative concern that commercial lenders not be disinclined to extend mortgages for fear of incurring legal responsibility and liability under the Act when they must take possession of mortgaged property to protect a security interest. Indeed, Env. § 4–401(i)(2)(i)(2) addresses those concerns by protecting lenders from remediation and clean up suits brought by the MDE when certain conditions are satisfied. The legislative history does not evidence an express or even an implied intention on the part of the General Assembly to abrogate, abolish, or preempt common law remedies against commercial lenders, however.

Finally, the Bank argues that we should affirm the circuit court's dismissal of the nuisance, trespass, negligence, and strict liability in tort claims against it because the facts alleged in the complaint do not support those causes of action. This argument was not raised in or decided by the circuit court. Accordingly, it is not properly before us for review. * * *

JUDGMENT REVERSED. CASE REMANDED TO CIRCUIT COURT
* * * FOR FURTHER PROCEEDINGS CONSISTENT WITH THIS
OPINION.

NOTE

This section illustrates that institutional lenders have generally succeeded in persuading Congress and many state legislatures to substantially exempt mortgagees from clean-up liability under CERCLA, RCRA, and similar state legislation. But *Edwards* suggests that such mortgagees, as foreclosure purchasers, remain liable to adjoining landowners for environmental contamination on a variety of common law theories. Should mortgagees now lobby for exemption from such common law liability?

In the absence of securing such blanket immunity, how should a mortgagee proceed as to a mortgage in default when it has reason to believe that the mortgaged premises are contaminated and potential owner liability exists to adjoining landowners or other third parties? To avoid becoming an owner of the contaminated premises and subject to the common law liabilities associated with ownership, should the mortgagee simply decline to foreclose? Should its decision be influenced by the amount of those potential liabilities? If the mortgagor or others who are personally liable for the mortgage debt have substantial other assets, should the mortgagee simply sue on the mortgage debt and avoid foreclosure entirely?

E. INSURANCE AND REAL ESTATE TAXES

Both the mortgagor and mortgagee have insurable interests for damage to the mortgaged property. The mortgagor's insurable interest is the value of the property; the mortgagee's insurable interest is the mortgage debt amount. See Nelson, Whitman, Burkhart & Freyermuth, Real Estate Finance Law § 4.14 (6th ed.2014). Of course, a mortgagee cannot collect both the proceeds of its casualty insurance policy and the full debt as well, because it would result in a windfall and unjust enrichment. The mortgagee is limited to a single recovery of the debt amount. See Bank of Richmondville v. Terra Nova Ins. Co. Ltd., 263 A.D.2d 786, 694 N.Y.S.2d 206 (1999); Sotelo v. Washington Mut. Ins. Co., 734 A.2d 421 (Pa. Super. 1999); Benton Banking Co. v. Tennessee Farmers Mut. Ins. Co., 906 S.W.2d 436, 438 (Tenn. 1995).

In principle, both the mortgagor and mortgagee can purchase their own casualty insurance policies. However, the mortgagee normally requires the mortgagor to carry casualty insurance insuring the interests of both parties. An older type of policy, known as a "loss payable" policy or "open" policy, contained a clause providing simply that the loss would be payable to the mortgagor and the mortgagee "as their interests may appear." Today, the "standard mortgage" or "union mortgage" policy is used nearly universally. It contains language along the following lines:

> Loss or damage, if any, under this policy shall be payable to the mortgagee as his interest may appear, and this insurance, as to the mortgagee only therein, shall not be invalidated by any act or neglect of the mortgagor or owner of the within described property, nor by any change in the title or ownership of the property, nor by the occupation of the premises for purposes more hazardous than are permitted by this policy, provided, that in case the mortgagor or owner shall neglect to pay any premium under this policy, the mortgagee shall on demand pay the same.

You can see why lenders prefer this form of policy and have pressed for its widespread adoption. In essence, it ensures that the lender can recover on the policy no matter what the borrower has done. The lender is covered even if the borrower intentionally demolishes improvements on the land. Wells Fargo Bank, NA v. Null, 304 Mich.App. 508, 847 N.W.2d 657 (2014); Home Sav. of Am., F.S.B. v. Continental Ins. Co., 87 Cal.App.4th 835, 104 Cal.Rptr.2d 790 (2001). For an excellent review of the "standard mortgage" clause see Patrick A. Randolph, Jr., The Mortgagee's Interest in Casualty Loss Proceeds: Evolving Rules and Risks, 32 Real Prop., Prob. & Tr. J. 1 (1997).

Under the "standard mortgage" clause, it is entirely possible that the lender will recover on the insurance policy though the borrower has engaged in acts, such as arson or fraud, that bar the borrower from recovery. In this situation, if the insurer pays the mortgage debt in full, it is subrogated to the debt and the mortgage and can enforce them against the mortgagor. See, e.g., The Money Store/Massachusetts, Inc. v. Hingham Mut. Fire Ins. Co., 430 Mass. 298, 718 N.E.2d 840 (1999) (mortgagor blew up insured building; insurer paid off the mortgage and could enforce it against the mortgagor); 16 Couch, Insurance § 224:27 (Russ ed. 2002). The subrogation principle derives from general legal principles and is usually stated explicitly in the insurance policy as well. A typical clause, which applied in West Suburban Bank v. Badger Mut. Ins. Co., 947 F.Supp. 333 (N.D.Ill.1996), provides:

> We may pay the mortgagee the remaining principal and accrued interest in return for a full assignment of the mortgagee's interest and any instruments given as security for the mortgage debt.

An additional benefit of the standard mortgage clause is that, if the mortgagor fails to pay the premium, the insurer cannot cancel the policy against the mortgagee without first notifying the mortgagee of the default and making a demand that the mortgagee pay the delinquent premium. See, e.g., Farmers Home Mut. Fire Ins. Co. v. Bank of Pocahontas, 355 Ark. 19, 129 S.W.3d 832 (2003).

Does the existence of insurance coverage paid for by the mortgagor benefit the mortgagee? It will do so if either of two sets of facts is true: (1) the mortgage contains a covenant requiring the borrower to carry the insurance, or (2) in most courts, the mortgagee is named as an insured or loss payee in the insurance policy.

Here is a little more detail on those points. Courts universally hold that, "if the mortgagor promised the mortgagee, in the mortgage or otherwise, to purchase the insurance," the mortgagee has a right to the insurance proceeds to the extent the casualty has impaired the mortgagee's security. Restatement (Third) of Property (Mortgages) § 4.7(a)(1). This is true even if the mortgagee is not named as a "loss payee" in the policy. See Conrad Bros. v. John Deere Ins. Co., 640 N.W.2d 231 (Iowa 2001); Castle Ins. Co. v. Vanover, 993 S.W.2d 509 (Ky.App. 1999); General Star Indemnity Co. v. Pike County Nat'l Bank, 706 So.2d 227 (Miss. 1997). Courts often describe the mortgagee's right as an "equitable lien" on the insurance proceeds. The mortgagee's right also doesn't depend on the mortgagor being personally liable for the debt; the mortgagee is entitled to the benefits of the insurance policy even if the loan is "non-recourse," see San Roman v. Atlantic Mut. Ins. Co., 250 A.D.2d 585, 672 N.Y.S.2d 396 (1998), and even if an antideficiency statute is applicable, see Redingler v. Imperial Sav. & Loan Ass'n, 47 Cal.App.3d 48, 120 Cal.Rptr. 575 (1975).

Nearly all mortgages contain clauses requiring the mortgagor to carry specified forms of insurance. However, the mortgagee may try to claim insurance proceeds for a loss not specified in the mortgage. For example, in Ziello v. Superior Court, 36 Cal.App.4th 321, 42 Cal.Rptr.2d 251 (1995), the mortgage stated that the mortgagor would carry a fire and "extended coverage" policy. In fact, the mortgagor also purchased earthquake coverage. The court held that, because the mortgage did not require that type of coverage, the mortgagee had no right to the insurance proceeds when the property was damaged by an earthquake.

If the mortgagee is named as an insured or loss payee in the policy, the mortgagee normally can benefit from the insurance proceeds to the extent necessary to pay the mortgage debt, even if neither the mortgage nor any other agreement required the borrower to carry the insurance. See, e.g., Singer v. American States Ins., 245 Mich.App. 370, 631 N.W.2d 34 (2001) (installment contract vendor was listed on declaration page of insurance policy as "contract vendor;" court held vendor could recover under the policy as a named insured). However, a California court has held that, unless the borrower promised to provide insurance for the mortgagee's benefit, the latter cannot claim the insurance proceeds even if it is a named insured in the policy. See Martin v. World Sav. & Loan Ass'n, 92 Cal.App.4th 803, 112 Cal.Rptr.2d 225 (2001).

The mortgagee's right to the insurance proceeds is only the beginning of the inquiry. Can the mortgagee elect to apply the proceeds toward a pay down of the mortgage debt, or must the mortgagee permit the mortgagor to use them to restore the damaged real estate, as most mortgagors doubtless expect? That is the issue in the following case.

STARKMAN V. SIGMOND
Superior Court of New Jersey, 1982
184 N.J.Super. 600, 446 A.2d 1249

DEIGHAN, J.S.C.

The question to be resolved herein is whether plaintiff mortgagors are entitled to the proceeds of a fire insurance policy (which insures the interest of both the mortgagors and the mortgagees) to rebuild the residence or must the proceeds be applied in reduction of the mortgage where the value of the vacant land exceeds the balance due on the mortgage which has been kept current. Research has revealed no New Jersey case which addresses this problem of payment of the fire insurance proceeds where the security is not impaired and the mortgage is not in default. It is held that under the facts of this case the mortgagors are entitled to the proceeds to rebuild the residence.

Plaintiff mortgagors Tami Starkman and Dora Birnbaum executed a purchase money mortgage to defendant mortgagees Robert Sigmond and Barbara Sigmond, his wife, in the amount of $60,000. A fire loss occurred on the mortgaged premises; mortgagees demand that the insurance proceeds be applied to the outstanding mortgage balance. Plaintiff mortgagors seek the proceeds of the fire insurance to rebuild the residence. The essential facts are not in dispute and both parties move for summary judgment.

After the complaint was filed and before filing an answer, defendant mortgagees moved for summary judgment. At the time the motion was heard the insurance company, Prudential Property and Casualty Insurance (Prudential), was not a party to the action. The court determined it should have the benefit of Prudential's position on its obligation under the insurance policy, and on August 23, 1981 denied defendants' motion. Thereafter, plaintiffs filed an amended complaint against Prudential; defendants Sigmond filed an answer and crossclaim against Prudential. Prudential filed its answer, including a third-party complaint against plaintiffs' husbands, Morris Starkman and Simon Birnbaum, asserting they were the real parties in interest.

Subsequently, Prudential agreed to issue a $135,000 check in settlement of all claims made under the insurance policy. After application by plaintiffs, the court on December 21, 1981, by consent of the parties, ordered Prudential to issue the $135,000 in two drafts: one in the sum of $60,000 payable to both mortgagees and mortgagors and the other in the sum of $75,000 payable to plaintiff mortgagors only. Thereafter, plaintiffs, defendants Sigmond, and Prudential entered into a consent order to invest the $60,000 pending a determination by the court of the rights of the parties. Prudential required a release from the Sigmonds before it would issue the $60,000 check. On February 16, 1982 the court entered another consent order which provided that payment of the $60,000 would be in [the] nature of an interpleader. The Sigmonds were to execute the release and assert any claims against the fund which may have been asserted against Prudential.

On January 6, 1981 plaintiffs purchased a house and lot located at 112 South Sacramento Avenue, Ventnor, New Jersey from defendants for $150,000. Defendants took back a purchase money mortgage in the sum of $60,000 with interest at the rate of 10% payable in monthly amortization installments of $525. The mortgage is for a 30-year term but has a "balloon" at the end which requires full payment to be made on January 6, 1986, i.e., the entire mortgage is payable within five years. The mortgage also required the mortgagors to maintain hazard insurance on the premises for the benefit of the mortgagees. Prudential issued the insurance policy to plaintiffs as the "insureds"; defendants are listed as mortgagees on the face of the insurance policy. The loss payable clause to the mortgagee appears in the body of the policy and provides:

> Loss, if any, under this policy, shall be payable to the mortgagee * * *, named on the first page of this policy, as interest may appear * * *, and this insurance as to the interest of the mortgagee * * *, shall not be invalidated by any act or neglect of the mortgagor * * * .

This clause is known as a "union mortgage clause" because it insulates the mortgagee from policy defenses which may be available against the mortgagor. 5A Appleman, Insurance Law and Practice, § 3401 at 282 (1970). The union mortgage clause is to be distinguished from an "open loss payable clause." Under an open loss clause the policy merely identifies who is to collect the proceeds. Ibid. "In the open form, the indemnity of the mortgagee is subject to the risk of every act and neglect of the mortgagor which would avoid the original policy in the mortgagor's hands." 5A Appleman, op. cit., § 3401 at 293.[1]

On February 23, 1981 the house was substantially destroyed by fire. On November 17, 1981 plaintiffs received notification from the building inspector of Ventnor to demolish the dwelling because the fire damage amounted to total destruction creating a dangerous situation—the walls could collapse and youngsters were playing on the rotting floors. Plaintiffs

---

[1]   For a short discussion of the two clauses, see 495 Corp. v. N.J. Ins. Underwriting Ass'n, 173 N.J.Super. 114, 117, n. 2, 413 A.2d 630 (App.Div.1980).

submitted a certification from a real estate appraiser evaluating the vacant land at approximately $71,500, an amount which is at least $10,000 in excess of the outstanding balance on the mortgage. Plaintiffs have kept the monthly mortgage payments current.

Plaintiffs argue that since the mortgage is not in default and the security is not impaired, defendants cannot insist on applying the proceeds of the insurance to pay off the mortgage debt. Plaintiffs place primary reliance on the terms and conditions for acceleration in the mortgage and note. Plaintiffs observe that the provisions of the note and mortgage were negotiated[2] and these documents are silent as to acceleration in the event of fire. They contend that if defendants use the proceeds to satisfy the mortgage debt, they will be deprived of the loan from defendants and defendants are currently getting what they bargained for, i.e., continuous monthly payments over a period of time.

In contrast, defendants rely on the terms of the insurance policy. They argue that the policy is an independent agreement between the insurer and the mortgagees and that their rights cannot be affected by any acts of the mortgagors in rebuilding. Defendants claim their rights under the insurance policy became vested at the time of the fire and no subsequent act of the mortgagor can defeat their right to the proceeds. Defendants suggest that payment of the $60,000 to plaintiffs will result in a windfall to plaintiffs.[3] Defendants maintain that plaintiffs will have realized $56,000 profit within a few months. While defendants acknowledge that part of the proceeds of the insurance represent a loss of contents by plaintiffs, they suggest that the contents claim would not in any way approximate $56,000.

The standard mortgage clause creates an independent contract of insurance, for the separate benefit of the mortgagee, engrafted upon the main contract of insurance contained in the policy itself. 495 Corp. v. N.J. Ins. Underwriting Ass'n, supra, 173 N.J.Super. at 123, 413 A.2d 630, citing Reed v. Firemen's Ins. Co., 81 N.J.L. 523, 526, 80 A. 462 (E. & A.1910); 5A Appleman, op. cit., § 3401 at 292. An independent agreement exists between the mortgagee and the insurer. Employers' Fire Ins. Co. v. Ritter, 112 N.J.Eq. 418, 420, 164 A. 426 (Ch.1933). There are two beneficiaries of the insurance policy, the owner and the mortgagee, each with distinct and dissimilar rights. Id. at 421, 164 A. 426.

---

[2] Various provisions of the note were deleted pursuant to the negotiations.

[3]

$135,000	(insurance proceeds)
+71,500	(value of lot) =
206,500	
-150,000	(purchase price) =
$56,500	(profit)

One line of cases and commentators state as a general rule that the mortgagee can recover the insurance proceeds regardless of the value of the remaining security once a fire loss occurs. E.g., Walter v. Marine Office of America, 537 F.2d 89, 97–99 (5 Cir.1976) (applying Louisiana law); Savarese v. Ohio Farmers' Ins. Co., 260 N.Y. 45, 53, 182 N.E. 665, 667 (Ct.App.1932); 5A Appleman, op. cit., § 3405 at 320; 29 N.J.Practice (Cunningham & Tischler, Law of Mortgages), § 164 at 756 (1975). The rationale of these cases results from a singular approach which focuses solely on the insurance policy. The policy is categorized as an independent contract[4] between the insurer and the mortgagee. Once a fire loss occurs, the mortgagee's right to the insurance proceeds vests. Any future act of the mortgagor which restores the property to its pre-fire condition is deemed irrelevant since the mortgagee is entitled to immediate payment after the fire.

Defendants Sigmond urge that the following section of the insurance policy requires direct payment to the mortgagee:

4. Mortgage Clause

Loss, if any, under this policy, shall be payable to the mortgagee (or trustee) named on the first page of this policy, as interest may appear, under all present or future mortgages upon the property herein described, in which the aforesaid may have an interest as mortgagee (or trustee), *in order of precedence of said mortgage * * * .* [Emphasis supplied]

The foregoing clause does not establish that losses are to be paid to the mortgagees, but rather sets the order of priority for payment if there is more than one mortgagee. The clause negatives proportionate payment by the insurer as between the mortgagees in the event that the mortgage claims exceed the amount to be paid by the insurance company or in the event both mortgagees make a claim for the proceeds of insurance.

Other courts and commentators adopt the opposite rule of law and allow the mortgagor to recover the insurance proceeds in order to rebuild the damaged property. E.g., Schoolcraft v. Ross, 81 Cal.App.3d 75, 146 Cal.Rptr. 57 (D.Ct.App.1978); Fergus v. Wilmarth, 117 Ill. 542, 7 N.E. 508 (Sup.Ct.1886); Cottman Co. v. Continental Trust Co., 169 Md. 595, 182 A. 551 (Ct.App.1936); Osborne, Nelson & Whitman, Real Estate Finance

---

4   See discussion of union mortgage clause, supra. One court has concluded that such a clause creates an *independent cause of action* by the mortgagee as a third-party beneficiary of the insurance policy, *not an independent contract:*

The fact that practically a limitless benefit is conferred by the standard clause [union clause] upon the mortgagee makes it none the less a benefit, and, however limitless a benefit may be, it can never reach the dignity of a contract. [Walker v. Queen Ins. Co., 136 S.C. 144, 160–163, 134 S.E. 263, 269 (1926), cited in 2 Williston, Contracts (3 ed. Jaeger 1959), § 401A at 1086, n. 6].

Law (3d ed. 1979), § 4.15 at 150; 46 C.J.S., Insurance, § 1147 at 29 (under authority of a covenant to repair).

Various analytical approaches allow courts to reach this result. Some courts conclude that the purpose of the insurance is to maintain the security for the mortgage debt—if the property is restored, the security has not been impaired. Therefore, the purpose of the insurance has been fulfilled as to the mortgagee's interest and the mortgagor recovers the proceeds. Cottman v. Continental Trust Co., supra.

Osborne, Nelson and Whitman, in their treatise Real Estate Finance Law (3d ed. 1979), § 4.15 at 150, comment:

> At least in the absence of mortgage provisions to the contrary, it would seem that in the modern standard mortgage policy context where the mortgage is not in default, the mortgagor normally should be able, where rebuilding is practical, to insist upon the application of the insurance proceeds to rebuild the premises. To be sure, to permit the mortgagor to defeat the mortgagee's right to recovery by rebuilding may force the mortgagee to litigate the extent and sufficiency of repairs. On the other hand, it is almost always the mortgagor who is paying the premiums on the casualty insurance policy. Moreover, while permitting the mortgagee to utilize the insurance proceeds to pay the mortgage debt presumably benefits the mortgagor by rendering the property free from the mortgage lien to the extent of the loss, in many cases the mortgagor probably cannot afford to rebuild or is unable to obtain new mortgage financing for that purpose. Thus, on balance, it would seem more equitable in most cases to permit the mortgagor to rebuild and have the insurance applied to that purpose.

There is precedent for this view. One leading case is Cottman Co. v. Continental Trust Co., supra. There, plaintiff mortgaged its tugboats to secure a debenture with defendants as trustee (mortgagee). Pursuant to the requirements of the mortgage, insurance was taken out to protect the interest of the trustee (mortgagee). Thereafter, several of the tugs were damaged and repaired at plaintiff's expense. The insurer paid the claim of the trustee, who refused to reimburse plaintiff. Plaintiff sued the trustee for the proceeds of the insurance. In reversing a judgment for defendant trustee and holding that plaintiff mortgagor was entitled to the proceeds of the insurance, the Maryland Court of Appeals stated:

> Few cases, apparently, have reached appellate courts where the use of the insurance money for the repair and restoration of the security has been combatted by the recipient mortgagee. In such cases the argument is made that by virtue of the replacement or restoration, the creditor is left in the same position as he was

before the loss, and therefore has no ground of complaint. It cannot be denied that if the restoration of the security, at the expense of the debtor, to the value it had before the loss or damage, leaves the parties in statu quo, then the retention of the insurance money by the creditor, mortgagee, or trustee, as additional security, would put the holder in a better position than he had originally bargained for. The theory of insurance, however, does not contemplate a resulting profit to the insured, or his mortgagee or other creditor. The interest of the mortgagee is to maintain the equilibrium of debt and security; and if, by the application of the insurance money to the upkeep of the security, that parity would be continued, it is not inequitable to require the payee of the fund to transfer the same to the debtor for that purpose, upon properly safeguarding its application to that end. [169 Md. at 601–02, 182 A. at 554]

In Schoolcraft v. Ross, supra, the deed of trust (mortgage) specifically gave the beneficiary (mortgagee) an option to use the insurance proceeds to rebuild or to apply in reduction of the mortgage debt. The mortgagee, relying on the option clause, elected to apply the proceeds to the debt despite the mortgagor's request to use the proceeds for rebuilding. The mortgagor could not afford to continue to pay the mortgage and also pay rent for an apartment, and thus defaulted in payment on the mortgage. In an action by the mortgagor for damages the California court held:

[T]he right of a beneficiary (e.g., mortgagee) to apply insurance proceeds to the balance of a note secured by a deed of trust must be performed in good faith and with fair dealing and that to the extent the security was not impaired the beneficiary *must* permit those proceeds to be used for the cost of rebuilding. [81 Cal.App.3d at 77, 146 Cal.Rptr. at 58; emphasis supplied]

Since there was no evidence of the impairment of the security, the court held the mortgagee had no right to the funds. The court, even in face of the mortgagee's option, observed:

Forcing the buyer to pay off in advance would result in a buyer losing certain property rights contemplated by the parties, *among them the benefit of a long term loan which permits the buyer to spread the purchase price of the property over a long time.* [81 Cal.App.3d at 81, 146 Cal.Rptr. at 60; emphasis supplied]

The court found no evidence of impairment of the security and concluded "To the extent the security was not impaired, [mortgagee] had no right to the funds." Ibid.

Cottman and *Savarese,* both supra, demonstrate a general principle that hazard insurance is to protect the mortgagee's interest if the security for the debt is impaired. Absent an impairment, the mortgagee has no right to insist on payment from the insurer. The proceeds are to be paid to the insured mortgagor to effect the repair. New Jersey has recognized impairment of security as a rationale for recovery by mortgagees in other situations. "[T]he theory of recovery by a mortgagee is indemnity against an impairment of the mortgaged property * * * ." 495 Corp. v. N.J. Ins. Underwriting Ass'n, supra, 173 N.J.Super. at 118, 413 A.2d 630 (foreclosure). A similar principle of impairment of security of mortgage has been applied to condemnation proceedings. In Transportation Comm'r v. Kastner, 179 N.J.Super. 613, 433 A.2d 448 (Law Div.1981), a part of the mortgaged property was taken by condemnation. The mortgage made no provision for payment of the condemnation award in the event of a partial taking. In holding that the mortgagees were not entitled to have the condemnation award paid the court stated:

> [A] lienholder cannot enforce his lien against the condemnation award unless the remaining property is of insufficient value to satisfy his lien. [at 615, 433 A.2d 448]

If the proceeds are paid to the mortgagees in the present case, mortgagors will be damaged to the extent that they will lose the benefit of a long-term loan which was bargained for. The court takes judicial notice of the current prevailing high interest rates and the general scarcity of mortgage money, particularly for construction mortgages. If plaintiffs were forced to obtain a mortgage in the open market, it certainly would be greatly to their disadvantage and at a much higher interest rate than that to which plaintiffs and defendants Sigmond had bargained for. If construction mortgage financing were not available, plaintiffs could not even rebuild their home.

Moreover, there is evidence that the parties did not intend to accelerate the debt in case of fire. Under the insurance policy the insurer has the option to repair, rebuild or replace the property destroyed or damaged within a reasonable time and on giving notice of its intention to do so within 30 days after the receipt of the proof of loss. The dissent in Savarese v. Ohio Farmers' Ins. Co., supra, focused on the insurer's policy option to repair the property or to pay the loss as evidence of the purpose of the policy to maintain the security.

> [T]his clause [option to repair] in the agreement furnishes some indication that the purpose of the policy and the provision therein contained [to pay the mortgagee] *was to protect the mortgagee's interest in the property* only if such damage was not repaired. [260 N.Y. at 60, 182 N.E. at 670 (Lehman, J. dissenting); emphasis supplied]

If the insurer had elected to exercise that option, both mortgagees and mortgagors would be bound. See 5A Appleman, op. cit., § 3405 at 317.

This provision, coupled with the covenant to repair in the mortgage, indicates that the purpose of the insurance was to protect the mortgagees' interest if the security was impaired. As a further indication of this intent the parties specifically deleted a provision in the note which would have permitted acceleration in the event of a breach of the covenant to repair. A similar provision in the mortgage was not deleted. Where acceleration provisions of a note and mortgage are in an irreconcilable conflict the note will prevail. See 55 Am.Jur.2d, Mortgages, § 176 at 304.

While a covenant to repair and a covenant to rebuild are not identical, the deletion of acceleration for breach of the covenant to repair in the note is indicative of the parties' intent. The mortgagees in the present case are attempting to accelerate the debt indirectly by demanding payment of the proceeds, a right which by negotiation they specifically gave up.

Lastly, defendant mortgagees are not prejudiced by permitting rebuilding of the residence and have sustained no damages. Property insurance is a contract of indemnity. 29 N.J.Practice, op. cit., § 164 at 737. The mortgagee collects the proceeds to compensate for its loss.

> It is an elementary principle of insurance law that fire insurance * * * is a contract of personal indemnity, not one from which a profit is to be realized * * * [T]he right to recover must be commensurate with the loss *actually* sustained. [Glens Falls Ins. Co. v. Sterling, 219 Md. 217, 222, 148 A.2d 453, 456 (Ct.App.1959); emphasis in original]

Since the vacant land remains as full security for the mortgage debt, it is difficult to identify any loss sustained by the mortgagee. This case differs from others in that, at the time the right to proceeds vested, unlike the *Savarese,* supra, rationale, the vacant land fully secured the debt. Cases which permit the mortgagee to recover refuse to take a hindsight view if the property has been restored by the trial date; the courts concentrate on the impairment of the security on the date of the fire. There has never been in this case impairment for purposes of the mortgagees interest.

> The court looks to the substance of the whole transaction *rather than to seek a metaphysical hypothesis upon which to justify a loss that is no loss.* [Ramsdell v. Insurance Co. of N. Amer., 197 Wis. 136, 139, 221 N.W. 654, 655 (Sup.Ct.1928); emphasis supplied]

The court finds that mortgagees have suffered no damage as a result of the fire, and until the building is commenced they have the security of the $60,000 fund which is in escrow. They have no loss for which indemnification is required nor have they been prejudiced. * * *

NOTES

1. *The significance of mortgage language.* An extremely important factual difference exists between the *Starkman* case and the *Schoolcraft* case, which the court discussed in *Starkman*. In *Starkman*, the mortgage was silent as to the disposition of the insurance proceeds between the mortgagor and mortgagee. In *Schoolcraft*, on the other hand, an express mortgage clause purported to give the mortgagee the right to capture the proceeds. Thus, the New Jersey court merely had to reverse the traditional "default rule" to reach its result, while the California court had to go farther and refuse to enforce the mortgage language.

Even *Starkman* is a minority view, though the Restatement (Third) of Property (Mortgages) § 4.6 adopts it. If the mortgagor promised the mortgagee to insure the premises, courts in most cases give the mortgagee the option of applying the insurance proceeds to the mortgage debt or to rebuilding the mortgaged premises, if no mortgage language is to the contrary. The mortgagee's right normally does not require a finding that rebuilding will jeopardize the mortgage security. See Nelson, Whitman, Burkhart & Freyermuth, Real Estate Finance Law § 4.15 (6th ed.2014).

The *Schoolcraft* approach, which endorses the use of insurance proceeds to rebuild in the face of specific mortgage language giving the mortgagee the option of compelling prepayment of the mortgage debt, is even more unusual; indeed, it may be unique. Most courts seem to interpret even less precise language in a more pro-mortgagee fashion. See, e.g., Giberson v. First Fed. Sav. & Loan Ass'n of Waterloo, 329 N.W.2d 9 (Iowa 1983) (clause allowed proceeds to be used for rebuilding "when authorized by the [mortgagee]"; court refused to give summary judgment for mortgagors who sought the funds for rebuilding without mortgagee's consent). Several courts have expressly rejected the *Schoolcraft* approach. See, e.g., English v. Fischer, 660 S.W.2d 521 (Tex.1983) (the "novel" doctrine of "good faith and fair dealing" is inapplicable when the mortgage language affords the mortgagee the prepayment option); Loving v. Ponderosa Systems, Inc., 479 N.E.2d 531 (Ind.1985).

On the other hand, California went even farther than *Schoolcraft*. In Kreshek v. Sperling, 157 Cal.App.3d 279, 204 Cal.Rptr. 30 (1984), the court required the lender to give the insurance proceeds to the borrower though the borrower did not intend to rebuild! Because the mortgage debt was $320,000 and the property was worth more than $2 million despite the fire, the court concluded that the fire did not impair the lender's security. The California legislature subsequently overruled *Kreshek*, but it left *Schoolcraft* intact. See Cal. Civ. Code § 2924.7. Hence, if the borrower does not want to rebuild, the lender is entitled to the insurance proceeds, up to the amount of the debt. See California Fair Plan v. Boktor, 2003 WL 22883998 (Cal.Ct.App.2003, not reported in Cal.Rptr.).

2. *When should rebuilding be permitted with insurance proceeds?* As a practical matter, mortgagors and mortgagees probably routinely agree to use

the insurance proceeds for rebuilding in most instances of casualty loss. The Fannie Mae/Freddie Mac Uniform Single-Family Mortgage form, reprinted as From 2 in Appendix A, is very widely used for residential mortgage loans nationwide. Clause 5 of that form provides: "Unless Lender and Borrower otherwise agree in writing, any insurance proceeds ... shall be applied to restoration or repair of the Property, if the restoration or repair is economically feasible and Lender's security is not lessened."

In a similar vein, Restatement (Third) of Property (Mortgages) § 4.7(b) (1997)* provides that:

> Unless the mortgage effectively provides to the contrary, if restoration of the loss or damage ... is reasonably feasible within the remaining term of the mortgage with the funds received by the mortgagee, together with any additional funds made available by the mortgagor, and if after restoration the real estate's value will equal or exceed its value at the time the mortgage was made, the mortgagee holds the funds received subject to a duty to apply them, at the mortgagor's request and upon reasonable conditions, toward restoration.

However, the view that restoration is a reasonable demand to which lenders should submit is not universal. In General G.M.C. Sales, Inc. v. Passarella, 195 N.J.Super. 614, 481 A.2d 307 (App.Div.1984), a sister court of the *Starkman* court rejected *Starkman's* reasoning:

> There may be cases in which the mortgagee will be adequately protected by a holding that allows the mortgagor to use the fire insurance proceeds to rebuild. But there will be times when the mortgagee will be placed at risk by having his mortgage on an existing building converted to a construction mortgage for a new building. The holding creates too much potential for dispute and litigation. ... The parties could dispute the value of the security after a fire, especially if the property is not insured at full market value. Disagreement could also arise as to the value of the repairs or the replacement structure, the amount of progress payments, and other matters. For example, in the case at hand a question was raised as to the right to reconstruct a nonconforming building. The trial judge said that the mortgagee should not be forced into partnership with the mortgagor in rebuilding the structure, and the mortgage loan should not be converted into a construction loan. We agree with these observations.

The New Jersey Supreme Court affirmed the *Passarella* holding as it applies to commercial property but expressly reserved judgment on its applicability to residential property. 101 N.J. 12, 499 A.2d 1017 (1985). Are these

---

*   © 1997 by The American Law Institute. Reprinted with permission.

objections to *Starkman* persuasive? Are the objections mitigated by the following, excerpt from § 4.7, comment d of the Restatement?*

> The mortgagee is entitled to impose reasonable conditions on the process of restoration of the real estate. For example, the mortgagee may reserve a power to review and approve the plans and specifications for the work to be done. Such a power is recognized if it is reasonably exercised. Likewise, the mortgagee may require reasonable provisions for the disbursal of the funds to ensure that they will in fact be used for restoration and not diverted to other purposes. If the mortgagee is experienced in construction lending, it may wish to administer the disbursal itself; alternatively, the mortgagee may require use of some external service, such as an escrow company, to disburse the funds and inspect the progress of the restoration. In either case, the reasonable administrative cost of these procedures may be charged against the funds.

Incidentally, the Restatement adopts *Starkman* but not necessarily *Schoolcraft*. The Restatement's provision for use of insurance proceeds for restoration is only a "default" rule, "unless the mortgage effectively provides the contrary." However, § 4.7 comment d observes that a mortgage clause allowing the mortgagee to capture the insurance proceeds when rebuilding is feasible may "be disregarded by the courts. For example, in jurisdictions following the Restatement, Second, Contracts the provision might be considered unenforceable on the ground that it is an unconscionable term of the contract (see Restatement, Second, Contracts § 208) or that enforcement would violate the mortgagee's duty of good faith and fair dealing (see Restatement, Second, Contracts § 205)."

3.   *How much of the insurance proceeds may the mortgagee capture?* Assume that rebuilding is not feasible, that the property is repaired without using the insurance proceeds, or that an effective mortgage clause provides that the lender need not allow rebuilding. Is the mortgagee entitled to *all* the insurance proceeds, up to the full amount of the mortgage debt? This is indeed the majority view. See Grange Mut. Cas. Co. v. Central Trust Co., 774 S.W.2d 838 (Ky.App.1989). In many cases, this rule puts the mortgagee in a *more* secure position than it would have occupied without the casualty.

Restatement (Third) of Property (Mortgages) § 4.7(a) (1997) takes the view, supported by a substantial minority of cases, that the lender is entitled to recover insurance proceeds only "to the extent that the mortgagee's security has been impaired by the loss or damage." This was the basis for the court's refusal to let the lender keep any of the insurance proceeds in Kreshek v. Sperling, note 1, *supra*. The Restatement measures impairment of security for this purpose in the same way as for waste—the mortgagee's recovery should be sufficient to restore the loan to its "scheduled" loan-to-value ratio. See the discussion in note 6 of Section C, Waste, in this chapter.

---

*   © 1997 by The American Law Institute. Reprinted with permission.

Here is an illustration of that principle on facts that parallel the illustration in note 6 of Section C. ME makes a loan of $80,000 to MR, secured by a mortgage on land with an appraised value of $100,000. MR purchases and maintains casualty insurance as required by the mortgage. During the next five years, MR makes all the scheduled payments, which reduces the mortgage debt balance to $70,000. At the same time, the land's value has increased to $120,000. A fire occurs, which reduces the land's value by $30,000 to $90,000. The insurer tenders $30,000. The scheduled loan-to-value ratio at the time of the fire was $70,000/$100,000 or 70 percent, so ME is entitled to a restoration of that loan-to-value ratio. Because the land is now worth $90,000, ME is entitled to a portion of the insurance proceeds necessary to reduce the debt balance to 70 percent of $90,000, or $63,000. Therefore, ME can claim $70,000 minus $63,000, or $7,000 of the fire insurance proceeds.

4. *Disposition of eminent domain awards.* When mortgaged property is taken in full by eminent domain, the mortgagee is entitled to the entire condemnation award, up to the debt balanced, in the absence of a contrary agreement. See Nelson, Whitman, Burkhart & Freyermuth, Real Estate Finance Law § 4.12 (6th ed. 2014). When only a partial taking occurs, the majority view is the same—the mortgagee may take the entire award, up to the debt balance. However, a growing and (we believe) well-reasoned trend suggests that the mortgagee should recover only enough to compensate for the impairment of its security. See People ex rel. Dept. of Transp. v. Redwood Baseline, Ltd., 84 Cal.App.3d 662, 149 Cal.Rptr. 11 (1978); State ex rel. Commr. of Transp. v. Kastner, 179 N.J.Super. 613, 433 A.2d 448 (Law Div.1981); Restatement (Third) of Property (Mortgages) § 4.7(a) (1997). However, confusion exists concerning how impairment of security should be measured. See note 6 in Section C of this chapter. Additionally, courts that limit the mortgagee's recovery to the impairment of its security are divided on whether a mortgage clause that purports to give the mortgagee the full award can override this result. See, e.g., First Western Fin. Corp. v. Vegas Continental, 100 Nev. 710, 692 P.2d 1279 (1984) (it cannot). See generally, David A. Leipziger, The Mortgagee's Remedies for Waste, 64 Cal.L.Rev. 1086, 1100 (1976); Harold Don Teague, Condemnation of Mortgaged Property, 44 Tex.L.Rev. 1535 (1966).

The Fannie Mae/Freddie Mac Uniform Single-Family Mortgage form that is reprinted as Form 2 in Appendix A, infra, takes quite a different approach to eminent domain awards than to casualty insurance proceeds. Clause 11 of the form allows the mortgagee to capture the full award, up to the debt amount, when a total taking occurs. When a partial taking occurs, the form allows the mortgagee to recover "the amount of the proceeds multiplied by the following fraction: (a) the total amount of the sums secured immediately before the partial taking, divided by (b) the fair market value of the Property immediately before the partial taking."

If the mortgagee is entitled to the eminent domain award, must it allow the funds to be used for rebuilding by analogy to the *Starkman* case? In many respects, eminent domain awards are similar to casualty insurance proceeds, but one obvious difference exists. In a total taking case, rebuilding is impossible because the real estate is gone! In a partial taking case, on the other hand, rebuilding may be feasible, though it is much less likely than with a casualty loss, because part of the real estate is unavailable. If rebuilding is feasible, the Restatement requires the lender to allow use of the eminent domain award for that purpose, in the absence of a contrary agreement. See Restatement (Third) of Property (Mortgages) § 4.7(b) (1997).

5.   *Effect of a full credit bid on insurance recovery.* Assume that, after a casualty loss, a mortgagee purchases the mortgaged premises at a foreclosure sale by bidding the full debt amount. Can the mortgagee later recover the casualty insurance proceeds? See Arkansas Teacher Retirement System v. Coronado Props., Ltd., 33 Ark.App. 17, 801 S.W.2d 50 (1990) ("If the mortgagee has bid in the full amount of its secured debt at the sale, it thereby satisfies its lien and loses all entitlement to any insurance proceeds."); Helmer v. Texas Farmers Ins. Co., 632 S.W.2d 194, 196 (Tex.App.1982) ("The law in most jurisdictions seems to be that if the mortgage debt is satisfied by the proceeds of sale, as reflected in the mortgage or deed of trust in this case, the mortgagee is entitled to no further payment on account thereof."); Norwest Mortg., Inc. v. State Farm Fire & Cas. Co., 118 Cal.Rptr.2d 367 (App. 2002) (depublished); Fire Ins. Exchange v. Bowers, 994 S.W.2d 110 (Mo.App. 1999).

The court in Whitestone Sav. & Loan Ass'n v. Allstate Ins. Co., 28 N.Y.2d 332, 321 N.Y.S.2d 862, 270 N.E.2d 694, (1971) gave an alternative explanation for this result: "[T]he mortgagee has voluntarily converted the debt into the property and has done so by taking the property in satisfaction of the debt. It could have bid less, thus leaving a deficiency for which the mortgagor would be obligated and from which there would survive an insurable interest." Restatement (Third) of Property (Mortgages) § 4.8(a) (1997) agrees.

Does this rule seem too harsh? If the mortgagee knows that a fire or other casualty has reduced the property's value to less than the outstanding debt amount, a full credit bid would be unwise. Thus, the rule seems to penalize a mortgagee that is stupid or that carelessly failed to check the property's condition before the foreclosure sale. Consider the court's comment in Whitestone Sav. & Loan Ass'n v. Allstate Ins. Co.:

> The rule is not harsh and it is eminently practical. None disputes that the mortgagee is entitled to recover only his debt. Any surplus value belongs to others, namely, the mortgagor or subsequent lienors. Indeed, it is not conceivable that the mortgagee could recover a deficiency judgment against the mortgagor if it had bid in the full amount of the debt at foreclosure sale. To allow the mortgagee, after effectively cutting off or discouraging lower bidders, to take the property—and then establish that it was worth less than the bid—encourages fraud, creates uncertainty as to the

mortgagor's rights, and most unfairly deprives the sale of whatever leaven comes from other bidders.

Of course, the mortgagee also cannot claim insurance proceeds if it voluntarily accepted full payment of the mortgage debt. See Benton Banking Co. v. Tennessee Farmers Mut. Ins. Co., 906 S.W.2d 436 (Tenn.1995) (mortgagee had no right to fire insurance proceeds after it accepted promissory note from insured mortgagors' parent in satisfaction of debt). Similarly, if the mortgagee makes a successful partial credit bid, it can take only enough insurance proceeds to pay the deficiency, even if the bid exceeded the damaged property's value. See Rodriguez v. First Union Nat'l Bank, 61 Mass.App.Ct. 438, 810 N.E.2d 1282 (2004); Lenart v. Ocwen Fin. Corp., 869 So.2d 588 (Fla. Ct.App.2004).

If damage to the mortgaged building is not visible from its exterior, should a court refuse to award insurance proceeds to the mortgagee after a full credit bid even if the mortgagor refused to let the mortgagee inspect the interior before foreclosure? See Universal Mortg. Co. v. Prudential Ins. Co., 799 F.2d 458 (9th Cir.1986) (denying recovery to mortgagee on similar facts). How should a prudent mortgagee handle this situation? Virtually all well-drafted mortgages give the lender a right of reasonable inspection of the premises. See Patrick A. Randolph, Jr., The Mortgagee's Interest in Casualty Loss Proceeds: Evolving Rules and Risks, 32 Real Prop., Prob. & Tr. J. 1 (1997).

A few courts have been more sympathetic to mortgagees:

The "foreclosure after loss" rule requires an election of remedies. This Court has held that when making an election between remedies, a party must make the election with the full and clear understanding of the problem, facts and remedies essential to the exercise of an intelligent choice.... We conclude that implicit in the "foreclosure after loss" rule is the requirement that the mortgagee or purchaser at the foreclosure sale have knowledge of the loss before making an election. However, the mortgagee or purchaser must diligently seek facts that would enable it to make an informed election.

Ex parte Chrysler First Fin. Servs. Corp., 608 So.2d 734, 737 (Ala.1992). In that case, the house on the property had been destroyed five days before the foreclosure sale, but the court concluded that the lender was not "dilatory" or at fault for failing to discover the loss.

Incidentally, if the mortgagee's full credit bid prevents it from making a claim on the casualty insurance, who gets the benefit of the "unused" insurance coverage? In Lee v. Royal Indemnity Co., 108 F.3d 651 (6th Cir.1997), the mortgagee "erroneously" made a full credit bid at foreclosure. Under Tennessee law, it was therefore precluded from recovering anything from the insurance company. The court held that the homeowner/mortgagor could therefore collect the full face amount of the policy, though his home had been heavily encumbered by the mortgage when the loss occurred. The court stated that, "once a mortgagee's interest in the policy is extinguished through subsequent acts, any interest it had in the policy reverts back to the [mortgagor] policy holder." The insurer, of course, argued that this unjustly enriched the mortgagor, but the court commented that it was as if the mortgagor's "rich uncle" had paid off his mortgage loan. The court in Rodriguez v. First Union Nat'l Bank, 61 Mass.App.Ct. 438, 810 N.E.2d 1282 (2004), reached the same result.

6. *Effect of full credit bid on other recovery by the mortgagee.* Full credit bids are dangerous for mortgagees in situations other than casualty loss. As we have already noted in Section C of this chapter concerning waste, a mortgagee who makes a full credit bid in foreclosure cannot recover anything for waste, even if it becomes apparent after the foreclosure that the property was not worth as much as the debt. See Evans v. California Trailer Court, Inc., 28 Cal.App.4th 540, 33 Cal.Rptr.2d 646 (1994).

Mortgagees sometimes sue their former mortgagors after foreclosure on a variety of other grounds: fraud in the mortgage application process, conversion of rents received before foreclosure ("waste of rents"), and improper receipt of eminent domain proceeds, to mention a few. Should a full credit bid also bar the mortgagee's recovery on these grounds? We will confront this question later in Chapter 6, Section H, infra.

7. *Insurance recovery for losses occurring after foreclosure.* Who is entitled to the insurance proceeds when the casualty loss occurs after a foreclosure purchase by the mortgagee? The mortgagee, of course, regardless of the amount it bid at the sale, because the mortgagee now owns the real estate and is insured by the policy. The policy may say that the proceeds are payable to the mortgagor and mortgagee "as their interests may appear," but the mortgagee's interest is now the fee title. See, e.g., Liberty Mut. Fire Ins. Co. v. Alexander, 374 N.J.Super. 340, 864 A.2d 1127 (App.Div.2005); Disrud v. Arnold, 167 Wis.2d 177, 482 N.W.2d 114 (App.1992); J. Burke McCormick, Note, Fire Insurance Recovery Rights of the Foreclosing Mortgagee: Is His Lien Lost in the Ashes?, 8 Ford.Urb.L.Rev. 857 (1980); Nelson, Whitman, Burkhart & Freyermuth, Real Estate Finance Law § 4.16 (6th ed.2014).

8. *Insurance purchased by the mortgagee.* Many mortgages provide that, if the mortgagor does not carry the required insurance, the mortgagee can purchase insurance to protect itself and charge the premiums to the mortgagor. This is often termed "force-placing" the insurance. See, e.g., Custer v. Homeside Lending, Inc., 858 So.2d 233 (Ala.2003), in which the court approved the lender's force-placing of flood insurance. However, the insurance obtained by the lender may be far from ideal from the borrower's viewpoint. One lender sent the following disclaimer to its borrower:

> Please note this is not a homeowners policy. * * * No attempt was made to duplicate any insurance you may have had in the past. The insurance coverage we have obtained may be more expensive, may

not be enough to cover your loss and provide less coverage than you could obtain from an agent or company of your choice.

Hickman v. SAFECO Ins. Co., 695 N.W.2d 365 (Minn.2005) (force-placed policy language evidenced intent to benefit borrower, as well as lender).

Escrow Accounts for Taxes and Insurance

The material above suggests that mortgagees have a strong and legitimate concern that their mortgagors maintain and pay the premiums for casualty insurance on the mortgaged premises. Mortgagees are perhaps even more insistent that mortgagors promptly pay the real estate taxes and special assessments accruing against the property. The reason for this concern, as Professor Durfee once aptly pointed out, is that "in most tax systems * * * the burden of the ordinary tax on land and the burden of special assessments for local improvements rest on both mortgagor and mortgagee in the sense that unless these charges are satisfied by someone before the axe falls, the interests of both parties will be rubbed out. The state goes after the land and its claim overrides *all* prior interests whatever their character." Edgar N. Durfee, Cases on Security 136 (1951) (emphasis added). In other words, even a "first" mortgage on real estate will be wiped out by a sale under a subsequently arising real estate tax lien.

For this reason, most mortgages include clauses that require the mortgagor to pay taxes and insurance premiums and make the failure to do so grounds for acceleration of the mortgage debt. As additional protection, many mortgagees demand that mortgagors set up accounts with the mortgagee into which the mortgagor will pay 1/12 of the annual taxes and insurance premiums each month (along with the regular monthly payment of principal and interest) and out of which the mortgagee will make the tax and insurance payments as they fall due. You can see the typical residential loan provision in Clause 3 of the Fannie Mae/Freddie Mac Uniform Mortgage Form, reproduced as Form 2 in Appendix A of this book. Loans on commercial real estate often have similar requirements.

These accounts are usually called "escrow," "impound," or "reserve" accounts. The usual obligations paid from escrow accounts are ad valorem property taxes, special assessments, and casualty insurance premiums. Sometimes other items are included, such as condominium or PUD homeowner association assessments and ground rents if the security property is ground-leased land. Use of escrow accounts ensures that the mortgagor will have enough money to pay these expenses and provides the lender with an "early warning system;" as soon as the mortgagor misses even one monthly payment, the lender is immediately aware of the default and can take measures to protect itself.

Escrow accounts are also an important source of revenue for loan servicers. If the mortgagee is not required to pay interest on the account to the mortgagor, it can invest the funds and earn interest on them for its own benefit until they need to be paid out. For an average account balance of, say, $1,000, the annual earnings at a 4% return would be $40. When a mortgagee sells a loan to a secondary market investor, such as Fannie Mae or Freddie Mac, the investor normally will employ the mortgagee to "service" the loan, which involves maintaining relations with the borrower, collecting and remitting to the investor the monthly payments, and administering the escrow account. Secondary market investors pay a fee to their servicers for these functions. A typical fee on a residential loan might be 25 to 50 "basis points." A "basis point" is one-hundredth of a percent. Twenty-five basis points would produce a servicing fee of $250 annually on a $100,000 loan. When this fee is combined with the "float" or investment income from the escrow account, an efficient servicer can earn a very attractive income from a portfolio of loans.

Mortgagee liability for interest on escrow accounts. Formerly, mortgagees often voluntarily paid interest on escrow accounts. Some lenders allowed their borrowers to set up interest-bearing savings accounts to receive the monthly escrow payments. Others credited the borrower's escrow payments to the mortgage loan balance and debited the loan balance when the lender paid the taxes and insurance premiums. This approach was very advantageous to borrowers, because it effectively allowed them to earn interest on their escrowed money at the mortgage debt rate.

However, these practices have largely faded away, and few lenders today pay or credit interest to their borrowers except when they are required by law to do so. During the 1970s, attorneys for borrowers filed a spate of class action suits in an attempt to establish that lenders have a duty to pay interest on escrowed funds though the mortgage documents do not clearly require them to do so. These plaintiffs employed a variety of creative theories, such as express trust, constructive trust, pledge, "special deposit," unjust enrichment, and quasi-contract. At first it seemed that they might be successful, because a few significant cases allowed borrowers to recover interest. See Derenco, Inc. v. Benjamin Franklin Fed. Sav. & Loan Ass'n, 281 Or. 533, 577 P.2d 477 (1978); Buchanan v. Brentwood Fed. Sav. & Loan Ass'n, 457 Pa. 135, 320 A.2d 117 (1974); Madsen v. Prudential Fed. Sav. & Loan Ass'n, 558 P.2d 1337 (Utah 1977).

However, this trend was short-lived. Lenders quickly revised their mortgage clauses concerning escrow accounts to delete words like "pledge," "trust," and "deposit." By the end of the 1970s, most state courts refused to order lenders to pay interest to borrowers. See Kronisch v. Howard Sav. Institute, 161 N.J.Super. 592, 392 A.2d 178 (1978); Michael E. Kaemmerer, Comment, Tax and Insurance Escrow Accounts in Mortgages—The Attack Presses On, 41 Mo.L.Rev. 133 (1976); Nelson, Whitman, Burkhart & Freyermuth, Real Estate Finance Law §§ 4.17– 4.18 (6th ed.2014).

To some extent, borrowers won in the legislatures what they lost in the courts. Several states enacted legislation regulating escrow accounts. The statutes are summarized in Nelson, Whitman, Burkhart & Freyermuth, Real Estate Finance Law § 4.19 (6th ed.2014). Little uniformity exists among them. They typically apply only to residential mortgages (one- to four-family dwellings). The required interest rate may be fixed by the statute or by a state regulatory agency, such as the Commissioner of Banking.

Federal preemption of state law requiring interest payment. No federal law or regulation requires lenders to pay interest on escrow accounts. To the contrary, a federal regulation provides that a federally-chartered savings and loan association "may extend credit as authorized under federal law, including this part, without regard to state laws purporting to regulate or otherwise affect their credit activities." 12 C.F.R. § 560.2. The types of state laws preempted specifically include "(6) Escrow accounts, impound accounts, and similar accounts." This regulation was held to preempt the New York statute requiring payment of interest on escrow accounts in Flagg v. Yonkers Sav. & Loan Ass'n, 396 F.3d 178 (2d Cir.2005). Another federal regulation preempts state laws concerning escrow accounts for national banks. 12 C.F.R. § 34.4. Is it good policy to place federal savings and loan associations and banks in this superior position to other types of lenders, which are bound by state law? Is it appropriate to preempt state consumer protections? See Nelson, Whitman, Burkhart & Freyermuth, Real Estate Finance Law § 11.6 (6th ed. 2014).

Escrow accounting under RESPA. When an escrow account is created (ordinarily, when the mortgage loan is made), the borrower normally must "fund" the account with a front-end payment. When the annual property taxes are due, the escrow account must have 12 months' worth of taxes. However, in most cases, a full year won't elapse between the date the loan is made and the date the taxes must be paid. Therefore, the borrower's regular monthly payments (1/12 of the annual taxes each month) will be inadequate to accumulate the necessary amount by the time the lender must pay the taxes. As a result, the lender requires a front-end payment. The amount of the front-end payment depends on how many months of regular monthly payments will be made between the date the loan is made and the date the taxes must be paid.

For example, assume that the loan is made on April 15 and that the taxes are assessed on a calendar year basis and are due and payable on December 15. (There are large variations in state tax practices, but these assumptions are plausible.) Further assume that the property taxes are $1,200 per year, or $100 per month. On these facts, the escrow account must have $1,200 by December 15. Where will this money come from?

Part of it will be derived from the borrower's regular payments of $100 per month into the escrow account. How many such payments will occur? Usually, the first loan payment is due at the beginning of the second full month after the loan is made. On our facts, that payment will be due on June 1. (Interest for the partial month from April 15 to April 30 will be paid by the borrower in cash at the closing; interest for the month of May will be paid as part of the June 1 loan payment.) The borrower will make additional loan and escrow payments on the first days of July, August, September, October, November, and December. Thus, when the taxes are due, the borrower will have made 7 monthly tax escrow payments of $100 each. That will put $700 in the escrow account. Where will the other $500 come from? The lender will require the borrower to "fund" the account at closing with $500. This money, when added to the $700 in monthly escrow payments, will equal $1,200 by the time the taxes are due.

This calculation leaves no margin for error. However, when the loan is made and the escrow account is set up, the tax authorities probably will not have fixed the precise tax amount. Suppose the taxes turn out to be higher than estimated or the buyer misses a monthly payment. To take care of such contingencies, the lender may require the buyer to put a "cushion" in the escrow account in addition to the amount we calculated above. A common requirement, which we will explore below, is a two-month contingency—an additional $200 at the closing in our example. Thus, the borrower must deposit $700 for taxes at the loan closing.

Adjustment between seller and buyer. The calculations we have just made do not affect the adjustment or "proration" of taxes for the year between the buyer and seller of the real estate. In our example, the seller owned the property for about 3½ months of the calendar year. Because the buyer will pay the taxes for the entire year in December, the seller needs to reimburse the buyer for 3½ months' worth of taxes—$350. Therefore, the settlement agent for the sale should debit the seller and credit the buyer with $350. (In practice, this calculation is usually done on a per diem basis, taking the precise number of days from January 1 to April 15 as the numerator of the fraction and 365 days as the denominator.)

Thus, the buyer gets $350 in the tax adjustment with the seller but must pay $700 to fund the new escrow account. In a sense, these two amounts offset each other, but we must keep in mind that they are completely separate conceptually. Their only relationship is that they both have some connection to the property taxes. The adjustment of $350 between the buyer and seller would occur even if the buyer paid all cash for the property and did not need to obtain a new loan or set up an escrow account.

Limitations on the lender's "cushion." Let's return to the "cushion" of $200 that the lender required the borrower to pay into the escrow account. The amount of the cushion is limited by a federal statute, the Real Estate Settlement Procedures Act, 12 U.S.C.A. § 2609, which provides:

> A lender, in connection with a federally related mortgage loan, may not require the borrower or prospective borrower—
>
> > (1) to deposit in any escrow account which may be established in connection with such loan for the purpose of assuring payment of taxes, insurance premiums, or other charges with respect to the property, in connection with the settlement, an aggregate sum (for such purpose) in excess of a sum that will be sufficient to pay such taxes, insurance premiums and other charges attributable to the period beginning on the last date on which each such charge would have been paid under the normal lending practice of the lender and local custom, provided that the selection of each such date constitutes prudent lending practice, and ending on the due date of its first full installment payment under the mortgage, plus one-sixth of the estimated total amount of such taxes, insurance premiums and other charges to be paid on dates, as provided above, during the ensuing twelve-month period.

Thus, the cushion is limited to 1/6 (two months' worth) of the estimated annual taxes and other escrowed items. This is the maximum cushion; a particular lender might only require one month's worth or none at all.

Accounting for multiple items. RESPA's requirements seem straightforward when only one item, such as property taxes, is being escrowed. However, most lenders escrow at least two items—taxes and casualty insurance premiums. If both items were paid from the escrow account at the same time, computing the allowable cushion under RESPA would still be simple. However, in most cases, they are not paid at the same time. Local law sets the date for property tax payments. In our example, it is December 15. On the other hand, casualty insurance premiums usually are paid annually, beginning approximately on the first anniversary of the date that the coverage began. Therefore, the escrow cycles for the property taxes and for the insurance premiums are usually "out of phase" with one another; their payouts do not come due simultaneously.

If the taxes and insurance are analyzed separately, the total escrow balance will never fall to zero, plus the "cushion," because when the escrow balance for taxes is low, the escrow balance for insurance will be relatively high and vice versa. This raises an interesting legal question. Does the RESPA section quoted above allow lenders to compute each item separately, so that each item will fall to zero, plus the "cushion," at its lowest point in the year? Or does it require an "aggregate" computation, so that the overall balance in the account will fall to zero, plus the "cushion," at its lowest point?

Lenders prefer the individual item approach for two reasons. First, it is easier to calculate. Although this is true, it is hardly an overwhelming argument in this computerized age. Second—and much more important—it creates higher average balances and larger investment earnings on the "float" in the accounts. Which is the correct interpretation of RESPA? The statute is ambiguous on the point and can equally easily be read either way.

HUD surveyed a sample of mortgage servicers in 1992 and determined that 90% of them were using individual item analysis. Lenders argued that RESPA did not require aggregate analysis. Lawyers for consumers, on the other hand, filed a number of class action lawsuits, arguing that their clients should not be required to tie up several hundred dollars unnecessarily in an escrow account for the life of their mortgage loans.

Both sides looked to the Department of Housing and Urban Development (HUD), which had authority to issue regulations interpreting RESPA, for a resolution of this controversy. For several years, HUD vacillated and held hearings and issued proposed regulations. In 1991, a group of seven state attorneys general issued a report criticizing HUD for apparently approving the use of individual item analysis and arguing that the statute required the use of aggregate analysis. See Kevin J. Skehan, Enforcement of the Federal Limitation Requirement on Advance Deposits in Escrow Accounts and the Potential Impact on Mortgage Lenders in Connecticut, 12 Bridgeport L. Rev. 789 (1992). Lender trade organizations, such as the Mortgage Bankers Association, vigorously disagreed.

Finally, in 1994, HUD, after much debate and confusion, published a regulation that resolved the debate. That regulation requires lenders to use the aggregate method. Making the change turned out to be more complex than HUD had anticipated, and it was forced to issue several more clarifying regulations during 1995. HUD estimated that the average family would save $250 because of the change.

On July 21, 2011, Congress transferred responsibility for the administration of RESPA to the Consumer Financial Protection Bureau. It also requires aggregate analysis. 12 C.F.R. § 1024.17.

Private actions under RESPA. Because the foregoing section, unlike several other RESPA provisions, is silent as to remedies, courts have held that no private cause of action exists under it for mortgagors who are required to make excessive escrow payments. See McAnaney v. Astoria Fin. Corp., 357 F.Supp.2d 578 (E.D.N.Y.2005). The Sixth Circuit has disagreed; see Vega v. First Fed. Sav. & Loan Ass'n, 622 F.2d 918 (6th Cir. 1980). See Seth M. Mott, Note, Tackling the Perplexing Sound of Statutory Silence: Why Courts Should Imply a Private Right of Action Under Section 10(A) of RESPA, 64 Wash. & Lee L. Rev. 1159 (2007); Christopher L. Sagers, An Implied Cause of Action under the Real Estate Settlement Procedures Act, 95 Mich. L. Rev. 1381 (1997).

CHAPTER FIVE

TRANSFER AND DISCHARGE

• • •

A. TRANSFER OF THE MORTGAGOR'S INTEREST

Most buyers of real estate cannot pay the entire purchase price in cash, but instead must obtain financing for a significant portion of the price. One way for a purchaser to do so is to obtain a new loan from a third-party lender, such as a bank or savings association. Another way, the subject of this section, is for the purchaser to "take over" an existing mortgage loan on the property. Here the title to the land is transferred to the purchaser, but the existing mortgage is not paid off or satisfied, but remains on the land. The purchaser is ordinarily given credit toward the purchase price in an amount equal to the outstanding balance of the loan being taken over. She may pay the remainder of the price in cash, or may finance part or all of it by other means, such as a second mortgage loan.

Why would a purchaser prefer to take over an existing mortgage loan rather than obtaining a new one? The most obvious reason is that, if interest rates have been rising, the rate on the old loan may be lower than on any comparable loan available in the current market. Of course, in that setting lenders are loath to see their loans "taken over" at existing rates; they would prefer to adjust those rates upward, or to have the loans paid off so the funds could be relent at a higher rate. Whether lenders have the legal power to gain these advantages depends largely on the existence and enforceability of "due on sale" clauses, which is the subject of Section B of this chapter.

But even if the existing mortgage loan does not have a lower interest rate than currently-available financing, or if that lower rate will be adjusted upward to a current market level by the lender, there may still be advantages to a real estate purchaser in taking over an existing mortgage loan. The purchaser can usually avoid payment of a number of "closing cost" items associated with obtaining a new loan, such as title insurance, an appraisal of the real estate, and perhaps some loan fees. The purchaser may also be able to take over the loan despite the fact that he or she does not meet the usual credit and income standards imposed by lenders for new loans, although this advantage, like the interest rate advantage mentioned in the previous paragraph, will likely not be

477

realized if the mortgage contains a "due on sale" clause, as virtually all modern mortgages do.

There are two distinct methods of taking over an existing mortgage loan: by *assuming* it and by merely *taking subject to* it. The economic aspects of these two methods are substantially identical, but as the material below shows, they have very different legal consequences.

⟨ MIDDLETON V. HANCOCK ▷

State of Equity Court of Appeal, 2014
1599 S.E.2d 1*

Per curiam. This is a sad case involving an unprofitable "strip mall"—a small shopping center named "Midgate Plaza" in the City of Equity. The original developer of Midgate Plaza was Fred Middleton, the plaintiff in this case. Construction on the shopping center was completed in 1985, and Middleton operated it successfully for a number of years. The original "permanent" or long-term loan on the property, in the amount of $1.7 million, was made by Equity Bank. It carried an interest rate of 8% per annum and a twenty-five year term, with monthly payments of $13,690. These payments were sufficient to amortize the original balance in full over the loan's term. All payments were made in a timely fashion during the period that Middleton owned the property.

Ten years after the loan was made, Middleton sold Midgate Plaza to Herb Hancock for $2.1 million. At that point the balance on the original mortgage loan had been reduced by regular amortization to about $1,390,000. Hancock is a local automobile dealer in the City of Equity. He wanted to acquire the shopping center as a first step in expanding his financial empire. The contract of sale signed by Middleton and Hancock contained the following provision:

> Purchaser agrees to take over payments on the existing loan, and to pay cash in the amount of $710,000 to Seller, representing the difference between the balance owing on the existing loan and the agreed purchase price of the Property.

Before the sale occurred, Middleton contacted Equity Bank to seek its approval for the sale. Such approval was necessary because of the presence in the Bank's mortgage of a "due-on-sale" clause, which would permit the Bank to accelerate the balance on the loan, making it immediately due and payable, if a sale of the property were made without the Bank's prior written consent. The Bank examined Hancock's personal balance sheet, reviewed the assets and liabilities of his automobile

---

*   This case is imaginary, although the opinion bears a close resemblance to many actual judicial opinions. The editors could not find a well-written opinion that covered all of the issues we wished to cover, so we wrote our own.

dealership, and judged that he was a satisfactory risk to take over the loan. It provided Middleton with a letter consenting to the sale. Because the 8 percent interest rate was quite close to current market rates in 1995, the Bank did not require any change in the rate or any other terms of the loan.

The sale was closed on April 1, 1995. The deed executed by Middleton and delivered to Hancock contained a clause stating: "The above-described real property is subject to a mortgage loan held by Equity Bank." There was no other document that made any reference to the mortgage; in particular, Hancock did not execute any "assumption agreement."

Hancock operated the property with apparent success for about five years. Unfortunately (for him), in 2000 a huge regional mall, known as the Upscale Equity Center, opened directly across the street from Midgate Mall. Upscale contains about ten times the leaseable square footage found in Midgate, and it seems that many of Midgate's former customers began shopping at Upscale instead. The leases of several of Midgate's retail tenants expired during this period. They were not renewed by their tenants, and Hancock was unable to find new tenants to fill most of these vacancies. Rents under percentage rent clauses from the remaining tenants also dropped as a result of slow sales caused by the general economic recession occurring during this period. As a result, Hancock's formerly positive cash flow from Midgate turned negative; he was not receiving sufficient rent from the property to pay his operating expenses (maintenance, property taxes, insurance, management costs, and the like) and to service the mortgage debt, which continued to require a monthly payment of $13,690.

Hancock began missing monthly payments, commencing in January 2002. During the past year (this opinion being prepared in January 2003), he has not made a single payment. Equity Bank contacted Middleton in March, 2002, when Hancock had missed three payments. The bank pointed out that Middleton had never been released from his personal liability on the mortgage loan and strongly "suggested" that he cure Hancock's default. In response, Middleton immediately paid the three months' worth of missed payments, or $41,070, plus late fees (which are four percent of any monthly payment that is made more than 5 days late) of $2,053, for a total of $44,123. (The Bank might also have demanded accrued interest on the late payments, but waived its right to do so in light of Middleton's prompt and favorable response.)

Middleton immediately contacted Hancock, demanding that he reimburse Middleton for the funds Middleton had paid to bring the loan current. Hancock was not helpful. His reply is captured in an e-mail he sent to Middleton, from which we quote:

When I bought this place, I sure intended to make the payments on the loan. But it just ain't bringing in enough money to do that, and I'll be danged if I'm going to put money into it out of my own pocket. The car business is pretty slack these days, and so far as I'm concerned the bank will just have to wait until times get better.

Although he tried on numerous occasions, Middleton was unable to get any better response from Hancock. Meanwhile Equity Bank continued to remind Middleton that he was still personally liable on the loan, and to threaten him with suit for the entire loan balance if he allowed further defaults to occur. To avoid this, Middleton began making all payments due on the loan, and has continued to do so up to the present time. He has made ten monthly payments in addition to the amount he paid to cure the loan default in March, 2002, as mentioned above, and at this point has paid the Bank a total of $181,023. Hancock remains in possession of Midgate Mall, and Middleton alleges that, given Hancock's total failure to make any mortgage payments during 2002, Hancock must have taken a substantial amount of cash out of the property during that time.

In June, 2002 Middleton filed this action against Hancock. He prayed for (1) a personal judgment against Hancock to reimburse him for the payments he has made on the mortgage loan (including any payments he may be required to make during the pendency of the litigation), and (2) foreclosure of the mortgage against Midgate Mall to assist him in recovery of those payments. Hancock filed a motion under Rule 12(b)(6) to dismiss the action for failure by Middleton to state a claim upon which relief could be granted. There were no disputed issues of fact. The district court determined that as a matter of law Middleton had no basis for recovery, and it dismissed Middleton's complaint with prejudice. Middleton then filed the present appeal.

DISCUSSION

A. *Did Hancock assume?* When an owner of mortgaged real property sells it without paying off and retiring the mortgage, the sale can be handled in either of two ways. The purchaser can either take "subject to" the mortgage (which is, in a sense, an inevitable conclusion, since the mortgage remains as an encumbrance on the land's title) or the purchaser can "assume" it. While people sometimes refer to "assumption of the mortgage, the "assumption" is really an assumption of liability on the debt, as represented by the promissory note in the present case. To be perfectly accurate, we should say that a sale or other transfer is always "subject to" the mortgage, and sometimes there is in addition an "assumption" of the debt.

An assumption is a promise by the purchaser to make the payments and perform the other covenants in the note and mortgage. It must be an express promise; in most states, including this one, we do not "imply" an assumption merely from the fact that the property was encumbered by the mortgage and the purchaser paid the difference between the agreed price and the mortgage balance in cash.[1] Even if the original mortgage contains a promise to pay (repeating the promise in the note, and even if the mortgage also contains "boiler-plate" language to the effect that it binds and benefits the "successors and assigns" of the property, the covenant to pay will not run with the land and become binding on a future owner in the absence of an assumption;[2] an express promise is required.

The promise need not be written, although it is obviously a good practice to use a writing.[3] The promise may be in a separate document, or it may appear in the contract of sale or the deed.[4] No separate consideration need be given for the assumption; it is simply part of the larger package of mutual promises, including the seller's promise to sell the real estate and the buyer's promise to pay the purchase price.

With this background in mind, we now examine the facts of the instant case to determine whether Hancock "assumed" the mortgage debt. As we have noted above, there was no express "assumption agreement." Middleton argues, however, that Hancock's assumption is expressed in two documents—the contract of sale and the deed by which Hancock acquired title.

The pertinent language of the contract of sale is "Purchaser agrees to take over payments on the existing loan." The question is whether an

---

[1] First Interstate Bank v. Nelco Enterprises, 822 P.2d 1260 (Wash.App. 1992). A few states, notably Pennsylvania and Oklahoma, differ, finding an "implied assumption" if the mortgage balance is deducted from the price. In those states, while a "subject to" conveyance creates no direct obligation to the mortgagee, the grantee is obligated by implication to indemnify the grantor if the latter is forced to pay the mortgage obligation. See Heaney v. Riddle, 23 A.2d 456 (Pa. 1942); Dick v. Vogt, 162 P.2d 325 (Ok. 1945).

[2] In re Ormond Beach Associates Limited Partnership, 184 F.3d 143 (2d Cir. 1999).

[3] One might suppose that an assumption agreement would fall within the section of the Statute of Frauds dealing with a promise "to answer for the debt, default, or misdoings of another." See Equity Rev. Stat. § 12–224. But the courts almost never so hold. They usually adopt the reasoning of the Virginia Supreme Court in Langman v. Alumni Assoc. of the University of Virginia, 247 Va. 491, 442 S.E.2d 669 (1994):

A grantee who assumes an existing mortgage is not a surety. The grantee makes no promise to the mortgagee to pay the debt of another, but promises the grantor to pay the mortgagee the debt the grantee owes to the grantor. This is an original undertaking.

However, many courts require that "the obligation of the grantee to assume and pay the mortgage debt be established by evidence which is clear and convincing." Cassidy v. Bonitatibus, 5 Conn.App. 240, 497 A.2d 1018 (1985). An oral assumption could be highly problematic under this standard.

[4] It is not necessary for the grantee to sign the deed, and grantees ordinarily do not do so. See Federal Nat. Mortg. Ass'n v. Carrington, 374 P.2d 153 (Wash. 1962). As the Virginia Supreme Court observed in Langman v. Alumni Assoc., note 3 supra, "A grantee who accepts a deed becomes contractually bound by its provisions and becomes liable to perform any promise or undertaking imposed by the deed on the grantee, including a promise to assume an existing mortgage."

agreement to "take over" the payments is the equivalent of an express promise to pay them. It is not easy to find authority on this point, since in most of the reported cases in which the term "take over" has been used, there is also an express "assumption," as when the purchaser agrees to "take over the property and assume the mortgage." See, e.g., Wilson v. Bob Wood & Associates, Inc., 633 S.W.2d 738 (Mo.App. 1981); Jolley v. Idaho Securities, Inc., 414 P.2d 879 (Idaho 1966). However, at least one court has held that the term "take over," standing alone, constitutes an assumption. In Commonwealth Land Title Ins. Co. v. Mattera, 616 N.Y.S.2d 798 (App.Div. 1994), the defendant signed an agreement providing "I agree to take over all of the obligations under the Notes and Mortgages as consolidated and modified by this Agreement as Borrower." The court found this language sufficient to impose personal liability on the defendant.

We must, somewhat reluctantly, disagree. There is no doubt that both Middleton and Hancock *expected* and *intended* Hancock to make the payments after he purchased Midgate Mall, but that is not the issue. The fundamental question is whether Hancock *promised* to do so. We do not consider "I agree to take over" to be the equivalent of "I promise to pay." The wording of the contract falls short of an express promise, and cannot sustain the conclusion that Hancock assumed the mortgage debt.[5]

If the contract of sale provides insufficient evidence of an assumption, the wording of the deed is even weaker. It merely recites that the property's title is "subject to a mortgage loan." That is a truism; of course the title is subject to the mortgage, since it was granted and recorded before the deed was delivered. That falls far short of an express promise by Hancock to pay the mortgage debt. Middleton has pointed to no other evidence, oral or written, that Hancock made an express promise to pay. In sum, there was no assumption on the facts before us.

B.   *The Suretyship Relationship.* When an owner of mortgaged real property sells it without paying off and retiring the mortgage, the mortgage (of course) continues to encumber the property's title in the hands of the purchaser. At the same time, the original mortgagor remains personally liable on the mortgage debt to the same extent that she or he was originally liable.[6] In the case of a loan that was originally "non-

---

[5]   That is not to suggest that the word "assumption" or "assume" must be employed. In Branch Banking and Trust Co. v. Kenyon Inv. Corp., 332 S.E.2d 186 (N.C.App. 1985), a letter sent by the lender to the grantees stated that "acceptance of payments made by [grantee] to the bank does not constitute a formal loan assumption by [grantee]." Nevertheless, the court found that the grantee had promised to make the loan payments, and thus that there was a "formal assumption." But "[t]here must be words importing that the grantee will pay the debt to make him personally liable;" Debral Realty, Inc. v. Marlborough Co-op. Bank, 717 N.E.2d 1023 (Mass.App.Ct.1999).

[6]   In some cases there is an argument that the original mortgagor is released, at least where the mortgage lender consents to the transfer under the authority of its due-on-sale clause. We refer to a regulation of the Office of Thrift Supervision (the OTS), issued under its authority

recourse," selling the property obviously does not create liability where none previously existed. But the loan in the instant case was a "recourse" loan, and Equity Bank was correct in advising Middleton that he remained liable on the note.

However, the original owner's liability is as a surety. The principal—that is, the party primarily liable—is the grantee who purchases the property if the grantee assumed the debt.[7] If, as in this case, the grantee did not assume, it is the real estate that is primarily liable.

This principal-surety relationship does not in any way tie the hands of the mortgagee. The mortgagee has the choice of foreclosing on the real estate,[8] suing the original mortgagor, or (if there is an assumption agreement) suing the grantee. The lender is not bound to proceed against these sources of recovery in any particular order.[9] If the foreclosure occurs first, and does not bring enough to fully satisfy the debt, the mortgagee can bring a deficiency claim against the mortgagor and (if she or he assumed) the grantee.[10]

The mortgagee may or may not have been a party to the assumption agreement. Even if it is not a party, it can bring a suit as a third-party

---

to regulate due-on-sale clauses granted by the Garn-St. Germain Depository Institutions Act of 1982, and found in 12 C.F.R. § 591.5(b)(4):

> A lender waives its option to exercise a due-on-sale clause as to a specific transfer if, before the transfer, the lender and the existing borrower's prospective successor in interest agree in writing that the successor in interest will be obligated under the terms of the loan and that interest on sums secured by the lender's security interest will be payable at a rate the lender shall request. Upon such agreement and resultant waiver, a lender shall release the existing borrower from all obligations under the loan instruments, and the lender is deemed to have made a new loan to the existing borrower's successor in interest.

On its face, this language, while hardly a model of clarity, seems to say that the lender that approves a transfer must also release the original borrower. Oddly, the General Counsel of the Federal Home Loan Bank Board, the predecessor agency of the OTS, concluded that it did not say that.

> The provisions * * * requiring the mandatory release of the original borrower from liability under the existing contract would not apply if the agreement to permit the assumption was expressly conditioned upon the original borrower's continued liability on the loan and the original borrower consented to such continued liability.

FHLBB General Counsel's Opinion Letter No. 1090 (Nov. 26, 1984). One federal court concluded that release of the borrower was indeed mandatory; see Gate City Fed. Sav. and Loan Ass'n v. Dalton, 808 P.2d 1117 (Utah App.1991). In the instant case the issue is not before us, since the regulation quoted applies only to loans on homes, not commercial property.

7   Investors Title Ins. Co. v. Montague, 543 S.E.2d 527 (N.C.Ct.App.2001).

8   The mortgage continues to encumber the real estate, notwithstanding the transfer. See Tomkus v. Parker, 224 S.E.2d 353 (Ga. 1976).

9   The State of Equity, unlike California and several other western states, does not have a "one action" or "security first" statute. Where such a statute is in effect, the lender will be required to proceed against the real estate by foreclosing the mortgage before seeking personal recovery against any person.

10   See Restatement (Third) of Property (Mortgages) § 5.1(b)(3) (1997). This assumes that the jurisdiction does not prohibit or limit deficiency judgments, and the State of Equity does not.

beneficiary of that agreement. Thus there is a technical difference between the lender's suing the mortgagor (which is an action on the promissory note) and suing the grantee (which is an action on the assumption agreement), but little practical difference.[11]

The principal-surety principle governs the relationship between the mortgagor and the grantee. Its fundamental purpose is to make the ultimate responsibility for the payment of the debt fall where it should. If the grantee assumed, the mortgagor who pays the debt has three avenues to proceed (usually referred to as forms of recourse) against the grantee: Subrogation, reimbursement, and exoneration. There follows a brief explanation of each, since all three are potentially pertinent to Middleton's claim in the present case.

1.   *Subrogation*.[12] The mortgagor-surety who pays the mortgage debt in full receives an assignment, by operation of law, of the mortgagee's note and mortgage. Hence, the mortgagor-surety can sue the grantee-principal on the note and can also foreclose the mortgage, provided that the mortgage has not already been foreclosed by the mortgagee. If the mortgagee *has* already foreclosed, and then seeks and recovers a deficiency from the mortgagor-surety, the latter is entitled to subrogation to the mortgagee's right to collect the deficiency from the grantee-principal. The major disadvantage of subrogation is that it is available only upon the surety-mortgagor's payment *in full*. There is no subrogation for a partial payment.

2.   *Reimbursement*.[13] If the mortgagor-surety pays the mortgage obligation in whole or in part when it is due or delinquent, he or she is entitled to reimbursement (or "indemnity," as some cases put it) from the grantee-principal, provided that the latter assumed the mortgage obligation. The mortgagor-surety is also entitled to reimbursement for any incidental costs of performance. Full payment of the debt is not necessary to the mortgagor-surety's right of reimbursement (unlike subrogation); a partial payment will suffice. However, reimbursement is an unsecured right; the mortgagor-surety can demand payment, but if the grantee-principal is insolvent or disappears, the real estate does not stand as collateral for the right of reimbursement.

3.   *Exoneration*.[14] If an assuming grantee does not pay the mortgage obligation when due, the mortgagor-surety may obtain a court order

---

[11] See Stalcup v. Easterly, 351 P.2d 735 (Okla. 1960), in which the distinction did make a difference. An Oklahoma statute required an action for a deficiency to be filed within 90 days after the date of the foreclosure sale. The court held that the mortgagor's action for reimbursement against the grantee was a suit on the assumption agreement, not a suit on the note or the debt, and therefore that the 90 limitation period was inapplicable.

[12] Restatement (Third) of Suretyship and Guaranty §§ 27–31 (1996).

[13] Restatement (Third) of Suretyship and Guaranty §§ 22–25 (1996).

[14] Restatement (Third) of Suretyship and Guaranty § 21 (1996).

compelling the grantee to pay.[15] One may think of this as specific performance of the assumption agreement. The mortgagor-surety need not pay in advance of getting such an order, since that burden has already been shifted to the grantee by the assumption agreement.

C. *Impact of the absence of an assumption agreement.* All three of the forms of recourse described above are available to the mortgagor/surety if the grantee/principal enters into an assumption agreement and later defaults on the secured debt. However, things change drastically if there is no assumption agreement, as in the present case.

In the absence of an assumption, the second and third forms of recourse mentioned above, reimbursement and exoneration, are simply not available, since they would involve personal judgments against the grantee and a non-assuming grantee has no personal liability. In addition, because Hancock did not assume, the first form of recourse, the mortgagor-surety's right of subrogation, is only to the mortgage (that is, against the real estate), and not to the note or personal obligation.[16] Hence, if the mortgagee has already foreclosed the mortgage and now recovers a deficiency from the mortgagor-surety, the mortgage is gone and subrogation in favor of the mortgagor-surety is simply unavailable.

That principle does not affect Middleton's claim of subrogation, since the mortgage in the present case has not been foreclosed. Of course, his subrogation would be only to the mortgage and not the note in any event, since as we have already seen, Hancock did not assume the obligation represented by the note and therefore has no personal liability. For that reason, his claim for money damages against Hancock must be rejected. Nonetheless, if he could claim subrogation to the mortgage and foreclose it, he would stand some chance of getting his money back.

However, another important principle states that subrogation is available only if the surety has paid the entire debt in full.[17] The reason is that if partial subrogation were available to a surety like Middleton, who has paid only part of the debt, the real estate collateral would be divided between two parties (here the Bank and Middleton) who may have quite divergent interests and views about when and how to foreclose. There is, after all, only one mortgage. The law simply will not impose on the Bank the burden of negotiating with Middleton about when and how the remedies under that unitary mortgage will be exercised.[18] To do so would,

---

[15] See Riedle v. Peterson, 560 N.E.2d 725 (Mass.App.1990).

[16] See Zastrow v. Knight, 229 N.W. 925 (S.D. 1930).

[17] Restatement (Third) of Suretyship and Guaranty § 28.

[18] See Sawyer v. Zacavich, 178 Cal. App. 2d 605, 611 (1960); Comment, Subrogation of Mortgages in California: A Comparison with the Restatement and Proposals for Change, 48 UCLA L. Rev. 1643 (2000).

in effect, force the Bank into a loan participation relationship without any participation agreement.

D.   *Conclusion*. Middleton is out of options.[19] Unless he is willing to prepay the entire mortgage debt (which is a large sum, and for all we know may involve prepayment fees as well as the balance owing), he cannot have subrogation. Since he did not obtain an assumption agreement from Hancock, he cannot have reimbursement or exoneration. This is an unfortunate consequence of what can only be described as Middleton's sloppy—even careless—handling of the sale transaction. If Middleton was represented by counsel in the sale transaction, he may now wish to consult an attorney about the possibility of a malpractice action against his former counsel. He may also wish to encourage Equity Bank to proceed with foreclosure against Midgate Mall if it has a value that exceeds the mortgage debt, since a foreclosure will end the continuing burden of the monthly payments that Middleton has been making.

The decision of the district court is affirmed. All concur.

NOTES

1.   *Mortgagor liability to government agencies*. Two major federal agencies, the Federal Housing Administration (FHA) and the Department of Veterans Affairs (VA), insure or guarantee some types of mortgage loans. Their role is explored in more detail in Chapter 8, Section E infra. For present purposes it is oversimplified but sufficient to say that they assure mortgage lenders that if a foreclosure of the real estate occurs, the lender will not sustain a loss.

If FHA or VA pays a lender's claim, the lender's right to a deficiency judgment is assigned to the government. For this reason, FHA and VA have a strong interest in assuring that, when property subject to one of their loans is sold, the buyer is a reliable and solvent individual. Both FHA and VA have developed procedures under which they can evaluate and approve (or reject) prospective buyers. The following is an excerpt from a notice given to all new HUD mortgagors to inform them of their rights:

> Even if you sell your home by letting an approved purchaser (that is, a creditworthy owner-occupant) assume your mortgage, you are still liable for the mortgage debt unless you obtain a *release from liability* from your mortgage lender. FHA-approved lenders have been instructed by HUD to prepare such a release when an original

---

[19] We understand that in some areas of the nation it is common for a mortgagor who sells the mortgaged real estate to demand that the purchaser sign not only an assumption agreement, but also a second mortgage securing the purchaser's performance of the assumption agreement. This rather ingenious idea would have been immensely helpful to Middleton in the present case, since it would have allowed him to make only partial payments on the debt (as he did), and then to have resort to the real estate to secure reimbursement to him from Hancock. Unfortunately, Middleton did none of these things.

homeowner sells his or her property to a creditworthy purchaser who executes an agreement to assume and pay the mortgage debt and thereby agrees to become the substitute mortgagor. The release is contained in Form HUD–92210–1, ("Approval of Purchaser and Release of Seller"). You should ask for it if the mortgage lender does not provide it to you automatically when you sell your home to a creditworthy owner-occupant purchaser who executes an agreement to assume personal liability for the debt. When this form is executed, you are no longer liable for the mortgage debt.

HUD Handbook 4330.1 REV–5, Appendix 13. See HUD Handbook 4155.1 7.1. The Veterans Administration has adopted a similar rule; see 38 C.F.R. §§ 36,4209, 36,4232, 36,4285. Both agencies permit the collection of an assumption fee by the lender.

The average seller of a house probably imagines that, once the buyer has assumed the mortgage loan, the seller need not worry about the matter further. But unless the buyer has been approved by FHA or VA and a release of the seller issued under the procedures described above, nothing could be farther from the truth. Suppose A obtains a VA-guaranteed loan. Subsequently A sells the house to B, who assumes the loan. VA does not issue (and may not even have been asked to issue) a release of liability to A. Five or ten years later, in a depressed housing market, B defaults on the loan. The lender forecloses, bids the amount estimated by VA to be the current market value of the property (which is significantly less than the loan balance), acquires title to the house, and conveys it to VA in return for VA's payment of the loan balance to the lender. VA then sues A for the deficiency—and prevails! See, e.g., In re Knevel, 100 B.R. 910 (Bankr.N.D.Ohio 1989).

2. *Assuming grantee's assertion of defenses.* Should an assuming grantee be able to assert defenses that would have been available to the original mortgagor against the collection of the mortgage debt or foreclosure of the mortgage? For example, suppose there is evidence that the mortgagee defrauded the original mortgagor, or even that the loan funds which the mortgagor promised to repay were never actually disbursed. Should such facts excuse the assuming grantee from paying the debt? The overwhelming answer of the courts is no. The grantee is said to be estopped to raise such defenses, because asserting them would allow the grantee to unjustly enrich himself or herself by getting the property for less than its agreed purchase price. The Michigan Supreme Court long ago explained this reasoning as follows:

> [The grantee] expressly assumes and agrees to pay the mortgage, and that irrespective of the value of the land covered by the mortgage. The amount of the mortgage is deducted from the consideration which he otherwise has assumed to pay for the land. That amount he has retained in his hands for that express purpose. His grantor, whose duty it was to pay, might have insisted upon payment to him of the entire consideration, and paid it himself. By

permitting his grantee to deduct this amount from the consideration and retain it, he has thereby rendered himself less able to meet the obligation, thereby reducing the mortgagee's personal security, but has at the same time to a corresponding amount aided the other to meet it.

Why then should not the grantee be held personally responsible to the mortgagee for the amount which he has thus assumed and agreed to pay? It is no injustice to the grantee to require him to pay it, because he has been permitted to deduct and retain that amount from the agreed consideration and value of the land. The consideration he agreed to pay at the time he made the purchase, should be paid by him at the time and in the manner agreed upon, and there is nothing inequitable in requiring him so to do.

Crawford v. Edwards, 33 Mich. 354, 359–360 (1876). This principle has been applied to many types of defenses that the original mortgagor might have raised: lack of capacity, fraud, mutual mistake, failure of consideration, the statute of limitations, and so on. See, e.g., Joyner v. Vitale, 926 P.2d 1154 (Alaska 1996) (grantee could not assert statute of limitations as a defense); Northeast Sav., F.A. v. Sennett, 161 A.D.2d 867, 555 N.Y.S.2d 915 (1990) (grantee who assumed a construction loan was not permitted to assert that some of the construction funds had been diverted to non-construction purposes through the mortgagee's negligence). The Restatement agrees; see Restatement (Third) of Property (Mortgages) § 5.1(c)(4) (1997).

Occasionally a court is a bit troubled about applying the estoppel principle. For example, a more recent Michigan opinion commented, "We are not entirely satisfied with the result we must reach, for the original mortgagee receives a windfall instead of the assuming buyer under this rule. That party is able to enforce an obligation which may be contrary to the public policy of this state merely because the party from whom the obligation was extracted has transferred his secured property." Michigan Wineries, Inc. v. Johnson, 68 Mich.App. 310, 313, 242 N.W.2d 568, 570 (1976), aff'd, 402 Mich. 306, 262 N.W.2d 651 (1978) (grantee not allowed to assert that original mortgage transaction violated state alcoholic beverage control statute).

Do you agree with the court's comment—that the estoppel principle will produce a windfall to the mortgagee? Suppose, for example, that the mortgage was obtained by the mortgagee by fraud. The mortgagor nonetheless sells the real estate to an assuming grantee, who is now bound to pay the mortgagee notwithstanding the fraud. Isn't the mortgagee subject to an action brought by the original mortgagor to recover the amount by which the mortgagee is unjustly enriched by the payment made by the grantee? And if such an action is brought and succeeds, doesn't everybody come out "even"?

3. *Subject-to grantee's assertion of defenses.* If the estoppel principle discussed in the previous note is sound, should it be limited to cases of mortgage assumption? Or should it apply equally to "subject to" transfers? After all, their economic consequences are identical, and the degree to which

the grantee is unjustly enriched if permitted to raise defenses against the mortgagee is the same. The courts have agreed with this reasoning; see Eurovest, Ltd. v. Segall, 528 So.2d 482 (Fla.App.1988); Pacific First Fed. Sav. & Loan Ass'n v. Lindberg, 64 Or.App. 140, 667 P.2d 535 (1983) ("The general rule is that a grantee of mortgaged property who takes the property "subject to" the mortgage cannot dispute its validity.") See Nelson, Whitman, Burkhart & Freyermuth, Real Estate Finance Law § 5.17 (6th ed.2014).

However, there are some situations in which the grantee should be allowed to raise defenses to the validity of the original mortgage or debt. For example, Restatement (Third) of Property (Mortgages) § 5.1 comment g suggests that if the transfer to the grantee is a gift, there's nothing unjust about the grantee's objecting to the mortgage's validity. The same is true if the grantee paid the full purchase price in cash, and the grantor promised to discharge the original debt. (Such an arrangement is rarely wise from the grantee's viewpoint, but it does occur occasionally.)

4. *The nature of the mortgagee's right against the grantee.* It is clear that the mortgagee can recover against an assuming grantee, either for the entire debt or for a deficiency after foreclosure of the mortgage, whether the mortgagee was a party to the assumption agreement or not. The simplest explanation is that the mortgagee is a third-party beneficiary of the assumption agreement, and the great majority of courts take this view.

There is an alternative explanation, the "suretyship subrogation" theory, which goes something like this: It is recognized that the mortgagor who transfers the property to an assuming grantee becomes a surety for the debt. If the mortgagor is called upon to pay the debt, he or she has a right of subrogation against the grantee (and the land) to recover reimbursement for the outlay. However, no suretyship relation can possibly exist unless the grantee is primarily liable to the mortgagee on the debt; hence, the grantee must indeed have a direct liability to the mortgagee. As the California Supreme Court once put it,

> * * * to avoid circuity of action, and to protect the mortgagor, as the intermediate party, from being compelled to pay the debt, and then to seek redress from his grantee who has assumed the mortgage debt, equity permits the mortgagee to bring all the parties who are liable for the debt, whether principally or ultimately, before the court, and have their rights adjusted in a single suit. In such an action the mortgagee represents the mortgagor for the purpose of enforcing this obligation of the purchaser to him, and his right to enforce this obligation has the same extent and is subject to the same limitations as would be that of the mortgagor in a separate action against his grantee.

Hopkins v. Warner, 109 Cal. 133, 41 P. 868, 869 (1895).

If this strikes you as circular logic, we can only agree. Professor Corbin once called this theory "a cumbrous intellectual expedient for holding that a contract between two parties can create an enforceable right in a third." Arthur L. Corbin, Contracts for the Benefit of Third Persons, 27 Yale. L.J. 1008, 1015 (1918). Calling the mortgagee a third party beneficiary seems a great deal more straightforward to us.

5. *Rescission of the assumption agreement.* Suppose the mortgagor/grantor demands an assumption agreement from the grantee at the time of the sale, but subsequently purports to rescind that agreement, to waive the grantee's duties under it, or to release the grantee from it. Is the mortgagee bound by this action, thus losing its claim against the grantee?

> Assuming that [the mortgagee has direct right of action against the grantee under a third party beneficiary theory], it can well be argued that the mortgage holder receives an immediate vested right under the assumption agreement which cannot be defeated by the grantor's subsequent release of the grantee. While there is authority for this view in other jurisdictions, the weight of authority requires acceptance or adoption of the assumption agreement for the mortgage holder's right to vest. What constitutes acceptance or adoption remains unsettled. Some courts require the mortgage holder to give notice of acceptance to the assuming grantee; others seem to require a material change of position making it inequitable to deprive the mortgage holder of his rights under the assumption agreement; still others presume acceptance, enabling the mortgage holder to acquire a vested right when the assumption occurs, subject, however, to a power of disaffirmance. But in no case would an attempted release be effective after the mortgage holder has begun an action on the assumption agreement.

Roger A. Cunningham & Saul Tischler, Transfer of the Real Estate Mortgagor's Interest, 27 Rutgers L.Rev. 46 (1973).* Restatement (Third) of Property (Mortgages) § 5.1(c)(5) also adopts the "material change of position" approach to this question. As an example of such a change of position, see Federal Land Bank of Wichita v. Krug, 253 Kan. 307, 856 P.2d 111 (1993).

6. *A break in the chain.* What is the effect of a chain of assumptions? If A, the original mortgagor, sells to B (who assumes), who later sells to C (who also assumes), it is clear that all three parties are personally liable to the mortgagee, who may elect to bring an action on the debt or for a deficiency against any or all of them. See Swanson v. Krenik, 868 P.2d 297 (Alaska 1994). In addition, if A or B pays the mortgage, either of them has suretyship rights (discussed below) against the person to whom they sold the land. In the final analysis, if A and B assert this right, C will and should be left "holding the bag."

---

* Reprinted with permission of Rutgers University, The State University of New Jersey, West Publishing Co. and the authors.

Matters get more complicated if there is a break in the chain of assumptions. Suppose we change the foregoing facts: A sells to B, who merely takes "subject to" and does not assume. B then resells to C, who gives B an assumption agreement. You may think this is irrational; if B has no personal liability on the debt to begin with, why should B bother to get C to assume such liability? But irrational or not, it sometimes happens.

The issue is subtle, and may depend on precisely what C's "assumption agreement" says. For example, suppose C merely promises "to keep, observe, and perform all of the terms, conditions, and provisions of A's agreement with the mortgagee that are to be kept, observed and performed by B." If B didn't assume, then the foregoing promise by C to assume B's duties is a promise to assume nothing at all! See Chambers v. Thomas, 123 Idaho 69, 844 P.2d 698 (1992), holding that C had no personal liability on these facts. Incidentally, much the same issue can arise when a grantee purports to "assume" a non-recourse mortgage debt. If the promise is to pay the note "according to the terms thereof," and the note's terms exclude personal liability, the "assuming" party has assumed nothing. See Schultz v. Weaver, 780 S.W.2d 323 (Tex.App.1989).

However, suppose the note provides for full personal recourse, and C's agreement is to pay the note itself, not merely B's (nonexistent) obligation. The courts have divided on the question whether C is liable to the mortgagee or not. Compare Carr v. Nodvin, 178 Ga.App. 228, 342 S.E.2d 698 (1986) (assuming grantee following break in chain is liable on debt) with Dail v. Campbell, 191 Cal.App.2d 416, 12 Cal.Rptr. 739 (1961) (assuming grantee, following break in chain of assumptions, has no personal liability). The difference may be explained by whether the jurisdiction follows the third-party beneficiary theory or the suretyship theory discussed in Note 4 supra. See generally Garrard Glenn, Mortgages § 271 (1943); Nelson, Whitman, Burkhart & Freyermuth, Real Estate Finance Law § 5.15 (6th ed. 2014); Annot., 12 A.L.R. 1529 (1921). Restatement (Third) of Property (Mortgages) § 5.1(c)(1) (1997) takes the view that the assuming grantee should be liable even if his or her predecessor was not.

––––––––––

The suretyship defenses. The law has traditionally been highly solicitous of sureties, and has taken the view that the surety ought not be held liable under a different "deal" than he or she originally made, unless the surety consents to the change in the terms of the "deal." Hence, a surety is generally discharged from his or her duties in a variety of situations in which actions of the obligee (here, the mortgagee) change the "deal" in a way that impairs the surety's position.[1] Such changes can include

––––––––––

[1] Indeed, traditional suretyship doctrine even discharged "uncompensated" sureties when the modification was *beneficial* to the surety; see Thomas-Sears v. Morris, 278 Ga.App. 152, 628 S.E.2d 241 (2006). But this view has now lost much of its weight.

- releasing the grantee from personal liability,
- releasing some or all of the real estate from the mortgage,
- impairing the mortgagee's right to realize on the security of the mortgage,
- modifying the interest rate or terms of payment, or
- extending the time to maturity of the mortgage loan.

The mortgagor-surety is said to have a "suretyship defense" in such cases. The mortgagor-surety's discharge is granted on the grounds that the actions of the mortgagee (1) have made it less likely that the grantee or the land will satisfy the debt, and (2) have made it more difficult for the mortgagor to assert recourse (that is, subrogation, reimbursement, and exoneration) against the grantee and the land if the mortgagor is required to pay the debt.

To see why these acts by the mortgagee (releasing the grantee or the real estate, or modifying or extending the time for payment on the mortgage debt) can impair the mortgagor's rights of recourse against the grantee, you must understand that such acts are *binding on the mortgagor in asserting recourse against the grantee* (unless the mortgagee has "preserved" the recourse of the mortgagor by an express agreement with the grantee, a technique that is probably seldom used). This conclusion may seem counterintuitive; why should the mortgagor be bound by an agreement or act to which she or he was not a party? But it is well established.

For example, if the mortgagee gives the grantee an additional year to pay the debt, the mortgagor may not assert recourse against the grantee until that extra year has elapsed. This may be extremely harmful to the mortgagor's position if, for example, the grantee becomes insolvent or the real estate declines precipitously in value during that year.

Similarly, if the mortgagee releases some of the real estate from the lien of the mortgage, the mortgagor may not assert recourse (by way of subrogation) against that part of the real estate. If the remaining real estate is not sufficient in value to fully cover the mortgage debt, the mortgagor is harmed, both because the risk of the grantee's defaulting is increased and because, if the mortgagor is required to pay the debt, the mortgagor's subrogation claim against the remaining real estate will be inadequate to reimburse the mortgagor's outlay.

While there is consensus that acts of the mortgagee that impair the mortgagor-surety's position should result in a discharge of the mortgagor-surety, there is great disagreement as to the *amount* of the discharge. Traditional suretyship law nearly always gave a complete discharge, even if the impairment of the surety's position was minor. However, an increasingly widespread viewpoint holds that a discharge should be recognized only to the extent that the surety would suffer loss as a result of the impairment. The Restatement (Third) of Suretyship and Guaranty § 37, Introductory Note (1997) and ensuing sections take this view, as does Restatement (Third) of Property (Mortgages) § 5.3 (1997). Consider how the court handles it in the following case. Pay particular attention to the footnotes.

Of course, if a mortgagor consents to a change in the terms of the loan by the grantee and the mortgagee, he or she cannot complain about continuing to be held liable as a surety. The mortgagee argued that such consent existed in the following case.

FIRST FEDERAL SAVINGS AND LOAN ASSOCIATION OF GARY V. ARENA

Court of Appeals of Indiana, Fourth District, 1980
406 N.E.2d 1279

CHIPMAN, JUDGE.

* * *

On May 26, 1965, the Arenas executed a note, mortgage, and supplemental agreement with First Federal. The note provided for a loan of $32,000 at an interest rate of 5¾%, and the mortgage securing this note provided for advances of up to $6,400. March 11, 1966, the Arenas were granted an advance of $5,100, and in consideration, they executed a modification and extension agreement which provided they would owe a new balance of $36,664.81, and the interest rate would be increased to 6%. A separate note, mortgage, and supplemental agreement were also executed by the Arenas in relation to this advance.

March 10, 1969, the Arenas conveyed the real estate which was the subject of both the May 26, 1965, and March 11, 1966, mortgages to Sanford G. Richardson by warranty deed subject to the two mortgages to First Federal.[1] The same day, without notice to or the consent of the Arenas, Mr. Richardson and First Federal entered into a modification and extension agreement, under the terms of which Richardson assumed both of the mortgages in question, and the time for payment was extended to twenty years; there was also a change in the interest rate from 6% to

---

[1] Although the grantee's preliminary offer to purchase provided Mr. Richardson would "assume" the existing mortgages on the property, the warranty deed evidencing the consummated contract recited the conveyance was "subject to" the Arenas' mortgages to First Federal. Based upon the general rule that any inconsistencies between the terms in the preliminary contract and the deed are to be settled by the deed alone, since all prior negotiations are considered merged in that instrument, *Wayne International Building & Loan Ass'n v. Beckner*, (1922) 191 Ind. 664, 134 N.E. 273; *Guckenberger v. Shank*, (1941) 110 Ind.App. 442, 37 N.E.2d 708, along with the fact none of the parties argued there was any mistake in drawing the deed or that they intended to make it read other than as in fact it was written, we have concluded, for purposes of this opinion, the conveyance was "subject to" the mortgage.

7¼%. Thus, this agreement, signed only by Richardson and First Federal, was designed to be a modification of First Federal's earlier agreement with the Arenas by extending the time of payment and modifying the terms of payment to which the Arenas and First Federal had agreed.

After June 27, 1975, Richardson failed to make the payments due under the March 10, 1969, modification and extension agreement. As a result, a default on the mortgages and notes occurred and a suit in foreclosure was filed on behalf of First Federal against the Arenas, Richardson, and several lienholders.

* * *

By reason of an expressed provision to that effect in the supplemental agreements between the Arenas and First Federal, the Arenas were not released from liability upon [the time] extension of the mortgage in the agreement between Mr. Richardson and First Federal; however, this agreement not only extended the time for payment, but it also modified the terms of payment by increasing the interest rate. It is our opinion the trial court properly found the Arenas had not consented to such a change in interest rates and, therefore, were released from liability.[3] Arenas' grantee and First Federal could not modify the original mortgagors' agreement without the mortgagors' consent.

The focal point in this controversy is the meaning to be accorded a reservation of rights clause which appeared in the supplemental agreement executed by the Arenas when they obtained the initial mortgage and later secured the advance. The agreement provided:

> * * * THE MORTGAGOR COVENANTS: 6. That in the event the ownership of said property or any part thereof becomes vested in a person other than the Mortgagor, the Mortgagee may, without notice to the Mortgagor, deal with such successor or successors in interest with reference to this mortgage and the debt hereby secured in the same manner as with the Mortgagor, and may

---

[3] If the full amount due on foreclosure did not exceed the value of the property at the time of the execution of the Modification and Extension Agreement, it was proper for the trial court to completely discharge the Arenas. *Mutual Ben. Life Ins. Co. v. Lindley*, (1932) 97 Ind.App. 575, 183 N.E. 127; Stevens, *Extension Agreements in the "Subject-To" Mortgage Situation*, 15 U.Cin.L.Rev. 58 (1941). As a corollary, if the value of the land at the time of this agreement was less than the amount of the mortgage on the property, the Arenas should have remained liable to the extent of this difference. Although it was improper for the trial court to hold there was a complete discharge without also holding the value of the land at the time of the March 10, 1969, agreement fully supported the mortgage loan, First Federal never raised any error regarding the extent to which the Arenas were discharged, see note 2 *supra*; consequently, we can only assume the amount due on foreclosure on March 10, 1969, would have been less than the value of the property at that time. We note, since Mr. Richardson offered to purchase the real estate in question for $37,000, and the aggregate balance remaining unpaid when Mr. Richardson and First Federal executed the Modification and Extension Agreement was $33,393.83, it appears the value of the land, in fact, did exceed the amount due, and thus, a complete discharge would have been proper.

forbear to sue or may extend time for payment of the debt, secured hereby, without discharging or in any way affecting the liability of the Mortgagor hereunder or upon the debt hereby secured.

First Federal asserts the reservation of rights language set out above permitted it, in dealing with Richardson, to increase the interest rate and extend the time of payment without first obtaining the Arenas' consent while still retaining their liability. Appellant takes the position that the portion of paragraph six providing for no discharge modified forbearing to sue and extending time for payment as well as dealing in the same manner as with the mortgagor; therefore, since the interest rate was increased when the Arenas were given their additional advance, according to First Federal, raising the interest rate in its agreement with Richardson would merely be dealing with him in the same manner as it had dealt with the Arenas and, consequently, should not result in a discharge.

The Arenas, on the other hand, contend the reservation of rights clause in the Supplemental Agreement made no reference to the alteration or modification of the interest rate but rather, referred only to an extension of the time for payment or the decision to forbear to sue.

While it is true paragraph six indicates First Federal could deal with successors in interest to the mortgage in the same manner as with the mortgagor, we hold the resolution of whether this meant First Federal and the Arenas' grantee would be permitted to increase the interest rate without affecting the Arenas' liability was a question of law for the trial court since the rules applicable to construction of contracts generally apply to the construction of an agreement whereby a purchaser of mortgaged premises assumes the payment of the mortgage. 20 I.L.E. Mortgages § 193.

* * *

The essence of the appeal before us then is whether the trial court correctly concluded that as a matter of law, the scope of the reservation of rights clause found in paragraph six did not include altering or modifying the interest rate, and consequently, First Federal did not reserve the right to modify and increase the interest rate from 6% to 7¼% without the consent of the Arenas. We hold the trial court's entry of summary judgment in favor of Arenas was proper.

When the Arenas conveyed the real estate to Richardson subject to the existing mortgages to First Federal, the land became as to said parties, the primary source of funds for payment of the debt. *Mutual Ben. Life Ins. Co. v. Lindley*, (1932) 97 Ind.App. 575, 183 N.E. 127. No technical relation of principal and surety arose between the Arenas and their grantee from this conveyance, but an equity did arise which bears a close resemblance to the equitable rights of a surety. As a result, the Arenas assumed a position analogous to that of a surety, and the grantee became the principal debtor to the extent of the value of the land conveyed. *Mutual Ben. Life Ins. Co. v. Lindley, supra*; Warm, *Some Aspects of the Rights and Liabilities of Mortgagee, Mortgagor and Grantee*, 10 Temple L.Q. 116 (1936).

While a mortgagor in such a situation may consent in advance to future modifications or agree his liability will not be discharged by subsequent agreements between his grantee and the mortgagee, such clauses are to be strictly construed against the mortgagee, see Friedman, *Discharge of Personal Liability on Mortgage Debts in New York*, 52 Yale L.J. 771, 788 (1943), since it would be unjust to subject the mortgagor to a new risk or material change to which he has not consented. Consequently, a reservation of rights clause will not prevent a discharge of liability where the modification in question exceeds the scope of the consent in the clause. This should come as no surprise since the mortgagor occupies the position of a surety, and the law of suretyship provides that a surety is entitled to stand on the strict letter of the contract upon which he is liable, and where he does not consent to a variation and a variation is made, it is fatal, see *American States Insurance Co. v. Floyd I. Staub, Inc.*, (1977) Ind.App., 370 N.E.2d 989; *White v. Household Finance Corp.*, (1973) 158 Ind.App. 394, 302 N.E.2d 828; therefore, an agreement between the principals for a higher interest than called for by the original contract will, if made without the surety's consent, release him from all liability. 74 Am.Jur.2d Suretyship § 47 (1974); see also 4 Am.Jur.2d Alteration of Instruments § 55 (1962).

The fact First Federal dealt with the grantee shows it knew of the Arenas' conveyance, and knowing of this conveyance, it was incumbent upon First Federal not to deal with the grantee in such a manner as would jeopardize or alter the surety-principal relationship. Warm, *Some Aspects of the Rights and Liabilities of Mortgagee, Mortgagor and Grantee*, 10 Temple L.Q. 116 (1936). The modification and extension agreement in question provided Mr. Richardson would personally assume the mortgage debt and thus, inured to the benefit of First Federal, but at the same time, the terms of the Arenas' earlier mortgage were changed to the detriment of the Arenas. If this increase in the interest rate was beyond the scope of the reservation of rights clause, the Arenas were thereby discharged, and the grantee became the sole debtor on the mortgages.

We hold the trial court properly rejected First Federal's argument that by increasing the interest rate it was merely dealing with Mr. Richardson in the same manner as it had dealt with the Arenas, and therefore, according to paragraph six, the Arenas should not have been discharged.

While it is true paragraph six indicated First Federal could deal with successors in interest to the mortgage in the same manner as with the mortgagor, this provision did not say First Federal could do so with impunity. We agree with the trial court that the portion of this paragraph providing for no discharge only modified forbearing to sue or extending the time for payment; consequently, the mortgagor would not be discharged from liability if the mortgagee simply extended the time for payment of the debt or opted not to bring suit, but these were the only situations where the mortgagee knew to a certainty his actions in dealing with the grantee would not discharge the mortgagor. The reservation of rights clause in paragraph six did not apply to activities which allegedly came within the ambit of dealing in the same manner as with the mortgagor. At the risk of being redundant, we again note, paragraph six stated in part: "6. (T)he Mortgagee may, without notice to the Mortgagor, deal with * * * successors in interest with reference to this mortgage and the debt hereby secured in the same manner as with the Mortgagor, and * * * ." The punctuation used clearly sets this portion of paragraph six apart from the remainder of the paragraph which then goes on to provide the mortgagee "may forbear to sue or may extend time for payment of the debt, * * * without discharging or in any way affecting the liability of the Mortgagor hereunder or upon the debt hereby secured."

In order to give the reservation of rights clause the expanded application urged by First Federal so that it also applied to dealing in the same manner as with the mortgagor, it would be necessary to ignore the punctuation used and the maxim that such clauses should be strictly construed against the mortgagee. Further, such a construction would change the reservation of rights provision from applying in two definite situations to an open-ended invitation to argue there was no discharge because the mortgagee either could have or in fact had dealt with the mortgagor in the same manner; the possible activities which arguably could then come within this clause's application would be indefinite.

We hold the construction of the supplemental agreement between the Arenas and First Federal was a question of law for the trial court, which correctly held paragraph six did not authorize First Federal and the Arenas' grantee to alter the terms of payment on the mortgage debt by increasing the interest rate without affecting the Arenas' liability.

Judgment affirmed.

MILLER, P. J., and YOUNG, J., concur.

NOTES

1.   *Scope of reservations of rights in the original mortgage.* It is perhaps amazing that a lender's lawyer, drafting a clause in a mortgage that reserves the mortgagee's rights against the mortgagor despite a modification entered into with a grantee, would fail to take into consideration *all* of the possible types of modifications—the whole range listed in the introductory note just prior to the *Arena* case! For another example of such sloppy drafting (or thinking), see Moss v. McDonald, 772 P.2d 626 (Colo.App.1988) (where original note language consented to extensions of time granted *after* maturity of the note, it did not serve as a consent to an extension granted *prior* to maturity).

2.   *The extent of the discharge.* A fundamental question raised by the *Arena* case is the *extent* to which the grantor should be discharged by a modification of the obligation, agreed to by the mortgagee and the grantee. The opinion holds that, after a "subject to" transfer, an increase in the interest rate without the grantor's consent discharges the grantor to the extent of the value of the property. The discharge would only be to the extent of the property's value because, in a "subject to" transfer, the Arenas would have had recourse only to the property. If Richardson had assumed the mortgage debt, the Indiana court's view is that the Arenas would have been totally discharged. This is the traditional approach.

But surely the Arenas would not have been harmed to this extent by the unconsented modification, which merely increased the interest rate from 6% to 7.25%. By the time of Richardson's default, about six years later, the mortgage balance was probably about $3,000 higher because of the increased interest than it would have been at the old interest rate. Why isn't this the proper limit of the Arenas' discharge? Restatement (Third) of Property (Mortgages) § 5.3 comment d and illustration 8 assert that it is.

To counter this argument, could the Arenas have asserted that the increased interest rate resulted in higher monthly payments due from Richardson, and that he would not (or at least, might not) have defaulted at all if his payments had remained at their original level? Hence, they should be completely discharged because they would (might?) never have been called upon to pay the debt if the interest rate had not increased. Is this position too speculative to be worth adopting?

The Restatements, as mentioned above, grant a discharge to the mortgagor/surety only to the extent that the modification of the loan's terms would otherwise harm him or her. Here's an additional illustration. Assume MR borrows $50,000 from ME on a one-year note secured by a mortgage on MR's house. MR then sells the house to GE, who does not assume the mortgage debt. GE then persuades ME to grant a time extension of one additional year to pay the loan. At the end of the second year, when the note falls due, GE defaults in payment and ME demands that MR pay the debt. The value of the house has fallen during the second year from $60,000 to $40,000. As a result of the time extension, the loan is now undersecured by

$10,000, and MR's recourse is impaired by that amount. Hence under the Restatement view, MR is discharged to the extent of $10,000, and is liable for only $40,000 to ME.

3. *The effect of modifications and time extensions on the mortgagor.* If the mortgagor is not completely discharged, the question arises as to how modifications of the loan's terms or maturity impact the mortgagor as against the mortgagee. The answer is that the mortgagor is entitled to the benefit of any advantageous modifications, but not bound by any disadvantageous modifications (unless the mortgagor consented to them, of course). In effect, the mortgagor is entitled to perform either the original or the modified version of the obligation. For example, if the interest rate is increased, the mortgagor can still pay off the loan at the original rate. Restatement of Suretyship & Guaranty § 41(c). If the loan maturity is extended, the mortgagor has the choice of paying on the original or the modified schedule. Restatement of Suretyship & Guaranty § 40(c).

4. *How can mortgagees avoid the suretyship defenses?* Mortgagees would naturally like to preserve their rights against original mortgagors when they elect to grant releases or modifications to grantees. There are three fairly obvious ways to do so:

(a) Include a clause in the mortgage preserving the mortgagee's claim against the mortgagor. That's what the drafter of the *Arena* mortgage tried to do; it just wasn't done very well. There's no doubt that this sort of provision (sometimes termed a "survival" clause or a "waiver of defenses" clause) is effective, but the courts tend to construe such clauses narrowly, as *Arena* illustrates.

(b) Obtain the mortgagor's consent to the modification after the mortgage is entered into, but before (or at the time that) the modification itself is made.

(c) Obtain the mortgagor's consent after the modification is made.

Think about choices (b) and (c). A common context is the situation in which the lender (acting under authority of a due-on-sale clause) has approved a grantee's assumption of a mortgage loan, but only on the condition that the interest rate be increased by, say, 1.5 percentage points. A simple way to obtain the mortgagor's consent to the increase is simply to ask the mortgagor to join in executing the amendment to the promissory note changing the rate. That implements choice (b) above. Without doubt the mortgagor/seller will be happy to cooperate; after all, she or he wants to sell the real estate.

On the other hand, suppose the lender fails get the mortgagor's consent at the time of the sale and modification. Instead the lender comes back to the mortgagor later, after the sale is completed, and asks the mortgagor to consent to the change of rate. Do you think the mortgagor will be cooperative now? At this point the sale is a "done deal" and the mortgagor is perfectly satisfied with the status quo. The lender no longer has any "leverage" to convince the mortgagor to sign a consent form.

B. RESTRICTIONS ON TRANSFER BY THE MORTGAGOR

The Due-on Clauses—Introduction*

The law of real property usually develops in an evolutionary fashion. Change is often measured in terms of decades and centuries rather than in months and years. Yet economic turmoil can accelerate this process. Just as the Great Depression of the 1930s spurred the enactment of mortgage moratoria and antideficiency legislation, so too the inflationary economic climate of the 1970s and early 1980s produced new mortgage law.

The major focus of this latter period was on the due-on-sale clause, a mortgage provision that affords the mortgagee the right to accelerate the mortgage debt and to foreclose if the mortgaged real estate is transferred without the mortgagee's consent.[2] Such clauses have two distinct functions from a lender's viewpoint. First, they are used to protect mortgagees against transfers that endanger mortgage security or increase the risk of default, typically because the proposed transfer is to a person with a poor credit rating or inadequate income to make the loan payments. Second and more importantly, they enable mortgagees to recall lower-than-market interest rate loans during periods of rising interest rates. Use of the due-on-sale clause in this context pits lenders against borrowers and real estate buyers, who would like to be able to sell and purchase mortgaged real estate by assuming existing loans. During the 1970s and early 1980s the due-on-sale clause became a major economic, political, and legal issue. It was confronted and evaluated by most state supreme courts, many legislatures, several federal regulatory agencies, the United States Supreme Court, and ultimately Congress. It was also the subject of a great deal of scholarly commentary.[3]

Given the prevailing economic conditions, this close scrutiny was hardly surprising. Due to exceptionally high interest rates and the

---

* This material is derived from Nelson, Whitman, Burkhart & Freyermuth, Real Estate Finance Law § 5.21 (6th ed. 2014), reprinted with permission of LEG, Inc. d/b/a West Academic.

[2] A typical due-on-sale clause provides, in part: "If all or any part of the Property or an interest therein is sold or transferred by Borrower without Lender's prior written consent, * * * Lender may, at Lender's option, declare all the sums secured by this mortgage to be due and payable." Federal National Mortgage Association/Federal Home Loan Mortgage Corporation Mortgage, Clause 18 (one to four family).

[3] See, e.g., Gorinson & Manishin, Garn-St. Germain: A Harbinger of Change, 40 Wash. & Lee L.Rev. 1313 (1983); Nelson & Whitman, Congressional Preemption of Mortgage Due-on-Sale Law: An Analysis of the Garn-St. Germain Act, 35 Hast.L.J. 241 (1983); Volkmer, The Application of the Restraints on Alienation Doctrine to Real Property Security Interests, 58 Iowa L.Rev. 747 (1973).

limited availability of home financing, large numbers of potential home buyers were excluded from the housing market. For many purchasers, the assumption of an existing lower-than-market interest mortgage represented one of the few practical financing alternatives. The financial climate also made it much more difficult for owners to sell. Many sellers were forced either to reduce significantly the price of their properties to enable buyers to qualify for institutional high-interest financing, or to suffer an effective price reduction by financing part of the purchase price themselves at lower-than-market interest rates. Thus, for those sellers with lower-than-market interest rate mortgages on their properties, assumability of the mortgage was a key to obtaining a higher price for the property.

On the other hand, the economic stake of institutional lenders in upholding due-on-sale clauses was also great. Institutional lenders, especially savings and loan associations, were experiencing severe economic difficulty. Because they held portfolios that included large numbers of fixed rate, lower-yielding mortgage loans, they were hard pressed to pay the higher short-term rates demanded by depositors. Many savings and loan associations and similar institutions failed, and others were left in precarious financial positions. Because the due-on-sale clause provided one means of eliminating lower-interest mortgage loans from institutional portfolios, and doing so without resort to expensive federal "bailout" or other subsidy schemes, federal regulators considered its enforceability critical to the economic health of the thrift industry.

Due-on-Encumbrance Restrictions

Mortgages may restrict mortgagor transfers by means other than a due-on-sale clause. For example, a mortgage may contain a clause authorizing the mortgagee to accelerate the debt if the mortgagor "further encumbers" the mortgaged real estate. Such language is usually referred to as a "due-on-encumbrance" provision. While due-on-encumbrance language is often included as part of a due-on-sale clause, it is not uncommon for a mortgage to contain a separate due-on-encumbrance clause. Unlike the due-on-sale situation, in which the mortgagee's desire to increase the interest rate predominates, due-on-encumbrance language is utilized mainly to protect against impairment of mortgage security by a debtor who incurs a junior mortgage debt and thus reduces his or her economic stake in the mortgaged real estate.

Increased-Interest-on-Transfer Clauses

Another provision closely related to the due-on-sale clause authorizes the mortgagee to increase or adjust the mortgage interest rate in the event of a transfer by the mortgagor. We refer to this as an "increased-interest-on-transfer" clause. This type of clause fulfills the same economic function as the due-on-sale clause in that it enables the mortgagee to use a transfer by the mortgagor as the basis for increasing the interest yield on the mortgage. However, unlike a due-on-sale clause, it does not confer on the mortgagee an absolute right to accelerate the mortgage debt upon a transfer; hence it gives no direct protection against transfer to an uncreditworthy buyer. Only if the transferee fails to pay the increased mortgage payments will there be grounds for declaration of a default and acceleration of the debt.

Installment Land Contract Prohibitions on Transfer

Transfer restrictions may also appear in installment land contracts, which are probably the most commonly used mortgage substitute. * * * Installment land contracts frequently include a provision that prohibits assignment by the vendee without the vendor's permission. Violation of such a provision constitutes a default and might result in vendor termination of the contract and loss of the purchaser's equity. In this respect the provision differs from a due-on-sale clause, under which an unapproved transfer will at most trigger an acceleration of the mortgage debt and, if the accelerated debt is unpaid, a public foreclosure sale of the mortgaged real estate.

Events Triggering Acceleration

A common question is what kind of event will trigger acceleration of a debt under a due-on-sale or other transfer restriction clause. While some early clauses used a "sale" alone as a triggering event, most of the recent forms employ broader language, often modeled after the mortgage form specified for use by lenders who sell mortgages to Fannie Mae and Freddie Mac. That form permits the lender to accelerate "if all or any part of the Property or any interest in it is sold or transferred (or if a beneficial interest in Borrower is sold or transferred and Borrower is not a natural person)." Under this language, standing alone, even a short-term lease or a grant of an easement or other limited interest in the land would suffice to trigger the lender's right to accelerate.

Perhaps the most significant question is whether a sale by installment land contract permits acceleration. The answer depends on the exact wording of the clause in question, but under broad language like that of the Fannie Mae/Freddie Mac clause the courts have nearly uniformly permitted acceleration.[4]

---

[4] See Income Realty & Mortgage, Inc. v. Columbia Savings and Loan Association, 661 P.2d 257, 259–60 (Colo.1983); Century Savings Association v. C. Michael Franke & Co., 9 Kan.App.2d 776, 689 P.2d 915 (1984) (contract for deed transfer deemed "transfer of title" for due-on-sale purposes); Mutual Federal Savings & Loan Association v. Wisconsin Wire Works, 58 Wis.2d 99, 101, 110, 205 N.W.2d 762, 769 (1973), appeal after remand, 71 Wis.2d 531, 239 N.W.2d 20 (1976). But see Fidelity Federal Savings and Loan Association v. Grieme, 112 Ill.App.3d 1014, 1019, 68 Ill.Dec. 558, 561, 446 N.E.2d 292, 295 (1983) (entering into agreement for deed held insufficient to trigger clause allowing lender to accelerate upon "change of ownership"); Peoples Federal Savings and Loan Association of East Chicago, Indiana v. Willsey, 466 N.E.2d 470

DUE-ON CLAUSES—PRE-GARN-ST. GERMAIN ACT STATE JUDICIAL AND LEGISLATIVE RESPONSE

Due-on-Sale Clauses

Due-on-sale clauses came under judicial attack as unreasonable restraints on alienation in many jurisdictions. While the results of these cases are now primarily of mere historical interest because of the federal legislation to be discussed below, a brief review of them will be helpful to an understanding the present legal context.

No court held that a due-on-sale clause was per se unlawful as a restraint on alienation. Indeed, some courts suggested that it was not a restraint on alienation at all. While many courts probably viewed the clause as an indirect restraint on alienation, all courts recognized that there were circumstances in which enforcement of the clause was reasonable and thus permissible. Some courts, however, were more sympathetic to enforcement than others, and two broad judicial approaches to the clause emerged.

Under the predominant judicial approach, the clause was deemed per se reasonable unless the borrower could show that the lender had engaged in unconscionable conduct.[5] The courts employing this approach recognized the desirability of protecting the mortgagee from the vagaries of the interest rate market. The mortgagee was not required to establish that a proposed transfer would impair security; the validity of the due-on-sale clause was not normally judged by the facts of an individual case. Under one variant of this approach, such facts were relevant only to the extent that the mortgagor attempted to meet the burden of proving that enforcement was unconscionable or inequitable in his or her case. An increase in the market interest rate was not thought sufficient to meet this burden, and due-on-sale clauses in such jurisdictions were usually enforced.

Under the minority approach, followed by about a dozen jurisdictions, the courts held that enforcement of due-on-sale clauses must be reasonable in individual cases, necessitating a case-by-case determination.[6] Under this approach, the mortgagee's desire to increase interest rates was not considered a sufficient reason to justify enforcement of the clause. The mortgagee had the burden to establish

---

(Ind.App.1984) (transfer by contract for deed not a sale or conveyance for purposes of due-on-sale clause).

[5] See, e.g., Tierce v. APS Co., 382 So.2d 485, 487 (Ala.1979); Income Realty & Mortgage Inc. v. Columbia Savings & Loan Association, 661 P.2d 257, 265 (Colo.1983).

[6] See, e.g., Baltimore Life Insurance Co. v. Harn, 15 Ariz.App. 78, 81, 486 P.2d 190, 193 (1971); Wellenkamp v. Bank of America, 21 Cal.3d 943, 953, 148 Cal.Rptr. 379, 385–86, 582 P.2d 970, 976–77 (1978); Magney v. Lincoln Mutual Savings Bank, 34 Wn.App. 45, 659 P.2d 537, 541 (1983).

reasonableness, which normally meant that the transfer would result in security impairment or an increased risk of default. Because this was usually hard to prove, lenders rarely sought due-on-sale enforcement in jurisdictions that followed this approach.

As noted above, majority or "automatic enforcement" jurisdictions often stated that due-on-sale clauses would be unenforceable if the mortgagor could establish that enforcement would be "unconscionable" or "inequitable." While it is difficult to articulate precisely when enforcement would be so categorized, it is probable that most courts would have been unwilling to enforce the clauses in "non-substantive" or "non-sale" transfers. For example, one court indicated that enforcement should be denied in situations such as transfers to a spouse who becomes a co-owner, transfers to a spouse incidental to a marriage dissolution proceeding or settlement, and transfers to an inter vivos trust of which the mortgagor was a beneficiary.

No-Transfer Provisions in Installment Land Contracts

While there was some early support for enforcement of "no-transfer" provisions in installment land contracts, later decisions were much less sympathetic. This attitude was reflected in two ways. First, "no-transfer" clauses were often construed narrowly against the vendor. Second, in contrast to the majority approach to due-on-sale clause enforcement, courts often eschewed an "automatic enforcement" approach; the "no-transfer" language was enforced only when it was established that the transfer would impair the vendor's security. Moreover, even when a vendor demonstrated such an impairment, it was likely that a court would avoid the imposition of forfeiture by permitting the transferee to pay off the contract balance, or by ordering that the real estate be foreclosed by public sale.

State Legislation

Several states imposed legislative limitations on due-on-sale clauses.[7] While the details of these statutes varied considerably, they commonly prohibited due-on-sale enforcement in residential mortgages unless the mortgagee could establish that a transfer would impair mortgage security. Most of the statutes permitted the mortgagee to condition transfer of the property upon payment of a limited "assumption fee" or upon an increase in the mortgage interest rate by a modest amount, usually no more than one percent. Some of the statutes imposed similar restrictions on increased-interest-on-transfer provisions.

---

7   See Ariz.Rev.Stat. § 33–806.02; West's Colo.Rev.Stat.Ann. § 38–30–165; O.C.G.A. § 44–14–5; Iowa Code Ann. § 535.8; N.M.Stat.Ann.1981, §§ 48–7–11 to 48–7–14; Minn.Stat.Ann. § 47.20; Utah Code Ann.1981, §§ 57–15–1 to 57–15–10.

DUE-ON CLAUSES—PRE-GARN-ST. GERMAIN ACT
FEDERAL REGULATION

In 1976 the Federal Home Loan Bank Board (the Board), the federal agency that regulated federally-chartered and federally-insured savings and loan associations, became concerned about the increasing controversy over whether federally-chartered associations had the authority to enforce due-on-sale clauses. The Board issued a regulation effective July 31, 1976 (the 1976 Regulation) which provided that a federal association "continues to have the power to include * * * a provision in its loan instrument whereby the association may, at its option, declare immediately due and payable sums secured by the association's security instrument if all or any part of the real property securing the loan is sold or transferred by the borrower without the association's prior written consent."[8]

In this regulation, the Board authorized federal associations to exercise the due-on-sale option (except in the case of certain types of "minor" transfers) and provided that all rights and remedies of the association and borrower "shall be exclusively governed by the terms of the loan contract." In the preamble to the 1976 Regulation the Board also expressed its intent that the due-on-sale practices of federal associations be governed exclusively by federal law, and emphasized that federal associations "shall not be bound by or subject to any conflicting state law which imposes different * * * due-on-sale requirements."[9]

While lower federal courts concluded that the 1976 Board Regulation preempted the application of state due-on-sale law to federal associations, a few state courts reached contrary results. Ultimately, this conflict was resolved by the United States Supreme Court in Fidelity Federal Savings & Loan Association v. de la Cuesta,[10] a case that addressed the effect of the 1976 Regulation on California law. California generally limited due-on-sale enforcement to situations in which impairment of mortgage security was established. In *de la Cuesta,* the Supreme Court held that: 1) the Board intended to preempt state law; 2) the 1976 Regulation in fact conflicted with California law, despite the fact that it merely authorized, and did not require, federal associations to utilize due-on-sale clauses; 3) the Board acted within its statutory authority under section 5(a) of the Home Owner's Loan Act, which authorized the Board to promulgate rules for the operation and regulation of federal associations; and 4) although the 1976 Regulation's merits might be debatable, it was a reasonable, and therefore a valid, exercise of the Board's authority.

---

8   12 C.F.R. § 545.8–3(f) (1983).

9   41 Fed.Reg. 18,286, 18,287.

10   458 U.S. 141, 102 S.Ct. 3014, 73 L.Ed.2d 664 (1982).

While *de la Cuesta* confirmed the validity of the Board's response to the needs of federally-chartered savings associations with respect to due-on-sale clauses, it did nothing for other types of lenders. Hence, these lenders, and particularly state-chartered savings and loan associations, sought a uniform national solution: congressional preemption of state laws restricting the enforcement of due-on-sale clauses. Their efforts culminated in the passage of the Garn Act.

SECTION 341, GARN-ST. GERMAIN DEPOSITORY INSTITUTIONS ACT OF 1982

96 Stat. 1505, 12 U.S.C.A. § 1701j–3, as amended, November 30, 1983, 97 Stat. 1237

Sec. 1701j–3. Preemption of due-on-sale prohibitions

(a) Definitions

For the purpose of this section—

(1) the term "due-on-sale clause" means a contract provision which authorizes a lender, at its option, to declare due and payable sums secured by the lender's security instrument if all or any part of the property, or an interest therein, securing the real property loan is sold or transferred without the lender's prior written consent;

(2) the term "lender" means a person or government agency making a real property loan or any assignee or transferee, in whole or in part, of such a person or agency;

(3) the term "real property loan" means a loan, mortgage, advance, or credit sale secured by a lien on real property, the stock allocated to a dwelling unit in a cooperative housing corporation, or a residential manufactured home, whether real or personal property; and

(4) the term "residential manufactured home" means a manufactured home as defined in section 5402(6) of Title 42 which is used as a residence; and

(5) the term "State" means any State of the United States, the District of Columbia, the Commonwealth of Puerto Rico, the Virgin Islands, Guam, the Northern Mariana Islands, American Samoa, and the Trust Territory of the Pacific Islands.

(b) Loan contract and terms governing execution or enforcement of due-on-sale options and rights and remedies of lenders and borrowers; assumptions of loan rates

(1) Notwithstanding any provision of the constitution or laws (including the judicial decisions) of any State to the contrary, a lender may, subject to subsection (c) of this section, enter into or enforce a contract containing a due-on-sale clause with respect to a real property loan.

(2) Except as otherwise provided in subsection (d) of this section, the exercise by the lender of its option pursuant to such a clause shall be exclusively governed by the terms of the loan contract, and all rights and remedies of the lender and the borrower shall be fixed and governed by the contract.

(3) In the exercise of its option under a due-on-sale clause, a lender is encouraged to permit an assumption of a real property loan at the existing contract rate or at a rate which is at or below the average between the contract and market rates, and nothing in this section shall be interpreted to prohibit any such assumption.

* * *

(d) Exemption of specified transfers or dispositions

With respect to a real property loan secured by a lien on residential real property containing less than five dwelling units, including a lien on the stock allocated to a dwelling unit in a cooperative housing corporation, or on a residential manufactured home, a lender may not exercise its option pursuant to a due-on-sale clause upon—

(1) the creation of a lien or other encumbrance subordinate to the lender's security instrument which does not relate to a transfer of rights of occupancy in the property;

(2) the creation of a purchase money security interest for household appliances;

(3) a transfer by devise, descent, or operation of law on the death of a joint tenant or tenant by the entirety;

(4) the granting of a leasehold interest of three years or less not containing an option to purchase;

(5) a transfer to a relative resulting from the death of a borrower;

(6) a transfer where the spouse or children of the borrower become an owner of the property;

(7) a transfer resulting from a decree of a dissolution of marriage, legal separation agreement, or from an incidental property settlement agreement, by which the spouse of the borrower becomes an owner of the property;

Limits on right to accelerate debts

(8) a transfer into an inter vivos trust in which the borrower is and remains a beneficiary and which does not relate to a transfer of rights of occupancy in the property; or

(9) any other transfer or disposition described in regulations prescribed by the Federal Home Loan Bank Board.

(e) Rules, regulations, and interpretations; future income bearing loans subject to due-on-sale options

(1) The Federal Home Loan Bank Board, in consultation with the Comptroller of the Currency and the National Credit Union Administration Board, is authorized to issue rules and regulations and to publish interpretations governing the implementation of this section.

(2) Notwithstanding the provisions of subsection (d) of this section, the rules and regulations prescribed under this section may permit a lender to exercise its option pursuant to a due-on-sale clause with respect to a real property loan and any related agreement pursuant to which a borrower obtains the right to receive future income.

* * *

THE GARN-ST. GERMAIN ACT*

The enactment of section 341 of the Garn-St. Germain Depository Institutions Act of 1982 ("the Act") signaled the dawn of a new era for due-on-sale clause enforcement. The Act broadly preempted state laws that restricted the enforcement of due-on-sale clauses, thereby making such clauses generally enforceable.

Congress delegated to the Federal Home Loan Bank Board (now the Office of Thrift Supervision) the authority to issue regulations interpreting the Act, and in April, 1983, the Board issued a final regulation entitled "Preemption of State Due-on-Sale Laws" ("the Regulation"). The following material analyzes the more important provisions of the Act and Regulation, their scope, and the complex problems of interpretation they have engendered.

Lenders Covered

The Act covers any "person or government agency making a real property loan." According to the Regulation, the foregoing definition includes,

without limitation, individuals, Federal associations, state-chartered savings and loan associations, national banks, state-

---

    * This material is based on Nelson, Whitman, Burkhart & Freyermuth, Real Estate Finance Law § 5.24 (6th ed. 2014), reprinted with permission of LEG, Inc. d/b/a West Academic.

chartered banks and state-chartered mutual savings banks, Federal credit unions, state-chartered credit unions, mortgage banks, insurance companies and finance companies which make real property loans, manufactured-home retailers who extend credit, agencies of the Federal government, [and] any lender approved by the Secretary of Housing and Urban Development for participation in any mortgage insurance program under the National Housing Act.[1]

However, the Act does not apply to a private bank; In re Black, 221 B.R. 38 (1998).

Loans Covered

The Act covers every "loan, mortgage, advance, or credit sale secured by a lien on real property, the stock allocated to a dwelling unit in a cooperative housing corporation, or a residential manufactured home, whether real or personal property." Thus it is not limited to residential loans. Although the Act makes no reference to mortgages on leasehold interests, the Regulation provides that a loan is secured by a lien on real property if it is made on the "security of any instrument * * * which makes * * * a leasehold or subleasehold * * * specific security for payment of the obligation secured by the instrument."[2]

* * *

Coverage of Installment Land Contracts

While the Act itself does not specifically mention installment land contracts, its preemption does apply to any "loan, mortgage, advance, or credit sale secured by a lien on real property." Does an installment contract vendor retain a "lien on real property," as well as legal title? The Regulation answers affirmatively,[3] and is probably correct. While a few courts have had conceptual difficulty with the notion that one can have legal title to land and a lien on it simultaneously, there is substantial authority that the installment land contract vendor retains a "vendor's lien" for the unpaid purchase price. Moreover, courts are increasingly equating installment land contracts with mortgages, and requiring foreclosure as the vendor's primary remedy. In such cases the vendor is surely foreclosing a "lien." Finally, while the analytical underpinnings for their decisions are not always clear, numerous courts routinely afford the vendor the option to foreclose an installment land contract as a mortgage.

---

[1]   48 Fed.Reg. 21,561 (codified at 12 CFR 591.2(g)).

[2]   48 Fed.Reg. 21,561 (codified at 12 CFR 591.2(h)).

[3]   48 Fed.Reg. 21,561 (codified at 12 CFR 591.2(h)) (" 'loan secured by a lien on real property' means a loan on the security on any instrument (whether a mortgage, deed of trust, or *land contract*) which makes the interest in real property (whether in fee or on a leasehold or subleasehold) specific security for the payment of the obligation secured by the instrument") (emphasis added). See Levine v. First Nat'l Bank, 948 So.2d 1051 (La.2006), agreeing.

This practice constitutes a persuasive argument that the contract vendor is also a "lienor."

The conclusion that the Act's preemption applies to installment land contracts does not mean that a violation of a contract prohibition on transfer will necessarily result in a forfeiture of the vendee's interest. When no-transfer provisions are upheld, it is likely that foreclosure of the contract will instead be ordered, and then only after the vendee has been afforded the opportunity to pay off the contract balance. The Act does not appear to change this. Literally, it only validates "due-on-sale" clauses—those that authorize the acceleration of the debt when the real estate is transferred without the lender's consent. A prohibition on transfer that purports to go beyond simple acceleration, and defines the remedies (such as forfeiture) to be imposed on the vendee, is unaffected by the Act and is thus still subject to pre-Act state law. It is highly improbable that a state court would enforce forfeiture, with its harsh consequences, simply because a transfer was made without the vendor's consent. A more likely judicial response would be to permit foreclosure of the contract as a mortgage. Such an approach would not be inconsistent with the policy inherent in the Act.

* * *

Transfers in Which Due-on-Sale Enforcement Is Prohibited

The Act expressly enumerates several types of transfers that may *not* be used as the basis for due-on-sale acceleration. The list is similar, though not identical, to the analogous provisions of the Fannie Mae/Freddie Mac mortgage form and the 1976 FHLBB regulations, and includes the creation of junior mortgages, transfers incident to divorce, at death and inter vivos to certain relatives, and leases for three years or less with no option to purchase.

When a transfer of one of these types is involved, the Act is preemptive: acceleration under a due-on-sale clause is prohibited even if permitted by state law. However, the above transfers are insulated from acceleration only if the mortgaged real estate contains "less than five dwelling units." The latter language was added to the Act on November 30, 1983. In its original form, the Act contained no such qualification.

The Regulation modifies the Act's exceptions to due-on-sale enforcement in other respects. For example, the Regulation adds to the further encumbrance exception by making it clear that a transfer by installment land contract does not constitute "[t]he creation of a lien or other encumbrance subordinate to the lender's security instrument."[4] This addition is probably unnecessary because installment land contract

---

4   48 Fed.Reg. 21,562 (codified at 12 CFR 591.5(b)(1)(i)).

transfers almost always entail the transfer of occupancy rights while, in order for the exception to apply, the Act states that the creation of the lien or encumbrance must "not relate to a transfer of rights of occupancy in the property."[5] In any event, the Board's interpretation of the exception is correct. The Act's "further encumbrance" exception is aimed at protecting mortgagors who have no intent to sell or transfer ownership, but want to create non-purchase money junior liens on their real estate for a variety of business or personal reasons.[6]

* * *

NOTES

1. *Non-sale transfers.* To what extent does the Act permit due-on-sale enforcement in "non-sale" or "non-substantive" family transfers that do not involve 1-to-4-family residences? For example, suppose a husband and wife own a store building in joint tenancy which is operated by them as a grocery store. Wife then dies and husband becomes the sole owner. If the building is mortgaged and the mortgage contains a due-on-sale clause, is it enforceable under the Act? Suppose a parent dies owning a 20 unit apartment building which, by the terms of the parent's will, is left to a daughter. A mortgage on the property contains a due-on-sale clause. Is it enforceable as a consequence of this probate transfer? See In re Smith, 469 B.R. 198, 202 (Bankr. S.D.N.Y. 2012) (the consent of lender was not required for the transfer of mother's interest in home to debtor-daughter, regardless of whether the mother was alive or whether an estate had been created); In re Cady, 440 B.R. 16, 20 (Bankr.N.D.N.Y.2010) (because parents transferred property to their son and daughter-in-law, the due-on-sale clauses contained in the mortgages were unenforceable).

2. *Farm land.* Note that the Act and Regulations omit any specific reference to transfers of farm land. For example, suppose husband and wife own a 640 acre farm in joint tenancy and husband dies. Assuming there is a mortgage on the land that contains a due-on-sale clause, does the transfer incident to his death trigger the clause? Should it make a difference whether the land contains a farm house? Would your answer be different if the land contained not only the farm house, but also 6 small houses for hired help? Finally, suppose the land is divided into non-contiguous parcels so that only one parcel contains the farm house. Is the due-on-sale clause enforceable under such circumstances? There seems to be no case law interpretation of these questions.

---

[5]   12 U.S.C.A. § 1701j–3(d)(1).

[6]   See Senate Committee Report, *supra* note 60, at 24. At least one case supports this conclusion. See Smith v. Frontier Fed. Sav. & Loan Ass'n, 649 P.2d 536 (Okl.1982); Darr v. First Fed. Sav. & Loan Ass'n of Detroit, 426 Mich. 11, 393 N.W.2d 152 (1986) (lien or encumbrance exception in due-on-sale clause construed not to include liens which are created only "as a result of the execution of an [installment land contract] which has as its primary purpose the transfer or sale of the security property').

3. *Involuntary transfers*. Suppose mortgaged real estate is transferred as a result of a foreclosure of a second mortgage, or a deed in lieu of foreclosure. May a due-on-sale clause contained in the first mortgage be validly invoked under the Act? See Blitz v. Marino, 786 P.2d 490 (Colo.App.1989) and Matter of Ruepp, 71 N.C.App. 146, 321 S.E.2d 517 (1984), both holding that foreclosure of the junior mortgage did not trigger acceleration; because the clause specifically permitted the creation of junior liens, the senior mortgagee was deemed to have impliedly waived the right to accelerate when a junior mortgagee later foreclosed. But see Barr Dev., Inc. v. Utah Mortg. Loan Corp., 106 Idaho 46, 675 P.2d 25 (1983) (suggesting that due-on-sale enforcement is not against public policy even where transfer is incident to foreclosure). What are the implications of the above cases for judicial interpretation of Section 1701j–3(d)(1) of the Act?

4. *Foreclosure of a prior mortgage as a transfer*. What about the opposite situation: will a foreclosure of a first mortgage act to trigger a due-on-sale clause in a second mortgage? See Executive Hills Home Builders, Inc. v. Whitley, 770 S.W.2d 507 (Mo.App.1989). Do you see why this is ordinarily a non-issue? What will happen to the second mortgage when the first mortgage is foreclosed?

5. *Non-standard transfers*. Here are a few more debatable "transfers." (a) One tenant in common transfers his or her interest to another tenant in common. See Davis v. Vecaro Dev. Corp., 101 N.C.App. 554, 400 S.E.2d 83 (1991) (due-on-sale clause triggered). (b) The mortgagor grants an option to purchase to an optionee, but the option has not yet been exercised. See Auernheimer v. Metzen, 98 Or.App. 722, 780 P.2d 796 (1989) (due-on-sale clause held triggered). Can this be correct? Is an option an interest in land?

6. *Transfers of stock or partnership interests*. Courts continue to confront transactions where a real estate transfer has occurred in substance but not in form. Suppose, for example, that the majority of shares of a closely-held corporate mortgagor are sold to a new owner. Assuming the mortgage contains a due-on-sale clause, is it enforceable in this setting even though the legal owner of the real estate is still the corporation? In light of the fact that a restraint on alienation is involved, that a corporation is a separate legal entity and that no actual conveyance has occurred, it seems likely that courts will construe the clause against due-on-sale enforcement. Such an approach has been applied in the limited partnership context involving a pre-Act transaction. See Fidelity Trust Co. v. BVD Assocs., 196 Conn. 270, 492 A.2d 180 (1985) (transfer by original limited partners of their partnership interest to new group of partners held not to constitute a violation of a due-on-sale clause because the general partner remained the same and the partnership was a separate legal entity).

A similar question arises if the title to the real estate is held by a trustee, and there is a change in the identity of the trust beneficiary. As a practical matter, beneficial ownership has been transferred, but legal title remains in the original trustee. Does such a transfer trigger a due-on-sale clause? This issue has been litigated extensively in Illinois, where land titles are often held in trust. See Mercado v. Calumet Fed. Sav. & Loan Ass'n, 196 Ill.App.3d 483, 143 Ill.Dec. 370, 554 N.E.2d 305 (1990), which summarizes the cases.

The due-on-sale clause (clause 18) in the most recent version of the uniform covenants in the FNMA/FHLMC mortgage form, reproduced in the Appendix of this book, begins:

> If all or any part of the Property or any interest in it is sold or transferred (or if a beneficial interest in Borrower is sold or transferred and Borrower is not a natural person) * * *

Does the parenthetical language solve the problems described above? Is a clause permitting acceleration upon the sale of corporate stock or a partnership interest really a "due-on-sale" clause as that term is defined in the Garn Act? If not, does the Federal preemption of the Act apply to such clauses?

7.   *Coverage of successive transfers.* Does a due-on-sale clause "run with the land?" Suppose A borrows money from a bank, giving it a mortgage on A's house. Subsequently A sells the house to B, who assumes (or takes subject to) the mortgage with the bank's consent. Later B desires to sell the house to C. Is further consent from the bank necessary? Or is the previous consent a relinquishment by the bank of the right to accelerate for the remainder of the life of the loan? Would it matter whether (a) the mortgage contained a statement that it bound the successors and assigns of the original mortgagor, or (b) the mortgagee, in granting consent to the A–B sale, expressly reserved the right to approve all future transfers? See Esplendido Apts. v. Metropolitan Condo. Ass'n, 161 Ariz. 325, 778 P.2d 1221 (1989), in which the court relied on the "successors and assigns" clause in finding that B's transfer to C triggered the due-on-sale clause; Howell v. Murray Mortg. Co., 890 S.W.2d 2d 78 (Tex.App.1994) (clause held binding on mortgagor's administrator). But see In re Ormond Beach Assocs. Ltd. Partn., 184 F.3d 143 (2d Cir. 1999).

8.   *Waivers by lenders.* Lenders can and frequently do waive their right to accelerate under due-on-sale clauses. Commonly a waiver is given in return for the payment to the lender of an "assumption fee," an increase in the interest rate on the loan, or both. See Gruber v. Federal Nat'l Mortg. Ass'n, 2003 WL 1091046 (Cal.App.2003) (not reported in Cal.Rptr.2d), upholding imposition of an assumption fee. Sometimes the grantee will argue that a waiver or estoppel should be implied from the lender's action, inaction, or ambiguous words. See In re Ramos, 357 B.R. 669 (Bankr.S.D.Fla.2006) (lender waived debtor's transfer of the property by failing to raise it properly in Chapter 13 bankruptcy proceeding); In re Mini, 2009 WL 3756827 (Bankr. N.D.Cal.2009) (finding it unfair and inequitable because of lender's prepetition conduct, to permit a due-on-sale provision to trump the debtor's attempts to reorganize in bankruptcy). Do you think a waiver or estoppel should be found on the following facts?

(a) A loan officer for the lender states "there will be no problem" with a loan assumption, provided that the purchaser's financial condition proves to be as represented to the lender. Compare Destin Sav. Bank v. Summerhouse of FWB, Inc., 579 So.2d 232 (Fla.App.1991) (no waiver found) with Great Northern Sav. Co. v. Ingarra, 66 Ohio St.2d 503, 423 N.E.2d 128 (1981), noted 11 Capital U.L.Rev. 380 (1981) (waiver found).

(b) The parties do not notify the lender of the sale, but the lender receives a hazard insurance binder that reflect the fact that the real estate has a new owner. The lender takes no action to enforce the due-on-sale clause for many months thereafter; see Rakestraw v. Dozier Assocs., Inc., 285 S.C. 358, 329 S.E.2d 437 (1985) (17-month delay; waiver and estoppel found); Cooper v. Deseret Fed. Sav. & Loan Ass'n, 757 P.2d 483 (Utah App.1988) (28 month delay; estoppel found). In cases such as this, should a court insist on some evidence that the purchaser has been damaged or harmed in some way by the lender's delay? Suppose that, immediately upon learning of the transfer, the lender demands that the purchaser assume the loan (which the purchaser refuses to do), but then delays for 12 months before accelerating and commencing foreclosure. If this is a waiver (as it was held to be; see Rubin v. Los Angeles Fed. Sav. & Loan Ass'n, 159 Cal.App.3d 292, 205 Cal.Rptr. 455 (1984)), isn't the court penalizing the lender for being patient and attempting to work out the dispute?

(c) Suppose the parties fail to notify the lender of the transfer, and lender does not receive any document disclosing the change of ownership. Should the lender be held to constructive notice of the fact that a deed to the property has been recorded? See Stenger v. Great Southern Sav. & Loan Ass'n, 677 S.W.2d 376 (Mo.App.1984) (no notice imputed).

9. *Concealment of transfers.* Most due-on-sale clauses contain no express covenant on the part of the borrower to disclose to the lender that a transfer is taking place. (Wouldn't a covenant of this sort make sense from the lender's viewpoint? One case holds that there is no implied duty to disclose transfers; see Medovoi v. American Sav. & Loan Ass'n, 89 Cal.App.3d 244, 152 Cal.Rptr. 572 (1979) (depublished). There are no cases imposing an implied duty to disclose). Borrowers are often tempted (and are sometimes advised by real estate brokers) to make transfers without reporting them to their lenders. They may go to some lengths to conceal sales; for example, they may arrange for the grantee to make the monthly payments to the grantor, and for the grantor to continue remitting them to the lender.

But concealment is tricky, and there is a good chance that the transaction will be "caught" by the lender sooner or later. Some lenders have contracted with title companies to "watch" their properties and report any recorded transfers. A lender may also discover that a transfer has occurred because it receives a tax bill or homeowner's insurance binder that shows the name of a new owner. Lenders may even have paid staff members visit properties to determine whether the original borrowers are still in residence.

A borrower may try to circumvent these means of detection; for example, the borrower may agree with the grantee that the deed will not be recorded, that the taxing authorities will not be notified of the sale, and that the hazard insurance will continue to be carried in the old owner's name. But these techniques are obviously risky and can give rise to serious problems.

If a lender discovers a transfer that has been concealed, what are its remedies? Obviously it can accelerate the loan if it acts within a reasonable time after the discovery. The acceleration itself might be quite devastating, particularly if interest rates have risen substantially or if the present owner cannot qualify for new financing. Might the lender also claim damages based, for example, on the lender's lost interest between the time of the transfer and the time of its discovery? Could a damages claim be predicated on some theory of breach of an implied covenant, such as the covenant of good faith and fair dealing? No reported case seems to have adopted such ideas, but it is certainly conceivable that a court could do so.

Suppose a lender discovers the concealed transfer and accelerates. The brunt of the lender's action falls on the grantee, of course. Could the grantee bring a successful action against the grantor, perhaps on the theory that the grantor had implicitly warranted that the financing taken over by the grantee would continue to be available for its full stated term? What if the grantee cannot qualify for any new financing, and ends up losing the property in foreclosure? Again, there is no case law imposing liability on the grantor in these situations, but the argument is not a frivolous one.

On the whole, we think concealment is a bad strategy, full of risks for both parties. The wiser course, we suggest, is to discuss the proposed transaction with the lender and make the best deal possible.

10. *Concealment by lawyers.* Should a lawyer be troubled by the ethical implications of counseling a client to conceal a transfer, or of arranging the details of the transaction? It is necessary to distinguish two issues: (a) Is the lawyer under an ethical obligation to inform, or not to inform, the lender that a transfer has occurred? (b) Is the lawyer under an ethical obligation to refrain from advising or assisting in the concealed transfer? The comments below are based on the Model Code of Professional Responsibility (1969) (MCPR), the Model Rules of Professional Conduct (1983) (MRPC), and the Restatement (Third) of the Law Governing Lawyers (2000) ("Restatement").

The lawyer's duty of disclosure or nondisclosure. A lawyer has a duty not knowingly to reveal a confidence of his or her client. See MCPR, D.R. 4–101(B) and (C); MRPC 1.6. Exceptions are made for disclosures necessary to prevent the client from committing a crime that would result in death or bodily harm, or that are based on "fraudulent" conduct by the client; see MCPR, D.R. 7–102(B); Restatement § 67(1). The relevant opinions consistently treat "fraudulent" as referring only to criminal conduct or something very close to it. Hence, there is probably a duty on the lawyer's part not to disclose a real estate transfer to a mortgage lender against the client's wishes.

The lawyer's duty to avoid advising or assisting in the transfer. The concealment of a transfer is at most a breach of contract (and perhaps not even that if the mortgage does not specifically require the borrower to report the transfer). However, the relevant rules require the lawyer to withdraw from representation only when the client's conduct is "illegal" or "fraudulent." MCPR, D.R. 7–102(A)(7); MRPC 1.2(d); Restatement § 94(2). There is no prohibition on advising a client to breach a contract. Again, the term "fraudulent" is generally taken to include only criminal or quasi-criminal activity. This approach is adopted in the due-on-sale situation by Oregon Ethics Opinion 464, exonerating a lawyer who assisted a client in a concealed real estate sale, and commenting that "the transaction, although legally precarious for both the buyer and seller, is not fraudulent or illegal." The "terminology" section of MRPC's Preamble provides:

> "Fraud" or "fraudulent" denotes conduct having a purpose to deceive and not merely negligent misrepresentation or failure to apprise another of relevant information.

It is difficult (though not impossible) to conceive of a court's finding nondisclosure of a real estate transfer to be fraudulent in this sense. State bar ethics opinions have generally agreed with Oregon. See Alaska Bar Ass'n Ethics Opinion #88–2; Illinois Bar Advisory Opinion No. 728; Virginia Bar Opinion 471 (1983).

A lawyer may nonetheless feel uncomfortable in assisting a client in a concealed transfer. If the client insists on proceeding contrary to the lawyer's advice, the lawyer is plainly entitled to withdraw from representation; see Restatement § 32(3)(f) (lawyer who considers the client's action "repugnant or imprudent" may withdraw). See Mark E. Roszkowski, Drafting Around Mortgage Due-on-Sale Clauses: The Dangers of Playing Hide-and-Seek, 21 Real Prop.Prob. and Tr. J. 23, 41–58 (1986).

C. TRANSFER OF THE MORTGAGEE'S INTEREST

In this section we discuss the legal aspects of transactions in which one lender (for example, the one who has "originated" or made a mortgage loan) sells or assigns the note and mortgage to another lender, typically termed an "investor." Such a transaction is known as a secondary sale, and the market in which transactions between lenders occur is called the secondary mortgage market. The economic aspects of the secondary market, and the involvement of government agencies in such transactions, are discussed in Chapter 8. Secondary market transactions can take many forms, but they generally fall into four categories.

1.   Outright sale to an investor who will hold the mortgage in its portfolio.

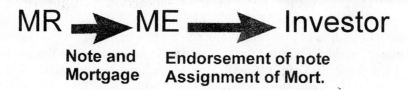

The transaction may involve a single (usually large) mortgage, or a pool of smaller (e.g., residential) mortgages. The investor is a company or institution with substantial funds to invest, such as a savings bank, a life insurance company, or a pension fund. In their earlier years as private entities, Fannie Mae and Freddie Mac acted as investors in this sort of transaction; they held in their portfolios a large share of the mortgages they purchased. The funds they invested were raised largely by selling debentures in the capital markets.

2.   Partial   assignments   (participations)   sold   to   multiple investors.

Here the investor typically retains a portion of ownership of the note and mortgage, but sells partial interests (literally tenancy in common interests) to other investors. For example, on a single large commercial loan, say $50 million, the investor might retain a 1/4 interest ($12.5 million) and sell the other three 1/4 ($12.5 million) shares to three other investors. Commercial banks and savings banks often engage in this sort of transaction as a way of diversifying their portfolios and reducing risk. Sometimes the original mortgagee will itself act as the "lead" lender in the participation, instead of selling the entire loan to a separate investor who will arrange the participation as shown above.

Instead of a single large commercial loan, the transaction may involve a pool of a large number of smaller (e.g., residential) mortgages. Fannie Mae and Freddie Mac currently use this method to raise a large proportion of their capital. They retain a small fraction of ownership in the pool (say, 5%) and sell the remaining 95% in the form of Participation Certificates (PCs) to investors in the capital markets. They often engage in "swap" transactions with the originating mortgagees, trading the mortgages for PCs, which the mortgagees then sell in the capital markets, usually to institutional investors such as pension funds, banks, and mutual funds.

Note that in either form of the transaction just described, the participants will ordinarily receive pro-rata pass-through shares of the payments of principal and interest made by the mortgagor(s), less certain fees earned by the PC issuer or lead lender. It is possible for the parties to agree that some participants will have a higher priority than others (or higher than the lead lender), and thus will have first right to the payments if a partial default by the mortgagor occurs. In addition, the lead lender may (or may not) guarantee receipt of the principal and interest payments to the participants; Fannie Mae and Freddie Mac generally do so.

3.   Sale of mortgage-backed pass-through securities.

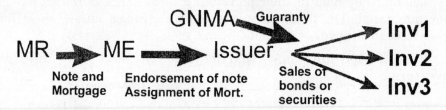

In this sort of transaction, the ultimate investors do not purchase fractional shares of ownership in the underlying mortgage or pool of mortgages. Instead, they purchase bonds or other securities, issued by the secondary market investor, and *collateralized* by the mortgage or mortgages. However, the payments received by the investors are "pass-throughs," meaning that they correspond on a pro-rata basis to the payments made on the underlying mortgages. That means that each payment an investor receives will be partly interest and partly a return of the invested principal.

This type of transaction was popularized by the Government National Mortgage Ass'n (GNMA or "Ginnie Mae"), a government agency and a part of the Department of Housing and Urban Development. For pools of residential mortgages that are individually insured by the Federal Housing Authority (FHA) or guaranteed by the Department of Veterans Affairs (VA), GNMA issues guaranties to the investors, assuring them that they will receive monthly payments corresponding to the payments due on the underlying mortgages even if some of the mortgages experience default. In essence, this places the full faith and credit of the United States behind the securities, making them highly liquid and salable at relatively low interest yields.

4. Sale of multiclass mortgage-backed securities.

When used with commercial mortgage loans, this type of transaction involves large pools (commonly 100 loans or more) of large mortgages (commonly $20 million each or more.) The securities, which are widely sold and traded in the capital markets, are not "pass-throughs," but instead represent a variety of combinations of principal and interest payments which, in the aggregate, can be covered by payments made by the borrowers on the underlying loans. For example, some classes of securities may pay interest only; some classes may pay out early in the life of the underlying loans, and some later; some classes may have priority over others. The securities are called "Commercial Mortgage-backed Securities" ("CMBS"), and the loans themselves are often called "conduit" loans. Each class of securities is called a "tranche," and a CMBS pool may give rise to as many as ten or twenty different tranches.

Issuers of these sorts of securities are often major Wall Street investment banks. The transactions are complex, and because the securities are "rated" prior to marketing, the details of the underlying mortgage transactions are largely governed by the requirements of the three Wall Street rating agencies (Moody's, Fitch's, and Standard and Poor). Substantial fees are captured by various parties, including the rating agencies and various trustees and loan servicers. (The diagram above is merely conceptual, and does not show all of these parties.)

Despite the cost of creation, complexity, and inflexibility of these loans, they are often sought by real estate entrepreneurs because they carry interest rates that are significantly lower than are usually available from other sources of funds. This is possible because the carving of the securities into multiple "tranches" allows the creation of security classes that appeal to a wide variety of investors.

The growth of residential mortgage-backed securities. The securitization of commercial mortgages, which became common in the 1990s, proved to be an effective and successful vehicle for raising commercial mortgage funds. Securitization of residential loans had a slower start. A relatively small proportion (less than 10%) of residential mortgage debt had been held in securitized pools since the mid-1980s. Beginning in 2003, an enormous increase in securitization of residential mortgages occurred, and by 2006 about 30% of home mortgages were held in securitized pools.

These "private-label" securitizations (to distinguish them from mortgage securities issued by Fannie Mae and Freddie Mac, and those guaranteed by GNMA) were strikingly different from the GNMA mortgage-backed securities discussed above. The mortgages in these new pools were nearly all conventional, not FHA and VA; the securities were not guaranteed by the federal government; and they were multiclass (like the commercial mortgage-backed securities discussed above), not pass-throughs as GNMA securities are. The GNMA program was carefully regulated and monitored by the federal government and had very few defaults. The new securitizations of the 2000s were quite the opposite.

In 2008 the residential mortgage market (and to a significant degree, the credit markets in general) collapsed, accompanied by drastically reduced liquidity, the de-privatization of Fannie Mae and Freddie Mac (which were placed in federal conservatorship), and the failure of a number of other large investment bankers and institutional lenders. The story of this collapse is complex, with many interlacing factors, some of which may yet only be dimly understood, but it revolves around the growth of private-label residential mortgage-backed securities.

Housing inflation and deflation. The problems arose because of the confluence of two factors. The first was a prolonged period of exceptionally low interest rates—rates that, beginning in 2001, were lower than at any time in the Twentieth Century. The low rates were a result of the exceptionally loose monetary policy pursued by the Federal Reserve Board. Because housing demand is highly influenced by (and negatively correlated to) interest rates, the result was a huge upswing in demand, which in turn drove housing prices into an extraordinary inflationary spiral, especially in the Sunbelt states. Such inflation tends to feed on itself, as people conclude, "I *have* to buy a house (or upgrade to a larger house) now, before price inflation puts houses out of my reach."

This inflationary spiral would, without doubt, have reversed itself within a few years, leading to a corrective period of price stagnation or deflation. After all, most people can only afford so much housing, and when prices get out of reach, demand has to drop. But the "correction" proved much more severe than might have been expected because of another factor: a fundamental structural realignment in the mortgage lending industry.

Mortgage industry restructuring. Traditionally, mortgage loans were made by "portfolio lenders," mainly banks and savings associations. All aspects of a loan were handled by the same—usually local—institution: loan application, loan closing, collection of payments, and maintenance of escrow accounts for taxes and insurance. In the 1970s this pattern began to change as more and more lenders began selling their loans on the "secondary market" to other investors, such as Fannie Mae and Freddie

Mac. But these secondary market investors generally maintained high quality standards, insisting that the loans they purchased be made only to borrowers who had a strong likelihood of making the payments.

This structure began to break down in two ways at the beginning of the Twenty-first Century. First, more and more loans were made by independent "mortgage brokers." These brokers would arrange to find and bring borrowers to "wholesale" lenders. The broker would take the applicant's loan application, "qualify" the borrower, and arrange for the loan closing. The broker received a commission, which was generated from the "yield spread premium"—in essence, the present value of the difference between the interest rate the borrower was paying and the (lower) interest yield demanded by the wholesale lender.

Commissions were fat during the early to mid-2000s. In high-cost areas like much of California, a broker might earn $20,000 or more on a single loan. And since the broker had no funds invested in the loan, many brokers simply did not care whether the borrower might later default or not; the emphasis was on making immediate commissions. The wholesale lenders and secondary market investors had (and tried to exercise) little control over the actions of loan brokers, who were typically small, very numerous, and able to enter and leave the market readily.

Some brokers were tempted to encourage borrowers to give "creative" answers to questions on the loan application (i.e., to lie), to help falsify information about income and ability to repay, and even to engage in outright fraud. See, e.g., In re First Alliance Mortg. Co., 471 F.3d 977 (9th Cir. 2006), in which Lehman Brothers, Inc., which issued mortgage-backed securities collateralized by a pool of residential mortgages, was charged with liability for "aiding and abetting" the fraudulent practices of the mortgage originator. The practice of making "Alt-A" loans (colloquially, "liar's loans") grew: loans which did not require the traditional forms of documentation of credit, employment and income for the borrower. And because interest rates and hence commissions were higher on "subprime" mortgages—those that did not require borrowers to meet traditional credit and income standards—brokers increasingly emphasized subprime lending, even pushing borrowers into subprime loans who could readily have qualified for prime loans.

At the same time, things were changing at the other end of the mortgage process, the secondary market, with the advent of residential mortgage securitizations noted above. Large numbers of pools of Alt-A and subprime mortgages were formed, in addition to pools of prime mortgages. Investors were dazzled by the high returns they could earn on these securities. In theory, they should have been concerned about the quality of the underlying mortgages, but it was impractical for them to investigate thousands of individual loans. As a fallback, the investors relied on the ratings given to the securities issues by the three New York rating agencies (Moody's, Standard and Poor, and Fitch's), but these agencies' methods of verifying loan quality were entirely inadequate. Moreover they were busy earning fees for providing high ratings and realized that down-rating a particular security could cost them in lost business as the issuer "shopped" the rating with the other agencies.

Thus a large share the residential mortgage industry had restructured itself into three components: mortgage brokers, wholesale lenders/securities issuers, and securities investors. Each of these components was making huge profits, but none of them cared much about mortgage quality; it was a far cry from the days when a single bank or savings association made the loan and took the loss if it went sour.

A perfect storm. This situation might have gone on for a very long time if housing prices had continued to rise, for rising prices can cover mortgage weaknesses very effectively, for several reasons. If prices rise, borrowers have increasing equity, and hence have an incentive to try very hard to avoid foreclosure. If they cannot continue to make the loan payments, they can usually sell the property for enough to fully cover the loan balance. And if lenders must foreclose in a rising market, they will usually recover enough to pay the loan balance and perhaps even make a profit.

But when prices began to stagnate or fall in 2006 and 2007, borrowers who had difficulty making their payments could no longer sell their houses for enough to cover their indebtedness. Moreover, many borrowers had obtained adjustable rate mortgages that carried artificially low "teaser" rates for the first two or three years. When these loans began to reset to market rates, the resulting higher payments made default inevitable in many cases.

Thus, the large upswing in foreclosures was caused by a combination of housing price deflation and an industry characterized by a huge "moral hazard"—a structure in which no one had a sufficient stake in ensuring that the mortgages being originated could and would be paid back. Anyone reasonably familiar with the mortgage business would have predicted that many of the loans made during the 2002–2006 period were headed for almost certain default. And of course, houses that were foreclosed were dumped back on the market, further increasing supply and driving down prices. It was a "perfect storm"—a set of conditions that would inevitably lead to disaster.

In many cases, these loans might have been "saved" by restructuring their payments in "workout" agreements. However, the loans were being serviced by professional servicers hired by the trustees of the securitized mortgage pools. These servicers typically had very limited authority to enter into modifications or workouts. In any event, they were overwhelmed by the volume of defaults and felt inadequately compensated for the huge amount of staff time that negotiating workouts would have required. Hence few loans were modified and saved from foreclosure.

The problems of loan default were not confined to the investors who purchased mortgage-backed securities. In many cases, institutional investors had attempted to hedge their default risk by entering into "credit default swap" agreements, mainly with commercial banks, insurance companies, and investment bankers. These providers of "swaps" were, in essence, selling insurance against mortgage default to the securities holders. So long as housing prices were rising, defaults were low and selling such insurance was highly profitable. But when the housing market turned negative and defaults began to rise, the institutions that had sold the credit default swaps were forced to begin paying off in amounts far beyond their expectations and capacities. The issuance of these swaps was completely unregulated, either by the Securities and Exchange Commission or by state insurance commissioners. The issuers had provided no, or inadequate, reserves to cover the claims they received, and they simply lacked the funds to pay them.

The size of the "credit default swap" market was difficult to grasp. There are no firm data (since the market was unregulated), but it is estimated that there were credit default swap agreements of $45 to $60 trillion by mid-2007—more than twice the size of the U.S. stock market! Perhaps it is fair to say that the issuers of these swaps had little idea of how to price the risk that they had assumed—a risk that was far greater than they had anticipated. Moreover, the credit default swap agreements themselves were widely traded, often with little attention to whether the original issuer had the financial strength to cover its obligations.

The results of this debacle were felt heavily by a wide group of investors in the private-label mortgage-backed securities market, such as pension funds, commercial banks, insurance companies, and sovereign wealth funds throughout the world, not to mention individuals who had acquired mortgage-backed securities for their own investment accounts. Some insurance companies and banks received a double hit, both as investors in mortgages or mortgage-backed securities and as issuers of credit default swap agreements. The devastation was widespread. As insurance companies weakened, concerns arose as to their ability to pay their obligations on other lines of insurance, such as municipal bond credit insurance.

The federal government's reaction to the mortgage crisis was complex, slow to develop, and initially inadequate. It is nicely summarized in U.S. Department of the Treasury, The Financial Crisis

Five Years Later: Response, Reform, and Progress (Sept. 2013). In Chapter 8 of this book you will encounter many of the federal initiatives.

5. Collateral or security transfer of notes and mortgages.

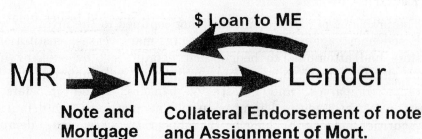

This type of transfer by the mortgagee, unlike all of the others described above, is not intended to be permanent. The mortgagee is seeking a loan from another lender, who demands collateral. The mortgagee pledges the note and mortgage as security for repayment of the new debt, documents by some form of loan and security agreement. The parties expect that, when the new debt is repaid, the security given by the mortgagee will be discharged and the note and mortgage returned to the mortgagee.

One of the most common users of this transaction is a mortgage banker who makes large numbers of residential loans, intending to sell them on the secondary market to Fannie Mae, Freddie Mac, or some other investor as described in examples 1 and 2 above, or to securitize them as described in examples 3 and 4. However, it may take the mortgage banker considerable time—several weeks or months, depending on its lending volume—to accumulate enough mortgages to form a pool of acceptable size. While the mortgage banker is accumulating a package of loans of sufficient size to sell, it may temporarily pledge the loans (i.e., the notes and mortgages) it has already originated to another lender, commonly a local commercial bank, as collateral for a line of credit. The funds drawn down on this line of credit will be used by the mortgage banker to continue to make additional loans. This is sometimes termed a "warehouse" line of credit, since the mortgage loans are "parked" in the bank's "warehouse" for a few days or weeks until the mortgage company is ready to sell them to secondary market investors or securitize them. The practice is nicely explained in Rodgers v. Seattle-First Nat'l Bank, 40 Wash.App. 127, 697 P.2d 1009 (1985).

Legal Aspects of Mortgage Transfer

While mortgage loans have been sold in secondary market transactions for centuries, it is surprising how widely courts and lawyers have misunderstood or misconceived the process. Indeed, a benefit of the otherwise dismal mortgage crisis, and the litigation that it spawned, was to clarify the law of mortgage transfer. One of the most helpful documents in achieving this clarification was published by the Permanent Editorial Board of the Uniform Commercial Code in November, 2011, entitled "Application of the Uniform Commercial Code to Selected Issues Relating to Mortgage Notes," and referred to here simply as the "PEB Report." It's an excellent source for those who need a carefully-written, thoughtful explanation of many aspects of the process. See also Whitman, What We Have Learned from the Mortgage Crisis about Transferring Mortgage Loans, 49 Real Prop., Prob. & Tr. J. 1 (2014).

What rights does the secondary market purchase of a mortgage want to obtain? Obviously, rights to both the promissory note and the mortgage, since without the mortgage, the note would be unsecured (making its collection more difficult and doubtful), and without the note, the mortgage would be unforeclosable (since the holder of the mortgage could not experience a default on the secured obligation). More about this in a moment.

But when we speak of rights to the note, we must recognize that there are two distinct set of rights that can be transferred: the *right to enforce*, and *ownership* (or "title") to the note. These two sets of rights are distinct from one another, and a great deal of confusion and nonsense has been created by muddling the two concepts.

Entitlement to enforce a note means that one can sue on it or (if applicable foreclosure requirements are met) foreclose the mortgage that secures it. The maker of the note (the mortgagor) is the party most concerned with who is entitled to enforce the note; the concept is designed to protect the maker against having to pay twice or defend against multiple claims on the note. If the maker pays in full the person entitled to enforce the note, it is discharged and the mortgage that secures it is extinguished.

On the other hand, *ownership* of the note means that one is entitled to its economic value. The owner of the note is the person who can claim the payments, including regular installment payments, a voluntary payoff, and the proceeds of a short sale or a foreclosure.

As the PEB Report (at p. 4, footnote 15) observes, "The concept of "person entitled to enforce" a note is not synonymous with "owner" of the note. * * * A person need not be the owner of a note to be the person entitled to enforce it, and not all owners will qualify as persons entitled to enforce." This is so because, as we will see, entitlement to enforce and ownership are governed by two separate legal regimes that establish different criteria. It is absolutely critical, when speaking or writing about note transfers, to make is clear whether one is referring to a transfer of ownership, a transfer of the right to enforce, or both. See Nationstar

Mortg., L.L.C. v. West, 2014 WL 820008 (Ohio App. 2014), in which the court did a nice job of explaining the distinction.

While people in casual conversation may talk generically about "transferring the note," doing so can easily lead to confusion, or even to nonsensical conclusions, if one does not specify whether ownership or the right of enforcement (or both) is to be transferred. For an excellent example, in which the legislature jumbled the two concepts but the court intelligently parsed them, see Trujillo v. Northwest Trustee Services, Inc., 326 P.3d 768 (Wash.App. 2014).

As we have indicated above, a secondary market purchaser of a mortgage loan ordinarily not only wants both ownership of the *note* and the right to enforce it, but also want both ownership of the *mortgage* and the right to foreclose it. As it happens, transfers of the right to enforce have been controversial and the subject of a great deal of litigation in recent years, while transfers of ownership have been straightforward and rarely litigated. We will consider transfers of the right to enforce at length below. First, however, two brief notes appear below—one on how ownership is transferred, and one on MERS.

Transferring ownership. U.C.C. Article 9 governs transfers of ownership of promissory notes (including those secured by real estate mortgages). A note an "instrument" in the lexicon of Article 9, and the definition is broad; under § 9–102(a)(47), an "instrument" is "a negotiable instrument or any other writing that evidences a right to the payment of a monetary obligation . . . and is of a type that in ordinary course of business is transferred by delivery with any necessary endorsement or assignment." Thus, both negotiable and nonnegotiable notes are covered.

Unfortunately for our purposes, Article 9 is written in the terminology of creation of security interests in collateral. The Code then (rather obliquely) defines "security interest" to include transfers of ownership; under § 1–201(b)(35), "security interest" includes "an interest of a *buyer* of . . . a promissory note." This peculiarity makes Article 9's wording confusing and difficult to follow as applied to outright sales of notes. To avoid this problem, we have rewritten § 9–203(b), the section dealing with creation of security interests, as though it were solely about sales of notes. As so rewritten, 9–203(b) reads as follows:

> a [sale of an interest in a promissory note] is enforceable against the [seller] and third parties with respect to the [note] only if:
>
> (1) value has been given;
>
> (2) the [seller] has rights in the [note] or the power to transfer rights in the [note] to a [buyer]; and

(3) one of the following conditions is met:

(A) the [seller] has authenticated a [sale] . . . agreement that provides a description of the [note] . . . ; [or]

(B) the [note] is in the possession of the [buyer] under Section 9–313 pursuant to the [seller's] agreement.

Thus, assuming the seller has rights in the note (or is an agent of someone who has such rights), and assuming the buyer gives value, ownership can be transferred in either of two ways: (A) by a signed, written agreement (or its electronic equivalent), such as a contract of sale or a written assignment, or (B) by delivering possession of the note to the buyer, provided that there is some agreement indicating that ownership is to be transferred.

What happens to the mortgage when ownership of a note is sold? Under 9–203(g) (also rewritten to focus on outright sales of notes) "The attachment of [ownership] in a right to payment or performance [i.e., a note] secured by a security interest or other lien on personal or real property is also attachment of [ownership] in the security interest, mortgage, or other lien." Thus, a sale of ownership rights in the note also automatically transfers the corresponding ownership rights in a real estate mortgage securing that note.

We haven't yet discussed transfers of the right of enforcement of notes; that comes next. But we can forecast a bit of that discussion by saying that, while a delivery of the original note will transfer *both* ownership and the right to enforce, the use of a separate document of assignment alone can be used to transfer ownership but will *not* transfer the right to enforce (at least if the note is negotiable).

MERS: A brief description. Because the next case deals with MERS (the Mortgage Electronic Registration System), we precede the case opinion with a bit of background on MERS. In the mid-1990s, the major players in the mortgage market (including Fannie Mae, Freddie Mac, the Mortgage Bankers Association, and several large banks) founded MERS to hold mortgages as a nominee for the note-holders. Under the MERS system, each residential mortgage either names MERS as the original mortgagee, or the original mortgagee assigns the mortgage to MERS immediately after origination. When the loan is subsequently transferred on the secondary market, MERS simply continues to be the holder of the mortgage, always serving as the nominee of the party who holds the note from time to time. MERS maintains a data base of note holders and servicers, and a borrower can query this data base to determine who holds and who services his or her mortgage loan.

The point of this system is to avoid the need for recording an assignment of the mortgage each time the loan is sold. This is an important objective, for recording assignments in the more than 3,600 local recording offices in the United States had become a major burden to secondary market investors. Under the MERS system, MERS is always the mortgage holder as shown in the local public records, and one needs to consult MERS' own records to determine who actually holds the loan. If a suit is filed that affects a MERS mortgage or the real estate it covers, MERS (as the mortgagee of record) is served with process, and it in turn notifies the actual holder of the note.

It is significant that MERS does not hold or take possession of the promissory notes (except in the case of electronic notes). Its responsibility is exclusively to hold the mortgages as nominee for the note holders. In most cases no further assignment of the mortgage is ever recorded by MERS, unless the note is transferred to a non-MERS member or an assignment is made to the servicer preparatory to foreclosure.

MERS served its function relatively smoothly and efficiently until the mortgage market largely collapsed in 2007. In the ensuing years, foreclosure defense lawyers launched a tide of litigation attacking numerous aspects of MERS' operations. Among the issues they raised were the following:

- Is MERS a "real party in interest" or otherwise entitled to notice of suits or administrative actions that might affect the interests of mortgagees?

- As a "nominee" for the mortgage holder, does MERS have authority to execute assignments or (in states using deeds of trust) to appoint substitute trustees.

- Does MERS have standing to foreclose mortgages in its own name? (This practice was dropped in 2011, but was remarkably controversial while it lasted.)

- Is MERS wrongfully depriving local recorders of the revenue they would earn if mortgage assignments were still being recorded locally?

- Does the placement of a mortgage with MERS somehow improperly separate the note from the mortgage, thus making the mortgage unenforceable?

- Are assignments by MERS valid, given the fact that they are typically executed by employees of the secondary market participants, who serve as nominal (and unpaid) officers of MERS? (There were also many attacks on the technical aspects of these assignments, often alleging them to be "robosigned.")

Most of the attacks on MERS were flimsy in terms of legal credibility, and MERS prevailed in court most of the time. But defending these attacks became extremely costly, and they took a real toll in terms of MERS' public reputation, as defaulting borrowers repeatedly claimed on blog posts that "MERS is taking my house."

U.S. BANK, N.A. v. BURNS
Missouri Court of Appeals, 2013
406 S.W.3d 495

GARY M. GAERTNER, JR., JUDGE.

Introduction

Jeana Burns (Appellant) appeals the trial court's summary judgment in favor of U.S. Bank National Association (U.S. Bank), as Indenture Trustee for the Registered Holders of Aegis Asset Back Securities Trust 2005–2, Mortgage Backed Notes (Securities Trust). Appellant also appeals the trial court's judgment on the pleadings in favor of Trustees of Wildhorse (Subdivision). Appellant argues that there are disputed issues of material fact that precluded summary judgment, and that the judgment on the pleadings erroneously included an unrelated party. We affirm the summary judgment and modify the judgment on the pleadings under Rule 84.14.

Background

On August 24, 1999, Appellant obtained title through a Missouri Warranty Deed to property located at 1536 Honey Locust Court in Chesterfield, Missouri (Property). Appellant recorded the warranty deed in the St. Louis County Records. The deed contained the Property's address as well as a correct legal description of the Property. Title to the Property is solely in Appellant's name. Also on August 24, 1999, Daryl Burns executed an Assent to Execution of Deeds and Waiver of Marital Rights, waiving any right to the Property. This document was also recorded in the St. Louis County Records.

On April 1, 2005, Appellant executed a promissory note (Note) in favor of Aegis Funding Corporation (Aegis) in the amount of $496,300.00. Attached to the Note was a deed of trust (Deed of Trust) for the Property that Appellant executed in favor of Aegis, to secure repayment of the loan. The Deed of Trust listed Mortgage Electronic Registration Systems, Inc. (MERS) as the beneficiary, and it stated that MERS acted as a nominee for Aegis. The Deed of Trust listed the Property's correct address but contained an incorrect legal description of the Property. Again, Daryl Burns executed an Assent to Execution of Deeds and Waiver of Marital Rights (Second Waiver), which was recorded in the St. Louis County

Records on April 8, 2005. This document contains the same incorrect legal description of the Property.

On January 31, 2008, MERS, as nominee for Aegis, executed an Assignment of Deed of Trust (Assignment) assigning all of its rights, title, and interest in the Deed of Trust "together with any and all notes and obligations therein described or referred to" to U.S. Bank, as Indenture Trustee for the Securities Trust. This Assignment was recorded in the St. Louis County Records, and it contained the same incorrect legal description of the Property.

On August 18, 2010, U.S. Bank filed suit against Appellant, Daryl Burns, and Subdivision, seeking in Counts I through III to reform the Deed of Trust, the Second Waiver, and the Assignment, respectively, to reflect the correct legal description of the Property. In Count IV, U.S. Bank requested that the trial court declare the Deed of Trust the first-priority lien against the Property and quiet title to the Property in Appellant's name, subject to the Deed of Trust.

In November 2011, Subdivision filed a cross-claim against Appellant and Daryl Burns requesting payment of outstanding subdivision assessments, late fees, and collection costs. Subdivision had previously recorded in the St. Louis County Records a lien against the Property for such fees, pursuant to Subdivision's policies applicable to the Property.

US Bank moved for summary judgment on all counts of its petition, and Subdivision moved for judgment on the pleadings regarding its cross-claim. The trial court granted both motions. In its summary judgment, the trial court ordered that the incorrect legal descriptions described above be reformed and declared the Deed of Trust a valid and enforceable lien against the Property. The trial court quieted title to the Property in the name of Appellant, subject to the Deed of Trust. In its judgment on the pleadings, the trial court ordered Appellant and Daryl Burns jointly and severally liable for subdivision fees and attorney's fees in the amount of $14,929.00. This appeal follows.

Discussion

Appellant raises two points on appeal. First, she argues that the trial court erred in granting summary judgment in favor of U.S. Bank, because a genuine dispute exists regarding a material fact, namely, whether U.S. Bank had an interest in the Property. In Point II, Appellant argues the trial court erred in granting Subdivision's motion for judgment on the pleadings against Daryl Burns, because he has no ownership interest in the Property. Subdivision agrees that Daryl Burns has no interest in the Property and should therefore have no liability for fees awarded by the trial court in its judgment on the cross-claim. Thus, Point II is granted. We consider Appellant's remaining point below.

Point I

Appellant argues the trial court erred in granting summary judgment because a genuine factual dispute exists regarding whether U.S. Bank was entitled to enforce the Deed of Trust. We disagree.

The trial court made the following finding:

> The Deed of Trust is held by [US Bank] and is a valid and enforceable lien against the Property and [US Bank] is entitled to enforce the provisions thereof.

Appellant's primary argument is that MERS' attempt in the Assignment to transfer the Deed of Trust together with the Note, when MERS was not a party to the Note, was ineffective. See *Bellistri v. Ocwen Loan Servicing, LLC*, 284 S.W.3d 619, 623 (Mo.App.E.D.2009) (invalidating attempted assignment of note with deed of trust where assignor was not party to note). However, given the circumstances here and applicable law, a different question requires threshold consideration.

In Missouri, "[a] deed of trust securing a negotiable note passes with it. . . ." *Goetz v. Selsor*, 628 S.W.2d 404, 405 (Mo.App.S.D.1982) (citing *Smith v. Holdoway Constr. Co.*, 129 S.W.2d 894, 899 (Mo.1939)). "[A] party entitled to enforce a note is also entitled to enforce the deed of trust securing that note. . . ." *In re Washington*, 468 B.R. 846, 853 (Bankr.W.D. Mo. 2011) (applying Missouri law). Thus, regardless of the Assignment, we first consider whether U.S. Bank is entitled to enforce the Note, and thereby the Deed of Trust with it.

Missouri has adopted the Uniform Commercial Code (UCC), which governs commercial transactions. Chapter 400, RSMo. (Supp.2012). Application of the UCC is straightforward regarding this question of who may enforce the Note. See *Washington*, 468 B.R. at 853. The holder of a negotiable instrument is entitled to enforce it. Section 400.3–301. A holder is one (1) who possesses the instrument, and (2) to whom the instrument is made payable. Section 400.1–201(20). Here, the Note was payable "to the order of Lender." "Lender," as defined by the Note, is Aegis. Aegis originally possessed the Note, and thus, Aegis was the original holder of the Note. Neither party disputes this fact.

US Bank contends it then became the holder of the Note by virtue of the endorsements on the Note made by Aegis. Endorsements made by the holder of a negotiable instrument are either "special" or "blank." Section 400.3–205. A special endorsement identifies a person to whom it makes the instrument payable. Section 400.3–205(a). Any endorsement by the holder that is not a special endorsement is a blank endorsement. Section 400.3–205(b). When an instrument is endorsed in blank, it becomes payable to its bearer and may be negotiated by transfer of possession alone until specially endorsed. Section 400.3–205(b); *Wohlschlaeger v. Dorsey*, 206 S.W.2d 677, 680 (Mo.App.1947).

US Bank attached a copy of the Note to its petition. U.S. Bank attached in its motion for summary judgment an affidavit by Nicole Melton, the Contract Management Coordinator of U.S. Bank's loan servicer, attesting that the copy of the Note attached to the petition was a "true and correct copy of the Note." That copy of the Note shows a special endorsement by Aegis, the original holder of the Note, to Aegis Mortgage Corporation. There is also a blank endorsement by Aegis Mortgage Corporation on the Note. U.S. Bank asserted in its reply memorandum in support of its motion for summary judgment that the Note was in its counsel's possession. U.S. Bank argues that the blank endorsement coupled with its possession of the Note makes U.S. Bank the holder of the Note. See Sections 400.3–205(b), 400.1–201(20).

Appellant disputes the validity of these endorsements. In her response to U.S. Bank's motion for summary judgment, Appellant offered a different copy of the Note. This copy did not contain any endorsements, and Appellant argues that a genuine factual dispute exists regarding whether the Note was endorsed to U.S. Bank. However, Appellant's copy of the Note had an attached allonge,[3] specially endorsing the Note to U.S. Bank, as Indenture Trustee of the Securities Trust.[4] Appellant also attached the affidavit of Johnna Miller, an authorized signer for Ocwen Loan Serving, LLC, the servicer for U.S. Bank. Ms. Miller attested that U.S. Bank was in physical possession of the Note and was the holder of the Note. Appellant does not dispute the validity of the allonge.[5]

Therefore, documents submitted by both parties in the record confirm U.S. Bank is in possession of the Note. Both copies of the Note contain endorsements: one specially to U.S. Bank on the attached allonge, and one in blank on the Note itself. Appellant has failed to establish the

---

[3] An allonge is "[a] piece of paper annexed to a negotiable instrument or promissory note on which to write endorsements for which there is no room on the instrument itself." *Bremen Bank & Trust Co. of St. Louis v. Muskopf*, 817 S.W.2d 602, 607 (Mo.App.E.D.1991) (quoting Black's Law Dictionary 100 (4th ed.1968)). An allonge is considered part of the note, and an endorsement on an allonge is effective even if there is room on the note for an endorsement. Section 400.3–204(a), Comment 1.

[4] Appellant also argues that U.S. Bank did not prove it was the Indenture Trustee for the Securities Trust, and therefore, U.S. Bank has no standing to enforce the Deed of Trust. In each document in the record relevant to the issue on appeal, where U.S. Bank appears, it is listed as the Indenture Trustee for the Securities Trust. Regardless, Appellant has not demonstrated how that fact, even if U.S. Bank was not the Indenture Trustee, is material to the determination of whether U.S. Bank is the holder of the Note under the UCC.

[5] In the summary judgment proceedings below, Appellant disputed the validity of the allonge based on its effective date in relation to a servicing agreement applicable to the Securities Trust. Appellant does not make this argument on appeal. Regardless, neither the date of any endorsement nor any provision of an outside servicing agreement is relevant to the determination under the UCC of whether U.S. Bank is the holder of the Note. See *Washington*, 468 B.R. at 852–53.

existence of a genuine factual dispute regarding either the endorsement of the Note to U.S. Bank or U.S. Bank's possession of the Note. These facts qualify U.S. Bank as the holder of the Note under the UCC. Section 400.1–201(20). As such, U.S. Bank is also the holder of the Deed of Trust, and therefore entitled to enforce the Deed of Trust. See *Washington*, 468 B.R. at 853. Thus, whether the Assignment effectively transferred the Deed of Trust to U.S. Bank is irrelevant. Point denied.

Conclusion

We find no genuine issue of material fact and no error of law in the trial court's conclusion that U.S. Bank was entitled to summary judgment as a matter of law. We affirm the summary judgment.

Regarding the trial court's judgment on the pleadings in favor of Subdivision, as neither the facts nor this Court's legal conclusion are in dispute, we exercise our ability to enter the proper judgment under Rule 84.14. See *Mitalovich v. Toomey*, 206 S.W.3d 361, 365 (Mo.App.E.D.2006) (modification of judgment is especially appropriate where there are no disputed facts). Therefore, we modify the trial court's judgment on the pleadings to remove Daryl Burns, and we affirm the judgment as modified in favor of Subdivision and against Appellant.

ROBERT M. CLAYTON, III, C.J., MICHAEL K. MULLEN, S.J., Concur.

NOTES

1. *The mortgage "follows the note."* The borrower's principal argument in the *Burns* case was that since MERS was not a party to the note, it had no right to assign the deed of trust securing it. This argument was consistent with the same court's earlier decision in Bellistri v. Ocwen Loan Servicing, LLC, 284 S.W.3d 619, 623 (Mo.App.E.D. 2009). There the court had said:

> When the holder of the promissory note assigns or transfers the note, the deed of trust is also transferred. An assignment of the deed of trust separate from the note has no "force." Effectively, the note and the deed of trust are inseparable, and when the promissory note is transferred, it vests in the transferee "all the interest, rights, powers and security conferred by the deed of trust upon the beneficiary therein and the payee in the notes." . . . MERS never held the promissory note, thus its assignment of the deed of trust to [the secondary market investor] separate from the note had no force.

But in the *Burns* case, the court's response to the borrower's argument that the assignment was ineffective was, "so what?" Since the note, which represents the debt, is the principal thing being sold, and since the mortgage is merely security for, or an accessory to, the note, any transfer of the right to enforce the note will *automatically* serve to transfer the right to enforce mortgage or deed of trust as well. No separate assignment of the mortgage or deed of trust is necessary in order to transfer the right to foreclose judicially (or in this case, nonjudicially). This is indeed the view of the vast majority of American courts. Dozens of cases could be cited; See, e.g., Deutsche Bank Nat. Trust Co. v. Matthews, 273 P.3d 43 (Okl. 2012); Restatement (Third) of Property (Mortgages) § 5.4(a). Sometimes courts explain this result by saying that a transfer of the right to enforce the note brings about an equitable assignment of the mortgage as well; see, e.g., Dow Family, LLC v. PHH Mortg. Corp., 838 N.W.2d 119 (Wis.App. 2013). Likewise, if there is an assignment of the mortgage but the note (assuming it is negotiable) is not delivered, the right of enforcement will not pass to the assignee; see In re American Equity Corp. of Pinellas, 332 B.R. 645 (Bankr. M.D. Fla. 2005).

Indeed, it is well nigh impossible to separate the mortgage from the note, and it is not clear why anyone would want to do so. After all, the note without the mortgage would be far less secure than with it, while the mortgage without the note would be essentially worthless, since the person who held the mortgage could not experience a default, and hence could never foreclose. The doctrine that the mortgage follows the note fulfills the important objective of keeping the two together, which is what the parties to the transfer want and expect in virtually all cases.

Observe carefully that here we are talking about the right to enforce: under the common law principle discussed in *Burns,* whoever obtains the right to enforce the note will also be able to enforce—that is, foreclose—the mortgage. This is quite distinct from the principle of U.C.C. § 9–203(g), discussed prior to the *Burns* case, which says that ownership of the mortgage will follow ownership of the note. That principle deals with the economic benefits of the note and mortgage, not the right to enforce them. In effect, it says that whoever is entitled to the financial proceeds of a suit on the note is also entitled to the financial proceeds of a foreclosure of the mortgage. Thus, just as there are two distinct aspects of the note (ownership and the right of enforcement) that can be transferred, there are two distinct ways (realization of the proceeds and the right of foreclosure) in which the mortgage can "follow the note." The right to enforce the mortgage follows the right to enforce the note under the common law principle used by the court in the *Burns* case. The ownership of the mortgage follows ownership of the note under U.C.C. § 9–203(g). This distinction between the two different ways that "the mortgage follows the note" is a subtlety that is often lost on lawyers and judges.

To say that a written assignment of a mortgage is unessential to foreclosure is not to say that it is a bad idea. On the contrary, use of mortgage assignments is an excellent practice, primarily because of the operation of the recording acts. Only a written mortgage assignment can be recorded, and recording, for reasons we will examine later, is very desirable from the viewpoint of the assignee. But an assignment is unnecessary to confer the right to foreclose judicially. Maine seems to be an exception with respect to judicial foreclosure; see Deutsche Bank Nat. Trust Co. v. Wilk, 76 A.3d 363 (Me. 2013) and Wells Fargo Bank, NA v. deBree, 38 A.3d 1257 (Me. 2012), apparently requiring proof of each link in the chain of mortgage assignments as a prerequisite to foreclosure. New Jersey has taken the same position by court rule, N.J. Ct. R. 4–64–1(b)(1–13), although the legal basis for the rule is uncertain, since the relevant statute, N.J. Stat. Ann. § 46:9–9, permits but does not require recording of assignments. But in nearly all other states, the note-holder can pursue judicial foreclosure without proof of an assignment of the mortgage. See, e.g., JP Morgan Chase Bank, N.A. v. Murray, 63 A.3d 1258 (Pa. Super. 2013) (holder of negotiable note can pursue foreclosure despite defects in chain of mortgage assignments).

Nonjudicial foreclosures are another matter. The Missouri court in *Burns* was quite willing to recognize the traditional rule that the right to foreclose the deed of trust follows the right to enforce the note, but at least a dozen nonjudicial foreclosure states have refused to do so, construing their statutes to require a chain of mortgage assignments as a prerequisite to foreclosure. We will return to this issue.

The other side of the coin, of course, is that one must have the right to enforce the note in order to foreclose the mortgage. See Kluge v. Fugazy, 536 N.Y.S.2d 92 (N.Y.App.Div. 1988) (where mortgage was assigned but note was excluded from assignment, assignee of mortgage could not foreclose); Restatement (Third) of Property (Mortgages) § 5.4(c): "A mortgage may be enforced only by, or in behalf of, a person who is entitled to enforce the obligation the mortgage secures." As we will see below, however, this concept is not always followed in nonjudicial foreclosures.

2. *Negotiability.* The *Burns* case seems to hold that the transfer of the right to enforce a note is governed by Article 3 of the Uniform Commercial Code. But this holding is correct only if the note in question is negotiable; Article 3 governs only negotiable notes, since it applies only to "instruments," and under UCC 3–104(b), " 'Instrument' means a negotiable instrument." Negotiability is a highly technical matter, and each note must be examined carefully to determine whether it is negotiable or not. It is disappointing, but not unusual, that the Missouri court simply assumed that the note before it was negotiable. That is a sloppy practice, but courts often do it. See Dale A. Whitman, How Negotiability Has Fouled Up the Secondary Mortgage Market, and What To Do About It, 37 Pepp.L.Rev. 737 (2010).

We will examine the requirements for negotiability in a moment. But suppose a particular note does not satisfy them, and therefore is not governed by UCC Article 3? In that case, a transfer of the right to enforce the note is presumably controlled by common law principles. There is, unfortunately, very little modern case law as to just what those principles are—a fact that may explain why courts so readily assume that notes are negotiable. Other examples of cases in which courts made that assumption without analysis include Provident Bank v. Community Home Mortg. Corp., 498 F.Supp.2d 558 (E.D.N.Y. 2007) and In re Woodberry, 383 B.R. 373 (D.S.C. 2008).

Now, back to Article 3. Under UCC § 3–104(a), in order to be negotiable, the instrument must:

- contain an unconditional promise * * * to pay a fixed amount of money, with or without interest or other charges;

- be payable to bearer or to order;

- be payable on demand or at a definite time;

- not state any other undertaking or instruction * * * to do any act in addition to the payment of money.

- Notwithstanding the foregoing, under UCC § 3–104(a)(3), a note can be negotiable even though it contains:

- an undertaking or power to give, maintain, or protect collateral;

- an authorization or power to the holder to confess judgment or realize on or dispose of collateral;

- a waiver of the benefit of any law intended for the advantage or protection of an obligor.

Finally, a note is considered conditional (hence, nonnegotiable) if it states an express condition, states that it is subject to or is governed by another writing, or states that rights or obligations with respect to its promise are stated in another writing. However, negotiability is not impaired by:

- a reference to another writing for a statement of rights with respect to collateral, prepayment, or acceleration;

- the fact that payment is limited to resort to a particular fund or source.

From these rules, one can see that, if negotiability is to be preserved, care must be taken in including references to mortgages in the notes they secure. A general statement that the note is secured by the mortgage is permissible, since it is merely a "statement of rights with respect to collateral." See Countrywide Home Loans, Inc. v. Randy St. Louis, 290 B.R. 1 (Bankr. E.D.N.Y.2003); Swindler v. Swindler, 355 S.C. 245, 584 S.E.2d 438 (Ct.App.2003). It is also acceptable to incorporate by reference in the note any specific terms of the mortgage that deal with "rights with respect to collateral, prepayment, or acceleration." See, e.g., In re Knigge, 479 B.R. 500 (8th Cir. 2012), finding that undertakings such as occupying the property, refraining from wasting or destroying the property, maintaining insurance on the property, and giving notice to lender of any losses related to the property were all within the Code's "give, maintain, or protect collateral" language and did not impair negotiability. But a general incorporation of the mortgage into the note will destroy negotiability, since Section 3–106 provides that the note is regarded conditional if "rights or obligations with respect to the promise or order are stated in another writing." See Resolution Trust Corp. v. 1601

Partners, Ltd., 796 F.Supp. 238 (N.D.Tex. 1992). The same is true of incorporation of other sorts of documents.

Nonrecourse notes, which provide that the maker has no personal liability and that the debt may be collected only from the real estate, were long held to be nonnegotiable on the ground that the promise to pay was not unconditional. However, the current version of Article 3, promulgated in 1990, reversed that rule, providing instead that a promise to pay is viewed as unconditional despite the fact that "payment is limited to resort to a particular fund or source." Likewise, under older versions of Article 3, adjustable rate notes were usually held nonnegotiable, but the current version of § 3–112(b) provides:

> Interest may be stated in an instrument as a fixed or variable amount of money or it may be expressed as a fixed or variable rate or rates. The amount or rate of interest may be stated or described in the instrument in any manner and may require reference to information not contained in the instrument.

3. *Is the standard residential note negotiable?* Virtually every residential mortgage loan made in the United States is written on the Fannie Mae/Freddie Mac Uniform Single Family Note. Hence, whether or not that particular note form is negotiable is a matter of crucial importance. In 1997 Professor Ronald Mann argued that the Fannie Mae/Freddie Mac Uniform Single-family Note form was nonnegotiable because Paragraph 4 of the note contains the statement, "When I make a prepayment, I will tell the Note Holder in writing that I am doing so." Mann observed,

> [T]hat provision appears to constitute an "undertaking . . . to do a[n] act in addition to the payment of money." For historical reasons codified in section 3–104(a)(3) of the U.C.C., a promissory note cannot be an instrument if it contains such an undertaking: the rules of negotiability apply only to promises to pay money, not to other, nonmonetary undertakings. Sending a notice certainly is an act "in addition to the payment of money," and the note's language seems to constitute an "undertaking" to perform that act (albeit only on certain conditions).

Ronald J. Mann, Searching for Negotiability in Payment and Credit Systems, 44 UCLA L.Rev. 951 (1997).

This argument went undiscovered by lawyers and the courts until 2010, but it has now been considered by perhaps a dozen courts, beginning with HSBC Bank USA, N.A. v. Gouda, 2010 WL 5128666 (N.J. Super. App.Div. 2010) (not reported in A.3d). All of them have rejected Mann's position and found the uniform residential note to be negotiable. They typically adopt this view on the grounds that (1) the borrower's decision to prepay principal is voluntary, not required; (2) the prepayment notification requirement imposes no additional financial liability on the borrower, and adds nothing to the promise to pay the debt; and (3) there is no penalty if the borrower fails to give the notification.

Whether this is correct in any ultimate sense is hard to say; none of the decisions is from the highest court of a state. The prepayment notice obligation in the Fannie Mae-Freddie Mac form is, by its nature, conditional; it applies only if the borrower elects to make a prepayment. As a matter of general principle, it is uncertain whether such an obligation falls under Section 3–104's proscription against "other undertakings" or not. But for the present, at least, it seems reasonable to assume that the standard residential note is negotiable.

The standard residential note form's negotiability has been attacked on a number of other grounds as well: that the note does not provide for a "sum certain" because it incorporates an obligation to pay property taxes and insurance premiums, and because it provides for collection of late charges; that the provision for application of payments in the note somehow constitutes an "other undertaking"; and that some forms of the note provide for adjustable interest. The courts have consistently rejected all of these challenges to the note's negotiability. See, e.g., In re Appponline.Com, Inc., 321 B.R. 614 (E.D.N.Y. 2003); Deutsche Bank Natl. Trust Co. v. Najar, 2013 WL 1791372 (Ohio App. 2013) (not published in N.E.2d).

4. *Transferring the right to enforce a negotiable note.* Reading the *Burns* case, one would likely conclude that under Article 3 the proper way to transfer the right of enforcement of a negotiable note is to endorse it (either in blank, or specially to the transferee) and deliver it, giving the transferee possession. This will work, but it is not the only way. Article 3 provides three methods of transferring the right of enforcement:

a. *Becoming a holder.* As *Burns* indicates, this will occur if the note has been delivered to and is in the possession of the person enforcing it, with an appropriate endorsement (either in blank—which makes the note a "bearer note," or specially—an endorsement that specifically identifies the person to whom the note is delivered). These actions will constitute the person who takes the note a "holder," entitling him or her to enforce the note. See, e.g., In re Walker, 466 B.R. 271, 280–81 (Bankr. E.D. Pa. 2012). No endorsement is necessary if the note was originally payable to "bearer;" see Bank of New York v. Raftogianis, 10 A.3d 236, 240 (N.J.Super.Ch.Div. 2010). Original bearer notes are virtually never used in real estate financing, but a note that has been endorsed in blank becomes a bearer note, so that the right of enforcement can then be further transferred by delivery of possession without the need for any additional endorsements.

b. *Becoming a nonholder who has the rights of a holder.* Under U.C.C. § 3–301(ii), this will occur if the note has been delivered to and is in the possession of the person enforcing it, but without an endorsement. In the absence of an endorsement, the person taking delivery cannot be a holder, but can still get the right of enforcement if the delivery was made for the purpose of transferring that right. The latter requirement may complicate enforcement or foreclosure, since the party in possession may be put to the burden of proving exactly how it acquired the note, and that the transfer to it was made for the purpose of giving the right of enforcement. See Leyva v. Nat'l Default Servicing Corp., 255 P.3d 1275, 1281 (Nev. 2011), requiring the servicer to provide specific, affirmative proof that the note was delivered to it for the purpose of transferring the right of enforcement. Avoiding this burden is the primary reason that endorsement of the note is wise and desirable. However, meeting the burden is usually possible; proof of the purpose of the delivery of the note might be provided through a mortgage assignment, a pooling and servicing agreement, or affidavits of the transferor's employees. See, e.g., Ulster Sav. Bank v. 28 Brynwood Lane, 41 A.3d 1077, 1085 (Conn.App. 2013).

c.   *Providing a "lost note affidavit."* Under U.C.C. § 3–309, a person who does not qualify to enforce the note under (a) or (b) above because of a lack of possession may still enforce it by providing a "lost note affidavit." See, e.g., Svrcek v. Rosenberg, 40 A.3d 494 (Md.App. 2012). However, the requirements for the affidavit are quite strict: the note must have been destroyed, its whereabouts not discoverable, or it must be in the wrongful possession of an unknown person or one who cannot be served. Before accepting such an affidavit, a court might well demand evidence as to the efforts that have been made to locate the note. See Correa v. U.S. Bank N.A., 118 So.3d 952 (Fla.App. 2013) (affidavit was insufficient, where foreclosure plaintiff did not prove the content of the note or the circumstances under which it was lost). In addition, the court can require the enforcing party to provide assurance (typically in the form of a bond or indemnity) against the possibility that the borrower will have to pay twice. See, e.g., First Const. Co. v. Tri-S. Mortg. Investors, 308 N.W.2d 298, 299 (Minn. 1981), approving requirement of a bond.

Florida, uniquely, has a statutory definition of what will constitute adequate protection against the borrower's having to pay twice. The list includes:

(a) A written indemnification agreement by a person reasonably believed sufficiently solvent to honor such an obligation;

(b) A surety bond;

(c) A letter of credit issued by a financial institution;

(d) A deposit of cash collateral with the clerk of the court; or

(e) Such other security as the court may deem appropriate under the circumstances.

Any security given shall be on terms and in amounts set by the court, for a time period through the running of the statute of limitations for enforcement of the underlying note, and conditioned to indemnify and hold harmless the maker of the note against any loss or damage, including principal, interest, and attorney fees and costs, that might occur by reason of a claim by another person to enforce the note.

Fla. Stat. 702.11. See Delia v. GMAC Mortg. Corp., 2014 WL 5284995 (Fla. App. 2014), refusing to grant foreclosure where the lender failed to produce proof that it had provided adequate protection.

5.   *Endorsement is essential to becoming a holder.* If one wishes to be a holder of negotiable note (method (a) above), an endorsement of the note, either in blank or special, is essential. A separate written assignment of the note or the mortgage plainly does not qualify; see Bremen Bank and Trust Co. of St. Louis v. Muskopf, 817 S.W.2d 602 (Mo.App. 1991); Bank of New York Mellon v. Deane, 970 N.Y.S.2d 427 (N.Y.Sup.Ct. 2013).

6.   *Transferring the right of enforcement of nonnegotiable notes.* On the other hand, if the note is not negotiable, and hence U.C.C. Article 3 does not apply, the right to enforce it can be transferred by assignment; see Kent v. Kent, 44 P.2d 445 (Cal.App. 1935). The assignment may be carried out in any of several ways: by endorsement on the note by the original payee-mortgagee; by the use of a separate document which the payee-mortgagee executes, stating that rights under the note are transferred to the assignee; or even by an oral statement to the assignee that a transfer is being made, at least if accompanied by a delivery. See Hill v. Alexander, 41 P. 1066 (Kan. App. 1895). Thus, the methods of transferring nonnegotiable notes are extremely flexible. However, there is very little modern authority on the transfer of nonnegotiable notes.

IN RE BASS

North Carolina Supreme Court, 2013
366 N.C. 464, 738 S.E.2d 173, 80 UCC Rep.Serv.2d 17

[The borrower (Bass) obtained a mortgage loan from Mortgage Lenders Network USA, which subsequently sold the loan to Emax Financial Group. After two additional secondary market transfers, the borrower defaulted and the current holder of the note commenced foreclosure proceedings. The borrower contested the validity of the transfer of the loan from Mortgage Lenders Network to Emax on the ground that the note was not properly endorsed because the endorsement lacked a valid signature.]

The UCC defines "signature" broadly, as "any symbol executed or adopted with present intention to adopt or accept a writing." N.C.G.S. § 25–1–201(b)(37) (2011). The official comment explains that, as the term "signed" is used in the Uniform Commercial Code, a complete signature is not necessary. The symbol may be printed, stamped or written; it may be by initials or by thumbprint. It may be on any part of the document and in appropriate cases may be found in a billhead or letterhead. No catalog of possible situations can be complete and the court must use common sense and commercial experience in passing upon these matters. The question always is whether the symbol was executed or adopted by the party with present intention to adopt or accept the writing.

Id. § 25–1–201 cmt. 37 (2011) (emphasis added). Thus, the UCC does not limit a signature to a long-form writing of an individual person's name. See 1B Lary Lawrence, Lawrence's Anderson on the Uniform Commercial Code § 1–201:385 (3d ed.2012) [hereinafter 1B Anderson]. Under this broad definition, "[t]he authenticating intent is sufficiently shown by the fact that the name of a party is written on the line which calls for the name of that party." *Id.* § 1–201:390. Even if there might be some irregularities in the signature, the necessary intent can still be found based on the signature itself and other attendant circumstances. Id. § 1–201:405. To the extent cases such as *Mayers v. McRimmon*, 140 N.C. 640, 53 S.E. 447 (1906), are superseded by the UCC in this context, they are overruled.

U.S. Bank was not the original lender with which Bass executed the Note. Therefore, each transfer required indorsement of the Note from one holder to the next. See N.C.G.S. § 25–3–201(b). Bass challenged the indorsement on the first transfer, which was evidenced by a stamp. While she acknowledges that a stamp can be a valid indorsement of a negotiable instrument, she asserts the stamp by Mortgage Lenders does not qualify as an indorsement under N.C.G.S. § 25–3–204(a). She relies on, inter alia, *Econo-Travel*, 301 N.C. at 204, 271 S.E.2d at 58, for the proposition that an indorsement must include some representation of an individual signature to be valid. Her reliance is misplaced, however, as *Econo-Travel* involved a promissory note lacking any indicia of indorsement to the plaintiff whatsoever. *Id.* at 203, 271 S.E.2d at 57. As such, *Econo-Travel* does not affect our analysis in the present case.

The contested stamp indicates on its face an intent to transfer the debt from Mortgage Lenders to Emax:

Pay to the order of:
Emax Financial Group, LLC
without recourse
By: Mortgage Lenders Network USA, Inc.

In addition, the stamp appears on the page of the Note where other, uncontested indorsements were placed. We also observe that the original

Note was indeed transferred in accordance with the stamp's clear intent. The stamp evidences that it was "executed or adopted by the party with present intention to adopt or accept the writing." N.C.G.S. § 25–1–201 cmt. 37. Under the broad definition of "signature" in N.C.G.S. § 25–1–201 and the accompanying official comment, the stamp by Mortgage Lenders constitutes a signature.

The stamp therefore was "an indorsement unless the accompanying words, terms of the instrument, place of the signature, or other circumstances unambiguously indicate that the signature was made for a purpose other than indorsement." Id. § 25–3–204(a) (emphasis added). With no unambiguous evidence indicating the signature was made for any other purpose, the stamp was an indorsement that transferred the Note from Mortgage Lenders to Emax.

Bass contends that U.S. Bank bore the burden of proving the indorsement was valid and authorized. We disagree. "[T]he authenticity of, and authority to make, each signature on the instrument is admitted unless specifically denied in the pleadings." Id. § 25–3–308(a) (2011). The official UCC comment to section 25–3–308 explains that "the signature is presumed to be authentic and authorized ... until some evidence is introduced which would support a finding that the signature is forged or unauthorized." Id. § 25–3–308 cmt. 1 (2011). Until the defendant produces such evidence, "the plaintiff is not required to prove that [the signature] is valid." Id. "The defendant is therefore required to make some sufficient showing of the grounds for the denial before the plaintiff is required to introduce evidence." Id.; see 6B Anderson § 3–308:9R; Hawkland §§ 3–308:2, 3–308:4.

The official comment explains the rationale behind the presumption in favor of the signature being authentic and authorized: "[I]n ordinary experience forged or unauthorized signatures are very uncommon, and normally any evidence is within the control of, or more accessible to, the defendant." N.C.G.S. § 25–3–308 cmt. 1. Under the UCC's General Definitions and Principles of Interpretation, "[w]henever this Chapter creates a 'presumption' with respect to a fact, or provides that a fact is 'presumed,' the trier of fact must find the existence of the fact unless and until evidence is introduced that supports a finding of its nonexistence." Id. § 25–1–206 (2011); see also 1B Anderson §§ 1–206:4, 1–206:5.

In the trial court, Bass made the bare assertion, "We don't know who had authority a[t] Mortgage Lenders Network to authorize the sale of (unintelligible) to E-max." She asserted, "[Y]ou have to have something more than a mere stamp." Yet Bass offered no evidence to demonstrate the actual possibility of forgery or error. Her bare assertions, with no supporting evidence, did not amount to a "sufficient showing of the grounds for the denial." N.C.G.S. § 25–3–308 cmt. 1; see also Dobson v.

Substitute Tr. Servs., Inc., 212 N.C.App. 45, ___, 711 S.E.2d 728, 731 (concluding the mortgagor's statement, "I cannot confirm the authenticity of the copy of the [n]ote produced by the Defendants," was insufficient to cast doubt upon the bank's status as holder of the promissory note), aff'd per curiam, 365 N.C. 304, 716 S.E.2d 849 (2011). Because Bass did not produce evidence to " support a finding that the signature [was] forged or unauthorized," the presumption in favor of the signature prevails and U.S. Bank was "not required to prove that it [was] valid." N.C.G.S. § 25–3–308 cmt. 1. Accordingly, Bass failed to overcome the presumption in favor of the signature, and the trial court erred in concluding the Note was not properly indorsed and transferred to Emax.

Tonya Bass stopped making payments on her mortgage and the loan went into default. In an attempt to prevent foreclosure, Bass asserted that U.S. Bank—which possessed the original Note—was not the holder of the Note. The indorsements on the Note unambiguously indicated the intent to transfer the Note from each preceding lender and finally to U.S. Bank. We hold that U.S. Bank is the holder of the Note and reverse the decision of the Court of Appeals.

NOTES

1. *Transferring the right to enforce a negotiable note (reprise).* While the court's treatment of the indorsement issues in *Bass* is correct and typical, it does make one error. The opinion states "each transfer required indorsement of the Note from one holder to the next." But as we have already seen, no indorsement is needed if the party seeking to enforce the note can qualify as a "non-holder with the rights of a holder" or can provide an acceptable lost note affidavit.

2. *Indorsement on an allonge.* People engaging in secondary mortgage market transactions often place their endorsements on an *allonge* rather than the original promissory note. An allonge is simply a separate piece of paper attached to the note. Allonges are usually more convenient to prepare from a mechanical point of view, and hence are very commonly used. Under earlier versions of U.C.C. Article 3, use of an allonge was permissible only if the there was insufficient space for the endorsement on the original note itself, but this is no longer a requirement; see Thomas v. Wells Fargo Bank, N.A., 116 So.3d 226 (Ala.Civ.App. 2012).

The allonge, to be effective, must be "affixed" to the note. See JP Morgan Chase Bank, N.A. v. Murray, 63 A.3d 1258 (Pa.Super. 2013) (loose allonge is insufficient to act as an endorsement). The decisions are surprisingly technical with respect to attachment to the note. It is clear that merely placing the allonge in the same file folder or envelope with the note is insufficient; see, e.g., Wells Fargo Bank, N.A. v. Freed, 2012 WL 6562819 (Ohio App. 2012) (not reported in N.E.2d). Gluing, pasting, or (probably) stapling is acceptable, but use of a paper clip or pin is not. See Wells Fargo

Bank, N.A. v. Bohatka, 112 So.2d 596 (Fla.App. 2013); Barry Hart Dubner, The Case of the $19 Million Staple, 6 Cooley L. Rev. 37 (1989). If the allonge was stapled to the note, but became detached in the process of photocopying it, the cases are divided; see In re Nash, 49 B.R. 254 (Bankr. D. Ariz. 1985).

Because of the risk that a stapled allonge can easily become detached from the note due to photocopying or handling, it is highly desirable that the allonge refer specifically to the note to which it is attached. Such a reference can easily make a difference in a court's determination that an allonge that has come loose constitutes an effective endorsement. See, e.g., SKW Real Estate Ltd. Partnership v. Gallicchio, 716 A.2d 903 (Conn.App. 1998). But this requires hand-tailoring of allonges, and it is plain from the descriptions of allonges in the cases that this is not usually done.

BOYCE v. AMERIHOME, INC. AND PLANETARY BANK N.A.*

Supreme Court of Erehwon, 2014
366 E.W.3d 489

A. NONYMOUS, C.J.

This case involves Ned and Charlotte Boyce, borrowers who claim that they were defrauded in their obtaining of a mortgage loan to purchase their house. The loan is currently held by Planetary Bank, which acts as trustee for a large securitized mortgage trust comprised of approximately 50,000 mortgage loans, of which the Boyces' is one. AmeriHome, Planetary's servicer, brought this action to foreclose the mortgage. We hold that, on account of Planetary Bank's status as a holder in due course under Article 3 of the Uniform Commercial Code, it is not subject to the Boyces' defense of fraud and may proceed to foreclose the mortgage.

This matter is before us on appeal from the denial by the district court of a motion for summary judgment made by the Boyces. The facts we recite are drawn from the parties' pleadings and affidavits. These documents are consistent with one another, and there is no material issue of fact. Hence the case is appropriate for disposition on summary judgment.

The Boyces purchased their house and entered into the loan transaction in February, 2007. The loan was arranged by Freddie Farmer, a residential mortgage broker, who placed the loan with Wonder Mortgage Co., a mortgage banking firm. The Boyces borrowed $357,000 for a 30 year term with an initial interest rate of 6.3%.

Farmer explained, and the Boyces understood, that the loan involved an adjustable interest rate (an "ARM" loan), that it would be adjusted

---

*   This case is imaginary, prepared by the editors of the book because we did not find an actual case that provided all of the elements we wished to include. —Eds.

annually, beginning at the start of the third year of the loan (sometimes called a 2/28 loan, since the rate is fixed for the first two years and adjustable thereafter), and that adjustments were to be based on an index equal to "the yield on United States Treasury Securities adjusted to a constant maturity of 1 year, as published by the Federal Reserve Board for the week preceding the date of interest rate adjustment." According to Bankrate.com, "Yields on Treasury securities at constant maturity are determined by the U.S. Treasury from the daily yield curve. That is based on the closing market-bid yields on actively traded Treasury securities in the over-the-counter market." This particular index is one of the most commonly-used indexes for ARM loans, and is commonly called the "one-year Treasury" index.

When the Boyces obtained the loan, the one-year Treasury rate was 5.05% and the starting rate on their loan was 6.3%. If their original interest rate had been a "fully-indexed rate," the "margin" (that is, the difference between their rate and the index) would thus have been 1.25%. During the first two years of their loan, U.S. Treasury yields fell precipitously, and by their first adjustment date, in February 2009, the one-year Treasury rate stood at only 0.62%. The Boyces (who are fairly literate in terms of financial matters) were aware of this decline in interest rates, and they expected their mortgage interest rate to be reduced accordingly when the first adjustment date arrived. They were shocked to receive a notice in early 2009, advising them that their rate was actually going up from 6.3% to 7.75%, and that their monthly payments would rise accordingly, from $2,210 to $2,535 per month.

The explanation for this increase was found in Paragraph 4(C) of their promissory note, which provided as follows:

> Before each Change Date, the Note Holder will calculate my new interest rate by adding SEVEN percentage point(s) (7.0%) to the Current Index. The Note Holder will then round the result of this addition up to the nearest one-fourth of one percentage point (0.25%).

Thus, at their first change date in February 2009, when the one-year Treasury rate stood at 0.62%, their new interest rate became 7.62%, which rounded up to 7.75%. By virtue the quoted language, their "margin" was not 1.25%, but was 7% instead.

The Boyces say that they did not realize it, but they had been given an "introductory" or "teaser" rate for the first two years of their loan. Their interest rate was certain to go up after the first two years, even if the Treasury bill index (and rates in general) did not change. Indeed, they were very fortunate that the index declined so much; if it had stayed the same, their new interest rate at the end of the introductory period would have been an astronomical 5.05% (the starting Treasury rate) plus 7%

(the margin), for a total of 12.05%, which would have rounded up to 12.25%!

But even the rate increase they actually received was too much for them. Mr. Boyce lost his position as a marketing director with a major oil company in 2008, and took a job as an assistant manager for a local grocery store at about half the salary. Mrs. Boyce, who had been employed as a public school teacher when the loan was obtained, had a child in late 2008 and quit her outside job. They struggled to pay the higher monthly payments that were imposed by the rate increase in 2009; they had half the income and a house payment that was more than $300 higher than when they bought the house. By this point their house had dropped in value by more than $100,000, and was worth at most $50,000 less than their mortgage balance. At the next subsequent interest rate adjustment date, in February 2010, their rate actually dropped to 7.5% but it was too little, too late. In mid-2010, they gave up, discontinuing making monthly payments on the loan. They have made no payments since.

Meanwhile, Wonder Mortgage Co. sold their loan to Maximum Finance Co. shortly after the loan was originated in 2007. A few months later, Maximum sold the loan into a so-called "private label" securitization, entitled "MaxMort Mortgage Certificates/Series 2007-AR10," with Planetary Bank as trustee. Planetary Bank employed AmeriHome, Inc. as servicer of the mortgages in the securitized pool.

In early 2011, AmeriHome commenced a judicial foreclosure proceeding against the Boyces in the Erehwon courts. The Boyces filed an answer raising various defenses, primarily praying for reformation of the mortgage documents on the ground of fraud. Both parties filed various affidavits relating to the origination, servicing, and transfer of the loan The Boyces then moved for summary judgment, and their motion was denied. This appeal followed.

The Borrowers' Defense. The Boyces base their defense to the foreclosure on the conduct of Freddie Farmer, the mortgage broker who arranged their loan from Wonder. Specifically, they allege that Farmer misrepresented the terms of the loan by telling them that their interest rate and monthly payments would go up only if the one-year Treasury index rate increased. In other words, he not only failed to tell them that they were receiving a "teaser rate" that was sure to increase even if the index rate did not, but he expressly stated that no such increase in their rate would occur.

They allege that he said this on several occasions. One of these was a telephone conversation on February 3, 2007, and Ms. Boyce was slow to answer the call, with the result that her answering machine turned on automatically and recorded the entire conversation. The Boyces provided a transcript of the conversation as an attachment to their pleading, and the following is an excerpt containing the relevant statements. AmeriHome does not dispute the accuracy of the transcript.

Ms. Boyce: I'm a little concerned about this adjustable rate thing. Are you sure that we don't have to worry about our interest rising in the future.

Mr. Farmer: Well, that could happen if the rates on Treasury debt go up, since that is the basis of your rate adjusting. Anyhow, you're locked in for the first two years.

Ms. Boyce: OK, I get the two-year thing. But after that, am I correct in understanding that our rate will go up only if the Treasury rate does?

Mr. Farmer: That's right. If there's no change in the Treasury rate, your rate can't change either. They are locked together.

Ms. Boyce: I guess this is all spelled out in the loan papers, right?

Mr. Farmer: It is, for sure. But they're written in the usual legal gobbledygook. I wouldn't bother trying to read them if I were you. After all, if you can't trust me, who can you trust?

These statements by Mr. Farmer were incorrect, and did not accurately portray the terms of the loan as stated in the Adjustable Rate Promissory Note that the Boyces signed.

In general, fraud can be established only by clear and convincing proof of the following elements:

> (1) the defendant made a false representation to the plaintiff, (2) the falsity of the representation was either known to the defendant or the representation was made with reckless indifference to its truth, (3) the misrepresentation was made for the purpose of defrauding the plaintiff, (4) the plaintiff relied on the misrepresentation and had the right to rely on it, and (5) the plaintiff suffered compensable injury as a result of the misrepresentation.

Frederick v. Hansen, 197 E.W.2d 29 (1964). See also Exxon Mobil Corp. v. Albright, 71 A.3d 30 (Md. 2013). Here most of these elements are obviously present. As we have already pointed out, the representation was false, and Farmer certainly should have been familiar with the terms of the loan he was arranging, and therefore should have known it was false. It was obviously made for the purpose of allaying the Boyce's concerns and thereby convincing them to take the loan. The tenor of Ms. Boyce's conversation makes it clear that the Boyces were relying on the information Farmer gave them, and the fact that their payments increased significantly, under circumstances in which Farmer said they would not increase, resulted in compensable injury to them. AmeriHome does not deny that Farmer made the quoted statements, nor does it contest any of these conclusions.

However AmeriHome argues that despite the falsity of Farmer's statements, they cannot constitute fraud because the true nature of the loan's terms was plainly spelled out in the documents the Boyces signed. Because of this fact, AmeriHome says the Boyces had no "right to rely" on Farmer's oral statements. The Boyces admit that they only looked over the note and other loan documents briefly and did not read them in detail. In oral argument, their counsel characterized the note as "filled with complicated legal and financial jargon that people can't understand even if they read it." (We observe that there is research tending to confirm this characterization; see Debra Pogrund Stark & Jessica M. Choplin, A License to Deceive: Enforcing Contractual Myths Despite Consumer Psychological Realities, 5 NYU J. Law & Bus. 617 (2009)).

There is no clear Erehwon precedent on this issue. Case law in other states is divided. A good illustration of reasoning denying the fraud claim is Evans v. Ameriquest Mortg. Co., 2003 WL 734169 (Mich.App. 2003) (not reported in N.W.2d). There the plaintiffs alleged that the defendant lender told them that the loan it was making would pay off both of the preexisting loans on their property. The court observed:

> However, even a cursory review of the documents signed by plaintiffs at closing would have revealed they continued to have a remaining balance on one of the existing mortgages after the refinancing. "[T]here can be no fraud where the means of knowledge regarding the truthfulness of the representation are available to the plaintiff and the degree of their utilization has not been prohibited by the defendant." Defendants did not prohibit plaintiffs from reading the documents, plaintiffs cannot claim fraud based on an alleged misrepresentation clearly contradicted by the documents.

> Plaintiffs also argue that defendants induced them not to read the documents. When a party's general fraudulent scheme prohibits the signer from reading the contract, then the signer's failure to read the contract provides no defense to the first party's fraud. However, taking plaintiffs' claim in the light most favorable to them, they have not shown a fraudulent scheme that induced them to sign the contract without reading the documents.

Similarly, in Vidal v. Liquidation Props., Inc., 104 So.3d 1274 (Fla.App. 2013), the court noted, "The second claim of 'fraud' is that the lender orally misrepresented the loan to be a fixed rate loan. However, the note and other documents the Vidals signed at the closing plainly indicate that the note had an adjustable rate. 'A party cannot recover in fraud for alleged oral misrepresentations that are adequately covered or expressly contradicted in a later written contract.' "

On the other hand, the California Court of Appeal found that fraudulent concealment might be established on facts considerably less compelling than those in the present case. In Boschma v. Home Loan Center, Inc., 129 Cal.Rptr.3d 874 (Cal.App. 2011), the borrowers entered into an "option ARM" loan with a "teaser rate," much like that in the present case. The consequence was that if the borrowers made payments on the schedule given to them at closing, their loan would experience "negative amortization"—that is, its outstanding balance would increase rather than be reduced over time—a fact that was never disclosed to them before closing, although it could be gleaned from a close reading of the complex language of the loan documents. Discussing the borrowers' fraud claim, the court said:

> The closer question is whether defendant can be deemed to have concealed or suppressed material facts even though at least some of these facts can be distilled from the loan documents through careful analysis of the Note and payment schedule. . . . [W]e conclude plaintiffs have adequately pleaded that material facts were concealed by inaccurate representations and half-truths. If plaintiffs can show defendant intentionally used its Option ARM forms to deceive borrowers, plaintiffs may be able to establish a fraud claim. Plaintiffs' actual interest rates and monthly payments sufficient to amortize the loan (or at least pay the accruing interest) were hidden in the complexity of the Option ARM contract terms. "The fact that a false statement may be obviously false to those who are trained and experienced does not change its character, nor take away its power to deceive others less experienced."

While the Boschma case was decided on a motion to dismiss, and the court recognized that the borrowers would still have the burden to prove the elements of fraud, the court's attitude toward borrowers who were lied to, but who could in theory have gained the truth by careful reading of the documents, is markedly more favorable than that of the Michigan and Florida courts.

We conclude, on the basis of the specific facts of the present case, that the Boyces have made out a defense of fraud. Several factors influence our decision: (a) The Boyces, while quite literate, are not financially or legally trained; (b) the language of the documents, as in Boschma, is complex and subtle; (c) Farmer encouraged them not to attempt to read the documents (although concededly he did not prevent them from doing so); and (d) Farmer's statement was an outright lie rather than merely a half-truth or concealment.

Responsibility of Wonder Mortgage for Farmer's fraudulent statements. What we have said thus far would be sufficient to establish Farmer's liability to the Boyces for fraud, but that is not the posture of this case. Farmer is not a party; his whereabouts are unknown and he could not be served or subpoenaed. We must therefore address the question of whether his misrepresentations can be attributed to Wonder Mortgage, the originator of the loan.

Under the principle of *respondeat superior*, an agent's actions within the scope of his or her authority are attributable to the principal. AmeriHome points out, as is undoubtedly true, that Farmer was an independent contractor, not an employee of Wonder. But that observation is beside the point; an independent contractor may have an agency relationship with a principal even though she or he is not an employee. See, e.g., LaSalle Bank Nat. Ass'n v. Bardales, 2009 WL 1312509 (Conn.Super. 2009) (not reported in A.2d); Zirkle v. Winkler, 585 S.E.2d 19 (W.Va. 2003). It is true that lenders have been held free of responsibility for the acts of the mortgage brokers when no agency relationship was shown to exist; see Menashe v. Bank of New York, 850 F.Supp.2d 1120 (D.Haw. 2012). But this conclusion is not inevitable, and depends on the facts. See, e.g., Mangindin v. Washington Mut. Bank, 637 F.Supp.2d 700 (N.D.Cal. 2009) ("Although a broker is customarily retained by the buyer, courts have rejected a bright line rule that a mortgage broker may never be the agent of a lender. Accordingly, general allegations of agency between a broker and lender are sufficient to survive a motion to dismiss on a negligence claim under California law."

In one case, cited in *Zirkel*, the court found that *respondeat superior* applied to a delivery driver for a newspaper, on the basis that

> when and how he was to perform his obligations was fixed in large measure by the terms of his "independent contractor" agreement; and the services he was required to render were "routine in nature, requiring diligence and responsibility, rather than discretion and skill."

In the present case, it is true that the Boyces originally contacted Farmer and asked him to help them arrange a loan. However, the Boyce's pleadings and affidavits point out the following uncontradicted facts relevant to Farmer's relationship to Wonder Mortgage. (1) While Farmer dealt with several lenders, approximately 65% of the loans he placed in 2006 and 2007 were with Wonder. (2) Farmer attended two seminars in 2006 put on by Wonder, the purpose of which was to train mortgage brokers in Wonder's loan requirements and underwriting standards. (3) Farmer received a daily "term sheet" by e-mail from Wonder, stating the terms on which it would accept loans, and he is alleged to have used that sheet in preparing the Boyce's loan documents. (4) Farmer used various disclosure forms provided by Wonder in preparing loan closings, including the Boyce's closing.

It is apparent that Farmer's discretion in making loans placed with Wonder was highly constrained by Wonder Mortgage's rules and policies. In light of these facts, we conclude that, with respect to the Boyces' loan, Farmer acted as an agent for Wonder, thereby making it equally responsible with Farmer for his fraudulent statements under the principle of *respondeat superior*.

The holder in due course doctrine. The present suit is not an action by the Boyces against Wonder, which is not a party to this action. Rather, they seek to use their fraud claim defensively, against the foreclosure action filed by AmeriHome as agent and servicer for Planetary Bank. They have prayed for reformation of the terms of their mortgage loan, and we assume that, if their fraud defense were recognized as against AmeriHome, they would be entitled to some relief along these lines. Unfortunately for them, it appears that they cannot assert the fraud against AmeriHome because it is protected by the holder in due course (HDC) doctrine. See the similar holding in Dauenhauer v. Bank of New York Mellon, 562 Fed.Appx. 473 (6th Cir. 2014). See also Short v. Wells Fargo Bank Minnesota, 401 F.Supp.2d 549 (S.D.W.Va.2005) (secondary market purchaser of note claimed insulation from defenses arising from fraudulent practices of originating mortgagee)

While the HDC doctrine has been recognized for centuries in Anglo-American common law, its modern form is expressed in Article 3 of the Uniform Commercial Code. In essence, an HDC is entitled to enforce an instrument notwithstanding certain defenses (termed "personal defenses") that the maker of the instrument might seek to raise. The core language is found in U.C.C. § 3–305(b), which states that "The right of a holder in due course to enforce the obligation of a party to pay the instrument is subject to defenses of the obligor stated in subsection (a)(1) ["real" defenses], but is not subject to defenses of the obligor stated in subsection (a)(2) ["personal" defenses] or claims in recoupment stated in subsection (a)(3) against a person other than the holder." We will return to the distinction between real and personal defenses later.

What proof must be satisfied for a party enforcing an instrument to be an HDC? First of all, *a fortiori* an HDC must be a "holder." According to U.C.C. § 1–201(21), " 'Holder' means the person in possession of a negotiable instrument that is payable either to bearer or to an identified person that is the person in possession." And under U.C.C. § 3–104(b), "Instrument" means a negotiable instrument. In the context of a mortgage note, these requirements add up to the following: to be a holder,

(a)   the note must be negotiable.

(b)   it must be in the possession of the person seeking to enforce it.

(c)   if the person seeking enforcement is not the original payee of the note, it must either have been endorsed specially to that person, or endorsed in blank.

In addition, the holder must be "in due course," which under U.C.C. § 3–302(a) requires the following:

(1)   the instrument when issued or negotiated to the holder does not bear such apparent evidence of forgery or alteration or is not otherwise so irregular or incomplete as to call into question its authenticity; and

(2)   the holder took the instrument (i) for value, (ii) in good faith, (iii) without notice that the instrument is overdue or has been dishonored or that there is an uncured default with respect to payment of another instrument issued as part of the same series, (iv) without notice that the instrument contains an unauthorized signature or has been altered, (v) without notice of any claim to the instrument described in Section 3–306, and (vi) without notice that any party has a defense or claim in recoupment described in Section 3–305(a).

With these requirements in mind, we examine the facts in the instant case. First, with respect to the negotiability of the note: the Boyce's loan was made using the standard Fannie Mae-Freddie Mac single-family residential note and mortgage. This note has been repeatedly held to be negotiable, and our research has disclosed no reported cases in opposition to this conclusion. See, e.g., In re Edwards, 76 UCC Rep.Serv.2d 220 (Bkrtcy.E.D.Wis. 2011); JP Morgan Chase Bank, N.A. v. Murray, 63 A.3d 1258 (Pa.Super. 2013). There is little point in repeating the analysis of prior cases on this point.

Second, AmeriHome is acting here as a servicing agent of Planetary Bank, which holds the note. It is generally agreed that an agent may act in a foreclosure proceeding on behalf of the note-holder; see, e.g., Arabia v. BAC Home Loans Servicing, L.P., 145 Cal.Rptr.3d 678 (Cal.App. 2012); Bank of America, N.A. v. Draper, 746 S.E.2d 478 (S.C.App. 2013). We see no reason not to follow this sensible rule in Erehwon. AmeriHome filed an affidavit stating that it has the original promissory note in its possession, with a photocopy of the note attached, and this assertion is uncontradicted. Thus, the requirement of possession is met.

Third, there is an appropriate endorsement on the note, as disclosed by the photocopy AmeriHome has provided. The original note was payable to Wonder Mortgage, Inc. The note bears an endorsement in blank, "Pay to the order of bearer," signed by Paul A. Morton in his capacity as Vice President of Wonder Mortgage. No further endorsement is necessary. (If the note had been endorsed specially to Maximum Finance, the intermediate holder, rather than in blank, then a further endorsement by Maximum Finance would have been necessary. But that is not the case here.)

Likewise, there is no dispute as to the "due course" with which Planetary Bank took the note. There is nothing on the note that suggests forgery or alteration, or indicates that it is irregular or incomplete. Planetary Bank took the note as part of a transfer of a large number of notes from Maximum Finance, for which a cash price was paid. At the time of the transfer, in May 2007, payments on the note were not in default. There is no indication in the record that Planetary Bank had any notice of Farmer's fraudulent statements, or of any other defense or claim to the note. In sum, Planetary Bank qualifies as a holder in due course.

Real and personal defenses. As mentioned above, HDC status gives Planetary Bank immunity from personal defenses, but not from real defenses. The defense of the Boyces here is based on fraud, which they stoutly argue is a real defense. Section 3–305(2) lists the real defenses. In brief, they are infancy, duress, lack of capacity, illegality, certain types of fraud, and discharge in insolvency proceedings. The personal defenses are not listed in the code, but consist essentially of all defenses except the "real" ones; they are generally thought to include lack of consideration, partial or total failure of consideration, accord and satisfaction, waiver, unconscionability, mutual mistake, and any sort of setoff or counterclaim which the debtor-mortgagor might raise against the original mortgagee. They also include fraud of a type other than that defined as a "real" defense in § 3–305.

The parties before us agree that the defense at issue in this case is fraud, but which sort of fraud is it? Under § 3–305(a)(1)(iii), "fraud that induced the obligor to sign the instrument with neither knowledge nor reasonable opportunity to learn of its character or its essential terms" is a real defense. This is roughly what is usually called "fraud in the execution;" the signer does not realize the nature of the document being signed, and cannot reasonably learn what it is or what it says.

The other type of fraud, which is a "personal" defense for HDC purposes, is usually termed "fraud in the inducement." Here the signer knows or can readily find out the nature and terms of the document, but is induced to enter into it by the other party's false representations.

Which of these characterizations best fits the present facts? The Official Comment to § 3–305 says that, in making this determination, "age, sex, education, intelligence, business experience, linguistic ability, relationship with the payee, and the urgency of the transaction should all be considered, as should the availability of some other person, perhaps a friend or relative, who might have been able to advise the maker."

We conclude that this case involves fraud in the inducement. The Boyces surely knew that the note they signed was indeed a promissory note, obligating them to repay their loan. They are both relatively young (in their 40s), college-educated, native English speakers, and fully competent. There is no indication in the record that they were rushed or pressured to hurry the transaction. If they had taken the time and trouble, they could have read the note in detail, and if they wished, sought advice about its terms from a lawyer or accountant. They did not do so, preferring instead to take the word of a lying mortgage broker about their obligations. While they were deceived by Farmer's statements, we must conclude that they had "reasonable opportunity to learn of [the note's] character or its essential terms."

The Boyces have a defense based on fraud, but it is not the sort of fraud that constitutes a "real" defense under § 3–305. Hence, it cannot be asserted against Planetary Bank and AmeriHome, Planetary's servicer, and we must disregard it in the present foreclosure action. It is well settled that, just as "the mortgage follows the note," the mortgage also partakes of the note's immunity from personal defenses; see, e.g., In re AppOnline.com, Inc., 290 B.R. 1 (Bankr.E.D.N.Y. 2003) and 321 B.R. 614 (E.D.N.Y. 2003); Hunt v. NationsCredit Financial Services Corp., 902 So.2d 75 (Ala.Civ.App. 2004); Yanfag v. Cyfred, Ltd., 2009 WL 5214891 (Guam Terr. 2009). Hence, if the defense would be irrelevant in an action to collect the note (as it would), it is also irrelevant in a proceeding to foreclose the mortgage.

Breaches of the Pooling and Servicing Agreement. When the securitization known as "MaxMort Mortgage Certificates/Series 2007-AR10" was created, Maximum Finance was established as a "special purpose entity," intended to be "bankruptcy-remote" from the sponsors of the securitization. All loans were to be transferred to Maximum Finance, and from it to Planetary Bank in its capacity as trustee for the bondholders. The rules governing these transfers were set out in a Pooling and Servicing Agreement (PSA), a complex legal document signed by Maximum Finance as "Depositor," Planetary Bank as "Trustee," and AmeriHome as "Servicer."

Article II of the PSA sets out the requirements for transfer of the loans to the Trustee. However, the parties agree that some of these requirements were not met. Specifically:

1. Within 90 days of the "start date" of the securitization (which was May 1, 2007), each promissory note was to have been delivered to Planetary Bank as Trustee. AmeriHome concedes that this was not done, and in fact the Boyce's note was not delivered until early in 2011).

2. Within the same period, each mortgage was to have an assignment of mortgage executed by the previous holder (in this case the originator, Wonder Mortgage) to Maximum Finance and recorded in the public records of the relevant local county or town. This was not done within the 90-day window required by the PSA, and so far as we can tell, it has never been done with the Boyce's mortgage. (We might mention here that under Erehwon law, no chain of mortgage assignments need be proved as a condition of foreclosing the mortgage.)

The Boyces argue that, because of these apparent breaches of the PSA, the transfers of the mortgage loans are void and consequently that Planetary Bank and its servicer cannot enforce them. However, this argument has been rejected repeatedly by the great majority of courts that have considered it, usually on the ground that borrowers are not parties to (or third-party beneficiaries of) the PSA, and therefore have no standing to enforce it. See, e.g., Dauenhauer v. Bank of New York Mellon, 562 Fed.Appx. 473 (6th Cir. 2014); Wells Fargo Bank, N.A. v. Strong, 89 A.3d 392 (Conn.App. 2014); HSBC Bank USA, N.A. v. Sherman, 2013 WL 5436540 (Ohio App. 2013) (not published in N.E.2d); Dernier v. Mortgage Network, Inc., 87 A.3d 465 (Vt. 2013).

Some courts have held that the standing issue turns on whether the transfer was void or voidable, with third parties having standing if the transfer was absolutely void. However, these same courts have virtually all held that a transfer in nonconformity with the PSA is merely voidable, thus denying standing to borrowers who seek to attack it. See, e.g., Rubio v. U.S. Bank, N.A., 2014 WL 1318631 (N.D.Cal. 2014) (not reported in F.Supp.2d); Calderon v. Bank of America N.A.; 941 F.Supp.2d 753 (W.D.Tex. 2013); Bank of America N.A. v. Bassman FBT, LLC, 981 N.E.2d 1 (Ill.App. 2012). This conclusion may seem difficult to reach if the trust is governed by New York law, since New York Estate Powers & Trusts Law § 7–2.4 states that "every act in contravention of the Trust is void." However, the courts have repeatedly held that "void" does not mean absolutely void under New York law, but rather means voidable. See, e.g., the *Dernier*, *Calderon* and *Bassman* cases cited above; Mooney v. Madden, 597 N.Y.S.2d 775 (N.Y.App.Div. 1993) (beneficiaries can ratify an act of the trustee that would otherwise be *ultra vires* and void under New York law).

There are dozens of cases denying borrowers standing to enforce a PSA, and to our knowledge, only two published cases that disagree. See Glaski v. Bank of America, N.A., 160 Cal.Rptr.3d 449 (Cal.App. 2013);[1]

---

[1] The purpose of the PSA's requirement for delivery within 90 days of the securitization's "start date" is evidently to ensure compliance with Internal Revenue Code Sec. 860. This section is popularly known as the "REMIC rule" (for "Real Estate Mortgage Investment Conduit.") Under Sec. 860, a mortgage securitization trust is treated as an income pass-though entity (rather than a taxable entity) if the rules are met. This status is, of course, extremely desirable.

Wells Fargo Bank, N.A. v. Erobobo, 2013 WL 1831799 (N.Y.Sup. 2013) (not reported in N.Y.S.3d). We note that *Glaski's* reasoning has been rejected by several other courts; see Moran v. HSBC Bank USA, N.A., 2014 WL 3851305 (N.D.Cal. 2014); Yvanova v. New Century Mortgage Corp., 172 Cal.Rptr.3d 104 (Cal.App. 2014); Keshtgar v. U.S. Bank, N.A., 172 Cal. Rptr. 3d 818 (2014), review granted 334 P.3d 686 (Cal. 2014). Likewise, Rajamin v. Deutsche Bank Nat. Trust Co., 757 F.3d 79 (2d Cir. 2014) has refused to follow *Erobobo*. We, too, decline to follow *Glaski* and *Erobobo*.

Moreover, we think all of these arguments are misconceived because they confuse ownership with the right of enforcement. The right to enforce the note (and therefore the mortgage) depends exclusively on compliance with Article 3's requirements. The nature and details of the underlying transaction are simply irrelevant, provided that the note is negotiable, was properly endorsed, and is in Planetary's possession. Given the fact that the note was endorsed in blank, Planetary could enforce it even if they had *stolen* it, unless the obligor could assert a defense based on proof that the note had been lost or stolen. See Washington Mut. Bank v. Roggio, 2012 WL 3600071 (N.J.Super. App.Div. 2012) (not reported in A.3d); U.C.C. § 3–305(c).

One requirement, found in § 860G(a)(3), is that the trust's mortgages must be "purchased by the REMIC within the 3-month period beginning on the startup day if . . . such purchase is pursuant to a fixed-price contract in effect on the startup day."

It thus appears that a REMIC trust that purchased mortgages outside the 3-month period might be at risk of losing its non-taxable status, a consequence that could be financially devastating to its bond-holders. However, it is not entirely clear whether the terms "purchase" and "transferred" refer to ownership or the right to enforce the note and mortgage. As we have already discussed, the right of enforcement can be transferred only by delivery of possession, which in the present case did not occur within the 90-day window. But transfer of ownership can be accomplished, under U.C.C. § 9–203(b), by "authenticating" (signing) a "security agreement" (an assignment of ownership) that describes the note, as well as by delivery of possession. In this case, Section 2.02 of the original PSA contained the following language of present transfer of ownership:

> "The Depositor, concurrently with the execution and delivery hereof, does hereby transfer, assign, set over and otherwise convey to the Trustee without recourse for the benefit of the Certificateholders all the right, title and interest of the Depositor in and to the Mortgage Loans identified on the Mortgage Loan Schedule."

Since the PSA itself was executed on the start date, the 90-day transfer requirement was easily complied with if the PSA identified the Boyces' note in the Mortgage Loan Schedule, and if it is ownership that must be transferred. But I.R.C. § 860G(3) and the accompanying regulations are obscure as to whether it is ownership or the right of enforcement (or both) that must be transferred within the 90-day window. It seems likely that Congress was unaware of the distinction when it adopted § 860.

We mention these matters only parenthetically. While they are potentially of crucial importance to the securitization, they must be resolved, if at all, between Planetary Bank and the Internal Revenue Service, and have no bearing on the bank's right to foreclose the mortgage in this case. The *Glaski* case treats them as relevant, in the sense that holding the transfer void, if it occurs outside the 90-day window, has the effect of protecting the securitization's tax status—but at the cost of denying it the right to enforce the mortgage, of course. We do not agree that these matters concerning the trust's tax status should be considered in a foreclosure case.

Note carefully that we are addressing the right to enforce the note, not its ownership. Whether the alleged breaches of the PSA are sufficient to deny Planetary's ownership is a question that is not before us. As we have already pointed out, the right to foreclose the mortgage attaches to the right to enforce the note, not to its ownership. Hence, for purposes of this foreclosure action, it does not matter whether the purported transfer of ownership of the note to Planetary was void or not.

Conclusion. We conclude that, despite the fraud with which the Boyces were victimized when they obtained their loan, they have no legal basis for resisting the foreclosure of the mortgage on their house.

We are not happy with this result. The HDC doctrine was originally designed to ensure that notes and other debt instruments issued by financial institutions would be acceptable in the stream of commerce. Indeed, until the 1860s, such bank notes were the only form of currency in circulation in the United States. It is obvious how disruptive it would be if the institutions issuing such notes could raise defenses when called upon to pay them.

But today, in cases like the present one, the HDC doctrine has been stood on its head. It is being used, not to protect consumers from defenses raised by banks, but to protect banks from defenses raised by consumers. See Kurt Eggert, Held up in Due Course: Codification and the Victory of Form over Intent in Negotiable Instrument Law, 35 Creighton L.Rev. 363 (2002). It is not apparent to us why investors who buy mortgage notes should not be held to investigate and stand behind the actions of those who originate the notes they buy, and to bear the risk of loss if they fail to do so. Given the fact that such investors have ample means and mechanisms for verifying the qualifications of both borrowers and loan originators with whom they do business, and that all except the most foolish investors actually do so, it is hard to see what essential role the HDC doctrine plays in the nation's economic life. And in some individual cases like this one, it bears harshly indeed on borrowers.

But the doctrine, while invented by the courts, is now statutory, and not within our province to change or question. Our task is to apply the law as it stands, and under the law, the Boyces are subject to foreclosure. The district court's order denying summary judgment for the Boyces is affirmed.

ALL CONCUR.

NOTES

1. *Defenses and claims.* The court in *Boyce* quotes U.C.C. § 3–305, which points out that a holder in due course is insulated from certain *defenses* that the maker of the instrument might raise. But a HDC also takes

free of *claims,* of which there are two different types. One is a "claim in recoupment," which is in essence an offset asserted by the maker of the note to an attempted enforcement. A claim in recoupment must arise from the transaction that gave rise to the instrument itself; see Hathorn v. Loftus, 726 A.2d 1278 (N.H. 1999). Under § 3–305(b), claims in recoupment are treated like personal defenses; hence, if a claim in recoupment is based on the conduct of someone other than the present holder, it can't be asserted against an HDC.

The other type of claim against which a HDC is protected (by U.C.C. § 3–306) is a claim *to the instrument.* By "claim," § 3–306 means "a claim of a property or possessory right in the instrument or its proceeds." Thus, HDCs are protected with respect to their ownership. Non-HDCs, on the other hand, take subject to preexisting claims; see In re Valentine, 146 B.R. 945 (Bankr. E.D.Va. 1991). Cases involving ownership claims against HDCs are not as common as those involving defenses, but they do arise.

One fairly recent example is In re AppOnline.com, Inc., 321 B.R. 614 (E.D.N.Y. 2003). A mortgage company that was in serious financial straits sent a check to a title company to fund a loan the mortgage company was making, with the title company acting as closing agent. The title company disbursed the funds, but the bank on which the check was drawn refused to pay it because the mortgage company had insufficient funds in its account. The title company sued, claiming that it was entitled to an equitable lien on the note and mortgage to help the title company reimburse itself for the loss that it had suffered as a result of the bad check. However, the mortgage company had transferred the note to an HDC, and on the basis of U.C.C. § 3–306 the court held that that HDC prevailed over the title company's claim.

Another example is Provident Bank v. Community Home Mortg. Corp., 498 F.Supp.2d 558 (E.D.N.Y. 2007). Community was a mortgage banker that obtained a warehouse line of credit from Southwest Bank. Community adopted a practice of having its residential borrowers execute two original copies of each promissory note, a practice known as "double-booking" the loans. It then delivered one copy of each note to Southwest as collateral for the line of credit, and at about the same time sold the other copies on the secondary market to Netbank. The court resolved the conflict by noting that the notes received by Netbank had been endorsed by Community, while the notes delivered by Southwest had not. Hence, it found that Netbank was a holder in due course, Southwest was not, and Netbank prevailed. Oddly, the court never cited § 3–306, although it seems directly applicable and supports the court's conclusion.

Because ownership of a note is ordinarily the province of Article 9, but claims of ownership against a HDC are governed by § 3–306, you might wonder whether these two provisions of the Uniform Commercial Code could lead to disparate or inconsistent results. For example, suppose the note had been delivered to a HDC, but the original payee had also assigned its ownership to a different party by a written assignment (as Article 9 would permit). As it turns out, no inconsistency is possible, for § 9–331(a) provides "This article does not limit the rights of a holder in due course of a negotiable instrument, a holder to which a negotiable document of title has been duly negotiated, or a protected purchaser of a security." Thus, if a claim against a HDC arises, § 3–306 will override Article 9.

2. *Non-holders in due course and patent equities.* Suppose a mortgage note is non-negotiable, or is negotiable but is transferred to one who does not qualify as a HDC. Under these circumstances the freedom from the maker's personal defenses granted by the U.C.C. to HDCs will not apply. If the note is negotiable but the holder is not a HDC, U.C.C. § 3–305(a)(2) makes the assignee subject to any "defense of the obligor that would be available if the person entitled to enforce the instrument were enforcing a right to payment under a simple contract." If the note is non-negotiable, the common law reaches the same result. See Lapis Enters., Inc. v. International Blimpie Corp., 84 A.D.2d 286, 445 N.Y.S.2d 574 (1981) (fraud defense can be asserted against assignee in good faith of a nonnegotiable note); Nelson, Whitman, Burkhart & Freyermuth, Real Estate Finance Law § 5.32 (6th ed. 2014).

The assignee of a note who believes that HDC protection may be lacking often wisely demands that the maker provide an "estoppel certificate" at the time of the transfer, averring that the note is valid and not subject to defenses by the maker. These certificates are generally effective; see Soler v. Klimova, 774 N.Y.S.2d 126 (N.Y.App.Div. 2004); Tinnes v. Immobilaire IV, Ltd., 2001 WL 122073 (Ohio App.2001) (not reported in N.E.2d) (person who relies on estoppel certificate may assert it whether or not identified in it). If they are broadly drafted, they can provide even better protection for the assignee than would the HDC doctrine, since they can insulate the assignee from both real and personal defenses of the maker. The maker's defenses in this context are often termed "patent" defenses or "patent equities," since by demanding an estoppel certificate the assignee of the note can bring them to light. By contrast, a "latent" defense or equity is a claim to the instrument, or a claim that will defeat it, by someone other than the maker—so that an estoppel statement by the maker is of no value in ferreting it out.

However, even for patent equities, an estoppel certificate is not always a panacea. As the New York Court of Appeals pointed out in Hammelburger v. Foursome Inn Corp., 54 N.Y.2d 580, 446 N.Y.S.2d 917, 431 N.E.2d 278 (1981), the assignee must actually rely on the certificate, and must not know that the facts differ from the certificate's recitations. Moreover, if the certificate itself was obtained by fraud or duress, the mortgagor will not be estopped by it and can later contradict its statements.

3. *The "close-connectedness" doctrine.* Certain other judge-made limitations on the holder-in-due course doctrine may have implications for the assignment of real estate mortgage debt. One such doctrine is the "close connectedness" concept. Under this theory holder-in-due-course status is lost if the purchaser of a negotiable note is too closely connected with the transferor; the purchaser is regarded as lacking "good faith." Professors

White and Summers have delineated several factors that tend to point toward "close connectedness." (The term "lender" refers to the assignee of the note.)

    (1)   Drafting by the lender of forms for the seller.

    (2)   Approval or establishment or both of the seller's procedures by the lender (e.g., setting of the interest rate, approval of a referral sales plan).

    (3)   An independent check by the lender on the credit of the debtor or some other direct contact between the lender and the debtor.

    (4)   Heavy reliance by the seller upon the lender (e.g., transfer by seller of all or a substantial part of his paper to one lender).

    (5)   Common or connected ownership or management of seller and lender.

See James J. White & Robert S. Summers, Uniform Commercial Code § 14–6 (6th ed. 2010); Schneberger v. Wheeler, 859 F.2d 1477 (11th Cir.1988) (applying Florida law); Miller v. Diversified Loan Serv. Co., 181 W.Va. 320, 382 S.E.2d 514 (1989). The doctrine was developed in the context of consumer credit transactions, and the courts have been quite reluctant to apply it in commercial loans. See, e.g., Equico Lessors, Inc. v. Ramadan, 493 So.2d 516 (Fla.App. 1986) ("In a commercial setting, more than just a close connection must be shown before an assignee will be denied the status of a holder in due course."); A.I. Trade Fin., Inc. v. Altos Hornos de Vizcaya, S.A., 840 F.Supp. 271 (S.D.N.Y. 1993) (in a commercial loan, "although a close connection may facilitate the holder's actual discovery and notice of fraud, the close relationship alone cannot create an issue of the holder's notice.)"

On the other hand, close-connectedness is alive and well in consumer transactions. Indeed, if the connection is close enough, one might ask whether it might form a basis, not merely for allowing the mortgagor to resist the lender's foreclosure action or suit on the note, but for permitting the mortgagor an affirmative recovery against the lender. That is precisely what happened in Union Mortg. Co. v. Barlow, 595 So.2d 1335 (Ala. 1992). The mortgagor was defrauded by a home improvement contract who had very close and long-standing ties to the mortgage company that purchased its mortgage loans. The jury awarded her $6 million in punitive damages against the mortgage company!

    4.   *The decline of the HDC doctrine.* During the past several decades, a number of states have reversed or modified the holder in due course doctrine in consumer transactions by individualized statutes. See e.g., 9 Vt.Stat.Ann. § 2455 ("indebtedness of a consumer"); West's Rev.Code Wash.Ann. § 63.14.020 (retail installment contracts). In addition, the Uniform Consumer Credit Code, drafted by the National Conference of Commissioners on Uniform State Laws, abolishes the HDC doctrine in "consumer loan" and "consumer credit sale" transactions. The UCCC was originally promulgated

in 1968, and that version has been adopted by at least seven states: Colorado, Indiana, Oklahoma, South Carolina, Utah, Wisconsin and Wyoming. A new draft was released in 1974 and has been adopted in Idaho, Iowa, Kansas and Maine.

The demise of the HDC doctrine in consumer credit transactions was predicted to be cataclysmic, but in fact was absorbed by credit providers with scarcely a hiccough. See Ralph J. Rohner, Holder in Due Course in Consumer Transactions: Requiem, Revival, or Reformation? 60 Cornell L.Rev. 503 (1975); James J. White & Robert S. Summers, Uniform Commercial Code § 14–1 (4th ed.1995).

The impact of the UCCC and the other state statutes mentioned above on mortgage transactions is rather marginal. Most mortgages are given to secure repayment of loans of money or payment for the real estate itself, rather than payment for goods or services; hence, they are not regarded as "consumer credit" transactions, and the statutes mentioned have no effect on them at all. Perhaps the UCCC's greatest mortgage-law consequences arise when a consumer enters into a contract for home improvement services (e.g., the installation of aluminum siding), and gives a note secured by a mortgage in payment.

5. *The FTC rule.* The Federal Trade Commission virtually eliminated the HDC doctrine in consumer credit transactions by a "trade regulation rule" adopted in 1975 entitled "Preservation of Consumers' Claims and Defenses." Under this rule, it is an unfair trade practice for a seller of goods or services to finance a sale without including in the note or other evidence of debt ("consumer credit contract") language that makes the seller and any subsequent assignee subject to the consumer's claims and defenses. 16 C.F.R. § 433 1–2. This language must be in at least ten point bold face type and reads as follows:

> **"NOTICE. ANY HOLDER OF THIS CONSUMER CREDIT CONTRACT IS SUBJECT TO ALL CLAIMS AND DEFENSES WHICH THE DEBTOR COULD ASSERT AGAINST THE SELLER OF GOODS OR SERVICES OBTAINED WITH THE PROCEEDS HEREOF. RECOVERY HEREUNDER BY THE DEBTOR SHALL NOT EXCEED AMOUNTS PAID BY THE DEBTOR HEREUNDER."**

See Hempstead Bank v. Babcock, 115 Misc.2d 97, 453 N.Y.S.2d 557 (1982). While the primary impact of the rule is on seller financing, third party purchase-money loans are also covered if a type of close-connectedness test is satisfied. Under this requirement, a third party lender comes within the rule if the seller of goods or services "refers consumers to the lender or is affiliated with the creditor by common control, contract, or business arrangement." 16 C.F.R. § 433.1(d).

The FTC rule covers only natural persons purchasing goods or services for personal, family or household use, and only purchases of $25,000 or less.

16 C.F.R. §§ 433.1(b), 433.1(d)(e). Real estate mortgages are affected only to the extent that they secure payment for such goods and services. 16 C.F.R. § 433.1(c); Associates Home Equity Servs., Inc. v. Troup, 343 N.J.Super. 254, 778 A.2d 529 (App.Div.2001). Consequently, a mortgage loan used to buy a house, whether it has first or junior lien status, is untouched by the rule.

6. *The federal holder-in-due-course doctrine.* A bulk purchaser of a lender's inventory of loans cannot be a holder in due course; see UCC § 3–302(c); Bankers Trust (Delaware) v. 236 Beltway Inv., 865 F.Supp. 1186 (1994). However, when a federally-insured financial institution becomes insolvent and its assets are transferred in bulk to the Federal Deposit Insurance Corp. (FDIC), a different rule obtains:

> The federal holder in due course doctrine bars makers of promissory notes from asserting personal defenses against the FDIC and its successors in connection with purchase and assumption transactions involving troubled financial institutions. * * * The FDIC enjoys this protection as a matter of federal common law so that it may achieve the congressional mandate of the "sound, effective, and uninterrupted operation of the [nation's] banking system with resulting safety and liquidity of bank deposits."

Sunbelt Savings FSB, Dallas v. Montross, 923 F.2d 353 (5th Cir.1991) (holding that *non*-negotiable notes are not protected by the federal HDC doctrine). The HDC doctrine protects the federal agencies both when they are acting as receivers for insolvent institutions and when, in their corporate capacities, they acquire ownership of an institution's assets. It has also been held to protect parties who acquire notes from the federal agencies; see Hudspeth v. Investor Collection Servs. Ltd. Partn., 985 S.W.2d 477 (Tex.App. 1998).

However, the opinion in O'Melveny & Myers v. F.D.I.C., 512 U.S. 79, 114 S.Ct. 2048, 129 L.Ed.2d 67 (1994) suggests that the only protection the FDIC enjoys against defenses is that arising from the federal statute, 12 U.S.C. § 1823(e). The circuits are split as to whether the federal holder in due course doctrine remains viable. Compare Murphy v. FDIC, 61 F.3d 34 (D.C. Cir. 1995) (only statutory protection available to FDIC) with Motorcity of Jacksonville v. Southeast Bank, 83 F.3d 1317 (11th Cir. 1996) (common law protections remain available to FDIC).

7. *Predatory lending.* Both federal and state statutes that attempt to control or penalize predatory mortgage lenders may withdraw the protection of the holder in due course doctrine from secondary market purchasers of predatory loans. The federal statute, the Home Equity and Ownership Protection Act of 1994 ("HOEPA") provides that:

> Any person who purchases or is otherwise assigned a mortgage referred to in section 1602(aa) of this title shall be subject to all claims and defenses with respect to that mortgage that the consumer could assert against the creditor of the mortgage, unless

the purchaser or assignee demonstrates, by a preponderance of the evidence, that a reasonable person exercising ordinary due diligence, could not determine, based on the documentation required by this subchapter, the itemization of the amount financed, and other disclosure of disbursements that the mortgage was a mortgage referred to in section 1602(aa) of this title.

15 U.S.C.A. § 1641(d)(1).

HOEPA's definition of covered loans was expanded by the 2010 Dodd-Frank Act and the ensuing regulations of the Consumer Financial Protection Bureau. Effective January 10, 2014, loans were covered if they met any of the following criteria (with the dollar figures adjusted annually for inflation):

- The transaction's annual percentage rate (APR) exceeds the applicable average prime offer rate by more than 6.5 percentage points for most first-lien mortgages, or by more than 8.5 percentage points for a first mortgage if the dwelling is personal property and the transaction is for less than $50,000;

- The transaction's APR exceeds the applicable average prime offer rate by more than 8.5 percentage points for subordinate or junior mortgages;

- The transaction's points and fees exceed 5 percent of the total transaction amount or, for loans below $20,000, the lesser of 8 percent of the total transaction amount or $1,000; or

- The credit transaction documents permit the creditor to charge or collect a prepayment penalty more than 36 months after transaction closing or permit such fees or penalties to exceed, in the aggregate, more than 2 percent of the amount prepaid.

More detail about HOEPA is found in Chapter 8, Section E of this book.

8.   *Possible changes.* The Holder in Due Course doctrine continues to be controversial. Consumer advocates generally oppose it, believe it should have been eliminated for mortgage loans by the FTC when it adopted its 1975 rule discussed above, and continue to press for its repeal or substantial weakening with respect to mortgage loans today. Secondary market investors, and especially the securitization industry, claim to view it as sacrosanct and predict dire consequences if it is weakened or eliminated. In 2014 the American Law Institute created an advisory group to consider possible significant changes in the HDC doctrine in the context of home mortgage notes. At the same time, the drafting committee for the Uniform Home Foreclosure Procedures Act, a project of the Uniform Law Commission, was also considering making changes in HDC. Where these efforts will lead, and whether they will come to fruition, is uncertain, but it seems likely that change is in the wind.

9.   *Nonjudicial foreclosures.* About 30 states, by statute, provide a procedure for foreclosing mortgages without the necessity of a judicial action. In about half of these states, the security document is a "deed of trust" instead of a mortgage, and the foreclosure is handled by the trustee named in the deed of trust. All of the U.S. states continue to allow traditional common-law judicial foreclosures as well, so the nonjudicial procedure is only an option. However, in most of the states permitting them, nonjudicial foreclosures are highly popular among lenders because they are regarded as cheaper and quicker than judicial proceedings. You'll learn a great deal more about nonjudicial foreclosures in Chapter 6 of this book.

Under most nonjudicial foreclosure procedures, having standing to foreclose is established in exactly the same way as in a judicial foreclosure—by producing proof that the party seeking to foreclose has the right of enforcement of the promissory note. The proof is commonly by means of an affidavit or a statement or notice that the foreclosing party must record in the public records and serve on the borrower. For example, in the *Burns* case above, you'll recall the court pointing out that in Missouri "a party entitled to enforce a note is also entitled to enforce the deed of trust securing that note. . . ." Most states using nonjudicial foreclosure continue to follow this perfectly sensible approach.

However, the past few years, the courts of eight states have construed their nonjudicial foreclosure statutes as *not* requiring any proof, evidence, or even allegation that the foreclosing party has the right to enforce the promissory note. In those states, all of our discussion above concerning the methods of transferring the right of enforcement under U.C.C. Article 3 are simply irrelevant in a nonjudicial foreclosure. The result is bizarre; it stems from inadequate drafting of the original statutes (whose drafters in most cases seem to have been unaware that secondary mortgage market existed), combined with an unwillingness on the part of the courts to recognize that the statutes should be read in *pari materia* with the Uniform Commercial Code.

The states reaching this result are Alabama, Arizona, California, Georgia, Idaho, Minnesota, Michigan, and Texas. The cases are discussed in Dale A. Whitman & Drew Milner, Foreclosing on Nothing: The Curious Problem of the Deed of Trust Foreclosure Without Entitlement to Enforce the Note, 66 Ark.L.Rev. 21 (2013). The conclusion these courts have reached is by no means inevitable; the Massachusetts Supreme Judicial Court, faced with the same issue, read its foreclosure statute as effectively incorporating U.C.C. Article 3's principles for transferring the right of enforcement of the note. See Eaton v. Federal Nat'l Mortg. Ass'n, 969 N.E.2d 1118 (Mass. 2012).

If holding the note is not the relevant indicium of the right to foreclose, what is? Surely there is *some* form of evidence that must exist to confer the right to foreclose—even if there is no court in which to present it unless the borrower brings an action to enjoin the foreclosure. The recent decisions in the group of eight states identified above often do not make this question easy to answer. Depending on the jurisdiction, it may be a photocopy of the note, a chain of assignments (possibly recorded, possibly not), or perhaps either a chain of assignments or possession of the note. California is a particular mystery, since it appears that neither the right to enforce the note nor a recorded chain of assignments is necessary to give one authority to instruct the trustee of a deed of trust to foreclose. See Debrunner v. Deutsche Bank Nat. Tr., 138 Cal.Rptr.3d 830 (Cal.App. 2012) (no proof of the right to enforce the note is required to foreclose nonjudicially); Haynes v. EMC Mortgage Corp., 140 Cal. Rptr. 3d 32 (Cal.App. 2012) (recorded assignment of deed of trust unnecessary to foreclose nonjudicially); Johnson v. PNC Mortgage, 2014 WL 6629585 (N.D. Cal. 2014) (party may foreclose even if assignment of deed of trust is defective).

NOTE ON SECONDARY MARKET REPURCHASE OBLIGATIONS

Contracts between mortgage originators and secondary market purchasers almost invariably contain numerous representations and warranties by the originator/seller. Among the common ones are the following:

- The seller is a properly formed entity, licensed to do business in the state where the loans were made, with legal authority to originate and to sell the loans.

- The seller is solvent and the information concerning its financial condition that has been provided to the purchaser is true and correct.

- The sale of the loans will not violate any law or breach any contract or duty of the seller, or any court order.

- The sale of the loans is in the ordinary course of business and is not a "bulk transfer."

- The seller's originating and servicing practices are legally proper, and the escrow accounts for taxes and insurance have been properly set up and maintained. The seller is an approved seller/servicer by Fannie Mae and Freddie Mac (even though this may be a sale to a private entity).

- The seller has not made any materially inaccurate or misleading statements concerning the loans to the purchaser.

- The seller is a member in good standing of MERS, and has complied and will comply with all MERS rules and procedures.

- All mortgages being sold have the priority (first or second) that has been attributed to them.

- All payments due from the loan escrow accounts for taxes, insurance, etc. have been paid.

- None of the notes or mortgages has been modified, and no mortgagor has been released from liability.

- The notes and mortgages are not subject to any defense or setoff; none of the mortgagors was in bankruptcy when the loan was originated.

- All of the properties are insured in a manner complying with Fannie Mae and Freddie Mac guidelines.

- The loans are not in default, or subject to any event that would become a default with the passage of time.

- None of the loans are "high cost" loans under HOEPA, and none are subject to any state or local predatory lending law.

There may be many more "reps and warranties," but these give a flavor of what can be expected. If the loans being sold are "subprime," the last of the reps and warranties listed above may need to be modified.

The agreement will typically provide that if a breach of the reps and warranties is discovered by the purchaser, it will give the seller a limited time (e.g., 60 days) to correct the breach. If the breach is not corrected within that time, the purchaser can require the seller to repurchase the loan.

Repurchase by the seller may also be required if the loan goes into "early default." Definitions of "early default" vary; under one version, the seller must buy back the loan if any of the first three mortgage payments after the sale becomes more than 30 days delinquent, or if the mortgagor files bankruptcy within the first three months after the sale of the loan.

Fannie Mae and Freddie Mac follow similar procedures, but with some variations. For example, if Freddie Mac determines that a loan is deficient and requests the seller to repurchase it, the seller has 30 days to file an appeal. If the appeal is denied, the repurchase must then take place within 15 days. See Freddie Mac, Industry Letter (Sept. 4, 2008).

A large number of lawsuits have been filed recently by secondary market purchasers who alleged that mortgage originators had failed to repurchase mortgage loans as required by their contracts. In some cases, however, the originators had become insolvent, so that it was unlikely that recovery by the secondary market investors would come close to equaling their losses. The claims were based on both loans in default when the secondary market sale occurred, thus breaching the warranties and representations in the contract, and loans that defaulted soon after the sale, triggering an "early default" repurchase obligation. See, e.g., DLJ Mortg. Capital, Inc. v. Fairmont Funding, Ltd., 920 N.Y.S.2d 1 (N.Y.App.Div. 2011) (court refused to find that purchaser had waived or was estopped to assert repurchase provision); Bank of America, N.A. v. Wells Fargo Bank, N.A. by and through Midland Loan Serv., 2014 WL 3639190 (N.D. Ill. 2014) (not reported in F.Supp.2d) (finding that the purchaser had a duty to mitigate its damages by proper servicing while it held the loan, and such duty could affect the amount it was entitled to recover in the repurchase transaction).

NOTE ON TRANSFERS OF MORTGAGE SERVICING

As we have already noted, the process of collecting and accounting for mortgage loan payments, maintaining escrow or reserve accounts to pay property taxes and hazard insurance, and dealing with defaults and foreclosures is known loosely as "servicing" of a loan. When a portfolio lender (e.g., a savings and loan association) makes a loan and retains it in portfolio, it is both the "investor" and the "servicer." But quite frequently the functions of investor and servicer are split from one another. For example, lender A may originate the loan, transfer ownership of it to B, and retain the servicing. Alternatively, lender A may originate the loan, transfer ownership to B, and sell the servicing rights to C.

The servicer is, of course, the agent of the owner or investor, and represents it in dealing with the borrower. Servicers earn fees for their work; a typical annual fee for a residential loan might be in the range of .0020 to .00375 (20 to 37½ "basis points") of the loan amount. Thus, a servicer might earn $200 to $375 per year for servicing a $100,000 loan. In addition to the servicing fee, the servicer earns interest on the balance in the tax and insurance escrow accounts it holds. This "float" can be quite significant, and is a material attraction to lenders who seek servicing contracts. Servicers are also allowed to keep late fees, inspection fees, and some other miscellaneous fees.

There are obvious economies of scale in servicing. In an age of computer-based systems, the expense of servicing a portfolio of 100,000 loans is much less than 100 times as great as servicing a portfolio of 1,000 loans. Hence there are economic incentives for large servicers to become even larger, purchasing servicing rights from smaller entities. Servicing can be freely transferred, and a very active market in servicing rights exists in the United States.

But transfers of servicing can be confusing and frustrating to borrowers. They may find that they can no longer deal with the "friendly" local institution that originated their loans, but instead must contend with faceless bureaucrats in Detroit or Dallas, reachable only by toll-free numbers that seem always to be busy or that connect to endless voice-mail chains. Payments may be miscredited or lost when servicing is transferred. Smooth, careful transfers seem the exception rather than the rule.

As a result of consumer complaints about servicing transfers, Congress, in the Cranston-Gonzalez Affordable Housing Act of 1990, added to RESPA (the Real Estate Settlement Procedures Act) a new Section 6 that deals with transfers of servicing. It requires that at the time of loan application, the borrower must be informed of the lender's practices in terms of servicing transfers—that is, how likely it is that servicing will be transferred. See Rochester Home Equity, Inc. v. Upton, 1 Misc.3d 412, 767 N.Y.S.2d 201

(Sup.Ct.2003). In addition, if an actual transfer of servicing occurs, the borrower must be given notice by the transferor 15 days before, and by the transferee 15 days after the transfer. Section 6 also contains a grievance procedure and a provision for civil damages and penalties against lenders who fail to comply with it.

In addition, Section 404(a) of the Helping Families Save Their Homes Act of 2009 requires an assignee of residential loan to notify the borrower of the transfer within 30 days after it occurs, even if there is no change of servicing. The borrower may recover actual or statutory damages for a breach of this duty. Note that this obligation to provide notice of loan transfers imposes a duty only on the transferee and not the transferor, and in this way differs from the 1990 statute discussed above requiring notification of changes in servicing, under which both parties must provide notice. Both statutes are analyzed carefully in Gale v. First Franklin Loan Services, 701 F.3d 1240 (9th Cir. 2012).

NOTE ON THE PAYMENT PROBLEM

Suppose you borrow money from a bank on a mortgage loan. Subsequently you desire to pay off the loan. You go to the bank and tender a check for the balance due, which the bank duly accepts. What you do not know is that the bank assigned your note and mortgage to another investor some months earlier. If the bank fails to remit your payment to the present holder of your note, are you liable to the holder to pay it again? At first blush, the question seems absurd; how can you be held responsible for failing to pay the assignee when you had not been informed that any assignment had been made or that any assignee existed? Surely you cannot be forced to pay again.

Amazingly, under traditional legal principles, this conclusion is wrong! Payment to the assignor is ineffective against the assignee, even though the payor had no idea that there *was* an assignee. Of course, the assignor is liable for failing to forward or refund the payment; see Hilgeman v. American Mortg. Securities, Inc., 994 P.2d 1030 (Ariz.App. 2000). But if the assignor is missing or insolvent, the payor is out of luck! The precise reason for this result depended on whether the promissory note was or was not negotiable.

Nonnegotiable notes. If the note was nonnegotiable, the common law of "symbolic writings" governed. Under this concept, the note was regarded as a physical reification of the debt itself. The Contracts Restatement put it this way:

> [A]n obligor who renders performance without requiring production of such a symbolic writing takes the risk that the person receiving performance does not have possession of the writing either because he has assigned it or because his right is defective. Nonproduction has the same effect as receipt of notification of assignment or reason to know of a defect in an assignee's right. In addition, the obligor who performs without surrender or cancellation of or appropriate notation on the writing takes the risk of further obligation to an

assignee who takes possession of the writing as a bona fide purchaser.

Restatement (Second) of Contracts § 338, cmt. h, at 80 (1981). In effect, this rule meant that the payor was expected to demand to see the note before making each payment, and demand its surrender before making a final payoff.

Negotiable notes. If the note was negotiable, U.C.C. Article 3 governed, and produced the same result. UCC § 3–602 (1990) provides that an instrument is paid, and the payor is discharged, "... to the extent that payment is made ... to a person entitled to enforce the instrument." Under § 3–301, the phrase "person entitled to enforce" includes a holder to whom the instrument has been negotiated. Significantly, it also includes any person to whom the instrument is delivered for the purpose of giving the right of enforcement, even if that person is not a holder; U.C.C. § 3–203(a), (b). Thus, a transfer by delivery of the instrument without an indorsement will not constitute the transferee a holder, but the transferee is still entitled to enforce the instrument. Comment 1 of U.C.C. § 3–203 explains the matter this way:

> [A negotiable] instrument is a reified right to payment. The right is represented by the instrument itself. The right to payment is transferred by delivery of possession of the instrument "by a person other than its issuer for the purpose of giving to the person receiving delivery the right to enforce the instrument."

The code never explicitly stated that delivery of the instrument vests the power to discharge the obligation *exclusively* in the person "entitled to enforce" the instrument, but that was the widespread understanding. Consequently, if the original payee delivered possession of the instrument to someone else for the purpose of transferring the right of enforcement, a subsequent payment to the original payee would not discharge the obligation. This result followed whether the new possessor of the instrument was a holder or was "in due course" or not. In effect, the payment had simply been made to the wrong person—a person who no longer had the power to discharge the obligation. See Whitehead v. American Security & Trust Co., 285 F.2d 282, 284 (D.C.Cir.1960).

Hence in theory no lawyer, title company, or escrow company should ever conduct a closing in which a mortgage loan is being paid off without first demanding to see the existing note. But it is often very inconvenient for the lender to produce the note. Remember that the original note, and not merely a photocopy, must be examined. It may be held in a vault in the lender's home office in another city, for example, or (more commonly these days) in the vault of a custodian in New York or Chicago. Producing it takes time and costs money. As a practical matter, closing agents usually don't bother; they trust the lender, and sometimes that trust is misplaced. And if the "payment" rule is impractical with regard to final payments, it is obviously even more out of touch with reality with respect to regular monthly payments. In Equity

Bank v. Gonsalves, 44 Conn.Supp. 464, 691 A.2d 1143 (1996), the court described the standard doctrine discussed above, and then commented:

> The reason given [for the payment rule] is that the maker can protect himself by demanding production of the instrument and refusing to pay a party not in possession of it. * * * To this court that reason does not make sense as to a mortgage note payable monthly. A mortgagor cannot be expected every month he makes a payment to ask a mortgagee bank to prove [its] possession of the note. See Dale A. Whitman, Reforming the Law: The Payment Rule as a Paradigm, 1998 B.Y.U. L. Rev. 1169 (1998).

Changing the rule: nonnegotiable notes. For a long time there was widespread agreement among real estate lawyers (and some courts) that the "payment" rule described above was undesirable and introduced unnecessary risk and complexity in financing transactions. However, changing it proved to be a slow process. When Restatement (Third) of Property (Mortgages) was issued in 1997, § 5.5 rejected the "payment" rule, providing instead that "performance of the obligation to the transferor is effective against the transferee if rendered before the obligor receives notice of the transfer." This language, if followed by the courts, should eliminate the "payment" rule with respect to nonnegotiable notes. Of course, only time will tell whether courts will do so; there are as yet no cases under § 5.5. See EMC Mortg. Corp. v. Chaudhri, 946 A.2d 578 (N.J.Super. App.Div.2008), purporting to reject the Restatement and finding that recording of the mortgage assignment gave constructive notice of the transfer. However, the case involves not payment to the transferor, but the right to foreclose of the transferee.

In addition, the Mortgages Restatement recognizes that the traditional rule continues to operate with respect to negotiable notes, since they are governed by U.C.C. Article 3, and Restatements can't repeal statutes. Only an amendment to U.C.C. Article 3 could accomplish that purpose.

Changing the rule: negotiable notes. In 2002, the Permanent Editorial Board of the U.C.C. adopted a change involving the first four subsections of U.C.C. § 3–602. The key change is in subsection (b).

> (a) Subject to subsection (e), an instrument is paid to the extent payment is made by or on behalf of a party obliged to pay the instrument, and to a person entitled to enforce the instrument.

> (b) Subject to subsection (e), a note is paid to the extent payment is made by or on behalf of a party obliged to pay the note to a person that formerly was entitled to enforce the note only if at the time of the payment the party obliged to pay has not received adequate notification that the note has been transferred and that payment is to be made to the transferee. A notification is adequate only if it is signed by the transferor or the transferee, reasonably identifies the transferred note, and provides an address at which payments subsequently are to be made. Upon request, a transferee shall

seasonably furnish reasonable proof that the note has been transferred. Unless the transferee complies with the request, a payment to the person that formerly was entitled to enforce the note is effective for purposes of subsection (c) even if the party obliged to pay the note has received a notification under this subsection.

(c) Subject to subsection (e), to the extent of a payment under subsections (a) and (b), the obligation of the party obliged to pay the instrument is discharged even if payment is made with knowledge of a claim to the instrument under Section 3–306 by another person.

(d) Subject to subsection (e), a transferee, or any party that has acquired rights in the instrument directly or indirectly from a transferee, including a party that has rights as a holder in due course, is deemed to have notice of any payment that is made under subsection (b) after the note is transferred to the transferee but before the party obliged to pay the note receives adequate notification of the transfer.

The need for subsection (d) might not be apparent in light of subsection (b), which seems to do the trick by itself. A new Official Comment to subsection (d) explains that its purpose is to prevent holders in due course from losing the other immunities from defenses that their status would otherwise give them:

> Subsection (d) assures that the discharge provided by subsection (c) is effective against the transferee and those whose rights derive from the transferee. By deeming those persons to have notice of any payment made under subsection (b), subsection (d) gives those persons "notice of the discharge" within the meaning of Section 3–302(b). Accordingly, the discharge is effective against those persons, even if any of them has the rights of a holder in due course. * * * The deemed notice provided by subsection (d) does not, however, prevent a person from becoming, or acquiring the rights of, a holder in due course. * * * Thus, such a person does not become subject to other defenses described in Section 3–305(a)(2), claims in recoupment described in Section 3–305(a)(3), or claims to the instrument under Section 3–306.

Unfortunately, this amendment has been enacted in only twelve states at this writing.

The effect of the "payment" rule. Although the "payment" rule may seem harsh, its practical effect is largely limited to transactions among natural persons rather than institutions. While the transfer of institutional mortgages on the secondary market is pervasively common, so also is the practice of designating the originating mortgagee or some other firm as the agent of the assignee for purposes of "servicing" the loan. As we have already seen, servicing entails, among other things, receiving the mortgage payments from the mortgagor. It is perfectly plain that the mortgagor will be protected in continuing to make payments to the servicer so long as an agency relationship exists. See Skott v. Bank of America Illinois, 468 S.E.2d 359 (Ga. 1996).

One might argue that the courts should be extremely aggressive in finding agency relationships even among non-institutional mortgagees and assignees—perhaps even implying an agency merely from the fact that the mortgagor continued making regular payments to the mortgagee after the assignment, and that the assignee made no objection to the mortgagor. For a good example of such aggressive lawmaking, see Rodgers v. Seattle-First Nat'l Bank, 697 P.2d 1009 (Wash.App. 1985).

NOTES ON RECORDATION OF MORTGAGE ASSIGNMENTS

Is it necessary or relevant to record an assignment of a mortgage? We have already seen that, as between the parties to a transfer of a note and mortgage, no assignment of the mortgage is necessary; a transfer of the note (usually by endorsement and delivery of it) will automatically transfer the mortgage rights as well. Nonetheless, use of an separate assignment of the mortgage is customary. As we have suggested above, the document may be either in the form of an outright transfer or an assignment for security purposes, depending on the nature of the transaction.

The notes below discuss whether and when recording of an assignment is significant. More detail on each of these situations is found in Nelson, Whitman, Burkhart & Freyermuth, Real Estate Finance Law § 5.33 (6th ed. 2014). For convenience of notation, we will use the following descriptions of the parties: MR is the original mortgagor and ME the mortgagee; A1 is the first assignee of the mortgage and A2 the second (from the original mortgagee). GE is a grantee who purchases the property from MR after the mortgage has been given and assigned. The relationship of these parties may be diagramed as follows:

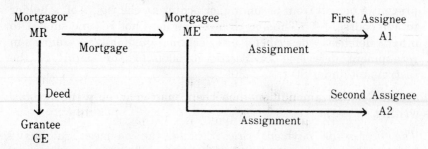

Bear in mind that not all of these parties are necessarily involved in each of the following situations. In fact, A2 and GE do not appear in most of them.

1. *Validity of the assignment as between the parties.* General principles of recording law make it clear that recordation is unnecessary to the validity of any instrument as between the parties to it. See Stoebuck & Whitman, Property § 11.9 (3d ed. 2000). Thus ME and A1 are bound by the assignment

whether it is recorded or not. In any event, as we have already discussed, that the assignment is not essential to A1's ability to foreclose the mortgage judicially; that ability follows from A1's having the right to enforce the note.

Perhaps it goes without saying that recordation of a mortgage assignment is not necessary to preserve the priority of the mortgage as against other interests in the land. That priority is established by the original recording of the mortgage itself, and simply continues if the loan is sold or pledged on the secondary market; see In re Cook, 457 F.3d 561 (6th Cir. 2006); In re Patton, 314 B.R. 826 (Bankr. D. Kan. 2004).

2. *Failure to record as excusing the mortgagor's default.* Assume MR mortgages land to ME, and ME assigns the mortgage to A1. The assignment is not recorded. Then MR defaults, A1 institutes foreclosure, and MR defends by pointing out A1's failure to record. This defense will fail, of course; the recording acts are intended to protect subsequent purchasers of either the land or (arguably) the mortgage, and MR is neither. As the court put it in Rowe v. Small Bus. Admin., 446 N.E.2d 991 (Ind.App.1983), "We fail to see how the [mortgagors] needed notice from the record to be aware of their obligations."

3. *Recording as giving notice of the assignment to the mortgagor.* If MR mortgages land to ME and ME gives a recorded assignment to A1, does the recordation act as constructive notice of the assignment to MR? Why do we care about notice? If the note is negotiated to A1, we have already seen that, under the payment rule embodied in UCC Article 3 (in states that have not adopted the 2003 amendments), MR is bound to discover the assignment by insisting on seeing the note before making each payment; recording the assignment can hardly add anything to this already burdensome duty.

But if the note is not negotiable or the traditional payment rule has been reversed by the 2002 amendments to UCC Article 3, the question whether MR has notice of the assignment becomes more important, since it is easier to argue that payment to ME is good until MR has such notice. Does recording the assignment give notice? The answer surely should be no, since finding notice on these facts would mean that MR would be expected to examine the title before making each payment on the loan. As one court put it,

> To require any [person] to run a title search before making any disbursements to a payee named in a note held for collection and secured by a deed of trust, or to pay at its peril, would impose an impractical and crushing burden.* * *

Giorgi v. Pioneer Title Ins. Co., 454 P.2d 104 (Nev. 1969). A few statutes and cases disagree and impose this burden; see Rucker v. State Exchange Bank, 355 So.2d 171 (Fla.App. 1978); EMC Mortg. Corp. v. Chaudhri, 946 A.2d 578 (N.J.Super. App.Div. 2008) (dictum); see Nelson, Whitman, Burkhart & Freyermuth, Real Estate Finance Law § 5.33 (6th ed. 2014). The far preferable and much more widely held view is represented by the following New York statute:

McKINNEY'S CONSOL. LAWS OF NEW YORK, Real Prop.Law, § 324 (1968): The recording of an assignment of a mortgage is not in itself a notice of such assignment to a mortgagor, his heirs or personal representatives, or to an owner of the mortgaged premises, where such assignment is recorded subsequent to the recording of the conveyances of such premises to such owner, so as to invalidate a payment made by either of them to the mortgagee or to a prior assignee of the mortgage.

4. *Recording as notice to a grantee taking title from the mortgagor.* Now add to the foregoing facts a deed of the land from MR to GE, delivered *after* the assignment to A1. If the mortgage note is nonnegotiable, so that it is relevant to determine whether GE has notice of the assignment, should the recordation be held to give GE notice? Here there is no great burden in so holding, since GE is expected to examine the public records anyway as part of the normal process of purchasing the land. GE is precisely the sort of third party who is held to notice of a previously-recorded conveyance. If the assignment is unrecorded on these facts, it is well established that GE is entitled to assume that ME still holds the note and mortgage, and a payoff by GE to ME is binding against A1. See Sixty St. Francis Street, Inc. v. American Sav. & Loan Ass'n, 554 So.2d 1003 (Ala.1989) (unclear whether note was negotiable or not).

5. *Failure to record as facilitating a wrongful release by the original mortgagee.* Read this note with extra care; it explains the most important reason that assignees of mortgages should record. Assume MR mortgages land to ME, who assigns the mortgage to A1. However, A1 fails to record. Now ME connives with MR to execute and record a release of the mortgage. There is in fact no payoff of the loan, and A1 is unaware of the scheme. The crooked MR, having now appeared to clear the land's title of the mortgage, sells it to a bona fide purchaser (GE) and splits his unlawful gains with ME. Is A1 bound by the release?

The answer is plainly that A1 is bound. The reason is that, if the assignment is unrecorded, it is entirely impossible for GE to protect herself against this form of skullduggery. See Kalen v. Gelderman, 66 S.D. 53, 278 N.W. 165 (1938); Brenner v. Neu, 28 Ill.App.2d 219, 170 N.E.2d 897 (1960). This is perhaps the best and most obvious reason that A1 should record an assignment.

A similar problem can arise if MR conveys title to the land to ME (i.e., as a deed in lieu of foreclosure) after ME has made an unrecorded assignment to A1. If ME now sells the land, the buyer who checks the records will find no assignment, and hence will naturally assume that the mortgage has merged with the title in ME's hands, and hence has been extinguished. This seems the proper result, but the cases are divided as to whether the buyer from ME will take free of or subject to the mortgage held by A1. See Curtis v. Moore, 152 N.Y. 159, 46 N.E. 168 (1897), discussed in Nelson, Whitman, Burkhart & Freyermuth, Real Estate Finance Law § 5.33 (6th ed. 2014).

6.　*Wrongful release by the trustee under a deed of trust.* Suppose that, instead of a mortgage, MR gives a deed of trust to T (a trustee) to secure a note to ME. ME then assigns the note and the beneficial interest in the deed of trust to A1. Subsequently T, who turns out to be a crook, improperly executes a reconveyance of the deed of trust to MR, even though MR has not paid the underlying debt. MR then sells the land to a GE, a bona fide purchaser.

Here, perhaps surprisingly, GE will prevail whether the assignment is recorded or not. The reason lies in the role of the trustee, who is in many jurisdictions the only party who *can* reconvey the title to MR. In effect, the trustee represents (for the limited purposes of reconveyance and foreclosure) whoever may hold the beneficial interest in the note from time to time. See Marsh v. Stover, 363 Ill. 490, 2 N.E.2d 559 (1936), noted 31 Ill.L.Rev. 350 (1936).

Note that this rule applies only if it is the trustee who issues the reconveyance. In some jurisdictions in which deeds of trust are used, satisfactions are customarily given by the beneficiary directly, rather than by the trustee. There the rule for mortgages discussed in the previous notes will govern.

7.　*Recording as ensuring notice to assignee of new litigation.* Suppose a secondary market investor buys a mortgage loan, but records no assignment. Then a suit is filed that could jeopardize the validity or priority of the mortgage. One obvious example is a foreclosure of a mortgage senior to the one in question, but there are many other possibilities: a quiet title action by someone claiming better title to the land, a building or housing code enforcement proceeding, or an action to force cleanup of hazardous waste on the land, for example. The plaintiff in that action may perform a title examination, discover the identity of the original mortgagee or previous holder of the mortgage, and make service of process on that party. But the actual (though unrecorded) holder of the mortgage will get no direct service (since there is no obvious way for the plaintiff to identify the holder), and hence the holder may not learn of the suit from the party who was actually served.

In Fifth Third Bank v. NCS Mortgage Lending Co., 860 N.E.2d 785 (Ohio App. 2006), a foreclosure action was filed by a prior mortgage holder. The court found the foreclosure judgment binding on the assignee of the junior mortgage, which had never learned of or entered an appearance in the litigation, despite its claim that it had instructed its predecessor to record an assignment of the mortgage—an act that was "inexplicably" never done. Because most secondary market investors use independent servicers to manage their mortgage portfolios, an investor may prefer to have a recorded assignment run to its servicer rather than itself. In this way, any notice issued will find its way directly to the entity that is responsible for management of the loan, rather than having to take the circuitous route of going first to the investor, who will then need to notify the servicer. But in

Fifth Third Bank, no assignment at all was recorded, and hence no notice of the litigation was directed either to the investor or its servicer. The case illustrates that failing to record a mortgage assignment can have disastrous consequences. For a similar example, in which the prior lien being foreclosed was a mechanics lien, see Rhode Island Const. Services, Inc. v. Harris Mill, LLC, 68 A.3d 450 (R.I. 2013).

As an alternative to recording an assignment to itself, the investor may prefer to have an assignment recorded to MERS, the Mortgage Electronic Registration Systems. MERS is merely a nominee for the investor, but it operates a "mail room" function, keeping a record of all investors and servicers, and redirecting to the relevant servicer any notice that it receives with respect to a particular mortgage. Unfortunately, this notion is not foolproof, for it depends on the courts taking the same view of MERS that MERS itself takes. In Landmark National Bank v. Kesler, 216 P.3d 158 (Kan. 2009), the original mortgagee named in the junior mortgage was MERS, as nominee for the actual lender. A senior mortgagee filed a foreclosure action, but never served either MERS or the junior lender, and a default judgment was entered against both of them, wiping out the second mortgage. The Kansas Supreme Court found no error in the trial judge's refusal to set aside the default judgment. The junior mortgagee was not entitled to notice because there was no assignment to it in the public records; the court found that MERS was not entitled to notice because it was merely a nominee, had advanced no funds under the mortgage loan, and was therefore not a real party in interest. This conclusion seems absurd, but Indiana and Arkansas courts have followed it.

8.   *Effect of recording on successive conflicting assignments by the mortgagee.* Assume MR mortgages land to ME. ME now makes two conflicting assignments of the mortgage, the first to A1 and the second to A2. Which of them is considered to hold the mortgage?

The first question is whether the mortgage note is negotiable. If this is so, we have already seen that under U.C.C. Article 3, the right of enforcement of both the note and the mortgage will normally follow possession of the note (provided the note is endorsed or the assignee can prove that possession was delivered for the purpose of transferring the right of enforcement). Obviously if A1 has obtained actual possession of the note, A2 cannot obtain it from ME; this should be enough to "tip off" A2 that the proposed assignment to A2 is of dubious validity, and A1 will prevail. All of this follows whether A1 records or not. A1's position will be buttressed by the "claims" language of U.C.C. § 3–306 if A1 is a HDC, but that factor doesn't seem necessary to A1's position.

In theory A2 could argue that he or she is just the sort of "subsequent purchaser" who is protected by the recording acts against a prior unrecorded assignment, but the courts, faced with this apparent conflict between the U.C.C. and the recording acts, should and usually will opt to apply the U.C.C. and disregard the recording act, reasoning (as always) that the mortgage follows the note. See American Bank of the South v. Rothenberg, 598 So.2d

289 (Fla.App. 1992); Jan Z. Krasnowiecki, J. Gregg Miller & Lloyd R. Ziff, The Kennedy Mortgage Co. Bankruptcy Case: New Light Shed on the Position of Mortgage Warehousing Banks, 56 Am.Bankr.L.J. 325, 333–39 (1982), arguing strenuously for the preeminence of the U.C.C. in this situation.

If the note is negotiable but A1 does not take possession of it (perhaps taking a mere written assignment rather than the endorsed note itself), and if A2 does take the note, A2 will prevail. Again, this result should, and usually does, follow irrespective of whether the first assignment is recorded. In other words, a recordation by A1 will not be considered constructive notice to A2, so as to deprive A2 of title to the note and mortgage. See Foster v. Augustanna College, 92 Okl. 96, 218 P. 335, 37 A.L.R. 854 (1923); Nelson, Whitman, Burkhart & Freyermuth, Real Estate Finance Law § 5.34 (6th ed. 2014). This conclusion is supported by UCC § 3–302(b), which provides:

> Public filing or recording of a document does not of itself constitute notice of a defense, claim in recoupment, or claim to the instrument.

Incidentally, in this setting A1, not getting possession of the note, obviously can't become a HDC, thus ruling out the protection against adverse claims provided by § 3–306.

Things change drastically if the note is nonnegotiable. Now U.C.C. Article 3 does not apply, and the state's recording act is usually held to control. If A1 fails to record and A2 qualifies as a BFP under the recording acts (and in notice-race states, records first), A2 will prevail. See Fannin Inv. & Dev. Co. v. Neuhaus, 427 S.W.2d 82 (Tex.Civ.App.1968); Second Nat'l Bank v. Dyer, 121 Conn. 263, 184 A. 386 (1936). Does this contravene the general notion that the note or indebtedness is the primary right of the mortgagee, and the mortgage is merely an adjunct which follows it? Should A2 prevail only if A2 gets actual possession of the original note from ME? The *Dyer* case did not so require; see Nelson, Whitman, Burkhart & Freyermuth, Real Estate Finance Law § 5.33 (6th ed. 2014).

Actual possession not req [handwritten margin note]

9. *Recording as a prerequisite to foreclosure.* In about a dozen states, by statute, a party who claims to hold a mortgage by virtue of an assignment cannot foreclose unless the assignment has been recorded. Except for Maine, virtually all of these statutes apply only to nonjudicial foreclosures. See, e.g., Minn.Stat.Ann. § 580.02(3), requiring that any assignments be recorded as a prerequisite to a nonjudicial foreclosure. Maine does indeed construe its statute to require a chain of recorded assignments for a judicial foreclosure; see Deutsche Bank Nat. Trust Co. v. Wilk, 76 A.3d 363 (Me. 2013).

It's not at all obvious what policy these statutes serve, other than to give title insurance companies some "comfort" by providing a clear public chain of title to rely upon when they insure the title of a foreclosure purchaser. There is no strong reason to regard recording of assignments as essential, and a number of other nonjudicial foreclosure states do not require it, along with nearly all judicial foreclosure states. Moreover, the presence or absence of a recorded assignment proves nothing about who holds or has the right to enforce the promissory note, which (properly understood) is the critical issue in a mortgage foreclosure.

The statutes requiring recording of assignments as a precondition to foreclosure amount to little more than a formality. The recording can take place immediately prior to the foreclosure, which may be many months or years after the actual assignment. Hence, these statutes are essentially useless in informing borrowers about who holds their mortgages. See, e.g., WM Specialty Mortg., LLC v. Salomon, 874 So.2d 680 (Fla.App.2004) (assignee may foreclose despite late-executed assignment). Moreover, courts tend to treat the recording requirement as irrelevant if no one is injured by the failure to record (as is usually the case); see Federal Home Loan Mortg. Ass'n v. Kelley, 2014 2014 WL 4232687 (Mich.App. 2014); Dixon v. Windsor, 596 So.2d 898 (Ala.1992).

NOTE ON THE CREATION OF A
NATIONAL MORTGAGE REGISTRY

Thus far in this chapter, we have spent a good deal of effort to explain the existing system for transferring mortgages (and notes secured by mortgages). In this note, we step back to appraise the system, and ask whether something better might not be created.

In theory, the requirement of U.C.C. Article 3 for delivery of possession of negotiable notes, as the exclusive way to transfer the right of enforcement, serves two purposes. First, it ensures that two (or more) competing parties cannot assert the same right of enforcement against the borrower (since there can be only one party in possession of the original note), and thus protects the borrower against double enforcement. Second, it allows the borrower to determine, by demanding to see the original note, whether a party attempting to enforce the note actually has the right of enforcement.

The system works reasonably well to achieve the first objective, except in the eight states (discussed in note 9 on page 564 supra) that don't require proof of the right to enforce the note as a prerequisite to nonjudicial foreclosure. At the same time, the system imposes significant costs on secondary market participants to move original notes around the country (with the attendant risks of lost notes) and to store them in a network of custodians' vaults.

Unfortunately, the system is almost completely useless to achieve the second objective. In an era in which nearly all mortgages are sold on the secondary market, and in which loans are managed by servicers who are seldom located near the borrowers, any request by a borrower to see the original note is likely to be met with incredulous silence or a polite chuckle. The note is likely held by a custodian for the secondary market investor, and is located far away in a vault to which the servicer has no simple means of access. If the borrower were insistent, the servicer might be able to e-mail or fax a copy of the note to the borrower, but a copy, of course, would prove nothing. As a practical matter, there is simply no convenient mechanism by which a borrower can verify that the servicer who is demanding payment of the note actually holds it or represents the holder.

Substantial additional costs grow from the need to record mortgage assignments in the local real estate records (which, as we saw above, is obligatory in order to use nonjudicial foreclosure in about a dozen states, and is a wise precaution everywhere). The party making the assignment must discover which local recording jurisdiction is applicable (of the more than 3,600 in the United States) and determine what its document standards and fees are. It must then hand tailor the assignment (which must, of course, bear the names of the parties to the original mortgage, its recording data, a signature of the assignor, and a notarial acknowledgment) and transmit it to the correct recording office with the appropriate fee. None of this is impossible, but it is sufficiently burdensome that it's easy to see why many secondary market participants forego recording of assignments unless and until it becomes necessary in order to foreclose the mortgage.

Both the process of physically shipping notes around the country and the need to record assignments in one of thousands of local jurisdictions seem archaic, rooted in the technology of the eighteenth and nineteenth centuries. Indeed, the whole idea of having one system (delivery) for transferring notes and another (recording assignments or MERS) for transferring mortgages seems dull-witted, when everyone agrees that the right to enforce the note and the mortgage should remain together. Couldn't transfers of notes and mortgages be tracked together with a single system. Surely in an era of nationwide digital networks and electronic documents we can do better.

At this point, no successor system is at hand. MERS was created as an attempt to ameliorate the problems of recording mortgage assignments, but MERS does not address the issue of note delivery at all (except in the case of electronic notes, currently a small subset of all notes), and as we have seen, MERS has had many problems of its own.

But some progress is being made. There have been serious academic efforts to describe an integrated nationwide system of registration for notes and mortgages traded on the secondary market. See Dale A. Whitman, A Proposal for a National Mortgage Registry: MERS Done Right, 78 Missouri L.Rev. 1 (2013); Adam Levitin, The Paper Chase: Securitization, Foreclosure, and the Uncertainty of Mortgage Title, 63 Duke L.J. 637 (2013).

More recently, the New York Federal Reserve Bank's office of General Counsel sponsored a series of meetings with mortgage industry participants and began development of a statute that would create a nationwide mortgage registry. This is still a work in progress, and the description below should be regarded as highly tentative. The registry would supplant the present system of transferring mortgage loans, including the delivery of original promissory notes and the recording of mortgage assignments in the local real estate records. The following material outlines the conceptual framework of the registry as it has been developed thus far.

Why is a registry needed? The existing rules may have been practical in an era in which secondary market transfers were relatively uncommon, but today they have become increasingly burdensome and productive of litigation, as participants in the industry are well aware. They also fail to provide borrowers a quick, simple, and accurate way of determining who holds and who services their mortgages at any given moment. The proposed national registry is intended to solve these problems by (1) providing for the making of secondary market transfers by an electronic "book entry" by the present mortgage holder, and (2) permitting borrowers to determine the identity of their mortgage's holder and servicer through a simple internet query.

Federal or state law and operation? One current draft assumes that the statute will be adopted by Congress. This is necessary in order to preempt conflicting state law with respect to the mechanisms of transfer (delivery of promissory notes and recording of mortgage assignment) and the prerequisites for foreclosure and discharge of mortgages. One can conceive of a program for addressing these issues though state statutes or a uniform act, but it seems likely that a great deal of time and effort would be needed to achieve nationwide uniformity in this way. If a federal statute is the approach taken, there would be a "regulator" with authority to adopt operating rules and standards for the registry. That regulator, which might be an existing federal agency or a newly-created one, might operate the registry itself, or it might provide oversight to a privately-operated registry that would serve as a utility to the mortgage industry. The present drafts leave these matters open for further discussion.

The role of existing law. As currently conceived, the registry would not supplant the role of local recording as a means of establishing the priority of mortgages. Thus, it is expected (and might even be required) that each mortgage would be recorded before being deposited in the national registry. Likewise, when a mortgage was foreclosed or paid off, an appropriate document would be recorded locally. However, all transfers made after the loan was deposited in the registry would be reflected only in the registry itself, and not in the local land records.

Who could use the registry? First, a word about terminology. A person or entity who is entitled to place a mortgage in the registry is termed a "depositor." A person or entity who is shown in the registry's records as holding the mortgage is a "registrant." Ordinarily, when a mortgage was deposited, the depositor would be the initial registrant. Depositors would be required to meet standards established by the regulator with respect to data quality, information security, and capital. If a party wished to deposit a mortgage but did not meet these standards, it could employ the services of a "third party service provider" that met them.

Access to data in the registry would be tiered. Basic information about the identity of the registrant and the registrant's servicer (if any) might be available via the internet to the general public, just as mortgage assignments are now available to the public in the local land records. Other details of the registry's information would be restricted to borrowers, registrants, and servicers as needed.

Interaction with the U.C.C. The system would be designed to work smoothly with the Uniform Commercial Code, and to preserve all of the options that parties to negotiable promissory notes now have under it. While the original promissory note would be destroyed when a mortgage was registered (in order to prevent "double selling" of the note), the registered obligation would be deemed to have the characteristics of the original note, and the registrant would be deemed to be in possession of it (as well as to be the assignee of a recorded mortgage assignment for state law purposes). Thus, the consequences of possession of a negotiable note in terms of right to enforce (under U.C.C. Article 3) and ownership (under U.C.C. Article 9) would continue to apply to the registered obligation. A registrant making a transfer would have the choice (as under current law) whether to endorse the registered obligation or not. "Transferrable records" under eSign and UETA, and even nonnegotiable paper notes, could be registered and would be subject to the existing concepts of Articles 3 and 9. No change would be made in the existing "Holder in Due Course" doctrine for negotiable notes. Security interests in mortgage notes could continue to be created in essentially the same manner as at present under U.C.C. Article 9, perfected either by filing of a financing statement in state records or by taking possession as reflected in the registry.

Foreclosure and discharge. Existing law varies considerably from state to state with respect to a party's ability to establish standing to foreclose a mortgage or deed of trust. The proposed registry would not change state foreclosure law, but it would make it clear that, with respect to a mortgage in the national registry, only the registrant or its servicer could pursue foreclosure, irrespective of existing state requirements. Likewise, a discharge of the mortgage could be given only by the registrant or its servicer. The registry would provide certificates as needed to record in the local land records or to produce in court in order to facilitate foreclosures or discharges.

Warranties. A party who deposits a mortgage with the registry would be required to warrant that it was in rightful possession of the original note and had the right to enforce it. It would also warrant that the instrument was genuine and had not been altered, and that the depositor had no knowledge of any adverse claims to it. If a "Third Party Servicer Provider" was used to make a deposit, it would be required to make those same warranties.

Conclusion. At this writing it is difficult to say when or whether a national registry system like that described above will become a reality. The barriers, both political and in terms of garnering industry support and consensus, are formidable. On the other hand, our experience with the existing system during the mortgage crisis that began in 2007 has demonstrated just how dysfunctional and inefficient it is. The need for change is strong.

NOTE ON COLLATERAL (SECURITY) ASSIGNMENTS
OF MORTGAGES

Collateral assignments and the "payment" rule. There are two quite distinct types of assignments of notes and mortgages. The first is an "outright" assignment—a sale of the loan, usually for cash, to an investor who plans to hold it for the long term or securitize it. The second is a "collateral" assignment, in which the loan is pledged by the mortgagee as collateral for *another* loan, one made by the assignee to the mortgagee. As mentioned above, "servicing" contracts, in which some entity (sometimes the local lender who originated the loan) is appointed an agent to collect payments and remit them to the secondary market investor are very common with outright assignments. However, such formal contracts for servicing are much less common in collateral assignments; instead, the originating mortgagee simply continues to service the loans.

As we have already noted, mortgage bankers frequently obtain much of their operating capital by borrowing funds from commercial banks on lines of credit. They then use these funds to originate mortgage loans, which they ultimately package and sell on the secondary mortgage market or securitize. While a mortgage banker is accumulating a package of loans of sufficient size to sell, it may temporarily pledge the loans (i.e., the notes and mortgages) it has already originated to the commercial bank as collateral for the line of credit.[11]

Suppose the mortgage banker receives a repayment on one of these loans while it is pledged or "warehoused" with the bank. If the mortgage banker has been designated as the bank's agent to receive such payments, all is well from the borrower's viewpoint. But if there is no formal agency agreement, and if the mortgage banker becomes insolvent and fails to pay off the bank's line of credit, the bank may claim that it is not bound by the payment made by the mortgagor, and that the note and mortgage are still in effect. In such cases, courts are inclined to work hard to find or imply an agency relationship; see In re Royal West Properties, Inc., 441 B.R. 158 (Bankr. S.D.Fla. 2010); Rodgers v. Seattle-First Nat'l Bank, 697 P.2d 1009 (Wash.App. 1985). As we saw in the previous section of this book, ultimately the combination of Restatement § 5.5 and the revisions to UCC § 3–602 should eliminate this problem, whether the notes are negotiable or nonnegotiable.

How does the pledgee of a mortgage "foreclose?" Assume that a default occurs in payment on the debt for which a note and mortgage have been pledged as security. How should the pledgee "foreclose" or realize on the

---

[11] The warehouse line of credit is not the only way mortgage bankers obtain financing. Some, especially smaller, mortgage bankers act as "correspondents" for commercial banks or other larger lenders. The correspondent will originate residential loans meeting the larger institution's specifications, and will fund the loan at closing; the larger institution will then immediately reimburse the correspondent for the loan amount and will take ownership of the loan. This approach is sometimes called "table funding" because the larger institution's check is available virtually at the closing table.

security? One approach is for the pledgee to put the underlying note and mortgage on the secondary mortgage market and sell them. This follows from UCC § 9–610, which provides that:

(a) After default, a secured party may sell, lease, license, or otherwise dispose of any or all of the collateral * * * .

(b) Every aspect of a disposition of collateral, including the method, manner, time, place, and other terms, must be commercially reasonable. If commercially reasonable, a secured party may dispose of collateral by public or private proceedings, by one or more contracts, as a unit or in parcels, and at any time and place and on any terms.

Another option is found in UCC § 9–607(a)(1), which provides:

If so agreed, and in any event upon default, a secured party may notify an account debtor or other person obligated on collateral to make payment or otherwise render performance to or for the benefit of the secured party.

Hence the pledgee of the note and mortgage may simply notify the mortgagor on the underlying debt to begin making payments on that debt directly to the pledgee. See Columbus Investments v. Lewis, 48 P.3d 1222 (Colo. 2002). Of course, if the mortgagor was unaware of the pledge or is unwilling to accept the pledgee's word that a default by the mortgagee has occurred, the pledgee may need to obtain a court order directing the mortgagor to make future payments to the pledgee.

Suppose the underlying mortgage debt is also in default. Can the pledgee foreclose the mortgage on the land, or must the pledgee first engage in some sort of "foreclosure" of the security interest *in* the note and mortgage? If the note is negotiable (and perhaps even if it is not), these questions should be answered by first inquiring who has possession of the note, the pledgor or the pledgee. This inquiry would fit with our earlier discussion of transfers of the right of enforcement of a negotiable note. If possession has been transferred to the pledgee, it's highly likely that a court would find the pledgee has the right to enforce the note and the mortgage. See Bank of Tokyo Trust Co. v. Urban Food Malls Ltd., 650 N.Y.S.2d 654 (N.Y.App.Div. 1996), agreeing with this conclusion, but requiring the pledgee to join the pledgor in the foreclosure action if the balance on the debt secured by the pledge is less than the balance owing on the mortgage. See also Prairie Properties, L.L.C. v. McNeill, 996 S.W.2d 635 (Mo.App.1999) (collateral assignee of mortgage who obtained possession of note had authority to release it).

Even if possession of the note has been transferred to the pledgee, the pledgor might still have the power to foreclose the mortgage under an agency or servicing agreement, express or implied, with the pledgee. Compare Poseidon Devel., Inc. v. Woodland Lane Estates, LLC, 62 Cal.Rptr.3d 59 (Cal.App. 2007), holding that a lender who had made an assignment of the mortgage could no longer foreclose or enforce it. The assignor claimed the assignment was only as collateral, but on its face the assignment appeared absolute.

NOTES ON PERFECTION OF SECURITY INTERESTS IN MORTGAGE NOTES AND MORTGAGES

Let us return briefly to the case of a collateral (security) assignment of a note and mortgage. We have already covered the rules for "attachment" of security interests in such notes when we discussed outright sales of mortgage notes beginning on page 526. Under UCC § 9–203(b), attachment can occur in either of two ways: (A) by a signed, written agreement (or its electronic equivalent), such as a contract of sale or a written assignment, or (B) by delivering possession of the note to the buyer, provided that there is also some agreement indicating that ownership is to be transferred. These rules are the same whether a collateral (security) transfer or an outright sale of the note is contemplated.

However, attachment is not the end of the story. As we shall see in a moment, it is highly desirable for the pledgee to be "perfected," a status that is also governed by UCC Article 9. Under Article 9, "perfection" gives the secured party (the pledgee) priority over competing secured parties who perfect later (see UCC § 9–322(a)), subsequent lien creditors (see UCC § 9–317(a)), and subsequent purchasers of the security property (see UCC § 9–317(b)). Thus, "perfection" under Article 9 has a significance much like that of recordation in real estate law.

When does "perfection" become important? Suppose the mortgagee makes two competing collateral assignments of the same note and mortgage. A mortgage banker that was in serious financial trouble might be tempted to do this, and not to mention the first assignment to the second assignee. Which assignee would be entitled to the payments made on the note?

Or suppose the mortgagee makes only one collateral assignment, but then files bankruptcy. In general a trustee in bankruptcy has the "strong-arm" power, under § 544(a) of the Bankruptcy Code, to act as a perfected judgment lien creditor of the bankrupt as of the date of bankruptcy. Acting under this power, the trustee might claim the note and mortgage as against pledgee. If the court found that the pledgee's claim was unperfected and thus the bankruptcy trustee prevailed, the payments on the note would go to the bankruptcy estate and benefit the mortgagee's general creditors, and the pledgee would be limited to a pro-rata share of those payments. In both of these situations, perfection under UCC Article 9 by the pledgee is of prime importance.

Incidentally, you may wonder why we did not mention perfection in our previous discussion of outright sales of ownership interests in notes. The reason is that perfection is not an issue with outright sales; under UCC § 9–309(4), when the sale "attaches," perfection is automatic.

However, when a collateral security interest attaches, perfection is *not* automatic and must be done separately. The previous version of Article 9, which was supplanted by the current version in 2001, stated that perfection could be accomplished only by transferring possession of the note, but it left some important questions unanswered. It wasn't clear whether perfection of a security interest in the note also perfected the security interest as to the mortgage, or whether some separate action was needed to perfect as to the mortgage. If a separate action was needed with respect to the mortgage, it wasn't clear what that action was. Frankly, the law was a mess. Compare Landmark Land Co. v. Sprague, 529 F.Supp. 971 (S.D.N.Y.1981) with In re Maryville Sav. & Loan Corp., 743 F.2d 413 (6th Cir.1984) and supplemental opinion, 760 F.2d 119 (6th Cir.1985).

Fortunately, revised Article 9 solves all of these problems in a neat and rational way. First, under § 9–308(g), "Perfection of a security interest in a right to payment or performance also perfects a security interest in a lien on personal or real property securing the right, notwithstanding other law to the contrary." In effect, perfection as to the note automatically takes care of the mortgage as well. It isn't necessary to record a mortgage assignment in order to perfect as to the real estate. See Provident Bank v. Community Home Mortg. Corp., 498 F.Supp.2d 558 (E.D.N.Y. 2007).

Now, how does the assignee perfect as to the note—since it is the main thing to be concerned about? Perfection by taking possession of the original note was the only method recognized by the previous version of Article 9. It still works under revised Article 9. A note is still an "instrument" in Article 9 parlance (whether it is negotiable or not), and a security interest in it can be perfected by taking possession; in fact, that's the best way to perfect. See § 9–313(a). However, revised Article 9 also provides an alternative: the assignee can perfect by filing a financing statement (a "UCC–1" form), typically with the Secretary of State's office. See § 9–312(a). Either method is acceptable. However, a later perfection by possession supersedes an earlier perfection by filing unless the later taker has actual knowledge of the earlier one. See § 9–330(d).

Why was this new procedure for perfection by filing a financing statement included? The reason is that many creditors find it extremely burdensome to go to the trouble of taking possession of their debtors' promissory notes, especially when the credit is being advanced for only a short term. Moving the notes back and forth causes serious record-keeping headaches and raises the risk of losing or mislaying notes. Filing is much easier and cheaper, and will presumably be equally effective as against a future trustee in bankruptcy of the debtor.

But perfection by filing is a sort of "second-rate" perfection, since it can be "trumped" by the debtor's later giving actual possession of the notes to a different creditor who pays value and lacks knowledge of the earlier transfer. UCC § 9–330(d). So a creditor won't want to perfect by filing unless the creditor has complete trust that the debtor will not "double-assign" the loan.

If the creditor has any qualms at all about the business ethics of the debtor, the creditor had better go to the extra trouble of taking possession of those notes. By the same token, if the creditor does get possession, the fact that there has been a prior filing is simply irrelevant; hence, there is no necessity for a creditor who is taking possession of the note to do a UCC search.

Incidentally (but very importantly), taking possession really does require the physical moving of the note. The courts are very disinclined to accept anything less than a manual transfer of possession to the secured party-assignee or to its agent or custodian. It is most unwise for the assignee to leave the note in the hands of the mortgagee-assignor as the assignee's "trustee," "nominee," "agent," or the like. See In re Executive Growth Investments, Inc., 40 B.R. 417 (Bkrtcy.C.D.Cal.1984). On the other hand, a trustee, nominee, or agent is fine so long as that party reports to the assignee; see In re McFadden, 471 B.R. 136 (Bankr. D.S.C. 2012); In re Butler, 512 B.R. 643 (Bankr. W.D.Wash. 2014).

Perfection and HDC status. It is worth noting that the transfer of possession of the instrument "kills two birds with one stone." It is an essential element of holder in due course status under Article 3, and also accomplishes perfection under Article 9. Which of these is more important to the usual lender who takes a collateral security interest in notes and mortgages? Put another way, which is the greater risk to the lender: that the original mortgagee will commit fraud or otherwise engage in behavior that gives rise to a defense by the mortgagor, or that the original mortgagee will become bankrupt, so that perfection will be necessary to forestall the claim of a trustee in bankruptcy? For the great majority of creditors who do business with reputable original mortgagees, holder in due course status is quite unimportant, while in periods of rising interest rates, the bankruptcy of such mortgagees is a very real and serious risk.

Mortgage notes and installment contracts. This is a good time to reflect an important difference between notes secured by mortgages and real estate installment contracts. As we saw earlier, an installment contract is not an "instrument" at all, but is instead an "account" under revised Article 9. Thus, while a security interest in a note is perfected either by the transfer of possession of the note or by the filing of a financing statement in the state's UCC records, perfection of a security interest in a vendor's rights under an installment contract can be accomplished only by filing. The distinction is nicely spelled out in In re Holiday Interval, Inc., 94 B.R. 594 (Bankr.W.D.Mo.1988). See also Chapter 3, Section B supra.

NOTES ON MORTGAGE PARTICIPATIONS

In a mortgage participation, a "lead lender" originates a mortgage loan and then sells fractional interests in it to one or more other lenders. For example, the lead lender may loan $10 million to a shopping center developer, and may then sell four $2 million participations to four other lenders, keeping a $2 million investment for itself. Similar arrangements are often made for packages of much smaller loans on residential properties.

Why do lenders engage in participations? In some cases, each lender may be limited by governmental regulation in the amount of lending it can make to a particular borrower or secured by a particular type of property. In the example above, the $2 million participation shares may be within this limit, while the entire $10 million loan, if made by a single lender, might exceed it. In addition each lender, by diversifying its portfolio, spreads the risk of loan default; it is generally safer for a lender to invest $2 million in each of five different projects (especially if they are located in five different market areas) than to invest $10 million in a single project.

A participation is not the only way for a group of lenders to pool their funds in making loans. Alternatively, they might form a partnership or a joint venture, or they might enter into a multi-lender agreement or "syndication," in which each lender has a direct relationship with the borrower, advancing part of the total loan funds and becoming a direct creditor of the borrower for repayment of these funds, with separate collateral. But in real estate lending, participations are much more commonly employed than these other approaches. See John C. Murray, Recharacterization Issues in Participating Loans, 19 Probate & Property 36 (Sept./Oct. 2005); Yoken, Loan Participations and Multibank Financing of California Real Estate, 9 Cal. Real Prop. J. 31 (No. 2, Spring 1991).

How is a participation structured mechanically? In the past a very common method involved one mortgage securing a series of notes or bonds, each one for a fractional part of the debt. Some or all of these notes or bonds were then sold to third party assignees. The most common method in use today, however, involves the use of a single note and mortgage for each loan. The originating mortgagee or "lead lender" will generally retain the original note and mortgage and sell "participation certificates" to the other institutions. These certificates will detail the fractional interests sold and the specific mortgage loan involved. Thus the participation is really a partial assignment of the note and mortgage.

If the participation involves the sale of fractional interests in a large pool of smaller mortgage loans, the originating mortgagee will sell "participation certificates" delineating the fractional interest being sold and specifically identifying which mortgage loans are involved. In both of the above situations the participation certificates will be governed more specifically by the terms of a detailed "participation agreement." The following material will highlight some of the legal issues that arise with participations and participation agreements.

Priority among the participants. Suppose the loan goes into default and foreclosure ensues. As among the participants, and as against the lead lender, who will have priority as to the foreclosure proceeds and any collectible deficiency judgment? Today, almost all courts grant a pro-rata priority among the participants in the absence of a contrary agreement. See generally Nelson, Whitman, Burkhart & Freyermuth, Real Estate Finance Law § 5.35 (6th ed. 2014). Likewise, the participants have no special priority vis á vis the lead lender unless the agreement provides otherwise; see Domeyer v. O'Connell, 364 Ill. 467, 4 N.E.2d 830 (1936).

However, these common law priority rules are seldom significant today, because participation agreements almost always deal with these matters in detail. Clauses that establish priorities between the participants themselves, and between them and the lead lender, are very common. But disputes can still arise if the language of the agreement is not entirely clear; see Bank of Chicago v. Park Nat'l Bank, 640 N.E.2d 1288 (Ill.App. 1994).

Managing the mortgage loan. In any participation, someone must be in charge. Decisions about management of the underlying loan or loans must be made. Who will have this authority? The following provision provides one possible answer:

> Seller [lead lender] shall give prompt notice to Purchaser as to any default under the terms of any mortgage in which the Purchaser has a participation interest. Seller may act upon any loan in default and the security property by any procedure which may be necessary in its sole discretion, including the acceptance of a deed in lieu of foreclosure or the purchase at a foreclosure sale or trustee's sale. Seller shall exercise the judgment of a prudent lender in Seller's lending area. Seller shall make an appraisal of the property within a reasonable time before taking any action affecting such loan in default. Seller may manage, maintain or dispose of property so acquired in any manner which it shall deem necessary, the parties hereto sharing ratably with Seller in the net proceeds of sale to the extent of Purchaser's share in the unpaid principal balance due on the loan. It is further understood that it shall be within the sole discretion of Seller, after 10 days written notice to Purchaser, to determine whether foreclosure shall be pursuant to a power of sale, or through court action, and as to whether or not a deficiency judgment shall be obtained.

While this language gives the lead lender full decision-making authority, one can easily imagine cases in which such an arrangement is unacceptable to the participants—particularly if the lead lender retains only a small fraction of ownership of the underlying loan. The participants may insist that the lead lender at least consult with them before making critical decisions. They may even want one of their number to have authority instead of the lead lender, or may want to subject all important decisions to majority vote.

Nevertheless, lenders sometimes enter into participation agreements that are vague or silent as to who will make managerial decisions concerning the loan. The question whether to be lenient or tough, to forbear or foreclose, is often a close one on which the participants may have very different opinions. For examples of such disputes, see Southern Pacific Thrift & Loan Ass'n v. Savings Ass'n Mortg. Co., 70 Cal.App.4th 634, 82 Cal.Rptr.2d 874

(1999); Capitol Sav. & Loan Ass'n v. First Fin. Sav. & Loan Ass'n, 364 N.W.2d 267 (Iowa App.1984). Even well-drafted agreements often end up in litigation. See, e.g., Mark Twain Bank v. Continental Bank, 817 F.Supp. 792 (E.D.Mo.1993), in which the agreement required the participant's agreement before the lead bank could "extend the final maturity" of the underlying loan. The court held that a decision by the lead bank to defer certain payments by the borrower was outside the scope of this phrase, and was proper even if the participant did not agree.

One implication of the participation's structure is that the individual participants cannot pursue independent remedies against the borrower, but rather must count on the lead lender (or other servicer hired by the lead lender) to do so. See Beal Savings Bank v. Sommer, 834 N.Y.S.2d 44 (N.Y. 2007).

Lead lender liability. When a participation goes sour, the participants often attempt to find some theory of liability that will allow them to shift their losses to the lead lender. Sometimes this is easy. For example, the lead lender in a participation ordinarily services the underlying mortgage loan or loans, collecting payments, escrowing taxes and insurance, maintaining accounts, and remitting to the participants their share of the payments received. Suppose the lead bank collects payments from the borrower(s) and simply refuses to forward to the participants a part of the share to which they are entitled under the agreement. Pretty obviously, this conduct will breach the lead lender's contractual duty. See Resolution Trust Corp. v. Heights of Texas FSB, 1991 WL 205040 (D.Kan.1991) (not reported in F.Supp.)

The participation agreement will sometimes state that the lead lender, in its capacity as servicer, will hold the funds collected from the borrower "in trust" for the participants. Again, it seems obvious that if the lead lender misappropriates these funds or deals with them negligently, liability for breach of fiduciary duty will result. However, the courts have been most reluctant to extrapolate from this limited "trust" language a general fiduciary duty that extends, for example, to the lead lender's management of relations with the borrower. See Southern Pacific Thrift & Loan Ass'n v. Savings Ass'n Mortg. Co., 70 Cal.App.4th 634, 82 Cal.Rptr.2d 874 (1999); First Citizens Fed. Sav. & Loan Ass'n v. Worthen Bank, 919 F.2d 510 (9th Cir.1990). Of course, a general fiduciary duty may be found if the language of the participation agreement is broad enough. See Guaranty Sav. & Loan Ass'n v. Ultimate Sav. Bank, 737 F.Supp. 366 (W.D.Va.1990), where the agreement stated, "Seller * * * is to act in all matters hereunder for the Buyer * * * as a trustee with fiduciary duties to administer the loans hereunder."

Participations as securities. Participants sometimes attempt to establish that their shares are securities under the federal securities acts, hoping that this characterization will make it easier for them to blame the lead lender for the failure of the underlying loan. However, virtually all of the cases refuse to treat a participation sold to a financial institution as a security. See, e.g., First Fin. Fed. Sav. & Loan Ass'n v. E.F. Hutton Mortg. Corp., 834 F.2d 685

(8th Cir.1987); McVay v. Western Plains Service Corp., 823 F.2d 1395 (10th Cir.1987). On the other hand, if the participation interest is sold to an unsophisticated private individual, it is relatively easy to convince a court that it is a security. See, e.g., Pollack v. Laidlaw Holdings, Inc., 27 F.3d 808 (2d Cir.1994). The details of the analysis are not within the scope of our present treatment; see J. Thomas Cookson, Loan Participation Agreements as Securities: Judicial Interpretations of the Securities Act of 1933 and the Securities Exchange Act of 1934, 24 Wm. & Mary L. Rev. 295 (1983). The unsophisticated consumer who invests in participation interests is at a particular disadvantage, often finding himself or herself in a swimming pool operated by a shark. See Braunreiter, Consumer Investing in Trust Deeds, 2 Cal.Real Prop.J. 29 (Winter 1984).

Misrepresentation or concealment by the lead lender. Many of the conflicts that arise between the lead lender and the participants revolve around the fact that the characteristics of the underlying borrower and the real estate never matched the participants' beliefs or assumptions. For example, the borrower may have had weaker credit, less real estate management experience, lower net worth, or a poorer track record in repaying past loans than the participants understood. The real estate may have had a lower value, been in a more risky location, or been more difficult to develop than the participants realized. Ideally the parties would make it perfectly clear whether the participants were relying on the lead lender's representations about such matters, or whether they had made their own investigation of the facts. But the extent of such reliance is often left quite unclear, and gives rise to litigation. See, e.g., Commonwealth Mortg. Corp. v. First Nationwide Bank, 873 F.2d 859 (5th Cir.1989); First Fed. Sav. & Loan Ass'n v. Twin City Sav. Bank, FSB, 868 F.2d 725 (5th Cir.1989).

Misdealing by the lead lender. As the foregoing material suggests, modern participation agreements are characterized by a high degree of flexibility and informality. The underlying loan documents, including notes and mortgages, are usually left in the hands of the lead lender. Normally neither the participation agreement nor the participation certificates are recorded in the real estate records, nor is a financing statement filed under Article 9 of the UCC. Indeed, no filing seems necessary, since a participation interest is evidently a "payment intangible" under Article 9, and perfection of security interests in payment intangibles is automatic under § 9–309(3). Moreover, the participants are clearly not holders in due course of the mortgage note or notes. Most of the time this informality simplifies what otherwise could be an inherently complex transaction. It creates few problems where, as is usual, the lead lender is a solvent, reputable and reasonably competent lending institution.

On the other hand, what if the lead lender is incompetent or crooked? Suppose, for example, that a lead lender reassigns the note or notes or sells additional participation interests in them? Or suppose the loan documents are pledged as security for unrelated borrowing by the lead lender? Even assuming that such acts are not conscious misdealing, what if they occur by mistake? What if the lead lender becomes insolvent and goes into bankruptcy? In each of these cases, a potential conflict exists between the claims of the participants and those of third parties whose interests arise through the lead lender.

These problems have the potential to arise simply because the lead lender continues to hold the underlying mortgage note or notes. Hence, one obvious precaution the participants can take is to relieve the lead lender of possession of the notes. Of course, it is not easy for the parties to agree that one of several participants will be the "lucky" one who holds the notes. A more even-handed approach is to appoint a custodian (typically a commercial bank that has no other connection with the transaction) and transfer the notes to it with an accompanying agreement. This will prevent the lead lender from improperly releasing the underlying mortgages or "double-selling" or "double-pledging" the notes. An alternative, somewhat simpler but less neat, is to mark the notes with a legend stating that participation shares in them have been sold, to whom they were sold, and in what amounts. This approach is more practical if the participation is of a single large mortgage loan rather than a pool of small loans.

Recharacterization of the participation as a loan. If the lead lender enters bankruptcy, the trustee in bankruptcy might argue that the participation "sales" are not sales at all, but instead are merely loans by the participants to the lead lender, with the interests in the mortgage notes serving as security for repayment. These supposed security interests are often unperfected, with the participants relying on the automatic perfection concept of § 9–309(3), which governs payment intangibles. The trustee in bankruptcy, acting under the "strong-arm" powers granted by Section 544(a)(1) of the Bankruptcy Code, could arguably assume the role of a perfected lien creditor and thus take priority over these unperfected security interests.

With a properly-drafted participation agreement, this argument has little substance. Ordinarily, the parties' agreement that a sale, not a loan, is intended, should control. However, the parties may add features which weaken the sale characterization. For example, if the participation agreement includes a guarantee by the lead lender of payment of the underlying obligation, or a repurchase provision which obliges the lead lender to buy back the participation interest in the event of default, the courts may conclude that the participants do not have the normal risks of ownership, and thus that the transaction is in reality a loan with the underlying mortgage and note serving as security for its repayment. See, e.g., In re Brooke Capital Corp., 2012 WL 4793010 (Bankr. D. Kan. 2012); In re Sackman Mortg. Corp., 158 B.R. 926 (Bankr. S.D.N.Y. 1993). The cases are mixed; contra, see In re Lemons & Associates, Inc., 67 B.R. 198 (Bankr.D.Nev.1986).

The risk that the participation will be recharacterized as a loan means that it is unwise for the participants to rely on the automatic perfection concept embodied in UCC § 9–309(3), since it will not apply if the transaction is deemed a loan. If that occurs, it's likely that the proper Article 9 characterization would be as "accounts"; the court in *Brooke Capital*, supra, seems to have reached that conclusion. Hence, as a precaution the participants should file financing statements, thereby perfecting under § 9–310(a).

D. DISCHARGE OF THE DEBT AND MORTGAGE: BY PAYMENT OR OTHERWISE

Everyone recognizes instinctively that when a borrower pays off the mortgage debt in full, the mortgage itself is extinguished. The popular mythology of the borrower "burning the mortgage" reflects this basic concept. The concept is indeed correct, but it is a bit more complex and requires some further explanation.

To begin with, a mortgage may be paid off by either of two classes of persons: those who are "primarily responsible" for paying it and those who are not. Who is "primarily responsible?" The concept is not dependent on the existence of personal liability on the debt. Most obviously, the mortgagor is "primarily responsible" if he or she still owns the real estate, whether the debt is recourse or not. Likewise, if the real estate is sold, the grantee becomes "primarily responsible," whether the grantee assumed personal liability on the debt or not. Even a tenant in common, a life tenant, or other holder of a limited interest in the real estate is "primarily responsible" except to the extent that someone else has a duty to reimburse him or her for part of the payment he or she might make.

If a complete payoff of the loan (including any valid accrued interest, prepayment fees, and other miscellaneous items) is made by somebody who is "primarily responsible," the mortgage is indeed extinguished. Legally, it doesn't exist anymore. Of course, that doesn't make it disappear from the public records. Hence, the mortgagee has a duty to provide a suitable document, recordable in form, showing that the mortgage has been released. The person making the payoff can then record it to clear the records. We can correctly refer to the payoff as a "redemption" of the land from the mortgage.

Incidentally, the great majority of states have statutes that formalize the mortgagee's duty to provide a recordable document discharging the mortgage. The name customarily given to the document varies from one jurisdiction to another; it may be called a release, a satisfaction-piece, a discharge, or (particularly where deeds of trust are commonly used) a reconveyance. The name has little significance. These statutes often provide a fixed time period (e.g., 10 to 90 days) within which the lender must provide the document of discharge. Many of them impose financial penalties on lenders who fail to comply, and in addition allow the payor to recover any actual damages resulting from the lender's failure to provide a discharge.

Most of the statutory penalties are imposed only after the borrower submits a specific request for the satisfaction, and their amounts are generally modest (say, $100 to $1,000), but some are quite Draconian. The Missouri statute, for example, imposes a penalty of the lesser of $300 per day or ten percent of the loan balance. In Oklahoma, it's one percent of the loan balance for each day after ten days; see Tucker v. FSB Mortgage of Little Rock, 886 P.2d 498 (Okl.App.1994), imposing a penalty of $16,400. In South Carolina, the trial court may in its discretion impose a penalty of up to one-half of the loan balance; such an order, imposing a fee of $72,500, was upheld in Kinard v. Fleet Real Estate Funding Corp., 319 S.C. 408, 461 S.E.2d 833 (App.1995). The worst (or best) jurisdiction is Pennsylvania, which provides (in Pa.Stat.Ann., tit.21, §§ 681–82) for a forfeiture by the mortgagee of any amount up to the full mortgage debt, in the court's discretion. The Uniform Residential Mortgage Satisfaction Act, promulgated by the National Conference of Commissioners on Uniform State Laws in 2004, imposes a flat penalty of $500 if the satisfaction is not provided within 30 days after a written demand; the demand may not be sent until 30 days after the payoff occurs, effectively giving the lender at least 60 days before the penalty becomes effective. Id. at § 203. The Act has been adopted in Alabama, North Carolina, Virginia and Wisconsin.

Ordinarily only a complete payoff will have the effect of extinguishing a mortgage. However, sometimes the parties to a mortgage loan will negotiate and include in their mortgage a "partial release" clause. Such an arrangement is particularly common where a lender has a blanket mortgage on a subdivision of lots, and is willing to allow the developer to sell individual lots "out from under" the blanket mortgage by paying the lender a specified amount for the release of each lot. A similar clause may be used when an apartment building is converted to condominiums.

What about payoffs by people who are not "primarily responsible?" Such people include an original mortgagor who has transferred the land subject to or with an assumption of the mortgage; the holder of a junior mortgage or other junior lien, a tenant under a subordinate lease, and conceivably even people holding easements or covenant rights subordinate to the mortgage. They too have the right to pay the mortgage in full (if it is due by its terms or has been accelerated by the mortgagee), and their act of payment is also properly known as a redemption. However, redemption by such a person has a very different consequence than redemption by one who is "primarily responsible." It doesn't *extinguish* the mortgage, but instead *assigns* both the obligation (the note or other evidence of debt) and the mortgage to the payor.

This assignment takes place by operation of law, and is based on the principle of subrogation. Its purpose is to avoid unjust enrichment by helping the payor get reimbursed by the person who *should* have paid—the person who is primarily responsible for payment. Although the assignment takes place automatically, the mortgagee is obligated upon request to give the payor an actual paper document of assignment showing that the payor now has the rights the mortgagee had before.

Perhaps the most common illustration of this principle involves the holder of a second mortgage who learns that the borrower has defaulted in payment on the first mortgage. The holder of the second may elect to go to the holder of the first and pay it off in full. Now the holder of the second mortgage also holds the first mortgage (and the right to enforce the first note personally, as well, if it is a recourse obligation). Why would the holder of second engage in this transaction? Principally to gain control of the timing and procedure of foreclosure. The second mortgagee can now determine whether and when to foreclose, and whether foreclosure will be judicial or by power of sale (if the jurisdiction permits the latter). If property values are presently low but the holder of the second expects them to rise in the near future, gaining this control may mean the difference between the second mortgagee's being wiped out by a foreclosure of the first and being able to recover, in the long run, at least part of its debt.

Tender. Suppose someone (in either of the two categories discussed above) approaches a mortgage lender and offers to pay off the mortgage debt in full, but the lender refuses to accept the money. This present offer (if it is in fact within the offeror's ability to carry out) is a tender. For many purposes, it is as good as an actual payment. It immediately stops the running of interest on the mortgage debt. It entitles the payor to a release or an assignment (as the case may be) of the mortgage.

Of course, the tender must be in cash or "good funds;" a tender of a new promissory note for the balance owing on the old note is completely ineffective to extinguish the mortgage; see FNMA v. McAuliffe, 226 A.D.2d 497, 641 N.Y.S.2d 115 (1996). Moreover, the tender must be "kept good" in the sense that the party who tenders must continue to be ready, willing, and able to pay. The tender must also be unconditional (except, of course, for the condition that the law imposes anyway—namely, that the lender provide a document of release or assignment).

On all of these matters involving discharge and tender, see Restatement (Third) of Property (Mortgages) § 6.4 (1997).

Mortgagees' disclosures. One who is ready to pay off a mortgage debt needs to know the amount to pay. Lenders often keep better records than borrowers, and even if the borrower has calculated the payoff amount, he or she would like to be certain that the lender agrees. Hence, it is customary for lenders to provide "payoff letters" or statements upon request, usually for a small fee.

In addition to the borrower who is paying off of the loan, there are a number of other persons who may have a legitimate need to know the balance and status of the mortgage debt. For example, a buyer who intends to assume or take subject to an existing debt will need to know its amount. A bidder at the foreclosure sale of a junior mortgage needs to know the amount of the senior mortgage debt. A junior lienholder who intends to redeem a senior mortgage in order to protect against its foreclosure will need to know the redemption amount.

Perhaps 15 or so jurisdictions have statutes requiring lenders to provide payoff statements, but they are often poorly drafted. The Restatement (Third) of Property (Mortgages) § 1.6 (1997) takes the view that lenders have a common-law obligation to provide a statement of the amount owing, the current interest rate and the basis of adjustment if it is adjustable, any additional fees and charges the lender claims, and whether the loan is in default or has been accelerated. The lender must also disclose the balance in any escrow account (held to pay taxes and insurance, for example), and the identity of any person whom the lender knows has acquired an interest in the mortgage or the debt.

A request for this information must be made for good cause by the mortgagor, someone else whose performance is secured by the mortgage, the holder of any interest in the real estate, or a prospective bidder at a foreclosure sale. A mortgagee who fails to disclose within a reasonable time after such a request is liable for damages. In addition, an incorrect disclosure may estop the lender to deny its accuracy as against someone who has reasonably and detrimentally relied on it. Note that it's hard for a mortgagor to claim detrimental reliance on an incorrect statement, since the mortgagor knows or should know at least the approximate balance owing on his or her own debt. See, e.g., In re Royal Meadows Stables, Inc., 187 B.R. 516 (Bankr.E.D.Va.1995) (borrower had at least "constructive knowledge" of the actual amount of the debt). Compare Freedom Fin. Thrift & Loan v. Golden Pacific Bank, 20 Cal.App.4th 1305, 25 Cal.Rptr.2d 235 (1993), in which a new lender paid off the old loan on the basis of a payoff statement which the old lender later claimed was erroneously low. The court held the old lender was estopped as against the new lender, but could still recover the remaining amount of the debt from the borrower.

Section 201(d) of the Uniform Residential Mortgage Satisfaction Act contains language similar to that of the Restatement. It requires the payoff statement to include "(1) the date on which it was prepared and the payoff amount as of that date, including the amount by type of each fee, charge, or other sum included within the payoff amount; (2) the information reasonably necessary to calculate the payoff amount as of the requested payoff date, including the per diem interest amount; and (3) the payment cutoff time, if any, the address or place where payment must be made, and any limitation as to the authorized method of payment."

Prepayment. Contrary to what is probably pervasive popular belief, a mortgagee has a common law right to refuse an early tender or "prepayment" of principal or interest. This rule is derived from the classic case of Brown v. Cole, 14 L.J. (N.S.) Ch. 167, Chancery, 1845, where the court stated that if mortgagors "were allowed to pay off their mortgage money at any time after the execution of the mortgage, it might be attended with extreme inconvenience to mortgagees, who generally advance their money as an investment." For many mortgagees, prepayment creates more than a problem of reinvesting the prepaid funds. If the mortgage is held by a vendor who desires installment sale reporting of his gain on the sale under § 453 of the Internal Revenue Code, unanticipated prepayment can result in greatly increased tax liability.

In an attempt to buttress their common law rights, mortgagees sometimes include "lock-out" mortgage provisions that specifically prohibit prepayment for a fixed period of time, or even for the entire life of the loan. See, e.g., Hartford Life Ins. Co. v. Randall, 283 Or. 297, 583 P.2d 1126 (1978), upholding a mortgage note provision which entirely prohibited any payoff for eleven years as not constituting an unreasonable restraint on alienation; George v. Fowler, 96 Wash.App. 187, 978 P.2d 565 (1999), upholding a lock-out for the full life of the loan. Of course, even if the loan is "locked out" and gives the borrower no prepayment privilege, the lender may still accept a prepayment voluntarily if the borrower "sweetens" the deal by agreeing to pay a negotiated fee. See Tyler v. Equitable Life Assur. Socy., 512 So.2d 55 (Ala.1987). But under common law principles, a "lock-out" clause is unnecessary, since no lender ever has a duty to accept a prepayment unless the mortgage or note expressly authorize the borrower to prepay.

The common law rule, termed "perfect tender in time," has been widely criticized as contrary to most borrowers' expectations. Restatement (Third) of Property (Mortgages) § 6.1 (1997) rejects it, providing instead that "In the absence of an agreement restricting or prohibiting payment of the mortgage obligation prior to maturity, the mortgagor has a right to make such payment in whole or in part." It seems little enough to ask of mortgagees, who are nearly always the drafters of the loan documents, that if they want to restrict prepayment they ought to say so. But only two jurisdictions have agreed; see Mahoney v. Furches, 503 Pa. 60, 468 A.2d 458 (1983); Skyles v. Burge, 789 S.W.2d 116 (Mo.App.1990). The arguments are nicely set out in Metropolitan Life Ins. Co. v. Promenade Towers Mut. Housing Corp., 84 Md.App. 702, 581 A.2d 846 (1990) which, like nearly all recent cases, continues to follow "perfect tender in time." See, e.g., Ex parte Brannon, 683 So.2d 994 (Ala.1996). See also Poommipanit v. Sloan, 1 Neb.App. 1132, 510 N.W.2d 542 (1993), applying the common law rule to a real estate installment contract.[12]

As a matter of practice, of course, many mortgagees permit prepayment and provide for it in their mortgage documents. However, they may exact a fee or "prepayment penalty" for the privilege of prepaying the loan. Much of the following material focuses on judicial and legislative attempts to deal with such fees. For comprehensive treatments of mortgage prepayment, see Megan W. Murray, Prepayment Premiums: Contracting for Future Financial Stability in the Commercial Lending Market, 96 Iowa L.Rev. 1037 (2011); Dale A. Whitman, Mortgage Prepayment Clauses: A Legal and Economic Analysis, 40 UCLA L.Rev. 851 (1993); Frank S. Alexander, Mortgage Prepayment: The Trial of Common Sense, 72 Cornell L.Rev. 288 (1987).

LOPRESTI V. WELLS FARGO BANK, N.A

Superior Court of New Jersey, Appellate Division, 2014
435 N.J.Super. 311, 88 A.3d 944

The opinion of the court was delivered by PARRILLO, P.J.A.D.

* * * On March 1, 2002, Body Max executed and delivered a Promissory Note to defendant's predecessor, First Union, as evidence of a $550,000 loan. The terms of this note included an interest rate of 6.75% and required Body Max to make "consecutive monthly payments of principal and interest in the amount of $4,898.00 commencing on April 1, 2002 and continuing on the same day of each month thereafter until fully paid." The total principal and interest accrued on the loan was "due and payable on March 1, 2007." In addition, this original note contained a prepayment provision setting a fee of 1% in the event Body Max paid the loan prior to the termination date:

---

[12] It is rare for a court to depart from "perfect tender in time," but it can occur. See Littlejohn v. Parrish, 163 Ohio App.3d 456, 839 N.E.2d 49 (2005), holding that if the borrower was willing to pay a fee that would fully compensate the lenders for their lost interest income, the lenders' refusal to accept prepayment breached the implied contractual duty of good faith and fair dealing.

PREPAYMENT COMPENSATION. Principal may be prepaid in whole or in part at any time; *provided, however,* if principal is paid before it is due under this Note, whether voluntary, mandatory, upon acceleration or otherwise, such prepayment shall include a fee equal to 1% of the amount prepaid.

Any prepayment in whole or in part shall include accrued interest and all other sums then due under any of the Loan Documents. No partial prepayment shall affect the obligation of Borrower to make any payment of principal or interest due under this Note on the due dates specified.

This note was executed by Salvatore Lopresti (Lopresti) in his capacity as President of Body Max.

In order to secure payment of its obligations under the original note, Body Max executed a Mortgage and Absolute Assignment of Leases dated March 1, 2002 to First Union. This mortgage covered Body Max's principal place of business, a gymnasium located on Delsea Drive in Washington Township. This document was also executed by Lopresti as President of Body Max.

Additionally, on March 1, 2002, Lopresti executed and delivered to First Union an Unconditional Guaranty to provide assurance that Body Max would fulfill its obligations under the original note. To secure payment and performance of the guaranty, plaintiffs executed and delivered a Mortgage and Absolute Assignment Agreement of Leases to First Union, covering the premises where their primary residence was located, also in Washington Township.

Pursuant to the loan transaction of March 1, 2002, First Union advanced the full $550,000 loan proceeds to Body Max. Body Max then transferred the funds to TD Bank in order to pay off a prior loan borrowed by Body Max. Plaintiffs did not personally receive any of the loan proceeds.

Thereafter, on December 20, 2005, Body Max modified the terms of its original note with Wachovia Bank, First Union's successor and Wells Fargo's immediate predecessor. Lopresti, as President of Body Max, executed and delivered the modified note of December 20, 2005 in the amount of $460,195.41. The modified note stated that it "renew[ed], extend[ed] and/or modifie[d] that [Original Note of March 1, 2002], evidencing an original principal amount of $550,000.00." The terms of the modified note included an interest rate of 7.25% and called for "consecutive monthly payments of principal and interest in the amount of $4,228.19 commencing on January 20, 2006, and continuing on the same day of each month thereafter until fully paid." All of the principal and interest on this modified note were "due and payable on December 20, 2020." Further, the modified note defined "loan documents" as "all documents executed in connection with or related to the loan evidenced by this Note and any prior notes which evidence all or any portion of the loan evidenced by this Note ... guaranty agreements, ... [and] mortgage instruments. . . ."

The December 20, 2005 modified note also contained a prepayment provision, structured to compensate Wachovia for an early payoff of the loan, in the event market interest rates had fallen. The provision states:

COMPENSATION UPON PREPAYMENT OR ACCELERATION.

In addition to principal, interest and any other amounts due under this Note, Borrower shall on demand pay to Bank any "Breakage Fee" due hereunder for any voluntary or mandatory prepayment or acceleration, in whole or in part, of principal of this Note occurring prior to the date such principal would, but for that prepayment or acceleration, have become due. For any date of prepayment or acceleration ("Break Date"), a Breakage Fee shall be due if the rate under "A" below exceeds the rate under "B" below and shall be determined as follows:

Breakage Fee = the sum of the products of ((A-B) x C) for each installment of principal being prepaid, where:

A = A rate equal to the sum of (i) the bond equivalent yield (bid side) of the U.S. Treasury security with a maturity closest to the Maturity Date as reported by *The Wall Street Journal* (or other published source) on the funding date of this Note, plus (ii) 1/2%.

B = A rate equal to the bond equivalent yield (bid side) of the U.S. Treasury security with a maturity closest to the Maturity Date as reported by *The Wall Street Journal* (or other published source) on the Break Date.

C = The principal installment amount being prepaid times (the number of days remaining until the scheduled due date for such installment divided by 360).

"Maturity Date" is the date on which the final payment of principal of this Note would, but for any prepayment or acceleration, have become due.

Breakage Fees are payable as liquidated damages, are a reasonable pre-estimate of the losses, costs and expenses Bank would incur in the event of any prepayment or acceleration of this Note, are not a penalty, will not require claim for, or proof of, actual damages, and Bank's determination thereof shall be conclusive and binding in the absence of manifest error.

Any prepayment in whole or in part shall include accrued interest and all other sums then due under any of the Loan Documents. No partial prepayment shall affect Borrower's obligation to make any payment of principal or interest due under this Note on the date specified in the Repayment Terms paragraph of this Note until this Note has been paid in full.

On May 19, 2010, Body Max attempted to refinance the original 2002 loan, as modified by the 2005 loan, in order to obtain a lower interest rate and to reduce the prepayment fees on the loan. However, about two months later, Wachovia declined Body Max's request due to the company's "negative equity positions and losses."

Subsequently, Body Max was able to obtain refinancing from TD Bank Commercial Lending (TD Bank) and requested a payoff amount from Wachovia for the balance of the loan. On July 21, 2010, Wachovia provided Body Max with a payoff of all amounts due on the loan. TD Bank then transferred the total payoff amount of $416,838.78 directly to Wells Fargo, which included $368,383.99 of principal, $148.38 of accrued interest and $48,306.41 in prepayment fees. A Settlement Statement was executed by TD Bank and Body Max evidencing the total amount of the loan owed to Wells Fargo, including the prepayment fee, that was advanced by TD Bank on behalf of Body Max.

According to Wells Fargo, plaintiffs did not issue any personal checks from any of their personal accounts to pay the principal loan or the $48,306.41 prepayment fee due to the Bank. Rather, as noted, the prepayment fees were paid by TD Bank directly to Wells Fargo out of the proceeds of its loan to Body Max.

As noted, plaintiffs filed a complaint alleging that defendant violated both the Prepayment Law and the New Jersey Consumer Fraud Act, *N.J.S.A.* 56:8–1 to –20, by assessing and collecting a prepayment charge as provided for in the promissory note executed in connection with the business loan to Body Max. In its summary judgment motion, defendant maintained that plaintiffs lacked standing because they did not have a sufficient stake in the matter inasmuch as Body Max paid the prepayment fee through its refinancing arrangement with TD Bank. Substantively, defendant argued that the protection of the Prepayment Law allowing for prepayment *without* penalty to any "mortgagor," other than a corporation, simply does not apply to commercial loans between sophisticated business parties, such as the transaction at issue here. Additionally, defendant contended that the formula used to calculate the prepayment fee was reasonable and designed to protect the Bank's interests in the event that interest rates had fallen prior to the maturity of the loan. Finally, defendant maintained that there was no evidence of unlawful conduct to support the consumer fraud count.

Plaintiffs countered that they have standing as personal guarantors of the bank loan; that the Prepayment Law applies to this transaction because the initial loan was secured by their personal residence and they were personally liable for the obligations under the loan; that the prepayment fee was unreasonable because the modification of more than 13% was greater than the initial bargained for prepayment fee of 1% and Wells Fargo failed to provide documentation evidencing how it reached the amount charged; and finally that the prepayment penalty amounted to a violation of the Consumer Fraud Act.

In granting summary judgment for defendant, dismissing plaintiffs' complaint in its entirety, the motion judge held that the Prepayment Law did not apply, reasoning:

> The corporation willingly negotiated the terms of [its] loan with the banks that were involved here. . . . There were sophisticated parties. Certainly the reason why a prepayment penalty cannot be imposed on the individual is to protect that individual, but it is not felt it was necessary when we have a corporation involved.

The court further explained "that there was a guaranty executed, which did involve the plaintiffs in this matter, but . . . the guaranty never came into play, the individuals never came into play in this matter, [because] there was no default."

The judge also found no Consumer Fraud Act violation:

> When we're dealing with the New Jersey Consumer Fraud Act, . . . a plaintiff must allege three elements under the Consumer Fraud Act. One, unlawful conduct by the defendant, and then we go on to an ascertainable loss and a causal relationship. . . .

> I find that the plaintiff in this matter is unable to provide the [c]ourt with any evidence whatsoever of unlawful conduct by the defendant in this matter and, therefore, that cause of action cannot be sustained either in this instance. They have failed on the first prong of the three-part test under the Act.

This appeal by plaintiffs followed. * * *

Pursuant to *N.J.S.A.* 46:10B–2, "[p]repayment of a mortgage loan may be made by or on behalf of a mortgagor at any time without penalty." Consequently, "[a]ny holder of a mortgage loan . . . who shall knowingly demand and receive prepayment fees . . . shall be liable to the mortgagor for the return of the whole amount of the prepayment fees so received, plus interest. . . ." *N.J.S.A.* 46:10B–5.

Thus, the Prepayment Law prohibits the charging of a prepayment fee on a "mortgage loan," which is defined as "a loan secured by an interest in real property consisting of land upon which is erected or to be erected, in whole or in part *with the proceeds of such loan,* a structure containing ... dwelling units...." *N.J.S.A.* 46:10B–1(a) (emphasis added). Moreover, a "mortgagor" is defined as "any person *other than a corporation* liable for the payment of a mortgage loan, and the owner of the real property which secures the payment of a mortgage loan[.]" *N.J.S.A.* 46:10B–1(b) (emphasis added).

The Prepayment Law applies to individual consumers, not commercial mortgagors, as the Legislature clearly "intended to protect individual mortgagors from being locked into long-term mortgages with excessive interest rates, but felt that more sophisticated commercial mortgagors needed no such protection." *Shinn v. Encore Mortg. Servs., Inc.,* 96 *F.Supp.*2d 419, 422 (D.N.J.2000). Indeed, we have upheld the use of prepayment fees negotiated on commercial loans between sophisticated parties. *See e.g., Westmark Commercial Mortg. Fund IV v. Teenform Assocs., L.P.,* 362 *N.J.Super.* 336, 347–48, 827 *A.*2d 1154 (App.Div.2003) (holding that the prepayment premium on a commercial loan was permissible where the debtor freely entered into the contract, the terms of the contract were clear and unambiguous, and the parties were experienced and sophisticated); *Mony Life Ins. Co. v. Paramus Parkway Building, Ltd.,* 364 *N.J.Super.* 92, 105, 834 *A.*2d 475 (App.Div.2003) (holding that a clear and unambiguous prepayment premium clause was "valid and enforceable under New Jersey law[ ]").

In *Westmark, supra,* the debtor challenged the prepayment premiums that were charged after the creditor accelerated the payout under the loan contract. 362 *N.J.Super.* at 343, 827 *A.*2d 1154. We noted, at the outset, that "[a] borrower does not have the right, under New Jersey law, to prepay a commercial loan, unless the documents afford that right." *Id.* at 343–44, 827 *A.*2d 1154 (citing *Norwest Bank Minnesota v. Blair Road Assocs.,* 252 *F.Supp.*2d 86, 97 (D.N.J.2003)). Thus, " '[s]ince a lender has the right not to have the loan prepaid but rely on collecting the interest contracted for, the lender is entitled to charge a penalty to the borrower for the privilege of the prepayment.' " *Id.* at 344, 827 *A.*2d 1154 (quoting *Norwest, supra,* 252 *F.Supp.*2d at 97). Further, we determined that prepayment clauses were "designed to protect a lender against potential losses it may incur if a loan is paid earlier than contracted for." *Ibid.* (citing *United States v. Harris,* 246 *F.*3d 566, 573 (6th Cir.2001)).

In holding that the prepayment fee in *Westmark, supra,* was enforceable, we relied, in part, on the *Restatement (Third) of Property: Mortgages* § 6.2 (1997). *Id.* at 347, 827 *A.*2d 1154. Specifically, the Restatement notes that "if the borrower fully understood and had the opportunity to bargain over the clause, either with the assistance of counsel or by virtue of the borrower's own experience and expertise, the clause will ordinarily be enforced." *Restatement (Third), supra,* § 6.2 comment c. In addition, we reasoned that "to deem the [prepayment] clause unenforceable[ ] . . . would be providing defendants with a better contract than they were able to negotiate for themselves. . . ." *Id.* at 347, 827 A.2d 1154; *see also Karl's Sales & Serv. v. Gimbel Bros., Inc.,* 249 *N.J.Super.* 487, 493, 592 A.2d 647 (App.Div.) (finding that courts may not "remake a better contract for the parties than they themselves have seen fit to enter into, or to alter it for the benefit of one party and to the detriment of the other [ ]"), *certif. denied,* 127 *N.J.* 548, 606 A.2d 362 (1991).

Here, it is undisputed that the subject matter of plaintiffs' complaint involves a commercial loan to a business, and the loan proceeds were used for business, and not personal, much less residential home, purposes. Plaintiffs offer no proof to the contrary.

Nevertheless, plaintiffs argue that they fall within the Prepayment Law's definition of "mortgagor" because they are "any person other than a corporation" and they were liable for payment of the loan in the event Body Max defaulted. Specifically, they point to the guaranty executed as part of the initial promissory note, which provided their residential property as collateral security in the event Body Max defaulted on the loan. Plaintiffs' statutory interpretation is simply wrong.

On March 1, 2002, Body Max executed and delivered a Promissory Note to First Union as evidence of a $550,000 loan. Significantly, the borrower under the promissory note was not plaintiffs but their business, Body Max. In fact, the 2002 and 2005 loan documents that contained the prepayment provisions explicitly designate Body Max as the borrower.

Just as significant, the full amount of the loan was advanced to Body Max under the original note. In other words, Wells Fargo transferred the loan proceeds directly to Body Max's corporate account, not to plaintiffs' personal accounts, and the proceeds were not used in connection with plaintiffs' real property. Also, to secure the amounts advanced under the original note, Body Max executed and delivered a mortgage on the commercial property where the corporation conducts business.

Even more fatal to plaintiffs' position, the mortgage referred to in their complaint, although it covers their residence, does not secure a personal loan, since, as noted, the loan proceeds were not used in connection with plaintiffs' real property. Rather, the mortgage secures plaintiffs' personal guarantee of the obligations of their business, Body Max, under the Wells Fargo commercial loan. As such, because the loan proceeds from the bank were not used in connection with plaintiffs' real property, their residential mortgage is not a "mortgage loan" within the definition of *N.J.S.A.* 46:10B–1(a), and therefore Wells Fargo is not the "holder of a mortgage loan" subject to the protections against prepayment fees in the Prepayment Law.

In fact, neither plaintiffs' guarantee nor the mortgage on their residence provide for a prepayment fee, and plaintiffs did not pay the prepayment fee in this matter. Rather, the prepayment fee is expressly provided for in the note executed by Body Max and naming Body Max as the borrower. Pursuant to that contractual provision, it was Body Max that was charged the prepayment fee, and Body Max that paid all accounts owed to Wells Fargo, including the prepayment fee, when Body Max refinanced the loan with TD Bank.

To reiterate then, Body Max was the actual borrower and "mortgagor" under the Wells Fargo loan. The 2002 initial loan and the 2005 loan modification were both executed by Body Max and required the corporation to fulfill the loan obligations, including the prepayment fee. And to that end, Body Max fulfilled its obligations to Wells Fargo, including payment of the contractual prepayment fee, through its refinanced loan with TD Bank. And because of Body Max's corporate status, Wells Fargo, as holder of the mortgage loan, was exempted from the Prepayment Law's proscription against charging such a fee. *N.J.S.A.* 46:10B–1(b). Thus, we concur with the motion judge's holding that the Prepayment Law is inapplicable to the instant transaction.

We are therefore left with plaintiffs' alternative contention that the prepayment fee in the 2005 modified loan was excessive. Specifically, plaintiffs argue that the modified prepayment provision, which increased the 1% fee to over 13%, was unreasonable, and that the $48,306.41 prepayment charge amounted to an unlawful penalty or stipulated damage clause.

Defendant maintains that the "breakage fee" formula used to calculate the prepayment charge was structured to do nothing more than compensate the Bank for the investment value lost in the event Body Max paid the loan off early at a time when interest rates had fallen. Specifically, Wells Fargo contends that if the interest rates at the time of refinancing were higher than the interest rates when Body Max received funding for the loan, there would have been no prepayment fee. Thus, Wells Fargo asserts that the formula was not an arbitrary penalty, but rather a mechanism to protect its investment. We agree.

In asserting that the prepayment charge was unreasonable, plaintiffs rely exclusively on *MetLife Capital Financial Corporation v. Washington Avenue Associates L.P.,* 159 *N.J.* 484, 495–501, 732 *A.*2d 493 (1998), which addressed the reasonableness of a 5% late fee on a commercial loan. At the outset, the Court determined that "liquidated damages provisions in a commercial contract between sophisticated parties are presumptively reasonable and the party challenging the clause bears the burden of proving its unreasonableness." *Id.* at 496, 732 *A.*2d 493. The Court found that the reasonableness of a stipulated damages provision requires a review of the totality of the circumstances. *Id.* at 495, 732 *A.*2d 493. After considering several factors regarding this late fee, including (1) the normal industry standard; (2) the use of the fee to compensate the lender for administrative costs; (3) the fact that the "loan involved an arms-length, fully negotiated transaction between two sophisticated commercial parties, each represented by counsel[,]"; and (4) the absence of fraud, duress or unconscionability on the part of the lender, the Court concluded that the borrower was unable to overcome the presumptive reasonableness of the fee. *Id.* at 500, 732 *A.*2d 493.

Here, too, plaintiffs have not overcome the presumptive reasonableness of the prepayment fee. As the trial court noted, the loan transaction involved sophisticated parties, who freely negotiated the terms of the loan, and the prepayment provision was "clearly spelled out" in the 2005 loan modification. In addition, as Wells Fargo asserts, the "breakage fee" was not an arbitrary penalty, but rather a carefully constructed formula used to protect the Bank's loan investment in the event interest rates dropped prior to the termination date. The formula sought to protect Wells Fargo's investment by accounting for the market interest rates at the time of prepayment in comparison to the interest rates at the time the loan was first advanced.[3] According to this formula, if the interest rates at the time Body Max prematurely paid the loan were higher than when it first received the loan, then there would have been no prepayment fee. Thus, the totality of the circumstances concerning the prepayment provision, including the sophistication of the parties involved, the use of the fee to compensate Wells Fargo, and considering that the formula used to calculate the breakage fee was "clearly spelled out," demonstrate that the charge was neither excessive nor unreasonable.

Finally, having found no violation by defendant of the Prepayment Law, and therefore no unlawful conduct or unconscionable commercial practice, plaintiffs simply have not established a viable, valid claim under the Consumer Fraud Act. Therefore, the dismissal of this count of plaintiffs' complaint was also proper.

Affirmed.

---

[3] For each monthly installment payment due on the loan, the breakage fee was calculated as the difference between the yield on Treasuries with the same maturity as the loan, as of the date the loan was originally funded, and the yield on Treasuries as of the date the loan was prepaid. The result is a measure of the difference in the investment value of funds on the date of the loan and the date of the prepayment. This figure was then multiplied by the amount of each principal installment being prepaid times the number of days remaining until the scheduled due date for such installment divided by 360.

NOTES

1. *Language permitting prepayment.* Even under the common law rule, lenders sometimes include language permitting prepayment without realizing that they've done it. If the promissory note provides for payments of X dollars per month "or more," or if it states that the entire balance must be paid by X date "if not sooner paid," the borrower can prepay the balance owing at any time. See Latimer v. Grundy County Nat'l Bank, 239 Ill.App.3d 1000, 180 Ill.Dec. 400, 607 N.E.2d 294 (1993); Acord v. Jones, 211 Ga.App. 682, 440 S.E.2d 679 (1994). The casual use of such "boilerplate" phrases can backfire against the lender.

2. *Types of prepayment clauses.* Many mortgages expressly permit prepayment, but only upon the borrower's paying of an additional fee or "penalty." Such fees are relatively rare in home mortgage loans, but are widely used in loans on commercial property. A variety of formulas may be used to calculate the fee. Examples include:

-   six months' interest on the amount by which prepayments in any 12 month period exceed 20% of the original principal amount. (This formula was widely used in home mortgages loans in the 1960s and 1970s.)

-   A fixed percentage (e.g., 2%) of the amount being prepaid. (This percentage may decline over time as the loan grows closer to maturity; e.g., 2% during the loan's first five years, and 1% thereafter.)

-   The present value of difference between the interest the lender would have earned on the mortgage loan for the remaining term and the interest it would earn on the same sum if invested in some alternative investment, such as U.S. government securities of an equivalent term. (This sort of clause is sometimes referred to as a "yield maintenance" fee.) The wording of such clauses tends to be complex and filled with mathematical jargon, unintelligible to many readers. Here is an example of a relatively clear and simple version (with the definitions of the terms omitted):

"Required Yield Maintenance" shall mean an amount equal to the positive excess of (i) the present value ("PV") of all future installments of principal and interest due under this Note including the principal amount due at maturity (collectively, "All Future Payments"), discounted at an interest rate per annum equal to the Treasury Constant Maturity Yield Index published during the second full week preceding the date on which such premium is payable for instruments having a maturity coterminous with the remaining term of this Note, over (ii) the principal amount of this Note outstanding immediately before such prepayment [(PV of All

> Future Payments)—(principal balance at time of prepayment) = prepayment fee].

This sort of clause is now widely used and enforced by the courts; see, e.g., Great Plains Real Estate Devel., L.L.C. v. Union Central Life Ins. Co., 536 F.3d 939 (8th Cir.2008); In re AE Hotel Venture, 321 B.R. 209 (Bankr. N.D.Ill.2005). The use of the yield on U.S. Treasury securities is obviously unrealistic; in all probability the lender is going to invest the prepaid funds in another mortgage loan, not in Treasury bonds. Nonetheless, the courts applying state law have nearly always approved the use of a "Treasury Flat" reference rate in yield maintenance clauses. See, e.g., River East Plaza, L.L.C. v. Variable Annuity Life Ins. Co., 498 F.3d 718 (7th Cir.2007).

3. *Attacking prepayment fees.* Borrowers have been almost completely unsuccessful in attacking prepayment fees in state courts. This doesn't seem surprising. After all, if a clause "locking out" the loan and allowing no prepayment at all is enforceable (as it clearly is), then *a fortiori* a clause allowing prepayment for a fee should be enforceable as well.

The usual statement is that a court will refuse to enforce a prepayment fee only if it "shocks the conscience," and fees that are shocking enough are so rare as to be virtually nonexistent. See, e.g., Shadoan v. World Sav. & Loan Ass'n, 219 Cal.App.3d 97, 268 Cal.Rptr. 207 (1990). Perhaps the most extreme case is Williams v. Fassler, 110 Cal.App.3d 7, 167 Cal.Rptr. 545 (1980), which provided (in a seller-financed mortgage) for a fee of 50% of the amount of the prepayment. The mortgagee-seller testified that he wished to avoid the negative income tax consequences that could have resulted if more than 30% of the total purchase price had been paid during the year of sale, and that his accountant advised him that the 50% fee would do the trick. The court said, "We * * * hold that in a transaction between private parties, an agreement specifying a 50 percent prepayment penalty is valid if the penalty is reasonably related to the obligee's anticipated risk of incurring increased tax liability upon the occurrence of the prepayment."

Other grounds for attack have been asserted, but not with much success. Sometimes borrowers argue that the clause is a form of liquidation of damages, and hence must be a reasonable advance estimate of the probable damages the lender will suffer from the prepayment. We agree that a prepayment fee is indeed a liquidation of damages. However, state courts have been quite unreceptive to the use of this liquidated damages/penalty analysis; see Lazzareschi Inv. Co. v. San Francisco Fed. Sav. & Loan Ass'n, 22 Cal.App.3d 303, 99 Cal.Rptr. 417 (1971). And even when they adopt the analysis, they nearly always find the fee to be a reasonable estimate and uphold it. See TMG Life Ins. Co. v. Ashner, 21 Kan.App.2d 234, 898 P.2d 1145 (1995).

Occasionally a borrower will try to convince a state court that a prepayment fee is a form of excessive interest, and is therefore a violation of the state's usury statute. But this argument nearly always fails, as it should. Interest is a charge for the *use* of money, while a prepayment fee is a charge for *giving back* the money, not using it. See C.C. Port, Ltd. v. Davis-Penn Mortg. Co., 891 F.Supp. 371 (S.D.Tex.1994).

In sum, attacks on prepayment fees in state courts seem doomed to failure. Restatement (Third) of Property (Mortgages) § 6.2 agrees; it provides that, except for the application of the general contract law principles of good faith, fair dealing, and unconscionability, "an agreement that prohibits payment of the mortgage obligation prior to maturity is enforceable, and * * * an agreement requiring the mortgagor to pay a fee or charge as a condition of such payment is enforceable."

4.   *Prepayment fees in bankruptcy.* It often happens that a prepayment is tendered by a borrower who is in bankruptcy—typically a Chapter 11 reorganization. Here the question is not so much whether the fee is enforceable under state law (although that question must be answered affirmatively in order for the lender to collect the fee) as whether the fee is collectible as a *secured* claim in bankruptcy. If the fee is recognized as enforceable but unsecured, the lender will stand in line with the debtor's general creditors, and may recover only a few cents on the dollar. But if the fee is regarded as a secured claim, and if the real estate has enough value above the amount of the mortgage debt itself, the lender will recover the full fee.

Whether the fee can be treated as a secured claim is governed by Bankruptcy Code § 506(b), which simply requires that such fees be "reasonable." But this is a far cry from the "shock the conscience" test usually employed under state law. The bankruptcy courts usually treat the fee as a species of liquidated damages, and they initially were quite aggressive in finding prepayment fees unreasonable. Indeed, yield maintenance clauses often came in for sharp criticism in the bankruptcy courts. For example, a rather crude and simplistic yield maintenance formula might set the fee as the amount prepaid, times the number of years remaining on the loan, times the difference between the contract interest rate and the interest rate on U.S. government securities of the same maturity as the remaining loan term. For example, assume a loan with a $1 million balance, an 8% interest rate, and a 10 year term is being prepaid. Further assume that the current interest yield on ten-year U.S. government bonds is 3%. Under the formula above, the prepayment fee would be $1 million x 10 years x 5%, or $500,000.

However, there are a number of features of this clause which tend to exaggerate the lender's damages, and which have incurred the wrath of bankruptcy judges in similar cases. The objectionable features include the following:

> a.   The formula above doesn't take the time value of money into account. It imposes the fee immediately, while the lender's interest yield would have been earned only over the next ten years. It thus overcompensates the lender. The interest differential should be discounted to present value terms.

b.   In most cases, the mortgage loan calls for monthly payments that will fully or at least partially amortize it over its term. Thus, if $1 million is being prepaid, that $1 million would not have been outstanding for the next ten years even in the absence of prepayment. A yield maintenance formula that assumes the amount being prepaid would otherwise have been the loan's balance for its full remaining term is usually unrealistic, and tends to overcompensate the lender.

Bankruptcy courts are highly unreceptive to formulas that tend to overcompensate lenders systematically in these ways. As one court put it, "The damage formula is simple and well established. It is the difference in the interest yield between the contract rate and the market rate at the time of prepayment, projected over the term of the loan and then discounted to arrive at present value. * * * Any prepayment charge should be wholly or largely dependent upon such a calculation." In re A.J. Lane & Co., 113 B.R. 821 (Bankr.D.Mass.1990). Similar criticisms are found in In re Kroh Bros. Dev. Co., 88 B.R. 997 (Bankr.W.D.Mo.1988); In re Skyler Ridge, 80 B.R. 500 (Bankr.C.D.Cal.1987). Even when the bankruptcy courts treat the enforceability issue as entirely one of state law, they often take an aggressively pro-borrower view of state law; see In re Wiston XXIV Ltd. Partn., 170 B.R. 453 (D.Kan.1994), aff'd, 45 F.3d 441 (10th Cir.1994).

A further objection to many yield maintenance clauses is that they use the current rate on U.S. Treasury obligations (of the same maturity as the remaining loan term) as a "reference" or discount rate in computing the present value of the fee. It is quite arguable that this is unreasonable; the lender will very likely relend the funds, not by purchasing government bonds, but by making another real estate loan. It may have a shortfall in return for a brief period until another real estate lending opportunity arises, but in the long run, it is the rate on similar mortgage loans, not the government bond rate, that is relevant.

However, more recently, yield maintenance provisions are faring better in bankruptcy courts. Several recent decisions accept the use of the U.S. obligation rate as a reference rate. See In re CP Holdings, Inc., 332 B.R. 380 (W.D.Mo.2005):

> The Court rejects CP Holdings' argument that the interest rate on commercial first-mortgage loans should be used when calculating the reinvestment yield, rather than the yield on a U.S. Treasury issue, for two reasons. First, this substitution would be offensive to the basic notion of freedom of contract as the parties agreed that the yield on a U.S. Treasury issue would be used to calculate the reinvestment yield CP Holdings and CALPERS, two "sophisticated and experienced business parties," contracted to have the prepayment premium calculated using the yield on a U.S. Treasury issue. (Hr'g Tr. 132:20–143:2; 138:7–140:1). The Court, in deference to long-standing principles of contract law, declines CP Holdings'

request to impermissibly rewrite the contract in contravention of the parties bargained-for agreement.

Second, the testimony of both experts supports a finding that the use of the yield on a U.S. Treasury issue to calculate the reinvestment yield is reasonable. Randolph, CALPERS expert, testified that the yield on a U.S. Treasury issue provides a stable and relatively secure interest rate. Pflaum, CP Holdings' expert, recognized that "only Treasury instruments are absolutely default free," can be "move[d] with the press of a button," "are held as reserve by central banks," and are used "to develop and structure financial derivatives." (Pflaum Test. 84:19–85:3). Accordingly, the parties made a reasonable attempt to forecast the damages anticipated by acceleration by using the yield on a U.S. Treasury in the prepayment premium formula because such an investment is safe, easy to obtain and provides a relatively stable and secure rate of return.

Do you think the borrower's expert witness did a good job in this case? The applicable U.S. Treasury yield was 3.8687%, while the current rate on new commercial mortgages was alleged to be 6.5%. The choice of rates had an enormous impact on the amount of the resulting fee. Unfortunately, there is no standard index of commercial mortgage loan rates, and it is arguable that such loans vary so widely that it would not be feasible to create such an index. By contrast, the market for U.S. Treasury obligations is extremely liquid and their rates are widely reported. Use of a U.S. Treasury rate was also sustained in In re Doctors Hospital of Hyde Park, 508 B.R. 697 (Bankr.N.D.Ill. 2014); In re Vanderveer Estates Holdings, Inc., 283 B.R. 122 (Bankr.E.D.N.Y.2002). For a state case upholding the use of a U.S. Treasury rate, see Santa Rosa KM Associates, Ltd., P.C. v. Principal Life Ins. Co., 41 Kan.App.2d 840, 206 P.3d 40, 48–49 (2009).

Incidentally, what happens if the bankruptcy court disallows the fee as a secured claim under § 506(b) on the basis of its unreasonableness? Does the court then substitute a fee of a reasonable amount? No such luck! There's simply no secured claim at all for a prepayment fee, and the lender must take its chances with the other unsecured creditors. It's a stiff penalty for the lender who was too greedy in the original drafting and negotiation of the loan.

5. *The* Lopresti *Case.* Even though the prepayment fee (breakage fee) in *Lopresti,* our principal case, refers to U.S. Treasury rates, it is not a yield maintenance provision and is almost the model of fairness. The use of the U.S. Treasury yield is for the sole purpose of determining the extent to which market interest rates declined since the inception of the loan. Moreover, the U.S. Treasury rate, unlike a rate on comparable commercial loans, is readily ascertainable by reference to the *Wall Street Journal.* Finally, if the applicable Treasury rates increase after the loan is executed, no prepayment

premium is collectable at all. Should borrowers' counsel look to *Lopresti,* in future commercial loan negotiations?

6.   *Prepayment caused by the mortgagee's acceleration.* An extremely important problem arises when a prepayment occurs, not because the borrower desires to prepay, but because lender accelerates the debt under the authority of a clause in the mortgage. Under the typical mortgage, at least four causes for such an acceleration may exist: (1) acceleration on account of the borrower's default; (2) acceleration under a due-on-sale clause when the borrower transfers the real estate without the lender's approval; (3) a payment of insurance proceeds due to a casualty that damages the property; and (4) a payment of an eminent domain award (or a settlement of an eminent domain claim) resulting from a governmental taking of the property.

In all of these settings, borrowers have usually argued that the prepayment was "involuntary" and thus not within the scope of the clause requiring payment of a fee. Several early cases agreed with this argument and denied the mortgagee the fee, but recent cases seem to reflect a change in attitude by the courts.

a.   *Acceleration upon default.* Where the mortgage clause clearly applies the fee to prepayments resulting from acceleration for default, the courts will enforce it. See Willow Grove, Ltd., v. Fed. Nat'l Mortgage Ass'n, 2013 WL 6865127 (D.Colo. 2013); Planned Pethood Plus, Inc., 228 P.3d 262 (Colo.App.2010); Feinstein v. Ashplant, 961 So.2d 1074 (Fla.App.2007); In re AE Hotel Venture, 321 B.R. 209 (Bankr. N.D.Ill.2005); Citicorp Mortg., Inc. v. Morrisville Hampton Village Realty Ltd. Partn., 443 Pa.Super. 595, 662 A.2d 1120 (1995); Biancalana v. Fleming, 45 Cal.App.4th 698, 53 Cal.Rptr.2d 47 (1996). If the clause is unclear, refusal to enforce is the likely result; see In re Denver Merch. Mart, Inc., 740 F.3d 1052 (5th Cir.2014); In re Tri-State Ethanol, LLC, 369 B.R. 481 (D.S.D.2007); Broadway Bank v. Star Hospitality, Inc., 695 N.W.2d 43 (Table) (Iowa Ct.App.2004); In re McClung, 2003 WL 23807834 (Bankr. D. Kan. 2003). This distinction is now so well understood that a lender's lawyer who failed to make the point clear in the documents would be suspected of having lived in a cave for the past twenty years!

Does imposition of the fee when a default exists violate any important public policy? If the purpose of the fee is to shift to the borrower the risk that a prepayment will occur and will damage the lender, isn't that the very risk that eventuates when the borrower defaults and the lender accelerates? After all, one can hardly expect the lender to forbear accelerating indefinitely in the face of a default.

b.   *Acceleration by virtue of payment of casualty insurance or eminent domain proceeds.* Mortgages usually provide that the lender, at its option, may insist that a payment of casualty insurance or eminent domain proceeds be applied toward the balance owing on the mortgage loan. Whether such clauses are enforceable is a matter of debate; see Chapter 4, Section E supra.

If such payments are applied toward the loan balance they are, in a sense, prepayments. Can the lender thus demand a prepayment fee as well?

The traditional attitude of the courts was to refuse enforcement of the fee in this situation. In several recent cases, however, the courts have dealt with clauses that were very clear in requiring a prepayment fee, and have enforced the fee; see, e.g., Melin v. TCF Fin. Corp., 1995 WL 265064 (Minn.Ct.App.1995) (not reported in N.W.2d).

Restatement (Third) Property (Mortgages) § 6.3 (1997) agrees that the fee should be collectible if the mortgage so provides, but with an important exception. Suppose the mortgagor requests that the insurance or eminent domain funds, instead of being paid on the mortgage, be used to restore the real estate. Further, suppose restoration would be economically feasible with the funds available, and would return the property to at least its original value, but the mortgagor refuses this request. On these facts, no prepayment fee should be collectible, for the lender really has no necessity, in terms of the loan's safety and security, for demanding the prepayment. The lender's demand is probably being made because interest rates have risen and the money can be relent at a higher rate. For the lender to collect the prepayment fee at the same time would be an unwarranted windfall.

c. *Acceleration under a due-on-sale clause.* If the loan in question is secured by a one-to-four-family home, the answer is given by federal regulation. Under 12 C.F.R. § 591.5(b)(2) and (b)(3), promulgated by the Office of Thrift Supervision pursuant to its authority under the Garn-St. Germain Act:

(2) A lender shall not impose a prepayment penalty or equivalent fee when the lender or party acting on behalf of the lender

(i) Declares by written notice that the loan is due pursuant to a due-on-sale clause or

(ii) Commences a judicial or nonjudicial foreclosure proceeding to enforce a due-on-sale clause or to seek payment in full as a result of invoking such clause.

(3) A lender shall not impose a prepayment penalty or equivalent fee when the lender or party acting on behalf of the lender fails to approve within 30 days the completed credit application of a qualified transferee of the security property to assume the loan in accordance with the terms of the loan, and thereafter the borrower transfers the security property to such transferee and prepays the loan in full within 120 days after receipt by the lender of the completed credit application.

A few states have statutes taking the same position; see, e.g., N.Y. Real Prop.L. § 254–a. Suppose, however, the property is not a 1-to-4-family residence and no state statute applies. Again, the cases usually treat the prepayment as "involuntary" and refuse to impose the fee. See, e.g., McCausland v. Bankers Life Ins. Co., 110 Wash.2d 716, 757 P.2d 941 (1988);

Tan v. California Fed. Sav. & Loan Ass'n, 140 Cal.App.3d 800, 189 Cal.Rptr. 775 (1983). However, in most of these cases the documents were not clear in imposing the prepayment fee when the lender accelerated under the due-on-sale clause.

If better-drafted (from the lender's viewpoint) documents make this clear, how should the courts respond? There seem to be no recent cases, but the correct analysis, by analogy to our discussion of insurance and condemnation proceeds above, is to ask why the lender accelerated. If the lender has a legitimate objection to the proposed real estate buyer's credit, income, or other factors that rendered the buyer unqualified for the loan, the lender should be entitled to the prepayment fee; after all, it isn't the lender's fault that the borrower decided to sell to an unqualified person. On the other hand,

> If a lender elects to accelerate the debt upon sale because interest rates have increased [and not because the proposed buyer is unqualified], the lender should not also be allowed to collect a prepayment fee. The function of the prepayment fee or prohibition is to protect lenders from borrower refinancing in times of falling interest rates and should not be used to penalize borrowers who refuse to accept lender's [sic] increased interest rates at resale in times of rising rates. It is only fair that the lender be prohibited from demanding prepayment fees upon acceleration of the debt since, in that instance, it is the lender who is insisting on prepayment.

Warrington 611 Assocs. v. Aetna Life Ins. Co., 705 F.Supp. 229 (D.N.J.1989).

7. *Statutory limitations on residential prepayment fees.* State legislation in this area is widespread but varies in content. One common element in all such legislation is that it is usually limited to loans secured by residential real estate, the latter being variously defined by such terminology as: "single family dwellings," "owner-occupied single family dwellings," "one to four family dwellings" or "an owner-occupied one to six family residence."

Within the context of this common qualification, the legislation varies considerably. For example, at one extreme is the Pennsylvania statute which simply prohibits all prepayment penalties in residential mortgage obligations entered into after the effective date of the statute. 41 Pa.Stat. § 405. New Jersey has similar legislation. N.J.Stat.Ann. 46:10B–1, 10B–3. See *Lopresti, supra.* Illinois achieves the same practical effect by prohibiting prepayment penalties in all residential mortgages carrying an interest rate in excess of 8%. 815 Ill. Comp. Ann. Stat. § 205/4. Missouri, on the other hand, prohibits the imposition of all prepayment penalties in residential real estate loans after five years from the date of the execution of the loan. Vernon's Ann.Mo.Stat. § 408.036. Michigan cuts off such penalties after three years for single family dwellings, but limits such charges within three years to 1% of the amount of any prepayment. Mich.Comp.Laws Ann. § 438.31c. In New York, any mortgage loan made by a savings and loan association may be prepaid. However, the loan agreement may provide for a period during which prepayment may not be made without penalty. Where the mortgage loan is an owner-occupied one to six family residence, the penalties may be imposed only during the first year of the loan and may not exceed interest for a period of three months on the principal so prepaid, or interest for the remaining months in the first year, whichever is the lesser amount. N.Y.—McKinney's Banking Law § 393(2). Similar New York legislation exists for mortgage loans made by mortgagees other than savings and loan associations. N.Y.— McKinney's Gen.Obl.Law § 5–501(3)(b). Mississippi permits prepayment penalties as to single family dwellings under the following conditions: if prepayment is made during the first year of the loan, the prepayment charge is 5% of the mortgage amount; thereafter, the charge drops by 1% annually until after five years no penalty may be collected. Miss.Code 1974, § 75–17–1(11). The California legislation is perhaps the least stringent on the mortgagee. West's Ann.Cal.Civ. Code § 2954–9(b). Prepayment charges may be assessed with respect to mortgages on residential real estate of four units or less within the first five years. Within such period, 20% of the unpaid balance may be prepaid free of penalty within a twelve month period. However, the maximum charge on a prepayment in excess of the 20% amount is six months' interest.

Currently a federally-chartered savings and loan association may, subject to disclosure requirements, "impose a penalty on prepayment of a loan as provided in the loan contract." 12 C.F.R. § 560.34. This regulation's effect is to preempt any contrary state law, and hence in some states to permit federal savings associations to charge prepayment fees on residential loans when state-chartered lenders in the same state cannot do so. Similarly, the Office of the Comptroller of the Currency has preempted application of state law on prepayment fees to national banks; see 12 C.F.R. § 34.23.

There are two major quasi-federal entities that purchase residential mortgage loans on the secondary market, Fannie Mae and Freddie Mac. They generally do not enforce prepayment clauses in mortgages they own, and their standard note and mortgage forms permit free prepayment. Mortgagees using the standard form may attach a prepayment clause by rider, but the rider must state that it becomes void upon purchase of the mortgage by Fannie or Freddie. The practices and rules of Fannie and Freddie tend to have a significant impact on mortgage lending practices because many mortgagees either sell mortgages to such entities or want to retain the option to do so. Hence, prepayment fees in prime home mortgage loans have become quite rare, although they are common in subprime loans.

Finally, prepayment fees in mortgage loans guaranteed by the Veterans Administration or insured by the Federal Housing Administration are prohibited and the loans may be prepaid at any time. See 38 C.F.R. § 36.4311; 24 C.F.R. § 203.22(b).

Mortgage lenders often attempt to provide incentives for their borrowers to pay loan installments on time. Two commonly-used incentives are late fees and default interest.

WESTMARK COMMERCIAL MORTGAGE FUND IV v. TEENFORM ASSOCIATES, L.P.

Superior Court of New Jersey, Appellate Division, 2003
362 N.J.Super. 336, 827 A.2d 1154

The opinion of the court was delivered by WEFING, J.A.D.

This is a mortgage foreclosure action in which defendants appeal from certain aspects of a Final Judgment of Foreclosure entered on January 15, 2002. After reviewing the record in light of the contentions advanced on appeal, we affirm but remand for entry of a corrected judgment.

On July 28, 1999 defendants executed a promissory note to plaintiff for the sum of $3,145,000. The note carried an interest rate of eight percent and called for equal monthly payments of $23,076.90 for a period of five years, at which point the balance was due in full. To secure their obligation, defendants granted plaintiff mortgages on three parcels of commercial property, one in Carlstadt, in Bergen County, one in Brick, in Ocean County and one in Phillipsburg, in Warren County.

Less than a year later, defendants fell behind in their payments. Plaintiff filed a complaint in foreclosure in July 2000 and venued the matter with the Chancery Division in Bergen County. In November 2000, plaintiff was granted partial summary judgment and the matter was forwarded to the Office of Foreclosure, where plaintiff sought entry of final judgment. Defendants disputed the amounts due under the note and mortgages and the matter was returned to the Chancery Division for a hearing. Following that hearing, the Chancery Division concluded that the amounts sought, in excess of $200,000, were reasonable and were due and owing. A Final Judgment of Foreclosure was entered thereafter, from which defendants have appealed.

The matters in dispute fall into four categories: late fees, default interest, prepayment fees and attorney fees. The July 28 note provided for all four items. Defendants contend that the amounts allowed in each category are unreasonable and unwarranted. For the reasons stated in this opinion, we disagree.

I

Paragraph 5 of the July 28, 1999 note provides as follows:

5. If any installment under this Note shall not be received by Holder on the date due, Holder may at its option impose a late

charge of six percent (6%) of the overdue amount. Considering all of the circumstances on the date of this Note, such late charge represents a fair and reasonable estimate of the costs that will be sustained by Holder due to the failure of Borrower to make a timely payment. The parties further agree that proof of actual damages would be costly or inconvenient. Such late charge shall be paid without prejudice to the right of Holder to collect any other amounts due or to declare a default under this Note or the other Loan Documents or to exercise any other rights and remedies of Holder. If the late charge provided for herein exceeds the maximum late charge provided by applicable law, such late charge shall be automatically reduced to the maximum late charge permitted by applicable law.

Defendants contend this paragraph is invalid, under the settled principle stated in *Westmount Country Club v. Kameny*, 82 N.J.Super. 200, 205, 197 A.2d 379 (App.Div.1964), that "[p]arties to a contract may not fix a penalty for its breach . . . . such a contract is unlawful."

Our analysis of the question presented must perforce begin with the Supreme Court's recent opinion in *MetLife v. Washington Avenue Associates, L.P.*, 159 N.J. 484, 732 A.2d 493 (1999). That also was a foreclosure action involving commercial property. The Note in question in that case called for the debtor to pay a late fee of five percent of any delinquent payments. The debtor challenged that as unreasonable. The Supreme Court, however, disagreed.

The Court noted that liquidated damages clauses in a commercial context between sophisticated parties are presumptively reasonable. *Id.* at 496, 732 A.2d 493. The Court held that the burden of establishing a particular clause as unreasonable rests upon the party challenging it as such. *Ibid.* No one factor is determinative whether a clause is reasonable; rather, a reviewing court must look at the totality of the circumstances. *Id.* at 495, 732 A.2d 493. In conducting its review, the Court deemed it appropriate to look to what is permitted by statute and what constitutes common practice within the industry. *Id.* at 497, 732 A.2d 493. After completing that survey, the Court concluded that late fees based upon a percentage of the delinquent installment are generally allowed and that five percent was not an unusually large or unreasonable fee in commercial transactions. The Court noted that defendants had presented no evidence to overcome the presumption of reasonableness or to suggest fraud, duress or unconscionability on the part of the lender. The Court thus concluded the five percent late charge was reasonable. *Id.* at 500, 732 A.2d 493.

Here, defendants argue that plaintiff did not present any evidence that the late fees charged were related to any actual or anticipated damages to plaintiff flowing from late payment. The argument misapprehends *MetLife*, however. The burden of proof rested squarely on defendants, who presented no evidence at all on the question of the reasonableness of the late fees. We recognize that the late fee in question here is six percent, as opposed to the five percent deemed reasonable in *MetLife*. In light of the defendants' total failure of proof, however, we have no basis to conclude that an increase of one percentage point is sufficient to overcome the presumption of reasonableness and, thus, affirm the decision of the Chancery Division judge that six percent was reasonable in the context of this case.

There is an additional aspect to defendants' challenge to the award of late fees. They cite *Crest Savings & Loan Ass'n v. Mason*, 243 N.J.Super. 646, 649, 581 A.2d 120 (Ch.Div.1990), for the proposition that a lender cannot collect late charges "for nonpayments of installments claimed to be due after the filing of the complaint." We have no quarrel with the principle, but it is inapplicable. This complaint was filed in July 2000 and we have no indication in this record of any late fees charged for any period after that date.

II

Paragraph 6 of the note provides as follows:

6.   If the unpaid balance hereof is not received by Holder on the Maturity Date, or on the Acceleration Date (defined below) such amount shall bear interest at the Note Rate plus two (2%) per annum (the "Default Rate") from such date until paid in full. Considering all of the circumstances on the date of this Note, such interest represents a fair and reasonable estimate of the costs and expenses that will result from the loss of use of the money due. The parties further agree that proof of actual damages would be costly or inconvenient. Interest at the Default Rate shall be paid without prejudice to the right of Holder to collect any other amounts due or to declare a default under this Note or the other Loan Documents or to exercise any other rights or remedies of Holder.

Defendants challenge this clause on default interest on the same basis that they challenged the clause on late fees. We apply the same analysis that we did to the question of the reasonableness of the late fees and reach the same conclusion.

The *MetLife* Court also considered the validity of a clause increasing the rate of interest upon default in payment. The Court found that default interest rates are a common tool utilized by lenders to offset a portion of the damages incurred as a result of delinquent loans. *Id.* at 501, 732 A.2d 493. The Court held that default interest rates should be measured for reasonableness and if found to be unreasonable, struck down as a penalty. *Ibid.* In *MetLife*, the default interest rate was 12.55%, three percentage points higher than the contract rate. The Court determined that the three percent increase in the interest rate was a reasonable estimate of the lender's potential costs of administering a defaulted loan, as well as the potential difference in interest rates between the defaulted loan and a replacement loan the lender may be able to place. *Ibid.*

Here, the note called for an increase of two percentage points in the interest rate upon default, raising it from eight percent to ten percent. Based upon the result reached in *MetLife* and defendants' total failure to present any proof to the contrary, the Chancery Division judge correctly determined the ten percent default interest rate to be reasonable.

[The court's discussion of the prepayment fee and attorney's fees is omitted.]

NOTES

1. *Theories of attack.* As *Westmark* illustrates, both late fees and default interest are subject to attack on the ground that they represent attempts to liquidate damages, but fail the test that requires such liquidation clauses to represent a reasonable advance estimate of the probable actual damages.

There is, however, another mode of analysis: that both late fees and default interest may make the loan usurious. Of course, not all states have usury statutes, and some states have statutes that don't apply to mortgage loans. Moreover, nearly all state usury ceilings on first lien loans secured by residential property are preempted by federal law; see 12 U.S.C.A. § 1735f–7, derived from § 501 of the Depository Institutions Deregulation and Monetary Control Act of 1980, as amended by § 324 of the Housing and Community Development Amendments of 1980. (A few states exercised the right to "un-preempt" their usury laws from this federal statute.)

But if a state usury statute is indeed applicable, it is easy to see how a court might find a default interest provision to violate it, and thus might strike it down, if the total interest is high enough to exceed the statutory limit. After all, default interest *is* interest, and interest is what usury statutes are all about. On the other hand, applying a usury analysis to a late fee is more subtle. Late fees are not denominated as interest, and they usually don't accrue on the basis of the number of days, weeks, or months that a payment is late, but rather apply in a fixed amount regardless of how late the payment is (after some brief grace period, commonly 5 to 15 days).

The Arkansas Supreme Court characterized a late fee as usurious interest in Bunn v. Weyerhaeuser Co., 268 Ark. 445, 598 S.W.2d 54 (1980). North Carolina agreed in Swindell v. FNMA, 330 N.C. 153, 409 S.E.2d 892

(1991) (5% late fee usurious). However, in Clermont v. Secured Inv. Corp., 25 Cal.App.3d 766, 102 Cal.Rptr. 340 (1972), the court concluded that "while the late charge here * * * must constitute either damages or interest, it may not * * * constitute both." Having determined that the clause was a liquidated damages provision, the court believed it was unnecessary to look at the usury allegation; it remanded the case for a decision on the liquidated damages issue.

A usury attack on a late fee may be difficult to sustain for another reason. Usury statutes often impose harsh penalties on usurious transactions, such as total loss of interest, or sometimes even loss of principal. Such severe consequences may make courts reluctant to take a broad view of the usury approach.

2. *Unconscionability as a standard.* The "reasonableness" approach used by the New Jersey court in *Westmark*, and drawn from the law of liquidated damages, is not the only mode of analysis of late fees and default interest. An alternative approach, not as widely employed, applies the doctrine of unconscionability, typically extrapolated from the well-known statement of that doctrine in UCC § 2–302.

Unconscionability may be substantive (e.g., an extreme and oppressive term), procedural (e.g., unfair surprise because the borrower did not realize the nature of the term agreed to), or a combination of the two. Use of the unconscionability standard is advocated in Steven W. Bender & Michael T. Madison, The Enforceability of Default Interest in Real Estate Mortgages, 43 Real Prop. Prob. & Trust J. 199 (2008).

It is usually more difficult to get a court to intervene and refuse enforcement if the unconscionability standard is employed. See, e.g., Four J. Funding v. Land Pres., L.L.C., 2004 WL 3130562 (Conn.Super. 2004) (default interest at 24% was not unconscionable); Bekins Bar V Ranch v. Huth, 664 P.2d 455 (Utah 1983) (default interest at 36% and 58% was not unconscionable). Sometimes a court will fail to draw a clear distinction between the reasonableness and unconscionability standards. See, e.g., Cantamar, L.L.C. v. Champagne, 142 P.3d 140 (Utah App. 2006) (default interest clause would be an unreasonable liquidation of damages if it were unconscionable; 30% default rate was not unconscionable).

3. *Rationales for late fees and default interest.* Late fees are perhaps most naturally understood as compensating the lender for past harm: the lender's administrative expense and difficulty in dealing with the borrower's default. Default interest, on the other hand, may be regarded as compensating for future harm growing out of the fact that the loan, having defaulted, is now riskier than had been anticipated. Losses may accrue to the lender due the necessity of placing reserves against the loan, the fact that the lender's balance sheet may be adversely affected, the potential for penalties from regulatory authorities, and the need to implement increased monitoring of the defaulted loan. See Bender & Madison, supra note 2, at 201–202. In addition, a loan that has defaulted may be regarded as "damaged goods,"

more difficult to sell on the secondary market, even if the default has been cured. See Harris Ominsky, Real Estate Lore: Modern Techniques and Everyday Tips for the Practitioner 68 (2006).

4. *What default interest rate is excessive?* A default interest clause that increases the contract rate by three or four percent is almost certain to be upheld. See, e.g., Flojo Int'l, Inc. v. Lassleben, 4 Cal.App.4th 713, 6 Cal.Rptr.2d 99 (1992) (4% increase upheld); Norwest Bank Minnesota v. Blair Road Assocs., L.P., 252 F.Supp.2d 86 (D.N.J.2003) (prime rate plus 4% upheld). Cases striking down default interest usually involve much larger increases. See, e.g., Feller v. Architects Display Bldgs., Inc., 54 N.J.Super. 205, 148 A.2d 634 (App.Div.1959) (increase from 17% to 33% struck down); Stuchin v. Kasirer, 237 N.J.Super. 604, 568 A.2d 907 (App.Div.1990) (increase from 9% to 24% struck down). But the cases are hard to reconcile, and some courts have approved quite high rates. See, e.g., In re Dixon, 228 B.R. 166 (W.D.Va.,1998) (increase from 18% to 36% upheld); Casaccio v. Habel, 14 Ill.App.3d 822, 303 N.E.2d 548 (1973) (increase from 18% to 24% upheld).

5. *What amount of late charge is excessive?* The *Westmark* case is typical; the cases routinely uphold late fees up to 5% or 6% of the missed installment. See McKeever v. Fiore, 78 Conn.App. 783, 829 A.2d 846 (2003) (5% fee upheld); Mattvidi Assocs. Ltd. Partn. v. NationsBank of Virginia, 100 Md.App. 71, 639 A.2d 228 (1994) (5% fee upheld, with a comprehensive listing of other decisions). Cases involving larger fees are rare.

However, suppose the fee is based not on the missed installment but on the *outstanding principal balance* of the loan! Here even a small percentage factor can produce a very large fee indeed. In Garrett v. Coast & Southern Fed. Sav. & Loan Ass'n, 9 Cal.3d 731, 108 Cal.Rptr. 845, 511 P.2d 1197 (1973), the court applied a liquidated damage/penalty analysis and concluded that the lender had "made no 'reasonable endeavor * * * to estimate a fair average compensation for any loss that might be sustained' by the delinquency in the payment of the installment." It struck down the fee.

Much the same result follows if the late fee is applied to a late "balloon" payment—that is, a payment of the full balance, as required by the loan documents. In 1300 Ave. P Realty Corp. v. Stratigakis, 186 Misc.2d 745, 720 N.Y.S.2d 725 (Sup.Ct.2000), a 4% fee clause was applied in such a setting, producing a fee of nearly $15,000, but the court nonetheless enforced it. Contrast Art Country Squire, L.L.C. v. Inland Mortg. Corp., 745 N.E.2d 885 (Ind.Ct.App.2001), in which the court worked hard to construe the fee as applicable only to monthly payments, and not to the balloon.

Sometimes the lender's own characterization of the fee may give the game away. In Hitz v. First Interstate Bank, 38 Cal.App.4th 274, 44 Cal.Rptr.2d 890 (1995), borrowers on credit card debts attacked the lender's charging of both late fees and "overlimit" fees (applicable to borrowers whose account balances exceeded their credit limits). A bank executive had written a memo when the fees were introduced, projecting "new revenue" of $250,000 annually from the fees without any mention of costs. The executive also testified that he considered the fees "a good source of revenue," and that he expected the bank to "make a profit" from the fees. That was enough to convince the court that the fees were not a "reasonable endeavor to estimate fair compensation for loss."

6.   *The effect of acceleration on late fees.* Assume that a mortgagor defaults in monthly payments and the mortgagee accelerates the loan. If the acceleration had not occurred, a number of additional monthly payments would have fallen due by the time the foreclosure is completed. Is the lender entitled to a late fee on these payments? It is generally held that no further fees are collectible after acceleration. As one court put it:

> Upon such acceleration, installment payments are no longer due, and [mortgagee] is entitled to the amount of the debt and interest provided for in the mortgage documents. There is then no basis for allowing [mortgagee] compensation for administrative expenses in connection with alleged late payments. [Mortgagee] is relegated to its rights in the foreclosure action.

Crest Sav. & Loan Ass'n v. Mason, 243 N.J.Super. 646, 581 A.2d 120 (1990). In agreement, see Shadhali, Inc. v. Hintlian, 41 Conn.App. 225, 675 A.2d 3 (1996); Fowler v. First Fed. Sav. & Loan Ass'n, 643 So.2d 30 (Fla.App.1994); Green Point Sav. Bank v. Varana, 236 A.D.2d 443, 653 N.Y.S.2d 656 (1997); Security Mut. Life Ins. Co. v. Contemporary Real Estate Assocs., 979 F.2d 329 (3d Cir.1992) (Pennsylvania law). Some of these cases suggest that contrary result would be reached if the mortgage documents clearly provided for the continued accrual of late fees after acceleration. Can this be correct?

Courts following the construction outlined above will sometimes assert that if a late fee *were* applied to a balloon payment or an accelerated balance, it would produce an unconscionable penalty. See Poseidon Devel., Inc. v. Woodland Lane Estates, L.L.C., 152 Cal.App.4th 1106, 62 Cal.Rptr.3d 59 (2007); LaSalle Bank N.A. v. Shepherd Mall Partners, L.L.C., 140 P.3d 559 (Okl.Civ.App.2006).

7.   *State statutory limitations on late fees.* A number of states impose statutory regulation of late payment charges. All of them require that the fee be calculated on the amount of the late installment, not on the principal amount of the loan. New York limits late payment penalties with respect to mortgages on owner-occupied one to six family dwellings to a maximum of 2% of the past due installment and requires a fifteen day grace period after an installment due date before penalty may be assessed. See N.Y.—McKinney's Real Prop.Law § 254–b. Massachusetts limits late penalties on first mortgages on owner-occupied dwellings of four or less households or on a residential condominium unit to 3% of the late installment and, as in New York, a fifteen day grace period is provided. Mass.Gen.Laws Ann. c. 183, § 59. In California, as to loans on single family, owner-occupied dwellings, the maximum late charge is the greater of 6% of each delinquent installment or

$5, and it may be imposed only after a ten day grace period. West's Cal.Civ.Code § 2954.4.

8. *Federal regulatory limitations on late fees.* Prior to 1984 a Federal Home Loan Bank Board Regulation, applicable to all federally-chartered savings and loan associations, prohibited late payment penalties on home loans in excess of 5% of the amount of the late installment. See 12 C.F.R. § 545.8–3(d) (1983). However, under the current regulation, no limitation exists on the amount of the fees. See 12 C.F.R. § 560.33. Moreover, the no-limitation regulation preempts any conflicting state law, so that federal savings associations may be able to charge larger late fees than other lenders in the state. See Collins v. Union Fed. Sav. & Loan Ass'n, 99 Nev. 284, 662 P.2d 610 (1983).

However, under 12 C.F.R. § 560.33 the OTS does impose certain procedural and notice limitations:

> A Federal savings association may not impose a late charge more than one time for late payment of the same installment, and any installment payment made by the borrower shall be applied to the longest outstanding installment due. An association shall not assess a late charge as to any payment received by it within fifteen days after the due date of such payment. No form of such late charge permitted by this paragraph shall be considered as interest to the Federal savings association and the Federal savings association shall not deduct late charges from the regular periodic installment payments on the loan, but must collect them as such from the borrower.

With respect to all loans made to consumers, federally-regulated lenders may not charge a late fee when the only delinquency is the borrower's failure to pay a previously-assessed late fee. See 12 C.F.R. § 227.15 (banks belonging to the Federal Reserve System); 12 C.F.R. § 535.14 (federal savings associations).

As to mortgages insured by the Federal Housing Administration (FHA), late payment penalties are limited to 4% of each installment due that is more than fifteen days late. 24 C.F.R. § 203.25. The maximum late charge for mortgages guaranteed by the Veterans Administration (VA) is 4% of any installment that is delinquent more than fifteen days. 38 C.F.R. § 36.4212(d).

Fannie Mae requires collection, on non-federally insured or guaranteed mortgages, of a late charge of 4% of the late installment (or such lesser amount as will comply with any state law limitation) after a 15 day grace period. Freddie Mac permits, but does not require, the collection of a maximum 5% late charge after a 15 day grace period.

9. *Late fees and default interest in bankruptcy.* When a late fee or default interest rate is imposed on a borrower who is in bankruptcy, the practical question for the lender is whether the added amount is recognizable as a *secured* claim by the bankruptcy court. If the claim is not secured, there

is little probability that the lender will be able to recover it in full. With respect to late fees, it is clear that to be treated as a secured claim, the additional amount must be "reasonable" under Bankruptcy Code § 506(b). "Reasonableness" boils down to the court's determination that the amount is a fair estimate of the lender's additional costs resulting from the default.

The bankruptcy cases usually recognize late fees up to 4% or 5% of the late installment, but disallow much larger fees. See, e.g., In re Presque Isle Apts., L.P., 112 B.R. 744 (Bankr.W.D.Pa.1990) (lender that assessed a 4% late fee was allowed it, but could not retroactively increase the fee to 6%, even though the latter percentage was called for by the promissory note); In re Penick, 108 B.R. 776 (Bankr.W.D.Okl.1989) ($5 late fee per installment allowed).

With respect to default interest, it is not so clear that the "reasonableness" standard of § 506(b) should govern, since it refers only to "fees, costs, and charges." Nonetheless, bankruptcy courts usually scrutinize default interest carefully. Default interest rates that exceed the pre-default contract rate by only 4% or 5% are usually treated as secured claims. See, e.g., In re Terry Ltd. Partn., 27 F.3d 241 (7th Cir.1994) (increase from 14.25% to 17.25% recognized); In re Holmes, 330 B.R. 317 (Bankr.M.D.Ga.2005) (increase to 18% recognized). Much larger increases are usually disallowed; see In re Phoenix Bus. Park Ltd. Partn., 257 B.R. 517 (Bankr.D.Ariz.2001), determining that an increase from 10.75% to 24% was an unenforceable penalty. But see In re K & J Properties, Inc., 2005 WL 2589862 (Bankr.D.Colo.2005) (upholding a 36% default rate).

DEVLIN V. WIENER

Connecticut Supreme Court, 1995
232 Conn. 550, 656 A.2d 664

CALLAHAN, ASSOCIATE JUSTICE.

This appeal requires us to determine whether a mortgage deed and the underlying obligation that the deed purports to secure are sufficiently definite to sustain the plaintiff's foreclosure action. The trial court concluded that a debt is owed the plaintiff and that the debt is secured by a valid mortgage. We agree.

The record reveals the following facts. The plaintiff, Gerald Devlin, owned a nine acre parcel of real estate in Branford, on which his residence was located. The defendants Pine Orchard Associates, Inc., and Pine Orchard Development Corporation (collectively, Pine Orchard), sought to acquire and then subdivide the plaintiff's land. On February 18, 1984, the plaintiff executed a written contract to sell the nine acre parcel and his residence to Pine Orchard. The agreement entered into by the parties, although convoluted, essentially provided that the plaintiff would convey his interest in his Branford real estate to Pine Orchard for a cash of $86,000 and a promise by Pine Orchard either (1) to convey to the plaintiff a finished three bedroom condominium, cooperative apartment unit or single-family residence in the planned subdivision, or (2) to transfer to the plaintiff a building lot in the planned subdivision together with sufficient building materials for the plaintiff to erect a three bedroom single-family residence on the lot, or (3) to return to the plaintiff his Branford residence together with one half of one acre of land. The agreement further provided that, as security for Pine Orchard's additional promise, Pine Orchard would mortgage the transferred property back to the plaintiff. Finally, the agreement provided that the mortgage would secure a debt of Pine Orchard to the plaintiff in the amount of $84,000.[3] The $86,000 was paid to the plaintiff at the time of the closing and, as required by the agreement, was used to extinguish an existing first mortgage held by the Branford Savings Bank. No other consideration has been paid to the plaintiff.

On February 29, 1984, the plaintiff conveyed his interest in the Branford real estate to Pine Orchard Development Corporation and, on the same date, that defendant mortgaged the same real estate to the plaintiff in accordance with paragraph twenty-nine of the purchase and sale agreement. Daniel J. Wiener executed the mortgage instrument in his capacity as president of the corporation. The mortgage deed expressly stated that it was given to secure the obligation of Pine Orchard to "transfer certain properties" to the plaintiff pursuant to "a contract dated February 18, 1984." Although the deed itself was silent as to the amount of the secured debt, paragraph twenty-nine of the purchase and sale agreement specifically indicated that the mortgage was to secure an obligation of the corporation in the amount of $84,000.

On July 8, 1985, Pine Orchard Development Corporation conveyed all of its interest in the Branford property to Pine Orchard Development Associates, a partnership in which Daniel J. Wiener was a general partner. Thereafter, Pine Orchard Development Associates transferred the property to Daniel J. Wiener and Gloria Maddox Wiener, jointly as husband and wife with a right of survivorship. On April 13, 1990, Daniel J. Wiener transferred his interest in the Branford property, by quitclaim deed for no consideration, to his wife, the named defendant, Gloria Maddox Wiener.

On January 31, 1992, the plaintiff filed suit against Pine Orchard Associates, Inc., Pine Orchard Development Corporation and Gloria Maddox Wiener for foreclosure of his mortgage, claiming that the

---

[3] The document itself, which was fashioned by the parties without the aid of counsel, is several pages in length and contains various crossouts, insertions and initialed modifications. As aptly noted by the trial court, the agreement "graphically demonstrates the potential for disaster in documents prepared by laypersons without the assistance of lawyers."

defendants' obligation to the plaintiff, as set forth in the February 18, 1984 purchase and sale agreement and as secured by the mortgage deed given by Pine Orchard Development Corporation to the plaintiff on February 29, 1984, was in default. The named defendant filed an answer and various special defenses, including the defense that the "Mortgage Deed does not refer to a 'Mortgage Note' and fails to define any other obligation or debt in sufficient detail," and therefore does not secure an enforceable obligation.

After a hearing, the trial court concluded that "[a]s between the parties . . . there is an indebtedness due to the plaintiff on the mortgage in the amount of $84,000. While the defendants have cited deficiencies in the document in question, the court notes that . . . the document is susceptible to 'a reasonable and precise interpretation.' . . . The court finds there is an underlying obligation due to the plaintiff in the amount of $84,000.00 and that this amount is secured by a valid mortgage." Thereafter, on motion by the plaintiff, the trial court ordered a foreclosure by sale and rendered judgment accordingly. The named defendant appealed from the judgment of the trial court to the Appellate Court, and we transferred the appeal to this court pursuant to Practice Book § 4023 and General Statutes § 51–199(c).

On appeal, the named defendant claims only that the trial court improperly concluded that the mortgage deed and the obligation purportedly secured by the mortgage deed were sufficiently definite to sustain the plaintiff's foreclosure action. At the outset, the named defendant challenges the trial court's finding that she was a party, or in privity with a party, to the mortgage transaction. She claims, therefore, that the trial court improperly applied the law governing the enforceability of mortgages between parties to the mortgage, instead of applying the law governing the enforceability of mortgages between mortgagees and nonparties. Moreover, the named defendant claims that the mortgage deed is invalid because it does not secure a note, but rather, the performance of affirmative acts by Pine Orchard under the February 18, 1984 purchase and sale agreement, and because the deed does not recite the specific amount of the debt allegedly owed. Finally, the named defendant contends that the obligation contained in paragraph twenty-eight of the purchase and sale agreement is insufficient because it is too indefinite as to time for performance, subject matter and method of performance. We conclude that the mortgage is sufficiently definite as to be enforceable against the named defendant even if she is properly viewed as a third party, and we therefore affirm the judgment of the trial court.

We begin by reviewing the well established common law governing the sufficiency of mortgage deeds as between a mortgagee and a nonparty to the mortgage. "In [*Dart & Bogue Co. v. Slosberg*, 202 Conn. 566, 578–79, 522 A.2d 763 (1987)], we stated that the dispositive question in examining the validity of a mortgage is whether it provides 'reasonable notice' to third parties of the obligation that is secured. . . . The purpose of such 'reasonable notice' is to prevent parties that are not privy to the transaction from being defrauded or misled. . . . A corollary of this proposition is that errors and omissions in the recorded mortgage that would not mislead a title searcher as to the true nature of the secured obligation do not affect the validity of the mortgage against third parties. . . . In other words, the recorded mortgage deed does not need to recite with particularity all of the details of the underlying transaction. . . .

> "In *Dart & Bogue Co.* [*v. Slosberg, supra*, 202 Conn. at 579, 522 A.2d 763], we defined 'reasonable notice' as notice of the nature and amount of the encumbrance which the mortgagor intends to place upon the land. . . . The 'nature' of a secured debt includes such fundamental characteristics as whether the debt is absolute or contingent, liquidated or unliquidated, or whether it is given to secure an existing liability or future advances. . . . The 'amount' of the debt is the dollar value of the obligation secured, to the extent that it can be ascertained at the time the mortgage is executed. If the debt cannot be definitively ascertained at that time, such data must be set out with respect to that debt as will put anyone interested in the inquiry upon a track leading to discovery. . . . Significantly, in *Dart & Bogue Co.* [*v. Slosberg, supra*, at 580, 522 A.2d 763], we recognized that [t]he record is the starting point for inquiry, not . . . the starting and ending point. . . . In sum, if a party is able by common prudence and by the exercise of ordinary diligence, [to] ascertain the extent of the encumbrance from information set out in the land records, then the mortgage is valid." (Citations omitted; internal quotation marks omitted.)

Connecticut National Bank v. Esposito, 210 Conn. 221, 227–28, 554 A.2d 735 (1989).

We initially note that we will not declare the mortgage deed invalid, as the named defendant urges us to do, simply because the deed itself lacks a statement of the specific amount of the debt secured. As in Esposito, the deed in the present case omits "documents that contain important details about the obligation but the existence of which documents [is] expressly referred to in the recorded mortgage deed. The mortgage deed does not affirmatively misidentify the characteristics of the obligation, thus leading a title searcher to believe that the obligation is something that it is not, nor does the omission of the documents leave a title searcher without any indication of the obligation's nature or without a reasonable direction to discover the terms of the mortgage." *Id.* at 230, 554 A.2d 735. In fact, the mortgage deed expressly states that the obligation secured is set forth in the February 18, 1984 purchase and sale agreement between the plaintiff and Pine Orchard Associates, Inc., and further states that the agreement is on file at the office of the attorney for Pine Orchard. Thus, because the mortgage deed sufficiently puts a title searcher on notice of the location of the underlying agreement that contains the substance of the secured debt, the efficacy of the mortgage deed may be determined by analyzing the sufficiency of the underlying agreement.

Moreover, the mortgage deed is not invalid simply because it purports to secure a "performance" instead of a stated monetary obligation. "The condition of a mortgage may be the payment of a debt, the indemnity of a surety, or the doing or not doing any other act. *Cook v. Bartholomew*, 60 Conn. 24, 25, 22 A. 444 (1891); see *State v. Hurlburt*, 82 Conn. 232, 236, 72 A. 1079 (1909); *Jarvis v. Woodruff*, 22 Conn. 548, 550–51 (1853); *Gagan v. Leary*, 14 Conn.Sup. 468, 470 (1946); see also 9 G. Thompson, Real Property (Grimes 1958) § 4659, p. 32." (Internal quotation marks omitted.) *Connecticut National Bank v. Esposito, supra,* 210 Conn. at 225–26, 554 A.2d 735. Thus, if we determine that the underlying agreement contains a sufficiently definite obligation, whether that obligation be for the payment of a specific dollar amount or for the performance of some act, we may also determine that the mortgage deed is adequate to sustain the plaintiff's foreclosure action.

We now turn to the parties' February 18, 1984 purchase and sale agreement. Although the named defendant contends that the agreement is insufficient to support the mortgage deed at issue because the obligation contained in paragraph twenty-eight is too indefinite as to time for performance, subject matter and method of performance, the trial court, after viewing all of the evidence, concluded otherwise. On appeal, we are limited to determining whether this legal conclusion finds support in the record and is "legally and logically correct." *Pandolphe's Auto Parts, Inc. v. Manchester*, 181 Conn. 217, 221–22, 435 A.2d 24 (1980); see also *RK Constructors, Inc. v. Fusco Corp.*, 231 Conn. 381, 384–85, 650 A.2d 153 (1994).

The trial court concluded that paragraph twenty-eight of the parties' purchase and sale agreement creates an obligation due the plaintiff in the amount of $84,000. Our review of the various subsections to paragraph twenty-eight of the original agreement, which was made a trial exhibit by the plaintiff, reveals that Pine Orchard agreed to compensate the plaintiff for the Branford property, in addition to the $86,000 payment made to extinguish the existing encumbrance, by one of three alternate methods.

First, under paragraph twenty-eight (a) Pine Orchard could have chosen to return to the plaintiff his Branford residence together with one half of one acre of land. Second, under paragraph twenty-eight (a)(i), Pine Orchard could have chosen to transfer to the plaintiff a building lot together with sufficient building materials for the plaintiff to erect a three-bedroom single-family residence on the lot. Third, under paragraph twenty-eight (a)(ii), Pine Orchard could have chosen to convey to the plaintiff a finished three bedroom condominium, cooperative apartment unit or single-family residence in the subdivision that the defendants planned to construct on the Branford property. We further note that paragraph twenty-nine of the agreement provides that, as security for Pine Orchard's obligations to the plaintiff under paragraph twenty-eight, Pine Orchard granted the plaintiff a mortgage interest in the Branford property in the amount of $84,000.

Our review of the agreement between the plaintiff and Pine Orchard, which was part of the record before the trial court, persuades us to conclude that the trial court properly found that Pine Orchard Development Corporation had executed a mortgage securing a debt to the plaintiff in the amount of $84,000. Although the named defendant claims that the agreement is insufficient because it does not specify a time for performance, we note that both subsections (a) and (b) of paragraph twenty-eight of the agreement refer to a requirement that any conveyance to the plaintiff be made within two years from the date of closing. Likewise, although the named defendant contends that the method of performance and the subject matter constituting the substance of the agreement are not sufficiently specified, the parties specifically agreed that each of the three options that Pine Orchard could have chosen to satisfy its obligation to the plaintiff had a value of $84,000. Thus, we conclude that the trial court's determination that there is an underlying obligation owed the plaintiff in the amount of $84,000, and that this amount is secured by a valid mortgage, is supported by the record and is "legally and logically correct." *Pandolphe's Auto Parts, Inc. v. Manchester, supra,* 181 Conn. at 221–22, 435 A.2d 24.

The judgment of the trial court is affirmed and the case is remanded to that court to set new law days and to order appropriate notice.

In this opinion the other justices concurred.

NOTES

1. *Definiteness of obligation.* There are two distinct issues in the *Devlin* case, and it is useful to consider them separately. One issue is whether the obligation that a mortgage secures is described with sufficient clarity. The Connecticut court (wisely, we think) takes the view that the obligation must be definite, but that the definition doesn't necessarily have to

appear in the mortgage itself, so long as the mortgage contains "data * * * with respect to that debt as will put anyone interested in the inquiry upon a track leading to discovery." The details may be in another agreement or set of agreements between the parties. Restatement (Third) of Property (Mortgages) § 1.5(a) (1997) is even more forgiving: "A mortgage need not describe the obligation whose performance it secures, provided the parties have otherwise reached agreement identifying that obligation." Obviously, describing the obligation, or at least identifying the documents that describe it, is a sound practice.

Not all courts are so accommodating as the Restatement and the Connecticut court. In Kalange v. Rencher, 136 Idaho 192, 30 P.3d 970 (2001), the parties entered into a note and a deed of trust, but also signed a separate "loan agreement," not mentioned in the deed of trust, which required the borrower to pay an additional $50,000 under certain circumstances. The court refused to recognize that the "loan agreement" was secured by the deed of trust, even though it was quite obvious that the parties understood it to be secured. See also, Wilson v. Ledger, 97 A.D. 1028, 949 N.Y.S.2d 515 (App.Div.2012) (the plans and specifications for the residence to be constructed, as well as the size and location of the lot upon which it would be built and conveyed to plaintiff, were essential terms of the note and mortgage inasmuch they represented the manner of repayment of the debt—the parties left these material terms for future negotiation and agreement and failed to set forth in the documents any objective method for supplying these missing terms, resulting in only an unenforceable agreement to agree).

2.   *Non-monetary obligations.* The second issue in *Devlin* is whether the non-monetary obligation is capable of being reduced to a money equivalent. If it cannot, it cannot be secured by a mortgage. See Nelson, Whitman, Burkhart & Freyermuth, Real Estate Finance Law § 2.2 (6th ed.2014); Restatement (Third) of Property (Mortgages) § 1.4 (1997). For example, a variety of construction agreements have been held capable of being mortgaged and the cost of completion of the contract has been deemed prima facie evidence of the mortgage debt. See Pawtucket Instn. for Sav. v. Gagnon, 475 A.2d 1028 (R.I.1984) (promise to build apartment house); Jeffrey Towers, Inc. v. Straus, 31 A.D.2d 319, 297 N.Y.S.2d 450 (1969) (promise to build driveway and sewer line). In *Devlin*, the parties made this issue relatively easy by stipulating to the $84,000 value for the obligation.

What's the reason for requiring that the obligation be reducible to a monetary equivalent? As the comment to Restatement § 1.4 observes,

> Mortgage enforcement would break down if mortgages were permitted to secure performance of obligations that could not be measured in terms of money. There would be no means of determining whether a foreclosure sale produced a surplus or a deficiency. If a junior lienholder desired to redeem, there would be

no means of determining the amount necessary to accomplish a redemption.*

3.   *Support mortgages.* Restatement (Third) of Property (Mortgages) § 1.4 (1997) Illustration 4 comments that when a mortgage is given both to secure a promise of financial support, and also a promise of "love, affection, and kindness," the mortgage is valid to secure the first obligation but not the second. The reason, of course, is that a promise of emotional support cannot be reduced to a monetary equivalent. Yet people fairly often enter into mortgages that purport to require such "emotional" obligations. See, e.g., Thompson v. Glidden, 445 A.2d 676 (Me.1982).

E. LOSS MITIGATION

When the real estate and mortgage bubbles burst in 2008, massive numbers of properties went into foreclosure. Lenders have foreclosed on millions of homes and other properties, which fueled the downward spiral of land values and community deterioration. The foreclosures have displaced massive numbers of families and shuttered many businesses. In an attempt to address these devastating outcomes, the federal, state, and local governments have been attempting to encourage lenders to engage in loss mitigation, rather than to foreclose. These loss mitigation programs are designed to get lenders to accept a deed in lieu of foreclosure, modify the loan terms to make the loan more affordable for the borrower, or agree to a "short sale" when the mortgaged property is worth less than the outstanding debt amount. The following materials examine each of these foreclosure alternatives.

1. DEEDS IN LIEU OF FORECLOSURE

When foreclosure is impending, the borrower may offer to deed the property to the lender, and the lender often will accept the deed for both commercial and residential mortgages. Deeds in lieu of foreclosure may seem attractive to the parties for several reasons. The mortgagee may seek to avoid the delay and expense associated with foreclosure. This motivation may be especially strong when a judicial proceeding is the only foreclosure remedy and in states with long post-foreclosure redemption periods. Moreover, if the mortgagor is of dubious solvency, the mortgagee may be perfectly willing to forego seeking a deficiency judgment. In any event, legislation in some jurisdictions prohibits or severely restricts deficiency judgments.

The mortgagor may want to avoid the possibility of a personal judgment that, though currently uncollectible, can create future problems if his or her financial fortunes ultimately improve. Sometimes, the mortgagor can persuade the mortgagee who accepts a deed in lieu not to

---

*   © 1997 by The American Law Institute. Reprinted with permission.

take action to impair the mortgagor's credit rating. In any event, a notation of a deed in lieu on a credit report is substantially less damaging than a notation of an actual foreclosure.

Due diligence. When a mortgagee is considering whether to accept a deed in lieu, it should take all the same precautions as any well-advised property purchaser. This is especially so in the case of income-producing rental real estate:

> The mortgagee's investigation should include an environmental audit to determine whether the property is or may be contaminated by hazardous waste; a determination whether the property complies with the Americans with Disabilities Act, is the subject of any existing lawsuits or tort claims, and complies with local zoning and other codes; a check for unpaid trade creditors and, if they exist, a determination whether the mortgagor or mortgagee will be responsible for paying them; and a review of the content and assignability of all vendor service contracts. The mortgagee also should identify any other liabilities or restrictions on the real estate.

Nelson, Whitman, Burkhart & Freyermuth, Real Estate Finance Law § 6.19 (6th ed. 2014).

Deed in lieu not a clog. The deed in lieu does not normally constitute an invalid clog on the equity of redemption, because the prohibition against clogging applies only to agreements given when the lender makes the loan and not to transactions designed to wind up and terminate the mortgage relationship. See Panagouleas Interiors, Inc. v. Silent Partner Group, Inc., 2002 WL 441409 (Ohio Ct.App.2002) (not reported in N.E.2d); Levenson v. Feuer, 60 Mass.App.Ct. 428, 803 N.E.2d 341 (2004).

Nonetheless, a court can recharacterize a deed in lieu as an equitable mortgage ("additional security for the loan"), though the borrower did not give the deed at the same time as the mortgage. This result is particularly likely if the borrower gave the deed as part of a "workout" agreement, in which the lender gave the defaulting borrower additional time to perform on the loan, and if the borrower kept possession of the property. The key fact is that the borrower did not give the deed as an immediate and final conveyance of the property.

The lender sometimes tries to pretty up this picture by putting the deed in lieu of foreclosure into escrow, with instructions that the escrow agent record and deliver it only if the borrower defaults again. This really doesn't improve matters at all. The borrower is still at risk of being persuaded by the mirage of hope to sign anything—including the deed—to keep the loan alive a little longer, which is exactly what the clogging doctrine won't allow. Courts sometimes invalidate the deed or give it effect only as "additional security" and not as an actual transfer of title.

See, e.g., Basile v. Erhal Holding Corp., 148 A.D.2d 484, 538 N.Y.S.2d 831 (1989); Panagouleas Interiors, Inc. v. Silent Partner Group, Inc., 2002 WL 441409 (Ohio App. 2002) (not reported in N.E.2d). Contra, see Ringling Joint Venture II v. Huntington Nat'l Bank, 595 So.2d 180 (Fla. Dist. Ct. App. 1992); Wensel v. Flatte, 27 Ark.App. 5, 764 S.W.2d 627 (1989). Courts in the latter cases stressed the facts that the borrower was a business and not a consumer, was represented by counsel, and was thoroughly advised concerning the deed's effect.

Inequitable deeds in lieu. Even if a court does not find an "equitable mortgage," as one commentator has noted, "there is an underlying idea that the mortgagor and mortgagee are not of equal bargaining strength. Therefore, it is entirely possible, especially if the consideration paid is disproportionately less than the value of the equity or if none is paid where the equity has value, that the whole transaction will be construed as unfair or unconscionable. The courts will either permit the mortgagor to redeem at this point or restore the original mortgagor-mortgagee relationship." Note, Mortgages—Improvements—Absolute Deed in Lieu of Foreclosure, 31 Mo.L.Rev. 312, 315 (1966); Francie Cohen Spahn, Deeds in Lieu of Foreclosure, 26 No. 4 Prac. Real Est. Law. 47 (2010). See, e.g., Robar v. Ellingson, 301 N.W.2d 653, 657–58 (N.D.1981).

To provide some protection against this possibility, a mortgagee frequently will accept a deed in lieu only if it also gets (1) a property appraisal and (2) the mortgagor's affidavit. What is the point of the appraisal? What should the affidavit say? Id.

Deed in lieu in bankruptcy. When a borrower is experiencing sufficient financial difficulties that it gives a deed in lieu, a significant chance exists that the borrower subsequently will declare bankruptcy. Under some circumstances, a deed in lieu may be avoidable under the Bankruptcy Code. It is arguably a *preference* under § 547 if the mortgagee was insolvent when it delivered the deed and entered bankruptcy within 90 days of delivery and if the outstanding debt was less than the property's value. Alternatively, it may be a *fraudulent transfer* under § 548 of the Bankruptcy Code if the mortgagor went into bankruptcy within two years after the conveyance and did not receive "reasonably equivalent value" for it. See Sensenich v. Molleur, 328 B.R. 675 (Bankr.D.Vt.2005) (treating a Vermont strict foreclosure like a deed in lieu for purposes of § 548); Ann M. Burkhart, Freeing Mortgages of Merger, 40 Vand.L.Rev. 283, 339–41 (1987). You should reconsider this problem in connection with the bankruptcy material in Chapter 6, Section J, infra.

Merger. In addition to the potential challenges described above, a mortgagee that is deciding whether to accept a deed in lieu must consider the impact of the doctrine of merger. Fortunately, a challenge based on the merger doctrine generally can be prevented by including a statement in the deed that the mortgagee does not intend the mortgage to merge into the fee title.

NELSON, WHITMAN, BURKHART & FREYERMUTH, REAL ESTATE FINANCE LAW
541–42 (6th ed.2014)*

Merger—General Considerations

The doctrine of merger is one of the most complex and confusing areas of the law of mortgages. The basic doctrine itself can be stated in a few sentences and is deceptively simple. When a mortgagee's interest and a fee title coincide and meet in the same person, the lesser estate, the mortgage, merges into the greater, the fee, and is extinguished. Courts state that "whether a merger has occurred depends on the intent of the parties, especially the one in whom the interests unite. If merger is against that party's best interest, it will not be deemed intended by the parties."

Once having stated the basic doctrine, the confusion begins. The confusion often arises because merger can be used either as a defense to the mortgage debt or as an argument that the mortgage no longer exists. For example, suppose that in lieu of a foreclosure action, a mortgagor agrees to convey the mortgaged property to the mortgagee. Does the merger of the two estates in the mortgagee extinguish the mortgage debt so that the mortgagee cannot pursue the mortgagor personally? On the other hand, the same facts may result in a merger problem with the focus on the *mortgage* and not on the debt. Suppose that our mortgagee was a first mortgagee and that, through inadvertence, took a deed in lieu of foreclosure without first checking to see if junior liens existed on the real estate. If a junior lienor did exist, is it now a senior lien because merger destroyed the former first mortgage or can the original first mortgagee foreclose it to eliminate the junior lien?

———————

Merger of the Mortgage

Merger of the *mortgage* is an important issue, especially when junior liens exist. Unlike foreclosure, a deed in lieu of foreclosure does not eliminate those liens. Therefore, a mortgagee that is considering accepting a deed in lieu should have the title examined to determine whether junior interests exist. If they do, the lender normally should foreclose, rather than accept a deed in lieu.

———————

*   Reprinted with permission of LEG, Inc. d/b/a West Academic.

If a senior mortgagee accepts a deed in lieu without having the title examined or if the title examiner misses a junior lien, the junior lienor may assert that the senior mortgage has merged into the fee title and that the junior lien now has first priority! This argument, while often made, seldom succeeds. Courts usually hold that the senior mortgage still exists and can be foreclosed to eliminate the subsequently-discovered junior lien. The Texas Supreme Court reached this conclusion in North Texas Bldg. & Loan Ass'n v. Overton, 126 Tex. 104, 86 S.W.2d 738 (1935):

> It is often true, as no doubt it was in the instant case, that it is decidedly to the advantage of the mortgagor and mortgagee to avoid the necessity of a foreclosure suit by a conveyance of the premises to the mortgagee. A rule penalizing them for so doing would be contrary to our policy that litigation is not to be encouraged. The junior lienholder suffers no injury thereby, but is in the same position as if there had been a foreclosure without his having been made a party. His equity of redemption is not affected, neither is his lien thereby elevated to a first lien.

* * *

> It is immaterial, as between the senior and junior lienholders, whether the mortgagee retains the note and mortgage in his possession or surrenders them to the mortgagor. It is likewise immaterial whether or not the deed of conveyance from the mortgagor to the mortgagee recites, as did the one in the instant case, that the cancellation of the note and mortgage was a part of the consideration for the conveyance.

Professor Durfee has described the theoretical justification for this result as follows: "[T]he classical approach to a case of this sort takes several steps. (1) At common law there is a merger of the mortgage in the equity of redemption. (2) Equity will prevent merger if the party in whom the interests unite is found to have intended to keep both interests on foot. (3) In the absence of evidence of a contrary intent, equity will presume the existence of that intent that is most beneficial to the party holding the two interests." Durfee, Cases on Security 396 (1951). These arguments are obviously sound, and courts widely accept them. Representative cases include Federal Land Bank v. Colorado Nat'l Bank, 786 P.2d 514 (Colo.App.1989); GBJ, Inc., II v. First Avenue Inv. Corp., 520 N.W.2d 508 (Minn.App.1994); London Bank & Trust Co. v. American Fidelity Bank & Trust Co., 697 S.W.2d 956 (Ky.App.1985); Altabet v. Monroe Methodist Church, 54 Wash.App. 695, 777 P.2d 544 (1989).

However, courts in deed in lieu cases hold that merger has extinguished the senior mortgage just often enough to entice some junior lienors to make that argument. See, e.g., Citizens State Bank of New Castle v. Countrywide Home Loans, Inc., 949 N.E.2d. 1195 (Ind. 2011);

Janus Properties, Inc. v. First Florida Bank, N.A., 546 So.2d 785 (Fla.App.1989) (court found merger and elevated the junior mortgage to first priority). In that case, the court placed some reliance on the fact that the first mortgagee, after accepting the deed in lieu, "solemnized its intent by executing and recording a satisfaction of mortgage." What should the mortgagee have done instead?

Eliminating the doctrine of merger. For an analysis of the merger doctrine's applicability to mortgages and arguments for its abolition, see Ann M. Burkhart, Freeing Mortgages of Merger, 40 Vand.L.Rev. 283 (1987). Indeed, the Restatement takes the position that the merger doctrine "does not apply to mortgages or affect the enforceability of a mortgage obligation." Restatement (Third) of Property (Mortgages) § 8.5 (1997). If a court adopts the Restatement approach and rejects the merger doctrine, will the intervening lien problem be obviated? "[A] conveyance of the equity of redemption by a mortgagor or subsequent grantee to a mortgagee will not, except in extremely rare circumstances, terminate the latter's mortgage as against liens or other interests that prior to the conveyance were junior to it." Restatement (Third) of Property (Mortgages) § 8.5 cmt. b (1997). Suppose the mortgagee who takes the deed in lieu assumes that an intervening lien exists or takes with actual knowledge of it. Should the mortgagee still be able to foreclose? See id.

Use of nominee. If a court is inclined to enforce the merger doctrine though a junior lien exists, can merger be avoided by having the deed in lieu run to a nominee of the mortgagee, such as its attorney or affiliated corporation, rather than to the mortgagee? See Alden Hotel Co. v. Kanin, 88 Misc.2d 546, 387 N.Y.S.2d 948 (1976).

Merger of the Debt

Merger is more often a *debt* problem when the controversy is between the person who holds the debt, mortgage, and property title and the person who is liable for the debt. These controversies arise in at least five settings: (1) The mortgagee acquires the property title (equity of redemption) from the mortgagor; (2) The mortgagee acquires title from the mortgagor's grantee; (3) The holder of more than one mortgage acquires title by purchasing at a foreclosure sale of one of those mortgages; (4) The mortgagee transfers the debt and mortgage to the mortgagor; and (5) The mortgagee transfers the debt and mortgage to the mortgagor's grantee. For a detailed consideration of these categories, see Nelson, Whitman, Burkhart & Freyermuth, Real Estate Finance Law § 6.16 (6th ed.2015).

MID KANSAS FEDERAL SAVINGS AND LOAN ASSOCIATION v. DYNAMIC DEVELOPMENT CORPORATION

Supreme Court of Arizona, 1991
167 Ariz. 122, 804 P.2d 1310

FELDMAN, VICE CHIEF JUSTICE.

A construction lender held notes secured by first and second deeds of trust on a residential developer's property. The lender acquired title to the property at a trustee's sale on the second trust deed and thereafter brought an action against the developer for the balance due on the first notes. The court of appeals held that the lender was precluded from doing so under A.R.S. § 33–814(G) and the rationale of our decision in *Baker v. Gardner*, 160 Ariz. 98, 770 P.2d 766 (1988).

We must determine whether the anti-deficiency statutes apply to a residential developer and whether a lender may recover the balance owing on the first notes after it has acquired title to the property at the foreclosure sale of its second deed of trust.

* * *

[W]e hold that by its terms, the anti-deficiency statute does not apply to Dynamic in this case and A.R.S. § 33–814(G) does not preclude Mid Kansas from waiving its security and bringing a debt action on the notes.

C.   The Doctrine of Merger and Extinguishment

Because we hold that the anti-deficiency statute does not apply, we must reach the merger and extinguishment issue that is the basis of the concurring opinion in the court of appeals. Dynamic listed that issue for our consideration under Rule 23(c), Ariz.R.Civ.App.P., 17B A.R.S., as an issue not decided by the court of appeals but that would need to be addressed if the court of appeals' opinion were reversed.

1.   Merger of Estates

As Dynamic has noted, the facts in this case provide the basis for two merger arguments. The first is the theory of merger of estates. Generally, when one person obtains both a greater and a lesser interest in the same property, and no intermediate interest exists in another person, a merger occurs and the lesser interest is extinguished. 3 R. Powell, The Law of Real Property § 459 (1990 Rev.). Thus, merger may occur when a mortgagee's interest and the fee title are owned by the same person. Id. The potential for merger arises whenever a mortgagee acquires the mortgagor's equity of redemption. However, even if a merger would otherwise occur at law, contrary intent or equitable considerations may preclude this result under appropriate circumstances. 2 L. Jones, The Law of Mortgages § 1080 (8th ed. 1928). This court has long recognized these general rules of merger of estates. *Bowman v. Cook*, 101 Ariz. 366, 419 P.2d 723 (1966); *Hathaway v. Neal*, 31 Ariz. 155, 251 P. 173 (1926).

We assume, therefore, no one arguing to the contrary, that when Mid Kansas acquired title on the foreclosure of its second lien, its rights under that lien were merged in the title. See *Bowman*, 101 Ariz. at 367, 419 P.2d at 724. The question before us, however, is somewhat different. Today we must consider if Mid Kansas's rights under the first lien were affected when it acquired title by foreclosure on its second lien.

2. Merger of Rights

Where the same mortgagee holds both a first and second mortgage on the mortgagor's land, and becomes the purchaser at the foreclosure sale of one of the mortgages, the question of merger of rights—often called extinguishment—arises. The merger of rights doctrine addresses the narrow question of whether the mortgagor's personal liability on the senior debt has been discharged. *Wright v. Anderson*, 62 S.D. 444, 253 N.W. 484, 487 (1934). The primary issue in the doctrine of merger of rights is whether the lender would be unjustly enriched if he were permitted to enforce the debt. See generally Burkhart, *Freeing Mortgages of Merger*, 40 Vand.L.Rev. 283, 382 (1987).

Although the mortgagee's purchase of the property at the foreclosure of the senior mortgage will not extinguish the debt secured by a junior mortgage, the reverse is true where the junior mortgage is foreclosed. If one holding both junior and senior mortgages forecloses the junior and purchases the property at the foreclosure sale, the long-standing rule is that, absent a contrary agreement, the mortgagor's personal liability for the debt secured by the first mortgage is extinguished. G. Nelson & D. Whitman, Real Estate Finance Law § 6.16, at 467 (2d ed. 1985). The rule has been followed for generations. See *Board of Trustees of the Gen. Retirement Sys. v. Ren-Cen Indoor Tennis & Racquet Club*, 145 Mich.App. 318, 377 N.W.2d 432 (1985), appeal denied, 425 Mich. 875, 388 N.W.2d 680 (1986); *Tri-County Bank & Trust Co. v. Watts*, 234 Neb. 124, 449 N.W.2d 537 (1989); Annotation, Union of Title to Mortgage and Fee in Same Person as Affecting Right to Personal Judgment for Mortgage Debt, 95 A.L.R. 89, 104–105 (1935) (citing *Belleville Sav. Bank v. Reis*, 136 Ill. 242, 26 N.E. 646 (1891)); *McDonald v. Magirl*, 97 Iowa 677, 66 N.W. 904 (1896); *Wright*, 253 N.W. 484; see also 2 G. Glenn, Mortgages § 337, at 1408 (1943).

The basis of the merger of rights doctrine is that the purchaser at a foreclosure sale of a junior lien takes subject to all senior liens. *Ren-Cen Club*, 377 N.W.2d at 434; *Wright*, 253 N.W. at 487; see also Burkhart, *supra*, 40 Vand.L.Rev. at 377. Although the purchaser does not become personally liable on the senior debt (as does an assuming grantee), the purchaser must pay it to avoid the risk of losing his newly acquired land to foreclosure by the senior lienholder. Therefore, the land becomes the primary fund for the senior debt, and the purchaser is presumed to have deducted the amount of the senior liens from the amount he bids for the land. *Tri-County Bank*, 449 N.W.2d at 541. As the court in *Wright* explained, when the same mortgagee holds both the junior and senior mortgages on the land and buys at the foreclosure sale of the junior mortgage:

> The mortgagor * * * has an equitable right to have the land pay the mortgage before his personal liability is called upon and the purchaser will not be permitted to retain the land * * * and enforce the same against the mortgagor personally.

253 N.W. at 487. Similarly, the court in *Ren-Cen Club* noted that

> [t]he indebtedness will be presumed to have been discharged so soon as the holder of it becomes invested with title to the land upon which it is charged, on the principle that a party may not sue himself at law or in equity. The purchaser is presumed to have bought the land at its value, less the amount of indebtedness secured thereon, and equity will not permit him to hold the land and still collect the debt from the mortgagor.

377 N.W.2d at 435 (quoting *Belleville Savings Bank v. Reis*, 136 Ill. 242, 26 N.E. 646, 647 (1891) (citations omitted)).

Thus, the merger of rights doctrine holds that the senior lien is merged into—or extinguished by—the title acquired by the lienholder when he acquires the mortgagor's equity of redemption under a sale on the junior lien. Of course, this rule comes into play only when the equity of redemption is extinguished. See *Wright*, 253 N.W. at 487; 2 Jones, *supra*, § 1080, at 514. Although the deed of trust is a relatively new instrument that postdates cases such as *Wright* and *Belleville*, we find the doctrine of merger and extinguishment even more compelling under a modern deed of trust statute, which cuts off the borrower's equity of redemption at the time of the trustee's sale. See A.R.S. § 33–811(B). In *Patton v. First Federal Savings & Loan Ass'n*, we commented on the unique features of the deed of trust that required a strict construction in favor of the borrower:

> Compared to mortgage requirements, the Deed of Trust procedures authorized by statute make it far easier for lenders to forfeit the borrower's interest in the real estate securing a loan, and also abrogate the right of redemption after sale guaranteed under a mortgage foreclosure. * * * [U]nder a Deed of Trust, the trustee holds a power of sale permitting him to sell the property out of court with no necessity of judicial action. The Deed of Trust statutes thus strip borrowers of many of the protections available under a mortgage. Therefore, lenders must strictly

> comply with the Deed of Trust statutes, and the statutes and
> Deeds of Trust must be strictly construed in favor of the
> borrower.

118 Ariz. 473, 477, 578 P.2d 152, 156 (1978).

As we have previously noted, even where a merger would otherwise
occur at law, an express agreement between the parties that no merger
shall occur often precludes such a finding by the court. Nelson &
Whitman, *supra*, § 6.16, at 467 (citing *Toston v. Utah Mortgage Loan
Corp.*, 115 F.2d 560 (9th Cir. 1940); *Continental Title & Trust Co. v.
Devlin*, 209 Pa. 380, 58 A. 843 (1904); *Van Woerden v. Union
Improvement Co.*, 156 Wash. 555, 287 P. 870 (1930)). Of course, where the
mortgagee acquires title to the property through an involuntary
conveyance, such as foreclosure, the parties obviously will not have
formed a mutual intent concerning the continued enforceability of the
debt. Burkhart, *supra*, 40 Vand.L.Rev. at 377.

However, such an intent may be implied under circumstances that
would make a finding of merger inequitable to the parties. The dissent in
Wright, for instance, argued that where the mortgagee paid the full value
of the property without deducting the amount of the prior lien, the rule of
merger should not apply. 253 N.W. at 489 (Polley, J., dissenting). This
argument was adopted by a recent decision that allowed a bank to retain
its claim for the unsecured deficiency remaining on the first mortgage
even though the bank purchased the property at the foreclosure sale on
the second mortgage. *In re Richardson*, 48 B.R. 141 (Bkrtcy.E.D.Tenn.
1985). The court found that the bank had not tried to take unfair
advantage of the debtor because its bid had reflected the value of the
property and the bank had, in addition, credited the debtors with the
amount beyond the bid it received on reselling the property. *Id.* at 142. A
different result would obtain where the mortgagee is permitted to keep
land that is worth as much as the two mortgage debts and also allowed to
collect on the senior debt. In the latter situation, the mortgagee would be
unjustly enriched, and the merger doctrine is appropriately applied to
destroy the senior debt. Nelson & Whitman, *supra*, § 6.16, at 467–68.

The facts in this case clearly illustrate and require application of the
doctrine of merger and extinguishment; they also demonstrate that no
equitable exception is appropriate here. Mid Kansas held the four first
deeds of trust and the second blanket deed of trust on the four lots. Mid
Kansas purchased all four pieces of property with a credit bid of the
amount due on the second lien, $101,986.67. Mid Kansas thus acquired
free and clear title to improved property apparently worth between
$555,750 and $608,000.[9] Even accepting the lower figure, it is apparent

---

[9] The value of the properties, as listed on the IRS Statements of Acquisition or
Abandonment of Secured Property filed by Mid Kansas, totalled $555,750. Mid Kansas
submitted appraisals to the trial court estimating the value of the lots, if completed in

that the sum of the junior and senior liens ($527,236.67 exclusive of interest and costs) on the property at the relevant time—the date of the foreclosure sale—was probably less than the value of the property. Mid Kansas obviously tendered a credit bid that was discounted by the amount of the senior liens. Therefore, Mid Kansas would be unjustly enriched were we to allow it to acquire, for $100,000, property worth over $500,000 and also sue Dynamic for another $400,000 under the first notes. Mid Kansas does not contend that the property it acquired was worth less than the total owed on the first and second liens.

On these facts, we hold that the doctrine of merger and extinguishment applies. See *Ren-Cen Club*, 377 N.W.2d at 436 (equity will not assist plaintiff in obtaining the price advantage of purchasing at a second mortgage sale without the disadvantage of having to satisfy the debt secured by the first mortgage). Because the holder of the senior lien acquired title, free from any equity of redemption, on the foreclosure of the junior lien, the doctrine of merger extinguishes the maker's liability on the senior notes.[10] This result is supported by other courts that have applied the doctrine of merger and extinguishment and held that the debt secured by the first mortgage is discharged when the senior mortgagee acquires the property at a sale on the second mortgage and the price at foreclosure sale is depressed to reflect the outstanding first mortgage. See, e.g., *Ren-Cen Club*, 377 N.W.2d 432; *Tri-County Bank*, 449 N.W.2d 537; see also authorities cited in Annot., supra, 95 A.L.R. at 104–105.

CONCLUSION

The anti-deficiency statute, A.R.S. § 33–814(G), does not apply to Dynamic in this case because the homes under construction were not utilized for single-family dwellings. We vacate the court of appeals' opinion and reverse the trial court's judgment. The case is remanded to the trial court for proceedings consistent with this opinion. On remand, the parties will have the opportunity to present evidence as to the value of the property at the time of the foreclosure sale. If the facts are as they appear on this record, equity will require no exception to the doctrine of merger and extinguishment. If Dynamic prevails, it will be eligible for its attorney's fees subject to Rule 21, Ariz.R.Civ.App.P., 17B A.R.S.

---

accordance with the plans and specifications, at $608,000. Ironically, the IRS statements filed by Mid Kansas stated that the "borrower was not personally liable for repayment of the debt," although Mid Kansas attributes this to "clerical error" and has since "corrected" the forms.

[10] We note that our legislature has specifically curtailed a lender's ability to obtain a judgment against the debtor in excess of the fair value of the land in those cases where a deficiency judgment is permitted. See A.R.S. § 33–814(A). We find this legislative proscription against unjust enrichment persuasive in our present holding.

GORDON, C.J., and MOELLER and CORCORAN, JJ., concur.

CAMERON, JUSTICE, dissenting in part, concurring in part. [Justice Cameron's dissenting opinion, which is based on the view that the majority misconstrued the antideficiency statute, is omitted.]

NOTES

1. *Understanding* Mid Kansas. You'll recall that Mid Kansas held two mortgages from Dynamic on the same property—a first mortgage with a balance owing of $425,000 and a second with a balance owing of $100,000. The property had a market value of $550,000. (The numbers have been rounded slightly to make them easier to follow.)

Mid Kansas foreclosed the second mortgage and was the successful bidder; it bought the property for $100,000. In this foreclosure sale, Mid Kansas had an advantage over other possible bidders. No other bidder could afford to bid more than $125,000, because it would be buying the property subject to the $425,000 first mortgage. Any bidder, other than Mid Kansas, would have to subtract the balance on that mortgage from the property's value in calculating its maximum bid.

Mid Kansas, on the other hand, was not limited in this way when bidding at its own foreclosure sale. For example, suppose Mid Kansas bid $150,000, which would easily allow it to outbid any other bidder. Of this bid, $100,000 would be applied to the second mortgage debt, fully discharging it, and the remaining $50,000 would be paid to any subordinate lienholders or, if none existed, to the mortgagor. Mid Kansas would now hold title to the real estate, and it would be free and clear of both mortgages. The reason, of course, is that the second mortgage would have been destroyed by its foreclosure, and the first mortgage would be eliminated because Mid Kansas owned the fee title and the first mortgage. In this context, it is sensible to say that a merger of the first mortgage and the fee title has occurred.

Mid Kansas would own a parcel of land worth $550,000 for a purchase price of $150,000—a "windfall" gain of $400,000. Because it doesn't have to pay off the first mortgage, as any other successful bidder would, it could bid without the inhibition that other bidders face. For that reason, courts do to Mid Kansas something that they wouldn't do to any other bidder. They force Mid Kansas to account for the windfall it has received when it sues on the first mortgage note. Although the first mortgage is gone, the first mortgage *note* is still alive and well. A suit on that note is similar to an action for a deficiency after a foreclosure of the first mortgage.

In our example, Mid Kansas has a $400,000 windfall. If it sues on the $425,000 first mortgage note, the court will offset that claim by the $400,000 windfall. Therefore, Mid Kansas can collect only $25,000 on the note.

In the actual case, Mid Kansas bid only $100,000, giving it a $450,000 windfall, which completely offset the $425,000 first mortgage note. The smaller the windfall, the more Mid Kansas can recover on the first note. If it had bid $550,000 at the foreclosure sale, it would have had no windfall, because the land was worth $550,000. It could have collected the full amount owing on the first mortgage note.

Here's one more example. Suppose Mid Kansas had bid $450,000 at the second mortgage foreclosure sale. By doing so, it would get $550,000 worth of property, giving it a $100,000 windfall. We subtract that windfall from the balance owing on the first mortgage debt, which is $425,000. So Mid Kansas can collect only the difference, or $325,000, on the first mortgage debt.

Incidentally, the same principle operates any time a first mortgagee bids at the foreclosure sale of a second mortgage, even if the two mortgages are initially held by two different lenders.

2. *Extensions of the* Mid Kansas *principle.* In Centennial Square, Ltd. v. Resolution Trust Co., 815 P.2d 1002 (Colo.App.1991), the court applied the merger principle discussed in *Mid Kansas* to prevent the lender, after foreclosure, from recovering pre-foreclosure profits earned by the property receiver. In Licursi v. Sweeney, 156 Vt. 418, 594 A.2d 396 (1991), the court applied the principle to the holder of the second and third mortgages that foreclosed the latter mortgage.

3. *What should the* Mid Kansas *mortgagee have done?* When a mortgagee holds two mortgages on the same property, and both are in default, how should he or she proceed? Does the solution lie in foreclosing both mortgages judicially at the same time and seeking a single deficiency judgment against the mortgagor? Assuming that both mortgages are in default, should the mortgagee instead foreclose on the senior mortgage and purchase at that foreclosure sale? See Nelson, Whitman, Burkhart & Freyermuth, Real Estate Finance Law § 6.16 (6th ed.2014).

4. *Is merger needed to reach the* Mid-Kansas *result?* If a court adopts the Restatement approach, what result would it reach in a case like *Mid Kansas*? What analysis would it use in reaching that result? See Restatement (Third) of Property (Mortgages) § 8.5 cmt. c(2) (1997).

5. *Deed in lieu and merger of the debt.* Similarly, if the mortgagee in *Mid Kansas* had accepted a deed in lieu, rather than foreclosing, would merger of the debt be an issue? If, as is usual, the conveyance to the mortgagee is made and accepted as payment of the mortgage debt, no question of merger of the *debt* is either possible or necessary. The debt is certainly eliminated but not because of merger. It was discharged by payment or, more accurately, by substituted performance or accord and satisfaction. Nelson, Whitman, Burkhart & Freyermuth, Real Estate Finance Law § 6.16 (6th ed.2014).

6. *Is a deficiency judgment available?* When negotiating with the mortgagee to accept a deed in lieu, the mortgagor should attempt to obtain the mortgagee's covenant not to sue on the note. If the mortgagee does not give the covenant and subsequently concludes that the property's value is less than the debt balance, can the mortgagee sue for the "deficiency?" Or

should merger of the *debt* always be inferred, even if a merger of the mortgage is not? See Nash Finch Co. v. Corey Dev., Ltd., 669 N.W.2d 546 (Iowa 2003); Prigal v. Kearn, 557 So.2d 647 (Fla.App.1990). The courts in both cases recognized that the deficiency liability continues to exist unless the parties specifically agree to cancel it. In contrast, Illinois statutorily provides that acceptance of a deed in lieu eliminates personal liability for the debt unless the parties expressly agree otherwise. 735 Ill.Comp.Stat. 5/15–1401.

In Volk v. Wisconsin Mortg. Assur. Co., 474 N.W.2d 40 (N.D.1991), the mortgagor was in default and asked the mortgagee to accept a deed in lieu of foreclosure. The mortgagee agreed to do so if the mortgagor paid $9,200, which was the mortgagee's estimate of the loss it would otherwise suffer from taking the deed in lieu. The mortgagor refused, and the mortgagee foreclosed. The mortgagor then brought a tort action for damages and argued that, because the lender was barred from obtaining a deficiency judgment after foreclosure, it had committed an abuse of process by attempting to condition acceptance of a deed in lieu on the payment of what was, in effect, a deficiency. The court conceded that the mortgagee had no duty to accept a deed in lieu but nevertheless agreed with the mortgagor's tort theory!

2. LOAN MODIFICATIONS

NELSON, WHITMAN, BURKHART & FREYERMUTH, REAL ESTATE FINANCE LAW
591–92 (6th ed. 2014)*

In 2008, Congress enacted the Emergency Economic Stabilization Act[167] to implement the Troubled Asset Relief Program ("TARP") and provided $700 billion to the Treasury Department to stabilize the financial markets. TARP directed the Secretary of the Treasury to "implement a plan that seeks to maximize assistance for homeowners and use the authority of the Secretary to encourage the servicers of the underlying mortgages . . . to take advantage of . . . programs to minimize foreclosures."[168] As part of this initiative, Treasury created the Making Home Affordable ("MHA") program in 2009 to address the huge increase in the number of home foreclosures. The MHA includes the Home Affordable Modification Program ("HAMP"), which creates national servicing standards and provides financial incentives for loan modifications. Fannie Mae, Freddie Mac, the Department of Housing and Urban Development, the Department of Veterans Affairs, and the Rural Housing Service all participate in HAMP. It currently is scheduled to expire on December 31, 2016. * * *

---

* Reprinted with permission of LEG, Inc. d/b/a West Academic.

[167] P.L. 110–343, 122 Stat. 3765.

[168] 12 U.S.C. § 5219(a).

Servicers for loans that Fannie Mae or Freddie Mac own or guarantee must participate in HAMP, but participation is voluntary for other servicers. However, almost every major servicer has agreed to participate by signing a Servicer Participation Agreement ("SPA") with Fannie Mae, which serves as the program's financial agent. A participating servicer must follow a uniform modification process and attempt to make the borrower's loan affordable through an interest rate reduction, term extension, principal forbearance, and principal forgiveness. However, the servicer need not consider a loan modification if the servicing agreement prohibits it.

HAMP has generated a great deal of litigation by frustrated homeowners because many servicers have been unable or unwilling to comply with its requirements. Courts repeatedly have held that homeowners who qualify for a HAMP loan modification don't have standing to enforce HAMP against servicers. Some courts also have held that HAMP preempts state law, including the common law of contracts. The court in the following case examines the most common claims that homeowners have made and correctly holds that HAMP doesn't preempt state law.

WIGOD v. WELLS FARGO BANK, N.A.

United States Court of Appeals, Seventh Circuit, 2012
673 F.3d 547

HAMILTON, CIRCUIT JUDGE.

We are asked in this appeal to determine whether Lori Wigod has stated claims under Illinois law against her home mortgage servicer for refusing to modify her loan pursuant to the federal Home Affordable Mortgage Program (HAMP). The U.S. Department of the Treasury implemented HAMP to help homeowners avoid foreclosure amidst the sharp decline in the nation's housing market in 2008. In 2009, Wells Fargo issued Wigod a four-month "trial" loan modification, under which it agreed to permanently modify the loan if she qualified under HAMP guidelines. Wigod alleges that she did qualify and that Wells Fargo refused to grant her a permanent modification. She brought this putative class action alleging violations of Illinois law under common-law contract and tort theories and under the Illinois Consumer Fraud and Deceptive Business Practices Act (ICFA). The district court dismissed the complaint in its entirety under Rule 12(b)(6) of the Federal Rules of Civil Procedure. *Wigod v. Wells Fargo Bank, N.A.,* No. 10 CV 2348, 2011 WL 250501 (N.D.Ill. Jan. 25, 2011). The court reasoned that Wigod's claims were premised on Wells Fargo's obligations under HAMP, which does not confer a private federal right of action on borrowers to enforce its requirements.

This appeal followed, and it presents two sets of issues. The first set of issues concerns whether Wigod has stated viable claims under Illinois common law and the ICFA. We conclude that she has on four counts. Wigod alleges that Wells Fargo agreed to permanently modify her home loan, deliberately misled her into believing it would do so, and then refused to make good on its promise. These allegations support garden-variety claims for breach of contract or promissory estoppel. She has also plausibly alleged that Wells Fargo committed fraud under Illinois common law and engaged in unfair or deceptive business practices in violation of the ICFA. Wigod's claims for negligent hiring or supervision and for negligent misrepresentation or concealment are not viable, however. They are barred by Illinois's economic loss doctrine because she alleges only economic harms arising from a contractual relationship. Wigod's claim for fraudulent concealment is also not actionable because she cannot show that Wells Fargo owed her a fiduciary or other duty of disclosure.

The second set of issues concerns whether these state-law claims are preempted or otherwise barred by federal law. We hold that they are not. HAMP and its enabling statute do not contain a federal right of action, but neither do they preempt otherwise viable state-law claims. We accordingly reverse the judgment of the district court on the contract, promissory estoppel, fraudulent misrepresentation, and ICFA claims, and affirm its judgment on the negligence claims and fraudulent concealment claim.

I.   *Factual and Procedural Background*

     * * *

A.   *The Home Affordable Mortgage Program*

In response to rapidly deteriorating financial market conditions in the late summer and early fall of 2008, Congress enacted the Emergency Economic Stabilization Act, P.L. 110–343, 122 Stat. 3765. The centerpiece of the Act was the Troubled Asset Relief Program (TARP), which required the Secretary of the Treasury, among many other duties and powers, to "implement a plan that seeks to maximize assistance for homeowners and . . . encourage the servicers of the underlying mortgages . . . to take advantage of . . . available programs to minimize foreclosures." 12 U.S.C. § 5219(a). Congress also granted the Secretary the authority to "use loan guarantees and credit enhancements to facilitate loan modifications to prevent avoidable foreclosures." *Id.*

Pursuant to this authority, in February 2009 the Secretary set aside up to $50 billion of TARP funds to induce lenders to refinance mortgages with more favorable interest rates and thereby allow homeowners to avoid foreclosure. The Secretary negotiated Servicer Participation Agreements (SPAs) with dozens of home loan servicers, including Wells Fargo. Under the terms of the SPAs, servicers agreed to identify homeowners who were in default or would likely soon be in default on their mortgage payments, and to modify the loans of those eligible under the program. In exchange, servicers would receive a $1,000 payment for each permanent modification, along with other incentives. The SPAs stated that servicers "shall perform the loan modification . . . described in . . . the Program guidelines and procedures issued by the Treasury . . . and . . . any supplemental documentation, instructions, bulletins, letters, directives, or other communications . . . issued by the Treasury." In such supplemental guidelines, Treasury directed servicers to determine each borrower's eligibility for a modification by following what amounted to a three-step process. * * *

B. *The Trial Period Plan*

Where a borrower qualified for a HAMP loan modification, the modification process itself consisted of two stages. After determining a borrower was eligible, the servicer implemented a Trial Period Plan (TPP) under the new loan repayment terms it formulated. The trial period under the TPP lasted three or more months, during which time the lender "must service the mortgage loan . . . in the same manner as it would service a loan in forbearance." Supplemental Directive 09–01. After the trial period, if the borrower complied with all terms of the TPP Agreement—including making all required payments and providing all required documentation—and if the borrower's representations remained true and correct, the servicer had to offer a permanent modification. See Supplemental Directive 09–01 ("If the borrower complies with the terms and conditions of the Trial Period Plan, the loan modification will become effective on the first day of the month following the trial period. . . .").

Treasury modified its directives on the timing of the verification process in a way that affects this case. Under the original guidelines that were in effect when Wigod applied for a modification, a servicer could initiate a TPP based on a borrower's undocumented representations about her finances. See Supplemental Directive 09–01 ("Servicers may use recent verbal [sic] financial information to prepare and offer a Trial Period Plan. Servicers are not required to verify financial information prior to the effective date of the trial period."). Those guidelines were part of a decision to roll out HAMP very quickly.

C. *Plaintiff's Loan*

In September 2007, Wigod obtained a home mortgage loan for $728,500 from Wachovia Mortgage, which later merged into Wells Fargo. (For simplicity, we refer only to Wells Fargo here.) Finding herself in financial distress, Wigod submitted a written request to Wells Fargo for a HAMP modification in April 2009. At that time, Treasury's original guidelines were still in force, so Wells Fargo could choose whether (A) to offer Wigod a trial modification based on unverified oral representations, or (B) to require her to provide documentary proof of her financial information before commencing the trial plan.

Wigod alleges that Wells Fargo took option (B). Only after Wigod provided all required financial documentation did Wells Fargo, in mid-May 2009, determine that Wigod was eligible for HAMP and send her a TPP Agreement. The TPP stated: "I understand that after I sign and return two copies of this Plan to the Lender, the Lender will send me a signed copy of this Plan if I qualify for the [permanent modification] Offer or will send me written notice that I do not qualify for the Offer." TPP ¶ 2.

On May 28, 2009, Wigod signed two copies of the TPP Agreement and returned them to the bank, along with additional documents and the first of four modified trial period payments. Wells Fargo then executed the TPP Agreement and sent a copy to Wigod in early June 2009. The trial term ran from July 1, 2009 to November 1, 2009. The TPP Agreement provided: "If I am in compliance with this Loan Trial Period and my representations in Section 1 continue to be true in all material respects, then the Lender will provide me with a [permanent] Loan Modification Agreement." TPP ¶ 1.

Wigod timely made, and Wells Fargo accepted, all four payments due under the trial plan. On the pleadings, we must assume that she complied with all other obligations under the TPP Agreement. Nevertheless, Wells Fargo declined to offer Wigod a permanent HAMP modification, informing her only that it was "unable to get you to a modified payment amount that you could afford per the investor guidelines on your mortgage." After the expiration of the TPP, Wells Fargo warned Wigod that she owed the outstanding balance and late fees and, in a subsequent letter, that she was in default on her home mortgage loan. Over the next few months, Wigod protested Wells Fargo's decision in a number of telephone conversations, but to no avail. During that time, she continued to make mortgage payments in the reduced amount due under the TPP, even after the trial term ended on November 1, 2009. In the meantime, Wells Fargo sent Wigod monthly notices threatening to foreclose if she failed to pay the accumulating amount of delinquency based on the original loan terms.

According to Wigod, Wells Fargo improperly re-evaluated her for HAMP after it had already determined that she was qualified and offered her a trial modification, and that it erroneously determined that she was ineligible for a permanent modification by miscalculating her property taxes. Wells Fargo responds that Treasury guidelines then in force allowed the servicer to verify, after initiating a trial modification, that the borrower satisfied all government and investor criteria for a permanent modification, and that Wigod did not. In the course of this proceeding, however, Wells Fargo has not identified the specific criteria that Wigod failed to satisfy, except to say that it could not craft a permanent modification plan for her that would be consistent with its investor guidelines. Because we are reviewing a Rule 12(b)(6) dismissal, we disregard Wells Fargo's effort to contradict the complaint.

D. *Procedural History*

On April 15, 2010, Wigod filed a class action complaint in the Northern District of Illinois on behalf of all homeowners in the United States who had entered into TPP Agreements with Wells Fargo, complied with all terms, and were nevertheless denied permanent modifications. Wigod's complaint contains seven counts: (I) breach of contract (and breach of implied covenants) for violating the TPP; (II) promissory estoppel, also based on representations made in the TPP; (III) breach of the Servicer Participation Agreement; (IV) negligent hiring and supervision; (V) fraudulent misrepresentation or concealment; (VI) negligent misrepresentation or concealment; and (VII) violation of the ICFA.

* * *

We first examine whether Wigod has adequately pled viable claims under Illinois law, and we conclude that she has done so for breach of contract, promissory estoppel, fraudulent misrepresentation, and violation of the ICFA. We then consider whether federal law precludes Wigod from pursuing her state-law claims, and we hold that it does not.

II. *State-Law Claims*

A. *Breach of Contract*

At the heart of Wigod's complaint is her claim for breach of contract. The required elements of a breach of contract claim in Illinois are the standard ones of common law: "(1) offer and acceptance, (2) consideration, (3) definite and certain terms, (4) performance by the plaintiff of all required conditions, (5) breach, and (6) damages." *Association Benefit Services, Inc. v. Caremark RX, Inc.,* 493 F.3d 841, 849 (7th Cir.2007), quoting *MC Baldwin Fin. Co. v. DiMaggio, Rosario & Veraja, LLC,* 364 Ill.App.3d 6, 300 Ill.Dec. 601, 845 N.E.2d 22, 30 (2006).

In two different provisions of the TPP Agreement, paragraph 1 and section 3, Wells Fargo promised to offer Wigod a permanent loan modification if two conditions were satisfied: (1) she complied with the terms of the TPP by making timely payments and disclosures; and (2) her representations remained true and accurate. Wigod alleges that she met both conditions and accepted the offer, but that Wells Fargo refused to provide a permanent modification. These allegations state a claim for breach of contract. Wells Fargo offers three theories, however, to argue that the TPP was not an enforceable contract: (1) the TPP contained no valid offer; (2) consideration was absent; and (3) the TPP lacked clear and definite terms. We reject each theory.

1. *Valid Offer*

In Illinois, the "test for an offer is whether it induces a reasonable belief in the recipient that he can, by accepting, bind the sender." To determine whether the TPP made a definite (though conditional) offer of permanent modification, we examine the language of the agreement itself and the surrounding circumstances. See Restatement (Second) of Contracts § 26, cmts. *a* & *c* (1981), citing *R.E. Crummer & Co. v. Nuveen,* 147 F.2d 3, 5 (7th Cir.1945).

Wells Fargo contends that the TPP was not an enforceable offer to permanently modify Wigod's mortgage because it was conditioned on Wells Fargo's further review of her financial information to ensure she qualified under HAMP. Under contract law principles, when "some further act of the purported offeror is necessary, the purported offeree has no power to create contractual relations, and there is as yet no operative offer." 1 Joseph M. Perillo, *Corbin on Contracts* § 1.11, at 31 (rev. ed. 1993) (hereinafter "*Corbin on Contracts* (rev. ed.)"), citing *Bank of Benton v. Cogdill,* 118 Ill.App.3d 280, 73 Ill.Dec. 871, 454 N.E.2d 1120, 1125–26 (1983). Thus, "a person can prevent his submission from being treated as an offer by [using] suitable language conditioning the formation of a contract on some further step, such as approval by corporate headquarters." *Architectural Metal Systems, Inc. v. Consolidated Systems, Inc.,* 58 F.3d 1227, 1230 (7th Cir.1995) (Illinois law). Wells Fargo contends that the TPP did just that by making a permanent modification expressly contingent on the bank taking some later action.

That is not a reasonable reading of the TPP. Certainly, when the promisor conditions a promise on *his own* future action or approval, there is no binding offer. But when the promise is conditioned on the performance of some act *by the promisee* or a third party, there can be a valid offer. See 1 Richard A. Lord, *Williston on Contracts* § 4:27 (4th ed. 2011) (hereinafter "*Williston on Contracts* ") ("[A] condition of subsequent approval by the promisor in the promisor's sole discretion gives rise to no obligation. . . . However, the mere fact that an offer or agreement is subject to events not within the promisor's control . . . will not render the agreement illusory).

Here the TPP spelled out two conditions precedent to Wells Fargo's obligation to offer a permanent modification: Wigod had to comply with the requirements of the trial plan, and her financial information had to remain true and accurate. But these were conditions to be satisfied by the promisee (Wigod) rather than conditions requiring further manifestation of assent by the promisor (Wells Fargo). These conditions were therefore consistent with treating the TPP as an offer for permanent modification.

Wells Fargo insists that its obligation to modify Wigod's mortgage was also contingent on its determination, after the trial period began, that she qualified under HAMP guidelines. That theory conflicts with the plain terms of the TPP. At the beginning, when Wigod received the unsigned TPP, she had to furnish Wells Fargo with "documents to permit verification of . . . [her] income . . . to determine whether [she] qualif[ied] for the offer." TPP ¶ 2. The TPP then provided: "I understand that after I sign and return two copies of this Plan to the Lender, the Lender will send me a signed copy of this Plan *if I qualify for the Offer* or will send me written notice that I do not qualify for the offer." TPP ¶ 2 (emphasis added). Wigod signed two copies of the Plan on May 29, 2009, and returned them along with additional financial documentation to Wells Fargo.

Under the terms of the TPP Agreement, then, that moment was Wells Fargo's opportunity to determine whether Wigod qualified. If she did not, it could have and should have denied her a modification on that basis. Instead, Wells Fargo countersigned on June 4, 2009 and mailed a copy to Wigod with a letter congratulating her on her approval for a trial modification. In so doing, Wells Fargo communicated to Wigod that she qualified for HAMP and would receive a permanent "Loan Modification Agreement" after the trial period, provided she was "in compliance with this Loan Trial Period and [her] representations . . . continue[d] to be true in all material respects." TPP ¶ 1.

In more abstract terms, then, when Wells Fargo executed the TPP, its terms included a unilateral offer to modify Wigod's loan conditioned on her compliance with the stated terms of the bargain. "The test for an offer is whether it induces a reasonable belief in the [offeree] that he can, by accepting, bind the [offeror]." *Architectural Metal Systems,* 58 F.3d at 1229, citing *McCarty,* 44 Ill.Dec. 570, 411 N.E.2d at 943; see also 1 *Williston on Contracts* § 4.10 (offer existed if the purported offeree "reasonably [could] have supposed that by acting in accordance with it a contract could be concluded"). Here a reasonable person in Wigod's position would read the TPP as a definite offer to provide a permanent modification that she could accept so long as she satisfied the conditions.

This is so notwithstanding the qualifying language in section 2 of the TPP. An acknowledgment in that section provided: "I understand that the Plan is not a modification of the Loan Documents and that the Loan Documents will not be modified unless and until (i) I meet all of the conditions required for modification, (ii) I receive a fully executed copy of the Modification Agreement, and (iii) the Modification Effective Date has passed." TPP § 2.G. According to Wells Fargo, this provision meant that all of its obligations to Wigod terminated if Wells Fargo itself chose not to deliver "a fully executed TPP *and* 'Modification Agreement' by November 1, 2009." In other words, Wells Fargo argues that its obligation to send Wigod a permanent Modification Agreement was triggered only if and when it actually sent Wigod a Modification Agreement.

Wells Fargo's proposed reading of section 2 would nullify other express provisions of the TPP Agreement. Specifically, it would nullify Wells Fargo's obligation to "send [Wigod] a Modification Agreement" if she "compl[ied] with the requirements" of the TPP and if her "representations . . . continue to be true in all material respects." TPP § 3. Under Wells Fargo's theory, it could simply refuse to send the Modification Agreement for any reason whatsoever—interest rates went up, the economy soured, it just didn't like Wigod—and there would still be no breach. Under this reading, a borrower who did all the TPP required of her would be entitled to a permanent modification only when the bank exercised its unbridled discretion to put a Modification Agreement in the mail. In short, Wells Fargo's interpretation of the qualifying language in section 2 turns an otherwise straightforward offer into an illusion.

The more natural interpretation is to read the provision as saying that no permanent modification *existed* "unless and until" Wigod (i) met all conditions, (ii) Wells Fargo executed the Modification Agreement, and (iii) the effective modification date passed. Before these conditions were met, the loan documents remained unmodified and in force, but under paragraph 1 and section 3 of the TPP, Wells Fargo still had an obligation to *offer* Wigod a permanent modification once she satisfied all her obligations under the agreement. This interpretation follows from the plain and ordinary meaning of the contract language stating that "the Plan is not a modification . . . unless and until" the conditions precedent were fulfilled. TPP § 2.G. And, unlike Wells Fargo's reading, it gives full effect to all of the TPP's provisions. See *McHenry Savings Bank v. Autoworks of Wauconda, Inc.,* 399 Ill.App.3d 104, 338 Ill.Dec. 671, 924 N.E.2d 1197, 1205 (2010) ("If possible we must interpret a contract in a manner that gives effect to all of the contract's provisions."), citing *Bank of America Nat'l Trust & Savings Ass'n v. Schulson,* 305 Ill.App.3d 941, 239 Ill.Dec. 462, 714 N.E.2d 20, 24 (1999). Once Wells Fargo signed the TPP Agreement and returned it to Wigod, an objectively reasonable person would construe it as an offer to provide a permanent modification agreement if she fulfilled its conditions.

2. *Consideration*

Under Illinois law, "consideration consists of some detriment to the offeror, some benefit to the offeree, or some bargained-for exchange between them." *Dumas v. Infinity Broadcasting Corp.,* 416 F.3d 671, 679

n. 9 (7th Cir.2005), quoting *Doyle v. Holy Cross Hospital,* 186 Ill.2d 104, 237 Ill.Dec. 100, 708 N.E.2d 1140, 1145 (1999). "If a debtor does something more or different in character from that which it was legally bound to do, it will constitute consideration for the promise." 3 *Williston on Contracts,* § 7:27.

Here the TPP contained sufficient consideration because, under its terms, Wigod (the promisee) incurred cognizable legal detriments. By signing it, Wigod agreed to open new escrow accounts, to undergo credit counseling (if asked), and to provide and vouch for the truth of her financial information. Wigod's complaint alleges that she did more than simply agree to pay a discounted amount in satisfaction of a prior debt. In exchange for Wells Fargo's conditional promise to modify her home mortgage, she undertook multiple obligations above and beyond her existing legal duty to make mortgage payments. This was adequate consideration, as a number of district courts adjudicating third-generation HAMP cases have recognized. See, *e.g., In re Bank of America Home Affordable Modification Program (HAMP) Contract Litigation,* No. 10–md–02193–RWZ, 2011 WL 2637222, at *4 (D.Mass. July 6, 2011) (multi-district litigation) ("The requirements of the TPP all constitute new legal detriments."); *Ansanelli v. JP Morgan Chase Bank, N.A.,* No. C 10–03892 WHA, 2011 WL 1134451, at *4 (N.D.Cal. Mar. 28, 2011) (same).

3. *Definite and Certain Terms*

A contract is enforceable under Illinois law if from its plain terms it is ascertainable what each party has agreed to do. *Academy Chicago Publishers v. Cheever,* 144 Ill.2d 24, 161 Ill.Dec. 335, 578 N.E.2d 981, 983 (1991). "A contract may be enforced even though some contract terms may be missing or left to be agreed upon, but if the essential terms are so uncertain that there is no basis for deciding whether the agreement has been kept or broken, there is no contract." *Id.,* 161 Ill.Dec. 335, 578 N.E.2d at 984. Wells Fargo contends that the TPP is unenforceable because it did not specify the exact terms of the permanent loan modification, including the interest rate, the principal balance, loan duration, and the total monthly payment. Because the TPP allowed the lender to determine the precise contours of the permanent modification at a later date, Wells Fargo argues, it reflected no "meeting of the minds" as to the permanent modification's essential terms, so that it was an unenforceable "agreement to agree."

It is true that Wigod's trial period terms were an "estimate" of the terms of the permanent modification and that Wells Fargo had some limited discretion to modify permanent terms based on its determination of the "final amounts of unpaid interest and other delinquent amounts." TPP §§ 2, 3. But this hardly makes the TPP a mere "agreement to agree."

This court, applying Illinois law, has explained that a contract with open terms can be enforced:

> In order for such a contract to be enforceable, however, it is necessary that the terms to be agreed upon in the future can be determined "independent of a party's mere 'wish, will, and desire' . . . , either by virtue of the agreement itself or by commercial practice or other usage or custom."

United States v. Orr Construction Co., 560 F.2d 765, 769 (7th Cir.1977), quoting 1 Arthur Linton Corbin, *Corbin on Contracts* § 95, at 402 (1960 ed.) (hereinafter "*Corbin on Contracts* (1960 ed.)") (internal quotation marks omitted). Professor Corbin's treatise continues: "This may be the case, even though the determination is left to one of the contracting parties, if he is required to make it 'in good faith' in accordance with some existing standard or with facts capable of objective proof." 1 *Corbin on Contracts* § 95, at 402 (1960 ed.).

In this case, HAMP guidelines provided precisely this "existing standard" by which the ultimate terms of Wigod's permanent modification were to be set. When one party to a contract has discretion to set open terms in a contract, that party must do so "reasonably and not arbitrarily or in a manner inconsistent with the reasonable expectations of the parties." *Cromeens, Holloman, Sibert, Inc. v. AB Volvo,* 349 F.3d 376, 395 (7th Cir.2003) (applying Illinois law). In its program directives, the Department of the Treasury set forth the exact mechanisms for determining borrower eligibility and for calculating modification terms— namely, the waterfall method and the Net Present Value (NPV) test. These HAMP guidelines unquestionably informed the reasonable expectations of the parties to Wigod's TPP Agreement, which is actually entitled "*Home Affordable Modification Program* Loan Trial Period." In Wigod's reasonable reading of the agreement, if she "qualif[ied] for the Offer" (meaning, of course, that she qualified under HAMP) and complied with the terms of the TPP, Wells Fargo would offer her a permanent modification. TPP ¶ 2. To calculate Wigod's trial modification terms, Wells Fargo was obligated to use the NPV test and the waterfall method to try to bring her monthly payments down to 31 percent of her gross income. Although the trial terms were just an "estimate" of the permanent modification terms, the TPP fairly implied that any deviation from them in the permanent offer would also be based on Wells Fargo's application of the established HAMP criteria and formulas.

Wells Fargo, of course, has not offered Wigod *any* permanent modification, let alone one that is consistent with HAMP program guidelines. Thus, even without reference to the HAMP modification rules, Wigod's complaint alleges that Wells Fargo breached its promise to provide her with a permanent modification once she fulfilled the TPP's conditions. Although Wells Fargo may have had some limited discretion to set the precise terms of an offered permanent modification, it was certainly required to offer *some* sort of good-faith permanent modification to Wigod consistent with HAMP guidelines. It has offered none. * * *

B. *Promissory Estoppel*

Wigod also asserts a claim for promissory estoppel, which is an alternative means of obtaining contractual relief under Illinois law. The doctrine is "commonly explained as promoting the same purposes as the tort of misrepresentation: punishing or deterring those who mislead others to their detriment and compensating those who are misled." Avery Katz, *When Should an Offer Stick? The Economics of Promissory Estoppel in Preliminary Negotiations,* 105 Yale L.J. 1249, 1254 (1996). To establish the elements of promissory estoppel, "the plaintiff must prove that (1) defendant made an unambiguous promise to plaintiff, (2) plaintiff relied on such promise, (3) plaintiff's reliance was expected and foreseeable by defendants, and (4) plaintiff relied on the promise to its detriment." *Newton Tractor Sales, Inc. v. Kubota Tractor Corp.,* 233 Ill.2d 46, 329 Ill.Dec. 322, 906 N.E.2d 520, 523–24 (2009).

Wigod has adequately alleged her claim of promissory estoppel. She asserts that Wells Fargo made an unambiguous promise that if she made timely payments and accurate representations during the trial period, she would receive an offer for a permanent loan modification calculated using the required HAMP methodology. She also alleges that she relied on that promise to her detriment by foregoing the opportunity to use other remedies to save her home (such as restructuring her debt in bankruptcy), and by devoting her resources to making the lower monthly payments under the TPP Agreement rather than attempting to sell her home or simply defaulting. A lost opportunity can constitute a sufficient detriment to support a promissory estoppel claim. See *Wood v. Mid-Valley Inc.,* 942 F.2d 425, 428 (7th Cir.1991) (noting that a "foregone . . . opportunity" would be "reliance enough to support a claim of promissory estoppel") (applying Indiana law). Wigod's complaint therefore alleged a sufficiently clear promise, evidence of her own reliance, and an explanation of the injury that resulted. She also contends that Wells Fargo ought to have anticipated her compliance with the terms of its promise. This was enough to present a facially plausible claim of promissory estoppel.[8]

C. *Negligent Hiring and Supervision*

Wigod's next claim is that Wells Fargo deliberately hired unqualified customer service employees and refused to train them to implement HAMP effectively "so that borrowers would become too frustrated to pursue their modifications." Wigod also alleges that Wells Fargo adopted policies designed to sabotage the HAMP modification process, such as a rule limiting borrowers to only one telephone call with any given employee, effectively requiring borrowers to start from scratch with an unfamiliar agent in any follow-up call.

The economic loss doctrine forecloses Wigod's recovery on this negligence claim. Known as the *Moorman* doctrine in Illinois, this doctrine bars recovery in tort for purely economic losses arising out of a failure to perform contractual obligations. See *Moorman Manufacturing Co. v. Nat'l Tank Co.,* 91 Ill.2d 69, 61 Ill.Dec. 746, 435 N.E.2d 443, 448–49 (1982). The *Moorman* doctrine precludes liability for negligent hiring and supervision in cases where, in the course of performing a contract between the defendant and the plaintiff, the defendant's employees negligently cause the plaintiff to suffer some purely economic form of harm. * * *

D. *Fraud Claims*

Illinois courts expressly recognize an exception to the Moorman doctrine "where the plaintiff's damages are proximately caused by a defendant's intentional, false representation, i.e., fraud." Catalan, 629 F.3d at 693, quoting First Midwest Bank, N.A. v. Stewart Title Guaranty Co., 218 Ill.2d 326, 300 Ill.Dec. 69, 843 N.E.2d 327, 333 (2006); see also Stein v. D'Amico, No. 86 C 9099, 1987 WL 4934, at *3 (N.D.Ill. June 5, 1987) (applying fraud exception to Moorman doctrine for claim of fraudulent concealment). Because of this exception, the economic loss doctrine does not bar Wigod's claim for fraudulent misrepresentation. She has adequately pled the elements of fraudulent misrepresentation but not fraudulent concealment.

1. *Fraudulent Misrepresentation*

The elements of a claim of fraudulent misrepresentation in Illinois are:

> (1) [a] false statement of material fact (2) known or believed to be false by the party making it; (3) intent to induce the other party to act; (4) action by the other party in reliance on the truth of the statement; and (5) damage to the other party resulting from that reliance.

Dloogatch v. Brincat, 396 Ill.App.3d 842, 336 Ill.Dec. 571, 920 N.E.2d 1161, 1166 (2009), quoting Soules v. General Motors Corp., 79 Ill.2d 282, 37 Ill.Dec. 597, 402 N.E.2d 599, 601 (1980). Under the heightened federal pleading standard of Rule 9(b) of the Federal Rules of Civil Procedure, a plaintiff "alleging fraud ... must state with particularity the circumstances constituting fraud." See Borsellino v. Goldman Sachs Group, Inc., 477 F.3d 502, 507 (7th Cir.2007) ("This heightened pleading requirement is a response to the great harm to the reputation of a business firm or other enterprise a fraud claim can do.") (internal quotation marks omitted). We have summarized the particularity requirement as calling for the first paragraph of any newspaper story: "the who, what, when, where, and how." E.g., Windy City Metal Fabricators & Supply, Inc. v. CIT Technology Financing Services, Inc., 536 F.3d 663, 668 (7th Cir.2008). Wigod's complaint satisfies that standard. She identifies the knowing misrepresentation as Wells Fargo's statement in the TPP that it would offer her a permanent modification if she complied with the terms and conditions of the TPP. She also alleges that Wells Fargo intended that she would act in reliance on promises it made in the TPP and that she reasonably did so to her detriment. Fraudulent intent may be alleged generally, see Fed.R.Civ.P. 9(b), so the only element seriously at issue on the pleadings is reasonable reliance.

* * *

Wigod alleges that she was a victim of a scheme to defraud: in her complaint, she accuses Wells Fargo of deliberately implementing a "system designed to wrongfully deprive its eligible HAMP borrowers of an opportunity to modify their mortgages." Whether she has alleged "specific, objective manifestations" of this scheme is a closer question, but we think it likely that Illinois courts would say yes.

The scheme alleged here does not rest solely on Wells Fargo's single broken promise to Wigod. She claims that thousands of HAMP-eligible homeowners became victims of Wells Fargo's "intentional and systematic failure to offer permanent loan modifications" after falsely telling them it would. Illinois courts have found as few as two broken promises enough to establish a scheme to defraud. See, e.g., General Electric Credit Auto Lease, Inc. v. Jankuski, 177 Ill.App.3d 380, 126 Ill.Dec. 676, 532 N.E.2d 361, 362–63 (1988).

2. *Fraudulent Concealment*

The heightened pleading standard of Rule 9(b) also applies to fraudulent concealment claims. To plead this tort properly, in addition to meeting the elements of fraudulent misrepresentation, a plaintiff must allege that the defendant intentionally omitted or concealed a material fact that it was under a duty to disclose to the plaintiff. Weidner v. Karlin, 402 Ill.App.3d 1084, 342 Ill.Dec. 475, 932 N.E.2d 602, 605 (2010). A duty to disclose would arise if "plaintiff and defendant are in a fiduciary or confidential relationship" or in a "situation where plaintiff places trust and confidence in defendant, thereby placing defendant in a position of influence and superiority over plaintiff." Connick v. Suzuki Motor Co., 174 Ill.2d 482, 221 Ill.Dec. 389, 675 N.E.2d 584, 593 (1996).

Wigod alleges that Wells Fargo knowingly concealed that it would (1) report her to credit rating agencies as being in default on her mortgage; and (2) reevaluate her eligibility for a permanent modification in contravention of HAMP directives. The district court dismissed this fraudulent concealment claim due to "the absence of any fiduciary or other duty to speak" on the part of Wells Fargo as a mortgagee. In the district court, Wigod apparently conceded that Wells Fargo was not a fiduciary under Illinois law, but she argued that she placed a special trust and confidence in the bank as her HAMP servicer. The district court rejected this theory on the ground that any special trust relationship between Wigod and Wells Fargo existed solely through the lender's participation in HAMP, which does not provide the borrower with a private right of action.

For two reasons, we affirm the dismissal of the fraudulent concealment claim. First, Wigod's special trust argument is waived: in this appeal, Wigod raised the issue only in her reply brief, and arguments raised for the first time in a reply brief are waived. Padula v. Leimbach, 656 F.3d 595, 605 (7th Cir.2011). Second, even if we overlooked the waiver, we would agree with the district court that no special trust relationship existed here. Wells Fargo's participation in HAMP is not sufficient to create a special trust relationship with Wigod and the roughly 250,000 other homeowners with whom it entered TPP Agreements. The Illinois Appellate Court has recently stated that the standard for identifying a special trust relationship is "extremely similar to that of a fiduciary relationship." Benson v. Stafford, 407 Ill.App.3d 902, 346 Ill.Dec. 828, 941 N.E.2d 386, 403 (2010).

* * *

E. *Negligent Misrepresentation or Concealment*

In the alternative to her fraudulent misrepresentation and concealment claims, Wigod alleges that Wells Fargo negligently or carelessly (rather than intentionally) misrepresented or omitted material facts. Negligent misrepresentation involves the same elements as fraudulent misrepresentation, except that (1) the defendant need not have known that the statement was false, but must merely have been negligent in failing to ascertain the truth of his statement; and (2) the defendant must have owed the plaintiff a duty to provide accurate information. See *Kopley Group V., L.P. v. Sheridan Edgewater Properties, Ltd.,* 376 Ill.App.3d 1006, 315 Ill.Dec. 218, 876 N.E.2d 218, 228 (2007).

Whether or not Wigod has successfully pled the elements of negligent misrepresentation and concealment, this claim is also barred by the economic loss doctrine. Any duty Wells Fargo may have had to provide accurate information to Wigod arose directly from their commercial and contractual relationship. Wigod is right that HAMP requires servicers to help borrowers understand the modification terms. But this obligation is not owed to the general public—only to mortgagors in the HAMP modification process. If Wells Fargo had such obligations to Wigod, then, it was only because it executed a TPP agreement with her under HAMP. Any disclosure duties owed here are contractual ones and therefore do not sound in the torts of negligent misrepresentation or negligent concealment. We affirm the dismissal of these claims, and proceed to Wigod's final cause of action.

F. The Illinois Consumer Fraud and Deceptive Business Practices Act (ICFA)

The ICFA protects consumers against "unfair or deceptive acts or practices," including "fraud," "false promise," and the "misrepresentation or the concealment, suppression or omission of any material fact." 815 ILCS 505/2. The Act is "liberally construed to effectuate its purpose." *Robinson v. Toyota Motor Credit Corp.*, 201 Ill.2d 403, 266 Ill.Dec. 879, 775 N.E.2d 951, 960 (2002). The elements of a claim under the ICFA are: "(1) a deceptive or unfair act or practice by the defendant; (2) the defendant's intent that the plaintiff rely on the deceptive or unfair practice; and (3) the unfair or deceptive practice occurred during a course of conduct involving trade or commerce." *Siegel v. Shell Oil Co.*, 612 F.3d 932, 934 (7th Cir.2010), citing *Robinson*, 266 Ill.Dec. 879, 775 N.E.2d at 960. In addition, "a plaintiff must demonstrate that the defendant's conduct is the proximate cause of the injury." *Id.* at 935.

Wigod accuses Wells Fargo of practices that are both deceptive and unfair. In her complaint, Wigod incorporates by reference her common-law fraud claims, alleging that Wells Fargo's misrepresentation and concealment of material facts constituted deceptive business practices. She also alleges that Wells Fargo dishonestly and ineffectually implemented HAMP, and that this conduct constituted "unfair, immoral, unscrupulous business practices." The district court dismissed Wigod's ICFA claim on two grounds: first, because Wigod did not allege that Wells Fargo acted with an intent to deceive her; and second, because Wigod did not plausibly plead that Wells Fargo's conduct caused her any actual pecuniary injury. On both points, we disagree.

First, "intent to deceive" is not a required element of a claim under the ICFA, which provides redress "not only for deceptive business practices, but also for business practices that, while not deceptive, are unfair." *Boyd v. U.S. Bank, N.A. ex rel. Sasco Aames Mortg. Loan Trust Series 2003–1*, 787 F.Supp.2d 747, 751 (N.D.Ill.2011) (holding that a loan servicer's alleged failure to consider the plaintiff's eligibility for a HAMP modification was a sufficient predicate for an ICFA claim); see 815 ILCS 505/2 ("[U]nfair *or* deceptive acts or practices . . . are hereby declared unlawful. . . .") (emphasis added). Wigod alleges that Wells Fargo engaged in both deceptive (fraudulent) and unfair business practices. Moreover, even if she had alleged only deceptive practices, pleading intent would still be unnecessary, since a "claim for 'deceptive' business practices under the Consumer Fraud Act does not require proof of intent to deceive." *Siegel v. Shell Oil Co.,* 480 F.Supp.2d 1034, 1044 n. 5 (N.D.Ill.2007), *aff'd,* 612 F.3d 932. It is enough to allege that the defendant committed a deceptive or unfair act and intended that the plaintiff rely on that act, and Wigod has done so.

The district court also concluded that Wigod did not identify any "actual pecuniary loss" that she suffered. Because Wigod's reduced trial plan payments were less than the amount she was legally obliged to pay Wells Fargo under the terms of her original loan documents, the court reasoned that Wigod was better off than she would have been without the TPP. This reasoning overlooks Wigod's allegations that she incurred costs and fees, lost other opportunities to save her home, suffered a negative impact to her credit, never received a Modification Agreement, and lost her ability to receive incentive payments during the first five years of the modification. Prior to entering the trial plan, Wigod also could have taken the path of "efficient breach" and defaulted immediately rather than executing the TPP and making trial payments. By the time Wigod realized she would not receive the permanent modification she believed she had been promised, late fees had mounted and she found herself in default on her loan and with fewer options than when the trial period began. Whether any of these alternatives might have saved her home, or at least cut her losses, is impossible to determine from the pleadings. Her allegations are at least plausible. She has alleged pecuniary injury caused by Wells Fargo's deception and successfully pled the elements of an ICFA violation.

* * *

IV. *Conclusion*

We predict that the Illinois courts would find some of Wigod's claims actionable under the laws of their state, and we can find no basis in the law of federal preemption that would bar those claims. The judgment of the district court is therefore REVERSED as to Counts I, II, and VII, and the fraudulent misrepresentation claim of Count V, and AFFIRMED as to Counts IV, VI, and the fraudulent concealment claim of Count V. The case is REMANDED for further proceedings on the surviving counts.

NOTES

1.   *CFPB loss mitigation servicing standards.* The Consumer Financial Protection Bureau (CFPB) promulgated national loss mitigation servicing standards that became effective on January 10, 2014. Like HAMP, these standards are intended to decrease the number of home foreclosures by further standardizing servicers' loss mitigation procedures. The standards apply when a "federally related mortgage loan" on the borrower's principal residence goes into default. Because early intervention has proven to be most

effective, servicers are required to make good faith efforts to speak with a borrower within 36 days after default. Servicers also must give the borrower a written notice that describes loss mitigation options and a statement encouraging the borrower to contact the servicer. The standards are only procedural; they do not impose a substantive duty to offer loss mitigation, which will undercut their effectiveness. However, unlike HAMP, borrowers have a private right of action to enforce the CFPB standards. Based on the large amount of HAMP litigation, despite courts' frequent holdings that borrowers do not have enforceable rights, the CFPB standards may prove to be a powerful tool for borrowers and may provide a strong incentive for servicers to comply.

2.   *State and local laws and programs.* Since the market meltdown in 2008, many state and local governments have attempted to facilitate the use of loss mitigation measures, including loan modifications. Unlike HAMP, many state programs give borrowers standing to enforce the servicers' duties. To provide additional time for borrowers to pursue loan modifications, several states have increased the time to foreclose and require written notice to borrowers concerning potential loss mitigation measures. E.g. Cal. Civ. Code § 2923.5; 735 Ill. Comp. Stat. 5/15–1502.5; Mich. Comp. Laws Ann. § 600.3205a(1)(e). To provide a structure for borrowers and servicers to discuss loss mitigation, many state and local governments have created mediation programs. E.g. Conn. Gen. Stat. § 8–265ee; Del. Code Ann. tit. 10, § 5062C; Md. Code Ann., Real Prop. § 7–105.1. The mediation process is especially important in states with nonjudicial foreclosure because it gives the borrower an opportunity to challenge the lender's right to foreclose and the amount in default.

3.   *Is mediation worthwhile?* Data on the number of successful mediations varies quite a bit. The variation undoubtedly is due at least in part to differences among the programs, such as whether the program (1) is voluntary or mandatory, (2) requires a neutral third party mediator or only negotiation between the borrower and servicer, and (3) requires the servicer to negotiate in good faith. However, a National Consumer Law Center report indicates that successful mediations are becoming more successful. The report states that the proportion of mediations that decreased the borrower's monthly payment by at least 20% increased from 18.81% in 2008 to 53.8% in 2011. Perhaps as a result, the default rate on modified loans decreased from 56.2% in 2008 to 25.7% in 2010. Geoff Walsh, Rebuilding America: How States Can Save Millions of Homes Through Foreclosure Mediation (Feb. 2012), available at www.nclc.org/foreclosures-and-mortgages/rebuilding-america.html. See also Alexander, Immergluck, Balthrop, Schaeffing & Clark, Legislative Responses to the Foreclosure Crisis in Nonjudicial Foreclosure States, 31 Rev. Banking & Fin. L. 341 (2011–2012) (up to 70% of mediations successful); Zacks, The Grand Bargain: Pro-Borrower Responses to the Housing Crisis and Implications for Future Lending and Homeownership, 57 Loy. L. Rev. 541 (2011) (42% of mediations successful).

Another study found that lenders lost about $124,000 for each residential foreclosure in November 2008, but only $23,610 when they participated in mediation and reduced the principal balance. Khader, Note, Mediating Mediations: Protecting the Homeowner's Right to Self-Determination in Foreclosure Mediation Programs, 44 Colum.J.L. & Soc. Probs. 109, 115 (2010). Moreover, even if the parties don't agree to a loan modification, they can negotiate another loss mitigation option to avoid foreclosure, such as a deed in lieu of foreclosure.

4. *Additional readings.* For additional information about loan modifications, see Nelson, Whitman, Burkhart & Freyermuth, Real Estate Finance Law § 7.9 (6th ed. 2014); Chiles & Mitchell, HAMP: An Overview of the Program and Recent Litigation Trends, 65 Consumer Fin. L.Q. Rep. 194 (2011); Mason, No One Saw It Coming—Again: Systemic Risk and State Foreclosure Proceedings: Why a National Uniform Foreclosure Law is Necessary, 67 U. Miami L. Rev. 41 (2012); McCormick, HAMP Litigation Update 2013: The Year of the Trial Period Plan, 43 Housing L. Bull. 203 (2013); Thompson, Foreclosing Modifications: How Servicer Incentives Discourage Loan Modifications, 86 Wash. L. Rev. 755 (2011).

3. SHORT SALES

During the recent recession, land values declined throughout the country and precipitously so in many areas. As a result, a massive number of parcels of real estate dropped in value to less than the debt that they secured. To sell the real estate, the owner has to convince the mortgagee and other lienors to release their liens in exchange for the sale proceeds, though the proceeds are insufficient to pay the secured debts in full. Because these "short sales" or "preforeclosure sales" can be advantageous for the lienors and for the landowner, they became as common as foreclosures, though the number of short sales now is declining. Brumfield, The "Short Cut" to the Stabilization of the Underwater Housing Market: How the New FHFA Short Sale Guidelines Promote Economic Efficiency, 41 Real Est. L.J. 456 (2013); Real Estate Economy Watch, Short Sales Peak, Then Plummet, available at www.real estateeconomywatch.com/2013/09/short-sales-peak-then-plummet/.

The biggest advantage of a short sale is that the real estate usually sells for more than it would at a foreclosure sale. A short seller typically lists the property for sale with a real estate agent, who actively markets the property. In contrast, foreclosure sales involve very limited, if any, marketing. Additionally, a short sale is safer for the purchaser than a foreclosure sale. For example, short sale purchasers can physically inspect the property before agreeing to buy it and, after agreeing to buy, have time to arrange financing and a title examination. In contrast, a foreclosure purchaser normally can't inspect the property before the sale and, in many states, must pay the purchase price immediately.

Another significant advantage of a short sale is that it often can occur much more quickly than a foreclosure sale. A lender can process a short sale request in 60–90 days after the seller has found a buyer. Dunaway, Babbitt, Gerth & McGrane, Law of Distressed Real Estate § 3B:8. In contrast, the average time for a foreclosure nationally is over a year; in some states, it is substantially longer. Notice, State-Level Guarantee Fee Pricing, Federal Housing Finance Agency (Sept. 25, 2012), 77 Fed. Reg. 58,991, 58,992 (average in New Jersey is 750 days; 820 days in New York). Even in states in which the speedier nonjudicial foreclosure is available, a statutory right of redemption may allow the borrower to retain possession of the property for six months to two years after the foreclosure. If the borrower can't redeem during that time, he may stop maintaining the property and paying the taxes and insurance premiums.

Short sales also are less expensive for lenders than foreclosure sales, especially in states that require judicial foreclosure. Because the foreclosing lender often purchases the property at the sale, the lender can incur not only the costs of foreclosure, but also of owning and selling the property.

Borrowers also can benefit from a short sale. They avoid the embarrassment and stigma of going through foreclosure. Additionally, some, though not all, commentators believe that a borrower's credit rating is not as adversely affected by a short sale as by a foreclosure sale. With a short sale, the borrower has actively attempted to sell the property and pay at least part of the debt, rather than putting the lender to the task of foreclosing. Dunaway, Babbitt, Gerth & McGrane, Law of Distressed Real Estate § 3B:8; Miller, Short Sales Overview with an Emphasis on Broker Issues, 26 No. 3 Prac. Real Est. Law. 9 (2010); John Skiba, What Will a Short Sale, Bankruptcy, or Foreclosure Do to My Credit Score?, JDSUPRA Law News, available at www.jdsupra.com/legalnews/what-will -a-short-sale-bankruptcy-or-f-69774/.

A common stumbling block to a short sale is getting every lienor to agree to release its lien. Particularly if a lienor won't receive any of the sale proceeds, it may be content to wait and see if the property's value increases in the future, rather than agreeing to a short sale now. Any private mortgage insurer also has to agree to the sale and also may prefer to wait for the property's value to increase. Moreover, the borrower has to get all these consents before the purchase agreement expires.

An additional concern for the borrower is whether it will be liable for a deficiency after the short sale. If so, the borrower may prefer foreclosure, so that it can keep possession of the property rent-free for a longer period of time. Courts are divided on whether a state's antideficiency statute protects a borrower after a short sale, as well as after a foreclosure.

ESPINOZA V. BANK OF AMERICA, N.A.

United States District Court, S.D. California, 2011
823 F.Supp.2d 1053

IRMA E. GONZALEZ, CHIEF JUDGE.

Presently before the Court is Defendants' motion to dismiss Plaintiffs' first amended complaint. For the reasons stated below, the Court **GRANTS** Defendants' motion.

BACKGROUND

In late 2004, Plaintiffs purchased property located in San Diego County at 397 Camino Elevado, Bonita, CA 91902. The purchase was financed with two mortgages, and the mortgages were secured by deeds of trust (DOT 1 and DOT 2) that were executed and recorded.

Over the next two years, Plaintiffs engaged in a series of additional finance transactions. By the end of 2007, Plaintiffs' property was secured by two deeds of trust, DOT 3 (with Washington Mutual Bank) and DOT 5 (with Bank of America); all other deeds of trusts had been terminated.

Some time later, Plaintiffs were unable to make their mortgage payments under DOT 3 and DOT 5. In July 2009, California Reconveyance Company, an agent of Chase Home Finance (as successor-in-interest to Washington Mutual Bank) filed a Notice of Default (NOD) with the San Diego County Recorder, thus initiating the nonjudicial foreclosure process under California Civil Code § 2924.

In October 2009, Plaintiffs entered into an agreement with a third party for a "short sale." Because the agreement was designed to alienate the property for less than the full amount owed on the property, it was contingent on the approval of the two lien holders, Chase Home Finance (as successor-in-interest to Washington Mutual Bank) and Bank of America. Plaintiffs obtained approval for the "short sale" from Chase Home Finance and Bank of America and then closed escrow on the "short sale." According to the terms of the approval, "[u]pon the bank's receipt of the $20,875.53 and a signed copy of the final Short Sale HUD–1 Form the bank will release the lien and charge off the remaining debt as a collectable balance." On March 25, 2010, Plaintiffs closed escrow on their short sale.

On April 1, 2010, Bank of America filed a Substitution of Trustee and Full Reconveyance, releasing its lien on the property. The reconveyance deed states, in bold letters:

> **This Release of Lien does not constitute a satisfaction of the underlying debt secured by the Mortgage described above, which remains in full force and effect. It serves**

only to release the lien of the Mortgage upon the above described property.

Plaintiffs then transferred ownership of the property to the new buyer.

In November 2010, Defendant SRA Associates, acting on behalf of Bank of America, sent a collection letter to Plaintiffs demanding payment of a $79,652.98 balance. Plaintiffs' obligation to pay the $79,652.98 balance is the subject of this action.

Plaintiffs filed suit in San Diego Superior Court, and Defendants removed the action to this Court on April 27, 2011. Shortly thereafter, Defendants moved to dismiss Plaintiffs' complaint. The Court granted Defendants' motion, dismissing the complaint with leave to amend. On July 27, 2011, Plaintiffs filed the first amended complaint (FAC), alleging three causes of action: (1) for declaratory relief under the California Code of Civil Procedure § 580d; (2) for declaratory relief under the California Code of Civil Procedure § 580e; and (3) for declaratory relief under common law antideficiency protection. Defendants now move to dismiss the FAC in its entirety.

* * *

DISCUSSION

I.   Declaratory Relief Under California Code of Civil Procedure § 580d

Claim one of the FAC alleges section 580d precludes Bank of America from collecting the remaining balance under DOT 5. Under California law, if a borrower defaults on a loan secured by a deed of trust containing a power of sale clause, the lender may pursue a nonjudicial foreclosure. A nonjudicial foreclosure is subject to the antideficiency statutes, which prevent the foreclosing lender from obtaining a judgment for any difference between the debt and the proceeds from the sale:

> No judgment shall be rendered for any deficiency upon a note secured by a deed of trust or mortgage upon real property or an estate for years therein hereafter executed in any case in which the real property or estate for years therein has been sold *by the mortgagee or trustee under power of sale contained in the mortgage or deed of trust.*

Cal.Civ.Proc.Code § 580d (emphasis added). By its terms, section 580d applies "only when a personal judgment against a debtor is sought *after a foreclosure." Dreyfuss v. Union Bank of Cal.,* 24 Cal.4th 400, 407, 101 Cal.Rptr.2d 29, 11 P.3d 383 (2000) (emphasis added).

Plaintiffs argue that, under § 580d, a secured lender waives its right to a deficiency by *initiating* nonjudicial foreclosure proceedings, whether or not a nonjudicial foreclosure sale actually occurs. Plaintiffs' assertion is incorrect under California law. "Mere commencement of nonjudicial foreclosure proceedings [is] not an election of remedy." *Bank of Am. v. Graves,* 51 Cal.App.4th 607, 614–15, 59 Cal.Rptr.2d 288 (1996) (citing *Carpenter v. Title Ins. & Trust Co.,* 71 Cal.App.2d 593, 596, 163 P.2d 73 (1945)); *Griffin v. Compere,* 114 Cal.App.2d 246, 247, 250 P.2d 1 (1952) (holding that, where a creditor brought a foreclosure action but then dismissed it, merely initiating the foreclosure action did not constitute an election of remedies that would preclude a later private sale and suit for the deficiency).

Plaintiffs, citing no authority on this point, argue that, because Bank of America secured a deed of trust with a power of sale provision, it effectively enforced the power of sale provision by approving Plaintiffs' short sale. A power of sale provision in a deed of trust grants a lender the right to conduct a nonjudicial foreclosure sale. *See Gomes v. Countrywide Home Loans, Inc.,* 192 Cal.App.4th 1149, 1158, 121 Cal.Rptr.3d 819 (2011). But no foreclosure sale occurred in this case. Section 580d does not apply here, because it only applies to protect a debtor from a deficiency judgment *after a foreclosure sale. Dreyfuss,* 24 Cal.4th at 407, 101 Cal.Rptr.2d 29, 11 P.3d 383.

Plaintiffs' allegations do not entitle them to relief under section 580d. Thus, the Court **DISMISSES WITH PREJUDICE** Plaintiffs' first cause of action.

II. Declaratory Relief Under California Code of Civil Procedure § 580e

California Civil Procedure Code Section 580e provides, in relevant part:

(a)(1) No deficiency shall be owed or collected, and no deficiency judgment shall be requested or rendered for any deficiency upon a note secured solely by a deed of trust or mortgage for a dwelling of not more than four units, in any case in which the trustor or mortgagor sells the dwelling for a sale price less than the remaining amount of the indebtedness outstanding at the time of sale, in accordance with the written consent of the holder of the deed of trust or mortgage, provided that both of the following have occurred:

(A) Title has been voluntarily transferred to a buyer by grant deed or by other document of conveyance that has been recorded in the county where all or part of the real property is located.

(B) The proceeds of the sale have been tendered to the mortgagee, beneficiary, or the agent of the mortgagee or beneficiary, in accordance with the parties' agreement.

In short, section 580e prevents a lender that consents to a short sale from pursuing the post-sale deficiency.[2] However, because section 580e became effective on January 1, 2011, and the amendment in July 2011, well after Plaintiffs executed their short sale, Plaintiffs are not protected by section 580e.

Plaintiffs closed escrow on their short sale on March 25, 2010, and Bank of America executed the reconveyance deed on April 1, 2010. Title was transferred to the new buyer shortly thereafter, and by November 3, 2010, Bank of America sought payment of the balance of Plaintiffs' debt— $79,652.98. But section 580e was not enacted until January 1, 2011.

The general rule is that statutes operate prospectively unless the statute includes a provision expressly stating otherwise. Moreover, California's Civil Procedure Code includes a provision stating that "[n]o part of [this code] is retroactive, unless expressly so declared." Cal.Civ.Proc.Code § 3.

Nothing in section 580e indicates that it should apply retroactively. Because it was enacted after Plaintiffs conducted their short sale, Defendants argue that section 580e does not preclude them from seeking the remaining balance of Plaintiffs' loan.

Plaintiffs attempt to avoid the retroactivity issue by reframing the focus of section 580e. They argue section 580e regulates *deficiencies* stemming from short sales, not the short sales themselves. Under Plaintiffs' theory, once enacted, section 580e extinguished any then-existing deficiencies. Because there remained a deficiency balance on Plaintiffs' loan at the time the new law took effect, Plaintiffs argue that section 580e bars Defendants from seeking the deficiency.

The practical effect interpreting the statute as Plaintiffs suggest would be to extinguish the rights to deficiency balances negotiated between parties prior to the enactment of section 580e. In other words, despite Plaintiffs attempt to interpret section 580e so that it would apply to this case without also operating retroactively, applying the statute as Plaintiffs' request would cause the precise harm courts seek to avoid with the presumption against applying statutes retrospectively: interference with parties' antecedent rights.

Plaintiffs' interpretation of section 580e also ignores the most plausible reading of the statutory text. Section 580e provides that a lender cannot collect a deficiency "in any case in which the trustor or mortgager *sells* the dwelling for a sale price less than the remaining

---

[2] Enacted on January 1, 2011, section 580e initially protected a debtor engaging in a creditor-approved short sale from liability for any deficiency owed on the *first deed of trust* only. *See* 2010 Cal. Stat., ch. 701 (S.B. 931). As amended on July 15, 2011, section 580e now applies to any lender that consents to a short sale, whether or not the lender is in the first position. *See* Cal. Civil Proc. Code § 580e; 2011 Cal. Stat., ch. 82.

amount of the indebtedness outstanding at the time of the sale." Cal. Civ. P. Code § 580e(a)(1) (emphasis added). The word "sells" is prospective in nature; it suggests the legislature intended section 580e's antideficiency protections to apply to future short sales, not to extinguish deficiencies remaining from short sales that occurred before the statute was enacted.

The legislative history also indicates that section 580e was intended to apply to short sales occurring after the statute took effect. Analyzing the July 2011 amendment to section 580e, the Assembly Committee on Judiciary stated:

> SB 458 [codified as amended at Cal.Civ.Proc.Code § 580e] . . . adds additional protections against post-short sale deficiency liability to junior note holders (seconds) when those lenders approve a short sale. It is important to note that the short sale process remains voluntary on every participant's part—only lenders that actually agree to the sale will be affected, and sellers that cannot put together an acceptable sale may still go to foreclosure and even bankruptcy.

Assembly Committee Bill Analysis of SB 458, June 28, 2011. As in the statute itself, the Committee's use of forward-looking language—"when those lenders approve a short sale," "only lenders that actually agree to the sale," "sellers that cannot put together an acceptable sale"—suggests the legislature intended section 580e to apply to future short sales, not those that had already occurred.

Section 580e applies only to short sales occurring after the statute was enacted. Here, the parties negotiated the terms of the short sale, and the short sale occurred, before section 580e was enacted. Accordingly section 580e does not apply to this case. Thus, the Court **DISMISSES WITH PREJUDICE** Plaintiffs' second cause of action.

* * * [The court then dismissed with prejudice the Plaintiffs' third cause of action.]

CONCLUSION

For the reasons stated above, the Court **GRANTS** Defendants' motion and **DISMISSES** Plaintiffs' claims **WITH PREJUDICE.** The Clerk shall terminate this case.

IT IS SO ORDERED.

NOTES

1. *Strict statutory interpretation.* Based on the *Espinoza* court's analysis, Bank of America could not have obtained a deficiency judgment if it had foreclosed but could get a deficiency after agreeing to a short sale. Is this decision appropriate? Other courts have been more lenient in their interpretation of an antideficiency statute. For example, in Enloe v. Kelso,

217 Cal. App. 4th 877, 158 Cal. Rptr. 3d 881 (2d Dist. 2013), the court held that the short seller was protected by the antideficiency statute because it should be "liberally construed to effect its purpose" and should be applied based on the transaction's substance, rather than its form. In Tanque Verde Anesthesiologists L.T.D. Profit Sharing Plan v. Proffer Group, Inc., 172 Ariz. 311, 836 P.2d 1021 (Ct. App. Div. 2 1992), the court assumed that the antideficiency statute applied to a short seller, though the statute provided that it applied when land is "sold pursuant to the trustee's power of sale." See Nelson, Whitman, Burkhart & Freyermuth, Real Estate Finance Law § 6.20 (6th ed. 2014).

2. *Short sale antideficiency statute.* As described in the opinion, California has enacted an antideficiency statute for short sales. Cal. Civ. Proc. Code § 580e. The statute also prohibits (1) lenders from requiring the borrower to pay any consideration, other than the sale proceeds, for the lender's consent to the short sale and (2) waiver of the borrower's protections under the statute. The stated statutory purposes are to limit the borrower's liability, to "mitigate the impact of the ongoing foreclosure crisis and to encourage the approval of short sales as an alternative to foreclosure." Some commentators have argued that prohibiting a deficiency judgment and additional compensation from the borrower will prevent the third goal from being achieved. Bernhardt, Short Sales and Deficiency Liability: The Pointlessness of Purposes, Sept. 2013 Real Prop. L. Rep. 1 (2013); Ornstein & Maree, California Senate Bill 458, 65 Consumer Fin. L.Q. Rep. 291 (2011).

3. *Short sale process.* To encourage the use of short sales in lieu of foreclosure and to speed up the process, the Federal Housing Finance Agency and other government agencies involved in housing finance have promulgated standard forms and servicing guidelines for short sales. The guidelines address a variety of issues, including seller eligibility, methods for processing short sale applications, and permitted closing costs. HUD, the Department of the Treasury, Fannie Mae, and Freddie Mac also provide financial incentives for borrowers and junior lienors to encourage the use of short sales. See Nelson, Whitman, Burkhart & Freyermuth, Real Estate Finance Law § 6.21 (6th ed. 2014). Additionally, some states now statutorily require lenders to respond in a timely manner to short sale requests. See, e.g., 735 Ill. Comp. Stat. 5/15–1401.1; Ind. Code §§ 24–4.4–2–201 & 24–9–3–6; Nev. Rev. Stat. § 668.051.

CHAPTER SIX

FORECLOSURE

■ ■ ■

A. ACCELERATION AND MARSHALING

1. ACCELERATION

GRAF v. HOPE BLDG. CORP.

Court of Appeals of New York, 1930
254 N.Y. 1, 171 N.E. 884

O'BRIEN, J. Plaintiffs, as executors of Joseph L. Graf, are the holders of two consolidated mortgages forming a single lien on real property the title to which is vested in defendant Hope Building Corporation. According to the terms of the agreement consolidating the mortgages, the principal sum is made payable January 1, 1935. Nevertheless, a clause provides that the whole shall become due after default for twenty days in the payment of any installment of interest. David Herstein is the controlling stockholder and also president and treasurer of defendant. He alone was authorized to sign checks in its behalf. Early in June, 1927, he went to Europe. Before his departure a clerical assistant who was also the nominal secretary of the corporation computed the interest due July 1, and through an error in arithmetic incorrectly calculated it. Mr. Herstein signed the check for the erroneous amount but before the date upon which the interest became due, the secretary discovered the error, notified the mortgagee of the shortage of $401.87, stated that on the president's return from Europe the balance would be paid and on June 30 forwarded to the mortgagee the check as drawn. It was deposited by the mortgagee and paid by defendant. On July 5 Mr. Herstein returned, but, through an omission in his office, he was not informed of the default in the payment of interest. At the expiration of twenty-one days this action of foreclosure was begun. Defendant made tender of the deficiency but the mortgagee, strictly insisting on his contract rights, refused the tender and elected to assert the power created by the acceleration clause in the consolidation agreement.

On the undisputed facts as found, we are unable to perceive any defense to the action and are, therefore, constrained to reverse the judgment dismissing the complaint. Plaintiffs may be ungenerous, but generosity is a voluntary attribute and can not be enforced even by a chancellor. Forbearance is a quality which under the circumstances of this case is likewise free from coercion. Here there is no penalty, no forfeiture (Ferris v. Ferris, 28 Barb. 29; Noyes v. Anderson, 124 N.Y. 175, 180), nothing except a covenant fair on its face to which both parties willingly consented. It is neither oppressive nor unconscionable. (Valentine v. Van Wagner, 37 Barb. 60.) In the absence of some act by the mortgagee which a court of equity would be justified in considering unconscionable, he is entitled to the benefit of the covenant. The contract is definite and no reason appears for its reformation by the courts. (Abrams v. Thompson, 251 N.Y. 79, 86.) We are not at liberty to revise while professing to construe. (Sun P. & P. Assn. v. Remington P. & P. Co., 235 N.Y. 338, 346.) Defendant's mishap, caused by a succession of its errors and negligent omissions, is not of the nature requiring relief from its default. Rejection of plaintiff's legal right could rest only on compassion for defendant's negligence. Such a tender emotion must be exerted, if at all, by the parties rather than by the court. Our guide must be the precedents prevailing since courts of equity were established in this State. Stability of contract obligations must not be undermined by judicial sympathy. To allow this judgment to stand would constitute an interference by this court between parties whose contract is clear. One has been unfortunately negligent but neither has committed a wrong. If defendant's president had left some person in charge with authority to deal with affairs as they might arise, the first error could have been immediately corrected and the second would not have occurred. Even after Mr. Herstein's return on July 5, two weeks remained before the expiration of the twenty days. The secretary's forgetfulness during this time is not sufficient excuse for a court of equity to refuse to lend its aid to the prosecution of an action based upon an incontestably plain agreement. Such a refusal would set at nought the rules announced and enforced for a century in such cases as Noyes v. Clark (7 Paige, 179); Hale v. Gouverneur (4 Edw.Ch. 207); Ferris v. Ferris (supra); Valentine v. Van Wagner (supra); Malcolm v. Allen (49 N.Y. 448); Bennett v. Stevenson (53 N.Y. 508); Hothorn v. Louis (52 App.Div. 218; affd., 170 N.Y. 576). The words of Chancellor Walworth in Noyes v. Clark (supra) express the rule which has since prevailed in respect to the rights of a mortgagee against a defaulting mortgagor under an acceleration clause: "The parties * * * had an unquestionable right to make the extension of credit dependent upon the punctual payment of the interest at the times fixed for that purpose. And if, from the mere negligence of the mortgagor in performing his contract, he suffers the whole debt to become due and payable, according to the terms of the mortgage, no court will interfere to relieve him from the payment thereof according to the conditions of his own agreement. (Steel v. Bradfield, 4 Taunt.Rep. 227; James v. Thomas, 5 Barn. & Adol. 40.)" Ferris v. Ferris (supra) illustrates the application of that rule when the court, holding that the acceleration clause works neither a forfeiture nor a penalty, rejected a defense founded upon the fact that the mortgagor was unacquainted with business and suffered the day of payment to arrive sooner in consequence of her own negligence than she would otherwise have done. This court has never departed from that rule. Cases can be found in other courts where the facts may be so distinguished as to take them out of the rule or where other theories have been applied in a way which fails to meet with our approval. We feel that the interests of certainty and security in real estate transactions forbid us, in the absence of fraud, bad faith or unconscionable conduct, to recede from the doctrine that is so deeply imbedded in equity.

Reliance is placed by respondent upon Noyes v. Anderson (supra), but we think that the reasoning in that case requires a reversal here. There the issue related to the effect upon a collateral agreement of a default in the payment of an assessment, and the court, giving full recognition to the principles of the cases above cited, decided that the breach of a condition subsequent in that agreement, unlike a default in the payment of interest on the principal of a mortgage debt, resulted in a forfeiture. * * *

The judgment of the Appellate Division and that of the Special Term should be reversed and judgment ordered in favor of plaintiff for the relief demanded in the complaint, with costs in all courts.

CARDOZO, CH. J. (dissenting). The action is one for the foreclosure of a consolidated mortgage.

The principal of the mortgage is $335,000, payable in quarter-annual installments of $1,500, beginning April 1, 1925, and continuing until January 1, 1935, when there is to be payment of the residue ($276,500). Interest computed at the rate of 5¾ per cent per annum is payable quarter-annually, like the installments of the principal. At the option of the mortgagee the whole of the principal is to become due after default for twenty days in the payment of any installment of the interest.

On July 1, 1927, there became due the quarterly installment of principal ($1,500), and interest ($4,621.56), in all $6,121.56. The interest payments were not constant in amount, for the debt on which interest was to be computed varied each quarter with the reduction of the principal. At this time, the owner of the equity of redemption was the Hope Building Corporation, which was not a signer of the bond nor personally bound for the payment of the debt. The corporation was owned and controlled by its president, Mr. Herstein, who sailed for Europe June 2, 1927, on a hurried trip for business. Before leaving he requested his bookkeeper, who was nominally the secretary of the corporation, to make out the checks for the principal and interest payable in July. Through an error in arithmetic, she computed the interest as $4,219.69, which was $401.87 short of the correct amount. Mr. Herstein signed a check for the interest so computed and also one for $1,500, the installment of the principal. After he had gone, the bookkeeper recalculated the interest and discovered her mistake. There was no one authorized to sign checks when the president was away. Accordingly on June 24 she mailed the two checks to the plaintiff mortgagee, stating that a mistake in arithmetic had been made, and that the president was expected to return about July 5, at which time a check for $401.87 would be promptly forwarded. The president of the corporation returned at the appointed time, but unfortunately the bookkeeper forgot about the error, and failed to bring it to his attention. The twenty-day period of grace expired July 21. On July 22, without warning or demand, the plaintiff began this action for the foreclosure of its mortgage, electing to declare the principal indebtedness to be due by reason of the default in the payment of the interest. Promptly the same day, the corporation, thus advised of its default, tendered the overdue installment. The tender, being rejected, was kept good by payment into court. These facts being proved, the trial judge held that there has been a mere mistake in computation, against which equity would relieve by refusing to cooperate with the plaintiff in the effort to collect the accelerated debt. The Appellate Division unanimously affirmed. Upon appeal by the plaintiff the case is now here by allowance of this court.

There is no undeviating principle that equity shall enforce the covenants of a mortgage, unmoved by an appeal *ad misericordiam*, however urgent or affecting. The development of the jurisdiction of the chancery is lined with historic monuments that point another course. * * *

To all this, acceleration clauses in mortgages do not constitute an exception. They are not a class by themselves, removed from interference by force of something peculiar in their internal constitution. In general, it is true, they will be enforced as they are written. In particular this has been held of a covenant in a mortgage accelerating the maturity of the principal in default of punctual payment of an installment of the interest. If the quality of a penalty inheres in such a covenant at all, it is not there to such a degree as to call, in ordinary circumstances, for mitigation or repression (Noyes v. Clark, 7 Paige, 179; Ferris v. Ferris, 28 Barb. 29; Malcolm v. Allen, 49 N.Y. 448; Bennett v. Stevenson, 53 N.Y. 508). Less favor has been shown to a provision for acceleration of a mortgage in default of punctual payment of taxes or assessments. We have held that such a provision, though not a penalty in a strict or proper sense, is yet so closely akin thereto in view of the forfeiture of credit that equity will relieve against it if default has been due to mere venial inattention and if relief can be granted without damage to the lender (Noyes v. Anderson, 124 N.Y. 175; followed in Ver Planck v. Godfrey, 42 App.Div. 16; Germania Life Ins. Co. v. Potter, 124 App.Div. 814, and of Trowbridge v.

Malex Realty Corp., 198 App.Div. 656). In the one case as in the other, in foreclosure for default of taxes just as in foreclosure for default of interest, the privilege of acceleration is absolute in the event of a default, if the privilege is to be measured by the language of the covenant. The distinction lies in this only, that the punctual payment of interest has an importance to the lender as affecting his way of life, perhaps the very means for his support, whereas the importance of payment of the taxes is merely as an assurance of security. The difference is not one of kind, for the provision is enforcible even as to taxes if the default is continuous or willful; it is a difference merely of degree, the purpose of the payment being referred to as a test wherewith to gauge the measure of the hardship, the extent of the oppression.

There is neither purpose nor desire to impair the stability of the rule, which is still to be enforced as one of general application, that nonpayment of interest will accelerate the debt if the mortgage so provides. The rule is well understood, and is fair to borrower and lender in its normal operation. Especially is it fair if there is a period of grace (in this case twenty days) whereby a reasonable leeway is afforded to inadvertence and improvidence. In such circumstances, with one period of grace established by the covenant, only the most appealing equity will justify a court in transcending the allotted period and substituting another. There is a difference, however, between a denial of power, without heed to the hardship calling for its use, and a definition of hardship that will limit the occasions upon which power shall be exercised. In none of the cases cited as indicative of lack of power was there any need to determine the effect of accident or mistake apparent to a mortgagee who has preferred default to payment. * * *

When an advantage is unconscionable depends upon the circumstances. It is not unconscionable generally to insist that payment shall be made according to the letter of a contract. It may be unconscionable to insist upon adherence to the letter where the default is limited to a trifling balance, where the failure to pay the balance is the product of mistake, and where the mortgagee indicates by his conduct that he appreciates the mistake and has attempted by silence and inaction to turn it to his own advantage. The holder of this mortgage must have understood that he could have his money for the asking. His silence, followed, as it was, by immediate suit at the first available opportunity, brings conviction to the mind that he was avoiding any act that would spur the mortgagor to payment. What he did was almost as suggestive of that purpose as if he had kept out of the way in order to avoid a tender (Noyes v. Clark, supra). Demand was, indeed, unnecessary to bring the debt to maturity at law. There is not a technical estoppel (Thompson v. Simpson, 128 N.Y. 270, 291; Spencer Bower on Estoppel by Representation, pp. 61, 352, 358; cf. Williston, Contracts, vol. 3, §§ 1497,

1548, 1557). The consequence does not follow that, in conditions so peculiar, the omission to make demand is without significance in equity. Significant it may then be in helping the court to a determination whether the conduct of a suitor in taking advantage of a default, so easily averted and so plainly unintentional, is consistent with good conscience (cf. Retan v. Clark, 220 Mich. 493). True, indeed, it is that accident and mistake will often be inadequate to supply a basis for the granting or withholding of equitable remedies where the consequences to be corrected might have been avoided if the victim of the misfortune had ordered his affairs with reasonable diligence (United States v. Ames, 99 U.S. 35, 47; Grymes v. Sanders, 93 U.S. 55; Noyes v. Clark, supra). The restriction, however, is not obdurate, for always the gravity of the fault must be compared with the gravity of the hardship (Noyes v. Anderson, supra; Lawrence v. American Nat. Bank, 54 N.Y. 432; Ball v. Shepard, 202 N.Y. 247, 253). Let the hardship be strong enough, and equity will find a way, though many a formula of inaction may seem to bar the path. * * *

* * * The court will stand aside when by intervening it will make itself an instrument of injustice (Thomas v. Brownville, etc., R.R. Co., supra). There is no occasion to define the situations in which it will be ready to go farther and stay the remedy at law. Enough for present purposes that it may withhold a remedy in equity. If justice exacts an acceptance of a tender, the relief to be granted will be subject to that condition, and the decree will be limited to the overdue installments, with costs accruing to the date of tender and refusal. * * *

POUND, CRANE and HUBBS, JJ., concur with O'BRIEN, J. LEHMAN and KELLOGG, JJ., concur with CARDOZO, J.

mC   *mR*

FEDERAL HOME LOAN MORTGAGE CORP. v. TAYLOR

District Court of Appeal of Florida, First District, 1975
318 So.2d 203

WILLIS, BEN C., ASSOCIATE JUDGE.

The appellant was plaintiff in the trial court in a suit to foreclose a real estate mortgage given by appellees to secure an installment promissory note by them. Appellant is the owner and holder of the note and mortgage. The parties will be referred to as the mortgagors and mortgagee.

The pleadings and other preliminaries to the entry of the Final Judgment are somewhat unique and will be mentioned further. In the Final Judgment, dated October 8, 1974, the trial judge declined the foreclosure of the mortgage, reciting: " * * * It being the opinion of the Court that it would not be equitable to allow foreclosure of said property because this action is the result of both parties' conduct". * * * In the final paragraph of the judgment it is provided that if the mortgagors comply with the payments required of them, as above mentioned, the note and mortgage shall be reinstated "and that the obligations and duties provided in the original note and mortgage will proceed under the original terms and conditions".

* * *

The note involved is a conventional FHA form monthly installment instrument in the principal amount of $13,600.00 with 8½% interest on the unpaid balance payable in monthly installments of $104.58 each commencing September 1, 1970 and falling due on the first day of each succeeding month. It has an acceleration clause to the effect that if default be made in the payment of any installment and "such installment is not made good prior to the due date of the next installment, the entire principal sum and accrued interest shall at once become due and payable without notice at the option of the holder of this note". * * *

* * *

The mortgage also provides:

"Any deficiency in the amount of such monthly payment shall, unless made good by the mortgagor prior to the due date of the next such payment, constitute an event of default under this mortgage. The mortgagee may collect a late charge not to exceed two cents (2) for each dollar ($1) of each payment more than fifteen (15) days in arrears to cover the extra expense involved in handling delinquent payments."

The net effect of the payment provisions is that the monthly installment is due on the first day of the month, but there is a grace period of fifteen days within which it may be paid without further obligation. If not paid within this period a "late charge" may be assessed, and further, if such payment is not "made good" prior to the first of the next month, the mortgagee has the option to declare the entire unpaid principal and accrued interest due and payable "at once" without notice.

The facts involved are not in serious dispute. The mortgagor, George B. Taylor, was during the events involved a noncommissioned officer in the U.S. Air Force and from about September 1972 until sometime shortly prior to the final hearing on October 8, 1974 was on active duty as a member of an Aerospace Rescue and Recovery Squadron at Clark Air Base in the Philippine Islands. His family, including his wife, the defendant Jo Ann Taylor, was with him in the Philippines. Apparently until April 1973 the monthly payments were seasonably made and received within the month. The May 1973 payment was a month and twenty days late but was accepted by the mortgagee. The next payment was on September 10, 1973 when payments of three installments were made. These were accepted and applied to the installments due on the first of June, July and August. Mail deliveries to and from the Philippines and the U.S. mainland require seven to eighteen days.

On September 29, 1973 the mortgagors mailed two money orders aggregating $121.38, which was the proper sum for the monthly payment due September 1, 1973. The payment includes the $104.58 installment as specified in the note, also escrow funds of $14.42 for accruing taxes and insurance as provided in the mortgage, and a late charge of $2.38. This payment was returned with a covering form letter dated October 4, 1973 stating the remittance is not sufficient to reinstate the delinquent account and that the sum of $240.38 is required "to eliminate the delinquency, which includes the regular installment due the first day of this month and *late* charge". Thereafter the mortgagor mailed payments which would have been sufficient to pay the accruals within the month but when received in the succeeding month another installment would have fallen due on the first. In each instance the mortgagee would mail it back because of the lack of the current installment. This continued each month until March 1974 with remittances and returns often crossing in the mail. In April 1974 and thereafter mortgagors discontinued payments as it was likely they would be returned or even misplaced in the mail. However, they set aside monies in an escrow account to be available for payments on the debt.

The Complaint seeking foreclosure, filed April 6, 1974, alleged default by failing to pay payments due September 1, 1973 and all subsequent payments. Pursuant to motion by plaintiff, an attorney ad litem was appointed for defendant mortgagors pursuant to the Soldiers' and Sailors' Civil Relief Act (50 U.S.C.A.App. Sec. 520), as defendant, George B. Taylor, was on active duty in the military services. Constructive service of process on defendants was apparently perfected. However, the attorney ad litem filed a motion to stay proceedings under 50 U.S.C.A.App. 521 until the serviceman should be able to return. An order staying proceedings for 30 days was entered June 10, 1974. Ultimately the final hearing was conducted in two parts with the plaintiff's evidence being received on August 29, 1974 in the absence of defendant but with the attorney ad litem present and participating and on October 8, 1974 the testimony of mortgagor George Taylor was taken, final arguments heard, and the court's ruling announced. It does not appear that any formal Answer was filed, but in the attorney ad litem's affidavit and motion for stay of proceedings it was set forth that defendants had made every good faith effort to pay plaintiff the sums due and they had all been returned. There were other statements of confusion in communications at such distance and a change in amount of monthly payments due to loss of homestead status of the property involved.

It is apparent that the cause was heard primarily on the issue of whether or not the acceleration of the due date of future mortgage installments with resultant foreclosure would be unconscionable and an inequitable result. * * *

The mortgagor, George Taylor, testified that the reason for the late payment in September was the necessity of having his daughter flown back to the mainland to a hospital in Texas. He further testified that in October and November he was still having financial problems as he had to pay rent for his wife in Texas, presumably in connection with the child's hospitalization, also pay for his living quarters in the Philippines, and pay the installment on the mortgage in Florida.

The mortgagee contends that the trial court abused its discretion in refusing to honor acceleration of the due date of the debt and accord a foreclosure for the full amount of the unpaid principal and accrued interest. It is fully established in the jurisprudence of this state that an acceleration clause or promise in an installment note or mortgage confers a contract right upon the note or mortgage holder which he may elect to invoke upon default and to seek enforcement. Treb Trading Co. v. Green, 102 Fla. 238, 135 So. 510 (1931); Campbell v. Werner, Fla.App.3rd 1970, 232 So.2d 252. It is essential that valid contracts be safeguarded and the right of enforcement in the event of breach be accorded. A mere offer or willingness of a mortgagor to cure a default, after a valid election to accelerate, is not deemed a sufficient ground to deny acceleration and foreclosure. Campbell v. Werner, supra. Furthermore, mere notions or concepts of natural justice of a chancellor which are not in accord with established equitable rules and maxims may not be applied in rendering judgment. The obligation of a mortgagor to pay and the right of a mortgagee to foreclosure in accordance with the terms of the note and mortgage are absolute and are not contingent on the mortgagor's health, good fortune, ill fortune, or other personal circumstances affecting his ability to pay. Home Owners' Loan Corp. v. Wilkes, 130 Fla. 492, 178 So. 161.

However, it is equally well established in our law that a court of equity may refuse to foreclose a mortgage when an acceleration of the due date of the debt would be an inequitable or unjust result and the circumstances would render the acceleration unconscionable. Kreiss Potassium Phosphate Co. v. Knight, 98 Fla. 1004, 124 So. 751; Lieberbaum v. Surfcomber Hotel Corp. (Fla.App.3rd 1960), 122 So.2d 28; Althouse v. Kenney (Fla.App.2nd 1966), 182 So.2d 270.

In the case sub judice the mortgagor had not prior to the return of his tendered payment received by the mortgagee subsequent to October 1, 1973, been aware of any purpose or inclination of the mortgagee to be uneasy about this account. After nearly three years of regular payments, there was one lapse of a month plus 20 days in making a payment followed by a three month lapse but immediately afterwards there were paid three installments with late charges. The September 10, 1973 payment did not include the installment which fell due September 1. However, prior to October 4 this installment was paid, but mortgagee refused to accept it because the October 1 installment was not included. The lag in mail deliveries was obviously a circumstance which contributed to much of the lack of communication and misunderstanding. It is to be noticed here that the mortgagors were not in the Philippines by mere choice but due to a military assignment. Though the personal hardship arising from the daughter's need of state-side hospitalization is not a circumstance to excuse payment of a debt when due, the distance between the mortgagors and mortgagee's agent because of military obligations of the mortgagor is not to be ignored as a factor impairing the ability of the parties to communicate demands and responses thereto. The total evidence indicates a good faith effort on the part of mortgagors to meet the mortgagee's conditions of bringing the account current. Perhaps the mortgagee would have been less adamant in returning tendered payments were it not for the fear that continued acceptance may have worked a waiver or estoppel to assert an accelerated default. Cited in support of such a concept is Criado v. Milgram, Fla.App.3rd 1970, 237 So.2d 596. This case is not in point as there the estoppel arose when the assignee of the mortgage knew that the mortgagors had continued to make payments to the assignor after the assignment, and thus assignee was estopped to assert that mortgagor was in default for not making payments to him. Here, the trial judge was well within his discretion in concluding that it would be unconscionable to precipitate the maturity of the entire balance of over $14,000 which could only result in the loss of the mortgaged property through foreclosure, all because of a technical default of one month's installment which well could arise from excusable misunderstanding and lack of effective and timely communication. We find no error in that portion of the judgment declining foreclosure and effecting reinstatement of the note and mortgage.

* * *

Affirmed.

McCord, Acting C.J., and Mills, J., concur.

NOTES

1.   *Tender before or after acceleration.* When or if acceleration occurs can have crucial consequences for the parties. If the mortgagor tenders the arrearages (past-due installments) before acceleration, the mortgage is reinstated. See, e.g., Delandro v. America's Mortg. Servicing, Inc., 674 So.2d 184 (Fla.App.1996); Kent v. Pipia, 185 Mich.App. 599, 462 N.W.2d 800 (1990). After acceleration, only tender of the full accelerated mortgage debt will suffice, unless a statute provides to the contrary. See, e.g., United Companies

Lending Corp. v. Hingos, 283 A.D.2d 764, 724 N.Y.S.2d 134 (2001); City Savings Bank of Bridgeport v. Dessoff, 3 Conn.App. 644, 491 A.2d 424 (1985); Dime Savings Bank of New York v. Glavey, 214 A.D.2d 419, 625 N.Y.S.2d 181 (1995). A mortgagee's post-acceleration acceptance of arrearages only reduces the mortgage obligation but does not defeat the acceleration. See Ryder v. Bank of Hickory Hills, 146 Ill.2d 98, 165 Ill.Dec. 650, 585 N.E.2d 46 (1991).

When does acceleration take place? Most acceleration clauses are "optional," as opposed to "automatic," in the sense that acceleration does not automatically occur when the mortgagor defaults. In some states, both notice of intent to accelerate and notice of acceleration itself are required unless the parties agree otherwise. See, e.g., Shumway v. Horizon Credit Corp., 801 S.W.2d 890 (Tex.1991); Ogden v. Gibraltar Sav. Ass'n, 640 S.W.2d 232 (Tex.1982). However, in most jurisdictions, notice is not mandatory. Rather, the mortgagee "must perform some affirmative, overt act evidencing his intention to take advantage of the accelerating provision. Such affirmative action must be taken before the debtor tenders what is actually due, or the creditor loses his right to treat the entire debt as due because of that particular default." Spires v. Lawless, 493 S.W.2d 65, 73 (Mo.App.1973). In some states, the affirmative action must be a notice to the mortgagor. See In re Crystal Properties, Ltd., 268 F.3d 743 (9th Cir.2001) (California law).

Mortgagees often use notice to the mortgagor to establish the requisite affirmative action. In many states, commencement of a foreclosure proceeding is sufficient evidence of an election to accelerate. See Nelson, Whitman, Burkhart & Freyermuth, Real Estate Finance Law § 7.6 (6th ed.2014). Under the Restatement, acceleration is "effective on the date specified in a written notice delivered by mortgagee to mortgagor after the latter's default. The notice may provide that the acceleration is effective immediately or at some future specified date." Restatement (Third) of Property (Mortgages) § 8.1, cmt. b (1997).

2. *Defaults other than failure to pay installments.* Depending on the language of the acceleration clause, acceleration may be triggered not only by failure to pay installments of principal or interest, but also by such derelictions as failure to insure or pay taxes. When a non-debt related default triggers acceleration, should reinstatement of insurance or payment of taxes before the foreclosure sale be sufficient to avoid acceleration, or must the mortgagor also pay the accelerated debt? Compare Jeffery v. Seven Seventeen Corp., 461 A.2d 1009 (Del.1983) and Parrott v. Wallace, 127 Idaho 306, 900 P.2d 214 (App.1995) with Balducci v. Eberly, 304 Md. 664, 500 A.2d 1042 (1985) and Eisen v. Kostakos, 116 N.J.Super. 358, 282 A.2d 421 (App.Div.1971).

Under the Restatement view, only tender of the accelerated debt will defeat acceleration in the non-debt related default context. See Restatement (Third) of Property (Mortgages) § 8.1(c) & cmt. c (1997). Interestingly, a few courts have held that impairment of security is needed to justify acceleration when the mortgagor fails to pay taxes or maintain casualty insurance on the mortgaged premises. See Mid-State Trust II v. Jackson, 42 Ark.App. 112, 854 S.W.2d 734 (1993) (insurance); Vonk v. Dunn, 161 Ariz. 24, 775 P.2d 1088 (1989) (taxes); Freeman v. Lind, 181 Cal.App.3d 791, 226 Cal.Rptr. 515 (1986) (insurance), *abrogated by* Cal. Civ. Code § 2924.7.

3. *Note and mortgage inconsistency.* Problems arise when the note and mortgage are inconsistent with respect to acceleration. Suppose the mortgage contains an acceleration clause, but the note does not. Most courts permit acceleration in the event of default and allow foreclosure for the full amount of the mortgage debt. This is the Restatement approach. See Restatement (Third) of Property (Mortgages) § 8.1(a) (1997). However, some courts do not permit a deficiency judgment under these circumstances. See Robert Kratovil, Modern Mortgage Law and Practice 84 (1988). Uniform Commercial Code § 3–105(c) provides that a mortgage note is negotiable though it includes a provision that allows acceleration for breach of a mortgage covenant. For an illustration of the potential pitfalls of failing to include that provision, see 2140 Lincoln Park West v. American Nat'l Bank & Trust Co. of Chicago, 88 Ill.App.3d 660, 43 Ill.Dec. 857, 410 N.E.2d 990 (1980).

4. *Judicial discretion to permit reinstatement.* If the mortgagee has validly accelerated, does a court have discretion to permit the mortgagor to defeat acceleration by paying just the arrearages? *Graf* and *Taylor* represent opposing perspectives on this issue. Many courts, like the *Graf* majority, hold that a mortgagor will not be relieved from enforcement of an acceleration clause if he defaulted as a result of his negligence or mistake or by accident, at least in the absence of fraud, bad faith, or other mortgagee conduct that renders use of the clause unconscionable. This judicial attitude is perhaps best exemplified by the following language from Verna v. O'Brien, 78 Misc.2d 288, 356 N.Y.S.2d 929 (1974), a post-*Graf* New York decision: "[M]ere improvidence or neglect or poverty or illness is not sufficient basis for relief in equity from foreclosure under a mortgage acceleration clause. A mortgagee may be ungenerous, perhaps even uncharitable, but generosity and charity are voluntary attributes and cannot be enforced by the court."

Under the Restatement, judicial discretion to defeat acceleration exists only if "the mortgagee has waived its right to accelerate" or "has engaged in fraud, bad faith, or other conduct making acceleration unconscionable." Restatement (Third) of Property (Mortgages) § 8.1(d)(2), (3) (1997). Thus, "a mortgagee who is guilty of no misconduct is *ex ante* permitted to rely on its contract acceleration right without being subject to the vagaries of mortgagor's financial and personal situation, a matter over which mortgagee usually has little control." Id., cmt. e.

Other courts, like *Taylor*, take the view that "equity has the power to relieve a mortgagor for an inadvertent default in the payment of principal or interest where acceleration would work extreme hardship upon him." Robert R. Rosenthal, The Role of Courts of Equity in Preventing Acceleration Predicated upon a Mortgagor's Inadvertent Default, 22 Syr.L.Rev. 897, 904 (1972). See also Steven W. Bender, Equity in Times of Mortgage Crisis, 48

Real Prop. Tr. & Est. L.J. 543, 550–51 (2014). Indeed, one court has specifically endorsed Justice Cardozo's characterization of the appropriate approach as a "balancing process;" when deciding whether equitable relief should be granted, "the gravity of the fault must be weighed against the gravity of the hardship." Redding v. Gibbs, 203 Neb. 727, 280 N.W.2d 53 (1979). Moreover, New York courts continue to have difficulty with *Graf.* Consider, for example, the language of Karas v. Wasserman, 91 A.D.2d 812, 458 N.Y.S.2d 280, 281–82 (1982):

> Plaintiffs mistakenly rely here on the continued vitality of the majority holding in Graf v. Hope Building Corp., 254 N.Y. 1, 171 N.E. 884, to the effect that acceleration clauses in mortgages will be strictly enforced irrespective of the circumstances and nature of the default. Rather, it seems clear that the evolving subsequent case law has largely adopted the reasoning of Chief Judge Cardozo's dissenting position in *Graf,* 254 N.Y. 1, 8–15, 171 N.E. 884, *supra,* that the equitable remedy of foreclosure may be denied in the case of an inadvertent, inconsequential default in order to prevent unconscionably overreaching conduct by a mortgagee (see Blomgren v. Tinton 763 Corp., 18 A.D.2d 979, 238 N.Y.S.2d 435; 100 Eighth Ave. Corp. v. Morgenstern, 4 A.D.2d 754, 164 N.Y.S.2d 812; More Realty Corp. v. Mootchnick, 232 App.Div. 705, 247 N.Y.S. 712; Scelza v. Ryba, 10 Misc.2d 186, 169 N.Y.S.2d 462; Domus Realty Corp. v. 3440 Realty Co., 179 Misc. 749, 40 N.Y.S.2d 69, aff'd, 266 App.Div. 725, 41 N.Y.S.2d 940). Indeed, the *Graf* dissent has recently been cited as authority for that proposition by the Court of Appeals in connection with a rent acceleration clause in a lease (Fifty States Mgt. Corp. v. Pioneer Auto Parks, 46 N.Y.2d 573, 577, 578–579, 415 N.Y.S.2d 800, 389 N.E.2d 113) and in other similar contexts (J.N.A. Realty Corp. v. Cross Bay Chelsea, 42 N.Y.2d 392, 398–400, 397 N.Y.S.2d 958, 366 N.E.2d 1313).

Which approach makes more sense from a judicial economy perspective? It has been asserted that the Restatement approach "avoids difficult and time-consuming judicial inquiries into such matters as the degree of mortgagor's negligence, the relative hardship that acceleration imposes, and other subjective concerns." Restatement (Third) of Property (Mortgages) § 8.1 cmt. e. Are you convinced?

5.　*Waiver, abandonment, and estoppel.* Virtually all courts recognize that acceleration may sometimes be defeated by mortgagee *waiver.* For examples in which acceleration was precluded by the mortgagee's consistent past pattern of accepting late payments, see Alderman v. Davidson, 326 Or. 508, 954 P.2d 779 (1998) (repeated acceptance of late installment payments constituted waiver of right to accelerate); Rosselot v. Heimbrock, 54 Ohio App.3d 103, 561 N.E.2d 555 (1988); McGowan v. Pasol, 605 S.W.2d 728 (Tex.Civ.App.1980). See generally, Nelson, Whitman, Burkhart & Freyermuth, Real Estate Finance Law § 7.7 (6th ed.2014).

Sometimes, mortgagors assert that the mortgagee has *abandoned* or *waived* an otherwise valid acceleration. As stated in Note 1, the mortgagee's post-acceleration acceptance of arrearages normally only reduces the mortgage debt and does not impair the validity of the acceleration and foreclosure. Of course, a mortgagor and mortgagee can agree to undo or "abandon" an earlier acceleration. To what extent, however, can the parties' post-acceleration actions cause abandonment? For example, suppose that, after acceleration, a mortgagee accepts arrearages and several monthly installment payments from the mortgagor but forecloses nonjudicially almost a year later for the then mortgage balance. In this situation, a court arguably could conclude that the parties' post-acceleration actions evidence an agreement to abandon the earlier acceleration and, therefore, that the foreclosure based on that acceleration is invalid. However, courts rarely find abandonment. See generally, Holy Cross Church of God in Christ v. Wolf, 44 S.W.3d 562 (Tex.2001); Fitzgerald v. Harry, 2003 WL 22147557 (Tex.App.2003, not reported in S.W.2d) (post-acceleration letter from mortgagee to mortgagor stating "in the event you do not pay your note payments . . . your unpaid note balance will be accelerated" together with a "vague assertion" that the mortgagee accepted subsequent note payments were insufficient to constitute abandonment).

Is it good public policy to be generous in finding waiver or abandonment? Will forbearance by mortgagees be discouraged? Suppose the note or mortgage contains "anti-waiver" language. According to the Restatement, while "such a provision may, in close cases, tip the balance against a finding of waiver, it usually is not dispositive on the waiver issue." Restatement (Third) of Property (Mortgages) § 8.1 cmt. e (1997). But see Gaul v. Olympia Fitness Center, Inc., 88 Ohio App.3d 310, 623 N.E.2d 1281 (1993) ("a mortgagee's past acceptance of late loan payments does not constitute a waiver of mortgagee's right to accelerate * * * following a subsequent default where the relevant loan documents contain 'anti-waiver' provisions."). Consider the following language of the Connecticut Supreme Court:

> [U]nder this court's interpretation of nonwaiver clauses * * * the plaintiff's conduct in affording the defendant eight additional days to stave off the consequences of acceleration and foreclosure by curing the default cannot be construed as a waiver of its option to accelerate the mortgage loan. Indeed, a conclusion by this court that a lender, by giving a borrower one more opportunity to cure a default, has not clearly and unequivocally exercised its right to accelerate the debt, ultimately would militate against persons in the defendant's position; such a conclusion surely would eviscerate any inclination or incentive that a lender might have to extend any kind of generosity or flexibility to borrowers in default, on the eve of commencing litigation. Moreover, the letter from the plaintiff's attorney was not contradictory, as the defendant claims, because beyond affording the defendant a few more days to cure her default, *it did not retract expressly the previous notice of acceleration.*

Webster Bank v. Oakley, 265 Conn. 539, 551, 830 A.2d 139, 147–48 (2003).

Even if no consistent prior pattern of forbearance exists, a mortgagee may sometimes be *estopped* to accelerate based on a single transaction. For example, a mortgagee may be estopped if it attempts to accelerate after orally assuring a mortgagor in default that acceleration and foreclosure will be postponed while the mortgagor attempts to sell the mortgaged property. Unless the mortgagee gives reasonable notice that it is withdrawing the extension, the mortgagor has a defense to acceleration if she detrimentally relied on the assurance. See Nelson, Whitman, Burkhart & Freyermuth, Real Estate Finance Law § 7.7 (6th ed. 2014).

6. *Arrearages legislation.* Many states have enacted "arrearages" legislation that permits the mortgagor to defeat acceleration by curing the default that existed before acceleration. Consider the following California statute:

> (a)(1) Whenever all or a portion of the principal sum of any obligation secured by deed of trust or mortgage on real property or an estate for years therein hereafter executed has, prior to the maturity date fixed in that obligation, become due or been declared due by reason of default in payment of interest or of any installment of principal, or by reason of failure of trustor or mortgagor to pay, in accordance with the terms of that obligation or of the deed of trust or mortgage, taxes, assessments, premiums for insurance, or advances made by beneficiary or mortgagee in accordance with the terms of that obligation or of the deed of trust or mortgage; the trustor or mortgagor or his or her successor in interest in the mortgaged or trust property or any part thereof, or any beneficiary under a subordinate deed of trust or any other person having a subordinate lien or encumbrance of record thereon, at any time within the period specified in subdivision (e), if the power of sale therein is to be exercised, or, otherwise at any time prior to entry of the decree of foreclosure, may pay to the beneficiary or the mortgagee or their successors in interest, respectively, the entire amount due, at the time payment is tendered, with respect to (A) all amounts of principal, interest, taxes, assessments, insurance premiums, or advances actually known by the beneficiary to be, and that are, in default and shown in the notice of default, under the terms of the deed of trust or mortgage and the obligation secured thereby, (B) all amounts in default on recurring obligations not · shown in the notice of default, and (C) all reasonable costs and expenses, subject to subdivision (c), which are actually incurred in enforcing the terms of the obligation, deed of trust or mortgage, and trustee's or attorney's fees, subject to subdivision (d), other than the portion of principal as would not then be due had no default occurred, and thereby cure the default theretofore existing, and thereupon, all proceedings theretofore had or instituted shall be dismissed or discontinued and the obligation and deed of trust or

mortgage shall be reinstated and shall be and remain in force and effect, the same as if the acceleration had not occurred. * * * For the purposes of this subdivision, the term "recurring obligation" means all amounts of principal and interest on the loan, or rents, subject to the deed of trust or mortgage in default due after the notice of default is recorded; all amounts of principal and interest or rents advanced on senior liens or leaseholds which are advanced after the recordation of the notice of default; and payments of taxes, assessments, and hazard insurance advanced after recordation of the notice of default.

* * *

(c) Costs and expenses which may be charged pursuant to Sections 2924 to 2924i, inclusive, shall be limited to the costs incurred for recording, mailing, publishing, and posting notices required by Sections 2924 to 2924i, inclusive, postponement pursuant to Section 2924g made to either the beneficiary or trustee not to exceed fifty dollars ($50) per postponement and a fee for a trustee's sale guarantee or, in the event of judicial foreclosure, a litigation guarantee. * * *

(d) Trustee's or attorney's fees which may be charged pursuant to subdivision (a), or until the notice of sale is deposited in the mail to the trustor as provided in Section 2924b, if the sale is by power of sale contained in the deed of trust or mortgage, or, otherwise at any time prior to the decree of foreclosure, are hereby authorized to be in a base amount that does not exceed three hundred dollars ($300) if the unpaid principal sum is one hundred fifty thousand dollars ($150,000) or less, or two hundred fifty dollars ($250) if the unpaid sum secured exceeds one hundred fifty thousand dollars ($150,000), plus one-quarter of 1 percent of any portion of the unpaid principal sum secured exceeding one hundred fifty thousand dollars ($150,000) up to and including five hundred thousand dollars ($500,000), plus one-eighth of 1 percent of any portion of the unpaid principal sum secured exceeding five hundred thousand dollars ($500,000). Any charge for trustee's or attorney's fees authorized by this subdivision shall be conclusively presumed to be lawful and valid where the charge does not exceed the amounts authorized herein. * * *

(e) Reinstatement of a monetary default under the terms of an obligation secured by a deed of trust, or mortgage may be made at any time within the period commencing with the date of recordation of the notice of default until five business days prior to the date of sale set forth in the initial recorded notice of sale.

West's Ann.Cal.Civ.Code § 2924c. See also Alaska Stat. § 34.20.070(b); Minn. Stat. Ann. § 580.30; 41 Pa.Stat. § 404; Utah Code Ann.1953, 57–1–31. Suppose that, in California, the mortgagor's failure to pay real estate taxes triggers acceleration. Can the mortgagor avert foreclosure simply by tendering the amount of the delinquent taxes?

Note that the California statute confers the right to cure on the "trustor or mortgagor or his or her successor in interest in the mortgaged or trust property or any part thereof." Does this language permit a junior lienor to exercise cure rights? The Alaska Supreme Court was confronted with this issue when interpreting Alaska Stat. § 34.20.070(b), which provides in pertinent part:

> At any time before the sale, if the default has arisen by failure to make payments required by the trust deed, the default may be cured by payment of the sum in default other than the principal that would not then be due if no default had occurred, plus attorney fees or court costs actually incurred by the trustee due to the default.

According to the court:

> [T]he language admits of two possible interpretations. The legislature may have omitted express mention of obligors because it assumed that the reference would apply only to obligors; alternatively, it may have omitted express mention because it wished to include other interested parties * * * . From the plain text either interpretation is plausible.
>
> Because the statute is written in the passive voice—it states that the "default may be cured"—its meaning is ambiguous. * * *
>
> Especially when statutory language and legislative history are ambiguous, we look to the common law as a useful tool to discern legislative intent and to interpret statutes. * * *
>
> The equity of redemption * * * is analogous to the right of cure granted [by § 34.20.070(b)]. If a lienholder is able to redeem the property, then that person should also be able to cure a default. * * * We have characterized cure as a type of redemption: "If the party who executes the deed of trust defaults the obligation, the party nonetheless has a right of redemption. In other words, the party has the opportunity to cure the default at any time *before* a nonjudicial sale." Therefore just as the junior lienholder has the right to redeem a mortgage, we determine that the junior lienholder also possesses the right to cure default on a deed of trust before the foreclosure sale. Our conclusion is further buttressed by the twin principles that redemption statutes should be construed liberally and that equity abhors a forfeiture.

Young v. Embley, 143 P.3d 936, 944–46 (2006). Is a similar interpretation of the California statute appropriate?

Under the Minnesota statute, the mortgagor can reinstate the mortgage by paying, before the foreclosure sale, "the amount actually due thereon and constituting the default actually existing in the conditions of the mortgage at the time of the commencement of the foreclosure proceedings * * * ." Minn.Stat.Ann. § 580.30. Do the terms "amount actually due" and "default actually existing" mean the amount due and the default existing now that the mortgagee has accelerated? See Davis v. Davis, 293 Minn. 44, 196 N.W.2d 473 (1972).

Are arrearages statutes subject to abuse by mortgagors who may default repeatedly, knowing they can defeat acceleration by simply tendering the arrearages? Will the requirement that, in addition to arrearages, the mortgagor pay statutory attorney's fees and certain other costs deter potential abuse? Will it in California? Should the number of reinstatements be limited? See Purdon's Pa.Stat.Ann. Tit. 41 § 404 (mortgagor limited to three reinstatements per year). Will commercial mortgagors be willing repeatedly to accept the economic penalties of reinstatement, especially in the case of mortgages of substantial dollar amount? Should statutory reinstatement rights be accorded only to residential mortgagors? See the Pennsylvania statute, supra.

The Federal Housing Administration (FHA) has issued regulations for foreclosing loans that it has insured. See 24 CFR §§ 203.600–616 (1995). Under its reinstatement provision:

> The mortgagee shall permit reinstatement of a mortgage, even after the institution of foreclosure proceedings, if the mortgagor tenders in a lump sum all amounts required to bring the account current, including foreclosure costs and reasonable attorney's fees and expenses properly associated with the foreclosure action, unless: (a) The mortgagee has accepted reinstatement after the institution of foreclosure proceedings within two years immediately preceding the commencement of the current foreclosure action, (b) reinstatement will preclude foreclosure following a subsequent default, or (c) reinstatement will adversely affect the priority of the mortgage lien.

24 CFR § 203.608. In addition, the regulations generally require the mortgagee to meet with the mortgagor in person before acceleration and authorize the mortgagee to enter into special forbearance agreements with the mortgagor. See 24 CFR §§ 203.604–203.614. Does the reinstatement regulation deal adequately with potential abuse by the mortgagor?

7. *Uniform Commercial Code § 1–309.* Mortgagors occasionally use Uniform Commercial Code § 1–309 in an attempt to defeat acceleration. Section 1–309 provides that a "term providing that one party or that party's successor in interest may accelerate payment or performance * * * 'at will' or when the party 'deems itself insecure', or words of similar import, means that the party has power to do so only if that party in good faith believes that the prospect of payment or performance is impaired." Thus, if a mortgage note authorizes a mortgagee to accelerate "at will" or when it deems itself "insecure" and acceleration is based on that language, the mortgagee is

governed by the good faith requirement. See e.g., Jackson v. State Bank of Wapello, 488 N.W.2d 151 (Iowa 1992).

However, mortgage notes rarely include "at will" or "insecurity" language and, even if they do, actual acceleration is almost always based on specific mortgagor defaults, such as failure to pay the debt, real estate taxes, or insurance premiums. Nevertheless, a few courts have applied the good faith requirement to accelerations based on those types of specific defaults. Some courts have even done so when the mortgage note apparently did not include an "at will" or "insecurity" provision. See Brown v. AVEMCO Inv. Corp., 603 F.2d 1367 (9th Cir.1979); Williamson v. Wanlass, 545 P.2d 1145 (Utah 1976). However, most courts interpret § 1–309 literally, rather than expansively, and hold that it cannot be used to defeat acceleration when the mortgagor actually has defaulted. See e.g., Greenberg v. Service Business Forms Indus., Inc., 882 F.2d 1538 (10th Cir.1989); Bowen v. Danna, 276 Ark. 528, 637 S.W.2d 560 (1982); Ben Franklin Fin. Corp. v. Davis, 226 Ill.App.3d 414, 168 Ill.Dec. 457, 589 N.E.2d 857 (1992); Don Anderson Enters., Inc. v. Entertainment Enters., Inc., 589 S.W.2d 70 (Mo.App.1979). See generally, Nelson, Whitman, Burkhart & Freyermuth, Real Estate Finance Law § 7.7 (6th ed. 2014).

8. *Bankruptcy Code.* Suppose a mortgagee accelerates the debt and the mortgagor does not have a statutory or contractual right to defeat acceleration by a pre-foreclosure tender of arrearages. If the mortgagor files a Chapter 13 bankruptcy proceeding before foreclosure, the bankruptcy court has ample authority to permit the mortgagor to reinstate the mortgage by paying the arrearages. See Section J of this Chapter, infra.

9. *Fannie Mae/Freddie Mac mortgage form language.* The Fannie Mae/Freddie Mac standard residential mortgage or deed of trust form contains important limitations on the acceleration process. It requires the mortgagee to give the mortgagor a detailed mailed notice and a thirty-day grace period before acceleration, and it permits the mortgagor to defeat acceleration until five days before foreclosure by paying the arrearages and the mortgagee's reasonable costs and attorney's fees. See Appendix A, Form 2, ¶ 19 and Forms 3 and 4, ¶ 22. Compare the California arrearages statute at Note 6 supra. These provisions may be omitted from the Fannie Mae/Freddie Mac form only if state law is more protective of the mortgagor. Because most institutional lenders want the option of selling their home mortgages to these two secondary market purchasers, the Fannie Mae/Freddie Mac form is very widely used. Therefore, even in states that do not statutorily regulate acceleration, vast numbers of mortgagors have substantial protection against abuse of the acceleration process.

10. *Absence of acceleration clause.* Suppose that the note and mortgage do not include an acceleration clause or that the clause is unenforceable for some reason. If the mortgagor defaults on its payment obligation, courts occasionally permit acceleration based on the contract concept of anticipatory repudiation. See Barnett v. Oliver, 18 Kan.App.2d 672, 858 P.2d 1228 (1993)

(trial court did not abuse its equitable discretion by accelerating balance in absence of acceleration clause). However, in the absence of an enforceable acceleration clause, the mortgagee normally can foreclose only for the installment in default. When this occurs, what does the foreclosure purchaser get? How much should he or she pay? What happens to the surplus, if any? See Nelson, Whitman, Burkhart & Freyermuth, Real Estate Finance Law § 7.8 (6th ed. 2014). Some jurisdictions address these issues statutorily. See e.g., Minn.Stat.Ann. § 580.09; West's Ann.Cal.Code Civ.Proc. § 728; Golden v. Ramapo Imp. Corp., 78 A.D.2d 648, 432 N.Y.S.2d 238 (1980) (interpreting New York statute).

2. MARSHALING

If a mortgage covers more than one parcel of land, should the mortgagee sell them together or separately at a foreclosure sale? If the mortgagee should sell them separately, which parcel should be sold first? These questions are particularly important if some parcels are encumbered by junior liens or other subordinate interests, while others are not. Naturally, the junior interest holders would like the mortgagee to foreclose first on the parcels without junior interests, because those foreclosures may generate enough money to satisfy the mortgagor's outstanding debt and thereby extinguish the mortgage on the other parcels.

Marshaling is an equitable doctrine that may dictate the order in which a mortgagee must foreclose. The first rule of marshaling, called the "two funds" rule, represents an attempt, where possible, to avoid the unnecessary elimination of junior interests. The term "two funds" is a bit misleading; it is more accurate to say that are two items of collateral. In the following case, the two items are (1) the surface estate in certain parcels of land and (2) the mineral estate in the same parcels.

MATTER OF ESTATE OF HANSEN
Supreme Court of North Dakota, 1990
458 N.W.2d 264

MESCHKE, JUSTICE.

* * *

In February 1975, Albert Hansen borrowed $53,000 from the Bank of North Dakota [BND] and, to secure the debt, mortgaged 1,040 acres of property in McKenzie County. The mortgage covered both the surface and minerals. In July 1981, Albert and Dianna Hansen gave the State Bank of Towner [SBT] a $200,000 promissory note in settlement of pending legal actions. See State Bank of Towner v. Hansen, 302 N.W.2d 760 (N.D.1981). To secure this debt, the Hansens gave SBT a second mortgage on the surface of the property earlier mortgaged to BND. The SBT mortgage expressly provided that the minerals "shall not be subject to this mortgage." The Hansens defaulted on the debt to SBT in November 1984. [Subsequently, Hansen also defaulted to BND. Albert Hansen died, and Dianna Hansen appears here representing his estate.—Eds]

* * *

BND began foreclosure of its mortgage in August 1988 when Hansen was indebted to it for more than $70,000. The BND mortgage covered both the minerals and the surface of the Hansen property. In its answer to the BND complaint, SBT requested that BND marshal its security under NDCC 13–01–04 and 35–01–15 and sell the minerals first at the foreclosure sale because SBT's junior mortgage covered only the surface. Hansen answered and requested that the surface be sold first in seven separate parcels and that the minerals be sold second in the same sequence. BND objected and argued that the minerals could not be sold separately from the surface.

The trial court ruled that the minerals could be sold separately from the surface and ordered that the minerals be sold before the surface, but in separate parcels and in the sequence designated by Hansen. At the foreclosure sale on April 28, 1989, the minerals were sold to Williams, Walter F. Gehrts, Kenneth Henry, and Raymond Sharkey for a total of $74,680. Because that amount equaled the foreclosure judgment, BND was not aggrieved and did not appeal. Hansen appealed, however, urging that the trial court erred in ordering the minerals sold before the surface. * * *

[W]e conclude that the trial court properly marshaled the mortgaged property for the protection of SBT as a junior lienholder in this case.

The rules for marshaling mortgaged property to pay distinct debts are codified in this state. NDCC 13–01–04 sets forth the basic principle:

> Marshaling funds—Rights of creditors. When a creditor is entitled to resort to each of several funds for the satisfaction of his claim and another person has an interest in, or is entitled as a creditor to resort to, some but not all of them, the latter may require the former to seek satisfaction from those funds to which the latter has no such claim so far as it can be done without impairing the right of the former to complete satisfaction and without doing injustice to third persons.

The pertinent part of NDCC 35–01–15 is to the same effect:

> Order of resort for payment—Marshaling securities. When a person has a lien upon several things and other persons have subordinate liens upon or interests in some but not all of the same things, the person having the prior lien, if he can do so without the risk of loss to himself or of injustice to other persons,

on the demand of any party interested, must resort to the property in the following order:

     1.   To the things upon which he has an exclusive lien.

These enactments codify the long-recognized equitable duty owed by a senior lienholder to a junior lienholder. See Aberle v. Merkel, 70 N.D. 89, 291 N.W. 913, 918 (1940); Union Nat'l Bank v. Milburn & Stoddard Co., 7 N.D. 201, 73 N.W. 527 Syllabus 4 (1897). The principle applies here.

Assuming that sale of the minerals separately from the surface was correct, these marshaling statutes entitled SBT to have the minerals, on which it had no lien, sold before the surface if it could be done without risk of loss to BND or injustice to Hansen. Hansen and SBT agreed that the surface and minerals should be sold separately and do not challenge this part of the decision on appeal.

The trial court partially granted Hansen's request as to the sequence of the sale of the parcels but, contrary to her request, ordered that the minerals be sold before the surface. Hansen asserts that this violated her right to designate the sequence of sale of the parcels authorized by 1987 N.D.Sess.Laws Ch. 194 and NDCC 28–23–07. See Footnote 1, supra. Section 5 of 1987 N.D.Sess. Laws Ch. 194 said that "[a]t the foreclosure sale, or in writing at least ten days prior to sale, the debtor may direct the division of the property into known lots or parcels and may direct the order in which the lots or parcels and the remaining property, or other property may be sold, as provided by section 28–23–07." NDCC 28–23–07 says that the "debtor, if present at the sale, may direct the order in which property, real or personal, shall be sold, when such property consists of several known lots or parcels or of articles which can be sold to advantage separately, and the sheriff or other officer must follow such directions."

These two statutory rights of the debtor to designate the sequence of sale "of known lots or parcels" do not differ substantially. See Production Credit Ass'n v. Henderson, 429 N.W.2d 421, 425 (N.D.1988). The purpose of these laws is "to give the [debtor] an opportunity to redeem from any, or all parcels or lots, to sell only so much of the property as is necessary to pay the debt, and to get the highest possible price for the land sold." Figenskau v. Wiege, 56 N.D. 768, 219 N.W. 471, 472 (1928). They are also intended to assist a debtor in protecting homestead rights. See First Security Bank, Underwood, N.D. v. Enyart, 439 N.W.2d 801, 806–807 (N.D.1989). Absent any other rights, these provisions authorized Hansen to direct that the surface be sold before the minerals if it could be sold to advantage separately.

Neither Hansen nor SBT has cited any precedent assessing the interplay between a marshaling statute and a like manner-of-sale statute, and we have not discovered any. However, "when two statutes relating to the same subject matter appear to be in conflict, they should, whenever possible, be construed to give effect to both if such can be done without doing violence to either." O'Fallon v. Pollard, 427 N.W.2d 809, 811 (N.D.1988); NDCC 1–02–07. Inconsistent statutes should be construed, if possible, to give effect to both.

This court has indicated that the manner-of-sale statute is not paramount in all events. In Michael v. Grady, 52 N.D. 740, 204 N.W. 182, 184 (1925), the court said that not every sale where property consisting of several known lots or parcels is sold en masse is subject to attack, "particularly in those cases where the several parcels are first offered separately but no bids are received thereon." Likewise we do not believe the Legislature intended that the debtor's right to designate the sequence of sale of parcels invariably overrides and defeats a junior lienholder's right to invoke equitable principles of marshaling.

The marshaling statutes and the manner-of-sale statutes are both designed to achieve equitable results for their intended beneficiaries. Where there exists more than one lien on the property, the trial court should balance the competing equities of the junior lienholder and of the debtor in settling the sequence of sale of parcels. We believe this approach harmonizes these provisions.

The trial court in this case properly weighed the equities in directing that the minerals be sold before the surface, in separate parcels and in the sequence requested by Hansen. Hansen was not injured by sale of the minerals first to pay the debt inasmuch as both the surface and minerals secured the BND mortgage. Hansen's attempt to free the minerals from the BND mortgage and make the junior lienholder, SBT, entirely subordinate to the BND debt would have placed SBT in a position nearly comparable to an unsecured creditor.

We are aware of statements in Douglas County State Bank v. Steele, 54 N.D. 686, 210 N.W. 657, 659 (1926), to the effect that, under the marshaling statutes, a homestead claimant could require a senior lienholder "to resort first to the nonhomestead quarter, even though to have done so would have wholly defeated the rights of the junior lienholder upon that quarter." However, Hansen's assertion that her homestead rights were violated is unpersuasive. In this case, we agree with the trial court that Hansen's homestead rights were adequately protected. Because the sale of minerals satisfied the BND mortgage, the surface was not sold and no redemption from the BND foreclosure was required for the mortgagors to retain the surface of the homestead parcel. Having requested a separate sale of the minerals, Hansen cannot object to the separate sale of the homestead minerals. Hansen did not request that the homestead minerals and the homestead surface be the very last parcels sold to satisfy the debt. * * * We conclude that the trial court's directions for the sequence of sale fairly balanced SBT's right to require marshaling and Hansen's right to specify the sequence of sale.

We therefore affirm the trial court's orders directing the sequence of sale and confirming the sheriff's sale.

NOTE: THE INVERSE ORDER OF ALIENATION RULE

The form of marshaling involved in *Hansen* is the "two funds" rule. See Nelson, Whitman, Burkhart & Freyermuth, Real Estate Finance Law § 10.9 (6th ed. 2014). Courts often apply another form of marshaling when an owner gives a mortgage on real estate and then sells a portion of that real estate. For example, suppose that mortgagor borrows money and gives a "blanket" mortgage on her land, which consists of three residential lots. She then sold parcel 1 to A; later, she sold parcel 2 to B. She retained parcel 3. Neither A nor B assumed the mortgage. Based on the mortgagor's promise to make the full payment on the mortgage debt, A and B both paid the full fair market value for their parcels, with no credit to the price for any part of the mortgage debt.

Is this a wise transaction for A or B? They have purchased land subject to a mortgage, but with no direct control of the payments due under it. If the mortgagor defaults, they may not even learn about the default until the foreclosure process is set in motion. Moreover, if A and B wish to redeem, they must pay the entire outstanding debt if the mortgagee has accelerated, which could be a great hardship or impossible for them. Most observers would conclude that, unless the mortgagor is exceptionally creditworthy and reliable, A and B have entered into a very risky transaction. Nevertheless, people sometimes agree to this arrangement. Can you see a safer way to structure it, assuming that the mortgagee will cooperate?

If the mortgagor defaults on the mortgage debt, in what order should the mortgagee foreclose on the three parcels?

> The traditional rule or doctrine of inverse order of alienation provides that where a portion of lands subject to a lien has been alienated, the grantees may insist that the land retained by the grantor or original owner be sold first to satisfy the lien * * * and that where the original owner has alienated all of the land subject to the lien in separate parcels successively, the parcels alienated or encumbered be sold in the reverse order of alienation. * * *

> The reason for this rule is that if the last parcel had been retained by the grantor, it would have been liable first to satisfy the judgment lien. * * * The purchaser of the parcel last alienated, who had notice of the prior alienation of other parcels encumbered by the judgment liens, "sits in the seat" of the common grantor, and has precisely the same rights and incurs the same obligations as the common grantor. Therefore, that purchaser's property must be sold first in order to satisfy the judgment lien.

Commonwealth Land Title Co. v. Kornbluth, 175 Cal.App.3d 518, 220 Cal.Rptr. 774 (1985). Under this reasoning, which is widely (but not universally) followed, the mortgagee must foreclose first on parcel 3, because the mortgagor still owns it. If this foreclosure does not produce sufficient funds to pay the mortgage debt in full, the mortgagee must foreclose next on B's parcel. If the debt is still unsatisfied, the mortgagee can foreclose on A's parcel.

Why does the grantor have to suffer foreclosure first? And why, as between the two grantees, should B suffer before A? Is this latter result harder to rationalize than the notion that the mortgagee should first foreclose on the mortgagor's land? Finally, do you see why a court will not protect A from immediate foreclosure if A assumed the entire debt or received credit for it against the purchase price for parcel 1?

Should the mortgagee be legally required to foreclose on B before A only if B had knowledge of A's position before buying parcel 2? Courts uniformly agree that B's knowledge is a prerequisite to marshaling. But how will B learn about A's position? The mortgagor obviously does not want to tell B, because doing so may discourage B from buying the land. If A's deed is recorded, should B be held to have constructive notice? The court in Commonwealth Land Title Co. v. Kornbluth, supra, commented: "The notice required is actual notice or notice presumed from circumstances and not constructive notice arising from recordation."

Why should this be the rule? If B does an ordinary title examination, B will discover the mortgage. Additionally, it will be obvious to B's title examiner that the mortgage covers more land than B is buying. Is it too much to ask that the title examiner make a further check of the records to determine whether the mortgagor has already transferred some of the mortgaged real estate to a person like A? Or does that assume that the title examiner will understand the doctrine of marshaling—not exactly a simple concept for anyone?

While we have described the "inverse order of alienation" rule with respect to deeds from the mortgagor to A and B, the same principle applies when the mortgagor executes a blanket first mortgage on parcels 1 and 2, then gives A a second mortgage on parcel 1, and then later gives B a second mortgage on parcel 2. In this situation, the "two funds" rule does not apply to A and B, because parcels 1 and 2 are both encumbered by the blanket first mortgage and by either A's or B's second mortgage. But the "inverse order" rule requires the first mortgagee to foreclose on parcel 2 before foreclosing on parcel 1. See In re Shull, 72 B.R. 193 (Bankr.D.S.C.1986).

The Restatement (Third) of Property (Mortgages) § 8.6 (1997) endorses both the "two funds" rule and the "inverse order of alienation" rule. The Restatement notes that a court should order marshaling only if it would benefit the holders of subordinate interests. For example, a court should not require marshaling when the total value of the parcels is less than the outstanding mortgage debt. Because the mortgagee will have to foreclose on all the parcels, the order of the foreclosures makes little difference to the junior lienholders. See Restatement § 8.6 cmt. d.

Putting marshaling aside for a moment, consider the foreclosure of a single mortgage that covers two or more parcels. Who should decide whether the mortgagee can sell them together ("in bulk") or separately? If the mortgagee will sell them separately, who should decide the order of sale? We consider this issue in Section D of this Chapter.

B. MISCELLANEOUS FORECLOSURE METHODS

As mentioned previously, two major methods of mortgage foreclosure are in use in the United States. The most pervasive method is judicial foreclosure in equity accompanied by a judicial sale. This type of foreclosure is available in every state and, in many states, is the only type of foreclosure permitted. In over half the states, the prevailing method is a non-judicial foreclosure under a power of sale. Depending on the state, the "power of sale" in a mortgage is vested in the mortgagee or in a public official, such as the sheriff or the "public trustee" in Colorado. In a deed of trust, which is used in most "power of sale" states, the power of sale is in the trustee. These two predominant methods, judicial sale and power of sale, will receive considerable emphasis in this Chapter.

Several other relatively minor foreclosure methods should be mentioned, including *strict foreclosure.* Under this method, foreclosure is in court, but no foreclosure sale is held. Instead, the court gives the defaulting mortgagor a period of time to pay the mortgage debt. If the mortgagor fails to do so, title to the mortgaged property vests in the mortgagee without a sale. If the property is worth more than the mortgage debt, the mortgagor has no right to the excess. On the other hand, if the mortgaged real estate is worth less than the mortgage debt, the mortgagor is liable for the deficiency. See e.g., Eichman v. J & J Bldg. Co., Inc., 216 Conn. 443, 582 A.2d 182 (1990). This method is still in use in Vermont and in Connecticut. See e.g., Conn.Gen.Stat.Ann. § 49–15; Farmers & Mechanics Bank v. Arbucci, 24 Conn.App. 486, 589 A.2d 14 (1991); Pacific Mut. Life Ins. Co. v. Broad Assocs. Ltd. Partn., 24 Conn.App. 42, 585 A.2d 115 (1991); Vt. Stat. Ann. tit. 12, § 4941; Vt.R.Civ.P., Rule 80.1(a)–(*l*); Stowe Center, Inc. v. Burlington Sav. Bank, 141 Vt. 634, 451 A.2d 1114 (1982). On the other hand, if the mortgagor or a junior lienholder makes a strong showing that the mortgaged real estate is worth more than the mortgage debt, the court may require a foreclosure sale. See, e.g., Brann v. Savides, 48 Conn.App. 807, 712 A.2d 963 (1998) (foreclosure by sale should have been ordered because the real estate's fair market value exceeded the obligation by more than $200,000). Strict foreclosure, as we shall see, is also available in many other jurisdictions to deal with the rather limited problem of how to handle a junior lienor who has been omitted from a judicial foreclosure suit.

Some New England states permit two related foreclosure methods—*Entry Without Process* and *Actions at Law for a Writ of Entry*. Under the former method, a mortgagee may take possession of the premises without legal help after the mortgagor defaults. If the mortgagee maintains possession for a time period varying from one to three years, the mortgagor's equity of redemption terminates. The mortgagee's entry must be peace-able. Its possession can be constructive, so that the mortgagor essentially becomes the mortgagee's tenant. In the *Action at Law for a Writ of Entry,* the mortgagee initiates a judicial action and alleges that the mortgage is in default. After an accounting for what is due and owing, the court enters a judgment for possession of the premises. If the mortgagee takes and maintains possession for one to three years, depending on the jurisdiction, the mortgagor's equity of redemption terminates. Both of these methods result in strict foreclosure, because they do not require a property sale. Moreover, the mortgagee can obtain a deficiency judgment if the property is worth less than the mortgage debt. See generally, George E. Osborne, Handbook on the Law of Mortgages § 314 (1970).

Scire Facias is a type of judicial foreclosure at law and is used, for the most part, only in Delaware. It is similar to the remedy at law available to the ordinary execution creditor. After a default, the mortgagee can obtain a judicial writ of *scire facias,* which is an order for the mortgagor to show cause why the land should not be taken in execution to satisfy the defaulted mortgage obligation. If the mortgagee prevails, the court issues a judgment for the amount owing and a writ of *levari facias,* which directs that the judgment be satisfied from the proceeds of a public execution sale. See Gelof v. First Nat'l Bank of Frankford, 373 A.2d 206 (Del.Super. 1977). See also Nelson, Whitman, Burkhart & Freyermuth, Real Estate Finance Law § 7.12 n.259 (6th ed. 2014).

NOTE

Constitutionality of strict foreclosure. Does vesting title to the mortgaged property in the mortgagee without a sale create constitutional problems? Does strict foreclosure violate the Due Process and Equal Protection Clauses of the United States Constitution because the mortgagee can obtain a deficiency judgment against the mortgagor if the mortgaged property's value is less than the mortgage debt, but the mortgagor has no claim if the property's value is greater than the debt?

In Dieffenbach v. Attorney General of Vermont, 604 F.2d 187 (2d Cir.1979), the United States Court of Appeals for the Second Circuit rejected both constitutional challenges to Vermont's strict foreclosure. The court emphasized that strict foreclosure does not violate substantive due process because it is rationally related to a legitimate state interest. According to the court, "[o]ne possible purpose of strict foreclosure is to make it easier for banks or other creditors to lend by giving them a speculative interest in the property, for the bank realizes that it may retain the excess if the property's value happens to exceed the debt. Another purpose might be to compensate the bank for its expense * * * in a foreclosure suit and subsequent sale. A third possibility is that, in an implicit quid pro quo, the legislature has granted the banks this speculative interest in return for requiring the banks to lend money at lower interest rates, and to permit prepayment without penalty." Id. at 196.

The court also rejected the equal protection challenge that strict foreclosure impermissibly burdens only those mortgagors whose property is worth more than the mortgage debt. The court reasoned that the "legislature may reasonably have concluded that strict foreclosure laws equitably distribute the commercial costs of mortgages because every mortgagor * * * is equally subject to the risk that his property's value will exceed the portion of his debt that he is unable to pay. The state's failure to 'insure' against the unequal actual incidence of this risk by permitting banks to absorb the risk in their interest rates does not amount to a violation of equal protection." Id. at 197.

C. JUDICIAL FORECLOSURE

NELSON, WHITMAN, BURKHART & FREYERMUTH, REAL ESTATE FINANCE LAW
605–606 (6th ed.2014)*

Judicial foreclosure, which is an equitable action, is a major method of foreclosure in the United States. It is the exclusive or generally used foreclosure method in 30% of the states. Moreover, it is available in every state, either by express statutory enactment or as an incident to the inherent jurisdiction of courts of equity. Even in jurisdictions where power of sale foreclosure is dominant, judicial foreclosure is necessary in certain special situations, such as when the mortgage does not authorize a power of sale foreclosure. For example, if a court holds that a document in the form of a deed is actually an equitable mortgage, the deed will not contain a power of sale clause and, therefore, must be foreclosed judicially. A mortgagee also should judicially foreclose when a lien priority is disputed. In that situation, a judicial determination of lien priority will enable potential foreclosure purchasers to know the state of the title they will be bidding on. On the other hand, if the mortgagee foreclosed by power of sale, uncertainty as to lien priority would discourage bidding and create title problems for the sale purchaser. In some jurisdictions, deficiency judgments are unavailable after a power of

*   Reprinted with permission of LEG, Inc. d/b/a West Academic.

sale foreclosure. Consequently, if the mortgagee believes that the foreclosure sale will yield less than the debt and wishes to retain the option of obtaining a deficiency judgment, judicial foreclosure is mandatory.

NOTES

1. *The "necessary-proper party" distinction.* Courts frequently use the terms "necessary" and "proper" to describe parties-defendant in judicial foreclosure proceedings. Unfortunately, no unanimity exists concerning their meaning. However, the terminology is useful in the context of the basic purposes of the foreclosure proceeding. Two purposes are often articulated. First, a successful foreclosure should terminate the rights of all holders of interests that are "subject to" the mortgage being foreclosed. However, to state this proposition begs the question "why"? The answer is found in the more fundamental and descriptive purpose of foreclosure, which is to give the foreclosure sale purchaser essentially the title to the land "as it stood at the time of the time of the execution of the mortgage." Scharaga v. Schwartzberg, 149 A.D.2d 578, 540 N.Y.S.2d 451 (1989). Or, as the Restatement puts it, the purpose of foreclosure is to put "the foreclosure purchaser into the shoes of the mortgagor at the time the mortgage being foreclosed was executed." Restatement (Third) of Property (Mortgages) § 7.1 cmt. a (1997). In this sense, a party is "necessary" if failing to join it will defeat this purposes.

If a junior interest holder is not joined, "that interest is neither terminated nor otherwise prejudiced by the foreclosure." Id. cmt. b. For example, if a first mortgagee judicially forecloses and does not join the second mortgagee, the latter's mortgage remains on the land. In that case, the sale purchaser's title to the land is fundamentally different than the mortgagor's title when he executed the first mortgage. Thus, as a general rule, "necessary parties" are all persons who hold an interest in the mortgaged real estate that is junior to the mortgage being foreclosed. For a catalogue of these persons, see Nelson, Whitman, Burkhart & Freyermuth, Real Estate Finance Law § 7.13 (6th ed. 2014). We will consider a little later in this section the rights of an omitted "necessary" party.

The reason judicial foreclosure does not terminate unjoined junior interests is constitutional. Consider the language of the following Kansas decision, holding that an unjoined junior lease is not terminated by foreclosure:

> There is no logic and no order to a theory which binds a tenant and automatically terminates his or her interest in real estate by a court decision to which he or she was not a party. Indeed, our sense of due process is offended by a rule which forecloses an interest in real estate where the holder of that interest is not given an opportunity to be heard on the issue. The Kansas rule is designed to ensure that a tenant may not have his or her leasehold interest in property automatically forfeited without the due process right of a day in

court. We reject the argument that expediency and the complexities of modern society require that we abandon our present process for one which would adjudicate the property interests of non-parties to an action and bind them without having an opportunity to present their claims in court.

Citizens Bank & Trust v. Brothers Const. & Mfg., Inc., 18 Kan.App.2d 704, 859 P.2d 394, 398 (1993). Accord Como, Inc. v. Carson Square, Inc., 648 N.E.2d 1247 (Ind.App.1995).

2. *Impact of foreclosure on senior interests.* What is the status of a *senior* lien or other *senior* interest when a junior lienor forecloses? A senior lienor is not a "necessary" party because it is not subject to or subordinate to the mortgage being foreclosed. The senior lienor's interest will not be terminated or otherwise prejudiced by the junior foreclosure. To omit the senior from a foreclosure suit by the junior lienor will not defeat the purposes of foreclosure, because the senior's lien existed when the mortgagor executed the mortgage being foreclosed. Indeed, it is often said that only junior interest holders can be made parties-defendant without their consent.

On the other hand, can a senior lienor be joined, against its will, as a "proper" party? If so, to what extent will it be bound by the proceeding? Clearly, the foreclosing mortgagee can join a senior lienor for certain limited purposes. For example, a foreclosing junior lienor can join a senior lienor to determine the amount and terms of the senior lien. Do you see why this would be important from the foreclosing junior lienor's perspective? The foreclosing lienor also can join a person who claims to hold a senior lien if the foreclosing lienor claims that its lien is senior. The foreclosure proceeding can be used to determine this priority dispute.

On the other hand, will a court ever force a senior lienor to be joined for the purpose of selling the property free and clear its lien, with the sale proceeds distributed according to lien priority? Normally, the answer is no. Should the result be different if the senior lien is in default? Even in that situation, shouldn't the senior mortgagee be able to choose its own time for selling and not be forced to do so in a market that, in its judgment, is unfavorable? Only a few courts have upheld such "free and clear" foreclosures over the senior lienor's objection, even when the senior mortgage is in default. For a discussion of these problems, see Nelson, Whitman, Burkhart & Freyermuth, Real Estate Finance Law § 7.15 (6th ed. 2014); Durfee, Cases on Security §§ 203–204 (1951). For a thoughtful argument that junior lienors should normally have the power to foreclose "free and clear" of senior liens, see David Gray Carlson, Simultaneous Attachment of Liens on After-Acquired Property, 6 Cardozo L.Rev. 505, 530–34 (1985).

3. *Junior lessee as a necessary party.* The presence of lessees in a foreclosure proceeding, judicial or otherwise, presents special problems. In this connection reconsider *Dover Mobile Estates* and its accompanying note at page 380, supra. If a lease is senior to the mortgage, the lessee and lease are unaffected by foreclosure. The sale purchaser obtains the mortgagor's interest

and becomes the lessee's landlord. See Annot., Effect of Foreclosure of Mortgage as Terminating Lease, 14 A.L.R. 664. Because the foreclosure does not affect the lease, the lessee is not a "necessary" party in a judicial foreclosure proceeding. On the other hand, if the mortgage is senior to the lease, the general rule is that the foreclosure of the leased premises:

> nullifies and extinguishes the lease * * *. No contract of lease which the mortgagor may make with respect to the mortgaged premises either inures to the benefit of the mortgagee or is binding on him. There is no privity of either estate or contract between the mortgagee and the lessee of the mortgagor to bind either, and the foreclosure of the mortgage avoids the lease and releases the lessee from any obligation. The tenancy created by attornment between the mortgagor's lessee and the purchaser under the foreclosure is an entirely new tenancy, and not a continuation of the old tenancy with the substitution of a new landlord. Whenever the estate which the lessor had at the time of making the lease is defeated or determined, the lease is extinguished with it.

Roosevelt Hotel Corp. v. Williams, 227 Mo.App. 1063, 56 S.W.2d 801, 802 (1933). Accord Reilly v. Firestone Tire & Rubber Co., 764 F.2d 167 (3d Cir.1985).

If a foreclosing mortgagee does not join a junior lessee, one would assume that the lessee's interest would be unaffected by the foreclosure. Indeed, that is the majority and clearly correct rule. See e.g., Como, Inc. v. Carson Square, Inc., 648 N.E.2d 1247 (Ind.App.1995); Citizens Bank & Trust v. Brothers Const. & Mfg., Inc., 18 Kan.App.2d 704, 859 P.2d 394 (1993); Nelson, Whitman, Burkhart & Freyermuth, Real Estate Finance Law § 7.13 (6th ed. 2014). However, a few courts hold that, while most unjoined junior interests survive foreclosure, junior leases do not. One Ohio court described the rationale for this holding:

> Where interests are of a type properly determinable in foreclosure proceedings, they survive the foreclosure if not joined. Among that type are title, liens, or similar interests. Where interests are not of that type, among which are to be found the personal rights of possession and quiet enjoyment conveyed by lessor to lessee, joinder is not necessary and they are foreclosed absolutely. * * *

> We agree with the analysis * * * that the rights of possession and quiet enjoyment through the lease are personal rights; their existence derives from the lessor's title, and they are extinguished upon the foreclosure of that title and the interests incident to it.

Hembree v. Mid-America Federal Sav. & Loan Ass'n, 64 Ohio App.3d 144, 154–55, 580 N.E.2d 1103, 1109–10 (1989). See Menard, Inc. v. 1945 Cornell, LLC, 991 N.E.2d 360 (App. Ct. 2013); New York Life Ins. Co. v. Simplex Products Corp., 135 Ohio St. 501, 21 N.E.2d 585 (1939). Does this reasoning satisfy you? Don't all junior interests "derive from" the mortgagor's title?

If, as most courts hold, an omitted junior lessee's interest is unaffected by a foreclosure sale, can the foreclosing mortgagee choose whether to sell the property subject to the lease or free and clear of it? Does this rule encourage mortgagees intentionally to omit a junior lessee whose lease is substantially more pro-landlord than would be possible if negotiated under current market conditions?

The cases are divided about equally on whether the mortgagee may "pick and choose" which leases "live" or "die." See Nelson, Whitman, Burkhart & Freyermuth, Real Estate Finance Law § 7.13 (6th ed. 2014). In states that don't allow the mortgagee to "pick and choose," the courts permit an unjoined tenant to intervene in the foreclosure proceeding to get its (presumably undesirable from the tenant's viewpoint) lease wiped out.

Do the "pick and choose" states confer "a bonus on a mortgagee that violates the normal foreclosure maxim encouraging joinder of all junior interest holders"? Nelson, Whitman, Burkhart & Freyermuth, Real Estate Finance Law 612 (6th ed. 2014). On the other hand, when a junior lessee enters into a lease for a fixed term, why should the fortuity of a default in the landlord's mortgage allow him or her to escape the lease obligation? If the mortgagor-landlord had voluntarily sold the reversion, the tenant would not be relieved of most lease obligations. Why should the result be different if the mortgagor-landlord's interest is transferred through the foreclosure process?

As *Dover Mobile Estates* and its note also illustrate, mortgagor-landlords, lessees, and mortgagees commonly adjust their relationships vis á vis each other through devices such as subordination, non-disturbance, and attornment agreements. Are these devices ultimately the better approach for dealing with the "pick and choose" issue?

MURPHY V. FARWELL

Supreme Court of Wisconsin, 1859
9 Wis. 102

By the Court, PAINE, J. This case has once been in this court on a demurrer to the complainant's bill. It was a bill to redeem certain premises from a sale on the foreclosure of a first mortgage, the complainant claiming under a second mortgage which he had owned and foreclosed, buying, himself, at the sale. He was not made a party to the first foreclosure suit, nor did he make those interested in the first mortgage nor *Farwell* the purchaser under it, parties to his foreclosure suit. The demurrer was urged on the ground that by foreclosing and selling on the second mortgage the complainant had so changed his position as to have lost the right to redeem and that his bill was in the nature of an ejectment in equity. The case is reported in 2 Wis. 533, from which it appears that this court held that the complainant upon the facts set forth in the bill, had a right to redeem; and the demurrer was overruled.

The case was sent back to the circuit where various proceedings were had; including answers by the defendants; a change of venue to Racine county; the taking of testimony and preparation for final hearing; when the defendant *Farwell* having filed a petition claiming the right to redeem the premises, by paying the amount of the decree in the second foreclosure suit, interest and costs, paid the money into court, except the costs in this suit; and the court entered a decree adjudging *Farwell* to be the owner of the fee, and *Murphy* to have only the rights of a subsequent mortgagee; that *Farwell* had the right to pay off *Murphy's* lien, and ordered the bill to be dismissed on payment of the costs in this suit, within ten days after notice of their taxation. The costs were paid, and from that decree the complainant appeals to this court.

It was urged by the counsel for the appellant, on the argument that inasmuch as neither of these parties was bound by the proceedings in the foreclosure suit of the other, that the result of the two foreclosures and sales was to vest in each a perfect title to the premises, as against all the world except the other, and that all that was necessary for either to perfect his title was to pay off the amount paid by the other. That this right was mutual, neither having any superiority over the other, but both standing originally on a footing of entire equality; and this being the case, he urged that the complainant, by his greater diligence in first offering to redeem, had acquired a superior equity over *Farwell,* who had delayed through several years of litigation to make any offer or attempt to exercise the right on his part.

But the counsel for the respondent contended that these parties did not stand on an equal footing after their respective sales. But that, on the contrary, *Farwell* purchasing at the sale under the first mortgage, acquired the entire right of the owner of the first mortgage, and the entire equity of redemption, subject only to the second mortgage, while *Murphy* purchasing at the sale under the second mortgage, in a proceeding against *Cady* alone, acquired nothing by his purchase, so far as the lots covered by both mortgages were concerned, for the reason that *Cady's* interest had been entirely divested by the previous sale on the first mortgage. So that *Farwell* owning the entire property in fee, subject only to the second mortgage, and *Murphy* owning only the interest represented by the second mortgage, *Farwell* had an absolute right to pay the second mortgage and extinguish its lien, as he was allowed to do by the court below. * * *

And we must confess at the outset that the proposition of the appellant's counsel seems to us difficult to comprehend, or to be arrived at. * * *

It would seem obvious that if the sale under the first mortgage was operative at all, that it would have conveyed to *Farwell,* the purchaser, the entire equity of redemption remaining in *Cady,* who was a party to that suit. If this was done, it is difficult to see how the same equity of redemption could have been conveyed to *Murphy* at the second sale. If it did remain to be conveyed to *Murphy* at that sale, it is equally difficult to understand by what process of reasoning it could still be shown to be in *Farwell.*

If such a complex condition of things could be produced at all, it must have been from one or both of the following reasons, as no others were suggested: First, because *Murphy* was not a party to the first suit; or, secondly, because the rule of *lis pendens* applied to the sale, at which *Farwell* purchased; the second foreclosure suit being pending at that time. Let us see if either of these reasons is sufficient to produce such a result.

It seems very clear that the first is not. For if *Murphy* had not commenced his foreclosure suit until after the first sale, there can be no doubt that the entire interest remaining in *Cady* would have been transferred by that sale to *Farwell,* not only as against all the world, except *Murphy,* but as against *Murphy* himself. Of course, he not being a party, his rights would not have been affected by the proceedings. *Farwell* would have taken *Cady's* interest just as *Cady* held it, that is, subject to *Murphy's* mortgage. But he would have taken it, the whole of it, as well against *Murphy* as against *Cady* himself. And it needs hardly be said, that this is not at all inconsistent with the doctrine that a person, not a party to a proceeding is not bound by it; for it is very obvious that *Murphy's* rights would have remained quite as perfect as before, only in pursuing them he would have to pursue a different party. For a subsequent foreclosure against *Cady,* and a sale under it, would, as to the lots covered by the first mortgage, have been a mere nullity. It seems very clear, therefore, that the fact that *Murphy* was not a party to the first suit, did not prevent the entire interest of *Cady* from being transferred to *Farwell* by the sale, as well against *Murphy* as everybody else.

Would the doctrine of *lis pendens,* applied to the first sale, have produced the result contended for? It seems to us clearly not; because the entire equity of redemption being still in *Cady* at the time of commencing the second suit; then if the doctrine of *lis pendens* applied to the sale to *Farwell* in the first suit, *Murphy* at the purchase in the second suit would have taken the entire interest of *Cady,* as well against *Farwell* as against *Cady,* because such we understand to be the precise effect of the rule of *lis pendens;* that is, that a purchaser within a rule, is just as much bound by the final decree or judgment rendered, as is the party whose right he purchases. And he cannot by such a purchase prevent the one pursuing the property by litigation from obtaining his judgment or decree with the same effect it would have had if no such purchase had been made.

* * * To apply the rule here, would be to say that after a first mortgagee has begun his foreclosure, and obtained his decree of sale, that a second mortgagee, by beginning his suit, arrests the proceedings of the first, or subjects him to the disability of being bound, or having a purchaser at his sale, bound by a judgment in a suit to which they are neither parties. It is plain that the reason of the rule does not exist here, and that to apply it, would be to subject a prior and a paramount right to an unjust and oppressive disability. * * *

What, then, were the rights of these purchasers? *Farwell* acquired the interest of all the parties to the first suit, including the interest represented by the first mortgage, and the equity of redemption subject only to the second mortgage. *Murphy* having proceeded in his suit against *Cady* alone, could by a sale, after *Cady's* entire interest had been divested by the first sale, only have acquired the interest represented by the second mortgage, so far as the two lots covered by the first were concerned. *Farwell* then, as owner of the fee, subject to the second mortgage, had the right to pay it, as he was permitted to do by the court below.

It has been urged upon us that this conclusion is contrary to the former decision of the court in this case, and that the decision settled the whole matter now presented, so that it is *res adjudicata*. We have examined it very carefully, and are unable to perceive that it had any such effect. A judgment makes only that which was in issue, *res adjudicata*. What was in issue in this suit when it was then before this court? There was a demurrer to the bill, which was urged principally for the reason that the sale to *Murphy* had so changed his rights, as to deprive him of the right to redeem. If he had the right still, of course the demurrer would have to be overruled. The court held that he had, and the demurrer was overruled, as, undoubtedly, it ought to have been. That decision, therefore, made it *res adjudicata,* that the bill was not without equity, and that *Murphy* had the right to redeem. But whether he had all the rights that he may have supposed he had, whether the effect of allowing him to redeem would have been all that he or his counsel may have thought as indicated by the bill, was not settled, because not in issue. * * *

They say, also, though it was not strictly presented by the issue, that *Farwell* had a right to redeem from the complainant. But whether the position of one was in any respect superior to that of the other; whether *Farwell* would have the right to do as he has since done, and pay off the amount of *Murphy's* mortgage, notwithstanding the latter had first filed his bill to redeem, neither of these things did they decide, because neither of them was presented. They are presented to us by this appeal, and we have determined them as already stated, as we deem it, not at all in conflict with the former decision of the court.

The judgment of the court below must be affirmed.

NELSON, WHITMAN, BURKHART & FREYERMUTH, REAL ESTATE FINANCE LAW
612–15 (6th ed.2014)*

The general rule is that lack of knowledge or notice of a subordinate interest in the mortgaged land does not excuse a foreclosing mortgagee from joining the holder of that interest to the suit. If the mortgagee does not join the subordinate interest holder, its interest, whether it is legal or equitable and whether it is an ownership interest or a lien, is not subject to the foreclosure decree. However, some exceptions exist. A foreclosure sale purchaser who pays value for the legal title without notice of the unjoined interest qualifies as a bona fide purchaser and takes free of that interest if it is only an equitable interest. Similarly, under a typical recording statute, a foreclosure sale purchaser who buys without knowledge or notice of an outstanding but unrecorded interest may take free and clear of it just as effectively as if its holder had been joined in the foreclosure action. Some courts have held that even the foreclosing mortgagee can qualify as a bona fide purchaser, though contrary authority exists. Some statutes, either explicitly or as interpreted, go further and terminate the unrecorded interest of an unjoined party as effectively as if he had been joined. Under the most extreme of these statutes, the foreclosure terminates the unrecorded interest though the mortgagee had actual knowledge of it when he began the foreclosure action. Protecting the foreclosing mortgagee and the foreclosure purchaser against unrecorded interests is very appropriate when they had no actual notice of the interest before suit or actual knowledge during the pendency of the litigation.

While the bona fide purchaser rule and the recording statutes aid the foreclosing mortgagee, the lis pendens doctrine also substantially serves his interests. That doctrine applies when a grantee acquires an interest in real estate that is the subject of a judicial action, such as a judicial foreclosure. If the property is within the court's jurisdiction and is specifically described, any grantee takes subject to the outcome of the judicial action, though she is not a party to it and had no actual knowledge of either the suit or the claim under litigation. Courts in some cases have erroneously failed to differentiate the lis pendens doctrine from situations in which the grantee had actual notice of the plaintiff's rights. Actual notice binds a grantee whether or not litigation is pending. Lis pendens also is different than the principle of privity of title, which applies to grantees after a judgment against a grantor, and the rule that property in judicial custody cannot be transferred in derogation of the

---

*   Reprinted with permission of LEG, Inc. d/b/a West Academic.

court's later order. Courts frequently describe the doctrine as resting on constructive notice, but its true basis is public policy. Lis pendens protects the court's jurisdiction. In the absence of lis pendens, a property owner could defeat the court's jurisdiction by transferring the property to a third party, which would force the plaintiff to commence a new action against the transferee.

However, the lis pendens doctrine can impose a hardship on innocent property purchasers who, as a practical matter, cannot discover the pending litigation concerning the property. Therefore, many states have enacted statutes that apply the lis pendens doctrine against third parties only if the plaintiff has filed a notice of the pendency of its suit ("lis pendens notice"). Nevertheless, even in those states, the doctrine can still create a trap for unwary purchasers who rely solely on a search for a lis pendens notice. Few of the statutes preempt the entire common law doctrine. As a result, it can still apply in many situations.

Even when the statute applies, the scope of its coverage can be problematic. The recorded lis pendens notice clearly binds subsequent mortgagees and grantees of the property, but what is its effect on prior unrecorded mortgages and other conveyances? If a foreclosing mortgagee has actual knowledge of an unrecorded mortgage when filing the lis pendens notice, the holder of the unrecorded mortgage will not be bound by the foreclosure proceeding unless joined to it. If the foreclosing mortgagee leans of the unrecorded mortgage after recording the notice but before judgment, at least one court has held that he must join the holder of the unrecorded mortgage. However, several other courts have held that the latter merely has a right to intervene and will be bound by the judgment if she fails to do so.

NOTE: OMITTED PARTY PROBLEM

When any party that has the right to redeem is omitted from a foreclosure action, his or her interest is not terminated by that action. So far as the omitted party is concerned, the foreclosure is void and his or her right of redemption is the same as before the foreclosure. The foreclosure sale purchaser acquires the foreclosing mortgagee's rights and the rights of all junior interest holders who were joined in the foreclosure.

Rights of omitted owner. If the omitted party is the property owner, she retains her title, but the foreclosure purchaser now owns the mortgage and may re-foreclose it against the omitted owner. See English v. Bankers Trust Co. of Cal., N.A., 895 So.2d 1120 (Fla.App.2005). The omitted owner may avoid foreclosure by exercising her equity of redemption and paying the mortgage debt to the foreclosure sale purchaser. See Pinto v. EMC Mortg. Corp., 700 So.2d 91 (Fla.App.1997). When the omitted owner redeems, she redeems the title to the land and, in doing so, cuts off the foreclosure sale purchaser's interest in the land. The foreclosure sale purchaser has no further right to redeem from or pay off the owner-mortgagor.

Rights of omitted lienor. If the omitted party is a junior lienor, the situation becomes more complicated. Like the owner, the junior lienor has an equitable right to redeem. When he is omitted from the foreclosure, his lien and his equity of redemption are unaffected.

Why would it be unfair to terminate the junior lien when the lienor was not joined to the foreclosure action? After all, a judicially supervised sale has occurred, and, in the great majority of cases, the high bid does not exceed the amount of the foreclosed mortgage. If the high bid was no more than the amount of the foreclosed lien, is the bid amount adequate proof that the property's value was insufficient to cover the amount owing to the junior and that the junior must and should go away empty-handed?

No. Although a sale occurred, the junior was not a participant. The junior did not have an opportunity to bid for the property or to try to find other bidders to maximize the sale price. It is well known that, in most foreclosure sales, the bidding is scarcely spirited. The foreclosing senior lienor often is the only bidder. Of course, it is possible that even if the junior had been a party and present at the sale, no amount of effort on his part would have generated a higher bid. But this fact cannot be established by speculation. Instead, the junior lienor is entitled to a process that will duplicate, as much as possible, his right to have the value of the property tested at a sale *in which he is a participant.*

How can this result be achieved? Courts have granted two principal remedies to omitted junior lienors—foreclosure and redemption. See Abdoney v. York, 903 So.2d 981 (Fla.App.2005). The first remedy is the junior foreclosing his lien, subject to the first mortgage, which is "revived" for this purpose. Courts sometimes say that, with respect to the junior lienor, the original foreclosure sale never occurred. At the senior foreclosure sale, the buyer acquired both the mortgagor's and senior mortgagee's rights. If the junior subsequently forecloses his lien, the sale will convey the original mortgagor's interest to the buyer at the second sale, but the buyer at the original sale retains the original mortgagee's interest, which is revived for this purpose. For an excellent example of an omitted junior's foreclosure, see Pease Co. v. Huntington Nat'l Bank, 24 Ohio App.3d 227, 495 N.E.2d 45 (1985).

It is entirely possible that no one will bid for the property under these conditions. If the property's value is less than the senior lien amount, this should always be true. But even if no one bids, the junior lienor has had an opportunity to prove whether the property is worth more than the senior lien amount.

The amount of the "revived" first lien is the balance that was owed before the first foreclosure sale, which may be more or less than the foreclosure purchaser paid. If it is more, the purchaser at the first foreclosure sale gets a windfall when the debt secured by the first mortgage is paid. This is not improper, because the sale purchaser would have gotten the same windfall if she had been allowed to keep the property and sell it. On the other hand, if the purchaser paid more than the senior lien amount, the second foreclosure sale will deprive her of title to the property and replace it with a lien for a smaller amount. This could be a serious detriment to the original purchaser and may discourage foreclosure sale bidders from bidding more than the amount of the lien being foreclosed. Arguably, this detriment is a reasonable penalty to impose on the purchaser for failing to discover the junior lienor's omission before bidding at the first foreclosure sale. However, this argument is premised on the incorrect assumption that a careful search of the public records will always reveal the junior lien. For example, the junior lien may be a mechanic's lien that was unrecorded at the time of the senior foreclosure sale but that subsequently was recorded and related back to a time before the sale.

The omitted junior lienor's other principal remedy is redemption. See e.g., United States Dept. of Hous. & Urban Dev. v. Union Mortg. Co., Inc., 661 A.2d 163 (Me.1995); Diamond Benefits Life Ins. Co. v. Troll, 66 Cal.App.4th 1, 77 Cal.Rptr.2d 581 (1998); Kuehl v. Eckhart, 608 N.W.2d 475 (Iowa 2000); Western Bank, Santa Fe v. Fluid Assets Dev. Corp., 111 N.M. 458, 806 P.2d 1048 (1991). Davis v. Cole, 193 Misc.2d 380, 747 N.Y.S.2d 722 (Sup.2002). The junior lienor may tender to the buyer at the senior foreclosure sale—in her capacity as the holder of the revived senior lien—the balance that was owed on the senior lien at the time of foreclosure. If the junior exercises this equity of redemption, he acquires the revived senior lien. As the holder of the senior and junior liens, he may foreclose either or both of them. Unlike the case in which an omitted *owner* redeems, the term "redemption" here does not refer to the vesting of the property title in the junior, but merely to the junior's power to acquire the senior lien. Sometimes it is said that, by tendering payment of the balance owing on the senior lien, the junior becomes subrogated to the senior mortgagee's rights—rights which have now, by the first sale, been vested in the sale purchaser.

Exercising the equity of redemption requires the omitted junior to come up with a substantial amount of money, and he cannot use the property itself as security to borrow the money. For this reason, omitted junior lienors do not commonly exercise the equity of redemption, and it certainly imposes a burden on a junior lienor that would not have existed if he had been named as a party to the original foreclosure action.

A third remedy is available to the omitted junior lienor, though it is seldom useable in practice. In some jurisdictions, if the foreclosure sale of the senior lien produced a surplus and if that surplus is still identifiable in the hands of the original mortgagor or of a lienor who is subordinate to the omitted junior, the junior can assert a lien on the surplus funds. Obviously, cases in which these circumstances exist are very rare indeed.

Rights of foreclosure purchaser. Let us now turn to the methods that are available to the purchaser at the senior sale to protect her interests if an omitted junior lienor forecloses or exercises the equity of redemption, as described above. The purchaser may have three options—the equity of redemption, re-foreclosure, and, in some states, strict foreclosure. Let us look first at redemption. If the omitted junior has not taken any action, the senior sale purchaser may pay off the junior lien and thereby clear the property title. As we noted earlier, the senior foreclosure purchaser succeeds not only to the rights of the senior mortgagee, but also to the rights of the foreclosed mortgagor. Because the mortgagor had the right to pay off the junior lien, the senior foreclosure purchaser has the same right, until the junior lienor forecloses his lien. Whether this is an attractive alternative to the senior purchaser obviously depends on how large the junior lien is. If the senior purchaser doubts that the property is worth the additional investment, she may be well-advised to allow the junior to foreclose, because she will still have a first mortgage on the property in the amount of the original senior lien.

Even if the junior lienor redeems the senior debt from the original sale purchaser, the parties' position is not significantly changed. The senior purchaser can simply pay off the senior lien in the junior's hands, using the very dollars that the junior paid the purchaser when the junior redeemed. The senior foreclosure purchaser's redemption has priority because the purchaser stands in the shoes of the foreclosed mortgagor. When an owner exercises her equity of redemption, the lienor's debt has been paid off and he no longer has an interest in the land. His only right is to be paid. Thus, the transaction is a wash. If the senior purchaser is willing to pay enough money out of her own pocket, she can also pay off the junior lien. Therefore, the senior sale purchaser can easily nullify an omitted junior lienor's redemption. If the senior purchaser does not wish to take the next step and pay off the junior lien as well, the omitted junior lienor still has the power to compel a test of the property's value in his own foreclosure sale.

An alternative route that the senior sale purchaser may take is to re-foreclose the first mortgage. See e.g., Ordones v. American Interstate Ins. Co., 950 So.2d 427 (Fla.App.2006); United States Dept. of Hous. & Urban Dev. v. Union Mortg. Co., Inc., 661 A.2d 163 (Me.1995); Western Bank, Santa Fe v. Fluid Assets Dev. Corp., 111 N.M. 458, 806 P.2d 1048 (1991); Ahern v. Pierce, 236 A.D.2d 343, 653 N.Y.S.2d 620 (1997); First Fed. Sav. & Loan Ass'n v. Nath, 839 P.2d 1336 (Okla.1992); U.S. Bank of Washington v. Hursey, 116 Wash.2d 522, 806 P.2d 245 (1991). This time, we may be sure that the senior sale purchaser will not omit the junior lienor. The purchaser takes this action in her capacity as the senior mortgagee. The junior can participate in the sale and thus has the right that he was denied when the senior mortgagee originally foreclosed. The proceeds of the sale will be used to pay off both liens in the order of their priority, with any additional surplus going to the re-foreclosing party in her capacity as the property owner.

However, if the original sale purchaser re-forecloses the first mortgage and if the successful bid at the second sale does not produce a surplus above the total of both liens, the original sale purchaser stands to lose any amount she bid at the first sale in excess of the balance owing on the senior lien. She should have the right to sue the original mortgagor for the loss, but such a right is not well-established. In any event, we may well imagine that it is not worth much as a practical matter in most cases.

The third method that may be available to the senior sale purchaser to deal with an omitted junior lienor is usually termed "strict foreclosure." In substance, it is a judicial decree that the junior lien will be canceled unless the junior pays off the senior debt within a court-specified time period. It is not available in all jurisdictions.

CITICORP MORTGAGE INC. v. PESSIN

Superior Court of New Jersey, Appellate Division, 1990
238 N.J.Super. 606, 570 A.2d 481

Before JUDGES PETRELLA, O'BRIEN and STERN.

The opinion of the court was delivered by

PETRELLA, P.J.A.D.

The issue in this case revolves around the effect of the failure of the first mortgagee to name the assignees of a second mortgagee in a foreclosure action. Citicorp Mortgage, Inc. (Citicorp) foreclosed on its first mortgage and thereafter brought a strict foreclosure action to cut off the rights of all lienholders who had not been joined in the original foreclosure action. Citicorp had been the successful bidder at the sheriff's sale which followed the first foreclosure. The Chancery Division Judge concluded that despite the fact there had been an omission to join the assignee of the second mortgage, he had to balance the rights acquired by the purchaser under the foreclosure action against those of the omitted party. He fashioned an equitable remedy and allowed the junior encumbrancer the opportunity to pay off the senior mortgage indebtedness to preclude strict foreclosure.

L. Steven Pessin, one of the assignees, appeals and argues that Citicorp, as purchaser of the property, was not entitled to equitable relief, that strict foreclosure here would violate the recording act and that strict foreclosure should not have been granted.

The property which is the subject of this action is located in Piscataway Township. It was owned by Glen A. Holcombe, Sr. who executed a first bond and mortgage to Citicorp for $123,700 on November 10, 1986. On the same date Holcombe executed a second mortgage to Rudy Grillo, Sr. in the amount of $19,000. Both mortgages were recorded on November 25, 1986. The second mortgage was expressly subordinate to that of Citicorp. * * * By assignment of mortgage dated September 18, 1987 Grillo assigned his mortgage to Theresa Klein, Richard Hollander and Pessin in consideration of payment of $10,500. * * * The assignment was recorded in the Middlesex County Clerk's office on October 16, 1987.

Three days later, on October 19, 1987, Citicorp filed a foreclosure action by a complaint dated October 13, 1987 which named the Holcombes and Grillo as defendants. Since the complaint was dated October 13, 1987, but not filed until October 19, the assignment to Pessin, which was recorded on October 16, 1987, was not only omitted from the complaint but could not have been discovered as of the date indicated that the complaint was signed. Cf. Gutermuth v. Ropiecki, 159 N.J.Super. 139, 148, 387 A.2d 385 (Ch.Div.1977). A notice of lis pendens was filed on November 6, 1987 under the caption of the foreclosure action. This lis pendens, captioned in the cause, was filed after the recordation of the assignment of the second mortgage.

The foreclosure action proceeded uneventfully. Eventually, the property was sold to Citicorp at a sheriff's sale on May 11, 1988 for $108,487. A sheriff's deed to Citicorp was recorded on June 20, 1988. It appears from a certification of Citicorp's attorney submitted to the trial court that on December 6, 1988 Pessin advised them that he and others were the assignees of the Grillo mortgage.

Citicorp then instituted an action against the assignees.[3] It moved for summary judgment and to strike Pessin's answer which was filed in that action. Judge Bachman in a March 23, 1989 written opinion refused to place the second mortgagee in a superior position to that of the first mortgagee. He accorded an equitable remedy to Pessin of the right to redeem the property and pay off the entire senior debt within 60 days. * * *

Essentially, Pessin's argument on this appeal is that if strict foreclosure were denied to Citicorp, then he should have a lien on the property in the amount of the second mortgage. He argues that the title searcher, if negligence could be proven against him, would be liable to Citicorp for the sum necessary to satisfy this mortgage. He concludes that if his mortgage was thus paid by Citicorp the lien would be discharged and title would be free and clear of liens.

Pessin also challenges the viability of strict foreclosure on the grounds that it is a harsh doctrine which is not followed in a majority of jurisdictions in this country. He acknowledges that it has not been seriously reexamined in this State in over 50 years. He buttresses his argument with a reference to the following findings of the trial court:

---

[3] Defendants Theresa Klein and Richard Hollander were named as assignees on the mortgage and were also named as defendants in Citicorp's strict foreclosure action. No answer or action was ever taken by the codefendants and they have not appeared on this appeal.

Where an omitted junior lienholder is involved, strict foreclosure has generally only been granted when some fault is present on the part of the junior lienholder. In N[ew] J[ersey] the remedy has been implemented when the junior lienor had actual knowledge of the defective foreclosure and delayed in asserting his claim, or when there has been fraud in the transaction. [Citations omitted.] In the instant case, there is no proof of fraud, prejudicial delay or other fault of the omitted party which warrants strict foreclosure at this juncture.

Since the trial judge found no fault on the part of the junior lienholder, Pessin argues that the remedy accorded should not have been ordered since it amounted to strict foreclosure against him. He again presses his argument that Citicorp should have been compelled to satisfy his mortgage and seek redress from its title searcher. We reject Pessin's arguments.

Aside from the fact that we do not consider it appropriate as an intermediate appellate court to overrule long-standing precedent, including decisions of the former Court of Errors and Appeals, we are satisfied that a complainant in a foreclosure action who purchases in good faith at the foreclosure sale is entitled to file a complaint to force an outstanding junior lienor to redeem its mortgage or be foreclosed of the equity of redemption.

In *Parker v. Child,* 25 *N.J.Eq.* 41 (Ch.Div.1874), it was held that where a first mortgagee forecloses his mortgage, but omits making the second mortgagee a party to the suit, the rights and equities of the parties not named are unaffected. The second mortgagee was thus entitled to redeem the property within a reasonable time or be foreclosed of the equity of redemption. Similarly, in *Sears, Roebuck & Co. v. Camp,* 124 *N.J.Eq.* 403, 1 *A.*2d 425 (E. & A.1938), the Court of Errors and Appeals held that strict foreclosure is available when a foreclosing mortgagee fails to discover an outstanding junior mortgagee. There the first mortgagee purchased the property at the foreclosure sale for a nominal amount and then resold it to an innocent third party. The court held:

> Yet strict foreclosure is still an appropriate remedy where, in the special circumstances, it will subserve equity and justice. This is particularly the case where, through the customary foreclosure by judicial sale or a conveyance by the mortgagor, the legal and equitable estates have become united in the mortgagee, who is also in possession under his legal title, and some outstanding junior interest has not, by reason of pure inadvertence, not aggravated by bad faith, been barred by the decree. Such is the established practice in this State. [Citations omitted.] *Id.* at 409, 1 *A.*2d 425.

The court also noted:

> It is not suggested that Camp is entitled, at his option to a
> foreclosure by judicial sale as an incident of his contract, . . . and
> the question is therefore not before us. *Id.* at 413, 1 *A.*2d 425.

Pessin has not urged that the proper remedy should have been a
judicial sale, rather than strict foreclosure. See *Powell v. Giddens,* 231
N.J.Super. 49, 53, 555 *A.*2d 4 (App.Div.1989). See also 30 *N.J.Practice*
(Cunningham and Tischler, Law of Mortgages) § 201 at 52 (1975). The
effect of Pessin's argument would be to elevate the second mortgage to a
position superior to the first mortgage as a result of the failure to include
the assignment of the mortgage in the original foreclosure action. Pessin's
rights as an assignee of the second mortgage cannot rise higher than
those of the second mortgage. See *Cressman v. Davis,* 57 *N.J.Eq.* 619,
621, 42 *A.* 768 (E. & A.1899); *S.D. Walker, Inc. v. Brigantine Beach Hotel
Corp.,* 44 *N.J.Super.* 193, 208, 129 *A.*2d 758 (Ch.Div.1957); *Rose v.
Kimball,* 16 *N.J.Eq.* 185 (Ch.Div.1863). We are satisfied that the
Chancery Division Judge appropriately concluded that there was an
inadequate remedy at law here under the circumstances.

Strict foreclosure is a recognized remedy in this State. *Sears,
Roebuck & Co. v. Camp, supra* (124 *N.J.Eq.* 403, 1 *A.*2d 425). The remedy
grew out of equitable concerns where there was a default on a mortgage.
Prior to the remedy of strict foreclosure, upon default the mortgagee was
entitled to a right of possession of the mortgaged property. *Id.* at 407, 1
*A.*2d 425. However, with the advent of strict foreclosure, the right to
redeem the property was recognized. *Ibid.* Eventually, foreclosure by
judicial sale became the usual practice with the passage of statutes
providing for this disposition. See *Steffel v. Grissler,* 129 *N.J.Eq.* 425, 19
*A.*2d 798 (E. & A.1941).

Generally, there are various remedies available to a purchaser of
property at a foreclosure sale when a junior lienor has been omitted from
the foreclosure proceedings. These remedies include:

> . . . proceedings de novo to foreclose, or a suit to compel the
> junior lienholder to redeem, and, upon his failure to do so, to
> forever bar him from redemption . . . [or] [i]f the purchaser
> prefers, he may pay the amount of the junior lien and thereby
> prevent redemption or foreclosure. [55 *Am.Jur.*2d, *Mortgages,*
> § 852 (1971).] [Footnotes omitted.]

The Chancery Division Judge did not consider in his opinion the date
of the foreclosure complaint as compared with the recording date of the
assignment and the filing date of the foreclosure action. The judge
essentially left the parties in the position they would have been in had
the error not occurred. He stated:

The rights of an omitted junior mortgagor are neither enlarged or diminished, but retained, when a defective foreclosure sale occurs. [*Camp*] *Clearwater* [*v. Plock*], *supra* [59 *N.J.Super.* 1, 157 A.2d 15 (1959)]. This principle is a two-edged sword. Although legal and equitable title merge in the purchasing senior lienholder, the omitted junior lienor's claims cannot rise higher than they were before the defective sale. [Citations omitted.]

We conclude that Judge Bachman's decision was consistent with the policy of the foreclosure statutes and the recording acts.

* * *

Here, Citicorp was aware of and joined the second mortgagee in the foreclosure. It was not actually aware of the existence of the assignment at the time it purchased the property at the foreclosure sale. The judge's determination is consistent with and protects the priorities in place prior to the foreclosure as best as possible. It is true that there are intangibles which cannot be measured after the fact, such as whether Pessin could have driven the price up sufficiently at the sheriff's sale to satisfy both liens. The remedy afforded Pessin here gives proper regard to the priorities prior to the sale, as well as according some relief to Pessin.

Affirmed.

NOTES

1. *Availability of strict foreclosure.* Courts take a variety of approaches to the use of strict foreclosure against an omitted lienor. Courts in some cases suggest that the remedy is automatically available, unless the senior mortgagee intentionally omitted the junior lienor. See Tejedo v. Secretary of Veterans Affairs, 673 So.2d 959 (Fla.App.1996). Other courts have held that strict foreclosure is unavailable to deal with an omitted junior lienor. See United States Dept. of Hous. & Urban Dev. v. Union Mortg. Co., Inc., 661 A.2d 163 (Me.1995) ("We conclude that any attempt to subsequently foreclose against the junior mortgagee must preserve the junior mortgagee's right to redeem from the senior mortgage and the right to participate in a second public sale.").

However, courts in most jurisdictions do not follow either extreme approach. In many jurisdictions, to have strict foreclosure against an omitted junior lienor, the original foreclosure purchaser must establish that (1) she bought in good faith without knowledge of the outstanding interest and (2) the junior lienor knew of the sale and permitted the purchaser to buy without disclosing the junior lien.

Courts in other decisions, like *Citicorp*, follow a flexible rule that requires equitable grounds for relief. These courts generally require that the foreclosing senior mortgagee omitted the junior through inadvertence or mistake untinged with bad faith. Moreover, some courts look at the property's value or the sale price at the prior foreclosure sale. If the premises are worth no more than the senior encumbrances, a court should allow strict foreclosure of the junior lien. See, e.g., Mesiavech v. Newman, 120 N.J.Eq. 192, 184 A. 538 (Ch.1936). According to the Restatement:

> Because strict foreclosure deprives the omitted junior of the right to participate in a public foreclosure sale and to receive any potential surplus from it, there is a presumption against this remedy. Thus, strict foreclosure should be available only where the senior purchaser can establish that the omission was the result of inadvertence or mistake and that the fair market value of the mortgaged real estate does not exceed the amount of encumbrances senior to the junior lien.

Restatement

Restatement (Third) of Property (Mortgages) § 7.1 cmt. b (1997).* Some states statutorily provide for strict foreclosure. See, e.g., 2035 Realty Co. v. Howard Fuel Corp., 77 A.D.2d 870, 431 N.Y.S.2d 57 (1980). For an excellent and extensive analysis of the omitted junior lienor problem and the rights and remedies of the parties, see George M. Platt, The Dracula Mortgage: Creature of the Omitted Lienholder, 67 Ore.L.Rev. 287 (1988).

Suppose that in the principal case, Pessin, the junior mortgagee, had sought judicial foreclosure of the junior lien. Would the result have been the same? Would his case have been helped if he could have introduced credible evidence that the property was worth more than the amount of the senior lien?

2.   *Equitable redemption vs. statutory redemption.* We have assumed in the foregoing discussion that, if the omitted junior lienor redeems, he is exercising the equitable right of redemption, rather than the statutory right of redemption. The court discussed this concept in Portland Mortgage Co. v. Creditors Protective Ass'n, which you are about to read. Some commentators have argued that the omitted junior should have a choice of proceeding under either form of redemption.

The choice can make a difference for several reasons. For example, a junior lienor who redeems under a statutory right of redemption normally gets fee title to the property, rather than just the revived first lien. Moreover, to exercise statutory redemption, the junior must usually pay the price paid at the original foreclosure sale, rather than the balance that was owed on the first lien. Unlike equitable redemption, the mortgagor in many states has the first right to statutorily redeem, and the junior lienors can redeem only if the mortgagor does not. Additionally, statutory redemption has a fixed time period, while equitable redemption is cut off only by the doctrine of laches or a foreclosure in which the person seeking to redeem is a party.

---

*   © 1997 by The American Law Institute. Reprinted with permission.

PORTLAND MORTGAGE CO. v. CREDITORS PROTECTIVE ASS'N

Supreme Court of Oregon, 1953
199 Or. 432, 262 P.2d 918

BRAND, JUSTICE.

This is an appeal by the Creditors Protective Association from an order denying a motion made by it for an order requiring the sheriff of Multnomah County to accept an offer of redemption made by it for the real property described in these proceedings.

The Portland Mortgage Company, a corporation, held a first mortgage upon the real property involved in this case. Katherine M. and Byron L. Randol were the mortgagors. The appellant Creditors Protective Association, a corporation, obtained a judgment against the Randols, which became a lien against said property, subsequent in time and inferior to the lien of the plaintiff's mortgage. The judgment was entered on 21 March 1950. On 24 March 1950 the plaintiff brought suit to foreclose its mortgage, but did not join the judgment lienholder as a party. The mortgage was foreclosed by decree on 25 May 1950 and the plaintiff purchased the property at the foreclosure sale for $6,214.72, being the amount of the mortgage plus costs. On 3 July 1950 the sheriff executed and delivered to the plaintiff a certificate of sale to the property. The sale was confirmed on 20 July 1950. On 17 August 1950 the plaintiff filed a suit in equity against the defendant Creditors Protective Association, the judgment lienholder. The complaint alleged that the judgment lien of the defendant, which had not been foreclosed in the original suit, constituted a cloud upon the plaintiff's title, and that it was subsequent in time and inferior to the interest of the plaintiff as purchaser at the mortgage foreclosure sale, except for the statutory right of redemption possessed by the defendant as a judgment lien creditor. The complaint prayed for the entry of an interlocutory judgment and decree requiring that the defendant redeem from the sheriff's sale to the plaintiff "within such time as the court shall deem reasonable in the manner and mode provided by statute for the redemption by a lien creditor from a sale of real property on execution, and in the event of the failure of the defendants so to redeem said property, that a final judgment and decree be entered herein forever barring * * * " the claim of the defendant in or to the real property.

On 16 July 1951, more than a year after the sale of the mortgaged property to the plaintiff, and pursuant to the foreclosure decree, the sheriff executed and delivered to the plaintiff a deed conveying the premises. On 20 August 1951 the circuit court entered an interlocutory decree reciting the entry of a default against the defendant and providing that said defendant should have a period of 60 days from the date of the decree within which to redeem the property "in the manner and mode provided by the statutes of the State of Oregon for redemption by a lien creditor from an execution sale of real property from the Sheriff's sale to plaintiff", and providing further that in the event of failure of the defendant to redeem within the time allowed, a final judgment would be entered, barring and foreclosing the right of the defendant in the property. On 20 September 1951 the defendant judgment lienholder filed with the sheriff of Multnomah County a notice addressed to the plaintiff, its attorneys, the contract purchasers from the plaintiff and the sheriff, by the terms of which the parties mentioned, were notified that the defendant claimed a judgment lien against the property, which was due and unpaid. The notice further provided:

> " * * * that pursuant to Chapter 6–1605, O.C.L.A.1940, you are hereby requested to account on or before the expiration of ten days of the receipt of this notice for all rents, issues and profits from the following described property * * * [describing it] and you are further notified of redemption of said property, and that on the 9th day of October, 1951, at 10:00 o'clock A.M., Creditors Protective Association, an Oregon corporation, will apply to the Sheriff of Multnomah County to redeem the above described real property pursuant to Chapter 6–1607, O.C.L.A.1940."

* * *

On 9 October 1951 at the hour of 9:30 a.m., being one-half hour before the time specified by the defendant as the time at which it would "apply to the sheriff of Multnomah County to redeem * * *" the property, the plaintiff paid to the clerk of Multnomah County the sum of $321.50 which was sufficient to constitute full satisfaction of the judgment of the defendant, and thereupon the clerk satisfied said judgment on the margin of the record. It is stipulated that said funds are still being held by the county clerk. At the hour of 10 o'clock a.m., being the time set in the so-called notice of redemption, the defendant applied to the sheriff to redeem the real property and tendered to the sheriff the sum of $7,037.88, being the amount set out in the accounting as the amount necessary to redeem the property. The plaintiff, through its attorney, then exhibited the receipt of the county clerk for the sum of $321.50, received as satisfaction of the defendant's judgment. The defendant, by its attorney, refused said sum of $321.50. The sheriff denied the application of the defendant to redeem, for the reason that the judgment records showed that the judgment held by the defendant had been satisfied in full prior to the tender of the redemption money by the defendant, basing his decision upon the provisions of O.C.L.A. §§ 6–1602, subsection (2), 6–1607, subsections (1)(b) and (1)(c). * * *

On 22 October 1951 the defendant filed a motion for an order requiring the sheriff to accept the offer of redemption made by it. That motion was made and filed in the case which the plaintiff had instituted on 17 August 1950 for the purpose of foreclosing the interest of the defendant judgment lienholder, and in which case the defendant had defaulted. The offer was accompanied by an affidavit reciting the facts and stating that the payment of $321.50 to the clerk by the plaintiff was made without the knowledge or consent of defendant. On 12 December 1951 the court denied the motion of the defendant, from which order the defendant appeals. * * *

Only one assignment of error is presented by the defendant for consideration here, namely, that the court erred in denying the motion of the defendant for an order directing the sheriff of Multnomah County to accept the tender of defendant and to allow it to redeem the subject real property. The defendant maintains that the right of a lien creditor to redeem is a valuable and absolute right granted by statute which cannot be abridged or defeated by the purchaser at a mortgage foreclosure sale without the consent of the lien creditor. He relies upon the provisions of O.C.L.A. §§ 6–1602 to 6–1607 inclusive as the basis of the asserted right.

* * *

The defendant intimates that a lien creditor is a necessary party to a mortgage foreclosure. This is true only in a limited sense. The statute provides that any person having a lien subsequent to the plaintiff upon the same property shall be made a defendant in a suit to foreclose a mortgage. O.C.L.A. §§ 9–501, 9–502. But it is established that although junior lien claimants are necessary parties if the decree is to affect them, nevertheless the decree of foreclosure is valid as to all parties who are properly joined even though other lienors are not joined. The omitted junior lienholder is in the same position as if no foreclosure had ever taken place, and he has the same rights, no more and no less, which he had before the foreclosure suit was commenced. * * * One of the rights available to the junior lienholder is to redeem the mortgage and thus become subrogated to the position of the senior mortgagee. Brown v. Crawford, D.C., 252 F. 248; Coughanour v. Hutchinson, 41 Or. 419, 69 P. 68. This right was therefore available to the defendant unless it was cut off by the act of the plaintiff in paying into court the amount of the judgment which was a lien on the mortgaged property. * * *

Just as the omitted junior lienholder retains the rights he had in the property subject to the lien, so the senior mortgagee retains rights with respect to the junior lienholder which are the equivalent of those held by him before the foreclosure of his mortgage. The purchaser at the foreclosure sale, whether he be the mortgagee or a third party, is vested with the rights of the mortgagee as against any omitted parties in the foreclosure suit, and may proceed to cut off the junior lien by suit for strict foreclosure. By the decree the junior lienor will be required to redeem or be barred of any rights in the property. This is the procedure sanctioned by the courts of this state. * * *

The defendant claims that his right to redeem in this case is granted by statute and relies on O.C.L.A. § 6–1602(2), which provides that a creditor having a lien by judgment may redeem property sold subject to redemption. It is evident from defendant's argument and brief that it has confused the equitable right of redemption or equity of redemption with the statutory right of redemption. A clear distinction must be made between these two concepts.

The difference between the equity of redemption and statutory redemption has been made clear by the decisions of this court. Higgs v. McDuffie, 81 Or. 256, 157 P. 794, 158 P. 953; and Sellwood v. Gray, supra. The classic statement is that of Mr. Justice Lord in Sellwood v. Gray [11 Or. 534, 5 P. 196]. We quote:

> " * * * His equity of redemption is the right to redeem from the mortgage—to pay off the mortgage debt—until this right is barred by a decree of foreclosure; but until this right is barred, his estate, in law or in equity, is just the same after as it was before default. It is a right, though, of which the law takes no cognizance, and is enforceable only in equity, and has nothing to do with our statute of redemptions. [Citing cases.] This is a valuable right, and exists not only in the mortgagor himself, but in every other person who has an interest in, or legal or equitable lien upon, the mortgaged premises, and includes judgment creditors, all of whom may insist upon a redemption of the mortgage. [Citing authorities.] Nor can one against his consent be deprived of this right without due process of law. To bar his right of redemption he must be made a party to the foreclosure, or the proceeding as to him will be a nullity. * * * "

The exercise of the equitable right of redemption has the effect of discharging the lien if the redemption is by the mortgagor or his successor in interest, but if a junior lien claimant redeems, the effect is to substitute the junior for the senior lienholder. In the latter case, the aggregate of the liens will be unchanged, but the persons holding the liens will be different. A junior lien, and the right of redemption which is an incident thereof, will remain in existence unless and until the same is foreclosed by a senior lienholder. When the junior lien is foreclosed, then the statutory right of redemption as to junior lien creditors given by O.C.L.A. § 6–1602(2) comes into existence. If there has never been a foreclosure of the junior lien, then there is no statutory right of redemption, only the equitable right of redemption. Concerning the rights of an omitted junior lienholder, a learned author states:

> "* * * This man's rights remain as they were, because the foreclosure does not bind him; and so, as a participant in the equity of redemption which, as to him, was never foreclosed, he can redeem in equity. That, indeed, is not only his proper course, but it is the only procedure that should be open to him. He cannot resort to statutory redemption, because he is not within the terms of the statute. The latter comes into effect at and with foreclosure, as we have seen, but the statute envisages those only whom the foreclosure has barred. It follows that one who has never been foreclosed cannot resort to statutory redemption. His remedy remains where it always was, regardless of whether the particular State had provided for statutory redemption. The remedy is redemption in equity after the ancient mode." 2 Glenn on Mortgages, § 238.

It is apparent, therefore, that the defendant cannot rely on the statutory provisions as a basis for his claim of an absolute right to redeem. The obvious purpose of the statutory right of redemption is to give an additional opportunity to the mortgagor to recover his land and to the subsequent lien creditors to protect their interests. But, as has been indicated, the defendant herein can protect his interests without resort to the statutory right of redemption, and we therefore hold that the defendant does not come within the provisions of O.C.L.A. § 6–1602(2). The provisions of O.C.L.A. § 6–1603 limiting the right of a lien creditor to redeem to the period of 60 days from date of sale clearly indicates that the statutory right of redemption does not apply in cases such as the one at bar. It was provided in the interlocutory decree that the defendant "shall have a period of sixty days from the date of this decree within which to redeem in the manner and mode provided by the statutes of the State of Oregon for redemption by a lien creditor from an execution sale of real property * * *." The quoted provision did not constitute a holding that the defendant had a statutory right of redemption. The decree only adopted the procedure of statutory redemption as that which should be followed by the defendant if it should choose to redeem.

The junior lienor, who was omitted in the foreclosure of the senior mortgage, still has the valuable right of redemption available to him, but, when such a right is exercised, the authorities are clear that the redeeming junior lienholder is not entitled to a conveyance of the property, but rather to an assignment of the security interest of the senior mortgage. Renard v. Brown, 7 Neb. 449; Smith v. Shay, 62 Iowa 119, 17 N.W. 444; O'Brien v. Perkins, Tex.Civ.App., 276 S.W. 308; Shelton v. O'Brien, Tex.Com.App., 285 S.W. 260. This rule is stated in 2 Jones, Mortgages, 8th ed, § 1376, as follows:

"A junior incumbrancer who, not having been made a party to a foreclosure of a prior mortgage, afterward redeems, redeems not the premises, strictly speaking, but the prior incumbrance; and he is entitled, not to a conveyance of the premises, but to an assignment of the security. Therefore if the prior mortgagee in such case has become the purchaser at the foreclosure sale, and has thus acquired the equity of redemption of the mortgaged premises, the junior mortgagee upon redeeming is not entitled to a conveyance of the estate, but to an assignment of the prior mortgage; whereupon the prior mortgagee, as owner of the equity of redemption, may, if he choose, pay the amount due upon the junior mortgage, redeeming that. * * * "

When a junior lienholder has redeemed the senior incumbrance and steps into the shoes of the prior mortgagee, he must foreclose his lien and have the property sold, in order to realize on his security, unless the purchaser at the prior foreclosure, who has acquired the mortgagor's equity of redemption, chooses to redeem from him. The equity of redemption acquired by the purchaser at the foreclosure sale, when perfected by delivery of a sheriff's deed, constitutes the basis of his right to re-redeem from a junior lienholder who by redemption from the purchaser has acquired the rights of the senior mortgagee but has not acquired the property. We quote:

"Redemption by a junior lienor, however, means a correlative privilege on the part of the senior whose mortgage has gone through foreclosure. The junior lien, in the beginning, was subject to redemption on the part of the mortgagor. The latter, of course, lost all his rights and interest when the decree of foreclosure was entered against him. But let us remember that the junior's security consisted only of the equity of redemption, or a share in it. Hence if he redeems after a foreclosure from which he has been omitted, he is not redeeming the premises as the mortgagor would have done, but is merely acquiring the senior mortgage for the protection of his own interest. It follows that he can be met at the gate by the purchaser at the sale, whether he be the senior mortgagee or a third party, with a tender of money in payment of his debt with interest. In other words, the purchaser at the sale can dispose of the junior mortgagee by redeeming the land from his lien." 1 Glenn, Mortgages, § 86.5.

* * *

The authorities cited control the decision in the pending case. Since the sheriff's deed to the plaintiff conveyed all the interests in the property except the judgment lien held by the defendant, the plaintiff acquired an owner's interest in the property entitling it to pay off the judgment of defendant and free the land of the lien. O.C.L.A. § 6–1001. No question is raised in this court as to the right of the clerk of the court to enter the satisfaction of judgment as permitted by O.C.L.A. § 6–1001. Since the purchaser, having a sheriff's deed, could redeem from the junior lienholder if the latter had redeemed from the senior mortgage, and could thereby acquire unencumbered and unclouded title, we can see no reason why such junior lienholder cannot be paid off prior to any redemption. In the view we take of this case, it therefore makes no difference whether the notice of redemption by the junior lienholder was given prior to the time plaintiff paid the judgment, or how far such proceedings had been carried.

* * *

We hold that the payment by the plaintiff to the county clerk pursuant to the provisions of O.C.L.A. § 6–1001 and the entry of satisfaction on the margin of the record discharged defendant's judgment and that thereupon the defendant ceased to be a lienholder. Having been fully paid he had no right to redeem.

The order of the trial court denying defendant's motion to require the sheriff to accept defendant's offer of redemption is affirmed.

LAND ASSOCIATES, INC. V. BECKER

Supreme Court of Oregon, 1982
294 Or. 308, 656 P.2d 927

CAMPBELL, JUSTICE.

* * *

Land Associates, the seller of real property on a land sales contract, brought an action for judgment against its buyer on June 26, 1979, naming several others who had interests in the property as defendants. Land Associates initially requested a strict foreclosure, but in an amended complaint asked for a judicial sale. Land Associates joined those who held junior liens and judgments of record at the time it filed the complaint. After the complaint was filed, two trust deeds and a judgment against the buyer went on record. The trust deeds were recorded June 27, 1979, and July 2, 1979. The judgment was entered October 31, 1979. The people holding these three above-mentioned liens were not joined in the foreclosure action and did not intervene. On November 19, 1979, Becker, the purchaser on the contract, conveyed his interest in the property by deed to respondent E & B Investors. On March 5, 1980, the trial court entered a stipulated decree that gave Land Associates judgment for the balance of the purchase price, attorney fees and costs and directed the sale of the property on execution by the sheriff to satisfy the judgment.

The decree provided for a possible deficiency and foreclosed all property interests or rights of all defendants, except for the statutory rights of redemption.

Land Associates bought the property at the sheriff's sale on April 17, 1980, and 27 days later, on May 14, 1980, obtained an ex parte order from the court directing the sheriff to issue a deed. The record in this court indicates that only the State of Oregon waived its rights to redeem. On this same day Land Associates assigned the certificate of sale to respondent E & B Investors and conveyed the property. The sheriff issued the deed the following day. The court confirmed the sale on May 15, 1980.

The three pendente lite lien creditors mentioned above then assigned their interests to appellant Bautista on June 13, 1980. On the same day, 57 days after the sale, Bautista served her notice of intent to redeem on Land Associates and its assignee E & B Investors. The sheriff refused to proceed with the redemption without direction from the court because he had already issued a deed to Land Associates. Bautista then intervened in this action, naming Land Associates and E & B Investors, Inc. as respondents, and filed allegations in the nature of a complaint asking to set aside the order which authorized the deed and directing the sheriff to permit her to exercise her statutory right of redemption. The trial court dismissed her second amended complaint and she appealed.

The Court of Appeals affirmed this dismissal. It held that Bautista, as the assignee of unjoined junior lien creditors, had no right to statutory redemption, relying on Portland Mtg. Co. v. Creditors Prot. Ass'n., 199 Or. 432, 262 P.2d 918 (1953).

* * *

The period for statutory redemption[2] starts after the foreclosure and sale itself and is one last chance for the previous owner and any lien

---

[2] Bautista claims a right to redeem under ORS 23.530 and 23.540:

"ORS 23.530. Property sold subject to redemption, as provided in ORS 23.520, or any part thereof separately sold, may be redeemed by the following persons:

"(1) The mortgagor or judgment debtor whose right and title were sold, or his heir, devisee or grantee, who has acquired, by inheritance, devise, deed, sale, or by virtue of any execution or by any other means, the legal title to the whole or any part of the property separately sold; provided, that in the event redemption is made by anyone acquiring the legal title after attachment, or after a judgment becomes a lien on the property, such person shall acquire no greater or better right thereby to the property so redeemed than the holder of the legal title at the time of such attachment or judgment.

"(2) A creditor having a lien by judgment, decree or mortgage on any portion of the property, or any portion of any part thereof separately sold, subsequent in time to that on which the property was sold. Such creditors, after having redeemed the property, are to be termed redemptioners."

"ORS 23.540. A lien creditor may redeem the property within 60 days from the date of the sale by paying the amount of the purchase money, with interest at the rate of 10 percent per annum thereon from the time of sale, together with the amount of any taxes which the purchaser may have paid thereon, and any other sum which the judgment debtor might be required to pay for redemption, with like interest, and if the purchaser creditors to regain the property. It is important to distinguish the two types of redemption—equitable redemption only exists until the interest is foreclosed, while statutory redemption only begins after the interest is foreclosed.

In the present case, the Court of Appeals relied on *Portland Mtg. Co.,* supra, indicating that while arguably Bautista might have an equitable right of redemption, she did not have a statutory right of redemption. In this it is mistaken. *Portland Mtg. Co.* concerned an attempted redemption by junior lien creditors who were not joined in the foreclosure action. This court held that they had no right to statutory right to redeem because their interest had not been foreclosed. Those creditors were lienholders of record when the initial petition was filed; because they were not joined they were not bound by the foreclosure, and a statutory right of redemption did not arise.

The present situation differs because Bautista's predecessors were not lienholders of record when the initial complaint was filed. The doctrine of lis pendens controls here. This doctrine states that the filing of a suit concerning real property is notice to people who obtain an interest in the property after the commencement of the suit that they will be bound by the outcome of the suit. Puckett v. Benjamin, 21 Or. 370, 381, 28 P. 65 (1891). It is a necessary doctrine; without it every change of ownership or lesser interest in real property would require a modification of the suit and would require continual checking of the records to be sure that someone else had not obtained property rights in the property in question. Respondents argue that the doctrine means that any change of ownership during the pendency of the suit does not have any legal effect until the outcome of the suit, but in this they are mistaken. Kaston v. Storey, 47 Or. 150, 154, 80 P. 217 (1905). The doctrine of lis pendens does not change a property owner's right to transfer interests in a property even though a foreclosure suit is pending, and it also does not stop another person from gaining an interest by becoming a lien creditor after the suit is filed, as did Bautista's predecessors in interest in the present case.

The doctrine of lis pendens, however, binds Bautista's predecessors in interest by the foreclosure suit. This is the major difference between the present case and *Portland Mtg. Co.* In *Portland Mtg. Co.,* because the lien creditors of record were not joined, they were not bound by the foreclosure; thus the statutory right of redemption did not arise and their only recourse would have been the equitable right of redemption.

[handwritten margin notes: "lis pendens"; "Portland"]

---

is also a creditor having a lien prior to that of the redemptioner, the amount of such lien, with interest; provided, that if objections to any sale are filed, a lien creditor may redeem within 60 days from the date of the order confirming the sale."

The situation in the present case is just the opposite; because the interests did not arise until after the foreclosure suit started, the doctrine of lis pendens means that the holders of these interests are bound by the decree of foreclosure and thus their interests were foreclosed along with those of the buyer and the lien creditors who were joined in the suit. Because their interests were foreclosed, their statutory right of redemption then came into existence. Bautista acquired these rights by the assignment. She thus is in the class of people who can exercise the rights of statutory redemption.

* * *

Reversed and remanded.

D. POWER OF SALE FORECLOSURE

1. SOME GENERAL CONSIDERATIONS

NELSON, WHITMAN, BURKHART & FREYERMUTH,
REAL ESTATE FINANCE LAW
634–38 (6th ed. 2014)*

The other main foreclosure method—power of sale foreclosure—is available in thirty-five jurisdictions. After varying types and degrees of notice, the property is sold at a public sale, either by a public official, such as a sheriff, by some other third party, or by the mortgagee. Almost no power of sale foreclosure statutes provide an opportunity for a hearing before the foreclosure sale. Power of sale foreclosure is also called nonjudicial foreclosure or foreclosure by advertisement.

In some states that authorize power of sale foreclosures, the deed of trust is the most commonly used mortgage instrument. The mortgagor-trustor conveys the real estate to a trustee who holds it in trust for the mortgagee-beneficiary until the mortgage debt is paid in full. In the event of foreclosure, the trustee exercises the power of sale by a public sale of the mortgaged property. The sale usually is not judicially supervised.

The notice requirements for a power of sale foreclosure vary but are usually less rigorous than for a judicial foreclosure. The required notice may simply be notice of foreclosure or notice of default or both. While some states require the foreclosing mortgagee to give notice by mail or personal service to every person that has a junior record interest in the real estate, many do not. A few states require only notice by publication. Some of these states require a newspaper advertisement, but others require only public posting. Other states require published notice and notice by mail or personal service to the mortgagor and to the owner of

---

*   Reprinted with permission of LEG, Inc. d/b/a West Academic.

the mortgaged real estate, but not to junior lienors and others holding an interest subordinate to the mortgage being foreclosed. A few states attempt to protect those interested parties who are neither mortgagors nor owners by requiring the foreclosing mortgagee to mail notice of foreclosure to any person who has previously recorded a request for such notice. In addition to the state notice requirements, federal legislation makes a power of sale foreclosure ineffective against a junior federal tax lien unless the foreclosing mortgagee gives the United States written notice by registered or certified mail or by personal service at least 25 days before the sale.

[Two federal statutes authorize power of sale foreclosure of all residential mortgages held by the Department of Housing and Urban Development ("HUD"). The Multifamily Mortgage Foreclosure Act (the "Multifamily Act") authorizes power of sale foreclosure for federally-insured and certain other mortgages on property, other than one- to four-family dwellings. 12 U.S.C.A. §§ 3701–3717. The Single Family Mortgage Foreclosure Act (the "Single Family Act") does the same for HUD-held mortgages on one- to four-family dwellings. 12 U.S.C.A. §§ 3751–3758. The Acts' provisions are similar. Regulations implementing both Acts were streamlined and consolidated in one regulation in 1996. 24 C.F.R. §§ 27.1–27.123, 61 Fed.Reg. 48546 (1996). The Acts authorize a power of sale foreclosure even if the mortgage was executed before the Act's effective date and, apparently, even if the mortgage does not include a power of sale clause. The Secretary of HUD designates a commissioner to conduct the foreclosure and sale.

Foreclosure under the Acts is initiated by service of a Notice of Default and Foreclosure Sale that contains information concerning the property being foreclosed, the date and place of sale, and related information. The notice must be published once a week for three consecutive weeks and posted on the property for at least seven days before the sale. Additionally, it must be sent by certified mail, return receipt requested, at least 21 days before the foreclosure sale to the original mortgagor, to those liable on the mortgage debt, and to the property "owner." At least 10 days before the sale, the notice must be sent to all persons having a lien on the property. Unless one takes a broad view of who is an "owner" under the statute, neither the Acts, nor the regulations promulgated thereunder require mailed notice to holders of leases, easements, and similar interests junior to the mortgage being foreclosed. The sale date must be at least thirty days "after the due date of the earliest unpaid installment or the occurrence of a nonmonetary default."

Though the Acts do not provide for a hearing, the regulations for multifamily foreclosures specify that "HUD will provide to the mortgagor [and current owner] an opportunity informally to present reasons why the mortgage should not be foreclosed. Such opportunity may be provided before or after the designation of the foreclosure commissioner but before service of the notice of default and foreclosure." 24 C.F.R. § 27.5. HUD is making substantial use of the Multifamily Act. See Patton, The Multifamily Mortgage Foreclosure Act Proves Effective, Title News, Oct.1992, at 8. For an analysis of the Acts, see Patrick A. Randolph, The New Federal Foreclosure Laws, 49 Okla.L.Rev. 123 (1996).]

The underlying theory of power of sale foreclosure is simple. By complying with the statutory requirements, the mortgagee can achieve the same results as judicial foreclosure without the substantial additional burdens that judicial foreclosure entails. Like judicial foreclosure, power of sale foreclosure terminates all interests junior to the mortgage being foreclosed and gives the sale purchaser the same title that the mortgagor had when she gave the mortgage. Moreover, where it is commonly employed, power of sale foreclosure has provided an effective foreclosure remedy that usually is substantially faster and cheaper than judicial foreclosure.

Although power of sale foreclosure generally works and is more efficient and less costly than judicial foreclosure, the titles it produces have been less stable than those resulting from judicial foreclosure for at least three reasons. First, court supervision in judicial foreclosure prevents many defects. Second, the defendants in a judicial foreclosure will bring possible defects to the court's attention, which provides additional protection. Finally, the concept of judicial finality insulates even technically defective judicial foreclosure proceedings against subsequent collateral attack. None of these protections are inherent in power of sale foreclosure. Moreover, as we will examine in detail later in this chapter, power of sale foreclosure has been subject to constitutional challenge because of its alleged notice and hearing deficiencies.

Another troubling distinction between judicial and power of sale foreclosures has been frequently litigated during the past several years. To have standing to foreclose a mortgage judicially, the plaintiff has to prove that it has the right to enforce the debt. However, courts in several states have held that the same standing requirement does not exist for power of sale foreclosures, as well illustrated by the decision in You v. JP Morgan Chase Bank, 293 Ga. 67, 743 S.E.2d 428 (2013). In that case, the borrowers borrowed money to buy a home and signed a note and deed to secure debt. The lender transferred the note to "an unidentified entity" and then assigned the security deed to JP Morgan Chase's predecessor. When the borrowers defaulted, Chase foreclosed nonjudicially and was the highest bidder. The borrowers then sued Chase for wrongful foreclosure.

In their suit, the borrowers argued that Chase could not foreclose because it did not own the note. The Georgia Supreme Court stated that the plaintiffs' argument would have been correct if Chase had foreclosed judicially, because Chase would have had to prove that it had the right to enforce the note. However, the court held that the same rule does not apply to a power of sale foreclosure because the Georgia power of sale statutes do not expressly include that requirement. The court stated that the owner of a security deed can foreclose by power of sale even if it does not hold the note *or have any beneficial interest in the debt.*

2. DEFECTS IN THE EXERCISE OF THE POWER

BASKURT v. BEAL

Supreme Court of Alaska, 2004
101 P.3d 1041

Before: BRYNER, CHIEF JUSTICE, MATTHEWS, EASTAUGH, and FABE, JUSTICES.

OPINION

MATTHEWS, JUSTICE.

* * *

FACTS

This case involves two parcels of land originally owned by Marion and Mortimer Moore. * * * In 1991 Mortimer and Marion simultaneously sold their respective parcels to Charles McAlpine. The following day, McAlpine conveyed the parcels to Annette Beal by quitclaim deed. These transactions were financed by two separate promissory notes signed by McAlpine: Note A for $95,000 payable to Mortimer; and Note B for $135,000 payable to Marion. Each note was to be paid to the respective seller through its own separate escrow account.

The two promissory notes were secured by a single deed of trust covering both parcels * * *. In 1994 Annette paid off the $95,000 owed on Note A for Parcel 1 to Mortimer. At that time, there was some discussion regarding paying off Note B, but Marion preferred to continue to receive monthly payments rather than being paid off in a single lump sum. Marion did agree to a reduction of the interest rate on Note B. The 1991 deed of trust was modified to reflect the payoff of the note to Mortimer and the change in interest rate on Marion's note.

In the fall of 1999, after an erratic payment history, Annette fell behind in her payments. Sarah Baskurt the Moores' daughter, took steps to commence foreclosure, including contacting attorney Jim Christie to conduct the foreclosure. Christie and Land Title Company of Alaska, Inc., made the arrangements for the foreclosure. At that time, Annette owed $26,780.81 on Parcel 2, having paid approximately eighty percent of the original $135,000 purchase price.

The foreclosure sale was held on April 26, 2000, inside the main entrance of the Nesbett Memorial Courthouse in Anchorage. Prior to arriving at the sale, Baskurt, who wanted to bid on the property but believed she lacked the financial strength and knowledge of property development to do so on her own, contacted friends to see if they would be interested in bidding on the property as her partner. Robert and Joyce Wainscott agreed and Baskurt and Joyce Wainscott formed a partnership for the purpose of acquiring and developing or reselling the property. Baskurt, who believed the property was worth at least $250,000, brought a check for $151,000 to the sale. The Wainscotts brought a check for $100,000 to the sale. The trio had at least $251,000 available to put toward the purchase price of the property.

At the sale Baskurt recognized her neighbor, Allen Rosenthal, whom Baskurt knew to have considerable experience in home construction. Rosenthal had learned of the foreclosure sale about a week earlier and had contacted Land Title, who referred him to Christie. Christie provided Rosenthal with general information about the property and the foreclosure. Rosenthal, who believed the property could be subdivided for family residences or condominiums, thought that if he could purchase the land for under $160,000 he would have gotten a "good deal." He had with him cashier's checks for $60,000 and $100,000.

Baskurt approached Rosenthal and asked why he was at the sale. Rosenthal testified that he told Baskurt he was interested in bidding on the property but denies that he told Baskurt how much he was willing to bid. Baskurt claims Rosenthal told her he would be willing to bid up to $95,000 on the property. Baskurt asked Rosenthal to join her partnership with Joyce, and Rosenthal tentatively agreed. Baskurt spoke with Joyce, and the three cemented their partnership. There was little discussion regarding bidding strategy or tactics, and the three assumed that each would be a one-third partner, contributing an equal portion to the sale price. Immediately following the expansion of the partnership, Leslie Plikat, Land Title's agent, inspected Baskurt's and Rosenthal's cashiers checks. Plikat registered two bidders, Baskurt and Rosenthal.

The foreclosure sale, conducted by Christie, was by public outcry. Baskurt made the opening and only bid for $26,781.81, a dollar over the remaining debt owed on the property, on behalf of the partnership. There were no other bids, and the property was sold to Baskurt, Joyce, and Rosenthal via a trustee's deed.

PROCEEDINGS

On May 17, 2000, Annette filed a complaint against Baskurt, Wainscott, Rosenthal, McAlpine, and Land Title seeking to have the foreclosure sale set aside.[2] * * * After a three-day bench trial, the superior court set aside the foreclosure sale as both void and voidable. Final judgment setting aside the foreclosure sale and awarding attorney's fees and costs to Annette was entered on February 28, 2003. Purchasers appeal. * * *

The Foreclosure Sale Was Voidable

Pursuant to AS 34.20.070 a trustee under a deed of trust executed as security for the payment of an indebtedness may, in the case of default or noncompliance with the terms of the deed, foreclose and sell the property according to the terms provided in the deed.[6] However, defects in the mechanics of the trustee's exercise of the power to foreclose may render the foreclosure sale voidable.[7] Generally, mere inadequacy of price is not sufficient by itself to require setting aside a foreclosure sale.[8] However, if the inadequacy of the sale price is (1) "so gross as to shock the conscience and raise a presumption of fraud or unfairness," or (2) is coupled with other irregularities in the sale procedures, then invalidation of the sale may be justified.[9]

Gross inadequacy is measured by reference to the fair market value of the property at the time of the sale.[10] Fair market value for these purposes has been defined as

> not the fair "forced sale" value of the real estate, but the price which would result from negotiation and mutual agreement, after ample time to find a purchaser, between a vendor who is

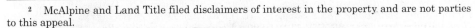

---

2   McAlpine and Land Title filed disclaimers of interest in the property and are not parties to this appeal.

6   AS 34.20.070(a) provides in pertinent part:

> If a deed of trust is executed conveying real property located in the state to a trustee as security for the payment of an indebtedness and the deed provides that in case of default or noncompliance with the terms of the trust, the trustee may sell the property for condition broken, the trustee, in addition to the right of foreclosure and sale, may execute the trust by sale of the property, upon the conditions and in the manner set forth in the deed of trust, without first securing a decree of foreclosure and order of sale from the court, if the trustee has complied with the notice requirements of (b) of this section.

7   *See Rosenberg v. Smidt,* 727 P.2d 778, 784 (Alaska 1986) (distinguishing void and voidable sales; in case of latter, alleged defect goes "not to the trustee's right to proceed with the foreclosure but only to the mechanics of exercising that power") (internal citations omitted).

8   *See McHugh v. Church,* 583 P.2d 210, 213 (Alaska 1978) (holding mere inadequacy of price insufficient to set aside foreclosure sale in context of judicial sale); *see also* GRANT S. NELSON & DALE A. WHITMAN, REAL ESTATE FINANCE LAW § 7.21, at 672 (4th ed. 2002) ("All jurisdictions adhere to the recognized rule that mere inadequacy of the foreclosure sale price will not invalidate a sale, absent fraud, unfairness or other irregularity.").

9   *McHugh,* 583 P.2d at 213–14.

10   RESTATEMENT 3D OF PROPERTY (MORTGAGES) § 8.3 cmt. b, at 584, 593 (1997).

willing, but not compelled to sell, and a purchaser who is willing to buy, but not compelled to take a particular piece of real estate.[11]

Courts determine adequacy of price by comparing the fair market value to the purchase price of the property at the foreclosure sale. Jurisdictions vary on what percentage of fair market value renders the purchase price grossly inadequate. Foreclosure sale prices of fifty percent or more of fair market value are routinely upheld.[12] Even prices garnering less than fifty percent of fair market value are often upheld.[13] However, several courts have upheld the invalidation of a foreclosure sale that produced a price of twenty percent of fair market value or less.[14] The New Mexico Supreme Court has enunciated the standard that when the price falls into the ten to forty percent range, it should not be confirmed "absent good reasons why it should be."[15]

The Restatement adopts the position that although "'gross inadequacy' cannot be defined in terms of a specific percentage of fair market value," generally, "a court is warranted in invalidating a sale where the price is less than twenty percent of fair market value and, absent other foreclosure defects, is usually not warranted in invalidating a sale that yields in excess of that amount."[16]

---

[11] *Id.* at 584; *see also BFP v. Resolution Trust Corp.,* 511 U.S. 531, 537–38, 114 S.Ct. 1757, 128 L.Ed.2d 556 (1994) ("The market value of . . . a piece of property is the price which it might be expected to bring if offered for sale in a fair market; not the price which might be obtained on a sale at public auction or a sale forced by the necessities of the owner, but such a price as would be fixed by negotiation and mutual agreement, after ample time to find a purchaser, as between a vendor who is willing (but not compelled) to sell and a purchaser who desires to buy but is not compelled to take the particular . . . piece of property.") (citing BLACK'S LAW DICTIONARY 971 (6th ed.1990)).

[12] *See, e.g., Fed. Deposit Ins. Corp. v. Villemaire,* 849 F.Supp. 116 (D.Mass.1994); *Kurtz v. Ripley County State Bank,* 785 F.Supp. 116 (E.D.Mo.1992); *Danbury Savings & Loan Ass'n v. Hovi,* 20 Conn.App. 638, 569 A.2d 1143 (1990); *Moody v. Glendale Fed. Bank,* 643 So.2d 1149 (Fla.3d DCA 1994); *Guerra v. Mutual Federal Savings & Loan Ass'n,* 194 So.2d 15 (Fla. 1st DCA 1967); *Long Island Sav. Bank v. Valiquette,* 183 A.D.2d 877, 584 N.Y.S.2d 127 (N.Y.App.Div.1992); *Glenville & 110 Corp. v. Tortora,* 137 A.D.2d 654, 524 N.Y.S.2d 747 (N.Y.App.Div.1988); *Zisser v. Noah Indus. Marine & Ship Repair, Inc.,* 129 A.D.2d 795, 514 N.Y.S.2d 786 (N.Y.App.Div.1987); *S & T Bank v. Dalessio,* 429 Pa.Super. 282, 632 A.2d 566 (1993); *Cedrone v. Warwick Fed. Sav. & Loan Ass'n,* 459 A.2d 944 (R.I.1983).

[13] *See, e.g., Moeller v. Lien,* 25 Cal.App.4th 822, 30 Cal.Rptr.2d 777 (1994) (25% of fair market value); *Shipp Corp., Inc. v. Charpilloz,* 414 So.2d 1122 (Fla. 2d DCA 1982) (33% of fair market value); *Hurlock Food Processors Inv. Assocs. v. Mercantile-Safe Deposit & Trust Co.,* 98 Md.App. 314, 633 A.2d 438 (Md.1993) (35% of fair market value); *Frank Buttermark Plumbing & Heating Corp. v. Sagarese,* 119 A.D.2d 540, 500 N.Y.S.2d 551 (N.Y.App.Div.1986) (30% of fair market value).

[14] *See, e.g., Ballentyne v. Smith,* 205 U.S. 285, 27 S.Ct. 527, 51 L.Ed. 803 (1907) (14% of fair market value); *Crown Life Ins. Co. v. Candlewood, Ltd.,* 112 N.M. 633, 818 P.2d 411 (1991) (15% of fair market value); *United Oklahoma Bank v. Moss,* 793 P.2d 1359 (Okla.1990) (approximately 20% of fair market value); *Rife v. Woolfolk,* 169 W.Va. 660, 289 S.E.2d 220 (1982) (14% of fair market value).

[15] *Armstrong v. Csurilla,* 112 N.M. 579, 817 P.2d 1221, 1234–35 (1991).

[16] RESTATEMENT § 8.3 cmt. b, at 584.

Even where the foreclosure sale price is not grossly inadequate, a low price coupled with some other irregularity in the foreclosure proceeding can be sufficient to render the sale voidable. As explained by the United States Supreme Court in *Schroeder v. Young*[17] and noted by this court in *McHugh:*

> While mere inadequacy of price has rarely been held sufficient in itself to justify setting aside a judicial sale of property, courts are not slow to seize upon other circumstances impeaching the fairness of the transaction, as a cause for vacating it, especially if the inadequacy be so gross as to shock the conscience. If the sale has been attended by any irregularity, as if several lots have been sold in bulk where they should have been sold separately, or sold in such manner that their full value could not be realized; if bidders have been kept away; if any undue advantage has been taken to the prejudice of the owner of the property, or he has been lulled into a false security; or, if the sale had been collusively, or in any other manner, conducted for the benefit of the purchaser, and the property has been sold at a greatly inadequate price, the sale may be set aside, and the owner may be permitted to redeem.[18]

Other commentators agree. Professors [Nelson and Whitman] explain that problems connected with foreclosure sales, including

> problems associated with the notice of the sale, sale by parcel or in bulk, and adequacy of the foreclosure price ... have their greatest impact in a cumulative sense. While one of these problems may not always be sufficient to set aside a sale, the more of them that are present in one fact situation, the greater the likelihood that a new sale will be ordered.[19]

The Restatement adopts a sliding-scale approach to the cumulative effect that price and irregular procedures have on the fairness of the sale:

> Even where the foreclosure price for less than fair market value cannot be characterized as "grossly inadequate," if the foreclosure proceeding is defective under local law in some other respect, a court is warranted in invalidating the sale and may even be required to do so. Such defects may include, for example, ... selling too much or too little of the mortgaged real estate. For example, even a slight irregularity in the foreclosure process coupled with a sale price that is substantially below fair market

---

[17]   161 U.S. 334, 337–38, 16 S.Ct. 512, 40 L.Ed. 721 (1896).

[18]   *McHugh v. Church,* 583 P.2d 210, 213 (Alaska 1978) (quoting *Schroeder,* 161 U.S. at 337–38, 16 S.Ct. 512).

[19]   GRANT S. NELSON & DALE A. WHITMAN, REAL ESTATE FINANCE LAW § 7.16, at 657 (4th ed.2002).

value may justify or even compel the invalidation of the sale. . . . On the other hand, even a sale for slightly below fair market value may be enough to require invalidation of the sale where there is a major defect in the foreclosure process.[20]

In *McHugh,* we considered the effect of selling property in bulk as opposed to by parcel.[21] Though we declined to adopt "a flat rule requiring the trustee to sell real property in separate lots or parcels, rather than as a whole unit,"[22] we recognized that a trustee under a deed of trust is a dual fiduciary owing duties to both the trustor and the beneficiary.[23] Among the duties owed by the trustee is the duty to take reasonable and appropriate steps to avoid sacrifice of the debtor's property and interest.[24]

Bearing these principles in mind, we turn to the facts of this case. Purchasers contend that there was no basis to set the foreclosure sale aside as voidable. They argue, among other things, that the sale should not have been set aside on the basis of an inadequate price since under *McHugh,* an inadequate price is an insufficient basis for setting aside a foreclosure sale. Further, they contend that the sale should not have been set aside on the ground that the parcels were sold together because under *McHugh,* the trustee was under no duty to sell the parcels separately.

We are not convinced by Purchasers' argument. The test for whether a sale is voidable based on price inadequacy is whether the price paid was *grossly* inadequate when compared to the fair market value of the property on the date of the foreclosure sale. The trial court found that the 1991 sales price of $225,000 was the best indicator of fair market value. The fact that the foreclosure purchase price of $26,781.10 was less than fifteen percent of the sale price indicates that the gross inadequacy standard was met.[25] The trial court so found, and Purchasers identify no circumstances indicating that this finding is erroneous.

The superior court also found that the sale of either parcel alone would likely have generated sufficient proceeds to satisfy the amount due. By conducting the sale in bulk rather than selling only one parcel, the court found that the trustee failed in its duty to act reasonably to protect Beal's interests. This finding is supported by the evidence and is in accordance with our observation in *McHugh* that a trustee has a duty to take reasonable steps to act impartially and in such a way as "not to sacrifice the debtor's property."[26] When coupled with the inadequacy of

---

[20] RESTATEMENT 3D OF PROPERTY (MORTGAGES) § 8.3, at 587.
[21] *See McHugh,* 583 P.2d at 213–18.
[22] *Id.* at 218.
[23] *Id.* at 214.
[24] *Id.* at 218.
[25] *See* discussion *supra* pp. 1044–1045.
[26] *McHugh,* 583 P.2d at 218.

the price, the trustee's unreasonable failure to sell only one parcel initially justifies invalidating the sale.[27]

We conclude that the superior court properly set aside the sale based on the grossly inadequate sale price and the trustee's failure to sell only one parcel in breach of its duty to act reasonably to protect Beal's interests.

For the above reasons we conclude that the sale was voidable and AFFIRM the decision of the superior court.

CARPENETI, JUSTICE, not participating.

NOTES

1. *State court remedies to attack power of sale foreclosure.* Three remedies normally are available to challenge the validity of a power of sale foreclosure: (1) an injunction suit against a pending foreclosure; (2) a suit in equity to set aside the sale, and (3) an action for damages against the foreclosing mortgagee or trustee. See Nelson, Whitman, Burkhart & Freyermuth, Real Estate Finance Law § 7.23 (6th ed.2014). Not only the mortgagor, but also the holders of interests that were junior to the foreclosed mortgage, can seek these remedies. A particular remedy's availability depends on several factors, including "whether the defect is discovered before or after the sale, the nature of the defect, and importantly, if the sale has already been completed, whether the sale purchaser or any subsequent grantee is a bona fide purchaser." Id.

2. *The tender requirement.* When a mortgagor seeks injunctive relief or to set aside a sale, some courts require him to tender into the court the outstanding mortgage debt. See, e.g., Ginther-Davis Center, Ltd. v. Houston Nat'l Bank, 600 S.W.2d 856 (Tex.Civ.App.1980); Smith v. Citizens & Southern Fin. Corp., 245 Ga. 850, 268 S.E.2d 157 (1980). When the amount is in dispute, these courts require the mortgagor to tender at least the amount he concedes is due. The tender requirement is premised on the maxim that one who seeks equity must do equity. Whatever the underlying equitable basis for the tender requirement, does it make sense when applied in this situation? Is it not implicit in the mortgagor's equity of redemption and in the prohibition against clogging it, that a mortgagor's interest can only be terminated by a foreclosure? See Nelson, Whitman, Burkhart & Freyermuth, Real Estate Finance Law § 3.1 (6th ed.2014). Is it not also implicit in the concept of foreclosure that a mortgagor, whatever his economic condition, is entitled to an orderly liquidation of the mortgage security? If so, shouldn't the mortgagor have the right to one valid foreclosure sale? See id. §§ 7.22–7.23.

A few courts apparently also require tender of the mortgage debt by junior lienors seeking equitable relief against a power of sale foreclosure. See

---

[27] *Id.* Our conclusion should not be read as implying that the gross inadequacy of the sale price alone would not be a sufficient ground to set aside the sale. It is not necessary to reach that question in this case because of the additional flaw in the sale process.

Arnolds Mgmt. Corp. v. Eischen, 158 Cal.App.3d 575, 205 Cal.Rptr. 15 (1984) (full tender required). Does a junior lienor have a stronger argument against tender than a mortgagor? Should it make a difference that the mortgagor normally is personally liable on the mortgage debt but the junior lienor is not?

3. *Common foreclosure defects.* A variety of defects are used with varying degrees of success to challenge power of sale foreclosures. Sometimes, the challenge is to the *mortgagee's right to foreclose.* For example, a mortgagor may assert that no default exists in the mortgage obligation or that the mortgagee did not have the right to accelerate. On the other hand, many challenges are to the *foreclosure process,* rather than to the mortgagee's substantive right to foreclose. Procedural challenges may be based on defects such as intentional and negligent chilled bidding, improper time or place of sale, defective notice of sale, and selling either too much or too little of the mortgaged land. For further consideration of these grounds, see Nelson, Whitman, Burkhart & Freyermuth, Real Estate Finance Law § 7.22 (6th ed.2014). The next two principal cases and the notes following them examine challenges based on an inadequate foreclosure sale price.

4. *The "void"-"voidable"-"inconsequential" distinction.* Defects in a power of sale foreclosure can be categorized in at least three ways. Some defects are so substantial that they render the sale *void.* In this situation, the sale transfers no title to the sale purchaser or subsequent grantees, except perhaps by adverse possession. A forged mortgage, for example, is in this category. Similarly, a foreclosure is void if the lender did not validly accelerate the debt or if the debt was otherwise not yet due.

Most defects render the foreclosure *voidable,* rather than void. See e.g., Rosenberg v. Smidt, 727 P.2d 778 (Alaska 1986). In a voidable sale, bare legal title passes to the sale purchaser, subject to the redemption rights of those who were injured by the sale defect. For example, a sale is voidable in some jurisdictions if the mortgagee purchases at its own power of sale foreclosure. However, if the defect only makes the sale voidable, the redemption rights can be eliminated if a bona fide purchaser acquires the land for value. In that situation, an action for damages against the foreclosing mortgagee or trustee may be the only remedy.

Finally, some defects are so *inconsequential* that the sale is neither void nor voidable. Such defects include minor typographical or similar errors that do not prejudice any of the affected parties. As such, they do not affect the validity of the sale. For a thorough consideration and classification of defects in the exercise of a power of sale, see Nelson, Whitman, Burkhart & Freyermuth, Real Estate Finance Law § 7.21 (6th ed. 2014).

5. *Who is a bona fide purchaser?* If the defective sale is only voidable, who should be treated as a bona fide purchaser ("BFP")? If the sale purchaser paid value and is unrelated to the mortgagee, she should take free of voidable defects if (a) she did not have actual notice of the defects and is not on reasonable notice from recorded documents and (b) the defects were not

noticeable by a person exercising reasonable care at the sale. If the foreclosing mortgagee purchases at the sale, can it qualify as a BFP? Can the mortgagee's attorney be a BFP? See Pizza v. Walter, 345 Md. 664, 694 A.2d 93 (1997) (mortgagee's attorney who purchased at foreclosure sale and aided in preparation of trustee's sale not a BFP).

When should a subsequent grantee qualify as a BFP and take free of defects that render the sale voidable? If the grantee did not attend the foreclosure sale, arguably she should be treated as a BFP unless she has actual notice or reasonable notice from recorded documents. If a BFP transfers the property to the foreclosing mortgagee, is it protected from a suit to redeem the land, if not for damages?

6. *Trustee as a fiduciary.* As in *Beal,* courts often stress that a trustee under a deed of trust is a fiduciary for both the mortgagor and mortgagee and must act impartially between them. See, e.g., Meyers Way Dev. Ltd. Partn. v. University Sav. Bank, 80 Wash.App. 655, 910 P.2d 1308 (1996); Nelson, Whitman, Burkhart & Freyermuth, Real Estate Finance Law § 7.22 (6th ed.2014). Yet the trustee clearly represents two parties whose interests are often antithetical. Consequently, he is not a traditional trustee, and courts do not universally accept the "fiduciary" label. Consider the following language of the California Supreme Court:

> The similarities between a trustee of an express trust and a trustee under a deed of trust end with the name. "Just as a panda is not a true bear, a trustee of a deed of trust does not have a true trustee's interest in, and control over, the trust property. Nor is it bound by fiduciary duties that characterize a true trustee."

Monterey S.P. Partn. v. W.L. Bangham, Inc., 49 Cal.3d 454, 261 Cal.Rptr. 587, 777 P.2d 623 (1989). Another California court characterized "the role of such trustee" as "more nearly that of a common agent of the parties to the instrument." Lancaster Sec. Inv. Corp. v. Kessler, 159 Cal.App.2d 649, 324 P.2d 634 (1958).

7. *Trustee obligation to verify default.* Before foreclosing, does a trustee have a duty to investigate whether the debt is in default? In Spires v. Edgar, 513 S.W.2d 372 (Mo.1974), the Missouri Supreme Court held that "in the absence of unusual circumstances known to the trustee, he may, upon receiving a request for foreclosure from the creditor, proceed upon that advice without making any affirmative investigation and without giving any special notice to the debtor."

8. *Trustee as foreclosure purchaser.* It is a widely accepted rule that a trustee may not purchase the premises at a sale she conducts, at least without the mortgagor-trustor's express consent. See e.g., Smith v. Credico Indus. Loan Co., 234 Va. 514, 362 S.E.2d 735 (1987) ("a co-trustee under a deed of trust cannot purchase property on behalf of herself or another at the foreclosure sale, even where that sale is conducted by another trustee, and even where the trustee who makes the purchase was not an active

participant in conducting the sale"); Nelson, Whitman, Burkhart & Freyermuth, Real Estate Finance Law § 7.22 (6th ed.2014). But see Stephens, Partain & Cunningham v. Hollis, 196 Cal.App.3d 948, 242 Cal.Rptr. 251 (1987) ("It has long been recognized that a trustee under a deed of trust is not absolutely prohibited from purchasing the trust property at the trustee's own sale.")

9. *Trustee closely related to mortgagee-purchaser.* The trustee sometimes is an officer or employee of the beneficiary or the beneficiary's attorney or the holder of an equity interest in it. In many jurisdictions, this close connection may cause closer judicial scrutiny of the sale, but it usually will not invalidate it. See, e.g., Perry v. Virginia Mortg. & Inv. Co., Inc., 412 A.2d 1194 (D.C.App.1980); Boatmen's Bank of Pulaski County v. Wilson, 833 S.W.2d 879 (Mo.App.1992) (sale upheld though trustee was officer of bank-mortgagee).

However, other courts will set aside the sale in these situations. These courts analyze the situation in at least two ways. Some courts take the position that, when a substantial connection exists between the trustee and beneficiary, the beneficiary's purchase in reality is an indirect purchase by the trustee that is voidable. See, e.g., Whitlow v. Mountain Trust Bank, 215 Va. 149, 207 S.E.2d 837 (1974). Alternatively, some courts hold that an "instrument—in form a deed of trust—executed to the chief executive officer of a corporation is, in effect, a mortgage, and the law relating to foreclosure of mortgage deeds rather than the law relating to trust deeds is applicable." Mills v. Mutual Bldg. & Loan Ass'n, 216 N.C. 664, 6 S.E.2d 549 (1940). The sale is voidable because the beneficiary is treated as if he had purchased from himself at his own foreclosure sale.

Other states have attempted to deal with the foregoing problem by statute. For example, a Utah statute authorizes a bank or savings and loan association to be both a trustee and beneficiary under the same deed of trust. Utah Code Ann. § 57–1–21. Another Utah statute states that "[a]ny person, including the beneficiary or trustee, may bid at the sale." Utah Code Ann. § 57–1–27. Consider the language of the following Virginia statute:

A. The fact that a trustee in a deed of trust to secure a debt due to a corporation is a stockholder, member, employee, officer, or director of, or counsel to, the corporation does not disqualify the trustee from exercising the powers conferred on him by the deed of trust so long as the trustee did not participate in the corporation's decision as to the amount to be bid at the sale of the trust property.

B. In addition to the provisions of subsection A, if the lender secured by the deed of trust bids the amount secured, including interest through the date of sale and costs of foreclosure, the trustee's participation in fixing the bid price by the lender shall not be deemed improper and the sale shall not be rendered voidable solely by reason of the trustee's participation.

Va.Code Ann. § 64.2–1423.

10. *Inadequate foreclosure price.* Perhaps the most commonly asserted, but least successful, challenge to power of sale foreclosure is inadequacy of the sale price. Nationally, "it is well-settled that in the absence of irregularity in the conduct of the foreclosure sale, mere inadequacy of price will not operate to set the sale aside, unless the consideration is so grossly inadequate as to shock the conscience of the court." Lake Hillsdale Estates, Inc. v. Galloway, 473 So.2d 461 (Miss.1985). As one commentator has noted with respect to his jurisdiction, "sales have been upheld where the price paid for the property was only one-half, one-third, one-fourth, one-fifth, or even one-twentieth of its reasonable value." Larry D. Dingus, Mortgages—Redemption After Foreclosure Sale in Missouri, 25 Mo.L.Rev. 261, 263–64 (1960). Indeed, one court, convinced that the "conscience shocking test" was "impractical and should be abandoned," held that "[i]f a foreclosure sale is legally held, conducted and consummated, there must be some evidence of irregularity, misconduct, fraud, or unfairness on the part of the trustee or the mortgagee that caused or contributed to an inadequate price, for a court of equity to set aside the sale." Holt v. Citizens Central Bank, 688 S.W.2d 414 (Tenn.1984). Finally, the Single Family Mortgage Foreclosure Act of 1994, which applies to one- to four-family mortgages held by HUD, provides that the foreclosure "sale price shall be conclusively presumed to be reasonable and equal to the fair market value of the property." 12 U.S.C.A. § 3760(e).

The *Beal* court adopted the Restatement's "grossly inadequate" standard. Under that standard, a court is "warranted in invalidating a sale where the price is less than 20 percent of fair market value and * * * is usually not warranted in invalidating a sale that yields in excess of that amount." Restatement (Third) of Property (Mortgages) § 8.3, cmt. b (1997). The Arizona Supreme Court has agreed. See Krohn v. Sweetheart Properties, Ltd., 203 Ariz. 205, 52 P.3d 774 (2002).

The "grossly inadequate" standard applies only if no other defects existed in the foreclosure process: "[E]ven where the foreclosure price * * * cannot be characterized as 'grossly inadequate,' if the foreclosure proceeding is defective under local law in some other respect, a court is warranted in invalidating the sale and may even be required to do so." Id. § 8.3 cmt. b (1997). See Pizza v. Walter, 345 Md. 664, 694 A.2d 93 (1997) (sale yielding slightly more than 50% of fair market value set aside when coupled with inadequate advertising).

Finally, "adequacy of the sale price looms larger on its own when the mortgagee is seeking to validate it for purposes of seeking a deficiency judgment. Courts scrutinize the sale price much more closely if the mortgagee wants a deficiency judgment in addition to the land." Nelson, Whitman, Burkhart & Freyermuth, Real Estate Finance Law 647 (6th ed.2014).

11. *Sales by parcel or in bulk.* As *Beal* illustrates, if a mortgage obligation is secured by more than one parcel of real estate, the trustee or

foreclosing mortgagee must choose whether to sell one parcel at a time or to sell the parcels in bulk. Many courts require the mode of sale that is most beneficial to the mortgagor.

> Normally, a presumption exists for selling in parcels, because "a sale in parcels or lots opens a field to a greater number of bidders, is conducive to a better price, tends to prohibit odious speculation upon the distress of the debtor, and enables him to redeem some of the property without being compelled to redeem it all." If selling only some of the parcels will yield enough money to pay the debt, the lender must sell just those parcels, though selling in bulk would yield more money than selling all the parcels separately. Courts usually hold that using the wrong method of sale makes the sale voidable. To have the sale set aside, the mortgagor must establish that the method of sale caused injury, normally by showing that a different sale method would have generated more proceeds. On the other hand, courts in a significant number of cases have upheld bulk sales on the ground that the sale method is discretionary, absent specific direction in the mortgage.

Nelson, Whitman, Burkhart & Freyermuth, Real Estate Finance Law 650–51 (6th ed.2014).

> Many states statutorily address the "parcel-bulk" issue. See e.g., Minn.Stat.Ann. § 580.08 ("If the mortgaged premises consist of separate and distinct farms or tracts, they shall be sold separately, and no more farms or tracts shall be sold than are necessary to satisfy the amount due on such mortgage."). Other statutes give the foreclosing party discretion as to the method of sale. See Or.Rev.Stat. § 86.782. Consider the language of the California statute:

> > When the property consists of several known lots or parcels, they shall be sold separately unless the deed of trust or mortgage provides otherwise. * * * The trustor, if present at the sale, may also, unless the deed of trust or mortgage otherwise provides, direct the order in which property shall be sold, when the property consists of several known lots or parcels which may be sold to advantage separately, and the trustee shall follow that direction.

Cal. Civ.Code § 2924g(b). Suppose the mortgagor and junior lienors, if any, differ as to the mode of sale. What should the rule be?

12. *Chilled bidding.* Irregular conduct by a mortgagee or trustee that suppresses bidding is often characterized as "chilled bidding" and is the basis for setting aside a sale. Chilled bidding can be categorized in two ways:

> The first occurs when the mortgagee or trustee and potential purchasers collude or engage in other intentional conduct to suppress the bidding. The second type encompasses inadvertent and unintentional acts by the trustee or mortgagee that suppress bidding.

The first type of chilled bidding occurs in a myriad of fact situations and arguably voids the sale, rather than merely rendering it voidable. For example, a mortgagee or trustee can attempt to guarantee that it will be the successful sale bidder by paying off potential third party bidders or by agreeing to share the resale profits with them. Alternatively, the mortgagee or trustee can discourage bidding by intentionally misrepresenting the state of the title or the property's physical condition.

Nelson, Whitman, Burkhart & Freyermuth, Real Estate Finance Law 652–53 (6th ed.2014). Even though the *Beal* opinion does not mention chilled bidding, would the "partnership" among Baskurt (the mortgagees' daughter), Joyce, and Rosenthal have provided an independent basis for setting aside the sale?

Chilled bidding issues can also arise in the context of inadvertent or "innocent" erroneous statements by the mortgagee or trustee at the foreclosure sale or in the foreclosure notice. See id. at 649.

13. *Junior federal tax liens.* As noted earlier in this section, power of sale foreclosure is ineffective against a junior federal tax lien unless written notice is provided to the United States at least 25 days before the sale by registered or certified mail or by personal service. See 26 U.S.C.A. § 7425(b) & (c). If such notice is not provided to the United States, should the foreclosure sale purchaser be permitted to set aside the sale and recover the purchase price? Consider the reasoning of the Minnesota Supreme Court in Gerdin v. Princeton State Bank, 384 N.W.2d 868 (Minn.1986):

> The [mortgagee] argue[s] that [purchaser] is deemed to have constructive knowledge of all recorded liens and encumbrances. Had [purchaser] checked the property's title, he would have found two tax liens which were *junior* to the mortgage. Because they were junior liens, [he] would have been justified in assuming they would be eliminated (subject only to a right of redemption) by the foreclosure sale. It should be emphasized that a search of title by [purchaser] would *not* have indicated whether notice had been sent to the state and federal governments. Because the failure to give notice to the government would not have been discovered by a title search, the doctrine of caveat emptor is inapplicable.

> While the power to foreclose by advertisement derives from a power of sale clause in the mortgage agreement, the exercise of that power must comply, at least substantially, with the statutory requirements. *See Lowell v. North,* 4 Minn. 32, Gil. 15 (1860) (failure to publish notice required by statute entitles mortgagor to damages or to have sale set aside); *Sheasgreen Holding Co. v. Dworsky,* 181 Minn. 79, 231 N.W. 395 (1930) (failure to record power of attorney before sale, as required by statute, renders sale void), *Clark v. Kraker,* 51 Minn. 444, 53 N.W. 706 (1892) (failure to separate homestead tract, as required by law, renders sale voidable, but not void). In this case, the mortgagee's failure to comply with

mandatory statutory language ("shall be mailed") should render the sale voidable by the purchaser because, as discussed above, failure to give notice to tax lienors makes the foreclosure sale fail its essential purpose.

Do you agree with the foregoing result and reasoning? Who should have standing to challenge the validity of the sale, the United States or the purchaser? In any event, should the fact that the federal tax lien was properly recorded have obligated the purchaser to inquire whether the notice was mailed?

IN RE EDRY

United States Bankruptcy Court, D. Massachusetts, 1996
201 B.R. 604

JAMES F. QUEENAN, JR., BANKRUPTCY JUDGE.

* * *

I.   FACTS

The Debtor, a divorced mother with adult children, lives alone at 41 Nashoba Road, Acton, Massachusetts, whose title stands in her name alone. She is self-employed in the operation of a cleaning agency, working out of her home. The defendant, Rhode Island Hospital Trust National Bank, is the holder by assignment of a mortgage on the home. * * *

Beginning in at least September of 1994, the Debtor experienced difficulty making timely payments on the Bank's mortgage. She was constantly late in her payments through all of 1995. This prompted the Bank to telephone her on numerous occasions, leaving messages on her recorder requesting a return call. It also sent her delinquency notices. The Debtor's response was to make the payment due, but to do so about a month late. She called the Bank on several occasions attempting to resolve the situation, but was unable to speak to anyone and left messages on the Bank's recorder. In November of 1995, the Bank accelerated the full balance due on the mortgage and gave the Debtor 30 days to make payment in full.

On February 13, 1996, the Bank sent the Debtor's most recent check back to her. That check was apparently for the payment due in January, although the Debtor testified she thought it was for the February payment. On February 22, 1996, the Bank instructed its lawyers to commence foreclosure. Upon receiving a letter from the Bank's law firm, the Debtor called the firm. The paralegal in charge of the foreclosure told her the Bank would not accept further monthly payments. The Debtor asked for current information on the balance of her account. The paralegal told her the information would be faxed to her at her home Fax machine, but that was never done.

The Bank commenced the foreclosure process and scheduled a sale for August 1, 1996. It hired as the auctioneer Paul E. Saperstein Co., Inc. ("Saperstein"). Saperstein is a firm of highly experienced auctioneers. It employs several auctioneers and conducts many hundreds of residential foreclosure auctions each year. The Bank's law firm instructed Saperstein not to promote the sale through so-called "display" advertisements. Display ads are placed in the real estate pages of a newspaper and measure two columns wide and four inches high. Saperstein advertises its auctions through such display ads in at least 80% of the residential mortgage foreclosures it conducts. The Bank, through its law firm, advertised the sale only by placing a statutorily prescribed notice of the sale in the legal section of the newspaper once a week for three successive weeks. See Mass.Gen.L. ch. 244, § 14. The Bank also gave the Debtor notice of the sale by mail, as required by the statute. On August 1, 1996, an auctioneer employed by Saperstein, Ronald P. Pelletier, arrived at the Debtor's home about one-half hour before the scheduled 10:00 a.m. sales time, hanging his auction flag on a tree in the front yard. Lee DeFillipio, the paralegal in charge of the foreclosure, arrived at about the same time. Four potential buyers appeared. Pelletier qualified three as bidders because they had the required $5,000 deposit with them. The Debtor did not appear. Pelletier made no effort to seek her permission for the potential bidders to inspect the inside of the home. As the bidding rose, DeFillipio made one bid of $85,535.81 on behalf of the Bank. This was the precise balance of the Bank's debt. The bidding continued and ended at $86,500, which was bid by the defendant Michael Gurtler. Pelletier and Gurtler then signed a memorandum of sale for $86,500, and Gurtler paid a $5,000 deposit. The memorandum states the balance is to be paid within thirty days.

The Bank made no effort to obtain a current appraisal indicating the fair market value of the property. Nor did it offer testimony at trial of the property's fair market value. William F. Curley, Jr., a highly qualified appraiser, testified for the Debtor. Based upon his testimony, I find the property had a fair market value of $190,000 at the time of foreclosure. On August 27, 1996, the Debtor filed with this court a chapter 13 petition and the present complaint. Her intention in the chapter 13 proceeding is to cure arrearages on the mortgage and make current payments. I immediately issued a temporary restraining order enjoining consummation of the sale pending a hearing on a preliminary injunction. On September 4, 1996, after a nonevidentiary hearing, I granted a preliminary injunction enjoining the sale until a trial could be held. * * *

II.　INVALIDITY OF FORECLOSURE

Under Massachusetts law, a foreclosing mortgagee must do more than comply with the procedure prescribed by statute. "It has been repeatedly held in this Commonwealth, and elsewhere, that a mortgagee who attempts to execute a power of sale contained in a mortgage is bound to exercise good faith, and to use reasonable diligence to protect the rights and interests of the mortgagor under the contract.... It is his duty, for the benefit of the mortgagor whom he represents, so to act in the execution of the power as to obtain for the property as large a price as possible." Clark v. Simmons, 150 Mass. 357, 359, 23 N.E. 108, 108 (1890). "Good faith and reasonable regard for the interest of the mortgagor will not permit him to make a sale when no one will offer a price which another could reasonably think of accepting if he were obliged to sell the property at a day's notice for what it would bring." Id., 150 Mass. at 360, 23 N.E. at 108.

A disparity between the foreclosure sales price and fair market value is not sufficient of itself to invalidate a foreclosure, but such disparity plus other circumstances can be. * * * The Supreme Judicial Court of Massachusetts has on several occasions voided a foreclosure sale when sufficient circumstances were present. For example, in Bon v. Graves, 216 Mass. 440, 103 N.E. 1023 (1914), the mortgagee chose to place the required legal notices in a newspaper which had a more limited circulation than five other local newspapers. And, although he knew that two owners of nearby properties were interested in purchasing the mortgaged property, he gave them no personal notice of the sale. Nor did he give notice of the sale to the plaintiff, who held a second mortgage on the property. The property sold at foreclosure for $2,900, much less than its fair market value of at least $5,000. * * * Chief Justice Rugg, writing for the court, held that the inadequate price, combined with the other circumstances, invalidated the foreclosure. In Sandler v. Silk, 292 Mass. 493, 198 N.E. 749 (1935), property worth $7,800 was sold at foreclosure for $1,200, subject to a small first mortgage. Having given the required personal notice to the owner and notice by publication, the mortgagee gave no personal notice of the sale to the plaintiff, an attaching creditor, despite the mortgagee's promise to do so. After ruling the plaintiff was not entitled to notice beyond publication, the court stated: "Nevertheless, the fact that in these circumstances no notice was sent to the plaintiff is evidence that good faith was not used to obtain the best reasonable possible price." 292 Mass. at 497, 198 N.E. at 751. The court held there was sufficient evidence to support the finding for the plaintiff made below and affirmed the damage judgment entered by the trial court. See also Union Market Nat'l Bank v. Derderian, 318 Mass. 578, 62 N.E.2d 661 (1945) (sale invalidated because of inadequate price and auctioneer's unadvertised requirements that potential purchasers must deposit $1,000 to qualify as bidders); Kavolsky v. Kaufman, 273 Mass. 418, 173 N.E. 499 (1930) (affirming verdict for defendant in mortgagee's deficiency action because property sold for $2,400 after auctioneer refused to sell to a $9,000 bidder due to bidder's failure to make a $1,000 deposit rather than the more usual deposit of $200.); Clark, 150 Mass. at 360–61, 357, 23 N.E.

at 108–09 (invalidating $1,200 foreclosure sale where property's value was at least $1,400 and mortgagee did not give junior mortgagee personal notice of sale despite a request for such notice).

In the present case, there is strong evidence the Bank did not use reasonable diligence to protect the Debtor's interests. The sales price of $86,500 is only 45% of the property's $190,000 fair market value. Moreover, the Bank made no attempt to ascertain the fair market value. Nor did it do anything to enhance the bidding beyond making its own bid at precisely the balance of its mortgage.

Most significant is the Bank's decision, despite the common practice to the contrary, to give only the bare notice required by statute. This consists of publishing once each week, for three successive weeks, a small notice, phrased in legalese, in the legal pages of a local newspaper, and sending a copy of the notice to the owner. See Mass.Gen.L. ch. 244 § 14. The only information about the property contained in the statutory notice is a metes and bounds description of the land area. Id. This is hardly a paradigm of marketing technique. Nor is it consistent with general practice. Based on the Saperstein testimony, I find that at least 80% of residential mortgage foreclosures in this area are advertised through so-called display ads, in addition to the required statutory publication. These ads are twice as large as the statutory notice, appear in the real estate section of the newspaper rather than in its legal section, contain much more information than does the legal notice, and generally are far better designed to sell the property. The Bank's failure to place such ads was a conscious decision on its part, not a mere lapse. Despite knowing that Saperstein normally promoted foreclosures through display ads, the Bank expressly instructed Saperstein not to do so in this instance.

The Supreme Judicial Court of Massachusetts has not dealt with a foreclosure that has been advertised through only the statutory notice in the face of a customary practice of more extensive advertising. But it has been faced with analogous circumstances. In Kavolsky, 273 Mass. at 420–23, 173 N.E. at 500–01, the court invalidated a foreclosure largely because the auctioneer required the high bidder to deposit $1,000 rather than the more customary $200. And in Union Market Nat'l Bank, 318 Mass. at 580–82, 62 N.E.2d at 661–63, potential purchasers had to first deposit $1,000 with the auctioneer. The published notice of the sale did not contain this requirement. It merely referred to a $500 deposit to be made by the winning bidder and stated other terms would be announced at the sale. The court found the $1,000 deposit requirement to be opposed to common practice and voided the sale. I believe the court would do the same here because of the Bank's conscious decision to place only minimal advertising. I therefore conclude the Bank did not make, in good faith, a diligent effort to protect the interest of the Debtor. I accordingly invalidate the foreclosure. * * *

III. RIGHTS OF HIGH BIDDER

It is of course true that a good faith purchaser for value takes property free of an unknown lien or interest held by another party, for example, free of an unrecorded lien. That doctrine does not protect the defendant Gurtler, for two reasons. First, Gurtler is an experienced purchaser at foreclosure sales who knew of the usual practice of advertising through display ads. Secondly, and more basically, never having completed the sales transaction, Gurtler is not a purchaser. He merely contracted to purchase. The contract being invalid, he is entitled to the return of his $5,000 deposit. In sum, he lacks the equities favoring a bona fide purchaser for value.

NOTES

1. *Bankruptcy court and state law.* Mortgagor-debtors, as in *Edry,* frequently use bankruptcy proceedings, rather than state court suits, as a vehicle for attacking power of sale foreclosures. Although bankruptcy courts are required to apply state law in this context, many believe that they do so with greater sympathy towards debtors. We will focus in greater detail on the use of bankruptcy for this purpose in Chapter 6, Section J, infra.

2. *Power of sale in mortgagee.* As we pointed out earlier, the deed of trust is the most commonly used land security instrument in most power of sale jurisdictions. Why use a deed of trust, which requires a trustee to foreclose, rather than a mortgage with a power of sale in the mortgagee? The reason is that courts in many of these states have held that, if a mortgagee exercises a power of sale and purchases the property at that sale, the sale is voidable. See Nelson, Whitman, Burkhart & Freyermuth, Real Estate Finance Law § 7.22 (6th ed.2014). In a few jurisdictions, including Massachusetts (as illustrated by *Edry*), Minnesota, and New Hampshire, a mortgage with a power of sale in the mortgagee is the primary financing device, and mortgagees can purchase at their own sales. Nevertheless, courts in some of these jurisdictions impose a relatively heavy burden of diligence on the mortgagee:

> The mortgagee "must act in good faith and must use reasonable diligence to protect the interests of the mortgagor." * * * The mortgagee's duty is more exacting when it becomes the buyer of the property. "When a party who is intrusted with a power to sell attempts to become the purchaser, he will be held to the strictest good faith and utmost diligence for the protection of the rights of his principal." * * * Consistent with these requirements, the mortgagee has a duty "to obtain for the property as large a price as possible."

Williams v. Resolution GGF OY, 417 Mass. 377, 630 N.E.2d 581 (1994). Accord: Murphy v. Financial Dev. Corp., 126 N.H. 536, 495 A.2d 1245 (1985).

In *Edry,* a third party purchased at the foreclosure sale. Should a foreclosing mortgagee be required to take steps beyond what the statute requires when it does not purchase at the sale?

3.   *Damages for wrongful foreclosure.* Suppose a defect renders a power of sale foreclosure "voidable," but the foreclosure purchaser (unlike in *Edry*) is a bona fide purchaser. The owner cannot recover the land and only has an action for damages against the foreclosing mortgagee. In these circumstances, what is the appropriate measure of damages? Many courts hold that the measure of damages is the difference between the property's fair market value and the aggregate amount of liens thereon as of the date of the sale. See Munger v. Moore, 11 Cal.App.3d 1, 89 Cal.Rptr. 323 (1970); Adkison v. Hannah, 475 S.W.2d 39, 43 (Mo.1972). Other courts describe the measure of damages as the value of the mortgagor's equity in the property at the time of the foreclosure sale. See, e.g., Guay v. Brotherhood Bldg. Ass'n, 87 N.H. 216, 177 A. 409 (1935). See generally, Annot., 97 A.L.R. 1059. Should the appropriate measure of damages instead simply be the property's fair market value at time of sale, less the value of any senior liens and the foreclosure sale price? Cf. Murphy v. Financial Dev. Corp., 126 N.H. 536, 495 A.2d 1245 (1985). Or should it be the fair market value, less any senior lien and the mortgage that was wrongfully foreclosed? See Nelson, Whitman, Burkhart & Freyermuth, Real Estate Finance Law 669–70 (6th ed.2014). Which measure of damages will make the mortgagor whole for her loss of the land?

Let's apply the foregoing variations to the following hypothetical. Suppose that a second mortgage foreclosure is voidable but that a bona fide purchaser now owns the land. Immediately before the sale, the title was encumbered by a first mortgage of $10,000, a second mortgage of $5,000, and a third mortgage of $3,000. Suppose the second mortgagee purchased at the foreclosure sale for $4,000. The land's fair market value was $20,000. How much should the mortgagor recover from the second mortgagee?

Suppose the land's value has increased since the defective foreclosure sale. In calculating damages, should the mortgagor be able to use the property's fair market value at the time of the damage action? Who should have the benefit of any appreciation in land value between the sale date and the damages action? See Nelson, Whitman, Burkhart & Freyermuth, Real Estate Finance Law § 7.23 (6th ed.2014).

Suppose a junior lienor brings the damages action. What is the proper measure of damages? What should the *maximum* recovery be? See id. at 667.

Should a plaintiff who succeeds in setting aside a foreclosure sale also be permitted to recover damages? Should she be able to recover permanent damages? See Calhoun First Nat'l Bank v. Dickens, 264 Ga. 285, 443 S.E.2d 837 (1994) (mortgagor may not recover both the property and the value of her equity). If not, what damages, if any, should be recoverable? Consider the following language from Clark v. West, 196 Ga.App. 456, 395 S.E.2d 884 (1990):

The gist of appellees' argument is that an injured party must elect between an equitable action for cancellation of the foreclosure sale and a suit for damages, and pursuit of one to satisfaction results in the exclusion of the other. We agree that this principle applies if the injured party is seeking to redress only the loss of the value of the property. That is, the injured party may not *both* set aside or cancel the foreclosure *and also* recover damages for the value of the property. However, this court has approved actions in which both cancellation and damages were sought. See *Andrews v. Holloway,* 140 Ga.App. 622, 231 S.E.2d 548 (1976); *Gilbert v. Cherry,* 136 Ga.App. 417, 221 S.E.2d 472 (1975). In those cases, cancellation was sought to recover the property, and *in addition,* damages were sought for other breaches of duty and other losses. The latter procedure applies in the case at bar, because appellant sought both cancellation of the foreclosure sale to recover the property and also damages for her mental anguish, which resulted from the intentional nature of defendant's acts, alleging that appellees clearly knew the note was not in default and they had no right to foreclose. It strains credulity to insist that the recovery of appellant's wrongfully foreclosed residence has made her whole, and we find no bar in law or in logic to a recovery of damages for her humiliation and emotional distress should evidence at trial establish the truth of the allegation in her pleadings that the foreclosure was instituted intentionally and without basis. Accordingly, we do not agree that because the foreclosure sale had been canceled, appellant could not pursue her separate claim for damages.

4.   *Action for damages vs. suit to set aside.* If a bona fide purchaser has not acquired the foreclosed property, should a mortgagor nevertheless have the option of a suit to set aside the sale or an action for damages? In Rogers v. Barnes, 169 Mass. 179, 47 N.E. 602, 604 (1897), the court stated the predominant view:

> On principle, we think it must be considered that in this commonwealth a mortgagee, when there has been no default or breach of the conditions of the mortgage, cannot sell the land mortgaged under the usual power of sale contained in a mortgage, so as to pass a good title even to a bona fide purchaser for value, or to any subsequent purchaser from him. * * * A majority of the court, however, do not think that the decision of this case necessarily depends upon the question whether Rice [a bona fide purchaser] took a good, absolute title or not. The case of the plaintiff, taken most favorably for the defendant, somewhat resembles that of a conversion of personal property, where the owner can sue the wrongdoer, and recover the full value of the property converted, even though the title to the property did not pass by the conversion, or can recover the property; or that of a misappropriation or

unauthorized investment or sale of trust property, where the cestui que trust can compel the trustee to account for the full value of the property, even although the property, or some of it, can be recovered. In neither of these cases can the plaintiff recover both the property and full damages for the conversion or misappropriation of it, but if he recover judgment for full damages, and they are paid, the title to the property passes to the wrongdoer and his grantees. A mortgagee, in executing the power of sale contained in a mortgage, is, in a sense, trustee for the mortgagor. So, in the present case, a majority of the court think that the plaintiff, if he so elect, can recover full damages of the defendant, whether he can or cannot redeem the premises from Rice. If the damages recovered are paid, the effect is to make Rice's title good as against the plaintiff's. The defendant, for the purpose of mitigating damages, cannot be heard to say that he has not done what he intended to do, and what, on the face of the transaction, he appears to have done, when what he has done will become valid and effectual if he pays the damages.

For a contrary view, see Bowen v. Bankers' Life Co., 185 Minn. 35, 239 N.W. 774, 776 (1931) ("to recover damages at law it is necessary to show that the land went to an innocent holder so that plaintiff's interest in it was lost"). Which position is preferable from a public policy perspective? For a general consideration of the cases, see Annot., 97 A.L.R. 1059.

Now consider the following puzzling language from a Missouri case:

When a foreclosure is wrongful because no default giving rise to a right to sell exists, the mortgagor has two remedies: it can let the sale stand and sue at law for damages or it can bring an equitable action to have it set aside. If the mortgagee did have the right to foreclose, but the sale was otherwise void or voidable, then the remedy is a suit in equity to set the sale aside.

Dobson v. Mortgage Elec. Registration Systems, Inc./GMAC Mortg. Corp, 259 S.W.3d 19, 22 (Mo.App.2008). Suppose that a mortgage was clearly in default so that the mortgagee had a right to foreclose but that a procedural defect in the foreclosure process rendered the sale voidable, but not void. For example, suppose that the trustee's oral statements at the sale negligently chilled the bidding. Suppose further that a bona fide purchaser later acquires title to the foreclosed real estate. Does this mean that the mortgagor does not have a remedy because a BFP intervened?

5. *Damages for "attempted wrongful foreclosure."* Suppose a power of sale foreclosure is commenced, but the sale never takes place, because a court enjoins it, a bankruptcy court stays it, or the mortgagee fails to complete the foreclosure process. If the mortgagor had been attempting to market the real estate, the pending foreclosure could have encouraged potential purchasers, who sensed a "distress" sale, to delay acting or to make "low-ball" offers. Moreover, the pending sale may have substantially harmed the mortgagor's credit rating. Although some courts have been willing to consider a cause of

action for "attempted wrongful foreclosure," many courts have been reluctant to extend liability into an area where damages claims may seem speculative and subject to abuse. See Nelson, Whitman, Burkhart & Freyermuth, Real Estate Finance Law 672 (6th ed.2014). Where recognized, what is the underlying theory of the cause of action? Is it a tort cause of action for slander on title? Interference with prospective economic advantage? What degree of fault or intent on the wrongdoer's part is required? See In re Hwang, 189 B.R. 786 (Bkrtcy.C.D.Cal.1995) ("A mortgage or trust deed holder who forecloses in the absence of a default under the promissory note, mortgage or deed of trust commits an offense against the property rights of the mortgagor. Liability for wrongful foreclosure arises without consideration of the *mens rea* of the foreclosing party.").

6.   *Suits for damages by others.* Should parties other than the mortgagor and the junior interest holders have an action for damages? Suppose, for example, that prospective third party bidders allege that the mortgagee and the trustee conspired to ensure that the mortgagee could purchase the real estate. See Block v. Tobin, 45 Cal.App.3d 214, 119 Cal.Rptr. 288 (1975).

7.   *Trustee or mortgagee liability to foreclosure purchaser.* To what extent is the trustee or mortgagee responsible to the foreclosure sale purchaser for title defects in the mortgaged real estate? Consider the language of Stuart v. American Sec. Bank, 494 A.2d 1333 (D.C.App.1985):

> The general rule is that a foreclosure purchaser takes a property subject to prior liens and interests accruing prior to consummation of the sale. *See Patron v. American National Bank of Jacksonville,* 382 So.2d 156, 158 (Fla.App.1980); 55 Am.Jur.2d *Mortgages* § 780 (1971); 3A R. Powell, The Law of Real Property, ¶ 466 at 696.64(4) (1984) (deed given without warranty). The recording of the assessments operates as constructive notice to all purchasers. *Ivrey v. Karr,* 182 Md. 463, 473, 34 A.2d 847, 852 (1943). Moreover, a trustee generally has no obligation to disclose liens or interests which the purchaser could have discovered by his own investigation. *Id.* at 852 (quoting *Wicks v. Westcott,* 59 Md. 270, 277 (1883)). Prior liens are not affected by a foreclosure sale and are normally not payable out of the proceeds of such sale. *Gunton v. Zantzinger,* 3 MacArthur (10 D.C.) 262, 264–65 (1879); *Baltimore Federal Savings & Loan Association v. Eareckson,* 221 Md. 527, 528–31, 158 A.2d 121, 123–24 (1960) (prior first mortgage). In other words, the doctrine of *caveat emptor* applies to foreclosure sales because a trustee makes no warranty of title and is generally subject to no duty to investigate or describe outstanding liens or encumbrances. *See Ivrey v. Karr, supra,* 182 Md. at 473, 34 A.2d at 852; *Feldman v. Rucker,* 201 Va. 11, 19–21, 109 S.E.2d 379, 385–86 (1959); G. Bogert & G. Bogert, The Law of Trust & Trustees, § 745 at 487 (rev. 2d ed. 1982). The purchaser must therefore make his own investigation and determine what liens or encumbrances may

exist against the property prior to turning over his deposit. *Cf. Garland v. Hill,* 28 Md.App. 622, 624, 346 A.2d 711, 713 (1975) (notice for purpose of allowing further investigation by interested person), *aff'd,* 277 Md. 710, 357 A.2d 374 (1976).

Should it make a difference if the trustee has actual knowledge of a title defect? According to McPherson v. Purdue, 21 Wash.App. 450, 585 P.2d 830 (1978):

> In this state, the rule of caveat emptor is no longer rigidly applied to the complete exclusion of any moral and legal obligation to disclose material facts not readily observable upon reasonable inspection by the purchaser. Hughes v. Stusser, 68 Wash.2d 707, 415 P.2d 89 (1966). The material fact here was the absence of any title to an easement which the deed of trust purported to convey. Examination of the chain of title would have revealed this defect. [The purchaser] could have readily discovered this material fact by an inspection of the chain of title in the object case, and he was not entitled to rely on the trustee's silence in this matter.

Courts have also applied this analysis to the failure to disclose physical defects in the mortgaged real estate. See Karoutas v. HomeFed Bank, 232 Cal.App.3d 767, 283 Cal.Rptr. 809 (1991) (mortgagee with actual knowledge of defective soil conditions liable for damages and rescission for failing to disclose conditions to a foreclosure purchaser who could not reasonably be expected to discover them).

GLIDDEN V. MUNCIPAL AUTHORITY OF TACOMA

Supreme Court of Washington, en banc., 1988
111 Wash.2d 341, 758 P.2d 487

DURHAM, JUSTICE.

In October 1986, Patricia Rourke, as trustee under a deed of trust, conducted a nonjudicial foreclosure sale of property in Pierce County. Appellant Municipal Authority of the City of Tacoma (Municipal Authority) was the successful bidder at the sale and received from Rourke a trustee's deed containing recitals that notice of the sale had been sent "to all persons entitled thereto", and that the sale complied in all respects to the notice requirements of Washington's deeds of trust act, RCW 61.24.

The issue presented for decision is what protection these recitals, and the "conclusive evidence" standard of RCW 61.24.040(7), afford Municipal Authority against a claim to the property asserted by respondent Old Stone Bank (OSB), a junior lienor who was not notified of the sale in the manner required by the deeds of trust act. Municipal Authority asserts that because it is a bona fide purchaser for value (BFP), RCW 61.24.040(7) vests it with clear title. OSB contends that because Municipal Authority is itself a junior lienor, the "conclusive evidence" rule of RCW 61.24.040(7) does not protect it from challenges based on flawed foreclosure procedures. OSB also asserts that Municipal Authority does not qualify as a BFP.

* * *

I

The property in dispute, by means of separate deeds of trust, secured debts owed by the Mount Bay Corporation to plaintiff Marian Glidden ($37,640.16), respondent OSB ($88,500), and appellant Municipal Authority ($38,605). Glidden is the senior lienholder, with OSB and Municipal Authority, respectively, occupying the second-and third-order lienholder positions. There are at least two other junior lienors.

When Mount Bay defaulted on its debt to Glidden in 1986, Rourke, as trustee, initiated foreclosure proceedings pursuant to the power of sale provision in the Glidden deed of trust. In May 1986, Rourke notified Mount Bay that it was in default. On June 5, Rourke served on Mount Bay notice that the trust property would be sold at public auction on October 17, 1986, if Mount Bay's default was not cured before October 7. Rourke recorded this notice with the county auditor and posted it on the property but did not notify any of the junior lienholders about the impending foreclosure sale as required by RCW 61.24.040(1)(b).

Municipal Authority learned of the sale from the posted notice, and called Rourke on June 16 to request copies of the notice and of her foreclosure report. Between June 16 and October 17, the scheduled date of Rourke's sale, Municipal Authority and Rourke communicated on several occasions. On at least two of these occasions, Bryan Chushcoff, an attorney for Municipal Authority, asked Rourke if she had given notice of the planned foreclosure sale to junior encumbrancers. Rourke responded each time by saying: "Of course, Bryan, I always do." On the day of the sale, another Municipal Authority official asked Rourke if she had notified junior lienholders. Again she said that she had.

While Rourke's foreclosure plans were going forward, OSB set in motion its own foreclosure of the property. OSB initiated foreclosure proceedings in June and scheduled a sale for December. Rourke first learned of OSB's sale on June 20 in a phone conversation with OSB's attorney and received further notice of it in September, when an updated title report disclosed the recording of a notice of trustee's sale under OSB's deed of trust. Municipal Authority in September of OSB's plans to foreclose when it received a copy of this notice of trustee's sale.

Municipal Authority and Glidden were the only bidders at Rourke's sale. Glidden bid $37,640.19, the amount of Mount Bay's indebtedness to her. Municipal Authority bid $37,845. Rourke accepted Municipal Authority's bid.

Immediately after the sale, Chushcoff appeared at Rourke's law office to tender the purchase price. He received a receipt for the payment, and returned later in the day to pick up the trustee's deed. During this second visit, Chushcoff and Rourke speculated as to why OSB had not entered a bid. Terry McCarthy, a partner in Rourke's firm, happened into the conversation and asked Rourke if she had served OSB with notice. Rourke asserted that she had and told McCarthy and Chushcoff that OSB representatives had indicated to her that they knew about the sale.

The trustee's deed Municipal Authority received contained the following recitals:

> 7.   The Trustee * * * in accordance with law, caused copies of the statutory "Notice of Trustee's Sale" to be transmitted by mail to all persons entitled thereto and either posted or served prior to ninety days before the sale * * *
>
>   * * *
>
> 9.   All legal requirements and all provisions of said Deed of Trust have been complied with, as to acts to be performed and notices to be given, as provided in Chapter 61.24 RCW.

On October 29, Rourke learned from OSB's title company that OSB had not received notice of the sale and after checking her records realized that other junior lienholders also had not received proper notice. Rourke immediately called Municipal Authority and asked that the sale be undone. After some weeks of discussions, Rourke tendered to Municipal Authority its purchase price and a quitclaim deed. Municipal Authority refused the tender.

Glidden and Rourke commenced this action in December 1986, seeking a judgment declaring void the October 17 sale and the trustee's deed Rourke issued to Municipal Authority following the sale on the basis that Rourke had failed to serve proper notice on the junior lienholders. In its answer, Municipal Authority asserted that as a BFP it acquired clear title to the sale property pursuant to RCW 61.24.040(7). Municipal Authority asked that title be quieted in its favor, or in the alternative that Rourke and her law firm be held liable for damages in the amount of the fair market value of the property, at a minimum of $146,000.

OSB, impleaded by Municipal Authority as a third party defendant, answered Municipal Authority's claims by contending that as a junior lienor it was entitled to, but did not receive, statutory notice of the foreclosure sale, and that Rourke's failure to comply with statutory notice requirements renders the sale void as to OSB's interests in the property. Had it known of the sale, OSB asserted, it would have cured Mount Bay's default and thus preserved its interests. OSB also refuted Municipal

Authority's claim to being a BFP and requested a ruling that Rourke's sale is void and that OSB's interests in the property remain valid.

On OSB's motion for summary judgment, the trial court ruled OSB's second priority lien to be "a valid, existing, enforceable lien" notwithstanding Municipal Authority's purchase because OSB "was an omitted junior lienor in that it was not notified of the sale[.]" Thus, the court held, OSB "may proceed to foreclose its Deed of Trust or exercise any rights under the Old Stone Deed of Trust and promissory note secured thereby." The trial court made no finding on Municipal Authority's status as a BFP. We granted Municipal Authority's petition for direct review.

II

Washington's deeds of trust act, RCW 61.24, authorizes nonjudicial foreclosures of deeds of trust as a time-efficient alternative to judicial mortgage foreclosure proceedings. *See* Gose, *The Trust Deed Act in Washington,* 41 Wash.L.Rev. 94 (1966). We have previously identified three principal goals of the deed of trust private sale program:

> First, the nonjudicial foreclosure process should remain efficient and inexpensive. Second, the process should provide an adequate opportunity for interested parties to prevent wrongful foreclosure. Third, the process should promote the stability of land titles.

(Citation omitted.) *Cox v. Helenius,* 103 Wash.2d 383, 387, 693 P.2d 683 (1985).

As this case well illustrates, these goals "are often difficult to reconcile." Comment, *Court Actions Contesting the Nonjudicial Foreclosure of Deeds of Trust in Washington,* 59 Wash.L.Rev. 323, 330 (1984). Permitting "omitted junior lienors" such as OSB to retain collateral interests in land that has been sold at auction, while advancing the second objective, would undermine the third. Conversely, preventing such omitted parties from challenging nonjudicial foreclosures in order to protect the title obtained by a sale purchaser such as Municipal Authority would favor the third objective over the second.

We would find the proper balance of objectives difficult to achieve in this case if it were not for RCW 61.24.040(7). That provision requires the foreclosing trustee to issue to the foreclosure sale purchaser a deed which:

> shall recite the facts showing that the sale was conducted in compliance with all of the requirements of this chapter and of the deed of trust, which recital shall be prima facie evidence of such compliance and conclusive evidence thereof in favor of bona fide purchasers and encumbrancers for value[.]

The deed Rourke issued to Municipal Authority contains recitals that notice was properly served "to all persons entitled thereto", "as provided in Chapter 61.24 RCW." Thus, if Municipal Authority is a BFP, RCW 61.24.040(7) renders these recitals conclusive as to the correctness of the foreclosure sale procedures and Municipal Authority would be entitled to clear title. If Municipal Authority is not a BFP, however, the deed recitals would be only prima facie evidence that the sale was conducted properly, subject to rebuttal by omitted junior lienholders seeking preservation of their interests.[3] *See Steward v. Good,* 51 Wash.App. 509, 512, 754 P.2d 150 (1988); Comment, 59 Wash.L.Rev. at 339; Comment, *In Deed An Alternative Security Device: The Nebraska's Trust Deeds Act,* 64 Neb.L.Rev. 92, 127–28 (1985).

In the posture in which this case comes to us, therefore, the issue we must decide is this: Viewed in a light most favorable to the nonmoving party (Municipal Authority), does the evidence on which the trial court based its ruling establish that Municipal Authority is not a BFP as a matter of law?

III

Before considering how the evidence bears out OSB's claim that Municipal Authority is not a BFP, we address two legal arguments advanced by OSB, which, if correct, would make resolution of the BFP issue unnecessary. First, OSB contends that, as an "omitted junior lienor", it is entitled to preservation of its interest regardless of whether Municipal Authority is a BFP. The trial court apparently accepted this argument, concluding, without addressing the BFP question:

1. That at the Trustee's sale, Old Stone Bank was an omitted junior lienor in that it was not notified of the sale;

2. As an omitted junior lienor, Old Stone Bank's lien was not affected by the Trustee's sale[.]

We cannot agree that OSB's interest may be sustained without consideration of Municipal Authority's status as a BFP. While lack of notice undeniably prejudices omitted junior lienors whose interests are extinguished by foreclosure, *see* RCW 61.24.050, the Legislature has determined that on balance the rights of the bona fide purchaser are paramount. See earlier discussion of RCW 61.24.040(7). Post-sale challenges are thus improper; the omitted lienors must seek other

---

[3] Ordinarily, a nonjudicial foreclosure sale would extinguish all junior liens. *See* RCW 61.24.050. As the trial court correctly observed, however, the "omitted junior lienor" rule of mortgage law may operate in the nonjudicial foreclosure context to preserve the interest of a junior lienor who has not had an opportunity to contest foreclosure or participate at the foreclosure sale. *See* RCW 61.24.020 (deeds of trust are "subject to all laws relating to mortgages on real property", except when the act provides otherwise).

remedies. *See* Comment, 59 Wash.L.Rev. at 337–40; Comment, 64 Neb.L.Rev. at 122.

OSB argues also that RCW 61.24.040(7) cannot protect Municipal Authority even if Municipal Authority is a BFP because the provision does not apply to "lienholder insiders". In support of this argument, OSB notes that "conclusive recitals" provisions such as that contained in RCW 61.24.040(7) have been interpreted as affording no protection to trust beneficiaries who purchase the trust property at a procedurally flawed nonjudicial foreclosure sale. *See Johnson v. Johnson,* 25 Wash.2d 797, 172 P.2d 243 (1946) (applying California law to "conclusive recitals" clause contained in deed of trust). Such recitals should also afford no protection to other junior lienholders, OSB asserts.

We find this argument to be without merit. The reason a trust beneficiary might be denied the benefits of "conclusive recitals" clauses is that the beneficiary is in a position to conduct the sale in a manner calculated to serve his own interests. *See Johnson,* at 840, 172 P.2d 243 ("conclusive recitals" clause should not protect "the beneficiary of the trust who purchased at the sale brought about by it"); Comment, 64 Neb.L.Rev. at 128 n. 150. But nothing inherent to the relationship between a junior lienholder and the foreclosing party, and certainly nothing that has been established about Municipal Authority's relationship to Glidden or Rourke here, enables the junior lienholder to rig a sale to its benefit. Thus, there is no cause to deny lienholders, as a class, the protection the "conclusive evidence" standard of RCW 61.24.040(7) affords.

We are persuaded against OSB's proposed "lienholder insider" exception to the recitals provision in RCW 61.24.040(7) also because such an exception is unnecessary to the proper operation of the statute. Textually, RCW 61.24.040(7) does not distinguish lienholders from other purchasers. The only distinction that is drawn is that between purchasers who are BFPs and those who are not, and this we find sufficient to protect third parties from prejudice caused by procedural flaws in foreclosures. A lienholder/purchaser who acts in reliance on flawed sale procedures would not be a BFP, and thus would not be insulated by the "conclusive evidence" rule.[4]

A broad brush exclusion of "lienholder insiders" is not only unjustified, it appears to be unwise. By limiting the availability of post-sale challenges to foreclosure, the "conclusive evidence" rule of RCW

---

[4] Significantly, scholarly discussions of conclusive recitals provisions make no mention of the need for a "lienholder insiders" exception. *See* G. Nelson & D. Whitman, *Real Estate Finance Law* § 7.20, at 537–39 (2d ed. 1985); Comment, *Court Actions Contesting the Nonjudicial Foreclosure of Deeds of Trust in Washington,* 59 Wash.L.Rev. 323, 339 (1984); Comment, *In Deed An Alternative Security Device: The Nebraska's Trust Deeds Act,* 64 Neb.L.Rev. 92, 127–28 (1985).

61.24.040(7) plays a critical role in removing the disincentives to investment that had existed under prior mortgage foreclosure laws. *See* Gose, 41 Wash.L.Rev. at 95–96. The promise of clear title helps attract purchasers to land sale auctions, and the swiftness and certainty of the nonjudicial foreclosure process encourages land-backed financing by assuring lenders a reliable method for realizing on their security interests. We would do almost certain damage to an essential aspect of the deed of trust program, therefore, if we were to deny post-sale protections to what is likely the broadest class of sale participants—the junior lienholders. *See Rosenberg v. Smidt,* 727 P.2d 778, 787 (Alaska 1986) (Moore, J., dissenting in part).

IV

We turn now to the bona fide purchaser question. A BFP is one who purchases property without knowledge, actual or constructive, of competing interests. *Miebach v. Colasurdo,* 102 Wash.2d 170, 175–76, 685 P.2d 1074 (1984). At issue here is Municipal Authority's knowledge that OSB had not received notice of Rourke's sale. OSB does not contend that Municipal Authority had actual knowledge of Rourke's failure to notify OSB, but argues that Municipal Authority should be charged with constructive knowledge of Rourke's error.

Two questions of fact must be answered to respond to OSB's contention. First, did the events surrounding Rourke's sale create in Municipal Authority a duty to inquire into possible flaws in the foreclosure process? Second, if Municipal Authority did have such a duty, did it satisfy that duty? *See generally Miebach,* at 175–77, 685 P.2d 1074 (discussing "inquiry notice"). Only the second of these questions is at issue here, since Municipal Authority concedes that "the circumstances surrounding the Glidden sale were such as to require it to make inquiry."

The question of whether Municipal Authority satisfied its duty of inquiry cannot properly be answered on summary judgment, however, because on this question, "the evidence is such that different inferences might reasonably be drawn therefrom". *Hudesman v. Foley,* 73 Wash.2d 880, 889, 441 P.2d 532 (1968) (quoting 92 C.J.S. *Vendor & Purchaser* § 374 (1955)); *see Fleming v. Stoddard Wendle Motor Co.,* 70 Wash.2d 465, 423 P.2d 926 (1967). That Municipal Authority had not received proper notice of Rourke's sale; that it knew about OSB's planned December sale; that junior lienholders did not attend the sale—these facts might suggest that Municipal Authority could not reasonably rely on Rourke's claim that she "always" notifies junior lienholders. On the other hand, knowing as much as Municipal Authority, Rourke persistently stood by her claims that she had notified OSB.

More also needs to be known about the communications between Municipal Authority and Rourke before it can be said with certainty that

Municipal Authority acted unreasonably in relying on her. For example, did Rourke have a reputation for carelessness in performing her duties as trustee? Was she known to respond hastily and incorrectly to inquiries put to her? What more can be determined about the timing and substance of Rourke's assurances that would reflect on the reasonableness of Municipal Authority's reliance? From a fuller appreciation of the circumstances of Rourke's interactions with Municipal Authority, the trial court will better be able to determine the reasonableness of Municipal Authority's reliance.

Urging us not to worry about this unresolved factual question, OSB offers the following principle of law: "Reasonable inquiry means inquiry of the party possessing the potential claim against the property." While obviously of value to OSB here, hard and fast rules of this sort are not generally recommended for questions of reasonableness. *Cf.* W. Keeton, D. Dobbs, R. Keeton, & D. Owen, *Prosser and Keeton on Torts* § 35 (5th ed. 1984) (disapproving rigid rules of conduct in tort law where reasonableness is in issue). What Municipal Authority reasonably should have done, and what a future foreclosure sale purchaser reasonably should do to prevent challenges to its title, can be determined only from the particular circumstances that obtain in each case.

We cannot accept OSB's proffered rule in any event because we find it to be unsupportable as a matter of law. The only case OSB cites for the rule is *Enterprise Timber, Inc. v. Washington Title Ins. Co.,* 76 Wash.2d 479, 457 P.2d 600 (1969), in which a mortgagee was charged with constructive knowledge of a fraud perpetrated by the mortgagor in acquiring the mortgaged property. The basis for the imputation of constructive knowledge was the mortgagee's actual knowledge of the mortgagor's bad reputation and prior illegal conduct in similar transactions.

> This knowledge apparently prompted [the mortgagee] to take unusual precautions to protect itself, and should have prompted a reasonable investigation of [the mortgagor's] purchase of the property. A simple inquiry of [the previous owner] would have revealed the fraud in procuring the conveyance. The record amply supports the [trial] court's finding that plaintiff unreasonably failed to make this investigation and was thus charged with constructive notice of the fraud . . .

Enterprise Timber, at 483, 457 P.2d 600.

OSB would read this language to mean that inquiry concerning other interests in property *must* be made of the interested parties themselves. We do not believe the holding of *Enterprise Timber* is that broad. The *Enterprise Timber* opinion merely observes that such inquiry would have disclosed a fraud in the transaction there at issue; at most, it suggests that inquiry of the previous owner was necessary under the circumstances that obtained in that case because whatever assurances the mortgagor might have made concerning the validity of his title were patently unreliable. Because there is no evidence that Rourke had a reputation for failing to give notice or being untruthful, this case is distinguishable.

The order on summary judgment is reversed and the case remanded for further proceedings.

PEARSON, C.J., and ANDERSEN, UTTER, BRACHTENBACH, CALLOW, GOODLOE, DOLLIVER and DORE, JJ., concur.

NOTES

1. *Presumption statutes.* Like Washington, several states have presumption statutes that are designed to enhance the finality of power of sale foreclosures and the marketability of titles that they produce. See, e.g., Ala. Code §§ 35–10–5, 12–21–99; West's Ann.Cal.Civ.Code § 2924; Mo. Ann. Stat. § 443.380; Nev.Rev.Stat.Ann. § 107.030(8); S.D.Codified Laws § 21–48–23; Utah Code Ann. § 57–1–28. Consider the following analysis of these statutes:

> Though these statutes vary significantly, they nevertheless seem to fall into three general categories. The first type, which we characterize as *"rebuttable presumption"* legislation, is exemplified by the Missouri statute: "[T]he recitals in the trustee or mortgagee's deed concerning the default, advertisement, sale or receipt of the purchase money, and all other facts pertinent thereto, shall be received as prima facie evidence in all courts of the truth thereof." [Mo.Rev.Stat. § 443.380] This type of statute, which is found, with minor variations, in over a dozen states, contains neither "conclusive presumption" language nor any specific protection for bona fide purchasers. Indeed, a few of these statutes claim to deal only with the *notice* requirements of the foreclosure and not with other aspects that might be carried out improperly. At most, the recitals create a rebuttable presumption that there was a valid basis for foreclosure and that the necessary procedural requirements have been satisfied. These statutes seem to do little more than restate the common law notion that the party attacking the validity of a foreclosure sale has the burden of proof. Presumably the rights of a bona fide purchaser under this type of statute would be no greater than those afforded under the common law "void-voidable" classification of power of sale foreclosure defects considered above. Such statutes contribute only slightly to the stability of power of sale titles.

> In the second category of statutes, the inclusion of appropriate recitals creates a conclusive presumption in favor of bona fide

purchasers, but this presumption extends only to notice requirements of the sale. We label this type of statute *"conclusive presumption for bona fide purchasers—notice only."* The California statute is typical; it states:

> [A] recital in the deed executed pursuant to the power of sale of compliance with all requirements of law regarding the mailing of copies of notices or the publication of a copy of the notice of default or the personal delivery of the copy of the notice of default or the posting of copies of the notice of sale or the publication of a copy thereof shall constitute prima facie evidence of compliance with these requirements and conclusive evidence thereof in favor of bona fide purchasers and encumbrancers for value and without notice.

[Cal.Civ.Code § 2924]. * * * [I]n the absence of such a statute, the failure to mail a statutorily required notice to a mortgagor renders the foreclosure sale void. That the property is sold to a bona fide purchaser is irrelevant. No title, legal or equitable, passes at the sale. The statute, however, reduces the impact of the notice defect. In effect, the notice defect is deemed to render the sale only *voidable.* Consequently, a foreclosure sale purchaser or subsequent grantee who qualifies as a bona fide purchaser will hold an indefeasible title despite the failure to give proper notice.

On the other hand, it is unclear whether the [foregoing] statute will benefit a bona fide purchaser when the defect in the sale process is *procedural* but does not deal with the statutory notice requirements. For example, suppose the person who conducts a foreclosure sale under a deed of trust was improperly replaced as trustee by another person a few days before the sale. Under the traditional analysis, the sale is void regardless of the sale purchaser's being a bona fide purchaser. The California statute does not appear to aid the purchaser in that context because a sale by an unqualified trustee does not constitute the type of notice defect that is within the literal purview of the statute. * * *

The third category, which we characterize as *"conclusive presumption for bona fide purchasers—all aspects of foreclosure"* affords the greatest protection for bona fide purchasers. At least fourteen states have this type of legislation. Washington's statute typifies this category. It requires the foreclosing trustee to issue the foreclosure purchaser a deed that

> shall recite the facts showing the sale was conducted in compliance with all of the requirements of this chapter and of the deed of trust, which recital shall be prima facie evidence of such compliance and conclusive evidence thereof in favor of bona fide purchasers and encumbrancers for value.

[Wash.Rev.Code Ann. § 61.24.040]. * * *

The literal language of this type of statute is breathtakingly broad in its impact on bona fide purchasers. Not only does it purport to protect a bona fide purchaser from notice and other procedural defects in the foreclosure process, it is arguably applicable even when the mortgagee had no substantive right to foreclose. * * * Suppose, for example, that a mortgage is foreclosed even though the obligation that it secures is not in default, or that the mortgage was forged. Under traditional state, the foreclosure would be void in either instance, and would be set aside even against a sale purchaser who was a bona fide purchaser. The literal language of ["category three"] statutes suggest a different result. * * *

Limiting the conclusive impact of [such statutes] to procedural defects in the foreclosure process clearly makes sense. To allow a bona fide purchaser to prevail over a mortgagor who was not in default or a person who never executed a mortgage to begin with would be fundamentally unfair, a normative result that legislatures adopting "category three" statutes probably did not intend.

Grant S. Nelson & Dale A. Whitman, *Reforming Foreclosure: The Uniform Nonjudicial Foreclosure Act*, 53 Duke L.J. 1399, 1503–07 (2004).

2. *Washington statute amended.* Shortly after *Glidden* was decided, the Washington legislature amended West's Rev.Code Wash.Ann. § 61.24.040(7) to provide that "these recitals shall not affect the lien or interest of any person entitled to notice under RCW § 61.24.040(1), if the trustee fails to give the required notice to such person. In such case, the lien or interest of such omitted person shall not be affected by the sale and such omitted person shall be treated as if such person was the holder of the same lien or interest and was omitted as a party defendant in a judicial foreclosure proceeding." Why do you think the response to *Glidden* was so swift?

3. *Intentional omission of junior parties in a power of sale foreclosure.* Earlier in our consideration of judicial foreclosure, we observed that in some jurisdictions a foreclosing mortgagee can keep a pro-landlord junior lease alive by intentionally not joining the lessee. Should this be possible in the power of sale context? Suppose, for example, a state power of sale statute requires a foreclosing mortgagee to mail notice to each person holding a junior interest in mortgaged land. Suppose further that the foreclosing mortgagee mails notice to everyone entitled to it except junior lessees that the mortgagee wants to keep. Should the foreclosure be effective against everyone but the "un-notified lessees"? Or should the foreclosure be invalid as to everyone? Does the amendment to the Washington statute discussed in Note 2 permit a foreclosing mortgagee to keep favorable junior leases alive after the power of sale foreclosure by intentionally failing to give them the required statutory notice?

3. CONSTITUTIONAL PROBLEMS WITH THE POWER OF SALE

As we noted earlier, power of sale foreclosure statutes vary considerably in the degree and nature of notice that the foreclosing mortgagee must give the mortgagor and other interested parties. Moreover, power of sale legislation almost never provides for a hearing, judicial or otherwise, before foreclosure. To what extent do these attributes of power of sale foreclosures create constitutional problems under the due process clauses of the Fifth and Fourteenth Amendments to the federal Constitution? The following materials examines these issues. It is important to remember that the Fourteenth Amendment's due process clause applies only when "significant state involvement" exists and that the due process clause of the Fifth Amendment applies only when sufficient "federal action" exists.

RICKER V. UNITED STATES

United States District Court, Maine, 1976
417 F.Supp. 133

GIGNOUX, DISTRICT JUDGE.

In this action, which is now before the Court on cross-motions for summary judgment, plaintiffs Ellie G. Ricker and Elizabeth Ricker seek to nullify the foreclosure sale of their farm by the Farmers Home Administration (FmHA). Named as defendants are the United States of America, the Secretary of Agriculture and three FmHA officials, and Ivan and Vivian Upton, who purchased the property at the foreclosure sale.

Plaintiffs allege that the foreclosure procedures utilized by FmHA failed to afford them notice and an opportunity to be heard and thus violated the Due Process Clause of the Fifth Amendment. They also charge that the Maine nonjudicial foreclosure statute, 14 Me.Rev.St.Ann. §§ 6203–04, pursuant to which the foreclosure was effected, is void because in violation of the Due Process Clause of the Fourteenth Amendment. Finally, they attack their underlying indebtedness to FmHA on the ground that the loans were improperly made and enforced by FmHA in violation of the agency's alleged obligations to make only sound loans to plaintiffs and to supervise plaintiffs' farming operations. See 7 U.S.C.A. §§ 1983(b), (d); 7 CFR §§ 1802.1–1802.67, 1831.3. As relief, plaintiffs seek a declaratory judgment that the foreclosure and subsequent sale of the property were void and without effect and an order enjoining defendants from removing plaintiffs from their land, "taking any action based upon the purported foreclosure," or seeking repayment of the outstanding loans.

* * *

For the reasons to be stated, the Court holds that the foreclosure and sale of plaintiffs' farm were effected in violation of their rights to due process under the Fifth Amendment, and hence are void and of no effect. The Court therefore does not reach the question whether the Maine nonjudicial foreclosure statute violates the Due Process Clause of the Fourteenth Amendment.[2] Nor does the Court deem it appropriate at this time to consider the validity of the loans secured by the FmHA mortgage.

I

Plaintiff Ellie G. Ricker is 74 years old; his wife, plaintiff Elizabeth Ricker, is 78 years old. Mr. Ricker purchased an 80-acre potato farm in Blaine, Aroostook County, Maine in 1943. He farmed the land until 1970, and he and his wife still reside on the property. Between April 1966 and March 1968 the Rickers executed a series of five promissory notes to FmHA in consideration of operating loans authorized by the Consolidated Farmers Home Administration Act of 1961, as amended, 7 U.S.C.A. § 1921 et seq. In August 1968 they applied for a sixth loan to harvest the 1968 potato crop. At that time substantial balances were due and owing on the first five notes, and FmHA required the Rickers to execute and deliver a mortgage deed on the farm to secure all six promissory notes.

By May 1970 the Rickers had retired from farming and were living on a small fixed income. Substantial unpaid balances remained on the six notes. An FmHA official visited the Rickers on at least four occasions in 1970 and 1971 to attempt to work out a resolution of the debt. He proposed that the Rickers voluntarily transfer the farm to FmHA or at least rent it to produce income that might pay off the debt. The Rickers rejected these proposals.

In the spring of 1972, on the recommendation of FmHA officials in Maine and after approval by the FmHA Office of General Counsel, FmHA decided to foreclose on the Ricker mortgage. At this time outstanding balances on the promissory notes totaled $17,676.84, plus substantial interest. On April 14, 1972 FmHA mailed each of the Rickers an identical "Notice of Acceleration of Indebtedness and Demand for Payment." These

---

[2] Nor can this opinion easily be extended to reach the question whether the use by a nonfederal mortgagee of the Maine nonjudicial foreclosure statute violates the Due Process Clause of the Fourteenth Amendment. Any challenge to the use of that procedure by such a mortgagee would have to clear the hurdle of establishing "state action," a consideration not involved in the present case. See, e.g., Northrip v. Federal National Mortgage Association, 527 F.2d 23 (6th Cir.1975). Further, the question whether a mortgagor has waived any right to due process can be determined only in the light of the facts of each case. See Swarb v. Lennox, 405 U.S. 191, 200, 92 S.Ct. 767, 31 L.Ed.2d 138 (1972); Bryant v. Jefferson Federal Savings & Loan Association, 166 U.S.App.D.C. 178, 509 F.2d 511, 515–16 (D.C.Cir.1974). See also Gunter v. Merchants Warren National Bank, 360 F.Supp. 1085 (D.Me.1973) (three-judge court) (invalidating prejudgment attachment statute); Kramer v. Inhabitants of the Town of Linneus, 144 Me. 239, 67 A.2d 536 (1949) (invalidating tax lien foreclosure statute as applied to nonresident); Henry and Cole, Are Maine's Real Property Mortgage Foreclosure Statutes Constitutional?, 8 Me.Bar Bull., May 1974, at 1.

were sent by certified mail, return receipt requested. The notices recited the promissory notes and past due indebtedness thereon, demanded immediate payment and concluded:

> Unless full payment of said indebtedness is received on or before May 15, 1972, appropriate measures will be taken to foreclose the said mortgage and pursue any other available remedies.

The agency received receipts for these letters signed by the Rickers and dated April 18, 1972. After expiration of the 30-day period allowed in the notices, FmHA instituted nonjudicial proceedings for foreclosure of the Rickers' mortgage pursuant to 14 Me.Rev.Stat.Ann. § 6203(1): that is, FmHA caused to be published a notice of foreclosure on three successive weeks in the Presque Isle, Maine *Star Herald* and recorded a copy of the notice and a certificate of publication in the Southern Aroostook Registry of Deeds on June 22, 1972. No written notice of the foreclosure sale was served on the Rickers, and FmHA did not utilize its option under 14 Me.Rev.Stat.Ann. § 6203(2) to have the Rickers served with an attested copy of the newspaper advertisement. The Rickers testified in their affidavits, which are uncontroverted, that they "heard that the Farmers Home Administration went through some kind of procedure with a newspaper concerning our farm" but did not see the notices themselves nor understand that FmHA had foreclosed.

Following publication of the notice of foreclosure, the Rickers had one year to redeem the property by satisfying the debt. 14 Me.Rev.Stat.Ann. § 6204. An FmHA official visited the farm shortly before the end of the period of redemption to appraise the property and warn the Rickers that sale was imminent. The Rickers state, however, that they remained unaware of the sale until afterward and then learned of it only by word of mouth. The Rickers made no further payments on the notes; and in July 1974 FmHA sold the farm to the Uptons for $15,600. FmHA delivered to the Uptons a quit claim deed and took back a purchase money mortgage in the amount of $14,400, which has not yet been discharged.

II

It cannot be doubted that the Rickers were "deprived of * * * property, without due process of law" in violation of the Fifth Amendment. First, the foreclosure and sale were initiated and carried out by federal employees acting on behalf of the federal government: they plainly were bound to observe the requirements of the Fifth Amendment. See, e.g., Arnett v. Kennedy, 416 U.S. 134, 164, 94 S.Ct. 1633, 40 L.Ed.2d 15 (1974) (Powell, J., concurring); Rudder v. United States, 96 U.S.App.D.C. 329, 226 F.2d 51, 53 (1955). Second, the Rickers as mortgagors retained under Maine law the right to undisturbed enjoyment of the farm until entry of foreclosure by the mortgagee. Pettengill v. Turo, 159 Me. 350, 359, 193 A.2d 367 (1963). The Government's foreclosure thus clearly deprived plaintiffs of an interest in property protected by the Fifth Amendment. See Fuentes v. Shevin, 407 U.S. 67, 84, 92 S.Ct. 1983, 32 L.Ed.2d 556 (1972); Law v. United States Department of Agriculture, supra, 366 F.Supp. at 1238 & n. 6; United States v. Certain Land in the City of Augusta, 220 F.Supp. 696, 699 (D.Me.1963). Finally, the procedures utilized by FmHA plainly failed to afford the Rickers the procedural safeguards which due process requires. Although the requirements of due process may vary with differing circumstances, Supreme Court decisions have fully established that procedural due process demands, at a minimum, notice and an opportunity to be heard. Fuentes v. Shevin, supra, 407 U.S. at 80–82, 92 S.Ct. 1983; Boddie v. Connecticut, 401 U.S. 371, 377–79, 91 S.Ct. 780, 28 L.Ed.2d 113 (1971); Armstrong v. Manzo, 380 U.S. 545, 550–52, 85 S.Ct. 1187, 14 L.Ed.2d 62 (1965); Mullane v. Central Hanover Bank & Trust Co., 339 U.S. 306, 313, 70 S.Ct. 652, 94 L.Ed. 865 (1950); Gunter v. Merchants Warren National Bank, 360 F.Supp. 1085, 1088 (D.Me.1973) (three-judge court). In the instant case, the Rickers were provided neither of these essential protections.

The Government asserts that the Rickers received satisfactory notice of the impending foreclosure. To be adequate, notice "must be such as is reasonably calculated to reach interested parties." Mullane v. Central Hanover Bank & Trust Co., supra, 339 U.S. at 318, 70 S.Ct. at 659. The newspaper foreclosure notices, which the Rickers did not see, plainly failed to meet this standard. "[N]otice by publication is not enough with respect to a person whose name and address are known or very easily ascertainable and whose legally protected interests are directly affected by the proceedings in question." Schroeder v. City of New York, 371 U.S. 208, 212–13, 83 S.Ct. 279, 282, 9 L.Ed.2d 255 (1962). Accord, Walker v. City of Hutchinson, 352 U.S. 112, 115–16, 77 S.Ct. 200, 1 L.Ed.2d 178 (1956); Mullane v. Central Hanover Bank & Trust Co., supra, at 314–19, 70 S.Ct. 652. The only communication received by the Rickers which could even remotely be construed as notice was the "Notice of Acceleration of Indebtedness and Demand for Payment." But this document merely stated that the Rickers' debt was accelerated, that payment was immediately due and demanded, and that unless full payment were forthcoming by May 15, 1972, "appropriate measures [would] be taken to foreclose the said mortgage and pursue any other available remedies." This threat of foreclosure simply did not give clear notice that foreclosure proceedings would in fact be instituted. More importantly, this "Notice of Acceleration" made no pretense of extending the Rickers any opportunity to challenge the decision to institute foreclosure proceedings.

Although "the formality and procedural requisites for the hearing can vary, depending upon the importance of the interests involved and the nature of the * * * proceedings," Boddie v. Connecticut, supra, 401 U.S. at 378, 91 S.Ct. 780 at 786, the Constitution requires a meaningful and timely opportunity to be heard. North Georgia Finishing, Inc. v. Di-Chem, Inc., 419 U.S. 601, 606, 95 S.Ct. 719, 42 L.Ed.2d 751 (1975); Mitchell v. W.T. Grant Co., 416 U.S. 600, 618, 94 S.Ct. 1895, 40 L.Ed.2d 406 (1974); Fuentes v. Shevin, supra, 407 U.S. at 80–82, 92 S.Ct. 1983. The Rickers were offered no opportunity for hearing, and no hearing was held, before their mortgage was foreclosed.

The Government argues that any opportunity to be heard would be mere surplusage in the context of a mortgage foreclosure. The issues are open and shut: the existence of overdue debt and of a valid mortgage agreement. But this argument must fail, for two reasons. First, the simplicity of the legal issues and the improbability of any colorable challenge to the Government's position does not of itself dispel the need that the party affected have an opportunity to be heard before a final deprivation takes place. See Mitchell v. W.T. Grant Co., supra, 416 U.S. at 609–10, 616–18, 94 S.Ct. 1895; Fuentes v. Shevin, supra, 407 U.S. at 87 & n. 17, 92 S.Ct. 1983; Turner v. Blackburn, 389 F.Supp. 1250, 1259 (W.D.N.C.1975) (three-judge court); Garner v. Tri-State Development Co., 382 F.Supp. 377, 380 (E.D.Mich.1974). Second, the Rickers have brought forward challenges to the foreclosure based not only on the validity of the mortgage but also on the propriety of FmHA's decision to foreclose. They claim that the notes held by the Government lacked consideration because FmHA failed to provide the managerial assistance to borrowers allegedly required by Department of Agriculture regulations, that FmHA abused its discretion by continuing to make loans which it knew or should have known the Rickers could never repay, and that the decision to foreclose was made in disregard of policy considerations in favor of compromising or postponing payment of the underlying debt. See generally 31 U.S.C.A. §§ 952–53; 7 CFR § 1867.1 et seq. The Rickers should have been afforded a reasonable opportunity to present these claims. At a minimum, such an opportunity would require express written notice of the impending foreclosure, informing them that they were entitled to a hearing at which they could challenge both the legal right of FmHA to foreclose and the propriety of the decision to do so. See generally Goldberg v. Kelly, 397 U.S. 254, 266–71, 90 S.Ct. 1011, 25 L.Ed.2d 287 (1970); Escalera v. New York City Housing Authority, 425 F.2d 853, 861–64 (2d Cir.), cert. denied, 400 U.S. 853, 91 S.Ct. 54, 27 L.Ed.2d 91 (1970); Turner v. Blackburn, supra, at 1259. Nothing approaching such an opportunity to challenge the Government's action was offered the Rickers in the present situation.

Finally, the Government contends that the Rickers waived their constitutional rights to notice and hearing by signing the mortgage in 1968. The Court disagrees. To be effective, waiver of a constitutional right must be "voluntary, knowing, and intelligently made." D.H. Overmyer Co. v. Frick Co., 405 U.S. 174, 185, 92 S.Ct. 775, 782, 31 L.Ed.2d 124 (1972); Swarb v. Lennox, 405 U.S. 191, 92 S.Ct. 767, 31 L.Ed.2d 138 (1972). No language in the mortgage signed by the Rickers amounted to a waiver of their due process right of prior notice and hearing. Paragraphs 12 and 18 of the mortgage, upon which the Government relies, do no more than state the Government's right to foreclose under Maine law upon the occurrence of certain events. Cf. Fuentes v. Shevin, supra, 407 U.S. at 96, 92 S.Ct. 1983; Turner v. Blackburn, supra, at 1255, 1260–61. Even if the mortgage had contained language which might be construed as a waiver, the Ricker mortgage was a contract of adhesion, and the Government has "made no showing whatever that the * * * [Rickers] were actually aware or made aware of the significance of the fine print now relied upon as a waiver of constitutional rights." Fuentes v. Shevin, 407 U.S. supra, at 95, 92 S.Ct. at 2002. It is undisputed that the Rickers are an elderly farming couple, now in their seventies; that neither of them received more than a sixth grade education; and that although they had many dealings with FmHA over the years, they were unfamiliar with legal documents and had no prior experience of a foreclosure proceeding. The Rickers have testified that they did not read the mortgage and that they had no understanding at the time they executed the mortgage that they were foregoing their rights to notice and hearing before foreclosure and sale of their farm. No attorney was advising them, and at no time did anyone explain to them that by signing the mortgage they were waiving their rights to notice and hearing. Under these circumstances, the signing of the mortgage plainly did not constitute a "voluntary, knowing, and intelligently made" waiver of the Rickers' due process rights.

Accordingly, the Court has concluded that the procedures by which FmHA effected the foreclosure and sale of the Rickers' farm violated their Fifth Amendment rights to due process.

III

Defendants Ivan and Vivian Upton, who purchased the Ricker farm at the foreclosure sale, contend that they are bona fide purchasers for value and are entitled to the property free of any claim by plaintiffs. See 33 Me.Rev.Stat.Ann. § 201 (1965); Hayden v. Russell, 119 Me. 38, 109 A. 485 (1920); Knapp v. Bailey, 79 Me. 195, 9 A. 122 (1887); IV American Law of Property § 17.10 (A. Casner ed. 1952). Under the applicable Maine law, however, a quit claim deed is only effective to convey whatever interest the grantor may have had in the land. Reed v. Knights, 87 Me. 181, 32 A. 870 (1895); Coe v. Persons Unknown, 43 Me. 432 (1857); Butman v. Hussey, 30 Me. 263 (1849). Consequently, if the Government's foreclosure was ineffective, the Government obtained no title to the Ricker farm which could be conveyed to the Uptons. In any event, it is clear that the Uptons were not bona fide purchasers. The quit claim deed they received from FmHA expressly recited that the premises had been acquired "by virtue of foreclosure proceedings." The proof of publication recorded in the Southern Aroostook Registry of Deeds disclosed that the foreclosure had been effected by nonjudicial process. The Rickers continued to occupy the property and to claim title. Under Maine law a purchaser at a foreclosure sale cannot claim protection as a bona fide purchaser where, as here, it appears from documents and facts known at the time of purchase that there may be a substantial defect in the seller's claim of title. See Rowe v. Hayden, 149 Me. 266, 101 A.2d 190 (1953); Devine v. Tierney, 139 Me. 50 (1942); Hopkins v. McCarthy, 121 Me. 27, 31, 115 A. 513 (1921); Knapp v. Bailey, supra. The sale by FmHA to the Uptons therefore did not cut off plaintiffs' interest in the property.

IV

The Court holds that the foreclosure of plaintiffs' mortgage was effected by FmHA in violation of plaintiffs' Fifth Amendment rights to due process and that the sale of plaintiffs' farm to defendants Upton was ineffective to divest plaintiffs' title to the premises. Accordingly, judgment will be entered for plaintiffs against defendants declaring that the foreclosure and sale of their property were void and without effect because the foreclosure procedures utilized violated plaintiffs' rights under the Due Process Clause of the Fifth Amendment, and further enjoining defendants from removing plaintiffs from their land or taking any other action based upon the purported foreclosure. In all other respects, plaintiffs' claims for relief are denied. Plaintiffs' counsel will prepare a proposed form of judgment, to be approved as to form by defendants' counsel and submitted for entry by the Court.

It is so ordered.

NOTES

1. *The notice requirement.* In Turner v. Blackburn, 389 F.Supp. 1250 (W.D.N.C.1975), a three judge federal court invalidated North Carolina power of sale legislation that required only notice by newspaper publication and posting. The court stated: "To propose to a homeowner that he trek to the courthouse or spend 20 cents to examine fine-print legal notices, *daily* for the duration of a twenty-year mortgage, as his sole protection against summary eviction, seems to us to offer him nothing of value."

In Mennonite Bd. of Missions v. Adams, 462 U.S. 791, 103 S.Ct. 2706, 77 L.Ed.2d 180 (1983), the United States Supreme Court relied on *Mullane* in holding that a mortgagee's due process rights were violated because notice that the mortgaged property was being sold for nonpayment of taxes was only published and posted in the county courthouse. The Court emphasized that "when the mortgagee is identified in a mortgage that is publicly recorded, constructive notice by publication must be supplemented by notice mailed to the mortgagee's last known available address, or by personal service. But unless the mortgagee is not reasonably identifiable, constructive notice alone does not satisfy the mandate of *Mullane.*" Id.

In Federal Deposit Ins. Corp. v. Morrison, 568 F.Supp. 1240 (N.D.Ala.1983), a federal district court invalidated a power of sale foreclosure conducted under Alabama legislation that afforded a mortgagor notice by publication only. The court emphasized that, if notice by publication is constitutionally deficient with respect to a mortgagee, as in *Mennonite,* it is *a fortiori* inadequate as to a mortgagor. According to the district court, under *Mennonite* "the notice published * * * 'simply was not such as one desirous of actually informing the [mortgagor] might reasonably adopt to accomplish it." Id. at 1244. However, the Eleventh Circuit reversed on the perplexing ground that foreclosure "did not deprive [the mortgagor] of his equity of redemption, but only terminated it," and hence that no taking had occurred. According to the court:

> The state in creating this interest commanded that it should exist only up to the moment when the mortgagee properly exercised the power of sale. That such a moment was undetermined when the parties signed the mortgage did not nullify the conditional nature of his equity of redemption, any more than the unpredictability of a life estate holder's death can prevent termination of his interest when he actually dies. The blame for turning the once-hypothetical foreclosure into reality lies solely with the mortgagors.

747 F.2d 610, 615. For the view that the Eleventh Circuit's opinion in *Morrison* reflects "an understanding of the practical problems faced by foreclosing mortgagees, practicalities not taken into account in * * * *Mennonite* or the district court in *Morrison,* and that it reflects 'a clarity of insight into the complexities of Alabama mortgage law rarely accorded the depth of analysis that body of law deserves,'" see Romaine S. Scott, *Mennonite:* What Does It Mean to Alabama Mortgagees After *Federal Deposit Insurance Corp. v. Morrison,* 36 Alabama L.Rev. 969, 998 (1985). On the other hand, the Fifth Circuit sharply criticized the Eleventh Circuit's approach in *Morrison:*

> The Eleventh Circuit's reasoning * * * illustrates the persistent difficulty of defining the rights in property that are subject to constitutional protections. Although the Supreme Court has recognized that the states have broad power to create and define the scope of property rights, the Court has also recognized that a purely positivist view of property rights threatens to render the Due Process Clause meaningless.
>
> * * *
>
> The simple act of labeling a condition "substantive" does not eliminate due process concerns. At some point, to hold that no due process attaches to the operation of a "substantive" condition that terminates a property right is to define the scope of that property

right by the *absence* of procedural protections attendant upon its termination. This too reduces the due process clause to a tautology.

Davis Oil Co. v. Mills, 873 F.2d 774, 782–84 (5th Cir.1989).

Are junior lienors constitutionally entitled to more than notice by publication? The junior lienor often has a greater financial stake in the mortgaged real estate than the mortgagor. If notice by publication or posting is insufficient when a tax lien sale will terminate a junior lien, shouldn't it also be insufficient when a senior mortgage foreclosure will do the same? Can commercial junior lienors keep themselves informed concerning the status of senior liens? What about non-commercial junior lienors? See generally, Nelson, Whitman, Burkhart & Freyermuth, Real Estate Finance Law § 7.25 (6th ed.2014). Consider the language of a Maryland decision in which the court held that *Mennonite* requires junior lienors to get at least mailed notice of a power of sale:

> A simple title scan from the time the property was acquired by the current owner to the initiation of the foreclosure proceedings would have provided notice of [the junior mortgagee's] interest in the property. Also, [the junior mortgagee's] name and address appear on the top page of the deed of trust which is recorded in the land records * * * . Certainly, this process is not oppressive to the foreclosing party in terms of the amount of time, money or effort expended.

Island Fin., Inc. v. Ballman, 92 Md.App. 125, 607 A.2d 76 (1992). Accord: USX Corp. v. H.H. Champlin, 992 F.2d 1380 (5th Cir.1993); Teschke v. Keller, 38 Mass.App.Ct. 627, 650 N.E.2d 1279 (1995).

2. *"Request for notice" statutes.* Some power of sale statutes require mailed notice not only to the mortgagor and the real estate owner, but also to any person who has recorded a request to receive it. See, e.g., Vernon's Ann.Mo.Stat. § 443.325. Does this type of statute obviate the constitutional notice problem with respect to junior lienors? Consider a typical judicial response to this question:

> The [request for notice] statute is designed to go hand in hand with [the] constitutional protection so that no property interest will be unfairly extinguished. In this instance [the junior lienor] did not receive notice solely for the reason that it had not filed a request for notice of sale. It is clear, however, that with little effort or diligence, [mortgagee] could have obtained [the junior lienor's] address and mailed notice to [it]. After taking into consideration the holdings of *Mennonite* and its progeny, we believe that [a request for notice statute] protects the due process rights of those parties whose interests and addresses are not "reasonably ascertainable," by providing a mechanism through which such parties can be assured that they will receive notice. If an interest of a party is reasonably ascertainable, however, the minimum requirements of due process

dictate that actual notice be given without a formal request for notice being filed.

Island Fin., Inc. v. Ballman, 92 Md.App. 125, 607 A.2d 76 (1992). Accord Davis Oil Co. v. Mills, 873 F.2d 774 (5th Cir.1989); USX Corp. v. H.H. Champlin, 992 F.2d 1380 (5th Cir.1993).

3. *Supplemental notice by foreclosing mortgagee.* To what extent can a foreclosing mortgagee obviate the notice argument by providing more extensive notice than the statute requires? Some courts and commentators have maintained that "the fact that mortgagees alert mortgagors to their rights will not satisfy the requirements of due process or cure a constitutionally infirm statute." Kathleen Barry, Comment, The Constitutionality of Maine's Real Estate Mortgage Foreclosure Statutes, 32 Maine L.Rev. 147, 171 (1980). See also Wuchter v. Pizzutti, 276 U.S. 13, 48 S.Ct. 259, 72 L.Ed. 446 (1928) (nonresident motorist service of process statute that required only service on the secretary of state violated the Fourteenth Amendment due process clause though the secretary of state actually mailed notice to the nonresident motorist). On the other hand, if notice is actually provided to all interested parties, does anyone have the requisite injury required by Article III of the Constitution to confer standing to litigate the statute's constitutional infirmity? See Nelson, Whitman, Burkhart & Freyermuth, Real Estate Finance Law § 7.26 (6th ed. 2014).

4. *The hearing requirement.* Several courts that have reached the hearing issue directly have cited *Fuentes* to invalidate power of sale statutes. See e.g., Turner v. Blackburn, 389 F.Supp. 1250 (W.D.N.C.1975); Garner v. Tri-State Dev. Co., 382 F.Supp. 377 (E.D.Mich.1974); Northrip v. Federal Nat'l Mortg. Ass'n, 372 F.Supp. 594 (E.D.Mich.1974), *rev'd on other grounds*, 572 F.2d 23 (6th Cir. 1975); Valley Dev. at Vail, Inc. v. Warder, 192 Colo. 316, 557 P.2d 1180 (1976). However, in Guidarelli v. Lazaretti, 305 Minn. 551, 233 N.W.2d 890 (1975), the Minnesota Supreme Court upheld that state's power of sale statute against a *Fuentes* hearing argument. The court stated:

> Unlike the due process problems raised by [*Sniadach* and *Fuentes*] the statutory scheme for mortgage foreclosure by advertisement, Minn.St. c. 580, provides for 4 weeks' prior notice before sale, it permits the mortgagor to redeem his property within either 6 months or 1 year, and most importantly, he is not deprived of the use and possession of the property prior to the public foreclosure sale.

Do you agree? Which is more burdensome to a debtor, being deprived of temporary possession of a refrigerator or automobile until a final hearing on the merits or being deprived of title to real estate with no statutory requirement of a hearing at all?

In many jurisdictions, a mortgagor or junior lienor often challenges a pending power of sale foreclosure by bringing a suit to enjoin it. The basis for the injunction suit is found either in the common law or in a general statutory authorization that is not part of the power of sale legislation. A few power of sale statutes specifically authorize an injunction suit by the mortgagor. See Wash. Rev.Code § 61.24.130. Does the ability to bring a suit satisfy the constitutional hearing requirement? Or do the power of sale statutes have to provide an opportunity for a hearing? See Nelson, Whitman, Burkhart & Freyermuth, Real Estate Finance Law § 7.26 (6th ed.2014).

The hearing probably does not have to be judicial. As the *Turner* court indicated, a hearing before a "clerk or a similar neutral official" is sufficient. Turner v. Blackburn, 389 F.Supp. 1250 (W.D.N.C.1975). Moreover, in United States v. Ford, 551 F.Supp. 1101 (N.D.Miss.1982), a federal district court held that a federal agency's administrative hearing procedure can supplement state power of sale legislation that fails to satisfy due process hearing requirements. The neutrality of the administrative official conducting the hearing is an important issue. Indeed, in reversing a trial court's refusal to issue preliminary injunctive relief against an FmHA power of sale foreclosure, the Eleventh Circuit said:

> A fair hearing requires an impartial arbiter. We have serious reservations about the neutrality of the hearing officers. The regulations establish that the hearing officer is a nearby district director. On its face, the regulation appears less than neutral. The nearby director will be evaluating a decision to foreclose made by a peer and already approved by his boss, the state director. * * * On the surface, the [mortgagors] have shown a substantial likelihood that a conflict may exist that impinges the hearing officer's impartiality.

Johnson v. U.S. Dept. of Agric., 734 F.2d 774 (11th Cir.1984).

5. *Waiver of due process rights.* Assuming that many power of sale statutes violate procedural due process requirements, is waiver a possible solution? In *Ricker,* the court held that the mortgagor's waiver was invalid because it was not voluntary, knowing, and intelligently made. In *Fuentes,* the Supreme Court recognized the possibility of waiver but rejected it on the facts of that case. The Court held that the waivers were ineffective for several reasons: (1) The contracts did not provide specifically for a waiver of constitutional rights, and they did not specify the process by which "the seller could take back the goods"; (2) The parties did not understand the significance of the waiver; and (3) The parties who negotiated the contract terms had unequal bargaining positions. For further consideration of waiver in power of sale foreclosures, see Johnson v. U.S. Dept. of Agric., 734 F.2d 774 (11th Cir.1984); Rau v. Cavenaugh, 500 F.Supp. 204 (D.S.D.1980).

If a valid waiver depends only on making the waiving party aware of what rights he is waiving, it could be argued that carefully drafted language in a mortgage or deed of trust can constitute a waiver of procedural due process rights. On the other hand, if a valid waiver depends on factors such as equality of bargaining power, doesn't a subsequent title examiner have an impossible burden? If bargaining inequality invalidates the power of sale clause in a particular mortgage, can this claim be used against any purchaser or only against the foreclosing lender if it buys at the sale? One commentator has pointed out:

> If as the *Fuentes* and *Overmyer* cases suggest, not all waivers will be effective, then the power of sale foreclosure may be rendered of doubtful utility because of the problems of establishing marketable title. Defects of the type described above will not appear of record. How will a title examiner be able to distinguish a valid exercise of a power for sale from an ineffective one? Would such a defect render a sale void or merely voidable? If the sale is rendered void, then no title passes in law or equity. Thus, the purchaser at the sale, whether the noteholder or a third party, cannot get title of any kind and *a fortiori* no title would pass to subsequent purchasers. If, however, the defect renders the sale only voidable the mortgagor or grantor's right to challenge is cut off as against any purchaser for value without notice. Thus the grantor or mortgagor will be able to set aside the sale as against the noteholder as purchaser, but not as against a sale purchaser or subsequent grantee who would otherwise qualify as a purchaser for value without notice.

Grant S. Nelson, Deed of Trust Foreclosure Under Power of Sale—Constitutional Problems—Legislative Alternative, 28 Mo.Bar J. 428, 434 (1972).

How could an effective waiver by subsequent junior mortgagees or judgment creditors be established? Is the mortgagor's waiver in recorded documents sufficient to bind junior interest holders? Can constitutional rights be waived in such an indirect fashion? See Nelson, Whitman, Burkhart & Freyermuth, Real Estate Finance Law § 7.27 (6th ed.2014).

6.   *Federal power of sale legislation.* As mentioned earlier, the federal Multifamily Mortgage Foreclosure Act ("Multifamily Act") and the Single Family Mortgage Foreclosure Act ("Single Family Act") authorize power of sale foreclosure of all residential mortgages held by the Department of Housing and Urban Development ("HUD"). Under the Acts, the Notice of Default and Foreclosure must be sent by certified mail, return receipt requested, at least twenty-one days before the foreclosure sale, to the original mortgagor, any other person liable for the mortgage debt, the property "owner," and, at least ten days before the sale, all lienors. 12 U.S.C.A. §§ 3708(1) & 3758(2). Unless one takes a broad view of who is an "owner," neither the Acts nor the related regulations require mailed notice to holders of leases, easements, and similar junior interests. Is this a constitutional defect? As we noted earlier, a junior interest holder who is not joined to judicial foreclosure is not bound by the proceedings, because of due process principles. Should we apply similar reasoning to power of sale foreclosures?

The Acts do not provide for a hearing. However, the regulations for the Multifamily Act require HUD to "provide to the mortgagor [and current owner] an opportunity informally to present reasons why the mortgage should not be foreclosed. Such opportunity may be provided before or after the designation of a foreclosure commissioner but before service of the notice of default and foreclosure." 24 C.F.R. § 27.5. The regulations for the Single Family Act do not include a similar requirement. Does even the Multifamily Act requirement satisfy due process? At least one court has held that is does with respect to mortgagors. See Lisbon Square v. United States, 856 F.Supp. 482 (E.D.Wis.1994) ("By offering a mortgagor a chance to explain the failure to make mortgage payments, HUD provides all the due process required by the Fifth Amendment. * * * A mortgagor who fails to respond to notices of delinquency waives the right to be heard.") Are you convinced? In any event, are the Acts constitutionally defective because other junior interest holders are not afforded a right to a hearing?

For an analysis of the Acts and of Congress' attempts to expand their coverage to other federally-held mortgages, see Patrick A. Randolph, The New Federal Foreclosure Laws, 49 Okla.L.Rev. 123 (1996).

NELSON, WHITMAN, BURKHART & FREYERMUTH,
REAL ESTATE FINANCE LAW

§ 7.28 (6th ed.2014).*

To trigger the Fourteenth Amendment's notice and hearing requirements, state action must exist. If a court does not find sufficient state action in connection with a power of sale foreclosure, it will not consider the notice or hearing issues, no matter how deficient the statutes are in those respects. Interestingly, courts in some early power of sale cases decided the constitutional issues without considering state action. However, the issue has become increasingly important, and the clear trend of the case law is against finding state action. This trend is significant because, as a practical matter, it means that power of sale statutes continue to provide an effective foreclosure method for nongovernmental mortgagees even when the statutes are noticeably deficient concerning notice and hearings.

For an analysis of how courts have handled the state action arguments, see Nelson, Whitman, Burkhart & Freyermuth, Real Estate Finance Law § 7.28 (6th ed. 2014).

WARREN V. GOVERNMENT NATIONAL
MORTGAGE ASSOCIATION

United States Court of Appeals, Eighth Circuit, 1980
611 F.2d 1229, cert. denied, 449 U.S. 847, 101 S.Ct. 133, 66 L.Ed.2d 57 (1980)

Before ROSS and STEPHENSON, CIRCUIT JUDGES, and MCMANUS, DISTRICT
JUDGE.

MCMANUS, DISTRICT JUDGE.

* * *

Plaintiff and her husband were the owners of a residence in Kansas City, Missouri, which they purchased in August of 1966 from the United States Department of Housing and Urban Development (HUD). As part of the purchase price, they executed a note, secured by a deed of trust, to the Federal National Mortgage Association (FNMA). Thereafter, by Congressional Act, FNMA was converted into GNMA, a private corporation wholly-owned by the federal government. 12 U.S.C.A. § 1716 et seq. Plaintiff's note and deed of trust were transferred and assigned to GNMA. The deed of trust included a "Power of Sale" clause, which in the event of default permitted the trustee to initiate an extrajudicial foreclosure sale in accordance with Missouri statutory procedures.

In September of 1970, the successor trustee under the deed of trust— a private attorney retained by GNMA and not otherwise employed by the federal government—mailed a letter, first class not registered nor certified receipt, to the plaintiff and her husband, notifying them that GNMA deemed the payments on the note to be in default and that, as holder of the note, GNMA had elected to declare the entire principal due. The letter, therefore, demanded payment of the entire balance but contained no mention or threat of foreclosure by a trustee's sale. For whatever reasons, plaintiff made no response to the letter.

Thereafter, GNMA foreclosed against plaintiff by causing the trustee to advertise in a newspaper, used almost exclusively for such legal notices, and to conduct a public sale, all in compliance with the power of sale clause in the deed of trust. GNMA was the purchaser at this sale.

* * *

Plaintiff's challenge rests essentially on her contention that she was denied fifth amendment due process rights to notice and hearing *prior to* the foreclosure sale. We affirm on the basis of no federal government action.

The Due Process Clause of the Fifth Amendment to the United States Constitution provides that: "No person shall * * * be deprived of * * * property, without due process of law; * * *" It applies to federal government not private action, Public Utilities Comm'n v. Pollak, 343

U.S. 451, 461, 72 S.Ct. 813, 96 L.Ed. 1068 (1952); while the fourteenth amendment due process clause applies to the states, see, e.g., Moose Lodge No. 107 v. Irvis, 407 U.S. 163, 172–73, 92 S.Ct. 1965, 32 L.Ed.2d 627 (1972); Shelley v. Kraemer, 334 U.S. 1, 13, 68 S.Ct. 836, 92 L.Ed. 1161 (1948). The standard for finding federal government action under the fifth amendment is the same as that for finding state action under the fourteenth amendment. See, e.g., Geneva Towers Tenants Org. v. Federated Mortgage Investors, 504 F.2d 483, 487 (9th Cir.1974); Ponce v. Housing Authority of Tulare County, 389 F.Supp. 635, 648 (E.D.Cal.1975). That standard is that there must exist "a sufficiently close nexus between the [government] and the challenged action of the regulated entity so that the action of the latter may be fairly treated as that of the [government] itself." Jackson v. Metropolitan Edison Co., 419 U.S. 345, 351, 95 S.Ct. 449, 453, 42 L.Ed.2d 477 (1974).

It is undisputed in this case that GNMA is a corporate entity, wholly-owned by the federal government, 31 U.S.C.A. § 846. It was created by the partition of the FNMA under the National Housing Act of 1968, 12 U.S.C.A. § 1716 et seq., and is under the management and control of the Secretary of HUD, 12 U.S.C.A. §§ 1723(a) & 1723a(d). It has no capital stock, 12 U.S.C.A. § 1717(a)(2)(A). The economic benefits and burdens of its administration inure to the Secretary of the Treasury, 12 U.S.C.A. § 1722. Moreover, under 12 U.S.C.A. § 1717(b)(1), it is authorized to purchase, service, sell or otherwise deal in mortgages insured under 12 U.S.C.A. §§ 1701–1750g by the Federal Housing Authority (FHA).[7] Thus, GNMA is not only wholly-owned by the federal government but it also operates under federal government authority.[8]

---

   7   GNMA is authorized to deal only in mortgages or deeds of trust insured under federal programs and is not, unlike FNMA, authorized to deal in "conventional mortgages". Compare 12 U.S.C.A. §§ 1717(a)(2)(A) & 1717(b)(1) with 12 U.S.C.A. § 1717(a)(2)(B) & 1717(b)(2). Thus, GNMA was authorized to deal in plaintiff's deed of trust in this case because that deed of trust was insured by FHA under § 203 of the National Housing Act, 12 U.S.C.A. § 1709.

   8   Although the pertinent legislative history is somewhat unclear with respect to Congress' intent in bifurcating the old FNMA into two distinct corporate entities—FNMA and GNMA—in 1968, it is fairly certain that Congress was primarily motivated by "the emphasis of recent years of increased reliance on private sponsorship under our housing programs and participation by private enterprises in the financing and production of housing." H.R.Rep. No. 1585, 90th Cong.2d Sess. reprinted in [1968] U.S.Code Cong. & Admin.News, pp. 2873, 2874. To that end, Congress decided to place the former FNMA's secondary market operation in a new privately owned corporation (with the continued designation FNMA) and its special assistance, management and liquidating functions in the new GNMA. Id., U.S.Code Cong., supra, at 2875; see also id., at 2943–48, 3004–09.

     Thus, if considered purely as a matter of statutory and organizational form the new GNMA could perhaps be viewed as more "governmental" than its counterpart FNMA. We, however, read the legislative history to indicate Congress' intent as being essentially to dissociate as far as possible the newly created entities, however characterized as to form, from the federal government in regard to their respective secondary mortgage market functions.

     In short, in terms of substance as opposed to form, we view the functions served by GNMA as being no more governmental than those served by the new FNMA, and accordingly we consider the cases holding the new FNMA's secondary mortgage market

To recognize these relational facts, however, does not end the federal government action inquiry for, as was the case in Public Utilities Comm'n. v. Pollak, 343 U.S. 451, 72 S.Ct. 813, 96 L.Ed. 1068 (1952), the deciding issue in this regard is not simply whether GNMA is a government-owned or authorized corporation; rather, it is whether as such GNMA's foreclosure action pursuant to the contractual power of sale clause in the deed of trust was so closely linked to federal government regulation that it can in actuality be viewed more as the action of the federal government itself than that of GNMA. Compare also Jackson v. Metropolitan Edison Co., 419 U.S. 345, 356–57 & n. 16, 95 S.Ct. 449, 42 L.Ed.2d 477 (1974).

In approaching the latter issue, we emphasize that the power of sale clause as contained in the deed of trust is a contractual power having its genesis in the deed of trust itself and as such exists independent of any statute otherwise governing it. * * * As a party to the contract, and even though it was a governmentally-owned and authorized entity, GNMA had a right to resort to its contractual remedies just as a purely private entity had. * * *

We therefore are of the general opinion that mortgage foreclosures through power of sale agreements such as the one at issue here are not in and of themselves powers of a governmental nature. Compare Northrip v. FNMA, 527 F.2d 23, 31 (6th Cir.1975); Bryant v. Jefferson Federal Savings and Loan Assoc., 166 U.S.App.D.C. 178, 180–81, 509 F.2d 511, 513–14 (D.C.Cir.1974). * * *

Plaintiff's major contention in this regard is that, all these considerations notwithstanding, federal government action is implicated in this case because the deed of trust form was specifically approved by HUD regulations, 24 CFR § 203.17, and therefore GNMA's foreclosure action pursuant to that deed of trust was by implication also specifically approved by HUD. If this court were to accept plaintiff's argument, every FHA guaranteed mortgage held either by GNMA, FNMA or a private lending agency would be placed in the same position of constitutional uncertainty simply by virtue of the fact that the mortgage form must also be approved by a federal agency under HUD regulations. Moreover, plaintiff's argument ignores the point that the central inquiry is not whether the form of the deed of trust is approved by federal regulations, but rather it is whether there exists a sufficiently close nexus between the government regulations and the challenged activity specifically at issue

---

functions to be essentially "private action" as persuasive authority on the federal government action issue presented in this case. Compare Roberts v. Cameron-Brown Co., 556 F.2d 356, 358–60 (5th Cir.1977); Northrip v. FNMA, 527 F.2d 23, 30–33 (6th Cir.1975).

so that the challenged activity itself may be fairly treated as truly that of the federal government directly. * * *

The challenged activity specifically at issue in this case is GNMA's extrajudicial foreclosure pursuant to the power of sale terms of the deed of trust, performed in accordance with Missouri laws. Plaintiff cites 24 CFR Pts. 200 & 203 generally as support for her argument that the Secretary of HUD, vicariously through GNMA, directly regulates GNMA's foreclosure procedures here. We find nothing in those general provisions, however, constituting direct federal government regulation of GNMA's servicing policies, including what methods it may use to protect its financial interest in the mortgage on default.

Concededly, the Commissioner of the FHA is required to approve the form of the mortgage or deed of trust before it is eligible for FHA insurance under 24 CFR § 203.17, but that regulation does not dictate what foreclosure provisions are to be included in the deed of trust. Indeed, 24 CFR § 203.17(b), (c) and (d) explicitly set forth certain provisions which must be included in any mortgage or deed of trust approved under subpart 203. If the Secretary of HUD had intended to regulate the specific *method* of foreclosure to be adopted by an investor in an insured mortgage, the regulations would certainly have directly and expressly set forth that method in 24 CFR § 203.17.

Moreover, it is admitted in this case that the foreclosure of plaintiff's deed of trust was according to its own terms and under the extrajudicial foreclosure statutes of Missouri. There is nothing in the record to indicate that the powers otherwise exercisable by officers or employees of the federal government were in any way applied or used in this foreclosure of plaintiff's deed of trust. In fact, the foreclosure was conducted by the successor trustee strictly in accordance with Missouri law pursuant to his position as the contractually appointed trustee and not as a government employee.

Further, the only direct government involvement in the relations with the mortgagor or grantor of the deed of trust after default can be found in 24 CFR § 203.355. The regulation contemplates that if a claim is to be made under the mortgage insurance certificate then the mortgagee must take whatever steps, including foreclosure if and as permitted under state law, that are necessary to vest title to the property in either its name, or in the name of the commissioner. The rule, however, does not make explicit what specific foreclosure methods or procedures are to be adopted by the mortgagee. Thus, we view it as insufficient to conclude that the power of sale foreclosure methods at issue here were that of the federal government itself.

We conclude generally, therefore, that the federal government has neither mandated nor approved the method of foreclosure to be followed in the event of default; nor could it since the foreclosure procedures must accord with Missouri law. Since federal government regulation was not directly and substantially linked to the challenged foreclosure activity complained of by plaintiff and at issue here, no "federal government action" exists and plaintiff has no cognizable constitutional claim under the fifth amendment.

For the foregoing reasons, we affirm the judgment of the District Court. We need not reach waiver and other issues raised by plaintiff.

ROSS, CIRCUIT JUDGE, concurring.

I concur in the determination that there was no federal government action for the reason that GNMA functions only in a traditionally nonsovereign capacity in providing secondary mortgages and enforcing them according to their terms. Northrip v. Federal Nat. Mtg. Ass'n, 527 F.2d 23 (6th Cir.1975); accord Roberts v. Cameron-Brown Co., 556 F.2d 356 (5th Cir.1977).

NOTES

1. *Analysis of* Warren. The *Warren* court held that GNMA "had a right to resort to its contractual remedies just as a purely private entity had," though GNMA is wholly owned by the United States and operates under federal governmental authority. Does the court intend by this language to create a "proprietary-governmental" distinction for state or federal action analysis? Is the court indirectly saying that mortgage foreclosure is essentially a proprietary or commercial function and, therefore, is not subject to the Fifth Amendment, even when the government is foreclosing? Should federal or state government ever be able to act *for its own account,* whether in a proprietary or governmental fashion, without being subject to the requirements of the Fifth or Fourteenth Amendments?

Would the *Warren* court have found federal action in the *Ricker* case (page 760 supra)? Should it matter that GNMA, though wholly owned by the United States, is nevertheless formally a corporate entity and not a direct instrumentality of the federal government?

Should it make a difference whether the government entity is foreclosing as original mortgagee, as in *Ricker,* or as a subsequent secondary market purchaser, as in *Warren*? What about the fact that, in *Warren,* a federal predecessor corporation to GNMA was the initial mortgagee?

2. *Impact of* Lebron *decision.* In an important "federal action" case, Lebron v. National R.R. Passenger Corp., 513 U.S. 374, 115 S.Ct. 961, 130 L.Ed.2d 902 (1995), the United States Supreme Court held that Amtrak should be treated as the federal government for First Amendment purposes. In *Lebron,* an Amtrak vice president had rescinded a billboard contract in Penn Station because the proposed billboard was political in nature. Justice Scalia's opinion for the Court held: "[W]here, as here, the Government creates

a corporation by special law, for the furtherance of governmental objectives, and retains for itself permanent authority to appoint a majority of the directors of that corporation, the corporation is part of the Government for purposes of the First Amendment." Id. at 974–75.

Consider *Lebron*'s impact on federal corporations that hold and foreclose mortgages and, in particular, on *Warren:*

> In *Lebron*, the Supreme Court established a two-prong test for determining if a federal government corporation is a federal government actor for purposes of evaluating federal action. The first prong considers the extent to which the corporation was formed for the furtherance of governmental objectives, which Amtrak satisfied based upon the purpose given by Congress in the legislation that created Amtrak. The second prong involves the extent to which the federal government retains control over the corporation's efforts to achieve its objectives, which Amtrak satisfied because of the structure of its board of directors.

> * * * The Government National Mortgage Association, * * * may now be subject to Fifth Amendment scrutiny where it had not been prior to *Lebron*. GNMA's status as a wholly-owned governmental corporation * * * makes GNMA a likely candidate for governmental actor status.

> If the *Lebron* test were used to analyze the facts in *Warren*, for example, it is likely that the court would reach a different result. The first prong of the test would easily be satisfied by the declaration of purpose in the statute. As for the second prong, when Congress partitioned GNMA and FNMA in 1968, GNMA stayed with the government when FNMA was established as a private corporation. As part of the government, GNMA is controlled by the Secretary of Housing and Urban Development. Therefore, if the *Lebron* test is to be expanded beyond the First Amendment, GNMA is certain to be considered a federal actor for Fifth Amendment purposes, thereby invalidating *Warren*.

Daniel E. Blegen, The Constitutionality of Power of Sale Foreclosures by Federal Government Entities, 62 Mo.L.Rev. 425, 440–41, 444–46 (1997).*

Blegen argued that *Lebron* did not have a similar impact on Fannie Mae and Freddie Mac, two government-created corporations that are the nation's largest secondary market purchasers of home mortgages:

> Both [Fannie Mae] and [Freddie Mac] will satisfy the first prong of [*Lebron*], because they were both formed by the government to further governmental objectives. The second prong, however, is probably not met by either Fannie Mae or Freddie Mac. Fannie Mae is entirely owned by the private sector and has only a minority of

---

*   Copyright 1997 by The Curators of the University of Missouri.

directors appointed by the government. Freddie Mac is also owned by the private sector and also has only a minority of directors appointed by the government.

Id.

Analysis of the second prong potentially changed in 2008 when the Federal Housing Finance Agency (FHFA) placed Fannie Mae and Freddie Mac into conservatorship with FHFA as the conservator. As conservator, the FHFA assumed the power of the board of directors and management of both corporations. New CEOs were appointed who reported to FHFA. In exchange for massive monetary infusions, senior preferred shares in each corporation were issued to the federal government with a 10% coupon. More important, the government received warrants to obtain stock for a few cents per share. If the warrants are exercised, the federal government will receive a 79.9% ownership stake in each corporation.

For these reasons and because FHFA clearly is a government agency, mortgagors have challenged Fannie Mae and Freddie Mac power of sale foreclosures on due process grounds. However, the federal courts uniformly have held that the conservatorship has not turned Fannie Mae and Freddie Mac into government actors for two reasons. First, the courts have held that "[FHFA's] 'control' is merely the same control that Freddie Mac had before the conservatorship." Federal Home Loan Mortgage Corp. v. Shamoon, 922 F.Supp.2d 641 (E.D.Mich. 2013). Another court stated this reason in a slightly different way: "Fannie Mae was not converted into a government entity when it was placed into conservatorship; instead, FHFA stepped into the shoes of Fannie Mae." Herron v. Fannie Mae, 857 F.Supp.2d 87 (D.D.C. 2012). For the same reason, courts have held that FHFA is not a government actor in this context. Second, the courts have focused on the words "permanent authority" in the second prong of the *Lebron* test and said that the conservatorship does not satisfy this element because it is not permanent. These cases may help put to rest any question about the necessity for Fannie Mae and Freddie Mac to comply with the Fifth Amendment's due process requirements even post-conservatorship.

Putting aside the constitutional questions, is it good public policy to make foreclosure more difficult for federal entities like GNMA than it is for their private counterparts? See Daniel E. Blegen, The Constitutionality of Power of Sale Foreclosures by Federal Government Entities, 62 Mo.L.Rev. 425, 446–47 (1997).

4. THE UNIFORM NONJUDICIAL FORECLOSURE ACT

While power of sale foreclosure has existed for at least 100 years, remarkably little national uniformity has been achieved. In 1974, the National Conference of Commissioners on Uniform State Laws adopted the Uniform Land Transactions Act (ULTA). ULTA covered numerous aspects of real property law, and a major portion was devoted to land security. In 1985, the Conference moved these mortgage-related provisions into a separate act, the Uniform Land Security Interest Act (ULSIA). Despite the Conference's aggressive advocacy, no state adopted either ULTA or ULSIA.

The Conference decided to try again to achieve uniformity in real estate foreclosures. The result was the Uniform Nonjudicial Foreclosure Act (Act). The Act is the product of years of drafting and reflects the thinking of many of the nation's prominent land finance scholars and practitioners. The major elements of the Act are described in the following excerpt from its Prefatory Note:

Methods of foreclosure. The Act provides for three methods of foreclosure and permits the secured creditor to elect the method to be used. The first is conventional foreclosure by means of an auction sale, conducted by a representative of the foreclosing creditor. In this foreclosure method, evaluation of the collateral (by means of the high bid at the sale) and liquidation (by means of a foreclosure deed to the high bidder) are combined.

The second and third methods of foreclosure authorized by the Act separate the evaluation and liquidation functions. The second method is foreclosure by negotiated sale. Such a sale will be consummated in much the same way as other real property sales; the property will probably be listed with a real estate broker and advertised extensively. This is usually an effective way of liquidating the property, but has not been used in this country as a method of evaluating the property for purposes of foreclosure because of concern about the potential for collusive price-setting between the secured creditor and the purchaser.

In the procedure for foreclosure by negotiated sale authorized in this Act, that concern is eliminated. The creditor notifies the debtor and junior lien holders of the "foreclosure amount" that it is willing to offer for the property, and they can simply disapprove the sale if they are dissatisfied with that amount. If the amount is reasonable, and is more than the debtor and junior lienors could expect to recover from an auction sale, they have every reason to permit the sale to proceed. If one or more of them disapproves, the foreclosing creditor has three choices: (1) to discontinue the negotiated sale and resort to a different method of foreclosure; (2) to exclude the objecting party from the effect of the foreclosure, so that the objector will be unaffected by the foreclosure; or (3) to pay off the objecting party, if that person holds a lien. This last alternative is likely to be employed only when the objecting party's lien is for a minor amount.

The third foreclosure method authorized by the Act is foreclosure by appraisal. This method accomplishes only the first function of foreclosure, namely the evaluation of the collateral. It does not liquidate the property, but rather leaves it in the hands of the secured creditor, who will have the burden of liquidating it after the foreclosure is completed.

In a sense, foreclosure by appraisal is similar to common law "strict foreclosure," but in this Act it is surrounded with much more extensive safeguards to protect the interests of the parties who are being foreclosed and to ensure the integrity of the appraisal's result. The lender selects the appraiser, but the appraiser must meet reasonable professional standards of qualification and may not be an employee of the lender. As with foreclosure by negotiated sale, the secured creditor notifies the debtor and junior lien holders of the "foreclosure amount" that it is willing to offer for the property. Any debtor or junior lienor who is dissatisfied with the amount can simply disapprove it and, as with a foreclosure by negotiated sale, the foreclosing creditor must either exclude the objector from the foreclosure, pay off the objector, or discontinue the foreclosure by appraisal and employ a different method of foreclosure.

In a foreclosure by negotiated sale or by appraisal, the "foreclosure amount" is, in effect, an offer by the creditor. That offer need not be identical to the property's selling price (in the case of a negotiated sale) or the property's appraised value (in the case of a foreclosure by appraisal), but it must be at least 85 percent of that amount. The 15% margin is intended to allow the creditor ample latitude to cover the expenses of holding and marketing the property. A foreclosure amount lower than 85 percent is impermissible, and would warrant a court in enjoining the foreclosure or, if the foreclosure has been completed, assessing damages against the foreclosing creditor or setting the foreclosure aside if title has not passed to a bona fide purchaser.

With all three of these foreclosure methods sufficient protections, outlined in more detail below, have been included to assure protection of the legitimate interests of debtors and subordinate interest holders. However, foreclosures by auction have traditionally been known for producing prices that are well below market values. The principal reason for the adoption of the new methods, foreclosure by negotiated sale and by appraisal, is the belief that they will produce higher effective prices. If this is true they will come to be widely used, lenders will realize more of the indebtedness owed to them, and borrowers will experience fewer deficiency claims and more surpluses.

At the same time, the Act aims to improve prices at auction sales by requiring foreclosing lenders to disclose title information (which they must necessarily obtain in any event in order to carry out the foreclosure process) and encouraging them to disclose other reports and information they possess. The Act also encourages debtors to permit pre-foreclosure inspection of the security property by prospective buyers, another feature intended to foster higher prices.

Systems of notice. The nonjudicial foreclosure statutes presently in effect may be divided into one-notice and two-notice systems. In a two-notice system, the secured creditor typically is required to send a notice of default, and after the passage of some time period, a second notice of foreclosure. Depending on the jurisdiction, the first notice may or may not coincide with an acceleration of the debt. If it does not, the period between the first and second notices (or some part of that period) may be thought of as a "cure" period, during which only arrearages need be paid to put the loan back "on stream."

The present Act creates a "two-notice" system. Debtors are given a notice of default and a 30-day period of cure before a notice of foreclosure may be issued to them. For nonresidential debtors this time period may be reduced to ten days by agreement. No provision is made for giving a notice of default to junior lien holders. Only after the cure period has expired can the foreclosing creditor accelerate the debt and give a notice of foreclosure.

After the cure period expires, an original notice of foreclosure must be given to all parties whose interests will be extinguished by the foreclosure. This is a departure from many of the existing nonjudicial foreclosure statutes that provide direct mailed notice of foreclosure only to the debtor. Under such statutes it is entirely possible for the foreclosure of a senior mortgage to terminate a junior mortgage without the holder of the junior lien even knowing that the termination has occurred. See, e.g., In re Ocwen Financial Services, Inc., 649 N.W.2d 854 (Minn.App.2002). That sort of unfair result cannot occur under this Act.

The foreclosure cannot occur earlier than an additional 90 days after the notice of foreclosure is given. Thus, a minimum of 120 days will ordinarily elapse between the debtor's default and the date of foreclosure. During the 90-day period, any affected persons have the right to redeem the collateral from the security interest, although they must usually pay the accelerated balance due to do so.

In addition to these two notices, all affected parties will receive further warning that the foreclosure is about to occur. In the case of foreclosure by auction, a copy of the advertisement of the sale must be given to them; it may be included with the notice of foreclosure or sent separately. If foreclosure is by negotiated sale, the affected parties must be given a notice informing them of the proposed sale. In the case of foreclosure by appraisal, they will receive a copy of the appraisal report, informing them of the date that the foreclosure will take effect.

Due process: notice and hearing. When a governmental entity forecloses a mortgage, judicial decisions make it reasonably clear that the entity must comply with the demands of the Due Process Clause, including the giving of notice reasonably calculated to inform those whose rights are affected, and the provision of a hearing at which such persons may present defenses to the foreclosure. See, e.g., Rau v. Cavenaugh, 500 F.Supp. 204 (D.S.D.1980); Ricker v. United States, 417 F.Supp. 133 (D.Me.1976); Turner v. Blackburn, 389 F.Supp. 1250 (W.D.N.C.1975). Contra, see Federal Deposit Insurance Corporation v. Morrison, 747 F.2d 610 (11th Cir.1984).

Whether these protections are also required when a private creditor forecloses is not settled. However, irrespective of the requirements of Due Process, fundamental fairness demands that all persons whose rights may be destroyed by a foreclosure should have advance notice of the proceeding and the opportunity to show why it should not go forward. As a three-judge federal court in North Carolina put it, "To propose to a homeowner that he trek to the courthouse or spend 20 cents to examine fine-print legal notices, daily for the duration of a twenty-year mortgage, as his sole protection against summary eviction, seems to us to offer him nothing of value." Turner v. Blackburn, supra, at 1258.

The Act therefore provides (in Sections 203 and 204) for notice to all those whose property rights are put at risk by foreclosure. It also provides, in Section 205, an opportunity for any other person who wishes to receive notice of the foreclosure to file a request for such notice in the public records.

In addition, Section 206 of the Act provides residential debtors the right to an informal meeting with a responsible representative of the secured creditor to present reasons why the foreclosure should not go forward. This meeting, which will be held only if it is affirmatively requested, is intended to guard debtors against the fundamental unfairness of a mistakenly-conducted foreclosure. The creditor's representative must have available at the meeting the evidence of the debtor's default. It is believed that right to a meeting will satisfy the hearing element of the due process requirement if a government agency is foreclosing under the Act. While the Act does not obligate creditors to hold a meeting with nonresidential debtors or with subordinate lienholders, neither does it preclude such a meeting.

It might be argued that the informal meeting process created by the Act is unnecessary because a debtor or junior lienor can always bring an action to enjoin an improper foreclosure. However, this step requires a good deal of affirmative effort by the plaintiff—the retaining of counsel, typically at significant cost, and the pursuit of litigation. It is not clear that this option is adequate to protect unsophisticated debtors.

* * *

Omitted parties. Mortgage law uniformly holds that a person who is not made a party to a judicial foreclosure is not bound by it, and such a person's interest survives the foreclosure. However, in foreclosures by power of sale there is little legal authority as to the effect of failure to provide notice to holders of junior interests. The Act explicitly provides that holders of junior interests who are entitled to notice are not bound by the foreclosure if they are not given notice. Hence their position is like that of an omitted party in a judicial foreclosure. See Nelson, Whitman, Burkhart & Freyermuth, Real Estate Finance Law § 7.16 (6th ed. 2015).

Sometimes a foreclosing lender wishes to avoid terminating a particular subordinate interest by the foreclosure. Case law is about evenly divided as to whether this can be done against the junior interest holder's wishes. Id. at § 7.13. The Act expressly permits the foreclosing creditor to give to any junior interest holder a "notice of preservation," effectively excluding that party from the effect of the foreclosure even though the party is given notice of the foreclosure. This sort of notice is most likely to be employed to preserve leases that the lender regards as advantageous.

Redemption. Mortgaged property may be redeemed in either of two ways: by equitable redemption before foreclosure and by statutory redemption for some fixed period of time after foreclosure. All states recognize equitable redemption, but only about half of the states have statutes permitting redemption after foreclosure. The Act recognizes the fundamental right to equitable redemption until the date of foreclosure, but does not permit post-foreclosure redemption. While post-sale redemption occasionally benefits a debtor or junior lienor, it is believed that in the aggregate such parties are disadvantaged by the depression in foreclosure bid prices that results from the uncertain status of title introduced by statutory redemption.

Title from foreclosures. No matter which method of foreclosure is employed, the Act provides that if the notice of foreclosure has been recorded, completion of the foreclosure process by recording an appropriate deed and affidavit conclusively establishes compliance with the Act in favor of good faith purchasers for value of the collateral. If a creditor fails to comply with the provisions of the Act in conducting a foreclosure, a court may, of course, assess damages against the creditor. In addition, a serious failure of compliance may warrant a court in setting aside the foreclosure if no bona fide purchaser's rights have intervened. The extent to which defects in the foreclosure process will cause a court to set aside a foreclosure is left to other law.

Deficiency liability. In general, no matter which of the three foreclosure methods is employed, the Act permits recovery of a deficiency by the foreclosing creditor if the obligation is a recourse debt. However, residential debtors who act in good faith are exempt from deficiency liability. In addition, deficiency liability is limited by the "fair market value" concept: a debtor may present proof of the property's fair market value, and may have the amount of the deficiency limited as though the foreclosure amount was at least 90 percent of fair market value. This limitation is available to all debtors if the foreclosure was by auction, but is available only to residential debtors in the case of a foreclosure by negotiated sale or by appraisal.

The "residential debtor" concept. The Act preserves, with some changes, the "residential debtor" concept employed (and termed the "protected party") in ULTA and ULSIA. It recognizes two classes of debtors: residential debtors and everyone else. Residential debtors are assumed to need additional legal protections from foreclosing creditors that are not essential to other persons.

"Residential debtor" includes both a person who owns a home on which a security interest exists, and anyone who is personally liable on an obligation that is secured by a home. "Home" is used here as a shorthand for "residential real property," which must be owner-occupied and contain no more than four dwelling units. Thus, "residential debtor" encompasses not only the usual consumer borrowers on home mortgage loans, but also relatives who guarantee their loans and purchasers who buy homes subject to, or with an assumption of, existing mortgages.

Several specific protections are provided for residential debtors in the Act. Some of them have been mentioned above, but all are catalogued here:

1.   In general, the terms of the security agreement may fix the standards by which performance of an obligation under the Act is to be measured, so long as those standards are not manifestly unreasonable. However, such provisions are not binding on residential debtors.

2.   The Act requires the foreclosing creditor to send debtors notices of default and foreclosure, as well as the advertisement or statement of the actual foreclosure. If these notices are given by mail, residential debtors are entitled to two copies, one of which must be given by registered or certified mail.

3.   After sending a required notice, a foreclosing creditor may discover that the recipient's address was incorrect. The creditor is required to make a reasonable effort to discover a correct address and, if one can be found, to send a new notice. For residential debtors, any time period that is counted from the date of giving notice will now run from the date of the new notice. This principle is applied to nonresidential debtors as well, but is limited by a provision that the time period ends no later than 45 days after the date it would have ended if counted from the date the original notice was given.

4.   The cure period allowed to debtors to reinstate their loans without acceleration is ordinarily thirty days after a notice of default is given. This period may be reduced by agreement of the parties to as little as ten days, but no reduction is permitted if any debtor is a residential debtor.

5.   Residential debtors are entitled to demand a meeting with a representative of the foreclosing creditor and to review in that meeting the evidence that the foreclosure is legally warranted.

6.   The Act prohibits the entry of deficiency judgments against residential debtors who have acted in good faith with

respect to the property and the foreclosure. This provision employs the risk of a deficiency judgment as an incentive to encourage residential debtors to act responsibly by avoiding fraud or waste, providing pre-foreclosure access to the property to prospective buyers, and relinquishing possession promptly after foreclosure. Deficiency claims may be asserted against guarantors of residential debtors.

7.   A debtor faced with a deficiency judgment is entitled present proof of the property's fair market value, and to have the amount of the deficiency limited as though the foreclosure amount was at least 90 percent of fair market value. This limitation protects residential debtors no matter which of the three methods of foreclosure was employed; nonresidential debtors may assert the limitation on the deficiency only if the foreclosure was by auction.

8.   A deficiency action against a residential debtor must be commenced within 90 days after the time of foreclosure; deficiency actions against nonresidential debtors are not thus limited, and are governed only by the jurisdiction's general statute of limitations.

9.   A residential debtor who files an action to enjoin a foreclosure on the ground that it is legally improper is not required to post a bond in order to obtain a temporary restraining order or a preliminary injunction, even if a bond would ordinarily be required under the jurisdiction's law.

Uniform Nonjudicial Foreclosure Act, Prefatory Note (2002). For a detailed analysis of the Act, see Grant S. Nelson & Dale A. Whitman, Reforming Foreclosure: The Uniform Nonjudicial Foreclosure Act, 53 Duke L.J. 1399 (2004).

What are the Act's prospects in state legislatures? Should Congress enact it? Consider the following commentary:

If the past is prologue, the Act's chances are slim indeed. While many commentators fervently hope otherwise, it seems highly likely that the Act will suffer the same fate as its ULSIA predecessor.

Why not then encourage Congress to enact it? Indeed, the hodgepodge of state real estate mortgage law and the need for uniformity have produced intermittent calls over the past three decades for the congressional enactment of a mortgage foreclosure code. In view of the enormous impact of mortgage financing on the national economy, this advocacy for federal action will at some point be compelling. Moreover, the adoption of the Act by Congress clearly would survive a Commerce Clause challenge under existing [standards].

Grant S. Nelson, A Commerce Clause Standard for the New Millennium: "Yes" to Broad Congressional Control over Commercial Transactions; "No" to Federal Legislation on Social and Cultural Issues, 55 Ark.L.Rev. 135–36 (2002).

E. DISBURSEMENT OF FORECLOSURE SALE PROCEEDS

NELSON, WHITMAN, BURKHART & FREYERMUTH, REAL ESTATE FINANCE LAW
698–700 (6th ed.2014)*

When a foreclosure sale produces surplus proceeds, the rules governing who gets the surplus and in what order are generally clear. The major underlying principle is that the surplus represents the remnant of the equity of redemption and the security that the foreclosure eliminated. Consequently, the surplus stands in the place of the foreclosed real estate and the liens and interests that previously attached to that real estate now attach to the surplus.[905] The junior interest holders are entitled to be paid out of the surplus in the order of priority that existed before foreclosure.[906] The foreclosed owner's claim normally is junior to the claims of lienors and others whose interest was eliminated by the foreclosure.[907]

---

* Reprinted with permission of LEG, Inc. d/b/a West Academic.

[905] United Bank v. Mani, 81 Mass. App. Ct. 75, 959 N.E.2d 452 (2011); Lynch v. Price Homes, Inc., 156 N.C. App. 83, 575 S.E.2d 543 (2003) ("As a general rule, proceeds of a foreclosure sale are, constructively at least, real property and stand in place of the land."); In re Schiphof, 192 N.C. App. 696, 666 S.E.2d 497 (2008) (*contra* surplus funds do not constitute real estate; they are foreclosed owner's general funds).

Under the Restatement, the "surplus stands in the place of the foreclosed real estate, and the liens and interests that previously attached to the real estate now attach to the surplus." Restatement Third, Property: Mortgages § 7.4 comment a.

[906] Restatement Third, Property: Mortgages § 7.4 comment a; see also Horizon Bank and Trust Co. v. Flaherty, 309 F. Supp. 2d 178 (D. Mass. 2004) ("Under both Massachusetts and federal law, the surplus proceeds of a foreclosure sale pass by equitable lien to junior lienors."); Hanley v. Pearson, 204 Ariz. 147, 61 P.3d 29 (Ct. App. Div. 1 2003) (citing Restatement, "the surplus from a trustee sale is applied to those liens that are extinguished by the sale in the order of their priority").

Under the foregoing principles, if an installment land contract vendor either chooses or is required to foreclose the contract, any surplus over the amount needed to satisfy the contract balance belongs to the vendee. See Davidson v. D.H. Hansen Ranch, Inc., 235 Mont. 204, 766 P.2d 258 (1988). Of course, if junior liens encumbered the vendee's interest, those lienors have priority over the vendee for any surplus.

[907] * * * See, e.g., Concord Enterprises, Inc. v. Binder, 710 A.2d 219 (D.C. 1998) ("[I]n the event of a surplus the trustee must satisfy subordinate mortgages, judgments, or liens against the property before turning it over to the mortgagor."); Spencer v. Jameson, 147 Idaho 497, 211 P.3d 106 (2009); Bank of America, N.A. v. BA Mortgage, LLC, 137 N.M. 368, 2005–NMCA–037,

* * *

Statutes often regulate the distribution of surplus, especially in the power of sale setting. Some statutes codify the principles described above.[909] Other statutes, by their express terms, give the surplus to the mortgagor and do not refer to the junior lienors' rights.[910] However, courts generally interpret this type of statute as giving junior lienors rights in the surplus that are superior to the property owner's rights.[911] A few statutes do not mention priorities but simply authorize the mortgagee or trustee to pay the surplus "to the person or persons legally entitled to the proceeds."[912]

BANK OF AMERICA, NA v. B.A. MORTGAGE, LLC

Court of Appeals of New Mexico, 2005
137 N.M. 368, 111 P.3d 226

VIGIL, JUDGE.

A fund was created when BA Mortgage, LLC foreclosed on its mortgage and the subsequent sale of the property resulted in a surplus of $28,467.43. This appeal requires us to determine whether a junior mortgagee or the debtor's assignee of her rights of redemption and surplus is entitled to the surplus. The district court ruled that the debtor's assignee was entitled to the surplus. * * *

---

111 P.3d 226 (Ct. App. 2005); Note: Rights in the Proceeds of a Foreclosure Sale—The Court Helps Those Who Help Themselves, 51 N.C. L. Rev. 1100 (1973).

Under the Restatement, "the claim of the holder of the foreclosed equity of redemption to the surplus is subordinate to the claims of all other holders of liens and interests terminated by the foreclosure." Restatement Third, Property: Mortgages § 7.4 comment b.

[909] See, e.g., Ariz.Rev.Stat. § 33–727(B): "If there are other liens on the property sold, or other payments secured by the same mortgage, they shall be paid in their order * * * "; Cal. Civ. Code § 2924j(e) (after payment of expenses, the lien being foreclosed, any excess goes to "satisfy the outstanding balance of obligations secured by any junior liens or encumbrances in order of their priority").

[910] See, e.g., Minn. Stat. Ann. § 580.10; Ind. Code Ann. § 32–30–10–14; Wash. Rev. Code Ann. § 61.12.150.

[911] See, e.g., White v. Shirk, 20 Ind. App. 589, 51 N.E. 126 (1898); United Bank v. Mani, 81 Mass. App. Ct. 75, 959 N.E.2d 452, 455 n.8 (2011) (mortgagee is mortgagor's success or assign); Brown v. Crookston Agr. Ass'n, 34 Minn. 545, 26 N.W. 907 (1886); Fuller v. Langum, 37 Minn. 74, 33 N.W. 122 (1887).

[912] See Utah Code Ann. § 57–1–29. Courts typically interpret this language to incorporate the common law of surplus. See Timm v. Dewsnup, 2003 UT 47, 86 P.3d 699 (Utah 2003) ("[A]lthough [the statute] does not specifically mention junior trust deeds or lienholders, the surplus from the sale stands in the place of the foreclosed real estate and is subject to the same liens and interests that were attached to it. . . . In other words, any excess left over from the nonjudicial foreclosure sale on the trust deed property belongs not to [mortgagor], but to other valid lienholders.").

Entitlement to the Surplus

G. Nelson and D. Whitman, *Real Estate Finance Law* § 7.31, at 588 (2d ed. 1985), states the rule regarding the right to surplus after foreclosure:

> The major underlying principle is that the surplus represents the remnant of the equity of redemption and security wiped out by the foreclosure. Consequently, the surplus stands in the place of the foreclosed real estate and the liens and interests that previously attached to that real estate now attach to the surplus. They are entitled to be paid out of the surplus in the order of priority they enjoyed prior to foreclosure. The claim of the foreclosed mortgagor or the owner of the equity of redemption normally is junior to those of all valid liens wiped out by the foreclosure. (footnotes omitted).

Restatement (Third) of Property: Mortgages § 7.4 (1997), states the same rule, providing that "the surplus is applied to liens and other interests terminated by the foreclosure in order of their priority and the remaining balance, if any, is distributed to the holder of the equity of redemption." Therefore, "the claim of the holder of the foreclosed equity of redemption to the surplus is subordinate to the claims of all other holders of liens and interests terminated by the foreclosure." *Id.* cmt. b.

It is undisputed that Junior Mortgagee recorded its lien before Assignee obtained its assignment of right of redemption and made a claim to the right to any surplus. Applying the foregoing rule, Junior Mortgagee has a higher priority claim to the surplus than Assignee. *See Pacific Loan Mgmt. Corp. v. Superior Court,* 196 Cal.App.3d 1485, 242 Cal.Rptr. 547, 551–52 (1987) (stating that a junior lienor had the right to have its secured debt paid from surplus); *W.A.H. Church, Inc. v. Holmes,* 46 F.2d 608, 611 (D.C.1931) (stating that surplus arising from foreclosure must be used to satisfy subordinate mortgages, liens, and judgments before any surplus can be turned over to the mortgagor); *Builders Supply Co. v. Pine Belt Sav. & Loan Ass'n,* 369 So.2d 743, 745 (Miss.1979) (stating that "the surplus arising from a sale under a senior lien should be applied on a junior lien"); *Morsemere Fed. Sav. & Loan Ass'n v. Nicolaou,* 206 N.J.Super. 637, 503 A.2d 392, 394 (Ct.App.Div.1986) (stating that "surplus funds take on the character of the land, at least with respect to junior encumbrancers whose liens existed at the time of the foreclosure").

Assignee persuaded the district court, and makes the argument on appeal, that Junior Mortgagee's failure to obtain a judgment on its lien means that Junior Mortgagee lost any right it had to the surplus. The court's view was that the junior lien was wiped out in the foreclosure, and because there was no judgment on the junior lien, the lien did not survive the foreclosure.

We disagree. Under the general rule, the surplus stands in the place of the foreclosed real estate and the liens and interests that previously attached to the real estate now attach to the surplus. Nelson & Whitman, *supra*, § 7.31, at 589; Restatement of Prop. § 7.4. Junior Mortgagee was timely and proactive in asserting its right to any surplus. It filed a cross-claim in the foreclosure action, appeared, and argued its position. When questioned by the court, it explained that it had not yet obtained a judgment because there was no reason to do so until after the foreclosure and after it became clear there was a surplus. It explained that to maintain its status as a lienor, it only needed to have a valid lien, not a judgment. We agree with this proposition. *See* Nelson & Whitman, *supra*, § 7.31, at 589 (stating, "[i]n order to qualify for lienor status, it must be established that the claim was reduced to a lien prior to the foreclosure sale." (footnote omitted)). Moreover, in addition to its express reservation of jurisdiction, the court's order granting foreclosure recognized that there still might be additional matters to resolve, including the parties' rights to any surplus that might result from the sale. This would include the distribution of any possible surplus that might result from the sale. Junior Mortgagee's decision to make its claim and lien known, but to wait and see how things developed, was reasonable. We therefore also reject Assignee's additional argument that Junior Mortgagee did not exercise the diligence required because it never served its cross-claim on the mortgagor.

Foreclosure is an equitable action, and the distribution of foreclosure proceeds should be governed by equitable considerations. *See Las Campanas Limited Partnership v. Pribble,* 1997–NMCA–055, ¶ 9, 123 N.M. 520, 943 P.2d 554; *see also Kankakee Federal Savings & Loan Association v. Mueller,* 134 Ill.App.3d 943, 89 Ill.Dec. 781, 481 N.E.2d 332, 334 (1985) (noting that the distribution of proceeds from foreclosure is equitable). Junior Mortgagee timely appeared and made its claim and lien known well before the sale, and continued to press its point before the surplus was distributed. We conclude that the steps taken by Junior Mortgagee, including filing its motion for judgment for foreclosure and priority claim to surplus money proceeds, were sufficient to preserve its claim to the surplus. *See id.* 89 Ill.Dec. 781, 481 N.E.2d at 333–34 (holding that junior mortgagee was entitled to its share of the surplus from foreclosure even though it initially defaulted in the senior's foreclosure action and did not appear until it filed a motion, after the foreclosure, where the junior mortgage had been set forth in the senior mortgagee's petition, the junior mortgage was admitted in the answer, and the court had preserved its right to control the future distribution of the surplus); *Morsemere,* 503 A.2d at 394–95 (allowing a junior claimant to share in the surplus even though it did not move to intervene in the senior mortgagee's foreclosure action until after the sale); *Cowan v. Stoker,* 100 Utah 377, 115 P.2d 153, 155 (1941) (holding that a motion made before the proceeds of the foreclosure sale have been distributed "and served on all parties to the suit who are thereafter given an opportunity to plead and be heard, is a proper means for opening up the judgment for the purpose of allowing a junior mortgagee to make claim to surplus funds" because the "law is interested not so much in form as in substance").

Hold.

We conclude that Junior Mortgagee is entitled to the surplus because it has a higher priority claim to the surplus than Assignee unless, on remand, it is determined that its lien is invalid. For these reasons, we reverse and remand for further proceedings.

IT IS SO ORDERED.

We concur: JAMES J. WECHSLER and JONATHAN B. SUTIN, JUDGES.

NOTES

Most foreclosures don't yield a surplus.

1. *Procedural requirements for junior lienor to preserve claim to surplus in judicial foreclosure.* Most foreclosures do not yield a surplus. Therefore, does it make sense to require a junior lienor to appear and plead in every senior foreclosure simply to preserve a possible claim to surplus? Do any policy reasons justify this expenditure of legal fees and other costs? Is this burden especially problematic for vendor purchase money junior lienors? Why not allow the foreclosed junior to assert its claim for the first time after the foreclosure sale, like in power of sale foreclosures?

2. *Effect of mortgage language on disposition of surplus.* Suppose a first mortgage provides that, after paying the sale costs and the first mortgage debt, any remaining foreclosure sale proceeds should be paid to the "mortgagor, his heirs, successors and assigns." As between a junior mortgagee and the mortgagor, who should be paid first? Is the junior mortgagee an "assign" of the mortgagor? See Webster v. Wishon, 675 F.Supp. 552 (W.D.Mo.1986) ("Junior encumbrancers will take precedence over the mortgagor, as regards the right to have their demands paid out of surplus, because the execution of a junior mortgage amounts to an assignment of the mortgagor's equity of redemption to the junior mortgagee and of the assignor's right in equity to the surplus in case of a sale under the prior encumbrance."). Accord Restatement (Third) of Property (Mortgages) § 7.4 cmt. d (1997).

Suppose, instead, that the first mortgage states: "In the event this mortgage is foreclosed, after the obligation of the mortgage is satisfied, any surplus shall be paid to the mortgagor and not to the holder of any lien or other interest subordinate to this mortgage." See id.

3. *Senior lien claim on junior surplus.* An important corollary of the above rules governing surplus is that only those whose interests were cut off by the foreclosure have a valid claim on surplus. Is that rule fair to senior lienors? Should a senior lienor be able to use the surplus produced by a junior

lien foreclosure sale to pay the senior debt? Should it make a difference if the foreclosed mortgagor is insolvent? See Armand's Engr., Inc. v. Town & Country Club, Inc., 113 R.I. 515, 324 A.2d 334 (1974). See generally, Bohra v. Montgomery, 31 Ark.App. 253, 792 S.W.2d 360 (1990) ("upon a sale of a junior mortgage, the surplus belongs to the mortgagor, and is not applied to the satisfaction of the prior mortgage"); Davis v. Huntsville Prod. Credit Ass'n, 481 So.2d 1103 (Ala.1985) ("a first mortgagee has no right to any surplus upon foreclosure of the second mortgage, particularly in the absence of default of the first mortgage"); Members Equity Credit Union v. Duefel, 295 Ill.App.3d 336, 229 Ill.Dec. 876, 692 N.E.2d 865 (1998); Restatement (Third) of Property (Mortgages) § 7.4 cmt. c (1997) ("Senior lienors have no claim to a surplus produced by the foreclosure of junior mortgage.").

4. *Payment of surplus to holders of non-possessory junior interests.* If a foreclosure terminates an easement, the easement holder has a valid claim to any foreclosure surplus. See Anderman v. 1395 E. 52nd Street Realty Corp., 60 Misc.2d 437, 303 N.Y.S.2d 474 (1969). Should the mortgagor or the easement holder have priority in the surplus? Should the surplus be allocated between them on some type of pro rata basis? Consider the same questions when the mortgagor and a lessee claim the surplus. According to the Restatement: "[S]uch persons are entitled to receive, in order of their pre-foreclosure priority, the fair market value of their interests as of the date of foreclosure. Fair market value for the foregoing purpose is determined in the same manner as in eminent domain proceedings." Restatement (Third) of Property (Mortgages) § 7.4 cmt. b.

[handwritten margin note: If FS terminates easement]

5. *Acceptance of surplus as ratifying foreclosure.* Suppose that a power of sale foreclosure yields a surplus but that the mortgagor believes grounds exist for having the sale set aside. Would you advise the mortgagor to accept the surplus? Consider the consequences for one mortgagor who did so:

> It has been held that acceptance of a surplus derived from a foreclosure sale waives the right of the mortgagor to attack the foreclosure. Flake v. High Point Perpetual Building and Loan Association, 204 N.C. 650, 169 S.E. 223 (1933); 55 Am.Jur.2d Mortgages § 665 (1971). By endorsing the check and reaping the benefits of the surplus toward the satisfaction of other debts, plaintiffs elected to ratify the sale. They may not now treat the sale as a nullity and have it set aside, or sue the trustee for wrongfully conducting the sale. *Flake,* supra.

Leonard v. Pell, 56 N.C.App. 405, 289 S.E.2d 140, 142 (1982).

6. *Effect of other security on competing surplus claims.* Suppose that a first mortgage foreclosure sale produces a surplus but that it is insufficient to satisfy the second and third mortgagees' claims. If the third mortgagee can prove that the second mortgage debt is more than adequately secured by other property, should the third mortgagee have a superior claim to the surplus if its debt is not otherwise secured? See United States v. Century Fed. Sav. and Loan Ass'n, 418 So.2d 1195 (Fla.App.1982). This argument is a

variation on the marshaling principle discussed in Section A of this chapter. Good authority exists for marshaling foreclosure surplus. See, e.g., Pongetti v. Bankers Trust Sav. & Loan Ass'n, 368 So.2d 819 (Miss.1979).

7.   *Separately owned parcels securing one obligation.* A and B both executed a promissory note, which is secured by separate mortgages on Blackacre, owned by A, and Whiteacre, owned by B. Upon default, the mortgagee first foreclosed on Blackacre, which sold for $135,000. The mortgagee then foreclosed on Whiteacre, which sold for $187,000. Subtracting the mortgage debt from the combined sale proceed leaves a surplus of $112,055. How should it be divided? Consider the court's approach in Hilfiker v. Preyer, 690 S.W.2d 451 (Mo.App.1985):

> We believe the distribution of the surplus should not turn here on which tract the trustee decides to sell first, but upon other criteria. Which is sold first might be determined by chance or the whim of the trustee. It would be unfair to base it on the order of sale absent some circumstances that might call for the burden of payment to primarily fall on one owner.

> Barring such circumstances, see *Weyant v. Murphy,* 78 Cal. 278, 20 P. 568 (1889); *Champlain Valley Federal Savings and Loan Ass'n v. Ladue,* 35 A.D.2d 888, 316 N.Y.S.2d 19 (1970); 3 Jones on Mortgages § 1630 (7th ed. 1915), which the trial court was not required to find here, the equitable way to divide the surplus is proportionate to the amount generated by each tract at the sale. This was the method used to divide the surplus where a mortgage covered two separately owned tracts. See *In re M. Dewing Co.,* 248 F. 605 (D.R.I.1917). See also 3 Wiltsie, Mortgage Foreclosure § 1016, p. 1605 (5th ed. 1939).

> Dividing the surplus in accordance with the amount generated by the separate tracts, [B] would receive 58% of the surplus, or $64,992.47. [A] would receive 42% or $47,063.52.

8.   *Junior lienor's right to surplus when mortgagor claims homestead rights.* Suppose a first mortgage foreclosure yields a surplus. Does a mortgagor who asserts homestead rights or the junior mortgage have a stronger claim to the surplus? Consider how a Washington appellate court resolved this issue under that state's homestead statute:

> Generally, a property owner's homestead interest in property takes priority over the interests of other creditors. Under Washington's Homestead Act, "the homestead is exempt from attachment and from execution or forced sale for the debts of the owner up to the amount specified in RCW 6.13.030." RCW 6.13.070(1). Usually, a creditor's lien on the property is for only an amount in excess of the homestead exemption * * * . At the time of the trustee's sale in this case, the homestead exemption was set at $30,000. RCW 6.13.030 (1995).

But this general rule has an exception—an owner's homestead interest in property is subordinate to the interest of a deed of trust beneficiary. RCW 6.13.080 provides:

> The homestead exemption is not available against an execution or forced sale in satisfaction of judgments obtained ... [o]n debts secured (a) by security agreements describing as collateral the property that is claimed as a homestead or (b) by mortgages or deeds of trust on the premises that have been executed and acknowledged by the husband and wife or by any unmarried claimant.

> The [mortgagors] concede that their homestead interest was subordinate to the first deed of trust beneficiary's interest. But they contend that their interest in the excess proceeds is superior to the second deed of trust beneficiary's interest. The [mortgagors] point out that once the first deed of trust beneficiary foreclosed on its loan and the trustee sold the property, [junior mortgagee] lost its security interest in the property. Once its loan was no longer secured by the real estate, the [mortgagors] argue, [junior mortgagee] became like any other creditor. As an ordinary creditor, the [mortgagors] conclude, [junior mortgagee's] interest in the excess sale proceeds was subordinate to the homestead interest.

* * *

> But even when the Homestead Act is liberally construed, it provides no basis to adopt the [mortgagors'] position regarding the relative priority of the parties' interests in the proceeds. Again, the Homestead Act provides that the homestead exemption is not available against an execution in satisfaction of judgments obtained on debts secured by deeds of trust. RCW 6.13.080. This provision does not distinguish between first and second deeds of trust. The provision does not require that a deed of trust beneficiary must satisfy the debt through a foreclosure sale in order to take priority over a homestead interest.

> Likewise, the deed of trust statute provides no basis to conclude that the second deed of trust beneficiary's interest in the excess proceeds is subordinate to the homestead interest. To the contrary, the statute provides that a creditor's interest in excess proceeds from a nonjudicial foreclosure sale pursuant to a deed of trust continues at the same priority as the creditor's interest in the property: "[i]nterests in, or liens or claims of liens against the property eliminated by sale under this section shall attach to the surplus in the order of priority that it had attached to the property." RCW 61.24.080(3).

> [Junior mortgagee's] interest in the real property was superior to the homestead interest. Under RCW 61.24.080(3), [junior

mortgagee] maintained its priority interest in the excess proceeds from the nonjudicial foreclosure sale. A contrary holding would discourage lenders from granting second deeds of trust and from entering subordination agreements. Both of these services are important to consumers. Moreover, our holding will not in effect extinguish the homestead right by operation of the deed of trust statute. Liens other than junior deeds of trust continue to be subordinate to the homestead interest.

In re Upton, 102 Wash.App. 220, 6 P.3d 1231, 1233–34 (2000).

F. REACQUISITION OF TITLE BY MORTGAGOR AND RELATED ISSUES

OLD REPUBLIC INSURANCE CO. v. CURRIE

Superior Court of New Jersey, 1995
284 N.J.Super. 571, 665 A.2d 1153

BOYLE, P.J.CH.

Allen and Ruthie Currie were the owners of property at #16 West End Avenue, Plainfield, New Jersey. On or about July 16, 1974, the Curries executed a home repair contract and mortgage of even date which was subsequently assigned to plaintiff, Old Republic Insurance Company ("Old Republic"). The Curries thereafter filed a petition in bankruptcy. On December 4, 1978, the U.S. Bankruptcy Court entered an order declaring the lien of plaintiff to the Plainfield property fixed in the amount of $6,476.

After the bankruptcy, Allen and Ruthie Currie lost the Plainfield property through a foreclosure. However, on January 19, 1981, defendant, Allen Currie, reacquired the property. Ruthie Currie was not named on this later deed. No payments have been made toward the satisfaction of this debt since the date of the bankruptcy order.

Sometime during the month of April 1984, plaintiff ran a search of the property which disclosed that the Secretary of the Department of Housing and Urban Development conveyed the property to an Allen Currie. Plaintiff claims that it was unable to ascertain whether this Allen Currie was the same Allen Currie who had been indebted to Old Republic because this time Ruth Currie was not on the deed. Plaintiff responded to this information by rerecording its mortgage. However, plaintiff made no further attempt to verify the identity of the new owner until May, 1993. At some point thereafter, plaintiff confirmed that Allen Currie had reacquired the property and commenced this action on August 10, 1994.

Plaintiff argues that, by operation of law, its mortgage is revived, and that it is entitled to simple interest on the $6,476, plus simple interest at the contract rate of 12.5% to the date of judgment, together with counsel fees and costs as allowed by the court rules.

Defendant's sole defense to this action is that the above bankruptcy proceeding extinguished defendant's indebtedness to plaintiff. However, there is no authority to support this proposition. Plaintiff asserts that defendant's answer has failed to interpose a validly recognized defense and therefore brings this motion to strike defendant's answer. * * *

* * *

Generally, the purchaser at a foreclosure sale acquires the entire interest of the mortgagor and mortgagee unaffected by the rights of junior mortgagees or encumbrancers who are parties to the foreclosure. Atlantic City National Bank v. Wilson, 108 N.J.Eq. 213, 154 A. 537 (E. & A.1931). However, if the mortgagor is the purchaser or subsequently reacquires the property, there is authority that the junior mortgages revive as liens on the property. For example, it is clear that if the mortgagor and the first mortgagee contrive to extinguish the second mortgage, the court will restore the second mortgage. Stiger v. Mahone, 24 N.J.Eq. 426 (Ch. 1874). But even in the absence of fraud, the reacquisition is held to revive the second mortgage on three distinct theories.

First, under the payment theory, when the mortgagor purchases the property at the sale, the mortgagor is in effect paying the first mortgage and the second mortgage moves into first position. This is what would have occurred if the mortgagor had paid the first mortgage when it became due. If payment after foreclosure were to alter this result, the mortgagor would be profiting by its own wrong in failing to pay when due. Elkind v. Pinkerton, 294 Mass. 502, 2 N.E. 2d 456 (1936).

Second, is the covenant to defend title theory. Under this approach, the second mortgage that is revived usually contains a warranty that the mortgagor agrees that he will defend the title against all lawful claims. Permitting the foreclosure of the first mortgage is a breach of the warranty to defend the title. Even if the second mortgagee takes subject to the first mortgage, it has been held that the warranty to defend is not affected by the reference to the first mortgage. Merchants' National Bank v. Miller, 229 N.W. 357 (N.D.1930); cf. Dorff v. Bornstein, 277 N.Y. 236, 14 N.E. 2d 51 (1938).

Third, the warranty of title theory is based upon the warranty of title contained in the second mortgage. The mortgagor has warranted that the mortgaged premises shall be security for the debt and that the mortgagor will produce the property if the debt is not paid. If, for some reason (such as the foreclosure of the first mortgage with the title vesting in a third party), the mortgagor is prevented from producing the security, the obligation remains and is merely postponed until the mortgagor can fulfill it. When the mortgagor reacquires the property, it then must provide the property as security for the debt. This after-acquired title doctrine is an ancient equitable remedy designed to effectuate the intention of the parties. It has long been settled that an after-acquired title inures to the benefit of the mortgagee. Decker v. Caskey, 3 N.J.Eq. 446 (Ch. 1836); Tully v. Taylor, 84 N.J.Eq. 459, 94 A. 572 (E. & A. 1915). It is also treated as an obligation founded on the warranty. Robinson-Shore Development Co. v. Gallagher, 26 N.J. 59, 138 A. 2d 726 (1958). Even if the mortgagor's personal liability for the debt which is secured by the mortgage has been extinguished by bankruptcy, the warranty obligation is not nullified and he must produce the property. Baird v. Chamberlain, 60 N.D. 784, 236 N.W. 724 (1931).

Based upon the foregoing, this court is satisfied that (1) plaintiff is entitled to have its mortgage revived and (2) that defendant's answer does not contest the validity or priority of plaintiff's mortgage. Accordingly, this court will grant plaintiff's motion to strike defendant's answer.

This court, on its own motion, has decided to address the issue as to the proper amount to which plaintiff is entitled. While plaintiff contends that it is entitled to simple interest at the contract rate of 12.5% to the date of judgment, this court cannot agree. Plaintiff was on notice in April, 1984 that Allen Currie had reacquired the subject property. At that point, plaintiff should have asserted its rights. Had plaintiff done so, defendant would have had the opportunity to satisfy his debt without paying an additional eleven years of accrued interest, totaling $8,904.50. Therefore, plaintiff's inaction prejudiced defendant by $8,904.50, as plaintiff concededly did not notify defendant that it had rerecorded its mortgage. There is no evidence to suggest that defendant had occasion to become aware of the lien. In light of the above, this court holds that it would be unconscionable to permit plaintiff to benefit from its own dereliction to the tune of 12.5% interest over a period of eleven years. Consequently, plaintiff's claim is barred in part by laches. Laches is a "delay for a length of time, which, unexplained and unexcused, is unreasonable under the circumstances and has been prejudicial to the other party." West Jersey Title and Guaranty Co. v. Industrial Trust Co., 27 N.J. 144, 153, 141 A. 2d 782 (1958) (citing Hinners v. Banville, 114 N.J.Eq. 348, 168 A. 618 (E. & A.1933)).

Plaintiff's entire claim is not barred by laches. Instead, its claim is barred to the extent defendant has been prejudiced. Defendant was prejudiced in this matter to the extent that plaintiff did not assiduously pursue its rights after the April 1984 title search. Accordingly, this court awards plaintiff interest on its claim from the date of the bankruptcy judgment (December 4, 1978), to January 1, 1985, which this court deems to be a reasonable time within which plaintiff could have asserted its right. Therefore, plaintiff's judgment is in the reduced amount of $11,395, plus attorney's fees and costs as provided in the Rules.

NOTES

1. *Moral issues.* The principal case, more than most, raises basic questions of fairness and morality. Although a senior lien foreclosure normally eliminates junior liens and other junior interests, should the rule apply when the mortgagor purchases at the senior sale? The principal case articulates three traditional reasons why it should not apply. However, this case boils down to an intuitive notion of fairness—a person should not profit by defaulting. The relief afforded the redeemed junior lienor is also constrained by an intuitive notion of fairness. Because the junior lienor unreasonable delayed in asserting its claim, the court substantially reduced the accrued interest on the revived mortgage. This is a classic application of the equitable principle of laches. For further exploration of the "fairness-morality" issue, see Grant S. Nelson, The Foreclosure Purchase by the Equity of Redemption Holder or Other Junior Interests: When Should Principles of Fairness and Morality Trump Normal Priority Rules?, 72 Mo.L.Rev. 1259 (2007).

For a subsequent New Jersey decision rejecting the reasoning of *Old Republic*, see Mooney v. Provident Sav. Bank, 308 N.J.Super. 195, 705 A.2d 816 (1997).

2. *Reacquisition by "nonrecourse" mortgagor or subsequent grantee.* If the mortgagor who reacquires title was not personally liable on the mortgage obligation, should the junior liens be revived? The usual answer is "yes." "Even where the mortgage obligation is completely" nonrecourse, "the mortgagor agrees to the satisfaction of that obligation out of the mortgaged real estate. Thus, actions by the mortgagor that undermine the ability of the mortgagee to realize on the benefits of that agreement should be discouraged." Restatement (Third) of Property (Mortgages) § 4.9 cmt. b (1997).

Should the answer be the same when the person who reacquired the title was a subsequent grantee? The answer clearly is "yes" in the case of an assuming grantee, but what about a "subject to" grantee? According to the Restatement:

> Strong policy considerations also compel the application of the same rule to transferees of the mortgagor who take subject to the mortgage, but who do not assume liability on existing liens. In this type of transaction, the purchase price paid by the transferee is almost always reduced by the value of any liens that the transferee agrees are to remain on the real estate. To permit the transferee under such circumstances to acquire title through a senior lien foreclosure and, in so doing, to destroy junior liens, would enable the transferee to acquire the real estate for less than originally

contemplated. Such unjust enrichment of the transferee should be discouraged.

Id.*

3. *Mortgagor reacquisition from bona fide purchaser.* The easiest cases for revival are when the mortgagor purchases at the foreclosure sale or when the purchaser acts on the mortgagor's behalf. On the other hand, if the sale purchaser is a bona fide purchaser who does not know the mortgagor or her plan to terminate junior interests and later sells the property to the mortgagor, should the junior interests revive? "[T]here are good reasons to allow the [mortgagor] to reacquire title from a bona fide purchaser free and clear of previously foreclosed interests." Restatement (Third) of Property (Mortgages) § 4.9 cmt. b (1997) What are they? See id; 1 Nelson, Whitman, Burkhart & Freyermuth, Real Estate Finance Law § 4.44 (6th ed. Practitioner Series 2014).

In the principal case, Curry, the mortgagor, did not reacquire title by purchasing at the foreclosure sale, but rather from the Secretary of HUD who apparently was the foreclosure purchaser and the original senior mortgagee. Usually, a mortgagee-purchaser does not qualify as a bona fide purchaser. See Nelson, Whitman, Burkhart & Freyermuth, id. Therefore, Curry probably could not qualify as a transferee from a bona fide purchaser.

4. *Junior interest holders acquire title.* Generally, when a junior interest holder purchases at a senior foreclosure sale, the other junior interests do not revive. Under the Restatement, "a purchase by a junior lienor or other junior interest at a validly conducted foreclosure of a senior lien cuts off the rights of both the holder of the equity of redemption and other junior interests as well." Restatement (Third) of Property (Mortgages) § 4.9(b) cmt. c (1997).

Greater controversy exists when the senior foreclosure is of a real estate tax lien. While the Restatement applies the foregoing rule in the tax foreclosure context, substantial case law disagrees. See id. comment c and the reporters' note. If a mortgagee purchases at a senior tax sale, shouldn't the sale terminate the mortgagor's and the juniors' interests?

G. STATUTORY REDEMPTION

When a valid foreclosure has taken place, the equitable right of redemption ends. However, about half of the states have provided for a statutory right of redemption which provides an additional time period for mortgagors, their successors in interest, and, in some instances, junior lienors, to pay a certain sum of money to redeem the title to the property. To some extent we have already considered the impact of such statutes in the omitted lienor situation. Under statutory redemption, the redemption amount is normally tied to the foreclosure sale price rather than to the

---

* © 1997 by The American Law Institute. Reprinted with permission.

mortgage debt, as is the case with respect to equitable redemption. During the period of statutory redemption the mortgagor usually will have the right to possession. A few states, however, require the mortgagor to post bond as a condition precedent to acquiring the right to redeem and the right to possession. See, e.g., Vernon's Ann.Mo.Stat. § 443.410. The statutes vary greatly from state to state both as to time period and as to whether parties other than mortgagors and their successors have redemption rights. Moreover, in some states statutory redemption is available only after a power of sale foreclosure (see, e.g., Vernon's Ann.Mo.Stat. § 443.410), whereas in others it is available only after judicial foreclosure (see, e.g., Utah Code Ann.1953, § 78B–6–906; West's Rev.Code Wash.Ann. § 61.24.050). In the majority of states, however, it is available in both types of foreclosure. See, e.g., Minn.Stat.Ann. §§ 580.23, 580.24 and 581.10.

While there is great variation in these statutes, most fall into two broad categories—the "strict priority" or "ordered redemption" approach and the "scramble method." The Minnesota statute, reprinted below, follows the "strict priority" approach.

MINN.STAT.ANN.
§§ 580.23, .24

580.23. Redemption by mortgagor * * *

Subdivision 1. Six-month redemption period. (a) When lands have been sold in conformity with the preceding sections of this chapter, the mortgagor, the mortgagor's personal representatives or assigns, within six months after such sale, except as otherwise provided in subdivision 2 or section 582.032 or 582.32, may redeem such lands, as hereinafter provided, by paying the sum of money for which the same were sold, with interest from the time of sale at the rate provided to be paid on the mortgage debt as stated in the certificate of sale and, if no rate be provided in the certificate of sale, at the rate of six percent per annum, together with any further sums which may be payable as provided in sections 582.03 and 582.031.

(b) Delivery of funds and documents for redemption must be made at the normal place of business of the recipient, on days other than Sunday, Saturday, and legal holidays, between the hours of 9:00 a.m. and 4:00 p.m.

* * *

Subd. 2. 12-month redemption period. Notwithstanding the provisions of subdivision 1 hereof, when lands have been sold in conformity with the preceding sections of this chapter, the mortgagor, the mortgagor's personal representatives or assigns, within 12 months after such sale, may redeem such lands in accordance with the provisions of payment of subdivision 1 thereof, if:

(1) the mortgage was executed prior to July 1, 1967;

(2) the amount claimed to be due and owing as of the date of the notice of foreclosure sale is less than 66–2/3 percent of the original principal amount secured by the mortgage;

(3) the mortgage was executed prior to July 1, 1987, and the mortgaged premises, as of the date of the execution of the mortgage, exceeded ten acres in size;

(4) the mortgage was executed prior to August 1, 1994, and the mortgaged premises, as of the date of the execution of the mortgage, exceeded ten acres but did not exceed 40 acres in size and was in agricultural use as defined in section 40A.02, subdivision 3;

(5) the mortgaged premises, as of the date of the execution of the mortgage, exceeded 40 acres in size; or

(6) the mortgage was executed on or after August 1, 1994, and the mortgaged premises, as of the date of the execution of the mortgage, exceeded ten acres but did not exceed 40 acres in size and was in agricultural use. * * *

* * *

Subd. 4. Waiver; 12-month redemption for ag use. A mortgagor, before or at the time of granting a mortgage executed on or after August 1, 1994, may waive in writing the mortgagor's right under subdivision 2, clause (6), to have a 12-month redemption period based upon the premises being in agricultural use as of the date of execution of the mortgage. The written waiver must be either a document separate from the mortgage or a separately executed and acknowledged addendum to the mortgage on a separate page. * * * Where there is a waiver of the rights under subdivision 2, clause (6), the redemption period in subdivision 1 applies.

580.24. Redemption by creditor

(a) If no redemption is made by the mortgagor, the mortgagor's personal representatives or assigns, the most senior creditor having a legal or equitable lien upon the mortgaged premises, or some part of it, subsequent to the foreclosed mortgage, may redeem within seven days after the expiration of the redemption period determined under section 580.23 or 582.032, whichever is applicable; and each subsequent creditor having a lien may redeem, in the order of priority of their respective liens, within seven days after the time allowed the prior lienholder by paying the amount required under this section. However, no creditor is entitled to redeem unless, one week or more prior to the expiration of the period allowed for redemption by the mortgagor, the creditor:

(1) records with each county recorder and registrar of titles where the foreclosed mortgage is recorded a notice of the creditor's intention to redeem;

(2) records with each county recorder and registrar of titles where the notice of the creditor's intention to redeem is recorded all documents necessary to create the lien on the mortgaged premises and to evidence the creditor's ownership of the lien, including a copy of any money judgment necessary to create the lien; and

(3) after complying with clauses (1) and (2), delivers to the sheriff who conducted the foreclosure sale or the sheriff's successor in office a copy of each of the documents required to be recorded under clauses (1) and (2), with the office, date and time of filing for record stated on the first page of each document.

* * *

(b) Saturdays, Sundays, legal holidays, and the first day following the expiration of the prior redemption period must be included in computing the seven-day redemption period. When the last day of the period falls on Saturday, Sunday, or a legal holiday, that day must be omitted from the computation. The order of redemption by judgment creditors subsequent to the foreclosed mortgage shall be determined by the order in which their judgments were entered as memorials on the certificate of title for the foreclosed premises or docketed in the office of the district court administrator if the property is not registered under chapter 508 or 508A, regardless of the homestead status of the property. All mechanic's lienholders who have coordinate liens shall have one combined seven-day period to redeem.

(c) The amount required to redeem from the holder of the sheriff's certificate of sale is the amount required under section 580.23. The amount required to redeem from a person holding a certificate of redemption is:

(1) the amount paid to redeem as shown on the certificate of redemption; plus

(2) interest on that amount to the date of redemption; plus

(3) the amount claimed due on the person's lien, as shown on the affidavit under section 580.25, clause (3).

The amount required to redeem may be paid to the holder of the sheriff's certificate of sale or the certificate of redemption, as the case may be, or to the sheriff for the holder.

For an excellent description of how the Colorado "ordered redemption" system operates, see Wyse Fin. Servs., Inc. v. National Real Estate Inv., LLC., 92 P.3d 918 (Colo.2004).

The second approach, the "scramble method," has been described as follows:

> Here again, once the mortgagor redeems, all others are preempted from exercising their right. The difference is that there is no priority order in which redemptions may be made from the purchaser. If a junior lienor redeems first, then the next redeeming party, whether it is the mortgagor or another junior lienor, must pay the previously redeeming lienor the foreclosure sale price and sometimes the amount of the lien of that junior lienor (depending on whether the prior redemptioner had preforeclosure priority over the second redemptioner). Once the previously redeeming junior lienor has been fully paid so that his lien is satisfied, he has no further redemption rights. If, however, the originally redeeming junior lienor had preforeclosure priority that was subordinate to the next redeeming junior lienor, then he may take another opportunity to redeem if his lien is still unsatisfied.

3 Richard R. Powell & Patrick A. Rohan, Powell on Real Property § 470 (1997). For a thorough examination of this redemption method, represented by the Iowa model, see Patrick B. Bauer, Statutory Redemption Reconsidered: The Operation of Iowa's Redemption Statute In Two Counties Between 1881 and 1980, 70 Iowa L.Rev. 343 (1985); Lee B. Blum, Iowa Statutory Redemption After Mortgage Foreclosure, 35 Iowa L.Rev. 72 (1949); Iowa Code Ann. Ch. 628.

UNITED STATES v. STADIUM APARTMENTS, INC.

United States Court of Appeals, Ninth Circuit, 1970
425 F.2d 358, cert. denied, 400 U.S. 926, 91 S.Ct. 187, 27 L.Ed.2d 185 (1970)

[FHA had insured the mortgage given by the developer of an apartment project to Prudential Insurance Co. When the developer defaulted, Prudential assigned the mortgage to FHA, as it was legally entitled to do under 12 U.S.C.A. § 1743, and FHA paid Prudential the balance owing on the mortgage. FHA then obtained a default judgment in federal district court foreclosing the mortgage. The district judge framed the foreclosure decree to allow a one-year period of redemption as provided by Idaho statute. FHA appealed this aspect of the decree, arguing that under principles of federal pre-emption and supremacy, it was not subject to the Idaho statutory redemption provisions. Although the developer did not participate in the appeal, the Ninth Circuit invited the attorneys general of the states within the circuit to submit amicus curiae briefs, and several did so. The court held that federal law should apply, and that no redemptive period should be permitted following foreclosure. The discussion of federalism is deleted from the portion of the opinion reproduced below, but the concepts are treated in Chapter 8, Section F of this book, infra.]

* * *

Reasons of policy dictate the same result. In the first place, only 26 of the states provide for post-foreclosure redemption. The periods of redemption vary widely. So do other conditions to redemption and the rules governing right to possession, right to rents, making repairs, and other matters arising during the redemption period.

* * *

There is a split of authority as to whether the right of redemption can be waived. Similarly, there is a split of authority as to the right of the mortgagee to recover the value of improvements made during the redemption period. It would be contrary to the teaching of every case that we have cited to hold that there is a different federal policy in each state, thus making FHA "subject to the vagaries of the laws of the several states." Clearfield Trust Co. v. United States, 1943, 318 U.S. 363, 367, 63 S.Ct. 573, 575, 87 L.Ed. 838. Which policy is to be the federal policy, that of the states which do not provide for a period of redemption, or that of those which do? And if the policy is to be the latter, is it to embrace, in each state, all of the special rules applicable in that state alone? Is it to be expanded to establish a federal right of redemption in each state where none exists under local law?

In response to our request, the government has informed us of the views of federal agencies involved in the lending or insuring of funds for private housing purposes. These include, in addition to the Federal Housing Administration, the Farmers Home Administration of the Department of Agriculture, acting under 42 U.S.C.A. § 1471 ff., and the Veterans Administration, acting under 38 U.S.C.A. § 1800 ff. We quote the government's response:

> "The Farmers Home Administration, the Federal Housing Administration, and the Veterans Administration have informed us that their experience has indicated that the imposition of post-foreclosure-sale redemption periods makes the foreclosure remedy more costly and administratively time-consuming in those states whose local law so provides. Generally, the reasons given in support of this conclusion are * * * that existence of a post-sale period for redemption chills bidding at the foreclosure

sale, forcing the United States to buy the property at the sale
and to hold it (paying meanwhile the costs of maintenance) until
the expiration of the period, when it finally can give good title to
a purchaser."

Additional reasons stated by the government are quoted in the margin.[7]
We do not find the policy arguments presented by California convincing.
First, it is argued that the purpose of the redemption statutes is to force
the mortgagee and others to bid the full market price at the sale. We
assume that this is the purpose; we are not convinced that the statutes
accomplish it. What third party would bid and pay the full market value,
knowing that he cannot have the property to do with as he wishes until a
set period has gone by, and that at the end of the period he may not get it,
but instead may be forced to accept a payment which may or may not
fully reimburse him for his outlays? In some states he cannot get
possession. E.g., California Code Civ.Proc. § 703, Mau, Sadler & Co. v.
Kearney, 143 Cal. 506, 77 P. 411; Haynes v. Treadway, 133 Cal. 400, 65
P. 892. In some states if he does get possession and collects rents, they
will be deducted from his reimbursement, e.g., Idaho, Clark Investment
Co. v. United States, supra. In some states, if he makes repairs, he will
not be repaid for his outlays. These are precisely the problems which the
federal government should not have to face. It is not in the real estate

---

[7] "The Farmers Home Administration has stated that where post-sale redemption periods
have been imposed, the mortgaged property may, after sale and before expiration of the
redemption period, 'stand unoccupied and unattended for considerable periods of time and
consequently [may] deteriorate substantially in value, to the detriment of the financial interest
of the United States and without concomitant benefit to any other party.' Similarly, the Veterans
Administration reported to us that where a post-sale redemption period is imposed unless the
former owner redeems timely, the mortgagee or his assignee are obligated to pay holding costs
during the redemption period, i.e., taxes, public improvements, if any, the cost of repairs to
preserve the security, and the cost of hazard insurance premium when necessary. There is also
for consideration the interest normally accruing on the outstanding investment. Moreover, many
of these properties have been abandoned and must remain vacant during redemption periods. In
many instances they are subject to extreme vandalism during these periods which is, of course,
costly to the holder."

"Most pertinent to the present case, of course, were the comments of the Federal Housing
Administration concerning foreclosures on multi-family projects like that involved here. The
Federal Housing Administration reported to us:

'It is perhaps the normal situation to find any project in foreclosure to be in need of
substantial repair. Many mortgagors, during a period of diminishing income, utilize the
net income to keep the mortgage current as long as possible, keeping maintenance
expenses to a bare minimum. When the evil day arrives that the income will no longer
cover the mortgage payments, he falls into default, and the subject of the foreclosure
action is a property which requires substantial expenditures to place it in properly
habitable condition, and to make it attractive to the rental market. With the notable
exception of Alabama, redemption statutes permit a foreclosure purchaser to receive
from a redemptioner little more than the price bid at the foreclosure sale, so that a
purchaser is well advised to keep rehabilitation expenses to an absolute minimum until
the redemption period expires. As a practical matter, this delays the day when FHA, as
such purchaser can safely embark on a program involving capital expenditures, thereby
delaying the day when the property may be placed in condition for its best use and for
advantageous sale which will reimburse the insurance fund for a portion of the loss
incurred as a result of the mortgagor's default.'"

business. It should not have to hold and manage properties for any period longer than is absolutely necessary for it to get back its money. It should not be subjected to the risk that the property will deteriorate, and it should not be left with no means to protect itself against such losses.

Our doubts as to whether the statutes accomplish the purpose is reinforced by the fact that in many states, partly because of those statutes, real estate financing is almost exclusively secured by trust deeds with power of sale. This is certainly true in California, and the statutory right of redemption does not apply to such sales. Py v. Pleitner, 1945, 70 Cal.App.2d 576, 161 P.2d 393; Roberts v. True, 1908, 7 Cal.App. 379, 94 P. 392. See also, as to Idaho, n. 5, supra. One is tempted to inquire why, if public policy so strongly favors a post-sale period of redemption, the legislature has not applied it to sales under trust deeds? Perhaps it is because the redemption statute has, in some states, made the use of mortgages almost a dead letter.

Moreover, the policy of FHA is to bid the fair market value at the foreclosure sale. For this purpose, it has the property carefully appraised before bidding. See Book 2, Volume VII, Sec. 72926 of the FHA Manual. It is authorized by 12 U.S.C.A. § 1713(k) to "bid any sum up to but not in excess of the total unpaid indebtedness secured by the mortgage, plus taxes, insurance, foreclosure costs, fees, and other expenses * * * ." It bids fair market value for its own protection as well as that of the mortgagor and other lienors. It is limited to the amount specified because the objective is to recover its loss on the mortgage insurance, not to put the government in the business of buying and speculating in real property. Presumably, if the property is worth more, others will increase the bid, the government will be paid in full, and the excess will go to junior lien holders and, if there be sufficient funds, to the mortgagor.

It is also suggested that a purpose of the redemption statutes is to protect junior lienors. Perhaps. But if the objective of the statutes is to obtain bids equal to market value, and if as is argued, the bidding would be lower in the absence of the statutes, then junior lienors could more easily protect themselves in the latter situation. They could buy the property at the sale for less. It is always open to the junior lienors to protect themselves by bidding. They take with notice of the senior lien. Here, the government's judgment was for $93,804.97; its bid was $55,100. The court found the value of the property to be $58,000. The deficiency judgment is for $37,728.88. This is a singularly inappropriate case in which to be concerned about junior lien holders. They simply have no equity in the property. * * *

Nor is it accurate to say that the application of state redemption rights does not tie up government funds; as this case illustrates, it does do so. Under 12 U.S.C.A. § 1743(c) the mortgagee has the option of assigning the mortgage to the Secretary and being paid the full amount of the guarantee, instead of itself foreclosing. As might be expected, that is what Prudential did in this case. Why would any mortgagee do otherwise, when by so assigning it can receive the full benefit of the insurance without having to incur the expense and risk attendant upon foreclosure? Under the statute, Prudential received the full benefit of the insurance—government obligations equal to the then total value of the mortgage, in this case more than $90,000. If the redemption period applies, the government must wait a year to get its money back—and it may not then get it all, or even as much as it bid.

We conclude that the Idaho statute providing for right of redemption is not here applicable.

* * *

ELY, CIRCUIT JUDGE (dissenting):

The statutes can best be understood through a brief review of their historical development. * * *

The harshness of strict foreclosure led to the concept of foreclosure by sale. Theoretically, the property was to be sold to the highest bidder with the mortgagee having first claim to the proceeds and the mortgagor obtaining his equity in the form of whatever surplus remained. This approach was expected to yield more even results by allowing the competitive market to set the value of the land instead of the "value" being set at the amount of the unpaid debt as was the fact under strict foreclosure. Unfortunately, this expectation was frustrated by reason of the immense advantages favoring the mortgagee at the sale. First, it was unnecessary for the mortgagee to raise and expend any cash up to the amount of the unpaid debt. Secondly, there would not often be an interested outside buyer, or junior lienholder with cash, at the precise time of the sale. Thus, the senior mortgagee was assured of being almost always the only bidder at the sale. The junior lienors, in particular, suffered under this method since their interests were cut off by the judicial sale. Since they had no weapons with which to force the sale price above the amount of the senior's claim, they often realized nothing on their claims.

The response of many jurisdictions to the unsatisfactory results of the foreclosure-by-sale procedure was the adoption of a statutory redemption period. The basic design of statutory redemption consists of giving the mortgagor and those claiming under him (including junior lienors) the right to redeem the property from the purchaser at the sale within a specified period by paying, *not* the balance of the debt secured, but the price paid at the sale. The objective of the redemption right is that the mortgagee or other bidders, if any, shall bid not less than the fair market value of the land, since otherwise the purchaser risks being divested of the land by redemption at less than its market value.

The key to understanding the statutory redemption right lies in the proposition that the statute's operation is in the nature of a threat. When redemption is exercised, it is thereby evidenced that the mortgagee has not bid adequately at the sale and the statute has not had its intended effect. On the other hand, if the threat functions successfully and the mortgagee does bid adequately, then the mortgagor and junior lienors, if any, will have been satisfied to the full value of the property and there will be no reason for exercising the redemption right. If he bids the full market value of the property, then the mortgagee may rest secure in the knowledge that it will not be redeemed. See generally Durfee & Doddridge, Redemption From Foreclosure Sale, 23 Mich.L.Rev. 825, 827–834 (1925); Note, Redemption From Judicial Sales, 5 U.Chi.L.Rev. 625, 626 (1938).

* * *

The Government, and also the majority, make several arguments designed to show that redemption statutes are neither important nor necessary. The first is that the statutes do not work because no third party will bid at the sale, knowing that he will be subject to redemption. The statutes, as I have tried to explain, are not the least bit concerned with the actions of third parties since they were necessitated by the observation that third parties do not ordinarily bid at foreclosure sales in any event. Instead of trying to stimulate bidding at the sale, they set up the more realistic possibility that the property will be redeemed if the mortgagee's bid is inadequate.

NOTES

1. *No statutory redemption under federal foreclosure acts.* As the foregoing indicates, the federal government views statutory redemption as contrary to its interest as a mortgagee. See generally, 12 U.S.C.A. sec. 1710. ("notwithstanding any state law to the contrary, there shall be no right of redemption * * * in the mortgagor or any other person subsequent to the foreclosure sale in connection with a Secretary-held single family mortgage"). Specifically, the Single Family Mortgage Foreclosure Act of 1994, which authorizes power of sale foreclosure of federally-insured mortgages on one-to-four family dwellings held by the Secretary of Housing and Urban Development, provides that, as to any foreclosure under it, "there shall be no [post-sale] right of redemption, or right of possession based upon a right of redemption in the mortgagor or others." 12 U.S.C.A. § 3763(e). Also, The Multifamily Mortgage Foreclosure Act of 1981, which authorizes power of sale foreclosure for HUD held mortgages on property other than one-to-four family dwellings, has an identical prohibition on statutory redemption. 12 U.S.C.A. § 3713(d).

2. *Federal government as junior lienor.* When the federal government finds itself in the role of a junior lienholder, it finds the statutory redemption concept much more to its liking. By federal statute the United States, as a foreclosed junior lienor, is generally afforded by statute "one year from the date of sale within which to redeem." 28 U.S.C.A. § 2410. As to federal tax liens, the redemption period is the longer of 120 days or the state redemption period, if any. 26 U.S.C.A. § 7425; 28 U.S.C.A. § 2410(c). To the extent that state legislation is less protective of the interests of junior lienors, it is preempted by the federal statutes. See United States v. John Hancock Mut. Life Ins. Co., 364 U.S. 301, 81 S.Ct. 1, 5 L.Ed.2d 1 (1960). Consider the following description of the aim of this federal redemption scheme:

> The statutory purpose is to encourage the lienholder to bid at least a fair price on the property being foreclosed by allowing the government to redeem the property at the same price that the lienholder pays for it (plus interest); if the superior lienholder pays the debtor at least a fair price, this somewhat inures to the benefit of the government as a creditor by reducing the debtor's obligations; the government is not obliged to redeem; if the lienholder pays less than a fair price, the government in redeeming the property is able to capture any differential between the price paid and the property's fair market value.

Delta Sav. & Loan Ass'n, Inc. v. IRS, 847 F.2d 248, 251 (5th Cir.1988). In view of the federal government's arguments in *Stadium Apartments,* do you see some irony in the foregoing language?

3. *Improvements by purchaser during the redemption period.* In a few states, the foreclosure sale purchaser has the right to possession during the redemption period. If you were such a purchaser in possession should you make repairs or improvements to the real estate? Should the foreclosed mortgagor redeem will you be reimbursed for such expenditures? Ultimately, this issue must be resolved by the language of redemption statute. Consider how the New Mexico Supreme Court approached this problem:

> There is no mention of improvements or betterments in the statute. Thus the only funds that a purchaser may recover under the redemption statute are those funds that the purchaser paid to acquire the property. Those funds include the amount the purchaser paid for the property, with interest [10% per annum], plus any taxes and penalties. Section 39–5–18(A)(1) * * * Those funds also include any amount paid by the purchaser to satisfy outstanding liens or mortgages on the property, with interest, plus taxes and penalties. Section 39–5–18(A)(1). The statute does not allow the purchaser to recover for any funds paid for improvements.
>
> We also agree * * * that requiring the redeemer to pay for such improvements would contravene the public policy embodied in the redemption statute. One of the purposes of the redemption statute is to give the property owner * * * a reasonable opportunity to

redeem the property. * * * This purpose would be defeated if redeemers were required to pay purchasers for improvements, in addition to those costs provided for in the redemption statute. Purchasers could make it more burdensome for redeemers to redeem their property by investing significant amounts of money into improvements, almost ensuring that the redeemer would be unable to redeem their property.

Chase Manhattan Bank v. Candelaria, 135 N.M. 527, 90 P.3d 985 (2004). On the other hand, a few state statutes appear to require the redeeming mortgagor to pay for improvements made by a sale purchaser while in possession. See e.g., Section 6–5–252, Ala.Code. Suppose the property is rental residential real estate and repairs are necessary during the redemption period. Is it good public policy to deny reimbursement for such repairs?

FARMERS PRODUCTION CREDIT ASSOCIATION v. McFARLAND

Supreme Court of Iowa, 1985
374 N.W.2d 654

Considered en banc.

SCHULTZ, JUSTICE.

In this appeal a mortgagors' assignee and a junior mortgage lienholder compete for final redemption rights in a senior mortgagee's foreclosure action. Daniel and Linda McFarland (mortgagors) owned real estate that was subject to two mortgages. On June 9, 1983, the junior mortgage-holder, Production Credit Association (PCA), filed an action to foreclose its mortgage. Shortly thereafter, the senior mortgage-holder, American Federal Savings & Loan Association (AFS), filed a separate foreclosure action against the McFarlands naming PCA as a junior lienholder and party defendant. On November 11, 1983, a decree of foreclosure was entered in the latter action in favor of AFS and it stated PCA had a valid second lien. The property was sold to AFS at a January 10, 1984, sheriff's sale and the mortgagors were granted a six-month period of redemption. See Iowa Code § 628.26. On April 6, 1984, the mortgagors conveyed their redemption rights to Daniel's mother, Dorothy McFarland. On that date Dorothy (assignee) tendered a check for redemption of the property. The junior mortgage holder, PCA, on May 3, 1984, tendered its own check in an attempt to redeem the property. No issue is advanced concerning the validity of either tender; however, the assignee claims her redemption precluded further redemptions.

In its June 9, 1983, petition for foreclosure PCA alleged Daniel and Linda McFarland had entered into a collateral agreement and mortgage in the amount of $40,000 to secure other notes contracted between the parties. PCA prayed for judgment in rem against the mortgaged premises in the amount of $40,000 plus interest and other costs and requested the mortgage be foreclosed. In their answer the mortgagors requested the court to determine the amount they owed PCA. Following PCA's attempt to redeem the property foreclosed in the AFS action, Dorothy McFarland intervened in PCA's foreclosure action and claimed her redemption in the AFS foreclosure had extinguished PCA's lien. At the same time, the mortgagors amended their answer and requested the court to enter a decree denying PCA's petition for foreclosure or, in the alternative, hold their mortgage obligation was limited to $40,000 if foreclosure was ordered.

* * *

On October 1, 1984, the trial court entered a three-pronged ruling: (1) PCA was entitled to recover the principal and interest on its note; (2) PCA could redeem the property from the mortgagors' assignee; and (3) PCA was entitled to a sheriff's deed to the property.

On appeal the mortgagors and assignee maintain the trial court erred in ruling PCA was entitled to redeem. They claim a junior lienholder cannot redeem after an assignee of the mortgagor has redeemed because a redeeming assignee takes the property unencumbered by liens on the property. Although we hold the junior lienholder cannot redeem in this case, the reason for our decision is different from that asserted by the mortgagors and assignee. Since the assignee redeemed within the exclusive statutory period granted a debtor, we hold the junior lienholder has no right to redeem. However, we further hold that a redemption by the debtor or assignee during the exclusive period does not allow either party to take the property free and clear of liens on the property.

Several sections of Iowa Code chapter 628 are relevant. Under section 628.3 the debtor's right to redeem is for a period of one year from the date of a sale "and for the first six months thereafter such right of redemption is exclusive." Section 628.5 provides for redemption by creditors: "If no redemption is made by the debtor as above provided, thereafter, and at any time within nine months from the day of sale, said redemption may be made by a mortgagee * * * " The "as above provided" is an obvious reference to the debtor's exclusive right to redeem pursuant to section 628.3. Section 628.26 permits an agreement to reduce the period of redemption, as in this case, so that the mortgagor's period of redemption set forth in section 628.3 is reduced from twelve to six months, the exclusive right to redeem is the first three months, and the creditors' period of redemption is after three months and within four months from the date of sale.

The plain language of section 628.3 gives the debtor the exclusive right to redeem during the appropriate six or three month period. "An exclusive right is one which only the grantee thereof can exercise, and from which all others are prohibited or shut out." *Black's Law Dictionary* 507 (rev. 5th ed. 1979). We interpret the use of the term "exclusive" to vest the right of redemption in the debtor only and to shut out all creditors. In the instant case the mortgagors have assigned their redemption rights to Dorothy McFarland. Such assignments are permitted under section 628.25 which provides "[t]he rights of a debtor in relation to redemption are transferable, and the assignee has the like power to redeem." "Like" is defined as "[e]qual in quantity, quality, or degree or exactly corresponding." *Black's Law Dictionary* at 834. The plain words of the statute give the assignee the same quantity and quality of rights as the debtor, which would include the "exclusive" right to redeem within three months of the sheriff's sale.

* * *

Although redemption by the mortgagor or assignee during the exclusive period prevents redemption by a junior lienholder, it does not provide the redeemer complete relief from junior liens. We do not agree with the claim of the mortgagors and assignee that the assignee is the owner of the property free and clear of liens. The trial court did not address this issue because it ruled PCA's redemption was valid. In equity our review is de novo and our responsibility is to decide as the trial court should have. *Farmers Savings Bank, Joice, Iowa v. Gerhart,* 372 N.W.2d 238, 242 (Iowa 1985). Consequently, we determine the respective rights of a mortgagor's assignee and junior lienholders in a foreclosure action.

Before addressing this issue, however, we find it necessary to review the rights of a junior lienholder. After the debtor's exclusive period of redemption has expired, any creditor can redeem the property as long as its claim against the debtor has matured into a lien before the creditor's period of redemption has ceased. Iowa Code § 628.5. A creditor's period of redemption is either after six months and within nine months from the date of sale pursuant to section 628.5 or after three and within four months from the sale under section 628.26. Creditors can even redeem from each other. Iowa Code § 628.8.

A judgment creditor who fails to redeem within the statutory period of time loses his lien on the property. *Paulsen v. Jensen,* 209 Iowa 453, 458, 228 N.W. 357, 359 (1929). Additionally, a junior mortgagee who is a party to the foreclosure action and fails to redeem has his lien on the property extinguished. *Anderson v. Renshaw,* 229 Iowa 93, 98–99, 294 N.W. 274, 277–78 (1940). A judgment lien, lost by the failure to redeem by the junior judgment lienholder, will attach again to the property when the debtor redeems the property, but the junior mortgage lien is not re-established. *Id.* at 99, 294 N.W. at 278. This is because a judgment lien automatically attaches to after acquired real estate of the debtor. *Id.; see* Iowa Code § 624.23(1). The extinguishment of the junior mortgage lien, however, does not destroy the debt itself and the mortgagee can later obtain a judgment against the debtor. *Anderson,* 229 Iowa at 99, 294 N.W. at 278.

There is no question that our decisions have distinguished between redemption by a mortgagor and that by an assignee with respect to the rights of junior lienholders that have failed to redeem within the statutory period. Under those circumstances we have indicated that while a judgment creditor's lien is re-established when the mortgagor redeems, neither the judgment creditor nor junior mortgagee's rights attach to property redeemed by the assignee. *Cadd v. Snell,* 219 Iowa 728, 733–35, 259 N.W. 590, 592–93 (1935); *Paulsen,* 209 Iowa at 458, 228 N.W. at 359 (1929); *Cooper v. Maurer,* 122 Iowa 321, 326–27, 98 N.W. 124, 125–26 (1904); *Moody v. Funk,* 82 Iowa 1, 4, 47 N.W. 1008, 1009 (1891). In *Cooper* we gave the reason for the distinction when we stated:

> If, when the process of redemption is complete, the property is again vested in the debtor either by his having been the last to redeem or by conveyance from the holder of a sheriff's deed, then the unsatisfied creditor may reach it, for the simple reason that all the debtor's property is liable for the payment of his debts unless specifically exempted by statute. If, however, when the last redemption has been made, the property is in a third person, it cannot be so subjected for the equally simple reason that the property of one man cannot be subjected to the payment of the debts of another.

122 Iowa at 327, 98 N.W. at 126.

These cases, however, do not benefit the assignee in this action. All those cases addressed the issue of whether liens that have been extinguished become re-established when the assignee redeems. Under the facts in the present action, the mortgagors had subjected their property to the PCA lien, which was in force at the time of the assignment. By redeeming within three months of the sheriff's sale the assignee prevented any redemption by the mortgagor's creditors. Therefore, PCA's lien was not extinguished because no creditor redemption period existed. PCA's lien remained viable and the assignee's right to the property is subject to the PCA lien. The titleholders could not divest PCA's lien on the property merely by assigning their redemption rights to Daniel's mother.

The mortgagors and assignee assert our language in *Tirrill* [v. Miller, 206 Iowa 426, 218 N.W. 303 (1928)] indicates that when a mortgagor's assignee redeems, the assignee takes the property free from liens and debts of the mortgagor and the property is subjected only to the debts of the assignee. 206 Iowa at 429, 218 N.W. at 304. Although the assignee's redemption in that case was within the exclusive period, we note again that the issue of the exclusive right to redeem was neither raised nor discussed in *Tirrill*. Additionally, under the facts in that case the court acknowledged the creditor had a right to redeem. *Id.* Therefore, statements made in the *Tirrill* decision were under circumstances in which the court recognized the lienholders could have protected themselves by redeeming. In the present case PCA attempted to redeem, but we determined PCA had no right of redemption. Despite language in *Tirrill* to the contrary, we hold the liens of a junior lienholder or creditor are not extinguished when a mortgagor or assignee redeems during the exclusive statutory period.

It could be argued that junior creditors' liens are extinguished either by the entry of the foreclosure decree or the completion of the sheriff's sale. Under such an argument the creditors then possess only a statutory right of redemption which is cut off when the debtor or the debtor's assignee redeems during the exclusive period. Although this cut-off theory was not advanced by either party at trial or on appeal, we deem it necessary to address it. We conclude, however, that such a theory is not in line with our statutory scheme and is contrary to our case law.

Our statutes indicate that junior creditors' liens are still in effect after the entry of a foreclosure decree and the sheriff's sale. Chapter 654 of the Code outlines procedures for the foreclosure of real estate mortgages and makes reference to "liens upon the property" at a time subsequent to the foreclosure decree and sale. *See* Iowa Code § 654.7 (disposal of over-plus "if there is no other lien upon the property"); § 654.8 (providing "a person having a lien on the property which is junior to the mortgage" can be assigned the interest of the holder of the mortgage); § 654.9 (provision for the payment of "any other liens on the property sold"). Likewise, the chapter on executions, chapter 626, recognizes liens on the property after the foreclosure and sale. *See* Iowa Code § 626.82 (overplus paid to the debtor "unless there are liens upon the property").

Our case law also supports the proposition that junior creditors' liens continue after the foreclosure decree and sheriff's sale. We have determined that the purchaser at a foreclosure sale acquires only an equitable lien for the amount of the purchase money, and legal title remains in the mortgagor and is not divested until the expiration of the statutory periods of redemption. *In re Jensen's Estate,* 225 Iowa 1249, 1252–53, 282 N.W. 712, 714 (1938); *Wissmath Packing Co. v. Mississippi River Power Co.,* 179 Iowa 1309, 1324, 162 N.W. 846, 851 (1917); *Greenlee v. North British & Mercantile Insurance Co.,* 102 Iowa 427, 429, 71 N.W. 534, 535 (1897). Language in our cases indicates that the junior lienholders' rights are extinguished with the expiration of their period of redemption. *See Anderson,* 229 Iowa at 99, 294 N.W. at 278 ("the lien of appellee's mortgage upon the foreclosed property was lost at the expiration of nine months"); *Paulsen,* 209 Iowa at 458, 228 N.W. at 359 ("[w]hen the junior creditor fails to redeem before the expiration of nine months, he loses his lien upon that property").

In light of our statutory scheme and case law addressed to mortgage foreclosures, we conclude that junior creditors' liens continue after the foreclosure decree and sheriff's sale. Junior lienholders can protect their claims either by bidding at the foreclosure sale or redeeming in a deliberate manner. *See* Iowa Code chs. 626 and 628; * * *

In summary, the trial court erred in allowing PCA to redeem the property from Dorothy McFarland, and PCA is not entitled to a sheriff's deed from the foreclosure sale in the AFS action. Although Dorothy McFarland has a right to title under the assignment, her title is subject to the rights of PCA against the property in this action. The district court should amend its order to allow foreclosure in rem on the PCA lien.

AFFIRMED IN PART, REVERSED IN PART AND REMANDED.

All Justices concur except UHLENHOPP, CARTER and WOLLE, JJ., who concur in part and dissent in part.

UHLENHOPP, JUSTICE, concurring in part, dissenting in part.

I concur in the holding of the majority that the junior mortgagee cannot redeem from the assignee, but dissent from the holding that the junior mortgagee can foreclose against the property. I join in Justice Carter's dissent, but add the following.

* * *

When the sheriff's sale was held under the senior mortgage foreclosure judgment, the junior mortgagee could have protected itself by bidding on the property if it believed the property had value in excess of the senior mortgage. It did not do so, and the senior mortgagee bid in the property. If the *mortgagor* had thereafter redeemed at any time during the six-month redemption period and if the junior mortgagee had meantime obtained judgment against the mortgagor on the mortgagor's note, the junior mortgagee would have had a lien on the property *under its judgment against the mortgagor by virtue of the statute which makes a judgment a lien against the debtor's real property.* Iowa Code § 624.23.

The *assignee,* however, redeemed. A judgment in favor of the junior mortgagee against the mortgagor would not be against the assignee, and would not be a lien on the assignee's real property. The junior mortgagee therefore would have no judgment lien to enforce against the property in the assignee's hands.

I would affirm the district court's judgment that the junior mortgagee is entitled to judgment on the mortgagor's note, but would otherwise reverse the judgment.

CARTER and WOLLE, JJ., join this concurrence in part and dissent in part.

CARTER, JUSTICE, dissenting.

I dissent.

The majority opinion unnecessarily and without articulating a single policy ground supporting its result significantly retracts the protection previously afforded mortgagors under our redemption laws. It is particularly unfortunate that this occurs at a time when, because of prevailing economic conditions, mortgagors are particularly in need of such protection.

* * *

Within the context of our established system of foreclosure by judicial sale, our decisions have followed a consistent course in declaring that junior liens are extinguished at the conclusion of the statutory redemption process. *E.g., Anderson v. Renshaw,* 229 Iowa 93, 98–99, 294 N.W. 274, 277–78 (1940); *Cadd v. Snell,* 219 Iowa 728, 733–35, 259 N.W. 590, 592–93 (1935); *Paulsen v. Jensen,* 209 Iowa 453, 458, 228 N.W. 357, 359 (1929); *Cooper v. Maurer,* 122 Iowa 321, 326–27, 98 N.W. 124, 125–26 (1904). In the present case, the statutory redemption process terminated upon redemption from sale by the mortgagor's assignee.

The majority seeks to escape from the inevitable consequence of the cited cases by completely ignoring the mechanics of foreclosure by judicial sale. It is axiomatic in a system of foreclosure by sale that any interest of the mortgagors in the real estate is extinguished by the sale in order that the purchaser at the sale may obtain a clear title. All that remained in the mortgagor or junior lienholders following the sale was a mere incorporeal hereditament derived from the statutes governing redemption from sale. The majority opinion misinterprets the language in some of our decisions as establishing the time for extinguishment of junior liens as the expiration of the redemption period for creditors. One need only recognize foreclosure by sale for what it is in order to realize that such reliance is misplaced. The extinguishment of all liens at the time of sale is essential to the successful operation of that system. 5 G. Thompson, *Real Property* § 4838 (1924); Comment, 27 Iowa L.Rev. 482, 485 (1942). Moreover, in reviewing the policy reasons underlying extinguishment of liens of junior lienholders upon foreclosure, there is absolutely no reason to turn the issue on the timing of the redemption made by the mortgagor or the mortgagor's assignee.

It is significant that, to the extent some courts have sought to establish the liens of junior creditors against property held by redeeming mortgagors, such cases do not suggest that the liens were not extinguished upon sale. The protection of liens in these cases has developed under theories in which the junior liens may be "revived." *See* Durfee & Doddridge, *Redemption from Foreclosure Sale—The Uniform Mortgage Act,* 23 Mich.L.Rev. 825, 850 (1925) (hereinafter cited as *Durfee & Doddridge*). There is no authority in our cases for holding as the majority does that, if a mortgagor or a mortgagor's assignee redeems during the exclusive period, they take the property subject to the junior liens. Indeed, as the majority concedes, *Tirrill v. Miller,* 206 Iowa 426, 429, 218 N.W. 303, 304 (1928) holds otherwise.

If the law really is as the majority suggests, this is a matter of critical importance in the functioning of mortgage foreclosure litigation. Vital property interests turn on the timing of the mortgagor's redemption. Given this circumstance, it is strange that in more than 100 years of litigation this court has never before suggested that the timing of the mortgagor's redemption is of any significance in determining the status of junior liens. Moreover, at least four critical examinations of our redemption system by legal commentators have been undertaken not one of which has suggested that the timing of the mortgagor's redemption makes any difference in determining the status of junior liens. *See* Bauer, *Statutory Redemption Reconsidered: The Operation of Iowa's Redemption Statute in Two Counties Between 1881 and 1980,* 70 Iowa L.Rev. 343, 379–84 (1985) (hereinafter cited as *Bauer*); *Osborne*[, *Mortgages,*] § 309, at 642–44; Blum, *Iowa Statutory Redemption After Mortgage Foreclosure,* 35 Iowa L.Rev. 72, 73 (1949); *Durfee & Doddridge* at 857.

Indeed, *Osborne* and *Durfee & Doddridge* suggest the contrary. The former states:

> The [preferred] scheme is designed to put pressure on the foreclosing mortgagee at the time of the sale to bid what he thinks the property is worth, up to the amount of his debt; and it puts pressure on a junior lienor during the period of his right to redeem to bid more than the price paid by the senior mortgagee. Iowa at the present time comes closest to this suggested solution. Under its statute the mortgagor's assignee on redemption clearly takes free of all liens against the mortgagor.

Osborne at 642 (footnotes omitted). Similarly, *Durfee & Doddridge* have suggested that under the Iowa decisions the redemptioner simply succeeds to the rights of the purchaser. *Durfee & Doddridge* at 857. They see this as a desirable result and suggest that junior lienors like senior lienors should be forced to bid at the sale at their peril in order to preserve their security interest. * * *

It is difficult to suggest any reason for the provisions of section 628.3 which give the mortgagor an exclusive right of redemption for the first six months, except as a vehicle for exerting pressure on junior lienors to bid at the sale. Under the majority's approach, the mortgagee's exclusive right now becomes meaningless in any case where there are junior liens. In addition, the presence of such an illusory right in our statutes creates a trap for the unwary debtor who will often be acting without advice of counsel.

A major flaw in the majority's approach is the resulting overbreadth of the category of creditors who will be afforded protection. The majority concedes that junior lienors who have been afforded an opportunity to redeem and have not done so should lose their liens, but holds that it is otherwise when the mortgagor's redemption during the exclusive period precludes redemption by creditors. This distinction is impossible to justify based on the realities of junior lien status. A recent study indicates that more than ninety percent of all junior lienholders fail to make redemption. *See Bauer,* 70 Iowa L.Rev. at 370, 377. Under the majority's holding in the present case, there is no method for distinguishing legitimate redemption rights from purely illusory redemption rights. The result will be to give a windfall to those junior lienors whose security interests are worthless based upon the value of the property and who would not have redeemed from the sale even if they had enjoyed an opportunity to do so.

If it were the intent of chapter 628 to protect junior lienholders in the manner that the majority proposes, they and not the mortgagor would logically have been given the exclusive right of redemption at the outset of the redemption process thereby permitting them to establish their position if the value of the property warranted such action but extinguishing their liens in those cases where it did not. The fact that our legislature has granted to the mortgagor an exclusive right to go forward in the redemption tug-of-war and has denied to junior lienors the right to redeem from a previously redeeming mortgagor leads to the inescapable conclusion that it had no intent to protect junior lienors in the situation presented in the present case.

UHLENHOPP and WOLLE, JJ., join this dissent.

NOTES

1. *Lien revival after statutory redemption.* Courts take a variety of approaches to lien revival when the mortgagor or her successor redeems. Many, for example, endorse revival of all junior liens in existence prior to the sale. See, e.g., Franklin v. Spencer, 309 Or. 476, 789 P.2d 643 (1990) ("redemption by the mortgagor * * * 'reinstates' the lien of any unsatisfied docketed judgment the instant that the mortgagor * * * redeems"); Newman v. American Nat'l Bank, 780 P.2d 336 (Wyo.1989) ("Public policy requires

[the] revival of junior mortgages. The potential for a mortgagor to eliminate junior mortgagees by allowing a foreclosure by the senior mortgagee and then [redeeming] is a solid basis for such public policy"). Indeed, in some states, even the lien of the foreclosed mortgage is revived to the extent of any unpaid deficiency. See Nelson, Whitman, Burkhart & Freyermuth, Real Estate Law § 8.6 (6th ed.2014).

At the opposite extreme are states like California, where its statute provides that "[l]iens extinguished by the sale * * * do not reattach to the property after redemption and the property that was subject to the extinguished lien may not be applied to the satisfaction of the claim or judgment under which the lien was created." West's Ann.Cal.Code Civ.Proc. § 729.080(e). According to its legislative history, the foregoing statute "changes the prior rule that liens subordinate to that under which the sale was held reattach upon redemption by the judgment debtor or a successor in interest. The prior rule that upon redemption by the judgment debtor the judgment lien under which the property was sold reattaches for the amount of the deficiency is also not continued. * * * This encourages the judgment creditor and subordinate lienholders to protect their interests by looking to the property sold. * * * [This legislation] makes it clear that once a lien is extinguished a lien may not be created on the same property to enforce the same claim or judgment. Hence, for example, a judgment creditor whose judgment lien is extinguished may not again record the judgment to create a lien on the same property, nor may the judgment creditor obtain an execution lien by levy of a writ of execution on the property." Cal.Legislative Committee Comment, § 729.080(e) (1982). See Cal.L.Rev.Comm. Reports 2001.

A few pages back we learned that where the mortgagor or other holder of the equity of redemption purchases the property at the foreclosure sale, junior liens and other interests are not terminated. See pages 796–799 supra. Is this policy subverted by the California's approach to lien revival in the statutory redemption context?

2. *Assignee of mortgagor as redeeming party.* In most jurisdictions, the mortgagor's statutory redemption right is assignable. See, e.g., Chess v. Burt, 87 So.3d 1201 (Ala.App. 2011); Western Bank of Las Cruces v. Malooly, 119 N.M. 743, 895 P.2d 265 (App.1995); 4 Richard R. Powell & Patrick A. Rohan, Powell on Real Property § 470 (1997). However, courts differ on the effect of a redemption by the assignee. In some, previously existing junior liens against the mortgagor revive against the redeeming assignee. See, e.g., Donovan v. Farmers Home Admin., 19 F.3d 1267 (8th Cir.1994) (applying South Dakota law). In others, the redeeming assignee takes free of such liens even though they revive where the mortgagor is the redeeming party. See, e.g., Turner v. Les File Drywall, Inc., 117 N.M. 7, 868 P.2d 652 (1994). Why should the mortgagor be able to transfer to her assignee a better title than she possessed? Is this good policy? See Nelson, Whitman, Burkhart & Freyermuth, Real Estate Finance Law § 8.6 (6th ed.2014).

Is the majority in *McFarland* influenced by *who* the mortgagor's assignee is? Would it have reached the same result had the assignee been unrelated to the mortgagor?

3.   *Redemption by junior lienor.* Suppose a junior lienor redeems under an applicable statutory redemption system. Do other junior liens revive? Under most statutes, redemption by a junior lienor gives it the same title the foreclosure sale purchaser would have obtained had there been no redemption. See Nelson, Whitman, Burkhart & Freyermuth, Real Estate Finance Law 758 (6th ed.2014). In other words, junior liens do not revive. Is this good policy?

H. ANTI-DEFICIENCY LEGISLATION AND RELATED PROBLEMS

Under the traditional approach followed in many jurisdictions, once the mortgage goes into default and the obligation is accelerated, the mortgagee has two options. The mortgagee may either (1) obtain a judgment on the personal obligation and enforce it by levying upon any of the mortgagor's property and, if a deficiency remains, foreclose on the mortgaged real estate for the balance or (2) foreclose on the real estate first and if the proceeds are insufficient to satisfy the mortgage obligation, obtain a deficiency judgment thereafter. Some jurisdictions following the above approach require the mortgagee to elect one of the two options. The Restatement agrees; see Restatement (Third) of Property (Mortgages) § 8.2 (1997). Other states, however, reject this "election of remedies" requirement; the mortgagee is permitted to follow both options simultaneously with the only limitation being that the mortgage obligation may only be satisfied once.

Under the traditional approach, a deficiency judgment is calculated by subtracting the foreclosure sale price from the mortgage obligation. If the foreclosure is judicial, the deficiency judgment is obtained in the same proceeding after the foreclosure sale. Where the foreclosure is by power of sale, the mortgagee obtains a deficiency judgment by filing a separate judicial action against the mortgagor.

As we have seen earlier in this chapter, a forced sale, even under stable economic conditions, normally will not bring a price that will reflect the reasonable market value of the property if it were marketed outside the foreclosure context. Moreover, in times of severe economic downturn, mortgaged property often sells for substantially depressed prices. To make matters worse, mortgagees occasionally purchase at the foreclosure sale for a deflated price, obtain a deficiency judgment and resell the real estate at a profit.

The great depression of the 1930's, as might be expected, produced a substantial amount of varied state legislation to provide relief for mortgagors. Perhaps best-known were the various moratoria statutes. Such legislation differed from state to state. Some statutes gave courts authority to grant foreclosure postponements on petition of mortgagors in individual cases. Other statutes extended the period of statutory redemption beyond the usual period or stretched out the periods of time in a foreclosure action. See generally George E. Osborne, Handbook on the Law of Mortgages § 331 (1970). Most of this legislation was upheld against federal and state constitutional attack. Constitutional law students are familiar with Home Building & Loan Ass'n v. Blaisdell, 290 U.S. 398, 54 S.Ct. 231, 78 L.Ed. 413 (1934), which upheld the Minnesota legislation, finding it not to be an unconstitutional impairment of the obligation of contracts.

However, as the economy recovered, most of the moratoria legislation either lapsed, was repealed, or became moribund. The more lasting legacy of the 1930's depression, as well as prior and subsequent economic downturns, is the wide variety of procedural and substantive limitations on deficiency judgments imposed by legislatures and, less frequently, by the courts. The following material is intended to provide you with a general overview of these limitations.

GRANT S. NELSON, DEFICIENCY JUDGMENTS AFTER REAL ESTATE FORECLOSURES IN MISSOURI: SOME MODEST PROPOSALS

47 Mo.L.Rev. 151, 152–54 (1982)*

The majority of states limits the mortgagee's right to a deficiency judgment. Some limitations are procedural. For example, many states impose strict notice requirements[5] and time limits[6] on the mortgagee. Failure by the mortgagee to comply with these limitations can destroy the right to obtain a deficiency judgment.[7]

Likewise, failure to comply with "one action" rules also can destroy the mortgagee's right to a deficiency judgment. Under such rules, the mortgagee's only remedy on default is foreclosure, and he must obtain any deficiency judgment incident to the foreclosure proceeding.[8] Two justifications are often cited for this rule:

---

*   Reprinted with permission of The Missouri Law Review.

5   *See, e.g.,* Me.Rev.Stat.Ann. tit. 14, § 6203–E (1980).

6   *See, e.g.,* Nev.Rev.Stat. § 40.455 (1979) (three months after sale); N.J.Stat.Ann. § 2A:50–2 (West Cum.Supp.1981–1982) (three months after sale or confirmation); N.D.Cent.Code § 32–19–06 (1976) (ninety days after sale). Some states limit the time for completing execution on a deficiency judgment. *See, e.g., id.* (three years).

7   *See* N.Y.Real Prop.Acts.Law § 1371(3) (McKinney 1979); Okla.Stat.Ann. tit. 12, § 686 (West 1960).

8   Cal.Civ.Proc.Code § 726 (West 1980) provides:

There can be but one form of action for the recovery of any debt, or the enforcement of any right secured by mortgage upon real property, which action must be in accordance

One is to protect the mortgagor against multiplicity of actions when the separate actions, though theoretically distinct, are so closely connected that normally they can and should be decided in one suit. The other is to compel a creditor who has taken a mortgage on land to exhaust his security before attempting to reach any unmortgaged property to satisfy his claim.[9]

Similar restrictions sometimes apply to power of sale foreclosures.[10] In such situations, the exercise of the power of sale is a condition precedent to a subsequent action at law for a deficiency. Some commentators refer to this restriction as the "security first" principle.[11]

There also are important substantive limitations on deficiency judgments. As a result of the depression of the 1930s, many states enacted "fair value" legislation, and most of this legislation is still in force. Fair value statutes usually define the deficiency as the difference between the mortgage debt and the fair value of the foreclosed land, rather than as the difference between the mortgage debt and the foreclosure sale price of the land.[12] Depending on the statute, a court[13] or a jury[14] may determine the fair value. Most of these statutes were designed to deal with depression conditions, when foreclosure sales typically yielded nominal amounts. This legislation, however, also assumes that even in a stable economic climate, a forced sale of real estate will yield a price significantly lower than otherwise would be obtained by private sale.

Closely related to the fair value approach are the appraisal statutes used in a few states.[15] This legislation requires the court or the person

---

with the provisions of this chapter. In such action the court may, by its judgment, direct the sale of the encumbered property * * * .

Four other states—Idaho, Montana, Nevada, and Utah—have one action statutes copied from California. *See* Idaho Code § 6–101 (1979); Mont.Code Ann. § 71–1–222 (1981); Nev.Rev.Stat. § 40.430 (1979); Utah Code Ann. § 78–37–1 (1977).

9   G. Osborne, G. Nelson & D. Whitman, Real Estate Finance Law § 8.2, at 526.

10   *See, e.g.,* Walker v. Community Bank, 10 Cal.3d 729, 733–34, 518 P.2d 329, 331–32, 111 Cal.Rptr. 897, 899–900 (1974); Nevada Land & Mortgage Co. v. Hidden Wells Ranch, Inc., 83 Nev. 501, 504, 435 P.2d 198, 200 (1967).

11   G. Osborne, G. Nelson & D. Whitman, *supra* note 9, § 8.2, at 527. Many states also have "election of remedies" statutes under which the mortgagee can foreclose and seek a deficiency judgment or sue on the note and then foreclose, but cannot bring both actions simultaneously. *See, e.g.,* N.Y.Real Prop.Acts.Law §§ 1301, 1401 (McKinney 1979). For a complete compilation of the 15 states with such statutes, see Washburn, *The Judicial and Legislative Response to Price Inadequacy in Mortgage Foreclosure Sales,* 53 S.Cal.L.Rev. 843, 928 n. 467 (1980).

12   *See, e.g.,* Cal.Civ.Proc.Code § 726 (West 1980); N.Y.Real Prop.Acts.Law § 1371 (McKinney 1979); Utah Code Ann. § 57–1–32 (1974).

13   *See, e.g.,* N.Y.Real Prop.Acts.Law § 1371 (McKinney 1979).

14   *See, e.g.,* N.D.Cent.Code §§ 32–9–04,–06,–07 (1979). For an analysis of this statute, see First State Bank v. Ihringer, 217 N.W.2d 857, 859–63 (N.D.1974).

15   *See, e.g.,* Ark.Stat.Ann. § 51–1112 (1971); La.Code Civ.Proc.Ann. art. 2336–2337 (West 1961); S.C.Code § 29–3–660 to –760 (1976).

conducting the foreclosure sale to appoint an appraiser, who determines the value of the property. For example, in South Carolina, a statute reduces the deficiency by the difference between the foreclosure sale price and the appraisal amount.[16] Other state appraisal statutes establish two-thirds of the appraisal value as an upset price and prohibit deficiency judgments if the upset price satisfies the mortgage debt and costs.[17]

Numerous other types of antideficiency legislation are common. For example, some states prohibit deficiency judgments after a power of sale[18] or a purchase money mortgage[19] foreclosure. Some of these latter statutes limit the definition of a purchase money mortgage to those held by the vendor as the mortgagee,[20] while others also include purchase money mortgages held by a variety of third party lenders.[21] Many such statutes also apply only to purchases of residential property.[22]

For a more detailed and comprehensive consideration of the antideficiency concepts treated in this subsection, see Robert M. Washburn, Judicial and Legislative Response to Price Inadequacy in Mortgage Foreclosure Sales, 53 So.Cal.L.Rev. 843 (1980). For an insightful economic analysis of anti-deficiency legislation, see Michael H. Schill, An Economic Analysis of Mortgagor Protection Laws, 77 Va.L.Rev. 489 (1991). For a strong brief for barring deficiency judgments in the home foreclosure setting, see John Mixon, Deficiency Judgments Following Home Mortgage Foreclosure: An Anachronism That Increases Personal Tragedy, Impedes Regional, Economic Recovery and Means Little to Lenders, 22 Tex.Tech.L.Rev. 1 (1991).

The California anti-deficiency regulatory scheme is probably more complex and pervasive than that of any other jurisdiction. Consequently, you should study carefully the description of this regulatory framework contained in Cornelison v. Kornbluth, 15 Cal.3d 590, 125 Cal.Rptr. 557, 542 P.2d 981 (1975):

> Prior to 1933, a mortgagee of real property was required to exhaust his security before enforcing the debt or otherwise to

---

[16] S.C.Code § 29–3–740 (1976).

[17] See, e.g., Ohio Rev.Code Ann. § 2329.19 (Page 1981); Wyo.Stat. § 1–17–316 (1977).

[18] See, e.g., Cal.Civ.Proc.Code § 580d (West 1976); Wash.Rev.Code Ann. § 61.24.100 (Cum.Supp.1981). For a discussion of the Washington statute, see Helbling Bros. v. Turner, 14 Wash.App. 494, 496–98, 542 P.2d 1257, 1258–59 (1975).

[19] See, e.g., N.C.Gen.Stat. § 45–21.38 (1976); S.D.Comp.Laws Ann. §§ 44–8–20 to –24 (1967).

[20] See, e.g., N.C.Gen.Stat. § 45–21.38 (1976).

[21] See, e.g., Ariz.Rev.Stat.Ann. § 33–729(A) (1974).

[22] See, e.g., id. §§ 33–729,–814; Or.Rev.Stat. §§ 88.070–.075 (1979).

waive all right to his security (§ 726; see Walker v. Community Bank (1974) 10 Cal.3d 729, 733–734, 111 Cal.Rptr. 897, 518 P.2d 329). However, having resorted to the security, whether by judicial sale or private nonjudicial sale, the mortgagee could obtain a deficiency judgment against the mortgagor for the difference between the amount of the indebtedness and the amount realized from the sale. As a consequence during the great depression with its dearth of money and declining property values, a mortgagee was able to purchase the subject real property at the foreclosure sale at a depressed price far below its normal fair market value and thereafter to obtain a double recovery by holding the debtor for a large deficiency. (Roseleaf Corp. v. Chierighino (1963) 59 Cal.2d 35, 40, 27 Cal.Rptr. 873, 378 P.2d 97; see Glenn, Mortgages (1943) § 156, pp. 857–861.) In order to counteract this situation, California in 1933 enacted fair market value limitations applicable to both judicial foreclosure sales (§ 726) and private foreclosure sales (§ 580a) which limited the mortgagee's deficiency judgment after exhaustion of the security to the difference between the fair value of the property at the time of the sale (irrespective of the amount actually realized at the sale) and the outstanding debt for which the property was security. Therefore, if, due to the depressed economic conditions, the property serving as security was sold for less than the fair value as determined under section 726 or section 580a, the mortgagee could not recover the amount of that difference in his action for a deficiency judgment. (See Hetland, Secured Real Estate Transactions (Cont.Ed.Bar 1974) § 9.3, pp. 183–184.)

In certain situations, however, the Legislature deemed even this partial deficiency too oppressive. Accordingly, in 1933 it enacted section 580b which barred deficiency judgments altogether on purchase money mortgages. "Section 580b places the risk of inadequate security on the purchase money mortgagee. A vendor is thus discouraged from overvaluing the security. Precarious land promotion schemes are discouraged, for the security value of the land gives purchasers a clue as to its true market value. [Citation.] If inadequacy of security results, not from overvaluing, but from a decline in property values during a general or local depression, section 580b prevents the aggravation of the downturn that would result if defaulting purchasers were burdened with large personal liability. Section 580b thus serves as a stabilizing factor in land sales." (Roseleaf Corp. v. Chierighino, supra, 59 Cal.2d 35, 42, 27 Cal.Rptr. 873, 877, 378 P.2d 97, 101; see also Spangler v. Memel (1972) 7

Cal.3d 603, 612, 102 Cal.Rptr. 807, 498 P.2d 1055; Bargioni v. Hill (1963) 59 Cal.2d 121, 123, 28 Cal.Rptr. 321, 378 P.2d 593.)

Although both judicial foreclosure sales and private nonjudicial foreclosure sales provided for identical deficiency judgments in nonpurchase money situations subsequent to the 1933 enactment of the fair value limitations, one significant difference remained, namely property sold through judicial foreclosure was subject to the statutory right of redemption (§ 725a), while property sold by private foreclosure sale was not redeemable. By virtue of sections 725a and 701, the judgment debtor, his successor in interest or a junior lienor could redeem the property at any time during one year after the sale, frequently by tendering the sale price. The effect of this right of redemption was to remove any incentive on the part of the mortgagee to enter a low bid at the sale (since the property could be redeemed for that amount) and to encourage the making of a bid approximating the fair market value of the security. However, since real property purchased at a private foreclosure sale was not subject to redemption, the mortgagee by electing this remedy, could gain irredeemable title to the property by a bid substantially below the fair value and still collect a deficiency judgment for the difference between the fair value of the security and the outstanding indebtedness.

In 1940 the Legislature placed the two remedies, judicial foreclosure sale and private nonjudicial foreclosure sale on a parity by enacting section 580d. Section 580d bars "any deficiency judgment" following a private foreclosure sale. "It seems clear that section 580d was enacted to put judicial enforcement on a parity with private enforcement. This result could be accomplished by giving the debtor a right to redeem after a sale under the power. The right to redeem, like proscription of a deficiency judgment, has the effect of making the security satisfy a realistic share of the debt. [Citation.] By choosing instead to bar a deficiency judgment after private sale, the Legislature achieved its purpose without denying the creditor his election of remedies. If the creditor wishes a deficiency judgment, his sale is subject to statutory redemption rights. If he wishes a sale resulting in nonredeemable title, he must forego the right to a deficiency judgment. In either case the debtor is protected." (Roseleaf v. Chierighino, supra, 59 Cal.2d 35, 43–44, 27 Cal.Rptr. 873, 878, 378 P.2d 97, 102.)

Now consider carefully a specific application of West's Ann.Cal.Code Civ.Proc. § 580b:

DeBERARD PROPERTIES, LTD. v. LIM

Supreme Court of California, 1999
20 Cal.4th 659, 85 Cal.Rptr.2d 292, 976 P.2d 843

MOSK, J.

We must decide whether, notwithstanding the protection against deficiency judgments conferred by Code of Civil Procedure section 580b (hereafter section 580b), a purchaser may waive, by contract term, that protection in exchange for new consideration following the original purchase money sale. * * *

In 1990, Myo Za Theresa Lim and Bun Raymond Lim agreed to buy a shopping center from DeBerard Properties, Ltd., for $3.2 million. The Lims tendered a $1,120,000 down payment, assumed a first trust deed securing an obligation of $1,913,266.92 held by a bank, and signed a promissory note for $170,000 secured by a second trust deed in favor of DeBerard.

By September 1993 the Lims could no longer make payments on the obligations secured by the first and second trust deeds. The Lims hired an accountant to renegotiate their obligations to the holders of the trust deeds. The accountant renegotiated both obligations. As a result, the parties to this case executed a forbearance agreement.

The agreement halved the monthly payments from $1,416.67 to $708.33 and the interest rate from 10 to 5 percent. Also, DeBerard agreed not to foreclose, and it agreed to subordinate its trust deed to any modification of the bank loan, in order to facilitate the Lims' renegotiations with the bank. In turn, the Lims waived the protection provided by section 580b.

Despite these changes, the Lims soon defaulted on their obligations to the bank and DeBerard. The bank foreclosed and extinguished DeBerard's junior security interest. DeBerard then filed this suit on the promissory note.

In a bench trial, the court concluded that section 580b may be waived as a matter of law and found that the Lims had voluntarily, knowingly, and intelligently waived it. The court awarded DeBerard $241,075.81 plus costs.

The Court of Appeal reversed. It concluded that section 580b's language precluded its protection from being waived.

We begin with section 580b's text. As relevant here, the statute provides: "No deficiency judgment shall lie in any event after a sale of real property . . . for failure of the purchaser to complete his or her contract of sale, or under a deed of trust or mortgage given to the vendor to secure payment of the balance of the purchase price of that real property . . . ”

The language of section 580b is plain. A vendor is barred from obtaining a deficiency judgment against a purchaser in a purchase money secured land transaction. “[I]n the case of a seller-financed loan for real property, i.e., a purchase money obligation, a deficiency judgment is prohibited.” (*Ghirardo v. Antonioli* (1996) 14 Cal.4th 39, 49, 57 Cal.Rptr.2d 687, 924 P.2d 996.) “The explicit language of section 580b brooks no interpretation other than that deficiency judgments are prohibited by the purchase money mortgagee so long as a purchase money mortgage or deed of trust is in effect on the original property. To allow a purchase money creditor to circumvent the absolute rule by enforcing a . . . waiver of section 580b in exchange for other concessions would [flout] the very purpose of the rule. If the purchase money creditor retains an interest in the original property, the debtor cannot be held for a deficiency. If the purchase money creditor does not wish to accept the risk that the property will be lost through foreclosure by another secured creditor, the remedy is to either foreclose himself or destroy the purchase money nature of the transaction . . . ” (*Palm v. Schilling,* 199 Cal.App.3d at p. 76, 244 Cal.Rptr. 600 * * *).

Historically we have discerned two reasons for the Legislature's decision to protect purchasers in purchase money secured land transactions. First, section 580b is a transaction-specific stabilization measure: it stabilizes purchase money secured land sales by keeping the vendor from overvaluing the property and by suggesting to the purchaser its true value. Second, it is a macroeconomic stabilization measure: if property values drop and the land is foreclosed upon, the purchaser's loss is limited to the land that he or she used as security in the transaction, purchasers as a class are harmed less than they might otherwise be during a time of economic decline, and the economy benefits. * * *

DeBerard correctly observes that in *Spangler v. Memel* (1972) 7 Cal.3d 603, 102 Cal.Rptr. 807, 498 P.2d 1055 (*Spangler*), we held that section 580b did not apply to the facts at issue, notwithstanding the statute's absolute bar to deficiency judgments in purchase money secured land sales. It contends that we should hold the statute may be waived in cases such as this.

Spangler, however, creates only a narrow exception to the scope of section 580b, and we decline to create another one here.

In *Spangler*, the vendor conveyed a single-family residence on Sunset Boulevard in Los Angeles to the purchaser for $90,000, consisting of $26,100 in cash and a $63,900 note secured by a purchase money deed of trust, which the vendor agreed to subordinate to future construction loans of as much as $2 million so that the residence could be replaced by an office building. The purchasers in turn agreed to waive the antideficiency judgment protection of section 580b, so that the vendor would have recourse against them should the lender of the construction loans foreclose on an anticipated higher priority encumbrance. The purchasers found a lender that, as expected, extended a $408,000 loan on condition that its deed of trust have priority over the vendor's.

Once built, the office building proved to be a commercial failure, and the lender foreclosed on its deed of trust, extinguishing the value of the vendor's subordinated security. The vendor sued the purchasers to recoup the deficiency, and we held that she could recover it.

We explained that section 580b's protection "applies automatically only to the standard purchase money situation. We are of the view that if the transaction in question is a variation on the standard purchase money mortgage or deed of trust transaction, it should be examined so as to determine whether it subserves the purposes of section 580b ... " (*Spangler, supra*, 7 Cal.3d at p. 611, 102 Cal.Rptr. 807, 498 P.2d 1055.) Thus, *Spangler* created a two-part inquiry: does the sale vary from a standard purchase money transaction, and if so, does applying section 580b's antideficiency protection comport with the Legislature's intent? Section 580b applies unless the answer to the first question is yes and the answer to the second question is no.

In *Spangler*, we held that "a sale of real property for commercial development in which the vendor agrees to subordinate his senior lien under the purchase money deed of trust to the liens of lenders of the construction money for the commercial development is a variation on the standard purchase money mortgage transaction." (*Spangler, supra*, 7 Cal.3d at p. 611, 102 Cal.Rptr. 807, 498 P.2d 1055.) And we held that applying section 580b would not comport with the Legislature's intent. "[T]he success of the commercial development depends upon the competence, diligence and good faith of the developing purchaser. It would seem proper, therefore, that the purchaser[—]not the vendor[—]bear the risk of failure, particularly since in the event of default, the junior lienor vendor will lose both the land and the purchase price." (7 Cal.3d at p. 613, 102 Cal.Rptr. 807, 498 P.2d 1055.)

Moreover, "[i]n the subordination clause context, the amount of the construction loan is usually extremely large. This is illustrated by the case at bench[,] where the subordination clause provided that the vendor would agree to subordinate for construction loans up to $2 million, and a loan of $408,000 was actually obtained. It is clear that the typical vendor in this context cannot possibly raise the astronomical sums needed to buy in at the senior sale and thereby protect his junior security interest. The only possible protection available to the vendor[,] other than careful and sometimes fortuitous choice of purchasers, is to allow a deficiency judgment against the commercial developer." (*Spangler, supra,* 7 Cal.3d at p. 614, 102 Cal.Rptr. 807, 498 P.2d 1055.)

The Court of Appeal has, in various decisions, properly recognized that *Spangler's* application is limited. "*Spangler* does not make the mere presence of a subordination agreement a push button that defeats the rule of automatic application of section 580b. It is only when a subordination agreement signals a pronounced change in the use to which the property is devoted—thus making it a variation on the standard purchase money security transaction—that the transaction is removed from the reach of the rule." (*Thompson v. Allert* (1991) 233 Cal.App.3d 1462, 1466, 285 Cal.Rptr. 367.) * * *

In sum, Spangler's rule is limited to those situations in which a pronounced intensification of the property's anticipated post-sale use both requires and eventually results in construction financing that dwarfs the property's value at the time of sale. Furthermore, the purchaser must be in a much better position than the vendor to assess the property's possible value and to understand the risks involved in capitalizing on the property's potential. Finally, under all the circumstances of the sale, including the property's development and the financing for that development, conferring section 580b's protection must unfairly thrust "the risk of the failure of the commercial development . . . upon the vendor" (*Spangler, supra,* 7 Cal.3d at p. 613, 102 Cal.Rptr. 807, 498 P.2d 1055), imposing on it a commercially unreasonable burden because "the success of the commercial development depends upon the competence, diligence and good faith of the developing purchaser" (*ibid.*). In a situation in which all three factors are found, stability in secured land transactions is deemed to be better maintained by creating an exception to section 580b's safe harbor.[3] * * *

This case, however, is unlike *Spangler.* DeBerard sold the Lims a shopping center. The Lims continued to operate a shopping center—they did not obtain a construction loan that dwarfed the property's value at the time of sale and then proceed to build a more intensive use. Merely renegotiating the sale's terms in an effort to salvage the transaction did

---

[3]   Significant risks attach to vendors' interests that are subordinated to construction loans. In *Budget Realty Inc. v. Hunter,* supra, 157 Cal.App.3d 511, 204 Cal.Rptr. 48, the court noted: "The subordination of a seller's purchase money lien to construction financing exposes the seller to unique risks. Construction financing is extremely short-term financing. Further, the amount financed for construction of improvements generally dwarfs the value of the land. Thus, for a seller to salvage his position from the foreclosing construction lender, the seller must pay a 'balloon payment' typically exceeding the entire value of the land he sold. Permanent or interim 'take out' financing is not accessible until the project is substantially completed. Further, the costs of the improvements are reflected only fractionally in the project's value until the improvements are substantially completed. A half-completed office building generally does not have one-half the market value of a completed office building. Subordination to construction financing substantially aggravates the jeopardy to the seller's security." (*Id.* at p. 516, 204 Cal.Rptr. 48.) * * *

not take it outside the scope the Legislature intended section 580b to have.

With commendable candor, DeBerard acknowledges that this case is different from *Spangler* in some respects, but nonetheless it advances several reasons in favor of its view that we should permit the Lims to waive section 580b.

First, DeBerard discerns that the Lims' agreement to waive section 580b's protection enabled the "dramatic" change in the terms of their obligation to DeBerard. "The workout agreement, and the renegotiation of the senior and junior loans, reallocated the risks and dramatically changed the financial nature of the commercial development. The success or failure of the workout agreement was in the hands of the borrowers and the senior lender."

As stated, however, we cannot justify permitting a waiver in disregard of the language of section 580b just because DeBerard eased the terms of the Lims' obligation to it. The fact is that the same property secured its note. * * * And there was no large construction loan in furtherance of an intensified use. Nor do we agree that there was a dramatic change in the financial arrangements that might conceivably bring this case within *Spangler's* ambit. DeBerard began with a relatively risky subordinated security interest, and ended in the same position. * * *

Next, DeBerard contends that we should take into account that the Lims were sophisticated purchasers and borrowers. The record supports its factual contention. Nevertheless, section 580b does not distinguish between sophisticated ˙ and unsophisticated purchasers, just as the relevant portion does not distinguish between residential and commercial sales. * * *

Next, DeBerard invokes policy. Enforcing "post-default waivers of [section] 580b would encourage vendors holding junior purchase money trust deeds to execute subordination agreements in favor of the senior lender, thus enabling the senior lender to modify the senior debt. Without such a subordination, the senior lender is forced to choose between a unilateral modification . . . or foreclosure." In sum, DeBerard argues that allowing waivers of section 580b's protection will encourage flexibility in negotiating modifications of purchase money secured land sales.

In our view, DeBerard's policy argument must be addressed to the Legislature, which can consider in detail the benefit, if any, of permitting a purchaser to waive section 580b's protection in exchange for easing the terms of its obligation to its secured creditor or creditors. * * *

Finally, DeBerard notes that *Russell v. Roberts,* 39 Cal.App.3d 390, 114 Cal.Rptr. 305, is authority for its view. We recognize that a few Court of Appeal decisions have declared that a purchaser's post-sale waiver of section 580b's protection in exchange for consideration is generally valid—i.e., even when, unlike the facts of Spangler, the property is not distinctly improved by means of a construction loan to which the vendor's interest is subordinated. * * *

The only decision to discuss the point is *Russell*. That court stated that section 580b may be waived "after the sale and deed of trust transaction are completed." (*Russell v. Roberts, supra,* 39 Cal.App.3d at p. 395, 114 Cal.Rptr. 305.) *Russell* drew an analogy to *Salter v. Ulrich* (1943) 22 Cal.2d 263, 138 P.2d 7, which stated: "Since necessity often drives debtors to make ruinous concessions when a loan is needed, [Code of Civil Procedure] section 726 should be applied to protect them and to prevent a waiver in advance. This reasoning, however, does not apply after the loan is made, when all rights have been established and there remains only the enforcement of those rights." (*Id.* at p. 267, 138 P.2d 7.)

Russell also found a policy reason to support its conclusion. "We note also ... *Spangler v. Memel,* 7 Cal.3d 603, 610 [102 Cal.Rptr. 807, 498 P.2d 1055], which expresses the conclusion, 'that section 580b automatically applied only to the standard purchase money transaction and that with respect to variants from this standard purchase money transaction, section 580b would apply only if the factual circumstances came within the purposes of the section ... ' It seems clearly not 'within the purposes of the section' to deny a vendee whose rights have long been established, and who is no longer subject to the coercion of the lender, the privilege of waiving for a new consideration one of those earlier attained rights." (*Russell v. Roberts, supra,* 39 Cal.App.3d at p. 395, 114 Cal.Rptr. 305.) * * *

With regard to the policy reasoning of *Russell v. Roberts, supra,* 39 Cal.App.3d 390, 114 Cal.Rptr. 305, we agree with Palm that " '[r]uinous concessions' are, if anything, easier to obtain when the debtor is in default. Then, the temptation to 'press the bet' is likely to be stronger than the poor decision to purchase the property in the first instance." (*Palm v. Schilling, supra,* 199 Cal.App.3d at p. 73, 244 Cal.Rptr. 600.) * * *

We therefore disapprove the discussion in *Russell v. Roberts, supra,* 39 Cal.App.3d at pages 394–395, 114 Cal.Rptr. 305, and the dicta in [prior Court of Appeal decisions].

We affirm the Court of Appeal's judgment.

GEORGE, C.J., AND BAXTER, J., WERDEGAR, J., CHIN, J., AND BROWN, J., concur.

Concurring Opinion by KENNARD, J.

I concur in the majority opinion. I write separately to comment further on the purposes of Code of Civil Procedure section 580b. As the majority notes, * * * this court [has] articulated two purposes for section 580b: preventing sellers from overvaluing real property and moderating the economic dislocation caused by downturns in property values.

As to the first purpose, commentators and the Court of Appeal have noted the lack of economic logic to the argument that Code of Civil Procedure section 580b reduces overvaluation of properties. (See *Budget Realty, Inc. v. Hunter* (1984) 157 Cal.App.3d 511, 515–516, 204 Cal.Rptr. 48; Harris, *California Code of Civil Procedure Section 580b Revisited: Freedom of Contract in Real Estate Purchase Agreements* (1993) 30 San Diego L.Rev. 509, 516–517; Bernhardt, Cal. Mortgage and Deed of Trust Practice (Cont. Ed. Bar 2d ed.1990) One-Action and Antideficiency Rules, § 4.27, pp. 207–208; Hetland, Cal. Real Estate Secured Transactions (Cont. Ed. Bar 1970) p. 270.) Assume the fair market value of the property is X. If the seller finds a buyer willing to pay 2X or 3X for the property, the seller is no worse off selling for that price (and often will be better off) than selling for X. In either case, if default occurs, the price the seller will be able to resell the property for is the same regardless of the initial selling price (assuming a stable property market, that price will be X). The seller gains nothing by refusing to sell its property for the higher price, and loses nothing by selling the property for more than its value as security. Although overvaluing may increase the risk of default in property bought for commercial purposes (by increasing the income stream the property must generate in order to pay for itself), the increased selling price may well compensate the seller for the increased risk. Moreover, section 580b encourages buyers to offer more than the market value of the property because they know that in the case of default they will not be personally liable for any deficiency. In my view, the criticisms of the overvaluation rationale * * * described above are well founded.

NOTES

1.   *Waivers of 580b. DeBerard* tells us that virtually all post-default waivers of section 580b are unenforceable. Thus, vendors may rely only on the *Spangler* construction lending exception and perhaps unique settings involving a "special relationship between the parties."

Nickerman v. Ryan, 93 Cal.App.3d 564, 155 Cal.Rptr. 830 (1979), represents a "special relationship" case. In that case the court limited the impact of section 580b on a mortgage transaction that was incident to a post-dissolution agreement adjusting the interests of an ex-wife and ex-husband in property held as tenants in common. The agreement provided for the conveyance of the ex-wife's interest in a motel and certain other real estate to the ex-husband. In return, ex-husband delivered to her a promissory note for $25,000 secured by a deed of trust on the motel and conveyed to her his interest in the former family home and certain other property. Later, foreclosure of a senior lien on the motel wiped out her junior deed of trust lien. She then sued him for a deficiency judgment on the note. The ex-husband asserted that section 580b barred such a judgment because the deed of trust was given to secure the "purchase" by him of her interest in the motel and other real estate.

The trial court found that the "note and deed of trust were not given to [ex-wife] to secure payment of the balance of the purchase price of the [motel], but rather to equalize a division of community property after a decree of divorce". In affirming this trial court finding, the Court of Appeal also determined that "the transaction * * * is such a variation on the standard purchase money mortgage or deed of trust transaction that it would not subserve the purposes of section 580b * * * to deny a deficiency judgment in this case." According to the court, "it would be ironic to hold that the [ex-wife] who entered into the transaction to be free of the vicissitudes of the commercial enterprises, and so surrendered her joint right of control, should find that her fair share of the joint property was lost because of the sole management of the [ex-husband] who assumed the risks of the motel and apartment business. She is deserving of the same consideration given the vendor in Spangler v. Memel."

2. *Refinancing purchase money home mortgages.* Perhaps more important to California homeowners is the fact that § 580b not only bars deficiency judgments in favor of vendor-mortgagees, but also "(3) *under a deed of trust, or mortgage, on a dwelling for not more than four families given to a lender to secure repayment of a loan which was in fact used to pay all or a part of the purchase price of that dwelling occupied, entirely or in part, by the purchaser.*" (emphasis supplied). As a result, virtually all California homeowners are protected against deficiency judgments on institutional purchase-money mortgages. In effect, such loans are "non-recourse;" mortgagors are not personally liable on them.

However, homeowners may have unwittingly lost this 580b protection when, due to falling interest rates, they refinanced their existing purchase money loans. Millions of California homeowners did so during the unusually low interest period during the past decade. Was the new loan "in fact used to pay all or a part of the purchase price"? Should the new loan be treated as a continuation of its predecessor for this purpose? While the California Supreme Court has not addressed these questions, one California Court of Appeals has determined that refinanced mortgages are not "purchase money" and represent a variation on the standard purchase money transaction to which 580b is inapplicable; see Union Bank v. Wendland, 54 Cal.App.3d 393, 126 Cal.Rptr. 549 (1976). For a comprehensive consideration of this potentially important problem, see Carol Burns, Comment, Will Refinancing Your Home Mortgage Risk Your Life Savings?: Refinancing and California Code of Civil Procedure Section 580b, 43 UCLA L.Rev. 2077 (1996).

In 2012, the California legislation resolved the foregoing issue in favor of the refinancing mortgagor:

> No deficiency judgment shall lie in any event on any loan, refinance, or other credit transaction (collectively a "credit transaction") which is used to refinance a purchase money loan, or subsequent refinances of a purchase money loan, except to the extent that in a credit transaction, the lender or creditor advances new principal (hereafter "new advance") which is not applied to any obligation owed or to be owed under the purchase money loan, or to fees, cost, or related expenses of the credit transaction. Any new credit transaction shall be deemed to be a purchase money loan except as to the principal amount of any new advance.

As a result, a refinancing of a purchase money mortgagor or deed of trust receives protection under section 580(b) except to the extent it is a "cash out" transaction. The foregoing language was effective January 1, 2013. It is partially retroactive because it applies to refinancing of a purchase money loans that existed prior to the effective date. Nevertheless it does not apply to any refinancing that was consummated prior to the January 1, 2013 effective date.

3. *The "short-sale" and deficiency judgment issues.* During the "Great Recession" of the past several years the "short-sale" has been a common foreclosure alternative. This practice is considered in detail elsewhere in this casebook. See pages 661–668 supra. Instead of conveying the real estate to the mortgagee in lieu of foreclosure, as is the practice in a deed in lieu transaction, the mortgagor, with lender's consent, sells the property to a third person for less than the mortgage balance. The mortgagee then releases its lien from the real estate. The lender finds this type of transaction advantageous because it avoids the expense and delay of foreclosure as well as the possessory obligations (repair and maintenance costs) associated with a deed in lieu of foreclosure. In most states the mortgagee will have the ability to recover from the mortgagor the difference between the short sale amount and the mortgage obligation. Consequently, prudent mortgagors will negotiate a release of this deficiency.

In 2011 the California legislature protected such mortgagors by enacting section 580(e) of the Code of Civil Procedure which bars deficiencies incident to short sales on all loans (whether purchase money or otherwise) on dwellings containing not more than four dwelling units "in any case in which the trustor or mortgagor sells the dwelling for a sale price less than the remaining amount of the indebtedness outstanding at the time of sale in accordance with the written consent of the holder of the deed of trust or mortgage * * * . Cal. Civ. Proc. Code sec. 580(e) (2011). This legislation is effective July 15, 2011 but is probably not retroactive. See Bank of America, N.A. v. Roberts, 217 Cal.App.4th 1386, 159 Cal.Rptr.3d 345 (Cal.App.2013).

4. *Guarantors and section 580b.* As the foregoing illustrates, most California purchase money mortgagors are protected against personal

liability on their mortgage obligations. But suppose a mortgagee insists that the purchase money mortgage obligation be guaranteed by a third party. To what extent are guarantors of such mortgages similarly shielded? The next principal case deals with this issue. We will also consider this issue in the national context later in this section. See pages 865–867 infra.

TALBOTT V. HUSTWIT

California Court of Appeal, Fourth District, Division 3, 2008
164 Cal.App.4th 148, 78 Cal.Rptr.3d 703

ARONSON, J.

* * *

The Hustwits are guarantors of a loan plaintiff Cynthia D. Talbott, trustee of the Cynthia D. Talbott Separate Property Trust (Talbott), made to Pacific West Investment Trust (Trust). A trust deed against certain Newport Beach real property secured the Trust's loan obligations. The Trust defaulted and Talbott instituted a nonjudicial foreclosure under the power of sale provision in the trust deed. A trustee sale was held in March 2005. Talbott purchased the property with a $900,000 credit bid, subject to a senior loan. Talbott then sued the Hustwits under their guaranty agreements for the difference between the $900,000 credit bid and the unpaid balance of the loan, $1,288,042.36, plus interest. After a bench trial on stipulated facts, the court issued a written statement of decision awarding Talbott $432,628.40, plus interest. The Hustwits now appeal.

A. Section 580a Does Not Apply to Guarantors

California's antideficiency statutes (§§ 580a, 580b, 580d, 726), enacted during the depression, limit or prohibit lenders from obtaining personal judgments against borrowers where the lender's sale of real property security produces proceeds insufficient to cover the amount of the debt. (See Cornelison v. Kornbluth (1975) 15 Cal.3d 590, 600–602, 125 Cal.Rptr. 557, 542 P.2d 981.) Section 580a provides in relevant part:

> Whenever a money judgment is sought for the balance due upon an obligation for the payment of which a deed of trust or mortgage with power of sale upon real property or any interest therein was given as security, following the exercise of the power of sale in such deed of trust or mortgage, the plaintiff shall set forth in his or her complaint the entire amount of the indebtedness which was secured by the deed of trust or mortgage at the time of sale, the amount for which the real property or interest therein was sold and the fair market value thereof at the date of sale and the date of that sale. . . .

Before rendering any judgment the court shall find the fair market value of the real property, or interest therein sold, at the time of the sale. The court may render judgment for not more than the amount by which the entire amount of the indebtedness due at the time of sale exceeded the fair market value of the real property or interest therein sold at the time of sale with interest thereon from the date of the sale. . . .

The Hustwits contend section 580a applied to them, and the trial court erred in failing to consider evidence that the property's fair market value exceeded the total amount owed Talbott. We disagree.

The Hustwits were held liable as guarantors of the Trust's loan obligation to Talbott. A guarantor is one who promises to answer for the debt or perform the obligation of another when the person ultimately liable fails to pay or perform. (Civ.Code, § 2787.) "A contract of guaranty gives rise to a separate and independent obligation from that which binds the principal debtor." (*Security-First Nat. Bank v. Chapman* (1940) 41 Cal.App.2d 219, 221, 106 P.2d 431.) "Since section 580a has to do solely with actions for recovery of deficiency judgments on the principal obligation [it] has no application to an action against a guarantor [citations]. . . ." (*Mariners Sav. & Loan Assn. v. Neil* (1971) 22 Cal.App.3d 232, 234, 99 Cal.Rptr. 238 (*Mariners*); *Bank of America etc. Assn. v. Hunter* (1937) 8 Cal.2d 592, 67 P.2d 99; *Loeb v. Christie* (1936) 6 Cal.2d 416, 57 P.2d 1303; *see also Dreyfuss v. Union Bank of California* (2000) 24 Cal.4th 400, 407, 101 Cal.Rptr.2d 29, 11 P.3d 383 ["a creditor's resort to any and all security on a debt does not implicate the antideficiency provisions"].)

The Hustwits do not address the case law holding that guarantors cannot claim the protection of section 580a, and concede they were unable to discover any case law to the contrary. Instead, they cite two cases which recognize a general state policy to prevent secured creditors from obtaining excess recoveries. (See *Bank of Hemet v. United States* (9th Cir.1981) 643 F.2d 661; *Walter E. Heller Western, Inc. v. Bloxham* (1985) 176 Cal.App.3d 266, 221 Cal.Rptr. 425.) Neither of these cases concern guarantors, and the general policy statements contained in them does not persuade us to abandon Supreme Court precedent.[2] Accordingly, we conclude section 580a has no application to guarantors.

---

[2] As the concurrence recognizes, the case law supporting liability here has remained unchanged for over 60 years. We can thus safely assume virtually all of the loan guaranties now in existence were made in reliance upon the current state of the law. Although we share our concurring colleague's observations and concerns, we believe any change in the law affecting liability of guarantors for deficiency judgments should originate with the Legislature, which is better able to measure the impact of altering commercial arrangements by into account the views of experts and affected parties.

B. *The Hustwits Are True Guarantors*

Although case law is uniform in holding section 580a does not apply to guarantors, the question remains whether the Hustwits were true guarantors. Courts have recognized a distinction between true, independent contracts of guaranty and guaranties executed by the primary obligor. (*Mariners, supra,* 22 Cal.App.3d at p. 234, 99 Cal.Rptr. 238.) "It is well established that where a principal obligor purports to take on additional liability as a guarantor, nothing is added to the primary obligation. [Citations omitted.] The correct inquiry set out by the authority is whether the purported debtor is anything other than an instrumentality used by the individuals who guaranteed the debtor's obligation, and whether such instrumentality actually removed the individuals from their status and obligations as debtors." (*Torrey Pines Bank v. Hoffman* (1991) 231 Cal.App.3d 308, 319–320, 282 Cal.Rptr. 354 (*Torrey Pines*); *Cadle Co. II v. Harvey* (2000) 83 Cal.App.4th 927, 933, 100 Cal.Rptr.2d 150.)

In *Torrey Pines,* a bank sued a husband and wife on personal guaranties signed in connection with a construction loan the bank made to a revocable living trust in which the defendants were the trustors, trustees, and primary beneficiaries. The court determined the structure of the trust made any distinction between the guarantors and the debtor insignificant, thus barring the bank from recovering on the guaranties. Specifically, the court noted that under the trust law at the time, trustees were personally liable on contracts entered into on behalf of their trusts. Accordingly, the trust was deemed a " 'mere instrumentality.' " (*Torrey Pines, supra,* 231 Cal.App.3d at p. 321, 282 Cal.Rptr. 354.) The court, however, did not enunciate a blanket rule applying to all living trusts, clarifying: "We emphasize that our holding is necessarily limited to these facts. While it would be possible in a living trust to create a greater degree of separation of interest between settlor, trustee, and beneficiary (e.g., by the use of a separate trustee), this particular trust device did not accomplish enough division between these interests to enable us to say that the purpose of the antideficiency law would be served by enforcing these personal guaranties as 'true' guaranties, as opposed to 'purported' guaranties." (*Id.* at p. 323, 282 Cal.Rptr. 354.)

Similarly, *Riddle v. Lushing* (1962) 203 Cal.App.2d 831, 836, 21 Cal.Rptr. 902, involved a situation in which partners had individually guaranteed a partnership note. Because the partners were already jointly and severally liable on the note as general partners, the court held the guaranty did not change the partners' status as principal obligors. (*Ibid.*)

In contrast, *Mariners, supra,* 22 Cal.App.3d 232, 99 Cal.Rptr. 238, involved a situation where the wife took out a loan secured by her separately-owned real property, and the husband signed a personal guaranty. The court recognized that in many ways a husband and wife are partners, but nonetheless held the husband became a true guarantor because he would not have been personally liable for the loan made to the wife absent the guaranty. (*Id.* at p. 235, 99 Cal.Rptr. 238.)

Here, the trust arrangement provided the Hustwits a significantly greater degree of separation than that in *Torrey Pines*. Although the Hustwits are the settlors of the Trust, they are secondary, not primary, beneficiaries. More importantly, the Hustwits are not trustees of the Trust; instead, the Hustwits used a limited liability company as trustee, thus limiting their personal liability for the Trust's obligations. The Hustwits became true guarantors because the Hustwits' trust arrangement "actually removed the[m] from their status and obligations as debtors." (*Torrey Pines, supra*, 231 Cal.App.3d at p. 320, 282 Cal.Rptr. 354.) Accordingly, we conclude the trial court did not err in holding the protections of section 580a inapplicable in the present case.

The judgment is affirmed. * * *

SILLS, P.J., Concurring.

I agree with the reasoning and result of the majority opinion, because both are compelled by Supreme Court authority. However, I write separately to voice concerns about the potential danger for the easy circumvention of the protections offered consumers under California's statutory antideficiency legislation by the use of loan guarantees. (See Code Civ., Proc., §§ 580a, 580b, 580d & 726.)[1] The current "subprime mortgage crisis" at a time of generally declining real estate prices illustrates the public importance of the issue.[2]

* * *

As the majority opinion correctly decides—well, correctly under the current state of the case law—the Hustwits simply outwitted themselves. They have to take the rough with the smooth, and, more specifically, cannot avail themselves of the protections of limited liability corporations

---

[1]   As explained by the California Supreme Court in *Cornelison v. Kornbluth* (1975) 15 Cal.3d 590, 600, 125 Cal.Rptr. 557, 542 P.2d 981, antideficiency was a Depression-era response to the potential for "double recovery" by lenders. At a time of declining property prices, lenders would be able to purchase the real property securing the debt at a price below normal market value, and then hold the debtor liable "for a large deficiency." Later, the incentive on the part of the lender to bid too low was removed by creating a right of redemption (bid too low and the debtor could get the property back for that amount!) and the right of redemption was extended to both private and judicial foreclosures. The point being: If a lender wanted a deficiency judgment, the lender would be subject to statutory redemption rights. (*Id.* at pp. 601–602, 125 Cal.Rptr. 557, 542 P.2d 981.)

[2]   See Posting of Gary Becker to The Becker-Posner Blog, http://www.becker-posner-blog.com/archives/2007/12 (Dec. 23, 2007) ["The vast majority of economists, including me, were surprised by the extent of the subprime mortgage crisis. This needs to be recognized when evaluating the numerous proposals about how to prevent the next housing crisis, and also about how to help those who are in danger of having their homes foreclosed."] (as of June 9, 2008).

and at the same time claim an obligation is really theirs at the same time. Sometimes piercing the veil can actually help you.

* * *

Given [the contemporary sharp decline in real estate values] there is a real danger that, under the effect of current case law, lenders will seize the non-coverage of guarantors as a loophole to circumvent antideficiency protections otherwise afforded homeowners: Just get the parents or other relatives to guarantee the loan. Since the guarantee obligation has been held "independent" of the loan, the lender can obtain a deficiency judgment under deflationary conditions.

The Legislature, of course, can readily cure this danger (as it can cure any non-Constitutionally created anomaly in the law with the right drafting). * * *

NOTES

1. *Section 580a fair value limitation.* Section 580a of the West's California Code of Civil Procedure, like its section 726(b) judicial foreclosure counterpart, imposes a fair value limitation on actions for a deficiency judgment following power of sale foreclosure. Section 580a is usually irrelevant because section 580d already bars a deficiency judgment in the latter setting. Moreover, as *Talbot* illustrates, it is also unavailable to guarantors.

However, section 580a has always had some potential for debtor protection in those situations where a junior lien is wiped out by a power of sale foreclosure of a senior interest. Suppose, for example, that a senior lien of $30,000 is foreclosed by power of sale, thus eliminating a $15,000 junior lien. Suppose further that the fair market value of the land at the time of the senior sale was $50,000 and that the foreclosed junior lienor seeks a deficiency judgment against the debtor for $15,000. Arguably, it is unfair to allow the junior lienor to recover because he could have protected himself by taking part at the foreclosure sale. By so doing, he either could have obtained land that was worth enough to cover his debt or, if someone else was the ultimate purchaser, the junior's bidding could have insured that the sale yielded enough of a surplus so that his lien would have been satisfied out of the sale proceeds. As we noted earlier, section 580d would not bar our foreclosed junior lienor from obtaining a deficiency judgment because he was not the foreclosing party. However, if the fair value concept of section 580a is applicable to non-foreclosing parties as well as to foreclosing lienors, it could be used to deny deficiency relief to the foreclosed junior to the extent that the fair value of the property exceeded the senior debt. Since in our fact situation, the fair value of the land exceeded the senior debt by $20,000, there was sufficient value to cover the junior debt and the junior arguably should be denied any deficiency judgment against the debtor.

This interpretation of section 580a was rejected by the California Supreme Court in 1963 in Roseleaf Corp. v. Chierighino, 59 Cal.2d 35, 27 Cal.Rptr. 873, 378 P.2d 97 (1963). The *Roseleaf* court stated:

> The position of a junior lienor whose security is lost through a senior sale is different from that of a selling senior lienor. A selling senior can make certain that the security brings an amount equal to his claim against the debtor or the fair market value, whichever is less, simply by bidding in for that amount. He need not invest any additional funds. The junior lienor, however, is in no better position to protect himself than is the debtor. Either would have to invest additional funds to redeem or buy in at the sale. Equitable considerations favor placing this burden on the debtor, not only because it is his default that provokes the senior sale, but also because he has the benefit of his bargain with the junior lienor who, unlike the selling senior, might otherwise end up with nothing.

More recently, the California Court of Appeal, Fourth District, in Walter E. Heller Western, Inc. v. Bloxham, 176 Cal.App.3d 266, 221 Cal.Rptr. 425 (1985), distinguished *Roseleaf* and held that section 580a applied "to limit the amount of the deficiency judgment recoverable by the purchasing junior. The amount is limited to the lesser of the excess of the combined debts of the senior and junior lienholders over 1) the fair market value of the property or 2) the selling price at the foreclosure sale." According to the *Bloxham* court,

> The [United States Court of Appeals for the Ninth Circuit] in *Bank of Hemet,* 643 F.2d 661 (9th Cir.1981) correctly perceived a real distinction between a sold-out junior and one who purchases at the senior's sale, a distinction that was not before our Supreme Court in *Roseleaf.* (See Benjamin, *California Fair Value Limitations Applied to Non-Foreclosing Junior Lienholder* (1982) 12 Golden Gate L.Rev. 317.) The junior in *Roseleaf* did not purchase at the senior's sale. To apply the fair value limitations to that junior would result in the amount of his deficiency being limited by the amount of someone else's bid, a factor over which he has no control. However, once a junior chooses to purchase, it is equitable to apply the fair value limitations to him. Any loss to him as creditor by his own underbidding is gained by him as purchaser for a bargain price. (California Mortgage and Deed of Trust Practice (Cont.Ed.Bar Supp.1985) § 4.31, p. 35.) "To so limit the deficiency judgment right is consistent with the general purpose of section 580a, *viz.,* to protect against a lienor buying in the property at a deflated price, obtaining a deficiency judgment, and achieving a recovery in excess of the debt by reselling the property at a profit * * * [¶] * * * The unmistakable policy of California is to prevent excess recoveries by secured creditors." (*Bank of Hemet v. United States, supra,* 643 F.2d at p. 669.)

2. *Impact of 580a on power of sale foreclosure of multiple parcels.* In Dreyfuss v. Union Bank of California, 24 Cal.4th 400, 101 Cal.Rptr.2d 29, 11 P.3d 383 (2000), the debtor granted the mortgagee a deed of trust on one parcel of real estate and guarantors provided two additional parcels as additional security for the mortgage obligation. Ultimately, the mortgagee foreclosed by power of sale on each of the three parcels. Mortgagee was the successful bidder at each sale and the total of its three bids was $3.75 million, the exact amount of the mortgage obligation. The guarantors then filed an action asserting that the prices obtained at the successive foreclosures were below market value. Had the mortgagee purchased each parcel at its fair market value, they argued, it would not have been necessary to foreclose on all of the parcels and there would have been land left over for the guarantors. The guarantors argued that the "spirit" if not the literal language of section 580a applied so that the mortgagee was required to credit them with the fair market value of the first parcel foreclosed before foreclosing against the remaining two parcels. This argument failed in the trial court and the court of appeals. The Supreme Court similarly rejected the guarantors' assertion. In the Supreme Court's view, "applying the fair market value provisions of [section 580a] in this context * * * by eliminating the finality of nonjudicial foreclosure and requiring judicial oversight, would derogate the legislative goal of providing a 'quick, inexpensive, and efficient remedy.'" Id. at 390. Thus section 580a seems largely irrelevant to California foreclosures except in the *Bank of Hemet* context.

3. *Actions for fraud and anti-deficiency legislation.* To what extent, if any, should California anti-deficiency legislation bar mortgagee actions against mortgagors based on fraudulently induced loan transactions? Suppose, for example, that in an application to a Bank for financing to acquire a $600,000 single family house, the borrower falsely represented that he or she owned over $300,000 in stocks and bonds. Indeed, the borrower submitted falsified statements from a brokerage house. The Bank then made $450,000 loan and took back a deed of trust on the house. Two years later, after a steep decline in real estate values, the loan went into default, the Bank foreclosed and the property sold at the foreclosure sale for $375,000. Suppose now the Bank files an action for fraud against the borrower to recover $75,000 on the theory that but for the fraudulent misrepresentation as to his or her net worth, Bank would not have made the loan and would not have suffered the foreclosure deficiency. Does the tort action violate California anti-deficiency prohibitions? Most California courts have been reluctant to allow anti-deficiency statutes to be a shield for fraud and have reasoned that "a suit for fraud is a completely separate remedy from a suit on a promissory note secured by a deed of trust. This [fraud] action is not a suit on a note. * * * It would be wrong to apply a bar of recovery against plaintiff based on a transaction that was fraudulently induced. To do so would be to condone the fraud." Manson v. Reed, 186 Cal.App.3d 1493, 231 Cal.Rptr. 446 (1986). On the other hand, at least one decision cast doubt on the viability of such fraud actions. See First Fed. Sav. & Loan Ass'n of Phoenix v. Lehman, 159 Cal.App.3d 537, 205 Cal.Rptr. 600 (1984) (fraud action barred by anti-

deficiency statutes because there was no causal relationship between the alleged fraud and the damages sustained).

In response to the foregoing apparent uncertainty, legislation was enacted specifying that notwithstanding anti-deficiency statutes "may bring an action for the recovery of damages, including exemplary damages not to exceed 50 percent of actual damages, against a borrower" based on fraud when the latter's conduct induced the making of the loan. West's Ann.Cal.Fin.Code §§ 1301, 7459, 7460, 15102. The legislation exempts single-family residential real property "when the property is actually occupied by the borrower as represented to the lender in order to obtain the loan and the loan is for $150,000 or less * * * ." Id. In 1987 the legislature added language to section 726 of the Code of Civil Procedure which not only restates the 1985 legislation, but also makes it clear that it covers "any person authorized by this state to make or arrange loans or any successor in interest thereto, that originates, acquires, or purchases * * * any loan secured * * * by a mortgage or deed of trust on real property." West's Ann.Cal.Code Civ.Pro. §§ 726(f), (g). To what extent does this legislation clarify the problem?

<h3 style="text-align:center">BOWEN V. YNIGUEZ</h3>

California Court of Appeal, First District, 2005
2005 WL 1324773 (Not officially published)

POLLAK, J.

     * * *

<h3 style="text-align:center">FACTUAL AND PROCEDURAL BACKGROUND</h3>

On March 4, 1997, plaintiff sold defendants the Pelican Inn (the Inn), a small inn located in Westport, California, on the Mendocino Coast. Under an "as is" commercial real estate purchase contract and escrow instructions, defendants agreed to purchase the property for $325,000. Defendants agreed to make a $50,000 down payment, and gave plaintiff a promissory note in the amount of $275,000, $20,000 of which was due on August 31, 1997, and the balance of which was payable in monthly installments of $2,051.79 for five years. Defendants also agreed to pay $10,000 for personal property located in the Inn, and $15,000 for the purchase of the liquor license.

After a delay in the close of escrow, defendants took possession of the property and began operating the Inn on June 26, 1997. Defendants made the monthly payments for July and August, but were unable to make the $20,000 payment due on August 31. The parties attempted unsuccessfully to renegotiate the terms of the promissory note and, on September 26, 1997, plaintiff recorded a notice of default in the amount of $22,762.94.

In February 1998, Richard Yniguez filed a petition in bankruptcy and obtained a stay prohibiting plaintiff from foreclosing on the property. One month later, Steven Yniguez also initiated personal bankruptcy proceedings. Defendants continued to occupy and operate the Inn while the bankruptcy proceedings were pending.

In early 1999, the bankruptcy stay was lifted and, on April 6, 1999, a nonjudicial foreclosure sale was held. At that time, $224,590.66 was due on the promissory note. Plaintiff was the only bidder and purchased the property for $124,000. She recorded the deed and took possession of the property the same day. The following day, plaintiff served on Steven Yniguez a three-day notice of eviction. When defendants returned to the Inn in May 1999 to recover their personal property, they found that some of their property was missing.

On June 3, 1999, plaintiff filed a complaint against defendants alleging causes of action for bad faith waste of her security interest, fraud, negligent misrepresentation, and suppression of fact. The complaint alleges that defendants "committed waste by willfully mismanaging, damaging, and despoiling the real property and allowing it to deteriorate from a failure to clean, repair, maintain, and do all other acts necessary to preserve it." The following day, defendants filed a cross-complaint against plaintiff alleging causes of action for fraud, negligent misrepresentation, concealment, conversion of personal property, wrongful eviction and trespass.

The matter was tried before the court in October 2003. The trial court rejected plaintiff's fraud claims, but found that defendants had committed bad faith waste and awarded plaintiff $55,000 in damages. The trial court rejected most of the defendants' cross-claims but found that plaintiff had unlawfully evicted defendants and converted their personal property, for which it awarded defendants $10,001 in actual damages and $1,000 in punitive damages. Thereafter, defendants filed a timely notice of appeal from the portion of the judgment entered in favor of plaintiff and awarding damages on her cause of action for waste.

DISCUSSION

1. *Substantial evidence supports the trial court's finding that defendants committed bad faith waste.* In *Cornelison v. Kornbluth* (1975) 15 Cal.3d 590, 602–603 (*Cornelison*), the California Supreme Court first recognized a cause of action for the bad faith waste of real property subject to a security interest. (See Civ.Code, § 2929.) The court held that a cause of action for bad faith waste requires evidence of the reckless, intentional or malicious destruction, misuse, alteration or neglect of real property. * * * The court distinguished such waste from neglect that occurs due to the owner's financial inability to properly maintain the property.

"For example, a purchaser caught in such circumstances may be compelled in the normal course of events to forego the general maintenance and repair of the property in order to keep up his payments on the mortgage debt. If he eventually defaults and loses the property, to hold him subject to additional liability for waste would seem to run counter to the purpose of [the anti-deficiency statute] and to permit the purchase money lender to obtain what is in effect a deficiency judgment."

(*Ibid.*)

Defendants contend there is no substantial evidence to support the finding that the Inn was damaged by their reckless or malicious conduct, rather than by unavoidable financial difficulties that made it impossible for them to properly maintain the Inn. They claim that despite their best efforts to profitably operate the Inn, they "faced multiple setbacks that had a negative impact upon the business." First, "a portion of the floor in the laundry area collapsed because of pre-existing water damage, and [defendants] had no funds available to make the necessary repairs." Then, "a serious water leak in the room above the dining room caused severe damage to the dining area, and caused the Inn to close for weeks for repairs." Finally, there was "a serious sewer leak in the kitchen in late-March, 1998, that resulted in severe water damage to the kitchen area, and caused the Inn to close for weeks before repairs could be made."

The trial court here found that "[v]isual evidence presented through photographs and videos as well as the testimony of numerous witnesses established the widespread destruction and degradation of the Pelican Inn during defendants' tenure as possessors. While there is evidence that the Inn had significant structural problems before transfer to the defendants, nothing in evidence can account for the seemingly wanton degradation of the property and grounds when recovered by the plaintiff." Photographs taken before and after defendants purchase of the property and a videotape made in April 1999, after defendants' had vacated the property, amply support the trial court's assessment. As the trial court noted, it appears from the videotape that "significant parts of the establishment had been removed and put in the yard" and the back yard looks as if "a disaster had hit." In addition to the gaping hole in the kitchen floor, the kitchen appears not to have been cleaned for months. Every available surface is littered with dirty dishes, moldy food, and empty liquor bottles. Similar filth is found throughout the bedrooms and common areas of the Inn. While the sewer leak and burst pipes may have been beyond defendants' control, they provide no excuse for having hacked the floor boards apart and failing to replace, or at least recover, them when the plumbing was repaired. Any financial difficulties caused by these unexpected repairs do not explain the complete disarray of the property. The filth and general disrepair depicted in the videotape was not caused by a lack of funds but by mismanagement and complete disregard for the property. A letter written by Richard Yniguez in May

1999 further supports the conclusion that the waste was not merely the product of financial constraints. In this letter, written after the foreclosure sale, Richard Yniguez wrote that Steven was using the Inn as a "party house." He refers to Steven's "mismanagement of the business," noting that "major spending was going on treating people to food, drink and board, at a time when money had to be saved for the important expenses such as the mortgage payments all other expenses that go along with the privilege of ownership." * * *

2. *Substantial evidence supports the trial court's finding that the value of the Inn declined while in defendants' possession.* Defendants contend there is no substantial evidence to support the trial court's finding that the value of the property declined while they were in possession of the Inn. They argue that the difference between the original sale price and the price for which the property sold at the foreclosure sale was insufficient to establish a decline in value. However, the evidence of the price that defendants paid for the Inn in 1997 is certainly a proper measure of the fair market value of the Inn at that time. (See *Dennis v. County of Santa Clara* (1989) 215 Cal.App.3d 1019, 1027–1028 [tax assessor can presume fair market value of property based on purchase price].) Likewise, as the court stated in *Cornelison, supra,* 15 Cal.3d at page 607, "a nonjudicial foreclosure sale, if regularly held, finally fixes the value of the property therein sold." Defendants fail to point to any evidence of irregularities in the foreclosure sale that would preclude plaintiff's reliance on the sales price as evidence of the value of the Inn at that time. * * * Considering the state of the property at the time of the foreclosure, it is understandable why no other party was interested in bidding on the Inn. Accordingly, substantial evidence supports the trial court's finding of diminution in the property value.

3. *Trial court did not err in calculating damages.* Defendants contend the trial court improperly calculated plaintiff's damages because it measured her damages based on the cost of repairs and loss of profit as opposed to the impairment of her security interest. In *Cornelison,* the court explained that "If the beneficiary or mortgagee at the foreclosure sale enters a bid for the full amount of the obligation owing to him together with the costs and fees due in connection with the sale, he cannot recover damages for waste, since he cannot establish any impairment of security, the lien of the deed of trust or mortgage having been theretofore extinguished by his full credit bid and all his security interest in the property thereby nullified. If, however, he bids less than the full amount of the obligation and thereby acquires the property valued at less than the full amount, his security has been impaired and he may recover damages for waste in an amount *not exceeding* the difference between the amount of his bid and the full amount of the outstanding indebtedness immediately prior to the foreclosure sale."

(*Cornelison, supra,* 15 Cal.3d at p. 607, italics added.) Accordingly, the formula prescribed in *Cornelison* establishes only the maximum recovery of damages for waste. (*Glendale Fed. Sav. Loan Assn. v. Marina View Heights Dev. Co.* (1977) 66 Cal.App.3d 101, 147.)

Within the *Cornelison* ceiling, it is " 'within the province of the trier of fact to determine on a case by case basis to what, if any, extent the impairment of the mortgagee's security has been caused . . . by the general decline of real property values and to what, if any, extent . . . by the bad faith acts of the mortgagor, such determination . . . being subject to review under the established rule of appellate review.' " (*Glendale Fed. Sav. Loan Assn. v. Marina View Heights Dev. Co., supra,* at p. 146.) Here, the trial court determined that the impairment of plaintiff's security was properly measured by the costs of repairing the property, including any profits lost during the time required to complete the repairs. In doing so, the trial court was "guided by the principle generally applicable to tortious conduct: that plaintiff should recover all of the detriment proximately caused by the injury."

We see no error in the trial court's calculation. Defendants do not suggest an alternative method for calculating plaintiff's damages. Instead, they state only that "[t]he court did not consider whether there had been an impairment to the value of the property subject to respondent's lien so as to render the property an inadequate security for [defendants'] mortgage debt." As evidenced by its statement of decision, the trial court considered that plaintiff's "damages are measured by the amount of injury to the security caused by the defendants' acts, i.e., by the substantial harm which impairs the value of the subject property so as to render it inadequate security for the mortgage debt." By basing plaintiff's damages on the cost of repairs and profits lost while the repairs were being performed, the trial court measured only the consequences of defendants' waste and excluded any impairment of the security interest caused by a general decline in the real estate market or other factors. The $55,000 award is little more than half the ceiling placed on the recoverable damages by the deficiency that remained after the foreclosure sale. * * *

The judgment is affirmed. Plaintiff is to recover her costs on appeal.

We concur: CORRIGAN, ACTING P.J., and PARRILLI, J.

NOTE

Anti-deficiency statutes and the "full credit bid" problem. The foregoing material tells us that anti-deficiency legislation does not bar most actions against the mortgagor for fraud or "bad faith" waste. See Gary L. Barr, Wasteland: The Antideficiency Rule in Foreclosures Does Not Apply in Cases of Bad Faith Waste, 30 L.A. Law 20 (2008). But this is not the end of the story. As *Bowen* explains, a mortgagee may be barred from recovery if it purchases the mortgaged real estate at the foreclosure sale by making a "full credit bid"—one that is an amount equal to or exceeds the mortgage obligation. The theory is that when the mortgagee purchases in such a fashion, the mortgage obligation is satisfied and no further claim against the mortgagor is justified. But should this be an iron-clad rule? Consider the language of a recent California Supreme Court opinion in which a mortgagee who purchased at the foreclosure sale by a full credit bid later sued not the mortgagor, but a real estate broker, an appraiser, and a title insurance company on the theory that they had conspired to defraud the lender by submitting inflated appraisals and other false information about the properties and borrowers in a series of loans:

> As with any purchaser at a foreclosure sale, by making a successful full credit bid or bid in any amount, the lender is making a generally irrevocable offer to purchase the property for that amount. The lender, perhaps more than a third party purchaser with fewer resources with which to gain insight into the property's value, generally bears the burden and risk of making an informed bid.

> It does not follow, however, that being intentionally and materially misled by its own fiduciaries or agents as to the value of the property prior to even making the loan is within the realm of that risk. * * * Most lenders, such as [plaintiff] in this case, are corporate entities, and rely on their agents to provide them material information. Here, [plaintiff] did obtain appraisals, and attempted to make informed loan decisions. It alleges, however, that its appraiser, Rothwell, in conspiracy with defendants, fraudulently misrepresented the nature of the properties and the existence and qualifications of the buyers, and that it did not discover the fraud until after it acquired title to the properties. The full credit bid rule was not intended to immunize wrongdoers from the consequences of their fraudulent acts.

> We conclude therefore that in order to establish reliance, [plaintiff] need only demonstrate that its full credit bids were a proximate result of defendants' fraud, and that in the absence of such fraud it would not, in all reasonable probability, have made the bids. * * * As for the question of whether this reliance was justifiable, a generally fact-based inquiry, we reiterate that "Negligence on the part of the plaintiff in failing to discover the falsity of a statement is no defense when the misrepresentation was intentional rather than negligent." * * * "Nor is a plaintiff held to the standard of precaution or of minimum knowledge of a hypothetical, reasonable man." * * * "If the conduct of the plaintiff in the light of his own intelligence and information was manifestly unreasonable, however, he will be denied a recovery." * * *

Thus, to the extent [plaintiff's] full credit bids were proximately caused by defendants' fraudulent misrepresentations, and this reliance without independent or additional inquiry was either appropriate given the context of the relationship or was not otherwise manifestly unreasonable, Alliance's bids cannot be deemed an admission of the properties' value. * * * Hence, the full credit bid rule would not apply.

In the alternative, to the extent [plaintiff's] full credit bids were not proximately caused by defendants' fraudulent misrepresentations, or its reliance without independent or additional inquiry was either inappropriate given the context of the relationship or was otherwise manifestly unreasonable, the full credit bid rule applies, and [plaintiff's] bid would then constitute an irrevocable offer to purchase the property for that amount. * * * Hence, under these circumstances, [plaintiff] would not be entitled to recover the difference between its bid, which by definition is "an amount equal to the unpaid principal and interest of the mortgage debt, together with the costs, fees and other expenses of the foreclosure," and the actual value of the property. (Cornelison, supra, 15 Cal.3d at p. 606, fn. 10, 125 Cal.Rptr. 557, 542 P.2d 981.) It would, however, still be able to recover any other damages flowing from the defendants' fraud.

Alliance Mortg. Co. v. Rothwell, 10 Cal.4th 1226, 44 Cal.Rptr.2d 352, 359–365, 900 P.2d 601, 608–614 (1995). What would those other damages be? See id. at 614–616. For a case where a mortgagee making a full credit bid was held to be unjustified in relying an allegedly fraudulent appraisal issued prior to the consummation of the loan, see Michelson v. Camp, 72 Cal.App.4th 955, 85 Cal.Rptr.2d 539 (1999).

California's "One-Action" Rule:
Code of Civil Procedure § 726(a)

NELSON, WHITMAN, BURKHART & FREYERMUTH,
REAL ESTATE FINANCE LAW
710–711, 722–724 (6th ed.2014)*

This rule means, in general, that in the event of a default, the mortgagee's sole remedy is a foreclosure action and that any deficiency claim must be sought in that proceeding. The purpose of this rule is two-fold. One is to protect the mortgagor against a multiplicity of actions when the separate actions, though theoretically distinct, are so closely connected that normally they can and should be decided in one suit. The other is to compel a creditor who has taken a mortgage on land to exhaust the security before attempting to reach any unmortgaged property to

---

* Reprinted with permission of LEG, Inc. d/b/a/ West Academic.

satisfy the claim. The mortgagee * * * cannot disregard the security even if it wishes to do so, and sue upon the note or debt. Nor may the requirement of the statute be waived by the mortgagor through a provision in the mortgage. * * *

Procedurally, a mortgagor may use the rule both defensively and as a sanction. If the mortgagor successfully raises the rule as an affirmative defence, the mortgagee will be required to exhaust the security before obtaining a deficiency judgment. On the other hand, suppose the mortgagor does not raise the rule in the personal action. As the California Supreme Court has stated, the mortgagor "may still invoke it as a sanction against the mortgagee on the basis that the latter by not foreclosing on the security in the action brought to enforce the debt, has made an election of remedies and waived the security."

* * *

Under what circumstances, if any, may mortgagee's violation of section 726a result in destruction of the underlying *debt* as well as the security? This issue has been raised in the context of recent litigation involving "setoffs" against the mortgage obligation of mortgagor's deposits with mortgagee. In Bank of America v. Daily, [152 Cal.App.3d 767, 199 Cal.Rptr. 557 (1984)] a mortgagee-bank set off approximately $10,000 from the mortgagor's checking account as partial payment on an obligation secured by mortgagor's real estate. When the mortgagee later filed an action to foreclose on the real estate, the mortgagor asserted that by exercising setoff, the mortgagee waived its rights against the security. Ultimately, the Court of Appeal held that the setoff violated section 726a and that the mortgagee had waived its right to foreclose on the security. However, in its analysis of the security loss question, the court quoted Professor Hetland's position that "the classic sanction against the creditor who fails to exhaust all his security for the same debt in a single action is harsh, yet it follows inescapably from the availability of but one action to the creditor—he waives the balance of the security *and he waives any claim to the unpaid balance of the debt.*" [quoting John R. Hetland, Cal.Real Estate Secured Transactions § 6.18, p. 258 (1970)].

The [supreme] court next confronted this issue in Security Pacific National Bank v. Wozab, [51 Cal.3d 991, 275 Cal.Rptr. 201, 800 P.2d 557 (1990)]. *Wozab* involved a setoff of approximately $2800 against an indebtedness secured by mortgagors' residence exceeding $1,000,000. The mortgagors (Wozabs) contended that the setoff caused mortgagee to lose its security in the residence. After considering this claim, mortgagee reconveyed the deed of trust to the Wozabs, but sought to recover the unpaid debt of approximately $976,000 from the Wozabs. The Wozabs then asserted that the setoff not only resulted in a waiver of the security, but in a destruction of the underlying debt as well. The Supreme Court disagreed, holding that the appropriate sanction was loss of the security only. In reaching this result, the court stressed that section 726a not only embodies a one-action rule, but a "security first" principle as well. The former rule was not violated in *Wozab* because a setoff was not deemed an "action," the latter being defined by the Civil Procedure Code as "an ordinary proceeding in a court of justice by which one party prosecutes another for the declaration, enforcement, or protection of a right, the redress or prevention of a wrong, or the punishment of a public offense." Presumably, had the setoff represented an "action," destruction of the underlying debt would have been an appropriate sanction. Rather, the court opted to find a violation of the security first concept. In so doing, it did not completely rule out loss of the underlying debt for a "security first" violation, but clearly was inclined to view such a sanction as acceptable only in extreme cases. According to the court:

> Allowing the bank to sue on the debt does not violate the two fundamental purposes of section 726: (1) preventing a multiplicity of lawsuits against the debtor, and (2) requiring exhaustion of the security before a resort to the debtor's unencumbered assets. The present action is the only lawsuit against the Wozabs, and they freely chose not to have the bank foreclose the security interest.

> Finally, the result advocated by the Wozabs—allowing them to evade their debt almost in its entirety—would be a gross injustice to the bank and a corresponding windfall to the Wozabs. * * *

> The result we reach is also fair and workable in future cases. Because a debtor can object to an improper setoff and require the bank to return it and proceed first against the security interest, a bank cannot *unilaterally* waive its security interest by taking an improper setoff and then proceeding directly on the underlying debt. The debto retains the right to require the bank to return the improper setoff and proceed against the security interest before bank attempts to recover on the underlying debt. Of course, if the bank refused the debtor's demand and retained the setoff funds, the security-first rule * * * would preclude the bank from foreclosing the security interest or proceeding on the underlying debt. Conversely, if the bank complied with the debtor's demand to return the funds and to proceed first against the security, the debtor could not thereafter assert the bank had waived its security interest. [Id. at 51 Cal.3d 991, 1005, 275 Cal.Rptr. 201, 210, 800 P.2d 557, 566.]

NOTES

1. *Letters of credit and section 726(a).* "Standby letters of credit" are increasingly used to partially secure obligations where the prime security is a mortgage or deed of trust on real estate. Professors White and Summers describe this device as follows:

> A standby letter of credit * * * acts as a "backup" against [debtor] defaults on obligations of all kinds. For example, it might be issued to a bank that financed a real estate transaction of the [debtor]. It might provide for payment of certain amounts on presentation of a document which stated that the [debtor] had defaulted and that a specific amount was owing to the beneficiary.

James J. White and Robert S. Summers, Uniform Commercial Code 703 (4th ed.1995). Such letters of credit are commonly issued by banks in favor of a mortgagee. The premium for its issuance is paid by the mortgagor-debtor. Thus, for example, suppose mortgagee lends $10,000,000 to mortgagor, the obligation being secured by a deed of trust on mortgagor's office building. As additional security mortgagee demands a $2,000,000 letter of credit from a bank acceptable to mortgagee. Thus, the mortgagee can look to the letter of credit as well as the real estate as security for the obligation. Note that the letter of credit is governed by something called the "independence principle." This means that the obligation of the issuer of the letter of credit to the mortgagee is independent of the mortgagee's performance under its agreement with mortgagor. In other words, the issuer normally must pay upon mortgagee presenting the appropriate written demand even though mortgagor may be justified in not performing its obligation to mortgagee. Id.

Note further how the obligation of the issuer of the letter of credit differs from that of a guarantor. "In the typical secondary guarantee, the guarantor can defend against a claim by the beneficiary [Lender] by showing that its customer [Debtor] had a justifiable basis for failing to perform." Id. at 704. Thus, a typical mortgagee would generally prefer to have their mortgagor's obligation backed up by a standby letter of credit than a guarantee.

To what extent does the presence of a letter of credit together with a deed of trust on real estate as security for an obligation raise section 726(a) problems? In 1994 California enacted legislation which provides that when an obligation is secured by both a deed of trust and a letter of credit, a draw against the letter of credit does not violate the one action rule. See West's Ann.Cal.Civ.Code § 580.5. See also 1111 Prospect Partners, L.P. v. Superior Court, 45 Cal.Rptr.2d 338 (App.1995) (a draw against a letter of credit followed by a nonjudicial foreclosure of the deed of trust is not a violation of section 726(a); thus pre-1994 law was held to be consistent with section 580.5).

2. *Obtaining the appointment of a receiver or enforcing an assignment of rents as a 726(a) problem.* Is a judicial action to obtain the appointment of a receiver an "action" for purposes of section 726(a)? Even if it is, it is a

provisional remedy and is almost always ancillary to a foreclosure proceeding. Hence there is no violation of the one-action rule in including a receivership request in a judicial foreclosure action. More important, the receivership statute, as amended in 1991, makes it clear that "[a]ny action by a secured lender to appoint a receiver pursuant to this section shall not constitute an action" for purposes of section 726(a). West's Ann.Cal.Code Civ.Proc. § 564(d).

Suppose, instead, that a mortgagee proceeds nonjudicially against the rents under an assignment of rents agreement and then conducts a power of sale foreclosure of its deed of trust against the building. Since mortgagee has proceeded in both instances nonjudicially, it would not seem to run afoul of section 726(a). There is early case law holding that the one-action rule is not violated where the mortgagee proceeds against its various pieces of security serially by nonjudicial foreclosure. See Hatch v. Security-First Nat'l Bank, 19 Cal.2d 254, 120 P.2d 869 (1942). Moreover, legislation provides that as to post-1996 assignments of rents, "an enforcement action * * * and a collection, distribution, or application of rents, issues or profits by the assignee following an enforcement action * * * shall not * * * [c]onstitute an action, render the obligation unenforceable, violate Section 726 * * * or * * * otherwise limit any rights available to the assignee with respect to its security." West's Ann.Cal.Civ.Code § 2938(e)(2).

3. *CERCLA and section 726(a).* As we already know, section 726(a) gives the mortgagor the right to force foreclosure of the mortgaged real estate as a condition precedent to seeking a deficiency judgment. However, until recently, foreclosure and purchase by a mortgagee of contaminated real estate created the concern that it would become liable for massive cleanup costs under CERCLA. This concern was allayed by the enactment of an amendment to section 726 that permits the mortgagee, subject to certain limitations, to waive its security interest in "environmentally impaired" real estate and proceed against the mortgagor as an unsecured creditor. This election is available to the mortgagee if (1) the costs of cleanup exceed 25% of the fair market value of the real estate (ignoring the impact of the contamination on that value) and (2) mortgagor had actual knowledge of the contamination when the obligation was created or mortgagor caused, contributed to or permitted it to occur. See West's Ann.Cal.Code Civ.Proc. § 726.5. Consequently, a mortgagee will often be able to obtain a judgment on the underlying debt while avoiding any potential CERCLA liability that could accrue from taking possession of contaminated real estate incident to foreclosure.

4. *The Nevada approach to the "one-action rule."* As the foregoing notes illustrate, both California courts and its legislature have taken an ad hoc approach to defining what is not an "action" for purposes of section 726(a). Nevada represents an interesting contrast. While the core of Nevada's one-action rule has its origin in California's section 726(a), the Nevada legislature has taken a more "global" approach in specifically identifying sixteen acts that do not constitute an action:

As used in this section, an "action" does not include any act or proceeding:

(a) To appoint a receiver for, or obtain possession of, any real or personal collateral for the debt or as provided in NRS 32.015.

(b) To enforce a security interest in, or the assignment of, any rents, issues, profits or other income of any real or personal property.

(c) To enforce a mortgage or other lien upon any real or personal collateral located outside of the State which does not, except as required under the laws of that jurisdiction, result in a personal judgment against the debtor.

(d) For the recovery of damages arising from the commission of a tort, including a recovery under NRS 40.750, or the recovery of any declaratory or equitable relief.

(e) For the exercise of a power of sale pursuant to NRS 107.080.

(f) For the exercise of any right or remedy authorized by chapter 104 of NRS or by the Uniform Commercial Code as enacted in any other state.

(g) For the exercise of any right to set off, or to enforce a pledge in, a deposit account pursuant to a written agreement or pledge.

(h) To draw under a letter of credit.

(i) To enforce an agreement with a surety or guarantor if enforcement of the mortgage or other lien has been automatically stayed pursuant to 11 U.S.C. § 362 or pursuant to an order of a federal bankruptcy court under any other provision of the United States Bankruptcy Code for not less than 120 days following the mailing of notice to the surety or guarantor pursuant to subsection 1 of NRS 107.095.

(j) To collect any debt, or enforce any right, secured by a mortgage or other lien on real property if the property has been sold to a person other than the creditor to satisfy, in whole or in part, a debt or other right secured by a senior mortgage or other senior lien on the property.

(k) Relating to any proceeding in bankruptcy, including the filing of a proof of claim, seeking relief from an automatic stay and any other action to determine the amount or validity of a debt.

(l) For filing a claim pursuant to chapter 147 of NRS or to enforce such a claim which has been disallowed.

(m) Which does not include the collection of the debt or realization of the collateral securing the debt.

(n) Pursuant to NRS 40.507 or 40.508.

(*o*) Pursuant to an agreement entered into pursuant to NRS 361.7311 between an owner of the property and the assignee of a tax lien against the property, or an action which is authorized by NRS 361.733.

(p) Which is exempted from the provisions of this section by specific statute.

(q) To recover costs of suit, costs and expenses of sale, attorneys' fees and other incidental relief in connection with any action authorized by this subsection.

Nev.Rev.Stat. § 40.430(6). The fact that Nevada's legislature found it necessary to create the foregoing "laundry list" of exceptions raises the question whether lawyers, rather than mortgagors, are the primary beneficiaries of the one-action rule. For an example of Nevada courts applying the rule in its traditional setting, see Bonicamp v. Vazquez, 120 Nev. 377, 91 P.3d 584 (2004) (where a debt incurred in Colorado was secured by a deed of trust on Nevada real estate, the mortgagee was barred from foreclosing on the deed of trust after it had previously obtained a default judgment on the debt against the debtor in Colorado).

5. *The "mixed collateral" problem.* When a debtor gives consensual liens on both real and personal property to secure *one obligation*, a "mixed collateral" situation arises. This normally raises the problem of reconciling the application of Article 9 of the California Commercial Code with the anti-deficiency legislation we are studying in this section. Note, however, that the principal case, while in a certain sense a mixed collateral situation, is not governed by the foregoing analysis because letters of credit are covered by Article 5, rather than Article 9, of the UCC.

Our concern in this note is with the relationship of Article 9 of the UCC with California anti-deficiency statutes. Prior to 1986, the real property statutes were dominant in this setting. Thus, as Professors Hetland and Hansen observed, "a creditor who took an interest in even a small quantity of the debtor's real property subjected the *entire debt to the protections of the real property system.*" John R. Hetland and Charles A. Hansen, The "Mixed Collateral" Amendments to California's Commercial Code—Covert Repeal of California's Real Property Foreclosure and Antideficiency Provisions or Exercise in Futility?, 75 Cal.L.Rev. 185, 190 (1987). For example, real estate foreclosure was deemed impermissible where the creditor proceeded first against personal property security without simultaneously seeking foreclosure of the real estate. See, e.g., Epstein v. Enterprise Leasing Corp., 189 Cal.App.3d 834, 234 Cal.Rptr. 676 (1987) (depublished) (where debt is secured by personality and realty, action for claim and delivery on the personalty bars creditor from foreclosing on realty deed of trust).

In 1986 and 2001, however, California adopted new "mixed collateral" amendments to its Commercial Code that substantially changed the dominance of the real property anti-deficiency statutes over personal property security remedies. See West's Cal.Comm.Code § 9604. This legislation provides that if an obligation is secured by both personal property (including fixtures) and real estate, the secured party may:

>(A) Proceed, in any sequence, (i) in accordance with the secured party's rights and remedies in respect of real property as to the real property security, and (ii) in accordance with this chapter as to the personal property or fixtures.

>(B) Proceed in any sequence, as to both, some, or all of the real property and some or all of the personal property or fixtures in accordance with the secured party's rights and remedies in respect of the real property, by including the portion of the personal property or fixtures selected by the secured party in the judicial or nonjudicial foreclosure of the real property in accordance with the procedures applicable to real property. In proceeding under this subparagraph, (i) no provision of this chapter other than this subparagraph, subparagraph (C) of paragraph (4), and paragraphs (7) and (8) shall apply to any aspect of the foreclosure; (ii) a power of sale under the deed of trust or mortgage shall be exercisable with respect to both the real property and the personal property or fixtures being sold; and (iii) the sale may be conducted by the mortgagee under the mortgage or by the trustee under the deed of trust. The secured party shall not be deemed to have elected irrevocably to proceed as to both real property and personal property or fixtures as provided in this subparagraph with respect to any particular property, unless and until that particular property actually has been disposed of pursuant to a unified sale (judicial or nonjudicial) conducted in accordance with the procedures applicable to real property, and then only as to the property so sold.

>(C) Proceed, in any sequence, as to part of the personal property or fixtures as provided in subparagraph (A), and as to other of the personal property or fixtures as provided in subparagraph (B).

West's Ann.Cal.Comm.Code § 9604(a)(1).

MID KANSAS FEDERAL SAVINGS & LOAN ASSOCIATION V. DYNAMIC DEVELOPMENT CORPORATION

Supreme Court of Arizona, 1991
167 Ariz. 122, 804 P.2d 1310

FELDMAN, VICE CHIEF JUSTICE.

A construction lender held notes secured by first and second deeds of trust on a residential developer's property. The lender acquired title to the property at a trustee's sale on the second trust deed and thereafter brought an action against the developer for the balance due on the first notes. The court of appeals held that the lender was precluded from doing so under A.R.S. § 33–814(G) and the rationale of our decision in *Baker v. Gardner,* 160 Ariz. 98, 770 P.2d 766 (1988).

We must determine whether the anti-deficiency statutes apply to a residential developer and whether a lender may recover the balance owing on the first notes after it has acquired title to the property at the foreclosure sale of its second deed of trust. Rule 23, Ariz.R.Civ.App.P., 17B A.R.S. We have jurisdiction under Ariz. Const. art. 6, § 5(3) and A.R.S. § 12–120.24.

FACTS AND PROCEDURAL HISTORY

A. *Factual Background*

Dynamic Development Corporation (Dynamic) is a developer that builds and sells residential and commercial property. In May 1985, Dynamic secured financing from Mid Kansas Federal Savings and Loan Association (Mid Kansas) for the construction of ten "spec" homes on lots Dynamic owned in a Prescott subdivision. The total loan, amounting to $803,250, was disbursed in the form of ten separate loans, each evidenced by a separate note and secured by a separate deed of trust on a single unimproved lot. Unable to complete construction with the amounts financed under the first notes, Dynamic obtained an additional $150,000 loan from Mid Kansas in January of 1986. This loan was evidenced by a single promissory note and a blanket deed of trust on the seven lots remaining unsold.

The first and second notes came due in the summer of 1986. Two more lots were sold and released from the liens. In the fall of 1986, Mid Kansas notified Dynamic that the five remaining properties would be sold at a trustee's sale if the total debt on the first and second notes was not paid. Dynamic was unable to pay the total balance due, but did sell one more lot prior to the trustee's sale and applied the proceeds to the second note.

Mid Kansas noticed a trustee's sale on the four remaining properties, each of which was by then improved by a substantially finished residence. At the time of the trustee's sale, Dynamic owed Mid Kansas approximately $102,000 on the second note and $425,000 on the four first notes. Originally, the sales on the first deeds were scheduled for the day after the sale on the second deed. On January 20, 1987, the second-position blanket deed of trust was foreclosed by the sale of the four parcels. Mid Kansas purchased the property with a credit bid of the balance owed on the second note. The four first-position sales were postponed and ultimately never held. Having thus acquired title to the property, Mid Kansas now seeks to waive the security of the first liens and sue for the balance due on the first notes.

B.   Procedural Background

Mid Kansas's amended complaint stated causes of action for recovery of the balance due under each of the four promissory notes. Mid Kansas moved for partial summary judgment on the four debt claims. The trial court granted the motion and entered judgment for Mid Kansas pursuant to Rule 54(b), Ariz.R.Civ.P., 16 A.R.S.

The court found that Dynamic was in default on the four construction notes in the principal amount of $425,250 plus interest at thirteen percent. The court rejected Dynamic's claim that Mid Kansas had "artificially created a deficiency and now seeks a deficiency judgment against the maker of the notes." The court determined that

> under the holding of *Southwest Savings and Loan v. Ludi,* 122 Ariz. 226 [594 P.2d 92 (1979)], Plaintiff can maintain an action on these notes notwithstanding there was a Trustee's Sale instituted by Plaintiff on a separate deed of trust involving the [same] subject properties.

On appeal, Dynamic argued that Mid Kansas was prohibited from recovering on the promissory notes by the Arizona anti-deficiency statute, A.R.S. § 33–814(G). After the release of our opinion in *Baker,* Dynamic filed a supplemental brief asserting that *Ludi* could no longer be read to permit a residential mortgage holder to waive its security and sue on the note. *See Southwest Sav. & Loan Ass'n v. Ludi,* 122 Ariz. 226, 594 P.2d 92 (1979). Dynamic argued that *Baker* prohibited any attempt to waive the security and sue on the note as a disguised action for deficiency. Therefore, Mid Kansas could not both foreclose the second deed by power of sale and elect to sue Dynamic on the first notes covering the same property.

The court of appeals reversed and remanded the case for entry of judgment for Dynamic. *Mid Kansas Fed. Sav. & Loan Ass'n v. Dynamic Dev. Corp.,* 163 Ariz. 233, 787 P.2d 132 (Ct.App.1989). The court held that under *Baker,* Mid Kansas's attempt to waive the security and sue on the debt was an action for a deficiency, barred after a trustee's sale under § 33–814(G).

* * *

Mid Kansas petitioned for review in this court, presenting the following issues for our consideration:

1.   Whether commercial developers of residential property who borrow for business purposes are entitled to the benefit of Arizona's consumer anti-deficiency statutes, A.R.S. §§ 33–729(A) and 33–814(G).

2.   Whether Arizona's anti-deficiency statutes apply when the encumbered properties are not actually used as residences.

3. Whether a lender's election to waive its security and sue upon a construction loan note secured by a deed of trust constitutes an action for a deficiency prohibited by Arizona's anti-deficiency statutes, A.R.S. §§ 33–729(A) and 33–814(G).

DISCUSSION

A. The Applicability of the Anti-deficiency Statutes

Arizona has two anti-deficiency statutes. A.R.S. § 33–729(A) applies to purchase money mortgages and purchase money deeds of trust foreclosed judicially pursuant to the authority of A.R.S. § 33–807(A). A.R.S. § 33–814(G) applies to deeds of trust that are foreclosed by trustee's sale, regardless of whether they represent purchase money obligations. Both sections prohibit a deficiency judgment after sale of a parcel of "property of two and one-half acres or less which is limited to and utilized for either a single one-family or single two-family dwelling." A.R.S. §§ 33–729(A), 33–814(G).

Arizona also has an election of remedies statute within the general law applicable to mortgages. Under A.R.S. § 33–722, a mortgagee can foreclose and seek a deficiency judgment or can sue on the note and then execute on the resultant judgment but cannot bring both actions simultaneously. *See* Washburn, *The Judicial and Legislative Response to Price Inadequacy in Mortgage Foreclosure Sales,* 53 S.Cal.L.Rev. 843, 928 (1980). The election statute is intended to protect the debtor from multiple suits and at the same time grant the creditor the benefit of the security.

The election statute alters the traditional common law rule that a holder of a note secured by a mortgage has the right to sue on the note alone, to foreclose on the property, or to pursue both remedies at once (although there may be only one recovery on the debt). *See Paramount Ins., Inc. v. Rayson & Smitley,* 86 Nev. 644, 472 P.2d 530, 533 (1970).[2] However, the reach of the statute, as applied to most mortgages, is quite limited. In *Smith v. Mangels,* 73 Ariz. 203, 207, 240 P.2d 168, 170 (1952), this court held the election statute does not preclude a subsequent foreclosure action after judgment on the debt, as is the case in some other states. *See, e.g.,* Neb.Rev.Stat. §§ 25–2140 and 25–2143 (1989); N.Y. Real Prop.Acts.Law § 1301 (McKinney 1979); S.D.Codified Laws Ann. §§ 21–47–5 and 21–47–6 (1987).

---

[2] Under the statutory scheme, the provisions within the law of mortgages (chapter 6 of A.R.S. Title 33) are not applicable to deeds of trust unless the deed of trust is judicially foreclosed as a mortgage pursuant to A.R.S. § 33–807(A). *See* A.R.S. § 33–805. The election statute is within chapter 6. Therefore, the election statute is not applicable to deeds of trust foreclosed by trustee's sale, and there is no analogous statute within the law applicable to deeds of trust. Dynamic does not contend that the lender lost its common law right to elect among its remedies. *See generally Universal Inv. Co. v. Sahara Motor Inn, Inc.,* 127 Ariz. 213, 215, 619 P.2d 485, 487 (Ct.App.1980) (deed of trust statute does not mandate foreclosure by trustee's sale, but allows option to foreclose as mortgage or bring action on debt).

In *Baker,* we held the election statute was limited by the subsequently enacted purchase money mortgage anti-deficiency statute, A.R.S. § 33–729(A), which barred the lender from waiving the security and suing on the debt. 160 Ariz. at 104, 770 P.2d at 772. In so holding, we joined the courts of California and North Carolina in finding that such an election is inconsistent with the anti-deficiency statutes, which limit the lender to recovery from the land itself. *Id.*

Baker held that the lender should not be allowed to circumvent the anti-deficiency statute by electing to sue the debtor on the note, thereby realizing any difference between the value of the real property and the amount owed on the debt. As our supplemental opinion pointed out, *Baker's* holding applies whenever the anti-deficiency statutes apply and therefore is not always limited to the purchase money situation. 160 Ariz. at 106–07, 770 P.2d at 774–75. Assuming that the deed of trust falls within one of the anti-deficiency statutes, an action for a deficiency is prohibited after a trustee's sale on any deed of trust and after judicial foreclosure on purchase money deeds of trust. *See* A.R.S. §§ 33–814(G) and 33–729(A). If a lender holds a non-purchase money deed of trust, he *may* recover a deficiency *if* he does so through an action for judicial foreclosure because A.R.S. § 33–729(A) applies only to purchase money liens. In this latter case, of course, the debtor receives the protections of judicial foreclosure, including a statutory redemption right.

Read together, therefore, the statutes enact the following scheme: when the holder of a non-purchase money deed of trust of the type described in A.R.S. § 33–814(G) forecloses by non-judicial sale, the statute protects the borrower from a deficiency judgment. The lender therefore may not waive the security and sue on the note. *Baker,* 160 Ariz. at 106, 770 P.2d at 774. The holder may, however, seek to foreclose the deed of trust as if it were a mortgage, as allowed by § 33–814(E); if he does so, the debtor is allowed redemption rights under §§ 33–726 and 12–1281 through 12–1289 and is thus protected from low credit bids, but the holder may recover a deficiency judgment—the difference between the balance of the debt and the sale price—unless the note is a purchase money obligation. In the latter case, the borrower is protected by the mortgage anti-deficiency statute, A.R.S. § 33–729(A), which applies only to purchase money obligations. *Baker,* 160 Ariz. at 106, 770 P.2d at 774.

Thus, if under *Baker* and the facts of this case Dynamic is protected by an anti-deficiency statute, Mid Kansas could not elect to waive its security and sue on the first notes after having already chosen to proceed by trustee's sale under the second deed of trust.

B.   Persons and Properties Included Within the Statutory Definitions

Mid Kansas argues that neither Dynamic, as a developer, nor the property under construction is protected by an anti-deficiency statute.

Neither of the statutes is limited to individual homeowners rather than residential developers. Rather, the statutes apparently protect any mortgagor, provided the subject property is a single one-or two-family residential dwelling on two and one-half acres or less.[4]

As we noted in *Baker,* both anti-deficiency statutes were enacted in 1971, along with several other laws designed to protect consumers. 160 Ariz. at 101, 770 P.2d at 769. As with virtually all anti-deficiency statutes, the Arizona provisions were designed to temper the effects of economic recession on mortgagors by precluding "artificial deficiencies resulting from forced sales." *Id.* (quoting Boyd and Balentine, *Arizona's Consumer Legislation: Winning the Battle But * * *,* 14 Ariz.L.Rev. 627, 654 (1972)). Anti-deficiency statutes put the burden on the lender or seller to fairly value the property when extending the loan, recognizing that consumers often are not equipped to make such estimations. *See generally Spangler v. Memel,* 7 Cal.3d 603, 102 Cal.Rptr. 807, 812–13, 498 P.2d 1055, 1060–61 (1972); Leipziger, *Deficiency Judgments in California: The Supreme Court Tries Again,* 22 U.C.L.A. L.REV. 753, 759–61 (1975). Indeed, the articulated purpose behind A.R.S. § 33–729(A) (and presumably behind its deed of trust counterpart, as we held in *Baker*) was to protect "homeowners" from deficiency judgments. *See Baker,* 160 Ariz. at 101, 770 P.2d at 769.

However, absent express limiting language in the statute or explicit evidence of legislative intent, we cannot hold that the statute excludes residential developers. Where the language of a statute is plain and unambiguous, courts must generally follow the text as written. *Mid Kansas,* 163 Ariz. at 238, 787 P.2d at 137 (citing *State Farm Mut. Ins. Co. v. Agency Rent-A-Car, Inc.,* 139 Ariz. 201, 203, 677 P.2d 1309, 1311 (Ct.App.1983); *cf. Ritchie v. Grand Canyon Scenic Rides,* 165 Ariz. 460, 799 P.2d 801 (1990) (rule inapplicable where it would produce absurd result)). While we can infer that the legislature's primary intent was to protect individual homeowners rather than commercial developers, neither the statutory text nor legislative history evinces an intent to *exclude* any other type of mortgagor. Indeed, the North Carolina Supreme

---

[4]   The statutes read as follows (relevant portions emphasized):

A.R.S. § 33–729(A):

> [I]f a mortgage is given to secure the payment of the balance of the purchase price, or to secure a loan to pay all or part of the purchase price, of *a parcel of real property of two and one-half acres or less which is limited to and utilized for either a single one-family or single two-family dwelling* . . . [there shall be no deficiency judgment] . . .

A.R.S. § 33–814(G):

> If *trust property of two and one-half acres or less which is limited to and utilized for either a single one-family or single two-family dwelling* is sold pursuant to the trustee's power of sale, no action may be maintained to recover any difference between the amount obtained by sale and the amount of the indebtedness and any interest, costs and expenses.

Court decided to apply a similar anti-deficiency statute to a commercial borrower, finding that the statute expressed no intent to exclude commercial transactions and therefore that the court could not read in such an intent. *Barnaby v. Boardman,* 313 N.C. 565, 330 S.E.2d 600, 603 (1985). Therefore, we hold that so long as the subject properties fit within the statutory definition, the identity of the mortgagor as either a homeowner or developer is irrelevant.

In contrast to the lack of legislative limitation as to the type of mortgagor protected, there is specific textual expression as to the type of property protected. Both statutes require that the property be (1) two and one-half acres or less, (2) limited to and utilized for a dwelling that is (3) single one-family or single two-family in nature. In applying a statute, we have long held that its words are to be given their ordinary meaning, unless the legislature has offered its own definition of the words or it appears from the context that a special meaning was intended. *State Tax Comm'n v. Peck,* 106 Ariz. 394, 395, 476 P.2d 849, 850 (1970).

A.R.S. § 33–814(g) calls for the property to be "limited to" a single one-or two-family dwelling. The word "dwelling" is susceptible to several interpretations, depending on the context of its use. *See* 28 C.J.S. *Dwelling* (1941 and 1990 Supp.). However, the principal element in all such definitions is the "purpose or use of a building for human abode," meaning that the structure is wholly or partially occupied by persons lodging therein at night or intended for such use. *Id.* * * *

The anti-deficiency statutes require not only that the property be limited to dwelling purposes, but also that it be "utilized for" such purposes. In *Northern Arizona Properties v. Pinetop Properties Group,* the court of appeals held that an investment condominium, which was occasionally occupied by the owners and occasionally rented out to third persons, fell within the statutory definition. 151 Ariz. 9, 725 P.2d 501 (Ct.App.1986). In deciding that the statute applied to a dwelling used for investment purposes and not as the mortgagor's principal residence, the court employed the definition of "dwelling" in Webster's Ninth New Collegiate Dictionary and in several housing codes as "a shelter * * * in which people live." Hence, although the condominium was held as an investment, it was also used (utilized) as a dwelling. *Id.* at 12, 725 P.2d at 504.

In contrast to the *Northern Arizona Properties* case, the property in question here had never been used as a dwelling, and was in fact not yet susceptible of being used as a dwelling. There is a difference between property intended for eventual use as a dwelling and property utilized as a dwelling. We hold that commercial residential properties held by the mortgagor for construction and eventual *resale* as dwellings are not within the definition of properties "limited to" and *"utilized* for" single-family dwellings. The property is not utilized as a dwelling when it is unfinished, has never been lived in, and is being held for sale to its first occupant by an owner who has no intent to ever occupy the property. *Cf. Northern Arizona Properties* (mortgagors intended to occupy property occasionally and rent it out).

Therefore, we hold that by its terms, the anti-deficiency statute does not apply to Dynamic in this case and A.R.S. § 33–814(G) does not preclude Mid Kansas from waiving its security and bringing a debt action on the notes.

[The court then held that Mid Kansas nevertheless was probably barred from recovering against Dynamic because of the merger doctrine. For a consideration of the merger aspect of this case, see pages 632–643, supra.]

GORDON, C.J., and MOELLER and CORCORAN, JJ., concur.

CAMERON, JUSTICE, dissenting in part, concurring in part.

I concur in the result the majority ultimately reaches. However, because of my dissent in *Baker v. Gardner,* 160 Ariz. 98, 770 P.2d 766 (1988), I write separately. * * * It was my belief then, and now, that *any* creditor has the right under § 33–722 to elect either to foreclose on the mortgage *or* to sue on the note. *Id.* at 105, 770 P.2d at 774. Once the creditor chooses to foreclose, the anti-deficiency statutes apply, and he cannot seek a deficiency judgment. *Id.*

The majority reiterates the rationale of *Baker,* noting that if the anti-deficiency statutes include Dynamic, Mid Kansas would be precluded from waiving its security and could not sue on the first note after having foreclosed on the second note. Next, the majority determines whether Dynamic, as a commercial developer, is protected by the anti-deficiency statutes. Noting the statutes' purpose was to protect "homeowners" from deficiency judgments and to protect consumers who were not sophisticated enough to value property when seeking a loan, the majority includes commercial developers as mortgagors within statutory protection. Commercial developers, however, are business people who are capable of valuing their business enterprises when seeking commercial or construction loans. They are neither unsophisticated consumers nor "homeowners."

After determining that Dynamic falls within the class of persons protected by the statutes, the majority then notes that the property in question does not fit the statutory language. The majority stated that "commercial residential properties held by the mortgagor for construction and eventual *resale* as dwellings are not within the definition of properties 'limited to' and '*utilized* for' * * * dwellings." At 129, 804 P.2d at 1317. Commercial developers are generously included as mortgagors covered under the statutes, but excluded due to the type of property they hold. Again, I believe this is wrong. The majority's interpretation of "dwelling" and "utilized for" means that a commercial developer's property will never meet the statutory language. By applying the reasoning of my dissent in *Baker,* we could have more easily and clearly reached the majority's result, without having to extend empty statutory protection. I believe that the anti-deficiency statutes were not intended to cover commercial developers and, therefore, Mid Kansas has the right to elect to foreclose or to sue on the first note.

NOTES

1. *Absence of "one-action" rule.* In *Baker*, the supreme court held that Arizona's purchase money anti-deficiency legislation barred a mortgagee election to waive the security and sue on the note. Should the absence of a "one-action" rule in Arizona have made its decision in *Baker* more difficult?

2. *Florida approach.* Consider the following description of Florida's unique and confusing deficiency legislation:

> Florida deficiency legislation is both unique and ambiguous.[15] Under its language, where a deficiency judgment is sought, "the amount bid at the sale may be considered by the court as one of the factors in determining a deficiency under the usual equitable principles."[16] This language[17] has created substantial difficulty for Florida appellate courts. While one court has taken the position that "if the value of the foreclosed property exceeds the debt, the chancellor is authorized in denying a deficiency,"[18] other decisions emphasize that the granting of a deficiency judgment based on the foreclosure sale price "is the rule rather than the exception" unless fraud or other inequitable conduct infects the sale process.[19] Even

---

[15] See West's Fla.Stat.Ann. § 45.031(7).

[16] Id.

[17] The statutory language was in response to R.K. Cooper Construction Co. v. Fulton, 216 So.2d 11 (Fla.1968), a Florida Supreme Court decision which held:

"The value of the property as established by the sale is conclusive insofar as consideration to support title to the property in the purchaser, but the statutory automatic approval cannot bind the trial court when a suit at law is filed to enforce collection of the remaining amount due on the note. A shockingly inadequate sale price in the foreclosure proceeding can be asserted as an equitable defense and the trial judge has the discretion and duty to inquire into the reasonable and fair market value of the property sold, the adequacy of the sale price, and the relationship, if any, between the foreclosing mortgagee and the purchaser at the sale, before entering a judgment on the note." Id. at 13.

[18] Hamilton Investment Trust v. Escambia Developers, Inc., 352 So.2d 883, 884 (Fla.App.1977). See Trustees of Central States Southeast and Southwest Areas, Pension Fund v. Indico Corp., 401 So.2d 904 (Fla.App.1981). Cf. Withers v. Flagship Peoples Bank, 473 So.2d 789 (Fla.App.1985); Fara Manufacturing Co., Inc. v. First Federal Savings and Loan Association of Miami, 366 So.2d 164 (Fla.App.1979).

[19] Federal Deposit Insurance Corp. v. Circle Bar Ranch, Inc., 450 So.2d 921 (Fla.App.1984); Lloyd v. Cannon, 399 So.2d 1095, 1096 (Fla.App.1981), review denied, 408 So.2d 1092 (Fla.1981); Flagship State Bank of Jacksonville v. Drew Equipment Co., 392 So.2d 609, 613 (Fla.App.1981); S/D Enterprises, Inc. v. Chase Manhattan Bank, 374 So.2d 1121 (Fla.App.1979).

these latter cases suggest that a deficiency judgment may be denied or reduced where the foreclosure sale price is "shockingly inadequate" or "unconscionable."[20] Moreover, there is some evidence that Florida trial courts allow mortgagors to introduce evidence of the fair market value of foreclosed real estate and that those courts use their determination of value, rather than the foreclosure sale price, to calculate the amount of the deficiency judgment.[21] Consequently, while it would be inaccurate to assert that Florida is a "fair value" jurisdiction, it would also be misleading to suggest that Florida trial courts have no flexibility in determining whether to use the foreclosure sale price or the market value of the foreclosed real estate as the crucial factor in deficiency judgment proceedings.

Nelson, Whitman, Burkhart & Freyermuth, Real Estate Finance Law 715–716 (6th ed. 2014).*

3. *Anti-deficiency statutes and installment land contracts.* To what extent will statutory prohibitions against purchase money mortgage deficiency judgments apply to installment land contracts? Suppose, for example, that a contract vendor, instead of invoking forfeiture, elects to seek specific performance in the form of a money decree for the contract price. For the view that such statutes do not prohibit "awarding specific performance by granting a money decree and further providing that in the event the decree is not paid the property shall be sold and the proceeds applied in satisfaction of the money decree", see Glacier Campground v. Wild Rivers, Inc., 182 Mont. 389, 597 P.2d 689 (1978); Renard v. Allen, 237 Or. 406, 391 P.2d 777 (1964).

Compare Venable v. Harmon, 233 Cal.App.2d 297, 43 Cal.Rptr. 490 (1965), in which the vendor repossessed the land after the purchaser's default, and then sued for damages. "[T]o allow the vendor to recover this judgment places him in a better position than under a trust deed or mortgage. It would allow him to recover a personal judgment and retain title to the land. This would accomplish the exact result which * * * the statute was designed to prevent." See also Ferguson v. Swanstrom, 2012 WL 3539123 (Cal.App. 2012).

4. *Rights of guarantors.* To what extent are guarantors of mortgage debt protected by anti-deficiency legislation? We have already examined the California situation. See pages 836–840, supra. Consider the following analysis:

Guarantors of the mortgage debt frequently attempt to invoke the protection of anti-deficiency legislation. While the case law is

---

[20] Id. See Wilson v. Adams & Fusselle, Inc., 467 So.2d 345 (Fla.App.1985).

[21] See e.g., Peoples Federal Savings & Loan Association of Tarentum, Pennsylvania v. Shoreline Garden Townhomes, II, Ltd., 538 So.2d 864 (Fla.App.1988); Coppola v. Housing Investment Corp. of Florida, 400 So.2d 112 (Fla.App.1981).

* Reprinted with permission of LEG, Inc., d/b/a/ West Academic.

substantial,[2] generalization in this area is hazardous for a variety of reasons. First, most of the cases involve questions of legislative intent and, in many instances, that intent is hardly apparent. Often cases will turn on the specific and sometimes unique language of a particular statute. Finally, all anti-deficiency legislation does not serve identical policy objectives and, consequently, courts may interpret certain types of statutes more broadly than others.

Notwithstanding these difficulties, certain observations are appropriate. There is some judicial predisposition to deny guarantors the protection of anti-deficiency legislation.[3] Courts typically reason that the liability of a guarantor is based on a separate and distinct contract of guaranty and not imposed by the note or the mortgage securing it.[4] Moreover, some courts stress that where the statute does not clearly encompass guarantors, they will be reluctant to extend statutory protection to them.[5] Guarantors are, however, sometimes successful.[6] Some statutes specifically protect guarantors.[7] Moreover, where a statute specifically applied to persons "directly or indirectly or contingently liable", courts have protected guarantors under it.[8] In addition, courts are sometimes responsive to "substance over form" arguments. Thus, anti-deficiency protection has been extended to persons who formally played the role of guarantor, but who were in substance the principal obligors of mortgage debt incurred by "dummy" or straw party mortgagors.[9] A somewhat similar approach has been utilized

---

[2] See generally Annot., 49 A.L.R.3d 554 (1973).

[3] See, e.g., Mariners Savings and Loan Association v. Neil, 22 Cal.App.3d 232, 99 Cal.Rptr. 238 (1971); First Security Bank of Idaho, N.A. v. Gaige, 115 Idaho 172, 765 P.2d 683 (1988); Bank of Kirkwood Plaza v. Mueller, 294 N.W.2d 640 (N.D.1980); Sumner v. Enercon Development Company, 307 Or. 579, 771 P.2d 619 (1989), on remand 98 Or.App. 18, 779 P.2d 150 (1989); Victory Highway Village, Inc. v. Weaver, 480 F.Supp. 71 (D.Minn.1979).

[4] See, e.g., Riverside National Bank v. Manolakis, 613 P.2d 438 (Okl.1980). Cf. Founders Bank and Trust Company v. Upsher, 830 P.2d 1355 (Okl.1992).

[5] See, e.g., First Security Bank of Idaho, N.A. v. Gaige, 115 Idaho 172, 765 P.2d 683 (1988); Bank of Kirkwood Plaza v. Mueller, 294 N.W.2d 640 (N.D.1980); Sumner v. Enercon Development Company, 307 Or. 579, 771 P.2d 619 (1989), on remand 98 Or.App. 18, 779 P.2d 150 (1989).

[6] See e.g., Bank of Southern California v. Dombrow, 46 Cal.Rptr.2d 656 (Cal.App.1995) (fair value statute protects guarantors as well as debtors); Adams v. Cooper, 340 N.C. 242, 460 S.E.2d 120 (N.C.1995) (purchase-money antideficiency statute protects guarantors as well as mortgagor). First Interstate Bank of Arizona, N.A. v. Tatum and Bell Center Associates, 170 Ariz. 99, 821 P.2d 1384 (App.1991); First Interstate Bank of Nevada v. Shields, 102 Nev. 616, 730 P.2d 429 (1986). See Freeman & Freeman Gurev, An Overview of Defenses Available to Guarantors of Real Property Secured Transactions under California Law, 38 Santa Clara L.Rev. 329 (1998).

[7] See e.g., Ariz.Rev.Stat.Ann. § 33–814(A); V.T.C.A., Prop.Code §§ 51.004, 51.005. For a consideration of the Arizona legislation, see Johnson, Guarantor Deficiency Judgment Liability Under Arizona Revised Statutes Annotated Section 33–814, 22 Ariz.St.L.J. 797 (1990).

[8] See Klinke v. Samuels, 264 N.Y. 144, 190 N.E. 324 (1934); Kramer v. Relgov Realty Co., 268 N.Y. 592, 198 N.E. 420 (1935).

[9] See, e.g., In re Wilton-Maxfield Management Co., 117 F.2d 913 (9th Cir.1941); Valinda Builders, Inc. v. Bissner, 230 Cal.App.2d 106, 40 Cal.Rptr. 735 (1964). In re Harstad, 136 B.R. 806 (Bkrtcy.Minn.1992). But see Paradise Land & Cattle Company v. McWilliams Enterprises,

in less obvious situations. Some courts have held, for example, that where an individual partner guarantees the debt of the partnership, she can assert anti-deficiency protection because, given the nature of the partnership entity, the guarantor is "nothing more than the principal obligor under another name."[10] Likewise there is case law that gives the benefit of anti-deficiency legislation to guarantors of the debt of a family trust where the guarantors were trustees and beneficiaries of the trust.[11]

Nelson, Whitman, Burkhart & Freyermuth, Real Estate Finance Law 720–721 (6th ed.2014).*

5. *Restatement approach.* Under the Restatement, the mortgagee, after acceleration, may either (1) obtain a judgment on the personal obligation and enforce it by levying upon any of the mortgagor's assets and, if a deficiency remains, foreclose on the mortgaged real estate or (2) foreclose first on the mortgaged real estate and, if necessary, seek a deficiency judgment. Restatement (Third) of Property (Mortgages) § 8.2 (1997). The Restatement rejects the "one-action" rule. On the other hand, the mortgagor is substantially protected against a multiplicity of actions because mortgagee may not proceed under the above options concurrently or consecutively. "Once the mortgagee opts to proceed under one of the two [options], it is prohibited from utilizing the other." Id. cmt. b.

The Restatement permits deficiency judgments even though the mortgage is "purchase-money" or is being foreclosed by power of sale. On the other hand, it rejects the traditional common law view that the foreclosure sale price should automatically be used in measuring the deficiency. Instead, it adopts the "fair value" approach by giving the mortgagor "the right to insist that the greater of the fair market value of the real estate or the foreclose sale price be used in calculating the deficiency." Restatement (Third) of Property (Mortgages) § 8.4 cmt. a (1997).

> This approach enables the mortgagee to be made whole where the mortgaged real estate is insufficient to satisfy the mortgage obligation, but at the same time protects against the mortgagee purchasing the property at a deflated price, obtaining a deficiency judgment and, by reselling the real estate at a profit, achieving a recovery that exceeds the obligation. Thus, it is aimed primarily at preventing the unjust enrichment of the mortgagee. [It] also

---

Inc., 959 F.2d 1463 (9th Cir.1992) (liability against guarantor-corporation upheld even though it was owned by mortgagors).

[10] See Union Bank v. Dorn, 254 Cal.App.2d 157, 61 Cal.Rptr. 893 (1967); Riddle v. Lushing, 203 Cal.App.2d 831, 21 Cal.Rptr. 902 (1962); First Interstate Bank of Fargo, N.A. v. Larson, 475 N.W.2d 538 (N.D.1991); Westinghouse Credit Corp. v. Barton, 789 F.Supp. 1043 (C.D.Cal.1992) (partner-guarantor given benefit of anti-deficiency laws even though loan to partnership was "non-recourse").

[11] Torrey Pines Bank v. Hoffman, 231 Cal.App.3d 308, 282 Cal.Rptr. 354 (1991).

* Reprinted with permission of LEG Inc., d/b/a/ West Academic.

protects the mortgagor from the harsh consequences of suffering both the loss of the real estate and the burden of a deficiency judgment that does not fairly recognize the value of that real estate.

Id.*

6.   *Should state anti-deficiency legislation be preempted by federal action?* Consider the following commentary:

> Strategic default—the practice of opting to default on an underwater home mortgage when the mortgagor has the ability to pay—has been a significant exacerbating factor in the mortgage crisis and its accompanying economic upheaval.[221] The practice is aided and abetted by states such as California that limit or prohibit personal recourse on mortgage obligations.[222] As a result, strategic default is a more pervasive problem in these states than in their recourse brethren.[223] In effect, such states grant home mortgagors an option with respect to the mortgaged real estate. If market forces cause the property to increase in value, that increase inures to the benefit of the mortgagor. On the other hand, if the property value decreases and the mortgage is underwater, a mortgagor is able to avoid any personal liability through a deficiency judgment.
>
> Where state law permits such strategic behavior, we find it difficult to conclude that a mortgagor is acting immorally. On the other hand, we believe that such activity should be made illegal. Thus, we conclude that Congress should preempt state non-recourse law by enacting legislation based on Section 8.4 of the Restatement (Third) of Property: Mortgages.[224] Should Congress choose to take this course of action, it would pose no greater threat to federalism principles than when it opted in 1982, through the Garn Act, to invalidate state judicial decisions and statutes that enabled home purchasers to take over a seller's existing low interest rate mortgage without obtaining the mortgagee's consent.[225] Indeed, the Garn Act was applicable to virtually all mortgages in the United States.[226]
>
> Should Congress find such preemption politically unappealing, we advocate that federal agencies such as FHFA accomplish the same result through the regulatory process.

Grant S. Nelson & Gabriel D. Serbulea, Strategic Defaulters Versus the Federal Taxpayer: A Brief for the Preemption of State Anti-Deficiency Law for Residential Mortgages, 66 Ark.L.Rev. 65, 108–109 (2013).

---

*   © 1997 by The American Law Institute. Reprinted with permission.

[221] *See* White, *Emotional Drivers*, *supra* note 6, at 1284.

[222] CAL. CIV. PROC. CODE § 580b (West 2012).

[223] Bhutta et al., *supra* note 147, at 25.

[224] RESTATEMENT (THIRD) OF PROP.: MORTGAGES § 8.4 (1996); *see supra* Part V.A–B.

[225] *See supra* Part V.C–E.

[226] *See supra* notes 169–72 and accompanying text.

I. THE SERVICEMEMBERS CIVIL RELIEF ACT

From our country's early days, state and federal legislators have appreciated the need to relieve from or modify certain legal responsibilities of those who answer the call to serve in the military. The justification for this approach has been to allow these persons to perform their military duties without being hindered unnecessarily by pressing legal concerns at home. For example, during the War of 1812, Louisiana suspended all civil legal actions against soldiers for four months as the British marched on New Orleans. See H.R. Rep. 108–81. 108th Cong. 1st Sess. (2003). Later, during the Civil War, "Congress recognized the need to protect service members from civil obligations while on military duty away from home, * * * [and] [f]or the duration of the war * * * passed a total moratorium on civil actions brought against Union soldiers and sailors." Terry M. Jarrett, The Servicemembers Civil Relief Act: Important New Protections for Those in Uniform, 60 J.Mo.B. 174, 174 (2004).

When the United States entered World War I, Congress again felt the need to protect members of the armed forces and thus enacted the Soldiers' and Sailors' Civil Relief Act of 1918. See Soldiers and Sailors Civil Relief Act of 1918, ch. 20, 40 Stat. 440. While World War I legislation was not as sweeping as its Civil War counterpart, it provided substantial protection to servicemembers on active duty against property seizure, foreclosure, bankruptcy or similar actions. As World War II loomed on the immediate horizon, Congress enacted the Soldiers' and Sailors' Civil Relief Act of 1940 (the "SSCRA"). This statute largely renewed the 1918 bill which had expired shortly after the end of World War I. However, the SSCRA did not contain an expiration date and thus it survived for 63 years having been amended at least 13 times. Most recently, the SSCRA was amended in 1991 and 2002 in response to massive activations of military reserve forces in connection with Operation Desert Storm (the first Iraq War) and Operation Enduring Freedom (the Afghanistan operation in response to the 9–11 attack). See Jarrett, *supra*, at 175.

In 2003, in response to the Iraq War, Congress renovated and modified the SSCRA by enacting the Servicemembers Civil Relief Act ("SCRA" or the "Act") "[t]o restate, clarify, and revise the Soldiers' and Sailors' Civil Relief Act of 1940." While the SCRA deals with a wide variety of commercial transactions entered into by servicemembers, it does not make significant changes in its predecessor's treatment of real estate mortgage transactions. We briefly describe SCRA's impact in several important areas of interest to real estate lawyers and mortgagees.

Statutes of Limitation

Section 526 automatically tolls all statutes of limitation during the period of service that would otherwise run against a serviceperson. See 50 U.S.C.A. App. § 526. It contains no language requiring that the serviceperson be prejudiced by his or her military service. This section tolls not only properly denominated statutes of limitation, but also to such periods relating to "the redemption of real estate sold or forfeited to enforce an obligation, tax, or assessment." Id. Thus, section 526 has been held to extend the time for redemption under state statutory redemption by a period equal to the mortgagor's period of service. See 1 Nelson, Whitman, Burkhart & Freyermuth, Real Estate Finance Law § 8.9 (6th ed. Practitioner Series 2014). Moreover, it also applies to redemption periods after real estate tax sales. See Hedrick v. Bigby, 228 Ark. 40, 305 S.W.2d 674 (1957). Equally important, the United States Supreme Court has unanimously rejected the contention that section 526 requires "career" servicepersons to establish that their military service prejudiced their ability to redeem—rather, the Court concluded that "Congress included a prejudice requirement whenever it considered it appropriate to do so, and * * * its omission of any such requirement in [§ 526] was deliberate." Conroy v. Aniskoff, 507 U.S. 511, 113 S.Ct. 1562, 123 L.Ed.2d 229 (1993).

Maximum Rate of Interest

Section 527 limits interest to six percent during military service on obligations incurred before entering service, even though a higher rate was originally agreed upon. 50 U.S.C.A. App. § 527. The interest rate is automatically reduced to the six percent maximum unless the mortgagee proves that military service has no material effect on the ability of the serviceperson to pay a higher rate. For example, suppose a mortgagor executes a 8% mortgage note and is then called into active duty in the military. The burden then falls on the mortgagee to justify a rate higher than six percent. Anecdotal evidence suggests that during both the 1991–92 Persian Gulf War and the later Iraq and Afghanistan hostilities institutional mortgage lenders frequently voluntarily agreed to collect six percent during the period of involuntary duty.

Installment Land Contracts (Contracts for Deed)

When a serviceperson defaults under an installment land contract entered into prior to military service, the vendor may not terminate or rescind the contract or repossess the land except by judicial action. 50 U.S.C.A. App. § 532. Forfeiture through nonjudicial means is a criminal act. Id. If the vendor files such a judicial action, the court may condition its order on repayment of all or part of the deposit and prior installments. If military service materially affected the serviceperson's ability to comply with the terms of payment, the court may order an absolute stay or one conditioned on partial payment. The court also has the option to order the judicial sale of the real estate and an appropriate division of the proceeds.

Mortgages and Deeds of Trust

Section 533 treats obligations secured by mortgages and deeds of trust in much the same fashion as its Section 532 counterpart deals with installment land contracts. After a default in payment or other breach in a mortgage or deed of trust obligation consummated prior to service, the mortgagee may not sell, foreclose, or seize the mortgaged real estate during the term of service or for one year thereafter except pursuant to a judicial order. The practical effect is that in states where power of sale foreclosure is the predominant foreclosure method mortgagees must, as a practical matter, foreclose judicially.

Waiver by Servicemember

A servicemember may waive the protections of the Act if the waiver is "made pursuant to a written agreement of the parties that is executed during or after the servicemember's period of military service. The written agreement shall specify the legal instrument to which the waiver applies * * * ." 50 U.S.C.A.App. § 517(a). This waiver may cover the rights conferred by the Act on both mortgagors under mortgages and deeds of trust and vendees under installment land contracts. 50 U.S.C.A.App. § 517(b)(1)(B). Note, however, that such a waiver is effective only if it is "executed *during or after* the servicemember's period of military service." 50 U.S.C.A.App. § 517(a) (emphasis added). Consequently, pre-service waivers are ineffective. Thus, for example, if a serviceperson purchases a home and executes a specific waiver of section 533 rights, and is later called to active duty, the waiver is unenforceable. On the other hand, if the same purchase transaction is entered into while the serviceperson is on active duty, the waiver is effective.

J. BANKRUPTCY

1. INTRODUCTORY CONCEPTS

When a mortgagor files for bankruptcy, the mortgagee's ability to enforce its lien becomes subject to the substantive and procedural limitations imposed by federal bankruptcy law. A variety of objectives motivate the bankruptcy system. The first is to provide an honest but unfortunate debtor with a "fresh start." See Jackson, The Fresh Start Policy in Bankruptcy Law, 98 Harv. L. Rev. 1393 (1985). For a consumer debtor, this means the ability to obtain a discharge from otherwise unmanageable pre-bankruptcy debts; for a business debtor, this means the ability to restructure pre-bankruptcy debts and continue in business. A second objective is to provide a collective remedy for creditors of an insolvent debtor. Outside of bankruptcy, a debtor's financial distress can trigger a "race to the courthouse" in which creditors compete for the debtor's limited assets in judicial or nonjudicial collection processes. This race is potentially counterproductive in several respects. The distraction of responding to creditor collection activity may compromise the debtor's ability to carry out its business operations. Further, as noted earlier in this Chapter, foreclosure sales often bring sale prices lower than the debtor might have obtained in an arms-length sale. By forcing creditors into a collective proceeding, bankruptcy seeks to protect the value of the debtor's assets for the benefit of the debtor (if reorganization is possible) or all creditors (if reorganization is impossible). In this way, bankruptcy law mitigates the adverse consequences of the "race to the courthouse" in a way that provides consistent treatment to similarly situated creditors. See generally Charles Tabb, The Law of Bankruptcy (2d ed. 2009); Elizabeth Warren, Bankruptcy Policy, 54 U. Chi. L Rev. 775 (1987); Thomas Jackson, The Logic and Limits of Bankruptcy Law (1986).

Enacted by Congress in 1978 and revised on several subsequent occasions (most recently in 2005 by the Bankruptcy Abuse Prevention and Consumer Protection Act, or BAPCPA), the Bankruptcy Code divides bankruptcy law into separate "Chapters." Three of these Chapters (1, 3, and 5) contain general provisions that apply in all types of bankruptcy cases. The remaining Chapters govern the specific types of bankruptcy cases. The most common is Chapter 7, which involves the liquidation of the debtor's non-exempt assets to satisfy his or her creditors according to the priority and amount of their claims, typically in exchange for a discharge of most of the debtor's pre-bankruptcy debts. Chapter 11 provides for the reorganization and rehabilitation of a business debtor through the negotiation and confirmation of a reorganization plan that typically restructures the rights of both secured and unsecured creditors. Chapter 13 provides a reorganization process that permits individual wage earners to restructure or reduce unsecured claims and certain secured claims by committing all of their net disposable income for a period of three to five years toward the payment of such claims. Chapter 12, enacted in 1986, provides a similar reorganization procedure for family farmers. In this Section, we will focus upon those aspects of bankruptcy law that have the most significant consequences for the mortgagor-mortgagee relationship.

The bankruptcy estate. The filing of a bankruptcy petition creates a bankruptcy estate. Subject to limited statutory exceptions, all of the interests in property (whether legal or equitable) owned by the debtor at the moment of the bankruptcy petition become part of the bankruptcy estate. 11 U.S.C.A. § 541(a)(1). If, at that time, the mortgagee has begun the foreclosure process but has not yet completed a foreclosure sale, the debtor's rights in the property have not yet been extinguished, and thus the mortgaged premises become property of the bankruptcy estate. In re Webb, 472 B.R. 665 (6th Cir. B.A.P. 2012).

The bankruptcy trustee/debtor-in-possession. The central figure in Chapter 7 bankruptcy cases is the trustee, who is the official representative of the bankruptcy estate. The Chapter 7 trustee collects and manages the property in the bankruptcy estate, investigates the bankrupt's financial affairs, invalidates any improper pre-bankruptcy transfers by the debtor, liquidates the property of the estate, and distributes the proceeds to those creditors entitled to payment under the Code's distributive scheme. 11 U.S.C.A. § 704. By contrast, in reorganization cases under Chapters 11, 12, and 13, property of the estate remains in the hands of the debtor—who is called the "debtor-in-possession" or "DIP"—and the debtor may use that property while formulating a plan to pay the claims of creditors using the debtor's post-bankruptcy earnings. 11 U.S.C.A. §§ 1107(a), 1203(a), 1303. In Chapter 12 and 13 cases, a trustee is appointed, but the trustee's role is primarily administrative, i.e., it collects the debtor's disposable post-bankruptcy income and uses it to make the payments due to creditors under the debtor's reorganization plan. 11 U.S.C.A. § 1202(b), 1302(b). In Chapter 11 cases, the court does not appoint a trustee at all, unless the debtor is engaging in fraudulent conduct or the court concludes that the appointment of a trustee is necessary to protect the bankruptcy estate and the interests of persons holding claims against the estate. 11 U.S.C.A. § 1104(a).

Contrasting secured and unsecured claims. Before making distributions to creditors, bankruptcy must identify those creditors holding valid claims against the debtor. Bankruptcy law respects most pre-bankruptcy claims,[1] but disallows claims that are not enforceable under nonbankruptcy law (such as a claim evidenced by a forged promissory note or that is barred by the applicable statute of limitations). 11 U.S.C.A. § 502(a), (b). Bankruptcy law also generally disallows claims for unmatured interest. 11 U.S.C.A. § 502(b)(2). Thus, if Debtor owed Bank $20,000 on an unsecured note bearing a 10% annual interest rate, the Bank's claim in bankruptcy would no longer accrue interest after the petition date.[2]

---

[1] Claims are deemed valid or "allowed" unless the trustee, the debtor, or some other party in interest raises a valid objection. 11 U.S.C.A. § 502(a); In re Hemingway Transport, Inc., 993 F.2d 915 (1st Cir. 1993). Once a proper objection is raised, the court must conduct a hearing and determine the allowed amount of the creditor's claim.

[2] The denial of claims for unmatured interest is based on administrative convenience. Usually, insolvent debtors cannot pay 100% of unsecured claims—much less interest on those claims. Disallowance of claims for unmatured interest permits the trustee/debtor-in-possession to avoid the accrual of interest (and the need to have to recompute claim amounts) as the bankruptcy case proceeds. Vanston Bondholders' Protective Comm. v. Green, 329 U.S. 156 (1946); In re Brooks, 323 F.3d 675 (8th Cir. 2003). Notwithstanding section 502(b)(2), however, creditors holding oversecured claims (claims secured by property with a value that exceeds the

The Code separates claims into two primary categories—*secured* and *unsecured*. Generally, bankruptcy law takes secured creditors as it finds them on the petition date—a security interest that is valid under nonbankruptcy law is generally respected in bankruptcy. Thus, a creditor with a valid mortgage lien upon the debtor's land is treated as the holder of a *secured claim*, and retains both its lien on the land and its pre-bankruptcy priority for any distribution from the proceeds of that land.[3] 11 U.S.C.A. § 506(a)(1). By contrast, the holders of *unsecured claims*—general creditors without any pre-bankruptcy lien against specific assets of the debtor—receive payment on their claims on a pro rata basis to the extent that assets remain after payment of secured claims and the expenses of bankruptcy administration. 11 U.S.C.A. §§ 507(b), 726(a).

In some cases, a mortgagee may hold an *undersecured claim*—i.e., one secured by a lien on land that is worth less than the total balance owed to the mortgagee. For example, suppose Bank holds a valid mortgage lien on Chapter 7 Debtor's land (worth $40,000) to secure a debt of $100,000. Outside of bankruptcy, the creditor would hold one legal claim against the debtor in the amount of $100,000. Section 506(a)(1) of the Bankruptcy Code, however, "bifurcates" Bank's claim, treating it as if it were two separate claims—a secured claim equal to the value of the collateral, and an unsecured claim to the extent of the deficiency balance of Bank's claim. In this example, Bank would thus have a secured claim of $40,000 and an unsecured claim of $60,000.

NOTE

Statutory redemption in bankruptcy. Suppose a petition for bankruptcy is filed after a foreclosure sale, but before the expiration of the bankrupt mortgagor's state law statutory redemption right. In this situation, the trustee has the power to exercise the mortgagor's redemption right for the time period remaining under the applicable state statute or 60 days after the bankruptcy petition, whichever is longer. See 11 U.S.C.A. § 108(b); In re Thom, Inc., 95 B.R. 261 (Bankr. D. Me. 1989). The bankruptcy petition, however, does not toll the running of the state statutory redemption period. See, e.g., In re Whispering Bay Campground, Inc., 850 F.2d 443 (8th Cir. 1988); Nelson, Whitman, Burkhart & Freyermuth, Real Estate Finance Law § 8.12, at 768 n.338 (6th ed. 2014). Under what circumstances would a trustee choose to exercise such rights? Where would the money come from?

---

balance of the debt) are entitled to collect post-petition interest as part of their allowed claim, up to but not exceeding the value of the collateral. 11 U.S.C.A. § 506(a)(1), (b).

[3] This principle is subject to two caveats, as discussed later in this section. First, even if the lien is valid, the bankruptcy petition prevents or "stays" the creditor from exercising its nonbankruptcy remedies during the bankruptcy. 11 U.S.C.A. § 362(a). Second, the Code gives the trustee/debtor-in-possession the power to avoid certain liens, including liens that the creditor failed to perfect prior to bankruptcy. 11 U.S.C.A. § 544(a).

2. THE AUTOMATIC STAY

The most immediate impact of a mortgagor's bankruptcy is the automatic stay. Under 11 U.S.C.A. § 362(a), any effort by a mortgagee to foreclose a mortgage against property of the estate, whether judicially or nonjudicially, is stayed by the bankruptcy petition. 11 U.S.C.A. § 362(a)(4); In re Kline, 472 B.R. 98 (10th Cir. B.A.P. 2012). The stay also prevents the mortgagee from taking any other collection efforts, such as suing for a personal judgment on the mortgage debt, seeking to execute on a judgment obtained prior to bankruptcy, seeking the appointment of a receiver for the mortgaged premises, or even sending a demand letter to the debtor. 11 U.S.C.A. § 362(a)(1), (2), (3), (6). The stay even prevents a mortgagee from recording a mortgage that debtor had granted (but that had not been recorded) prior to bankruptcy. 11 U.S.C.A. § 362(a)(4). The stay thus brings collection activity against the mortgagor to a halt, essentially forcing the mortgagee and other creditors to resolve claims against the debtor through the collective bankruptcy process.

If the mortgagee violates the automatic stay, the mortgagor's rights in the property are unaffected; creditor actions in violation of the stay are void,[4] even if the creditor in question lacked knowledge or notice of the bankruptcy filing. See, e.g., In re Cueva, 371 F.3d 232 (5th Cir. 2004) (foreclosure sale in violation of stay invalid regardless of mortgagee's lack of knowledge of stay). Further, a creditor that knowingly violates the stay (i.e., that commits a "willful" violation) is liable for actual damages, including costs and attorney fees, and potentially punitive damages if the conduct is egregious or outrageous. 11 U.S.C.A. § 362(k)(1); Jones v. Wells Fargo Home Mortg., Inc., 489 B.R. 645 (E.D. La. 2013) (upholding $3.17 million punitive damage award for lender's willful violation of stay). Unless the court grants a creditor relief from the automatic stay, the stay remains in effect until the bankruptcy case is closed or dismissed or until the debtor receives a discharge, whichever occurs first. 11 U.S.C.A. § 362(c)(2).

---

[4] Most federal circuits have held that actions taken in violation of the stay are void *ab initio*. In re Smith Corset Shops, Inc., 696 F.2d 971 (1st Cir.1982); Rexnord Holdings v. Bidermann, 21 F.3d 522 (2d Cir.1994); In re Graves, 33 F.3d 242 (3d Cir.1994); Matthews v. Rosene, 739 F.2d 249 (7th Cir.1984); In re Vierkant, 240 B.R. 317 (8th Cir.1999); Hillis Motors, Inc. v. Hawaii Auto. Dealers' Ass'n, 997 F.2d 581 (9th Cir.1993); Ellis v. Consolidated Diesel Elec. Corp., 894 F.2d 371 (10th Cir.1990); In re Albany Partners, 749 F.2d 670 (11th Cir.1984). The Fifth, Sixth, and Federal Circuits, by contrast, have held that actions taken in violation of the automatic stay are voidable, based on the power of the bankruptcy court to retroactively annul the automatic stay. Picco v. Global Marine Drilling Co., 900 F.2d 846 (5th Cir.1989); Easley v. Pettibone Michigan Corp., 990 F.2d 905 (6th Cir.1993); Bronson v. United States, 46 F.3d 1573 (Fed.Cir.1995).

Suppose that Mortgagee files a judicial foreclosure complaint shortly after Mortgagor files a bankruptcy petition. Mortgagee later obtains relief from stay to proceed with foreclosure. If the initial complaint was void (the majority approach), Mortgagee would have to refile the complaint altogether; by contrast, if the complaint was merely voidable, the court's grant of relief from stay could validate the initial complaint (in which case Mortgagee would not have to refile the complaint).

Relief from the automatic stay. In some circumstances, the interest of the bankruptcy estate or the debtor in having the stay remain in effect does not outweigh a mortgagee's interest in foreclosing its lien. The Code thus provides a mechanism to allow the court, at the request of an affected creditor, to grant relief from the stay to permit that creditor to take action that would otherwise violate section 362(a). Section 362(d) sets forth four standards for relief from the stay that are relevant to mortgagees; each is discussed in turn below.

Relief from stay: Lack of equity and capacity for reorganization. Under section 362(d)(2), a mortgagee can obtain relief from stay if "the debtor does not have an equity" in the collateral and the collateral "is not necessary to an effective reorganization." If these grounds are present, relief from stay is appropriate; neither the debtor nor general creditors would benefit if the mortgaged premises remained property of the estate. [Can you see why?]

In a Chapter 7 case, there is by definition no possibility of effective reorganization; thus, if a Chapter 7 debtor lacks equity in the mortgaged premises, the mortgagee is entitled to relief under section 362(d)(2). See, e.g., In re McFadden, 471 B.R. 136 (Bankr. D. S.C. 2012). We will give further consideration to section 362(d)(2) later in this Chapter, when discussing Chapter 11 and the requirements for confirming a Chapter 11 plan of reorganization.

Relief from stay: Relief for "cause" and lack of "adequate protection." Section 362(d)(1) provides that the court shall grant relief from the stay if a creditor demonstrates "cause, including the lack of adequate protection of an interest in property" held by that creditor. Outside of bankruptcy, a mortgagee could foreclose, sell the mortgaged premises and apply the proceeds to the debt. By preventing such a foreclosure and allowing the trustee or debtor-in-possession to retain and use the collateral during the bankruptcy,[5] the stay imposes upon the mortgagee the risk that its collateral may depreciate during that period. This depreciation could result from market fluctuations in the value of the premises, use of the premises that reduces or exhausts its economic value, or from damage to the premises by an uninsured casualty. Such depreciation could ultimately result in a reduced recovery for the mortgagee.

Section 362(d)(1) allows the mortgagee to obtain "adequate protection" against this depreciation risk. The mortgagee can file a motion requesting that the court terminate the stay and permit the mortgagee to foreclose its lien immediately, or condition the continuation of the stay upon its receiving "adequate protection" of its lien. Once the

---

[5]   The trustee generally may use property of the estate in the ordinary course of business, without the need for prior court approval. 11 U.S.C.A. § 363(c). The debtor-in-possession in a Chapter 11 case, or the debtor in a Chapter 12 or 13 case, also has a comparable power of use. 11 U.S.C.A. §§ 1107(a), 1203, 1303.

mortgagee makes this request, the trustee/debtor-in-possession must either provide mortgagee with adequate protection of its lien or surrender the premises to the mortgagee; if neither occurs, the bankruptcy court must lift the stay and permit the mortgagee to foreclose. The trustee/debtor-in-possession can provide adequate protection by any action that eliminates the risk that the stay will impose a depreciation loss upon the mortgagee. Thus, for example, if the risk arises from the mortgagor's failure to maintain casualty insurance on the premises, the court should lift the stay unless the trustee or debtor-in-possession puts adequate casualty insurance coverage in place. See, e.g., In re Jones, 189 B.R. 13 (Bankr. E.D. Okla. 1995).

Section 361 provides an illustrative list of the ways that the trustee/debtor-in-possession can provide adequate protection. These could include periodic cash payments during the bankruptcy in an amount sufficient to offset expected depreciation in the collateral's value,[6] a "replacement lien" upon other property,[7] or anything else that would provide the secured party with the "indubitable equivalent" of its interest in the collateral. The term "indubitable equivalent" includes the existence of an "equity cushion," meaning any surplus value (or "equity") in the collateral above the balance of the debt. Thus, suppose that Bank holds a mortgage on Debtor's land to secure an unpaid debt of $200,000, and that during Debtor's bankruptcy, the value of the land is expected to depreciate by as much as 20% due to local market conditions. If the value of the mortgaged land is $400,000, even a 20% depreciation of the collateral (e.g., a reduction in value to $320,000) would leave Bank more than fully secured. Under these circumstances, the Bank's "equity cushion" would provide adequate protection for the continuation of the automatic stay, and the trustee/debtor-in-possession would not need to make cash payments or provide a replacement lien on other property.

Should the requirement for "adequate protection" encompass the mortgagee's lost opportunity cost? When a mortgagor files for bankruptcy, it often ceases making payments on its mortgage debt (if it had not already done so prior to bankruptcy). This means that the mortgagee is not collecting the interest that would otherwise have accrued on the mortgage debt. Outside of bankruptcy, the mortgagee could foreclose, sell the premises, and reinvest the sale proceeds in an alternative investment (e.g., a loan to a solvent borrower capable of paying interest). By delaying the mortgagee in pursuing this remedy, the stay imposes a lost opportunity cost upon the mortgagee, and bankruptcy law generally

---

[6]   11 U.S.C.A. § 361(1). Cash payments to the mortgagee would reduce the amount of the mortgagee's claim, thus maintaining the value of the depreciated collateral relative to the unpaid balance of the mortgage debt.

[7]   11 U.S.C.A. § 361(2). For the replacement lien to provide adequate protection, the property subject to the replacement lien must be either unencumbered or the estate must have equity in the property that exceeds the expected depreciation loss in the original collateral.

compounds this burden by disallowing claims for unmatured interest. 11 U.S.C.A. § 502(b)(2).

For some mortgagees, bankruptcy mitigates this burden. Section 506(b) provides that an oversecured creditor (one with an equity cushion) may collect interest on its secured claim, up to (but not beyond) the total value of the collateral. But what about undersecured mortgagees?

UNITED SAVINGS ASSOCIATION OF TEXAS v. TIMBERS OF INWOOD FOREST ASSOCIATES, LTD.

Supreme Court of the United States, 1988
484 U.S. 365, 108 S. Ct. 626, 98 L.Ed.2d 740

JUSTICE SCALIA delivered the opinion of the Court. . . .

I

On June 29, 1982, respondent Timbers of Inwood Forest Associates, Ltd., executed a note in the principal amount of $4,100,000. Petitioner is the holder of the note as well as of a security interest created the same day in an apartment project owned by respondent in Houston, Texas. The security interest included an assignment of rents from the project. On March 4, 1985, respondent filed a voluntary petition under Chapter 11. . . .

On March 18, 1985, petitioner moved for relief from the automatic stay of enforcement of liens triggered by the petition, see 11 U.S.C. § 362(a), on the ground that there was lack of "adequate protection" of its interest within the meaning of 11 U.S.C. § 362(d)(1). At a hearing before the Bankruptcy Court, it was established that respondent owed petitioner $4,366,388.77, and evidence was presented that the value of the collateral was somewhere between $2,650,000 and $4,250,000. The collateral was appreciating in value, but only very slightly. It was therefore undisputed that petitioner was an undersecured creditor. Respondent had agreed to pay petitioner the postpetition rents from the apartment project (covered by the after-acquired property clause in the security agreement), minus operating expenses. Petitioner contended, however, that it was entitled to additional compensation. The Bankruptcy Court agreed and on April 19, 1985, it conditioned continuance of the stay on monthly payments by respondent, at the market rate of 12% per annum, on the estimated amount realizable on foreclosure, $4,250,000—commencing six months after the filing of the bankruptcy petition, to reflect the normal foreclosure delays. The court held that the postpetition rents could be applied to these payments. Respondent appealed to the District Court and petitioner cross-appealed on the amount of the adequate protection payments. The District Court affirmed but the Fifth Circuit en banc reversed.

We granted certiorari to determine whether undersecured creditors are entitled to compensation under 11 U.S.C. § 362(d)(1) for the delay caused by the automatic stay in foreclosing on their collateral.

II

When a bankruptcy petition is filed, § 362(a) of the Bankruptcy Code provides an automatic stay of, among other things, actions taken to realize the value of collateral given by the debtor. The provision of the Code central to the decision of this case is § 362(d), which reads as follows:

> On request of a party in interest and after notice and a hearing, the court shall grant relief from the stay provided under subsection (a) of this section, such as by terminating, annulling, modifying, or conditioning such stay—
>
> (1) for cause, including the lack of adequate protection of an interest in property of such party in interest; or
>
> (2) with respect to a stay of an act against property under subsection (a) of this section, if—
>
>> (A) the debtor does not have an equity in such property; and
>>
>> (B) such property is not necessary to an effective reorganization.

The phrase "adequate protection" in paragraph (1) of the foregoing provision is given further content by § 361 of the Code, which reads in relevant part as follows:

> When adequate protection is required under section 362 . . . of this title of an interest of an entity in property, such adequate protection may be provided by—
>
> (1) requiring the trustee to make a cash payment or periodic cash payments to such entity, to the extent that the stay under section 362 of this title . . . results in a decrease in the value of such entity's interest in such property;
>
> (2) providing to such entity an additional or replacement lien to the extent that such stay . . . results in a decrease in the value of such entity's interest in such property; or
>
> (3) granting such other relief . . . as will result in the realization by such entity of the indubitable equivalent of such entity's interest in such property.

It is common ground that the "interest in property" referred to by § 362(d)(1) includes the right of a secured creditor to have the security applied in payment of the debt upon completion of the reorganization; and that that interest is not adequately protected if the security is depreciating during the term of the stay. Thus, it is agreed that if the apartment project in this case had been declining in value petitioner would have been entitled, under § 362(d)(1), to cash payments or additional security in the amount of the decline, as § 361 describes. The crux of the present dispute is that petitioner asserts, and respondent denies, that the phrase "interest in property" also includes the secured party's right (suspended by the stay) to take immediate possession of the defaulted security, and apply it in payment of the debt. If that right is embraced by the term, it is obviously not adequately protected unless the secured party is reimbursed for the use of the proceeds he is deprived of during the term of the stay.

The term "interest in property" certainly summons up such concepts as "fee ownership," "life estate," "co-ownership," and "security interest" more readily than it does the notion of "right to immediate foreclosure." Nonetheless, viewed in the isolated context of § 362(d)(1), the phrase could reasonably be given the meaning petitioner asserts. Statutory construction, however, is a holistic endeavor. A provision that may seem ambiguous in isolation is often clarified by the remainder of the statutory scheme—because the same terminology is used elsewhere in a context that makes its meaning clear, or because only one of the permissible meanings produces a substantive effect that is compatible with the rest of the law. That is the case here. Section 362(d)(1) is only one of a series of provisions in the Bankruptcy Code dealing with the rights of secured creditors. The language in those other provisions, and the substantive dispositions that they effect, persuade us that the "interest in property" protected by § 362(d)(1) does not include a secured party's right to immediate foreclosure.

Section 506 of the Code defines the amount of the secured creditor's allowed secured claim and the conditions of his receiving postpetition interest. In relevant part it reads as follows:

(a) An allowed claim of a creditor secured by a lien on property in which the estate has an interest ... is a secured claim to the extent of the value of such creditor's interest in the estate's interest in such property, ... and is an unsecured claim to the extent that the value of such creditor's interest ... is less than the amount of such allowed claim. ...

(b) To the extent that an allowed secured claim is secured by property the value of which ... is greater than the amount of such claim, there shall be allowed to the holder of such claim, interest on such claim, and any reasonable fees, costs, or charges provided for under the agreement under which such claim arose.

In subsection (a) of this provision the creditor's "interest in property" obviously means his security interest without taking account of his right to immediate possession of the collateral on default. If the latter were included, the "value of such creditor's interest" would increase, and the proportions of the claim that are secured and unsecured would alter, as the stay continues—since the value of the entitlement to use the collateral from the date of bankruptcy would rise with the passage of time. No one suggests this was intended. The phrase "value of such creditor's interest" in § 506(a) means "the value of the collateral." H.R.Rep. No. 95–595, pp. 181, 356 (1977); see also S.Rep. No. 95–989, p. 68 (1978), U.S. Code Cong. & Admin. News 1978, pp. 5787, 5854, 6141, 6312. We think the phrase "value of such entity's interest" in § 361(1) and (2), when applied to secured creditors, means the same.

Even more important for our purposes than § 506's use of terminology is its substantive effect of denying undersecured creditors postpetition interest on their claims—just as it denies *over* secured creditors postpetition interest to the extent that such interest, when added to the principal amount of the claim, will exceed the value of the collateral. Section 506(b) provides that *"[t]o the extent that* an allowed secured claim is secured by property the value of which . . . is greater than the amount of such claim, there shall be allowed to the holder of such claim, interest on such claim." (Emphasis added.) Since this provision permits postpetition interest to be paid only out of the "security cushion," the undersecured creditor, who has no such cushion, falls within the general rule disallowing postpetition interest. See 11 U.S.C. § 502(b)(2). If the Code had meant to give the undersecured creditor, who is thus denied interest on his *claim,* interest on the value of his *collateral,* surely this is where that disposition would have been set forth, and not obscured within the "adequate protection" provision of § 362(d)(1). Instead of the intricate phraseology set forth above, § 506(b) would simply have said that the secured creditor is entitled to interest "on his allowed claim, or on the value of the property securing his allowed claim, whichever is lesser." Petitioner's interpretation of § 362(d)(1) must be regarded as contradicting the carefully drawn disposition of § 506(b).

Petitioner seeks to avoid this conclusion by characterizing § 506(b) as merely an alternative method for compensating oversecured creditors, which does not imply that no compensation is available to undersecured creditors. This theory of duplicate protection for oversecured creditors is implausible even in the abstract, but even more so in light of the historical principles of bankruptcy law. Section 506(b)'s denial of postpetition interest to undersecured creditors merely codified pre-Code bankruptcy law, in which that denial was part of the conscious allocation of reorganization benefits and losses between undersecured and unsecured creditors. "To allow a secured creditor interest where his security was worth less than the value of his debt was thought to be inequitable to unsecured creditors." *Vanston Bondholders Protective Committee v. Green,* 329 U.S. 156, 164, 67 S.Ct. 237, 240, 91 L.Ed. 162 (1946). It was considered unfair to allow an undersecured creditor to recover interest from the estate's unencumbered assets before unsecured creditors had recovered any principal. See *id.,* at 164, 166, 67 S.Ct. at 240, 241; *Ticonic Nat. Bank v. Sprague,* 303 U.S. 406, 412, 58 S.Ct. 612, 615, 82 L.Ed. 926 (1938). We think it unlikely that § 506(b) codified the pre-Code rule with the intent, not of achieving the principal purpose and function of that rule, but of providing over-secured creditors an alternative method of compensation. Moreover, it is incomprehensible why Congress would want to favor undersecured creditors with interest if they move for it under § 362(d)(1) at the inception of the reorganization process—thereby probably pushing the estate into liquidation—but not if they forbear and seek it only at the completion of the reorganization.

Second, petitioner's interpretation of § 362(d)(1) is structurally inconsistent with 11 U.S.C. § 552. Section 552(a) states the general rule that a prepetition security interest does not reach property acquired by the estate or debtor postpetition. Section 552(b) sets forth an exception, allowing postpetition "proceeds, product, offspring, rents, or profits" of the collateral to be covered only if the security agreement expressly provides for an interest in such property, and the interest has been perfected under "applicable nonbankruptcy law." See, *e.g., In re Casbeer,* 793 F.2d 1436, 1442–1444 (CA5 1986); *In re Johnson,* 62 B.R. 24, 28–30 (CA9 Bkrtcy.App. Panel 1986); cf. *Butner v. United States,* 440 U.S. 48, 54–56, 99 S.Ct. 914, 917–18, 59 L.Ed.2d 136 (1979) (same rule under former Bankruptcy Act). Section 552(b) therefore makes possession of a perfected security interest in postpetition rents or profits from collateral a condition of having them applied to satisfying the claim of the secured creditor ahead of the claims of unsecured creditors. Under petitioner's interpretation, however, the undersecured creditor who lacks such a perfected security interest in effect achieves the same result by demanding the "use value" of his collateral under § 362. It is true that § 506(b) gives the *over* secured creditor, despite lack of compliance with the conditions of § 552, a similar priority over unsecured creditors; but that does not compromise the principle of § 552, since the interest payments come only out of the "cushion" in which the oversecured creditor *does have* a perfected security interest.

Third, petitioner's interpretation of § 362(d)(1) makes nonsense of § 362(d)(2). On petitioner's theory, the undersecured creditor's inability to take immediate possession of his collateral is always "cause" for conditioning the stay (upon the payment of market rate interest) under § 362(d)(1), since there is, within the meaning of that paragraph, "lack of adequate protection of an interest in property." But § 362(d)(2) expressly provides a different standard for relief from a stay "of an act against property," which of course includes taking possession of collateral. It provides that the court shall grant relief "if . . . (A) the debtor does not have an equity in such property [*i.e.,* the creditor is undersecured]; *and* (B) such property is not necessary to an effective reorganization." (Emphasis added.) By applying the "adequate protection of an interest in property" provision of § 362(d)(1) to the alleged "interest" in the earning power of collateral, petitioner creates the strange consequence that § 362 entitles the secured creditor to relief from the stay (1) if he is undersecured (and thus not eligible for interest under § 506(b)), *or* (2) if he is undersecured *and* his collateral "is not necessary to an effective reorganization." This renders § 362(d)(2) a practical nullity and a theoretical absurdity. If § 362(d)(1) is interpreted in this fashion, an undersecured creditor would seek relief under § 362(d)(2) only if his collateral was not depreciating (or he was being compensated for depreciation) and it was receiving market rate interest on his collateral, but nonetheless wanted to foreclose. Petitioner offers no reason why Congress would want to provide relief for such an obstreperous and thoroughly unharmed creditor.

Section 362(d)(2) also belies petitioner's contention that undersecured creditors will face inordinate and extortionate delay if they are denied compensation for interest lost during the stay as part of "adequate protection" under § 362(d)(1). Once the movant under § 362(d)(2) establishes that he is an undersecured creditor, it is the burden of the *debtor* to establish that the collateral at issue is "necessary to an effective reorganization." See § 362(g). What this requires is not merely a showing that if there is conceivably to be an effective reorganization, this property will be needed for it; but that the property is essential for an effective reorganization *that is in prospect.* This means, as many lower courts, including the en banc court in this case, have properly said, that there must be "a reasonable possibility of a successful reorganization within a reasonable time." 808 F.2d, at 370–371, and nn. 12–13, and cases cited therein. The cases are numerous in which § 362(d)(2) relief has been provided within less than a year from the filing of the bankruptcy petition. And while the bankruptcy courts demand less detailed showings during the four months in which the debtor is given the exclusive right to put together a plan, see 11 U.S.C. §§ 1121(b), (c)(2), even within that period lack of any realistic prospect of effective reorganization will require § 362(d)(2) relief.

III

A

Petitioner contends that denying it compensation under § 362(d)(1) is inconsistent with sections of the Code other than those just discussed.

Petitioner principally relies on the phrase "indubitable equivalent" in § 361(3), which also appears in 11 U.S.C. § 1129(b)(2)(A)(iii). Petitioner contends that in the latter context, which sets forth the standards for confirming a reorganization plan, the phrase has developed a well-settled meaning connoting the right of a secured creditor to receive present value of his security—thus requiring interest if the claim is to be paid over time. It is true that under § 1129(b) a secured claimant has a right to receive under a plan the present value of his collateral. This entitlement arises, however, not from the phrase "indubitable equivalent" in § 1129(b)(2)(A)(iii), but from the provision of § 1129(b)(2)(A)(i)(II) that guarantees the secured creditor "deferred cash payments . . . of a value, *as of the effective date of the plan,* of at least the value of such [secured claimant's] interest in the estate's interest in such property." (Emphasis added.) Under this formulation, even though the undersecured creditor's "interest" is regarded (properly) as solely the value of the collateral, he must be rendered payments that assure him that value *as of the effective date of the plan.* In § 361(3), by contrast, the relief pending the stay need only be such *"as will result in the realization* . . . of the indubitable equivalent" of the collateral. (Emphasis added.) It is obvious (since §§ 361 and 362(d)(1) do not entitle the secured creditor to immediate payment of the principal of his collateral) that this "realization" is to "result" not at once, but only upon completion of the reorganization. It is *then* that he must be assured "realization . . . of the indubitable equivalent" of his collateral. To put the point differently: similarity of outcome between § 361(3) and § 1129 would be demanded only if the former read "such other relief . . . as will give such entity, *as of the date of the relief,* the indubitable equivalent of such entity's interest in such property." . . .

Petitioner also contends that the Code embodies a principle that secured creditors do not bear the costs of reorganization. It derives this from the rule that general administrative expenses do not have priority over secured claims. See §§ 506(c), 507(a). But the general principle does not follow from the particular rule. That secured creditors do not bear one kind of reorganization cost hardly means that they bear none of them. The Code rule on administrative expenses merely continues pre-Code law. But it was also pre-Code law that undersecured creditors were not entitled to postpetition interest as compensation for the delay of reorganization. Congress could hardly have understood that the readoption of the rule on administrative expenses would work a change in the rule on postpetition interest, which it also readopted.

Finally, petitioner contends that failure to interpret § 362(d)(1) to require compensation of undersecured creditors for delay will create an inconsistency in the Code in the (admittedly rare) case when the debtor proves solvent. When that occurs, 11 U.S.C. § 726(a)(5) provides that postpetition interest is allowed on unsecured claims. Petitioner contends it would be absurd to allow postpetition interest on unsecured claims but not on the secured portion of undersecured creditors' claims. It would be disingenuous to deny that this is an apparent anomaly, but it will occur so rarely that it is more likely the product of inadvertence than are the blatant inconsistencies petitioner's interpretation would produce. Its inequitable effects, moreover, are entirely avoidable, since an undersecured creditor is entitled to "surrender or waive his security and prove his entire claim as an unsecured one." *United States Nat. Bank v. Chase Nat. Bank,* 331 U.S. 28, 34, 67 S.Ct. 1041, 1044, 91 L.Ed. 1320 (1947). Section 726(a)(5) therefore requires no more than that undersecured creditors receive postpetition interest from a solvent debtor on equal terms with unsecured creditors rather than ahead of them— which, where the debtor is solvent, involves no hardship.

B

Petitioner contends that its interpretation is supported by the legislative history of §§ 361 and 362(d)(1), relying almost entirely on statements that "[s]ecured creditors should not be deprived of the benefit of their bargain." H.R.Rep. No. 95–595, at 339; S.Rep. No. 95–989, at 53, U.S. Code Cong. & Admin. News 1978, pp. 5839, 6295. Such generalizations are inadequate to overcome the plain textual indication in §§ 506 and 362(d)(2) of the Code that Congress did not wish the undersecured creditor to receive interest on his collateral during the term of the stay. If it is at all relevant, the legislative history tends to subvert rather than support petitioner's thesis, since it contains not a hint that § 362(d)(1) entitles the undersecured creditor to postpetition interest. Such a major change in the existing rules would not likely have been made without specific provision in the text of the statute, cf. *Kelly v. Robinson,* 479 U.S. 36, 47, 107 S.Ct. 353, 359–360, 93 L.Ed.2d 216 (1986); it is most improbable that it would have been made without even any mention in the legislative history. . . .

The Fifth Circuit correctly held that the undersecured petitioner is not entitled to interest on its collateral during the stay to assure adequate protection under 11 U.S.C. § 362(d)(1). Petitioner has never sought relief from the stay under § 362(d)(2) or on any ground other than lack of adequate protection. Accordingly, the judgment of the Fifth Circuit is

Affirmed.

NOTES

1. *Understanding the context of* Timbers. In a Chapter 11 case, there is typically a delay between the petition date and the date that the debtor proposes and confirms a reorganization plan. As discussed later in this Chapter, once the debtor begins to perform its confirmed plan of reorganization, the Code requires the debtor to repay any secured claim with

interest. 11 U.S.C.A. § 1129(b)(2)(A)(i). Thus, *Timbers* focuses only whether an undersecured creditor is entitled to interest on the secured portion of its claim during the "pendency of bankruptcy," i.e., the period between the petition date and the effective date of the debtor's confirmed plan.

2.   *The economic premises of* Timbers. Section 506(a) provides that a mortgagee's claim is secured "to the extent of the value of such creditor's interest in the estate's interest in the property." In interpreting this language, the Court defines the phrase "value of such creditor's interest" to mean "the value of the collateral." In other words, if the value of the mortgaged premises is $4 million, then the value of the mortgagee's interest is also $4 million. In light of the stay (and the court's reasoning), is this correct?

While commentators have criticized the *Timbers* decision both for its economic premises and its method of statutory interpretation, see, e.g., Douglas G. Baird, The Elements of Bankruptcy 204 (rev. ed. 1993); David Gray Carlson, Adequate Protection Payments and the Surrender of Cash Collateral in Chapter 11 Reorganizations, 15 Cardozo L. Rev. 1357 (1994), the Court's subsequent bankruptcy decisions have never questioned *Timbers*.

3.   *Nonpayment of taxes as "cause" for relief from stay.* Suppose Bank holds a mortgage on the land of Mortgagor, who has filed a bankruptcy petition. On the petition date, Mortgagor owes Bank $1 million, and the mortgaged land has a value of $800,000. While the land is not depreciating in value, Mortgagor has not paid real estate taxes for the most recent year (totalling $20,000). Can Bank obtain relief from stay based on Mortgagor's nonpayment of taxes? Why or why not? See, e.g., In re Biltwood Properties, LLC, 473 B.R. 70 (Bankr. M.D. Pa. 2012).

Relief from stay under 11 U.S.C.A. § 362(d)(3). Frequently, commercial real estate projects are structured as "single-asset" projects, i.e., the mortgagor is a business entity that owns no other assets and engages in no other business. Many have questioned whether bankruptcy law should provide any protection for such owners. The critique asserts that bankruptcy should facilitate the reorganization of active business concerns—ones that could not realistically negotiate a collective restructuring with hundreds or thousands of individual creditors without judicial intervention. By contrast, the "single asset" real estate project typically involves one debtor (the mortgagor) and few if any creditors other than the mortgagee—calling into question whether reorganization requires the need for an intrusive (and expensive) federal judicial process. The Bankruptcy Code did not exclude owners of "single asset" properties from seeking bankruptcy protection, however, and the owners of single-asset projects frequently sought bankruptcy protection during the real estate downturn of the late 1980s and early 1990s.

This seriously frustrated mortgage lenders, particularly after *Timbers* confirmed that an undersecured mortgagee could not collect interest during the pendency of the bankruptcy. With no obligation to pay such interest, single-asset mortgagors would frequently "drag their feet" in proposing a plan of reorganization, often hoping that market conditions would improve in the interim. Mortgagees complained bitterly about this pattern, arguing that the owner of a "single-asset" project should have a limited amount of time to "fish or cut bait."

In 1994, Congress responded by adding § 362(d)(3), which now provides:

> On request of a party in interest and after notice and a hearing, the court shall grant relief from the stay ... with respect to a stay of an act against single asset real estate[8] under subsection (a), by a creditor whose claim is secured by an interest in such real estate, unless, not later than the date that is 90 days after the entry of the order for relief (or such later date as the court may determine for cause by order entered within that 90-day period) or 30 days after the court determines that the debtor is subject to this paragraph, whichever is later—
>
> > (A) the debtor has filed a plan of reorganization that has a reasonable possibility of being confirmed within a reasonable time; or
> >
> > (B) the debtor has commenced monthly payments that (i) may, in the debtor's sole discretion ... be made from rents or other income generated before, on, or after the date of the commencement of the case by or from the property to each creditor whose claim is secured by such real estate (other than a claim secured by a judgment lien or by an unmatured statutory lien); and (ii) are in an amount equal to interest at the then applicable nondefault contract rate of interest on the value of the creditor's interest in the real estate. ...

As a result, once the mortgagee of single asset real estate moves for relief from stay under § 362(d)(3), the debtor must either (1) propose a feasible reorganization plan within 90 days or (2) begin making monthly payments of interest on the secured portion of the mortgagee's claim (calculated using the nondefault interest rate specified in the mortgage note). If the debtor does neither, the court must grant relief from the stay and permit the mortgagee to foreclose. See, e.g., In re RYYZ, LLC, 490 B.R.

---

[8]   The term "single asset real estate" means "real property constituting a single property or project, other than residential real property with fewer than 4 residential units, which generates substantially all of the gross income of a debtor who is not a family farmer and on which no substantial business is being conducted by a debtor other than the business of operating the real property and activities incidental thereto." 11 U.S.C.A. § 101(51B).

29 (Bankr. E.D.N.Y. 2013); In re RIM Development, LLC, 448 B.R. 280 (Bankr. D. Kan. 2010). Query: Should Congress have required pendency interest payments at the default contract rate, or at the prevailing market rate if that rate would be higher? Why or why not?

When Congress first enacted § 362(d)(3), the term "single asset real estate" included only projects with a value of $4 million or less. Obviously, many actual single-asset projects did not meet this definition, and creditors holding mortgages on these larger single-asset projects could not qualify for protection under § 362(d)(3). In 2005, Congress removed the $4 million limit.

Relief from stay: Bankruptcy abuse. During the 1980s and early 1990s, mortgagees often complained that mortgagors abused the bankruptcy process by filing "serial" bankruptcies—i.e., filing to prevent a foreclosure, confirming a reorganization plan, seeking bankruptcy protection again when the plan failed, and so on repeatedly. In 1994, Congress addressed this concern (whether real or perceived) by enacting section 362(d)(4), which now provides that the court shall grant a motion by a mortgagee for relief from stay:

> if the court finds that the filing of the petition was part of a scheme to delay, hinder, or defraud creditors that involved either (A) transfer of all or part ownership of, or other interest in, such real property without the consent of the [mortgagee] or court approval; or (B) multiple bankruptcy filings affecting such real property.

Further, if the court grants a mortgagee relief under section 362(d)(4), the mortgagee may record the order granting relief in the local real property records, and that recorded order will provide *in rem* relief from stay in any other bankruptcy filed in the ensuing two years.

NOTES

1. *Other serial filings.* Many creditors complained that section 362(d)(4) did not sufficiently address the "serial filing" problem. Thus, in BAPCPA in 2005, Congress also limited the protection of the automatic stay for some "repeat" filers. BAPCPA limits the stay for individual debtors in Chapters 7, 11, or 13 who, on the petition date, had been the debtor in another bankruptcy case that had been pending within the previous year but since dismissed. In such cases, the stay terminates with respect to the debtor 30 days after the filing of the later case, unless the court continues the stay upon motion of the debtor and the debtor establishes that the new filing was in "good faith as to the creditors to be stayed." 11 U.S.C.A. § 362(c)(3)(B). For cases in which the debtor failed to establish the requisite "good faith," see, e.g., In re Cannon, 375 B.R. 908 (Bankr. E.D. Mo. 2007); In re Kurtzahn, 337 B.R. 356 (Bankr. D. Minn. 2006); In re Collins, 335 B.R. 646 (Bankr. S.D. Tex. 2005).

2. *Relief from stay—procedural considerations.* If a secured creditor files a motion seeking relief from the stay, the court must act upon the motion within thirty days; if not, the moving party automatically receives the requested relief. 11 U.S.C.A. § 362(e)(1). During this thirty-day period, the court conducts a preliminary hearing, after which it either (a) enters an order granting or denying the requested relief, or (b) continues the stay temporarily pending a later final hearing and determination. If the court continues the stay pending a final hearing, the court must conclude that final hearing within thirty days of the preliminary hearing, unless the court extends that thirty-day period with the consent of the parties or based upon "compelling circumstances." *Id.*

The moving party (usually the secured creditor) bears the burden of proof on the issue of the debtor's equity in the collateral (and thus on the value of the collateral). 11 U.S.C.A. § 362(g)(1). The party opposing relief (typically the trustee/debtor-in-possession) bears the burden of proof on all other issues. 11 U.S.C.A. § 362(g)(2). In exceptional circumstances, the court can order relief from the stay without notice, if the party seeking relief would suffer "irreparable damage" by the delay occasioned by notice and a hearing. 11 U.S.C.A. § 362(f).

In 2005, Congress amended section 362 to place an additional constraint upon an individual debtor's ability to delay a final determination of a secured party's motion for relief from stay. In the Chapter 7, 11, or 13 case of an individual debtor, the stay terminates sixty days after the secured party's motion, unless the court renders a final determination of the motion within that sixty-day period or the sixty-day period is extended by the secured party's consent or by the court—but the court may only extend this sixty-day period "for such *specific* time as the court finds is required for good cause," and the court must make specific factual findings justifying the extension. 11 U.S.C.A. § 362(e)(2) (emphasis added).

3. THE TRUSTEE'S AVOIDING POWERS

Because the trustee represents the interests of the bankrupt's unsecured creditors, the trustee's primary goal is to maximize the size of the estate available to satisfy those claims. The trustee will thus carefully investigate the debtor's financial affairs to discover any legal basis to challenge the validity of a creditor's claim or the validity of liens against property of the estate. The Code provides the trustee with an impressive arsenal of weapons in this effort. The most basic is 11 U.S.C.A. § 558, which gives the trustee "the benefit of any defense available to the debtor" against a creditor. Thus, to the extent that a debtor could have invalidated a mortgage based on fraud, usury, lack of capacity, or other grounds, so too can the trustee.

The Code also endows the trustee with a series of *avoiding powers*— causes of action that allow the bankruptcy trustee (or the debtor-in-possession in reorganization proceedings)[9] to invalidate (or "avoid") certain dispositions of property by the debtor or obligations incurred by the debtor during some period of time prior to bankruptcy or during bankruptcy. This section discusses the avoiding powers of greatest potential consequence to mortgagees.

The "strong-arm" power. Bankruptcy Code section § 544(a) provides that the trustee has the status, as of the petition date, of a judgment lien creditor as to the debtor's personal property and a bona fide purchaser as to the debtor's land (other than fixtures). 11 U.S.C.A. § 544(a)(1) (personalty), § 544(a)(3) (land other than fixtures). Outside of bankruptcy, a bona fide purchaser of land would take that land free of an unrecorded mortgage. Section 544(a)(3) thus permits the trustee to invalidate (or "avoid") any mortgage against property of the estate if, on the petition date, that mortgage was not recorded under the applicable state recording statute. Thus, courts have permitted the trustee/debtor in possession to avoid a mortgage in cases where the mortgagee:

- failed to record until after the bankruptcy petition. See, e.g., In re Garrido Jimenez, 370 B.R. 878 (1st Cir. B.A.P. 2007). [Note that the mortgagee's action of recording the mortgage after the petition date would also constitute a violation of the automatic stay. 11 U.S.C.A. § 362(a)(4).]

- failed to record altogether. See, e.g., In re Sullivan, 387 B.R. 353 (1st Cir. B.A.P. 2008).

- tried to record the mortgage, but did not properly do so within the chain of title. See, e.g., In re Ramos, 493 B.R. 355 (Bankr. D. P.R. 2013); In re Thulis, 474 B.R. 668 (Bankr. W.D. Wis. 2012).

- filed the mortgage for recording in the wrong county. See, e.g., In re Morgan, 449 B.R. 821 (Bankr. N.D. Ga. 2010).

- erroneously recorded a release of the mortgage prior to bankruptcy. See, e.g., In re Mammola, 474 B.R. 23 (Bankr. D. Mass. 2012).

---

[9] In Chapter 11 and Chapter 12 cases, the debtor in possession receives the powers of a trustee, including the avoiding powers. 11 U.S.C.A. §§ 1107(a), 1203. The Code does not expressly delegate the avoiding powers to a Chapter 13 debtor, 11 U.S.C.A. § 1303, but the legislative history indicates that section 1303 "does not imply that the debtor does not also possess other powers concurrently with the trustee," 124 Cong. Rec. 32,409 (floor statement of Rep. Edwards). As a result, numerous courts have concluded that a Chapter 13 debtor can exercise the avoiding powers. See, e.g., In re Dickson, 427 B.R. 399 (Bankr.6th Cir.2010); In re Fitzgerald, 237 B.R. 252 (Bankr.D.Conn.1999); In re Hernandez, 150 B.R. 29 (Bankr.S.D.Tex.1993). The trend in recent decisions, however, suggests a growing doubt that a Chapter 13 debtor can exercise the avoiding powers. See, e.g., In re Stangel, 219 F.3d 498 (5th Cir. 2000); In re Barbee, 461 B.R. 711 (6th Cir. B.A.P. 2011); In re Hansen, 332 B.R. 8 (10th Cir. B.A.P. 2005); In re Merrifield, 214 B.R. 362 (8th Cir. B.A.P. 1997).

Under section 544(a)(3), the trustee's knowledge is irrelevant; the strong-arm power bestows on the trustee the status of a bona fide purchaser *even if* the trustee has actual knowledge of the unrecorded mortgage.

Avoidance of the mortgage typically allows the trustee to liquidate the mortgaged property and use the proceeds to pay administrative expenses and unsecured creditors. While the debtor's underlying obligation to the mortgagee remains valid, the mortgagee's claim is treated as unsecured, which will significantly reduce the mortgagee's recovery.

NOTES

1. *Defects in the execution or acknowledgment of mortgages.* The trustee/debtor-in-possession often invokes the strong-arm power in cases involving some defect in the execution of a mortgage. In these cases, the result turns on whether the defect defeats the ability of the mortgage to provide constructive notice to subsequent purchasers under applicable state law.[10] Thus, similar defects can produce different results in different states. Compare In re Bunn, 578 F.3d 487 (6th Cir. 2009) (under Ohio law, mortgage was sufficient to provide constructive notice even it described the property using only a street address rather than a legal description) with In re Hiseman, 330 B.R. 251 (Bankr. D. Utah 2005) (contrary result under Utah law).

During the recent real estate crisis, trustees have frequently attempted to use the strong-arm power to avoid mortgages that were improperly acknowledged. Again, whether the trustee may avoid such a mortgage depends upon whether state law treats it as sufficient to provide constructive notice to subsequent purchasers. If not, the trustee may use the strong-arm power to invalidate the mortgage. See, e.g., In re Kelley, 498 B.R. 342 (1st Cir. B.A.P. 2013); In re Kebe, 469 B.R. 778 (Bankr. S.D. Ohio 2012). Does it make sense to allow the trustee/debtor-in-possession to avoid such a

---

[10] See, e.g., In re McCormick, 669 F.3d 177 (4th Cir.2012) (where mortgage covered two parcels but only described one parcel properly, trustee may avoid mortgage as to improperly described parcel); In re Gilmore, 468 B.R. 896 (Bankr.W.D.Mo.2012) (trustee may avoid lien of lender that did not record original executed deed of trust; affidavit recorded by lender did not give constructive notice to subsequent purchasers); In re Berg, 387 B.R. 524 (Bankr.N.D.Ill.2008) (trustee may avoid mortgage that failed to indicate principal amount of the debt or the applicable interest rate); In re Skumpija, 494 B.R. 822 (Bankr.E.D.N.C.2013) (trustee may avoid deed of trust that failed properly to identify the obligation it secured).

Because the trustee's strong-arm power depends upon underlying state law, similar sets of facts can produce different results from state to state. For example, in Bank of America v. Greene, 465 B.R. 789 (E.D.Tenn.2012), the register of deeds accepted a mortgage for recording and assigned it book and page numbers, but subsequently and mistakenly voided the mortgage and removed it from the records (assigning a different unrelated document to the same book and page number). Based on its understanding of Tennessee law, the court ruled that the mortgage was not recorded within the chain of title and thus could be avoided by the trustee. *Greene,* 465 B.R. at 800–01. By contrast, the Florida courts have ruled on similar facts that a mortgage improperly removed from the records by the recording official nevertheless gives constructive notice to subsequent purchasers. Mayfield v. First City Bank of Florida, 95 So.3d 398 (Fla.Ct.App.2012).

mortgage? A defective acknowledgment does not defeat the validity of the mortgage between the mortgagor and the mortgagee; does it affect the ability of searchers to locate the mortgage in the land records?

2.   *Preservation of an avoided mortgage lien for the benefit of the estate.* Suppose that First Bank takes a mortgage on Debtor's land but fails to record it. Debtor later grants a mortgage to Second Bank, which properly records. Debtor subsequently files a Chapter 7 case; on the petition date, Debtor owes each bank $100,000 but the mortgaged land is worth only $150,000. In this circumstance, Second Bank might try to argue that First Bank's failure to record the mortgage should result in Second Bank being promoted to first priority.

Under 11 U.S.C.A. § 551, however, the avoided transfer—i.e., the lien created by the unrecorded First Bank mortgage—is "preserved for the benefit of the estate." Section 551 thus allows the trustee to assert the lien of First Bank as if that lien did still have priority over Second Bank. The trustee would thus be entitled to receive the first $100,000 of sale proceeds from the land—and could devote that sum to payment of administrative expenses and unsecured claims—before the remaining proceeds could be distributed to Second Bank on account of its junior lien. See, e.g., In re Guido, 344 B.R. 193 (Bankr. D. Mass. 2006).

The power to avoid fraudulent transfers. Sometimes, debtors deliberately frustrate the collection efforts of their creditors by giving property (or transferring it at bargain prices) to friends, relatives, or third parties. The common law has always allowed an injured creditor to invalidate an intentionally fraudulent transfer, and both the Uniform Fraudulent Conveyance Act (UFCA) and the Uniform Fraudulent Transfer Act (UFTA) contain provisions that permit creditors to avoid transfers made by a debtor with the intent to hinder, delay, or defraud creditors. UFCA § 7; UFTA § 4(a)(1). Because such transfers also disadvantage an insolvent debtor's unsecured creditors, the Code permits the trustee to avoid intentionally fraudulent transfers made by the debtor within the two-year period prior to bankruptcy. 11 U.S.C.A. § 548(a)(1)(A).

More commonly, debtors make transfers by gift or for insufficient consideration without a specific intent to hinder, delay, or defraud creditors. Because these transfers nevertheless have the same impact as intentionally fraudulent transfers, the common law has long deemed such transfers by *insolvent* debtors to be *constructively* fraudulent transfers. Both the UFCA and the UFTA allow creditors to avoid constructively fraudulent transfers. UFCA § 4; UFTA § 4(a)(2), The Bankruptcy Code provides a similar rule in section 548(a)(1)(B), which permits the trustee to avoid any transfer of the debtor's property if the transfer was made within two years prior to the debtor's bankruptcy, the debtor received less than a "reasonably equivalent value" in exchange, and the debtor was insolvent at the time the transfer was made or was rendered insolvent as a result. 11 U.S.C.A. § 548(a)(1)(B)(i), (ii)(I). The trustee can recover the property from the transferee, even if the transferee acted in good faith and without knowledge that the transfer was fraudulent.[11]

For the most part, the trustee's power to avoid constructively fraudulent transfers does not present a substantial threat to the typical mortgagee. The trustee cannot avoid pre-petition installment payments by the mortgagor as constructively fraudulent transfers, even if the debtor was insolvent, because the debtor received equivalent value for those payments—*pro tanto* satisfaction of the debt. Likewise, because section 548 defines "value" to include "securing . . . [an] antecedent debt," 11 U.S.C.A. § 548(d)(2)(A), the trustee cannot use section 548 to avoid a mortgage simply because the debtor granted it to secure what previously had been an unsecured debt. If a debtor granted a mortgage to secure the debt of an unrelated borrower, however, the debtor would not have received "value," and thus the trustee could avoid the mortgage as a fraudulent transfer if the debtor was insolvent or was rendered insolvent by granting the mortgage. See, e.g., In re Scheffler, 471 B.R. 464 (Bankr. E.D. Pa. 2012).[12]

The primary context in which section 548 has affected mortgagees involves attempts by trustees/debtors-in-possession to invalidate pre-bankruptcy foreclosure sales. For example, suppose that Bank foreclosed on its mortgage against Mortgagor's land and conducted a public sale at which Bank purchased the land for a full credit bid of $100,000. Three months later, Bank contracted to sell the land to a third person for $180,000, but before that sale can close, Mortgagor files a bankruptcy petition. One might argue that this foreclosure sale should be viewed as constructively fraudulent, at least if the $180,000 resale price accurately reflected the land's fair market value at the time of the foreclosure sale (in which case Mortgagor received $80,000 less than equivalent value for its interest in the land at foreclosure). In this instance, the foreclosure

---

[11] 11 U.S.C.A. §§ 548(a)(1), 550(a)(1). Because this result may be harsh to the transferee, the Code provides some protection; if the transferee purchased the property in good faith, it receives a lien on the property to the extent of the amount paid to the debtor. 11 U.S.C.A. § 548(c). In addition, if the initial transferee has already conveyed the property to a third party, the trustee cannot recover the property from the third party if it took the property for value, in good faith, and without knowledge of the fact that the initial transfer from the debtor was fraudulent. 11 U.S.C.A. § 550(b).

[12] In determining whether a debtor is insolvent, the court must take into account both the debtor's fixed and contingent liabilities. In valuing the debtor's contingent liabilities, the court must consider the probability that the contingency will occur. See Covey v. Commercial Nat'l Bank of Peoria, 960 F.2d 657 (7th Cir.1992). Thus, if the debtor grants a mortgage to secure the obligation of a third party, valuation of this contingent liability requires the court to consider the likelihood of default by the third party.

sale would have diminished Mortgagor's bankruptcy estate to the detriment of other creditors.

For many years, the weight of authority held that the trustee/debtor-in-possession could invalidate a pre-bankruptcy foreclosure sale as constructively fraudulent if the foreclosure sale price was less than 70% of the property's fair market value. The leading case for this view was Durrett v. Washington Nat'l Ins. Co., 621 F.2d 201 (5th Cir. 1980). While *Durrett* was widely followed, reaction from the real estate community was hostile. Opponents argued that because *Durrett* created a long period of uncertainty about the validity of title purchased at a foreclosure sale, it "naturally inhibit[ed] a purchaser other than the mortgagee from purchasing at foreclosure," Abramson v. Lakewood Bank & Trust Co., 647 F.2d 547, 549 (5th Cir. 1981) (Clark, J., dissenting), and in turn resulted in reduced sale prices and increased likelihood of deficiency judgments.[13]

In 1994, the United States Supreme Court rejected *Durrett* and its progeny in BFP v. Resolution Trust Corp., 511 U.S. 531, 114 S.Ct. 1757, 128 L.Ed.2d 554 (1994). In a 5–4 decision, the Court held that "a fair and proper price, or a 'reasonably equivalent value,' for foreclosed property, is the price in fact received at the foreclosure sale, so long as all the requirements of the State's foreclosure law have been complied with." *BFP*, 511 U.S. at 544. As a result, section 548 no longer provides a basis to invalidate a noncollusive foreclosure sale based on inadequacy of the price, so long as all other requirements of state foreclosure law have been satisfied.

NOTES

1.　*The impact of* BFP *on installment land contract forfeitures.* Does *BFP* preclude a determination that forfeiture under an installment land contract may be a fraudulent conveyance under section 548? For example, suppose Vendee defaults under an installment land contract on which Vendee owes a balance of $50,000, and Vendee's interest is forfeited. At the time, the land in question is worth $100,000. Six months later, Vendee files a Chapter 7 bankruptcy petition. Can the trustee set aside the contract termination as constructively fraudulent to Vendee's creditors? Some courts have held that *BFP* does not preclude the trustee from avoiding an installment contract forfeiture. See, e.g., In re Houston, 385 B.R. 268 (Bankr. N.D. Iowa 2008). Other courts have held that *BFP* prevents the trustee from setting aside contract forfeitures, however, concluding that "absent a debt so small as to shock the conscience, the cancellation of the remaining debt . . . through a

---

[13] For comprehensive criticism of *Durrett*, see, e.g., Zinman, Houle & Weiss, Fraudulent Transfers According to Alden, Gross & Borowitz: A Tale of Two Circuits, 39 Bus. Law. 977 (1984); Baird & Jackson, Fraudulent Conveyance Law and Its Proper Domain, 38 Vand. L. Rev. 829 (1985); Zinman, Noncollusive Regularly Conducted Foreclosure Sales: Involuntary Nonfraudulent Transfers, 9 Cardozo L. Rev. 581 (1987); Note, Nonjudicial Foreclosure Under Deed of Trust May Be a Fraudulent Transfer of Bankrupt's Property, 47 Mo. L. Rev. 345 (1982).

forfeiture proceeding regularly conducted pursuant to state law is 'reasonably equivalent value' for the debtor's interest in the property." See, e.g., In re Vermillion, 176 B.R. 563 (Bankr. D. Or. 1994); In re Butler, 552 N.W.2d 226 (Minn. 1996). Note that *BFP* involved a public auction foreclosure sale (which ostensibly serves as an opportunity for public valuation of the land). Should *BFP* apply to an installment contract forfeiture, where no such public valuation takes place?

2. *The impact of* BFP *on strict foreclosure.* One bankruptcy court in Connecticut held that "the value received by the debtors for their transfer of their interest in the property [pursuant to strict foreclosure] ... is the 'reasonably equivalent value' of the interest transferred." In re Talbot, 254 B.R. 63, 71 (Bankr. D. Conn. 2000). The court noted that "Connecticut strict foreclosure law provides a debtor with sufficient procedural safeguards to render it analogous to the foreclosure sale context of *BFP*." *Talbot*, 254 B.R. at 70. By contrast, another Connecticut bankruptcy court concluded that the mortgagee's compliance with strict foreclosure procedures did not conclusively establish that the mortgagor received "reasonably equivalent value." In re Fitzgerald, 255 B.R. 807 (Bankr. D. Conn. 2000). Which approach is more sensible? What sort of "procedural safeguards" are needed to make the context sufficiently analogous to *BFP*?

3. *The impact of* BFP *on deeds in lieu of foreclosure.* Suppose that Mortgagor executes and delivers to Bank a deed in lieu of foreclosure following default. Six months later, Mortgagor files a Chapter 7 case. Does BFP preclude the trustee from setting aside the deed in lieu of foreclosure as constructively fraudulent? See, e.g., In re 4100 West Grand LLC, 481 B.R. 444 (Bankr. N.D. Ill. 2012). Why or why not?

4. *Avoidance of fraudulent transfers under section 544(b).* The Code allows the trustee to set aside any transfer of the debtor's property that an actual unsecured creditor could have avoided under state law. 11 U.S.C.A. § 544(b)(1). As discussed earlier, state fraudulent transfer laws (typically either the UFTA or the UFCA) permit a creditor harmed by an intentionally or constructively fraudulent transfer to invalidate that transfer. Thus, if the trustee can identify an actual unsecured creditor of the debtor that is capable of asserting a state law fraudulent transfer claim, the trustee can use section 544(b) to assert that claim on behalf of the bankruptcy estate.

After *BFP*, the applicable standards for a fraudulent transfer are essentially the same under both section 548(a) and most applicable state fraudulent transfer laws. Thus, the trustee will use section 544(b) to attack a fraudulent transfer only if it occurred more than two years prior to bankruptcy (and thus outside section 548's two-year reach-back period). State law may provide a longer reach-back period for fraudulent transfers. For example, the UFTA generally allows creditors a period of four years in which to avoid a fraudulent transfer. UFTA § 9(a), (b).

The power to avoid preferential transfers. Suppose Debtor has only $1,000 in assets but has two unsecured creditors, X and Y, to whom Debtor owes $1,000 each. X reduces its claim to judgment and levies upon the $1,000 in assets shortly before Debtor files for bankruptcy. In this situation, X receives payment in full, and Y gets nothing; X has received a "preferential" payment relative to Y. Outside of bankruptcy, commercial law does not invalidate preferential transfers, but leaves creditors to their own collection efforts—"the race goes to the swiftest." Bankruptcy law cares about such transfers, however, because it seeks to discourage creditors from engaging in "eve-of-bankruptcy" collection activities and thus triggering the "race to the courthouse" that bankruptcy seeks to avoid or mitigate. Thus, section 547 allows the trustee or debtor-in-possession to avoid any voluntary or involuntary transfer of an interest in the debtor's property if the transfer:

- was made to a creditor or benefitted a creditor, 11 U.S.C.A. § 547(b)(1);

- was made on account of an antecedent debt, 11 U.S.C.A. § 547(b)(2);

- took place while the debtor was insolvent, 11 U.S.C.A. § 547(b)(3);[14]

- took place during the ninety-day period prior to bankruptcy (or within one year prior to bankruptcy if the benefitted creditor was an "insider"), 11 U.S.C.A. § 547(b)(4); and

- made the creditor better off than it would have been if the transfer had not occurred and the creditor had instead received payment on the debt only through a Chapter 7 liquidation of the debtor's assets, 11 U.S.C.A. § 547(b)(5).

For mortgagees, section 547 presents a risk in four discrete contexts: (1) payments by the mortgagor on the debt during the preference period; (2) mortgages taken during the preference period to secure previously unsecured debt; (3) delayed recording of the mortgage during the preference period; and (4) foreclosure sales during the preference period.

Preferences—payments on the mortgage debt. Suppose that on June 1, Debtor repays Bank the full $50,000 balance of an outstanding mortgage loan covering Blackacre. On July 1, Debtor files for bankruptcy. If Blackacre has a fair market value of $50,000 or more, Debtor's repayment to Bank was not a preference, because it did not improve Bank's position vis-à-vis other creditors. If the Debtor had not made the payment and had instead filed a Chapter 7 case, Bank (as a fully secured creditor) would

---

[14] 11 U.S.C.A. § 547(b)(3). The Code applies a "balance sheet" test—the debtor is insolvent if the sum of its debts exceed the value of its assets. 11 U.S.C.A. § 101(32). Section 547(f) provides that in any preference action, the debtor is presumed to have been insolvent during the ninety days prior to bankruptcy. 11 U.S.C.A. § 547(f).

have received full payment anyway. See, e.g., In re EDC, Inc. 930 F.2d 1275 (7th Cir. 1991); Braniff Airways, Inc. v. Exxon Co., U.S.A., 814 F.2d 1030 (5th Cir. 1987). By contrast, if Blackacre has a fair market value of only $30,000, then the trustee can avoid the $50,000 payment to Bank as a preference. In a Chapter 7 liquidation, Bank would have received less than $50,000; its $50,000 claim would have been bifurcated into a $30,000 secured claim (which would have been paid in full) and a $20,000 unsecured claim (on which Bank would have received only a pro rata dividend). The trustee could thus recover the entire $50,000 payment from Bank.

What about the more typical situation in which the debtor makes regular monthly payments of principal and interest? Can the trustee successfully recover any installment payments made by the debtor during the 90 days prior to bankruptcy as preferences? If the payments were in the scheduled amount and were made in a timely fashion, the answer is no. The Code provides an exception from the preference rule for payments made by the debtor if the debt was "incurred by the debtor in the ordinary course of business or financial affairs of the debtor and the transferee" and the payments were made "in the ordinary course of business or financial affairs of the debtor and the transferee" or "according to ordinary business terms." 11 U.S.C.A. § 547(c)(2).[15]

Preferences—mortgage to secure previously unsecured debt. Section 547 permits the trustee to avoid a mortgage granted by the mortgagor within the preference period if the mortgage secures a pre-existing and previously unsecured debt. For example, suppose Debtor is in default in repayment of a $50,000 unsecured debt owed to Bank. Rather than seeking a judgment against Debtor, Bank agrees to forbear when Debtor executes a mortgage covering Blackacre (which is unencumbered and has a value exceeding $50,000). Two weeks later, Debtor files a bankruptcy petition. In this example, the mortgage (which is a transfer of an interest in Debtor's property) improved Bank's position vis-à-vis other creditors by securing an otherwise unsecured claim (on which Bank would have received only a pro rata dividend in a Chapter 7 liquidation). Thus, the trustee can avoid Bank's mortgage lien as a preference, leaving Bank with an entirely unsecured claim.

Preferences—the late-recorded mortgage. There is often a delay between the execution of a mortgage and its recording. In ideal

---

[15] Prior to 1984, this exception provided that payments could not qualify as "ordinary course" unless they were made within forty-five days of the date the debt arose. As a result, payments on long-term debt could not qualify for "ordinary course" protection. In 1984, Congress removed the forty-five-day limitation, which triggered a debate in the courts as to whether payments on long-term debt could qualify for protection as ordinary-course transfers. This debate was ultimately resolved in Union Bank v. Wolas, 502 U.S. 151 (1991), in which the Supreme Court held that payments on long-term debt can qualify for protection under section 547(c)(2).

circumstances, this delay is a matter of mere minutes or hours; however, due to inadvertence or neglect, the delay could extend for a greater period. During this delay, the mortgagee has a "secret" lien and third parties are at risk of transacting with the mortgagor in ignorance of the as-yet unrecorded mortgage. Bankruptcy policy discourages such secret liens, and this policy is reflected in the "timing" rule by which Section 547 establishes when a transfer is deemed to occur for purposes of the preference rule. Section 547(e)(2) provides that a "transfer" is made for the purposes of section 547:

> (A) at the time such transfer takes effect between the transferor and the transferee, if such transfer is perfected at, or within 30 days after, such time . . . ;

> (B) at the time such transfer is perfected, if such transfer is perfected after such 30 days; or

> (C) immediately before the date of the filing of the petition, if such transfer is not perfected at the later of—

>> (i) the commencement of the case; or

>> (ii) 30 days after such transfer takes effect between the transferor and the transferee.

A transfer of real property is "perfected" when "a bona fide purchaser of such property from the debtor against whom applicable law permits the transfer to be perfected cannot acquire an interest that is superior to the interest of the transferee." 11 U.S.C.A. § 547(e)(1)(A). Thus, under any type of state recording act, a mortgage is "perfected" at the moment it is recorded.

This timing rule places a premium upon timely recording of a mortgage in the event of the mortgagor's bankruptcy. For example, suppose that on July 1, Debtor borrows $100,000 from Bank and grants Bank a mortgage on Blackacre. On September 1, Debtor files a bankruptcy petition. If Bank recorded its mortgage on or before July 31 (within thirty days after its execution), the mortgage is deemed to have been granted on July 1. 11 U.S.C.A. § 547(e)(2)(A). Thus, Debtor will not have granted the mortgage on account of an antecedent debt and the trustee cannot set aside the mortgage as a preference. By contrast, if the Bank did not record its mortgage until August 10, section 547(e)(2)(B) will deem the mortgage to have been granted on August 10 (even though the mortgage debt was actually incurred on July 1). As a result, Debtor will be deemed to have granted the mortgage on account of an antecedent debt and the trustee could avoid the mortgage as a preference (assuming it satisfies all of the other requirements of section 547(b)). See, e.g., In re Lee, 530 F.3d 458 (6th Cir. 2008) (mortgage recorded 72 days after loan proceeds disbursed); In re Panzarino, 469 B.R. 286 (Bankr. N.D. Ill. 2012) (mortgage executed four years prior to preference period but only recorded during 90 days prior to bankruptcy); In re Norsworthy, 373 B.R. 194 (Bankr. N.D. Ga. 2007) (mortgage recorded more than 30 days after its execution). As a matter of policy, why allow the trustee to set aside a late-recorded mortgage as a preference? See, e.g., Nelson, Whitman, Burkhart & Freyermuth, Real Estate Finance Law § 8.16 (6th ed. 2014).

Preferences—pre-bankruptcy foreclosure sales. As discussed earlier, *BFP* diminished the trustee's ability to avoid a pre-bankruptcy foreclosure sale as constructively fraudulent based on an inadequate sale price. After *BFP*, however, a number of courts have allowed the trustee to set aside pre-bankruptcy foreclosure sales at inadequate prices as preferences, at least where the mortgagee is the foreclosure sale purchaser. To appreciate the problem, consider the facts in In re Villareal, 413 B.R. 633 (Bankr. S.D. Tex. 2009). The mortgagee foreclosed following the debtor's default and purchased the premises for a credit bid of $70,000, even though the mortgagee's own appraiser had valued the premises at *$4.02 million!* Less than two months later, the debtor filed a Chapter 13 petition and sought to set aside the foreclosure sale as a preference. The debtor argued that by virtue of the foreclosure sale, the mortgagee received a transfer of the debtor's property than enabled the mortgagee to receive land worth $4.02 million—more than it would have received in a Chapter 7 liquidation, in which it would have received (at most) only the amount of the unpaid debt. The foreclosure sale in *Villareal* technically meets each element of section 547(b); should the trustee be able to use section 547 to set aside the sale when the *BFP* case would not allow the sale to be set aside under section 548?

IN RE EHRING

United States Court of Appeals, Ninth Circuit, 1990
900 F.2d 184

FARRIS, CIRCUIT JUDGE. . . . This case raises an issue of first impression:

Did the purchase of real property security at a noncollusive, nonjudicial foreclosure sale by the secured creditor, within 90 days prior to the bankruptcy petition, constitute an avoidable preference under 11 U.S.C. § 547(b)?

A. For purposes of calculating the 90 day preference period, what was the transfer and when did it occur?

B. If the transfer occurred within the 90 day period before the petition, did the creditor receive more than would have been received in a Chapter 7 liquidation?. . .

The facts are uncontested. Ehring borrowed $145,000 from Coast Home Loans, Inc. and executed a promissory note in that amount to

Coast. The Note was secured by a second deed of trust on real property dated March 2, 1983. Ehring was the Trustor and Coast was the Beneficiary. Coast assigned its trust deed to Western Community Moneycenter, which recorded on March 15, 1983.

Ehring defaulted on his note and Western caused a trustee's sale to be held pursuant to the power of sale provision in the deed of trust. A valid trustee's (nonjudicial foreclosure) sale was held on February 22, 1985 and Western purchased the property for the amount of Ehring's indebtedness in the second deed of trust—$199,746.41. Western recorded its purchase on March 21, 1985.

On April 18, 1985 Western entered into a purchase contract with the Millers to sell the property for $390,000. There was an escrow closing in July, 1985.

On May 21, 1985, Ehring filed a bankruptcy petition under Chapter 11. Both the foreclosure sale and the resale to the Millers occurred within 90 days of that petition. Ehring commenced an action against Western under section 547 of the Bankruptcy Code, seeking the return of $110,000 as an avoidable preference transfer. The $110,000 represents the difference between the $390,000 sale price to the Millers and the amount due under the first and second deeds of trust and associated costs of foreclosure. Ehring does not challenge the validity of the sale.

The bankruptcy court granted summary judgment for Western, finding no preference in either the trustee's sale or the resale to the Millers. The BAP affirmed and Ehring appeals. . . .

The first question is what constitutes a transfer for purposes of § 547(b). If the relevant transfer occurred when Western recorded its deed of trust, then the transfer occurred before the 90 day period and the transfer is not avoidable. However, if a transfer occurred at the time of the foreclosure sale or at the recording of the foreclosure sale, then the transfer would be within the 90 day period and the court would have to determine if Western received more than it should have under § 547(b)(5). . . .

Whether a particular occurrence is a transfer for purposes of bankruptcy is a matter of federal characterization. *McKenzie v. Irving Trust Co.*, 323 U.S. 365, 369–70, 65 S.Ct. 405, 407–08, 89 L.Ed. 305 (1945). When a transfer occurs is defined by state law as directed by the Code. See id.; *Evans v. Valley West Shopping Center, Inc.*, 567 F.2d 358, 360 (9th Cir.1978) (per curiam); 11 U.S.C. § 547(e).

Western argues that a nonjudicial foreclosure sale is not a transfer, citing *In re Madrid*, 725 F.2d 1197 (9th Cir.1984). . . .

However, the Code definition of "transfer" has since been amended to explicitly include "foreclosure of the debtor's equity of redemption." 11

U.S.C. § 101(50). . . . See *In re Verna*, 58 B.R. 246 (Bankr.C.D.Cal.1986) (foreclosure is a transfer for purposes of fraudulent conveyances (11 U.S.C. § 548)); *In re Christian*, 48 B.R. 833 (D.Colo.1985); 5 Collier on Bankruptcy ¶ 1300.12(32) (15th ed. 1989) ("This amendment [101(50)] . . . will make it difficult if not impossible to conclude, as had other courts before the amendment, that a foreclosure sale does not involve the transfer of any interest of the debtor."); 2 J. White & R. Summers, Uniform Commercial Code § 25–7, at 449 (3rd ed. 1988) ("it is hard to escape the conclusion that there is a 'transfer of an interest of a debtor in property' at the time of the foreclosure").

Section 547(e) more specifically defines when a "transfer" occurs for purposes of measuring if it is within the 90 day period. Section 547(e)(2) states that there is a transfer made "(A) at the time such transfer takes effect between the transferor and the transferee, if such transfer is perfected at, or within 10 days after, such time," or "(B) at the time such transfer is perfected, if such transfer is perfected after such 10 days," or (C) just before the filing of the petition, if neither (A) or (B) is satisfied. Under California law, a transfer of real property, for purposes of § 547(e), is perfected at the time of recording. See Cal.Civ.Code §§ 1213–1215 (West 1982). Here, both the foreclosure sale and the recording of the trustee's deed occurred within 90 days of the petition. . . .

Assuming the foreclosure qualifies as a transfer, we must then consider the antecedent debt requirement. When the debtor (involuntarily) transfers this limited interest, i.e. the right of redemption and possession, what does he get in return? Presumably, the outstanding debt will be retired (depending on the applicability of any deficiency judgment). That debt obligation is an antecedent debt, thus the requirement is met. But see *In re Park North Partners, Ltd.*, 85 B.R. 916, 918 (Bankr.N.D.Ga.1988). Professors White and Summers agree with this analysis, rejecting as metaphysical the argument that "the abolition of the mortgage [is] a giving of present value to the debtor." 2 J. White & R. Summers, Uniform Commercial Code § 25–7, at 450. They rightly point out that the foreclosure sale does not always even wipe out the mortgage. . . .

As a result of the foreclosure the creditor is paid some or all of the money it is due or gains possession of the collateral, satisfying section 547(b)(1). Section 547(f) creates a presumption, unrebutted in this case, that the debtor is insolvent during the 90 days prior to filing its petition. Section 547(b)(3) is satisfied as well. . . .

The final requirement that must be met for there to be a "preference" is that the creditor "received more" than it would have under Chapter 7 liquidation and distribution. This means that we must look at what the debtor transfers to the creditor when the creditor forecloses. This task is made more difficult by the fact that the Code does not say what "more" the creditor should not receive. In one hand, at the end of the foreclosure sale the creditor appears to have a piece of property. In the other hand, at the end of a Chapter 7 liquidation it would have money in satisfaction of its claim, to the extent of its security. How do we decide if the property is "more" than the money?

If the petition had been filed before the foreclosure sale was complete, the automatic stay (11 U.S.C. § 362) would have prevented the sale. The creditor might have been able to lift the stay or might have had to wait for the trustee to liquidate the collateral. To the extent that the creditor is secured, it would receive 100% of its claim in dollar value—$199,746.41. The property appears to be worth $390,000 because the creditor sold it at that price a short time later, and it is well recognized that for various reasons foreclosure sales (and liquidation sales) do not bring the same value as a non-distress (fair market) sale. Because the creditor appears to have received value greater than the debt that was secured, it could be argued that the creditor has received "more" from the foreclosure than it would have under Chapter 7 liquidation.

This analysis, however, fails to consider the reality of the transaction. If the creditor received "more" it is only because the creditor elected to purchase the property at the foreclosure sale rather than simply accepting the receipts of a sale to a third party. Had the third party outbid the creditor, there could be no preference because the price paid would not have been transferred for an antecedent debt. Since section 547 does not reach a third-party purchaser, it is difficult to see why the existence of a preference should turn on the status of the purchaser as a creditor. If the sale was defective or the purchaser otherwise took unfair advantage of the debtor, the transfer may be voided under section 548, regardless of whether the purchaser was the creditor or a third party. We see no reason to construe section 547 to permit avoidance of an otherwise properly conducted sale based solely on the creditor being the highest bidder.

Furthermore, a close analysis of a foreclosure proceeding supports treating the creditor the same as the third-party buyer. Foreclosure is not a unitary event, but in fact two separate legal events. First, the creditor must exert its power or right to foreclose—to force the sale of the property. The creditor has no obligation to buy, let alone, bid at the sale. Moreover, the creditor in purchasing the property at the foreclosure sale assumes the risk of not being able to dispose of it for the amount of the debt. The sale is a separate, second transaction, the receipts of which will be used to satisfy the creditor.

A preference exists only when the creditor has received more under the foreclosure than it would have under Chapter 7 liquidation. There is nothing in the statute that prohibits the creditor from purchasing the property in a liquidation sale—just as at foreclosure. In fact, section 547(b)(5) likely presumes a liquidation sale similar to the foreclosure sale forced by the mortgagee. See 2 J. White & R. Summers, Uniform Commercial Code § 25–7, at 450. We conclude therefore that a creditor who purchases at a regularly conducted foreclosure sale has not received more than it would have under a Chapter 7 liquidation sale. . . .

NOTE

The rationale of BFP *in the preference context.* A number of decisions have concurred with *Ehring*. See, e.g., In re Free, 449 B.R. 461 (Bankr. W.D. Pa. 2011); In re Cottrell, 213 B.R. 378 (Bankr. M.D. Ala. 1996). By contrast, a significant number of decisions have rejected *Ehring* and hold that the trustee can avoid a pre-bankruptcy foreclosure sale under section 547(b). See, e.g., In re Whittle Development, Inc., 463 B.R. 796 (Bankr. N.D. Tex. 2011); In re Villareal, 413 B.R. 633 (Bankr. S.D. Tex. 2009); In re Andrews, 262 B.R. 299 (Bankr. M.D. Pa. 2001); In re Park North Partners, Ltd., 80 B.R. 551 (N.D. Ga. 1987), on remand, 85 B.R. 916 (Bankr. N.D. Ga. 1988).

Some courts have argued that BFP's policy of promoting finality also justifies prohibiting the trustee/DIP from using section 547(b) to set aside a pre-bankruptcy foreclosure sale. See, e.g., In re Pulcini, 261 B.R. 836, 844 (Bankr. W.D. Pa. 2001) (decision to set aside sheriff's sale as a preference would "profoundly affect Pennsylvania's interest in making title to real property stable and secure" because "title to real property purchased at a foreclosure sale 'would be under a federally created cloud' "). Is this concern legitimate? Would section 547(b) have the same potential chilling effect on foreclosure sale bidding as section 548? Why or why not? See generally Kenneth M. Misken & Juliana Bell, Preference Actions Arising Out of Foreclosure Sales, 31 Am.Bankr.Inst.J. 24 (April 2012); Averch & Berryman, Mortgage Foreclosure as a Preference: Does *BFP* Protect the Lender?, 7 J.Bankr.L. & Prac. 281 (1988).

Some commentators have argued that the *Ehring* approach is correct because preference law should address only those situations where a creditor gets paid up to the full amount of the debt, but not where the creditor receives a transfer in excess of full payment. Under this reasoning, the excess is not a preference but a fraudulent transfer—and thus avoidable only as a fraudulent transfer. In other words, if a creditor who is owed $1,000 would have received $300 in a Chapter 7 liquidation, but is paid $1,200 by the insolvent debtor within 90 days of bankruptcy, $1,000 of the transfer is preferential while the $200 excess can only be a fraudulent transfer. See, e.g., Kennedy, Involuntary Fraudulent Transfers, 9 Cardozo L.Rev. 531, 563–564 (1987); Zinman, Houle & Weiss, Fraudulent Transfers According to Alden, Gross & Borowitz: A Tale of Two Circuits, 39 Bus.Law. 977, 985 (1984). Is this argument persuasive? Is it consistent with the statutory language of the Bankruptcy Code? Can you make a persuasive argument for why bankruptcy policy justifies treating the entire $1,200 payment as a preference? See, e.g., Nelson, Whitman, Burkhart & Freyermuth, Real Estate Finance Law § 8.16 (6th ed. 2014).

4. THE MORTGAGEE IN A CHAPTER 7 CASE

Chapter 7 is "liquidation" or "straight" bankruptcy. A Chapter 7 debtor must turn over all of its nonexempt property[16] to the trustee in exchange for a discharge of most of its pre-bankruptcy debts. The trustee gathers the debtor's nonexempt property, unless an item is valueless or burdensome to the estate, in which case the trustee will abandon it under 11 U.S.C.A. § 554(a).[17] The trustee then liquidates the property of the estate and distributes the proceeds in accordance with the Code's distribution scheme. 11 U.S.C.A. §§ 725, 726.

One can best understand how Chapter 7 affects the rights of a mortgagee by considering a series of hypotheticals. Suppose Mortgagor owns a home subject to a recorded mortgage held by Bank. After being laid off from work, Mortgagor cannot make mortgage payments for several months and ultimately files a Chapter 7 petition. On the petition date, Mortgagor owes Bank $150,000, but the home is worth only $100,000. In this situation, the outcome is straightforward. The trustee will abandon the home, as there is no equity in it that could benefit the estate. Because Mortgagor is in default, Bank can move for relief from stay under § 362(d)(2) and will receive that relief as the debtor has no equity in the home.[18] Upon receiving relief from stay, Bank can foreclose its lien under applicable state law.

Suppose instead that on the petition date, the home is worth $300,000 and is located in a state in which debtors may claim a $30,000 exemption in a residence. In this situation, the trustee will not abandon the home, as there is substantial equity in the home that could benefit the

---

[16] Under the laws of each state, debtors are permitted to keep some amount of property free of the claims of general (unsecured) creditors seeking execution of a judgment. Each state's exemption law varies (and some are more generous than others), but the exemption permits the debtor to retain a certain amount of equity in a home, a car, clothing and household goods, personal effects such as jewelry, "tools of the trade," and some rights to payment (such as for child support or social security benefits). Thus, for example, if the applicable exemption allowed the debtor an exemption not to exceed $20,000 in its residence, and the debtor's residence was a manufactured home valued at $15,000, then the debtor could exempt the residence from the bankruptcy estate. 11 U.S.C.A. § 522(b). This means that the trustee could not take possession of the home, sell it, and apply the proceeds to expenses of bankruptcy administration and payment of unsecured creditor clams.

[17] When the trustee abandons property of the estate, title to that property is vested back into the debtor. If the abandoned property is subject to a security interest, the creditor holding that security interest can enforce that security interest, but only after first obtaining relief from stay as described earlier in Part J2.

[18] As explained in Part J2, section 362(d)(2)'s second prong—that the property not be "necessary to an effective reorganization" of the debtor—is irrelevant in Chapter 7 cases, in which the debtor is liquidating and not reorganizing. See, e.g., In re J & M Salupo Dev. Co., Inc., 388 B.R. 809 (Bankr. N.D. Ohio 2008).

estate. Instead, using power granted by 11 U.S.C.A. § 363(f),[19] the trustee will sell the home free and clear of liens, with Bank's mortgage lien being transferred to the proceeds of the sale. Thus, if the trustee sells the home for $300,000, Bank will receive the first $150,000 of proceeds to satisfy its secured claim; Debtor will receive the next $30,000 in proceeds on account of its exemption, and Trustee will apply the remaining $120,000 in proceeds to expenses of sale and then toward the claims of unsecured creditors.[20]

Can the Chapter 7 mortgagor keep her home? In some cases, a mortgagor may file a Chapter 7 petition even if she is current on her mortgage, can afford to keep paying it, and wants to retain her home. This may occur, for example, if she is employed and can pay her ordinary expenses as they come due, but has become insolvent due to a catastrophic medical expense or a large tort or contract liability. The mortgagor's ability to retain her home in this situation will depend upon its value relative to the balance of the mortgage debt and any exemption. For example, suppose Mortgagor's home is worth $300,000 but the remaining balance of the mortgage debt owed to Bank is only $150,000. In this situation, Mortgagor cannot retain its ownership of the home; the trustee will use its power under § 363(f) to sell the home (to capture Mortgagor's equity and apply it to payment of unsecured claims), and Mortgagor will be left with only the cash value of her residence exemption.

By contrast, suppose the home is worth $120,000 but Mortgagor owes Bank $150,000 on the mortgage debt. In this situation, the trustee will abandon the home. Yet under state law, Bank cannot foreclose if

---

[19] Section 363(f) provides:

The trustee may sell property . . . free and clear of any interest in such property of an entity other than the estate, only if—

(1) applicable nonbankruptcy law permits sale of such property free and clear of such interest;

(2) such entity consents;

(3) such interest is a lien and the price at which such property is to be sold is greater than the aggregate value of all liens on such property;

(4) such interest is in bona fide dispute; or

(5) such entity could be compelled, in a legal or equitable proceeding, to accept a money satisfaction of such interest.

[20] What if the home was worth only $200,000 on the petition date? In this situation, the trustee's decision may depend upon how quickly (and at what price and cost) the trustee believes it can sell the home. If the trustee can sell the home immediately for $200,000 at a cost of only $10,000, the sale could net $10,000 for the benefit of unsecured creditors. But what if the trustee expects it to take six months to sell the home due to market conditions? In this situation, the trustee must recall that Bank, as an oversecured creditor, is entitled to post-petition pendency interest as part of its secured claim under § 506(b). Thus, the longer it takes trustee to sell the home, the higher Bank's claim will grow as that interest accrues! Thus, if the trustee is not confident in its ability to sell the home quickly and for an amount sufficient to generate a surplus for the estate, the trustee may instead abandon the home and allow Bank to foreclose (after Bank obtains relief from the automatic stay).

Mortgagor is not in default under the mortgage.[21] Further, if Mortgagor can keep making her payments, Bank may prefer not to foreclose anyway, as foreclosure now would result in a deficiency (for which Mortgagor's liability will be discharged in Chapter 7). Thus, in this situation, as long as Mortgagor keeps making her regular monthly payments in a timely fashion, she can keep her home. [Of course, if Mortgagor is "underwater" on the mortgage, she might rationally choose to "walk away," not make further payments, let Bank foreclose on the mortgage, and take her Chapter 7 discharge of any personal liability to Bank. Given that, why might Mortgagor keep the home and continue making monthly payments?]

In this situation, Mortgagor ideally would like to stay in her home and reduce the principal amount of her mortgage to $120,000 (probably reducing the corresponding amount of her monthly mortgage payments). Outside of bankruptcy, Mortgagor cannot restructure the mortgage in this way without Bank's consent. Can Mortgagor use the bankruptcy process to accomplish this result?

At first blush, the Bankruptcy Code seems to provide plausible authority in 11 U.S.C.A. § 506(d), which provides in pertinent part that "[t]o the extent that a lien secures a claim against the debtor that is not an allowed secured claim, such lien is void. . . ." Recall that § 506(a) would "bifurcate" Bank's claim into a secured claim for $120,000 and an unsecured claim for $30,000. Mortgagor thus might argue that Bank's lien is valid to the extent it secures the repayment of $120,000, but invalid to the extent that it would secure the $30,000 unsecured claim. If Mortgagor was correct, Mortgagor could thus "strip down" Bank's lien— meaning that once Mortgagor had repaid $120,000 to Bank, Bank's mortgage would be extinguished! Unfortunately for the Mortgagor, the Supreme Court has rejected this argument.

DEWSNUP V. TIMM

Supreme Court of the United States, 1992
502 U.S. 410, 112 S.Ct. 773, 116 L.Ed.2d 903

JUSTICE BLACKMUN delivered the opinion of the Court. We are confronted in this case with an issue concerning § 506(d) of the Bankruptcy Code, 11 U.S.C. § 506(d). May a debtor "strip down" a creditor's lien on real property to the value of the collateral, as judicially determined, when that value is less than the amount of the claim secured by the lien?

---

[21] You might ask: "Doesn't a mortgage typically provide that the mortgagor's bankruptcy would be an event of default?" Indeed, mortgages and other contracts typically provide that bankruptcy is an event of default, but the Bankruptcy Code typically does not give effect to such clauses (known as "ipso facto" clauses).

I

On June 1, 1978, respondents loaned $119,000 to petitioner Aletha Dewsnup and her husband, T. LaMar Dewsnup, since deceased. The loan was accompanied by a Deed of Trust granting a lien on two parcels of Utah farmland owned by the Dewsnups.

Petitioner defaulted the following year. Under the terms of the Deed of Trust, respondents at that point could have proceeded against the real property collateral by accelerating the maturity of the loan, issuing a notice of default, and selling the land at a public foreclosure sale to satisfy the debt. See also Utah Code Ann. §§ 57–1–20 to 57–1–37 (1990 and Supp.1991).

Respondents did issue a notice of default in 1981. Before the foreclosure sale took place, however, petitioner sought reorganization under Chapter 11 of the Bankruptcy Code, 11 U.S.C. § 1101 *et seq.* That bankruptcy petition was dismissed, as was a subsequent Chapter 11 petition. In June 1984, petitioner filed a petition seeking liquidation under Chapter 7 of the Code, 11 U.S.C. § 701 *et seq.* Because of the pendency of these bankruptcy proceedings, respondents were not able to proceed to the foreclosure sale. See 11 U.S.C. § 362 (1988 ed. and Supp. II).

In 1987, petitioner filed the present adversary proceeding in the Bankruptcy Court for the District of Utah seeking, pursuant to § 506, to "avoid" a portion of respondents' lien. Petitioner represented that the debt of approximately $120,000 then owed to respondents exceeded the fair market value of the land and that, therefore, the Bankruptcy Court should reduce the lien to that value. According to petitioner, this was compelled by the interrelationship of the security-reducing provision of § 506(a) and the lien-voiding provision of § 506(d). Under § 506(a) ("An allowed claim of a creditor secured by a lien on property in which the estate has an interest . . . is a secured claim to the extent of the value of such creditor's interest in the estate's interest in such property"), respondents would have an "allowed secured claim" only to the extent of the judicially determined value of their collateral. And under § 506(d) ("To the extent that a lien secures a claim against the debtor that is not an allowed secured claim, such lien is void"), the court would be required to void the lien as to the remaining portion of respondents' claim, because the remaining portion was not an "allowed secured claim" within the meaning of § 506(a).

The Bankruptcy Court refused to grant this relief. *In re Dewsnup,* 87 B.R. 676 (1988). After a trial, it determined that the then value of the land subject to the Deed of Trust was $39,000. It indulged in the assumption that the property had been abandoned by the trustee pursuant to § 554, and reasoned that once property was abandoned it no longer fell within the reach of § 506(a), which applies only to "property in which the estate has an interest," and therefore was not covered by § 506(d).

The United States District Court, without a supporting opinion, summarily affirmed the Bankruptcy Court's judgment of dismissal with prejudice. App. to Pet. for Cert. 12a.

The Court of Appeals for the Tenth Circuit, in its turn, also affirmed. *In re Dewsnup,* 908 F.2d 588 (1990). Starting from the "fundamental premise" of § 506(a) that a claim is subject to reduction in security only when the estate has an interest in the property, the court reasoned that because the estate had no interest in abandoned property, § 506(a) did not apply (nor, by implication, did § 506(d)). *Id.,* at 590–591. The court then noted that a contrary result would be inconsistent with § 722 under which a debtor has a limited right to redeem certain personal property. *Id.,* at 592. . . .

II

[T]he parties and their *amici* are not in agreement in their respective approaches to the problem of statutory interpretation that confronts us. Petitioner-debtor takes the position that §§ 506(a) and 506(d) are complementary and to be read together. Because, under § 506(a), a claim is secured only to the extent of the judicially determined value of the real property on which the lien is fixed, a debtor can void a lien on the property pursuant to § 506(d) to the extent the claim is no longer secured and thus is not "an allowed secured claim." In other words, § 506(a) bifurcates classes of claims allowed under § 502 into secured claims and unsecured claims; any portion of an allowed claim deemed to be unsecured under § 506(a) is not an "allowed secured claim" within the lien-voiding scope of § 506(d). Petitioner argues that there is no exception for unsecured property abandoned by the trustee.

Petitioner's *amicus* argues that the plain language of § 506(d) dictates that the proper portion of an undersecured lien on property in a Chapter 7 case is void whether or not the property is abandoned by the trustee. It further argues that the rationale of the Court of Appeals would lead to evisceration of the debtor's right of redemption and the elimination of an undersecured creditor's ability to participate in the distribution of the estate's assets.

Respondents primarily assert that § 506(d) is not, as petitioner would have it, "rigidly tied" to § 506(a). They argue that § 506(a) performs the function of classifying claims by true secured status at the time of distribution of the estate to ensure fairness to unsecured claimants. In contrast, the lien-voiding § 506(d) is directed to the time at which foreclosure is to take place, and, where the trustee has abandoned the property, no bankruptcy distributional purpose is served by voiding the lien.

In the alternative, respondents, joined by the United States as *amicus curiae,* argue more broadly that the words "allowed secured claim" in § 506(d) need not be read as an indivisible term of art defined by reference to § 506(a), which by its terms is not a definitional provision. Rather, the words should be read term-by-term to refer to any claim that is, first, allowed, and, second, secured. Because there is no question that the claim at issue here has been "allowed" pursuant to § 502 of the Code and is secured by a lien with recourse to the underlying collateral, it does not come within the scope of § 506(d), which voids only liens corresponding to claims that have *not* been allowed and secured. This reading of § 506(d), according to respondents and the United States, gives the provision the simple and sensible function of voiding a lien whenever a claim secured by the lien itself has not been allowed. It ensures that the Code's determination not to allow the underlying claim against the debtor personally is given full effect by preventing its assertion against the debtor's property.

Respondents point out that pre-Code bankruptcy law preserved liens like respondents' and that there is nothing in the Code's legislative history that reflects any intent to alter that law. Moreover, according to respondents, the "fresh start" policy cannot justify an impairment of respondents' property rights, for the fresh start does not extend to an *in rem* claim against property but is limited to a discharge of personal liability.

III

The foregoing recital of the contrasting positions of the respective parties and their *amici* demonstrates that § 506 of the Bankruptcy Code and its relationship to other provisions of that Code do embrace some ambiguities. Hypothetical applications that come to mind and those advanced at oral argument illustrate the difficulty of interpreting the statute in a single opinion that would apply to all possible fact situations. We therefore focus upon the case before us and allow other facts to await their legal resolution on another day.

We conclude that respondents' alternative position, espoused also by the United States, although not without its difficulty, generally is the better of the several approaches. Therefore, we hold that § 506(d) does not allow petitioner to "strip down" respondents' lien, because respondents' claim is secured by a lien and has been fully allowed pursuant to § 502. Were we writing on a clean slate, we might be inclined to agree with petitioner that the words "allowed secured claim" must take the same meaning in § 506(d) as in § 506(a). But, given the ambiguity in the text, we are not convinced that Congress intended to depart from the pre-Code rule that liens pass through bankruptcy unaffected.

1. The practical effect of petitioner's argument is to freeze the creditor's secured interest at the judicially determined valuation. By this approach, the creditor would lose the benefit of any increase in the value of the property by the time of the foreclosure sale. The increase would accrue to the benefit of the debtor, a result some of the parties describe as a "windfall."

We think, however, that the creditor's lien stays with the real property until the foreclosure. That is what was bargained for by the mortgagor and the mortgagee. The voidness language sensibly applies only to the security aspect of the lien and then only to the real deficiency in the security. Any increase over the judicially determined valuation during bankruptcy rightly accrues to the benefit of the creditor, not to the benefit of the debtor and not to the benefit of other unsecured creditors whose claims have been allowed and who had nothing to do with the mortgagor-mortgagee bargain. . . .

2. This result appears to have been clearly established before the passage of the 1978 Act. Under the Bankruptcy Act of 1898, a lien on real property passed through bankruptcy unaffected. This Court recently acknowledged that this was so. See *Farrey v. Sanderfoot,* 500 U.S. 291, 297, 111 S.Ct. 1825, 1829, 114 L.Ed.2d 337 (1991) ("Ordinarily, liens and other secured interests survive bankruptcy"); *Johnson v. Home State Bank,* 501 U.S. 78, 84, 111 S.Ct. 2150, 2154, 115 L.Ed.2d 66 (1991) ("Rather, a bankruptcy discharge extinguishes only one mode of enforcing a claim—namely, an action against the debtor *in personam*—while leaving intact another—namely, an action against the debtor *in rem*").

3. Apart from reorganization proceedings, see 11 U.S.C. §§ 616(1) and (10) (1976 ed.), no provision of the pre-Code statute permitted involuntary reduction of the amount of a creditor's lien for any reason other than payment on the debt. . . .

Congress must have enacted the Code with a full understanding of this practice. See H.R.Rep. No. 95–595, p. 357 (1977), U.S.Code Cong. & Admin. News 1978, pp. 5787, 6313 ("Subsection (d) permits liens to pass through the bankruptcy case unaffected").

4. When Congress amends the bankruptcy laws, it does not write "on a clean slate." See *Emil v. Hanley,* 318 U.S. 515, 521, 63 S.Ct. 687, 690–691, 87 L.Ed. 954 (1943). Furthermore, this Court has been reluctant to accept arguments that would interpret the Code, however vague the particular language under consideration might be, to effect a major change in pre-Code practice that is not the subject of at least some discussion in the legislative history. See *United Savings Assn. of Texas v. Timbers of Inwood Forest Associates, Ltd.,* 484 U.S. 365, 380, 108 S.Ct.

626, 634, 98 L.Ed.2d 740 (1988). See also *Pennsylvania Dept. of Public Welfare v. Davenport*, 495 U.S. 552, 563, 110 S.Ct. 2126, 2133, 109 L.Ed.2d 588 (1990); *United States v. Ron Pair Enterprises, Inc.*, 489 U.S. 235, 244–245, 109 S.Ct. 1026, 1032–1033, 103 L.Ed.2d 290 (1989). Of course, where the language is unambiguous, silence in the legislative history cannot be controlling. But, given the ambiguity here, to attribute to Congress the intention to grant a debtor the broad new remedy against allowed claims to the extent that they become "unsecured" for purposes of § 506(a) without the new remedy's being mentioned somewhere in the Code itself or in the annals of Congress is not plausible, in our view, and is contrary to basic bankruptcy principles.

The judgment of the Court of Appeals is affirmed.

JUSTICE SCALIA, with whom JUSTICE SOUTER joins, dissenting. With exceptions not pertinent here, § 506(d) of the Bankruptcy Code provides: "To the extent that a lien secures a claim against the debtor that is not an allowed secured claim, such lien is void. . . ." Read naturally and in accordance with other provisions of the statute, this automatically voids a lien to the extent the claim it secures is not both an "allowed claim" and a "secured claim" under the Code. In holding otherwise, the Court replaces what Congress said with what it thinks Congress ought to have said—and in the process disregards, and hence impairs for future use, well-established principles of statutory construction. I respectfully dissent. . . .

This case turns solely on the meaning of a single phrase found throughout the Bankruptcy Code: "allowed secured claim." Section 506(d) unambiguously provides that to the extent a lien does not secure such a claim it is (with certain exceptions) rendered void. See 11 U.S.C. § 506(d). Congress did not leave the meaning of "allowed secured claim" to speculation. Section 506(a) says that an "allowed claim" (the meaning of which is obvious) is also a "secured claim" "to the extent of *the value of [the] creditor's interest in the estate's interest in [the securing] property.*" (Emphasis added.) (This means, generally speaking, that an allowed claim "is secured only to the extent of the value of the property on which the lien is fixed; the remainder of that claim is considered unsecured." *United States v. Ron Pair Enterprises, Inc.*, 489 U.S. 235, 239, 109 S.Ct. 1026, 1029, 103 L.Ed.2d 290 (1989).) When § 506(d) refers to an "allowed secured claim," it can only be referring to that allowed "secured claim" so carefully described two brief subsections earlier.

The phrase obviously bears the meaning set forth in § 506(a) when it is used in the subsections of § 506 other than § 506(d)—for example, in § 506(b), which addresses "allowed secured claim[s]" that are oversecured. Indeed, as respondents apparently concede, even when the phrase appears outside of § 506, it invariably means what § 506(a) describes: the portion of a creditor's allowed claim that is secured after the calculations required by that provision have been performed. See, *e.g.*, 11 U.S.C. § 722 (permitting a Chapter 7 debtor to redeem certain tangible personal property from certain liens "by paying the holder of such lien the amount of the *allowed secured claim* of such holder that is secured by such lien"); § 1225(a)(5) (prescribing treatment of *"allowed secured claim[s]"* in family farmer's reorganization plan); § 1325(a)(5) (same with respect to *"allowed secured claim[s]"* in individual reorganizations). (Emphases added.) The statute is similarly consistent in its use of the companion phrase *"allowed unsecured claim"* to describe (with respect to a claim supported by a lien) that portion of the claim that is treated as "unsecured" under § 506(a). See, *e.g.*, 11 U.S.C. § 507(a)(7) (fixing priority of *"allowed unsecured claims* of governmental units"); § 726(a)(2) (providing for payment of *"allowed unsecured claim[s]"* in Chapter 7 liquidation); § 1225(a)(4) (setting standard for treatment of *"allowed unsecured claim[s]"* in Chapter 12 plan); § 1325(a)(4) (setting standard for treatment of *"allowed unsecured claim[s]"* in Chapter 13 plan). (Emphases added.) When, on the other hand, the Bankruptcy Code means to refer to a secured party's entire allowed claim, *i.e.*, to both the "secured" and "unsecured" portions under § 506(a), it uses the term *"allowed claim"*—as in 11 U.S.C. § 363(k), which refers to "a lien that secures an allowed claim." Given this clear and unmistakable pattern of usage, it seems to me impossible to hold, as the Court does, that "the words 'allowed secured claim' in § 506(d) need not be read as an indivisible term of art defined by reference to § 506(a)." We have often invoked the normal rule of statutory construction that identical words used in different parts of the same act are intended to have the same meaning. That rule must surely apply, *a fortiori,* to use of identical words *in the same section of the same enactment.*

The Court makes no attempt to establish a textual or structural basis for overriding the plain meaning of § 506(d), but rests its decision upon policy intuitions of a legislative character, and upon the principle that a text which is "ambiguous" (a status apparently achieved by being the subject of disagreement between self-interested litigants) cannot change pre-Code law without the *imprimatur* of "legislative history." Thus abandoning the normal and sensible principle that a term (and especially an artfully defined term such as "allowed secured claim") bears the same meaning throughout the statute, the Court adopts instead what might be called the one-subsection-at-a-time approach to statutory exegesis. . . .

The principal harm caused by today's decision is not the misinterpretation of § 506(d) of the Bankruptcy Code. The disposition that misinterpretation produces brings the Code closer to prior practice and is, as the Court irrelevantly observes, probably fairer from the standpoint of natural justice. (I say irrelevantly, because a bankruptcy law has little to do with natural justice.) The greater and more enduring damage of today's opinion consists in its destruction of predictability, in the Bankruptcy Code and elsewhere. By disregarding well-established and oft-repeated principles of statutory construction, it renders those principles less secure and the certainty they are designed to achieve less attainable. When a seemingly clear provision can be pronounced "ambiguous" *sans* textual and structural analysis, and when the assumption of uniform meaning is replaced by "one-subsection-at-a-time" interpretation, innumerable statutory texts become worth litigating. In the bankruptcy field alone, for example, unfortunate future litigants will have to pay the price for our expressed neutrality "as to whether the words 'allowed secured claim' have different meaning in other provisions of the Bankruptcy Code." Having taken this case to resolve uncertainty regarding one provision, we end by spawning confusion regarding scores of others. I respectfully dissent.

NOTES

1. Dewsnup *and the undersecured mortgagee*. Thanks to *Dewsnup,* an undersecured mortgagee in Chapter 7 still possesses the right to collect the full amount of the debt from the mortgaged property itself, even though the mortgagor's personal liability on the debt is discharged. Thus, the mortgagee will retain its lien on the mortgaged property until the mortgage is foreclosed or the mortgagor repays the mortgage debt in full. Full payment presumably would occur only if the mortgagor continues making all regularly scheduled installments, or if the mortgagor makes a full prepayment (as would occur if the mortgagor refinanced the mortgage, which might occur if the property subsequently appreciated in value to the point that the loan was no longer "underwater").

As the facts in *Dewsnup* make clear, this principle applies not only if the mortgagor is not in default at the time of the bankruptcy petition, but also when the mortgagor is in default. In this regard, does *Dewsnup* help mortgagors by giving the mortgagee an incentive to delay foreclosure (hoping for a possible post-bankruptcy increase in the value of the land)?

2. Dewsnup *and "wholly underwater" junior liens*. Suppose that Mortgagor files a Chapter 7 petition. Mortgagor owns a home subject to two mortgages: a senior mortgage held by Bank1 (securing an unpaid balance of $200,000) and a junior mortgage held by Bank2 (securing an unpaid balance of $50,000). On the petition date, the home is worth only $150,000. Bank1's undersecured mortgage lien passes through the Chapter 7 case unaffected under *Dewsnup.* But what about Bank2's mortgage, which is entirely underwater on the petition date? Does *Dewsnup* also prohibit a Chapter 7 debtor from using section 506(d) to invalidate (or "strip-off") an underwater junior lien?

Prior to *Dewsnup,* the Eleventh Circuit had ruled that section 506(d) permitted a Chapter 7 debtor to invalidate an entirely underwater junior lien. Folendore v. United States Small Bus. Admin., 862 F.2d 1537 (11th Cir. 1989). After *Dewsnup,* however, the overwhelming weight of judicial authority has held that section 506(d) does not permit "strip-off." As the Sixth Circuit reasoned:

> As in the case of a "strip down," to permit a "strip off" would mark a departure from the pre-Code rule that real property liens emerge from bankruptcy unaffected. Also, as in the case of a "stripdown," a "strip-off" would rob the mortgagee of the bargain it struck with the mortgagor, i.e., that the consensual lien would remain with the property until foreclosure. . . . Finally, as was true in the context of "strip downs," Chapter 7 "strip offs" also carry the risk of a "windfall" to the debtors should the value of the encumbered property increase by the time of the foreclosure sale.

In re Talbert, 344 F.3d 555, 560 (6th Cir. 2003). See also Palomar v. First Am. Bank, 722 F.3d 992 (7th Cir. 2013); Ryan v. Homecomings Fin. Network, 253 F.3d 778 (4th Cir. 2001); In re Concannon, 338 B.R. 90 (9th Cir. B.A.P. 2006); In re Richins, 469 B.R. 375 (Bankr. D. Utah 2012).

Nevertheless, the Eleventh Circuit has repeatedly ruled that its *Folendore* decision survived *Dewsnup* and that section 506(d) permits a Chapter 7 debtor to invalidate a junior creditor's entirely underwater lien. In re Malone, 564 Fed.Appx. 991 (11th Cir. 2014); In re McNeal, 477 Fed. Appx. 562 (11th Cir. 2012). Is there a good reason to prohibit Chapter 7 debtors from stripping down undersecured liens but allow them to strip off wholly underwater liens? Compare Note, Lien-Stripping in Consumer Bankruptcy: Debtors Cannot Strip Liens Down Partially, But Can They Strip Them Off Entirely? The Answer Should Be No, 21 Am. Bankr. Inst. L.J. 257 (2013) with Ponoroff, Hey, The Sun Is Hot and the Water's Fine: Why Not Strip Off That Lien?, 30 Emory Bankr. Dev. J. 13 (2013).

As this book is in press, the Supreme Court has heard argument in two cases, Bank of America, N.A. v. Toledo-Cardona and Bank of America, N.A. v. Caulkett, in which the Court granted certiorari to resolve this split of authority. Initially, it was expected that the Court would either extend *Dewsnup* to prohibit strip-off of underwater liens, or narrow *Dewsnup* to apply only to the "strip-down" of undersecured liens. Based on questioning by the Justices at the oral argument, however, some bankruptcy scholars have speculated that the Court may overrule *Dewsnup* and conclude that section 506(d) permits a Chapter 7 debtor to strip-down an undersecured lien.

5. THE MORTGAGEE IN A CHAPTER 13 CASE

Chapter 13 is to certain salaried or wage-earning individuals[22] what Chapter 11 is to the corporation or other business entity. A Chapter 13 debtor can retain her pre-bankruptcy property and repay her creditors

---

[22] A Chapter 13 debtor cannot have secured debts exceeding $1,149,525 or unsecured debt exceeding $383,175. 11 U.S.C.A. § 109(e). These amounts are effective as of April 1, 2013, and they are automatically adjusted at three-year intervals based on the Consumer Price Index. 11 U.S.C.A. § 104(b). Individuals with debts exceeding these limits must seek reorganization in Chapter 11.

through a reorganization plan confirmed by the court and funded by her post-bankruptcy income. The debtor pays this income to a Chapter 13 trustee, who in turn makes payments to creditors in accordance with the confirmed plan. When the debtor completes performance of the plan, the debtor receives a discharge of her debts (even if the creditors did not receive payment in full).[23] The following section addresses the impact of Chapter 13 on mortgagees.

The automatic stay and relief from stay in Chapter 13. In Chapter 13 cases, mortgagees are subject to the automatic stay of section 362. In addition, Chapter 13 also provides a special stay protecting third parties who have guaranteed a debtor's consumer debt[24] or put up collateral to secure such a debt. 11 U.S.C.A. § 1301(a)(1) ("a creditor may not act, or commence or continue any civil action, to collect all or any part of a consumer debt of the debtor from any individual that is liable on such debt with the debtor, or that secured such debt unless such individual became liable on or secured such debt in the ordinary course of such individual's business"). Thus, suppose Bank holds a purchase money mortgage on Mortgagor's home, and Mortgagor's father both guaranteed Mortgagor's repayment of the mortgage debt and executed a mortgage on his own home to secure that guaranty. The general automatic stay prevents Bank from foreclosing against Mortgagor's home, and section 1301 prevents Bank from suing Mortgagor's father on the guaranty or foreclosing on the father's home.

As explained earlier, section 362(d)(1) authorizes relief from the stay "for cause, including the lack of adequate protection of an interest in property of [the mortgagor]," and section 362(d)(2) authorizes relief if "(A) the [mortgagor] does not have an equity in such property; and (B) such property is not necessary to an effective reorganization." Courts have disagreed about whether both subsections apply in Chapter 13 cases. While a few courts have held that a mortgagee may seek relief in Chapter 13 only under section 362(d)(1), see, e.g., In re Fischer, 136 B.R. 819 (D. Alaska 1992),[25] the substantial weight of authority holds that a mortgagee can also seek relief under section 362(d)(2). See, e.g., In re McNeely, 366 B.R. 542 (Bankr. N.D. W.Va. 2007); In re Mellino, 333 B.R.

---

[23] 11 U.S.C.A. § 1328(a). Section 1328(a) excludes certain debts from discharge, including domestic support obligations, student loan indebtedness, and installment debts where the final contract payment extends beyond the expiration of the plan (such as a mortgage debt where the remaining mortgage term exceeds the plan period). See 8 Collier on Bankruptcy ¶ 1328.02[3], at 1328–11 to 1328–24 (16th ed.).

[24] In this context, "consumer debt" means a debt incurred primarily for personal, family, or household purposes. 11 U.S.C.A. § 101(7).

[25] One commentator has argued that because section 362(d)(2) refers to a "reorganization," it should apply only to Chapter 11 (which is entitled "Reorganization") and not to Chapter 13 (which is entitled "Adjustment of Debts of an Individual with Regular Income"). Comment, Home Foreclosures Under Chapter 13 of the Bankruptcy Reform Act, 30 UCLA L.Rev. 637, 648 (1983). Can you explain why this argument is unpersuasive?

578 (Bankr. D. Mass. 2005); In re Herrin, 325 B.R. 774 (Bankr. N.D. Ind. 2005). Where the mortgage covers the debtor's home, relief from stay under section 362(d)(2) is unlikely; courts will treat the debtor's home as being "necessary" to the debtor's ability to rehabilitate in Chapter 13. See, e.g., 3 Collier on Bankruptcy ¶ 362.07[4][b], at 362–121 (16th ed.).

Repayment under a Chapter 13 plan. Chapter 13 requires the debtor to propose a plan to repay creditor claims over a period of five years (reduced to three if the debtor's income is below the state's median income for households of similar size). 11 U.S.C.A. § 1325(b)(4)(A). Chapter 13 does not specify how much of her post-bankruptcy income the debtor must pay to the trustee; it merely requires that the debtor pay "such portion of future earnings or other future income ... as is necessary for the execution of the plan." 11 U.S.C.A. § 1322(a)(1). This means that the debtor's contribution depends upon the plan's repayment terms, which must satisfy the confirmation requirements set forth in section 1325.

The debtor does not have to pay unsecured claims in full; however, the court may not confirm a Chapter 13 plan unless unsecured creditors will receive as much or more than they would have received in a Chapter 7 liquidation. 11 U.S.C.A. § 1325(a)(4). In addition, if the debtor does not pay unsecured claims in full, the court cannot confirm the plan over the objection of an unsecured creditor unless the debtor contributes *all* of her "disposable income" to fund the plan. 11 U.S.C.A. § 1325(b)(1). The court also may not confirm the plan unless it concludes that the debtor filed her petition and proposed her plan in good faith, 11 U.S.C.A. § 1325(a)(3), (7), and the plan is feasible, i.e., "the debtor will be able to make all payments under the plan and to comply with the plan." 11 U.S.C.A. § 1325(a)(6).

Modification of secured claims, cure of prepetition defaults and "de-acceleration." Sections 1322 and 1325 address how a Chapter 13 plan may treat secured claims. In particular, section 1322(b) provides that a Chapter 13 plan may:

> (2) modify the rights of holders of secured claims, other than a claim secured only by a security interest in real property that is the debtor's principal residence, or of holders of unsecured claims, or leave unaffected the rights of holders of any class of claims;

> (3) provide for the curing or waiving of any default; . . .

> (5) notwithstanding paragraph (2) of this subsection, provide for the curing of any default within a reasonable time and maintenance of payments while the case is pending on any unsecured claim or secured claim on which the last payment is due after the date on which the final payment under the plan is due. . . .

To understanding the impact of these sections, consider this common example. Suppose Smith obtained a 30-year mortgage on a vacation home, at 8% annual interest. Five years into the mortgage, Smith lost his job and stopped making his $1,000 monthly mortgage payments. Bank (which holds the mortgage on the home) accelerated the mortgage and started a foreclosure proceeding. When Smith found a new job with an income sufficient to allow him to resume making mortgage payments, he filed a Chapter 13 petition to stop Bank's foreclosure. On the petition date, Smith had not paid his mortgage payment in six months ($6,000 total). Outside of bankruptcy, Smith could not keep the home and avoid foreclosure without either (1) paying off the accelerated balance of the debt in full or (2) paying the $6,000 arrearage to reinstate the mortgage, if applicable state law or the mortgage permitted reinstatement. Section 1322(b), however, permits Smith to "de-accelerate" the loan, resume making his $1,000 monthly installment payment, and cure the $6,000 arrearage by making an additional monthly installment payment under the Chapter 13 plan (e.g., by paying Bank an additional $100 each month for the 60 months of the plan).

"Cramdown." As noted above, section 1322(b)(2) also permits a plan to modify the rights of creditors holding secured claims (other than a claim secured only by real property that is the debtor's principal residence). In the previous example, this means that if prevailing interest rates are now 4%, Smith's plan might propose to modify the terms of Bank's mortgage to reduce the interest rate from 8% (the original contract rate) down to 5%—which would lower Smith's monthly payment amount.

If the plan proposes to modify a secured claim, the court can confirm the plan only if it satisfies one of the following requirements:

- the mortgagee accepts the plan, 11 U.S.C.A. § 1325(a)(5)(A);
- the plan proposes to surrender the property to the mortgagee, 11 U.S.C.A. § 1325(a)(5)(C); or
- the mortgagee will retain its lien on the collateral and the debtor will make future payments that have a present value that equals or exceeds the amount of the mortgagee's secured claim. 11 U.S.C.A. § 1325(a)(5)(B).

This third approach is known as "cramdown," i.e., the debtor crams its repayment plan down the throat of the unconsenting mortgagee.

The impact of the cramdown requirement is best understood through an another example. Assume that Smith owns a vacation condo subject to a mortgage loan held by Bank. The loan bears an 8% annual interest rate, is repayable in equal monthly installments of $1,400, has 20 years remaining to maturity, and an unpaid balance of $200,000. On the date Smith files a Chapter 13 petition, he is current on the mortgage, but due to market conditions, the vacation home has a value of only $120,000. As discussed earlier, section 506(a) bifurcates Bank's claim into a secured claim of $120,000 and an unsecured claim of $80,000. Bank will be paid on account of its unsecured claim to the same extent as other unsecured creditors. As for the Bank's secured claim, sections 1322(b)(2) and 1325 effectively permit Smith to "strip-down" that claim to the home's $120,000 current value. If Smith wants to strip-down the Bank's claim and retain the vacation home, Smith has two alternatives:

- Smith can make a lump-sum payment of $120,000 to Bank in full satisfaction of Bank's secured claim, thereby extinguishing Bank's lien.

- Smith can amortize the $120,000 secured claim through installment payments over five years under his plan. These payments must be in "equal monthly amounts," 11 U.S.C.A. § 1325(a)(5)(B)(iii)(I),[26] and must have a present value of $120,000 or more. Once Smith makes all installment payments under the plan in a timely fashion, Bank's mortgage lien will be extinguished—and if the condo should appreciate in value in the future, all of that appreciation will insure to the benefit of Smith.

Of course, Smith may be unable to accomplish either alternative. Smith may lack the ability to make a lump-sum payment of $120,000, or the post-bankruptcy income to make the installment payments necessary to amortize the full $120,000 balance in only five years. [At an 8% interest rate, the plan would require monthly installments of $2,433.] If so, Smith will be unable to modify or "strip-down" Bank's secured claim—at least over Bank's objection. In that case, to keep the house, Smith will have to continue to make all of the payments required under the original amortization schedule, unless he can convince the Bank to agree to modify the loan terms voluntarily. [This is often referred to as providing for payment of the mortgage "outside the plan."]

NOTES

1. *Determining the cram-down rate.* Because cram-down requires the court to calculate the present value of the debtor's plan payments, the court must determine what interest rate to use in making that calculation. The Code provides no explicit guidance, and courts have struggled to identify the appropriate rate. Because cram-down effectively forces the mortgagee to extend credit to a bankrupt debtor (rather than allowing the mortgagee to sell the collateral and reinvest the loan proceeds), mortgagees would prefer a

---

[26] Congress added this requirement in 2005, which prevents a Chapter 13 debtor from proposing to pay a secured creditor (over its objection) interest-only payments during the plan with a balloon payment of the entire secured claim in the plan's final month. See, e.g., In re Hamilton, 401 B.R. 539 (1st Cir. B.A.P. 2009). Why prohibit Debtor from proposing such a "balloon" plan?

"market" or "coerced loan" approach that would approximate the rate that a comparable debtor would have to pay to borrow an amount equal to the secured claim. By contrast, debtors have argued for a "cost of funds" rule that would set the cram-down rate based on the interest rate the creditor would have to pay to borrow a comparable amount. One might also take the view that the court should presumptively use the pre-bankruptcy contract rate as the cram-down rate, but allow either the debtor or the mortgagee to present evidence that might justify an upward or downward adjustment based upon the circumstances.

The Supreme Court attempted to resolve the confusion in Till v. SCS Credit Corp., 541 U.S. 465, 124 S. Ct. 1951 (2004). That case involved an attempt by a Chapter 13 debtor to modify its secured car loan from the pre-bankruptcy contract interest rate of 21% to a cram-down rate of 9.5%. The debtor proposed this as an appropriate cram-down rate because the existing "prime" rate was 8%, and an additional 1.5% adjustment was appropriate to account for the risk of the debtor's default. The Court's plurality decision ultimately upheld the bankruptcy court's confirmation of the plan, but it added little clarity. Four justices (Justices Stevens, Souter, Ginsburg, and Breyer) concurred with the bankruptcy court's "prime plus" formula approach, while the four dissenting judges (Justices Scalia, Kennedy, O'Connor and Rehnquist) would have adopted the presumptive contract rate approach. Justice Thomas did not agree with either approach, but concurred in the result (the 9.5% rate) because he believed that the Code did not require any adjustment for risk and thus that the secured creditor had no grounds to complain if the plan proposed any rate above the prime rate.

Commentators have roundly criticized *Till*, and justifiably so. The Court's opinions discuss the "prime" rate as if it were a "risk-free" rate (on top of which the court should then add an appropriate adjustment to account for the debtor's risk), but the prime rate is not a "risk-free" rate. The plurality opinion also provided no meaningful guidance as to how to calculate an appropriate risk premium, noting merely that courts have generally approved adjustments of 1% to 3%, and stating:

> Together with the cramdown provision, [the feasibility] requirement obligates the court to select a rate high enough to compensate the creditor for its risk but not so high as to doom the plan. If the court determines that the likelihood of default is so high as to necessitate an "eye-popping" interest rate, the plan probably should not be confirmed. [*Till*, 541 U.S. at 480–481.]

2. *Cure and interest on arrearages*. Returning to the first example on page 917, section 1322(b)(5) would permit Smith to cure the unpaid arrearage of $6,000 by paying it off in monthly installments under the plan. Prior to 1993, most courts held that the Chapter 13 debtor did not have to pay interest on the arrearage being cured. See, e.g., Landmark Fin. Servs. v. Hall, 918 F.2d 1150 (4th Cir. 1990). In 1993, the Supreme Court held in Rake v. Wade, 508 U.S. 464 (1993), that an oversecured creditor was entitled to post-

petition interest on arrearages as a matter of right under section 506(b) (regardless of whether the creditor's contract provided for interest). In 1994, Congress added section 1322(e), which superseded *Rake* and provides that notwithstanding section 506(b), a creditor may collect interest on the arrearage being cured "in accordance with the underlying agreement and applicable nonbankruptcy law." Thus, because the loan in the example provided for 8% annual interest, Smith's cure of the $6,000 arrearage would require monthly installments under the plan of $121.66.

Mortgages on primary residences and the anti-modification rule. While section 1322(b)(2) generally allows a Chapter 13 plan to modify secured claims, the plan cannot modify a claim that is "secured only by a security interest in real property that is the debtor's principal residence." Without the mortgagee's consent, a Chapter 13 debtor cannot reduce the principal amount of the mortgage on its primary residence, regardless of its value. Likewise, the debtor can neither reduce the interest rate (even if market rates have declined) nor extend the loan term so as to reduce the monthly payment amount. Further, under the weight of authority, a junior mortgage enjoys the same protection against modification, as long as there is some equity in the home above the amount of the senior obligations. Congress adopted this anti-modification rule "in response to perceptions, or to suggestions advanced in the legislative hearings ... that home-mortgagor lenders, performing a valuable social service through their loans, needed special protection against modification." Grubbs v. Houston First American Savings Ass'n, 730 F.2d 236, 246 (5th Cir. 1984).

Suppose Debtor owes $200,000 to Bank, secured by a mortgage on its primary home (worth only $150,000). Can Debtor modify the $50,000 unsecured portion of Bank's claim, or does section 1322(b)(2) protect the *entire claim* against modification? Relying upon section 506(d)—which invalidates a lien to the extent it "secures a claim against the debtor other than an allowed secured claim"—Debtor might propose to continue making the same monthly payment as before, but with that payment being applied toward a secured claim with a stripped-down balance of $150,000. If the Code permitted this approach, Debtor could get a release of the mortgage lien once Debtor had amortized the $150,000 balance of the secured claim.

Initially, the majority of courts upheld the ability of the debtor to bifurcate undersecured home mortgage claims and modify the unsecured portion of those claims. See, e.g., Bellamy v. Federal Home Loan Mortg., 962 F.2d 176 (2d Cir. 1992); In re Hart, 923 F.2d 1410 (10th Cir. 1991); Wilson v. Commonwealth Mortg. Corp., 895 F.2d 123 (3d Cir. 1990); Lomas Mortgage USA v. Wiese, 980 F.2d 1279 (9th Cir. 1992). These courts held that "other than" as used in section 1322(b)(2) referred only to secured claims and thus did not prevent modification of the unsecured portion of the mortgagee's claim. The leading case for the minority view was In re Nobleman, 968 F.2d 483 (5th Cir. 1992), in which the United States Court of Appeals for the Fifth

Circuit held that section 1322(b)(2) prevented modification of any portion of the mortgagee's claim. See also, e.g., Landmark Financial Services v. Hall, 918 F.2d 1150 (4th Cir. 1990). The Fifth Circuit in *Nobleman* noted that section 1322(b)(2) authorized modification of the "rights of holders of secured claims" rather than modification of secured claims themselves, and thus reasoned that the anti-modification rule prevented the debtor from modifying any of the rights of the mortgagee even if its claim was undersecured.

The Supreme Court unanimously resolved the split of authority by affirming the Fifth Circuit's reasoning and result. Nobleman v. American Savings Bank, 508 U.S. 324, 113 S. Ct. 2106 (1993). The *Nobleman* approach certainly treats the undersecured mortgagee more favorably than it would be treated under state law outside of bankruptcy. [Can you explain why?] Nevertheless, given the fragile state of lending institutions in the early 1990s and real estate values during that period, *Nobleman* may have represented a small judicial contribution to the solvency of the mortgage lending industry. See generally Scarberry & Reddie, Home Mortgage Stripdown in Chapter 13 Bankruptcy: A Contextual Approach to Sections 1322(b)(2) and (b)(5), 20 Pepperdine L.Rev. 425 (1993); Nassen, Bankruptcy Code § 1322(b)(2)'s No-Modification Clause: Who Does It Protect?, 33 Ariz.L.Rev. 979 (1991).

In 1994, Congress added section 1322(c)(2), which did not modify *Nobelman* but did affect its application in certain Chapter 13 cases. Section 1322(c)(2) permits the debtor to modify a secured claim despite the anti-modification rule if "the last payment on the original payment schedule . . . is due before the final payment under the plan is due. . . ." Most courts and commentators take the view that section 1322(c)(2) permits a debtor to bifurcate an undersecured home mortgage in this situation and cram-down the unsecured component of the claim. See, e.g., In re Paschen, 296 F.3d 1203 (11th Cir.), cert. denied, 537 U.S. 1097, 123 S. Ct. 696 (2002); 8 Collier on Bankruptcy ¶ 1322.17 (16th ed.). Contra: In re Witt, 113 F.3d 508 (4th Cir. 1997). But section 1322(c)(2)'s practical effect is limited. In the typical Chapter 13 case, the debtor will have more than five years remaining on its mortgage term, and section 1322(c)(2) will not displace the anti-modification rule. As a result, section 1322(c)(2) will permit modification only for short-term mortgages, mortgages that are nearly paid off, and mortgages with impending balloon payments. Why might Congress have thought it appropriate to permit the debtor to modify the mortgage in these contexts, but not on the facts of *Nobleman*? See 8 Collier on Bankruptcy ¶ 1322.17; Nelson, Whitman, Burkhart & Freyermuth, Real Estate Finance Law § 8.18 (6th ed. 2014).

NOTES

1. *Is de-acceleration and cure an impermissible "modification"?* Frequently, by the time a Chapter 13 filing occurs, the debtor has already defaulted on her home mortgage and the mortgagee has already accelerated the maturity of the debt. As noted previously, section 1322(b)(5) permits cure of a prepetition arrearage on a "secured claim on which the last payment is

due after the date on which the final payment is due under the plan." If the mortgagee has already accelerated the debt pre-petition, however, the mortgagee might argue that the "last payment" is now due immediately, not at the originally scheduled maturity date. On this reading, section 1322(b)(5) would be unavailable, and an attempted cure of the arrearage would be an impermissible modification!

Initially, some courts adopted this argument. See, e.g., In re Britton, 35 B.R. 373 (N.D. Ind. 1982); In re Williams, 11 B.R. 504 (Bankr. S.D. Tex. 1981). In 1982, however, the United States Court of Appeals for the Second Circuit held that a Chapter 13 plan could defeat a pre-petition mortgage acceleration by cure and reinstatement. In re Taddeo, 685 F.2d 24 (2d Cir. 1982). As the court held, "we think the power to cure must comprehend the power to de-accelerate," Taddeo, 685 F.2d at 26, and "the power to 'cure any default' granted in § 1322(b)(3) and (b)(5) is not limited by the ban against 'modifying' home mortgages in § 1322(b)(2) because we do not read 'curing defaults' under (b)(3) or 'curing defaults and maintaining payments' under (b)(5) to be modifications of claims." Taddeo, 685 F.2d at 27. The near unanimous weight of judicial authority and scholarly commentary has endorsed Taddeo, and for good reason:

> As the Taddeo court itself stressed, "conditioning a debtor's right to cure on its having filed a Chapter 13 petition prior to acceleration would prompt unseemly and wasteful races to the courthouse. Worse, there would be races in which mortgagees possess an unwarranted and likely insurmountable advantage: wage earners seldom will possess the sophistication in bankruptcy matters that financial institutions do, and often will not have retained counsel in time to do much good." Moreover, even assuming a relatively high level of debtor sophistication, an anti-Taddeo approach may well encourage premature bankruptcy petitions rather than debtor attempts to resolve their financial problems by negotiation, mediation or other extrajudicial means. Finally, a refusal to permit de-acceleration would "encourage mortgagees to declare defaults and accelerate earlier to avoid the necessity of dealing with a Chapter 13 debtor."

Nelson, Whitman, Burkhart & Freyermuth, Real Estate Finance Law § 8.18, at 826 (6th ed. 2014) (quoting Zaretsky, Some Limits on Mortgagees' Rights in Chapter 13, 50 Brooklyn L. Rev. 433, 443 (1984)).

2.   Taddeo and balloon payments. Suppose that at the time Smith files a Chapter 13 petition, the entire $100,000 balance of the mortgage on his primary home is due—not by virtue of acceleration, but because Smith's note provided for a "balloon payment" that is now due. Can Smith use Taddeo to "deflate" the balloon and pay it off in installments under the plan? That would appear to be a "modification," and for this reason, the weight of authority prior to 1994 held that the answer was no. See, e.g., In re Seidel, 752 F.2d 1382 (9th Cir. 1985). But in 1994, Congress added section

1322(c)(2), which (as noted in the text) would explicitly allow Smith to take the $100,000 balloon debt and pay it off in installments during the Chapter 13 plan. See, e.g., In re Paschen, 296 F.3d 1203 (11th Cir. 2002); In re Kelly, 283 B.R. 808 (Bankr. M.D. Fla. 2002).

But suppose Smith's home is worth only $75,000. Does section 1322(c)(2) only permit Smith to modify the *repayment period* for paying the entire balloon, or does it also allow Smith to modify the *entire claim* through cram-down under section 1325(a)(5)? On this question, courts have disagreed. Compare In re Witt, 113 F.3d 508 (4th Cir. 1997) (section 1322(c)(2) only permits modification of the repayment period, not the claim itself) with In re Paschen, 296 F.2d 1203 (11th Cir. 2002) (section 1322(c)(2) permits modification of the claim). The weight of subsequent authority and commentary is consistent with *Paschen.* 8 Collier on Bankruptcy ¶ 1322.17, at 1322–57 (16th ed.). Is that sensible?

3.   *When is the debtor's cure right extinguished?* Section 1322(c)(1) provides that "a default with respect to . . . a lien on the debtor's principal residence may be cured . . . until such residence is sold at a foreclosure sale that is conducted in accordance with applicable nonbankruptcy law." Clearly, if a sale has divested the mortgagor of all interest in the property, cure is unavailable. But when is the residence "sold"? When the auctioneer's hammer falls? When the court enters an order confirming the sale? When a deed is delivered to the purchaser? What if the state allows statutory post-sale redemption?

The language of section 1322(c)(1) could have addressed these questions more explicitly. The most literal reading appears to prevent cure after a foreclosure sale has occurred—even if state law provides a post-sale redemption right—and the weight of judicial authority so holds. See, e.g., In re Cain, 423 F.3d 617 (6th Cir. 2005); In re McKinney, 344 B.R. 1 (Bankr. D. Me. 2006). Can you explain why cure during the statutory redemption period would be inappropriate? See Nelson, Whitman, Burkhart & Freyermuth, Real Estate Finance Law § 8.18 (6th ed. 2014).

There remains judicial disagreement, however, regarding when the sale is final within the meaning of section 1322(c)(1). Some courts hold that the section established a federal "gavel" rule under which the cure right terminates when the hammer falls at the sale auction, as long as the sale complied with state law. See, e.g., In re Connors, 497 F.3d 314 (3d Cir. 2007); In re Cain, 423 F.3d 617 (6th Cir. 2005); In re Woodford, 354 B.R. 153 (Bankr. W.D. Ky. 2006). The weight of authority requires that the court look to state law to determine whether any "post-gavel" actions—such as execution and delivery of a deed, or judicial confirmation of the sale—were required for the property to have been "sold." See, e.g., In re Jenkins, 422 B.R. 175 (Bankr. E.D. Ark. 2010) (execution and delivery of deed); In re Howard, 351 B.R. 251 (Bankr. M.D. Ga. 2006) (delivery of deed); In re Wescott, 309 B.R. 308 (Bankr. E.D. Wis. 2004) (judicial confirmation of foreclosure sale).

4. *The limits of the anti-modification rule.* Section 1322(b)(2) prohibits modification of a claim that is secured *"only* by a security interest in real property that is the debtor's principal residence." This means that if a mortgage loan on the debtor's principal residence is also secured by other real estate or personal property, modification is permitted! See, e.g., In re Lafata, 483 F.3d 13 (2d Cir. 2007) (modification permitted where debtor's residence was primarily located on an adjacent lot and merely encroached on mortgaged real estate); In re Potts, 421 B.R. 518 (8th Cir. B.A.P. 2010) (modification permitted where mortgage covered both home and separate parcel used for grazing and growing crops). Under the weight of authority, modification is also permitted where the mortgaged premises includes not only the debtor's principal residence, but other rental property as well (i.e., a duplex in which the debtor occupies one unit as its principal residence but rents out the other unit). See, e.g., In re Scarborough, 461 F.3d 406 (3rd Cir. 2006); Lomas Mortg. v. Louis, 82 F.3d 1 (1st Cir.1996); In re Picchi, 448 B.R. 870 (1st Cir. B.A.P. 2011). Can you identify a discernible rationale for this limitation?

Section 1322(b)(2)'s "only" qualification has proven to be a dangerous trap for many home mortgagees. The inclination of secured lenders is to take as much security as possible; indeed, it is normally considered prudent to do so. A mortgagee that succumbs to this temptation and takes an additional mortgage on other real estate or a security interest in the debtor's automobiles, boats or other chattels loses its protection against mortgage modification.

Prior to 2005, lenders often unwittingly threatened their anti-modification protection by including in the mortgage boilerplate language that extended the lender's security to include items reasonably related to the real estate, such as appliances, machinery, furniture, equipment, and fixtures installed on the mortgaged premises; rents, issues and profits of the mortgaged premises; and tax and insurance escrow funds held by the mortgagee. See, e.g., Wilson v. Commonwealth Mortg. Corp., 895 F.2d 123 (3d Cir. 1990) (appliances); In re Jackson, 136 B.R. 797 (Bankr. N.D. Ill. 1992) (rents); In re Hughes, 333 B.R. 360 (Bankr. M.D.N.C. 2005) (escrow funds). In 2005, in BAPCPA, Congress redefined "debtor's principal residence" to include "incidental property," which includes as "(A) property commonly conveyed with a principal residence in the area where the real property is located; (B) all easements, rights, appurtenances, fixtures, rents, royalties, mineral rights, oil or gas rights or profits, water rights, escrow funds, or insurance proceeds; and (C) all replacements or additions." 11 U.S.C.A. §§ 101(13A)(A) ("debtor's principal residence"); 101(27B) ("incidental property"). Thus, while additional security such as a mortgage on another tract of real estate or a security interest in the debtor's car will continue to destroy the mortgagee's protection against modification, the normal boilerplate provisions found in most residential mortgage forms should not have this effect. How about a mortgage that also covers appliances such as a refrigerator? Could the mortgagee avoid the potential consequences of the "only" limitation by releasing the additional security before the debtor's Chapter 13 petition? See, e.g., In re Baker, 398 B.R. 198 (Bankr. N.D. Ohio 2008). What if the release comes after the petition? See, e.g., Wilson v. Commonwealth Mortg. Corp., 895 F.2d 123, 129 (3d Cir.1990).

5.   *The timing of the "principal residence" determination.* For purposes of the anti-modification rule, must the home be the debtor's principal residence at the time the loan is made, on the petition date, or both? Courts have not reached consensus. See, e.g., In re Scarborough, 461 F.3d 406 (3d Cir. 2006) (date of loan); In re Proctor, 494 B.R. 833 (Bankr.E.D.N.C.2013) (same); In re Lebrun, 185 B.R. 665 (Bankr.D.Mass.1995) (petition date); In re Abdelgadir, 455 B.R. 896 (9th Cir. B.A.P. 2011) (using petition date in interpreting Chapter 11's analogous anti-modification rule). In 2010, Congress amended the definition of "debtor's principal residence" to read "if used as the principal residence by the debtor." 11 U.S.C.A. § 101(13A). Does this language provide a clear answer to the question? Why or why not?

6.   *Does the anti-modification rule reflect sound policy?* In the wake of the economic crisis that began in 2007, home values in many markets plummeted, leaving many homeowners "underwater" (owing more than their homes were worth). The anti-modification rule effectively meant that homeowners could not use Chapter 13 as a way to modify their mortgage loans and remain in their homes. The resulting foreclosure crisis prompted significant responses by both states (foreclosure reform and the implementation of mediation programs designed to facilitate negotiations that might encourage loan modifications) and the federal government (including the HAMP and HARP programs designed to facilitate modification of home mortgage loans). Would these objectives be better facilitated by doing away with the anti-modification rule? Why or why not?

7.   *Junior liens and "strip-off" of wholly unsecured junior liens.* Under the weight of authority, a junior mortgage on the debtor's primary residence enjoys the same protection against modification, as long as there is some equity in the home above the amount of the senior obligations. See, e.g., In re Brenneke, 441 B.R. 625 (Bankr. E.D. Mo. 2010); In re Rubottom, 134 B.R. 641 (9th Cir. B.A.P. 1991). But what about the creditor holding a wholly "underwater" junior mortgage on the primary residence? Can the Chapter 13 debtor modify the mortgagee's claim, or does the anti-modification rule prohibit that result?

Following *Nobleman*, a few courts ruled that section 1322(b)(2) prohibited modification in this context. See, e.g., In re Hughes, 402 B.R. 325 (Bankr. D. Minn. 2009); In re Diggs, 228 B.R. 611 (Bankr. W.D. La. 1999); In re Lewandowski, 219 B.R. 99 (Bankr. W.D. Pa. 1998). However, the near-unanimous weight of recent authority permits the Chapter 13 debtor to use section 1322(b)(2) to strip-off a wholly underwater lien. See, e.g., In re Zimmer, 313 F.3d 1220 (9th Cir. 2002); In re Lane, 280 F.3d 663 (6th Cir. 2002); In re Pond, 252 F.3d 122 (2d Cir. 2001); In re Tanner, 217 F.3d 1357 (11th Cir. 2000); In re Bartee, 212 F.3d 277 (5th Cir. 2000); In re Frazier, 448

B.R. 803 (Bankr.E.D.Cal.2011), aff'd sub nom. Frazier v. Real Time Resolutions, Inc., 469 B.R. 889 (E.D.Cal.2012); TD Bank, N.A. v. Landry, 479 B.R. 1 (D.Mass.2012); In re Hall, 495 B.R. 393 (Bankr.N.D.Ill.2013). These decisions have reasoned that under *Nobelman*, the anti-modification rule cannot apply unless the mortgagee has a secured claim, and the wholly underwater junior lienor has no secured claim at all thanks to section 506(a).

Courts have disagreed, however, whether the authority for this strip-off lies within section 506(d) or section 1322(b)(2)'s anti-modification rule. As discussed earlier, the Supreme Court in *Dewsnup* concluded that a Chapter 7 debtor may not use section 506(d) to strip-down an undersecured lien. Following *Dewsnup*, there has been debate as to whether the Court's interpretation of section 506(d) applied outside of Chapter 7 cases. Some courts have concluded that *Dewsnup* does not apply in Chapter 13, and that a Chapter 13 debtor can use section 506(d) to strip-off an underwater junior lien. See, e.g., Carroll v. Key Bank, 2011 WL 6338912 (D.Utah 2011); Hart v. San Diego Credit Union, 449 B.R. 783 (S.D.Cal.2010). The Tenth Circuit, however, has ruled that section 1322(b)(2) provides the exclusive authority for lien stripping in Chapter 13. In re Woolsey, 696 F.3d 1266 (10th Cir. 2012). From a pleading perspective, a Chapter 13 debtor thus must take care to plead the correct statutory basis for stripping-off an underwater junior lien.

8. *Manufactured homes.* Does the anti-modification rule apply where the debtor's principal residence is a manufactured home? Section 1322(b)(2) makes clear that the mortgagee must have a "security interest in real property that is the debtor's principal residence" to qualify for the protection of the anti-modification rule. A new mobile or manufactured home begins its life as personal property; in most states, upon the sale of a new manufactured home, the state issues a certificate of title for the home (as if the home were a vehicle). The home does not become "real property" under state law unless it has become a fixture or the owner complies with the state's "conversion" statute (which involves the surrender of the certificate of title and the permanent or quasi-permanent attachment of the home to a parcel of land). Thus, a lender or seller that provides purchase money financing for the purchase of a manufactured home takes (at least initially) a security interest in personal property and would not qualify for the protection of the antimodification rule unless and until the home becomes "real property." Compare In re Williamson, 400 B.R. 917 (Bankr. M.D. Ga. 2009) (mobile home deemed realty; lender's interest not modifiable) with In re Ennis, 558 F.3d 343 (4th Cir. 2009) (mobile home deemed personalty under Virginia law; lender's interest subject to modification).

In 2005, BAPCPA amended the definition of "debtor's principal residence" to include a "mobile or manufactured home" used as the principal residence by the debtor, "without regard to whether it is attached to real property." 11 U.S.C.A. § 101(13A). At first blush, this might appear to give manufactured home lenders the benefit of the anti-modification rule, without regard to whether the home was attached to the land. However, BAPCPA did not modify the language of section 1322(b)(2), which requires the lender to have a security interest in *"real property* that is the debtor's principal residence" to qualify for the anti-modification rule. As a result, most courts have held that unless the manufactured home has become a fixture or the lender has complied with the state's conversion statute (if any), a Chapter 13 debtor can modify the claim of a lender with a security interest in the home. See, e.g., In re Coleman, 392 B.R. 767 (8th Cir. B.A.P. 2008).

What are the policy implications of this result? On the one hand, unlike normal single family real estate, many manufactured homes tend to depreciate over time regardless of market conditions. Thus, the reasoning of *Coleman* subjects manufactured home lenders to a significant risk of strip-down if the borrower files a Chapter 13. On the other hand, after such a strip-down, it may be less likely that the home will appreciate in value in the future, and therefore it will be less likely that the debtor could reap an "undeserved" windfall. In the wake of the recent real estate crisis, given the demand and need for affordable housing alternatives, should manufactured home lenders receive the same protection from modification as lenders holding liens on traditional "stick-built" homes? See Ann M. Burkhart, Bringing Manufactured Housing into the Real Estate Finance System, 37 Pepperdine L. Rev. 427 (2010).

9.   *"Chapter 20" cases: strip-off of a wholly unsecured junior lien by a Chapter 13 debtor after obtaining a discharge in a prior Chapter 7 case.* Some debtors are not eligible for Chapter 13 relief because their debts exceed the statutory debt limits for Chapter 13 relief. For example, suppose Smith owns a principal residence subject to an $800,000 first mortgage and a $200,000 second mortgage. Because of a severe drop in real estate values, the home is now valued at only $700,000. Because Smith also has $800,000 in unsecured debt due to catastrophic medical expenses, he is not eligible for Chapter 13 relief. Smith would like to discharge the medical debt and retain the home while "stripping-off" the underwater second mortgage lien. A Chapter 7 filing would permit Smith to discharge the medical debt but, as discussed previously, most authority holds that *Dewsnup* prevents a debtor from stripping-off a wholly underwater junior lien in Chapter 7.

Thus, Smith may react strategically by attempting two successive bankruptcy filings. First, Smith might file a Chapter 7 petition to discharge the unsecured medical debt (and thereby bring himself within the permissible Chapter 13 debt limits). Then, after getting a Chapter 7 discharge, Smith might file a Chapter 13 petition and try to use section 1322(b)(2) to strip-off the underwater second mortgage lien (even though that relief was not available in his prior Chapter 7). In the bankruptcy vernacular, Smith's conduct is often called "Chapter 20" bankruptcy.

In 2005, BAPCPA amended the Code by adding section 1328(f), which prohibits a Chapter 13 debtor from obtaining a discharge of debt in Chapter 13 if the debtor has obtained a Chapter 7 discharge during the preceding four years. But the Code does not prohibit a debtor from filing a Chapter 13 in this situation—it only prohibits the debtor from obtaining a Chapter 13 discharge. So can Smith use "Chapter 20" to strip-off the underwater junior lien?

IN RE CAIN

United States Bankruptcy Appellate Panel, Sixth Circuit, 2014
513 B.R. 316

MARIAN F. HARRISON, Bankruptcy Appellate Panel Judge. Debtor Andrea M. Cain (the "Debtor") appeals the August 9, 2013 order of the United States Bankruptcy Court for the Northern District of Ohio (the "Bankruptcy Court") denying the Debtor's unopposed Motion to Avoid the Mortgage Lien of Amerifirst Home Improvement Financial Company ("Amerifirst"). For the reasons that follow, the Panel REVERSES the Bankruptcy Court's denial of the Debtor's Motion to Avoid the Mortgage Lien of Amerifirst. . . .

The Debtor first filed a Chapter 7 petition and received a discharge on February 1, 2008. On July 3, 2008, the Debtor filed the present Chapter 13 case to pay an outstanding auto loan and tax obligations, to cure the default on her first mortgage, and to avoid a wholly unsecured second mortgage on her residence. The Debtor's Amended Chapter 13 Plan, dated August 21, 2008, was confirmed on September 18, 2008. The confirmed Chapter 13 plan included the following provision:

> Debtors will avoid the mortgage and/or judgment liens of Amerifirst Home Improvement Finance, Squires Construction Company, & Ohio Department of Taxation, which [are] wholly unsecured pursuant to 11 U.S.C. §§ 506(a), 1322(b)(2) & 1325(a)(5)(B), and which wholly impairs Debtors' exemption in their residence home pursuant to 11 U.S.C. § 522(f). Any unsecured claim filed by said creditor(s) shall be disallowed as discharged in Debtors' Chapter 7 Bankruptcy Case No. 08–10687 filed February 1, 2008 unless otherwise allowed by a separate order of the Court.

Because the Debtor had received a Chapter 7 discharge within the preceding four years, the Debtor was not eligible for a discharge in her Chapter 13 case. *See* 11 U.S.C. § 1328(f)(1). Accordingly, upon completion of the Debtor's payments under the plan, the Chapter 13 Trustee filed his Motion for Order Releasing Wages and Closing Case Without a Discharge. The Chapter 13 Trustee's motion was granted on May 6, 2013. On May 17, 2013, the Debtor filed a Motion to Avoid Mortgage Lien on Real Estate against Amerifirst in order to effectuate the provisions of her confirmed Chapter 13 Plan and to avoid Amerifirst's second mortgage lien on her residence. At the time of the Chapter 13 filing, the Debtor's residence was valued at not more than $100,800. The residence was encumbered by Everhome Mortgage Company's first mortgage in the amount of $106,306.38 and by Amerifirst's second mortgage in the amount of $9,415.28.

No party-in-interest objected to the Debtor's Motion to Avoid Mortgage Lien on Real Estate, however, the Bankruptcy Court denied the motion by order, dated August 9, 2013. The Bankruptcy Court held:

> The lien stripping power of 11 U.S.C. § 506 is unavailable to Debtor. She received a Chapter 7 discharge within four years of filing this case and is therefore ineligible for a Chapter 13 discharge. 11 U.S.C. § 1328(f)(1). Pursuant to § 1325(a)(5), the lien stays in place until discharge or payment of the underlying debt. Because the Debtor is ineligible for a discharge, the mortgage lien will stay in place until payment of the underlying debt.

The determinative issue in this appeal concerns the interplay between various provisions of the Bankruptcy Code affecting "Chapter 20" debtors. Specifically, the issue is whether a debtor may strip off a wholly unsecured, inferior mortgage lien on the debtor's primary residence in a Chapter 13 case filed less than four years after having received a Chapter 7 discharge.

This question has not been addressed by the Sixth Circuit. Two Circuit Courts and one Bankruptcy Appellate Panel have considered it, finding that a valueless lien can be stripped, regardless of discharge eligibility. *Wells Fargo Bank, N.A. v. Scantling (In re Scantling),* [754] F.3d [1323], 2014 WL 2750349, at *5 (11th Cir. June 18, 2014); *Branigan v. Davis (In re Davis),* 716 F.3d 331 (4th Cir.2013); *Fisette v. Keller (In re Fisette),* 455 B.R. 177, 185 (B.A.P. 8th Cir.2011). Bankruptcy courts, however, are split on the question and on their approach. . . .

Courts utilizing the first approach refuse to allow stripping off wholly unsecured liens in Chapter 20 cases because doing so would amount to a "de facto discharge." *Lindskog v. M & I Bank,* 480 B.R. 916, 919 (E.D.Wis.2012). These courts rely on an interpretation of *Dewsnup v. Timm,* 502 U.S. 410, 417, 112 S.Ct. 773, 778, 116 L.Ed.2d 903 (1992) (holding that Section 506(d) does not allow a party to "strip down" a partially secured lien), and on Congress' inclusion of a discharge requirement in 11 U.S.C. § 1325(a)(5)(B)(i)(II). *See, e.g., In re Gerardin,* 447 B.R. 342, 352 (Bankr.S.D.Fla.2011) ("[D]ebtor who is ineligible for a chapter 13 discharge may not strip down or strip off a lien."), *abrogated by In re Scantling,* 2014 WL 2750349; *In re Fenn,* 428 B.R. 494, 500 (Bankr.N.D.Ill.2010) (allowing permanent strip off of junior mortgage lien after Chapter 20 debtor completes plan "results in a de facto discharge") (citation omitted); *Orkwis v. MERS (In re Orkwis),* 457 B.R. 243, 252 (Bankr.E.D.N.Y.2011) (holding that junior lien is not removed until entry of discharge); *In re Winitzky,* No. 1:08–bk–19337–MT, 2009 WL 9139891, at *5 (Bankr.C.D.Cal. May 7, 2009) (holding that Code does not allow court to strip lien where debtor cannot receive a discharge).

Those courts adopting the second approach allow Chapter 20 lien stripping but hold that the parties' pre-bankruptcy rights are reinstated by operation of law after the plan has been consummated. *See, e.g., Victorio v. Billingslea,* 470 B.R. 545, 556 (S.D.Cal.2012) (finding that a Chapter 20 debtor must pay debt in full during course of Chapter 13 plan to permanently avoid liability on wholly unsecured lien); *In re Jarvis,* 390 B.R. 600, 605–06 (Bankr.C.D.Ill.2008) (holding that discharge is a necessary prerequisite to permanency of lien avoidance); *In re Lilly,* 378 B.R. 232, 236 (Bankr.C.D.Ill.2007) (citation omitted) ("Where a debtor does not receive a discharge . . . any modifications to a creditor's rights imposed in the plan are not permanent and have no binding effect once the term of the plan ends."); *In re Trujillo,* No. 6: 10–bk–02615–ABB, 2010 WL 4669095, at *2 (Bankr.M.D.Fla. Nov.10, 2010) (same), *aff'd sub nom. Trujillo v. BAC Home Loan Servicing, L.P. (In re Trujillo),* 2012 WL 8883694 (M.D.Fla. Aug.10, 2012), *abrogated by In re Scantling,* 2014 WL 2750349.

Courts applying the third approach "allow chapter 20 lien stripping because nothing in the Bankruptcy Code prevents it." *In re Jennings,* 454 B.R. at 257 (citations omitted). These courts contend that the mechanism that voids the lien is plan completion, and that Chapter 20 cases end in administrative closing rather than dismissal. *See, e.g., In re Scantling,* 2014 WL 2750349, at *5 (strip off of unsecured mortgage on debtor's principal residence "is accomplished through the § 506(a) valuation procedure that determines that the creditor does not hold a secured claim"); *In re Davis,* 716 F.3d at 338 (holding that Chapter 20 debtor can strip a worthless lien permanently upon completion of plan); *Zeman v. Waterman (In re Waterman),* 469 B.R. 334, 339 (D.Colo.2012) ("Chapter 20 debtor may strip off a wholly unsecured lien from his principal residence, despite being ineligible for a discharge."); *In re Fair,* 450 B.R. 853, 858 (E.D.Wis.2011) (citations omitted) ("[T]here is nothing in the bankruptcy code which ties the modification of an unsecured lien to obtaining a discharge under chapter 13."); *In re Fisette,* 455 B.R. at 185 (citations omitted) ("[N]othing in the Bankruptcy Code conditions a Chapter 13 debtor's ability to modify a wholly unsecured creditor's lien under § 1322(b) on his eligibility for a discharge."); *In re Wapshare,* 492 B.R. 211, 217–18 (Bankr.S.D.N.Y.2013) (citations omitted) ("[U]nsecured junior mortgage lien is permanently avoided in chapter 20 cases once a chapter 13 plan is confirmed and all plan payments have been made."); *Wong v. Green Tree Serv., LLC (In re Wong),* 488 B.R. 537, 551 (Bankr.E.D.N.Y.2013) (holding that where claim is unsecured under § 506(a), then claim is unsecured with respect to § 1322(b)(2) and § 1325(a)(5)); *In re Dolinak,* 497 B.R. 15, 22–23 (Bankr.D.N.H.2013) (citation omitted) ("Section 1328(f)(1) only prevents a chapter 20 debtor from receiving a discharge; it does not limit a chapter 20 debtor's rights under § 1322(b)."); *In re Gloster,* 459 B.R. 200, 205 (Bankr.D.N.J.2011) (holding that lien stripping allowed in "Chapter 20 setting so long as a subsequent Chapter 13 is filed in good faith and a plan is successfully completed.").

A growing consensus of courts have followed the third approach, holding that nothing in the Code prevents a Chapter 20 debtor from stripping a wholly unsecured junior lien on the debtor's principal residence. This approach is most consistent with the Sixth Circuit's decision in *In re Lane,* 280 F.3d 663, 669, because it starts by determining the status of the claim under 11 U.S.C. § 506(a).

In the present case, the Bankruptcy Court based its holding on 11 U.S.C. § 1325(a)(5)(B), which requires that the holder of a secured claim retain the lien securing the claim until the mortgage is satisfied or the debtor receives a discharge, whichever comes first. Thus, the Bankruptcy Court determined that because of the Debtor's ineligibility for a discharge, she must satisfy Amerifirst's lien in full. By failing to first determine the proper classification of Amerifirst's claim, the Bankruptcy Court's decision disregarded the road map set forth in *Nobelman* and *Lane.*

It is undisputed that under 11 U.S.C. § 506 Amerifirst's lien has no value because the amount owed under the first mortgage exceeds the value of the property. Consequently, pursuant to the holding in *Lane,* Amerifirst's claim is "unsecured" under 11 U.S.C. § 506(a). *Id.* at 669. Thus, Amerifirst's lien cannot be treated as a secured claim under 11 U.S.C. § 1322(b)(2) (protecting holders of "secured claims" secured only by a security interest in a debtor's principal residence). *In re Wong,* 488 B.R. at 551. Nor do the requirements of 11 U.S.C. § 1325(a)(5) (protecting the holder of a secured claim until the debt is paid or the debtor is discharged) apply. *Id.*

Applying the reasoning set forth in *Lane* to the facts of this case, the wholly unsecured status of Amerifirst's claim, rather than the Debtor's eligibility for a discharge, is determinative. *See In re Scantling,* 2014 WL 2750349, at *5 ("[S]trip off is accomplished through the § 506(a) valuation procedure that determines that the creditor does not hold a secured claim."). Nothing in 11 U.S.C. § 1328(f)(1) prohibits a Chapter 20 debtor from taking advantage of the protections and benefits (other than discharge) of Chapter 13. *Frazier v. Real Time Resolutions, Inc. (In re Frazier),* 469 B.R. 889, 899 (E.D.Cal.2012) (citation omitted). Lien-stripping is an important tool in the Chapter 13 toolbox, and it is not conditioned on being eligible for a discharge. *In re Jennings,* 454 B.R. at 258 (citations omitted). *See also In re Frazier,* 469 B.R. at 895–96

("[W]holly unsecured junior lien on the debtor's principal residence may be removed in Chapter 20 action despite the operation of § 1328(f)(1)."). Accordingly, a Chapter 20 debtor may avoid a wholly unsecured lien on the debtor's principal residence.

Based on the above, the Bankruptcy Court erred by denying the Debtor's Motion to Avoid the Mortgage Lien of Amerifirst. . . .

NOTE

Which approach is preferable? At first blush, the *Cain* approach appears to sanction an end run around *Dewsnup*'s prohibition on lien-stripping. As one bankruptcy court noted, "allowing a debtor to file chapter 7, discharge all dischargeable debts and then immediately file chapter 13 to strip off a second mortgage lien would not be much different than simply avoiding the mortgage lien in the chapter 7 itself." In re Blosser, 2009 WL 1064455 (Bankr. E.D. Wis. 2009). Nevertheless, there are legitimate reasons why a "Chapter 20" debtor might want to use the restructuring tools of Chapter 13 even if she is not eligible for a discharge. Further, the Supreme Court has explicitly recognized that "Congress did not intend to categorically foreclose the benefit of Chapter 13 lien reorganization to a debtor who previously filed for Chapter 7 relief." Johnson v. Home State Bank, 501 U.S. 78, 87 (1991). As a result, courts should be properly reluctant to presume Congress intended for section 1328(f) to limit the availability of Chapter 13's other lien restructuring tools.

Still, it is worth noting that 11 U.S.C.A. § 1325(a)(3) requires that a court may not confirm a Chapter 13 plan unless "the plan has been proposed in good faith and not by any means forbidden by law." If the debtor has no good reason for using "Chapter 20" other than stripping-off an underwater junior lien that could not have been avoided in Chapter 7, can the court properly conclude that the debtor's Chapter 13 plan lacks good faith and thus cannot be confirmed? See, e.g., In re Okosisi, 451 B.R. 90 (Bankr. D. Nev. 2011); In re Tran, 431 B.R. 230 (Bankr. N.D. Cal. 2010).

6.   THE MORTGAGEE IN A CHAPTER 11 CASE

Chapter 11 establishes the process for reorganization of business debtors and individual debtors with debts that exceed the permissible limits for Chapter 13. As in Chapter 13, the Chapter 11 debtor-in-possession must propose a plan that explains how and to what extent it will pay its creditors on account of their claims. In Chapter 13 cases, all plans are either 3 or 5 years, and it is typical for the debtor to submit a plan at the same time he or she files the bankruptcy petition. By contrast, in Chapter 11, there is no fixed plan period, and there can be a significant delay between the petition date and the date that debtor proposes and seeks confirmation of a plan. The debtor has the exclusive right to submit a plan for the first 120 days of a Chapter 11 case, 11 U.S.C.A. § 1121(b), and for longer if the court extends this exclusivity period for "cause." 11 U.S.C.A. § 1121(d).[27] The need for this period derives from several factors. First, the financial affairs of Chapter 11 debtors are often more complex (and thus potentially more difficult to restructure) than those of individual debtors in Chapter 13. For this reason, Chapter 11 debtors often need time to adjust their operations to respond to the circumstances that resulted in the bankruptcy filing. Second, unlike in Chapter 13— where approval of the plan rests solely with the bankruptcy court— Chapter 11's provisions require that creditors vote on the plan, and judicial confirmation requires that the plan meet certain creditor approval thresholds. Thus, while the debtor negotiates with its creditors, a significant amount of time may pass between the petition date and the date on which the debtor begins repaying creditors under the terms of a confirmed plan.

Chapter 11, classification of mortgage claims, and nonrecourse mortgages. As discussed earlier, if the unpaid balance of the mortgage debt exceeds the value of the mortgaged property, section 506(a) "bifurcates" the mortgagee's claim into two claims—a secured claim equal to the value of the mortgaged property, and an unsecured claim for the difference between the value of the mortgaged property and the unpaid balance of the debt. Initially, one might assume that a commercial mortgagee might have no unsecured claim at all if the mortgage loan was "nonrecourse" (meaning that the mortgagor and mortgagee agreed in the loan documents that the mortgagor would have no personal liability on the debt). For distribution purposes in Chapter 11, however, nonrecourse mortgages are treated as if the mortgagee had recourse against the debtor. 11 U.S.C.A. § 1111(b)(1)(A) ("A claim secured by a lien on property of the estate shall be allowed or disallowed . . . the same as if the holder of such claim had recourse against the debtor on account of such claim, whether or not such holder has such recourse. . . ."). Thus, suppose Debtor owns an office building that is subject to a nonrecourse mortgage held by First Life Insurance Co. (First Life) that secures an unpaid balance of $20 million. On the Chapter 11 petition date, the office building is worth $15 million. Even though First Life could not have obtained a deficiency judgment against Debtor outside of bankruptcy, First Life still has an allowed unsecured claim of $5 million, and is entitled to receive a distribution in bankruptcy on account of that claim, along with other unsecured creditors. Can you explain why bankruptcy gives the nonrecourse mortgagee the right to assert an unsecured claim?

There are only two situations in which an undersecured nonrecourse mortgagee cannot assert an unsecured claim in Chapter 11. The first arises when the debtor proposes to sell the mortgaged property rather

---

[27] If the debtor fails to file a plan, any other party (including a creditor) can file a plan after the exclusive period has expired.

than to retain ownership of it. 11 U.S.C.A. § 1111(b)(1)(A)(ii). This exception makes sense, because in that case the mortgagee receives exactly what it bargained for in making a nonrecourse loan. The second arises when the undersecured mortgagee makes a "section 1111(b) election," choosing to waive its unsecured claim and have its entire claim treated as fully secured. 11 U.S.C.A. §§ 1111(b)(1)(A)(i), 1111(b)(2). In the above example, if First Life makes this election, First Life is deemed to have a secured claim of $20 million. It will retain its lien on the office building to secure the repayment of that entire amount, but it must forgo any right to share in any distribution made to unsecured creditors. The section 1111(b) election thus allows an undersecured mortgagee like First Bank to avoid having its lien "stripped-down" in Chapter 11.[28]

The Chapter 11 plan. Section 1123 of the Code specifies in elaborate detail the contents of the plan, but two elements merit primary attention here. First, the plan must sort creditor claims into "classes"; second, the plan must describe in detail how it will treat each class of creditors (i.e., how it proposes to repay claims within that class). The debtor can place a claim into a particular class only if it is "substantially similar" to other claims in the same class. 11 U.S.C.A. § 1122(a). Thus, a Chapter 11 plan must classify secured and unsecured claims separately, and cannot place a senior mortgage claim and a junior mortgage claim on the same property in the same class. [This typically means that each secured claim must be placed in its own separate class.]

As in Chapter 13, a Chapter 11 plan may propose to repay unsecured creditors less than the full amount of their claims, and may modify a secured claim (unless the debtor is an individual debtor and the claim is secured only by the debtor's primary residence). 11 U.S.C.A. § 1123(b)(1), (5). In Chapter 11 vernacular, a claim that is modified by the debtor's plan is said to be "impaired." 11 U.S.C.A. § 1124 (a class is not "impaired" if the plan "leaves unaltered the legal, equitable or contractual rights" of all claims in the class). Importantly, a plan's mere cure of a pre-bankruptcy default and de-acceleration of a pre-bankruptcy acceleration is not impairment. 11 U.S.C.A. § 1124(2).[29] Thus, as in Chapter 13, the Chapter 11 debtor may cure the default by paying any arrearages in installments under its plan. However, if the plan proposes to modify the interest rate, extend the repayment term, or "strip-down" the principal

---

[28] A mortgagee cannot make an 1111(b) election if the creditor's interest is of "inconsequential value." 11 U.S.C.A. § 1111(b)(1)(B)(i). Thus, if a junior mortgagee's debt is entirely "underwater" (i.e., the collateral's value is lower than the balance owed to the senior mortgagee), the junior cannot make an 1111(b) election. As a result, as in Chapter 13, the Chapter 11 debtor can "strip-off" the lien of an entirely underwater junior mortgagee. In re Heritage Highgate, Inc., 679 F.3d 132 (3d Cir. 2012); In re Johnson, 386 B.R. 171 (Bankr. W.D. Pa. 2008).

[29] If the plan proposes to pay the arrearage in installments, the debtor must pay interest on the arrearage "in accordance with the underlying agreement and applicable nonbankruptcy law." 11 U.S.C.A. § 1123(d).

balance to the current value of the collateral, such a modification impairs the mortgagee's secured claim.

Once the debtor files its proposed plan, the debtor must solicit the requisite creditor acceptance needed for court approval (or "confirmation") of the plan. Each creditor must receive a copy of the plan (or a plan summary) and a judicially-approved disclosure statement, and then each creditor votes whether to accept the plan. In general (and subject to the possibility of approval by "cram-down" as discussed later in this section), for the debtor to confirm its plan, each class of creditors must either (1) accept the plan or (2) not be impaired by it. 11 U.S.C.A. § 1129(a)(8). If a class is unimpaired, it is deemed to have accepted the plan. 11 U.S.C.A. § 1126(f). If the plan impairs a class of claims, the class is deemed to accept the plan if a majority in number and two-thirds in total amount of the claims in the class vote to approve the plan. 11 U.S.C.A. § 1126(c).

The confirmation requirements. Section 1129 establishes the requirements for the court to confirm a plan. As explained above, each class must accept the plan or must not be impaired. In addition, if even one creditor in an impaired class votes not to accept the plan, then the court may not confirm the plan unless it pays each creditor in that class an amount not less than the creditor would have received in a Chapter 7 liquidation. 11 U.S.C.A. § 1129(a)(7). Moreover, *at least one class* of impaired claims must accept the plan. 11 U.S.C.A. § 1129(a)(10). Finally, the court cannot confirm the plan unless it concludes that the plan was proposed in good faith, 11 U.S.C.A. § 1129(a)(3), and is "feasible," i.e., that confirmation "is not likely to be followed by the liquidation, or the need for further financial reorganization, of the debtor . . . unless such liquidation or reorganization is proposed in the plan." 11 U.S.C.A. § 1129(a)(11). Under this standard, the court must examine the adequacy of the debtor's capital structure, its earning power, economic conditions, the ability of debtor's management and the probability of its continuation, and any other factors related to the debtor's ability to perform its plan successfully. See, e.g., In re Waterford Hotel, Inc., 497 B.R. 255 (Bankr. E.D. Mich. 2013).

Cram-down. If a plan satisfies all of the other requirements of section 1129, but an impaired class still fails to approve it, the court may nevertheless confirm or "cram-down" the plan over the objection of that class, as long as the plan "does not discriminate unfairly, and is fair and equitable" to that class. 11 U.S.C.A. § 1129(b)(1). To understand the implications of cram-down for the mortgagee, suppose Debtor owns a shopping center subject to a mortgage held by First Life Insurance Company (First Life) that secures an outstanding balance of $12 million. After losing several major tenants, Debtor files a Chapter 11 petition. The shopping center's current value is $10 million. First Life does not make a section 1111(b) election, so it has a secured claim of $10 million and an unsecured claim of $2 million. As a result, First Life will have two votes on the plan: one as the only claimant in the class that contains its secured claim, and another as a member of a class of unsecured creditors. If First Life votes to reject the plan, then the class containing its secured claim will reject the plan; further, because of the size of its unsecured claim, its rejection may preclude Debtor from obtaining the necessary approval (two-thirds in amount) needed from the class of unsecured creditors. Thus, if First Life votes to reject the plan, Debtor cannot confirm it unless it satisfies the cram-down standards. The "fair and equitable" cram-down standard, however, applies differently to secured and unsecured claims.

Cram-down: The "fair and equitable" standard and secured claims. Section 1129(b)(2)(A) provides three standards under which a cram-down plan is considered "fair and equitable" in its treatment of an objecting mortgagee's secured claim, depending on how the plan proposes to treat the mortgagee. The first standard applies if the debtor plans to retain the mortgaged property; if so, the mortgagee must retain its lien and must receive present or deferred cash payments under the plan that (1) are at least equal to the amount of the total unpaid mortgage debt and (2) have a present value that is not less than the value of the mortgaged real estate. 11 U.S.C.A. § 1129(b)(2)(A)(i). Thus, in the above example, if Debtor wants to retain the shopping center over First Life's objection, First Life must retain its lien on the shopping center to secure the $10 million secured claim, the plan must make payments to First Life over the life of the plan that total at least $12 million, and these payments must have a present value of at least $10 million.

The second standard applies if the debtor's plan proposes to sell the real estate free and clear of the mortgage. In that case, the plan is considered "fair and equitable" as long as the mortgagee's lien is transferred to the sale proceeds, 11 U.S.C.A. § 1129(b)(2)(A)(ii), and the mortgagee has the opportunity (unless the court orders otherwise for cause) to "credit bid" at the sale—i.e., to bid by offsetting its successful bid against the unpaid balance of the debt. 11 U.S.C.A. § 363(k). The mortgagee's ability to credit-bid protects the mortgagee against the risk that the collateral is sold at a price below what the mortgagee considers to be the collateral's fair market value.

The third standard focuses on whether the debtor's cram-down plan provides for the mortgagee to realize the "indubitable equivalent" of its claim. 11 U.S.C.A. § 1129(b)(2)(A)(iii). The Code does not define "indubitable equivalence," but the Code's legislative history indicates that this term was intended to "give[ ] the parties and the courts flexibility by allowing such other relief as will result in the realization by the protected entity of the value of its interest in the property involved." H.R. Rep. No. 95–595, at 340 (1977), reprinted in 1978 U.S. Code Cong. & Admin. News 5962, 6296. The debtor will rely on this standard only when it cannot satisfy one of the other two standards. For example, in In re River East Plaza, LLC, 669 F.3d 826 (7th Cir. 2012), the debtor owned mortgaged real estate worth only $13.5 million in a case in which the mortgagee (which was owed $38.3 million) made a section 1111(b) election. The debtor's plan proposed to "substitute" collateral, such that the debtor would keep the real estate free of the mortgagee's lien, while instead giving the mortgagee a first lien on $13.5 million in 30-year Treasury bonds. The court held that the bonds were not the "indubitable equivalent" of the mortgaged land (can you explain why not?) and that the plan's treatment of the mortgagee's secured claim was not fair and equitable.[30]

Section 1129(b) provides that the "fair and equitable" standard "includes" the three standards discussed above. The nonexclusive nature of the word "including" suggests that a court might conclude that a plan technically satisfies one of these standards and yet is still not "fair and equitable." See In re D & F Constr., Inc., 865 F.2d 673 (5th Cir. 1989) ("technical compliance with all the requirements in § 1129(b)(2) does not assure that the plan is 'fair and equitable.' . . . A court must consider the entire plan in the context of the rights of creditors under state law and the particular facts and circumstances in determining whether a plan is 'fair and equitable.' "). Thus, suppose that in the prior example, Debtor's plan proposes to pay First Life interest-only payments on its $10 million secured claim for 20 years, and then to pay the entire principal balance in a balloon payment after 20 years. The shopping center will need substantial refurbishment within the next 20 years, but the plan does not address how Debtor will accumulate the necessary reserves or obtain financing for such refurbishment. In such a case, a court will likely conclude that the plan is not fair and equitable because it defers repayment for too long a period and subjects the mortgagee to an unjustified risk of nonpayment. See, e.g., In re VIP Motor Lodge, 133 B.R. 41 (Bankr. D. Del. 1991).

Cram-down: The "fair and equitable" standard, unsecured claims, and the "absolute priority rule." If a class of unsecured creditors rejects a plan, the plan cannot satisfy the "fair and equitable" standard unless it also satisfies the "absolute priority rule." This rule—which is the product of early pre-Code case law and is now codified in section 1129(b)(2)(B)—

---

[30] Sometimes, debtors have proposed to sell mortgaged property free and clear of the mortgagee's lien, but via sales in which the mortgagee would not be allowed to credit bid. A few federal courts of appeal ruled that such sales offered the mortgagee the "indubitable equivalent" of its secured claim, as long as the asset was for a price at or above the judicially-determined value or in an arms-length public auction sale. See, e.g., In re Philadelphia Newspapers, 599 F.3d 298 (3d Cir. 2010); In re Pacific Lumber Co., 584 F.3d 229 (5th Cir. 2009). In 2012, however, the Supreme Court rejected these cases, holding that a plan that proposes to sell the collateral free and clear of the mortgagee's lien, but does not give the mortgagee the right to credit bid at that sale, cannot satisfy the indubitable equivalent standard. See, e.g., RadLAX Gateway Hotel, LLC v. Amalgamated Bank, 132 S.Ct. 2065 (2012).

requires that the claims of a class of unsecured creditors must be paid *in full* before any junior class of creditors or interest holders (including those holding ownership interests in the debtor) receives any property on account of those junior interests. Thus, in our prior example, suppose Debtor's plan proposes to retain full ownership of the shopping center without making any additional equity investment, but to pay only 50% of First Life's $2 million unsecured claim. The plan would violate the absolute priority rule and could not be crammed-down over First Life's objection, even if every other class had voted to accept the plan.

As a result, a debtor normally cannot retain ownership of property of the estate solely on account of its pre-bankruptcy ownership interest unless unsecured creditors consent or receive full payment of their claims. Pre-Code case law, however, permitted deviation from the absolute priority rule if the holder of the junior interest injected new capital, in the form of money or money's worth, that was a reasonable equivalent of the ownership interest being received by the reorganized debtor. The Bankruptcy Code codified the absolute priority rule but did not explicitly codify the pre-Code "new value" exception. The Seventh and Ninth Circuits have ruled that a "new value" exception exists, see, e.g., In re 203 N. LaSalle St. Partn., 126 F.3d 955 (7th Cir. 1998); In re Bonner Mall Partn., 2 F.3d 899 (9th Cir. 1993), while the Second and Fourth Circuits have expressed doubt (but without definitively stating that it does not exist). See, e.g., In re Coltex Loop Central Three Partners, L.P., 138 F.3d 39 (2d Cir. 1998); In re Bryson Props., XVIII, 961 F.2d 496 (4th Cir. 1992). The remaining circuits have not ruled definitively, and the district and bankruptcy courts are divided. 7 Collier on Bankruptcy ¶ 1129.03[4][c], at 1129–94 n.166 (16th ed.) (collecting cases).

The Supreme Court has yet to rule directly on the question. Its most recent consideration of the "new value" exception came in Bank of America Nat'l Trust & Sav. Ass'n v. 203 North LaSalle St. Partnership, 526 U.S. 434 (1999). In that case, an undersecured mortgagee held a $38.5 million unsecured deficiency claim for which the plan proposed to pay only a 16% dividend. Under the debtor's plan, certain pre-bankruptcy partners of the debtor were to contribute $6.125 million in new capital in exchange for the full ownership interest in the reorganized debtor. Further, the plan was subject to the condition that the debtor's partners had the exclusive right to contribute the new capital. The mortgagee argued that the plan was not fair and equitable, because it proposed to vest ownership of the property in the reorganized debtor and its partners without giving anyone else (including the mortgagee) the opportunity to propose a larger investment or a competing reorganization plan. Without definitively addressing whether the Code contained a "new value" exception, the Court agreed that the plan could not be confirmed:

> If the price to be paid for the equity interest is the best obtainable, old equity does not need the protection of exclusiveness (unless to trump an equal offer from someone else); if it is not the best, there is no apparent reason for giving old equity a bargain. There is no reason, that is, unless the very purpose of the whole transaction is, at least in part, to do old equity a favor. And that, of course, is to say that old equity would obtain its opportunity, and the resulting benefit, because of old equity's prior interest within the meaning of subsection [1129](b)(2)(B)(ii).

203 N. LaSalle St., 526 U.S. at 456. See also In re Castleton Plaza, LP, 707 F.3d 821 (7th Cir. 2013) ("Competition is essential whenever a plan of reorganization leaves an objecting creditor unpaid yet distributes an equity interest to an insider."). For further discussion of the "new value" exception, see Hoang, The New Value Exception to the Absolute Priority Rule After *In re 203 N. Lasalle Street Partnership*: What Should Bankruptcy Courts Do, and How Can Congress Help?, 149 U. Pa. L. Rev. 581, 612 (2000); Carlson & Williams, The Truth About the New Value Exception to Bankruptcy's Absolute Priority Rule, 21 Cardozo L. Rev. 1303 (2001); Watson, Left for Dead?: The Supreme Court's Treatment of the New Value Exception, 78 N.C. L. Rev. 1190 (2000); Markell, Owners, Auctions, and Absolute Priority in Bankruptcy Reorganizations, 44 Stan. L. Rev. 69 (1991).

Cram-down: "Unfair discrimination." As noted earlier, the cram-down standard also requires that the plan must not "discriminate unfairly" with respect to the claims of an objecting impaired class. 11 U.S.C.A. § 1129(b)(1). The prohibition against unfair discrimination prevents the debtor from treating similar classes of claims differently, at least without appropriate justification for doing so. See, e.g., Markell, A New Perspective on Unfair Discrimination in Chapter 11, 72 Am. Bankr. L.J. 227 (1998); Polivy, Unfair Discrimination in Chapter 11: Comprehensive Compilation of Current Case Law, 72 Am. Bankr. L.J. 191 (1998).

The starting point for Chapter 11 claim classification is section 1122(a), which provides that "a plan may place a claim or interest in a particular class only if such claim or interest is substantially similar to the other claims or interests of such class." Thus, the debtor could typically classify unsecured claims in the same class, "whether [arising from] trade, tort, publicly held debt or a *deficiency of a secured creditor.*" In re Pine Lake Village Apt. Co., 19 B.R. 819, 830 (Bankr. S.D.N.Y. 1982). Nevertheless, the Code allows the debtor to create a separate class for unsecured claims that are "less than or reduced to an amount that the court approves as reasonable and necessary for administrative convenience." 11 U.S.C.A. § 1122(b). Thus, for example, Debtor's plan could have one class of unsecured creditors with claims over $500 (which it would pay in quarterly installments over a ten-year period) and another class for unsecured creditors with claims under $500 (which it would pay in full in a lump sum immediately after confirmation). The Code permits this treatment—even though it discriminates between smaller unsecured claims and larger ones—as a matter of convenience, permitting the debtor to avoid the administrative costs of paying small claims in small installments over a long period. See, e.g., 7 Collier on Bankruptcy ¶ 1122.03[4] (16th ed.).

Implicitly, the "unfair" discrimination standard suggests that a debtor can separately classify certain unsecured claims if the debtor can offer a sufficient justification for doing so. What justification would be sufficient? In considering this question, it is important to keep in mind that the cram-down standard requires that *at least one* impaired class must vote to confirm the plan. Thus, returning to our continuing example, suppose that Debtor's unsecured creditors include First Bank (which holds a $2 million unsecured deficiency claim) and twelve employees and trade creditors (which hold claims totalling $200,000 and ranging from $5,000 to $25,000). If Debtor classifies all of the unsecured creditors together in the same class, the two-thirds-in-amount requirement means that a "no" vote by First Bank will cause the class to reject the plan—and if there is no other impaired class that approves the plan, Debtor cannot cram-down the plan over First Bank's objection, even if a court would conclude that it was "fair and equitable." For this reason, Debtor may attempt to classify First Bank's deficiency claim in one class and the employees and trade creditors in a different class, hoping that the employees and trade creditors will approve the plan and thus facilitate Debtor's cram-down.[31]

This type of classification is sometimes pejoratively called "artificial classification" or "gerrymandering." Some courts have traditionally demonstrated substantial hostility towards gerrymandering, most notably the Fifth Circuit in In re Greystone III Joint Venture, 995 F.2d 1274 (5th Cir. 1991). In *Greystone*, the debtor owed the mortgagee approximately $9,325,000 and trade creditors approximately $145,000. The bankruptcy court valued the mortgaged real estate at $5,825,000, leaving the mortgagee with an unsecured claim of $3,500,000. The debtor's plan classified the mortgagee's unsecured deficiency claim

---

[31] As discussed previously, an undersecured mortgagee may elect under § 1111(b) to waive its unsecured claim and have its claim treated as fully secured notwithstanding the current value of the collateral. Thus, the decision of an undersecured mortgagee like First Life whether to make a § 1111(b) election is not a simple one. If First Life makes the election, it must forgo any distribution on account of unsecured claims, but its lien will remain effective against the land until the entire $12 million unpaid debt is satisfied. However, because the election would leave First Life with no unsecured claim, First Bank will be unable to vote as an unsecured creditor, meaning it would have less leverage to prevent the cram-down of a plan to which it objects.

separately from the claims of trade creditors; the debtor would pay each class approximately 4% of their claims, but the plan also provided that the debtor's general partner would pay the balance of the trade creditors' claims in full. The mortgagee rejected the plan, but the trade creditor class voted to accept it, and the bankruptcy and district courts approved the plan (even though the mortgagee had proposed to fund a competing plan that would have paid all unsecured creditors in full). The Fifth Circuit reversed, holding that the debtor had classified the claims separately only to gerrymander an affirmative vote for plan and not for independent substantive reasons, pithily stating "thou shalt not classify similar claims differently in order to gerrymander an affirmative vote on a reorganization plan." *Greystone*, 995 F.2d at 1279. The court noted that the record did not demonstrate the debtor's inability to obtain services if trade creditors did not receive preferential treatment, and thus concluded that the bankruptcy court was clearly erroneous to have found a good business reason for the separate classification. *Greystone*, 995 F.2d at 1281.

Consistent with *Greystone*, a number of courts have concluded that the debtor may not classify the unsecured deficiency claim of a mortgagee separately from the claims of other unsecured creditors (other than administrative convenience creditors). See, e.g., In re Bryson Props., XVIII, 961 F.2d 496 (4th Cir. 1992); In re Lumber Exchange Bldg. Partn., 968 F.2d 647 (8th Cir. 1992). Nevertheless, a few courts have reached the opposite result and have *required* the debtor to separately classify unsecured claims that would have been nonrecourse claims outside of bankruptcy, reasoning that these are significantly different from the claims of other unsecured creditors and thus cannot be classified together under section 1122. See, e.g., In re Woodbrook Assocs., 19 F.3d 314 (7th Cir.1994); Beal Bank SSB v. Waters Edge Ltd. Partn., 248 B.R. 668 (D. Mass.2000). See also In re Loop 76, LLC, 465 B.R. 525 (9th Cir. B.A.P. 2012) (claim guaranteed by a third party was not "substantially similar" to other claims that were not guaranteed; thus, not only could the claims be separately classified, they had to be separately classified). As a policy matter, which approach seems more sensible to you?

NOTES

1. *The cram-down interest rate.* When the Chapter 11 plan proposes to repay the mortgagee's secured claim in deferred installments, the cram-down standard requires that the installments have a present value equal to or exceeding the amount of the secured claim. To calculate the present value of the debtor's plan payments, the court must determine what interest rate to use in making that calculation. As discussed earlier in this section, in Till v. SCS Credit Corp., 541 U.S. 465, 124 S.Ct. 1951, 158 L.Ed.2d 787 (2004), a plurality of the Supreme Court held that the Chapter 13 cram-down standard required the use of a "formula approach" that starts with the prime rate and

adjusts that rate upwards to account for the debtor's risk of nonpayment. While *Till* was a Chapter 13 case, the plurality's opinion viewed the formula approach as applicable in the Chapter 11 cram-down context as well, and the weight of subsequent authority has used the *Till* formula approach in Chapter 11 cram-downs. See, e.g., In re Texas Grand Prairie Hotel Realty, L.L.C., 710 F.3d 324 (5th Cir. 2013); In re LMR, LLC, 496 B.R. 410 (Bankr. W.D.Tex. 2013); In re Texas Star Refreshments, LLC, 494 B.R. 684 (Bankr.N.D.Tex.2013).

2. *Curing pre-bankruptcy arrearages—does interest accrue at the pre-default contract rate or the default rate?* If the plan proposes to cure a pre-bankruptcy arrearage, then "[n]otwithstanding ... section 506[ ](b) ... the amount necessary to cure the default shall be determined in accordance with the underlying agreement and applicable nonbankruptcy law." 11 U.S.C.A. § 1123(d). Section 1123(d) thus makes clear that if the debtor cures the mortgage arrearage in installments, it must pay interest on the arrearage whether or not the mortgagee is oversecured. Courts have disagreed, however, over whether interest would accrue at the pre-default contract rate or at any post-default contract rate. The Ninth Circuit has held that the debtor could effect a cure by repaying the arrearage at the pre-default contract rate, In re Entz-White Lumber & Supply, 850 F.2d 1338 (9th Cir. 1988), but the weight of recent authority holds that cure would require repayment of the arrearage at the applicable post-default rate. See, e.g., In re Moody Nat'l SHS Houston H, LLC, 426 B.R. 667 (Bankr. S.D. Tex. 2010); In re Sweet, 369 B.R. 644 (Bankr. D. Colo. 2007); In re 139–141 Owners Corp., 313 B.R. 364 (S.D.N.Y. 2004). Does the Code's language adequately resolve the question?

3. *Cram-down—some examples.* Consider the following examples of proposed plans. In which, if any, should a court be willing to cram-down the plan over the objection of the mortgagee?

(a) Debtor owns an office building that is subject to a mortgage held by First Life Insurance Co. (First Life) that secures an unpaid balance of $20 million. On the date Debtor files its Chapter 11 petition, the office building is more than half vacant and is worth only $10 million. Debtor's plan proposes to make interest only payments on First Life's secured claim at 10% interest for fifteen years (assume the prevailing market interest rate is 8%), with a balloon payment of all outstanding principal at the end of fifteen years. However, due to current vacancy levels, net operating rentals are not sufficient to permit Debtor to pay the full amount of interest that will accrue on First Life's secured claim. Thus, Debtor's plan proposes to capitalize the unpaid portion of the interest, which will cause the total principal balance to increase each month until the property produces net rents sufficient to pay full debt service. [For reasons that should be clear, this is referred to as a "negative amortization" plan.] Can the court cram-down this plan over First Life's objection? Why or why not? What additional information, if any, would you want to ascertain in making this judgment? See, e.g., Great Western Bank v. Sierra Woods Group, 953 F.2d 1174, 1177–78 (9th Cir. 1992); In re D

& F Constr. Inc., 865 F.2d 673, 675–76 (5th Cir. 1989); In re Spanish Lake Assocs., 92 B.R. 875 (Bankr. E.D. Mo. 1988); In re Edgewater Motel, Inc., 85 B.R. 989 (Bankr. E.D. Tenn. 1988); Schermer & Bartz, Negative Amortization and Plan Confirmation: Is It Fair and Equitable Under Section 1129(b) of the Bankruptcy Code?, 8 Bankr. Dev. J. 1 (1991).

(b)   Debtor owns a 16-acre parcel of undeveloped land that is subject to a mortgage held by Bank that secures an unpaid balance of $1.4 million. Debtor's Chapter 11 plan proposes to transfer 5.6 acres of the land to Bank in full satisfaction of the debt. [This is referred to as a "dirt-for-debt" plan or an "eat dirt" plan.] Debtor offers an appraisal indicating that the 5.6 acre parcel is worth $1.6 million. Can the court cram-down this plan over Bank's objection? Why or why not? What additional information, if any, would you want to ascertain in making this judgment? See, e.g., In re Arnold & Baker Farms, 85 F.3d 1415 (9th Cir. 1996); In re Richfield 81 Partners II, LLC, 447 B.R. 653 (Bankr. N.D. Ga. 2011); In re Riddle, 444 B.R. 681 (Bankr. N.D. Ga. 2011); Lurey & Berlin, When Can Less Than All of a Creditor's Collateral Serve as the Indubitable Equivalent of the Creditor's Secured Claim?, 28 Cumb. L. Rev. 333 (1998).

(c)   Debtor owns a shopping center that is subject to a mortgage held by First Life that secures an unpaid balance of $12 million. On the date Debtor files its Chapter 11 petition, the center is worth only $10 million; First Life does not make a section 1111(b) election. In its plan, Debtor separates its unsecured creditors into two classes—a "convenience" class of unsecured creditors holding claims under $1,500, and a "general" unsecured class (which is dominated by First Life's $2 million unsecured deficiency claim). Debtor has cash available to pay the convenience class creditors in cash in full on the effective date of its proposed plan, but if it does that, those creditors will not be impaired (and thus cannot vote on the plan). To obtain the approval of the convenience class (and thus obtain the approval of one class as required for cram-down), Debtor proposes to pay the convenience class creditors in full, but to delay that payment for 90 days after the plan's effective date. The convenience class is the only class of creditors that votes to approve the plan. First Life argues that the creditors in the convenience class were not truly "impaired" and thus were not entitled to vote, such that the court should hold Debtor ineligible to cram-down the plan. Should the court permit the Debtor's "artificial impairment" of the convenience class so as to allow cram-down? Compare In re Windsor on the River Assocs., Ltd., 7 F.3d 127, 132 (8th Cir. 1993) (no) with In re Village at Camp Bowie I, L.P. 710 F.3d 239 (5th Cir. 2013) and In re L&J Anaheim Assocs., 995 F.2d 940 (9th Cir. 1993) (yes). See also Brubaker, Artificial Impairment and the Single-Asset Real Estate Debtor, 33 Bankruptcy Law Letter 1 (No. 4, April 2013); Markell, Clueless on Classification: Toward Removing Artificial Limits on Chapter 11 Claim Classification, 11 Emory Bankr. Dev. J. 1 (1995); Carlson, Artificial Impairment and the Single Asset Chapter 11 Case, 23 Cap. U. L. Rev. 339 (1994).

4. *The absolute priority rule and individual debtors.* Traditionally, the absolute priority rule applied in Chapter 11 cases involving individual debtors as well as those involving business entities. In 2005, BAPCPA amended the cramdown standard for unsecured claims to state:

> the holder of any claim or interest that is junior to the claims of such class [of unsecured claims] will not receive or retain under the plan on account of such junior claim or interest any property, *except that in a case in which the debtor is an individual, the debtor may retain property included in the estate under section 1115* . . . .[32]

11 U.S.C.A. § 1129(b)(2)(B)(ii) (amendment language in italics). Section 1115 provides that in addition to property included within the estate under section 541, in individual Chapter 11 cases property of the estate also includes property and earnings received by the debtor post-petition.

This amendment produced an interpretive quandary: Did Congress intend that an individual Chapter 11 debtor that did not pay unsecured creditors in full could keep only its post-petition property and earnings (not its pre-bankruptcy property)? Or did Congress instead mean that the individual Chapter 11 debtor could keep any property of the estate— including pre-bankruptcy property—even if it did not pay unsecured creditors in full? Under the former interpretation, the absolute priority rule would still apply to prevent the individual Chapter 11 debtor from retaining pre-bankruptcy property unless it paid unsecured creditors in full; under the latter interpretation, the absolute priority rule would no longer apply in individual Chapter 11 cases.

A few courts have concluded that BAPCPA abolished the absolute priority rule in individual Chapter 11 cases. See, e.g., In re Friedman, 466 B.R. 471 (9th Cir. B.A.P. 2012); In re O'Neal, 490 B.R. 837 (Bankr. W.D. Ark. 2013). The growing weight of authority, however, has concluded that the absolute priority rule still applies to an individual Chapter 11 debtor proposing to retain pre-bankruptcy property. See, e.g., Ice House America, LLC v. Cardin, 751 F.3d 734 (6th Cir. 2014); In re Lively, 717 F.3d 406 (5th Cir. 2013); In re Stephens, 704 F.3d 1279 (10th Cir. 2013); In re Maharaj, 681 F.3d 558 (4th Cir. 2012).

5. *The automatic stay and stay relief in Chapter 11.* From the moment of the petition, the stay prohibits the mortgagee from foreclosing or otherwise seeking to enforce the mortgage debt unless the court grants relief from stay based on one of the grounds discussed earlier in Part J2. Mortgagees frequently file a motion for relief from the stay as quickly as possible after the petition is filed. The mortgagee may have a number of objectives in seeking relief. The mortgagee may want to proceed with foreclosure immediately, or may simply want to force the debtor to pay interest on the mortgagee's secured claim during bankruptcy. Alternatively, the mortgagee

---

[32] 11 U.S.C.A. § 1129(b)(2)(B)(ii) (amendment language in italics).

may file the motion to obtain leverage against the debtor in negotiations over the terms of the debtor's plan.

It is relatively rare for a mortgagee to obtain relief from stay under section 362(d)(1)'s "cause, including lack of adequate protection" standard. As discussed earlier, this standard protects the mortgagee against the risk of depreciation in the value of the collateral during bankruptcy. Unless the mortgagee can demonstrate that the debtor's use of the real estate poses this risk, relief under section 362(d)(1) will not be forthcoming. Instead, a real estate mortgagee is more likely to seek relief under either section 362(d)(2) or 362(d)(3).

If the mortgaged property is single-asset real estate, the mortgagee will certainly seek relief under section 362(d)(3). As explained earlier, the debtor of single-asset real estate must either (1) propose a feasible reorganization plan within 90 days or (2) begin making monthly payments of interest on the secured portion of the mortgagee's claim. If the debtor does neither, the court must grant relief from the stay and permit the mortgagee to foreclose. Section 362(d)(3) thus forces the single-asset real estate debtor to propose its plan quickly, or to at least pay interest to the secured party to the extent that the debtor takes longer than 90 days to propose its plan.

Most frequently, the mortgagee will seek relief under section 362(d)(2), which entitles the mortgagee to relief if the debtor does not have an equity in the mortgaged property (i.e., the property is worth less than the outstanding balance of all encumbrances on the property) and the property is "not necessary to an effective reorganization." In this situation, the court should lift the stay and allow the mortgagee to foreclose, as continuing the stay would serve no purpose for either the secured creditor or unsecured creditors.

When a mortgagee seeks relief under section 362(d)(2), the burden is on the debtor to demonstrate that the collateral is "necessary to an effective reorganization." 11 U.S.C.A. § 362(g)(2). To meet this burden, the debtor need not actually have a finalized reorganization plan, but still must show that there exists "a reasonable likelihood of a successful reorganization within a reasonable time." United Savings Ass'n v. Timbers of Inwood Forest Assocs., Ltd., 484 U.S. 365, 375, 108 S.Ct. 626, 632, 98 L.Ed.2d 740 (1988). If the debtor has only been in Chapter 11 for a month, however, and is still negotiating its plan with creditors, how does the court make this determination? *Timbers* made clear that the court could and should grant relief from stay—even early in the case, during the debtor's "exclusivity" period—if the debtor has no equity and cannot demonstrate any realistic prospect of reorganization. But in the early stages of a Chapter 11 case, bankruptcy courts tend to give the debtor the "benefit of the doubt" and are reluctant to conclude that a successful reorganization is unlikely. By contrast, if the debtor has been in Chapter 11 for longer than the exclusivity period and has not yet managed to negotiate a feasible plan with creditors, relief under section 362(d)(2) becomes more likely. See, e.g., In re Ashgrove Apts. of DeKalb Cty., Ltd., 121 B.R. 752, 756 (Bankr.S.D.Ohio 1990) ("[A]s the case progresses, so too does the debtor's burden of proving that successful reorganization may be reasonably expected. . . . [T]he test should be viewed as a continuum with the scales tipping in favor of the debtor in the early stages and the burden of proof becoming greater in the later stages."). See also In re Gunnison Center Apts., L.P., 320 B.R. 391 (Bankr. D. Colo. 2005); In re Holly's, Inc., 140 B.R. 643 (Bankr.W.D.Mich.1992).

6. *Valuation of mortgaged property in Chapter 11.* The value of mortgaged property is relevant in Chapter 11 for several reasons. In the context of a motion for relief from stay, it may be relevant in determining whether the mortgagee is oversecured or the debtor has equity in the collateral. In the context of plan confirmation, it may be relevant in terms of whether the debtor's plan meets the cram-down standard.

Unfortunately, the Code is not explicit as to the timing of such valuation. A few courts applied a "single valuation" approach that valued the collateral for all purposes as of the petition date. See, e.g., In re Torcise, 187 B.R. 18 (S.D. Fla. 1995); In re Hulen Park Place Ltd., 130 B.R. 39 (N.D. Tex. 1991). Others used a "dual valuation approach" that valued the collateral at the petition date relief from stay purposes and again at plan confirmation for evaluating the debtor's plan. See, e.g., In re Addison Props. Ltd. Partn., 185 B.R. 766 (Bankr. N.D. Ill. 1995); In re Kennedy, 177 B.R. 967 (Bankr. S.D. Ala. 1995). The weight of recent authority adopts a flexible approach under which "valuation of the collateral and the creditor's claim should be flexible and not limited to a single point in time, such as the petition date or confirmation date." In re T-H New Orleans Ltd. Partn., 116 F.3d 790 (5th Cir. 1997) (claim that was initially undersecured on petition date held to become oversecured by virtue of post-bankruptcy appreciation in land value; mortgagee became entitled to post-petition interest only at the point the mortgagee became oversecured); In re SW Boston Hotel Venture, LLC, 479 B.R. 210 (1st Cir. B.A.P. 2012). This approach seems most consistent with section 506(a)(1), which states that the value of a creditor's collateral "shall be determined in light of the purpose of the valuation and of the proposed disposition or use of such property, and in conjunction with any hearing on such disposition or use or on a plan affecting such creditor's interest."

7. THE MORTGAGEE IN A CHAPTER 12 CASE

NELSON, WHITMAN, BURKHART & FREYERMUTH, REAL
ESTATE FINANCE LAW
861–867 (6th ed. 2014)*

For farmers unable to cope with the economic hardship of the severe agricultural recession of the 1980s, Chapters 11 and 13 provided little meaningful relief. Pursuing Chapter 11 reorganization involves substantial administrative expense, and the substantial creditor

---

*   Reprinted with permission of LEG, Inc., d/b/a/ West Academic.

influence over the content of the reorganization plan made it extremely difficult for a family farmer to obtain approval of a plan that offered any significant chance of a successful rehabilitation. Further, while Chapter 13 could have provided an advantageous reorganization vehicle for family farmers, most were ineligible for Chapter 13 relief because they had secured and/or unsecured debts that far exceeded the eligibility limits.

In 1986, Congress responded by enacting a new Chapter 12 of the Bankruptcy Code entitled "Adjustment of Debts of a Family Farmer with Regular Annual Income" (hereinafter "Chapter 12").[860] In large measure, Chapter 12 extends Chapter 13-like protections to family farmers, and thus the substance and structure of the two chapters are very similar. In general, Chapter 12 affords important powers to the debtor, including the ability to reduce secured indebtedness to the *current* value of the underlying security, to repay the reduced amount of those secured claims over an extended period of time, and to satisfy unsecured claims— including those that became unsecured by the foregoing "write down" of the security—by paying to the plan only his "disposable income" (income which is not reasonably necessary for family support and business operations). Further, the Chapter 12 debtor need not satisfy the absolute priority rule that would be applicable in Chapter 11, permitting the debtor to retain a family farm even without full repayment to objecting unsecured creditors.[861] Upon successful completion of the plan, the debtor is discharged of his or her unsecured indebtedness.[862]

---

[860] 11 U.S.C.A. §§ 1201 to 1231. Chapter 12 was set to expire in 1993, but was temporarily extended several times. In 2005, despite the relative rarity of Chapter 12 cases, Congress made Chapter 12 permanent and extended its provisions to cover family fishermen, incorporating aquaculture operations and effectively reversing prior decisions, such as In re Watford, 898 F.2d 1525 (11th Cir.1990), in which courts held that fishing operations were not "farming operations" within the meaning of Chapter 12. This section of the text will focus only upon family farmers.

For further discussion of Chapter 12, see Porter, Phantom Farmers: Chapter 12 of the Bankruptcy Code, 79 Am.Bankr.L.J. 729 (2005); Van Patten, Chapter 12 in the Courts, 38 S.Dak.L.Rev. 52 (1993); Flaccus, A Comparison of Farm Bankruptcies in Chapter 11 and the New Chapter 12, 11 Ark.L.R.L.Rev. 49 (1989); Armstrong, The Family Farmer Bankruptcy Act of 1986: An Analysis for Farm Lenders, 104 Banking L.J. 189 (1987); King, Chapter 12: Adjustment of Debts of a Family Farmer with Regular Income, 29 So.Tex.L.Rev. 615 (1988); Matson, Understanding the New Family Farmer Bankruptcy Act, 21 U.Rich.L.Rev. 521 (1987); Norton, the New Family Farmer Bankruptcy Act, 3 Prac.Real Est.Law. 37 (1987); Wilson, Chapter 12: Family Farm Reorganization, 8 J.Agric.Tax. & L. 299 (1987); Comment, Protecting America's Farmers Under State Mediation Laws and Chapter 12: Who's Being Protected?, 72 Marq.L.Rev. 466 (1989); Comment, Bankruptcy Chapter 12: How Many Family Farms Can It Salvage?, 55 U.M.K.C.L.Rev. 639 (1987); Note, An Analysis of the Family Farmer Bankruptcy Act of 1986, 15 Hofstra L.Rev. 353 (1987). Comment, 57 Miss.L.J. 185 (1988), Note, 27 Washburn L.J. 495 (1988).

[861] 8 Collier on Bankruptcy ¶ 1200.01[4], at 1200–8 (16th ed.). Courts have even confirmed plans in which all disposable income was allocated to payment of secured claims, with no payment at all on unsecured claims. See In re Kjerulf, 82 B.R. 123 (Bankr.D.Or.1987).

[862] 11 U.S.C.A. § 1228(a).

Who qualifies for Chapter 12 relief?

Debtors are eligible to seek relief under Chapter 12 only if they are "a family farmer ... with regular annual income."[863] The term "family farmer" can include an individual (or married couple), as well as a corporation or partnership in which more than 50% of the stock or equity is held by family members (including relatives) who conduct farming operations.[864] For individuals to be eligible, at least 50% of their debts must have arisen out of their farming operations;[865] for a corporation or partnership, the eligibility threshold is 80%.[866] In any event, the debtor's aggregate debts cannot exceed $4,031,575;[867] a debtor exceeding the debt limitations must seek reorganization, if at all, in Chapter 11. These eligibility requirements reflect Congress's intent to exclude "large" farming operations, whether or not family-owned.

The debtor, the Chapter 12 trustee, and control of the farming operation

While a trustee is appointed in all Chapter 12 cases,[868] the farmer remains in possession of property of the bankruptcy estate (including any mortgaged real estate) and continues to operate the farm as a debtor-in-possession.[869] The debtor-in-possession has the rights, powers and duties of a Chapter 11 trustee, including the ability to assert any of the avoiding powers.[870] The Chapter 12 trustee has limited duties[871] unless the debtor-

---

[863] 11 U.S.C.A. § 109(f).

[864] 11 U.S.C.A. § 101(18). If the debtor is a corporation, its stock cannot be publicly traded. 11 U.S.C.A. § 101(18)(B)(iii). The term "farming operation" includes, inter alia, "farming, tillage of the soil, dairy farming, ranching, production or raising of crops, poultry, or livestock, and production of poultry or livestock products in an unmanufactured state." 11 U.S.C.A. § 101(21).

[865] 11 U.S.C.A. § 101(18)(A). In determining whether the debtor satisfies this threshold, a debt for the debtor's principal residence is excluded unless that debt arises out a farming operation. Courts have concluded that a mortgage debt on the debtor's principal residence arises out of a farming operation if the purpose of the debt has some connection to the debtor's farming activity. See, e.g., In re Woods, 465 B.R. 196 (Bankr.10th Cir.2012) (debtor's farmhouse was an integral part of farm operation when farm's books and records were maintained in there, and its proximity to the farming operation allowed debtor to take care of their livestock and irrigation system); In re Marlatt, 116 B.R. 703 (Bankr.D.Neb.1990) (mortgage on debtor's farmhouse arose out of farming operation where mortgage loan enabled debtor to retain farm in divorce settlement).

[866] 11 U.S.C.A. § 101(18)(B)(i). A debt for a dwelling owned by the debtor and used as a principal residence by a shareholder/partner is excluded unless the debt arises out of a farming operation.

[867] 11 U.S.C.A. § 101(18)(A). This amount is effective as of April 1, 2013, and is automatically adjusted at three-year intervals based on the Consumer Price Index. 11 U.S.C.A. § 104(b).

[868] 11 U.S.C.A. § 1202(a).

[869] 11 U.S.C.A. § 1203.

[870] 11 U.S.C.A. § 1203. See, e.g., In re McClintock, 75 B.R. 612 (Bankr.W.D.Mo.1987) (Chapter 12 debtor-in-possession entitled to avoid fraudulent transfer under section 548); In re Jardine, 120 B.R. 559 (Bankr.D.Id.1990) (Chapter 12 debtor-in-possession entitled to avoid preferential transfer under section 547). For further discussion of the avoiding powers, see §§ 8.13 to 8.16 supra.

in-possession is removed from control of the farming operation and replaced by the Chapter 12 trustee, which can occur only for cause, including "fraud, dishonesty, incompetence, or gross mismanagement."[872] As in the Chapter 11 context, it is extremely rare for the debtor-in-possession to be removed.[873]

The automatic stay, relief from stay, and "adequate protection" in Chapter 12

As in other Chapters, section 362(a)'s automatic stay against enforcement of creditor claims applies in Chapter 12 cases,[874] thus precluding (for example) a mortgagee from foreclosing a mortgage on the debtor's farmland without first obtaining relief from stay. In addition, as in Chapter 13, Chapter 12 also extends the automatic stay to cover actions to collect consumer debts from co-debtors,[875] thus protecting the debtor from the risk of pressure from family members or friends who may have agreed to guarantee the debtor's obligations. The co-debtor stay applies only to individual family farmers, and does not cover debts arising from the debtor's farming operations.[876]

As explained previously, section 362(d)(2) requires the bankruptcy court to grant a secured creditor relief from stay if the debtor has no equity in the collateral and the collateral is not "necessary to an effective reorganization" of the debtor. Because the family farmer's reorganization will require its possession of the farmland and other farm-related collateral, a secured creditor can obtain relief from stay under section 362(d)(2) only if the court concludes that the debtor has no prospect for successful reorganization. As in the Chapter 11 context, courts are extremely reluctant to reach such a conclusion, particularly early in a case before the debtor has an opportunity to formulate a plan.

As also explained previously, section 362(d)(1) requires the bankruptcy court to grant a secured creditor relief from stay "for cause, including the lack of adequate protection" of the creditor's interest in the collateral. This permits a secured party to protect itself against the risk that the debtor's possession and use of the collateral during the pendency

---

[871] See generally 8 Collier on Bankruptcy ¶ 1202.03 (16th ed.). Where the debtor in possession remains in control of farming operations, courts have held that the Chapter 12 trustee lacks standing to exercise the avoiding powers. See, e.g., In re Colvin, 2012 WL 1865562 (Bankr.W.D. Tex.2012); In re Tiegen, 123 B.R. 887 (Bankr.D.Mont.1991).

[872] 11 U.S.C.A. § 1204(a). By contrast, the Chapter 13 trustee may not displace the debtor from possession.

[873] See In re Jessen, 82 B.R. 490 (Bankr.S.D.Iowa 1988); 8 Collier on Bankruptcy ¶ 1204.01 (16th ed.).

[874] 11 U.S.C.A. § 362(a).

[875] 11 U.S.C.A. § 1201(a).

[876] 11 U.S.C.A. § 1201(a)(1). Relief from the Chapter 12 co-debtor stay is governed by 11 U.S.C.A. § 1201(c).

of the stay results in depreciation of the collateral to the creditor's detriment. In section 1205, however, Congress provided standards for providing adequate protection, applicable only in Chapter 12,[880] that could make it easier than in Chapter 11 for the debtor-mortgagor to keep the stay in effect. Like section 361, section 1205(b) permits the Chapter 12 debtor to provide adequate protection against depreciation of the collateral through cash payments, a replacement lien on other property, or other action deemed sufficient to provide adequate protection. However, section 1205(b) also permits the debtor to provide adequate protection to a mortgagee by paying the mortgagee the use value of the farmland, measured by "the reasonable rent customary in the community where the property is located, based upon the rental value, net income, and earning capacity or the property,"[881] even if that amount would not fully account for all anticipated depreciation in the farmland's value.[882] Thus, to keep the stay in place, the Chapter 12 debtor will need to provide the mortgagee with *no more* than the fair rental value of the land.[883] As the legislative history notes, "[i]f the lender cannot resell the property [after foreclosure], it typically will rent the property at a market rate. If the debtor pays market rent while he reorganizes, the lender will be getting only what it would realistically get as a result of a foreclosure."[884]

The Chapter 12 plan and treatment of creditor claims

The requirements for a Chapter 12 plan are largely similar to those for a Chapter 13 reorganization. The plan's term is typically three years, but can be extended to five years if the court approves with cause.[885] During the plan period, unless the plan will pay unsecured creditors in full, the court may not confirm the plan over the objection of an unsecured

---

[880] 11 U.S.C.A. § 1205(a) ("Section 361 does not apply in a case under this chapter.").

[881] 11 U.S.C.A. § 1205(b)(3).

[882] At first blush, it is curious that section 1205(b)(3) should treat "use value" in the form of reasonable rental value as a measure of adequate protection—especially given the Supreme Court's *Timbers* decision . . . which held that "adequate protection" within the meaning of section 361 protects the creditor against depreciation of the collateral and does not require the debtor to pay an undersecured creditor interest on the secured portion of its claim. The explanation is that Congress added Chapter 12 in 1986—two years prior to *Timbers*—and at that time, there was substantial judicial authority that adequate protection of an undersecured claim *did* require payment of interest during the pendency of the stay, even if the collateral was not depreciating in value. See, e.g., In re American Mariner Indus., Inc., 734 F.2d 426 (9th Cir.1984). In that context of uncertainty, Congress might have viewed a "reasonable rental value" standard for adequate protection as more "pro-farmer" than a standard based upon prevailing interest rates—particularly at a time when mortgage interest rates were relatively high and farm rental values were relatively low. After *Timbers*, there is general agreement that the Chapter 12 debtor would need to pay rent as adequate protection only as necessary to protect the mortgagee against depreciation in the value of the mortgaged premises. Zink v. Vanmiddlesworth, 300 B.R. 394 (N.D.N.Y.2003); Van Patten, Chapter 12 in the Courts, 38 S.Dak.L.Rev. 52 (1993).

[883] In re Kocher, 78 B.R. 844, 850 (Bankr.S.D.Ohio 1987).

[884] 132 Cong.Rec. S3529 (daily ed. March 26, 1986) (statement of Sen. Grassley).

[885] 11 U.S.C.A. § 1222(c).

creditor unless the debtor pays to the trustee all of its "projected disposable income" to fund the plan.[886]

A Chapter 12 plan may modify the claim of an unsecured creditor, who need not be paid in full as long as the creditor receives no less under the plan that the creditor would have received in a Chapter 7 liquidation of the debtor.[887] Likewise, a Chapter 12 plan may modify secured claims (including claims secured only by the debtor's principal residence),[888] such as by extension of the maturity of the loan term, reduction of principal,[889] or a reduction of the interest rate.[890] The court cannot confirm the plan, however, unless the plan is feasible.[891] Furthermore, if the plan modifies a secured claim, the court cannot confirm the plan unless the secured creditor accepts it, the debtor surrenders the collateral, or the plan allows the creditor to retain its lien and makes payments to the creditor the present value of which equal or exceed the amount of the creditor's secured claim.[892]

The foregoing is more readily understood in the context of the facts of Travelers Insurance Company v. Bullington.[893] In that case, the farmers owed the mortgagee approximately $645,000, secured by land worth only $475,000 on the petition date. The indebtedness was due in a balloon payment after five years and carried an interest rate that was fixed for

---

[886] 11 U.S.C.A. § 1225(b). A plan under which the debtor contributes all of its net disposable income satisfies this standard even if the debtor projects that it will have no net disposable income. See In re Rowley, 143 B.R. 547 (Bankr.D.S.D.1992); see also Gribbins v. Farm Credit Servs. of Mid-America, ACA, 43 Fed.Appx. 861 (6th Cir.2002) (where Chapter 12 debtor failed to comply with plan by making disposable income available to unsecured creditors, bankruptcy court was justified in dismissing the case).

[887] 11 U.S.C.A. §§ 1222(b)(2), 1225(a)(4). See also In re Borg, 88 B.R. 288 (Bankr.D.Mont. 1988). The court must make this determination based upon the value of the collateral as of the effective date of the plan, not the petition date. See, e.g., In re Novak, 252 B.R. 487 (Bankr.D.N.D. 2000); In re Hopwood, 124 B.R. 82 (E.D.Mo.1991).

[888] Unlike home mortgagees in Chapter 13, mortgagees of Chapter 12 debtors do not have the benefit of an anti-modification rule.

[889] In other words, a Chapter 12 debtor may "strip-down" an undersecured mortgage, reduce its principal balance to the then-current value of the land, and (after completing its plan and receiving a discharge) avoid the creditor's lien to the extent of the unpaid portion of the mortgagee's unsecured claim. See, e.g., In re Stidham, 292 B.R. 204 (Bankr.W.D.Okla.2003).

[890] 11 U.S.C.A. § 1222(b)(2). See, e.g., In re Citrowske, 72 B.R. 613 (Bankr.D.Minn.1987). Courts have even confirmed "negative amortization" plans of the type sometimes proposed in Chapter 11 . . . See In re Nauman, 213 B.R. 355 (Bankr.9th Cir.1997).

[891] 11 U.S.C.A. § 1225(a)(6) (debtor must "be able to make all payments under the plan and comply with the plan"). For cases interpreting this requirement, see, e.g., In re Chambers, 2008 WL 5649690 (Bankr.E.D.Tenn.2008) (plan not feasible where debtor's projected income unreasonably exceeded historical income); In re Tofsrud, 230 B.R. 862 (Bankr.D.N.D.1999) (plan not feasible where debtor proposed to grow crop with which debtor had no experience); In re Sauer, 223 B.R. 715 (Bankr.D.N.D.1998) (plan not feasible where debtor's projected expenses were unreasonably low).

[892] 11 U.S.C.A. § 1225(a)(5). As in Chapters 11 or 13, this is referred to as the "cramdown" standard. See, e.g., In re Chickosky, 2013 WL 5434131 (Bankr.D.Conn.2013) (Chapter 12 plan could not eliminate cross-collateralization rights of lender that funded debtor's farming operations); In re Heath, 483 B.R. 708 (Bankr.E.D.Ark.2012) (same).

[893] 878 F.2d 354 (11th Cir.1989).

the first year at 12.5% and thereafter floated at one point above an index of AAA-rated corporate bonds. The farmers' Chapter 12 plan bifurcated the mortgagee's claim into a secured claim of $475,000 and an unsecured claim for $170,000. The plan converted the pre-existing five-year obligation into a thirty-year fixed rate mortgage of $475,000 carrying a fixed interest rate of 10.75%. The $170,000 unsecured claim was to be discharged at the end of the four-year plan period after having any disposable income applied proportionately to its payment along with the farmers' other unsecured debts. The bankruptcy court approved the plan (and the Eleventh Circuit affirmed) notwithstanding the mortgagee's objections to the extension of the secured claim to thirty years and the mandated fixed interest rate.[894] The court held that the section 1222(b)(9) authorized the extension of the mortgage.[895] Moreover, it concluded:

> [S]imply because a creditor subjectively would not extend a mortgage on the same terms does not mean that objectively the mortgage does not have a given value. Given that [mortgagee] has pointed to no record evidence to show that the 10.75% interest rate does not give the mortgage a present value of $475,000, while [mortgagors'] chart does tend to support the interest rate, the bankruptcy court's finding . . . is supported by sufficient evidence.[896]

There is substantial authority that the bifurcation and strip-down of undersecured claims reflected by *Bullington* does not operate as an unconstitutional taking of the mortgagee's property.[897]

A Chapter 12 plan may "provide for the curing or waiving of any default."[898] Thus, as in Chapters 11 and 13, pre-foreclosure mortgage

---

[894] This example is not meant to suggest that a Chapter 12 debtor could necessarily impose a thirty-year amortization schedule on the objecting mortgagee. As one commentator has noted, "[t]he court should not approve a thirty-year amortization if the debtor is capable of paying the claim over a 20-year period. A long-term payment should be permitted only to the extent that it is necessary to preserve the debtor's farming operation." 8 Collier on Bankruptcy ¶ 1225.03[4][b], at 1225–17 (16th ed.). As a result, Chapter 12 plans commonly may provide for long-term amortization but require the debtor to make a balloon payment at the end of a specified period. See, e.g., In re Schreiner, 2009 WL 924418 (Bankr.D.Neb.2009) (plan payments based on 20-year amortization but with 5-year balloon payment); In re Torelli, 338 B.R. 390 (Bankr.E.D.Ark.2006) (plan payments based on 10-year amortization but with 5-year balloon payment).

[895] 11 U.S.C.A. § 1222(b)(9) (plan may "provide for payment of allowed secured claims . . . over a period exceeding [the duration of the plan]").

[896] Travelers Ins. Co. v. Bullington, 878 F.2d 354, 359 (11th Cir.1989). As in Chapters 11 and 13, calculating the present value of plan payments to a secured creditor requires selecting an appropriate interest rate. Because the Chapter 12 and 13 cramdown standards are comparable, it seems appropriate to conclude that the Supreme Court's analysis in *Till* will govern determination of the appropriate rate. The limited case authority so far has concluded that *Till*'s formula approach applies in Chapter 12. See, e.g., In re Woods, 465 B.R. 196 (Bankr.10th Cir.2012).

[897] See, e.g., Travelers Ins. Co. v. Bullington, 878 F.2d 354 (11th Cir.1989); Dahlke v. Doering, 94 B.R. 569 (D.Minn.1989); In re Kerwin-White, 129 B.R. 375 (Bankr.D.Vt.1991), aff'd, 996 F.2d 552 (2d Cir.1993).

[898] 11 U.S.C.A. § 1222(b)(3).

accelerations may be de-accelerated and the original payment schedule reinstated.[899] Moreover, the "absolute priority" rule applicable in Chapter 11—which requires that a plan pay unsecured creditors in full before the debtor can retain property of the estate on account of the debtor's interest—does not apply in Chapter 12. A farmer-debtor in Chapter 11 could not keep its land after completion of its plan unless the plan paid unsecured creditors in full or the unsecured creditors agreed to accept the plan; thus, an undersecured mortgagee could use the threat of withholding its consent to obtain higher plan payments on the unsecured portion of its claim. Farmer-debtors in Chapter 12 are not subject to such mortgagee bargaining leverage.

Under Chapter 11, a mortgagee has the option to give up the unsecured part of his claim and instead have the mortgage treated as if it were fully secured. If the real estate goes up in value during the Chapter 11 case, the mortgagee who takes this election gets the benefit of that appreciation.[901] Under Chapter 12, the mortgagee loses this option. An appraisal at the time of plan confirmation will establish the amount of the secured claim. If the land goes up in value, the farmer-debtor will get the benefit of that appreciation at the completion of the plan.

NOTE

Write-downs of debt in the Farm Credit System. In addition to Chapter 12, many farm mortgagors can take advantage of the Agricultural Credit Act of 1987 (the "Act"). See 7 U.S.C.A. § 2001 et seq.; 12 U.S.C.A. § 2202 et seq. The Act affords delinquent borrowers from the Farmers Home Administration ("FmHA") significant substantive rights to have their mortgage loans "restructured," which generally entails the "write-down" of principal and interest. To be eligible for this assistance,

> (1) the delinquency must be due to circumstances beyond the control of the borrower * * * ;

> (2) the borrower must have acted in good faith with the Secretary * * * ;

> (3) the borrower must present a preliminary plan * * * that contains reasonable assumptions [with respect to the borrower's ability to meet living, farming and debt servicing expenses]; and

> (4) the loan, if restructured, must result in a net recovery to the Federal Government, during the term of the loan as restructured,

---

[899] If the foreclosure sale has already occurred prior to the petition, de-acceleration is more problematic. While there is authority under Chapter 13 that de-acceleration is permissible, at least in statutory redemption states, at least one decision has held that such relief is unavailable in Chapter 12. See Justice v. Valley Nat'l Bank, 849 F.2d 1078 (8th Cir.1988). See also In re McKinney, 84 B.R. 748 (Bankr.D.Kan.1987) (de-acceleration not permitted after entry of foreclosure judgment).

[901] 11 U.S.C.A. § 1111(b).

that would be more than or equal to the net recovery to the Federal Government from an involuntary liquidation or foreclosure on the property securing the loan.

7 U.S.C.A. § 2001. If the borrower meets the foregoing requirements, the Secretary must "offer to restructure the loan obligations of the borrower . . . through primary loan service programs that would enable the borrower to meet the obligations (as modified) under the loan and to continue the farming operations of the borrower." *Id.* The Act confers similar rights on Farm Credit System borrowers, a large group of agricultural debtors who obtain land operational financing from Federal Land Bank Associations and Production Credit Associations. 12 U.S.C.A. § 2202a.

To the extent that the foregoing legislation mandates write-downs of delinquent farm mortgages, does it represent a form of "non-bankruptcy" bankruptcy? To what extent will eligible farm borrowers be able to achieve a bankruptcy result without having to suffer the possible stigma attached to a public filing of a Chapter 12 petition?

8. RENTS IN BANKRUPTCY

As we noted in Chapter 4, mortgagees frequently rely not only on the real estate itself as security, but also on the rents, issues and profits it produces. Thus, mortgagees frequently rely on assignments (or more accurately, "mortgages") of "rents, issues and profits" to create that desired additional security. Once a mortgagor files a bankruptcy petition, a dispute may arise between the mortgagee and the bankruptcy trustee (or the debtor in possession in a Chapter 11 proceeding) as to who has a prior claim to rents collected during the bankruptcy proceeding.

Throughout the litigation concerning rental assignments during the past two decades, state law has traditionally governed the enforceability in bankruptcy of security interests in rents. In 1979, in Butner v. United States, 440 U.S. 48, 99 S.Ct. 914, 59 L.Ed.2d 136 (1979), the Supreme Court held that state law governed in determining whether a mortgagee had a valid security interest in rents collected during bankruptcy. According to the Court, the bankruptcy court "should take whatever steps are necessary to ensure that the mortgagee is afforded * * * the same protection he would have under state law if no bankruptcy had ensued." Although *Butner* was decided under an earlier bankruptcy statute, courts have uniformly followed it in applying the current Code. See, e.g., Matter of Village Properties, Ltd., 723 F.2d 441 (5th Cir.1984); In re Rancourt, 123 B.R. 143 (Bankr.D.N.H.1991); In re Mid-City Hotel Assocs., 114 B.R. 634 (Bankr.D.Minn.1990). Consequently, at this point, you should now go back to Chapter 4, Section A and review carefully state law on rental assignments. Especially, refresh your understanding concerning the difference between "perfection" and "enforcement" concepts. The rest of this section addresses the specific impact of bankruptcy on the mortgagee's interest in rents.

The applicable provisions governing the security in rents in bankruptcy are found in Sections 363 and 552 of the Code:

§ 363. Use, sale, or lease of property

(a) In this section, "cash collateral" means cash . . . or other cash equivalents whenever acquired in which the estate and an entity other than the estate have an interest and includes the proceeds, products, offspring, rents, or profits of property and the fees, charges, accounts or other payments for the use or occupancy of rooms and other public facilities in hotels, motels, or other lodging properties subject to a security interest as provided in section 552(b) of this title, whether existing before or after the commencement of a case under this title. . . .

(c)(1) . . . [U]nless the court orders otherwise, the trustee . . . may use property of the estate in the ordinary course of business without notice or a hearing.

(c)(2) The trustee may not use, sell, or lease cash collateral under paragraph (1) of this subsection unless—

    (A) each entity that has an interest in such cash collateral consents; or

    (B) the court, after notice and a hearing, authorizes such use, sale, or lease in accordance with the provisions of this section. . . .

(c)(4) Except as provided in paragraph (2) of this subsection, the trustee shall segregate and account for any cash collateral in the trustee's possession, custody, or control. . . .

(e) Notwithstanding any other provision of this section, at any time, on request of an entity that has an interest in property used, sold, or leased, or proposed to be used, sold, or leased, by the trustee, the court, with or without a hearing, shall prohibit or condition such use, sale, or lease as is necessary to provide adequate protection of such interest. . . .

§ 552. Postpetition effect of security interest

(a) Except as provided in subsection (b) of this section, property acquired by the estate or by the debtor after the commencement of the case is not subject to any lien resulting from any security agreement entered into by the debtor before the commencement of the case.

(b)(1) Except as provided in sections 363, 506(c), 522, 544, 545, 547, and 548 of this title, if the debtor and an entity entered into a security agreement before the commencement of the case and if the security interest created by such security agreement extends to property of the debtor acquired before the commencement of the case and to proceeds, products, offspring, or profits of such property, then such security interest extends to such proceeds, products, offspring, or profits acquired by the estate after commencement of the case to the extent provided by such security agreement and applicable nonbankruptcy law, except to any extent that the court, after notice and a hearing and based on the equities of the case, orders otherwise.

(b)(2) Except as provided in sections 363, 506(c), 522, 544, 545, 547, and 548 of this title, and notwithstanding section 546(b) of this title, if the debtor and an entity entered into a security agreement before the commencement of the case and if the security interest created by such security agreement extends to property of the debtor acquired before the commencement of the case and to amounts paid as rents of such property or the fees, charges, accounts, or other payments for the use or occupancy of rooms and other public facilities in hotels, motels, or other lodging properties, then such security interest extends to such rents and such fees, charges, accounts, or other payments acquired by the estate after the commencement of the case to the extent provided in such security agreement, except to any extent that the court, after notice and a hearing and based on the equities of the case, orders otherwise.

Post-petition rents: Mortgagee vs. trustee or debtor-in-possession. When a mortgagor files a Chapter 11 petition, the mortgagor hopes to control post-petition rents and use them to help fund its efforts to reorganize (e.g., by using them to pay operating expenses, marketing expenses needed to secure new tenants, and the attorney fees needed to secure experienced bankruptcy counsel). By contrast, the mortgagee views the post-petition rents as its cash collateral and wants to prevent their use, preserving them for application to the unpaid balance of the debt—particularly where the mortgagee is undersecured and accumulated post-petition rents can reduce the mortgagee's deficiency claim.

Mortgagees and trustee or debtors-in-possession have acted vigorously to protect their respective interests in post-petition rents, and these efforts have produced an enormous volume of litigation regarding the parties' respective rights to post-petition rents. The cases tend to fall into one of three basic scenarios, each discussed below.

Scenario 1. The mortgagee takes an assignment of rents, but fails to record it prior to the mortgagor's bankruptcy. In this relatively rare instance, the avoiding powers will permit the trustee or debtor in possession to invalidate the assignment and control post-petition rents. Under section 544(a)(3), the trustee or debtor in possession has the status of a hypothetical bona fide purchaser of land. Under state law in all states, a bona fide purchaser of an interest in land takes that interest free of the unrecorded interest of third parties, such as the lien created by an unrecorded mortgage or assignment of rents. As a result, the mortgagee in this scenario will not have a security interest in the post-petition rents under section 552(b), and they will not constitute "cash collateral" under section 363(a). The trustee or debtor in possession can thus use them in its reorganization as it sees fit, without regard to the mortgagee's objection.

Scenario 2. The mortgagee takes and properly records an assignment of rents. After default, and before the mortgagor files a bankruptcy petition, the mortgagee takes the steps required under state law to enforce the assignment and begins collecting rents. In Scenario 2, courts have taken one of two basic approaches. Under the majority (and correct) approach, the post-petition rents constitute the mortgagee's cash collateral under sections 552(b)(2) and 363(a); thus, the trustee or debtor-in-possession cannot control or use the post-petition rents without the mortgagee's consent or court approval, and the court cannot approve that use over the mortgagee's objection unless the mortgagee receives adequate protection of its interest in the cash collateral or unless the court determines that the "equities of the case" justify that use under section 552(b)(2). Under the minority (and incorrect) view, the post-petition rents do not constitute property of the estate, but instead belong to the mortgagee (who may apply them in reduction of the unpaid debt).

Courts adhering to the minority approach have concluded that "[w]hen a mortgagee completes all steps necessary to enforce its rights under an assignment of rent clause pre-petition, all interests of the [mortgagor] in the rents are extinguished and the rents do not become property of the estate or cash collateral." See, e.g., Sovereign Bank v. Schwab, 414 F.3d 450 (3rd Cir. 2005); In re Cordova, 500 B.R. 701 (D. N.J. 2013); In re Soho 25 Retail, LLC, 2011 WL 1333084 (Bankr. S.D.N.Y. 2011); In re Robin Assocs., 275 B.R. 218 (Bankr. W.D. Pa. 2001). Many of the decisions adhering to this view involve assignments that the court characterized as "absolute" assignments rather than assignments intended for security. See, e.g., In re Jason Realty, L.P., 59 F.3d 423 (3d Cir. 1995); In re Village Props, Ltd., 723 F.2d 441 (5th Cir. 1984); 460 Tennessee Street, LLC v. Telesis Community Credit Union, 437 B.R. 306 (W.D. Tenn. 2010). Practically, a court following this approach must automatically deny the debtor in possession access to post-petition rents, regardless of the equities or whether the mortgagee's interest is or could be adequately protected.

The minority approach is both counter-intuitive and analytically unsound. Suppose the mortgagee had obtained the appointment of a receiver prior to bankruptcy (an action sufficient to enforce the assignment of rents in every state). This does not turn the receiver or the mortgagee into the beneficial owner of the rents. The receiver is accountable to the mortgagor for its management, and the net rents (after necessary expenses of the receivership) must be applied to the debt. Because the mortgagor retains a beneficial interest in the rents accruing during the receivership, even if it lacks control over them, the mortgagee's right is still appropriately characterized as a security interest. As a result, it is inappropriate to conclude that the mortgagor in Scenario 2 retains no interest in the rents that constitutes property of the estate. Under the correct view, the post-petition rents in Scenario 2 constitute property of the estate, but they also constitute the mortgagee's cash collateral (for which the mortgagee is entitled to adequate protection). See, e.g., In re Millette, 186 F.3d 638 (5th Cir. 1999); In re Buttermilk Towne Center, LLC, 442 B.R. 558 (6th Cir. B.A.P. 2010); In re MRI Beltline Industrial, L.P., 476 B.R. 917 (Bankr. N.D. Tex. 2012); In re South Side House, LLC, 474 B.R. 391 (Bankr. E.D.N.Y. 2012); In re Senior Housing Alternatives, Inc., 444 B.R. 386 (Bankr. E.D. Tenn. 2011); In re Village Green I, GP, 435 B.R. 525 (Bankr. W.D. Tenn. 2010).

Scenario 3. The mortgagee takes and properly records an assignment of rents. After the mortgagor's default, but before the mortgagee has taken steps sufficient to enforce its assignment, the mortgagor files a bankruptcy petition. In Scenario 3, the relative rights of the mortgagee and the trustee or debtor in possession depend upon whether state law on assignment of rents governs the mortgagee's rights and, if so, whether the mortgagee's lien on rents is considered "perfected" (by virtue of the recorded assignment) or "unperfected" (because the mortgagee has not yet taken steps to enforce the assignment).

The traditional "common law" approach in Scenario 3. If state law governs the mortgagee's rights, and the applicable state law follows the traditional "common law" view that an assignment of rents is not perfected—and is thus inchoate and ineffective—until the assignee has taken steps to activate that interest after default, then the trustee or debtor-in-possession in Scenario 3 may invalidate the mortgagee's unperfected interest under the strong-arm clause. Under this view, the post-petition rents would not constitute the mortgagee's cash collateral, and the trustee or debtor-in-possession could control and use the post-petition rents despite mortgagee's objection. As discussed in Chapter 4, during the 1980s and 1990s, a substantial number of federal courts reached this conclusion. See, e.g., In re Century Inv. Fund VIII L.P., 937 F.2d 371 (7th Cir. 1991) (applying Wisconsin law); In re Sam A. Tisci, Inc., 133 B.R. 857 (N.D. Ohio 1991); In re Turtle Creek, Ltd., 194 B.R. 267 (Bankr. N.D.Ala. 1996); In re Mews Assocs., L.P., 144 B.R. 867 (Bankr. W.D.Mo. 1992); In re Kurth Ranch, 110 B.R. 501 (Bankr. D. Mont. 1990); In re Neideffer, 96 B.R. 241 (Bankr. D. N.D. 1988); In re Ziegler, 65 B.R. 285 (Bankr. D. S.D. 1986).

Some court decisions in cases comparable to Scenario 3 followed the traditional common law rule, but nevertheless allowed the mortgagee to enforce its assignment of rents *after the bankruptcy petition* pursuant to section 546(b). Section 546(b)(1) provides that

> The [trustee's avoiding powers] are subject to any generally applicable law that (A) permits perfection of an interest in property to be effective against an entity that acquires rights in such property before the date of perfection. . . .

Section 546(b)(2) further provides that if that generally applicable law "requires seizure of such property or commencement of an action to accomplish such perfection . . . [and] such property has not been seized or such action has not been commenced before the date of the filing of the petition . . . [then] such interest in such property shall be perfected . . . by giving notice within the time fixed by such law for such seizure or such commencement." If section 546(b) applies, then the automatic stay does not prevent a mortgagee from perfecting its security interest after the petition date. 11 U.S.C.A. § 362(b)(3).

Mortgagees facing Scenario 3 have often asserted that section 546(b)(2) permitted them to perfect post-petition by seeking possession or a receivership in bankruptcy court or by giving notice of their intention to enforce the assignment of rents. By doing so, they argued, they thus perfected their interest in rents, making the post-petition rents "cash collateral." A substantial number of courts have accepted this argument. See, e.g., Virginia Beach Fed. Sav. & Loan Ass'n v. Wood, 901 F.2d 849 (10th Cir. 1990); Saline State Bank v. Mahloch, 834 F.2d 690 (8th Cir. 1987); In re Casbeer, 793 F.2d 1436 (5th Cir. 1986). The argument is incorrect, however, and a substantial number of decisions have properly rejected it. See, e.g., In re Kurth Ranch, 110 B.R. 501 (Bankr. D. Mont. 1990); In re Wynnewood House Assocs., 121 B.R. 716 (Bankr. E.D. Pa. 1990); In re Multi-Group III Ltd. Partn., 99 B.R. 5 (Bankr. D. Ariz. 1989). By its terms, section 546(b)(1) permits post-petition perfection only when the relevant state perfection law allows the perfection to "relate back" so as to prevail over the interests of intervening third parties. Because state laws governing rent assignments do not provide this relation-back attribute, section 546(b) does not authorize a mortgagee to perfect its interest in rents after the petition date.

The modern majority approach in Scenario 3. Under the majority (and correct) view, as explained earlier, the recorded assignment is sufficient under state law to "perfect" the mortgagee's security interest in rents, see, e.g., In re Millette, 186 F.3d 638 (5th Cir. 1999), and thus the trustee or debtor-in-possession may not invalidate that security interest altogether using the strong-arm power. As a result, the post-petition rents constitute the mortgagee's cash collateral even if the mortgagee had not taken steps to begin collecting rents prior to bankruptcy. While this appears to permit post-petition enforcement of the mortgagee's interest in rents, the language of the Bankruptcy Code contemplates this result. As one court has observed:

> Section 363(c)(2) provides, in effect, for the automatic sequestration of rents that are subject to a perfected security interest. Under § 361(3), the bankruptcy court may provide adequate protection by "granting such other relief . . . as will result in the realization by such entity of the indubitable equivalent of such entity's interest," while § 105(a) grants the bankruptcy court the power to "issue any order . . . necessary or appropriate to carry out the provisions of [the Code]." We hold that under these authorities, the bankruptcy court's powers are sufficiently broad to allow it to enforce a mortgagee's security interest in rents when and to the extent a state court would do so.

In re Park at Dash Point L.P., 121 B.R. 850, 859 (Bankr. W.D. Wash. 1990).

Use of post-petition rents that constitute cash collateral. If the mortgagee's perfected security interest extends to post-petition rents under section 552(b)(2), those rents constitute "cash collateral" under section 363(a). Under section 363(c), the trustee or debtor in possession cannot use rents that are cash collateral without the consent of the mortgagee or court approval following notice and a hearing. If the mortgagee requests adequate protection of its cash collateral, the court must prohibit or condition use of the cash collateral "as is necessary to provide adequate protection of such interest." 11 U.S.C.A. § 363(e).

This does not mean that the mortgagee is automatically entitled to prevent the trustee or debtor from using the rents. If, for example, the mortgagee is oversecured and has a sizable equity cushion, the court will permit the debtor to use the post-petition rents so long as the equity cushion provides adequate protection of the mortgage debt. More commonly, however, the mortgagee finds itself undersecured. In that scenario, the Code permits the trustee or debtor-in-possession to use the post-petition rents only if either (a) the trustee or debtor in possession can provide adequate protection of the mortgagee's interest in the cash collateral or (b) the court concludes that the "equities of the case" justify the mortgagee's use.

As a result, the debtor's ability to use the post-petition rents may depend upon the debtor's intended use for them. If the debtor proposes to use a portion of the rents to pay the reasonable expenses of operating the property (i.e., paying the utilities, providing common area maintenance services), the court may well conclude that payment of these expenses is "necessary to protect the value of the creditor's interest in future rents and the real property, and therefore is not inconsistent with providing the creditor adequate protection, even if the creditor is undersecured." In re Park at Dash Point L.P., 121 B.R. 850, 859 (Bankr. W.D. Wash. 1990). See also In re Murray, 2011 WL 5902623 (Bankr. E.D.N.C. 2011); In re Cavros, 262 B.R. 206 (Bankr. D. Conn. 2001). Alternatively, the court might conclude that the "equities of the case" justify allowing the debtor to use the post-petition rents to pay for reasonable expenses of operating the property because the mortgagee would have to incur those expenses if it took over the property and became a mortgagee in possession. By contrast, if the debtor is proposing to use the post-petition rents to pay its Chapter 11 attorneys or other reorganization expenses unrelated to maintenance of the mortgaged premises, the court is unlikely to permit that use unless the debtor can provide adequate protection (such as some form of substitute collateral).

Debtors have sometimes argued that they should be allowed to use the current month's rent, even if it constitutes cash collateral, as long as the mortgagee retains its lien on future rents. Most recent decisions, however, reject the view that future rents from the same property are an appropriate form of substitute collateral. As one court has noted:

> Where . . . there is a specific assignment of rents given as security, a diversion of any portion of the rents to a party other [than] the secured party is clearly a diminution of the secured party's interests in the assignment of rents portion of the security. . . . The secured party has a security interest in the full amount of the future rents. Therefore, this court cannot accept that the use of future rents to replace the expenditure of the prior months rents somehow provides adequate protection for the secured party.

In re River Oaks Ltd. Partn., 166 B.R. 94, 99 (E.D. Mich. 1994). See also Putnal v. SunTrust Bank, 489 B.R. 285 (M.D. Ga. 2013); In re MRI Beltline Indus., L.P., 476 B.R. 917 (Bankr. N.D. Tex. 2012).

9.   INSTALLMENT LAND CONTRACTS
IN BANKRUPTCY

Suppose the party filing a bankruptcy petition is a vendor or vendee under an installment land contract rather than a mortgagee or mortgagor under a traditional mortgage or deed of trust. Here our starting point is section 365(a) of the Bankruptcy Code. This section permits the trustee or debtor-in-possession to "assume" or "reject" any "executory contract" of the debtor. 11 U.S.C.A. § 365(a).

Vendor bankruptcy. Assume that a vendor and vendee executed an installment land contract 7 years ago that provided for a purchase price of $100,000, payable in equal annual installments over 20 years. The vendee took possession immediately and has paid seven of the installments. Now the vendor experiences financial distress and files a bankruptcy petition. If the trustee or debtor-in-possession "rejects" the contract under section 365, what are the vendee's options?

Assuming that the vendee is in possession, as will almost always be the case, the right to reject the contract is trumped by the vendee's right to complete the payments over the term of the contract and to obtain legal title. See 11 U.S.C.A. § 365(i). In the unlikely event the vendee is not in possession, rejection means that he or she will not be able to complete the contract and obtain title to the land. Rather, the vendee will be left as an unsecured creditor with a claim for damages against the bankruptcy estate.

Vendee bankruptcy. In the more common scenario, it is the installment contract vendee that seeks bankruptcy protection. In this setting, the crucial question is whether the contract is an "executory contract" for purposes of section 365(a) or rather as a "mortgage" or "security device" not governed by section 365.

IN RE HEWARD BROTHERS
United States Bankruptcy Court, District of Idaho, 1997
210 B.R. 475

JIM D. PAPPAS, CHIEF JUDGE. . . . On March 22, 1990, FCB [Farm Credit Bank of Spokane] agreed to sell a 320 acre farm located in Cassia County, Idaho, to Debtor for $165,000. Debtor agreed to pay FCB $41,250 at the time of purchase, and the remainder of the purchase price in annual installments. The Contract provides that FCB remain the record owner of the property until Debtor makes the final payment, at which time FCB is required to provide Debtor a warranty deed to the property. A title insurance policy was purchased for Debtor, and a memorandum of contract was recorded, both at the inception of the Contract.

Debtor made the down payment of $41,250 and six annual installments. While Debtor still owes FCB over $120,000 on the purchase price, the parties have stipulated that Debtor has $80,000 in equity in the property. Debtor did not pay the March 1, 1997, installment, and on April 23, 1997, filed for Chapter 11 relief.

Executory contracts receive special treatment in bankruptcy cases. If a contract is "executory" for purposes of the Bankruptcy Code, a debtor may preserve its rights under the contract solely by assuming it and performing its terms, only after curing any default existing at the time the bankruptcy case was filed, and providing the other party to the contract with adequate assurance of the debtor's future performance of the contract. 11 U.S.C. §§ 365(a), (b)(1). As compared to most security agreements, for example, if a contract is executory, a Chapter 11 debtor's right to modify its terms in a Chapter 11 reorganization plan is extremely limited by the statutes. Upon request, the Court may fix a deadline by which a debtor must assume or reject the contract. 11 U.S.C. § 365(d)(2).

FCB asserts its installment land sales contract with Debtor is an executory contract for the purposes Section 365. Debtor argues that the Contract is not executory, but is instead a secured financing device, analogous to a mortgage. Debtor seeks an opportunity to modify the terms of the Contract through its forthcoming reorganization plan.

The Bankruptcy Code contains no precise definition of an executory contract. The legislative history to Section 365, tersely provides that an executory contract is a contract on which performance remains due to some extent on both sides. * * * The Ninth Circuit uses the widely referenced "Countryman" definition [Countryman, Executory Contracts in Bankruptcy: Part 1, 57 Minn.L.Rev. 439 (1973)] for guidance in determining whether a contract is executory for bankruptcy purposes. See, e.g., In re Robert L. Helms Constr. & Dev. Co. Inc., 110 F.3d 1470, 1472 (9th Cir.1997) (citations omitted). Under Countryman,

> [a contract is executory if] the obligations of both parties are so far unperformed that the failure of either party to complete performance would constitute a material breach and thus excuse the performance of the other.

Id. at 1472 n. 2 (citations omitted). While the determination of whether a contract is executory for bankruptcy purposes is a matter of federal law, whether a party's failure to perform its remaining obligations under a contract constitutes a material breach is an issue of state contract law. * * *

However, the Ninth Circuit has also created an exception to the general rule that the Countryman definition controls whether a contract is executory for bankruptcy purposes. In re Pacific Express, Inc., 780 F.2d

1482 (9th Cir.1986). There the Court declined to apply Countryman to a security agreement disguised as a lease. The court held that

> [a] "lease" which is really a disguised security agreement does not require assumption or rejection under section 365. Courts have declined to apply section 365 to security agreements, even where those agreements have taken on the surface formalities of contracts or unexpired leases that might otherwise come within the apparent reach of that section. [citations omitted]

> The conclusion that section 365 does not apply to a security interest disguised as a lease makes sense. Otherwise, Congress' grant of avoiding powers under section 544 and other sections of the Bankruptcy Code would conflict with its mandate under section 365. Both are designed to protect and conserve the [debtor's] estate.

In re Pacific Express, 780 F.2d at 1487. * * * In addition, the Ninth Circuit Bankruptcy Appellate Panel applied the same reasoning to an installment land sale contract, where the seller places a deed in escrow, in In re Rehbein, 60 B.R. 436, 440–441 (9th Cir.BAP 1986).

Nationwide, there is a distinct division of authority on the issue presented by this case, whether an installment land sale contract is an executory contract for purposes of the Bankruptcy Code. Compare In re Streets & Beard Farm Partnership, 882 F.2d 233 (7th Cir.1989) (treating installment land sale contract as a security device, not an executory contract), and In re Rehbein, 60 B.R. 436 (9th Cir.BAP 1986) (same), and In re Vinson, 202 B.R. 972 (Bankr.S.D.Ill.1996) (same), and In re Kratz, 96 B.R. 127 (Bankr.S.D.Ohio 1988) (same), and In re McDaniel, 89 B.R. 861 (Bankr.E.D.Wash.1988) (same), and In re Fox, 83 B.R. 290 (Bankr. E.D.Pa.1988) (same), and In re Sennhenn, 80 B.R. 89 (Bankr.S.D.Ohio 1987) (same), and In re Britton, 43 B.R. 605 (Bankr.E.D.Mich.1984) (same), and In re Booth, 19 B.R. 53 (Bankr.D.Utah 1982) (same), with In re Speck, 798 F.2d 279 (8th Cir.1986) (viewing installment land contracts as executory), and In re Scanlan, 80 B.R. 131 (Bankr.S.D.Iowa 1987) (same), and In re Aslan, 65 B.R. 826 (Bankr.C.D.Cal.1986) (same), and Shaw v. Dawson, 48 B.R. 857 (D.N.M.1985) (same), and In re Anderson, 36 B.R. 120 (Bankr.D.Haw.1983) (same). The critical component in the reasoning of each of the various decisions concerns whether the Countryman definition should be mechanically applied in every instance to determine if the land sale contract is executory under Section 365. In each case where Countryman is imposed literally, the land sale contract is found to be executory. * * *

As the Ninth Circuit has recognized, taken literally, the Countryman definition would render almost all agreements executory since it is the rare contract indeed that does not encompass some unperformed obligations on each side.[1] Because of this, rote classifications of contracts under Countryman should be avoided. Rather, the individual characteristics of each contract should be analyzed under the peculiar facts of each bankruptcy case in order to determine whether the contract is executory. In re Robert L. Helms Constr. & Dev. Co., Inc., 110 F.3d 1470 (9th Cir.1997). And, as explained in *Pacific Express*, it makes better sense to find that Section 365 does not apply to the real estate contract which in reality is merely a security device. This Court also long ago recognized that many installment land sale contracts will not be eligible for protection as executory contracts under Section 365. In re Cox, 83 I.B.C.R. 45 (Young, J.).

Under the Ninth Circuit approach, given the facts of this case, and considering relevant state law, the outcome is clear. Under Idaho law, when the parties entered their contract, Debtor became the equitable owner of the farm property under the time-honored doctrine of equitable conversion. Holscher v. James, 124 Idaho 443, 860 P.2d 646 (1993); Rush v. Anestos, 104 Idaho 630, 661 P.2d 1229 (1983). Debtor was entitled to immediate possession and use of the property with all the benefits of ownership. Likewise, Debtor assumed all responsibilities for the property including the duty to maintain the property, and to pay relevant taxes and assessments. Simply put, Debtor was the owner of the farm in all respects, except that legal title to the property remained vested in FCB. FCB, on the other hand, has but one obligation to perform under the contract: to transfer legal title to Debtor upon completion of the Contract payments.

Under Idaho law, if upon default by the buyer, the equity subject to forfeiture under an installment land contract exceeds the seller's reasonable damages suffered on account of the buyer's breach, the contract must be foreclosed in the same manner as a mortgage through judicial sale. See, e.g., Thomas v. Klein, 99 Idaho 105, 577 P.2d 1153 (1978). Here, the parties have agreed that Debtor has $80,000 in equity over and above the balance due to FCB, a fact which suggests that a strict forfeiture under the contract may not be available to FCB upon Debtor's default.

In addition to the duty to physically tender a deed to Debtor, FCB stresses that its obligation to convey "marketable" title is a critical future obligation in this case, constituting the Contract executory. * * * The Court is not persuaded. While it is true FCB could cloud title to this property during the term of the agreement, the likelihood of this seems

---

[1] For example, even in the case of the classic land sale secured by a mortgage, at the conclusion of the buyer's payments, the seller is obliged to tender a satisfaction or release of the mortgage, the failure to do so likely constituting an actionable breach of contract. Dohrman v. Tomlinson, 88 Idaho 313, 399 P.2d 255 (1965); Idaho Code § 45–915 (providing for penalties upon failure to release a satisfied mortgage).

remote. FCB, an institutional lender and part of the federal farm credit system, offers no facts to show the circumstances under which it may, or its motivation to, cloud Debtor's title. To the contrary, by obtaining a title insurance policy for Debtor at closing showing the property free and clear of encumbrances, and by recording a public notice of the existence of Debtor's rights under the Contract to gain the protection for Debtor of the recording acts, the notion that FCB will be tempted to wrongfully breach its contract and encumber this property deserves little credence. Every indication in the record is that FCB does not intend to encumber the property. Therefore, under these facts, the obligation not to cloud title is hardly the sort of "performance" that Congress had in mind when it enacted the special protections of Section 365 of the Bankruptcy Code.

In reaching this decision, the Court does not hold that all installment land sale contracts are security devices. As observed above, this is a fact-specific inquiry. Each contract must be analyzed based upon its own terms to see if the obligations created therein amount to more than a mere security device. For example, in the contract in In re Cochise College Park, Inc., 703 F.2d 1339 (9th Cir.1983), the seller had obligations remaining that were not related to security for payment of the purchase price. There, the seller was required to construct a subdivision on the property in question, clearly constituting an appropriate basis to render the contract executory. Another good example is In re Frontier Properties, Inc., 979 F.2d 1358 (9th Cir.1992). In that case, the seller not only retained title under the contract, but also agreed to pay off the underlying debt on the property, and to pay insurance, taxes and assessments. Id. at 1365.

When the seller has remaining obligations not related to the security function served by the typical title-retaining land sales contract, the contract is more than a mere security device, and application of the Countryman test is appropriate. But where, as here, the remaining "obligations" of the seller amount solely to the ministerial duty inherent in all security agreements in connection with releasing the lien upon full payment, the contract is a security device and Section 365 does not apply.

FCB also argues that the Contract is executory because the parties so contracted. However, this Court is not bound by the contract's terms. Generally, a prepetition agreement to waive a benefit of bankruptcy is void as against public policy. See Fallick v. Kehr, 369 F.2d 899 (2d Cir.1966) (prepetition agreement to waive benefit of bankruptcy not specifically enforceable); In re Freeman, 165 B.R. 307 (Bankr.S.D.Fla. 1994) (same) * * *. Accordingly, this Court looks beyond the parties' agreement, and examines the Contract's true nature under applicable law to determine whether it is in fact executory.

* * * Because the Contract is in essence a security agreement, the Contract is not executory for purposes of Section 365, and the Court concludes that FCB's motion to require Debtor to assume or reject the contract as executory should be denied. A separate order will be entered.

NOTES

1. *Significance of the "security device-executory contract" distinction.* In general, what are the implications of a court treating an installment land contract as a security device in a vendee bankruptcy? Consider the following commentary:

> [I]f the installment land contract is characterized as a mortgage or security interest, Vendor may not invoke section 365 and will be afforded the status of a mortgagee in Vendee's bankruptcy. If the land is worth more than the unpaid balance, the trustee will sell the land; Vendor will receive the unpaid balance and the surplus will be available for distribution to Vendee's unsecured creditors.

> Having the installment land contract characterized as a security device rather than an executory contract can be even more crucial in a Chapter 11, 12, or 13 case. In these Chapters, if the contract is treated as a mortgage, it can be made a part of the reorganization plan and serve to enhance the likelihood of the plan's success. Consider, for example, the impact of mortgage treatment in a Chapter 12 farm reorganization. If the land has declined in value, the farmer-debtor may be able to reduce the installment contract balance to the land's current market value and have the excess over that value ultimately discharged after modest payments under the plan. By contrast, if the contract is treated as an "executory contract," then if the farmer-debtor lacks the funds to cure the default and compensate the vendor for damages flowing from the default, the farmer-debtor will likely have to forfeit the land to the vendor and this will substantially diminish the likelihood of a successful reorganization. Indeed, where the contract real estate is the debtor's sole or major asset, treatment of the contract as "executory" may well mean the failure of the reorganization and the inevitability of liquidation.

Nelson, Whitman, Burkhart & Freyermuth, Real Estate Finance Law 882–883 (6th ed. 2014).*

Should mortgage lenders in jurisdictions that treat installment land contracts as "executory" consider recasting their mortgage loan transactions so that they become installment land contract vendors rather than mortgagees? What would you advise?

---

* Reprinted with permission of LEG, Inc., d/b/a/ West Academic.

2. *"Executoriness" as a matter of state or federal law.* The *Heward* court notes that "the determination of whether a contract is executory for bankruptcy purposes is a matter of federal law." Should this issue instead be determined by state law? Should an installment land contract be characterized as a mortgage or security device only to the extent that state law treats it as such in other contexts? If so, a bankruptcy court in Kentucky or Indiana, where installment land contracts are essentially deemed mortgages, would reach a different result than in New Mexico, where state courts continue to resist such a characterization. On the one hand, if bankruptcy courts uniformly take the position that installment land contracts are security or devices or mortgages as a matter of federal law, it may hasten the day when such contracts are uniformly treated as mortgages for all purposes (a result which we would generally applaud). See Grant S. Nelson & Dale A. Whitman, Installment Land Contracts—The National Scene Revisited, 1985 B.Y.U.L.Rev. 1, 63. On the other hand, does it unduly upset the expectations of the parties for a bankruptcy court to treat an installment land contract as a mortgage when local law clearly does not?

3. *Impact of contract provisions classifying contract as "executory."* What other doctrine does the *Heward* court's refusal to enforce the parties' contract language characterizing the contract as "executory" call to mind? See Chapter 3, Section A supra.

CHAPTER SEVEN

SOME PRIORITY PROBLEMS

■ ■ ■

A. PURCHASE MONEY MORTGAGES

A purchase money mortgage is a mortgage that the mortgagor grants to enable the mortgagor to acquire ownership of the mortgaged land. A *vendor purchase money mortgage* can arise when the seller of land agrees to extend credit to the buyer for some portion of the land's purchase price, and the buyer grants a mortgage on the land to secure the buyer's obligation to pay the remaining purchase price. There can also be a *third party purchase money mortgage*; this would arise when the buyer of land obtains a loan from a third party (typically a bank, savings and loan, or other institutional lender), uses the loan proceeds to pay the purchase price of the land, and grants the third party a mortgage to secure the buyer's repayment of the loan.

Suppose that Jones purchases Blackacre from Seller using the proceeds of a loan obtained from First Bank and grants First Bank a purchase money mortgage. Shortly thereafter, First Bank discovers that Cathy Creditor asserts a judgment lien against Blackacre based on an unpaid judgment obtained against Jones two years earlier. How should the law resolve a priority contest between First Bank and Cathy Creditor? Should it matter whether and/or when First Bank recorded its mortgage? Should it matter whether First Bank knew or should have known about the claims of Creditor?

KENTUCKY LEGAL SYSTEMS CORP. v. DUNN

Court of Appeals of Kentucky, 2006
205 S.W.3d 235

TACKETT, J. Kentucky Legal Systems Corporation (KLS) appeals from the judgment of the Fayette Circuit Court finding that its judgment lien against all property owned by N.E. Dunn and George E. "Ged" Dunn was inferior to the mortgage held by Community Trust Bank, where the mortgage enabled the purchase of the subject real property. KLS argues that Kentucky law requires that its first-recorded judgment lien have priority over the Community Trust mortgage. We disagree and affirm.

The property in question was purchased in October 2000, by Dunn, and the loan enabling the purchase was given by Community Trust Bank in exchange for a mortgage on the property. The judgment held by KLS was entered in 1992, and the judgment lien filed and properly recorded in 1998 against all real property owned by Dunn. KLS argues that the bank was on constructive notice of its judgment lien and that it failed to exercise due care before giving Dunn a loan. Dunn later defaulted on the mortgage and the bank sought foreclosure and a declaration that its mortgage held priority over the judgment lien. The circuit court agreed that the mortgage should be considered a purchase money mortgage in accord with the Restatement (Third) of Property, *Mortgages* § 7.2 (1997), quoting the following section:

> Under this section the vendor's purchase money mortgage is senior to any previous judgment liens that arise against the purchaser-mortgagor. This is true even though a judgment attaches as a lien to the judgment debtor's after-acquired real estate and the vendor takes the mortgage with actual knowledge of the judgment. . . .
>
> Because this long-established rule makes it unnecessary for a purchase money lender to examine for preexisting judgments and other liens against the purchaser-mortgagor, it reduces title risk in connection with such transactions and thus encourages purchase money financing by vendors. Moreover, the rule is justified on grounds of fundamental fairness. The vendor-mortgagee should prevail because the lien creditor has not extended credit or perfected the lien in reliance on the right to be repaid out of any specific property, much less out of the real estate previously owned by the vendor. This is obvious, since the judgment was obtained before the debtor acquired the real estate to which the judgment lien attached. . . .
>
> This section extends the same priority preference to third party purchase money lenders. . . . While it is true that such lenders, unlike vendors, do not give up ownership of specific real estate, they nevertheless part with money with the expectation that they will have security in that real estate. Without this advance of money, the purchaser-mortgagor would never have received the property and the other claimants would never have had the opportunity to satisfy their claims from such a convenient source. As in the vendor purchase money context, this section seeks to avoid conferring a windfall on those claimants. [Restatement (Third) of Property (Mortgages) § 7.2 cmt. b.]

The circuit court adopted the Restatement's reasoning and held the bank's mortgage was superior to KLS's judgment lien. This appeal followed.

KLS's argument for its priority rests entirely on two statutes, KRS 382.270 which requires recording of all instruments affecting real property, and KRS 382.280, which provides that deeds and mortgages take effect in the order in which they are legally acknowledged and recorded. Coupled with the dearth of Kentucky cases on the subject, KLS argues that in the absence of a statutory mandate to do so, the courts should look only at the recording dates of instruments for guidance as to priority. Community Trust, citing the Restatement (Third) and other treatises, argues that the judgment was correct because without its grant of a loan with a mortgage reserved, the debtor would have no interest in the property at all to which KLS's judgment lien could attach, and cites many cases in other jurisdictions which follow this rule. KLS responds by saying that Kentucky only recognizes a limited exception to the ordinary rules on priority for purchase money mortgages, narrowly defining such an interest as a 'vendor's lien" where the grantor himself retains the mortgage.

KLS cites only two Kentucky cases, *Purdom v. Broach*, 210 Ky. 161, 275 S.W. 365 (1925) and *Minix v. Maggard*, 652 S.W.2d 93 (Ky.App.1983), in support of the above proposition. On closer examination, neither case is particularly useful to this determination. *Purdom* mentions vendor's liens only by saying 'no distinction can be made between a vendor's lien and a mortgage, as the former is simply a purchase-money mortgage, and therefore equivalent in legal effect." *Purdom* at 366. *Minix*, meanwhile, deals with an extraordinary set of facts involving an unrecorded purchase money mortgage from the grantor, but of which all of the relevant parties had actual notice, and a federal tax lien, and this Court held that due to the actual notice the purchase money mortgage had priority even though it was unrecorded. Neither case specifically defines a purchase money mortgage in the narrow way suggested by KLS, in that they do not involve a third-party lender at all.

Nor do the two statutes foreclose the possibility of an exception for purchase money mortgages to the ordinary rules of priority. The statutes are quite general and do not address the specific situation at all. In fact, the statutes only specifically mention mortgages and deeds, and not other interests created by liens such as the one held by KLS. We hold in the absence of definite guidance from case law or statute, the circuit court properly decided the question of priority based on guidance from the Restatement, which serves as a guiding star for courts and scholars alike on the state of the law. Considering also the many states which have adopted the Restatement (Third)'s view on this question,[1] either

---

[1]   *See, Guffey v. Creutzinger*, 984 S.W.2d 219 (Tenn.Ct.App.1998); *see also, Belland v. O.K. Lumber Co., Inc.*, 797 P.2d 638 (Alaska 1990); *Garrett Tire Center, Inc. v. Herbaugh*, 294 Ark. 21, 740 S.W.2d 612 (1987); *Citibank Mortgage Corp. v. Carteret Savings Bank, F.A.*, 612 So.2d 599 (Fla.Dist.Ct.App.1992); *Aetna Cas. & Sur. Co. v. Valdosta Federal Savings & Loan Ass'n*, 175 Ga.App. 614, 333 S.E.2d 849 (1985).

specifically by reference to the Restatement or by holding in accord with the reasoning behind the section, we hold that Kentucky should adopt this logical rule that third parties who lend money used to purchase real estate in exchange for a mortgage hold special priority over all other recorded liens and judgments except where agreed otherwise by the parties or specified by statute.

With respect to KLS's argument that Community Trust did not exercise due care in failing to discover its judgment lien, for the reasons stated in the Restatement (Third) we hold that Community Trust, as a purchase money lender, did not need to search for judgment liens, as they should be given first priority over a judgment lien regardless of whether they had notice of any kind of the interest. Even had Community Trust discovered the lien by exercise of due diligence, it should be granted priority over the judgment creditor's lien due to its status as a purchase money lender. . . .

NOTES

1.   *The general priority for purchase money mortgages.* Real estate law has traditionally accorded the purchase money mortgagee with a special priority over all other recorded liens and judgments. As noted in Fleet Mtge. Corp. v. Stevenson, 241 N.J.Super. 408, 575 A.2d 63 (1990):

> [P]riority of purchase money mortgages has been a fixture of N.J. law since 1820. . . . [T]heir special priority can be asserted against: (1) claims of dower [or] curtesy by the purchaser's spouse, (2) the lien of judgments, (3) mechanics liens, (4) mortgages executed before the purchase of the land, and (5) federal tax liens filed against the purchaser before he acquired title. The rationale behind such an historic and thoroughgoing priority is found essentially in the equity which results from providing the wherewithal to purchase the property. . . .

2.   *Construction loan as a purchase money mortgage.* Suppose the proceeds of a mortgage loan are used not only to acquire title to Blackacre, but also to construct a building on it. Clearly, the part of the loan used to acquire title to Blackacre qualifies for purchase money mortgage treatment. But what about the part used for construction? The cases disagree. Compare Resolution Trust Corp. v. Bopp, 18 Kan.App.2d 271, 850 P.2d 939 (1993) ("[T]o split the mortgage would deny the lender its expected security interest and would, under modern lending practices, have a chilling effect on this type of building activity.") with Westinghouse Elec. Co. v. Vann Realty Co., 568 S.W.2d 777 (Mo.1978) (where part of the loan proceeds were used to acquire land and the rest to build apartment buildings on the land, the part that was used to acquire title was purchase money, but the rest was not). The Restatement treats the entire amount of the loan as "purchase money." Restatement (Third) of Property (Mortgages) § 7.2 cmt. c (1997). In a state

like Missouri that does not provide the construction lender with purchase money priority for those funds directed to improvements, how might the lender structure the transaction to obtain the desired priority?

Suppose Jones purchases Blackacre (an undeveloped parcel) with previously saved cash, and then obtains a $300,000 construction mortgage loan which she uses to build a home on Blackacre. Should any of the loan proceeds be treated as "purchase money"? According to the Restatement, "[e]ven where the proceeds of the loan are used exclusively for improving the mortgaged real estate, the mortgage will receive purchase money treatment so long as it is given as part of the same transaction in which title to the real estate is acquired." Id. cmt. c. Is this a sensible position? Why or why not? What if Jones had purchased Blackacre six months before obtaining the construction loan? Id. (construction mortgage is part of the acquisition transaction only if the mortgagor commences "negotiations with the construction lender prior to mortgagor's acquisition of title, and the actual loan [is] 'made incident to the mortgagor's acquisition of title or within a reasonable time thereafter' ").

3.　*Judgment searches against prospective mortgagors.* Purchase money lenders commonly conduct a search for judgments against prospective borrowers prior to making a loan. Given the result in the principal case, why bother? Would it be malpractice for a lawyer who represents such a lender to fail to make a search? See Belland v. O.K. Lumber Co., Inc., 797 P.2d 638 (Alaska 1990).

———————

The Impact of Recording Acts; Priority Among Competing Purchase Money Mortgages. Remarkably, a purchase money mortgage need *never* be recorded to protect the mortgagee against judgment liens or other claims attaching to the real estate that arose against the purchaser-mortgagor before it acquired title. Restatement (Third) of Property (Mortgages) § 7.2 cmt. c (1997). However, *subsequent* interests that arise through the purchaser-mortgagor are another matter. Here the recording acts can be crucial. Under some circumstances, given a negligent purchase money mortgagee, it is conceivable that a purchase money mortgage will be superior to a prior judgment lien against the mortgagor, but inferior to a subsequent mortgage. For example, suppose J has an outstanding judgment lien against P. L lends money to P to purchase Blackacre from S. S conveys Blackacre to P, which deed is recorded. At the same time P gives a mortgage for the purchase money to L, but L fails to record. A few days later X lends money to P and takes and records a mortgage on Blackacre, without actual knowledge of L's mortgage. In all probability, L's purchase-money mortgage will be prior to J's lien, but junior to X's subsequent mortgage. See Thorpe v. Helmer, 275 Ill. 86, 113 N.E. 954 (1916) (intervening judgment lien); Trigg v. Vermillion, 113 Mo. 230, 20 S.W. 1047 (1892) (intervening mortgage). See Restatement

(Third) of Property (Mortgages) § 7.2 cmt. b and illus. 8 (1997). For a thoughtful analysis, albeit in a slightly different context, of how such a lien circularity problem could be resolved, see Santa Cruz Lumber Co. v. Bank of America, 160 Cal.App.3d 858, 207 Cal.Rptr. 28 (1984).

In some circumstances, a buyer of land may grant more than one purchase money mortgage. For example, suppose P buys Blackacre from S for a total price of $200,000. P pays $180,000 of the price in cash and executes to S both an installment note for the $20,000 balance and a mortgage to secure repayment of the note. But P obtained the $180,000 in cash by virtue of a mortgage loan from Bank. Both S and Bank have purchase money mortgages: which has priority? The Restatement, which reflects the substantial weight of authority, takes the view that a vendor purchase money mortgage has priority over its third party counterpart, unless the parties themselves have demonstrated a contrary intent (such as by a subordination agreement) or the state's recording act provides otherwise. Restatement (Third) of Property (Mortgages) § 7.2(c) (1997); ALH Holding Co. v. Bank of Telluride, 18 P.3d 742 (Colo.2000); Rothermich v. Weber's St. Charles Lanes, Inc., 957 S.W.2d 509 (Mo.App.1997). The rationale for this rule is that the vendor (S) presumably would not have sold the property in the first place without a firm understanding that she would get first priority if the buyer (P) defaulted.

By contrast, as demonstrated by the following case, courts in a few states accord no special priority to the vendor mortgagee and instead resolve priority based upon the first-in-time principle and the state's recording act. As you read Insight LLC v. Gunter, which rejects the Restatement (wrongly, we believe), consider whether the court's approach is coherent and workable.

INSIGHT LLC v. GUNTER
Supreme Court of Idaho, 2013
302 P.3d 1052

[Editors' Note: We have included this opinion, although we believe Part C is wrongly decided, because one can learn valuable lessons from making mistakes or seeing others make them. As you read Part C, consider how the court's rule would encourage vendor and third-party purchase money mortgagees to behave in documenting similar transactions (particularly by comparison to the Restatement approach.)]

W. JONES, Justice. . . . This is an appeal from a district court trial regarding a dispute over two liens on real property: a deed of trust and a mortgage. Appellants ("Insight") are assignees of a mortgage secured by 160 acres of real property owned by Summitt, Inc. ("Summitt"), which includes an 18-acre parcel of land that Summitt purchased from the

Respondents ("the Gunters"). The Gunters hold a deed of trust on the Gunter property. . . .

Summitt owned a 142-acre parcel of land that it intended to develop into a residential subdivision. Respondents, Pat and Monica Gunter owned an 18-acre plot of land that adjoined Summitt's 142 acres ("the Gunter property"). Not wanting to live next to a residential development, the Gunters solicited Summitt's president, Ron Hazel, to purchase the Gunter property; the parties agreed to a price of $799,000. On April 21, 2006, the Gunters and Summitt, through its president, Hazel, entered into a purchase and sale agreement for the Gunter property. The agreement, prepared by Summitt, identified EasyWay Escrow ("EasyWay") as the closing agent for the transaction. The agreement provided $1,000 earnest money and the balance of the purchase price was to be paid in "cash at closing." Possession of the land was to be delivered at closing on June 19, 2006.

After executing the purchase and sale agreement, Hazel contacted Independent Mortgage Ltd. Co. ("IM"), seeking a loan of $799,000. IM agreed to loan Summitt $616,000 so long as Summitt's principals executed personal guarantees and secured the mortgage with 160 acres of land including *both* the 142 acres already owned by Summitt and the 18 acres comprising the Gunter property.

Shortly after the execution of the agreement, Hazel contacted Monica Gunter and revealed that Summitt was unable to come up with the full amount of the purchase price. Hazel informed her Summitt could pay $599,000 and asked the Gunters to finance the remaining $200,000 of the purchase price, which the Gunters agreed to do. This conversation was documented by notes taken by Monica Gunter and delivered to EasyWay. These notes do not mention any other loan or financing contemplated by Summitt for the purchase of the Gunter property.

Sandpoint Title was responsible for recording and providing title insurance for both the IM mortgage and the Gunters' deed of trust. Stephanie Brown prepared the documents related to the IM/Summitt mortgage. Carol Sommerfeld, owner of EasyWay Escrow, prepared the documents related to the Gunter/Summitt deed of trust. The district court found that Sommerfeld was not aware of the mortgage executed between IM and Summitt. The district court also found that the Gunters lacked knowledge of the IM/Summitt mortgage at the time of the closing, because they were never informed of any financing by Summitt other than their own deed of trust. Also, there was no reference to the IM mortgage in any part of the closing file. As to the dispute of whether Hazel informed the Gunters or Sommerfeld of the IM/Summitt mortgage, the district court found credible Sommerfeld's and Monica Gunter's testimony that they were not informed of the IM/Summitt mortgage. It also found that IM knew of the Gunters' deed of trust because IM considered seeking a subordination agreement from the Gunters.

Hazel signed the IM/Summitt mortgage on June 19, 2006, at IM's offices in Sandpoint, Idaho. Later that same day Summitt executed a deed of trust in favor of the Gunters at EasyWay's office. All of the documents were delivered to Sandpoint Title by IM and EasyWay for recordation. IM instructed Sandpoint that the IM/Summitt mortgage was to be recorded first. The deed from the Gunters to Summitt was recorded on June 20, 2006, at 4:16 p.m. The IM/Summitt mortgage was recorded that same day at 4:17 p.m., and the Gunter/Summitt deed of trust was recorded at 4:18 p.m.

In 2007, Summitt defaulted on its obligations to both IM and the Gunters. Insight[1] filed a Complaint on August 27, 2008, naming Summitt, Summitt's principals, and the Gunters as defendants. On November 26, 2008, the Gunters answered and denied that their deed of trust was junior to the IM/Summitt mortgage. On February 17, 2009, Insight filed a motion for summary judgment. The district court denied the motion because there was an issue as to who was the initial encumbrancer. Insight filed a motion for reconsideration, which the district court denied. . . .

After trial, the district court found that the closing of the Gunter/Summitt deed of trust was a separate and independent transaction from the IM/Summitt mortgage. The court found that the separate closings were not part of "one continuous transaction." The district court further found that the Gunters' deed of trust effectively encumbered the Gunter property at the time the transaction between Summitt and the Gunters closed. However, it found the IM mortgage on the combined 160-acre parcel of land did not create an encumbrance on the Gunter property until after the Gunter/Summitt transaction closed. The rationale was that the mortgage could not encumber property that is not owned by the mortgagor. As a result, the Gunters' deed of trust was determined to be the "first encumbrance" on the Gunter property. The court also found that IM was not a good faith purchaser—even though it recorded first—because it was aware of the financing agreement between Summitt and the Gunters.

On appeal, Insight argues that the IM mortgage has priority as a matter of law because it was a purchase money mortgage that was first recorded thus rendering its "good faith" irrelevant. Insight also contends that the Gunters were not good faith purchasers and had imputed knowledge of IM's mortgage through the escrow agent, EasyWay. Respondents counter that the Gunters' deed of trust was the first encumbrance on the Gunter property; the IM mortgage was not a

---

[1] The IM/Summitt mortgage was assigned to Insight.

purchase money mortgage; and even if it was a purchase money mortgage, the Gunters' deed of trust effectively encumbered the land first and therefore had priority. . . .

A. The district court's finding that IM had notice of the Gunters' Deed of Trust is Clearly Erroneous. The district court found that IM had actual notice of the Gunters' deed of trust, because IM considered a subordination agreement and instructed Sandpoint Title to record the IM mortgage first. This finding is clearly erroneous.

The district court found that Summit executed the IM mortgage on June 19, 2006. The district court further found that Summit executed the Gunters' deed of trust also on June 19, 2006, but later in the day. It is not technically possible for IM to have notice of an encumbrance on property before that encumbrance actually comes into existence. Though IM knew that Summitt was intending to execute a deed of trust, that was notice of an intent to subsequently encumber property, not notice of an actual encumbrance on property. Therefore, the district court's finding that IM had notice of the Gunters' deed of trust is clearly erroneous.

B. The IM/Summitt Mortgage Was a Purchase Money Mortgage. . . . Idaho Code § 45–112 requires that a purchase money mortgage be given "at the time of [the land's] conveyance." This statutory language reflects the commonly recognized requirement that a purchase money mortgage be granted as a part of "one continuous transaction involving the purchase" of land. The execution of the mortgage and the transfer of the deed need not be strictly contemporaneous. When a deed and mortgage are executed as part of the same transaction, the mortgage is not granted to the mortgagee after the mortgagor has obtained title; rather, the mortgagor takes title already encumbered by the mortgage.

Insight argues that the IM mortgage was part of one continuous transaction because security instruments were signed on the same day within hours of each other, the mortgage funds were sent to EasyWay, and all the documents were recorded together by Sandpoint Title. In other words, the mortgage was merely one step of several necessary to accomplish a single transaction. Respondents, however rely on the district court's finding that the IM mortgage closed separately from the Gunters' deed of trust, because the "IM mortgage could not encumber property before it is owned by the buyer." Thus, they argue the Gunter/Summitt deed of trust must have occurred before the IM mortgage.

The district court concluded that the IM mortgage was not a purchase money mortgage because it was not part of one continuous transaction. The district court reasoned that the mortgage and deed of trust closed at different times and at different locations. The district court noted that Carol Sommerfeld closed the Gunter/Summitt transaction at the office of EasyWay, while Stephanie Brown prepared all the documents related to the IM/Summitt transaction at the IM offices. This evidence, to the district court, did "not reflect coordination of a single closing effort" on the part of the parties. The district court noted that the Gunters did not have knowledge of the IM mortgage and were not informed of the mortgage. This conclusion was clearly erroneous.

The primary inquiry is whether the mortgage was intended as part of a single transaction. [*Estate of Skvorak v. Security Union Title Ins. Co.*, 89 P.3d 856 (Idaho 20014)] demonstrates that mortgages need not be executed in unison to be part of the same transaction. In *Skvorak*, the two mortgages were executed at different times on the same day and were not executed in the presence of all of the parties. In the current matter, Hazel executed the IM/Summitt mortgage on June 19 and the Gunter/Summitt deed of trust later that day. Also, the mere fact that the IM mortgage was signed at IM's offices and not in the presence of the Gunters is not fatal to the purchase money mortgage status of the IM mortgage, because in *Skvorak*, both parties had purchase money mortgages even though one of them was not signed in the presence of both the parties. Likewise, the present case involves one transaction with two mortgages enabling Summitt to purchase the Gunter property. A land-sale transaction concludes upon the delivery of the deed. Here, before the deed was delivered to Summitt, the proceeds and documents were delivered in escrow to the title company. Therefore, there was only one transaction.

The district court also found that the IM mortgage was not a purchase money mortgage because it was only able to encumber the Gunter property at the time Summitt gained an ownership interest in the Gunter property. But the district court's reasoning neglects the very nature of a purchase money mortgage, and presupposes that the mortgage was not a purchase money mortgage in order to find that IM did not encumber the property when executed. Under this standard, no purchase money mortgage could effectively encumber property before title passes to the mortgagor, because the purchase money *enables* the mortgagor to acquire title to the property. Insight rightly notes that applying the district court's reasoning—that "[the IM] mortgage could not encumber the Gunter property, because Summitt did not own the Gunter property when the mortgage was signed,"—would preclude any purchase money mortgage from being a purchase money mortgage. In a purchase money mortgage, title does *not* first pass to the mortgagor, which is then encumbered; rather, title passes to the mortgagor *already* encumbered. Nothing in Idaho's jurisprudence precludes more than one purchase money mortgage from being executed on land. Therefore, since the IM mortgage provided the funds necessary to enable Summitt to purchase the Gunter property, and since the money was not paid directly to Summitt but to EasyWay, the Gunter property passed to Summitt already encumbered by the Gunters' deed of trust *and* the IM mortgage.

In sum, the district court's finding that the IM mortgage and Gunters' deed of trust were not part of one continuous transaction is clearly erroneous. The mortgage granted by IM was a purchase money mortgage because it was executed to enable Summitt to purchase the property in question, in the same transaction as the acquisition of title. The question next becomes whether the taking of additional security by IM on the mortgage destroyed the purchase money status of the IM mortgage. . . .

Whether the taking of additional security on a mortgage, beyond the land being purchased, destroys the purchase money status of a mortgage, is a question of first impression. As early as the 1800s, courts have recognized purchase money mortgages, even though additional security was taken on a note. This additional security was often in the form of an assignment or a deed of trust. *See, e.g., Farmers' & Mech. Sav. Co. v. McCabe,* 73 Mo.App. 551, 553 (1898); *Bliss v. Crosier,* 159 Mass. 498, 34 N.E. 1075 (1893). One particular New York case from 1912 involved land given as additional security. *See Hubbard v. Lydecker,* 78 Misc. 80, 137 N.Y.S. 714, 716 (N.Y.S.1912). In *Hubbard,* a purchase money mortgage was given to purchase a lot on Prospect Street. The purchase money mortgage also included a lien on a lot on Greenridge Avenue as additional security. The court held that the mortgage was primarily a lien on the Prospect Street lot and that the Greenridge Avenue lot merely stood in the position of a guarantor.

The loan given by IM was given with the intent to enable Summitt to purchase the Gunter property. But after examining the property, Insight wanted additional security. Insight agreed to take a second mortgage on the adjoining 142 acres of Summitt property to guarantee the loan. The IM mortgage was primarily a purchase money mortgage designed to enable Summitt to purchase the property.

In sum, the IM mortgage was a purchase money mortgage that was not destroyed by the taking of additional security by IM.

C. The District Court Erred in Concluding the Gunter Deed of Trust Took Priority. Since both the IM/Summitt mortgage and the Gunter/Summitt deed of trust are purchase money mortgages, the next issue is which security interest has priority.

Insight argues that the IM mortgage has priority as a matter of law. Insight reads *Skvorak* as holding that as between two purchase money mortgages, the first to record has priority. Insight contends that the first party to record is the initial encumbrancer, and that the initial encumbrancer's knowledge is irrelevant. Second, Insight argues that the Gunters, even if they lacked actual knowledge, had constructive notice of IM's mortgage because it was recorded first, and constructive notice under I.C. § 55–811 is imparted at the time it is deposited with the recorder. Also, Insight contends that the Gunters had imputed inquiry notice of the IM mortgage, because EasyWay should have known from its past transactions with Summitt that Summitt was securing the purchase money with a mortgage from IM.

The Gunters contend that even if the IM mortgage is a purchase money mortgage, *Skvorak* does not support Insight's argument. The Gunters read *Skvorak* as only applicable when both mortgages were part of one continuous transaction, and where both parties knew of the other's mortgage. The Gunters contend they are the initial encumbrancer based on the district court's finding that the IM mortgage and the Gunters' deed of trust were not part of one continuous transaction. In the alternative, the Gunters urge this Court to reconsider its earlier rejection of § 7.2 of the Restatement.

The parties dispute who is the initial encumbrancer under *Skvorak*. Insight contends IM was the initial encumbrancer on the Gunter property, because the IM mortgage and the Gunters' deed of trust were not separate transactions, but one continuous transaction. IM was, therefore, the initial encumbrancer because it was the first to record. The Gunters argue the first encumbrancer is the first lien to be executed in one continuous transaction. Therefore, they argue IM was not the first encumbrancer, because it had knowledge of the Gunters' deed of trust, and its mortgage was a separate transaction. The district court concluded that because the IM mortgage was a separate transaction, it was not valid upon its execution but only after the Gunters' deed of trust closed and transferred title of the Gunter property. Consequently, the district court held that the Gunters' deed of trust was necessarily the first to encumber the property, and since IM had knowledge of the Gunters' deed of trust, its mortgage was subsequent to the Gunters' deed of trust.

In *Skvorak*, "initial encumbrancer" is merely the characterization of the party against whom subsequent purchasers are tested under the recording statutes. The court noted that the good faith of the initial encumbrancer is irrelevant. It should be clarified that the good faith of the initial encumbrancer is irrelevant as to subsequent encumbrancers, because the initial encumbrancer cannot technically have notice of an encumbrance before it comes into existence. But the issue presented in *Skvorak* was "the priority between a vendor purchase money mortgage and a third party purchase money mortgage, where the vendor has notice of the third party's mortgage and it was recorded first." 140 Idaho at 22, 89 P.3d at 862 (emphasis added). In *Skvorak*, "each party knew or had constructive notice of the other party's mortgage." Id. at 21, 89 P.3d at 861. Quite simply, in a dispute involving priority between two mortgages in a single transaction, where both parties are good faith encumbrancers of property for value, the first to record has priority against all other subsequent mortgages. *Id.* at 23, 89 P.3d at 863.

A purchase money mortgage is given priority against other liens subject to the recording laws. I.C. § 45–112. Idaho's race-notice statute provides that "[e]very conveyance of real property is . . . void as against any subsequent purchaser or mortgagee of the same property, or any part thereof, in good faith and for a valuable consideration, whose conveyance is first duly recorded." I.C. § 55–812. Our race-notice statute only voids a prior conveyance if (1) the subsequent conveyance was made in good faith and for valuable consideration; and (2) the subsequent conveyance is the first duly recorded. Idaho law defines "conveyance" as "the instrument in writing by which any estate or interest in real property is created, alienated, mortgaged or encumbered." I.C. § 55–813. A conveyance does not depend upon when it is recorded.

Here, the Summitt/IM mortgage was executed on June 19, 2006, before the Summitt/Gunter deed of trust was executed. Therefore, the IM mortgage was the prior conveyance and the Gunters' deed of trust was the subsequent conveyance. Since the Gunters' deed of trust was the subsequent encumbrance, the only way it could take priority over the IM mortgage as the first encumbrance—where IM by default is a good faith encumbrancer against subsequent encumbrancers—is if the Gunters were the first to record. The Gunters were not the first to record. Therefore, their deed of trust is junior to the IM mortgage. . . .

NOTES

1. *The rationale for vendor purchase money priority.* In providing priority for the vendor purchase money mortgagee over the third party purchase money mortgagee, the Restatement is consistent with Uniform Commercial Code Article 9, which provides comparable priority for a vendor purchase money secured party. See U.C.C. § 9–324(g)(1). As the Restatement explains:

> The preference for vendor purchase money mortgagees is arguably counterintuitive, at least from an economic perspective. After all, both the third party lender and the vendor make the sale transaction possible, and both rely upon the security of the same specific property for payment. Moreover, third party purchase money mortgagees, especially in residential transactions, often invest a substantially greater economic stake in the mortgaged property than that retained by the vendor.

> Nevertheless, the equities favor the vendor. Not only does the vendor part with specific real estate rather than money, but the vendor would never relinquish it at all except on the understanding that the vendor will be able to use it to satisfy the obligation to pay the price. This is the case even though the vendor may know that the mortgagor is going to finance the transaction in part by borrowing from a third party and giving a mortgage to secure that

obligation. In the final analysis, the law is more sympathetic to the vendor's hazard of losing real estate previously owned than to the third party lender's risk of being unable to collect from an interest in real estate that never previously belonged to it.

Restatement (Third) of Property (Mortgages) § 7.2, cmt. d (1997).

2. *Rethinking* Gunter. The court in *Gunter* does not adopt Restatement § 7.2, but instead concludes that the priority of competing mortgages is governed by the state recording act. Under this approach, the court must decide which mortgagee was "first in time," as that mortgagee would have temporal priority unless the recording statute protected the latter-in-time mortgagee. The *Gunter* court concluded that because the third-party IM mortgage was executed first, it was entitled to priority unless the Gunters' seller mortgage qualified for the protection of the recording statute—which it did not, because the IM mortgage was recorded first. In the context of this transaction, does it make sense to ascribe significance to which mortgage was executed first? See Restatement (Third) of Property (Mortgages) § 7.2 cmt. d (1997) (answering "no," where both mortgages arise in the context of the same transaction). Is the court's opinion internally consistent in this regard? How would you expect the result in *Gunter* to influence how third-party lenders like IM behave in similar transactions?

3. *Understanding the appropriate impact of notice and the recording acts on vendor vs. third party priority.* Suppose that both the vendor and the third party lender are aware of each other. This is often the case, especially when the earnest money contract (which the third party lender routinely examines as part of reviewing the purchaser's loan application) mentions that the vendor is to finance a portion of the price. In this situation, the vendor's mortgage should be senior; the third party cannot gain priority simply by recording first. This is because in most states the recording acts confer priority only on a subsequent purchaser *without notice* and, in our situation, each party has notice of the other. Likewise, if *neither* party has notice of the other's mortgage, again vendor should prevail. The state's recording act should not change this result because it grants priority only to a *subsequent* purchaser without notice, and as discussed above, it makes little sense to treat the third-party lender as holding a subsequent mortgage if both mortgages arise in the same transaction. Restatement (Third) of Property (Mortgages) § 7.2 cmt. d (1997).

But suppose that only one of the parties has notice of the other. In this situation, even the Restatement agrees that the recording act rather than vendor preference should govern, and the party lacking notice should prevail. "Even though delivery of the mortgages is essentially simultaneous, the party lacking notice must in fairness be treated as the subsequent taker and thus eligible for the protection of the recording acts. Thus, in a jurisdiction having a notice type recording act, the lender who takes its mortgage without notice of the other's mortgage prevails. . . . In a race-notice type jurisdiction, the lender who takes without notice must also record first in order to prevail." Id.

Many institutional third party lenders are either required by law or the dictates of prudence to hold first mortgages. How can they obtain certain priority over the vendor?

> The normal method is to have the vendor subordinate his lien to that of the third party lender. Ideally, this is usually done by including language in the vendor's mortgage specifically referring to the third party lender's mortgage and declaring its subordination to it. Normally, a vendor will agree to this for at least two reasons. First, he wants the third party mortgage transaction to be approved so that he can sell his property. Second, a vendor who takes a mortgage under such circumstances probably assumes, at the time of the initial transaction at least, that his will be a second mortgage.

Nelson, Whitman, Burkhart & Freyermuth, Real Estate Finance Law § 9.2, at 895 (6th ed. 2014). A third party lender may also prevail if a court finds that the vendor's oral statements and conduct indicate an intent to subordinate the vendor's lien to the third party mortgage. See Pulse v. North Am. Land Title Co., 218 Mont. 275, 707 P.2d 1105 (1985). Suppose that there is no express subordination agreement, but the vendor has notice of the third party's mortgage and the third party mortgage is recorded before the vendor's mortgage. In this situation, should a court hold that the vendor has impliedly subordinated to the third party lender? See Restatement (Third) of Property (Mortgages) § 7.2 cmt. d (1997).

4.　*Competing third party purchase money mortgages.* Sometimes the purchase money for a residential transaction is supplied by two third party lenders, one institutional (e.g., a bank) and one noninstitutional (e.g., a parent or employer). Suppose that the buyer, for example, is able to supply 5% of the purchase price. Then buyer arranges for a mortgage loan from a savings and loan association for 75% of the purchase price and a mortgage loan for the remaining 20% from his father. Should there be any underlying assumptions as to the priority of institutional lenders against private lenders? Should both mortgages share equal priority? While Article 9's "pure race" filing system gives priority to the first of the third party purchase money secured parties to file or perfect its security interest, § 9–324(g)(2), the case law provides little in the way of a common law answer in the mortgage law context. How do you assume this problem is handled in practice? Will recording first necessarily create priority? Should the savings and loan association require the father to take an explicit second mortgage or otherwise to subordinate? What happens if the savings and loan association is led to believe that the full 25% of the purchase price is to be supplied from purchaser's personal resources when in fact purchaser covertly gives a mortgage to father for part of the 25%? See Nelson, Whitman, Burkhart & Freyermuth, Real Estate Finance Law § 9.2 (6th ed. 2014).

B. THE AFTER-ACQUIRED PROPERTY CLAUSE AND THE DRAGNET CLAUSE

Article 9 of the Uniform Commercial Code, with limited exceptions, authorizes a debtor to grant a security interest in both present and after-acquired personal property. See U.C.C. § 9–204(a). This provides significant transactional efficiencies for many business debtors. The classic example would be a retail seller of inventory such as a furniture store. Such a seller would typically finance its inventory of furniture either using a loan from a local bank or credit extended by furniture manufacturers. A creditor financing the seller's inventory may wish to take a security interest in the seller's furniture inventory to secure repayment of this credit.

In this situation, the *nemo dat* principle—which establishes that A cannot grant B any rights in an object of property that A does not have in the first place—presents a potential problem. Obviously, the seller will be selling items from its furniture inventory to customers, and then acquiring new items of furniture to replenish its inventory. The creditor may wish to take a security interest in this new inventory; however, at the time of the original loan, the seller doesn't own that new inventory yet. Without an "after-acquired property clause," the seller and the creditor would have to enter into a new security agreement each time the seller obtained a new shipment of inventory. U.C.C. § 9–204(a) instead permits the seller and the creditor to enter into one security agreement that is sufficient to cover both the seller's existing on-hand inventory and all inventory subsequently acquired by the seller. By virtue of the after-acquired property clause, the creditor's security interest will attach to each new item of inventory the seller acquires in the future as the seller acquires it.

Perhaps not surprisingly, it is much less common for a real estate mortgage to contain an after-acquired property clause. Nevertheless, suppose that Jones borrows $250,000 from First Bank and grants First Bank a mortgage that covers not only Blackacre but "all other real property that Jones shall acquire in the future until the mortgage debt is repaid." Three years later, while the mortgage remains unpaid, Jones acquires Whiteacre. Should the First Bank mortgage also cover Whiteacre? If Jones granted Second Bank a purchase money mortgage at the time Jones acquired Whiteacre, which bank's mortgage would have priority as to Whiteacre?

HICKSON LUMBER CO. V. GAY LUMBER CO.

Supreme Court of North Carolina, 1909
150 N.C. 282, 63 S.E. 1045

BROWN, J. The controversy presented by this appeal is clearly stated in the brief of the learned counsel for appellants, in these words: "The only question which we desire to present on this appeal is whether the mortgage to James H. Pou covers the property specifically described in the mortgage to the Hickson Lumber Company by virtue of the following language contained in the Pou mortgage: 'also all the property, real, personal, or mixed, wheresoever the same is situated, now owned by the Gay Lumber Company or shall be owned during the continuance of the liability hereinafter mentioned.' We insist that it does not." The Pou mortgage was executed 24 February, 1903, and duly recorded 6 March, 1903. The Hickson mortgage was executed 24 September, 1903, recorded 16 October, 1903, and embraces five tracts of land, therein described, and one locomotive, all of which property was acquired by the Gay Lumber Company after the Pou mortgage was recorded. The several tracts of land were conveyed by deeds to the Gay Lumber Company, by the grantors therein named, some little time before the execution of the Hickson mortgage and after the recording of the Pou mortgage. Upon the hearing the Hickson Lumber Company offered to prove that the tracts of timber described in the mortgage, and which were acquired subsequently to the execution of the mortgage executed to James H. Pou, were purchased with funds advanced for the purpose by the said Hickson Lumber Company. This evidence was excluded, and the appellant excepted.

For the purposes of this appeal, we will consider the fact offered to be proved as established.

The questions to be considered are:

First, the sufficiency of the terms of the Pou mortgage to embrace after-acquired property.

Second, the validity of a mortgage which undertakes to bind after-acquired property.

Third, whether or not the fact that the Hickson Lumber Company furnished money to the Gay Lumber Company, which money was used by the latter company in the purchase of these lands, gives the lumber company a priority over the lien of the Pou mortgage.

1. Although the after-acquired property clause in the Pou mortgage might have been expressed with greater fullness of language, nevertheless there is manifested an undoubted intention upon the part of the mortgagor to bring within the lien of the instrument all property, both real and personal, which the mortgagor shall acquire at any time after the execution of the mortgage and during the continuance of the liability

created by it. From its very nature, such a clause cannot usually describe with accuracy the property the mortgagor will thereafter acquire, for that is unknown. But upon the principle of *"Id certum est quod certum reddi potest,"* the after-acquired property may be easily identified and brought within the terms of the instrument.

The substance of the authorities is to the effect that when the mortgage is intended to cover subsequently acquired property, either express terms should be used to that end or else it must clearly appear from the language of the deed that such was the manifest intention of the parties. . . .

Our researches have discovered but one case where words similar to those in the Pou mortgage were held not to cover an after-acquired grant of lands, but we think the decision, which is extremely voluminous, as it covers many points, is evidently based upon the fact that the lands were granted on certain terms or trusts, the object of which would be defeated if the property granted could be subjected to the mortgage lien. Meyer v. Johnston, 53 Ala. 323, and same case, 64 Ala. 606. The consensus of authority leads us to conclude that the terms employed in the Pou mortgage are sufficient to embrace the after-acquired lands and personal property of the mortgagor.

2.   The words used being sufficient, we will next consider the validity of such a mortgage.

It is well understood that at common law nothing can be mortgaged that is not in existence and does not at the time belong to the mortgagor, for a person cannot convey that which he does not own; but it is now well settled that equity will give effect to a contract to convey future-acquired property, whether real or personal. Equity considers that done which the mortgagor has agreed to do, and treats the mortgage as already attaching to the newly acquired property as it comes into the mortgagor's hands. "It is settled that such a clause is valid," says Mr. Justice Brewer, in Trust Co. v. Kneeland, 138 U.S. 419. "A clause in a mortgage which subjects subsequently acquired property to the lien of the mortgage is a valid clause," says Mr. Justice Peckham, in Bear Lake Co. v. Garland, 164 U.S. 15. Galveston v. Cowdrey, 11 Wallace 459; 1 Jones on Mortgages, sec. 153; Pingrey on Mortgages, sec. 453; Brown v. Dail, 117 N.C. 41; Perry v. White, 111 N.C. 197; Cooper v. Rouse, 130 N.C. 202.

[Editors' Note: The appellant argued that the effectiveness of an after-acquired property clause in a mortgage should be limited to mortgages granted by railroad corporations, and that the after-acquired property clause in the Pou mortgage was not effective because Gay Lumber Company was not a railroad corporation. The court rejected this argument, stating that the after-acquired property doctrine "is not confined in its application to railroad corporations, as is manifest from an examination of the text writers and the cases cited from our own and other courts."]

3.   Having determined that the Pou mortgage is a valid lien upon the after-acquired property of the mortgagor, we will next consider if there is any principle of equity which forbids its enforcement against the appellants. The courts will not enforce the after-acquired property clause in a mortgage against anyone who can set up an equity of equal dignity in his own behalf, for where equities are equal the law will prevail. Therefore the clause will not be enforced against subsequent purchasers for value and without notice.

The appellant cannot avail itself of that protection, as the Pou mortgage was recorded in apt time. In North Carolina a mortgage upon after-acquired property, being enforceable inter partes, becomes, upon registration, valid and enforceable against subsequent purchasers, because the registration is an effectual notice as against the world. Hence, the Hickson Lumber Company advanced their money, with which to buy new timber lands, with a knowledge of the Pou mortgage and with notice of Pou's equities. The fact that the appellant loaned money to the mortgagor to buy the lands which the mortgagor purchased from others will not raise an equity to defeat the Pou mortgage, of which appellant had notice. Coe v. Railroad, 10 Ohio St., 372; Galveston v. Cowdrey, 78 U.S., 459; Bank v. Doud, 52 L.R.A., 481; Locomotive Works v. Truesdale, 9 L.R.A., 140.

It is undoubtedly true that if the appellant had a lien on these lands at the date they were acquired by the Gay Lumber Company, which it could enforce against that corporation, it could enforce it against Pou, for the after-acquired property clause only attaches to such interest as the mortgagor acquires; and it would be immaterial whether Pou had notice of such lien or not. Jones on Mortgages, sec. 158. But the appellant had no lien when the Gay Company acquired the lands by deed. It never had any lien until its mortgage was subsequently executed, and that is secondary to the Pou mortgage.

The money advanced to purchase the lands cannot well be classified as "purchase money," for the purchase money was paid to the vendors at the time they executed their deeds to the Gay Lumber Company. It was simply money borrowed with which to pay for the lands, and until the execution of the mortgage by the Gay Company to appellant it was only a simple contract debt, with nothing to secure it; but assuming that the money advanced constituted "the purchase money," in the strict sense of those words, that would give appellants no lien on the lands. Ever since the leading case of Womble v. Battle, 38 N.C., 182, decided in 1844, it has been settled in this State that a vendor of real estate who has conveyed it by deed has no lien upon the land for the purchase money, and that the

English doctrine of the purchase-money lien does not obtain here. We therefore conclude that, assuming the facts to be as claimed, they establish no equity in appellant which is paramount to the Pou mortgage.

Let the costs of this appeal be paid by the Hickson Lumber Company. The judgment of the Superior Court is affirmed.

NOTES

1. *Is an after-acquired property provision in a mortgage effective to cover after-acquired personal property?* Traditionally, some mortgages have commonly included not only a description of the specific real estate being mortgaged, but also a clause purporting to cover all after-acquired realty and personalty. Summarizing existing case law in 1963, Roger Cunningham and Saul Tischler noted:

> [In some states], the after-acquired property clause is effective to create an equitable lien upon both real and personal property subsequently acquired by the mortgagor regardless of the character of the business in which the mortgagor is engaged, provided the new property bears a functional relation to the property originally mortgaged. In other states, the after-acquired property clause is effective to create an equitable lien upon both realty and personalty if the mortgagor is a railroad company or other public utility company, but is effective only with respect to realty if not within that class.

Roger Cunningham & Saul Tischler, Equitable Real Estate Mortgages, 17 Rutgers L. Rev. 679, 718 (1963). Today, because U.C.C. Article 9 applies in all 50 states, and because U.C.C. § 9–204(a) generally validates after-acquired property clauses in personal property security agreements, a mortgagee that wants an enforceable lien upon after-acquired personal property would also have the mortgagor sign a personal property security agreement containing a suitable after-acquired property clause. While a real estate mortgage could also constitute an effective Article 9 security agreement if it met the necessary standards of Article 9 (i.e., if it sufficiently indicated the intent of the debtor to create a security interest in personal property and sufficiently identified that personal property), most prudent lenders would simply have the borrower execute both a real estate mortgage covering the land and an Article 9 security agreement covering the personal property.

2. *The general validity of an after-acquired property provision as to after-acquired land.* Consistent with the weight of authority, the Restatement recognizes the validity of an after-acquired property provision as between the mortgagor and the mortgagee. See Restatement (Third) of Property (Mortgages) § 7.5 (1997). It defines an after-acquired property provision as encompassing tracts or parcels of real estate that the mortgagor subsequently acquires. See id. cmt. a. The provision is effective between the parties even if the later-acquired parcels are in a different county or state than the real

estate originally mortgaged. Id. cmt. b. The rationale for enforcement is grounded in a specific performance theory; the provision is viewed as a promise by mortgagor to mortgage after-acquired parcels which will be specifically enforced as soon mortgagor acquires title to them. Id.

Note that in the *Hickson Lumber* case, the appellant attempted to limit the effectiveness of an after-acquired property clause to mortgages executed by railroad corporations. What might be the rationale for such a limitation? Was the court correct to reject such a limitation?

3. *Relationship to accession and the law of fixtures*. Suppose X grants a mortgage upon Blackacre, which is undeveloped land. X then builds a home on the land. Does the mortgage cover the home if the mortgage does not contain an after-acquired property clause? Yes; because of the doctrine of accession or the law of fixtures, an after-acquired property clause is normally not necessary for a mortgage on Blackacre to attach to subsequent improvements made on Blackacre. Hoyle v. Plattsburgh & M.R.R., 54 N.Y. 314 (1873); 3 Glenn, Mortgages, 1450 (1943).

An important warning, however, is in order. To state the foregoing principles does not resolve numerous substantial and complex priority questions. To say that X's home becomes covered by the mortgage does not resolve the problem of what happens if X's building contractor is not paid. The question then becomes one of priority between the mortgage and a possible mechanic's lien. See generally Chapter 9, Section C infra. Or suppose that X installs a furnace in the home. The furnace is likely a fixture covered by the real estate mortgage, but this alone does not resolve priority as between the real estate mortgagee and the holder of a purchase-money security interest in the furnace. We consider these problems in our treatment of fixtures in Chapter 7, Section D infra.

4. *Recording act and "chain of title" problems*. To say that after-acquired property provisions are generally effective between the parties begs a more difficult question: when are they effective against those who take subsequent interests in the after-acquired parcels? As *Hickson Lumber* illustrates, priority disputes under after-acquired property clauses often boil down to interpretations of what constitutes constructive notice under state recording acts. To oversimplify the problem, suppose that R gives a mortgage (containing an after-acquired property clause) on Blackacre to X. R then acquires Whiteacre with his own money. Two months later R borrows money from Z who takes and records a mortgage on Whiteacre. X has a valid mortgage on Whiteacre, but is it senior or junior to Z's mortgage?

Hickson Lumber implies that X's mortgage is senior to Z's mortgage, because the recording of the mortgage on Blackacre is "effectual notice as against the world." But this implication is doubtful. First, suppose that Whiteacre and Blackacre are located in different counties. As you learned in Chapter 2, the land records in each county relate only to land within that county, so the recording of the mortgage on Blackacre in one county cannot provide constructive notice to Z when Z is searching title to Whiteacre in a different county.

Even if Blackacre and Whiteacre *are* in the same county, the implication that X's mortgage should be senior to Z's mortgage is potentially problematic. Would a reasonable person in the position of Z (who is searching title to Whiteacre) be expected to find X's mortgage against Blackacre and realize that it contains an after-acquired property clause that might also cover Whiteacre? On the one hand, both mortgages would be recorded in the grantor index under the name 'R'; thus, one might argue that Z should review any mortgage granted by R—including the mortgage on Blackacre—because any such mortgage could cover Whiteacre, either directly or by virtue of an after-acquired property clause. On the other hand, one might also argue that it would be unreasonable to expect Z (who, again, is searching title to Whiteacre) to search the records any further back in time than the date on which R acquired Whiteacre. If Z begins his search on the date R acquired Whiteacre and searches forward, of course, Z will not discover the mortgage against Blackacre (recorded at an earlier date) and thus likely will not discover the after-acquired property clause.

Courts have often stated that "to constitute constructive notice to third persons an instrument must be in the chain of title to the property and will not be considered to be notice of record simply because it has been recorded at some time prior to acquisition of title [by such third parties]." Glen Ellyn Sav. & Loan Ass'n v. State Bank of Geneva, 65 Ill.App.3d 916, 22 Ill.Dec. 569, 575, 382 N.E.2d 1267, 1273 (1978). Should Z be required to search the grantor-grantee index for other mortgages made by R? Should it make a difference if R is a large corporation? See Nelson, Whitman, Burkhart & Freyermuth, Real Estate Finance Law § 9.3 (6th ed. 2014); 3 Glenn, Mortgages, 1659–1660 (1943).

The Restatement resolves this question by treating a recorded mortgage containing an after-acquired property provision as unrecorded as against those who later purchase interests in the after-acquired real estate. Restatement (Third) of Property (Mortgages) § 7.5 cmt. d (1997). Under this approach, if a state has either a "notice" or "race-notice" recording act, and Z takes its mortgage on Whiteacre without *actual* knowledge of X's mortgage, Z's mortgage will have priority. The opposite will be the case if Z takes with *actual* knowledge.

5.   *After-acquired property provision vs. purchase money mortgage.* Now suppose that in the problem in Note 4, the money supplied by Z was used by R to acquire Whiteacre, so that Z's mortgage on Whiteacre is a third party purchase money mortgage. Suppose further that when Z took his mortgage, he had *actual* knowledge of X's mortgage before advancing the funds to R. Here Z's mortgage should be senior to X's mortgage by virtue of the purchase money mortgage doctrine which, in this setting, trumps the recording act. See Restatement (Third) of Property (Mortgages) § 7.5(b) cmt. e (1997). Is this good policy?

Is the *Hickson Lumber* decision consistent with the Restatement? Why didn't the court rule that Hickson Lumber Co. had purchase money priority over the Pou mortgage? Is it because Hickson Lumber Co. was a third party and not a vendor (i.e., does the case limit the purchase money doctrine to vendors)? If not, what explains the result? Cf. U.C.C. § 9–103 cmt. 3.

Just as a mortgage may contain an after-acquired property clause that contemplates an expansion of the mortgage security, a mortgage can also contain a "future advances" provision that envisions an expansion of the original mortgage debt (i.e., additional borrowings). Future advances provisions are most commonly used in construction mortgage financing, which we discuss in detail in Chapter 9 infra. At this point, however, it is worth mentioning another type of "future loan" provision, the *dragnet clause*. In essence, a dragnet clause states that the real estate covered by the mortgage will stand as security not only for the loan being made contemporaneously with the mortgage, but also for any other debt for which the borrower (1) is already liable to the lender or (2) may become liable to the lender in the future, until the mortgage is satisfied. Note that the lender is not promising to make any future loans; so far as the lender is concerned, any subsequent indebtedness is entirely optional. But if any such debt is later created, the dragnet clause (if given effect) says that this mortgage will secure it.

FIRST SEC. BANK OF UTAH v. SHIEW

Supreme Court of Utah, 1980
609 P.2d 952

MAUGHAN, JUSTICE. Utah Farm Bureau Insurance Company appeals from a judgment of the District Court awarding to First Security Bank of Utah the sum of $4,369.25, plus interest and costs, for the wrongful disbursement of fire insurance proceeds. The bank's claim is contingent on whether the insured premises were security by reason of a dragnet clause in a mortgage thereon for a subsequent, unrelated business transaction of the mortgagors. The judgment is reversed, and the cause is remanded with an order to enter judgment in favor of the insurance company.

In 1972, Bill and Linda Shiew purchased a home in Monticello, Utah. Plaintiff's branch in Monticello, Utah, loaned $6,342.48 to the Shiews; this loan was secured by a mortgage on the home. A standard printed provision in the mortgage recited it was "to secure the payment of any and all claims or demands now due or to become due now or hereafter contracted or incurred which the said mortgagee or the holder hereof, from time to time, may have or hold against the mortgagors or either of them, whether as maker, surety, guarantor, partner or otherwise, and whether contracted directly with or purchased by the holder hereof: . . ."

In 1974, in connection with a cattle-raising venture, the Shiews obtained a loan of $8,900.00 from plaintiff's branch in Price, Utah. The parties entered into a security agreement (Farm Products Chattel Mortgage) to secure this loan. The recited security was certain specified cattle and feed as well as all after acquired cattle and feed. The security agreement made no reference to the mortgage on the debtor's home as additional security. In fact, the security agreement recited: "This agreement constitutes the entire agreement between the parties."

In 1975, the Shiews were divorced, and Linda Shiew was awarded the home in Monticello. In April 1976, plaintiff filed an action against the Shiews in connection with the cattle business transaction. Plaintiff alleged that the security for payment of the note had *all* been disposed of in accordance with the terms of the security agreement, and the collateral was totally exhausted. Plaintiff claimed a deficiency of $4,369.25 and demanded judgment for that amount, plus interest and attorneys fees. It is significant that at the time of filing this action plaintiff did not claim the loan was further secured by a mortgage on the home in Monticello. Further, if the cattle loan were secured by the real estate mortgage as later claimed by plaintiff, under Section 78–37–1 (the single action rule), plaintiff would have been compelled to foreclose the real estate mortgage and exhaust that security rather than attempting to recover the debt directly by a money judgment.

Linda Shiew answered the complaint, but a judgment by default was entered against Bill Shiew on September 1, 1976. This judgment recited the facts concerning the loan transaction in 1974 in Price, Utah, and reiterated that the collateral securing the loan had been exhausted and a deficiency of $4,369.25 remained, and judgment against Bill Shiew was awarded in this amount to plaintiff.

Subsequently, on October 14, 1976, plaintiff filed a motion for leave to file an amended complaint and for an order making Utah Farm Bureau Insurance Company a defendant. This motion was granted.

The home in Monticello had been destroyed by fire in 1976. Plaintiff was a loss payee under the insurance policy. The insurance company issued a check payable to Linda Shiew and plaintiff in the sum of $10,000. The plaintiff requested Mrs. Shiew's endorsement so that it could satisfy the outstanding balance due on both the Price and Monticello loans. Mrs. Shiew refused to pay off the Price loan out of the fire insurance proceeds. Plaintiff notified the insurance company of this dispute.

On May 11, 1976, the insurance company issued two separate checks. One was payable to plaintiff in the amount of $2,843.80, the unpaid balance on the loan on the home in Monticello. The other check, payable to Linda Shiew, was in the amount of $7,156.20.

On November 10, 1976, plaintiff filed an amended complaint. In the first cause of action, plaintiff alleged the same facts and pleaded for a judgment against the Shiews, jointly and severally for the deficiency. In the second cause of action, plaintiff for the first time asserted that the dragnet provision in the mortgage on the home in Monticello made the mortgage security for any other indebtedness of Shiews. Plaintiff alleged that the insurance policy issued on the home contained a mortgage clause, and the house and its contents were destroyed by fire. Plaintiff alleged that the insurance company wrongfully paid the proceeds of the insurance to Linda Shiew, while Shiews were indebted to plaintiff in the sum of $4,369.25, together with interest and costs; plaintiff demanded judgment against the insurance company.

Upon trial before the court, plaintiff was awarded judgment against the insurance company and Linda Shiew. The insurance company alone appeals therefrom.

The primary issue submitted by defendant to the trial court and then to this Court concerns the proper interpretation of a dragnet clause in a mortgage. Defendant vigorously urged the dragnet clause should be interpreted according to the Kansas[1]-Hawaiian[2] rule, which provides:

> " * * * in the absence of clear, supportive evidence of a contrary intention a mortgage containing a dragnet type clause will not be extended to cover future advances unless the advances are of the same kind and quality or relate to the same transaction or series of transactions as the principal obligation secured or unless the document evidencing the subsequent advance refers to the mortgage as providing security therefor. * * * "[3]

This Court has not previously undertaken a definitive interpretation of dragnet clauses in mortgages.

In Osborne, Nelson, Whitman, Real Estate Finance Law (1979), Section 12.8, p. 772, a dragnet clause is described as a mortgage provision which purports to make the real estate security for other, usually unspecified debts which the mortgagor may already owe or may owe in the future to the mortgagee. The lender usually has no particular future advances in mind and merely includes the clause for its potential future utility. Frequently, as in this case, the clause is included in the printed language of mortgages drafted by the mortgagee. These clauses are

---

[1]   *Emporia State Bank and Trust Company v. Mounkes*, 214 Kan. 178, 519 P.2d 618 (1974).

[2]   *Akamine & Sons, Ltd. v. American Security Bank*, 50 Hawaii 304, 440 P.2d 262 (1968).

[3]   Note 1 supra, at p. 623 of 519 P.2d.

seldom the subject of negotiation and may go entirely unnoticed by the mortgagor until the mortgagee asserts them.

Osborne explains:

"* * * Dragnet clauses are generally upheld, but because their apparent coverage is so broad, and because the mortgagor is often unaware of their presence or implications, the courts tend to construe them narrowly against the mortgagee. Generalizations are difficult, since the language of the particular clause may be a decisive factor. However, the following illustrations show numerous ways in which the courts have narrowed the application of dragnet clauses. Sometimes such holdings are said to be based on the intention of the parties, but in reality they usually represent the court's conceptions of fairness and equity. These illustrations are not intended to represent any majority rule, as there are many conflicting or contrary cases. They merely show the sort of judicial treatment dragnet clauses often receive.

"1. The mortgage will only secure advances made or debts incurred in the future. If the mortgagor already owes debts to the mortgagee at the time the mortgage is executed, it would supposedly be easy to identify those existing debts specifically; if they are not so identified, it is assumed that the parties did not intend to secure them.

"2. Only debts of the same type or character as the original debt are secured by the mortgage. For example, if the original loan is for home repairs, a future loan or advance for more repairs would be secured by the mortgage but a loan for an automobile purchase would not. It is easy to imagine grey areas in such a test. For example, what if the second loan were for adding a room to the house? The resolution of the matter is made easier if the documents on the second loan state that it is to be secured under the dragnet clause of the existing mortgage.

"3. As an extension of the foregoing concept, it is sometimes held that the dragnet clause will cover future debts only if the documents evidencing those debts specifically refer back to the clause.

"4. If the future debt is separately secured, whether by another mortgage or by a personal property security agreement, it may be assumed that the parties did not intend that it also be secured by the dragnet mortgage.

"5. The clause is inapplicable to debts which were originally owed by the mortgagor to third parties, and which were assigned to or purchased by the mortgagee.

"6. If there are several joint mortgagors, only future debts on which all of the mortgagors are obligated (or at least of which all were aware) will be covered by the dragnet clause.

"7. Once the original debt has been fully discharged, the mortgage is extinguished and cannot secure future loans.

"8. If the real estate is transferred by the mortgagor to a third party, any debts which the original mortgagor incurs thereafter are not secured by the mortgage. * * * "

Osborne further admonishes:

"While the dragnet clause is usually regarded as advantageous to mortgagees, that is not necessarily the case. One reason is that the types of judicial limitations on the clause discussed above are very much open to debate and further development in most states; in this sense, the clause is an invitation to litigation. * * * "

The foregoing illustrations indicate the diverse and numerous consequences which may flow from a dragnet clause. Although a clear majority rule has not evolved concerning the interpretation of these clauses, there is a consensus that dragnet clauses are not favored in equity and that they should be carefully scrutinized and strictly construed. As the court observed in the *Akamine* case: "Completely unrestricted enforcement of such mortgages would tend to reduce the borrower to the status of economic serf. * * * "

In the *Akamine* case the court ruled that unless the prior or subsequent advance related to the same transaction or series of transactions, the mortgage must specifically refer to it for the advance to be secured. The court explained it would not assist a lending institution in an attempt to captivate a borrower by inclusion in a mortgage of a broad all inclusive dragnet clause. The court observed contracts requiring one party to deal exclusively with one supplier have been viewed with great suspicion under the antitrust laws. The court stated:

"* * * to attempt to foreclose, for example, on the mortgagor's home for debts incurred in operating a business and which debts are not specifically covered by the mortgage would be unconscionable and contrary to public policy."

* * *

In the instant case the dragnet clause was a standard boiler plate provision inserted by the mortgagee in the mortgage on the Shiews' home in Monticello, Utah. There was no evidence this clause was a subject of negotiation between the parties, or that the attention of the mortgagors was directed to this provision. The mortgage was to secure a loan for the purchase of their home, and this transaction was with plaintiff's branch in Monticello, Utah, in 1972. In 1974, the Shiews entered into an entirely different type of transaction, a security agreement to finance a business venture, cattle raising. This transaction was conducted with a branch of plaintiff's bank in Price, Utah. The cattle and feed were recited as the security for this subsequent loan. Furthermore, the security agreement failed to mention the obligation was also secured by the real estate mortgage, and, in fact, refuted such a consequence by an integration clause which recited it constituted the entire agreement between the parties. The legal effect of this integration clause was the preclusion of any claim by the bank that it had accepted the mortgagors' continuing offer to secure future advances with the real estate mortgage on their home.

There is not a scintilla of evidence to support the inference the parties intended the second loan to be under the security of the first loan. The second loan was of an entirely different nature and type of transaction. The self-serving statements of the bank officer that he relied on the defendants' financial statement which specified their home as an asset is of no evidentiary value, for he did not claim he communicated an acceptance of the mortgagors' offer of the home as security, and, in fact, the integration clause of the security agreement would negate such an agreement.

In the instant case, when the dragnet clause is strictly construed against the mortgagee, who drafted it, and interpreted in accordance with afore-cited authority, there is an insufficient evidentiary basis to sustain the determination of the trial court that the mortgage on the Shiews' home constituted security for the subsequent security agreement concerning the financing of their cattle venture. . . .

[The dissenting opinion of JUSTICE HALL is deleted.]

NOTES

1. *Future advances under the Restatement.* Restatement (Third) of Property (Mortgages) § 2.4(b) agrees with the thrust of the *Shiew* case. It provides that, to be secured under a dragnet clause: "The advances must be made in a transaction similar in character to the mortgage transaction, unless (1) the mortgage describes with reasonable specificity the additional type or types of transactions in which advances will be secured; or (2) the parties specifically agree, at the time of the making of the advances, that the mortgage will secure them." A large body of case law agrees. See, e.g., In re Wollin, 249 B.R. 555 (Bankr. D. Or. 2000) (motor vehicle loan agreement did not secure credit card debt); In re Ballarino, 180 B.R. 343 (D.Mass.1995)

(home mortgage containing dragnet clause did not secure later business loan). There is a bit of contrary authority. See, e.g., In re Willie, 157 B.R. 623 (Bankr.M.D.Tenn.1993) (under Tennessee law, dragnet clause in mortgage for personal purposes caused it to secure later loan for business purposes); First Commonwealth Bank v. West, 55 S.W.3d 829 (Ky.App. 2000) (dragnet clause in mortgage on home and business real estate secured later debt to purchase tractor-trailer).

See generally Ryan A. Hackney, Ripping Holes in the Dragnet: The Failings of U.C.C. § 9–204(c) as Applied to Consumer Transactions, 87 Tex. L.Rev. 1249 (2009); David I. Cisar, The Enforceability of Dragnet Clauses, 18 Am.Bankr.Inst.J. 18 (1999); Michael P. Pearson & Robert G. Reedy, Note, Enforceability of "Dragnet Clauses" in Deeds of Trust: The Current State of the Law in Texas, 56 Tex. L.Rev. 733 (1978); Nelson, Whitman, Burkhart & Freyermuth, Real Estate Finance Law § 12.8 (6th ed. 2014); Annot., Debts Included in Provision of Mortgage Purporting to Cover All Future and Existing Debts (Dragnet Clause)—Modern Statutes, 3 A.L.R.4th 690 (1980).

2. *Statutory limitations on dragnet clause coverage.* Many states have statutes governing mortgages for future advances. A table describing them is found in Restatement (Third) of Property (Mortgages) § 2.1 (1997). The statutes typically require that a maximum amount be stated in the mortgage, and withdraw priority for any advances over that amount. Under such a statute, the "other" indebtedness secured under a dragnet clause could not, when added to the outstanding balance still due under the mortgage note itself, exceed the original face amount of the note and mortgage. See, e.g., Mark Twain Kansas City Bank v. Cates, 248 Kan. 700, 810 P.2d 1154 (1991).

About a dozen statutes contain a "cutoff notice" provision, under which the debtor may record and/or serve on the lender a notice to the effect that he or she no longer wishes the future advances clause to be effective. See, e.g., Mo.Ann.Stat. § 443.055; Fla.Stat.Ann. § 697.04; Nev.Rev.Stat. §§ 106.300–.400. Advances or loans made previously will still continue to be secured by the mortgage, of course, but no further advances will be secured. The result is that the debtor may "escape" from the dragnet clause whenever desired. However, a debtor who is initially unaware of the dragnet clause's existence or meaning is unlikely to assert this right until it is "too late"—that is, until after incurring a large amount of other debt which is swept under the mortgage by the dragnet clause. The "cutoff notice" concept is discussed in more detail in Chapter 9, Section C infra.

3. *Court-made limitations on dragnet clauses.* The material quoted in the *Shiew* case points out a number of limitations courts frequently impose on enforcement of dragnet clauses. Here is one more. Suppose property is subject to a mortgage containing a dragnet clause. The original mortgagor sells the property to a grantee who assumes the mortgage. The grantee then incurs an unrelated debt to the mortgagee. Is that debt secured by the mortgage? See Matter of Barnard, 1 B.R. 640 (Bankr.M.D.Fla.1979). The Restatement does not recognize such advances as being secured; it provides:

"If mortgaged real property is transferred, the mortgage will secure only advances made prior to the mortgagee's gaining actual knowledge of the transfer." Restatement (Third) of Property (Mortgages) § 2.4(c) (1997). Note that this also eliminates coverage of advances made to the original mortgagor after the lender learns that the real estate has been transferred.

4. *Waiver of court-created protections for borrowers.* Should it be possible for the debtor to waive these limitations in the clause itself? Suppose the clause provides that future loans shall be secured by the mortgage

> regardless of whether or not this instrument is specifically referred to in the evidence of indebtedness executed by Mortgagors with regard to such future advances, and further regardless of whether or not such future advances may be for purposes related or unrelated to the purpose for which the original indebtedness secured hereby is loaned.

In Union Nat'l Bank of Little Rock v. First State Bank & Trust Co., 16 Ark.App. 116, 697 S.W.2d 940 (1985), this language was found to be an effective waiver of the judicial rules which would otherwise apply. The court observed, "[n]or do we find merit in the argument that the second quoted provision was in 'fine print.' The print was no different from any of the other printed portion of the mortgage in issue."

5. *Estoppel by payoff statement.* Suppose a lender whose mortgage contains a dragnet clause issues a payoff statement. The statement gives only the balance owing on the direct mortgage debt, and fails to mention the additional non-mortgage debt that is swept under the mortgage by its dragnet clause. One court held the lender estopped by such a statement; in effect, it had eliminated the effectiveness of its own dragnet clause! See Regions Bank v. Wachovia Bank, 248 B.R. 201 (Bankr.S.D.Ga.2000).

C. REPLACEMENT AND MODIFICATION OF SENIOR MORTGAGES: IMPACT ON JUNIOR LIENORS

SOVEREIGN BANK V. GILLIS

Superior Court of New Jersey, Appellate Division, 2013
432 N.J.Super. 36, 74 A.3d 1

SABATINO, J.A.D. This appeal concerns whether a refinancing lender that discharges its own previous mortgage and issues another mortgage loan for a higher amount, and which simultaneously pays off the balance owed on a junior lienor's line of credit without having it closed, can rely upon equitable principles to maintain its priority over that junior lienor. This question of priority arises here in a context in which the borrowers, after obtaining the refinancing, drew additional funds on the line of credit and then defaulted on both the refinanced mortgage loan and the line of credit.

Applying principles of replacement and modification recognized in the Restatement (Third) of Property—Mortgages (1997) ("the Third Restatement"), we reverse the trial court's decision allowing the junior lienor that extended the line of credit to vault over the priority of the refinancing mortgage lender. We consequently direct the trial court, on remand, to determine the proper extent of the refinancing lender's priority, in an amount that avoids material prejudice to the junior lienor. . . .

The essential facts are substantially undisputed. On May 28, 1998, defendants Joseph and Eulalia Gillis ("the Gillises") borrowed $650,000 from Washington Mutual Bank, FA ("WaMu") to finance the purchase of a residential property in Warren Township. The mortgage loan had a thirty-year term through June 2028, with an adjustable interest rate initially set at 6.625%. WaMu secured the May 1998 loan with a purchase-money mortgage, which was recorded in the first position of priority.

Subsequently, in December 1998, the Gillises obtained a home-equity line of credit from Broad National Bank, secured by a mortgage recorded in the second position. In October 2001, the Gillises obtained additional funding from Crown Bank, NA ("Crown"), secured by a mortgage recorded in the third position.

On March 18, 2003, the Gillises obtained yet another home-equity line of credit, this time from Independence Community Bank ("Independence"), for the sum of $500,000, also secured by a mortgage. As a condition of closing, Independence required that the proceeds from the funds borrowed on the line of credit be used to discharge the two preexisting debts that the Gillises held with Broad and Crown. The amount remaining after the discharge (i.e., $58,252.58) was applied to pay down a portion of the outstanding purchase-money mortgage with WaMu, which at the time had a principal balance of about $534,000. Both the Broad and Crown mortgages were discharged shortly thereafter the payoff. Consequently, the March 18, 2003 line of credit with Independence stood in a second lien position behind the May 1998 WaMu purchase-money mortgage.

In January 2005, the Gillises sought to refinance their existing mortgage loans. To that end, they borrowed $1.19 million from WaMu, secured by another mortgage on their property ("the WaMu refinanced mortgage") dated January 13, 2005. The WaMu refinanced mortgage loan had a thirty-year term through February 2035, with an adjustable interest rate initially set at 4.027%. The WaMu refinanced mortgage was recorded on January 31, 2005. The principal amount from this refinancing was used to pay off the Gillises' remaining debt of $482,023.67 that the original May 1998 WaMu purchase-money mortgage secured, as well as the remaining debt of $499,921.93 that the Independence line of credit mortgage secured. . . .

For reasons that are not clear from the appellate record, WaMu failed to obtain written authorization from the Gillises to close out the Independence line of credit. Consequently, the mortgage on that line of credit was not discharged of record, despite an alleged intent to do so. The WaMu refinanced mortgage was instead recorded behind the Independence line of credit mortgage, which remained a lien of record even though the balance on that loan existing at the time of the January 2005 refinancing had been paid off by WaMu in full.

Thereafter, the Gillises continued to borrow funds under the Independence line of credit, starting on February 14, 2005 and continuing at least until August 15, 2006. Ultimately, however, the Gillises defaulted on both the WaMu refinanced mortgage loan and the Independence line of credit.

Pursuant to a January 2010 assignment, appellant Deutsche Bank National Trust Company ("Deutsche Bank") began holding the WaMu refinanced mortgage as the Trustee for WaMu Mortgage Pass Through Certificates, WAMU 2005–AR9. In addition, the mortgage on the Independence line of credit was assigned to respondent Sovereign Bank ("Sovereign").

In January 2010, Deutsche filed a foreclosure action in the Chancery Division against the Gillises on the defaulted WaMu refinanced mortgage. Sovereign likewise filed a foreclosure action in the Chancery Division in October 2010 on the defaulted line of credit. The trial court jointly managed the two foreclosure actions, but did not consolidate them. Consequently, the parties litigated their dispute under the caption of Sovereign Bank's foreclosure action.

Deutsche moved for summary judgment against Sovereign, arguing that, based upon equitable principles, the WaMu refinanced mortgage loan had priority over the Independence line of credit. Deutsche argued that the WaMu refinanced mortgage should be granted priority over the Independence line of credit mortgage under the doctrine of equitable subrogation because the debt on the line of credit existing at the time of the refinancing had been paid in full and was, in any case, intended to be discharged.

Sovereign cross-moved for summary judgment against Deutsche, conversely maintaining that the Independence line of credit, which had been recorded first, had priority over the WaMu refinanced mortgage loan. Among other things, Sovereign argued that the doctrine of equitable subrogation cannot be invoked to give the WaMu refinanced mortgage priority over the Independence line of credit because WaMu had actual knowledge of that pre-existing and recorded line of credit when the refinancing occurred. Sovereign further argued that because the line of credit had not been properly closed and that because the Gillises had subsequently withdrawn additional funds on it, the Independence mortgage should instead maintain priority over the WaMu refinanced mortgage.

Upon considering the lenders' competing arguments, the trial court granted summary judgment to Sovereign and held that the Independence line of credit has priority over the WaMu refinanced mortgage. In its written decision, the court applied case law instructing that a new mortgagee is not entitled to equitable subrogation if it "possesses actual knowledge of the prior encumbrance." First Union Nat'l Bank v. Nelkin, 354 N.J.Super. 557, 565–66, 808 A.2d 856 (App.Div.2002). Because WaMu obviously had such actual knowledge of the Independence line of credit when it paid off the balance on that loan in January 2005 as part of the refinancing, the court concluded that WaMu could not equitably maintain any priority over the Independence loan.

On appeal, Deutsche urges that we reverse the trial court and grant it an equitable remedy of priority, despite WaMu's admitted awareness of the Independence loan at the time of the refinancing. Deutsche contends that the "actual knowledge" exception recognized in *Nelkin* and other case law, at least as applied in these circumstances, unfairly bestows a windfall upon the original junior lienor, Independence, and its assignee, Sovereign. Deutsche argues that the actual knowledge principle wrongfully penalizes a refinancing lender such as WaMu that knowingly pays down a junior debt in full.

As part of its arguments, Deutsche relies upon principles of equity set forth in the Third Restatement, including comment (e) to Section 7.6, which states that "where a mortgage loan is refinanced by the same lender, a mortgage securing the new loan may be given the priority of the original mortgage under the principles of replacement and modification of mortgages." Because we endorse that approach, we reverse the trial court's decision and remand for further proceedings to determine the appropriate extent of appellant's priority. . . .

[Editors' Note: The court's discussion of whether a refinancing lender with actual knowledge of an intervening lien should be equitably subrogated to the priority of the refinanced mortgage is omitted. We focus on this issue in the context of third-party financing beginning on page 1008.]

We did not need to decide in [Investors Sav. Bank v. Keybank Nat'l Ass'n, 424 N.J.Super. 439, 443, 38 A.3d 638 (App.Div.2012)] whether to endorse the Third Restatement's recommended approach to equitable subrogation, because the facts in that case, unlike the present one, did not involve a refinancing lender's actual knowledge of an intervening lien. Although the Third Restatement, and the newer out-of-state cases that have adopted it, raise significant doctrinal and policy issues, we do not need to resolve them here, either. That is because there is an alternative method for analyzing and resolving the priority question before us. Specifically, because the refinanced mortgage loan in 2005 was provided by the same lender—WaMu—as the original 1998 senior mortgage loan, the priority analysis can be guided by principles of "replacement" and "modification."

As Judge Berman correctly recognized in [UPS Capital Bus. Credit v. Abbey, 408 N.J.Super. 524, 530, 975 A.2d 548 (Ch.Div.2009)], the modification of a mortgage loan by the same lender does not necessarily have to be treated in the same fashion, with respect to priority over an intervening lienor, as a new loan that has been made by a third party. Factually in *Abbey,* the defendant had initially borrowed $187,450 from Washington Mutual, which the bank then secured with a mortgage against the defendant's property recorded in the first position. A second bank, UPS Capital, held a subordinated mortgage on the property, recorded in the second position. The defendant later sought to refinance his original loan from Washington Mutual, and the bank lent him $185,000 with terms that carried a lower interest rate and a longer payoff period. The defendant ultimately defaulted on these loans. In the foreclosure proceeding, the two banks, UPS Capital and Washington Mutual, sought to gain a superior lien position over the other.

As Judge Berman correctly observed in that case, Washington Mutual's "'new' loan was in effect a 'modification' as well as a 'renewal' [because] a lower interest rate was applied and the lien was to be paid over a longer period of time." *Id.* at 528–29, 975 A.2d 548. Nevertheless, despite recognizing that Washington Mutual's mortgage was indeed a replacement mortgage, the judge elected to decide the case on the basis of equitable subrogation. He noted that the bank did not have actual knowledge that UPS Capital held an intervening lien on the property. Based on this, the judge held that equitable subrogation applied to permit Washington Mutual to maintain its first priority lien.

The same result as in *Abbey,* i.e., priority for the refinancing lender, should obtain here, but specifically under principles of modification and replacement. In this context, the lender's actual knowledge of an intervening lien is not a bar to its reliance upon equitable principles of priority. As the Third Restatement explains, "subrogation cannot be involved unless the second loan is made by a different lender than the holder of the first mortgage; one cannot be subrogated to one's own previous mortgage." *Id.* at § 7.6 cmt. e. The Third Restatement further instructs in comment e to Section 7.6 that "[w]here a mortgage loan is refinanced by the same lender, a mortgage securing the new loan may be given the priority of the original mortgage under the principles of replacement and modification of mortgages." *Ibid.* This is in keeping with similar commentary within a leading New Jersey treatise on mortgages, which observes that "equitable subrogation" is doctrinally confined to cases "[w]hen a third party who is not a surety and who has no interest to protect loans [ ] advances money to pay off a mortgage[.]" 29 N.J. Practice (Weinstein, Mortgages) (2001) § 13.9.

In this present distinct context of modification and replacement, we conclude that the critical question of priority must revolve around whether the junior lienor, here Sovereign, has been materially prejudiced. As Section 7.3 of the Third Restatement provides as to replacement:

> (a) If a senior mortgage is released of record and, as part of the same transaction, is *replaced* with a new mortgage, the latter mortgage *retains the same priority* as its predecessor, except
>
>> (1) to the extent that any change in the terms of the mortgage or the obligation it secures is *materially prejudicial* to the holder of a junior interest in the real estate, or
>>
>> (2) to the extent that one who is protected by the recording act acquires an interest in the real estate at a time that the senior mortgage is not of record. [Emphasis added.]

Similar principles apply if the refinancing causes a modification of the original loan, as set forth in Section 7.3(b) and (c):

> (b) If a senior mortgage or the obligation it secures is *modified* by the parties, the mortgage as modified *retains priority* as against junior interests in the real estate, except to the extent that the modification is *materially prejudicial* to the holders of such interests and is not within the scope of a reservation of right to modify as provided in Subsection (c).
>
> (c) If the mortgagor and mortgagee reserve the right in a mortgage to modify the mortgage or the obligation it secures, the mortgage as modified retains priority even if the modification is *materially prejudicial* to the holders of junior interests in the real estate, except as provided in Subsection (d). [Emphasis added.]

We regard this as a sound approach. A proper judicial analysis of material prejudice will examine such aspects as the respective loan amounts involved, the interest rates, and, potentially the loan terms.[13]

---

[13] Without resolving the issue conclusively, we tend to agree with the Third Restatement that an extension of the loan term in the refinanced loan is not likely to cause material prejudice to a junior lienor because the refinancing usually is staving off foreclosure on the senior loan.

Actual or constructive knowledge by the refinancing lender, if it is the same original lender or its corporate successor, should be irrelevant. Consequently, summary judgment entered here in favor of Sovereign, which was predicated on a finding of WaMu's actual knowledge, must be reversed as a matter of law. To do otherwise would allow Sovereign to reap an undeserved windfall, particularly since WaMu paid off not only its original mortgage but also paid down in full the balance on the Independence line of credit.

That said, the priority of Deutsche, as WaMu's assignee, must be equitably calibrated to take into account the fact that the $1.19 million in refinancing provided by WaMu in 2005 exceeded the balance then due on WaMu's original $650,000 loan from 1998. A pro tanto "cap" on the new loan's priority appears to be appropriate in this respect, though we do not decide in the abstract on this record whether the cap should be (1) the original $650,000 loan amount, (2) the $534,000 balance at the time of the Independence loan in 2003, or (3) the roughly $482,000 balance when the refinancing occurred in 2005. Although the refinanced loan was extended at a lower interest rate than the 1998 loan, an analysis of the comparative adjustable rates also may have equitable implications.

We defer these equitable considerations to the trial court on remand, directing that the court evaluate these (and any other identified) matters of potential "material prejudice" to Sovereign, and then to ascertain an appropriate priority amount for Deutsche's lien that comports with these principles. . . .

NOTES

1. *Replacement of senior mortgages: impact on junior interests.* Replacement mortgages arise frequently in the construction lending context. Frequently the construction lender for a project also becomes the permanent lender. As a result, the construction lender will release the construction mortgage of record and either immediately or shortly thereafter record a permanent or "long term" mortgage. This will occur even though the original construction mortgage obligation remained unsatisfied.

Priority disputes can arise when the foregoing transaction takes place if there are intervening liens on the real estate, e.g., mortgages or judgment liens that arose after the recording of the construction mortgage but before the recording of the permanent mortgage. Once the construction mortgage is released of record, the intervening lienholders may assert opportunistically that because of the replacement transaction, they have been promoted in priority and are now senior to the permanent mortgage.

Normally, this assertion by the junior interests will be fruitless. The *Gillis* court articulates the pervasive rule that a senior mortgagee who discharges its mortgage of record and takes and records a replacement mortgage nevertheless retains the priority of the original mortgage except to the extent that any change in the terms of the mortgage or the obligation it secures is materially prejudicial to the holder of the junior interest. What type of "material prejudice" must exist to trigger a loss of priority? There is one obvious situation where priority should be lost. Suppose that First Bank releases its construction mortgage *before* recording its permanent mortgage, and during the interim the borrower grants another mortgage to Second Bank, which does not know that First Bank has not been fully repaid. Here Second Bank's mortgage will trump the replacement mortgage because of the operation of the recording acts. Restatement (Third) of Property (Mortgages) § 7.3(a)(2) (1997).

Putting aside this rather easy example, in what other situations will there be a loss of priority?

a.　*Extension of time for payment of the senior debt.* Generally, where the replacement mortgage extends the due date for repayment of the indebtedness, the extension is not deemed to create "material prejudice" and therefore no loss of priority occurs. Comment b to Restatement § 7.3 explains:

> There is a strong presumption under this section that a time extension on a senior mortgage or obligation, standing alone, is not materially prejudicial to intervening interests. A finding of material prejudice is justified only in the rare situation where the time extension can fairly be said to place the junior interest in substantially weaker position. The typical junior lienholder is normally grateful to have a time extension forestall the destruction of its lien by a senior foreclosure.

Can you articulate circumstances under which a time extension would "place the junior interest in a substantially weaker position"?

b.　*Increase in interest rate or principal balance of the senior debt.* Where the replacement mortgage secures an increased principal amount or there is an increase in the interest rate, there often will be a loss of priority vis a vis junior interests. See, e.g., Skaneateles Savings Bank v. Herold, 50 A.D.2d 85, 376 N.Y.S.2d 286 (1975). Why should this be so? Note we say "often" and not "always." The original mortgage may be a "future advances" mortgage, a concept we explore in great detail in Chapter 9, Section C infra. In general terms, a future advances mortgage contemplates later advances of money by the lender to the mortgagor. Thus to the extent that such a mortgage states that it secures future advances, a junior lienor is on notice of its nature and usually should not be in a position to complain that the principal balance is increasing. In our context, for example, if the original mortgage was clearly designated to secure "future advances," a holder of a junior interest may not be justified in complaining that the replacement mortgage is for a larger principal amount.

Should the mortgagee attempt to avoid the "intent to subordinate problem" by including language in the replacement document that it represents a continuation and not a payment and discharge of the original debt and mortgage, and that no subordination to junior interests is intended? See Nelson, Whitman, Burkhart & Freyermuth, Real Estate Finance Law § 9.4 (6th ed. 2014).

Don't worry that our consideration of "material prejudice" at this point seems rather sketchy. We will explore these issues further in only a slightly different context in the next Note.

2.   *Modification of senior mortgages: impact on junior interests.* It is common for a mortgagee and the mortgagor to agree to a variety of modifications in the terms of the mortgage or its obligation. Note that here, there is no "new" replacement mortgage. The original mortgage remains of record and the modifications are reflected in an amendment agreement. The latter agreement is usually recorded. Often these modifications arise because the mortgagor is in financial distress and the modification agreement is part of a "workout" agreement. In other cases, the mortgagor will be financially healthy and the modifications may simply reflect business needs or changes in market conditions.

Whatever the cause of such modifications, the priority questions they create are largely the same as in the replacement mortgage context. To what extent do such modifications result in a loss of priority vis a vis intervening junior interests?

> "It is well established that while a senior mortgagee can enter into an agreement with the mortgagor modifying the terms of the underlying note or mortgage without first having to notify any junior lienors or to obtain their consent, if the modification is such that it prejudices the rights of the junior lienors or impairs the security, their consent is required." *Shultis v. Woodstock Land Dev. Assocs.*, 188 A.D.2d 234, 594 N.Y.S.2d 890, 892 (N.Y.App.Div.1993); *see Fleet Bank v. County of Monroe Ind. Dev. Agency*, 224 A.D.2d 964, 637 N.Y.S.2d 870, 871 (N.Y.App.Div.1996); *Empire Trust Co. v. Park-Lexington Corp.*, 243 App. Div. 315, 321, 276 N.Y.S. 586, 592 (1934); *Shane v. Winter Hill Fed. Sav. and Loan Ass'n.*, 397 Mass. 479, 492 N.E.2d 92, 95 (1986). "Failure to obtain the consent in these cases results in the modification being ineffective as to the junior lienors and the senior lienor relinquishing to the junior lienors its priority with respect to the modified terms." *Shultis*, 594 N.Y.S.2d at 892 (citations omitted). "While this sanction ordinarily creates only the partial loss of priority noted above, in situations where the senior lienor's actions in modifying the note or mortgage have substantially impaired the junior lienors' security interest or effectively destroyed their equity, courts have indicated an inclination to wholly divest the senior lien of its priority and to elevate the junior liens to a position of superiority." *Id.* (citation omitted); *see* cases cited in FRIEDMAN, CONTRACTS & CONVEYANCES, 6th ed., Vol. 2, § 6.5 n. 13 (1998).

Burney v. McLaughlin, 63 S.W.3d 223, 230–232 (Mo.App.S.D.2001). Consistent with this view, Restatement § 7.3(b) provides that "[i]f a senior mortgage or the obligation it secures is modified by the parties, the mortgage as modified retains priority as against junior interests in the real estate, except to the extent that the modification is materially prejudicial to the holders of such interests. . . ." A determination of when material prejudice occurs is a fact-specific inquiry. As discussed in the preceding note, a court would be unlikely to find material prejudice where the modification of the senior mortgage was merely an extension of time for payment. Restatement (Third) of Property (Mortgages) § 7.3 cmt. b (1997); Lennar Northeast Partners v. Buice, 49 Cal.App.4th 1576, 57 Cal.Rptr.2d 435 (1996).

By contrast, where the modification involves an increased interest rate and/or an increase in the principal amount of the indebtedness, a court is more likely to find material prejudice to the junior lienholder and grant the junior lienholder priority over the earlier mortgage to the extent of the modification. Restatement (Third) of Property (Mortgages) § 7.3 cmt. c (1997); Shultis v. Woodstock Land Dev. Assocs., 188 A.D.2d 234, 594 N.Y.S.2d 890 (1993). Can you explain why? Suppose that a senior mortgage is a 30-year amortizing mortgage with an original principal balance of $120,000 and an original interest rate of 10%. Now suppose that the mortgagor defaults when the outstanding balance of the senior mortgage debt has been reduced to $100,000. After six months of negotiations, the mortgagor and senior mortgagee agree to modify the senior mortgage debt, restating the principal balance at $105,000 (to "capitalize" the $5,000 in unpaid interest that accrued during their negotiations) and increasing the interest rate to 12%. If this modification occurred without the consent of the junior lienholder, is the junior lienholder materially prejudiced by the modification? If so, how would you calculate the extent to which the junior lienholder was materially prejudiced? What additional information, if any, would you need to obtain to make this calculation?

Courts sometimes suggest that a modification of a senior mortgage can be so substantial that complete loss of priority will result. See, e.g., Lennar Northeast Partners v. Buice, 49 Cal.App.4th 1576, 57 Cal.Rptr.2d 435 (1996); Shultis v. Woodstock Land Dev. Assocs., 188 A.D.2d 234, 594 N.Y.S.2d 890 (1993). Suppose, for example, the modification of the senior mortgage obligation is so substantial that there is no value left in the real estate to secure the junior lien. Can you think of other similar situations?

3. *Senior mortgage language reserving the right to modify.* Can the priority problems created by modifications be avoided by thoughtful drafting techniques? Suppose the original mortgage contains the following language: "All those claiming by, through or under the mortgagor consent to any extensions, amendments, modifications, or alterations of the mortgage obligation agreed to by the mortgagor and mortgagee and their successors, including those that increase the its principal amount or interest rate." Under the Restatement, this language is effective against junior interests. See Restatement (Third) of Property (Mortgages) § 7.3(c) (1997). Is this good

policy? For the view that such a provision should be unenforceable, see Robert Kratovil & Raymond J. Werner, Mortgage Extensions and Modifications, 8 Creighton L.Rev. 595, 610 (1975). See generally, Robert P. Giesen, "Routine" Mortgage Modifications: Lenders Beware, 17 Real Estate L.J. 221 (1989).

If such a provision is enforceable, will a mortgagor be able later to obtain junior mortgage financing? Will junior lenders be deterred from lending to mortgagor when the amount of the senior mortgage is uncertain because of the potential for its later modification? The Restatement deals with this problem by permitting the mortgagor to issue a "cut-off notice" to the mortgagee that terminates the right to modify conferred by the above senior mortgage provision. Restatement (Third) of Property (Mortgages) § 7.3(d). Once this notice becomes effective, any future modifications will again be governed by the "material prejudice" standard. Id. cmt. e.

Note that the modification provision quoted in the foregoing paragraph operates in much the same fashion as an optional future advance provision in a mortgage to secure future advances. See Chapter 9, Section C, infra; Nelson, Whitman, Burkhart & Freyermuth, Real Estate Finance Law § 12.7 (6th ed. 2014).

Refinancing of senior mortgage by new lender. Suppose Jones owns Blackacre subject to a recorded first mortgage in favor of First National Bank and a recorded second mortgage in favor of State Savings Bank. Jones decides to refinance her first mortgage with a new lender, Regional Mortgage, to get the benefit of a particularly favorable interest rate. In the process of refinancing, Jones pays off the debt to First National Bank using the loan proceeds obtained from Regional Mortgage. Jones executes a new mortgage on Blackacre to Regional Mortgage, which records it promptly. First National Bank's mortgage is released of record.

Several months later, Jones loses her job and soon thereafter defaults to both Regional Mortgage and State Savings Bank. Both lenders institute foreclosure proceedings. Having paid off First National Bank's mortgage (which had priority over the State Savings Bank mortgage) through the refinancing, Regional Mortgage argues that it should be subrogated to the priority First National Bank would have enjoyed prior to the refinancing. By contrast, State Savings Bank argues that it now has priority under the recording acts, because it now holds the first-recorded mortgage of record. So which lender is entitled to priority? Should it matter whether Regional Mortgage knew or should have known of the existence of the State Savings Bank mortgage? Should the intent of Jones and Regional Mortgage at the time of the refinancing be relevant?

In resolving similar cases, courts have disagreed regarding whether the refinancing lender is subrogated into the priority of the refinanced senior lender. The next two cases are illustrative. The first adopts the view of the Restatement, under which Regional Mortgage would be subrogated to the first priority position formerly held by First National Bank. The second rejects the Restatement approach, and would instead grant priority to State Savings Bank based upon the operation of the recording act. In reading these two excerpts, which view do you think is more persuasive, and why?

HOUSTON V. BANK OF AMERICA FEDERAL SAVINGS BANK

Supreme Court of Nevada, 2003
119 Nev. 485, 78 P.3d 71

PER CURIAM. . . . Appellants, Edward R. Houston and Regina Houston, paid David Boone $740,000 for investment services. Boone converted the $740,000 to his own use. Shortly thereafter, on May 13, 1998, Boone and his wife Donna divorced. Pursuant to their property settlement agreement, Boone quitclaimed to Donna the real property located at 2100 Marina Bay Court, Las Vegas, Nevada (the property). At the time of the divorce, Norwest Mortgage, Bank of America's predecessor, held a deed of trust on the property for approximately $342,000.

On May 14, 1998, the Houstons filed a complaint against Boone to recover their $740,000. On June 1, 1998, the Houstons filed a notice of lis pendens on the property in the Clark County Recorder's Office. The Houstons also filed an ex parte motion for an order directing the issuance of a prejudgment writ of attachment, which the district court granted. Early on June 26, 1998, the writ of attachment was filed in the Clark County Recorder's Office. Ultimately, the Houstons obtained a judgment against Boone for $740,000. Boone filed for bankruptcy, but eventually stipulated that the money he owed the Houstons was a nondischargeable debt. The district court granted the Houstons a writ of execution on the property and scheduled a sale of the property. Bank of America intervened and the sale was enjoined.

Bank of America had refinanced the property for Donna on June 26, 1998, after the Houstons' writ of attachment was recorded. Bank of America had hired Nevada Title Company to perform a title search of the property, which was conducted on May 29, 1998, over a month before the refinancing.

After the district court enjoined the sale, both Bank of America and the Houstons filed motions for summary judgment. Bank of America argued that it held the priority lien on the property because it succeeded to the rights of Norwest. The Houstons contended, among other things, that Bank of America was negligent in failing to discover their interest in the property and that they would suffer an injury if the district court allowed Bank of America to succeed to Norwest's priority position. However, the Houstons did not provide the district court with the terms of the former deed of trust or any other evidence of prejudice. The district court granted summary judgment in favor of Bank of America and denied the Houstons' motion for summary judgment. The Houstons appeal. . . .

Equitable subrogation permits "a person who pays off an encumbrance to assume the same priority position as the holder of the previous encumbrance."[4] We have previously applied the doctrine of equitable subrogation, but not in the context presented by this case.[5] Other jurisdictions have adopted three different approaches[6] in determining whether to apply equitable subrogation under circumstances in which a third party held a lien on the property at the time the second lender paid off the former encumbrance.

The first approach, which a majority of states follow, is that actual knowledge of an existing lien precludes the application of equitable subrogation, but constructive knowledge does not.[8] The reasoning underlying this approach is that if a mortgagee did not possess actual notice of a junior lien holder, the mortgagee expected to step into the shoes of the previous creditor it had paid off.[9] In our view, however, this rule promotes willful ignorance; it encourages prospective mortgagees to avoid conducting title searches. Under this approach, if a prospective mortgagee performs a title search and discovers a junior lien holder, it will be barred from being subrogated. However, if a prospective mortgagee forgoes conducting a search, which would have uncovered a junior lien holder, and puts on blinders, it nevertheless will be subrogated. Thus, we decline to adopt this approach.

The second approach bars the application of equitable subrogation when a lien holder possesses either actual or constructive notice of an

---

4   *Mort v. U.S.*, 86 F.3d 890, 893 (9th Cir.1996).

5   *See, e.g., Laffranchini v. Clark*, 39 Nev. 48, 55–56, 153 P. 250, 251–52 (1915) (concluding that the holder of an invalid mortgage was not a volunteer, and thus, entitled to be equitably subrogated to the priority position of the lender whose loan it had paid).

6   Although there are generally three approaches the courts have adopted, some courts refuse to adopt a bright-line rule and simply consider constructive or actual knowledge as a factor in weighing the equities. *See, e.g., East Boston Sav. Bank v. Ogan*, 428 Mass. 327, 701 N.E.2d 331, 335 (1998) (refusing to adopt a bright-line rule regarding subrogee knowledge).

8   *Osterman v. Baber*, 714 N.E.2d 735, 739 (Ind.Ct.App.1999) (recognizing that the majority of jurisdictions hold that actual knowledge bars equitable subrogation, but constructive notice does not, but declining to adopt the majority view); *Rusher v. Bunker*, 99 Or.App. 303, 782 P.2d 170, 172 (1989) (acknowledging that the weight of authority is that constructive knowledge alone does not preclude equitable subrogation); *Restatement (Third) of Property: Mortgages* § 7.6 cmt. e (1997); *see, e.g., U.S. v. Baran*, 996 F.2d 25, 29 (2d Cir.1993) (applying New York law); *Dietrich Industries, Inc. v. U.S.*, 988 F.2d 568, 572 (5th Cir.1993) (applying Texas law); *Brooks v. Resolution Trust Corp.*, 599 So.2d 1163, 1165 (Ala.1992); *Smith v. State S & L Ass'n*, 175 Cal.App.3d 1092, 223 Cal.Rptr. 298, 301 (1985); *United Carolina Bank v. Beesley*, 663 A.2d 574, 576 (Me.1995); *Enterprise Bank v. Federal Land Bank*, 139 S.C. 397, 138 S.E. 146, 148–50 (1927).

9   George E. Osborne, *Mortgages* § 282, at 573 (2d ed.1970).

existing lien.[10] However, precluding equitable subrogation when a mortgagee discovered or could have discovered a junior lien holder runs contrary to the purposes underlying the doctrine. Equitable subrogation is an equitable remedy to avoid a person's receiving an unearned windfall at the expense of another. If there were no subrogation, a junior lien holder would be promoted in priority, giving that creditor/lien holder an unwarranted and unjust windfall. Neither negligence nor constructive notice of an existing lien is relevant as to whether the junior lien holder will be unjustly enriched or prejudiced. The "basis for subrogation in [the mortgage] context is the lender's justified expectation of receiving [a] security" interest in the property.[13] Even a lender with knowledge of an existing lien on the property ordinarily expects to step into the shoes of the creditor it paid off. Therefore, we also decline to adopt this approach.

The third approach, the view adopted by section 7.6 of the Restatement (Third) of Property: Mortgages, disregards actual or constructive notice if the junior lien holder is not prejudiced.[15] Under the Restatement, a mortgagee will be subrogated when it pays the entire loan of another as long as the mortgagee "was promised repayment and reasonably expected to receive a security interest in the real estate with the priority of the mortgage being discharged, and if subrogation will not materially prejudice the holders of intervening interests in the real estate."[16] Because the Restatement approach is the most persuasive, we adopt the view expressed by it.

---

[10] *See Harms v. Burt*, 30 Kan.App.2d 263, 40 P.3d 329, 332 (2002); *see also Independence One Mortg. v. Katsaros*, 43 Conn.App. 71, 681 A.2d 1005, 1007–08 (1996). Additionally, some courts hold a sophisticated party to a higher standard in determining whether to apply equitable subrogation. *See, e.g., Universal Title Ins. Co. v. U.S.*, 942 F.2d 1311, 1317 (8th Cir.1991) (noting that "Minnesota courts impose stricter standards on professionals than lay persons in assessing whether mistakes are 'excusable' for purposes of the doctrine of legal subrogation"). Also, other courts hold that negligence in discovering an existing encumbrance bars equitable subrogation or at least consider a party's negligence in determining whether to apply equitable subrogation. *See Bankers Trust Co. v. U.S.*, 29 Kan.App.2d 215, 25 P.3d 877, 882 (2001); *Landmark Bank v. Ciaravino*, 752 S.W.2d 923, 929 (Mo.Ct.App.1988); *USLife Title Ins. Co. of Dallas v. Romero*, 98 N.M. 699, 652 P.2d 249, 252 (N.M.Ct.App.1982); *Kim v. Lee*, 145 Wash.2d 79, 31 P.3d 665, 671–72, as corrected, 43 P.3d 1222 (Wash.2001). However, in a number of these cases negligence merely appears to be another rationale for holding that constructive notice bars equitable subrogation. *See, e.g., Kim*, 31 P.3d at 671–72.

[13] 2 Grant S. Nelson & Dale A. Whitman, *Real Estate Finance Law* § 10.6, at 15–16 (4th ed. 2002).

[15] *See Suntrust Bank v. Riverside Nat. Bank*, 792 So.2d 1222, 1227 n. 3 (Fla.Dist.Ct.App.2001) (citing section 7.6 of the Restatement to support its decision that negligence in failing to discover an existing lien does not preclude the application of equitable subrogation as long as the existing interest does not suffer prejudice); *see also Trus Joist Corp. v. Nat'l Union Fire Ins. Co.*, 190 N.J.Super. 168, 462 A.2d 603, 609 (1983) (subrogating mortgagee notwithstanding its possessing actual knowledge of an existing intervening interest), *overruled on other grounds by Trus Joist Corp. v. Treetop Associates, Inc.*, 97 N.J. 22, 477 A.2d 817 (1984); *Klotz v. Klotz*, 440 N.W.2d 406, 407–10 (Iowa Ct.App.1989) (subrogating party to senior lien position despite party's having actual knowledge of junior lien holder). These latter two cases do not adopt the Restatement, but their holdings are similar to the Restatement view.

[16] *Restatement (Third) of Property: Mortgages* § 7.6(a)(4).

Under the Restatement, notice of an intervening lien is not necessarily pertinent to whether a party should be subrogated, and a party can be subrogated even if the party possessed actual knowledge of the other lien holder.[17] Pursuant to the Restatement, "[t]he question in such cases is whether the payor reasonably expected to get security with a priority equal to the mortgage being paid."[18] Further, "[a] refinancing mortgagee should be found to lack such an expectation only where there is affirmative proof that the mortgagee intended to subordinate its mortgage to the intervening interest."[19]

The Restatement reasons that an intervening lien holder will not be materially prejudiced by the application of equitable subrogation because the intervening lien holder will remain in the same position. The Restatement notes that "[t]he holders of intervening interests can hardly complain about this result, for they are no worse off than before the senior obligation was discharged."[21] Subrogation will not be granted if it would result in injustice or prejudice to an intervening lienor.

In this case, Bank of America fully paid off the former deed of trust on the property held by Norwest. In the district court's order granting Bank of America's motion for a preliminary injunction, it found that Bank of America paid off the entire former mortgage "with the intention and belief that it would acquire Norwest Mortgage's first-position deed of trust lien on the Property." Further, the record does not contain any evidence that Bank of America intended to subordinate its mortgage to the Houstons.[23]

The Houstons argue that there are issues of fact as to whether they will be prejudiced by the equitable subrogation of Bank of America to the priority lien position. Yet the Houstons did not produce any evidence that they would be prejudiced by equitably subrogating Bank of America, nor did they request time to produce such evidence. Both parties agree that Bank of America's loan is $5,000 more than the Norwest deed of trust, and therefore Bank of America is not entitled to equitable subrogation with regard to the $5,000 increase in its loan.

The mortgagor changed from Boone and Donna, to Donna alone, but the Houstons did not offer any evidence that this change prejudiced them. The Houstons did not show that Donna has a poor credit rating, makes so

---

[17] *Id.* § 7.6 cmt. e.

[18] *Id.*

[19] *Id.*

[21] *Id.* § 7.6 cmt. a.

[23] The Houstons maintain that Bank of America should not be equitably subrogated to the priority position because it negligently failed to discover the lis pendens and writ of attachment the Houstons filed. Alternatively, they contend that there are issues of fact as to whether Bank of America was reasonable in relying on a twenty-seven day old title report. However, since we adopt the Restatement view, Bank of America's negligence in discovering the lis pendens and writ of attachment or its knowledge thereof is irrelevant.

little money, or has so few assets that Bank of America will likely have to foreclose on the property, resulting in the Houstons' loss of their interest in the property. The Houstons did not provide the district court with the previous loan's terms to compare with the new loan's terms to determine if there were modifications that materially prejudice the Houstons. Because there is no evidence in the record that the Houstons will be in a worse position than if Bank of America did not pay off the Norwest deed of trust, the district court did not err by granting Bank of America's motion for summary judgment and denying the Houstons' motion.

We affirm the judgment of the district court.

COUNTRYWIDE HOME LOANS, INC. v. FIRST NAT'L BANK OF STEAMBOAT SPRINGS

Supreme Court of Wyoming, 2006
144 P.3d 1224

KITE, JUSTICE. . . . [Editors' Note: Elmer and Anita Ketcham owned a parcel of land that was subject to a recorded 1997 mortgage held by the Bank of New York and referred to in the decision as the "AWL mortgage." In 2002, the Ketchams granted another mortgage on the same parcel to First National Bank to secure a business loan. In 2003, the Ketchams obtained a $97,500 refinancing loan from Countrywide. At the time of the refinancing loan, Countrywide obtained a title insurance commitment, which listed the two previous mortgages as prior liens. The Ketchams executed a mortgage to Countrywide, which was recorded on April 15, 2003. The Ketchams used the Countrywide loan proceeds to pay off the AWL mortgage.

In June of 2003, the Ketchams defaulted to First National Bank, which instituted a foreclosure action. In this action, both First National Bank and Countrywide sought summary judgment as to their respective lien priorities—First National Bank claiming first priority under the state's recording statute, and Countrywide claiming first priority based upon equitable subrogation to the prior position of the AWL mortgage. The district court ruled in favor of First National Bank, and Countrywide appealed.]

In declining to apply the Restatement, the district court relied on § 34–1–121, which provides in relevant part as follows:

§ 34–1–121. Recorded instrument as notice to subsequent purchasers; recordation of instruments issued by United States or state of Wyoming.

(a) Each and every deed, mortgage, instrument or conveyance touching any interest in lands, made and recorded, according to the provisions of this chapter, shall be notice to and take precedence of any subsequent purchaser or purchasers from the time of the delivery of any instrument at the office of the register of deeds (county clerk), for record.

Reading this provision strictly to mean that lien priority is determined by the date of recording, the district court held First National Bank's 2002 mortgage had priority over Countrywide's subsequent 2003 mortgage.

In reaching this result, the district court concluded application of the Restatement was not appropriate:

> where a lender has actual and constructive notice of a junior mortgagee and could have taken any one of a number of steps to protect its interests. [Countrywide] could have asked for a subordination agreement or an assignment of the AWL mortgage; it did neither of these things and now seeks to rely upon the concept that it "expected" to step into AWL's priority without anything more. The argument goes that, in recognizing the doctrine of equitable subrogation, [First National Bank] is not prejudiced and "loses nothing" because it remains second in priority (before it was behind AWL; now it would be behind [Countrywide]). But, this Court believes equity requires looking at things from a different perspective: [Countrywide] entered into the third mortgage on the property with knowledge of [First National Bank's] prior loan to Ketcham. Why should [Countrywide] get the benefit (and be unjustly enriched) by leaping over [First National Bank] to assume AWL's priority status. [Countrywide] has done nothing to deserve this advantage.

Countrywide argues the district court's approach does not account for the equities of this case and ignores the purpose equitable "subrogation serves in the modern mortgage re-financing context." Countrywide contends the modern trend among courts is to apply equitable subrogation as set forth in the Restatement. Countrywide asserts the district court's approach is contrary to the purpose served by applying the doctrine because: 1) the Ketchams, Countrywide and AWL reasonably expected Countrywide would have first priority; 2) Countrywide would not have agreed to re-finance the 1997 AWL mortgage if it had known it would not have first priority; 3) First National Bank's position would not change if subrogation were allowed; 4) First National Bank should not be moved forward in priority simply because Countrywide knew of the 2002 mortgage when it paid off the AWL mortgage; 5) First National Bank accepted the risks inherent in accepting a second priority lien when it demanded additional collateral from the Ketchams; and 6) giving the 2002 mortgage priority results in an inappropriate windfall to First

National Bank. Before addressing these assertions, we consider § 34–1–121 and our precedent on the doctrine of equitable subrogation.

By statute and case decision, Wyoming is a filing date priority jurisdiction. Section 34–1–121; *Barnhart Drilling Co., Inc. v. Petroleum Fin., Inc.*, 807 P.2d 411, 413 (Wyo.1991) citing *Marple v. Wyo. Prod. Credit Ass'n*, 750 P.2d 1315 (Wyo.1988); *Crozier v. Malone*, 366 P.2d 125 (Wyo.1961). That is, as the Wyoming legislature expressly provided in § 34–1–121, a mortgage properly recorded in the county clerk's office provides notice to subsequent purchasers and takes precedence over later conveyances. As stated in *Crozier*, 366 P.2d at 127, a subsequent purchaser (or mortgagee) has constructive notice of any burden upon title from the date of recordation.

Countrywide asks this Court to recognize an equitable exception to Wyoming's "first in time" statutory provision. Specifically, Countrywide asks us to recognize the doctrine of equitable subrogation as set forth in the Restatement and apply it in this case so Countrywide, by extending a loan to the Ketchams in 2003 to pay off their 1997 mortgage with AWL, is subrogated to AWL's primary lien position. In other words, by executing the 2003 mortgage which allowed the Ketchams to pay off the 1997 mortgage, Countrywide seeks to stand in the shoes of AWL and be given priority over all post-1997 encumbrances.

This Court has not previously considered the Restatement version of equitable subrogation. However, in addressing the concept of subrogation, this Court long ago stated:

> The right of subrogation may arise and sometimes must arise from contract. This is conventional subrogation. The right is sometimes given in the absence of contract, is then a creation of the court of equity, and is given when otherwise there would be a manifest failure of justice. This is legal subrogation. It is a mode which equity adopts to compel the ultimate payment of a debt by one who in justice, equity, and good conscience ought to pay it, though it is not exercised in favor of a mere intermeddler. This principle, adopted from the Roman law and at first sparingly exercised, has come to be one of the great principles of equity of our jurisprudence, and courts incline to extend it rather than restrict it. One instance in which legal subrogation is applied is in connection with the protection of a lien, and the rule is universal that one who has an interest in property by lien or otherwise, in making payment of prior liens, including taxes, is not a mere volunteer, and that he will be entitled, upon payment of a superior lien in order to protect his own lien, to be subrogated to the rights of the superior lienholder.

Wyoming Bldg. & Loan Ass'n v. Mills Const. Co., 38 Wyo. 515, 269 P. 45, 48–49 (1928) (citations omitted).

We applied this reasoning in *Gaub v. Simpson*, 866 P.2d 765, 768 (Wyo.1993) to uphold the application of legal subrogation under the following facts: Gaub sold real property to Cook; Simpson purchased Cook's interest in the property by paying Gaub the amount Cook owed; Gaub failed to record the deed to Simpson; with Gaub still appearing as the record owner, the IRS filed an income tax lien against the property for income taxes Gaub owed; Simpson paid the taxes in order to avoid the lien on his property; and Simpson sought reimbursement from Gaub.

In upholding the application of equitable subrogation to these facts, we said:

> [W]e are satisfied with the legal propriety of the ruling by the district court, in accordance with Wyoming law, that Simpson paid a tax bill, which Gaub owed, in order to protect Simpson's property from an IRS lien. The law justifies this action on the part of Simpson; makes Simpson a subrogee to the rights of the IRS; and demonstrates that, in pursuing the course he chose, Simpson did not act as a volunteer.

Gaub, 866 P.2d at 768. We cited with approval the following excerpt from 73 Am.Jur.2d, *Subrogation*, § 25, "Persons acting in self-protection," p. 614,

> The right of subrogation is not necessarily confined to those who are legally bound to make the payment, but extends as well to persons who pay the debt in self-protection, since they might suffer loss if the obligation is not discharged. A person who has an interest to protect by making the payment is not regarded as a volunteer. * * * The extent or quantity of the subrogee's interest which is in jeopardy is not material. If he had any palpable interest which will be protected by the extinguishment of the debt, he may pay the debt and be entitled to hold and enforce it just as the creditor could. * * * It would seem that one acting in good faith in making his payment, and under a reasonable belief that it is necessary to his protection, is entitled to subrogation, even though it turns out that he had no interest to protect.

Gaub, 866 P.2d at 768.

Thus, we have recognized equitable subrogation in Wyoming as a creation of courts of equity to prevent manifest injustice. *Wyo. Bldg. & Loan*, 269 P. at 48–49. We have specifically applied it to compel payment of a debt by one who in justice, equity, and good conscience ought to pay it and to allow one who pays a superior lien in order to protect his own lien to be subrogated to the rights of the superior lien holder. *Id.; Gaub*, 866 P.2d at 768. We have recognized the appropriateness of the doctrine where one pays the debt of another under a reasonable belief that such payment is necessary for his own protection. *Id.* We have not, however, applied the doctrine of equitable subrogation as set forth in the Restatement to allow a refinancing mortgagee to step into the shoes of a prior mortgagee for purposes of obtaining lien priority.

Having considered our statute and the cases from other states in which courts have applied equitable subrogation in the context of mortgage re-financing, we decline to adopt the Restatement. Unlike the trend in other courts, we are not persuaded any manifest injustice results from applying the express language of § 34–1–121 and adhering to the clear legislative intent that lien priority in Wyoming is to be determined by the date of recording. Here, the AWL mortgage was recorded in 1997, the First National Bank mortgage was recorded in 2002 and Countrywide's mortgage was recorded in 2003. Countrywide knew of the existence of First National Bank's lien before it extended the loan to the Ketchams. Thus, Countrywide knew First National Bank had a prior recorded lien on the property when it executed the 2003 mortgage. Countrywide was charged with knowing Wyoming is a "first in time" jurisdiction. We are charged with the duty of giving effect to the statutes our legislature has enacted. Where the language of a statute is plain and unambiguous and conveys a clear and definite meaning, the court has no right to look for and impose another meaning, but has the duty to give full force and effect to the legislative product. Contrary to Countrywide's assertion, it had no reason to expect under Wyoming law that its 2003 mortgage would be given priority over First National Bank's 2002 mortgage. Although Countrywide makes the policy argument that equitable subrogation will make refinancing more readily available to the public and thereby, serves the public interest, those arguments are properly directed to the legislature. In addition, the primary purpose of our recording statute is to secure certainty of title. *Condos v. Trapp*, 717 P.2d 827, 832 (Wyo.1986). This countervailing public policy interest in clarity and certainty in matters of land title arguably outweighs the interests of private lending institutions which can be protected by simple due diligence.

As this Court stated in *Wyoming Bldg. & Loan Ass'n*, 269 P. at 48, equitable subrogation is "a creation of the court of equity, and is given when otherwise there would be a manifest failure of justice." "It is a mode which equity adopts to compel the ultimate payment of a debt by one who in justice, equity and good conscience ought to pay it, though it is not exercised in favor of a mere intermeddler." *Id.* These factors, which may compel application of the doctrine of equitable subrogation in other contexts, simply are not present in the case of a mortgagee who agrees to refinance a prior mortgage. In this context, the mortgagee does not pay the debt (or extend the loan) because "in justice, equity and good conscience he ought to pay it." Nor in the context of mortgage re-financing does the mortgagee pay the debt because, as in *Gaub*, he must do so in order to protect his own interest. To the contrary, the mortgagee who refinances a prior mortgage more closely resembles a volunteer or intermeddler in whose favor courts have not been inclined to apply equitable subrogation. In our view equitable subrogation simply has no application where a financial institution extends a loan for the purpose of enabling a mortgagor to pay off an existing mortgage, knowing that a subordinate lien exists on the real estate. Other mechanisms are available for a re-financing lender to obtain first priority without invoking equity to achieve that result. * * *

NOTES

1. *The Restatement approach and its impact on refinancing costs.* When a mortgage is refinanced, it is customary for the refinancing lender, as a condition of making the loan, to obtain a new mortgagee's title insurance policy, the cost of which is borne by the borrower. The average cost of this title insurance to the refinancing homeowner on a $130,000 new mortgage is currently approximately $400. The cumulative cost nationally to homeowners runs in the billions of dollars annually, particularly during periods when large numbers of owners refinance because of falling interest rates. One of the major reasons a refinancing mortgagee requires title insurance is to be protected against the risk that intervening liens or other interests in real estate that may have been created since the original mortgage was recorded will have priority over the new refinancing mortgage. We have argued that the pervasive adoption of the *Restatement* approach has the potential to reduce or eliminate the title insurance company's risk in this situation. Would title insurers be forced by market pressures to pass the benefit of this reduced risk to homeowners in the form of substantially lowered title insurance premiums? See Grant S. Nelson & Dale A. Whitman, Adopting Restatement Mortgage Subrogation Principles: Saving Billions of Dollars for Refinancing Homeowners, 2006 B.Y.U. L.Rev. 305.

Why did the Wyoming court ignore these potential benefits and reject the Restatement approach? Is the court's analysis persuasive? Note that Countrywide could have solved this priority problem in advance through careful planning, either by (a) conditioning its willingness to make a refinancing loan upon First National Bank's execution and delivery of a subordination agreement, or (b) taking an express assignment of the AWL mortgage. If Countrywide could have avoided the problem so easily, should the court be sympathetic to Countrywide's subrogation argument?

2. *Expanding subrogation to new purchasers.* Suppose a home or other real estate is sold and the proceeds of a loan from the purchaser's lender are used to pay off the seller's prior senior mortgage. As part of this transaction,

the prior senior mortgage is released and the purchaser's lender records a new mortgage. Suppose the new lender or its title insurer fails to discover a pre-existing lien. Should the junior mortgage be promoted? Or should subrogation protect the new mortgagee? Generally subrogation has not been available because it is assumed to apply only to debts incurred by the original debtor. However, the Massachusetts Supreme Court has adopted a broad, "no-fault" Restatement view of subrogation:

> Because we find that the equities are substantially similar in refinancing and sales transactions, and that application of equitable subrogation to a sale is consistent with our precedent, we hold that equitable subrogation applies in this case. * * * [T]he distinction between a sale and a refinancing exists, but subrogation arising out of either context yields the same result.

East Boston Sav. Bank v. Ogan, 428 Mass. 327, 701 N.E.2d 331, 335–36 (1998). As in the refinancing context, lenders to new home purchasers always require a separate title insurance policy insuring the priority and validity of its mortgage. The premium for this policy is usually paid for by the new home purchaser. Would pervasive adoption of the Restatement subrogation approach substantially reduce this cost to purchasers?

Suppose that the new purchaser does not obtain institutional financing but instead pays the purchase price in cash, part of which is used to pay off the seller's mortgage. If the purchaser later discovers the intervening lien, can the purchaser be equitably subrogated to the lien of the paid-off mortgage and thus claim priority over the intervening lien creditor? See, e.g., Sourcecorp, Inc. v. Norcutt, 229 Ariz. 270, 274 P.3d 1204 (2012).

D. FIXTURES

This section deals with the difficult problems of priorities that arise when otherwise moveable chattels (e.g., furnaces, machinery, central air conditioning, silos or grain bins) are annexed or affixed to real estate so as to become fixtures. Although the problems are complex and varied, one of the most common fact situations involves a conflict between the seller or third party lender who takes a purchase money security interest in the article and a mortgagee who holds a mortgage on the real estate. Until the adoption of the Uniform Commercial Code, such problems were handled in a dozen or so states by section 7 of the Uniform Conditional Sales Act and elsewhere by the common law or by other specific state statutes. See Nelson, Whitman, Burkhart & Freyermuth, Real Estate Finance Law § 9.6 (6th ed. 2014).

Today, Article 9 of the Uniform Commercial Code has been adopted in all 50 states, and it addresses fixture priority questions in section 9–334. The following excerpts provide an overview of the rules by which Article 9 resolves priority disputes between a real estate mortgagee and another person holding an Article 9 security interest in an item that has become a fixture.

NELSON, WHITMAN, BURKHART & FREYERMUTH, REAL ESTATE FINANCE LAW
(6th ed.2014)*

. . . [C]onflicts may arise between a creditor holding a claim against a fixture under personal property law (e.g., Article 9) and a creditor holding a claim against fixtures under real property law. The purpose of the UCC fixture provisions is to specify the order of priority in these disputes, based on state law definitions of what is a fixture.[154] In theory, there was no intent to promulgate a uniform definition of fixtures which would encroach upon local realty laws. Thus, much of the pre-UCC case law regarding whether a good has become a fixture remains relevant.[156] Two reasons were asserted for perpetuating this local law: (1) the generalized nature of a uniform law was inadequate to meet the needs of diverse local circumstances; and (2) laws pertaining to traditionally unique real property were deeply entrenched; a wholesale attempt at displacement would simply have caused omission of the fixture provisions from states' enactments of the UCC.

To maximize understanding of the ensuing topics, the fixture provisions of the Revised Article 9 are set out below.[158]

---

* Reprinted with permission of LEG, Inc. d/b/a West Academic.

[154] See, e.g., White and Summers, Uniform Commercial Code § 25.5 (6th ed.); In re Shelton, 35 B.R. 505, 508–509 (Bankr. E.D. Va. 1983).

[156] See, e.g., Alamosa Nat. Bank v. San Luis Valley Grain Growers, Inc., 756 P.2d 1022, 7 U.C.C. Rep. Serv. 2d 285 (Colo. App. 1988); Sears, Roebuck & Co. v. Bay Bank & Trust Co., 537 So. 2d 1041 (Fla. 1st DCA 1989); Community Bank of Homestead v. Barnett Bank of the Keys, 518 So. 2d 928, 5 U.C.C. Rep. Serv. 2d 239 (Fla. 3d DCA 1987); C.I.T. Financial Services v. Premier Corp., 1987 OK 101, 747 P.2d 934 (Okla. 1987); Courtright Cattle Co. v. Dolsen Co., 94 Wash. 2d 645, 619 P.2d 344 (1980); Wyoming State Farm Loan Bd. v. Farm Credit System Capital Corp., 759 P.2d 1230, 7 U.C.C. Rep. Serv. 2d 243 (Wyo. 1988); In re Black, 95 B.R. 223 (Bankr. N.D. Ala. 1988); Matter of Farrier, 61 B.R. 950, 1 U.C.C. Rep. Serv. 2d 1379 (Bankr. W.D. Pa. 1986); In re Shelton, 35 B.R. 505 (Bankr. E.D. Va. 1983); In re Boden Mining Corp., 11 B.R. 562, 33 U.C.C. Rep. Serv. 1550 (Bankr. S.D. W.Va. 1981); In re Avery, 7 B.R. 28 (Bankr. D. S.C. 1980); White and Summers, supra note 1 at 1055.

[158] The full text of the fixtures provision of Revised Article 9 is as follows:

§ 9–334. Priority of Security Interests in Fixtures * * *

(a) **[Security interest in fixtures under this article.]** A security interest under this article may be created in goods that are fixtures or may continue in goods that become fixtures. A security interest does not exist under this article in ordinary building materials incorporated into an improvement on land.

(b) **[Security interest in fixtures under real-property law.]** This article does not prevent creation of an encumbrance upon fixtures under real property law.

(c) **[General rule: subordination of security interest in fixtures.]** In cases not governed by subsections (d) through (h), a security interest in fixtures is subordinate to a conflicting interest of an encumbrancer or owner of the related real property other than the debtor.

(d) **[Fixtures purchase-money priority.]** Except as otherwise provided in subsection (h), a perfected security interest in fixtures has priority over a conflicting interest of an encumbrancer or owner of the real property if the debtor has an interest of record in or is in possession of the real property and: (1) the security interest is a purchase-money security interest; (2) the interest of the encumbrancer or owner arises before the goods become fixtures; and (3) the security interest is perfected by a fixture filing before the goods become fixtures or within 20 days thereafter.

(e) **[Priority of security interest in fixtures over interests in real property.]** A perfected security interest in fixtures has priority over a conflicting interest of an encumbrancer or owner of the real property if: (1) the debtor has an interest of record in the real property or is in possession of the real property and the security interest: (A) is perfected by a fixture filing before the interest of the encumbrancer or owner is of record; and (B) has priority over any conflicting interest of a predecessor in title of the encumbrancer or owner; (2) before the goods become fixtures, the security interest is perfected by any method permitted by this article and the fixtures are readily removable: (A) factory or office machines; (B) equipment that is not primarily used or leased for use in the operation of the real property; or (C) replacements of domestic appliances that are consumer goods; (3) the conflicting interest is a lien on the real property obtained by legal or equitable proceedings after the security interest was perfected by any method permitted by this article; or (4) the security interest is: (A) created in a manufactured home in a manufactured-home transaction; and (B) perfected pursuant to a statute described in Section 9–311(a)(2).

(f) **[Priority based on consent, disclaimer, or right to remove.]** A security interest in fixtures, whether or not perfected, has priority over a conflicting interest of an encumbrancer or owner of the real property if: (1) the encumbrancer or owner has, in an authenticated record, consented to the security interest or disclaimed an interest in the goods as fixtures; or (2) the debtor has a right to remove the goods as against the encumbrancer or owner.

(g) **[Continuation of paragraph (f)(2) priority.]** The priority of the security interest under paragraph (f)(2) continues for a reasonable time if the debtor's right to remove the goods as against the encumbrancer or owner terminates.

(h) **[Priority of construction mortgage.]** A mortgage is a construction mortgage to the extent that it secures an obligation incurred for the construction of an improvement on land, including the acquisition cost of the land, if a recorded record of the mortgage so indicates. Except as otherwise provided in subsections (e) and (f), a security interest in fixtures is subordinate to a construction mortgage if a record of the mortgage is recorded before the goods become fixtures and the goods become fixtures before the completion of the construction. A mortgage has this priority to the same extent as a construction mortgage to the extent that it is given to refinance a construction mortgage.

§ 9–102(a) Definitions

(40) "Fixture filing" means the filing of a financing statement covering goods that are or are to become fixtures and satisfying Section 9–502(a) and (b). The term includes the filing of a financing statement covering goods of a transmitting utility which are or are to become fixtures.

(41) "Fixtures" means goods that have become so related to particular real property that an interest in them arises under real property law.

(53) "Manufactured home" means a structure, transportable in one or more sections, which, in the traveling mode, is eight body feet or more in width or 40 body feet or more in length, or, when erected on site, is 320 or more square feet, and which is built on a permanent chassis and designed to be used as a dwelling with or without a permanent foundation when connected to the required utilities, and includes the plumbing, heating, air-conditioning, and electrical systems contained therein. * * *

(54) "Manufactured-home transaction" means a secured transaction: (A) that creates a purchase-money security interest in a manufactured home, other than a manufactured home held as inventory; or (B) in which a manufactured home, other than a manufactured home held as inventory, is the primary collateral.

Although local law defining fixtures is still applicable, the UCC has to some extent influenced these local fixture concepts by its apparent recognition of three classes of goods. Authorities uniformly accept this so-called "tri-partite" concept, which consists of the three following classes situated on a continuum: (1) incorporated building materials; (2) fixtures; and (3) purely personal property.[159]

Under the UCC, no security interest exists in "ordinary building materials incorporated into an improvement on land" irrespective of whether local law classifies such materials as fixtures.[160] This prohibition does not affect rights of enforcement against the debtor personally as opposed to against the actual materials.[161] This provision derives from the [old] Uniform Conditional Sales Act and the policy underlying it is to prevent waste by prohibiting the dismantling of a completed structure.[162]

At the opposite extreme of the continuum is purely personal property. Upon first reading the UCC fixture scheme, one may form a common misconception that realty claimants can somehow prevail as to such property. Goods that are purely personal property do not become part of a real estate mortgage, even though a chattel security interest is never perfected, merely because the goods are located on the mortgaged property. For example, personalty such as stereo components or household furniture would not be subject to a real estate mortgage simply because they were situated inside a mortgaged home.[163]

For the intermediate class of fixtures, Article 9 defers to state real estate law the question of when a good becomes a fixture,[164] and instead adopts in U.C.C. § 9–334 a set of rules to resolve priority conflicts between real estate mortgagees and parties holding conflicting interests arising under Article 9. . . .

---

[159] U.C.C. § 9–334, Comment 3; Adams, Security Interests in Fixtures Under Mississippi's Uniform Commercial Code, 47 Miss.L.J. 831, 836 (1976).

[160] U.C.C. § 9–334(a). The concept of "ordinary building materials" should be understood to cover lumber, wires, paint, nails, and other types of materials that would effectively lose their identity during the building process. Cf. In re Ryan, 360 B.R. 50, 62 U.C.C. Rep. Serv. 2d 58 (Bankr. W.D. N.Y. 2007) (specialty bathtub did not qualify as ordinary building material; security interest of seller continued in bathtub even after it became a fixture in debtor's home); In re Troutt, 62 Collier Bankr. Cas. 2d (MB) 1413, Bankr. L. Rep. (CCH) ¶ 81632, 70 U.C.C. Rep. Serv. 2d 424 (Bankr. S.D. Ill. 2009) (segments of insulation stapled into debtor's attic was a fixture).

[161] U.C.C. § 9–334(a).

[162] Henning, The Impact of Revised Article 9 on Missouri's Fixture Financing Scheme, 48 Mo.L.Rev. 63, 69–71 (1983).

[163] The mortgagee could obtain a security interest in these items if the mortgage contained language sufficient to create a security interest in them under U.C.C. § 9–203(b).

[164] U.C.C. § 9–102(a)(41) (" 'Fixtures' means goods that have become so related to particular real property that an interest in them arises under real property law.").

NOTE

State law of fixtures. The traditional hornbook definition of a fixture is "a former chattel which, while retaining its separate physical identity, is so connected with the realty that a disinterested observer would consider it a part thereof." 5 Am. Law of Prop. § 19.1 at 3–4 (1952). Professor Steve Knippenberg has offered a more informal and intuitive (if somewhat impractical) definition: "You take the world, you shake it, and everything that doesn't fall off is [a fixture]." Lopucki & Warren, Secured Credit: A Systems Approach 350 (7th ed. 2012). But the precise point at which a chattel becomes a fixture is left to the law of each state, and state court decisions have proven somewhat unpredictable. To the extent generalization is possible:

> Courts use a facts-and-circumstances test to determine whether a particular asset qualifies as a fixture, typically focusing upon three elements: (1) the intent of the annexor, (2) the degree of physical affixation to the realty, and (3) the degree of adaptation of the asset to the particular characteristics of the real estate. The first factor—the intent of the annexor—is important in disputes between a secured party and the party that owned the land at the time of affixation, but courts largely ignore this factor in disputes between a secured party and a subsequent purchaser of the land. In deciding whether to buy or lend, a purchaser typically will have relied upon the appearance that the fixture was part of the land, and the reasonable expectations of the purchaser outweigh the hidden intentions of the annexor. Accordingly, in most disputes involving whether goods constitute a fixture, the issue turns on the degree of affixation and adaptation. Goods that are plugged into the wall are "affixed" to the land, but a court is not likely to characterize the goods as a fixture. If a couple of screws connect goods to the land to keep the goods from vibrating, the goods may or may not be a fixture. If the goods are so extensively attached to or embedded in the land that the goods cannot be removed without intensive labor, the goods are almost certainly a fixture. Adaptation comes into play if the physical connection between the goods and the land is slight, but the goods have been specially designed to fit into a particular area. For example, drapes that are loosely attached but are specifically designed for a particular room may qualify as fixtures.

Lawrence, Henning & Freyermuth, Understanding Secured Transactions 304 (5th ed. 2012).

NELSON, WHITMAN, BURKHART & FREYERMUTH, REAL ESTATE FINANCE LAW

(6th ed.2014)[*]

Subsequent Real Estate Mortgages

[T]he default rule in U.C.C. § 9–334 is that an Article 9 security interest in fixtures is subordinate to the conflicting interest of a real estate mortgagee,[168] but the drafters provided a number of exceptions under which the Article 9 fixture secured party can establish first priority. The first such exception governs disputes between an Article 9 fixture security interest and the claim of a mortgagee whose lien arises after the goods become a fixture. In this situation, a "first to file" rule applies: as between a subsequent mortgagee and a prior Article 9 security interest in fixtures, the first party to make a fixture filing or record his real estate mortgage attains priority.[169] As a result, a subsequent realty mortgagee cannot obtain priority over an Article 9 security interest in fixtures so long as the Article 9 secured party has properly perfected its interest by a fixture filing. The fixture filing, as it appears in the land records, alerts subsequent purchasers and mortgagees. . . .

Prior Real Estate Mortgagees

Even if a real estate mortgage precedes the creation of an Article 9 security interest in a good that is later affixed to the real estate, Article 9 nevertheless awards priority to the Article 9 fixture security interest if (1) it is a purchase money security interest, and (2) a fixture filing is made before or within 20 days after the goods become fixtures.[170] Thus, suppose that Bank holds a recorded mortgage on P's home. On March 1, P purchases a furnace from X and grants S a security interest in the furnace to secure the unpaid balance of the purchase price. On March 2, P installs the furnace in his home, and the furnace becomes a fixture under applicable state law. On March 3, S makes a fixture filing in the appropriate real estate records. In this situation, S's purchase money security interest in the furnace takes priority over Bank's interest in the furnace as a mortgagee.

---

[*]   Reprinted with permission of LEG, Inc. d/b/a West Academic.

[168] U.C.C. § 9–334(c).

[169] U.C.C. § 9–334(e)(1); Corning Bank v. Bank of Rector, 265 Ark. 68, 576 S.W.2d 949, 26 U.C.C. Rep. Serv. 1367 (1979); C.I.T. Financial Services v. Premier Corp., 1987 OK 101, 747 P.2d 934 (Okla. 1987); Matter of Farrier, 61 B.R. 950, 1 U.C.C. Rep. Serv. 2d 1379 (Bankr. W.D. Pa. 1986).

[170] U.C.C. § 9–334(d) and Comment 7; Yeadon Fabric Domes, Inc. v. Maine Sports Complex, LLC, 2006 ME 85, 901 A.2d 200, 60 U.C.C. Rep. Serv. 2d 367 (Me. 2006); WSFS v. Chillibilly's, Inc., 57 U.C.C. Rep. Serv. 2d 692 (Del. Super. Ct. 2005); M & M Development, Inc. v. LS Monticello JV Inc., 190 A.D.2d 392, 599 N.Y.S.2d 137, 21 U.C.C. Rep. Serv. 2d 1195 (3d Dep't1993); Parsons v. Lender Service, Inc., 1990 OK CIV APP 72, 801 P.2d 739, 13 U.C.C. Rep. Serv. 2d 1332 (Ct. App. Div. 3 1990); First Wisconsin Nat. Bank of Milwaukee v. Federal Land Bank of St. Paul, 849 F.2d 284, 6 U.C.C. Rep. Serv. 2d 975 (7th Cir. 1988); Schroeder, Security Interests in Fixtures, 1975 Ariz.St.L.J. 319, 320–329.

The historical preference for purchase money financing explains this "purchase-money" exception. In the above hypothetical, because the furnace was not part of the home at the time Bank took its mortgage, Bank did not rely upon the furnace as part of its security in the mortgage agreement. Further, the furnace likely enhances the value of the home and thus benefits the Bank by increasing the value of its security. To award Bank priority over S as to the furnace would arguably give Bank an undeserved, unbargained-for windfall.[171] . . .

In rare circumstances, an Article 9 security interest is created in a good after it has already become a fixture. For example, suppose that Bank holds a recorded mortgage on P's home. P purchases a furnace (paying in cash) and installs the furnace in his home, such that the furnace becomes a fixture under applicable state law. Later, P borrows money from X and grants X a security interest in the furnace. Even if X makes a timely fixture filing, Bank's mortgage takes priority, because X does not have a purchase money security interest and thus does not qualify for protection under U.C.C. § 9–334(d).[172] This result makes sense, because P is not buying and affixing new goods to improve the freehold, but is borrowing against existing property on which a lender could have relied in taking a real estate mortgage.[173]

Construction Mortgages

Construction mortgagees, for a variety of reasons, pay out the proceeds of their loans on an installment basis as the construction of the building progresses. In an attempt to ensure that these subsequent advances relate back to the original date of the mortgage for priority purposes, construction mortgagees include "future advances" clauses in construction mortgages. In the typical construction loan, the borrower and construction lender expect that the borrower will use some of the construction funds advanced to acquire goods that will become fixtures upon installation. Naturally, therefore, the construction mortgagee wants to claim such fixtures as part of its security.

The "purchase money" priority rule discussed above, however, would create a potential trap for the construction mortgagee. For example, suppose that Bank holds a construction loan mortgage on an office building being constructed by P. During construction, P purchases $20,000 worth of cabinetry on credit from S, who takes a purchase money

---

[171] Lawrence, Henning & Freyermuth, Understanding Secured Transactions 308 (5th ed. 2012).

[172] Schroeder, supra note 170, at 320–321. See McIlroy Bank & Trust Fayetteville v. Federal Land Bank of St. Louis, 266 Ark. 481, 585 S.W.2d 947 (1979). However, real estate mortgagees sometimes lose because of an inability to establish that the goods became fixtures. See, e.g., In re Avery, 7 B.R. 28 (Bankr. D. S.C. 1980).

[173] Schroeder, supra note 170, at 321. See McIlroy Bank & Trust Fayetteville v. Federal Land Bank of St. Louis, 266 Ark. 481, 585 S.W.2d 947 (1979).

security interest to secure the purchase price. P then installs the cabinets into the building, and the cabinets become a fixture under applicable state law. On the same day, S makes an appropriate fixture filing covering the cabinets. In this situation, U.C.C. § 9–334(d) would give S priority over Bank as to the cabinets. Such a result may be inappropriate, however, because Bank may well have expected to finance all of the building's fixtures; granting priority to S would effectively allow P to "double-finance" the cabinets.

Article 9 addresses this dilemma by providing a special rule that provides the expected priority to the construction mortgagee so long as the mortgage is recorded before the goods are affixed.[175] As one commentator has noted, "as to any goods that become fixtures during the course of construction, the construction mortgagee enjoys priority to the extent of all advances made under the mortgage to finance the construction, including the cost of acquiring the land."[176] The construction mortgagee has priority for such advances even as against a purchase money security interest in fixtures;[177] moreover, it makes no difference whether the advances are "optional" or "obligatory."[178] The benefit of this priority is available to both assignees of the construction mortgage and to refinancing mortgagees.[179]

Exceptions Favoring Fixture Financers

A real estate mortgagee with priority may consent to subordinate his claim to the security interest of the fixture financier.[180] The mortgagee might agree to give such consent where the mortgagee has reasons to maintain the good will of the mortgagor, or where the mortgagee reasonably did not expect to have priority as to a particular fixture. For example, suppose that Bank holds a recorded construction mortgage on P's office building. P now wants to install certain fixtures during construction that were not part of the original construction budget and for which the Bank will not be advancing funds under its construction loan agreement. In such a case, the Bank might decide to consent to subordinate its priority to another secured party willing to provide financing for those particular fixtures.

In certain limited situations, U.C.C. § 9–334(e) enables an Article 9 fixture secured party to obtain priority over certain conflicting real estate

---

[175] U.C.C. § 9–334(g).

[176] Adams, supra note 159, at 908. To qualify as a construction mortgage, a mortgage must secure "an obligation incurred for the construction of an improvement on land." U.C.C. § 9–334(h).

[177] U.C.C. § 9–334(h); Funk, The Proposed Revision of Article 9 of the Uniform Commercial Code, 26 Bus.Law. 1465, 1472 (1972).

[178] U.C.C. § 9–334, Comment 11.

[179] U.C.C. § 9–334(h); Schroeder, supra note 170, at 332.

[180] U.C.C. § 9–334(f)(1).

interests by perfecting under Article 9's regular perfection rules rather than by making a fixture filing. For example, a security interest in fixtures has priority over a real estate mortgagee with respect to "readily moveable factory or office machines," "equipment that is not primarily used or leased for use in the operation of the real property," or "replacements of domestic appliances that are consumer goods" as long as that security interest is perfected "by any method permitted" in the UCC.[181] The drafters included this provision to alleviate the confusion in various jurisdictions as to whether these types of items are fixtures or pure personalty. In the drafters' judgment, commercial actors view office machines, stoves, refrigerators, and similar domestic appliances as being in the nature of chattels, even if a jurisdiction's real estate laws might characterize them as fixtures. The exception thus protects the expectations of an Article 9 secured party "who, perhaps in the mistaken belief that the readily removable goods will not become fixtures, makes a UCC filing ... rather than a fixture filing."[182] Note, however, that the priority guarantee for Article 9 secured parties as to domestic appliances extends only to replacement appliances, not original installations.[183] This limitation protects a construction lender that may have relied upon having a lien on the original appliances when it financed the home's construction.[184]

Likewise, the fixture secured party need not make a fixture filing to attain priority *vis-a-vis* lien creditors, including a trustee in bankruptcy.[185] Because such creditors typically do not rely on the real estate records, a fixture filing is not necessary and perfection by any other method is effective against them.[186] If the Article 9 secured party incorrectly assumes that goods will not become fixtures, she will be protected against nonreliance creditors as long as she takes the normal steps to perfect her interest under Article 9, even though she will be subordinated to recorded real estate mortgages because of her failure to make a fixture filing.

Finally, if fixtures are installed by a mortgagor's tenant, the UCC gives priority to the holder of an Article 9 security interest in those fixtures over conflicting interests in the realty if the tenant has the right

---

[181] U.C.C. § 9–334(e) and Comment 8. Perfection would ordinarily occur under Article 9 by the filing of a financing statement covering the goods in the appropriate filing office. U.C.C. § 9–310(a). However, if the security interest in question is a purchase-money security interest in consumer goods, that security interest is automatically perfected without the filing of a financing statement. U.C.C. § 9–309(1).

[182] U.C.C. § 9–334, Comment 8.

[183] U.C.C. § 9–334, Comment 8.

[184] Lawrence, Henning & Freyermuth, supra note 171, at 312.

[185] U.C.C. § 9–334(e)(3) and Comment 9. The term "lien creditor" is defined in U.C.C. § 9–102(a)(52) and includes creditors who acquire a lien on property "by attachment, levy, or the like." U.C.C. § 9–102(a)(52)(A).

[186] U.C.C. § 9–334(e)(3).

as against the mortgagor to remove the fixtures from the mortgaged property.[187] This priority continues for a reasonable time even after the tenant/debtor's right of removal terminates.[188]

NOTES

1. *Some priority problems.* Test your understanding of the provisions of UCC § 9–334 by ascertaining how that section resolves the following priority problems:

(a) Bank holds a recorded mortgage on Butcher's land and building. On February 1, Manufacturer sells Butcher a walk-in refrigerator on credit, taking a purchase-money security interest in the refrigerator. On February 3, Butcher installs the refrigerator in its building, thereby rendering it a fixture. On February 9, Manufacturer makes a proper fixture filing covering the refrigerator. Who has priority in the refrigerator: Bank or Manufacturer?

(b) Same as problem (a), but now assume that Manufacturer simply files a regular Article 9 financing statement rather than making a fixture filing. Who has priority in the refrigerator: Bank or Manufacturer?

(c) On February 1, Manufacturer sells Butcher a walk-in refrigerator on credit, taking a purchase-money security interest in the refrigerator. On February 3, Butcher installs the refrigerator in its building, thereby rendering it a fixture. On February 5, Butcher borrows $500,000 from Bank and grants Bank a mortgage on its building, which Bank records that same day. On February 8, Manufacturer makes a proper fixture filing covering the refrigerator. Who has priority in the refrigerator: Bank or Manufacturer?

(d) On July 1, Manufacturer sells Butcher a walk-in refrigerator on credit, taking a purchase-money security interest in the refrigerator. On July 3, Butcher installs the refrigerator in its building, rendering it a fixture. Manufacturer does not make a fixture filing, but does file an Article 9 financing statement covering the refrigerator. On September 1, Customer obtains a judgment against Butcher arising out of a food-poisoning incident, and the judgment constitutes a lien against Butcher's building. Who has priority in the refrigerator: Manufacturer or Customer?

(e) ABC Corp. (ABC) is building an office building financed by a construction loan from Bank, which holds a recorded mortgage. On November 1, Carpenter sells ABC 100 sets of cabinets for installation in the building; Carpenter takes a purchase-money security interest to secure ABC's

---

[187] U.C.C. § 9–334(f)(2). This provision is consistent with the so-called "trade fixtures" doctrine, under which goods affixed to leased premises are treated as personal property as between the lessor and the lessee. Lawrence, Henning & Freyermuth, supra note 171, at 315; see also FL Receivables Trust 2002–A v. Arizona Mills, L.L.C., 210 Ariz. 388, 111 P.3d 430, 57 U.C.C. Rep. Serv. 2d 625 (Ct. App. Div. 1 2005), review denied and ordered depublished, 212 Ariz. 43, 127 P.3d 59 (2006).

[188] U.C.C. § 9–334(g). Although it could not remove the fixture, the Article 9 fixture secured party could still reduce its claim against the debtor to judgment and enforce that claim against the debtor's other assets (assuming that the debtor has personal liability on the debt).

obligation to pay the purchase price of the cabinets. On November 20, the cabinets are installed in the building and become fixtures. On November 22, Carpenter files a fixture filing covering the cabinets. Who has priority as to the cabinets: Carpenter or Bank?

(f) Same as problem (e), but assume that ABC had completed construction of the building on October 15. Would this change your answer? Why or why not?

2.　*The fixture secured party's right to remove fixtures.* The priority recognized by UCC § 9–334 becomes critical in the event of default—either a default on the mortgage obligation or the obligation owed to the fixture secured party (or both). Suppose that Manufacturer has a security interest in Butcher's walk-in refrigerator (which is a fixture under state law) and Bank holds a recorded mortgage on the building in which the refrigerator is installed. If Butcher defaults, Manufacturer wants to be able to remove the refrigerator (i.e., to "unaffix" it, thereby restoring its character as personalty) and conduct a foreclosure sale governed by Article 9. Manufacturer's ability to do so is governed by section 9–604, which provides:

(a) **[Enforcement: personal and real property.]** If a security agreement covers both personal and real property, a secured party may proceed: (1) under this part as to the personal property without prejudicing any rights with respect to the real property; or (2) as to both the personal property and the real property in accordance with the rights with respect to the real property, in which case the other provisions of this part do not apply.

(b) **[Enforcement: fixtures.]** Subject to subsection (c), if a security agreement covers goods that are or become fixtures, a secured party may proceed: (1) under this part; or (2) in accordance with the rights with respect to real property, in which case the other provisions of this part do not apply.

(c) **[Removal of fixtures.]** Subject to the other provisions of this part, if a secured party holding a security interest in fixtures has priority over all owners and encumbrancers of the real property, the secured party, after default, may remove the collateral from the real property.

(d) **[Injury caused by removal.]** A secured party that removes collateral shall promptly reimburse any encumbrancer or owner of the real property, other than the debtor, for the cost of repair of any physical injury caused by the removal. The secured party need not reimburse the encumbrancer or owner for any diminution in value of the real property caused by the absence of the goods removed or by any necessity of replacing them. A person entitled to reimbursement may refuse permission to remove until the secured party gives adequate assurance for the performance of the obligation to reimburse.

Thus (as should be intuitive), Manufacturer cannot remove the refrigerator if it lacks priority over Bank's mortgage. In other words, if Manufacturer is not first in line, its security interest in the refrigerator is of little value. Instead, Manufacturer could only (a) wait to enforce its lien until after Bank's senior mortgage lien is satisfied, (b) assert its lien against any surplus proceeds if Bank subsequently forecloses its senior mortgage, or (c) assert any rights it may be able to claim against the land under the jurisdiction's laws governing mechanics' liens (discussed in Chapter 9, Section C infra).

By contrast, if Manufacturer has priority, it may remove the fixture and proceed to sell it in a foreclosure sale governed by Article 9, even over the objection of Bank. Bank could not complain that the removal of the refrigerator would lower the value of the land because of the absence of the refrigerator. If, however, removal of the refrigerator would do other physical damage to the building (e.g., if removal of the refrigerator would require removing and then replacing a wall at a cost of $1,500), Manufacturer would have to reimburse Bank for the cost to repair that damage.

3. *The fixture secured party's rights in a real estate foreclosure sale.* Suppose that in the example in note 2, Butcher defaults to both Manufacturer and Bank, and Bank schedules a foreclosure sale of the building. Suppose further that Manufacturer has first priority in the walk-in refrigerator. Manufacturer could remove the refrigerator, but does not want to do that because it fears the refrigerator would bring a low price if removed and sold as used equipment. Instead, Manufacturer wants to leave the refrigerator in the building, allow the building to be sold at foreclosure, and then claim first priority against the foreclosure sale proceeds. Can Manufacturer do this?

Prior to the revision of Article 9 in 2000, the answer was no, at least according to the leading case, Maplewood Bank & Trust v. Sears, Roebuck & Co., 265 N.J.Super. 25, 625 A.2d 537 (App.Div. 1993). In *Maplewood*, the court held that a secured party's right to priority in a fixture was limited to its removal and that a secured party had no claim against the land itself— and thus no claim to the proceeds of the foreclosure sale. Instead, the court held, the secured party continued to have its priority in the fixture and could enforce its security interest by removing the fixture (even after the foreclosure sale).

This decision was understandably criticized, because in some cases certain fixtures (especially ones that are particularly adapted to a building) may be worth substantially more "in place" than they would be if removed. Thus, in the 2000 Article 9 revisions, the drafters of the UCC overruled *Maplewood* by enacting section 9–604(b) (quoted in note 2 above). Section 9–604(b) allows a fixture secured party to choose to enforce its interest either under Article 9's enforcement provisions or under applicable state real estate law. If the secured party enforces its interest under real estate law, none of

Article 9's enforcement provisions apply. Thus, if the state's real estate laws permitted Manufacturer to join in Bank's foreclosure action and enforce its interest in that proceeding, Manufacturer could claim first priority against the foreclosure-sale proceeds. By contrast, if the state's real estate law does not permit Manufacturer to join in the Bank's foreclosure, then the buyer at Bank's foreclosure sale would take title to the land subject to Manufacturer's security interest in the fixture, which Manufacturer could enforce pursuant to Article 9.

E. RIGHTS IN CROPS

FLETCHER V. STILLMAN

Missouri Court of Appeals, Southern District, 1996
934 S.W.2d 597

SHRUM, JUDGE. . . . On September 28, 1992, Plaintiffs bought a New Madrid County farm at a foreclosure sale. Located on the farm at the time of the foreclosure sale was a matured but unharvested soybean crop that had been planted by a renter. When the renter harvested the soybeans after September 28, 1992, the landlord's one-third share of the crop sale proceeds was placed in a joint account pending resolution of the dispute. Plaintiffs then filed this suit in which they claimed entitlement to the crop proceeds on the theory that any crops not yet harvested passed with the land. Contrarily, Defendant claims that she is entitled to the crop proceeds because the crops had matured before the foreclosure sale, i.e., they were ready for harvest even though they had not yet been severed. The trial court concluded that it was bound by the case of *Holdsworth v. Key*, 520 S.W.2d 637 (Mo.App.1975), and found for Plaintiffs.

Holdsworth contains this language:

> "In Missouri, it is a settled legal principle of longstanding that unless otherwise provided in the deed of trust, unsevered crops standing on mortgaged land at the time of a foreclosure sale are subject to the lien of the deed of trust and pass to the purchaser of the land at the foreclosure sale. *Hayden v. Burkemper*, 101 Mo. 644, 14 S.W. 767 (1890); *Farmers' Bank of Hickory v. Bradley*, 315 Mo. 811, 288 S.W. 774 (banc 1926). The only way a growing crop can be relieved of the lien of a deed of trust is by an actual severance of the crop from the ground prior to the foreclosure sale."

Id. at 639[1–2].

Nevertheless, Defendant insists that the trial court erred in granting judgment for Plaintiffs because *Holdsworth* and other Missouri cases analyzed in her brief dealt with crops that were still growing at the time of sale and did not involve a matured crop as existed here. Defendant asserts that crop maturity distinguishes this case from any heretofore decided in Missouri, thus this is a case of first impression. With that as her premise, Defendant urges this court to adopt "the more equitable and fair rule, applied by numerous jurisdictions, [which] is that if the crop is mature and no longer drawing any nutrients or sustenance from the real estate, it is personalty, and does not pass with the land." Jurisdictions that adhere to this rule do so on the theory that once a crop matures and is no longer being supported by the soil, a constructive severance occurs so that the crop thereafter bears the same relation to the land on which it stood as it would if stored in a warehouse or barn. *See, e.g. Wood v. Wood*, 116 Colo. 593, 183 P.2d 889 (1947); *First National Bank v. Beegle*, 52 Kan. 709, 35 P. 814 (1894); *Hecht v. Dittman*, 56 Iowa 679, 7 N.W. 495 (1880). * * *

In response, Plaintiffs contend that this is not a case of first impression and that indeed the concept of constructive severance as contended for by Defendant is a doctrine that has been rejected by Missouri courts. In support of their argument, Plaintiffs cite *Farmers' Bank of Hickory v. Bradley*, 315 Mo. 811, 288 S.W. 774 (banc 1926); *Starkey v. Powell*, 315 Mo. 846, 288 S.W. 776 (banc 1926); and *Vogt [v. Cunningham]*, 50 Mo.App. 136 [(1892)]. We find that the three cases Plaintiffs rely on, when read together, settle the issue contrary to Defendant's contentions. * * *

In *Farmers' Bank of Hickory v. Bradley*, landowners gave a deed of trust on their farm to secure a note. After defaulting on the real estate note, they gave a chattel mortgage to [Bank] for "75 acres of corn located on the farm. . . ." After the chattel mortgage was given and while the corn was still standing and unharvested, the farm was sold to Bradley at foreclosure. Bradley took possession of the farm and its crops, which prompted [Bank] to file an action in replevin against Bradley to recover the corn. In effect, the trial court instructed the jury to return a verdict for [Bank]. When Bradley appealed, the Kansas City Court of Appeals reversed, holding that the deed of trust lien was superior to that of the chattel mortgage lien since the "growing corn crop" had not actually been severed from the ground at the time of the foreclosure sale. * * * Once *Bradley* was transferred [to the Supreme Court], the Supreme Court * * * sustained the decision of the Kansas City Court of Appeals and disapproved the contrary doctrine of constructive severance * * *. *Bradley*, 288 S.W. at 776. In so doing, the *Bradley* court said: "We have uniformly held that neither the owner of the land nor his grantee could free the growing crop of the lien of the deed of trust, except by an actual severance from the soil before possession taken or foreclosure had under the deed of trust." *Id.* at 775[2].

Starkey v. Powell was a case handed down on the same day as *Bradley*. In *Starkey*, a landowner gave a deed of trust on his farm in 1922.

Later, in September 1923, while the farm was still subject to the lien of the deed of trust, the landowner sold a corn crop that was on the farm to Starkey at a public sale. On October 22, 1923, the holder of the deed of trust caused a foreclosure sale to be held and Powell bought the farm. When Powell bought the farm, a part of the corn crop purchased earlier by Starkey remained unsevered in the field. Within "a few days after November 1, 1923," Powell gathered and removed the corn, prompting Starkey to sue him for trespass and conversion. The trial court gave the jury a peremptory instruction to find for Starkey. Powell appealed, charging that the trial court "erred in holding that there was a constructive severance of the crop." *Id.* at 777. The Kansas City Court of Appeals agreed and reversed * * * . On transfer the Supreme Court held that the case was controlled by *Bradley*, thus clearly rejecting the doctrine of constructive severance of crops.

* * * *Bradley* and *Starkey* require that we reject Defendant's urging that she was entitled to the crop proceeds because the soybeans had matured prior to the foreclosure sale, an argument which is grounded upon the doctrine of constructive severance, a theory clearly rejected in *Bradley* and *Starkey*. Although Defendant claims her case is distinguishable from *Bradley* and *Starkey* because the crops in those cases were not matured at the time of the foreclosure sale, it is a distinction without a difference. *Bradley* and *Starkey* did not turn on the narrow question of crop maturity, but rather were decided on the broader basis that Missouri would not recognize the doctrine of constructive severance of crops and that a crop can only be freed from the lien of a deed of trust by actual severance. *Bradley*, 288 S.W. at 775[2]; *Starkey*, 288 S.W. at 777. The judgment is affirmed.

NOTES

1. *Foreclosure purchaser vs. mortgagor. Fletcher* represents the normal view that in a dispute about growing crops between a foreclosure sale purchaser and a mortgagor, the former usually prevails "on the theory that the mortgagor has pledged the crops, as well as the land itself, as security for the loan." 9 Richard R. Powell & Patrick J. Rohan, Powell on Real Property § 58.03(2) (1997). Some courts, as *Fletcher* also points out, temper the foregoing by applying "constructive severance" after the crop has matured.

2. *Foreclosure purchaser vs. mortgagor's lessee.* Suppose in *Fletcher* that the foreclosure purchasers had claimed the *tenant's* share of the soybean crop. Should the foreclosure purchasers prevail in that context? Here a somewhat different analysis is often applied. If the lease was senior to the foreclosed mortgage, the tenant is entitled to the crops because his or her lease rights were unaffected by the foreclosure. Where, however, a subordinate lease is destroyed by foreclosure, the results are less predictable. On the one hand, some courts reject the lessee's post-foreclosure claim to the

crop by utilizing the severance analysis reflected in *Fletcher* and other foreclosure purchaser vs. mortgagor cases. On the other hand, many courts use the "emblements" concept to defeat the foreclosure purchaser. Under this approach, unsevered annual crops "produced primarily through the labor and industry of the land's possessor" are treated for this purpose as "personalty." 9 Richard R. Powell & Patrick J. Rohan, Powell on Real Property § 58.03 (1997). The latter concept is relied on because of the "uncertainty in the duration of the possessory right injected by the foreclosure of the mortgage." Id. at § 58.03(2).

3.   *Foreclosure purchaser vs. holder of Article 9 security interest in crops.* The crop entitlement question becomes more complex when a claim of a holder of an Article 9 security interest in crops is asserted against a real estate foreclosure purchaser. Note that the *Bradley* case, discussed in *Fletcher*, followed a traditional common law approach that the deed of trust lien trumped the chattel mortgage lien of the crop financer because "the 'growing corn crop' had not actually been severed from the ground at the time of the foreclosure sale." Under this approach, the creation of the chattel security interest in the crops did not represent a "constructive severance."

This analysis, however, pre-dated the adoption in every state of Article 9 of the Uniform Commercial Code. Article 9 governs security interests in "goods," and the drafters of Article 9 defined "goods" to include crops. Thus, Article 9 clearly contemplated that a lender could take and enforce a security interest in a farmer's crops under Article 9. This left open the question, however, of whether a lien could still arise against growing crops under real estate law—and, if so, the respective priority of a real estate mortgagee and a person holding an Article 9 security interest in crops.

Some courts and commentators took the view that by defining "goods" to include crops, the drafters of Article 9 intended for Article 9 to be the exclusive means of creating and enforcing a security interest in crops. See, e.g., Barkley Clark, The Law of Secured Transactions Under the Uniform Commercial Code ¶ 8.05[1] (1993) ("Article 9 is the exclusive statutory scheme to cover security interests in growing crops, and the mortgagee should not be able to claim a security interest under real estate law."); 4 White & Summers, Uniform Commercial Code § 30–7, at 44–45 (4th ed. 1995) ("Under a proper interpretation of Article 9, a real estate mortgagee cannot subject crops to his mortgage merely by complying with real estate mortgage law."). Certainly, it makes sense to conclude that by defining "goods" to include crops, the drafters of Article 9 intended for any priority conflicts as to crops to be governed by Article 9. Otherwise, farmers might have difficulty obtaining crop financing, because suppliers and farm lenders "would be forced to gamble upon the timing of foreclosure proceedings and even the weather in a race to sever crops" before a foreclosure sale of the land became final. Moritz Implement Co. v. Matthews, 265 Kan. 179, 959 P.2d 886 (1998). However, the statements of Clark and White and Summers may be overbroad to the extent they suggest that a real estate mortgagee could never claim an interest in crops under a mortgage. If a foreclosure sale occurs, there is a crop growing on the land at the time of the sale, and there is no conflicting Article 9 security interest in that crop, there is no good reason why ownership of the crop should not pass to the foreclosure sale purchaser under the general principle articulated in *Fletcher v. Stillman.*

To a significant extent, any lingering confusion has now been resolved by the 2000 amendments to Article 9, which provide clearly that a perfected security interest in crops has priority over the conflicting interest of the holder of a mortgage on the real property on which the crops are growing. U.C.C. § 9–334(i). Comment 12 to section 9–334 acknowledges that "[i]n some jurisdictions, a mortgage of real property may cover crops" under real estate law, but the mortgagee's interest is subordinate to a perfected Article 9 security interest in the crop. Given this clear statutory directive, a creditor "would be foolish indeed to rely on uncertain remnants of real estate law for creating consensual crop encumbrances." Eldon H. Reiley, Security Interests in Personal Property § 25:14 (3d ed. 2003).

F. FEDERAL TAX LIENS

NELSON, WHITMAN, BURKHART & FREYERMUTH, REAL ESTATE FINANCE LAW
(6th ed.2014)*

The Federal Tax Lien Act (FTLA) grants to the United States a lien on all property belonging to a taxpayer who fails to pay federal taxes following proper demand.[242] This lien relates back to the date on which the taxes became due,[243] and attaches to all existing and after-acquired real and personal property in which the taxpayer has an interest.[244] Because the lien arises by operation of law, it is a "secret lien" of which third parties dealing with the taxpayer may be unaware. Thus, the FTLA requires the IRS to file a public notice of the lien to make it effective against the rights of subsequent purchasers, judgment creditors, mechanics' lienholders, and holders of consensual security interests.[245]

The first-in-time, first-in-right principle provides the baseline for establishing the priority of conflicting property interests, including federal tax liens. Nevertheless, there are several situations in which a federal tax lien may take priority over a prior-in-time lien. One situation involves an unperfected security interest. A security interest arising under state law is deemed to exist for FTLA purposes only if the collateral is "in existence" and the interest "has become protected under local law as against a subsequent judgment lien arising out of an unsecured

---

*   Reprinted with permission of Thomson Reuters/West.

[242] 26 U.S.C.A. § 6321.

[243] 26 U.S.C.A. § 6322.

[244] 26 U.S.C.A. § 6321; Treas. Reg. § 301.6321–1.

[245] 26 U.S.C.A. § 6323(a).

obligation."[246] Thus, for example, the holder of an unperfected Article 9 security interest—whose claim is subordinate to a judgment lien creditor[247]—would have no "security interest" within the meaning of the FTLA, and thus would be subordinate to a later-filed federal tax lien.

By contrast, the priority of an unrecorded real estate mortgage *vis-a-vis* a federal tax lien depends upon the state's recording act. If the state's law requires recording to make a mortgage effective as against later judgment creditors, then the holder of an unrecorded mortgage would have no "security interest" within the meaning of the FTLA and would be subordinate to a later-filed federal tax lien.[248] In many states, however, even an unrecorded mortgage is effective against later judgment creditors, either because the judgment creditor is not considered to have paid value as a "purchaser" under the recording act or because the judgment lien statute imposes a lien only on the judgment debtor's actual real property, not his ostensible property as disclosed by a title examination.[249] In those states, an unrecorded mortgage would still have priority against a later-filed federal tax lien.

The "Choateness" Doctrine and Construction Financing

Another circumstance in which a federal tax lien may obtain priority over a prior-in-time lien involves lending secured by future advances. An understanding of this potential concern requires an explanation of the "choateness" doctrine under federal tax law. Even if a secured party has a perfected security interest before the government files notice of its tax lien, the secured party will not have priority over the tax lien unless its security interest is "choate." As explained in United States v. McDermott,[250] a security interest is choate if the identity of the secured party, the property to which the interest attaches, and the amount of the debt are all "established." In a typical residential mortgage transaction involving a single mortgage loan and a security interest in the borrower's home, the choateness doctrine poses no problem. For example, suppose Bank holds a recorded mortgage on Taxpayer's home securing repayment of the mortgage loan Taxpayer used to acquire the home. When Taxpayer fails to pay federal income taxes, the IRS files a tax lien notice. In this situation, the secured party (Bank), the collateral (the home), and the outstanding balance of the mortgage debt are all known.[251] Thus, Bank's mortgage unquestionably has priority over the federal tax lien.

---

[246] 26 U.S.C.A. § 6323(h)(1)(A).

[247] U.C.C. § 9–317(a)(2)(A).

[248] See, e.g., Citizens State Bank v. United States, 932 F.2d 490 (6th Cir.1991) (applying Kentucky law).

[249] Stoebuck & Whitman, Property § 11.10 nn.13–16 (3d ed.2000).

[250] 507 U.S. 447 (1993).

[251] The fact that the balance of the debt might increase in the future with the accrual of interest is irrelevant to the choateness analysis. If the Bank has priority over the federal tax lien

The choateness doctrine presents a conceptual challenge, however, when a secured party attempts to enforce a lien against property securing future advances. For example, suppose that Bank holds a perfected security interest in all of the assets of ABC Company (ABC), securing a $2 million line of credit. At the time ABC fails to pay its payroll taxes and the IRS files a tax lien notice, the outstanding balance on the line of credit is $1.1 million. Over the next week, before Bank learns of the tax lien filing, ABC borrows another $200,000 under its line of credit, increasing the balance to $1.3 million. In this situation, the advances to ABC after the tax lien filing would not satisfy the choateness doctrine, as the debt had not been "established" at $1.3 million prior to the tax lien filing. As a result, under the FTLA, Bank would not have a "security interest" in the collateral to the extent of the $200,000 in future advances[252] on the date of the tax lien notice. Thus, without some exception to the choateness doctrine, while Bank would have priority in the collateral to the extent of the $1.1 million balance on the date of the tax lien filing, Bank's interest would be subordinate to the IRS to the extent of the additional advances.

The choateness doctrine thus creates a substantial practical problem for a construction mortgagee. As discussed in greater detail elsewhere,[253] a construction mortgagee typically advances the loan proceeds in stages (or "draws") as construction actually proceeds. Because the typical construction mortgage provides that the mortgage secures future advances, the construction mortgagee expects that it will have the same priority for each and every draw under the construction loan agreement. But the choateness doctrine creates the potential that the filing of a tax lien notice could "freeze" the mortgagee's priority as of the date of the tax lien notice and subordinate the mortgagee's lien with respect to later advances. This might seem particularly unwelcome to the mortgagee to the extent that the mortgagee made advances after the tax lien notice was filed but without actual knowledge of that filing.

To ameliorate the effect of the choateness doctrine and protect the reasonable expectations of the construction lender, the FTLA provides that a federal tax lien will not have priority over a conflicting security interest to the extent that it (a) secures certain post-tax-lien-notice advances under a "real property construction or improvement financing agreement" and (b) "is protected under local law against a judgment lien

---

as to the principal amount of the debt, the Bank will likewise have priority as to interest accruing on that debt. 26 U.S.C.A. § 6323(e)(1).

[252] Under 26 U.S.C.A. § 6323(h)(1), a security interest exists only to the extent that "[its] holder has parted with money or money's worth."

[253] See infra § 12.1.

arising, as of the time of tax lien filing, out of an unsecured obligation."[254] Thus, suppose that O enters into a construction loan agreement with Bank to finance the construction of O's home on Blackacre, and grants Bank a construction mortgage on Blackacre. The mortgage, recorded on February 1, provides that Bank will make advances to O as construction proceeds. On March 1, the IRS files a tax lien notice against O based upon O's nonpayment of federal taxes. Construction continues, with Bank making advances on June 1, September 1, and upon completion on December 1. If under applicable state law, Bank would have had priority for these three advances over a hypothetical judgment creditor who had acquired her lien as of March 1, then Bank's security interest will have priority over the federal tax lien.[255]

Non-Construction-Related Future Advances

In some cases, a mortgage may cover future advances even though such advances are unrelated to the construction of improvements on land. For example, suppose that Owner grants Bank a second mortgage on her home on February 1 to secure the repayment of a home equity line of credit that Owner intends to use to pay her child's college tuition expenses. Then, on March 1, the IRS files a tax lien notice against Owner. In this situation, the FTLA's exception for a "real property construction or improvement financing agreement" would not apply to protect any advances made by Bank after March 1 to pay the child's tuition expenses. Nevertheless, the choateness doctrine would present the same essential risks to Bank in this situation; Bank might expect its priority to date from February 1, but the March 1 tax lien filing could potentially "freeze" the Bank's priority as of that date and subordinate the Bank's lien with respect to advances made thereafter. Again, this would be unwelcome news to the Bank, particularly if the Bank made future advances without actual knowledge of the March 1 tax lien filing.

The FTLA also ameliorates the impact of the choateness doctrine in this situation, but only as to certain future advances. The FTLA provides that a federal tax lien does not have priority over

> a security interest which came into existence after tax lien filing by reason of disbursements made before the 46th day after the date of tax lien filing, or (if earlier) before the person making such disbursements had actual notice or knowledge of tax lien filing, but only if such security interest (1) is in property . . . covered by the terms of a written agreement entered into before

---

[254] 26 U.S.C.A. § 6323(c)(1). The term "real property construction or improvement financing agreement" includes "an agreement to make cash disbursements to finance (i) the construction of improvement of real property, [or] (ii) a contract to construct or improve real property . . . ." 26 U.S.C.A. § 6323(c)(3)(A).

[255] See Treas. Reg. § 301.6323(c)–2(d), Example 1. For a detailed discussion of the state law rules governing future advances priority vis à vis intervening lien creditors, see § 12.7 infra.

tax lien filing, and (2) is protected under local law against a judgment lien arising, as of the time of tax lien filing, out of an unsecured obligation.[256]

This provision establishes a maximum 45-day window period in which a lender can obtain protection for future advances, subject to being shortened by actual knowledge of the tax lien filing. For example, suppose that when IRS files its tax lien notice against Owner on March 1, there is a zero balance on Owner's home equity line of credit. On April 1, Bank (which does not have knowledge of the tax lien) allows Owner to draw $5,000 on the line of credit to pay her child's tuition bill. On May 1, Bank (again without knowledge of the tax lien) allows Owner to draw an additional $5,000 on the line of credit to pay other college-related expenses. Further, assume that under state law, Bank would have priority over a judgment lien creditor as of March 1 with respect to both advances.[257] Under 26 U.S.C. § 6323(d), Bank will have priority over the IRS to the extent of the $5,000 advance of April 1, but not with respect to the $5,000 advance of May 1, which fell outside the 45-day window period. By contrast, suppose instead that on March 15, Bank had received a letter from the IRS advising Bank of its tax lien and providing a copy of its tax lien filing. In this situation, the Bank's knowledge of the tax lien terminates the window period for future advance priority, and thus Bank's mortgage would be subordinate to the federal tax lien with respect to both the April 1 and May 1 advances.

How can a mortgagee protect itself against this risk? Obviously, the lender can simply refuse to make advances to the borrower once the lender has knowledge of the federal tax lien. But because the window period never exceeds 45 days, the lender's mere lack of knowledge is not sufficient beyond that period. The lender thus cannot be certain of priority for a future advance unless it has checked the appropriate filing office within the preceding 45 days and did not find a tax lien notice on file against the borrower.[258]

NOTE

The Choateness Doctrine and Rents. Suppose that Developer owns a building subject to a recorded deed of trust and assignment of rents in favor of Bank. The building is partially occupied by Tenant A, who is paying rent to Developer under a long-term lease entered into several years ago. Now

---

[256] 26 U.S.C.A. § 6323(d).

[257] For a detailed discussion of the state law rules governing future advances priority vis à vis intervening lien creditors, see § 12.7 infra.

[258] In the case of real property, the IRS must file a tax lien notice in the office designated by the law of the state in which the property is situated. 26 U.S.C.A. § 6323(f)(1)(A)(i). Under the Uniform Federal Lien Registration Act (UFLRA), enacted in 39 states, the IRS must file a tax lien notice with respect to real estate in the real property recording office for the municipality where the land is located. UFLRA § 2(b).

suppose that the IRS files a notice of tax lien against Developer in the appropriate filing office, only days before Developer enters into a new lease for the remaining space in the building with Tenant B. As between Bank and the IRS, which has priority as to rents collected from Tenant A? From Tenant B?

As explained above, the FTLA recognizes a security interest only if the collateral is "in existence" and the interest "has become protected under local law as against a subsequent judgment lien arising out of an unsecured obligation." Developer's right to collect the rents accruing under Tenant A's lease arose upon the signing of the lease, prior to the tax lien. Because Bank holds a prior recorded assignment of rents, Bank has priority over the IRS as to those rents. But what about the rents accruing under Tenant B's lease? That lease did not come into existence until after the IRS filed its tax lien notice. In this situation, the IRS may argue that the choateness doctrine was not satisfied and that the IRS thus had priority over Bank as to the rents arising under Tenant B's lease.

In making this argument, the IRS analogizes a lender's interest in post-tax-lien rents to a lender's interest in after-acquired accounts receivable. If the taxpayer sells goods or provides services on credit (and thus becomes entitled to be paid) after the IRS files a tax lien, the right to payment did not exist at the time of the tax lien notice. Thus, even if a lender had a prior perfected security interest in all of the taxpayer's present and after-acquired accounts receivable, the lender's lien would be "inchoate" as to the accounts that arose after the IRS tax lien filing. As a result, the lender's prior-perfected security interest in those particular accounts would not take priority over the tax lien, except to the limited extent provided in FTLA § 6323(c).

Technically, the right to collect rents under a lease of land does fit within the definition of "account" under UCC Article 9. U.C.C. § 9–102(a)(2)(i) ("account" includes "a right to payment of a monetary obligation . . . for property that has been or is to be sold, leased, licensed, assigned, or otherwise disposed of . . ."). Does this mean that rents arising under the lease with Tenant B were like after-acquired accounts and thus inchoate so as to give the IRS priority as to those rents? Or should Bank's prior recorded assignment of rents give it priority over the IRS as to the rents arising under Tenant B's lease?

In Bloomfield State Bank v. United States, 644 F.3d 521 (7th Cir.2011), Judge Richard Posner provided the first and only reported appellate opinion addressing the issue, concluding that the prior recorded assignee of rents would have priority over the federal tax lien. Judge Posner rejected the argument that the rents were akin to after-acquired accounts receivable, instead treating the rents as "proceeds" of the land without regard to the timing of the lease:

> The real estate that generated the rental income at issue in this case existed when the mortgage was issued and thus before the

tax lien attached; the rental income was proceeds of that property, which preexisted the tax lien. . . .

. . . [B]ecause the bank had a lien on the real estate, the rentals were proceeds. By virtue of the rental-income provision in the mortgage [*i.e.*, the assignment of rents], the bank had a separate lien on the rents, but that is not the lien on which it is relying to trump the tax lien. The lien on which it is relying is the lien on the real estate. If an asset that secures a loan is sold and a receivable generated, the receivable becomes the security, substituting for the original asset. The sort of receivable to which the statute denies priority over a federal tax lien is one that does not match an existing asset; a month's rent is a receivable that matches the value of the real property for that month. [644 F.3d at 525–526.]

Do you agree with Posner's analysis? Why might it be appropriate to equate "rents" and "proceeds"? See R. Wilson Freyermuth, Of Hotel Revenues, Rents, and Formalism in the Bankruptcy Courts: Implications for Reforming Commercial Real Estate Finance, 40 UCLA L. Rev. 1461, 1533 (1993).

G. WRAP-AROUND MORTGAGES

The owner of income-producing real estate in a rising-interest market may be faced with a dilemma. Assume the property has appreciated in value since the owner originally purchased and financed it. Now the owner would like to recover in cash some of that increment in value, while at the same time retaining ownership of the property. The classic solution, of course, is refinancing—that is, obtaining a new mortgage loan and using part of the proceeds to discharge the old loan, with the remainder being available for the owner's other purposes.

However, if interest rates have risen substantially since the original loan was obtained, the owner will be most reluctant to pay it off. Indeed, it would be economically foolish to do so, for the low-interest loan has substantial intrinsic value. As an alternative, the owner may consider seeking second mortgage financing, but may be dissatisfied at the prospect of paying the very high interest rates usually demanded by second mortgage lenders.

In other market conditions, an owner of real estate may be faced with a similar problem for a different reason. If the existing financing carries a high interest rate relative to current market rates, the owner would probably like to pay it off, but may be deterred from doing so by a large prepayment penalty; worse, the loan may be "locked-in", with the lender having no obligation (and no inclination) to accept prepayment at all.

The economics of the wraparound mortgage. Under either set of conditions described above, a possible solution to the owner's problem is the *wrap-around mortgage*, sometimes termed the "all-inclusive mortgage" or (in states where the deed of trust is the common land security instrument) the "all-inclusive deed of trust." Its operation in the rising market situation is illustrated as follows. Assume the owner's present financing is a first mortgage loan obtained from a savings and loan association 10 years ago. Its original principal amount was $124,000, and it carries an 8% interest rate and an original term of 25 years. Its monthly payment is $957. 15 years remain on this mortgage, and its principal balance has been paid down to about $100,000. The owner's property is now worth $300,000, and if it were unencumbered, the owner would be able to obtain a conventional loan of $240,000 (80% of the property's value) from a bank. However, the owner wants to retain the existing financing if possible, because current rates on first mortgages are (let us stipulate) 14%.

The owner's banker suggests the following transaction. The bank will advance $140,000 to the owner in cash, and will take back from the owner a mortgage on the property. Because the existing mortgage will remain in effect, this new mortgage to the bank will be technically a second mortgage. The bank will have the owner execute a promissory note for $240,000, which is the sum of (a) the amount the bank will advance and (b) the balance on the existing mortgage. As payments on the existing (or "underlying") mortgage to the savings and loan association fall due each month, the bank will pay them out of the payments it receives from the owner. The new loan thus "wraps around" the old one. The note to the bank will earn interest at 12% and will call for level payments of $2,880 per month over a 15-year term.

From the bank's viewpoint, the transaction seems not so risky as a traditional second mortgage. If the owner defaults, the bank has a "very early warning" system (because all payments are being made directly to it). It can continue to make payments on the first mortgage if it wishes, thus ensuring that no default will occur on that mortgage. And it can foreclose its wrap-around mortgage with the confidence that the property's value is sufficient to support the bank's debt even with the continued existence and priority of the first mortgage. Because of this tight control exercised by the wrap lender, the wraparound loan is widely regarded as more closely analogous to a first than a second mortgage.

From an economic viewpoint the bank is also well-satisfied. It will receive payments from the owner each month of $2,880—the standard payments on a 15-year 12% loan of $240,000. It will transmit to the first mortgagee $957 each month, the full payment due on the senior loan. The difference, $1,923, will be retained by the bank. Because the bank has advanced only $140,000 of its own funds, the $1,923 net payment it retains is the equivalent of the payment on a loan with an interest rate of about 14.6%! (You may easily verify these figures with any standard mortgage payment table.) In effect, the bank has "leveraged" itself into a very attractive yield. If one thinks of the bank as having made a $240,000, 12% loan, it has been able to "borrow" $100,000 of that capital at an 8% rate. The owner is not dissatisfied with this arrangement. The owner's overall interest cost of the funds is still below the prevailing rate in the commercial loan market, and the owner has $140,000 in tax-free cash.

The wrap-around approach is obviously better for the owner than refinancing, because a new first mortgage would carry an interest rate of 14% rather than 12%. Is the wraparound also better than merely obtaining a second mortgage for $140,000 while leaving the existing first mortgage in place? If the owner could obtain a second mortgage for $140,000 with a 14% interest rate and a 15-year term, its payments would be $1,864 per month. Because the payments on the first mortgage are $957 per month, the total cash outlay toward debt service would be the sum of these two payments, or $2,821 per month. Compared with the wraparound approach's monthly payment of $2880, the second mortgage seems more attractive.

But this conclusion is fallacious, because a "straight" second mortgage probably will not be available at a 14% rate; if that is the "prime" rate for first mortgages, the rate on a second mortgage loan will probably be 3% or 4% higher. To illustrate, if the rate charged on the second mortgage were 17%, the payments on it would be $2,155. If this amount is added to the payment on the first mortgage of $957, the total monthly outlay would be $3,112, considerably more than the payment using the wraparound approach. Because the wraparound is seen by most lenders as being nearly as safe as a first mortgage, it is a way to get second mortgage financing on interest terms approaching those of first mortgages.

The foregoing example shows how the wrap-around mortgage can be used in refinancing by an existing owner. Essentially the same technique can be employed to finance a purchase by O of property which is already subject to an existing mortgage. O may obtain a new loan from the bank, which will agree to make the payments on the existing loan and will collect installments from O sufficient to cover the payments on both loans.

Alternatively, such a transaction may be structured without any involvement by a third-party lender; the seller may take back a mortgage and note from O, and will undertake to make the payments on the existing first mortgage. This arrangement may be termed a purchase-money wrap-around. In many areas of the nation a similar concept is commonly employed by sellers of land on installment contracts; the buyer makes payments on the contract to the seller, while the seller continues to make payments on a preexisting mortgage loan. The purchase-money wrap-around raises several unique issues which are explored in the notes below.

In cases in which the existing first mortgage carries a rate at or above the current market, but cannot be paid off on acceptable terms, the wrap-around mortgage will not produce the yield leverage described in the example above. But even so, it may be the only feasible means of refinancing or financing a sale without the payment of inordinately high rates for junior financing.

Treatments of the wrap-around concept include Gunning, The Wrap-Around Mortgage ... Friend or U.F.O.?, 2 Real Est.Rev. 35 (Summer 1972); Leider, How to Wrap Around a Mortgage, 4 Real Est.Rev. 29 (Winter 1975); Comment, The Wrap-around Mortgage: A Critical Inquiry, 21 U.C.L.A.L.Rev. 1529 (1974); Annot., Validity and Effect of "Wrap-around" Mortgages Whereby Purchaser Incorporates into Agreed Payments to Grantor Latter's Obligation on Initial Mortgage, 36 A.L.R. 4th 144 (1985).

Foreclosing wrap-around mortgages. Of all issues surrounding wrap-around mortgages, perhaps the most perplexing revolve around the mechanics of foreclosure. If the wrap borrower defaults and the wrap lender forecloses, what is the balance on the debt? How much should an intelligent buyer bid? What is the proper disposition of the sale proceeds?

To put these questions in context, assume the following facts. (The names and amounts in the actual cases we cite below have been adjusted to conform to these hypothetical facts.) ME1 holds the underlying mortgage with a balance of $300,000. ME2 holds the wrap loan, with a balance of $800,000. The unencumbered fair value of the property is $1 million. If MR (the wrap borrower) defaults and ME2 forecloses, the first question is whether the balance on the loan, as announced in advertisements and at the sale, should be $500,000 (the wrap debt minus the underlying debt) or $800,000 (the full wrap debt). It would be desirable if this question were answered in the wrap mortgage itself. As one treatise puts it,

> Since the beneficiary of the overriding [wrap] deed of trust is obligated to pay the senior included [underlying] debt, it should be provided expressly that a failure to pay the overriding note by its terms is a default under the overriding note and deed of trust only. The documents should also provide that the purchaser at the foreclosure sale is only purchasing the [wrap] beneficiary's equity, and that the amount of the defaulted debt, and therefore the beneficiary's bid at the sale, is only the amount of his equity, after deduction of the amount due on the senior included debt; therefore the purchaser at the sale receives his title subject to the senior included lien.

Harry D. Miller & Marvin B. Starr, Current Law of California Real Estate § 3.22 (1975), as quoted in Armsey v. Channel Associates, Inc., 184 Cal.App.3d 833, 229 Cal.Rptr. 509 (1986).

But suppose no such language appears in the wrap note or deed of trust. In FPCI RE-HAB 01 v. E & G Investments, Ltd., 207 Cal.App.3d 1018, 255 Cal.Rptr. 157 (1989), ME2 announced that the full wrap debt ($800,000) was owed. ME2 then became the successful bidder, making a full credit bid of $800,000. A junior lienholder (we'll call it ME3) attacked the propriety of this procedure.

[ME3] contends that had the trustee not advertised the total indebtedness under the [wraparound mortgage] was required in cash to cure the default, other purchasers would probably have bid at the foreclosure sale, and [ME3] would have received, from a fair sale, at least the amount due it under its note and deed of trust. In support of this argument, it points out that [ME2] sold the property shortly after the foreclosure sale for $1,125,000 to Dennis Waldman who, although present, had not bid at the foreclosure sale.

[ME3] also asserts that under the terms of [ME2's] wraparound mortgage, ME2's] credit bid should have been reduced in an amount equivalent to the then unpaid principal balance of the included notes. Since the notice of foreclosure specified that the amount required to purchase the property was [$800,000, ME2] should have had to pay the amount over its unpaid principal balance in cash and the senior lienors should have been paid off. Consequently, [ME3] asserts that [ME2] alleged the total indebtedness due only to prevent prospective purchasers from attending the sale who might have bid [$300,000] and taken the property subject to the senior encumbrances. * * *

[ME2's wraparound mortgage] provided that the total indebtedness was all due and payable in the event of default. Consequently, the notice of amount due at the foreclosure sale was correct. Although the [mortgage] also provided that the beneficiary must deduct from its credit bid the amount of principal owing on the senior encumbrances, we fail to ascertain how the discrepancy between the terms of the [mortgage] and the manner in which the sale was conducted aids [ME3's] cause. Its theory of damages is based upon speculation. [207 Cal.App.3d at 1020–1023, 255 Cal.Rptr. at 159–161.]

To the same effect is Concept Management, Ltd. v. Carpenter, 199 Ga.App. 503, 405 S.E.2d 119 (1991). Are these courts right? Would any intelligent third party bidder have been willing to bid $800,000, knowing that there was a preexisting $300,000 debt that would be unaffected by the foreclosure of the wrap mortgage? Surely not, unless the bidder had assurance that ME2 would take $300,000 of the sale proceeds and apply them to ME1's debt, thus paying it off. Could ME2 be counted on to do that? Indeed, would that be a legally permissible disposition of the sale proceeds? And yet, if ME2 has no duty to make such a payoff, isn't ME2 receiving an enormous advantage in bidding, as against any third party bidder?

What is the duty of the foreclosing wrap mortgagee (or trustee under a deed of trust) with respect to the sale proceeds? The typical (perhaps not-too-carefully-drafted) wrap mortgage will contain the usual clause stating that foreclosure proceeds will be applied to (1) expenses of sale and attorney's fees, (2) principal and interest owing on the [wrap] loan, with the remaining balance to (3) the mortgagors and their assigns. (The term "assigns" is routinely taken to include junior mortgagees and other subordinate lienholders.) Note that nothing is said about applying the sale proceeds toward payment of the underlying mortgage debt. But this is not the end of the inquiry. Consider the holding of Summers v. Consolidated Capital Special Trust, 783 S.W.2d 580 (Tex.1989):

> Absent an express agreement between the purchaser [the wrap borrower] and wrap note holder, the law should imply a covenant into the parties' agreement requiring the trustee to apply the proceeds first to the satisfaction of pre-existing debt before making any distribution to the mortgagor. *See J.M. Realty Inv. Corp. v. Stern*, 296 So.2d 588, 589 (Fla.App.1974). Texas law permits the insertion of an implied covenant when necessary to effectuate the parties' actual intent. * * *

> Thus, when a deed of trust lien securing a wraparound note is foreclosed, the amount bid for the property at the sale, net of expenses, is to be credited to the entire outstanding balance, including wrapped indebtedness, due on that note. If the bid exceeds such balance, a surplus results; if the balance exceeds the bid, a deficiency results. The trustee acting for the note holder is obliged by implied covenant to apply the net sales proceeds to discharge the entire wrapped indebtedness reflected in the note to the fullest extent possible. [783 S.W.2d at 583.]

To the same effect is Armsey v. Channel Associates, Inc., 184 Cal.App.3d 833, 229 Cal.Rptr. 509 (1986). Observe that the rationale of *Summers* does not appear to depend on the wrap lender's being personally liable on the underlying debt. If the wrap lender is a third-party lender, rather than the vendor of the property (as in a purchase-money wraparound), it will probably not be a signatory on or have personal liability on the underlying note. In that situation, who is benefitted by the "implied covenant" mentioned in *Summers?* Could a claim under the covenant be enforced by the underlying noteholder? See Downs v. Zeigler, Chapter 3, Section A, supra (which appears to have involved a wraparound mortgage, although it was not so identified by the court.) Comments on *Summers* are found in 47 Wash. & Lee L.Rev. 1059 (1990); 21 Tex.Tech.L.Rev. 873 (1990); 51 Tex.B.J. 1051 (1988).

A brief recapitulation may be helpful here. The usual wrap note and mortgage contain language requiring the wrap lender to make payments on the underlying loan, but only on the condition that the wrap borrower also makes its payments on the wrap loan. The *Summers* case, along with *J.M. Realty* and *Armsey,* holds that this principle, requiring the wrap lender to "pass through" the payments it receives on the wrap loan, also applies to the proceeds of a foreclosure sale, and that a covenant to that effect should be implied. What about yet a third form of payment that might be received by the wrap lender—the collection of a deficiency judgment from the wrap borrower? Should a court also infer a similar covenant by the wrap lender to pass through these funds to the underlying mortgage holder? The dissenting judge in *Summers* appeared to assume that the court would recognize no such covenant with respect to a deficiency recovery.

Where does the law now stand? Restatement (Third) of Property (Mortgages) § 7.8 flatly rejects the holding of the *Summers* case discussed above. Instead, it provides that the foreclosing wraparound lender may recover only the "net" debt—that is:

> the amount by which the balance owing on the obligation secured by the mortgage being foreclosed exceeds the balance owing on the mortgage obligation that the mortgagee has a duty to pay [i.e., the underlying mortgage] together with appropriate fees and costs. Any surplus remaining after application of this sum is distributed [to junior lienholders or the mortgagor].

The Restatement's comment observes that this result is subject to variation by the terms of the wraparound mortgage or other agreement among the parties.

Whether the Restatement's rule will ultimately prevail is uncertain. The Arizona Court of Appeals took the same approach in Midyett v. Rennat Properties, Inc., 171 Ariz. 492, 831 P.2d 868 (App.1992). Perhaps, in the absence of any language in the documents resolving the issues, the wrap lender has a choice: If the wrap lender forecloses only for its "net" or "true" debt (the difference between the balance on the wrap loan and the balance on the underlying loan), it need not apply any of these funds against the underlying debt. But if it forecloses for the full wrap loan balance, it is subject to the "implied covenant" (as in the *Summers* case) to pass through to the underlying noteholder the balance due to that party.

Observe that the notion of "passing through" large lump sums, such as those collected through foreclosure or enforcement of a deficiency judgment, is problematic. Suppose the underlying loan is "locked in" and cannot legally be prepaid. Suppose it can be prepaid only with a large accompanying fee. Suppose (as is quite likely) it has a relatively low interest rate, so that prepayment of it tends to defeat the wrap lender's expectation of profits on the wrap loan. Should a court, in any of these circumstances, modify the *Summers* holding to permit the foreclosing wrap lender to hold the proceeds (in escrow? in trust?) and pay them out to the underlying lender only over time, as the underlying debt comes due in the ordinary course? See In re Park North Partners, Ltd., 72 B.R. 79 (Bankr.N.D.Ga.1987):

> Defendant, as the holder of the wrap note, became obligated upon foreclosure to pay the difference between the amount bid and its wrap equity [$800,000—$500,000 = $300,000] over to the holders of the underlying debts as *they became due.* Therefore, there was no surplus, and Plaintiff-Debtor is entitled to no recovery against Defendants. [72 B.R. at 84 (emphasis added).]

What consequences will ensue if the wrap lender subsequently ceases making payments on the underlying debt, becomes insolvent, or files bankruptcy? The buyer at the foreclosure sale will be understandably concerned about these possibilities, because the buyer's title continues to be subject to the lien of the underlying mortgage until it is paid in full. Should a court impose some protective measures to ensure that those payments will in fact be made, at least if someone other than the wrap lender is the buyer at the sale?

Return for a moment to the problem of how to announce and advertise a wrap-around foreclosure sale. If the foreclosing wrap mortgagee or trustee recognizes that it has a duty to pay off the underlying loan, and a corresponding right to foreclose for the full balance on the wrap loan, shouldn't it make its intent to pay off the underlying loan very clear to bidders at the sale? Surely they need to know that this will be done.

In Quality Inns Int'l Inc. v. Booth, Fish, Simpson, Harrison & Hall, 58 N.C.App. 1, 292 S.E.2d 755 (1982), the attorney for Quality, the wrap lender, was also the trustee responsible for foreclosing the wrap deed of trust. When the fee owner (Greenway) defaulted, the attorney-trustee proceeded to foreclose it. The notice of sale he published stated that the sale would be "subject to" the underlying first deed of trust, but did not mention that the wrap lender was obligated to (and intended to) apply the proceeds of the foreclosure to the outstanding balance due on the underlying first deed of trust.

At the time of the sale, the balance on the wrap loan was about $600,000, while the balance on the underlying first loan was about $550,000. Quality, the wrap lender, was the successful bidder at the sale, bidding $585,000. It consciously chose this figure to be less than the balance on the wrap loan, believing that it would thereby avoid paying any surplus to the fee owner. After the sale, Quality indeed paid off the underlying first loan. However, to its surprise, Greenway made a claim for a surplus of $505,000. Greenway argued that in light of the "wrap" nature of the deed of trust which had been foreclosed, the true balance owing to Quality had been only the *difference* between the nominal balances on the two loans, or about $50,000. Greenway asserted that taking this figure (plus expenses) from Quality's bid left a surplus of $505,000.

After some initial litigation, Quality compromised this claim with Greenway for $30,000. It then filed a malpractice action against its attorney and his law firm to recover the $30,000 settlement payment plus the expenses it had incurred in the litigation with Greenway. The court held:

> Plaintiff seeks to proceed against defendants on two theories, or types, of malpractice: one, that defendants lacked that degree of knowledge and skill ordinarily possessed by attorneys handling real estate transactions, and two, that defendants failed to use reasonable care and diligence in handling plaintiff's problems with respect to recovering the personal property in the motel. The forecast of evidence presented by defendants in support of their summary judgment motion clearly shows that the genesis of plaintiff's problems with respect to plaintiff's entitlement to the personal property in the motel was in plaintiff's uncertainty as to how to proceed with the foreclosure of the real property. Defendant's forecast shows that defendants were aware that plaintiff regarded the Watts deed of trust as a "wrap-around" mortgage, or at least intended it to be such, but that plaintiff was uncertain as to how to effectively foreclose such a mortgage so as to not create a surplus to which Greenway might assert claim or which Greenway might use to retain possession of the personal property of the motel. Plaintiff's own forecast of evidence also reflects uncertainty of the law and appropriate strategy on plaintiff's part. Affidavits and depositions of skilled lawyers for both parties reflect that the so-called "wrap-around" mortgage is an area of real property law not well understood by property lawyers in North Carolina, and

further, that the foreclosure of such a mortgage is fraught with questions and uncertainty. * * *

The forecast of evidence shows that there was no bad faith on defendant's part, and that the problem with which defendants were entrusted grew from an uncertain and unsettled area of law. Defendants were therefore entitled to judgment as a matter of law on plaintiff's malpractice claim. [292 S.E.2d at 762–63.]

This holding was doubtless a great relief to the attorney-defendant, but would you want to rely on it? Can you see any steps that a competent attorney, advising a trustee under a wrap-around deed of trust, could take to avoid this sort of malpractice claim?

NOTES

1. *Drafting considerations.* How should a wrap-around mortgage be drafted? See Gunning, The Wrap-Around Mortgage ... Friend or U.F.O.?, Real Est.Rev., Summer 1972, at 35. The following excerpts from an actual wraparound note will suggest some additional drafting issues, beyond those discussed in the text above dealing with the foreclosure process. (The "Note Holder" is the wrap lender.)

(a) *Payments on Prior Note.* Until this Note is paid in full or otherwise canceled, I agree not to make any more payments directly to the holder of the Prior Note. So long as I make my monthly payments as described below and have not violated any other provision of this Note or the Security Instrument [mortgage], the Note Holder will make the monthly payments of principal and interest as they become due and payable under the Prior Note. However, if I do not make the payments described below, or if I violate any other provision of this Note or the Security Instrument, the Note Holder at its option can stop making these payments for me. If the Note Holder continues to make these payments despite my failure to make the payments due on this Note, the Note Holder may add these sums, with interest, to the indebtedness of this Note.

(b) *Notice of Holder of Prior Note.* I will notify the holder of the Prior Note to accept payments due under the Prior Note or Prior Security Instrument from the Note Holder. I will also instruct the holder of the Prior Note to send any notices under the Prior Note or Prior Security Instrument to the Note Holder's address. (The Note Holder will provide me with a copy of any notices it receives.) If I receive any notices from the holder of the Prior Note, I will promptly forward them to the Note Holder.

(c) *Subrogation to Prior Note.* If the Note Holder takes any actions or pays any sums on my behalf to the holder of the Prior Note under the terms of the Prior Note or Prior Security Instrument, the Note Holder will have the rights which the holder of the Prior Note would have had against me under the Prior Note and Prior Security Instrument. This is known as "subrogation."

(d) *Rights and Liabilities under Prior Note.* By its acceptance of this note and its agreements hereunder, the Note Holder has not assumed any of my liabilities or obligations to the holder of the Prior Note, or given that holder any additional rights or affected my liability under the Prior Note and the Prior Security Instrument. So long as this Note is outstanding, I agree to perform all obligations under the Prior Note and Prior Security Instrument except the obligation to make payments, and my failure to do so will be a violation of my obligations under this Note. I also agree not to modify or amend the Prior Note or Prior Security Instrument or to do or fail to do anything that results in an increase of the amount owed under the Prior Note and Prior Security Instrument.

(e) *Prepayments.* I can make payments of all or any part of the principal owing under this Note at any time before they are due without paying any penalty to the Note Holder. The Note Holder will use any prepayments I make first to reduce that part of the principal of this Note not consisting of sums due under the Prior Note. If that part of the principal has been reduced to zero, the Note Holder will cancel this Note and release the Security Instrument that secures this Note. The Note Holder will no longer make payments due under the Prior Note, will return any sums I have prepaid if not applied to this Note or to the Prior Note, and I will again be responsible to make payments directly to the holder of the Prior Note.

Clause (a) above makes the wrap lender's duty to make payments on the underlying loan conditional upon receiving the wrap borrower's payments. But suppose the wrap lender's duty is not expressly made conditional; instead, the wrap lender and borrower agree that the lender "shall be obligated to pay any and all installments falling due" on the underlying loan. Should a condition be implied in this language? If the wrap borrower defaults, may the wrap lender also default with impunity? In Hampton v. Minton, 785 S.W.2d 854 (Tex.Ct.App.1990), the wrap borrower defaulted, and so did the wrap lender. The court refused to find the wrap lender liable to the borrower for damages for its default; in effect, it implied a condition in language like that in Clause (a).

For additional drafting considerations, see R. Kymn Harp, When Wrap-Around Mortgages Return? The Time to Plan Is Now, Probate & Property, Jul./Aug. 2004, at 42.

2. *Consent of underlying noteholder and the impact of a due-on-sale clause in the underlying note.* Ideally, the underlying lender will consent to the creation of the wrap mortgage. The original lender ideally will also agree to send the wrap lender copies of all notices of default or foreclosure, will

agree to accept tender of payments from the wrap lender, will give the wrap lender an additional period of grace to cure any defaults, and will consent to any prepayment which the wrap lender desires to make on the original loan.

If prevailing interest rates are now higher than the interest rate on the underlying loan, however, the underlying lender may want to use the creation of the wrap mortgage as an excuse to accelerate the underlying loan. Consider the impact of an existing mortgage's due-on-sale clause on a proposed wrap-around loan. If the wrap is not associated with a sale of the property, it is simply a second mortgage. Whether it will trigger the due-on-sale clause depends on the clause's wording. For example, if the clause is actuated by the "transfer" of "any interest in" the subject property, the wrap-around mortgage will very probably trigger it. However, bear in mind that the Garn Act provides a specific exemption from due-on-sale acceleration for the placing of a junior mortgage on a one- to-four-family home. See Chapter 5, Section B, supra.

If the proposed wrap-around loan is associated with a sale of the property (i.e., it is a purchase-money wrap-around), the transfer of title to the realty itself will be sufficient to trigger the clause. Hence, consent of the underlying noteholder will be essential, and in the absence of such consent the use of wrap-around financing will be impossible. See Daniel Schwarz, The Wrap-Around Mortgage: Cold Comfort in the Winter of the Due-on-Sale Clause, 4 Ann. Rev. of Bank. L. 429 (1985).

There appears to be nothing unique to the wrap-around concept which bears on the underlying validity of due-on-sale clauses. See generally Chapter 5, Section B, supra. A due-on-encumbrance clause, if valid, would be equally inhibiting. See, e.g., Mills v. Nashua Fed. Sav. & Loan Ass'n, 121 N.H. 722, 433 A.2d 1312 (1981); Sanford M. Guerin, Selected Problems in Wrap-Around Financing: Suggested Approaches to Due-on-Sale Clauses and Purchaser's Depreciable Basis, 14 U.Mich.J.L.Reform 401 (1981).

3. *Some problems.* Consider the following problems and their implications for the proper drafting of a wrap-around note:

(a) Suppose that A holds Blackacre subject to a deed of trust in favor of Bank. Further suppose the following chain of events: (1) With Bank's consent, A sells Blackacre to B, taking back a wrap-around note and deed of trust as part of the price. (2) Without Bank's consent, B later resells Blackacre to C, taking a purchase money deed of trust from C for part of the purchase price. (3) When Bank discovers the sale to C, Bank accelerates the senior indebtedness pursuant to the due-on-sale clause in its deed of trust, and conducts a foreclosure sale which extinguishes the junior liens of A and B. (4) B then sues A for breach of contract, arguing that under the language of the wrap note, A was obligated to B to pay the indebtedness owed to Bank "as and when the same became due and payable." Suppose that A makes the following argument: "Under the wrap note, I agreed to make only the regular installment payments on the debt to Bank, which I did; I did not agree to pay off the full balance of the debt in the event of acceleration." Should A's argument succeed? It did not succeed in Stroh-Mc Investments v. Bowens, 725 P.2d 33 (Colo.App.1986) (wrap note containing quoted language unconditionally obligated wrap lender to pay full amount of underlying loan if accelerated). How would this hypothetical be resolved under the language of the wrap note in Note 1?

(b) Suppose A holds Blackacre subject to a deed of trust in favor of Bank. With Bank's consent, A sells Blackacre to B, taking back a wrap-around note and deed of trust as part of the price. B later wants to sell Blackacre to C and prepays the wrap note, but A refuses to prepay the underlying note to Bank. If the language of the wrap note is silent, must A prepay the underlying note to Bank? See Carroll v. Miller, 166 A.D.2d 492, 561 N.Y.S.2d 47 (1990), appeal dismissed, 78 N.Y.2d 951, 573 N.Y.S.2d 646, 578 N.E.2d 444 (1991). How would this hypothetical be resolved under the language of the wrap note in Note 1?

(c) Suppose that A holds Blackacre subject to a deed of trust in favor of Bank. Without Bank's consent, A sells Blackacre to B, taking back a wrap-around note and deed of trust as part of the price. When Bank discovers the sale to B, Bank accelerates the senior indebtedness pursuant to the due-on-sale clause in its deed of trust, and institutes a foreclosure proceeding. To get Bank to stop the foreclosure, B agrees to modify the terms of the underlying loan to increase the interest rate from 6% to 10%; A, however, does not participate in or agree to this modification and refuses to pay the higher payments on the underlying loan. If B makes these payments directly to Bank, is B entitled to have these payments credited against its obligation on the wrap note? See Holevas v. Mills, 124 N.H. 292, 469 A.2d 1329 (1983) (yes). How would this hypothetical be resolved under the language of the wrap note in Note 1?

4. *Term of the wrap-around loan.* Although in many cases the due dates of the wrap-around mortgage and the original loan were identical, this is not necessary; the wrap-around might have a shorter or a longer term. See Jerry Bronner, The Wraparound Mortgage: Its Structure, Uses, and Limitations, 12 J. Real Est.Tax 315, 323 n. 28 (1985). It is also possible to use the wrap-around technique to reduce the debt service payments on an existing loan. In such a case, the wrap-around lender might make no advance of funds to the borrower at all, but would instead simply agree to make the payments due on the original loan, and would permit the borrower to pay smaller installments over a longer term. See Zumpano, Wrap-around Financing: Can It Increase the Productivity of Income Property?, 50 Appraisal J. 283 (1982); Lane, The "Wrap-Around" Mortgage: Tax Problems Related to Its Use in Connection with the Refinancing or Sale of Real Estate, 33d Ann.N.Y.U.Inst. on Fed.Tax 1235 (1975).

5. *First lien status.* Is a wrap-around mortgage, which is technically a second lien, really as safe as a first lien? How will the wrap-around lender know about, or cure, non-monetary defaults such as waste by the borrower? Can it reasonably expect the original lender to notify it of such defaults? The

wrap lender should, of course, provide in the wrap-around documents that any default of a non-monetary nature (such as waste) under the first mortgage is automatically a default on the wrap mortgage (as in clause (d) of the wrap note reproduced in Note 1).

Title V of the Depository Institutions Deregulation and Monetary Control Act of 1980, Pub.L. No. 96–221, operates to preempt state usury ceilings on interest for loans secured by first liens on residential property. See Chapter 8, Section G, infra. Could a wrap loan be considered a first lien for this purpose? In 1980, the Federal Home Loan Bank Board issued a proposed regulation, 45 Fed.Reg. 86500 (Dec. 31, 1980), which would have classified wrap loans as first liens if they matured no earlier than the maturity date of the senior loan and the wrap lender maintained "at all times" sufficient funds to satisfy the senior loan. However, this proposed regulation was never made final. The present regulations, found in 12 C.F.R. Part 590, define "first lien" rather elliptically to include an "instrument * * * of such a nature that, in the event of default, the real estate described in the instrument could be subject to the satisfaction of the obligation with the same priority as a first mortgage or a first deed of trust in the jurisdiction where the real estate is located." 12 C.F.R. § 590.2(c). Could a wrap-around loan meet this definition? Holding that one did not, see Mitchell v. Trustees of U.S. Mutual Real Estate Inv. Trust, 144 Mich.App. 302, 375 N.W.2d 424 (1985), discussed in Luis F. Fernandez, Wraparound Mortgages and Usury Exemption, 65 Mich.B.J. 150 (1986).

Formerly the federal financial regulatory agencies generally required banks and savings associations to invest primarily in first liens. This is no longer the case, but a few state statutes and regulations continue to require first lien status. Would a wrap-around loan qualify? Assuming that a wrap-around is treated as the equivalent of a first mortgage, what is its loan-to-value ratio for purposes of regulations that restrict that ratio? Is it necessary for the wrap-around lender to count both loans? If so, the loan-to-value ratio will often far exceed 100%.

6.   *Non-institutional wrap-around lenders.* The purchase money wrap-around raises special problems. Here it is the seller of the property (who is typically not a financial institution) who is obligated to make the payments on the original loan. Suppose the seller does not do so, through neglect or malice. For an example, see Holland v. McCullen, 764 So.2d 810 (Fla.Ct.App.2000). How will the wrap borrower learn of the seller's default? Can the wrap borrower cure it? One solution is to create an escrow arrangement, with the escrowee receiving the borrower's payments, disbursing the payments on the original loan, and remitting the balance to the seller.

An alternative way of dealing with this problem requires the wrap borrower to approach the holder of the underlying first lien and secure its promise to notify the borrower in the event of a default in payments on the first loan. (Of course, the holder normally has no obligation to make such a promise, and may well refuse to do so.) If this promise is obtained, the borrower may then insert a clause in the wrap note, providing that if a first mortgage default occurs the borrower may immediately cure it by making payments on the first loan, and that such payments will count toward the obligation on the wrap loan. See Illinois State Bank v. Yates, 678 S.W.2d 819 (Mo.App.1984), in which the court held that such language in the note deprived it of negotiability.

A clause of this sort, however, is emphatically not the equivalent of a general right of the wrap borrower to make direct prepayments on the underlying mortgage loan. Such payments would have the effect of depriving the wrap lender of its investment expectations, and are ordinarily prohibited by the terms of the wrap note and mortgage. See clause (a) of the wrap note reproduced in Note 1 supra. This prohibition is certainly enforceable; see Gutzi Assocs. v. Switzer, 215 Cal.App.3d 1636, 264 Cal.Rptr. 538 (1989).

Incidentally, suppose the holder of the underlying loan makes a promise to notify the wrap borrower if a default occurs in payments on the underlying loan, and to give the wrap borrower an opportunity to cure. Is that sort of promise binding on the underlying lender? Has it received any consideration? Absent consideration, could the promise still be enforced on the basis of promissory estoppel? The court so held in Miles Homes Division v. First State Bank, 782 S.W.2d 798 (Mo.App.1990).

7. *Taxation of interest.* In a wrap-around situation, what is the amount of interest which the borrower pays? What amount does the wrap lender receive? Both questions are significant for tax purposes, because interest may be deductible to the borrower and is ordinary income to the lender. If the wrap loan is taken at face value, it may offer a way for the borrower to claim significantly increased interest deductions. In the example in the text above, the annual interest is roughly the same whether the borrower obtains a wrap-around mortgage or simply a new second mortgage. But suppose the original loan has been outstanding for a long time, and its payments are now mostly principal. The borrower obtains a new wrap-around loan, and by agreement between the borrower and the wrap lender, the payments on the wrap loan are all (or nearly all) interest. Can the borrower deduct all of this interest? Or should the wrap lender be considered as merely the agent of the borrower for purposes of making the payments on the original loan?

The agency theory was adopted by the IRS in Rev.Rul. 75–99, 1975–1 Cum.Bull. 197, which dealt with the lender's, not the borrower's, tax position. It held that, as to the amount the wrap lender passed along to the original lender, the wrap lender had neither interest income nor a deduction for interest paid. From the borrower's viewpoint, the wrap lender was merely a conduit for the portion of the payment ultimately received by the original lender. See 1975 Ruling Poses Problem for Wrap-around Mortgages, 48 J.Tax. 127 (1978). If the borrower pays substantial prepaid interest, front-end loan fees, etc. on the obtaining of the wrap-around mortgage, they must probably be amortized over the life of the (wrap?) loan under Sec. 451(g); see Gerald J. Robinson, The Lender's Line, 4 J.Real Est.Tax. 165 (1977).

8. *Personal liability of the wrap borrower.* Is a wrap borrower considered to have assumed, or merely taken subject to, the underlying mortgage? In the usual form of document, as reproduced in Note 1 supra, the borrower promises to pay only the wrap mortgage. While the borrower's title is obviously "subject to" the underlying mortgage, the borrower expressly promises *not* to pay (or at least, not to prepay) it. If the borrower defaults, the wrap lender is privileged to default on the underlying mortgage payments, because the wrap lender's promise to pay the underlying mortgage is conditional. Under these circumstances, suppose the holder of the underlying mortgage forecloses; is the wrap borrower liable for a deficiency? The court held not in Adams v. George, 119 Idaho 973, 812 P.2d 280 (1991). Would it matter if the borrower had in fact been splitting her payment, paying part of it to the holder of the underlying mortgage directly? In the *Adams* case, the court said:

> the mere fact that the purchaser makes payments on the existing mortgage does not establish that the purchaser has assumed personal liability for the debt. In *Siekman v. Moler*, this Court held that the evidence failed to demonstrate that the purchaser had assumed an existing debt despite the fact that the purchaser had made a number of payments directly to the holder of the mortgage. The Court wrote: We attach no special importance to the circumstance that appellant [the purchaser] paid interest later becoming due and that nothing was paid by the mortgagors [the sellers]. The land, the title to which had passed to appellant, was primarily liable for the payment of the debt and payment of interest by him was entirely consistent with his position that he accepted the title incumbered by the mortgage but without personal responsibility. *Siekman*, 47 Idaho at 456, 276 P. at 312–13. [*Adams*, 812 P.2d at 284.]

9. *Wrap lender's payments as future advances.* You will learn that in most states, optional future advances made by a mortgagee may lose their priority as against any intervening liens of which the mortgagee has notice. See Chapter 9, Section C, infra. Will this doctrine operate against a wrap lender? Are the wrap lender's payments on the original loan the equivalent of "advances" to the fee owner? If so, are they optional or obligatory? Consider the type of clause described in Note 1(a), supra. On this ground, title companies will sometimes refuse to insure the priority of wrap mortgages for more than the amount of the wrap lender's actual cash disbursement.

10. *Adding new underlying mortgages.* It is possible for a wrap mortgage to include authorization for its holder to place additional "included" or "underlying" mortgages on the fee title, despite the fact that the holder of the mortgage obviously does not hold that title. Such a provision might be thought of as a power of attorney, designating the wrap mortgage holder as

the fee owner's agent for purposes of executing additional mortgages. Similar provisions are sometimes found in installment land contracts that wrap around existing mortgages. (That context makes it a bit easier to conceptualize the wrap lender's authority to impose additional mortgages, because the wrap lender is still the technical owner of legal title to the realty.)

Clauses of this sort are obviously perilous from the viewpoint of the fee owner of the property. Perhaps the owner should "just say no" to such a clause. At a minimum, the owner would want to provide that the total balance on all "included" mortgages could not exceed the balance on the wrap mortgage, because if this occurred, paying off the wrap mortgage would not produce enough money to retire all of the underlying debt. In addition, the owner would want to ensure that additional mortgages will not increase the cash flow obligations of the wrap mortgage holder so much that they exceed the payments it is receiving on the wrap mortgage.

As an alternative to spelling out these detailed restrictions in the wrap mortgage itself, the owner might instead insert a clause requiring her or his consent to any additional "underlying" mortgages. Drafting such a clause can be quite tricky, especially if the payments being made on the wrap mortgage can vary as a function of the income generated by the real estate (say, a shopping center). See Official Ltd. Partners Comm. of 1981 Equidyne Props., I v. Credit Alliance Corp., 59 B.R. 930 (Bankr.S.D.N.Y.1986).

11. *Undisclosed underlying mortgages.* We ordinarily assume that in a sale with wrap-around financing, the buyer is fully aware of the existence of the underlying mortgage. But a buyer who is unsophisticated and does not examine the title might well take the property without actual knowledge of the underlying mortgage. Of course, the covenants of title in a warranty deed would be breached in such a transaction. But suppose the seller dutifully makes the payments on the underlying mortgage loan, and eventually pays it off. How has the buyer been harmed? The court held that a buyer in this situation had no damages at all in Man Ngok Tam v. Hoi Hong K. Luk, 154 Wis.2d 282, 453 N.W.2d 158 (App.1990), rev. denied, 454 N.W.2d 806 (1990).

Similarly, suppose the wrap-around lender defaults in payment on the underlying loan, it is accelerated, and the wrap lender then pays it off to prevent foreclosure. Is the wrap borrower damaged in any way? The court held not in Szenay v. Schaub, 496 So.2d 883 (Fla.App.1986).

12. *Usury.* Consider whether a wrap-around loan may violate state usury statutes. As mentioned in Note 5, supra, if the loan is regarded as secured by a first lien on residential property, federal law will preempt the state usury ceiling in most states. But suppose this is not the case.

If the wrap mortgage is taken by a land seller as part of a purchase-money transaction, it is probable that no usury violation will be found. Most states recognize a so-called "time-price differential" exemption to their usury statutes; in substance, it provides that seller financing of a sale of property can never be usurious, because the interest reserved by the seller on the unpaid portion of the price is simply part of the price itself. The fact that the seller charges a higher price when the sale price is paid over time rather than when title is transferred is irrelevant for usury purposes. See Hool v. Rydholm, 467 So.2d 1038 (Fla.App.1985); Patrick A. Randolph, Home Finance in the Shadow World: Unsolved Usury Problems Affecting Adjustable Rate and Wrap-around Mortgages in Missouri, 51 UMKC L.Rev. 41, 66–68 (1982).

But the "time-price" exemption is unavailable when the wrap loan is made by a third-party lender. The question then becomes: what is the interest rate? In the illustration in the text preceding these notes, for example, is it 12% (the nominal rate stated in the wrap loan documents) or 14.6% (the effective yield realized by the wrap lender, taking into account that the wrap lender is, in a sense, "borrowing" part of the capital it is lending from the preexisting first lender at a below-current-market rate)?

Ordinarily in assessing compliance with usury statutes we pay no attention to the *source* of the lender's funds or the *cost* of those funds to it. Why should the wrap-around loan be different? Is it because the lender has, in effect, taken the borrower's low-rate first loan balance away from him, in order to loan it back to him at a higher interest rate? (Note that this occurs only with third-party wrap-around financing, and not in a wrap-around sale of real estate.) Should this be thought morally or legally objectionable? Of course, the borrower has voluntarily agreed to "cede" the first loan to the wrap lender. But the voluntary nature of the borrower's intent is no defense to the charge of usury; if it were, usurious loans would be scarce indeed. The whole point of the usury concept is to protect borrowers from their own willingness to pay exorbitant interest rates.

A couple of cases have held third-party wrap loans to be usurious despite the fact that their nominal interest rates were below the usury ceiling. Unfortunately, their approaches to the calculation of the "true" interest rate are disappointingly vague; they tend to regard usury, like obscenity, as something that one simply knows when one sees! See In re Hamlett, 63 B.R. 492 (Bankr.M.D.Fla.1986); Mindlin v. Davis, 74 So.2d 789 (Fla.1954). See generally Note, Wrap-Around Financing: A Technique for Skirting the Usury Laws, 1972 Duke L.J. 785; Note, Wrap-around Deed of Trust: An Answer to the Allegation of Usury, 10 Pac.L.J. 923 (1979). Cf. Patrick A. Randolph, Home Finance in the Shadow World: Unsolved Usury Problems Affecting Adjustable Rate and Wrap-around Mortgages in Missouri, 51 UMKC L.Rev. 41 (1982).

13. *Mortgage recording taxes.* In many states, a tax is imposed on the recordation of a mortgage, and is based on the amount of the obligation the mortgage secures. What is the relevant amount in a wrap-around mortgage? Is it the total stated balance of the wrap loan, or only the difference between the wrap loan and the underlying loan balances? Does the answer to this question depend on whether the wrap is financing a sale, or is merely being

obtained to raise new cash for an existing owner? See Prince George's County v. McMahon, 59 Md.App. 682, 477 A.2d 1218 (1984), cert. denied, 301 Md. 639, 484 A.2d 274 (1984), applying the tax only to the difference between the two loan balances.

14. *Installment sale reporting of gain in wrap-around sales.* Under Internal Revenue Code § 453, a seller of property who receives the price in installments over more than one year is permitted to spread the reporting of the taxable gain on the sale over the same period. This is often highly advantageous to sellers. However, if the buyer "assumes or takes subject to" an existing mortgage loan, the full balance on that loan is regarded as having been received in the year of the sale. Under the rather complex formula for calculating the gain on installment payments (which we won't trouble to explain here), such a mortgage balance reduces the "contract price," and thus significantly diminishes the taxpayer's ability to spread the gain over into future years.

Several cases supported the notion that if the sale was financed with a wrap-around mortgage the buyer was *not* considered to have "assumed or taken subject to" the underlying mortgage. See, e.g., Stonecrest Corp. v. Comm'r, 24 T.C. 659 (1955). The IRS disagreed with these cases, and in 1981 it promulgated regulations under the purported authority of the Installment Sales Revision Act of 1980, asserting that if the sale employed wrap-around financing, it would be treated in the same way as an ordinary assumption or subject-to transaction. Temp. Treas. Reg. § 15A.453–1(b)(3)(ii). However, two Tax Court cases held these regulations invalid on the ground that they were outside the authority of the 1980 statute. See Professional Equities, Inc. v. Commissioner, 89 T.C. 165 (1987); Vincent E. Webb v. Commissioner, 54 T.C.M. 443 (1987). As the *Professional Equities* case put it,

> In the 30 years since *Stonecrest* we have identified wrap-around sales, in part, by the fact that in those sales the purchase price is paid in full directly to the seller. It is true that in wrap-around sales the seller may service the underlying mortgage out of the payments received from the buyer, but he is not obligated to do so and instead is free to discharge that mortgage however he chooses. The fact that he may normally choose to use the sale proceeds to service the underlying obligation does not justify the Commissioner's treating those proceeds as not, in fact, received by the seller. The seller in a wrap-around sale receives neither "current payment nor the practical benefit of current payment of the underlying debt." Hunt v. Commissioner, 80 T.C. 1126, 1142–1143 (1983). He receives instead the full payment price directly. If the seller did not receive unrestricted use of the full payment price directly but was merely a conduit for the mortgagee, we would not treat that sale under the method of taxing gain prescribed for wrap-around sales, but would apply the "subject to" and "assumed" regulations. [89 T.C. at 179–180.]

Thus, a wrap-around sale continues to be advantageous in assisting taxpayers to take maximum advantage of installment reporting. See Anna C. Fowler & Robert W. Wyndelts, Installment Sales: Wrap-around Mortgage Regulation Invalidated by the Tax Court, 15 J.Real Est.Tax. 203 (1988); Burton W. Kanter & Sheldon I. Banoff, Should Real Estate Be Sold Via Wrap-around Mortgages?, 70 J.Tax. 255 (1989).

CHAPTER EIGHT

GOVERNMENT INTERVENTION AND PRIVATE RISK-SPREADING IN THE MORTGAGE MARKET

■ ■ ■

The preceding chapters of this casebook have developed the doctrines of real estate conveyancing and security law. The remaining chapters will describe how these doctrines are employed in the financing and development of land. In this chapter, we will discuss the real estate finance market and its regulation and support by government. The following chapters will address various types of real estate development.

A. MORTGAGE LENDING IN AMERICA: AN OVERVIEW

Mortgage debt in the United States exceeded $13.3 trillion dollars in mid-2014; this was nearly half of all outstanding debt. Clearly, mortgage finance is critically important for the economy and for effectuating certain policy goals, such as fostering homeownership. Unsurprisingly, the government is actively involved in regulating and facilitating the mortgage market in a number of ways. However, developing and implementing an optimal set of regulations and interventions has proven difficult, and failures in the government's regulatory system substantially contributed to the credit and real estate market crises that occurred in 2007 and succeeding years. Hence, a consideration of the government's role is an essential part of evaluating the real estate finance system.

This chapter begins with an overview of mortgage lending. This section of the book describes the various types of mortgage lenders, the government-sponsored mortgage market support institutions, and their regulators, with particular focus on the changes that occurred in response to the 2007 market failures. The next section examines governmental efforts to prevent lending abuses, such as class-based lending discrimination and predatory lending. The following section deals with government and private programs to spread mortgage risk by means of mortgage insurance and guarantees. Finally, this chapter considers the balance of regulatory power between the federal and state governments as it is adjusted through federal preemption of state law.

As we begin to look at the structure of the mortgage market, we must keep certain distinctions in mind. One is the difference between the *origination* and *holding* of mortgages. By origination, we mean the acts necessary to put the loan "on the books." Somewhat simplified, they include receiving the prospective borrower's loan application, making the necessary appraisal, credit, and employment checks, seeing that the documents (such as the note, mortgage, and Truth-in-Lending and RESPA disclosures) are prepared and executed, providing for title (and perhaps mortgage) insurance, recording of documents, and disbursing the loan funds to the borrower or, in the case of a purchase-money mortgage, to the seller.

When these steps have been completed, the mortgage has been "originated." What will the originating institution do with this new investment? It may continue to hold the note and the mortgage that secures it in its own portfolio, collect the monthly payments, and use them for its other business activities. Obviously, this is feasible only if the institution has a source of investment funds, such as savings account deposits, life insurance premium receipts, or pension fund contributions, that it can devote to investment in mortgages. For example, savings associations traditionally held most of the loans they originated in their own portfolios.

As a second alternative, the originator may sell the note and mortgage (i.e., "sell the loan") to another institution. Indeed, a whole class of businesses, called mortgage bankers, exists for the purpose of originating loans with the expectation of selling all of them to other investors. Depository institutions, such as commercial banks and savings associations, also sell loans, particularly when their deposit inflows are slow and demand for new loans is high in their market areas.

The business arrangements under which originators obtain the funds they need, and by which they transfer the loans they create to secondary market investors, can take several different forms, as the following excerpt illustrates.

CONSUMER FINANCIAL PROTECTION BUREAU
EXAMINATION PROCEDURES: MORTGAGE ORIGINATION

(2012)

Mortgage lending generally occurs through retail, wholesale, or correspondent lending channels. Sometimes there are no clear lines of demarcation among the channels, as a participant may operate in more than one of them. Each channel is described in more detail below.

1. Retail Channel

In the retail channel, the lender conducts the origination process directly with the consumer, either in person or through an online application. An employee of the lender, generally called a loan officer, solicits the loan, takes the application, and tracks the application through to the closing process.

2. Wholesale Channel—Mortgage Brokers

In the wholesale channel, a mortgage broker solicits the loan and takes the application from the consumer. Mortgage brokers are independent contractors and are not employees of the lender. The broker establishes relationships with multiple mortgage lenders and offers different mortgage loan products from these lenders. Mortgage brokers generally do not make underwriting decisions and do not actually fund the loans. In this channel, it is the mortgage lender that makes the underwriting decision, based on information provided by the broker. These mortgage lenders, called wholesale lenders, often are divisions of larger depository institutions. Generally, a wholesale lender requires a broker to enter into a wholesale lending agreement before the broker may originate loans on the lender's behalf.

In a variant of standard wholesale mortgage originations, some brokers "table fund" loans. In a table-funded transaction, the mortgage broker closes the loan as the lender of record and then assigns the loan to a purchaser at or immediately after the closing. The loan purchaser provides the funding for the loan, but the documents name the mortgage broker as the creditor.

3. Correspondent Channel—Small Mortgage Lenders

Correspondent lending, a hybrid of retail channel and wholesale channel lending, often features smaller institutions, acting as correspondent lenders. Correspondent lenders are the primary interface with consumers, conducting all steps in the mortgage origination process and funding their own loans. They generally originate and deliver loans pursuant to underwriting standards set by other lenders or investors, usually larger depository lenders, upon advance commitment on price. In addition to soliciting consumers directly, correspondent lenders may receive applications and mortgage documents from mortgage brokers and subsequently speak directly with the consumer. Generally, a wholesale lender requires a correspondent to enter into a written correspondent lending agreement before the correspondent may originate loans for sale to the wholesale lender.

The graphic below shows the number of lenders of various types who originated residential mortgages in the U.S. in 2012. It is based on data collected under the Home Mortgage Disclosure Act. See Neil Bhutta and Glenn B. Canner, Mortgage Market Conditions and Borrower Outcomes: Evidence from the 2012 HMDA Data and Matched HMDA-Credit Record Data, 99 Fed. Reserve Bull. No. 4 (Nov. 2013). It reflects a total of about 7,400 originators. Most of the largest originators are banks; Wells Fargo Bank alone closed 19% of all residential loans made in 2013, and the four largest bank mortgage lenders (Wells Fargo, J.P. Morgan Chase, Bank of America, and U.S. Bank) together made about 39% of all loans originated (a total of about $1.8 trillion) in that year.

Originators of U.S. Residential Mortgage Debt
2012

What sorts of institutions buy loans from originators? Three government sponsored enterprises (GSEs) have been active buyers in the so-called secondary mortgage market: Fannie Mae (formerly known as the Federal National Mortgage Association), Freddie Mac (formerly known as the Federal Home Loan Mortgage Corporation), and the Government National Mortgage Association ("GNMA" or "Ginnie Mae"). We will examine the activities of these entities in more depth later. Life insurance companies and pension funds have seen mortgage loans, especially on large income-producing projects, as attractive investments. Because they usually do not have local personnel outside the home office trained in loan origination, a symbiotic relationship often exists between a mortgage banker and the life insurance companies, pension funds, or other investors that buy its commercial loans. Depository institutions, especially those in capital-rich areas such as New England, also have been important mortgage loan purchasers.

A third alternative for the mortgage loan originator (or an investor to whom the originator sells the loan) is to place the loan in a pool with others having similar characteristics and to "securitize" them. This can be done in one of several ways. One method is to sell "participation certificates" or "PCs" to investors. Each of these certificates transfers a fractional share of ownership in the pool of loans, much like stock certificates in a corporation. The lender issuing the PCs may guarantee payment of them to the investors. A second method is to pledge the loans as collateral for securities that the entity creating the pool will issue and sell in the capital markets. In this way, a lender can raise capital for mortgage lending from sources that are unlikely to invest directly in individual mortgages, such as pension plans and individual investors. This sort of security is known as a mortgage-backed security ("MBS"). Many different types of MBS exist. You will learn more about them in Section C of this chapter.

Two other distinctions must be kept in mind as we study the mortgage market. One is the difference between construction loans and long-term (sometimes called "permanent" or "take-out") loans. A construction loan is normally a short-term or demand loan made to the developer, who may or may not be the long-term owner of the building or subdivision being built. When the construction is completed, the permanent lender or an originator who will sell the loan to the permanent lender disburses the permanent loan funds, and the builder uses these funds to pay off (or "take out") the construction loan. The "permanent" loan is not literally permanent; it is a long-term loan (typically 8- to 20-year maturity for commercial property) made to the long-term owner of the property. Although permanent loans often are sold on the secondary market or are securitized, construction loans rarely are.

The other important distinction to consider is that between home loans (traditionally defined as loans on one-to four-family residential property) and loans on other types of real estate, such as apartment buildings, office buildings, shopping centers, industrial parks, farms, or undeveloped land. When we examine statistics about the mortgage market, we must be clear about the kind of property securing a particular loan. The following table, taken from data provided by the Federal Reserve Board, shows mortgage debt outstanding in the United States as of the end of the second quarter of 2014 by property type.

	Amount of Debt (Billions)	Percentage of Total Debt
Total Mortgage Debt, All Properties:	$13,323	
Farm Properties	179	.8%
Nonfarm Properties by Type of Property:		
1- to 4-Family Houses	9,855	74.4%
Multifamily Housing	958	7.2%
Commercial Property	2,330	17.6%
Total Nonfarm Property	13,143	99.2%

These data show that approximately three-fourths of all mortgage debt is represented by what is undoubtedly the most familiar category to most Americans—the 1-to-4-family home mortgage. Mortgage loans on commercial properties are next largest in importance, while both farm mortgages and mortgages on apartment projects are far less significant in the overall picture.

The following chart shows the types of mortgage debt holders and the percentage of overall mortgage debt that each type holds.

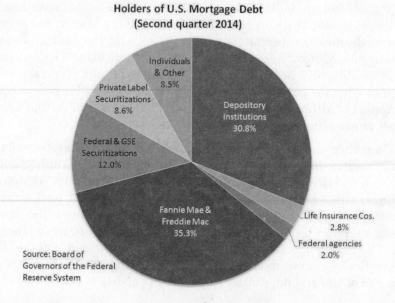

Holders of U.S. Mortgage Debt
(Second quarter 2014)

Individuals & Other 8.5%

Private Label Securitizations 8.6%

Depository Institutions 30.8%

Federal & GSE Securitizations 12.0%

Fannie Mae & Freddie Mac 35.3%

Life Insurance Cos. 2.8%

Federal agencies 2.0%

Source: Board of Governors of the Federal Reserve System

The allocation of commercial and multifamily mortgage debt among investors is a bit different than overall mortgage debt a shown above. According to Mortgage Bankers Association data, at the end of 2013 holders of commercial and multifamily mortgages were as follows:

commercial banks and thrifts held 35.5 percent of the total, life insurance companies held 13.3 percent, and government agencies and the GSEs together held 15.4 percent (including mortgage-backed securities they issued). Commercial mortgage-backed securities conduits accounted for 22.4 percent of the total commercial and multifamily debt. Private sources of funds accounted for the remainder.

It is interesting to see how overall mortgage debt has grown in the United States since the Great Depression. The following chart, which is derived from Federal Reserve Board data, shows total outstanding mortgage debt at five-year intervals.

Mortgage debt increased massively after the Second World War, especially during the 2000–2007 period, until the virtual collapse of the market in 2007. Growth since then has been very slow or negative. The rapid increase before 2007 was a result of many factors, including inflating land prices and construction costs, added real values as more real estate was developed, and increased loan-to-value ratios that would have created more outstanding debt even if property values had remained constant.

B. MORTGAGE ORIGINATORS AND THEIR REGULATORS

MARK JICKLIN & EDWARD V. MURPHY, WHO REGULATES
WHOM? AN OVERVIEW OF U.S FINANCIAL SUPERVISION
Congressional Research Service Report to Congress
December 8, 2010

Banking Regulators. Banking regulation in United States has evolved over time into a system of multiple regulators with overlapping jurisdictions. There is a dual banking system, in which each depository institution is subject to regulation by its chartering authority: state or federal. In addition, because virtually all depository institutions are federally insured, they are subject to at least one federal primary regulator (i.e., the federal authority responsible for examining the institution for safety and soundness and for ensuring its compliance with federal banking laws). The primary federal regulator of national banks is their chartering authority, the OCC [Office of the Comptroller of the Currency, within the U.S. Department of the Treasury]. The primary federal regulator of state-chartered banks that are members of the Federal Reserve System is the Board of Governors of the Federal Reserve System. State-chartered banks that are not members of the Federal Reserve System have the FDIC as their primary federal regulator. Thrifts (both state and federally chartered) had the Office of Thrift Supervision as their primary federal regulator, until the Dodd-Frank Act abolished the OTS and distributed its responsibilities among the OCC, the FDIC, and the Fed. All of these institutions, because their deposits are covered by FDIC deposit insurance, are also subject to the FDIC's regulatory authority. Credit unions—federally chartered or federally insured—are regulated by the National Credit Union Administration, which administers a deposit insurance fund separate from the FDIC's.

In general, lenders are expected to be prudent when extending loans. Each loan creates risk for the lender. The overall portfolio of loans extended or held by a lender, in relation to other assets and liabilities, affects that institution's stability. The relationship of lenders to each other, and to wider financial markets, affects the financial system's stability. The nature of these risks can vary between industry sectors, including commercial loans, farm loans, and consumer loans. Safety and soundness regulation encompasses the characteristics of (1) each loan, (2) the balance sheet of each institution, and (3) the risks in the system as a whole. Each loan has a variety of risk characteristics of concern to lenders and their regulators. Some of these risk characteristics can be estimated at the time the loan is issued. Credit risk, for example, is the risk that the borrower will fail to repay the principal of the loan as promised. Rising interest rates create another risk because the shorter-term interest rates that the lender often pays for its funds rise (e.g., deposit or CD rates) while the longer-term interest rates that the lender will receive from fixed-rate borrowers remain unchanged. Falling interest rates are not riskless either: fixed-rate borrowers may choose to repay loans early, reducing the lender's expected future cash flow. Federal financial regulators take into account expected default rates, prepayment rates, interest-rate exposure, and other risks when examining the loans issued by covered lenders.

Each lender's balance sheet can reduce or enhance the risks of the individual loans that make it up. A lender with many loans exposed to prepayment risk when interest rates fall, for example, could compensate by acquiring some assets that rise in value when interest rates fall. One example of a compensating asset would be an interest-rate derivative contract. Lenders are required to keep capital in reserve against the possibility of a drop in value of loan portfolios or other risky assets. Federal financial regulators take into account compensating assets, risk-based capital requirements, and other prudential standards when examining the balance sheets of covered lenders.

When regulators determine that a bank is taking excessive risks, or engaging in unsafe and unsound practices, they have a number of powerful tools at their disposal to reduce risk to the institution (and ultimately to the federal deposit insurance fund). They can require banks to reduce specified lending or financing practices, dispose of certain assets, and order banks to take steps to restore sound balance sheets. Banks have no alternative but to comply, since regulators have "life-or-death" options, such as withdrawing deposit insurance or seizing the bank outright. The federal banking agencies are briefly discussed below.

Office of the Comptroller of the Currency. The OCC was created in 1863 as part of the Department of Treasury to supervise federally chartered banks ("national" banks) and to replace the circulation of state bank notes with a single national currency (Chapter 106, 13 Stat. 99). The OCC regulates a wide variety of financial functions, but only for federally chartered banks. The head of the OCC, the Comptroller of the Currency, is also a member of the board of the FDIC and a director of the Neighborhood Reinvestment Corporation. The OCC has examination powers to enforce its responsibilities for the safety and soundness of nationally chartered banks. The OCC has strong enforcement powers, including the ability to issue cease and desist orders and revoke federal bank charters.

In addition to institution-level examinations, the OCC oversees systemic risk among nationally chartered banks. One example of OCC systemic concerns is the regular survey of credit underwriting practices. This survey compares underwriting standards over time and assesses whether OCC examiners believe the credit risk of nationally chartered bank portfolios is rising or falling. In addition, the OCC publishes regular reports on the derivatives activities of U.S. commercial banks.

Pursuant to Dodd-Frank, the OCC [is now] the primary regulator for federally chartered thrift institutions.

Federal Deposit Insurance Corporation. The FDIC was created in 1933 to provide assurance to small depositors that they would not lose their savings if their bank failed (P.L. 74–305, 49 Stat. 684). The FDIC is an independent agency that insures deposits, examines and supervises financial institutions, and manages receiverships, assuming and disposing of the assets of failed banks. The FDIC manages the deposit insurance fund, which consists of risk-based assessments levied on depository institutions. The fund is used for various purposes, primarily for resolving failed or failing institutions. The FDIC has broad jurisdiction because nearly all banks and thrifts, whether federally or state-chartered, carry FDIC insurance.

Deposit insurance reform was enacted in 2006 (P.L. 109–173, 119 Stat. 3601), including raising the coverage limit for retirement accounts to $250,000 and indexing both its limit and the general deposit insurance coverage ceiling to inflation. The reform act made changes to the risk-based assessment system to determine the payments of individual institutions. Within a range set by the reform act, the FDIC uses notice and comment rulemaking to set the designated reserve ratio (DRR) that supports the Deposit Insurance Fund (DIF). The FDIC uses its power to examine individual institutions and to issue regulations for all insured depository institutions to monitor and enforce safety and soundness. The FDIC is the primary federal regulator of state banks that are not members of the Federal Reserve System and state-chartered thrift institutions.

In 2008, as the financial crisis worsened, Congress enacted a temporary increase in the deposit insurance ceiling from $100,000 to $250,000 for most accounts. The increase was made permanent by Dodd-Frank.

Using emergency authority it received under the Federal Deposit Insurance Corporation Improvement Act of 1991 (FDICIA, P.L. 102–242), the FDIC made a determination of systemic risk in October 2008 and announced that it would temporarily guarantee (1) newly issued senior unsecured debt of banks, thrifts, and certain holding companies, and (2) non-interest bearing deposit transaction accounts (e.g., business checking accounts), regardless of dollar amount.

Under Dodd-Frank, the FDIC's authority to guarantee bank debt is made explicit. The Dodd-Frank Act also expanded the FDIC's role in liquidating troubled financial institutions. Under Dodd-Frank, the FSOC

[Financial Stability Oversight Council] will designate certain financial institutions—banks and nonbanks—as systemically important. In addition to more stringent capital regulation, those firms will be required to draw up "living wills," or plans for orderly liquidation. The Federal Reserve, with the concurrence of two-thirds of the FSOC, may determine that a firm represents a "severe threat" to financial stability and may order it closed. The FDIC will administer the resolution process for nonbanks as well as banks.

The Federal Reserve. The Board of Governors of the Federal Reserve System was established in 1913 to provide stability in the banking sector through the regulation of bank reserves (P.L. 63–43, 38 Stat. 251). The System consists of the Board of Governors in Washington and 12 regional reserve banks. In addition to its authority to conduct national monetary policy, the Federal Reserve has safety and soundness examination authority for a variety of lending institutions including bank holding companies; U.S. branches of foreign banks; and state-chartered banks that are members of the federal reserve system. Under the Gramm-Leach-Bliley Act (GLBA, P.L. 106–102), the Fed serves as the umbrella regulator for financial holding companies, which are defined as conglomerates that are permitted to engage in a broad array of financially related activities.

The Dodd-Frank Act made the Fed the primary regulator of all financial firms (bank or nonbank) that are designated as systemically significant by the Financial Stability Oversight Council (of which the Fed is a member). Capital requirements for such firms may be stricter than for other firms. In addition, Dodd-Frank made the Fed the principal regulator for savings and loan holding companies and securities holding companies, a new category of institution formerly defined in securities law as an investment bank holding company.

In addition to institution-level examinations of covered lenders, the Federal Reserve oversees systemic risk. This role came about not entirely through deliberate policy choices, but partly by default, as a result of the Fed's position as lender of last resort and its consequent ability to inject capital or liquidity into troubled institutions. The Federal Reserve's standard response to a financial crisis has been to announce that it stood ready to provide liquidity to the system. Until 2007, this announcement was sufficient: a number of crises—the Penn Central bankruptcy, the stock market crash of 1987, the junk bond collapse, sovereign debt crises, the Asian crises of 1997–1998, the dot.com crash, and the 9/11 attacks—were quickly brought under control, in most cases without doing harm to the U.S. economy. In 2007, however, the Fed's statements and its actual provision of liquidity failed to restore stability. As a result, the Fed's role as the primary systemic risk regulator was closely scrutinized and the Financial Stability Oversight Council was created.

Finally, Title VIII of Dodd-Frank gave the Fed new safety and soundness authority over payment, clearing, and settlement systems that the FSOC determines to be systemically important. The utilities and institutions that make up the U.S. financial infrastructure process millions of transactions daily, including bill payments, loans, securities purchases, and derivatives trades, representing trillions of dollars. The Federal Reserve is authorized to write risk management standards (except for clearing entities subject to appropriate rules of the CFTC or SEC) and to participate in supervisory examination and enforcement activities in coordination with prudential regulators.

National Credit Union Administration. The NCUA, originally part of the Farm Credit Administration, became an independent agency in 1970 (P.L. 91–206, 84 Stat. 49). The NCUA regulates all federal credit unions and those state credit unions that elect to be federally insured. It administers a Central Liquidity Facility, which is the credit union lender of last resort, and the National Credit Union Share Insurance Fund, which insures credit union deposits. Credit unions are member-owned financial cooperatives, and must be not-for-profit institutions. As such, they receive preferential tax treatment compared to mid-sized banks.

NOTE ON OTHER PRIVATE MORTGAGE LENDERS

Life insurance companies. The general insurance function of life insurance companies creates a steady and sizeable inflow of funds with a steady but relatively small and predictable outflow, which leaves large sums continually available for long-range investment. The investment pattern for these funds is based primarily upon the available return. As a result, mortgages must compete with other financial assets for life insurance companies' funds.

Until the 1950s, life insurance companies were significant lenders on single-family owner-occupied housing, but since then they have gradually withdrawn from this market and are now almost totally absent from it. However, life insurance companies remain a significant source of funding for commercial and multifamily apartment lending, accounting for 13.3% of all such mortgages held at the end of 2013.

Mortgage banking companies. Mortgage bankers originate loans in order to sell them to other investors or to securitize them. Hence, they hold loans only for the short term. While mortgage bankers make both residential and commercial loans, many specialize in single-family residential lending. The bulk of their business traditionally involved the origination of FHA-insured and VA-guaranteed mortgage loans. However, with the growth of private mortgage insurance companies, mortgage bankers increasingly expanded their activities into the field of conventional mortgages, and the share of their business represented by FHA and VA loans declined markedly.

Because mortgage bankers are not depository institutions, they cannot fund loans from deposited money like banks and savings associations. Instead, mortgage bankers fund loans with corporate capital and, more importantly, from warehouse loans, which are short-term lines of credit, usually from commercial banks. Some mortgage bankers have been started by or become affiliated with large financial institutions, such as bank holding companies.

Mortgage bankers sell their loans by soliciting commitments from large institutions to purchase substantial blocks of single-family loans and multifamily loans, and by selling mortgage-backed securities. Both Fannie Mae and Freddie Mac purchase large numbers of loans from mortgage bankers, and GNMA has had a great influence over mortgage bankers' operations through their use of the GNMA mortgage-backed security program. The bankers' income is earned from borrower fees, servicing fees, profits from loan sales, and indirectly from large tax and insurance escrow deposits, which are often used as compensating balances for bank lines of credit. A mortgage banker also may earn income from sidelines, such as land development and construction loans and standby commitments.

Mortgage banks are typically corporations and, as such, are subject to state corporate laws and regulations. Historically, federal and state supervision of mortgage bankers was minimal. However, many states have now adopted licensing laws for mortgage bankers, and they have become subject to much heavier regulation. In addition, the FHA must approve mortgage bankers that deal in FHA loans, and FHA periodically examines and audits these bankers to ensure that they are adequately capitalized and can properly service their loans.

Mortgage brokers. During the past thirty years, the United States has witnessed huge growth in the use of mortgage brokers to originate residential loans. A mortgage broker, unlike a mortgage banker, does not actually fund the loan. Rather, the broker acts as an intermediary that finds a lender for the borrower. This has become an increasingly valuable service as the array of mortgages has become more varied. The broker takes the borrower's loan application, performs a preliminary financial and credit evaluation based on the lender's underwriting standards, produces the necessary documents, and supervises the loan closing. The lender may be a bank, mortgage company, or thrift institution. The loan is closed in the lender's name, and the lender underwrites, funds, and often services the loan.

Until the enactment of the Dodd-Frank financial reform legislation by Congress in 2010, most mortgage brokers' income came from loan origination fees and from receiving "yield spread premiums" from the lender. A yield spread premium (YSP) is the additional compensation that a lender pays the broker if the borrower accepts a loan with an interest rate (the "retail" rate) that exceeds the minimum interest yield that the lender will accept (the "wholesale" rate). The spread between the two rates is typically 1/4% to 1/2%. The YSP increases as the difference between the retail and wholesale interest rates increases.

The YSP was controversial as a means of broker compensation for two reasons. First, borrowers often believed that the broker owed them a duty to obtain a loan at the lowest possible interest rate. In reality, there was no such duty, and the broker had an economic incentive to maximize the YSP by placing the retail loan at the highest possible rate. Second, borrowers often did not realize that they were paying the fee, because it was included in the interest rate on the loan. HUD construed RESPA was requiring disclosure of the broker's fee, but form of disclosure was obscure and often ineffective. Commentators disagreed on whether yield spread premium payments harmed borrowers, but there was widespread criticism of the practice.

The Dodd-Frank Act flatly YSPs prohibited in residential lending; see Dodd-Frank § 1403(c)(4)(A), amending section 129B of the Truth in Lending Act to prohibit any YSP that would "permit the total amount of direct and indirect compensation from all sources permitted to a mortgage originator to vary based on the terms of the loan (other than the amount of the principal)." Dodd-Frank also prohibited "dual compensation," in which the broker would be compensated both by the borrower and the lender; see Dodd-Frank § 1403(c)(2). The Consumer Financial Protection Bureau was given authority to implement, and to waive application of, these statutory provisions. The CFPB's final rule on loan originator compensation was issued January 20, 2013 and appears as 12 C.F.R. Part 1026. It continues the prohibition on dual compensation, and it prohibits the payment of compensation to a mortgage originator based on any term of the loan except its dollar amount. The final rule was designed primarily to protect consumers by reducing incentives for loan originators to steer consumers into loans with particular terms and by ensuring that loan originators are adequately qualified. See Nicole Olvera, Why the CFPB Should Reconsider Dodd-Frank's Prohibition on Yield Spread Premiums, 16 N.C. Banking Inst. 323 (2012).

C. GOVERNMENT-SPONSORED MORTGAGE MARKET SUPPORT INSTITUTIONS

HOUSING AMERICA'S FUTURE: NEW DIRECTIONS FOR NATIONAL POLICY

Housing Commission, Bipartisan Policy Center
February 2013, pages 40–46

Historical Context: The Path to Today's Housing Finance System. The Great Depression was a watershed period in the history of housing in the United States. Up until the mid-1930s, residential mortgages generally had short terms (usually three to ten years), variable interest rates, and featured "bullet" payments of principal at term. Borrowers would normally refinance these loans when they became due or pay off the outstanding loan balance. At the time, large down payments were common, and mortgages typically had very low loan-to-value (LTV) ratios of 60 percent or less. The homeownership rate, however, was significantly lower than it is today—around 45 percent, compared with 64.6 percent— as fewer families had the financial wherewithal to enter into mortgages with these more stringent terms. Homeownership was generally reserved for the wealthy or, in rural areas, for those who lived on and farmed their land.

As the Great Depression swept the nation, housing values declined by as much as 50 percent. Banks that held the mortgages on these homes refused to or were unable to refinance when the loans came due. Thousands of borrowers then defaulted, having neither the cash nor the home equity available to repay the loans. The consequence was a wave of about 250,000 foreclosures annually between 1931 and 1935.

In response to these events, the federal government established the Federal Home Loan Bank system in 1932 to increase the supply of mortgage funds available to local financial institutions and to serve as a credit reserve. Two years later, in 1934, the government created the FHA to help stabilize the mortgage market through its insurance programs. By insuring only mortgages that met certain limits on the maximum principal obligation, interest rate, LTV ratio, and loan duration, the FHA helped set the foundation for the modern standardized single-family mortgage. In 1944, the government established the VA loan guarantee program, similar in approach to the FHA loan-level insurance programs but targeted to helping military veterans and their families secure homeownership. In the years following World War II, the homeownership rate rose steadily, from 43.6 percent in 1940 to 55 percent in 1950 and to 66.2 percent in 2000, as measured by the Decennial Census.

In addition to ownership housing, the FHA also provides credit support for multifamily rental housing through a separate reserve fund first established by the National Housing Act of 1938. The FHA's authority to support multifamily housing was not widely exercised until the 1960s when several programs were created to encourage the construction and preservation of rental housing for moderate-income households.

In 1934, the government also authorized the FHA to create national mortgage associations to provide a secondary market to help mortgage lenders gain access to capital for FHA-insured loans. Only one such association was established, when the FHA chartered the Federal National Mortgage Association in 1937. In 1968, the Federal National Mortgage Association was partitioned into two separate entities—the Government National Mortgage Association, or Ginnie Mae, which remained in the government, and Fannie Mae, which became a privately owned company charged with the public mission of supporting the mortgage market by purchasing conventional (i.e., non-government-insured) mortgages. Until the 1980s, Fannie Mae carried out its mission by issuing debt—first as a government agency and after 1968 as a government-sponsored enterprise (GSE)—and using it to buy mortgages from their originators. In 1970, the secondary market grew with the creation of Freddie Mac, which was initially owned by the Federal Home Loan Banks and, with passage of the Financial Institutions Reform, Recovery and Enforcement Act (FIRREA) in 1989, reorganized as a private, for-profit corporation with a charter similar to that of Fannie Mae.

Over the years, Fannie Mae, Freddie Mac, and Ginnie Mae helped bring greater transparency and standardization to both the single-family and multifamily housing finance system, which has lowered mortgage costs. By setting clear benchmarks for loans eligible for securitization, the three institutions also helped improve the overall credit quality of the system. Moreover, by linking local financial institutions with global investors in the secondary market, they helped expand access to mortgage credit.

However, the companies' role was a sore point for the lending industry almost from the start. Acting as a giant thrift, Fannie Mae profited from the spread it earned between its cost of funds, which was lower than other private companies because of its government ties, and the interest rates on mortgages. The creation of the first MBS by Ginnie Mae in the 1970s led Fannie Mae and Freddie Mac, and then private Wall Street firms, to engage in securitization. Depositories viewed Fannie Mae as a competitor for balance-sheet lending, and, after MBS became the prevalent funding source, private-sector competitors likewise saw the GSEs as unfairly competing with them in the securities markets. Both institutions did enjoy a number of benefits because of their unique charters, including a line of credit with the U.S. Treasury, exemptions from certain state and local taxes, which provided favorable treatment for their portfolio business, and most importantly, an implied government guarantee of their securities as well as their own corporate debt. In return, the charters restricted Fannie Mae and Freddie Mac only to residential mortgage finance in the United States, and the companies were expected to support mortgage markets throughout all market cycles, an obligation that did not apply to other fully private investors or guarantors.

In the wake of the Savings and Loan crisis in 1989, Congress imposed new capital requirements and strengthened the GSEs' mission requirements. But the pressure to deliver returns to shareholders, along with the mistaken view shared by actors throughout the mortgage market that housing prices would continue to rise without interruption, encouraged Fannie Mae and Freddie Mac to leverage their businesses to unsustainable levels. With insufficient capital buffers, both institutions suffered catastrophic losses when the housing market collapsed and the credit markets froze, leading to their conservatorship by the government in 2008. Notably, during the housing crisis, the multifamily businesses of Fannie Mae and Freddie Mac continued to generate a profit for both institutions, as the default rates on their multifamily loans were substantially lower than the loans in their single-family portfolios. It is also worth noting that the 12 Federal Home Loan Bank cooperatives, which were designed to provide countercyclical liquidity for U.S. mortgage and housing market participants, remained a reliable source of liquidity for their more than 7,700 member institutions during the crisis. The Home Loan Banks provide a reliable flow of funds and liquidity to local lenders for housing and community development through advances funded by debt the banks issue and collateralized by mortgages or mortgage bonds exchanged by members in return for the advances. In late 2008, while other sources of credit froze, Federal Home Loan Bank advances increased by $400 billion (reaching $1 trillion) as the Home Loan Banks continued to support their members' participation in the housing market.

Despite our current difficulties, households in the United States have enjoyed a wider range of mortgage financing options than those in most other nations of the world. For instance, the most common mortgage product in the United States—the long-term, fixed-rate mortgage—is relatively rare in other countries where shorter-term and variable-rate mortgages are the norm. The long-term, fixed-rate mortgage has been a tremendous boon to consumers who are provided with cost certainty and protection from the risks associated with fluctuating interest rates. The process of securitization has played an instrumental role in setting the standards for these mortgages and making them widely available on affordable terms for millions of American families. By taking individual mortgages—inherently illiquid and difficult-to-price assets—and combining them with millions of other loans in stable securities based on cash flows from a broadly diversified portfolio of assets, securitization has opened the residential finance market to investors who otherwise could not participate in this market. The flow of cash has helped fuel one of the most stable, transparent, and efficient capital markets in the world and assured American consumers of a steady and reliable source of mortgage credit.

Single-Family Housing Finance Trends. In the wake of the collapse of privately funded and nongovernment-insured mortgages, the federal government has emerged as a dominant presence in the housing finance market, a role it has played before when private capital has fled the mortgage market. The federal government currently insures and guarantees the largest share of mortgage-backed securities and assumes the major portion of credit risk in the U.S. mortgage market.

In 2011, securities backed by Fannie Mae, Freddie Mac, and Ginnie Mae (with credit insurance from the FHA and the VA) constituted 97 percent of all MBS, with non-agency funds less than 3 percent. By comparison, Fannie Mae, Freddie Mac, and Ginnie Mae accounted for 78 percent of the MBS market in 2000, with non-agency funds at 22 percent. Government and GSE shares of MBS remained relatively steady through the 1990s, a period of strong economic growth and stable interest rates.

The same general situation is true for all mortgage originations (whether originated to be held in portfolio or sold into the MBS market). In 2010, private-sector-related originations including jumbo loans, loans originated for private-label securities, and adjustable-rate mortgages (ARMs) to be held in portfolio constituted only 12 percent of originations (compared with 53 percent in 2000 and 44 percent in 1990), while FHA/VA loans and Fannie Mae and Freddie Mac conforming loans constituted 88 percent of originations (versus 47 percent in 2000 and 56 percent in 1990).

While there are nascent signs that we have turned a corner, the U.S. system of single-family housing finance continues to face serious challenges as significant problems related to the Great Recession persist. Sustained high unemployment, an unprecedented collapse in house prices—especially in certain highly affected states and metropolitan areas—the large volume of foreclosures, and a prolonged foreclosure process in some states continue to stand in the way of a full market recovery. Further, while in most of the country the cost of buying a home has never been more affordable, stringent underwriting requirements prevent many would-be borrowers from taking advantage of these conditions. Borrowers' credit scores at origination have increased by 40 to 50 points since 2001.

The foregoing report proposes a program for future legislation under which the GSEs would be gradually phased out, and a new office, termed the "Public Guarantor," which would provide a "limited and explicit government guarantee for catastrophic risk for certain mortgage-backed securities." There is fairly general agreement that the GSEs should not be left in their current state of conservatorship—essentially as wards of the federal government—indefinitely. But no consensus has developed around any specific plan. Other proposals, made by a variety of individuals and interest groups, run along the following lines:

1.   Establishing a fully federal agency that would purchase and guarantee qualifying mortgages;

2.   Moving to a hybrid public/private approach that would involve explicit federal guarantees of some privately issued MBSs; or

3.   Promoting a fully private secondary mortgage market with no federal guarantees.

Reaching agreement on GSE reform has proven difficult, not only because of the usual philosophical differences between the political parties, but also because the housing finance system and the proposals for reform are so complex, and the reactions of other parts of the system to a change in the role of the GSEs is so uncertain, that no one has much real confidence that any plan, including their own, will have the desired results. See Andrea J. Boyack, Laudable Goals and Unintended Consequences: The Role and Control of Fannie Mae and Freddie Mac, 60 Am. U. L. Rev. 1489 (2011); Reginald T. O'Shields, Reforming America's Mortgage Market: What Comes After Fannie Mae And Freddie Mac?, 16 N.C. Banking Inst. 99 (2012); Richard Boyd, Bringing the GSE's Back In?: Bailouts, U.S. Housing Policy, and The Moral Case for Fannie Mae, 11 Geo. J. L. & Pub. Pol'y 457 (2013).

HOUSING FINANCE SYSTEM: A FRAMEWORK FOR ASSESSING POTENTIAL CHANGES

U.S. General Accountability Office
October 2014, pages 9–11

The Federal Home Loan Bank System is a government-sponsored enterprise that consists of 12 FHLBanks and the Office of Finance, the FHLBanks' fiscal agent. Each FHLBank is cooperatively owned by member financial institutions, typically commercial banks and thrifts. The FHLBanks borrow funds by issuing debt securities in capital markets and provide low-cost, long- and short-term advances (loans) to member institutions, which use the loans to fund mortgages and maintain liquidity for their operations.

Member institutions provide the FHLBanks with mortgages or other qualifying loans and securities, as collateral for the advances. If a member institution fails, the FHLBank generally gets repaid before many other creditors; depending on the agreement, the FHLBank may be able to draw on the majority of the financial institution's assets in addition to the collateral provided for the advances for repayment.

Private financial institutions and the federal government facilitate mortgage lending by insuring mortgages that meet certain criteria against default or guaranteeing lenders payment of principal and interest. Generally, lenders require borrowers to purchase private mortgage insurance when the initial loan-to-value (LTV) ratio of the mortgage (the amount of the mortgage loan divided by the value of the home) exceeds 80 percent. The enterprises require that loans they purchase with LTV ratios in excess of 80 percent have a credit enhancement mechanism, such as private mortgage insurance. Generally, loans with higher LTV ratios have a greater risk of default and may experience greater loss severity in the event of a default.

FHA operates the largest federal mortgage insurance program, which is backed by the full faith and credit of the federal government. FHA insures the full value of mortgages made by private lenders for borrowers making down payments of at least 3.5 percent. The purpose of FHA's mortgage insurance is to encourage lenders to make mortgages available to borrowers, including those who would not otherwise qualify, such as low-income and first-time homebuyers. Congress has set limits on the size of loans eligible for FHA insurance, and these limits have varied over time. For example, when the recent financial crisis and economic recession set in and other segments of the mortgage market contracted, Congress increased the loan amounts eligible for FHA insurance. In 2014, FHA's mortgage limits for single-family houses ranged from the national standard of $271,050, to $625,500 for other higher cost areas, and to $938,250 for certain areas outside of the 48 contiguous states such as Alaska, Hawaii, and Guam.

Borrowers pay up-front and ongoing insurance premiums that go to FHA's Mutual Mortgage Insurance Fund to cover the estimated long-term costs of the program. In fiscal year 2013, FHA reported that it insured more than 1.3 million new mortgages representing approximately $240 billion in mortgage insurance coverage on forward mortgages. This brought the total loans insured to more than 7.8 million, and FHA reported that its total amortized insurance-in-force on mortgages at the end of fiscal year 2013 was $1.09 trillion.

The federal government also administers two other mortgage insurance programs, through VA and USDA. The VA Home Loan Guaranty program provides financial incentives for private lenders to offer eligible service-members and veterans of the U.S. armed forces mortgages with certain favorable terms, such as not requiring a down payment or private mortgage insurance. Depending on the size of the loan, VA guarantees between 25 and 50 percent of the mortgage loan in the event that a borrower defaults, providing lenders with protection against some of the losses that may be associated with making these loans. Most veterans receiving guaranteed loans pay a funding fee of up to 3.3 percent of the loan amount, but the program also receives funding through federal appropriations. As of September 30, 2013, the outstanding principal of VA's guaranteed loans was $339 billion, but VA had only guaranteed $89 billion of that amount. USDA administers the

Section 502 Guaranteed Rural Housing Loan Program, which is designed to serve rural residents who have low or moderate incomes and are able to afford mortgage payments but are unable to obtain adequate housing through conventional financing, by guaranteeing loans made by commercial lenders. In 2013, the principal of new loans supported by USDA guarantees was $22.3 billion and the outstanding principal of all guaranteed loans was $89.7 billion.[14]

State and Local Housing Finance Agencies. The creation by state governments of mortgage market support agencies is a relatively recent phenomenon. In 1960 New York became the first state to do so; by 1970 twelve more states had acted, and now nearly all states have such agencies. The underlying concept of all of the agencies is similar. They sell bonds and other debt instruments that, because of their state government status, are exempt from federal and often state income taxation, and which therefore bear relatively low interest rates. The funds raised by these bond and note sales are then used to finance housing for low-income and moderate-income families and individuals, with the lower interest rates being passed on in the form of lower mortgage interest to the home-buyers (in the case of owner-occupied housing) or sponsor-landlords (in the case of rental apartments).

The mechanisms by which the state agencies funnel their money into the residential mortgage market are varied. Some make direct loans to housing developers, sponsors, and individual buyers. Others act as secondary market purchasers, issuing advance commitments to lending institutions to purchase loans which meet prescribed criteria. Still others make loans to lending institutions, on the condition that the funds be employed in mortgage lending on housing of the type the agency desires to assist. Some employ two or more of the foregoing methods. Whether single-family or multi-family housing is involved, the agencies usually impose limitations on the household income of the occupants and on the cost of the housing. A variety of other programmatic variations exist, including working cooperatively with the Department of Housing and Urban Development, supplying mortgage loans for projects subsidized by HUD under its Section 8 program.

As the success of the state housing finance agencies grew in the late 1970's, some cities and counties began to emulate their example, either creating local financing agencies or issuing mortgage-backed bonds

---

[14] USDA's guarantee provides coverage for eligible losses of up to 90 percent of the original principal, including unpaid principal and interest; principal and interest on USDA approved advances for protection and preservation of the property; and the costs associated with selling the foreclosed property. USDA and VA also make direct mortgage loans, though the total amount of loans made under these programs is far lower than the amount of loans that are guaranteed.

themselves. In most of these situations, single-family home loans to owner-occupants were involved. Viewing this increased activity, Congress became concerned that the implicit federal subsidy was being abused. There were reports of loans to wealthy individuals to buy expensive houses. Since the bonds represented a significant loss of revenue to the federal government, they could hardly be justified in social policy terms except in cases of needy borrowers who could not otherwise afford decent housing.

Congress' objections to this free-wheeling use of tax-free financing found expression in the Mortgage Subsidy Bond Tax Act of 1980, which added Section 103A to the Internal Revenue Code. It deems the interest on mortgage subsidy bonds to be taxable income unless the criteria set out in the Act are met. To qualify, 90% of the mortgage loans in the program must be to persons who have not owned a home during the previous three years, and 20% of the funds must be directed to economically distressed areas. Each state is given an annual "quota" in terms of dollar volume of bonds that can be issued; half of this amount is allocated to the state agency, and half to local agencies, unless the state chooses a different allocation. Prices of the homes financed must not exceed certain limits, and the IRS is authorized to publish "safe harbor" figures for these limits.

The Tax Reform Act of 1984 added a new twist in an attempt to respond to the long-expressed criticism that tax-exempt bonds are an inherently inefficient and costly technique for subsidizing housing, since much of the lost federal revenue benefits wealthy bond-holders and the various underwriters, lawyers, and other professionals who create and market the bonds. The 1984 Act allows state housing finance agencies to "trade in" a portion of their unused tax-exempt bond-issuing authority in return for authority to issue taxable bonds tied to "mortgage credit certificates", or MCC's. These MCC's can then be issued to qualified home buyers, and allow them to take a tax credit (not merely a deduction) for a portion of the interest they pay on their mortgage loans. The credit may vary from 10% to 50% of the interest paid, and has the obvious effect of reducing the cost of home ownership. Thus, the benefit to the home buyer is economically analogous to that which results from issuance of tax-free bonds, although under the MCC program, the interest on the agency's corresponding bonds is taxable rather than tax-exempt.

The MCC program was further complicated by the Technical and Miscellaneous Revenue Act of 1988, which set in place a system for recapturing the tax credits of homeowners whose incomes rise or who sell their houses at a profit. The recapture amount may be as great as the lesser of 6.25% of the highest mortgage balance or 50% of the mortgagor's gain on disposition of the property. The 6.25% figure is a maximum percentage, and is adjusted downward depending on the time the mortgagor has held the home; only 20% of it is applied if the home is disposed of in the first year; that percentage rises by 20% a year to 100% in the fifth year, and then declines by 20% per year through the ninth year. If the home is held for ten years or more, there is no recapture. A downward adjustment in the recapture amount is also made for low-income families.

A final important program operated by state housing finance agencies is known as the low income housing tax credit program. The agencies are authorized to allocate tax credits to developers and investors for the construction and rehabilitation of apartments for tenants. Developers are required, at a minimum, to rent 40 percent of their units to tenants with incomes equal to or less than 60 percent of the area median income, or to rent 20 percent of their units to tenants with incomes equal to or less than 50 percent of the area median income. Each state has a tax credit cap based on its population. The credit is claimed over a ten-year period, and requires the developer to set aside the housing units in question for low-income use for 30 years. The program is the largest federal government initiative subsidizing low-income privately-owned housing, and in recent years has provided subsidies for 70,000 to 100,000 dwelling units per year, or more than 1.3 million units since its inception in 1986. About a dozen states offer a similar credit against state income tax.

D. LENDING DISCRIMINATION

Class-based discrimination by mortgage lenders has been an ongoing problem in the United States. Some lenders have refused to make loans or have offered loans on less favorable terms to certain classes or races of loan applicants, or for homes in areas where the residents are predominantly members of racial minorities. Because of the perceived fundamental importance of housing and the usual need for financing to purchase it, a number of federal, state, and local laws prohibit lenders from engaging in these practices.

At the federal level, four principal statutes prohibit various types of discrimination in residential mortgage lending:

1. *The Fair Housing Act*, 42 U.S.C. § 3605, which is part of the Civil Rights Act of 1968, provides:

> (a) It shall be unlawful for any person or other entity whose business includes engaging in residential real estate-related transactions to discriminate against any person in making available such a transaction, or in the terms or conditions of such a transaction, because of race, color, religion, sex, handicap, familial status, or national origin.

(b) As used in this section, the term "residential real estate-related transaction" means any of the following:

(1) The making or purchasing of loans or providing other financial assistance—

(a) for purchasing, constructing, improving, repairing, or maintaining a dwelling; or

(b) secured by residential real estate.

2. *The Fair Housing Act.* The Fair Housing Act's prohibition on sex discrimination was added by the Housing and Community Development Act of 1974, which also contains the following provision, 12 U.S.C. § 1735f–5:

No federally related mortgage loan, or Federal insurance, guaranty, or other assistance in connection therewith (under this chapter or any other Act), shall be denied to any person on account of sex; and every person engaged in making mortgage loans secured by residential real property shall consider without prejudice the combined income of both husband and wife for the purpose of extending mortgage credit in the form of a federally related mortgage loan to a married couple or either member thereof.

A "federally related mortgage loan" is defined as including loans on one-to four-family residences in which any federal, federally-chartered, or federally-insured financial institution or any federal mortgage insurance or guaranty is involved or that is eligible for purchase by a government sponsored enterprise, such as Fannie Mae. This definition includes virtually all home mortgage loans.

3. *The Civil Rights Act of 1866*, 42 U.S.C. §§ 1981–1982, provides in substance that all citizens have the same right to buy, sell, and own property and to make and to enforce contracts as white citizens. For a century, this language was interpreted to prohibit only governmental action. But, in Jones v. Alfred H. Mayer Co., 392 U.S. 409, 88 S.Ct. 2186, 20 L.Ed.2d 1189 (1968), the Supreme Court construed it to apply to private action as well—in that case, a real estate developer's refusal to sell houses to black citizens.

4. *The Equal Credit Opportunity Act*, 15 U.S.C. § 1691 ("ECOA"), which was adopted in 1974, provides:

It shall be unlawful for any creditor to discriminate against any applicant, with respect to any aspect of a credit transaction—

(1) on the basis of race, color, religion, national origin, sex or marital status, or age (provided the applicant has the capacity to contract);

(2) because all or part of the applicant's income derives from any public assistance program; or

(3) because the applicant has in good faith exercised any right under this chapter.

The Federal Reserve Board has the principal authority to issue regulations under ECOA. Fourteen different federal agencies have enforcement powers depending on the type of creditor involved.

Two other federal statutes address the problem of lending discrimination, though they do not substantively prohibit it:

5. *The Home Mortgage Disclosure Act of 1975*, 12 U.S.C. §§ 2801–2810 ("HMDA"), requires depository financial institutions to maintain and to publish records showing, by census tract, the locations of the properties that secure their loans. These requirements enable community organizations to determine whether savings institutions are (as has frequently been charged) taking savings funds out of central-city minority areas and relending them in "safe" all-white suburbs. The information is also useful to the examiners from the various federal and state agencies that audit financial institutions' overall performance.

The Financial Institutions Reform, Recovery, and Enforcement Act of 1989, Pub. L. No. 101–73, 103 Stat. 183 ("FIRREA"), amended HMDA in 1989 to include within its coverage not only depository institutions, but also mortgage bankers that have at least $10 million in assets and an office in a metropolitan statistical area. FIRREA also expanded the reporting requirements; loan applications, as well as actual loans, must now be reported. The data to be reported now includes loan amount, property location, type of loan, and the race, sex, and income of loan applicants. Lenders with assets of less than $30 million need not collect or report these last three items. The reporting institutions are not required to cross-tabulate or analyze the data; the Federal Financial Institutions Examination Council prepares summary tabulations for each lender.

6. *The Community Reinvestment Act of 1977*, 12 U.S.C. §§ 2901–2908 ("CRA"), requires each federally-related financial institution to adopt a delineation of the community that it serves and a statement of policy indicating how it will serve that community, with particular reference to meeting mortgage lending needs. The federal agencies that supervise financial institutions are instructed to take this information and the institution's performance under its statement into account in making decisions relevant to the institution's future plans, such as establishing new branch offices and closing offices. See generally Craig E. Marcus, Note, Beyond the Boundaries of the Community Reinvestment Act and the Fair Lending Laws: Developing a Market-Based Framework

for Generating Low- and Moderate-Income Lending, 96 Colum.L.Rev. 710 (1996).

FIRREA amended CRA to require that the federal financial regulatory agencies publicly release their ratings and evaluation reports of the lenders' performance under CRA. Lenders are rated on the basis of their awareness of community credit needs, marketing of credit availability, actual extension of credit to serve the needs, and community development activities. See Deanna Caldwell, An Overview of Fair Lending Legislation, 28 J. Marshall L. Rev. 333 (1995); Peter E. Mahoney, The Community Reinvestment Act: Storm Clouds Clearing, 10 Prob. & Prop. (Jan.-Feb. 1996), at 53.

Some commentators placed much blame on CRA for the mortgage crisis of 2007, arguing that the statute had pressured banks into making risky loans to less-than-creditworthy borrowers in order to meet their obligations under the Act. There may be a small element of truth in this assertion, but it seems largely overdrawn. See Raymond H. Brescia, Part of the Disease or Part of the Cure: The Financial Crisis and the Community Reinvestment Act, 60 S.C. L. Rev. 617 (2009).

A final legal element bearing on discrimination in mortgage lending is the "disparate impact" concept. The Supreme Court first applied this concept in Griggs v. Duke Power Co., 401 U.S. 424, 91 S.Ct. 849, 28 L.Ed.2d 158 (1971). The case involved a company's employment and promotion practices under Title VII of the Civil Rights Act of 1964, which prohibits racial discrimination in employment. The company used intelligence and aptitude tests to determine which employees would be promoted. Black employees were less likely than whites to be promoted under this system, though no direct evidence existed that the employer intended to discriminate against blacks. The Court held that, if the plaintiffs could show that the company's tests and procedures had the *effect* of screening out disproportionate numbers of minorities, the burden would then shift to the employer to show that its practices were required by "business necessity" or by "genuine business need." Subsequent case development has indicated that the employer's burden is to show that it could not use other tests or criteria with a less discriminatory impact to accomplish the same business goal.

The Supreme Court has implied that this concept may apply to discrimination under the Fair Housing Act as well. Arlington Heights v. Metropolitan Hous. Dev. Corp., 429 U.S. 252, 97 S.Ct. 555, 50 L.Ed.2d 450 (1977), *on remand*, 558 F.2d 1283 (7th Cir.1977). But whether this is correct, and how it would apply to mortgage lending practices, is still being developed by case law and by regulation. We will explore this topic more below. Many commonly-used mortgage lending criteria, such as length of time in present employment, length of residence in the community, and previous homeownership, probably have the effect of screening out more minorities than whites. The same may be true of traditional property appraisal standards, because members of racial minorities tend to have lower incomes and, hence, to seek housing in older and less costly neighborhoods. If it can be shown that these criteria have no or only slight power to predict mortgage loan default, does their use violate the Fair Housing Act? *See* David E. Teitelbaum & Clarke D. Camper, Developments in Fair Lending, 51 Bus.Law. 843 (1996) (suggesting that the statistical relevance of some factors used in credit scoring are questionable).

MORTGAGE FINANCING: ACTIONS NEEDED TO HELP FHA MANAGE RISKS FROM NEW MORTGAGE LOAN PRODUCTS

U.S. General Accountability Office
Report GAO–05–194, Feb. 2005, at 23–26

The mortgage industry is increasingly using mortgage scoring and automated underwriting. During the 1990s, private mortgage insurers, the GSEs, and larger financial institutions developed automated underwriting systems. Mortgage scoring is a technology-based tool that relies on the statistical analysis of millions of previously originated mortgage loans to determine how key attributes such as the borrower's credit history, the property characteristics, and the terms of the mortgage note affect future loan performance. Automated underwriting refers to the process of collecting and processing the data used in the underwriting process. FHA has developed and recently implemented a mortgage scoring tool, called the FHA TOTAL Scorecard, to be used in conjunction with existing automated underwriting systems. * * * The mortgage industry also uses credit scoring models for estimating the credit risk of individuals—these methodologies are based on information such as payment patterns.

Statistical analyses identifying the characteristics of borrowers who were most likely to make loan payments have been used to create a weight or score associated with each of the characteristics. According to Fair, Isaac and Company sources, credit scores are often called "FICO scores" because most credit scores are produced from software developed by Fair, Isaac and Company. FICO scores generally range from 300 to 850 with higher scores indicating better credit history. The lower the credit score, the more compensating factors lenders might require to approve a loan. These factors can include a higher down payment and greater borrower reserves.

The characteristics and standards for low and no down payment mortgage products vary among mortgage institutions. Standards to determine a borrower's eligibility differ from lender to lender. For example, one mortgage institution might have a limit on household income where another might not. Each of these mortgage products requires some form of borrower investment. Most mortgage institutions use automated systems to underwrite loans but differ on how they consider factors such as the borrower's credit score and credit history. Finally, mortgage institutions also try to mitigate the increased risk associated with these products by employing tools like prepurchase counseling and greater insurance coverage.

Economic research we reviewed indicated that LTV ratios and credit scores are among the most important factors when estimating the risk level associated with individual mortgages. We identified and reviewed 45 papers that examined factors that could be informative. Of these, 37 examined if the LTV ratio was important and almost all of these papers (35) found the LTV ratio of a mortgage important and useful. Nineteen research papers evaluated how effective a borrower's credit score was in predicting loan performance, and all but one reported that the credit score was important and useful. In addition, a number of the papers reported that other factors were useful when estimating the risk level. For example, characteristics of the borrower—such as qualifying ratios— were cited in several of the papers we reviewed. Finally, other research evaluated additional factors; however, we identified very few papers that investigated the same variables or corroborated these findings. Collectively, the research we reviewed appeared to concur that considering multiple factors was important and useful in estimating the risk level of individual mortgages. For example, some of the papers (7) reported that considering LTV ratio and credit score concurrently was important and useful when estimating the risk level of individual mortgages.

Many studies found that a mortgage's LTV ratio was an important factor when estimating the risk level associated with individual mortgages. In theory, LTV ratios are important because of the direct relationship that exists between the amount of equity borrowers have in their homes and the likelihood of risk of default. The higher the LTV ratio, the less cash borrowers will have invested in their homes and the more likely it is that they may default on mortgage obligations, especially during times of economic hardship (e.g., unemployment, divorce, home price depreciation). And, according to one study, "most models of mortgage loan performance emphasize the role of the borrower's equity in the home in the decision to default." We identified 45 papers that examined the relationship between default and one or more predictive variables; of these, 37 examined if LTV ratio was important and useful. Almost all of these papers (35) determined that LTV ratio was effective in predicting loan performance—specifically, when predicting delinquency, default, and foreclosure. Several papers reported that there was a strong positive relationship between LTV ratio and default. Specifically, one paper reported that the default rates for mortgages with an LTV ratio above 95 percent were three to four times higher than default rates for mortgages with an LTV ratio between 90 to 95 percent. Another paper found that, at the end of 5 years, the cumulative probability of default risks for mortgages with an LTV ratio less than 95 percent was 2.48 percent; however, the cumulative probability of default for mortgages with an LTV ratio greater than or equal to 95 percent was 3.53 percent.

While the majority of the empirical research found that LTV ratio mattered, four of the research efforts did not find that LTV ratio is important when estimating the risk level associated with individual mortgages. For example, one paper found that, for subprime loans, delinquency rates were relatively unaffected by the LTV ratio. Generally, subprime loans are loans made to borrowers with past credit problems at a higher cost than conventional mortgage loans. Additionally, some (7) research efforts examined the relationship between the LTV ratio and severity (losses), and all found that there was a positive relationship between the LTV ratio and severity. * * *

Despite the relatively recent use of credit score information in the mortgage industry, several studies found that credit score was an important and useful factor when estimating the risk level associated with individual mortgages. In general, credit scores represent a borrower's credit history.[33]

Credit histories consist of many items, including the number and age of credit accounts of different types, the incidence and severity of payment problems, and the length of time since any payment problems occurred. The credit score reflects a borrower's historic performance and is an indication of the borrower's ability and willingness to manage debt payments. Of the 45 papers we reviewed, 19 evaluated how effective a borrower's credit score was in predicting loan performance. Eighteen research efforts evaluated how effective a borrower's credit score was in predicting delinquency, default, and foreclosure; all of these efforts found that a borrower's credit score was important. Generally, the papers reported that higher credit scores were associated with lower levels of defaults. Specifically, one study found that a mortgage with a credit score of 728 (indicating an applicant with excellent credit) had a default probability of 1.26 percent, while a mortgage with a credit score of 642 had a default probability of 3.41 percent—or more than two times higher.

Additionally, four research efforts examined the relationship between credit score and severity (losses), and three reported that there was a negative relationship between credit score and severity. For example, one

---

[33] Generally, the mortgage industry began widely using credit score information in the late 1990s; therefore, considering credit score in empirical loan performance analysis is very recent. Further, there was a particularly strong housing market during this period.

study found that credit scores were also helpful in predicting the amount of losses resulting from foreclosed mortgages. In particular, the paper reported the loss rate for defaulted mortgages with high credit scores was lower than foreclosed mortgages with low credit scores.

CITY OF LOS ANGELES V. BANK OF AMERICA CORPORATION

U.S. District Court, Central District of California
2014 WL 2770083 (2014)

PERCY ANDERSON, DISTRICT JUDGE.

Before the Court is a Motion to Dismiss filed by defendants Bank of America Corporation, Bank of America, N.A., Countrywide Financial Corporation, Countrywide Home Loans, and Countrywide Bank FSB ("Defendants") (Docket No. 27). Plaintiff City of Los Angeles ("Plaintiff") has filed an Opposition. The parties also filed supplemental briefing. Pursuant to Rule 78 of the Federal Rules of Civil Procedure and Local Rule 7–15, the Court finds this matter is appropriate for decision without oral argument.

I. Factual & Procedural Background

This suit is brought pursuant to the Fair Housing Act of 1968 ("FHA"), as amended, 42 U.S.C. §§ 3601, et seq., to seek redress for injuries allegedly caused by Defendants' pattern or practice of illegal and discriminatory mortgage lending. Specifically, Plaintiff seeks injunctive relief and damages for financial injuries due to foreclosures on Defendants' loans in minority neighborhoods and to minority borrowers that are the result of Defendants' discriminatory lending practices. Plaintiff alleges that beginning in 2004, Defendants began to flood historically under-served minority communities with high cost and other "predatory" loans, allegedly constituting "reverse redlining." The Complaint refers to Defendants as "BoA/Countrywide," "BoA" or "the Bank."

Plaintiff alleges that Defendants engaged in both redlining and reverse redlining. Plaintiff further alleges that Defendants' pattern and practice of reverse redlining has caused an excessive and disproportionately high number of foreclosures on the loans it has made in the minority neighborhoods of Los Angeles. According to the Complaint, Defendants' practice of traditional redlining has also caused an excessive and disproportionately high number of foreclosures in the minority neighborhoods. The Complaint alleges that Defendants have engaged in a continuous pattern and practice of mortgage discrimination in Los Angeles since 2004 by imposing different terms or conditions on a discriminatory basis.

In addition, Plaintiff alleges that Defendants would have had comparable foreclosure rates in minority and white communities if they had properly and uniformly applied underwriting practices in both areas. The Complaint alleges that Defendants' practice of failing to underwrite minority borrowers' applications properly, and of putting these borrowers into loans which: (1) have more onerous terms than loans given to similarly situated white borrowers; and (2) the borrowers cannot afford, leads to foreclosures.

Plaintiff's 68-page Complaint includes data and statistical analysis, as well as statements from Confidential Witnesses in support of its claims. Plaintiff alleges that Defendants have intentionally targeted predatory practices at African-American and Latino neighborhoods and residents. "The predatory practices include charging excessively high interest rates and fees that are not justified by borrowers' creditworthiness; providing teaser rate loans with bogus refinance opportunities; requiring large prepayment penalties while deliberately misleading borrowers about the penalties; refusing to refinance or modify predatory loans; and more." Further, the Complaint alleges that the discretionary lending policies and practice of targeting of minorities, who received predatory loan terms regardless of creditworthiness, have caused and continue to cause foreclosures in Los Angeles.

The Complaint additionally alleges that minority borrowers would have continued to make payments on the mortgage and remained in possession of the premises if Defendants had not improperly steered the borrower into a subprime loan, and that steering borrowers in this manner causes foreclosures and vacancies. Plaintiff further alleges that the discriminatory practices and resulting foreclosures in the minority neighborhoods have inflicted significant, direct, and continuing financial harm to the City. Plaintiff seeks damages based on reduced property tax revenues based on: (a) the decreased value of the vacant properties themselves; and (b) the decreased value of properties surrounding the vacant properties. In addition, Plaintiff seeks damages based on the cost of municipal services that have been and will be required to remedy the blight and unsafe and dangerous conditions which exist at vacant properties that foreclosed as a result of Defendants' discriminatory lending practices.

Defendants now move to dismiss the Complaint on the grounds that (1) Plaintiff lacks standing; (2) Plaintiff's FHA claim is barred by the statute of limitations; and (3) the Complaint fails to state a claim upon which relief can be granted. Plaintiff has filed an Opposition. The parties have also submitted supplemental briefs on the "zone of interests" issue. For the reasons set forth below, the Court denies Defendants' Motion to Dismiss.

II. Legal Standards

A. Standing

Article III of the United States Constitution requires that a litigant have standing to invoke the power of a federal court. Because Article III's standing requirements limit subject matter jurisdiction, a lawsuit is properly challenged by a rule 12(b)(1) motion to dismiss. See Chandler v. State Farm Mut. Auto. Ins. Co., 598 F.3d 1115, 1122 (9th Cir.2010).

The Supreme Court has held that to have standing under the Constitution, a party must show she has suffered an " 'injury in fact,' " that there is a "causal connection between the injury" and the defendant's complained-of conduct, and that it is likely " 'that the injury will be redressed by a favorable decision.' " Lujan v. Defenders of Wildlife, 504 U.S. 555, 560–61, 112 S.Ct. 2130, 2136–37, 119 L.Ed.2d 351 (1992). To demonstrate an "injury in fact," a plaintiff must establish an "invasion of a legally protected interest which is (a) concrete and particularized [citations] and (b) 'actual or imminent, not "conjectural" or 'hypothetical.' " Lujan, 504 U.S. at 560. To meet this test, the "line of causation" between the alleged conduct and injury must not be "too attenuated," and "the prospect of obtaining relief from the injury" must not be "too speculative." Allen v. Wright, 468 U.S. 737, 752, 104 S.Ct. 3315, 82 L.Ed.2d 556 (1984); Maya v. Centex Corp., 658 F.3d 1060, 1070 (9th Cir.2011). * * *

At the pleading stage, general factual allegations of injury resulting from the defendant's conduct may suffice, for on a motion to dismiss we "presum[e] that general allegations embrace those specific facts that are necessary to support the claim." National Wildlife Federation, 497 U.S. at 889. In response to a summary judgment motion, however, the plaintiff can no longer rest on such "mere allegations," but must "set forth" by affidavit or other evidence "specific facts," Fed. Rule Civ. Proc. 56(e), which for purposes of the summary judgment motion will be taken to be true. At the final stage, those facts must be "supported adequately by the evidence adduced at trial." Gladstone, 441 U.S. at 115, n. 31; Lujan, 504 U.S. 555, 112 S.Ct. 2130, 119 L.Ed.2d 351. * * *

Defendants argue that Plaintiff failed to plead an injury in fact and that Plaintiff cannot show an injury fairly traceable to Defendants' conduct. Defendants first argue that the injury alleged is not concrete and particularized. Defendants assert that the primary claimed injury is that values of properties nearby foreclosed homes have decreased, leading to a direct reduction in municipal revenue that otherwise would have been collected, which is pure speculation based on Plaintiff's tax scheme. Defendants further assert that the City Services theory of injury is equally deficient in setting out a non-speculative injury. The Opposition argues that Plaintiff has alleged two different types of damages that are concrete and particularized and that Plaintiff has satisfied the requirements of Article III standing.

As to the injury in fact requirement, Plaintiff alleges decreased property tax revenues and increased city services. Specifically, the City experienced decreased tax revenues due to reduced property values and had to increase spending on police and fire protection and other services to secure foreclosed homes that are abandoned. The four other district courts to look at this specific issue have found injury in fact based on these financial injuries. See City of Birmingham v. CitiGroup, Inc., No. 09–BE–467–S, 2009 WL 8652915 (N.D.Ala. Aug.19, 2009); Mayor and City of Baltimore v. Wells Fargo Bank, N.A., 677 F.Supp.2d 847 (D.Md.2010); Mayor and City of Baltimore v. Wells Fargo Bank, N.A., No. CIV JFM–08–62, 2011 WL 1557759 (D.Md. Apr.22, 2011); City of Memphis v. Wells Fargo Bank, N.A., No. 09–2857–STA, 2011 WL 1706756 (W.D.Tenn. May 4, 2011); and Dekalb Cnty., v. HSBC N. Am. Holdings, Inc., No. 1:12–CV–03640–JCJ, 2013 WL 7874104 (N.D.Ga. Sept.25, 2013). Those courts agreed that under the Supreme Court's decision in *Gladstone*, decreases in property tax revenues and/or increases in municipal services due to vacancies constitute injury in fact.

In *Gladstone*, the Supreme Court held that economic injury to the village as a consequence of alleged violations of the Fair Housing Act satisfied Article III. 441 U.S. at 92. "A significant reduction in property values directly injures a municipality by diminishing its tax base, thus threatening its ability to bear the costs of local government and to provide services." *Id.* at 110–11. Here, Plaintiff alleges reduced property values and decreased tax revenues due to Defendants' alleged violations of the FHA. Therefore, the Court finds that Plaintiff has satisfied the injury in fact element of standing at this stage of the proceedings.

As to the traceability or causation element of standing, Defendants raise several arguments as to why Plaintiff lacks standing. While Defendants are correct that many circumstances may cause foreclosures, including changes in borrowers' ability to repay due to personal life events, the conduct of intervening third parties, and the effect of general economic factors, the allegations of the Complaint limit Plaintiff's claim in this case to only those damages arising from foreclosures caused by Defendants' discriminatory loans. The Court acknowledges that only certain discriminatory loans are at issue because not all discriminatory loans result in foreclosure, not all foreclosures are caused by discriminatory lending practices, and not all foreclosures result in vacant properties. Despite the problems that Plaintiff may ultimately face in proving each link in the causal chain, at this stage Plaintiff has pled factual allegations of injury resulting from the Defendants' conduct.

In *City of Birmingham*, the court found no standing based on lack of traceability or that the causation was too speculative due to the other factors involved, such as the local and national economy, job loss, health problems, and changes in the housing market. 2009 WL 8652915 at *5. In *City of Baltimore*, the court granted a motion to dismiss with leave to amend, and ultimately found that the city had standing based on the third amended complaint. 2011 WL 1557759 at *5. In *City of Memphis*, the court found that the city plausibly alleged a causal connection between their injuries and the conduct of Defendants and the limited damages alleged were fairly traceable to defendants' illegal conduct. 2011 WL 1706756 at *9.6 Finally, in *Dekalb County*, the court found that the complaint satisfied the fairly traceable component of standing "in that the government and industry findings, as well as the empirical data contained in the Complaint raise the pleadings above the speculative level." 2013 WL 7874104 at *7.

The Supreme Court has found organizational standing under the FHA, Havens Realty Corp., et al. v. Sylvia Coleman, 455 U.S. 363, 379, 102 S.Ct. 1114, 71 L.Ed.2d 214 (1982), and has held that a nonprofit development corporation had standing to assert that a denial of rezoning was racially discriminatory and violated the FHA. Arlington Heights v. Metro. Hous. Dev. Corp., 429 U.S. 252, 263, 97 S.Ct. 555, 50 L.Ed.2d 450 (1977). Here, the Complaint contains allegations that Defendants' acts caused the homes to lose value beyond those losses caused by general economic conditions. For example, Plaintiff alleges that "[i]f these unaffordable refinance and home equity loans had not been made, the subject properties would not have become vacant." (Compl.¶ 167.)

Plaintiff argues its injuries are fairly traceable to Defendants' conduct where Plaintiff has performed statistical analyses establishing that loans with predatory terms issued to minorities were more likely to result in foreclosure. A regression analysis of loans issued by BoA/Countrywide in Los Angeles from 2004–2011, controlling for objective risk characteristics such as credit history, loan-to-value ratio, and the ratio of loan amount to income, demonstrates that a predatory loan is 2.382 times more likely to result in foreclosure than a nonpredatory loan. (Compl.¶ 168.)

Defendants respond that, despite what a regression analysis may show, if the individual circumstances of the borrowers or properties in question would have led to foreclosure despite the allegedly unfavorable terms of the loans or if Plaintiff cannot prove recoverable damages it allegedly suffered as the result of the vacancy of the properties, then Plaintiff cannot prevail in this law suit. Defendants are correct that Plaintiff will ultimately have to prove each link in the causal chain. However, at this stage of the proceedings, Plaintiff has sufficiently alleged factual support for each link.

Defendants also argue that the Ninth Circuit's decisions in Maya and Kaing v. Pulte Homes, Inc., 2010 WL 625365, at *6 (N.D.Cal. Feb.18, 2010), aff'd, 464 F. App'x 630, 631 (9th Cir.2011), support their position. While *Maya* and *Kaing* are instructive, these cases are factually distinct because the defendants in those actions were engaged in the business of building and selling homes, as well as financing the purchase of homes by its customers. Even if the decreased home value allegations in *Maya* are similar to the allegations here, the Ninth Circuit remanded that action to permit plaintiffs to amend in order to provide an expert report distinguishing the effect of defendants' actions from general economic influences. "Expert testimony can be used to explain the causal connection between defendants' actions and plaintiffs' injuries, even in the context of other market forces." *Maya*, 635 F.3d at 1073. Here, the Complaint contains detailed regression analysis, statistical evidence and statements from confidential witnesses. Further, the Complaint alleges that Plaintiff can do Hedonic regression analysis to control for other causes. At this stage, these allegations are sufficient to make the links in the causal chain plausible and not merely hypothetical.

Additionally, Plaintiff does not appear to dispute that there were other factors that led to foreclosures or other factors that caused a decline in the City's revenue. The Complaint only seeks to recover for those financial injuries attributable to Defendants' alleged discriminatory lending practices. The Complaint alleges that a Hedonic regression analysis can control for other variables and calculate damages precisely. While social and economic factors affecting the value of real estate may have relevance to Plaintiff's damage claims, these factors do not break the fairly traceable causal chain between Defendants' lending practices and Plaintiff's narrow damages allegations. See *City of Baltimore*, 2011 WL 1557759 at *15. [After extended additional discussion, the court concluded that the City had the requisite standing.]

* * *

B. Statute of Limitations

"An aggrieved person may commence a civil action in an appropriate United States district court or State court not later than 2 years after the occurrence or termination of an alleged discriminatory housing practice . . . to obtain appropriate relief with respect to such discriminatory housing practice. . . ."). 42 U.S.C. § 3613(a)(1)(A). An FHA claim for discrimination begins to run from the date of loan closing. Silva v. G.E. Money Bank, 449 F. App'x 641, 644 (9th Cir.2011); Davenport v. Litton Loan Servicing, LP, 725 F.Supp.2d 862 (N.D.Cal.2010) (same as to reverse redlining claim).

Defendants argue that Plaintiff's FHA claim is time-barred. Defendants assert that Plaintiff limits its FHA cause of action to the consequences of alleged "reverse redlining" by Countrywide, i.e. targeting minority communities for high-priced loans, alleging that conduct ended in 2008, prior to BoA's acquisition and beyond the statutory two-year limitations period. Defendants further assert that to the extent the Complaint alleges Defendants have engaged in different discriminatory conduct, "traditional redlining," i.e. refusing to make loans, this different allegation does not toll limitations as to the prior conduct.

[The court found that the complaint was filed within the limitations period, both because some specific loans were made within 2 years prior to the filing date and because the Plaintiff had alleged an eight-year continuing practice, extending into the 2-year limitations period, of making discriminatory loans.]

* * *

C. Failure to State a Claim

1. Fair Housing Act

Under the FHA, "[i]t shall be unlawful for any person or other entity whose business includes engaging in residential real estate-related transactions to discriminate against any person in making available such a transaction, or in the terms or conditions of such a transaction, because of race, color, religion, sex, handicap, familial status, or national origin." 42 U.S.C. § 3605(a). The making or purchasing of loans or proving other financial assistance is included in the definition of a "residential real estate-related transaction." 42 U.S.C. § 3605(b)(1).

Defendants first argue that Plaintiff cannot pursue FHA violations under a disparate impact theory; and that even if it could, Plaintiff has failed to state a disparate impact claim in this case. In Smith v. City of Jackson, 544 U.S. 228, 125 S.Ct. 1536, 161 L.Ed.2d 410 (2005), the Supreme Court found that whether a federal statute allows for recovery based on disparate impact depends on its text, and specifically on whether "the text focuses on the effects of the action . . . rather than the motivation for the action." Id. at 236. In a footnote in their Motion to Dismiss, Defendants acknowledge that the Ninth Circuit has recognized disparate impact FHA claims after Smith, but Defendants argue that those decisions are not persuasive here.[10] There are numerous decisions recognizing disparate impact claims under the FHA following the decision in Smith and declining to hold that Smith overturned Ninth Circuit precedent recognizing such disparate impact theories.[11] Accordingly,

---

[10] The FHA prohibits not just intentional discrimination "but also actions that have a discriminatory effect based on race (disparate-impact discrimination)." Ojo v. Farmers Grp., Inc., 600 F.3d 1205, 1207 (9th Cir.2010); see also Pfaff v. U.S. Dep't of Hous. & Urban Dev., 88 F.3d 739, 745–46 (9th Cir.1996).

[11] See Budnick v. Town of Carefree, 518 F.3d 1109 (9th Cir.2008) (providing elements necessary to establish a prima facie case of disparate impact under the FHA); NAACP v.

Plaintiff may pursue its discrimination claims under a theory of disparate impact.

Additionally, the Court finds that Plaintiff has sufficiently alleged a claim for disparate impact discrimination. Plaintiff has numerous factual allegations relying on both statistical data and statements of confidential witnesses. For example, the Complaint alleges, "[d]ata reported by the Bank, and available through public databases, shows that in 2004–2011, 14.7% of loans made by BoA/Countrywide to African-American and Latino customers in Los Angeles were high-cost, but only 4.2% of loans made to white customers in Los Angeles were high-cost. This data demonstrates a pattern of statistically significant differences in the product placement for high cost loans between minority and white borrowers." The Complaint also alleges that Defendants targeted minority neighborhoods in Los Angeles for predatory loans and that the result of these lending practices was a materially greater number of foreclosures and vacancies at those specific properties.

Furthermore, the Complaint asserts that statistical data shows that a borrower in a predominantly minority census tract was 1.676 times more likely to receive a predatory loan as was a borrower with similar credit characteristics in a predominantly white neighborhood. A plaintiff is not required to make out a prima facie case at this stage of the proceedings; instead, a plaintiff must sufficiently plead a disparate impact claim. See Gilligan v. Jamco Dev. Corp., 108 F.3d 246 (9th Cir.1997). Here, allegations based on regression analysis and confidential witness statements provide facts sufficient to allege a cause of action for disparate impact under the FHA. Construing all inferences in Plaintiff's favor, the Court finds Plaintiff has alleged Defendants' policy resulted in a disproportionately adverse impact on African Americans and Latinos in Los Angeles. Thus, Defendants' Motion to Dismiss on this ground is denied.

Next, Defendants argue that Plaintiff has failed to state a claim for intentional discrimination. Defendants assert that the Complaint fails to allege that reverse redlining or redlining was intentionally designed and implemented so as to disadvantage minority borrowers because of their minority status. "[A] plaintiff makes out a prima facie case of intentional discrimination under the FHA merely by showing that a protected group has been subjected to explicitly differential—i.e., discriminatory-treatment." Pack v. Fort Wash. II, 689 F.Supp.2d 1237, 1243 (E.D.Cal. 2009). Intentional discrimination requires a party to allege that the lender treated borrowers differently because of their protected status. See

---

Ameriquest Mortg. Co., 635 F.Supp.2d 1096, 1105 (C.D.Cal.2009); Taylor v. Accredited Home Lenders, Inc., 580 F.Supp.2d 1062, 1067 (S.D.Cal.2008) (finding Smith has not overruled prior precedent recognizing the FHA permits disparate impact claims).

Gamble v. City of Escondido, 104 F.3d 300, 305 (9th Cir.1997) ("Proof of discriminatory motive is crucial to a disparate treatment claim.").

Plaintiff argues that the Complaint includes factual allegations that Defendants targeted African-American and Latino borrowers for unfair loan terms on the basis of their race. The Complaint provides numerous allegations from confidential witnesses, including allegations that Defendants pressured loan salespeople to target minority groups and superiors told salespeople to target minorities. Based on the factual allegations in the Complaint, Plaintiff has plausibly stated a claim for intentional discrimination in violation of the FHA. Therefore, Defendants' Motion to Dismiss on this issue is denied.

2. Restitution/Unjust Enrichment

Defendants argue that there is no independent cause of action for "restitution," and Plaintiff has no claim that would allow it to receive restitution as an equitable remedy. In its Opposition, Plaintiff argues that it properly states a claim for restitution where it has conferred a benefit on Defendants by paying for the externalities or costs of harm caused by Defendants' discriminatory mortgage lending. Plaintiff argues that the Ninth Circuit has acknowledged that there is a "claim for the equitable remedy of restitution" where defendants have money or property that belongs to the plaintiff. Walker v. Geico Gen. Ins. Co., 558 F.3d 1025, 1027 (9th Cir.2009). Plaintiff further argues that it is asserting a claim for restitution based on unjust enrichment.

Restitution is a remedy, and there is no independent cause of action for "restitution." Munoz v. MacMillan, 195 Cal.App.4th 648, 661, 124 Cal.Rptr.3d 664 (2011); Melchior v. New Line Productions, Inc., 106 Cal.App.4th 779, 793, 131 Cal.Rptr.2d 347 (2003). California courts are split as to whether unjust enrichment is an independent cause of action. However, the split in the authorities on the existence of a "cause of action" for "unjust enrichment" under California law appears to be founded on semantics, drawing a distinction between unjust enrichment, restitution, and quasi-contract, without a difference. Nordberg v. Trilegiant Corp., 445 F.Supp.2d 1082, 1099–1100 (N.D.Cal.2006). The Supreme Court of California and California Courts of Appeal have recognized actions for relief under the equitable doctrine of unjust enrichment. Ohno v. Yasuma, 723 F.3d 984 (9th Cir.Cal.2013). Here, the second claim for relief is titled, "Common Law Claim For Restitution Based On California Law," and Plaintiff's Opposition argues that it has stated a claim for unjust enrichment.

The Complaint alleges, "[a]s a direct and proximate result of Defendants' predatory lending practices, Defendants have been enriched at Plaintiff's expense. Defendants have failed to remit those wrongfully obtained benefits or reimburse the City for their costs improperly caused by Defendants, and retention of the benefits by Defendants would be unjust without payment." Further, the Complaint alleges that "to its detriment the City has paid for the Defendants' externalities, or Defendants' costs of harm caused by its mortgage lending discrimination, in circumstances where Defendants are and have been aware of this obvious benefit and retention of such benefit would be unjust." Based on these allegations, Plaintiff has stated a claim that survives a motion to dismiss.

Although Plaintiff mislabels its second cause of action as one for restitution, the Court finds that Plaintiff's allegations are sufficient to state a claim under California law. See In re TFT-LCD (Flat Panel) Antitrust Litig., No. M 07–1827 SI, 2011 WL 4345435, at *3 (N.D.Cal. Sept.15, 2011). Even though the allegations survive at this stage, Defendants may argue and submit evidence at the summary judgment or trial stage that Plaintiff did not confer a benefit upon Defendants, that Defendants had no knowledge of such benefit, that retention of that benefit is not unjust, or that the benefit was conferred incidentally to the performance of the City's duties. The Court notes once again that Plaintiff will ultimately need to prove all the elements of its claims.

Conclusion

Based on the foregoing, the Court finds that Plaintiff has standing at the pleading stage. Therefore, Defendants' Motion to Dismiss for lack of standing is denied. Since Plaintiff bears the burden of proof as to standing and must support each element with "the manner and degree of evidence required at the successive stages of the litigation," Lujan, 504 U.S. at 561, the Court stresses that its holding on Plaintiff's standing at the pleading stage does not preclude Defendants from developing a factual record and revisiting the standing issue at a later stage of the case.

Further, Defendants' Motion to Dismiss based on the statute of limitations under the FHA is denied because Plaintiff has sufficiently alleged discriminatory loans originating through December 31, 2011, a pattern or practice of discriminatory lending that occurred from 2004 through 2011, and has also alleged continuing violations. While the face of the Complaint alleges continuing violations of the FHA and a broad practice of discriminatory lending, Defendants may raise the statute of limitations affirmative defense at a later stage of the proceedings once a factual record has been developed. Additionally, the Court finds that Plaintiff has adequately stated a claim under the FHA and stated a claim for unjust enrichment. * * *

NOTES

1. *Intentional racial discrimination.* When race is a motivating factor in denial of mortgage financing for a home, the Fair Housing Act clearly has been violated. For example, in Green v. Rancho Santa Margarita Mortg. Co., 28 Cal.App.4th 686, 33 Cal.Rptr.2d 706 (1994), a mortgage broker failed to place a loan for a black couple though many lenders would have considered the couple to be qualified and though the broker had placed loans for less-qualified white couples in the same development. The court concluded that the broker's half-hearted efforts could be explained only by racial bias. See also Barber v. Rancho Mortg. & Inv. Corp., 26 Cal.App.4th 1819, 32 Cal.Rptr.2d 906 (1994).

However, such bias normally is difficult to prove. In Simms v. First Gibraltar Bank, 83 F.3d 1546 (5th Cir.1996), an apartment project owner, Simms, attempted to convince a lender to finance the conversion of the project into a cooperative that probably would be predominantly minority-owned. The bank refused, and the owner sued, claiming that the decision was racially motivated. The court was unconvinced:

> The fundamental flaw in this evidence is that Simms * * * presented absolutely no evidence that other, "non-protected" applicants or applications were treated any differently around the time of Simms' rejection. * * * Simms also did not present any evidence from which it might be inferred that First Gibraltar had a poor record of lending in minority areas or to minorities; furthermore, there was not the slightest evidence of racial bias presented on the part of any of First Gibraltar's personnel. Although Simms' expert, Smith, testified that it was industry custom to provide written notification of a rejection, and the district court ruled that First Gibraltar was required to give written notification of the rejection under Regulation B of the Equal Credit Opportunity Act, failure to provide written notification to Simms is insufficient to infer a racial motive on the part of First Gibraltar without some showing that other, "non-protected" applications were treated differently. In other words, failing to follow industry custom or federal regulations is not evidence from which a jury could infer racial animus unless Simms showed that First Gibraltar normally conformed with industry custom or complied with federal regulations in handling similar, "non-protected" applications. [83 F.3d at 1558.]

The difficulty of proving that the defendant's actions are motivated by racial bias often leads plaintiffs to attempt to prove their case on the basis of disparate racial impact instead.

2. *Disparate impact.* The Supreme Court has never clearly held the disparate impact theory applicable in a Fair Housing Act case, although numerous lower federal courts have done so. Several of those cases have involved mortgage lending standards or practices with a disparate impact on

minorities. See, e.g., Miller v. Countrywide Bank, N.A., 571 F.Supp.2d 251, 253 (D. Mass. 2008); Beaulialice v. Federal Home Loan Mortg. Corp., 2007 WL 744646 (M.D.Fla. 2007); Hargraves v. Capitol City Mortg., 140 F.Supp.2d 7, 20–21 (D.D.C. 2000).

However, the issue is not quite as clear as the court in the *City of Los Angeles* case seemed to believe. The reason is that the statutory language is arguably lacking. Specifically, Title VII, prohibiting discrimination in employment (the context in which the disparate impact theory originated) provides that "It shall be an unlawful employment practice for an employer: (2) to limit, segregate, or classify his employees or applicants for employment in any way which would deprive or tend to deprive any individual of employment opportunities or *otherwise adversely affect* his status as an employee, because of such individuals race, color, religion, sex, or national origin." By comparison, in the Fair Housing Act, discrimination is prohibited but there is no language referring the "effects" or "results" of a party's actions. It's arguable that this lack indicates that Congress did not intend to penalize acts that had a disparate impact based on race. See Kirk D. Jensen and Jeffrey P. Naimon, The Fair Housing Act, Disparate Impact Claims, and *Magner v. Gallagher*: An Opportunity to Return to the Primacy of the Statutory Text, 129 Banking L.J. 99 (2012). The disparate impact test was rejected as inapplicable in a Fair Housing Act case on this ground in American Insurance Assoc. v. U.S. Dep't of Housing and Urban Development, 2014 WL 5702711 (D.D.C. 2014).

The Supreme Court seems eager enough to resolve this issue. In recent years it granted certiorari in three cases raising it, although the first two were never heard by the court: Gallagher v. Magner, 636 F.3d 380 (8th Cir. 2010), cert. granted 132 S.Ct. 548 (2011), and Mt. Holly Gardens Citizens in Action, Inc. v. Twp. of Mount Holly, 658 F.3d 375 (3d Cir. 2011), cert. granted 133 S.Ct. 2824 (2013). Both of these cases were settled before they could be argued to the Court, leaving the question undecided. Certiorari has been granted in a third case, which is pending at this writing: Texas Department of Housing and Community Affairs v. The Inclusive Communities Project, 747 F.3d 275 (5th Cir. 2014), cert. granted 82 USLW 3686. None of these cases involved mortgage lending. The Texas case, for example, was brought by ICP, an organization whose goal is to help minority families in Dallas relocate to predominantly white neighborhoods. They are aided in working toward this goal if apartment projects built with Low Income Housing Tax Credits (LIHTC) are available, but ICP argues that the state agency responsible for allocating LIHTC funds tends to set them aside predominantly for projects in minority areas, thus perpetuating minority concentration there. Thus, it is not entirely clear that the Supreme Court's resolution of the case will clarify the issues of disparate impact in mortgage lending raised by the *City of Los Angeles* case.

There is no doubt that many lenders and mortgage loan servicers intensely dislike the disparate impact test. It can easily have the effect of illegitimizing credit standards and servicing practices that they have used for decades and that they consider essential to good lending practice. If they are attacked by a regulatory agency or the Department of Justice, they are faced with an unattractive choice—to spend the necessary time and resources to defend against the claim, perhaps unsuccessfully, or to settle, often for a substantial sum. Settlement is often the more attractive option.

3. *Federal agency interpretations.* The federal agencies responsible for administering the Fair Housing Act are clearly of the view that the disparate impact test applies. For example, the CFPB's examination manual for financial institutions provides:

> When an Agency finds that a lender's policy or practice has a disparate impact, the next step is to seek to determine whether the policy or practice is justified by "business necessity." The justification must be manifest and may not be hypothetical or speculative. Factors that may be relevant to the justification could include cost and profitability. Even if a policy or practice that has a disparate impact on a prohibited basis can be justified by business necessity, it still may be found to be in violation if an alternative policy or practice could serve the same purpose with less discriminatory effect. Finally, evidence of discriminatory intent is not necessary to establish that a lender's adoption or implementation of a policy or practice that has a disparate impact is in violation of the FHAct or ECOA.

Consumer Financial Protection Bureau, Supervision and Examination Manual, Oct. 2011, at IFLP4. HUD has also issued a statement along similar lines; see 78 Fed.Reg. 11460 (Feb. 15, 2013), codified at 24 CFR part 100. Illustrative mortgage lending practices cited by HUD as having a discriminatory impact include mortgage pricing policies that give lenders or brokers discretion to impose additional charges or higher interest rates unrelated to a borrower's creditworthiness; credit scoring overrides provided by a purchaser of loans; and credit offered on predatory terms.

But many common underwriting rules bear more heavily on minority than on white loan applicants. These include the usual 28% to 32% housing expense-to-income ratio, and probably such requirements as previous homeownership, a specific time in the present residence or on the present job, and the like. The relatively lower incomes and higher mobility of minorities in the United States mean that such criteria will result in more loan rejections than will be experienced by whites. The issue then becomes the nature of the proof that a lender must offer to rebut the prima facie case. Most of the underwriting guidelines now in use probably have *some* predictive validity in assessing risk of future default, but some of them are far weaker than others. Perhaps the courts will hold that those with only marginal predictive power cannot be used if they produce a disparate impact on racial minorities, but there are no clear holdings to that effect yet. Despite all the talk about disparate impact, this is largely unexplored territory.

4.   *The "Qualified Mortgage" regulations.* The introduction of the Qualified Mortgage (QM) concept by the 2010 Dodd-Frank Act added a further layer of complexity to the equation. The applicable regulation was issued by CFPB on January 10, 2013; see 12 CFR Part 1026.

Adopted to implement Dodd-Frank's "ability to repay" concept, the definition of a QM, as formulated by the CFPB, includes a provision that the ratio of the borrower's total installment debt to income cannot exceed 43 percent. While this percentage is relatively liberal, and is identical to the current Federal Housing Administration requirement, there is little doubt that, because minority borrowers tend to have lower incomes and carry heavier debt service burdens that whites, the use of a 43% ratio will have the effect of rationing out more minority than white households. Home mortgage lenders are not required to confine their lending to QMs, but the definition represents a safe harbor in the sense that QM loans are automatically deemed to satisfy the "ability to repay" requirement.

Lenders who expected to limit their lending to loans complying with the QM standards worried that they might be open to a charge of illegal discrimination under a disparate impact analysis. The CFBP and the federal financial regulators attempted to quell these fears, issuing a joint statement that they did "not anticipate that a creditor's decision to offer only Qualified Mortgages would, absent other factors, elevate a supervised institution's fair lending risk." Many lenders were less than fully satisfied; HUD and the Department of Justice did not join in the statement, and in any event, a policy adopted by the federal agencies would not preclude a private action under ECOA or the Fair Housing Act. Nonetheless, it would be somewhat bizarre if a lender were charged with illegal discrimination for operating within a "safe harbor" established by its regulators. See Nicholas Cassidy, The Fair Housing Act, Disparate Impact, and the Ability-to-Repay: A Compliance Dilemma for Mortgage Lenders, 32 Rev. Banking & Fin. L. 43 (2013).

E.   PREDATORY LENDING

In recent decades concern has grown about the practice of "predatory" mortgage lending. Predatory loans may have terms that are highly disadvantageous—high interest rates, high front-end "points," excessive fees for front-end services, high prepayment penalties, and sometimes a "balloon" obligation after only a small portion of the original loan balance has been amortized. Some predatory loans are made to borrowers who could not qualify for more "normal" mortgage financing, but this is not always the case; sometimes the borrowers have had good credit and adequate income and would have been able to obtain a loan from other sources on much better terms. But, like a large number of borrowers, rich and poor, they did not shop the market to try to find better terms.

Should such loans be illegal, regardless of whether they have a discriminatory effect on racial minorities? In recent years, an increasing number of states and cities have adopted legislation making "predatory" loans illegal. But the meaning of the term "predatory" is not self-evident, and a wide variety of definitions have been adopted.

There is only one federal statute addressing predatory lending: The Home Ownership and Equity Protection Act, or HOEPA. The statute was substantially modified by the Dodd-Frank financial reform legislation of 2010. Its application is governed by rules promulgated by the Consumer Financial Protection Bureau (CFPB). The following excerpt will provide background on its operation.

RECENT CHANGES TO HOEPA

Angela J. Cheek[*]
Business Law Today, April, 2013

On January 10, 2013, the Bureau of Consumer Financial Protection (Bureau) issued a final rule amending Regulation Z by expanding the types of transactions subject to the Home Ownership and Equity Protection Act of 1994 (HOEPA), revising and expanding HOEPA thresholds, and imposing additional requirements on HOEPA loans. The final rule also amends Regulation Z and Regulation X (RESPA) by imposing homeownership counseling requirements. These changes are effective for all loans applied for on and after January 10, 2014. This article focuses on the final rule's expanded coverage, thresholds, requirements, and its impact on creditors, brokers, purchasers, and consumers.

Expanded Coverage. Transactions eligible for HOEPA coverage now include purchase-money loans and home-equity lines of credit (HELOCs). Transactions excluded from coverage include: reverse mortgage loans, loans to finance the initial construction of a dwelling, loans originated by a Housing Finance Agency, and loans under USDA's Section 502 Direct Loan Program. While this expanded coverage may improve consumers' understanding of the terms and features of a high-cost mortgage, it also may limit their access to credit, since most lenders are reluctant to make high-cost mortgages. Further, creditors will incur additional costs in identifying these types of loans, including, but not limited to, those costs related to changing or upgrading automated systems and disclosures, legal and compliance review, and staff training. Creditors also may lose revenue as a greater number of their loans are subject to HOEPA, and there is limited secondary market demand for high-cost mortgages.

---

[*]   Copyright © 2013 by the American Bar Association; Angela J. Cheek.

What is a High-Cost Mortgage? A "High-Cost Mortgage" is a consumer credit transaction secured by a consumer's 1–4 unit principal dwelling, including purchase and non-purchase money closed-end credit transactions and HELOCs, in which

1. The annual percentage rate (APR) exceeds the average prime offer rate (APOR) for a comparable transaction by more than:

    a. 6.5 percentage points for first liens;

    b. 8.5 percentage points for first liens less than $50,000 secured by a dwelling that is personal property (e.g., manufactured home); or

    c. 8.5 percentage points for junior liens;

2. The total points and fees exceed:

    a. 5 percent of the total loan amount if the loan amount is $20,000 or more; or

    b. The lesser of 8 percent of the total loan amount or $1,000 for a loan amount less than $20,000 (the $1,000 and $20,000 figures are adjusted annually); or

3. A prepayment penalty may be charged more than 36 months after consummation or account opening, or may exceed, in total, more than 2 percent of the amount prepaid.

Although the thresholds seem straight-forward, the devil is in the details. Let's dive into those details.

New High-Cost APR and Index. Creditors may use one of three methods to determine the interest rate for the APR calculation. For a fixed-rate transaction, a creditor must use the interest rate in effect as of the date the interest rate for the transaction was set. For a variable-rate transaction which varies according to an index, a creditor must use the higher of the index plus margin or the introductory interest rate in effect as of the date the interest rate for the transaction is set. For a variable-rate transaction which does not vary according to an index (e.g., step-rate mortgage), a creditor must use the maximum interest rate that may be imposed during the term of the transaction.

In order to determine the applicable rate threshold, a creditor must now use the APOR index for a comparable transaction. APOR tables and guidance are available at www.ffiec.gov/ratespread/aportables.htm and www.ffiec.gov/ratespread. There are three factors to consider when determining a "comparable transaction": (1) whether the transaction is a fixed-rate or variable-rate, (2) the date the interest rate for the transaction was set, and (3) the term of the transaction. The "date the interest rate was set" means the date on which the loan's interest rate is set for the final time before closing. If there is a rate lock agreement, it is the lock date specified in the agreement. If a rate is reset after execution of a rate lock agreement (e.g., float-down option exercise date), then the relevant date is the date the rate is re-set for the final time before closing. If there is no rate lock agreement, the relevant date is the date on which the rate is set for the final time before closing. In the case of a fixed-rate transaction, the "term of the transaction" is the transaction's term to maturity. In the case of a variable-rate transaction, the "term of the transaction" is the initial fixed-rate period, rounded to the nearest number of whole years (or, if the initial fixed-rate period is less than one year, one year). A creditor originating a fixed-rate, evergreen HELOC should use a term of 30 years.

What is the potential impact of the revised APR threshold? First, the Bureau estimates a 20 percent increase in refinance and home improvement loans that will be High-Cost Mortgages. Second, FHA recently extended its monthly mortgage insurance premium requirement. This will cause the APR for FHA loans to be higher, since the APR reflects costs other than interest on closed-end transactions, which in turn could make more FHA loans High-Cost Mortgages. Third, the APR calculated from a fully-indexed rate will be higher than the composite APR calculated according to Regulation Z Section 1026.17.

New High-Cost Points and Fees Threshold and Definition. Which points and fees threshold applies depends on whether the face amount of the note, in a closed-end transaction, or the credit limit, in an open-end transaction, is $20,000 or more. In contrast, for the points and fees threshold calculation, the final rule uses a "total loan amount." In a closed-end transaction the "total loan amount" is calculated by starting with the amount financed and subtracting (1) any financed item listed in 1026.4(c)(7) which is unreasonable or is paid to the creditor or an affiliate; (2) any upfront financed credit insurance premium; and (3) the prior loan's prepayment penalty if it is financed, subject to certain limitations. The HELOC "total loan amount" is the credit limit.

The final rule also amends the definition of points and fees to remove certain items previously included (e.g., certain upfront mortgage insurance premiums and bona fide discount points) and to add other items (e.g., the maximum prepayment penalty). Under the final rule, "points and fees" mean the following fees or charges that are known at or before consummation:

1.   All items included in the finance charge under 1026.4(a) and (b).

2.   All compensation paid directly or indirectly by a consumer or creditor to a loan originator that can be attributed to the transaction at the time the interest rate is set. This requirement, as currently drafted, would double-count loan originator compensation under certain

circumstances. There is a Concurrent Proposal that would address this issue. Stay tuned.

3. All items listed in 1026.4(c)(7) if unreasonable, or the creditor or its affiliate receives compensation, direct or indirect, in connection with the charge.

4. Upfront credit life, disability, unemployment insurance premiums.

5. The maximum prepayment penalty. (Note: The following state high cost points and fees calculations also may include some or all of the prepayment penalty amount: Arkansas, Georgia, Massachusetts, New Jersey, New Mexico, North Carolina, and South Carolina.)

6. The prior loan's prepayment penalty, subject to certain limitations. (Note: Georgia, Massachusetts, New Jersey, and New Mexico have a similar requirement.)

7. For HELOCs only, any participation fee payable at or before account opening and any minimum or per-transaction fee (assume at least one draw).

The following items known at or before consummation are excluded from the calculation of "points and fees":

1. Interest or time-price differential

2. Any premium or similar charge imposed in connection with a federal or state agency program (i.e., FHA Mortgage Insurance, VA Funding Fee, or USDA RHS Upfront Guarantee Fee).

3. Any premium or similar charge that protects the creditor against the consumer's default or other credit loss (e.g., private mortgage insurance), but only to the extent the upfront amount does not exceed the FHA upfront mortgage insurance premium for a comparable loan and the upfront guarantee or premium is automatically refundable on a pro rata basis upon satisfaction of the mortgage.

4. Any bona fide third-party charge not retained by the creditor, loan originator, or an affiliate of either, unless the charge is required to be included;

5. Up to 2 bona fide discount points, if the undiscounted interest rate does not exceed the comparable APOR by more than 1 percentage point, or up to 1 bona fide discount point if the undiscounted interest rate does not exceed the APOR by more than 2 percentage points. For transactions secured by personal property, a creditor would use the average rate for a loan insured under Title I of NHA. A discount point is considered bona fide if it reduces the undiscounted rate by at least .25 basis points. (The following states have some form of bona fide discount

point exclusion in their high cost thresholds: Indiana, New Jersey, New Mexico, North Carolina, South Carolina, and Tennessee.)

Based upon the lower points and fees threshold, smaller loan amounts may easily exceed the 5 percent threshold. If this occurs, access to small loan credit may be limited, as creditors and the secondary market have little appetite for High-Cost Mortgages.

New Prepayment Penalty Threshold. The new threshold limits when a penalty may be imposed to the first 36 months of the transaction, and limits the penalty amount to 2 percent of the amount prepaid. For purposes of this threshold, a prepayment penalty does not include (1) certain conditionally-waived upfront bona fide third-party closing costs; and (2) until January 21, 2015, interest charged consistent with the monthly interest accrual amortization method for FHA insured transactions.

The Bureau believes the number of transactions affected by the prepayment threshold will be small, since the maximum prepayment penalty is included in the points and fees calculation, and a creditor would have to forgo some or all of the other charges included in the points and fees calculation, in order to originate a "qualified mortgage" which caps points and fees at 3 percent. In addition, limiting the penalty to the first 36 months will impact lenders in California, Louisiana, Minnesota, New Hampshire, and Ohio, all of which allow prepayment penalties to be charged for a longer period (60/84, 60, 42, 60, and 60 months respectively). This threshold also impacts the allowable prepayment penalty amount in Illinois, 3 percent, and Louisiana, which allows a 5 percent penalty in the first year.

New High-Cost Mortgage Restrictions. Sections 1026.32 and 1026.34 provide that once a transaction is a High-Cost Mortgage:

- Balloon payments are generally prohibited.
- Prepayment penalties are prohibited.
- Financing points and fees are prohibited.
- Late fees cannot exceed 4 percent of the past due payment or be imposed until after 15 days past due.
- Payoff statement must be provided within 5 days of request and fees are restricted.
- Modification and Deferral Fees are prohibited.
- Ability-to-Repay assessment is required for HELOCs. Closed-end loans must meet the 2013 Ability-to-Repay Final Rule requirements.
- No default may be recommended or encouraged.

Revised High-Cost Mortgage Disclosures. Section 1026.32(c) revises the High-Cost Mortgage disclosure and distinguishes closed-end and HELOC requirements. A creditor must provide the disclosure to the consumer not less than 3 business days prior to consummation or account opening. * * *

Corrections of Unintentional Violations. New Section 1026.32(h) allows a creditor or assignee, who, when acting in good faith, fails to comply with any Section 1026.32 requirement, to take steps to cure the "violation" by providing written notice of available choices. For notice to be adequate, the consumer should have at least 60 days to consider the options and communicate a choice. The creditor or assignee must satisfy either of the following sets of conditions:

1.   Within 30 days of consummation or account opening and prior to the institution of any action, the consumer discovers the violation or the creditor or assignee notifies the consumer, and the creditor or assignee (a) provides appropriate restitution within 30 days; (b) adjusts the transaction's terms, within 30 days, by either, at the choice of the consumer (i) making the transaction satisfy Section 1026.32 requirements; or (ii) Changing the transaction's terms so it will no longer be a High-Cost Mortgage.

2.   Within 60 days of the creditor's discovery or receipt of notification of an unintentional violation or bona fide error and prior to the institution of any action, the creditor (a) notifies the consumer of the compliance failure; (b) provides appropriate restitution within 30 days; and (c) adjusts the transaction's terms, within 30 days, by either, at the choice of the consumer (i) making the transaction satisfy Section 1026.32 requirements; or (ii) changing the transaction's terms so it will no longer be a High-Cost Mortgage.

Regulation X (RESPA) Homeownership Counseling Organization List. 12 CFR 1026.20 requires a lender to provide a written list of homeownership counseling organizations (the List) to the applicant of a federally related mortgage loan, which includes a loan (other than temporary financing, e.g., construction loan) secured by a 1–4 unit dwelling, including purchase and non-purchase money closed-end credit and HELOCs. The creditor must retrieve the List information from the Bureau's website or from data made available by the Bureau or HUD no more than 30 days prior to delivery.

A lender must provide the List no later than 3 business days after the lender or mortgage broker receives an application. If there is more than one applicant, the lender may provide the List to the applicant with primary liability. If the lender does not provide the List in person, the lender must mail or deliver it by other means, including electronically, subject to the E-Sign Act. Although the lender is ultimately responsible for compliance, a mortgage broker or dealer also may provide the List. If there is more than one lender, only one List is required. Unless otherwise prohibited, the lender may provide the List with other required disclosures. For a HELOC subject to Regulation Z, a lender that provides the applicant with the List may comply with the timing and delivery requirements of either 1024.20(a) or 1026.40(b).

A lender does not need to provide the List if before the end of the 3 business days, the application is denied or withdrawn, or the application is for a reverse mortgage or loan secured by a timeshare.

High-Cost Mortgage Counseling Requirements. Section 1026.34(a)(5) requires a creditor, prior to making a High-Cost Mortgage, to receive written certification from an unaffiliated HUD-certified or -approved or state housing finance authority-certified or -approved counselor that the consumer received counseling on the advisability of the transaction. The certification must contain the elements specified in 1026.34(a)(5). The creditor may receive the certification by mail, e-mail, or facsimile. A creditor may process the application, order the appraisal or title search, prior to receiving the certification.

A consumer may not obtain counseling until after receiving the initial good faith estimate on a closed-end transaction or the initial HELOC disclosures required by Regulation Z. A creditor cannot direct a consumer to a particular counselor or organization. A consumer may pay a bona fide third-party counseling fee and it may be financed. A creditor may pay the fee, but cannot condition payment on loan consummation or account opening. A creditor may confirm counseling prior to paying the fee; however, if the consumer withdraws the application, a creditor may not condition the payment on receipt of the certification.

Negative Amortization Counseling Requirements. Section 1026.36(k) requires a creditor, prior to making a closed-end loan secured by a 1–4 unit dwelling which may result in negative amortization, to obtain confirmation that a first-time borrower received counseling on the risks of negative amortization from a HUD-certified or -approved counselor or counseling organization. Acceptable confirmation includes a certificate, letter, or e-mail. This requirement does not apply to reverse mortgages or loans secured by a timeshare. A creditor cannot direct a consumer to choose a particular counselor or organization. Although a creditor cannot make the loan prior to receiving this confirmation, a creditor may engage in other activities, such as processing the application or ordering the appraisal or title search.

Conclusion. Although originations of High-Cost Mortgages are a small percentage of the market as a result of special disclosure requirements, restrictions, enhanced borrower remedies, and assignee liability, the expansion of HOEPA coverage will increase the number of loans subject to HOEPA and the new and lower thresholds will increase the number of loans classified as High-Cost Mortgages. What percentage of loans this will include is difficult to determine.

This article just begins to scratch the surface of the issues this final rule raises for lenders, brokers, and their compliance or legal experts. Lenders will want to review 30 state and local high cost coverage and threshold requirements to determine any necessary changes. Lenders will want to review rates and fees on smaller loans, in order to determine how to price these loans appropriately to avoid a High-Cost Mortgage designation. Lenders and brokers will want to review their loan originator compensation policies. Lenders will want to review state prepayment penalty riders to ensure compliance with federal and state law. Lenders will want to consider creating new procedures to handle unintentional Section 32 violations, to meet the timing and other cure requirements. Finally, lenders will need to plan for the additional costs they will incur in updating automated systems, disclosures and documents, employee training, and outside legal advice. Will these HOEPA changes ultimately help consumers or reduce access to credit? Only time will tell.

NOTES

1. *Compliance costs.* The new HOEPA rules are, to put it mildly, complex, and they illustrate the difficulties of formulating rules to curb abusive lending practices. Lenders who make HOEPA loans (and those who wish to avoid making such loans) will incur substantial training and supervision expenses to ensure compliance with the law, and those costs will be passed on to all borrowers in the form of higher loan costs. Lenders particularly complained about the provisions for including originator compensation (including salaries) as a loan fee; they argued that compensation was often formula-driven and that it was not easy to allocate it to individual loans.

2. *The market impact of HOEPA.* There is little doubt that most institutional lenders are not eager to make HOEPA loans, and that the expanded definitions of the CFBP's new rule will reduce the availability of low-balance mortgage loans. Lenders generally decried this result; see, e.g., Joseph A. Woodruff and Chris Driskill, Say Goodbye to Small Loans, Mortgage Banking, July 2013. But is that a good thing or a bad thing? The question is not easy to answer. By definition, HOEPA loans have onerous terms, but if they are not available, where will consumers go for comparable credit? Perhaps to small loan companies or "payday" lenders? Will the terms of the alternative forms of credit be better or worse than HOEPA loans? These are questions to which we have seen no systematic or conclusive answers.

HOEPA was designed to curtail abusive and unfair practices by lenders in making new mortgage loans. There are, however, numerous other schemes for cheating homeowners, as the following excerpt indicates.

SOUTH BROOKLYN LEGAL SERVICES, PREDATORY LENDING INVESTIGATION CHECKLIST

Practicing Law Institute Real Estate Law and Practice Course Handbook Series
(May 13, 2008)*

First-Time Home-Buyer Scams/Property Flipping

Property flipping scams are a common abusive lending practice, often targeted at first-time and minority home-buyers. Property flipping occurs when a real estate speculator purchases a property cheaply, and then quickly "flips" or resells the property to an unsuspecting home-buyer at a price that exceeds the market value. Typically, the real estate speculator steers the home buyer to a group of real estate professionals (attorneys, lenders, etc.), all of whom are working in concert to deceive the home buyer (often known as a "one-stop shop"). In this way, the real estate speculator ensures that the home-buyer does not receive any independent advice regarding the terms of the purchase, the condition of the property, or the nature of the mortgage. In some cases, real estate speculators are selling houses for the fair market value to home buyers who will not be able to sustain the mortgage debt.

Loan Flipping

Many unsuspecting homeowners, predominantly minority and/or seniors, are victims of loan flipping. Loan flipping is equity stripping through refinances that have no tangible benefit to the homeowner.

In most loan flipping cases, homeowners are led to believe that they will get a reduction in their mortgage payment from the previous loan, a lower rate, debt consolidation, and cash-out. However, most homeowners end up in a higher-cost mortgage without the promised benefit; they lose significant home equity through exorbitant costs and fees; their previously unsecured debt is refinanced into a secured mortgage; and they are placed at increased risk of foreclosure.

Refinance/Home Improvement Scams

Like unscrupulous mortgage brokers, contractors also aggressively solicit homeowners by mail, phone calls and door-to-door solicitations. Unscrupulous contractors are known to provide financing through dishonest lenders, and typically get paid out of the loan closing before doing any work. In some cases, the contractor begins work on the home

---

*   Reprinted with permission of the author.

before financing is made available, a tactic known as spiking, in order to pressure the homeowner to secure financing. It is not unusual for contractors to stop doing work or never begin any work after they receive payment.

Deed Theft/Foreclosure Rescue Scams

Foreclosure is public record information. Foreclosure rescue companies (which often operate out of real estate agencies) obtain these records and bombard homeowners with solicitations that promise foreclosure prevention assistance. Homeowners in foreclosure are often desperate and confused about the foreclosure process, and are therefore more susceptible to foreclosure rescue scams. Foreclosure rescue companies typically target low income and minority neighborhoods. Foreclosure rescue scams work in a few ways. Some homeowners are told that they can save their home from foreclosure with an affordable refinance mortgage, when in fact, the rescue entity tricks the homeowners into signing over the deed to their house to a straw-buyer who takes out a loan for significantly more than what the homeowner owed. Indeed, the new mortgage is frequently 100% of the property value. The unsuspecting homeowners no longer own the home, receive little or no money from the deed transfer, are forced to pay a much higher mortgage every month, and are eventually threatened with eviction.

The other type of rescue scam is when homeowners are instructed by a foreclosure rescue entity to sign the house over to a straw-buyer for a certain period of time, usually a year. The homeowners are then told that after that time expires, title will be transferred back into their name and their credit will be fixed. Instead, the foreclosure rescue entity takes out a mortgage for the full value of the home in the name of a straw-buyer, stealing all the equity and making it impossible for the homeowners to repurchase their home. Thus, the homeowners lose title to their home, receive little to no money from the transaction, and are placed at risk of eviction.

NOTES

1. *Licensing loan originators.* To help combat predatory lending, Congress enacted the Secure and Fair Enforcement for Mortgage Licensing Act ("S.A.F.E. Act") as part of the Housing and Economic Recovery Act of 2008, Pub. L. No. 110–289. The S.A.F.E. Act requires all residential mortgage originators, including mortgage brokers, to be licensed. To obtain a license, the originator must provide fingerprints, a personal history, including work experience, and permission for a background check. A license will be granted only if the applicant has not previously had a loan originator license revoked or been convicted of a felony and has demonstrated financial responsibility and good character. An applicant also must satisfy educational and testing requirements. The Act requires the creation of a mandatory nationwide

registration system for mortgage originators that will provide publicly-accessible information concerning the status of every originator's license.

2. *State anti-predatory lending laws.* The great majority of states have anti-predatory lending laws. The laws vary widely with respect to the types of loans they cover and the types of practices they prohibit. Several state statutes prohibit or regulate prepayment penalties, balloon payments, mandatory arbitration clauses, and mortgage broker fees. The most common type of state law is a "mini-HOEPA" law. Some of these laws include the same or similar terms as the federal HOEPA, but others apply to a wider range of loans.

The state laws also differ on the available remedies. Some allow private actions, but others allow only government enforcement. Some allow damage multipliers, and loan assignees are liable for violations under some state laws but not others.

Commentators have disagreed on the efficacy and desirability of state anti-predatory lending laws. Opponents argue that these laws are counterproductive, because they restrict access to credit and increase loan costs. However, a number of studies indicate that the laws are effective. In one national study, the researchers found that, although weak state laws do not significantly affect lenders' behaviors, more restrictive state laws reduce subprime originations and increase the likelihood that a lender will reject a subprime loan application. Raphael W. Bostic, Kathleen C. Engel, Patricia A. McCoy, Anthony Pennington-Cross & Susan M. Wachter, State and Local Anti-Predatory Lending Laws: The Effect of Legal Enforcement Mechanisms (Aug. 7, 2007), *available at* http://ssrn.com/abstract=1005423.

REGULATORY ACTIONS BY THE CONSUMER FINANCIAL PROTECTION BUREAU

Since its creation in 2010 by the Dodd-Frank financial reform legislation, the CFPB has taken a number of regulatory actions that bear directly on the mortgage industry. Two have already been mentioned above: the HEOPA rules and the "ability to repay" (ATR) and "qualified mortgage" (QM) regulations.

The table below lists the major CFPB rules affecting mortgages. Each of them is complex, and any summary presentation like this omits many important details. CFPB has published a variety of charts and guides to help industry participants comply with them. The Federal Register citations given in the table represent the original publication of each final rule, but in most cases there have been (or may be in the future) additional Federal Register publications of modifications or clarifications to each rule; these are not listed below. Both the modifications and the charts and guides are readily available at www.consumerfinance.gov/.

Rule	Federal Register cite	Subject matter
HOEPA	78 FR 6855 1/31/13	Defines "high-cost" loans and explains the limitations imposed on such loans.
Ability to Repay/ Qualified Mortgage	78 FR 6855 1/31/13	Sets out factors to be considered by lenders making closed-end mortgage loans to assess the borrower's ability to repay (ATR). Defines "qualified mortgages" (QM), which represent a safe harbor for compliance with ATR. In brief, a QM must meet the following: • Points and fees do not exceed 3% • Loan term no greater than 30 years • No negative amortization, interest-only, or balloon features • Total household debt payment-to-income ratio not exceeding 43%
Loan originator	78 FR 11279 2/15/13	Defines "loan originator." Prohibits a loan originator's compensation from being based on the terms of a transaction (with limited exceptions) or a proxy for a transaction term. Imposes record-keeping requirements.
ECOA Valuations	78 FR 7215 1/31/13	Requires creditors to automatically send a free copy of home appraisals and other written valuations to the borrower promptly after they are completed, regardless of whether a loan is ultimately made.
HPML Appraisals	78 FR 10367 2/13/13	Establishes standards with which appraisers and appraisals must comply. Applies to "higher priced" mortgage loans ("HPMLs") having an interest rate that exceeds the "Average Prime Offer Rate" by a fixed percentage.
HPML Escrows	78 FR 4725 1/22/13	Requires lenders to maintain an escrow account for property taxes and insurance premiums for 5 years if the loan is an HPML.
Servicing (TILA and RESPA)	78 FR 10901 2/14/13	These rules address many aspects of mortgage servicing, including: • General servicing policies and procedures

		▪ Error resolution and information requests ▪ Force-placed insurance ▪ Early intervention with delinquent borrowers ▪ Continuity of contact with delinquent borrowers ▪ Loss mitigation ▪ Interest rate adjustment notices for ARMs ▪ Prompt crediting of mortgage payments and responses to requests for payoff amounts
Loan Estimate and Closing Statement	78 FR 79730 11/20/2013 12 CFR 1024, 1026	Replaces the TILA disclosures and the RESPA "good faith estimate" and "HUD–1 Settlement Statement" with a new "Loan Estimate" and "Closing Statement"

One more important administrative rule prompted by the Dodd-Frank Act was promulgated not by the CFPB, but by six federal financial regulatory agencies (the FRB, OCC, FDIC, SEC, HUD, and FHFA). It is usually described as the "risk retention" rule. The Dodd-Frank Act § 941(b) generally requires an issuer of asset-backed securities to retain at least 5% of the credit risk of the assets collateralizing the securities. This is sometimes called the "skin in the game" requirement; Congress believed that securitizers would be much more careful about the quality of the underlying assets if they had to retain ownership of 5% of those assets for their own accounts.

However, there is an exemption from these requirements for securities that are collateralized exclusively by "Qualified Residential Mortgages" (QRMs). Dodd-Frank did not define QRMs, but left this task to the six federal agencies mentioned above. In their final rule, issued in November 2014, the agencies, somewhat surprisingly, simply adopted the CFPB's QM definition as the definition for QRMs as well. Thus, a QRM must have points and fees that do not exceed 3%, a loan term no greater than 30 years, and no negative amortization, interest-only, or balloon features. Most significantly, the borrower's total household debt payment-to-income ratio may not exceed 43%.

Earlier proposals by the agencies had included a number of additional elements in the QRM definition, including restricting QRMs to owner-occupied houses and first lien mortgages. Borrower credit standards and a maximum loan-to-value ratio of 70% were also proposed. But all of these extra requirements were dropped in the final QRM rule in favor of a QRM definition that simply "borrowed" CFPB's QM definition.

The final rule will be effective one year after publication in the Federal Register for residential mortgage-backed securitizations (RMBS) and two years after publication for all other securitization types. It is not yet clear how the rule will affect lending in the primary market, but in general securities issuers are not eager to retain any risk on the assets they use as collateral. Hence, it seems likely that many lenders will offer only loans that meet the QM/QRM standards.

F. SPREADING MORTGAGE RISK—INSURERS AND GUARANTORS

MORTGAGE FINANCING: ACTIONS NEEDED TO HELP FHA MANAGE RISKS FROM NEW MORTGAGE LOAN PRODUCTS

U.S. General Accountability Office
Report GAO–05–194, Feb. 2005, at 7–13, 23–26*

Mortgage insurance, a commonly used credit enhancement, protects lenders against losses in the event of default. Lenders usually require mortgage insurance when a homebuyer has a down payment of less than 20 percent of the value of the home. FHA, VA, the USDA's Rural Housing Service (RHS), and private mortgage insurers provide this insurance. * * *

Private mortgage insurers generally offer first loss coverage—that is, they will pay all the losses from a foreclosure up to a stated percentage of the claim amount. Generally, these insurers limit the coverage that they offer to between 25 percent and 35 percent of the claim amount.

The insurance offered by the government varies in the amount of lender incurred losses it will cover. For example, VA guarantees losses up to 25 percent to 50 percent of the loan, while FHA's principal single-family insurance program insures almost 100 percent. FHA plays a particularly large role in certain market segments, including low-income and first-time homebuyers. * * * To cover lenders' losses, FHA collects insurance premiums from borrowers. These premiums, along with proceeds from the sale of foreclosed properties, pay for claims that FHA pays lenders as a result of foreclosures. * * *

Each mortgage institution we studied limits in some way the mortgages or the borrowers that may be eligible for their low and no down payment products, but the specific limits and criteria differ among institutions. Fannie Mae and Freddie Mac are constrained in the size of the mortgages they may purchase. Specifically, the Housing and Community Development Act of 1980 requires a limit (conforming loan limit) on the size of mortgages that can be purchased by either Fannie

---

*   Most footnotes, graphs, and charts have been omitted.

Mae or Freddie Mac. In [2014], the conforming mortgage limit for Fannie Mae and Freddie Mac is [$417,000] for most of the nation.

FHA is also limited in the size of mortgages it may insure. The FHA loan limit varies by location and property type, depending on the cost of homes in an area and the number of units in a property. * * * [For a single-family home in 2014, the normal loan limit is $214,050.] FHA also has higher limits in Alaska, Hawaii, Guam, and the U.S. Virgin Islands because these are considered to be high cost areas.

Although VA does not have a mortgage limit, lenders generally limit VA mortgages to four times the VA guaranty amount, which is now set at 25 percent of the conforming loan limit. Since the maximum guaranty currently is legislatively set at $104,250, VA-guaranteed mortgages will rarely exceed $417,000.

OVERVIEW OF GAO'S PAST WORK ON FHA'S SINGLE-FAMILY MORTGAGE INSURANCE PROGRAMS

U.S. General Accountability Office, Letter Report of Mathew J. Scirè,
Director, Financial Markets and Community Investment
GAO–13–400R, March 7, 2013*

FHA Loan Volume. FHA's loan volume grew considerably from 2006 to 2010 and has since remained high. FHA insured almost half a million loans, totaling $70 billion in mortgage insurance, in 2006. (This was low compared to prior years; from 2000 to 2005, FHA's loan volume ranged from about 521,000 to about 1.2 million loans.) For 2009, the agency insured about 1.9 million loans, totaling more than $361 billion in mortgage insurance. The number of loans dropped in 2012 to about 1.2 million, or about $227 billion in mortgage insurance.

FHA Market Share. Looking at all mortgages (both insured and uninsured), FHA's overall market share, in terms of number of loans, increased from 3.3 percent in 2006 to a high of 21.1 percent in 2009 and decreased in 2011 to 14 percent. (These data do not include reverse mortgages; as we discuss later, FHA currently insures nearly 100 percent of reverse mortgages.)

Similarly, FHA's market share of all purchase mortgages increased from 4.5 percent in 2006 to a high of 32.6 percent in 2009. (In the 5 years prior to 2006, FHA's share of purchase mortgages was as high as 14.2 percent.) In 2011, FHA's market share of purchase mortgages was 26.5 percent. In recent years, the contraction of other segments of the mortgage market and legislated increases in the loan amounts eligible for FHA insurance resulted in higher demand for FHA-insured mortgages.

---

*   The text has been edited, and graphics and footnotes omitted.

FHA's Customers. The agency has played a particularly large role among first-time and minority homebuyers. Over the last 4 years, FHA has insured more than 3.5 million home purchase loans, 2.8 million of which were for first-time homebuyers. In 2012 about 78 percent of these loans went to first-time homebuyers, about 32 percent of whom were minorities. * * * While FHA insurance was used for approximately 27 percent of all home purchases in 2011, FHA-insured loans accounted for 50 percent of loans to African-American borrowers and 49 percent of loans to Hispanic borrowers.

[Unsurprisingly, FHA's huge upswing in business during the recession years of 2007–12, combined with declining housing market prices, resulted in large losses to its insurance fund.] The Omnibus Budget Reconciliation Act of 1990 required the HUD Secretary to ensure that FHA's Mutual Mortgage Insurance Fund attained a capital ratio (the ratio of the insurance fund's economic value to insurance obligations) of at least 2 percent by November 2000 and maintained at least that ratio at all times thereafter. * * The insurance fund's capital ratio dropped sharply in 2008 and fell below the statutory minimum in 2009, when economic and market developments created conditions that simultaneously reduced the insurance fund's economic value (the numerator of the capital ratio) and increased the insurance-in-force, or insurance obligations (the denominator of the capital ratio). According to annual actuarial reviews of the insurance fund, the capital ratio fell from about 7 percent in 2006, to 3 percent in 2008, and below 2 percent in 2009. In 2012, the capital ratio fell below zero to negative 1.44 percent.

NOTE: UPDATE ON MORTGAGE INSURANCE PREMIUMS

FHA mortgage insurance premiums. In recent years, FHA has taken several steps to restore its insurance fund's capital ratio to better than the statutory minimum. It tightened its underwriting standards, and it increased the minimum down payment for large loans—those above $625,000 (available only in high-cost areas)—from 3.5% to 5%. In 2013 it also imposed significant increases in its mortgage insurance premiums (MIPs). FHA charges both an up-front MIP, paid at closing of the loan (although it may be financed as part of the mortgage debt), and an annual MIP, paid in twelve monthly installments along with principal and interest. The increased up-front MIP is 1.75% of the base loan amount. (It was formerly 1.0%.) The annual MIP, computed as a percentage of the base loan amount, depends on the loan-to-value ratio and the loan's term, as indicated in the following table. (MIPs are higher for loans exceeding $625,000.)

L/V ratio	Term 15 years or less	Term more than 15 years
Below 90%	0.45%	1.30%
90% to 95%	0.70%	1.30%
Above 95%	0.70%	1.35%

FHA formerly permitted borrowers to cancel their FHA mortgage insurance when the outstanding principal balance of an FHA loan reached 78 percent of the original balance. However, in 2013 FHA changed its policy, and no longer allows cancellation for the entire life of the loan if the loan's starting loan balance was higher than 90% of its appraised value. For loans in which the loan-to-value began at 90% or less, mortgage insurance premiums must be paid for 11 years.

VA funding fee. VA charges a "funding fee" for its guaranty. The fee may be as high as 3.3% of the amount borrowed, and is based on a variety of factors, including the type of military service in which the borrower was engaged, the loan-to-value ratio, and whether the loan is new or a refinance. For example, for a regular military veteran obtaining a first-time loan with no down payment, the fee is 2.15% of the loan amount.

PMI loan limits and mortgage insurance premiums. PMI's may impose maximum loan amounts or loan-to-value ratio limits as a consequence of their own internal policies or the statutes and regulations of the states in which they are chartered and operate. In addition, PMI-insured conventional loans must comply with the regulations governing the financial institutions that make them, and with the guidelines of the purchasing investor if they are sold on the secondary mortgage market. For these reasons, PMI loans are generally limited to 95% loan-to-value ratios or lower, although in some cases PMI insurers will cover loans up to 97% or even 100% of value.

Premiums charged by the PMIs vary from one company to another, and may also depend on whether the loan-to-value ratio is 85% or below, between 86% and 90%, or between 91% and 95%, or above 95%. Premiums are usually paid along with the principal and interest payment as a monthly fee. For a 30-year fixed-rate loan up to 85% of value, the premium might be 0.32% per year, divided into 12 monthly installments; on a $100,000 loan, this would amount to $29.17 per month. For a loan exceeding 95% of value, a typical premium would be 0.90% per year, or $75 per month on a $100,000 loan. Higher premiums are usually charged for graduated-payment and adjustable rate loans, since they are believed to carry greater risk of default and loss. Rates may also vary on the basis of the borrower's credit score and the percentage of the original loan amount that the insurance contract covers. Some insurers offer single-premium up-front rates as an alternative to monthly payments.

G. FEDERAL PREEMPTION OF STATE MORTGAGE LAW

Although the vast preponderance of mortgage law is state law, we have seen in this chapter that the federal government is heavily involved in the mortgage market in a variety of ways: chartering and insuring mortgage lenders' deposits, purchasing mortgages on the secondary market, guaranteeing payment of securities backed by mortgages, and insuring or guaranteeing the repayment of individual mortgage loans. To what extent do federal contacts such as these permit the federal government or the courts to substitute federal law for state law when a mortgage is made, foreclosed, or otherwise the subject of legal action? If federal law is to be applied, what is its source? What is the effect on state law of the regulations of federal agencies that supervise financial institutions? These are the questions to be answered in this section.

Preemption of state mortgage law occurs in three distinct contexts: (1) when a federal agency is a market participant as the holder and enforcer of a note and mortgage; (2) when Congress adopts a statute that expressly preempts state law or creates an irreconcilable conflict with it; and (3) when a federal financial agency, acting under the authority given it by Congress, adopts a regulation that preempts state law or conflicts with it to such an extent that the state law must be deemed preempted.

1. FEDERAL AGENCIES AS MARKET PARTICIPANTS

No serious question exists that, when the federal government or its agencies foreclose a federally-held mortgage, federal law governs essentially all controversial aspects of the foreclosure, including confirmation of the sale, deficiency judgment liability, redemption rights, and rent assignments. The key question is not whether federal law applies, but rather what *is* the federal law? Should the court adopt the existing state rule as the federal rule, fashion a federal court-made rule, or derive a rule from the agency's regulations or documents? *See generally* Nelson, Whitman, Burkhart & Freyermuth, Real Estate Finance Law § 11.6 (6th ed. 2014).

The Supreme Court's controlling decision involving the federal government's preemptive rights as the holder of a debt or mortgage is United States v. Kimbell Foods, Inc., 440 U.S. 715, 99 S.Ct. 1448, 59 L.Ed.2d 711 (1979). The Court stated that, in deciding whether to adopt state law as the federal rule of decision when the government is enforcing an obligation, a court must determine:

1. Whether the federal program is one that, by its nature, requires nationwide uniformity;

2.   Whether adopting the state law would frustrate the federal program's specific objectives; and

3.   Whether applying a uniform federal rule would disrupt existing commercial relations predicated on state law.

See In re Bubert, 61 B.R. 362 (W.D.Tex.1986). *Kimbell Foods* has often been viewed as embodying a strong preference for adopting state law as the federal rule. *See, e.g.,* United States v. Stump Home Specialties Mfg., Inc., 905 F.2d 1117, 1119 (7th Cir.1990). Much the same attitude is expressed in Frank S. Alexander, Federal Intervention in Real Estate Finance: Preemption and Federal Common Law, 71 N.C.L.Rev. 293 (1993):

> When the federal government is acting simply as a market participant in real estate finance, and Congress has not expressly declared otherwise, state law should apply to the transaction. The federal interest in protecting the security and recovering the indebtedness is federal only because it identifies the holder of the interest; it is not federal because of any attribute of sovereignty. There is no inherent or obvious reason to displace state law and create judicially a federal rule which prefers the position of the government as creditor. To the contrary, when acting in the same capacity as a private creditor, the federal government "should fare no better, and no worse, than a private lender."

Nonetheless, the outcomes of the cases since *Kimbell Foods* have been varied, unpredictable, and chaotic. Typical points of controversy that arise when a federal agency forecloses a mortgage include:

> 1.   Does the agency have to observe the same formalities for establishing lien priority as other lenders under state law?
>
> 2.   Can the agency collect a deficiency judgment from a debtor under conditions in which state law would ordinarily bar deficiencies?
>
> 3.   Does the agency have to recognize a post-foreclosure statutory right of redemption provided by state law?
>
> 4.   Can the agency require a borrower to waive rights that are ordinarily nonwaivable under state law?
>
> 5.   Does the agency have to provide all notices required by state law, such as a notice of default to borrowers?

Similar questions may arise after the FHA or VA pays a claim to a private lender. For example, if the VA pays a claim on a guaranteed loan, can it obtain reimbursement from the defaulting borrower despite a state antideficiency statute? Courts have been inconsistent in answering these types of questions, and we do not take the space here to summarize the case law. A good starting point is Professor Alexander's excellent article, cited above.

The notion that there should be general federal mortgage foreclosure statute has floated about the federal housing and financial regulatory agencies for many years. The idea is attractive to the agencies because they often find themselves taking losses on foreclosures as a consequence of slow and, in their view, outmoded state procedures. But despite this benefit, Congress has not enacted a comprehensive federal foreclosure statute.

However, Congress enacted a narrower bill, the Multifamily Mortgage Foreclosure Act, 12 U.S.C. §§ 3701–3717, in 1981. The Act created a nonjudicial foreclosure process for mortgages held by HUD on multifamily housing projects. It expressly preempts any state law granting post-foreclosure redemption rights. In 1994, Congress enacted a parallel act, the Single Family Mortgage Foreclosure Act, 12 U.S.C. §§ 3751–3768, which applies to HUD-held single-family home mortgages. For HUD's regulations under both acts, *see* 24 C.F.R. pt. 27, which was promulgated in 61 Fed.Reg. 48,546 (1996). *See generally* Patrick A. Randolph, Jr., The New Federal Foreclosure Laws, 49 Okla.L.Rev. 123 (1996); Nelson, Whitman, Burkhart & Freyermuth, Real Estate Finance Law § 11.4 (6th ed. 2014).

2. EXPRESS CONGRESSIONAL PREEMPTION

Congress clearly has the power to preempt state law by direct statutory enactment if the subject matter is within the federal government's constitutional power. The Commerce Clause is the usual basis asserted for such action. During the 1980s, Congress preempted several aspects of state mortgage law:

1.   Section 501 of the Depository Institutions Deregulation and Monetary Control Act of 1980, 12 U.S.C. § 1735f–7, preempts all state usury laws for "federally-related" loans secured by first liens on residential real estate. Grunbeck v. Dime Sav. Bank, 848 F.Supp. 294 (D.N.H. 1994) (§ 501 preempts New Hampshire statute requiring that interest on residential mortgage loans be computed on simple interest basis as a state law limiting rate or amount of interest).

2.   Section 341 of the Garn-St. Germain Depository Institutions Act of 1982, 12 U.S.C. § 1701j–3, preempts state law restrictions on the enforceability of due-on-sale clauses in mortgages. The OCC regulations implementing the Act are in 12 C.F.R. pt. 591. *See* Chapter 5, Section B supra, for a complete discussion of the preemption.

3.   The Alternative Mortgage Transactions Parity Act of 1982, 12 U.S.C. §§ 3801–3806 (the "AMTPA"), preempts state law restrictions on the structure of "alternative" mortgage instruments. The Act authorizes

state-chartered financial institutions to make mortgage loans of types that the federal financial regulators have approved, even if state law does not allow them. See the following section of this chapter for a more thorough discussion of such mortgage formats.

In these statutes preempting state law, Congress permitted state legislatures, within some limited time period after enactment of the federal statute, to regain control of the field by "opting out" of the federal preemption. In each of the cases above, a few states did so. See, e.g., Doyle v. Southern Guaranty Corp., 795 F.2d 907 (11th Cir.1986) (discussing Georgia's override of the 1980 federal usury preemption).

3. CONFLICT PREEMPTION

NELSON, WHITMAN, BURKHART & FREYERMUTH, REAL ESTATE FINANCE LAW
Section 11.6 (6th ed. 2014)*

The term "conflict preemption" refers to cases in which a federal statute or program's purposes cannot be achieved if state law is also followed. The conflict may be purely statutory, as in cases in which federal law specifically approves conduct that state law prohibits. However, most of the litigation has dealt with the question whether a federal banking regulator may issue regulations that preempt state law and thereby may immunize conduct that state law would prohibit or punish. Historically there was a sharp difference between the treatment of national banks under the Office of the Comptroller of the Currency (OCC) and savings associations under the Office of Thrift Supervision (OTS). Savings associations were governed by the 1933 Home Owners Loan Act,[332] which permitted the OTS to grant them a remarkably comprehensive form of preemption, governing every aspect of their operations "from the cradle to the grave,"[333] and fully occupying the field. This "field preemption," however, did not apply to national banks. The 1864 National Bank Act[334] under which they operated contained no

---

*   Reprinted with permission of LEG, Inc., d/b/a West Academic.

[332] 12 U.S.C. §§ 1461–1468.

[333] A good illustration is Fidelity Fed. Sav. & Loan Ass'n v. De la Cuesta, 458 U.S. 141 (1982), upholding, under the authority of the Home Owners Loan Act, the regulation of the Federal Home Loan Bank Board preempting state law with respect to due-on-sale clauses. See Meyers v. Beverly Hills Fed. Sav. & Loan Ass'n, 499 F.2d 1145 (9th Cir. 1974). When state courts "deal with the internal affairs of federal savings and loan associations * * * they are nonetheless applying federal law." Murphy v. Colonial Federal Savings and Loan Association, 388 F.2d 609, 612 (2d Cir. 1967). See Community Title Co. v. Roosevelt Federal Savings & Loan Association, 670 S.W.2d 895, 903 (Mo.App. 1984). On control by OTS' predecessor, the FHLBB, of S & L mergers, see Federal Home Loan Bank Board: Preemptive Rights or Unbridled Powers?, 12 Cap.U.L.Rev. 529 (1983).

[334] 12 U.S.C. §§ 85–86.

specific preemption language, and the courts were forced to develop principles to guide the OCC in its preemptive efforts.

The standard statement governing the OCC's preemptive authority is found in the Supreme Court's opinion in Barnett Bank of Marion County v. Nelson.[335] The Court held that a Florida statute prohibiting banks from selling insurance in certain towns was preempted by a 1916 federal law which authorized such actions because the state insurance law stood as an "obstacle to the accomplishment and execution of the full purposes and objectives of Congress." This is a classic example of "conflict preemption." As applied to OCC, it would mean that agency had authority to preempt state law that "prevents or significantly interferes" with a national bank's exercise of its powers.

In practice, the OTS (and its predecessor, the Federal Home Loan Bank Board) pressed its preemptive authority over savings associations very broadly. As early as 1994, its implementing regulation[336] listed a large number of examples of preempted features of loan transactions and lender operations, and the courts upheld its authority in each instance. For example, regulations concerning prepayment penalties,[337] interest on tax escrow accounts[338] on home loans, and many other mortgage law topics[339] were held to prevail over contrary state law. Consumer advocates complained of these rules, for the federal regulations often granted savings associations latitude and power that would have been denied them under state law.

---

[335] 517 U.S. 25, 116 S.Ct. 1103 (1996). See also Association of Banks in Ins., Inc. v. Duryee, 270 F.3d 397 (6th Cir. 2001) (federal statute preempted state insurance regulation as applied to national banks).

[336] 12 CFR § 560.2(a).

[337] Toolan v. Trevose Federal Savings & Loan Association, 462 A.2d 224 (Pa. 1983); Meyers v. Beverly Hills Federal Savings and Loan Association, 499 F.2d 1145 (9th Cir. 1974); see generally § 6.4, supra.

[338] First Federal Savings & Loan Association v. Greenwald, 591 F.2d 417 (1st Cir. 1979); Wisconsin League of Financial Institutions, Ltd. v. Galecki, 707 F.Supp. 401 (W.D.Wis. 1989); Olsen v. Financial Federal Savings & Loan Association, 434 N.E.2d 406 (Ill.App. 1982). See generally § 4.19 supra.

[339] The following cases found the indicated state laws preempted by 12 CFR § 560.2, the OTS preemption regulation, or its predecessors: Flagg v. Yonkers Sav. and Loan Ass'n, 396 F.3d 178 (2d Cir. 2005) (state law requiring payment of interest on escrow account balances); State Farm Bank v. Burke, 445 F.Supp.2d 207 (D.Conn. 2006) (state law regulating use of agents by lender to perform marketing, solicitation, and customer service activities); Silvas v. E*Trade Mortg. Corp., 421 F.Supp.2d 1315 (S.D.Cal. 2006) (false advertising in violation of California unfair competition law); Stoneking v. Bank of America, 43 P.3d 1089 (N.M.App. 2002) (state law restricting collection of prepayment fees); Washington Mutual Bank v. Superior Court, 115 Cal.Rptr.2d 765 (Cal.App .2002) (state law restrictions on the charging of pre-closing interest); Bright v. Washington Mut. Bank, 2002 WL 453725 (Cal.App. 2002) (not published in Cal.Rptr.) (state law restricting hazard insurance requirements); Chaires v. Chevy Chase Bank, F.S.B., 748 A.2d 34 (Md.App. 2000) (state law limitations on front-end loan fee charges); Turner v. First Union Nat. Bank, 740 A.2d 1081 (N.J. 1999) (state law restricting lender from charging borrower for attorney review of documents). * * *

The OCC was determined not be left behind in the preemption race. In 2004 it followed the lead of OTS, adopting its own broad preemption of state law for national banks.[340] The list of preempted areas of the law was nearly identical to that of the OTS discussed above,[341] and it was far from nuanced; there was little or nothing to support the notion that application of state law in these categories would "prevent or significantly interfere" with the proper functioning of the banks' federal powers. Indeed, the OCC virtually adopted the OTS's concept of "field preemption."[342] Whether this sort of blunderbuss preemption was justified, in light of the OCC's weaker statutory foundation[343] and the Supreme Court's holding in *Barnett Bank*, was doubtful.[344]

In any event, by 2010 Congress concluded that both banking regulators had gone too far. Perhaps influenced by the spate of unbridled subprime and sometimes predatory loans that had contributed to the collapse of the housing and mortgage markets in 2007,[345] Congress, in the Dodd-Frank Act, elected to rein in the regulators' preemptive efforts.[346] It restated the *Barnett Bank* "prevents or significantly interferes" standard, but it declared that determinations of preemption of "state consumer financial laws"[347] must now be made on the basis of "substantial

---

[340] 69 Fed.Reg. 1904 (Jan. 13, 2004), amending 12 CFR § 7.4007–.4009 (non-real estate loans); 12 CFR § 34.3–.4 (real estate loans).

[341] 12 CFR § 34.4(a). See also Beneficial Nat'l Bank v. Anderson, 539 U.S. 1 U.S. (2003) (National Bank Act preempts state law usury claims against national banks). See Keith R. Fisher, Toward a Basal Tenth Amendment: A Riposte to National Bank Preemption of State Consumer Protection Laws, 29 Harv. J.L. & Pub. Pol'y 981 (2006); Mark A. Olthoff, National Bank Act Preemption in the Secondary Market, 123 Banking L.J. 401 (2006). As with the OTS, the OCC excluded from the preemption, "to the extent that they only incidentally affect the exercise of national banks' real estate lending powers," state laws governing contracts, torts, criminal law, homestead laws, rights to collect debts, acquisition and transfer of real property, taxation, and zoning. 12 CFR § 34.4(b). See Charter One Mortg. Corp. v. Condra, 847 N.E.2d 207 (Ind.App. 2006) (Indiana rule barring unauthorized practice of law was not preempted by the National Bank Act or 12 C.F.R. § 7.4002, even though it prevented national banks from charging document preparation fees for legal instruments prepared by non-attorneys).

[342] See Jared Elosta, Dynamic Federalism and Consumer Financial Protection: How the Dodd-Frank Act Changes the Preemption Debate, 89 N.C.L.Rev. 1273, 1280 (2011).

[343] See, e.g., Aguayo v. U.S. Bank. 653 F.3d 912 (9th Cir. 2011) ("The OTS. unlike the OCC, has explicit full field preemption.").

[344] See Watters v. Wachovia Bank, N.A., 550 U.S. 1, 22, 127 S.Ct. 1559, 1573 (2007) (Stevens, J., dissenting); Arthur E. Wilmarth Jr., The OCC's Preemption Rules Exceed the Agency's Authority and Present a Serious Threat to the Dual Banking System and Consumer Protection, 23 Ann. Rev. Banking & Fin. L. 225 (2004).

[345] See F. Paul Bland, Freedom from Abusive Preemption under Dodd-Frank, 49 Trial 18 (Dec. 2013).

[346] See Debra Lee Hovatter, Preemption Analysis under the National Bank Act: Then and Now, 67 Consumer Fin. L.Q. Rep. 5 (2013); Matthew Dyckman, Financial Regulatory Reform— The Dodd-Frank Act Rolls Back Federal Preemption, 64 Consumer Fin. L.Q. Rep. 129 (2010).

[347] A "state consumer financial law" is defined as one that "does not directly or indirectly discriminate against national banks and that directly and specifically regulates the manner, content, or terms and conditions of any financial transaction (as may be authorized for national banks to engage in), or any account related thereto, with respect to a consumer." 12 U.S.C.A. § 25b(a)(2). Thus, the banking regulators are free to preempt any state law that discriminates against federally-chartered institutions. In Cline v. Bank of America, N.A., 823 F. Supp.2d 387

evidence," and rendered on a case-by-case basis rather than by blanket regulation.[348]

Dodd-Frank limited the banking regulators' preemptive actions in several other ways. Preemption must be based on "substantial evidence" that the conflict meets the *Barnett Bank* standard.[349] If the regulator finds that law of another state has "substantively equivalent" terms as one that it is now preempting, it must first consult with the CFPB and take its views into consideration.[350] The OCC is also required to conduct a review of each preemption determination every five years, and to report to Congress on the outcome of these reviews.[351] Further, preemption determinations must now be "made by a court, or by regulation or order," rather than by informal letter rulings as had often been used in the past.[352] Finally, Dodd-Frank requires the OCC to publish, and update at least quarterly, a list of all of its preemption determinations.[353] One might have expected a wholesale revision by the OCC of its preemption regulation after Dodd-Frank went into effect, but in fact its revision made no changes in the listing of categories of states laws that were preempted; OCC took the position that Congress had no intent to force changes in this basic list.[354]

Two structural changes were also made to the banking regulators' preemptive authority by Dodd-Frank. First, the Supreme Court had previously held that the OCC had authority to preempt state law with respect to subsidiaries of national banks,[355] but under Dodd-Frank, subsidiaries and affiliates are entitled to no preemption at all.[356] Second, Congress completely eliminated the "field preemption" language of the Home Owners Loan Act, so that now federal savings associations are

---

(S.D.W.Va. 2011), the court found that a West Virginia statute designed to curb abusive debt collection practices was not a "state consumer financial law," since it did not regulate the original debt transaction.

[348] 12 U.S.C.A. § 25b(b)(3)(A). "Case by case" determination means that the regulators must make a determination "concerning the impact of a particular State consumer financial law on any national bank that is subject to" it.

[349] 12 U.S.C.A. § 25b(c).

[350] 12 U.S.C.A. § 25b(b)(3)(B).

[351] 12 U.S.C.A. § 25b(d).

[352] 12 U.S.C.A. § 25b(b)(1)(B).

[353] 12 U.S.C.A. § 25b(g).

[354] See OCC commentary to its final revised regulation, 76 Fed.Reg. 43549, 43557 (July 21, 2011): "The types and terms of laws that are set out in the 2004 preemption rules were based on the OCC's experience with the potential impact of such laws on national bank powers and operations. We have re-reviewed those rules in connection with this rulemaking to confirm that the specific types of laws cited in the rules are consistent with the standard for conflict preemption in the Supreme Court's *Barnett* decision." See Raymond Natter & Katie Wechsler, Dodd-Frank Act and National Bank Preemption: Much Ado About Nothing, 7 Va. L. & Bus. Rev. 301, 303 (2012) (asserting that Dodd-Frank's changes are "relatively minor").

[355] Watters v. Wachovia Bank, N.A., 550 U.S. 1 (2007).

[356] 12 U.S.C.A. § 25b(e).

entitled to OTS preemption under exactly the same standards as are national banks under the OCC.[357]

The fact that Congress ratcheted up the procedures for preemption, but did so only with respect to "state consumer financial laws," is perplexing. What is now the preemption standard for state laws that are not "consumer financial laws?"[358] *Barnett Bank* is still in effect, and indeed seems to have received the imprimatur of Congress,[359] and its holding is not confined to "consumer financial laws." How the courts will respond when faced with attempted OCC preemption of such laws remains to be seen.[360]

H. ALTERNATIVE MORTGAGE INSTRUMENTS

In Section G of Chapter 1 of this book, we described and illustrated the operation of the traditional fixed-interest-rate level-payment fully-amortized mortgage loan. For many years, beginning during the depression of the 1930s, such loans constituted the great bulk of mortgage lending in the United States. But during the past 45 years or so a whole new set of mortgage instruments—"alternative mortgages"—has developed. This section will describe those instruments.

First, however, we need to identify the reasons alternative mortgages were created. One important reason was the dilemma of portfolio lenders, such as savings associations and the GSEs, that historically "borrowed short and lent long." These lenders obtained short-term funds from savers or investors and loaned those funds as relatively long-term fixed-interest mortgage loans. That is, they engaged in "term intermediation." If short-term interest rates rose rapidly, the lender's borrowing costs dramatically increased, while the interest yields on the lender's portfolio of mortgages remained relatively constant. This risk was more than theoretical, as

---

[357] Dodd-Frank Act, Pub.L. 111–203 (2010), at § 1046, adding new § 6 to HOLA, stating: "Notwithstanding the authorities granted under sections 4 and 5, this Act does not occupy the field in any area of State law." Oddly, there is no mention at all of the National Credit Union Administration, the regulator of federal credit unions. Presumably it remains subject to the *Barnett Bank* standard, but without all of the additional restrictions to which OTS and OCC are now subject.

[358] See, e.g., Cline v. Bank of America, supra note 35.

[359] See, e.g., Baptista v. JPMorgan Chase Bank, N.A., 640 F.3d 1194 (11th Cir. 2011), applying *Barnett Bank* and concluding that there was an "irreconcilable conflict" between an OCC regulation expressly allowing banks to charge check-cashing fees and a Florida statute prohibiting such fees.

[360] See New Mexico v. Capital One Bank (USA) N.A., 980 F.Supp.2d 1314 (D.N.M. 2013) (state unfair trade practice laws prohibiting misrepresentation are not preempted except to the extent that they involve debt cancellation or suspension agreements, a field that OCC has expressly preempted); Sacco v. Bank of America, N.A., 2012 WL 6566681 (W.D.N.C. 2012) (not reported in F.Supp.2d) (OCC regulations preempted bank's "right to collect debts," but did not preempt state law governing abusive collection practices); Michael Bolos, The Application of Dodd-Frank's Dual Preemption Standard to State UDAP Laws, 14 U. Pa. J. Bus. L. 289 (2011), discussing preemption of state unfair and deceptive practices acts, and concluding that they are probably not "consumer financial laws."

shown by the disastrous results for the thrift industry during the 1980–82 period of rapidly increasing interest rates. The perils of lending on long-term fixed-interest mortgages was starkly clear to the many lenders that did not survive that experience.

The obvious approach to this problem was to reduce the average term of the loan portfolio. One way for lenders to do this is to shift out of mortgage lending partially or entirely and to make other types of loans that, by their nature, have shorter terms. Both the Depository Institutions Deregulation and Monetary Control Act of 1980 and the Garn-St. Germain Depository Institutions Act of 1982 moved in this direction by authorizing thrift institutions to invest more of their assets in consumer and commercial loans, which tend to have shorter terms and higher interest rates than mortgage loans. However, this approach was fairly disastrous to the industry, in part because its management had no experience with this type of lending and made many bad loans.

The other major approach to reducing the risk of term intermediation is the main subject of this section of the book—the first and most important of the alternative mortgage instruments, the adjustable rate mortgage ("ARM"). If interest rates on mortgage loans change when market rates change, the result is far more attractive to the institutions. In an ideal portfolio of this sort, the overall yield on the portfolio would always be precisely equal to the current market interest rate, so that the effective maturity of loans and of savings would match. In a rough way, this is the purpose for adjustable rate mortgages, which mortgage lenders now widely offer.

Interest rates and mortgage affordability. If one assumes constant risks, maturities, and liquidities, mortgage interest rates are directly related to the inflation lenders anticipate will occur during the loan's term. This is reasonable, because if inflation occurs, lenders will receive repayment in devalued dollars. A 4 percent loan in a non-inflationary economy provides the same real return to the lender as a 14 percent loan in an economy with an inflation rate of 10 percent. From 1955–65, inflation averaged roughly 1.5% per year and mortgage interest rates averaged about 5.5%; both were relatively stable. This suggests that mortgage investors were demanding a real rate of return (after inflation) on the order of 4% and that interest rates above this level constituted an inflation premium. Other loan characteristics have changed since that era, so one should not take the 4% return figure as more than a rough estimate of the real rate lenders will demand today, but it is useful to bear in mind.

Most mortgage lenders will make loans only to those who "qualify" in terms of some standard ratio of housing expense to income. "Housing expense" generally includes the debt service on the mortgage, plus the annual property taxes, mortgage insurance and hazard insurance premiums, and any home owners association dues or special assessments. Various lenders and secondary market investors have adopted different expense-to-income ratios, but they commonly range from about 28% to 33%. For simplicity's sake, ignore the taxes, insurance premiums, and other minor expenses and assume that the lender requires the mortgage payment-to-income ratio to be no more than 30%. This means that a family with a monthly income of $4,000 could not qualify for a loan with monthly payments exceeding $1,200. Even if the family were willing to make higher payments, the lender would simply refuse to make the loan.

The result is that rising interest rates tend to "ration" borrowers out of the market. The on the next page shows the approximate principal amount a family with an income of $48,000 per year can qualify to borrow at various interest rates. It is based on a 30-year level-payment loan and a 30% payment-to-income ratio rule, so that the maximum monthly payment for principal and interest is $1,200.

Interest Rate	Principal Amount
6%	$200,000
8%	$163,500
10%	$136,700
12%	$116,700
14%	$101,300

Another way of looking at the problem is to examine how much income a family would need to qualify for, say, a $150,000 loan at various interest rates. The table below shows the answer, based on the same assumptions stated above.

Interest Rate	Monthly Payment	Annual Income Required
6%	$900	$36,000
8%	$1,100	$44,000
10%	$1,316	$52,640
12%	$1,543	$61,720
14%	$1,777	$71,080

The rationing effect of increasing interest rates is apparent. Ironically, many families' income will increase with inflation (or nearly as rapidly) over time if the lenders' expectations are correct. In a few years, a family that was clearly unqualified for a given loan may have increased its income sufficiently to pay the same loan with relative ease. However, because the payments are level, the family is unqualified in the only year that matters—the year in which they would like to borrow. They simply will not get the loan.

One might argue that if inflation and concomitant high interest rates are only temporary, the problem is not so bad. Unlike food, owner-occupied housing is a good whose consumption can be deferred. People can continue to rent, to live with relatives, and to double up in other ways. But high interest rates that persist over the long run indisputably have a harsh impact on large numbers of households.

The rationing effect of high interest rates leaves its mark on the supply side of the housing market as well. When rates rise and buyers cannot qualify, the effective demand for housing diminishes. Housing builders and sellers of existing housing units are often hard-hit. They find themselves with unsold properties on which mortgage interest and other expenses continue to accrue. Builders must lay off workers and cancel relationships with subcontractors and materials suppliers, and they may be forced to hold land that cannot be developed (and pay taxes and insurance costs on it) because the market demand has disappeared.

Arguably, the housing construction industry is in some ways an ideal one to be affected in this way, because it is not characterized by large investments in plant and equipment and, therefore, can reduce the scope of its operations with relative ease. But this is to some degree a self-fulfilling prophecy. The highly cyclical nature of the industry strongly discourages major capital investments in such potentially promising trends as factory-built housing. The "boom and bust" cycles that have impacted the housing industry since 1966 have carried a price in terms of efficiency and innovation.

Since 1968, the nation's mortgage markets have undergone great changes that facilitate the easy flow of funds from the general capital markets into mortgage lending. These innovations in the secondary mortgage market and in mortgage securitizations have been strikingly successful in ameliorating the structural problems of housing finance. It is no longer common during periods of "tight money" for borrowers to find that local institutions simply have no lendable funds. But these institutional relationships do not solve the problem of affordability of high interest rates. So long as cycles of inflation and monetary stringency continue to occur, interest rates will continue to reach high levels from time to time. This explains the search for new forms of mortgage instruments that may soften the impact of high rates.

Affordability issues do not arise only because of high interest rates. During the first half of the 2000s, many regions of the nation experienced very rapid price appreciation in housing. Even though interest rates were very low, high prices made housing unaffordable for many families. Lenders adopted changes in the structure of their mortgage loans—in many case, ill-advised and poorly designed changes—in order to address this issue.

We have now introduced two of the principal problems of housing finance—the difficulty lenders have in mediating between savers and borrowers in a rising-interest market and the difficulty borrowers have in qualifying for loans when interest rates or housing prices are high. We are ready to turn to the innovations in mortgage instruments that may help to resolve these problems. For most of the new mortgage forms (other than the ARM), we have provided only a brief description without extensive citations to the relevant federal regulations. However, agencies have authorized virtually all these forms. As you read about each of them, consider whether it is useful in protecting lenders from rate risk, making housing more affordable to borrowers, or both.

ARMs. ARMs are intended to deal with the lender's difficulties. They enable the lender to periodically modify the interest rate over the life of the loan as market rates change. Thus, the risk of rate fluctuations is shifted from the lender to the borrower. From the lender's viewpoint, the loan's rate of return will approximate the return on a series of short-term loans.

However, ARMs raise questions from the borrower's viewpoint. The most significant is whether the borrower will be able to pay higher rates in the future. The answer depends in part on how a rate increase will be implemented. There are at least three methods:

1.   Monthly payments can be increased by an amount that fully amortizes the loan at the new, higher rate;

2.   The loan maturity can be increased, but even very large increases in maturity can accommodate only small rate increases if the loan begins with a 30-year term; or

3.   The increased interest can be capitalized (added to principal). This may result in "negative amortization," in which the loan balance increases, rather than decreases, each month.

Of course, combinations of these three methods are possible.

The federal financial regulatory agencies permit their regulated lenders to make ARM loans with relatively few limitations. The OTS rules for federal savings associations are promulgated in 12 C.F.R. § 226.19; the lender must give the borrower disclosures about the nature of the index, the adjustment frequency, and a historical example that shows how payments can change. Under 12 C.F.R. § 560.35, the interest rate must correspond directly with the movement of an index, formula, or schedule that is specified in the loan contract and that is "readily available and independently verifiable." For national banks, the Office of the Comptroller of the Currency requires similar disclosures for ARM loans on owner-occupied homes and use of an index that is "readily available to and verifiable by the borrower and beyond the control of the bank." 12 C.F.R. § 34.22.

The following article describes the key features that a borrower should consider when evaluating an adjustable rate mortgage loan.

JOHN E. JACOBS, EVERYTHING THE HOME OWNER'S COUNSEL WANTED TO KNOW ABOUT ADJUSTABLE RATE MORTGAGE LOANS—BUT WAS AFRAID TO ASK
65 Mich.B.J. 156 (1986)

* * *

1. **Index.** A variety of Indexes may be used by lenders, which include: (i) U.S. Treasury security yields, (ii) long-term fixed rate mortgages, (iii) lender's cost of funds, or (iv) prime rate of the lender or a third party. The practitioner should advise his/her client on the relative merits of the various Indexes available. * * *

Generally, the Index will be the rate in effect on a certain date prior to the date upon which the interest rate changes. This date may be 30 to 45 days before the change date, thereby providing the lender with an adequate period of time to notify the borrower of the adjustment. Usually the promissory note provides that, if the Index is no longer available, the holder of the promissory note may choose a new Index, based upon comparable information.

The "change date" is the date upon which the interest begins to accrue at the new interest rate. The first installment, based on the new interest rate, will generally be due 30 days after the change date.

2. **Margin.** The Margin is the amount the lender adds to the Index in order to determine the interest rate. Generally, the Margin is the same amount throughout the term of the loan.

Lenders may, however, provide a Margin which is lower at the first adjustment than at subsequent adjustments. Most lenders charge a Margin between one and three percentage points. The existence of Interest Rate Caps, described below, may cause the Margin to be greater.

Promissory notes provide that the sum of the Margin plus the Index is either rounded to the "nearest one-eighth of one percent" or "up to the nearest one-eighth of one percent." The former clause will generally result in a lower interest rate.

3. **Initial Interest Rate.** The Initial Interest Rate is the rate charged during the first portion of the term of the loan, such as the first year. The Initial Interest Rate is generally one to three percentage points below the interest rate for fixed rate mortgage loans. It may also be less than the sum of the Margin plus the Index.

The Initial Interest Rate may be further reduced as the result of a "buy down." In this case, the home seller, builder or borrower pays a sum of money to the lender in order to reduce the Initial Interest Rate otherwise offered by the lender. The "bought down rate," however, may not be the rate applicable in calculating interest rate caps described below.

The lower Initial Interest Rate provides the lender with an ability to qualify the borrower for a loan for which the borrower may not otherwise be able to qualify. A low Initial Interest Rate is sometimes referred to as a "teaser" rate. Borrower's counsel should consult with the borrower as to whether the borrower's income will increase sufficiently to pay the increased installment payments after the Initial Interest Rate is no longer effective. * * *

4. **Adjustment Interval.** The Adjustment Interval is the period between changes in the interest rate. Most commonly, Adjustment Intervals are one, three or five years. A larger Adjustment Interval will generally result in a higher Initial Interest Rate. In addition, the Index may be tied to the Adjustment Interval. For example, if the Adjustment Interval is three years, the lender may require an Index of the yield on U.S. Treasury securities with a maturity of three years instead of one year. * * * [G]enerally, U.S. Treasury securities with a maturity of three years bear a higher interest rate than such securities with a maturity of one year.

5. **Interest Rate Caps.** An ARM may provide that the interest rate will not increase by more than a certain number of percentage points at each Adjustment Interval. Typically, the cap is one or two percentage points. Borrower's counsel should determine whether the cap applies to the initial adjustment of the interest rate. If the ARM has a teaser rate or the Initial Interest Rate has been bought down, the cap may not be applicable to the adjustment after this reduced interest rate is no longer applicable. The application of the cap to the first adjustment may avoid an increase in the monthly installment, which is substantially more than the increase in the borrower's income.

ARMs may also provide an interest rate cap over the life of the loan. The limitation may be expressed as a specified number of percentage points above the Initial Interest Rate or a specified rate of interest. The most common limitation is five percentage points above the Initial Interest Rate, assuming no teaser or bought down rate. Again, the practitioner should determine whether the cap is applied to the introductory interest rate or only after the first adjustment.

These caps result in limiting the rate of interest charged to the borrower. Therefore, the interest lost as a result of the cap is lost forever.

6. **Monthly Payment Cap.** The borrower may be given the option to limit the increase which would occur in the amount of the monthly installment as a result of the increase in the interest rate. Typically, the

option will be to limit the increase in the monthly payment to 7–1/2% each year until the payment reaches the amount required to pay the loan in full over the remaining term at the current interest rate.

As opposed to the Interest Rate Cap, although the increase in the monthly payment is limited, interest continues to accrue at the new interest rate. Therefore, if the limited monthly payment is less than the amount of interest which accrues in the month, the accrued and unpaid portion of the interest will be added to the principal amount of the loan. This results in "negative amortization."

Such programs generally do not permit the principal balance of the loan to exceed a specified amount, often 125% of the original loan balance. If the principal balance would exceed the maximum amount, the monthly payment is then increased to the amount required to pay the then principal balance in full over the remaining term of the loan, at the interest rate currently in effect.

NOTES

1.   *The yield curve.* Under normal economic conditions, and with all other variations held equal, a debt with a longer term to maturity will carry a higher interest rate than a debt of shorter maturity. The usual explanation of this phenomenon is that a lender that ties up its money for a longer term will, by doing so, ensure that it will miss out on any opportunities to reinvest the money at a higher interest if shorter-term rates move upward during the loan's term. Lenders demand compensation for this lost potential opportunity in the form of a higher rate on the loan being made.

One can make a graph showing interest rates as a function of loan maturity. Such a graph, called a "yield curve," appears below. Of course, it is important not to compare apples with oranges; a yield curve graph is meaningful only if all of the other characteristics of the debts on the graph are essentially similar. The graph below is based on U.S. Treasury debt instruments of various maturities. They meet our criteria of similarity; they carry virtually no credit risk, since it is assumed that the United States government will always pay its debts, and there is an active secondary market for all U.S. debt obligations, irrespective of their maturity.

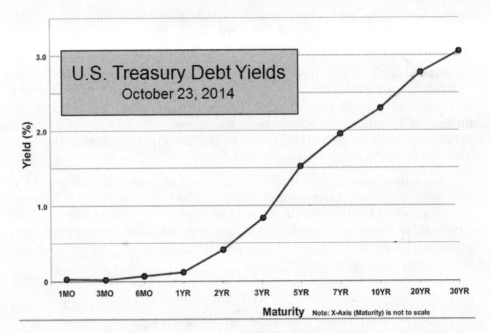

Obviously, if lenders consider current rates to be abnormally high, so that there is an expectation that shorter-term rates will actually decline in the future, the yield curve will have a different shape, sloping downward to the right; this is called an "inverted yield curve." The period 1980–82, when interest rates were extremely high, was characterized by inverted yield curves.

One implication of the normal yield curve is that adjustable rate mortgage loans generally carry lower interest rates that fixed-rate loans. The reason is that an ARM is economically equivalent to a series of shorter-term loans, each with its own interest rate that will approximate current market rates. (We say "approximate" because, if market rates change rapidly, the annual and lifetime rate caps on an ARM may prevent it from fully following the market rate changes.) Moreover, the frequency with which an ARM's interest can be adjusted has a strong impact on the initial rate. Thus, for example, an ARM which adjusts annually will, in normal economic times, have a lower initial interest rate that an ARM which adjusts every two years.

2. *Variations on ARMS.* It has become fairly common for lenders to provide a longer period of fixed interest before beginning to make rate adjustments. For example, the loan might have a fixed rate for 3, 5, or 7 years, and thereafter adjust annually. These loans would be known colloquially as 3/1, 5/1, and 7/1 hybrid ARMS. The longer the period during which the rate is fixed, the more the loan resembles a standard fixed-rate loan, and hence (assuming a normal yield curve), the higher the initial rate is likely to be.

Many indexes are used in constructing ARMs, but those mentioned below are the most popular:

- *Constant Maturity Treasury (CMT) indexes.* Each day the Treasury plots a yield curve of Treasury securities. This curve, which (as explained above) relates the yield on a security to its time to maturity, is based on the closing market bid yields on actively traded Treasury securities in the over-the-counter market. The information is gathered by the New York Federal Reserve Bank. These are not newly-issued securities, but rather those traded on the secondary market, and hence they may have a very wide range of remaining maturities. After the curve is created, the yield values are interpolated from the curve at fixed maturities of 1, 3 and 6 months and 1, 2, 3, 5, 7, 10, 20, and 30 years. This method provides a yield for a 10 year maturity, for example, even if no outstanding security traded on that date has exactly 10 years remaining to maturity. The most common ARM index is the 1-year CMT yield; about half of all ARMS use this index. Such ARMS usually adjust their rates annually.

- *Treasury Bill (T-Bill) indexes.* These indexes are based on the yields at the weekly auctions of new (original issue) debt securities by the Treasury. Monthly averages are then computed from the weekly auctions held during the previous month. The monthly 6-Month Treasury Bill index ("6-month T-Bill") is the index most often used for ARMs, and such ARMs usually adjust every six months.

- *Twelve-month moving Treasury average (MTA) index.* This index is calculated by averaging the monthly yields of the 1-year CMT yield (see above) for the previous twelve months. Because it is 12-month average, it tends to move more slowly and is less volatile that the CMT and T-Bill indexes mentioned above. For ARMs based on this index, the rate is usually adjusted every month and the monthly payment is adjusted either monthly or annually.

- *Eleventh District cost-of-funds (11th Dist. COFI) index.* A cost-of-funds index (COFI) is a weighted average of the interest rates paid by financial institutions to borrow money from their depositors, mainly on checking accounts, savings accounts, and certificates of deposit. This particular COFI is based on institutions that are members of the Eleventh Federal Home Loan Bank District, which includes California, Arizona, and Nevada. Because rates paid to depositors and savers tend to change relatively slowly, this index is less volatile than CMT and T-Bill indexes. On many loans based on this index, the rate is adjusted every month but the monthly payment is adjusted only once a year.

- *London Interbank Offered Rate (LIBOR) index.* This index is based on the interest rates paid by London banks to borrow each other's reserves. The rates are set by the market and are highly volatile. LIBOR rates have various maturities, but those most commonly used as ARM indexes are one-month, six-month, and one-year terms. The ARMs using these indexes would likewise adjust every month, six months, or year.

3. *The Mortgage Disclosure Improvement Act of 2008 and the CFPB Integrated Disclosures.* In 2008 Congress ratcheted up the disclosures that lenders must give to borrowers for residential ARM loans. See the Mortgage Disclosure Improvement Act of 2008, found in sections 2501 through 2503 of the Housing and Economic Recovery Act of 2008, Pub. L. 110–289 (2008). Under this Act, ARM and other TILA disclosures must be provided within three business days after an application is received and before the consumer has paid any fee (other than a fee for obtaining the consumer's credit history). For ARM loans, the disclosure form must tell the borrower that payments will vary based on interest rate changes, the date on which the first change can occur, and that the borrower may be unable to refinance at a lower rate in the future. The disclosure form must include examples of possible payment changes, including the maximum payment amount that the loan documents allow.

In Section 1032(f) of the 2010 Dodd-Frank Act, Congress instructed the Consumer Financial Protection Bureau to develop a disclosure statement and set of accompanying rules that would combine the disclosures previously required by both TILA (including its ARM disclosures) and RESPA. CFPB did so, and ultimately promulgated a final integrated disclosure rule to take effect on August 1, 2015. See 12 C.F.R. Parts 1024 and 1026. The integrated disclosure form, both blank and filled-out, and compliance guides are presented on the CFPB's web page entitled "TILA-RESPA Integrated Disclosure rule implementation."

The Home Equity Conversion Mortgage (HECM)

The home equity conversion mortgage (HECM) is sometimes called a "reverse mortgage." It is designed to allow elderly or retired persons who have large equities in their home to borrow against the equity to help pay living expenses. In the simplest form, the lender makes monthly disbursements to the homeowner, and the outstanding balance on the loan increases to reflect both the disbursements and the accrued interest on those disbursements. When the balance reaches the maximum loan amount, the borrower has to repay the loan, which generally requires that the property be sold.

FHA introduced a HECM program in 1989; see 24 C.F.R. Part 206. While the program has been popular, significant concerns have also been raised about it, as the following excerpt suggests.

REVERSE MORTGAGES: PRODUCT COMPLEXITY AND CONSUMER PROTECTION ISSUES UNDERSCORE NEED FOR IMPROVED CONTROLS OVER COUNSELING FOR BORROWERS*

U.S. General Accountability Office
Report No. GAO–09–606, June 2009

According to industry sources, almost all reverse mortgages are currently made under the Home Equity Conversion Mortgage (HECM) program, which is administered by the Department of Housing and Urban Development (HUD). * * * The volume of HECMs made annually has grown from 157 loans in fiscal year 1990 to more than 112,000 loans in fiscal year 2008. In addition, recent years have seen a rapid increase in the number of lenders participating in the HECM program, with more than 1,500 lenders originating their first HECM in 2008, bringing the total number of HECM lenders to over 2,700.

A reverse mortgage is a loan against the borrower's home that the borrower does not need to repay for as long as the borrower meets certain conditions. These conditions, among others, require the borrower to live in the home, pay property taxes and homeowners' insurance, maintain the property, and retain the title in his or her name. Reverse mortgages typically are "rising debt, falling equity" loans, in which the loan balance increases and the home equity decreases over time. As the borrower receives payments from the lender, the lender adds the principal and interest to the loan balance, reducing the homeowner's equity. This is the opposite of what happens in forward mortgages, which are characterized as "falling debt, rising equity" loans. With forward mortgages, monthly loan payments made to the lender add to the borrower's home equity and decrease the loan balance. See fig. 1.

---

*   Some material has been reordered and brought up to date to reflect fees as of 2014. –Eds.

Figure 1: Comparison of 30-Year Forward and Reverse Mortgages

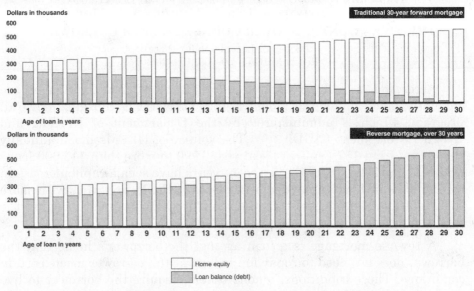

The Housing and Community Development Act of 1987 (Pub. L. No. 100–242) authorized HECMs as a demonstration program in HUD. It was the first nationwide reverse mortgage program—available in all 50 states, the District of Columbia, and Puerto Rico—that offered the possibility of lifetime home occupancy to elderly homeowners. Homeowners aged 62 or over with a significant amount of home equity are eligible, as long as they live in the house as the principal residence, are not delinquent on any federal debt, and live in a single-family residence. If the borrower has any remaining balance on a forward mortgage, this generally must be paid off first (typically, taken up-front from the reverse mortgage). In addition, the condition of the house must meet HUD's minimum property standards, but a portion of the HECM can be set aside for required repairs. The borrower makes no monthly payments, and there are no income or credit requirements to qualify for the mortgage.

The amount of money that a lender can advance to a HECM borrower (loan amount) depends on three main factors. First, the loan amount is based on the "maximum claim amount," which is defined as the lesser of the appraised value of the house or the Federal Housing Administration (FHA) loan limit (the highest mortgage value HUD will insure). [The current maximum amount of an FHA HECM is $625,500 in high-cost areas. —Eds.] Second, the age of the borrower affects the borrower's loan amount—the older the borrower, the higher the loan amount. However, if there is more than one homeowner, the loan amount is based on the age of the youngest borrower. Third, the interest rate also affects the loan amount. Typically, the lower the interest rate, the higher the loan amount.

The complicated nature of the product and the concern that older consumers can be more vulnerable to unscrupulous sales practices have brought reverse mortgages to the attention of consumer advocates, regulators, and policymakers. Since the inception of the HECM program, Congress has required prospective borrowers to obtain adequate counseling by an independent third party so that they could make informed decisions about whether to obtain a HECM. Borrowers must complete counseling with a HUD-approved housing counseling agency before obtaining the loan. Nevertheless, concerns about consumer protections persist. For example, some consumer advocates have expressed concern about misleading marketing and inappropriate cross-selling—the practice of encouraging borrowers to use reverse mortgage funds to purchase insurance or other products that may be unsuitable to the borrower's financial situation. The Housing and Economic Recovery Act of 2008 (HERA) acknowledged some of these concerns by putting in place additional consumer protection measures.

There are substantial fees in connection with obtaining a HECM, including the following:

- *Origination fee:* Prior to HERA, HECM borrowers were charged an origination fee equal to 2 percent of the maximum claim amount with a minimum fee of $2,000. Since the implementation of HERA, HECM borrowers are charged an origination fee calculated as 2 percent of the maximum claim amount up to $200,000 plus 1 percent of the maximum claim amount over $200,000, with a maximum fee of $6,000 and a minimum fee of $2,500.

- *Mortgage insurance premium:* Borrowers are charged an up-front mortgage insurance premium, ordinarily equal to 0.5 percent of the maximum claim amount. However, an additional upfront MIP of another 2% (bringing total up to 2.5%) is charged if, pursuant to mandatory obligations of the borrower, more than 60% of the available Principal Limit is drawn upon at closing or within the first 12 months Additionally, borrowers are charged a monthly mortgage insurance premium on their loan balance at an annual rate of 1.25 percent.

- *Interest:* Borrowers are charged interest, which generally includes a base interest rate plus a fixed lender margin rate, on the loan balance. Lenders can offer HECMs with fixed, annually adjustable, or monthly adjustable base interest rates. The adjustable rates can be tied to either the 1-Year Constant Maturity Treasury Rate or 1-Year London Interbank Offered Rate Index. Most HECMs have adjustable interest rates.

- *HECM counseling fee*: The HECM program requires prospective borrowers to receive counseling to ensure an understanding of the loan.

HUD allows counseling providers to charge borrowers up to $125 for HECM counseling.

- *Loan servicing fee*: Borrowers pay a monthly servicing fee of up to $35.

There is a secondary market for HECMs, as most lenders prefer not to hold the loans on their balance sheets. Fannie Mae has purchased 90 percent of HECM loans and holds them in its portfolio. In 2007, Ginnie Mae developed and implemented a HECM Mortgage Backed Security product, in which Ginnie Mae-approved issuers pool and securitize a small proportion of HECMs. Fannie Mae and Ginnie Mae's involvement in the HECM secondary market helps to provide liquidity so that lenders can continue offering HECM loans to seniors.

NOTE: LESS FREQUENTLY USED ALTERNATIVE MORTGAGES

Lenders have developed a wide variety of alternative mortgages, though the availability of any particular type at a given time depends on market conditions. In addition to the alternative mortgages that we already have described, the following types are sometimes available:

The Price Level Adjusted Mortgage (PLAM). This mortgage format offers a different approach to the problem of mismatch between the maturities of a lender's loans and its funds sources. The PLAM is widely used in several other countries and presents an interesting alternative to the ARM. As we discussed earlier, mortgage interest rates reflect a component of real rate-of-return (perhaps 3% to 4%), plus an additional component for the lender's estimate of future inflation. In the PLAM, the lender charges only the real rate for interest, but the loan's outstanding principal balance is adjusted periodically (say, annually) to reflect changes in the nation's overall price levels. In the United States, the Consumer Price Index could be used for this purpose.

With a PLAM, payments are very low in the mortgage's early years, because they are based on the real interest rate of, say, 4%. If inflation occurs, however, payments will increase each year because the 4% rate will be applied to a higher outstanding balance. Note that *actual* inflation, rather than *expectations* about inflation, is relevant for the PLAM. For borrowers who believe that their income will increase, the PLAM might be quite attractive. *See* Michael S. Knoll, The Second Generation of Notes Indexed For Inflation, 39 Emory L.J. 499 (1990); Michael S. Knoll, Taxation, Negative Amortization and Affordable Mortgages, 53 Ohio St. L.J. 1341 (1992); Joel J. Goldberg, Note, Alternative Mortgage Instruments: Authorizing and Implementing Price Level Adjusted Mortgages, 16 U.Mich.J.L.Reform 115 (1982). For a review of other nations' experiences with the PLAM, *see* Harold Robinson, Readjustable Mortgages in an Inflationary Economy, 4 Fed. Home Loan Bank Bd. J. 19 (Feb. 1971).

PLAMs have occasionally been used on nonresidential mortgages in the United States. However, they make the most sense in a highly inflationary economy, and inflation has been relatively low in the U.S. in recent years, so there has been little interest in PLAMs. In Aztec Properties, Inc. v. Union Planters Nat'l Bank, 530 S.W.2d 756 (Tenn.1975), *cert. denied*, 425 U.S. 975, 96 S.Ct. 2175, 48 L.Ed.2d 799 (1976), the Tennessee Supreme Court held that the increases in principal under a PLAM were in reality interest, which triggered the usury statute. *See* Mildred B. Dodson, Note, Inflation and Indexing—Usury in Commercial Loans: *Aztec Properties, Inc. v. Union Planters National Bank*, 11 Tulsa L.J. 450 (1976).

The Shared Appreciation Mortgage (SAM). With this mortgage, a portion of the interest rate is payable only from increases in the mortgaged property's value. In effect, the lender holds an equity interest, as well as a security interest, in the real estate. For example, suppose a lender makes a ten-year loan with a 10 percent fixed interest rate and an additional 5 percent contingent rate. The borrower would make regular monthly payments based on the 10 percent rate. At the end of ten years or when the borrower sells the property, whichever occurs first, the 5 percent contingent interest is due. However, it is payable from only 40 percent of the property's increase in value since the loan was made.

If the property is sold, the selling price establishes its appreciated value. If it is not sold, it is appraised after ten years to determine its value. In calculating the net appreciation, the borrower receives credits for the property's original cost and for any improvements made during the loan term. If the borrower has not sold the property before the ten-year term expires, the lender may have to refinance it, including the accrued contingent interest, for a new 30-year term at the current fixed interest rate.

SAMs have been used in the United States mainly for commercial mortgage loans, but occasionally a lender offers SAM residential loans. *See generally* Anthony B. Sandersa & V. Carlos Slawson, Shared Appreciation Mortgages: Lessons from the UK, 14 J. Hous. Econ. 178 (Sept. 2005).

The Graduated Payment Mortgage (GPM). The graduated payment mortgage is designed to make housing more affordable. The interest rate is fixed for the life of the loan, but the payments increase, typically by X percent each year for the first Y years of the loan, and then remain constant for the remainder of the term. The result is heavier payments in the later years to compensate for the reduced payments in the early years of the loan. If the annual payment increase is not too steep, the borrower's income should have increased enough to cover it. Note, however, that the payment increases will occur even if the borrower's income diminishes or disappears.

FHA is authorized to insure GPM loans by Section 245 of the National Housing Act. Of the five FHA GPM plans, three allow mortgage payments to increase at a rate of 2.5 percent, 5 percent, or 7.5 percent each year for the first 5 years of the loan. In the other two plans, payments increase at a rate of 2 to 3 percent annually over a 10-year period. Beginning in the sixth year of the 5 year plans and in the eleventh year of the 10 year plans, payments stay the same for the remaining years of the mortgage. FHA plans that have a greater rate of increase over a longer period will have lower payments in the early years.

NOTE: PREEMPTION OF STATE LAW LIMITATIONS ON ALTERNATIVE MORTGAGE INSTRUMENTS

In the 1970s and 1980s, the federal agencies that regulate financial institutions began to authorize the use of numerous new types of mortgage instruments that involved features such as adjustable interest rates and graduated payments. However, this authority extended only to federally-chartered institutions, because state law and regulations govern state-chartered banks, savings associations, and credit unions, even if they had federal deposit insurance. Some state regulators promulgated regulations similar to the federal regulations, but frequently their efforts were comparatively slow, were inhibited by state statutes, and included limitations not found in the federal regulations. As a result, state-chartered lenders operated under a competitive disadvantage with the federal lenders.

Congress addressed this problem in Title VIII of the Depository Institutions Amendments of 1982, which are known as the Alternative Mortgage Transaction Parity Act of 1982 ("AMTPA"). It authorizes all state-chartered financial institutions to make the same types of mortgage loans as federally-chartered lenders. Thus, state law limitations on alternative mortgage loans became irrelevant except to the extent that they were broader than the analogous federal regulations.

AMTPA's main features include:

Property types covered. To be covered by the AMTPA, the loan must be secured by residential real estate, co-op stock, or a manufactured home. Thus, loans on commercial or other nonresidential property are excluded.

Mortgage types covered. The AMTPA covers all forms of adjustable-interest loans, whether the adjustment is explicit or is in the form of a renegotiation or roll-over provision. It covers loans with variations in term, repayment, or other features and, therefore, probably applies to GPMs. *See* Grunbeck v. Dime Sav. Bank, 74 F.3d 331 (1st Cir. 1996) (AMTPA preempts state law prohibition on "interest on interest").

Lenders covered. The AMTPA includes all depository institutions, HUD-approved lenders, and persons who regularly engage in the business of extending credit on the security of property of the types described above. Transferees from these lenders are also covered. Note that this definition includes mortgage bankers and similar businesses that are typically unregulated by either state or federal law.

Federal regulations apply. State-chartered banks must conform to OCC regulations. State credit unions must conform to NCUA regulations. All other lenders, including savings associations and unregulated lenders, such as mortgage bankers, must conform to OTS regulations, now merged with the OCC.

Reimposition of state law. States were given authority to reimpose state law by either a legislative act or a referendum vote before October 15, 1985. Several states readopted state law, see, e.g., N.Y.-McKinney's Banking Law § 6–g; Me.Rev.Stat. § 1–110; S.C.Code 1976, § 34–1–110. Arizona and Wisconsin partially readopted state law.

See generally D. Edwin Schmelzer, The Preemptions for Alternative Mortgage Transactions and Due-on-Sale Clauses in the Garn-St. Germain Act, 102 Bank. L.J. 256 (1985).

The scope of the AMTPA was controversial. During the early 2000s, several federal courts held that all aspects of alternative mortgages, including features having nothing to do with their "alternative" character, were preempted. See, e.g., National Home Equity Mortg. Ass'n v. Face, 239 F.3d 633 (4th Cir. 2001) (Virginia law on prepayment penalties preempted); Shinn v. Encore Mortgage Services, Inc., 96 F.Supp.2d 419 (D.N.J. 2000) (N.J. law on prepayment penalties preempted). Congress reversed these holdings in the 2010 Dodd-Frank Act, clarifying that the only state laws preempted were those dealing with adjustments to interest rate or finance charge, and not those "that regulate mortgage transactions generally, including any restriction on prepayment penalties or late charges." See Dodd-Frank Act, Pub.L. 111–203, at § 1083(a)(2)(A)(iv).

PART 3

REAL ESTATE DEVELOPMENT

■ ■ ■

CHAPTER NINE

SUBDIVISIONS AND DETACHED HOUSE DEVELOPMENTS

■ ■ ■

At this point, we begin the first of three chapters that examine the legal aspects of specific types of real estate developments. This chapter covers subdivisions. The next chapter treats "common interest communities"—planned unit developments, condominiums, and cooperatives. The third chapter covers income-producing properties, such as apartments and shopping centers. Our objective is to provide a reasonably comprehensive picture of the legal issues relating to planning, financing, constructing, and marketing these kinds of developments and of the parties' legal rights when the developer does not meet its obligations. For the most part, we will not consider public controls over land use, such as zoning and subdivision regulations. These matters are highly complex and are frequently covered in separate law school courses with titles such as "land use planning law." We will also largely leave consideration of tax issues to your tax law courses.

A. OVERVIEW OF THE SUBDIVISION PROCESS

In purest form, a subdivider is a person who buys a relatively large tract of land and divides it into smaller parcels for resale. In most cases, the land's ultimate use (at least according to the subdivider's advertisements) will be residential or recreational. Within this general characterization, we can identify three categories of subdividers:

1. *The remote subdivider's* land is usually rather far from any major urban area. Marketing efforts are often aimed toward persons who may wish to camp on their lots or to build smaller houses or cabins for weekend or summer use. The developer's sales force will often emphasize the subdivision's supposedly attractive investment opportunities and will cite figures predicting large capital value appreciation for the lots. The subdivider rarely builds any houses or cabins in this sort of development, and the other facilities it installs are often meager; paved roads, utility connections, waste disposal facilities, schools, and other parts of the infrastructure may be missing or promised for an indefinite future that never arrives.

2.   *The suburban lot seller,* like the remote subdivider, does not build houses. But two factors distinguish this type of developer from the sometimes-disreputable recreational lot seller. First, the land is located in the developing fringe of an urban area and, therefore, is desirable for immediate residential use. Most lot buyers plan to build homes in the near future. Second, the subdivider typically provides most or all of the normal public facilities required for a viable residential neighborhood, such as streets and sidewalks, street lighting, storm and sanitary sewers, utility connections, and sometimes parks or other recreational facilities. Many of these facilities are the developer's responsibility based on applicable city or county ordinances. In contrast, the remote subdivider usually operates in more remote jurisdictions that are not accustomed to major urban development and, therefore, do not require significant infrastructure improvements.

3.   *The merchant builder* is probably the most familiar type of subdivider, because a large proportion of Americans live in homes these builders have constructed. Merchant builders usually operate in the same areas and provide the same range of facilities as the suburban lot seller, but they also build a house on each lot. The development may take the traditional form, with detached houses on quarter-acre to half-acre rectangular lots on rectilinear streets. In recent years, merchant builders increasingly have constructed curved streets and cul-de-sacs, semi-detached or attached houses, and relatively small private lots with larger common areas for children's play, swimming pools, and other recreational facilities. This newer format is typically called a "planned unit development" ("PUD") or simply "planned development," but many of the legal issues it raises are similar to those of the more traditional grid-street subdivision.

The categories we have described above are not, of course, quite as neat as they seem. The distinction between remote subdividers and suburban lot sellers is sometimes hard to discern. Moreover, some suburban operators sell a portion of their lots without houses and build on the remainder. Even remote subdividers, in a few cases, sell finished houses on their lots. But for the most part, it is fairly easy to identify a particular subdivider with one of these categories.

In this section, we will focus principally on merchant builders, but many of the legal problems raised by their operations are applicable to the other two categories of subdividers as well. We begin by presenting a general overview of the merchant builder's operations. We will examine a typical subdivision from initial land acquisition to final sale of completed houses. The following sections of this chapter will analyze in detail the legal issues raised by various phases of the subdivider's operations, such as construction financing and mechanic's liens.

Most subdividers are small businesspersons. The great majority probably build fewer than 50 houses per year. Although there has been some trend toward greater scale and concentration, it is by no means dominant. Perhaps the most salient fact about typical small builders is that they are very thinly capitalized. Even builders who have operated successfully for many years often operate with little equity capital. Builders prefer to employ borrowed money and to use as little of their own funds as possible. In the parlance of the industry, they are "highly leveraged" and prefer to come as close as possible to "mortgaging out," using no money of their own.

A sophisticated merchant builder's work begins well before it has identified any particular land for the subdivision. Because houses can be sold only where there are willing buyers, market research is necessary to demonstrate that homes of a particular design and price range can be sold in a given locality. Both construction and permanent lenders will be interested in this market data, but the developer must review it first to determine that going forward makes business sense.

Of course, many small builders do not perform or contract for formal market surveys. They rely instead on their own instincts and experience; they feel that they know what is selling and where. Indeed, in some metropolitan areas, housing demand appears to be so strong that market research seems superfluous. But housing demand is notoriously volatile, and even areas like these can become overbuilt, with unsold houses sitting for long periods of time in a saturated market. Market demand is also a function of interest rates and of the availability of financing. The builder's sales projections must be reviewed in the light of probable financial trends and buyers' ability to obtain mortgage loans at acceptable interest rates.

After determining market demand, the builder is ready to choose a specific site for the development. Sites for new subdivisions are typically in the developing urban fringe, although occasionally land may become available in already-urbanized areas as a result of urban renewal land clearance, the development of a "new town in town," or because a municipal, state, or the federal government makes land available that had previously been restricted to governmental use. In the usual suburban case, the land has been previously used for agriculture, although the subdivider does not always buy directly from the farmer. Often, land speculators will have purchased agricultural land that they anticipated would become desirable for subdivision in the near future, and the developer must then deal with them. In other cases, the subdivider is also a speculator and has decided that the market is ready for a subdivision on the land that it purchased some years earlier.

As the development process progresses, land prices increase. Land used for agricultural purposes may have a value of only a few thousand dollars per acre. A developer, however, will usually have to pay a substantial premium above that amount to acquire the land when it is ready for development. After the developer has obtained the necessary land use approvals, including any necessary rezoning, has invested in the necessary infrastructure, such as streets and sewers, and has paid the necessary fees for water, sewer, and other utility hookups and for local school, park, and other funds, the final market price of a finished lot will be many times its value as raw land. For this reason, if the developer does not already own the land, it often prefers reserving the right to buy with an option to purchase, rather than entering into a binding purchase agreement. With an option agreement, the developer can buy the land in the future if it decides to do so and will forfeit a relatively small amount of money if it decides not to exercise the option because the project turns out to be infeasible.

During the option period, the developer pursues a variety of matters more or less simultaneously, such as surveys, soil tests, and environmental investigations. The planning and engineering of the subdivision is a first concern, because both lenders and local governments will review the subdivision layout and design before giving their approvals. Additionally, in almost all cases, a local government agency must approve the subdivision. As part of this review and approval process, the subdivider prepares a subdivision plat, which is a map that shows the layout of streets, lots, easements, and other features of the subdivision. After the plat is approved, it is recorded with the county recorder or another appropriate government office and then provides the basis for legal descriptions of lots in the subdivision. In most jurisdictions, the plat also constitutes a dedication of the streets and other public facilities that it shows. Because the developer may not actually construct these facilities for some time, many local governments require the developer to escrow funds, post a bond, or otherwise provide assurances that the improvements will be completed and that the developer will be financially responsible for their construction.

Before exercising the option, the subdivider also must attempt to obtain financing for the project. As described in the next section, the subdivider normally must arrange financing to acquire the land (purchase money land financing), to build the project (construction loan), and to finance the new home purchases and pay the construction loan (permanent or take-out financing). In addition to the loan costs, the subdivider usually is responsible for the fees of the attorneys, planners, and other professionals involved in the project, although it can sometimes persuade the original owner of the land to share the expenses.

The subdivider will buy the land only after obtaining the necessary government approvals and arranging financing. Although these contingencies could have been included in a firm purchase agreement as preconditions to the subdivider's obligation to purchase the land, such a contract would be long and complex. Therefore, as described above, most developers prefer to use the option agreement. When all the necessary planning is completed and the government approvals have been obtained, the developer will exercise the option, thus creating a binding contract to purchase the land.

B. FINANCING THE PROJECT

1. PURCHASE MONEY LAND FINANCING

Subdividers rarely are willing or able to pay cash for the land to be developed. A cash purchase is feasible if the subdivider is willing to proceed very slowly; it can enter into option agreements with the owner that allow it to purchase a few lots at a time with the proceeds from sales of lots that it has previously developed. But a subdivider that wants to operate on a substantial scale must arrange credit to finance the land acquisition.

One possibility is to enter into a loan agreement with a single lender, such as a commercial bank or savings association, for enough funds to cover the entire project, including land acquisition, site development, and construction. Such loans are usually called "ADC" loans ("acquisition, development, and construction" loans). Although some lenders make them, the FDIC has warned that "ADC lending is a highly specialized field with inherent risks that must be managed and controlled to ensure that this activity remains profitable." FDIC Financial Institution Letter FIL–110–98 (Oct. 8, 1998). Because of this perception of risk, ADC loans tend to be made only by large institutions to large developers. Obtaining only a land acquisition loan from an institutional lender also can be difficult.

Therefore, the subdivider often persuades the seller to extend credit for a large part of the land's purchase price. For the most common form of seller financing, the seller deeds the property to the developer, and the developer gives the seller a small down payment and a promissory note and purchase money mortgage on the property for the balance of the purchase price. Alternatively, the land can be sold by means of an installment contract pursuant to which the seller retains title to the land until the entire purchase price is paid. The subdivider adjusts the maturity of the purchase money obligation to reflect the development plans; the longer the construction time contemplated, the longer the maturity of the obligation.

Persuading the land seller to defer receipt of part of the purchase price often is possible because Internal Revenue Code § 453 permits sellers to spread the tax on the gain from the sale across the years in which the proceeds are actually received, rather than paying the entire tax in the year of sale. This treatment is available whether the sale is by installment contract or by deed with a note and mortgage back to the seller.

When completed homes are sold, the developer must be able to convey them free of the purchase money lien. Therefore, the loan documents usually include a partial release clause. Under this type of clause, the purchase money lien on a lot is released when the lot is sold and a specified fraction of the loan is paid to the lien holder. Alternatively, the land may be placed in a "subdivision trust" with a title company or other trustee who is instructed to convey each lot free of the purchase money lien when the portion of the loan attributable to that lot is paid to the lien holder. The developer may also reserve a right to prepay all or part of the land purchase obligation if more favorable interim financing becomes available.

2.   CONSTRUCTION AND PERMANENT FINANCING

A construction loan is the usual source of funds for building the improvements on the land. The construction loan is a short-term loan that usually is secured by a mortgage or deed of trust on the property. The construction lender will take all the precautions normally associated with the acquisition of a mortgage lien. For example, the lender normally requires a title search and title insurance for the lender's construction mortgage, and the developer usually must be personally liable for the debt if the nominal developing entity is a thinly-capitalized corporation or limited liability company. The construction loan is repaid as each improved lot is sold.

The most important construction lenders for commercial developments are commercial banks, insurance companies, and pension funds. Fannie Mae, Freddie Mac, and government agencies, such as the Federal Housing Administration, also are important construction lenders, but only for multi-family/apartment construction. Because these lenders almost always insist on first lien position, the purchase money land lien and the lien for any site development loan normally must be subordinated to the construction mortgage. This is best accomplished by language in the purchase money and site development loan security documents or in a separate agreement that the construction loan will have first priority.

Subordination substantially increases the risk for the subordinated liens, a fact that the subordinated lienors may not fully appreciate.

From the construction lender's viewpoint, it is also important that a long-term permanent loan is available to pay off the entire construction loan when construction is complete or to provide financing for individual home buyers. If buyers cannot obtain financing to purchase a home, the developer will have few sales. Therefore, unless the construction lender is very confident concerning the developer's solvency and the homes' marketability, it often requires the developer to obtain a permanent loan commitment as a condition to the construction loan being funded. For some types of construction lenders, an advance take-out commitment is a legal requirement. Sometimes, the construction lender also provides the permanent loan commitment. However, since the most recent recession, many large permanent lenders generally will not issue a permanent loan commitment until the construction is complete.

Another major concern of the construction lender is that the value of the improvements constructed with the loan proceeds at least equals those proceeds. Two common situations exist in which this expectation may not be fulfilled. First, the builder may "draw down" the construction funds but divert them to some use other than labor and materials on the construction site. For an unscrupulous builder, the funds' ultimate destination might be an offshore bank account. More frequently, the builder needs the money for other business purposes. For example, the builder may have another subdivision that has run into financial difficulties and may hope to "bail it out" with the construction funds diverted from the present project.

Second, even if the developer is completely honest, the property's security value may be less than the amount of funds disbursed because of normal construction risks. During labor strikes, bad weather, and other delays, costs continue to accrue even though little or no work of value is being accomplished on the site. Similarly, material costs may rise substantially and unexpectedly. Although some kinds of hazards, such as fire, can be insured against, delays and some other types of risks are uninsurable. Therefore, a subdivision into which one million dollars in construction loan funds have been poured very well may be worth only $800,000 or less.

If the builder becomes bankrupt, is unable to complete construction, or otherwise defaults on the construction loan, the construction lender may decide to foreclose and take title to the partially-completed property. But this simply shifts to the construction lender all the risks that the builder could not manage, and most construction lenders have little desire to place themselves in that situation. On the contrary, the construction lender's principal goal is to have the builder successfully complete the project within the limits of the funds committed, so that it can sell the homes and repay the construction loan.

To achieve this goal, construction lenders have developed several techniques for insuring that the disbursed loan proceeds are used for improvements on the construction site. When the loan is made, the lender and builder execute a "construction loan agreement" that specifies the loan disbursement procedures and conditions. For a very complete and well-designed illustration, *see* Nelson, Whitman, Burkhart & Freyermuth, Real Estate Finance Law § 14:2 (6th ed. Practitioner Series 2014). *See also* Dianne S. Coscarelli, The Construction Loan Agreement: Six Provisions Important to Lender's Counsel, Prob. & Prop., Jan./Feb. 2001, at 30; Richard E. Strauss, Construction Financing: An Additional Dimension, 54 The Secured Lender, Nov./Dec. 1998, at 34. Various approaches are used by lenders in different areas of the nation, but the most common include the following:

1. *Progress payments.* Under this approach, the lender advances funds as specific stages of construction are completed. For example, the lender might advance 1/7th of the funds on a particular house when the excavation is completed and the foundation is poured, the next 1/7th when the exterior walls are framed, the next 1/7th when the roof is on, and so on.

2. *The voucher system.* The lender may require the developer to pay the workers and suppliers directly and then to present those bills, marked "paid," to the lender for reimbursement. In principle, this assures the lender that the funds it disburses represent work already done on the property. However, the developer may be tempted to persuade or to coerce workers and suppliers to mark bills as being paid when they are not. This practice gives the developer some additional cash, but it violates the construction loan agreement and increases the lender's risk.

3. *Direct disbursements to workers and suppliers.* As a variant of the voucher system, the lender may require that the workers' and suppliers' bills be presented directly to it. The lender then pays them and debits the builder's construction loan account accordingly.

4. *Third party disbursing agents.* Rather than managing the construction loan itself, the lender may employ a third party, such as a title insurance company, a "construction control company," an escrow company, or some other independent entity, to make all disbursements to the workers and suppliers. The disbursing agent may be willing to guarantee that the funds have been disbursed only for work actually done on the project.

No matter which approach the construction lender uses, it is likely to require that a certain fraction of the total cost, typically 5 to 10 percent, be "held back" until the construction on a particular house is completed and the local government issues a certificate of occupancy.

Construction loans do not always cover the entire cost of construction. For example, they frequently do not cover off-site improvements, such as storm and sanitary sewers and street paving. To pay for these items, the builder may have to invest some of its own cash in the project. Lenders also often require the builder to post a cash deposit with the lender to provide assurance that the builder is sufficiently solvent to complete the project. Additionally, the lender may require the builder to post a payment and performance bond, which obligates the bonding company to complete the project within the agreed-upon budget if the builder cannot. However, bonds are uncommon in subdivision work because most small builders cannot qualify for them and because larger builders that can qualify are usually sufficiently solvent that a bond is thought to add little protection.

Both before and during construction, the construction lender takes a close interest in the plans and specifications for the houses and for the off-site improvements. The lender frequently inspects the improvements to ensure that they are being completed in accordance with those plans and specifications. The construction lender is motivated by self-interest; if the development does not meet the specifications, the permanent lender may refuse to honor its loan commitment, and the construction lender may have a "white elephant" on its hands if the houses are unmarketable because they are out of compliance.

To provide additional protection, many construction lenders use "demand" notes, which allow the lender to require repayment of the note at any time and to foreclose if the builder is unable to comply. In the normal course of construction, the lender would not make such a demand. However, if the builder runs into serious difficulties, the lender can call the loan due, take over the project, and complete construction. This rarely occurs, but its threat can be an effective means of spurring the builder to more vigorous action.

For the reasons described above, construction lending is far more complex and burdensome than long-term lending, but it can also be more lucrative. Interest rates on construction loans are typically several percentage points higher than on permanent loans. Moreover, construction lenders use a variety of techniques for boosting the yields on these loans. "Loan fees" and "points" are often charged in addition to interest. Lenders sometimes charge interest on the entire construction loan for the total construction period, though the funds are actually disbursed over a period of several months. *See* Hoffman v. Key Federal

Sav. & Loan Ass'n, 286 Md. 28, 416 A.2d 1265 (1979). The lender may also pay little or no interest on the funds that the builder is required to deposit with the lender to ensure financial responsibility.

When construction on a house is completed and a home buyer is found, the buyer obtains a permanent loan and pays the purchase price to the builder. The builder, in turn, uses the purchase price to pay off a pro rata share of the construction loan, the purchase money land loan, and any site development loan, including accrued interest. The lenders then release their liens on the lot, which enables a clear conveyance of title.

A few decades ago, subdividers often took second mortgages from home buyers to reduce the down payment to a level that more people could afford. Because the subdivider usually needed cash and could not afford to hold second mortgages, it almost always sold this paper at a rather deep discount to some other lender. This practice has become less common for urban subdivision developers, but recreational subdividers still routinely provide financing for their customers by taking installment contracts or purchase-money mortgages and then usually selling or "discounting" them to finance companies or other investors.

The excerpt below illustrates in a concrete way some of the problems that can arise with construction lending. While it deals with an apartment project, rather than a subdivision, most of the issues are similar.

HENRY S. KESLER, CONSTRUCTION LENDING RISKS AND RETURNS
Mortgage Banking, Jan. 1989, at 62

The Apartments at Purple Creek is an example of a construction lending project that involved many of the risks facing a construction lender. This was a $3,400,000 construction loan on a 96-unit garden apartment project in rural Evanston, Wyoming. Evanston was in the midst of the oil boom and had a housing shortage and prospects for continued expansion. The project had obtained a commitment for FHA-insured IRB (Industrial Revenue Bond) term financing sponsored by the city with a letter of credit enhancement from a major bank in a neighboring state.

The developers had only done one other apartment property. The partnership included a construction foreman who had worked for a successful apartment developer. To further simplify the construction, the project was a copy of a previously built apartment and was to be modular construction with pre-fabricated apartment units delivered to the site by a major home fabricator. The borrowers' net worth was modest and illiquid with the required cash equity being contributed from numerous limited partners, some closely related to the borrowers. A nine-month construction loan was approved and closed in December with substantial fees and course-of-construction, FHA inspections required.

The loan production officer was so optimistic that he failed to objectively present the borrowers' experience or financial status. Instead, the construction lender relied upon the existence of the FHA-insured take-out commitment to influence final approval. At loan closing, the loan officer casually approved the change of construction method from prefabricated, modular construction to onsite framing. Yet, no change was made to the construction budget. The loan was then turned over to the lender's construction loan administration division.

During an early inspection by the lender's independent architect not only was the construction method a surprise but the borrower/contractor had redesigned the project and was using unapproved plans.

Because of the lack of available skilled labor in this rural community and unusually severe weather conditions, construction costs skyrocketed. The borrower hid the cost increases from the lender until costs were out of control. Lien laws gave all laborers and suppliers priority over the construction loan. The foreman was diverting funds to his personal benefit and several subcontractors went bankrupt. The construction lender finally had to forcibly take control of the security pledged from the borrowers (their homes), and funded cost overruns by increasing the loan $700,000.

The project was ultimately completed nine months late. By that time, the Evanston economy had severely deteriorated and conventional financing would only support a $2,800,000 loan and the IRB could not be increased. Fortunately for the construction lender, the FHA commitment and the IRB had been extended but their funding prohibited any subordinate financing. As a result, the construction lender was forced to look only to the additional collateral pledged by the borrowers for satisfaction of a $700,000 loan increase. Thus, the lender ultimately experienced a loss in excess of $500,000.

This loan had it all: lack of thorough underwriting; undercapitalized inexperienced borrower/developers; multiple borrowers; underestimated costs; changes to the construction method; failure of subcontractors; fraudulent diversion of funds; loss of rental market; subsidized term financing; and the involvement of a supervising governmental agency. In addition, there was the poor judgment of the loan officer, the failure of early identification of the problems and lack of immediate control measures by the construction lender. Ultimately the letter-of-credit-issuing bank was required to fund to satisfy the bonds and also suffered a major loss.

NOTES ON CONSTRUCTION LENDER LIABILITY

1. *Liability for construction defects.* New home builders are now widely held liable for defects in design or construction on the basis of an implied warranty of habitability. Should such liability be imposed on a construction lender as well, if it reviewed and approved the defective plans and specifications or if it inspected the property and became aware of the defects? In many cases, the builder is judgment-proof or nearly so, while the lender is a "deep pocket." Most such claims against lenders have failed. *See* Chapter 2, Section D supra; Craig R. Thorstenson, Comment, Mortgage Lender Liability to the Purchaser of New or Existing Homes, 1988 Ill.L.Rev. 191; Nelson, Whitman, Burkhart & Freyermuth, Real Estate Finance Law § 12.11 (6th ed. 2014).

2. *Liability for hazardous waste contamination.* Consider a construction lender's potential liability for a violation of CERCLA (Comprehensive Environmental Response, Compensation and Liability Act of 1980, 42 U.S.C.A. §§ 9601–9675). A more thorough treatment of CERCLA's impact on mortgage lenders is found in Chapter 4, Section D supra, but that section deals primarily with the lender's role as a mortgagee in possession or as a foreclosure sale purchaser. What is the liability of a construction lender that makes a loan for a residential subdivision on a site that was previously used for industrial purposes and is contaminated by industrial waste? Is the lender liable by virtue of its role in the construction process? At least one court has held that it is. Tanglewood East Homeowners v. Charles-Thomas, Inc., 849 F.2d 1568 (5th Cir.1988). However, no other court has reached the same conclusion.

3. *Liability for discontinuance of loan funding.* During the 1980s, a great flurry of litigation involved what was loosely termed "lender liability." Most of the cases involved lines of credit granted to businesses or to farming operations. The loan documents provided for short-term loans (typically one year). When the borrower's business began to falter or to fail, the lender refused to renew the line of credit. *See, e.g.*, K.M.C. Co., Inc. v. Irving Trust Co., 757 F.2d 752 (6th Cir.1985); State Nat'l Bank v. Farah Mfg. Co., 678 S.W.2d 661 (Tex.App.1984). Borrowers usually asserted damages on the ground that the lender's termination of the credit line caused the business to fail or, at least, drove the nails into its coffin. They often based their claim on breach of a contractual duty of good faith and fair dealing, breach of a fiduciary relationship, tortious interference with contractual relations, or on the argument that the short-term credit agreement had been changed by the parties' course of conduct into a longer-term obligation to lend.

In recent years, nearly all these cases failed to establish liability. In the absence of highly improper or misleading statements by the lender, courts generally enforced the loan documents as written, permitted acceleration of the debt because it was in default or because the loan's term ended, and refused to find a continuing duty to lend. *See, e.g.*, Mitsui Manufacturers Bank v. Superior Court, 212 Cal.App.3d 726, 260 Cal.Rptr. 793 (1989);

Batterman v. Wells Fargo Ag Credit Corp., 802 P.2d 1112 (Colo.App.1990); Lachenmaier v. First Bank Systems, Inc., 246 Mont. 26, 803 P.2d 614 (1990); Bloomfield v. Nebraska State Bank, 237 Neb. 89, 465 N.W.2d 144 (1991); Kathleen S. McLeroy, Note, Lender Liability and Discretionary Lending: Putting the Good Faith Performance Standard in Perspective, 46 Wash. & Lee L.Rev. 1067 (1989).

A few of these "lender liability" cases involved development or construction loans. For example, in Storek & Storek v. Citicorp Real Estate, Inc., 100 Cal.App.4th 44, 122 Cal.Rptr.2d 267 (2002), the developer argued that the construction lender had "set up" the developer for default on a loan to complete a partially-finished development. The construction loan agreement provided that a default existed if the loan was "out of balance" (i.e., if insufficient funds remained in the construction account to complete the project) when the lender knew that the loan was "out of balance" from the outset. The court held that, if the lender had reasonable evidence that the loan was out of balance, it could declare a default and foreclose regardless of its alleged bad motives.

However, if a lender cannot provide reasonable evidence of a default, it may indeed be liable for "calling" the loan. In Shaughnessy v. Mark Twain State Bank, 715 S.W.2d 944 (Mo.App.1986), Mark Twain State Bank gave a developer, Shaughnessy, a $50,000 line of credit to perform preliminary site development on a real estate project. The loan was secured by a deed of trust. After some funds were advanced and expended, the bank became dissatisfied with the project, refused to advance more funds, and "called" the loan. The developer sued for damages and prevailed. In rejecting the bank's defense, the court stated:

> Mark Twain argues that . . . three events of default occurred . . . : (1) the bank deemed itself insecure; (2) the bank determined that a material adverse change had occurred in the financial condition of Shaughnessy; and (3) material falsehood in the loan application. Thus, Mark Twain argues that since one or more of these three conditions were met the note was in default and breach of the contract to lend occurred. We disagree.
>
> These are factual issues. Mark Twain vigorously asserts that after it visited the Questover Canyon site, it discovered that things were not as it had thought. Thus, Mark Twain then could have considered itself insecure or that a materially adverse change had occurred, thus triggering default by Shaughnessy. However, Shaughnessy's evidence was that the bank never gave him any reason for cutting him off. Certainly had the bank felt it was insecure it would have articulated its reasons to Shaughnessy. It did not and therefore, we cannot say the trial court was clearly in error in finding no default occurred.
>
> Mark Twain also claims that Shaughnessy defaulted by filing a materially false loan application. Mark Twain urges us to reverse

based on the fact that Shaughnessy's 1978 income was $24,000 when in fact, according to his income tax return it was only $684.06. We disagree. First, the record shows that Shaughnessy's income from insurance sales in 1978 was not a crucial factor in the loan process as was Shaughnessy's equity in Questover Canyon and the prospect for payoff through sales. Secondly, there is no evidence that Mark Twain was aware of this discrepancy until after it refused to disburse.

The promissory note at issue in *Shaughnessy* was a demand note. That type of note provides that the lender can demand payment at any time. Section 1–309 of the Uniform Commercial Code deals with a similar yet distinct type of note. It specifies the circumstances under which a lender can accelerate a loan with a defined maturity date based on the lender's insecurity:

> A term providing that one party or that party's successor in interest may accelerate payment or performance or require collateral or additional collateral . . . when the party "deems itself insecure," or words of similar import, means that the party has power to do so only if that party in good faith believes that the prospect of payment or performance is impaired. The burden of establishing lack of good faith is on the party against which the power has been exercised.

3. LOAN COMMITMENTS

Both construction and permanent loans are generally preceded by a loan commitment—a lender's written promise to make the loan when certain conditions are met. For example, in a permanent loan commitment in which the lender agrees to finance the purchase of homes in a subdivision, the lender will reserve the right to review the loan applicants' credit and income, because these future buyers cannot usually be identified when the commitment is given (before the construction begins). Before giving a commitment, the permanent lender usually reviews the available market research concerning the proposed subdivision and the plans and specifications for it. The commitment will be conditioned on the construction being completed in accordance with the plans and specifications.

Loan commitments made by major lenders on major projects, such as a life insurance company's permanent loan commitment on a multimillion-dollar shopping center, are usually lengthy (say, 20 to 30 pages), carefully negotiated, and well-drafted. On the other hand, commitments made by local lenders to local builders are often cursory and haphazard and give rise to numerous problems of interpretation. The following example of a construction loan commitment is somewhere in between.

EQUITY NATIONAL BANK

August 14, 2015

Mr. Edward Jones
1270 Sloan Street
Evergreen, Colorado 80439

    Re: Construction Loan

Dear Mr. Jones:

    We are pleased to inform you that Equity National Bank ("Lender") has conditionally approved your application for a loan ("Loan") to construct a home on certain real estate located in Evergreen, Jefferson County, Colorado, and being more commonly known as "Longbourne" (the "Project"). The Loan and this Commitment are subject to the terms and conditions contained herein and the terms and conditions contained in the Standard Terms and Conditions attached hereto as <u>Schedule "A"</u> and made a part hereof (this commitment letter and the Standard Terms and Conditions being collectively referred to herein as the "Commitment").

1.   **Identification of Borrower:**

    Edward Jones, having a mailing address of 1270 Sloan Street, Evergreen, Colorado 80439 ("Borrower"). Borrower is/are [*choose one*]:

[x]   a single adult individual over 18 years of age.
[ ]   a married couple.
[ ]   a _____ partnership.
[ ]   a _____ corporation.
[ ]   a _____ limited liability company.
[ ]   other: _____

2.   **Loan Amount:**

    The amount of the Loan shall be equal to the lesser of (a) Three Hundred Thousand and 00/100 Dollars ($300,000.00) and (b) [*choose applicable paragraph*]:

[ ]   Eighty percent (80%) of the lesser amount of the appraised value or the sales price of the Project, pursuant to an appraisal acceptable to Lender and otherwise satisfying the requirements of state and federal statutes and regulations.
[x]   Ninety percent (90%) of the purchase price of the Project provided that the Loan shall be modified to a permanent Loan upon completion of the Project.

3.   **Loan Term:**

    The Loan shall be due and payable on July 1, 2016 (the "Expiration Date"), without notice or demand.

4. **Interest Rate:**

The Loan shall be a variable rate loan. The outstanding principal balance of the Loan shall bear interest at a variable per annum rate equal to two percent (2%) above the prime rate of interest from time to time published in the Wall Street Journal. Interest shall be calculated on the basis of a three hundred sixty (360) day year applied to the actual number of days involved ("Applicable Interest Rate").

Default interest at a per annum rate equal to four percent (4%) above the then Applicable Interest Rate shall be applied under circumstances of default and situations in which Lender advances any monies on behalf of Borrower as more particularly described and provided in the Loan Documents.

5. **Payments:**

Interest only shall be due and payable, in arrears, each month during the Loan term, with payments commencing on the first day of the second month following the date of the Loan closing.

In any and all events, the Loan's entire unpaid principal balance, together with all accrued and unpaid interest thereon, shall be due and payable on the Expiration Date.

6. **Disbursements and Other Terms of Loan:**

Unless otherwise agreed in writing by Lender, the Loan shall be closed before construction commences on the Project. The Project shall be constructed in accordance with the proposal and other documentation submitted to Lender. Construction of the Project shall be completed on or before June 20, 2016 in strict accordance with the plans and specifications (the "Plans and Specifications"), construction contract, and cost breakdown approved in advance by Lender. Each request by Borrower for a disbursement of the Loan must be made pursuant to the procedures required from time to time by Lender.

Before Closing, Borrower shall deliver to Lender a detailed project budget and cost breakdown for the purchase of the real estate, if applicable, and the construction of the Project, including the extension of all utilities and the completion of all necessary landscaping. As soon as available, but in any event within five (5) days of execution, Borrower shall deliver to Lender copies of executed contracts from the general contractor that support the budget and cost breakdown, acceptable to Lender, and that specify the source of funds, if any, necessary to cover all costs in excess of the Loan. Unless waived by Lender, all construction contracts shall be fixed-price contracts containing no-lien provisions, shall be in recordable form, and shall otherwise comply with all applicable statutes.

Each request by Borrower for disbursement of proceeds from the Loan must (i) be made on Lender's form Request for Disbursement, executed by Borrower, and certified by an engineer or engineering firm acceptable to Lender but employed at the Borrower's expense, (ii) include such lien waivers as the Lender may require, all on forms and in substance satisfactory to Lender, and (iii) comply with all other conditions and requirements contained in the other Loan Documents. No disbursement shall be made on work requiring government inspections until all appropriate approvals have been obtained. Final disbursement of the Loan proceeds shall be made when construction has been fully completed, inspected, and approved by the inspecting architect, engineer, or appraiser. All construction draws must be supported by a title insurance endorsement that updates Lender's loan policy through the date of each requested disbursement and reflects a status of title satisfactory to Lender. All disbursements shall be made based on the percentage of work completed. Lender shall not be obligated to disburse more than the amounts listed as being funded by Lender on the Project budget and construction cost breakdown, nor shall Lender be obligated to fund any items not shown on the Project budget and construction cost breakdown.

The Project must be constructed in compliance with all ordinances, codes, statutes, and regulations applicable to the Project and in a professional manner in strict accordance with the Plans and Specifications. All construction work is subject to final inspection by Lender's representative, which inspection shall be for Lender's sole benefit and may not be relied on by Borrower.

7. **Security:**

(a) Borrower's obligations with respect to the Loan shall be secured by:

First Mortgage. A first mortgage on the Project, together with a security interest in all fixtures and equipment, now owned or hereafter acquired and used or held for use in connection with the construction, equipping, operation, or maintenance thereof.

(b) In addition to (a) above, the Borrower's Loan obligations may, in Lender's sole discretion, be secured by one or more of the following:

Fixture Filing. A separate fixture filing providing a lien on all elements that are or may become fixtures to the Project;

General Assignment. An assignment of all Borrower's right, title, and interest in and to the Plans and Specifications and all construction contracts and subcontracts and contractor's, subcontractor's, and supplier's warranties relating to the construction, equipping, operation, or maintenance of the Project;

> and any other additional security and/or instruments as may be set forth elsewhere herein or otherwise required by Lender and/or its counsel to fully and effectively secure Lender's Loan and its priority in such security and the Project.

8. <u>Unconditional Guaranty</u>:

Payment of the Loan and all obligations of Borrower shall be unconditionally guaranteed by _____ Not applicable_____ ("Guarantor(s)"), in form and substance approved by Lender (the "Guaranty(ies)"). Further, at Lender's sole discretion, the spouse of each married Guarantor who is not otherwise a Guarantor of the Loan, may be required to complete and deliver Lender's form Spousal Waiver, wherein Guarantor's spouse waives and subjects his or her rights in jointly held property to the rights of Lender under the Guaranty.

9. <u>Loan Documents</u>:

The Loan shall be evidenced by this Commitment, a construction loan agreement, a promissory note, a mortgage, and such other documents as Lender may require, including such consents and other evidences of due organization, authority, and/or power of Borrower and/or Guarantors, as applicable, to enter into, deliver, and perform the obligations contemplated by this Commitment and the other loan documents (collectively, the "Loan Documents"). All instruments, documents, and other terms required in connection with the Loan shall be in form and content satisfactory to Lender and its counsel.

10. <u>Payment of Expenses</u>:

Borrower shall pay all costs incidental to the Loan, including, but not limited to, title insurance (including all updates of title required by Lender), survey charges, the cost of environmental inspections, appraisals, insurance premiums for all required insurance coverages, inspecting engineer's, architects', or appraiser fees, and any and all other incidental expenses of Lender, whether or not the Loan is closed, including Lender's reasonable attorneys' fees and costs incurred in connection with the review and documentation of the Loan or otherwise.

11. <u>Default</u>:

Any one or more of the following shall constitute an event of default: (a) failure to pay when due any principal or interest on the Loan or any other obligation or liability owed to Lender by Borrower; (b) failure to observe or perform any agreement or covenant contained in the Loan Documents; (c) breach of any warranty, representation, certification, or statement contained in the Loan Documents or in any certification or other agreement or document executed or delivered in connection with the Loan Documents, (d) death of any individual who is a Borrower or Guarantor; (e) assignment by Borrower or any guarantor for the benefit of its creditors; (f) appointment of a receiver or a trustee for Borrower or Guarantor or any of its assets; (g) the filing of a petition to adjudicate Borrower or Guarantor as bankrupt; (h) default by Borrower or Guarantor under any agreement with or undertaking to Lender whether or not related to the Loan; (i) Lender in good faith deems itself insecure; (j) any material adverse change in the financial, operating, or other condition of Borrower or Guarantor; or (k) Lender believes the prospect of payment or performance of the Loan is impaired.

The foregoing constitutes a list of the basic events of default and is not intended to be an exhaustive list. It shall be supplemented by such additional events of default as provided in the other Loan Documents.

After an event of default, at Lender's option and without further notice or demand to Borrower, the Loan shall become immediately due and payable. All rights and remedies of Lender herein specified and/or otherwise provided in the other Loan Documents, are cumulative and in addition to, not in limitation of, any rights and remedies that it may have by law or at equity.

12. **Commitment and Construction Loan Fee:**

(a) Borrower shall pay to Lender as a commitment fee in respect of the Loan the sum of One Thousand and 00/100 Dollars ($1,000.00). Such commitment fee shall be earned upon acceptance of this Commitment Letter and shall not be refunded even if the Loan is not approved. Lender shall apply the commitment fee to the construction loan fee charged by the Lender at the closing of the Loan.

(b) In consideration for the Loan, Borrower shall pay to Lender a construction loan fee of Three Thousand and 00/100 Dollars ($3,000.00), which shall be paid at the closing of the Loan.

13. **Other Conditions:**

In addition to all other terms, conditions, and requirements hereof, Borrower shall provide Lender before closing of the Loan evidence acceptable to Lender that Borrower has obtained a firm commitment for financing in amount sufficient to pay off the Loan at maturity (the "Take-Out Commitment"). In so doing, Borrower shall take all actions necessary and provide all information required by the terms of such Take-Out Commitment.

14. **Acceptance:**

This Commitment is not binding upon Lender unless an executed copy hereof is returned to the undersigned on or before August 21, 2015, together with the commitment fee provided in paragraph 12(a) above, which shall be paid to Lender in the form of a cashier's or certified check. In the event the Loan committed hereunder is not closed on or before September 9, 2015, this Commitment shall be null and void and have no further force or effect. Closing of the Loan is subject to the condition that, in Lender's sole discretion, there is no material deterioration of Borrower's or, if applicable, Guarantor's financial position, that Borrower has the power and financial capacity to repay all amounts owing or to be owed in connection with the Loan, and that all conditions have been satisfied, approvals have been obtained, and all documents, reports, surveys, and inspections are satisfactory to Lender. Any extension of this Commitment shall be made only with Lender's written approval.

15. **Inconsistencies:**

The terms and provisions of this Commitment and those contained in the other Loan Documents shall, to the fullest extent possible, be read and applied as supplementary to each other to fulfill the intents and purposes of the Loan Documents. Notwithstanding the foregoing, if any inconsistencies exist between the terms and conditions of this Commitment and any other Loan Document, the terms and conditions of this Commitment shall control and be binding.

Very truly yours,

EQUITY NATIONAL BANK

By: *Elizabeth Darcy*

Elizabeth Darcy
Its President

ACCEPTED AND AGREED to this ____ day of _____, 2015.

By:_____

Edward Jones

NOTES

1. *Additional readings.* For a more detailed consideration of loan commitments, *see* John N. Oest, Negotiating the Loan Commitment: The Borrower's Perspective, 19 Bus. L. Today 61 (Jan./Feb. 2010); Susan G. Talley, Key Issues in Construction Lending (With Sample Forms), ALI-ABA Business Law Course Materials Journal, June 2007, at 15; George A. Nation, III, The *Clardy* Case: Lessons For Lenders Concerning Commitment Letters and Other Pre-loan Contracts, 114 Banking L.J. 347 (1997).

2. *Representing Edward Jones.* Mr. Jones has asked you to review the commitment letter for him. Please advise him on the following issues:

a. Does the commitment letter obligate the bank to lend $300,000 to Mr. Jones? Does the letter obligate Mr. Jones to borrow the funds from Equity National Bank?

b. Under what circumstances can the bank refuse to make loan advances? What changes would you like to make?

c. If the construction costs more than anticipated, is the bank obligated to advance enough funds to complete construction?

d. Under what circumstances can the bank make the entire loan due and payable? Does Mr. Jones have the right to cure defaults? What changes would you like to make?

e. What other changes to the commitment letter would you recommend?

3. *Oral commitments.* The commitment above is written. Would it be enforceable if it had been given orally? *See* Coastland Corp. v. Third Nat'l Mortg. Co., 611 F.2d 969 (4th Cir.1979) (oral commitment enforceable). *Compare* Leeper v. Weintraub, 273 N.J.Super. 532, 642 A.2d 1032 (App.Div.1994); Ed Schory & Sons, Inc. v. Society Nat'l Bank, 75 Ohio St.3d 433, 662 N.E.2d 1074 (1996); Bridges v. Reliance Trust Co., 205 Ga.App. 400, 422 S.E.2d 277 (1992) (all holding that the Statute of Frauds barred enforcement). Of course, the wording of the particular Statute of Frauds is a critical factor. *See* Rhode Island Hospital Trust Nat'l Bank v. Varadian, 419 Mass. 841, 647 N.E.2d 1174 (1995) (the borrowers, who were sophisticated real estate developers, could not reasonably have understood the bank's promises to be a binding commitment).

4. *Reliance on the permanent loan commitment.* If the construction lender requires a take-out commitment before funding the construction loan, does it need to be concerned with the adequacy of the builder's plans and specifications or with the project's marketability or can it rely on the permanent lender's review of these matters? If it does so, what risks does it incur?

5. *Construction changes.* Construction projects rarely are built in exact accordance with the original plans and specifications. Changes result from materials shortages, unexpected conditions encountered in construction, shifts in market demand, and sometimes simply better ideas. If the builder and construction lender agree that a particular change is appropriate, is it necessary to get the permanent lender's approval? Is it reasonable for the permanent lender to insist upon a right to approve? *See* John P. McNearney & Jude J. Beller, Did Your Construction Lender Ask for That?, 18 Prob. & Prop. 58 (Nov./Dec. 2004).

6. *Commitment fees.* A lender will usually charge a fee for a permanent loan commitment, especially if it includes a definite interest rate, because the

lender is assuming the risk that market rates may increase. Typical charges are in the range of 0.50%–1% of the amount committed. Because construction loans normally are variable rate, the fee for that type of loan commitment is normally somewhat less.

7. *Lender's retention of the fee.* If a developer pays a commitment fee but later obtains financing elsewhere, the lender that issued the commitment will usually retain the fee. The commitment letter often expressly permits the lender to do so. Is this legally sound? Courts usually regard the fee as a form of reasonable liquidated damages. *See* Capital Holding Corp. v. Octagon Dev. Co., 757 S.W.2d 202 (Ky.App.1988); B.F. Saul Real Estate Inv. Trust v. McGovern, 683 S.W.2d 531 (Tex.App.1984). *See also* Annot., Enforceability of Provision in Loan Commitment Agreement Authorizing Lender to Charge Standby Fee, Commitment Fee, or Similar Deposit, 93 A.L.R.3d 1156.

8. *Specific performance of loan commitments.* If the lender reneges on the commitment, can the builder or house purchaser get specific performance? Courts usually say that promises to loan money are not specifically enforceable but that contracts to sell or purchase land are. Which type is a permanent loan commitment? A construction loan commitment? *See* Southampton Wholesale Food Terminal, Inc. v. Providence Produce Warehouse Co., 129 F.Supp. 663 (D.Mass.1955). To obtain specific performance, does the remedy at law have to be inadequate? Are there situations in which damages are an inadequate remedy for the permanent lender's refusal to honor its commitment? What is the proper measure of damages? *See* Higgins v. Arizona Sav. & Loan Ass'n, 85 Ariz. 6, 330 P.2d 504 (1958). Can the construction lender get damages or specific performance against the reneging permanent lender? *See generally* Robert Shadur, Avoiding Lender Liability at the Loan Commitment Stage, 6 Prac.Real Est.Law. 47 (No. 6, May 1990).

In a few cases, courts have granted specific performance against a lender. *See* Selective Builders, Inc. v. Hudson City Sav. Bank, 137 N.J.Super. 500, 349 A.2d 564 (Ch.Div.1975); First Nat'l State Bank of New Jersey v. Commonwealth Fed. Sav. & Loan Ass'n, 610 F.2d 164 (3d Cir.1979) (construction lender can enforce permanent lender's commitment). *See* Michael J. Mehr & Lawrence Kilgore, Enforcement of the Real Estate Loan Commitment: Improvement of the Borrower's Remedies, 24 Wayne L.Rev. 1011 (1978); Roger D. Groot, Specific Performance of Contracts to Provide Permanent Financing, 60 Cornell L.Rev. 718 (1975); Nelson, Whitman, Burkhart & Freyermuth, Real Estate Finance Law § 12.3 (6th ed. 2014).

9. *Actions by lenders against borrowers.* If a loan applicant obtains a commitment but then refuses to borrow the funds (usually because it found a lower interest rate elsewhere), can the lender that issued the commitment recover damages for breach of contract? The answer depends on whether the commitment is a bilateral contract or merely gives the applicant an option to borrow. Every commitment should, of course, make this clear, but many do not. *Compare* Lincoln Nat'l Life Ins. Co. v. NCR Corp., 603 F.Supp. 1393

(N.D.Ind.1984) (contract bound borrower to draw down funds), *with* Capital Holding Corp. v. Octagon Dev. Co., 757 S.W.2d 202 (Ky.App.1988) (commitment did not bind borrower to draw funds). Often, the term "standby commitment" is a clue that the applicant has only an option, and not a duty, to take the loan.

Even if the commitment is bilateral and imposes a duty to borrow, the applicant who fails to do so does not always lose the commitment fee. In Woodbridge Place Apts. v. Washington Square Capital, Inc., 965 F.2d 1429 (7th Cir.1992), the borrower's obligation to take the loan was subject to the condition that the subject apartment building reach 93% occupancy before the loan was to close. The building failed to do so. The court held that the borrower's refusal to draw the funds was due to a failure of the condition and was not a breach of the loan commitment. Hence, the court ordered the lender to refund the borrower's deposit. On the other hand, if the commitment had expressly made the deposit nonrefundable, the court would have reached the contrary result.

Even if the commitment imposes a duty to borrow, it seems settled that the lender cannot obtain a decree of specific performance against a loan applicant who refuses to borrow the funds. A recovery of damages, the remedy at law, is adequate. *See* City Centre One Assocs. v. Teachers Ins. & Annuity Ass'n, 656 F.Supp. 658 (D.Utah 1987).

10. *Conditions in commitments.* Permanent loan commitments are usually filled with conditions that must be met before the lender is obligated to fund the loan. Completion of the improvements is the most obvious example. Courts typically strictly enforce the conditions. If they are not met, the commitment expires, and, if the agreement so provides, the borrower loses the commitment fee. *See, e.g.,* Johnson v. American Nat'l Ins. Co., 126 Ariz. 219, 613 P.2d 1275 (App.1980) (project not completed by commitment's expiration date); Mellon Bank v. Aetna Bus. Credit, Inc., 619 F.2d 1001 (3d Cir.1980) (permanent loan on office building project conditioned on borrower's solvency; borrower was insolvent). *Cf.* Hall v. W. L. Brady Inv., Inc., 684 S.W.2d 379 (Mo.App.1984) (substantial, but not perfect, completion of building satisfies requirements of permanent loan commitment).

C. LIEN PRIORITY

1. SUBORDINATION OF THE PURCHASE MONEY MORTGAGE

If the subdivider is to obtain a construction loan from an institutional lender, the lender usually requires a first mortgage or deed of trust to secure the loan. Some states statutorily require state-chartered banks and other financial institutions to obtain first liens on real estate loans. Even without a statutory requirement, lending institutions usually demand a first priority lien as a matter of policy. Therefore, the relative priorities of the construction and purchase money mortgages must be adjusted so that the construction mortgage is senior. While this adjustment is usually a simple task, it is essential because, without an explicit reversal of priorities, the law everywhere presumes that the purchase money mortgage is senior. *See* Cal.Civ.Code § 2898; Restatement (Third) of Property (Mortgages) § 7.2 (1997); Nelson, Whitman, Burkhart & Freyermuth, Real Estate Finance Law §§ 9.1–9.2 (6th ed. 2014); Chapter 7, Section A supra.

How is this reversal of priorities accomplished? If the subdivider has completed arrangements for the construction loan before acquiring the land, the purchase money mortgage can expressly provide that it is subordinate to the construction mortgage. The purchase money mortgage can incorporate the construction mortgage by reference or can include it as an attachment.

Another approach that is sometimes employed is to omit any reference in the mortgages to their relative priorities and instead to make certain that the documents are recorded in the following order: (1) deed from land seller to subdivider; (2) construction loan mortgage from subdivider to lender; and (3) purchase money mortgage from subdivider to land seller. To many actors in the real estate community, it seems obvious that the order of recording dictates the priority of the two mortgages, but this assumption is false. The typical recording statute provides: "All conveyances are void until recorded as against subsequent purchasers or creditors without notice and for valuable consideration [who record first]." (The last phrase is added in race-notice jurisdictions.) Hence, if all the parties know of one another's interest, as is usually the case, no one is "without notice," and it does not matter which mortgage is recorded first!

Courts sometimes treat the order of recording as representing the parties' intentions about priority and give effect to those intentions. *See, e.g.,* BB & T of South Carolina v. Kidwell, 350 S.C. 382, 565 S.E.2d 316 (App.2002); Estate of Skvorak v. Security Union Title Ins. Co., 140 Idaho 16, 89 P.3d 856 (2004). But one cannot count on this result; the court may well (and quite properly) disregard the order of recording and base priority instead on the order that the mortgages were delivered and on the presumption of priority for purchase money mortgages. Hence, reliance on the order of recording to determine priority is a risky business indeed. Express agreements stating the intended priority, signed by all affected parties, are far preferable. *See* Nelson, Whitman, Burkhart & Freyermuth, Real Estate Finance Law § 9.2 (6th ed. 2014); Chapter 7, Section A supra.

Suppose, however, that negotiations for the construction loan have not been completed before the subdivider takes title to the land. One possibility is for the subdivider to forbear from getting a subordination agreement from the land seller based on the assumption that the seller's self-interest will induce it to subordinate when a construction loan has been arranged. After all, if the seller does not subordinate, there will be no construction, no cash flow to the developer, and no payments to the land seller. Thus, perhaps the land seller can be expected to cooperate in subordinating to a reasonable construction loan when the time comes. The subdivider might even include language in the purchase money mortgage by which the land seller agrees to negotiate in good faith for subordination or words to that effect. Such language may be legally unenforceable as an "agreement to agree" but still worth having as a practical matter. But can you think of situations in which the land seller might have good economic reasons for refusal to cooperate?

For this reason, the subdivider might be quite reluctant to rely on the land seller's future good faith. As an alternative, the subdivider might insert language in the purchase money mortgage or in a side agreement that the land seller agrees to be subordinate to a construction loan to be made in the future, the elements of which may be spelled out with greater or lesser specificity. This is the so-called "automatic subordination"—that is, subordination to a loan that can't yet be precisely identified or described. From the land seller's viewpoint, such a subordination should set off flashing red lights. If the future construction loan proves to be unduly burdensome, the result may be a default by the developer and a foreclosure on the construction mortgage that wipes out the land seller's mortgage.

Should the law protect land sellers from entering into automatic subordination agreements that don't spell out the terms of the future loan specifically? Some courts have thought so. Consider the following description in Roskamp Manley Assocs., Inc. v. Davin Dev. & Inv. Corp., 184 Cal.App.3d 513, 519–20, 229 Cal.Rptr. 186, 189–90 (1986) of an important California Supreme Court case:

> In Handy v. Gordon, 65 Cal.2d 578, 55 Cal.Rptr. 769, 422 P.2d 329 [1967], defendant vendor agreed to sell land to plaintiff developer for $1,200,000 at 2 percent interest per year, payable in annual installments of $120,000, beginning three years after close of escrow, the balance due in ten years. Sellers agreed to subordinate their trust deed to other trust deeds securing construction loans. Terms of subordination were: loans in maximum amounts of $10,000 and $52,000 per lot, and maximum interest rate of 7 percent and 6.6 percent, to mature in not less than 6 and 35 years respectively. The contract did not specify the number of lots. Plaintiff sued for specific performance, and judgment on the pleadings for defendants was affirmed. The court stated: "Although the parties to a contract of sale containing a subordination clause may delegate to the

vendee or third party lenders power to determine the details of subordinating loans, an enforceable subordination clause must contain terms that will define and minimize the risk that the subordinating liens will impair or destroy the seller's security. [ ] Such terms may include limits on the use to which the proceeds may be put to insure that their use will improve the value of the land, maximum amounts so that the loans will not exceed the contemplated value of the improvements they finance, requirements that the loans do not exceed some specified percentage of the construction cost or value of the property as improved, specified amounts per square foot of construction, or other limits designed to protect the security. Without some such terms, however, the seller is forced to rely entirely on the buyer's good faith and ability as a developer to insure that he will not lose both his land and the purchase price. Even if we were to assume that a contract of sale contemplating subdivision by the vendee is sufficiently different from the usual land sale contract to take it out of the operation of the anti-deficiency legislation [ ], the personal liability alone of the vendee would not constitute sufficient protection to the vendor to permit specific performance." (*Id.*, at p. 581, 55 Cal.Rptr. 769, 422 P.2d 329.)

In *Handy*, the court found the contract did not afford defendants any additional protection since not all of the loan proceeds were to be used for construction, there was no assurance that the amounts of the loans would not exceed the value the improvements added to the security, and defendants were not assured that the total amount of the subordinating loans would be kept low enough to enable them to protect themselves by bidding on the property if the senior liens were foreclosed. (*Id.*, at p. 582, 55 Cal.Rptr. 769, 422 P.2d 329.) The court agreed with defendants, that as to them, the contract was not "just and reasonable" as a matter of law. (*Id.*, at p. 581, 55 Cal.Rptr. 769, 422 P.2d 329.)

While fairness is no doubt a good thing, there is by no means universal agreement that courts should impose it in automatic subordination cases. As Professor Patrick Randolph of the University of Missouri-Kansas City School of Law has observed: "*Handy*, in fact, suggests that the court must be satisfied overall that the contract is fair, which of course means that no buyer, short of a lawsuit, can ever be confident that it has an enforceable subordination agreement."

Nonetheless, the reasoning in opinions like *Handy* has been highly influential, and courts in many cases have held subordination agreements to be unenforceable because of ambiguity or unfairness. Do you think that the following clauses should be enforceable?

a.   "Buyer to obtain loan in the amount of $63,500 from lending institution of their choice. Seller to carry $24,000 at 8.69% interest amortized over 30 years to balloon in 5 years. Seller may pay off Contract early without penalty." Linderkamp v. Hoffman, 562 N.W.2d 734 (N.D. 1997).

b.   "Twenty acres of said land are subordinated to the purchasers for immediate improvement, and such other tracts shall be subordinated to use as the occasion may arise." Grooms v. Williams, 227 Md. 165, 175 A.2d 575 (1961).

c.   "[Seller] agrees to carry 2nd Deed of Trust in the amount of $25,000 for 10 yrs., equal payments with 6% interest per annum." Hux v. Raben, 74 Ill.App.2d 214, 219 N.E.2d 770 (1966), *aff'd*, 38 Ill.2d 223, 230 N.E.2d 831 (1967).

d.   "[Seller agrees to subordinate] to any deed of trust that [buyer] might give to an FDIC insured lending institution." Stenehjem v. Kyn Jin Cho, 631 P.2d 482 (Alaska 1981).

e.   "[Seller] agrees to execute a deed of subordination upon the request of [buyer] in such amount as may be reasonably requested by the [seller] so as to allow the [seller] to procure a construction loan on the above-described real property." MCB Ltd. v. McGowan, 86 N.C.App. 607, 359 S.E.2d 50 (1987).

In all five cases, the court held that the agreement was unenforceable. However, other courts have enforced very similar subordination clauses. *See, e.g.,* North Shore Realty Corp. v. Gallaher, 114 So.2d 634 (Fla.App.1959). *See also* Warren H. McNamara, Jr., Subordination Agreements as Viewed by Sellers, Purchasers, Construction Lenders, and Title Companies, 12 Real Est.L.J. 347 (1984).

The Restatement (Third) of Property (Mortgages) § 7.7 (1997) provides that if the subordination is to an interest to be created in the future, that interest must be described in the subordination "with reasonable specificity." According to comment b of that section:

> [R]easonable specificity requires at a minimum an identification of the new lender or the type of lender, an upper limit on the initial amount of that debt, and an upper limit on its interest rate. If the parties contemplate that the proceeds of the later mortgage will be used to improve the real estate, and that those improvements are part of the bargained-for security on which the subordinating mortgagee is relying, then reasonable specificity requires a statement requiring use of the subsequent loan proceeds for that purpose and a reasonable description of the improvements.

Compare Smith v. Martin, 124 N.C.App. 592, 478 S.E.2d 228 (N.C.App.1996) (subordination to a future mortgage must, at a minimum, state the loan's maximum amount and maximum interest rate).

NOTES

1.   *Waiver of the courts' protection.* Can a land seller waive the type of protection given in *Handy*? Suppose the subordination clause describes in rather vague terms the first deed of trust loan to which the land seller is subordinating and then provides that this first deed of trust shall:

> * * * constitute a lien or charge on said land prior and superior to the lien or charge of this deed of trust as to any and all loans or advances which shall be made under such hereafter executed deed of trust * * * and without regard to the application or use of the proceeds of such loan or advances insofar as the validity of this subordination is concerned.

See Weiss v. Brentwood Sav. & Loan Ass'n, 4 Cal.App.3d 738, 84 Cal.Rptr. 736 (1970); Schneider v. Ampliflo Corp., 148 Cal.App.3d 637, 196 Cal.Rptr. 172 (1983), in which the courts enforced similar language. Does this make sense? If the subordination is unfair because it is so vague, is it any more fair when the land seller admits in writing that she or he knows it is unfair?

2.   *Remedies.* In *Handy* and in *Roskamp*, the developer wanted specific performance of the subordination agreement. Suppose the developer had sued the land seller for damages instead. Is there any reason that a vague or unfair subordination should be "more enforceable" at law than in equity?

If a court determines that a subordination clause is unenforceable under *Handy*, what is the result?

a.   The seller is not obligated to convey the land?

b.   The seller must convey the land but is entitled to cash?

c.   The seller must convey the land and take back the agreed security instrument, but it has first priority?

See Gluskin v. Atlantic Sav. & Loan Ass'n, 32 Cal.App.3d 307, 108 Cal.Rptr. 318 (1973). Does it matter, in determining which remedy is appropriate, whether the subordination agreement was a part of the contract of sale, of the mortgage or deed of trust, or in a separate document? Where would you put the agreement if you represented a California subdivider who insisted on having an automatic-type subordination?

3.   *Statutory regulation of subordination clauses.* Cal.Civ.Code §§ 2953.1–.5 require that instruments that contain subordination agreements must call attention to them by prescribed legends in 10-point bold type. Failure to do so permits the clause to be declared void at the election of the person whose interest is subordinated. However, these provisions apply only when both the purchase money obligation and the maximum loan to which it

may be subordinated do not exceed $25,000. How many such cases do you suppose there are?

An opposing approach is represented by Conn.Gen.Stat.Ann. § 49–31c, which provides that subordination to a future mortgage is valid "notwithstanding that [it] does not contain any of the terms or provisions of the future mortgage."

4.   *Conditional subordination.* The protections that *Handy* requires in subordinations are really *conditions.* In effect, the subordinating party says: "I agree that my lien will become subordinate, but only if the lien that is gaining priority over mine satisfies certain specifications. Otherwise, I retain my priority." If the condition isn't met, there's no subordination. There is no doubt that a court will uphold express conditions in a subordination agreement. *See* Bank v. Crumley, 699 S.W.2d 164 (Tenn.App.1985); Life Sav. & Loan Ass'n v. Bryant, 125 Ill.App.3d 1012, 81 Ill.Dec. 577, 467 N.E.2d 277 (1984); Riggs Nat'l Bank v. Wines, 59 Md.App. 219, 474 A.2d 1360 (1984); Hugh B. Lambe, Enforceability of Subordination Agreements, 19 Real Prop. Prob. & Tr.J. 631 (1984).

However, if the conditions are not met, a total denial of subordination may be inappropriate. Restatement (Third) of Property (Mortgages) § 7.7 comment c (1997) suggests that "in many cases in which the conditions are unsatisfied, justice can be done by imposing a *pro tanto* loss of priority to reflect the loss suffered by the subordinating mortgagee as a result of deviation from the conditions."

To illustrate, suppose ME1 agrees to subordinate to ME2's mortgage if the interest rate on ME2's loan is no higher than 10%. In fact, ME2 makes a loan to the borrower at 12%. Should ME2 get priority to the extent of the balance that would have been owing to ME2 if the rate had been 10%, with ME1 having priority thereafter? Or can ME1 successfully argue that ME2 should lose priority entirely, because the higher interest rate made it more probable that the borrower would default?

The *pro tanto* approach suggested by the Restatement was not followed in Friarsgate, Inc. v. First Fed. Sav. & Loan Ass'n, 317 S.C. 452, 454 S.E.2d 901 (App.1995), in which the vendors agreed to subordinate on the condition that total future loans not exceed 75% of the fair market value of the lot and improvements. The future loans in fact exceeded 75%, and the court held that the subordination was completely ineffective.

5.   *Implied conditions.* Suppose the mortgagee who has initial top priority enters into a subordination agreement but fails to include any protective conditions of the sort discussed in *Handy* and in *Roskamp.* Should a court *imply* reasonable conditions to protect the subordinating party? That is precisely what the California Court of Appeal did in Middlebrook-Anderson Co. v. Southwest Sav. & Loan Ass'n, 18 Cal.App.3d 1023, 1037, 96 Cal.Rptr. 338 (1971), *discussed in* Frederick D. Minnes, Note, Purchase Money

Subordination Agreements in California: An Analysis of Conditional Subordination, 45 S.Cal.L.Rev. 1109 (1972). The court stated:

> An implied agreement in the instant case can and, in equity, should be spelled out from lender's alleged actual knowledge of the provisions of the seller's lien in general, and of the subordination therein in particular. In the superior position of a financial institution constantly engaged in professional construction lending, [the lender] had no reason to believe their trust deed conferred any lien to which the fee was subordinate other than to the extent of money spent for construction purposes. Its loan under the circumstances cannot be viewed other than as subject to the fair application of the construction funds. Accordingly, we conclude that such lien as the trust deed might have conferred on the lender should not be advanced or preferred over the seller.

Accord Burkons v. Ticor Title Ins. Co., 168 Ariz. 345, 813 P.2d 710 (1991); Peoples Bank v. L & T Developers, Inc., 434 So.2d 699 (Miss.1983), *noted* 53 Miss.L.J. 691 (1983). In Ban-Co Inv. Co. v. Loveless, 22 Wash.App. 122, 587 P.2d 567 (1978), a land seller used a similar theory to support an action in *damages* against the developer.

Courts in many other cases have rejected the *Middlebrook* approach and refused to imply subordination conditions. *See, e.g.,* Connecticut Bank & Trust Co. v. Carriage Lane Assocs., 219 Conn. 772, 595 A.2d 334 (1991); Home Sav. Ass'n v. State Bank of Woodstock, 763 F.Supp. 292 (N.D.Ill.1991). *See generally* Nelson, Whitman, Burkhart & Freyermuth, Real Estate Finance Law § 12.10 (6th ed. 2014). The courts in these cases generally hold that the lender has no duty to junior lienors to use any particular care in ensuring that disbursements are used for construction, unless there are express conditions in the agreement, the junior lienor has been defrauded, or the lender and the developer colluded.

A few courts have held that construction lenders have an implied duty to use reasonable care in supervising disbursements to prevent diversion of the funds to other purposes. *See* Fikes v. First Federal Sav. & Loan Ass'n, 533 P.2d 251 (Alaska 1975); Cambridge Acceptance Corp. v. Hockstein, 102 N.J.Super. 435, 246 A.2d 138 (App.Div.1968). But this represents a small minority viewpoint. *See* Philip L. Bruner & Patrick J. O'Connor, Jr., Lender Liability in Construction Financing, Construction Briefings No. 2003–10; Annot., Construction Mortgagee-Lender's Duty to Protect Interest of Subordinated Purchase-Money Mortgagee, 13 A.L.R.5th 684.

6. *What are "improvements"?* Under an express or implied clause that subordinates a mortgage only to advances "for improvements," what sorts of disbursements by the construction lender are included? Disbursements often do not pay directly for labor or materials on the site. Consider the following possibilities:

a.   The lender makes an advance that it knows the developer will use to buy a new cabin cruiser.

b.   The lender makes an advance that it believes will be used for construction. However, the lender's methods for verifying application of the funds are less rigorous than those of most construction lenders, and the subdivider diverts the funds to unrelated uses.

c.   The facts are the same as in (b), except that the lender's methods are the same as those of most other lenders. Nonetheless, by fraud, forgery, or other artifice, the developer diverts the funds to unrelated uses.

d.   The lender makes an "advance" to cover the "loan fee" on the construction loan by charging the subdivider's loan account with the fee but with no money changing hands. Does it matter whether the loan fee is 2% or 13%? What about an advance to cover the commitment fee on the permanent loan commitment?

e.   The lender makes an advance for attorney's fees, title insurance, and other closing costs in connection with the construction loan.

f.   Uninsured damage occurs to the improvements when the construction is partially completed. The lender advances additional funds, which the construction loan agreement does not require, to repair the damage.

Several cases deal with these issues, but little consistency exists among them. The court in Ban-Co Inv. Co. v. Loveless, 22 Wash.App. 122, 587 P.2d 567 (1978) held that the following were improper disbursements: (1) rent on the developer's ground lease; (2) payments for the developer's overhead and profit; and (3) payments to a general contractor that was working for the developer on another project. The last holding seems indisputable! *See also* Hyatt v. Maryland Fed. Sav. & Loan Ass'n, 42 Md.App. 623, 402 A.2d 118 (1979); G. Credit Co. v. Mid-West Land Dev., Inc., 207 Kan. 325, 485 P.2d 205 (1971).

If you were drafting a subordination agreement, how would you define "construction"? What items are legitimate because they add permanent value to the land and, thus, do not increase the subordinated party's risk?

7.   *Drafting subordinations.* Suppose you are representing a land vendor in a sale to a subdivider who needs subordination. What protective clauses would you try to insert? You might consider conditioning the subordination on some or all of the following:

a.   The construction lender's identity or type;

b.   The type of improvements to be constructed;

c.   The loan characteristics to which your client will subordinate;

d.   The requirement that loan funds are used for construction;

e.   A listing of the types of disbursements that will constitute payment for "construction;"

f.   The lender's method of disbursement;

g.   Your client's right to approve detailed plans and specifications;

h.   Procurement of a permanent loan commitment on terms that are satisfactory to your client;

i.   A requirement that the developer carry appropriate insurance;

j.   Your client's right to inspect the work progress and the developer's and lender's books; and

k.   Your client's rights to notice by the construction lender of any default on the loan and to cure within a reasonable time.

Of course, no substitute exists for the developer's integrity and experience. How could you help your client verify these qualities before signing a subordination agreement?

2. MECHANIC'S LIENS

A problem that can haunt the construction lender, the permanent lender, and the knowledgeable home buyer is the mechanic's lien. The contractor, the workers, and the materials supplier can file a mechanic's lien on the property if the developer fails to pay them. In some states, the lien even extends to undisbursed construction loan funds. In many jurisdictions, the liens have priority as of the date that work began on the property, though the lien does not have to be filed until several months after the work is completed.

The relative priority of the mortgage and the mechanic's liens is critically important in the construction context because, if the improved land has to be sold to pay the debts, it usually isn't worth enough to pay both the lender and the mechanic's lienors. The problem is compounded because title insurance companies often exclude mechanic's liens from the coverage of their policies because a title search can't disclose a lien that has not yet been recorded. For these reasons, construction lenders usually take great pains to ensure that their construction loan mortgage is recorded before any work is done on the property, though even this precaution does not protect the mortgage's priority from mechanic's liens in a few jurisdictions. Unsurprisingly, the priority of mechanic's liens over construction and permanent loans is one of the most frequently litigated issues in cases concerning subdivisions.

NELSON, WHITMAN, BURKHART & FREYERMUTH, REAL ESTATE FINANCE LAW

§ 12.4 (6th ed. 2014)*

Mechanic's liens give unpaid contractors, workers, and materials suppliers a security interest in the real estate that they have improved. They can foreclose the lien to recover the money owed them. A form of mechanic's lien seems to have existed in the Roman law, was well developed in the civil law, and was incorporated in the Code Napoleon. However, the mechanic's lien was unknown in England, either at common law or in equity. Our present laws are of native origin in the United States, dating back to the Maryland statute of 1791. Today, mechanic's lien legislation exists in every state.[163] Generalizations about mechanic's liens are problematic and always must be checked against local law, because the laws creating the liens and judicial interpretations of the laws are extremely varied and because legislatures frequently amend the laws. Furthermore, case law is unreliable on this subject because a decision generally is meaningful only with respect to the precise language of the statute that existed when the cause of action arose. The variability has been justified on the ground that the problems involved are dissimilar in different parts of the country, even perhaps from state to state. This assertion is dubious, but efforts to secure uniform legislation on the subject have failed. The resulting state-by-state complexity makes comprehensive treatment of mechanic's liens in this section impossible. However, this section does describe the principal statutory groups and their general features.

The basic idea of a mechanic's lien is that a person whose work or materials improve real estate[167] and who has not been paid should be

---

* Reprinted with permission of LEG, Inc. d/b/a West Academic.

[163] See Armour & Co. v. Western Const. Co., 36 Wash. 529, 78 P. 1106 (1905). At least three states' constitutions provide for mechanic's liens. Cal. Const. Art. XIV, § 3; N.C. Const. Art. X, § 3; Tex. Const. Art. XVI, § 37; see Youngblood, Mechanics' and Materialmen's Liens in Texas, 26 Sw. L.J. 665, 687 (1972). There has been no serious move to federalize mechanic's lien law. See Glass, Old Statutes Never Die . . . Nor Do They Fade Away: A Proposal for Modernizing Mechanics' Lien Law by Federal Action, 27 Ohio N.U. L. Rev. 67 (2000).

[167] Even work done off-site may be lienable if it directly benefits the property. See In re Trilogy Development Co., 468 B.R. 854 (Bankr. W.D. Mo. 2011); John Wagner Associates v. Hercules, Inc., 797 P.2d 1123 (Utah Ct. App. 1990) (modular buildings, although removable, are part of real estate and provide basis for mechanic's lien); Alaska Cascade Financial Services, Inc. v. Doors Northwest, Inc., 52 Wash. App. 588, 762 P.2d 362 (Div. 2 1988) (modular buildings lienable, though constructed off-site); Vulcraft, a Div. of Nucor Corp. v. Midtown Business Park, Ltd., 1990–NMSC–095, 110 N.M. 761, 800 P.2d 195 (1990) (steel fabrication performed off-site); Northlake Concrete Products, Inc. v. Wylie, 34 Wash. App. 810, 663 P.2d 1380 (Div. 1 1983) (sewer line). But mere maintenance or repair work is usually non-lienable. In re Payless Cashways, Inc., 230 B.R. 120 (B.A.P. 8th Cir. 1999), aff'd, 203 F.3d 1081, 35 Bankr. Ct. Dec. (CRR) 191 (8th Cir. 2000). See also Negvesky v. United Interior Resources, Inc., 32 A.D.3d 530, 821 N.Y.S.2d 107 (2d Dep't 2006) (installation of modular work stations not lienable); TPST Soil Recyclers of Washington, Inc. v. W.F. Anderson Const., Inc., 91 Wash. App. 297, 957 P.2d 265 (Div. 2 1998), opinion amended on reconsideration, 967 P.2d 1266 (Wash. Ct. App. Div. 2 1998) (Utah law) (cleanup of contaminated soil not lienable).

permitted to recover from that real estate.[168] Beginning with the original
Maryland statute, "[t]hese laws grew, and their validity became
established, as the courts held that the building business did not have the
protection inherent in the widespread distribution of credit risk common
to other businesses, and therefore needed this broader and special
protection. Contractors, subcontractors, materialmen, and other building
groups were frequently obliged to extend credit in larger amounts, and for
longer time, than other businesses. Such parties might have their entire
capital, or a substantial part of it, tied up in one or two, or ten or twenty,
projects under construction."[169]

Originally, the mechanic's lien laws protected only general
contractors or master-builders. But today "practically every segment
composing the construction industry—including contractors,
subcontractors, material dealers, laborers, artisans, architects, landscape
architects, engineers, surveyors—is granted liens of varying extent under
varying conditions for the labor, services, or materials furnished or
contracted to be furnished for the particular improvement."[171] Because
mechanic's lien statutes are in derogation of the common law, courts often
state that they should be strictly construed. However, courts also often
state that, because mechanic's lien statutes are remedial, they should be
liberally construed to protect workers and materials suppliers. The court
in *Ferguson Enterprises, Inc. v. Keybuild Solutions, Inc.*, 275 P.3d 741,
745 (Colo. App 2011), articulated the correct approach: "The mechanics'

In most jurisdictions, the lien is on the entire parcel of real estate, including land and
improvements. However, in a few states, the improvement is legally separate from the land, and
the lien attaches only to the improvement. See Provident Bank v. Tri-County Southside Asphalt,
Inc., 804 N.E.2d 161 (Ind. Ct. App. 2004), on reh'g in part, 806 N.E.2d 802 (Ind. Ct. App. 2004).

[168] This does not necessarily mean that the contract price can be recovered; if the work was
done improperly, the lien may be for less or even zero. See Cashway Concrete & Materials v.
Sanner Contracting Co., 158 Ariz. 81, 761 P.2d 155 (Ct. App. Div. 2 1988) (lien is for reasonable
value of materials furnished; contract price is evidence of reasonable value).

The lien is not the contractor's sole remedy. The contractor may get a personal judgment for
the amount due or recover in quantum meruit or for unjust enrichment, though she failed to
properly perfect a lien. See Brown Sprinkler Corp. v. Somerset-Pulaski County Development
Foundation, Inc., 335 S.W.3d 455, 458 (Ky. Ct. App. 2010); Craft v. Stevenson Lumber Yard, Inc.,
179 N.J. 56, 843 A.2d 1076 (2004). The contractor may not recover both on the lien and in
quantum meruit. See KC Excavating and Grading, Inc. v. Crane Const. Co., 141 S.W.3d 401 (Mo.
Ct. App. W.D. 2004).

[169] Stalling, Mechanics' Lien Laws as They Exist Today, 4 F.H.L.B. Rev. 232 (1938); see
Cook v. Carlson, 364 F. Supp. 24 (D.S.D. 1973).

[171] Stalling, Mechanics' Lien Laws as They Exist Today, 4 F.H.L.B. Rev. 232 (1938); Smith,
Note, Mechanic's Lien Priority Rights for Design Professionals, 46 Wash. & Lee L. Rev. 1035
(1989); Survey of Illinois Law for the Years 1951–1952: Property, 31 Chi.-Kent L. Rev. 61, 71
(1952). See In re Premier Hotel Development Group, 271 B.R. 813 (Bankr. E.D. Tenn. 2002)
(engineers and architects are entitled to lien, but liens have priority over mortgage only if lien
claimant gave notice of work to mortgagee, either directly or by recording notice, before mortgage
recorded); Mark Twain Kansas City Bank v. Kroh Bros. Development Co., 14 Kan. App. 2d 714,
798 P.2d 511 (1990) (architect may have lien only if building is constructed); Mutual Savings
Ass'n v. Res/Com Properties, L.L.C., 32 Kan. App. 2d 48, 79 P.3d 184 (2003) (engineering
company entitled to lien for preliminary surveying and staking).

lien statute should be strictly construed with respect to those acts necessary to perfect the lien and should be construed liberally as to the provisions of the statute that are remedial in nature."

If the mechanic's lien was available only to those with whom the owner dealt directly, little question would exist as to the amount of the lien—it would be for the unpaid contract amount. When the acts extended their coverage to persons that had no direct dealings with the owner, they divided into two main types. One type, generally designated the "Pennsylvania" type,[175] gives the subcontractor a direct right for the value of its contributions. Some statutes in this group provide that the claims cannot exceed the contract price, less payments properly made to the contractor, or provide a method for the owner to limit them to that amount. However, other states permit the subcontractors' claims to exceed the contract price and to be payable though the owner has paid the general contractor in full. The other type of act, usually called the "New York" system, gives the subcontractor a derivative lien based on the contractor's rights. Because the lien rights are based on the contract between the owner and general contractor, the liability of the owner's property is limited to the contract price, less payments properly made to the contractor.[180]

The procedure that a lien claimant must follow varies widely among the states but typically requires filing a claim notice within a specified period of time, typically 60 to 180 days, after completing the work.[181] The notice usually must be recorded, served personally on the owner, published in a newspaper, or some combination of these methods. If the claim is not paid within an additional specified period, typically six months to one year, the claimant usually must bring a judicial action to foreclose the lien in a manner similar to a mortgage foreclosure.

When the claimant perfects the lien by giving or recording the required notice, the lien's priority usually relates back to an earlier time. This relation-back feature is frequently litigated between construction mortgagees and mechanic's lienors that are attempting to prove senior priority status. Nearly half the states provide that mechanic's liens take

---

[175] See Pa. Stat. Ann. tit. 49, § 1301. Approximately thirty states follow the Pennsylvania approach. See Comment: Mechanics' Liens and Surety Bonds in the Building Trades, 68 Yale L.J. 138, 144 n.30 (1958); Maurice T. Brunner, Annotation, Release or waiver of mechanic's lien by general contractor as affecting rights of subcontractor or materialman, 75 A.L.R.3d 505.

[180] See N.Y. Lien Law § 4; Fla. Stat. Ann. § 713.06(1); Ga. Code Ann. § 44–14–361(b).

[181] The date of completion is not always easy to determine. Suppose the owner calls the mechanic back to correct defective work that she discovered after nominal completion? See In re Jennerwein, 309 B.R. 385 (Bankr. M.D. Fla. 2004) (contractor's return to site to inspect fence and make list of unfinished items extended time to file); Creme de la Creme (Kansas), Inc. v. R & R Intern., Inc., 32 Kan. App. 2d 490, 85 P.3d 205 (2004) ("call-back" work was performed as a courtesy and did not extend contractor's time to file); Interstate Electrical Services Corp. v. Cummings Properties, LLC, 63 Mass. App. Ct. 295, 825 N.E.2d 1059 (2005) (call-back work was part of original contract and extended time to file); Rossi v. Pawiroredjo, 2004 MT 39, 320 Mont. 63, 85 P.3d 776 (2004) (contractor's return to site to remove floor stain extended time to file).

priority from the date the building project began. In theory, this rule seems unobjectionable, because a property inspection will presumably disclose whether construction has begun. As a practical matter, however, commencement is often an ambiguous event. Courts disagree whether it has occurred when lumber is piled on the property, trees and brush have been cleared or grading has begun, or an electrical service pole and box are erected. In an attempt to ensure their priority over mechanic's liens that might be filed later, well-advised construction lenders photograph the property on the day they record their mortgage to establish that construction has not begun.

The second most popular priority date is the day the particular lienor began furnishing labor or materials. The difficulties of determining the beginning of service or materials deliveries are considerably greater than those of determining when the whole building operation started. Additionally, an intervening mortgage can divide the lien claimants into prior and subsequent groups, which creates a problem when the mechanic's lien statute provides that all lien claimants have the same priority.

The third most common priority date, which exists in about six jurisdictions, is the day the claimant files the lien. In a few other states, the liens attach as of the date of the general contract or of the lienor's contract or when a notice of the contract is recorded. In some states, the liens attach at different times depending on various factors. In Missouri, the relative priorities of the construction mortgage and the mechanic's liens can differ for the land and for the improvements for which the lienors supplied labor or materials. Mechanic's liens on the land take priority from the date that work began, but the mechanic's liens on the improvement have first priority, regardless of when the construction mortgage is recorded. In some states, the mortgage is senior to the mechanic's liens if the loan proceeds were used to pay for the construction.

The statutes usually provide that property is lienable only if the improvements were constructed with the owner's consent. "Owner" is defined in a variety of ways. A tenant or life tenant often does not have the requisite power to consent. The owner "consents" if she signs a construction contract. Courts in some jurisdictions have held that a formal contract is not required and that the owner's acquiescence or even mere knowledge of the construction is sufficient. A number of these jurisdictions provide a procedure by which an owner who has not contracted for the improvement can record or post on the property a notice or disclaimer of responsibility within some fixed time after construction began. Depending on the statute, the notice can shift the burden of proving actual consent to the lienor or can entirely bar the filing of liens on the owner's property interest.[200]

NOTES

1. *Additional reading.* For further discussion of mechanic's liens from a national perspective, *see* Ethan Glass, Old Statutes Never Die . . . Nor Do They Fade Away: A Proposal for Modernizing Mechanics' Lien Law by Federal Action, 27 Ohio N.U. L. Rev. 67 (2000); Michael G. Walsh, A Mechanics' Lien Primer for the General Practitioner, 37 Prac.Law. 77 (July 1991); Nelson, Whitman, Burkhart & Freyermuth, Real Estate Finance Law § 12.4 (6th ed. 2014).

2. *Risks for purchasers.* Although the material reprinted above focuses on the plight of the landowner, consider the position of a *purchaser.* Whether the improvements on the land are new or used, potential mechanic's lien claimants may exist. If the lien need not be filed until some months after the last work is done, how can a purchaser avoid taking title subject to a mechanic's lien? Obviously, a record title search is insufficient. The owner may try to obtain lien waivers from all the workers and materials suppliers, but how can the purchaser be certain that the owner knows the identity and location of all of them? And, as described above, title insurance may not protect against mechanic's liens.

In some states, unrecorded mechanic's liens are binding on bona fide purchasers only if the contractor has filed a notice of the construction contract with the register of deeds or if the improvements are "visually evident." But the "visually evident" requirement is no panacea for buyers because it may provide little guidance. For example, if the seller has recently hired a heating contractor to replace the furnace, is that improvement "visually evident" to the buyer?

The courts' interpretation of the standard also can be difficult to predict. For example, in Carlson-Grefe Const., Inc. v. Rosemount Condo. Group Partn., 474 N.W.2d 405 (Minn.App.1991), the court found that neither the presence of a construction trailer containing plumbing supplies on the site nor a ceremonial groundbreaking was a sufficiently visible activity to establish the priority of a mechanic's lien. Many other cases deal with activities such as architectural, engineering, surveying, and legal work on the project. *See also* Himmighoefer v. Medallion Indus., Inc., 302 Md. 270, 487 A.2d 282 (1985), in which the court discusses the Maryland mechanic's lien statute amendments that protect bona fide purchasers who enter into contracts before the mechanic's lien is reduced to judgment.

Note that the problem of unrecorded mechanic's liens affects not only purchasers, but also anyone else acquiring an interest in the land. For

---

[200] Some statutes permit the lienor to remove the improvement notwithstanding the owner's notice of nonresponsibility, which may compel the owner to pay for the improvement to keep it. See, e.g., American Transit Mix Co. v. Weber, 106 Cal. App. 2d 74, 234 P.2d 732 (3d Dist. 1951).

example, a lender that takes a mortgage may find that it is subject to a mechanic's lien that was unrecorded and, therefore, undiscoverable when the mortgage was given.

3. *Lien waivers.* Can mechanic's liens be waived? The question must be divided into two contexts. First, what about a "no lien" clause in the construction agreement between the owner and the contractor? In most states, little doubt exists that this agreement binds the general contractor, but does it also bind the workers and suppliers? The jurisdictions are divided. In some states, the general contractor's agreement binds them; in other states, their rights are independent of the general contractor's and cannot be waived without their consent. *E.g.* Cal. Civ. Code § 8122 (waiver in construction contract binds workers and suppliers only if they give written waiver and release); 49 Pa. Stat. § 1402 (waiver in construction contract binds workers and suppliers if they had notice of it); Lehrer McGovern Bovis, Inc. v. Bullock Insulation, Inc., 197 P.3d 1032 (Nev. 2008) (lien waiver in construction agreement does not bind subcontractor). Similarly, several states invalidate a lien waiver if the worker or supplier has not been paid. *E.g.* Nev. Rev. Stat. §§ 108.2453 & 108.2457; Wis. Stat. § 779.135(1).

Second, is a waiver enforceable if the worker or supplier gave it either during the course of construction or after the construction is completed? Courts in virtually all jurisdictions sustain these waivers, which is fortunate because they are extremely useful. For example, if you are buying a newly-constructed house or one on which work has recently been done, you would be very wise to get a list of the people that had worked on the project or had supplied materials and to insist that they provide you with lien waivers. Of course, a court might refuse to enforce a waiver if it was obtained by fraudulent representations or by bad faith conduct. *See, e.g.,* Stringert & Bowers, Inc. v. On-Line Systems, Inc., 236 Pa.Super. 196, 345 A.2d 194 (1975).

Some jurisdictions prohibit the waiver of a lien arising from an *executory* contract. *See* the Maryland statute discussed in National Glass, Inc. v. J.C. Penney Properties, Inc., 336 Md. 606, 650 A.2d 246 (1994). New York, Pennsylvania, and Florida have similar statutes. In effect, this means that a worker or materials supplier can waive a lien for work already performed or materials already delivered but not for work or materials to be provided in the future. Hence, a buyer or lender must obtain waivers at the conclusion of the construction process to be certain that no lien claims will be filed.

A variation on this theme is the so-called "pay-if-paid" provision, which a general contractor may include in its contract with the workers and materials suppliers. Under this provision, the worker or supplier is entitled to payment only if the owner pays the contractor. Some states invalidate this type of provision because they believe it is contrary to the public policy underlying mechanic's lien statutes. *E.g.* 770 Ill. Comp. Stat. 60/21(e); Nev. Rev. Stat. §§ 624.624 & 624.626; N.C. Gen. Stat. § 22C–2; Wis. Stat. § 779.135(3); West-Fair Elec. Contractors v. Aetna Cas. & Sur. Co., 87 N.Y.2d 148, 638 N.Y.S.2d

394, 661 N.E.2d 967 (1995). Other states enforce them. *E.g.* MidAmerica Constr. Mgmt., Inc. v. MasTec N. America, Inc., 436 F.3d 1257 (10th Cir. 2006) (pay-if-paid provisions enforceable under New Mexico and Texas law).

4.   *The stop notice.* If a construction lender uses sufficient care, it will usually be able to preserve the priority of its mortgage against mechanic's liens in most jurisdictions. This situation is highly unsatisfactory to mechanic's lien claimants because foreclosure of the construction mortgage will eliminate their liens and will leave them with only the tenuous hope that the foreclosure sale will generate some surplus proceeds. This hope is particularly tenuous because the construction lender usually is the only bidder at the sale, and it rarely will bid more than it is owed.

Recognizing the dilemma that mechanic's lienors face, several states have provided the stop notice as an alternative means of recovery for them. Under stop notice statutes, a mechanic's lienor (usually excepting the general contractor) may make a claim on any undisbursed construction funds in the hands of the lender and, under some statutes, of the borrower. This remedy is perhaps most fully developed in California, Cal.Civ.Code §§ 8500–60, but is also available in Alabama, Indiana, Mississippi, North Carolina, Rhode Island, Texas, and Washington.

5.   *Equitable lien on the land.* Although an unpaid worker or materials supplier can generally file a mechanic's lien, the filing may be unavailing. For example, a construction mortgage that is recorded before work commenced on the project will have priority over mechanic's liens in most jurisdictions. Alternatively, the worker or supplier may have failed to file the required lien notice within the statutorily prescribed time or may have otherwise failed to comply with the lien statute. Finally, if the construction is on public land, it is exempt from mechanic's liens.

In these types of situations, a creative lawyer may try to rectify the thwarted lienor's problem by filing a suit that asserts an "equitable lien" against the land. As a practical matter, this sort of lien has little value unless a court will elevate its priority over that of the construction mortgage. But, far from giving priority to such a lien, a court might ordinarily be expected to hold that the mechanic's lien statute is the claimant's only remedy. *See, e.g.,* Hill Behan Lumber Co. v. Marchese, 1 Ill.App.3d 789, 275 N.E.2d 451 (1971) ("We are unable to find any authority which would grant an equitable lien in a situation where it would have been appropriate to impose a mechanic's lien had there been compliance with the statute."); All State Plumbing, Inc. v. Mutual Security Life Ins. Co., 537 So.2d 598 (Fla.App.1988) (lien on land refused).

However, suppose there is evidence that the lien claimant (let's say, a framing subcontractor) had the following sort of conversation with the construction lender's loan officer before the construction mortgage was foreclosed:

Sub: We've been working on this project for several months now, but I have begun hearing rumors that the project is over-budget and may be foreclosed on.

Loan officer: I wouldn't be worried about that if I were you. The project is in good standing.

Sub: I would certainly want to know if the construction loan was in trouble. I don't want to keep working on the site if I'm not going to get paid. Can you assure me that I will get my money on this job?

Loan officer: Absolutely. Don't worry about a thing.

This conversation isn't entirely hypothetical. Consider the court's description of the facts in Rinker Materials Corp. v. Palmer First Nat'l Bank & Trust Co., 361 So.2d 156 (Fla.1978):

> At one time or another, [the construction lender] assured all petitioners that there were sufficient funds in the loan account to complete the project; that they should continue to furnish labor and materials; that there was no need to file mechanic's liens; and that the bank would do everything it could to see that the subcontractors were paid, including the issuance of joint checks to the contractor and subcontractors if necessary. In reliance on the bank's statements, petitioners continued to furnish labor and materials.

Note that the loan officer in our little scene has a real dilemma. If the loan officer is candid and tells the subcontractor that the project is over-budget and that the lender is actively considering foreclosure, the sub probably will walk off the job, rather than throw good work after bad. That action by the sub would cause the other subs to walk off the job, too, which could virtually assure the project's failure and foreclosure. Obviously, the loan officer has no wish to hasten these events if there is any chance at all that the project can be saved. Candor obviously is contrary to the loan officer's self-interest. The temptation to lie, or at least to exaggerate the project's status, is strong.

Now assume that the construction loan mortgage for the project involved in the foregoing scenario is in fact foreclosed and that the mechanic's liens are subordinate to it. Can the subcontractor reasonably assert that the loan officer's statements were misleading or even fraudulent and that as a result the lender is estopped from denying that the mechanic's lien has priority over the mortgage? Such holdings are not uncommon. See Trout's Inv., Inc. v. Davis, 482 S.W.2d 510 (Mo.App.1972). A court accepted a similar argument in principle but rejected it for lack of evidence of such assurances in FDIC v. Key Biscayne Dev. Ass'n, 858 F.2d 670 (11th Cir.1988).

Alternatively, the subcontractor might argue that the misleading statements created an equitable lien that is senior to the mortgage. The subcontractor also can attempt to gain senior priority by arguing that the loan officer's statements amount to an oral or equitable subordination of the mortgage to the mechanic's liens. This approach was endorsed by the court in In re 200 Woodbury Realty Trust, 99 B.R. 184 (Bankr.D.N.H.1989), and was recognized in principle but rejected on the facts by the court in In re Commercial Inv., Ltd., 92 B.R. 488 (Bankr.D.N.M.1988).

But don't be too sanguine about the chances of a mechanic's lien claimant winning one of these cases. In Rinker Materials Corp. v. Palmer First Nat'l Bank, *supra*, the Florida Supreme Court held that "a party may successfully maintain a suit under the theory of equitable estoppel only where there is proof of fraud, misrepresentation, or other affirmative deception." Amazingly, it found that the statements described in the indented paragraph above did not meet this test: "The trial court in this case found that the bank's statements were neither fraudulent nor untrue." It denied the lien. Because the loan was indeed foreclosed and the mechanic's liens were wiped out, isn't it obvious that the statements were, at a minimum, misleading? Isn't the mechanic's lienor equally harmed by the statements whether they were made with conscious falsity or in perfect good faith? *See also* Curly Customs, Inc. v. Bank of Boston, 49 Mass.App.Ct. 197, 727 N.E.2d 1212 (2000) (requiring false or misleading representations by the lender).

Some theories have been suggested that might give unpaid workers and suppliers prime equitable liens without proof of the construction lender's fraudulent or false statements. One is unjust enrichment based on the notion that the lender has title to the improvements through foreclosure and that the contractor has not been paid for them. *See generally* Jeffrey Murray, Comment, Owner/Lender Liability to Unpaid Subcontractors, 29 Duq. L. Rev. 661 (1991); Nelson, Whitman, Burkhart & Freyermuth, Real Estate Finance Law § 12.6 (6th ed. 2014). This theory makes considerable sense if the real estate is worth more than the construction lender's investment, so that it has received a windfall by foreclosing. Still, little judicial authority supports it. *See, e.g.,* Bane-Nelson, Inc. v. Heritage Bank & Trust, 855 F.Supp. 280 (E.D.Wis.1994) (rejecting this theory under Wisconsin law).

6.   *Equitable lien on undisbursed construction funds.* A second type of equitable lien might be asserted against the undisbursed funds remaining in the construction lender's loan account. This remedy is roughly analogous to a stop notice, except that it might be asserted in states with no stop notice statute or in cases in which the contractor has failed to satisfy the procedural requirements for a stop notice. It depends, of course, on the existence of undisbursed funds. If the construction project is already over-budget at the time of the foreclosure, as is often the case, there won't be any funds to assert the lien against.

The fundamental premise of a successful equitable lien against undisbursed funds is unjust enrichment. If the lender has foreclosed the construction mortgage and has acquired title to the project without spending the entire loan amount, it has gotten the project for less than its market value and has done so at the expense of the unpaid workers and suppliers.

A model case of this sort is Morgen-Oswood & Assocs. v. Continental Mortg. Investors, 323 So.2d 684 (Fla.App.1975), *cert. dismissed,* 342 So.2d 1100 (Fla.1977). Other examples include DeKalb County v. J & A Pipeline Co., Inc., 263 Ga. 645, 437 S.E.2d 327 (1993) (public project); Ten Hoeve Bros., Inc. v. City of Hartford, 1996 WL 285540 (Conn.Super. 1996) (not reported in A.2d) (public project); Twin City Constr. Co. v. ITT Indus. Credit Co., 358 N.W.2d 716 (Minn.App.1984). *See generally* Annot., Building and Construction Contracts: Contractor's Equitable Lien Upon Percentage of Funds Withheld by Contractee or Lender, 54 A.L.R.3d 848 (1974); George Lefcoe & Mark Schaffer, Construction Lending and the Equitable Lien, 40 S.Cal.L.Rev. 439 (1967).

Should it matter whether the contractor has completed the job? Can't the lender be unjustly enriched even if the contractor has not performed all its work or if the entire project is incomplete? *Compare* McBain v. Santa Clara Sav. & Loan Ass'n, 241 Cal.App.2d 829, 51 Cal.Rptr. 78 (1966)[1] (completion of project irrelevant) *with* Pioneer Plumbing Supply Co. v. Southwest Sav. & Loan Ass'n, 102 Ariz. 258, 428 P.2d 115 (1967); J. G. Plumbing Serv. Inc. v. Coastal Mortg. Co., 329 So.2d 393 (Fla.App.1976); Town Concrete Pipe of Washington, Inc. v. Redford, 43 Wash.App. 493, 717 P.2d 1384 (1986) (completion of project essential to lien). What does completion have to do with it? Isn't the issue whether the construction lender obtained excess value for its money while the workers and suppliers are unpaid?

Note that, unlike assertions of an equitable lien on the land, the existence of a misrepresentation by the construction lender to the mechanic's lien claimant is usually irrelevant when an equitable lien is asserted against undisbursed funds. *See* Emerald Designs, Inc. v. Citibank, 626 So.2d 1084 (Fla.App.1993); Swinerton & Walberg Co. v. Union Bank, 25 Cal.App.3d 259, 101 Cal.Rptr. 665 (1972).

7. *The mechanic as a third party beneficiary.* Suppose an unpaid worker or supplier can show that the construction lender did not follow the loan disbursement procedures in the construction loan agreement or procedures that are considered to be standard or prudent in the industry and that, as a result, the owner or prime contractor was able to divert the funds to other purposes. (There's an old joke about the developer who owns a beautiful boat named "First Draw" moored in the local marina.) Can the unpaid mechanic successfully argue that the construction lender owed it a duty to disburse the funds properly and, therefore, is liable to the mechanic up to the amount of the diverted funds?

In a few states, courts have held that the mechanic's liens have priority over the construction mortgage to the extent that the construction lender

---

[1] The California cases imposing equitable liens are of only academic interest; a statute that became effective in 1971 limits all claims against construction loan funds to those permitted by stop notice. See Cal.Civil Code § 3264; Nibbi Bros., Inc. v. Brannan St. Investors, 205 Cal.App.3d 1415, 253 Cal.Rptr. 289 (1988). In contrast, the Washington Court of Appeals refused to read its state's stop notice statute as barring equitable liens. Town Concrete Pipe of Washington, Inc. v. Redford, 43 Wash.App. 493, 717 P.2d 1384 (1986).

knowingly permitted diversion of construction funds to non-construction purposes. *See* Spickes Bros. Painting Contractors, Inc. v. Worthen Bank & Trust Co., N.A., 299 Ark. 79, 771 S.W.2d 258 (1989). But courts in most jurisdictions have refused to find that the lender has a duty to workers and suppliers to disburse the construction funds carefully. *See, e.g.,* Peterson v. First Clayton Bank & Trust Co., 214 Ga.App. 94, 447 S.E.2d 63 (1994); Comet Dev. Corp. v. Prudential Ins. Co., 579 So.2d 355 (Fla.App.1991).

Alternatively, the mechanics might argue that they are third party beneficiaries of the construction loan agreement and can recover if the lender breaches it by using sloppy disbursement practices or by improperly refusing to disburse funds to pay them. Only rarely has a court accepted the third party beneficiary argument. *See, e.g.,* United States v. Mill Ass'n, Inc., 480 F.Supp. 3 (E.D.N.Y.1978) (based on loan agreement's reference to state lien law). Courts in the great majority of cases hold that workers and suppliers are only incidental beneficiaries of the loan agreement and cannot enforce it. *See, e.g.,* Van-Tex, Inc. v. Pierce, 703 F.2d 891 (5th Cir.1983); Silverdale Hotel Assocs. v. Lomas & Nettleton Co., 36 Wash.App. 762, 677 P.2d 773 (1984) (rejecting the third party beneficiary argument but awarding the unpaid contractor an equitable lien based on estoppel arising from the lender's assurances to the contractor that it would be paid).

To prevent a court from finding that mechanics can enforce the loan agreement as third party beneficiaries, lenders now usually insert language in the loan agreement that expressly disclaims intent to benefit workers or suppliers. Such language nearly always has the desired effect. *See* Howard Sav. Bank v. Lefcon Partn., 209 A.D.2d 473, 618 N.Y.S.2d 910 (1994). *See generally* Jeffrey Murray, Comment, Owner/Lender Liability to Unpaid Subcontractors, 29 Duq. L.Rev. 661 (1991); Nelson, Whitman, Burkhart & Freyermuth, Real Estate Finance Law § 12.6 (6th ed. 2014); Robert K. Jordan, Construction Lender Liability to Third Parties, Prob. & Prop., Mar./Apr. 1991, at 45.

3. OPTIONAL AND OBLIGATORY LOAN ADVANCES

A construction mortgage is one type of mortgage that secures "future advances;" the construction lender advances the loan proceeds only as and when the improvements are built. Other examples of future advance mortgages are "line of credit" loans, such as home equity loans, and mortgages that include a dragnet clause, as described in Chapter 7, Section B supra.

Under standard doctrine, a mortgage secures future advances only if the parties to the mortgage so agree and:

1.   The mortgage states that it secures repayment of future advances;

2.   The subsequent purchaser of an interest in the real estate otherwise has prior notice of the parties' agreement; or

3. The mortgage states a monetary amount to be secured, and the advances do not cause the total indebtedness to exceed that amount.

Restatement (Third) of Property (Mortgages) § 2.1 (1997).*

Some items of indebtedness that the mortgage secures are so common that we do not usually think of them as future advances. They include interest on the unpaid balance, costs of collection, and attorneys' fees if the mortgage so provides. *See* Restatement § 2.1(e). In addition, advances by a mortgagee to protect the value of the real estate are routinely added to the mortgage debt without labeling them "future advances" and without adhering to the three-part test described above. Such advances include payments for property taxes, payments on senior liens, costs of curing waste, and expenses for defending the property's title.

By the terms of state recording statutes, all the advances that the mortgage secures share the mortgage's original priority. Therefore, if the mortgage has priority as of June 30, 2009, the advances made in the future all have priority as of June 30, 2009. Despite the clear statutory language, courts in many states have created an exception that can change this result if the loan advances are "optional," rather than "obligatory." Based on this judicial rule, if the lender is obligated to make a future loan advance, the advance shares the mortgage's original priority. On the other hand, if a future advance was optional and if the lender knew that a subsequent lien had attached before making the advance, that optional advance has priority only as of the date it is made.

If a future advance loses priority to an intervening lien, the result looks something like an Oreo cookie. For example, if the future advance mortgage has first priority, any advances that are obligatory or that are made before the lender has notice of an intervening lien share first priority with the mortgage. The intervening lien has second priority. The optional advances that were made with notice of the intervening lien have third priority. In effect, the future advance mortgagee holds both a first mortgage and a third mortgage, with the intervening lienor in between.

In most reported cases, the intervening lien is a mechanic's lien, but the rule works the same way if it is second mortgage to a land vendor or any other statutory or consensual lien. The result is much like the case of a first mortgage that is modified to increase its principal amount without the second mortgage holder's consent. Obviously, the second mortgagee isn't subordinate to the added amount. *See* Lennar Northeast Partners v. Buice Revocable Living Trust, 49 Cal.App.4th 1576, 57 Cal.Rptr.2d 435 (1996).

What is the rationale for determining priority based on whether an advance is optional or obligatory? In La Cholla Group, Inc. v. Timm, 173 Ariz. 490, 492–93, 844 P.2d 657, 659–60 (Ariz. Ct. App. 1992), a case of first impression, the court gave this explanation:

> [B]y giving absolute priority to recorded obligatory advances, the rule provides security to lenders who are under contractual obligations to advance funds even if the borrower has subsequently overencumbered the collateral. *See* Comment, *Priority Disputes in Future Advance Mortgages: Picking the Winner in Arizona*, 1985 Ariz. St. L.J. 537. In addition, if optional advances were given an absolute preference, "the mortgagor could not demand the contemplated additional loan funds and could not obtain financing from another lender, because no one will lend on security that will be reduced or eliminated if the first mortgagee decides to make subsequent advances." G. Nelson and D. Whitman, *Real Estate Finance Law*, § 12.7, at 887 (2d ed. 1985). Finally, by awarding priority only to obligatory advances disclosed on the title record, secondary creditors are given notice of the full extent of encumbrances on the property prior to extending credit against it. *Priority Disputes in Future Advance Mortgages, supra.*

The Restatement (Third) of Property (Mortgages) § 2.3, Reporters' Note to Comment a (1997) suggests that the doctrine is an exceedingly blunt instrument for accomplishing its purposes, particularly because distinguishing between optional and obligatory advances has proven to be difficult and often unpredictable. Other commentators have argued that courts are too prone to characterize advances as optional. What factors should a court consider in characterizing loan advances? As shown in the next case, the terms of the loan agreement are crucially important.

IRWIN CONCRETE, INC. v. SUN COAST PROPERTIES, INC.

Washington Court of Appeals, 1982
33 Wash.App. 190, 653 P.2d 1331

WORSWICK, JUDGE

This litigation arose out of an unfortunate but familiar occurrence: a grand plan for real estate development gone awry.

In 1972, Olympic Mall Co. borrowed $350,000 from Continental, Inc., to purchase and develop 179 acres of land near Gig Harbor. A deed of trust secured the note. In April 1973, Olympic conveyed 7 of the 179 acres to Sun Coast Properties, Inc., to build a shopping center. The sale contract required Olympic to install a water system on its remaining 172 acres to provide water for the center. Sun Coast then borrowed $1.5 million from Continental for completion of the center.

By April 1974, Olympic was in default on its $350,000 loan from Continental and Continental notified the trustee of default. In September 1974, Continental gave notice of the trustee's sale of the 172 acres to all whose liens were then of record. * * * Hernando Chaves and Associates, engineered the water system, working first for Olympic and later for Sun Coast. Chaves filed a lien on all the land on December 5, 1974.

At the trustee sale on January 24, 1975, Continental bid in and bought Olympic's interest in the 172 acres.

* * *

Chaves contends that his lien was not foreclosed by the trustee sale because it was senior to that of Continental. He argues that the loan agreement between Continental and Olympic made advances optional with Continental; thus, he claims, to the extent of monies advanced after he started work, his lien claim was senior, citing National Bank of Washington v. Equity Investors, 81 Wash.2d 886, 506 P.2d 20 (1973). We disagree.

Chaves cites *Equity Investors* for the correct proposition but he does not come within it. In *Equity Investors,* the court restated the Washington rule that a mortgage to secure future advances takes priority over mechanic's liens accruing after recording of the mortgage, unless the future advances are optional. Where the advances are optional, priority is determined when the advances are made. *Equity Investors*, 81 Wash.2d at 897, 506 P.2d 20. The court found that the bank's advances to Equity Investors were optional, because the bank had discretion whether to disburse funds or not, and could not have been compelled by court decree to advance any money. The court came to this conclusion based on language in the contract which stated that money would be advanced to Equity Investors, " ' . . . *at such times and in such amounts as the Lender shall determine*'." The court stated:

> Although in a given case there may be difficulty in ascertaining from the circumstances and the language of the mortgage and loan papers covering the whole agreement whether the advances are to be regarded as optional or mandatory, we think that the contractual reservations giving the lender the broad discretion of deciding when and in what amounts, *or if at all,* he must advance the money render the advances optional rather than obligatory where the purpose is to decide construction lien priorities arising after the initial filing for record of the lender's security documents.

81 Wash.2d at 899, 506 P.2d 20.

Unlike *Equity Investors,* the contract between Continental and Olympic did not allow Continental to disburse funds based on its own criteria. Subsection (2)(c) of the contract stated:

> The remaining $80,000 shall be disbursed after said lease to a national retail grocery chain has been secured and approved by Continental, for the purpose of site developments, plans for which shall be approved by Continental, and disbursements for which shall be made monthly against actual development costs, based on cost verification as site preparation progresses. Disbursements hereunder shall be subject to approval of Continental.

Disbursements were subject to Continental's approval. However, Continental was not free to advance or retain the money as it saw fit. The quoted language specifies the conditions under which Continental could approve or disapprove of disbursements: "disbursements for which shall be made monthly against actual development costs, based on cost verification as site preparation progresses." Continental's control over disbursements was limited to verifying each advance requested for the cost of work completed on the land. If the amount requested of Continental was verified, Continental had no option, but was required to disburse the money. Continental was obligated to loan $350,000 to Olympic. The only control Continental had over future advances was the ability to see that Olympic spent the loan money for improvements to the land. That control did not render the future advances optional.

Because Continental's advances were mandatory, its deed of trust securing the future advances was perfected on June 9, 1972, the date of filing. Chaves' mechanic's lien arose on June 16, 1972, the date he commenced work, and consequently was junior to the deed of trust.

Affirmed.

PETRIE and PETRICH, JJ., concur.

NOTES

1. *Lender's failure to use loan agreement protections.* In *Irwin Concrete,* the court held that the future advances maintained the priority of the mortgage because the conditions in the loan agreement were nondiscretionary. In some cases, nondiscretionary conditions were insufficient to preserve the priority of future advances. For example, in J.I. Kislak Mortg. Corp. v. William Matthews Builder, Inc., 287 A.2d 686 (Del.Super.1972), *aff'd*, 303 A.2d 648 (Del.1973), the construction loan agreement provided:

> None of the said respective installments or any part thereof, not theretofore paid over shall be required to be made by Lender unless and until Borrower shall procure and deliver to Lender original

receipts or such other evidence as shall be satisfactory to Lender, showing that any installment received theretofore under this Agreement has been disbursed fully and properly to materialmen, laborers, subcontractors, and to any other person, firm or corporation providing or furnishing materials or labor or both, in connection with the construction of said improvements on the above mentioned premises.

Despite this language, the lender made advances without first demanding to see paid receipts for the work on the project. Because it was not obligated to make the advances without the receipts, the court held the advances were optional and, therefore, subordinate to the mechanic's liens. *See also* New York & Suburban Fed. Sav. & Loan Ass'n v. Fi-Pen Realty Co., 133 N.Y.S.2d 33 (Sup.Ct.1954). These cases indicate that the lender must *use* all the protections it has reserved; if it waives any of them, it may also be waiving its priority! *Contra, see* Home Lumber Co. v. Kopfmann Homes, Inc., 535 N.W.2d 302 (Minn.1995).

2. *Advances to protect security.* Despite their optional character, certain types of advances that are necessary to protect the lender's security interest have the same legal advantages as obligatory advances. These include advances to pay property taxes, insurance premiums, and prior liens. *See* Southern Trust Mortg. Co. v. K & B Door Co., 104 Nev. 564, 763 P.2d 353 (1988); Gerald L. Blackburn, Mortgages to Secure Future Advances, 21 Mo.L.Rev. 209, 220–21 (1956); Restatement (Third) of Property (Mortgages) § 2.2(b) (1997).

3. *Continued funding of the over-budget project.* Perhaps the most common form of optional advance occurs when the project has drawn down the full amount of the construction loan but is not yet complete. The lender clearly has no obligation to advance additional funds, *see* Kinner v. World Sav. & Loan Ass'n, 57 Cal.App.3d 724, 129 Cal.Rptr. 400 (1976), but it may reasonably believe that investing additional funds to complete the project is desirable and preferable to foreclosure from everyone's viewpoint. Can the lender plausibly argue that the additional advance is not optional because it is compelled by economic necessity and because all other courses of action are likely to produce much greater economic loss? Perhaps surprisingly, the additional advance may lose priority. *See* Percy Galbreath & Son, Inc. v. Watkins, 560 S.W.2d 239 (Ky.App.1977); Larry Skipworth, Should Construction Lenders Lose Out on Voluntary Advances If a Loan Turns Sour?, 5 Real Est.L.J. 221 (1977). In light of that possibility, what should the lender do before advancing the additional funds?

4. *What constitutes notice?* A further problem with the optional/obligatory advance doctrine is determining when the lender has "notice" that another lien has "attached." The application of these rules is far from certain. For example, as of what date does the mechanic's lien "attach" for this purpose? Is it:

    a.   The date the first work is done or materials supplied?

    b.   The date the lienor notifies the owner that a lien is claimed?

    c.   The date the notice of lien is filed of record?

Similarly ambiguous is the issue of what "notice" is necessary to subject an optional advance to a loss of priority:

    a.   Knowledge that work has been done or materials supplied to the project?

    b.   Knowledge that payment to the potential lienor has not been made?

    c.   Knowledge that payment to the potential lienor is in default?

    d.   Knowledge that a lien is claimed or that a notice of lien has been filed of record?

    e.   Constructive notice from the filing of a notice of lien in the public records?

The cases are divided. *See* Lincoln Fed. Sav. & Loan Ass'n v. Platt Homes, Inc., 185 N.J.Super. 457, 449 A.2d 553 (Ch.Div.1982) (constructive notice from public records is sufficient); J.I. Kislak Mortg. Corp., *supra* note 1. But the majority view appears to be that actual knowledge of the intervening lien is required. In re Johnson, 124 B.R. 648 (Bankr.E.D.Pa.1991) (holding that Pennsylvania courts would no longer recognize constructive notice from the public records and would require actual notice of the intervening lien); National Bank of Waterloo v. Moeller, 434 N.W.2d 887 (Iowa 1989); Drilling Serv. Co. v. Baebler, 484 S.W.2d 1 (Mo.1972); Grider v. Mutual Fed. Sav. & Loan Ass'n, 565 S.W.2d 647 (Ky.App.1978), *noted* 68 Ky.L.J. 681, 691–94 (1980). Ohio and several other states statutorily require written notice. Ohio Rev.Code § 5301.232.

If the competing junior lien is a land vendor's purchase money mortgage, rather than a mechanic's lien, usually it clearly has "attached" and the construction lender had notice of it. For other types of junior mortgages, this is not necessarily the case. *See, e.g.,* Bank of Ephraim v. Davis, 559 P.2d 538 (Utah 1977) (senior lender not bound by recording of junior mortgage; no duty to search the records before each advance). *See* Aaron E. Michel, Note, *Capital Mortgage Service Co. v. Southard:* A Change in Policy Concerning the Priority of Advances Over Intervening Liens in Protecting Mortgages, 9 Cap.U.L.Rev. 383 (1979).

    5.   *The Restatement's approach.* Restatement (Third) of Property (Mortgages) § 2.3(a) (1997) flatly rejects the optional advance doctrine. It provides: "If a mortgage secures repayment of future advances, all advances have the priority of the original mortgage." If adopted by the courts, this will certainly simplify life for construction lenders.

But what about the concern for the borrower's ability to obtain new financing if the construction lender refuses to make additional optional advances? The Restatement deals with that problem by adopting a "cutoff notice" procedure, under which the mortgagor may at any time issue a notice to the mortgagee terminating or subordinating the mortgage to any further advances. About a dozen states have statutes providing for such a procedure. *See, e.g.,* Mo.Ann.Stat. § 443.055; Fla.Stat.Ann. § 697.04; Nev.Rev.Stat.Ann. § 106.400. Most of these statutes also contain statements, like the Restatement, that all advances have the priority of the original mortgage. But the Restatement's view is that *courts* should accept the "cutoff notice" procedure and the concomitant granting of full priority to all future advances as a matter of common law, whether the jurisdiction has approved it by statute or not.

How does the cutoff notice help the landowner who has given a mortgage providing for future advances? If the lender refuses to make advances when the borrower requests them, the borrower can issue the notice and thus can cap the outstanding principal amount at its present level. The borrower can then go to other lenders, seek second mortgage financing from them, and assure them that the amount of the first priority lien will not increase. If the borrower's credit is good and if the land has substantial value over and above the first mortgage balance, the borrower should be able to obtain junior financing. Thus, it's unnecessary to subordinate the future advances under the first mortgage to allow the landowner to get financing elsewhere. *See* Grant S. Nelson & Dale A. Whitman, Rethinking Future Advance Mortgages: A Brief for the Restatement Approach, 44 Duke L.J. 657 (1995).

Ironically, the Restatement and several of the statutes after which it was patterned probably will *not* allow the borrower to issue a cutoff notice for a construction loan. As the Restatement puts it, a cutoff notice cannot be issued if "a termination or subordination of advances would unreasonably jeopardize the mortgagee's security for advances already made." The underlying principle is that a half-finished construction project isn't worth half the value of a finished project. Thus, a borrower who completes part of the work and terminates receipt of advances might never find the funds to complete the project, and the lender might end up seriously undersecured. Of course, under the Restatement a court might recognize the validity of a cutoff notice on a construction loan if the borrower provided satisfactory assurances to the lender that the project would indeed be completed with funds from other sources. Note that, even if the notice itself is effective, the borrower's refusal to draw down the remainder of the loan funds may breach the borrower's loan commitment or loan agreement, giving rise to liability for damages.

Does the Restatement expect too much lawmaking of the courts? Is recognition of a cutoff notice procedure in a state that does not statutorily provide for it beyond the proper province of judges? We would suggest not. After all, the present optional/obligatory advance doctrine was invented by the courts with no help from legislation. May they not just as well invent or adopt a better approach?

6. *Statutory abolition of the optional advance doctrine.* Several states have statutorily given all future advances priority without providing a "cutoff

notice" procedure. Why? Perhaps because it seemed a simple solution and because they concluded that the problem of the landowner with equity, but with no way to borrow against it, was too minor an issue to worry about. This is essentially the view taken in James B. Hughes, Jr., Future Advance Mortgages: Preserving the Benefits and Burdens of the Bargain, 29 Wake Forest L.Rev. 1101 (1994). Or perhaps they never realized that the issue existed. Washington took this action in the wake of the *Equity Investors* case, described in the *Irwin Concrete* decision. *See* Wash.Rev.Code § 60.04.226. The Restatement (Third) of Property (Mortgages) § 2.1 Statutory Note includes a comprehensive table of the statutes.

7. *Should mechanic's liens have priority over construction loans?* As we have seen, a construction lender that records its mortgage before any work is done and that administers the loan carefully, without reserving too much discretion, can maintain priority over subsequently-filed mechanic's liens in most states. However, as described in the treatise excerpt reprinted in the section on mechanic's liens, this may not work in Missouri and in a few other states; the mechanic's liens can be prior to the construction mortgage no matter what the lender does. Professor Ronald Mann surveyed a group of lenders and asked whether the Missouri rule discouraged them from making construction loans in Missouri:

> All had the same general response: they are willing to make loans in Missouri despite the lower priority, but they are more careful about risk there than they are in jurisdictions where they have a better priority position. That increased care is exactly what the system should seek because that increased attention to risk results in pricing that more accurately reflects the value of individual construction projects.

Ronald J. Mann, The First Shall Be Last: A Contextual Argument for Abandoning Temporal Rules of Lien Priority, 75 Tex.L.Rev. 11, 40 (1996). Professor Mann argued that construction lenders are far better positioned to control and manage construction risks than are individual contractors and suppliers and, therefore, that it is more efficient for the law to impose the primary risk of loss from defaulted projects on lenders. Do you agree? Adoption of his position would require a major restructuring of mechanic's lien statutes in most states.

8. *Interaction of subordination agreements and the optional advance doctrine.* What is the effect of a subordination agreement on the optional advance doctrine? In *Equity Investors*, the construction lender was also competing with a group of subordinated land vendors. Their subordination agreement said "[the subordinator] does hereby unconditionally subordinate the lien of his mortgage * * * to the lien of the lender's mortgage * * * and all advances or charges made or accruing thereunder." The court held that this language subordinated the vendors to even the Bank's *optional* advances. National Bank of Washington v. Equity Investors, 83 Wash.2d 435, 518 P.2d 1072 (1974).

9. *Future advances under home equity loans.* The Tax Reform Act of 1986 gave added significance to the problem of optional future advances. The Act disallows interest deductions on non-business debt unless the debt is secured by the taxpayer's residence. The Act thus caused a sharp surge of interest in the "home equity loan," which is simply a second mortgage loan secured by a residence. Some home equity loans are for fixed amounts and are disbursed in a single payment, raising no future advance problems. But others are of the "home equity line of credit" ("HELOC") type, under which the borrower executes and records a mortgage on her home and then borrows and repays the loan in various amounts and at various times over many years, with the mortgage purporting to secure all disbursements up to some specified maximum. *See generally* Julia Patterson Forrester, Mortgaging the American Dream: A Critical Evaluation of the Federal Government's Promotion of Home Equity Financing, 69 Tulane L.Rev. 373 (1994).

If the lender is obligated to permit the borrower to draw down funds at any time under this sort of secured line of credit, the priority of the advances is probably beyond question. But if the lender has too much discretion to cease making advances, they might all be deemed optional and potentially subordinate to intervening liens. Several states have adopted statutes to protect lenders against this possibility. *See, e.g.*, Mont.Code Ann. § 71–1–206; N.Y. Real Prop.Law § 281. While these statutes were enacted primarily with homeowner-mortgagors in mind, they may also apply to commercial lines of credit secured by real property as well.

Consider the lender who is thinking of making a junior mortgage loan on property already encumbered by a "home equity" mortgage. The junior lender may legitimately be very concerned that subsequent advances under the home equity loan might "eat up" so much of the property's value as to leave the junior mortgagee undersecured. While the optional advance doctrine is supposed to protect the junior mortgagee, its uncertainties with respect to what is "obligatory," what notice is required to the senior lender, and so on, make it an uncertain protection. However, if the state has adopted a cutoff notice statute of the sort discussed in note 5 above, the junior lender can insist as a condition of making the junior loan that the mortgagor give an appropriate notice to the senior lender, thereby limiting advances under the senior loan to those already made or perhaps to some additional amount acceptable to the junior lender.

CHAPTER TEN

COMMON INTEREST OWNERSHIP

■ ■ ■

In this chapter we examine the financing and development of "common interest communities" such as condominiums, cooperatives, and planned communities. In many ways these developments are similar to detached-house subdivisions, for they involve the sale of individual units to purchasers, usually for use as personal residences. In this respect they differ from the types of projects to be discussed in Chapter 11—shopping centers, office buildings, and the like—which are usually constructed with rental use rather than sales of units in mind. But common interest communities differ from conventional subdivisions in two important ways. The first difference might be termed "density," for these developments usually have a larger number of units packed into a smaller physical space than do subdivisions. They may take the form of town-house or row-house buildings, clustered but detached houses, or low-rise or high-rise multi-unit buildings. Often they will include some "common areas" (such as parks, pools, or other recreational facilities) which are open for all of the owners to use, perhaps as a way of compensating for the lack of large private yards associated with individual units. The second difference is the presence of some organized association of owners. This association may take one of several legal forms, and it may engage in numerous functions, but one of its purposes is nearly always the management of the common areas and the making and enforcement of rules and procedures for their use.

The growth in the development of common interest communities over the past four decades is staggering. According to the Community Associations Institute, in 1970, there were only 10,000 community associations in the United States, covering 701,000 residential units and housing a total of 2.1 million (about 1% of the population of the U.S.). By contrast, as of 2013, there were 26.3 million residential units in the United States governed by 328,500 community associations, housing a total of 65.7 million people. See Community Associations Institute Research Foundation, National and State Statistical Review for 2013, http://www.cairf.org/research/factbook/2013_statistical_review.pdf. As most modern residential real estate development now occurs within common interest communities, this trend is expected to continue for the foreseeable future. As a result, the modern real estate lawyer must have a firm grasp of the law governing the creation, financing, and governance of common interest communities.

This chapter begins with an introduction to the basic types of common interest developments—the condominium, the cooperative, and the planned community with a homeowners' association. This introduction will compare and contrast these forms of common interest developments, focusing upon the original legal framework upon which each developed while also highlighting recent law reform efforts to unify the law governing common interest development under the "common interest community" rubric. The chapter will then discuss a number of the practical and legal issues arising out of the creation, operation, and governance of common interest communities. As in the previous chapter on subdivisions, the reader is cautioned that we have intentionally omitted any detailed discussion of local public land-use controls, such as zoning and subdivision ordinances. These are of great importance in higher-density developments, but because of their complexity must be left for coverage in a separate course.

A. TYPES OF COMMON INTEREST OWNERSHIP

1. CONDOMINIUMS

The condominium is a legal format for "unit ownership"—that is, ownership of a specific portion of a larger parcel or structure. There is considerable interdependence among the unit owners in a condominium project, because they must usually be concerned with maintenance and management of "common areas" of the project. Although most condominiums are residential apartment buildings, it is possible to create an office building condominium (or even a campsite condominium in the woods!). Nevertheless, these materials will focus upon the housing condominium.

A condominium is created by the execution and recording of a "declaration." The declaration typically includes a legal description of the underlying land, a description of the improvements on the land (including both the housing units and any common facilities), and a statement identifying each unit owner's fraction of the rights and obligations associated with the common facilities. For each unit owner, this fraction establishes her ownership share of the common facilities of the condominium project, her obligation for the project's common expenses, and her proportionate voice and vote in managing the project. The declaration also commonly includes a set of covenants, conditions, and restrictions (often called CC&Rs) applicable to each unit. The CC&Rs establish both affirmative obligations binding on each unit owner (such as the obligation to pay assessments to fund the maintenance of common areas) and negative covenants and restrictions (such as limitations on the permitted use of units).

The specific content of a declaration is established by a particular state's condominium statute. The first and most important function of these statutes is to make it clear that one can own a fee simple absolute interest in a housing unit even though it cannot be described purely by reference to boundaries on the surface of the earth. For example, if one owns a unit on the 10th floor of a high rise building, that ownership is essentially of air space. Of course, the statutes (even the most rudimentary ones) go far beyond this. For example, condominium statutes generally provide that the unit owners will own the common areas personally as tenants in common. In a condominium, the common areas are not only specific land areas such as the swimming pools and tennis courts; the applicable statute may well provide that all parts of the buildings except the portions within the interior walls of the individual units are deemed common areas. Under this view, common areas would include the exterior walls, roof, lobbies and hallways, and perhaps even some plumbing, heating, and electrical equipment.

The Evolution of Condominium Acts. Section 234 of the National Housing Act, enacted in 1960, authorized the Federal Housing Administration (FHA) to insure mortgages on residential condominium units. Shortly thereafter, FHA drafted and promulgated a model state condominium statute based heavily on Puerto Rico's condominium statute. By 1968, all American states had adopted condominium statutes, and most of them were close copies of the FHA Model Act.

This "first generation" of condominium acts was both narrow in scope and very inflexible—and thus unsatisfactory in key respects for both developers and consumers. As development of a condominium proceeds, developers sometimes want to make changes to development plans, as dictated by marketing considerations. The first generation condominium acts, however, did not readily permit a developer to make such changes after recording the declaration. Likewise, during periods of economic difficulty, condominium projects under development may go into default, often to be taken over by the lender that has provided construction financing for the project. The first generation condominium acts did not adequately address the question of what happens to the developer's rights and obligations when a project is taken over by a successor such as the construction lender. Finally, first generation condominium acts were not "consumer friendly," and unsophisticated or uncounseled consumers often had difficulty adequately evaluating the nature of the rights they would obtain when purchasing a condominium unit.

These experiences led the Uniform Law Commission to draft the Uniform Condominium Act (UCA), first promulgated in 1977 and amended in 1980. The UCA, which became the template for the "second generation" of condominium acts, was heavily influenced by contemporaneous revision of the existing condominium acts in Virginia and Florida. The UCA incorporated the concept of the "flexible condominium," making it possible for the declaration to provide clearly for the addition or removal of real estate from a condominium and the creation of additional units. The UCA also provided detailed provisions regarding the voluntary and involuntary transfer of the developer's rights, the extent of the developer's ability to control the unit owners' association during development, and the operation and governance of the unit owners' association (including the association's ability to impose liens for unpaid assessments). In exchange for this flexibility and certainty to the developer and the owners' association, the UCA also mandated more substantial consumer protections, including (among many others) mandatory and more thorough consumer disclosures, a fifteen-day "cooling off" period in which a purchaser may cancel, statutory damages for failure to provide required disclosure, insurance requirements, and limitations upon the developer's ability to enter into contracts binding upon the unit owners' association following completion of the project. For a more complete discussion of the UCA's consumer protection provisions, see David A. Thomas, The New Uniform Condominium Act, 64 A.B.A.J. 1370 (1978).

Condominium states based upon the UCA have been enacted in Alabama, Arizona, Louisiana, Maine, Minnesota, Missouri, Nebraska, New Hampshire, New Mexico, North Carolina, Pennsylvania, Rhode Island, Texas, Virginia, and Washington. See http://www.law.cornell.edu/uniform/vol7.html#condo. For more detailed treatment of the UCA, see N. Walter Graff, Minnesota Uniform Condominium Act: The View of Developer's Counsel, 10 Wm. Mitchell L. Rev. 71 (1984); John B. Lundquist, Mixed Use Condominiums Under the Minnesota Uniform Condominium Act, 10 Wm. Mitchell L.Rev. 97 (1984); Kent H. Roberts, Uniform Condominium Act—New Flexibility for Developers, 40 J. Mo. Bar 177 (1984); William S. Ohlemeyer, Comment, The Uniform Condominium Act in Missouri, 49 Mo. L. Rev. 595 (1984).

After 1980, law reform organizations began working to integrate the law of condominiums with the laws governing other forms of common interest communities, including cooperatives and planned communities. This law reform effort has included both the Restatement (Third) of Property—Servitudes, approved by the American Law Institute in 2000, and the Uniform Common Interest Ownership Act (UCIOA), first promulgated by NCCUSL in 1982 and amended in 1994, 2008, and 2014. Both the Restatement of Servitudes and UCIOA are discussed further in Section A4 of this chapter.

2. COOPERATIVES

Consumer and agricultural cooperatives are familiar to many Americans, especially in rural areas. In these organizations persons join together as buyers or sellers, creating a group which will have greater power in the marketplace than any of its individual members. If profits result from the enterprise, they are distributed to the cooperators (or "members") on an equitable basis.

Housing cooperatives serve a similar purpose, typically in densely populated urban areas (such as New York and Chicago) where land scarcity makes the construction of detached homes impossible or cost-prohibitive. A cooperative association is organized (typically in a not-for-profit form of business organization), and the cooperators are shareholders in this organization, which acquires and holds title to an apartment building or complex of buildings (the "project"). Each member is also a tenant of a particular apartment, with the cooperative organization as landlord. The member's lease is sometimes called a "proprietary lease," indicating that the member is in a sense an owner.

The cooperative organization must pay directly the various costs associated with the purchase and operation of the project. Typically the largest single monthly outlay is the debt service (payments of principal and interest) on the mortgage, which covers the entire project. Other outlays of the cooperative organization include real estate taxes, maintenance and repairs, management and administrative expenses, insurance, and reserves for future replacements of items which may be expected to wear out over time. All of these charges are budgeted on a monthly basis and divided among the members in proportion to the shares of stock allocated to each apartment. Each member's share of these charges is payable by him as rent under the member's proprietary lease. However, the member may deduct the portion of those monthly payments attributable to mortgage interest and real estate taxes on the member's federal income tax return, provided that at least 80% of the gross income of the cooperative organization is derived from payments by tenant-shareholders. I.R.C. § 216.

There are certain hazards and limitations intrinsic in the nature of a housing cooperative. The presence of the blanket mortgage precludes the kind of flexible financing that would be possible if each apartment unit were considered a separate parcel of real estate. [Financing of individual cooperative units is discussed in more detail in Section B of this chapter.] Furthermore, the interdependence of the cooperative requires each member to place heavy reliance and trust on other members. If a member defaults on his monthly rent, the cooperative organization may dispossess the member through eviction and may foreclose on the member's ownership share of the organization. See, e.g., Village Green Mut. Homes,

Inc. v. Randolph, 361 Md. 179, 760 A.2d 716 (2000). An occasional default is not too troublesome. However, if several members default at about the same time, perhaps as a result of adverse economic conditions, the organization risks going into default on the blanket mortgage, thus jeopardizing the interests of those members who are entirely current in their payments. Nevertheless, there are significant reasons why a cooperative may be preferred over a condominium:

> Three of the strongest are the following: cooperative unit owners have a greater say in choosing their co-owners than do condominium unit owners; a cooperative corporation can raise money by borrowing against its assets, and usually at a good rate, whereas there is no convenient mechanism for condominium unit owners as a group to obtain funds for common purposes; and each cooperative unit owner, unlike his condominium counterpart in most instances, enjoys the extremely valuable benefit of limited liability that comes from operating in the corporate form. [Joel E. Miller, Congress Grants Co-op Limited and Uncertain Relief from General Utilities Repeal, 5 Tax Mgmt. Real Est.J. 15 (1989).]

Cooperative housing is quite popular in several areas of the United States. By far the largest concentration exists in New York City. Significant numbers of cooperatives also exist in Detroit, Minneapolis-St. Paul, and several other major cities, and occasionally rural housing cooperatives are found. The major concentrations of cooperative housing are principally a result of efforts by labor unions and nonprofit organizations, aided in New York by the state's Mitchell-Lama Act, which provides property tax abatement as well as low-interest loans for cooperative housing, and throughout the United States by Section 213 of the National Housing Act, which permits FHA to insure blanket mortgages on cooperatives. Only a small percentage of the new housing projects developed in the United States each year are cooperatives, and their importance has been eclipsed in the past few years by the burgeoning development of condominiums.

In 1981, the Uniform Law Commission promulgated the Model Real Estate Cooperative Act (MRECA). Although enacted in Virginia, MRECA's relevance was diminished by the subsequent promulgation of the Uniform Common Interest Ownership Act (UCIOA), which subsumes condominiums, cooperatives, and planned communities under the broader "common interest community" rubric.

NOTE

Condominium or cooperative? Legal form and unit value. To what extent should the form of common interest ownership affect the value of an owner's unit investment? In a recent empirical study of the New York City residential market, Michael Schill, Ioan Voicu and Jonathan Miller concluded that the typical New York City condominium unit was more valuable than a comparable cooperative unit. This "condominium premium" varied, depending upon the extent to which the cooperative owner was able to finance her purchase under the cooperative's rules and whether the cooperative was subject to a transfer fee covenant or "flip tax" (i.e., a fee payable to the cooperative association upon the approved resale of a cooperative unit). Where a cooperative apartment was subject to no financing restriction and no flip tax (the situation most comparable to the typical condominium unit), the condominium value premium was 13.4%. This premium decreased to 10.6% for cooperative units on which the unit owner could finance 60–79% of the purchase, and 8.8% for all cooperative units. However, for cooperatives in buildings that allow no financing by unit owners, the authors found no condominium premium at all; instead, in those situations, comparable condominium units were worth 25.4% less. What might explain these data?

 Armed with this result, we now turn to the puzzle that motivated our study—why do cooperative apartment buildings vastly outnumber condominium buildings in New York City, a pattern that is in direct contrast to what exists in other parts of the United States? Certainly, part of the answer is the fact that until the 1960s, the housing cooperative was the only legal form available for common-interest homeownership in the city. Nevertheless, with the advent of the condominium and the diffusion of knowledge and familiarity with the condominium form, why do cooperative apartment buildings persist in light of the sizable premium value that our results suggest is associated with condominiums? This concluding section will discuss three possible answers to this question: (1) social exclusivity, (2) monetized transaction costs, and (3) collective-decision-making costs.

 . . . [T]he existence of both cooperative and condominium buildings may be partly explained by the desire for social exclusivity. A landlord of a building catering to affluent tenants might seek to charge monopoly rents to tenants for the privilege of living in this type of unique environment. Collective ownership—through cooperative or condominium form—would provide a way to avoid this type of exploitation.

 Indeed, our results showing that cooperative owners in buildings that prohibit mortgage financing enjoy a price premium relative to condominiums provides some support for this thesis. A large proportion (77.3 percent) of the apartment sales in buildings with rules prohibiting financing were also in the top quartile of cooperative apartment values. This suggests that affluent New Yorkers may be using the no-financing restriction to maintain an affluent living environment and that the benefits of social exclusiveness themselves generate value for these purchasers. . . .

. . . [The social exclusivity thesis] does not explain why the vast majority of cooperative apartments that serve nonaffluent households continue to exist. One possible reason concerns the transaction, or "switching" costs of moving from one form of ownership to the other. Liquidation of the corporation and distribution to share owners of interests in the real property could lead to a taxable event for the corporation as well as for its shareholders. Each shareholder would be required to contribute to the satisfaction of the blanket mortgage loan, renegotiate the terms of his or her individual cooperative share mortgage, and have new financing documents prepared and recorded. The new condominium association would also probably need to take steps to arrange financing for owners whose credit may have deteriorated between the time they took out their share mortgages and the time of conversion or who cannot qualify for the additional debt needed to pay off their shares of the underlying mortgage. A variety of other costs would be entailed, including fees for real estate consultants and attorneys, closing costs, and recording taxes. [The authors estimated these costs to be $31,000 per unit, or roughly 67% of the expected "condominium premium."]

Relatively high monetary transaction costs are compounded by . . . the "costs of collective decision making." The law and economics literature suggests that there are many barriers of a strategic nature to bargaining to an efficient outcome (in our case, the conversion), especially when the number of bargainers is greater than two. Given that a conversion involves tens or hundreds of people, it is easy to imagine them failing to reach an efficient outcome, even if the potential gains are very high.

This collective-action problem is likely to be particularly severe in urban communities where residents are not homogenous. It is highly likely that not all cooperative owners have similar time horizons or financial characteristics. For example, the members of households on a fixed income who wish to remain as occupants might prefer not to pay the high transaction costs of conversion for a speculative gain that would be realized only on sale. In addition, some households with bad credit might find themselves in a situation in which they are unable to qualify for a condominium unit loan.

The problem of collective action is exacerbated by statutory and contractual supermajority requirements. For example, New York State law requires that the owners of at least two-thirds of the shares must approve a proposed dissolution, and the bylaws of many cooperative corporations have thresholds as high as 80 percent. . . .

In the end, despite the premium typically associated with condominium status, it is much too early to sound the death knell for the cooperative apartment, at least in New York. While it is likely that new apartment buildings will be built as condominiums to take advantage of the economic benefits of this legal form, problems of collective action combined with inertia and substantial transaction costs suggest that at least for the foreseeable future the housing cooperative will remain a dominant feature of our nation's largest city.*

Michael H. Schill, Ioan Voicu & Jonathan Miller, The Condominium Versus Cooperative Puzzle: An Empirical Analysis of Housing in New York City, 36 J. Leg. Stud. 275, 312–316 (2007).

3. PLANNED COMMUNITIES

The "planned community" melds the concept of subdivision (introduced in Chapter 9) with the concept of shared ownership of common facilities. The following materials discuss the evolution of the modern planned community, highlighting both its common law origins and the key structural differences between the planned community and condominiums or cooperatives.

MICHAEL L. UTZ, COMMON INTEREST OWNERSHIP IN PENNSYLVANIA: AN EXAMINATION OF STATUTORY REFORM AND IMPLICATIONS FOR PRACTITIONERS
37 Duquesne L. Rev. 465, 468–477 (1999)**

The planned community with homeowners' association is second only to the condominium in popularity as a model for common interest ownership. In many areas of the country, the planned community with a homeowners' association is quickly becoming synonymous with suburban residential development. Unfortunately, courts, commentators, the American Law Institute ("ALI"), and even the [Uniform Law Commission] have been inconsistent in the use of terms to describe this model. However, it is not terminology but the method of common interest ownership that distinguishes the planned community from the condominium and the cooperative.

Unlike the condominium form of ownership, owners of individual units in a planned community do not own an undivided interest in common areas. Also, unlike the cooperative, all of the real estate is not owned by an entity separate and apart from the individual unit owners.

---

*   Reprinted with the permission of The University of Chicago Press.
**   Reprinted with the permission of the Duquesne Law Review.

Instead, ownership of common areas is typically vested in an incorporated homeowners' association, and residents retain fee simple ownership in their individual units. It is this unique legal structure that gives rise to the growing popularity of the planned community. * * *

The importance of the planned community cannot be overstated. The Urban Land Institute ("ULI") is credited with first describing the prototypical planned community in its landmark publication, The Homes Association Handbook.[49] The ULI describes how the basic model of the planned community evolved, tracing its origin to early seventeenth-century England.[51] Samuel Ruggles introduced the concept to the United States in 1831, when he developed Gramercy Park in Manhattan for which he used a trust arrangement whereby legal title to the park was vested in a trustee for the benefit of the surrounding owners. At the same time, the property owners of Louisburg Square in Boston drafted and recorded a land agreement to provide for maintenance of the park area in the center of the Square, thus becoming the first homeowners' association in the United States.[53]

The first modern example of the typical suburban planned community to use covenants running with the land to enforce contractual arrangements between homeowners was Roland Park in Baltimore, which Edward H. Bouton developed in 1891. Another important development came with the development of Kensington in Great Neck, Long Island in 1909. This community helped establish the concept of automatic membership in a homeowners' association and concomitant assessments for maintenance of common areas, the obligation for which ran with the land. Kensington became the modern archetype of the planned community.

The planned community concept has proven exceptionally popular for many reasons. Homeowners overwhelmingly endorse the concept of shared ownership and association management of common areas.[58] Volunteer members who serve on boards of directors of homeowners' and

---

[49] Urban Land Institute, The Homes Association Handbook, Technical Bulletin 50 (1964) [hereinafter Homes Association Handbook].

[51] The ULI states "[the planned community] originated . . . when the Earl of Leicester built his London townhouse and laid out Leicester Square in front of it. By 1700 the Square was surrounded by buildings and, by 1743, the property owners had employed a legal device to assure the exclusive use and maintenance of this park." Homes Association Handbook, at 39.

[53] Id. Other early examples of this type of arrangement include Ocean Grove (New Jersey); Squirrel Island (Maine); and Delano Park (Maine). Id.

[58] A recent survey conducted by the Research Foundation of the Community Associations Institute indicated that homeowners were satisfied with community association home ownership (common interest ownership coupled with a condominium association or homeowners' association). When asked the question whether "[homeowners] think that community association homeownership [sic] is a satisfactory housing choice," thirty percent agreed completely, fifty-two percent mostly agreed, and seven percent slightly agreed. * * *

condominium associations[59] also express satisfaction with the arrangement.[60] One of the reasons for the success of the planned community concept may be the feeling of community or belonging that this type of arrangement engenders. Although these concepts may be somewhat nebulous and certainly have different degrees of importance and meaning to different individuals, there is, nevertheless, empirical support for this proposition.[61]

This is not to suggest, however, that shared ownership coupled with community association management is an Edenic solution. Such problems as apathy, misunderstanding or deliberate disregard of covenants or community rules, failure to pay association fees, and interpersonal conflict among homeowners are all problems that associations face.[62] Notwithstanding these inherent shortcomings, the planned community managed by a homeowners' association continues to enjoy an unprecedented level of popularity and growth. The innate flexibility of this arrangement may have contributed to its growing importance. Developers, home purchasers, city planners, and the zoning and land use legal community have long sought solutions that provide a greater degree of flexibility. * * *

Planned Communities and the Common Law

Although the condominium model of common interest ownership is largely a product of statutory law, * * * it was the common law that gave recognition to the planned community and controlled its operation and function. * * *

Under the common law, the developer created a common interest community by filing [a set of covenants, conditions and restrictions (CC & R's)].[68] Once the developer established the common interest community,

---

[59] Both the condominium model and the planned community model of common interest ownership typically rely on residents voluntarily serving on a board of directors. In smaller communities, this board of directors assumes management functions, while in larger communities the board of directors may employ a professional management company.

[60] The Community Associations Institute asked board members whether "[s]erving on an association board of directors has been a good experience." Thirty-five of the respondents indicated that they completely agreed, forty-eight percent mostly agreed, and seven percent slightly agreed. * * *

[61] Id. When asked "[h]ow would you describe the level of community feeling in your development?" fifty-eight percent of residents indicated that their community was "friendly," and eight percent believed their community was "neighborly." * * *

[62] Id. Eighty percent of residents indicated that apathy or lack of interest was a problem, sixty-nine percent indicated that not understanding rules was a problem, thirty-four percent indicated that fiduciary irresponsibility was a problem, and thirty-two percent indicated that interpersonal conflict was a problem. * * *

[68] The ALI defines declaration as "the recorded document or documents containing the servitudes that create and govern the common interest community." Restatement (Third) of the Law of Property: Servitudes § 6.2(5) (Tentative Draft No. 7, 1998). A servitude is "[a] charge or burden resting upon one estate for the benefit or advantage of another." Black's Law Dictionary 1370 (6th ed. 1990). Most declarations are called condominium declarations if the common

he or she typically provided for an association to manage the common property; however, if the [CC & R's] failed to establish the association, a majority of the lot or unit owners, the courts, or the local government had the ability to form an association to manage such common property. In addition to specific powers, the common law vested the common interest community with all powers reasonably necessary to carry out the management and enforcement of the servitude framework established by the declaration. Specific powers available to the association included the power to levy assessments, charge fees, and borrow money; manage, acquire, and improve common property; make rules and regulations for protection of lot or unit owners; and to enforce these provisions through the courts or via the imposition of fines, penalties, late fees, and withdrawal of privileges. The board did not, however, have the power to impose architectural restrictions either on the home itself or on landscaping. * * *

The common law also evolved to define certain duties owed by the common interest community to its members. In addition to the duties expressly stated in the governing documents, the common law imposed standards quite similar to those imposed on boards of directors under the laws pertaining to corporations. The association was required to meet an ordinary care standard, treat its members fairly, use its discretionary powers in a reasonable manner, and disclose to members information regarding association affairs. In any suit against the association, the member had the burden of proving both a breach of duty on the part of the association and actual or potential damage to the interests of the community. The common law placed similar duties on the individual members of the board of directors. Any breach of the foregoing duties usually did not subject the individual owners to joint and several liability; rather liability was limited to the individual owners [sic] proportionate share of association expenses.

The common law also addressed the issue of governance of common interest communities and required that it be a representative form of government with a board of directors entitled to exercise the powers given to the association in the governing documents or via judicial decision. Usually, each lot or unit owner was entitled to one vote absent an express provision to the contrary. In addition, the law gave members the right to attend board meetings and present their opinions on issues concerning the community.

Courts were also called upon to fashion a body of law concerning the relationship between the developer and the association. Typically, at the beginning of the development process, the developer formed and retained

---

interest community uses the condominium model or declaration of covenants, conditions, and restrictions ("CC & Rs") if the common interest model is the planned community.

control over the association. At some point in the process, the developer ceded control to a duly elected board of directors. The common law imposed on the developer the duty to create the association and to turn over control of association affairs to the board of directors after a time sufficient to protect the interests of the developer. Once this formal change of control had taken place, the association gained the ability to treat as voidable many self-dealing contracts with the developer. Before the transfer of control, the developer owed certain duties to the association including the duties to use (1) reasonable care in managing common property, (2) ensure that association finances were handled responsibly, (3) enforce the servitude regime, including payment of assessments, and (4) to disclose certain matters to the association. The developer could not modify the [CC & R's] if such a modification would have a material effect on the character of the development or place an unfair burden on existing owners unless the declaration specifically put the unit or lot owners on notice that the developer retained such an ability to modify.

NOTES

1. *The Uniform Planned Community Act.* As market conditions created additional demand for planned communities, developers and law reformers sought to provide a more solid statutory foundation for the development of planned communities. In 1980, the Uniform Law Commission (ULC) promulgated the Uniform Planned Community Act (UPCA):

> UPCA not only codified the law of homeowner associations but also provided statutory enablement for a common-interest housing regime (defined in UPCA as a "planned community") in which title to all common areas (including hallways and other interior spaces in a high-rise building) could be held in the name of the governing association instead of being fragmented among its members.

Norman Geis, Beyond the Condominium: The Uniform Common-Interest Ownership Act, 17 Real Prop. Prob. & Trust J. 757, 758 (1982). As Geis noted, UPCA thus addressed a significant flaw in the early-generation condominium legislation, which had assumed that a condominium regime had to be operated by the unit owners acting collectively as an unincorporated association. Id.

UPCA has been enacted in North Carolina and Pennsylvania. However, as discussed in the next section, coverage of planned communities is now subsumed within the Uniform Common Interest Ownership Act, promulgated by the ULC in 1982 and subsequently amended in 1994, 2008, and 2014.

2. *Distinguishing planned communities and planned unit developments (PUDs).* It can be easy to confuse the term "planned community" with the "planned unit development" (or PUD). The planned community arises and is governed by virtue of private law; by contrast, PUD

is a concept of zoning law. Most zoning schemes are based upon segregation of residential, commercial, and industrial uses, with the idea that commercial development cannot take place within a residential zone. However, a zoning ordinance can incorporate PUDs, in which a developer proposes a self-contained community within a particular zone. Zoning approval for a PUD permits a developer to build "mixed-use" developments that feature a combination of both high-and low-density residential and commercial development. With increasing concern that traditional zoning has exacerbated "urban sprawl," modern planners have manifested a renewed enthusiasm for PUDs as a means for municipalities to achieve "smart growth." For further background on PUDs, see Daniel R. Mandelker, Legislation for Planned Unit Developments and Master-Planned Communities, 40 Urb. Law. 419 (2008).

A PUD could (and often does) include one or more planned communities. For example, a PUD might include several different subdivisions of detached single-family homes (each governed by a separate homeowners' association and thus each a separate planned community), as well as several different condominium projects (each governed by a separate unit owners' association).

4. MODERN LAW REFORM: SYNTHESIZING COMMON INTEREST OWNERSHIP

a.   *The Uniform Common Interest Ownership Act.* Because of the structural differences in the legal forms of condominiums, cooperatives, and planned communities, early-generation common interest ownership statutes tended to be form-specific. As discussed in the previous sections, the Uniform Law Commission (ULC) originally promulgated separate uniform acts for each type of development—the Uniform Condominium Act (UCA) (1977, amended in 1980), the Uniform Planned Community Act (UPCA) (1980), and the Model Real Estate Cooperative Act (MRECA) (1981). In preparing these separate acts, however, the drafters were cognizant of the fact that there existed a coherent and consistent set of rights and obligations that were shared by all common interest developments, regardless of their organizational form. In 1982, this led the ULC to draft and promulgate the Uniform Common Interest Ownership Act (UCIOA), which was "based on the broad premise that all common-interest housing regimes have the same essential characteristics, and on the corollary notion that the various forms are differentiated from each other only by the scheme of ownership of the common elements and the units." Norman Geis, Beyond the Condominium: The Uniform Common-Interest Ownership Act, 17 Real Prop. Prob. & Trust J. 757, 759 (1982).

UCIOA incorporated the existing substantive provisions of its three predecessors, while creating the new defined term "common-interest community" which included the condominium, the cooperative, and the planned community:

> The defined term, common-interest community, expresses the central legal concept in UCIOA. The definition of this term provides a functional description of all regimes which are subject to the act and thereby establishes the outer reaches of the jurisdiction of the act. The wording of this key definition is deceptively simple:

>> "Common-Interest Community" means real estate with respect to which any person, by virtue of his ownership of a unit, is obligated to pay for real estate taxes, insurance premiums, maintenance or improvement of other real estate described in a declaration.

> The important components of this definition are: (1) there must exist a "unit" within the common-interest community (consisting of a physical portion of the real estate "designated for separate ownership or occupancy") whose owner must make the designated payments with respect to "other real estate described in a declaration;" and (2) those payments must be mandatory and not optional. These threshold requirements thus exclude from UCIOA any development where there is no division of the property into "units" and "other real estate" and any such development organized on a voluntary rather than compulsory membership basis. . . .

> Derived from the general definition of common-interest community are three subsidiary definitions which articulate the three different species into which all common-interest communities are divided: the "condominium," the "cooperative" and the "planned community." Each of these forms is differentiated from the other two by the manner in which title to the units and common elements comprising the real estate within the regime is divided between the managing association and its members.

> Thus, "condominium" is defined as a common-interest community in which "portions of the real estate are designated for separate ownership and the remainder of the real estate is designated for common ownership solely by the owners of those portions." This definition is subject to the further proviso that "a common-interest community is not a condominium unless the undivided interest in the common elements are vested in the unit owners."

> A "cooperative" is defined as a common-interest community in which "the real estate is owned by an association, each of

whose members is entitled by virtue of his ownership interest in the association to exclusive possession of a unit." This definition is supplemented by a special refinement in the meaning of the term "unit" when that term is applied to a cooperative. Since the cooperative association holds legal title to both the units and common elements, it would be a misnomer to characterize each member as a "unit owner" of the cooperative real estate. Therefore, UCIOA provides that, in certain contexts, references to a cooperative "unit" will denote the legal interest in that unit rather than the parcel of real estate within the unit boundaries. This legal interest consists of the member's "right to possession of a unit under a proprietary lease coupled with the allocated interests of that unit." For this purpose, "allocated interests" is a defined term which means "the common expense liability and the ownership interest and votes in the association."

These interlocking definitions neatly and precisely describe the trilateral relationship between the members of a cooperative, the cooperative association, and the cooperative real estate. At the same time they allow all the provisions of UCIOA derived from UCA and UPCA relating to the ownership, conveyance and encumbrance of condominium and planned community units, to apply with equal force to cooperative units.

All other common-interest communities (i.e., those which do not fall within the statutory definitions of condominium or cooperative) are denominated "planned communities." Thus, "planned community" is a residual term which sweeps into the jurisdiction of UCIOA any regime falling within the generic definition of common-interest community which is neither a condominium nor a cooperative. Examples include a homeowner association regime which owns and administers the roads or recreational facilities in a planned unit development or cluster subdivision project, a "master association" which administers the inter-condominium facilities in a multi-condominium project, and any other form of multi-ownership development (containing "units" and "other real estate") administered by a mandatory-membership association that has the right to assess its members.*

Geis, 17 Real Prop. Prob. & Trust J. at 759–761. As Geis noted, this eliminated the need for UCIOA to repeat the provisions that were identical in its three predecessor acts, and provided states with flexibility in enactment. States without any common interest legislation could simply enact UCIOA, while the numerous states that had already

---

adopted the UCA could transform their existing statute into UCIOA through amendments to key definitions and incorporation of selected provisions unique to cooperatives and planned communities.

UCIOA has been modestly successful in gaining adoptions. It has been enacted (with some modifications) in Alaska, Colorado, Connecticut, Minnesota, Nevada, Vermont, and West Virginia. See LII: Uniform Business and Financial Laws Locator, http://www.law.cornell.edu/uniform/vol7.html#comin. Although California did not adopt UCIOA, the Davis-Stirling Common Interest Development Act, enacted in 1985, is similar in purpose and scope. See West's Ann. Cal. Civ. Code §§ 4000–6150.

In 1994, the ULC substantially amended UCIOA, requiring additional consumer disclosures to purchasers, providing for greater developer flexibility as to future expansion or modification of the development, and giving greater power to owners associations in dealing with unruly and disruptive owners and their tenants. The ULC amended UCIOA again in 2008, most particularly incorporating a "homeowner bill of rights" (the Uniform Common Interest Owners Bill of Rights Act), which was prompted by concerns that developers or others in control of the decision-making apparatus of an association might abuse or take advantage of the rights of individual unit owners. The most recent amendments occurred in 2014, and focused solely upon issues associated with the priority of the association's lien for common expense assessments (to which we return in Section D of this chapter).

b. *The Restatement (Third) of Property—Servitudes.* As you should recall from your Property course, the laws of easements and covenants (or promissory servitudes) arose as two distinct bodies of law. As a result, while easements and covenants serve similar purposes—facilitating and enhancing land use by tying rights and duties to ownership of land—laws governing easements and covenants developed independently and in ways that were not internally consistent. For example, while the holder of an easement in gross (such as a utility service easement) could continue to enforce that easement following a transfer of the servient estate, the common law held that a person holding the benefit of a covenant in gross could not do so following a transfer of the burdened land. Another example involves the "privity" requirement, which the common law applied to efforts to enforce covenants against successors at law (in actions for damages), but did not apply in cases involving the enforcement of easements. By way of review, consider two neighboring landowners, Smith and Jones, who previously entered an agreement to limit their respective uses to residential purposes only. Further, assume that Jones later sold his land to Davis, who opened a bar on the land. Under the common law of covenants, Smith could not have recovered damages against Davis for breaching the agreement—even if the agreement had explicitly stated that it bound the successors of Smith and Jones—because no horizontal privity had existed between Smith and Jones at the time the easement was created. By contrast, if Jones had granted Smith an easement to cross Jones's parcel, the lack of horizontal privity between Jones and Smith would not have prevented Smith from crossing the land following its transfer from Jones to Davis.

Over the last half-century, courts and commentators began to question whether the common law rules of easements and covenants—as traditionally articulated in the original Restatement of Property in 1944—were ideally suited to modern land transfer and development patterns. These concerns became increasingly significant as more and more development began to occur in common interest developments, which (as discussed in the previous section) rely substantially upon the use of covenants as a means of land use control. These concerns ultimately led the ALI to undertake a new restatement of the law of easements and covenants. This effort, which occurred roughly contemporaneously with ULC's promulgation and later amendment of UCIOA, culminated in 2000 with the approval of the Restatement (Third) of Property—Servitudes.

The Restatement of Servitudes overtly attempts to modernize the law of easements and covenants in an integrated and coherent fashion under the rubric of "servitudes":

> [The Restatement's goal is] to present[ ] servitudes law as an integrated body of doctrine encompassing the rules applicable to profits, easements, and covenants. The draft reflects the modern analytical perception that all the servitude devices are functionally similar, and that for the most part they are, or should be, governed by the same rules. Only in the relatively few instances where there are real differences among the servitude devices are different rules justifiable. Treating all the servitude devices together, rather than dividing the subject into a division for each, not only avoids substantial repetition of identical rules, but also promotes thoughtful consideration of the reasons why different rules may be required. . . .

Restatement (Third) of Property—Servitudes, Tent. Draft No. 1 (April 5, 1989). Since its enactment, the new Restatement has proven increasingly influential in sparking substantial academic and practical commentary about the laws of easements and covenants.

In restating the laws governing owners associations, the Restatement takes an approach that is analytically similar to UCIOA, adopting the concept of the "common-interest community":

> A "common-interest community" is a real-estate development or neighborhood in which individually owned lots or

units are burdened by a servitude that imposes an obligation that cannot be avoided by nonuse or withdrawal

> (1) to pay for the use of, or contribute to the maintenance of, property held or enjoyed in common by the individual owners, or

> (2) to pay dues or assessments to an association that provides services or facilities to the common property or to the individually owned property, or that enforces other servitudes burdening the property in the development or neighborhood. [Restatement (Third) of Property—Servitudes § 6.2(1) (2000).]

Like the comparable definition in UCIOA, this definition is inclusive of all of the traditional forms of common interest ownership. The Restatement also elaborates upon the powers and duties of a common-interest community as well as the relationship between the developer and the community (albeit in slightly less detail than UCIOA). In jurisdictions that have not adopted UCIOA, UCA, or some comparably detailed common interest ownership statute, the Restatement is likely to have increasing significance as a source for resolving disputes arising within common interest communities.

B. FINANCING OF PROJECTS AND UNITS*

There is no special novelty in the financing of planned developments; in general, they are treated like other subdivisions, and both construction and permanent loans are made on them. The construction lender will often be willing to advance sufficient funds to cover most or all of the cost of the recreational facilities and other common area improvements as well as the construction of the units themselves.

While the same general types of financing arrangements are made for condominiums, lenders tend to be somewhat more cautious than with conventional subdivisions. Construction lenders virtually always require that a permanent loan commitment be obtained before construction commences. Many permanent lenders attempt to protect themselves against market failures by stipulating that no permanent loans will be made unless and until some specified portion of the units have been "pre-sold"—that is, the developer has signed agreements with buyers for them. Because of the pre-sale requirement, a condominium developer may launch its sales program at a very early stage, possibly even before construction begins.

With construction lending on condominiums, market surveys and other evidences of salability are of critical importance. The construction

---

* This material is derived from 2 Grant S. Nelson, Dale A. Whitman, Ann M. Burkhart & R. Wilson Freyermuth, Real Estate Finance Law §§ 13.5 and 13.6 (6th ed. Practitioners' Series 2014), reprinted with permission of Thomson Reuters.

and permanent lenders will need to be satisfied with the documentation, including the declaration, bylaws, and any leases or other supporting instruments; reviewing these papers is commonly a rather massive task. Often the same institution will make both the construction and permanent loans, an arrangement which simplifies the review process. Under many statutes the condominium declaration can be recorded even before construction begins, but most construction lenders will not permit its filing until construction is nearly completed or at least until a high percentage of units has been sold. In this way, if sales are slow, the lender may require the developer to change the project to rental use, at which point the developer will not file a declaration of condominium status and will refund the deposits of the early unit buyers. The UCA compels delayed filing. UCA § 2–101 (1980) (declaration may not be recorded until all structural components and mechanical systems are substantially completed).

Permanent Financing of Condominium Units

Institutional lenders generally may make permanent mortgage loans on condominium units on the same terms as loans on detached houses or other buildings. However, the permanent lender on a condominium unit must consider many factors which are unimportant or nonexistent in the financing of subdivision houses. Most of these factors are related to the importance of the owners association and the common areas to the success (and thus the future security value) of the project. While the discussion which follows concentrates on the permanent lender's concerns, construction lenders must also consider these factors, because construction lenders may be forced into a permanent lending role if the developer defaults on the construction loan or the permanent lender refuses to honor its loan commitment. Indeed, unit purchasers themselves should also consider these factors, although unit purchasers often lack the sophistication to realize the potential dangers.

Certain precautions are particularly significant to the permanent lender if it finances the sale of some units while other units or the common areas are still under construction or remain in the developer's hands. Obviously, the unit being financed should itself be completed. To ensure that the project will be successfully marketed as a condominium, many permanent lenders impose a "pre-sale requirement;" that is, they will refuse to close any loans until the developer has entered into binding sale contracts for some fixed percentage of the units. The permanent lender will also be legitimately concerned with the developer's financial ability to complete the project, and may wish to verify that sufficient funds remain in the construction loan account for this purpose.

The payment of assessments to the association for unsold units can also pose a problem. Many statutes make no distinction between sold and unsold units, and require that assessments be collected uniformly from all.[1] This approach seems unreasonable from the developer's viewpoint, because unoccupied units obviously contribute little or nothing to certain variable costs of the association's operations; for example, they supply no users for the swimming pool, tennis courts, or equestrian trails. However, many fixed costs are independent of the number of users. A fair resolution of this problem may require a somewhat smaller assessment for units still owned by the developer than for occupied units. While a two-level assessment system is not permitted under many statutes, the same result may be achieved if the developer pays a full assessment but is entitled to reimbursement of a portion from the other owners under a separate contract. Alternatively, the developer might pay the full assessment amounts and attempt to recover the outlays through higher sale prices for the later-sold units. In any event, the permanent lender should ascertain that the developer is obligated to pay a fair share of the costs of operating the association during the marketing period and has the financial strength to do so; a default might result in deteriorating physical facilities or a financially weakened or even insolvent association. The lender may even require a cash deposit or letter of credit from the developer to secure these payments.

The permanent lender must also be concerned with the developer's attempts to retain control over the association until most of the units have been sold. Developers often create two classes of stock, attached to unsold and sold units respectively, with the former having a greater voting power. For example, if the first class has three votes per share and the second only one vote per share, the developer can maintain effective control until the project is three-fourths sold. This degree of retention of control is probably reasonable to protect the developer against the enactment of rules or procedures that might make the project unattractive to some buyers and thus impair the developer's marketing program.[2] The permanent mortgagee, however, may refuse to lend if the period of developer control will extend past some given percentage of units transferred, and may also insist on the fixing of an outside date by which control must pass to the unit owners irrespective of the number of sales.

Virtually every important aspect of the association's ongoing functions concerns the permanent lender, because operational inadequacies may diminish the security value of the units. The lender will want a satisfactory answer to the following questions: Is membership in the association automatic? Has a lien for unpaid assessments been

---

[1] UCA § 3–115 requires that once any units have been assessed, all units (including those still owned by the developer) must be assessed under the same formula. Until that time, however, the developer is free to pay all common area expenses.

[2] A few statutes expressly limit the period of developer control; see, e.g., UCA § 3–103; West's Fla.Stat.Ann. §§ 718.301 (condominiums), 719.301 (cooperatives).

created by proper language in the declaration or master deed? Has the association established a reasonable budget, supported by adequate assessment amounts? Is the assessment delinquency rate reasonably low? Has the association established adequate reserves for repairs and replacements, with provision that they not be used except for specified items? Has the association hired a competent management firm (if the project is large enough to justify it)? Is the project subject to unreasonable management contracts or recreational facility leases? Is there provision for an independent annual audit of the association's books? Has the association arranged adequate blanket insurance for the common areas and exteriors of units, with provision for increased coverage to match inflation?

Many permanent lenders insist on certain types of protection in the condominium documentation. For example, the lender may want: notice from the association of default in assessments by any of its mortgagors; exemption (if the lender becomes the owner of a unit through foreclosure) from the usual clause giving the association a right of first refusal or other right to control the subsequent transfer of the unit, and from any restriction on leasing of units; notice of cancellation of any insurance policies on the project; the right to examine the association's books at reasonable times; notice of association meetings and the right to attend; notice of any substantial loss or damage to common areas; and the right to vote on, or even to veto, such major policy decisions as the hiring or firing of a management firm, amendments to the declaration or bylaws, expansion or contraction of the project, or use of hazard insurance proceeds other than for repairs.

Finally, the lender will often revise its usual mortgage and note forms to add special provisions relating to condominiums. These revisions will usually include covenants by the mortgagor to pay association assessments when due, to notify the lender of any delinquency notices received from the association, and to abide by all provisions of the condominium's declaration, bylaws, and rules. The documents may require that the mortgagor pay assessments to an escrow or impound account. The mortgagor may also be required to covenant not to vote in favor of major policy changes in the project without the mortgagee's consent. Failure of the association to maintain adequate insurance coverage may be made a condition of default, and the lender may reserve the right to pay delinquent assessments and to charge them against the mortgagor's loan balance.

Authority of Lenders, Insurers, and Investors

There is little controversy concerning the power of lenders to make permanent mortgage loans on condominium units. Both federally-chartered and state-chartered institutions are generally permitted to treat them as the equivalent of single-family houses, although the lending powers of state-chartered institutions are a matter of state law and some variations exist.

The Federal Housing Administration (FHA) insures permanent mortgages on condominium units under the same general terms and conditions as mortgages on detached houses.

The Department of Veterans Affairs (VA) was first given authority to guarantee loans on condominium units in 1970, but could do so only when at least one unit in the project had been insured by FHA. In 1975 this statutory limitation was dropped, and the VA now guarantees such loans regardless of prior FHA involvement.[3] VA imposes a number of requirements to protect its interests, including a seventy percent presale requirement (which may be reduced in special circumstances)[4] and limitations on reservations of rights by developers (such as the retention of a veto over the association after unit owners obtain majority control).[5] In addition, VA regards projects as unacceptable if they prohibit leasing of units, or impose a right of first refusal upon resale.[6] As with FHA, the terms of the VA loan guarantee are identical to those on detached houses.

Both Fannie Mae and Freddie Mac purchase permanent mortgage loans on condominium units. The two agencies have similar, but not identical, requirements; they are too numerous and complex to be set out in detail here, but generally deal with the issues and concerns discussed earlier in this section. The precise requirements depend on the nature of the project: primary residence, second home, or investor (rental) use. Among the matters covered by Fannie Mae and Freddie Mac rules are the following: the completion of common area improvements; the adequacy of reserves for repairs and replacements; the percentage of occupancy by year-round residents; the percentage of units pre-sold; the existence of reasonable provisions for transfer of control of the association from the developer to the residents; freedom for mortgagees from any rights of the association to restrict sales of units; and a power in the association to terminate management contracts by notice. This list is merely illustrative, and Fannie Mae and Freddie Mac consider many other matters as well.

Permanent Financing of Cooperative Units

Traditionally the only permanent financing encumbering a cooperative project was its blanket mortgage. In most respects lenders

---

[3]   Veterans Housing Act of 1974, Pub.L. No. 93–569, § 3, 88 Stat. 1863 (presently codified at 38 U.S.C.A. §§ 3710–3714; statutory authorization for the guaranty of loans on condominium units appears at 38 U.S.C.A. § 3710(a)(6)).

[4]   38 C.F.R. § 36.4365(c).

[5]   38 C.F.R. § 36.4363(a).

[6]   38 C.F.R. § 36.4362(c)(6) (leasing restrictions). The disapproval of rights of first refusal applies only to projects established after December 1, 1976; see 38 C.F.R. § 36.4362(c)(5).

have viewed blanket mortgages as similar to loans on rental apartment buildings, although they have been concerned to some extent with the governance, internal procedures, and financial stability of cooperative corporations. Permanent blanket mortgages (as well as construction loans) on cooperative projects can be insured by FHA under section 213 of the National Housing Act.[7] Loan-to-value ratios may be as high as ninety-eight percent, a feature that makes section 213 more attractive than conventional loans, which are generally limited to eighty percent of value. While the time and complexity of FHA processing under section 213 reduce its usefulness, the program was for a time very active in those jurisdictions in which cooperatives are popular. FHA also insures cooperative blanket mortgages under National Housing Act sections 221(d)(3) and 221(d)(4), with 100 percent of replacement cost available under the d(3) program and 90% under d(4). Conventional blanket loans on co-ops are also widely available.

Beginning with the New York statute enacted in 1971,[8] many states have authorized institutional lenders to make loans, often called "share loans," on the security of individual cooperative units.[9] Prior to this development, lack of institutional financing was a major impediment to the financial success of cooperatives. Purchasers of units were obliged to pay cash, obtain personal loans from external sources, or negotiate installment contracts or promissory notes with unit sellers to cover the difference between the selling price of the unit and the unit's pro rata portion of the blanket mortgage.

Institutional financing of individual co-op units was given further impetus by section 4(b) of the Emergency Home Purchase Act of 1974, which added a new subsection (n) to section 203 of the National Housing Act, authorizing FHA to insure individual unit loans.[10] Under FHA's regulations, the loan must be secured by a first lien on the corporate stock certificate and the "occupancy certificate" or proprietary lease. The loan maturity is limited to thirty years, the remaining term of the blanket mortgage, or 75% of the remaining economic life of the building

---

[7]   12 U.S.C.A. § 1715e.

[8]   N.Y. McKinney's Bank. Law §§ 103(5) (banks), 235(8–a) (savings banks), 380(2–a) (savings and loan associations). These statutes have undergone a series of liberalizing amendments since their enactment in 1981. They now permit maturities and loan-to-value ratios as generous as on loans made to owner-occupants of single-family homes. See generally Charles A. Goldstein, Institutional Purchase Money Financing of Cooperative Apartments, 46 St. John's L.Rev. 632 (1972).

[9]   See, e.g., West's Ann. Cal. Fin. Code § 1494; Mass. Gen. Laws Ann. ch. 157B, § 13; Minn. Stat. Ann. § 47.20, subd. 3; N.J. Stat. Ann. § 17:2–6(d).

[10]   12 U.S.C.A. § 1709(n). See 24 C.F.R. § 203.43c(f). Initially, FHA could insure unit loans only in buildings that were subject to blanket mortgages insured by FHA under section 213, but this limitation was removed by § 419 of the Housing and Urban-Rural Recovery Act of 1983, Pub.L. No. 98–181, with respect to projects completed for more than one year. See 49 Fed.Reg. 40188 (Oct. 15, 1984).

improvements, whichever is less.[11] The FHA regulations recognize that a unit purchaser is always taking, in effect, subject to the blanket mortgage; thus, a lien on the unit is economically analogous to a second mortgage. The regulations limit the share loan to no more than the normal FHA amount, less the unit's pro-rata share of the blanket mortgage.[12]

Several of the other major federal agencies involved in housing have followed FHA's example and included cooperative share loans in their programs. The Office of Comptroller of the Currency authorizes federally-chartered savings and loan associations to make share loans on the same basis as loans on detached housing.[13] The Veterans Administration authorizes share loans under its loan guaranty program, although it reserves the right to make project-by-project determinations of acceptability, rather than issuing detailed regulations specifying what loans will be approved.[14] Fannie Mae has a program for purchasing share loans originated by local lending institutions.[15] In the aggregate, these changes represent a vast increase in institutional borrowing opportunities over those available before the 1970s.

Creating and Foreclosing Share Loan Security Interests

Despite the great expansion in institutional lending on cooperative apartments, there is still confusion as to the proper method for a lender to acquire, perfect, and foreclose on a security interest in the stock and proprietary lease that represent ownership of a co-op unit.[16] The problem stems from the fact that the cooperator holds two inseparable rights—a share of stock, which seems undeniably personal property, and a leasehold which may be viewed either as realty or personalty.[17] This dichotomy has proven troublesome in a variety of contexts: whether the federal securities laws govern cooperative apartment sales,[18] whether the usual rights and duties associated with landlord-tenant law apply,[19] and

---

[11]　24 C.F.R. § 203.43c(h)(4).

[12]　See 24 C.F.R. § 203.43c(g).

[13]　12 C.F.R. § 560.30.

[14]　See 38 C.F.R. § 36.4346.

[15]　See Fannie Mae Selling Guide, B4–2.3–04: Loan Eligibility for Co-op Share Loans, available at https://www.fanniemae.com/content/guide/selling/b4/2.3/04.html#Co-op.20Share.20 Loan.20Eligibility.20Requirements.

[16]　For an excellent review of New York law on these issues, see Robert E. Parella, Real Property, 1998–99 Survey of New York Law, 50 Syr. L. Rev. 863 (2000).

[17]　The leasehold estate was traditionally regarded as a "chattel real," a species of personal property; see William B. Stoebuck & Dale A. Whitman, Property § 6.11 (3d ed. 2000).

[18]　They do not; see United Housing Foundation, Inc. v. Forman, 421 U.S. 837, 95 S.Ct. 2051, 44 L.Ed.2d 621 (1975), rehearing denied, 423 U.S. 884, 96 S.Ct. 157, 46 L.Ed.2d 115 (1975).

[19]　Compare Linden Hill No. 1 Cooperative Corp. v. Kleiner, 124 Misc.2d 1001, 478 N.Y.S.2d 519 (1984) (statute protecting tenant ownership of pets applies to cooperatives) and Suarez v. Rivercross Tenants' Corp., 107 Misc.2d 135, 438 N.Y.S.2d 164 (1981) (implied warranty of habitability for residential tenants applies to cooperatives) with Earl W. Jimerson Hous. Co. v.

whether real estate or personal property concepts govern sales contracts[20] and distribution of decedents' estates.[21]

On the specific problem of perfection of a security interest in a cooperative apartment, the case law is helpful but not fully satisfactory. The New York courts approached the question by drawing an analogy to the cases that involve enforcement of sales contracts on cooperative apartments; those cases take the position that the principal rights of the cooperative tenant stem from the ownership of shares, and thus that the UCC controls. This suggests that the UCC should govern issues relating to security interests as well. The New York Court of Appeals adopted this view in 1977 in State Tax Commission v. Shor.[22] It held that, because the cooperative apartment was not realty, a creditor who obtained a judgment against an apartment owner would not thereby acquire an automatic lien on the apartment. In dictum, the *Shor* court asserted that a lender could perfect a security interest in the apartment merely by taking possession of the shares and the lease, in a manner analogous of the taking of a pledge of chattel paper or a promissory note. The share of stock was viewed as the primary indicium of ownership, with the lease being merely ancillary. Based upon the language of Article 9 in effect at the time of the case, the court concluded that the share certificate was an "instrument," that perfection of a security interest in the share certificate could be accomplished by possession, and that no filing of a financing statement would be necessary. Subsequent New York state and federal court decisions confirmed this view.[23]

Butler, 97 Misc.2d 563, 412 N.Y.S.2d 560 (1978) (summary possession procedure, normally applicable to landlord-tenant relationship, does not apply to cooperatives).

[20] Compare Firth v. Lu, 103 Wash.App. 267, 12 P.3d 618 (2000) (sale of cooperative unit is a transfer of an interest in real property and is covered by the statute of frauds); Presten v. Sailer, 225 N.J.Super. 178, 542 A.2d 7 (1988) (same); and Moloney v. Weingarten, 118 A.D.2d 836, 500 N.Y.S.2d 320 (1986) (same) with Weiss v. Karch, 62 N.Y.2d 849, 850, 477 N.Y.S.2d 615, 615, 466 N.E.2d 155 (1984) (sale of cooperative apartment is analogous to a sale of securities, governed by Article 2 of the Uniform Commercial Code); Friedman v. Sommer, 63 N.Y.2d 788, 481 N.Y.S.2d 326, 471 N.E.2d 139 (1984) (same); and Silverman v. Alcoa Plaza Assocs., 37 A.D.2d 166, 323 N.Y.S.2d 39 (1971) (U.C.C. Article 2 governs, prohibiting forfeiture of purchaser's earnest money deposit). See also Star v. 308 Owners Corp., 130 Misc.2d 732, 497 N.Y.S.2d 282, 283 (1985) (building code enforceable against cooperative unit, as holder of interest in real estate); In re Carton, 4 B.R. 401, 403 (Bankr. D. Md. 1980) (under Maryland law, owner's interest in cooperative apartment is real estate for purposes of attachment of judgment lien).

[21] In re Jack's Estate, 126 Misc.2d 1060, 484 N.Y.S.2d 489 (1985) (cooperative apartment interest treated as personalty); In re Miller's Estate, 205 Misc. 770, 130 N.Y.S.2d 295 (1954) (same). See also In re Levenhar, 24 B.R. 331 (Bankr. E.D.N.Y. 1982) (cooperative apartment interest is personalty, and hence cannot be held in tenancy by the entirety).

[22] 43 N.Y.2d 151, 400 N.Y.S.2d 805, 371 N.E.2d 523 (1977).

[23] Superior Fin. Corp. v. Haskell, 556 F.Supp. 199 (S.D.N.Y. 1983) (upholding priority of lender's unfiled security interest in cooperative apartment, perfected by possession of documents, against a subsequently-filed federal tax lien); Brief v. 120 Owners Corp., 157 A.D.2d 515, 549 N.Y.S.2d 706 (1990) (same, as against all subsequent liens including federal tax liens).

Lenders outside New York may well be uncomfortable with these conclusions, which would no longer be appropriate in a transaction governed by revised Article 9 of the Uniform Commercial Code, which became effective in 2001. Under revised Article 9, the owner's rights in the cooperative entity, even if evidenced by a share certificate, are not an "instrument" under U.C.C. § 9–102(a)(47), because the certificate is not a "writing that evidences a right to the payment of a monetary obligation." Instead, these rights would be characterized either as a "general intangible" under U.C.C. § 9–102(a)(42) or a "security" governed by U.C.C. Article 8. A security interest in a general intangible must be perfected by the filing of a financing statement. U.C.C. § 9–310(a). A security interest in a certificated security can be perfected by delivery of the certificate under U.C.C. § 9–313(a).

Likewise, if the proprietary lease is viewed as the principal indicator of ownership and the share certificate is viewed as the ancillary item, then by its terms Article 9 would not apply to a security interest in the lease. See U.C.C. § 9–109(d)(11) (Article 9 does not apply to "the creation or transfer of an interest in or lien on real property, including a lease"). Thus, under this view, a security interest in the lease should be viewed as a real estate interest subject to perfection by recordation in the real property records. This view was followed in In re McGuinness.[24] Thus, to be certain that its interest in the proprietary lease is perfected, the lender may wish to obtain and record a real estate mortgage on the cooperator's leasehold estate, in addition to taking possession of the documents and filing a financing statement under Article 9.

A related question arises as to how a creditor can properly foreclose upon a security interest in a cooperative apartment. In FDIC v. Evans,[25] the secured lender, which had taken a possessory pledge of the shares and lease, conducted a nonjudicial sale to a bona fide purchaser, relying on Article 9's authorization to secured parties to dispose of collateral in a "commercially reasonable" manner. The court found this action proper, and rejected the argument of the preceding paragraph that a security interest in the proprietary lease is excluded from UCC Article 9.[26] In another case, the New York Appellate Division indicated that a judicial foreclosure under Article 9 would also be proper.[27] But a Bankruptcy

---

[24] 139 B.R. 3 (Bankr. D. N.J. 1992).

[25] No. 75–C–1947 (E.D.N.Y. Apr. 14, 1976), unreported. The opinion is reprinted in full in Patrick J. Rohan & Melvin A. Reskin, Cooperative Housing Law & Practice § 5A.12 (1984). See also Mehralian v. Riverview Tower Homeowners Ass'n, 464 N.W.2d 571 (Minn. Ct. App. 1990) (statute governing redemption following real estate mortgage foreclosure does not apply to foreclosure of stock in cooperative apartment).

[26] The court also rejected an argument that the sale was a violation of Due Process because it was held without a prior hearing. This is consistent with the usual attitude of the courts in reviewing power-of-sale foreclosures of real estate mortgages.

[27] Fundex Capital Corp. v. Reichard, 172 A.D.2d 420, 568 N.Y.S.2d 794 (1991) (foreclosure of security interest in stock and proprietary lease is governed by Article 9, which authorizes the

Court applying Illinois law disagreed, noting that the proprietary lease was real property, so that a collateral assignment of it was not within the scope of Article 9 and would have to be foreclosed as a real estate mortgage. The court conceded that Article 9 would control a foreclosure on shares of stock alone as collateral, but concluded that it would be improper to permit the severance of the lease and stock rights in a cooperative to subject the stock to Article 9.[28]

Because of the bifurcated nature of cooperative apartment ownership, questions of perfection and foreclosure of security interests are not easily answered within the framework of existing law. Clarifying legislation is badly needed, and has been enacted in two of the states where many cooperatives are located. A 1988 New York statute adopted the view of prior case law that cooperative apartments are personal property, but declared that security interests in them must be perfected by the filing of an Article 9 financing statement in the local government office in which real estate mortgages are recorded.[29] New York has likewise enacted special foreclosure procedures for foreclosing on cooperative interests; while Article 9 governs the foreclosure, New York has amended its version of Article 9 to require an additional pre-foreclosure notice at least 90 days prior to the foreclosure sale.[30] New Jersey took a different approach, but with much the same ultimate result; its statute treats cooperative units as a special type of real estate, with transfers of title and perfection of security interests accomplished through recordation in the county recorders' offices.[31] Such documents are recorded in the same way as real estate deeds and mortgages, and are also indexed in a master register maintained for each cooperative project.

---

secured party to "reduce his claim to judgment, foreclose or otherwise enforce the security interest by any available judicial procedure").

[28] In re McNair, 90 B.R. 912 (Bankr. N.D. Ill. 1988). These problems are largely resolved if the cooperative is of the type in which each owner holds a fractional share in the project as a tenant in common. Such interests are readily mortgageable and may be foreclosed upon. See Future Fed. Sav. & Loan Ass'n v. Daunhauer, 687 S.W.2d 871 (Ky. Ct. App.1985).

[29] N.Y. U.C.C. § 9–501(1)(c). New York has also amended its version of Article 9 to specify the particular content of a financing statement covering a cooperative unit, N.Y. U.C.C. § 9–502(a)(4), (e). Such a filing is effective for 50 years until terminated, without the need for periodic continuation statements. N.Y. U.C.C. § 9–515(h).

[30] N.Y. U.C.C. § 9–611(f)(1). The statute dictates the form and content of this additional pre-foreclosure notice. N.Y. U.C.C. § 9–611(f)(2) to (5). Where a lender fails to comply with these requirements, a court can stay a nonjudicial sale of the cooperative unit under Article 9 until the lender does comply. See, e.g., Stern-Obstfeld v. Bank of America, 30 Misc. 3d 901, 915 N.Y.S.2d 456 (Sup. 2011). Finally, New York has also amended its version of Article 9 to permit "strict foreclosure" of a cooperative interest, which is the Article 9 analogue for a deed in lieu of foreclosure. N.Y. U.C.C. § 9–620(h).

[31] N.J. Rev. Stat. § 46:8D–1 et seq. The statute has been construed to apply only to post-act cooperatives; see Drew Assocs. v. Travisano, 235 N.J.Super. 194, 561 A.2d 1177 (A.D.1989), aff'd in part, rev'd in part on other grounds, 122 N.J. 249, 584 A.2d 807 (1991). See also In re McGuinness, 139 B.R. 3 (Bankr. D. N.J. 1992), comparing pre-act law with the act.

This legislation has been extremely helpful in New York and New Jersey, but cooperatives in other states remain in a legally ambiguous position. An amendment to the UCC, adopted nationally, seems the best way to solve the problem, although no action on it has been taken at this writing.[32]

NOTES

1.   *Foreclosure of cooperative unit and occupancy.* Keep in mind that the high bidder following the foreclosure of a cooperative unit has no guarantee of being able to occupy the unit. A sale of a cooperative unit is subject to the cooperative's governing documents, which typically require board approval of prospective purchasers.

2.   *Mechanic's liens.* Mechanic's liens raise unique problems in condominiums. If a contractor performs work on an individual unit, there is no serious doubt that the lien for unpaid work attaches only to that unit. But suppose the work is performed on the common elements, either at the behest of the developer or the owners association. Many of the statutes explicitly disallow liens on the common elements; see UCA § 3–117(a); FHA Model Act § 9(a). Instead, the lien may attach to all affected units. Should this result follow even if the work was performed (or the lien attached) prior to the recording of the declaration? See Stevens Constr. Corp. v. Draper Hall, Inc., 73 Wis.2d 104, 242 N.W.2d 893 (1976). The acts often provide that each unit owner can satisfy and discharge the lien as to his or her unit by a pro rata payment; see UCA § 3–117(b); FHA Model Act § 9(b); 2 Nelson, Whitman, Burkhart & Freyermuth, Real Estate Finance Law § 13.3 (6th ed., Practitioner Series 2014); E.D. McGillicuddy Constr. Co., Inc. v. Knoll Recreation Ass'n, Inc., 31 Cal.App.3d 891, 107 Cal.Rptr. 899 (1973).

C. CONFLICTS BETWEEN DEVELOPER AND UNIT PURCHASERS

To a significant extent, the developer of a common interest community and the purchasers of units in that community have economic interests that converge. For example, it is in the best interest of the unit purchasers to have facilities, covenants, rules and regulations that will facilitate the orderly management of the community and thus help to preserve the value of each unit purchaser's investment. Likewise, if such facilities, covenants, rules and regulations exist, the developer should find it easier to sell units in the community.

Nevertheless, the interests of the developer and the unit purchasers are not identical. A developer's primary interest is in marketing units at a profit on its investment. As a result, the developer will want to retain the

---

[32] See Robert M. Zinman, Report on Condominium Communities to the Advisory Group on Real Estate Related Collateral, UCC Article 9 Study Group.

flexibility to make changes to the community during the development and marketing phase if warranted by market conditions. For example, the developer of a condominium building originally planned for 250 units may wish to expand to 350 units if area demand for new condominium units is high. Such an expansion may come as an unwelcome or unexpected surprise, however, to early unit purchasers, who may feel that the larger community will devalue their units and create more stress upon shared facilities (e.g., more residents using the pool, clubhouse, or tennis courts).

In this section, we explore a variety of settings in which conflicts can arise between the developer and unit purchasers. One common conflict involves the extent to which a developer is subject to assessment for units that have not yet been built, or that are built but remain unsold. For example, suppose that Developer places a declaration upon 100 acres of land creating the Shady Acres Condominium, including 200 units (in 20 10-unit buildings), a pool and tennis courts, and parking. Developer built four of the buildings (40 units) along with the pool, tennis courts, and a portion of the parking, and sold all 40 units, but then ran out of financing. Must the owners of the 40 units bear all the cost of maintaining the pool and tennis courts, or must the Developer pay assessments on the 160 units that remain unbuilt? Can the declaration expressly relieve the Developer of the obligation to pay assessments on unbuilt or unsold units?

TARA MANATEE, INC. v. FAIRWAY GARDENS AT TARA CONDOMINIUM ASS'N, INC.

District Court of Appeal of Florida, Second District, 2003
870 So.2d 32

FULMER, JUDGE. Tara Manatee, Inc. (Developer) was the developer of a twenty-building, eighty-unit condominium project in Manatee County that is now operated by Fairway Gardens at Tara Condominium Association, Inc. (Association). Prior to turnover of control of the association, the Developer was operating under the developer guarantee provision of section 718.116(9)(a)(2), Florida Statutes (1995), which states in relevant part:

A developer ... who owns condominium units ... may be excused from the payment of his share of the common expense which would have been assessed against those units during the period of time that he has guaranteed to each purchaser in the purchase contract, declaration, or prospectus ... that the assessment for common expenses of the condominium imposed upon the unit owners would not increase over a stated dollar amount and has obligated himself to pay any amount of common expenses incurred during that period and not produced by the assessments at the guaranteed level receivable from other unit owners.

The premise of the developer guarantee provision is that a developer should be excused from paying assessments on its units during the initial sales phase when its units are typically unsold and, thus, not consuming services of the association. Joseph E. Adams, *Community Associations: 1998 Survey of Florida Law,* 23 Nova L.Rev. 65, 75 (1998). Otherwise, the developer would bear a disproportionate burden in the maintenance of the condominium. *Id.* However, the developer must guarantee that assessments against nondeveloper unit owners will not exceed a stated dollar amount and the developer must also agree to fund any deficit incurred in the operation of the condominium (including funding of reserves, unless properly waived) during the guarantee period. *Id.*

In this case, the Developer contended that there was no deficit at turnover. However, the Association contended that there was a deficit of $44,009 because the Developer failed to fund maintenance reserves for the units that had not yet been built. The Developer refused to pay the $44,009 and sought a declaratory judgment interpreting its obligations under the Declaration of Condominium and applicable statutes. The Association answered and filed a counterclaim seeking a money judgment for $44,009. Both parties filed motions for summary judgment. The trial court granted the Association's motion and entered a final judgment in the amount of $52,794.77, which represented the Association's claim for $44,009 plus prejudgment interest.

At the summary judgment hearing the Association argued that when the Declaration of Condominium was recorded the Developer became obligated to fund reserves for the maintenance of all eighty proposed units. In support, the Association first cited section 718.104(2), Florida Statutes (1995), which provides that "[u]pon the recording of the declaration . . . all units described in the declaration . . . as being located in or on the land then being submitted to condominium ownership shall come into existence, regardless of the state of completion of planned improvements in which the units may be located."

Next, the Association cited section 718.112(2)(f)(2), which contains a requirement that the annual budget of common expenses include reserve accounts for capital expenditures and deferred maintenance. The same subsection provides that "prior to turnover of control of an association . . . the developer may vote to waive the reserves or reduce the funding of reserves for the first 2 years." § 718.112(2)(f)(2). The Association argued that the Developer was obligated to fund maintenance reserves for all eighty units described in the declaration because the units came into existence when the declaration was recorded and the Developer did not vote to waive or reduce the reserves. Finally, the Association acknowledged that the condominium was being operated under a developer guarantee authorized by section 718.116(9)(a)(2) and asserted that the Developer's obligation under this provision included funding reserves for unbuilt units because maintenance reserves are a common expense incurred upon the recording of the declaration. And, if the Developer did not wish to fund these reserves, it should have built a phased condominium or should have voted to waive or reduce the reserves.

The Developer agreed that its unbuilt units came into existence when the declaration was recorded, and therefore, all proposed units were subject to assessments as they became due for the maintenance of common elements and built units. The Developer also agreed that as part of the developer guarantee it was obligated to ensure that reserves for constructed units and common elements such as the pool and roads were fully funded. However, with respect to reserves for deferred maintenance, the Developer argued that it was only obligated to fund reserves for the maintenance of constructed buildings and common elements.

On appeal, the Developer frames the issue as whether maintenance reserves for unbuilt units are an "incurred" common expense for which the Developer is liable under the developer guarantee provision. The determination of whether these reserves are an incurred common expense turns on a determination of what event triggers the requirement that they be funded. The trial court cited *Hyde Park Condominium Ass'n v. Estero Island Real Estate, Inc.*, 486 So.2d 1 (Fla. 2d DCA 1986), and concluded that the Developer became obligated to fund full reserves for all eighty units at the time the declaration was recorded because at that time "the eighty units came into existence." While we agree that the units came into legal existence upon the recording of the declaration, we do not agree that the obligation to fund deferred maintenance reserves for the unbuilt units also arose at that time.

In *Hyde Park,* the Hyde Park Condominium Association filed suit against the owners of Units D1–7 for failure to pay assessments for common expenses.... The owners denied responsibility for paying assessments because the property owned consisted of lots rather than constructed units. *Id.* The trial court found that lots 1–7 of Unit D were unimproved property and were not "units" subject to assessments. *Id.* This court reversed. *Id.* We noted that the Hyde Park Condominium declaration provided that all units were liable for a proportionate share of the common expenses in the same proportion as such units share in the common elements. *Id.* We concluded that the unimproved lots were units:

> Under the 1969 Act, condominium property includes land, all improvements, all improvements on the land, and all easements and rights with the condominium. § 711.03(9) [Fla. Stat. (1969)].

> A "unit" is that part of the condominium property "which is *to be
> subject to private ownership.*" § 711.03(13) (emphasis added).
> "Common elements" are defined as "portions of the condominium
> property *not included in the units.*" § 711.03(4) (emphasis added).
> Therefore, under the 1969 Act, the only type of private
> ownership available within a condominium is a "unit."

Id.. Hyde Park stands for the proposition that all units, whether built or
unbuilt, must share in assessments for common expenses of the
condominium. For example, if only five units are constructed and sold in a
fifty-unit condominium, assessments for the expense of maintaining the
roads, landscaping, and common elements, such as a pool, would be levied
against all fifty units and not just the five that were already constructed.
Hyde Park does not stand for the proposition that deferred maintenance
reserves for unbuilt units become an incurred common expense at the
time a declaration is recorded and, therefore, does not support the trial
court's order in this case.

We conclude that the requirement to fund reserves for deferred
maintenance is not triggered by the recording of a declaration of
condominium. We reach this conclusion by construing section
718.112(2)(f), which addresses what must be included in an annual
budget, and more specifically subsection 718.112(2)(f)(2), which addresses
reserve accounts. This subsection provides in part:

> In addition to annual operating expenses, the budget shall
> include reserve accounts for capital expenditures and deferred
> maintenance. These accounts shall include, but are not limited
> to, roof replacement, building painting, and pavement
> resurfacing, regardless of the amount of deferred maintenance
> expense or replacement cost, and for any other item for which
> the deferred maintenance expense or replacement cost exceeds
> $10,000. The amount to be reserved shall be computed by means
> of a formula which is based upon estimated remaining useful life
> and estimated replacement cost or deferred maintenance
> expense of each reserve item. The association may adjust
> replacement reserve assessments annually to take into account
> any changes in estimates or extension of the useful life of a
> reserve item caused by deferred maintenance. This subsection
> does not apply to budgets in which the members of an
> association have, by a majority vote at a duly called meeting of
> the association, determined for a fiscal year to provide no
> reserves or reserves less adequate than required by this
> subsection. However, prior to turnover of control of an
> association by a developer to unit owners other than a developer
> pursuant to § 718.301, the developer may vote to waive the
> reserves or reduce the funding of reserves for the first 2 years of

the operation of the association, after which time reserves may only be waived or reduced upon the vote of a majority of all nondeveloper voting interests voting in person or by limited proxy at a duly called meeting of the association.

§ 718.112(2)(f)(2).

We conclude that, based on the wording of this statute, a developer is not required to fund deferred maintenance reserves for unbuilt units. The formula prescribed to determine amounts to be reserved is based in part on the "remaining useful life" of each reserve item. The phrase "remaining useful life" suggests that the "useful life" of an improvement has already begun. The useful life of a unit in terms of maintenance does not commence until it is built because unbuilt units do not deteriorate and accrue maintenance needs. Furthermore, the provisions of section 718.112(2)(f)(2) whereby a developer may vote to waive or reduce the funding of reserves must be read to apply only to reserves that are required to be funded. We find no requirement to fund maintenance reserves for unbuilt units and, therefore, no waiver was necessary. . . .

NOTES

1. *Developer liability for assessments on unbuilt or unsold units.* Sometimes, a developer may provide in the declaration that developer-owned lots or units are exempt from assessments. In the condominium context, a developer's flexibility to pay reduced assessments (or none at all) may be limited by the language of the applicable condominium statute. See FHA Model Act § 23; Palm Bay Towers Corp. v. Brooks, 466 So.2d 1071 (Fla. Ct. App. 1984) (terms of declaration do not overrule statutory obligation of developer to pay assessments on units it owns). For example, UCA and UCIOA provide that common expenses must be assessed against all units in accordance with the allocations established in the declaration, UCA § 3–115(b), UCIOA § 3–115(b), and further provide that the developer may not allocate assessments among units in a fashion that discriminates in favor of the developer. UCA § 2–107(a), UCIOA § 2–107(b). See also Bodily v. Parkmont Village Green Home Owners Ass'n, Inc., 104 Cal.App.3d 348, 163 Cal.Rptr. 658 (1980) (agreement between association and developer to reduce developer's assessment liability on unsold units held to violate California Subdivided Lands Act); Alma Investments, Inc. v. Bahia Mar Co-owners Ass'n, 999 S.W.2d 820 (Tex. Ct. App. 1999) (provisions allowing developer to exempt certain units from paying assessment charges were void as against public policy).

Is there a meaningful difference between unsold units and unbuilt units? To the extent that assessments are based generally on the idea that those using common elements should pay for the maintenance of those elements, is it fair to hold the developer liable for assessments on unbuilt or "phantom" units? Why or why not? How does the Florida "guarantee" statute try to address this problem, and does it do so adequately? How else might a developer attempt to minimize its obligation for assessments on unbuilt or unsold units? Consider the following alternatives:

(a) *Amendment of declaration.* In some cases, the declaration may permit its terms to be modified upon approval by a majority or supermajority of the unit owners. [In a few states, including California, a declaration may be modified by majority approval unless the declaration is made unamendable by its express terms, or unless the declaration expressly requires a supermajority. See Cal. Civ. Code § 4260.] Returning to the hypothetical immediately prior to *Tara Manatee*, suppose that the declaration for Shady Acres Condominium contains a provision allowing a majority of owners to modify the declaration, with voting determined by "one unit, one vote." Developer proposes to amend the declaration to relieve all Developer-owned units from common area assessments, and the amendment is approved when Developer (who owns the 160 unbuilt units) casts its votes in favor of the amendment. Should such an amendment enforceable? Why or why not? Compare Investors Ltd. v. Sun Mountain Condominium, 683 P.2d 891 (Idaho Ct. App. 1984) (developer/owner of unbuilt units was not "owner" entitled to vote on amendment seeking to add additional building to condominium) with Mountain View Condominium Homeowners Ass'n, Inc. v. Scott, 883 P.2d 453 (Ariz. 1994) (ownership of completed units indistinguishable from ownership of uncompleted units for assessment purposes).

(b) *Annexation/phasing.* Now suppose that in the original declaration for Shady Acres Condominium, Developer only subjected the first 40 units, pool, tennis courts, and parking to the declaration, but that the declaration also provided: "Annexation by Developer. Developer shall have the unilateral privilege to subject all or any portions of real property owned by Developer to this Declaration." Developer plans to build the remaining 160 units in phases, as financing and market conditions permit. Now would the Developer have any assessment liability for the unbuilt units?

2. *Funding of reserves.* Governing documents typically require the maintenance of a reserve fund for capital expenditures and deferred maintenance of common elements. If created and managed properly, a portion of the assessment against each unit is placed in a reserve account each assessment period, and these reserves are typically invested by the association until needed. This is sensible, as the cost of certain major repairs (e.g., replacing a condominium's roof) may well exceed the amount that an association could expect to raise through assessments in any one year. If the creation and funding of reserves is sensible, can you explain why the court in *Tara Manatee* concluded that the developer was not obligated to pay reserves on unbuilt units?

3. *"Lowballing" of assessments.* Sometimes, a developer may subsidize the cost of maintaining common elements during development and marketing. This may permit the developer to establish artificially low assessments on unit purchasers, thereby enhancing the developer's ability to

sell units. Of course, the piper must eventually be paid, and when the developer subsidies stop, assessment amounts may increase dramatically. Suppose that Smith purchases a home from such a developer, only to discover that when the developer stops subsidizing common expenses six months later, the association must triple its annual assessment amount. Should Smith be able to rescind the contract? Why or why not? What additional information, if any, would you like to discover before reaching a conclusion?

4.   *Tardy completion of units and failure to complete common facilities.* Under all types of unit ownership plans, the developer often sells units prior to construction, or sells constructed units before completing common recreational facilities. The buyers may rely on the developer's promise, oral or written, that completion will occur. Where the problem is failure to complete a unit, courts have held that if the developer does not finish the unit within a reasonable time of the agreed closing date, the buyer may rescind and recover the deposit. See, e.g., Reider v. P-48, Inc., 362 So.2d 105 (Fla. Ct. App. 1978).

Should the same be true if the developer runs out of money and fails to complete common facilities? What protections can be devised for unit purchasers in this situation? In Moss Dev. Co. v. Geary, 41 Cal.App.3d 1, 115 Cal.Rptr. 736 (1974), the California Department of Real Estate, as a condition of approval of a PUD, required the developer to place in a neutral escrow $1000 from the sale of each lot in the development. These funds were to assure completion of the common area improvements, and could be released to the developer only if 500 lots were sold within 5 years; otherwise the funds would be refunded to the lot buyers. The developer did not in fact sell 500 lots within the five-year period, but nonetheless completed the improvements and conveyed them to the owners association. The court held that the agreement with the Department of Real Estate should be construed to permit release of the funds to the developer under these conditions.

5.   *Expansion of the project.* Suppose that the Developer of Village Green, a planned community expected to include 200 homes, is in the early stages of marketing. Early sales are very slow, due to market concerns that low- and moderate-income housing will be constructed on an adjoining parcel of land. In response, Developer acquires the adjoining parcel of land and announces plans to expand the planned community to incorporate this land. The new plans include the construction of a golf course, the maintenance of which would be subsidized through assessments, along with the construction of an additional 100 homes surrounding the golf course. Can Developer make such a change without the unanimous consent of all existing owners within the community?

As discussed earlier in this chapter, first generation condominium acts (such as the original FHA Model Act) did not satisfactorily address the extent to which the developer could expand the project after beginning construction and sales. This created great uncertainty for developers, with some courts suggesting that expansion was improper absent unanimous approval of all unit owners. See Suprenant v. First Trade Union Sav. Bank, FSB, 40 Mass.

App. Ct. 637, 666 N.E.2d 1026 (1996) (amending declaration to extend original seven-year time period for adding additional phases was improper without the approval of 100% of all unit owners whose percentage interests in common areas were affected).

Second generation statutes such as UCA and UCIOA expressly permit a developer to amend or modify the declaration to permit expansion of a project, but this flexibility is not without limits. See, e.g., Restatement (Third) of Property—Servitudes § 6.21 ("A developer may not exercise a power to amend or modify the declaration in a way that would materially change the character of the development or the burdens on the existing community members unless the declaration fairly apprises purchasers that the power could be used for the kind of change proposed."). Should Developer be able to convert Village Green into a golf course community? What if Developer did not plan to build a golf course on the additional land, but only to add an additional 100 homes (increasing the community to 300 homes), without adding any recreational facilities to the existing pool and four tennis courts? How specific must the declaration be before Developer should be able to make such changes? See UCIOA §§ 2–105, 2–110.

Court decisions have been solicitous of disappointed purchasers of condominium units, particularly where the purchase was made prior to completion of construction and where the developer made material changes to the project after the purchaser signed a contract. In such cases, courts have permitted the disappointed purchaser to rescind the contract. See, e.g., Barber v. Chalfonte Dev. Corp., 369 So.2d 983 (Fla. Ct. App. 1979) (changes in documents eliminating certain recreational facilities and imposing further restrictions on decoration of units); Aaronson v. Susi, 296 So.2d 508 (Fla. Ct. App. 1974) (developer converted part of the advertised recreational space into an additional apartment unit).

6. *Developer control of the association.* Developers frequently attempt to maintain control over the owners' association even after selling the majority of the units, either by retaining all powers of the association or by establishing voting rules that give disproportionate weight to the developer (e.g., unsold units retained by the developer have five times the votes of sold units) and thus allow the developer to "outvote" other owners within the association. This is motivated (at least in part) by fear that once the developer turns over control to the owners' association, the owners may make changes in the declaration or rules that would make it more difficult for the developer to market the remaining units. Such extensive developer control may prove very frustrating to unit purchasers when the developer and unit purchasers do not see eye-to-eye on matters of importance to the community residents.

Frequently, permanent lenders will refuse to make a mortgage loan on a project if the period of developer control will extend past some given percentage of units transferred, and may also insist on specifying a fixed date on which control will pass to the unit owners regardless of unit sales. At what point, even though still in the minority, should unit purchasers be entitled to some representation in the management of the condominium? Consider the Florida approach to this question and to the question of control:

(1) If unit owners other than the developer own 15 percent or more of the units in a condominium that will be operated ultimately by an association, the unit owners other than the developer are entitled to elect at least one-third of the members of the board of administration of the association. Unit owners other than the developer are entitled to elect at least a majority of the members of the board of administration of an association, upon the first to occur of any of the following events:

(a) Three years after 50 percent of the units that will be operated ultimately by the association have been conveyed to purchasers;

(b) Three months after 90 percent of the units that will be operated ultimately by the association have been conveyed to purchasers;

(c) When all the units that will be operated ultimately by the association have been completed, some of them have been conveyed to purchasers, and none of the others are being offered for sale by the developer in the ordinary course of business;

(d) When some of the units have been conveyed to purchasers and none of the others are being constructed or offered for sale by the developer in the ordinary course of business; . . . [or]

(g) Seven years after [recordation of the declaration or the recordation of a transfer of title to a unit purchaser].

The developer is entitled to elect at least one member of the board of administration of an association as long as the developer holds for sale in the ordinary course of business at least 5 percent, in condominiums with fewer than 500 units, and 2 percent, in condominiums with more than 500 units, of the units in a condominium operated by the association.

West's Fla. Stat. Ann. § 718.301(1). For interesting interpretations of the foregoing, see Bishop Assocs. Ltd. Partn. v. Belkin, 521 So.2d 158 (Fla. Ct. App. 1988); Department of Bus. Reg., Div. of Land Sales v. Siegel, 479 So.2d 112 (Fla. 1985).

Frequently, the struggle for control is not against the original developer, but against the developer's mortgagee who has acquired the developer's remaining units through foreclosure or a deed in lieu. To what extent should the mortgagee be treated as the "developer" for purposes of control? See McKnight v. Board of Directors, 32 Ohio St.3d 6, 512 N.E.2d 316 (1987). See

2 Nelson, Whitman, Burkhart & Freyermuth, Real Estate Finance Law § 13.3 (6th ed. Practitioner Series 2014), at 366–367.

7.   *Rental of units by developer.* If unit sales are slow, the developer may decide to hold some units for rental purposes. Persons who have already purchased units may have strong objections to this practice, arguing that it produces a fundamental change in the character of the project and that tenants are less concerned, careful, quiet, etc., than are owners. If the declaration gives the association clear authority to restrict or prohibit rentals, there seems no reason not to enforce the association's decisions. See, e.g., Le Febvre v. Osterndorf, 87 Wis.2d 525, 275 N.W.2d 154 (Ct. App. 1979) (court enjoined developer from rental use of unsold units without permission of association's board of directors where permission was required under bylaws); Spratt v. Henderson Mill Condo. Ass'n, 224 Ga. App. 761, 481 S.E.2d 879 (1997) (where association had discretion to allow rental use, its decision to deny such use was upheld). Even if there is no authority for the association to control renting of units, a resolution of the association restricting rentals may be upheld anyway on the ground that it has a general authority to restrict use of the units. See Breezy Point Holiday Harbor Lodge-Beachside Apt. Owners' Ass'n v. B.P. Partn., 531 N.W.2d 917 (Minn. Ct. App. 1995).

8.   *Defects in design and construction.* The same sort of protection given to buyers of detached houses for defects in design and construction is generally also extended to buyers of condominiums, cooperatives, and units in planned communities. See generally Chapter 2, Section D supra. See, e.g., Jablonsky v. Klemm, 377 N.W.2d 560 (N.D. 1985); Rouse v. Glascam Builders, Inc., 101 Wash.2d 127, 677 P.2d 125 (1984); Gable v. Silver, 264 So.2d 418 (Fla. 1972). See generally Robert M. Diamond and Deborah K. Raines, Consumer Warranty Issues in the Sale of Residential Condominiums, 20 Real Prop. Prob. & Tr. J. 933 (1985); Mark D. Pearlstein, Developer Liability for Defects in Condominiums, 74 Ill. Bar. J. 18 (Sept. 1985); Comment, Caveat Venditor in Maryland Condominium Sales: Cases and Legislation Imposing Implied Warranties in Sales of Residential Condominiums, 14 U. Balt. L. Rev. 116 (1984); Annot., 50 A.L.R.3d 1071. The UCA contains express and implied warranty provisions similar to those of the ULTA; see UCA §§ 4–113 to 4–116 (1980).

9.   *Condominiums and the Interstate Land Sales Full Disclosure Act.* In 1968, in response to perceptions of widespread misrepresentation and fraud by developers in the subdivision of vacant land and sale of lots to out-of-state purchasers for future development (i.e., the proverbial sales of "Florida swampland"), Congress enacted the Interstate Land Sales Full Disclosure Act (commonly referred to as ILSA). 15 U.S.C.A. § 1701 et seq. ILSA imposed upon developers stringent registration and disclosure requirements concerning the sale of subdivision "lots," and gave purchasers the ability to rescind purchase contracts for a period of two years if the developer failed to comply with these requirements.

At the time ILSA was enacted, it was not contemplated that ILSA would apply to the typical condominium development (where the unit buyer is not anticipating a long delay prior to the construction of the unit). Nevertheless, in 1978, Congress added the term "condominium" to ILSA's "improved land" exclusion, see 15 U.S.C.A. § 1702(a)(2) (ILSA does not apply to "the sale or lease of any improved land on which there is a . . . condominium . . . building, or the sale or lease of land under a contract obligating the seller or lessor to erect such a building thereon within a period of two years"). Because condominium sale contracts often exculpate the developer from responsibility for delays in completing construction, federal courts began interpreting ILSA as applying to the sale of condominium units unless the condominium fell within one of ILSA's other exclusions (such as its exclusion for projects with fewer than 100 lots). See, e.g., Cruz v. Leviev Fulton Club, LLC, 711 F.Supp.2d 329, 331 (S.D.N.Y. 2010) (citing cases); James L. Olivier, Beyond Consumer Protection: The Application of the Interstate Land Sales Full Disclosure Act to Condominium Sales, 37 U. Fla. L. Rev. 945 (1985). As a result, developers of large condominium projects had to comply with ILSA's registration and disclosure requirements.

During the recent recession, as condominium values plummeted in many markets, numerous condominium buyers (remorseful over the rapid decline in the value of the resale value of units they had contracted to purchase) began raising technical violations of ILSA's disclosure requirements in an attempt to escape liability on their purchase contracts. See Joseph Einav, Read Between the Lines: Why Recent ILSA Litigation Is Bad for Business and Contravenes Congressional Intent, 33 Cardozo L. Rev. 2139 (2012). In response to pressure from developers, Congress finally reacted in 2014, amending ILSA to make clear that effective March 26, 2015, ILSA's registration and disclosure requirements will not apply to the sale or lease of a condominium unit. Pub. L. 113–167, Sept. 26, 2014, 128 Stat. 1882. For further background on the 2014 ILSA amendments and their potential implications, see Mark A. Romance, ILSA Amendment Could Turn Out to Be All Smoke, No Fire, http://www.law360.com/articles/591195/ilsa-amendment-could-turn-out-to-be-all-smoke-no-fire; Robert S. Freedman, Richard C. Linquanti & William P. Sklar, New Condominium Exemption to the Interstate Land Sales Full Disclosure Act, http://www.cfjblaw.com/new-condominium-exemption-to-the-interstate-land-sales-full-disclosure-act/.

Suppose that shortly after purchasing and moving into a unit in Shady Acres Condominium, Smith learns two things that disturb him greatly. First, Smith learns that while Developer was still in control of the association, Developer entered into a contract with the association under which a related corporation (of which Developer is the sole shareholder) will manage the condominium for 25 years, at a property management fee that is 2% higher than that charged by comparable property managers. Second, Smith learns that the pool and tennis courts are not in fact owned by the unit owners, but by Developer, and are leased by Developer to the association for 99 years at a rental amount which, on an annual basis, is roughly equal to the fee simple value of the facilities! If Smith tries to mobilize the association to challenge the validity of these "sweetheart" contracts, should the law intervene to protect the owners, or are such deals the unavoidable consequence of freedom of contract?

While early decisions were unsympathetic to purchaser attacks on developer self-dealing, more recent decisions have allowed owners associations either to rescind sweetheart contracts or to recover from the developer for the benefit of the association unreasonable profits gained from such agreements. One good example of this judicial approach is Avila South Condo. Ass'n, Inc. v. Kappa Corp., 347 So.2d 599 (Fla. 1977). In that case a developer, while an officer and in control of the owners association, caused the association to enter into a 20-year lease to use recreational facilities owned by the developer's spouse. After unit owners took control of the association, they filed suit against the developer to recover for the association's benefit the difference between the rent reserved in the lease and the fair rental value of the facilities. The association claimed that the developer had a fiduciary obligation to it and had violated that duty. The Florida Supreme Court ruled that the complaint stated a cause of action. It stated: "[A]ny officer or director of a condominium association who has contracted on behalf of the association with himself, or with another corporation in which he is, or becomes substantially interested, or with another for his personal benefit may be liable to the association for that amount by which he was unjustly enriched as a result of the contract." *Id.* at 607. On the other hand, "no director or officer shall be required to return any portion of moneys paid by the association where it is shown that he received the funds with the consent of the association or with the consent of a substantial number of the individuals comprising the association." *Id.*

Although regulation of real estate transactions is typically a matter of state law, it is not surprising that Congress has gotten involved in these issues given the volume of real estate marketed across state lines. In 1980, Congress adopted the Condominium and Cooperative Abuse Relief Act (CCARA), which addresses the above issues as well as other problems presented by the conversion of apartments to condominiums and cooperatives (and the concomitant displacement of tenants). The pertinent provisions of the CCARA (without the extensive definitions) are reproduced below.

CONDOMINIUM AND COOPERATIVE ABUSE RELIEF
ACT OF 1980

15 U.S.C. § 3601 et seq.

§ 3607. Termination of self-dealing contracts

(a) **Operation, maintenance, and management contracts; penalty.** Any contract or portion thereof which is entered into after October 8, 1980, and which—

(1) provides for operation, maintenance, or management of a condominium or cooperative association in a conversion project, or of property serving the condominium or cooperative unit owners in such project;

(2) is between such unit owners or such association and the developer or an affiliate of the developer;

(3) was entered into while such association was controlled by the developer through special developer control or because the developer held a majority of the votes in such association; and

(4) is for a period of more than three years, including any automatic renewal provisions which are exercisable at the sole option of the developer or an affiliate of the developer,

may be terminated without penalty by such unit owners or such association.

(b) **Time of termination.** Any termination under this section may occur only during the two-year period beginning on the date on which (1) special developer control over the association is terminated; or (2) the developer owns 25 per centum or less of the units in the conversion project, whichever occurs first.

(c) **Vote of owners of units.** A termination under this section shall be by a vote of owners of not less than two-thirds of the units other than the units owned by the developer or an affiliate of the developer.

(d) **Effective date of termination.** Following the unit owners' vote, the termination shall be effective ninety days after hand delivering notice or mailing notice by prepaid United States mail to the parties to the contract.

§ 3608. Judicial determinations respecting unconscionable leases

(a) **Lease characteristics; authorization by unit owners; conditions precedent to action.** Cooperative and condominium unit owners through the unit owners' association may bring an action seeking a judicial determination that a lease or leases, or portions thereof, were unconscionable at the time they were made. An action may be brought under this section if each such lease has all of the following characteristics:

(1) it was made in connection with a cooperative or condominium project;

(2) it was entered into while the cooperative or condominium owners' association was controlled by the developer either through special developer control or because the developer held a majority of the votes in the owners' association;

(3) it had to be accepted or ratified by purchasers or through the unit owners' association as a condition of purchase of a unit in the cooperative or condominium project;

(4) it is for a period of more than twenty-one years or is for a period of less than twenty-one years but contains automatic renewal provisions for a period of more than twenty-one years;

(5) it contains an automatic rent increase clause; and

(6) it was entered into prior to June 4, 1975.

Such action must be authorized by the cooperative or condominium unit owners through a vote of not less than two-thirds of the owners of the units other than units owned by the developer or an affiliate of the developer, and may be brought by the cooperative or condominium unit owners through the units owners' association. Prior to instituting such action, the cooperative or condominium unit owners must, through a vote of not less than two-thirds of the owners of the units other than units owned by the developer or an affiliate of the developer, agree to enter into negotiation with the lessor and must seek through such negotiation to eliminate or modify any lease terms that are alleged to be unconscionable; if an agreement is not reached in ninety days from the date on which the authorizing vote was taken, the unit owners may authorize an action after following the procedure specified in the preceding sentence.

(b) **Presumption of unconscionability; rebuttal.** A rebuttable presumption of unconscionability exists if it is established that, in addition to the characteristics set forth in subsection (a) of this section, the lease—

(1) creates a lien subjecting any unit to foreclosure for failure to make payments;

(2) contains provisions requiring either the cooperative or condominium unit owners or the cooperative or condominium association as lessees to assume all or substantially all obligations and liabilities associated with the maintenance, management and use of the leased property, in addition to the obligation to make lease payments;

(3) contains an automatic rent increase clause without establishing a specific maximum lease payment; and

(4) requires an annual rental which exceeds 25 per centum of the appraised value of the leased property as improved: *Provided,* That, for purposes of this paragraph "annual rental" means the amount due during the first twelve months of the lease for all units, regardless of whether such units were occupied or sold during that period, and "appraised value" means the appraised value placed upon the leased property the first tax year after the sale of a unit in the condominium or after the sale of a membership or share interest in the cooperative association to a party who is not an affiliate of the developer.

Once the rebuttable presumption is established, the court, in making its finding, shall consider the lease or portion of the lease to be unconscionable unless proven otherwise by a preponderance of the evidence to the contrary.

(c) **Presentation of evidence after finding of unconscionability.** Whenever it is claimed, or appears to the court, that a lease or any portion thereof is, or may have been, unconscionable at the time it was made, the parties shall be afforded a reasonable opportunity to present evidence at least as to—

(1) the commercial setting of the negotiations;

(2) whether a party has knowingly taken advantage of the inability of the other party reasonably to protect his interests;

(3) the effect and purpose of the lease or portion thereof, including its relationship to other contracts between the association, the unit owners and the developer or an affiliate of the developer; and

(4) the disparity between the amount charged under the lease and the value of the real estate subject to the lease measured by the price at which similar real estate was readily obtainable in similar transactions.

(d) **Remedial relief; matters considered; attorneys' fees.** Upon finding that any lease, or portion thereof, is unconscionable, the court shall exercise its authority to grant remedial relief as necessary to avoid an unconscionable result, taking into consideration the economic value of the lease. Such relief may include, but shall not be limited to rescission, reformation, restitution, the award of damages and reasonable attorney fees and court costs. A defendant may recover reasonable attorneys' fees if the court determines that the cause of action filed by the plaintiff is frivolous, malicious, or lacking in substantial merit.

(e) **Actions allowed after termination of special developer control.** Nothing in this section may be construed to authorize the bringing of an action by [a] cooperative and condominium unit owners' association, seeking a judicial determination that a lease or leases, or portions thereof, are unconscionable, where such unit owners or a unit owners' association representing them has, after the termination of special developer control, reached an agreement with a holder of such lease or leases which either—

(1) sets forth the terms and conditions under which such lease or leases is or shall be purchased by such unit owners or associations; or

(2) reforms any clause in the lease which contained an automatic rent increase clause, unless such agreement was entered into when the leaseholder or his affiliate held a majority of the votes in the owners' association.

§ 3609. Void lease or contract provisions. Any provision in any lease or contract requiring unit owners or the owners' association, in any conversion project involving a contract meeting the requirements of section 3607 of this title or in any project involving a lease meeting the requirements of section 3608 of this title, to reimburse, regardless of outcome, the developer, his successor, or affiliate of the developer for attorneys' fees or money judgments, in a suit between unit owners or the owners' association and the developer arising under the lease or agreement, is against public policy and void.

§ 3610. Relationship of statutory provisions to State and local laws. Nothing in this title may be construed to prevent or limit the authority of any State or local government to enact and enforce any law, ordinance, or code with regard to any condominium, cooperative, or conversion project, if such law, ordinance, or code does not abridge, deny, or contravene any standard for consumer protection established under this title. Notwithstanding the preceding sentence, the provisions of this title, except for the application of section 3608 of this title and the prohibition included in section 3609 of this title as it relates to a lease with respect to which a cause of action may be established under section 3608 of this title, shall not apply in the case of any State or local government which has the authority to enact and enforce such a law, ordinance, or code, if, during the three-year period following October 8, 1980, such State or local government enacts a law, ordinance, or code, or amendments thereto, stating in substance that such provisions of this title shall not apply in that State or local government jurisdiction.

NOTES

1. *Litigation under CCARA.* The CCARA has frequently been used, albeit with varying success, to challenge leases entered into by cooperative associations with developers when the former were developer-controlled. See e.g., 605 Park Garage Assocs., LLC v. 605 Apt. Corp., 412 F.3d 304 (2d Cir. 2005) (CCARA does not apply to renewals of garage lease where original lease was executed prior to CCARA's effective date); Bleecker Charles Co. v. 350 Bleecker Street Apt. Corp., 327 F.3d 197 (2d Cir. 2003) (failure to act within two years after developer loses control); Cromwell Assocs. v. Oliver Cromwell Owners, Inc., 941 F.2d 107 (2d Cir. 1991) (lease of portion of project to affiliate of developer not a "contract" covered by § 3607 where leased premises were not used for benefit of unit owners); Park South Tenants Corp. v. 200 Central Park South Assocs., L.P., 941 F.2d 112 (2d Cir. 1991) (developer not obligated to disgorge profits earned under sweetheart lease prior to termination); 2 Tudor City Place Assocs. v. 2 Tudor City Tenants Corp., 924 F.2d 1247 (2d Cir. 1991) (association had authority to terminate garage lease); West 14th St. Comm. Corp. v. 5 West 14th Owners Corp., 815 F.2d 188 (2d Cir. 1987) (association could terminate garage and laundry leases); Coliseum Park Apts. Co. v. Coliseum Tenants Corp., 742 F.Supp. 128 (S.D.N.Y. 1990) (association termination of garage lease); see generally Salvatore LaMonica, Note, Developer Leases Under the Condominium and Cooperative Abuse Relief Act of 1980, 15 Hofstra L. Rev. 631 (1987).

CCARA does not apply to planned communities; is there a reason? Do the same potential abuses exist? Do you think CCARA will provide remedies for the traditional problems of recreational leases and management contracts, so that state law and alternative federal law theories will become irrelevant?

2. *Management contract vs. recreational lease: remedies.* Is there a fundamental difference in the nature of appropriate remedies for management contracts as compared to recreational leases? If the owners association cancels a management contract, it will usually be easy to find another manager. But if a recreational lease is canceled, where will the owners swim or play tennis? Note that the presence of these facilities may have been a major factor motivating the purchase of units.

3. *State legislation.* State legislation has attempted to address the self-dealing problem. Florida legislation not only grants broad authority to the association to terminate leases and contracts entered into by the association while it was controlled by the developer, it also delineates certain minimum provisions that all such agreements must contain. West's Fla. Stat. Ann. §§ 718.302, 718.3025. For interesting interpretations of the Florida legislation, see Wash-Bowl Vending Co., Inc. v. No. 3 Condo. Ass'n, Village Green, Inc., 485 So.2d 1307 (Fla. Ct. App. 1986) (laundry space lease); Tri-Properties, Inc. v. Moonspinner Condo. Ass'n, Inc., 447 So.2d 965 (Fla. Ct. App. 1984) (management contract). New Jersey has similar legislation. See N.J. Stat. Ann. § 46:8B–12.2. See also Va. Code § 55–79.74(C), providing that the term of such a lease or contract cannot exceed two years and may be

terminated by the association without penalty by 90 days written notice given no later than 60 days after expiration of developer control.

4. *UCA and UCIOA.* UCA § 3–103(a) (1980) provides: "In the performance of their duties, the officers and members of the executive board are required to exercise (i) if appointed by the declarant, the care required of fiduciaries of the unit owners and (ii) if elected by the unit owners, ordinary and reasonable care." Section 3–105 provides that certain contracts or leases (including those covering management, recreation or parking facilities, those to which the declarant is a party, and those which are not bona fide or are unconscionable) may be terminated by the board after the unit owners take over. UCIOA contains comparable provisions. UCIOA §§ 3–103(a), 3–105. Query: if the new board can always cancel objectionable contracts or leases, is it possible that the original execution of those contracts or leases can be regarded as a breach of a fiduciary duty?

5. *Antitrust concerns.* If a developer sells condominium units and also leases recreational facilities to the association, has it engaged in an illegal tying agreement in violation of the Sherman and Clayton Acts? Is there a sufficient connection with interstate commerce to provide a basis for federal jurisdiction over such a claim? The court so held in Chatham Condo. Ass'ns v. Century Village, Inc., 597 F.2d 1002 (5th Cir. 1979).

On the merits of the tying agreement claim, the Florida courts, acting under state antitrust law, have been unimpressed. See Avila South Condo. Ass'n, Inc. v. Kappa Corp., 347 So.2d 599 (Fla. 1977); Point East One Condo. Corp., Inc. v. Point East Developers, Inc., 348 So.2d 32 (Fla. Ct. App. 1977). The Fifth Circuit in *Chatham, supra,* was not so sure whether or not two products were involved:

> At one end of the spectrum, we feel certain that the requirement that purchasers of condominiums also buy an undivided interest in certain common areas does not involve two separate products. At the other end of the spectrum, however, it would clearly be improper to require condominium purchasers to patronize, for example, a local shopping center owned by the condominium developers; in this hypothetical situation, two separate products are clearly involved. Somewhere in between these two extremes the line between which products constitute part of the condominium "leisure living" package and which products are separate must be drawn. We are unable to do so at this juncture in the present case, however.

597 F.2d at 1013. Cf. Terre Du Lac Ass'n, Inc. v. Terre Du Lac, Inc., 772 F.2d 467 (8th Cir.1985) (complaint challenging practice of recreational subdivision developer requiring lot owners to pay a $3,000 initiation fee to join country club if they purchased their lot from someone other than the developer, while offering free memberships to persons who purchase lots from the developer, held to state a valid claim under the Sherman Act).

6. *Recreational leases—rent increases.* Recreational leases are commonly for very long terms, and developers often insert clauses which cause the rents to increase in accordance with the Consumer Price Index or some similar measure of inflation. The Florida statute prohibiting this device was upheld in Schlytter v. Baker, 580 F.2d 848 (5th Cir. 1978). See West's Fla. Stat. Ann. § 718.4015. See also Association of Golden Glades Condo. Club, Inc. v. Security Mgmt. Corp., 557 So.2d 1350 (Fla. 1990) (statute only partially retroactive); Moonlit Waters Apts., Inc. v. Cauley, 666 So.2d 898 (Fla. 1996) (statute did not apply to a ground lease of land on which the entire project was constructed, as distinct from a lease of recreational facilities). Is there anything inherently unconscionable or offensive in such a clause? The same sort of device is very widely employed in long-term commercial leases.

7. *Recreational leases—additional readings.* See generally John R. Lewis & Kenneth A. Jessell, The Condominium Recreational Lease Controversy, 9 Real Est. L.J. 7 (1980); Thomas G. Krebs, The Legislative Response to "Sweetheart" Management Contracts: Protecting the Condominium Purchaser, 55 Chi.-Kent L. Rev. 319 (1979); William Griffith Thomas, Guiding the Condominium Developer Through the Control Period, 6 Real Est. L.J. 132 (1977); Annot., Self-dealing by developers of condominium project as affecting contracts or leases with condominium association, 73 A.L.R.3d 613 (1977).

8. *Standing issues.* Who has standing to assert against the developer the various claims discussed above? May the association do so, or is it necessary for each individual unit owner to do so? See generally Paul S. Jacobsen, Standing of Condominium Associations to Sue: One for All or All for One?, 13 Hamline L. Rev. 15 (1990). In interpreting state condominium statutes, procedural rules and case law, most decisions recognize that the association or its management committee has standing to assert a variety of claims against the developer. See, e.g., Orange Grove Terrace Owners Ass'n v. Bryant Props., Inc., 176 Cal.App.3d 1217, 222 Cal.Rptr. 523 (1986) (negligent repair of common areas prior to formal organization of the owners' association); Queen's Grant Villas Horizontal Prop. Regimes I-V v. Daniel Int'l Corp., 286 S.C. 555, 335 S.E.2d 365 (1985) (construction defects in common areas); Towerhill Condo. Ass'n v. American Condo. Homes, Inc., 66 Or.App. 342, 675 P.2d 1051 (1984) (breach of warranty and negligence with respect to defects in the common areas); Brickyard Homeowners' Ass'n Mgmt. Comm. v. Gibbons Realty Co., 668 P.2d 535 (Utah 1983) (negligent design and breach of warranty with respect to common areas and certain units); Mission Hills Condo. Ass'n M-1 v. Corley, 570 F.Supp. 453 (N.D. Ill. 1983) (association has standing to pursue antitrust claim under Sherman Act, but not under Clayton Act). But see Summerhouse Condo. Ass'n, Inc. v. Majestic Sav. & Loan Ass'n, 44 Colo.App. 495, 615 P.2d 71 (1980) (association lacks standing on claims based on breach of warranty and fiduciary duty); Commodore Plaza at Century 21 Condo. Ass'n, Inc. v. Saul J. Morgan Enters., Inc., 301 So.2d 783 (Fla. Ct. App. 1974) (association lacks standing to

complain under statute requiring management contracts to be "fair and reasonable").

To what extent does an individual unit owner have standing to assert claims against the developer, contractors or board members? Consider the language of Frantz v. CBI Fairmac Corp., 229 Va. 444, 331 S.E.2d 390 (1985):

> Hence, while a unit owner may assert a claim under the provisions of the Condominium Act for the violation of some individual right, [the Act] contemplates that a violation of a right held in common by all unit owners shall be maintained by a unit owners' association, unless the association fails or refuses to assert the common right.

Accord Cigal v. Leader Dev. Corp., 408 Mass. 212, 557 N.E.2d 1119 (1990) (negligent construction claim against contractor and breach of fiduciary duty action against condominium board directors could be raised by association only).

9.   *Disclosure as remedy for self-dealing?* Is full disclosure the answer to self-dealing? Several of the "second-generation" statutes require extensive disclosure of documents (and summaries of them, as they are often too voluminous and technical for most unit purchasers). For example, the Florida statute, West's Fla. Stat. Ann. § 718.504, requires buyers to be given as many as twenty documents. UCA requires the distribution of a "public offering statement" by the developer, and gives buyers a right to cancel their purchaser contracts for 15 days after receiving it, UCA §§ 4–101 to 4–106 (1980). UCIOA contains comparable provisions. UCIOA §§ 4–101 to 4–108. Much of the debate about the federal legislation also centered around disclosure, although the CCARA did not adopt this approach. See Comment, Condominium Regulation: Beyond Disclosure, 123 U. Pa. L. Rev. 639 (1975).

Is any of this likely to be meaningful? If disclosure is to be compelled, is it better to disclose the original documents themselves, a summary-type of offering statement, or both? Should buyers be permitted to waive disclosure? What about buyers in industrial or commercial condominiums? Should disclosure rules apply to cooperatives and planned communities as well as condominiums?

———————

Suppose that 100 buyers enter into pre-construction contracts for the purchase of a unit in the proposed Harbor View Condominiums, each making a $10,000 deposit. Partway through construction, the developer encounters unexpected cost overruns. The developer spends the accumulated purchasers' deposits, but still cannot complete construction. The developer then defaults on its construction loan, the lender forecloses its mortgage, and the lender acquires the partially completed project at the foreclosure sale. Have the buyers lost their deposits and/or the contractual rights to purchase their units, or can the buyers enforce their contracts against the lender?

STATE SAVINGS & LOAN ASS'N V. KAUAIAN DEVELOPMENT CO.

Supreme Court of Hawaii, 1968
50 Hawaii 540, 445 P.2d 109

LEVINSON, JUSTICE. . . . [The developer entered into pre-construction contracts of sale with a number of condominium unit purchasers. These contracts were unrecorded, but the construction lender, State Savings, had actual knowledge of them when it recorded its construction mortgage. Construction was completed, but sales were apparently slow and the developer defaulted on the construction loan. State Savings sought to foreclose on the property, including the interests of buyers under the pre-construction contracts.]

Except as modified by statute with respect to registered land, the proposition is well established that one who takes an interest in real property with knowledge of the existence of contracts of sale of other interests in the property is subject to the terms of the contracts, Hurst v. Kukahi, 25 Haw. 194 (1919). Furthermore, Hawaii recognizes the present transferability of interests in futuro which would have been invalid at common law, Puukaiakea v. Hiaa, 5 Haw. 484 (1885).

But the purchasers cite no authority, and we have found none, indicating that a contract for the sale of an interest in land and a building to be constructed on the land creates an equitable interest in the building superior to a mortgage securing a construction loan for the building. . . .

State Savings . . . contends that since the contracts were not specifically enforceable they did not convey an interest in real property. We recognize that equity courts generally refrain from issuing decrees which they cannot enforce, and that equity courts will not order acts requiring continuous supervision, such as construction of building. But State Savings cites no authority which supports the conclusion that the inability, or refusal, of equity courts to grant a particular remedy indicates that no interest in real property has been conveyed. Recognition of an interest in real property does not necessarily depend on the availability of a specific remedy to protect such interests.

The question, then, is whether we ought to extend the protection equity historically has given to rights arising under an executory contract for the sale of land to interests of contract purchasers in a unit in a condominium to be built. Both parties agree that this case, and the issues involved in it, ought to be resolved in a manner which most effectively will implement the legislative desire to encourage the development of condominium projects in Hawaii. They disagree, obviously, as to the resolution which will best effectuate that purpose. The legislative enactment with which we are dealing in this case has profound social and economic overtones, not only in Hawaii but also in every densely populated area of the United States. Our construction of such legislation must be imaginative and progressive rather than restrictive.

We conclude that the overall objectives of [Hawaii's Horizontal Property Regimes Act, or H.P.R.A.] will best be effectuated by recognizing the rights of purchasers under the contracts as superior to those of a subsequent mortgagee receiving his mortgage with knowledge of those interests. First, equity courts long have recognized the basic unfairness of permitting a person to take an interest in property with knowledge that other interests, prior in time, exist, and permitting the subsequent interest to be free from those interests. As a general rule, a vendor can convey no more of an interest than he has at the time of the conveyance.

Second, and perhaps even more important, condominiums were developed as a method of ownership under which the individual purchaser's interest could be well protected. A significant part of the H.P.R.A. is devoted to ensuring that purchasers or potential purchasers will be well-informed of their rights and of the interests and liabilities they assume in purchasing a condominium unit. Obviously the purchasers cannot reasonably expect to receive their interests without paying for them or arranging for financing. Where an independent construction loan is necessary, it is a relatively small task to require the mortgagee to obtain subordination agreements from the purchasers as a condition of advancing the funds for construction. The burden cast upon the lending institution is light in comparison to the obvious virtue of this procedure in making clear to the unit purchaser his position. Undoubtedly this procedure would have been followed had State Savings hired an attorney to draw up the mortgage and advised him of the existing contracts of sale. It would be unconscionable for a lending institution to assume that it could ignore preexisting contract rights. The additional step of obtaining subordination agreements is consonant with the legislature's desire to protect the purchasers and to enable them to keep informed as to their rights and obligations. . . .

II. Mechanic's and Materialman's Liens

On August 24, 1964, the architect sent a letter to [Kauaian] certifying that construction was substantially completed. [Kauaian] refused to publish and file the notice of completion even after the contractor's formal demand. On August 18, 1965, the contractor and a supplier filed notices of mechanic's and materialman's liens. The architect filed notice of its lien more than one year after, but within one year and 45 days from, the date of actual completion. The appellants asserted that the statutory liens were invalid for failure to file within the statutory period and that even if they were timely filed, they could not attach to the individual purchasers' interests.

1. *Mechanic's and Materialman's Liens Under the H.P.R.A.* The appellants contend that the mere filing of the declaration prevented the liens from attaching to the interests of purchasers of the individual units. They do not refer to any provision of the statute and they do not cite any authority to support this broad assertion. The H.P.R.A. specifically provides that it is supplementary to all other provisions of the Revised Laws and that only laws inconsistent with the H.P.R.A. are repealed. It is silent on the subject of mechanics' liens, and therefore R.L.H.1955, § 193–40 et seq., is inapplicable only if, and to the extent that, it is inconsistent with the H.P.R.A.

The only section which even arguably could be inconsistent with the enforcement of mechanics' liens is section 4 of Act 180 which is entitled "Status of apartments within an horizontal property regime." It provides:

> Once the property is submitted to the horizontal property regime, an apartment in the building may be individually conveyed and encumbered and may be the subject of ownership, possession or sale and of all types of juridic acts inter vivos or mortis causa, as if it were sole and entirely independent of the other apartments in the building of which they form a part, and the corresponding individual titles and interests shall be recordable.

We construe this section merely to make the individual units legal entities equivalent to a dwelling built as an individual structure. It cannot reasonably be construed to give the condominium unit owner any greater interest than the owner of a single-family dwelling.

The law in Hawaii clearly gives a mechanic a lien on the improvement he constructs as well as on the interest of the owner of the improvement in the land, R.L.H.1955, § 193–41. It is also clear that the mechanic's lien attaches to equitable interests arising under a contract of sale, Hofgaard & Co. v. Smith, 30 Haw. 882 (1929). Applying those principles to this case, it is clear that the mechanics' and materialmen's liens attached to the purchasers' equitable interest. . . .

GLENVIEW STATE BANK v. SHYMAN

Appellate Court of Illinois, First District, 1986
146 Ill.App.3d 136, 100 Ill.Dec. 13, 496 N.E.2d 1078

JUSTICE JIGANTI delivered the opinion of the court. This is an appeal by Glenview State Bank . . . from a trial court order finding that the interest of Leon Shyman . . . in condominium Unit A of Lakeshore Terrace has priority over two construction loan mortgages executed subsequent to the conveyance of Unit A, but recorded before the recordation of the deed as to Unit A. Whether the trial court erred in finding that Shyman's interest is free and clear of Glenview State Bank's claim of priority depends upon whether Glenview State Bank had notice of Shyman's interest at the time it executed the mortgages.

This action arose when Glenview State Bank filed a complaint to foreclose two mortgages on Lakeshore Terrace, Inc. Lakeshore Terrace was the mortgagor and the proceeds of the loan were to be used for the construction of the condominiums within the Lakeshore Terrace development. The mortgages were executed on March 28, 1981, and August 25, 1981, and were recorded on April 20, 1981, and August 31, 1981, respectively. In response to Glenview State Bank's complaint Shyman filed an answer and counterclaim in which he argued that Glenview State Bank had knowledge of his previously acquired interest in Unit A. This issue raised by the counterclaim was resolved by a bench trial.

At trial Shyman testified that in November of 1980 he signed a contract to purchase Unit R from Lakeshore Terrace. Thereafter Shyman was informed that Unit R was not available but that he could choose from one of the other condominium units. Shyman chose Unit A. However, that unit was also tentatively under agreement to be purchased. Nevertheless, Shyman testified that he and James Howard, president and developer of Lakeshore Terrace, orally agreed that if Unit A became available, and if Shyman contracted for Unit F and paid for Unit F, Shyman would be able to obtain Unit A. Although the parties entered into a contract for Unit F, no contract existed with respect to Unit A. It is important to note that the contract for Unit F contained a rider which provided that if the seller conveyed a unit prior to substantial completion, the title to that unit would be subject to the construction loan mortgage. This rider was also in the contracts used with regard to other units that had been sold before substantial completion.

In February of 1981 Shyman tendered the agreed-upon purchase price for Unit F and in return received a receipt which acknowledged the amount paid and recited that Units A through F could be selected at a later date. Soon thereafter Unit A was in fact conveyed to Shyman. The deed for Unit A was dated January 30, 1981, and was recorded on November 18, 1982, one year and three months after the mortgages. After the condominium unit was completed Shyman took possession of Unit A and began renting that unit.

With regard to the loans issued by Glenview State Bank, it was the opinion of Shyman's expert that because Glenview State Bank had knowledge that other condominium units had been presold the bank had inquiry notice of Shyman's interest in Unit A. Shyman argued that this inquiry notice would charge Glenview State Bank with notice of all facts that a diligent investigation or inquiry would have revealed and that in this case the investigation would have revealed Shyman's interest in Unit

A. This also was the rationale underlying the trial court's decision. We disagree, however, that the evidence supports a finding that Glenview State Bank was put on notice of any prior interest in Unit A.

The contention in this case is that Glenview State Bank must be charged with inquiry notice of the prior unrecorded conveyance of Unit A. A person will be charged with notice when that person has knowledge of facts or circumstances that would cause a person of prudence to make further inquiry. If that person does not investigate further he or she will be charged with notice of any facts that may have been discovered by the inquiry. *Bryant v. Lakeside Galleries, Inc.* (1949), 402 Ill. 466, 478, 84 N.E.2d 412; *Burnex Oil Co. v. Floyd* (1969), 106 Ill.App.2d 16, 24, 245 N.E.2d 539.

In this case there was no documentation available to Glenview State Bank that would have placed it on notice that some interest in Unit A was affected. Although there were presale contracts pertaining to other units of Lakeshore Terrace of which Glenview State Bank had knowledge, no contract existed with regard to Unit A. Moreover, these other contracts made no reference to Unit A or to any fact that would have caused Glenview State Bank to inquire further into any potential interest in Unit A. On the contrary, these contracts would have caused one to believe that no further investigation was required as the rider specifically states that if the seller conveyed any of the units prior to substantial completion, as was done in this case, those units would be subject to the construction loan mortgages. We believe that Glenview State Bank had a right to rely on this provision and was under no duty to contact each presale purchaser to ascertain whether the terms of the contracts had been altered. To conclude otherwise would place an undue burden of inquiry on prospective purchasers and mortgagees. Consequently, we believe that the trial court's finding that Glenview State Bank had notice was against the manifest weight of the evidence and therefore must be reversed. . . .

For the foregoing reasons the order of the trial court declaring Shyman to be the owner in fee simple of Unit A free and clear of any claims of priority of Glenview State Bank as mortgagee is reversed. . . .

NOTES

1. Kauaian *and* Shyman *compared.* Are *Kauaian* and *Shyman* consistent? Do you believe the appellate court in *Shyman* was correct to reverse the trial court's determination that the construction lender was on inquiry notice of the unit purchaser's interest? Do you suppose the *Kauaian* mortgagee had a greater degree of knowledge than its *Shyman* counterpart? See 2 Nelson, Whitman, Burkhart & Freyermuth, Real Estate Finance Law § 13.3 (6th ed., Practitioner Series 2014).

2. *Use of subordination clauses in sales contracts.* In light of the *Kauaian* case's holding about priorities as between contract purchasers and construction lenders, would you advise construction lender-clients to insist that developers insert subordination clauses in their pre-construction sales contracts? How likely is it that the average unit buyer will understand the significance of the clause? How specific must the language of the clause be? Cf. Handy v. Gordon, 65 Cal.2d 578, 55 Cal.Rptr. 769, 422 P.2d 329 (1967), discussed in Chapter 9, Section C, supra, and related cases.

Consider the following subordination clause in a condominium purchase agreement:

> Purchaser agrees that the provisions of this Agreement are and shall be subject and subordinate to the lien of any mortgages heretofore or hereafter made and any payments or expenses already made or incurred or which hereafter may be made or incurred pursuant to the terms thereof . . . or to protect the security thereof, to the full extent, without the execution of any further legal documents by Purchaser.

Purchase Agreement for Seaview Estates Condominium ¶ 26(b), 1 Patrick J. Rohan & Melvin A. Reskin, Condominium Law and Practice—Forms, Appendix C-19. Does this pass the *Handy* test?

How do you think the *Shyman* court would have ruled if the construction mortgagee had conceded that it possessed the requisite knowledge and the purchaser had actually executed a purchase agreement on Unit A? Would it have used the subordination language in the agreement to find in favor of the construction lender? Would it have been justified in doing so? Why does the *Kauaian* court suggest that it would be unconscionable for a lending institution to assume that it can ignore pre-existing contract rights of unit purchasers, but that it is not unconscionable for mechanic's lienors to do so?

3. *Kauaian—subsequent history.* The *Kauaian* case returned to the Hawaii Supreme Court twelve years later. Construing the construction loan mortgage, which stated that it was "subject to" the condominium declaration, the court held that State Savings's priority was inferior to the equitable liens of the unit purchasers who signed their contracts after the construction mortgage was recorded as well as before. State Sav. & Loan Ass'n v. Kauaian Dev. Co., 62 Hawaii 188, 613 P.2d 1315 (1980).

4. *Washington approach.* The courts of Washington state have been unwilling to adopt the concept of equitable conversion in real estate sales contracts; see Ashford v. Reese, 132 Wash. 649, 233 P. 29 (1925). However, they have held, for purposes of the attachment of a judgment lien to the purchaser's interest, that it is indeed an "interest in real property." See Cascade Sec. Bank v. Butler, 88 Wash.2d 777, 567 P.2d 631 (1977). How should all of this affect priorities as between a construction loan deed of trust and an earlier purchaser's rights under a contract of sale? See Nelson v. Great Northwest Fed. Sav. & Loan Ass'n, 37 Wash.App. 316, 679 P.2d 953

(1984), holding the purchaser inferior despite the absence of any subordination language in the contract. The court simply held that the contract created no rights to the real estate.

5. *Non-condominium context.* The problem of priority for purchasers' earnest money deposits is not uniquely related to condominiums, but can arise whenever a project is "pre-sold" prior to completion. The "equitable lien" for deposits has been recognized in other cases; compare Dunson v. Stockton, Whatley, Davin & Co., 346 So.2d 603 (Fla. Ct. App. 1977) with Armetta v. Clevetrust Realty Investors, 359 So.2d 540 (Fla. Ct. App. 1978). See 2 Nelson, Whitman, Burkhart & Freyermuth, Real Estate Finance Law § 13.3 (6th ed. Practitioner Series 2014).

6. *Post-closing foreclosure of construction mortgage.* Suppose the construction loan goes into default and foreclosure occurs after title to some units has passed to individual purchasers. Will their percentage interests in the common areas be protected from foreclosure? See FHA Model Act § 9. Even if so, can the lender foreclose on the percentage of the common areas attributable to unsold units? If it does, can the buyer at the foreclosure sale convert the unsold units into rental units? Can the buyer convert the recreational facilities to community-wide or even city-wide use? Must the buyer permit the owners' association to manage the recreational facilities? [Note that if the buyer has purchased enough unsold units, the buyer may well be able to control the association, and even to amend the bylaws if desired.] Can the purchasers of the early units guard against any of these eventualities?

7. *Escrow of earnest money.* An increasingly common method of protecting purchasers against loss of their earnest money deposits is to require the developer to hold them in escrow until construction is completed and the units are conveyed to their purchasers. This has long been an FHA requirement, and many "second-generation" statutes also require it. See e.g., West's Fla. Stat. Ann. § 718.202. The UCA also mandates escrowing of such funds; see UCA § 4–110 (1980), which applies even to money given to the developer under a non-binding "reservation agreement."

D. OPERATING THE COMMON INTEREST COMMUNITY

1. FINANCING COMMUNITY OPERATIONS

In the public sector, most municipalities depend (at least in part) on the ability to levy taxes and assessments against real estate as needed to fund public services and improvements. Common interest communities provide a private sector analogue; to be viable, common interest communities require efficient and enforceable assessment mechanisms sufficient to fund the present and future maintenance of common facilities. Ever since the New York Court of Appeals upheld the enforcement of an assessment covenant as a covenant running with the land in the landmark case of Neponsit Property Owners' Ass'n, Inc. v. Emigrant Indus. Sav. Bank, 278 N.Y. 248, 15 N.E.2d 793 (1938), the ability of a common interest community to provide for and collect assessments for common facilities has been well-accepted.

Accordingly, the declaration creating a common interest community typically establishes the initial and/or maximum amounts of assessments, procedures for increasing assessments or levying special assessments, the allocation of reserves for future capital needs, and mechanisms to facilitate the ability of the owners association to collect unpaid assessments. In the typical declaration, these mechanisms may include fines or the accrual of interest upon overdue assessments, as well as a lien in favor of the owners association on any assessed lot for which assessments remain unpaid. The foreclosure of such a lien, and the subsequent sale of the assessed parcel with the application of sale proceeds to satisfy the unpaid assessments, provides the association (at least theoretically) with the fiscal strength necessary to satisfy its responsibilities to provide services and maintain common facilities.

Nevertheless, collection of unpaid assessments (particularly through foreclosure) presents owners associations with a number of practical and legal problems. The following case and notes address some of these problems, including: whether the association can foreclose its lien through private sale or must instead use judicial foreclosure; whether the sale is subject to standards of commercial reasonableness; how significant a default must exist before a foreclosure can proceed; and the priority of the association's lien vis-à-vis a mortgage lien against the assessed lot.

WILL V. MILL CONDOMINIUM OWNERS' ASSOCIATION

Supreme Court of Vermont, 2004
176 Vt. 380, 848 A.2d 336

AMESTOY, C.J. Appellant owned a residential condominium unit at The Mill Condominiums in Ludlow, Vermont. After appellant failed to pay her condominium dues over a period of time, the officers of the Mill Condominium Owners' Association instructed attorney Martin Nitka to foreclose on the property. Attorney Nitka thereafter commenced a nonjudicial foreclosure pursuant to 27A V.S.A. § 3–116. Appellant had notice of the foreclosure sale and discussed the matter with attorney Nitka. She informed him that she would wire him the unpaid dues and asked him to postpone the sale scheduled for July 12, 2001, to a later time. Appellant's recollection of the discussion was that the sale would not take place if she wired the money to attorney Nitka's account by the close of the business day, July 16. According to attorney Nitka, he agreed to delay the sale only until July 13, but after the telephone conversation with appellant realized that he had other commitments, and moved the sale to July 16, 2001. At 10:00 a.m. on July 16, 2001, attorney Nitka proceeded with the auction of appellant's condominium. Appellant's wire transfer of funds sufficient to cover the dues, fees, and costs owed arrived at 11:00 a.m. By that time, the property had been sold to defendants Allen and Linda Seiple for $3510.10, the amount necessary to pay the delinquent dues, attorney's fees, and the costs of foreclosure. The trial court found that, at the time of the sale, attorney Nitka and the Seiples apparently believed that the unit was subject to a mortgage of $45,000. It was later determined that the mortgage had been earlier discharged. The trial court found that the fair market value of the condominium at the time of sale was approximately $70,000. Attorney Nitka delivered the deed to the Seiples on August 31, 2001.

In October 2001, appellant filed a complaint seeking a declaratory judgment setting aside the nonjudicial foreclosure. In December 2001, after trial, the court entered judgment for defendants on the record. * * *

[Appellant] claims that the condominium association and attorney Nitka breached their duties when they failed to maximize the sale price of the condominium. The trial court rejected this claim after concluding that there is no statutory requirement to conduct the sale in a commercially reasonable manner, and that neither the condominium association, nor Nitka, owed appellant a fiduciary duty. Nevertheless, appellant argues that 12 V.S.A. § 4532(g) imposes on the mortgagee an affirmative duty to conduct the nonjudicial sale in a commercially reasonable manner or in such a manner as to maximize the sales price of such property. * * *

* * * Appellees' resort to the nonjudicial foreclosure statute arises not as a result of a mortgagor-mortgagee relationship—but rather because of the provisions of the Uniform Common Interest Ownership Act, 27A V.S.A. §§ 1–101–4–120 (UCIOA), which provides a statutory right to the Condominium Association to institute a nonjudicial foreclosure proceeding for nonpayment of condominium dues. Thus, the extent of the duty owed by the Condominium Association and its agent to the appellant is first established by discerning the obligations and rights of the parties under the Act.

The Association's commencement of a nonjudicial foreclosure was made pursuant to 27A V.S.A. § 3–116(i), which states, "The association's lien may be foreclosed pursuant to section 4531a of Title 12 in which case the association shall notify all the lienholders of the affected unit of its action."

The official comment to § 3–116 reveals the Legislature's intent to provide condominium associations with adequate mechanisms to collect unpaid dues while offering alternatives to the radical remedy of foreclosure. Thus, the comment notes that subsection (1) "makes clear that the association may have remedies short of foreclosure of its lien that can be used to collect unpaid assessments. The association, for example, might bring an action in debt or breach of contract against a recalcitrant unit owner rather than resorting to foreclosure." On the other hand, the Legislature reserves what it considers the more expeditious procedures for foreclosure on units belonging to a cooperative, since in these associations assessments are used to pay each unit's share of the common mortgage, and nonpayment may force the whole community into default. Thus, the statute allows for the treatment of units in cooperatives as personal property instead of realty, so that they can be foreclosed under the generally less expensive and faster procedure provided for under Article 9 of the Uniform Commercial Code (UCC). The comment points out that condominium communities are generally not burdened by a substantial underlying mortgage and therefore,

> failure to pay assessments on time will have less serious consequences for the association than in the case of cooperatives. The section provides that the association lien in a condominium or planned community is to be foreclosed according to the rules generally applicable to real estate mortgages . . . rather than setting out a special faster method of foreclosure in the statute.

* * * Although the rules "generally applicable to real estate mortgages" do not impose a commercial reasonableness standard on foreclosure sales, the UCIOA does provide for this additional layer of protection. Section 1–113 of the UCIOA states that "[e]very contract or duty governed by this title imposes an obligation of good faith on all parties in its performance or enforcement." * * *

The UCC and Uniform Simplification of Land Transfers Act sections alluded to in the official comment define and refer to the observance of "reasonable commercial standards of fair dealing in the trade." 9A V.S.A. § 2–103(1)(b)(UCC). Hence, the official comment to § 1–113 expresses in unequivocal terms the Legislature's intent to import the commercial reasonableness standard into the UCIOA.

While the intent of the Legislature to impose the commercial reasonableness standard on all common interest communities created after the effective date of the law is clear, the application of the standard to common interest communities created before the enactment of the statute is less certain. * * *

The issue is relevant to the instant case because it appears that the Mill Condominium Association predated the January 1, 1999 effective date of the UCIOA. It would be irrational, however, to conclude that the commercial reasonableness standard need not to be observed in a § 3–116 foreclosure because the condominium association predated the statute. The foreclosure action deals with appellant's unpaid assessments occurring after January 1, 1999, and neither appellant nor appellees contest the applicability of the UCIOA in part to preexisting common interest communities "with respect to events and circumstances occurring after the effective date of [the Act]." 27A V.S.A. § 1–204(a). * * *

It is conceivable that the Legislature omitted § 1–113 from the enumeration of sections applicable to pre-existing common interest communities because of concerns that applying the commercial reasonableness standard to previously acquired rights and obligations "would unduly alter the legitimate expectations of [pre-existing] unit owners and declarants." 27A V.S.A. § 1–201 (official comment). It is inconceivable, however, that the Legislature intended its omission to insulate pre-existing communities from their obligations under the UCIOA when they are availing themselves of a remedy provided by the very same act, because the parties could not expect that their obligations would be defined by any standard other than the one supplied by the statute. We presume that "the Legislature [did] not intend an interpretation that would lead to absurd or irrational consequences." *Braun v. Bd. of Dental Exam'rs,* 167 Vt. 110, 117, 702 A.2d 124, 128 (1997). Therefore, we hold that the enforcement mechanisms provided for in § 3–116 must be conducted in good faith as defined in § 1–113, that is, in a commercially reasonable manner.

The "commercial reasonableness" standard is well defined in Vermont. A secured party's disposition of collateral is governed by Part 6 of Article 9 of Vermont's Uniform Commercial Code. Title 9A, § 9–610(b) imposes a positive duty on the secured party to act in a commercially reasonable manner in every aspect of the disposition of collateral. 9A V.S.A. § 9–610(b). * * *

The commercial reasonableness of a sale must be determined on a case-by-case basis. *Fed. Fin. Co. v. Papadopoulos,* 168 Vt. 621, 623, 721 A.2d 501, 503 (1998) (mem.). The secured party bears the burden "to prove that the disposition of collateral was commercially reasonable." *Id.* * * *

The evidence in the record, however, does not support summary judgment under this standard; rather, it supports a finding that, as a matter of law, the sale did not conform with the requirements of good faith and commercial reasonableness set forth by § 1–113 of the UCIOA. First, the disparity between the condominium's sale price and its fair market value, although not dispositive, must be taken into account in the assessment of the reasonableness of the sale. See *Papadopoulos,* 168 Vt. at 623, 721 A.2d at 503. In this case the discrepancy suggests that no efforts were made to attain the best price for the unit. The trial court found the fair market value of the condominium to be "approximately $70,000." Although the court observed that attorney Nitka and the Seiples apparently thought that the property was subject to an undischarged $45,000 mortgage, the purchase price—even under such an assumption—was less than 15% of the value found by the trial court.

In addition, this Court has found that, in private sales, the seller's exclusive reliance on one bid may be a factor against a finding of reasonableness. *Id.* Although this was a public sale, it weighs against such a finding in this case as well, considering the alleged statement from Mr. Nitka to Mr. Seiple informing him that the minimum acceptable bid for this property would be $3510.50. Although there is no suggestion that this was done in bad faith, giving this information to the only bidder was certainly not a way to maximize the value of the collateral; rather, it was an assurance that the condominium would be sold for exactly that low amount.

Summary judgment is vacated, and the case remanded to the trial court for entry of judgment voiding foreclosure sale of appellant's condominium unit.

NOTES

1. *The assessment lien.* Under some first-generation legislation, it was often unclear that an association's lien could cover matters other than common expenses. See, e.g., FHA Model Act § 23; Elbadramany v. Oceans Seven Condo. Ass'n, Inc., 461 So.2d 1001 (Fla. Ct. App. 1984) (fine for parking boat in condominium parking lot could not be a lien because it was not a common expense under state condominium legislation). As a result, some courts refused to permit fees or charges not specifically authorized by the declaration. See, e.g., Westbridge Condo. Ass'n, Inc. v. Lawrence, 554 A.2d 1163 (D.C. Ct. App. 1989) ($150 move-in fee impermissible because not authorized by condominium documents, which required pro rata allocation of costs of operating common areas absent specific owner negligence or misconduct). By contrast, the UCA and UCIOA expressly provide that the association's lien covers fees, charges, late charges, fines, and interest unless the declaration provides otherwise. UCA § 3–116, UCIOA § 3–116.

2. *Controversy over lien foreclosure.* There have been numerous stories in the popular media concerning alleged abuses of the lien foreclosure process. Most commonly, owners complained of foreclosures for relatively minor amounts, or for charges such as uncollected fines rather than the usual unpaid monthly assessments. See, e.g., Paul Quinlan & Will Rothschild, "Home Lost Over $1,380 Dues," Sarasota Herald-Tribune p. A1, August 3, 2005; Shonda Novak, "Bill Targets Homeowner Association Foreclosures," Austin American Statesman, p. F1, February 5, 2005; Cary Aspinwall, "Homeowners' Rights Groups Fight Back; New State Laws Give More Power to Residents Facing Conflicts with Associations," The Arizona Republic, p. 1A, August 15, 2005. For an overview of these issues, see Gemma Giantosmasi, A Balancing Act: The Foreclosure Power of Homeowners' Associations, 72 Ford. L. Rev. 2503 (2004).

In an attempt to respond to these concerns, the 2008 amendments to UCIOA articulate clearer limits upon an association's ability to enforce its lien via foreclosure. First, the association may not begin a foreclosure unless the owner owes a sum equal to at least three months of regularly scheduled common expense assessments, the owner has failed to accept or comply with a payment plan offered by the association, and the association board has voted to commence foreclosure against the specific unit in question. UCIOA § 3–116(n). Second, nonjudicial foreclosure is permissible only when the unpaid sums include past due assessments; if the unpaid sums consist of fines or sums other than assessments, the association cannot foreclose without first obtaining a judgment for those sums and a judgment lien against the unit. UCIOA § 3–116(p). Finally, UCIOA now expressly resolves the interpretive question addressed in *Will*, requiring that any sale foreclosing an association's lien must be commercially reasonable in all respects, "including the method, advertising, time, place and terms." UCIOA § 3–116(q). These changes were inspired by similar limitations previously imposed by individual state legislatures. See, e.g., Ariz. Rev. Stat. Ann. § 33–1807(A) (limiting automatic lien to assessments and costs directly related to them, and requiring judicial process for enforcement as to other fines and penalties); West's Ann. Cal. Civ. Code § 5720(b) (prohibiting association from foreclosing for unpaid assessment if the amount due is less than $1,800; lower amounts must be recovered in small claims court); Fla. Stat. Ann. § 720.305 (lien not available for fines less than $1,000).

An argument can be made that assessment liens are to owners associations what real estate tax liens are to government entities. Most tax lien foreclosure systems allow long redemption periods for delinquent taxpayers. Should such long periods be available to defaulting unit owners? Is it one thing to provide long redemption periods for delinquent real estate taxes (where the costs can be spread over the entire taxpaying public) and yet another to do so in common interest communities (where the shortfall may have to be borne by increased assessments on relatively few owners)?

3. *Commercial reasonableness and advertisement.* As you learned in Chapter 6, mortgage law has typically not required a foreclosing mortgagee to conduct a commercially reasonable sale. As a result, foreclosure sales often involve little or no advertising beyond the legal notices required by most foreclosure statutes. The *Will* decision concluded that under Vermont's version of UCIOA, the association's duty of good faith and fair dealing effectively required the association to conduct its foreclosure sale in a commercially reasonable manner. Did the court inappropriately conflate "good faith" and "commercial reasonableness"?

As indicated in note 2, the 2014 amendments to UCIOA explicitly incorporate a requirement of commercial reasonableness for sales to enforce association liens. In the context of personal property foreclosure sales—for which Article 9 provides a comparable "commercial reasonableness" requirement in U.C.C. § 9–610(b)—courts have sometimes looked dimly upon a secured party that conducted a foreclosure sale involving minimal advertisement. For example, in Contrail Leasing Partners, Ltd. v. Consolidated Airways, Inc., 742 F.2d 1095 (7th Cir. 1984), the court held that a secured party that sold a corporate jet after publishing only one small advertisement failed to meet the "commercially reasonable" standard. The court suggested that the secured party's advertisement should have been more conspicuous and should have been placed in additional trade publications to expose the collateral to additional potential buyers.

Because the term "commercially reasonable" has long been incorporated within the UCC, to what extent should UCC case law interpreting the term influence the evaluation of foreclosure sales involving association liens? What implications would this have for associations in collecting unpaid assessments? What advertisement or marketing should an association have to undertake prior to conducting a foreclosure sale?

4. *Personal liability for assessments.* A unit owner has more to fear from an unpaid assessment than loss of his or her unit through foreclosure of the association lien. Each unit owner is also *personally liable* for assessments that are attributable to his or her period of ownership. See UCA § 3–116(f) and comment 3; UCIOA § 3–116(g) (2008). Moreover, where a unit is owned by more than one person, there often is joint and several liability for the assessment against the unit. See Chattahoochee Chase Condo. Ass'n v. Ruben, 221 Ga.App. 724, 472 S.E.2d 520 (1996) (unit owner with only a one percent interest in the unit held jointly and severally liable for the entire assessment against the unit). This personal liability can be discharged, however, if the unit owner goes through bankruptcy; this has proven to be a problem for some associations. See James L. Winokur, Critical Assessment: The Financial Role of Community Associations, 38 Santa Clara L. Rev. 1135 (1998).

5. *Assessment lien priority vs. mortgage liens.* Under most first-generation condominium statutes, first mortgage liens on a unit have priority over the association's lien for unpaid assessments against that unit. FHA Model Act § 23(a); Ariz. Rev. Stat. § 33–1807(B); N.Y. Real Prop. Law § 339z. Is this appropriate, given that liens for unpaid real estate taxes are senior to all mortgage liens? By contrast, both the UCA and UCIOA provide that an association's assessment lien has priority over a mortgage on the assessed unit to the extent of unpaid assessments due during the six months immediately prior to the lien enforcement proceeding (and attorneys' fees and costs incurred by the association in foreclosing its lien). See UCA § 3–116; UCIOA § 3–116(b), (c). Professor Winokur explains the rationale for this approach:

> In addition to giving community associations a share—albeit a limited share—of the sale proceeds when residences in common interest communities are foreclosed, the more important consequence of limited "super-priority" for a portion of association assessment defaults may be in providing the association much needed leverage in getting the property more quickly into

foreclosure, leading to purchase by a solvent owner (often the mortgagee), or by encouraging the senior mortgagee to pay assessments it might not technically be obligated to pay in order to gain control over the timing and mode of foreclosure. . . .

Winokur, supra note 4, at 1135. There has been disagreement, however, as to the meaning of UCIOA's lien priority provision. Compare Andrea J. Boyack, Community Collateral Damage: A Question of Priorities, 43 Loy. U. Chi. L. Rev. 53, 99 (2011) ("The six-month capped "super priority" portion of the association lien does not have a true priority status under UCIOA since this six-month assessment lien cannot be foreclosed as senior to a mortgage lien. Rather, it either creates a payment priority for some portion of unpaid assessments, which would take the first position in the foreclosure repayment "waterfall," or grants durability to some portion of unpaid assessments, allowing the security for such debt to survive foreclosure.") with Report of the Joint Editorial Board for Uniform Real Property Acts, The Six-Month "Limited Priority Lien" for Association Fees Under the Uniform Common Interest Ownership Act (association's six-month limited priority lien constitutes a true lien priority and not merely a distributional preference in favor of the association). If the association forecloses its assessment lien, and the "first" mortgagee does not step forward and pay off the priority portion of the association's lien prior to the association's sale, does the sale extinguish the first mortgage lien? Does it matter whether the association foreclosed its lien in a judicial proceeding rather than a nonjudicial proceeding?

SFR INVESTMENTS POOL 1, LLC v. U.S. BANK, N.A.

Supreme Court of Nevada, 2014
334 P.3d 408

PICKERING, J. NRS 116.3116 gives a homeowners' association (HOA) a superpriority lien on an individual homeowner's property for up to nine months of unpaid HOA dues. With limited exceptions, this lien is "prior to all other liens and encumbrances" on the homeowner's property, even a first deed of trust recorded before the dues became delinquent. NRS 116.3116(2). We must decide whether this is a true priority lien such that its foreclosure extinguishes a first deed of trust on the property and, if so, whether it can be foreclosed nonjudicially. We answer both questions in the affirmative and therefore reverse. . . .

This dispute involves a residence located in a common-interest community known as Southern Highlands. The property was subject to Covenants, Conditions, and Restrictions (CC & Rs) recorded in 2000. In 2007 it was further encumbered by a note and deed of trust in favor of, via assignment, respondent U.S. Bank, N.A. By 2010, the former homeowners, who are not parties to this case, had fallen delinquent on their Southern Highlands Community Association (SHHOA) dues and also defaulted on their obligations to U.S. Bank. Separately, SHHOA and U.S. Bank each initiated nonjudicial foreclosure proceedings.

Appellant SFR Investments Pool 1, LLC (SFR) purchased the property at the SHHOA's trustee's sale, which took place on September 5, 2012. SFR received and recorded a trustee's deed reciting compliance with all applicable notice requirements. In the meantime, the trustee's sale on U.S. Bank's deed of trust had been postponed to December 19, 2012. Days before then, SFR filed an action to quiet title and enjoin the sale. SFR alleged that the SHHOA trustee's deed extinguished U.S. Bank's deed of trust and vested clear title in SFR, leaving U.S. Bank nothing to foreclose.

. . . Ultimately, the district court denied SFR's motion for a preliminary injunction and granted U.S. Bank's countermotion to dismiss. It held that an HOA must proceed judicially to validly foreclose its superpriority lien. Since SHHOA foreclosed nonjudicially, the district court reasoned, U.S. Bank's first deed of trust survived the SHHOA trustee's sale and was senior to the trustee's deed SFR received. . . .

The HOA lien statute, NRS 116.3116, is a creature of the Uniform Common Interest Ownership Act of 1982, § 3–116, 7 U.L.A., part II 121–24 (2009) (amended 1994, 2008) (UCIOA), which Nevada adopted in 1991, 1991 Nev. Stat., ch. 245, § 1–128, at 535–79, and codified as NRS Chapter 116. . . .

NRS 116.3116(1) gives an HOA a lien on its homeowners' residences—the UCIOA calls them "units," see NRS 116.093—"for any construction penalty that is imposed against the unit's owner . . ., any assessment levied against that unit or any fines imposed against the unit's owner from the time the construction penalty, assessment or fine becomes due." NRS 116.3116(2) elevates the priority of the HOA lien over other liens. It states that the HOA's lien is "prior to all other liens and encumbrances on a unit" except for:

> (a) Liens and encumbrances recorded before the recordation of the declaration [creating the common-interest community] . . . ;

> (b) A first security interest on the unit recorded before the date on which the assessment sought to be enforced became delinquent . . . ; and

> (c) Liens for real estate taxes and other governmental assessments or charges against the unit or cooperative.

NRS 116.3116(2) (emphasis added). If subsection 2 ended there, a first deed of trust would have complete priority over an HOA lien. But it goes on to carve out a partial exception to subparagraph (2)(b)'s exception for first security interests:

The [HOA] lien is also prior to all security interests described in paragraph (b) to the extent of any [maintenance and nuisance-abatement] charges incurred by the association on a unit pursuant to NRS 116.310312 and to the extent of the assessments for common expenses [i.e., HOA dues] based on the periodic budget adopted by the association pursuant to NRS 116.3115 which would have become due in the absence of acceleration during the 9 months immediately preceding institution of an action to enforce the lien, unless federal regulations adopted by the Federal Home Loan Mortgage Corporation or the Federal National Mortgage Association require a shorter period of priority for the lien. . . . This subsection does not affect the priority of mechanics' or materialmen's liens, or the priority of liens for other assessments made by the association.

NRS 116.3116(2) (emphases added).

As to first deeds of trust, NRS 116.3116(2) thus splits an HOA lien into two pieces, a superpriority piece and a subpriority piece. The superpriority piece, consisting of the last nine months of unpaid HOA dues and maintenance and nuisance-abatement charges, is "prior to" a first deed of trust. The subpriority piece, consisting of all other HOA fees or assessments, is subordinate to a first deed of trust. . . .

U.S. Bank maintains that NRS 116.3116(2) merely creates a payment priority as between the HOA and the beneficiary of the first deed of trust. If so, then the dues and maintenance and nuisance-abatement piece of the HOA lien does not acquire superpriority status until the beneficiary of the first deed of trust forecloses, at which point, to obtain clear, insurable title, the foreclosure-sale buyer would have to pay off that piece of the HOA lien. But if the superpriority piece is a true priority lien, then it is senior to the first deed of trust. As such, it can be foreclosed and its foreclosure will extinguish the first deed of trust. See, e.g., Restatement (Third) of Prop.: Mortgages § 7.1 (1997) ("A valid foreclosure of a mortgage terminates all interests in the foreclosed real estate that are junior to the mortgage being foreclosed and whose holders are properly joined or notified under applicable law.").

Nevada's state and federal district courts are divided on whether NRS 116.3116 establishes a true priority lien. Compare *7912 Limbwood Court Trust v. Wells Fargo Bank, N.A.*, 979 F.Supp.2d 1142, 1149 (D.Nev.2013) ("[A] foreclosure sale on the HOA super priority lien extinguishes all junior interests, including the first deed of trust."), *Cape Jasmine Court Trust v. Cent. Mortg. Co.*, No. 2:13CV–1125APG–CWH, 2014 WL 1305015, at *4 (D.Nev. Mar. 31, 2014) (same), and *First 100, LLC v. Burns*, No. A677693 (8th Jud.Dist.Ct. May 31, 2013) (order denying motion to dismiss) (same), with *Bayview Loan Servicing, LLC v. Alessi & Koenig, LLC*, 962 F.Supp.2d 1222, 1225 (D.Nev.2013) ("The super-priority amount is senior to an earlier-recorded first mortgage in the sense that it must be satisfied before a first mortgage upon its own foreclosure, but it is in parity with an earlier-recorded first mortgage with respect to extinguishment, i.e., the foreclosure of neither extinguishes the other.") (emphasis in original); *Weeping Hollow Ave. Trust v. Spencer*, No. 2:13–CV–00544–JCM–VCF, 2013 WL 2296313, at *6 (D.Nev. May 24, 2013) (same), and *Diakonos Holdings, LLC v. Countrywide Home Loans, Inc.*, No. 2:12–CV–00949–KJD–RJJ, 2013 WL 531092, at *3 (D.Nev. Feb. 11, 2013) (similar).

Textually, NRS 116.3116 supports the *Limbwood, Cape Jasmine*, and *First 100* view that it establishes a true priority lien. NRS 116.3116(2) does not speak in terms of payment priorities. It states that the HOA "lien . . . is *prior to* " other liens and encumbrances "except . . . [a] first security interest," then adds that, "The lien is *also prior to* [first] security interests" to the extent of nine months of unpaid HOA dues and maintenance and nuisance-abatement charges. *Ibid.* (emphases added). "Prior" refers to the lien, not payment or proceeds, and is used the same way in both sentences, a point the phrase "*also* prior to" drives home. And "priority lien" and "prior lien" mean the same thing, according to *Black's Law Dictionary* 1008 (9th ed.2009): "A lien that is superior to one or more other liens on the same property, usu. because it was perfected first."

The official comments to UCIOA § 3–116 confirm its text. Payment priority proponents insist that the statute cannot mean what it says because the result—a split lien, a piece of which has priority over a first deed of trust—is unprecedented. *Cf. Bayview Loan Servicing*, 962 F.Supp.2d at 1226 (observing that, "the real estate community in Nevada clearly understands the statutes to work the way the Court finds," that is to say, as establishing only a payment priority). But the official comments to UCIOA § 3–116 forthrightly acknowledge that the split-lien approach represents a "significant departure from existing practice." 1982 UCIOA § 3–116 cmt. 1; 1994 & 2008 UCIOA § 3–116 cmt. 2. It is a specially devised mechanism designed to "strike[ ] an equitable balance between the need to enforce collection of unpaid assessments and the obvious necessity for protecting the priority of the security interests of lenders." *Id.* The comments continue: "As a practical matter, secured lenders will most likely pay the 6 [in Nevada, nine] months' assessments demanded by the association rather than having the association foreclose on the unit." *Id.* (emphasis added). If the superpriority piece of the HOA lien just established a payment priority, the reference to a first security holder paying off the superpriority piece of the lien to stave off foreclosure would make no sense.

"An official comment written by the drafters of a statute and available to a legislature before the statute is enacted has considerable weight as an aid to statutory construction." *Acierno v. Worthy Bros. Pipeline Corp.*, 656 A.2d 1085, 1090 (Del.1995). The comments to the 1982 UCIOA were available to the 1991 Legislature when it enacted NRS Chapter 116. Even though the comments emphasize that the split-lien approach is "[a] significant departure from existing practice," 1982 UCIOA § 3–116 cmt. 1, the Legislature enacted NRS 116.3116(2) with UCIOA § 3–116's superpriority provision intact. From this it follows that, however unconventional, the superpriority piece of the HOA lien carries true priority over a first deed of trust.

The Uniform Law Commission (ULC) has established a Joint Editorial Board for Uniform Real Property Acts (JEB), made up of members from the ULC; the ABA Section of Real Property, Probate and Trust Law; and the American College of Real Estate Lawyers, which "is responsible for monitoring all uniform real property acts," of which the UCIOA is one. The JEB's 2013 report entitled, The Six-Month "Limited Priority Lien" for Association Fees Under the Uniform Common Interest Ownership Act, also supports that § 3–116(b) establishes a true priority lien. Addressing the recent foreclosure crisis and the incentives the crisis created for first security holders to strategically delay foreclosure, this report canvasses the case law construing the UCIOA's superpriority lien. It endorses the decision in *Summerhill Village Homeowners Ass'n v. Roughley*, 289 P.3d 645, 647–48 (2012), which, addressing a statute using the same superpriority language as NRS 116.3116(2), holds that an HOA's judicial foreclosure of the superpriority piece of its lien extinguished the first deed of trust. JEB, The Six-Month "Limited Priority Lien," at 8–9. The report then criticizes by name two of the three Nevada federal district court cases cited above as being on the payment-priority side of the NRS 116.3116(2) split—*Weeping Hollow* and *Diakonos*—saying they "misread and misinterpret the Uniform Laws limited priority lien provision, which . . . constitutes a true lien priority, [such that] the association's proper enforcement of its lien . . . extinguish[es] the otherwise senior mortgage lien." *Id.* at 10 n. 9.

The comments liken the HOA lien to "other inchoate liens such as real estate taxes and mechanics liens." 1994 & 2008 UCIOA § 3–116 cmt. 1. An HOA's "sources of revenues are usually limited to common assessments." JEB, The Six-Month "Limited Priority Lien," at 4. This makes an HOA's ability to foreclose on the unpaid dues portion of its lien essential for common-interest communities. *Id.* at 1–2. Otherwise, when a homeowner walks away from the property and the first deed of trust holder delays foreclosure, the HOA has to "either increase the assessment burden on the remaining unit/parcel owners or reduce the services the association provides (e.g., by deferring maintenance on common amenities)." *Id.* at 5–6. To avoid having the community subsidize first security holders who delay foreclosure, whether strategically or for some other reason, UCIOA § 3–116 creates a true superpriority lien:

> A foreclosure sale of the association's lien (whether judicial or nonjudicial) is governed by the principles generally applicable to lien foreclosure sales, i.e., a foreclosure sale of a lien entitled to priority extinguishes that lien and any subordinate liens, transferring those liens to the sale proceeds. Nothing in the Uniform Laws establishes (or was intended to establish) a contrary result.

Id. at 9 (footnotes omitted).

U.S. Bank's final objection is that it makes little sense and is unfair to allow a relatively nominal lien—nine months of HOA dues—to extinguish a first deed of trust securing hundreds of thousands of dollars of debt. But as a junior lienholder, U.S. Bank could have paid off the SHHOA lien to avert loss of its security; it also could have established an escrow for SHHOA assessments to avoid having to use its own funds to pay delinquent dues. 1982 UCIOA § 3116 cmt. 1; 1994 & 2008 UCIOA § 3–116 cmt. 2. The inequity U.S. Bank decries is thus of its own making and not a reason to give NRS 116.3116(2) a singular reading at odds with its text and the interpretation given it by the authors and editors of the UCIOA. . . .

Since NRS 116.3116(2) establishes a true superpriority lien, the next question we must decide is whether the lien may be foreclosed nonjudicially or requires judicial foreclosure. NRS Chapter 116 answers this question directly: An HOA may foreclose its lien by nonjudicial foreclosure sale. Thus, NRS 116.3116(1) defines what an HOA lien covers, while NRS 116.31162(1) states that "in a planned community"—a "planned community" is any type of "common-interest community that is not a condominium or a cooperative," NRS 116.075—"the association may foreclose its lien by sale." To "foreclose [a] lien by sale" under NRS 116.31162(1) encompasses an HOAs conducting a nonjudicial foreclosure sale. This is evident from the remainder of NRS 116.31162, which speaks to the statutory notices of delinquency, default and election to sell required of a nonjudicial foreclosure sale, and the sections that follow, NRS 116.31163 through NRS 116.31168, all of which concern the mechanics and requirements of nonjudicial foreclosure sales of HOA liens. The only limits Chapter 116 places on HOA lien foreclosure sales appear in NRS 116.31162(5) and (6), which restrict foreclosure of HOA liens for certain fines and penalties and liens on homes in Nevada's foreclosure mediation program (FMP). Given this statutory text, we cannot agree with our dissenting colleagues that NRS Chapter 116 requires judicial foreclosure of the superpriority piece of an HOA lien but authorizes nonjudicial foreclosure of everything else.

Together, NRS 116.3116(1) and NRS 116.31162 provide for the nonjudicial foreclosure of the whole of an HOA's lien, not just the subpriority piece of it. U.S. Bank and our dissenting colleagues do not come to terms with NRS 116.31162. Instead, they focus on a single phrase in NRS 116.3116(2) which defines the superpriority piece of the lien as comprising "assessments for common expenses . . . which would have become due in the absence of acceleration during the 9 months immediately preceding *institution of an action to enforce the lien.*" (Emphasis added.) Not acknowledging that NRS 116.3116(2) only discusses lien priority, not foreclosure methods, they maintain that the phrase "institution of an action to enforce the lien" suggests a civil action, a lawsuit brought in a court of law. But the phrase is not so narrow that it excludes nonjudicial foreclosure proceedings. *Black's Law Dictionary* 869 (9th ed.2009) defines "institution" as "[t]he commencement of something, *such as* a civil or criminal action." (Emphasis added.) As *Black's* recognizes, "foreclosure" proceedings are "instituted" and include both "judicial foreclosure" and "nonjudicial foreclosure" methods. *Id.* at 719 (defining "foreclosure," "judicial foreclosure," and "nonjudicial" or "power-of-sale foreclosure"). And in the context of foreclosures, "action" appears to be commonly used in connection with nonjudicial as well as judicial foreclosures. *See In re Bonner Mall P'ship*, 2 F.3d 899, 902 (9th Cir.1993) (referring to a bank "commenc[ing] a nonjudical foreclosure action"); *Santiago v. BAC Home Loans Servicing, L.P.*, ___ F.Supp.2d ___, ___, 2014 WL 2075994, at *3 (W.D.Tex.2014) (holding an assignee to be "an appropriate party to initiate a nonjudicial foreclosure action against the Property").

The argument that NRS 116.3116(2)'s use of the word "action" means "that an HOA must foreclose judicially to invoke the superpriority" lien provision was considered and rejected in *Nationstar Mortgage, LLC v. Rob and Robbie, LLC*, No. 2:13–cv–01241–RCJ–PAL, 2014 WL 3661398, at *4 (D.Nev. July 23, 2014). The court gave "two independent reasons" for its holding. "First, 'action' does not include only civil actions. The Legislature could easily have said 'civil action' or 'judicial action,' but it used the broader term 'action.' " *Id.* In the lien foreclosure context, "where the statutes . . . provide for either judicial or non judicial foreclosure, 'action' is most reasonably read to include either." *Id.* Second, NRS 116.3116(2) does not "use the word 'action' in a way that makes the super-priority status depend[e]nt upon whether an 'action' has been instituted. Rather, the word 'action' is used (in the subjunctive mode, not the indicative mode) as a way to measure the portion of an HOA lien that has super-priority status." *Id.*

UCIOA § 3–116(b) uses the phrase "institution of an action to enforce the lien" in describing the superpriority lien, exactly as NRS 116.3116(2) does. Section 3–116(j) of the 1982 and 1994 UCIOA (and with minor alteration, section 3–116(k) of the 2008 UCIOA) prompt the adopting state to choose and insert its authorized foreclosure method, be it judicial or nonjudicial:

(j)   The association's lien may be foreclosed as provided in this subsection:

(1)   In a condominium or planned community, the association's lien must be foreclosed in like manner as a mortgage on real estate [or by power of sale under [insert appropriate state statute]];

(2)   In a cooperative whose unit owners' interests in the units are real estate (Section 1–105), the association's lien must be foreclosed in like manner as a mortgage on real estate [or by power of sale under [insert appropriate state statute]] [or by power of sale under subsection (k)]; or

(3)   In a cooperative whose unit owners' interests in the units are personal property (Section 1–105), the association's lien must be foreclosed in like manner as a security interest under [insert reference to Article 9, Uniform Commercial Code.]

[(4) In the case of foreclosure under [insert reference to state power of sale statute], the association shall give reasonable notice of its action to all lien holders of the unit whose interest would be affected.]

1982 UCIOA § 3–116(i). If the UCIOA meant "institution of an action to enforce the lien" in § 3–116(b) to signify that all superpriority HOA lien foreclosures must proceed judicially, § 3–116(j)'s repeated references to the foreclosure of "the association's lien" by judicial or nonjudicial foreclosure, depending on the enacting state's local laws, is inexplicable. And, indeed, the Joint Editorial Board for Uniform Real Property Acts has confirmed that, in the context of an HOA's superpriority lien specifically, "[a] foreclosure sale of the association's lien (whether judicial or nonjudicial) is governed by the principles generally applicable to lien foreclosure sales, i.e., a foreclosure sale of a lien entitled to priority extinguishes that lien and any subordinate liens." JEB, The Six-Month "Limited Priority Lien," at 9 (emphasis added) (footnote omitted).

Nevada did not enact subsection (j) of § 3–116. Instead, it enacted a series of separate, consecutively numbered statutes, NRS 116.31162 through NRS 116.31168, each addressing a specific aspect of the nonjudicial foreclosure process NRS 116.31162 authorizes for HOA liens. These statutes use "enforce" throughout with reference to an HOA's nonjudicial foreclosure of its lien. See NRS 116.31162(l)(b)(2) (the notice of delinquent assessment must identify "the person authorized by the association to enforce the lien by sale"); NRS 116.31162(1)(c); NRS 116.31164(2) (discussing costs, fees, and expenses incident to an HOA's nonjudicial "enforcement of its lien"). Nothing in these statutes suggests that, by adopting them in lieu of the more abbreviated § 3–116(j), Nevada was *sub silentio* rejecting the UCIOA's use of "institution of an action to enforce the lien" as applying to either judicial or nonjudicial foreclosures—much less distinguishing, though without saying so, between the subpriority piece of an HOA's lien, to which the nonjudicial foreclosure procedures detailed in NRS 116.31162 through NRS 116.31168 would apply, and the superpriority piece of an HOA's lien, which would require a judicial foreclosure proceeding not actually mentioned in Chapter 116. If anything, Nevada's elaborate nonjudicial foreclosure provisions signal the Legislature's embrace of nonjudicial foreclosure of HOA liens, not the opposite.

Recall that, unlike § 3–116(b), which currently limits the superpriority piece of an HOA's lien to six months of unpaid dues, Nevada's superpriority lien covers nine months of dues as well as maintenance and nuisance-abatement charges "incurred . . . pursuant to NRS 116.310312." NRS 116.3116(2). Addressing maintenance and nuisance-abatement charges, NRS 116.310312(4) expressly cross-references Chapter 116's nonjudicial foreclosure provisions, stating that "[t]he lien may be foreclosed under NRS 116.31162 to 116.31168, inclusive." The maintenance and nuisance-abatement statute borrows the phrase "institution of an action to enforce the lien" from NRS 116.3116 in explaining that even if federal law requires a shorter period of priority, "the period of priority of the lien must not be less than the 6 months immediately preceding the institution of an action to enforce the lien." NRS 116.310312(6). This phrasing is underinclusive and beyond confusing unless read to encompass judicial and nonjudicial foreclosures alike, both in NRS 116.310312(6) and in its statute of origin, NRS 116.3116(2).

The Nevada Real Estate Division of the Department of Business and Industry (NRED) is charged with administering Chapter 116. NRS 116.623(l)(a) tasks NRED with issuing "advisory opinions as to the applicability or interpretation of . . . [a]ny provision of this chapter." On December 12, 2012, NRED issued Advisory Opinion No. 1301. The opinion addresses, among other questions, whether NRS 116.3116(2) requires a civil action by an HOA to foreclose the superpriority piece of its lien. NRED opines that it does not: "The association is not required to institute a civil action in court to trigger the 9 month look back provided in NRS 116.3116(2)." 13–01 Op. Dep't of Bus. & Indus., Real Estate Div. 18 (2012). Elaborating, the NRED opinion states, "NRS 116 does not require an association to take any particular action to enforce its lien, but [only] that it institutes 'an action,'" which includes the HOA taking action under NRS 116.31162 to initiate the nonjudicial foreclosure process. *Id.* at 17–18. NRED's interpretation is persuasive, as it comports with both the statutory text and the JEB's interpretation of the UCIOA. *See Int'l Game Tech., Inc. v. Second Judicial Dist. Court*, 122 Nev. 132, 157, 127 P.3d 1088, 1106 (2006).

U.S. Bank and the dissent argue that judicial foreclosure should be required as a matter of policy because of the safeguards it offers—notice and an opportunity to be heard, court supervision of the sale, judicial review of the amount of the lien comprising the superpriority piece, and a one-year redemption period. See NRS 40.430.463; NRS 21.190–.210. But this argument assumes that requiring the superpriority piece of an HOA lien to be judicially foreclosed will actually afford such protections without need of further amendment to Chapter 116, and this is far from clear. To allow nonjudicial foreclosure of the subpriority piece, which is where the dissent would draw the judicial v. nonjudicial foreclosure line, produces the same difficulties for the homeowners and junior lienholders that are cited as policy reasons for requiring judicial foreclosure of the superpriority piece of the lien; the only difference is the benefit that would inure to first security holders under the dissent's interpretation of Chapter 116. Surely, if the Legislature intended such an unusual distinction, it would have said so explicitly, but it did not.

We recognize that "there has been considerable publicity across the country regarding alleged abuse in the foreclosure process when unit owners fail to pay sums due" their HOA, prompting amendments to the UCIOA that "propose [ ] new and considerable restrictions on the foreclosure process as it applies to common interest communities." Prefatory Note to the 2008 Amendments to the UCIOA, 7 U.L.A., part IB, at 225 (2009). But the choice of foreclosure method for HOA liens is the Legislature's, and the Nevada Legislature has written NRS Chapter 116 to allow nonjudicial foreclosure of HOA liens, subject to the special notice requirements and protections handcrafted by the Legislature in NRS 116.31162 through NRS 116.31168. Countervailing policy arguments exist in favor of allowing nonjudicial foreclosure, including that judicial foreclosure takes longer to accomplish, thereby delaying the common-interest community's receipt of needed HOA funds. The consequences of such delays can be "devastating to the community and the remaining residents," who must either make up the dues deficiencies, arguably unjustly enriching the delaying lender, or abandon amenities and maintenance, thereby impairing the value of their homes. JEB, The Six-Month "Limited Priority Lien," at 4–5. If revisions to the foreclosure methods provided for in NRS Chapter 116 are appropriate, they are for the Legislature to craft, not this court. . . .

U.S. Bank makes two additional arguments that merit brief discussion. First, the lender contends that the nonjudicial foreclosure in this case violated its due process rights. Second, it invokes the mortgage savings clause in the Southern Highlands CC & Rs, arguing that this clause subordinates SHHOA's lien to the first deed of trust. Neither argument holds up to analysis. . . .

The contours of U.S. Bank's due process argument are protean. To the extent U.S. Bank argues that a statutory scheme that gives an HOA a superpriority lien that can be foreclosed nonjudicially, thereby extinguishing an earlier filed deed of trust, offends due process, the argument is a nonstarter. As discussed in *7912 Limbwood Court Trust*, 979 F.Supp.2d at 1152.

> Chapter 116 was enacted in 1991, and thus [the lender] was on notice that by operation of the statute, the [earlier recorded] CC & Rs might entitle the HOA to a super priority lien at some future date which would take priority over a [later recorded] first deed of trust. . . . Consequently, the conclusion that foreclosure on an HOA super priority lien extinguishes all junior liens, including a first deed of trust recorded prior to a notice of delinquent assessments, does not violate [the lender's] due process rights.

Accord Nationstar Mtg., 2014 WL 3661398, at *3 (rejecting a due process challenge to nonjudicial foreclosure of a superpriority lien).

U.S. Bank further complains about the content of the notice it received. It argues that due process requires specific notice indicating the amount of the superpriority piece of the lien and explaining how the beneficiary of the first deed of trust can prevent the superpriority foreclosure sale. But it appears from the record that specific lien amounts were stated in the notices, ranging from $1,149.24 when the notice of delinquency was recorded to $4,542.06 when the notice of sale was sent. The notices went to the homeowner and other junior lienholders, not just U.S. Bank, so it was appropriate to state the total amount of the lien. As U.S. Bank argues elsewhere, dues will typically comprise most, perhaps even all, of the HOA lien. And from what little the record contains, nothing appears to have stopped U.S. Bank from determining the precise superpriority amount in advance of the sale or paying the entire amount and requesting a refund of the balance. *Cf. In re Medaglia*, 52 F.3d 451, 455 (2d Cir.1995) ("[I]t is well established that due process is not offended by requiring a person with actual, timely knowledge of an event that may affect a right to exercise due diligence and take necessary steps to preserve that right."). . . .

U.S. Bank last argues that, even if NRS 116.3116(2) allows nonjudicial foreclosure of a superpriority lien, the mortgage savings clause in the Southern Highlands CC & Rs subordinated SSHOA's superpriority lien to the first deed of trust. The mortgage savings clause states that "no lien created under this Article 9 [governing nonpayment of assessments], nor the enforcement of any provision of this Declaration shall defeat or render invalid the rights of the beneficiary under any Recorded first deed of trust encumbering a Unit, made in good faith and for value." It also states that "[t]he lien of the assessments, including interest and costs, shall be subordinate to the lien of any first Mortgage upon the Unit."

NRS 116.1104 defeats this argument. It states that Chapter 116's "provisions may not be varied by agreement, and rights conferred by it may not be waived . . . [e]xcept as *expressly* provided in" Chapter 116. (Emphasis added.) "Nothing in [NRS] 116.3116 expressly provides for a waiver of the HOA's right to a priority position for the HOA's super priority lien." *See 7912 Limbwood Court Trust*, 979 F.Supp.2d at 1153: The mortgage savings clause thus does not affect NRS 116.3116(2)'s application in this case. . . .

NRS 116.3116(2) gives an HOA a true superpriority lien, proper foreclosure of which will extinguish a first deed of trust. Because Chapter 116 permits nonjudicial foreclosure of HOA liens, and because SFR's complaint alleges that proper notices were sent and received, we reverse the district court's order of dismissal. In view of this holding, we vacate the order denying preliminary injunctive relief and remand for further proceedings consistent with this opinion.

[The opinion of GIBBONS, C.J., concurring in part and dissenting in part, is omitted.]

NOTES

1.   *Considering the implications of* SFR Investments *and the UCIOA assessment lien superpriority.* Under the first-generation common interest statutes, the association's lien is entirely subordinate to the lien of a first mortgage on the unit or lot. As a policy matter, one might justify such an approach by arguing that (a) the first mortgage lien frequently secures purchase money credit that was extended to enable the owner to acquire the unit or lot, and (b) without having the assurance of first priority, institutional lenders might be reluctant to extend mortgage credit on common interest units or lots. According full priority to the first mortgagee, however, creates a significant risk to the association in "down" markets. For example, suppose that Smith purchases a unit in Shady Acres Condominiums in 2006 for a price of $250,000, using the proceeds of a $225,000 mortgage loan from Bank. Three years later, as a result of the collapse in land values, Smith's unit declines in value to only $125,000, at which point Smith defaults on both the mortgage and the payment of association dues. In such a down market, Bank may choose to delay implementing a foreclosure of its mortgage. If Bank

purchases the unit in a foreclosure sale, Bank becomes liable for assessments that accrue following its purchase (by contrast, Bank is not personally liable for assessments that accrue before it acquires title at foreclosure). Understandably, Bank may not wish to pay the cost of assessments for a period in which Bank is "stuck" with title to a unit that it cannot sell for an acceptable price in a down market. Instead, Bank might choose to delay the foreclosure, hoping that the market will recover—hopefully enabling the Bank to recover a larger portion of the unpaid balance in a future foreclosure sale, and in the meantime saving the Bank from liability for assessments that accrue during the period of delay.

But the Bank's ostensibly reasonable choice to delay foreclosure may be financially devastating for the association. If Smith is not paying his assessments, the association can theoretically foreclose its lien and have Smith's unit sold. But because Smith's unit is worth less than the balance owed to Bank, no buyer will be willing to pay anything to take the unit subject to Bank's mortgage lien! In a down market such as those experienced in the late 2000s and early 2010s, the association's ability to foreclose is an empty threat. As a result, associations are left with a dilemma—maintain the association's existing budget by increasing assessments on the nondefaulting unit owners, or cut the association's budget (and the common area maintenance funded by the budget).

By contrast, by giving the association a priority for six months of unpaid assessments, UCA and UCIOA preserve the association's leverage, even in a down market. If the association's lien has a true priority, and its sale would thus extinguish the otherwise-first mortgage lien, the association can now conduct a foreclosure of its lien with confidence that buyers (who would receive clear title at the sale) will be prepared to pay an amount sufficient to satisfy at least the priority portion of the unpaid assessment balance.

Is the result in *SFR Investments* unduly harsh to U.S. Bank? Should U.S. Bank and other mortgage lenders refrain from making mortgage loans in UCIOA states, or charge increased interest rates on common interest unit loans? Look at the Fannie/Freddie Uniform Instrument (Appendix A). What might U.S. Bank have done differently to protect itself against the risks posed by the association's superpriority lien?

2. *2014 amendments to UCIOA § 3–116.* In 2014, the Uniform Law Commission made a number of amendments to UCIOA § 3–116. These amendments clarified that § 3–116 did in fact create a "true" lien priority (effectively codifying the result in *SFR Investments*). They also clarified that this priority existed regardless of the method by which the association foreclosed its lien (again, confirming the result in *SFR Investments*).

In addition, the amendments modified the operation of the six-month priority rule in cases of a mortgagee's extended delay in foreclosure. Consider another variation of the Smith hypothetical from note 1. Suppose that by the time the association forecloses its lien, Smith has paid neither his mortgage payment nor his monthly association assessment for 24 consecutive months.

Under original UCIOA § 3–116, Bank could satisfy the priority portion of the association's lien by paying the association an amount equal to only six months of unpaid assessments. Under revised UCIOA § 3–116, the association's priority is extended to six months of unpaid assessments for each annual budget year of the association (meaning that in the hypothetical, the association's priority would extend to 12 months of unpaid assessments).

Finally, the amendments would permit the association to use forcible entry and detainer to recover possession of the defaulting owner's unit. This would permit the association to rent the unit to another occupant pending the association's foreclosure (or to condition the defaulting owner's continued occupancy on payment of the assessments).

3.   *For what expenditures can members be assessed?* There is little doubt that an association can use assessments to fund customary maintenance and management expenses. See, e.g., Telluride Lodge Ass'n v. Zoline, 707 P.2d 998 (Colo. Ct. App. 1985) (upholding assessment for a roof that was significantly different from the original). Note, however, that normally the association may assess unit owners only for maintenance and improvements on the common areas. Association funds may not be used, for example, to maintain individual units. See, e.g. Montgomery v. Columbia Knoll Condo. Council, 231 Va. 437, 344 S.E.2d 912 (1986) ($125,000 expenditure to replace all windows impermissible because windows were a part of individual units and not common areas).

What if the association's board decides to make some capital improvements in the common areas? For example, suppose that the board decides to spend $500 for new landscaping at the entrance to the community and $750,000 for an indoor pool and a gym with modern exercise equipment. Should these expenditures require a majority vote of the board, a majority vote of the owners themselves, or the unanimous vote of all owners? The answer may depend on both the statute and the declaration governing the community. See, e.g., San Antonio Villa Del Sol Homeowners Ass'n v. Miller, 761 S.W.2d 460 (Tex. Ct. App. 1988) (upholding $61,500 special assessment for plumbing as permitted capital improvement under condominium documents); Trafalgar Towers Ass'n No. 2, Inc. v. Zimet, 314 So.2d 595 (Fla. Ct. App. 1975) (upholding association's authority to assess members for acquisition of a unit in the building for use as a residence by the resident manager); Amoruso v. Board of Mgrs. of Westchester Hills Condo., 38 A.D.2d 845, 330 N.Y.S.2d 107 (1972) (upholding assessment for construction of a basketball court costing $500). See Annot., 77 A.L.R.3d 1290. Assessments for new recreational facilities are often controversial, because some owners may expect to make heavy use of them while others do not plan to use them at all.

Now consider a different scenario. Suppose that Shady Acres (a planned community) was created 40 years ago, with homes surrounding a lake owned by an owners association. Under the original declaration, membership in the owners association was voluntary; only members of the association paid assessments to maintain the lake, and nonmembers were not permitted to use the lake for boating, fishing, swimming, etc. Over time, however, the expenses of maintaining the lake and monitoring its use increased to the point that the board recommended that the association vote to impose mandatory assessments on all owners. If a majority of the owners vote to impose mandatory assessments, can such assessments be enforced against objecting owners?

EVERGREEN HIGHLANDS ASS'N V. WEST
Supreme Court of Colorado, 2003
73 P.3d 1

JUSTICE RICE. . . . Petitioner Evergreen Highlands Association, a Colorado non-profit corporation ("Association"), is the homeowner association for Evergreen Highlands Subdivision—Unit 4 ("Evergreen Highlands") in Jefferson County. The subdivision consists of sixty-three lots, associated roads, and a 22.3 acre park area which is open to use by all residents of the subdivision. The Association holds title to and maintains the park area, which contains hiking and equestrian trails, a barn and stables, a ball field, a fishing pond, and tennis courts. The park area is almost completely surrounded by private homeowners' lots, with no fence or other boundary separating the park area from the homes. Respondent Robert A. West owns one of the lots bordering directly on the park area, and has used the facilities there to play tennis, fish, and walk his dog.

Evergreen Highlands Subdivision was created and its plat filed in 1972. The plat indicated that the park area was to be conveyed to the homeowners association. Protective covenants for Evergreen Highlands were also filed in 1972, but did not require lot owners to be members of or pay dues to the Association. The Association, however, was incorporated in 1973 for the purposes of maintaining the common area and facilities, enforcing the covenants, paying taxes on the common area, and determining annual fees. The developer conveyed the park area to the Association in 1976. Between the years of 1976 and 1995, when the modification of the covenants at issue in this case occurred, the Association relied on voluntary assessments from lot owners to pay for maintenance of and improvements to the park area. Such expenses included property taxes, insurance for the park area and its structures, weed spraying, tennis court resurfacing, and barn and stable maintenance.

Article 13 of the original Evergreen Highlands covenants provides that a majority of lot owners may agree to modify the covenants, stating in relevant part as follows:

> [T]he owners of seventy-five percent of the lots which are subject
> to these covenants may release all or part of the land so

restricted from any one or more of said restrictions, *or may change or modify any one or more of said restrictions*, by executing and acknowledging an appropriate agreement or agreements in writing for such purposes and filing the same in the Office of the County Clerk and Recorder of Jefferson County, Colorado.

Protective Covenants for Evergreen Highlands—Unit 4, art. 13 (Nov. 6, 1972) (emphasis added) (hereinafter "modification clause"). In 1995, pursuant to the modification clause, at least seventy-five percent of Evergreen Highlands' lot owners voted to add a new Article 16 to the covenants. This article required all lot owners to be members of and pay assessments to the Association, and permitted the Association to impose liens on the property of any owners who failed to pay their assessment. Assessments were set at fifty dollars per year per lot.

Respondent purchased his lot in 1986 when membership in the Association and payment of assessments was voluntary, a fact that Respondent contends positively influenced his decision to purchase in Evergreen Highlands. Respondent was not among the majority of homeowners who approved the 1995 amendment to the covenants, and he subsequently refused to pay his lot assessment. When the Association threatened to record a lien against his property, Respondent filed this lawsuit challenging the validity of the 1995 amendment. The Association counterclaimed for a declaratory judgment that it had the implied power to collect assessments from all lot owners in the subdivision, and accordingly sought damages from West for breach of the implied contract. The district court ruled in favor of the Association on the ground that the amendment was valid and binding; therefore, it never reached the merits of the Association's counterclaims.

The court of appeals reversed, finding that the terms "change or modify" as set forth in the modification clause of the covenants did not allow for the addition of a wholly new covenant, but only for modifications to the existing covenants. . . . The court of appeals did not address the issue of whether the Association had the implied power to collect assessments from lot owners, and therefore whether Respondent was in breach of an implied contract. We granted certiorari and now reverse and remand. . . .

[Editors' Note: We have omitted the portion of the court's opinion in which it held that the covenant had been properly modified under the terms of the modification provision.]

The Association additionally argues that, even in the absence of an express covenant imposing mandatory assessments, it has the implied power to collect assessments from its members. To this end, the Association brought a counterclaim against West for breach of an implied contract obligating him to pay a proportionate share for repair, upkeep, and maintenance of the common area. The Association now argues that, based on West's breach of the implied contract, it is entitled as a matter of law to collect the unpaid assessments from Respondent.

We agree. Our review of case law from other states, the Restatement of Property (Servitudes), and the declarations for Evergreen Highlands in effect when West purchased his property, as supported by our understanding of the purpose of the Colorado Common Interest Ownership Act ("CCIOA"), convinces us that such an implied power exists in these circumstances. We therefore hold that Evergreen Highlands is a common interest community by implication, and that the Association has the implied power to levy assessments against lot owners to provide for maintenance of and improvements to common areas of the subdivision.

This being a question of first impression in Colorado, we first examine case law from other jurisdictions and find it largely in concurrence with our holding. When faced with this issue, a substantial number of states have arrived at the conclusion that homeowner associations have the implied power to levy dues or assessments even in the absence of express authority. *See, e.g., Spinnler Point Colony Ass'n, Inc. v. Nash,* 689 A.2d 1026, 1028–29 (Pa.Commw.Ct.1997) (holding that where ownership in a residential community allows owners to utilize common areas, "there is an implied agreement to accept the proportionate costs for maintaining and repairing these facilities."); *Meadow Run & Mountain Lake Park Ass'n v. Berkel,* 409 Pa.Super. 637, 598 A.2d 1024, 1026 (1991) (same); *Seaview Ass'n of Fire Island, N.Y., Inc. v. Williams,* 69 N.Y.2d 987, 517 N.Y.S.2d 709, 510 N.E.2d 793, 794 (1987) (holding that when lot purchaser has knowledge that homeowners association provides facilities and services to community residents, purchase creates an implied-in-fact contract to pay a proportionate share of those facilities and services); *Perry v. Bridgetown Cmty. Ass'n, Inc.,* 486 So.2d 1230, 1234 (Miss.1986) ("A landowner who willfully purchases property subject to control of the association and derives benefits from membership in the association implies his consent to be charged assessments and dues common to all other members."). *But see Popponesset Beach Ass'n, Inc. v. Marchillo,* 39 Mass.App.Ct. 586, 658 N.E.2d 983, 987–88 (1996) (holding that where lot owner had no notice in his chain of title of assessments and had not used the common areas, there existed no implied-in-fact contract to pay past and future assessments).[7]

Reflecting this considerable body of law, the newest version of the Restatement of Property (Servitudes) provides that "a common-interest community has the power to raise the funds reasonably necessary to carry out its functions by levying assessments against the individually

---

[7] We note that in contrast to *Marchillo,* testimony in this case showed that West had, in fact, availed himself of the benefits of the park area.

owned property in the community. . . ." Restatement of Servitudes § 6.5(1)(a) (2000). In addition, as explained in a comment to that section, the power to levy assessments "will be implied if not expressly granted by the declaration or by statute." *Id.* at § 6.5 cmt. b; *see also* Wayne S. Hyatt, *Condominium and Homeowner Association Practice: Community Association Law* 36 (1981) ("The assessment is not equivalent to membership dues or some other discretionary charge. . . . As long as legitimate expenses are incurred, the individual member must bear his or her share.").

We find the Restatement and case law from other states persuasive in analyzing the issue before us today. In addition, these authorities are in harmony with the legislative purpose motivating the enactment of CCIOA. *See, e.g.,* § 38–33.3–102(1)(b), 10 C.R.S. (2002) ("That the continuation of the economic prosperity of Colorado is dependent upon the strengthening of homeowner associations . . . through enhancing the financial stability of associations by increasing the association's powers to collect delinquent assessments"); § 38–33.3–102(1)(d) ("That it is the policy of this state to promote effective and efficient property management through defined operational requirements that preserve flexibility for such homeowner associations").

Respondent, however, argues that the implied power to mandate assessments can only be imputed to "common interest communities," which both CCIOA and the Restatement define as residential communities in which there exists a mandatory obligation or servitude imposed on individual owners to pay for common elements of the community. Respondent therefore contends that because the original covenants did not impose such a servitude, Evergreen Highlands is not a common interest community, and accordingly cannot have the implied power to levy assessments against its members pursuant to these authorities.

Respondent's argument, however, relies on the assumption that the servitude or obligation to pay which would have defined Evergreen Highlands as a common interest community was required to have been made express in the covenants or in his deed. This assumption is incorrect. CCIOA provides only that the obligation must arise from the "declarations," which are defined as "any recorded instruments however denominated, that create a common interest community, including any amendments to those instruments and also including, but not limited to, plats and maps." § 38–33.3–103(13), 10 C.R.S. (2002); *see also* Restatement of Servitudes § 6.2(5)(2000) ("'Declaration' means the recorded document or documents containing the servitudes that create and govern the common-interest community.").

The declarations in effect for Evergreen Highlands in 1986 incorporated all documents recorded up to that date, and included not only: (1) the covenants, but also; (2) the 1972 plat, which noted that the park area would be conveyed to the homeowners association; (3) the 1973 Articles of Incorporation for the Association stating that the Association's purposes were to "own, acquire, build, operate, and maintain" the common area and facilities, to pay taxes on same, and to "determine annual membership or use fees"; and (4) the 1976 deed whereby the developer quit-claimed his ownership in the park area to the Association.

At the time Respondent purchased his lot in 1986, the Evergreen Highlands' declarations made clear that a homeowners association existed, it owned and maintained the park area, and it had the power to impose annual membership or use fees on lot owners. These declarations were sufficient to create a common interest community by implication. As explained by the Restatement:

> An implied obligation may . . . be found where the declaration expressly creates an association for the purpose of managing common property or enforcing use restrictions and design controls, but fails to include a mechanism for providing the funds necessary to carry out its functions. When such an implied obligation is established, the lots are a common-interest community within the meaning of this Chapter.

Restatement (Third) of Property: Servitudes § 6.2 cmt. a (2000); *see also id.* at illus. 2 (citing an example virtually identical to that of Evergreen Highlands and finding it a common interest community by judicial decree).

We accordingly adopt the position taken by the Restatement and many other states, and hold that the declarations for Evergreen Highlands were sufficient to create a common interest community by implication. The Association therefore has the implicit power to levy assessments against lot owners for the purpose of maintaining the common area of the subdivision. Respondent, as a lot owner, has an implied duty to pay his proportionate share of the cost of maintaining and operating the common area. We therefore remand the case to the court of appeals with orders to return it to the trial court to calculate Petitioner's damages in a manner consistent with this opinion. . . .

NOTE

Identifying the limits of the association's assessment power. Are you persuaded by the *West* court's analysis that a CIC has the implied power to levy assessments? Do you believe a reasonable purchaser in West's position would have appreciated the possibility of the future adoption of mandatory assessments? Would West's position be more reasonable if the declaration had not been amendable, and the association had been relying solely on its (alleged) implied power to impose mandatory assessments?

In considering this question, compare the situation in *West* with the hypothetical in note 3 prior to *West*. Suppose that originally, Shady Acres did not have a pool or exercise gym. Suppose further that over 80% of the owners vote to approve the expenditure of funds, but Pushaw (one of the dissenting owners) files a lawsuit arguing that the association lacks the power to do this. Does the analysis in *West* suggest that the association would prevail? Why or why not? What additional information, if any, would you want to ascertain in making your judgment?

_____

2.　MANAGEMENT OF COMMUNITY LIFE AND AFFAIRS

As the preceding section suggests, common interest communities are analytically comparable to municipalities in the sense that they provide community services paid for through the imposition of community "taxes" (assessments). Common interest communities also typically place a variety of contractual restrictions on owners within the community, as a means to protect community members from uses that might threaten their financial investment and/or their peaceful enjoyment of their units. In this regard, common interest communities also resemble municipalities, which commonly use zoning and other police powers to regulate life within municipal boundaries.

As common interest communities increasingly proliferate, disputes inevitably arise between neighbors over the extent to which the community should be able to control or prevent certain uses or activities within the community, either by direct limitations in the declaration itself or by rulemaking by the association board. When such disputes arise, what rule should courts play in interpreting and applying a community's declaration and rules? For example, would a residential-use-only covenant permit the community to prohibit a resident from operating a freelance website design business within her home, or from providing home-based day care for neighborhood children? To what extent can a community's declaration or rules prohibit an owner from transferring her interest, either by lease or outright fee transfer? To what extent do constitutional principles or public policy provide a basis for limiting a community's ability to enforce its declaration or rules? To what extent can an association, its board, or its members be held liable to individual members of the community harmed by an association or board decision? The following materials explore these and related questions.

BOARD OF DIRECTORS OF 175 E. DELAWARE PLACE
HOMEOWNERS ASS'N V. HINOJOSA

Illinois Court of Appeals, 1997
287 Ill.App.3d 886, 223 Ill.Dec. 222, 679 N.E.2d 407

JUSTICE RAKOWSKI delivered the opinion of the court. . . . 175 East Delaware Place was organized as a condominium in 1973 by the recording of a declaration and bylaws. The property includes floors 45 through 92 of the John Hancock building and contains 705 condominium units. The declaration and bylaws were silent on the issue of pet ownership in the building. In 1976, the Board adopted a rule allowing owners to have pets, including dogs, only with the permission of the Board. On January 21, 1980, during a regular board meeting, the Board adopted a rule barring unit owners from bringing additional dogs onto the premises. In October of 1985, defendants Nancy Lee Carlson and Benjamin Tessler purchased a unit in the building. At this time, they signed a pet agreement acknowledging the no-dog rule. In February of 1993, while leasing out another one of their units, they signed the same agreement again. In March of 1993, the no-dog rule was reincluded in the Board's rules and regulations.

In June of 1993, defendants Carlson and Tessler acquired a dog. This same month, a group of owners brought suit against the Board challenging the no-dog rule. This suit was eventually abandoned and is not part of this appeal. In September of 1993, defendants Carlson and Tessler received notice of a hearing for their violation of the no-dog rule. The hearing was held on November 30, 1993, and the committee recommended to the Board that Carlson and Tessler be ordered to remove the dog within 30 days. If the dog remained on the premises after 30 days, defendants Carlson and Tessler should be assessed a fine of $100 per day for each day the dog remained. The Board adopted the committee's recommendation and on January 23, 1994, began assessing fines on defendants Carlson and Tessler. On April 20, 1994, after Carlson and Tessler failed to pay the fines, the Board recorded a notice and claim of statutory lien.

In August of 1994, defendants Carlson and Tessler sold the unit to defendants Jorge and Donna Hinojosa subject to the lien. In November of 1994, the Board filed the instant action seeking to foreclose on the lien. Defendants moved to dismiss the suit. . . . The trial court ruled that the Board had the power to promulgate the rule but held that the rule was unreasonable.

A.   Legal Background. . . .

A condominium comes into being by the recording of a declaration. The declaration is prepared and recorded by either the developer or association. . . . Its primary function is to provide a constitution for the condominium—to guide the condominium development throughout the years. The declaration contains the property's legal description, defines the units and common elements, provides the percentage of ownership interests, establishes the rights and obligations of owners, and contains restrictions on the use of the property. R. Otto, *Illinois Act in Condominium Titles*, in Illinois Condominium Law § 1.15, at 1–27 (Ill.Inst. for Cont.Legal Educ.1994). All restrictions contained in the declaration are covenants that run with the land and bind each subsequent owner. They are given a strong presumption of validity. M. Kurtzon, *Representing the Condominium Association*, in Illinois Condominium Law § 10.19, at 10–17 (Ill.Inst. for Cont.Legal Educ.1994). Section 4 of the Act details what elements must be contained in the declaration. Paragraph (i) states: "Such other lawful provisions not inconsistent with the provisions of this Act as the owner or owners may deem desirable in order to promote and preserve the cooperative aspect of ownership of the property and to facilitate the proper administration thereof." 765 ILCS 605/4(i) (West 1994).

The second document is the bylaws, which deal with administration and procedural matters concerning the property. Bylaws may be embodied in the declaration or be a separate document. In either case, the bylaws must be recorded with the declaration. 765 ILCS 605/17(a) (West 1994). Should the bylaws conflict with the declaration, the declaration prevails. Section 18 of the Act sets forth certain provisions that shall be included in the bylaws. Relevant to the issue before us is paragraph (k), which states: "[R]estrictions on and requirements respecting the use and maintenance of the units and the use of the common elements, not set forth in the declaration, as are designed to prevent unreasonable interference with the use of their respective units and of the common elements by the several unit owners." 765 ILCS 605/18(k) (West 1994).

The third item governing condominium conduct is the board rules and regulations. Section 18.4 of the Act deals with powers and duties of the board and provides that the board may:

> "[A]dopt and amend rules and regulations covering the details of the operation and use of the property, after a meeting of the unit owners called for the specific purpose of discussing the proposed rules and regulations."

765 ILCS 605/18.4(h) (West 1994). Under this rule, "a board of managers may not take any action that is beyond the authority granted it under the condominium instruments and the Condominium Property Act." 765 ILCS 605/18.4, Historical & Practice Notes, at 129 (West 1993). The board shall exercise for the association all powers, duties, and authority vested in the association by law or the condominium documents. It generally has broad powers and its rules govern the requirements of day-to-day living

in the association. Board rules must be objective, evenhanded, nondiscriminatory, and applied uniformly. See J. Shifrin, *Cooperative, Condominium, and Homeowners' Association Litigation*, in Real Estate Litigation § 11.20, at 11–17 (Ill.Inst. for Cont.Legal Educ.1994).

B.   Power of the Board to Promulgate the No-Dog Rule.

As noted, pursuant to section 18.4 the Board has the power to adopt rules and regulations. Section 18(k) does discuss restrictions that shall be included in the bylaws. However, this provision merely gives the association the authority to include restrictions in the condominium instruments that will clothe the restrictions with a strong presumption of validity and make them less susceptible to attack. The provision does not state that if a restriction is not contained in the bylaws it will be unenforceable. We thus conclude that the Board's no-dog rule is not in conflict [with] the Act.

The 175 East Delaware Place declaration and bylaws do not make any reference to pet ownership or dogs, in particular. As to the Board's powers, the declaration provides:

> The Board, may adopt such reasonable rules and regulations as it may deem advisable for the maintenance, conservation and beautification of the Property, and for the health, comfort, safety and general welfare of the Owners and occupants of the Property. Written notice of such rules and regulations shall be given to all Owners and Occupants and the entire Property shall at all times be maintained subject to such rules and regulations.

The declaration clearly gives the Board authority to promulgate rules regarding use of and restrictions on the use of units. Because the Board is authorized to promulgate reasonable rules for the general welfare of the owners and the declaration is silent on the issue of dog ownership, the instant rule does not conflict with either the declaration or the bylaws.

Courts that have addressed the issue have held that dogs may be prohibited or restricted by provisions in the declaration or bylaws. See *Nahrstedt v. Lakeside Village Condominium Ass'n*, 8 Cal.4th 361, 878 P.2d 1275, 33 Cal.Rptr.2d 63 (1994) (restriction in recorded declaration barring all pets except fish and birds enforceable unless unreasonable); *Chateau Village North Condominium Ass'n v. Jordan*, 643 P.2d 791 (Colo.App.1982) (rule barring all pets appended to bylaws and recorded enforceable); *Parkway Gardens Condominium Ass'n v. Kinser*, 536 So.2d 1076 (Fla.App.1988) (board rule barring pets unenforceable because declaration allowed them); *Zeskind v. Jockey Club Condominium Apartments, Unit II, Inc.*, 468 So.2d 1021 (Fla.App.1985) (no-pet rule in declaration enforceable); *Wilshire Condominium Ass'n v. Kohlbrand*, 368 So.2d 629 (Fla.App.1979) (restriction in declaration barring replacement of lap dogs enforceable); *Johnson v. Keith*, 368 Mass. 316, 331 N.E.2d 879

(1975) (board rule barring all pets unenforceable; rule must be included in bylaws); *Noble v. Murphy*, 34 Mass.App.Ct. 452, 612 N.E.2d 266 (1993) (restriction barring all pets incorporated in original recorded documents enforceable); but see *Dulaney Towers Maintenance Corp. v. O'Brey*, 46 Md.App. 464, 418 A.2d 1233 (1980) (board rule limiting number of pets enforceable). The issue before us, however, is whether the Board may promulgate a rule restricting dog ownership. This issue has not been addressed in Illinois.

Apple II Condominium Ass'n v. Worth Bank & Trust Co., 277 Ill.App.3d 345, 659 N.E.2d 93, 213 Ill.Dec. 463 (1995), addresses use restrictions under the Act. In *Apple II*, we set forth standards for evaluating such restrictions and adopted the analysis set forth in *Hidden Harbour Estates, Inc. v. Basso*, 393 So.2d 637 (Fla.App.1981). We differentiated use restrictions that are contained in the declaration or bylaws from those promulgated by board rule. The restrictions in the first category "are clothed in a very strong presumption of validity and will not be invalidated absent a showing that they are wholly arbitrary in their application, in violation of public policy, or that they abrogate some fundamental constitutional right. * * * '[R]easonableness' is not the appropriate test for such restrictions." *Apple II*, 277 Ill.App.3d at 350–51, 659 N.E.2d 93, 213 Ill.Dec. 463. However, when the board promulgates a rule restricting the use of property, the second category, "the board must affirmatively show the use it wishes to prohibit or restrict is 'antagonistic to the legitimate objectives of the condominium association.'" *Apple II*, 277 Ill.App.3d at 351, 659 N.E.2d 93, 213 Ill.Dec. 463, quoting *Basso*, 393 So.2d at 640. Thus, "[w]hen such a rule [use restriction] is adopted by the board alone or requires the board to exercise discretion, we will scrutinize the restriction and uphold it only if it is affirmatively shown to be reasonable in its purpose and application." *Apple II*, 277 Ill.App.3d at 352, 659 N.E.2d 93, 213 Ill.Dec. 463.

Based on the above, we conclude that the Board had the power to promulgate a reasonable no-dog rule.

C. Reasonableness of Rule.

Because the rule was promulgated by the Board, it is not clothed with a strong presumption of validity. Thus, we must carefully scrutinize the rule to determine if it is reasonable in its purpose and application. Because the facts are not in dispute, the issue is one of law.

In *Dulaney Towers Maintenance Corp. v. O'Brey*, 46 Md.App. 464, 418 A.2d 1233 (1980), the court stated:

"The rationale for allowing the placing of restrictions in, or the barring of pets by way of, house rules is based on potentially offensive odors, noise, possible health hazards, clean-up and maintenance problems, and the fact that pets can and do defile hallways, elevators, and other common areas." *Dulaney Towers Maintenance*, 46 Md.App. at 466, 418 A.2d at 1235.

The above factors, in conjunction with the specific facts of this case, lead us to conclude the Board's no-dog rule is a reasonable exercise of the Board's rule-making power. The John Hancock building is located in a very urban and densely populated area of the city where parks, grass, and other recreational areas for dogs are scarce. The 705 residences are located on the 45th through 92nd floors. In order to take a dog out, one must access elevators and descend anywhere from 45 to 92 floors.

The rule was adopted to prevent possible injury or harm. The original purpose for promulgating the rule was due to an incident in which one dog killed another dog in the building. The Board had tried less restrictive measures to regulate dogs in the past. However, these measures did not cure or alleviate what the Board reasonably perceived to be potential and real problems. It should also be noted that when the no-dog rule was adopted, owners were allowed to retain existing dogs. The rule only prohibited additional and/or replacement dogs.

Because the Board applied the rule to all owners and the purpose for the rule was rational, we conclude that the rule is reasonable under the specific facts of this case.

Reversed and remanded. . . .

NOTES

1. *The association governing board as legislator or "city council."* The principal case does a good job of spelling out the hierarchy of the governing documents of a common interest community: (1) the applicable common interest ownership statute; (2) the declaration; (3) the bylaws; and (4) the rules and regulations adopted by the association board. Thus, a declaration provision carries a "strong presumption of validity" and may be invalidated only if it is inconsistent with the governing statute, other legislation or overriding public policy concerns. A similar analysis is applied to a bylaw provision, except, of course, that a bylaw may also be invalidated if it is inconsistent with the declaration. Thus, for example, a pet restriction contained in the declaration carries a strong presumption of validity and is likely to be upheld. See, e.g., Nahrstedt v. Lakeside Village Condo. Ass'n, 8 Cal.4th 361, 878 P.2d 1275, 33 Cal.Rptr.2d 63 (1994). By contrast, a board rule will fall if it contravenes statutes, the declaration or bylaws. Moreover, the board must establish that its rule is "reasonable."

The Restatement of Servitudes likewise distinguishes between provisions contained in the declaration and rules enacted by the governing board. Recorded declaration provisions "are valid unless illegal, unconstitutional, or against public policy." Restatement (Third) of Property—Servitudes § 6.7 cmt. b (2000). By contrast, board-promulgated rules are invalid "unless they are also reasonable." *Id.* See generally Paula A. Franzese, Building Community in Common Interest Communities: The Promise of the Restatement (Third) of Servitudes, 38 Real Prop. Prob. & Tr. J. 17 (2003).

In assessing the validity of a bylaw amendment or a board rule, it is helpful to use the following analysis:

a.   *Were applicable procedural requirements satisfied?* The failure to comply with notice and hearing requirements mandated by state statutes, the declaration or bylaws may invalidate rules promulgated by the board. Alternatively, a rule or bylaw may fall because it did not obtain the requisite number of votes from the unit owners. See, e.g., Ridgely Condo. Ass'n, Inc. v. Smyrnioudis, 343 Md. 357, 681 A.2d 494 (1996) (bylaw amendment revoking right of commercial unit owners to have customers and clients use lobby was not merely a "use" restriction requiring a 2/3 vote of unit owners, but rather a restriction on an "interest in property" requiring consent of all unit owners).

b.   *Do the governing documents provide substantive authority for the rule or regulation?* Unless the governing statutes, declaration or bylaws authorize a board rule, it may be *ultra vires.* See, e.g., Carney v. Donley, 261 Ill.App.3d 1002, 199 Ill.Dec. 219, 633 N.E.2d 1015 (1994) (board lacks authority to authorize unit balcony extensions into common area); Makeever v. Lyle, 125 Ariz. 384, 609 P.2d 1084 (Ct. App. 1980) (board may not deprive an owner of his or her interest in common areas absent authorization by statute, the declaration or bylaws).

c.   *Does the rule satisfy a "reasonableness" test?* Even if the Board's action satisfies the prior two requirements, a court must ultimately determine, as the principal case illustrates, whether the board action is "reasonable." Do you agree with the *Hinojosa* court's conclusion that a ban on dogs is reasonable? Would it matter if the rule had been adopted in the absence of any complaints or incidents involving dogs? Suppose instead that the Board had adopted a rule banning smoking anywhere in the building, including inside individual units. Would that rule be reasonable? Should it matter whether the rules were adopted only after consideration by the board, or instead were ratified by a vote of association members? What if the state's condominium statute authorizes association bylaws to provide restrictions regarding the use of the units, which "may include other prohibitions on, or allowance of, smoking tobacco products"? Utah Code Ann. § 57–8–16(7)(b). See, e.g., Cara L. Thomas, Butt Out! Controlling Environmental Tobacco Smoke in Condominiums, Prob. & Prop. 15–16 (May/June 2008); Staci Semrad, A New Arena in the Fight Over Smoking: The Home, N.Y. Times, Nov. 5, 2007, at A18 (detailing efforts within condominiums across the country to ban smoking inside units); David C. Drewes, Note, Putting the "Community" Back in Common Interest Communities: A Proposal for Participation-Enhancing Procedural Review, 101 Colum. L. Rev. 314 (2001) (suggesting judges should be more reluctant to find rules reasonable if adopted in a "hierarchical, exclusive process," so as to encourage boards to obtain broader participation of individual residents in rulemaking). For a thoughtful consideration of the factors a court should consider in evaluating whether a unit owner should be relieved from the impact of a rule enacted by an association, see Patrick A. Randolph, Changing the Rules: Should Courts Limit the Power of Common Interest Communities to Alter Unit Owners' Privileges in the Face of Vested Expectations?, 38 Santa Clara L.Rev. 1081 (1998). For further consideration of these issues, see Andrea J. Boyack, Common Interest Community Covenants and the Freedom of Contract Myth, 22 J. L. & Pol'y 767 (2014); Lee Anne Fennell, Contracting Communities, 2004 U. Ill. L. Rev. 829; Michael R. Fierro, Note, Condominium Association Remedies Against a Recalcitrant Unit Owner, 73 St. John's L. Rev. 247 (1999); Paula A. Franzese, Common Interest Communities: Standards of Review and Review of Standards, 3 Wash. U.J.L. & Pol'y, 663, 667 (2000); Vincent Di Lorenzo, Judicial Deference to Management Decisions in Planned Unit Developments, 15 Prob. & Prop. 20 (Jan.-Feb. 2001); Wayne Hyatt, Common Interest Communities: Evolution and Reinvention, 31 J. Marshall L. Rev. 303 (1998).

2. *New York's "business judgment" rule.* In Levandusky v. One Fifth Ave. Apt. Corp., 75 N.Y.2d 530, 554 N.Y.S.2d 807, 553 N.E.2d 1317 (1990), the court upheld the authority of a cooperative board to withdraw prior approval of an apartment renovation, notwithstanding substantial expenditures by the lessee, where the lessee had failed initially to disclose fully the impact of the renovation on the building's heating system:

> It is apparent, then, that a standard for judicial review of the actions of a cooperative or condominium governing board must be sensitive to a variety of concerns—sometimes competing concerns. Even when the governing board acts within the scope of its authority, some check on its potential powers to regulate residents' conduct, life-style and property rights is necessary to protect individual residents from abusive exercise, notwithstanding that the residents have, to an extent, consented to be regulated and even selected their representatives (*see*, Note, *The Rule of Law in Residential Associations,* 99 Harv.L.Rev. 472 [1985]). At the same time, the chosen standard of review should not undermine the purposes for which the residential community and its governing structure were formed: protection of the interest of the entire community of residents in an environment managed by the board for the common benefit.

> We conclude that these goals are best served by a standard of review that is analogous to the business judgment rule applied by courts to determine challenges to decisions made by corporate directors (*see, Auerbach v. Bennett,* 47 N.Y.2d 619, 629, 419 N.Y.S.2d 920, 393 N.E.2d 994). . . .

> Developed in the context of commercial enterprises, the business judgment rule prohibits judicial inquiry into actions of

corporate directors "taken in good faith and in the exercise of honest judgment in the lawful and legitimate furtherance of corporate purposes." (*Auerbach v. Bennett,* 47 N.Y.2d 619, 629, 419 N.Y.S.2d 920, 393 N.E.2d 994, *supra.*) So long as the corporation's directors have not breached their fiduciary obligation to the corporation, "the exercise of [their powers] for the common and general interests of the corporation may not be questioned, although the results show that what they did was unwise or inexpedient." (*Pollitz v. Wabash R.R. Co.,* 207 N.Y. 113, 124, 100 N.E. 721.)

Application of a similar doctrine is appropriate because a cooperative corporation is—in fact and function—a corporation, acting through the management of its board of directors, and subject to the Business Corporation Law. There is no cause to create a special new category in law for corporate actions by coop boards.

... For present purposes, we need not, nor should we determine the entire range of the fiduciary obligations of a cooperative board, other than to note that the board owes its duty of loyalty to the cooperative—that is, it must act for the benefit of the residents collectively. So long as the board acts for the purposes of the cooperative, within the scope of its authority and in good faith, courts will not substitute their judgment for the board's. Stated somewhat differently, unless a resident challenging the board's action is able to demonstrate a breach of this duty, judicial review is not available. ...

As applied in condominium and cooperative cases, review of a board's decision under a reasonableness standard has much in common with the rule we adopt today. A primary focus of the inquiry is whether board action is in furtherance of a legitimate purpose of the cooperative or condominium, in which case it will generally be upheld. The difference between the reasonableness test and the rule we adopt is twofold. First—unlike the business judgment rule, which places on the owner seeking review the burden to demonstrate a breach of the board's fiduciary duty—reasonableness review requires the board to demonstrate that its decision was reasonable. Second, although in practice a certain amount of deference appears to be accorded to board decisions, reasonableness review permits—indeed, in theory requires—the court itself to evaluate the merits or wisdom of the board's decision (*see, e.g., Hidden Harbour Estates v. Basso,* 393 So.2d 637, 640 [Fla.Dist.Ct.App.]), just as the Appellate Division did in the present case.

How would a board's decision to adopt a no-dog rule, or a no-smoking rule, be evaluated under this rule? Do you think such a rule would be more likely to be upheld? Less likely? Equally likely? We will revisit the "business judgment" rule in additional detail later in this chapter. See Lamden v. La Jolla Shores Clubdominium Homeowners Ass'n, infra.

3.   *Planned communities and sexual offenders.* A vote by the residents of Panther Valley, a New Jersey gated community of more than 2,000 homes, amended its declaration and bylaws to prohibit certain sex offenders from living in the community—specifically, any individual registered as a "Tier 3" offender (individuals deemed to pose a high risk of re-offending) under New Jersey's "Megan's Law." Plaintiff, a homeowner in the community, challenged the amendment's validity. The trial court upheld the validity of the amendment; on appeal, the court of appeals reversed the trial court's judgment:

> Because these amendments all reflect changes adopted substantially after plaintiff took up residence at Panther Valley, and because the governing documents require no more than a simple majority vote, we are unwilling to afford them the presumption of validity for which defendants contend. We are satisfied that plaintiff is entitled in the context of this case to have these amendments judged on their reasonableness. . . .

> Plaintiff . . . contends that [the amendment] is contrary to public policy. . . . Although not contained within the record before us, we are aware that other similar common interest communities within the State have passed similar restrictions upon residency by Tier 3 registrants. 156 N.J.L.J. 361 (May 3, 1999). We do not know from the record how many common interest communities exist within the State and we do not know from the record how many of those communities have seen fit to adopt comparable restrictions and whether they have determined to include a broader group than Tier 3 registrants. We are thus unable to determine whether the result of such provisions is to make a large segment of the housing market unavailable to one category of individual and indeed perhaps to approach "the ogre of vigilantism and harassment," the potential dangers of which the Supreme Court recognized even while upholding the constitutionality of Megan's Law. *Doe v. Poritz*, 142 N.J. 1, 110, 662 A.2d 367 (1995).

> We recognize, of course, that Tier 3 registrants (and indeed convicted criminals) are not a protected group within the terms of New Jersey's Law Against Discrimination. N.J.S.A. 10:5–3. Nor have we been pointed to any authority deeming them handicapped. In this regard, however see *Arnold Murray Constr., L.L.C. v. Hicks*, 621 N.W.2d 171 (S.D.2001), in which the court upheld the eviction of a handicapped tenant who posed a direct threat to the health and safety of other tenants without the necessity of attempting to provide reasonable accommodations under the federal Fair Housing Act. It does not necessarily follow, however, that large segments of the State could entirely close their doors to such individuals,

confining them to a narrow corridor and thus perhaps exposing those within that remaining corridor to a greater risk of harm than they might otherwise have had to confront.

Common interest communities fill a particular need in the housing market but they also pose unique problems for those who remain outside their gates, whether voluntarily or by economic necessity. The understandable desire of individuals to protect themselves and their families from some of the ravages of modern society and thus reside within such communities should not become a vehicle to ensure that those problems remain the burden of those least able to afford a viable solution.

We hasten to add that we recognize that not all gated communities are refuges for the wealthy. They are a spreading phenomenon that can be found among all economic strata. Owens, *supra*, 34 Am.Crim. L.Rev. at 1136–37. Their growth has been fueled by the public's fear of crime and need for safety. *Ibid.*; Kennedy, *supra*, 105 Yale L.J. at 766.

The Supreme Court has long cautioned against the dangers inherent in courts, presented with a meager record, ruling upon questions having a broad social and legal impact. . . . Although the Supreme Court concluded in *Doe v. Poritz, supra*, that it had no basis to overturn the legislative judgment "that public safety was more important than the potential for [an] unfair . . . impact . . .", 142 N.J. at 110, 662 A.2d 367, it did so on the basis of a fully-formed record. We decline to write a solution for a problem that has not been fully stated.

Because we have concluded, for the reasons we have set forth, that the record was insufficient to permit determination of the issue, we reverse that portion of the trial court's judgment upholding the validity of the . . . amendment to the Association's Declaration.

Mulligan v. Panther Valley Property Owners Ass'n, 337 N.J.Super. 293, 766 A.2d 1186, 1190–1193 (App. Div. 2001). Nevertheless, the court refused to order a remand, stating "[w]e see no reason to depart from the general practice that a plaintiff who failed initially to present sufficient evidence to the trial court is, ordinarily, not entitled to a remand to cure that deficiency." Do you find the denial of a remand in this instance somewhat disingenuous? Plaintiff also argued that the amendment was an invalid restraint on alienation. The court easily rejected this argument: "that there may be 80 individuals out of a total of 8.4 million to whom plaintiff may not sell her home cannot . . . seriously be considered an unlawful restriction upon her right to sell or lease her home." *Id.* at 1192. We consider restraints on an owner's ability to alienate his or her unit later in this section.

4.   *Age and disability discrimination.* Age restrictions on condominium residency have proved to be a fertile source of litigation, especially restrictions on children and those under the age of majority. Prior to 1988, court decisions generally upheld such restrictions. See, e.g., Pearlman v. Lake Dora Villas Mgmt., Inc., 479 So.2d 780 (Fla. Ct. App. 1985), Everglades Plaza Condo. Ass'n Inc. v. Buckner, 462 So.2d 835 (Fla. Ct. App. 1984). But see O'Connor v. Village Green Owners Ass'n, 33 Cal.3d 790, 191 Cal.Rptr. 320, 662 P.2d 427 (1983), in which the California Supreme Court invalidated a condominium restriction against occupancy by children as a violation of California's Unruh Civil Rights Act, even though "age" was not a protected class (note that in Marina Point, Ltd. v. Wolfson, 30 Cal.3d 721, 180 Cal.Rptr. 496, 640 P.2d 115 (1982), the California Supreme Court had earlier invalidated a landlord's "no children" policy as a violation of the Unruh Civil Rights Act, concluding that Act's identification of protected classes was "illustrative," not "exclusive," and that the Act prohibited all "arbitrary" discrimination by business establishments).

Since 1988, however, discrimination against occupancy by children has been, in substantial degree, prohibited by the federal Fair Housing Act (FHA). The FHA makes it unlawful for most persons and entities engaged in residential real estate transactions to discriminate on the basis of "familial status," as well as on the previously forbidden grounds of race, color, religion, sex, handicap, or national origin. See 42 U.S.C.A. § 3605. "Familial status" is defined to mean families which include children under the age of 18. See 42 U.S.C.A. § 3602(k). See Martin v. Palm Beach Atlantic Ass'n, Inc., 696 So.2d 919 (Fla. Ct. App. 1997) (even though rules prohibiting occupancy by children under the age of 12 were not enforced, their publication by the association was a violation of the FHA).

However, the FHA creates an exception for "housing for older persons" in which familial status discrimination is not prohibited. See 42 U.S.C.A. § 3607(b)(1). "Housing for older persons" includes housing which is "intended and operated for occupancy by at least one person 55 years of age or older per unit." This in turn means that at least 80% of the units are in fact occupied by at least one person over 55, and that the project has published and adheres to "policies and procedures which demonstrate an intent . . . to provide housing for persons 55 years of age or older." See 42 U.S.C.A. § 3607(b)(2)(C). HUD's regulations are found in 24 C.F.R. §§ 100.300 to 100.308. A requirement in the original statute that the project have "significant facilities and services" for older residents was deleted by Congress in 1995. For a complete discussion of the Act and the 1995 Amendments, see Nicole Napolitano, Note, The Fair Housing Act Amendments and Age Restrictive Covenants in Condominiums and Cooperatives, 73 St. John's L. Rev. 273 (1999); Jonathan I. Edelstein, Family Values: Prevention of Discrimination and the Housing for Older Persons Act of 1995, 52 U. Miami L. Rev. 947 (1998); James A. Kushner, Fair Housing Amendments Act of 1988: The Second Generation of Fair Housing, 42 Vand. L. Rev. 1049 (1989).

Unless a common interest community can satisfy the "housing for older persons" exception, rules and regulations that prohibit residency by families containing persons under 18 will be unenforceable. See, e.g., Simovits v. Chanticleer Condo. Ass'n, 933 F.Supp. 1394 (N.D. Ill. 1996). In Westwood Community Two Ass'n, Inc. v. Lewis, 687 So.2d 296 (Fla. Ct. App. 1997), the court found that the association did not comply with the "housing for older persons" definition in the Florida equivalent of the FHA, and that it had no authority to amend its bylaws to come into compliance.

Note that the FHA also prohibits discrimination based on "handicap." Consider the implications of this Act for developers of common interest communities:

> Section 804 . . . states that discrimination includes "a refusal to make reasonable accommodations in rules, policies, practices, or services when such accommodations may be necessary to afford [a disabled person] equal opportunity to use and enjoy a dwelling. . . . The starting point for determining what constitutes a reasonable accommodation . . . is an understanding that the purpose of the law is to end the unnecessary exclusion of persons with handicaps from the American mainstream. The reasonable accommodation requirement does not entail, however, an obligation to do everything humanly possible to accommodate a disabled person; cost (to the defendant) and benefit (to the plaintiff) merit consideration as well. Similarly, the concept of necessity, at a minimum, must illustrate that the desired accommodation will affirmatively enhance a disabled person's quality of life by ameliorating the effects of the disability.

Gary A. Poliakoff, The Effect of the Fair Housing Act on Deed Restrictions and Rules and Regulations Within Common Interest Ownership Housing Communities, 17 Prob. & Prop. 36 (May/June 2003). One area where associations often must make accommodations is on the issue of service animals; obviously, an otherwise valid "no dog" rule could not be enforced against a blind resident whose mobility depended upon a seeing-eye dog. See, e.g., Rebecca J. Huss, No Pets Allowed: Housing Issues and Companion Animals, 11 Animal L. 69 (2005).

5.   *Association sanctions against owner.* Consider the range of possible sanctions against an owner who either refuses to comply with valid behavioral rules or becomes delinquent in paying assessments. They include: (a) the usual dunning letters and telephone calls; (b) denial of use of the common recreational facilities; (c) imposition of fines; (d) denial of voting rights; (e) publication of the delinquency in a project newsletter or on a community bulletin board; (f) injunctive relief; or (g) foreclosure of the association's lien on the unit. Many of these actions are difficult for the association to take, especially if there is no professional management in the project to encourage the taking of a "tough" line. Members are often reluctant to take seemingly severe action against their own neighbors, and continuing

infractions and delinquencies are common in many projects. Some of the actions mentioned raise serious legal issues as well. See generally James J. Scavo & Richard P. Voss, Community Association Late Fees and Publication of Delinquencies: Are They Legal?, 7 Real Est. L.J. 216 (1979); Jackson, Homeowners Associations: Remedies to Enforce Assessment Collections, 51 L.A. Bar J. 423 (1976).

Some condominium documents authorize the association to compel the sale of a member's unit as a sanction for violation of condominium rules. Are such provisions valid? Are they workable? See Michael C. Kim, Involuntary Sale: Banishing an Owner from the Condominium Community, 31 John Marshall L. Rev. 429 (1998) (taking the position that, subject to rudimentary due process protections, courts "should not be reluctant to execute the involuntary sale remedy"). See also Amos B. Elberg, Note, Remedies for Common Interest Development Rule Violations, 101 Colum. L. Rev. 1958 (2001).

Should disputes between unit owners and the association be resolved by arbitration or mediation? For example, Florida legislation requires non-binding arbitration prior to the institution of litigation. The state is mandated to employ full-time attorneys to conduct arbitration hearings. Fla. Stat. Ann. § 718.1255. See Scott E. Mollen, Alternative Dispute Resolution of Condominium and Cooperative Conflicts, 73 St. John's L. Rev. 75 (1999).

6. *Discipline and sanctions against cooperative members.* Theoretically, it should be easier to discipline a cooperative resident for violation of the rules or delinquencies in payment of assessments than in a condominium or planned community. Remember that each cooperator is "merely" a tenant, holding possession of the apartment under a proprietary lease. The cooperative managers, then, may conclude that ordinary landlord-tenant remedies and rules apply, so that the association may remove the cooperator after some short period of statutory notice, with unlawful detainer available in the event the cooperator does not leave voluntarily. There is indeed authority that such remedies are applicable to a defaulting cooperator.

The difficulty with landlord-tenant reasoning, of course, is that cooperators often have thousands of dollars in "equity" in their units, and the courts are not likely to approve forfeitures of such investments in a cavalier manner. In the context of rules violations, the courts nearly always refuse to terminate a proprietary lease unless the rule is reasonable and without first giving the tenant a generous grace period to come into compliance. See, e.g., Moss v. Elofsson, 194 Ill.App.3d 256, 141 Ill.Dec. 182, 550 N.E.2d 1228 (1990) (forfeiture of lease impermissible where there is no evidence of willful breach of provision requiring lessee to permit management access at reasonable hours and where lessee's efforts to cure were reasonable); 520 East 86th St., Inc. v. Leventritt, 127 Misc.2d 566, 486 N.Y.S.2d 854 (Civ. Ct. 1985) (rule providing for termination of lease for two months' rent arrearage deemed unenforceable as unreasonable forfeiture unless reasonable provision is made for cure); Patrick J. Rohan & Melvin A. Reskin, Cooperative Housing Law &

Practice § 11.05[1]. An Arizona court completely rejected the landlord-tenant characterization and refused to permit the use of the forcible entry and detainer statute to evict a defaulting cooperator, instead characterizing the relationship as one "akin to that found in a deed of trust arrangement" under which the cooperator's interest "is clearly in the nature of an ownership or fee interest." Kadera v. Superior Court, 187 Ariz. 557, 931 P.2d 1067 (Ct. App. 1996).

40 West 67th Street v. Pullman, 100 N.Y.2d 147, 760 N.Y.S.2d 745, 790 N.E.2d 1174 (2003), is a recent illustrative case that demonstrates the appropriate standard for judicial review of a decision to terminate a cooperator's proprietary lease for violation of cooperative rules. The defendant in *Pullman*, shortly after purchasing a cooperative apartment, began engaging in numerous forms of disruptive and outrageous conduct, including: (a) sending harassing letters to the residents of a neighboring apartment containing false accusations of unneighborly and illegal activity; (b) distributing flyers to other residents referring to another resident, by name, as a potential "psychopath in our midst," accusing that resident of cutting the defendant's telephone lines, and suggesting that resident's wife and the board president's wife were having "intimate personal relations"; (c) making alterations to his apartment without Board approval; (d) having construction work performed on the weekend in violation of cooperative rules; (e) refusing to allow an inspection of his apartment; and (f) commencing repetitive lawsuits against the neighbor and the cooperative board. In reaction to this behavior, the cooperative called a special meeting pursuant to the provisions of the defendant's proprietary lease agreement, which provided for termination of the tenancy if the cooperative by a two-thirds vote determined that "because of objectionable conduct on the part of the Lessee . . . the tenancy of the Lessee is undesirable." After a timely-noticed meeting at which owners of more than 75% of the outstanding shares in the cooperative were present, the shareholders in attendance unanimously voted that defendant's conduct was "objectionable" and directed the Board to terminate his proprietary lease and cancel his shares.

After the Board sent a notice of termination and ordered the defendant to vacate, the defendant remained in the apartment, prompting the cooperative to sue to eject him and obtain a declaratory judgment cancelling his shares in the cooperative. The trial court denied the cooperative's motion for summary judgment, holding that the cooperative could only eject the defendant by proving his "objectionable conduct" by competent evidence to the satisfaction of the court under N.Y. Real Prop. Actions & Proc. Law § 711(1). A divided Appellate Division reversed, granting the cooperative summary judgment on its causes of action for ejectment and the cancellation of defendant's stock. The Court of Appeals of New York affirmed:

> In *Matter of Levandusky v. One Fifth Ave. Apt. Corp.*, 75 N.Y.2d 530, 554 N.Y.S.2d 807, 553 N.E.2d 1317, we held that the business judgment rule is the proper standard of judicial review when

evaluating   decisions   made   by   residential   cooperative
corporations. . . .

[RPAPL § 711(1)] requires "competent evidence" to show that a
tenant is objectionable. Thus, in this context, the competent
evidence that is the basis for the shareholder vote will be reviewed
under the business judgment rule, which means courts will
normally defer to that vote and the shareholders' stated findings as
competent evidence that the tenant is indeed objectionable under
the statute. As we stated in *Levandusky,* a single standard of review
for cooperatives is preferable, and "we see no purpose in allowing
the form of the action to dictate the substance of the standard by
which the legitimacy of corporate action is to be measured" . . .

Despite this deferential standard, there are instances when
courts should undertake review of board decisions. To trigger
further judicial scrutiny, an aggrieved shareholder-tenant must
make a showing that the board acted (1) outside the scope of its
authority, (2) in a way that did not legitimately further the
corporate purpose or (3) in bad faith. [*Pullman,* 790 N.E.2d at 1178–
1180.]

The Court upheld the termination decision, concluding that the defendant
had failed to demonstrate that the board had exceeded its authority or had
acted in bad faith or so as not to legitimately further the interests of the
cooperative. [Note that the termination of a proprietary lease does not
necessarily imply the cooperator also loses the accumulated "equity" in his
unit. In *Pullman,* the cooperative conceded that upon resale of the
apartment, it was obligated to return the sale proceeds to the defendant after
deduction of costs of sale and expenses incurred in the litigation.]

7. *Is the association a "state actor" for federal or state constitutional
purposes?* A city council ordinance must pass federal and state constitutional
muster because such an ordinance constitutes "state action." Thus, severe
First Amendment problems would arise if a city council prohibited the
display of flags from apartment balconies. However, the First Amendment
applies to government action to limit speech, and is typically understood not
to govern private action. Thus, for example, a private employer can typically
impose and enforce even content-based speech restrictions on its employees.

So suppose a community association board prohibits a unit owner from
displaying an American flag from the balcony of his unit, or from displaying
political yard signs. Is this state action in violation of the First Amendment,
or private action free of constitutional constraints? Some academic
commentators and many pro-homeowners advocates have argued strongly
that the law should treat community associations as state actors subject to
constitutional constraints. See, e.g., Weakland, Condominium Associations:
Living Under the Due Process Shadow, 13 Pepp. L. Rev. 297 (1986). While an
occasional decision has agreed, see, e.g., Gerber v. Longboat Harbour North
Condo., Inc., 724 F.Supp. 884 (M.D. Fla. 1989), most courts have refused to

treat community associations as state actors under either the U.S. Constitution or its state counterparts. See, e.g., Rosenberry, The Application of the Federal and State Constitutions to Condominiums, Cooperatives, and Planned Developments, 19 Real Prop., Prob. & Tr. L.J. 1 (1984); Natelson, Law of Property Owners Associations § 4.6.5 (1989).

In 2006, "community association as state actor" advocates were heartened by a temporary victory in a case involving Twin Rivers, a planned community of over 10,000 residents in East Windsor, New Jersey. The Twin Rivers Homeowners Association board adopted rules that restricted the posting of signs by residents, limiting residents to one sign per lawn and one per window and prohibiting the posting of signs on utility poles, trees, and other natural features within the community. The board also adopted policies with regard to the use of the Twin Rivers community room and with respect to the publication of the Association's monthly newspaper. Some number of Twin Rivers residents—unhappy with the board's governance (including the sign restrictions and the community room access policy) and unable to obtain "equal access" to the editorial pages of the Association's newspaper— established a committee known as the Committee for a Better Twin Rivers. When their efforts to achieve desired changes in community governance were unsuccessful, the Committee filed a lawsuit challenging the validity of the Association's policies regarding signs, community room access, and access to the editorial pages of the Association's newspaper based upon the guarantees of free speech and association protected by the New Jersey constitution. The trial court awarded summary judgment to the Association as to the validity of its sign policy and its newspaper editorial policies, holding that the Association was not a "quasi-municipality" subject to the state constitution's free speech and association clauses. The intermediate appellate court reversed, however, concluding that the Association was subject to state constitutional standards with respect to its internal rules and regulations.

In late 2007, the New Jersey Supreme Court unanimously reversed and reinstated the trial court's judgment. The court acknowledged that "the vast majority of other jurisdictions that have interpreted a state constitutional provision with language similar to our constitution's free speech provision require 'state action' as a precondition to imposing constitutional obligations on private property owners." The court noted, however, that under the New Jersey constitution, "the rights of free speech and assembly under our constitution are not only secure from interference by governmental or public bodies, but under certain circumstances from the interference by the owner of private property as well." The court then evaluated the Twin Rivers restrictions under its prior decisions in State v. Schmid, 84 N.J. 535, 423 A.2d 615 (1980), and New Jersey Coalition Against War in the Middle East v. J.M.B. Realty Corp., 138 N.J. 326, 650 A.2d 757 (1994), cert. denied, 516 U.S. 812 (1995).

The first *Schmid* factor requires that we consider the nature, purposes, and primary use of the property. Twin Rivers is a common interest community "in which the property is burdened by servitudes requiring property owners to contribute to maintenance of commonly held property or to pay dues or assessments to an owners association that provides services or facilities to the community." *Restatement (Third) of Property: Servitudes* § 6 (2000). We have recognized that "[a] common-interest community is distinguishable from any other form of real property ownership because 'there is a commonality of interest, an interdependence directly tied to the use, enjoyment, and ownership of property.'" *Fox v. Kings Grant Maint. Ass'n,* 167 N.J. 208, 222, 770 A.2d 707 (2001) (quoting Wayne S. Hyatt, *Condominium and Homeowner Association Practice: Community Association Law* § 2.01 at 25 (2d ed.1988)).

The primary use of the property in Twin Rivers is residential. There are privately owned businesses within the borders of Twin Rivers, but the Association derives no revenue from them. East Windsor Township, not Twin Rivers, provides for the school system, the police and fire departments, the municipal court system, and the first aid services. Twin Rivers offers its residents services in the form of landscape maintenance, upkeep of trust-owned roads, removal of trash from certain sections of the community, and cleaning of snow. Thus, we find the nature, purposes, and primary use of Twin Rivers's property is for private purposes and does not favor a finding that the Association's rules and regulations violated plaintiffs' constitutional rights.

The second *Schmid* factor requires that we examine the extent and nature of the public's invitation to use the property. A public invitation to use the premises may be express or implied. As we explained in *Coalition,* an implied invitation can be inferred where the property owner permits and encourages public use of the property. Here, the Association has not invited the public to use its property. Although Twin Rivers is not a gated community and its roads are accessible to public traffic, we agree with the Association's position that "Trust-owned property and facilities are for the exclusive use of Twin Rivers residents and their invited guests." Moreover, the mere fact that owners may sell or rent property to members of the public who are invited to come into Twin Rivers and inspect such property hardly implicates a public invitation. We conclude that the limited nature of the public's invitation to use the property does not favor a finding that the Association's rules and regulations violated plaintiffs' constitutional rights.

The third *Schmid* factor concerns the purpose of the expressional activity in relation to both the private and public use of the property. This part of the test requires that we examine "the compatibility of the free speech sought to be exercised with the uses of the property." Essentially, we must look to the fairness of the restrictions imposed by the Association in relation to plaintiffs' free speech rights. In this case, plaintiffs' expressional activities—posting political signs, free use of the community room, and access to the community newspaper—involve political-like speech aimed at affecting the manner in which Twin Rivers is managed.

We find that plaintiffs' expressional activities are not unreasonably restricted. As the Association points out, the relationship between it and the homeowners is a contractual one, formalized in reasonable covenants that appear in all deeds. Moreover, unlike the university in *Schmid,* and the shopping center in *Coalition,* Twin Rivers is not a private forum that invites the public on its property to either facilitate academic discourse or to encourage public commerce. Rather, Twin Rivers is a private, residential community whose residents have contractually agreed to abide by the common rules and regulations of the Association. The mutual benefit and reciprocal nature of those rules and regulations, and their enforcement, is essential to the fundamental nature of the communal living arrangement that Twin Rivers residents enjoy. We further conclude that this factor does not weigh in favor of finding that the Association's rules and regulations violated plaintiffs' constitutional rights. . . .

The outcome of the balancing of the expressional rights and the privacy interests is obvious. "We do not interfere lightly with private property rights." *Coalition, supra,* 138 N.J. at 371, 650 A.2d 757. We find that the minor restrictions on plaintiffs' expressional activities are not unreasonable or oppressive, and the Association is not acting as a municipality. The Association's restrictions concerning the placement of the signs, the use of the community room, and access to its newspaper are reasonable "concerning the time, place, and manner of" such restrictions. Neither singularly nor in combination is the *Schmid/Coalition* test satisfied in favor of concluding that a constitutional right was infringed here. Consequently, we conclude that in balancing plaintiffs' expressional rights against the Association's private property interest, the Association's policies do not violate the free speech and right of assembly clauses of the New Jersey Constitution.

Committee for a Better Twin Rivers v. Twin Rivers Homeowners' Ass'n, 192 N.J. 344, 365–368, 929 A.2d 1060, 1072–1074 (2007). The court also suggested that the interest of residents in free speech and assembly were adequately protected by the business judgment rule, public policy limitations on the enforceability of covenants, and the ability of the residents to influence community decisions through participation in community governance. If these protections are sufficient, under what circumstances might an association's conduct transgress constitutional limits?

8.   *A homeowner "bill of rights"?* Should a developer make sure that the common interest community declaration contains an owner's bill of rights? If

so, what rights should be included? Suppose a condominium association enacts a rule banning use of a condominium for religious services. See Neuman v. Grandview at Emerald Hills, Inc., 861 So.2d 494 (Fla.App.2003) (upholding such a ban). Professor French has advocated the "bill of rights" approach, see Susan F. French, The Constitution of a Private Residential Government Should Include a Bill of Rights, 27 Wake Forest L. Rev. 345, 351–52 (1992). The 2008 amendments to UCIOA also include a "homeowners bill of rights."

9.   *Statutory responses to intrusive association regulation.* Following the public outcry over association attempts to use sign restrictions to prevent the display of flags, and the outpouring of patriotism experienced in the wake of the events of September 11, 2001, several states have enacted legislation that prevents homeowner and condominium associations from restricting the ability of their residents to display the American flag. Consider the following California statute:

> Except as required for the protection of the public health or safety, no governing document shall limit or prohibit, or be construed to limit or prohibit, the display of the flag of the United States by a member on or in the member's separate interest or within the member's exclusive use common area.

Cal. Civ. Code § 4705(a). See also Fla. Stat. Ann. § 720.304(2); Ariz. Rev. Stat. § 33–1261(A), (B). For a consideration of these statutes, see Note, 117 Harv. L. Rev. 2047 (2004).

Likewise, in the wake of the uproar following the California Supreme Court's decision in Nahrstedt v. Lakeside Village Condo. Ass'n, Inc., 8 Cal.4th 361, 33 Cal.Rptr.2d 63, 878 P.2d 1275 (1994) (enforcing as reasonable a no-pet restriction contained in the condominium declaration), the California legislature enacted Cal. Civ. Code § 4715(a), which provides that "[n]o governing documents shall prohibit the owner of a separate interest within a common interest development from keeping at least one pet within the common interest development, subject to reasonable rules and regulations of the association."

10.   *Restrictions on transfer.* In many common interest communities, the declaration or rules may contain restrictions upon a resident's ability to transfer her interest. Such restrictions may range from narrowly-tailored restrictions on leasing all the way up to complete prohibition on sale without the prior written consent of the association board. To what extent should an association be able to exercise control over a member's ability to transfer her interest in a unit or lot within the community?

AQUARIAN FOUNDATION, INC. v. SHOLOM HOUSE, INC.

District Court of Appeal of Florida, Third District, 1984
448 So.2d 1166

DANIEL S. PEARSON, JUDGE. All is not peaceful at the Sholom House Condominium. In disregard of a provision of the declaration of condominium requiring the written consent of the condominium association's board of directors to any sale, lease, assignment or transfer of a unit owner's interest, Bertha Albares, a member of the board of directors, sold her condominium unit to the Aquarian Foundation, Inc. without obtaining such consent. Eschewing its right to ratify the sale, the association, expressly empowered by the declaration to "arbitrarily, capriciously, or unreasonably" withhold its consent, sued to set aside the conveyance, to dispossess Aquarian, and to recover damages under a clause in the declaration which provides that:

> In the event of a violation by the condominium [sic] by the unit owner of any of the covenants, restrictions and limitations, contained in this declaration, then in that event the fee simple title to the condominium parcel shall immediately revert to the association, subject to the association paying to said former unit owner, the fair appraised value thereof, at the time of reversion, to be determined as herein provided.

The trial court, after a non-jury trial, found that Albares had violated the declaration of condominium, thus triggering the reverter clause. Accordingly, it entered a judgment for the association, declaring the conveyance to Aquarian null and void, ejecting Aquarian, and retaining jurisdiction to award damages, attorneys' fees and costs after a determination of the fair appraised value of the property. Aquarian appeals. We reverse.

The issue presented by this appeal is whether the power vested in the association to arbitrarily, capriciously, or unreasonably withhold its consent to transfer constitutes an unreasonable restraint on alienation, notwithstanding the above-quoted reverter clause which mandates that the association compensate the unit owner in the event, in this case, of a transfer of the unit in violation of the consent requirement.

It is well settled that increased controls and limitations upon the rights of unit owners to transfer their property are necessary concomitants of condominium living. *See Hidden Harbour Estates, Inc. v. Norman,* 309 So.2d 180 (Fla. 4th DCA 1975); *Holiday Out in America at St. Lucie, Inc. v. Bowes,* 285 So.2d 63 (Fla. 4th DCA 1973); *Chianese v. Culley,* 397 F.Supp. 1344 (S.D.Fla.1975). . . .

Accordingly, restrictions on a unit owner's right to transfer his property are recognized as a valid means of insuring the association's ability to control the composition of the condominium as a whole. . . .

However, despite the law's recognition of the particular desirability of restrictions on the right to transfer in the context of condominium living, such restrictions will be invalidated when found to violate some external public policy or constitutional right of the individual. *Hidden Harbour Estates, Inc. v. Basso,* 393 So.2d at 639–40. *See Pepe v. Whispering Sands Condominium Association, Inc.,* 351 So.2d 755 (Fla. 2d DCA 1977). Merely because a declaration of condominium is in the nature of a private compact and a *restriction* contained therein is not subject to the same reasonableness requirement as a restriction contained in a public regulation, *see White Egret Condominium, Inc. v. Franklin,* 379 So.2d 346, 350 (Fla.1979), where the restriction constitutes a restraint on alienation, condominium associations are not immune from the requirement that the *restraint* be reasonable. Thus, while a condominium association's board of directors has considerable latitude in withholding its consent to a unit owner's transfer, the resulting restraint on alienation must be reasonable. In this manner the balance between the right of the association to maintain its homogeneity and the right of the individual to alienate his property is struck.

The basic premise of the public policy rule against unreasonable restraints on alienation, *see 7 Thompson On Real Property,* § 3161 (1962); 31 C.J.S. *Estates* 8(b)(2) (1964), is that free alienability of property fosters economic growth and commercial development. *Davis v. Geyer,* 151 Fla. 362, 9 So.2d 727 (1942); *Seagate Condominium Association, Inc. v. Duffy,* 330 So.2d 484. Because "[t]he validity or invalidity of a restraint depends upon its long-term effect on the improvement and marketability of the property," *Iglehart v. Phillips,* 383 So.2d 610, 614 (Fla.1980), where the restraint, for whatever duration, does not impede the improvement of the property or its marketability, it is not illegal. *Id.* at 615. Accordingly, where a restraint on alienation, no matter how absolute and encompassing, is conditioned upon the restrainer's obligation to purchase the property at the then fair market value, the restraint is valid. *Id.* at 614–15, and cases collected.

The declaration of condominium in the present case permits the association to reject perpetually any unit owner's prospective purchaser for any or no reason. Such a provision, so obviously an absolute restraint on alienation, can be saved from invalidity only if the association has a corresponding obligation to purchase or procure a purchaser for the property from the unit owner at its fair market value. Otherwise stated, if, as here, the association is empowered to act arbitrarily, capriciously, and unreasonably in rejecting a unit owner's prospective purchaser, it must in turn be accountable to the unit owner by offering payment or a substitute market for the property. When this accountability exists, even an absolute and perpetual restraint on the unit owner's ability to select a purchaser is lawful. *See Chianese v. Culley,* 397 F.Supp. 1344 (notwithstanding association's right to approve any transfer except one to an existing unit owner, requirement that within sixty days association provide another purchaser or approve original purchaser creates a preemptive right in association and saves declaration of condominium from being an unlawful restraint on alienation).

The declaration of condominium involved in the instant case contains no language requiring the association to provide another purchaser, purchase the property from the unit owner, or, failing either of these, approve the proposed transfer. What it does contain is the reverter clause, which the association contends is the functional equivalent of a preemptive right and, as such, makes the restraint on alienation lawful.

In our view, the problem with the association's position is that the reverter clause imposes no obligation upon the association to compensate the unit owner within a reasonable time after the association withholds its consent to transfer, and the clause is not therefore the functional equivalent of a preemptive right. *Cf. Chianese v. Culley,* 397 F.Supp. 1344. Instead, the clause and the association's obligation do not come into effect until a violation of the restriction on an unapproved transfer occurs. . . .

The association's accountability to the unit owner is illusory. There is no reasonable likelihood that a potential purchaser, apprised by the condominium documents that the consent of the association is required and that a purchase without consent vitiates the sale, would be willing to acquire the property without the association's consent. Without a sale, there is no violation of the reverter clause. Without a violation of the reverter clause, the association has no obligation to pay the unit owner.

Effectively, then, the power of the association to arbitrarily, capriciously, and unreasonably withhold its consent to transfer prevents the activation of the reverter clause and eliminates the accountability of the association to the unit owner. Therefore, we conclude that the power of the association to arbitrarily, capriciously, and unreasonably withhold its consent to transfer is not saved by the reverter clause from being declared an invalid and unenforceable restraint on alienation. Accordingly, the judgment of the trial court is

Reversed.

NOTES

1. *Restraints on alienation in the condominium setting.* For an excellent analysis of the competing policy concerns inherent in the application of restraints on alienation doctrine in the condominium setting, see Vincent DiLorenzo, Restraint on Alienation in a Condominium Context— An Evaluation and Theory for Decision Making, 24 Real Prop. Prob. & Tr. J. 403 (1989).

2.　*Rights of first refusal*. Rights of first refusal (or "preemptive" rights) give the association the right to purchase the unit should the unit owner decide to sell it. Usually, the language of such a provision will give the association a fixed period of time to either meet the terms of an offer that the unit seller is otherwise willing to accept or to allow the proposed transfer. Such provisions normally are not deemed to be unreasonable restraints on alienation. See e.g., Ritchey v. Villa Nueva Condo. Ass'n, 81 Cal.App.3d 688, 146 Cal.Rptr. 695 (1978); Chianese v. Culley, 397 F.Supp. 1344 (S.D. Fla. 1975). However, all courts require that the right be exercised reasonably. See e.g., Lyons v. King, 397 So.2d 964 (Fla. Ct. App. 1981). Consequently, the use of the right to exclude purchasers on the basis of race, creed, gender, age, familial status or national origin will be deemed "unreasonable" and will often run afoul of federal or state statutes or local ordinances that prohibit discrimination in the sale of housing. See e.g., Lippman v. Bridgecrest Estates I Unit Owners Ass'n, Inc., 991 S.W.2d 145 (Mo. Ct. App. 1998) (association's exercise of right of first refusal constituted familial status discrimination in violation of federal Fair Housing Act); Wolinsky v. Kadison, 114 Ill.App.3d 527, 70 Ill.Dec. 277, 449 N.E.2d 151 (1983) (allegation that right of first refusal was exercised to exclude an unmarried female stated a valid cause of action under Chicago ordinance); Olin L. Browder, Restraints on Alienation of Condominium Units (The Right of First Refusal), 1970 U. Ill. L.F. 231, 257–259 (1970).

Suppose that a condominium association amends its bylaws to provide that the development's 10 studio-size units can be sold only to owners of larger units. [Assume that the studio units were all initially sold to affluent buyers of larger units, who used them either for storage or as quarters for their servants.] If an owner of one of the studio units contracts to sell that unit to a current nonresident, should the court enforce the amended bylaw and enjoin the sale? Consider the following answer:

> [It cannot] be said that the purpose of the restrictions of sale of studio units—to preserve the character of the Condominium—is unreasonable. Although the duration of the restriction appears to be unlimited on its face, the restriction can be modified at any time by a duly called meeting of the unit owners to further amend the bylaws.

Demchick v. 90 East End Ave. Condo., 18 A.D.3d 383, 384, 796 N.Y.S.2d 62, 63 (2005). Is this a satisfactory answer?

3.　*Rights of first refusal and the rule against perpetuities*. Do rights of first refusal run afoul of the rule against perpetuities? The common law rule against perpetuities invalidates a contingent future interest in property that may vest more than 21 years after some life in being at the time the interest was created. A right of first refusal, if it is deemed a contingent future interest and is unlimited as to time, literally violates the rule because the owner of the burdened property could decide to sell (and the holder of the right decide to purchase) at any time in the future—potentially, after everyone alive at the time the right was created has died and an additional 21 years has passed.

While there is case authority invalidating such rights, see, e.g., Hensley-O'Neal v. Metropolitan Nat'l Bank, 297 S.W.3d 610 (Mo. Ct. App. 2009) (right of first refusal violated rule against perpetuities), many states have by statute exempted them from the rule, either generally or with particular reference to condominiums. Moreover, most commentators agree that the rule should be inapplicable to such rights in the condominium context. See Olin L. Browder, Restraints on the Alienation of Condominium Units (The Right of First Refusal), 1970 U. Ill. L.F. 231, 248–256 (1970); Lawrence E. Allison, Comment, The Mississippi Condominium Act: An Analysis of Potential Problems, 44 Miss. L.J. 261 (1973). Professor Browder, for example, suggested several bases for sustaining the typical condominium right of first refusal against a rule against perpetuities attack. Among these are arguments that such a right: (1) is only a contractual one until exercised and is thus not a contingent future interest in property; (2) is fully justified by the social values inherent in condominium housing; and (3) is subject to the rule against perpetuities exception applicable to possibilities of reverter and rights of entry. Browder, supra, at 255–256.

4. *Restrictions on leasing.* It has become increasingly common for condominium documents to place significant restrictions on the unit owner's ability to lease her unit. For example, there may be a flat prohibition on the creation of all leaseholds. Alternatively, the prohibition may be effective only for a fixed time period, such as for 10 or 20 years. Why might an owners association find such restrictions desirable? What may happen to a condominium development where the majority of owners are absentee landlords?

Courts have shown support for such restrictions on leasehold creation. See Four Brothers Homes at Heartland Condo. II v. Gerbino, 262 A.D.2d 279, 691 N.Y.S.2d 114 (1999) (total prohibition on leasing units not an unreasonable restraint on alienation); Apple II Condo. Ass'n v. Worth Bank & Trust Co., 277 Ill.App.3d 345, 213 Ill.Dec. 463, 659 N.E.2d 93 (1995) (leasing prohibition in condominium declaration is presumed valid and will be upheld unless it can be shown that prohibition is arbitrary, contrary to public policy, or violates some fundamental constitutional right of unit owners); City of Oceanside v. McKenna, 215 Cal.App.3d 1420, 264 Cal.Rptr. 275 (1989) (a ten-year restriction on leasing condominium units in a publicly-financed project deemed reasonable and enforceable by injunctive relief); Worthinglen Condo. Unit Owners' Ass'n v. Brown, 57 Ohio App.3d 73, 566 N.E.2d 1275 (1989) (amendment to condominium declaration prohibiting unit owners from leasing their units is not *per se* unenforceable against unit owners who purchased their units prior to the amendment; restriction must be judged by a reasonableness standard in light of the surrounding circumstances). For other decisions upholding leasing restrictions, see Flagler Fed. Sav. & Loan Ass'n v. Crestview Towers, 595 So.2d 198 (Fla. Ct. App. 1992); Seagate Condo. Ass'n v. Duffy, 330 So.2d 484 (Fla. Ct. App. 1976).

Professor Susan French has advocated declaration language providing that "the association shall not adopt rules that prohibit transfer of any lot or unit, or require consent of the association for transfer of any lot or unit, for any period greater than [two] months." Susan F. French, The Constitution of a Private Residential Government Should Include a Bill of Rights, 27 Wake Forest L.Rev. 345, 352 (1992). Do you agree? What concerns might justify placing this limitation upon an owners association? See also David E. Grassmick, Minding the Neighbor's Business: Just How Far Can Condominium Owners' Associations Go in Deciding Who Can Move Into the Building?, 2002 U. Ill. L. Rev. 185, 213.

5.   *Other limitations on a unit owner's right to transfer.* Consider the following types of limitations on a unit owner's right to transfer her interest.

(a)   *Restrictions on immediate resale or "flipping."* Suppose that Wells purchases a new condominium unit from the developer of a 250-unit project. The declaration provides:

> The original purchaser of any unit is prohibited from selling that unit for a period of two years following that purchase without the prior written consent of Developer. If Developer grants its consent to any sale within such two-year period, Developer is entitled to receive 50% of any profit received by the original purchaser of the unit in the approved sale, after deduction of any real estate commissions and other necessary expenses of sale.

Six months later, Wells is transferred to another state and signs a contract to sell her unit to Lambert, without obtaining Developer's prior consent. Can Developer get an injunction to prevent the closing of the sale? If the sale closes, can Developer recover 50% of Wells's profit from the sale? How would you evaluate the reasonableness of this restriction, and what additional information (if any) do you think might be relevant to this evaluation?

(b)   *Transfer fee covenants.* Suppose that the declaration imposes a covenant, binding upon the owner of each lot/unit (and their heirs, successors, and assigns), that specifies that the owner must pay a fee to the owners association upon a sale of the lot/unit equal to 1% of the sale price. Is there any problem enforcing such a covenant? In evaluating the reasonableness of this fee, is the fee qualitatively any different from a homeowners' association assessment?

Now suppose that the declaration imposes a comparable 1% resale fee, but specifies that the owner must pay the fee to *the developer* upon resale. Can this fee be upheld as reasonable? Why or why not? Compare Cal. Civ. Code § 1098.5 (yes, subject to statutory disclosure requirements) with Fla. Stat. Ann. § 689.28 and Mo. Rev. Stat. § 442.558 (no). Note that Federal Housing Finance Agency regulations now preclude Fannie Mae and Freddie Mac from purchasing mortgages on land subject to most "private" transfer fee covenants created after February 8, 2011. 12 C.F.R. §§ 1228.1 to 1228.4. Why should such private transfer fees be considered unreasonable? See, e.g., Joint

Editorial Board for Uniform Real Property Acts, Position Paper on Private Transfer Fee Covenants, http://www.uniformlaws.org/shared/docs/jeburpa/ 2010apr_JEBURPA_Position%20paper_Private%20transfer%20fee%20coven ants.pdf.

6. *Restrictions on cooperative transfer.* In cooperatives, control over transfer frequently takes the form of an express prohibition on the member's alienation of her corporate shares and leasehold interest. While courts would deem such a direct restraint an unreasonable restraint on alienation in the context of a fee simple transfer of real estate, the assumption has been that the cooperative member's ownership interest is governed in this context by landlord-tenant law. Under the latter rules, courts generally uphold tenant covenants not to assign or sublease without the landlord's consent. William B. Stoebuck & Dale A. Whitman, The Law of Property 386–387 (3d ed. 2000).

Consequently, courts have afforded cooperative boards broad power to refuse consent to prospective transferees. See, e.g., Rossi v. Simms, 119 A.D.2d 137, 506 N.Y.S.2d 50 (1986); Patrick J. Rohan & Melvin A. Reskin, Cooperative Housing Law and Practice § 7.02[3]. Indeed, as one commentator has pointed out, "such individuals as Richard Nixon, Gloria Vanderbilt, Calvin Klein and Madonna have all been refused memberships in cooperatives." Stuart S. Moskowitz, Co-op Transfer Restrictions: Business Judgment, Board of Discretion and Bankruptcy—Part II, 62 N.Y. State Bar J. 28, 31 (Dec. 1990). Importantly, however, the power to refuse consent is often limited by fair housing legislation and ordinances. For example, a New York statute prohibits a cooperative corporation from withholding "its consent to the sale or proposed sale of certificates of stock or other evidence of ownership of an interest in such corporation because of the race, creed, national origin, or sex of the purchaser." N.Y. McKinney's Civ. Rts. L. § 19–a(1). The federal Fair Housing Act will have the same effect.

Professor Rohan's observations regarding this power to refuse consent are informative:

> Even if the board acts in good faith, its ability to exercise broad discretion places the entire financial and social burden back on the outgoing unit owner, who, upon having his proffered buyer rejected, must now start the process of seeking an acceptable purchaser all over again. In recent years, this has worked an extreme hardship on unit sellers relocated to another city by their employers or whose units have become substantially devalued as a consequence of radical downturns in the co-op market. This evil is compounded by the fact that in most co-ops the cooperator has no right, or a very limited right, to lease out his unit to enable him to carry the unit pending its resale. This double blow to departing unit owners plays havoc with their finances and may impair their credit rating or even push them into insolvency.

Patrick J. Rohan, Preparing Community Associations for the Twenty-First Century: Anticipating the Legal Problems and Possible Solutions, 73 St. John's L. Rev. 3, 18 (1999).

Recognizing this potential for abuse of a cooperator, courts may refuse to allow the enforcement of transfer restrictions to the extent that enforcement would work a forfeiture of the member's ownership interest. For example, in In re Bentley, 26 B.R. 69 (Bankr. S.D.N.Y. 1982), the cooperative board refused to approve a proposed transfer by Bentley, a resident and former member of the board who had filed a Chapter 11 bankruptcy petition, under which Bentley would sell his apartment to an investor who would lease the apartment back to Bentley for two years. The board refused the transfer (even though at the time, 30% of the units were still owned by the developer and leased to tenants). As a result of this refusal, Bentley was unable to confirm his Chapter 11 plan and could not make the payments necessary to cure the defaults on his proprietary lease, placing him in jeopardy of having his lease terminated. Bentley sued challenging the enforceability of the provisions of his proprietary lease, which purported to give absolute discretion to the board in approval decisions. The court held:

> This Court finds the provisions of [the proprietary lease] to be unconscionable as a matter of law at the time the lease was made to the extent that those provisions are applied to prevent Bentley from selling the Apartment because the result would be a forfeiture of the Apartment to the Lessor cooperative corporation. This Court is of the view that even without the authority granted to it by [New York statutes], it would find, as a matter of contract construction, an implied covenant in the proprietary lease that the consent provision would not be utilized so as to cause a forfeiture of an apartment to the cooperative corporation and consequent benefit to other shareholders to the detriment of the apartment owner. [*Bentley*, 26 B.R. at 72.]

Does this mean a cooperator can effectively use bankruptcy to force a transfer over the objection of the board? Suppose that a bankrupt cooperator finds a prospective purchaser who can afford to pay market value for the apartment in cash, but whose personality and lifestyle are offensive to the cooperative board. Does the board have no alternative but to accept this purchaser? According to one commentator, "if the debtor was able to bring someone forward who was willing to pay a fair sum for the apartment, it is arguable that a bankruptcy court could require a board to either come up with another purchaser, or with valid and persuasive reasons why the debtor's proffered candidate was not acceptable to it. Absent this justification, it is likely that the court would allow the transfer to proceed. On the other hand, if the proffered candidate was truly and objectively unacceptable to the board, the board was able to articulate its reasons for rejection, and the court accepted those reasons as valid ones, the court could side with the board." Stuart S. Moskowitz, Co-op Transfer Restrictions: Business Judgment, Board of Discretion and Bankruptcy—Part II, 62 N.Y. St. Bar J. 28, 31–32 (Dec. 1990).

Management of daily life within a common interest community depends upon the exercise of judgment by the association board (or some other authorized decision-making group). For example, many modern residential common interest developments are subject to covenants that prohibit lot owners from building a new home or modifying an existing one without obtaining prior approval of the building plans and specifications (either by the association board or an architectural control committee). An association board might have to make a decision between relying upon neighborhood residents to volunteer to mow grass or tend landscaping in common areas or to expend association funds to hire a private contractor to perform the job.

Our lived experience with the democratic process tells us that people of good will often disagree regarding how to govern or regulate life within the community. If a unit owner in a common interest development disagrees with a board's decision, should the law respond by deferring to the judgment as a product of the community's democratic process? Or should unit owners have recourse to judicial review—and, if so, what standard should govern that review?

LAMDEN V. LA JOLLA SHORES CLUBDOMINIUM HOMEOWNERS ASS'N

Supreme Court of California
21 Cal.4th 249, 87 Cal.Rptr.2d 237, 980 P.2d 940 (1999)

WERDEGAR, J. ... Plaintiff Gertrude M. Lamden owns a condominium unit in one of three buildings comprising the La Jolla Shores Clubdominium condominium development (Development). Over some years, the Board of Governors (Board) of defendant La Jolla Shores Clubdominium Homeowners Association (Association), an unincorporated community association, elected to spot treat (secondary treatment), rather than fumigate (primary treatment), for termites the building in which Lamden's unit is located (Building Three).

In the late 1980's, attempting to remedy water intrusion and mildew damage, the Association hired a contractor to renovate exterior siding on all three buildings in the Development. The contractor replaced the siding on the southern exposure of Building Three and removed damaged drywall and framing. Where the contractor encountered termites, a termite extermination company provided spot treatment and replaced damaged material.

Lamden remodeled the interior of her condominium in 1990. At that time, the Association's manager arranged for a termite extermination company to spot treat areas where Lamden had encountered termites.

The following year, both Lamden and the Association obtained termite inspection reports recommending fumigation, but the Association's Board decided against that approach. As the Court of Appeal explained, the Board based its decision not to fumigate on concerns about the cost of fumigation, logistical problems with temporarily relocating residents, concern that fumigation residue could affect residents' health and safety, awareness that upcoming walkway renovations would include replacement of damaged areas, pet moving expenses, anticipated breakage by the termite company, lost rental income and the likelihood that termite infestation would recur even if primary treatment were utilized. The Board decided to continue to rely on secondary treatment until a more widespread problem was demonstrated.

In 1991 and 1992, the Association engaged a company to repair water intrusion damage to four units in Building Three. The company removed siding in the balcony area, repaired and waterproofed the decks, and repaired joints between the decks and the walls of the units. The siding of the unit below Lamden's and one of its walls were repaired. Where termite infestation or damage became apparent during this project, spot treatment was applied and damaged material removed.

In 1993 and 1994, the Association commissioned major renovation of the Development's walkway system, underpinnings of which had suffered water and termite damage. The $1.6 million walkway project was monitored by a structural engineer and an on-site architect.

In 1994, Lamden brought this action for damages, an injunction and declaratory relief. She purported to state numerous causes of action based on the Association's refusal to fumigate for termites, naming as defendants certain individual members of the Board as well as the Association. Her amended complaint included claims sounding in breach of contract (viz., the governing Declaration of Restrictions [Declaration]), breach of fiduciary duty and negligence. She alleged that the Association, in opting for secondary over primary treatment, had breached Civil Code section 1364, subdivision (b)(1) and the Declaration in failing adequately to repair, replace and maintain the common areas of the Development. . . .

After both sides had presented evidence and argument, the trial court rendered findings related to the termite infestation affecting plaintiff's condominium unit, its causes, and the remedial steps taken by the Association. The trial court found there was "no question from all the evidence that Mrs. Lamden's unit . . . has had a serious problem with termites." In fact, the trial court found, "The evidence . . . was overwhelming that termites had been a problem over the past several years." The court concluded, however, that while "there may be active infestation" that would require "steps [to be] taken within the future years," there was no evidence that the condominium units were in imminent structural danger or "that these units are about to fall or something is about to happen."

The trial court also found that, "starting in the late '80's," the Association had arranged for "some work" addressing the termite problem to be done. Remedial and investigative work ordered by the Association included, according to the trial court, removal of siding to reveal the extent of damage, a "big project . . . in the early '90's," and an architect's report on building design factors. According to the court, the Board "did at one point seriously consider" primary treatment; "they got a bid for this fumigation, and there was discussion." The court found that the Board also considered possible problems entailed by fumigation, including relocation costs, lost rent, concerns about pets and plants, human health issues and eventual termite reinfestation.

As to the causes of the Development's termite infestation, the trial court concluded that "the key problem came about from you might say a poor design" and resulting "water intrusion." In short, the trial court stated, "the real culprit is not so much the Board, but it's the poor design and the water damage that is conducive to bringing the termites in."

As to the Association's actions, the trial court stated, "the Board did take appropriate action." The court noted the Board "did come up with a plan," viz., to engage a pest control service to "come out and [spot] treat [termite infestation] when it was found." The trial judge opined he might, "from a personal relations standpoint," have acted sooner or differently under the circumstances than did the Association, but nevertheless concluded "the Board did have a rational basis for their decision to reject fumigation, and do what they did." Ultimately, the court gave judgment for the Association, applying what it called a "business judgment test." Lamden appealed.

Citing *Frances T. v. Village Green Owners Association* (1986) 42 Cal.3d 490, 229 Cal.Rptr. 456, 723 P.2d 573 (*Frances T.*), the Court of Appeal agreed with Lamden that the trial court had applied the wrong standard of care in assessing the Association's actions. In the Court of Appeal's view, relevant statutes, the governing Declaration and principles of common law imposed on the Association an objective duty of reasonable care in repairing and maintaining the Development's common areas near Lamden's unit as occasioned by the presence of termites. The court also concluded that, had the trial court analyzed the Association's actions under an objective standard of reasonableness, an outcome more favorable to Lamden likely would have resulted. Accordingly, the Court of Appeal reversed the judgment of the trial court. . . .

The Association would have us decide this case through application of "the business judgment rule." As we have observed, that rule of judicial deference to corporate decisionmaking "exists in one form or another in every American jurisdiction." (*Frances T., supra*, 42 Cal.3d at p. 507, fn. 14, 229 Cal.Rptr. 456, 723 P.2d 573.)

"The common law business judgment rule has two components—one which immunizes [corporate] directors from personal liability if they act in accordance with its requirements, and another which insulates from court intervention those management decisions which are made by directors in good faith in what the directors believe is the organization's best interest." (*Lee v. Interinsurance Exchange* (1996) 50 Cal.App.4th 694, 714, 57 Cal.Rptr.2d 798) A hallmark of the business judgment rule is that, when the rule's requirements are met, a court will not substitute its judgment for that of the corporation's board of directors. . . . According to the Association, uniformly applying a business judgment standard in judicial review of community association board decisions would promote certainty, stability and predictability in common interest development governance. Plaintiff, on the other hand, contends general application of a business judgment standard to board decisions would undermine individual owners' ability, under Civil Code section 1354, to enforce, as equitable servitudes, the CC & R's in a common interest development's declaration. Stressing residents' interest in a stable and predictable living environment, as embodied in a given development's particular CC & R's, plaintiff encourages us to impose on community associations an objective standard of reasonableness in carrying out their duties under governing CC & R's or public policy. . . .

Our existing jurisprudence specifically addressing the governance of common interest developments is not voluminous. While we have not previously examined the question of what standard or test generally governs judicial review of decisions made by the board of directors of a community association, we have examined related questions.

Fifty years ago, in *Hannula v. Hacienda Homes* (1949) 34 Cal.2d 442, 211 P.2d 302, we held that the decision by the board of directors of a real estate development company to deny, under a restrictive covenant in a deed, the owner of a fractional part of a lot permission to build a dwelling thereon "must be a reasonable determination made in good faith." Sixteen years ago, we held that a condominium owners association is a "business establishment" within the meaning of the Unruh Civil Rights Act, section 51 of the Civil Code. (*O'Connor v. Village Green Owners Association* (1983) 33 Cal.3d 790, 796, 191 Cal.Rptr. 320, 662 P.2d 427.) And 10 years ago, in *Frances T., supra*, 42 Cal.3d 490, 229 Cal.Rptr. 456, 723 P.2d 573, we considered "whether a condominium owners association and the individual members of its board of directors may be held liable for injuries to a unit owner caused by third-party criminal conduct." (*Id.* at p. 495, 229 Cal.Rptr. 456, 723 P.2d 573.)

In *Frances T.*, a condominium owner who resided in her unit brought an action against the community association, a nonprofit corporation, and the individual members of its board of directors after she was raped and robbed in her dwelling. She alleged negligence, breach of contract and breach of fiduciary duty, based on the association's failure to install sufficient exterior lighting and its requiring her to remove additional lighting that she had installed herself. The trial court sustained the defendants' general demurrers to all three causes of action. (*Frances T.*, *supra*, 42 Cal.3d at p. 495, 229 Cal.Rptr. 456, 723 P.2d 573.) We reversed. A community association, we concluded, may be held to a landlord's standard of care as to residents' safety in the common areas, and the plaintiff had alleged particularized facts stating a cause of action against both the association and the individual members of the board. The plaintiff failed, however, to state a cause of action for breach of contract, as neither the development's governing CC & R's nor the association's bylaws obligated the defendants to install additional lighting. The plaintiff failed likewise to state a cause of action for breach of fiduciary duties, as the defendants had fulfilled their duty to the plaintiff as a shareholder, and the plaintiff had alleged no facts to show that the association's board members had a fiduciary duty to serve as the condominium project's landlord. . . .

More recently, in *Nahrstedt v. Lakeside Village Condominium Assn.* (1994) 8 Cal.4th 361, 375, 33 Cal.Rptr.2d 63, 878 P.2d 1275 (*Nahrstedt*), we confronted the question, "When restrictions limiting the use of property within a common interest development satisfy the requirements of covenants running with the land or of equitable servitudes, what standard or test governs their enforceability?"

In *Nahrstedt*, an owner of a condominium unit who had three cats sued the community association, its officers and two of its employees for declaratory relief, seeking to prevent the defendants from enforcing against her a prohibition on keeping pets that was contained in the community association's recorded CC & R's. In resolving the dispute, we distilled from numerous authorities the principle that "[a]n equitable servitude will be enforced unless it violates public policy; it bears no rational relationship to the protection, preservation, operation or purpose of the affected land; or it otherwise imposes burdens on the affected land that are so disproportionate to the restriction's beneficial effects that the restriction should not be enforced." Applying this principle, and noting that a common interest development's recorded use restrictions are "enforceable equitable servitudes, unless unreasonable" (Civ.Code, § 1354, subd. (a)), we held that "such restrictions should be enforced unless they are wholly arbitrary, violate a fundamental public policy, or impose a burden on the use of affected land that far outweighs any benefit."

In deciding *Nahrstedt*, we noted that ownership of a unit in a common interest development ordinarily "entails mandatory membership in an owners association, which, through an elected board of directors, is empowered to enforce any use restrictions contained in the project's declaration or master deed and to enact new rules governing the use and occupancy of property within the project." "Because of its considerable power in managing and regulating a common interest development," we observed, "the governing board of an owners association must guard against the potential for the abuse of that power." We also noted that a community association's governing board's power to regulate "pertains to a 'wide spectrum of activities,' such as the volume of playing music, hours of social gatherings, use of patio furniture and barbecues, and rental of units."

We declared in *Nahrstedt* that, "when an association determines that a unit owner has violated a use restriction, the association must do so in good faith, not in an arbitrary or capricious manner, and its enforcement procedures must be fair and applied uniformly." Nevertheless, we stated, "Generally, courts will uphold decisions made by the governing board of an owners association so long as they represent good faith efforts to further the purposes of the common interest development, are consistent with the development's governing documents, and comply with public policy." . . .

[H]aving reviewed the record in this case, and in light of the foregoing authorities, we conclude that the Board's decision here to use secondary, rather than primary, treatment in addressing the Development's termite problem, a matter entrusted to its discretion under the Declaration and Civil Code section 1364, falls within [this pronouncement from] *Nahrstedt.* . . . Moreover, our deferring to the Board's discretion in this matter, which, as previously noted, is broadly conferred in the Development's CC & R's, is consistent with *Nahrstedt*'s holding that CC & R's "should be enforced unless they are wholly arbitrary, violate a fundamental public policy, or impose a burden on the use of affected land that far outweighs any benefit."

Here, the Board exercised discretion clearly within the scope of its authority under the Declaration and governing statutes to select among means for discharging its obligation to maintain and repair the Development's common areas occasioned by the presence of wood-destroying pests or organisms. The trial court found that the Board acted upon reasonable investigation, in good faith, and in a manner the Board believed was in the best interests of the Association and its members.

Contrary to the Court of Appeal, we conclude the trial court was correct to defer to the Board's decision. We hold that, where a duly constituted community association board, upon reasonable investigation, in good faith and with regard for the best interests of the community association and its members, exercises discretion within the scope of its authority under relevant statutes, covenants and restrictions to select among means for discharging an obligation to maintain and repair a development's common areas, courts should defer to the board's authority and presumed expertise. . . .

Plaintiff warns that judicial deference to the Board's decision in this case would not be appropriate, lest every community association be free to do as little or as much as it pleases in satisfying its obligations to its members. We do not agree. Our respecting the Association's discretion, under this Declaration, to choose among modes of termite treatment does not foreclose the possibility that more restrictive provisions relating to the same or other topics might be "otherwise provided in the declaration[s]" (Civ.Code, § 1364, subd. (b)(1)) of other common interest developments. As discussed, we have before us today a declaration constituting a general scheme for maintenance, protection and enhancement of value of the Development, one that entrusts to the Association the management, maintenance and preservation of the Development's common areas and confers on the Board the power and authority to maintain and repair those areas. Thus, the Association's obligation at issue in this case is broadly cast, plainly conferring on the Association the discretion to select, as it did, among available means for addressing the Development's termite infestation. Under the circumstances, our respecting that discretion obviously does not foreclose community association governance provisions that, within the bounds of the law, might more narrowly circumscribe association or board discretion. . . .

Finally, plaintiff contends a rule of judicial deference will insulate community association boards' decisions from judicial review. We disagree. As illustrated by *Fountain Valley Chateau Blanc Homeowner's Assn. v. Department of Veterans Affairs* (1998) 67 Cal.App.4th 743, 754–755, 79 Cal.Rptr.2d 248 (*Fountain Valley*), judicial oversight affords significant protection against overreaching by such boards.

In *Fountain Valley*, a homeowners association, threatening litigation against an elderly homeowner with Hodgkin's disease, gained access to the interior of his residence and demanded he remove a number of personal items, including books and papers not constituting "standard reading material," claiming the items posed a fire hazard. The homeowner settled the original complaint, but cross-complained for violation of privacy, trespass, negligence and breach of contract. The jury returned a verdict in his favor, finding specifically that the association had acted unreasonably. . . . [T]he Court of Appeal held that, in light of the operative facts found by the jury, it was "virtually impossible" to say the association had acted reasonably. The city fire department had found no fire hazard, and the association "did not have a good faith, albeit mistaken, belief in that danger." In the absence of such good faith belief, the court determined the jury's verdict must stand, thus impliedly finding no basis for judicial deference to the association's decision. . . .

Common sense suggests that judicial deference in such cases as this is appropriate, in view of the relative competence, over that of courts, possessed by owners and directors of common interest developments to make the detailed and peculiar economic decisions necessary in the maintenance of those developments. A deferential standard will, by minimizing the likelihood of unproductive litigation over their governing associations' discretionary economic decisions, foster stability, certainty and predictability in the governance and management of common interest developments. Beneficial corollaries include enhancement of the incentives for essential voluntary owner participation in common interest development governance and conservation of scarce judicial resources.

For the foregoing reasons, the judgment of the Court of Appeal is reversed.

NOTES

1. *The enforceability of assessments for community facilities/services and the quality of services provided.* Suppose that an owners association generally provides snow removal services, but fails to do so on two occasions during the year—and that as a result, several residents in a low-lying area of the development are unable to get to work. May those residents withhold some or all of their assessment payments? The majority view suggests that the answer is no; each landowner's assessment obligation is independent (*i.e.*, without regard to the association's performance of those services or her satisfaction with that performance). See, e.g., Kay v. Via Verde Homeowners Ass'n, Inc., 677 So.2d 337 (Fla. Ct. App. 1996) and Panther Lake Homeowner's Ass'n v. Juergensen, 76 Wash.App. 586, 887 P.2d 465 (1995) (denying offsets); but see Kirktown Homes Ass'n v. Arey, 812 S.W.2d 198 (Mo. Ct. App. 1991) (allowing offset). Some states protect association finances in this setting by statute. *See, e.g.*, Ga. Code Ann. § 44–3–80(d). Can you explain why the law should view the landowner's assessment obligation as independent? To what extent should the language of the declaration control this determination?

2. *Judicial review of association decisions—"reasonableness" vs. "business judgment."* When an owner raises a challenge to a board decision or action, courts have applied one of two standards of review: the "business judgment" rule, applied by analogy in *Lamden*, or the "reasonableness" standard typified by *Hidden Harbor Estates, Inc. v. Basso*, 393 So.2d 637 (Fla. App. 1981). In *Basso*, a couple sought permission to drill a well on their lot. The board of the Hidden Harbor Estates owners association denied their request because of concerns that the proposed well might (a) increase the

salinity of two existing wells that supplied water to unit owners, (b) result in staining of sidewalks and other common areas, and (c) cause a proliferation of wells by other unit owners. When the Bassos drilled a well anyway, the board sued to enjoin its operation. The trial court denied an injunction, and the appellate court affirmed. The court admitted that the board's stated reasons for denial were "legitimate objectives which would have promoted the aesthetic appeal of the condominium development." 393 So.2d at 640. The court nevertheless concluded that the board had failed to demonstrate that its denial was reasonable:

> The requirement of "reasonableness" in these instances is designed to somewhat fetter the discretion of the board of directors. By imposing such a standard, the board is required to enact rules and make decisions that are reasonably related to the promotion of the health, happiness and peace of mind of the unit owners.... [W]here the decision to allow a particular use is within the discretion of the board, the board must allow the use unless the use is demonstrably antagonistic to the legitimate objectives of the condominium association, *i.e.*, the health, happiness and peace of mind of the individual unit owners. [*Id.*]

Do you think that Ms. Lamden would have prevailed under this standard? Why was the court in *Lamden* willing to provide such strong deference to the Association's judgment as to how to address the termite infestation problem? Are you persuaded by the court's explanation? If you were representing Ms. Lamden, what facts (if true) might strengthen her case that the board's decision breached its duty to her as a lot owner?

3. TORT LIABILITY OF ASSOCIATIONS AND OWNERS

MARTINEZ v. WOODMAR IV CONDOMINIUMS HOMEOWNERS ASS'N, INC.

Supreme Court of Arizona En Banc, 1997
189 Ariz. 206, 941 P.2d 218

FELDMAN, JUSTICE. . . . Plaintiff was attending a graduation party at Defendant's 152-unit condominium complex. Plaintiff was a guest of the tenant of a unit owner. After fifteen minutes at the party, he and two other party-goers returned to the complex's parking lot to check on their cars. One of his friends found a group of local ruffians sitting in and on his car. A discussion ensued. As Plaintiff was running away from the altercation, he was shot in the back. The group scattered and no one has yet been apprehended and charged with the shooting.

From the descriptions given by Plaintiff and his friends, the live-in security officer for the complex recognized the group as a gang of young people from a neighboring complex that often would gather in the parking lot to sell drugs and participate in other unsavory activities. Usually, the security guard would disperse them when he saw them. However, because of budget constraints, Defendant employed only one guard, who patrolled the complex for eight hours a day—usually between eight or nine in the evening and five or six in the morning. The shooting occurred about an hour before the guard came on duty.

Plaintiff brought a damage action against Defendant, claiming it retained control of the parking lot and arguing that had Defendant hired a second guard for an earlier shift, the group would have been sent on its way before the altercation could have occurred. The trial court found no duty and granted Defendant's motion for summary judgment, which the court of appeals affirmed. . . .

Apparently, the court of appeals saw this case as one of a landlord's duty to protect Plaintiff from the tortious acts of a third party—the gang. The court found Plaintiff was only a social guest and therefore to be treated as a licensee. The court concluded Plaintiff could not recover under the rubric of the Restatement (Second) of Torts § 315 (1965), which says there is

> no duty so to control the conduct of a third person as to prevent him from causing physical harm to another unless (a) a special relation exists between the [defendant] and the third person which imposes a duty upon the [defendant] to control the third person's conduct, or (b) a special relation exists between the [defendant] and the [plaintiff] which gives to the [plaintiff] a right of protection.

Martinez, 187 Ariz. at 409, 930 P.2d at 486, citing Restatement § 315. The court then held, "Woodmar did not assume a duty to protect plaintiff, create or encourage his contact with the group in the parking lot, or act in any other way so as to justify imposing on Woodmar a duty to protect plaintiff . . . " *Id.* at 410, 930 P.2d at 487.

We believe the court of appeals improperly characterized the case. Because no special relation of the type contemplated by Restatement § 315 existed between Plaintiff and Defendant or Defendant and the shooter, Defendant had no § 315 responsibility to control the shooter. This does not, however, free Defendant from liability for breach of any duty it might have had as the owner or possessor of land. That duty would exist because of Defendant's status with respect to the land and consequent power to prevent harm by exercising control over its property. We agree with the court of appeals' conclusion that Defendant had no § 315 responsibility or duty to control the shooter but do not believe Defendant was without a duty to use care to control its property. . . .

We focus on Defendant's status with relation to the land rather than the presence or absence of a special relationship between it and the tortfeasor or Plaintiff. We are concerned only with the question of whether Defendant, occupying a status similar to that of a landlord, had a duty of reasonable care to maintain the safety of its common areas because it had control over the land. In *Petolicchio v. Santa Cruz County Fair & Rodeo Ass'n*, we cited *Frances T. v. Village Green Owners Ass'n*, 42 Cal.3d 490, 229 Cal.Rptr. 456, 723 P.2d 573 (1986), for the proposition that in response to changed social conditions, courts may recognize a landowner's duty of reasonable care to protect against another's foreseeable criminal acts. 177 Ariz. 256, 261, 866 P.2d 1342, 1347 (1994). In *Frances T.*, the California court found a condominium association could be held liable as a landlord when it had actual knowledge of inadequate lighting and the hazardous condition it created, yet failed to remedy the condition that led to the plaintiff's rape and robbery. In the present case, the court of appeals noted *Frances T.* and stated: "Assuming without deciding that Woodmar acted like a landlord in controlling the complex common areas, it might have had some duty to protect an owner of a condominium unit or the owner's tenant." *Martinez*, 187 Ariz. at 409, 930 P.2d at 486. However, the court distinguished between a condominium owner and a social guest/licensee, holding any duty owed to a unit owner would not extend to Plaintiff. *Id.*

We believe this distinction is contrary to existing law when, as in this case, the danger causing the injury is located on property in the exclusive control of the landlord or condominium association. In Arizona, if there is no statute or case law on a particular subject, we have traditionally followed the Restatement of Laws. Restatement § 360 states:

> A possessor of land who leases a part thereof and retains in his own control any other part which the lessee is entitled to use as appurtenant to the part leased to him, is subject to liability to his lessee *and others lawfully upon the land with the consent of the lessee or a sublessee* for physical harm caused by a dangerous condition upon that part of the land retained in the lessor's control, if the lessor by the exercise of reasonable care could have discovered the condition and the unreasonable risk involved therein and could have made the condition safe.

(Emphasis added.) Restatement (Second) of Property § 17.3 contains an almost identical provision. With respect to common areas, § 360 was followed in *Dolezal v. Carbrey*, 161 Ariz. 365, 778 P.2d 1261 (App.1989) (landlord's duty of care extended to social guests of tenant). As was noted by Prosser & Keeton, landlord liability extends to areas where "the landlord has retained control over that aspect of the premises responsible for the injury." W. Page Keeton, et al., Prosser and Keeton on the Law of Torts § 63, at 442 (5th ed.1984).

We note Defendant in this case is not a lessor but a new type of possessor—a condominium association that has retained in its control common areas, such as the parking lot, that unit owners are entitled to use as appurtenant to their unit. We couple this with the introduction to Part Six of the Restatement (Second) of Property, which addresses the tort liability of landlords, stating: "In condominiums, the tort problem is the same as in any other case of the tort liability of the possessor of land to others."

The element of control, we believe, is essential to a finding of duty for the condominium association. Like a landlord who maintains control and liability for conditions in common areas, the condominium association controls all aspects of maintenance and security for the common areas and, most likely, forbids individual unit owners from taking on these chores. Thus, if the association owes no duty of care over the common areas of the property, no one does because no one else possesses the ability to cure defects in the common area. We do not believe the law recognizes such a lack of responsibility for safety. We therefore hold that with respect to common areas under its exclusive control, a condominium association has the same duties as a landlord. *Frances T.*, 229 Cal.Rptr. at 461, 723 P.2d at 578.

Thus, if we apply the rules of Restatement § 360 and Restatement (Second) of Property § 17.3, a condominium association has a duty not only to the unit owners and their tenants but also to those who are on the land with their consent and who will inevitably be expected to use common areas such as the parking lot. *See* Restatement § 360 cmt. d (the rule stated in § 360 applies to all common areas the lessee is expected to use, such as the yard). On this point, we believe the case law is quite clear and supports the Restatement view. Traditionally—Prosser & Keeton cites cases as early as 1880, *e.g., Looney v. McLean*, 129 Mass. 33 (1880)—common areas were considered under the control of the landlord, although open and necessary for use by tenants. This element of control creates an "affirmative obligation to exercise reasonable care to inspect and repair such parts of the premises for the protection of the lessee; and the duty extends also to members of the tenant's family, his employees, his invitees, his guests, and others on the land in the right of the tenant. . . ." Prosser & Keeton § 63, at 440. This, of course, is the duty enumerated in Restatement § 360. We hold that Defendant's duty with respect to the common areas, like that of a landlord, extends not only to the unit owners but also to those on the land with consent of the owners and their tenants.[6]. . .

---

6   No other rule, we believe, makes sense. Suppose, for example, that a unit owner and his visiting brother were in the complex elevator and were injured when it malfunctioned because of the association's negligence in repair or maintenance. It would be a strange rule that would allow the injured unit owner to recover for his injuries while the brother, a guest equally expected and invited to use the elevator, could not. It would be possible, of course, to argue that the guest would recover if the defect were hidden but not if it were obvious. Could the association then escape responsibility simply by posting a sign stating "caution, elevator may malfunction"?

The duty to maintain the safety of common areas applies not only to physical conditions on the land but, we believe, also to dangerous activities on the land. See Restatement § 344; Restatement (Second) of Property § 17.3. Thus, the condominium association, like a landlord and certain other land possessors, has a duty to maintain the common areas it controls in a safe condition and protect both owners and their guests from dangerous conditions or activities.

The court of appeals noted the Restatement rule but stated that "given plaintiff's legal status [as a licensee], Woodmar only owed a duty to 'refrain from knowingly letting him run upon a hidden peril or wantonly or wilfully causing him harm.'" *Martinez*, 187 Ariz. at 410, 930 P.2d at 487. The court found the gang hanging out in the parking lot was not a hidden danger, stating the "transient harm created by third persons who commit crimes" is distinguishable from a dangerous physical condition that a landowner must make safe. *Id.* at 410, 930 P.2d at 487. Again, we disagree. *See Robertson v. Sixpence Inns*, 163 Ariz. 539, 544, 789 P.2d 1040, 1045 (1990) (land possessor's duty encompasses reasonable care to protect from or warn of danger of criminal attacks); Restatement § 344. The duty to those using the common areas with consent of the association, its unit owners, and their tenants, includes the use of reasonable care to prevent harm from criminal intrusion. *See* Restatement (Second) of Property § 17.3 cmt. 1. . . .

It is well recognized at present that failure to provide adequate lighting, door locks, or other security measures may subject certain landowners to liability for harm caused by a criminal attack on persons to whom the owner owes a duty of care. . . . Restatement (Second) of Property § 17.3, illus. 18.

Logically, it cannot be otherwise. If one owes a duty of reasonable care to those on one's land with permission, then the circumstances will dictate what is reasonable to protect others from foreseeable and preventable danger. The category of danger neither creates nor eradicates duty; it only indicates what conduct may be reasonable to fulfill the duty. As Prosser & Keeton acknowledges, since 1970 courts have recognized the landlord's duty of care may include measures to protect others from criminal attacks, provided the attacks are reasonably foreseeable and preventable. Prosser & Keeton § 63, at 442–43 (citing *Kline v. 1500 Massachusetts Ave. Apartment Corp.*, 439 F.2d 477 (D.C.Cir.1970) (owner of urban multiple-unit apartment dwelling had duty of reasonable care to protect tenants from foreseeable criminal assaults)); *see also Robertson*, 163 Ariz. at 544, 789 P.2d at 1045 (duty to independent contractor

---

We refuse to embrace such arcane and illogical distinctions. With respect to the common areas, the possessor—landlord or association—invites all tenants, owners and their guests, as users. See Restatement § 343.

foreseeably attacked by criminal); *Rosenbaum v. Security Pacific Corp.*, 43 Cal.App.4th 1084, 50 Cal.Rptr.2d 917 (1996); *Frances T.*, 229 Cal.Rptr. at 475–76, 723 P.2d at 593; *Doud v. Las Vegas Hilton Corp.*, 109 Nev. 1096, 864 P.2d 796, 798 (1993); *Berry Property Management, Inc. v. Bliskey*, 850 S.W.2d 644, 653 (Tex.App.1993).

Our case is the type in which courts are tempted to blur the concepts of duty and negligence. As we have previously indicated, we disapprove of attempts to equate the concepts of duty with specific details of conduct. *Markowitz v. Arizona Parks Bd.*, 146 Ariz. 352, 355, 706 P.2d 364, 367 (1985). Duty is an issue "of the relation between individuals which imposes upon one a legal obligation for the benefit of the other. . . ." *Id.* (quoting *Coburn v. City of Tucson*, 143 Ariz. 50, 52, 691 P.2d 1078, 1080 (1984)); Prosser & Keeton § 53, at 356. As the possessor of the common areas, Defendant had a relationship, similar to that of a landlord, with unit owners, their tenants, and persons on the land with consent and permission to use the common areas. That relationship required Defendant to use reasonable care to avoid causing the injury to those it permitted to use the property under its control. *Markowitz*, 146 Ariz. at 355, 706 P.2d at 367 (citing Restatement § 343 and quoting Prosser & Keeton § 61, at 419). The relationship between Defendant, its unit owners, and persons given permission to enter the common areas thus imposed an obligation on Defendant to take reasonable precautions for the latter's safety. The type of foreseeable danger did not dictate the existence of duty but only the nature and extent of the conduct necessary to fulfill the duty. The true issue on summary judgment in this case, therefore, was not the question of duty but rather the question of negligence. We turn, then, to the specific facts to determine whether the trial judge correctly granted summary judgment. . . .

In the response to the motion for summary judgment, there is evidence presented that Defendant knew of the incursion by gangs in the parking lot and other common areas of its property, knew the gangs engaged in drug dealing and other criminal activity, was warned by its own security guard of the need for 24-hour patrols, had hired a second guard for a short period but terminated him because of expense considerations, and knew a neighboring condominium complex had hired off-duty Phoenix police officers to patrol. We therefore hold there is sufficient evidence from which a jury could find the danger foreseeable and Defendant negligent.

On this record, also, we cannot say as a matter of law Defendant could not have taken reasonable measures that probably would have prevented the attack. It may be that increased security patrols, better fencing, calls for police control, or other measures might have prevented injury. This question of causation in fact is, of course, one especially for the jury. . . .

The record in this case provides sufficient evidence from which a jury could find negligence and causation. Accordingly, summary judgment was improper. Therefore, we vacate the court of appeals' opinion, reverse the trial court's grant of summary judgment, and remand to the trial court for proceedings consistent with this opinion. . . .

NOTES

1.   *Torts on the common areas.* What is the nature of the liability for torts occurring on common elements of a common interest community? Potential victims include the unit owners, their family members, invitees, and strangers. Negligent acts which cause injury may be committed by the same categories of persons, including (because they may be of particular importance) the officers, directors, or employees of the owners association. A matrix of possible litigation parties might look like this (with the plaintiff being the first-mentioned in each case):

Unit owner vs. association

Unit owner vs. other unit owners

Third parties vs. association

Third parties vs. unit owner or owners

We may be tempted to place great emphasis on whether the association is or is not incorporated, recalling that traditionally the shareholders of a corporation are not personally liable for its torts. In the condominium context, however, this conclusion is quite misleading; title to the common areas is with the individual members, who arguably have a legal duty to maintain "their" property in a reasonably safe condition—a duty which they cannot escape merely by employing an association (whether incorporated or not) to manage the property. In a cooperative, the insulation from liability may well have greater meaning, especially because the cooperative corporation holds legal title to real estate in which it may have substantial equity, a factor which diminishes the probability that a court will "pierce the corporate veil."

2.   *Association liability for the criminal acts of third parties.* One critique of *Martinez* takes the position that "given the nature and form of a condominium, and in light of the fact that a significant number of jurisdictions have refused to expand the liability of a landlord in the context of protecting tenants and guests, it seems unreasonable and illogical to expand a condominium association's liability in such a broad manner." Irene S. Mazun, Comment, Condo Associations—New Cop on the Beat: *Martinez v. Woodmar IV Condominium Homeowners Association*, 73 St. John's L. Rev. 325, 344 (1999). Mazun argued that the court instead should have imposed a duty on a condominium association "when there is a physical defect in the common areas that causes criminal activity, the association's act or omissions enhances criminal activity, or the association voluntarily assumes a duty to protect." Id. Would the result have been the same in any event?

3.   *Liability of directors of association board.* If the association has tort liability with respect the common areas, what about its directors? In *Francis T.*, the plaintiff owned a unit in a condominium project in an area that had been subject to increased criminal activity. Concerned for her own safety, the plaintiff complained about inadequate exterior lighting on the units, and installed an exterior security light on her own unit. The board required her to remove the light on the ground that it violated the covenants governing the project. The night after the plaintiff removed the lighting, an intruder entered into the plaintiff's unit, where the plaintiff was raped and robbed. The plaintiff sued the individual directors of the association board, arguing that they breached a duty of care they owed to her by ordering her to remove the external lighting she had installed for her protection and by failing to provide adequate lighting within a reasonable period of time. The Supreme Court of California held:

> It is well settled that corporate directors cannot be held *vicariously* liable for the corporation's torts in which they do not participate. Their liability, if any, stems from their own tortious conduct, not from their status as directors or officers of the enterprise. . . .

> Directors are liable to third persons injured by their own tortious conduct regardless of whether they acted on behalf of the corporation and regardless of whether the corporation is also liable. This liability does not depend on the same grounds as "piercing the corporate veil," on account of inadequate capitalization for instance, but rather on the officer or director's personal participation or specific authorization of the tortious act. . . .

> To maintain a tort claim against a director in his or her personal capacity, a plaintiff must first show that the director specifically authorized, directed or participated in the allegedly tortious conduct; or that although they specifically knew or reasonably should have known that some hazardous condition or activity under their control could injure plaintiff, they negligently failed to take or order appropriate action to avoid the harm. The plaintiff must also allege and prove that an ordinarily prudent person, knowing what the director knew at that time, would not have acted similarly under the circumstances. . . .

> Under the facts as alleged by plaintiff, the directors named as defendants had specific knowledge of a hazardous condition threatening physical injury to the residents, yet they failed to take any action to avoid the harm; moreover, the action they did take may have exacerbated the risk by causing plaintiff's unit to be without any lighting on the night she was attacked. Plaintiff has thus pled facts to support two theories of negligence, both of which state a cause of action under the standard stated above. . . .

In this case plaintiff's amended complaint alleges that each of the directors participated in the tortious activity. Under our analysis, this allegation is sufficient to withstand a demurrer. However, since only "a director who actually votes for the commission of a tort is personally liable, even though the wrongful act is performed in the name of the corporation," plaintiff will have to prove that each director acted negligently as an individual. Of course, the individual directors may then present evidence showing they opposed or did not participate in the alleged tortious conduct.

Frances T. v. Village Green Owners Ass'n, 42 Cal.3d 490, 229 Cal.Rptr. 456, 723 P.2d 573 (1986) (citations omitted).

Many (if not most) condominium association officers and directors serve without compensation, unlike many of their corporate counterparts. In light of the language of *Frances T.,* would you be willing to serve on an association board or as an officer? California's statute insulates volunteer officers or directors of an association from acts or omissions liability in excess of insurance coverage for acts or omissions performed in good faith and within the scope of the officer's or director's duties if the act or omission was not "willful, wanton, or grossly negligent" and the association maintains liability coverage in the amount required by the statute ($500,000 in communities with 100 or fewer units and $1 million in communities with more than 100 units). Cal. Civ. Code § 5800. Would this statute allay your concerns about serving as an association officer or director? Does it go too far to protect volunteer officers or directors?

4. *Should some condominium associations have sovereign immunity?* Condominium projects are often immense in size. In *Martinez,* the project consisted of 142 units. The Village Green Condominium project in *Frances T.* consisted of 92 buildings, each containing several units. Given the project's size, would it be appropriate to characterize the relationship between the association and the unit owner as one of municipal government to citizen or property owner rather than as one between landlord and tenant? Similarly, is a director or officer of the association more like a city council member or municipal officer than a director or officer of a corporation? Earlier in this section, we noted that some would treat the association as the government for 14th Amendment "state action" purposes. Should the governmental analogy also be used in the condominium tort liability context? If so, should the traditional immunities afforded municipal government and its officials apply as well to the association, its officers and directors? For a general consideration of governmental and official immunities, see Sandra M. Stevenson, Understanding Local Government § 9.2 (2003); Prosser and Keeton on Torts §§ 131–132 (5th ed.1984).

5. *Necessity of insurance coverage.* Obviously, the question of insurance protection becomes extremely important. The problems of adequately insuring a common interest community are extraordinarily complex. At a minimum, the following types of insurance seem to be

essential: (a) insurance against loss through fire and other casualties to both the common areas and the individual units; (b) liability insurance for wrongful acts imputed to both the association, its officers and directors and the occupants of the units; (c) insurance against casualty loss to personal property located in the units and in the common areas; (d) fidelity insurance to cover losses through dishonesty or defalcation by the association's officers, directors, and employees; (e) liability insurance for the association's officers and directors; (f) workman's compensation coverage for employees of the association; and (g) title insurance for the unit purchasers. See generally James M. Pedowitz, Condominium Unit Title Insurance, 73 St. John's L. Rev. 183 (1999); 1 Patrick J. Rohan & Melvin A. Reskin, Condominium Law & Practice Ch. 11; John T. Even, The Administration of Insurance for Condominiums, 1970 U. Ill. L.F. 204.

PEKELNAYA V. ALLYN

Supreme Court, New York, Appellate Division, First Department, 2005
802 N.Y.S.2d 669

TOM, J.P. The novel issue raised on this appeal is whether the proportionate interest in the common elements of a condominium held by the owners of the individual units subjects them to liability for injuries sustained by a third party as the result of a defective condition in a common element. . . .

Plaintiffs Aba and Michael Taratuta are father and son. Defendants are the individual owners of the 11 units comprising the Park 106 Condominium, located at 69 West 106th Street in Manhattan (collectively, the unit owners). While walking on the sidewalk, Aba and Michael Taratuta were struck and seriously injured by a section of chain-link fence, measuring approximately 4 feet by 5 feet, that fell from the roof of the condominium. The dislodged section was part of a security fence erected along the parapet wall of the roof to prevent access from adjoining buildings. It was installed prior to the time the condominium acquired the building and, thus, before the unit owners acquired their interest in the common elements upon taking possession of their respective apartments.

Michael Taratuta's injuries included traumatic brain injury, open comminuted skull fractures and multiple intracerebral hemorrhages and contusions, which rendered him severely and permanently disabled. His father sustained blunt head trauma and fractures of the vertebral column, among other injuries. Plaintiffs commenced a previous action against the condominium's board of managers on the theory that the board is responsible for the maintenance of common elements, including the rooftop security fence. Allegedly because damages will exceed the $2 million in insurance carried by the board, plaintiffs commenced this action against the unit owners. . . .

The unit owners hold title to their respective condominium apartments in fee simple absolute (Real Property Law § 339–e). The condominium declaration accords each unit an ownership interest of approximately 9% in the common elements, which comprises the unit owner's "common interest" (Real Property Law § 339–e [ii]). The roof of the premises is included in the common elements. However, it is designated a "limited" common element because its use is restricted to the owners of the fifth-floor apartments, defendants Hinojosa and Ragues, each of whom is allotted a 50% ownership interest in the limited common element. The provisions of the declaration notwithstanding, plaintiffs assert that "the 'access' to the roof is not exclusive to the owners of Units 5A and 5B since such units do not have 'direct and exclusive access from the interior of [their] respective units.' " Rather, all unit owners have the same access to the roof, which can only be reached by way of a common interior stairway leading to a common doorway at roof level. Thus, for purposes of this appeal, the unit owners are all in the same legal position.

The unit owners appeal from the denial of their motions for accelerated judgment dismissing the complaint and all cross claims against them (CPLR 3211; 3212). . . .

Supreme Court denied the motions, reasoning that Multiple Dwelling Law § 78 places the responsibility to maintain the premises in safe condition upon the "owner." Because the unit owners have not relinquished their collective ownership of the common elements, the court concluded that they are statutorily liable to plaintiffs.

On this appeal, the unit owners argue that the Condominium Act (Real Property Law § 339–d, *et seq.*) places the duty to maintain the common elements on the condominium's board of managers. They further contend that the court improperly applied the doctrine of res ipsa loquitur to subject them to liability.

Plaintiffs concede that the parapet-wall fence forms part of the common elements of the condominium. Plaintiffs also acknowledge that the board has the power and the duty to maintain the common elements. Nevertheless, plaintiffs contend that because of the part interest held by each individual unit owner in the condominium's common elements, Multiple Dwelling Law § 78 imposes upon them, as their collective owner, a nondelegable "duty to persons on its premises to maintain them in a reasonably safe condition.". . . Plaintiffs argue that statutory liability is abated only if an owner has parted with all possession and control of the premises. . . .

The issue to be decided on this appeal—whether liability should be imposed on the owners of individual condominium units for injuries to third persons resulting from a defect in a common element—is apparently a case of first impression. Plaintiffs note that, unlike some other jurisdictions, New York State has not provided for the allocation of responsibility for injury to third persons as the result of negligence in the maintenance and repair of common elements. . . .

[Plaintiffs contend] that Multiple Dwelling Law § 78 imposes liability on the unit owners by virtue of their ownership interest in the common elements. As previously noted, § 78 makes an "owner" responsible "for the safe maintenance of the building and its facilities". . . . The term "owner" is defined in Multiple Dwelling Law § 4(44) to "include the owner or owners of the freehold of the premises or lesser estate therein, a mortgagee or vendee in possession, assignee of rents, receiver, executor, trustee, lessee, agent, or any other person, firm or corporation, directly or indirectly in control of a dwelling." Plaintiffs argue that the unit owners, by virtue of their aggregate, respective minority ownership interests, are the "owner or owners" of the common elements. Alternatively, plaintiffs maintain that because the unit owners have surrendered less than complete ownership and control of the common elements to the board of managers, they cannot escape the liability imposed on owners by Multiple Dwelling Law § 78.

As this Court has stated, "The controlling tenet of statutory construction is that an act shall be given the effect intended by the Legislature (McKinney's Cons. Laws of NY, Book 1, Statutes § 92[a])" (*Thoreson v. Penthouse Intl.*, 179 A.D.2d 29, 33, 583 N.Y.S.2d 213, *affd.* 80 N.Y.2d 490, 591 N.Y.S.2d 978, 606 N.E.2d 1369). It is inconceivable that the Legislature intended the definition of the term "owner" contained in the Multiple Dwelling Law to apply to individual condominium unit owners because the Multiple Dwelling Law (L. 1929, ch. 713) preceded the enactment of the Condominium Act (L. 1964, ch. 82) by some 35 years. In addition, the nature of the ownership interest in the common elements bestowed on the unit owner by the Condominium Act is materially dissimilar to the freehold interest necessary to subject a person to liability as an "owner" under Multiple Dwelling Law § 78.

To qualify as an "owner" based on a property interest in the premises, a person must be "the owner . . . of the freehold of the premises or lesser estate therein" (Multiple Dwelling Law § 4). The unit owners' interests in their respective condominium units clearly subject them to liability as "owners" under Multiple Dwelling Law § 78 because ownership in fee simple absolute (Real Property Law § 339–e) is an interest in the freehold (*see* Garner, A Dictionary of Modern Legal Usage, at 252). By contrast, a unit owner's interest in the common elements—the "common interest"—is defined as the "proportionate undivided leasehold interest in the common elements appertaining to each unit, as expressed in the declaration" (Real Property Law § 339–e[ii]). This minority proportionate *leasehold* interest is not an interest in the freehold necessary to subject the condominium unit owner to liability as an owner of the common elements under the Multiple Dwelling Law (*cf. People v. Reyes,* 75 N.Y.2d 590, 594, 555 N.Y.S.2d 30, 554 N.E.2d 67 [retention of interest in freehold and control over premises rendered defendant liable for condition of premises despite net lease]).[4]

Plaintiffs correctly note that the condominium form of ownership is purely a creature of statute. As a legislative enactment in derogation of the common law, the Condominium Act is subject to strict construction. . . . Plaintiffs do not point to any provision of the Condominium Act that imposes liability on a unit owner for injury caused by the defective condition of a common element; nor do they suggest that the common law recognizes liability based upon such a premise. Indeed, they concede that the Condominium Act does not address the apportionment of tort liability involving a common element.

The condominium being a creature of statute, the Legislature is the appropriate body to weigh the interest of an injured party in recovering damages against the interest of the individual unit owners in avoiding liability for the consequences of acts or omissions beyond their control. The failure of the Legislature to provide for liability in the absence of control by condominium unit owners over the maintenance and repair of the common elements precludes the courts from imposing responsibility by implication. Statutes which create such vicarious liability are narrowly construed. . . . "The Legislature is presumed to be aware of the law in existence at the time of an enactment and to have abrogated the common law only to the extent that the clear import of the language of the statute requires" (*B & F Bldg. Corp. v. Liebig,* 76 N.Y.2d 689, 693, 563 N.Y.S.2d 40, 564 N.E.2d 650). The condominium form of ownership being purely a creation of statute, in the absence of any provision in the Condominium Act holding the unit owners vicariously liable for the acts and omissions of the board of managers, it cannot be said that the Legislature intended to provide a means of recovery to an injured third person predicated solely upon the interest of the unit owners in the common elements.

Plaintiffs advance the argument that the unit owners should be held liable for the board's negligence in the maintenance of the common elements based upon a principal-agent relationship. Multiple Dwelling Law § 4(44) defines "owner" to include "any . . . person . . . directly or indirectly in control of a dwelling." Thus, plaintiffs suggest, the unit

---

4 Multiple Dwelling Law § 4(44) includes a "lessee" within the definition of "owner." However, it is clear from the context that the provision contemplates a lessee of the entire premises who, like the other enumerated categories of "owner" ("mortgagee or vendee in possession, assignee of rents, receiver, executor, trustee, lessee, agent") functions in a capacity that affords direct or indirect control of the premises (*see Reyes,* 75 N.Y.2d at 594, 555 N.Y.S.2d 30, 554 N.E.2d 67; *Worth Distribs. v. Latham,* 59 N.Y.2d 231, 238, 464 N.Y.S.2d 435, 451 N.E.2d 193 [right to enter for inspection and repair under net lease constitutes sufficient retention of control to subject owners to liability]).

owners are responsible for maintenance and repairs to the common elements because the condominium board acts on their behalf.

While this argument is superficially plausible, it is unsupported by either common law, the Condominium Act or practical experience. Where, as here, the putative agent (the board of managers) is not a servant, vicarious liability will not be imposed on the principal (the unit owners, collectively). "Since an agent who is not a servant is not subject to any right of control by his employer over the details of his physical conduct, the responsibility ordinarily rests upon the agent alone, and the principal is not liable for the torts which [the agent] may commit" (Prosser and Keeton, Torts § 70, at 508).

Vicarious liability of a principal for an agent's negligence is predicated on "the general common law notion that one who is in a position to exercise some general control over the situation must exercise it or bear the loss" (*id.* § 69, at 500). In the extreme, where the principal's control is exclusive, liability may be imposed under the doctrine of res ipsa loquitur. . . .

Where control is lacking, however, liability is not imposed even when, in the context of a motion for summary judgment to dismiss the complaint, it is presumed that the putative principal's negligence can be established. . . .

It is clear that condominium common elements are solely under the control of the board of managers. The Condominium Act provides that the cost of materials and labor incurred in connection with the common elements is payable out of common charges (Real Property Law § 339–e), which "shall constitute trust funds for the purpose of paying the cost of such labor or materials performed or furnished at the express request or with the consent of the manager, managing agent or board of managers, and the same shall be expended first for such purpose before expending any part of the same for any other purpose" (Real Property Law § 339–*l*). Implicit in the statutory requirement that work on the common elements be performed "at the express request or with the consent of the . . . board of managers" is the recognition that the board exercises exclusive control over the common elements.

The control purportedly exercised by the unit owners, as collective principal, over the board of managers, as purported agent, is flatly contradicted by case law reflecting general experience with residential forms of common and cooperative ownership. A board of managers

> "takes on the burden of managing the property for the benefit of the proprietary lessees. As one court observed, 'Every man may consider his home his castle and himself as the king thereof; nonetheless his sovereign fiat to use his property as he pleases must yield, at least in degree, where ownership is in common or

cooperation with others. The benefits of condominium living demand no less'" (*Matter of Levandusky v. One Fifth Ave. Apt. Corp.,* 75 N.Y.2d 530, 537, 554 N.Y.S.2d 807, 553 N.E.2d 1317).

The prerogative of a board of managers to conduct business as it sees fit is well established. If a condominium or cooperative board were the mere instrumentality of its constituent unit owners, as plaintiffs suggest, the Court of Appeals would not have been moved to note that "some check on its potential powers to regulate residents' conduct, life-style and property rights is necessary to protect individual residents from abusive exercise, notwithstanding that the residents have, to an extent, consented to be regulated and even selected their representatives" (*Levandusky,* 75 N.Y.2d at 537, 554 N.Y.S.2d 807, 553 N.E.2d 1317). However, judicial restraint of the board's powers is not permitted to abrogate "the purposes for which the residential community and its governing structure were formed: protection of the interest of the entire community of residents in an environment managed by the board for the common benefit" (*id.*). Under the applicable standard of review afforded by the business judgment rule, so long as a managing board acts without discriminatory intent, actions taken "in furtherance of a legitimate purpose of the cooperative or condominium ... will generally be upheld" (*Levandusky*). . . .

The realities of cooperative and condominium governance simply do not comport with plaintiffs' attribution of control to the unit owners based on the board's designation as their agent. Since the unit owners have no control over, or direct responsibility for, the common elements and neither statutory nor common law renders an individual condominium unit owner liable for injuries sustained as the result of defects in the common elements, the unit owners are not liable for plaintiffs' damages. . . . As this Court stated in *Aarons v. 401 Hotel,* 12 A.D.3d 293, 293–294, 785 N.Y.S.2d 73, "An undivided interest in the common elements, including the land, does not equate with a proprietary interest in the portion of the building where the accident occurred sufficient to impose liability."

Plaintiffs further argue that the unit owners should be held liable as a matter of policy to afford a means of recovery to a person injured by a defect in the common elements. They note that unlike the cooperative form of ownership, in which the corporation is the owner of the premises and thus provides a source of payment for damages in excess of insurance coverage, the condominium is owned by the unit owners. Therefore, if the condominium's board of managers does not carry insurance against injury to third persons, the effect is to render the condominium judgment proof under circumstances such as these.

While the concern voiced by plaintiffs is sound, it is not material to the matter before us. Here, the condominium board has obtained substantial insurance coverage. Plaintiffs' grievance is not that the amount of liability insurance is inconsequential but that it will be insufficient to cover their damages. Be that as it may, the law only affords a means of recovery; it does not guarantee that the defendant will have sufficient resources to provide full compensation for any and all losses sustained. The situation confronting plaintiffs in this regard is no different than that faced by a plaintiff who is severely injured by a motorist carrying only the minimum liability insurance required by the Vehicle and Traffic Law.

We note that the Condominium Act, while setting forth minimum insurance requirements for property damage (Real Property Law § 339–bb), makes no provision for minimum liability coverage. Defendant ... points out that California Civil Code § 1365.9(b)(2)(A) requires a condominium to obtain minimum liability insurance in the amount of $2 million if it contains 100 or fewer units. This is precisely the amount of liability coverage obtained by the board of managers in this case. Thus, the board cannot be faulted for unreasonably disregarding the interests of third parties who might sustain injury as the result of the condition of the premises. Nor can it be said that the board failed to exercise good faith in deciding the appropriate amount of liability coverage or that its decision was not the product of honest judgment in furtherance of a legitimate purpose of the condominium. . . .

Whether a judgment awarding damages for personal injury sustained as the result of the defective condition of the common elements of a condominium should be enforceable against the individual dwelling units and whether the board of managers of a condominium should be required to carry a minimum amount of general liability insurance, and the amount of such coverage, are matters appropriately addressed by the Legislature. Balancing the resulting public benefit against the financial impact upon the individual condominium unit owners and the infringement upon the discretion of the board of managers to exercise its business judgment involves competing policy considerations that are within the particular province of the legislative branch of government. . . . We urge legislation to require a condominium to obtain a minimum amount of liability insurance coverage in such amount as may be deemed adequate to protect the public. . . .

NOTES

1. *An alternative judicial solution.* The Texas Supreme Court took another approach to the question of unit owner liability for torts on the common areas:

> We hold ... that because of the limited control afforded a unit owner by the statutory condominium regime, the creation of a regime effects a reallocation of tort liability. The liability of a condominium co-owner is limited to his *pro rata* interest in the regime as a whole, where such liability arises from those areas held in tenancy-in-common.

Dutcher v. Owens, 647 S.W.2d 948 (Tex.1983). To what extent would the Texas approach have helped the unit owners in *Pekelnaya?*

2. *Legislative approaches.* While several states have attempted to resolve legislatively the question of unit owner liability for torts arising out of the common areas, there is hardly a uniform approach, as the following commentary illustrates:

> Several states. have solved the problem without specifically addressing the issue by requiring that all suits are to be brought against the association. Thus, the question of the tort liability of a unit owner is never raised. The best example of this type of statute can be found in Alaska's Horizontal Property Regimes Act. [Alaska Stat. § 34.07.] It provides that "[a] cause of action relating to the common areas and facilities for damages arising out of tortious conduct shall be maintained only against the association of apartment owners" ... [*Id.* § 34.07.260.] These states allow a plaintiff to recover from the association by providing that a "[j]udgment for money against the association shall become a lien against any property owned by the association and against each of the condominium units." [Wis. Stat. Ann. § 703.25(3).] By allowing a unit owner to remove a lien from a unit by paying a pro-rata share of the judgment, these statutes limit the unit owner's liability to the actual interest he owns.

> Both Mississippi and New Jersey have included provisions in their respective condominium acts that stipulate that a unit owner "shall have no personal liability for any damages in connection with the use of the common elements." [Miss. Code § 89–9–29(B); N.J. Stat. Ann. § 46:8B–16(c).] The attempt of these states to eliminate a unit owner's liability, however, results only in a limitation of such liability, since a judgment against the association would result in a lien on the condominium units. A unit owner would still have to pay a pro-rata amount of the judgment to remove the lien from his unit.

> Other states have not specified who an injured plaintiff may sue but have specifically limited each unit owner's liability to a proportionate amount based on the fractional ownership in the common elements.... Although these states do not require a plaintiff to sue the association, to do otherwise would necessitate the joinder of every unit owner as a defendant in order for the plaintiff to collect the full recovery. To ensure recovery, then, a suit against the association would be a more attractive alternative.

Alison Holladay, Note, Condominium Unit Owner Tort Liability: *Owens v. Dutcher*, 35 Baylor L. Rev. 189, 200–201 (1983).* Under the UCA, "an action alleging a wrong done by the association must be brought against the association and not against any unit owner." UCA § 3–111. According to UCA § 3–117, "a judgment for money against the association . . . is a lien in favor of the judgment lienholder against all of the units in the condominium at the time at which the judgment is entered." The owner "of an affected unit may pay to the lienholder the amount of the lien attributable to his unit, and the lienholder, upon receipt of payment, promptly shall deliver a release of the lien covering that unit. The amount of payment must be proportionate to the ratio which that unit owner's common expense liability bears to the common expense liabilities of all unit owners whose units are subject to the lien." UCA § 3–117(c).

In California, an important appellate case, Ruoff v. Harbor Creek Community Ass'n, 10 Cal.App.4th 1624, 13 Cal.Rptr.2d 755 (1992), endorsed a joint and several liability approach to unit owner liability. In response, California enacted 1995 legislation that provided civil liability protection to individual unit owners if the owners association maintains insurance coverage for the association's general liability of "at least two million dollars if the common interest development consists of 100 or fewer separate interests" or "at least three million dollars if the common interest development consists of more than 100 separate interests." Cal. Civ. Code § 5805. Presumably, if the association fails to carry the requisite insurance, there is joint and several liability for unit owners. See Jerry C.M. Orten & John H. Zacharia, Allocation of Damages for Tort Liability in Common Interest Communities, 31 Real Prop. Prob & Tr. J. 647 (1997).

3.   *An alternative approach.* Professor Eric Freyfogle has suggested the following condominium tort liability scheme:

- An association should be liable only to the extent of its liability insurance, but states should require associations to have liability insurance with required minimum coverage amounts, and states should also consider requiring associations to set aside, in escrow, a sum equal to its insurance deductible.

- To the extent of insurance coverage, states should require claimants to sue the association and should prohibit a suit against a unit owner unless the owner actively participated in the tort.

- Unit owners at the time a tort is committed should be personally liable for any portion of a judgment not covered by the association's insurance policy. Later buyers of units should enjoy immunity. Liability of unit owners should be joint (allocated in the same manner as common expenses), not several.

---

* Reprinted with permission of the Baylor Law Review.

- Unit owners should have the same right to sue the association as do third parties.

- The association should have full power to defend the litigation on behalf of all unit owners, and plaintiffs should have not have to join unit owners individually except as needed to satisfy due process requirements. A unit owner should not be able to challenge a judgment against the association, but should be allowed to settle any claim for the unit owner's pro-rata share of any excess liability.

- The standard of care for management of common areas should be the standard applicable to owners of private residences, and it should apply to all plaintiffs (whether unit owners or outsiders).

Eric T. Freyfogle, A Comprehensive Theory of Condominium Tort Liability, 39 U.Fla.L.Rev. 877, 920–923 (1987). How would you evaluate the benefits and detriments of Freyfogle's proposal, both in terms of the unit owners themselves and the public at large?

E. CONVERSION OF RENTAL HOUSING TO CONDOMINIUMS AND COOPERATIVES

Sometimes a developer seeking a new project will convert an existing apartment building into a condominium (or, less commonly, a cooperative) rather than undertake construction of a new project. There are a number of reasons the developer may prefer conversion; these may include:

- *Initial cost.* The developer may find it cheaper to buy and renovate an existing building than to undertake new construction.

- *Location.* An existing apartment building may occupy a desirable location that is preferable to sites available for new construction.

- *Aesthetic concerns.* An existing building may have architectural or design features that cannot be reproduced in new construction, or at least not without significant expense.

- *Legal constraints.* The developer of a newly-constructed condominium would typically hold warranty liability to the purchaser; by contrast, conversion of an existing building may only require a disclosure of the property's condition and may carry no warranty. Likewise, while new construction requires strict adherence to current building codes, renovation of existing buildings may not. From a cost perspective, these lesser constraints may mean that conversion is more profitable for the developer than new construction, and converted units may in some cases be more affordable to unit purchasers than newly-constructed units.

- *Relative profitability of rental vs. sale markets.* During a long and sustained period of low mortgage interest rates, homeownership becomes more affordable and it becomes easier for consumers to shift from rental to ownership. In a market with increasing demand for homeownership and decreasing demand for tenancies, owners of apartments may conclude that they can earn a greater return by converting and selling the units than by continuing to operate them as apartments. The relative profitability of conversion can also be accentuated by state and local tax policy, particularly in jurisdictions where real property tax assessment rates are higher for rental real property than for owner-occupied property.

The first significant wave of conversions began in the 1970s, and it presented two basic problems. The first was that first-generation common interest ownership statutes did not adequately address or regulate the conversion process and the rights of existing tenants in that process. Must existing tenants get notice of the developer's intent to convert and, if so, how much? Must existing tenants have an option to purchase their existing unit and/or to renew their existing leases? What disclosures must the developer provide to purchasers regarding building condition and operating costs? The second problem was a perception that conversion displaced existing lower-income tenants and resulted in a reduction in the availability of affordable housing. One commentator addressed the perceived impact of the conversion phenomenon in the Chicago area:

Illinois and its rental housing stock have proven to be fertile ground for condominium conversions. In 2005, the most active year for conversions, the metropolitan Chicago area ranked ninth in the country for condominium conversions. That same year, 3,965 units were converted to condominiums in downtown Chicago alone, more than any other year since 1979. Chicago suburbs also experienced similar trends, with approximately 4,500 suburban units converted to condominiums in 2006. Chicago's recent conversion craze is the city's third wave of conversions within the past thirty-five years. The first occurred in the late 1970s and early 1980s, and the second swept the city in the early 1990s.

This latest conversion craze has had a detrimental effect upon the supply of affordable housing. Nearly 5,000 rental units in Chicago were sold for conversion in 2005, while the creation of new rental units hovered at just around 2,000, resulting in a net loss of approximately 3,000 rental units. This continued a larger trend in which Chicago lost at least 34,400 units of housing between 2000 and 2003. This reduction in the overall supply of available apartments placed upward pressure on rents, making affordable housing more difficult to find. Affordable rental units are already scarce, with 53% of Chicago renters spending 30% or more of their income on rent. The cost of supplying affordable rental housing has also increased in light of rising land values and increased density restrictions. Against the backdrop of a particularly tight rental market, condominium conversions present a stark example of the removal of affordable rental units from the market.*

Kathryn B. Richards, Note, The Illinois Condominium Property Act: An Analysis of Legislative Efforts to Improve Tenants' Rights in the Condominium Conversion Process, 57 DePaul L. Rev. 829, 832–834 (2008).

As these concerns struck the public consciousness, state and local governments began responding through regulatory legislation designed to limit condominium conversions or their negative impacts.

JENNIFER SILVER AND CATHY SHREVE, CONDOMINIUM CONVERSION CONTROLS

(An Information Bulletin of the Community and Economic Development Task Force of the Urban Consortium) 1979

Because of the relative newness of both the conversion phenomenon and the legislative responses developed in reaction to it there is an absence of case law dealing directly with conversion legality issues at the local level. A 1976 National Institute of Municipal Law Officers Report suggests that court decisions related to rent control legislation are the most analogous, and discussed four legal issues raised in relation to rent control, and applicable to conversion control legislation. The first is whether restrictions on the use of private property are a valid exercise of municipal police power in housing situations which threaten the public health, safety or welfare. With respect to rent control provisions, courts have consistently upheld the right to regulate rents under certain housing market conditions which constitute an emergency situation. Generally, emergencies have been found when there is a low or zero vacancy rate,[6] or exorbitant increases in rents[7] or when there is an imbalance in the housing market caused by abnormal events.[8] It should

---

*   Reprinted with the permission of the DePaul Law Review.

[6]   Albigese v. Jersey City, 127 N.J.Super. 101, 316 A.2d 483 (1974).

[7]   Birkenfeld v. City of Berkeley, 49 Cal.App.3d 464, 122 Cal.Rptr. 891 (1975).

[8]   Edgar A. Levy Leasing Co. v. Siegel, 258 U.S. 242, 42 S.Ct. 289, 66 L.Ed. 595 (1922); Chastleton Corp. v. Sinclair, 264 U.S. 543, 44 S.Ct. 405, 68 L.Ed. 841 (1924).

not be assumed, however, that regulations adopted in some areas will be valid in others, since the circumstances which define legitimate use of police power vary with local circumstances and conditions. It is likely, however, that in areas which already have rent control legislation on the books, condominium conversion restrictions are likely to be more easily accepted.

A second legal issue common to both rent control and conversion control is whether these kinds of regulations result in a taking of private property without just compensation, or an "unconstitutional taking" which violates due process of law. Generally, courts have held that these types of regulations fall within municipalities' legitimate police power, the exercise of which does not require compensation. In one case, it was held that "a prohibition simply upon the use of property for purposes that are declared, by valid legislation, to be injurious to health, morals or safety of the community cannot . . . be deemed a taking . . . of property for the public benefit."[9] Overall, case law has upheld the notion that property owners do not have a right to the most beneficial use of their property, and that restrictions which limit profitability are valid, when they are in the interest of the public welfare.

A third legal issue is whether rent control or conversion restrictions on private property violate the Equal Protection Clause of the Fourteenth Amendment because they discriminate against certain classes of owners. Again, in rent control decisions courts have given municipalities fairly broad latitude in defining restrictions, and have found that equal protection is not violated as long as some reasonable or rational basis exists for the restrictions in question. In one particular case, courts upheld the validity of rent control restrictions which affect certain classes of property owners more than others with the following language:

> Regulatory need in a particular field may appear to the legislative mind in different dimensions and proportions, as more acute in one area than in another. Consequently, the reform may proceed one step at a time, addressing itself to the aspects of the problem which seems the most pressing.[10]

A fourth legal issue is whether local conversion regulations conflict in any way with existing state condominium statutes. If locally adopted

---

9   Goldblatt v. Hempstead, 369 U.S. 590, 593, 82 S.Ct. 987, 989, 8 L.Ed.2d 130 (1962), quoting from Mugler v. Kansas, 123 U.S. 623, 8 S.Ct. 273, 31 L.Ed. 205 (1887).

10   Albigese v. Jersey City, supra. [The conclusion in the text has been reinforced by Pennell v. City of San Jose, 485 U.S. 1, 108 S.Ct. 849, 99 L.Ed.2d 1 (1988), in which the U.S. Supreme Court held that a provision in a rent control ordinance that allowed a hearing officer to consider tenant hardship in fixing a reasonable rent violated neither due process nor equal protection provisions of the United States Constitution. The Court also concluded that it was premature to consider whether the provision created a "taking" of private property without just compensation. See also Yee v. City of Escondido, 503 U.S. 519, 112 S.Ct. 1522, 118 L.Ed.2d 153 (1992) (upholding mobile home rent control physical taking claim).—Eds.]

restrictions have the effect of circumscribing or prohibiting what is expressly permitted by State Law, they may be struck down.*

Overall, there is ample precedent in case law to support the validity of municipal regulations restricting condominium conversions, provided that:

—the laws are adopted as a valid exercise of police power in a clearly defined emergency housing situation in the interest of public welfare;

—the nature of the restrictions is not so onerous or confiscatory as to constitute a taking of private property without just compensation;

—the basis for the restrictions is rational in relation to the specific objective of the regulatory legislation;

—the restrictions do not conflict with existing state statutes.

———————

Silver and Shreve proceeded to discuss the types of local legislative controls which have been imposed by various ordinances throughout the nation. They itemized these controls under three headings: consumer protection (for purchasers), tenants' rights (for existing tenants), and protection against displacement. The following is a summary of the controls identified by the report in each of these areas.

A. Consumer Protection

1. Disclosure requirements.

2. Property reports, prepared by independent engineers, on the buildings and systems.

3. Compliance with building and/or housing codes.

4. Estimates of projected operating costs and other cost factors.

5. Minimum standards with respect to laundry, storage, sound transmission, and other qualities.

6. Limitations on the converter's control of the owners association.

———————

* [In Claridge House One, Inc. v. Borough of Verona, 490 F.Supp. 706 (D. N.J. 1980), the borough had adopted an ordinance imposing a one-year moratorium on condominium conversions. The court held the ordinance void on two grounds. First, the legislature of the state had adopted a set of comprehensive protections for tenants in buildings being converted, N.J. Stat. Ann. § 2A:18–61, thereby preempting the field of conversion regulation. Second, the legislature had enacted an "antidiscrimination" statute for condominiums: "All laws, ordinances and regulations concerning planning, subdivision and zoning, shall be construed and applied with reference to the nature and use of the condominium without regard to the form of ownership." N.J. Stat. Ann. § 46:8B–29. The borough's ordinance would discriminate against condominiums in violation of this statute, the court concluded.—Eds.]

7.   Warranties and associated escrow accounts.

8.   A cooling-off period following signing of a contract of purchase.

9.   Penalties for the converter's failure to comply with the foregoing.

B.   Tenants' Rights

1.   Notification to tenants of intent to convert, and possibly a right to a hearing or even a requirement that a specified percentage of tenants consent to the conversion or agree to purchase their units.

2.   Lengthy periods of notice to vacate (from 90 days to 3 years).

3.   A right of first refusal to purchase one's present unit.

4.   A requirement that the converter honor existing fixed-term leases, although the tenants may be given an option to terminate them after notification of the conversion.

5.   Relocation assistance, either by cash payment or by finding alternate rental accommodations.

6.   Prohibition on coercion and harassment.

C.   Protection Against Displacement

1.   Conversion moratoria.

2.   Requirements that vacancy rates or surpluses exceed specified levels before conversion may proceed.

3.   Protection for low-income housing, either by requiring that the converter price a given percentage of the units for low-income buyers or by prohibiting conversions which will adversely affect the overall supply of low-income housing.

NOTES

1.   *Tenant displacement and federal inaction.* Despite widespread concern regarding the extent to which conversion activity produces tenant displacement, Congress has never enacted federal legislation addressing or regulating conversions. In fact, Section 606 of the Condominium and Cooperative Abuse Relief Act of 1980 provided that:

It is the sense of the Congress that, when multifamily rental housing projects are converted to condominium or cooperative use, tenants in those projects are entitled to adequate notice of the pending conversion and to receive the first opportunity to purchase units in the converted projects and that State and local governments which have not already provided for such notice and opportunity for purchase should move toward that end. The Congress believes it is the responsibility of state and local governments to provide for such notice and opportunity to purchase in a prompt manner. The Congress has decided not to intervene and therefore leaves this responsibility to state and local governments to be carried out. [15 U.S.C.A. § 3605.]

2. *Uniform Condominium Act.* The UCA contains two sections dealing with conversion issues. Section 4–106 requires the converter to provide additional information in the public offering statements, including an engineering report on structural, mechanical, and electrical systems, the converter's estimate of the useful life of these items (or a statement that no representations in that respect are made), and a list of outstanding code violations and the estimated cost of curing them. Section 4–112 deals with protection of existing tenants. It gives them a right to 120 days written notice before they must vacate their apartments. For 60 days after receiving this notice, they have the right of first refusal to purchase their units at the public offering price. Following the tenant's 60-day period, the converter may not sell a unit on more favorable terms to an outsider within the following 180 days.

3. *State legislation.* Many states have enacted conversion legislation that is more sweeping and restrictive than the UCA. Increasingly, legislation has focused on protecting elderly and disabled tenants who become involved in the conversion process. See, e.g., Mo. Rev. Stat. § 448.4–112(3) (limiting a converter's right to evict low-and moderate-income elderly and the disabled for up to 15 years if state Housing Development Commission money is available for "acquisition, planning, rehabilitation or other expenses" in connection with the conversion). On the other hand, consider the far-reaching and restrictive nature of the New York statute:

> No eviction proceedings will be commenced at any time against non-purchasing tenants for failure to purchase or any other reason applicable to expiration of tenancy; provided that such proceedings may be commenced for non-payment of rent, illegal use or occupancy of the premises, refusal of reasonable access to the owner or a similar breach by the non-purchasing tenant of his obligations to the owner of the dwelling unit or the shares allocated thereto; and provided further that an owner of a unit or of the shares allocated thereto may not commence an action to recover possession of a dwelling unit from a non-purchasing tenant on the grounds that he seeks the dwelling unit for the use and occupancy of himself or his family.

N.Y. Gen. Bus. Law § 352–eeee(2)(c)(ii). New York courts have had difficulty deciding which tenants are protected from eviction upon conversion. Compare Paikoff v. Harris, 185 Misc.2d 372, 713 N.Y.S.2d 109 (1999) (tenants who had sublet from a coop purchaser post-conversion entitled to protection against eviction) with Park West Village Assocs. v. Nishoika, 187 Misc.2d 243, 721

N.Y.S.2d 459 (2000) (tenant who leased from condominium conversion purchaser five years after conversion not entitled to protection of statute). Another example of restrictive regulation of the conversion process can be found in New Jersey and is described in Troy Ltd. v. Renna, 727 F.2d 287 (3d Cir. 1984).

4. *Conversion literature.* There has been an enormous output of law review work on the conversion topic. See, e.g., Leighton J. Hyde, Rethinking *Roth*: Why the Florida Legislature Should Empower Local Governments to Regulate Condominium Conversions, 42 Stetson L. Rev. 751 (2013); Julie D. Lawton, Tenant Purchase as a Means of Creating and Preserving Affordable Homeownership, 20 Georgetown J. on Poverty L. & Pol'y 55 (2012); Sarah Comeau, Judicial Sponsored Gentrification of the District of Columbia: The Tenant Opportunity to Purchase Act, 19 Amer. U.J. Gender Soc. Pol'y & L. 401 (2011); Aaron O'Toole & Benita Jones, Tenant Purchase Laws as a Tool for Affordable Housing Preservation: The D.C. Experience, 18 J. Affordable Hous. & Comm. Dev. L. 367 (Summer 2009); Kathryn B. Richards, Note, The Illinois Condominium Property Act: An Analysis of Legislative Efforts to Improve Tenants' Rights in the Condominium Conversion Process, 57 DePaul L. Rev. 829 (2008); Douglas E. Chabot, Note, Casting New Light on a Continuing Problem: Reconsidering the Scope and Protections Offered by Massachusetts's Condominium Conversion Regulations, 42 Suffolk U.L. Rev. 101 (2008); Jonathan Feldman, Regulating Condominium Conversions: The Constitutionality of Tenant Approval Provisions, 21 Urb. L. 85 (1989); Bernard V. Keenan, Condominium Conversion of Residential Rental Units: A Proposal for State Regulation and a Model Act, 20 U. Mich. J.L. Ref. 639 (1987); David James Burge, Statutory Protection Against Condominium Conversions for North Carolina Residential Tenants, 62 N.C. L. Rev. 1346 (1984); David A. Fine, Comment, The Condominium Conversion Problem: Causes and Solutions, 1980 Duke L.J. 306; Gurdon H. Buck, What to Do for Tenants and Purchasers in a Condominium Conversion, 26 Prac. Law. 45 (July 1980); Constance W. Cranch, Comment, The Regulation of Rental Apartment Conversions, 8 Ford. Urb. L.J. 507 (1980); Note, The Validity of Ordinances Limiting Condominium Conversions, 78 Mich. L. Rev. 124 (1979); Randy Wynn, Condominium Conversion and Tenant Rights—Wisconsin Statutes Section 703.08: What Kind of Protection Does It Really Provide?, 63 Marq. L. Rev. 73 (1979); Roger J. Illsley, Note, Municipal Regulation of Condominium Conversions in California, 53 So. Cal. L. Rev. 225 (1979); G. Gregory Handschuh & Victor A. Cohen, Note, Tenant Protection in Condominium Conversions: The New York Experience, 48 St. John's L. Rev. 978 (1974).

HORNSTEIN v. BARRY

District of Columbia Court of Appeals, En Banc, 1989
560 A.2d 530

SCHWELB, ASSOCIATE JUDGE. Appellants challenge the constitutionality of the District's Rental Housing Conversion and Sale

Act, D.C.Code §§ 45–1601 *et seq.* (1986 and 1988 Supp.) (hereinafter the RHCSA or the Act). This statute provides in substance that an owner of rental housing may not convert it to condominium use unless fifty per cent of the eligible tenants consent to such conversion. . . .

I

Appellants own the Savoy, a 203-unit apartment complex in northwest Washington. For many years, they have sought to convert the Savoy into a condominium. In May, 1981, they filed this action in the Superior Court against the Mayor and other District of Columbia officials (the District), alleging that the defendants had unlawfully denied their application for conversion, in violation of their statutory and constitutional rights. In January, 1983, Judge John F. Doyle granted the District's motion for summary judgment and dismissed all of the owners' claims.

The owners appealed to this court. On September 11, 1987, a three-judge panel affirmed Judge Doyle's dismissal of the owners' statutory claims, but held that the tenant consent requirement constitutes an improper delegation of legislative authority and deprives the owners of property without due process of law. The panel found that there was a genuine issue of material fact which precluded the entry of summary judgment as to the uncompensated taking claim and remanded for further development of that issue. . . .

II

The RHCSA forbids the conversion of a rental apartment complex into condominium units unless the Mayor certifies that a majority of the tenants qualified to vote have consented. §§ 45–1611(a), 45–1612.

In enacting the RHCSA, the Council made a number of findings, summarized below, in which it explained the need for the legislation. According to the Council, there exists a continuing housing crisis in this city, with a severe shortage of rental housing and a low vacancy rate, particularly in relation to units which lower income tenants can afford. § 45–1601(2). The conversion of rental units to condominiums or cooperatives depletes the rental housing stock. § 45–1601(3). Lower income tenants, particularly the elderly, feel the bite of this depletion most severely, for post-conversion costs are usually beyond their means, a condition which results in forced displacement, serious overcrowding, and disproportionally high housing costs. § 45–1601(4). Experience with prior conversion controls has demonstrated that such restrictions have not been sufficiently effective, and tenants who are most directly affected by conversion should be given a voice in the determination whether their rental housing should be converted. § 45–1601(7). . . .

In § 45–1602, the Council enumerated the purposes of the legislation, which parallel and complement the legislative findings summarized above. The Act was designed, among other things,

> [t]o discourage the displacement of tenants through conversion or sale of rental property, and to strengthen the bargaining position of tenants toward that end without unduly interfering with the rights of property owners to the due process of law.

§ 45–1602(1).

III . . .

Delegation, Standardlessness, and Due Process.

Although they acknowledge the applicability of the presumption of constitutionality, the owners contend that the tenant consent requirement impermissibly delegates legislative authority to private citizens. They claim, in effect, that the RHCSA relegates their right to use their property as they see fit to the caprice of tenants who are free to act to promote their own private advantage rather than in the public interest. They argue that no standards are provided for the granting or withholding of consent, so that a majority of the tenants can bar conversion for a good reason, a capricious reason, a selfish reason, or no reason at all. This standardlessness, say the owners, renders the legislation unconstitutional and denies them property without due process of law.

It cannot be gainsaid that, under this statutory scheme, a tenant majority may act arbitrarily, and that there is no objective standard to which they must conform. Indeed, the Council, by making it an explicit purpose of the Act to strengthen the bargaining power of tenants, undoubtedly recognized that the residents of a particular rental complex might well act in their own financial interest and consent to conversion only if the owners would sweeten the pie by buying them out at an attractive price. Where the residents of one complex agree to conversion in response to their landlord's financial largesse, their parochial interest in allowing the landlord to take the affected units off the rental market may collide with the needs of tenants city-wide and with the prime goal of the legislation, which is to avoid the erosion of affordable rental housing.

These criticisms of the Act may be thought plausible or persuasive, and perhaps the give and take of the political process has, in this instance as in others, produced less than perfect legislation. Perfection, however, is neither constitutionally required nor practically achievable.[8] . . . The Act

---

[8] Given the Council's stated purposes, we know of no flawless legislative solution that would achieve all of them. The Council could have made the ban on conversion absolute, *see Griffin Development Co. v. City of Oxnard,* 39 Cal.3d 256, 217 Cal.Rptr. 1, 703 P.2d 339 (1985), but this would have placed further restrictions on the choices available both to owners and to their tenants. Another alternative would have been to fashion legislative standards, with the

permits tenants to dispense with the protection provided by the general ban on conversions if they can negotiate a better bargain for themselves. It may not be pretty, but we do not think it is unconstitutional.

Allowing a group of intended beneficiaries of legislation to waive its protection is not an impermissible delegation of legislative functions to private decisionmakers. "An otherwise valid regulation is not rendered invalid simply because those whom the regulation is designed to safeguard elect to forgo its protection." *New Motor Vehicle Board v. Orrin W. Fox Co.,* 439 U.S. 96, 109, 99 S.Ct. 403, 411, 58 L.Ed.2d 361 (1978), citing *Thomas Cusack Co. v. City of Chicago,* 242 U.S. 526, 37 S.Ct. 190, 61 L.Ed. 472 (1917). Where, as here, the City Council has made an appropriate finding that conversion to condominium use is presumptively contrary to the public interest and should be proscribed, it may constitutionally allow the primary beneficiaries of such a proscription to waive its benefits, even though this allows the units in question to be used in a manner which would otherwise be impermissible. *Cusack, supra.* Although such an arrangement countenances some private sovereignty over the fate of others and a concomitant lack of standards, the due process clause is not thereby transgressed. . . .

Uncompensated Taking.

The owners claim that by enacting the RHCSA and the rent control laws, and by effecting "delays through the use of illegal ordinances," the District has taken their property for public use without just compensation, in violation of the Fifth Amendment. . . .

To prove a taking under the Fifth Amendment, it is not necessary to demonstrate that the property was "taken" in the narrow sense of the word, nor need the government have directly appropriated the title, possession, or use of the property. *Richmond Elks Hall Assn. v. Richmond Redevelopment Agency,* 561 F.2d 1327, 1330 (9th Cir.1977). A land use regulation effects a taking if it denies an owner any economically viable use of his land. *Agins v. Tiburon,* 447 U.S. 255, 260, 100 S.Ct. 2138, 2141, 65 L.Ed.2d 106 (1980); *Nollan v. California Coastal Com'n,* 483 U.S. 825, 833–34, 107 S.Ct. 3141, 3146, 97 L.Ed.2d 677 (1987). The just compensation clause does not, however, require that a landowner be permitted to make the most profitable use of his property. Quite the contrary, diminution in property value, standing alone, does not establish a taking, especially where the property is capable of earning a reasonable return within the governmental restrictions. *Penn Central Transp. Co. v. New York City,* 438 U.S. 104, 129, 131, 98 S.Ct. 2646, 2661, 2662, 57 L.Ed.2d 631 (1978); *see Keystone Bituminous Coal Ass'n v. DeBenedictis,*

---

wishes of tenants being one factor, but the Council could reasonably conclude that this would have necessitated more administrative hearings, more bureaucracy, more litigation and more delay.

480 U.S. 470, 495–96, 107 S.Ct. 1232, 1247, 94 L.Ed.2d 472 (1987); *900 G Street Assoc. v. Dept. of Housing,* 430 A.2d 1387, 1390–91 (D.C.1981).

These principles have been applied to situations similar to the one that confronts us here. In *Griffin Development Co. v. City of Oxnard, supra,* the Supreme Court of California upheld, against a Fifth Amendment challenge, a regulation which effectively prohibited condominium conversion. The court noted that the owner was "free to continue to rent its apartments, unaffected by the ordinance; the regulations apply only to its plans to convert the apartments to condominiums." 39 Cal.3d at 259, 217 Cal.Rptr. at 1, 703 P.2d at 344–45. The court observed that most land use regulations have the effect of reducing the value of regulated properties, but concluded that even a significant diminution in value is insufficient to establish a prohibited taking. *Id.* at 2, 217 Cal.Rptr. at 260, 703 P.2d at 345. . . .

In the present case, as in *Griffin, supra,* the owners are free to continue to use the Savoy as rental property. They complain in conclusory fashion that the District's rent control laws promote expropriation, but the Supreme Court declined, only last term, to reconsider *Block v. Hirsh,* 256 U.S. 135, 41 S.Ct. 458, 65 L.Ed. 865 (1921) and its progeny, upholding the constitutionality of rent control. *Pennell, supra,* 485 U.S. at 11–12, 108 S.Ct. at 857–58 n. 6. Moreover, the District permits a landlord to file a hardship petition and obtain an upward adjustment of the rent if his rate of return has been less than 12% per year, § 45–2522, a provision which appears to make the law anything but confiscatory. Given these circumstances, as well as the presumption of constitutionality, the difficulties with the owners' contention that the District has taken their property without compensation may not be easy to surmount.

[The court affirmed the judgment with respect to the owners' statutory and due process claims, but concluded that summary judgment was not appropriate on the takings claim, because the record had focused entirely on the owners' statutory claims, and "did not address the factual context of the issue of uncompensated taking." The court thus remanded the case to the D.C. Superior Court for further proceedings with respect to the uncompensated taking claim.]

[The concurring and dissenting opinion of JUDGE NEWMAN and the concurring and dissenting opinion of JUDGES FERREN and TERRY are omitted.]

REILLY, SENIOR JUDGE, dissenting in part. In my view, the basic premise that an absolute prohibition of condominium conversion is within the power of our local government to enact rests upon shaky grounds. Only one judicial authority is cited by the majority for that proposition: a decision of the California Supreme Court, a somewhat dubious source for guidance on questions of constitutional law. Such legislation . . . might be questionable as tending over time to reduce the supply of rental units, because anti-condominium legislation, like rent control laws, creates a powerful disincentive to the construction of new rental apartment buildings. In any event, as such a statute is not before us, it is scarcely within our province to pass upon its constitutionality.

The real fallacy of this rationale, however, is that even though a general prohibition of conversions to condominia might survive a due process challenge, the tenant election provision would be enough to render such a statute unconstitutional.

In my view, the basic reliance of the circuit court and the majority opinion upon *Thomas Cusack Co. v. City of Chicago,* 242 U.S. 526, 37 S.Ct. 190, 61 L.Ed. 472 (1917), is badly misplaced. It was not *Cusack,* but *Washington ex rel. Seattle Title Trust Co. v. Roberge,* 278 U.S. 116, 49 S.Ct. 50, 73 L.Ed. 210 (1928) whose controlling precedential weight was reaffirmed by the recent *Eastlake* opinion, and it is to the latter case that this court should look in deciding the delegation issue.

In *Roberge,* as we pointed out in the panel opinion, 530 A.2d at 1183, the Supreme Court struck down an *amendment* to a general zoning ordinance, which revision allowed the operation of a philanthropic home for children and the elderly, provided the owners of two-thirds of the property in an adjacent area gave their written consent, on the ground that such an "arbitrary" (*i.e.,* standardless) delegation of power was repugnant to the due process clause. . . .

In short, what the *Roberge* Court held was that even though a municipality might have authority to pass a law restricting a particular district to purely private residential use, a waiver provision which could be invoked only by a small segment of voters made the presumed validity of a general prohibition irrelevant. . . .

Apparently refusing to concede our point that a referendum limited only to a small segment of the community can be upheld only when the legislation is directed at some kind of nuisance, *e.g.,* unsightly billboards, the majority contends that because the tenant election process here was expressly intended to confer greater bargaining power on the occupants of the rental units and to encourage the formation of tenant organizations for negotiating purposes, such Council findings justify a delegation of legislative power to a narrow group for whose protection the statute was enacted. The challenged provision, however, goes far beyond conferring reasonable bargaining power on the favored few in electorates thus limited. It grants them an absolute power of veto, and thus cannot be equated with statutes like the National Labor Relations Act which confer collective bargaining powers on workers. That statute, in order to insure that the delegation of such power could pass constitutional muster, provides that "the obligation [to bargain] does not compel either party to agree to a proposal or require the making of a concession." 29 U.S.C. § 158(d) (1982).

The majority candidly notes that, under the challenged statutory scheme, a majority of tenants in a particular complex may bar conversion for purely arbitrary or capricious reasons, or may agree to it, only because the financial offer of the landlords to buy them out appeals to selfish reasons. It then concedes that such parochial reasons for responding to their landlord's largesse "may collide with the needs of tenants city wide and with the prime goal of legislation, which is to avoid the erosion of affordable rental housing.". . .

So far as the separate issue of an unconstitutional taking without compensation is concerned, I also believe that in this posture of the case a remand for the purpose of an evidentiary proceeding is required. Although the petitioners for rehearing dispute this part of the order entered by the panel, it is plain that this argument is premature under the holding of the Supreme Court in *Pennell v. City of San Jose,* 485 U.S. 1, 108 S.Ct. 849, 99 L.Ed.2d 1 (1988). I see no reason for the extended comments of the majority on this issue, which are almost tantamount to an advisory opinion against plaintiff. Surely cases like *Nollan v. California Coastal Commission,* 483 U.S. 825, 107 S.Ct. 3141, 97 L.Ed.2d 677 (1987), which vindicated the rights of thalatarian landholders to exclusive access to their shore property in the absence of compensation for a public easement, show that the issue is anything but frivolous.

NOTES

1. *Preemption challenges.* Statutory preemption challenges to city conversion ordinances have met with mixed success. The probability of success of such a challenge will depend largely on the language and scope of the state conversion legislation. For example, a city ordinance that imposes a moratorium on conversion may be held to conflict with state legislation that seems to authorize conversion, but merely requires notice to tenants as a condition precedent to conversion. Or, where the state has enacted a comprehensive set of protections for tenants in a conversion building, a court may hold that the state legislature has "occupied the field" or preempted the entire area so as to prohibit municipal conversion limitations of any kind. See, e.g., Claridge House One, Inc. v. Borough of Verona, 490 F.Supp. 706 (D. N.J. 1980), aff'd, 633 F.2d 209 (3d Cir. 1980) (one year local moratorium preempted by comprehensive state regulatory scheme). Contra: Griffin Dev. Co. v. City of Oxnard, 39 Cal.3d 256, 217 Cal.Rptr. 1, 703 P.2d 339 (1985) (condominium moratorium ordinance not preempted by Subdivision Map Act).

Sometimes the local government may simply lack power under its state constitution or statutes to enact the conversion regulation. See Greater Boston Real Estate Bd. v. City of Boston, 397 Mass. 870, 494 N.E.2d 1301

(1986) (city lacked authority under rent control enabling statute to enact condominium and cooperative conversion ordinance); Bannerman v. City of Fall River, 391 Mass. 328, 461 N.E.2d 793 (1984) (ordinance permitting conversion only with approval of housing conversion board held to violate constitutional provision prohibiting cities from enacting a private or civil law governing civil relationships except as an incident to exercise of an independent municipal power).

For a comprehensive analysis of constitutional problems of conversion ordinances, see Lori S. Roback, Comment, Regulating Condominium Conversions: Do Municipal Ordinances Adequately Protect Tenants' and Owners' Constitutional Rights?, 1985 Ariz. St. L.J. 935 (1985). For more specific analysis of the tenant approval issue, see Jonathan Feldman, Regulating Condominium Conversions: The Constitutionality of Tenant Approval Provisions, 21 Urban Lawyer 85 (1989).

2. *The tenancy in common as a device for avoiding conversion restrictions.* In some cities, owners of rental buildings who are stymied by local ordinances restricting condominium conversions eschew the conversion route entirely. Instead, they sell tenancy in common interests in the building to would-be unit purchasers. As part of this transaction, the purchaser receives the right to occupy a particular apartment. The purchaser, in turn, is able to finance the purchase by giving a mortgage on his or her undivided interest in the building. [For a description of such an arrangement, referred to in California as a "community apartment" or a "deed plan," see Adler v. Elphick, 184 Cal.App.3d 642, 229 Cal.Rptr. 254 (1986).] In San Francisco, this practice led the city council to enact an ordinance extending its regulation of condo conversions to the tenancy in common approach, prohibiting exclusive occupancy agreements between the co-tenants. The ordinance was challenged by building owners on privacy and state preemption grounds. The challenge succeeded at the trial court level and was upheld by the California Court of Appeals. Tom v. City and County of San Francisco, 120 Cal.App.4th 674, 16 Cal.Rptr.3d 13 (2004).

2 NELSON, WHITMAN, BURKHART & FREYERMUTH, REAL ESTATE FINANCE LAW

§ 13.4, at 390–393 (6th ed. Practitioner Series 2014)*

Occasionally an apartment building owner is able to manage a conversion without resort to new blanket financing, but this can be accomplished only if the existing mortgage lender is agreeable. If the mortgage contains a due-on-sale clause, the lender must waive it. The lender must also be willing to join in the condominium declaration, and must modify the existing mortgage documents by inserting a partial release clause to facilitate the sale of individual units free of the blanket lien. Often the lender is uninterested in taking these steps, or will do so

---

* Reprinted with permission of Thomson Reuters.

only in return for financial concessions that the converter finds unacceptable. The alternate approach for the converter is to obtain an interim loan from a different lender that will contain the necessary language, and to use its proceeds to pay off the existing loan. The attractiveness of this technique will depend on numerous factors, including the interest rate and other costs associated with the interim loan and the prepayment charge that may be demanded by the existing lender.

Interim loans to finance conversions usually do not require regular principal amortization, but do require the reduction of the principal by some agreed amount for each condominium unit sold, much in the same manner as blanket construction loans on subdivisions. They are usually limited to 75 or 80% of the property's value *as a condominium,* but if this would result in a loan approaching 100% of the value as a rental project, the interim lender will often require some cash investment by the converter (thus limiting the loan to perhaps 90% of the rental value). In any event, the "value" on which the loan is based will generally include the cost of the renovations that the converter plans to make. A portion of the interim loan may even be disbursed in installments as these improvements are put in place, as with a construction loan.

The interim lender is intensely concerned with the converter's cash flow projections for the conversion period. The building must generate enough cash to cover any periodic interest payments due on the interim loan as well as the usual operating, maintenance, and management costs of a rental building, plus the converter's obligation to pay assessments to the new owners' association. Because a shortfall can easily result in default and foreclosure of the interim mortgage, the interim lender must be confident that it can complete the conversion successfully if necessary. . . .

Conversion of rental buildings to cooperatives is far less common than conversion to condominiums except in New York, where it has been a frequent and closely regulated occurrence.[7] . . . [T]he financing problems are much simpler because, absent a due-on-sale clause, the agreement of the existing lender is generally not needed and the conversion can proceed without its participation.[9] Often the outstanding balance on the

---

[7] See N.Y. Gen. Bus. Law § 352e (conversions in New York State generally), § 352ee (conversions of nonresidential property), § 352eee (conversions in municipalities of Westchester, Nassau & Rockland Counties which adopt it), and § 352eeee (conversions in New York City). These rules are summarized in 2 P. Rohan & M. Reskin, Cooperative Housing Law & Practice § 6.04; Comment, Examining Cooperative Conversion: An Analysis of Recent New York Legislation, 11 Fordham Urb. L.J. 1089 (1982). See Richards v. Kaskel, 32 N.Y.2d 524, 347 N.Y.S.2d 1, 300 N.E.2d 388 (1973).

[9] This may not be true, however, if the rental project was insured under a HUD-subsidized housing program. See Boston Five Cents Sav. Bank v. Secretary of Dept. of Housing & Urban Development, 768 F.2d 5 (1st Cir. 1985) (conversion might constitute a "change of use" as that phrase was used in the HUD regulatory agreement).

existing financing will be too low to make conversion feasible. In such cases the existing loan may be refinanced, or if its interest rate is so low that it is worth preserving, a wrap-around or second mortgage may be arranged to provide cash for refurbishing the building and to lower the required down payments of the apartment purchasers. Separate original, interim, and permanent loans are not necessarily required, however; if the existing financing on the rental building is satisfactory, there is usually no reason that it cannot be carried through the conversion period and become the permanent financing for the cooperators.

NOTE

1.   *Federal income tax treatment of conversion.* Federal income tax treatment of condominium conversion has been significantly affected by the twists and turns that have marked federal tax policy since the mid-1980s. Until 1986, condominium conversion faced a major federal income tax question. When an apartment building was sold outside of the conversion context, unless there was depreciation recapture under section 1250 of the Internal Revenue Code, the gain on the sale was treated as a long-term capital gain. By contrast, in a new condominium development, the developer was traditionally treated as holding the condominium units "primarily for sale to customers in the ordinary course" of her "trade or business." Consequently, the gain on the sale of the units was classified as ordinary income by section 1221(1) and thus taxable at rates higher than for capital gains. However, classification of the gain on the sale of units in a condominium conversion was less clear. Would the IRS treat the converted units as the developer's "inventory" (and thus subject the gain on sales to ordinary income treatment), or instead conclude that the converted project retained its original status as an asset used in the developer's trade or business (thus allowing the developer to treat gain on sales as capital gain)?

The Tax Reform Act of 1986, Pub.L. No. 99–514, §§ 301(a), 311(a), repealed preferential capital gain tax treatment for gains realized in taxable years beginning after 1986. Thus long-term capital gains were taxed at the rates applied to ordinary income. As a practical matter, this eliminated the importance of whether the profit from a condominium conversion project is characterized as either ordinary income or capital gain (although capital gains were still important in that they could be offset by capital losses).

To some extent, Congress remuddied the waters by enacting the Revenue Reconciliation Act of 1990, which restored a small 3% capital gains preference (a 28% maximum capital gains rate versus a 31% maximum ordinary income rate). Because the differential in the two rates was small, condominium tax treatment issues remained in the background. However, with the passage of the Taxpayer Relief Act of 1997, Congress reopened these issues by reinstating a significant capital gains preference. In the 1997 Act, Congress reduced the top tax rate for long term capital gains from 28% to 20%, for individuals in a tax bracket above the lowest 15% bracket. Thus, for investments sold after May 6, 1997, there was a capital gains preference of 19.6% (a 20% maximum capital gains rate versus a 39.6% maximum ordinary income rate). Moreover, that 20% rate was reduced to 18% after the year 2000 for assets held more than 5 years. Finally, depreciation recapture under section 1250 of the Internal Revenue Code was taxed at a maximum rate of 25%, which still provided a 13% maximum capital gains preference for tax planning purposes.

The Jobs and Growth Tax Relief Reconciliation Act of 2003 ("2003 Act") further widened the capital gains tax preference. The 2003 Act decreased the capital gains tax rate from 20% to 15%. In addition, the top ordinary income tax rate was lowered to 35% from 39.6%. The rate reductions under the 2003 Act expired on December 31, 2012. Consequently, the tax treatment of condominium conversions continues to be an important issue.

One current approach to this characterization problem is to distinguish between appreciation in the building prior to conversion and the amount of profit realized from post-conversion activities (the sale of the individual units). The aim is to have pre-conversion appreciation in the building qualify for capital gains treatment while the profit attributable to post-conversion activities is treated as ordinary income. This involves selling the building to a conversion entity to recognize a capital gain on the appreciation in the building. If, of course, the building owner wants to participate in post-conversion profit, he or she should acquire an interest in that entity, but one that does not exceed 50% of the entity. If the owner violates the 50% test, he or she runs the risk that the profit on the sale to the entity will be treated as ordinary income. For further consideration of this transaction and its complexities, see James R. Hamill & Craig G. White, Choice of Entities for Real Estate Development, 1 Business Entities 26, 33 (Sept–Oct. 1999).

2.   *Conversion from cooperative to condominium.* Recently there is something of a trend for cooperatives to convert to condominium status. See, e.g., Stuart M. Saft, Financing Coop-to-Condo Conversion, 16 Real Est. Fin. J. 45 (2001); Richard Siegler, The Feasibility of Co-op to Condo Conversion, N.Y. Law J., March 5, 1997 p.3. This trend was driven by several factors. There is a perception that condominiums sell for significantly more than their coop counterparts. See, e.g. Saft, supra, at 49 ("brokers have been suggesting that a condominium unit sells for 10 percent to 20 percent more than a similar cooperative apartment"); Michael H. Schill, Ioan Voicu & Jonathan Miller, The Condominium v. Cooperative Puzzle: An Empirical Analysis of Housing in New York City, 36 J.Leg.Stud. 275, 312 (2007) ("According to our results, the typical condominium apartment is 8.8 percent more valuable than the typical cooperative apartment."). As one commentator noted,

> [S]ince co-op maintenance charges are fixed to cover debt service on the underlying mortgage, all of the real estate taxes and other common charges, they frequently exceed the common charges for a condominium, which exclude debt service and taxes. By unbundling these elements, there is a perception of lower common charges. Such

charges invariably are inversely related to apartment values. This disparity in stating the costs of co-op and condominium units may help to explain why buyers are willing to pay higher prices for condominium units than for co-ops.

Siegler, supra. Moreover, there is the problem of transferability. As we noted earlier in this chapter, coop associations wield much more substantial control over an owner's ability to sell or rent his or her apartment than do most condominium associations. After all, condo associations seldom have the money or inclination to exercise their rights of first refusal when unit owners choose to sell. While the coop's ability to control transfer may be reassuring to those who purchase an apartment with the intent to stay for a long period, for those who are seeking to sell the control reduces the pool of potential buyers and makes sale more difficult. In New York City, in particular, there have been frequent press articles about what are perceived to be arbitrary and capricious refusals of boards to approve coop transfers. See, e.g., "Co-op Board Hell," *New York Magazine,* Nov. 6, 1995, at 27; "Co-op Market Goes to Hell," *New York Post*, Jan. 26, 1997 at 12. A good friend of the authors, also a law professor, wished to purchase a New York City co-op in 2002, but was rejected by the board. He believed that the board suspected that he planned to rent out the unit rather than living in it, but since the board had no duty to provide a reason for its decision, he was unsure what its reason was.

Once the decision to convert from coop to condo is made, the lawyer's job just begins. What steps are necessary? Consider the following checklist delineated in a recent and useful article:

[I]n order to convert from a cooperative to a condominium, the cooperative would be required to take the following steps:

1.   Negotiate among the cooperative's shareholders the terms of the declaration of condominium and by-laws;

2.   Allocate the common interests among the various apartments;

3.   Obtain shareholder approval;

4.   Have an architect draw plans of the entire building, which would probably need the approval of the appropriate municipal agencies;

5.   Satisfy the mortgage on the building;

6.   Obtain the approval of all of the banks who hold liens against the individual apartments to convert the share loans to mortgages on condominium units;

7.   Obtain agreement of the Department of Taxation or other municipal authority to the allocation of real property taxes among the unit owners pursuant to the allocation of common interests;

8.   File with state agency;

9.   Possibly pay a real property transfer tax;

10. Close the transaction for the transfer of the building and each of the units.

Stuart M. Saft, Financing Coop-to-Condo Conversion, 16 Real Est. Fin. J. 45, 48 (2001). Where will the money be found to pay off the blanket mortgage on the building? Why do you think the lenders to the apartment owners might be favorably inclined to convert their loan documents to mortgages? See id. at 48–49. See also Joel E. Miller, Probable Income Tax Effects of New York City Cooperative-to-Condominium Conversion, 24 Tax Mgmt. Real Est. J. 328 (2008).

F. VACATION AND RESORT PROJECTS

Many of us would like to own an interest in an apartment unit at an attractive vacation spot, but few of us have the means to make this possible. Further, most of us would not want to carry the costs of owning such a unit 52 weeks each year merely to enjoy it for a few weeks (or weekends) in our busy schedules.

One solution to this problem is "time-sharing" or "interval ownership." These phrases indicate that the "owner" owns only the right to possess the unit for a specified period of time each year—say, from June 1 to June 14. If the interval is two weeks in length, there may be 24 other owners, each of which also has an assigned time slot, making a total of 50 weeks of use each year. [The two remaining weeks may be reserved for cleaning and refurbishing by the management.] Obviously, the purchase of a two-week time interval is much less costly than the purchase of the entire unit. Time-share units are often sold for as little as a few thousand dollars, although in places where recreational activities are seasonal (such as skiing), the price may vary quite widely with the time of year in which the interval is placed.

COMMENT, LEGAL CHALLENGES TO TIME SHARING OWNERSHIP
45 Mo. L. Rev. 423, 426–28 (1980)*

The generic term "time sharing ownership" is used to describe the two distinct techniques which have been developed to permit fee simple ownership of vacation homes on a time share basis. Each technique involves a separate and distinct real property concept and thus is identified by a different name. An *interval estate* is defined by the Uniform Condominium Act [Sec. 4–103] as:

A combination of (i) an estate for years in a unit, during the term of which title to a unit rotates among the time-share owners thereof, vesting in each of them in turn for periods established

---

* Reprinted with the permission of the Missouri Law Review.

by a fixed recorded schedule, with the series thus established recurring regularly until the term expires, coupled with (ii) a vested undivided fee simple interest in the remainder in that unit, the magnitude of that interest having been established by the declaration or by the deed creating the interval estate.

The second technique for conveying a time sharing estate, the *time span estate,* is defined as:

A combination of (i) an undivided interest in a present estate in fee simple in a unit, the magnitude of that interest having been established by the declaration or by the deed conveying the time span estate, coupled with (ii) the exclusive right to possession and occupancy of that unit during a regularly recurring period designated by that deed or by a recorded document referred to therein.

In both the interval estate and the time span estate a purchaser is also a tenant in common with all other purchasers of the common areas of the complex.

In essence the time span estate makes all unit owners tenants in common in fee simple absolute, with each tenant in common having title to the undivided interest specified in his deed. The undivided right to possession and use of the whole property in its entirety is the one unity among tenants in common. Therefore, to maintain the viability of time sharing ownership, the time span method necessitates that a separate agreement delineating each unit owner's specific period of occupancy be entered into by all co-tenant-purchasers. Each co-tenant also waives his right to seek partition. The time span estate is freely alienable, either inter vivos by deed or by testamentary transfer.

The interval estate technique is conceptually more difficult than the time span method. Purchasers do not take title to each condominium unit as tenants in common; rather, the purchaser receives two separate and distinct vested interests in the unit. First, the interval estate owner acquires a defeasible fee in the form of an estate for years for the time period in each year during which he is entitled to occupancy. This defeasible fee will continue to vest in the owner for a period of years equal to the expected useful life of the building as a resort complex. For example, an interval estate owner may purchase a defeasible fee for the first two weeks in July for the next forty years. The owner's fee, being defeasible, is subject to a shifting executory interest which passes the fee to the next owner upon commencement of a subsequent time period, such as the third week of July in the above example.

The second interest acquired by the owner of an interval estate is a vested remainder as a tenant in common with the other interval estate owners of the unit, upon the termination of the defeasible fee interest.

This collective remainder interest was added to the defeasible fee arrangement in an attempt to eliminate any possible violation of the Rule Against Perpetuities. At the remote date when the interval estate owners become tenants in common, they may, if they choose, repeat the cycle for another period of years. The interval estate differs from the time span estate in that the right of occupancy and title of ownership coincide; the interval owner is the sole owner of the unit during his period of occupancy. Also, the right of occupancy arises by reason of the ownership interest, and not by reason of some contract or lease as under the time span estate.

The primary advantage of time sharing ownership is the low cost of the property interest purchased. A time-share estate owner also experiences the intangible satisfaction of owning a place of his own. He need not be concerned with making vacation reservations months ahead of time, nor is he subject to escalating motel costs. Additional advantages of owning a vacation time-share estate include interest and real estate tax deductions, equity buildup, and the possibility of leveraged appreciation leading to a profit upon resale.

For the developer, the advantage of time share estates results from the higher sales price he receives from each unit. In fact, the price markup of a unit sold as time share estates may be from 15 to 100% higher than the selling price of a comparable non-time sharing unit.

NOTES

1.   *The fee simple estate.* A third method of creating a time-share interest is simply to convey a fee simple estate which is described as giving possession for a specified period each year. Such estates are not included in the traditional corpus of estates in land recognized by the common law, and for this reason, many attorneys are reluctant to take this approach. At least one state, however, specifically recognizes this approach by statute. See Utah Code Ann. § 57–8–6. A fourth approach encompasses a variety of non-fee ownership concepts, such as licenses, leases and club memberships. See Patrick J. Rohan & Daniel A. Furlong, Timesharing and Consumer Protection: A Precis for Attorneys, 10 Wm. Mitchell L. Rev. 13, 17 (1984).

2.   *State legislation.* Numerous states have enacted time-sharing legislation. A significant number of these statutes are comprehensive in scope. See, e.g., Fla. Stat. Ann. §§ 721.01 to 721.32; Haw. Rev. Stat. Ann. §§ 514E–1 to 514E–31; Tenn. Code Ann. §§ 66–32–101 to 66–32–139; S.C. Code §§ 27–32–10 to 27–32–250; Neb. Rev. Stat. §§ 76–1701 to 76–1741; Va. Code §§ 55–360 to 55–365.1.

Two model timeshare acts have served as the impetus and guide for much of the foregoing legislation. In 1980, NCCUSL issued the Model Real Estate Time-Share Act (MRETSA). This act is detailed and comprehensive and includes within the concept of "time share estate" any right to occupy a unit "during [5] or more separated time periods over a period of at least [5] years." MRETSA § 1–102(18). Moreover, the drafters intended to include within the foregoing definition each of the four ownership methods described above. MRETSA § 1–102, cmt. 4. In organization, the act parallels the UCA and extends much of the latter's consumer protection provisions to time-share purchasers. States that have adopted MRETSA or its substantial equivalent include Louisiana, Maryland and Rhode Island. See La. Stat. Ann. §§ 9–1131.1 to 9–1131.30; Md. Code Real Prop. §§ 11A–101 to 11A–129; R.I. Gen. Laws §§ 34–41–1.01 to 34–41–5.07.

The National TimeSharing Council of the American Land Development Association and the National Association of Real Estate License Law Officials jointly drafted a Model Timeshare Act. This Act is less complex and detailed than MRETSA and affords developers greater flexibility in structuring their documents. See Patrick J. Rohan & Daniel A. Furlong, Timesharing and Consumer Protection: A Precis for Attorneys, 10 Wm. Mitchell L. Rev. 13, 32–33 (1984). Several states patterned their legislation in whole or in part on the Model Timeshare Act, including Florida, Hawaii, Tennessee, Nebraska and Virginia. Id.

Law review commentary on time-sharing and the foregoing legislation is substantial. See, e.g., Elizabeth A. Cameron & Salina Maxwell, Protecting Consumers: The Contractual and Real Estate Issues Involving Timeshares, Quartershares, and Fractional Ownerships, 37 Real Est. L.J. 278 (2009); David A. Bowen. Note, Timeshare Ownership: Regulation and Common Sense, 18 Loy. Cons. L. Rev. 459 (2006); Mary Lou Savage, Colin M. Lancaster & Nicholas C. Bougopoulos, Time Share Regulation: The Wisconsin Model, 77 Marq. L. Rev. 719 (1994); Cynthia J. Bart, From the Legislatures: The New Mexico Time Share Act, 16 Real Est. L.J. 181 (1987); Robert M. Kessler, Note, The North Carolina Time Share Act, 62 N.C. L. Rev. 1356 (1984); Joseph M. Meier, Note, Timesharing: Oregon's Legislation, 20 Willamette L. Rev. 283 (1984); Ellen R. Peirce & Richard A. Mann, Time-Share Interests in Real Estate: A Critical Evaluation of the Regulatory Environment, 59 Notre Dame L. Rev. 9 (1983).

3. *Time-sharing legal issues.* A number of legal questions exist with respect to time-sharing. They are discussed in the law review comments cited above and will be mentioned only briefly here. They are more acute in the case of plans which make the owners of a given unit tenants in common.

(a) Can a federal tax lien (or other type of lien under state law) against one owner be asserted against the entire unit, jeopardizing the rights of the other owners?

(b) Can the interest of one of the owners of a unit be levied upon to satisfy judgments for torts committed in the common areas or in a unit by another owner, or for damage to the unit itself which injures the enjoyment of another owner?

(c) Is the agreement of the owners of a given unit not to seek partition of that unit an enforceable agreement?

(d) To what extent do covenants not to partition, to share expenses, etc., run with the land and bind future owners?

4.   *The partition problem.* Where the time-share owner is a tenant in common with other weekly owners, serious partition problems arise. Typically tenants in common have a right to partition. In other words, in the time-share context, the owner of week 10 could seek partition and the entire unit (all 52 weeks) could be sold to the highest bidder at a public auction. This could give enormous leverage and potential for mischief to the owner of a single week. Consequently, many time-share declarations prohibit such partition actions. Should such language be enforceable? What if the time-share documents are silent as to this issue? Consider the following North Carolina statute:

> When a time share is owned by two or more persons as tenants in common or as joint tenants either may seek a partition by sale of that interest but no purchaser of a time share may maintain an action for partition by sale or in kind of the unit in which such time share is held.

N.C. Gen. Stat. § 93A–43. For similar statutes, see, e.g., Nev. Rev. Stat. Ann. § 119A.500; N.M. Stat. Ann. § 47–11–3.

5.   *The time-share as an "executory contract."* Under each of the first three time-share ownership methods described earlier, the purchaser receives some type of fee interest. Consequently, her ownership is not jeopardized by subsequent developer bankruptcy. However, where the ownership falls into the fourth category, developer bankruptcy in the past has sometimes proved to be fatal to the time-share owner. To the extent that the purchaser's ownership right was characterized as merely contractual and executory, it was capable of being terminated by a bankruptcy trustee who asserted the power to avoid executory contracts under section 365 of the Bankruptcy Code. See Sombrero Reef Club, Inc. v. Allman, 18 B.R. 612 (Bankr. S.D. Fla. 1982); Mark C. Eriks, Note, Treatment of Time-Share Interests Under the Bankruptcy Code, 59 Ind.L.J. 223 (1984).

In response to this problem, Congress in 1984 amended section 365 to give such time-share purchasers essentially the same protection in developer bankruptcy as is afforded an installment land contract vendee when her vendor goes into bankruptcy:

> (i)(1) If the trustee rejects an executory contract of the debtor for the sale of real property or for the sale of a timeshare interest under a timeshare plan, under which the purchaser is in possession, such purchaser may treat such contract as terminated, or, in the alternative, may remain in possession of such real property or timeshare interest.

(2) If such purchaser remains in possession—

(A) such purchaser shall continue to make all payments due under such contract, but may offset against such payments any damages occurring after the date of the rejection of such contract caused by the nonperformance of any obligation of the debtor after such date, but such purchaser does not have any rights against the estate on account of any damages arising after such date from such rejection, other than such offset; and

(B) the trustee shall deliver title to such purchaser in accordance with the provisions of such contract, but is relieved of all other obligations to perform under such contract.

11 U.S.C.A. § 365(i). See Terry L. Arnold, Note, Real Estate Timesharing: Construction of Non-Fee Ownership, 27 Wash. U.J. Urb. & Contemp. Law 215, 246–47 (1984).

Because purchasers of time-shares feel more comfortable receiving some type of deed of a fee simple estate, most developers tend to use that type of ownership. From the developer's perspective, however, there are strong arguments in favor of the "license" or club ownership approach. See Robert E. Dady & Robert S. Freedman, To Deed or Not to Deed: That Is the Timeshare Question, 15 Prob. & Prop. 49 (March–April 2001).

6.   *Governance of a time-share development.* In a sense, time-sharing is inconsistent with the "miniature democracy" concept of the condominium owners association. The owners of a given unit may be scattered over a number of states or even countries, and only a small fraction of them will be in residence in the condominium project at any given time. Their ability to organize and to exchange information and views is obviously very limited. The professional management (usually affiliated with the developer) occupies a position of far greater power than in a project designed for year-around residence. In many cases the owners are asked to give their proxies to the management, and most presumably do so. The MRETSA attempts to encourage owner participation by providing for initiative, referendum, and recall so that owners can institute major policy changes in the project's operation. Is this sort of effort likely to be successful? See Stephen G. Johnakin, Self-Governance in Timeshare Projects: Mail-Order Democracy, 19 Real Prop. Prob. & Tr. J. 705 (1984).

7.   *The regular/time-share condominium "hybrid."* Occasionally a developer will create a condominium project that consists partially of "normal" condominium units and partially of time-share units. Usually the developer did not plan to create this arrangement at the outset. Rather, it typically arises out of an attempt to salvage a traditional condominium development that has not sold well. For example, a developer may have sold only 40–50% of the units and may decide to sell the balance as time-shares. Does this arrangement pose special problems for owners of the regular units? Should time-share owners also be concerned? How should voting and

governance be allocated between the two types of owners? Should there be two owners associations? For a good example of how these latter issues can be the source of significant conflict, see Lake Arrowhead Chalets Timeshare Owners Ass'n v. Lake Arrowhead Chalets Owners Ass'n, 51 Cal.App.4th 1403, 59 Cal.Rptr.2d 875 (1996) (by-law amendment that permitted time-share owners to elect only 3 out of 7 directors disadvantaged that class of members, and was ineffective under applicable corporation code because it was not approved by the members of that class).

Sometimes the "hybrid" condominium raises difficult assessment issues. Expenses associated with timeshare units are frequently more costly because maintenance (for example, furniture must be replaced by the association in timeshare units) and marketing costs can be higher for such units than for "regular units." Consider the following language from a recent Missouri decision:

> A condominium association may only exercise its powers within the constraints of its condominium declaration. . . . [O]ur review of . . . the Declaration convinces us that the association can only assess a maintenance fee against a Unit Week Purchaser. Imogene was a Unit Owner, not a Unit Week Purchaser. Moreover, the trial court could have found from the evidence presented that the Association was assessing a "maintenance fee" against Imogene, based on the various component charges that were included in her assessment. For example, . . . the Declaration specifies that, in addition to true common expenses, the "maintenance fee" assessed against a Unit Week Purchaser can include his or her pro rata share of the cost of repainting the unit, replacing furniture and carpeting, etc. Imogene's assessment was calculated using a "reserve fund" charge, which included anticipated expenses for refurbishing interval ownership units. As a Unit Owner, Imogene received no benefit from such expenditures. The same is true of the charges included in her assessment for time-share sales parties, credit card fees and liability for other interval owners' maintenance fees. . . . Because the Association may exercise its authority to levy and collect assessments only in the manner provided in the Declaration, it did not have the authority to assess a maintenance fee against a Unit Owner like Imogene.

Surrey Condo. Ass'n, Inc. v. Webb, 163 S.W.3d 531, 536 (Mo. Ct. App. 2005).

From the developer's perspective, the failure of the original documents in a "regular" condominium development to authorize the subsequent conversion of unsold units to time share status can sometimes pose an insurmountable hurdle to such a conversion. See e.g., Colo. Rev. Stat. 38–33–111(1) ("No time share estates shall be created with respect to any condominium unit except pursuant to provisions in the project instruments expressly permitting the creation of such estates."). Thus, a prudent developer who wants to retain the option to convert some or all of the units to time share status should include such an authorization in the original project documents.

8. *Regulation of brokers.* In most states a Real Estate Commission (or similarly-named agency) regulates the activities of real estate brokers. In a few states its authority extends to the regulation or approval of the substantive content of real estate offerings. Is a time-share condominium real estate for this purpose? Does the answer depend on the legal structure of the time-sharing program? Suppose it is a club-type or license-type arrangement in which owners do not have rights in specific units? Compare Cal-Am Corp. v. Department of Real Estate, 104 Cal.App.3d 453, 163 Cal.Rptr. 729 (1980) (agency had jurisdiction) with State v. Carriage House Assocs., 94 Nev. 707, 585 P.2d 1337 (1978) (no jurisdiction). See Terry L. Arnold, Note, Real Estate Timesharing: Construction of Non-Fee Ownership, 27 Wash. U.J. Urb. & Contemp. Law 215, 230–37 (1984).

A more recent phenomenon is the condominium hotel. The following excerpt explains the basic operations of such a project.

ALVIN L. ARNOLD, 2 REAL ESTATE TRANSACTIONS: STRUCTURE AND ANALYSIS
§ 16:214*

Condominium (condo) hotels have become an increasingly popular format for development, particularly in resort-oriented locations. Nightly rental of units placed in a rental pool by condo owners is nothing new, as this practice has occurred for years in resorts and a few urban locations. What has changed, however, are the scope and nature of these properties and the relationships among the condo owners, property managers, customers, and project developers. . . .

Management of the facility. Previously, condo facilities were managed and maintained either by the project developer or a homeowners association. Rooms were rented on a best-efforts basis (at times, by a hired local operator) without the benefit of aggressive marketing or a widespread reach to attract vacationers. Today, the industry has shifted its strategy toward the outright sale of the hotel management opportunity to nationally-affiliated hotel companies that operate the properties like a conventional hotel operation. This has been achieved by separately deeding all of the hotel-like features mentioned above as individual commercial condominium units (including maids' closets on each floor). The commercial condos are then sold to a hotel operating company. Along with rental agreements from the individual condo buyers, this allows the property to be managed as if it were a hotel. From the traveler's

---

* Reprinted with permission of Thomson Reuters/West and HVS International.

perspective, the property (other than having larger guest room facilities) seems to offer an experience identical to that of a luxury resort hotel in terms of services and amenities.

Financial benefits. From the condominium unit buyer's point of view, this type of development can offer enhanced financial returns if his unit is placed in a rental pool. During periods when the owner is not using the unit, the hotel operator manages it. By capitalizing on the operator's national affiliation, reservation system, brand recognition, and management expertise, unit owners are more likely to receive a higher amount of rental income despite having to surrender a portion of the unit's revenues to the operator.

This also is an interesting approach for hotel operators. In some respects, it is similar to owning a hotel outright, because the operator does own some real estate (i.e., the commercial condominium units appurtenant to running hotel services). However, individual condo buyers own the actual guest rooms. As a result, the overall cash investment by the operator is less than that in typical hotel deals. To a certain extent, the operator essentially is given a long-term management contract, because a long-term relationship is expected to exist with the condo owners. The difference lies in the fact that condo hotel operators are able manage the properties without a specified termination date, since they actually own real property in the form of the commercial condominium units.

Terms of management agreement. In order to place a unit in the rental pool, a management and rental agreement is signed between the unit owner and the hotel management company. The agreement has the following key provisions. A portion of the revenues received from the nightly sales of rental pool units is to flow through to the condo owners with the hotel management company retaining the balance. A usage provision stipulates frequency and notice requirements for owner usage of condos. An FF & E (furniture, fixtures and equipment) reserve is to be maintained by the hotel operator. The FF & E furnishing packages (including replacements) within the individual units must comply with specified standards. Failure to comply with the standards may either necessitate immediate refurbishment (at the unit owner's expense) or the expulsion of the non-conforming unit from the rental pool. An owner is not obligated to place his unit in the rental pool. Directly renting a unit to others or hiring a third-party property manager to do so is possible. However, this option usually is not a viable approach, since guests may not have full privileges in areas controlled by the hotel operator.

Financial responsibility for maintenance and repairs of common space is pro-rated among unit owners based on the number of their shares. A homeowners association normally oversees the collection of dues from unit owners. The dues typically cover reserves, common area maintenance, property insurance, and utilities. Real estate taxes are paid directly by unit owners and the hotel operator pays the costs of its operations (e.g., salaries and other direct hotel expenses).

Attractions for developers. Developers of condo hotel projects are attracted to the owner/operator approach because it enables them to quickly monetize the management function of the property. In essence, the sale of the hotel management opportunity is akin to a condo unit that can be sold for immediate profit. If the hotel management opportunity is sold upfront (during the sell-out phase of the residential units), the developer may be able to receive revenues from renting the completed but unsold units to hotel guests.

G. REAL ESTATE INTERESTS AS SECURITIES

In this section we consider whether those who offer to sell interests in real estate are considered as selling "securities" and thus become subject to federal and state securities laws. The subject is an important one, although the detailed consequences of classification of an offering as a security are far beyond the scope of this book. In general, several results follow. The offering may become subject to the rather onerous registration requirements of the Securities Act of 1933 or to similar state laws in some jurisdictions. In some states, a state agency may exercise even more direct supervision over the offering, requiring that it be found "fair, just, and reasonable" or in compliance with some similar standard before it can be sold. Further, the Securities Exchange Act of 1934 may raise problems for the offeror; the sales people may need to be licensed by the SEC, the offeror may be subject to certain record-keeping requirements, and may be limited by law in the ability to offer financing for the units. Finally, the stringent antifraud provisions of federal and some state securities acts may subject the offeror to a much stronger probability of liability for misstatements or half-truths than would be the case under common law fraud rules.

The result is that real estate developers are exceedingly reluctant to have their offerings considered securities. Our present concern is to discover the circumstances under which that label will be attached to them. Although this section appears in the chapter of the casebook dealing with condominiums and other forms of unit ownership, the securities question is not limited to these ownership formats. It is conceivable that even a sale of raw land might be regarded as a security under some circumstances. It is in the condominium context, however, that the question has been most widely considered and debated.

Our discussion here focuses on the sales of real estate interests which give the purchaser the right to personal possession, at least for part of each year. If the property is to be rented out to others full-time, and the offeror of the interest or his affiliates will be involved in managing or renting it, there is scarcely any question that a security is being offered. Thus limited partnership interests, or even tenancies in common, in rental apartment buildings and commercial properties are quite obviously securities if there is some centralized management (as is nearly always the case). But property which the purchaser can occupy personally certainly is not a security in most cases. It would be, to say the least, quite a surprise if the courts began to hold that the typical suburban homebuilder was actually selling securities!

The matter might be thought a bit more debatable in the case of cooperatives, since a co-op buyer does receive a share of stock, an instrument traditionally associated with the concept of a security. But in United Housing Foundation, Inc. v. Forman, 421 U.S. 837, 95 S.Ct. 2051, 44 L.Ed.2d 621 (1975), the Supreme Court rejected such an argument. It held that a security was an "investment contract," and that no such contract was involved when a cooperative unit was sold:

> There is no doubt that purchasers in this housing cooperative sought to obtain a decent home at an attractive price. But that type of economic interest characterizes every form of commercial dealing. What distinguishes a security transaction—and what is absent here—is an investment where one parts with his money in the hope of receiving profits from the efforts of others, and not where he purchases a commodity for personal consumption or living quarters for personal use.

The entity which sponsored and developed the cooperative in *Forman* was a non-profit organization, but it is doubtful that this matters. In Grenader v. Spitz, 537 F.2d 612 (2d Cir.1976), the court reached the same result with respect to a conversion cooperative sponsored by a profit-oriented converter.

The extremes of characterization are thus defined. If one purchases solely for one's own use and occupancy, there is no security, while if one purchases for the purpose of making money through the efforts of others, a security is being sold. Between these poles, however, many intermediate situations exist.

SECURITIES AND EXCHANGE COMMISSION V. KIRKLAND

United States District Court, Middle District of Florida, 2007
521 F. Supp. 2d 1281

JOHN ANTOON II, DISTRICT JUDGE. . . . If it sounds too good to be true, you may be listening to Patrick Kirkland. While to investors he boasted thirty years' experience in the real estate development business and seven years' experience developing senior triplexes—a dormitory-style, shared living concept for senior citizens—he failed to mention investors' class action and individual lawsuits, two Desist and Refrain Orders and a Temporary Restraining Order issued by the state of California against him and his companies, falsified leases, inflated appraisal values, and relatively nonexistent leasing patterns in the units he was selling as a "sure thing" investment opportunity. His investors, who were assured an estimated annual net cash profit of, in some cases, $31,000, were losing money quickly because the little rental income taken in was insufficient to cover the expenses of operating the developments, much less cover the mortgages on the properties. As his investors were sinking, Kirkland was buying houses, apartments, and two engagement rings, each of which cost as much as a luxury car. He was traveling in a "corporate plane" flown by a private pilot; driving a Rolls Royce, a Porsche, and three Lexuses; and living in a home worth more than $4 million. His lavish lifestyle was funded by his investors' initial deposits in his "sure thing" investment concept.

On February 16, 2006, the SEC filed the instant Complaint against Kirkland and his companies. . . . The SEC brings four counts against Kirkland. In Count I, the SEC alleges that Kirkland sold unregistered securities in violation of sections 5(a) and 5(c) of the Securities Act of 1933 ("the Securities Act"), 15 U.S.C. §§ 77e(a) and (b). In Counts II–IV, the SEC alleges that Kirkland committed securities fraud in violation of section 17(a)(1) of the Securities Act, 15 U.S.C. § 77q(a)(1); sections 17(a)(2) and 17(a)(3) of the Securities Act, 15 U.S.C. §§ 77q(a)(2) and (a)(3); and section 10b of the Securities Exchange Act of 1934 ("the Exchange Act"), 15 U.S.C. § 78j(b), and its subsequently promulgated Rule 10b–5, 17 C.F.R. § 240.10b–5. . . .

The primary legal issue and threshold matter for each of the counts asserted against Kirkland is whether his senior triplex offerings constitute an offer or sale of securities within the meaning of the Securities Act. Kirkland admits that he did not register his triplex investments with the SEC, and he has not claimed that he is entitled to any exemption of the registration requirement. Thus, if the offerings are securities, Kirkland violated sections 5(a) and 5(c) of the Securities Act, 15 U.S.C. §§ 77e(a) and (b).[3] Kirkland argues that the triplex offerings

---

[3]   Sections 5(a) and (c) of the Securities Act "make it unlawful, absent an exemption from registration, for any person to make use of the means or instruments of transportation or communication in interstate commerce or of the mails to offer to sell [or] to sell . . . any security . . . when no registration statement has been filed or is in effect as to the security." *SEC v. Chem. Trust*, No. 00–8015–CIV, 2000 WL 33231600, at *9 (S.D.Fla. Dec. 19, 2000); *see also* 15 U.S.C. §§ 77e(a) & (b). In addition to admitting that he did not register his offerings, Kirkland also admits advertising in the Wall Street Journal and Money Magazine, admits utilizing a website generally available to the public, admits sending prospective investors packages detailing the investment opportunity, and admits calling prospective investors, who were located all across the country. Thus, if Kirkland's offerings constitute securities, he has violated the provisions of the Securities Act raised in Count I.

were not securities but instead were fee simple real estate transfers that are not regulated by the SEC. For the following reasons, the Court determines that Kirkland was engaged in the offering and sale of unregistered securities and that summary judgment must be entered as to Count I.

The definition of a security includes stock, of course, and, among other things, investment contracts. 15 U.S.C. § 77b(a)(1). Congress intentionally defined "the term 'security' in sufficiently broad and general terms so as to include within the definition the many types of instruments that in our commercial world fall within the ordinary concept of a security." *United Hous. Found., Inc. v. Forman,* 421 U.S. 837, 847–48, 95 S.Ct. 2051, 44 L.Ed.2d 621 (1975) (quoting H.R.Rep. No. 85, at 11, 73d Cong. (1st Sess.1933)). This broad construction was designed "to afford the investing public a full measure of protection." *SEC v. W.J. Howey Co.,* 328 U.S. 293, 298, 66 S.Ct. 1100, 90 L.Ed. 1244 (1946). Courts are therefore called upon to look at the substance and "economic realit[ies]" of the underlying transaction rather than its label or form. *Id.* at 298–99, 66 S.Ct. 1100; *see also Tcherepnin v. Knight,* 389 U.S. 332, 336, 88 S.Ct. 548, 19 L.Ed.2d 564 (1967).

The Securities Act does not define 'investment contract,' but the United States Supreme Court has defined it as:

> a contract, transaction or scheme whereby a person invests his money in a common enterprise and is led to expect profits solely from the efforts of the promoter or a third party, it being immaterial whether the shares in the enterprise are evidenced by formal certificates or by nominal interests in the physical assets employed in the enterprise.

Howey, 328 U.S. at 298–99, 66 S.Ct. 1100. "It embodies a flexible rather than a static principle, one that is capable of adaptation to meet the countless and variable schemes devised by those who seek the use of the money of others on the promise of profits." *Id.* at 299, 66 S.Ct. 1100. It reaches "[n]ovel, uncommon, or irregular devices, whatever they appear to be." *SEC v. C.M. Joiner Leasing Corp.,* 320 U.S. 344, 351, 64 S.Ct. 120, 88 L.Ed. 88 (1943). An investment contract may be present even "where the tangible interest which is sold has intrinsic value independent of the success of the enterprise as a whole." *Howey,* 328 U.S. at 301, 66 S.Ct. 1100.

Real estate transactions do not typically constitute investment contracts or securities, particularly when the purchaser is "interested in acquiring housing rather than making an investment for profit." *Forman,* 421 U.S. at 860, 95 S.Ct. 2051. Certain real estate investments may constitute securities that must be registered, however, when the sale itself is tied to a collateral rental or service agreement, when the purchase is motivated by economic inducements and expected profits, when the purchaser expects to participate in a profit-sharing or rental pooling arrangement upon completing the transaction, or when the transaction includes restrictions limiting the owner's control over the property. *Guidelines as to the Applicability of the Federal Securities Laws to Offers and Sales of Condominiums or Units in a Real Estate Development, Securities Act*, 1973 WL 158443, Release No. 33–5347, 1 Fed. Sec. L. Rep. (CCH) ¶ 1049 (Jan. 4, 1973), *available at* 1973 WL 158443 (hereinafter Release, 1973 WL 158443); *see also Howey*, 328 U.S. 293, 299–301, 66 S.Ct. 1100. The SEC has advised that "the offering of [real estate] units in conjunction with any one of the following will cause the offering to be viewed as an offering of securities in the form of investment contracts":

> 1. The condominiums, with any rental arrangement or other similar service, are offered and sold with emphasis on the economic benefits to the purchaser to be derived from the managerial efforts of the promoter, or a third party designated or arranged for by the promoter, from rental of the units[;]
>
> 2. The offering of participation in a rental pool arrangement; and
>
> 3. The offering of a rental or similar arrangement whereby the purchaser must hold his unit available for rental for any part of the year, must use an exclusive rental agent or is otherwise materially restricted in his occupancy or rental of his unit.

Release, 1973 WL158443, at *3. By contrast, when real estate units "are not offered and sold with emphasis on the economic benefits to the purchaser to be derived from the managerial efforts of others, and assuming that no plan to avoid the registration requirements of the Securities Act is involved," the unit owner "may enter into a non-pooled rental arrangement with an agent not designated or required to be used as a condition of purchase" and the transaction will not involve the sale of a security. *Id.*

With these guidelines in mind, the Court analyzes Kirkland's triplex offerings under the three-pronged *Howey* test to determine if they are investment contracts. Under this test, an offering is an "investment contract" if there is: "(1) an investment of money, (2) a common enterprise, and (3) the expectation of profits to be derived solely from the efforts of others." *SEC v. Unique Fin. Concepts, Inc.*, 196 F.3d 1195, 1199 (11th Cir.1999) (quoting *Villeneuve v. Advanced Bus. Concepts Corp.*, 698 F.2d 1121, 1124 (11th Cir.1983)); *see also Hocking v. Dubois*, 885 F.2d 1449, 1455 (9th Cir.1989).

     1. An Investment of Money. Howey's first prong requires that there be a "commitment of assets in such a manner as to subject oneself to

financial loss." *SEC v. Comcoa Ltd.*, 855 F.Supp. 1258, 1260
(S.D.Fla.1994) (citing *Stowell v. Ted S. Finkel Inv. Servs., Inc.*, 489
F.Supp. 1209, 1223 (S.D.Fla.1980)). One hundred nineteen people
invested $70.3 million into Kirkland's scheme. These funds represent
either deposits on reserved triplex units or outright purchases made
between 1999 and February 2006. Some developments were sold out of
triplex units, others had more than half of the units sold before the SEC
initiated its action against Kirkland.

Investors' deposit money was not placed in escrow as in the typical
real estate transaction, but was instead placed in Kirkland's bank
accounts, from which he withdrew his employees' salaries and
commissions, funds for new construction projects and real estate, and
money to provide for his own lavish lifestyle. Also unlike a typical real
estate transaction, the same units were often promised to multiple
investors. James Johnson, Tropical Village's accountant, stated that
sometimes more than one name would be assigned to a unit because the
first deposit would fall through, so the unit would be resold. Other times,
however, the same unit would be inexplicably double-sold to different
investors at the direction of Kirkland. At closing, the contracted units
were shuffled around depending on actual availability.

Kirkland solicited investors with nationally-run ads placed in The
Wall Street Journal, The New York Times, Money Magazine, Smart
Money, The Los Angeles Times, and the San Francisco Chronicle. The ads
marketed the triplexes as investment opportunities, not as places to live.
Cf. Forman, 421 U.S. at 858, 95 S.Ct. 2051 ("What distinguishes a
security transaction—and what is absent here—is an investment where
one parts with his money in the hope of receiving profits from the efforts
of others, and not where he purchases a commodity for personal
consumption or living quarters for personal use.").

Although Kirkland does not assert any argument with respect to the
first prong of *Howey,* it is instructive to detail a typical transaction. If an
investor wanted to purchase a triplex unit, he or she would initially put
up $6,000 as partial payment of the 10% deposit of the total purchase
price of the unit.[6] Later, the remainder of the 10% would be due. As an
incentive for investors to close on a unit, Kirkland would offer to "rent
out" the buyer's unit for either 6 months or 12 months, in order to cover
the investor's mortgage payments until the unit was rented; Kirkland
promised investors positive cash flow. Kirkland also had Tropical Village
pay 3% of the closing costs to offset the time it took to build the triplexes.

---

[6]   The purchase price of a unit, containing 5–7 bedrooms available to rent, ranged from
$595,000 to $825,000. At times, a lower price would be offered, but just prior to closing, Kirkland
would represent to the investor that the value of the investment had just increased. Kirkland
sometimes "purchased" a unit from Tropical Village at a higher price to serve as a comparable,
though inflated, sale for the next appraisal.

In some instances, he also held a second mortgage on the property, which was not disclosed in the HUD statements.

Kirkland promised and contracted to return the entirety of an investor's deposit if the investor was unable to secure funding or if the investor visited the units and changed his or her mind about the investment. Many investors wanted out for either of these reasons, but Kirkland did not refund their money easily. He told investors that they were in breach of contract and that he was entitled to keep the deposit as damages. Sometimes, when threatened with a lawsuit, Kirkland would refund deposits. Others still wait for their earnest money to be returned.

Investors made their "purchases" with the expectation of returning a profit. The investors' risk of financial loss was exacerbated by their lack of control over the investments and by their complete dependence on the efforts of Kirkland, his staff, and the management companies he hired for the endeavor's success. A large number of people invested a great deal of money into Kirkland's failing scheme. The first prong of the *Howey* test is satisfied.

2.   *Common Enterprise.* Two types of commonality may satisfy *Howey's* second prong, the common enterprise element. Vertical commonality exists where " 'the fortunes of the investor are interwoven with and dependent on the efforts and success of those seeking the investment or of third parties.' " *Unique Fin. Concepts,* 196 F.3d at 1199 (quoting *Villeneuve,* 698 F.2d at 1124). Horizontal commonality exists where there is "a pooling of interests or profits" in the transaction. *See Hocking,* 885 F.2d at 1459.

The Eleventh Circuit has held that vertical commonality is sufficient to satisfy *Howey's* common enterprise element, finding it more "flexible" and less "stringent" than horizontal commonality. *Unique Fin. Concepts,* 196 F.3d at 1200 n. 4. As the SEC has pointed out, however, Kirkland's triplex investment scheme satisfies the Eleventh Circuit's standard as well as the stricter standard of horizontal commonality, thus easily meeting *Howey's* second requirement that the scheme involve a common enterprise.

a.   *Vertical Commonality.* If the investors' money is tied to the efforts and success of someone else—whether it be the promoter or a third party—vertical commonality is present in the scheme. *Id.* This inquiry largely overlaps with *Howey's* final prong. " 'The thrust of the common enterprise test is that the investors have no desire to perform the chores necessary for a return.' " *Id.* at 1200 (quoting *Eberhardt v. Waters,* 901 F.2d 1578, 1580–81 (11th Cir.1990)). They are passive as opposed to active investors.

Kirkland's triplex offerings satisfy the vertical commonality test because the investors had little to no control over the success of the endeavor or the future of their investments. That control rested in the hands of Kirkland and the management company that he chose and controlled. Together, they advertised for tenants, chose and approved tenants, collected rent, and maintained the premises. Investors could neither assume control of the rental process nor choose the rate at which their units were rented. Indeed, the investors purchased their units under the expectation that a certain rate would be charged to tenants, but some found that the rental rates were unilaterally and surreptitiously lowered in an attempt to attract tenants to an undesirable living arrangement. Kirkland and the management company controlled the offering of rental incentives, which lowered any expected or projected return the investors would hope to earn. Kirkland decided to stop requiring background checks of tenants, which, together with the incentives offered, harmed the reputations of the developments because such decisions attracted a less than desirable tenant population. Kirkland, the management company, and the sales agents intentionally concealed information about occupancy rates and tenant interest from investors. Some investors were not even allowed to see the units they owned when they visited the property because they were told that the tenants did not want to be disturbed.

Kirkland urges the Court to look at the purchase contracts and at the existence of homeowners' associations and determine that the investors maintained ultimate control of their units. However, any control held by the investors or by the homeowners' association was illusory; the management company took care of everything. Indeed, it was this promise that lured the distantly-located, unsophisticated investors into Kirkland's scheme.

    b.   *Horizontal Commonality.* A scheme has horizontal commonality if the investors pool their assets and "give up any claim to profits or losses attributable to their particular investments in return for a pro rata share of the profits of the enterprise." *Hocking,* 885 F.2d at 1459. Such investors "make their collective fortunes dependent on the success of a single common enterprise." *Id.* Rental pooling agreements meet the standard for horizontal commonality. *Release,* 1973 WL 158443, at *3.

    Kirkland's senior triplex investments were offered with the promise of a rental pooling agreement. Although Kirkland disputes that he played any role in implementing the pooling arrangement, ample evidence indicates otherwise. The pooling arrangement, in which investors theoretically stood to profit from the development as a whole even if their individual units remained unoccupied, was a major selling point and a strong incentive for investors. Kirkland's accountant testified that "because the project wasn't working as planned, [Kirkland] came up with the pooling idea to make it sound like there's gonna be some revenue coming out. But, it didn't matter how you . . . cut it, there was never going to be revenue—There wasn't enough revenue to support the expenses. . . .

And so, yes, there is a pooling system. All it means is that the losses are shared equally.". . .

The record evidence reveals that the pooling arrangement went hand-in-hand with the purchase of a triplex. The promise of rental income even in times of vacancy was a major selling point to hesitant investors. Based on the horizontal commonality evidenced by the rental pooling agreement, Kirkland's triplex offerings satisfy the second *Howey* element of common enterprise.

3. *Expectation of Profits Produced by the Efforts of Others.* Kirkland's primary argument centers on the last prong of the *Howey* test, which he correctly identifies as the most litigated of the three. Although *Howey* indicated that the expectation of profits must "come *solely* from the efforts of others," 328 U.S. at 301, 66 S.Ct. 1100 (emphasis added), many courts, including the Eleventh Circuit, have rejected a literal or strict interpretation and have instead interpreted "solely" to mean substantially or primarily. The Eleventh Circuit's inquiry asks " 'whether the efforts made by those other than the investor are the undeniably significant ones, those essential managerial efforts which affect the failure or success of the enterprise.' " *Unique Fin. Concepts,* 196 F.3d at 1201 (citing *SEC v. Koscot Interplanetary, Inc.,* 497 F.2d 473, 479 (5th Cir.1974), and quoting *Glenn W. Turner Enters.,* 474 F.2d at 482). In *Forman,* the Supreme Court removed the emphasis from the word "solely" and held that "the touchstone" of the test is "an investment in a common venture premised on a reasonable expectation of profits to be derived from the entrepreneurial or managerial efforts of others." 421 U.S. at 852, 95 S.Ct. 2051. An investor's degree of control over his investment is to be determined practically. *See Hocking,* 885 F.2d at 1460; *SEC v. Merch. Capital, LLC,* 483 F.3d 747, 754–55 (11th Cir.2007). Even under a strict interpretation of "solely," however, Kirkland's scheme satisfies the final element of *Howey.*

In an investment contract scheme, "the investor is 'attracted solely by the prospects of a return on his investment . . . [and is not] motivated by a desire to use or consume the item purchased—to occupy the land or to develop it themselves.' " *Forman,* 421 U.S. at 852–53, 95 S.Ct. 2051 (quoting *Howey,* 328 U.S. at 300, 66 S.Ct. 1100). The level of control that investors have over their properties is key to determining whether the scheme involves an investment contract. *Unique Fin. Concepts,* 196 F.3d at 1201. "If the investor retains the ability to control the profitability of his investment, the agreement is no security." *Albanese v. Fla. Nat'l Bank of Orlando,* 823 F.2d 408, 410 (11th Cir.1987). If the scheme is designed so that the investor can remain passive while reaping the benefits of the investment, it is likely that *Howey's* third prong has been satisfied. *See Hocking,* 885 F.2d at 1461.

Kirkland's sales agents report that while an investor could live in one of the units he or she owned if the investor had no children and could perhaps decorate the unit, the investor could not modify it, control the price at which the unit was rented, or hire an independent rental management company. The investors were not involved in any aspect of purchasing the land or of designing, constructing, furnishing, or decorating the units. They were not involved in advertising, collecting rent, or doing anything beyond making mortgage and expense payments. The advertisements indicated that the purchase price included management and financing.

Investor Adams was told that the management company was in place and doing everything—running ads, managing the properties, collecting rent, and issuing checks to the Investors. Investor Shanahan was also assured that he would not have to do any work to maintain his investment because the onsite management company handled everything. Investor Dimapasok was told that he did not "even need to manage the property" and that it "was being done" for him. The motto of the company appeared to be that investors just had to sit back and collect their checks.

A sales letter to a potential investor stated:

> Tropical Village, Inc. oversees the management company and does this on a not-for-profit basis. **Each owner *will not* be required to be involved in the day-to-day operation of the triplex.** The management staff will be responsible for advertising, showing potential residents the available bedrooms, [and] maintenance of the interiors/exteriors and the grounds. The management company will also be responsible for the collection of rents, paying bills, remitting checks to the investor(s) and will handle the day-to-day bookkeeping operation.

As indicated above in the vertical commonality analysis, any control held by the investors "was illusory and insufficient to disqualify the investment as a security." *See Eberhardt,* 901 F.2d at 1581: *see also Albanese,* 823 F.2d at 412; *Plunkett v. Francisco,* 430 F.Supp. 235, 239 (N.D.Ga.1977). Although there is little evidence regarding the relative sophistication of the investors, the very distance at which they lived from the developments underscores the fact that the investors never intended to manage their units. *See Howey,* 328 U.S. at 299–300, 66 S.Ct. 1100 ("They are offering this opportunity to persons who reside in distant localities and who lack the equipment and experience requisite to the cultivation, harvesting and marketing of the citrus products. Such persons have no desire to occupy the land or to develop it themselves; they are attracted solely by the prospects of a return on their investment."); *Hocking,* 885 F.2d at 1461. Investors' sole purpose was to provide funding for Kirkland's myriad schemes; in return, they were assured substantial returns on their cash investments.

Although the investment scheme in *Howey* concerned a stake in a citrus fruit enterprise and Kirkland's involves triplex units for seniors, there is little to substantively distinguish either setup. As the Supreme Court in *Howey* concluded:

> Thus all of the elements of a profit-seeking business venture are present here. The investors provide the capital and share in the earnings and profits; the promoters manage, control and operate the enterprise. It follows that the arrangements whereby the investors' interests are made manifest involve investment contracts, regardless of the legal terminology in which such contracts are clothed. The investment contracts in this instance take the form of land sales contracts, warranty deeds and service contracts which respondents offer to prospective investors. And respondents' failure to abide by the statutory and administrative rules in making such offerings . . . cannot be sanctioned under the Act.

Howey, 328 U.S. at 300, 66 S.Ct. 1100. Kirkland offered and sold unregistered securities in violation of sections 5(a) and 5(c) of the Securities Act. . . .

[The court proceeded to conclude that Kirkland committed securities fraud in violation of section 17(a) of the Securities Act, section 10(b) of the Securities Exchange Act, and Rule 10b–5, pointing to the following omissions and misrepresentations by Kirkland: (1) baseless profit projections based on false tenant occupancy rates, (2) false statements regarding high tenant demand for the triplexes, (3) failure to disclose California Desist and Refrain Orders and a Temporary Restraining Order, and (4) failure to disclose investor lawsuits.]

NOTES

1.   *Rental agreements and the SEC Release.* The SEC issued Securities Act Release No. 5347 (January 4, 1973), referred to in *Kirkland*, in response to its concern that few developers were registering condominium projects even though it believed many such offerings qualified for registration. The Release states that a condominium is an investment contract if it is offered in conjunction with a rental pooling arrangement or a mandatory or restrictive rental contract. In addition, the SEC added an "economic emphasis" test that requires a condominium to be registered if it is offered with "any rental arrangement or other similar service [that is] offered and sold with *emphasis on the economic benefits* to the purchaser to be derived from the managerial efforts of the promoter, or a third party designated or arranged for by the promoter, from rental of the units."

Suppose a buyer contacts a real estate broker for aid in finding a condominium for purchase as an investment. With the encouragement of the broker, the buyer signs an agreement to purchase a condominium unit in a resort complex from a third party who is not the original developer. In the course of the purchase transaction, the broker informs the buyer that a rental pooling arrangement ("RPA") is available from another third party (perhaps an affiliate of the project's developer) and supplies the buyer with information concerning the unit's daily average rental. The broker also assures the buyer that all future rentals of the unit can be handled by the RPA. Shortly after the buyer executes the purchase agreement, the broker presents an RPA agreement which the buyer also signs. Is the broker engaged in the sale of a security or investment contract for purposes of the *Howey* test? See Hocking v. Dubois, 885 F.2d 1449 (9th Cir. 1989) (en banc) (Ninth Circuit held, in 6–5 decision, that purchase of condominium unit and execution of RPA agreement constituted one transaction for purposes of *Howey* and, assuming all of the three *Howey* standards are satisfied, an investment contract would exist). Accord: Adams v. Hyannis Harborview, Inc., 838 F.Supp. 676 (D. Mass. 1993), aff'd and modified, 73 F.3d 1164 (1st Cir. 1996).

In Revak v. SEC Realty Corp., 18 F.3d 81 (2d Cir. 1994), the Court of Appeals for the Second Circuit held that the sale of Tennessee condominium units marketed primarily to New York investors failed to qualify as securities either under Release 5347 or the application of the *Howey* factors. The developer in *Revak* emphasized to potential purchasers the tax shelter advantages, the appreciation potential and the rental income that units could produce. Purchasers were also offered the option of an on-site management contract with a Tennessee corporation. The Court of Appeals ruled that the "common enterprise" requirement had not been satisfied. It observed that the management contract with the Tennessee firm did not entail the pooling of rental income and that there was no evidence that the developer, as opposed to the Tennessee firm, shared in the profits with the purchasers. Thus neither "horizontal commonality" nor "strict vertical commonality" were present. Because both of these elements were missing, the *Revak* concluded that the common enterprise prong was not satisfied. Accordingly, the sale of the condominium units did not constitute the sale of an "investment contract."

For further consideration of *Hocking, Revak* and related issues, see Elena Marty-Nelson, When Is a Real Estate Interest a "Security"?, 17 Prac. Real Est. Law. 7 (May 2001); Edward T. DeSilva, Comment, *Hocking v. Dubois*: Applying the Securities Laws to Condominium Resales, 58 Ford. L. Rev. 1121 (1990); Peter A. MacLaren, Note, Profits in Paradise: When Resort Condominiums Qualify as Investment Contracts, 19 Golden Gate U.L. Rev. 177 (1989); William J. Ohle, Note, *Hocking v. Dubois*: The Ninth Circuit Finds a Security in the Secondary Resort Condominium Market, 27 Willamette L. Rev. 147 (1991). With respect to condominium hotels, see James McGuire & Daniel Brown, Are Condo Hotels Subject to SEC

Regulations?, 20 N.Y. Real Est. L. Rep. (Feb. 2006), at 1; SEC No-Action Letter, Intrawest Corp., Nov. 8, 2002, http://www.404.gov/divisions/corpfin/cf-noaction/intrawt110802.htm (last visited Dec. 23, 2008).

2. *Time-shares as "securities."* Is there something about time-sharing that makes it more susceptible to the "security" characterization than an offering of year-round condominiums? Bear in mind the much more powerful role which the professional manager (often related to the developer) has in a time-sharing project. Even so, a security must involve some hope or expectation of profits from the efforts of management. Would any (or all) of the following types of hoped-for profits suffice?

(a) The developer assures buyers that their units will be salable on the market at greatly appreciated prices in the future. [Is this any different from assurances sometimes made by salespeople with respect to all types of real estate, including detached houses?]

(b) The developer points out that, by buying a time-share unit now, one can save large sums over the years in vacation expenses, because the time-share unit's cost will be relatively stable while alternative types of vacations are likely to rise rapidly in price.

(c) The developer, by the terms of the time-sharing documents, has the right to rent out the unit if the owner does not occupy it during his or her scheduled interval; if this occurs, some portion of the rent collected will be applied against the owner's annual assessment.

(d) A program for the exchange of units in various projects is offered.

See Patrick J. Rohan & Daniel A. Furlong, Timesharing and Consumer Protection: A Precis for Attorneys, 10 Wm. Mitchell L. Rev. 13, 20–25 (1984); Joseph W. Byrne, Securities Regulation of Time-Sharing Resort Condominiums, 7 Real Est. L.J. 3 (1978); Peter M. Gunnar, Regulation of Resort Time-Sharing, 57 Or. L. Rev. 31 (1978).

Initially, the SEC indicated a willingness to issue no-action letters for time-sharing condominiums. See, e.g., Jockey Club Inc., 1974 WL 7206 (May 10, 1974). [A "no-action" letter is a letter in which the SEC responds to a written inquiry from an investor by indicating that the SEC would take "no action" if an offering proceeds without registration.] However, in June 1974, the SEC directed its staff not to issue no-action letters concerning time-sharing plans because of the possibility of misunderstandings of the SEC's position in "this rapidly evolving area." The Innisfree Corporation, CCH Fed. Sec. L. Rep. 74–75 ¶ 79,935 (June 19, 1974). This ban on time-sharing no-action letters continues to be SEC policy. See SEC Release No. 33–6253 (October 28, 1980).

In Wals v. Fox Hills Dev. Corp., 24 F.3d 1016 (7th Cir. 1994), the Walses purchased "Week 5" (a week in February) of an apartment in the Fox Hills Golf Villa Condominium from its developer. At the same time, the Walses entered into a "flexible time" agreement with the developer (renewable annually) under which the Walses could swap their February week for a summer week. The plaintiffs also entered into another agreement, called the "4-share" program and also renewable annually, under which the plaintiffs agreed not to occupy the unit during the summer week (despite the swap agreement) but to instead allow the developer to rent that unit. The plaintiffs would receive the rent collected, minus the developer's 30% fee. The plaintiffs argued that this agreement converted the sale of the condominium into the sale of an investment contract which developer failed to register under the Securities Act of 1933, thus entitling the plaintiffs to rescind the sale. The Seventh Circuit disagreed, concluding that the 1933 Act required both vertical commonality (satisfied by the combined sale and rental agreement) and horizontal commonality (lacking because there was no pooling of interest among the investors):

> It makes no difference that the rental received by the plaintiffs was not the rental of their own property, which was week 5 of "their" condominium unit. In effect they swapped week 5 for a subsequent week, then rented the subsequent week and received the rental (if there was any, for of course the developer might be unsuccessful in his effort to rent it). Still, they did not receive an undivided share of some pool of rentals or profits. They received the rental on a single apartment, albeit one not owned by them (for it was not their week).

> There was a pooling of weeks, in a sense, because the plaintiffs selected their summer swap week from a "pool" of available weeks. But there was not a pooling of profits, which is essential to horizontal commonality.

Fox Hills, 24 F.3d at 1019. For the contrary view that only vertical commonality should be sufficient to satisfy the *Howey* test, see Jonathan E. Shook, Note, The Common Enterprise Test: Getting Horizontal or Going Vertical in *Wals v. Fox Hills Development Corp.*, 30 Tulsa L.J. 727 (1995). One federal appellate decision has found "horizontal commonality" in a relatively unusual variant on time-sharing. See Teague v. Bakker, 35 F.3d 978 (4th Cir. 1994) (trial court erred in directing verdict in favor of the Reverend Jim Bakker on plaintiff's claim that sale of "lifetime partnerships" in Heritage Grand Hotel constituted the sale of an "investment contract" under the federal Securities Act).

   3.   *Tenancy-in-common (TIC) interests: "securities" or not?* A seller of commercial real estate can face a significant federal tax burden (with capital gains taxed at 15% and recaptured depreciation at 25%). Internal Revenue Code § 1031 permits a taxpayer to defer federal taxation on such a transfer if the property is "exchanged solely for property of like kind." 26 U.S.C.A. § 1031(a)(1). All commercial real estate is considered like-kind, so a taxpayer could exchange an apartment building for an office building without recognition of tax liability. But if the taxpayer sold an office building and invested the proceeds in a real estate investment trust or a real estate

limited partnership, such an exchange is not a like-kind exchange for purposes of § 1031.

Suppose instead that the taxpayer sells an office building and instead purchases a fractional share in another office building, held in tenancy in common (TIC) with 15 other investors. Has the taxpayer acquired an interest in real estate qualifying for § 1031 nonrecognition, or has the taxpayer acquired an interest in a business entity that does not qualify as a like-kind exchange? Prior to 2002, sponsors of such TIC investments found marketing such interests difficult because of the perceived risk that the IRS might treat such investments as failing to qualify for like-kind exchange with direct ownership of real estate interests. In 2002, however, the IRS issued Revenue Procedure 2002–22, which sets forth the conditions under which a TIC interest qualifies as direct ownership of real estate rather than a security for § 1031 purposes. These conditions include:

- each owner must hold title as a tenant in common under state law;

- the number of co-owners must be 35 or fewer;

- while the co-owners may enter into periodic management agreements, the co-owners must retain the right to approve the hiring of any manager and any lease or sale of the property

- each co-owner must approve the creation of any lien on the property and must share in the indebtedness secured by that lien in proportion to their undivided interest; and

- each co-owner must share in all revenues and costs of the property in proportion to their undivided interest.

Rev. Proc. 2002–22, 2002–1 C.B. 733. With the certainty associated with Rev. Proc. 2002–22, the volume of TIC offerings has exploded.

Just because a TIC offering is not a security for § 1031 exchange purposes, however, does not mean that a TIC offering is not a security for purposes of the federal securities laws. In some TIC offerings, the TIC investors buy the property subject to a long-term lease with the sponsor or an affiliate. As one commentator explains:

> The sponsor or its affiliate leases the whole property from the TIC owners in exchange for an agreed upon amount of monthly income or rent payable to the TIC owners. Under this master lease, the sponsor or its affiliate is the only tenant. As the master lessee, the sponsor or its affiliate is ultimately responsible for all maintenance, leasing, and management-related obligations that arise in the operation of syndicated TIC investments. The master lease TIC structure requires little or no management on the part of the TIC owners. Because those who invest in an affiliated TIC depend on the undeniably significant entreprenurial and managerial efforts of the sponsor or its affiliate for the profitability of their investment,

players on both sides of the turf war generally agree that this structure is inherently a security.

David Rich, Betting the Farm: The TIC Turf War and Why TICs Constitute Investment Contracts Under Federal Securities Laws, 1 Wm. & Mary Bus. L. Rev. 451 (2010). See also Frederick Rosenberg, TICs—What Attorneys Need to Understand, 20 No. 2 PIABA B.J. 175 (2013); Elizabeth Ayres Whitman, A "Tic"ing Time Bomb: Rule 506 Meets Section 1031, 12 Ford. J. Corp. & Fin. L. 121 (2007); OMNI Brokerage, Inc. Argus Realty Investors, L.P. PASSCO Companies, LLC, SEC No-Action Letter, 2009 WL 153818 (Jan. 14, 2009) (noting that based upon facts presented, the sale of undivided TIC interests would constitute the sale of securities). TIC interests that constitute securities would have to be registered under Section 5 of the 1933 Act unless their sale satisfies the requirements of the safe harbor under Rule 506 of Regulation D, 17 C.F.R. § 230.506. Under this safe harbor, a TIC offering made only to accredited investors could not involve general solicitation or general advertisement in connection with the offering, and resales of the TIC interests are not available without registration or an exemption. Whitman, supra, at 131–132.

4. *Impact of state securities laws.* State securities statutes or "blue sky" laws may impose registration requirements on developers similar to those in the federal setting. See, e.g., West's Ann. Cal. Corp. Code §§ 25000 et seq.; N.Y. McKinney's Gen. Bus. Law § 352–e(1)(a). Compare All Seasons Resorts, Inc. v. Abrams, 68 N.Y.2d 81, 506 N.Y.S.2d 10, 497 N.E.2d 33 (1986) (seller of memberships in campgrounds not required to register its offering because memberships held not to constitute "participation interests or investments" in real estate ventures, "cooperative interests in realty," or "securities") with State v. Shade, 104 N.M. 710, 726 P.2d 864 (1986) (time-shares can be securities under state securities law that uses the *Howey* standard).

CHAPTER ELEVEN

INCOME-PRODUCING PROPERTY

• • •

A. FUNDAMENTAL INVESTMENT CONCEPTS

In this chapter, we will study the development and financing of income-producing properties. The income is usually rent. The properties may range from a small house, held by a landlord for rent to a single family, to a regional shopping center with more than a hundred tenants and a floor area of a million square feet. The most common income-producing properties are residential rental apartment buildings. Other types include office buildings, retail buildings, such as shopping centers and "strip malls," industrial parks, free-standing commercial and industrial buildings, hotels, senior and student housing, and manufactured home communities.

Unlike the subdivisions, condominiums, and cooperatives we have already studied, the properties with which we are concerned in this chapter are not built for sale to end users, but to keep as investments. The developer usually anticipates retaining ownership for a number of years after construction is completed to obtain the income and the tax deductions that the project will generate. Unlike the land speculator, the developer is not looking principally toward appreciation in property values as a source of investment return. Rather, the investment return will be derived from tenants' rent payments and from the favorable tax treatment afforded commercial properties. Appreciation in capital value is a welcome side benefit if it occurs.

Therefore, we begin by examining the concepts of cash flow and tax shelter. We will then examine the internal rate of return, which is one of the tools investors use to compare competing investment opportunities. Because an investor's return on a project is substantially affected by the amount of financing that lenders provide ("leverage") and by the type of business entity that the investors use to hold the property, those topics will be analyzed next. The final section of the chapter describes a number of creative financing techniques, including participating mortgages, ground leases, mezzanine loans, and sale-leasebacks, that real estate investors commonly use to increase their return and to make an otherwise unworkable project possible.

1. CASH FLOW

A rental project can generate a return for its owner in two basic ways: *cash flow* and *income tax shelter*. Once the project is completed and is occupied by tenants, the owner expects to receive a fixed amount of gross rent or a variable amount if rent is based on a percentage of the tenants' sales. The owner usually must spend part of the rent on *operating expenses*, such as maintenance, management fees, property taxes, insurance, and utilities. Different types of projects involve different allocations of these expenses between the tenant and landlord. For example, in the usual residential rental project, most or all of the expenses are the landlord's responsibility. In contrast, in a single-tenant free-standing commercial building, the parties may agree that the tenant will reimburse the landlord for all the expenses. This type of lease is called a "net lease" because the landlord need not apply any of the gross rents to operating expenses. Other types of leases may require the tenant to pay some expenses, while the landlord pays others. The difference between the landlord's income, including tenant expense reimbursements, and the property's operating expenses is an important income statement subtotal known as "net operating income."

For nearly all landlords, the gross rent is used to pay the *debt service,* which is the principal and interest on the permanent loan that is secured by the property. The debt service payment amount depends on the principal amount borrowed, the interest rate, the loan maturity, and the structure of the payment schedule. There may be more than one outstanding loan on which payments must be made. Normally, the landlord structures the leases so that rental payments are received with the same frequency that debt service payments are due.

The mathematical relationship among the elements discussed above may be expressed as follows:

	Gross Rents and Expense Reimbursements (if any)
–	Operating Expenses
=	Net Operating Income
–	Debt Service
=	Cash Flow

The illustration we have given is somewhat oversimplified, and other elements may come into play. For example, if the developer has leased, rather than purchased, the land on which the project is constructed (a highly useful technique in some situations, as we shall see later), periodic ground rent payments will be necessary. These payments may be categorized as operating expenses, although economically they are more analogous to debt service payments.

You should study the above equation carefully, because it is fundamentally important in the development and operation of all types of income-producing properties. Although many equity investors in income properties focus on cash flow, it is an imperfect measure of the investment's value because it fails to account for certain factors. For example, a portion of the landlord's debt service payment may reduce the debt's outstanding balance, which would increase the owner's equity. Such a benefit is not reflected in the cash flow. Moreover, fluctuations in the development's capital value due to physical and economic depreciation, changed location values, and other factors often do not affect cash flow in the short term, though they may have great significance in the long term. Some real estate investors tend to discount or ignore these matters, but more sophisticated investors focus on net operating income, because it is the primary driver of real estate market value.

2. TAX SHELTER

Do not make the mistake of assuming that the project's cash flow is identical to income for federal income tax purposes. On the contrary, the taxable income is likely to be very different from the cash flow for two principal reasons. First, while the project's operating expenses are usually entirely deductible from gross rents in computing taxable income, only the interest component of the debt service is deductible. Although the portion of debt service attributable to principal amortization reduces cash flow, it does not reduce taxable income.

Second, the owner of a building that is held for income production is entitled to federal income tax deductions for depreciation (technically termed "cost recovery") of the structure even if the property's value has not actually decreased. We will see later how such depreciation deductions are calculated. They may greatly exceed any actual diminution in the property's value. Therefore, the project's taxable income may be much less than its cash flow and may even produce a net tax loss despite the generation of considerable cash flow in a particular year.

Thus, debt amortization payments make taxable income higher than cash flow, while depreciation deductions make taxable income lower than cash flow. These two factors pull in opposite directions, and the balance between them is critical to many investors. That balance normally changes over time.

While the right to depreciate exists, the amount remains constant, because real estate structures depreciate for tax purposes on a "straight line" basis. For example, the cost of residential rental property is recovered over 27.5 years, which allows the owner to claim an annual cost recovery deduction of 1/27.5 of the building's value. Therefore, if the cost of an apartment building, excluding land and personal property, is

$1,000,000, the building's owner may claim a cost recovery deduction of 1/27.5 of $1 million, or $36,364, in each of the first 27.5 years of its life. The cost of nonresidential property is recovered over 39 years in the same manner.

While the depreciation amount doesn't vary, the portion of each debt service payment that is applied to reduce ("amortize") the outstanding principal balance increases with each succeeding payment on a level-payment fully-amortized mortgage. In the early years of operation, depreciation usually exceeds amortization so that some or all of the property's cash flow is tax-free. At some point in time, however, amortization may exceed depreciation and eventually both may end.

Under earlier versions of the Internal Revenue Code, owners of buildings placed in service before 1987 could use a variety of "accelerated" depreciation deduction formats, some of which allowed much larger deductions in the earlier years than in the later years of a building's life. In the early years, the accelerated depreciation deductions were often large enough to fully "shelter" or offset the project's cash flow and a substantial amount of the taxpayer's other income as well. The 1986 Tax Reform Act, which allows only straight line depreciation for real property, caused rental real estate values to decline sharply. However, the change does not apply to buildings that already were being depreciated at an accelerated rate.

The 1986 Tax Reform Act also adversely affected real estate investment by imposing severe limits on the deductibility of tax losses by "passive" investors in real estate or other business activities—i.e., activities in which the taxpayer does not "materially participate." I.R.C. § 469. Rental activity is defined as being passive. Section 469's basic concept is that losses from passive activities may be used to offset income from passive activities but not from active income, such as salary and business income, or from portfolio income, such as interest and dividends. Because a major function of tax-oriented real estate syndications traditionally has been to generate losses that high-bracket passive investors (typically, limited partners) could employ to offset their active income in the form of salaries and professional fees, § 469 at first was feared to be the death knell of such syndications. However, it includes two exceptions. It doesn't apply to individuals who materially participate in real property trades or businesses if they perform more than one-half of their personal services and more than 750 hours of services during the taxable year in those trades or businesses. Section 469 also includes a $25,000 exception, though this exception phases out for taxpayers whose taxable income exceeds $100,000 and fully phases out for taxpayers whose taxable income exceeds $150,000.

The complexities of the passive loss rules are considerable and are well beyond the scope of this book. *See generally* Thomas A. Coughlin & Tersh Boasberg, How the Tax Reform Act of 1986 Affects Real Estate, 2 Prac.Real Est.Law. 11 (Nov. 1986). But the net effect of these changes has been reduced reliance by real estate syndicators and their investors on the tax benefits of rental real estate ownership and increased focus on the economic benefits of cash flow, pre-tax profitability, and capital value appreciation.

3.   INTERNAL RATE OF RETURN

Most investors consider the available income tax deductions, as well as the cash flow, when making real estate investment decisions. Yet their decisions are often surprisingly unsophisticated. The only accurate method of comparing alternative investments, whether in real estate or other fields, is to take account of all sums, including taxes, that the investor must pay into the venture and all sums that the venture will return to the investor, including tax savings. This analysis must include a consideration of the timing of the inflows and outflows of cash. The ultimate gain or loss when the property is sold and the tax on the sale proceeds must be considered as well. With this information, a "discounted internal rate of return" can be computed that takes into account the time value of money.

The discounted internal rate of return ("IRR") is the rate that is used to discount future economic benefits to present value to make them equal the project's initial capital cost. It is described in many publications, *see, e.g.*, Leslie Kent Beckhart, Note, No Intrinsic Value: The Failure of Traditional Real Estate Appraisal Methods to Value Income-Producing Property, 66 S. Cal. L. Rev. 2251 (1993), but some investors are unfamiliar with it. While a detailed consideration of rate-of-return analysis is beyond the scope of this book, you should always remember that raw information about cash flow or anticipated tax benefits is not a substitute for a computation of the discounted rate of return.

A brief illustration of IRR analysis may be helpful. Suppose that one can invest in a real estate project by putting up $100,000 cash at the beginning of year one. The project will be held for only two years and will be rented continuously to a tenant during that period. For the sake of simplicity, assume that all rents, taxes, maintenance, and other expenses are due and are paid only at the end of each year. At the end of year one, the combination of cash flow and tax shelter (i.e., tax reductions on other income that result from losses on this project) amounts to $70,000. This is our investor's after-tax net benefit from the project in year one. In year two, the benefit is only $60,000, because our tax shelter has declined as a result of a smaller interest deduction. At the end of year two, the investor sold the project and paid tax on the gain realized on that sale. Taking into consideration both the cash generated by the sale (which may be large, small, or even zero if the investor simply abandons the property) and the tax due on the gain from the sale, let us assume that the sale's net effect is to cost $10,000. Hence, the overall benefit to our investor at the end of year two is the $60,000 net benefit from operations, minus the $10,000 in costs and taxes incurred in the sale, or $50,000.

In summary, our transaction looks like this:

Beginning year one	– $100,000	input
End year one	+ 70,000	output
End year two	+ 50,000	output

An unsophisticated investor might say that he or she had earned $20,000 in two years on a $100,000 investment, which isn't bad. But exactly how good is it? How can we compare it with alternative investments? For example, suppose the investor had placed the $100,000 in an interest-bearing savings account in a financial institution. What rate of interest would the account have to pay to permit a $70,000 withdrawal at the end of year one and to leave exactly $50,000 in the account at the end of year two? This rate is the IRR for our investment.

IRR calculations for real estate investments are usually done with a spreadsheet program on a computer. However, because our illustration is simple, we can do it with a hand calculator that performs "present value" computations. The approach is simply one of trial and error. First, we assume some interest rate and apply it to the two "output" figures above to see what amount of "input" cash would have produced them at that interest rate. Then add these two input amounts to see if they equal $100,000, our actual input. If they do, we have (luckily) chosen the correct interest rate. If they do not (as is more likely), we can choose a different interest rate and try again. Eventually, we can close in on the exact interest rate that makes the sum of the present values of the outputs equal to the input. That is the IRR for the project.

Let's try it first with 12%. What present values would give us $70,000 in one year and $50,000 in two years with a 12% rate compounded annually? If our calculator will not do present value calculations directly, we can do them using the formula:

$$\text{Present value} = \frac{\text{Future value}}{(1 + i)^n}$$

in which i is the interest rate per period (in this example, per year) and n is the number of periods. Let's try it with the $50,000 to be earned at the end of the second year. With a 12% interest rate, the formula becomes:

$$\text{Present value} = \frac{\$50,000}{(1 + .12)^2} = \frac{\$50,000}{(1.12)^2} = \frac{\$50,000}{1.2544}$$

$$\text{Present value} = \$39,859$$

In effect, if we invest $39,859 in a savings account that bears 12% interest compounded annually and leave the money there for 2 years, the account will contain $50,000, including interest.

Now let's try it systematically with the two outputs our illustrative project is going to produce for us. At 12 percent interest, we get the following results:

	Future value	Present value
Year 1	$70,000	$62,500
Year 2	$50,000	$39,860
		$102,360

Our total is too high; it exceeds our actual investment of $100,000. This suggests that we need to try a higher interest rate, which will decrease the total present value. Let's try the same process with 15% interest:

	Future value	Present value
Year 1	$70,000	$60,869
Year 2	$50,000	$37,807
		$98,676

Since this amount is lower than our actual $100,000, the interest rate we tried is too high. We now know that the correct rate is somewhere between 12% and 15%. We can keep trying until we get the correct answer. If we use 13.9%, here are the results:

	Future value	Present value
Year 1	$70,000	$61,457
Year 2	$50,000	$38,541
		$99,998

This is close enough to satisfy even the most meticulous! The internal rate of return from our project is 13.9%, because that rate makes the present value of all future earned amounts equal to the present amount invested. The 13.9% figure is extremely useful in comparing this investment with alternatives available to our investor.

As you see, this process is tedious even for a case with only two cash outflows. If we had dozens or hundreds of outflows, calculating the IRR by hand or by calculator would be extremely difficult, and we would likely make a mistake somewhere along the way even if we were very persistent. A computer, of course, can do such computations in a matter of a few seconds, though the process it follows is virtually the same as that illustrated above.

Some analysts use a refinement that may be of interest, but you need not be unduly concerned with it. The above approach implicitly assumes that the investor can reinvest the intermediate benefits received from the project at the same rate of return that the project itself produces. But this may not be true. For example, the investor may have to place the proceeds of year one in some lower-yielding investment, such as a bank savings account. Many computer models take this factor into account, because an IRR calculation that considers the so-called "reinvestment rate" may significantly differ from one that does not if the reinvestment rate is substantially different than the "straight" IRR as described above. *See* Edward J. Farragher, Clarifying the Confusion about IRR Reinvestment Assumptions, 13 Real Est.Rev. 56 (Summer 1983).

Note that an internal rate of return can be calculated in two ways. The method described above is called an "equity IRR" calculation, because it calculates the equity investor's return from the real estate based on the actual cash flows to the owner, including only the owner's down payment to purchase the real estate and deducting each year's debt service to determine the project's cash flow.

Another common IRR calculation is the "project IRR." It is often helpful for an investor to review the real estate investment's return potential on its own, before considering the investor's choice of financing, such as the down payment amount versus the loan amount, the interest rate for which the investor can qualify, and the debt's amortization period. In a project IRR calculation, the entire purchase price of the real estate is included as the initial cash outlay. Debt service isn't deducted from the annual cash flow; instead, the calculation uses the net operating income. The pay-off amount for any debt on the real estate is not deducted from the sale price. If the investor pays all cash for the project, the equity IRR equals the project IRR.

4. LEVERAGE

A project's rate of return to its equity investors depends on the ratio of debt to equity in the project's financing. If the project's overall rate of return on total investment (debt plus equity) exceeds the debt's interest rate, the equity investor can maximize the return by borrowing as much as possible to minimize the equity he or she must invest. Obtaining loans with high loan-to-value ratios is typically a principal objective of income property developers, though some risk-averse developers see the inherent risks in that strategy. The concept of using borrowed money to develop and hold real estate is known as leverage, and a project that is financed largely with debt capital is said to be highly leveraged.

A simple illustration will show the advantage of leverage. Assume that a developer decides to build a rental project for $1 million and that the project's gross rents, less operating expenses, will be $150,000 for the first year. Assume also that debt capital can be borrowed at 10% interest and that payments in the first year are interest only. The table below shows the cash flow as a percentage of equity investment if the developer finances the project entirely with personal funds, borrows 50% of the necessary funds, or borrows 90%.

Mortgage debt	0	$500,000	$900,000
Equity investment	$1,000,000	$500,000	$100,000
Gross rents less operating expenses	$150,000	$150,000	$150,000
Less debt service @ 10% of mortgage	0	$50,000	$90,000
amount			
Cash flow to developer	$150,000	$100,000	$60,000
Cash flow as a percent of equity investment	15%	20%	60%

The figures labeled "Cash flow as a percent of equity investment" are not the equivalent of a discounted rate of return on the investment, because they do not include tax benefits, mortgage amortization, or the tax consequences when the property is sold or otherwise transferred. Nonetheless, leverage produces the same basic impact on rate of return as it does on cash flow. Note that the tax benefits are essentially unaffected by mortgaging the property, because the depreciable basis includes the mortgage, as well as the equity investment. Crane v. Commissioner, 331 U.S. 1, 67 S.Ct. 1047, 91 L.Ed. 1301 (1947). The *Crane* decision's significance can hardly be overemphasized; in its absence, leverage would utterly defeat tax shelter. *See* Donald J. Weidner, Realty Shelters, Nonrecourse Financing, Tax Reform, and Profit Purpose, 32 Sw.L.J. 711 (1978).

Although leverage can provide benefits, it also creates risk for equity investors. In the foregoing example, suppose that the project's gross rents, less operating expenses, drop to $80,000 per year because of vacancies or local economic conditions. The debt service on the 90% mortgage is still $90,000, so the developer either has to pay the $10,000 deficit from some other source, if it can, or face foreclosure. By contrast, if the developer had paid all cash or had borrowed only 50%, the project would still be generating a positive cash flow. Similarly, a decrease in the property's value can have a negative effect on a highly-leveraged project. For example, if the project's value declines to $800,000 due to a recession, the 90% mortgaged property would be "under water," and a lender would be unwilling to extend the loan at its maturity without a substantial pay-down of the principal balance. In general, the more highly leveraged the investment, the greater the risk that an unforeseen reduction in the project's cash-generating capacity or market value will place the equity investor in a negative cash-flow or equity posture. The investor's rate of return will be similarly adversely affected.

In some transactions, distinguishing debt from equity can be difficult. For example, if the developer builds the project on land that it has ground-leased for 40 years at a fixed rental, the rent is equivalent to debt service. In contrast, some institutional mortgage lenders recently have been more prone to contract with developers for a "piece of the action" in addition to the fixed interest rate on the loan. Such arrangements may take the form of a joint venture or partnership between the developer and lender or an additional payment to the lender based on the collected rents, the gross or net sales in a commercial project, such as a shopping center, the net operating income of the property, or some other indicator of the project's financial success. In transactions of this type, the line between debt and equity investments becomes blurred, and the risk of failure and the reward for success are shared by the developer and lender. However, the developer has to pay the fixed interest on the "debt" even if the project is unsuccessful.

5.   CHOICE OF ENTITY

The tax benefits of a real estate investment are substantially affected by the type of legal entity that the investors use to hold the property. A vast lore of legal and accounting literature addresses the tax considerations in choosing a business entity and the allocation of tax losses to the entity's investors.

The corporate form is generally unattractive to real estate investors because corporate earnings are taxed twice; the corporation has to pay a corporate tax on its earnings, and the shareholders have to pay personal income tax on dividends. Moreover, shareholders cannot take advantage of the corporation's tax losses. In contrast, if a partnership's loan on real estate is nonrecourse, all gains and losses can be allocated to the individual partners, and the partnership is not separately taxed. This is an extremely advantageous arrangement for the partners.

As between general and limited partnerships, limited partnerships are more commonly used for real estate investments. A limited partner is liable for partnership activities only up to the amount of the partner's contribution, whereas a general partner has unlimited liability. Moreover, the limited partnership is particularly useful for real estate "syndications." In a syndication, groups of investors, most of whom are passive, place their funds with a general partner who builds or operates a real estate project. In contrast, a general partnership generally involves shared management rights and responsibilities.

The IRS's rules for determining whether an entity is taxed as a partnership or as a corporation were traditionally complex, subtle, and frustrating. During the 1980s and 1990s, a large number of states enacted statutes permitting the formation of limited liability companies (LLCs) and limited liability partnerships (LLPs). In a surprising turn-around, the IRS in 1996 announced a new approach to the taxation of such entities. It adopted a regulation that permits LLCs, LLPs, and limited and general partnerships to "check the box" and elect to be taxed as a partnership. *See* 26 C.F.R. §§ 301.7701–1 to –3. Exceptions exist to this favorable treatment for entities that are labeled "corporations" under state law, for entities that are publicly traded, and for insurance companies, banks, and foreign entities. But adoption of the regulation greatly simplified the task of creating a real estate investment vehicle that could pass its tax benefits to its investors and made LLCs the most popular and attractive entity for real estate investment.

As described in the next excerpt, the real estate investment trust (REIT) is another popular vehicle for holding income-producing properties.

MICHAEL G. FRANKEL & THAYNE T. NEEDLES, REAL ESTATE INVESTMENT TRUSTS: A GUIDE TO THEIR HISTORY, FORMATION AND TAXATION

Practicing Law Institute, Second Annual Real Estate Tax Forum (Feb.-Mar. 2000)

In simplest terms, a REIT is a corporation or business trust (taxable as a corporation) formed to generate income from the leasing of real estate or from interest collected on notes secured by real estate. The REIT's principle advantage over other publicly-traded entities is that it may avoid paying federal (and in many instances state) income tax as a result of deducting dividends paid to shareholders from pre-tax income. To qualify for the right to deduct its dividends, a REIT must satisfy a series of ownership, income, asset, distribution and organizational requirements.

Since the income of a REIT is typically taxed only at the shareholder level, a REIT may sometimes be thought of as a pass-through entity similar to a partnership. However, a REIT is governed by the principles of corporate taxation except for the special REIT provisions. A primary example of how REITs differ from partnerships is a REIT's inability to pass through losses to its shareholders. * * *

Legislation creating real estate investment trusts (REITs) was enacted in 1960. While various forms of REITs have existed since that time, the modern REIT industry traces its roots to the formation of Kimco

Realty Corporation in 1991. From the beginning of 1991 through the year ended 1996, the industry's market capitalization (outstanding shares times trading price) grew from $9 to nearly $90 billion. This figure only represents the approximately 200 publicly-traded REITs. In addition, there are more than 100 non-publicly traded (or private) REITs who hold assets valued in the tens of billions of dollars.

Overwhelmingly, the REITs formed in the 1990's are so-called "equity" REITs whose assets are comprised of ownership interests in actual brick & mortar buildings, which are leased to third parties. At year end 1996, equity REITs accounted for almost 90% of the industry's $90 billion of public market capitalization. The remaining market capitalization was represented by "mortgage" REITs, those REITs that hold or originate mortgage loans as their primary business, and "hybrid" REITs whose assets are a mixture of mortgages and buildings.

Equity REITs may be further broken down by their principal asset. REITs with at least a 75% concentration in a particular asset class comprise nearly 97% of equity REITs. Among these companies, the most common asset types for equity REITs (by their percentage of overall market capitalization) are:

Retail (malls, strip & outlet centers)	26%
Residential (apartments and manufactured homes)	24%
Office	11%
Industrial & Mixed Use	10%
Hotel	8%
Self Storage	7%
Health Care	6%
Other (Triple Net, Golf Course)	5%

* * *

The wave of new REITs created in the 1990's generally share certain characteristics. In addition to the already discussed attributes of being property owners that focus on a particular asset class, today's REITs generally have a geographic focus, have substantial insider ownership, and carry lower than normal levels of debt in comparison with private real estate companies, and are self-advised and self-managed.

As noted above, an important factor in the formation of a public REIT in today's environment is the participation of the REIT's sponsors. REIT insiders typically will own 10% to 35% of the REIT immediately following its IPO. Public investors see this as an important sign of management's vested interest in the REIT's performance and an indication that management's goals will be in line with their own. * * *

With respect to geography, Wall Street has typically required that REITs have a concentration in both asset type and location. Most publicly-traded REITs generally acquire properties within a defined metropolitan area or region of the country. Wall Street believes that this focus is necessary for management to provide expert management in the context of a real estate company. However, a recent trend shows a growing number of the REITs expanding into more than one city or region of the country, and some successful REITs make investments across asset classes in their search of strong investment opportunities.

A final trait of most publicly-traded REITs is a lower than normal debt-to-equity ratio when compared with private real estate owners. A REIT's total capitalization is generally comprised of 5% to 50% debt, with the higher figure typically limited to mall REITs. An industry average across product types is generally in the range of 30 to 35% of total capitalization.

NOTE

Typical operating expenses. The relationship between rents and operating expenses varies considerably based on factors such as property type, the region of the nation in which the property is located, and the property's age. Nevertheless, it is instructive to examine the following data, which was derived from reports by members of the National Apartment Association for 2013. Bear in mind that this ratio and the breakdown below do not necessarily apply to shopping centers, industrial buildings, or other nonresidential projects.

Median Operating Expense as a Percentage of Total Annual Rental Income

	Dollar Amount Per Unit	Percent of Gross Rent
Total Rental Income	$11,278	100%
Salaries and benefits	$1,171	10.4%
Insurance	$250	2.2%
Property taxes	$1,137	10.1%
Utilities	$535	4.7%
Management fees	$352	3.1%
Administrative (office, telephone)	$259	2.3%
Marketing	$163	1.4%
Contract services, such as lawn care	$266	2.4%
Repair and maintenance	$457	4.1%
Total Operating Expenses	**$4,589**	**40.7%**

Source: National Apartment Association 2013 Survey of Operating Income & Expenses in Rental Apartment Communities.

B. ALTERNATIVE FINANCING METHODS

In earlier chapters, we have examined the two most common land finance devices—a mortgage on the fee title and the installment land contract. In this section, we will explore a variety of creative financing techniques that are used for income-producing properties, including joint ventures, participating mortgages, ground leases, mezzanine loans, and the sale-leaseback. One commentator has described the purpose for these creative techniques as follows:

> Creative financing techniques exist because the marketplace demands that they exist. These arrangements make transactions come together that otherwise would not work. Creative lenders are constantly looking for ways to invest funds profitably and safely. Developers that have excellent projects, great track records and viable ideas sometimes need creative approaches to make a deal work that wouldn't work using traditional approaches.

Daniel B. Lewis, Creative Financing Techniques in Commercial Real Estate, 72 A.B.A. J. 60, 61 (Feb. 1986).

1. JOINT VENTURES AND PARTICIPATING MORTGAGES

JOHN W. HANLEY, JR., MORE IMPORTANT THAN EVER: THE REAL ESTATE JOINT VENTURE
23 Prob. & Prop. 12 (2009)[*]

What Is a Joint Venture?

A real estate joint venture is a vehicle for co-investment in a real estate property or interest by two or more parties. Typically structured as a limited liability company (or, occasionally, a limited or general partnership), the real estate joint venture raises the equity capital needed to complete a purchase or investment. In the case of a development or redevelopment project, the joint venture may combine that capital with real estate industry services from providers that prefer to receive an ownership-like interest in the asset, on a tax-efficient basis, rather than fees for their nonmonetary contributions to the success of the development or redevelopment.

State laws governing formation and operation of limited liability companies and partnerships, especially the laws of Delaware, provide co-owners with great flexibility in creating a structure and setting terms and

---

[*] Reprinted with permission of John W. Hanley, Jr., of Davis Wright Tremaine LLP, Seattle, Washington.

conditions to meet the goals and objectives of all the co-owners. See, e.g., Del. Code Ann. tit. 6, §§ 17–1101(c), 18–1101(b). * * *

The joint venture is often the preferred form of ownership structure for the purchase of a site and development of a new project or redevelopment of an existing property. The development company sponsor can use the joint venture to aggregate the required equity from other investors and to set the terms under which it will contribute to the enterprise its own expertise, contract rights, project entitlements, services, and, perhaps, a small amount of capital. A development joint venture agreement is typically more complex than the governing agreement for a joint venture whose sole purpose is to pool equity capital from similar investors and purchase a stabilized, income-producing commercial real estate property that will continue under third-party management. * * *

Advantages and Disadvantages of the Joint Venture

When the current owner or the prospective purchaser of commercial real estate [needs more capital than it can borrow from the first mortgagee, it] may find that it has at least a few choices among capital sources to close part of the equity gap. The choice may be among small and deeply subordinated second mortgage financing, expensive mezzanine debt financing, and additional equity raised in a joint venture from other like-minded investors. What are the advantages and disadvantages of using a joint venture to raise that extra measure of capital needed to recapitalize or purchase commercial real estate?

Typically, the sponsor's principal advantage in using a real estate joint venture to raise additional capital is that it promises a lower cost of capital than other sources. The joint venture agreement can and must meet the risk and reward expectations of each new investor. Frequently, that agreement can be structured to give the investor a preferred call on project net cash flow to a certain target rate of return; a pari passu return (that is, a call on equal footing with the rights of all other investors in the venture) to a second, higher target rate of return; and beyond that, a return that is often reduced to allow the sponsor to receive an additional amount based on its promoted interest. The cost to the sponsor of capital raised in this manner is more bearable than the financial burden of a market-priced subordinated second mortgage loan or a mezzanine loan from a third party, because joint venture capital becomes expensive only if the project is financially successful and the venture can afford to make premium distributions.

Frequently, another advantage of the joint venture is that it will be more likely to satisfy the requirements and expectations of the first mortgage lender. First mortgage loan documents prohibit or severely restrict the property owner's use of subordinated mortgage financing and mezzanine loans, but mortgage lenders are more willing to accommodate arrangements by a joint venture borrower that raises its additional equity capital internally. The economic terms of the relationship between a project sponsor and a new capital source, embedded in their joint venture agreement, can be similar to those that would govern a mezzanine loan or subordinated second mortgage loan. The first mortgage lender, however, is often more accepting of a new funding relationship "inside" a joint venture than a hard money loan to the borrower from an "outside" source, for at least two reasons. First, if the project fails to perform as expected and the investor never receives its expected preferred return, the investor may have remedies under the joint venture agreement, but exercise of these remedies usually does not require a foreclosure or other public proceeding that highlights the asset's financial distress. The investor's recourse is usually removal of the sponsor from management of the joint venture, further subordination of the sponsor's economic interest, or a call for additional capital, potentially leading to dilution of the sponsor's interest. From the mortgage lender's perspective, however, there is no interruption of its relationship with the borrower entity, even though the internal governance or economics of the venture have been altered. Second, historically capital market requirements for securitization of first mortgage loans have imposed programmatic prohibitions or limits on the use of second mortgage loans and management loans. These requirements impose fewer limitations on changes in governance or economics within a first mortgage borrower that is a joint venture.

In addition, in the case of a purchase transaction, when confronted by capital constraints or a hesitant project site seller, the new real estate project sponsor may find that under current market conditions the most effective way to complete the acquisition and launch its project is to include the prospective seller in the enterprise. This can be done by including the landowner in a new joint venture.

The principal disadvantage of using a joint venture to raise additional capital is the complexity and associated expense of structuring and documenting a joint venture agreement that will give the new funding source a preferred return, as well as protections and remedies, approximating the position typical of a junior lender.

Considerations in Forming the Joint Venture

Federal tax and state laws give the founders of a commercial real estate joint venture enormous flexibility in setting terms and conditions that will satisfy the competing objectives of the co-owners. This flexibility permits the prospective owners to establish an economic relationship inside the investment vehicle that has mutually accepted rules of capitalization, operation, governance, and liquidation. Flexibility breeds complexity, and a joint venture agreement often establishes intricate arrangements for capital formation and profit sharing. These agreements also address difficult issues and esoteric concepts arising from state and local laws governing limited liability companies (or partnerships), fiduciary duties, agency, commercial relations, intangible interests, contract rights, and real and personal property. * * *

It is beyond the scope of this article to address every topic and element to be negotiated, or at least considered, in the formation of a joint venture to acquire commercial real estate. The two subjects that are of the greatest importance in framing the real estate joint venture, subjects deserving the earliest possible consideration by the prospective investors, are the economics of the business organization and its management.

The Economic Terms of the Joint Venture

Prospective joint venturers are eager to discuss the finances and anticipated profits of the proposed relationship—often well before they bring legal advisors to the table. Indeed, working alone, the principals may hammer out a preliminary term sheet that identifies the target real estate to be owned by the proposed venture, the anticipated capital structure of the enterprise, the projected financial results to the partners, and little else. Of course, the definitive joint venture agreement must fully and accurately describe all of the economics of the proposed joint venture relationship. This subject permeates many terms in the well-crafted joint venture agreement, including at least the elements discussed below.

Planned Contributions

What are each investor's anticipated contributions to the capital or operations of the enterprise and when and how will each contribution be received and used? A contribution to capital may take the form of a transfer to the joint venture of cash or property. If the contribution is a transfer of property, secondary but important questions must be addressed. How will the property be valued for purposes of recognizing the transferor's investment in the venture? What are the legal requirements, formalities, and costs associated with transfer of the asset to the venture's balance sheet? Are there liabilities associated with the asset, and must the venture assume those liabilities? Does the asset have federal income tax attributes ("built-in" tax gain or loss, for example) that will carry over to the joint venture and be problematic?

A prospective venturer may be expected or required to contribute to the success of the joint venture in other ways. For example, a partner may be required to make its balance sheet strength available for the benefit of the joint venture by providing a limited or unlimited guaranty to the project's mortgage lender, or available to support the issuance of a letter of credit or other financial accommodation needed by the venture.

How is the venturer that provides such credit support to be recognized or compensated for this financial support?

Finally, the sponsor of the joint venture may be planning to provide, or cause an affiliate to provide, services necessary to execute the business plan of the venture in exchange for an economic stake in the venture. These services might include real estate brokerage services related to acquisition of the real estate, consulting services to secure necessary development or construction permits and approvals, construction management services for new improvements or the redevelopment of existing improvements, mortgage brokerage services for the placement of the anticipated first mortgage debt for the project, or leasing brokerage services to obtain the tenants for the completed development or redevelopment project. How are such services to be described, measured, and rewarded? Thorny federal income tax issues relate to the receipt of an economic interest in a real estate joint venture in exchange for services. The draftsman of the joint venture agreement must proceed cautiously in these areas.

Planned Rewards

Once the parties have reached agreement on their respective planned contributions to the venture, they must establish the financial return that each contribution will earn if the venture is successful. This process requires the parties to reach a mutual understanding of the degree of risk of financial failure associated with their common enterprise—at each stage of acquisition, development (or redevelopment), and operation of the real estate asset. The redevelopment of an existing commercial property in a transitional neighborhood that will need both novel land use approvals and a new class of tenants to succeed will naturally bear a greater risk of failure than the routine purchase of a fully occupied and well-maintained apartment building in a community known for strong job growth and an attractive lifestyle. The sponsor must offer a greater financial return to attract equity to the more risky venture than to the safer, more established property.

Once they have agreed on the appropriate financial return for each equity investment in the joint venture, the partners must determine how those returns will be realized. They must set the formulas for periodic or special cash distributions to some or all of the joint venturers out of cash proceeds realized from operations or capital events (for example, refinancings, condemnations, casualty losses, partial sales, or a complete sale of the real estate). In establishing these formulas, the flexibility of the joint venture is an invitation for creativity—constrained only to some extent by the federal partnership tax laws. To meet their respective economic objectives, the prospective joint venturers can provide for different priorities and different formulas for determining distribution amounts to each partner under a variety of circumstances. Complex "waterfalls" of distribution levels can be devised. In this fashion, each significant equity investor can be given a priority right to certain kinds of distributions if necessary, until it has received (or made significant progress toward receiving) the projected risk-adjusted return on its investment.

Planning for the Unexpected

The prospective partners will also want to address the possibility that the venture will fail or stall. They should try to agree on procedures—and requirements—by which unexpected project difficulties will be confronted and (hopefully) overcome. Once launched, the venture may require more equity capital than was originally contemplated, and one of the venturers may be unable or unwilling to make further capital contributions. Will the joint venture agreement require all, or permit less than all, of the joint venturers to provide proportionate funding for unanticipated future capital needs? Will the contributing investors enjoy an added measure of preferred return on an additional investment made in these circumstances? Will a noncontributing venturer suffer an economic disadvantage or penalty if it is unable or unwilling to contribute to the capital shortfall? The parties can include a wide range of possible mechanisms by which the venture's future capital requirements can be satisfied.

The Ultimate Business Terms

By working through these topics, formally or informally, prospective joint venturers can establish the fundamental economic terms of their proposed co-owned venture. When fully developed, the financial terms will determine how each investor providing capital or services, or both, will be rewarded for its contributions if the venture is successful, and what the nature and potential extent of its financial losses will be if the venture fails. Of course, the exact formula for sharing the prospective profits and losses earned by the joint venture will depend on many circumstances, including property and market conditions, the availability of other capital sources to the sponsor, and the availability of other investment opportunities to the investor.

Management Terms

The other major subject that should be addressed, at least conceptually, before the partners embark on the details of a definitive joint venture agreement is the subject of governance. How will this co-owned real estate enterprise be managed?

This subject is addressed in depth in an article by Richard R. Spore III, which discusses several threshold choices that should be made by the founders of a real estate joint venture if they are to have a centralized management structure that gives them the best chance of economic success. See *Management and Governance of Real Estate Joint Ventures: Avoiding Surprises and Resolving Conflict in Tough Times*, 23 Prob. & Prop. 33 (2009). Just as they did in crafting their economic blueprint (capitalization and the sharing of economic gains and losses), so also do the prospective joint venturers have enormous flexibility in crafting a management structure that best meets their respective needs and concerns. No one approach to centralized management is required for all ventures, as illustrated by three points.

First, as noted by Mr. Spore, an initial threshold choice is usually whether the owners will co-manage the enterprise by means of a management committee or board of directors composed of representatives of all, or the primary, venturers; or whether, instead, they will concentrate management authority in a single designated manager, usually the sponsor or an affiliate, whose duties and authorities will be circumscribed in various ways. In the commercial real estate industry, the latter structure is more typical, but the management plan chosen for a particular venture will be determined largely by the facts and circumstances surrounding that particular opportunity. For example, in the case of a venture being formed by a sponsor to exploit a new construction or redevelopment opportunity, the management burden may be quite substantial until the project is finished and placed in service. The venture may need a nimble, decisive manager who can make many timely decisions and deal with the unexpected, as the venture passes through the high-risk phases of permitting, development, construction, and lease-up to a lower-risk phase. Certainly if the sponsor hopes to earn a large promotional interest for the successful development of the project, it will negotiate for a clear and broad delegation of management authority having few checks and balances. In all likelihood, the other principal funding source—the construction lender—will also prefer that kind of governance structure. By contrast, if a joint venture is being formed by several similar, experienced investors to co-own a stabilized multifamily asset being managed by a reputable property management company, they will probably gravitate to the use of a board of directors or management committee for governance. This is particularly true if no one investor will be asked to make a substantially larger investment than the others or to provide other unique financial support, such as a guaranty to the mortgage lender.

Second, Mr. Spore notes the two alternative or complementary means typically used to check the authority of a designated managing member, in order to protect minority interests in the venture: approval rights (sometimes called "veto rights") for various potential future decisions by the manager and the use of an approved annual budget to establish limits on spending authority and revenue-related decisions. Again, the extent to which prospective partners rely on each of these mechanisms will depend on a host of considerations unique to that particular venture opportunity. In a new construction or redevelopment venture, use of annual budgets may not be practical until after the project has been built and leased, although the investors will no doubt comb through the proposed development/construction budget, require approval of that budget before investments will be made, and tightly control subsequent changes to that budget. Much more typically, the prospective venturers will develop a list of approval rights tied very closely to the anticipated permitting, development, construction, and leasing process—for example, selection of the architect, selection of the general contractor, issuance of the notice to proceed, and material change orders. By contrast, a venture being formed to acquire a stabilized real estate asset with well-understood and measurable operating revenues and expenses (for example, a successful hotel or apartment building) may lend itself to use of a management structure heavily dependent on review and approval of annual operating budgets and other periodic financial measurements to confine management's authority.

Third, Mr. Spore describes the wide range of choices to be made concerning future removal of the initial managing member. Again, the circumstances surrounding each particular joint venture will guide the venturers to a set of accountability terms acceptable to both the manager and the other venturers. Most significant is the manager's own investment in the venture as an equity partner, if the manager makes a monetary investment. What are the potential sources of economic loss for the venture? Of these potential losses, which are appropriately attributable to bad management, in light of the scope of the manager's delegated authority, its professed expertise, and the rewards offered to the manager for successful avoidance of those losses? Which are more appropriately borne proportionately by all the members as an enterprise risk?

As Mr. Spore so ably demonstrates, careful and thorough advance planning is required to launch a joint venture with a governance structure that will enhance, rather than undermine, the chance for economic success.

Conclusion

The real estate joint venture is a powerful and flexible tool to assemble equity capital, including land and other assets, and to attract the necessary real estate industry skills. Because of the great flexibility offered by this vehicle, the real estate joint venture is typically governed by a complex and dense joint venture agreement. Potential joint venturers should place their main focus on the economics and management of the enterprise to build the foundation needed for a successful real estate joint venture.

NOTE

A participating mortgage can take a variety of forms, but it often involves the lender taking a partial ownership interest in the mortgaged land or being entitled to a share of the income from the property in exchange for a loan at a lower interest rate and a higher loan-to-value ratio than otherwise would be available. This device was particularly popular in the 1980s and 1990s when interest rates were high and capital availability was constricted. Today, the joint venture is more commonly used, in part because of lower interest rates and concerns that a participating mortgage might be characterized as a clog on the equity of redemption. For further discussion of the financing methods mentioned above, *see* John C. Murray, Recharacterization Issues in Participating and "Equity Kicker" Mortgages, ALI-ABA Commercial Real Estate Defaults, Workouts & Reorganizations (Apr. 20–22, 2006); John C. Murray, Clogging Revisited, 33 Real Prop. Prob. & Tr. J. 279 (1998); Report, Legal Restrictions on Equity Participation Financings, 20 Real Prop.Prob. & Tr.J. 1139 (1985); James P. Gaines & Forrest E. Huffman, Negotiating the Terms of Participation Mortgages, 12 Real Est.Rev. 38 (Fall 1982); Laurence G. Preble & David W. Cartwright, Convertible and Shared Appreciation Loans: Unclogging the Equity of Redemption, 20 Real Prop.Prob. & Tr.J. 821 (1985).

2. GROUND LEASES

The ground lease is typically made to the developer by a long-time owner of the land or a land speculator who has previously purchased from such an owner. Occasionally, however, a pension fund or other institutional investor will purchase land with an advance commitment to lease it to a developer. The term of the ground lease must be at least as long as the term of the permanent mortgage loan that the developer will use to finance the improvements; typical terms range from 30 to 99 years. The lease usually provides that the buildings and other improvements will remain the developer's property until termination of the lease, at which time they will revert to the ground lessor. Almost invariably, ground leases are "net" leases that obligate the lessee to pay taxes, insurance, maintenance costs, and all other expenses related to the property.

Economically, the developer views the ground lease as a substitute for financing to purchase of the land. Although purchasing the land would give the developer title in perpetuity, while leasing gives possession for only a limited (although long) time, this difference is relatively unimportant to the developer, because the reversion's present value is very small when the lease commences.

From the developer's viewpoint, the ground lease has several attractions as a land acquisition vehicle. The developer will own and take depreciation deductions on the improvements. The ground rent paid to the lessor will be fully deductible. By contrast, if the land were purchased with a purchase money mortgage, a portion of the payments would be non-deductible principal amortization. Aside from a modest security deposit, the ground lease usually requires no front-end cash investment by the developer. If the ground lessor is willing to subordinate the lease to the developer's construction and permanent loan mortgages (technically, to subject the fee interest to those mortgages), the developer often can obtain significantly greater leverage than if it purchased the land.

The following example will illustrate the leverage advantages of both subordinated and unsubordinated ground leases. Assume a developer wishes to acquire land worth $1 million and to construct a shopping center on it at a cost of an additional $3 million. A lending institution is willing to make a 25-year mortgage loan at 10% interest in an amount equal to 70% of the property's value. The developer must decide whether to acquire the land in fee or to ground lease it with or without subordination by the lessor. If the lessor subordinates, the lender is willing to treat the value of the security as equal to the $4 million value of the land and improvements in fee, but if no subordination is obtained, the lender will base its loan on the $3 million value of the improvements alone. If the term of the unsubordinated ground lease is not suitably long, the lender may refuse to make the loan because the loan security could revert to the lessor.

Assume that gross rents from shopping center operations will be $800,000 per year and that the operating expenses will be $300,000. If a ground lease is employed, the lessor will demand a ground rent of $80,000 per year if the lessor's interest is subordinated or $100,000 if it is not.

	Land Purchased in Fee	Unsubordinated Ground Lease	Subordinated Ground Lease
Total Project Cost	$4,000,000	$4,000,000	$4,000,000
Less leased land	–0–	(1,000,000)	(1,000,000)
Less mortgage loan	(2,800,000)	(2,100,000)	(2,800,000)
Developer's equity investment	1,200,000	900,000	200,000

* * * * * *

Gross rents received	$800,000	$800,000	$800,000
Less operating expenses	(300,000)	(300,000)	(300,000)

Less debt service	(305,328)	(228,996)	(305,328)
Less ground rent	–0–	(80,000)	(100,000)
Net cash flow	194,672	191,004	94,672
Net cash flow as a percent of invested equity	16.2%	21.2%	47.3%

* * * * * *

Tax Treatment in First Year of Operation

Gross income	$800,000	$800,000	$800,000
Operating expense deduction	(300,000)	(300,000)	(300,000)
Interest deduction	(278,806)	(209,105)	(278,806)
Ground rent deduction	–0–	(80,000)	(100,000)
Depreciation deduction (straight line 39 years)	(76,923)	(76,923)	(76,923)
Taxable income	144,271	133,972	44,271

* * * * * *

After-Tax Benefit in First Year of Operation
(Assuming developer is in 28% marginal tax bracket)

Net cash flow	194,672	191,004	94,672
Less tax liability (28% of taxable income)	(40,396)	(37,512)	(12,396)
After-tax cash flow	154,276	153,492	82,276
After-tax cash flow as a percent of invested equity	12.86%	17.05%	41.14%

While the above analysis considers only the first year of operation and does not reflect the project's overall internal rate of return over a longer holding period, it is sufficient to suggest the substantial benefit available to the lessee under a subordinated ground lease. This benefit is primarily the result of leverage—i.e., the developer's ability to minimize equity investment in the project while building it largely with the capital of others, specifically the ground lessor and the mortgage lender.

If a ground lessor is unwilling to subordinate the lease to the mortgage, the lender almost certainly will require notice of any default by the lessee and the right to cure it. Otherwise, the lessee's default could cause its interest in the land to revert to the land lessor, which would extinguish the lender's rights to the collateral under the mortgage. A tri-party agreement among the land lessor, land lessee/borrower, and the lender is normally used. Based on the agreement, the lender has privity of contract with the ground lessor and can cure any default by the borrower on the land lease.

For the owner of a valuable tract of land who is not a developer, being a ground lessor has several benefits. First, by leasing rather than selling, the lessor avoids the tax liability on the long-term gain in the land's value which, even with installment reporting, might be quite onerous. In addition, the lessor converts his or her land holdings into a long-term investment with a determinable rate of return. The lessor may well anticipate dying before the lease expires, in which case the lessor's heirs will have the benefits of a stepped-up basis in the land and, hopefully, significant appreciation in value during the lease term as well. The improvements that will revert to the lessor or to the lessor's heirs on lease termination will, of course, be old and well-used, but they may still have substantial residual value.

The parties to a ground lease must be made acutely aware during the negotiation and drafting process that the lease must be acceptable to the developer's construction and permanent lenders, especially if the ground lease is unsubordinated. If the mortgage does not cover the lessor's fee simple interest, the foreclosing lender or other foreclosure purchaser will step into the developer's shoes as ground lessee.

Lenders want specific kinds of protection, some of which we will explore below. If they do not get it, they will not lend, and the lease will be essentially worthless to the developer. The safest course in most transactions is to work closely with the lender as the lease is being negotiated and to secure the lender's approval before it is finalized.

JOSHUA STEIN, A GUIDE TO GROUND LEASES

42–45, 50, 52–54, 71–72, 132, 139–40, 162,
167–68, 170, 198–99, 205–08, 227–31, 233 (2005)*

SUBORDINATION OF FEE MORTGAGES TO LEASEHOLD MORTGAGES

Any mention of fee mortgages in any lease transaction typically leads to complex discussions about the relative priorities of fee mortgages and leasehold mortgages. Leasehold mortgagees often say they want to know that any fee mortgage is "subordinate to" any leasehold mortgage, and that any leasehold mortgage is "prior to" any fee mortgage. While such a

---

request seems intuitively reasonable, it oversimplifies and misconstrues the relationship between fee mortgages and leasehold mortgages.

* * *

The relationship between fee mortgages and leasehold mortgages can best be understood by focusing on the relationship between fee mortgages and the lease. As between those two estates in the premises, the lease must typically be "superior" and the fee mortgage must typically be "subordinate." This means the fee mortgage can't hurt the leasehold, and the leasehold will survive any foreclosure of the fee mortgage.

Once the parties correctly define the priority of the lease, those priorities will benefit anyone who owns or holds any rights under the lease—the original tenant, a leasehold mortgagee, or a judgment creditor that acquires the lease at an execution sale. The leasehold mortgage creates an interest in the leasehold, and the leasehold is prior to fee mortgages. The fee mortgage can do no more damage to the leasehold mortgagee's estate than it can do to the leasehold itself. As long as the fee mortgagee can't damage the leasehold, it can't damage anyone whose interest in the premises arises from the leasehold.

The same principles also travel through to the benefit of subtenants. If a fee mortgagee is subordinate to the leasehold, then nothing the fee mortgagee does can impair the estate of any subtenant.

* * *

The tenant should agree, in the leasehold mortgage, not even to try to subordinate the lease to any fee mortgage. And the lease (as well as the memorandum of lease) should state that any such subordination is invalid without the leasehold mortgagee's consent.

SUBORDINATION OF THE FEE

In some leasehold financing transactions, the landlord joins in the leasehold mortgage to give the lender the fee estate as additional security for what would otherwise be purely a leasehold loan. These transactions are commonly referred to as "subordination of the fee," a label that is not technically correct. A landlord cannot "subordinate" a fee estate. A landlord can merely "join in" a leasehold mortgage, so the fee estate stands as additional collateral for the leasehold mortgagee's loan. The transaction may be called "subordination of the fee" because a foreclosure of the mortgage will terminate the landlord's interest in the fee estate, a relationship not too different from the relationship between the leasehold mortgagee and the holder of any estate subordinate to the leasehold mortgage.

In one of these transactions, the leasehold mortgagee is really also a fee mortgagee and cares much less—in theory, perhaps not at all—about what the lease says. In a foreclosure against a fee/leasehold collateral package, the fee/leasehold mortgagee should be able to take over both the fee and the leasehold. The mortgagee could, for example, collapse the lease through merger immediately after a foreclosure or conveyance in lieu of foreclosure. For that reason, the lease could in theory say almost anything at all, because the lender could make it all go away after a loan default and foreclosure. If the lack of leasehold protections caused the lease to terminate prematurely, the lender would simply foreclose on the fee estate and own everything at the end of the day anyway. Therefore such a lender might in theory not care about leasehold mortgagee protections.

* * *

In the author's experience, today's landlords (unless affiliated with the tenant) rarely agree to "subordinate the fee," any more than they would agree to pledge their stock portfolio, car, vacation house, or collection of priceless miniature tea sets to give the tenant's leasehold mortgagee additional collateral. The whole concept is inconsistent with the purpose and structure of a ground lease as generally understood in today's world. But one still sees it sometimes, even in modern transactions.

* * *

IDENTITY OF LEASEHOLD MORTGAGEE

... Neither a tenant nor a leasehold mortgagee will tolerate any general right for a landlord to approve leasehold mortgages or leasehold mortgagees.

A tenant and a leasehold mortgagee will, however, often agree to reasonable qualifications and restrictions on the identity of leasehold mortgagees and their transferees. For example, they might live with limitations like the following.

- The leasehold mortgagee cannot be an affiliate of the tenant, as this would in effect give the tenant all the added protections of a leasehold mortgagee—without the logical justification to do so. A tenant might, however, argue that good business reasons may exist for an affiliate to make a Leasehold Mortgage. On that basis, the Lease should allow it, but deny the affiliated Leasehold Mortgagee the right to exercise any Leasehold Mortgagee Protections beyond the right to hold a foreclosure sale.

- The leasehold mortgagee must meet certain "institutional" tests (for example, it must be an institutional lender, have a minimum net worth or a minimum level of other investments in real estate debt or equity or real estate assets under management, and satisfy other objective and appropriate standards). Without such a limitation, the landlord runs a number of risks, such as the possibility that the leasehold mortgagee may itself enter bankruptcy proceedings and hence the automatic stay may prevent the landlord from giving such leasehold mortgagee a notice necessary so the landlord can exercise rights or remedies against the tenant.

* * *

ESTOPPEL CERTIFICATES

Closing Requirement. For any leasehold mortgage closing, the leasehold mortgagee will typically require the landlord to deliver an estoppel certificate, confirming the status of the lease and potentially covering certain other matters. . . .

* * *

■ *Estoppel Certificate For A New Lease?* A leasehold mortgagee will often want an estoppel certificate even if the lease is being signed at closing, at least to confirm that the lease represents the entire agreement between the landlord and the tenant and that the landlord recognizes the existence of this particular leasehold mortgagee as opposed to leasehold mortgagees generally. A contemporaneous estoppel certificate also helps give the lender comfort that no unresolved issues exist between the landlord and the tenant. It may not ferret out any consideration that the landlord is paying the tenant, or vice versa, for entering into the lease. If the existence of such consideration would affect the leasehold mortgagee's underwriting, the leasehold mortgagee may want to investigate further.

■ *Separate Contract.* The leasehold mortgagee may also want to expand the estoppel certificate to confirm, expressly, that mortgagee protections constitute a separate contractual obligation from the landlord to the leasehold mortgagee, enforceable independently from the lease (and even, for example, if the lease has been rejected or terminated and does not adequately provide for "survival" of the leasehold mortgagee's "new lease" rights). A leasehold mortgagee may want to go a step further and require a separate recorded agreement to such effect.

■ *Loan Transfers.* Any estoppel certificate should look ahead to the high likelihood that the lender will transfer the loan. Therefore, the estoppel certificate should run in favor of not only the lender, but also its successors and assigns. The landlord will always want to say that any future reliance does not change the effective date of the certificate.

* * *

PERCENTAGE RENT

Usually, a ground lease establishes a formula for ground rent that does not depend on the tenant's income, but instead on a formulaic schedule or a value-based adjustment that reflects the general value of the site (considered as if vacant) rather than any value that arises from the tenant's efforts. The tenant essentially pays a negotiated purchase price (albeit in the form of a long-term ground rent instead of a cash payment at closing) and then the tenant's exploitation of the leased premises is the tenant's business.

A landlord may prefer to convert some component of the ground rent into percentage rent, if for example, the landlord: (a) anticipates dramatic but unpredictable success of the tenant's development project; (b) believes actual rental income is a better measure of the landlord's compensation than hypothetical land value as it may be estimated many years in the future and adjusted only infrequently; or (c) cannot assess the value of the site or the appropriate ground rent when the lease is signed, perhaps because the actual development potential cannot be reliably calculated.

In these cases, a landlord will occasionally insist on receiving a formulaic base rent (lower than it might otherwise be) plus a percentage of the tenant's gross income. Percentage rent of this type rapidly creates a litany of difficult issues and, in part for that reason, is disfavored for long-term ground leases.

* * *

TRANSFER RESTRICTIONS

Any leasehold mortgagee will, as a general proposition, want any lease to be freely transferable. Free transferability is in fact the "market standard" in ground leasing transactions, with a few exceptions. Remarkably, the rating agencies do not consistently and unambiguously require absolute free assignability of the leasehold. Instead, they seem willing to live with some landlord consent requirements, as long as any necessary consents for the current tenant and the current financing have already been granted.

Under black letter law, a lease is typically assignable unless it says it's not. Many leasehold mortgagees and their counsel will, however, want to see an express right to assign. Therefore, any lease that is intended to be "financeable" should contain such a provision, to avoid leaving a basis for any leasehold mortgagee, its counsel, or a future investor to raise questions or request a "clarification" from the landlord.

Transfer Approval Requirements. If a lease contemplates that the tenant will undertake major construction, the landlord may legitimately want the tenant to agree not to assign its position (other than to an affiliate in a way that preserves the landlord's credit package) until the major construction has been completed. Leasehold mortgagees will typically live with that restriction, as long as it carves out transfers to leasehold mortgagees and certain related transfers.

If the landlord is a governmental or not-for-profit entity, this often represents another circumstance when a tenant or leasehold mortgagee may be relatively willing to tolerate transfer restrictions, based on the assumption (or at least the hope or likelihood) that the landlord will not take maximum advantage of every available profit opportunity. Of course, it may depend on exactly what type of not-for-profit is involved and how it perceives its mission and fiduciary obligations. If the landlord ever transfers its position to a private investor, the tenant and leasehold mortgagee may want any landlord approval rights to vanish. . . .

Leasehold Mortgagee's Transfers. . . . If the lease contains any restrictions on transfer, then the tenant and the leasehold mortgagee should add language to exempt a foreclosing leasehold mortgagee from those restrictions, or at least as many of them as possible. The exemption should ideally apply to a leasehold mortgagee's foreclosure sale, the first subsequent transfer, and all subsequent transfers after that—as much as can be negotiated. If the transfer restrictions merely exempt the mortgage itself or only the foreclosure sale, but then come back to bite the next transfer (or perhaps the transfer after that), a leasehold mortgagee may have a problem, unless its business strategy contemplated the possibility of long-term ownership of the collateral.

* * *

Permitted Transfers. To the extent that the tenant and the leasehold mortgagee agree to tolerate any assignment restrictions in a lease, the landlord must consider all the usual issues that arise for any set of assignment restrictions. For example, any savvy landlord will remember that a prohibition on lease assignment usually does not limit a transfer of equity interests in the tenant, and therefore the landlord will add such a limitation. In response, the tenant and the leasehold mortgagee will think about the need to exempt certain transfers from the prohibitions in the lease, such as transfers:

- To affiliates;

- As part of a portfolio transaction or the sale of a business;

- For estate planning purposes or as the result of death;

- Among existing owners;

- Within the family (including domestic partners whether or not recognized as spouses under state law); or

- Arising from the admission of passive investors or not producing a change of control or management.

* * *

SUBLEASES

Importance of Subleasing. In addition to having the ability to freely transfer a lease, any leasehold mortgagee will also often want to assure that the lease allows subletting without limitation. This issue falls in the short list of issues that many leasehold mortgagees regard as "leasehold mortgagee protections" even though they relate to issues that are hardly unique to leasehold mortgagees—but instead affect the value and desirability of the lease as considered from any careful tenant's point of view.

* * *

SNDAs [Subordination, Nondisturbance, and Attornment Agreements] For Subtenants. For the tenant to be able to mount a successful subleasing program, the tenant may need assurances that the landlord will agree to recognize commercial subtenants as direct tenants if the lease ever terminates, and not disturb the subtenants' possession. Attorneys practicing in this area vary in how they label these agreements. "Recognition" may be the term used more commonly in the context of protecting subtenants against adverse consequences from possible termination of a ground lease. The word "nondisturbance" probably applies more to protection of tenants after foreclosure of a mortgage. Nevertheless, the words are used interchangeably in common practice and here.

* * *

USE

In a perfect world for any tenant and leasehold mortgagee, any ground lease will allow the tenant to conduct "any lawful use" in the premises. Tenants and leasehold mortgagees will, however, usually tolerate a narrower permitted use. Any such narrowing affects the value of the lease more than its basic financeability, provided that the scope of permitted uses still makes sense, allows reasonable flexibility, and will not intolerably limit a leasehold mortgagee's resale of the lease after a foreclosure event. . . . If . . . the landlord owns other operating real property near the leased premises and desires to maintain a coordinated set of land uses in the entire area, the landlord's position becomes particularly compelling. In these cases, the landlord may even want the tenant to promise to operate the leased premises for a certain use. The tenant may reluctantly accept such an obligation, at least for some period. If the tenant ever stops operating, the landlord may want a right to recapture (in which case the tenant will expect to be paid at least the book value of its improvement). Any such leasehold mortgagee would want to treat the possibility of any such recapture as the functional equivalent of a lease default.

* * *

CHANGE OF ZONING

Because of the likelihood of neighborhood change and other changed circumstances over the long term of a ground lease, a tenant may want the right to change the zoning of the premises. Absent unusual circumstances, the landlord should agree to cooperate as needed.

The landlord may want to limit the tenant's right to change zoning, if only to prevent the tenant from "downzoning" from a more valuable use to a less valuable use. As long as the tenant is willing to live with such a limitation, a typical generic landlord will generally have no legitimate basis to refuse to agree to cooperate with a change of zoning, particularly if the next rent adjustment under the lease will take the change of zoning into account. On the other hand, if the lease restricts the tenant's change of use—for example, because the landlord owns adjacent property and wants to achieve a certain mix of uses over a larger area or is a municipality or university whose agenda goes beyond rent maximization—the landlord would probably not want to agree to accommodate any change of zoning. The tenant would have to live with this restriction as part of the fundamental structure of the deal, an extension of the restrictive use clause.

* * *

LOSS (CASUALTY OR CONDEMNATION)

The possibility of a loss (a casualty or a condemnation) and its endless variations often consume many pages in a lease or a set of loan documents. The parties can negotiate and fine-tune this topic, and create new categories, conditions, and distinctions, to whatever degree they want or can stand (and whatever they dream up will, in all likelihood, bear little similarity to whatever actually happens in the real world in the unlikely event that the property suffers any loss).

Of all the issues any leasehold mortgagee protections cover, treatment of a loss may constitute the one issue least suited to a "one size fits all" resolution, but also the one where cost-benefit considerations most cry out for it. . . .

A lease must treat casualty and condemnation rather differently. After the former occurs, the improvements can typically be rebuilt and the parties can, at least in theory, be put back to exactly the same physical position that they were in before the casualty. (If, however, all the leases go away and the leasing market has worsened, the parties will not find themselves in the same financial position.) After a condemnation occurs, in contrast, neither the landlord nor the tenant retains an interest in the premises, and the premises—the shared asset—has changed its character from real estate into cash or a claim for payment against the condemning authority. That cash or claim should ultimately give each party something as close as possible (under the circumstances) to their interest in the premises before the condemnation occurred.

The rest of the world may consider real estate lawyers rather odd for spending so much time thinking about these things. Casualties and condemnations do happen, though, particularly in the long run, such as the 50-year or 99-year term of a lease. If a lease does not handle these events correctly, the defect may represent more than a minor anomaly. Instead, it may lead a conservative lender to reject an entire transaction, merely because under one particular unlikely hypothetical circumstance (a loss) the value that the lender counted on will simply vanish—with nothing to replace it.

Partial Condemnation. The various issues and inquires relating to loss proceeds become particularly complex as they relate to application of a condemnation award that arises from an insubstantial or partial condemnation, especially where parts of the project have special characteristics that may require special treatment depending on when, where, and how a particular loss occurs. The permutations and variations are endless, if one thinks long and hard enough about them.

Casualty. The landlord will argue that even though someone else (the tenant and its lender) paid for the improvements, one reason the landlord signed the lease was the fact that the landlord expected to inherit (or that the landlord's children or grandchildren would inherit) the improvements at the end of the term; hence, all property insurance proceeds should go to the landlord or be applied to restore in all circumstances whatsoever. The outcome of this issue will vary from lease to lease. In some cases, the treatment or allocation of proceeds might reflect a formula depending on the remaining term.

A leasehold mortgagee (unlike a typical fee mortgagee) will usually be willing to agree that loss proceeds must always be applied to restore, provided that the leasehold mortgagee is happy with who will hold the funds and the disbursement arrangements. In general, the leasehold mortgagee will recognize that the landlord's arguments in favor of restoring in all cases (where feasible) are substantially valid. In other words, because three parties—not just two—have an interest in restoring, the leasehold mortgagee cannot simply take the money and run, as a typical fee mortgagee might be able to do.

* * *

OPTIONS

A tenant may desire options to extend the lease or to purchase the premises at certain points. Therefore, almost every ground lease includes extension options—often many extension options. And perhaps a majority of ground leases give the tenant at least a "right of first refusal" to purchase the premises if the landlord ever decides to sell.

In the common case where an individual landlord wants to use a lease because the landlord would suffer a tax disaster upon a sale, the parties will often give the tenant a purchase option effective for some reasonable period after the landlord's death, based on the fact that the landlord's heirs would take a stepped-up basis at that point.

A leasehold mortgagee should scrutinize the language of any option to understand the conditions that must be satisfied to exercise the option. Can the leasehold mortgagee control the satisfaction of those conditions? Should the leasehold mortgagee have the right to exercise the option even if the conditions are not satisfied? These questions become particularly important if the option pricing is attractive or other elements of the transaction will effectively force the tenant (or the leasehold mortgagee) to exercise the option.

The landlord, on the other hand, may want to make the options in a lease harder to exercise, such as by attaching conditions (starting with the absence of any default as opposed to the absence of any event of default) and by stating that time is of the essence.

* * *

DEFAULTS, RIGHTS, AND REMEDIES—BETWEEN LANDLORD AND TENANT

Leasehold mortgagee protections concern themselves in large part with defaults, events of default, and the landlord's rights and remedies. These are the concepts that ultimately allow a landlord to terminate a lease and hence cause leasehold mortgagees to lose sleep. Here are some thoughts that landlords, tenants, and leasehold mortgagees may sometimes want to consider in dealing with landlords' remedies under leases and, particularly, the risk of termination upon default.

* * *

Why Termination? The possibility that a lease might terminate upon the tenant's default drives most of the concerns of any leasehold mortgagee. If a lease could not terminate upon the tenant's default, most of those concerns would vanish.

Must a landlord always have the right to terminate a lease for a default? Why not limit the landlord to an action for damages or for injunctive relief? Or why not say that only a court can terminate the lease—after a full litigation in which both the tenant and any leasehold mortgagees have been served? Why should the lease give the landlord an absolute nonjudicial right to "terminate" a lease upon a default (whether through a "conditional limitation" or other termination procedure)? Why shouldn't the lease termination be deferred until a court hearing or some other protracted procedure to assure that the tenant has full opportunity to cure its default and tell a court why the lease should not be terminated? Why not make it just as hard for a landlord to terminate a ground lease as it is for a mortgagee to foreclose a mortgage? Any of these measures would substantially diminish the need for many of the typical leasehold mortgagee protections and would substantially increase the stability and reliability of a ground lease as collateral for a loan.

* * *

Duty To Mitigate Damages. . . . Any landlord under a ground lease is supposed to receive an annuity, terminate any active management of the property, and never need to think about the property again until the lease expires. In such a case, mitigation requirements seem less appropriate than in the case of a landlord that actively manages commercial property leased for a short term or to multiple tenants. The landlord might also argue that both the passive landlord and the tenant have equal access to the leasing market, and the burden should fall on the tenant—not the landlord—to find a replacement tenant, as long as the terms of the lease make any such replacement feasible and practical (which they usually will, by allowing relatively free assignment and subletting).

* * *

CURE RIGHTS

The Limits of Cure Rights. Every prospective leasehold mortgagee always remembers that any lease needs to require the landlord to give leasehold mortgagees notice of any tenant default and opportunity to cure. But leasehold mortgagees may forget that cure rights merely allow the leasehold mortgagee to cure the default. They don't prevent a default from occurring. They still leave the leasehold mortgagee exposed to the possible risk of needing to "go out of pocket" to perform the tenant's obligations under the lease to save the lender's collateral.

If the lease contains—or might ever contain—any obligation that a leasehold mortgagee might find unpalatable or overly expensive, "cure rights" do not protect the leasehold mortgagee. If the tenant does not perform, the leasehold mortgagee will simply need to cure the unpalatable or overly expensive default, or lose the lease. Cure rights do not solve all problems. They simply give the leasehold mortgagee an opportunity to either (a) turn the defaulting borrower/tenant's problem into the leasehold mortgagee's problem or (b) lose all the collateral for the loan. Hence, a leasehold mortgagee's underwriting process must include a thorough review of the entire lease, to confirm that nothing in it can ever create an unpleasant surprise.

* * *

Cash Requirements. Do leasehold mortgagees fully understand the potential extent of their exposure and cash requirements if they ever need to cure defaults under a lease? Will they be willing and able to come up with substantial sums of money if needed to cure possible major defaults? Are they prepared to fund into a default or a dispute situation at a time when they might not have certainty regarding all the facts, or time to analyze them? These questions are reminders that even the world's most financeable lease is still a lease. It is still "collateral that eats." Leasehold mortgagees need to be ready to feed it if necessary. Are they? And are they institutionally capable of acting as quickly as may become necessary?

The issues in the preceding paragraph take on particular significance for any leasehold mortgagee that does not itself have a substantial balance sheet, or does not have quick access to any additional cash, such as an indenture trustee. How will the leasehold mortgagee quickly obtain the money it needs to save the lease? Sometimes the parties try to solve this problem by giving the leasehold mortgagee an escrow fund to draw upon if needed to cure defaults. In a true meltdown, though, will the cash suffice? If the leasehold mortgagee's cure periods are too short, issues like these may vitiate the leasehold mortgagee's cure rights entirely.

* * *

Bottom Line. As a bottom line matter, although every leasehold mortgagee always wants extensive cure rights, any leasehold mortgagee is highly unlikely to exercise them, for any number of reasons, including: (a) liability and other fears; (b) institutional inertia and delays; (c) bank group dissension; (d) lack of funds; (e) unrecoverability; and (f) an inclination to rely on a court-appointed receiver.

How often do leasehold mortgagees actually exercise cure rights? In the real world, these rights probably amount to a monitoring mechanism more than a practical lease preservation mechanism.

* * *

NEW LEASE

Overkill? Leasehold mortgagee protections [often] include, to one degree or another, traditional language requiring the landlord to enter into a "new lease" if the lease terminates. Some commentators believe "new lease" provisions are overkill. Whether that is true or not, most leasehold mortgagees, their counsel, and the rating agencies still expect to see new lease provisions in any "financeable" ground lease. Such provisions deliver a backup measure of protection from unexpected surprises (primarily the tenant's rejection of the lease in bankruptcy without the leasehold mortgagee's consent, but also the possibility that the leasehold mortgagee somehow fails to exercise its cure rights adequately, or the possibility of some weird left-field event that the parties cannot imagine—a recurring theme in the world of ground leases).

NOTES

1. *Subordinating the fee title.* Mr. Stein is undeniably correct that "subordination" is an inapt term to describe a ground lessor's agreement to subject the fee title to what would otherwise be a leasehold mortgage, but the term is so widely used that it seems inescapable. However, decisions in several recent cases have raised serious questions as to whether a mere "subordination" by the lessor is enough to subject the fee title to the mortgage. *See* Culberson Transp. Serv., Inc. v. John Alden Life Ins. Co., 1997 WL 358857 (Ohio App.1997), *review denied* 80 Ohio St.3d 1437, 685 N.E.2d 546 (1997); Travelers Ins. Co. v. Holiday Village Shopping Center Ltd. Partn., 280 Mont. 217, 931 P.2d 1292 (1996); Balch v. Leader Fed. Bank for Sav., 315 Ark. 444, 868 S.W.2d 47 (1993). *Contra see* In re Perrysburg Marketplace Co., 208 B.R. 148 (Bankr.N.D.Ohio 1997) (mere use of word "subordinate" is sufficient). In any event, mere use of the term "subordination" is a very poor practice. If the lessor is to subordinate the fee title, the mortgage should describe that interest, and the lessor should sign the mortgage.

2. *Subordination agreement in the ground lease.* Suppose the developer/lessee obtains a ground lease in which the lessor agrees to subordinate to any financing that the developer obtains. Does any problem exist by analogy to *Handy v. Gordon*, 422 P.2d 329 (1967) ("an enforceable subordination clause must contain terms that will define and minimize the risk that the subordinating liens will impair or destroy the seller's security")? *See* Dugan v. First Nat'l Bank, 227 Kan. 201, 606 P.2d 1009 (1980). Should the law protect the lessor from the results of acting incautiously? *See generally* Steve A. Bovell, The Subordinated Ground Lease, 23 Prac.Law. 41 (Sept. 1977).

3. *Protecting against inflation.* On the problem of protecting the ground lessor's cash flow against inflation, *see* Joshua Stein, The Most Important Issue in Every Ground Lease, 29 No. 1 Prac. Real Est. Law. 35 (2013). One approach is to provide that rent will be an agreed percentage of the land's appraised value and that the land periodically will be reappraised. In Eltinge & Graziadio Dev. Co. v. Childs, 49 Cal.App.3d 294, 122 Cal.Rptr. 369 (1975), the lease's stated purpose was for the construction of a shopping center, but it did not require that a shopping center be maintained on the land for any specific period of time. The ground tenant argued that the term

"appraised value" in the rent clause meant the property's value in light of its actual use as a shopping center. The court held that fair market value was the intended standard. What other problems can you envision in reappraisal clauses?

EMANUEL B. HALPER, MORTGAGEABILITY OF
UNSUBORDINATED GROUND LEASES (PART IV)

16 Real Est. Rev. 64, 68–69 (Fall 1986)*

Bankruptcy Clauses Don't Belong in Unsubordinated
Ground Leases

Including a bankruptcy clause in an unsubordinated ground lease is like dropping a starving shark in a tropical fish tank. If you insert a shark in the tank on Tuesday, expect some material changes by Wednesday. Possibly, the tropical fish will eat the shark. But don't bet on it.

Of course the principal goal of the bankruptcy clause of a lease is to terminate the leasehold estate in case the tenant becomes a debtor pursuant to a case commenced under the Bankruptcy Code.

A leasehold mortgagee would be more worried about the possible termination of the leasehold estate as a result of a bankruptcy than about its termination as a result of a default were it not for one of the delightful provisions of Section 365(e) of the Bankruptcy Code, which reads as follows:

(e)(1) Notwithstanding a provision in an executory contract or unexpired lease, or in applicable law, an executory contract or unexpired lease of the debtor may not be terminated or modified, and any right or obligation under such contract or lease may not be terminated or modified, at any time after the commencement of the case solely because of a provision in such contract or lease that is conditioned on—

(A) the insolvency or financial condition of the debtor at any time before the closing of the case;

(B) the commencement of a case under this title; or

(C) the appointment of or taking possession by a trustee in a case under this title or a custodian before such commencement.[3]

In short, Section 365(e) of the Bankruptcy Code clearly blocks a landlord from terminating a leasehold estate as a result of most of the events described in bankruptcy clauses.

---

    3   11 U.S.C.A. § 365(e).

If Section 365(e) works this wonder, why do some prospective leasehold mortgagees still find bankruptcy clauses so disagreeable? One reason may be that lenders fear the possibility that the statute could be amended to permit landlords to cancel leases as a result of bankruptcy or insolvency. A much greater irritant to leasehold mortgagees is the fact that the wording of most bankruptcy clauses extends their scope to circumstances that have no (or only a peripheral) relationship to bankruptcy.

The inclusion of nonbankruptcy events in the bankruptcy clause is traditional rather than logical. The work of some less-than-knowledgeable legal draftsman of the distant past has found its way into the form books. Given the curious predilection of lawyers to copy the work of earlier generations (no matter how ineptly or illiterately drafted), the ancient form still troubles negotiators.

Here are four events that, although not directly related to bankruptcy, smelled like bankruptcy to the long-forgotten author of the poorly drafted ground lease forms that are still used.

- An assignment for the benefit of creditors

- The failure to discharge a judgment or an attachment

- The dissolution of the tenant

- The appointment of a receiver or a trustee of any of the tenant's property

A leasehold mortgagee can't stop a tenant from assigning its assets for the benefit of creditors. Assignments for the benefit of creditors are not governed by the federal Bankruptcy Act; so Section 365(e) won't protect the leasehold mortgagee against a termination.

The failure of a tenant to discharge a judgment or an attachment and the appointment of a receiver or trustee of any of the tenant's assets (in a nonbankruptcy proceeding) as a foundation for lease termination fall into the silly category. By itself, a tenant's failure to discharge a judgment does no harm to a ground lessor and doesn't even indicate that the tenant's financial position has deteriorated. Many shopping center owners have default judgments outstanding for no reason other than a failure of their liability insurance companies to have answered a summons and complaint properly.

The appointment of a state court receiver to take control of one apartment house owned by a tenant who owns another fifty buildings is not significant in this context and should not trouble a landowner.

Dissolution of a tenant is no big deal, and it shouldn't bother a landowner at all. Many partnerships are ground lease tenants. If a partnership dissolves, the partners become tenants in common, or a reconstituted partnership becomes the tenant. So what! On the other hand, if the dissolution of the tenant can cause a termination of the leasehold estate, the ground lease will not be mortgageable.

A leasehold mortgagee does not have the power to stop these events from happening or the power to cure them in case they do happen. A lender that would accept a ground lease that includes such provisions as security would risk losing its investment without the opportunity to protect itself.

NOTE

Additional readings. For an excellent general treatment of the subject of ground leases, see Gerald T. Grenert, Ground Lease Practice (Calif.Cont.Ed. of the Bar 1971). *See also* Jerome D. Whalen, Commercial Ground Leases (2d ed. 2008); Bernard H. Goldstein, Ground-Lease Provisions for the Construction of a New Building, 1 Prac.Real Est.Law. 55 (Jan. 1985); Steve A. Bovell, The Subordinated Ground Lease, 23 Prac.Law. 41 (Sept. 1977); Noel Nellis, Drafting or Reviewing a Ground Lease to Make it "Mortgageable," 1 Cal.C.E.B. Real Prop.L.Rptr. 49 (May 1978).

3. MEZZANINE LOANS AND PREFERRED EQUITY INVESTMENTS

As described earlier in this chapter, investors generally prefer to have as little of their own money invested in a real estate project as possible. Their rate of return increases as the loan-to-value ratio (LTV) of the project's financing increases. However, first mortgage loans on income-producing properties usually have an LTV of not more than 75%. John C. Murray & Randall L. Scott, Title and UCC Insurance for Mezzanine-Financing Transactions, 43 Real Prop. Tr. & Est. J. 83, 84 (2008). Therefore, investors often want to borrow additional funds for the project. A frequent obstacle is a due-on-encumbrance clause in the first mortgage. As described in Chapter 5, Section B supra, that clause authorizes the mortgagee to accelerate the loan if a second mortgage is granted.

Mezzanine loans and preferred equity investments are methods of obtaining financing that do not create a new encumbrance on the land. A mezzanine loan is to the equity holders of the entity that owns the project, and they pledge their equity shares as security for the loan. For example, if a limited partnership owns the project, the loan is to the limited partners, and they pledge their partnership interests as security. The security interest is subordinate to the mortgage but is superior to the borrowers' ownership interest. In a preferred equity investment, the lender receives an ownership interest in the borrowing entity.

A diligent first mortgage lender's loan documents require the lender's prior consent to either of these arrangements and make a pledge of the ownership interests in the borrower without the lender's prior consent an event of default. A first mortgage lender normally also will require an inter-creditor agreement with the mezzanine lender. Additionally, the first mortgage lender should reserve the right to approve all members/owners of the borrower in the case of a preferred equity arrangement. A responsible first mortgage lender will understand the sources and structure of any equity, preferred equity, and mezzanine debt in the capital stack before the closing of the first mortgage loan.

ANDREW R. BERMAN, "ONCE A MORTGAGE, ALWAYS A MORTGAGE"—THE USE (AND MISUSE) OF MEZZANINE LOANS AND PREFERRED EQUITY INVESTMENTS

11 Stan. J.L. Bus. & Fin. 76, 80, 105–12 (2005)*

The rapid success of mezzanine loans and preferred equity investments indicates more than just market demand for new and popular financial products. These new financings are quickly (and quietly) replacing conventional junior mortgages as the principal means to provide property owners with additional financing. In so doing, these new financing techniques have not only fundamentally transformed the real estate capital markets but also marked a new chapter in the history of real estate finance. The conventional wisdom on real estate finance is no longer true: real estate finance is not limited simply to the many varieties of mortgage products in the primary and secondary mortgage market. Now, commercial property owners have a new array of new financing techniques some of which are neither directly secured by real estate nor even directly involve land.

* * *

A major NYC real estate developer recently completed a real estate refinancing of The Daily News Building—one of the many properties held in his vast real estate portfolio. The Daily News Building, located on East 42nd Street in midtown Manhattan, is what real estate brokers like to refer to as a "trophy" office building. It contains over one million square feet of office space, and was recently estimated to be worth approximately $250 million dollars. Unable to sell The Daily News Building at the price he desired, the owner instead chose to refinance the property for about $240 million dollars. After paying off the existing first mortgage from the loan proceeds of this refinancing, the owner was able to pocket almost $80 million dollars.

---

* Reprinted with permission of Andrew R. Berman and the Stanford Journal of Law, Business & Finance.

How did the owner of The Daily News Building achieve this alchemy? He was able to structure a transaction that actually consisted of several separate real estate financings: (i) a first mortgage loan for $155 million made by Deutsche Bank; (ii) a mezzanine loan for $30 million made by Capital Trust, a New York investment fund; and (iii) a preferred equity investment in the amount of $53 million made by SL Green, a New York real estate investment trust. While no longer unusual, this real estate owner combined conventional mortgage debt with two new non-traditional financing techniques: mezzanine financing and preferred equity investments.

A. Mezzanine Loans.

* * *

In the real estate capital markets, the term "mezzanine financing" refers to debt that sits between senior debt and the borrower's equity. In this case, mezzanine debt is junior to the mortgage loan but senior to the borrower's equity. A mezzanine loan in the real estate industry typically refers to debt that is secured solely by the mezzanine borrower's indirect ownership of the mortgage borrower—the entity that actually owns the income producing real property. This same underlying real property also serves as collateral for the senior mortgage lender.

In a mezzanine loan, neither the mezzanine borrower nor lender actually holds any direct real property interest in the underlying land serving as collateral. Rather, their respective interests are derived solely from the mezzanine borrower's (direct or indirect) ownership of the equity in the underlying mortgage borrower. The mezzanine borrower grants to the mezzanine lender a lien on its equity in the mortgage borrower pursuant to a written instrument (typically a security agreement), and thereafter the mezzanine lender holds an effective lien on the collateral at least vis-à-vis the mezzanine borrower.

Similar to junior mortgage financing, the national rating agencies also dictate to a large extent the form and structure of mezzanine financing. For instance, in a typical mezzanine financing, the rating agencies require that the underlying organizational documents of the mezzanine borrower only permit certain specified activities. As a corporate law matter, the mezzanine borrower may only own the direct or indirect equity in the mortgage borrower and it is typically prohibited from undertaking any other corporate or business activity. Because of these organizational limitations, this type of entity is referred to as a "special purpose" entity (SPE).

The rating agencies often also require the underlying organizational documents of the mezzanine borrower to prohibit or significantly curtail its ability to file any type of petition for bankruptcy, insolvency, or reorganization. These types of provisions and limitations are optimistically considered to make an entity "bankruptcy remote," and the industry refers to such an entity as a bankruptcy remote entity (BRE). In order to qualify as a SPE/BRE, the rating agencies also require strict limits on the type and amount of permitted additional indebtedness and require their approval of the identity of, and the review of the management, finances, and experience of, the mezzanine lender. These limitations represent, in part, the agencies' attempt to avoid the substantive consolidation of the mezzanine borrower's assets with another bankrupt but related entity.

Since the mezzanine lender's collateral is equity in another entity, the collateral is technically personal property; therefore Article 9 of the Uniform Commercial Code (UCC) applies rather than local mortgage law. By recording a UCC–1 Financing Statement in the appropriate recording office, the mezzanine lender can also generally ensure that its lien is effective and superior to most other third-parties'. Similar to mortgage law, once the Financing Statement describing the collateral is properly recorded, the mezzanine lender's security interest becomes perfected and is thereafter generally superior to that of subsequent lien holders, judgment lien creditors and bona fide purchasers.

Mezzanine loans differ significantly from traditional loans secured by real estate where the mortgage borrower directly owns income producing real property. With a mortgage loan, the mortgage borrower grants a lien on its real property pursuant to a written instrument (typically a mortgage or in some states, a deed of trust), and thereafter the lender holds an effective mortgage lien on the collateral. In addition, since the rights and remedies of a mortgagee are inextricably linked to the mortgaged real property, the law of the state where the real property is located typically governs the enforceability of the lender's principal remedies (i.e., lender's right to obtain a receiver or foreclose the mortgage lien). By recording the mortgage in the land records where the property is located, mortgage lenders can also generally ensure that its lien is effective and superior to most other third-parties'.

In addition, because of the interplay between federal bankruptcy law and mortgage law, a mortgagee may typically assert a powerful arsenal of rights and remedies against both the mortgage borrower and any third party claiming any of the bankrupt debtor's assets, including any junior secured lender, unsecured creditor, or equity investor. The mortgage law of most states, for example, permits a mortgagee to appoint a receiver for the property, foreclose the mortgage and sell the real property, and eliminate many subordinate junior liens and encumbrances adversely affecting the value of the collateral. By granting the mortgagee the power to eliminate certain junior liens and encumbrances, the mortgage foreclosure process typically enables a mortgagee to sell the property at the foreclosure sale for a higher price, thereby increasing the cash available to repay the outstanding debt.

Compared to the senior mortgage lender's right to foreclose its senior mortgage, the mezzanine lender's right to foreclose on the equity interests of the mezzanine borrower is both riskier and of somewhat limited value. Whereas a mortgagee's foreclosure rights derive from its mortgage on the borrower's real property, a mezzanine lender's remedies derive solely from its lien on personal property (i.e., the equity in the mezzanine borrower). And unlike a mortgagee's right to foreclose all junior liens and encumbrances on the underlying real property, a mezzanine lender has no rights to foreclose any other liens on the underlying real property—a mezzanine lender's rights are limited solely to foreclosing junior liens on the equity in the mezzanine borrower and not the real property. Even after a successful foreclosure of a mezzanine loan, therefore, the underlying mortgage property remains subject to the lien of the senior mortgage as well as any other liens, leases, and other encumbrances previously recorded against the mortgage property. Furthermore, the existence of a default under the mezzanine loan suggests that there is probably inadequate cash flow or some other problem with the fundamentals of the real estate venture; therefore, it is likely that there will also be new tax liens, mechanics liens, and perhaps even judgment liens recorded against the underlying mortgaged property. These other liens only further deteriorate the value of the mezzanine lender's collateral.

Unfortunately for many mezzanine lenders, even their right to foreclose junior liens on their own collateral—the equity in the mezzanine borrower—is often of little value. Since the mezzanine loan documents typically prohibit any other liens on the lender's collateral and because of its limited marketability, it is unlikely (except in the case of fraud or willful violation of the mezzanine loan documents) that there are any other junior liens on the equity anyway. Oftentimes, the mezzanine lender's sole remedy is to foreclose its lien on the equity and then attempt to sell the equity at a UCC foreclosure sale. But the rating agencies also restrict the mezzanine lender's ability to foreclose on its collateral without compliance with many conditions. For example, the agencies all require that the mezzanine lender obtain a "No Downgrade Letter"— written confirmation from the rating agencies that the mezzanine lender's enforcement actions will not cause a downgrade of the rating of the related CMBS issuance which is secured or contains the related senior mortgage on the underlying real property. In addition, mezzanine lenders typically must also deliver to the rating agencies a new non-consolidation bankruptcy opinion. This opinion is typically prepared by a nationally recognized law firm and concludes that it is unlikely that the assets of the mortgage borrower will be substantively consolidated with the mezzanine borrower (or any other affiliated entities) in case of a bankruptcy.

In addition, since there is typically no active market for the purchase and sale of the equity in the mezzanine borrower and no other bidders, the mezzanine lender often has no choice other than to bid-in and "buy" the equity at the foreclosure sale. In such a case, the mezzanine lender still has not received any cash proceeds, although after the foreclosure sale, the mezzanine lender at least has direct day-to-day control of the mezzanine borrower (and, therefore, also indirect control of the mortgage borrower and the underlying real property). Only then may the mezzanine lender (in its new capacity as the indirect owner of the mortgage borrower) attempt to force a sale of the mortgaged property. But as discussed above, this right is of limited value since the underlying real property remains subject to the senior mortgage, which generally prohibits the sale of the real property and contains an extensive set of restrictive covenants and other prohibitions. The fact remains that even after a successful foreclosure on its collateral—the equity of the mezzanine borrower—the mezzanine lender is still just an owner in the underlying mortgage borrower. As equity, the mezzanine lender's claims are structurally subordinated and junior to every other secured or unsecured creditor of the mortgage borrower.

B. Preferred Equity Financing.

In a preferred equity transaction, the financing source (the Preferred Member) typically makes an investment (generally in the form of a capital contribution) in the underlying mortgage borrower. In exchange for its investment, the financing source receives equity in the mortgage borrower, and if the senior mortgage prohibits such an investment directly in the mortgage borrower, the financing source makes an investment in a newly formed entity that indirectly owns the underlying mortgage borrower.

The Preferred Member has special rights including a preferred rate of return on its investment and accelerated repayment of its capital. The organizational documents of the investment entity (i.e., the Preferred Equity Borrower) typically provide that the Preferred Member receives its preferred return (representing the interest component) before any other member receives any cash distributions. In addition, if the real estate venture is successful, the Preferred Member typically also has the right to receive certain cash distributions of excess cash flow. Since these distributions are usually applied to reduce the recipient's capital account, the Preferred Member typically also receives the repayment of its initial investment prior to the other equity investors. Because of these special rights, preferred equity transactions are analytically similar to traditional loans since the preferred rate of return basically reflects interest and the accelerated repayment of the capital reflects repayment of principal.

Although these preferential payments make the Preferred Member senior to the other equity investors, the Preferred Member is still just an equity owner in the Preferred Equity Borrower. As a result, it usually remains junior to all secured or unsecured creditors. Because of this unique structure, a Preferred Member in a preferred equity financing "occupies an identical position in the capital structure and in relation to the property cash flow as a mezzanine financing. . . ." However, a Preferred Member "differs significantly because it already has an equity ownership interest and does not need to foreclose any pledge to gain an equity ownership interest . . . in the borrower."

The national rating agencies usually require that the underlying senior mortgage and/or mezzanine loan prohibit or otherwise severely restrict any distributions to equity unless there is sufficient excess cash flow from the underlying income producing property. And typically there is excess cash flow only after the payment of a wide variety of expenses and obligations of the mortgage borrower (e.g., (i) interest and principal under the mortgage or mezzanine loan; (ii) required cash reserves for debt service, principal prepayment, capital improvements, tenant leasing expenses, and taxes and insurance operating expenses of the mortgage property; and (iii) trade creditors, taxing authorities, judgment lien and other creditors). Consequently, the Preferred Member doesn't ordinarily receive any cash distribution unless the enterprise is successful, there is excess cash flow, and all other expenses and debt obligations have been satisfied in full. No matter that a preferred equity transaction is substantively similar to a loan—since preferred equity is not legally structured as debt, a Preferred Member does not have the same rights as a creditor of the mortgage borrower. Given these structural realities, a Preferred Member is likely to receive its preferred rate of return and the repayment of its initial investment only if the mortgage borrower realizes its lofty economic projections, generates sufficient cash flow, and repays in full all its outstanding debt obligations.

On the other hand, if the venture fails to earn sufficient cash flow to repay the senior mortgage, it is likely that the Preferred Equity Borrower will default since there will also be insufficient funds to pay the Preferred Member its preferred return or capital. In order to maintain the fiction that preferred equity is not debt, however, the transaction documents typically refer to these "defaults" as "Change of Control Events." And, if a Change of Control Event occurs, most preferred equity arrangements provide that day-to-day control and management of the Preferred Equity Borrower automatically and immediately shifts to the Preferred Member. This "change of control" mechanism effectively makes the Preferred Member's remedies similar to a mezzanine lender. As discussed above, a mezzanine lender in order to enforce its rights typically would foreclosure its lien on the equity interests, thereby seizing day-to-day control of the mezzanine borrower. In this way, the mezzanine lender gains indirect but effective control of the mortgage borrower and the underlying mortgaged property. Unlike the mezzanine loan, however, the Preferred Member's financing arrangement is structured as an equity investment rather than secured debt. Therefore, there is no collateral and the Preferred Member has no foreclosure rights. However, after a Change of Control Event occurs, the Preferred Member effectively controls the mortgage borrower by virtue of the contractual provisions contained in the organizational documents of the borrower.

Although the Preferred Member will effectively control the mortgage borrower after a Change of Control Event occurs, the shift in control does nothing to eliminate any of the liens, contractual obligations, mortgages, and other obligations binding upon the mortgage borrower. Similar to a mezzanine lender, therefore, the Preferred Member also takes the "collateral" (i.e., control of the mortgage borrower) subject to the senior mortgage and any other existing liens and obligations. And unlike a mortgage lender, neither the mezzanine lender nor Preferred Member may foreclose upon and thereby eliminate any of these liens or encumbrances. In addition, preferred equity investments are also subject to certain bankruptcy risks such as the possibility that a bankruptcy court would recharacterize its equity investment as debt.

Furthermore, many senior mortgages prohibit any change in the composition of the direct equity investors in the mortgage borrower or a material change in the parties exercising effective control over the mortgage borrower. If the Preferred Member begins to exercise control of the mortgage borrower as a result of the occurrence of a Change in Control Event, therefore, it is likely that there would also be a default under the senior mortgage. Any default under the senior mortgage or the commencement of a mortgage foreclosure action substantially reduces the value of the Preferred Member's investment in the mortgage borrower. As a result, these mortgage prohibitions often leave the mezzanine lender and Preferred Member without any effective remedy.

NOTES

1. *Equitable mortgages?* In the article from which the preceding reading was excerpted, Professor Berman concludes that mezzanine loans and preferred equity financing are mortgage substitutes and that lenders use them, in part, to eliminate the borrower's equity of redemption. Based on the long-standing judicial refusal to allow lenders to "clog the equity of redemption," see Chapter 3, Section A supra, Professor Berman states that courts should apply mortgage law to mezzanine loans and preferred equity financing. For a contrary view, see Jon S. Robins, David E. Wallace & Mark

Franke, Mezzanine Finance and Preferred Equity Investment in Commercial Real Estate: Security, Collateral & Control, 1 Mich. J. Private Equity & Venture Cap. L. 93 (2012).

2. *Problems that a second mortgage creates.* Why do first mortgagees dislike second mortgages? After all, the first mortgagee has a superior lien. There are a number of reasons. For example, if the first mortgagee modifies its loan, the second mortgage may acquire priority, and it may be prior to optional loan advances on the first mortgage. A foreclosure on the second mortgage will eliminate junior leases. The second mortgagee may go bankrupt, which could result in a stay on the first mortgagee's ability to foreclose. *See* Joseph Philip Forte, Mezzanine Finance: A Legal Background, ALI-ABA Commercial Securitization for Real Estate Lawyers (Mar. 27–28, 2008) for an extensive list of potential problems that a second mortgage creates for first mortgagees.

3. *Risks for the mezzanine lender.* As described in the excerpt, mezzanine lenders occupy a far riskier position than a first mortgagee. For this reason, the interest rate on a mezzanine loan is substantially higher and the loan term is substantially shorter than for a first mortgage. The mezzanine loan term generally is five years or less. Michael T. Madison, Jeffry R. Dwyer & Steven W. Bender, The Law of Real Estate Financing (2007).

4. SALE-LEASEBACK

MICHAEL A. YUHAS & JAMES A. FELLOWS, SALE-LEASEBACKS REVISITED: THE OLD AND THE NEW OF FEDERAL TAX LAW
31 Real Est. L.J. 9 (Summer 2002)*

The sale-leaseback transaction is uniquely different from the traditional sales transaction, because the seller retains a property interest in the asset sold. Upon the sale of the real estate, the seller possesses a leasehold interest in the property, generally retaining an option to renew the lease as well as an option to repurchase the property at the expiration of the lease term. Typically, though not exclusively, the sale-leaseback transaction is attractive to those who are interested in constructing a new building, but who are unable to obtain conventional construction financing.

The Typical Sale-Leaseback

Under a typical sale-leaseback arrangement, the seller-lessee (hereinafter sometimes referred to as simply the "seller") agrees to transfer the legal title to unimproved real estate to the buyer-lessor (hereinafter sometimes referred to as simply the "buyer"). The buyer then agrees to finance the construction costs of a commercial building on the

---

* Reprinted with permission of the authors.

property, by obtaining a mortgage from a third party financial intermediary. Simultaneous to the sale, the buyer leases the property back to the seller. The terms of the lease are usually a long-term "triple net lease" arrangement, with the seller-lessee responsible for property taxes, insurance, and operating expenses. Such an arrangement shifts the benefits and burdens of ownership back to the seller-lessee. In addition, the lease agreement may also allocate the risk of destruction or condemnation back to the seller, by having the seller reimburse the buyer-lessor for any loss in property value due to casualties, or governmental seizures and regulatory edicts.

The seller-lessee's rental payments will usually approximate the amount the buyer-lessor will need to service the construction mortgage. The lease agreement will typically provide the seller with a lease renewal option at a fixed rental, along with the option to repurchase the property either during or at the end of the lease term for a price that may or may not approximate the fair market value of the property at that time.

* * *

Why the Sale-Leaseback?

Why arrange for a sale-leaseback in the first place? One reason is that the sale-leaseback may be the only way for the seller to obtain construction financing, especially if there exist contractual or regulatory restrictions against conventional borrowing. Furthermore, during tight credit conditions, the sale-leaseback may be the only source of financing available. The financial drawback here is that the cost of a sale-leaseback may be higher to the seller-lessee than conventional financing. Instead of paying interest to a financial institution, the seller will be making rental payments for the right to use property. The "implied interest" in the form of rental payments may be higher than the stated interest rate from a financial institution, as the buyer-lessor cannot usually spread the risk of financing a large number of properties over numerous lessees. In many cases, the buyer-lessor may be assuming substantial risk in financing the construction of the property for the seller-lessee. In addition to this risk element driving up the "implied interest" in the rental payments, the buyer, because it is not ostensibly charging interest, can circumvent local and state usury laws.

The sale-leaseback transaction may also prove to be more attractive than conventional financing for the seller in another respect. Unlike conventional financing, which generally provides the debtor with a maximum of 80 percent of the property's value, a sale-leaseback can provide the seller with a cash sales price equal to the full fair market value of the property. Moreover, if the lease agreement is structured properly, the rental obligations will not show up on the books of the seller-lessee as a debt obligation. Thus, a sale-leaseback provides a benefit to those entities that are under contractual limits as to how much debt they can carry on their books.

In addition to arranging favorable financing for construction, a sale-leaseback may be an easy method for the seller to generate some quick cash flow for commercial property already owned and constructed. Desiring immediate cash, the owner sells real estate (to include a commercial building and underlying land) to a buyer for cash, and then immediately leases the property (at least the building) back from the buyer. In effect, the seller-lessee is obtaining the equivalent of a loan for the full value of the property, generating cash for other purposes, with repayment to occur in the form of rental payments to the buyer-lessor.

Federal Income Tax Issues of the Sale-Leaseback

Whether the IRS and the courts respect the sale-leaseback as such, or reclassify the transaction as a financing device, can have dramatic income tax consequences for both the seller and buyer. If the sale-leaseback form is respected, the buyer-lessor is treated as the true owner, i.e., the "tax owner" of the property. As such, the buyer reports rental income and is entitled to depreciation deductions on the building, in addition to an interest deduction for repayments on any mortgage to the financial institution. The seller-lessee is entitled to a rental deduction for the amount of rents paid to the buyer, as well as deductions for any operating expenses such as property taxes, insurance, and maintenance costs. In addition, the seller reports gain or loss on the sale of the property to the buyer should the sale price be more or less than the property's cost basis.

You Are In Good Hands

Consider the following example, which succinctly summarizes the issues, and the difference between a true sale and an implicit financing arrangement.

Example: Profit, Inc. wants to construct a new retail store on undeveloped real estate that it already owns. Due to a tight money market and the desire to keep a conventional loan off its books, the company consummates a sale-leaseback agreement with Realty, LLC. Profit sells Realty the undeveloped land, and Realty agrees to construct the retail store on the land, leasing it back to Profit under a triple net lease arrangement over 36 years. The total construction cost is estimated to be $10,000,000, and Good Hands Insurance Company agrees to loan Realty $9,500,000 of the construction costs, with Realty financing the remaining $500,000. The terms of the loan are set at 8 percent interest per annum, with equal loan payments over 36 years. The lease terms are set so that the rental payments from Profit approximate the payments of interest and principal by Realty, LLC to Good Hands Insurance Company. Assuming that the sale-leaseback passes muster as a true sale under Federal tax law, Realty,

LLC is entitled not only to a deduction for interest paid on the loan, but is also entitled to depreciation on the building. Realty will of course have to report rental income from Profit, Inc., which is allowed a tax deduction for the rental payments, as well as any insurance, taxes, and operating expenses. Profit, Inc. must also report a gain or loss on the sale of the underlying land.

What are the tax consequences from the above scenario? The rental payments by Profit, set to coincide with the loan amortization payments by Realty to Good Hands, are $810,788 per year. Tax depreciation per year is $256,410, based on a 39-year tax life, with no salvage value. The interest for the first year, paid by Profit to Good Hands, as part of the first year loan payment, is $9,500,000 x .08 = $760,000. For the first year of the sale-leaseback period, Realty, LLC, the buyer-lessor, reports the following:

Rental income	$810,788
Depreciation	(256,410)
Interest expense	(760,000)
Tax loss	$(205,622)

Assuming that the investors of Realty, LLC (taxed as a partnership under Federal tax law) are all in the 40 percent tax bracket (when both Federal and state income taxes are considered), this tax loss provides an "up front" tax savings (reduction in tax liability) of $82,249. Profit, Inc. of course will deduct the $810,788 rental payment as an expense, along with any normal operating expenses.

On the other hand, if the agreement between Profit, Inc. and Realty, LLC is deemed a financing arrangement under extant tax law, then the sale is ignored for tax purposes, and Profit remains the "tax owner" of the property. Realty, LLC becomes a mere tax conduit, indirectly arranging financing from Good Hands Insurance Company. In this case, it is Profit, Inc., the seller-lessee and still the "tax owner" of the property, that is allowed the depreciation deduction for tax purposes. On the balance sheet of Profit, the capitalized present value of the future lease payments is considered an explicit liability. Moreover, the payments by Profit to Realty are treated as a repayment of an implicit loan by Realty to Profit. The first year's payment of $810,788 by Profit is now bifurcated between a $760,000 interest payment (and tax deduction) and a $50,788 reduction in loan principal. Profit, Inc. is also allowed the depreciation deduction of $256,410.

Realty, LLC reports interest income of $760,000, which should approximate the interest that it pays to Good Hands Insurance Company. Thus Realty has no tax profit or loss, and in effect loses the tax benefits for the year. These have been passed back to Profit, Inc. Under a true sale, Profit had tax deductions of $810,788, under the lease agreement, equal to the full rental payment to Realty. Its tax deductions now, under an implied financing arrangement, are:

Depreciation	$256,410
Interest	760,000
Total deductions	$1,016,410

The difference between Profit's total deductions under a financing arrangement, vis-à-vis the true sale arrangement in the preceding scenario, is $205,622, which equals the tax loss to Realty, LLC under a true sale scenario. Thus, a characterization of the sale-leaseback as a financing arrangement effectively passes the tax benefits (in the form of the depreciation deduction) back to the seller-lessee. There is certainly a conflict of tax interest here, so both the seller and buyer will have to negotiate the type of lease arrangement they desire. For example, a buyer-lessor in a high tax bracket may be willing to forgo some income, especially if it is a related party to the seller-lessee. But even if the two parties try to arrange a tax result that is mutually beneficial to both, it is not the intent of the parties, but the prevailing tax law, that will determine whether or not a true lease, or a financing agreement, exists. Notwithstanding the hopes or expectations of the parties, the sale-leaseback will be disregarded, and a financing transaction results, if the transaction is entered into without any economic, commercial, or legal purposes other than the avoidance of Federal income taxes.

APPENDIX A

LAND FINANCING FORMS

■ ■ ■

1. FANNIE MAE/FREDDIE MAC MULTISTATE FIXED RATE NOTE—SINGLE FAMILY

This Note, together with the Fannie Mae/Freddie Mac Uniform Mortgage and Deed of Trust Instruments, also reproduced in this Appendix, constitute the core of the most pervasively used single family residential financing document package. Because use of these documents is required for secondary market purchase by Fannie Mae and Freddie Mac, they have established a nationwide norm on numerous substantive issues, many of which are considered elsewhere in this volume.

NOTE

_____, _____ _____ _____
        [Date]   [City]   [State]

_____
[Property Address]

1. BORROWER'S PROMISE TO PAY

In return for a loan that I have received, I promise to pay U.S. $_____ (this amount is called "Principal"), plus interest, to the order of the Lender. The Lender is _____. I will make all payments under this Note in the form of cash, check or money order.

I understand that the Lender may transfer this Note. The Lender or anyone who takes this Note by transfer and who is entitled to receive payments under this Note is called the "Note Holder."

2. INTEREST

Interest will be charged on unpaid principal until the full amount of Principal has been paid. I will pay interest at a yearly rate of _____%.

The interest rate required by this Section 2 is the rate I will pay both before and after any default described in Section 6(B) of this Note.

3. PAYMENTS

(A) Time and Place of Payments

I will pay principal and interest by making a payment every month.

I will make my monthly payment on the _____ day of each month beginning on _____, _____. I will make these payments every month until I have paid all of the principal and interest and any other charges described below that I may owe under this Note. Each monthly payment will be applied as of its scheduled due date and will be applied to interest before Principal. If, on _____, 20_____, I still owe amounts under this Note, I will pay those amounts in full on that date, which is called the "Maturity Date."

I will make my monthly payments at _____ or at a different place if required by the Note Holder.

(B) Amount of Monthly Payments

My monthly payment will be in the amount of U.S. $_____.

4. BORROWER'S RIGHT TO PREPAY

I have the right to make payments of Principal at any time before they are due. A payment of Principal only is known as a "Prepayment." When I make a Prepayment, I will tell the Note Holder in writing that I am doing so. I may not designate a payment as a Prepayment if I have not made all the monthly payments due under the Note.

I may make a full Prepayment or partial Prepayments without paying a Prepayment charge. The Note Holder will use my Prepayments to reduce the amount of Principal that I owe under this Note. However, the Note Holder may apply my Prepayment to the accrued and unpaid interest on the Prepayment amount, before applying my Prepayment to reduce the Principal amount of the Note. If I make a partial Prepayment, there will be no changes in the due date or in the amount of my monthly payment unless the Note Holder agrees in writing to those changes.

5. LOAN CHARGES

If a law, which applies to this loan and which sets maximum loan charges, is finally interpreted so that the interest or other loan charges collected or to be collected in connection with this loan exceed the permitted limits, then: (a) any such loan charge shall be reduced by the amount necessary to reduce the charge to the permitted limit; and (b) any sums already collected from me which exceeded permitted limits will be refunded to me. The Note Holder may choose to make this refund by reducing the Principal I owe under this Note or by making a direct payment to me. If a refund reduces Principal, the reduction will be treated as a partial Prepayment.

6. BORROWER'S FAILURE TO PAY AS REQUIRED

(A) Late Charge for Overdue Payments

If the Note Holder has not received the full amount of any monthly payment by the end of _____ calendar days after the date it is due, I will pay a late charge to the Note Holder. The amount of the charge will be _____% of my overdue payment of principal and interest. I will pay this late charge promptly but only once on each late payment.

(B) Default

If I do not pay the full amount of each monthly payment on the date it is due, I will be in default.

(C) Notice of Default

If I am in default, the Note Holder may send me a written notice telling me that if I do not pay the overdue amount by a certain date, the Note Holder may require me to pay immediately the full amount of Principal which has not been paid and all the interest that I owe on that amount. That date must be at least 30 days after the date on which the notice is mailed to me or delivered by other means.

(D) No Waiver By Note Holder

Even if, at a time when I am in default, the Note Holder does not require me to pay immediately in full as described above, the Note Holder will still have the right to do so if I am in default at a later time.

(E) Payment of Note Holder's Costs and Expenses

If the Note Holder has required me to pay immediately in full as described above, the Note Holder will have the right to be paid back by me for all of its costs and expenses in enforcing this Note to the extent not prohibited by applicable law. Those expenses include, for example, reasonable attorneys' fees.

7. GIVING OF NOTICES

Unless applicable law requires a different method, any notice that must be given to me under this Note will be given by delivering it or by mailing it by first class mail to me at the Property Address above or at a different address if I give the Note Holder a notice of my different address.

Any notice that must be given to the Note Holder under this Note will be given by delivering it or by mailing it by first class mail to the Note Holder at the address stated in Section 3(A) above or at a different address if I am given a notice of that different address.

8. OBLIGATIONS OF PERSONS UNDER THIS NOTE

If more than one person signs this Note, each person is fully and personally obligated to keep all of the promises made in this Note, including the promise to pay the full amount owed. Any person who is a guarantor, surety or endorser of this Note is also obligated to do these things. Any person who takes over these obligations, including the obligations of a guarantor, surety or endorser of this Note, is also obligated to keep all of the promises made in this Note. The Note Holder may enforce its rights under this Note against each person individually or against all of us together. This means that any one of us may be required to pay all of the amounts owed under this Note.

9. WAIVERS

I and any other person who has obligations under this Note waive the rights of Presentment and Notice of Dishonor. "Presentment" means the right to require the Note Holder to demand payment of amounts due. "Notice of Dishonor" means the right to require the Note Holder to give notice to other persons that amounts due have not been paid.

10. UNIFORM SECURED NOTE

This Note is a uniform instrument with limited variations in some jurisdictions. In addition to the protections given to the Note Holder under this Note, a Mortgage, Deed of Trust, or Security Deed (the "Security Instrument"), dated the same date as this Note, protects the Note Holder from possible losses which might result if I do not keep the promises which I make in this Note. That Security Instrument describes how and under what conditions I may be required to make immediate payment in full of all amounts I owe under this Note. Some of those conditions are described as follows:

If all or any part of the Property or any Interest in the Property is sold or transferred (or if Borrower is not a natural person and a beneficial interest in Borrower is sold or transferred) without Lender's prior written consent, Lender may require immediate payment in full of all sums secured by this Security Instrument. However, this option shall not be exercised by Lender if such exercise is prohibited by Applicable Law.

If Lender exercises this option, Lender shall give Borrower notice of acceleration. The notice shall provide a period of not less than 30 days from the date the notice is given in accordance with Section 15 within which Borrower must pay all sums secured by this Security Instrument. If Borrower fails to pay these sums prior to the expiration of this period, Lender may invoke any remedies permitted by this Security Instrument without further notice or demand on Borrower.

Witness the Hand(S) and Seal(S) of the Undersigned.

_____

_____
(Seal)
- Borrower

_____

(Seal)
- Borrower

_____

_____

(Seal)
- Borrower

[Sign Original Only]

2.   FANNIE MAE/FREDDIE MAC UNIFORM MORTGAGE—DEED OF TRUST COVENANTS—SINGLE FAMILY

Fannie Mae and Freddie Mac have prepared a uniform mortgage or deed of trust (whichever is locally customary) for each U.S. state. The Uniform Covenants (clauses 1 through 21) reproduced below are contained in all Fannie Mae/Freddie Mac single-family mortgages and deeds of trust, and serve to foster national uniformity on a variety of significant substantive mortgage law issues. We also include here an introductory "Definitions" section which defines the terms used in the Uniform Covenants. The Fannie Mae/Freddie Mac forms also include non-uniform covenants for each state to take into account local real estate security formats, substantive law requirements and foreclosure methods. The Uniform Covenants as reprinted here were last revised in January, 2001; the non-uniform covenants in several states have been revised more recently to reflect changes in state law.

DEFINITIONS

Words used in multiple sections of this document are defined below and other words are defined in Sections 3, 11, 13, 18, 20 and 21. Certain rules regarding the usage of words used in this document are also provided in Section 16.

(A) "Security Instrument" means this document, which is dated _____, _____, together with all Riders to this document.

(B) "Borrower" is _____. Borrower is the trustor under this Security Instrument.

(C) "Lender" is _____. Lender is a _____ organized and existing under the laws of _____. Lender's address is _____. Lender is the beneficiary under this Security Instrument.

(D) "Trustee" is _____.

(E) "Note" means the promissory note signed by Borrower and dated _____, _____. The Note states that Borrower owes Lender _____ Dollars (U.S. $_____) plus interest.

Borrower has promised to pay this debt in regular Periodic Payments and to pay the debt in full not later than _____.

(F) "Property" means the property that is described below under the heading "Transfer of Rights in the Property."

(G) "Loan" means the debt evidenced by the Note, plus interest, any prepayment charges and late charges due under the Note, and all sums due under this Security Instrument, plus interest.

(H) "Riders" means all Riders to this Security Instrument that are executed by Borrower. The following Riders are to be executed by Borrower [check box as applicable]:

- ☐ Adjustable Rate Rider
- ☐ Balloon Rider
- ☐ 1–4 Family Rider
- ☐ Condominium Rider
- ☐ Planned Unit Development Rider
- ☐ Biweekly Payment Rider
- ☐ Second Home Rider
- ☐ Other(s) [specify] _____

(I) "Applicable Law" means all controlling applicable federal, state and local statutes, regulations, ordinances and administrative rules and orders (that have the effect of law) as well as all applicable final, non-appealable judicial opinions.

(J) "Community Association Dues, Fees, and Assessments" means all dues, fees, assessments and other charges that are imposed on Borrower or the Property by a condominium association, homeowners association or similar organization.

(K) "Electronic Funds Transfer" means any transfer of funds, other than a transaction originated by check, draft, or similar paper instrument, which is initiated through an electronic terminal, telephonic instrument, computer, or magnetic tape so as to order, instruct, or authorize a financial institution to debit or credit an account. Such term includes, but is not limited to, point-of-sale transfers, automated teller machine transactions, transfers initiated by telephone, wire transfers, and automated clearinghouse transfers.

(L) "Escrow Items" means those items that are described in Section 3.

(M) "Miscellaneous Proceeds" means any compensation, settlement, award of damages, or proceeds paid by any third party (other than insurance proceeds paid under the coverages described in Section 5) for: (i) damage to, or destruction of, the Property; (ii) condemnation or other taking of all or any part of the Property; (iii) conveyance in lieu of condemnation; or (iv) misrepresentations of, or omissions as to, the value and/or condition of the Property.

(N) "Mortgage Insurance" means insurance protecting Lender against the nonpayment of, or default on, the Loan.

(O) "Periodic Payment" means the regularly scheduled amount due for (i) principal and interest under the Note, plus (ii) any amounts under Section 3 of this Security Instrument.

(P) "RESPA" means the Real Estate Settlement Procedures Act (12 U.S.C. § 2601 et seq.) and its implementing regulation, Regulation X (24 C.F.R. Part 3500), as they might be amended from time to time, or any additional or successor legislation or regulation that governs the same subject matter. As used in this Security Instrument, "RESPA" refers to all requirements and restrictions that are imposed in regard to a "federally related mortgage loan" even if the Loan does not qualify as a "federally related mortgage loan" under RESPA.

(Q) "Successor in Interest of Borrower" means any party that has taken title to the Property, whether or not that party has assumed Borrower's obligations under the Note and/or this Security Instrument.

[Here non-uniform covenants applicable to a particular state are inserted]

1. Payment of Principal, Interest, Escrow Items, Prepayment Charges, and Late Charges. Borrower shall pay when due the principal of, and interest on, the debt evidenced by the Note and any prepayment charges and late charges due under the Note. Borrower shall also pay funds for Escrow Items pursuant to Section 3. Payments due under the Note and this Security Instrument shall be made in U.S. currency. However, if any check or other instrument received by Lender as payment under the Note or this Security Instrument is returned to Lender unpaid, Lender may require that any or all subsequent payments due under the Note and this Security Instrument be made in one or more of the following forms, as selected by Lender: (a) cash; (b) money order; (c) certified check, bank check, treasurer's check or cashier's check, provided any such check is drawn upon an institution whose deposits are insured by a federal agency, instrumentality, or entity; or (d) Electronic Funds Transfer.

Payments are deemed received by Lender when received at the location designated in the Note or at such other location as may be designated by Lender in accordance with the notice provisions in Section 15. Lender may return any payment or partial payment if the payment or partial payments are insufficient to bring the Loan current. Lender may accept any payment or partial payment insufficient to bring the Loan current, without waiver of any rights hereunder or prejudice to its rights to refuse such payment or partial payments in the future, but Lender is not obligated to apply such payments at the time such payments are accepted. If each Periodic Payment is applied as of its scheduled due date, then Lender need not pay interest on unapplied funds. Lender may hold such unapplied funds until Borrower makes payment to bring the Loan current. If Borrower does not do so within a reasonable period of time, Lender shall either apply such funds or return them to Borrower. If not applied earlier, such funds will be applied to the outstanding principal balance under the Note immediately prior to foreclosure. No offset or claim which Borrower might have now or in the future against Lender shall relieve Borrower from making payments due under the Note and this Security Instrument or performing the covenants and agreements secured by this Security Instrument.

2. **Application of Payments or Proceeds.** Except as otherwise described in this Section 2, all payments accepted and applied by Lender shall be applied in the following order of priority: (a) interest due under the Note; (b) principal due under the Note; (c) amounts due under Section 3. Such payments shall be applied to each Periodic Payment in the order in which it became due. Any remaining amounts shall be applied first to late charges, second to any other amounts due under this Security Instrument, and then to reduce the principal balance of the Note.

If Lender receives a payment from Borrower for a delinquent Periodic Payment which includes a sufficient amount to pay any late charge due, the payment may be applied to the delinquent payment and the late charge. If more than one Periodic Payment is outstanding, Lender may apply any payment received from Borrower to the repayment of the Periodic Payments if, and to the extent that, each payment can be paid in full. To the extent that any excess exists after the payment is applied to the full payment of one or more Periodic Payments, such excess may be applied to any late charges due. Voluntary prepayments shall be applied first to any prepayment charges and then as described in the Note.

Any application of payments, insurance proceeds, or Miscellaneous Proceeds to principal due under the Note shall not extend or postpone the due date, or change the amount, of the Periodic Payments.

3. **Funds for Escrow Items.** Borrower shall pay to Lender on the day Periodic Payments are due under the Note, until the Note is paid in full, a sum (the "Funds") to provide for payment of amounts due for: (a) taxes and assessments and other items which can attain priority over this Security Instrument as a lien or encumbrance on the Property; (b) leasehold payments or ground rents on the Property, if any; (c) premiums for any and all insurance required by Lender under Section 5; and (d) Mortgage Insurance premiums, if any, or any sums payable by Borrower to Lender in lieu of the payment of Mortgage Insurance premiums in

accordance with the provisions of Section 10. These items are called "Escrow Items." At origination or at any time during the term of the Loan, Lender may require that Community Association Dues, Fees, and Assessments, if any, be escrowed by Borrower, and such dues, fees and assessments shall be an Escrow Item. Borrower shall promptly furnish to Lender all notices of amounts to be paid under this Section. Borrower shall pay Lender the Funds for Escrow Items unless Lender waives Borrower's obligation to pay the Funds for any or all Escrow Items. Lender may waive Borrower's obligation to pay to Lender Funds for any or all Escrow Items at any time. Any such waiver may only be in writing. In the event of such waiver, Borrower shall pay directly, when and where payable, the amounts due for any Escrow Items for which payment of Funds has been waived by Lender and, if Lender requires, shall furnish to Lender receipts evidencing such payment within such time period as Lender may require. Borrower's obligation to make such payments and to provide receipts shall for all purposes be deemed to be a covenant and agreement contained in this Security Instrument, as the phrase "covenant and agreement" is used in Section 9. If Borrower is obligated to pay Escrow Items directly, pursuant to a waiver, and Borrower fails to pay the amount due for an Escrow Item, Lender may exercise its rights under Section 9 and pay such amount and Borrower shall then be obligated under Section 9 to repay to Lender any such amount. Lender may revoke the waiver as to any or all Escrow Items at any time by a notice given in accordance with Section 15 and, upon such revocation, Borrower shall pay to Lender all Funds, and in such amounts, that are then required under this Section 3.

Lender may, at any time, collect and hold Funds in an amount (a) sufficient to permit Lender to apply the Funds at the time specified under RESPA, and (b) not to exceed the maximum amount a lender can require under RESPA. Lender shall estimate the amount of Funds due on the basis of current data and reasonable estimates of expenditures of future Escrow Items or otherwise in accordance with Applicable Law.

The Funds shall be held in an institution whose deposits are insured by a federal agency, instrumentality, or entity (including Lender, if Lender is an institution whose deposits are so insured) or in any Federal Home Loan Bank. Lender shall apply the Funds to pay the Escrow Items no later than the time specified under RESPA. Lender shall not charge Borrower for holding and applying the Funds, annually analyzing the escrow account, or verifying the Escrow Items, unless Lender pays Borrower interest on the Funds and Applicable Law permits Lender to make such a charge. Unless an agreement is made in writing or Applicable Law requires interest to be paid on the Funds, Lender shall not be required to pay Borrower any interest or earnings on the Funds. Borrower and Lender can agree in writing, however, that interest shall be paid on the Funds. Lender shall give to Borrower, without charge, an annual accounting of the Funds as required by RESPA.

If there is a surplus of Funds held in escrow, as defined under RESPA, Lender shall account to Borrower for the excess funds in accordance with RESPA. If there is a shortage of Funds held in escrow, as defined under RESPA, Lender shall notify Borrower as required by RESPA, and Borrower shall pay to Lender the amount necessary to make up the shortage in accordance with RESPA, but in no more than 12 monthly payments. If there is a deficiency of Funds held in escrow, as defined under RESPA, Lender shall notify Borrower as required by RESPA, and Borrower shall pay to Lender the amount necessary to make up the deficiency in accordance with RESPA, but in no more than 12 monthly payments.

Upon payment in full of all sums secured by this Security Instrument, Lender shall promptly refund to Borrower any Funds held by Lender.

4.   Charges; Liens. Borrower shall pay all taxes, assessments, charges, fines, and impositions attributable to the Property which can attain priority over this Security Instrument, leasehold payments or ground rents on the Property, if any, and Community Association Dues, Fees, and Assessments, if any. To the extent that these items are Escrow Items, Borrower shall pay them in the manner provided in Section 3.

Borrower shall promptly discharge any lien which has priority over this Security Instrument unless Borrower: (a) agrees in writing to the payment of the obligation secured by the lien in a manner acceptable to Lender, but only so long as Borrower is performing such agreement; (b) contests the lien in good faith by, or defends against enforcement of the lien in, legal proceedings which in Lender's opinion operate to prevent the enforcement of the lien while those proceedings are pending, but only until such proceedings are concluded; or (c) secures from the holder of the lien an agreement satisfactory to Lender subordinating the lien to this Security Instrument. If Lender determines that any part of the Property is subject to a lien which can attain priority over this Security Instrument, Lender may give Borrower a notice identifying the lien. Within 10 days of the date on which that notice is given, Borrower shall satisfy the lien or take one or more of the actions set forth above in this Section 4.

Lender may require Borrower to pay a one-time charge for a real estate tax verification and/or reporting service used by Lender in connection with this Loan.

5.   Property Insurance. Borrower shall keep the improvements now existing or hereafter erected on the Property insured against loss by fire, hazards included within the term "extended coverage," and any other hazards including, but not limited to, earthquakes and floods, for which Lender requires insurance. This insurance shall be maintained in the amounts (including deductible levels) and for the periods that Lender requires. What Lender requires pursuant to the preceding sentences can change during the term of the Loan. The insurance carrier providing the insurance shall be chosen by Borrower subject to Lender's right to disapprove Borrower's choice, which right shall not be exercised unreasonably. Lender may require Borrower to pay, in connection with this Loan, either: (a) a one-time charge for flood zone determination, certification and tracking services; or (b) a one-time charge for flood zone determination and certification services and subsequent charges each time remappings or similar changes occur which reasonably might affect such determination or certification. Borrower shall also be responsible for the payment of any fees imposed by the Federal Emergency Management Agency in connection with the review of any flood zone determination resulting from an objection by Borrower.

If Borrower fails to maintain any of the coverages described above, Lender may obtain insurance coverage, at Lender's option and Borrower's expense. Lender is under no obligation to purchase any particular type or amount of coverage. Therefore, such coverage shall cover Lender, but might or might not protect Borrower, Borrower's equity in the Property, or the contents of the Property, against any risk, hazard or liability and might provide greater or lesser coverage than was previously in effect. Borrower acknowledges that the cost of the insurance coverage so obtained might significantly exceed the cost of insurance that Borrower could have obtained. Any amounts disbursed by Lender under this Section 5 shall become additional debt of Borrower secured by this Security Instrument. These amounts shall bear interest at the Note rate from the date of disbursement and shall be payable, with such interest, upon notice from Lender to Borrower requesting payment.

All insurance policies required by Lender and renewals of such policies shall be subject to Lender's right to disapprove such policies, shall include a standard mortgage clause, and shall name Lender as mortgagee and/or as an additional loss payee and Borrower further agrees to generally assign rights to insurance proceeds to the holder of the Note up to the amount of the outstanding loan balance. Lender shall have the right to hold the policies and renewal certificates. If Lender requires, Borrower shall promptly give to Lender all receipts of paid premiums and renewal notices. If Borrower obtains any form of insurance coverage, not otherwise required by Lender, for damage to, or destruction of, the Property, such policy shall include a standard mortgage clause and shall name Lender as mortgagee and/or as an additional loss payee and Borrower further agrees to generally assign rights to insurance proceeds to the holder of the Note up to the amount of the outstanding loan balance.

In the event of loss, Borrower shall give prompt notice to the insurance carrier and Lender. Lender may make proof of loss if not made promptly by Borrower. Unless Lender and Borrower otherwise agree in writing, any insurance proceeds, whether or not the underlying insurance was required by Lender, shall be applied to restoration or repair of the Property, if the restoration or repair is economically feasible and Lender's security is not lessened. During such repair and restoration period, Lender shall have the right to hold such insurance proceeds until Lender has had an opportunity to inspect such Property to ensure the work has been completed to Lender's satisfaction, provided that such inspection shall be undertaken promptly. Lender may disburse proceeds for the repairs and restoration in a single payment or in a series of progress payments as the work is completed. Unless an agreement is made in writing or Applicable Law requires interest to be paid on such insurance proceeds, Lender shall not be required to pay Borrower any interest or earnings on such proceeds. Fees for public adjusters, or other third parties, retained by Borrower shall not be paid out of the insurance proceeds and shall be the sole obligation of Borrower. If the restoration or repair is not economically feasible or Lender's security would be lessened, the insurance proceeds shall be applied to the sums secured by this Security Instrument, whether or not then due, with the excess, if any, paid to Borrower. Such insurance proceeds shall be applied in the order provided for in Section 2.

If Borrower abandons the Property, Lender may file, negotiate and settle any available insurance claim and related matters. If Borrower does not respond within 30 days to a notice from Lender that the insurance carrier has offered to settle a claim, then Lender may negotiate and settle the claim. The 30-day period will begin when the notice is given. In either event, or if Lender acquires the Property under Section 22 or otherwise, Borrower hereby assigns to Lender (a) Borrower's rights to any insurance proceeds in an amount not to exceed the amounts unpaid under the Note or this Security Instrument, and (b) any other of Borrower's rights (other than the right to any refund of unearned premiums paid by Borrower) under all insurance policies covering the Property, insofar as such rights are applicable to the coverage of the Property. Lender may use the insurance proceeds either to repair or restore the Property or to pay amounts unpaid under the Note or this Security Instrument, whether or not then due.

6. Occupancy. Borrower shall occupy, establish, and use the Property as Borrower's principal residence within 60 days after the execution of this Security Instrument and shall continue to occupy the Property as Borrower's principal residence for at least one year after the date of occupancy, unless Lender otherwise agrees in writing, which consent shall not be unreasonably withheld, or unless extenuating circumstances exist which are beyond Borrower's control.

7. Preservation, Maintenance and Protection of the Property; Inspections. Borrower shall not destroy, damage or impair the Property, allow the Property to deteriorate or commit waste on the Property. Whether or not Borrower is residing in the Property, Borrower shall maintain the Property in order to prevent the Property from deteriorating or decreasing in value due to its condition. Unless it is determined pursuant to Section 5 that repair or restoration is not economically feasible, Borrower shall promptly repair the Property if damaged to avoid further deterioration or damage. If insurance or condemnation proceeds are paid in connection with damage to, or the taking of, the Property, Borrower shall be responsible for repairing or restoring the Property only if Lender has released proceeds for such purposes. Lender may disburse proceeds for the repairs and restoration in a single payment or in a series of progress payments as the work is completed. If the insurance or condemnation proceeds are not sufficient to repair or restore the Property, Borrower is not relieved of Borrower's obligation for the completion of such repair or restoration.

Lender or its agent may make reasonable entries upon and inspections of the Property. If it has reasonable cause, Lender may inspect the interior of the improvements on the Property. Lender shall give Borrower notice at the time of or prior to such an interior inspection specifying such reasonable cause.

8. Borrower's Loan Application. Borrower shall be in default if, during the Loan application process, Borrower or any persons or entities acting at the direction of Borrower or with Borrower's knowledge or consent gave materially false, misleading, or inaccurate information or statements to Lender (or failed to provide Lender with material information) in connection with the Loan. Material representations include, but are not limited to, representations concerning Borrower's occupancy of the Property as Borrower's principal residence.

9. Protection of Lender's Interest in the Property and Rights Under this Security Instrument. If (a) Borrower fails to perform the covenants and agreements contained in this Security Instrument, (b) there is a legal proceeding that might significantly affect Lender's interest in the Property and/or rights under this Security Instrument (such as a proceeding in bankruptcy, probate, for condemnation or forfeiture, for enforcement of a lien which may attain priority over this Security Instrument or to enforce laws or regulations), or (c) Borrower has abandoned the Property, then Lender may do and pay for whatever is reasonable or appropriate to protect Lender's interest in the Property and rights under this Security Instrument, including protecting and/or assessing the value of the Property, and securing and/or repairing the Property. Lender's actions can include, but are not limited to: (a) paying any sums secured by a lien which has priority over this Security Instrument; (b) appearing in court; and (c) paying reasonable attorneys' fees to protect its interest in the Property and/or rights under this Security Instrument, including its secured position in a bankruptcy proceeding. Securing the Property includes, but is not limited to, entering the Property to make repairs, change locks, replace or board up doors and windows, drain water from pipes, eliminate building or other code violations or dangerous conditions, and have utilities turned on or off. Although Lender may take action under this Section 9, Lender does not have to do so and is not under any duty or obligation to do so. It is agreed that Lender incurs no liability for not taking any or all actions authorized under this Section 9.

Any amounts disbursed by Lender under this Section 9 shall become additional debt of Borrower secured by this Security Instrument. These amounts shall bear interest at the Note rate from the date of disbursement and shall be payable, with such interest, upon notice from Lender to Borrower requesting payment.

If this Security Instrument is on a leasehold, Borrower shall comply with all the provisions of the lease. If Borrower acquires fee title to the Property, the leasehold and the fee title shall not merge unless Lender agrees to the merger in writing.

10. Mortgage Insurance. If Lender required Mortgage Insurance as a condition of making the Loan, Borrower shall pay the premiums required to maintain the Mortgage Insurance in effect. If, for any reason, the Mortgage Insurance coverage required by Lender ceases to be available from the mortgage insurer that previously provided such insurance and Borrower was required to make separately designated payments toward the premiums for Mortgage Insurance, Borrower shall pay the premiums required to obtain coverage substantially equivalent to the Mortgage Insurance previously in effect, at a cost substantially equivalent to the cost to Borrower of the Mortgage Insurance previously in effect, from an alternate mortgage insurer selected by Lender.

If substantially equivalent Mortgage Insurance coverage is not available, Borrower shall continue to pay to Lender the amount of the separately designated payments that were due when the insurance coverage ceased to be in effect. Lender will accept, use and retain these payments as a non-refundable loss reserve in lieu of Mortgage Insurance. Such loss reserve shall be non-refundable, notwithstanding the fact that the Loan is ultimately paid in full, and Lender shall not be required to pay Borrower any interest or earnings on such loss reserve. Lender can no longer require loss reserve payments if Mortgage Insurance coverage (in the amount and for the period that Lender requires) provided by an insurer selected by Lender again becomes available, is obtained, and Lender requires separately designated payments toward the premiums for Mortgage Insurance. If Lender required Mortgage Insurance as a condition of making the Loan and Borrower was required to make separately designated payments toward the premiums for Mortgage Insurance, Borrower shall pay the premiums required to maintain Mortgage Insurance in effect, or to provide a non-refundable loss reserve, until Lender's requirement for Mortgage Insurance ends in accordance with any written agreement between Borrower and Lender providing for such termination or until termination is required by Applicable Law. Nothing in this Section 10 affects Borrower's obligation to pay interest at the rate provided in the Note.

Mortgage Insurance reimburses Lender (or any entity that purchases the Note) for certain losses it may incur if Borrower does not repay the Loan as agreed. Borrower is not a party to the Mortgage Insurance.

Mortgage insurers evaluate their total risk on all such insurance in force from time to time, and may enter into agreements with other parties that share or modify their risk, or reduce losses. These agreements are on terms and conditions that are satisfactory to the mortgage insurer and the other party (or parties) to these agreements. These agreements may require the mortgage insurer to make payments using any source of funds that the mortgage insurer may have available (which may include funds obtained from Mortgage Insurance premiums).

As a result of these agreements, Lender, any purchaser of the Note, another insurer, any reinsurer, any other entity, or any affiliate of any of the foregoing, may receive (directly or indirectly) amounts that derive from (or might be characterized as) a portion of Borrower's payments for Mortgage Insurance, in exchange for sharing or modifying the mortgage insurer's risk, or reducing losses. If such agreement provides that an affiliate of Lender takes a share of the insurer's risk in exchange for a share of the premiums paid to the insurer, the arrangement is often termed "captive reinsurance." Further:

(a) Any such agreements will not affect the amounts that Borrower has agreed to pay for Mortgage Insurance, or any other terms of the Loan. Such agreements will not increase the amount Borrower will owe for Mortgage Insurance, and they will not entitle Borrower to any refund.

(b) Any such agreements will not affect the rights Borrower has—if any—with respect to the Mortgage Insurance under the Homeowners Protection Act of 1998 or any other law. These rights may include the right to receive certain disclosures, to request and obtain cancellation of the Mortgage Insurance, to have the Mortgage Insurance terminated automatically, and/or to receive a refund of any Mortgage Insurance premiums that were unearned at the time of such cancellation or termination.

11. Assignment of Miscellaneous Proceeds; Forfeiture. All Miscellaneous Proceeds are hereby assigned to and shall be paid to Lender.

If the Property is damaged, such Miscellaneous Proceeds shall be applied to restoration or repair of the Property, if the restoration or repair is economically feasible and Lender's security is not lessened. During such repair and restoration period, Lender shall have the right to hold such Miscellaneous Proceeds until Lender has had an opportunity to inspect such Property to ensure the work has been completed to Lender's satisfaction, provided that such inspection shall be undertaken promptly. Lender may pay for the repairs and restoration in a single disbursement or in a series of progress payments as the work is completed. Unless an agreement is made in writing or Applicable Law requires interest to be paid on such Miscellaneous Proceeds, Lender shall not be required to pay Borrower any interest or earnings on such Miscellaneous Proceeds. If the restoration or repair is not economically feasible or Lender's security would be lessened, the Miscellaneous Proceeds shall be applied to the sums secured by this Security Instrument, whether or not then due, with the excess, if any, paid to Borrower. Such Miscellaneous Proceeds shall be applied in the order provided for in Section 2.

In the event of a total taking, destruction, or loss in value of the Property, the Miscellaneous Proceeds shall be applied to the sums secured by this Security Instrument, whether or not then due, with the excess, if any, paid to Borrower.

In the event of a partial taking, destruction, or loss in value of the Property in which the fair market value of the Property immediately before the partial taking, destruction, or loss in value is equal to or greater than the amount of the sums secured by this Security Instrument immediately before the partial taking, destruction, or loss in value, unless Borrower and Lender otherwise agree in writing, the sums secured by this Security Instrument shall be reduced by the amount of the Miscellaneous Proceeds multiplied by the following fraction: (a) the total amount of the sums secured immediately before the partial taking, destruction, or loss in value divided by (b) the fair market value of the Property immediately before the partial taking, destruction, or loss in value. Any balance shall be paid to Borrower.

In the event of a partial taking, destruction, or loss in value of the Property in which the fair market value of the Property immediately before the partial taking, destruction, or loss in value is less than the amount of the sums secured immediately before the partial taking, destruction, or loss in value, unless Borrower and Lender otherwise agree in writing, the Miscellaneous Proceeds shall be applied to the sums secured by this Security Instrument whether or not the sums are then due.

If the Property is abandoned by Borrower, or if, after notice by Lender to Borrower that the Opposing Party (as defined in the next sentence) offers to make an award to settle a claim for damages, Borrower fails to respond to Lender within 30 days after the date the notice is given, Lender is authorized to collect and apply the Miscellaneous Proceeds either to restoration or repair of the Property or to the sums secured by this Security Instrument, whether or not then due. "Opposing Party" means the third party that owes Borrower Miscellaneous Proceeds or the party against whom Borrower has a right of action in regard to Miscellaneous Proceeds.

Borrower shall be in default if any action or proceeding, whether civil or criminal, is begun that, in Lender's judgment, could result in forfeiture of the Property or other material impairment of Lender's interest in the Property or rights under this Security Instrument. Borrower can cure such a default and, if acceleration has occurred, reinstate as provided in Section 19, by causing the action or proceeding to be dismissed with a ruling that, in Lender's judgment, precludes forfeiture of the Property or other material impairment of Lender's interest in the Property or rights under this Security Instrument. The proceeds of any award or claim for damages that are attributable to the impairment of Lender's interest in the Property are hereby assigned and shall be paid to Lender.

All Miscellaneous Proceeds that are not applied to restoration or repair of the Property shall be applied in the order provided for in Section 2.

12. Borrower Not Released; Forbearance By Lender Not a Waiver. Extension of the time for payment or modification of amortization of the sums secured by this Security Instrument granted by Lender to Borrower or any Successor in Interest of Borrower shall not operate to release the liability of Borrower or any Successors in Interest of Borrower. Lender shall not be required to commence proceedings against any Successor in Interest of Borrower or to refuse to extend time for payment or otherwise modify amortization of the sums secured by this Security Instrument by reason of any demand made by the original Borrower or any Successors in Interest of Borrower. Any forbearance by Lender in exercising any right or remedy including, without limitation, Lender's acceptance of payments from third persons, entities or Successors in Interest of Borrower or in amounts less than the amount then due, shall not be a waiver of or preclude the exercise of any right or remedy.

13. Joint and Several Liability; Co-signers; Successors and Assigns Bound. Borrower covenants and agrees that Borrower's obligations and liability shall be joint and several. However, any Borrower who co-signs this Security Instrument but does not execute the Note (a "co-signer"): (a) is co-signing this Security Instrument only to mortgage, grant and convey the co-signer's interest in the Property under the terms of this Security Instrument; (b) is not personally obligated to pay the sums secured by this Security Instrument; and (c) agrees that Lender and any other Borrower can agree to extend, modify, forbear or make any accommodations with regard to the terms of this Security Instrument or the Note without the co-signer's consent.

Subject to the provisions of Section 18, any Successor in Interest of Borrower who assumes Borrower's obligations under this Security Instrument in writing, and is approved by Lender, shall obtain all of Borrower's rights and benefits under this Security Instrument. Borrower shall not be released from Borrower's obligations and liability under this Security Instrument unless Lender agrees to such release in writing. The covenants and agreements of this Security Instrument shall bind (except as provided in Section 20) and benefit the successors and assigns of Lender.

14. Loan Charges. Lender may charge Borrower fees for services performed in connection with Borrower's default, for the purpose of protecting Lender's interest in the Property and rights under this Security Instrument, including, but not limited to, attorneys' fees, property inspection and valuation fees. In regard to any other fees, the absence of express authority in this Security Instrument to charge a specific fee to Borrower shall not be construed as a prohibition on the charging of such fee. Lender may not charge fees that are expressly prohibited by this Security Instrument or by Applicable Law.

If the Loan is subject to a law which sets maximum loan charges, and that law is finally interpreted so that the interest or other loan charges collected or to be collected in connection with the Loan exceed the permitted limits, then: (a) any such loan charge shall be reduced by the amount necessary to reduce the charge to the permitted limit; and (b) any sums already collected from Borrower which exceeded permitted limits will be refunded to Borrower. Lender may choose to make this refund by reducing the principal owed under the Note or by making a direct payment to Borrower. If a refund reduces principal, the reduction will be treated as a partial prepayment without any prepayment charge (whether or not a prepayment charge is provided for under the Note). Borrower's acceptance of any such refund made by direct payment to Borrower will constitute a waiver of any right of action Borrower might have arising out of such overcharge.

15. Notices. All notices given by Borrower or Lender in connection with this Security Instrument must be in writing. Any notice to Borrower in connection with this Security Instrument shall be deemed to have been given to Borrower when mailed by first class mail or when actually delivered to Borrower's notice address if sent by other means. Notice to any one Borrower shall constitute notice to all Borrowers unless Applicable Law expressly requires otherwise. The notice address shall be the Property Address unless Borrower has designated a substitute notice address by notice to Lender. Borrower shall promptly notify Lender of Borrower's change of address. If Lender specifies a procedure for reporting Borrower's change of address, then Borrower shall only report a change of address through that specified procedure. There may be only one designated notice address under this Security Instrument at any one time. Any notice to Lender shall be given by delivering it or by mailing it by first class mail to Lender's address stated herein unless Lender has designated another address by notice to Borrower. Any notice in connection with this Security Instrument shall not be deemed to have been given to Lender until actually received by Lender. If any notice required by this Security Instrument is also required under Applicable Law, the Applicable Law requirement will satisfy the corresponding requirement under this Security Instrument.

16. Governing Law; Severability; Rules of Construction. This Security Instrument shall be governed by federal law and the law of the jurisdiction in which the Property is located. All rights and obligations contained in this Security Instrument are subject to any requirements and limitations of Applicable Law. Applicable Law might explicitly or implicitly allow the parties to agree by contract or it might be silent, but such silence shall not be construed as a prohibition against agreement by contract. In the event that any provision or clause of this Security Instrument or the Note conflicts with Applicable Law, such conflict shall not affect other provisions of this Security Instrument or the Note which can be given effect without the conflicting provision.

As used in this Security Instrument: (a) words of the masculine gender shall mean and include corresponding neuter words or words of the feminine gender; (b) words in the singular shall mean and include the plural and vice versa; and (c) the word "may" gives sole discretion without any obligation to take any action.

17. Borrower's Copy. Borrower shall be given one copy of the Note and of this Security Instrument.

18. Transfer of the Property or a Beneficial Interest in Borrower. As used in this Section 18, "Interest in the Property" means any legal or beneficial interest in the Property, including, but not limited to, those beneficial interests transferred in a bond for deed, contract for deed, installment sales contract or escrow agreement, the intent of which is the transfer of title by Borrower at a future date to a purchaser.

If all or any part of the Property or any Interest in the Property is sold or transferred (or if Borrower is not a natural person and a beneficial interest in Borrower is sold or transferred) without Lender's prior written consent, Lender may require immediate payment in full of all sums secured by this Security Instrument. However, this option shall not be exercised by Lender if such exercise is prohibited by Applicable Law.

If Lender exercises this option, Lender shall give Borrower notice of acceleration. The notice shall provide a period of not less than 30 days from the date the notice is given in accordance with Section 15 within which Borrower must pay all sums secured by this Security Instrument. If Borrower fails to pay these sums prior to the expiration of this period, Lender may invoke any remedies permitted by this Security Instrument without further notice or demand on Borrower.

19. Borrower's Right to Reinstate After Acceleration. If Borrower meets certain conditions, Borrower shall have the right to have enforcement of this Security Instrument discontinued at any time prior to the earliest of: (a) five days before sale of the Property pursuant to any power of sale contained in this Security Instrument; (b) such other period as Applicable Law might specify for the termination of Borrower's right to reinstate; or (c) entry of a judgment enforcing this Security Instrument. Those conditions are that Borrower: (a) pays Lender all sums which then would be due under this Security Instrument and the Note as if no acceleration had occurred; (b) cures any default of any other covenants or agreements; (c) pays all expenses incurred in enforcing this Security Instrument, including, but not limited to, reasonable attorneys' fees, property inspection and valuation fees, and other fees incurred for the purpose of protecting Lender's interest in the Property and rights under this Security Instrument; and (d) takes such action as Lender may reasonably require to assure that Lender's interest in the Property and rights under this Security Instrument, and Borrower's obligation to pay the sums secured by this Security Instrument, shall continue unchanged. Lender may require that Borrower pay such reinstatement sums and expenses in one or more of the following forms, as selected by Lender: (a) cash; (b) money order; (c) certified check, bank check, treasurer's check or cashier's check, provided any such check is drawn upon an institution whose deposits are insured by a federal agency, instrumentality or entity; or (d) Electronic Funds Transfer. Upon reinstatement by Borrower, this Security Instrument and obligations secured hereby shall remain fully effective as if no acceleration had occurred. However, this right to reinstate shall not apply in the case of acceleration under Section 18.

20. Sale of Note; Change of Loan Servicer; Notice of Grievance. The Note or a partial interest in the Note (together with this Security Instrument) can be sold one or more times without prior notice to Borrower. A sale might result in a change in the entity (known as the "Loan Servicer") that collects Periodic Payments due under the Note and this Security Instrument and performs other mortgage loan servicing obligations under the Note, this Security Instrument, and Applicable Law. There also might be one or more changes of the Loan Servicer unrelated to a sale of the Note. If there is a change of the Loan Servicer, Borrower will be given written notice of the change which will state the name and address of the new Loan Servicer, the address to which payments should be made and any other information RESPA requires in connection with a notice of transfer of servicing. If the Note is sold and thereafter the Loan is serviced by a Loan Servicer other than the purchaser of the Note, the mortgage loan servicing obligations to Borrower will remain with the Loan Servicer or be transferred to a successor Loan Servicer and are not assumed by the Note purchaser unless otherwise provided by the Note purchaser.

Neither Borrower nor Lender may commence, join, or be joined to any judicial action (as either an individual litigant or the member of a class) that arises from the other party's actions pursuant to this Security Instrument or that alleges that the other party has breached any provision of, or any duty owed by reason of, this Security Instrument, until such Borrower or Lender has notified the other party (with such notice given in compliance with the requirements of Section 15) of such alleged breach and afforded the other party hereto a reasonable period after the giving of such notice to take corrective action. If Applicable Law provides a time period which must elapse before certain action can be taken, that time period will be deemed to be reasonable for purposes of this paragraph. The notice of acceleration and opportunity to cure given to Borrower pursuant to Section 22 and the notice of acceleration given to Borrower pursuant to Section 18 shall be deemed to satisfy the notice and opportunity to take corrective action provisions of this Section 20.

21. Hazardous Substances. As used in this Section 21: (a) "Hazardous Substances" are those substances defined as toxic or hazardous substances, pollutants, or wastes by Environmental Law and the following substances: gasoline, kerosene, other flammable or toxic petroleum products, toxic pesticides and herbicides, volatile solvents, materials containing asbestos or formaldehyde, and radioactive materials; (b) "Environmental Law" means federal laws and laws of the jurisdiction where the Property is located that relate to health, safety or environmental protection; (c) "Environmental Cleanup" includes any response action, remedial action, or removal action, as defined in Environmental Law; and (d) an "Environmental Condition" means a condition that can cause, contribute to, or otherwise trigger an Environmental Cleanup.

Borrower shall not cause or permit the presence, use, disposal, storage, or release of any Hazardous Substances, or threaten to release any Hazardous Substances, on or in the Property. Borrower shall not do, nor allow anyone else to do, anything affecting the Property (a) that is in violation of any Environmental Law, (b) which creates an Environmental Condition, or (c) which, due to the presence, use, or release of a Hazardous Substance, creates a condition that adversely affects the value of the Property. The preceding two sentences shall not apply to the presence, use, or storage on the Property of small quantities of Hazardous Substances that are generally recognized to be appropriate to normal residential uses and to maintenance of the Property (including, but not limited to, hazardous substances in consumer products).

Borrower shall promptly give Lender written notice of (a) any investigation, claim, demand, lawsuit or other action by any governmental or regulatory agency or private party involving the Property and any Hazardous Substance or Environmental Law of which Borrower has actual knowledge, (b) any Environmental Condition, including but not limited to, any spilling, leaking, discharge, release or threat of release of any Hazardous Substance, and (c) any condition caused by the presence, use or release of a Hazardous Substance which adversely affects the value of the Property. If Borrower learns, or is notified by any governmental or regulatory authority, or any private party, that any removal or other remediation of any Hazardous Substance affecting the Property is necessary, Borrower shall promptly take all necessary remedial actions in accordance with Environmental Law. Nothing herein shall create any obligation on Lender for an Environmental Cleanup.

[Here non-Uniform Covenants applicable to a particular state are inserted]

3. FANNIE MAE/FREDDIE MAC DEED OF TRUST—SINGLE FAMILY—CALIFORNIA

California, like many western and Midwestern states, uses the deed of trust with power of sale as the predominant land financing instrument. While deeds of trust differ from mortgages in certain minor respects, most substantive mortgage law is applicable to them. Mortgages seldom are used in such states because they can be foreclosed only by judicial action.

DEED OF TRUST

[Here insert definitions from Form 2, supra]

TRANSFER OF RIGHTS IN THE PROPERTY This Security Instrument secures to Lender: (i) the repayment of the Loan, and all renewals, extensions and modifications of the Note; and (ii) the performance of Borrower's covenants and agreements under this Security Instrument and the Note. For this purpose, Borrower irrevocably grants and conveys to Trustee, in trust, with power of sale, the following described property located in the _____ of

[Type of Recording Jurisdiction]

_____: which currently has the address of

   [Name of Recording Jurisdiction]

_____   _____, California _____

      [Street]   [City]   [Zip Code]

("Property Address"):

TOGETHER WITH all the improvements now or hereafter erected on the property, and all easements, appurtenances, and fixtures now or hereafter a part of the property. All replacements and additions shall also be covered by this Security Instrument. All of the foregoing is referred to in this Security Instrument as the "Property."

BORROWER COVENANTS that Borrower is lawfully seised of the estate hereby conveyed and has the right to grant and convey the Property and that the Property is unencumbered, except for encumbrances of record. Borrower warrants and will defend generally the title to the Property against all claims and demands, subject to any encumbrances of record.

THIS SECURITY INSTRUMENT combines uniform covenants for national use and non-uniform covenants with limited variations by jurisdiction to constitute a uniform security instrument covering real property.

UNIFORM COVENANTS. Borrower and Lender covenant and agree as follows:

[Uniform covenants appear here. See Form 2, supra]

NON-UNIFORM COVENANTS. Borrower and Lender further covenant and agree as follows:

22. Acceleration; Remedies. Lender shall give notice to Borrower prior to acceleration following Borrower's breach of any covenant or agreement in this Security Instrument (but not prior to acceleration under Section 18 unless Applicable Law provides otherwise). The notice shall specify: (a) the default; (b) the action required to cure the default; (c) a date, not less than 30 days from the date the notice is given to Borrower, by which the default must be cured; and (d) that failure to cure the default on or before the date specified in the notice may result in acceleration of the sums secured by this Security Instrument and sale of the Property. The notice shall further inform Borrower of the right to reinstate after acceleration and the right to bring a court action to assert the non-existence of a default or any other defense of Borrower to acceleration and sale. If the default is not cured on or before the date specified in the notice, Lender at its option may require immediate payment in full of all sums secured by this Security Instrument without further demand and may invoke the power of sale and any other remedies permitted by Applicable Law. Lender shall be entitled to collect all expenses incurred in pursuing the remedies provided in this Section 22, including, but not limited to, reasonable attorneys' fees and costs of title evidence.

If Lender invokes the power of sale, Lender shall execute or cause Trustee to execute a written notice of the occurrence of an event of default and of Lender's election to cause the Property to be sold. Trustee shall cause this notice to be recorded in each county in which any part of the Property is located. Lender or Trustee shall mail copies of the notice as prescribed by Applicable Law to Borrower and to the other persons prescribed by Applicable Law. Trustee shall give public notice of sale to the persons and in the manner prescribed by Applicable Law. After the time required by Applicable Law, Trustee, without demand on Borrower, shall sell the Property at public auction to the highest bidder at the time and place and under the terms designated in the notice of sale in one or more parcels and in any order Trustee determines. Trustee may postpone sale of all or any parcel of the Property by public announcement at the time and place of any previously scheduled sale. Lender or its designee may purchase the Property at any sale.

Trustee shall deliver to the purchaser Trustee's deed conveying the Property without any covenant or warranty, expressed or implied. The recitals in the Trustee's deed shall be prima facie evidence of the truth of the statements made therein. Trustee shall apply the proceeds of the sale in the following order: (a) to all expenses of the sale, including, but not limited to, reasonable Trustee's and attorneys' fees; (b) to all sums secured by this Security Instrument; and (c) any excess to the person or persons legally entitled to it.

23. Reconveyance. Upon payment of all sums secured by this Security Instrument, Lender shall request Trustee to reconvey the Property and shall surrender this Security Instrument and all notes evidencing debt secured by this Security Instrument to Trustee. Trustee shall reconvey the Property without warranty to the person or persons legally entitled to it. Lender may charge such person or persons a reasonable fee for reconveying the Property, but only if the fee is paid to a third party (such as the Trustee) for services rendered and the charging of the fee is permitted under Applicable Law. If the fee charged does not exceed the fee set by Applicable Law, the fee is conclusively presumed to be reasonable.

24. Substitute Trustee. Lender, at its option, may from time to time appoint a successor trustee to any Trustee appointed hereunder by an instrument executed and acknowledged by Lender and recorded in the office of the Recorder of the county in which the Property is located. The instrument shall contain the name of the original Lender, Trustee and Borrower, the book and page where this Security Instrument is recorded and the name and address of the successor trustee. Without conveyance of the Property, the successor trustee shall succeed to all the title, powers and duties conferred upon the Trustee herein and by Applicable Law. This procedure for substitution of trustee shall govern to the exclusion of all other provisions for substitution.

25. Statement of Obligation Fee. Lender may collect a fee not to exceed the maximum amount permitted by Applicable Law for furnishing the statement of obligation as provided by Section 2943 of the Civil Code of California.

BY SIGNING BELOW, Borrower accepts and agrees to the terms and covenants contained in this Security Instrument and in any Rider executed by Borrower and recorded with it.

Witnesses: _____(Seal)

_____Borrower

_____(Seal)

_____Borrower

4. FANNIE MAE/FREDDIE MAC MORTGAGE—SINGLE FAMILY—KANSAS

Kansas, like such other states as Florida, Illinois, Iowa, and New York uses the mortgage as the perdomininant financing device and permits only foreclosure by judicial action. Consequently, the Kansas form makes no reference to a power of sale or non-judicial foreclosure.

MORTGAGE

[Here insert definition from Form 2, supra]

TRANSFER OF RIGHTS IN THE PROPERTY This Security Instrument secures to Lender: (i) the repayment of the Loan, and all renewals, extensions and modifications of the Note; and (ii) the performance of Borrower's covenants and agreements under this Security Instrument and the Note. For this purpose, Borrower mortgages and warrants to Lender and Lender's successors and assigns the following described property located in the _____ of

[Type of Recording Jurisdiction]

_____: which currently has the address of

[Name of Recording Jurisdiction]

_____ _____, Kansas _____
     [Street]   [City]   [Zip Code]

("Property Address"):

TOGETHER WITH all the improvements now or hereafter erected on the property, and all easements, appurtenances, and fixtures now or hereafter a part of the property. All replacements and additions shall also be covered by this Security Instrument. All of the foregoing is referred to in this Security Instrument as the "Property."

BORROWER COVENANTS that Borrower is lawfully seised of the estate hereby conveyed and has the right to mortgage, grant and convey the Property and that the Property is unencumbered, except for encumbrances of record. Borrower warrants and will defend generally the title to the Property against all claims and demands, subject to any encumbrances of record.

THIS SECURITY INSTRUMENT combines uniform covenants for national use and non-uniform covenants with limited variations by jurisdiction to constitute a uniform security instrument covering real property.

UNIFORM COVENANTS. Borrower and Lender covenant and agree as follows:

[Uniform Covenants appear here. See Form 2, supra]

22. Acceleration; Remedies. Lender shall give notice to Borrower prior to acceleration following Borrower's breach of any covenant or agreement in this Security Instrument (but not prior to acceleration under Section 18 unless Applicable Law provides otherwise). The notice shall specify: (a) the default; (b) the action required to cure the default; (c) a date, not less than 30 days from the date the notice is given to Borrower, by which the default must be cured; and (d) that failure to cure the default on or before the date specified in the notice may result in acceleration of the sums secured by this Security Instrument, foreclosure by judicial proceeding and sale of the Property. The notice shall further inform Borrower of the right to reinstate after acceleration and the right to assert in the foreclosure proceeding the non-existence of a default or any other defense of Borrower to acceleration and foreclosure. If the default is not cured on or before the date specified in the notice, Lender at its option may require immediate payment in full of all sums secured by this Security Instrument without further demand and may foreclose this Security Instrument by judicial proceeding. Lender shall be entitled to collect all expenses incurred in pursuing the remedies provided in this Section 22, including, but not limited to, costs of title evidence.

Lender shall be entitled to collect all reasonable expenses incurred in pursuing the remedies provided in this Section 22, including, but not limited to, reasonable attorneys' fees, to the extent allowed by Applicable Law.

23. Release. Upon payment of all sums secured by this Security Instrument, Lender shall release this Security Instrument. Lender may charge Borrower a fee for releasing this Security Instrument, but only if the fee is paid to a third party for services rendered and the charging of the fee is permitted under Applicable Law.

24. Waiver of Redemption. Borrower waives all rights of redemption to the extent allowed by law.

BY SIGNING BELOW, Borrower accepts and agrees to the terms and covenants contained in this Security Instrument and in any Rider executed by Borrower and recorded with it.

Witnesses: _____(Seal)

        _____Borrower

        _____(Seal)

        _____Borrower

5. FANNIE MAE/FREDDIE MAC MORTGAGE WITH POWER OF SALE—SINGLE FAMILY—MINNESOTA

Minnesota uses a mortgage with power of sale as the most common land financing device. While judicial foreclosure is, of course, permissible (see Minn.Stat.Ann. § 581.01 et seq.) foreclosure is almost always by power of sale, or, as it is referred to locally, by "advertisement." See Minn.Stat.Ann. § 581.01 et seq. The power of sale is exercised by the sheriff. see Minn.Stat.Ann. § 581.06.

MORTGAGE

Here insert definitions from Form 2, supra]

TRANSFER OF RIGHTS IN THE PROPERTY This Security Instrument secures to Lender: (i) the repayment of the Loan, and all renewals, extensions and modifications of the Note; and (ii) the performance of Borrower's covenants and agreements under this Security Instrument and the Note. For this purpose, Borrower does hereby mortgage, grant and convey to Lender and Lender's successors and assigns, with power of sale, the following described property located in the _____ of _____:

    [Type of Recording Jurisdiction]   [Name of Recording Jurisdiction]

which currently has the address of _____

                              [Street]

_____, Minnesota _____ ("Property Address"):

     [City]   [Zip Code]

TOGETHER WITH all the improvements now or hereafter erected on the property, and all easements, appurtenances, and fixtures now or hereafter a part of the property. All replacements and additions shall also be covered by this Security Instrument. All of the foregoing is referred to in this Security Instrument as the "Property."

BORROWER COVENANTS that Borrower is lawfully seised of the estate hereby conveyed and has the right to mortgage, grant and convey the Property and that the Property is unencumbered, except for encumbrances of record. Borrower warrants and will defend generally the title to the Property against all claims and demands, subject to any encumbrances of record.

THIS SECURITY INSTRUMENT combines uniform covenants for national use and non-uniform covenants with limited variations by jurisdiction to constitute a uniform security instrument covering real property.

UNIFORM COVENANTS. Borrower and Lender covenant and agree as follows:

[Uniform Covenants appear here, See Form 2, supra]

22. Acceleration; Remedies. Lender shall give notice to Borrower by certified mail to the address of the Property or another address designated by Borrower prior to acceleration following Borrower's breach of any covenant or agreement in this Security Instrument (but not prior to acceleration under Section 18 unless Applicable Law provides otherwise). The notice shall specify: (a) the default; (b) the action required to cure the default; (c) a date, not less than 30 days from the date the notice is given to Borrower, by which the default must be cured; and (d) that failure to cure the default on or before the date specified in the notice may result in acceleration of the sums secured by this Security Instrument and sale of the Property. The notice shall further inform Borrower of the right to reinstate after acceleration and the right to bring a court action to assert the non-existence of a default or any other defense of Borrower to acceleration and sale. If the default is not cured on or before the date specified in the notice, Lender at its option may require immediate payment in full of all sums secured by this Security Instrument without further demand and may invoke the power of sale and any other remedies permitted by Applicable Law. Lender shall be entitled to collect all expenses incurred in pursuing the remedies provided in this Section 22, including, but not limited to, reasonable attorneys' fees.

If Lender invokes the power of sale, Lender shall cause a copy of a notice of sale to be served upon any person in possession of the Property. Lender shall publish a notice of sale, and the Property shall be sold at public auction in the manner prescribed by Applicable Law. Lender or its designee may purchase the Property at any sale. The proceeds of the sale shall be applied in the following order: (a) to all expenses of the sale, including, but not limited to, reasonable attorneys' fees; (b) to all sums secured by this Security Instrument; and (c) any excess to the person or persons legally entitled to it.

23. Release. Upon payment of all sums secured by this Security Instrument, Lender shall discharge this Security Instrument. Borrower shall pay any recordation costs. Lender may charge Borrower a fee for releasing this Security Instrument, but only if the fee is paid to a third party for services rendered and the charging of the fee is permitted under Applicable Law.

24. Waiver of Homestead. Borrower waives all right of homestead exemption in the Property.

25. Interest on Advances. The interest rate on advances made by Lender under this Security Instrument shall not exceed the maximum rate allowed by Applicable Law.

BY SIGNING BELOW, Borrower accepts and agrees to the terms and covenants contained in this Security Instrument and in any Rider executed by Borrower and recorded with it.

Witnesses: _____(Seal)

_____Borrower

_____(Seal)

_____Borrower

6.   FANNIE MAE/FREDDIE MAC ADJUSTABLE RATE NOTE

The drafter of a mortgage note with an adjustable interest rate provision must address a variety of issues. A major factor is the *index* itself. Another is the *frequency* of rate adjustment. In practice, these two factors are often tied together; for example, if the index is the rate on three-year U.S. Treasury securities, the adjustment frequency will typically be every three years. In addition, the documents may or may not have an *interest rate cap*—a limit above which the rate will not be raised, irrespective of the movement of the index rate. Similarly, a *payment cap* may be imposed, so that monthly payments will not exceed a given amount, notwithstanding index rate fluctuations.

The particular form presented here, prepared by Fannie Mae and Freddie Mac, adopts a "one-year index"—that is, the weekly average yield of U.S. Treasury securities, adjusted to a constant maturity of one year. The reader is cautioned that transactions which employ different parameters than these will require considerable redrafting, or the adoption of different Fannie Mae and Freddie Mac forms if such are available as to fit the transaction.

ADJUSTABLE RATE NOTE

(One-Year Treasury Index—Rate Caps)

THIS NOTE PROVIDES FOR A CHANGE IN MY FIXED INTEREST RATE TO AN ADJUSTABLE INTEREST RATE. THIS NOTE LIMITS THE AMOUNT MY ADJUSTABLE INTEREST RATE CAN CHANGE AT ANY ONE TIME AND THE MAXIMUM RATE I MUST PAY.

_____, _____ _____ _____
       [Date]   [City]   [State]

_____
                        [Property Address]

1. BORROWER'S PROMISE TO PAY

In return for a loan that I have received, I promise to pay U.S. $_____ (this amount is called "Principal"), plus interest, to the order of Lender. Lender is _____. I will make all payments under this Note in the form of cash, check or money order.

I understand that Lender may transfer this Note. Lender or anyone who takes this Note by transfer and who is entitled to receive payments under this Note is called the "Note Holder."

2. INTEREST

Interest will be charged on unpaid principal until the full amount of Principal has been paid. I will pay interest at a yearly rate of _____%. The interest rate I will pay may change in accordance with Section 4 of this Note.

The interest rate required by this Section 2 and Section 4 of this Note is the rate I will pay both before and after any default described in Section 7(B) of this Note.

3. PAYMENTS

(A) Time and Place of Payments

I will pay principal and interest by making a payment every month.

I will make my monthly payments on the first day of each month beginning on _____, ____. I will make these payments every month until I have paid all of the principal and interest and any other charges described below that I may owe under this Note. Each monthly payment will be applied as of its scheduled due date and will be applied to interest before Principal. If, on _____, ____, I still owe amounts under this Note, I will pay those amounts in full on that date, which is called the "Maturity Date."

I will make my monthly payments at _____ or at a different place if required by the Note Holder.

(B) Amount of My Initial Monthly Payments

Each of my initial monthly payments will be in the amount of U.S. $_____. This amount may change.

(C) Monthly Payment Changes

Changes in my monthly payment will reflect changes in the unpaid principal of my loan and in the interest rate that I must pay. The Note Holder will determine my new interest rate and the changed amount of my monthly payment in accordance with Section 4 of this Note.

4. ADJUSTABLE INTEREST RATE AND MONTHLY PAYMENT CHANGES

(A) Change Dates

The initial fixed interest rate I will pay will change to an adjustable interest rate on the first day of _____, ____, and the adjustable interest rate I will pay may change on that day every 12th month thereafter. The date on which my initial fixed interest rate changes to an adjustable interest rate, and each date on which my adjustable interest rate could change, is called a "Change Date."

(B) The Index

Beginning with the first Change Date, my adjustable interest rate will be based on an Index. The "Index" is the weekly average yield on United States Treasury securities adjusted to a constant maturity of one year, as made available by the Federal Reserve Board. The most recent Index figure available as of the date 45 days before each Change Date is called the "Current Index."

If the Index is no longer available, the Note Holder will choose a new index that is based upon comparable information. The Note Holder will give me notice of this choice.

(C) Calculation of Changes

Before each Change Date, the Note Holder will calculate my new interest rate by adding _____ percentage points (_____%) to the Current Index. The Note Holder will then round the result of this addition to the nearest one-eighth of one percentage point (0.125%). Subject to the limits stated in Section 4(D) below, this rounded amount will be my new interest rate until the next Change Date.

The Note Holder will then determine the amount of the monthly payment that would be sufficient to repay the unpaid principal that I am expected to owe at the Change Date in full on the Maturity Date at my new interest rate in substantially equal payments. The result of this calculation will be the new amount of my monthly payment.

(D) Limits on Interest Rate Changes

The interest rate I am required to pay at the first Change Date will not be greater than _____% or less than _____%. Thereafter, my adjustable interest rate will never be increased or decreased on any single Change Date by more than two percentage points from the rate of interest I have been paying for the preceding 12 months. My interest rate will never be greater than _____%.

(E) Effective Date of Changes

My new interest rate will become effective on each Change Date. I will pay the amount of my new monthly payment beginning on the first monthly payment date after the Change Date until the amount of my monthly payment changes again.

(F) Notice of Changes

The Note Holder will deliver or mail to me a notice of any changes in my initial fixed interest rate to an adjustable interest rate and of any changes in my adjustable interest rate before the effective date of any change. The notice will include the amount of my monthly payment, any information required by law to be given to me and also the title and telephone number of a person who will answer any question I may have regarding the notice.

5. BORROWER'S RIGHT TO PREPAY

I have the right to make payments of Principal at any time before they are due. A payment of Principal only is known as a "Prepayment." When I make a Prepayment, I will tell the Note Holder in writing that I am doing so. I may not designate a payment as a Prepayment if I have not made all the monthly payments due under this Note.

I may make a full Prepayment or partial Prepayments without paying any Prepayment charge. The Note Holder will use my Prepayments to reduce the amount of Principal that I owe under this Note. However, the Note Holder may apply my Prepayment to the accrued and unpaid interest on the Prepayment amount before applying my Prepayment to reduce the Principal amount of this Note. If I make a partial Prepayment, there will be no changes in the due dates of my monthly payments unless the Note Holder agrees in writing to those changes. My partial Prepayment may reduce the amount of my monthly payments after the first Change Date following my partial Prepayment. However, any reduction due to my partial Prepayment may be offset by an interest rate increase.

6. LOAN CHARGES

If a law, which applies to this loan and which sets maximum loan charges, is finally interpreted so that the interest or other loan charges collected or to be collected in connection with this loan exceed the permitted limits, then: (a) any such loan charge shall be reduced by the amount necessary to reduce the charge to the permitted limit; and (b) any sums already collected from me that exceeded permitted limits will be refunded to me. The Note Holder may choose to make this refund by reducing the Principal I owe under this Note or by making a direct payment to me. If a refund reduces Principal, the reduction will be treated as a partial Prepayment.

7. BORROWER'S FAILURE TO PAY AS REQUIRED

(A) Late Charges for Overdue Payments

If the Note Holder has not received the full amount of any monthly payment by the end of _____ calendar days after the date it is due, I will pay a late charge to the Note Holder. The amount of the charge will be _____% of my overdue payment of principal and interest. I will pay this late charge promptly but only once on each late payment.

(B) Default

If I do not pay the full amount of each monthly payment on the date it is due, I will be in default.

(C) Notice of Default

If I am in default, the Note Holder may send me a written notice telling me that if I do not pay the overdue amount by a certain date, the Note Holder may require me to pay immediately the full amount of Principal that has not been paid and all the interest that I owe on that amount. That date must be at least 30 days after the date on which the notice is mailed to me or delivered by other means.

(D) No Waiver By Note Holder

Even if, at a time when I am in default, the Note Holder does not require me to pay immediately in full as described above, the Note Holder will still have the right to do so if I am in default at a later time.

(E) Payment of Note Holder's Costs and Expenses

If the Note Holder has required me to pay immediately in full as described above, the Note Holder will have the right to be paid back by me for all of its costs and expenses in enforcing this Note to the extent not prohibited by applicable law. Those expenses include, for example, reasonable attorneys' fees.

8. GIVING OF NOTICES

Unless applicable law requires a different method, any notice that must be given to me under this Note will be given by delivering it or by mailing it by first class mail to me at the Property Address above or at a different address if I give the Note Holder a notice of my different address.

Unless the Note Holder requires a different method, any notice that must be given to the Note Holder under this Note will be given by mailing it by first class mail to the Note Holder at the address stated in Section 3(A) above or at a different address if I am given a notice of that different address.

9. OBLIGATIONS OF PERSONS UNDER THIS NOTE

If more than one person signs this Note, each person is fully and personally obligated to keep all of the promises made in this Note, including the promise to pay the full amount owed. Any person who is a guarantor, surety or endorser of this Note is also obligated to do these things. Any person who takes over these obligations, including the obligations of a guarantor, surety or endorser of this Note, is also obligated to keep all of the promises made in this Note. The Note Holder may enforce its rights under this Note against each person individually or against all of us together. This means that any one of us may be required to pay all of the amounts owed under this Note.

10. WAIVERS

I and any other person who has obligations under this Note waive the rights of Presentment and Notice of Dishonor. "Presentment" means the right to require the Note Holder to demand payment of amounts due. "Notice of Dishonor" means the right to require the Note Holder to give notice to other persons that amounts due have not been paid.

11. UNIFORM SECURED NOTE

This Note is a uniform instrument with limited variations in some jurisdictions. In addition to the protections given to the Note Holder under this Note, a Mortgage, Deed of Trust, or Security Deed (the "Security Instrument"), dated the same date as this Note, protects the Note Holder from possible losses that might result if I do not keep the promises that I make in this Note. That Security Instrument describes how and under what conditions I may be required to make immediate payment in full of all amounts I owe under this Note. Some of those conditions read as follows:

(A) Until my initial fixed interest rate changes to an adjustable interest rate under the terms stated in Section 4 above, Uniform Covenant 18 of the Security Instrument shall read as follows:

Transfer of the Property or a Beneficial Interest in Borrower. As used in this Section 18, "Interest in the Property" means any legal or beneficial interest in the Property, including, but not limited to, those beneficial interests transferred in a bond for deed, contract for deed, installment sales contract or escrow agreement, the intent of which is the transfer of title by Borrower at a future date to a purchaser.

If all or any part of the Property or any Interest in the Property is sold or transferred (or if Borrower is not a natural person and a beneficial interest in Borrower is sold or transferred) without Lender's prior written consent, Lender may require immediate payment in full of all sums secured by this Security Instrument. However, this option shall not be exercised by Lender if such exercise is prohibited by Applicable Law.

If Lender exercises this option, Lender shall give Borrower notice of acceleration. The notice shall provide a period of not less than 30 days from the date the notice is given in accordance with Section 15 within which Borrower must pay all sums secured by this Security Instrument. If Borrower fails to pay these sums prior to the expiration of this period, Lender may invoke any remedies permitted by this Security Instrument without further notice or demand on Borrower.

(B) When my initial fixed interest rate changes to an adjustable interest rate under the terms stated in Section 4 above, Uniform Covenant 18 of the Security Instrument described in Section 11(A) above shall then cease to be in effect, and Uniform Covenant 18 of the Security Instrument shall instead read as follows:

Transfer of the Property or a Beneficial Interest in Borrower. As used in this Section 18, "Interest in the Property" means any legal or beneficial interest in the Property, including, but not limited to, those beneficial interests transferred in a bond for deed, contract for deed, installment sales contract or escrow agreement, the intent of which is the transfer of title by Borrower at a future date to a purchaser.

If all or any part of the Property or any Interest in the Property is sold or transferred (or if Borrower is not a natural person and a beneficial interest in Borrower is sold or transferred) without Lender's prior written consent, Lender may require immediate payment in full of all sums secured by this Security Instrument. However, this option shall not be exercised by Lender if such exercise is prohibited by Applicable Law. Lender also shall not exercise this option if: (a) Borrower causes to be submitted to Lender information required by Lender to evaluate the intended transferee as if a new loan were being made to the transferee; and (b) Lender reasonably determines that Lender's security will not be impaired by the loan assumption and that the risk of a breach of any covenant or agreement in this Security Instrument is acceptable to Lender.

To the extent permitted by Applicable Law, Lender may charge a reasonable fee as a condition to Lender's consent to the loan assumption. Lender also may require the transferee to sign an assumption agreement that is acceptable to Lender and that obligates the transferee to keep all the promises and agreements made in the Note and in this Security Instrument. Borrower will continue to be obligated under the Note and this Security Instrument unless Lender releases Borrower in writing.

If Lender exercises the option to require immediate payment in full, Lender shall give Borrower notice of acceleration. The notice shall provide a period of not less than 30 days from the date the notice is given in accordance with Section 15 within which Borrower must pay all sums secured by this Security Instrument. If Borrower fails to pay these sums prior to the expiration of this period, Lender may invoke any remedies permitted by this Security Instrument without further notice or demand on Borrower.

WITNESS THE HAND(S) AND SEAL(S) OF THE UNDERSIGNED.

_____(Seal)
-Borrower

_____(Seal)
-Borrower

_____(Seal)
-Borrower

7. FANNIE MAE/FREDDIE MAC CONDOMINIUM RIDER

Permanent mortgage loans on condominium units are usually made on much the same terms as loans on detached residential real estate. However, the condominium mortgage confronts a variety of concerns that are unimportant or non-existent in more traditional financing contexts. Most of these concerns relate to the importance of the owners association and the common areas to the long term success of the project and, thus, to the security value of the units themselves. See Chapter 10 supra. The Condominium Rider reflects an attempt to deal with many of these special problems. A separate rider is also required in connection with planned unit development mortgage loans; however, because it is virtually identical to the Condominium Rider, we chose not to include it in this volume. See Fannie Mae/Freddie Mac Multistate PUD Rider Single Family—Form 3150.

CONDOMINIUM RIDER

THIS CONDOMINIUM RIDER is made this _____ day of _____, _____, and is incorporated into and shall be deemed to amend and supplement the Mortgage, Deed of Trust, or Security Deed (the "Security Instrument") of the same date given by the undersigned (the "Borrower") to secure Borrower's Note to _____ (the "Lender") of the same date and covering the Property described in the Security Instrument and located at: _____

[Property Address]

The Property includes a unit in, together with an undivided interest in the common elements of, a condominium project known as:

_____

[Name of Condominium Project]

(the "Condominium Project"). If the owners association or other entity which acts for the Condominium Project (the "Owners Association") holds title to property for the benefit or use of its members or shareholders, the Property also includes Borrower's interest in the Owners Association and the uses, proceeds and benefits of Borrower's interest.

CONDOMINIUM COVENANTS. In addition to the covenants and agreements made in the Security Instrument, Borrower and Lender further covenant and agree as follows:

A. **Condominium Obligations.** Borrower shall perform all of Borrower's obligations under the Condominium Project's Constituent Documents. The "Constituent Documents" are the: (i) Declaration or any other document which creates the Condominium Project; (ii) by-laws; (iii) code of regulations; and (iv) other equivalent documents. Borrower shall promptly pay, when due, all dues and assessments imposed pursuant to the Constituent Documents.

B. **Property Insurance.** So long as the Owners Association maintains, with a generally accepted insurance carrier, a "master" or "blanket" policy on the Condominium Project which is satisfactory to Lender and which provides insurance coverage in the amounts (including deductible levels), for the periods, and against loss by fire, hazards included within the term "extended coverage," and any other hazards, including, but not limited to, earthquakes and floods, from which Lender requires insurance, then: (i) Lender waives the provision in Section 3 for the Periodic Payment to Lender of the yearly premium installments for property insurance on the Property; and (ii) Borrower's obligation under Section 5 to maintain property insurance coverage on the Property is deemed satisfied to the extent that the required coverage is provided by the Owners Association policy.

What Lender requires as a condition of this waiver can change during the term of the loan.

Borrower shall give Lender prompt notice of any lapse in required property insurance coverage provided by the master or blanket policy.

In the event of a distribution of property insurance proceeds in lieu of restoration or repair following a loss to the Property, whether to the unit or to common elements, any proceeds payable to Borrower are hereby assigned and shall be paid to Lender for application to the sums secured by the Security Instrument, whether or not then due, with the excess, if any, paid to Borrower.

C. **Public Liability Insurance.** Borrower shall take such actions as may be reasonable to insure that the Owners Association maintains a public liability insurance policy acceptable in form, amount, and extent of coverage to Lender.

D. **Condemnation.** The proceeds of any award or claim for damages, direct or consequential, payable to Borrower in connection with any condemnation or other taking of all or any part of the Property, whether of the unit or of the common elements, or for any conveyance in lieu of condemnation, are hereby assigned and shall be paid to Lender. Such proceeds shall be applied by Lender to the sums secured by the Security Instrument as provided in Section 11.

E. **Lender's Prior Consent.** Borrower shall not, except after notice to Lender and with Lender's prior written consent, either partition or subdivide the Property or consent to: (i) the abandonment or termination of the Condominium Project, except for abandonment or termination required by law in the case of substantial destruction by fire or other casualty or in the case of a taking by condemnation or eminent domain; (ii) any amendment to any provision of the Constituent Documents if the provision is for the express benefit of Lender; (iii) termination of professional management and assumption of self-management of the Owners Association; or (iv) any action which would have the effect of rendering the public liability insurance coverage maintained by the Owners Association unacceptable to Lender.

F. **Remedies.** If Borrower does not pay condominium dues and assessments when due, then Lender may pay them. Any amounts disbursed by Lender under this paragraph F shall become additional debt of Borrower secured by the Security

Instrument. Unless Borrower and Lender agree to other terms of payment, these amounts shall bear interest from the date of disbursement at the Note rate and shall be payable, with interest, upon notice from Lender to Borrower requesting payment.

BY SIGNING BELOW, Borrower accepts and agrees to the terms and covenants contained in this Condominium Rider.

_____(Seal)
-Borrower

_____(Seal)
-Borrower

8. CONTRACT FOR DEED—INDIVIDUAL SELLER—MINNESOTA

Even though Minnesota authorizes nonjudicial foreclosure of mortgages containing a power of sale, installment land contracts (contracts for deed) are frequently used in vendor financing settings. A major reason for this use is to avoid statutory redemption rights that mortgagors and junior lienors enjoy after power of sale foreclosure in Minnesota. See Minn.Stat.Ann. §§ 580.23 & 530.24. The forfeiture clause is enforceable by complying with Minn.Stat.Ann. § 559.21. The following contract for deed form (30.1.1) is part of a compilation published following Minn.Stat.Ann. ch. 507 and has semi-official" status.

Form 30.1.1 (2011)

DATE: _____
                    (month/day/year)

THIS CONTRACT FOR DEED (the "Contract") is made on the above date by _____ (insert name and marital status of each Seller) _____ ("Seller"), And _____ (insert name of each Purchaser) _____, ("Purchaser"). (*Check box if* ❏ *joint tenancy.*)

Seller and Purchaser agree to the following terms:

1.   Property Description. Seller hereby sells and Purchaser hereby buys real property in _____ County, Minnesota, described as follows:

_____

Check here if all or part of the described real property is Registered (Torrens) ❏

together with all hereditaments and appurtenances belonging thereto (the "Property"). Unless otherwise specified, Seller hereby delivers possession of the Property to Purchaser on the date hereof.

Check applicable box:

❏ The Seller certifies that the Seller does not know of any wells on the described real property.

❏ A well disclosure certificate accompanies this document or has been electronically filed. (If electronically filed, insert WDC number:) _____

❏ I am familiar with the property described in this instrument and I certify that the status and number of wells on the described real property have not changed since the last previously filed well disclosure certificate.

2.   **Title.** Seller warrants that title to the Property is, on the date of this Contract, subject only to the following exceptions:

   (a)   Covenants, conditions, restrictions (without effective forfeiture provisions) and declarations of record, if any;

   (b)   Reservation of minerals or mineral rights by the State of Minnesota, if any;

   (c)   Utility and drainage easements which do not interfere with present improvements;

   (d)   Applicable laws, ordinances, and regulations;

   (e)   The lien of real estate taxes and installments of special assessments which are payable by Purchaser pursuant to paragraph 6 of this Contract; and

   (f)   The following liens or encumbrances:

3.   **Delivery of Deed and Evidence of Title.** Upon Purchaser's full performance of this Contract, Seller shall:

   (a)   Execute, acknowledge, and deliver to Purchaser a _____ Deed, in recordable form, conveying marketable title to the Property to Purchaser, subject only to the following exceptions:

      (i)   Those exceptions referred to in paragraph 2(a), (b), (c), (d), and (e) of this Contract;

      (ii) Liens, encumbrances, adverse claims or other matters which Purchaser has created, suffered or permitted to accrue after the date of this Contract; and

      (iii) The following liens or encumbrances:

   (b)   Deliver to Purchaser the abstract of title to the Property, without further extension, to the extent required by the purchase agreement (if any) between Seller and Purchaser.

4.   **Purchase Price.** Purchaser shall pay to Seller at _____ the sum of _____ Dollars ($ _____), as and for the purchase price (the "Purchase Price") for the Property, payable as follows:

5.   Prepayment. Unless otherwise provided in this Contract, Purchaser shall have the right to fully or partially prepay this Contract at any time without penalty. Any partial prepayment shall be applied first to payment of amounts then due under this Contract, including unpaid accrued interest, and the balance shall be applied to the principal installments to be paid in the inverse order of their maturity. Partial prepayment shall not postpone the due date of the installments to be paid pursuant to this Contract or change the amount of such installments.

6.   Real Estate Taxes and Assessments. Real estate taxes and installments of special assessments which are due and payable in the year in which this Contract is dated shall be paid as follows:

Purchaser shall pay, before penalty accrues, all real estate taxes and installments of special assessments assessed against the Property which are due and payable in all subsequent years. Seller warrants that the real estate taxes and installments of special assessments which were due and payable in the years preceding the year in which this Contract is dated are paid in full. If the Property is subject to a recorded declaration providing for assessments to be levied against the Property by any owners' association, Purchaser shall promptly pay, when due, all assessments imposed by the owners' association or other governing body as required by the provisions of the declaration or other related documents.

7.   Property Insurance.

(a)   Insured Risks and Amounts. Purchaser shall keep all buildings, improvements, and fixtures now or later located on or a part of the Property insured against loss by fire, lightning and such other perils as are included in a standard "all-risk" endorsement, and against loss or damage by all other risks and hazards covered by a standard extended coverage insurance policy, including, without limitation, vandalism, malicious mischief, burglary, theft and, if applicable, steam boiler explosion. Such insurance shall be in an amount no less than the full replacement cost of the buildings, improvements, and fixtures, without deduction for physical depreciation. If any of the buildings, improvements, or fixtures are located in a federally designated flood prone area, and if flood insurance is available for that area, Purchaser shall procure and maintain flood insurance in amounts reasonably satisfactory to Seller.

(b)   Other Terms. The insurance policy shall contain a loss payable clause in favor of Seller which provides that Seller's right to recover under the insurance shall not be impaired by any acts or omissions of Purchaser or Seller, and that Seller shall otherwise be afforded all rights and privileges customarily provided a mortgagee under the so-called standard mortgage clause.

(c)   Notice of Damage. In the event of damage to the Property by fire or other casualty, Purchaser shall promptly give notice of such damage to Seller and the insurance company.

8.   Damage to the Property.

(a)   Application of Insurance Proceeds. If the Property is damaged by fire or other casualty, the insurance proceeds paid on account of such damage shall be applied to payment of the amounts payable by Purchaser under this Contract, even if such amounts are not then due to be paid, unless Purchaser makes a permitted election described in the next paragraph. Such amounts shall be first applied to unpaid accrued interest and next to the installments to be paid as provided in this Contract in the inverse order of their maturity. Such payment shall not postpone the due date of the installments to be paid pursuant to this Contract or change the amount of such installments. The balance of insurance proceeds, if any, shall be the property of Purchaser.

(b)   Purchaser's Election to Rebuild. If Purchaser is not in default under this Contract, or after curing any such default, and if the mortgagees in any prior mortgages and sellers in any prior contracts for deed do not require otherwise, Purchaser may elect to have that portion of such insurance proceeds necessary to repair, replace, or restore the damaged Property (the "Repairs") deposited in escrow with a bank or title insurance company qualified to do business in the State of Minnesota, or such other party as may be mutually agreeable to Seller and Purchaser. The election may only be made by written notice to Seller within sixty (60) days after the damage occurs. Also, the election will only be permitted if the plans and specifications and contracts for the Repairs are approved by Seller, which approval Seller shall not unreasonably withhold or delay. If such a permitted election is made by Purchaser, Seller and Purchaser shall jointly deposit, when paid, such insurance proceeds into such escrow. If such insurance proceeds are insufficient for the Repairs, Purchaser shall, before the commencement of the Repairs, deposit into such escrow sufficient additional money to insure the full payment for the Repairs. Even if the insurance proceeds are unavailable or are insufficient to pay the cost of the Repairs, Purchaser shall at all times be responsible to pay the full cost of the Repairs. All escrowed funds shall be disbursed by the escrowee in accordance with generally accepted sound construction disbursement procedures. The costs incurred or to be incurred on account of such escrow shall be deposited by Purchaser into such escrow before the commencement of the Repairs. Purchaser shall complete the Repairs as soon as reasonably possible and in a good and workmanlike manner, and in any event the Repairs shall be completed by Purchaser within one (1) year after the damage occurs. If, following the completion of and payment for the Repairs, there remains any undisbursed escrow funds, such funds shall be applied to payment of the amounts payable by Purchaser under this Contract in accordance with paragraph 8(a) above.

(c) Owners' Association. If the Property is subject to a recorded declaration, so long as the owners' association maintains a master or blanket policy of insurance against fire, extended coverage perils and such other hazards and in such amount as are required by this Contract, then: (i) Purchaser's obligation in the Contract to maintain hazard insurance coverage on the Property is satisfied; (ii) the provisions of paragraph 8(a) of this Contract regarding application of insurance proceeds shall be superseded by the provisions of the declaration or other related documents; and (iii) in the event of a distribution of insurance proceeds in lieu of restoration or repair following an insured casualty loss to the Property, any such proceeds payable to Purchaser are hereby assigned and shall be paid to Seller for application to the sum secured by this Contract, with the excess, if any, paid to Purchaser.

9. Injury or Damage Occurring on the Property.

(a) Liability. Seller shall be free from liability and claims for damages by reason of injuries occurring on or after the date of this Contract to any person or persons or property while on or about the Property. Purchaser shall defend and indemnify Seller from all liability, loss, cost, and obligations, including reasonable attorneys' fees, on account of or arising out of any such injuries. However, Purchaser shall have no liability or obligation to Seller for such injuries which are caused by the negligence or intentional wrongful acts or omissions of Seller.

(b) Liability Insurance. Purchaser shall, at Purchaser's own expense, procure and maintain liability insurance against claims for bodily injury, death and property damage occurring on or about the Property in amounts reasonably satisfactory to Seller and naming Seller as an additional insured.

10. Insurance Generally. The insurance which Purchaser is required to procure and maintain pursuant to paragraphs 7 and 9 of this Contract shall be issued by an insurance company or companies licensed to do business in the State of Minnesota and acceptable to Seller. The insurance shall be maintained by Purchaser at all times while any amount remains unpaid under this Contract. The insurance policies shall provide for not less than ten (10) days written notice to Seller before cancellation, non-renewal, termination or change in coverage, and Purchaser shall deliver to Seller a duplicate original or certificate of such insurance policy or policies.

11. Condemnation. If all or any part of the Property is taken in condemnation proceedings instituted under power of eminent domain or is conveyed in lieu thereof under threat of condemnation, the money paid pursuant to such condemnation or conveyance in lieu thereof shall be applied to payment of the amounts payable by Purchaser under this Contract, even if such amounts are not then due to be paid. Such amounts shall be applied in the same manner as a prepayment as provided in paragraph 5 of this Contract. Such payments shall not postpone the due date of the installments to be paid pursuant to this Contract or change the amount of such installments. The balance, if any, shall be the property of Purchaser.

12. Waste, Repair, and Liens. Purchaser shall not remove or demolish any buildings, improvements, or fixtures now or later located on or a part of the Property, nor shall Purchaser commit or allow waste of the Property. Purchaser shall maintain the Property in good condition and repair. Purchaser shall not create or permit to accrue liens or adverse claims against the Property which constitute a lien or claim against Seller's interest in the Property. Purchaser shall pay to Seller all amounts, costs and expenses, including reasonable attorneys' fees, incurred by Seller to remove any such liens or adverse claims.

13. Compliance with Laws. Except for matters which Seller has created, suffered, or permitted to exist prior to the date of this Contract, Purchaser shall comply or cause compliance with all laws and regulations of any governmental authority which affect the Property or the manner of using or operating the same, and with all restrictive covenants, if any, affecting title to the Property or the use thereof.

14. Recording of Contract; Deed Tax. Purchaser shall, at Purchaser's expense, record this Contract in the Office of the County Recorder or Registrar of Titles in the county in which the Property is located within four (4) months after the date hereof. Purchaser shall pay any penalty imposed under Minn. Stat. 507.235 for failure to timely record the Contract. Seller shall, upon Purchaser's full performance of this Contract, pay the deed tax due upon the recording of the deed to be delivered by Seller.

15. Notice of Assignment. If either Seller or Purchaser assigns its interest in the Property, the assigning party shall promptly furnish a copy of such assignment to the non-assigning party.

16. Protection of Interests. If Purchaser fails to pay any sum of money required under the terms of this Contract or fails to perform any of the Purchaser's obligations as set forth in this Contract, Seller may, at Seller's option, pay the same or cause the same to be performed, or both, and the amounts so paid by Seller and the cost of such performance shall be payable at once, with interest at the rate stated in paragraph 4 of this Contract, as an additional amount due Seller under this Contract. If there now exists, or if Seller hereafter creates, suffers or permits to accrue, any mortgage, contract for deed, lien or encumbrance against the Property which is not herein expressly assumed by Purchaser, and provided

Purchaser is not in default under this Contract, Seller shall timely pay all amounts due thereon, and if Seller fails to do so, Purchaser may, at Purchaser's option, pay any such delinquent amounts or take any actions reasonably necessary to cure defaults thereunder and deduct the amounts so paid together with interest at the rate provided in this Contract from the payments next coming due under this Contract.

17. Defaults and Remedies. The time of performance by Purchaser of the terms of this Contract is an essential part of this Contract. If Purchaser fails to timely perform any term of this Contract, Seller may, at Seller's option, elect to declare this Contract cancelled and terminated by notice to Purchaser in accordance with applicable law or elect any other remedy available at law or in equity. If Seller elects to terminate this Contract, all right, title, and interest acquired under this Contract by Purchaser shall then cease and terminate, and all improvements made upon the Property and all payments made by Purchaser pursuant to this Contract (including escrow payments, if any) shall belong to Seller as liquidated damages for breach of this Contract. Neither the extension of the time for payment of any sum of money to be paid hereunder nor any waiver by Seller of Seller's rights to declare this Contract forfeited by reason of any breach shall in any manner affect Seller's right to cancel this Contract because of defaults subsequently occurring, and no extension of time shall be valid unless agreed to in writing. After service of notice of default and failure to cure such default within the period allowed by law, Purchaser shall, upon demand, surrender possession of the Property to Seller, but Purchaser shall be entitled to possession of the Property until the expiration of such period. Failure by Seller to exercise one or more remedies available under this paragraph 17 shall not constitute a waiver of the right to exercise such remedy or remedies thereafter.

18. Binding Effect. The terms of this Contract shall run with the land and bind the parties hereto and the successors in interest.

19. Headings. Headings of the paragraphs of this Contract are for convenience only and do not define, limit, or construe the contents of such paragraphs.

20. Additional Terms: Check here if ❑ an addendum to this Contract containing additional terms and conditions is attached hereto.

9.   FHA MODEL SECURITY INSTRUMENT FORM

The FHA Model Security Instrument Form can be found in HUD Handbook 4155.2 12.A. Although the form is titled "Model Mortgage Form" in the Handbook and references a mortgage in the first line, the form is meant to serve as a general security instrument, and is therefore useable for either a mortgage or deed of trust. This intent is evidenced by all future references being to a "Security Instrument."[104] The form consists of three parts.

The introductory portion is predominantly the same language found in a given state's Fannie Mae or Freddie Mac security instrument. This portion has not been reprinted below due to its nearly uniform character. This portion must provide a space for the FHA Case Number. The model form HUD provides in the handbook is useable in Michigan.[105]

The middle portion of the form consists of 16 covenants entitled "Uniform Covenants" that are specific to FHA. These covenants apply in all states. The language of the uniform covenants is styled after the Fannie Mae and Freddie Mac forms, but is not the same as the uniform covenants used in the Fannie Mae and Freddie Mac forms, and Fannie Mae or Freddie Mac uniform covenants may not be substituted.[106] This portion of the form has been reprinted below.

The final portion of the form, which is reprinted below in skeletal form, consists of Non-Uniform Covenants.[107] The first such covenant is an Assignment of Rents provision. FHA has provided specific language to use, unless it is inconsistent with state law. The final covenant provided by FHA deals with foreclosure. This covenant uses state-specific Fannie Mae or Freddie Mac language modified to reflect HUD policy.[108] Certain states have specific language provided by HUD that they must implement, which can be found in HUD Handbook 4155.2 6.B. California has no such special provisions.

After these two Non-Uniform Covenants, a lender will include state-specific Fannie Mae or Freddie Mac Non-Uniform Covenants. California specific provisions may be seen in section 3 of this Appendix: FANNIE MAE/FREDDIE MAC DEED OF TRUST—SINGLE FAMILY—CALIFORNIA starting with Non-Uniform Covenants (paragraph 22). Finally there is a portion for the Family Mortgage Foreclosure Act of 1994, and a portion for any Riders.

UNIFORM COVENANTS

1. Payment of Principal, Interest and Late Charge

Borrower shall pay when due the principal of, and interest on, the debt evidenced by the Note and late charges due under the Note.

---

[104] HUD Handbook 4155.2 12.A.1.a
[105] *Id.*
[106] HUD Handbook 4155.2 12.A.2.c
[107] HUD Handbook 4155.2 12.A.2.d
[108] HUD Handbook 4155.2 12.A.2.e

2. Monthly Payment of Taxes, Insurance, and Other Charges

Borrower shall include in each monthly payment, together with the principal and interest as set forth in the Note and any late charges, a sum for

(a) taxes and special assessments levied or to be levied against the Property.

(b) leasehold payments or ground rents on the Property, and

(c) premiums for insurance required under Paragraph 4. In any year in which the Lender must pay a mortgage insurance premium to the Secretary of Housing and Urban Development ("Secretary"), or in any year in which such premium would have been required if Lender still held the Security Instrument, each monthly payment shall also include either

   (i) a sum for the annual mortgage insurance premium to be paid by the Lender to the Secretary, or

   (ii) a monthly charge instead of a mortgage insurance premium if this Security Instrument is held by the Secretary, in a reasonable amount to be determined by the Secretary. Except for the monthly charge by the Secretary, these items are called "Escrow Items" and the sums paid to Lender are called "Escrow Funds."

Lender may, at any time, collect and hold amounts for Escrow Items in an aggregate amount not to exceed the maximum amount that may be required for Borrower's escrow account under the Real Estate Settlement Procedures Act of 1974, 12 U.S.C. sec. 2601 et seq. and implementing regulations, 24 CFR Part 3500, as they may be amended from time to time (RESPA), except that the cushion or reserve permitted by RESPA for unanticipated disbursements or disbursements before the Borrower's payments are available in the account may not be based on amounts due for the mortgage insurance premium.

If the amounts held by Lender for Escrow Items exceeds the amounts permitted to be held by RESPA, Lender shall deal with the excess funds as required by RESPA. If the amounts of funds held by Lender at any time are not sufficient to pay the Escrow Items when due, Lender may notify the Borrower and require Borrower to make up the shortage as permitted by RESPA.

The Escrow Funds are pledged as additional security for all sums secured by this Security Instrument. If Borrower tenders to Lender the full payment of all such sums, Borrowers account shall be credited with the balance remaining for all installment items (a), (b), and (c) and any mortgage insurance premium **installment** that Lender has not become obligated to pay to the Secretary, and Lender shall promptly refund any excess funds to Borrower. Immediately prior to a foreclosure sale of the Property or its acquisition by Lender, Borrower's account shall be credited with any balance remaining for all installments for items (a), (b), and (c).

3. Application of Payments

All payments under Paragraphs 1 and 2 shall be applied by Lender as follows:

- First, to the mortgage insurance premiums to be paid by Lender to the Secretary or to the monthly charge by the Secretary instead of the monthly mortgage insurance premiums;

- Second, to any taxes, special assessments, leasehold payments or ground rents, and fire, flood and other hazard insurance premiums, as required;

- Third, to interest due under the Note;

- Fourth, to amortization of the principal of the Note; and

- Fifth, to late charges due under the Note.

4. Fire, Flood, and Other Hazard Insurance

Borrower shall insure all improvements on the Property, whether now in existence or subsequently erected, against any hazards, casualties, and contingencies, including fire, for which Lender requires insurance. This insurance shall be maintained in the amounts and for the periods that Lender requires. Borrower shall also insure all improvements on the Property, whether now in existence or subsequently erected, against loss by floods to the extend required by the Secretary. All insurance shall be carried with companies approved by Lender. The insurance policies and any renewals shall be held by Lender and shall include loss payable clauses in favor of, and in a form acceptable to, Lender.

In the event of loss, Borrower shall give Lender immediate notice by mail. Lender may make proof of loss if not made promptly by Borrower. Each insurance company concerned is hereby authorized and directed to make payment for such loss directly to Lender, instead of to Borrower and to Lender jointly. All or any part of the insurance proceeds may be applied by Lender at its option, either

(a) To the reduction of the indebtedness under the Note and this Security Instrument, first to any delinquent amounts applied in the order in Paragraph 3, and then to prepayment of principal, or

(b) to the restoration or repair of the damaged Property. Any application of the proceeds to the principal shall not extend or postpone the due date of the monthly payments which are referred to in Paragraph 2, or change the amount of such payments. Any excess insurance proceeds over an amount required to pay all outstanding indebtedness under the Note and this Security Instrument shall be paid to the entity shall be paid to the entity legally entitled thereto.

In the event of foreclosure of this Security Instrument or other transfer of title to the Property that distinguishes the indebtedness, all right, title and interest of Borrower in and to insurance policies in force shall pass to the purchaser.

5.   Occupancy, Preservation, Maintenance and Protection of the Property; Borrower's Loan Application; Leaseholds

Borrower shall occupy, establish, and use the Property as Borrower's principal residence within sixty days after the execution of this Security Instrument (or within sixty days of a later sale or transfer of the Property) and shall continue to occupy the Property as Borrowed principal residence for at least one year after the date of occupancy, under Lender determines that requirement will cause undue hardship for Borrower, or unless extenuating circumstances exist which are beyond Borrower's control. Borrower shall notify Lender of any extenuating circumstances. Borrower shall not commit waste or destroy, damage or substantially change the Property or allow the Property to deteriorate, reasonable wear and tear excepted. Lender may inspect the Property if the Property is vacant or abandoned or the loan is in default. Lender may take reasonable action to protect and preserve such vacant or abandoned property. Borrower shall also be in default if borrower, during the loan application process, gave materially false or inaccurate information or statements Lender (or failed to provide Lender with any material information) in connection with the loan evidenced by the Note, including, but not limited to, representations concerning Borrower's occupancy of the Property as a principal residence. If this Security Instrument is on a leasehold, Borrower shall comply with the provisions of the lease. If Borrower acquires fee title to the Property, the leasehold and fee title shall not be merged unless the lender agrees to the merge in writing.

6.   Condemnation

The proceeds of any award or claim for damages, direct or consequential, in connection with any condemnation or other taking of any part of the Property, or for conveyance in place of condemnation, are hereby assigned and shall be paid to Lender to the extent of the full amount of the indebtedness that remains unpaid under the Note and this Security Instrument. Lender shall apply such proceeds to the reduction of the

Indebtedness under the Note and this Security Instrument, first to any delinquent amounts applied in the order provided in Paragraph 3, and then to prepayment of principal. Any application of the proceeds to the principal shall not extend or postpone the due date of the monthly payments, which are referred to in Paragraph 2, or change the amount of such payments. Any excess proceeds over an amount requirement to pay all outstanding indebtedness under the Note and this Security Instrument shall be paid to the entity legally entitled thereto.

7.   Charges to Borrower and Protection of Lender's Rights in the Property

Borrower shall pay all governmental or municipal charges, fines and impositions that are not included in Paragraph 2. Borrower shall pay these obligations on time directly to the entity which is owed the payment. If failure to pay would adversely affect Lender's interest in the Property, upon Lender's request Borrower shall promptly furnish to Lender receipts evidencing these payments.

If Borrower fails to make these payments or the payments required by Paragraph 2, or fails to perform any other covenants and agreements contained in this Security Instrument, or there is a legal proceeding that may significantly affect Lender's rights in the Property (such as a proceeding in bankruptcy, for condemnation or to enforce laws or regulations), then Lender may do and pay whatever is necessary to protect the value of the Property and Lender's right in the Property, including payment of taxes, hazard insurance and other items mentioned in Paragraph 2.

Any amounts disbursed by Lender under this Paragraph shall become an additional debt of Borrower and be secured by this Security Instrument. These amounts shall bear Interest from the date of disbursement at the Note rate, and at the option of Lender shall be immediately due and payable.

Borrower shall promptly discharge any lien which has priority over this Security Instrument unless Borrower:

    (a)   agrees in writing to the payment of the obligation secured by the lien in a manner acceptable to lender;

    (b)   contests in good faith the lien by, or defends against enforcement of the lien in, legal proceedings which in the Lender's opinion operate to prevent the enforcement of the lien; or

    (c)   secures from the holder of the lien an agreement satisfactory to Lender subordinating the lien to this Security Instrument. If Lender determines that any part of the Property is subject to a lien which may attain priority over this Security Instrument, Lender may give Borrower a notice identifying the lien. Borrower shall satisfy the lien or take one or more of the actions set forth above within 10 days of the giving of notice.

8. Fees

Lender may collect fees and charges authorized by the Secretary.

9. Grounds for Acceleration of Debt

(a) **Default.** Lender may, except as limited by regulations issued by the Security in the case of payment defaults, require immediate payment in full of all sums secured by this Security Instrument if:

    (i) Borrower defaults by failing to pay in full any monthly payment required by this Security Instrument prior to or on the due date of the next monthly payment, or

    (ii) Borrower defaults by failing for a period of thirty days, to perform any other obligations contained in this Security Instrument.

(b) **Sale Without Credit Approval.** Lender shall, if permitted by applicable laws (including Section 341(d) of the Garn-St. Germain Depository Institutions Act of 1982, 12 U.S.C. 1701j–3(d)) and with the prior approval of the Secretary, requirement immediate payment in full of all sums secured by this security Instrument if:

    (i) All or part of the Property, or a beneficial interest in a trust owning all or part of the Property, is sold or otherwise transferred (other than by devise or descent), and

    (ii) The Property is not occupied by the purchaser or grantee as his or her principal residence, or the purchaser as grantee does so occupy the Property, but his or her credit has not been approved in accordance with the requirements of the Secretary.

(c) **No Waiver.** If circumstances occur that would permit Lender to require immediate payment in full, but Lender does not require such payments, Lender does not waive its rights with respect to subsequent events.

(d) **Regulations of HUD Secretary.** In many circumstances regulations issued by the Secretary will limit Lender rights, in the case of payment defaults, to require immediate payment in full and foreclose if not paid. This Security Instrument does not authorize acceleration or foreclosure if not permitted by regulations of the Secretary.

(e) **Mortgage Not Insured [OPTIONAL].** Borrower agrees that if this Security Instrument and the Note are not determined to be eligible for insurance under the National Housing Act within _____ from the date hereof, Lender may, at its option require immediate payment in full of all sums secured by this Security Instrument. A written statement of any authorized agent of the Secretary dated subsequent to from the date hereof, declining to insure this Security Instrument and the Note, shall be deemed conclusive proof of such ineligibility. Notwithstanding the foregoing, this option may not be exercised by Lender when the unavailability of insurance is solely due to Lender's failure to remit a mortgage insurance premium to the Secretary.

Note: Lenders are authorized, but not require, to add Paragraph 9(e). Any period may be inserted in the two blanks, expressed either in number of days or months, which is not shorter than sixty days and not longer than either months.

10. Reinstatement

Borrower has a right to be reinstated if Lender has required immediate payment in full because of Borrower's failure to pay an amount due under the Note or this Security Instrument. This right applies even after foreclosure proceedings are instituted. To reinstate the Security Instrument, Borrower shall tender in a lump sum all amounts required to bring Borrower account current including, to the extent they are obligations of borrower under this Security Instrument, foreclosure costs and reasonable and customary attorney's fees and expenses properly associated with the foreclosing proceeding. Upon reinstatement by Borrower, this Security Instrument and the obligations that it secures shall remain in effect as if Lender had not required immediate payment in full. However, Lender is not required to permit reinstatement if:

(i) Lender has accepted reinstatement after the commencement of foreclosure proceedings within two years immediately preceding the commencement of a current foreclosure proceeding,

(ii) reinstatement will preclude foreclosure on different grounds in the future, or

(iii) reinstatement will adversely affect the priority of the lien created by this Security Instrument.

11. Borrower Not Released: Forbearance by Lender Not a Waiver

Extension of the time of payment or modification of amortization of the sums secured by this Security Instrument granted by Lender to any successor in interest of Borrower shall not operate to release the liability of the original Borrower or Borrower's successor in interest. Lender shall not be required to commence proceedings against any successor in interest or refuse to extend time for payment or otherwise modify amortization of the sums secured by this Security Instrument by reason of any demand made by the original Borrower or Borrower's successors in interest. Any forbearance by Lender in exercising any right or remedy shall not be a waiver of or preclude the exercise of any right or remedy.

12. Successors and Assigns Bound; Joint and Several Liability; Co-Signers

The covenants and agreements of this Security Instrument shall bind and benefit the successors and assigns of Lender and Borrower, subject to the provisions of Paragraph 9(b). Borrower's covenants and agreements shall be joint and several. Any Borrower who co-signs this Security Instrument but does not execute but does not execute the Note:

(a) is co-signing this Security Instrument only to mortgage, grant and convey that Borrower's interest in the Property under the terms of this Security Instrument;

(b) is not personally obligated to pay the sums secured by this Security Instrument;

(c) agrees that Lender and any other Borrower may agree to extend, modify, forbear or make any accommodations with regard to the term of this Security Instrument or the Note without that Borrower's consent.

13. Notices

Any notice to Borrower provided for in this Security Instrument shall be given by delivering it or by mailing it by first class mail unless applicable law requires use of another method. The noticed shall be directed to the Property Address or any other address Borrower designates by notice to Lender. Any notice to Lender shall be given by first class mail to Lender's address stated herein or any address Lender designates by notice to Borrower. Any notice provided for in this Security Instrument shall be deemed to have been given to Borrower or Lender when given as provided in this paragraph.

14. Governing Law; Severability

This Security Instrument shall be governed by Federal law and the law of the jurisdiction in which the Property is located. In the event that any provisions or clause of this Security Instrument or the Note conflicts with applicable law, such conflict shall not affect other provisions of this Security Instrument or the Note which can be given effect without the conflicting provision. To this end, the provisions of this Security Instrument and the Note are declared to be severable.

15. Borrower's Copy

Borrower shall be given one conformed copy of the Note and of this Security Instrument

16. Hazardous Substances

Borrower shall not cause or permit the presence, use, disposal, storage, or release of any Hazardous Substances on or in the Property. Borrower shall not do, nor allow anyone else to do, anything affecting the Property that is in violation of any Environmental law. The preceding two sentences shall not apply to the presence, use, or storage on the Property of small quantities of Hazardous Substances that are generally recognized to be appropriate to normal residential uses and to maintenance of the Property.

Borrower shall promptly give Lender written notice of any Investigation, claim, demand, lawsuit or other action by any governmental or regulatory agency or private party involving the Property and any Hazardous Substance or Environmental Law of which Borrower has actual knowledge. If Borrower learns, or is noticed by any governmental or regulatory authority, that any removal or other remediation of any Hazardous Substances affecting the Property is necessary, Borrower shall promptly take all necessary remedial actions in accordance with Environmental Law.

As used in this paragraph 16, "Hazardous Substances" are those substances defined as toxic or hazardous substances by Environment law and the following substances: gasoline, kerosene, other flammable or toxic petroleum products, toxic pesticides and herbicides, volatile solvents, material containing asbestos or formaldehyde, and radioactive materials. As used in the paragraph 16, "Environmental law" means federal laws and laws of the jurisdiction where the Property is located that related to health, safety or environmental protection.

NON-UNIFORM COVENANTS. Borrower and Lender further covenant and agree as follows:

17. Assignment of Rents

Use the following language unless prohibited by state law:

Note: If changes are necessary to create an assignment of rents enforceable under state law, the lender should make necessary changes but the revised paragraph should grant the lender the maximum interest in rents permitted by law.

18. Foreclosure Procedure

For illustration only. The text needs state adaption, as provided in 4155.2 6.B.2.d.

The following language is mandatory in all cases:

If the Lender's interest in this Security Instrument is held by the Secretary and the Secretary requires immediate payment in full under Paragraph 9, the Secretary may invoke the nonjudicial power of sale provided in the single Family Mortgage Foreclosure Act of 1994 ("Act") (12 U.S.C. 3751 et seq.) by requesting a foreclosure commissioner designated under the Act to commence foreclosure and to sell the Property as provided in the Act. Nothing in the preceding sentence shall deprive the Secretary of any rights otherwise available to a Lender under this Paragraph 18 or applicable law

State Specific Paragraphs

For California specific language, see supra section 3. FANNIE MAE/FREDDIE MAC DEED OF TRUST—SINGLE FAMILY—CALIFORNIA starting with Non-Uniform Covenants (paragraph 22)

Riders to This Security Instrument

If one or more riders are executed by Borrower and recorded together with this Security Instrument, the covenants of each such rider shall be incorporated into and shall amend and supplement the covenants and agreements of this Security Instrument as if the rider(s) were a part of this Security Instrument. [Check applicable box(es)].

___ Condominium Rider ___ Growing Equity Rider ___ Other [specify]

___ Planned Unit Development Rider ___ Graduated Payment Rider

BY SIGNING BELOW, Borrower accepts and agrees to the terms contained in this Security Instrument and in any rider(s) executed by Borrower and recorded with it.

INDEX

References are to Pages